Endsheet Pictures

INSIGHT
ON THE SCRIPTURES

Volume 1: Aaron - Jehoshua

Copyright © 1988 by
WATCH TOWER BIBLE AND TRACT SOCIETY OF PENNSYLVANIA
INTERNATIONAL BIBLE STUDENTS ASSOCIATION

Publishers
WATCHTOWER BIBLE AND TRACT SOCIETY OF NEW YORK, INC.
INTERNATIONAL BIBLE STUDENTS ASSOCIATION
Brooklyn, New York, U.S.A.

First Printing in English: 1,000,000 copies

Insight on the Scriptures English (it-1-E)
Made in the United States of America

What This Publication Contains

The objective of this publication is to help you to acquire insight on the Scriptures. How is it done? By bringing together from all parts of the Bible the details that relate to subjects being discussed. By drawing attention to original-language words and their literal meaning. By considering related information from secular history, archaeological research, and other fields of science and evaluating this in the light of the Bible. By providing visual aids. By helping you to discern the value of acting in harmony with what the Bible says.

The Bible tells about the dealings of Jehovah God with mankind, and it does so in a context that convincingly reflects real life. It names people and places, refers to contemporary nations and rulers, and mentions specific types of plants and animals. Background knowledge can help you to benefit more fully from Bible references to such people and things. To assist you, *Insight on the Scriptures* contains informative articles about more than 3,000 persons named in the Scriptures as well as facts concerning 97 nations, tribes, and peoples. There are over 1,000 articles discussing specific geographic places, 96 about various plants, and 106 that deal with birds and animals. Besides these, there are articles on many other vital Scriptural subjects.

Each book of the Bible is given special attention. An outline of each one of the books draws attention to the principal ideas that are developed by the writer, and it does so in a form that is easy to read and remember. Unless otherwise indicated, the Bible translation quoted in this reference work is the *New World Translation of the Holy Scriptures—With References*, 1984 Edition, although over 40 other translations are also cited and quoted.

Visual aids include scores of maps, many of which isolate key locations on the basis of historical time periods. There are also a large number of pictures to help you to visualize the Bible lands and events that took place there. A few are artists' portrayals of important historical events. Many more are photographs of specific locations and of museum displays that relate to the Bible record. Acknowledgments for pictures from museum displays and for other pictures are shown in Volume 2, on page 1276.

In-depth articles discuss Hebrew, Greek, and Aramaic—the languages in which the Bible was originally written. Articles are developed in line with the meaning of relevant expressions in the original languages, not simply the way those terms are understood in other tongues popularly used today. Meanings of Bible names in this publication are based on the way the original-language components of the names are actually used elsewhere in the Bible.

How can you find answers to your Bible questions? (1) Is it the meaning of a particular *Bible expression* that you want? Is your question about a *person*, a *place*, or perhaps a *quality?* Keep in mind that all the articles are arranged alphabetically and that Bible names and expressions are according to the rendering of the *New World Translation.* Turn to the article that has as its heading the name or subject that you have in mind. If you do not readily find what you need, try the Subject Index in the back of Volume 2; it pinpoints valuable material that may be in an unexpected place. (2) If you need the explanation of a specific *scripture*, turn directly to the Scripture Index in Volume 2.

It is our earnest desire that this publication will deepen your appreciation for the Bible's Author, Jehovah God, and give you greater insight as to the meaning of his Word, and that it will move you to apply its contents more fully in your own life and to share its vital truths with others.

Special Features in Color

Maps are listed in
Volume 1 on page 8.

Examples of Helpful Features

Headings in all-capital letters designate main articles

> **AARON** (Aar'on). A son of Amram and Jochebed of the tribe of Levi, born in Egypt in 1597 B.C.E. Levi was Aaron's great-grandfather. (Ex 6:13, 16-20) Miriam was his elder sister, and Moses was his younger brother by three years.

Bold lettering with capital letters is used for principal subheadings

> **During the Kingships of David and Solomon.** It appears that when David finally gained the throne, Abiathar was made the high priest. Some scholars suggest that, after High Priest Ahimelech's death, King Saul had Zadok installed as high

Bold italics indicate a subdivision of material under the principal subheading

> ***Christian principles regarding strangers.***   In the Christian Greek Scriptures love toward the stranger (Gr., *xe'nos*) is strongly emphasized as a quality the Christian must exercise. The apostle Paul says: "Do not forget hospitality [Gr., *phi·lo-*

Pronunciation guide

> **ABEDNEGO** (A·bed'ne·go) [probably, Servant of Nebo [a Babylonian god]]. The name given to Azariah, one of the youths of the Jewish royalty or nobility taken captive by Nebuchadnezzar in

Meaning of name

> **ELIJAH** (E·li'jah) **[My God Is Jehovah].**
> 1. One of the foremost prophets of Israel. Evidently his home was in Tishbeh, thought by some to be a village in the land of Gilead, E of the Jordan River. (1Ki 17:1) He started his long

Question that is answered in the following paragraph(s)

> ***Why was Aaron not punished for making the golden calf?***
>
> Despite his privileged position, Aaron had his shortcomings. During Moses' first 40-day stay on Mount Sinai, "the people congregated themselves

A boldface number at the beginning of a paragraph indicates a different person or place with the same name

> **1.** A gatekeeper of the Korahites appointed by David; the seventh son of Meshelemiah of the tribe of Levi.—1Ch 26:1-3.
>
> **2.** The son of Zerahiah who, accompanied by 200 males of the paternal house of Pahath-moab, returned from Babylon to Jerusalem with Ezra.

Cross-references direct attention to articles that have valuable additional information or to visual aids

> firmed by the finding of a silver denarius coin bearing the head of Tiberius and put in circulation about the year 15 C.E. **(PICTURE, Vol. 2, p. 544)** (Compare Lu 3:1, 2.) The fact that Pontius Pilate was then Roman governor of Judea is also demonstrated by a stone slab found at Caesarea bearing the Latin names *Pontius Pilatus* and *Tiberieum.* **—See PILATE; PICTURE, Vol. 2, p. 741.**

Modern-day equivalents are given for Biblical weights, measures, and money

> Hosea paid 15 silver pieces **(if shekels, $33)** and one and a half homer measures **(330 L; 300 dry qt)** of barley to buy back the adulterous woman Gomer as his wife (Ho 1:3; 3:1, 2), a price that some commentators consider to total the price of a slave, 30 silver shekels **($66)**. (Ex 21:32) The "offering of jealousy" required by the

All abbreviations are explained in Volume 1, on pages 1277, 1278

> **(Isa** 40:11) The expression "wife of [one's] bosom," as in some translations (*KJ; Ro; RS; AT*), is given clearer meaning when rendered, "wife thou dost cherish in thy bosom" (*Kx*), "your cherished wife."

Geographic names in parentheses are equivalents in another language (usually in modern Hebrew)

> In the period of the Judges, the Canaanite city was situated on a mound identified with Tell el-Fukhkhar **(Tel 'Akko),** about 1 km (0.6 mi) from the bay and 1.8 km (1 mi) E of the present-day Old City walls. During the Persian period, from the sixth century B.C.E., the city spread westward to

Geographic locations are shown on an accompanying map; scriptures tell what happened there during the period of history under consideration

LOCATIONS ON MAP With Related Scriptures	
Ai	Ge 12:8; 13:3, 4
Beer-sheba	Ge 21:31-33; 22:19
Bethel	Ge 12:8
Damascus	Ge 14:15
Dan	Ge 14:14
Gerar	Ge 20:1-18

Maps

Index of locations on all maps:
Volume 1, pages 1273-1276.

A

AARON (Aar'on). A son of Amram and Jochebed of the tribe of Levi, born in Egypt in 1597 B.C.E. Levi was Aaron's great-grandfather. (Ex 6:13, 16-20) Miriam was his elder sister, and Moses was his younger brother by three years. (Ex 2:1-4; 7:7) Aaron married Elisheba, daughter of Amminadab, and had four sons, Nadab, Abihu, Eleazar, and Ithamar. (Ex 6:23) He died in 1474 B.C.E. at the age of 123 years.—Nu 33:39.

Owing to Moses' reluctance because he found it difficult to speak fluently, Jehovah assigned Aaron to act as Moses' spokesman before Pharaoh, saying of Aaron: "I do know that he can really speak." Aaron went to meet Moses at Mount Sinai and was informed of the far-reaching proportions of the divinely outlined program of action involving Israel and Egypt, and the brothers then journeyed back to Egypt.—Ex 4:14-16, 27-30.

Aaron now began serving as "a mouth" to Moses, speaking for him to the older men of Israel and performing miraculous signs as proof of the divine origin of their messages. When the time came for their appearance at Pharaoh's court, the 83-year-old Aaron, as Moses' spokesman, had to face up to that arrogant ruler. As Jehovah thereafter told Moses: "See, I have made you God to Pharaoh, and Aaron your own brother will become your prophet." (Ex 7:1, 7) It was Aaron who performed the first miraculous sign before Pharaoh and his magic-practicing priests; and, later, it was Aaron who, at Moses' order, stretched forth Moses' rod and signaled the start of the Ten Plagues. (Ex 7:9-12, 19, 20) He continued to work in united coordination with Moses and in obedience to God during the succeeding plagues, until liberation finally came. In this he was a good example for Christians who serve as "ambassadors substituting for Christ, as though God were making entreaty through us."—Ex 7:6; 2Co 5:20.

Aaron's activity as spokesman for Moses evidently diminished during the 40 years of wandering in the wilderness, since Moses appears to have done more of the speaking himself. (Ex 32:26-30; 34:31-34; 35:1, 4) The rod also returned to Moses' hands after the third plague. And Aaron, along with Hur, merely supported Moses' arms at the battle of Amalek. (Ex 9:23; 17:9, 12) However, Jehovah generally continued to associate Aaron with Moses when giving instruction, and they are spoken of as acting and speaking together, right up to the time of Aaron's death.—Nu 20:6-12.

Aaron, in his subordinate position, did not accompany Moses to the top of Mount Sinai to receive the Law covenant, but, together with two of his sons and 70 of the older men of the nation, he was permitted to approach the mountain and behold a magnificent vision of God's glory. (Ex 24:9-15) In the Law covenant Aaron and his house received honorable mention, and God designated Aaron for the position of high priest.—Ex 28:1-3.

High Priest. By a seven-day installation ceremony Aaron was invested with his sacred duties by Moses as God's agent, and his four sons were also installed as underpriests. Moses dressed Aaron in beautiful garments of gold, blue, purple, and scarlet materials, including shoulder pieces and a breastpiece that was adorned with precious gems of varied colors. On his head was placed a turban of fine linen. Attached to it was a plate of pure gold, engraved with the words "Holiness belongs to Jehovah." (Le 8:7-9; Ex 28) Aaron was then anointed in the manner described at Psalm 133:2 and could thereafter be called the *ma·shi'ach,* or messiah (*khri·stos', LXX*), that is, the "anointed one."—Le 4:5, 16; 6:22.

Aaron not only was placed over all the priesthood but also was divinely declared to be the one from whose line, or house, all future high priests must come. Yet Aaron himself had not received the priesthood by inheritance, and so the apostle Paul could say of him: "A man takes this honor, not of his own accord, but only when he is called by God, just as Aaron also was. So too the Christ did not glorify himself by becoming a high priest, but was glorified by him who spoke with reference to him: 'You are my son; I, today, I have become your father.'" (Heb 5:4, 5) Paul thereafter demonstrates the way in which the priestly office, first filled by Aaron, was typical of that which Christ Jesus fills as a superior and heavenly high priest. This being so, the priestly functions of Aaron's high office take on added meaning for us.—Heb 8:1-6; 9:6-14, 23-28.

As high priest, Aaron was responsible for directing all features of worship at the tabernacle

9

and supervising the work of the thousands of Levites engaged in its service. (Nu 3:5-10) On the annual Day of Atonement he presented sin offerings for the priesthood and Levites and for the people of Israel, and he alone was permitted to enter the Most Holy of the tabernacle with the sacrificial blood of the animals. (Le 16) The daily offering up of incense, the presentation of the firstfruits of the grain harvest, and many other features of the worship were exclusive prerogatives of Aaron and his sons as priests. (Ex 30:7, 8; Lu 1:8-11; Le 23:4-11) His anointing, however, sanctified him to perform not only sacrificial duties for the nation but other duties as well. He was responsible to teach the nation the Word of God. (Le 10:8-11; De 24:8; Mal 2:7) He, as well as his successors, served as the chief officer under Jehovah the King. On high state occasions he wore the costly garments and the "shining plate" of gold on his linen turban. He also wore the breastpiece that contained the Urim and Thummim, enabling him to receive Jehovah's "Yes" or "No" to national problems; although, for the duration of Moses' life and mediatorship, this feature appears to have received little use.—Ex 28:4, 29, 30, 36; see HIGH PRIEST.

Aaron's devotion to pure worship was early put to the test by the death of his sons Nadab and Abihu, who suffered destruction by God for making profane use of their priestly positions. The record says: "And Aaron kept silent." When he and his two surviving sons were instructed not to mourn over the dead transgressors, "they did according to Moses' word."—Le 10:1-11.

During nearly 40 years Aaron represented the 12 tribes before Jehovah in his capacity as high priest. While in the wilderness, a serious rebellion broke out against the authority of Moses and Aaron. It was led by a Levite named Korah, together with the Reubenites Dathan, Abiram, and On, who complained against their leadership. Jehovah caused the earth to open beneath the tents of Korah, Dathan, and Abiram, swallowing them up along with their households, while Korah himself and 250 of his coconspirators were destroyed by fire. (Nu 16:1-35) Murmuring broke out now on the part of the congregation against Moses and Aaron; and in the divine plague that ensued, Aaron showed great faith and courage in obediently going out with his fire holder and making atonement for the people while "standing between the dead and the living," until the scourge was stopped.—Nu 16:46-50.

God now directed that 12 rods, each representing one of the 12 tribes, be placed in the taberna-

cle, and the rod for the tribe of Levi was inscribed with Aaron's name. (Nu 17:1-4) On the following day Moses entered the tent of the Testimony and found that Aaron's rod had budded, blossomed with flowers, and bore ripe almonds. (Nu 17:8) This established beyond dispute Jehovah's choice of the Levite sons of Aaron for priestly service and His authorization of Aaron as high priest. Thereafter, the right of Aaron's house to the priesthood was never seriously challenged. The budded rod of Aaron was placed in the ark of the covenant as "a sign to the sons of rebelliousness," though it appears that after the death of these rebellious ones and the entry of the nation into the Land of Promise the rod was removed, having served its purpose.—Nu 17:10; Heb 9:4; 2Ch 5:10; 1Ki 8:9.

Why was Aaron not punished for making the golden calf?

Despite his privileged position, Aaron had his shortcomings. During Moses' first 40-day stay on Mount Sinai, "the people congregated themselves about Aaron and said to him: 'Get up, make for us a god who will go ahead of us, because as regards this Moses, the man who led us up out of the land of Egypt, we certainly do not know what has happened to him.'" (Ex 32:1) Aaron acceded and cooperated with these rebellious ones in making a golden calf statue. (Ex 32:2-6) When later confronted by Moses, he gave a weak excuse. (Ex 32:22-24) However, Jehovah did not single him out as the prime wrongdoer but told Moses: "So now let me be, that my anger may blaze against *them* and I may exterminate *them*." (Ex 32:10) Moses brought the matter to a showdown by crying: "Who is on Jehovah's side? To me!" (Ex 32:26) All the sons of Levi responded, and this undoubtedly included Aaron. Three thousand idolaters, probably the prime movers of the rebellion, were slain by them. (Ex 32:28) Nevertheless, Moses later reminded the rest of the people that they, too, bore guilt. (Ex 32:30) Aaron, therefore, was not alone in receiving God's mercy. His subsequent actions indicated that he was not in heart harmony with the idolatrous movement but simply gave in to the pressure of the rebels. (Ex 32:35) Jehovah showed that Aaron had received his forgiveness by maintaining as valid Aaron's appointment to become high priest.—Ex 40: 12, 13.

After having loyally supported his younger brother through many difficult experiences and having recently been installed as high priest by

Moses as God's representative, Aaron foolishly associated himself with his sister Miriam in criticizing Moses for his marriage to a Cushite woman and in challenging Moses' unique relationship and position with Jehovah God, saying: "Is it just by Moses alone that Jehovah has spoken? Is it not by us also that he has spoken?" (Nu 12:1, 2) Jehovah swiftly took action, brought the three before him in front of the tent of meeting, and strongly castigated Aaron and Miriam for disrespecting God's appointment. The fact that only Miriam was stricken with leprosy may mark her as the instigator of the action and may indicate that Aaron again had shown weakness by being induced to join her. However, if Aaron had been similarly struck with leprosy, it would have invalidated his appointment as high priest, according to God's law. (Le 21:21-23) His right heart attitude manifested itself by his immediate confession and apology for the foolishness of their act and by his agonized plea for Moses' intercession on leprous Miriam's behalf.—Nu 12:10-13.

Aaron again shared responsibility for wrong when he, along with Moses, failed to sanctify and honor God before the congregation in the incident involving the providing of water at Meribah in Kadesh. For this action God decreed that neither of them would enjoy the privilege of bringing the nation into the Land of Promise.—Nu 20:9-13.

On the first day of the month Ab, in the 40th year following the Exodus, the nation of Israel lay encamped on the frontier of Edom before Mount Hor. Within a matter of months they would be crossing over the Jordan; but not the 123-year-old Aaron. At Jehovah's instruction, and with all the camp watching, Aaron, his son Eleazar, and Moses went climbing to the top of Mount Hor. There Aaron let his brother remove his priestly garments from him and put them on his son and successor to the high priesthood, Eleazar. Then Aaron died. He was probably buried there by his brother and his son, and for 30 days Israel mourned his death.—Nu 20:24-29.

It is noteworthy that in each of his three deflections, Aaron does not appear as the principal initiator of the wrong action but, rather, seems to have allowed the pressure of the circumstances or the influence of others to sway him from a course of rectitude. Particularly in his first trespass, he could have applied the principle underlying the command: "You must not follow after the crowd for evil ends." (Ex 23:2) Nevertheless, his name is thereafter used in the Scriptures in an honorable way, and God's Son, during his earthly lifetime, recognized the legitimacy of the Aaronic priesthood.—Ps 115:10, 12; 118:3; 133:1, 2; 135:19; Mt 5:17-19; 8:4.

Aaron's Priestly Descendants. The expression "Aaronites" appears in the *King James Version* and *Moffatt* at 1 Chronicles 12:27; 27:17. (The Masoretic text in Hebrew simply uses the name Aaron. *LXX* [Lagardian edition, at 1Ch 12:27] says "of the sons of Aaron.") It is evident that the word "Aaron" is here used in a collective sense, much as is the name Israel, and stands for the house of Aaron or his male descendants in David's time who were of the tribe of Levi and were serving as priests. (1Ch 6:48-53) The *New World Translation* reads: "And Jehoiada was the leader [of the sons] of Aaron, and with him were three thousand seven hundred" (1Ch 12:27), bracketing the words "of the sons" to denote that they are supplied.

AB. The postexilic name of the 5th lunar month of the Jewish sacred calendar, but the 11th of the secular calendar. It corresponds to part of July and part of August.

The meaning of the name Ab is uncertain. In the Bible it is mentioned, not directly by name, but only as "the fifth month." The name does appear, however, in the Mishnah (*Ta'anit* 4:6) and other postexilic Jewish writings.

Ab was a month of summer heat, a time when the harvesting of grapes began in Israel.—See Calendar.

It was on the first day of Ab that Aaron died on Mount Hor. (Nu 33:38) Second Kings 25:8 says that it was on the seventh day of this month that Nebuzaradan, the servant of the king of Babylon, "came to Jerusalem." However, Jeremiah 52:12 tells us that it was on the tenth day of this month that Nebuzaradan "came into Jerusalem." The *Soncino Books of the Bible* comments on this, saying: "The interval of three days may be accounted for as representing the date of Nebuzaradan's arrival on the scene and the commencement of operations." (Edited by A. Cohen, London, 1949) It would appear, then, that Nebuzaradan arrived at Jerusalem on the seventh day, made his survey from his camp outside the city walls, and gave directions for the demolition of the city fortifications and the plundering of its treasures; finally, on the tenth day of the month, he entered the city and its holy temple. According to Josephus (*The Jewish War*, VI, 250, 268 [iv, 5, 8]), Herod's temple was burned by the Romans on the tenth day of the fifth month (70 C.E.), and Josephus makes note of the precise correspondency of this date with the burning of the first temple on the same day by the Babylonians.

During the following 70-year Babylonian exile, this fifth month was a time of fastings and wailings by the Jews in memory of the destruction of the temple in Jerusalem. (Zec 7:3, 5; 8:19) It was also in the month Ab that Ezra returned to the restored Jerusalem to instruct the Jews in the Law of Jehovah.—Ezr 7:8, 9, 25.

ABADDON (A·bad′don) [from Heb., meaning "Destruction"]. At Revelation 9:11 this Hebrew word is transliterated into the English text. There we read concerning the symbolic plague of locusts that they have "a king, the angel of the abyss. In Hebrew his name is Abaddon, but in Greek he has the name Apollyon."

In Hebrew the word 'avad·dohn' means "destruction" and may also refer to "the place of destruction." It appears in the original Hebrew text a total of five times, and in four of the occurrences it is used to parallel "the burial place," "Sheol," and "death." (Ps 88:11; Job 26:6; 28:22; Pr 15:11) The word 'avad·dohn' in these texts evidently refers to the destructive processes that ensue with human death, and these scriptures indicate that decay or destruction takes place in Sheol, the common grave of mankind. At Job 31:12 'avad·dohn' designates the damaging effect of an adulterous course. Job declared: "That [adulterous course] is a fire that would eat clear to destruction ['adh-'avad·dohn'], and among all my produce it would take root."—Compare Pr 6:26-28, 32; 7:26, 27.

Abaddon, the angel of the abyss —who is he?

At Revelation 9:11, however, the word "Abaddon" is used as the name of "the angel of the abyss." The corresponding Greek name Apollyon means "Destroyer." In the past century there were efforts made to show that this text prophetically applied to individuals such as Emperor Vespasian, Muhammad, and even Napoleon, and the angel was generally regarded as "satanic." It should be noted, however, that at Revelation 20:1-3 the angel having "the key of the abyss" is shown to be God's representative from heaven, and rather than being "satanic," he binds and hurls Satan into the abyss. Commenting on Revelation 9:11, *The Interpreter's Bible* says: "Abaddon, however, is an angel not of Satan but of God, performing his work of destruction at God's bidding."

In the Hebrew scriptures just considered, it is evident that 'avad·dohn' is paralleled with Sheol and death. At Revelation 1:18 we find Christ Jesus stating: "I am living forever and ever, and I have the keys of death and of Hades." His power with regard to the abyss is shown at Luke 8:31. That he has destroying power, including the power of destruction over Satan, is evident from Hebrews 2:14, which says that Jesus partook of blood and flesh in order that "through his death he might bring to nothing the one having the means to cause death, that is, the Devil." At Revelation 19:11-16 he is clearly represented as God's appointed Destroyer or Executioner.—See APOLLYON.

ABAGTHA (A·bag′tha). The name of one of seven court officials who ministered to the Persian king Ahasuerus, the husband of the Jewess Esther, in his palace in Shushan, then capital of Persia.—Es 1:10.

In the *King James Version,* Abagtha is said to be one of seven "chamberlains," and the marginal reading says "eunuchs." While eunuchs were frequently used as trusted servants within royal households in Middle Eastern countries, the original Hebrew word *sa·ris'* primarily has the meaning of "court official" and only secondarily has reference to a castrated person. Since these seven court officials were attendants of the king and apparently not assigned as guardians of the women (as was Hegai, the king's eunuch mentioned at Esther 2:3), they may not have been eunuchs in the physical sense.

ABANAH (A·ba′nah). One of the two rivers of Damascus referred to by the Syrian army commander Naaman when scorning Elisha's instructions to bathe himself in the waters of the Jordan as a cure for his leprosy.—2Ki 5:12.

This river is generally identified with the Nahr Barada, which rises in the Anti-Lebanon mountains to the NW of Damascus and, after traversing the mountains, emerges from a gorge just to the W of Damascus. Then it courses through the northern part of the city and fans out to irrigate a large area before finally losing itself in a body of marshes to the E of the city. Its waters, used to irrigate fields and orchards by means of canals and conduits, create an extensive verdant oasis. It can well be said that Damascus owes its existence to the Barada. It has long been the source of water for the city's cisterns, fountains, and baths. Classical writers called it Golden River (Chrysorrhoas). So, Naaman's high opinion of the river appears to have had a solid basis.

The word "Amana" or "Amanah" is used instead of "Abanah" at 2 Kings 5:12 in *An American Translation,* also in the translation published by The Jewish Publication Society of America, and the margin of the Masoretic text as well as the Syriac *Peshitta* so read. At Song of Solomon 4:8 reference is made to "Amana" in many translations, and it is understood to refer to the Anti-Lebanon mountains in which the river here discussed has its source. Hence, the river may have taken on the name of the mountains in which it originated.

ABARIM (Ab′a·rim) [Fords (Crossings); Borderland (Regions Beyond)]. This name doubtless applies to a region E of the Jordan River and, more particularly, E of the Dead Sea. At Jeremiah 22:20 it is mentioned along with regions of Lebanon and Bashan.

In the other instances where it appears in the Bible record, it is connected with a range or system of mountains. The term "Abarim," as referring to the "regions beyond," may indicate that the ones originating the term were located on the *western* side of the Jordan; and it is possible that this term was originally used by Abraham and was still retained by the Israelites on leaving Egypt.

It was near the end of the 40-year trek through the wilderness that the Israelites reached this territory and encamped "in the mountains of Abarim." (Nu 33:47, 48) Thereafter they descended to the Plains of Moab, which lie E of the Jordan at the N end of the Dead Sea. Here they made their final encampment before crossing the Jordan River. Here, too, Jehovah said to Moses: "Go up into this mountain of Abarim, Mount Nebo, which is in the land of Moab, which fronts toward Jericho, and see the land of Canaan, which I am giving to the sons of Israel as a possession."—De 32:49; Nu 27:12.

It would appear from this that the region of Abarim, together with its range of mountains, was in the NW part of the territory of Moab. However, it may possibly have extended the full length of the chain of mountain bluffs that rise along the entire E side of the Dead Sea from N to S. At Numbers 21:11 and 33:44 reference is made to a stopping point on the route of the Israelites called "Iye-abarim," and the context places this to the S of Moab and at the S end of the Dead Sea. It may have marked the southernmost point of the region called Abarim.—See IYE-ABARIM.

Mount Nebo was evidently one of the higher mountains of Abarim, if not the highest.—See NEBO No. 3.

ABBA (Ab′ba). The word *'ab·ba′′* in Aramaic corresponds to the emphatic or definite form of *'av*, literally meaning "the father," or "O Father." It

was the intimate name used by children for their fathers and combines some of the intimacy of the English word "papa" while retaining the dignity of the word "father," being both informal and yet respectful. It was, therefore, an endearing form of address rather than a title and was among the first words a child learned to speak.

This Aramaic word appears three times in the Scriptures. It is always in transliterated form in the original Greek and usually is transliterated in English translations. Each time the term is followed immediately by the translation *ho pa·ter′* in Greek, which literally means "the father" or, used as the vocative, "O Father." In each case it is used with reference to the heavenly Father, Jehovah.

Mark records that Jesus used the term when praying to Jehovah God in Gethsemane shortly before his death, saying: *"Abba,* Father, all things are possible to you; remove this cup from me. Yet not what I want, but what you want." (Mr 14:36) Here is the fervent appeal of a son to a beloved father, followed quickly by an assurance that, in any event, he would remain obedient.

The two other occurrences are in Paul's letters, at Romans 8:15 and Galatians 4:6. In both places the word is used in connection with Christians called to be spirit-begotten sons of God and indicates the intimacy of their relationship with their Father. While they are "slaves to God" and "bought with a price," yet they are also sons in the house of a loving Father, and they are made positively aware of this status by holy spirit through their Lord Jesus.—Ro 6:22; 1Co 7:23; Ro 8:15; Ga 4:6.

Rather than as just a translation from Aramaic into Greek, some see in the use of both *'Ab·ba′′* and "Father" together, first, the trust, confidence, and submissiveness of a child, followed by a mature appreciation of the filial relationship and its responsibilities. It seems evident from these texts that, in apostolic times, the Christians made use of the term *'Ab·ba′′* in their prayers to God.

The word *'Ab·ba′′* came to be applied as a title of honor to the Jewish rabbis in the early centuries of the Common Era and is found as such in the Babylonian Talmud. (*Berakhot* 16*b*) The one acting in the capacity of vice-president of the Jewish Sanhedrin already held the title of *'Av*, or Father of the Sanhedrin. In later periods the title was also applied to the bishops of the Coptic, Ethiopic, and Syrian churches and, more particularly, became the title of the Bishop of Alexandria, thereby making him the "papa" or "pope" of that part of the Eastern church. The English words "abbot" and "abbey" are both derived from the Aramaic 'ab·ba'. Jerome, the translator of the Latin *Vulgate,* objected to the use of the title "abbot" as applied to the Catholic monks in his time and did so on the basis that it violated Jesus' instructions at Matthew 23:9: "Moreover, do not call anyone your father on earth, for one is your Father, the heavenly One."

ABDA (Ab'da) [Servant].

1. The father of Adoniram. (1Ki 4:6) His son, Adoniram, was a prince over those conscripted for forced labor during David's and Solomon's reigns, and is evidently the Adoram, or Hadoram, referred to in other texts. (2Sa 20:24; 1Ki 12:18; 2Ch 10:18) Hence, Abda probably was a contemporary of King David.

2. A descendant of Jeduthun, of the tribe of Levi. (Ne 11:17, 18) Abda the Levite is evidently the same as the "Obadiah" mentioned at 1 Chronicles 9:16. He was among the exiles to return to Jerusalem from Babylon.

ABDEEL (Ab'de·el) [Servant of God]. Father of Shelemiah, one of three men sent by King Jehoiakim to seize the prophet Jeremiah and his secretary Baruch.—Jer 36:26.

ABDI (Ab'di) [shortened form of Abdiel].

1. A Levite of the house of Merari. He was the father of Kishi and probably a contemporary of Saul, whose reign ran from 1117 to 1078 B.C.E. —1Ch 6:31, 33, 39, 44.

2. Also a Levite of the house of Merari. He was the father of Kish. (2Ch 29:12) Because of the similarity of their sons' names, this Abdi and the one described above are represented in some Bible dictionaries as being the same person. However, the fact that this second Abdi's son, Kish, lived in the time of King Hezekiah some 250 years after David's time, makes such a conclusion illogical. This second Abdi was probably a contemporary of Kings Jotham and Ahaz, whose reigns cover the period from 777 B.C.E. to about 746 B.C.E.

3. A man of the family of Elam who lived in postexilic times. (Ezr 10:26) He was among those Israelites who had taken foreign wives but who put them away in response to Ezra's exhortation following his return to Jerusalem in the seventh year of King Artaxerxes (Longimanus) (468 B.C.E.).—Ezr 7:8; 10:1-4, 10-12, 26, 44.

ABDIEL (Ab'di·el) [Servant of God]. The son of Guni and the father of Ahi, of the tribe of Gad. (1Ch 5:15) He lived in the region of Gilead and Bashan, E of the Jordan, an area prominent for cattle raising.—1Ch 5:16.

ABDON (Ab'don) [from a root meaning "servant"].

1. A judge, the son of Hillel the Pirathonite of Ephraim. (Jg 12:13-15) According to Josephus (*Jewish Antiquities,* V, 273 [vii, 15]), his rule of eight years was one of peace, and the Bible record makes no mention of wars during that period. Abdon's 40 sons and 30 grandsons all "rode on seventy full-grown asses," a sign of considerable wealth and rank at that time. At the end of his judgeship, Abdon was buried in his native Ephraim.

Some would connect Abdon with "Bedan," mentioned at 1 Samuel 12:11; however, Bedan is more likely identified with Barak, whose name appears in this text in both the Greek *Septuagint* and the Syriac *Peshitta.*

2. A Benjamite, firstborn son of Jeiel and evidently a brother of Ner, Saul's grandfather.—1Ch 8:30; 9:36, 39.

3. An official in King Josiah's court (2Ch 34: 20), called Achbor at 2 Kings 22:12.—See Achbor No. 2.

4. A son of Shashak of the tribe of Benjamin; a headman dwelling in Jerusalem.—1Ch 8:23-28.

5. One of four cities in the territory of Asher given to the Levites of the family of Gershon. (Jos 21:27-30; 1Ch 6:71-74) It is probably Khirbet 'Abdeh (Tel 'Avdon) about 6 km (3.5 mi) E of Achzib. This site lies on the N side of the Wadi Qarn (Nahal Keziv) and at the foot of the hills of Galilee and hence near the N end of the Plain of Asher.

ABEDNEGO (A·bed'ne·go) [probably, Servant of Nebo [a Babylonian god]]. The name given to Azariah, one of the youths of the Jewish royalty or nobility taken captive by Nebuchadnezzar in 617 B.C.E.—Da 1:3, 4, 7.

Some scholars believe "Nego" to be an intentional corruption of the name Nebo, a Babylonian god, so as not to offend Azariah. (See Nebo No. 4.) The name Azariah means "Jehovah Has Helped," and it appears that these Hebrews, among themselves, continued to use their original names. (Da 2:17) In Babylon he, along with Daniel, Hananiah, and Mishael, passed, with high honors, a three-year training course and a regal examination personally conducted by Nebuchadnezzar, after having first demonstrated religious integrity in matters of food and drink. (Da 1:4, 5, 8-20) Later, at Daniel's request, the king made Azariah and his two companions administrators over the jurisdictional district of Babylon.—Da 2:49.

Abednego (Azariah), along with his two Hebrew companions, was subsequently denounced before the king by certain Chaldeans for refusing to bow down to the king's golden image in response to particular music. (Da 3:5, 8, 12) When they were questioned by the enraged king, their firm refusal to violate their conscience and their expression of faith in Jehovah resulted in the king's having them thrown into a superheated furnace, where they were miraculously protected by God's angelic representative. Following their release by the shaken king, and after members of the royal court saw that the three men had escaped unharmed, they were restored to royal favor.—Da 3:15-30; see MESHACH; SHADRACH.

ABEL (A'bel).

1. [possibly, Exhalation; Vanity]. The second son of Adam and his wife Eve, and the younger brother of their firstborn son, Cain.—Ge 4:2.

It is probable that, while yet alive, Abel had sisters; the record mentions the birth of daughters to his parents, but their names are not recorded. (Ge 5:1-4) As a man, he became a herder of sheep; his brother, a farmer.—Ge 4:2.

After an indefinite period of time, Abel made an offering to Jehovah God. Cain did likewise. Each brought of what he had: Abel, of the firstlings of his flocks; Cain, of his produce. (Ge 4:3, 4) They both had belief in God. They undoubtedly learned of Him from their parents and must have known why they all were outside the garden of Eden and denied entry to it. Their offerings indicated a recognition of their alienated state and of their desire for God's favor. God expressed favor toward Abel's offering but not Cain's. How the approval and the rejection were manifested the record does not show, but it was undoubtedly evident to both men. The reason for God's approval of only Abel's offering is made clear by later writings. The apostle Paul lists Abel as the first man of faith, at Hebrews 11:4, and shows that this resulted in his sacrifice being of "greater worth" than Cain's offering. By contrast, 1 John 3:11, 12 shows Cain's heart attitude to have been bad; and his later rejection of God's counsel and warning, as well as his premeditated murder of his brother Abel, demonstrated this.

While it cannot be said that Abel had any foreknowledge of the eventual outworking of the divine promise at Genesis 3:15 concerning the promised "seed," he likely had given much thought to that promise and believed that blood would have to be shed, someone would have to be 'bruised in the heel,' so that mankind might be uplifted again to the state of perfection that Adam

and Eve had enjoyed before their rebellion. (Heb 11:4) In the light of this, Abel's offering of the firstlings of his flock certainly was appropriate and undoubtedly was a factor in God's expression of approval. To the Giver of life, Abel gave as his gift life, even though it was only from among the flock.—Compare Joh 1:36.

Jesus shows Abel to have been the first martyr and object of religious persecution waged by his intolerant brother Cain. In doing so, Jesus speaks of Abel as living at "the founding of the world." (Lu 11:48-51) The Greek word for "world" is ko'smos and in this text refers to the world of mankind. The term "founding" is a rendering of the Greek ka·ta·bo·le' and literally means "throwing down [of seed]." (Heb 11:11, Int) By the expression "the founding of the world," Jesus manifestly referred to the birth of children to Adam and Eve, thereby producing a world of mankind. Paul includes Abel among the "cloud of witnesses" of pre-Christian times.—Heb 11:4; 12:1.

How does the blood of Jesus 'speak in a better way than that of Abel'?

Because of his faith and divine approval, the record of which continues to bear witness, it could be said that Abel, "although he died, yet speaks." (Heb 11:4) At Hebrews 12:24 the apostle refers to "Jesus the mediator of a new covenant, and the blood of sprinkling, which speaks in a better way than Abel's blood." Though shed in martyrdom, Abel's blood did not ransom or redeem anyone, any more than did the blood of his sacrificed sheep. His blood in effect cried to God for vengeance upon assassin Cain. The blood of Jesus, here presented as validating the new covenant, speaks in a better way than Abel's in that it calls to God for mercy upon all persons of faith like Abel, and is the means by which their ransoming is possible.

Since Seth was evidently born shortly after Abel's death and when Adam was 130 years of age, it is possible that Abel may have been as much as 100 years old at the time of his martyrdom.—Ge 4:25; 5:3.

2. [Watercourse]. A town also called Abel-beth-maacah or Abel of Beth-maacah. Elsewhere used as a prefix to the names of various places.—2Sa 20:18; see ABEL-BETH-MAACAH.

3. At 1 Samuel 6:18 the *King James Version* refers to "the great stone of Abel," while the marginal reading says, "Or, great Abel, that is, mourning." However, modern translations generally read

here simply "the great stone." (Compare *AT, NC* [Spanish], *NW, JB,* and others.) While the Masoretic Hebrew text uses the word *'A·vel'* in this verse, the Greek *Septuagint* and the Aramaic Targums translate it as if it were *'e·ven,* that is, "stone." This agrees with verse 14 of the same chapter. It could not refer to Abel of Beth-maacah, since the incident recorded at 1 Samuel 6:18 took place near Beth-shemesh in Judah.

ABEL-BETH-MAACAH (A'bel-beth-ma'a-cah), **ABEL OF BETH-MAACAH** [Watercourse of the House of Maacah]. A fortified city of Naphtali in northern Palestine probably 7 km (4 mi) WNW of Dan, identified with Tell Abil (Tel Avel Bet Ma'akha). It was favorably located on the road from Hazor northward at the intersection of the E-W route from Damascus to Tyre.

David's men under Joab besieged the city when the rebel Sheba fled there. Thereupon, a wise woman, speaking for "the peaceable and faithful ones of Israel," pleaded with Joab not to destroy Abel, from of old the place to inquire for wise judgments, hence "a mother in Israel"; meaning also, probably, a metropolis or city having dependent towns. Heeding this woman's advice, the inhabitants pitched Sheba's head over the wall, and the city was spared.—2Sa 20:14-22.

Instigated by Asa of Judah, Syrian Ben-hadad I struck down Abel-beth-maacah to divert Baasha of Israel from building Ramah. (1Ki 15:20; see RAMAH No. 1.) Abel of Beth-maacah was captured by Tiglath-pileser III of Assyria during the reign of Pekah, and its inhabitants were sent into exile. (2Ki 15:29) This city, called in Assyrian texts Abilakka, appears in the inscriptions of Tiglath-pileser III in the list of cities he conquered. The surrounding fertile, well-watered fields doubtless gave rise to another merited name, Abel-maim (meaning "Watercourse of Waters"). Its situation made it a good storage place.—2Ch 16:4.

ABEL-KERAMIM (A'bel-ker'a·mim) [Watercourse of the Vineyards]. The most distant point to which Jephthah pursued the Ammonites in their defeat. (Jg 11:33) It is generally held to be situated between Heshbon and Rabbah, or Rabbah Ammon (modern 'Amman). It is generally identified today with Khirbet es-Suq, about 8 km (5 mi) S of Rabbah ('Amman), which possibly fits Eusebius' description. (*Onomasticon* 32, 15-16) Some recommend Na'ur, about 14 km (9 mi) SW of Rabbah Ammon as the probable location.

ABEL-MAIM. See ABEL-BETH-MAACAH.

ABEL-MEHOLAH (A'bel-me·ho'lah) [Watercourse of Dancing]. The home of Elisha, where Elijah found him plowing and anointed him prophet successor.—1Ki 19:16-19.

At an earlier date Abel-meholah figures in the account of the defeat of the Midianites by Gideon's small band of warriors. The disorganized flight of the Midianites is reported to have carried them "as far as the outskirts of Abel-meholah by Tabbath." —Jg 7:22.

Because Tabbath lies E of the Jordan River, effort has been made since 1951 to identify Abel-meholah with Tell el-Maqlub on the Wadi el-Yabis. Additional argument adduced for this identification has been that Elijah, after leaving Horeb, stopped at Abel-meholah to anoint Elisha and had the further commission to travel to "the wilderness of Damascus" to anoint Hazael as king over Syria. (1Ki 19:15) The major ancient highway leading from Horeb to Damascus was E of the Jordan, although at times this route was controlled by nomads.

However, the account of Gideon's pursuit of the Midianites in reality indicates that they were W (rather than E) of the Jordan at the point of Judges 7:22. (See Jg 7:24.) And, as regards Elijah's trip to the Wilderness of Damascus, the record shows that this was not effected immediately but, rather, was made sometime later by his successor, Elisha. (1Ki 19:15-19; 2Ki 8:7-13) In view of this, some geographic texts continue to recommend a site W of the Jordan rather than E of it. (*The Geographical and Topographical Texts of the Old Testament,* by J. Simons, Leiden, 1959; *The Geography of the Bible,* by D. Baly, 1957; and the *Atlas of the Bible,* by L. H. Grollenberg, 1956) Both Jerome and Eusebius of the early centuries of the Common Era identified Abel-meholah with a site 10 Roman miles (15 km; 9 mi) S of Beth-shean (W of the Jordan). *The Land of the Bible,* by Y. Aharoni, states: "Abel-meholah has now been identified with much confidence with Tell Abu Sus on the [west] bank of the Jordan, 15 km. south of Beth-shean." (Translated and edited by A. Rainey, 1979, p. 313) The nearby plain of Beth-shean is well suited for large-scale farming.—Compare 1Ki 19:19.

Further indication in favor of such a site W of the Jordan is the fact that Abel-meholah later formed part of Solomon's fifth administrative district and is listed with other places W of the Jordan. (1Ki 4:12) It was evidently the home of Adriel the Meholathite, a son-in-law of Saul. (1Sa 18:19; 2Sa 21:8) Festal dancing in harvest celebrations perhaps accounts for this name Abel-meholah.

ABEL-MIZRAIM. See ATAD.

ABEL OF BETH-MAACAH. See ABEL-BETH-MAACAH.

ABEL-SHITTIM. See SHITTIM No. 1.

ABHORRENT THING. The Hebrew word *nid·dah'* occurs 30 times in the Hebrew Scriptures and is possibly derived from the root word *na·dhah'*, which means "exclude; put out of mind (refuse to think of)." (Isa 66:5; Am 6:3) *Nid·dah'* indicates impurity, something abhorrent, whether physically, as for example, from menstruation (Le 12:2, 5; 15:20, 24, 25, 33), or morally, as from idolatry. (Ezr 9:11; 2Ch 29:5) The same Hebrew word is used with regard to the "water for *cleansing*" (Nu 19:9-21; 31:23, *NW*; "water used in case of menstruation," Nu 19:9, *NW*, ftn; "water of separation," *KJ*; "water for impurity," *RS, AT*; "lustral water," *JB*), indicating water used to remove that which is impure or unclean.

Thus, at Lamentations 1:17 Jeremiah says that Jerusalem in her desolation "has become an abhorrent thing ["as a menstruous woman," *KJ*; "*objeto de abominación*," *NC* (Spanish); "abhorrent," *AT*] in among them [that is, among the surrounding nations]."

Prior to Jerusalem's destruction by Babylon, Jehovah said of the people of Israel through his prophet Ezekiel: "The house of Israel were dwelling upon their soil, and they kept making it unclean with their way and with their dealings. Like the uncleanness of menstruation [*nid·dah'*] their way has become before me." (Eze 36:17) Due to idolatrous practices, Israel was spiritually impure and would thus be avoided by her husbandly owner, Jehovah God, and would be reunited with him spiritually only after cleansing. Thus, at verse 25, Jehovah says: "And I will sprinkle upon you clean water, and you will become clean; from all your impurities and from all your dungy idols I shall cleanse you."—Compare Eze 18:6.

At Ezekiel 7:19, 20 God expresses his anger against Israel for having made religious images with their silver and their gold and says that he will, therefore, cause them to throw their silver and their gold into the streets as an "abhorrent thing [*nid·dah'*]."—Compare Isa 30:22; see DISGUSTING THING, LOATHSOME THING.

Abhorrence. Other Hebrew expressions having the sense of "abhorrence" are *quts*, referring to the emotional reaction and defined as "abhor; have an abhorrence of; feel a sickening dread of" (Ge 27:46; 1Ki 11:25; Nu 22:3), and *ga·al'*, also meaning "abhor," but indicating a rejection of the object abhorred. (Le 26:11, 15, 30; 2Sa 1:21, ftn) In the Greek *Septuagint* these Hebrew words at times are rendered *pro·so·khthi'zo*, signifying "become disgusted" (Ge 27:46; Le 26:15; compare Heb 3:10), and *bde·lys'so·mai*, conveying the sense of "express abhorrence of; have disgust for."—Le 20:23; 26:11; compare Ro 2:22.

Because the Canaanites were guilty of sexual immorality and perversion, idolatry, and spiritistic practices, the Most High abhorred them, and this resulted in his decreeing their destruction. (Le 20:2-23) The Israelites were warned that, if they became disobedient, Jehovah would also abhor them, withdrawing his protection and blessing. By reason of loyalty to his covenant made with Israel, however, he would not abhor them to the point of bringing about their complete extermination. (Le 26:11-45) In the case of those who will prove to be wicked, the resurrection will turn out to be one to eternal "abhorrence" (Heb., *de·ra·'ohn'*). It will be a resurrection to condemnatory judgment resulting in everlasting cutting-off.—Da 12:2; Joh 5:28, 29.

Deliberate rejection of Jehovah's commands, reproof, and provisions constitutes an improper abhorrence. The Israelites were guilty of this when they refused to follow Jehovah's commands, as well as when they came to abhor the manna as "contemptible bread." (Nu 21:5; Le 26:15) Proverbs 3:11 counsels against 'abhorring Jehovah's reproof.'

At Romans 12:9 Christians are admonished: "Abhor what is wicked." The Greek term here rendered "abhor" (*a·po·sty·ge'o*) is the intensive form of the Greek verb meaning "hate," and thus literally means "hate intensely." A person's failing to abhor what is wicked, no longer loathing it, can result in his becoming an object of Jehovah's abhorrence.

ABI. See ABIJAH No. 7.

ABI-ALBON (A'bi-al'bon). A Benjamite and an outstanding warrior listed among 37 of King David's most valiant fighters. (2Sa 23:31) He is evidently the Abiel referred to in a parallel passage at 1 Chronicles 11:32. He is called the Arbathite, perhaps because of coming from the city of Betharabah, which lay near the frontier between Benjamin and Judah above the N end of the Dead Sea. (Jos 15:6; 18:18, 21, 22) His fighting valor was in accord with Jacob's deathbed prophecy concerning the tribe of Benjamin.—Ge 49:27.

ABIASAPH (A·bi'a·saph) [(My) Father Has Gathered]. One of the three sons of Korah the Levite, and a descendant of Kohath. (Ex 6:16-24) His brothers were Elkanah and Assir. He is apparently referred to as Ebiasaph at 1 Chronicles 6:37 and perhaps at 1 Chronicles 9:19 and 1 Chronicles 6:23.

It appears that Korah's sons did not join their father in his rebellion, along with Dathan and Abiram, against Moses and Aaron. Hence, these sons did not die with their father at that time. (Nu 26:9-11) Thus, at a later period, we find reference made to "the sons of Korah" in the superscriptions of many of the Psalms (42, 44-49, 84, 85, 87, 88), although this term has, basically, the meaning of "the descendants of Korah," or "the house of Korah."

ABIATHAR (A·bi'a·thar) [Father of Excellence; Father of More Than Enough (Overflow)]. A son of High Priest Ahimelech, of the tribe of Levi and of the line of Eli. (1Sa 14:3; 22:11; 23:6) He lived during the reigns of Saul, David, and Solomon, and during David's reign he became high priest. He had two sons, Jonathan and Ahimelech (the same name as Abiathar's father).—2Sa 15:27, 36; 8:17.

Abiathar was living in Nob, "the city of the priests," a short distance from Jerusalem, when King Saul had Doeg the Edomite slaughter Abiathar's father, the high priest, and other priests (85 in all), because of their supposed support of David. Doeg also struck down with the sword all the other residents of the city. Only Abiathar escaped. He fled to David, himself a fugitive, evidently at Keilah, several miles to the SW. David, feeling a certain personal responsibility for the tragedy, told Abiathar: "I well knew on that day, because Doeg the Edomite was there, that he would without fail tell Saul. I personally have wronged every soul of the house of your father. Just dwell with me. Do not be afraid, for whoever looks for my soul looks for your soul, for you are one needing protection with me."—1Sa 22:12-23; 23:6.

Abiathar now traveled with David during the remainder of his outlawed state and served as priest for David's forces. First Samuel 23:6 shows that Abiathar had brought with him an ephod, and while the priests in general wore an ephod of linen (1Sa 22:18), verses 9-12 of chapter 23 indicate that this was apparently the ephod of Abiathar's father, the high priest, containing the Urim and Thummim.

During the Kingships of David and Solomon. It appears that when David finally gained the throne, Abiathar was made the high priest. Some scholars suggest that, after High Priest Ahimelech's death, King Saul had Zadok installed as high priest to replace Ahimelech, thereby not recognizing Abiathar, who was in the company of Saul's future successor, David. They hold that, following his ascension to the throne, David made Abiathar an associate high priest along with Zadok. Such

view is evidently taken due to the fact that Zadok and Abiathar are regularly mentioned together as though sharing a high position in the priesthood. (2Sa 15:29, 35; 17:15; 19:11; 20:25; 1Ki 1:7, 8, 25, 26; 4:4; 1Ch 15:11) However, the inspired record nowhere mentions any appointment of Zadok as high priest under King Saul. It is possible that Zadok's prominence is due to his being a seer or prophet, just as the prophet Samuel received greater mention in the divine record than the high priest of his time. (2Sa 15:27) The evidence indicates that Abiathar was the sole high priest during David's reign and that Zadok then occupied a position secondary to him.—1Ki 2:27, 35; Mr 2:26.

The text at 2 Samuel 8:17 has caused some question in this regard, since it says that "Zadok the son of Ahitub and Ahimelech the son of Abiathar were priests" then, but does not mention Abiathar as high priest. Some suggest that the names of Ahimelech and Abiathar were transposed by a scribal error so that the text should read "Abiathar the son of Ahimelech," even as it does in the Syriac *Peshitta*. However, the record at 1 Chronicles (18:16; 24:3, 6, 31) confirms the order of the names in this verse as found in the Masoretic text. It therefore appears more likely that Zadok and Ahimelech are mentioned simply as secondary priests under High Priest Abiathar, and that Abiathar's position was, in this instance, assumed to be understood.—1Ch 16:37-40; compare Nu 3:32.

Abiathar, along with other priests, shared in the privilege of bringing the ark of Jehovah up from Obed-edom's home to Jerusalem. (2Sa 6:12; 1Ch 15:11, 12) In addition to being high priest he was included in David's group of advisers.—1Ch 27:33, 34.

Toward the latter part of his father David's reign, Absalom formed a conspiracy against him. Abiathar again stayed by David when circumstances forced the king to flee from Jerusalem. As part of a plan to thwart the counsel of traitorous Ahithophel, David's previous counselor, Abiathar and Zadok as loyal priests were sent back to Jerusalem to serve as liaison officers to keep David advised of his rebellious son's plans. (2Sa 15:24-36; 17:15) After Absalom's death, Abiathar and Zadok served as intermediaries to arrange David's return to the capital.—2Sa 19:11-14.

In view of his faithful record of enduring many hardships in David's company during his time as a fugitive from Saul and again during Absalom's rebellion, and considering his having enjoyed David's confidence, friendship, and favor during some four decades, it is surprising to find Abiathar linking himself up with another son of David,

Adonijah, in a later conspiracy for the throne. Though the plot also had the support of Joab as head of the army, it failed; and Solomon was appointed as king, with loyal priest Zadok doing the anointing at David's instruction. (1Ki 1:7, 32-40) Abiathar's son Jonathan, who had previously served as a runner to bear news to David during Absalom's insurrection, now went to advise Adonijah of the plot's miscarriage. King Solomon took no immediate action against Abiathar, but when evidence showed that the plot was still smoldering, he ordered Adonijah's and Joab's death and banished priest Abiathar from Jerusalem, saying: "Go to Anathoth to your fields! For you are deserving of death; but on this day I shall not put you to death, because you carried the ark of the Sovereign Lord Jehovah before David my father, and because you suffered affliction during all the time that my father suffered affliction." (1Ki 2:26) Zadok was now assigned to replace Abiathar in his priestly position, and with this the office of high priest passed again to the line of Aaron's son Eleazar; and the priestly line of the house of Eli came to a complete end, in fulfillment of the prophecy at 1 Samuel 2:31.—1Ki 2:27; 1Sa 3: 12-14.

While the record later, at 1 Kings 4:4, again refers to "Zadok and Abiathar" as priests of Solomon's reign, it is likely that Abiathar is listed only in an honorary capacity or in a historical sense. Some scholars suggest that Solomon, after demoting Abiathar, then assigned him to serve as Zadok's deputy, and that while one officiated on Mount Zion, where the Ark was kept, the other served at the tabernacle, which continued in Gibeon prior to the building of the temple. (See 1Ch 16:37-40.) However, 1 Kings 2:26 shows that Solomon sent Abiathar to his fields in Anathoth, and while Anathoth was not far from Gibeon, Solomon's order indicates that Abiathar was being removed from any active participation in the priesthood.

At Mark 2:26 most translations have Jesus saying that David went into the house of God and ate the showbread "when Abiathar was high priest." Since Abiathar's father, Ahimelech, was the high priest when that event took place, such translation would result in a historical error. It is noteworthy that a number of early manuscripts omit the above phrase, and it is not found in the corresponding passages at Matthew 12:4 and Luke 6:4. However, a similar Greek structure occurs at Mark 12:26 and Luke 20:37, and here many translations use the phrase "in the passage about." (*RS; AT; JB*) So, it appears that Mark 2:26 properly allows

for the translation given in the *New World Translation*, which reads: "How he entered into the house of God, *in the account* about Abiathar the chief priest." Since the account of the first exploits of Abiathar begins immediately following the record of David's entering the house of God to eat the showbread, and since Abiathar did later become Israel's high priest in David's reign, this translation maintains the historical accuracy of the record.

ABIB (A'bib) [Green Ears]. The original name of the first lunar month of the Jewish sacred calendar and of the seventh month of the secular calendar. (Ex 13:4; 23:15; 34:18; De 16:1) It corresponds, generally, with part of March and part of April.

The name Abib is understood to mean "Green Ears," the ears of grain being ripe but still soft. (Compare Le 2:14.) It was during this month that the barley harvest took place, followed some weeks later by the wheat harvest. The latter, or spring, rains also began and these helped to bring the Jordan River to flood stage. (Jos 3:15) It was designated by Jehovah as the initial month of the sacred year at the time of the Exodus from Egypt. (Ex 12:1, 2; 13:4) Following the Babylonian exile this name was replaced by the name Nisan.—See NISAN.

ABIDA (A·bi'da) [Father Has Known (Me)]. Abida was a son of Midian and a grandson of Abraham by his wife Keturah. He had four brothers, named Ephah, Epher, Hanoch, and Eldaah. —Ge 25:1, 2, 4; 1Ch 1:33.

ABIDAN (Ab'i·dan) [(My) Father Has Judged]. The chieftain of the tribe of Benjamin at the time of the census of Israel in the second year following the Exodus from Egypt. (Nu 1:11, 16) He was the head over the 35,400 men of Benjamin over 20 years of age who camped on the W side of the tabernacle.—Nu 2:18, 22, 23.

At the completion of the tabernacle and its inauguration (1512 B.C.E.), during 12 days each chieftain presented a noncompetitive offering of silver and gold dishware, worth about $1,720, in addition to offerings of grain, oil, incense, and livestock, and it was on the ninth day that Abidan did so. (Nu 7:10, 60-65) He died during the 40-year journey in the wilderness.—Nu 14:29, 30.

ABIEL (A·bi'el) [(My) Father Is God].

1. A son of Zeror, and descendant of Bechorath and Aphiah, of the tribe of Benjamin. A comparison of 1 Chronicles 8:29-33 and 9:35-39 with 1 Samuel 9:1, 2 and 14:50, 51 gives basis for

believing that Abiel is also called "Jeiel" in the Chronicles account, since Jeiel is there shown to be the father of Ner, who became the father of Kish, Saul's father. First Samuel 14:50, 51 also shows Abiel (or Jeiel) to be the father of Ner. The record in Chronicles indicates that Jeiel (or Abiel) had nine other sons, of whom one was named Kish, and this older Kish would thus be the uncle of the son of Ner who bore the same name.

Assuming Abiel and Jeiel both to be names of the same person, we arrive at a genealogy such as is set forth in this chart.

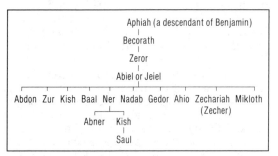

Therefore, when we read at 1 Samuel 9:1 that Kish (that is, the second Kish, the father of Saul) was "the son of Abiel," it appears that the meaning is that he was the grandson of Abiel, as is often the case in Bible genealogy where one or more links in the genealogy are simply omitted. (Thus, while "the family of the Matrites" is mentioned at 1 Samuel 10:21 as including Kish and Saul, the name of Matri does not appear in the accounts we are considering, nor in the rest of the Bible.)

The record in 1 Chronicles (8:33; 9:39) seems quite definite in presenting Ner as the immediate father of the second Kish, and this is clearly the more explicit of the two accounts.—See KISH Nos. 2 and 3.

2. Also a Benjamite.—See ABI-ALBON.

ABI-EZER (Abi-e′zer) [(My) Father Is a Helper].

1. One of "the sons of Gilead" the grandson of Manasseh, Joseph's firstborn. A comparison of the accounts at Numbers 26:28-30 and Joshua 17:1, 2 shows that he is also called Iezer (Jeezer, *KJ*), which is a shortened form of Abi-ezer, the prefix "Ab" (father) being removed.

Abi-ezer was a family head and an ancestor of Judge Gideon. (Jg 6:11, 24, 34; 8:2) It appears that after the division of land among the tribes of Israel, Abi-ezer's family either originally or at a later time settled in the area of Ophrah, in the territory of Manasseh W of the Jordan.

The name is also used to stand for the house of Abi-ezer in a collective sense.—Jg 8:2; see ABI-EZRITE.

2. A son of Hammolecheth, who was sister of Manasseh's grandson Gilead. (1Ch 7:18) Some commentators view this Abi-ezer as being the same as No. 1.

3. A Benjamite from Anathoth, one of King David's 37 most valiant fighters. (2Sa 23:27, 39) He was head of a paternal house and divisional head over a force of 24,000 fellow tribesmen, serving the king during the ninth month of each year. (1Ch 11:28; 27:1, 12) Along with other Benjamites, by his valor in war he fulfilled the prophecy at Genesis 49:27. His town of Anathoth lay a few miles NNE of Jerusalem, within the territory of Benjamin.—1Ch 6:60.

ABI-EZRITE (Abi-ez′rite) [Of (Belonging to) Abi-ezer]. A descendant of Abi-ezer; of the family of Abi-ezer. (Jg 6:11, 24; 8:32) Numbers 26:30 reads "Iezerites" ("Jeezerites," *KJ*), which is a contraction of Abi-ezrites. This term is applied in the Bible to those descended from Abi-ezer the 'son of Gilead,' rather than to the Abi-ezer of David's time.—See ABI-EZER No. 1.

ABIGAIL (Ab′i·gail) [(My) Father Has Made Himself Joyful].

1. A wife of David. Originally, the wife of wealthy Nabal from Maon, a city on the edge of the Wilderness of Judah, W of the Dead Sea. (1Sa 25:2, 3; Jos 15:20, 55) She was "good in discretion and beautiful in form," while her first husband, whose name means "Senseless; Stupid," was "harsh and bad in his practices."

Following the prophet Samuel's death, David and his men moved into the area where the flocks of Abigail's husband were pastured. David's men thereafter were like a protective "wall" around Nabal's shepherds and flocks, night and day. So, when shearing time came, David sent some young men up to Carmel to call Nabal's attention to the good service rendered him and to request an offering of food from him. (1Sa 25:4-8, 15, 16) But miserly Nabal screamed rebukes at them and insulted David as if he were an inconsequential person, and all of them as if they were possibly runaway slaves. (1Sa 25:9-11, 14) This so angered David that he girded on his sword and led about 400 men toward Carmel to wipe out Nabal and the men of his household.—1Sa 25:12, 13, 21, 22.

Abigail, hearing of the incident through a disturbed servant, showed her wise perception by immediately rounding up an ample supply of food and grain and then sent these ahead of her in care of her servants, much as Jacob had done before making contact with Esau. (1Sa 25:14-19; Ge 32:13-20) Without saying anything to her husband, she rode to meet David, and in a long and fervent plea, which manifested wisdom and logic as well as respect and humility, she convinced David that her husband's senseless words did not justify the unrighteous shedding of blood or the failure to trust in Jehovah to settle the matter in a right way himself. (1Sa 25:14-20, 23-31) David thanked God for the woman's good sense and quick action.—1Sa 25:32-35; compare Pr 25:21, 22; 15:1, 2.

Returning home, Abigail waited for her husband to sober up from a drunken feast and then informed him of her actions. Now "his heart came to be dead inside him, and he himself became as a stone," and after ten days Jehovah caused him to expire. When the news reached David, he sent a marriage proposal to Abigail, which she did not hesitate to accept. She shared David's affections along with Ahinoam, a Jezreelitess, whom David had previously taken as wife. David's first wife, Michal, had already been given by her father Saul to another man.—1Sa 25:36-44.

Abigail was with David in Gath on the western edge of the Shephelah and later down in the NW Negeb at Ziklag. During David's absence a raiding party of Amalekites from the S burned Ziklag and carried off all the women and children, including Abigail and Ahinoam. Assured by Jehovah of success, David led his men in pursuit and, in a surprise attack, overcame the Amalekites and retrieved the captives and possessions.—1Sa 30:1-19.

Back at Ziklag, three days later, the news of Saul's death arrived. (2Sa 1:1, 2) Abigail now accompanied her husband to Hebron of Judah, where David was first anointed as king. Here she gave birth to a son, Chileab (2Sa 3:3), also called Daniel at 1 Chronicles 3:1. David's wives increased to six in Hebron, and neither Abigail nor her son receive further mention in the account.—2Sa 3:2-5.

2. One of David's two sisters. (1Ch 2:13-17) Some scholars believe that she was only a half sister, being related by mother but not by father. At 2 Samuel 17:25 Abigail is called "the daughter of Nahash." Rabbinic tradition holds that Nahash is simply another name for Jesse, David's father. The Greek *Septuagint* (Lagardian edition) has "Jesse" instead of "Nahash" in this verse. A number of modern translations also read this way. (See *AT; JB; NC* [Spanish].) However, it is noteworthy that the record at 1 Chronicles 2:13-16 does not

call Abigail and Zeruiah 'daughters of Jesse' but rather "sisters" of Jesse's sons, including David. This allows for the possibility that their mother had first been married to a man named Nahash, to whom she bore Abigail and Zeruiah before becoming Jesse's wife and the mother of his sons. It cannot, therefore, be stated dogmatically that Abigail was the daughter of Jesse.—See NAHASH No. 2.

Abigail, David's sister, is mentioned as giving birth to only one son, Amasa. Her husband is referred to as Ithra the Israelite at 2 Samuel 17:25 but elsewhere is called Jether (1Ki 2:5, 32) and at 1 Chronicles 2:17 is spoken of as "Jether the Ishmaelite." (See JETHER No. 6.) It is possible that Abigail contracted marriage with Jether during the time Jesse and his family were dwelling in the land of Moab. (1Sa 22:3, 4) Her son, Amasa, received no apparent attention during David's reign until Absalom's rebellion. His cousin Absalom then made him the head of his armed forces. Nevertheless, following Absalom's death, Abigail's brother, King David, dealt with her son Amasa in obtaining support for his return to the throne, and thereafter made Amasa the head of the army, replacing Joab. (2Sa 19:11-14) This appointment soon brought death to Abigail's son, at the hands of his embittered cousin Joab.—2Sa 20:4-10.

ABIHAIL (Ab'i·ha·il) [(My) Father Is Vital Energy]. A name used in the Bible for three men and two women.

1. A man of the tribe of Levi and of the family (or clan) of Merari. He was the father of Zuriel, chieftain of the paternal house of the clan at the time of the Exodus.—Nu 3:35.

2. The wife of Abishur, who was of the tribe of Judah. (1Ch 2:29) She had two sons, Ahban and Molid.

3. A man of the tribe of Gad who settled in Bashan and Gilead. He was the son of Huri and a family chief or head.—1Ch 5:14-17.

4. The daughter of Eliab, David's oldest brother. (Though the Hebrew word *bath* [daughter] at 2 Chronicles 11:18 may also mean "granddaughter.")

The *King James Version* at 2 Chronicles 11:18 says: "And Rehoboam took him Mahalath the daughter of Jerimoth the son of David to wife, and Abihail the daughter of Eliab the son of Jesse." This would make Abihail appear to be the second wife of Rehoboam. However, the original Hebrew allows for a different rendering, and hence many modern translations here read: "Mahalath the daughter of Jerimoth the son of David, *and of*

Abihail the daughter of Eliab the son of Jesse." (See *RS, AT, JP, NW, JB.*) Concerning this, the *Soncino Books of the Bible* says in a footnote on 2 Chronicles 11:18: "The conjunction is implied. Mahalath was the daughter of Jerimoth and Abihail. Some commentators regard Abihail as the name of another of Rehoboam's wives." (Edited by A. Cohen, London, 1952) The singular pronouns used in the following verses (19, 20) support the view that only one wife of Rehoboam is meant in verse 18. It therefore appears most probable that Abihail was the mother of Rehoboam's wife Mahalath.

5. The father of Queen Esther and a descendant of Benjamin. He was the uncle of Esther's cousin, Mordecai. (Es 2:5, 15; 9:29) Esther 2:7 indicates that he and his wife died when their daughter Esther was quite young and thus sometime before her marriage to King Ahasuerus.

ABIHU (A·bi′hu) [He Is Father]. One of Aaron's four sons by his wife Elisheba; the brother of Nadab, Eleazar, and Ithamar. (Ex 6:23; 1Ch 6:3; 24:1) Born in Egypt, Abihu, as the second son of Aaron, was a mature man by the time of the Exodus, his father then being 83.—Nu 33:39.

As older sons, Nadab and Abihu were permitted by Jehovah to accompany their father and 70 of the older men of Israel in approaching Mount Sinai and there to see from a distance a magnificent vision of God's glory. (Ex 24:1, 9-11) Jehovah honored Aaron's sons, appointing them to serve as priests with their father, the high priest, and ordaining that from among them should come Aaron's eventual successor. They would wear priestly robes and headgears "for glory and beauty." Moses was to "anoint them and fill their hand with power and sanctify them" for their service to God. (Ex 28:1, 40-43) The priesthood would become theirs "as a statute to time indefinite."—Ex 29:8, 9.

Thereafter they were continually included in God's instructions regarding the priesthood and its functions. (Ex 29:10-46; 30:26-38) Also, God emphatically impressed upon them, as well as upon the entire nation, the vital importance of respecting the sanctity of the things related to his worship, including the altar of incense and incidental equipment. Their lives depended upon their respecting the divine regulations.

Now, one year from the start of the Exodus, came the time for setting up of the tabernacle and the installation of the priesthood (1512 B.C.E.). The entire nation assembled before the entrance of the tent of meeting for the installation ceremonies and saw Aaron and Abihu and his brothers, washed and turbaned, receive the anointing as priests of God to represent the nation before Him. Thereafter the newly installed priests remained at the entrance of the tent of meeting for seven days to complete their installation and, as Moses said, "'to fill your hand with power.' . . . And Aaron and his sons proceeded to do all the things that Jehovah had commanded by means of Moses."—Le 8:1-3, 13-36.

On the eighth day Aaron began to officiate, with Abihu and his brothers assisting. (Le 9:1-24) They witnessed the glorious manifestation of God's presence. But, evidently before the day was over, the account says that "Nadab and Abihu took up and brought each one his fire holder and put fire in them and placed incense upon it, and they began offering before Jehovah illegitimate fire, which he had not prescribed for them. At this a fire came out from before Jehovah and consumed them, so that they died before Jehovah." (Le 10:1, 2) Their corpses were carried outside the camp by Aaron's cousins at Moses' instruction. Their father and remaining brothers were instructed by God to refrain from any display of grief over their being thus cut off from the congregation.—Le 10:4-7.

Immediately thereafter God gave Aaron a warning against the use of intoxicating liquor by him or his sons at the time of serving at the tabernacle, "that you may not die." Commenting on verse 9, *The Pentateuch and Haftorahs* says: "The Rabbis connected the incident of Nadab and Abihu with this injunction against intoxicating liquors before officiating in the Sanctuary." (Edited by J. H. Hertz, London, 1972, p. 446) So, the matter of intoxication may have been involved in their grave sin, but the actual cause of their death was the violation of God's requirement for pure worship by their offering "illegitimate fire, which he had not prescribed for them."

Abihu enjoyed great honor from God and outstanding prominence before all the nation for a short while; but, whether from ambition, an inflated ego, or due to a trifling attitude toward God's instructions, his privileges were short-lived, and he died childless.—Nu 3:2-4; 26:60, 61; 1Ch 24:1, 2.

ABIHUD (A·bi′hud) [possibly, Father Is Dignity]. A descendant of Benjamin through his firstborn, Bela.—1Ch 8:1-3.

ABIJAH (A·bi′jah) [My Father Is Jehovah]. In 2 Kings 18:2 Abi occurs as an abbreviation of this name. Abijam is another variant found in the Masoretic text at 1 Kings 14:31; 15:1, 7, 8. However, in 1 Kings 14:31 about 12 Hebrew manuscripts and the Bomberg edition of the Hebrew Bible of Jacob ben Hayim (1524-1525) read "Abijah."

1. A grandson of Benjamin, listed in seventh position among Becher's nine sons.—1Ch 7:8.

2. According to the Masoretic text, the wife of Hezron, a grandson of Judah by his daughter-in-law Tamar. This Abijah may have been the mother of Ashhur the father of Tekoa.—1Ch 2:4, 5, 24; see HEZRON No. 2.

3. The prophet Samuel's second son, who, together with his elder brother Joel, was appointed by his aging father to be a judge of Israel at Beer-sheba. Because they perverted judgment, accepted bribes, and extorted unjust profits, the older men of Israel demanded that Samuel appoint a king to rule over them.—1Sa 8:1-5; 1Ch 6:28.

4. A priestly descendant of Aaron, who in King David's day was recognized as head of one of the paternal houses of Israel. David divided the priesthood into 24 divisions, each to serve at the sanctuary for a one-week period every six months. The paternal house of Abijah was chosen by lot to head the eighth division and thereafter it was known as "the division of Abijah." (1Ch 24:3-10; Lu 1:5) So it is said that priest Zechariah, the father of John the Baptizer, belonged to "the division of Abijah."

5. One of Rehoboam's 28 sons, also called Abijam, who became the second king of the two-tribe kingdom of Judah and reigned from 980 to 978 B.C.E. (1Ki 14:31–15:8) He was a regal descendant of David on both his father's and his mother's side, the 16th generation from Abraham in the royal lineage of Jesus Christ. (1Ch 3:10; Mt 1:7) Of Rehoboam's 18 wives and 60 concubines, Maacah (called Micaiah in 2 Chronicles 13:2), the granddaughter of Absalom, was his most beloved and was favored above the others by having her son Abijah chosen as successor to the throne, although he was not Rehoboam's firstborn son.—2Ch 11:20-22.

With the ascension of Abijah to the throne in the 18th year of King Jeroboam I of Israel, the hostilities between the northern and southern kingdoms resumed, and war ensued. Drawn up in battle formation against Judah's chosen army of 400,-000 mighty men of war were Jeroboam's 800,000 warriors. Undaunted by such odds, Abijah, in an impassioned speech, addressed himself to Jeroboam's crowd, condemning their idolatrous calf worship and reminding them that Jehovah's covenant with David was for a never-ending kingdom. "With us there is at the head the true God," declared Abijah, therefore "do not fight against Jeho-

vah . . . for you will not prove successful."—2Ch 12:16–13:12.

In the violent battle that ensued, Jeroboam's ambush was providentially thwarted and half a million of his men were destroyed, thus breaking Jeroboam's military power. Even the city of Bethel, where one of the detestable golden calves together with an apostate priesthood had been installed, was captured. And all of this, because Abijah had "leaned upon Jehovah." (2Ch 13:13-20) Nevertheless, Abijah went on walking in the sins of his father Rehoboam by allowing the high places, sacred pillars, and even the male temple prostitutes to continue in the land. "His heart did not prove to be complete with Jehovah his God." (1Ki 14:22-24; 15:3) During his lifetime he had 14 wives and 38 children, and upon his death his son Asa succeeded him upon the throne.—2Ch 13:21; 14:1.

6. The son of King Jeroboam I of Israel who died in his youth as a judgment from Jehovah. With Jeroboam's apostasy, adversity began plaguing his house, including the desperate sickness of young Abijah. Thereupon Jeroboam disguised the identity of his queen and sent her to consult the aged and blind prophet Ahijah at Shiloh. But Jehovah cannot be deceived. Through his prophet Ahijah, Jehovah declared that He would exterminate the male heirs of Jeroboam "just as one clears away the dung until it is disposed of." (1Ki 14:10; 15:25-30) Abijah, however, was the only descendant of Jeroboam who was honorably buried "for the reason that something good toward Jehovah" had been found in him.—1Ki 14:1-18.

7. The wife of King Ahaz of Judah and the mother of King Hezekiah. She was the daughter of Zechariah. At 2 Kings 18:2 her name is abbreviated as Abi.—2Ch 29:1.

8. One of the family heads of priests in the days of Zerubbabel and Jeshua following the Babylonian exile. Abijah is listed among more than 20 "heads of the priests and their brothers" who returned to Jerusalem with Zerubbabel. (Ne 12:1-7) Quite likely he was on hand at the laying of the temple foundation in the second year when the priestly services were reorganized. (Ezr 3:8-10) A generation later, in the days of Joiakim and Nehemiah, Abijah's priestly family was represented by Zichri.—Ne 12:12, 17, 26.

9. A priest, or the forefather of one, who, in the days of Nehemiah, participated in the sealing of the "trustworthy arrangement" or resolution to Jehovah. (Ne 9:38–10:8) If this was the same Abijah listed as No. 8, as suggested by some, then he would have been more than 100 years old.

ABIJAM. See ABIJAH No. 5.

ABILENE (Ab·i·le′ne). A Roman district, or tetrarchy, in the region of the Anti-Lebanon mountains N of Mount Hermon. It was named after its capital, Abila, a city situated in a picturesque gorge by the bank of the river Abanah (modern Barada).

At Luke 3:1 we are told that in the 15th year of Tiberius Caesar (28/29 C.E.) the district was ruled by Lysanias. This fact is confirmed by an inscription found at Abila in connection with a temple dedication dating from the reign of Tiberius. This inscription bears the name "Lysanias the tetrarch." Previously, Abilene had formed part of the kingdom of Herod the Great, but following his death, about the year 1 B.C.E., it was included in the province of Syria. Josephus records that the tetrarchy of Lysanias was joined to Palestine, in 37 C.E., under Herod Agrippa I, and that it was thereafter bestowed upon Herod Agrippa II by Claudius, in 53 C.E.

ABIMAEL (A·bim′a·el). A descendant of Shem through Arpachshad. His father was Joktan, whose brother, Peleg, was an ancestor of Abraham. (Ge 10:28; 1Ch 1:17-27) It is likely that Abimael and his 12 brothers were the progenitors of 13 different Arabian tribes that settled in the Arabian Peninsula.

ABIMELECH (A·bim′e·lech) [My Father Is King]. Either a personal name or an official title of several Philistine kings, perhaps similar to the title Pharaoh among the Egyptians and Caesar among the Romans.

1. The king of the city of Gerar, where Abraham and Sarah took up temporary residence in about 1919 B.C.E. Thinking the couple were brother and sister, he took Sarah to become his wife but, providentially, did not touch her. Warned by Jehovah in a dream, the king returned Sarah to Abraham together with compensation consisting of livestock and slaves and, in addition, a thousand shekels of silver (c. $2,200) as a guarantee of Sarah's chastity. Sometime later this king concluded a covenant of peace and mutual confidence with Abraham at Beer-sheba.—Ge 20:1-18; 21:22-34.

2. Possibly another king of Gerar at the time Isaac went there because of a famine. This was after the death of Abraham in 1843 B.C.E. Isaac, like his father Abraham, attempted to pass Rebekah off as his sister, but when the king, by accident, discovered she was Isaac's wife, he issued a public decree granting them protection. Isaac's God-given prosperity, however, became the object of

envy, and so the king requested Isaac to move out. Sometime later this king of Gerar concluded a covenant of peace with Isaac similar to the one his predecessor had made with Abraham.—Ge 26:1-31.

3. The Philistine king of the city of Gath in David's day.—Ps 34:Sup; see ACHISH.

4. A son of Judge Gideon born to his concubine at Shechem. After his father's death, Abimelech with presumptuous impudence sought to make himself king. Cunningly, he appealed to the landowners of Shechem through his mother's influential family. Upon obtaining their financial support he hired some ruffians, went to his father's house at Ophrah, and there massacred his half brothers upon a single stone. Of the 70 half brothers, only the youngest, Jotham, escaped the slaughter.

Abimelech was then proclaimed king, but Jehovah allowed a bad spirit to develop between the Shechemites and their new "king," in order to avenge the bloodguilt of all those connected with the conspiracy. A revolt was organized by Gaal. Abimelech quickly crushed it, captured and destroyed the city of Shechem, and sowed it with salt. Then he attacked the vault of the house, or sanctuary, of El-berith and set it afire, and in the conflagration about a thousand of his previous collaborators, the landowners of the tower of Shechem who had taken refuge there, were burned to death. Immediately Abimelech followed up this success by attacking Thebez to the N, only to have a woman on the city tower hurl an upper millstone down upon his head. Abimelech's three-year "reign" came to an end when his armor-bearer, in compliance with his dying request, ran him through with the sword, so that it could not be said that a woman had killed him.—Jg 8:30, 31; 9:1-57; 2Sa 11:21.

5. The Masoretic text, followed by the *King James Version,* reads "Abimelech" in 1 Chronicles 18:16. The Greek *Septuagint,* Latin *Vulgate,* Syriac *Peshitta,* and 12 Hebrew manuscripts read "Ahimelech," which is in agreement with 2 Samuel 8:17.

ABINADAB (A·bin′a·dab) [Father Is Willing (Noble; Generous)].

1. An inhabitant of the city of Kiriath-jearim in the territory of Judah about 14 km (8.5 mi) WNW of Jerusalem, in whose home the ark of the covenant was kept for a time.

When the sacred Ark was brought up from Beth-shemesh after its disastrous seven-month sojourn among the Philistines, it was deposited in the home of Abinadab, and his son Eleazar was sanctified to guard it. Here in this home the Ark remained for some 70 years, until David arranged to transfer it to Jerusalem. During the transfer another of Abinadab's sons, Uzzah, dropped dead in his tracks when Jehovah's anger blazed against him, because of his touching the Ark in disregard of the command at Numbers 4:15.—1Sa 6:20–7:1; 2Sa 6:1-7; 1Ch 13:6-10.

2. The second son of Jesse, and one of David's three older brothers who went to war with Saul against the Philistines.—1Sa 16:8; 17:13.

3. One of the sons of King Saul who was slain by the Philistines at Mount Gilboa.—1Sa 31:2; 1Ch 9:39.

4. The father of one of King Solomon's 12 food-supply deputies. This deputized "son of Abinadab," who is also called Ben-abinadab, married Solomon's daughter Taphath, and was assigned to provide food for Solomon's household one month out of the year from all the mountain ridge of Dor. —1Ki 4:7, 11.

ABINOAM (A·bin′o·am) [Father Is Pleasantness]. The father of Judge Barak, and a descendant of Naphtali. He was evidently a resident of the refuge city of Kedesh in the territory of Naphtali.—Jg 4:6, 12; 5:1, 12.

ABIRAM (A·bi′ram) [Father Is High (Exalted)].

1. A Reubenite, the son of Eliab and brother of Dathan and Nemuel. He was a family head and one of the principal men in Israel at the time of the Exodus from Egypt.—Nu 26:5-9.

Abiram and his brother Dathan supported Korah the Levite in his rebellion against the authority of Moses and Aaron. A third Reubenite, named On, is also included in the initial stage of the rebellion but thereafter receives no mention. (Nu 16:1) Having gathered a group of 250 chieftains, who were "men of fame," these men accused Moses and Aaron of arbitrarily elevating themselves over the rest of the congregation. (Nu 16:1-3) From Moses' words to Korah it is clear that Korah and his followers among the Levites sought the priesthood that had been conferred on Aaron (Nu 16:4-11); but this was evidently not the case with Abiram and Dathan, who were Reubenites. Moses dealt separately with them, and their rejection of his call for them to appear before him contains accusations directed solely against Moses, with no mention made of Aaron. They decried Moses' leadership of the nation and said that he was 'trying to play the prince over them to the limit,' and that he had failed in making good the promise of leading them into any land flowing with milk and honey. Moses' prayer to Jehovah in answer to

these accusations likewise contains a defense of his own actions, not those of Aaron.—Nu 16:12-15.

From this it would appear that the rebellion was two-pronged and aimed not only at the Aaronic priesthood but also at Moses' position as administrator of God's instructions. (Ps 106:16) The situation may have seemed opportune for organizing popular sentiment toward a change, since shortly before this the people had severely complained against Moses, had talked of appointing a new head to lead the nation back to Egypt, and had even talked of stoning Joshua and Caleb for upholding Moses and Aaron. (Nu 14:1-10) Reuben was Jacob's firstborn son but lost his right to the inheritance as such because of wrong action. (1Ch 5:1) Thus, Dathan and Abiram may have been expressing resentment at Moses the Levite's exercise of authority over them, because of desiring to regain the lost primacy of their forefather. Numbers 26:9, however, shows that their struggle was not only against Moses and Aaron but also "against Jehovah," who had divinely commissioned Moses and Aaron to occupy positions of authority.

Since the family of the Kohathites (in which Korah's family was included) encamped on the S side of the tabernacle, the same side as did the Reubenites, it is possible that Korah's tent was nearby those of Dathan and Abiram. (Nu 2:10; 3:29) At the time of God's expression of judgment, Dathan and Abiram stood at the entrances of their tents, while Korah and 250 rebel supporters were gathered at the entrance of the tent of meeting with their incense holders in their hands. Then, following Moses' call to the rest of the people to withdraw from around the tents of the three ringleaders of the rebellion, God manifested his condemnation of their disrespectful course by causing the ground to open up beneath the tents of these men, swallowing up Dathan and Abiram, and their households. (Nu 16:16-35; De 11:6; Ps 106:17) Korah's household, with the exception of his sons, likewise perished. Korah himself died with the 250 rebels, destroyed by fire before the tabernacle. (Nu 16:35; 26:10, 11) Thus the rebellion against divinely assigned authority came to a swift termination, and for his share in it, Abiram's name was wiped out of Israel.

2. The firstborn son of Hiel the Bethelite. At Joshua 6:26 Joshua's oath is recorded concerning the destroyed city of Jericho, foretelling that whoever should rebuild it would do so at the loss of his firstborn son. Abiram's father, Hiel, ignored this oath and, during the reign of King Ahab

(c. 940-920 B.C.E.) some five centuries after Joshua's time, he laid Jericho's foundations. Abiram, his son, died, evidently prematurely as a historically recorded fulfillment of the prophecy.—1Ki 16:34.

ABISHAG (Ab'i·shag). A young virgin from the town of Shunem, N of Jezreel and Mount Gilboa, in the territory of Issachar. (Jos 19:17-23) She was "beautiful in the extreme" and was chosen by David's servants to become the nurse and companion of the king during his final days.—1Ki 1:1-4.

David was now about 70 years of age (2Sa 5:4, 5), and as a result of debilitation he had little body heat. Abishag waited on him during the day, doubtless brightening the surroundings with her youthful freshness and beauty, and at night she 'lay in the king's bosom' to give him warmth, but "the king himself had no intercourse with her." Nevertheless, the attitude later manifested by Solomon regarding her indicates that Abishag was viewed as being in the position of wife or concubine of David. As such, by a rule in the ancient East, she would become the property of David's heir at the time of his death.

The account concerning Abishag directly precedes the account of the attempt at gaining the crown by the one who was probably David's oldest surviving son, Adonijah, and would seem to be so placed to give understanding to Adonijah's subsequent action during Solomon's reign. Solomon, after ascending the throne, had placed Adonijah on conditional pardon. Now Adonijah persuaded Solomon's mother, Bath-sheba, to ask Solomon to give him Abishag as his wife. Solomon, convinced that Adonijah's request was not due alone to Abishag's beauty but, rather, indicated a subtle effort to strengthen Adonijah's claim to the throne, reacted angrily, revoked Adonijah's pardon, and ordered his death. (1Ki 2:13-25) No further mention is made of Abishag, but it is probable that she continued as one of Solomon's wives or concubines.—See ADONIJAH No. 1.

ABISHAI (A·bish'ai) [possibly, Father Is (Exists)]. The son of David's sister or half sister Zeruiah and brother of Joab and Asahel.—2Sa 2:18; 1Ch 2:15, 16.

Abishai came to be more distinguished for his prowess than the 30 mighty warriors over whom he served as chief, his reputation even rivaling those of David's three most mighty men, for he once struck down 300 of the enemy single-handed, but "to the rank of the first three he did not come."—2Sa 23:18, 19.

Abishai loyally supported his uncle David in all his military campaigns but tended to be impulsive and ruthless and on occasion had to be restrained. For example, when he and David stole into Saul's military camp by night he would have pinned sleeping Saul, "the anointed of Jehovah," to the earth with Saul's own spear had not David restrained him. (1Sa 26:6-9) When Absalom rebelled, Abishai had to be held back twice from executing king-cursing Shimei. However, David was not able to prevent Abishai from collaborating in the death of Abner.—2Sa 3:30; 16:9-11; 19:21-23.

Abishai was noted for his taking the lead in striking down 18,000 Edomites and, again, in leading in the rout of the Ammonites. He also cooperated in putting down the rebellion of Sheba, a good-for-nothing Benjaminite. In David's last recorded battle had it not been for Abishai, he would have lost his life at the hand of a Philistine of great stature.—1Ch 18:12; 19:11-15; 2Sa 20:1, 6; 21:15-17.

ABISHALOM. See ABSALOM.

ABISHUA (Ab·i·shu'a) [possibly, Father Is Help].

1. A Benjamite of the family of Bela. (1Ch 8:1-4) Though he appears to be a son of Bela, the variance between the accounts at Numbers 26:40, 1 Chronicles 7:7, and 1 Chronicles 8:1-4 causes some to believe the word "sons" may mean, rather, "descendants."

2. The son of Phinehas and a great-grandson of Aaron. He was the father of Bukki. (1Ch 6:4, 5, 50, 51) At Ezra 7:1-5 he is shown to have been one of Ezra's forefathers. Josephus (*Jewish Antiquities*, V, 361, 362 [xi, 5]; VIII, 12 [i, 3]) refers to Abishua (called Abiezer in Book V) as the high priest, which, if accepted, would make him the fourth high priest of Israel. This would harmonize with Jehovah's promise made to Abishua's father, Phinehas, that the priesthood would remain in his family.—Nu 25:11-13.

ABISHUR (A·bi'shur) [Father Is a [Protective] Wall]. A descendant of Judah through the family line of Hezron, of the house of Jerahmeel. He was evidently the second son of Shammai and became the father of two sons by his wife Abihail.—1Ch 2:28, 29.

ABITAL (A·bi'tal) [Father Is Dew]. One of six wives through whom David had sons during the seven and a half years he reigned in Hebron (1077-1070 B.C.E.). Her son was named Shephatiah.—2Sa 3:4; 1Ch 3:3.

ABITUB (A·bi′tub) [Father Is Goodness]. A Benjamite, evidently the son of Shaharaim by his wife Hushim.—1Ch 8:8, 11.

ABIUD (A·bi′ud) [possibly, Father Is Dignity]. The Grecized or Anglicized form of the Hebrew name Abihud. A descendant of Zerubbabel and an ancestor of Christ Jesus. (Mt 1:13) The term "father" as used by Matthew may have the meaning of "forefather." Some scholars suggest that he may be the same as "Joda" at Luke 3:26. However, it is not necessary to relate these persons as being the same individual, since the genealogical lines given by Matthew and Luke are only parallel, not identical, while those at First Chronicles are independent. Abiud's son, Eliakim, is also included in the line of descent of the Messiah.—Mt 1:13.

ABNER (Ab′ner) [Father Is a Lamp]. Son of Ner, of the tribe of Benjamin. First Samuel 14:50, 51 evidently refers to Abner as "the uncle of Saul," though this phrase in the Hebrew can be applied either to Abner or to Ner, his father. Josephus speaks of Abner as Saul's cousin, and of their fathers, Ner and Kish, as brothers. (*Jewish Antiquities,* VI, 129, 130 [vi, 6]) However, the inspired history at 1 Chronicles 8:33 and 9:39 seems to weigh heavily in favor of Kish as being the son of Ner and, hence, the brother of Abner. This would make Abner the uncle of Saul.—See also the chart under ABIEL No. 1.

Abner served as chief of the army for Saul, and his fighting force sometimes assumed major proportions, upwards of 200,000 men. (1Sa 15:4) On special occasions he sat next to the king at the banquet table. (1Sa 20:25) Though Abner was undoubtedly a powerful and valiant man, Abner was chided by David, when the latter was a fugitive in the Wilderness of Ziph, for having failed to guard Saul's person properly as his lord and "the anointed of Jehovah."—1Sa 26:14-16.

Following Saul's death in the crushing defeat administered by the Philistines, Abner withdrew across the Jordan to Mahanaim in Gilead, taking Saul's son Ish-bosheth with him. Though David had been proclaimed king in Hebron by the tribe of Judah, Abner set up Ish-bosheth as a rival king in Mahanaim. Abner was clearly the power behind the throne and in time obtained the support of all the tribes except Judah on behalf of Ish-bosheth.—2Sa 2:8-10.

Eventually, the armies of the two opposing kings met in a test of strength at the Pool of Gibeon in the territory of Benjamin, about a third of the way from Hebron to Mahanaim. After the two armies had sized each other up, Abner pro-posed a contest between a dozen young warriors from each side. The sides were so evenly matched that a mutual slaughter resulted, provoking a full-scale combat between the two armies. Abner's forces lost 18 men for every one of Joab's soldiers and retreated toward the wilderness.—2Sa 2:12-17, 30, 31.

Abner, pursued by Joab's fleet-footed brother Asahel, urged him repeatedly to turn his attention elsewhere and avoid a deadly encounter with him. When Asahel kept refusing, Abner finally made a powerful backstroke and killed Asahel with the butt end of his spear, running him through in the abdomen. (2Sa 2:18-23) At Abner's appeal, Joab finally called a halt to the pursuit at sundown, and the two armies began marches back to their respective capitals. Their stamina can be seen from the 80 km (50 mi) or more that Abner's forces marched, down into the basin of the Jordan, fording the river, then up the Jordan Valley to the hills of Gilead, where they made their way to Mahanaim. After burying Asahel in Bethlehem (perhaps on the following day), Joab's men had a night-long march of over 22 km (14 mi) through the mountains to Hebron.—2Sa 2:29-32.

Abner supported Ish-bosheth's declining regime but also strengthened his own position, perhaps with an eye on the kingship, since he was, after all, the brother of Saul's father. When taken to task by Ish-bosheth for having relations with one of Saul's concubines (an act allowable only to the dead king's heir), Abner angrily announced the transfer of his support to David's side. (2Sa 3:6-11) He made overtures to David, stressing his own position as virtual ruler of the rest of Israel outside Judah. Satisfying David's requirement of the return of his wife Michal, Abner now privately approached the heads of the 11 tribes separated from Judah to build up their favor toward Jehovah's appointed king, David. (2Sa 3:12-19) Thereafter he was warmly received by David at his capital in Hebron, and that same day set out to persuade all the tribes to make a covenant with David. But Joab, absent on a raid, returned and, after denouncing Abner as a conniving spy, personally called him back and tricked Abner into a position where he could kill him.—2Sa 3:20-27.

With Abner's death, any hoped-for support for Ish-bosheth collapsed and Ish-bosheth was soon assassinated by traitorous men. With this the rule of the house of Saul came to a complete end.—2Sa 4:1-3, 5-12.

Many years later, while nearing the time of his own death, David remembered Abner's death (as well as Amasa's) and charged Solomon with the responsibility of removing the stain of bloodguilt that Joab had brought on David's house. (1Ki 2:1, 5, 6) Shortly thereafter, Abner's slayer, Joab, was executed at Solomon's order.—1Ki 2:31-34.

Only one son of Abner is listed, Jaasiel, who was a leader in the tribe of Benjamin during David's reign. (1Ch 27:21) First Chronicles 26:28 also mentions Abner's contributions toward the tabernacle from spoils won as chief of the army.

ABOMINATION OF DESOLATION. See DISGUSTING THING, LOATHSOME THING.

ABORTION.
The expulsion of an embryo or fetus before it can live on its own. Common use often distinguishes between *abortion* and *miscarriage,* the former being defined as the deliberate and induced emptying of a pregnant uterus, the latter being considered as the accidental and unavoidable interruption of pregnancy. The distinction between abortion and miscarriage is not made in the Bible; there the terms are used in a broader and interchangeable sense. The Hebrew *sha·khal',* meaning "suffer an abortion" (Ex 23:26), is also rendered "bereave" (De 32:25), 'bereave of children' (Le 26:22), 'miscarry' (Ho 9:14), and "prove fruitless" (Mal 3:11). The Hebrew word *yoh·tse'th,* rendered "abortion" in Psalm 144:14, is from a root meaning "come out." (Compare Ge 27:30.) The expressions "miscarriage" and "one prematurely born" (Ps 58:8; Ec 6:3) render the Hebrew word *ne'phel,* which comes from the root *na·phal',* meaning "fall."—Compare Isa 26:18.

Unavoidable abortion or miscarriage may be caused by accident, infectious disease, mental or physical stress and strain, or because of a general organic weakness on the part of the mother. The waters near Jericho were death dealing, causing miscarriages, until Jehovah's prophet Elisha healed them.—2Ki 2:19-22.

Deliberately to induce abortion or miscarriage by artificial means, by the use of drugs, or by medical operation, the sole purpose of which is to avoid the birth of an unwanted child, is an act of high crime in the sight of God. Life as a precious gift from God is sacred. Hence God's law to Moses protected the life of an unborn baby against more than criminal abortion, for if in a fracas between men a pregnant woman suffered an accident fatal to her or the child, "then you must give soul for soul." (Ex 21:22-25) Of course, before applying that penalty, the circumstances and degree of deliberateness were taken into consideration by the judges. (Compare Nu 35:22-24, 31.) But emphasizing the seriousness of any deliberate attempt to cause injury, Dr. J. Glenn comments:

"The viable embryo in the uterus *IS* a human individual, and therefore destroying it, is a violation of the sixth commandment."—*The Bible and Modern Medicine,* 1963, p. 176.

Properly viewed, the fruitage of the womb is a blessing of Jehovah. (Le 26:9; Ps 127:3) Hence, in promising to prosper Israel, God gave assurance of successful culmination of pregnancy and the bringing forth of children, saying: "Neither a woman suffering an abortion nor a barren woman will exist in your land." (Ex 23:26) As indicated in the prayer of the righteous, on the other hand, evidence of God's disfavor to his enemies would be their having miscarrying wombs and their becoming like miscarriages that never see the sun.—Ps 58:8; Ho 9:14.

Job in his misery contemplated that it would have been better had he been "a hidden miscarriage." "Why from the womb did I not proceed to die?" this tormented man cried out. (Job 3:11-16) Solomon, too, reasoned that a prematurely expelled fetus is better off than the person who lives a long time but who never comes to enjoy life.—Ec 6:3.

Contagious abortion, a disease characterized by premature birth, may occur among animals such as cattle, horses, sheep, and goats. Accidental abortion due to neglect or disease of domestic animals has also been known since the days of the patriarchs Jacob and Job.—Ge 31:38; Job 21:10.

ABRAHAM
(A'bra·ham) [Father of a Crowd (Multitude)]. The name given by Jehovah to Abram (meaning "Father Is High (Exalted)") when he was 99 years old, and when God was reaffirming His promise that Abraham's offspring would become many.—Ge 17:5.

Family Origin and Early History. Abraham was the tenth generation from Noah through Shem and was born 352 years after the Deluge, in 2018 B.C.E. Although listed first among the three sons of Terah, at Genesis 11:26, Abraham was not the firstborn. The Scriptures show that Terah was 70 years old when his first son was born, and that Abraham was born 60 years later when his father Terah was 130 years old. (Ge 11:32; 12:4) Evidently Abraham is listed first among his father's sons because of his outstanding faithfulness and prominence in the Scriptures, a practice that is followed in the case of several other outstanding men of faith such as Shem and Isaac.—Ge 5:32; 11:10; 1Ch 1:28.

Abraham was a native of the Chaldean city of Ur, a thriving metropolis located in the land of Shinar, near the present junction of the Euphrates and Tigris rivers. It was about 240 km (150 mi) SE of Nimrod's onetime royal city of Babel, or Babylon, so notorious for its unfinished Tower of Babel.

In Abraham's time, the city of Ur was steeped in Babylonish idolatry and the worship of its patron moon-god Sin. (Jos 24:2, 14, 15) Nevertheless, Abraham proved to be a man of faith in Jehovah God, even as his forefathers Shem and Noah; and as a consequence, he earned the reputation "the father of all those having faith while in uncircumcision." (Ro 4:11) Since true faith is based on accurate knowledge, Abraham may have received his understanding by personal association with Shem (their lives overlapped by 150 years). Abraham knew and used the name of Jehovah; to quote him: "Jehovah the Most High God, Producer of heaven and earth," "Jehovah, the God of the heavens and the God of the earth."—Ge 14:22; 24:3.

While Abraham was still living in Ur, "before he took up residence in Haran," Jehovah commanded him to move out to a strange land, leaving behind friends and relatives. (Ac 7:2-4; Ge 15:7; Ne 9:7) There in that country that He would show Abraham, God said he would make out of him a great nation. At the time, Abraham was married to his half sister Sarah, but they were childless and both were old. So it would take great faith to obey, but obey he did.

Terah, now around 200 years old and still the family's patriarchal head, agreed to accompany Abraham and Sarah on this long journey, and it is for this reason that Terah as father is credited with making the move toward Canaan. (Ge 11:31) It appears that fatherless Lot, Abraham's nephew, was adopted by his childless uncle and aunt and so accompanied them. Northwestward the caravan moved, some 960 km (600 mi), until they reached Haran, which was an important junction on the E-W trade routes. Haran is located where two wadis join to form a stream that reaches the Balikh River in the winter, about 110 km (68 mi) above where the Balikh empties into the Euphrates River. Here Abraham remained until the death of his father Terah.—MAP, Vol. 1, p. 330.

Sojourn in Canaan. Now 75 years old, Abraham began to move his household out of Haran to the land of Canaan, where he lived out the remaining hundred years of his life in tents as an alien and migratory resident. (Ge 12:4) It was following the death of his father Terah that Abraham went out from Haran in 1943 B.C.E. and crossed the Euphrates River, evidently on the 14th day of the month that later became known as Nisan. (Ge 11:32; Ex 12:40-43, *LXX*) It was at that time that the covenant between Jehovah and Abraham went into effect, and the 430-year period of temporary residence until the making of the Law covenant with Israel began.—Ex 12:40-42; Ga 3:17.

Evidently Abraham, with his flocks and herds, traveled down through Damascus and on to Shechem (located 48 km [30 mi] N of Jerusalem), near the big trees of Moreh. (Ge 12:6) Here Jehovah appeared again to Abraham, confirming and enlarging His covenant promise by declaring: "To your seed I am going to give this land." (Ge 12:7) Abraham not only built an altar to Jehovah there but, as he moved southward through the land, he built other altars along the way; and he called on the name of Jehovah. (Ge 12:8, 9) In time a severe famine compelled Abraham to move temporarily to Egypt, and to protect his life, he represented Sarah as his sister. This resulted in Pharaoh's taking beautiful Sarah into his household to be his wife, but before he could violate her, Jehovah had Pharaoh give her back. Abraham then returned to Canaan to the campsite between Bethel and Ai and again called "on the name of Jehovah."—Ge 12:10–13:4.

It now became necessary, because of the increasing size of their flocks and herds, for Abraham and Lot to separate. Lot selected the basin of the lower Jordan, a well-watered region "like the garden of Jehovah," and later established his camp near Sodom. (Ge 13:5-13) Abraham, for his part, after being told to travel about through the length and breadth of the land, came to dwell among the big trees of Mamre in Hebron, 30 km (19 mi) SSW of Jerusalem.—Ge 13:14-18.

When four allied kings, headed by the Elamite king Chedorlaomer, were successful in crushing a revolt of five Canaanite kings, Sodom and Gomorrah were sacked, and Lot was taken captive together with all of his property. Abraham, upon learning of this, quickly mustered 318 of his trained household servants. With his confederates Aner, Eshcol, and Mamre, he made a forced march in hot pursuit perhaps as much as 300 km (190 mi) northward to beyond Damascus and, with Jehovah's help, defeated a far superior force. Lot was thus rescued, and the stolen property was recovered. (Ge 14:1-16, 23, 24) As Abraham was returning from this great victory a "priest of the Most High God," Melchizedek, who was also the king of Salem, came out and blessed him, and Abraham, in turn, "gave him a tenth of everything."—Ge 14:17-20.

Appearance of the Promised Seed. Since Sarah continued to be barren, it appeared that Eliezer the faithful house steward from Damascus would receive Abraham's inheritance. Nevertheless, Jehovah again reassured Abraham that his own offspring would become uncountable, as the stars of heaven, and so Abraham "put faith in Jehovah; and he proceeded to count it to him as righteousness," even though this occurred years before Abraham was circumcised. (Ge 15:1-6; Ro 4:9, 10) Jehovah then concluded a formal covenant over animal sacrifices with Abraham, and at the same time, he revealed that Abraham's offspring would be afflicted for a period of 400 years, even being taken into slavery.—Ge 15:7-21; see COVENANT.

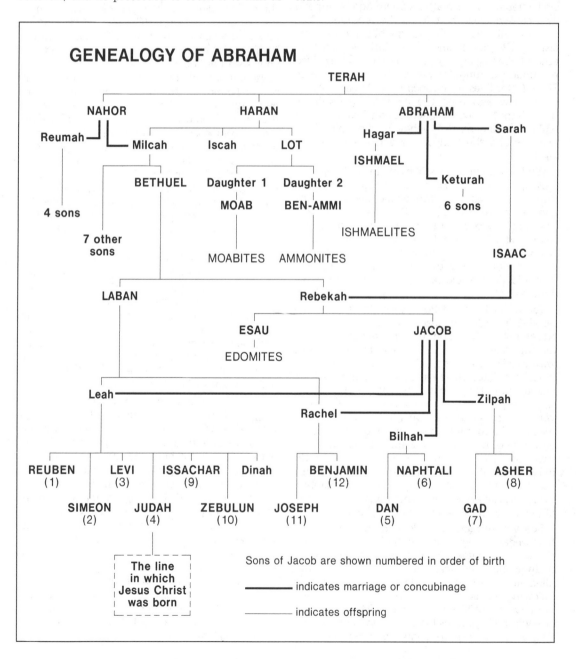

GENEALOGY OF ABRAHAM

The line in which Jesus Christ was born

Sons of Jacob are shown numbered in order of birth

——— indicates marriage or concubinage

——— indicates offspring

Time passed. They had now been in Canaan for about ten years, yet Sarah continued barren. She therefore proposed to substitute her Egyptian maidservant Hagar so that she might have a child by her. Abraham consented. And so in 1932 B.C.E., when Abraham was 86 years old, Ishmael was born. (Ge 16:3, 15, 16) More time passed. In 1919 B.C.E., when Abraham was 99 years old, as a sign or seal to testify to the special covenant relationship existing between himself and Abraham, Jehovah commanded that all the males of Abraham's household be circumcised. At the same time Jehovah changed his name from Abram to Abraham, "because a father of a crowd of nations I will make you." (Ge 17:5, 9-27; Ro 4:11) Soon after, three materialized angels, whom Abraham received hospitably in the name of Jehovah, promised that Sarah herself would conceive and give birth to a son, yes, within the coming year!—Ge 18:1-15.

And what an eventful year it proved to be! Sodom and Gomorrah were destroyed. Abraham's nephew and his two daughters barely escaped. A famine drove Abraham and his wife to Gerar, only to have the king of that Philistine city take Sarah for his harem. Jehovah intervened; Sarah was released; and at the appointed time, 1918 B.C.E., Isaac, the long-promised heir, was born when Abraham was 100 years old and Sarah was 90. (Ge 18:16–21:7) Five years later, when Isaac's 19-year-old half brother Ishmael poked fun at him, Abraham was compelled to dismiss Ishmael and his mother Hagar. It was then, in 1913 B.C.E., that the 400 years of affliction upon Abraham's offspring began.—Ge 21:8-21; 15:13; Ga 4:29.

The supreme test of Abraham's faith came about 20 years later. According to Jewish tradition, Isaac was now 25 years old. (*Jewish Antiquities,* by F. Josephus, I, 227 [xiii, 2]) In obedience to Jehovah's instructions Abraham took Isaac and traveled N from Beer-sheba at the Negeb to Mount Moriah, situated directly N of Salem. There he built an altar and prepared to offer up Isaac, the promised seed, as a burnt sacrifice. And indeed Abraham "as good as offered up Isaac," for "he reckoned that God was able to raise him up even from the dead." Only at the last moment did Jehovah intervene and provide a ram as a substitute for Isaac on the sacrificial altar. It was, therefore, this implicit faith backed up by complete obedience that moved Jehovah to reinforce his covenant with Abraham with a sworn oath, a special legal guarantee.—Ge 22:1-18; Heb 6:13-18; 11:17-19.

When Sarah died at Hebron in 1881 B.C.E. at the age of 127, it was necessary for Abraham to pur-chase a burial plot, for indeed he was only an alien resident owning no land in Canaan. So he bought a field with its cave at Machpelah near Mamre from the sons of Heth. (Ge 23:1-20; see PURCHASE.) Three years later, when Isaac reached the age of 40, Abraham sent his oldest servant, likely Eliezer, back to Mesopotamia in order to find a suitable wife, one who was also a true worshiper of Jehovah, for his son. Rebekah, who was the grandniece of Abraham, proved to be Jehovah's choice.—Ge 24:1-67.

"Furthermore, Abraham again took a wife," Keturah, and thereafter fathered six additional sons, so that from Abraham sprang not only the Israelites, Ishmaelites, and Edomites but also Medanites, Midianites, and others. (Ge 25:1, 2; 1Ch 1:28, 32, 34) Thus it was that Jehovah's prophetic utterance was fulfilled in Abraham: "A father of a crowd of nations I will make you." (Ge 17:5) Finally, at the good old age of 175, Abraham died, in 1843 B.C.E., and was buried by his sons Isaac and Ishmael in the cave of Machpelah. (Ge 25:7-10) Prior to his death Abraham gave gifts to the sons of his secondary wives and sent them away, so that Isaac would be the sole heir of "everything he had."—Ge 25:5, 6.

Patriarchal Head and Prophet. Abraham was a very wealthy man with great flocks and herds, much silver and gold, and a very large household numbering many hundreds of servants. (Ge 12:5, 16; 13:2, 6, 7; 17:23, 27; 20:14; 24:35) For this reason the kings of Canaan considered him a powerful "chieftain" and one with whom covenants of peace should be made. (Ge 23:6; 14:13; 21:22, 23) Yet at no time did Abraham allow materialism to blind his vision of Jehovah and His promises or cause him to become proud, high-minded, or selfish.—Ge 13:9; 14:21-23.

The first occurrence of the word "prophet" in the Hebrew Scriptures refers to Abraham, though others like Enoch prophesied before him. (Ge 20:7; Jude 14) The first identified in the Scriptures as a "Hebrew" is Abraham. (Ge 14:13) Abraham, like Abel, Enoch, and Noah, was a man of faith. (Heb 11:4-9) But the first occurrence of the expression "put faith in Jehovah" is in reference to Abraham. —Ge 15:6.

Indeed, this man of unusual faith walked with God, received communications from him by means of visions and dreams, and entertained his angelic messengers. (Ge 12:1-3, 7; 15:1-8, 12-21; 18:1-15; 22:11, 12, 15-18) He was well acquainted with the name of God even though Jehovah had not at that time revealed the full significance of His name. (Ex 6:2, 3) Time after time Abraham built altars and offered up sacrifices in the name of and to the praise and glory of his God Jehovah. —Ge 12:8; 13:4, 18; 21:33; 24:40; 48:15.

As patriarchal head, Abraham allowed no idolatry or ungodliness in his household but constantly taught all his sons and servants to "keep Jehovah's way to do righteousness and judgment." (Ge 18: 19) Every male member of Abraham's household was bound by Jehovah's law to submit to circumcision. The Egyptian slave girl Hagar called on Jehovah's name in prayer. And Abraham's oldest servant in a very heart-touching prayer to Jehovah demonstrated his own faith in Abraham's God. Isaac too, in his early manhood, proved his faith and his obedience to Jehovah by allowing himself to be bound hand and foot and placed atop the altar for sacrifice.—Ge 17:10-14, 23-27; 16:13; 24:2-56.

Historicity.   Jesus and his disciples referred to Abraham more than 70 times in their conversations and writings. In his illustration of the rich man and Lazarus, Jesus referred to Abraham in a symbolic sense. (Lu 16:19-31) When his opponents boasted that they were the offspring of Abraham, Jesus was quick to point out their hypocrisy, saying: "If you are Abraham's children, do the works of Abraham." (Joh 8:31-58; Mt 3:9, 10) No, as the apostle Paul said, it is not fleshly descent that counts, but, rather, faith like that of Abraham that enables one to be declared righteous. (Ro 9:6-8; 4:1-12) Paul also identified the true seed of Abraham as Christ, along with those who belong to Christ as "heirs with reference to a promise." (Ga 3:16, 29) He also speaks of Abraham's kindness and hospitality to strangers, and in his long list in Hebrews chapter 11 of illustrious witnesses of Jehovah, Paul does not overlook Abraham. It is Paul who points out that Abraham's two women, Sarah and Hagar, figured in a symbolic drama that involved Jehovah's two covenants. (Ga 4:22-31; Heb 11:8) The Bible writer James adds that Abraham backed up his faith by righteous works and, therefore, was known as "Jehovah's friend."—Jas 2:21-23.

Archaeological discoveries have also confirmed matters related in the Biblical history of Abraham: The geographic locations of many places and customs of that period of time, such as the purchase of the field from the Hittites, the choice of Eliezer as heir, and the treatment of Hagar.

ABRAM.   See ABRAHAM.

ABRONAH   (A·bro′nah). The site of one of the encampments of the Israelites on their wilderness trek from Egypt. It is listed between Jotbathah

and Ezion-geber and has been identified with the oasis 'Ain Defiyeh ('En 'Avrona), which lies 14.5 km (9 mi) NNE of Ezion-geber.—Nu 33: 34, 35.

ABSALOM   (Ab′sa·lom) [Father [that is, God] Is Peace]. The third of six sons born to David at Hebron. His mother was Maacah the daughter of Talmai the king of Geshur. (2Sa 3:3-5) Absalom fathered three sons and one daughter. (2Sa 14:27) He is evidently called Abishalom at 1 Kings 15:2, 10.—See 2Ch 11:20, 21.

Physical beauty ran strong in Absalom's family. He was nationally praised for his outstanding beauty; his luxuriant growth of hair, doubtless made heavier by the use of oil or ointments, weighed some 200 shekels (2.3 kg; 5 lb) when annually cut. His sister Tamar was also beautiful, and his daughter, named for her aunt, was "most beautiful in appearance." (2Sa 14:25-27; 13:1) Rather than being of benefit, however, this beauty contributed to some ugly events that caused immense grief to Absalom's father, David, as well as to others, and produced great turmoil for the nation.

Murder of Amnon.   The beauty of Absalom's sister Tamar caused his older half brother Amnon to become infatuated with her. Feigning illness, Amnon contrived to have Tamar sent to his quarters to cook for him, and then he forcibly violated her. Amnon's erotic love turned to contemptuous hate and he had Tamar put out into the street. Ripping apart her striped gown that had distinguished her as a virgin daughter of the king, and with ashes on her head, Tamar was met by Absalom. He quickly sized up the situation and voiced immediate suspicion of Amnon, indicating a prior alertness to his half brother's passionate desire. Absalom instructed his sister to raise no accusation, however, and took her into his home to reside.—2Sa 13:1-20.

According to John Kitto, Absalom's taking charge of Tamar, rather than her father's doing so, was in harmony with the Eastern custom, whereby, in a polygamous family, children of the same mother are the more closely knit together and the daughters "come under the special care and protection of their brother, who, . . . in all that affects their safety and honor, is more looked to than the father himself." (*Daily Bible Illustrations,* Samuel, Saul, and David, 1857, p. 384) Much earlier, it was Levi and Simeon, two of Dinah's full brothers, who took it upon themselves to avenge their sister's dishonor.—Ge 34:25.

Hearing of his daughter's humiliation, David reacted with great anger but, perhaps due to the fact that no direct or formal accusation was made with the support of evidence or witnesses, took no judicial action against the offender. (De 19:15) Absalom may have preferred not to have an issue made of Amnon's violation of the Levitical law (Le 18:9; 20:17), to avoid unsavory publicity for his family and name, but he, nevertheless, nursed a murderous hatred for Amnon while outwardly controlling himself until the propitious moment for exacting vengeance in his own way. (Compare Pr 26:24-26; Le 19:17.) From this point forward his life is a study in perfidy, occupying the major part of six chapters of Second Samuel.—2Sa 13: 21, 22.

Two years passed. Sheepshearing time came, a festive occasion, and Absalom arranged a feast at Baal-hazor about 22 km (14 mi) NNE of Jerusalem, inviting the king's sons and David himself. When his father begged off from attending, Absalom pressed him to agree to send Amnon, his first-born, in his stead. (Pr 10:18) At the feast, when Amnon was in "a merry mood with wine," Absalom ordered his servants to slay him. The other sons headed back to Jerusalem, and Absalom went into exile with his Syrian grandfather in the kingdom of Geshur to the E of the Sea of Galilee. (2Sa 13:23-38) The "sword" foretold by the prophet Nathan had now entered David's "house" and would continue there for the rest of his life.—2Sa 12:10.

Restoration to Favor. When three years' time had eased the pain of the loss of his firstborn, David felt paternal longing for Absalom. Joab, reading his royal uncle's thoughts, by means of stratagem opened the way for David to extend a probationary pardon allowing Absalom to be repatriated but without the right to appear in his father's court. (2Sa 13:39; 14:1-24) Absalom endured this ostracized status for two years and then began maneuvering for full pardon. When Joab, as an official of the king's court, refused to visit him, Absalom peremptorily had Joab's barley field burned and, when the indignant Joab came, told him he wanted a final decision by the king and said, "If there is any error in me, he must then put me to death." When Joab relayed the message, David received his son, who thereupon fell on the ground in symbol of complete submission, and the king gave him the kiss of full pardon.—2Sa 14:28-33.

Treasonous Activity. Any natural or filial affection that Absalom had for David, however, had apparently vanished during the five years of separation from his father. Three years of association with pagan royalty may have cultivated the cor-

roding influence of ambition. Absalom might have viewed himself as destined for the throne because of being descended from royalty on both sides of the family. Since Chileab (Daniel), who was second in line of David's sons, is not mentioned after the account of his birth, it is also possible that he had died, thereby leaving Absalom as David's oldest surviving son. (2Sa 3:3; 1Ch 3:1) Nevertheless, God's promise to David of a future "seed" to inherit the throne was given *after* Absalom's birth, and hence he should have known that he was not Jehovah's choice for the kingship. (2Sa 7:12) At any rate, once restored to royal rank, Absalom began an underhanded political campaign. With consummate skill he feigned great concern for the public welfare and presented himself as a man of the people. He carefully insinuated to the people, particularly those of the tribes outside Judah, that the king's court was lacking in interest in their problems and was greatly in need of a warmhearted man like Absalom.—2Sa 15:1-6.

The phrase "at the end of forty years" found at 2 Samuel 15:7 is uncertain in its application, and in the Greek *Septuagint* (Lagardian edition), Syriac *Peshitta,* and Latin *Vulgate* it is rendered as "four years." But it is not likely that Absalom would wait a total of six years to fulfill a vow, if the "four years" were viewed as counting from the time of his complete reinstatement. (2Sa 14:28) Since a three-year famine, a war with the Philistines, and Adonijah's attempt at the throne all took place during David's reign but after the events now considered, it is evident that the writer's starting point of "forty years" would have to have begun considerably prior to the beginning of David's 40-year reign, and perhaps means 40 years from his first anointing by Samuel. This would then allow for Absalom's being still a "young man" at this point (2Sa 18:5), since he was born sometime between 1077 and 1070 B.C.E.

Absalom, feeling satisfied that he had built up a strong following throughout the realm, obtained permission from his father by means of a pretext to go to Hebron, the original capital of Judah. From there he quickly organized a full-scale conspiracy for the throne, including a nationwide web of spies to proclaim his kingship. After having invoked God's blessing on his rule by offering sacrifices, he obtained the support of his father's most respected counselor, Ahithophel. Many now swung to Absalom's side.—2Sa 15:7-12.

Faced with a major crisis and anticipating a large-scale attack, David chose to evacuate the palace along with all his household, although he had the loyal support of a large body of faithful men, including the principal priests, Abiathar and Zadok. These two he sent back to Jerusalem to serve as liaison agents. While ascending the Mount of Olives, barefoot, head covered, and weeping, David was met by Hushai, the king's "companion," whom he likewise dispatched to Jerusalem to frustrate Ahithophel's counsel. (2Sa 15:13-37) Beset by opportunists, one seeking favor, another filled with partisan spirit and venting stored-up hatred, David stands in sharp contrast to Absalom by his quiet submission and refusal to render evil for evil. Rejecting his nephew Abishai's plea for permission to cross over and 'take off the head' of the stone-throwing, cursing Shimei, David reasoned: "Here my own son, who has come forth out of my own inward parts, is looking for my soul; and how much more now a Benjaminite! Let him alone that he may call down evil, for Jehovah has said so to him! Perhaps Jehovah will see with his eye, and Jehovah will actually restore to me goodness instead of his malediction this day."—2Sa 16:1-14.

Occupying Jerusalem and the palace, Absalom accepted Hushai's apparent defection to his side after first making a sarcastic reference to Hushai's being the faithful "companion" of David. Then, acting on Ahithophel's counsel, Absalom publicly had relations with his father's concubines as proof of the complete break between himself and David and of his unrelenting determination to maintain control of the throne. (2Sa 16:15-23) In this way the latter part of Nathan's inspired prophecy saw fulfillment.—2Sa 12:11.

Ahithophel now urged Absalom to charge him with authority to lead a force against David that very night so as to administer the deathblow before David's forces could get organized. Pleased, Absalom still thought it wise to hear Hushai's opinion. Realizing David's need for time, Hushai painted a vivid picture, possibly designed to play on any lack of genuine courage in Absalom (who, till now, had displayed more arrogance and craftiness than manly valor), as well as to appeal to Absalom's vanity. Hushai recommended the taking of time first to build up an overwhelming force of men to be then commanded by Absalom himself. By Jehovah's direction, Hushai's counsel was accepted. Ahithophel, evidently realizing that Absalom's revolt would fail, committed suicide.—2Sa 17:1-14, 23.

As a precautionary measure, Hushai sent word to David of Ahithophel's counsel, and despite Absalom's efforts to catch the clandestine couriers, David received the warning and crossed over the Jordan and went up into the hills of Gilead to Mahanaim (where Ish-bosheth had had his capital). Here he was received with expressions of generosity and kindness. Preparing for the conflict, David organized his expanding forces into three divisions under Joab, Abishai, and Ittai the Gittite. Urged to remain in the city, as his presence would be of more value there, David submitted and again displayed an amazing lack of rancor toward Absalom by publicly requesting his three captains to "deal gently for my sake with the young man Absalom."—2Sa 17:15–18:5.

Decisive Battle and Death. Absalom's newly formed forces were administered a crushing defeat by David's experienced fighters. The battle reached into the forest of Ephraim. Absalom, riding away on his royal mule, passed under the low branches of a large tree and apparently got his head enmeshed in the fork of a branch so that he was left suspended in the air. The man who reported to Joab that he had seen him said he would not have disobeyed David's request by slaying Absalom for "a thousand pieces of silver [if shekels, c. $2,200]," but Joab felt no such restraint and drove three shafts into Absalom's heart, after which ten of his men joined their captain in sharing the responsibility for Absalom's death. Absalom's body was thereafter thrown into a hollow and covered with a mound of stones as unworthy of burial.—2Sa 18:6-17; compare Jos 7:26; 8:29.

When messengers reached David in Mahanaim, his first concern was for his son. Learning of Absalom's death, David paced the floor of the roof chamber, crying: "My son Absalom, my son, my son Absalom! O that I might have died, I myself, instead of you, Absalom my son, my son!" (2Sa 18:24-33) Only Joab's blunt, straightforward speech and reasoning brought David out of his great grief due to the tragic course and end of this physically attractive and resourceful young man, whose driving ambition led him to fight against God's anointed, thus bringing himself to ruin. —2Sa 19:1-8; compare Pr 24:21, 22.

Psalm 3 was written by David at the time of Absalom's revolt, according to the superscription that heads the psalm.

Absalom's Monument. A pillar had been erected by Absalom in "the Low Plain of the King," also called "the Low Plain of Shaveh," near Jerusalem. (2Sa 18:18; Ge 14:17) He had erected it because of having no sons to keep his name alive after his death. It thus appears that his three sons mentioned at 2 Samuel 14:27 had died when young. Absalom was not buried at the place of his monument but was left in a hollow in the forest of Ephraim.—2Sa 18:6, 17.

There is a pillar cut out of the rock in the Kidron Valley that has been called the Tomb of Absalom, but its architecture indicates it is from the Greco-Roman period, perhaps of the time of Herod. So there is no basis for associating the name of Absalom with it.

ABUSIVE SPEECH. The original Greek word *bla·sphe·mi'a* and the verb *bla·sphe·me'o* basically indicate defamatory, calumnious, abusive language. As noted under the heading BLASPHEMY, the Greek word *bla·sphe·mi'a* has a broader meaning than the present English word "blasphemy." In English, only when such speech is directed against God, not against his creatures, is it properly termed "blasphemy." (Mt 12:31) Concerning this, *The Popular and Critical Bible Encyclopædia and Scriptural Dictionary* says: "Our English translators [that is, primarily those of the *KJ*] have not adhered to the right use of the term. They employ it with the same latitude as the Greek; but it is generally easy to perceive, from the connection and subject of a passage, whether *blasphemy*, properly so called, be meant, or only defamation." —Edited by S. Fallows, 1912, Vol. I, p. 291.

Thus, while the *King James Version* uses "blasphemy" and "blasphemed" in Acts 18:6, Colossians 3:8, 1 Timothy 6:1, and Titus 2:5, later translations say "slander," "abusive talk [or "speech"]," "reviled," "defamed," "abused," "spoken of abusively," and similar expressions. (See *RS, AT, NW,* and others.) However, the *King James Version* does recognize this distinction elsewhere in the Greek Scriptures.

As the following texts and surrounding verses show, at the time of his impalement abusive speech was directed against Christ by passersby, who said, "Bah! You would-be thrower-down of the temple and builder of it in three days' time, save yourself by coming down off the torture stake." Similar words came from one of the evildoers alongside. (Mr 15:29, 30; Mt 27:39, 40; Lu 23:39) Paul and his fellow Christians were objects of such speech by those who falsely construed their purpose, message, and Christian conscience (Ac 18:6; Ro 3:8; 14:16; 1Co 10:30; 1Pe 4:4), yet they themselves were to "speak injuriously of no one," and by their conduct gave no true grounds for their work or message to be spoken of abusively. (Eph 4:31; Col 3:8; 1Ti 6:1; Tit 2:5; 3:2; compare 2Pe 2:2.) Even the angels "do not bring . . . an accusation in abusive terms, not doing so out of respect for Jehovah." (2Pe 2:11) But such talk *can* be expected from those who indulge in loose con-

duct, those who are proud and mentally diseased over questionings and debates, and those who disregard or disrespect God's appointments.—1Ti 6:4; 2Pe 2:10-12; Jude 8-10.

The word *ga·dhaph'* is used in a corresponding way in the Hebrew Scriptures. Evidently originally referring to inflicting violent physical injury, it is used figuratively to mean "speak abusively," that is, harm with reproachful words. (Nu 15:30; 2Ki 19:6; Eze 20:27) The Hebrew word *na·qav'*, basically meaning "pierce; bore" (2Ki 12:9; 2Ki 18:21), has the sense of blaspheming in the account where the son of an Israelite woman was said to have 'abused' Jehovah's name. (Le 24: 11, 16) In these cases harsh or coarse speech is indicated, directed against either Jehovah God himself or his people. A study of the context makes clear the nature of such "abusive speech." —See EXECRATION; MALEDICTION; REVILING.

ABYSS. According to Parkhurst's *Greek and English Lexicon to the New Testament* (London, 1845, p. 2), the Greek *a'bys·sos* means "very or exceedingly deep." According to Liddell and Scott's *Greek-English Lexicon* (Oxford, 1968, p. 4), it means "unfathomable, boundless." The Greek *Septuagint* uses it regularly to translate the Hebrew *tehohm'* (watery deep), as at Genesis 1:2; 7:11.

A'bys·sos occurs nine times in the Christian Greek Scriptures, seven of them being in the book of Revelation. It is from "the abyss" that the symbolic locusts come forth under the headship of their king, Abaddon or Apollyon, "the angel of the abyss." (Re 9:1-3, 11) "The wild beast" that makes war against the "two witnesses" of God and kills them is also spoken of as coming "out of the abyss." (Re 11:3, 7) Revelation 20:1-3 describes the future casting of Satan into the abyss for a thousand years; something that a legion of demons urged Jesus not to do to them on a certain occasion.—Lu 8:31.

Scriptural Significance. It is noteworthy that the Greek *Septuagint* does not use *a'bys·sos* to translate the Hebrew *she'ohl'*, and in view of the fact that spirit creatures are cast into it, it cannot properly be *limited* in meaning to Sheol or Hades, inasmuch as these two words clearly refer to the common earthly grave of mankind. (Job 17:13-16; see HADES; SHEOL.) It does not refer to "the lake of fire," since it is after Satan's release from the abyss that he is thereupon hurled into the lake of fire. (Re 20:1-3, 7-10) Paul's statement at Romans 10:7, in which he speaks of Christ as being in the abyss, also precludes such possibility and shows as well that the abyss is not the same as Tartarus. —See TARTARUS.

Romans 10:6, 7 aids in clearing up the meaning of "the abyss" in stating: "But the righteousness resulting from faith speaks in this manner: 'Do not say in your heart, "Who will ascend into heaven?" that is, to bring Christ down; or, "Who will descend into the abyss?" that is, to bring Christ up from the dead.'" (Compare De 30:11-13.) It is evident that "the abyss" here refers to the place in which Christ Jesus spent part of three days and from which place his Father resurrected him. (Compare Ps 71:19, 20; Mt 12:40.) Revelation 20:7 refers to the abyss as a "prison," and the confinement of absolute restraint resulting from death in the case of Jesus certainly harmonizes with this. —Compare Ac 2:24; 2Sa 22:5, 6; Job 38:16, 17; Ps 9:13; 107:18; 116:3.

Concerning the root meaning "unfathomable" as characteristic of "the abyss," it is of interest to note the statement in Hastings' *Encyclopædia of Religion and Ethics* (1913, Vol. I, p. 54), which, in commenting on Romans 10:6, 7, says: "The impression conveyed by St. Paul's language is of the vastness of that realm, as of one that we should vainly attempt to explore." Paul contrasts the inaccessibility of "heaven" and of the "abyss" with the accessibility of righteousness by faith. The use of the related word *ba′thos* made by Paul at Romans 11:33 illustrates this: "O the depth [*ba′thos*] of God's riches and wisdom and knowledge! How unsearchable his judgments are and *past tracing out* his ways are!" (See also 1Co 2:10; Eph 3:18, 19.) So, in harmony with Romans 10:6, 7, the place that is represented by "the abyss" would also evidently imply being out of the reach of anyone but God or his appointed angel with "the key of the abyss." (Re 20:1) Liddell and Scott's *Greek-English Lexicon* (p. 4) gives as one of the meanings of the word *a′bys·sos* "the infinite void."

The plural form of the Hebrew word *metsoh·lah′* (or *metsu·lah′*) is translated "large abyss" in Psalm 88:6 and literally means "abysses," or "depths." (Compare Zec 10:11.) It is related to *tsu·lah′*, meaning "watery deep."—Isa 44:27.

ACACIA [Heb., *shit·tah′*]. A tree that grew well in the wilderness, where the Israelites sojourned. It was capable of providing rather large boards (nearly 4.5 m; 15 ft long, according to Ex 36:20, 21), which the Israelites used in constructing the portable tabernacle. Since this tree practically disappears from the Bible record after the entry into the Promised Land, this may also indicate a tree not commonly found throughout Palestine. Such description fits the acacia types known as *Acacia*

seyal and *Acacia tortilis* far better than any other plant life in the area. These acacia trees are still common in the Negeb and the Sinai area and some are found along the Jordan Valley S of the Sea of Galilee, but not in northern Palestine.

It is interesting to note that the word *seyal* is Arabic for "torrent," and the habitat of the acacia is in the torrent valleys, or wadis, down which water rushes during the rainy season and which are found in the otherwise arid, desert regions around the Dead Sea area and southward into the Arabian Desert and the Sinai Peninsula. Thus Joel's prophecy (3:18) says: "Out of the house of Jehovah there will go forth a spring, and it must irrigate the torrent valley of the Acacia Trees," which is clearly a place that would otherwise usually be dry. (See SHITTIM.) At Isaiah 41:19 Jehovah says: "In the wilderness I shall set the cedar tree, the acacia and the myrtle and the oil tree." Here three trees that normally grow in rich and fertile soils are prophesied to become the companions of the desert-loving acacia, as a result of divine provision for irrigation.—Isa 41:17, 18.

The acacia has many long thorns extending out from the widely spreading branches. These branches usually interlace with those of the neighboring acacias to form tangled thickets; this fact doubtless explains why the plural form *shittim′* is almost always used in the Bible record. The acacia may grow to heights of 6 to 8 m (20 to 26 ft), but often is bushlike in appearance. It has soft, feathery leaves and is covered with pleasingly fragrant yellow blossoms, producing curved tapering pods as its fruit. The rough, black bark covers a very hard, fine-grained, heavy wood that is immune to insect attack. These characteristics and its availability in the desert made the acacia especially well suited as a building material for the tabernacle and its furnishings. It was employed to construct the ark of the covenant (Ex 25:10; 37:1), the table of showbread (Ex 25:23; 37:10), altars (Ex 27:1; 37:25; 38:1), poles for carrying these items (Ex 25:13, 28; 27:6; 30:5; 37:4, 15, 28; 38:6), pillars for the curtain and screen (Ex 26:32, 37; 36:36), and the panel frames (Ex 26:15; 36:20) and their connecting bars (Ex 26:26; 36:31).

Acacia is still prized for cabinetwork because of its fine grain, rich orange-brown color, and durability. The ancient Egyptians clamped their mummy coffins shut with acacia and used it in the construction of their boats. Certain types of the tree also produce the gum arabic of commerce.

ACCAD (Ac′cad). One of the four cities founded by Nimrod that formed "the beginning of his kingdom." (Ge 10:10) Accad (Akkad) has been identi-

Acacia trees, common in the Sinai area, provided wood for the tabernacle

fied with the ancient city of Agade. The precise location is uncertain.

The name Akkad is also applied to the whole northern region of what later was called Babylonia. Akkad appears to have received prominence as the principal or royal city of that region under Sargon I (not the Sargon of Isa 20:1). The southern region of Mesopotamia was known as Sumer. Babylonia grew out of these two areas, and in Babylonian texts her rulers were still called "king of Akkad" down to the time of Babylon's fall in 539 B.C.E. On the Cyrus Cylinder, Babylon's conqueror takes over the title "King of Babylon, king of Sumer and Akkad."

The Akkadians appear to have surpassed the Sumerians in fine sculpture and intricate seal cutting. The name Akkadian (Accadian) today is used to describe the ancient Assyrian and Babylonian languages.

ACCEPTABLE TIME. At 2 Corinthians 6:2 the apostle Paul quotes from the prophecy of Isaiah 49:8, which says: "This is what Jehovah has said: 'In a time of goodwill I have answered you, and in a day of salvation I have helped you; and I kept safeguarding you that I might give you as a covenant for the people, to rehabilitate the land, to bring about the repossessing of the desolated hereditary possessions.'" In its original setting this statement was evidently made to Isaiah as representing or personifying the nation of Israel. (Isa 49:3) It was clearly a restoration prophecy and, hence, had its first fulfillment at the time of the liberation of Israel from Babylon when the call went to the Israelite prisoners, "Come out!" They thereafter returned to their homeland and rehabilitated the desolated land.—Isa 49:9.

However, the words "that I might give you as a covenant for the people" in verse 8 of this chapter and the preceding statement in verse 6 that this "servant" of Jehovah would be given as "a light of the nations, that [God's] salvation may come to be to the extremity of the earth," definitely mark the prophecy as Messianic and as therefore applying to Christ Jesus as God's "servant." (Compare Isa 42:1-4, 6, 7 with Mt 12:18-21.) Since the "time of goodwill" was a time when Jehovah would 'answer' and 'help' his servant, it must apply to Jesus' earthly life when he "offered up supplications and also petitions to the One who was able to save him out of death, with strong outcries and tears, and he was favorably heard for his godly fear." (Heb 5:7-9; compare Joh 12:27, 28; 17:1-5; Lu 22:41-44; 23:46.) It was, therefore, "a day of salvation" for God's own Son, during which period of opportunity he demonstrated perfection of integrity and, as a result, "became responsible for everlasting salvation to all those obeying him."—Heb 5:9.

Additionally, Paul's quotation from this prophecy indicates a still further application to those Christians whom Paul urges "not to accept the undeserved kindness of God and miss its purpose," and to whom he says (after quoting Isa 49:8): "Look! Now is the especially acceptable time. Look! Now is the day of salvation." (2Co 6:1, 2) Such Christians had become the spiritual "Israel of God" from Pentecost of 33 C.E. forward (Ga 6:16), but there was a need for them to prove worthy of God's undeserved kindness, so that the "acceptable time" might indeed prove to be "a day of salvation" for them.

The fact that the prophecy in its original application was one of restoration would likewise indicate an application to a time of release from spiritual captivity and of restoration to full favor with God.—Compare Ps 69:13-18.

To natural Jews who failed to appreciate the favorableness of the time and the opportunity that was theirs for entry into 'spiritual Israel,' Paul announced that he was turning to the non-Jewish nations, and he quoted Isaiah 49:6 in support, saying: "In fact, Jehovah has laid commandment upon us in these words, 'I have appointed you as a light of nations, for you to be a salvation to the extremity of the earth.'" (Ac 13:47) Since "time" and "day" are terms indicating temporariness, they imply urgency and the need to use wisely an opportune period or season of favor before its end comes bringing the withdrawal of divine mercy and offer of salvation.—Ro 13:11-13; 1Th 5:6-11; Eph 5:15-20.

ACCIDENT, ACCIDENTAL.

Unforeseen occurrences that result from ignorance, carelessness, or unavoidable events and that cause loss or injury are commonly called accidents. The Hebrew word *'a·sohn'* evidently literally means "a healing" and is used as a euphemism for "a fatal accident." (Compare Ge 42:4, ftn.) The Hebrew *miq·reh'*, which is derived from a root that means "meet; befall" (Ge 44:29; De 25:18), is rendered not only "accident" (1Sa 6:9) but also "eventuality" (Ec 2:14, 15; 3:19) and "by chance."—Ru 2:3.

Jacob feared that a fatal accident might befall his beloved son Benjamin if allowed to go to Egypt with his brothers. (Ge 42:4, 38) The Philistines returned the ark of Jehovah to prove whether the plague of piles they suffered really was from Jehovah or was just "an accident." (1Sa 6:9) Solomon recognized that anyone may become a victim of unforeseen occurrence.—Ec 9:11.

The Mosaic Law differentiated between an accident that proved fatal and one that was not. (Ex 21:22-25) It also distinguished between killing intentionally and unintentionally. For deliberate murder, capital punishment was mandatory; for those guilty of accidental homicide, cities of refuge were set up. (Nu 35:11-25, 31; see CITIES OF REFUGE.) The law applied equally to native Israelite and alien resident, and instructions for the necessary sacrifices to atone for accidental or unintentional sins were provided.—Le 4:1-35; 5:14-19; Nu 15:22-29.

ACCO

(Ac′co). A seaport city also known as Accho, Acre, and Ptolemais. It is located at the northern point of the yawning crescent-shaped Bay of Acco (or Bay of Haifa [Mifraz Hefa]). This bay is formed by the cape of Mount Carmel jutting out into the Mediterranean Sea about 13 km (8 mi) to the S.

In the period of the Judges, the Canaanite city was situated on a mound identified with Tell el-Fukhkhar (Tel 'Akko), about 1 km (0.6 mi) from the bay and 1.8 km (1 mi) E of the present-day Old City walls. During the Persian period, from the sixth century B.C.E., the city spread westward to include the peninsula that forms the N end of the Bay of Haifa. The port of the city was located there from the Persian period onward. By the time of the Christian Era, the location of Acco had come to include the peninsula and is included in the area of modern 'Akko.

Situated about 39 km (24 mi) S of Tyre, Acco was the most important seaport on the harbor-shy Palestinian coast until Herod the Great ran seawalls out from the shore to produce an artificial

Acco (later known as Ptolemais). The apostle Paul stopped at this seaport city on his final trip to Jerusalem

port at Caesarea. Acco was inferior to the Phoenician ports to the N and provided but poor shelter from the sea winds. However, it was strategically located close to the approach to the rich Plain of Jezreel (Esdraelon), and several commercial trade routes connected the port with Galilee, the Jordan Valley, and other points to the east. Timber, artistic commodities, and grain were exported through Acco.

Acco pertained to the territorial division assigned to Asher in the Promised Land, but Asher failed to drive out the Canaanites who were then living there. (Jg 1:31, 32) Mentioned only once in the Hebrew Scriptures, the city is more frequently referred to in non-Biblical records. Its name occurs several times in the Amarna Tablets. Other records show that it was subjugated by the Assyrian kings Sennacherib and Ashurbanipal. The city is mentioned in the Apocrypha as a center of opposition during the rule of the Maccabees. (1 Maccabees 5:15, 22, 55; 12:45-48; 13:12) By then its name had been changed to Ptolemais, a name originated by Ptolemy II Philadelphus of Egypt.

Under Emperor Claudius, the city of Ptolemais (Acco) became a Roman colony, and in apostolic times there was a group of Christians there. When returning from his third missionary tour, Paul put in at Acco (then known as Ptolemais) and spent the day visiting the brothers there before traveling on to Caesarea and Jerusalem.—Ac 21:7.

Today 'Akko is eclipsed in importance by the modern city of Haifa, located directly across the bay.

ACCUSATION.

A charge of wrongdoing. The one accused is called to account.

One Hebrew word rendered "accusation" (*sit-nah'*) comes from the root verb *sa·tan'*, meaning "resist." (Ezr 4:6; compare Zec 3:1.) The most common Greek word for "accuse" is *ka·te·go·re'o*, carrying the idea of 'speaking against' someone, usually in a judicial or legal sense. (Mr 3:2; Lu 6:7) At Luke 16:1 the Greek word *di·a·bal'lo*, rendered 'accuse,' may also be translated 'slander.' (*Int*) It is related to *di·a'bo·los* (slanderer), root of the word "Devil."

The Greek term translated 'accuse falsely' in Luke 3:14 (*sy·ko·phan·te'o*) is rendered 'extort by false accusation' in Luke 19:8. It literally means "take by fig-showing." Of the various explanations of the origin of this word, one is that in ancient Athens the exporting of figs from the province was prohibited. One who denounced others, accusing them of attempting to export figs, was termed a "fig-shower." The term came to designate a malignant informer, a person who accused others out of a love of gain, a false accuser, a blackmailer.

One might be called to account and charged with wrong, yet be entirely innocent, blameless, the victim of a false accuser. Hebrew law, therefore, set forth the responsibility each one in the nation had to bring to account wrongdoers, and at the same time it adequately provided protection for the accused. A few examples from the Mosaic Law will serve to illustrate these principles. If a person had any knowledge respecting a crime, he had to bring the accusation before the proper authorities. (Le 5:1; 24:11-14) The authorities, in turn, were to "search and investigate and inquire thoroughly" into the accusations to determine their validity before administering punishment. (De 13:12-14) An observer was not to hide wrongdoing or fail to bring an accusation against a guilty one, even if the person was a close relative like a brother, son, daughter, or marriage mate. (De 13:6-8; 21:18-20; Zec 13:3) The testimony of two or three witnesses was required, and not just the word of a single accuser.—Nu 35:30; De 17:6; 19:15; Joh 8:17; Heb 10:28.

The Law of Moses also gave the accused the right to face his accuser before a court of justice in order that the truth of the charges might be fully established. (De 19:16-19; 25:1) A classic instance of this was the case of the two prostitutes who, with a baby, appeared before wise King Solomon for him to decide which one was its mother.—1Ki 3:16-27.

Roman law likewise required the accusers to appear in court. So, when the Roman citizen Paul stood trial before governors Felix and Festus, his accusers were ordered to appear also. (Ac 22:30; 23:30, 35; 24:2, 8, 13, 19; 25:5, 11, 16, 18) Paul's appearance before Caesar in Rome, however, was on his own appeal that he might win an acquittal, and not that he might accuse his own nation. (Ac 28:19) Not Paul, not even Jesus, but Moses, by his conduct and by what he wrote, accused the Jewish nation of wrongdoing.—Joh 5:45.

Three Hebrews were accused of not worshiping Nebuchadnezzar's gold image and were pitched into the furnace. The accusation was true, though based on a bad law. However, they were innocent of wrongdoing, and upon appeal to the Supreme Court of Heaven they were cleared of any guilt by Jehovah. (Da 3:8-25) Similarly, Daniel was delivered from death, and the accusers who hatched the plot against him were thrown to the lions. (Da 6:24) The word "accused" in these two accounts translates an Aramaic phrase literally meaning "had eaten the pieces [of flesh torn from the body]," and it may also be rendered "slandered." (Da 3:8; 6:24; ftns) Opposers of the reconstruction of the temple in Jerusalem wrote a letter accusing the builders of wrongdoing, and a ban against the work based on the false accusation was imposed, a ban that was later proved unlawful. (Ezr 4:6–6:12) In like manner the religious leaders sought out ways of accusing Jesus as a lawbreaker. (Mt 12:10; Lu 6:7) They finally succeeded in having the innocent man arrested, and at the trial they were most vehement in their false accusation of the Righteous One, Jesus. (Mt 27:12; Mr 15:3; Lu 23:2, 10; Joh 18:29) These examples show how wrong it is to accuse others falsely, especially if the accusers are in positions of authority.—Lu 3:14; 19:8.

In the Christian congregation, overseers and ministerial servants not only should be innocent of bearing false witness against others but must be free from accusation themselves. (1Ti 3:10; Tit 1:6) Hence, if accusations are brought against an older man, there should be two or three witnesses to back them up. (Mt 18:16; 2Co 13:1; 1Ti 5:19) The whole congregation must be free from accusation (1Co 1:8; Col 1:22), though this does not mean they will be free from false accusations, for, indeed, the great Adversary, Satan the Devil, is "the accuser of our brothers . . . who accuses them day and night before our God!"—Re 12:10.

ACHAIA (A·cha′ia). Prior to the Roman conquest in 146 B.C.E., Achaia properly referred only to a small region in the Peloponnesus, stretching across the southern coast of the Gulf of Corinth, in a position somewhat similar to that occupied today by the section of the same name.

In Homeric poetry Greeks in general are spoken of under the name of Achaians. Due to the prominence of the Achaean League, a confederacy of cities, as the most powerful political body in Greece at the time of its conquest, the Romans thereafter generally spoke of all Greece as Achaia.

In 27 B.C.E., when Caesar Augustus reorganized the two provinces of Greece, Macedonia and Achaia, the name Achaia then applied to all the Peloponnesus and to part of continental Greece. The province of Achaia was under the administration of the Roman Senate and was ruled through a proconsul from its capital, Corinth. (2Co 1:1) Other cities of the province of Achaia mentioned in the Christian Greek Scriptures were Athens and Cenchreae. Achaia and its neighboring province to the N, Macedonia, were often linked together in common usage.—Ac 18:1, 18; 19:21; Ro 15:26; 16:1; 1Th 1:7, 8.

In the year 15 C.E., in response to complaints over the severity of taxation, Tiberius placed Achaia and Macedonia under imperial control, to be governed from the province of Moesia. This continued until 44 C.E. when Emperor Claudius restored these provinces to senatorial control, thereby causing a proconsul again to take up governing powers in Corinth. Due to ignorance of these facts, in the past some critics objected to the Bible's reference to Gallio as the "proconsul of Achaia," before whom Paul was brought. (Ac 18:12) However, the discovery of an inscription at Delphi made it evident that there was indeed a proconsul at Achaia named Gallio at the time described by the historian Luke, writer of Acts.—See GALLIO.

At Romans 15:26 the apostle Paul speaks of the generosity of the Christians in the province of Achaia in providing help for their needy brothers in Jerusalem. During Paul's second and third missionary journeys a considerable part of his time was spent in Achaia, and he expressed strong love for the brothers of that region.—2Co 11:10.

ACHAICUS (A·cha′i·cus) [Of (Belonging to) Achaia]. One of the mature associates of the Corinthian congregation, who, together with Stephanas and Fortunatus, visited Paul while he was at Ephesus.—1Co 16:17, 18.

ACHAN (A'chan) [related through a play on words to Achar, meaning "Bringer of Ostracism (Trouble)"]. The son of Carmi of the household of Zabdi of the family of Zerah of the tribe of Judah; also called Achar.—1Ch 2:7.

When the Israelites crossed the Jordan, Jehovah explicitly commanded that the firstfruits of the conquest, the city of Jericho, "must become a thing devoted to destruction; . . . it belongs to Jehovah." Its silver and gold were to be given to the treasury of Jehovah. (Jos 6:17, 19) Achan, however, upon finding a costly garment from Shinar and a 50-shekel gold bar (worth some $6,400) and 200 silver shekels ($440), secretly buried them beneath his tent. (Jos 7:21) Actually he had robbed God! Because of this violation of Jehovah's explicit instructions, when the next city, Ai, was attacked Jehovah withheld his blessing, and Israel was put to flight. Who was guilty? No one confessed. All Israel was then put on trial. Tribe by tribe, then family by family of the tribe of Judah, and finally, man by man of the house of Zabdi, they passed before Jehovah until Achan "got to be picked." (Jos 7:4-18) Only then did he admit his sin. Execution quickly followed. Achan, his family (who could hardly have been ignorant of what he had done), and his livestock were first stoned to death, and then burned with fire, together with all his possessions, in the Valley of Achor, meaning "Ostracism; Trouble."—Jos 7:19-26.

ACHAR. See ACHAN.

ACHBOR (Ach'bor) [Jerboa; Jumping Rodent].

1. The father of Baal-hanan, who is listed as the seventh king of Edom.—Ge 36:38, 39; 1Ch 1:49.

2. The son of Micaiah and a trusted official of King Josiah's court. (2Ki 22:12) He is called "Abdon the son of Micah" at 2 Chronicles 34:20. Upon learning of Jehovah's burning rage expressed in the ancient book of the Law, only recently discovered, Josiah sent Achbor as one of a committee of five to the prophetess Huldah to learn what should be done. (2Ki 22:8-14) Achbor was the father of Elnathan, a prince of the court of King Jehoiakim and very likely the great-grandfather of King Jehoiachin.—Jer 26:22; 36:12; 2Ki 24:8.

ACHIM (A'chim) [possibly from Heb., meaning "May [Jehovah] Firmly Establish; [Jehovah] Has Firmly Established"]. A royal descendant of David through Solomon and an ancestor of Joseph the adoptive father of Jesus.—Mt 1:14.

ACHISH (A'chish). A Philistine king of Gath who reigned during the time of David and Solomon. He was the son of Maoch or Maacah, and in the superscription of Psalm 34 is called Abimelech, perhaps a title similar to Pharaoh or Czar.—1Sa 27:2; 1Ki 2:39.

Twice when David was in flight from Saul he found refuge in the domain of King Achish. On the first occasion, when suspected of being an enemy, David feigned insanity, and Achish let him go as a harmless idiot. (1Sa 21:10-15; Ps 34:Sup; 56:Sup) On the second visit David was accompanied by 600 warriors and their families, and so Achish assigned them to live in Ziklag. During the year and four months that they were there Achish believed that David's band was making raids on Judean towns, whereas David was actually pillaging the Geshurites, Girzites, and Amalekites. (1Sa 27:1-12) So successful was the deception that Achish actually made David his personal bodyguard when the Philistines were organizing an attack on King Saul, and only at the last moment, upon the insistence of the other "axis lords" of the Philistines, were David and his men sent back to Ziklag. (1Sa 28:2; 29:1-11) When David became king and warred against Gath, Achish apparently was not killed. He lived into Solomon's reign.—1Ki 2:39-41; see GATH.

ACHOR (A'chor) [Ostracism; Trouble]. A valley or low plain forming part of the NE boundary of the tribal territory of Judah. (Jos 15:7) The valley's name, meaning "Ostracism; Trouble," resulted from its being the place where Achan and his household were stoned to death. Achan, by his stealing and hiding some booty from the capture of Jericho, had brought ostracism on the nation of Israel, including defeat at the first attack on Ai. —Jos 7:5-26.

Some have identified the Valley of Achor with the Wadi el Qilt, a ravinelike torrent valley that passes near Jericho. However, the description of its position as given at Joshua 15:7 appears to place it more to the S, and the statement at Isaiah 65:10 would indicate a broader, more spacious area. In view of this it is tentatively identified with el Buqei'a (Biq'at Hureqanya), a barren, low-lying plateau or basin, that stretches N and S across the Wadi Qumran (Nahal Qumeran) near the NW corner of the Dead Sea. Archaeological investigation there has revealed sites of ancient towns or forts as well as systems of dams.

At Hosea 2:15 Jehovah recalls Israel's youth at the time of the Exodus, and in a prophecy of restoration from future captivity, he promises that "the low plain of Achor," once a place of ostracism, will then become "as an entrance to hope." And, although the area is one of wilderness, in a similar restoration prophecy God foretells that the low plain of Achor will become "a resting-place for cattle."—Isa 65:10.

ACHSAH (Ach'sah) [Anklet; Bangle]. The daughter of the Judean spy Caleb whom he offered in marriage as a prize to whoever captured the stronghold of Debir in Judah's newly acquired territory. Caleb's nephew Othniel, who evidently became the first judge after Joshua (Jg 3:9, 10), captured it and, as a reward, married his cousin Achsah.—See OTHNIEL.

When Achsah left for her new home, she requested and received from her father an additional choice gift, a section containing the Upper and Lower Gulloth. (Jos 15:15-19; Jg 1:12-15) Achsah may have been the mother of Hathath.—1Ch 4:13.

ACHSHAPH (Ach'shaph) [Place of Practicing Sorcery]. A royal city of Canaan whose king responded to the call of Jabin, king of Hazor, and joined the encampment of kings at the waters of Merom to fight against Israel. (Jos 11:1, 5) He was killed in the battle that followed. (Jos 12:7, 20) The city of Achshaph was later included in the territory assigned as an inheritance to the tribe of Asher. —Jos 19:25.

Some scholars propose identifying Achshaph with Tell Kisan (Tel Kison), a site about 10 km (6 mi) SE of Acco (Acre). However, others favor Khirbet el-Harbaj (Tel Regev) about 11 km (7 mi) SE of Haifa.

ACHZIB (Ach'zib) [Deceitful Place]. The name of two cities.

1. A city in the southern part of the Promised Land, in the territory of Judah. (Jos 15:44) It is understood to be the same as "Chezib" (Ge 38:5, KJ), the birthplace of Judah's son Shelah. Joshua 15:33 shows it to be in the hilly country of the Shephelah, and it is tentatively identified with Tell el-Beida (Horvat Lavnin) 5 km (3 mi) WSW of Adullam. Lachish, Moresheth-gath, and Mareshah (mentioned along with Achzib in Mic 1:13-15) are all in that area. Cozeba, in 1 Chronicles 4:22, is generally considered to be the same as Achzib.

2. A Phoenician coastal city in the territory of the tribe of Asher. (Jos 19:29) Asher, however, never succeeded in conquering it, nor the more important city of Acco (Acre) to the S, perhaps due to hindering action on the part of the Phoenician fleet. (Jg 1:31, 32) Sennacherib of Assyria overran it in King Hezekiah's time and mentions it in his annals under the name Akzibi. In Greek and Roman times it was called Ecdippa. It has been identified with ez-Zib (Tel Akhziv), some 14 km

(9 mi) N of Acco at the mouth of the Wadi Qarn (Nahal Keziv).

ACRE. As used in the Scriptures, "acre" is understood to denote the measure of land that a span of bulls can plow in a day. The Hebrew word thus rendered (tse'medh) literally means "span" (1Sa 14:14, ftn; 1Ki 19:19) and is also rendered "couple" (Jg 19:3), "pair" (1Sa 11:7), and 'team' (2Ki 9:25). Likely the measure of land referred to was somewhat less than 0.4 ha (1 acre). The word jugerum, found in the Latin Vulgate, refers to an area of 0.25 ha (0.62 acre).

ACTS OF APOSTLES. This is the title by which one of the Bible books has been called since the second century C.E. It covers primarily the activity of Peter and Paul, rather than that of all the apostles in general; and it provides us with a most reliable and comprehensive history of the spectacular beginning and rapid development of the Christian organization, first among the Jews and then among the Samaritans and the Gentile nations.

The overriding theme of the entire Bible, Jehovah's Kingdom, dominates the book (Ac 1:3; 8:12; 14:22; 19:8; 20:25; 28:31), and we are constantly reminded of how the apostles bore "thorough witness" concerning Christ and that Kingdom and fully accomplished their ministry. (2:40; 5:42; 8:25; 10:42; 20:21, 24; 23:11; 26:22; 28:23) The book also provides a superb historical background against which to view the inspired letters of the Christian Greek Scriptures.

The Writer. The opening words of Acts refer to the Gospel of Luke as "the first account." And since both accounts are addressed to the same individual, Theophilus, we know that Luke, though not signing his name, was the writer of Acts. (Lu 1:3; Ac 1:1) Both accounts have a similar style and wording. The Muratorian Fragment of the late second century C.E. also attributes the writership to Luke. Ecclesiastical writings of the second century C.E. by Irenaeus of Lyons, Clement of Alexandria, and Tertullian of Carthage, when quoting from Acts, cite Luke as the writer.

When and Where Written. The book covers a period of approximately 28 years, from Jesus' ascension in 33 C.E. to the end of the second year of Paul's imprisonment in Rome about 61 C.E. During this period four Roman emperors ruled in succession: Tiberius, Caligula, Claudius, and Nero. Since it relates events through the second year of Paul's imprisonment in Rome, it could not have been completed earlier. Had the account been written later, it is reasonable to expect that Luke would have provided more information about Paul; if written after the year 64 C.E., mention surely would have been made of Nero's violent persecution that began then; and if written after 70 C.E., as some contend, we would expect to find Jerusalem's destruction recorded.

The writer Luke accompanied Paul much of the time during his travels, including the perilous voyage to Rome, which is apparent from his use of the first-person plural pronouns "we," "our," and "us" in Acts 16:10-17; 20:5-15; 21:1-18; 27:1-37; 28:1-16. Paul, in his letters written from Rome, mentions that Luke was also there. (Col 4:14; Phm 24) It was, therefore, in Rome that the writing of the book of Acts was completed.

As already observed, Luke himself was an eyewitness to much of what he wrote, and in his travels he contacted fellow Christians who either participated in or observed certain events described. For example, John Mark could tell him of Peter's miraculous prison release (Ac 12:12), while the events described in chapters 6 and 8 could have been learned from the missionary Phil-ip. And Paul, of course, as an eyewitness, was able to supply many details of events that happened when Luke was not with him.

Authenticity. The accuracy of the book of Acts has been verified over the years by a number of archaeological discoveries. For example, Acts 13:7 says that Sergius Paulus was the proconsul of Cyprus. Now it is known that shortly before Paul visited Cyprus it was ruled by a propraetor, or legate, but an inscription found in Cyprus proves that the island did come under the direct rule of the Roman Senate in the person of a provincial governor called a proconsul. Similarly in Greece, during the rule of Augustus Caesar, Achaia was a province under the direct rule of the Roman Senate, but when Tiberius was emperor it was ruled directly by him. Later, under Emperor Claudius, it again became a senatorial province, according to Tacitus. A fragment of a rescript from Claudius to the Delphians of Greece has been discovered, which refers to Gallio's proconsulship. Therefore, Acts 18:12 is correct in speaking of Gallio as the "proconsul" when Paul was there in Corinth, the

---

HIGHLIGHTS OF ACTS

The beginning of the Christian congregation and a record of its zealous public witnessing in the face of fierce opposition

Time covered: 33 to c. 61 C.E.

Before ascending to heaven, Jesus commissions followers to be witnesses of him as Jehovah's Messiah (1:1-26)

After receiving holy spirit, disciples boldly witness in many languages (2:1-5:42)

Jews in Jerusalem from many lands are given witness in their own languages; about 3,000 baptized

Peter and John are arrested and taken before Sanhedrin; fearlessly declare they will not stop witnessing

Filled with holy spirit, all the disciples speak the word of God boldly; multitudes become believers

Apostles are arrested; an angel releases them; brought before the Sanhedrin, they declare: "We must obey God as ruler rather than men"

Persecution results in expansion of the witness (6:1-9:43)

Stephen is seized, gives fearless witness, dies a martyr

Persecution scatters all but apostles; witness given in Samaria; Ethiopian eunuch baptized

Jesus appears to the persecutor Saul; Saul is converted, baptized, begins zealous ministry

Under divine direction the witness reaches uncircumcised Gentiles (10:1-12:25)

Peter preaches to Cornelius, his family, and his friends; these believe, receive holy spirit, and are baptized

Apostle's report of this prompts further expansion among nations

Paul's evangelizing tours (13:1-21:26)

First tour: To Cyprus, Asia Minor. Paul and Barnabas boldly witness publicly and in synagogues; thrown out of Antioch; mobbed in Iconium; first treated like gods in Lystra, then Paul is stoned

Circumcision issue decided by governing body at Jerusalem; Paul and Barnabas assigned to inform brothers that circumcision is not required but that believers must abstain from things sacrificed to idols, from blood, and from fornication

Second tour: Back through Asia Minor, into Macedonia and Greece. Imprisoned in Philippi, but jailer and his family get baptized; Jews stir up trouble in Thessalonica and Beroea; in Athens, Paul preaches in synagogue, in the marketplace, then on the Areopagus; 18-month ministry in Corinth

Third tour: Asia Minor, Greece. Fruitful Ephesian ministry, then uproar by silversmiths; apostle admonishes elders

Paul is arrested, witnesses to officials, is taken to Rome (21:27-28:31)

After mobbing in Jerusalem, Paul before Sanhedrin

As prisoner, Paul gives fearless witness before Felix, Festus, and King Herod Agrippa II, also on boat en route to Rome

A prisoner in Rome, Paul continues to find ways to preach about Christ and the Kingdom

capital of Achaia. (See GALLIO.) Also, an inscription on an archway in Thessalonica (fragments of which are preserved in the British Museum) shows that Acts 17:8 is correct in speaking of "the city rulers" ("politarchs," governors of the citizens), even though this title is not found in classical literature.

To this day in Athens the Areopagus, or Mars' Hill, where Paul preached, stands as a silent witness to the truthfulness of Acts. (Ac 17:19) Medical terms and expressions found in Acts are in agreement with the Greek medical writers of that time. Modes of travel used in the Middle East in the first century were essentially as described in Acts: overland, by walking, horseback, or horse-drawn chariots (23:24, 31, 32; 8:27-38); overseas, by cargo ships. (21:1-3; 27:1-5) Those ancient vessels did not have a single rudder but were controlled by two large oars, hence accurately spoken of in the plural number. (27:40) The description of Paul's voyage by ship to Rome (27:1-44) as to the time taken, the distance traveled, and the places visited is acknowledged by modern seamen familiar with the region as completely reliable and trustworthy.

Acts of Apostles was accepted without question as inspired Scripture and canonical by Scripture catalogers from the second through the fourth centuries C.E. Portions of the book, along with fragments of the four Gospels, are found in the Chester Beatty No. 1 papyrus manuscript (P^{45}) of the third century C.E. The Michigan No. 1571 manuscript (P^{38}) of the third or fourth century contains portions of chapters 18 and 19, and a fourth-century manuscript, Aegyptus No. 8683 (P^8), contains parts of chapters 4 through 6. The book of Acts was quoted from by Polycarp of Smyrna about 115 C.E., by Ignatius of Antioch about 110 C.E., and by Clement of Rome perhaps as early as 95 C.E. Athanasius, Jerome, and Augustine of the fourth century all confirm the earlier listings that included Acts.

ADADAH (A·da′dah). One of the cities in the southern part of the territory originally assigned to Judah, lying toward the border of Edom. (Jos 15:22) The Vatican Manuscript No. 1209 of the Greek *Septuagint* here reads *A·rou·el.* On this basis, as well as 1 Samuel 30:28, some scholars favor identifying it with Aroer in Judah.—See AROER No. 3.

ADAH (A′dah) [shortened form of Eleadah or Adaiah].

1. The first of Lamech's two living wives. She was the mother of Jabal and Jubal, the founders of nomadic herdsmen and musicians respectively. —Ge 4:19-23.

2. A Canaanite daughter of Elon the Hittite, and one of Esau's wives. As such she was "a source of bitterness of spirit to Isaac and Rebekah." Her son's name was Eliphaz, the father of Amalek. She may be the one called Basemath in Genesis 26:34. —Ge 26:35; 36:2, 4, 10, 12.

ADAIAH (A·dai′ah) [Jehovah Has Decked [the nameholder]].

1. A descendant of Levi's son Gershom and an ancestor of Asaph.—1Ch 6:39-43.

2. A Benjaminite, son of Shimei.—1Ch 8:1, 21.

3. The father of Maaseiah, who was one of "the chiefs of hundreds" that helped Jehoiada the priest overthrow wicked Athaliah's rule and set Jehoash upon the throne of Judah.—2Ch 23:1.

4. The father of Jedidah, who was the mother of King Josiah. (2Ki 22:1) He was a native of Bozkath, located in the Shephelah in the territory of Judah.—Jos 15:21, 33, 39.

5. A son of Joiarib of the tribe of Judah.—Ne 11:4, 5.

6. A priest dwelling in Jerusalem after the return from Babylonian exile, the son of Jeroham. —1Ch 9:10-12; Ne 11:12.

7. An Israelite, one of the descendants of Bani who divorced their foreign wives and sent away their sons after the Babylonian exile.—Ezr 10:29, 44.

8. Another of the Israelites who sent away their foreign wives and sons, his ancestral head being Binnui.—Ezr 10:38, 39, 44.

ADALIA (A·da′li·a). One of Haman's ten sons. —Es 9:7-10; see HAMAN.

ADAM (Ad′am) [Earthling Man; Mankind; Humankind; from a root meaning "red"]. The Hebrew word occurs as "man," "mankind," or "earthling man" over 560 times in the Scriptures and is applied to individuals and mankind in general. It is also used as a proper name.

1. God said: "Let us make *man* in our image." (Ge 1:26) What a historic pronouncement! And what a singular position in history Adam, the "son of God," holds—the first human creature! (Lu 3:38) Adam was the crowning glory of Jehovah's earthly creative works, not only because of the timing near the close of six creative epochs but, more importantly, because "in God's image he created him." (Ge 1:27) This is why the perfect man Adam, and his degenerate offspring to a much lesser degree, possessed mental powers and abilities far superior to all other earthly creatures.

In what way was Adam made in the likeness of God?

Made in the likeness of his Grand Creator, Adam had the divine attributes of love, wisdom, justice, and power; hence he possessed a sense of morality involving a conscience, something altogether new in the sphere of earthly life. In the image of God, Adam was to be a global administrator and have in subjection the sea and land creatures and the fowl of the air.

It was not necessary for Adam to be a spirit creature, in whole or in part, to possess Godlike qualities. Jehovah formed man out of the dust particles of the ground, put in him the force of life so that he became a living soul, and gave him the ability to reflect the image and likeness of his Creator. "The first man is out of the earth and made of dust." "The first man Adam became a living soul." (Ge 2:7; 1Co 15:45, 47) That was in the year 4026 B.C.E. It was likely in the fall of the year, for mankind's most ancient calendars began counting time in the autumn around October 1, or at the first new moon of the lunar civil year.—See YEAR.

Adam's home was a very special paradise, a veritable garden of pleasure called Eden (see EDEN No. 1), providing him with all the necessary physical things of life, for "every tree desirable to one's sight and good for food" for his perpetual sustenance was there. (Ge 2:9) All around Adam were peaceful animals of every kind and description. But Adam was alone. There was no other creature 'according to his kind' with which to talk. Jehovah recognized that "it is not good for the man to continue by himself." So by divine surgery, the first and only case of its kind, Jehovah took a rib from Adam and fashioned it into a female counterpart to be his wife and the mother of his children. Overjoyed with such a beautiful helper and constant companion, Adam burst forth in the first recorded poetry, "This is at last bone of my bones and flesh of my flesh," and she was called *woman* "because from man this one was taken." Later Adam called his wife Eve. (Ge 2:18-23; 3:20) The truthfulness of this account is attested to by Jesus and the apostles.—Mt 19:4-6; Mr 10:6-9; Eph 5:31; 1Ti 2:13.

Furthermore, Jehovah blessed these newlyweds with plenty of enjoyable work. (Compare Ec 3:13; 5:18.) They were not cursed with idleness. They were to keep busy and active dressing and taking care of their garden home, and as they multiplied

and filled the earth with billions of their kind, they were to expand this Paradise to earth's limits. This was a divine mandate.—Ge 1:28.

"God saw everything he had made and, look! it was very good." (Ge 1:31) Indeed, from the very beginning Adam was perfect in every respect. He was equipped with the power of speech and with a highly developed vocabulary. He was able to give meaningful names to the living creatures all around him. He was capable of carrying on a two-way conversation with his God and with his wife.

For all these reasons and many more, Adam was under obligation to love, worship, and strictly obey his Grand Creator. More than that, the Universal Lawgiver spelled out for him the simple law of obedience and fully informed him of the just and reasonable penalty for disobedience: "As for the tree of the knowledge of good and bad you must not eat from it, for in the day you eat from it you will positively die." (Ge 2:16, 17; 3:2, 3) Notwithstanding this explicit law carrying a severe penalty for disobedience, he did disobey.

Results of Sin. Eve was thoroughly deceived by Satan the Devil, but "Adam was not deceived," says the apostle Paul. (1Ti 2:14) With full knowledge Adam willfully and deliberately chose to disobey and then as a criminal he tried to hide. When brought to trial, instead of showing sorrow or regret or asking for forgiveness, Adam attempted to justify himself and pass the responsibility off on others, even blaming Jehovah for his own willful sin. "The woman whom *you* gave to be with me, she gave me fruit from the tree and so I ate." (Ge 3:7-12) So Adam was cast out of Eden into an unsubdued earth that was cursed to produce thorns and thistles, there to sweat out an existence, harvesting the bitter fruits of his sin. Outside the garden, awaiting death, Adam fathered sons and daughters, the names of only three being preserved—Cain, Abel, and Seth. To all of his children Adam passed on hereditary sin and death, since he himself was sinful.—Ge 3:23; 4:1, 2, 25.

This was the tragic start Adam gave the human race. Paradise, happiness, and everlasting life were forfeited, and in their place sin, suffering, and death were acquired through disobedience. "Through one man sin entered into the world and death through sin, and thus death spread to all men because they had all sinned." "Death ruled as king from Adam down." (Ro 5:12, 14) But Jehovah in his wisdom and love provided a "second man," "the last Adam," who is the Lord Jesus Christ. By means of this obedient "Son of God" the way was opened up whereby descendants of the disobedient "first man Adam" could regain Paradise and everlasting life, the church or congregation of Christ even gaining heavenly life. "For just as in Adam all are dying, so also in the Christ all will be made alive."—Joh 3:16, 18; Ro 6:23; 1Co 15:22, 45, 47.

After sinner Adam's expulsion from Eden he lived to see the murder of his own son, banishment of his killer-son, abuse of the marriage arrangement, and profanation of Jehovah's sacred name. He witnessed the building of a city, the development of musical instruments, and the forging of tools out of iron and copper. He watched and was condemned by the example of Enoch, "the seventh one in line from Adam," one who "kept walking with the true God." He even lived to see Noah's father Lamech of the ninth generation. Finally, after 930 years, most of which was spent in the slow process of dying, Adam returned to the ground from which he was taken, in the year 3096 B.C.E., just as Jehovah had said.—Ge 4:8-26; 5:5-24; Jude 14; see LAMECH No. 2.

2. A city mentioned at Joshua 3:16 as being at the side of Zarethan. It is generally identified with Tell ed-Damiyeh (Tel Damiya'), a site E of the Jordan River about 1 km (0.6 mi) S of the confluence of the Jordan and the torrent valley of Jabbok; it is about 28 km (17 mi) NNE of Jericho. The name of the city may be derived from the color of the alluvial clay, which is abundant in that region. —1Ki 7:46.

The Bible record indicates that the damming up of the Jordan's waters at the time of Israel's crossing the river took place at Adam. The Jordan Valley narrows considerably, beginning at the site of Tell ed-Damiyeh (Tel Damiya') northward, and history records that in the year 1267 a blockage of the river occurred at this very point due to the falling of a lofty mound across the river, stopping the flow of water for some 16 hours. In modern times, earth tremors in the summer of 1927 again caused landslides that dammed up the Jordan so that the flow of water was cut off for 21½ hours. (*The Foundations of Bible History: Joshua, Judges,* by J. Garstang, London, 1931, pp. 136, 137) If this was the means God saw fit to employ, then such a damming of the river in the days of Joshua was miraculously timed and effected so as to synchronize with the crossing of the Jordan on the day previously announced by Jehovah through Joshua.—Jos 3:5-13.

ADAMAH (Ad'a·mah) [Ground]. One of the fortified cities in the territory assigned to the tribe of Naphtali. Its location is not definitely known. —Jos 19:32, 36.

ADAMI-NEKEB (Ad'a·mi-ne'keb) [Ground of Piercing (Boring)]. A place in the southern part of Naphtali. (Jos 19:33) Its site is generally identified as Khirbet et-Tell (Tel Adami), above and W of Khirbet ed-Damiyeh, about 16 km (10 mi) ENE of Nazareth and approximately midway between Tiberias and Mount Tabor. Its position commanded a pass on an old caravan route between Gilead and the Plain of Acco.

ADAR (A'dar). The postexilic name of the 12th Jewish lunar month of the sacred calendar, but the 6th of the secular calendar. (Es 3:7) It corresponds to part of February and part of March. It is after the month Adar that the intercalary month, called Veadar, or the second Adar, is added in certain years.

During this month, which came at the close of the winter season and led into spring, the carob trees began to blossom in parts of Palestine, and in the warm lowlands the orange and lemon trees were ready for harvesting.

By a royal decree of King Ahasuerus of Persia the 13th day of Adar was to mark the destruction of all the Jews in the jurisdictional districts of his domain, this at the instigation of his prime minister, Haman. A new decree, issued through Queen Esther's mediation, enabled the Jews to gain a victory over their would-be assassins, and thereafter Mordecai ordered the 14th and 15th days of Adar to be celebrated in commemoration of their deliverance. (Es 3:13; 8:11, 12; 9:1, 15, 20, 21, 27, 28) This Jewish festival is known as Purim, a name derived from "Pur, that is, the Lot."—Es 9:24-26; see PURIM.

Adar is also the month in which Governor Zerubbabel finished the reconstruction of the temple in Jerusalem. (Ezr 6:15) Elsewhere in the Bible it is mentioned only as "the twelfth month."—2Ki 25:27; 1Ch 27:15; Jer 52:31; Eze 32:1.

ADBEEL (Ad'be·el). A grandson of Abraham, listed third among the 12 sons of Ishmael, his mother being an Egyptian. He was the chieftain of a tribal clan bearing his name.—Ge 21:21; 25:13-16; 1Ch 1:29.

ADDAR (Ad'dar).

1. A son of Bela, a Benjaminite.—1Ch 8:1, 3.

2. A southern border town of Judah located near Kadesh-barnea. (Jos 15:3) In Joshua's account it is listed as lying between Hezron and Karka, but at Numbers 34:4 it appears that the name Hezron (meaning "Courtyard; Settlement") is combined with Addar to form Hazar-addar, since the accounts are parallel. The book *Biblical*

Archaeology (by G. E. Wright, 1963, p. 71) suggests as a possible location that of 'Ain el-Qudeirat, where a perennial spring waters a small but fertile valley. It lies about 8 km (5 mi) NNW of 'Ain Qedeis, the possible location of Kadesh-barnea.

ADDI (Ad'di). The son of Cosam and father of Melchi. As a descendant of David through Nathan, Addi was an ancestor of Jesus.—Lu 3:28, 31.

ADDON (Ad'don). Apparently an unidentified location in Babylonia, from which some returning to Jerusalem in 537 B.C.E., at the end of the 70-year desolation of Judah, were unable to establish their genealogy from the public records. As a consequence, they were disqualified from serving in the priesthood. Some scholars think Addon was an individual who was unable to prove his ancestry.—Ezr 2:59-62; Ne 7:61-64.

ADIEL (Ad'i·el) [God Is an Ornament].

1. The father of Azmaveth, whom King David appointed to be over his royal treasure house. —1Ch 27:25, 31.

2. One of the chieftains of the tribe of Simeon, who, in the days of King Hezekiah of Judah in the eighth century B.C.E., shared in the dispossession of the Hamites from the region near Gedor.—1Ch 4:36, 38-41.

3. An Aaronic priest of the paternal house of Immer whose father was Jahzerah. His son Maasai served at Jerusalem after the Babylonian exile. —1Ch 9:12.

ADIN (A'din) [Pleasure-Given]. One of the paternal heads of Israel, several hundred of whose descendants returned from Babylonian exile with Zerubbabel. (Ezr 2:15; Ne 7:20) Later, 51 more of his lineage returned with Ezra in 468 B.C.E. (Ezr 8:6) A princely representative of Adin's paternal house was among those who attested to the "trustworthy arrangement" drawn up in the days of Nehemiah.—Ne 9:38; 10:1, 16.

ADINA (Ad'i·na) [from a root meaning "luxuriate" [that is, get pleasure]]. The son of Shiza, and an officer over 30 other Reubenites in David's army.—1Ch 11:26, 42.

ADINO. See JOSHEB-BASSHEBETH.

ADITHAIM (Ad·i·tha'im). One of the cities of Judah located in the Shephelah, or lowland. (Jos 15:33, 36) The exact site is uncertain.

ADJUTANT. The Hebrew word *sha·lish'* (third man, referring to the third warrior in a war chariot) has been translated in various Bible versions as "captain," "chariot-leader," "lord," "warrior," "adjutant."

Some monumental inscriptions illustrating "Hittite" and Assyrian war chariots show three men: one, the driver; another, the fighter with the sword, lance, or bow; and a third, the carrier of the shield. Though Egyptian monuments usually do not show three-manned chariots, the term is used at Exodus 14:7 with respect to Pharaoh's charioteers. The third chariot warrior, usually the one carrying the shield, was an assistant commander in the war chariot, an adjutant. The English word "adjutant" literally means "one that helps; assistant."

After mentioning that none of the sons of Israel were constituted slaves by Solomon, 1 Kings 9:22 states: "For they were the warriors and his servants and his princes and his adjutants and chiefs of his charioteers and of his horsemen." Commenting on this text, C. F. Keil states that the term *sha·li·shim'* (plural), used in this passage, could be understood as "royal adjutants."—*Commentary on the Old Testament*, 1973, Vol. III, 1 Kings, p. 146.

In the days of King Jehoram of Israel, the Syrians put Samaria under siege, which in time caused famine conditions within the city. When Elisha prophesied that there would be plenty of food, Jehoram's special adjutant ridiculed the prophecy. As Elisha had foretold, the adjutant saw the fulfillment of the prophecy but did not get to eat any of the food, being trampled to death in the gateway.—2Ki 7:2, 16-20.

At Jehu's command, his runners and adjutants, likely including Bidkar, struck down the Baal worshipers. (2Ki 9:25; 10:25) Pekah, another adjutant

Three men in an Assyrian war chariot

referred to in the Scriptures, assassinated Pekahiah the king of Israel and succeeded him to the throne.—2Ki 15:25; see Eze 23:15, ftn.

ADLAI (Ad'lai). Father of Shaphat, who served as overseer of the herds of David in the low plains. —1Ch 27:29.

ADMAH (Ad'mah) [Ground]. One of the five cities in the region of "the Low Plain of Siddim" inhabited by Canaanites. (Ge 10:19; 14:1-3) This low plain, or vale, was probably near the southern end of the Salt Sea.

Along with the neighboring cities of Sodom, Gomorrah, Zeboiim, and Bela (Zoar), Admah and its king, Shinab, suffered defeat at the time of the invasion by four eastern kings. (Ge 14:8-11) Deuteronomy 29:23 shows that Admah was later destroyed along with Sodom, Gomorrah, and Zeboiim when Jehovah caused a rain of fire and sulfur to descend upon the entire basin. (Ge 19:25) At Hosea 11:8 it is referred to, along with Zeboiim, as a warning example.

Many scholars believe that the original sites of Admah and the other "cities of the District" now lie submerged beneath the waters of the Salt Sea, though some others recently have claimed that the ruins of the cities may be identified with sites along wadis to the E and SE of the Dead Sea.—Ge 13:12.

ADMATHA (Ad·ma'tha) [from Persian, meaning "Unconquered"]. One of the seven princes in the kingdom of Persia and Media who had access to King Ahasuerus. These princes concurred in the judgment against Queen Vashti, and apparently such a committee of seven regularly served the Persian kings as counselors.—Es 1:14; Ezr 7:14.

ADMINISTRATION. A managerial procedure or an arrangement for supervision in the fulfilling of a responsibility or the attaining of a goal.

The Hebrew word translated "administration" in 1 Chronicles 26:30 (pequd·dah') comes from the root pa·qadh', meaning "visit; turn attention to." (Ru 1:6, ftn) It is also rendered "care; oversight." —2Ch 24:11; Nu 3:32; compare 2Ki 11:18, ftn; see OVERSEER.

From the start of human history God authorized perfect man to care for the earth and have in subjection its creatures. (Ge 1:26-28) After man's rebellion, particularly from the Flood forward, a patriarchal system of administration developed and became prominent. It managed family affairs and property and enforced standards of conduct.

The handling of Israel's national affairs by Moses according to the divine will during the 40-year wilderness trek provides a brilliant example of administration, including the delegation of authority to reliable subordinates. (Ex 18:19-26) Within the priesthood the prime responsibility for administration rested on the high priest (Nu 3:5-10); however, others were given the responsibility of the oversight and supervision of certain departments of service. (Nu 3:25, 26, 30-32, 36, 37; 4:16) Following Israel's entry into the Promised Land, judges acted as administrators of the nation, with divine backing.—Jg 2:16, 18; Ru 1:1.

Upon the establishment of the kingdom in Israel, a more complete system of administration developed. Under King David the administrative structure was quite detailed, with officials directly under the king and with divisional administrators serving throughout the country. (1Ch 26:29-32; 27:1, 16-22, 25-34) The priesthood was also thoroughly organized during David's reign, with supervisors for the tabernacle work, officers and judges, gatekeepers, singers and musicians, and the setting up of 24 priestly divisions for handling the service at the tabernacle. (1Ch 23:1-5; 24:1-19) Solomon's administration was even more extensive and provides an outstanding example of capable administration in the construction of the temple.—1Ki 4:1-7, 26, 27; 5:13-18.

Other nations also developed complex systems of administration, as indicated by the classes of officials assembled by King Nebuchadnezzar at the time of inaugurating his golden image. (Da 3:2, 3) Daniel himself was 'made ruler' (from Aramaic, shelet') over the jurisdictional district of Babylon and under him civil "administration" (Aramaic, 'avi·dhah') was given to Shadrach, Meshach, and Abednego.—Da 2:48, 49.

In the Christian Greek Scriptures, proper use of the delegated authority and responsibility resting upon those charged with overseeing the application and execution of God's expressed will among his people is often discussed; and this is done by references to stewardship and oversight. (Lu 16:2-4; 1Co 9:17; Eph 3:2; Col 1:25; Tit 1:7) While responsibility to God is shown to be of paramount importance (Ps 109:8; Ac 1:20), the interests of those who serve under such administration are also stressed.—1Pe 4:10; see STEWARD.

What is the "administration" that God has put into operation since 33 C.E.?

In his undeserved kindness God has purposed to have "an administration [Gr., oi·ko·no·mi'an, literally, "household management"] at the full limit of the appointed times, namely, to gather all things together again in the Christ, the things in the heavens and the things on the earth." (Eph 1:10; compare Lu 12:42, ftn.) This "administration," or managerial procedure, which God has been carrying on since the day of Pentecost of 33 C.E., has as its objective the unification of all his intelligent creatures. The first stage of God's "administration" is the gathering together again of "the things in the heavens," preparing the congregation of Kingdom heirs who are to live in the heavens under Jesus Christ as the spiritual Head. (Ro 8:16, 17; Eph 1:11; 1Pe 1:4) The second stage of this "administration" is the gathering together again of "the things on the earth," preparing those who are to live in an earthly paradise.—Joh 10:16; Re 7:9, 10; 21:3, 4.

ADNA (Ad′na) [Pleasure].

1. An Israelite, descendant of the paternal house of Pahath-moab, among those who agreed to send their non-Israelite wives away during the cleansing that took place following the counsel of Ezra the priest.—Ezr 10:30, 44.

2. A priest belonging to the paternal house of Harim, during the days of High Priest Joiakim and of Nehemiah and of Ezra the priest.—Ne 12: 12-15, 26.

ADNAH (Ad′nah) [Pleasure].

1. A valiant military officer of Manasseh who deserted from Saul to David's army at Ziklag. He fought at David's side in the pursuit of the marauding band of Amalekites that ravaged David's camp at Ziklag, and he came to be a chief in David's army.—1Ch 12:20, 21; 1Sa 30:1, 2, 17-19.

2. A Judean general of the armies during the reign of King Jehoshaphat, commanding 300,-000 valiant, mighty warriors, and exercising control over an additional 480,000 troops under the command of generals Jehohanan and Amasiah, all of whom ministered to the king at Jerusalem. —2Ch 17:13-16, 19.

ADONI-BEZEK (A·do′ni-be′zek) [Lord of Bezek]. A powerful ruler who, prior to the Israelite attack at Bezek, had humbled 70 pagan kings by cutting off their thumbs and great toes.

A similar practice was employed at one time by the ancient Athenians, who decreed that prisoners of war should lose their thumbs. Thereafter they could row but were unfit to handle a sword or spear. Soon after Joshua's death the combined forces of Judah and Simeon clashed with 10,-000 troops of the Canaanites and Perizzites at Bezek, causing Adoni-bezek to flee from the de-

feat. Upon being captured, his thumbs and great toes were also severed, at which time he declared: "Just the way I have done, so God has repaid me." He was transported to Jerusalem, where he died. —Jg 1:4-7.

ADONIJAH (Ad·o·ni′jah) [Jehovah Is Lord].

1. David's fourth son, born of Haggith in Hebron.—2Sa 3:4, 5.

Though of a different mother, Adonijah was quite similar to Absalom in being "very goodlooking in form" and in his ambition. (1Ki 1:5, 6; compare 2Sa 14:25; 15:1.) He becomes prominent in the Bible record during David's waning years. Despite Jehovah's declaration that the kingship would go to Solomon (1Ch 22:9, 10), Adonijah began boasting that he would be Israel's next king. Since Amnon and Absalom, and probably Chileab, were dead, Adonijah doubtless founded his claim to the throne on the basis of his being the eldest son. Like Absalom, he made a showy display of his pretensions and went uncorrected by his father. He built up party support by gaining the favor of the head of the army, Joab, and the head of the priesthood, Abiathar. (1Ki 1:5-8) He then held a sacrificial feast near En-rogel, a short distance from the city of Jerusalem, inviting most of the royal household, but not Solomon, Nathan the prophet, and Benaiah. His obvious purpose was to have himself declared king.—1Ki 1:9, 10, 25.

Nathan the prophet acted promptly to block Adonijah's scheme. He counseled Solomon's mother Bath-sheba to remind David of his oath in favor of Solomon's kingship and then appeared after her at the king's quarters to confirm her words and alert David to the gravity of the situation, also, in effect, indicating that he felt David may have been acting behind the backs of his close associates. (1Ki 1:11-27) This stirred the old king to action, and he promptly gave orders for the immediate anointing of Solomon as coregent and successor to the throne. This action provoked a joyful uproar by the people, which was heard at Adonijah's banquet. Soon a runner, priest Abiathar's son, appeared with the disquieting news of David's proclamation of Solomon as king. Adonijah's supporters quickly dispersed, and he fled to the tabernacle courtyard seeking refuge. Solomon then granted him pardon on the provision of his good behavior.—1Ki 1:32-53.

However, following David's death, Adonijah approached Bath-sheba and induced her to act as his agent before Solomon to request David's youthful nurse and companion, Abishag, as his wife.

Adonijah's statement that "the kingship was to have become mine, and it was toward me that all Israel had set their face for me to become king" indicates that he felt he had been deprived of his right, even though he professedly acknowledged God's hand in the matter. (1Ki 2:13-21) While his request may have been based solely on the desire for some compensation for the loss of the kingdom, it strongly suggested that the fires of ambition continued in Adonijah, since by a rule in the ancient East the wives and concubines of a king would only become those of his legal successor. (Compare 2Sa 3:7; 16:21.) Solomon so viewed this request made through his mother and ordered Adonijah's death, which order was promptly carried out by Benaiah.—1Ki 2:22-25.

2. A Levite sent by Jehoshaphat to teach in the cities of Judah.—2Ch 17:7-9.

3. One of "the heads of the people" whose descendant, if not he himself, joined certain princes and Levites in attesting by seal the confession contract made by the returned Israelites in the days of Nehemiah and Ezra. (Ne 9:38; 10:1, 14, 16) He is suggested by some to be the same as Adonikam at Ezra 2:13, whose descendants, numbering 666, returned from Babylon under Zerubbabel in 537 B.C.E. A comparison of the names of those whose representatives sealed the resolution at Nehemiah 10 and of those listed as heads of the returning exiles at Ezra 2 seems to bear this out.

ADONIKAM (Ad·o·ni′kam) [(My) Lord Has Raised Himself Up [that is, to help]]. A founder of one of the paternal houses of Israel. More than 600 members of this family returned to Jerusalem with Zerubbabel after the exile at Babylon. (Ezr 2:13; Ne 7:18) An additional 63 members of this paternal house accompanied Ezra to Jerusalem in 468 B.C.E. (Ezr 8:13) When the representatives of the paternal houses attested to the "trustworthy arrangement," or resolution drawn up in Nehemiah's day, this family was apparently listed by the name Adonijah.—Ne 9:38; 10:16.

ADONIRAM (Ad·o·ni′ram) [(My) Lord Is High (Exalted)]. A prince, able administrator, and the son of Abda. Adoniram served as overseer of those conscripted for forced labor during the reigns of David, Solomon, and Rehoboam, playing an important part in Solomon's many building projects. Later, when the ten tribes revolted against the harsh dictates of Rehoboam at Shechem in 997 B.C.E., the king sent this conscriptor for forced labor to the people, but they "pelted him with stones, so that he died." (2Ch 10:18) He is variously referred to as Adoniram (1Ki 4:6; 5:14),

as Adoram (2Sa 20:24; 1Ki 12:18), and as Hadoram.—2Ch 10:18.

ADONI-ZEDEK (A·do′ni-ze′dek) [(My) Lord Is Righteousness]. A king of Jerusalem at the time of the Israelite conquest of the Promised Land. Adoni-zedek joined with other petty kingdoms W of the Jordan in a consolidated effort to halt Joshua's conquering forces. (Jos 9:1-3) However, the Hivite inhabitants of Gibeon made peace with Joshua. In a retaliatory measure designed to stop further desertion to the enemy, Adoni-zedek united his army with those of four additional kings of the Amorites, and he laid siege against Gibeon and warred against it. Joshua's spectacular rescue of the Gibeonites and the shattering defeat of these combined forces caused the five kings to flee to Makkedah, where they were trapped in a cave. Joshua himself slew Adoni-zedek and the other four kings before his troops, and hung them upon stakes. Their corpses were finally thrown back into the cave, which came to be their tomb.—Jos 10:1-27.

ADOPTION. The taking or accepting as a son or daughter one who is not such by natural relationship. The Greek word translated "adoption" (hui·o·the·si′a) is a technical legal term that literally means "a placing as son."—Compare Ro 8:15, ftn.

In the Hebrew Scriptures adoption is not dealt with from the viewpoint of legal procedure, but the basic idea is set forth in several cases. It appears that Abraham, prior to the birth of Ishmael and Isaac, considered his slave Eliezer as at least in line for a position similar to that of an adopted son and as the likely inheritor of Abraham's house. (Ge 15:2-4) The practice of adopting slaves as sons has long been a common Middle Eastern practice, and as such they had inheritance rights, though not above those of children descended naturally from the father.

Rachel and Leah both considered the children born to Jacob by their handmaids as their own sons, 'born upon their knees.' (Ge 30:3-8, 12, 13, 24) These children inherited along with those born directly of Jacob's legal wives. They were natural sons of the father, and since the slave girls were property of the wives, Rachel and Leah had property rights in these children.

The child Moses was later adopted by Pharaoh's daughter. (Ex 2:5-10) Since men and women had equal rights under Egyptian law, Pharaoh's daughter was in position to exercise the right of adoption.

Within the nation of Israel adoption does not appear to have been widely practiced. The law of levirate marriage doubtless eliminated to a great extent a basic reason for adoption of children: the continuance of the parental name.—De 25:5, 6.

A Christian Significance. In the Christian Greek Scriptures adoption is mentioned several times by the apostle Paul with regard to the new status of those called and chosen by God. Such ones, born as descendants of the imperfect Adam, were in slavery to sin and did not possess inherent sonship of God. Through purchase by means of Christ Jesus, they receive the adoption as sons and also become heirs with Christ, the only-begotten Son of God. (Ga 4:1-7; Ro 8:14-17) They do not come by such sonship naturally but by God's choice and according to his will. (Eph 1:5) While acknowledged as God's children, or sons, from the time of God's begetting them by his spirit (1Jo 3:1; Joh 1:12, 13), their full realization of this privilege as spirit sons of God is dependent on their ultimate faithfulness. (Ro 8:17; Re 21:7) Thus, Paul speaks of them as "earnestly waiting for adoption as sons, the release from our bodies by ransom."—Ro 8:23.

Such adopted state brings benefits of freedom from "a spirit of slavery causing fear," replacing it with the confidence of sons; of hope of a heavenly inheritance assured by the witness of God's spirit. At the same time these spiritual sons are reminded by their adoption that such position is by God's undeserved kindness and selection rather than by their inherent right.—Ro 8:15, 16; Ga 4:5-7.

At Romans 9:4 Paul speaks of the fleshly Israelites as those "to whom belong the adoption as sons and the glory and the covenants and the giving of the Law," and this evidently refers to the unique position granted Israel while they were God's covenant people. Thus, God, on occasion, spoke of Israel as "my son." (Ex 4:22, 23; De 14:1, 2; Isa 43:6; Jer 31:9; Ho 1:10; 11:1; compare Joh 8:41.) Actual sonship, however, awaited the ransom provision made through Christ Jesus and was dependent on acceptance of that divine arrangement and faith in it.—Joh 1:12, 13; Ga 4:4, 5; 2Co 6:16-18.

ADORAIM (A·do·ra'im). One of the cities of Judah rebuilt and fortified by King Rehoboam in the tenth century B.C.E. (2Ch 11:9) It is identified with the modern village of Dura, located on a hillside about 8 km (5 mi) W of Hebron.

ADORAM. See ADONIRAM.

ADORNMENT. That which is put on to decorate, beautify, embellish, add luster to, and make the person himself, or that which he represents, pleasing or attractive. It may be for a good or for a deceptive purpose. The Hebrew word for "adornment" is hadha·rah', evidently from the root ha·dhar', meaning "honor." (1Ch 16:29; La 5:12) At 1 Peter 3:3 "adornment" translates the Greek word ko'smos, elsewhere rendered "world." The related verb ko·sme'o is translated "adorn."—Tit 2:10.

The Scriptures do not condemn physical adornment if it is properly done, and they highly recommend spiritual adornment. Jehovah himself is described as clothed in light and surrounded by beauty. (Ps 104:1, 2; Eze 1:1, 4-28; Re 4:2, 3) He has richly ornamented his creation with color, variety, and majestic magnificence.—Lu 12:27, 28; Ps 139:14; 1Co 15:41.

In Bible times the bridegroom and the bride adorned themselves for the marriage feast. In preparation the bride decked herself with the finest clothing and the best of the ornamental things that she possessed to present herself before the bridegroom. (Ps 45:13, 14; Isa 61:10) Jehovah speaks to Jerusalem, figuratively describing her as a girl whom he decked with fine, costly clothing and jewelry but who used her beauty and adornment unfaithfully as a prostitute. (Eze 16:10-19) Jehovah's prophet Hosea condemned Israel for adorning herself for the wrong purpose of attracting passionate lovers and engaging in false worship. (Ho 2:13) Through his prophets Jehovah foretold a restoration of Israel when she would come out of Babylonian exile and again adorn herself to express her joy and exultation.—Isa 52:1; Jer 31:4.

The temple in Jerusalem and Solomon's governmental buildings were beautifully adorned, to the delight of the queen of Sheba. (1Ki chaps 6, 7, 10) The temple rebuilt by Herod was a magnificent edifice adorned with fine stones and dedicated things. But Jesus showed that these material adornments would be of no avail when God's judgment came upon Jerusalem for her unfaithfulness.—Lu 21:5, 6.

The Proverbs show that if a great number of people choose to live under and delight in the rule of a king, this is one measure of his success. It is an adornment to him, recommending and adding luster to him as a ruler. (Pr 14:28) Jehovah is such a ruler by his Messianic Kingdom.—Ps 22:27-31; Php 2:10, 11.

Christian Counsel on Personal Adornment. Jesus and his apostles counseled constantly against putting trust in physical things and putting on a false show by means of material adornment. The apostle Paul said that Christian women should "adorn themselves in well-arranged dress, with modesty and soundness of mind, not with styles of hair braiding and gold or pearls or very expensive garb." (1Ti 2:9) During the days of the apostles it was a custom among women in that world of Greek culture to go in for elaborate coiffures and other adornment. How appropriate, therefore, is Peter's counsel to women in the Christian congregation not to put emphasis on 'the external braiding of the hair and the putting on of gold ornaments or the wearing of outer garments' but to let their adornment be, as with the faithful women of old, "the secret person of the heart in the incorruptible apparel of the quiet and mild spirit"!—1Pe 3:3-5.

The apostle Paul points out that the Christian can, by fine works of incorruptibleness in his teaching, seriousness, wholesome speech, and right conduct in all his ways of life, adorn the teachings of God, making them attractive to others. (Tit 2:10) In this spiritual way, the Christian congregation, the bride of Christ, eventually appears in her full beauty to her husband Jesus Christ. She is similarly described at Revelation 21:2 as "prepared as a bride adorned for her husband." Her spiritual beauty is a direct contrast to the adornment of Babylon the Great, spoken of as adorned with material things, the wage of her prostitution.—Re 18:16; see COSMETICS; DRESS; JEWELS AND PRECIOUS STONES; ORNAMENTS.

ADRAMMELECH (A·dram'me·lech).

1. A son of King Sennacherib of Assyria. Adrammelech and his brother Sharezer killed their father while he was bowing down at the house of his god Nisroch at Nineveh. They then escaped to the land of Ararat, apparently in the location of ancient Armenia in the mountainous region to the W of what is now known as the Caspian Sea. (2Ki 19:35-37; Isa 37:36-38) An inscription of Esar-haddon, another son of Sennacherib, relates that as his father's successor he engaged and defeated the armies of his father's murderers at Hanigalbat in that region.

2. A god worshiped by the Sepharvites, one of the subjugated peoples the king of Assyria brought into the territory of Samaria after his taking the Israelites of the ten-tribe kingdom into exile. It was to Adrammelech and Anammelech that the Sepharvites sacrificed their sons in the fire.—2Ki 17:22-24, 31, 33.

ADRAMYTTIUM (Ad·ra·myt'ti·um). A seaport city on the Aegean Sea, located in Mysia at the NW corner of Asia Minor, N of Pergamum. In modern Turkey the inland town of Edremit (E of the harbor) preserves the earlier name.

Adramyttium was part of the province of Asia under Roman rule and was evidently at one time a maritime commercial center of some importance, since it lay on the Roman road that passed through Pergamum and Ephesus to the S and Assos, Troas, and the Hellespont to the W and N. It is likely that Paul passed through Adramyttium on his third missionary tour. The only direct Bible reference to the place, however, is at Acts 27:2. At Caesarea, Paul, as a prisoner in the custody of the Roman officer Julius, boarded a ship from Adramyttium that was sailing to points along the coast of Asia Minor. Paul's party left the ship at Myra in Lycia, transferring to a grain boat from Alexandria that was sailing for Italy.—Ac 27:3-6.

ADRIA (A'dri·a). At Acts 27:27 reference is made to "the sea of Adria," in which Paul spent 14 turbulent days before being shipwrecked on the island of Malta. Strabo says this name is derived from the city of Atria, located at the mouth of the Po River on what is now called the Gulf of Venice. (*Geography*, 5, I, 8) The present Italian city of Adria lies somewhat back from the coast. It appears that the name Adria came to apply to the waters in that vicinity and was progressively extended to include all the present Adriatic Sea, the Ionian Sea, and those waters of the Mediterranean E of Sicily (and Malta) and W of Crete. So the name covered some waters that today are considered as outside the Adriatic Sea; but in Paul's day the island of Malta could properly be said to be bounded by "the sea of Adria."

ADRIEL (A'dri·el). The son of Barzillai, from the city of Abel-meholah.

Adriel was given Saul's oldest daughter Merab as wife, though she had previously been promised to David. (1Sa 18:17-19) All of Adriel's five sons were later surrendered for execution to help atone for Saul's attempted annihilation of the Gibeonites. (2Sa 21:8, 9) In this account Michal rather than Merab is spoken of as the mother of Adriel's five sons. Since Michal died childless (2Sa 6:23) and is nowhere spoken of as having been the wife of Adriel, some translators view the appearance of Michal's name as a scribal error. Nearly all Hebrew manuscripts, however, use Michal's name, and the traditional explanation is that Merab, Michal's older sister, died early after having borne five sons to Adriel and that Michal thereafter undertook the bringing up of her sister's five boys, thus resulting in their being spoken of as her sons. Isaac Leeser's translation reads at 2 Samuel 21:8: "And the five sons of Michal the daughter of Saul, whom she had brought up for Adriel."

ADULLAM (A·dul'lam). A city of Judah in the fertile lowland or Shephelah, about halfway between Bethlehem and Lachish. (Jos 15:35) It is identified with Tell esh-Sheikh Madhkur (Horvat 'Adullam), about 26 km (16 mi) WSW of Jerusalem. The original name seems to be preserved in the name of the nearby ruins of 'Id el-Ma (Miyeh). The site of Adullam dominates the Wadi es-Sur and the approach from that part of the Shephelah into the interior of Judah, thus making it a strategic location. It is primarily known for "the cave of Adullam," where David fled before King Saul. There are numerous limestone caves in this area.—2Sa 23:13.

Adullam was evidently an ancient city. Its first Biblical mention is in connection with Hirah "the Adullamite," who became a companion of Judah prior to the transfer of Jacob's family to Egypt. (Ge 38:1, 2, 12, 20) At the time of Joshua's invasion some three centuries later, Adullam was one of the 31 petty kingdoms that were vanquished by him. (Jos 11:1-15; 12:15) Adullam was thereafter allotted to Judah along with other cities of the Shephelah.—Jos 15:33-35.

David, as a fugitive from King Saul, escaped from the Philistine king Achish of Gath and went up to Adullam to a cave, where he was eventually joined by some 400 men. (1Sa 22:1-5) About 19 km (12 mi) WSW of Bethlehem, the area may have been known to David from his shepherd days. Its relative inaccessibility appears to have recommended it as David's stronghold. In later times, during his reign David used it as an operational site in wars against the Philistines. It was from this point that the three warriors made their sortie into Bethlehem to obtain the cistern water that David later refused to drink as representing their blood risked to obtain it.—1Ch 11:15-19; 12:16; 2Sa 5:17, 18.

Adullam was one of the chain of 15 fortress cities reinforced by Rehoboam of Judah. (2Ch 11:5-12) This chain, intended to provide protection from the W and S, was overrun by Sennacherib's troops during Hezekiah's rule (732 B.C.E.). (2Ki 18:13) Adullam is mentioned in the days of Nehemiah as among the cities resettled by the repatriated Jews who returned from the Babylonian exile.—Ne 11:30.

ADULTERY. As used in the Bible, adultery generally refers to voluntary sexual intercourse by a married person with one of the opposite sex other than one's mate, or, during the time that the Mosaic Law was in effect, such intercourse by any man with a married or a betrothed woman. The Hebrew root meaning "commit adultery" is na-'aph', while its Greek counterpart is moi·kheu'o.—Eze 16:32, ftn; Mt 5:32, ftn.

Certain primitive societies allow free relations within the same tribe, but promiscuity outside tribal bounds is considered adultery. On the history of adultery, *Funk & Wagnalls Standard Dictionary of Folklore, Mythology and Legend* (1949, Vol. 1, p. 15) says: "It occurs in all parts of the world and though it is considered reprehensible by many cultures it has enjoyed a considerable popularity in all cultures and at all times." Monuments attest to its prevalence in ancient Egypt; Potiphar's wife, who proposed that Joseph have relations with her, was such an Egyptian. (Ge 39:7, 10) Historically as well as at present, adultery is generally forbidden, but penalties are seldom imposed.

Jehovah's law separated Israel and raised the moral status of marriage and family life to a much higher level than that of the surrounding nations. The seventh commandment of the Decalogue stated in direct, unmistakable language: "You must not commit adultery." (Ex 20:14; De 5:18; Lu 18:20) Adulterous invasion of another man's domain was prohibited, as were other forms of sexual misconduct.—See FORNICATION; PROSTITUTE.

Under the Law of Moses the penalty for adultery was severe—death for both guilty parties: "In case a man is found lying down with a woman owned by an owner, both of them must then die together." This applied even to a betrothed woman, it being considered that she had committed adultery if she had relations with a man other than the one to whom she was duly engaged. (De 22:22-24) If suspected of adultery, a wife had to stand trial.—Nu 5:11-31; see THIGH.

Christians, though not under Mosaic Law, must also refrain from adultery. "For the law code, 'You must not commit adultery,' . . . is summed up in this word, namely, 'You must love your neighbor as yourself.'" There can be no hypocrisy in this matter. (Ro 13:9; 2:22) In teaching Bible principles, Jesus raised the moral standard still higher for Christians. He broadened out the matter of adultery, saying it was not limited to sexual contact a man might have with a woman not his mate: "Everyone that keeps on looking at a woman so as to have a passion for her has already committed adultery with her in his heart." Such men are among those who "have eyes full of adultery."—Mt 5:27, 28; 2Pe 2:14.

Jesus also pointed out that if a divorce was obtained by either husband or wife, except on the ground of fornication (Gr., por·nei'a), the remarriage of either one would constitute adultery. Even a single man who took such a divorced woman as his wife would be guilty of adultery.—Mt 5:32; 19:9; Mr 10:11, 12; Lu 16:18; Ro 7:2, 3.

Adultery is "actually sin against God." (Ge 39:9) Jehovah will judge those guilty of adultery, and none who persist in such a course "will inherit God's kingdom." (Mal 3:5; 1Co 6:9, 10; Heb 13:4) How true the proverb: "Anyone committing adultery with a woman is in want of heart; he that does it is bringing his own soul to ruin."—Pr 6:32-35.

How could one become guilty of spiritual adultery?

In a spiritual sense, adultery denotes unfaithfulness to Jehovah on the part of those who are joined to him in a covenant. Natural Israel in the Law covenant was, therefore, guilty of spiritual adultery because of false religious practices, some of which included sex-worship rites and disregard for the seventh commandment. (Jer 3:8, 9; 5:7, 8; 9:2; 13:27; 23:10; Ho 7:4) For similar reasons Jesus denounced as adulterous the generation of Jews in his day. (Mt 12:39; Mr 8:38) Likewise today, if Christians who are dedicated to Jehovah and who are in the new covenant defile themselves with the present system of things, they commit spiritual adultery.—Jas 4:4.

ADUMMIM   (A·dum′mim) [from a root meaning "red"; possibly, Red Rocks]. The ascent of Adummim is a steep pass about 12 km (7.5 mi) ENE of Jerusalem and midway between the cities of Jericho and Jerusalem. It leads up from the low Jordan Valley to the mountainous region of Judah. From ancient times till the present the road between the two cities has gone through this pass. It is mentioned in the Bible record, however, only as a boundary mark between the territories of Judah and Benjamin.—Jos 15:7; 18:17.

In Arabic the pass is called Tal'at ed-Damm (meaning "Ascent of Blood") and in Hebrew Ma'ale Adummim (meaning "Ascent of Adummim"). While some ancient writers have ascribed the name's origin to the spilling of blood by robbers and highwaymen, the more likely explanation is the reddish color of the soil due to exposed patches of ocher. The route was always a dangerous one because of the desolateness of the region and the prevalence of thievery, and from early times a fort was maintained there to protect travelers. Because of this, the site has been suggested as the scene of the attack on the traveler 'on his way down to Jericho,' as mentioned in Jesus' illustration of the neighborly Samaritan.—Lu 10:30-37.

"The torrent valley" mentioned at Joshua 15:7, in relation to which the ascent of Adummim lay to the S, is evidently the Wadi el Qilt, which runs fairly parallel to the road and passes just to the S of Jericho on its way to the Jordan River.

ADVERSARY.   An enemy that contends with or resists; an antagonist or opponent. The Hebrew word for "adversary" (tsar) comes from a root meaning "harass; show hostility to." (Nu 25:18; Ps 129:1) The Greek word an·ti′di·kos primarily refers to an "adversary at law" in a legal case (Lu 12:58; 18:3), but it can refer to others who are adversaries, or enemies, as in 1 Peter 5:8.

The most wicked Adversary, Satan the Devil, caused men and angels (see DEMON) to join his opposition to God and man. Satan first showed his opposition in the garden of Eden, where, through cruel and underhanded action, he led Eve and then Adam into a course of rebellion that brought sin and death upon all mankind. In the courts of heaven Satan displayed his antagonism, charging Jehovah with bribing Job for his loyalty, a charge which became an issue of universal importance. —Job 1:6-11; 2:1-5; see SATAN.

Worshipers of Jehovah in all ages have endured similar opposition from the Adversary by means of his agents. For example, when the remnant of God's people returned from Babylon, there were those who tried to prevent rebuilding the temple and the city wall. (Ezr 4:1; Ne 4:11) Hateful Haman, having the spirit of the Devil, proved to be a wicked adversary of the Jews in the days of Queen Esther. (Es 7:6) Christians today must be alert, watchful, on guard, and must put up a hard fight for the faith against the Adversary's machinations. (Eph 6:11, 12; Jude 3) Peter counsels: "Keep your senses, be watchful. Your adversary, the Devil, walks about like a roaring lion, seeking to devour someone. But take your stand against him, solid in the faith." (1Pe 5:8, 9) Eventually Jehovah's power will triumph over all opposers.—Jer 30:16; Mic 5:9.

When God's people were unfaithful he allowed their adversaries to plunder and defeat them. (Ps 89:42; La 1:5, 7, 10, 17; 2:17; 4:12) The enemy, however, drew wrong conclusions from these victories, taking credit for themselves and praising their gods or feeling that they would not be called to account for the way they treated Jehovah's people. (De 32:27; Jer 50:7) Jehovah was therefore obliged to humble these proud and boasting adversaries (Isa 1:24; 26:11; 59:18; Na 1:2); and this he did for his holy name's sake.—Isa 64:2; Eze 36:21-24.

AENEAS (Ae·ne′as) [Praised]. A man of Lydda, alongside the Plains of Sharon, healed by Peter after being paralyzed for eight years.—Ac 9:32-35.

AENON (Ae′non). A place having "a great quantity of water" available, where John the Baptizer performed immersions after the Passover of 30 C.E. (Joh 3:23) It was near the apparently better known place named Salim. The exact locations of these places are uncertain; however, Eusebius, bishop of Caesarea in the third and fourth centuries C.E., indicates a location in the Jordan Valley about 8 Roman miles (12 km; 7.5 mi) S of Beth-shean. In this area is Tell Ridgha (Tel Shalem), tentatively identified with Salim. Nearby are several springs that might fit Eusebius' description of the place called Aenon.

AFFECTION. A strong, warm, personal attachment, such as that existing between genuine friends.

The Hebrew word *cha·shaq′*, translated 'show affection' in Deuteronomy 7:7, has the root meaning "be attached to." (Ge 34:8) The Greek verb *phi·le′o* is translated 'have affection,' "like," 'be fond of,' and "kiss." (Mt 10:37; 23:6; Joh 12:25; Mr 14:44) 'To have affection' expresses a very close bond, of the kind that exists in close families between parents and children. Jesus felt such a deep affection for his friend Lazarus, so that he "gave way to tears" in connection with the death of Lazarus. (Joh 11:35, 36) The same expression is used to show the strong, warm, personal attachment Jehovah has for his Son and for his Son's followers, as well as the warm feeling of the disciples for God's Son.—Joh 5:20; 16:27; compare 1Co 16:22.

It is to be noted that there is a distinction between the Greek verbs *phi·le′o* and *a·ga·pa′o*, although many translators do not differentiate between these words. (See LOVE.) Regarding the difference between these words, F. Zorell (*Lexicon Graecum Novi Testamenti,* Paris, 1961, col. 1402) says: "[*A·ga·pa′o*] signifies a kind of love for someone or something occasioned freely and of our own accord because of clearly perceived reasons; [*phi·le′o*] differs from this in that it indicates a tender and affectionate kind of love such as arises spontaneously in our souls towards relatives or friends, and towards things we deem delightful."

The use of these two verbs in John 21 is worthy of note. Twice Jesus asked Peter if he loved him, using the verb *a·ga·pa′o*. Both times Peter earnestly affirmed that he had affection for Jesus, using the more intimate word *phi·le′o*. (Joh 21:15, 16) Finally, Jesus asked: "Do you have affection for me?" And Peter again asserted that he did. (Joh 21:17) Thus, Peter affirmed his warm, personal attachment for Jesus.

Brotherly love (Gr., *phi·la·del·phi′a,* literally, "affection for a brother") should exist among all members of the Christian congregation. (Ro 12:10; Heb 13:1; see also 1Pe 3:8.) Thus, the relationships within the congregation should be as close, strong, and warm as in a natural family. Even though the members of the congregation already show brotherly love, they are urged to do it in fuller measure. —1Th 4:9, 10.

The Greek word *phi·lo′stor·gos,* meaning "having tender affection," is used of a person who is close to another in warm intimacy. One of the roots of this compound term, *ster′go,* is frequently used to denote a natural affection, as between family members. The apostle Paul encouraged Christians to cultivate this quality. (Ro 12:10) Paul also indicated that the last days would be characterized by people "having no natural affection" (Gr., *a′stor·goi*) and that such persons are deserving of death.—2Ti 3:3; Ro 1:31, 32.

The Greek noun *phi·li′a* (friendship) is found only once in the Christian Greek Scriptures, where James warns that "the friendship with the world is enmity with God . . . Whoever, therefore, wants to be a friend [Gr., *phi′los*] of the world is constituting himself an enemy of God."—Jas 4:4.

Fondness for Money. One may develop a love of money (Gr., *phi·lar·gy·ri′a,* literally, "fondness of silver") and cause much damage to himself. (1Ti 6:10, *Int*) In the first century C.E. the Pharisees were money lovers, and this would be a characteristic of people in the last days. (Lu 16:14; 2Ti 3:2) In contrast, a Christian's manner of life should be "free of the love of money" (Gr., *a·phi·lar′gy·ros,* literally, "having no fondness of silver"). (Heb 13:5) To attain the office of overseer in the Christian congregation, one of the qualifications that has to be met is to be "not a lover of money." —1Ti 3:3.

Tender Affections (Tender Compassions). Strong emotions often have an effect on the body. Hence, the Greek word for intestines (*splag′khna*) is often used to denote "tender affections" or "tender compassions."—See 2Co 6:12; 7:15; Php 2:1; Col 3:12; Phm 7, 12, 20; 1Jo 3:17; see PITY.

AGABUS (Ag′a·bus). A Christian prophet who, together with other prophets, came down from Jerusalem to Antioch of Syria during the year of Paul's stay there.

Agabus foretold through the spirit "that a great famine was about to come upon the entire inhabited earth." (Ac 11:27, 28) As the account states, the prophecy was fulfilled during the reign of Emperor Claudius (41-54 C.E.). The Jewish historian Josephus refers to this "great famine."—*Jewish Antiquities,* XX, 51 (ii, 5); XX, 101 (v, 2).

Toward the close of Paul's last missionary tour (about 56 C.E.), he was met in Caesarea by Agabus, who illustrated a prophecy of Paul's future arrest in Jerusalem by binding his own hands and feet with Paul's girdle.—Ac 21:8-11.

AGAG (A'gag). The name or title applied to more than one king of the Amalekites.

1. Balaam, in his third prophetic utterance, foretold that a king of Israel would be "higher than Agag, and his kingdom will be lifted up." (Nu 24:7) These words were spoken about 1473 B.C.E., and no subsequent reference is made to Agag until the reign of King Saul (1117-1078 B.C.E.). Because of this some scholars suggest that "Agag" was a title used by the kings of the Amalekites similar to the title of Pharaoh used by the kings of Egypt. It may also be simply a case of the repeated use of a personal name. At any rate the manner of Balaam's reference to Agag indicates that his kingdom was at that time a powerful one.—Nu 24:20; see AMALEK, AMALEKITES.

2. The king of Amalek who was defeated by King Saul in fulfillment of Jehovah's decree. (Ex 17:14; De 25:17-19; 1Sa 15:1-7) However, Saul failed to execute Agag and allowed the people to keep some of the spoil, and this resulted in Samuel's pronouncement of God's rejection of Saul as king. (1Sa 15:8-29) Agag was then executed by Samuel, who told him: "Just as your sword has bereaved women of children, in that way your mother will be most bereaved of children among women."—1Sa 15:32, 33; compare Jg 1:5-7.

AGAGITE (Ag'ag·ite) [Of (Belonging to) Agag]. A term applied to Haman and to his father, Hammedatha, at Esther 3:1, 10; 8:3, 5; 9:24. It apparently designates them as descendants of Agag and hence of Amalekite descent. The Jews traditionally have understood the expression in this way and take the Agag to be the monarch mentioned at 1 Samuel 15:8-33. Josephus refers to Haman as "of Amalekite descent." (*Jewish Antiquities,* XI, 209 [vi, 5]) Mordecai was a descendant of Kish of the tribe of Benjamin, thus making him and Haman, in a sense, traditional enemies.—Es 2:5.

AGATE. A precious ornamental stone that is a form of chalcedony, a variety of colored quartz.

Most agates form as nodules in stratified deposits of silica found in certain rock cavities. The agate layers vary from clear to opaque, and they assume many shades of color because of the presence of microscopic particles of iron salts. The colors appear in combinations of yellow, brown, gray, blue, or black, and these may be attractively distributed in patterns of stripes, bands, or cloudy blends. Agate is slightly harder than steel and can be polished to a high gloss.

Agate used by the Israelites in the wilderness may have been brought from Egypt. According to Pliny the Elder, red agates veined with white were found in the vicinity of Thebes. Such a red agate may have been the variety that was mounted on the high priest's "breastpiece of judgment" to represent one of the 12 tribes of Israel. The center stone of the third row on Aaron's breastpiece was an agate (Heb., *shevoh',* a kind of precious stone).—Ex 28:2, 15, 19, 21, ftn; 39:12.

AGE. The time one has lived, usually counted by years, months, and days. The Hebrew idiom to describe the physical age of an individual was to say one was the "son of" so many years. Thus, Joseph is literally said to have died a "son of one hundred and ten years," that is, "at the age of a hundred and ten years." (Ge 50:26) Age may also refer to maturity. The Hebrew word *sehv* or *seh·vah'* (age; old age) comes from a root meaning "grow gray" and is also rendered "grayheadedness." (1Sa 12:2; Pr 20:29) A number of Hebrew words relating to old age and aging are derived from the noun *za·qan',* meaning "beard." (Le 19:27) The Greek word *he·li·ki'a* primarily denotes the "life span" or "age" of an individual but can also refer to one's "physical growth" or "size." (Mt 6:27; Joh 9:21; Lu 2:52; Lu 19:3) Also occurring in the Greek Scriptures are *ge'ras* ("old age"; Lu 1:36), *pre·sby'tes* ("aged man"; Phm 9), and *pre·sby'tis* ('aged woman'; Tit 2:3). The latter two words are related to *pre·sby'te·ros,* meaning "older man; elder."—See OLDER MAN.

Under the Law, at the age of 20 years the men qualified for military service. (Nu 1:3) The man blind from his birth to whom Jesus gave sight must have been at least 20 years old, since his parents told their interrogators: "Ask him. He is of age. He must speak for himself." (Joh 9:21, 23) Sarah is spoken of as being "past the age limit" for the bearing of children, as she was then some 90 years of age.—Heb 11:11.

An age limit was set for qualification to temple service, as was an age limit at which obligatory service ceased. Some have alleged a discrepancy in the statements at Numbers 4:3, 30, 31 and 8:24-26, since the age for beginning Levitical service is stated first as from 30 years of age and thereafter as from 25 years. However, the case seems to be that of two categories of service involved. Thus, certain rabbinic sources present the view that at the age of 25 a Levite was introduced into the tabernacle service but only to perform lighter tasks, and then, on reaching the full age of 30, he entered into the heavier tasks. They point out that the references to "the work" and "laborious service and the service of carrying loads" mentioned in Numbers 4:3, 47 do not appear at Numbers 8:24, where the age limit is 25. Others add the suggestion that those serving from the age of 30 years up had to do with the transporting of the tabernacle and its equipment when on the move, while those serving between the ages of 25 and 30 served only when the tabernacle was erected and standing at an encampment site. Those favoring the view that assignments to heavier tasks were given only at the age of 30 advance the reason that at that age greater strength, intellectual maturity, and soundness of judgment would have been attained. The Greek *Septuagint* gives the age as 25 at both Numbers 4:3 and 8:24. Later, in David's day, the age limit was dropped to 20 years for beginning tabernacle service, which was in time replaced by temple service.—1Ch 23:24-32; compare also Ezr 3:8.

As to retirement from obligatory service, this took place when the Levites reached the age of 50. The statement at Numbers 8:25, 26 indicates that at this age the Levites could still voluntarily assist those still eligible for assigned duties, but they themselves were given no direct assignment nor were they held accountable to fill such. The suggestion is made that the reason for the retirement limit for Levitical service was not merely out of consideration for their age but to prevent overcrowding of such offices. This age limit for Levites did not apply to the Aaronic high priest, for the high priest himself served in his holy office until death if he continued capable. (Nu 35:25) Aaron, Israel's first high priest, was chosen for service when he was more than 80 and served for almost 40 years.—Ex 7:7; Nu 33:39.

The Greek "Aion." "Age" may also refer to a period of time in man's history, whether having or not having datable bounds. It is frequently used to translate the Greek word *ai·on'* (plural, *ai·o'nes*) in some translations. Greek lexicographers show the word to mean *"space of time clearly defined and marked out, epoch, age,"* and also "lifetime, life," or "age, generation." Since an epoch, or age, can begin and end or it can go on forever, it follows that *ai·on'* could refer to a period of time that is endless, though having a beginning. Thus, as recorded at Mark 3:29, Jesus said that the blas-

phemer against the holy spirit was guilty of "everlasting [agelong, perpetual, eternal] sin," or a sin never to be canceled out at any future time. A similar expression was used with regard to the fruitless fig tree, where "forever" in the Greek is literally "to [for] the age." (Mt 21:19) At Jesus' birth the angelic promise was that "he will rule as king over the house of Jacob forever [literally, into the ages]."—Lu 1:33; see TIME INDEFINITE.

However, *ai·on'* can also refer more particularly to the consistent state of things or the current state of affairs or features that distinguish a certain period of time, epoch, or age rather than to the matter of time itself. As R. C. Trench states in *Synonyms of the New Testament* (London, 1961, p. 203): "Thus signifying time, it comes presently to signify all which exists in the world under conditions of time; . . . and then, more ethically, the course and current of this world's affairs." —See SYSTEMS OF THINGS; WORLD.

AGEE (A'gee). A Hararite, the father of Shammah, who was one of David's mighty men.—2Sa 23:8, 11.

AGRICULTURE. Farming; the cultivating of the soil and producing of crops, also the raising of livestock. Agriculture had its beginning in Eden, since Adam, after his creation by God, was placed in the garden "to cultivate it and to take care of it." (Ge 2:5, 15) However, due to the unfaithfulness of the first human pair, extension of the Edenic Paradise did not result; on the contrary, the ground came under God's curse. Sweat and toil were required for one to eke out a living from the soil. —Ge 3:17-19.

Adam and Eve's first son, Cain, became "a cultivator of the ground"; Abel, a herder of sheep. (Ge 4:2-4) Following the Flood, "Noah started off as a farmer" and planted a vineyard. (Ge 9:20) At a later period Abraham, Isaac, and Jacob led essentially a nomadic and pastoral life with their flocks, somewhat like pre-Flood Jabal (Ge 4:20), though in the case of Isaac and Jacob there is also evidence of their raising crops, wheat being specifically mentioned.—Ge 26:12; 27:37; 30:14; 37:7.

Israelite Agriculture. Excavations by archaeologists show the Palestine area to have been one of the earliest centers of agriculture. The Land of Promise was a very fertile land. In Lot's day the district of the Jordan was "like the garden of Jehovah, like the land of Egypt as far as Zoar." (Ge 13:10) Prior to the Exodus, the nation of Israel had been well acquainted with agriculture down in Egypt, where wheat, flax, barley, cucumbers, watermelons, leeks, onions, garlic, and other products were grown. (Ex 9:25, 26, 31, 32; Nu 11:5; De 11:10) Then for 40 years the nation led an unsettled way of life in the wilderness, though relatively free from the corrupting association of pagan peoples.

Upon their entry into the Land of Promise, the nation settled down to a life of cultivation of crops and of herding. There was definite advantage to their possessing a land already under cultivation. The great majority of the Hebrews familiar with agriculture in Egypt had by now perished in the wilderness, and hence, few if any qualified, proficient farmers with practical experience were available to begin farming in a land that was new and strange to them. (Nu 14:22-30; Heb 3:16, 17) So, it was greatly to their advantage now to inherit 'houses full of all good things, cisterns hewn out, vineyards and olive trees already planted and producing.'—De 6:10, 11; 8:6-9.

Following the division of the land into tribal territories, plots of ground were apportioned out, evidently by use of a measuring rope. (Ps 78:55; Eze 40:3; Am 7:17; Mic 2:4, 5) Once established, such boundaries were to be honored and respected.—De 19:14; 27:17; Pr 22:28; Ho 5:10; compare Job 24:2.

Agriculture occupied an important place in the legislation given Israel. The land belonged to Jehovah and so was not to be abused. (Le 25:23) The land could not be sold in perpetuity, and with the exception of properties within walled cities, land sold due to misfortunes and economic reverses was to be returned to the original possessor in the Jubilee year. (Le 25:10, 23-31) A sabbath rest was required every seventh year, during which the land lay fallow and its fertility was restored, thus accomplishing what is today done by rotation of crops. (Ex 23:10, 11; Le 25:3-7) Such a requirement might have appeared hazardous and was certainly a test of the nation's faith in God's promise to provide in sufficient abundance to carry them through till the harvest of the succeeding year. At the same time, it encouraged prudence and foresight. The Jubilee year (every 50th year) was also a year of rest for the land.—Le 25:11, 12.

The three annual festivals that Israel was commanded to celebrate were timed to coincide with agricultural seasons: the Festival of Unfermented Cakes at the time of the barley harvest, Pentecost at the time of the wheat harvest, and the Festival of Booths at the time of the completion of the harvesting of crops of the outgoing year. (Ex 23:14-16) For the Israelites the seasons and harvest were date factors and time indicators and were used more commonly as such than the names of the calendar months. Such agricultural life also protected the Israelites in a spiritual way, since it made them largely independent of other peoples for their needs and maintained at a minimum the need for commercial intercourse with the surrounding nations.

Though it was to be a land "flowing with milk and honey" for them under God's blessing, nevertheless, there were agricultural problems to be worked out. On condition of their obedience, there would be no need for large-scale irrigation. (De 8:7; 11:9-17) The rainy season began with the early rains about the middle of October and continued until the time of the later rains, which ended about the middle of April. (De 11:14) Then followed five generally rainless months, the heat and dryness of which were alleviated by heavy dews that settled at night and refreshed the soil and plants.—Ge 27:28; De 33:28; see DEW.

For soil conservation on slopes, terraces were apparently employed with stone walls to contain them and prevent the washing away of the vital topsoil. Archaeological excavations show as many as 60 or more of such terraces rising one above another on some hillsides. To ensure the safety of the

A terraced hillside, common in Israelite agriculture

crops, booths or huts or even permanent towers were built in the vineyards and fields so that a watchman could be stationed to survey the surrounding areas.—Isa 1:8; 5:2; Mt 21:33.

King Uzziah is particularly mentioned as "a lover of agriculture [literally, the ground]."—2Ch 26:10.

Though subsequent disobedience led to a withdrawal of God's blessing and brought as a consequence agricultural disasters through crop failures, droughts, locust plagues, mildew, and other problems, and though the destruction of much of the woodlands and the failure to maintain systems of terracing over a period of many centuries have led to a washing away of vast amounts of topsoil in much of Palestine, the remaining soil generally continues to be of great fertility to the present time.—See HARVEST; SOWER, SOWING; THRESHING; and similar related subjects under their individual headings.

AGRIPPA.   See HEROD No. 3.

AGUR   (A'gur). The son of Jakeh and writer of the 30th chapter of the book of Proverbs. (Pr 30:1) Nothing further is stated to enable further identification. He probably lived sometime during the period from Solomon's reign (1037-998 B.C.E.) to Hezekiah's reign (745-717 B.C.E.).

Some rabbinic scholars have considered the name Agur to be allegorical, applying to Solomon. Thus the footnote on Proverbs 30:1 in the *Soncino Books of the Bible* quotes from the Midrash as saying: "He was called *Agur* because he stored up (*agar*) knowledge of Torah, and *the son of Jakeh* because he spewed it out (*hikki*) in that he ignored the warning against multiplying wives." (Edited by A. Cohen, London, 1952) Even among the Jewish commentators, however, this view was not unanimous, many holding that the change of style, language, and content indicates a different writer.

AHAB   (A'hab) [Father's Brother].
1. Son of Omri and a king of the northern kingdom of Israel. He ruled in Samaria 22 years, from about 940 B.C.E.—1Ki 16:28, 29.

Condones False Worship.   Ahab's record was one of the worst as regards the vital area of true worship. Not only did the corrupted worship of Jehovah by means of Jeroboam's golden calves continue but Ahab also allowed Baal worship to infect Israel on an unprecedented scale due to his early marriage to Jezebel, the daughter of Ethbaal, king of Sidon. Josephus, quoting ancient historian Menander, refers to Ethbaal as Ithobal, and the

account (*Against Apion,* I, 123 [18]) relates that he was the priest of Astarte before ascending the throne by murdering the king.

Ahab allowed his pagan wife Jezebel to lead him into Baal worship, to build a temple for Baal, and to erect a sacred pole in honor of Ashtoreth (Astarte). (1Ki 16:30-33) Before long there were 450 prophets of Baal and 400 prophets of the sacred pole, all being fed from Jezebel's royal table. (1Ki 18:19) True prophets of Jehovah were slain by the sword, and only the action of Ahab's house manager Obadiah, a man of faith, preserved the lives of 100 of them by hiding them in caves, where they subsisted on bread and water.—1Ki 18:3, 4, 13; 19:10.

As a result of his turning to Baal worship, Ahab was informed by Elijah of the coming of a severe drought that, according to Luke 4:25 and James 5:17, covered a period of three years and six months. (1Ki 17:1; 18:1) The rains would return only at Elijah's word, and though Ahab searched for him in all the surrounding nations and kingdoms, Elijah stayed out of his reach until the due time. (1Ki 17:8, 9; 18:2, 10) Ahab now endeavored to place the blame on Elijah for the drought and famine, an accusation that Elijah refuted, showing the real cause to be the Baal worship patronized by Ahab. A test held on top of Mount Carmel proved Baal to be a nonentity and manifested Jehovah as the true God; the prophets of Baal were slain at Elijah's command, and shortly thereafter a drenching downpour brought an end to the drought. (1Ki 18:17-46) Ahab headed back to Jezreel and to his wife, whom he informed of Elijah's actions against Baalism. Jezebel reacted with a violent threat to Elijah, resulting in his flight to Mount Horeb.—1Ki 19:1-8.

Capital Construction; Victories Over Syria. It is believed that Ahab's construction works included the completing of Samaria's fortifications, shown by archaeology to have consisted of three immensely strong walls of superior workmanship. Excavations have revealed a rectangular palace platform measuring about 90 m (295 ft) by 180 m (590 ft), with an enclosing wall of fine ashlar masonry. Numerous ivory panels for decorating furniture and wall panels were found, perhaps connected with Ahab's "house of ivory" mentioned at 1 Kings 22:39.—PICTURE, Vol. 1, p. 948; also compare Am 3:15; 6:4.

The wealth of the city and the strength of its position were soon put to the test by a siege set against Samaria by Syrian Ben-hadad II at the head of a coalition of 32 kings. At first meekly acquiescing to the aggressor's demands, Ahab then balked at agreeing to allow the virtual plunder of his palace voluntarily. Peace negotiations fell through, and by divine direction Ahab employed a battle stratagem that caught the enemy off guard and led to their slaughter, though Ben-hadad escaped.—1Ki 20:1-21.

Convinced that Jehovah was a 'mountain god' only, Ben-hadad returned the following year with a military force of equal size, but drew up for battle on the generally flat tableland near Aphek in the territory of Manasseh, rather than advancing into the mountainous region of Samaria. (See APHEK No. 5.) The Israelite forces advanced to the battle site but looked like "two tiny flocks of goats" compared to the massive Syrian encampment. Reassured by Jehovah's promise to demonstrate that his power was not controlled by geography, Ahab's forces dealt a crushing defeat to the enemy. (1Ki 20:26-30) However, much like King Saul with Agag the Amalekite, Ahab let Ben-hadad survive and concluded a covenant with him by which captured cities would be returned to Israel and streets in Damascus would be assigned to Ahab, evidently for the establishment of bazaars, or markets, to promote Ahab's commercial interests in that Syrian capital. (1Ki 20:31-34) Similar to Saul, Ahab was condemned by Jehovah for this, with future calamity foretold for him and his people.—1Ki 20:35-43.

Murder of Naboth, and Consequences. During a three-year interval of peace, Ahab turned his attention to the acquisition of the vineyard of Naboth of Jezreel, a piece of land much desired by Ahab because it bordered his residential palace grounds there. When Naboth refused the request on the basis of God's law regarding the inviolability of hereditary possessions, Ahab petulantly withdrew to his house, where he lay on his couch with his face to the wall, refusing to eat. Learning the cause of his dejection, pagan Jezebel arranged the murder of Naboth under guise of a trial for blasphemy, using letters written in Ahab's name. When Ahab went to take possession of the coveted plot of ground, he was met by Elijah, who scathingly denounced him as a murderer and as one who sold himself to do wickedness at the constant prodding of his pagan wife. As the dogs had licked up Naboth's blood so dogs would lick up Ahab's blood, and Jezebel herself and Ahab's descendants would become food for dogs and scavenger birds. These words hit home, and in deep grief Ahab fasted in sackcloth, alternately sitting and pacing the floor in despondence. On this basis a measure of mercy was extended to him as regards the time when the calamity would come on his house.—1Ki 21:1-29.

Ahab's relations with Judah to the S were strengthened through a marriage alliance in which Ahab's daughter Athaliah was married to King Jehoshaphat's son Jehoram. (1Ki 22:44; 2Ki 8:18, 26; 2Ch 18:1) During a friendly visit by Jehoshaphat to Samaria, Ahab induced him to support him in an effort to retake Ramoth-gilead from the Syrians, who evidently had not carried out to the full the terms of the covenant made by Ben-hadad. While a body of false prophets chorused their assurances of success, at Jehoshaphat's insistence the prophet Micaiah, hated by Ahab, was called and predicted certain calamity. Ordering Micaiah's arrest, Ahab stubbornly went ahead with the attack, though taking the precaution to disguise himself, but he was hit by a random arrow so that he slowly died. His body was brought to Samaria for burial and when "they began to wash off the war chariot by the pool of Samaria . . . the dogs went licking up his blood." A large artificial basin has been excavated in the NW corner of the spacious palace courtyard in Samaria, and this may be the location of this fulfillment of prophecy.—1Ki 22:1-38.

Moabite and Assyrian Inscriptions. Mention is made of the rebuilding of Jericho during Ahab's reign, perhaps as part of a program for strengthening Israel's control over Moab. (1Ki 16:34; compare 2Ch 28:15.) The Moabite Stone by King Mesha of Moab speaks of the domination of Moab by King Omri and his son.

Assyrian inscriptions describing the battle waged between Shalmaneser III and a coalition of 12 kings at Karkar include the name *A-ha-ab-bu* as a member of the coalition. This is generally accepted by most scholars as a reference to King Ahab of Israel; however, for evidence showing that such a claim is subject to question, see the article on SHALMANESER No. 1.

2. A false prophet among the exiles in Babylon; son of Kolaiah. Jeremiah predicted that this immoral and lying prophet and his associate would be roasted in the fire by Nebuchadnezzar.—Jer 29:21-23.

AHARAH (A·har′ah). The third son of Benjamin. (1Ch 8:1) Probably the same as Ehi in Genesis 46:21 and Ahiram in Numbers 26:38.

AHARHEL (A·har′hel). Descendant of Judah, a son of Harum.—1Ch 4:8.

AHASBAI (A·has′bai). A Maacathite whose "son" Eliphelet was an outstanding fighter for David. (2Sa 23:34) The Maacah from which Ahasbai came could refer to Abel-beth-maacah in the territory of Naphtali or to the Syrian kingdom of Maacah. (2Sa 20:14; 10:6, 8) In the parallel list at 1 Chronicles 11:35, 36 the name Ur appears in place of Ahasbai.

AHASUERUS (A·has·u·e′rus). The name or title applied in the Hebrew Scriptures to three different rulers.

1. The father of Darius the Mede mentioned at Daniel 9:1. It is not presently possible to make any conclusive identification of this Ahasuerus with any person in secular history.

2. The Ahasuerus of Ezra 4:6, in the beginning of whose reign an accusation was written against the Jews by their enemies, may have been Cambyses, the successor of Cyrus the conqueror of Babylon and liberator of the Jews. Cambyses reigned from 529 to 522 B.C.E.

3. The Ahasuerus of the book of Esther is believed to be Xerxes I, the son of the Persian king Darius the Great (Darius Hystaspis). Ahasuerus (Xerxes I) is shown as ruling over 127 jurisdictional districts, from India to Ethiopia. The city of Shushan was his capital during major portions of his rule.—Es 1:1, 2.

In the book of Esther the regnal years of this king apparently are counted from the coregency with his father Darius the Great. This would mean that Xerxes' accession year was 496 B.C.E. and that his first regnal year was 495 B.C.E. (See PERSIA, PERSIANS.) In the third year of his reign, at a sumptuous banquet, he ordered lovely Queen Vashti to present herself and display her beauty to the people and princes. Her refusal caused his anger to flare up, and he dismissed her as his wife. (Es 1:3, 10-12, 19-21) In the seventh year of his reign he selected Esther, a Jewess, as his choice out of the many virgins brought in as prospects to replace Vashti. (Es 2:1-4, 16, 17) In the 12th year of his reign he allowed his prime minister Haman to use the king's signet ring to sign a decree that would result in a genocidal destruction of the Jews. This scheme was thwarted by Esther and her cousin Mordecai, Haman was hanged, and a new decree was issued, allowing the Jews the right to fight their attackers.—Es 3:1-9, 11; 7: 9, 10; 8:3-14; 9:5-10.

Subsequently, "King Ahasuerus proceeded to lay forced labor upon the land and the isles of the sea." (Es 10:1) This activity fits well with the pursuits of Xerxes, who completed much of the construction work his father Darius initiated at Persepolis.

Xerxes I also appears to be the "fourth [king]" mentioned at Daniel 11:2, the three preceding ones being Cyrus the Great, Cambyses II, and Darius Hystaspis. While seven other kings followed Xerxes on the throne of the Persian Empire, Xerxes was the last Persian emperor to carry war into Greece, whose rise as the dominant world power is described in the verse immediately following.—Da 11:3.

AHAVA (A·ha′va). The name given to a river or canal located in Babylonia, NW of Babylon, where Ezra gathered together certain Jews and held a fast before undertaking the trek to Jerusalem. (Ezr 8:15, 21, 31) It evidently was a journey of about eight or nine days from Babylon. (Compare Ezr 7:9; 8:15, 31.) Herodotus (I, 179) speaks of a little river named Is, which flows into the Euphrates, and states that the city of Is on this river is about eight days' journey from Babylon. Is has been identified with the modern Hit, and some suggest this as the probable location of Ahava.

Concerning the town of Hit, *The New Encyclopædia Britannica* (1987, Vol. 5, p. 949) says: "On the Euphrates River, Hit is a small walled town built on two mounds on the site of an ancient city; bitumen wells in the vicinity have been utilized for at least 3,000 years and were used in the building of Babylon." This source of bitumen may correspond to the Biblical account of the construction of the Tower of Babel, in which bitumen served for mortar.—Ge 11:3.

AHAZ (A′haz) [shortened form of Jehoahaz, meaning "May Jehovah Take Hold; Jehovah Has Taken Hold"].

1. The son of King Jotham of Judah. Ahaz began to reign at the age of 20 and continued for 16 years.—2Ki 16:2; 2Ch 28:1.

Since Ahaz' son Hezekiah was 25 when he began to reign, this would mean that Ahaz was less than 12 years old when fathering him. (2Ki 18:1, 2) Whereas puberty in males is usually reached between the ages of 12 and 15 in temperate climates, it may come earlier in warmer climates. Marriage customs also vary. *Zeitschrift für Semitistik und verwandte Gebiete* (edited by E. Littmann, Leipzig, 1927, Vol. 5, p. 132) reported that child marriage is frequent in the Promised Land even in modern times, one case being cited of two brothers aged 8 and 12 who were married, the wife of the older attending school with her husband. However, one Hebrew manuscript, the Syriac *Peshitta*, and some manuscripts of the Greek *Septuagint* at 2 Chronicles 28:1 give "twenty-five years" as the age of Ahaz when beginning to reign.

Whatever his exact age, Ahaz died relatively young and left a record of consistent delinquency.

Despite the fact that Isaiah, Hosea, and Micah all actively prophesied during Ahaz' time, rank idolatry marked his reign. He not only allowed it among his subjects but also personally and regularly engaged in pagan sacrificing, to the extent of offering up his own son(s) in fire in the Valley of Hinnom. (2Ki 16:3, 4; 2Ch 28:3, 4) Because of this abandonment to false worship, Ahaz' rule was beset by a flood of troubles. Syria and the northern kingdom of Israel combined to attack Judah from the N, the Edomites seized the opportunity to hit from the SE, and the Philistines invaded from the W. The valuable port of Elath on the Gulf of 'Aqaba was lost. Zichri, a mighty Ephraimite, killed a son of the king and two of Ahaz' principal men during the northern kingdom's raid that resulted in the slaughter of 120,000 in Judah and the taking captive of some 200,000 Judeans. Only the intervention of the prophet Oded, with the support of certain leading men of Ephraim, caused these captives to be released to return to Judah. —2Ch 28:5-15, 17-19; 2Ki 16:5, 6; Isa 7:1.

Ahaz' 'quivering heart' should have been strengthened by the prophet Isaiah's message from God assuring him that Jehovah would not allow the Syro-Israelite combine to destroy Judah and place a man not of the Davidic line upon the throne. But, when invited to request a sign from God, idolatrous Ahaz replied: "I shall not ask, neither shall I put Jehovah to the test." (Isa 7:2-12) Nevertheless, it was foretold that, as a sign, a maiden would give birth to a son, Immanuel (With Us Is God), and that before the boy grew up the Syro-Israelite combine would have ceased to pose a threat to Judah.—Isa 7:13-17; 8:5-8.

With regard to the "sixty-five years" at Isaiah 7:8, which Isaiah prophesied would be the period within which Ephraim would be "shattered to pieces," the *Commentary on the Whole Bible* (by Jamieson, Fausset, and Brown) states: *"One* deportation of Israel happened within one or two years from this time [the time of Isaiah's prophecy], under Tiglath-pileser (2 Kings 15. 29). *Another* in the reign of Hoshea, under Shalmaneser (2 Kings 17. 1-6), was about twenty years after. But the final one which utterly 'broke' up Israel so as to be 'not a people,' accompanied by a colonization of Samaria with foreigners, was under Esar-haddon, who carried away Manasseh, king of Judah, also, in the twenty-second year of his reign, sixty-five years from the utterance of this prophecy (cf. Ezra 4.2, 3, 10, with 2 Kings 17.24; 2 Chronicles 33.11)."

Vassalage to Assyria, and Death. Rather than put faith in Jehovah, however, Ahaz, out of fear of the Syro-Israelite conspiracy, chose the shortsighted policy of bribing Tiglath-pileser III of Assyria to come to his aid. (Isa 7:2-6; 8:12) Whatever relief the ambitious Assyrian king now brought to Ahaz by smashing Syria and Israel was only temporary. In the end it "caused him distress, and did not strengthen him" (2Ch 28:20), since Ahaz had now brought the heavy yoke of Assyria on Judah.

As a vassal king, Ahaz was apparently summoned to Damascus to render homage to Tiglath-pileser III and, while in that city, admired the pagan altar there, copied its design, and had priest Urijah build a duplicate to be placed before the temple in Jerusalem. Ahaz then presumed to offer sacrifices on this "great altar." The original copper altar was set to one side until the king should decide what use to make of it. (2Ki 16:10-16) Meanwhile he mutilated much of the copper temple equipment and rearranged other features in the temple area all "because of the king of Assyria," perhaps to pay the heavy tribute imposed on Judah or possibly to conceal some of the temple wealth from the greedy Assyrian's eyes. The temple doors were closed and Ahaz "made altars for himself at every corner in Jerusalem."—2Ki 16:17, 18; 2Ch 28:23-25.

After 16 years of misrule and rank apostasy Ahaz died, and though buried as his forefathers were "in the City of David" (2Ki 16:20), his body was not placed in the royal burial places of the kings. (2Ch 28:27) His name is listed in the royal genealogies.—1Ch 3:13; Mt 1:9.

The name of Ahaz appears in an inscription of Tiglath-pileser III as Yauhazi.

2. A great-grandson of Jonathan, son of King Saul.—1Ch 8:35, 36.

AHAZIAH (A·ha·zi'ah) [Jehovah Has Taken Hold]. The name of two kings, one of Israel, the other of Judah.

1. Son of Ahab and Jezebel, and king of Israel for two years beginning in about 919 B.C.E. He followed his idolatrous parents in Baal worship. (1Ki 22:51-53) Upon the death of Ahaziah's father, Moab seized the opportunity to revolt and thereby free itself from the heavy tribute of 100,000 lambs and an equal number of male sheep with their wool. (2Ki 1:1; 3:4, 5) This revolt is described by King Mesha of Moab in the Moabite Stone inscription. Perhaps due to his subsequent accident and early death, Ahaziah made no effort to subjugate the Moabites.

Ahaziah did form a maritime alliance with Jehoshaphat of Judah for a shipbuilding enterprise at Ezion-geber on the Gulf of ʿAqaba. The project was disapproved by God because of Ahaziah's wickedness, and the ships were wrecked. (2Ch 20:35-37) The account at 1 Kings 22:48, 49 shows that Ahaziah wanted Jehoshaphat's authorization for Israelite mariners to man the ships jointly with those of Judah, a request that Jehoshaphat refused. If this request was made prior to the wrecking of the ships, it may simply indicate Jehoshaphat's distrust of Ahaziah and caution against encroachment by the northern kingdom. If the request came after the failure of the fleet, it may have been an insinuation on Ahaziah's part that Jehoshaphat's men were lacking in ability and were responsible for the wreckage of the ships and hence the suggestion that the ships be refitted and sent out again with Israelite sailors also on board. In that case Jehoshaphat's refusal may have been in acknowledgment of God's manifest disapproval of the project.

A house accident, in which the king fell through a grating (perhaps one covering a daylight shaft) in his roof chamber, left him bedridden and seriously ill. (2Ki 1:2) As if the true God no longer existed, Ahaziah sent messengers to inquire of the Philistine god Baal-zebub (meaning "Owner of the Flies") as to his prospects of recovery. Intercepted by the prophet Elijah, the messengers turned back and delivered the message to the king that his sickbed would become his deathbed. Instead of humbling himself, Ahaziah sent a force of 50 men under their captain to bring Elijah in to him. That force and a second one, after giving Elijah the king's order to "come down" from the mountain where he was sitting, were both destroyed by fire. A third force sent by the stubborn king escaped only by virtue of the captain's respectful plea that he and his men's lives "be precious in [Elijah's] eyes." Elijah thereafter descended and delivered the death message to Ahaziah's face. Ahaziah gradually died and, being sonless, was succeeded by his brother Jehoram.—2Ki 1:2-17.

2. Son of Jehoram and Athaliah and listed as king of Judah for one year (c. 906 B.C.E.). During his father's reign the Philistines and Arabs invaded Judah and took captive all of Jehoram's sons except Jehoahaz (Ahaziah), the youngest. (2Ch 21:16, 17; 22:1) He was a young man of 22 years when ascending the throne, and his domineering mother Athaliah, daughter of Ahab and Jezebel, influenced him to wickedness. (2Ki 8:25-27; 2Ch 22:2-4) He accompanied King Jehoram of Israel (his maternal uncle) in a fight against Syria at Ramoth-gilead, which resulted in Jehoram's being wounded. Later, Ahaziah visited the convalescing

Jehoram at Jezreel.—2Ki 8:28, 29; 9:15; 2Ch 22:5, 6.

Coordinating the two accounts (2Ki 9:21-28; 2Ch 22:7-9), the following evidently took place: Jehu, on nearing Jezreel, met Jehoram and Ahaziah. Jehu struck down Jehoram, but Ahaziah fled. At this time Jehu did not pursue Ahaziah but continued to Jezreel to finish his executional work there. Meanwhile the fleeing Ahaziah tried to make his way back to Jerusalem; however, he only got as far as Samaria, where he tried to hide himself. Jehu's men, pursuing Ahaziah, discovered him in Samaria and captured him, and he was brought to Jehu, who was near the town of Ibleam, not far from Jezreel. When Jehu saw Ahaziah, he ordered his men to kill him in his chariot. They struck and wounded him on the way up to Gur, near Ibleam; but Ahaziah was allowed to escape, and he fled to Megiddo, where he died of his wounds. He was then taken to Jerusalem and buried there. The accounts of his death are not contradictory but complementary.

Second Chronicles 22:7 points out that Ahaziah's death "was from God," and thus Jehu acted as God's executioner in slaying this man who fellowshipped with the condemned house of Ahab. Ahaziah is also referred to as "Azariah" at 2 Chronicles 22:6 (though here 15 Hebrew manuscripts read "Ahaziah"), and as "Jehoahaz" at 2 Chronicles 21:17; 25:23 (a case of transposing the divine name to serve as a prefix instead of as a suffix).

AHBAN (Ah′ban). Son of Abishur and Abihail of the tribe of Judah.—1Ch 2:29.

AHER (A′her) [Another]. A descendant of Benjamin (1Ch 7:12), likely the same as Ahiram (Nu 26:38) or Aharah (1Ch 8:1), for which names Aher could be a contracted form.

AHI (A′hi) [from a root meaning "brother"].

1. Son of Abdiel, a family head from the tribe of Gad.—1Ch 5:15.

2. One of four sons of Shemer, a chieftain of the tribe of Asher from the family of Beriah.—1Ch 7:30, 31, 34.

AHIAM (A·hi′am). The son of Sharar (Sacar) the Hararite; one of David's 30 mighty men of the military forces.—2Sa 23:33; 1Ch 11:35.

AHIAN (A·hi′an) [Little Brother]. A son of Shemida, from the tribe of Manasseh.—1Ch 7:14, 19.

AHIEZER (A·hi·e′zer) [My Brother Is a Helper].

1. Son of Ammishaddai and chieftain of the tribe of Dan, selected a year after the Exodus. (Nu

1:1, 4, 12) In this capacity he assisted Moses with the census, commanded the rearguard three-tribe division when on the march, and presented his offering on the tenth day of the inauguration of the altar at the tabernacle.—Nu 2:25; 7:66, 71; 10:25.

2. A son of Shemaah the Gibeathite, and head of the mighty Benjamites that came to David's support at Ziklag.—1Ch 12:1-3.

AHIHUD (A·hi'hud). Despite differences in Hebrew spelling and vowel pointing, the names of the two different individuals below are spelled the same in English.

1. ['Achi·hudh', possibly, "Brother Is Dignity"]. Son of Shelomi; as chieftain of the tribe of Asher, he was chosen to assist in dividing the Promised Land among the people.—Nu 34:18, 27, 29.

2. ['Achi·chudh']. Brother of Uzza, of the tribe of Benjamin.—1Ch 8:7.

AHIJAH (A·hi'jah) [Jehovah Is (My) Brother].

1. The fifth-named son of Jerahmeel, of the tribe of Judah.—1Ch 2:25.

2. A family head in the tribe of Benjamin. (1Ch 8:6, 7) Some think he is the same as Ahoah in verse 4.

3. Son of Ahitub and great-grandson of Eli. He served as high priest in Shiloh when Saul was king. (1Sa 14:3, 18) Some suggest that he was either a brother of Ahimelech or, by substituting "melech" for "jah" in his name, was Ahimelech. —1Sa 22:9.

4. One of the mighty men in David's army, a Pelonite.—1Ch 11:36.

5. A Levite appointed over the treasures of Jehovah's house in David's reign.—1Ch 26:20.

6. Son of Shisha. He and his brother Elihoreph were Solomon's princely secretaries.—1Ki 4:2, 3.

7. A prophet of Jehovah residing in Shiloh who foretold how Solomon's kingdom would be split. Ripping a new garment into 12 parts, Ahijah gave 10 pieces to Jeroboam, promising that if Jeroboam proved faithful, Jehovah would build him "a lasting house." (1Ki 11:29-39; 12:15; 2Ch 10:15) After years of wicked rule Jeroboam sent his wife to inquire of Ahijah concerning the welfare of his sick son. The prophet, now old and blind, foretold that the boy would soon die and that Jehovah would "make a clean sweep behind the house of Jeroboam, just as one clears away the dung." (1Ki 14:2-18; 15:29) "The prophecy of Ahijah," one of the written records including Solomon's affairs, survived to the time of Ezra's compilation of Chronicles.—2Ch 9:29.

8. Father of Baasha, who conspired against Nadab and made himself king of Israel; of the tribe of Issachar.—1Ki 15:27, 33; 2Ki 9:9.

9. One of the 44 heads of the people whose descendant, if not he himself, joined in sealing Nehemiah's "trustworthy arrangement" to walk in Jehovah's laws.—Ne 10:26; 9:38.

AHIKAM (A·hi'kam) [(My) Brother Has Raised Himself Up [that is, to the battle]]. Son of Shaphan the royal secretary during Josiah's reign. Ahikam was one of the five sent to the prophetess Huldah by Josiah to inquire concerning what they had read in the recently discovered book of the Law. (2Ki 22:12-14; 2Ch 34:20-22) Later he protected Jeremiah's life when it was threatened. (Jer 26: 24) Ahikam's son Gedaliah was governor of Judah after Jerusalem's destruction in 607 B.C.E.—2Ki 25:22; Jer 40:5.

AHILUD (A·hi'lud). Father of David's royal recorder Jehoshaphat. (2Sa 8:16; 1Ch 18:15) Likely the father of Baana, a deputy of food supplies under Solomon.—1Ki 4:7, 12.

AHIMAAZ (A·him'a·az).

1. Father of Saul's wife Ahinoam.—1Sa 14:50.

2. Son of the priest Zadok and father of Azariah. (1Ch 6:8, 9, 53) When Absalom rebelled against his father David and usurped the throne, young Ahimaaz served a vital role in communicating intelligence to David. When about to be caught on one occasion, he and his companion hid in a well, the mouth of which a woman camouflaged with grain. (2Sa 15:27, 36; 17:17-21) When Absalom was killed, a Cushite runner was picked to take the news to David. Ahimaaz kept insisting that he too be allowed to run. Permission granted, he overtook the first runner and, upon approaching the city, was recognized by his running style. "This is a good man, and with good news he should come," exclaimed David. It proved to be so; Ahimaaz reported good news and left the bad for the second courier to deliver. (2Sa 18:19-32) Whether Ahimaaz was ever high priest is not certain. Some suggest he may have died before his father, thereby allowing Ahimaaz' son Azariah to succeed Zadok.—1Ki 4:2; 1Ch 6:8-10.

3. Husband of Solomon's daughter Basemath, and one of the 12 deputies appointed to provide food for the king's household one month out of the year from the territory of Naphtali. (1Ki 4:7, 15) Some suggest that he was the same individual as No. 2.

AHIMAN (A·hi'man).

1. Brother of Sheshai and Talmai. Likely Ahiman, Sheshai, and Talmai are to be understood as

representing three families of Anakim residing in Hebron when Canaan was spied out by the Israelites in 1512 B.C.E. (Nu 13:22, 28, 33) Many years later these Anakim were dispossessed by Caleb and the conquering Judeans.—Jos 14:10-15; 15: 13, 14; Jg 1:10.

2. A Levite and one of the trusted gatekeepers of Jerusalem after the return from Babylonian exile.—1Ch 9:17, 18.

AHIMELECH (A·him′e·lech).

1. Son of Ahitub and great-grandson of Eli; high priest at the tabernacle located at Nob. Because of giving aid to David, not knowing he was a fugitive from Saul, Ahimelech (along with 84 other priests of Jehovah as well as the men, women, and children of Nob) was massacred by the Edomite Doeg. Abiathar was the only son of Ahimelech to escape. (1Sa chaps 21, 22) David, later composing Psalm 52, recounted Doeg's heinous act. (Ps 52:Sup) Jesus too recalled David's experience with Ahimelech.—Mt 12:3, 4; Mr 2:25, 26; Lu 6:3, 4; see AHIJAH No. 3.

2. Son of Abiathar and grandson of Ahimelech, whom Doeg killed.—1Ch 18:16; 24:3, 6, 31.

3. A Hittite who was invited but who did not accompany David when he slipped into Saul's camp at night.—1Sa 26:6, 7.

AHIMOTH (A·hi′moth) [possibly, Brother of Death]. A Levite son of Elkanah of the family of Kohath.—1Ch 6:25.

AHINADAB (A·hin′a·dab) [Brother Is Willing (Noble; Generous)]. One of the 12 deputies responsible to provide food for Solomon's royal household on a monthly rotation basis. (1Ki 4:7, 14) Headquartered in Mahanaim, his assigned territory was located in southern Gilead.

AHINOAM (A·hin′o·am) [Brother Is Pleasantness].

1. King Saul's wife, daughter of Ahimaaz, and apparently the mother of Jonathan.—1Sa 14: 49, 50.

2. The Jezreelite wife of David. (1Sa 25:43; 2Sa 2:2) She accompanied David in his exile to Philistia, was captured by Amalekite raiders at Ziklag, and was rescued unharmed. (1Sa 27:3; 30:5, 18) Later, in Hebron, she became the mother of David's firstborn, Amnon.—2Sa 3:2; 1Ch 3:1.

AHIO (A·hi′o) [shortened form of Ahijah; or, possibly, Little Brother].

1. Apparently a son of Beriah and grandson of Elpaal, of the tribe of Benjamin.—1Ch 8:12-16.

2. A Benjamite, son of Jeiel by his wife Maacah. —1Ch 8:29, 31; 9:35-37.

3. Son of Abinadab of Kiriath-jearim. The ark of the covenant was being moved to Jerusalem on a new wagon; Ahio was walking ahead when his brother Uzzah was struck down for touching the Ark.—2Sa 6:3, 4; 1Ch 13:7-10.

AHIRA (A·hi′ra) [possibly, My Brother Is a Companion (Friend)]. The son of Enan, and the chieftain of the tribe of Naphtali during the wilderness wandering. Following the other chieftains, he made his own contribution at the inauguration of the altar.—Nu 1:15; 2:29; 7:1-3, 78; 10:27.

AHIRAM (A·hi′ram) [My Brother Is High (Exalted)]. A son of Benjamin and founder of a family. (Nu 26:38) Apparently the same as Ehi at Genesis 46:21 and Aharah at 1 Chronicles 8:1.

AHIRAMITES (A·hi′ram·ites) [Of (Belonging to) Ahiram]. A family descended from Ahiram, a son of Benjamin.—Nu 26:38.

AHISAMACH (A·his′a·mach) [My Brother Has Supported]. Danite father of Oholiab, who was the skilled craftsman associated with Bezalel in constructing the tabernacle.—Ex 31:2-6; 35:34; 38:23.

AHISHAHAR (A·hish′a·har) [Brother of the Dawn]. Last-named son of Bilhan and descendant of Benjamin.—1Ch 7:6, 10, 11.

AHISHAR (A·hi′shar). The princely steward in charge of Solomon's palace household.—1Ki 4:2, 6.

AHITHOPHEL (A·hith′o·phel). A native of Giloh in the hills of Judah (2Sa 15:12), father of one of David's mighty men named Eliam, and possibly the grandfather of Bath-sheba. (2Sa 11:3; 23:34) As David's personal adviser, Ahithophel's sagacious counsel was esteemed as if it were the direct word of Jehovah. (2Sa 16:23) Later this once-close companion treacherously turned traitor and joined David's son Absalom in a coup against the king. As a ringleader in the rebellion, he advised Absalom to violate David's concubines, and he asked permission to raise an army of 12,000 and immediately hunt down and kill David while David was in a disorganized and weakened state. (2Sa 15:31; 16:15, 21; 17:1-4) When Jehovah thwarted this bold scheme, and the counsel of Hushai was followed, Ahithophel evidently realized that Absalom's revolt would fail. (2Sa 15:32-34; 17:5-14) He committed suicide and was buried with his forefathers. (2Sa 17:23) Apart from wartime, this is the only case of suicide mentioned in the Hebrew Scriptures. His traitorous act is apparently recalled in Psalm 55:12-14.

AHITUB (A·hi′tub) [My Brother Is Goodness].

1. A descendant of Aaron's son Ithamar; son of Phinehas and grandson of High Priest Eli. (1Sa 14:3; 1Ch 24:3) Following the death of his father and grandfather on the same day, Ahitub possibly officiated as high priest. (1Sa 4:17, 18) His son, High Priest Ahimelech, was slain at Saul's command.—1Sa 22:9-20.

2. Son of Amariah, a descendant of Aaron's son Eleazar. (1Ch 6:3-8) There is no indication that he acted as high priest; this office was in the line of Ithamar at the time. Ahitub's son Zadok served as a secondary priest, not as high priest, during the reign of David, and then was assigned to replace Abiathar as high priest during the reign of Solomon.—2Sa 8:17; 1Ch 18:16; 1Ki 1:8; 2:27.

3. Another priest who descended from Ahitub No. 2. Genealogical listings are interrupted to call him "a leader of the house of the true God." (1Ch 9:11; Ne 11:11) His father's name was also Amariah, and from 1 Chronicles 9:11 and Nehemiah 11:11 it appears that his son was Meraioth and his grandson was Zadok.—1Ch 6:11, 12; Ezr 7:2.

AHLAB (Ah′lab). This Canaanite town was located in Asher's territory. (Jg 1:31) The tribe, however, failed to drive out the Canaanites, who subsequently continued to inhabit the city. The location is at present uncertain.

AHLAI (Ah′lai).

1. Likely the daughter of Sheshan of the tribe of Judah, given in marriage to her father's Egyptian servant Jarha for whom she bore Attai. However, Ahlai, if actually a *son* of Sheshan, may have died early.—1Ch 2:31, 34, 35.

2. Father of Zabad, who was a mighty man in David's army.—1Ch 11:41.

AHOAH (A·ho′ah), **AHOHI** (A·ho′hi), **AHOHITE** (A·ho′hite). A descendant of Benjamin through Bela. (1Ch 8:1-4) Perhaps the same as Ahijah in 1 Chronicles 8:7. Some of his descendants, Ahohites, were prominent fighters in David's army.—2Sa 23:9, 28; 1Ch 11:12, 29; 27:4.

AHUMAI (A·hu′mai). First-named son of Jahath in the genealogies of Judah.—1Ch 4:1, 2.

AHUZZAM (A·huz′zam) [from a root meaning "take hold"]. First-named son of Ashhur, of the tribe of Judah, by his wife Naarah.—1Ch 4:5, 6; 2:3-5, 24.

AHUZZATH (A·huz′zath) [Possession]. The "confidential friend" who accompanied Abimelech, Philistine king of Gerar, on a visit to Isaac at Beer-sheba. (Ge 26:23, 26) This is the first reference in the Bible to a "confidential friend," the trusted inner-circle position of one consulted for advice or authorized as spokesman.—See FRIEND (Friend [Companion] of the King).

AHZAI (Ah′zai) [shortened form of Ahaziah, meaning "Jehovah Has Taken Hold"]. Son of Meshillemoth and ancestor of certain priests in Jerusalem after the Babylonian exile. (Ne 11:13) Some believe he is the Jahzerah listed in 1 Chronicles 9:12.

AI (A′i) [Heap of Ruins]. In the *King James Version* also called "Hai," with the definite article prefixed, as it is in the Hebrew. The name also occurs in the feminine forms Aiath and Aija.—Isa 10:28; Ne 11:31.

1. A royal city of the Canaanites, the second city taken during the Israelite invasion. Ai was situated "close by Beth-aven, to the east of Bethel," with a valley plain to the N. (Jos 7:2; 8:11, 12) Michmash apparently lay to the S.—Isa 10:28.

Shortly after arrival in Canaan, Abraham had pitched his tent "with Bethel on the west and Ai on the east." He built an altar there and revisited the place after his sojourn in Egypt.—Ge 12:8; 13:3.

In 1473 B.C.E., following the victory over Jericho, Ai was attacked by a small force of about 3,000 Israelite soldiers, since the spies said of the inhabitants of Ai, "They are few." (Jos 7:2, 3) However, because of Achan's sin Israel suffered defeat. (Jos 7:4-15) After correction of this matter, Joshua employed a stratagem against Ai, setting an ambush at the rear of the city on its W side. The main force was deployed before the city to the N, where a valley or low desert plain lay, and from here Joshua prepared for a frontal attack on Ai. Having lured the king of Ai and a body of men out of Ai, Joshua's force feigned retreat until their pursuers were far from their fortress. Then the ambush was signaled into action, and the city was captured and set on fire. (Jos 8:1-27) Ai's king was executed, and the city was reduced to "an indefinitely lasting mound [Heb., *tel*], as a desolation down to this day."—Jos 8:28.

By Isaiah's time, in the eighth century B.C.E., the city, or perhaps an adjoining site, was inhabited and it was prophesied that it would be the first to be taken by the king of Assyria in his march on Jerusalem. (Isa 10:28) Following the Babylonian exile, Benjamites from Ai returned with Zerubbabel's caravan.—Ezr 2:28; Ne 7:32; 11:31.

Low Plain of Aijalon. When fighting the Amorites, Joshua called for the moon to be motionless "over the low plain of Aijalon"

Ai has been generally identified with the site Khirbet et-Tell (Horvat et-Tel), which preserves the meaning of the ancient name (et-Tell means "The Mound; The Heap of Ruins"). It is 2.3 km (1.4 mi) ESE of Bethel (modern Beitin). However, excavations made there in 1933-1935 and in 1964-1972 indicate that it was a large city, devastated about 2000 B.C.E. and thereafter uninhabited until about 1050 B.C.E. (according to archaeological methods of dating). Because of this, various attempts have been made by archaeologists to alter the sense of the Scriptural references to Ai. However, archaeologist J. Simons finds the identification with Khirbet et-Tell unacceptable on the basis of the city's size (Jos 7:3), the fact that there is no broad valley to the N of Khirbet et-Tell (Jos 8:11), and on other grounds. (*American Journal of Archaeology*, July-September 1947, p. 311) If the archaeological dating is correct, then the site must be located elsewhere. The name itself would not necessarily identify the place, since as Sir Frederic Kenyon states: "The transference of a name from a ruined or abandoned site to another near by is a common phenomenon in Palestine." —*The Bible and Archæology*, 1940, p. 190.

2. A city mentioned along with Heshbon in Jeremiah's prophecy against the Ammonites. (Jer 49:3) The location is unknown.

AIAH (A'iah) [Black Kite].

1. First named of two sons of the Hivite sheik Zibeon and uncle to one of Esau's wives, Oholibamah.—Ge 36:2, 20, 24, 29; 1Ch 1:40.

2. Father of Saul's concubine Rizpah. His two grandsons from this union were executed.—2Sa 3:7; 21:8-11.

AIATH.   See Ai No. 1.

AIJA.   See Ai No. 1.

AIJALON (Ai'ja·lon) [Place of the Hind; Place of the Stag].

1. A city of the Shephelah or hilly lowland of Palestine, on a hill at the S end of the beautiful low plain, or valley, of Aijalon. The village at this site is now called Yalo and is situated just N of the road from Jerusalem to Tel Aviv-Yafo, about 21 km (13 mi) WNW of Jerusalem.

The Valley of Aijalon is the northernmost of several valleys cutting across the hills of the Shephelah and was an important pass leading from the coastal plains up into the central mountainous region. Joshua was evidently near this plain when he called for the sun and the moon to stand "motionless" over Gibeon and over "the low plain of Aijalon," when he was completing his victorious battle against the five Amorite kings who had warred against Gibeon. (Jos 10:12-14) After Joshua's conquest of Canaan, Aijalon was assigned to the tribe of Dan. (Jos 19:40-42) It was later

assigned to the sons of Kohath as a Levite city.
—Jos 21:24.

The Danites at first proved unable to oust the Amorites from Aijalon, but it appears that Ephraim from the N came to their aid and "the hand of the house of Joseph got to be so heavy that they [the Amorites] were forced into task work." (Jg 1:34, 35) This may be the reason 1 Chronicles 6:69 lists Aijalon as belonging to Ephraim and as given by them to the Kohathites. (See, however, the corresponding case of GATH-RIMMON No. 1.) Later on, perhaps after the division of the kingdom, it is spoken of as the city of certain prominent Benjamites.—1Ch 8:13.

At Aijalon, Saul won his first victory over the Philistines, when Israel "kept striking down the [fleeing] Philistines from Michmash to Aijalon." (1Sa 14:31) Many years after that, when the kingdom had been divided after King Solomon's death (c. 998 B.C.E.), his son and successor Rehoboam fortified Aijalon and made it one of his strongholds against the N and W. (2Ch 11:5-12) Almost two and a half centuries later, Aijalon was lost to the Philistines during the reign of unfaithful King Ahaz (761-746 B.C.E.).—2Ch 28:18.

Aijalon is mentioned in one of the Amarna Tablets as Aialuna.

2. A place in the territory of Zebulun, where Judge Elon of that tribe was buried. (Jg 12:12) Its site is uncertain.

AIN   (A′in) [Fountain; Spring]. The word literally means "eye" but by analogy is used to mean a natural spring or fountain as distinguished from a man-made well or tank, which latter water source is expressed by the Hebrew terms *be'er′* and *bohr.* (Ge 49:22; De 8:7; see CISTERN; WELL.) It is often written "En-" when used in compounds, as En-rimmon, En-gedi, En-gannim.

1. A place mentioned by Jehovah when setting out the E boundary of Israel to Moses. (Nu 34:11) The "Riblah" mentioned in this text as being "on the east of Ain" evidently does not refer to the Riblah in the land of Hamath considerably to the N of Damascus, inasmuch as Ain is named in relation to the Sea of Chinnereth (Galilee). It lay to the N of that sea, but its exact location is uncertain.

2. One of the southernmost cities originally assigned to the tribe of Judah (Jos 15:32), then assigned to the tribe of Simeon when part of Simeon's allotment was taken out from Judah's overly large territory. (Jos 19:1, 7, 9; 1Ch 4:24, 32) Ain was near the city of Rimmon, and it appears that when it was resettled following the exile in

Babylon, the names of the two places were combined as one: En-rimmon. (Ne 11:29) As such, it is usually identified with Khirbet Umm er-Ramamin (Horvat Remalya), lying about 15 km (9 mi) N of Beer-sheba.—See RIMMON No. 2.

3. At Joshua 21:16 Ain is listed as one of the cities given to the Levites. A comparison of this text with Joshua 15:42; 19:7 and 1 Chronicles 6:59 indicates that the city here referred to is elsewhere called Ashan.—See ASHAN.

AKAN   (A′kan). Last named of three sons of Sheik Ezer of the Seirites. (Ge 36:20, 21, 27) The Masoretic text reads "Jaakan" at 1 Chronicles 1:42, but the Greek *Septuagint* (Codex Alexandrinus) and 22 Hebrew manuscripts read "Akan" in agreement with Genesis 36:27.

AKELDAMA   (A·kel′da·ma) [Field of Blood]. The name applied by the Jews to the plot of land, the purchase of which resulted from "the wages for unrighteousness" paid to Judas Iscariot for his betrayal of Christ Jesus. (Ac 1:18, 19) It has been identified as the Haqq ed-Dumm (meaning "Price of Blood") on the S side of the Valley of Hinnom, on the "Hill of Evil Counsel," which is a level plot of land a short distance up the slope. Upon this spot are ruins of a charnel house. A little to the SE is the Minzar Haqal Dema' (Akeldama Monastery) erected over the remains of cave tombs.

The statement at Acts 1:18 that Judas "purchased a field" indicates that he furnished the means for purchasing the field, or was the occasion of doing so. The record at Matthew 27:3-10 shows that the priests used the 30 pieces of silver (if shekels, $66) thrown into the temple by Judas to make the actual purchase and that this "Field of Blood" was previously a potter's field and was obtained by the priests "to bury strangers." (See POTTER'S FIELD.) The suggested location has been used as a burial site from early centuries.

Why does Matthew attribute the prophecy of Zechariah 11:12, 13 to Jeremiah?

The fulfillment of prophecy recorded by Matthew is based on "what was spoken through Jeremiah the prophet." Jeremiah was at times placed first in "the book of the prophets," and this section of prophecies therefore included not only Jeremiah's writings but also those of Zechariah. (Compare Lu 24:44.) The quotation made by Matthew appears to be drawn principally from Zechariah 11:12, 13, but paraphrased by Matthew and applied to the circumstances fulfilling it, this under inspiration by God's spirit. As a potter's field the land would be considered as worn out and of little value, worth only the price of a slave.

AKKUB (Ak'kub) [probably, One Seizing the Heel; Supplanter].

1. Father of a family of Nethinim who returned from Babylon with Zerubbabel, 537 B.C.E.—Ezr 2:1, 2, 45.

2. A postexilic Levitical gatekeeper and family head of gatekeepers.—1Ch 9:17; Ezr 2:42; Ne 7:45; 11:19; 12:25.

3. One of the 13 Levites who assisted Ezra with "explaining the law to the people."—Ne 8:7, 8.

4. Fourth named of seven sons of Elioenai, among the last descendants of David enrolled in Hebrew Scripture genealogy.—1Ch 3:24.

AKRABBIM (A·krab'bim) [Scorpions]. An upward slope or ascent on the SE frontier of Judah that constituted a boundary division when Canaan was apportioned to Israel. (Nu 34:4; Jg 1:36) It was situated about 29 km (18 mi) SW of the southern end of the Dead Sea and near the Wilderness of Zin. The area has been identified with present-day Naqb es-Safa (Ma'ale 'Aqrabbim), where the road from Beer-sheba to the Arabah descends abruptly into the Wadi Murra (Nahal Zin). The name may have been derived from the abundance of scorpions in this desert country or perhaps from the way the road repeatedly curves back on itself like the tail of a scorpion. It was evidently an ancient route used to go down to Edom and S to 'Aqaba on the Gulf of 'Aqaba.

ALABASTER. The name of small perfume vaselike vessels originally made of a stone found near Alabastron, Egypt. The stone itself, a form of calcium carbonate, also came to be known by the same name. David collected "alabaster [Heb., sha'-yish] stones in great quantity" for the building of Jehovah's temple in Jerusalem.—1Ch 29:2.

This ancient or "Oriental" alabaster should not be confused with a modern alabaster, a hydrated calcium sulfate that is easily scratched. The original alabaster is usually white and, because it is a stalagmite formation, sometimes has streaks of various colors. It approaches the hardness of marble but will not receive quite as high a polish. The solid alabaster was bored or drilled out to contain as much as a Roman pound (0.33 kg; 0.72 lb) of liquid. (Joh 12:3) The alabaster case (Gr., a·la'ba-stron) was usually fashioned with a narrow neck that could be effectively sealed to prevent the escape of the precious scent.

When less costly materials such as gypsum were used to make such cases, these too were called alabasters simply because of the use to which they were put. However, cases made from genuine alabaster were used for the more costly ointments and perfumes, like those with which Jesus was anointed on two occasions—once in the house of a Pharisee in Galilee (Lu 7:37) and once in the house of Simon the leper in Bethany.—Mt 26:6, 7; Mr 14:3.

ALAMOTH (Al'a·moth) [Maidens; Young Women]. Evidently a term of musical execution. It probably refers to the soprano voices of young women or the falsetto of boys. In 1 Chronicles 15:20, stringed instruments are described as being "tuned to Alamoth," the term being transliterated. However, in the superscription to Psalm 46 'ala·mohth' is translated "Maidens."

At 1 Chronicles 15:21, the verse following the above citation, another musical expression is transliterated, namely, shemi·nith', referring to "harps tuned to Sheminith." In the superscriptions of Psalms 6 and 12 this word is translated "lower octave." While the two terms Alamoth and Sheminith are not necessarily opposites in meaning, some scholars believe they do stand in contrast to each other. The contents of the respective psalms seem to indicate this also: Both psalms (6 and 12) containing shemi·nith' in their superscriptions are somewhat plaintive and would accordingly be accompanied in a more somber, lower range; whereas Psalm 46, containing 'ala·mohth' in its superscription, is joyous and reasonably would have accompaniment or be sung in a higher register.—See HARP; MUSIC.

ALEMETH (Al'e·meth).

1. Listed as the last of nine sons of Becher born in Egypt some time after 1728 B.C.E.—1Ch 7:8; Ge 46:21, 26.

2. A son of Jehoaddah (or Jarah) and a direct descendant of King Saul. His two brothers were Azmaveth and Zimri.—1Ch 8:36; 9:42.

3. A town of Benjamin.—See ALMON.

'ALEPH [א] ('A'leph). The first letter of the Hebrew alphabet. The name assigned to this letter is the same as the Hebrew word for "ox; cow." —Compare Ps 8:7; De 7:13.

In Hebrew 'a'leph is not a vowel but a consonant and has no true equivalent in English. It is transliterated in writing by a raised comma ('). As pronounced in Hebrew it is the softest of guttural sounds (that is, sounds pronounced in the throat) and is like the slight guttural sound given to the silent "h" at the beginning of the English word "hour," or like with the second "o" in "cooperate."

In the Hebrew, the first eight verses in Psalm 119 begin with *'a'leph.*

ALEXANDER (Al·ex·an'der) [Defender of Man].

1. Alexander the Great, son of Philip II of Macedonia and his wife Olympias, born at Pella in 356 B.C.E. Although not mentioned by name in the Bible, his rule of the fifth world empire was foretold two centuries before his birth.—Da 8:5-7, 20, 21.

In his early 20's, two years after ascending the throne following the assassination of his father, Alexander set out to conquer the world. (Da 8:5) This dashing young military strategist deployed his comparatively small army in deep-ranked phalanx formation, a tactic that was introduced by his father and that Alexander developed to a high degree of efficiency.

Instead of pursuing the fleeing Persians after two decisive victories in Asia Minor (the first at the Granicus River; the second on the Plain of Issus, where a great Persian army estimated at half a million met utter defeat), Alexander turned his attention to the island city of Tyre. Centuries earlier it had been foretold that the walls, towers, houses, and the very dust of Tyre would be pitched into the sea. (Eze 26:4, 12) It is, therefore, quite significant that Alexander took the rubble of the old mainland city destroyed by Nebuchadnezzar some years before and built with it an 800-m (0.5 mi) causeway out to the island city. The pounding by his navy and engines of war destroyed that proud mistress of the sea in July 332 B.C.E.

Jerusalem, on the other hand, opened its gates in surrender, and according to Josephus (*Jewish Antiquities*, XI, 337 [viii, 5]), Alexander was shown the book of Daniel's prophecy, presumably chapter 8, where a mighty Greek king would subdue and conquer the Persian Empire. Thereupon, Alexander spared Jerusalem and pushed S into Egypt, where he was greeted as a deliverer. There he founded the city of Alexandria, the seat of learning where the Greek *Septuagint* was made. Looking eastward, Alexander returned from Egypt through Palestine, and with 47,000 men, overpowered a reorganized Persian army of 1,000,000 near Gaugamela. In quick succession Darius III was murdered by onetime friends, Babylon surrendered, and Alexander pushed on to secure Susa and Persepolis. From there he continued his campaign into India before looking westward again.

Postconquest Events. Alexander had great plans for rebuilding Babylon and making it his capital, but they were never realized. As Daniel had foretold, he was cut down and broken in death. (Da 8:8) Alexander's ambition to rebuild

ALEXANDER THE GREAT AND BIBLE PROPHECY

Prophecy	Fulfillment
"A male of the goats . . . proceeded to strike down the ram and to break its two horns." "The ram that you saw possessing the two horns stands for the kings of Media and Persia. And the hairy he-goat stands for the king of Greece." (Da 8:5, 7, 20, 21)	After defeating the Medo-Persian forces twice in Asia Minor, Alexander's army pushed first to the S and then to the E, completely conquering the Medo-Persian Empire
"And your [Tyre's] dust they will place in the very midst of the water." (Eze 26:4, 12)	In 332 B.C.E., Alexander used the rubble of the old mainland city of Tyre to build a causeway to the island city, which he destroyed
"As soon as it became mighty, the great horn was broken." (Da 8:8)	In 323 B.C.E., at 32 years of age, he was stricken and died
"Desolate wastes to time indefinite are what [Babylon] will become." (Jer 51:26)	His grandiose plans to rebuild Babylon as his capital thus failed, and finally its site became a desolate waste
"His kingdom will be broken and be divided . . . but not to his posterity." (Da 11:4)	Alexander's heirs were murdered, and the kingdom fell apart
"The great horn was broken, and there proceeded to come up . . . four instead of it." (Da 8:8, 22)	By 301 B.C.E., four of Alexander's generals had taken over separate sections of the former empire

Babylon failed to materialize not simply because in 323 B.C.E. at 32, in the prime of life, he suddenly died of malarial fever complicated by his reckless living but because Jehovah had long before determined that Babylon would never be rebuilt. —Jer 50:35-40.

During his short career Alexander married Roxana, the daughter of the conquered Bactrian king, and also Statire, a daughter of the Persian king Darius III. By Roxana he had a son who was named Alexander (Allou). And by a certain Barsine he had an illegitimate son named Heracles (Hercules). However, the prophecy of Daniel had foretold that "not to his posterity" would his empire be left; so it was that all Alexander's family and heirs were done away with before many years passed. (Da 11:3, 4) Furthermore, it was written: "And that one having been broken, so that there were four that finally stood up instead of it, there are four kingdoms from his nation that will stand up, but not with his power." (Da 8:22) It was, therefore, no mere historical coincidence that the empire was divided among four of Alexander's generals: Seleucus Nicator taking Mesopotamia and Syria; Cassander, Macedonia and Greece; Ptolemy Lagus, Egypt and Palestine; and Lysimachus, Thrace and Asia Minor.

Alexander's conquest left its greatest mark on history by spreading the Greek language and culture far and wide. Common Greek (Koine) became the international language, hence the latter portion of the Bible was written in Koine rather than in Hebrew.

2. Son of Simon of Cyrene and brother of Rufus. Their father was compelled to carry Jesus' torture stake.—Mr 15:21; Lu 23:26.

3. A relative of Chief Priest Annas present at the trial of Peter and John.—Ac 4:6.

4. A Jew in Ephesus present when the silversmiths stirred up a riot against Paul. When Alexander attempted to speak to them, the wild mob shouted him down.—Ac 19:33, 34.

5. One who, with Hymenaeus, 'experienced shipwreck concerning his faith,' and was disfellowshipped because of his blasphemy. (1Ti 1:19, 20) Possibly the same as No. 6, below.

6. The coppersmith against whom Timothy was warned, because of his inflicting "many injuries" on Paul.—2Ti 4:14, 15.

ALEXANDRIA (Al·ex·an′dria). Chief city and famed metropolis of Egypt during the time of Jesus and his apostles. Modern Alexandria (called in Arabic Al-Iskandariyah) stands on the ancient

Medal bearing what is claimed to be the likeness of Alexander the Great

site and is a seaport but has little of the ancient splendor.

The city derived its name from Alexander the Great, who ordered it to be built in 332 B.C.E. In time it became the principal city of Egypt, and under the Ptolemies, the Hellenistic kings of Egypt, Alexandria was made Egypt's capital. It remained such when Rome took control in 30 B.C.E. and served as the administrative center of Egypt on through the Roman and Byzantine epochs down to the Arabic conquest in the seventh century C.E.

The Jews for long had formed a sizable portion of the population of Alexandria, which, at its height, reached perhaps 500,000 persons. Many of the Jews were descendants of the refugees who fled to Egypt after Jerusalem's fall in 607 B.C.E. In Tiberius' time they were said to compose about one-third of the city's total population. With their own section or quarter called Regio Judæorum, the Jews were allowed to live according to their own laws and have their own governor, or Alabarch.

It was here in Alexandria that the Greek *Septuagint*, the first translation of the Hebrew Scriptures, was made. It was produced by Alexandrian Jews, evidently beginning during the reign of Ptolemy (II) Philadelphus (285-246 B.C.E.).

Only brief reference is made to Alexandria in the Bible. Among those disputing with Stephen

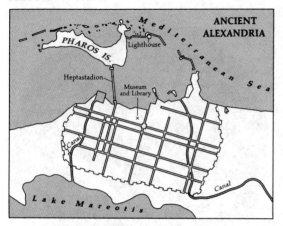

ANCIENT ALEXANDRIA

before his trial were "Alexandrians," or Jews from Alexandria. Alexandria was the native city of the eloquent Apollos. And two of the ships on which Paul traveled as a prisoner headed for Rome were out of Alexandria, doubtless large grain ships of the great Alexandrian fleet that crossed the Mediterranean Sea to Puteoli, Italy, though at times doing coastwise sailing to the ports of Asia Minor. —Ac 6:9; 18:24; 27:6; 28:11.

ALGUM [Heb., 'al·gum·mim' (2Ch 2:8; 9:10, 11); 'al·mug·gim' (1Ki 10:11, 12)]. A tree included by Solomon in his request to Hiram of Tyre for timbers for the construction of the temple and from which stairs and supports as well as harps and stringed instruments were constructed.

The algum tree of this account cannot be identified with certainty. It is traditionally suggested to be the red sandalwood (Pterocarpus santalinus) now found in India and Ceylon, although some favor the white sandalwood (Santalum album), perhaps because of Josephus' statement that it is like pine wood "but . . . whiter and more gleaming." (Jewish Antiquities, VIII, 177 [vii, 1]) The red sandalwood grows to heights of about 7.5 to 9 m (25 to 30 ft) and has a hard, fine-grained, reddish-brown wood that takes a high polish. It is suggested as suitable for musical instruments of the type mentioned in the Bible account. The wood has a sweet scent and is highly resistant to insects.

The red sandalwood does not grow in Lebanon at the present time. However, the record is not definite whether the "algum" trees were native to Lebanon or not. At any rate, Hiram later saw fit to bring them from Ophir, and here again, the timbers may have been imports even in Ophir, as it was in position to act as a trading center dealing with India, Egypt, and other places in Africa. (1Ki 10:11, 22) The rarity and preciousness of the wood

delivered by Hiram is indicated by the statement that "timbers of algum trees like this have not come in nor have they been seen down to this day."—1Ki 10:12.

ALIEN RESIDENT. In its general meaning the Hebrew noun ger refers to anyone who is residing as an alien outside his native land and who is restricted in civil rights. He may or may not have religious connections with the natives of the land in which he resides. Abraham, Isaac, Jacob, and their descendants were referred to as such before they were given legal title to the Promised Land.—Ge 15:13; 17:8; De 23:7.

When the Bible refers to a person of non-Israelite origin in relation to the Israelite commonwealth, the designation "alien resident" sometimes applies to one of these who had become a proselyte or a full worshiper of Jehovah. At times it refers to a settler in the land of Palestine who was content to live among the Israelites, obeying the fundamental laws of the land but not fully accepting the worship of Jehovah. The context determines to which class the term applies.

The Greek Septuagint translates ger as proselyte (Gr., pro·se'ly·tos) more than 70 times. Some suggest that often the alien resident attached himself to a Hebrew household for protection and was somewhat of a dependent but still distinguished from a slave. This is inferred from the expression "your alien resident."—De 5:14; compare De 1:16; also Le 22:10, where the term toh·shav', meaning "settler," is used.

When the Law covenant was transmitted at Mount Sinai, special legislation was embodied governing, in a very loving spirit, the relationship of the alien resident to the natural Israelite. Being at a disadvantage because of not being a natural-born Israelite, the alien resident was given special consideration and protection under the Law covenant, which had many provisions for the weak and vulnerable. Regularly Jehovah called Israel's attention to the fact that they themselves knew the afflictions that beset an alien resident in a land not his own and hence should extend to the alien residents among themselves the generous and protective spirit that they had not received. (Ex 22:21; 23:9; De 10:18) Basically, the alien resident, especially the proselyte, was to be treated as a brother.—Le 19:33, 34.

Although the terms of the Law covenant allowed for persons of all national backgrounds to come into membership of the congregation of Israel by accepting the true worship of Jehovah and becoming circumcised, there were exceptions and restrictions. The Egyptians and Edomites could not enter into the congregation until the third generation, that is, the third generation living in the land of Israel. (De 23:7, 8) Illegitimate sons and their descendants were denied entry into the congregation "to the tenth generation." (De 23:2) Ammonites and Moabites were prohibited "to the tenth generation . . . to time indefinite . . . You must not work for their peace and their prosperity all your days to time indefinite." (De 23:3-6) These restrictions all applied to males of these nations. Also, no male mutilated in his sexual parts could ever become a member of the congregation.—De 23:1.

The alien resident who had become a circumcised worshiper was bound to one law with the Israelites, that is, to obey all the terms of the Law covenant. (Le 24:22) A few examples are: He was required to keep the Sabbath (Ex 20:10; 23:12) and to celebrate the Passover (Nu 9:14; Ex 12:48, 49), the Festival of Unfermented Cakes (Ex 12:19), the Festival of Weeks (De 16:10, 11), the Festival of Booths (De 16:13, 14), and the Day of Atonement (Le 16:29, 30). He could offer sacrifices (Nu 15:14) and had to do so in the same manner as prescribed for the natural Israelite. (Nu 15:15, 16) His offerings were to be unblemished (Le 22:18-20) and brought to the entrance of the tent of meeting just as was done by the natural Israelite. (Le 17:8, 9) He could not engage in any false worship. (Le 20:2; Eze 14:7) He was required to drain blood out of game killed in hunting and would be "cut off" if he ate it undrained. (Le 17:10-14) He could receive forgiveness along with natural Israel for community responsibility for sins. (Nu 15:26, 29) He had to observe the purification procedures, for example, if unclean by touching a human corpse. (Nu 19:10, 11) The alien resident who could be given the body of an animal that had died of itself was evidently one who had not become a full-fledged worshiper of Jehovah.—De 14:21.

Judicially, the alien resident was guaranteed impartial justice in judgments involving a natural Israelite. (De 1:16, 17) He was not to be defrauded or subjected to perverted judgment. (De 24:14, 17) Curses were laid on those who rendered injustice to alien residents. (De 27:19) The cities of refuge for the unintentional manslayer were available for the alien resident and the settler as well as the natural Israelite.—Nu 35:15; Jos 20:9.

Alien residents, not having any land inheritance, might be merchants or hired laborers. Some were slaves. (Le 25:44-46) There was a possibility of their becoming wealthy. (Le 25:47; De 28:43) Generally, however, the Law classified

them as among the poor and outlined arrangements for protecting and providing for them. The alien resident could share in the tithes provided every third year. (De 14:28, 29; 26:12) Gleanings of the field and of the vineyard were to be left for him. (Le 19:9, 10; 23:22; De 24:19-21) He could receive the benefits of what grew during Sabbath years. (Le 25:6) He was given equal protection with a native Israelite as a hired laborer. A poor Israelite might sell himself to a wealthy alien resident, in which case the Israelite was to be treated kindly, like a hired laborer, and could be repurchased at any time by himself or by a kinsman or, at the latest, was released on the seventh year of his service or at the Jubilee.—Le 25:39-54; Ex 21:2; De 15:12.

During the period of the kings the alien residents continued to enjoy favorable relations. At the time of the construction of the temple at Jerusalem, they were drawn on as construction workers. (1Ch 22:2; 2Ch 2:17, 18) When King Asa acted to restore true worship in Judah, alien residents from all over the Promised Land assembled at Jerusalem along with natural Israelites, to enter jointly into a special covenant to search for Jehovah with all their heart and soul. (2Ch 15:8-14) After cleansing the temple, King Hezekiah declared a Passover celebration in Jerusalem in the second month. He sent the invitation throughout Israel, and many alien residents responded.—2Ch 30:25.

Following the restoration of the remnant of Israelites from the Babylonian exile, alien residents, comprised of such groups as the Nethinim (meaning "Given Ones"), slaves, professional male and female singers, and the sons of the servants of Solomon, were again found associated with them in true worship at the temple. The Nethinim included the Gibeonites who had been assigned by Joshua to permanent temple service. (Ezr 7:7, 24; 8:17-20; Jos 9:22-27) Down to the last mention of them these alien residents were inseparable adherents to the true worship of Jehovah, serving with the remnant of faithful natural Israelites who had returned from Babylon. (Ne 11:3, 21) In the postexilic period, prophets of Jehovah reiterated the principles of the Law covenant that safeguarded the rights of the alien resident.—Zec 7:10; Mal 3:5.

The prophet Ezekiel foretold a time when the alien resident would receive an inheritance in the land like a native among the sons of Israel. (Eze 47:21-23) After the coming of Jesus Christ the good news of the Kingdom was preached to Jews and proselytes, and these could equally become members of the Christian congregation. Then, in the time of Cornelius (36 C.E.), an uncircumcised Gentile and his household were accepted by Jehovah, receiving gifts of the spirit. (Ac 10) From that time on, uncircumcised Gentiles, upon accepting Christ, were admitted into the Christian congregation, "where there is neither Greek nor Jew, circumcision nor uncircumcision, foreigner, Scythian, slave, freeman, but Christ is all things and in all." (Col 3:11; Ga 3:28) Revelation 7:2-8 describes spiritual Israel as made up of 12 tribes of 12,000 each. Then verses 9 to 17 tell of a great crowd that no man could number, people out of all nations, tribes, peoples, and tongues who hail the enthroned King and his Lamb and receive God's favor and protection.

Settler. A settler was an inhabitant of a land or country not his own. The Hebrew word for settler (toh·shav´) comes from the root verb ya·shav´, meaning "dwell." (Ge 20:15) Evidently some of the settlers in Israel became proselytes; others were content to dwell with the Israelites and to obey the fundamental laws of the land but did not become worshipers of Jehovah as did circumcised proselytes. The settler was distinguished from the foreigner, who was generally a transient and was only extended the hospitality that is usually accorded guests in the Orient.

The settler who was an uncircumcised dweller in the land did not eat of the Passover or of anything holy. (Ex 12:45; Le 22:10) He received benefits along with the alien residents and the poor during the Sabbath year and the Jubilee year by being able to share in what the land produced. (Le 25:6, 12) He or his offspring could be purchased as slaves by the Israelites and passed on as a permanent inheritance without the right of repurchase or benefit of Jubilee release. (Le 25:45, 46) On the other hand, an Israelite might sell himself as a slave to a settler or to members of the settler's family, maintaining the right of repurchase at any time, as well as release in his seventh year of servitude or at the Jubilee.—Le 25:47-54; Ex 21:2; De 15:12.

While only the natural Israelites had a hereditary possession in the land, Jehovah was the actual owner and could put them in or out of the land as it suited his purpose. Regarding the sale of land he said: "So the land should not be sold in perpetuity, because the land is mine. For you are alien residents and settlers from my standpoint."—Le 25:23.

Stranger. The Hebrew word for stranger (zar) evidently comes from the root zur, meaning "turn aside; become estranged" (Ps 78:30; 69:8)

and thus has the basic meaning "one who distances or removes himself."—*Theological Dictionary of the Old Testament,* edited by G. Botterweck and H. Ringgren, 1980, Vol. 4, p. 53.

The considering of persons as strangers was done in matters pertaining to the Aaronic family and the tribe of Levi, and it affected the natural Israelite and the alien resident, as well as all other persons. Priestly functions were committed by the Law to the family of Aaron (Ex 28:1-3), and other temple matters were assigned to the tribe of Levi in general. (Nu 1:49, 50, 53) All other persons, including the natural Israelites of the 12 non-Levitical tribes, were likened to strangers with respect to the Levitical tribe in certain affairs. (Ex 29:33, *NW* ftn, "'non-Aaronite,' that is, a man not of the family of Aaron"; *KJ* margin, "every one not a Levite"; Nu 3:38, *NW* ftn, "that is, a non-Levite"; *JB,* "layman." See also Le 22:10; Nu 3:10.) According to the context "stranger," in most occurrences in the Pentateuch, refers to anyone not of the family of Aaron or not of the tribe of Levi, because priestly or ministerial privileges and duties were not assigned to him.

The stranger (non-Aaronite) could not eat of the installation sacrifice (Ex 29:33), nor be anointed with holy anointing oil (Ex 30:33), nor eat anything holy (Le 22:10). A non-Aaronite stranger could not handle any priestly duties. (Nu 3:10; 16:40; 18:7) A non-Levite stranger, that is, even those of any of the other 12 tribes, could not come near the tabernacle to set it up or for any purpose except to offer sacrifices or to approach the priests at the gate of the tent of meeting. (Le 4:24, 27-29) The daughter of a priest who married a non-Aaronite stranger could not eat of the contribution of the holy things, nor could her "stranger" husband.—Le 22:12, 13.

The word "stranger" was also applied to those who turned aside from what was in harmony with the Law and so were alienated from Jehovah. Thus the prostitute is referred to as a "strange woman." (Pr 2:16; 5:17; 7:5) Both the worshipers of false gods and the deities themselves are termed "strangers."—Jer 2:25; 3:13.

Strangers in the sense of persons with whom one is unacquainted, or foreigners, are also referred to in the Hebrew Scriptures.—1Ki 3:18; Job 19:15.

Christian principles regarding strangers. In the Christian Greek Scriptures love toward the stranger (Gr., xe´nos) is strongly emphasized as a quality the Christian must exercise. The apostle Paul says: "Do not forget hospitality [Gr., phi·lo·xe·ni´as, "fondness for strangers"], for through it some, unknown to themselves, entertained angels." (Heb 13:2) Jesus showed that he counts hospitality extended to his brothers, strangers or unacquainted though they may be at the time, as having been extended toward him. (Mt 25:34-46) The apostle John wrote commending Gaius for his good works toward Christian men, strangers to Gaius, sent to visit the congregation of which Gaius was a member, and he condemns Diotrephes, who showed them no respect.—3Jo 5-10; 1Ti 5:10.

Christians are termed "aliens" and "temporary residents" in the sense that they are no part of this world. (Joh 15:19; 1Pe 1:1) They are aliens in that they do not conform to the practices of the world hostile to God. (1Pe 2:11) Those of the Gentile nations, once "strangers to the covenants of the promise," without hope and "without God in the world," are, through Christ, "no longer strangers and alien residents," but "fellow citizens of the holy ones and are members of the household of God." (Eph 2:11, 12, 19) The "other sheep" that Jesus said he would gather into the "one flock" likewise take a position separate from the world, with favor of God and hope of life.—Joh 10:16; Mt 25:33, 34, 46; compare Re 7:9-17.

One who attempts to gather religious followers to himself is termed by Christ as "a thief" and "a stranger," one dangerous to Christ's "sheep," and is considered a false shepherd. Jesus' true "sheep" will give no recognition to a false shepherd's voice, just as the faithful Israelites kept themselves separate from the foreigner who advocated strange gods.—Joh 10:1, 5; see FOREIGNER.

ALKALI. See LAUNDRYMAN.

ALLAMMELECH (Al·lam′me·lech) [Massive Tree of the King]. A town in the territory allotted the tribe of Asher (Jos 19:26), N of the torrent valley of Kishon. The exact site is unknown but was probably in the S part of the Plain of Acco, perhaps on the Wadi el-Melek (Nahal Zippori), which empties into the Kishon.

ALLIANCE. A uniting together of different parties, families, individuals, or states, whether by marriage, mutual agreement, or legal compact. An alliance usually implies resultant mutual benefit or the joint pursuit of a desired purpose. The Hebrew word cha·var′ literally means "be joined" but is used figuratively to mean "be allied; have partnership." (Ex 28:7; Ps 94:20; 2Ch 20:35) The related cha·ver′ denotes an ally or partner.—Jg 20:11; Ps 119:63.

Abraham entered into an early alliance with Mamre, Eshcol, and Aner of the Amorites. The nature of the confederacy is not stated, but they joined him in his march to rescue his nephew Lot from invading kings. (Ge 14:13-24) Abraham was then dwelling as an alien in land controlled by petty kingdoms, and in this case, some formal declaration in the form of a covenant may have been required of him as a prerequisite for peaceful residence in their midst. However, Abraham avoided unnecessarily obligating himself to such political rulers, as is manifest by his statement to the king of Sodom at Genesis 14:21-24. Later, at Gerar, the Philistine king Abimelech reminded Abraham of his alien status and that he resided in the land of Philistia by Abimelech's consent, and he requested of him the swearing of an oath guaranteeing faithful conduct. Abraham acquiesced and later, following a water-rights dispute, made a covenant with Abimelech.—Ge 20:1, 15; 21:22-34.

Abraham's son Isaac also came to dwell in Gerar, although he was later asked by Abimelech to move out of the immediate vicinity, and he willingly complied. Disputes over water rights again occurred, but thereafter Abimelech and his chief associates approached Isaac requesting an oath of obligation and a covenant, doubtless as a renewal of that made with Abraham. Sworn statements were made by both parties guaranteeing reciprocal peaceful conduct. (Ge 26:16, 19-22, 26-31; compare Ge 31:48-53.) The apostle Paul states that these early patriarchs publicly declared themselves strangers and temporary residents tenting in the land, awaiting a city having real foundations, whose builder and maker is God. —Heb 11:8-10, 13-16.

A different situation prevailed with the entry of the nation of Israel into Canaan, the Land of Promise. The Sovereign God had given Israel full right to the land in fulfillment of his promise to their forefathers. They were, therefore, not entering as alien residents, and Jehovah prohibited their making alliances with the pagan nations in the land. (Ex 23:31-33; 34:11-16) They were to be subject only to God's laws and statutes, not to those of the nations due for eviction. (Le 18:3, 4; 20:22-24) They were particularly warned against forming marriage alliances with such nations. Such alliances would intimately involve them not only with pagan wives but with pagan relatives and their false religious practices and customs, and this would result in apostasy and a snare.—De 7:2-4; Ex 34:16; Jos 23:12, 13.

Marriage Alliances. The Hebrew verb cha·than′, meaning "form a marriage alliance," is related to cho·then′ (father-in-law), cha·than′ (bridegroom; son-in-law), cho·the′neth (mother-in-law), and *chathun·nah'* (marriage).—1Sa 18:22; Ex 3:1; 4:25; Ge 19:14; De 27:23; Ca 3:11.

Abraham insisted that Isaac's wife not be taken from among the Canaanites. (Ge 24:3, 4) Isaac gave similar instruction to Jacob. (Ge 28:1) At the time of Dinah's violation by Shechem the Hivite, the family of Jacob was urged by Hamor, Shechem's father, to enter into marriage alliances with that tribe. Though Jacob's sons did not follow through with their apparent acceptance, they did take the Hivite women and children captive after avenging Dinah's honor. (Ge 34:1-11, 29) Judah later married a Canaanite woman (Ge 38:2), and Joseph's wife was an Egyptian. (Ge 41:50) Moses married Zipporah, a Midianite, evidently called a "Cushite" at Numbers 12:1. (Ex 2:16, 21) These marriages, however, were contracted before the giving of the Law and hence could not be considered a violation of its requirements.

In the battle with Midian, the Israelites preserved alive only virgins from among the women and girls. (Nu 31:3, 18, 35) The Law allowed for the taking of a wife from among such parentless female war captives. (De 21:10-14) Within the Promised Land itself God's warning concerning marriage alliances with pagans was often ignored, with resulting problems and apostasy.—Jg 3:5, 6.

Marriage alliances were sometimes arranged with a view to achieving certain ends, as when David was invited by King Saul to form a marriage alliance with him by taking his daughter Michal as wife. (1Sa 18:21-27) One of the six wives who later bore David sons at Hebron was the daughter of the king of Geshur (2Sa 3:3), and some consider this to be a marriage alliance entered into by David with a view to weakening the position of rival Ish-bosheth, since Geshur was a petty kingdom lying on the other side of Mahanaim, Ish-bosheth's capital. Early in his reign King Solomon formed a marriage alliance with Pharaoh, taking his daughter as wife. (1Ki 3:1; 9:16) This marriage, along with others to Moabite, Ammonite, Edomite, Sidonian, and Hittite women, eventually caused Solomon to succumb to gross idolatry. (1Ki 11:1-6) King Ahab's marriage alliance with the king of Sidon by marrying his daughter Jezebel brought similar disastrous results for the northern kingdom of Israel. (1Ki 16:31-33) King Jehoshaphat thereafter formed an unwise marriage alliance with the idolatrous house of Ahab, with lasting bad consequences for the kingdom of Judah.—2Ch 18:1; 21:4-6; 22:2-4.

Following the exile, Ezra was shocked to find that even the priests and Levites had made marriage alliances with the Canaanites and others, a situation that was promptly corrected. (Ezr 9:1-3, 12-14; 10:1-5, 10-14, 44) Yet, in Nehemiah's time Tobiah the Ammonite again used marriage alliances to develop strong relations with the priestly family in Jerusalem and foster a strong faction of allies among the nobles of Judah, to the point that, in defiance of the Law (De 23:3), the priest Eliashib made a dining hall in the temple courtyard for this Ammonite. Nehemiah, however, indignantly threw all of Tobiah's furniture outside.—Ne 6:18; 13:4-9, 25-27; see MARRIAGE.

Covenants. Other alliances aside from marriage alliances were made, and these were generally in the form of a covenant. The covenant made with the Gibeonites was, of course, entered into by Israel because of a deception. (Jos 9:3-15) Nevertheless, once made, the covenant was thereafter respected so that Israel was willing to fight to protect the Gibeonites. (Jos 9:19-21; 10:6, 7) A personal alliance by covenant existed between Jonathan and David (1Sa 18:3; 20:11-17), a relationship that Saul condemned as a conspiracy. (1Sa 22:8) King Hiram of Tyre showed friendship toward David when David succeeded Saul as king, and Hiram became "a lover of David." (2Sa 5:11; 1Ki 5:1) Friendly relations continued, and on Solomon's accession to the throne a contract was made with King Hiram that called for the supplying of much of the material needed for the temple construction. (1Ki 5:2-18) Under this contract thousands of Israelite laborers were allowed entry into Lebanon and its forests. Hiram even addressed Solomon as "my brother." (1Ki 9:13) Tyre furnished seamen for Solomon's fleet of ships operating out of Ezion-geber. (1Ki 9:26, 27) When the kingdom of Tyre later turned against Israel and handed over Israelite exiles to Edom, it was accused of having violated "the covenant of brothers."—Am 1:9.

Unwise Alliances With Other Nations. Though God's prophets gave strong warnings against the forming of alliances with other nations, in times of danger or under the pressure of ambition the kings of Judah and Israel frequently ignored such warnings. (Isa 30:2-7; Jer 2:16-19, 36, 37; Ho 5:13; 8:8-10; 12:1) The end results were never good, as the following examples show.

King Asa of Judah used the royal treasures to buy King Ben-hadad I of Syria out of a covenant with King Baasha of Israel. (1Ki 15:18-20) As a result of this 'leaning on Syria' instead of on Jehovah, Asa was rebuked by the prophet Hanani with the words: "You have acted foolishly respecting this, for from now on there will exist wars against you." (2Ch 16:7-9) King Ahab of Israel later made a covenant with defeated Ben-hadad II and received similar condemnation from a prophet of God. (1Ki 20:34, 42) Jehoshaphat allied himself with Ahab in an unsuccessful attack against Syria and was thereafter asked by the prophet Jehu: "Is it to the wicked that help is to be given, and is it for those hating Jehovah that you should have love? And for this there is indignation against you from the person of Jehovah." (2Ch 18:2, 3; 19:2) Later Jehoshaphat made a commercial shipbuilding partnership with wicked King Ahaziah of Israel, but prophetic condemnation was fulfilled when the ships were wrecked. (2Ch 20:35-37) Obeying divine counsel, Amaziah of Judah wisely decided against the use of mercenary troops from Israel though it meant a loss of 100 talents of silver ($660,600) paid to them as a fee.—2Ch 25:6-10.

In the eighth century B.C.E. as Assyria began to rise as a dominant world power, its menacing shadow drove lesser kingdoms into many alliances and conspiracies. (Compare Isa 8:9-13.) A buildup of new weapons of warfare among the nations also caused increased fear. (Compare 2Ch 26:14, 15.) Menahem of Israel bribed the attacking Pul (Tiglath-pileser III) of Assyria. (2Ki 15:17-20) Rezin of Syria and Pekah of Israel formed a conspiratorial alliance against Ahaz of Judah, who, in turn, used the royal treasures and those from the temple to buy protection from Assyrian Tiglath-pileser III, resulting in the fall of Syrian Damascus. (2Ki 16:5-9; 2Ch 28:16) Hoshea of Israel made a conspiratorial alliance with King So of Egypt in the false hope of throwing off the Assyrian yoke imposed by Shalmaneser V, with the consequent fall of Israel in 740 B.C.E. (2Ki 17:3-6) Faithful Hezekiah of Judah, however, though falsely accused of trusting in Egypt, relied solely on Jehovah and was saved from the Assyrian Sennacherib's attack.—2Ki 18:19-22, 32-35; 19:14-19, 28, 32-36; compare Isa 31:1-3.

In its closing years, the kingdom of Judah fluctuated between Egypt and Babylon, "prostituting" itself to both powers. (Eze 16:26-29; 23:14) It came under the dominance of Egypt during Jehoiakim's reign (2Ki 23:34) but was soon made subject to Babylon. (2Ki 24:1, 7, 12-17) The last king, Zedekiah, made a futile attempt to free Judah from Babylon by a vain alliance with Egypt. Destruction of Jerusalem resulted. (2Ki 24:20; Eze 17:1-15) They had failed to accept Isaiah's inspired advice: "By coming back and resting you people will be saved. Your mightiness will prove to be simply in keeping undisturbed and in trustfulness."—Isa 30:15-17.

During the Maccabean period many treaties and alliances were made with the Syrians and the Romans for political advantage, but freedom from bondage did not result for Israel. In a later period the religious Sadducees were especially prominent in favoring political collaboration as a means toward ultimate national independence. Neither they nor the Pharisees accepted the Kingdom message proclaimed by Christ Jesus but allied themselves with Rome, declaring: "We have no king but Caesar." (Joh 19:12-15) Their religiopolitical alliance with Rome, however, ended in the disastrous destruction of Jerusalem in 70 C.E.—Lu 19:41-44; 21:20-24.

Political and religious alliances are indicated in the symbolisms of Revelation 17:1, 2, 10-18; 18:3. (Compare Jas 4:1-4.) Thus, throughout the Scriptural record the principle stated by Paul is stressed: "Do not become unevenly yoked with unbelievers. For what fellowship do righteousness and lawlessness have? Or what sharing does light have with darkness? . . . Get out from among them, and separate yourselves."—2Co 6:14-17.

ALLON (Al′lon) [Massive Tree]. A Simeonite, descendant of Shemaiah.—1Ch 4:37.

ALLON-BACUTH (Al′lon-bac′uth) [Massive Tree of Weeping]. A massive tree at the foot of Bethel, below the hill occupied by the city, named thus because under it Jacob buried "Deborah the nursing woman of Rebekah."—Ge 35:8; see BIG TREE, MASSIVE TREE.

ALMIGHTY. The word "Almighty" is translated from the Hebrew word Shad·dai′ and the Greek word Pan·to·kra′tor. Both words evidently convey the idea of strength or power.

The Hebrew Term. In the Hebrew text Shad·dai′ is used seven times along with 'El (God), forming the title "God Almighty." (Ge 17:1; 28:3; 35:11; 43:14; 48:3; Ex 6:3; Eze 10:5) In the other 41 occurrences it stands alone and is translated "the Almighty" or "the Almighty One." Similar to 'Adho·nai′ (Sovereign Lord) and 'Elo·him′ (God), Shad·dai′ is in the plural to denote excellence.—Ge 49:25; Nu 24:4; Ps 68:14.

The exact derivation of the word Shad·dai′ is a matter of discussion. The translators of the Septuagint used several Greek words in translating it, but in the book of Job they did employ the word Pan·to·kra′tor (All Powerful) 16 times for Shad·dai′. In a few cases they rendered it by a Greek term (hi·ka·nos′) meaning "sufficient" or "fit" (Ru 1:20, 21; Job 21:15; 31:2; 40:2), and later Greek translators such as Aquila and Symmachus followed this interpretation, thereby presenting *Shad·dai'* as the "Sufficient (Fit) One."

The view of some modern critics is expressed in the comment on Genesis 17:1 in the Catholic translation known as *The Jerusalem Bible* (ftn *b*), which states: "The usual translation 'Almighty God' is inaccurate; 'Mou[n]tain God' is the probable meaning." Such extreme view, however, is based on an imagined linkage of *Shad·dai'* with the Akkadian term *shadu* (mountain). *Unger's Bible Dictionary* (1965, p. 1000) comments: "This view, however, is unacceptable and Shaddai is best taken from the root *shadad* [*sha·dhadh'*], 'to be strong or powerful,' as in Arabic."—See also *The Analytical Hebrew and Chaldee Lexicon*, by Benjamin Davidson, p. 702.

Sha·dhadh' in the Bible text commonly implies violent power, as used in despoiling. (Compare Ps 17:9; Pr 11:3.) Isaiah 13:6 states: "Howl, you people, for the day of Jehovah is near! As a despoiling [*keshodh'*] from the Almighty [*mish·Shad·dai'*] it will come." While the idea of violent action is basic in the Biblical use of this root word, some scholars suggest that its original sense or primary meaning was simply "be strong" or "act strongly." *The Jewish Encyclopedia* (1976, Vol. IX, p. 162) states: "It is possible, however, that the original significance was that of 'overmastering' or 'overpowering strength,' and that this meaning persists in the divine [title]."

Jehovah used the title "God Almighty" (*'El Shad·dai'*) when making his promise to Abraham concerning the birth of Isaac, a promise requiring that Abraham have great faith in God's power to carry out that promise. It was thereafter used when God was spoken of as the one who would bless Isaac and Jacob as heirs of the Abrahamic covenant.—Ge 17:1; 28:3; 35:11; 48:3.

In harmony with this, Jehovah could later say to Moses: "I used to appear to Abraham, Isaac and Jacob as God Almighty [*be'El' Shad·dai'*], but as respects my name Jehovah I did not make myself known to them." (Ex 6:3) This could not mean that the name Jehovah was unknown to these patriarchs, since it was frequently used by them as well as by others before them. (Ge 4:1, 26; 14:22; 27:27; 28:16) In fact, in the book of Genesis, which relates the lives of the patriarchs, the word "Almighty" occurs only 6 times, whereas the personal name Jehovah was written 172 times in the original Hebrew text. Yet, while these patriarchs had come to appreciate by personal experience God's right to and qualifications for the title of "the Almighty One," they had not had opportunity to appreciate the full meaning and implications of his

personal name, Jehovah. In this regard, *The Illustrated Bible Dictionary* (Vol. 1, p. 572) comments: "The former revelation, to the Patriarchs, concerned promises belonging to a distant future; it supposed that they should be assured that He, Yahweh, was such a God (*'el*) as was competent (one possible meaning of *sadday*) to fulfill them. The revelation at the bush was greater and more intimate, God's power and immediate and continuing presence with them being all wrapped up in the familiar name of Yahweh."—Edited by J. D. Douglas, 1980.

Might implies strength or power to perform and to accomplish a thing purposed, as well as to overcome obstacles or opposition, and Jehovah's almightiness manifests his irresistible power to accomplish his purpose. At times violent action is presented in connection with God's title of "the Almighty One," as at Psalm 68:14, when he 'scatters abroad the kings'; at Joel 1:15, which describes the "despoiling [*shodh*] from the Almighty One [*mish·Shad·dai'*]" to come in "the day of Jehovah"; and at Isaiah 13:6, quoted earlier. It also gives assurance of his ability to bless (Ge 49:25) and is a guarantee of security to those trusting in him: "Anyone dwelling in the secret place of the Most High will procure himself lodging under the very shadow of the Almighty One."—Ps 91:1.

In the book of Job, *Shad·dai'* occurs 31 times, being used by all the characters in the drama there presented. Jehovah's power to punish or to afflict are set forth (Job 6:4; 27:13-23), so that the ones who say, "What does the Almighty amount to, that we should serve him, and how do we benefit ourselves in that we have come in touch with him?" and who therefore trust in their own power, can expect to drink of "the rage of the Almighty." (Job 21:15, 16, 20) The Almighty, therefore, merits awe, even dread, since his will cannot be ignored nor his law violated with impunity (Job 6:14; 23:15, 16; 31:1-3), even though the expression of his might is not immediately seen. (Job 24:1-3, 24; compare Ex 9:14-16; Ec 8:11-13.) Yet his power and might are always used in strict accord with justice and righteousness, never in an uncontrolled, wanton, erratic, or irresponsible manner. (Job 34:10, 12; 35:13; 37:23, 24) Hence, there is no just cause for men to contend or find fault with him. (Job 40:2-5) Those practicing righteousness can confidently approach him and enjoy a personal relationship with him. (Job 13:3; 29:4, 5; 31:35-37) As the Creator, he is the Source of life and wisdom.—Job 32:8; 33:4.

In the prophecy at Isaiah 9:6 concerning the Messiah, the title "Mighty God" is applied to the promised Prince of Peace. This expression, however, translates the Hebrew *'El Gib·bohr'*, not *'El Shad·dai'*, as in the above scriptures.

The Greek Term. In the Christian Greek Scriptures the word *Pan·to·kra'tor* occurs ten times, nine of them in the book of Revelation. The word basically means "Almighty," or "All Powerful." Its use in the Christian Greek Scriptures lends weight to the understanding of the Hebrew term *Shad·dai'* as meaning "Almighty One," since otherwise there would be no corresponding term for *Pan·to·kra'tor* in the Hebrew Scriptures.

At 2 Corinthians 6:18 Paul quotes from the Hebrew Scriptures in urging Christians to avoid false worship and the use of lifeless, powerless idols, thus qualifying as children of "the Almighty [*Pan·to·kra'tor*]." In view of the apostle's quotations, it is obvious that the title here applies to Jehovah God.

Similarly, throughout Revelation the title *Pan·to·kra'tor* is applied to the Creator and King of Eternity, Jehovah, as in "the song of Moses the slave of God and the song of the Lamb [Jesus Christ]," which acclaims Jehovah God as the one worthy of worship and fear by all nations. (Re 15:3; compare Re 21:22.) The title's application to Jehovah God is made obvious at Revelation 19:6 by the use of the expression Hallelujah (Praise Jah, you people!). Likewise, the expression "the One who is and who was and who is coming" (Re 1:8; 4:8) clearly points to the God of eternity (Ps 90:2), who not only "was" the Almighty in ancient times but continues to be so and "is coming" as such with an expression of his all-powerfulness. Again violent action is indicated, following his 'taking his great power' to rule as king, by the expression of his wrath against the opposing nations at "the war of the great day of God the Almighty." (Re 11:17, 18; 16:14) His Son, Christ Jesus, "The Word of God," is shown as expressing this "wrath of God the Almighty" against the nations in his position as king anointed by God. (Re 19:13-16) Yet such mighty expressions of God's judicial decisions continue to be in full accord with his standards of truth and righteousness.—Re 16:5-7; see GOD.

ALMODAD (Al·mo'dad). First of Joktan's 13 sons; fourth generation after Shem; nephew of Peleg, through whom the Messianic lineage is traced. Almodad fathered one of the 70 post-Flood families, settling in Arabia. (Ge 10:26, 32; 1Ch 1:20) Arabian tradition has him chief of the tribe Jurham and father of a wife of Ishmael.

ALMON (Al'mon). A Levite city within the territory of Benjamin; assigned to the sons of Aaron in the days of Joshua and of Eleazar the priest. (Jos 21:1, 18) It is called Alemeth in 1 Chronicles 6:60. The ancient site is at the village ruins of Khirbet 'Almit (Horvat 'Almit), about 6 km (3.5 mi) NE of Jerusalem and about 2 km (1 mi) ENE of Anathoth, another Levite city.

ALMOND [Heb., *luz* (Ge 30:37); *sha·qedh'* (Ge 43:11)]. The almond (*Amygdalus communis*) is a tree native to Palestine, Lebanon, and some areas of Mesopotamia. A member of the peach family, it grew both wild and as a cultivated fruit tree.

The Hebrew name *sha·qedh'* means, literally, "awakening one," and this is quite fitting since the almond is one of the earliest trees to bloom following the winter rest, blossoming as early as late January or early February. Note the play on words at Jeremiah 1:11, 12, where the Hebrew word for "almond tree" (*sha·qedh'*) is followed by the expression "keeping awake" (*sho·qedh'*). The tree may grow up to 5 m (16 ft) in height and, when blossoming, is covered with lovely pink and sometimes white flowers arranged in pairs. At Ecclesiastes 12:5 the blossoming almond tree is used to picture the white-headedness of old age. The leaves are oval shaped and serrated on the edges. The almond fruit has an oblong shape, rounded on one end and pointed on the other. It has always been considered a delicacy and was used by Jacob as part of a gift sent to Egypt with his returning sons. (Ge 43:11) The kernel is a source of desirable oil, 45 kg (100 lb) of the fruit producing some 20 kg (44 lb) of oil.

Doubtless due to their delicate beauty, the flowers of the almond were used as a pattern for the cups on the branches of the tabernacle lampstand. (Ex 25:33, 34; 37:19, 20) Aaron's rod was also an almond branch and miraculously budded overnight, producing ripe almonds as proof of God's approval on him as anointed high priest.—Nu 17:8.

ALMON-DIBLATHAIM (Al'mon-dib·la·tha'-im). A place between Dibon-gad and the mountains of Abarim where the Israelites encamped in the 40th year after their going out from Egypt (1473 B.C.E.). It was one of the last encampments during their wanderings. (Nu 33:46, 47) The site is not certain, but some scholars identify it with Khirbet Deleilat esh-Sherqiyeh, about 16 km (10 mi) NNE of Dibon (Dhiban). Possibly identical with Beth-diblathaim.—Jer 48:22.

ALMUG. See ALGUM.

ALOE, ALOESWOOD [Heb., *'aha·lim'* (plural) and *'aha·lohth'* (plural); Gr., *a·lo'e*]. A name applied to a variety of tree containing a fragrant, or

*Almond blossoms. The almond
is among the first trees to bloom as
winter ends; thus its Hebrew name
means "awakening one"*

aloe trees resembling an encampment of tents. (Nu 24:6) This text, however, has occasioned some discussion, since the *Aquilaria agallocha* trees are not found in Palestine. Their absence today, of course, would not necessarily prove that such trees were not present in that land nearly 3,500 years ago. On the other hand, Balaam's reference to the trees does not require that they be growing right in the area where he spoke. If the "cedars" mentioned immediately afterward in this text were cedars of Lebanon, then they would be trees growing outside that area, and the same could be true of the aloes. The other texts dealing with aloes refer only to their aromatic qualities and would allow for them to have been foreign imports.

Following the death of Christ Jesus, Nicodemus brought "a roll of myrrh and aloes" weighing about 100 Roman pounds (33 kg; 72 lb), to be used in preparing Jesus' body for burial. (Joh 19:39) Nicodemus' contribution must have represented a considerable outlay of money on his part, although the proportion of the less expensive myrrh included in the 100 pounds is not stated. While some apply the term "aloes" in this text to the plant of the lily family that now bears the botanical name of *Aloe vera*, the product of this plant (a thick juice from the leaves) is employed not for its aroma but as a purgative and for other health-related purposes. The aloes brought by Nicodemus was likely the same aloeswood product as that referred to in the Hebrew Scriptures.

aromatic, substance used as a perfume in the Biblical period. (Ps 45:8; Pr 7:17; Ca 4:14) Most commentators consider the aloe tree of the Bible to be the *Aquilaria agallocha*, sometimes called the eaglewood tree and now found principally in India and neighboring regions. The tree is large and spreading, at times reaching a height of 30 m (c. 100 ft). The inner core of the trunk and of branches is impregnated with resin and an odoriferous oil, from which comes the highly prized perfume. Apparently attaining its most aromatic state when in decay, the wood is sometimes buried in the ground to hasten the decaying process. In a finely powdered condition it is then sold commercially as "aloes."

The prophet Balaam's comparison of the tents of Israel with "aloe plants that Jehovah has planted, like cedars by the waters," may relate to the spreading shape of these lofty trees, a cluster of

ALPHA AND OMEGA. These are the names of the first and last letters of the Greek alphabet and are used as a title three times in the book of Revelation. The additional occurrence of this phrase in the *King James* rendering of Revelation 1:11, however, does not receive support from some of the oldest Greek manuscripts, including the Alexandrine, Sinaitic, and Codex Ephraemi rescriptus. It is, therefore, omitted in many modern translations.

While many commentators apply this title both to God and to Christ, a more careful examination of its use restricts its application to Jehovah God. The first verse of Revelation shows that the revelation was given originally by God and through Jesus Christ, hence the one speaking (through an angelic representative) at times is God himself, and at other times it is Christ Jesus. (Re 22:8) Thus Revelation 1:8 (*RS*) says: "'I am the Alpha and the Omega,' says the Lord God ["Jehovah God," *NW*], who is and who was and who is to come, the Almighty." Although the preceding verse speaks of Christ Jesus, it is clear that in verse 8 the application of the title is to "the Almighty" God. In this regard *Barnes' Notes on the New Testament* (1974) observes: "It cannot be absolutely certain that the writer meant to refer to the Lord Jesus specifically here . . . There is no real incongruity in supposing, also, that the writer here meant to refer to God as such."

The title occurs again at Revelation 21:6, and the following verse identifies the speaker by saying: "Anyone conquering will inherit these things, and I shall be his God and he will be my son." Inasmuch as Jesus referred to those who are joint heirs with him in his Kingdom as "brothers," not "sons," the speaker must be Jesus' heavenly Father, Jehovah God.—Mt 25:40; compare Heb 2:10-12.

The final occurrence of the title is at Revelation 22:13, which states: "I am the Alpha and the Omega, the first and the last, the beginning and the end." It is evident that a number of persons are represented as speaking in this chapter of Revelation; verses 8 and 9 show that the angel spoke to John, verse 16 obviously applies to Jesus, the first part of verse 17 is credited to "the spirit and the bride," and the one speaking in the latter part of verse 20 is manifestly John himself. "The Alpha and the Omega" of verses 12-15, therefore, may properly be identified as the same one who bears the title in the other two occurrences: Jehovah God. The expression, "Look! I am coming quickly," in verse 12, does not require that these aforementioned verses apply to Jesus, inasmuch as God also speaks of himself as "coming" to execute judgment. (Compare Isa 26:21.) Malachi 3:1-6 speaks of a *joint* coming for judgment on the part of Jehovah and his "messenger of the covenant."

The title "the Alpha and the Omega" carries the same thought as "the first and the last" and "the beginning and the end" when these terms are used with reference to Jehovah. Before him there was no Almighty God, and there will be none after

him. He will bring to a successful conclusion the issue over Godship, forever vindicated as the one and only Almighty God.—Compare Isa 44:6.

ALPHAEUS (Al·phae′us).

1. The father of the apostle Matthew Levi, the tax collector.—Mt 9:9; Mr 2:14.

2. The father of James the Less, the 9th listed of the 12 apostles. (Mt 10:3; Mr 3:18; Lu 6:15; Ac 1:13) Many scholars are supported by tradition in the general belief that Alphaeus was the same person as Clopas (Joh 19:25), which would also make him the husband of "the other Mary." (Mt 27:56; 28:1; Mr 15:40; 16:1; Lu 24:10) Either a variation in pronunciation of the root word or the individual's having had two names, a common thing in those days, would explain this difference.

ALTAR. Basically, a raised structure or place on which sacrifices are offered or incense is burned in worship of the true God or of another deity. The Hebrew word *miz·be′ach* (altar) comes from the root verb *za·vach′* (slaughter; sacrifice) and thus basically refers to a place of slaughtering or sacrificing. (Ge 8:20; De 12:21; 16:2) Similarly, the Greek *thy·si·a·ste′ri·on* (altar) comes from the root verb *thy′o*, also meaning "slaughter; sacrifice." (Mt 22:4; Mr 14:12) The Greek word *bo·mos′* refers to the altar of a false god.—Ac 17:23.

The first mention of an altar occurs after the Flood when "Noah began to build an altar to Jehovah" and offered burnt offerings thereon. (Ge 8:20) The only offerings mentioned prior to the Flood were those of Cain and Abel, and though it is likely that they did so, it is not stated whether they used altars or not.—Ge 4:3, 4.

Abraham built an altar at Shechem (Ge 12:7), at a point between Bethel and Ai (Ge 12:8; 13:3), at Hebron (Ge 13:18), and also evidently on Mount Moriah, where he sacrificed a ram given him by God in substitution for Isaac. (Ge 22:9-13) Only in this last case is a sacrifice specifically mentioned as being offered on these altars by Abraham. However, the basic meaning of the Hebrew word indicates that offerings were likely made in each case. Isaac later built an altar at Beer-sheba (Ge 26:23, 25), and Jacob built altars at Shechem and at Bethel. (Ge 33:18, 20; 35:1, 3, 7) These altars made by the patriarchs were doubtless of the type later mentioned by God in the Law covenant, either mounds of earth or platforms consisting of natural (unhewn) stones.—Ex 20:24, 25.

Moses constructed an altar following the victory over Amalek, naming it Jehovah-nissi (Jehovah Is My Signal Pole). (Ex 17:15, 16) At the making of the Law covenant with Israel, an altar was built by

Moses at the foot of Mount Sinai, and sacrifices were offered up on it. Blood from the sacrifices was sprinkled on the altar, on the book, and on the people, thereby validating and putting in force the covenant.—Ex 24:4-8; Heb 9:17-20.

Tabernacle Altars. With the setting up of the tabernacle, two altars were constructed according to divine pattern. The altar of burnt offering (also called "the altar of copper" [Ex 39:39]) was made of acacia wood in the form of a hollow chest, apparently without top or bottom. It was 2.2 m (7.3 ft) square and 1.3 m (4.4 ft) high with "horns" projecting from the upper four corners. All its surfaces were overlaid with copper. A grating, or network, of copper was placed below the altar's rim "down within," "toward the center." Four rings were placed at the four extremities near the grating, and these appear to be the same rings through which the two copper-sheathed acacia-wood poles were passed for carrying the altar. This might mean that a slot was cut through two sides of the altar allowing for a flat grating to be inserted, with the rings extending out on both sides. There is considerable difference of opinion among scholars on the subject, and many consider it likely that two sets of rings were involved, the second set, for insertion of the carrying poles, being attached directly to the outside of the altar. Copper equipment was made in the form of cans and shovels for the ashes, bowls for catching the blood of the animals, forks for handling the flesh, and fire holders.—Ex 27:1-8; 38:1-7, 30; Nu 4:14.

This copper altar for burnt offerings was placed before the entrance of the tabernacle. (Ex 40:6, 29) While it was of relatively low height, thus not necessarily requiring a means of approach, for ease of handling the sacrifices placed within it the earth may have been raised around it or there may have been a ramp leading up to it. (Compare Le 9:22, which states that Aaron "came down" from making offerings.) Since the animal was sacrificed "at the side of the altar to the north" (Le 1:11), "the place for the fatty ashes" removed from the altar was to the E (Le 1:16), and the basin of copper for washing was located to the W (Ex 30:18), this would logically leave the S as the open side on which such a means of approach might be placed.

Altar of incense. The altar of incense (also called "the altar of gold" [Ex 39:38]) was likewise made of acacia wood, the top and sides being overlaid with gold. A border of gold ran around the top. The altar measured 44.5 cm (17.5 in.) square and 89 cm (2.9 ft) high, and also had "horns" extending out from the four top corners.

Two gold rings were made for the insertion of the carrying poles made of acacia overlaid with gold, and these rings were placed underneath the gold border on opposite sides of the altar. (Ex 30:1-5; 37:25-28) A special incense was burned on this altar twice daily, in the morning and in the evening. (Ex 30:7-9, 34-38) The use of a censer, or a fire holder, is elsewhere mentioned for burning incense, and evidently such was employed also in connection with the altar of incense. (Le 16:12, 13; Heb 9:4; Re 8:5; compare 2Ch 26:16, 19.) The position of the altar of incense was within the tabernacle just before the curtain of the Most Holy so that it is spoken of as being "before the ark of the testimony."—Ex 30:1, 6; 40:5, 26, 27.

Sanctification and use of tabernacle altars. At the time of the installation ceremonies, both altars were anointed and sanctified. (Ex 40:9, 10) At that time, as also in subsequent sacrifices of certain sin offerings, blood of the sacrificed animal was put upon the horns of the altar of burnt offering, and the rest was poured out at its base. (Ex 29:12; Le 8:15; 9:8, 9) Some of the anointing oil and blood on the altar was spattered upon Aaron and his sons and their garments to sanctify them toward the conclusion of the installation ceremony. (Le 8:30) In all, seven days were required for the sanctification of the altar of burnt offering. (Ex 29:37) In other burnt offerings, communion sacrifices, and guilt offerings, the blood was sprinkled about upon the altar, while the blood of fowls sacrificed was spattered or drained at the side of the altar. (Le 1:5-17; 3:2-5; 5:7-9; 7:2) Grain offerings were made to smoke upon the altar as "a restful odor" to Jehovah. (Le 2:2-12) Remaining portions of the grain offering were eaten by the high priest and his sons alongside the altar. (Le 10:12) Annually on Atonement Day the altar was cleansed and sanctified by the high priest's placing some of the sacrificial animals' blood on the horns of the altar and by spattering it seven times upon the altar.—Le 16:18, 19.

In all the animal sacrifices presented, portions of the animal were made to smoke upon the altar, and for this purpose a fire was maintained on the altar and was never allowed to go out. (Le 6:9-13) From here the fire was obtained for the burning of incense. (Nu 16:46) Only Aaron and those of his descendants who were free from defects were permitted to serve at the altar. (Le 21:21-23) The other Levites were only assistants. Any man not of the seed of Aaron drawing near was to be put to death. (Nu 16:40; 18:1-7) Korah and his assembly were destroyed for failing to recognize this divine assignment, and the copper fire holders that they had taken were made into thin metal plates and overlaid on the altar as a sign that no one not of the offspring of Aaron should draw near.—Nu 16:1-11, 16-18, 36-40.

Once a year the golden altar of incense was also atoned for by the placing of sacrificial blood upon its horns. Other occasions on which it was so treated were when the sin offerings were made for members of the priesthood.—Ex 30:10; Le 4:7.

When being transported by the sons of Kohath both the altar of incense and the altar of burnt offerings were covered, the first with a blue cloth and sealskins, the second with a reddish-purple wool cloth and sealskins.—Nu 4:11-14; see TABERNACLE.

Temple Altars. Prior to the dedication of Solomon's temple, the copper altar made in the wilderness served for Israel's sacrificial offerings at the high place in Gibeon. (1Ki 3:4; 1Ch 16:39, 40; 21:29, 30; 2Ch 1:3-6) The copper altar thereafter made for the temple covered an area 16 times as large as the one made for the tabernacle, measuring about 8.9 m (29.2 ft) square and about 4.5 m (14.6 ft) high. (2Ch 4:1) In view of its height, some means of approach was essential. God's law prohibited the use of steps to the altar to prevent exposure of nakedness. (Ex 20:26) Some believe that the linen drawers worn by Aaron and his sons served to obviate this command and thus made steps allowable. (Ex 28:42, 43) However, it seems likely that an inclined ramp was used to approach the top of the altar of burnt offering. Josephus (*The Jewish War*, V, 225 [v, 6]) indicates that such an approach was used for the temple altar later built by Herod. If the arrangement of the altar of the temple followed that of the tabernacle, the ramp was probably on the S side of the altar. "The molten sea," where the priests washed, would thus be convenient, as it also lay toward the south. (2Ch 4:2-5, 9, 10) In other respects the altar constructed for the temple apparently was modeled after that of the tabernacle, and no detailed description of it is given.

It was located where David had earlier built his temporary altar on Mount Moriah. (2Sa 24:21, 25; 1Ch 21:26; 2Ch 8:12; 15:8) This is also traditionally held to have been the location where Abraham had attempted to offer up Isaac. (Ge 22:2) The blood of sacrificial animals was poured out at the altar's base, and it is likely that some kind of conduit existed for carrying the blood away from the temple area. Herod's temple is reported to have had such a conduit connected with the SW horn of the altar, and in the rock of the temple area, an opening has been found that leads to an underground channel going out to the Kidron Valley.

The altar of incense for the temple was made of cedarwood, but this seems to have been the only difference between it and that of the tabernacle. It was likewise overlaid with gold.—1Ki 6:20, 22; 7:48; 1Ch 28:18; 2Ch 4:19.

At the inauguration of the temple Solomon's prayer was offered before the altar of burnt offering, and at its conclusion fire came down from the heavens and consumed the sacrifices on the altar. (2Ch 6:12, 13; 7:1-3) Despite the fact that it covered an area of over 79 sq m (850 sq ft), this copper altar proved too small for the immense quantity of sacrifices made then, and so a portion of the courtyard was sanctified for that purpose. —1Ki 8:62-64.

In the latter part of Solomon's reign, and in the reigns of Rehoboam and Abijam, the altar of burnt offerings came into neglect so that King Asa found it necessary to renew it. (2Ch 15:8) King Uzziah was stricken with leprosy for attempting to burn incense on the golden altar of incense. (2Ch 26:16-19) King Ahaz moved the copper altar of burnt offering to one side and put a pagan altar in its place. (2Ki 16:14) His son Hezekiah, however, had the copper altar and its utensils cleansed, sanctified, and restored to service.—2Ch 29:18-24, 27; see TEMPLE.

Postexilic Altars. The first thing built in Jerusalem by the returning exiles under Zerubbabel and High Priest Jeshua was the altar for burnt offerings. (Ezr 3:2-6) In due time a new altar of incense was also made.

The Syrian king Antiochus Epiphanes carried off the golden altar of incense, and two years later (168 B.C.E.) he built an altar over the great altar of Jehovah and offered up a sacrifice to Zeus thereon. (1 Maccabees 1:20-64) Judas Maccabaeus thereafter built a new altar of unhewn stones and also restored the altar of incense.—1 Maccabees 4:44-49.

The altar of burnt offerings of Herod's temple was made of unhewn stones and, according to Josephus (*The Jewish War*, V, 225 [v, 6]), was 50 cubits square and 15 cubits high, though the Jewish Mishnah (*Middot* 3:1) gives smaller dimensions for it. It was to this altar, therefore, that Jesus made reference in his day. (Mt 5:23, 24; 23:18-20) The altar of incense of that temple is not described, but Luke 1:11 shows that an angel was standing to the right of it when he appeared to John's father Zechariah.

Altar of Ezekiel's Temple. In the visionary temple seen by Ezekiel, the altar for burnt offerings was similarly positioned before the temple (Eze 40:47), but it had a different design from that of the previous altars. The altar consisted of several sections successively indented or recessed. Its dimensions are given in measurements of the long cubit (51.8 cm; 20.4 in.). The base of the altar was one cubit thick and had a "lip" of one span (perhaps 26 cm; 10 in.) as a border around the top, thus forming a sort of gutter or channel, perhaps for receiving blood poured out. (Eze 43:13, 14) Resting on the base itself, but set in one cubit from its outer edge, was another section, and it measured two cubits (c. 104 cm; 41 in.) in height. A third section was stepped in one cubit and was four cubits (c. 207 cm; 82 in.) in height. It also had a border surrounding it of a half cubit (c. 26 cm; 10 in.), perhaps forming a second channel or a protective ledge. Finally, the altar hearth extended up yet another four cubits and was also stepped in one cubit from the preceding section; out from it extended four "horns." Stairs from the E provided approach to the altar hearth. (Eze 43:14-17) As with the altar built in the wilderness, a seven-day period of atonement and installation was to be observed. (Eze 43:19-26) Annual atonement was to be made for the altar along with the rest of the sanctuary on the first day of Nisan. (Eze 45:18, 19) The river of healing waters seen by Ezekiel flowed eastward from the temple and passed S of the altar.—Eze 47:1.

The altar of incense is not mentioned by name in the vision. However, the description of "the wooden altar" at Ezekiel 41:22, particularly the reference to it as "the table that is before Jehovah," indicates that this corresponded to the altar of incense rather than to the table of showbread. (Compare Ex 30:6, 8; 40:5; Re 8:3.) This altar was three cubits (c. 155 cm; 61 in.) high and evidently two cubits (c. 104 cm; 41 in.) square.

Other Altars. Since the post-Flood population did not continue with Noah in pure worship, it follows that many altars for false worship were produced, and excavations in Canaan, Mesopotamia, and other sites indicate that these existed from the earliest periods. Balaam had seven altars erected successively at three different sites in his vain attempts at calling down a curse on Israel. —Nu 22:40, 41; 23:4, 14, 29, 30.

The Israelites were instructed to tear down all pagan altars and destroy the sacred pillars and poles customarily built alongside them. (Ex 34:13; De 7:5, 6; 12:1-3) They were never to imitate these nor offer up their children by fire as did the Canaanites. (De 12:30, 31; 16:21) Instead of a multiplicity of altars, Israel was to have just *one* altar for the worship of the one true God, and this would be located at the place Jehovah would

choose. (De 12:2-6, 13, 14, 27; contrast this with Babylon, where there were 180 altars to the goddess Ishtar alone.) They were at first instructed to make an altar of unhewn stones following the crossing of the Jordan River (De 27:4-8), and this was built by Joshua on Mount Ebal. (Jos 8:30-32) Following the division of the conquered land, the tribes of Reuben and Gad and the half tribe of Manasseh built a conspicuous altar by the Jordan, which provoked a temporary crisis among the other tribes until it was determined that the altar was no sign of apostasy but only a memorial of faithfulness to Jehovah as the true God.—Jos 22:10-34.

Other altars were constructed, but these appear to have been built for specific occasions, not for continual use, and they were usually built in connection with angelic appearances or at angelic instruction. The one at Bochim and those of Gideon and Manoah were such. (Jg 2:1-5; 6:24-32; 13:15-23) The record concerning the altar set up at Bethel by the people when considering how to prevent the disappearance of the tribe of Benjamin does not indicate whether such had divine approval or was simply a case of their 'doing what was right in their own eyes.' (Jg 21:4, 25) As God's representative, Samuel offered sacrifice at Mizpah and also built an altar at Ramah. (1Sa 7:5, 9, 10, 17) This may have been due to the fact that Jehovah's presence was no longer in evidence at the tabernacle in Shiloh, following the removal of the Ark.—1Sa 4:4, 11; 6:19-21; 7:1, 2; compare Ps 78:59-64.

Use of temporary altars. On a number of occasions temporary altars were constructed. For example, Saul offered sacrifice at Gilgal and built an altar at Aijalon. (1Sa 13:7-12; 14:33-35) In the first case he was condemned for not waiting for Samuel to do the sacrificing, but the propriety of the locations as places for sacrificing was not considered.

David instructed Jonathan to explain his absence at Saul's table on the day of the new moon by saying that David was attending an annual family sacrifice at Bethlehem; however, since this was a subterfuge, it cannot definitely be known whether such was really celebrated. (1Sa 20:6, 28, 29) Later, as king, David built an altar on the threshing floor of Araunah (Ornan), and this was at divine command. (2Sa 24:18-25; 1Ch 21:18-26; 22:1) The statement at 1 Kings 9:25 with regard to Solomon's 'offering up sacrifices on the altar' clearly refers to his *causing* such to be done through the authorized priesthood.—Compare 2Ch 8:12-15.

With the setting up of the temple at Jerusalem, it appears that the altar was now definitely at "the place that Jehovah your God will choose . . . and there you must come." (De 12:5) Aside from the altar used by Elijah on Mount Carmel in the fire test with the Baal priests (1Ki 18:26-35), only apostasy now caused the setting up of other altars. Solomon himself was the first to be guilty of such apostasy, because of the influence of his foreign wives. (1Ki 11:3-8) Jeroboam of the newly formed northern kingdom endeavored to divert his subjects from going to the temple in Jerusalem by setting up altars at Bethel and Dan. (1Ki 12:28-33) A prophet then foretold that in the reign of King Josiah of Judah priests officiating at the altar in Bethel would be slaughtered and that the bones of dead men would be burned on the altar. The altar was ripped apart as a sign, and the prophecy was later completely fulfilled.—1Ki 13:1-5; 2Ki 23:15-20; compare Am 3:14.

During King Ahab's rule in Israel, pagan altars flourished. (1Ki 16:31-33) In the time of King Ahaz of Judah, there were altars "at every corner in Jerusalem," as well as many "high places." (2Ch 28:24, 25) Manasseh went so far as to build altars within the house of Jehovah and altars for worshiping "the army of the heavens" in the temple courtyard.—2Ki 21:3-5.

Though faithful kings periodically destroyed these idolatrous altars (2Ki 11:18; 23:12, 20; 2Ch 14:3; 30:14; 31:1; 34:4-7), prior to Jerusalem's fall Jeremiah could still say: "Your gods have become as many as your cities, O Judah; and as many altars as the streets of Jerusalem you people have placed for the shameful thing, altars to make sacrificial smoke to Baal."—Jer 11:13.

During exile and in apostolic period. During the period of the exile, the Jews who fled to Elephantine in Upper Egypt set up a temple and an altar, according to the Elephantine Papyri; and some centuries later the Jews near Leontopolis did likewise. (*Jewish Antiquities,* XIII, 62-68 [iii, 1]; *The Jewish War,* VII, 420-432 [x, 2, 3]) This latter temple and altar were built by Priest Onias in an attempt to fulfill Isaiah 19:19, 20.

In the Common Era, the apostle Paul in speaking to the Athenians referred to an altar inscribed "To an Unknown God." (Ac 17:23) Ample historical information is available to corroborate this. Apollonius of Tyana, who visited Athens sometime after Paul, is reported to have said: "It is a much greater proof of wisdom and sobriety to speak well of all the gods, especially at Athens, where altars are set up in honour even of unknown gods." (Philostratus, *The Life of Apollonius of Tyana,*

VI, III) Geographer Pausanias in the second century C.E. reported that on the road from the Phaleron Bay harbor to the city of Athens he had observed "altars of the gods named Unknown, and of heroes." He also spoke of "an altar of Unknown Gods" at Olympia. (*Description of Greece,* Attica, I, 4; Elis I, XIV, 8) A similar altar was discovered in 1909 at Pergamum in the precincts of the temple of Demeter.

Significance of Altars. In Hebrews chapters 8 and 9 the apostle Paul clearly shows that all the things related to the tabernacle and temple service were typical. (Heb 8:5; 9:23) The significance of the two altars is made evident by information in the Christian Greek Scriptures. The altar of burnt offerings represented God's "will," that is, his willingness to accept the perfect human sacrifice of his only-begotten Son. (Heb 10:5-10) Its location in front of the entrance to the sanctuary emphasizes the requirement of faith in that ransom sacrifice as a prerequisite for acceptance by God. (Joh 3:16-18) The insistence upon a single altar of sacrifice is in harmony with Christ's declaration: "I am the way and the truth and the life. No one comes to the Father except through me," as well as with the many texts declaring the unity to be manifest in the Christian faith.—Joh 14:6; Mt 7:13, 14; 1Co 1:10-13; Eph 4:3-6; note also Isaiah's prophecy, at Isa 56:7; 60:7, that people of all nations would come to God's altar.

It is notable that, though some individuals fled to the altar, taking hold of its horns, in hope of gaining protection, God's law prescribed that the willful murderer was to be taken "even from being at my altar to die." (Ex 21:14; compare 1Ki 1:50-53; 2:28-34.) The psalmist sang: "I shall wash my hands in innocency itself, and I will march around your altar, O Jehovah."—Ps 26:6.

Although Hebrews 13:10 has been used as basis for erection of literal altars by professed Christians, the context shows that the "altar" spoken of by Paul is not literal but symbolic. (Heb 13:10-16) M'Clintock and Strong's *Cyclopædia* (1882, Vol. I, p. 183) says concerning the early Christians: "When the ancient apologists were reproached with having no temples, no altars, no shrines, they simply replied, 'Shrines and altars we have not.'" Commenting on Hebrews 13:10, M. R. Vincent's *Word Studies in the New Testament* (1957, Vol. IV, p. 567) says: "It is a mistake to try to find in the Christian economy some specific object answering to *altar*—either the cross, or the eucharistic table, or Christ himself. Rather the ideas of approach to God,—sacrifice, atonement, pardon and acceptance, salvation,—are gathered up and generally represented in the figure of an altar, even as the Jewish altar was the point at which all these ideas converged." The multiplying of altars was strongly condemned by the Hebrew prophets. (Isa 17:7, 8) Hosea said that Ephraim "multiplied altars in order to sin" (Ho 8:11; 10:1, 2, 8; 12:11); Jeremiah stated that the sin of Judah was engraved "on the horns of their altars" (Jer 17:1, 2); and Ezekiel foretold the slaughter of false worshipers "all around their altars" (Eze 6:4-6, 13).

Expressions of divine judgment are also prophetically associated with the true altar. (Isa 6:5-12; Eze 9:2; Am 9:1) It is from "underneath the altar" that the souls of those slaughtered for witnessing for God symbolically cry out: "Until when, Sovereign Lord holy and true, are you refraining from judging and avenging our blood upon those who dwell on the earth?"—Re 6:9, 10; compare 8:5; 11:1; 16:7.

At Revelation 8:3, 4 the golden altar of incense is expressly related to the prayers of the righteous. It was customary among the Jews to pray at "the hour of offering incense." (Lu 1:9, 10; compare Ps 141:2.) The single altar for offering incense also corresponds with the one avenue of approach outlined in the Christian Greek Scriptures.—Joh 10:9; 14:6; 16:23; Eph 2:18-22; see OFFERINGS.

ALUSH (A'lush). A place on the Sinai Peninsula, between Dophkah and Rephidim, where the Israelites encamped. The site is not known.—Nu 33:13, 14.

ALVAH (Al'vah). A sheik of Edom and descendant of Esau. (Ge 36:40, 43; 1Ch 1:51) Possibly a place and a tribe were also called Alvah.—See TIMNA No. 3.

ALVAN (Al'van). First-named son of Sheik Shobal, a Seirite.—Ge 36:20, 23, 29; 1Ch 1:40.

AMAD (A'mad). A city of the fertile coastal plain N of the Carmel Range, assigned to the tribe of Asher. (Jos 19:26) Although there are several ruins in this area called 'Amud, the exact location of this city is not known.

AMAL (A'mal) [Hard Work]. Last named of four sons of Helem listed among "the sons of Asher, heads of the house of the forefathers, select, valiant, mighty men, heads of the chieftains." —1Ch 7:35, 40.

AMALEK (Am'a·lek), **AMALEKITES** (A·mal'-ek·ites). Son of Esau's firstborn Eliphaz, by his concubine Timna. (Ge 36:12, 16) Amalek, a grandson of Esau, was one of the sheiks of Edom. (Ge

36:15, 16) Amalek's name also designated his tribal descendants.—De 25:17; Jg 7:12; 1Sa 15:2.

The belief of some that the Amalekites were of a much earlier origin and not descendants of Esau's grandson Amalek is not founded on solid factual ground. The idea that the Amalekites predated Amalek was based on Balaam's proverbial utterance: "Amalek was the first one of the nations, but his end afterward will be even his perishing." (Nu 24:20) However, Balaam was not speaking here of history in general and the origin of nations seven or eight centuries earlier. He was speaking of history only in connection with the Israelites, whom he was hired to curse and who were about to enter the Promised Land. Hence, after listing Moab, Edom, and Seir as Israel's opponents, Balaam declares that the Amalekites were actually "the first one of the nations" to rise up in opposition to the Israelites on their march out of Egypt toward Palestine, and for this reason, the end of Amalek "will be even his perishing."

Moses, therefore, in relating events of Abraham's day before Amalek was born, spoke of "the whole field of the Amalekites," evidently describing the *region* as understood by people of Moses' time, instead of implying that Amalekites predated Amalek. (Ge 14:7) The center of this Amalekite territory was N of Kadesh-barnea in the Negeb desert in the southern part of Palestine, with their tributary camps radiating out into the Sinai Peninsula and northern Arabia. (1Sa 15:7) At one time their influence may have extended into the hills of Ephraim.—Jg 12:15.

The Amalekites were "the first one of the nations" to launch an unprovoked attack on the Israelites after the Exodus, at Rephidim near Mount Sinai. As a consequence, Jehovah decreed ultimate extinction for the Amalekites. (Nu 24:20; Ex 17:8-16; De 25:17-19) A year later, when the Israelites attempted to enter the Promised Land contrary to Jehovah's word, they were repulsed by the Amalekites. (Nu 14:41-45) Twice during the days of the Judges these adversaries of Israel shared in assaulting Israel. They did it in the days of Eglon king of Moab. (Jg 3:12, 13) Again, with the Midianites and Easterners, they pillaged the land of Israel seven years before Gideon and his 300 men dealt them a smashing defeat.—Jg 6:1-3, 33; 7:12; 10:12.

Because of this persistent hatred, during the period of the kings Jehovah 'called to account' the Amalekites, commanding King Saul to strike them down, which he did "from Havilah as far as Shur, which is in front of Egypt." However, Saul, overstepping Jehovah's order, spared Agag their king.

But God was not mocked, for "Samuel went hacking Agag to pieces before Jehovah in Gilgal." (1Sa 15:2-33) Some of David's raids included Amalekite villages, and when they in return attacked Ziklag and carried off David's wives and goods, he and 400 men overtook them, recovering all that had been stolen. (1Sa 27:8; 30:1-20) During the reign of Hezekiah, some of the tribe of Simeon annihilated the remnant of the Amalekites.—1Ch 4:42, 43.

There is no further direct mention of the Amalekites in Biblical or secular history. However, "Haman the son of . . . the Agagite" was probably a descendant, for "Agag" was the title or name of certain Amalekite kings. (Es 3:1; Nu 24:7; 1Sa 15:8, 9) Thus the Amalekites, along with others mentioned by name, were exterminated in order "that people may know that you, whose name is Jehovah, you alone are the Most High over all the earth."—Ps 83:6-18.

AMAM (A'mam). A village in the Negeb, in the southern part of the territory of Judah.—Jos 15:26.

AMANAH (A·ma'nah) [from a root meaning "trustworthy; faithful; long-lasting"]. This name appears in the Hebrew at Song of Solomon 4:8 in connection with Lebanon and Mount Hermon. Most translations simply transliterate the Hebrew word; however, some scholars understand it to refer to the Anti-Lebanon Range, while others apply it to that portion of the Anti-Lebanons in which the Nahr Barada has its source.—See ANTI-LEBANON.

AMARIAH (Am·a·ri'ah) [Jehovah Has Said].

1. A priestly descendant of Aaron's son Eleazar through Phinehas; son of Meraioth; father of Ahitub; grandfather of Zadok, who served as a secondary priest during the reign of David and high priest during the reign of Solomon. (1Ch 6:7, 52) It cannot be stated definitely that Amariah officiated as high priest, since the office temporarily switched to the house of Eli at about that time.

2. A Levite descendant of Kohath's son Hebron, listed in David's reorganization of temple service. —1Ch 23:1, 12, 19; 24:23.

3. Chief priest "for every matter of Jehovah," especially legal cases, during Jehoshaphat's reign. —2Ch 19:11.

4. Another descendant of Eleazar who lived at a later time than No. 1 above. Son of Azariah and father of another Ahitub.—1Ch 6:11; Ezr 7:3.

5. A Levite who assisted in distributing the tithes to the priests in their cities during the reign of Hezekiah.—2Ch 31:14, 15.

6. Son of Hezekiah (probably the king of Judah) and great-grandfather of the prophet Zephaniah. —Zep 1:1.

7. One of the principal priests returning from Babylon with Zerubbabel, 537 B.C.E. (Ne 12:1, 2, 7) In the days of Governor Nehemiah there was a 'paternal house' of priests by his name.—Ne 12:12, 13, 26.

8. A descendant of Binnui; one of those who sent away their pagan wives and sons in the days of Ezra.—Ezr 10:10-12, 38, 42, 44.

9. A priest, or the forefather of one, who attested to the "trustworthy arrangement" during Nehemiah's governorship. (Ne 9:38; 10:1, 3) He would have been more than 112 years old if the same as No. 7 above.

10. Ancestor of residents of Jerusalem in Nehemiah's time; of the tribe of Judah.—Ne 11:4.

AMASA (A·ma'sa) [shortened form of Amasiah].

1. Son of David's sister or half sister Abigail and Jether (Ithra), and cousin of Absalom and Joab. (2Sa 17:25; 1Ch 2:16, 17) Jether is called an Israelite in Samuel and an Ishmaelite in Chronicles, perhaps because he lived in Ishmaelite territory. Some contend that Amasa is to be identified with Amasai, one of those who joined David's army at Ziklag, but such an identification is uncertain.—1Ch 12:18.

Years later, when Amasa threw in his lot with Absalom's rebellion against David, he was put over Absalom's army in place of Joab. (2Sa 17:25) The rebellion was suppressed, David's son Absalom was killed by Joab, and Amasa was offered the place of Joab as David's army chief, for as David said, he is "my bone and my flesh."—2Sa 18:9-15; 19:13.

Again rebellion broke out, this time Sheba wanted no share in David. (2Sa 20:1, 2) Amasa was given three days to assemble an army. When he did not come at the fixed time, Abishai was told to take David's servants and pursue the rebels. Abishai's brother Joab and his men went with them in the pursuit of Sheba. Finally, when the latecomer Amasa met them, Joab, pretending to give an affectionate kiss, grabbed Amasa by the beard with one hand and used the sword in his other hand to rip Amasa's abdomen open. (2Sa 20:4-12) This may have been deserved recompense for Amasa's siding with Absalom but certainly not at the hand from which it came. David therefore commanded Solomon that Amasa should be avenged through the death of Joab. —1Ki 2:5, 32.

2. Son of Hadlai. Following victory over Judah, when Israelite warriors were bringing their brothers back as servants, Amasa was one of four headmen of Ephraim who heeded the plea of the prophet Oded to return the captives. He also assisted those of Judah with supplies and transportation needed for their repatriation.—2Ch 28:8-15.

AMASAI (A·ma′sai) [shortened form of Amasiah].

1. A Levite of the family of Kohath; son of Elkanah and ancestor of the prophet Samuel and the temple singer Heman of David's day.—1Ch 6:25, 35, 36.

2. The head of 30 men from the tribes of Judah and Benjamin who joined David at Ziklag. To allay David's fear of treachery, "spirit itself enveloped Amasai" as he pledged their wholehearted support, acknowledging that Jehovah was David's helper.—1Ch 12:16-18.

3. One of seven priests "loudly sounding the trumpets before the ark of the true God" when David had it brought to Jerusalem.—1Ch 15:24.

4. A Levite of the family of Kohath whose son Mahath assisted in cleansing and sanctifying the temple in the days of Hezekiah.—2Ch 29:12-18.

AMASHSAI (A·mash′sai). Son of Azarel and one of the priests residing in Jerusalem in Nehemiah's time.—Ne 11:13.

AMASIAH (Am·a·si′ah) [Jah Has Carried the Load]. Son of Zichri. During Jehoshaphat's reign he headed one of the Judean army divisions numbering 200,000.—2Ch 17:16.

AMAZIAH (Am·a·zi′ah) [Jehovah Is Strong].

1. A Levite of the family of Merari; son of Hilkiah, father of Hashabiah. One of his descendants shared in directing the singing before the tabernacle in David's time.—1Ch 6:31, 32, 45.

2. King of Judah who, in 858 B.C.E., came to the throne at 25 and ruled for 29 years from the assassination of his father Jehoash. His mother was Jehoaddin (Jehoaddan), his wife Jecoliah. (2Ki 14:1, 2; 15:2; 2Ch 25:1; 26:3) With the kingdom firm in his hand, he executed those that had murdered his father, but he heeded the law of Moses not to punish their sons. (2Ki 14:5, 6; De 24:16) His reign was marked by some enthusiasm for true worship but not with "a complete heart" and not without serious shortcomings that brought disaster both to himself and to the nation of Judah. The record of his rule deals primarily with two military campaigns.—2Ch 25:2.

Amaziah was first successful against Edom, or Seir, using a force of 300,000 from Judah and Benjamin. He had also hired 100,000 mercenaries from Israel, but upon the advice of a man of God he paid them off and sent them home. Jehovah gave Amaziah a smashing victory in the Valley of Salt, allowing him to kill off 20,000 of the enemy and to capture Sela, which he renamed Joktheel. However, Amaziah brought the gods of Seir back with him and began worshiping them, causing Jehovah's anger to blaze against him: "Why have you searched for the people's gods that did not deliver their own people out of your hand?" Amaziah only compounded the injury by silencing Jehovah's prophet.—2Ki 14:7; 2Ch 25:5-16.

Amaziah's second campaign was tragic from start to finish. The 100,000 from Israel who were dismissed raided towns of Judah on their return north. Perhaps it was this that provoked Amaziah foolishly to challenge Jehoash of the strong northern kingdom, saying: "Do come. Let us look each other in the face." Jehoash's response: How foolish for a thorny weed to confront a massive cedar only to be trampled by a wild beast! Amaziah refused to listen; he was apparently puffed up with his recent victory, and Jehovah had doomed Amaziah to defeat because of his idolatry. The battle was joined at Beth-shemesh, Judah fled, Amaziah was captured, a breach of about 178 m (584 ft) was made in Jerusalem's wall, and much temple treasure and many hostages were carried back to Samaria.—2Ki 14:8-14; 2Ch 25:13, 17-24.

From the time that Amaziah turned away from Jehovah's worship, a conspiracy was formed against him that finally forced Amaziah to flee to Lachish. There the conspirators put him to death. Amaziah was succeeded by his 16-year-old son Azariah (Uzziah).—2Ki 14:17-21; 2Ch 25:25-28.

3. A priest of the calf worship at Bethel who complained to Jeroboam II that the prophet Amos was a seditionist. He personally tried to frighten Amos into going back to Judah. The prophet, however, stood his ground, telling Amaziah that his wife would become a prostitute, his children would fall by the sword, and Amaziah himself would die on unclean ground.—Am 7:10-17.

4. Father of Joshah; of the tribe of Simeon. Joshah was one of the chieftains numbered among those clearing the valley near Gedor of the Meunim and of the Hamitic settlers in the days of Hezekiah.—1Ch 4:24, 34, 38-41.

AMBASSADOR. In Biblical usage, an official representative sent out by a ruler on a special occasion for a specific purpose. Older, mature men usually served in this capacity. Thus, the Greek words *pre·sbeu′o* ('act as an ambassador' [Eph

6:20]; 'be an ambassador' [2Co 5:20]) and *pre-sbei'a* ("body of ambassadors" [Lu 14:32]) are both related to the word *pre-sby'te-ros,* meaning "older man; elder."—Ac 11:30; Re 4:4.

Jesus Christ came as Jehovah God's "apostle," or "sent one." He it is who "shed light upon life and incorruption through the good news."—Heb 3:1; 2Ti 1:10.

After Christ had been resurrected to the heavens, being no longer on earth in person, his faithful followers were appointed to act in his place, "substituting for Christ" as ambassadors of God. Paul specifically mentions his office of ambassadorship. (2Co 5:18-20) He, like all the anointed followers of Jesus Christ, was sent to nations and people who were alienated from Jehovah God the Supreme Sovereign—ambassadors to a world not at peace with God. (Joh 14:30; 15:18, 19; Jas 4:4) As an ambassador, Paul bore a message of reconciliation to God through Christ and therefore spoke of himself while in prison as "an ambassador in chains." (Eph 6:20) His being in chains is a demonstration of the hostile attitude of this world toward God, Christ, and the Messianic Kingdom government, for ambassadors have since time immemorial been considered inviolate. It revealed the greatest hostility and was the grossest of insults on the part of the nations when they disrespected the ambassadors sent to represent the Kingdom of God under Christ.

In fulfilling his role as an ambassador, Paul respected the laws of the land but remained strictly neutral toward the world's political and military activities. This was in harmony with the principle that ambassadors of worldly governments must obey the law but are exempt from allegiance to the country to which they are sent.

Like the apostle Paul, all of Christ's faithful, anointed, spirit-begotten followers, who have a heavenly citizenship, are "ambassadors substituting for Christ."—2Co 5:20; Php 3:20.

How a person receives these ambassadors of God determines how God will deal with him. Jesus Christ set forth the principle in his illustration of the man who owned a vineyard and who first sent his slaves, then his son, as his representatives. The cultivators of the vineyard brutally mistreated those slaves and killed the owner's son. For this the owner of the vineyard brought destruction on the hostile cultivators. (Mt 21:33-41) Jesus gave another illustration, of the king whose slaves were killed while acting as messengers inviting guests to a marriage feast. The ones receiving his representatives in such a manner were counted as enemies of the king. (Mt 22:2-7) Jesus stated the

principle clearly when he said: "He that receives anyone I send receives me also. In turn he that receives me, receives also him that sent me."—Joh 13:20; see also Mt 23:34, 35; 25:34-46.

Jesus also used the peace-promoting work of an ambassador to illustrate our individual need to sue for peace with Jehovah God and give up all to follow in the footsteps of his Son in order to get God's favor and everlasting life. (Lu 14:31-33) Conversely, he illustrated the folly of being associated with those sending ambassadors to speak against the one on whom God confers kingly power. (Lu 19:12-14, 27) The Gibeonites are good examples of taking action in a tactful, successful suit for peace.—Jos 9:3-15, 22-27.

Pre-Christian Envoys. In the pre-Christian period there was no official governmental office corresponding exactly to the modern-day ambassador. There was no resident official representing a foreign government. Hence, the terms "messenger" (Heb., *mal·'akh'*) and "envoy" (Heb., *tsir*) more accurately describe their duties in Bible times. However, their rank and status were in many respects similar to those of ambassadors, and some of these aspects will be considered here. Such men were official representatives who carried messages between governments and individual rulers.

Unlike modern-day ambassadors, ancient envoys, or messengers, did not reside in foreign capitals but were dispatched only on special occasions for specific purposes. Often they were persons of rank (2Ki 18:17, 18), and their office was highly respected. Consequently, they were accorded inviolability of person when they visited other rulers.

The treatment accorded a ruler's messengers, or envoys, was regarded as treatment given the ruler and his government. Thus, when Rahab showed favor to the messengers sent as spies to Jericho by Joshua, she really was acting as she did because she recognized that Jehovah was the God and King of Israel. Jehovah, through Joshua, showed her favor accordingly. (Jos 6:17; Heb 11:31) A flagrant violation of the unwritten international custom of respect toward envoys was the action of Hanun the king of Ammon, to whom King David sent some servants in a gesture of friendship. The king of Ammon listened to his princes, who falsely called the messengers spies, and he publicly humiliated the messengers, demonstrating his disrespect for David and his government. This disgraceful action led to war.—2Sa 10:2–11:1; 12:26-31.

Instead of recalling an ambassador, which is what modern-day nations do when diplomatic relations are broken, the people of ancient times sent messengers, or envoys, as spokesmen to one another during times of strain in an effort to reestablish peaceful relations. Isaiah speaks of such "messengers of peace." (Isa 33:7) Hezekiah sent a peace appeal to Sennacherib the king of Assyria. Although Sennacherib was threatening the fortified cities of Judah, the messengers were given freedom of passage by the Assyrians because they were acting as Hezekiah's envoys. (2Ki 18:13-15) Another example of this can be seen in the record about Jephthah, a judge in Israel. By messengers he dispatched a letter to the king of the Ammonites to remonstrate against wrong action on his part and to clear up a dispute over territorial rights. If possible, Jephthah, through his envoys, would have settled the matter without war. These messengers were permitted to pass back and forth between the armies without hindrance.—Jg 11:12-28; see MESSENGER.

AMBUSH. A lying in wait in a concealed place to attack by surprise. Three Hebrew words for "ambush" ('e'rev, 'o'rev, and ma·'arav') come from the root 'a·rav', meaning "lie in wait." (Job 37:8; Jer 9:8; Ps 10:8; Jg 9:32) Similarly, the Greek word for "ambush" (e·ne'dra) is related to the verb e·ne·dreu'o, meaning "lie in wait."—Ac 25:3; 23:21.

Joshua skillfully employed an ambush against Ai, posting 5,000 men to the W of the city at night, while deploying the main body of his forces to the N. The following morning he drew the city's defenders away from the city by feigning defeat, thus allowing the ambush to rise up and take the city. (Jos 8:2-21) Ambushes were involved in the dispute between the landowners of Shechem and Gideon's son Abimelech. (Jg 9:25, 31-45) Samson was the object of ambushes by the Philistines. (Jg 16:1-12) Saul set an ambush against Amalek and later accused David of lying in ambush for him. (1Sa 15:5; 22:8) Other ambushes were those in the fight of Israel against the tribe of Benjamin (Jg 20:29-44), the unsuccessful ambush of Judah by Jeroboam (2Ch 13:13-19), the ambush producing confusion among Judah's attackers in the days of Jehoshaphat (2Ch 20:22, 23), those mentioned in describing the fall of Jerusalem (La 4:19), and the ambush decreed against Babylon by Jehovah (Jer 51:12). The returning Jewish exiles were protected by Jehovah from ambush.—Ezr 8:31; see WAR.

The Hebrew noun 'e'rev, meaning "ambush," is used in describing hunting tactics. (Job 37:8; 38: 40) The Hebrew verb 'a·rav' is used figuratively to describe the prostitute as she waylays men (Pr 7:12; 23:28) and to describe the tactics of wicked ones against the innocent as well as the righteous.

(Ps 10:9; Pr 1:11, 18; 12:6; 24:15; Mic 7:2; compare Job 31:9.) In Israel the death penalty was decreed for the man found guilty of killing another after lying in wait to do it.—De 19:11, 12.

The more than 40 Jews who "bound themselves with a curse" plotted an ambush against the apostle Paul but were foiled by Paul's nephew.—Ac 23:12-35.

AMEN. This word in both English and Greek is a transliteration from the Hebrew 'a·men'. The meaning is "so be it," or "surely." The Hebrew root word from which it is drawn ('a·man') means "be faithful; be trustworthy."

In the Hebrew Scriptures the word is used as a solemn expression to obligate oneself legally to an oath or covenant and its consequences (Nu 5:22; De 27:15-26; Ne 5:13), also as a solemn expression to subscribe to an expressed prayer (1Ch 16:36), to an expression of praise (Ne 8:6), or to an expressed purpose (1Ki 1:36; Jer 11:5). Each of the first four books, or collections, of the Psalms concludes with this expression, perhaps indicating that it was customary for the congregation of Israel to join in at the end of the song or psalm with an "Amen."—Ps 41:13; 72:19; 89:52; 106:48.

The Hebrew word 'a·man' is applied to Jehovah as "the *faithful* God" (De 7:9; Isa 49:7) and describes his reminders and promises as "trustworthy" and "faithful." (Ps 19:7; 89:28, 37) In the Christian Greek Scriptures the title "Amen" is applied to Christ Jesus as "the faithful and true witness." (Re 3:14) Jesus made singular use of the expression in his preaching and teaching, using it very often to preface a statement of fact, a promise, or a prophecy, thereby emphasizing the absolute truthfulness and reliability of what he said. (Mt 5:18; 6:2, 5, 16; 24:34) In these cases the Greek word (a·men') is translated as "truly" (*KJ*, "verily") or, when doubled, as throughout the book of John, "most truly." (Joh 1:51) Jesus' use of "amen" in this way is said to be unique in sacred literature, and it was consistent with his divinely given authority.—Mt 7:29.

However, as Paul shows at 2 Corinthians 1:19, 20, the title "Amen" applies to Jesus not merely as a truth speaker or as a true prophet and spokesman of God but also as the one in whom all of God's promises find fulfillment. His course of faithfulness and obedience even to a sacrificial death confirms and makes possible the bringing to reality of all the promises and declarations of God's purpose. He was the living Truth of those revelations of God's purpose, the things to which God had sworn.—Compare Joh 1:14, 17; 14:6; 18:37.

The expression "Amen" is used many times in letters, especially those of Paul, when the writer has expressed some form of praise to God (Ro 1:25; 16:27; Eph 3:21; 1Pe 4:11) or expresses the wish that God's favor be manifested in some manner toward the recipients of the letter. (Ro 15:33; Heb 13:20, 21) It is also used where the writer earnestly subscribes to what is expressed.—Re 1:7; 22:20.

The prayer expressed at 1 Chronicles 16:36 and those contained in the Psalms (41:13; 72:19; 89:52; 106:48), as well as the expressions contained in the canonical letters, all indicate the correctness of the use of "Amen" at the close of prayers. It is true that not all the prayers recorded show such conclusion, such as David's closing prayer for Solomon (1Ch 29:19) or Solomon's dedication prayer at the inauguration of the temple (1Ki 8:53-61), although such expression may well have been made. (Note 1Ch 29:20.) Similarly, its use is not recorded in Jesus' prayers (Mt 26:39, 42; Joh 17:1-26) or in the prayer of the disciples at Acts 4:24-30. However, the weight of the prior evidence presented strongly indicates the rightness of the use of "Amen" as a conclusion to prayer, and Paul's statement at 1 Corinthians 14:16 in particular shows that it was customary for those in Christian assembly to join in the Amen to a prayer. Additionally, the examples of those in heaven, recorded at Revelation 5:13, 14; 7:10-12; and 19:1-4, all give support to its use in subscribing to prayers or solemn statements and thereby, through the use of this one word, expressing the confidence, strong approval, and earnest hope that is in their hearts.

AMETHYST.   A semiprecious variety of crystallized quartz, purple or violet in color and used for jewelry. It occurs in the form of hexagonal crystals, and the color is attributed to traces of manganese or iron. One type of amethyst is the quartz variety (Occidental), whereas precious amethyst (Oriental) is a variety of corundum or sapphire. The name amethyst is taken from the Greek word *a·me'thy·stos* (meaning "not to intoxicate"), which is employed in the Greek *Septuagint* to render the Hebrew word *'ach·la·mah'* in Exodus 28:19 and 39:12.

Israel's high priest wore an amethyst stone in the third position of the third row of stones on his embroidered "breastpiece of judgment." (Ex 28:2, 15, 19, 21; 39:12) In his vision of "New Jerusalem," John observed that the 12th foundation of the holy city's wall was amethyst.—Re 21:2, 10, 19, 20.

'AM HA-'A'RETS.   See PEOPLE OF THE LAND (EARTH).

AMI.   See AMON No. 3.

AMITTAI   (A·mit'tai). Father of the prophet Jonah, from Gath-hepher in Zebulun.—2Ki 14:25; Jon 1:1.

AMMAH   (Am'mah) [possibly, Cubit]. A hill "in front of Giah on the way to the wilderness of Gibeon." Here Abner, Saul's former chief of the army and now fighting for Saul's son and heir, Ish-bosheth, made his last stand against the pursuing forces of Joab and Abishai, after they had defeated Abner in the battle at the Pool of Gibeon. At this hill Abner persuaded Joab to stop pursuing him, and the battle ended. (2Sa 2:12-32) While Ammah probably lay to the E of Gibeon, it is not known exactly which of the hills of this region bore this name.

AMMIEL   (Am'mi·el) [People of God].

1. Son of Gemalli of the tribe of Dan. One of 12 sent out by Moses to spy out the land of Canaan. (Nu 13:12) He was among the ten spies who gave a bad report of the Promised Land; he died by the scourge from Jehovah.—Nu 14:36, 37.

2. Father of Machir of Lo-debar, E of the Jordan. It was in the house of Machir that Mephibosheth, son of Jonathan, was lodging when David desired to extend loving-kindness to him.—2Sa 9:4, 5, 7; 17:27.

3. Father of Bath-sheba, Uriah's wife later taken by David. (1Ch 3:5) At 2 Samuel 11:3, he is called Eliam, which is simply a transposition of the components of the name Ammiel and means "God of the People." He was possibly the son of Ahithophel, the Gilonite, who was David's counselor but who turned traitor.—2Sa 23:34; 15:31.

4. A Levite, the sixth son of Obed-edom. He was a gatekeeper who shared responsibility for the storehouses of the house of Jehovah during David's time.—1Ch 26:4, 5, 12-15.

AMMIHUD   (Am·mi'hud) [My People Is Dignity].

1. An Ephraimite, father of Elishama, who was chieftain of the tribe of Ephraim in the second year after coming out of Egypt (1512 B.C.E.). (Nu 1:10; 2:18) He was an ancestor of Joshua (Jehoshua).—1Ch 7:26, 27.

2. A Simeonite, father of the Shemuel who was the chieftain for the tribe of Simeon appointed to share in dividing Canaan among the tribes of Israel (c. 1467 B.C.E.).—Nu 34:20.

3. Of the tribe of Naphtali, and father of Pedahel, who was the chieftain appointed shortly before Moses' death to share in dividing the land of Canaan among the tribes of Israel.—Nu 34:28.

4. Father of Talmai, king of Geshur, and grandfather of Maacah the mother of Absalom, David's son. Absalom fled to Geshur after killing his half brother Amnon.—2Sa 3:3; 13:37.

5. Son of Omri and a descendant of Perez, the son of Judah. He was the father of Uthai, who is listed as being among the first inhabitants to dwell in Jerusalem following the exile in Babylon.—1Ch 9:2, 4.

AMMINADAB (Am·min'a·dab) [My People Are Willing (Noble; Generous)].

1. A son of Ram of the family of Hezron, tribe of Judah. (1Ch 2:10) His son, Nahshon, was chieftain of Judah during the wilderness trek (Nu 1:7; 7:11, 12); his daughter, Elisheba, became Aaron's wife. (Ex 6:23) Amminadab was an ancestor of King David and of Christ Jesus.—Ru 4:19-22; Mt 1:4-16; Lu 3:23-33.

2. Perhaps an alternative name for Izhar, a son of Kohath and father of Korah. (1Ch 6:22; compare vss 2, 18, 37, 38; Ex 6:18, 21; Nu 3:19, 27.) Some copies of the Greek *Septuagint* give "Izhar" instead of "Amminadab" at 1 Chronicles 6:22 (6:7, *LXX*).

3. A Levite, of the sons of Uzziel; a family head in David's time. He helped to bring the ark of the covenant to Jerusalem.—1Ch 15:10-12.

AMMISHADDAI (Am·mi·shad'dai) [People of the Almighty]. Father of Ahiezer, who, as chieftain of the tribe of Dan, was with Moses when he numbered the assembly of Israel in the second year after coming out of Egypt (1512 B.C.E.).—Nu 1:12; 2:25.

AMMIZABAD (Am·miz'a·bad) [My People Have Endowed]. Son of Benaiah, who was King David's mighty man over the 30 outstanding fighters. Ammizabad acted for his father, Benaiah, in overseeing the third royal service group, for the third month of the year.—1Ch 27:5, 6.

AMMON (Am'mon) [The People]. Lot's son by his younger daughter; the progenitor of the Ammonites. (Ge 19:38) As in the case of the older daughter, so also Lot's younger daughter had relations with her father while they were residing in a cave in a mountainous region—after Lot's daughters had given him much wine to drink. (Ge 19:30-36) The name given to Ammon by his mother was Ben-ammi, meaning, "Son of My People [that is, relatives]" and not of foreigners like the Sodomites. The name thus evidently was associated with the concern voiced by the older daughter that the two daughters could not find anyone of their own people or family line to marry in the land they were inhabiting.

"Ammon" is also used at Psalm 83:7 to refer to the nation of his descendants. The expression "sons of Ammon" would recall to the Israelites the relationship existing between them and the Ammonites, a relationship that even Jehovah took into account, as evidenced by his directing the Israelites not to molest Ammon or to engage in strife with them, since they were sons of Lot, Abraham's nephew.—De 2:19; see AMMONITES.

AMMONIM (Am'mon·im) [The Peoples]. At 2 Chronicles 20:1 the Masoretic text refers to some of the "Ammonim [Heb., *'Am·moh·nim'*]" as being joined with the sons of Moab and of Ammon in war against Jehoshaphat king of Judah. The *King James Version* inserts the word "other" to make the text read, "the children of Moab, and the children of Ammon, and with them *other* beside the Ammonites"; while some other translations render the phrase in question as reading "some of the Ammonites" (*MR, JP, Dy*), though this seems illogical since the Ammonites are already mentioned in the verse. *Biblia Hebraica Stuttgartensia* (ftn) and most modern translations (*Ro, Mo, AT, RS, JB*) regard the text as referring to the Meunim of 2 Chronicles 26:7. This view supposes that a scribal error resulted in the first two consonants (מע) of the Hebrew *Me'u·nim'* being transposed, thus giving *'Am·moh·nim'*. This identification with the Meunim may find support in the fact that the remainder of the account of the fight against Jehoshaphat refers to "the mountainous region of Seir" (in place of "the Ammonim") as joined with the Ammonite-Moabite forces. (2Ch 20:10, 22, 23) The translators of the *Septuagint* used the same Greek word (*Mi·nai'on*) to render the Hebrew term at 2 Chronicles 20:1 as they did in the texts referring to the Meunim, showing that they understood them to be the same.—See MEUNIM.

Since the matter is not certain, however, some translations, such as that of Isaac Leeser and the *New World Translation*, prefer simply to transliterate the term into English, thereby retaining the wording found in the Masoretic text.

AMMONITES (Am'mon·ites) [Of (Belonging to) Ammon]. Descendants of Ammon, Lot's son by the younger of his two daughters. (Ge 19:36-38) They were close relatives of the Moabites, descended from Lot's other son, Moab, and are regularly mentioned in Biblical and ancient secular history along with the Moabites. They were also more distantly related to the Israelites, and this Biblical relationship is supported by the fact that the Ammonite language was a dialect or variant of Hebrew. With rare exceptions, however, the

Ammonites displayed violent enmity toward the nation of Israel.

Territory Occupied. Evidently out of consideration for their faithful forefather Lot, Jehovah God enabled the Ammonites to take possession of the territory previously held by the Rephaim, a towering people called the Zamzummim by the Ammonites. (De 2:17-21) This land lay E of the southern end of the Jordan River, and at one time, the territory of the Ammonites joined with that of the Moabites in the plateau region on the eastern side of the Dead Sea. Sometime prior to Israel's entry into Canaan, however, the Amorites had dispossessed the Ammonites of some of their land and pushed them to the N and E, thereby driving a wedge between them and the Moabites (who also suffered the loss of considerable territory). (Nu 21:26; Jos 12:2; Jg 11:13, 22) Thereafter the land of the sons of Ammon generally extended from the upper reaches of the curving torrent valley of Jabbok eastward toward the desert (Nu 21:24; Jos 12:2), with their capital located at Rabbah (modern 'Amman) by the Jabbok's headwaters. (De 3:11) Archaeologists have discovered ancient Ammonite sites and border fortresses in this region.

Under divine orders, the Israelites were careful not to trespass on the landholdings of the Ammonites when conquering the neighboring Amorites. (De 2:37; Jos 13:8-10) Thus, whereas Joshua 13:25 states that the tribe of Gad received "half of the land of the sons of Ammon" as part of their tribal inheritance, the reference is evidently to that portion of land previously taken from the Ammonites by the Amorites, territory apparently situated between the Jordan River and the upper Jabbok.

Conflicts With Israel. It was not until the time of King Eglon of Moab that the Ammonites, together with the Amalekites, joined with the Moabites in attacking Israel, driving westward to Jericho W of the Jordan. (Jg 3:12-14) After Judge Ehud erased the effects of this assault (Jg 3:26-30), the Ammonites did not again constitute a major threat to Israel until the days of Jephthah. By then the Israelites had returned to serving the gods of the nations and an 18-year period of oppression had ensued, with the Ammonites pushing at Israel from the E, while the Philistines menaced from the west. Ammonite forces not only terrorized the Israelites living in Gilead but even sallied W of the Jordan to harass the tribes of Benjamin, Judah, and Ephraim. (Jg 10:6-10) Finally cleansed of false worship, the Israelites rallied under the headship of Jephthah, and after Jephthah legally refuted the Ammonite charges of a

usurpation of land rights by Israel, the Ammonites were severely defeated.—Jg 10:16–11:33; see JEPHTHAH.

Some scholars have viewed Jephthah's reference to "Chemosh your god" as erroneous, claiming that Chemosh was the national god of Moab, not Ammon. (Jg 11:24; Nu 21:29) While the god of the Ammonites is variously referred to as Molech, Milcom, or Malcam (1Ki 11:5, 7; Jer 49:1, 3), these terms (all related to the root "king") are considered by some scholars to be titles rather than proper names, and they could have been applied to the god Chemosh. At any rate, the Ammonites were polytheistic (Jg 10:6), and the worship of Chemosh may have been nearly as prominent among them as among their relatives, the Moabites.

According to the Greek *Septuagint,* about one month after Saul's being designated king of Israel, King Nahash of Ammon besieged the city of Jabesh in Gilead, demanding the city's surrender, with the cruel requirement that his men could have peace only by each one's allowing his right eye to be bored out. (See NAHASH No. 1.) Learning of the siege, Saul proved his merit as king, marshaling the Israelite forces and routing the Ammonites. (1Sa 11:1-4, 11-15) Samuel's later statement reveals that it was the growing menace of the Ammonites under Nahash that ultimately provoked the Israelites' request for a king.—1Sa 12:12.

During David's rule. The Ammonites also suffered defeat at the hands of David, spoils or tribute being taken from them. (1Ch 18:11) The account of this at 2 Samuel 8:11, 12 forms part of a summary of David's conquests, and this summary may not necessarily be in complete chronological order with the preceding and subsequent accounts. Thus 2 Samuel 10:1, 2 suggests a comparatively peaceful relationship existing between Ammon and Israel during David's rule up to the time of King Nahash's death. Hanun, Nahash's son and successor, greatly angered David, however, by humiliating the messengers David sent to him as bearers of consolation. Becoming aware of the seriousness of the affront committed, the Ammonites sought out mercenary troops from the Syrians and prepared for an offensive against Israel, but they were outmaneuvered and defeated by the Israelite general Joab and his brother Abishai. —2Sa 10:1-14; 1Ch 19:6-15.

The following spring Rabbah, the capital city of Ammon, came under siege by David's forces. During one desperate sally by the besieged Ammonites, Uriah the Hittite died. (2Sa 11:1, 17, 24, 26, 27; see RABBAH No. 1.) The length of the siege is difficult to determine. The record of the birth of the adulterine child to Bath-sheba and the later birth of Solomon may fit chronologically within the period of the siege or may simply be given in complete form in order to terminate the account involving Bath-sheba, even though one or both of the births could have taken place after the siege. While the account at 1 Chronicles 20:1, 2 does not seem to indicate a protracted period, it would not be unusual if the siege had lasted into the following year. The full conquest of the Ammonite capital was finally effected by David.—2Sa 12:26-29.

"The crown of Malcam," referred to in the capture of Rabbah, was evidently a crown placed on the head of the Ammonite idol god, elsewhere called Molech or Milcom. While the *Revised Standard Version* translates the Hebrew term *Mal·kam'* here as "their king," it does not seem logical that a human king is referred to, inasmuch as the crown weighed "a talent of gold" (c. 34 kg; 92 lb t). It also seems likely that the crown's being placed on David's head was only a momentary act, perhaps to demonstrate the victory over this false god. —2Sa 12:30.

Because of some renderings of 2 Samuel 12:31 (*KJ, AS, Dy*), many have understood that the defeated Ammonites were cruelly sawed, axed, and burned to death by David. Later translations (*RS, AT, NW, JB*), however, evidently give the correct sense, showing that the Ammonites were put to forced labor working with saws and axes and in making bricks. This is substantiated by the fact that the Hebrew term rendered "brickkiln" in some translations is now known to refer instead to a wooden mold in which the clay was formed into a brick shape.

That not all Ammonites were bitter enemies of Israel is evident from the presence of Zelek the Ammonite among David's mighty men. (2Sa 23: 37) King Solomon had Ammonite women, including the mother of Rehoboam, among his foreign wives. (1Ki 11:1; 14:31) This, however, contributed to Solomon's apostasy and his setting up of "high places" for the worship of Milcom and other gods, these places being finally ruined by faithful King Josiah.—1Ki 11:5; 2Ki 23:13.

During the divided kingdom. The Ammonites regained their independence from the Davidic kings and during Jehoshaphat's reign (936-c. 911 B.C.E.) joined the Moabites and the inhabitants of the mountainous region of Seir in a combined offensive against Judah, but the alliance suffered a crushing defeat. (2Ch 20:1-4, 10-26) The inscriptions of Assyrian King Shalmaneser III, who ruled in the time of King Jehu

(c. 904-877 B.C.E.) of Israel, claim that the forces of "Ba'sa, son of Ruhubi, from Ammon" were among a coalition of kings opposing Assyria in the battle of Karkar. (*Ancient Near Eastern Texts,* edited by J. B. Pritchard, 1974, p. 279) One of the conspirators in the death of King Jehoash of Judah (c. 859 B.C.E.) was Zabad, the son of the Ammonitess Shimeath. (2Ch 24:22, 26) The strong government of Uzziah (829-778 B.C.E.) once more made the Ammonites tributaries of Judah (2Ch 26:8), and Uzziah's son Jotham reimposed this dominance over Ammon, exacting from them 100 silver talents ($660,600) and 10,000 cor measures (2,200 kl; 62,500 bu) of wheat and 10,000 of barley. (2Ch 27:5) The ability of the Ammonites to pay this large sum during three successive years may have been due to their favorable position along one of the major trade routes from Arabia to Damascus and to the relative fertility of the Jabbok Valley region, wheat and barley still being principal products in this area.

Evidently the increasing intervention of Assyrian power in Palestine during the reign of Jotham's successor Ahaz (761-746 B.C.E.) allowed the Ammonites to break free of Judean domination but only to exchange it for Assyrian oppression, for the records of Tiglath-pileser III list "Sanipu of Bit-Ammon [the house of Ammon]" as paying tribute to Assyria, along with Ahaz of Judah and Salamanu of Moab. Sennacherib's Prism, recounting his invasion of Judah in Hezekiah's time, likewise shows Ammon bringing gifts to the Assyrian invader, while Sennacherib's son Esarhaddon, a contemporary of Manasseh, includes "Puduil, king of Beth-Ammon," among those providing materials for building the city of Nineveh.

It appears likely that, following the deporting of the people of the northern kingdom of Israel by Tiglath-pileser III and one of his successors (2Ki 15:29; 17:6), the Ammonites began occupying the territory of the tribe of Gad, for which they had unsuccessfully fought against Jephthah. (Compare Ps 83:4-8.) Thus, in Jehovah's prophetic message through Jeremiah, the Ammonites are rebuked for seizing the Gadites' inheritance and are warned of a coming desolation upon Ammon and its god Malcam (Milcom). (Jer 49:1-5) The Ammonites went yet further by sending marauder bands to harass Judah under King Jehoiakim during the closing years of the Judean kingdom.—2Ki 24:2, 3.

Babylonian Invasion. With the Babylonian overthrow of Judah (607 B.C.E.), some Jews fled into Ammon, Moab, and Edom but returned upon hearing of the appointment of Gedaliah over the land. (Jer 40:11, 12) King Baalis of Ammon, however, conspired with the Judean army chief Ishmael in the assassination of Gedaliah (2Ki 25:23; Jer 40:14; 41:1-3), and Ishmael thereafter took refuge in Ammon.—Jer 41:10-15.

Although Ammon rejoiced at the fall of Jerusalem, Jehovah's day of accounting with the circumcised Ammonites finally came upon them because of their uncircumcised hearts. (Jer 9:25, 26) True to the prophecies proclaimed by Jeremiah, Ezekiel, and Amos, the Ammonites began to drink the cup of Jehovah's wrath, experiencing sword, famine, pestilence, and the desolation of their land.—Jer 25:17, 21; 27:1-8; Eze 25:1-10; Am 1:13-15.

That Ammon did not willingly submit to the Babylonian yoke is indicated by Ezekiel's description of the king of Babylon (Nebuchadnezzar) standing at the crossways and using divination to decide whether to go against Rabbah of Ammon or against Judah. (Eze 21:19-23, 28-32) Though the choice came out for attack first upon Jerusalem, Jewish historian Josephus records that, in the fifth year after desolating Jerusalem, Nebuchadnezzar returned to war against Coele-Syria, Ammon, and Moab. (*Jewish Antiquities*, X, 181 [ix, 7]) As foretold, Ammon would become "a resting-place of a flock" and Rabbah "a pasture ground of camels." (Eze 25:5) The camel-riding Orientals were to possess the land and tent therein.—Eze 25:4.

It is likely that Ammonite exiles, along with those of other nations, were allowed to return to their homeland by Cyrus, the conqueror of Babylon, in fulfillment of Jeremiah 49:6.

Intermarriage With Israelites. Following the return of the Jews from exile (537 B.C.E.), an Ammonite named Tobiah took a leading part in endeavoring to obstruct the rebuilding of Jerusalem's walls. (Ne 4:3, 7, 8) Yet later he had the audacity to make use of a dining hall within the temple precincts, until Nehemiah indignantly threw his furniture out. (Ne 13:4-8; see TOBIAH No. 2.) Many of the returned Jewish exiles also had taken wives of Ammonite and other foreign extraction and were severely rebuked for this, resulting in a general dismissal of such wives. —Ezr 9:1, 2; 10:10-19, 44; Ne 13:23-27.

After Tobiah's ejection from the temple grounds, God's law at Deuteronomy 23:3-6 prohibiting the entry of Ammonites and Moabites into the congregation of Israel was read and applied. (Ne 13:1-3) This restriction, imposed some 1,000 years earlier because of the Ammonite and Moabite refusal to succor the Israelites when they were approaching the Promised Land, is generally understood to mean that these people could not enter into full legal membership in the nation of Israel with all the concomitant rights and privileges that such membership would signify. It does not mean, of necessity, that Ammonite and Moabite individuals could not associate themselves with or reside among the Israelites and thereby benefit from the divine blessings upon God's people, and this is evident from the inclusion of Zelek, mentioned earlier, among David's chief warriors, as well as from the record concerning Ruth the Moabitess.—Ru 1:4, 16-18.

As to this latter case, Ruth's marriage to Boaz shows that females of these nations, upon turning to the worship of the true God, could be acceptable for marriage by Jewish males. Because the terms "Ammonite" and "Moabite" in the Hebrew text of Deuteronomy 23:3-6 are in the masculine gender, the Jewish Mishnah (*Yevamot* 8:3) argues that only male Ammonites and Moabites were excluded from Israel. Nevertheless, Ezra's insistence that the Jewish men send away their foreign wives and Nehemiah's similar attitude, previously mentioned, indicate that the admission of Ammonite and Moabite females into association with Israel was dependent upon their acceptance of true worship.

Though historical evidence, including the Apocryphal book of 1 Maccabees (5:6), shows that Ammon continued to be a distinct territory down till the second century B.C.E., by the first century B.C.E. the region appears to have become part of the Nabataean kingdom, and by the third century C.E. the Ammonites as a people disappear from history, doubtless absorbed by the Arabic tribes. As Zephaniah had prophesied, the sons of Ammon had become "like Gomorrah, . . . a desolate waste." —Zep 2:8-10.

In view of the disappearance of the Ammonites early in the Common Era, Daniel's mention of Ammon in his prophecy of "the time of the end" must apply in a spiritual sense and would logically refer to those who are among the hard-set enemies of the spiritual Israel of God, the Christian congregation.—Da 11:40, 41.

AMNESTY. At Esther 2:18 it is related that the Persian monarch Ahasuerus, after making Esther his queen, held a great banquet in her honor and granted "an amnesty for the jurisdictional districts" of his domain. The Hebrew word *hanachah'* here used occurs but once in the Scriptures. It is variously rendered as "amnesty" (*LXX*), "release" (*KJ*), "remission of taxes" (one Targum and *RS*), "holiday" (*Vg, AT*); and commentators suggest that the release, or amnesty, may have involved a remission of tribute, a remission of military service, release from prison, or a combination of these. A different Hebrew word (*shemittah'*) is used elsewhere in the Scriptures to describe a releasing from debt or suspension of labor.—De 15:1, 2, 9; 31:10; see SABBATH YEAR.

As to a release of prisoners, it may be noted that during the reign of Xerxes I, believed to be the Ahasuerus of the book of Esther, a number of revolts occurred. An inscription from Persepolis attributed to Xerxes states: "After I became king, there were (some) among these countries . . . which revolted (but) I crushed (lit.: killed) these countries, . . . and I put them (again) into their (former political) status." (*Ancient Near Eastern Texts,* edited by J. B. Pritchard, 1974, p. 317) Political prisoners doubtless resulted from such suppression of uprisings, and the festive time of Esther's being made queen may have been the occasion for Ahasuerus to efface the charges against such ones and grant them amnesty, or release. (Compare Mt 27:15.) The precise nature of the amnesty, however, remains undetermined.

AMNON (Am'non) [Trustworthy; Faithful; Long-Lasting].

1. David's firstborn son by Ahinoam the Jezreelitess, born at Hebron.—2Sa 3:2; 1Ch 3:1.

Amnon developed a passionate desire for lovely Tamar, Absalom's sister, to the point of lovesickness. Following the advice of his cousin Jehonadab, Amnon feigned illness and induced King David to send Tamar to Amnon's private quarters to prepare "bread of consolation" in his presence. He then used the opportunity to violate his half sister forcibly, despite her pleading and reasoning with him. His case illustrates how extremely selfish erotic love can be, for, having satisfied his desire, Amnon then had Tamar put out into the street as someone repugnant to him, someone whose very presence doubtless made him feel unclean.—2Sa 13:1-19.

Tamar's full brother, Absalom, nursed a hatred of Amnon for this act, and two years later at a sheepshearing festival Absalom had his servants murder Amnon when he was "in a merry mood with wine." (2Sa 13:20-29) Since Amnon, as David's eldest son, was heir apparent to the throne, his death may also have been viewed as desirable by Absalom as a means to better his own possibilities of gaining the kingship. With this event the prophecy made by Nathan following David's own misconduct with the wife of Uriah began to undergo fulfillment.—2Sa 12:10; see ABSALOM.

2. The first in the list of four sons of Shimon, of the tribe of Judah.—1Ch 4:1, 20.

AMOK (A'mok) [Deep; Unintelligible]. A principal priest who returned with Zerubbabel from exile in Babylon. (Ne 12:1, 7) His family was represented by his son Eber in the time of Joiakim.—Ne 12:12, 20.

AMON (A'mon).
[1-3: Trustworthy; Faithful; Long-Lasting]

1. A chief of the city of Samaria when Ahab, king of Israel, was ruling (c. 940-920 B.C.E.). The prophet Micaiah was put in his care while Ahab warred against Ramoth-gilead.—1Ki 22:10, 26; 2Ch 18:25.

2. A king of Judah (661-660 B.C.E.), and son of wicked King Manasseh. He began to rule at the age of 22 and followed the idolatrous course of his father's earlier years. The bad conditions described at Zephaniah 1:4; 3:2-4 doubtless were developing at this time. After two years on the throne, he was murdered by his own servants. "The people of the land ['am ha·'a'rets]" put the conspirators to death, placed his son Josiah on the throne, and buried Amon in "the garden of Uzza." (2Ki 21:19-26; 2Ch 33:20-25) The genealogy of Jesus includes his name.—Mt 1:10.

3. The family head of certain returned exiles included among "the sons of the servants of Solomon." (Ne 7:57-59) He is referred to as "Ami" in Ezra 2:57.

4. A local god of Thebes, or No-Amon, who rose to the position of "king of the gods" under the name Amon-Ra and whose high priest became head of all the Egyptian priesthoods. Amon is generally represented as a man wearing a crown surmounted by two tall parallel plumes. Like many of the other Egyptian deities, he is frequently shown holding the crux ansata, the "sign of life." Amon, his wife Mut, and Khonsu (his adopted son) made up the Theban triad.

A large part of Egypt's spoils of war found its way into the treasury of Amon, whose priesthood became very powerful and wealthy. In his work *A History of Egypt* (1902, Vol. V, pp. 205-217), E. A. W. Budge suggests that the priesthood may actually have encouraged warfare for their own benefit. In time the high priests of Amon, whose office had become hereditary, exercised even greater power than the pharaohs. One of them, Herihor, succeeded the last of the Ramses to the throne. According to J. H. Breasted's *History of Egypt,* under Hrihor (Herihor) "whatever the High Priest wished legally to effect could be sanctioned by special oracle of the god [Amon] at any time, and by prearrangement the cultus image before which the High Priest made known his desires invariably responded favourably . . . Priestly jugglery, ruling if necessary in utter disregard of law and justice, thus enabled the High Priest to cloak with the divine sanction all that he wished to effect."—1937, p. 523.

A number of adversities came to Thebes and her god Amon. Two of these are mentioned in the Scriptures. In the seventh century B.C.E., the conquering Assyrians under the command of Ashurbanipal razed Thebes to the ground, stripping her of all her wealth. The prophet Nahum refers to this event, using it as an illustration of Nineveh's coming destruction. (Na 3:8) Thebes recovered somewhat from the blow meted out to her by Assyria, regaining a measure of prosperity, but even this was to be short-lived. Jeremiah indicated that Jehovah's judgment was against Egypt and her gods, including Thebes and her god Amon. Into the hand of Nebuchadnezzar, Egypt would be given, bringing shame to her and to her gods, especially to Amon from No (Thebes).—Jer 46:25, 26; see No, No-Amon.

AMORITE (Am′or·ite). "The Amorite" appears among the list of the sons of Canaan, but elsewhere this term, always in the singular in the Hebrew text, is used collectively of the Canaanite tribe descended from the original Amorite. They were, therefore, a Hamitic race.—Ge 10:6, 15, 16; 1Ch 1:13, 14.

In Abraham's time the king of Elam in coalition with three other kings raided to the S of Canaan and defeated some of the Amorites dwelling at Hazazon-tamar, thought to be located SW of the Dead Sea. Three Amorite men living near or in Hebron were then "confederates of Abram" and as such aided him in pursuing and defeating the invading kings, thereby rescuing his nephew Lot. (Ge 14) Still, sometime thereafter God advised Abraham that when the error of the Amorites had finally "come to completion," Abraham's descendants would return to Canaan from an alien land and would take possession of the Amorites' land. —Ge 15:13-21.

Shortly before Jacob's death in Egypt, that patriarch promised Joseph: "I do give you one shoulder of land more than to your brothers, which I took from the hand of the Amorites by my sword and by my bow." (Ge 48:22) Since the word rendered "shoulder" in this text is *shekhem′* in Hebrew, some have claimed that Jacob was here referring to the plot of ground he had purchased near Shechem (Heb., *Shekhem′*). (Ge 33:18, 19) The purchase was a peaceable transaction, how-

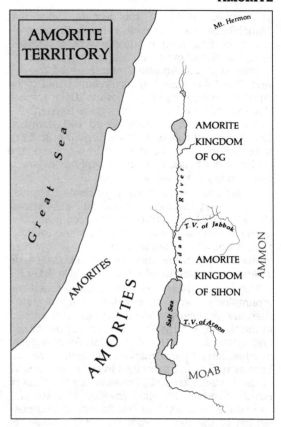

ever, and there is no record of any battle waged by Jacob in connection with the land. While Jacob's sons later did make a savage attack on the people of Shechem, Jacob disavowed responsibility for the act at the time (Ge 34:30); and on his deathbed he cursed the anger of Simeon and Levi that had motivated the attack. (Ge 49:5-7) Thus, it seems more reasonable to understand Jacob's promise as a prophetic utterance in which he envisioned by faith the future conquest of Canaan as though it were already effected, with Jacob 'taking the land of the Amorites' vicariously through the sword and bow of his descendants.

A Dominant Tribe in Canaan. Some commentators consider the term "Amorites" as used at Genesis 15:16 and 48:22 to represent the peoples of Canaan as a whole. The Amorites do appear to have been the principal or dominant tribe in Canaan at the time of the Israelite Exodus from Egypt. (Compare De 1:6-8, 19-21, 27; Jos 24:15, 18; Jg 6:10.) If this is so, then it would be understandable that, at times, other subordinate and related tribes should be referred to under the name of the dominant tribe of the Amorites. Thus, at Numbers 14:44, 45 the account states that "Amalekites" and "Canaanites" handed the Israelites their first military defeat, whereas Moses' recapitulation of events at Deuteronomy chapter 1 simply says "the Amorites" administered the defeat. (De 1:44) Likewise, Jerusalem is said to be ruled by an Amorite king at Joshua 10:5 (compare Eze 16:3, 45) but is shown elsewhere to be inhabited by Jebusites. (Jos 15:8, 63; Jg 1:21; compare also the case of Gibeon at Jos 9:7 and 2Sa 21:2.) In a similar manner, the name of one tribe of the nation of Israel, Judah, came to apply to all Israelites through the appellative "Jew."

Nevertheless, the Amorites are also listed separately among the independent Canaanite tribes. (Ex 3:8; 23:23, 24; 34:11-15) They composed one of the "seven nations more populous and mighty" than Israel, all devoted to destruction, with whom Israel was to make no covenant, form no marriage alliance, nor share in false worship.—De 7:1-4.

The 12 spies Moses sent into Canaan found the mountainous region occupied by Amorites, Hittites, and Jebusites, while the Amalekites resided in the Negeb, and the Canaanites dwelt by the sea and by the Jordan. (Nu 13:1, 2, 29) As previously in Abraham's time, Amorites still resided at Hebron as well as in other cities in the mountains W of the Jordan. (Jos 10:5) However, by the time of Israel's Exodus, they had invaded Moabite and Ammonite territory E of the Jordan, taking possession of the region from the torrent valley of Arnon in the S (thereafter the border of Moab), up to the torrent valley of Jabbok in the N (the border of Ammon). (Nu 21:13, 24, 26; Jos 12:2; Jg 11:22) This was the realm of Amorite King Sihon, described by Josephus the Jewish historian as "a region situated between three rivers [the Jordan, the Arnon, and the Jabbok], which give it something of the nature of an island." (*Jewish Antiquities*, IV, 95 [v, 2]) Additionally, to the N of Sihon's realm, there was another Amorite kingdom centered in Bashan under King Og. The southern border of his kingdom seems to have been contiguous with the territories of Sihon and of the Ammonites, thus extending from the Jabbok in the S up to Mount Hermon in the N.—De 3:1, 8.

Conquest by Israel. Drawing near the Promised Land and under divine orders not to trespass on the territories of Moab and Ammon (De 2:9, 37), the Israelites requested a transit permit from King Sihon at his capital city, Heshbon, offering stringent guarantees: "Let me pass through your land. We shall not turn off into a field or a vineyard. We shall drink water of no well. On the king's road we shall march until we pass through your territory." Instead, Sihon struck at Israel with

his combined forces and was summarily defeated a short distance from Heshbon, at Jahaz, his entire territory falling into Israelite possession. (Nu 21:21-32; De 2:24-36; see SIHON.) Invading neighboring King Og's territory, Israel also vanquished this Amorite ruler, capturing 60 fortified cities. (Nu 21:33-35; De 3:1-7; see OG.) The fall of these powerful Amorite kingdoms to Israel caused a sense of sickening dread to pervade Moab (Nu 22:2-4) and also the people of Canaan, as is revealed by Rahab's words to the Israelite spies. (De 2:24, 25; Jos 2:9-11) The territory of the two defeated Amorite kings now became the inheritance of the tribes of Reuben and Gad and half the tribe of Manasseh.—Nu 32:31-33, 39; De 3:8-13.

As for the Amorites W of the Jordan, "their hearts began to melt" upon hearing of the Israelites' miraculous crossing of the Jordan. This miracle, combined with the smashing victories Israel had already obtained, may explain, in part, why the Amorites made no attack upon the Israelite camp during the ensuing period in which the Israelite males were circumcised or while the Passover was celebrated. (Jos 5:1, 2, 8, 10) However, after the destruction of Jericho and Ai, a massive alliance of the tribes of Canaan was formed to present a united front against Israel. (Jos 9:1, 2) When the Hivite men of Gibeon elected to seek peace with Israel, they were promptly attacked by "five kings of the Amorites" and escaped destruction only because of an all-night march by Joshua's forces and Jehovah's miraculous intervention.—Jos 10:1-27; 11:19.

After this battle and after Joshua's succeeding campaign throughout the land, the power of the Amorites in the S of Palestine was evidently broken. Still, the Amorites in the northern regions joined with other tribes in an alliance that engaged Israel in battle at "the waters of Merom." Disastrously overwhelmed, the Amorites are never again mentioned as constituting a major danger to Israel. (Jos 11:1-9) A remnant remained, but their territory was greatly reduced, and in course of time they came into forced labor under Israelite domination. (Jos 13:4; Jg 1:34-36) Amorite women were taken as wives by Israelites, resulting in apostasy (Jg 3:5, 6), and the Amorites generally seem to have continued to be troublesome for some time, for it is mentioned that in Samuel's day, after a decisive defeat of the Philistines, "there came to be peace between Israel and the Amorites." (1Sa 7:14) Amorites were again among those put to forced labor during Solomon's reign. (1Ki 9:20, 21) Their idolatry and wickedness, evidently representative of that of all the Canaanites, was proverbial. (1Ki 21:26; 2Ki 21:11) The taking of Amorite wives still constituted a thorny problem among the returned Israelites after the Babylonian exile. (Ezr 9:1, 2) Eventually, however, the Amorite people, once the foremost ones of all Canaan, passed completely out of existence, like a tall, massive tree with its fruit removed and its roots destroyed.—Am 2:9, 10.

The "Amurru." Secular historians regularly associate the Amorites of the Bible with the people called the *Amurru* in early Akkadian (Assyro-Babylonian) cuneiform texts. The *Amurru* are represented as invading Mesopotamia early in the second millennium B.C.E. and as having had a kingdom in Babylonia for several centuries. Hammurabi, famed lawgiver of that period, is often referred to as of "Amorite" origin.

The evidence concerning the *Amurru,* however, does not appear to warrant the strong conclusions that are advanced as to their positive identification with the Biblical Amorites. *Amurru* in the ancient cuneiform texts basically meant "west" as referring to the region W of Mesopotamia. A. H. Sayce, in *The International Standard Bible Encyclopedia,* says that the name *Amurru* is "a purely geographical indication of their immediate origins, from the perspective of Mesopotamia, and conveys no information about their ethnic composition or their real name." (Edited by G. W. Bromiley, 1979, Vol. 1, p. 113) While Mari, an ancient city on the Euphrates in northern Mesopotamia, is referred to by modern secular historians as a center of the expansion of the *Amurru* into Mesopotamia, the thousands of tablets recovered there were almost all in the Semitic Akkadian (Assyro-Babylonian) language, with some names of West Semitic origin. As noted, however, the Biblical Amorites were Hamitic, not Semitic, and while the adoption of a Semitic tongue by some branch of them is not an impossibility, it is equally possible that the early *Amurru* were simply "westerners" from among the Semitic peoples living to the W of Babylonia. Professor John Bright in *A History of Israel* (1981, p. 49) says: "For some centuries [of the late third millennium and early second millennium B.C.E.] the people of northwestern Mesopotamia and northern Syria had been referred to in cuneiform texts as Amurru, i.e., 'Westerners.' This became, apparently, a general term applying to speakers of various Northwest-Semitic dialects found in the area including, in all probability, those strains from which later sprang both Hebrews and Arameans."

AMOS (A'mos) [Being a Load; Carrying a Load].

1. A prophet of Jehovah and writer of the book bearing his name, who lived in the ninth century B.C.E. (See AMOS, BOOK OF.) He was not, however, born as the son of a prophet, nor was he one of "the sons of the prophets."—1Ki 20:35; 2Ki 2:3; 4:1; Am 7:14.

His home was the town of Tekoa, some 16 km (10 mi) S of Jerusalem, at an elevation of about 820 m (2,700 ft). To the E, and sloping toward the Dead Sea, which lay about 1,200 m (4,000 ft) below, was the bleak wilderness of Judah, where, in his early life, the prophet found employment as a humble sheep raiser. (Am 1:1) The Hebrew word *no-qedhim'* here translated "sheep raisers" occurs in only one other place in the Bible (2Ki 3:4) and is related to *naqqad,* the Arabic word for a special breed of sheep, rather unattractive but highly valued for its fleece. Out in that wild country Amos also engaged in menial seasonal work as a nipper of sycamore figs, a variety considered food only for the poor. The practice of pinching or puncturing the figs was to hasten the ripening and increase the size and sweetness of the fruit.—Am 7:14; see SYCAMORE.

Like the shepherd David, who was called to public service by God, so also "Jehovah proceeded to take [Amos] from following the flock" and made him a prophet.—Am 7:15.

From the solitude in the wilderness of the south, Amos was sent to the idolatrous ten-tribe kingdom in the north with its capital Samaria.

Amos began his career as a prophet two years before the great earthquake that occurred during the reign of Uzziah, king of Judah. At the same time Jeroboam II, son of Joash, was king of Israel. (Am 1:1) Amos' prophecy is, therefore, placed sometime within the 26-year period from 829 to about 804 B.C.E., when the reigns of these two kings of Judah and Israel overlapped. The great earthquake that occurred two years after Amos was commissioned to be a prophet was of such magnitude that nearly 300 years later Zechariah made particular mention of it.—Zec 14:5.

How long Amos served as a prophet in the northern kingdom is uncertain. Amaziah, the wicked calf-worshiping priest of the state religion centered at Bethel, attempted to have him thrown out of the country on the grounds he was a threat to the security of the state. (Am 7:10-13) Whether Amaziah succeeded is not disclosed. At any rate, when Amos' prophetic mission to Israel was completed, he presumably returned to his native tribal territory of Judah. Jerome and Eusebius report that the prophet's sepulcher was located at Tekoa in their day. It also seems that after returning to Judah, Amos wrote down the prophecy, which at first had been delivered orally. He is often called one of the 12 "minor" prophets (his book is cataloged 3rd among the 12), yet the message he delivered is by no means of minor significance.

2. One of Jesus' ancestors, the eighth generation before Mary.—Lu 3:25.

AMOS, BOOK OF. The prophecy of this Hebrew book of the Bible was directed primarily to the northern kingdom of Israel. Apparently it was first delivered orally during the reigns of Jeroboam II and Uzziah, kings of Israel and of Judah respectively, whose periods of kingship overlapped between 829 and about 804 B.C.E. (Am 1:1) By about 804 B.C.E. it was committed to writing, presumably after the prophet returned to Judah. For details about the prophet himself, see AMOS No. 1.

The canonicity of this book, or its claim to a rightful place in the Bible, has never been questioned. From early times it has been accepted by the Jews, and it appears in the earliest Christian catalogs. Justin Martyr of the second century C.E. quoted from Amos in his *Dialogue With Trypho, a Jew* (chap XXII). The book itself is in complete agreement with the rest of the Bible, as is shown by the writer's many references to Bible history and the laws of Moses. (Am 1:11; 2:8-10; 4:11; 5:22, 25; 8:5) Christians of the first century accepted the writings of Amos as inspired Scripture. For example, the martyr Stephen (Ac 7:42, 43; Am 5:25-27) and James the half brother of Jesus (Ac 15:13-19; Am 9:11, 12) noted the fulfillment of some of the prophecies.

Other historical events likewise attest to the truthfulness of the prophet. It is a matter of history that all the nations condemned by Amos were in due time devoured by the fire of destruction. The highly fortified city of Samaria itself was besieged and captured in 740 B.C.E., and the Assyrian army took the inhabitants "into exile beyond Damascus," as foretold by Amos. (Am 5:27; 2Ki 17:5, 6) Judah to the south likewise received her due punishment when she was destroyed in 607 B.C.E. (Am 2:5) And true to Jehovah's word through Amos, captive descendants of both Israel and Judah returned in 537 B.C.E. to rebuild their homeland.—Am 9:14; Ezr 3:1.

Biblical archaeology also confirms that Amos was a truthful historian of his time, when, in describing the ostentatious luxury of the rich, he referred to their "houses of ivory" and "couches of ivory." (Am 3:15; 6:4) Commenting on some of these findings, Jack Finegan states: "It is of much interest that numerous ivories were found in the excavation of Samaria. These are mostly in the

---

HIGHLIGHTS OF AMOS

Prophecy directed especially to Israel, the northern ten-tribe kingdom, with its centers for calf worship at Dan and at Bethel

Written about 804 B.C.E., while Jeroboam II was king in Israel

Execution of Jehovah's judgment is certain not only against surrounding nations but especially against Israel (1:1–2:16)

Syria, Philistia, and Tyre for cruel treatment to Israel

Edom (related through Esau) and Ammon (related through Lot) for hatred and mistreatment of their brother Israelites; Moab for burning the bones of the king of Edom for lime

Judah for rejecting the law of Jehovah

Israel for oppressing the poor, for immorality, also for treating disrespectfully prophets and Nazirites raised up by God; no escape from divine punishment

Jehovah's message of judgment against Israel (3:1–6:14)

Israel has been specially favored by God; this results in special accountability

When Jehovah reveals his purpose to his servants, they prophesy; thus Amos warns that Jehovah will hold an accounting for false religious practices at Bethel and defrauding by luxury lovers in Samaria

Israel has not returned to Jehovah despite punishments already meted out; now warned, "Get ready to meet your God"

Even while warning of woes to come, Jehovah urges: "Search for me, and keep living," "Hate what is bad, and love what is good"

Visions and prophecies show Israel's end is near (7:1–8:14)

Vision of desolation by locusts; prophet intercedes

Vision of destructive fire; Amos again intercedes

Jehovah with a plummet to test Israel; no further excusing of Israel

Priest of Bethel commands Amos to stop prophesying there; Amos prophesies calamity for him

Basket of perishable summer fruit, signifying Israel's end near

Famine for hearing the words of Jehovah

Punishment and restoration (9:1-15)

No place that they can go to escape; nothing is beyond the reach of the Sovereign Lord Jehovah

Booth (royal house) of David to be rebuilt; regathered captives to enjoy lasting security

form of plaques or small panels in relief and presumably were once attached to furniture and inlaid in wall paneling."—*Light From the Ancient Past,* 1959, pp. 187, 188.

Jehovah's spirit moved Amos to employ simple, direct, picturesque language in a dignified manner befitting a prophet of God. Simple words, powerful words, words full of meaning, were chosen so both the high and the low could understand and get the sense of what he said. He used a variety of illustrations, some with rural flavor, to give vitality and force to his message. (Am 2:13; 4:2; 9:9) Historical events are accurately recalled. (1:9, 11, 13; 4:11) Allusions are made to familiar practices and customs of the people. (2:8; 6:4-6) The whole is a well-ordered composition with definite form and purpose.

As one of Jehovah's servants, Amos magnified the word and name, the righteousness, and the sovereignty of the Almighty. He describes how "the Sovereign Lord, Jehovah of the armies," is infinitely great, that nothing is beyond His reach or power. (Am 9:2-5) Even the sun, moon, constellations, and the elements are subject to Jehovah's commands. (5:8; 8:9) It is, therefore, a small matter for God to demonstrate his supremacy over the nations.—1:3-5; 2:1-3; 9:7.

In keeping with the meaning of his name, Amos bore a weighty message laden with woe and denunciation against the pagan nations as well as against Judah and Israel. He also carried a comforting message of restoration in which those faithful to Jehovah could put their hope.

AMOZ (A'moz) [Strong]. Father of Isaiah the prophet.—2Ki 19:2; Isa 1:1.

AMPHIPOLIS (Am·phip'o·lis) [Around the City]. A city of Macedonia, about 5 km (3 mi) from the Aegean Sea and the seaport of Eion. Paul passed through here on his second missionary tour. (Ac 17:1) It was built on a hill surrounded on three sides (N, W, and S) by the curving river Strymon, which situation doubtless gave name to the city. Amphipolis lay about 50 km (30 mi) WSW of Philippi and, due to its position on the famous Roman highway *Via Egnatia* and its control of the bridge over the river Strymon, was of considerable importance strategically and commercially. Originally founded as an Athenian colony in the fifth century B.C.E., it later came under the Macedonians. Thereafter Rome took control and made it a free city and the capital of the first district of Macedonia. The village of Neochori is now found there.

AMPLIATUS (Am·pli·a'tus) [from Lat., meaning "Enlarged"]. A beloved Christian brother in the congregation at Rome, to whom the apostle Paul sent greetings.—Ro 16:8.

AMRAM (Am'ram) [People High (Exalted)].

1. A grandson of Levi through Kohath. (Ex 6:16, 18, 20; Nu 3:19; 26:58; 1Ch 6:18) It is stated that he married "his father's sister" Jochebed, an act then allowable but later prohibited in the Mosaic Law. (Le 18:12) Some translations, however, endeavor to show her to be his cousin. (See JOCHEBED.) His children were Aaron, Miriam, and Moses.—Ex 6:20; Nu 26:59; 1Ch 6:2, 3; 23:12, 13.

2. One of "the sons of Bani," who, along with other returned exiles, responded to the call to put away foreign wives in 468 B.C.E.—Ezr 10:34, 44.

3. Name given to a Seirite, a son of Dishon, in the *King James Version* rendering of 1 Chronicles 1:41.—See HEMDAN.

AMRAMITES (Am'ram·ites) [Of (Belonging to) Amram]. The descendants of Amram, the grandson of Levi by Kohath. They composed a subdivision of the family of Kohathites. During the trek through the wilderness, they encamped on the S of the tabernacle with all the families of the sons of Kohath. The service assignment of the Kohathites was the Ark, the table, the lampstand, the altars, and the utensils, as well as the screen between the Holy and the Most Holy.—Nu 3:27-31; 1Ch 26:23.

AMRAPHEL (Am'ra·phel). King of Shinar in southern Mesopotamia, and an ally and supporter of King Chedorlaomer of Elam in the invasion and victory over five kings at the Low Plain of Siddim. Amraphel and his allies were later overtaken by Abram, in his rescue of Lot, and were completely routed. (Ge 14:1-16) There have been attempts to identify Amraphel with Hammurabi, but the identification is not certain.

AMUSEMENTS. As expressed by the writer of Ecclesiastes: "For everything there is an appointed time, . . . a time to weep and a time to laugh; a time to wail and a time to skip about." (Ec 3:1, 4) The word "laugh" here translates the Hebrew verb *sa·chaq'*. Though the basic meaning is "laugh," this word and the related words *sechoq'* and *tsa·chaq'* are also translated by expressions such as "celebrate," "play," "make sport," 'offer amusement,' and "have a good time." (2Sa 6:21; Job 41:5; Jg 16:25; Ex 32:6; Ge 26:8) Forms of the verb *sa·chaq'* are used at Proverbs 8:30, 31 with regard to the "master worker" as "being glad" before Jehovah following the earth's creation, as well as to describe the "play" of the animal creation in the sea and in the fields.—Ps 104:26; Job 40:20.

Expressions of Joy and Pleasure. The amusements and diversion of the Israelites are not prominently portrayed in the Bible record. Nevertheless, it shows them to be viewed as both proper and desirable when in harmony with the religious principles of the nation. The principal forms of recreation were the playing of musical instruments, singing, dancing, conversation, as well as some games. The propounding of riddles and difficult questions was much esteemed. —Jg 14:12.

Singing, dancing, and the use of tambourines broke forth in praise of Jehovah right after Israel's deliverance at the Red Sea. (Ex 15:20, 21) Later, when Aaron proclaimed "a festival to Jehovah" after having made the golden calf, the people ate and drank and then got up "to have a good time [letsa·cheq']." Their dancing and singing in this case, however, were coupled with false worship, causing disgrace.—Ex 32:5, 6, 18, 19, 25.

The three annual festivals provided occasion for enjoyment along with the observance of the requirements of worship set forth in the Law. "Circle dances" are mentioned with regard to the yearly festival held in Shiloh. (Jg 21:21) Other occasions were the victory celebrations (Jg 11:34; 1Sa 18:6, 7) and the coronation of a king. (1Ki 1:40) While dancing was engaged in more particularly by women, men also danced on occasion, as did David when bringing the Ark up to Jerusalem. (2Sa 6:5, 14, 21; 1Ch 13:8; 15:29) The vintage time and also sheepshearing time were occasions of joy and feasting. (Jer 25:30; 2Sa 13:23-28) Marriages, too, were times for enjoyment, and Jesus contributed toward such at a marriage held in Cana. (Jer 7:34; 16:9; Joh 2:1-10) At Luke 15:25 a music concert and dancing are mentioned as part of the festivities celebrating the return of the prodigal son.

In Egypt slaves were taught music and dancing to entertain the family and their guests. The Greeks also employed professional female dancers and musicians to entertain guests. There was dancing for entertainment on Herod's birthday when he was asked for the head of John the Baptizer. (Mt 14:6-8) Dancing was popular among the Greeks as an amusement, though Greek dancing was originally associated with religious worship.

Proper Balance in Amusement. Warnings against improper forms of amusement and the need for keeping entertainment in its place are set forth in certain texts. Proverbs describes the stupid one to whom the carrying on of loose conduct is like "sport [sechohq']" and the man who tricks his fellow and says, "Was I not having fun [mesacheq']?" (Pr 10:23; 26:19) Showing amusement's relative worth to be small, Proverbs 14:13 says: "Even in laughter [bi·sechohq'] the heart may be in pain; and grief is what rejoicing ends up in." (Compare Ec 2:2; 7:2, 3, 6.) The merry Philistines called out blind Samson to offer them amusement (sa·chaq'), only to have him bring the house down on them.—Jg 16:25-30.

Jeremiah, aware of the seriousness of the times and undergoing persecution for his preaching, states that he did not sit down with "those playing jokes [mesa·chaqim']" and exulting. (Jer 15:17) Though he foretold doom for Jerusalem, he also prophesied of the time when her inhabitants would again go forth with rejoicing in the dance of those laughing, decked with tambourines. (Jer 30:19; 31:4) Zechariah similarly foretold the day when the public squares of restored Jerusalem would be filled with children playing.—Zec 8:5; see DANCING; GAMES; THEATER.

AMZI (Am'zi) [shortened form of Amaziah, meaning "Jehovah Is Strong"].

1. A Levite of the family of Merari and an ancestor of Ethan, who was one of the singers at Jehovah's house appointed by David.—1Ch 6:31, 44-47.

2. A priest, son of Zechariah, and an ancestor of Adaiah, who is listed as residing in Jerusalem and doing service at the temple in the time of Nehemiah.—Ne 11:12.

ANAB (A'nab) [Grape]. A town in the S part of the hill country of Judah from which the giant Anakim were expelled by Joshua. (Jos 11:21; 15:48, 50) The site is identified with Khirbet 'Anab es-Saghireh, 1.5 km (1 mi) W of Edh Dhahiriya, about halfway between Hebron and Beer-sheba. The original name of the city may have been Kiriath-anab, since Egyptian texts apparently mention it as Qrt 'nb.

ANAH (A'nah). A son of Zibeon and the father of Esau's wife Oholibamah. (Ge 36:2, 14, 18, 20, 24, 25; 1Ch 1:34, 40, 41) At Genesis 36:2 the Hebrew text reads "Oholibamah the daughter of Anah the daughter of Zibeon." The Syriac Peshitta, the Samaritan Pentateuch, and the Greek Septuagint here all read "son of Zibeon," in agreement with Genesis 36:24, which shows Anah to be Zibeon's son. Some modern translations follow this rendering and say "son of Zibeon" in both verse 2 and verse 14. (*RS, AT, JB*) However, the Hebrew word for "daughter" here also allows for the broader meaning of granddaughter and may thus apply to Oholibamah rather than to Anah. Hence the *New World Translation* at Genesis 36:2 reads: "Oholibamah the daughter of Anah, the granddaughter of Zibeon the Hivite."

Some believe the name Anah applies to two persons, inasmuch as Anah is spoken of as a "Hivite" in verse 2 while the Anah of verses 20 and 29 is called a "Horite." However, if the term "Horite" means simply a "cave dweller," it could be used to describe the cave-dwelling habits of the Seirites rather than being used in a genealogical sense. The word "sons" in verse 20 thus appears to have the more general meaning of descendants. As M'Clintock and Strong's *Cyclopædia* (1882, Vol. I, p. 212) states: "The intention of the genealogy plainly is not so much to give the lineal descent of the Seirites as to enumerate those descendants who, being heads of tribes, came into connection with the Edomites. It would thus appear that Anah, from whom Esau's wife sprang, was the head of a tribe independent of his father, and ranking on an equality with that tribe."

ANAHARATH (An·a·ha′rath). A city of the tribe of Issachar, evidently in the eastern part of the Plain of Jezreel. (Jos 19:18, 19) Its exact location is at present uncertain.

ANAIAH (A·nai′ah) [Jah Has Answered].

1. One of the men who stood at Ezra's right hand when he read the Law to the people, on the first day of the seventh month. Probably a priest or prince.—Ne 8:2, 4.

2. One of the headmen of the people whose descendant, if not he himself, attested to the confession contract of Nehemiah.—Ne 10:1, 22.

ANAK (A′nak) [probably, Long-Necked [that is, of tall stature]]. The name applied to a tribe of unusually tall men and perhaps to their progenitor. At Numbers 13:22 and 28 the article is used with the name in Hebrew (ha·'Anaq′). If it is the personal name of the son of "Arba . . . the father of Anak" (Jos 15:13), the name thereafter was also applied to his progeny. (Compare Jos 15:14 with 14:15, where Arba is called "the great man among the Anakim.")—See ANAKIM.

ANAKIM (An′a·kim) [Those of (Belonging to) Anak]. A race of people of extraordinary size who inhabited the mountainous regions of Canaan as well as some coastal areas, particularly in the S thereof. At one time three prominent men of the Anakim, that is, Ahiman, Sheshai, and Talmai, resided at Hebron. (Nu 13:22) It was here that the 12 Hebrew spies first saw the Anakim, and 10 of the spies subsequently gave a frightening report of the experience, alleging that these men were descendants of the pre-Flood Nephilim and that, by comparison with them, the Hebrews were like "grasshoppers." (Nu 13:28-33; De 1:28) Their great stature caused them to be used as a standard of comparison in describing even the giantlike men of the Emim and the Rephaim. Their strength apparently produced the proverbial saying: "Who can make a firm stand before the sons of Anak?"—De 2:10, 11, 20, 21; 9:1-3.

In Joshua's rapid sweep through Canaan, he gained victories over the Anakim in the mountainous regions, destroying their cities, but others remained in the Philistine cities of Gaza, Ashdod, and Gath. Whether the Anakim were related to the Philistines, as some suggest, or were only associated with them is not stated in the record. (Jos 11:21, 22) Later, Caleb requested the city of Hebron (Kiriath-arba) and its territory, as promised him by God. (Jos 14:12-15; Nu 14:24) It appears that the Anakim had reestablished themselves in this area, perhaps while Joshua and his army were continuing their conquest in the northern parts of Canaan, and hence Caleb was now obliged to reconquer the territory.—Jg 1:10, 20.

Egyptian execration texts (from pottery on which the names of enemies of the pharaoh were written and which was then broken as a curse) might make reference to a tribe of Anak in Palestine as *Iy-'anaq*.

ANAMIM (An′a·mim). Hamitic descendants of Mizraim. Since Mizraim became synonymous with Egypt, it is probable that the Anamim settled there or in that area. (Ge 10:13; 1Ch 1:11) A cuneiform text of the time of Sargon II of Assyria (second half of the eighth century B.C.E.) apparently refers to them under the name "Anami."

ANAMMELECH (A·nam′me·lech) [possibly from Babylonian, meaning "Anu Is King"]. A deity of the Sepharvites that proved unable to deliver them from the Assyrian aggressors. (2Ki 18:34) The worship of Anammelech included the revolting practice of child sacrifice.—2Ki 17:31.

ANAN (A′nan) [possibly, Cloud]. One of the heads of the people of Israel, whose representative, if not he himself, together with Nehemiah and others, sealed the nation's resolution to serve Jehovah faithfully (455 B.C.E.).—Ne 10:1, 26.

ANANI (A·na′ni) [possibly a shortened form of Ananiah]. A son of Elioenai; a postexilic descendant of King David.—1Ch 3:24.

ANANIAH (A·na·ni′ah) [Jah Has Answered Me].

1. Father of Maaseiah and grandfather to Azariah, who assisted Nehemiah in rebuilding the walls of Jerusalem.—Ne 3:23.

2. A city inhabited by members of the tribe of Benjamin after the return from exile. (Ne 11:32) It is believed to be the same as Bethany (el-'Azariyeh [El 'Eizariya]) 2.5 km (1.5 mi) ESE of the Temple Mount in Jerusalem.—See BETHANY No. 1.

ANANIAS (An·a·ni′as) [Gr. form of the Heb. name Hananiah, meaning "Jehovah Has Shown Favor; Jehovah Has Been Gracious"].

1. A member of the early Christian congregation of Jerusalem. Following Pentecost of 33 C.E. the physical needs of the believers who remained in Jerusalem were cared for by mutual assistance among the Christians. A common fund was set up for this purpose. It was sustained by contributions representing the price of fields and houses sold by members of the congregation and then voluntarily donated. (Ac 4:34-37) Ananias sold a field and, with his wife's full knowledge, presented a part of the money obtained, while giving the appearance of turning in the entire sum, no doubt to gain a measure of commendation and esteem within the congregation. However, through a special gift of knowledge by the spirit, Peter discerned his pretense, exposed him as 'playing false to the holy spirit and to God,' and Ananias fell down and expired. When the men who buried him returned in about three hours, they found his wife Sapphira also dead for having tried to keep up the same false pretense.—Ac 5:1-10.

2. A Christian disciple of Damascus. Following the conversion of Saul, Ananias was given a vision in which Jesus gave him Saul's name and address with instructions to visit him. Though at first hesitant because he knew of Saul's fiery persecution of the Christians, Ananias thereafter responded and went to Saul, caused him to recover his sight, informed him of his commission to be God's witness, and arranged for his baptism. Saul (Paul), in a later defense before opposing Jews, referred to Ananias as a man "reverent according to the Law, well reported on by all the Jews dwelling there [in Damascus]." In view of his being a Christian, such Jewish commendation was indeed a remarkable testimony to his right conduct.—Ac 9:10-18; 22:12-16.

3. Jewish high priest from about 48 to 58 C.E. He was the son of Nedebaeus and was appointed to office by Herod, king of Chalcis, the brother of Herod Agrippa I. (Josephus' *Jewish Antiquities,* XX, 103 [v, 2]) He was sent to Rome in 52 C.E. to stand trial because of certain difficulties that had arisen between the Jews and the Samaritans, but he was acquitted by Claudius I, the emperor.

In about 56 C.E., while presiding at Paul's trial before the Sanhedrin, Ananias ordered Paul to be struck in the face. Paul reacted to this by predicting that God would repay such wrong action, and he referred to Ananias as a "whitewashed wall." Called to account for this, Paul excused himself as being unaware of the fact that the source of the order to strike him was the high priest and quoted Exodus 22:28 in acknowledgment of his obligation to show due respect. Some suggest that Paul's plea of ignorance was because Ananias' position as high priest was not legally certain after his return from Rome, but proof for this is not substantial. It could be simply an additional evidence of poor eyesight on Paul's part, as appears to be indicated in other texts. Ananias' command may have been brief enough and sufficiently charged with emotion to make it difficult for Paul to identify the speaker.—Ac 23:2-5.

Following the Sanhedrin trial Ananias, accompanied by certain older men and a public orator, traveled to Caesarea to press charges against Paul before Governor Felix. (Ac 24:1) No further mention of him is made in the Scriptural record. Secular history, however, represents him as a haughty and cruel person, whose conduct, both during his high priesthood and in the years following his removal, was marked by greed. Toward the beginning of the Jewish revolt of 66-70 C.E., Ananias was pursued by elements of the Jewish population because of his collaboration with the Roman authorities. Though hiding out in an aqueduct, he was discovered and murdered.

ANATH (A′nath).

1. The father of one of Israel's judges, Shamgar. —Jg 3:31; 5:6.

2. One of the three principal Canaanite goddesses. She is presented both as the sister and spouse of Baal and as a symbol of lustful sex and war. There is no evidence, however, to show that the name of Shamgar's father was drawn from that of the goddess Anath, although the apostasies of Israel during this period could allow for that. —Compare the case of Gideon at Jg 6:25-27.

ANATHOTH (An′a·thoth).

1. A Benjamite, son of Becher.—1Ch 7:8.

2. One of the heads of the people whose descendant, if not he himself, attested to and sealed

a trustworthy arrangement in the days of Nehemiah, to walk in the path of true worship of Jehovah.—Ne 9:38; 10:1, 19.

3. A Levite city in the territory of Benjamin. (Jos 21:17, 18; 1Ch 6:60) The name continues in that of the small village of 'Anata under 5 km (3 mi) NNE of Jerusalem, while the original site has been identified with Ras el-Kharrubeh about 800 m (0.5 mi) to the SW of the village. From its position on the hills, a view can be had of the Jordan Valley and the northern part of the Salt Sea. Anathoth was the home of two of David's mighty men. (2Sa 23:27; 1Ch 12:3) It was to Anathoth that Solomon banished Abiathar, thus bringing to an end the line of high priests from the house of Eli. (1Ki 2:26) Anathoth was one of the afflicted cities in the line of attack of invading Assyrian armies.—Isa 10:30.

Jeremiah was from Anathoth but became a 'prophet without honor' among his own people, as they threatened his life for speaking Jehovah's message of truth. (Jer 1:1; 11:21-23; 29:27) As a result, Jehovah foretold calamity for the city, and this came in due time when Babylon overran the land. (Jer 11:21-23) Prior to Jerusalem's fall, Jeremiah exercised his legal rights to purchase his cousin's tract of land at Anathoth as a sign that there would be a restoration from exile. (Jer 32:7-9) Among the first group of those returning from exile with Zerubbabel were 128 men of Anathoth; and Anathoth is included among the towns that were resettled, thus fulfilling Jeremiah's prophecy.—Ezr 2:23; Ne 7:27; 11:32.

ANATHOTHITE (An'a·thoth·ite) [Of (Belonging to) Anathoth]. An inhabitant of Anathoth, a priestly city in the territory of Benjamin.—2Sa 23:27; 1Ch 11:28; 12:3; 27:12.

ANCHOR. See SHIP.

ANCIENT OF DAYS. A translation of the Aramaic expression 'at·tiq' yoh·min', which indicates "one advanced (or aged) in days." This title of Jehovah appears only at Daniel 7:9, 13, and 22 and alternates with the title "Supreme One." (Da 7:18, 22, 25, 27) The scene is a courtroom where the Ancient of Days sits to judge the world powers, described under the symbolism of huge beasts. Their lease of rulership over the earth is taken away, and the "rulership and dignity and kingdom" are given to one "like a son of man" to whom all peoples are commanded to render obedience. —Da 7:10-14.

The title "Ancient of Days" appropriately contrasts the everlasting God with the successive world powers that rise and fall, and it portrays Jehovah in his role as the majestic and venerable Judge of all.—Ps 90:2; 75:7.

ANDREW (An'drew) [from a Gr. root meaning "man; male person"; probably, Manly]. A brother of Simon Peter and son of Jonah (John). (Mt 4:18; 16:17) While Andrew's native city was Bethsaida, he and Simon were living together in Capernaum at the time Jesus called them to become "fishers of men." (Mr 1:16, 17, 21, 29; Joh 1:44) Both cities were on the N shore of the Sea of Galilee, where the two brothers engaged in the fishing business in partnership with James and John.—Mt 4:18; Mr 1:16; Lu 5:10.

Andrew was first a disciple of John the Baptizer. (Joh 1:35, 40) In the fall of 29 C.E. he was at Bethany on the E side of the Jordan River and heard John the Baptizer introduce Jesus as "the Lamb of God." (Joh 1:29) He, along with another disciple (likely John), followed Jesus to his residence and was soon convinced he had found the Messiah. He then found and informed his brother Simon and led him to Jesus. (Joh 1:36-41) The two brothers returned to their fishing business, but between six months and a year later, after the arrest of John the Baptizer, they, along with James and John, were invited by Jesus to become "fishers of men." They immediately abandoned their nets and began accompanying Jesus. (Mt 4:18-20; Mr 1:14, 16-20) In time these four became apostles, and it is notable that Andrew is always listed as among the first four in all the apostolic lists.—Mt 10:2; Mr 3:18; Lu 6:14.

Andrew thereafter receives but brief mention. He and Philip discuss with Jesus the problem of feeding a crowd of about 5,000 men, and Andrew offers a suggestion that he himself considers of little practical value about some available food. (Joh 6:8, 9) At the time of the last Passover festival that they celebrated, Philip comes to Andrew for advice about a request of some Greeks to see Jesus, and the two then approach Jesus on the matter. (Joh 12:20-22) He is among the four on the Mount of Olives who ask Jesus for the sign that would mark the conclusion of the existing system of things. (Mr 13:3) The final mention of Andrew by name is shortly after Jesus' ascension.—Ac 1:13.

ANDRONICUS (An·dron'i·cus) [Man-Conquering]. A faithful Jewish Christian in the congregation at Rome to whom Paul sent greetings. Paul calls Andronicus and Junias "my relatives." While the Greek word used here (syg·ge·nes') in its broader sense can mean "fellow-countrymen," the primary meaning is "blood relatives of the same generation." The context indicates that Andronicus likely was so related to Paul. Like Paul, Andronicus had suffered imprisonment, was now a 'man of note' among the apostles, and had become a Christian prior to Paul.—Ro 16:7.

ANEM (A'nem). A city near the S border of Issachar, given as a Levite city to the Gershonites. (1Ch 6:71, 73) In the corresponding list at Joshua 21:29, Anem appears to be referred to as Engannim, probably the complete name.—See ENGANNIM No. 2.

ANER (A'ner).

1. A Canaanite. He and his two brothers, Mamre the Amorite and Eshcol, were "confederates" ("allies," *AT; RS*) of Abraham. (Ge 14:13) The word "confederates" is here translated from the Hebrew *ba·'aleh' verith'*, which literally means "owners (masters) of the covenant"; but "confederate" is from the Latin *confoederatus,* meaning "united," or "joined by a league," and hence properly translates the idea, the word *foedus* occurring in Genesis 14:13 in the Latin *Vulgate.* As to the terms of this agreement between these three brothers and Abraham, little indication is given in the record as to whether it was one of mutual defense against their warlike neighbors or simply one of peaceful coexistence. When Abraham's nephew Lot was taken captive by a league of kings, this confederacy saw action, as Aner with his brothers accompanied Abraham and his 318 trained servants from the big trees of Mamre (where Abraham was tenting) up to Dan, about 200 km (120 mi) to the NNE, and then on beyond Damascus. After the victory, Abraham refused any part of the spoil but saw to it that the three confederates were given a share for honoring this "confederacy."—Ge 14:24; see ALLIANCE.

2. A town of the territory of Manasseh given to the families of the sons of Kohath. (1Ch 6:70; Jos 21:26) Some scholars believe it is the same as Taanach at Joshua 21:25.—See TAANACH.

ANGEL.

Both the Hebrew *mal·'akh'* and the Greek *ag'ge·los* literally mean "messenger." From the first book of the Bible to the last, these words occur nearly 400 times. When spirit messengers are indicated, the words are translated "angels," but if the reference definitely is to human creatures, the rendering is "messengers." (Ge 16:7; 32:3; Jas 2:25; Re 22:8; see MESSENGER.) However, in the highly symbolic book of Revelation certain references to 'angels' may apply to human creatures.—Re 2:1, 8, 12, 18; 3:1, 7, 14.

Angels are sometimes termed spirits; that which is spirit is invisible and powerful. Thus we read: "A spirit came out and stood before Jehovah"; "Are they not all spirits for public service?" (1Ki 22:21; Heb 1:14) Having invisible spiritual bodies, they make their abode "in the heavens." (Mr 12:25; 1Co 15:44, 50) They are also termed "sons of the true God," "morning stars," and "holy myriads" (or "holy ones").—Job 1:6; 2:1; 38:7; De 33:2.

Not being creatures that marry and reproduce their own kind, the angels were individually created by Jehovah through his firstborn Son, "the beginning of the creation by God." (Mt 22:30; Re 3:14) "By means of him [this firstborn Son, the Word] all other things were created in the heavens . . . the things invisible . . . Also, he is before all other things and by means of him all other things were made to exist." (Col 1:15-17; Joh 1:1-3) The angels were created long before man's appearance, for at the 'founding of the earth' "the morning stars joyfully cried out together, and all the sons of God began shouting in applause."—Job 38:4-7.

As for the number of the angelic hosts of heaven, Daniel said he saw "a thousand thousands that kept ministering to [God], and ten thousand times ten thousand that kept standing right before him."—Da 7:10; Heb 12:22; Jude 14.

Order and Rank. As with the visible creation, so also in the invisible realm there is order and rank among the angels. The foremost angel, both in power and authority, is Michael, the archangel. (Da 10:13, 21; 12:1; Jude 9; Re 12:7; see ARCHANGEL; MICHAEL No. 1.) Because of his preeminence and his being called "the great prince who is standing in behalf of the sons of [God's] people," he is presumed to be the angel that led Israel through the wilderness. (Ex 23:20-23) Ranking very high among the angels in privileges and honor are the seraphs. (Isa 6:2, 6; see SERAPHS.) More frequently (some 90 times), the Scriptures mention the cherubs, and from the description of their duties and responsibilities it is apparent that they, too, hold a special position among the angels. (Ge 3:24; Eze 10:1-22; see CHERUB No. 1.) Then there is the great body of angelic messengers who serve as a means of communication between God and man. However, they do more than simply relay messages. As agents and deputies of the Most High God, they serve as responsible executioners of the divine purpose, be it protection and deliverance of God's people or destruction of the wicked.—Ge 19:1-26.

Personality. Some may deny distinct personality of individual angels, claiming they are impersonal forces of energy dispatched to accomplish the will of God, but the Bible teaches otherwise. Individual names imply individuality. The fact that two of their names, Michael and Gabriel, are given establishes the point sufficiently. (Da 12:1; Lu 1:26) The lack of more names was a safeguard against giving undue honor and worship to these creatures. Angels were dispatched by God as agents to act in his name, not in their own name. Hence, when Jacob asked an angel for his name, he refused to give it. (Ge 32:29) The angel that approached Joshua, when asked to identify himself, replied only that he was "prince of the army of Jehovah." (Jos 5:14) When Samson's parents asked an angel for his name, he withheld it, saying: "Just why should you ask about my name, when it is a wonderful one?" (Jg 13:17, 18) The apostle John attempted to worship angels and was twice rebuked: "Be careful! Do not do that! . . . Worship God."—Re 19:10; 22:8, 9.

As personalities, angels have the power to communicate with one another (1Co 13:1), the ability to talk various languages of men (Nu 22:32-35; Da 4:23; Ac 10:3-7), and the thinking ability with which to glorify and praise Jehovah (Ps 148:2; Lu 2:13). It is true that angels are sexless, because Jehovah made them so, not because they are impersonal forces. Angels are generally represented as males, and when materializing it was always in the male form, because God and his Son are spoken of as males. However, when certain materialized angels indulged in the pleasure of sex in the days of Noah, they were expelled from Jehovah's heavenly courts. Here was a display of angelic individuality, for, like humankind, they too are free moral agents, with the power of personal choice between right and wrong. (Ge 6:2, 4; 2Pe 2:4) By personal choice, hordes of angels joined Satan in his rebellion.—Re 12:7-9; Mt 25:41.

Powers and Privileges. Since God created man "a little lower than angels" (Heb 2:7), it follows that angels have a greater mental capacity than man. They are superhuman in power too. "Bless Jehovah, O you angels of his, mighty in power, carrying out his word." Angelic knowledge and power were displayed when two angels brought flaming destruction upon Sodom and Gomorrah. A single angel killed 185,000 of the Assyrian army.—Ps 103:20; Ge 19:13, 24; 2Ki 19:35.

Angels too can travel at tremendous speeds, far exceeding the limits of the physical world. Thus when Daniel was praying, God dispatched an angel to answer his prayer; and the angel arrived within moments, even before the prayer was concluded.—Da 9:20-23.

But for all their higher mental and spiritual powers, angels have their limitations. They did not know the "day and hour" when this system of things would be swept away, Jesus said. (Mt 24:36) They take a keen interest in the outworking of Jehovah's purposes, yet there are some things they do not understand. (1Pe 1:12) They rejoice at the repentance of a sinner, and they watch the "theatrical spectacle" furnished by Christians here on the world stage of public activity. They also observe the proper example of Christian women who wear a sign of authority upon their heads. —Lu 15:10; 1Co 4:9; 11:10; see IMMORTALITY (Kingdom Heirs Granted Immortality).

As Jehovah's ministers, the angels have enjoyed many privileges during the aeons of passing time. Angels ministered on behalf of Abraham, Jacob, Moses, Joshua, Isaiah, Daniel, Zechariah, Peter, Paul, and John, to mention but a few. (Ge 22:11; 31:11; Jos 5:14, 15; Isa 6:6, 7; Da 6:22; Zec 1:9; Ac 5:19, 20; 7:35; 12:7, 8; 27:23, 24; Re 1:1) Their messages contributed toward the writing of the Bible. In Revelation angels are mentioned far more times than in any other Bible book. Innumerable angels were seen around the great throne of Jehovah; seven blew the seven trumpets, while another seven poured out the seven bowls of God's anger; an angel flying in midheaven had "everlasting good news"; but another proclaimed, "Babylon the Great has fallen."—Re 5:11; 7:11; 8:6; 14:6, 8; 16:1.

Support of Christ and followers. From beginning to end, the holy angels of God followed the earthly sojourn of Jesus with extreme interest. They announced his conception and birth, and they ministered to him after the 40-day fast. An angel strengthened him when he prayed in Gethsemane on his final night as a human. When the mob came to arrest him, he could have called for no less than 12 legions of angels had he chosen to do so. Angels also announced his resurrection and were present at his ascension into heaven.—Mt 4:11; 26:53; 28:5-7; Lu 1:30, 31; 2:10, 11; 22:43; Ac 1:10, 11.

Thereafter, God's spirit messengers continued ministering to his servants on earth, even as Jesus promised: "Do not despise one of these little ones; for I tell you that their angels in heaven always behold the face of my Father." (Mt 18:10) "Are they not all spirits for public service, sent forth to minister for those who are going to inherit salvation?" (Heb 1:14) No longer do these mighty angelic ones appear visibly in behalf of Jehovah's servants on earth, as when they delivered the apostles from prison; nevertheless, God's servants are assured of the ever-present, invisible protecting armies, as real as those that surrounded the prophet Elisha and his servant. "He will give his own angels a command concerning you, to guard you in all your ways." Yes, "the angel of Jehovah is camping all around those fearing him, and he rescues them."—Ps 91:11; 34:7; Ac 5:19; 2Ki 6:15-17.

Angels are further shown accompanying Jesus Christ when he comes for judgment, separating "the wheat" from "the weeds" and "the sheep" from "the goats." Angels joined with Michael in his war on the dragon and the demons at the birth of God's Kingdom in heaven. They will also support the King of kings in fighting the war of the great day of God the Almighty.—Mt 13:41; 25:31-33; Re 12:7-10; 19:14-16.

ANGER. In the Bible several different Hebrew and Greek words are used to denote anger. The most common Hebrew word for anger is 'aph, basically meaning "nose; nostril" but often used figuratively for "anger" because of the violent breathing or snorting of an enraged person. (Compare Ps 18:7; Eze 38:18.) Related to 'aph is 'a·naph', meaning "be incensed." Anger is also often associated in the Hebrew Scriptures with heat and thus is said to blaze. Other Hebrew words are rendered "rage," "fury," and "indignation." In the Christian Greek Scriptures orge' is generally translated "wrath," while thy·mos' is usually rendered "anger."

God's Anger. Anger may be justified or unjustified. On God's part, his anger is always justified, being based on principle dictated by his right to exclusive devotion and his constancy in upholding truth; it is governed by his love for righteousness and for those practicing righteousness. Divine anger does not stem from a momentary whim, to be later regretted. Jehovah sees all the issues involved in a matter and has complete, entire knowledge of a situation. (Heb 4:13) He reads the heart; he notes the degree of ignorance, negligence, or willful sin; and he acts with impartiality.—De 10:17, 18; 1Sa 16:7; Ac 10:34, 35.

Principles controlling divine wrath. God's anger is always under control and in harmony with his attributes of love, wisdom, and justice. Because of his almighty power it is expressible to the degree he desires. (1Jo 4:8; Job 12:13; 37:23) God's anger is not futile. It is fully based on sufficient cause and always takes effect. His anger is satisfied and quieted only by the application of his principles. For example, in Israel a willful murderer could not be ransomed. Only by the shedding of his blood could the land be cleansed and freed from God's displeasure. (Nu 35:16-18,

30-33) But an arrangement was made on the basis of sacrifices and the services of the high priest to satisfy justice and to allay the anger of the God-ordained avenger of blood, whose heart may have been "hot." This was the provision of the cities of refuge.—De 19:4-7.

The anger of Jehovah can be allayed or satisfied only when justice is fully carried out. God's wrath is against all unrighteousness. He will not tolerate unrighteousness or exempt from punishment one deserving it. (Ex 34:7; Hab 1:13) However, on the basis of the sacrifice of Jesus Christ, who bore the pains and chastisement justly due mankind, God's anger may be relieved and turned away for those who come to exercise faith. (Isa 53:5) By means of this arrangement, Jehovah God is able to exhibit his own righteousness, "that he might be righteous even when declaring righteous the man that has faith in Jesus." (Ro 3:26) In this way justice is fully satisfied, and yet God has a basis on which to extend mercy. Anyone who is disobedient has the wrath of God remaining upon him. (Joh 3:36) But when a person exercises faith, the sacrifice of Jesus Christ saves him from the wrath of God. —1Th 1:10.

Means for expressing and the causes of anger. God's anger may be expressed directly or indirectly. He may use his laws governing natural things, or he may use other persons as instruments to express his anger. Those who violate his moral laws are under his wrath and receive in themselves "the full recompense, which was due for their error." These suffer a disapproved mental state, degradation, diseases, strife, and death. (Ro 1:18, 24, 27-32) When a person violates laws of the land that are in harmony with God's laws and is punished by the governmental authority, this is an indirect expression of God's wrath against that one. (Ro 13:1-4) Jesus Christ is the chief executioner of God's anger, and he will completely express God's wrath to fulfill his anger against the wicked.—Jer 30:23, 24; Re 19:7-16, 19-21.

Wrong attitudes and actions toward God's chosen ones will provoke his anger. The Egyptians were plagued because of not letting Israel worship Jehovah. (Ps 78:43-50) Miriam and Aaron felt the heat of divine anger because of disrespect for Moses' God-appointed position. (Nu 12:9, 10) Jehovah's anger was against judges who oppressed the lowly. (Isa 10:1-4) Those who hinder the preaching of the good news are in line for God's wrath. —1Th 2:16.

Jehovah is provoked to anger by false worship, especially when his professed people turn away to other gods. (Ex 32:7-10; Nu 25:3, 4; Jg 2:13, 14, 20; 1Ki 11:8, 9) His anger is aroused by immorality, suppression of the truth, unrepentance, disobedience to the good news, the despising of his words, mocking at his prophets, covetousness, injuriousness, envy, murder, strife, deceit, malicious disposition; by those who are whisperers, backbiters, haters of God, insolent, haughty, self-assuming, inventors of injurious things, disobedient to parents, false to agreements, merciless, spiritists, and liars. All of these and the practice of any other unrighteousness provoke God's anger. —Col 3:5, 6; 2Th 1:8; Ro 1:18, 29-31; 2:5, 8; 2Ch 36:15, 16; Re 22:15.

Anger not a dominant quality. However, Jehovah God is "slow to anger and abundant in loving-kindness." (Ex 34:6; Nu 14:18) If one fears Jehovah and works righteousness, he will receive mercy from Jehovah, for the Almighty recognizes man's inherited imperfection and shows mercy to him on this account and on the basis of Jesus' sacrifice. (Ps 103:13, 14; Ge 8:21; see also Zep 2:2, 3.) He checks his anger in behalf of his name and in order to carry out his purpose toward his chosen people. (Isa 48:9; Joe 2:13, 14) Jehovah's anger in time passes from those who truly serve him, acknowledge their sin, and repent. (Isa 12:1; Ps 30:5) He is not an angry God but a happy God, not unapproachable but pleasant, peaceful, and calm toward those who properly approach his presence. (1Ti 1:11; Ps 16:11; compare Re 4:3.) This is in contrast to the angry, merciless, cruel characteristics ascribed to the false gods of the pagans and portrayed in images of these gods.

What place does anger have in the life of a servant of God?

Man's expression of anger may be proper if it is based on principle. One may rightly express righteous indignation. We are commanded to "abhor what is wicked." (Ro 12:9) The Bible provides numerous examples of righteous indignation.—Ex 11:8; 32:19; Nu 16:12-15; 1Sa 20:34; Ne 5:6; Es 7:7; see also 2Sa 12:1-6.

However, the anger of man is more often unjustified and is many times uncontrolled. It is often based on insufficient cause and expressed without due regard for the consequences. After Jehovah had spared Nineveh, Jonah was displeased, "and he got to be hot with anger." Jonah lacked mercy and had to be corrected by Jehovah. (Jon 4:1-11) King Uzziah of Judah became enraged when corrected by the priests of Jehovah and went ahead in his presumptuous course, for which he was punished. (2Ch 26:16-21) Naaman's ill-advised pride caused indignation and rage on his part,

almost resulting in the loss of a blessing from God. —2Ki 5:10-14.

Vital need for control. Unjustified and uncontrolled anger has led many persons into greater sin, even acts of violence. "Cain grew hot with great anger" and slew Abel. (Ge 4:5, 8) Esau wanted to kill Jacob, who received the blessing of their father. (Ge 27:41-45) Saul in his rage hurled spears at David and Jonathan. (1Sa 18:11; 19:10; 20:30-34) Those in attendance at the synagogue in Nazareth, aroused to anger by Jesus' preaching, endeavored to hurl him from the brow of a mountain. (Lu 4:28, 29) Angered religious leaders "rushed upon [Stephen] with one accord" and stoned him to death.—Ac 7:54-60.

Anger, even when justified, if not controlled, may be dangerous, producing bad results. Simeon and Levi had reason to be indignant at Shechem for violating their sister Dinah, though some of the blame was hers. But the wanton slaughter of the Shechemites was an excessive penalty to inflict. Hence their father Jacob denounced their uncontrolled anger, cursing it. (Ge 34:1-31; 49:5-7) When under heavy provocation a person should control his anger. The complaint and rebelliousness of the Israelites provoked Moses, the meekest man on the earth, to an uncontrolled act of anger in which he failed to sanctify Jehovah, and for which he was punished.—Nu 12:3; 20:10-12; Ps 106:32, 33.

Fits of anger are classified along with other detestable works of the flesh, such as loose conduct, idolatry, practice of spiritism, and drunken bouts. Such will keep one from inheriting God's Kingdom. (Ga 5:19-21) Angry talk is to be kept out of the congregation. Men representing the congregation in prayer should be free from feelings of anger and ill will. (1Ti 2:8) Christians are commanded to be slow about wrath, being told that man's wrath does not work out God's righteousness. (Jas 1:19, 20) They are counseled to "yield place to the wrath" and to leave vengeance to Jehovah. (Ro 12:19) A man cannot be used as an overseer in the congregation of God if he is prone to wrath.—Tit 1:7.

While a person may on occasion be angry and sometimes justifiably so, he should not let it become sin to him by harboring it or maintaining a provoked state. He should not let the sun set with him in such a condition, for he would thereby allow place for the Devil to take advantage of him. (Eph 4:26, 27) Especially if it is a case of anger between Christian brothers, he should take proper steps to make peace or get the matter settled in the God-provided way. (Le 19:17, 18; Mt 5:23, 24;

18:15; Lu 17:3, 4) The Scriptures counsel that we should watch our associations in this regard, not having companionship with anyone given to anger or fits of rage, thereby avoiding a snare for our souls.—Pr 22:24, 25.

Jesus Christ, when a man on earth, gave us the perfect example. The records of his life do not recount one occasion where he had a fit of uncontrolled anger or where he allowed the lawlessness, rebelliousness, and harassment of the enemies of God to upset his spirit and cause him to reflect such a thing toward his followers or others. On one occasion he was "thoroughly grieved" at the insensibility of the hearts of the Pharisees and looked upon them with indignation. His next act was an act of healing. (Mr 3:5) When he, in another instance, drove out those who were defiling God's temple as well as violating the Law of Moses by making Jehovah's house a house of merchandise, it was through no uncontrolled, unjustified fit of anger. Rather, the Scriptures show that it was properly directed zeal for the house of Jehovah. —Joh 2:13-17.

Avoiding the damaging effects. Not only does anger have an adverse effect upon our spiritual health but it produces profound effects on the physical organism. It can cause rise in blood pressure, arterial changes, respiratory trouble, liver upsets, changes in the secretion of gall, effects on the pancreas. Anger and rage, as strong emotions, have been listed by physicians as contributing to, aggravating, or even causing such ailments as asthma, eye afflictions, skin diseases, hives, ulcers, and dental and digestive troubles. Rage and fury can upset thinking processes so that one cannot form logical conclusions or pass sound judgment. The aftermath of a fit of rage is often a period of extreme mental depression. It is therefore wisdom not only in a religious sense but in a physical sense to keep anger under control and to pursue peace and love.—Pr 14:29, 30; Ro 14:19; Jas 3:17; 1Pe 3:11.

According to the Scriptures, the time of the end is a time of rage and fury, with the nations becoming angry at Jehovah's taking over his power to reign, and the Devil being hurled to the earth, "having great anger, knowing he has a short period of time." (Re 11:17, 18; 12:10-12) With such strenuous conditions, the Christian will do well to control his spirit, avoiding the destructive emotion of anger.—Pr 14:29; Ec 7:9.

ANIAM   (A·ni'am) [I Am [of the] People [that is, a kinsman]]. A son of Shemida of the tribe of Manasseh.—1Ch 7:14, 19.

ANIM   (A'nim). A city in the mountainous region of southern Judah, mentioned in the distribution of land in the days of Joshua. (Jos 15:48, 50) It has been identified with Khirbet Ghuwein et-Tahta (Horvat 'Anim), a double ruin situated about 5 km (3 mi) S of Eshtemoa and about 19 km (12 mi) SSW of Hebron.

ANIMALS.   Living souls that are not human. (Compare Nu 31:28.) The Hebrew word *behe·mah'* refers to larger four-footed creatures, usually domestic animals but occasionally wild beasts. It is rendered "domestic animals," "beasts," "livestock," and "cattle." (Ge 1:26; 9:10; 34:23; Ps 107:38) The Hebrew *re'mes* denotes "moving animals" or "creeping things" and comes from the root *ra·mas'*, meaning "move; creep." (Ge 6:20; Eze 8:10; Ge 1: 28, ftn) Also, the Hebrew term *chai·yah'*, literally meaning "living creature," is used to refer to "wild beasts" or "wild animals." (Ge 1:28; 3:14; Isa 56:9) The parallel Greek term *zo'on* (living creature), also rendered 'animal.'—Re 4:7; 2Pe 2:12.

Jehovah God formed all the animals, each family kind having its own originally created representatives, for the record assures us that God made them each one "according to its kind." (Ge 1:25) In this article we shall consider particularly land animals.

In view of God's granting perfect man dominion over the various creatures of the earth, it was most appropriate that Adam be privileged to name these creatures. (Ge 1:26; 2:19, 20) Man's having the animals in subjection placed upon him a stewardship for which he would always be accountable to God.—Lu 12:48.

Animals were so created that they would have a fear and dread of man as their superior. (Ge 9:2, 3) According to naturalists, wild creatures, such as the leopard and the king cobra, normally prefer to retreat from man's presence, although they do attack when provoked, wounded, cornered, or suddenly surprised. It has been suggested that tigers become man-eaters, for example, by force of circumstances, such as old age or injury that would greatly limit the tiger's ability to procure its normal game, or the depletion of the tiger's game through man's hunting.

Already prior to the Flood, animals were killed to provide clothing for man and for sacrificial purposes. (Ge 3:21; 4:4) However, not until after the Deluge did Noah and his family receive permission from Jehovah to add flesh to their diet, with the stipulation that it must be drained of its blood. (Ge 9:3, 4) While this made it proper for man to kill animals for necessary food, he was not authorized thereby to indulge in needless slaughter for the sheer thrill of the hunt or to display personal prowess, as Nimrod, the rebel against God, undoubtedly did.—Ge 10:9.

Some have contended that the presence of animals on isolated islands like Australia and New Zealand is an indication that not all land animals outside the ark perished in the Deluge. However, the findings of oceanographers indicate that at one time land ridges connected what are now isolated land areas. For example, oceanographic studies indicate that the Mid-Atlantic Ridge may have crossed that ocean above the surface. Possibly there were also other ridges, and animals could have migrated by means of these before such ridges sank below the surface of the ocean. Other oceanographic studies have turned up evidence that once there existed a huge South Pacific continent that took in Australia and many of the South Sea isles. If such was the case, then, of course, the animals had no difficulty in migrating to these lands.

Clean and Unclean Animals. A classification of animals is to be noted in God's instructions to Noah to take with him into the ark seven of each clean animal and two of each unclean animal. (Ge 7:2, 3, 8, 9) Since a flesh diet had not yet been authorized, this distinction between clean and unclean was probably determined on the basis of what was acceptable to Jehovah as a sacrifice. Hence, on emerging from the ark, Noah knew which creatures were clean and suitable for offering upon the altar. (Ge 8:20) At that time no restriction existed with respect to the type of animals that Noah and his family could eat, as is indicated by Jehovah's words: *"Every* moving animal that is alive may serve as food for you."—Ge 9:3.

God's law to the Israelites, therefore, introduced a new distinction when it classified certain animals as clean and fit for food and others as unclean and prohibited as food. The scripture specifies: "Every creature that splits the hoof and forms a cleft in the hoofs and chews the cud among the beasts, that is what you may eat." (Le 11:3) And again: "You must eat no detestable thing of any sort. This is the sort of beast that you may eat: the bull, the sheep and the goat, the stag and gazelle and roebuck and wild goat and antelope and wild sheep and chamois; and every beast that splits the hoof and that forms a cleft into two hoofs, chewing the cud among the beasts."—De 14:3-6.

Animals lacking one or both of the above-mentioned features were not to be eaten by those under the terms of the Law covenant. The prohibited animals included the rock badger, the hare,

the pig, the camel. Also, creatures 'going upon their paws' were prohibited, this doubtless embracing such creatures as the lion, the bear, and the wolf.—Le 11:4-8, 26, 27; De 14:7, 8.

These dietary limitations applied only to those who were under the Mosaic Law, for the statement of Leviticus 11:8 is: "They are unclean for you," that is, for the Israelites. With the abrogation of the Law on the basis of the sacrificial death of Christ Jesus, the prohibitions were canceled, and once more all humans could consider themselves under the same broad provision announced to Noah following the Deluge.—Col 2:13-17; Ge 9:3, 4.

Since the restriction concerning unclean foods was taken out of the way with the rest of the Law, a question may arise as to why Peter, about three and a half years later, still had not eaten any "unclean" animals. (Ac 10:10-15) It must be remembered that the cancellation of the Law resulted in great changes in the lives of Christ's followers, and therefore, it reasonably took some time for them to appreciate all that was involved.

Illustrative Usage. The outstanding traits of animals are alluded to and used by Bible writers to symbolize a variety of qualities and powers. At times animal features may portray excellent qualities, divine as well as human. (Eze 1:10, 11; Re 4:6, 7) In other instances animals may be employed to represent wild, beastlike ruling powers that oppress and crush peoples.—Da 7:2-7; 8:5-8, 20, 21; Re 13:1-17; see BEASTS, SYMBOLIC.

Proper Use and View of Animal Creation. In connection with worship under the Mosaic Law, cattle, sheep, and goats were among the creatures acceptable for sacrifice. Such animals were to be sound ones, and no castrated animal was admissible. (Le 22:23-25) The use of animal blood for food or for any purpose other than sacrifice was prohibited. (Le 17:13, 14) Worship of any representation of an animal or other created thing was strictly forbidden.—Ex 20:4, 5.

The Bible inculcates just and merciful treatment of the lower creatures. Indeed, Jehovah represents himself as the Loving Provider for their lives and well-being. (Pr 12:10; Ps 145:15, 16) The Mosaic Law enjoined proper care of domestic animals. When found straying, domestic animals were to be returned safely to their owner; when crushed under a burden, they were to be relieved. (Ex 23:4, 5) They were to be worked humanely. (De 22:10; 25:4) They, as well as man, were to benefit from the Sabbath rests. (Ex 20:10; 23:12; De 5:14) Dangerous animals were to be controlled or destroyed. (Ge 9:5; Ex 21:28, 29) Crossbreeding of different sorts was forbidden.—Le 19:19.

God-fearing men see in animals part of God's generous provision for human welfare. Animals have served man as burden bearers, as sources of food and clothing, as sanitation agents, and as helpers in the vital activities of plowing and harvesting. Their variety of form and color has delighted his eye; their habits and instincts have been and still are an extensive field for inquiry into the marvels of God's creative work. Though animals die in the same manner as man, they do not share his hope of a resurrection.—2Pe 2:12; additionally, see individual animals, birds, insects, reptiles by name; also BIRDS; FISH; INSECTS.

ANKLET. The Hebrew words for "ankle chainlets" (*'ets·'a·dhah'*; Nu 31:50) and "step chains" (*tse·'a·dhah'*; Isa 3:20) both come from the root *tsa·'adh'*, meaning "take steps; march." (Jer 10:5; Pr 7:8) The Hebrew *'e'khes* (bangle; anklet) comes from the root *'a·khas'*, meaning "make a tinkling sound" or "shake bangles." (Isa 3:16, 18, ftns) Ankle bracelets or ornamental rings worn on the legs above the ankles were in common use in the ancient Middle East. They were made of such materials as brass, gold, silver, iron, glass, and ivory. On Egyptian monuments persons of both sexes are depicted as wearing them, and in Egypt anklets and bracelets were frequently made as matching ensembles.

Heavy anklets might make a ringing sound as they knocked together while the wearer walked along. However, at times pebbles were placed in hollow bangles or anklets in order to produce a sound, and Arabian girls of more recent times have also occasionally worn anklets with small bells attached to them. Too, ankle chainlets were sometimes fastened to the anklets worn by a woman, thus tying these ornaments together. The chainlets would make tinkling sounds as the wearer walked, and of course, they and the anklets themselves would attract attention. Ankle chainlets or step chains would also restrict or shorten the woman's step, so that she would walk with tripping steps and what might be considered a graceful or genteel feminine gait.—Isa 3:16.

"Ankle chainlets" were among pieces of jewelry the Israelites took from the Midianites as war booty and contributed as "Jehovah's offering." (Nu 31:50, 51) The haughty "daughters of Zion" of later times are described as women who "go walking with tripping steps, and with their feet they make a tinkling sound," or "on their feet they shake bangles." Through Isaiah, Jehovah warned them that he would take away their ornamental articles

and "the beauty of the bangles," or anklets, as well as their "step chains." (Isa 3:16, 18, 20) The Babylonian conquest of Judah and Jerusalem in 607 B.C.E. surely made inroads into the lives of these women, resulting in the loss of their many ornaments and of their freedom.—See ORNAMENTS.

ANNA (An'na) [from Heb., meaning "Favor; Grace"]. A prophetess, daughter of Phanuel of the tribe of Asher. Her name is the Greek form of Hannah.

Anna had become a widow after just seven years of married life and, at the time of the child Jesus' presentation at the temple, was 84 years of age. Nevertheless, she was constant in her attendance at the temple, evidently from the time of the morning service until the evening service and, as a result, was privileged to see the young child Jesus and bear witness about him. Her "fastings and supplications" indicate a mourning attitude and an earnest longing on her part. The centuries-long period of Jewish subjection, coupled with the deteriorating religious conditions that reached even to the temple and its priesthood, could well explain this. At any rate, though she might not have expected to be alive when the child became grown, she now joyfully witnessed to others of the liberation due to be effected through this coming Messiah.—Lu 2:36-38.

ANNAS (An'nas) [from Heb., meaning "Showing Favor; Gracious"].

Appointed high priest about 6 or 7 C.E. by Quirinius, the Roman governor of Syria, and serving until about 15 C.E. (Lu 2:2) Annas was therefore high priest when Jesus, at the age of 12, amazed the rabbinic teachers at the temple. (Lu 2:42-49) For reportedly overstepping his Roman-assigned jurisdiction, Annas was removed as high priest by Procurator Valerius Gratus. Though he no longer had the official title, it was quite evident that he continued to exercise great power and influence as high priest emeritus and predominant voice of the Jewish hierarchy. Five of his sons, as well as his son-in-law Caiaphas, each held the office of high priest. Because of his prominent position, Annas is rightly designated in the Scriptures as one of the chief priests. (Mt 26:3; Lu 3:2) When Jesus was arrested, he was first taken to Annas for questioning and then was sent to Caiaphas for trial. (Joh 18:13) The name of Annas heads the list of the foremost opponents of the apostles of Jesus Christ.—Ac 4:6.

The wealthy and powerful house of Annas was of the tribe of Levi, and the sale of sacrifices within the temple grounds was one of their chief sources of income—reason enough why they sought to kill Jesus, who twice cleansed the temple, which they had made "a cave of robbers." (Joh 2:13-16; Mt 21:12, 13; Mr 11:15-17; Lu 19:45, 46) An additional reason for Annas' hatred of Jesus and his apostles was likely Jesus' teaching of the resurrection, the raising of Lazarus in living proof, and the preaching and teaching of the same doctrine by the apostles, for if Annas was indeed a Sadducee, he did not believe in the resurrection. —Ac 23:8; compare 5:17.

ANOINTED, ANOINTING. The Bible often uses the Hebrew *sukh* and the Greek *a·lei'pho* for the commonplace greasing, or rubbing on of oil. (Da 10:3; Ru 3:3; Joh 11:2) But for a special anointing with oil, it generally uses the Hebrew word *ma·shach'*, from which the word *ma·shi'ach* (Messiah) comes, and the Greek word *khri'o*, from which comes *khri·stos'* (Christ). (Ex 30:30; Le 4:5, ftn; Lu 4:18; Ac 4:26) This distinction is maintained quite consistently both in the Hebrew and in the Greek. Some versions of the Bible do not maintain this fine distinction but translate all such words by the one term "anoint."

Rubbing or Greasing With Oil. In the lands of the Middle East it was a common practice to rub oil on the body, and among other things, this helped to protect the exposed portions from the intense rays of the sun. The oil also helped to keep the skin supple. Olive oil was generally used, and often perfume was added to it. The customary practice was to apply the oil after bathing. (Ru 3:3; 2Sa 12:20) Esther underwent a course of massage treatment for six months with oil of myrrh and for six months with oil of balsam before being presented to King Ahasuerus. (Es 2:12) Oil was also rubbed on the body in preparing a person for burial.—Mr 14:8; Lu 23:56.

When Jesus sent the 12 apostles out by twos, they greased with oil many whom they healed. The healing of the ailment was due to, not the oil itself, but the miraculous operation of God's holy spirit. Oil, which did have some healing and refreshing properties, was symbolic of the healing and refreshing experienced.—Mr 6:13; Lu 9:1; compare Lu 10:34.

Greasing the head with oil was a sign of favor. (Ps 23:5) The headmen of Ephraim took favorable action toward the captured Judean soldiers by greasing them and returning them to Jericho, as advised by the prophet Oded. (2Ch 28:15) Jehovah spoke of bringing about a lack of oil for rubbing as a sign of his displeasure. (De 28:40) To refrain from rubbing one's body with oil was regarded as a sign of mourning. (2Sa 14:2; Da 10:2, 3) To

grease the head of a guest with oil was regarded as an act of hospitality and courtesy, as is indicated by Jesus' words regarding a woman who greased his feet with perfumed oil.—Lu 7:38, 46.

Jesus told his disciples to grease their heads and wash their faces when fasting in order to appear normal, not making a show of sanctimoniousness and self-denial as the hypocritical Jewish religious leaders did to impress others.—Mt 6:16, 17.

James speaks of a spiritual 'greasing with oil' in the name of Jehovah for spiritually sick ones as the proper procedure for one needing spiritual help. That he refers to spiritual sickness is indicated by his statements: "Let him call the older men of the congregation," not doctors, and, "if he has committed sins, it will be forgiven him." (Jas 5:13-16) Jesus makes a spiritual application of the practice when he tells the Laodicean congregation to "buy from me . . . eyesalve to rub in your eyes that you may see."—Re 3:18.

Anointing. When a person was anointed with oil, the oil was put on his head and allowed to run down on his beard and onto the collar of his garments. (Ps 133:2) During the times of Biblical history, both the Hebrews and some of the non-Hebrews ceremonially anointed rulers. This constituted the confirmation of their official appointment to office. (Jg 9:8, 15; 1Sa 9:16; 2Sa 19:10) Samuel anointed Saul as king after God had designated Saul as his choice. (1Sa 10:1) David was anointed as king on three different occasions: once by Samuel, later by the men of Judah, and finally by all the tribes. (1Sa 16:13; 2Sa 2:4; 5:3) Aaron was anointed after his appointment to the office of high priest. (Le 8:12) Afterward, Aaron and his sons had some of the anointing oil along with the blood of the sacrifices spattered upon their garments, but Aaron was the only one who had the oil poured over his head.—Le 8:30.

Things dedicated as sacred were also anointed. Jacob took the stone on which he rested his head when he had an inspired dream, set it up as a pillar, and anointed it, thus marking that place as sacred; and he called the place Bethel, meaning "House of God." (Ge 28:18, 19) A short time later Jehovah acknowledged that this stone had been anointed. (Ge 31:13) In the wilderness of Sinai, at Jehovah's command, Moses anointed the tabernacle and its furnishings, indicating that they were dedicated, holy things.—Ex 30:26-28.

There are instances in which a person was regarded as being anointed because of being appointed by God, even though no oil was put on his head. This principle was demonstrated when Jehovah told Elijah to anoint Hazael as king over

Syria, Jehu as king over Israel, and Elisha as prophet in place of himself. (1Ki 19:15, 16) The Scriptural record goes on to show that one of the sons of the prophets associated with Elisha did anoint Jehu with literal oil, to be king over Israel. (2Ki 9:1-6) But there is no record that anyone anointed with oil either Hazael or Elisha. Moses was called a Christ, or Anointed One, although not anointed with oil, because Moses was appointed by Jehovah to be his prophet and representatve, the leader and deliverer of Israel. (Heb 11:24-26) Another case in point is the Persian king Cyrus, whom Isaiah had foretold that Jehovah would use as His anointed. (Isa 45:1) Cyrus was not actually anointed with oil by one of Jehovah's representatives, but because he was appointed by Jehovah to do a certain work, he could be said to be anointed.

In the Law Jehovah gave to Moses, he prescribed a formula for the anointing oil. It was of a special composition of the choicest ingredients —myrrh, sweet cinnamon, sweet calamus, cassia, and olive oil. (Ex 30:22-25) It was a capital offense for anyone to compound this mixture and to use it for any common or unauthorized purpose. (Ex 30:31-33) This figuratively demonstrated the importance and sacredness of an appointment to office that had been confirmed by anointing with sacred oil.

Fulfilling many prophecies in the Hebrew Scriptures, Jesus of Nazareth proved to be the Anointed One of Jehovah and could properly be called Messiah, or Christ, which titles convey that thought. (Mt 1:16; Heb 1:8, 9) Instead of being anointed with literal oil, he was anointed with Jehovah's spirit. (Mt 3:16) This was Jehovah's appointment of him as King, Prophet, and High Priest, and so he was referred to as Jehovah's Anointed. (Ps 2:2; Ac 3:20-26; 4:26, 27; Heb 5:5, 6) In his hometown of Nazareth, Jesus acknowledged this anointing when he applied to himself the prophecy of Isaiah 61:1, where the phrase appears: "Jehovah has anointed me." (Lu 4:18) Jesus Christ is the only one in the Scriptures who holds an anointing to all three offices: prophet, high priest, and king. Jesus was anointed with "the oil of exultation more than [his] partners" (the other kings of the line of David). This was by reason of his receiving the anointing directly from Jehovah himself, not with oil but with holy spirit, not to an earthly kingship but to a heavenly one combined with the office of heavenly High Priest.—Heb 1:9; Ps 45:7.

Like Jesus, his footstep followers who have been spirit begotten and anointed with holy spirit can be spoken of as anointed ones. (2Co 1:21) Just as Aaron was directly anointed as head of the priesthood, but his sons did not have the oil poured on their heads individually, so Jesus was anointed directly by Jehovah, and his congregation of spiritual brothers receive their anointing as a body of people through Jesus Christ. (Ac 2:1-4, 32, 33) They have thereby received an appointment from God to be kings and priests with Jesus Christ in the heavens. (2Co 5:5; Eph 1:13, 14; 1Pe 1:3, 4; Re 20:6) The apostle John indicated that the anointing by holy spirit that Christians receive teaches them. (1Jo 2:27) It commissions and qualifies them for the Christian ministry of the new covenant.—2Co 3:5, 6.

Jehovah has great love and concern for his anointed ones and watches over them carefully. (1Ch 16:22; Ps 2:2, 5; 20:6; 105:15; Lu 18:7) David recognized that God was the one who chose and appointed His anointed ones and that it was God who would judge them. To raise one's hand to do harm to Jehovah's anointed ones or any whom he appoints would bring Jehovah's displeasure.—1Sa 24:6; 26:11, 23; see CHRIST; INSTALLATION; KING (Divinely appointed representatives); MESSIAH.

ANOINTED ONE. See CHRIST.

ANT [Heb., nema·lah']. A small but extremely numerous and widespread insect, living in colonies, and noted in the Bible for its industriousness and instinctive wisdom. (Pr 6:6-8; 30:24, 25) It is estimated that there are over 10,000 varieties of ants, these insects being found in all parts of the earth with the exception of the polar regions.

"A People." The ants are called "a people" [Heb., 'am] in Proverbs 30:25, even as Joel referred to the locusts as "a nation" (Joe 1:6), and this expression is very suitable for these small creatures. While some ant colonies may contain only a few dozen ants, others have a huge population running into the hundreds of thousands. Although generally of moderate size, the nest or tunneled area may grow until it is as much as an acre in size. Within each colony there are three basic castes: the queen or queens, the males, and the workers (sexually undeveloped females). Yet, as the proverb states, the ant "has no commander, officer or ruler." (Pr 6:7) The queen is not such in a governmental sense and more fittingly can be called the mother ant, for her essential function is that of egg laying. Whereas a queen ant may live as much as 15 years, the males live only long enough to mate and then die. The worker ants, whose life span may reach six years, have various duties to perform, such as searching for and gathering in food for the colony, feeding the queen, acting as nurses for the larvae, cleaning the nest, digging new chambers as expansion is needed, and defending the nest. Worker ants may be of different sizes and proportions, even within the same colony, in some cases the larger ones acting as soldiers in the event of invasion of the nest. Still, despite the fairly precise division of work (which in some colonies is arranged according to the age of the workers and in others according to size) and the relatively complex social organization existent, there is no sign of any superior officer, or taskmaster.

'Instinctive Wisdom.' The 'wisdom' of the ants is not the product of intelligent reasoning but results from the instincts with which they are endowed by their Creator. The Bible makes reference to the ant as 'preparing its food in the summer and gathering its supplies in the harvest.' (Pr 6:8) One of the most common varieties of ants found in Palestine, the harvester, or agricultural, ant (*Messor semirufus*), stores up a large supply of grain in the spring and summer and makes use of it in seasons, including winter, when the obtaining of food becomes difficult. This ant is often found in the vicinity of threshing floors, where seeds and grain are plentiful. If rain causes dampness to reach the stored seeds, the harvester ant will thereafter carry the grains out into the sun for drying. It is even known to bite off the germ part of the seed so that it will not germinate while stored. Colonies of harvester ants are made conspicuous by well-worn paths as well as by seed husks that are left outside the entrance.

Exemplary Characteristics. Thus, a brief investigation of the ant gives force to the exhortation: "Go to the ant, you lazy one; see its ways and become wise." (Pr 6:6) Not only is their instinctive preparing for the future notable but also their persistence and determination, often carrying or tenaciously dragging objects weighing twice their own weight or more, doing everything possible to fulfill their particular task, and refusing to turn back even though they may fall, slide, or roll down some steep precipice. Remarkably cooperative, they keep their nests very clean and show concern for their fellow workers, at times assisting injured or exhausted ants back to the nest.

ANTELOPE [Heb., *di·shon'*]. A cud-chewing animal and a splitter of the hoof, sole mention of which is made at Deuteronomy 14:5, where it is included in the list of animals permitted to the Israelites for food. There is uncertainty as to which animal is meant by the Hebrew word *di·shon'*.

The addax antelope (*Addax nasomaculatus*), still surviving in the desert regions of North Afri-

ca, is often suggested as corresponding to the *di·shon'* of the Hebrew Scriptures. This antelope measures about 1 m (40 in.) high at the shoulder. Its spreading, cloven hooves equip it admirably for travel in the loose sands of the desert, where it can survive without water for extremely long periods. The widespread horns of this animal are twisted like a screw, making from one and a half to nearly three turns, and measuring about 1 m (40 in.) along the curve. With the exception of the belly, tail, hindquarters, and facial markings, which always remain white, the color of the addax antelope becomes darker in winter, changing from a sandy color to brownish. Another possibility is the Arabian oryx (*Oryx gazella leucoryx*), also a desert antelope.

ANTHOTHIJAH (An·tho·thi'jah). A son of Shashak of the tribe of Benjamin.—1Ch 8:24, 25.

ANTICHRIST. This word means "against (or instead of) Christ." It occurs a total of five times, singular and plural, all of them in two of John's epistles.

The subject was not new among the Christians when John wrote his letters (c. 98 C.E.). First John 2:18 states: "Young children, it is the last hour, and, just as you have heard that antichrist [Gr., *an·ti'khri·stos*] is coming, even now there have come to be many antichrists; from which fact we gain the knowledge that it is the last hour." John's statement shows that there are many individual antichrists, though all together they may form a composite person designated "the antichrist." (2Jo 7) The use of the expression "hour" as referring to a period of time, either relatively brief or of undetermined length, is exemplified in other writings of John. (See Joh 2:4; 4:21-23; 5:25, 28; 7:30; 8:20; 12:23, 27.) He thus did not restrict the appearance, existence, and activity of such antichrist to some future time only but showed that the antichrist was then present and would continue on.—1Jo 4:3.

Identification. Although there has been much effort in the past to identify "the antichrist" with an individual, such as Pompey, Nero, or Muhammad (this latter person being suggested by Pope Innocent III in 1213 C.E.), or with a specific organization, as in the Protestant view of "the antichrist" as applying to the papacy, John's inspired statements show the term to be broad in its application, embracing all those who deny that "Jesus is the Christ," and who deny that Jesus is the Son of God who came "in the flesh."—1Jo 2:22; 4:2, 3; 2Jo 7, *NE, NIV;* compare Joh 8:42, 48, 49; 9:22.

Denial of Jesus as the Christ and as the Son of God of necessity embraces the denial of any or all of the Scriptural teachings concerning him: his origin, his place in God's arrangement, his fulfillment of the prophecies in the Hebrew Scriptures as the promised Messiah, his ministry and teachings and prophecies, as well as any opposition to or efforts to replace him in his position as God's appointed High Priest and King. This is evident from other texts, which, while not using the term "antichrist," express essentially the same idea. Thus, Jesus stated: "He that is not on my side is against me, and he that does not gather with me scatters." (Lu 11:23) Second John 7 shows that such ones might act as deceivers, and hence the "antichrist" would include those who are "false Christs" and "false prophets," as well as those who perform powerful works in Jesus' name and yet are classed by him as "workers of lawlessness." —Mt 24:24; 7:15, 22, 23.

In view of Jesus' rule that what is done to his true followers is done to him (Mt 25:40, 45; Ac 9:5), the term must include those who persecute such ones, which means it would include the symbolic "Babylon the Great" and those described as the "evil slave" in Jesus' parable.—Lu 21:12; Re 17:5, 6; Mt 24:48-51.

John specifically mentions apostates as among those of the antichrist by referring to those who "went out from us," abandoning the Christian congregation. (1Jo 2:18, 19) It therefore includes "the man of lawlessness" or "son of destruction" described by Paul, as well as the "false teachers" Peter denounces for forming destructive sects and who "disown even the owner that bought them." —2Th 2:3-5; 2Pe 2:1; see MAN OF LAWLESSNESS.

Kingdoms, nations, and organizations are similarly shown to be part of the antichrist in the symbolic description at Revelation 17:8-15; 19:19-21.—Compare Ps 2:1, 2.

In all the above cases those composing the antichrist are shown to be headed for eventual destruction as a recompense for their opposing course.

ANTI-LEBANON (Anti-Leb'a·non). The easternmost of the two ranges forming the mountain system of Lebanon. The Anti-Lebanon Range parallels the Lebanon Range for about 100 km (60 mi), extending from the plateau of Bashan, E of Dan, up to the great Plain of Emesa, not far from the site of Riblah. Between the two ranges lies a long valley formed by the Orontes and Litani rivers and called Coele-Syria ("Hollow Syria") or the Beqa'.—Jos 11:17.

In the N the ridge is narrow and broken by a series of prominent peaks. The central mass is broader, higher, and rougher, while the southern zone is cut by long torrent valleys that lead off to the E and S. To the E of the main ridge there is a series of descending plateaus that gradually drop to the level of the Plains of Damascus. The southern zone includes Mount Hermon, which reaches 2,814 m (9,232 ft). The geology of these mountains is similar to that of the Lebanon Range, and they are composed mainly of limestone, having gray cliffs and round gray summits.

The Anti-Lebanon Range is evidently referred to in the Hebrew by the name "Amanah" at Song of Solomon 4:8, where it is mentioned in connection with Mount Hermon. While some have considered Amanah to be a particular mountain peak, it appears rather to refer either to the entire Anti-Lebanon Range or some part of it. The mountain ranges of "Libana" and "Ammanana" are mentioned jointly in inscriptions of Assyrian monarchs Tiglath-pileser III and Sennacherib. The Abanah River (modern Barada) is also called "Amanah" at 2 Kings 5:12 in the Syriac *Peshitta* and the Aramaic Targums, and this river, the principal one of Damascus, has its source in the southern part of the Anti-Lebanon mountains. Hence the name may refer either to that part of the range or to the range as a whole.

Since the major part of the Anti-Lebanon Range is not snowcapped, it has few rivers or streams. Little vegetation grows, but thin forests of dwarf oak and juniper trees are seen on various parts of the slopes. Few cedars remain today. The lower slopes still support vineyards, olive groves, and orchards, as they did in Bible times.

ANTIOCH (An'ti·och).

1. The city of Antioch in Syria was founded by Seleucus I (Nicator) shortly after he and Generals Cassander and Lysimachus won the decisive battle of Ipsus in Phrygia, Asia Minor, in 301 B.C.E. He selected the site because of its military advantages and named it after his father Antiochus. At the location of what today is called Antakya in Turkey, Antioch was founded on the S side of the navigable Orontes River at a bend some 32 km (20 mi) from the Mediterranean Sea. It was so situated geographically that it could easily dominate the trade of all NW Syria that traversed the routes between the Euphrates River and the Mediterranean Sea. It soon became a commercial center, and its manufacture of luxury goods brought prosperity and wealth to the cosmopolitan city. As a seaport for Antioch, Seleucus also founded the coastal city of Seleucia, named after himself. Before he was assassinated in 281 B.C.E., he trans-

ferred his seat of government from Babylon to his new Syrian capital, Antioch, where the Seleucid dynasty of kings continued in power until 64 B.C.E., when Roman General Pompey made Syria a Roman province. Not only was Antioch made the capital of the Roman province of Syria but it also became the third-largest city in the empire, after Rome and Alexandria.

The physical structure of the city had been laid out according to the plan of Alexandria, with great colonnaded streets that intersected, lending impressive beauty to the splendor of the surrounding buildings. It was called "The Queen of the East," "Antioch the Beautiful," "The Third Metropolis of the Roman Empire," and was unique in possessing a regular system of street lighting. Despite this outward show of beauty and industriousness, it gained a reputation for being morally corrupt because of the defiling practice of orgiastic rites in the name of religion. Juvenal said that 'the Orontes River had flowed into the Tiber River flooding Rome with the superstition and immorality of the East.'—*Juvenal and Persius,* Satire III, 62-65.

Biblical Connections and Later History. Josephus records that the Seleucids encouraged Jews to settle in Antioch and gave them full citizenship rights, thus establishing a sizable Jewish population. The first mention of Antioch in the Bible is in connection with Nicolaus from Antioch, who became a Christian after becoming a proselyte to the Jewish religion. (Ac 6:5) Direct Christian activity began there when some of the disciples were scattered as far as Antioch by the tribulation that arose following Stephen's death. (Ac 11:19, 20) When the congregation at Jerusalem heard that many Greek-speaking people were becoming believers, they dispatched Barnabas as far as Antioch, and when he observed the thriving interest manifested there, he brought Paul in from Tarsus to help. (Ac 11:21-26) They both dwelt there for a year teaching the people, and Paul thereafter used Antioch as a home base for his missionary tours. It was in Antioch that, by divine providence, the disciples were first called "Christians." (Ac 11:26) The generosity of the congregation was expressed when they sent a relief ministration (Ac 11:29) by the hands of Paul and Barnabas to the governing body in Jerusalem about 46 C.E. This coincided with a great famine occurring in the time of Claudius, as prophesied by Agabus. (Ac 11:27, 28) After they returned to Antioch, the holy spirit directed that Paul and Barnabas be set aside for special work, so they were sent on Paul's first missionary tour, about 47-48 C.E. Before he started on his second mis-

sionary tour and while he was in Antioch, the matter of circumcision for Gentiles arose in about 49 C.E., and the decree of the governing body at Jerusalem was delivered by Paul and Barnabas to the congregation at Antioch. (Ac 15:13-35) Paul's second missionary journey, about 49-52 C.E., likewise began and ended at Antioch, and here also was where Paul corrected Peter's compromising action of discriminating between Jews and Gentiles.—Ga 2:11, 12.

2. Antioch in Pisidia was also founded by Seleucus I (Nicator) and named in honor of his father, Antiochus. The ruins of the city are located near Yalvac in modern Turkey. (PICTURE, Vol. 2, p. 748) It was situated on the border of Phrygia and Pisidia and so might be considered part of one or the other of these provinces at different times. Thus, Greek geographer Strabo refers to it as a city of Phrygia toward Pisidia (*Geography,* 12, VIII, 13, 14), but, as *Funk and Wagnalls New Standard Bible Dictionary* (1936, p. 51) observes, "the majority of writers speak of it as Pisidian," even as did Luke. This identification served to distinguish it from Antioch in Syria. (See PISIDIA.) Because of its location, Antioch in Pisidia became part of the trade route between Cilicia and Ephesus and contained a mixed population including many Jews, who had established a synagogue there. It was a thoroughly Hellenized Greek-speaking city. Paul twice visited it with Barnabas on his first evangelistic journey about 47-48 C.E. and preached in the synagogue, finding much interest. (Ac 13: 14; 14:19-23) However, becoming jealous of the crowds that were attending, certain Jews stirred up some of the leading men and women of the city and threw Paul and Barnabas outside.—Ac 13:45, 50; 2Ti 3:11.

ANTIPAS (An'ti·pas) [shortened form of Antipater, meaning "Instead of [His] Father"].

1. A martyr of the early Christian congregation at Pergamum in the first century C.E.—Re 2:12, 13; see PERGAMUM.

2. Herod Antipas, son of Herod the Great.—See HEROD No. 2.

ANTIPATRIS (An·tip'a·tris) [Of (Belonging to) Antipater]. A city rebuilt by Herod the Great in 9 B.C.E. and named after his father Antipater (II). It is identified with Ras el-'Ain (Tel Afeq) in a well-watered and fertile section of the Plain of Sharon. Antipatris is believed to have been the location of the earlier city of Aphek, mentioned at 1 Samuel 4:1. Excavations conducted there in 1946, 1961, and 1974 appear to confirm this.—See APHEK No. 3.

It was to here that the main body of the Roman army escort conducted Paul, traveling some 50 km (30 mi) down the mountains from Jerusalem by night. (Ac 23:31) The place lay at the junction of the Roman military roads leading from Jerusalem and Lydda respectively to the Roman capital of Caesarea. From Antipatris the 70 cavalrymen took Paul the remaining distance of some 40 km (25 mi) across the plain to Caesarea.

ANTONIA, TOWER OF.

A fortified structure in Jerusalem, serving as soldiers' quarters. According to Josephus, it had apartments, baths, barracks, and courtyards.—PICTURE, Vol. 2, p. 535.

The Tower of Antonia was situated at the NW corner of the temple court and evidently occupied the site where Nehemiah earlier had constructed the Castle (or fortress) mentioned at Nehemiah 2:8. Herod the Great did extensive and costly repair work on it and increased its fortifications. Previously known as the Baris, Herod named it Antonia in honor of Mark Antony. As the Jewish high priest and ruler John Hyrcanus had done before him, Herod had the priestly garments kept there, apparently as a means of maintaining a certain check or control on the high priest.

According to Josephus, the fortress was built on a rocky eminence 50 cubits (c. 22 m; 73 ft) high. Above the rock, it had stone walls 40 cubits (c. 18 m; 58 ft) high and four corner towers, three of them 50 cubits (c. 22 m; 73 ft) high and the other, at the southeast corner overlooking the whole temple area, 70 cubits (c. 31 m; 102 ft) high. (*The Jewish War*, V, 238-247 [v, 8]) Prior to Herod's time the fortress served primarily against incursions from the N, but thereafter it mainly served as a point of control over the Jews and a means of policing the activities in the temple area, to which there was direct access from the fortress.

The square layout of the fortress would indicate that it had a central court. Some believe that it was in such a central court within this tower that Jesus appeared before Pilate for judgment. (Joh 19:13) They suggest that a stone pavement found in this area was the one referred to as *"Gabbatha."* Others, however, believe that Jesus' judgment by Pilate took place before Herod's palace.—See STONE PAVEMENT.

A more certain reference to the Tower of Antonia is that recorded in the account at Acts 21:30-40 and 22:24. Paul appears to have delivered his defense and witness to a religious mob from the steps of the fortress and thereafter was taken into the soldiers' quarters for examining. Probably Paul was returned to this place after his

stormy session with the Sanhedrin and was here when his nephew came to warn him of the conspiracy against his life.—Ac 23:10, 16.

The Tower of Antonia came to final ruin when it was destroyed along with the temple and city by Roman General Titus in 70 C.E.

ANUB

(A'nub). A descendant of Judah and son of Koz.—1Ch 4:1, 8.

ANXIETY.

A number of Hebrew words convey the sense of anxiety or worry. One of these (*tsa·rar'*) means to be confined in a physical sense and is thus rendered 'wrap up,' 'shut up,' and 'be cramped.' (Ex 12:34; Pr 26:8; Isa 49:19) In a figurative sense it means "grow anxious; be in sore straits." (Ge 32:7; 1Sa 28:15) Another is *da·'agh'*, rendered "become anxious; become frightened"; it is related to *de'a·ghah'*, meaning "anxious care." (1Sa 9:5; Isa 57:11; Pr 12:25) The Greek noun *me'ri·mna* is rendered "anxiety," while the related verb *me·ri·mna'o* means "be anxious."—Mt 13:22; Lu 12:22.

Anxiety can be damaging to one's well-being. It can lead to depression, robbing one of strength and the initiative to act. Says the inspired proverb: "Anxious care in the heart of a man is what will cause it to bow down." (Pr 12:25) There can be serious physical manifestations from worry. Observes the book *How to Master Your Nerves*: "Doctors know how anxiety can affect the body's functions. It can raise (or lower) blood pressure; it can elevate the white blood cell count; it can suddenly affect the blood sugar by the action of adrenalin on the liver. It can even change your electrocardiogram. Dr. Charles Mayo said: 'Worry affects the circulation, the heart, the glands, the whole nervous system.'"—By Drs. P. Steincrohn and D. La-Fia, 1970, p. 14.

Far more serious is the spiritual harm to which undue anxiety may lead. Jesus Christ indicated that appreciation for "the word of God" can be completely choked out by worry over the problems that are often part of life in the present system of things. Just as thorns can stop seedlings from reaching maturity and bearing fruit, so such anxiety can prevent spiritual development and the bearing of fruitage to God's praise. (Mt 13:22; Mr 4:18, 19; Lu 8:7, 11, 14) Because of having permitted these worries to dominate their lives, to the exclusion of spiritual interests, many will find themselves in a disapproved state before the Son of God upon his return in glory, to their everlasting loss.—Lu 21:34-36.

Proper Anxieties or Concerns. It is right to be anxious about doing what is pleasing to Jehovah God in order not to miss out on the blessings to be enjoyed by his devoted servants. One guilty of serious wrongdoing should feel as did the psalmist: "I began to be anxious over my sin." (Ps 38:18) A proper concern over sin leads to confession, repentance, and turning around from the wrong course, restoring a good relationship with the Most High.

All Christians should be anxious, or should truly care, about the spiritual, physical, and material welfare of fellow believers. (1Co 12:25-27) This kind of concern is reflected in the apostle John's letter to Gaius: "Beloved one, I pray that in all things you may be prospering and having good health, just as your soul is prospering." (3Jo 2) The apostle Paul spoke of "the anxiety for all the congregations." (2Co 11:28) He was deeply concerned that all remain faithful disciples of the Son of God to the end.

The Scriptures refer to being "anxious for the things of the Lord," that is, concerned for everything that will promote the interests of the Son of God. Free from the responsibilities and cares for a mate and children, single Christians are in a better position than are married people to minimize concern over "the things of the world" and so give greater attention to "the things of the Lord."—1Co 7:32-35.

The apostle Paul wrote that Christian husbands and wives would be "anxious for the things of the world," having distractions not shared by single Christians. In the case of an unmarried person, what may be ample for personal and home care and life's necessities—food, clothing, shelter—may fall far short of what is needed for a family. Because of the intimate relationship of husband and wife, both are rightly anxious or concerned about pleasing each other in providing that which will contribute to the physical, mental, emotional, and spiritual welfare of the entire family. Even without having to contend with sickness, emergencies, limitations, or handicaps, married couples with children are required to devote much more time to "things of the world," that is, to nonspiritual activities related to human life, than would usually be true of single Christians.

Still, mundane concerns should not be permitted to take on too much importance. Jesus Christ made this clear to Lazarus' sister Martha. Anxious about the entertainment of her guest, she could not see how it was possible to take time to listen to Jesus. Mary, on the other hand, was able to choose "the good portion," the receiving of spiritual nourishment from God's Son.—Lu 10:38-42.

Avoiding Undue Anxiety. Implicit trust in Jehovah's loving concern for the welfare of his servants can help one to avoid giving in to needless worry. (Jer 17:7, 8) Jesus Christ made the same observation in his Sermon on the Mount. He concluded his counsel regarding anxiety with the words: "Never be anxious about the next day, for the next day will have its own anxieties. Sufficient for each day is its own badness." (Mt 6:25-34) For a Christian, there are enough problems each day without one's adding to them by anxiety over what might happen the next day and may, in fact, never take place.

Even if a Christian is brought before interrogating authorities in times of persecution, his trust in God's help can liberate him from anxiety. By means of His spirit, Jehovah will sustain the Christian in this trialsome situation and make it possible for him to bear witness in a fine way. —Mt 10:18-20; Lu 12:11, 12.

Whenever a Christian is assailed by anything that could make him anxious, filling him with uneasiness and apprehension, he should turn to his heavenly Father in prayer. Thus he can 'throw his anxiety on Jehovah,' confident that he will be heard by the One who cares for him. (1Pe 5:7) The result will be an inner calm, the peace of God, that will guard the heart and the mental powers. Deep within himself, in his heart, the Christian will be freed from uneasiness, foreboding, and alarm, and the mind will not be unsettled by the distractions and perplexities resulting from anxiety.—Php 4:6, 7.

APE [Heb., *qohph*]. The apes imported by King Solomon may have been a species of long-tailed monkeys referred to by ancient writers as being native to Ethiopia. (1Ki 10:22; 2Ch 9:21) The fact that the Hebrew word *qohph* may be related to the Sanskrit word *kapi* and that peacocks are considered to be native to SE Asia has given rise to the conclusion that the apes were brought by Solomon's fleet from India or Ceylon. However, the imported items need not necessarily have come directly from the country of origin nor from the same land, in view of the indications that commercial intercourse existed between India and Africa even before Solomon's time.—See PEACOCK; TARSHISH No. 4.

APELLES (A·pel′les) [from Lat., *appello*, "call"]. A Christian in the congregation at Rome to whom Paul sent greetings as "the approved one in Christ."—Ro 16:10; compare 2Co 10:18; 2Ti 2:15.

APHEK (A′phek) [Streambed].

1. A town evidently N of Sidon mentioned to Joshua by Jehovah as among the places yet to be conquered. (Jos 13:4) It is presently identified

with Afaka (modern Afqa) about 39 km (24 mi) ENE of Beirut. It lies at the source of the Nahr Ibrahim, anciently known as the river Adonis, which flows down to Byblos on the Mediterranean Coast.

2. A town within the territory of Asher but which the tribe was unsuccessful in possessing. (Jos 19:24, 30) It is called Aphik at Judges 1:31. It has been identified with Tell Kurdaneh (Tel Afeq), about 8 km (5 mi) SSE of Acco.

3. A city that, on the basis of the cities mentioned with it, was evidently in the Plain of Sharon. Its king was among those slain by Joshua. (Jos 12:18) Centuries later, but prior to Saul's kingship, the Philistines encamped here before their victory over Israel, drawn up at nearby Ebenezer. (1Sa 4:1) Its location is considered to be at Ras el-'Ain (Tel Afeq; different from No. 2 above) at the source of the Yarkon River. Aphek is mentioned in Egyptian and Assyrian texts. It is believed that the town of Antipatris, mentioned at Acts 23:31, was built at the site of ancient Aphek. Josephus mentions "a tower called Apheku" in connection with Antipatris. (*The Jewish War,* II, 513 [xix, 1]) Shiloh, from which the Israelites brought the ark of the covenant, is about 35 km (22 mi) to the E.

4. A town apparently located in the Plain of Jezreel between the towns of Shunem and Jezreel. In the battle between the Philistines and the Israelites that resulted in King Saul's death, the original position of the Philistines was at Shunem, while the Israelites took a position on Mount Gilboa. (1Sa 28:4) The account thereafter indicates that the Philistines advanced to Aphek while Israel descended to the spring at Jezreel. At Aphek the axis lords of the Philistines now reviewed their marshaled forces and discovered David and his men accompanying Achish in the rear. David's forces were ordered to leave on the following morning, and then the Philistines advanced to the battle site at Jezreel. (1Sa 29:1-11) From there they pushed the defeated Israelites back up into Mount Gilboa, where the slaughter was completed and Saul and his three sons died.—1Sa 31:1-8.

Some scholars suggest that the events leading up to this battle are not written in chronological order and, therefore, identify this Aphek with the one in the Plain of Sharon. (See APHEK No. 3.) Yohanan Aharoni favors this view, stating: "The narrative of this war has been truncated to some degree by the insertion of the story about David. But one can still follow its general line. The Philistine rulers assembled their forces at Aphek at the sources of the Yarkon (1 Sam. 29.1) preparatory to

marching on Jezreel (vs. 11). Saul's troops 'were encamped by the fountain which is in Jezreel' (vs. 1); on the eve of the battle they ranged themselves on Mount Gilboa. The Philistines made camp across from them at Shunem (1 Sam. 28.4). The conflict ended in Philistine victory, while Saul and his three sons fell during the retreat at Gilboa."—*The Land of the Bible,* translated and edited by A. Rainey, 1979, pp. 290, 291.

5. A city mentioned at 1 Kings 20:26 as the site of the defeat of the Syrian Ben-hadad II. The retreating Syrians pulled back to the city, only to have its wall fall upon 27,000 of them. (1Ki 20:29, 30) It likewise seems to be the place prophetically indicated to King Jehoash by the dying prophet Elisha as the point where the Syrians would suffer future defeats at the hands of Israelites. (2Ki 13:17-19, 25) Some scholars would place the Aphek mentioned in these texts about 5 km (3 mi) E of the Sea of Galilee, where the modern village of Afiq or Fiq is found. However, so far no remains older than the fourth century B.C.E. have been found at the site. But at nearby 'En Gev on the shore of the Sea of Galilee remains of a large fortified city of the tenth to eighth centuries B.C.E. have been discovered.

APHEKAH (A·phe'kah) [Streambed]. A city in the mountainous region of southern Judah, mentioned as in the neighborhood of Hebron. (Jos 15:48, 53) Some scholars propose identifying it with Khirbet el-Hadab, about 6 km (3.5 mi) SW of Hebron. There are two water sources nearby, and archaeological remains of the Israelite period have been found at the site.

APHIAH (A·phi'ah). A Benjamite and one of King Saul's ancestors.—1Sa 9:1, 2.

APHIK. See APHEK No. 2.

APHRAH (Aph'rah) [probably, Dust]. A place mentioned by Micah (1:10) apparently in the Shephelah or the Plains of Philistia, according to the other towns mentioned in the context. Micah evidently makes a play on words in saying: "In the house of Aphrah [Heb., *'Aph·rah'*] wallow in the very dust [Heb., *'a·phar'*]."

APOCRYPHA (A·poc'ry·pha). The Greek word *a·po'kry·phos* is used in its original sense in three Bible texts as referring to things "carefully concealed." (Mr 4:22; Lu 8:17; Col 2:3) As applied to writings, it originally referred to those not read publicly, hence "concealed" from others. Later, however, the word took on the meaning of spurious or uncanonical, and today is used most commonly to refer to the additional writings declared part of the Bible canon by the Roman Catholic Church at the Council of Trent (1546). Catholic writers refer to these books as *deuterocanonical,* meaning "of the second (or later) canon," as distinguished from *protocanonical.*

These additional writings are Tobit, Judith, Wisdom (of Solomon), Ecclesiasticus (*not* Ecclesiastes), Baruch, 1 and 2 Maccabees, supplements to Esther, and three additions to Daniel: The Song of the Three Holy Children, Susanna and the Elders, and The Destruction of Bel and the Dragon. The exact time of their being written is uncertain, but the evidence points to a time no earlier than the second or third century B.C.E.

Evidence Against Canonicity. While in some cases they have certain historical value, any claim for canonicity on the part of these writings is without any solid foundation. The evidence points to a closing of the Hebrew canon following the writing of the books of Ezra, Nehemiah, and Malachi in the fifth century B.C.E. The Apocryphal writings were never included in the Jewish canon of inspired Scriptures and do not form part of it today.

The first-century Jewish historian Josephus shows the recognition given only to those few books (of the Hebrew canon) viewed as sacred, stating: "We do not possess myriads of inconsistent books, conflicting with each other. Our books, those which are justly accredited, are but two and twenty [the equivalent of the 39 books of the Hebrew Scriptures according to modern division], and contain the record of all time." He thereafter clearly shows an awareness of the existence of Apocryphal books and their exclusion from the Hebrew canon by adding: "From Artaxerxes to our own time the complete history has been written, but has not been deemed worthy of equal credit with the earlier records, because of the failure of the exact succession of the prophets." —*Against Apion,* I, 38, 41 (8).

Inclusion in "Septuagint." Arguments in favor of the canonicity of the writings generally revolve around the fact that these Apocryphal writings are to be found in many early copies of the Greek *Septuagint* translation of the Hebrew Scriptures, which translation was begun in Egypt about 280 B.C.E. However, since no original copies of the *Septuagint* are extant, it cannot be stated categorically that the Apocryphal books were originally included in that work. Many, perhaps most, of the Apocryphal writings were admittedly written *after* the commencement of the translation work of the *Septuagint* and so were obviously not on the original list of books selected for trans-

lation by the translating body. At best, then, they could rate only as accretions to that work.

Additionally, while the Greek-speaking Jews of Alexandria eventually inserted such Apocryphal writings into the Greek *Septuagint* and apparently viewed them as part of an enlarged canon of sacred writings, the statement by Josephus quoted earlier shows that they were never brought into the Jerusalem or Palestinian canon and were, at the most, viewed as only secondary writings and not of divine origin. Thus, the Jewish Council of Jamnia (about 90 C.E.) specifically excluded all such writings from the Hebrew canon.

The need for giving due consideration to the Jewish stand in this matter is clearly stated by the apostle Paul at Romans 3:1, 2.

Additional ancient testimony. One of the chief external evidences against the canonicity of the Apocrypha is the fact that none of the Christian Bible writers quoted from these books. While this of itself is not conclusive, inasmuch as their writings are also lacking in quotations from a few books recognized as canonical, such as Esther, Ecclesiastes, and The Song of Solomon, yet the fact that not one of the writings of the Apocrypha is quoted even once is certainly significant.

Not without weight also is the fact that leading Bible scholars and "church fathers" of the first centuries of the Common Era, on the whole, gave the Apocrypha an inferior position. Origen, of the early third century C.E., as a result of careful investigation made such a distinction between these writings and those of the true canon. Athanasius, Cyril of Jerusalem, Gregory of Nazianzus, and Amphilocius, all of the fourth century C.E., prepared catalogs listing the sacred writings in accord with the Hebrew canon and either ignored these additional writings or placed them in a secondary class.

Jerome, who is described as "the best Hebrew scholar" of the early church and who completed the Latin *Vulgate* in 405 C.E., took a definite stand against such Apocryphal books and was the first, in fact, to use the word "Apocrypha" explicitly in the sense of noncanonical as referring to these writings. Thus, in his prologue to the books of Samuel and Kings, Jerome lists the inspired books of the Hebrew Scriptures in harmony with the Hebrew canon (in which the 39 books are grouped as 22) and then says: "Thus there are twenty-two books . . . This prologue of the Scriptures can serve as a fortified approach to all the books which we translate from the Hebrew into Latin; so that we may know *that whatever is beyond these must be put in the apocrypha.*" In writing to a lady named

Laeta on the education of her daughter, Jerome counseled: "Let her avoid all the apocryphal books, and if she ever wishes to read them, not for the truth of their doctrines but out of respect for their wondrous tales, let her realize that they are not really written by those to whom they are ascribed, that there are many faulty elements in them, and that it requires great skill to look for gold in mud."—*Select Letters,* CVII.

Differing Catholic views. The trend toward including these additional writings as canonical was primarily initiated by Augustine (354-430 C.E.), although even he in later works acknowledged that there was a definite distinction between the books of the Hebrew canon and such "outside books." However, the Catholic Church, following Augustine's lead, included such additional writings in the canon of sacred books determined by the Council of Carthage in 397 C.E. It was, however, not until as late as 1546 C.E., at the Council of Trent, that the Roman Catholic Church definitely confirmed its acceptance of these additions into its catalog of Bible books, and this action was deemed necessary because, even within the church, opinion was still divided over these writings. John Wycliffe, the Roman Catholic priest and scholar who, with the subsequent help of Nicholas of Hereford, in the 14th century made the first translation of the Bible into English, did not include the Apocrypha in his work, and the preface to this translation declared such writings to be "without authority of belief." Dominican Cardinal Cajetan, foremost Catholic theologian of his time (1469-1534 C.E.) and called by Clement VII the "lamp of the Church," also differentiated between the books of the true Hebrew canon and the Apocryphal works, appealing to the writings of Jerome as an authority.

It is to be noted as well that the Council of Trent did not accept all the writings previously approved by the earlier Council of Carthage but dropped three of these: the Prayer of Manasses and 1 and 2 Esdras (not the 1 and 2 Esdras that, in the Catholic Douay Bible, correspond with Ezra and Nehemiah). Thus, these three writings that had appeared for over 1,100 years in the approved Latin *Vulgate* were now excluded.

Internal evidence. The internal evidence of these Apocryphal writings weighs even more heavily against their canonicity than does the external. They are completely lacking in the prophetic element. Their contents and teachings at times contradict those of the canonical books and are also contradictory within themselves. They are rife with historical and geographic inaccuracies and anachronisms. The writers in some cases are guilty of dishonesty in falsely representing their works as those of earlier inspired writers. They show themselves to be under pagan Greek influence, and at times resort to an extravagance of language and literary style wholly foreign to the inspired Scriptures. Two of the writers imply that they were not inspired. (See the Prologue to Ecclesiasticus; 2 Maccabees 2:24-32; 15:38-40, *Dy*.) Thus, it may be said that the best evidence against the canonicity of the Apocrypha is the Apocrypha itself. A consideration of the individual books here follows:

Tobit (Tobias). The account of a pious Jew of the tribe of Naphtali who is deported to Nineveh and who becomes blinded by having bird's dung fall in both of his eyes. He sends his son, Tobias, to Media to collect a debt, and Tobias is led by an angel, impersonating a human, to Ecbatana (Rages). En route he acquires the heart, liver, and gall of a fish. He encounters a widow who, though married seven times, remains a virgin because of each husband's having been killed on the marriage night by Asmodeus, the evil spirit. Encouraged by the angel, Tobias marries the widowed virgin, and by burning the fish's heart and liver, he drives away the demon. Upon returning home he restores his father's sight by use of the gall of the fish.

The story was probably written originally in Aramaic and is estimated to be of about the third century B.C.E. It is obviously not inspired by God because of the superstition and error found in the narrative. Among the inaccuracies it contains is this: The account states that in his youth Tobit saw the revolt of the northern tribes, which occurred in 997 B.C.E. after Solomon's death (Tobit 1:4, 5, *JB*), also that he was later deported to Nineveh with the tribe of Naphtali, in 740 B.C.E. (Tobias 1:11-13, *Dy*) That would mean that he lived more than 257 years. Yet Tobias 14:1-3 (*Dy*) says he was 102 years old at the time of his death.

Judith. This is the account of a beautiful Jewish widow of the city of "Bethulia." Nebuchadnezzar sends his officer Holofernes on a campaign to the W to destroy all worship except that of Nebuchadnezzar himself. The Jews are besieged in Bethulia, but Judith pretends to be a traitoress to the Jews' cause and is admitted to the camp of Holofernes, where she gives him a false report of the conditions in the city. At a feast, in which Holofernes becomes drunk, she is able to behead him with his own sword and then return to Bethulia with his head. The following morning the enemy camp is thrown into confusion, and the Jews gain complete victory.

As the Catholic translation *The Jerusalem Bible* comments in its Introduction to the Books of Tobit, Judith and Esther: "The book of Judith in particular shows a bland indifference to history and geography." Among the inconsistencies pointed out in that introduction is this: The events are stated as occurring during the reign of Nebuchadnezzar, who is called the king "who reigned over the Assyrians in the great city of Nineveh." (Judith 1:1, 7 [1:5, 10, *Dy*]) The introduction and footnotes of this translation point out that Nebuchadnezzar was king of Babylonia and never reigned in Nineveh, since Nineveh had been destroyed earlier by Nebuchadnezzar's father Nabopolassar.

Concerning the traveling itinerary of the army of Holofernes, this Introduction states that it is "a geographical impossibility." *The Illustrated Bible Dictionary* (Vol. 1, p. 76) comments: "The story is frank fiction—otherwise its inexactitudes would be incredible."—Edited by J. D. Douglas, 1980.

The book is thought to have been written in Palestine during the Greek period toward the end of the second century or the start of the first century B.C.E. It is believed to have been originally written in Hebrew.

Additions to the Book of Esther. These form six additional passages. Preceding the first chapter in some ancient Greek and Latin texts (but Es 11:2–12:6 in *Dy*) is the first portion, of 17 verses, presenting a dream of Mordecai and his exposing a conspiracy against the king. Following 3:13 (but 13:1-7 in *Dy*) the second addition presents the text of the king's edict against the Jews. At the close of chapter 4 (but 13:8–14:19 in *Dy*) prayers by Mordecai and Esther are related as the third addition. The fourth is made to follow 5:2 (but 15:1-19 in *Dy*) and recounts Esther's audience with the king. The fifth comes after 8:12 (but 16:1-24 in *Dy*) and consists of the king's edict allowing the Jews to defend themselves. At the close of the book (but 10:4–11:1 in *Dy*) the dream presented in the Apocryphal introduction is interpreted.

The placement of these additions varies in different translations, some placing them all at the end of the book (as did Jerome in his translation) and others interspersing them throughout the canonical text.

In the first of these Apocryphal sections Mordecai is presented as having been among the captives taken by Nebuchadnezzar, in 617 B.C.E., and as being an important man in the king's court in the second year of Ahasuerus (Gr. says Artaxerxes) over a century later. This statement that Mordecai occupied such an important position so early in the king's reign contradicts the canonical part of Esther. The Apocryphal additions are believed to be the work of an Egyptian Jew and to have been written during the second century B.C.E.

Wisdom (of Solomon). This is a treatise extolling the benefits to those seeking divine wisdom. Wisdom is personified as a celestial woman, and Solomon's prayer for wisdom is included in the text. The latter part reviews the history from Adam to the conquest of Canaan, drawing upon it for examples of blessings for wisdom and calamities for lack of it. The folly of image worship is discussed.

Though not mentioning him directly by name, in certain texts the book presents Solomon as its author. (Wisdom 9:7, 8, 12) But the book cites passages from Bible books written centuries after Solomon's death (c. 998 B.C.E.) and does so from the Greek *Septuagint,* which began to be translated about 280 B.C.E. The writer is believed to have been a Jew in Alexandria, Egypt, who wrote about the middle of the first century B.C.E.

The writer manifests a strong reliance on Greek philosophy. He employs Platonic terminology in advancing the doctrine of the immortality of the human soul. (Wisdom 2:23; 3:2, 4) Other pagan concepts presented are the preexistence of human souls and the view of the body as an impediment or hindrance to the soul. (8:19, 20; 9:15) The presentation of the historical events from Adam to Moses is embellished with many fanciful details, often at variance with the canonical record.

While some reference works endeavor to show certain correspondencies between passages from this Apocryphal writing and the later works of the Christian Greek Scriptures, the similarity is often slight and, even where somewhat stronger, would not indicate any drawing upon this Apocryphal work by the Christian writers but, rather, their drawing upon the canonical Hebrew Scriptures, which the Apocryphal writer also employed.

Ecclesiasticus. This book, also called The Wisdom of Jesus, the Son of Sirach, has the distinction of being the longest of the Apocryphal books and the only one whose author is known, Jesus ben-Sirach of Jerusalem. The writer expounds upon the nature of wisdom and its application for a successful life. Observance of the Law is strongly emphasized. Counsel on many areas of social conduct and daily life is given, including comments on table manners, dreams, and travel.

The concluding portion contains a review of important personages of Israel, ending with the high priest Simon II.

Contradicting Paul's statement at Romans 5:12-19, which places the responsibility for sin upon Adam, Ecclesiasticus says: "From the woman came the beginning of sin, and by her we all die." (25:33, *Dy*) The writer also prefers "any wickedness, but the wickedness of a woman." —25:19, *Dy*.

The book was originally written in Hebrew in the early part of the second century B.C.E. Quotations from it are found in the Jewish Talmud.

Baruch (Including the Epistle of Jeremias). The first five chapters of the book are made to appear as though they were written by Jeremiah's friend and scribe, Baruch; the sixth chapter is presented as a letter written by Jeremiah (Jeremias) himself. The book relates the expressions of repentance and prayers for relief on the part of the exiled Jews in Babylon, exhortations to follow wisdom, encouragement to hope in the promise of deliverance, and the denunciation of Babylonish idolatry.

Baruch is represented as being in Babylon (Baruch 1:1, 2), whereas the Bible record shows he went to Egypt, as did Jeremiah, and there is no evidence that Baruch was ever in Babylon. (Jer 43:5-7) Contrary to Jeremiah's prophecy that the desolation of Judah during the Babylonian exile would last 70 years (Jer 25:11, 12; 29:10), Baruch 6:2 tells the Jews that they will be in Babylon for seven generations and then experience release.

Jerome, in his preface to the book of Jeremiah, states: "I have not thought it worth while to translate the book of Baruch." The introduction to the book in *The Jerusalem Bible* (p. 1128) suggests that sections of the composition may have been written as late as the second or first century B.C.E.; hence by an author (or authors) other than Baruch. The original language was probably Hebrew.

The Song of the Three Holy Children. This addition to Daniel is made to follow Daniel 3:23. It consists of 67 verses presenting a prayer supposedly uttered by Azariah within the fiery furnace, followed by an account of an angel's putting out the fiery blaze, and finally a song sung by the three Hebrews inside the furnace. The song is quite similar to Psalm 148. Its references to the temple, priests, and cherubim, however, do not fit the time to which it alleges to conform. It may have been originally written in Hebrew and is considered to be of the first century B.C.E.

Susanna and the Elders. This short story relates an incident in the life of the beautiful wife of Joakim, a wealthy Jew in Babylon. While bathing, Susanna is approached by two Jewish elders who urge her to commit adultery with them and, upon her refusal, frame a false charge against her. At the trial she is sentenced to die, but youthful Daniel adroitly exposes the two elders, and Susanna is cleared of the charge. The original language is uncertain. It is considered to have been written during the first century B.C.E. In the Greek *Septuagint* it was placed before the canonical book of Daniel, and in the Latin *Vulgate* it was placed after it. Some versions include it as a 13th chapter of Daniel.

The Destruction of Bel and the Dragon. This is a third addition to Daniel, some versions placing it as a 14th chapter. In the account King Cyrus requires of Daniel that he worship an idol of the god Bel. By sprinkling ashes on the floor of the temple and thus detecting footprints, Daniel proves that the food supposedly eaten by the idol is really consumed by the pagan priests and their families. The priests are killed, and Daniel smashes the idol. Daniel is asked by the king to worship a living dragon. Daniel destroys the dragon but is thrown into the lions' den by the enraged populace. During the seven days of his confinement, an angel picks up Habakkuk by his hair and carries him and a bowl of stew from Judea to Babylon to provide Daniel with food. Habakkuk is then returned to Judea, Daniel is released from the den, and his opponents are thrown in and devoured. This addition is also considered to be from the first century B.C.E. These additions to Daniel are referred to in *The Illustrated Bible Dictionary* (Vol. 1, p. 76) as "pious legendary embroidery."

First Maccabees. A historical account of the Jewish struggle for independence during the second century B.C.E., from the beginning of Antiochus Epiphanes' reign (175 B.C.E.) to the death of Simon Maccabaeus (c. 134 B.C.E.). It deals particularly with the exploits of priest Mattathias and his sons, Judas, Jonathan, and Simon, in their battles with the Syrians.

This is the most valuable of the Apocryphal works because of the historical information it supplies for this period. However, as *The Jewish Encyclopedia* (1976, Vol. VIII, p. 243) comments, in it "history is written from the human standpoint." Like the other Apocryphal works, it did not form part of the inspired Hebrew canon. It was evidently written in Hebrew about the latter part of the second century B.C.E.

Second Maccabees. Though placed after First Maccabees, this account relates to part of the same time period (c. 180 B.C.E. to 160 B.C.E.) but was not written by the author of First Maccabees. The writer presents the book as a summary of the previous works of a certain Jason of Cyrene. It describes the persecutions of the Jews under Antiochus Epiphanes, the plundering of the temple, and its subsequent rededication.

The account represents Jeremiah, at the destruction of Jerusalem, as carrying the tabernacle and the ark of the covenant to a cave in the mountain from which Moses viewed the land of Canaan. (2 Maccabees 2:1-16) The tabernacle had, of course, been replaced by the temple some 420 years previously.

Various texts are employed in Catholic dogma as support for doctrines such as punishment after death (2 Maccabees 6:26), intercession by the saints (15:12-16), and the propriety of prayers for the dead (12:41-46, *Dy*).

In its Introduction to the Books of Maccabees, *The Jerusalem Bible* says concerning Second Maccabees: "The style is that of hellenistic writers, though not of the best: at times it is turgid, frequently pompous." The writer of Second Maccabees makes no pretense of writing under divine inspiration and devotes part of the second chapter to justifying his choice of the particular method used in handling the subject material. (2 Maccabees 2:24-32, *JB*) He concludes his work by saying: "Here, then, I will make an end of writing; if it has been done workmanly, and in historian's fashion, none better pleased than I; if it is of little merit, I must be humoured none the less." —2 Maccabees 15:38, 39, *Kx*.

The book was evidently written in Greek sometime between 134 B.C.E. and the fall of Jerusalem in 70 C.E.

Later Apocryphal Works. Particularly from the second century C.E. forward there has developed an immense body of writings making claim to divine inspiration and canonicity and pretending to relate to the Christian faith. Frequently referred to as the "Apocryphal New Testament," these writings represent efforts at imitating the Gospels, Acts, letters, and the revelations contained in the canonical books of the Christian Greek Scriptures. A large number of these are known only through fragments extant or by quotations from them or allusions to them by other writers.

These writings manifest an attempt to provide information that the inspired writings deliberately omit, such as the activities and events relating to Jesus' life from his early childhood on up to the time of his baptism, or an effort to manufacture support for doctrines or traditions that find no basis in the Bible or are in contradiction to it. Thus the so-called Gospel of Thomas and the Protevangelium of James are filled with fanciful accounts of miracles supposedly wrought by Jesus in his childhood. But the whole effect of the picture they draw of him is to cause Jesus to appear as a capricious and petulant child endowed with impressive powers. (Compare the genuine account at Lu 2:51, 52.) The Apocryphal "Acts," such as the "Acts of Paul" and the "Acts of Peter," lay heavy stress on complete abstinence from sexual relations and even depict the apostles as urging women to separate from their husbands, thus contradicting Paul's authentic counsel at 1 Corinthians 7.

Commenting on such postapostolic Apocryphal writings, *The Interpreter's Dictionary of the Bible* (Vol. 1, p. 166) states: "Many of them are trivial, some are highly theatrical, some are disgusting, even loathsome." (Edited by G. A. Buttrick, 1962) *Funk and Wagnalls New Standard Bible Dictionary* (1936, p. 56) comments: "They have been the fruitful source of sacred legends and ecclesiastical traditions. It is to these books that we must look for the origin of some of the dogmas of the Roman Catholic Church."

Just as the earlier Apocryphal writings were excluded from among the accepted pre-Christian Hebrew Scriptures, so also these later Apocryphal writings were not accepted as inspired nor included as canonical in the earliest collections or catalogs of the Christian Greek Scriptures.—See CANON.

APOLLONIA (Ap·ol·lo'ni·a) [Of (Belonging to) Apollo; Place of Apollo]. A city of Macedonia, named after the Greek sun-god Apollo, as were a number of other cities in the Mediterranean area. It was situated in the district of Mygdonia about 44 km (27 mi) from Amphipolis and 56 km (35 mi) from Thessalonica, or about one day's travel from each. It lay on the great Roman highway *Via Egnatia*, S of Lake Bolbe, but it does not receive prominence in history. Paul and Silas passed through it on Paul's second missionary tour, most likely in the spring or early summer of the year 50 C.E.—Ac 17:1.

APOLLOS (A·pol'los) [Destroyer; abbreviation of Apollonius]. A Jew of Alexandria, Egypt, possessed of notable eloquence in speaking and a sound knowledge of the Hebrew Scriptures. He seems to have been witnessed to by disciples of John the Baptizer or else by Christian witnesses prior to Pentecost, since he was "acquainted with only the baptism of John." (Ac 18:24, 25) Yet he was fired with conviction, and on arriving in Ephesus about 52 C.E., he began witnessing in the local synagogue. This brought him in contact with Aquila and Priscilla, who filled in some of the gaps in his understanding of Christian teaching. From Ephesus he went over to Achaia, supplied with a letter of introduction, and there he seems to have centered his activity in Corinth, where Paul had preceded him. His intensity and his powerful Scriptural confutations of the arguments of the unbelieving Jews proved of great aid to the brothers there. He thus 'watered what Paul had planted.'—Ac 18:26-28; 19:1; 1Co 3:6.

Unfortunately, by the time Paul wrote his first letter to the Corinthians (c. 55 C.E.), factions had developed in the Corinth congregation, with some viewing the eloquent Apollos as their leader, while others favored Paul or Peter or held only to Christ. (1Co 1:10-12) Paul's letter corrected their wrong thinking, showing the vital need for unity and the relative unimportance of individuals as only ministers serving under God and Christ. (1Co 3:4-9, 21-23; 4:6, 7) It appears that Apollos must then have been in or near Ephesus, where Paul evidently wrote First Corinthians, for Paul tells of his urging Apollos to visit the Corinth congregation. (1Co 16:12) Apollos' reluctance to go may have been due to the improper attitudes existing in Corinth or simply due to his having a field of activity that he felt required his continued attention a while longer. At any rate, Paul's brief statement shows that these two active missionaries had not allowed matters to produce a breach in their own unity. The final mention of Apollos is at Titus 3:13, where Paul asks Titus, then in Crete, to supply Apollos' needs for a certain trip.

APOLLYON (A·pol'lyon) [Destroyer]. The Greek name used by the apostle John to translate the Hebrew "Abaddon" at Revelation 9:11. Apollyon means "Destroyer," and is given as the name of "the angel of the abyss." Though most reference works apply this name to some evil personage or force, the whole setting of the apocalyptic vision is to the contrary, as it consistently portrays angels being used by God to bring woes upon His enemies.

The use of the related verb a·pol'ly·mi illustrates this, as at James 4:12, which says of God: "One there is that is lawgiver and judge, he who is able to save and to *destroy*." (Compare Mt 10:28.) The unclean spirit cast out of a man by Jesus in a synagogue at Capernaum acknowledged Jesus as God's agent and said: "What have we to do with you, Jesus you Nazarene? Did you come to *destroy* us?" (Mr 1:24; Lu 4:34) Jesus warned unrepentant opposers among his listeners of the danger of being destroyed. (Lu 13:3-5; 20:16) These and other texts point to the glorified Christ Jesus as the one referred to by this title.—Compare Re 19:11-16; Lu 8:31; see ABADDON.

APOSTASY. This term in Greek (a·po·sta·si'a) comes from the verb a·phi'ste·mi, literally meaning "stand away from." The noun has the sense of "desertion, abandonment or rebellion." (Ac 21:21, ftn) In classical Greek the noun was used to refer to political defection, and the verb is evidently employed in this sense at Acts 5:37, concerning Judas the Galilean who "drew off" (a·pe'ste·se, form of a·phi'ste·mi) followers. The Greek Septuagint uses the term at Genesis 14:4 with reference to such a rebellion. However, in the Christian Greek Scriptures it is used primarily with regard to religious defection; a withdrawal or abandonment of the true cause, worship, and service of God, and hence an abandonment of what one has previously professed and a total desertion of principles or faith. The religious leaders of Jerusalem charged Paul with such an apostasy against the Mosaic Law.

It may properly be said that God's Adversary was the first apostate, as is indicated by the name Satan. He caused the first human pair to apostatize. (Ge 3:1-15; Joh 8:44) Following the Flood, there was a rebellion against the words of the God of Noah. (Ge 11:1-9) Job later found it necessary to defend himself against the charge of apostasy on the part of his three supposed comforters. (Job 8:13; 15:34; 20:5) In his defense Job showed that God grants no audience to the apostate (Job 13:16), and he also showed the hopeless state of one cut off in apostasy. (Job 27:8; compare also Elihu's statement at 34:30; 36:13.) In these cases the Hebrew noun cha·neph' is used, meaning "[one] alienated from God," that is, an apostate. The related verb cha·neph' means "be inclined away from the right relation to God," or "pollute, lead to apostasy."—*Lexicon in Veteris Testamenti Libros,* by L. Koehler and W. Baumgartner, Leiden, 1958, p. 317.

Apostasy in Israel. The first two commandments of the Law condemned all apostasy. (Ex 20:3-6) And before Israel's entry into the Promised Land, they were warned against the grave danger of apostasy resulting from marriages with the people of the land. (De 7:3, 4) Even though a person who was inciting others to apostasy was a close relative or a marriage mate, he was to be put to death for having "spoken of revolt against Jehovah your God." (De 13:1-15) The tribes of Reuben, Gad, and Manasseh were quick to exonerate themselves of a charge of apostasy that arose because of their construction of an altar.—Jos 22:21-29.

Many of the kings of Israel and of Judah followed an apostate course—for example, Saul (1Sa 15:11; 28:6, 7), Jeroboam (1Ki 12:28-32), Ahab (1Ki 16:30-33), Ahaziah (1Ki 22:51-53), Jehoram (2Ch 21:6-15), Ahaz (2Ch 28:1-4), and Amon (2Ch 33:22, 23). In due time a nation of apostates developed because the people listened to apostate priests and prophets (Jer 23:11, 15) and other unprincipled men who, by smooth words and false sayings, led them into loose conduct, immorality, and desertion of Jehovah, "the source of living water." (Isa 10:6; 32:6, 7; Jer 3:1; 17:13) According to Isaiah 24:5, the very land became "polluted [*cha·nephah'*] under its inhabitants, for they have bypassed the laws, changed the regulation, broken the indefinitely lasting covenant." No mercy was to be granted them in the predicted destruction.—Isa 9:17; 33:11-14; Zep 1:4-6.

What characteristics identify apostates as distinct from true Christians?

An apostasy among professed Christians was foretold by the apostle Paul at 2 Thessalonians 2:3. He specifically mentioned certain apostates, such as Hymenaeus, Alexander, and Philetus. (1Ti 1:19, 20; 2Ti 2:16-19) Among the varied causes of apostasy set forth in apostolic warnings were: lack of faith (Heb 3:12), lack of endurance in the face of persecution (Heb 10:32-39), abandonment of right moral standards (2Pe 2:15-22), the heeding of the "counterfeit words" of false teachers and "misleading inspired utterances" (2Pe 2:1-3; 1Ti 4:1-3; 2Ti 2:16-19; compare Pr 11:9), and trying "to be declared righteous by means of law" (Ga 5:2-4). While still making profession of faith in God's Word, apostates may forsake his service by treating lightly the preaching and teaching work that he assigned to followers of Jesus Christ. (Lu 6:46; Mt 24:14; 28:19, 20) They may also claim to serve God but reject his representatives, his visible organization, and then turn to 'beating' their former associates to hinder their work. (Jude 8, 11; Nu 16: 19-21; Mt 24:45-51) Apostates often seek to make others their followers. (Ac 20:30; 2Pe 2:1, 3) Such ones willfully abandoning the Christian congregation thereby become part of the "antichrist." (1Jo 2:18, 19) As with the apostate Israelites, destruction is likewise foretold for apostates from the Christian congregation.—2Pe 2:1; Heb 6:4-8; see ASSOCIATION.

During the period of persecution that the early Christian congregation experienced at the hands of the Roman Empire, professed Christians were at times induced to deny their Christian discipleship, and those who did so were required to signify their apostasy by making an incense offering before some pagan god or by openly blaspheming the name of Christ.

It is evident that there is a distinction between a 'falling' due to weakness and the 'falling away' that constitutes apostasy. The latter implies a definite and willful withdrawal from the path of righteousness. (1Jo 3:4-8; 5:16, 17) Whatever its apparent basis, whether intellectual, moral, or spiritual, it constitutes a rebellion against God and a rejection of his Word of truth.—2Th 2:3, 4; see MAN OF LAWLESSNESS.

APOSTLE. The Greek word *a·po'sto·los* is derived from the common verb *a·po·stel'lo*, meaning simply "send forth (or off)." (Mt 10:5; Mr 11:3) Its basic sense is clearly illustrated in Jesus' statement: "A slave is not greater than his master, nor is one that is sent forth [*a·po'sto·los*] greater than the one that sent him." (Joh 13:16) In this sense the word also applies to Christ Jesus as "the apostle and high priest whom we confess." (Heb 3:1; compare Mt 10:40; 15:24; Lu 4:18, 43; 9:48; 10:16; Joh 3:17; 5:36, 38; 6:29, 57; 7:29; 8:42; 10:36; 11:42; 17:3, 8, 18, 21-25; 20:21.) Jesus was sent forth by God as his appointed and commissioned representative.

The term is principally applied, however, to those disciples whom Jesus personally selected as a body of 12 appointed representatives. The names of the original 12 selected are given at Matthew 10:2-4; Mark 3:16-19, and Luke 6:13-16. One of the original 12, Judas Iscariot, proved to be a traitor, thereby fulfilling earlier prophecies. (Ps 41:9; 109:8) The remaining 11 faithful apostles are again listed at Acts 1:13.

Some of the apostles had been disciples of John the Baptizer before becoming Jesus' disciples. (Joh 1:35-42) Eleven of them were evidently Galileans (Ac 2:7), Judas Iscariot being considered the sole Judean. They were from the working class; four were definitely fishermen by trade; one had been a tax collector. (Mt 4:18-21; 9:9-13) At least two of them appear to have been cousins of Jesus (James and John, the sons of Zebedee). They were men who were viewed by the religious leaders as "unlettered and ordinary," indicating that their education was elementary and not from the schools of higher learning. A number of them, including Peter (Cephas), were married men.—Ac 4:13; 1Co 9:5.

Of the 12, Peter, James, and John seem to have enjoyed the closest relationship with Jesus. They alone witnessed the resurrection of Jairus' daughter (Mr 5:35-43) and the transfiguration of Jesus

(Mt 17:1, 2), and they accompanied him farther into the garden of Gethsemane than the other apostles on the night of his arrest. (Mr 14:32, 33) A special affinity appears to have existed between Jesus and John, and John is accepted as being the one referred to as "the disciple whom Jesus used to love."—Joh 21:20-24; 13:23.

Selection and Early Ministry. The 12 were selected out of a larger group of disciples and were designated "apostles" by Jesus, "that they might continue with him and that he might send them out [a·po·stel′lei] to preach and to have authority to expel the demons." (Mr 3:13-15) Thereafter they did "continue with him" in very close association during the remainder of his earthly ministry, receiving extensive personal instruction and ministerial training. (Mt 10:1-42; Lu 8:1) Since they continued to be Jesus' pupils, they were still called "disciples," particularly in accounts of events prior to Pentecost. (Mt 11:1; 14:26; 20:17; Joh 20:2) Thereafter they are consistently called "apostles." At the time of their appointment, Jesus gave them miraculous powers to heal, as well as to expel demons, and they used these powers to some extent during Jesus' ministry. (Mr 3:14, 15; 6:13; Mt 10:1-8; Lu 9:6; compare Mt 17:16.) This activity, however, is shown to be always subordinate to their principal work of preaching. Though forming an inner circle of followers, their instruction and training included no mysterious rituals or ceremonies.

Human Weaknesses. Though greatly favored as apostles of God's Son, they manifested normal human failings and weaknesses. Peter was inclined to be rash and impetuous (Mt 16:22, 23; Joh 21:7, 8); Thomas was slow to be convinced (Joh 20:24, 25); James and John manifested youthful impatience (Lu 9:49, 54). They quarreled over the issue of their future greatness in the earthly kingdom that they expected Jesus to establish. (Mt 20:20-28; Mr 10:35-45; compare Ac 1:6; Lu 24:21.) They acknowledged their need for greater faith. (Lu 17:5; compare Mt 17:20.) Despite their years of intimate association with Jesus and though knowing him to be the Messiah, they all abandoned him at the time of his arrest (Mt 26:56); the matter of his burial was handled by others. The apostles were slow at first to accept the testimony of the women who first saw Jesus after his resurrection. (Lu 24:10, 11) Because of fear they met behind locked doors. (Joh 20:19, 26) The resurrected Jesus gave them further enlightenment, and following his ascension to heaven on the 40th day from his resurrection, they manifested great joy and "were continually in the temple blessing God."—Lu 24:44-53.

Activity in Christian Congregation. The outpouring of God's spirit upon them at Pentecost greatly strengthened the apostles. The first five chapters of the Acts of Apostles testify to the great fearlessness of the apostles and their boldness in declaring the good news and the resurrection of Jesus in spite of jailing, beatings, and threats of death from their rulers. During those early days after Pentecost, the dynamic leadership of the apostles, under the power of the holy spirit, resulted in amazing expansion in the Christian congregation. (Ac 2:41; 4:4) Their ministry was at first concentrated in Jerusalem, then extended to Samaria, and in time, throughout the known world.—Ac 5:42; 6:7; 8:5-17, 25; 1:8.

Their primary function as apostles was to be witnesses as to Jesus' fulfillment of Jehovah God's purposes and prophecies, particularly of his resurrection and exaltation, and to do a discipling work among all nations; and this commission was emphasized to them by Jesus just before his ascension to heaven. (Mt 28:19, 20; Ac 1:8, 22; 2:32-36; 3:15-26) Their testimony concerning the resurrection was that of eyewitnesses.—Ac 13:30-34.

Miraculous powers. Additionally, to fortify their testimony, the apostles continued to exercise the miraculous powers previously granted them by Jesus, and also other gifts of the spirit received from Pentecost forward. (Ac 5:12; 9:36-40; see GIFTS FROM GOD [Gifts of the Spirit].) While others, too, received such miraculous gifts of the spirit, the account shows that such was the case only when one or more of the apostles were present, or by the laying on of the hands of the apostles. Paul, though not one of the 12, also served in this way as an apostle personally appointed by Jesus Christ. (Ac 2:1, 4, 14; 8:14-18; 10:44; 19:6) Thus the power to transmit such gifts was unique with these apostles. Such miraculous gifts would therefore pass away with the passing away of these apostles and of those who had received these gifts through the apostles (1Co 13:2, 8-11), and thus we read that these powers were "missing in the 2nd-century church, the writers of those days speaking of them as a thing in the past—in the apostolic age, in fact."—*The Illustrated Bible Dictionary,* edited by J. D. Douglas, 1980, Vol. 1, p. 79.

Administrative position. In the formation, organization, and subsequent direction of the Christian congregation, the apostles occupied a primary position. (1Co 12:28; Eph 4:11) Although they were joined by others of the "older men" in such supervision, they formed a principal part of the governing body of the expanding Christian congregation, and this body was recognized by the early Christians everywhere as the channel of communication used by God to render decisions and direct the affairs of the congregation throughout the earth. (Ac 2:42; 8:14-17; 11:22; 15:1, 2, 6-31; 16:4, 5) This was possible for these men only because of the fulfillment of the promises about guidance by God's holy spirit. (Joh 15:26, 27) Such help enabled them to recall Jesus' instructions and teachings, to clarify points of doctrine, and to be progressively guided "into all the truth" revealed through them at that apostolic period. (Joh 14:26; 16:13-15; compare Joh 2:22; 12:16.) They made appointments to positions of service within the congregation and also designated areas in which certain ones would engage in missionary activity. —Ac 6:2, 3; Ga 2:8, 9.

The apostles, therefore, served as a foundation, resting on Christ Jesus himself as the cornerstone, for the building up of the "holy temple for Jehovah." (Eph 2:20-22; 1Pe 2:4-6) There is no evidence of the primacy of any one apostle in the established Christian congregation. (See PETER.) Peter and John appear to have been especially prominent at Pentecost and immediately thereafter, with Peter acting as the principal spokesman. (Ac 2:14, 37, 38; 3:1, 4, 11; 4:1, 13, 19; 5:3, 8, 15, 29) However, in the decisions made at that time neither of these appears to have had a superiority over the others of the governing body, and when news arrived of the baptisms taking place in Samaria, the apostles in Jerusalem "dispatched [a·pe'stei·lan] Peter and John to them," so that these two served, in effect, as apostles of the apostles. (Ac 6:2-6; 8:14, 15) Following the death of the apostle James, the disciple of the same name, James the half brother of Jesus, appears to have presided in the governing body. Paul speaks of this James and also Peter (Cephas) and John as "the ones who seemed to be pillars." (Ac 12:1, 2, 16, 17; Ga 1:18, 19; 2:9, 11-14) It was James who announced the final decision on the important issue of circumcision as involving the Gentile believers, at which meeting Peter and Paul both presented testimony.—Ac 15:1, 2, 6-21.

Who replaced Judas Iscariot as a twelfth apostle?

Because of the defection of Judas Iscariot, who died unfaithful, there were only 11 apostles remaining, and during the 40 days from Jesus' resurrection until his ascension to heaven he made no appointment of a replacement. Sometime during the ten days between Jesus' ascension and the day

of Pentecost it was viewed as necessary that another be selected to fill the vacancy left by Judas, not simply on the basis of his death but, rather, on the basis of his wicked defection, as the Scriptures quoted by Peter indicate. (Ac 1:15-22; Ps 69:25; 109:8; compare Re 3:11.) Thus, by contrast, when the *faithful* apostle James was put to death, there is no record of any concern to appoint anyone to succeed him in his position of apostle.—Ac 12:2.

It is evident from Peter's statements that it was then considered that any individual filling the position of an apostle of Jesus Christ must have the qualifications of having been personally conversant with him, having been an eyewitness of his works, his miracles, and particularly his resurrection. In view of this it can be seen that any apostolic succession would in course of time become an impossibility, unless there were divine action to supply these requirements in each individual case. At that particular time before Pentecost, however, there were men meeting these requirements, and two were put forth as suitable for replacing unfaithful Judas. Doubtless having in mind Proverbs 16:33, lots were cast, and Matthias was selected and was thereafter "reckoned along with the eleven apostles." (Ac 1:23-26) He is thus included among "the twelve" who settled the problem concerning the Greek-speaking disciples (Ac 6:1, 2), and evidently Paul includes him in referring to "the twelve" when speaking of Jesus' postresurrection appearances at 1 Corinthians 15:4-8. Thus, when Pentecost arrived, there were 12 apostolic foundations on which the spiritual Israel then formed could rest.

Congregational Apostleships. Matthias was not a mere apostle of the Jerusalem congregation, any more than the remaining 11 apostles were. His case is different from that of the Levite Joseph Barnabas who became an apostle of the congregation of Antioch, Syria. (Ac 13:1-4; 14:4, 14; 1Co 9:4-6) Other men also are referred to as "apostles of congregations" in the sense that they were sent forth by such congregations to represent them. (2Co 8:23) And, in writing to the Philippians, Paul speaks of Epaphroditus as "your envoy [a·po'sto·lon] and private servant for my need." (Php 2:25) The apostleship of these men was clearly not by virtue of any apostolic succession, nor did they form part of "the twelve" as did Matthias.

The correct understanding of the wider application of the term "apostle" can help to clear away any apparent discrepancy between Acts 9:26, 27 and Galatians 1:17-19, when applied to the same occasion. The first account states that Paul, on arriving in Jerusalem, was led "to the apostles" by

Barnabas. In the account in Galatians, however, Paul states that he visited with Peter and adds: "But I saw no one else of the apostles, only James the brother of the Lord." James (not the original apostle James the son of Zebedee nor James the son of Alphaeus, but the half brother of Jesus) was evidently viewed as an "apostle" in the wider sense, namely, as "one sent forth" by the Jerusalem congregation. This would allow for the Acts account to use the title in the plural in saying that Paul was led "to the apostles" (that is, Peter and James).—Compare 1Co 15:5-7; Ga 2:9.

The Selection of Paul. Probably about the year 34 C.E., Saul of Tarsus was converted and is later referred to as Paul. He did become a true apostle of Jesus Christ and was the direct choice of the resurrected and ascended Jesus Christ. (Ac 9:1-22; 22:6-21; 26:12-23; 13:9) He argued on behalf of his apostleship and presented as his qualification the fact that he had seen the resurrected Lord Jesus Christ, that he had performed miracles, and that he had served as a channel for imparting the holy spirit to baptized believers. (1Co 9:1, 2; 15:9, 10; 2Co 12:12; 2Ti 1:1, 11; Ro 1:1; 11:13; Ac 19:5, 6) Since the apostle James (the brother of John) was not killed until about the year 44 C.E., "the twelve" were yet alive at the time of Paul's becoming an apostle. He nowhere includes himself among such "twelve," while at the same time he acknowledges no inferiority in his apostleship compared with that of such ones. —Ga 2:6-9.

Matthias' and Paul's apostleships were both valid for the purpose for which those men were "sent forth," yet when the apostle John saw the vision of the heavenly New Jerusalem in the Revelation (given about 96 C.E.) he saw only 12 foundation stones and on them inscribed "the twelve names of the twelve apostles of the Lamb." (Re 21:14) The testimony of the Holy Scriptures is clear that the apostle Paul was never referred to as one of "the twelve." Therefore, it logically follows that one of "the twelve names of the twelve apostles of the Lamb" inscribed on the foundation stones of the New Jerusalem is that of Matthias and not that of Paul. This means that the vision of the apostle John reflects the situation that existed at the start of the Christian congregation on the day of Pentecost in the year 33 C.E.—See PAUL.

End of the Apostolic Period. Though the Bible does not relate the death of the 12 apostles, aside from that of James, the evidence available indicates that they maintained their faithfulness until death and therefore needed no replacement. Concerning history in the following centuries, the observation is made that "whenever it [the term "apostle"] is applied to individuals in later Christian literature, the use of the term is metaphorical. The church has never had apostles in the N[ew] T[estament] sense since the first century."—*The Interpreter's Dictionary of the Bible*, edited by G. A. Buttrick, 1962, Vol. 1, p. 172.

During their lifetime the apostles' presence served as a restraint upon the influences of apostasy, holding back the forces of false worship within the Christian congregation. It is evidently to this "restraint" that the apostle Paul referred at 2 Thessalonians 2:7: "True, the mystery of this lawlessness is already at work; but only till he who is right now acting as a restraint gets to be out of the way." (Compare Mt 13:24, 25; Ac 20:29, 30.) This apostolic influence, including the authority and powers unique with them, continued until the death of John about 100 C.E. (1Jo 2:26; 3Jo 9, 10) The rapid influx of apostasy and false doctrine and practices after the death of the apostles shows that any pretended apostolic successors had none of the restraining influence of the apostles.

The reference to Andronicus and Junias at Romans 16:7 as "men of note among the apostles" indicates, not that they were apostles, but, rather, that they were held in high repute *by* the apostles. That some made false pretenses of being "apostles of Christ" is shown at 2 Corinthians 11:5, 13; 12:11, 12; Revelation 2:2.

APPAIM (Ap′pa·im) [from a root meaning "nose; nostrils"]. A son of Nadab and descendant of

Jerahmeel of the tribe of Judah.—1Ch 2:25, 30, 31.

APPARITION. The Greek word *phan'ta·sma* occurs only in the two accounts of Jesus' walking over the waters of the Sea of Galilee to his disciples who were in a boat. (Mt 14:26; Mr 6:49) The frightened disciples are quoted as saying: "It is an apparition!" The word *phan'ta·sma* is variously translated as "spirit" (*KJ*), "ghost" (*AS, AT, RS, Mo*), "phantom" (*Fn*), "false vision" (*La*), and "apparition" (*Da, ED, Dy, Kx, MR, NW*).

An apparition is an illusion; something actually not present but temporarily believed in because of excited imagination or other cause. Assuring the disciples that such was not the case and that he was real, Jesus said: "It is I; have no fear."—Mt 14:27; Mr 6:50.

This was, therefore, a different situation from the occasion when the resurrected Jesus suddenly appeared in the midst of his disciples, causing them to imagine they beheld "a spirit [Gr., *pneu'-ma*]." (Lu 24:36, 37) Jesus' words in this situation evidently were not designed to convince them merely of his *reality* but to assure them that he was appearing before them in a fleshly human form and not in spirit form; hence, he told them to "feel me and see, because a spirit does not have flesh and bones just as you behold that I have." (Lu 24:38-43; compare Ge 18:1-8; 19:1-3.) There was, therefore, no need for them to be fearful, which was the effect produced on Daniel by an awesome angelic appearance of a completely different nature. (Compare Da 10:4-9.) The situation was likewise very different from that of Saul of Tarsus, who was later blinded by Jesus' appearance to him on the road to Damascus.—Ac 9:1-9; 26:12-14; see TRANSFIGURATION; VISION.

APPHIA (Ap'phi·a). A Christian woman mentioned along with Philemon and Archippus in Paul's letter directed to these three and the congregation in Philemon's house. (Phm 2) It is possible she was the wife of Philemon.

APPIUS, MARKETPLACE OF (Ap'pi·us). A marketplace 74 km (46 mi) SE of Rome. It was a well-known station on the famous Roman highway *Via Appia,* running from Rome to Brundusium (now called Brindisi) by way of Capua. Both the road and the marketplace draw their name from the founder, Appius Claudius Caecus, of the fourth century B.C.E.

As the usual point at which travelers halted at the close of the first day's journey out of Rome, this post station became a busy trading center. Adding to its importance was its location at the northern terminus of a canal that ran alongside the road, traversing the Pontine Marshes. Travelers reportedly were conveyed over this canal by night in barges pulled by mules. The Roman poet Horace describes the discomforts of the journey, complaining of the frogs and gnats and depicting the Marketplace of Appius as crammed with "boatmen and stingy tavern-keepers."—*Satires,* I, v, 1-6.

It was at this busy junction that the apostle Paul, traveling from Puteoli to Rome as a prisoner, first met the delegation of Christian brothers who, on hearing the news of his coming, had journeyed from Rome to meet him. Part of the delegation waited at Three Taverns (15 km [9 mi] closer to Rome) while the rest proceeded as far as the Marketplace of Appius.—Ac 28:15.

Today there is a place still known as the *Foro Appio,* or Appian Forum, on the Appian Way. A signpost indicates the area where the Marketplace of Appius once stood. There is a small rural town called Faiti across the Appian Way.

APPLE [Heb., *tap·pu'ach*]. There is much conjecture as to the identification of the tree and fruit denoted by the Hebrew word *tap·pu'ach.* The word itself indicates that which is distinguished by its *fragrance,* or *scent.* It comes from the root *na·phach',* meaning "blow; pant; struggle for breath." (Ge 2:7; Job 31:39; Jer 15:9) Regarding this, M. C. Fisher wrote: "Relationship [to *na·phach'*] seems at first semantically strained, but the ideas of 'breathe' and 'exhale an odor' are related. The by-form *puah* means both 'blow' (of wind) and 'exhale a pleasant odor, be fragrant.'" —*Theological Wordbook of the Old Testament,* edited by R. L. Harris, 1980, Vol. 2, p. 586.

Several fruits have been suggested in place of the apple, including the orange, the citron, the quince, and the apricot. The main objection raised to the apple is that the hot, dry climate of most of Palestine is unfavorable to apple culture. However, the related Arabic word *tufah* primarily means "apple," and it is notable that the Hebrew place-names Tappuah and Beth-tappuah (probably so named because of the prevalence of this fruit in their vicinity) have been preserved in their Arabic equivalents by the use of this word. (Jos 12:17; 15:34, 53; 16:8; 17:8) These places were not in the lowlands but in the hill country, where the climate is generally somewhat moderated. Additionally, the possibility of some climatic variations in the past cannot be completely ruled out. Apple trees do grow in Israel today and thus seem to fit the Bible description satisfactorily. William Thomson, who spent many years in Syria and Palestine in the past century, even reported finding apple orchards in the area of Ashkelon on the Plains of Philistia.—*The Land and the Book*, revised by J. Grande, 1910, pp. 545, 546.

The apple tree (*Pyrus malus*) is mentioned mainly in The Song of Solomon, where the expressions of love by the Shulammite's shepherd companion are likened to the pleasant shade of the apple tree and the sweetness of its fruit. (Ca 2:3, 5) In turn, he compares her breath to the fragrance of apples. (Ca 7:8; see also 8:5.) In the Proverbs (25:11) appropriate, opportune speech is likened to "apples of gold in silver carvings." The only other reference to the apple is at Joel 1:12. The common tradition as to the apple's being the forbidden fruit of Eden is without any Scriptural basis whatsoever. Similarly, the expression "apple of the eye" is found in the *King James Version* (Ps 17:8; Pr 7:2; and others) but is not a Hebrew expression, the literal translation being "the pupil of [one's] eyeball."

APPOINTED TIMES OF THE NATIONS.

After discussing the destruction due to come upon the city of Jerusalem, Jesus made the statement: "And Jerusalem will be trampled on by the nations, until the appointed times of the nations ["times of the Gentiles," *KJ, RS*] are fulfilled." (Lu 21:24) The period indicated by the expression "appointed times of the nations [Gr., *kai·roi' e·thnon'*]" has occasioned considerable discussion as to its meaning and implication.

Meaning of "Appointed Times." The expression "appointed times" here comes from the Greek word *kai·ros'* (plural, *kai·roi'*), which, according to *Vine's Expository Dictionary of Old and New Testament Words* (1981, Vol. 4, p. 138), "signified a fixed or definite period, a season, sometimes an opportune or seasonable time." Liddell and Scott's *Greek-English Lexicon* (1968, p. 859) gives the further definition of *"exact* or *critical time."* Thus, *kai·ros'* is used to refer to the harvest "season," "the season" of the fruits, and "the season" of figs (Mt 13:30; 21:34; Mr 11:13); "the proper time" for dispensing food (Mt 24:45; Lu 12:42); "the appointed time" for Jesus' ministry to begin and the period of opportunity it brought (Mr 1:15; Mt 16:3; Lu 12:56; 19:44); and the "appointed time" of his death. (Mt 26:18) The demons, about to be cast out of certain men, screamed at Jesus: "Did you come here to torment us before the appointed time?"—Mt 8:29.

Kai·ros' is also used with reference to future times or occasions within God's arrangement or timetable, particularly in relation to Christ's presence and his Kingdom. (Ac 1:7; 3:19; 1Th 5:1)

Thus, the apostle Paul speaks of "the sacred secret" revealed by God "for an administration at the full limit *of the appointed times* [*kai·ron'*], namely, to gather all things together again in the Christ, the things in the heavens and the things on the earth." (Eph 1:9, 10) In view of the meaning of the word *kai·ros'* as used in the Bible text, it can properly be expected that the expression "appointed times of the nations" refers, not to something vague or indefinite, but, rather, to a "fixed or definite period," an "exact or critical time," one having a definite beginning and a definite end.

"The Nations" and "Jerusalem." The significance of Jesus' statement is necessarily bound up in his reference to the 'trampling on Jerusalem,' which he stated would continue until the fulfillment of "the appointed times of the nations." The term "nations" or "Gentiles" translates the Greek word *e'thne*, which means "nations" and was used by the Bible writers to refer specifically to the non-Jewish nations. On this basis some have considered the prophecy to apply to the period of time during which the geographic site of the ancient city of Jerusalem would be under Gentile domination and control.

While the literal city of Jerusalem is obviously referred to in Jesus' description of the destruction that was to come and did come upon that city in the year 70 C.E. when the Romans demolished Jerusalem, the statement concerning "the appointed times of the nations" carries the prophecy far beyond that point, as many commentators have noted. Thus, the well-known *Commentary* by F. C. Cook says of Luke 21:24: "It serves to separate the strictly eschatological portion [that is, the portion relating to the last days] of the great prophecy, from the part belonging properly to the destruction of Jerusalem." So, it becomes essential to determine what significance the inspired Scriptures attach to "Jerusalem" in order to ascertain whether "the appointed times of the nations" relate only to the literal city of Jerusalem or to something additional and greater.

Jerusalem was the capital of the nation of Israel, whose kings of the line of David were said to "sit upon Jehovah's throne." (1Ch 29:23) As such, it represented the seat of the divinely constituted government or typical kingdom of God operating through the house of David. With its Mount Zion, it was "the town of the grand King." (Ps 48:1, 2) Hence, Jerusalem came to stand for the kingdom of the dynasty of King David, much as Washington, London, Paris, and Moscow represent the ruling powers of present-day nations and are so referred to in news communiqués. After Jerusalem was trampled on by the Babylonians, its king being taken into exile and the land laid desolate, no member of the Davidic dynasty again ruled from earthly Jerusalem. But the Scriptures show that Jesus, the Messiah, who was born in the line of David, would rule from heavenly Mount Zion, from heavenly Jerusalem.—Ps 2:6, 7; Heb 5:5; Re 14:1, 3.

Beginning of 'trampling.' The 'trampling' on that kingdom of the dynasty of Davidic rulers did not begin with the Roman devastation of the city of Jerusalem in 70 C.E. It began centuries earlier with the Babylonian overthrow of that dynasty in 607 B.C.E. when Nebuchadnezzar destroyed Jerusalem and took captive the dethroned king Zedekiah and the land was left desolate. (2Ki 25:1-26; see CHRONOLOGY.) This accorded with the prophetic words directed to Zedekiah at Ezekiel 21:25-27, namely: "Remove the turban, and lift off the crown. This will not be the same. . . . A ruin, a ruin, a ruin I shall make it. As for this also, it will certainly become no one's until he comes who has the legal right, and I must give it to him." The one who has "the legal right" to the Davidic crown lost by Zedekiah is demonstrated in the Christian Greek Scriptures to be Christ Jesus, of whom the angel, announcing his future birth, said: "Jehovah God will give him the throne of David his father, and he will rule as king over the house of Jacob forever, and there will be no end of his kingdom." —Lu 1:32, 33.

With Jerusalem's fall in 607 B.C.E. the Gentile powers exercised domination over the entire earth. The Davidic dynasty and rule suffered interruption, and so Jerusalem, or what it stood for, would continue to be "trampled on" as long as God's kingdom, as functioning through David's house, was kept in a low, inoperative condition under the Gentile powers. Observing this connection with rulership *Unger's Bible Dictionary* (1965, p. 398) comments: "Consequently Gentiles move on as 'the nations' to the end of their stewardship as earth rulers. The termination of this period will be the end of the 'times of the Gentiles.' (Luke 21:24; Dan. 2:36-44)."—Compare Eze 17:12-21; also the description of Medo-Persia's fall at Da 8:7, 20.

Relation to Daniel's Prophecies. At least twice in this prophecy concerning the time of the end, Jesus referred to the contents of the book of the prophet Daniel. (Compare Mt 24:15, 21 with Da 11:31; 12:1.) In the book of Daniel we find a picture drawn of the domination of the earth by the Gentile powers during their "appointed times." The second chapter of Daniel contains the prophetic vision (received by King Nebuchadnezzar) of the great image that Daniel by inspiration showed to represent the march of Gentile world powers, ending with their destruction by the Kingdom set up by "the God of heaven," which Kingdom then rules earth wide. (Da 2:31-45) It is of note that the image begins with the Babylonian Empire, the first world power to 'trample Jerusalem' by overthrowing the Davidic dynasty and leaving "Jehovah's throne" in Jerusalem vacant. This also confirms the start of "the appointed times of the nations" in the year of Jerusalem's destruction, 607 B.C.E.

Dream vision of tree in Daniel chapter 4. Again in the book of Daniel we find a close parallel to Jesus' use of the word "times" with regard to "the nations," or Gentile powers. And again it is Nebuchadnezzar, the dethroner of David's descendant Zedekiah, who was given another vision interpreted by Daniel as relating to divinely appointed kingship. The symbolic vision was of an immense tree; an angel from heaven commanded that it be chopped down. Its stump was then banded with iron and copper and had to stay that way among the grass of the field until "seven times" passed over it. "Let its heart be changed from that of mankind, and let the heart of a beast be given to it, and let seven times pass over it . . . to the intent that people living may know that the Most High is Ruler in the kingdom of mankind and that to the one whom he wants to, he gives it and he sets up over it even the lowliest one of mankind."—Da 4:10-17; see 4:16, ftn.

Related to "appointed times of the nations." The vision definitely had a fulfillment in Nebuchadnezzar himself. (See Da 4:31-35.) Therefore, some view it as having direct prophetic application only to him and see in this vision merely the presentation of the eternal verity of 'God's supremacy over all other powers—human or supposedly divine.' They acknowledge the application of that *truth* or *principle* beyond Nebuchadnezzar's own case but do not see it as relating to any specific time period or divine schedule. Yet, an examination of the entire book of Daniel reveals that the element of time is everywhere prominent in the visions and prophecies it presents; and the world powers and events described in each such vision are shown, not as isolated or as occurring at random with the time element left ambiguous, but, rather, as fitting into a historical setting or time sequence. (Compare Da 2:36-45; 7:3-12, 17-26; 8:3-14, 20-25; 9:2, 24-27; 11:2-45; 12:7-13.) Additionally, the book repeatedly points toward the conclusion that forms the theme of its prophecies: the establishment of a universal and eternal

Kingdom of God exercised through the rulership of the "son of man." (Da 2:35, 44, 45; 4:17, 25, 32; 7:9-14, 18, 22, 27; 12:1) The book is also distinctive in the Hebrew Scriptures for its references to "the time of the end."—Da 8:19; 11:35, 40; 12:4, 9.

In view of the above, it does not seem logical to evaluate the vision of the symbolic "tree" and its reference to "seven times" as having no other application than to the seven years of madness and subsequent recovery and return to power experienced by one Babylonian ruler, particularly so in the light of Jesus' own prophetic reference to "the appointed times of the nations." The *time* at which the vision was given: at the critical point in history when God, the Universal Sovereign, had allowed the very kingdom that he had established among his covenant people to be overthrown; the *person* to whom the vision was revealed: the very ruler who served as the divine instrument in such overthrow and who thereby became the recipient of world domination by divine permission, that is, without interference by any representative kingdom of Jehovah God; and the whole *theme* of the vision, namely: "that people living may know that the Most High is Ruler in the kingdom of mankind and that to the one whom he wants to, he gives it and he sets up over it even the lowliest one of mankind" (Da 4:17)—all of this gives strong reason for believing that the lengthy vision and its interpretation were included in the book of Daniel because of their revealing the duration of "the appointed times of the nations" and the time for the establishment of God's Kingdom by his Christ.

The tree symbolism and God's sovereignty. The symbolisms used in this prophetic vision are by no means unique. Trees are elsewhere used to represent ruling powers, including that of God's typical kingdom at Jerusalem. (Compare Jg 9:6-15; Eze 17:1-24; 31:2-18.) A stump's being caused to sprout and the symbol of "a twig" or "sprout" are found a number of times as representing the renewal of rulership in a certain stock or line, particularly in the Messianic prophecies. (Isa 10:33–11:10; 53:2-7; Jer 23:5; Eze 17:22-24; Zec 6:12, 13; compare Job 14:7-9.) Jesus spoke of himself as both "the root and the offspring of David."—Re 5:5; 22:16.

The fact is evident that the key point of the vision is Jehovah God's exercise of irresistible sovereignty in "the kingdom of mankind," and this provides the guide to the full meaning of the vision. The tree is shown to have an application to Nebuchadnezzar, who at that point in history was the head of the dominant World Power, Babylon. Yet, prior to Nebuchadnezzar's conquest of Jerusa-

lem, the typical kingdom of God ruling out of that city was the agency by which Jehovah expressed his rightful sovereignty toward the earth. It thus constituted a divine block or impediment for Nebuchadnezzar in attaining his goal of world domination. By allowing that typical kingdom at Jerusalem to be overthrown, Jehovah permitted his own visible expression of sovereignty through the Davidic dynasty of kings to be cut down. The expression and exercise of world domination in "the kingdom of mankind," unhindered by any representative kingdom of God, now passed into the hands of the Gentile nations. (La 1:5; 2:2, 16, 17) In the light of these facts "the tree" is seen to represent, beyond and above its application to Nebuchadnezzar, world sovereignty or domination by God's arrangement.

Renewal of world domination. God, however, here makes clear that he has not forever delivered up such world domination to the Gentile powers. The vision shows that God's self-restraint (represented by the bands of iron and of copper around the stump of the tree) would continue until "seven times pass over it." (Da 4:16, 23, 25) Then, since "the Most High is Ruler in the kingdom of mankind," God would give world domination "to the one whom he wants to." (Da 4:17) The prophetic book of Daniel itself shows that one to be the "son of man" to whom are given "rulership and dignity and kingdom, that the peoples, national groups and languages should all serve even him." (Da 7:13, 14) Jesus' own prophecy, in which the reference to "the appointed times of the nations" occurs, points definitely toward Christ Jesus' exercise of such world domination as God's chosen King, the heir of the Davidic dynasty. (Mt 24:30, 31; 25:31-34; Lu 21:27-31, 36) Thus, the symbolic stump, representing God's retention of the sovereign right to exercise world domination in "the kingdom of mankind," was due to sprout again in his Son's Kingdom.—Ps 89:27, 35-37.

Seven Symbolic Times. In Nebuchadnezzar's personal experience of the vision's fulfillment the "seven times" were evidently seven years, during which he became mad, with symptoms like those of lycanthropy, abandoning his throne to eat grass like a beast in the field. (Da 4:31-36) Notably, the Biblical description of the exercise of world domination by the Gentile powers is presented through the figure of beasts in opposition to the holy people of God and their "Prince of princes." (Compare Da 7:2-8, 12, 17-26; 8:3-12, 20-25; Re 11:7; 13:1-11; 17:7-14.) Concerning the word "times" (from Aramaic 'id·dan'), as used in Daniel's prophecy, lexicographers show it here to mean "years."

(See *Lexicon in Veteris Testamenti Libros,* by L. Koehler and W. Baumgartner, Leiden, 1958, p. 1106; *A Hebrew and English Lexicon of the Old Testament,* by Brown, Driver, and Briggs, 1980, p. 1105; *Lexicon Linguae Aramaicae Veteris Testamenti,* edited by E. Vogt, Rome, 1971, p. 124.) The duration of a year as so used is indicated to be 360 days, inasmuch as three and a half times are shown to equal "a thousand two hundred and sixty days" at Revelation 12:6, 14. (Compare also Re 11:2, 3.) "Seven times," according to this count, would equal 2,520 days. That a specific number of days may be used in the Bible record to represent prophetically an equivalent number of years can be seen by reading the accounts at Numbers 14:34 and Ezekiel 4:6. Only by applying the formula there expressed of "a day for a year" to the "seven times" of this prophecy can the vision of Daniel chapter 4 have significant fulfillment beyond the day of now extinct Nebuchadnezzar, as the evidence thus far presented gives reason to expect. They therefore represent 2,520 years.

It is a historical fact worth noting that, on the basis of the points and evidence above presented, the March 1880 edition of the *Watch Tower* magazine identified the year 1914 as the time for the close of "the appointed times of the nations" (and the end of the lease of power granted the Gentile rulers). This was some 34 years before the arrival of that year and the momentous events it initiated. In the August 30, 1914, edition of *The World,* a leading New York newspaper at that time, a feature article in the paper's Sunday magazine section commented on this as follows: "The terrific war outbreak in Europe has fulfilled an extraordinary prophecy. For a quarter of a century past, through preachers and through press, the 'International Bible Students' . . . have been proclaiming to the world that the Day of Wrath prophesied in the Bible would dawn in 1914."

The events that took place from and after the year 1914 C.E. are well-known history to all, beginning with the great war that erupted, the first *world* war in mankind's history and the first to be fought over the issue, not of the domination of Europe alone, nor of Africa, nor of Asia, but of *the domination of the world.*—Lu 21:7-33; Re 11:15-18; see LAST DAYS; PRESENCE.

APPROACH TO GOD.

In an ancient Oriental court any approach to the presence of the monarch by an individual could be made only in accord with established regulations and with the monarch's permission. In most cases an intermediary acted for petitioners desiring an audience with the ruler, introducing them and vouching for the genuineness of their credentials. To enter the inner courtyard of Persian King Ahasuerus without being called meant death; but Queen Esther, when risking her life to gain access to the king's presence, was favored with approval. (Es 4:11, 16; 5:1-3) The actions and words of Joseph's brothers illustrate the care employed to avoid causing offense before a king, for Judah said to Joseph: "It is the same with you as with Pharaoh." (Ge 42:6; 43:15-26; 44:14, 18) Thus, to gain access to the presence of an earthly ruler, though only an imperfect human, was often a very difficult matter and a rare privilege.

Sanctity of God's Presence. Although Paul stated in Athens that God "is not far off from each one of us" (Ac 17:27), and his accessibility is presented throughout his Word the Bible, the one approaching Him must also meet definite requirements and have His divine permission or approval. Daniel's vision of the majestic heavenly court of "the Ancient of Days" to whom the "son of man" "gained access" and was "brought . . . up close even before that One," illustrates the dignity, respect, and order associated with the presence of the Sovereign Ruler of the universe. (Da 7:9, 10, 13, 14; compare Jer 30:21.) The record at Job 1:6 and 2:1 indicates that God's angelic sons are also invited into his immediate presence at appointed times, and Satan's appearance among them must reasonably have been only by Sovereign permission.

Man, having been made in his Creator's image and likeness by being endowed with a measure of the divine attributes and having the responsibility of caring for the planet Earth and the animal creation on it, would need to be in communication with his God and Father. (Ge 1:26, 27) Such communication is described at Genesis 1:28-30; 2:16, 17.

As perfect creatures, and hence with no guilt complex or consciousness of sin, Adam and Eve could originally approach God in conversation without feeling the need for an intercessor between them and their Creator, doing so as children would approach their father. (Ge 1:31; 2:25) Their sin and rebellion lost for them this relationship, bringing condemnation of death. (Ge 3:16-24) Whether they made future attempts at approaching God is not stated.

Through Faith, Right Works, and Sacrifices. The account of the approach to God on the basis of offerings by Cain and by Abel shows that prerequisites for access to God were faith and right works. Hence, Cain was debarred from divine acceptance until he should "turn to doing good."

(Ge 4:5-9; 1Jo 3:12; Heb 11:4) The start that was later made of "calling on the name of Jehovah" in Enosh's time does not appear to have been sincere (Ge 4:26), inasmuch as the next man of faith mentioned after Abel is not Enosh but Enoch, whose 'walking with God' shows his approach was approved. (Ge 5:24; Heb 11:5) Enoch's prophecy, recorded at Jude 14, 15, however, indicates that rampant disrespect for God existed in his day. —See ENOSH, ENOS.

Noah's righteous and faultless course among his contemporaries gained him access to God and preservation. (Ge 6:9-19) Following the Flood, he approached God on the basis of a sacrifice, as had Abel; he was blessed and was advised of added requirements for divine approval as well as of God's covenant with all flesh guaranteeing that there would be no future global deluge. (Ge 8:20, 21; 9:1-11) The expression "Jehovah, Shem's God," apparently indicates that this son had gained a position of greater favor with God than had his two brothers.—Ge 9:26, 27.

Melchizedek's priesthood. Although Noah officiated at the altar on behalf of his family, there is no specific mention of a "priest" as acting on behalf of men in their approach to God until Melchizedek's time. Melchizedek's priesthood was recognized by Abraham, who "gave him a tenth of everything." (Ge 14:18-20) Melchizedek is presented as a prophetic type of Christ Jesus at Hebrews 7:1-3, 15-17, 25.

Approach by other patriarchs. Abraham's relations with God qualified him to be called 'God's friend' (Isa 41:8; 2Ch 20:7; Jas 2:23), and his faith and obedience, coupled with his respectful approach through altars and offerings, are emphasized as the basis for this. (Ge 18:18, 19; 26:3-6; Heb 11:8-10, 17-19) He was taken into covenant relationship with God. (Ge 12:1-3, 7; 15:1, 5-21; 17:1-8) Circumcision was given as a sign of this, for a time becoming a requirement for divine acceptance. (Ge 17:9-14; Ro 4:11) Abraham's position qualified him to make supplication even on behalf of others (Ge 20:7), yet his deep respect is always manifest before Jehovah's presence or his representative. (Ge 17:3; 18:23-33) Job, a distant relative of Abraham, acted as priest for his family, offering up burnt sacrifices for them (Job 1:5), and made supplication on behalf of his three "companions," and "Jehovah accepted Job's face."—Job 42:7-9.

Isaac and Jacob, heirs of the promise to Abraham, approached God by calling on "the name of Jehovah" in faith, and by the construction of altars and the presentation of offerings.—Heb 11:9, 20, 21; Ge 26:25; 31:54; 33:20.

Moses was instructed by God's angel not to approach the burning bush and was ordered to remove his sandals because of standing on "holy ground." (Ex 3:5) As God's appointed representative in the nation of Israel, Moses had unique access to Jehovah's presence during his life, as Jehovah spoke "mouth to mouth" with him. (Nu 12:6-13; Ex 24:1, 2, 12-18; 34:30-35) Moses, like Melchizedek, served as a prophetic type of Christ Jesus.—De 18:15; Ac 3:20-23.

Importance of approved approach stressed. Prior to the giving of the Law covenant, Jehovah instructed the entire nation of Israel to sanctify themselves for three days, washing their clothes. Bounds for approach were set and no one, man or beast, was to touch the mountain of Sinai under penalty of death. (Ex 19:10-15) Moses then "brought the people out of the camp to meet the true God," stationing them at the base of the mountain, and he ascended the mountain to receive the covenant's terms amid the thunder and lightning, smoke and fire, and trumpet sounds. (Ex 19:16-20) Moses was ordered not to let "the priests and the people break through to come up to Jehovah, that he may not break out upon them." (Ex 19:21-25) "The priests" here mentioned were perhaps a principal male of each family of Israel and as such would "regularly come near to Jehovah," like Job, on behalf of the family.

Under the Law Covenant. Through the Law covenant an arrangement was set up that provided for individual and national approach to God through an appointed priesthood and with legally prescribed sacrifices, connected with a sacred tabernacle and later a temple. The sons of Aaron the Levite acted as priests on behalf of the people. For others, even the Levites not of Aaron's line, to presume to draw near to the altar or the holy utensils to effect such service would result in death. (Le 2:8; Nu 3:10; 16:40; 17:12, 13; 18:2-4, 7) The priests had to meet strict requirements as to both physical and ceremonial cleanness, and they had to have on approved attire when approaching the altar or "the holy place." (Ex 28:40-43; 30:18-21; 40:32; Le 22:2, 3) Any disrespect or violation of divine instructions in approaching the Sovereign God brought the death penalty, as in the case of two of Aaron's own sons. (Le 10:1-3, 8-11; 16:1) Of the entire nation only Aaron, and those who succeeded him as high priest, could enter the Most Holy before the ark of the covenant, which was associated with Jehovah's presence; but even he was allowed to enter on but one day in the year, on Atonement Day. (Le 16:2, 17) In this privileged position Aaron prefigured Christ Jesus as God's High Priest.—Heb 8:1-6; 9:6, 7, 24.

At the dedication of the temple in Jerusalem, King Solomon approached Jehovah on behalf of the nation. His prayer was that Jehovah's eyes would prove to be opened day and night toward that house where He had placed His name and that He would hear the entreaties made by the king, the nation, and also foreigners joining themselves to Israel, whoever would "pray *toward this house.*" Thereby, Jehovah was accessible to all, from the king to the least person in the nation. —2Ch 6:19-42.

In Israel, approach to God on matters affecting the entire nation was made by king, priest, and prophet. The Urim and Thummim of the high priest were employed on certain occasions to determine God's direction. (1Sa 8:21, 22; 14:36-41; 1Ki 18:36-45; Jer 42:1-3) Violation of Jehovah's law regarding proper approach brought punishment, as in the case of Uzziah (2Ch 26:16-20), and could result in a complete cutting off of communication with God, as in the case of Saul. (1Sa 28:6; 1Ch 10:13) That Jehovah would permit no trifling with regard to his Sovereign Presence and objects associated with it is illustrated in the case of Abinadab's son Uzzah, who took hold of the ark of the covenant to steady it, with the result that "Jehovah's anger blazed against Uzzah and the true God struck him down there for the irreverent act."—2Sa 6:3-7.

Mere ritual and sacrifice insufficient. While it has been argued that the worship of Jehovah developed from one of ritual and sacrifice to one of moral requirement, the evidence is all to the contrary. Mere ritual and sacrifice in themselves never sufficed but provided only a token legal basis for approach to God. (Heb 9:9, 10) In the final analysis Jehovah himself decided whom to receive; thus Psalm 65:4 states: "Happy is the one you choose and cause to approach, that he may reside in your courtyards." Faith, righteousness, justice, freedom from bloodguilt, truthfulness, and obedience to God's expressed will were continually stressed as the credentials required for approach to God, so that not simply the one bearing gifts to the Universal Sovereign but the one "innocent in his hands and clean in heart" could ascend into the mountain of Jehovah. (Ps 15:1-4; 24:3-6; 50:7-23; 119:169-171; Pr 3:32; 21:3; Ho 6:6; Mic 6:6-8) Where these qualities were lacking, sacrifices, fasting, and even prayers became detestable and worthless in God's eyes. (Isa 1:11-17; 58:1-9; 29:13; Pr 15:8) When wrongdoing had been committed, a broken spirit and a crushed heart had to be first manifested before approach was approved. (Ps 51:16, 17) Priestly office could not gain favorable reception by God if such priests despised his name and offered unacceptable sacrifices.—Mal 1:6-9.

Approach to God is also described as the presenting of oneself before a court and coming near before the judge for judgment. (Ex 22:8; Nu 5:16; Job 31:35-37; Isa 50:8) At Isaiah 41:1, 21, 22 Jehovah tells the national groups to approach, with their controversial case and arguments, for judgment by him.

Basis for Approach Under New Covenant. The Law covenant arrangement with its animal sacrifices, as a pictorial legal basis, pointed toward a superior basis for approach to God. (Heb 9:8-10; 10:1) This came by means of the new covenant through which all were to 'know Jehovah, from the least one even to the greatest one.' (Jer 31:31-34; Heb 7:19; 8:10-13) As the sole Mediator of that new covenant, Christ Jesus became "the way." He said, "No one comes to the Father except through me." (Joh 14:6, 13, 14) The barrier separating the Jews from the uncircumcised Gentile nations outside God's national covenant with Israel was removed by means of Christ's death, so that "through him we, both peoples, have the approach to the Father by one spirit." (Eph 2:11-19; Ac 10:35) Faith in God as "the rewarder of those earnestly seeking him" and in the ransom is the prerequisite for peaceful approach and a kindly reception by God through Jesus Christ. (Heb 11:6; 1Pe 3:18) Those approaching through Christ Jesus as their High Priest and Intercessor know that "he is always alive to plead for them" (Heb 7:25), and they can confidently "approach with freeness of speech to the throne of undeserved kindness." (Heb 4:14-16; Eph 3:12) They do not approach in fear of condemnation. (Ro 8:33, 34) Yet they retain the godly fear and awe that such approach to God, "the Judge of all," merits. —Heb 12:18-24, 28, 29.

The Christian's approach to God involves sacrifices and offerings of a spiritual kind. (1Pe 2:4, 5; Heb 13:15; Ro 12:1) Material temples and gold, silver, and stone images are shown to be of no benefit in approaching the true God. (Ac 7:47-50; 17:24-29; compare Eph 2:20-22.) Friends of the world are God's enemies; the haughty he opposes, but humble ones with 'clean hands' and a 'pure heart' can "draw close to God, and he will draw close to [them]."—Jas 4:4-8.

Anointed Christians called to a heavenly hope have a "way of entry into the holy place by the blood of Jesus," and, knowing well the "great priest over the house of God," they can "approach with true hearts in the full assurance of faith." —Heb 10:19-22.

As to the importance of one's trustfully approaching God, the psalmist aptly sums up the matter in saying: "For, look! the very ones keeping away from you will perish. You will certainly silence every one immorally leaving you. But as for me, the drawing near to God is good for me. In the Sovereign Lord Jehovah I have placed my refuge, to declare all your works."—Ps 73:27, 28; see PRAYER.

APRON. The Greek word *si·mi·kin'thi·on* denotes a thing girded around half the body, a half-girding and a narrow covering. (Ac 19:12) It seems to have been tied around the waist to cover part of the body for a distance below the waist. It may have been worn to protect other garments, perhaps by tradesmen such as fishermen, potters, water carriers, grocers, bakers, and carpenters. The ephod of the priests was considerably different, being an apronlike garment that hung from the shoulders, having front and back sections. —Ex 28:6-8; see HIGH PRIEST.

The Greek word translated "put on an apron" in Luke 17:8 (*pe·ri·zon'ny·mai*) literally means "gird oneself about."—Compare Eph 6:14.

'AQABA, GULF OF. See RED SEA.

AQUILA (Aq'ui·la) [from Lat., meaning "Eagle"]. A natural Jew and native of Pontus in northern Asia Minor. Priscilla, his wife and loyal companion, is always mentioned in association with him. Banished from Rome by Emperor Claudius' decree against Jews sometime in the year 49 or early 50 C.E., they took up residence in Corinth. (Ac 18:1, 2) When Paul arrived there in the autumn of 50 C.E., Aquila and Priscilla kindly received him into their home. A very close friendship developed among them as they worked together at their common trade of tentmaking and as Aquila and Priscilla doubtless aided Paul in building up the new congregation there.—Ac 18:3.

When Paul sailed for Syria at the end of his second missionary tour in the spring of about 52 C.E., Aquila and Priscilla went as far as Ephesus with him. (Ac 18:18, 19) They remained there at least until Paul wrote to the Corinthians from there about 55 C.E. Their home was used as the local meeting place for the congregation, and there they had the privilege of assisting the eloquent Apollos to a more accurate understanding of the way of God. (1Co 16:19; Ac 18:26) By the time Paul wrote to the Romans, about 56 C.E.,

Claudius' rule had ended and Aquila and Priscilla had returned to Rome, for Paul conveyed his greetings to them, his "fellow workers." (Ro 16:3) Here, also, the congregation met in their house. (Ro 16:5) Sometime during their relationship with Paul, Aquila and Priscilla had "risked their own necks" in behalf of Paul, thus meriting the thanks of all the congregations. (Ro 16:4) Later they moved back to Ephesus, for Paul, while in Rome just before suffering martyrdom (c. 65 C.E.), asked Timothy to convey his greetings to them there. —1Ti 1:3; 2Ti 4:19.

AR [probably, City]. A city of Moab, possibly its capital. It was on the S side of the Arnon Valley, but its precise location is uncertain. (Nu 21:15) At times Ar is used as synonymous with Moab. (De 2:18, 9, 29) At one time the limits of Moab extended N of the Arnon, but this region was taken from them by King Sihon of the Amorites. (Nu 21:26-28) The Israelites did not attack Moab, since Jehovah had forbidden them to do so, having given "the territory of Moab, that is, Ar," to the sons of Lot as "a holding." (De 2:9, 18, 29) In his pronouncement of desolations against Moab, Isaiah foretold that Ar would be "silenced" along with the other principal cities of Moab.—Isa 15:1.

Since the name Ar probably means "City," some suggest that the "city of Moab" (Heb., *'ir Moh·'av'*) mentioned at Numbers 22:36 and also the "city" of Deuteronomy 2:36 both refer to Ar.

ARA (A'ra). A son of Jether of the tribe of Asher.—1Ch 7:30, 38.

ARAB, I (A'rab) [Ambush]. A town in the mountains of Judah, mentioned along with Hebron, Dumah, and other cities. (Jos 15:48, 52) It is identified with Khirbet er-Rabiyeh, lying between Dumah and Carmel, about 12 km (7.5 mi) SW of Hebron. Paarai the Arbite (2Sa 23:35) was evidently from this town.

ARAB, II. See ARABIAN.

ARABAH (Ar'a·bah) [Desert Plain]. That part of the extraordinary depression, or rift valley, that extends toward the S from the slopes of Mount Hermon, cradles the Sea of Galilee and the Jordan River, drops far below sea level to form the basin of the Dead Sea, and then continues on southward to the Gulf of 'Aqaba at the Red Sea.—De 3:17; Jos 3:16; 11:16; Jer 52:7.

This long, narrow, N-S valley, often dry, and containing few cities, is limited on each side by a long row of mountains. It varies in width from less than 1 km to 16 km (0.5 to 10 mi) and is 435 km (270 mi) long, owing its existence to a fault line, or long fracture in the earth's crust. The Jordan winds through the northern part of this straight valley, and its steady flow waters a green belt down the center of the valley's floor. South of the Dead Sea, however, the Arabah is fed only by seasonal torrent streams that are insufficient to bring life to the dry soil.

Some commentators limit the word "Arabah" to the part of this great rift valley that is S of the Dead Sea, but it also refers to the region at least as far N as the Sea of Galilee, or Chinnereth. (Jos 12:3; 2Sa 2:29) The part of this valley N of the Dead Sea is now called the Ghor, meaning "Depression," while the word "Arabah" is more particularly applied to the far drier region to the S.

The Dead Sea is called "the sea of the Arabah." (De 3:17; 4:49; 2Ki 14:25) Without the definite article the word 'ara·vah' is also used in a general sense and may be properly translated as "desert plain." The plural ('ara·vohth') is frequently applied to the desert plains of Jericho and Moab, the part of the Jordan Valley just N of the Dead Sea. —Nu 22:1; 26:3, 63; 31:12; Jos 4:13; 5:10; Jer 39:5.

ARABAH, TORRENT VALLEY OF. At Amos 6:14 the prophet warns the kingdoms of Judah and Israel that the land will be oppressed by a foreign power all the way from "Hamath down to the torrent valley of the Arabah [Desert Plain]." (Compare 2Ki 14:25.) While the term "Arabah" is applied to the entire Rift Valley region from the Sea of Galilee on down to the Red Sea, here it has particular application to the area from S of the Dead Sea down to the Gulf of 'Aqaba. Thus, while the expression "torrent valley of the Arabah" might have reference to a wadi such as the torrent valley of Zered, which empties into the S end of the Dead Sea ("the sea of the Arabah," De 3:17), it is notable that the expression used by Amos is the exact equivalent of the Arabic name applied to the region running from the S end of the Dead Sea to the Gulf of 'Aqaba, namely "Wadi el-'Arabah." Amos' prophecy indicated a complete overrunning of the entire land once controlled by Judah and Israel, from N to S. During the following century this prophecy saw fulfillment in the invasions of Assyrian kings, including Tiglath-pileser III, Shalmaneser V, Sargon II, and Sennacherib.

ARABIA. The Arabian Peninsula forms part of the Asiatic continent at its extreme SW corner. It is bounded on the E by the Persian Gulf and the Gulf of Oman, on the S by the Arabian Sea and the Gulf of Aden, and on the W by the Red Sea, while the Fertile Crescent of Mesopotamia, Syria, and Israel curves around its northern end. Surrounded as it is on three sides by water, in part it resembles a huge island and is commonly called by its people the "Island of the Arabs" (*Jazirat al-'arab*).

With an area of about 2,600,000 sq km (1,000,000 sq mi), or the equivalent of about one third the land surface of the continental United States, Arabia is the world's largest peninsula. The western coastline stretches some 2,900 km (1,800 mi), and at its widest point the peninsula is about 1,900 km (1,200 mi) across.

The peninsula consists of a rocky tableland sloping eastward down toward the Persian Gulf from its backbone formed by the mountain range running parallel to the W coast. One peak in the SW corner reaches an altitude of over 3,600 m (12,000 ft). Across the interior of the southern end of the peninsula lies the great desert called Rub' al-Khali, the largest continuous stretch of sandy area on earth, known as the Empty Quarter. To the N of the Nejd or central plateau is the smaller An Nafud Desert region, which culminates in the Syrian Desert.

The small streams found along the outer edges of the peninsula and in the high central plateau (or Nejd) are not numerous, and their flow is only during certain seasons. Job, who evidently lived in what is today the Syrian Desert region, describes the drying up of such "winter torrents."—Job 6:15-20.

Though so much of this vast tableland is arid, sufficient rainfall does occur along the western mountain range, the central plateau, and in the S to sustain a considerable population. Here and around the larger oases the fellahin, or peasant farmers, can produce crops of millet, wheat, barley, and corn, and here date palms (Ex 15:27) and fig trees grow. Acacia trees, producing the resinous gum known as gum arabic, and other aromatic trees and plants formed a major part of the ancient Arabian economy, as they do to a lesser extent in modern times, being eclipsed today by the black gold of petroleum.—Ge 2:12.

Because of a general scarcity of water, animal and bird life is necessarily reduced, yet sheep, goats, camels, wild asses, jackals, falcons, and eagles live there today, as they did in Bible times. (Eze 27:21; 2Ch 17:11; Jg 6:5; Job 39:5-8, 26, 27; Isa 60:7; 34:13) Some wildlife, such as the lion, the wild bull, and the ostrich, have now become extinct in this territory. (Job 38:39, 40; 39:9-18) Arabian horses are renowned for their beauty and strength to this day.—Compare Job 39:19-25.

Arabian Tribes. Arabia eventually became the home of many of the post-Flood families listed at Genesis chapter 10. In the Semitic branch, Joktan fathered the heads of some 13 different Arabian tribes; while three of Aram's descendants, Uz, Gether, and Mash, appear to have settled in the area of N Arabia and the Syrian Desert. (Ge 10:23, 26-29) The tent-dwelling Ishmaelites ranged from the Sinai Peninsula, across N Arabia and as far as Assyria. (Ge 25:13-18) The Midianites were located mainly in the NW part of Arabia just E of the Gulf of 'Aqaba. (Ge 25:4) Esau's descendants were based in the mountainous region of Edom to the SE of the Dead Sea. (Ge 36:8, 9, 40-43) From the Hamitic branch several descendants of Cush, including Havilah, Sabtah, Raamah and his sons Sheba and Dedan, and Sabteca, seem to have occupied mainly the southern part of the Arabian Peninsula.—Ge 10:7.

Ancient Assyrian and Babylonian inscriptions make mention of various tribes of Arabia. Shalmaneser III lists "Gindibu', from Arabia." Zabibe and Samsi are mentioned as Arabian queens in the inscriptions of Tiglath-pileser III. Sargon II mentions "Samsi, queen of Arabia (and) It'amar the Sabaean." Other cuneiform inscriptions refer to the Sabai, the Nabaiti, the Qidri, and the Idibaili, the Masai, and the Temai.—Compare Ge 25:3, 13-15.

Biblical References. Hadhramaut, one of the four major ancient kingdoms of South Arabia, is usually identified with Hazarmaveth of Genesis 10:26. The Wadi Hadhramaut, a long valley running parallel to the S coast of Arabia, was the center of the kingdom with its capital at Shabwa. Other Biblical names occurring as places in Arabia are Dedan, Tema, Dumah, and Buz.—Isa 21:11-14; Jer 25:23, 24.

Abraham skirted around Arabia in migrating from Ur of the Chaldeans to the land of Canaan. When later obliged to go down to Egypt, he may have passed through part of Arabia by traversing the northern portion of the Sinai Peninsula (instead of following the route along the Mediterranean Coast), as also on his return trip. (Ge 12:10; 13:1) The drama of the book of Job has its setting in the land of Uz in northern Arabia (Job 1:1), and the Sabean raiders who attacked the property of this "greatest of all the Orientals" were an Arabian tribe perhaps descended from Joktan. (Job 1:3; Ge 10:26-28) Job's three "comforters" and Elihu also appear to have come from Arabian sectors. (Job 2:11; 32:2) Moses spent 40 years in Arabia when sojourning with the Midianite Jethro. (Ex 2:15–3:1; Ac 7:29, 30) The next event of

major importance to occur in Arabia was the giving of the Law covenant at Mount Sinai in the southern part of the Sinai Peninsula, where the liberated nation of Israel had congregated. (Ex 19:1, 2) Thus, the apostle Paul some 15 centuries later referred to the event as taking place at "Sinai, a mountain in Arabia."—Ga 4:25.

In view of the present state of Arabia in general, the picture of perhaps some three million Israelites living for 40 years in the wilderness may seem a near impossibility. (Ex 12:37, 38) The major factor, of course, was the miraculous provision of food and water assured them by Jehovah. (De 8:2-4; Nu 20:7, 8) Although the conditions were clearly difficult and the scarcity of water is obviously indicated in the Scriptural account (Nu 20:4, 5), there is, nevertheless, reason to believe that at that time, some 3,500 years in the past, the water supply in Arabia was to some extent superior to what it is at the present time. The existence of many deep dry wadis, or valleys, which were once riverbeds, gives evidence that at some time in the past there was sufficient rainfall to produce streams of water coursing through them. The disappearance of certain forms of animal life may be due in part to the decrease in the water supply. Yet, basically, Arabia was then just what it is now: an arid land, or steppe.

Out of Arabia during the period of the Judges came hordes of camel-riding Midianites, Amalekites, and "Easterners" to ravage the land of Israel. (Jg 6:1-6) Such razzias, or sudden raids, have always been the principal method of warfare in Arabia. (2Ch 22:1) The camel, whose domestication is believed to have been effected in Arabia, was in use as a mode of transportation at least as early as the time of Abraham. (Ge 24:1-4, 10, 61, 64) Because of the great superiority of the camel over the ass for extended desert travel, its domestication is considered to have accomplished somewhat of an economic revolution for Arabia, contributing to the development of the so-called "Spice Kingdoms" of South Arabia.

Camel caravans out of the more fertile S wound along the desert routes that ran parallel to the Red Sea, moving from oasis to oasis and from well to well until reaching the Sinai Peninsula, from which point they could branch off to Egypt or continue up into Palestine or to Damascus. Besides their highly prized spices and aromatic resins, such as frankincense and myrrh (Isa 60:6), they might carry gold and algum wood from Ophir (1Ki 9:28; 10:11) and precious gems, as did the queen of Sheba on her visit to King Solomon. (1Ki 10:1-10, 15; 2Ch 9:1-9, 14) The waters of the Persian Gulf abound with pearl oysters. Since the

SW corner of Arabia is separated from Africa by a narrow strait of water only about 32 km (20 mi) across, products from Ethiopia (2Ch 21:16), such as ivory and ebony, could also have been included in the wares of these traveling merchants.—Eze 27:15.

Nabonidus, the Babylonian king whose son Belshazzar was ruling in Babylon at the time of its fall (539 B.C.E.), spent ten years in the oasis city of Taima (Tema) in the northern part of the central plateau of Arabia.—See TEMA No. 2.

During the fifth century B.C.E., Palestine was subject to considerable influence from Arabia, as is seen by the references to "Geshem the Arabian" at Nehemiah 2:19 and 6:1-7.

The Himyarite Kingdom, which gained control of South Arabia about 115 B.C.E., had its capital at Zafar (suggested by some to be the Sephar of Genesis 10:30). To the N the Nabataeans (possibly descended from Nebaioth of Genesis 25:13), with their capital at Petra in the rocky gorges of Edom, became powerful from the fourth century B.C.E. onward. In time they extended their control throughout the S part of the Negeb and up through Moab and the region E of the Jordan. During some years of the first century B.C.E. and again in the first century C.E. they ruled over Damascus. Their king Aretas IV (c. 9 B.C.E.–40 C.E.) is mentioned at 2 Corinthians 11:32 with regard to Paul's escape from Damascus, described at Acts 9:23-25. Herod Antipas married the daughter of Aretas IV but divorced her in order to marry Herodias.—Mr 6:17; see ARETAS.

Paul says that following his conversion he "went off into Arabia, and . . . came back again to Damascus." (Ga 1:17) Such a journey may have been into the neighboring area of the Syrian Desert, though the term would also allow for its being in any part of the Arabian Peninsula.

During the first century B.C.E., Palmyra to the NE of Damascus began to develop as an Arab center and in time surpassed Petra as a trading state. In 270 C.E., under Queen Zenobia, the Palmyrene army occupied Egypt and became a serious rival to Rome until defeated in 272 C.E.

Language. The language of the peoples of Arabia is a member of the South Semitic group and has remained more stable than the other Semitic languages. It has, therefore, proved helpful in improving the understanding of many expressions and words in the ancient Hebrew of the Bible.

ARABIAN (A·ra′bi·an).

The names Arab and Arabian in the Scriptures are used chiefly in a broad sense as applying to an inhabitant of Arabia, that immense land to the E and S of Palestine. At times the context and use imply a specific tribe or ethnic group.—1Ki 10:15; 2Ch 9:14; 21:16.

A number of Arabian tribes were Semitic, descending from Shem through Joktan; others were Hamitic, descending through Ham's son Cush. (Ge 10:6, 7, 26-30) Some of Abraham's descendants by Hagar and Keturah also came to dwell in Arabia, as the sons of Ishmael who "took up tabernacling from Havilah near Shur, which is in front of Egypt, as far as Assyria." (Ge 25:1-4, 12-18) Esau's offspring, dwelling in the mountainous region of Seir, also came within the general classification of Arabian.—Ge 36:1-43.

For the most part the Arabians were a wandering people who led a pastoral life, dwelling in tents. (Isa 13:20; Jer 3:2) Others, however, were traders, and some are mentioned as merchants for Tyre. (Eze 27:21) God's servants had numerous contacts with them. The Midianite merchants on their way to Egypt to whom Joseph was sold were Arabian, as were the Sabeans from S Arabia who raided Job's cattle and she-asses. (Ge 37:28; Job 1:1, 15) During their 40-year trek in the wilderness the Israelites came into calamitous contact with the Baal-worshiping Midianites (Nu 25:6, 14-18), and during the period of the Judges, hordes of camel-riding Arabians regularly raided Israel for seven years, until Judge Gideon severely defeated them.—Jg 6:1-6; 7:12-25.

Rulers of Arabian kingdoms paid tribute to King Solomon. (1Ki 10:15; 2Ch 9:14) The Arabs paid Jehoshaphat a tribute of 7,700 rams and an equal number of he-goats, but they later allied themselves with the Philistines against Jehoshaphat's son and successor Jehoram, their marauder bands killing many of his sons. (2Ch 17:11; 21:16; 22:1) Uzziah waged successful warfare against them during his reign. (2Ch 26:1, 7) Arabian opposers were among those causing difficulty to Nehemiah during the restoration of Jerusalem's walls.—Ne 2:19; 4:7, 8; 6:1.

Though nomadic, generally independent, and often quite isolated from the mainstream of activity of those times, the Arabs came in for prophetic attention and judgment by God. (Isa 21:13; Jer 25:17-24) Centuries later, some Arabians were perhaps among those becoming members of the early Christian congregation at Pentecost.—Ac 2:11, 41; see ARABIA.

ARAD (A′rad).

1. One of the headmen of the tribe of Benjamin who at one time lived in Jerusalem.—1Ch 8:15, 28.

2. A city on the southern border of Canaan, whose king attacked Israel as they approached Canaan. The Israelites devoted the district to destruction and called it "Hormah," meaning "A Devoting to Destruction." (Nu 21:1-3; 33:40) They did not then settle there, however, and evidently some of the inhabitants escaped destruction. Hence, the king of Arad is included in the list of 31 kings later vanquished in Joshua's whirlwind campaign. (Jos 12: 14) The Kenites later settled in the wilderness area to the S of Arad.—Jg 1:16.

Israelite Arad is generally identified with Tel 'Arad, one of the most imposing mounds in the Negeb region. It lies on a somewhat rolling plain about 28 km (17 mi) E of Beer-sheba. Excavations at Tel 'Arad uncovered some 200 ostraca, about half of them in Hebrew and the rest in Aramaic. One such Hebrew

Ruins of a fortress at Tel 'Arad. Among the Hebrew ostraca found near here is one that mentions "the house of Jehovah"

potsherd, said to be from the second half of the seventh century B.C.E., reads: "To my lord Eliashib: May Jehovah ask for your peace. . . . He dwells in the house of Jehovah."—PICTURE, Vol. 1, p. 325.

Because of the absence of late Canaanite remains at Tel 'Arad, Y. Aharoni suggests that Canaanite Arad was located at Tell el-Milh (Tel Malhata), 12 km (7 mi) SW of Tel 'Arad.

ARAH (A'rah).

1. A son of Ulla of the tribe of Asher.—1Ch 7:30, 39.

2. Head of a family whose members returned to Jerusalem from Babylon with Zerubbabel. (Ezr 2:1, 2, 5; Ne 7:6, 7, 10) Father, or forefather, of Shecaniah, the father-in-law of Tobiah the Ammonite.—Ne 6:18.

ARAM (A'ram).

1. The last son listed of Shem's five sons. Aram and his four sons, Uz, Hul, Gether, and Mash, constituted 5 of the 70 post-Flood families, and their descendants were the Aramaeans and Syrians.—Ge 10:22, 23; 1Ch 1:17.

2. The son of Kemuel and a grandson of Nahor, the latter being Abraham's brother. Aram was, therefore, a grandnephew of Abraham and a first cousin once removed of Isaac. Rebekah, the daughter of Aram's uncle Bethuel, was Aram's first cousin. Nahor's family did not leave Mesopotamia with Abraham, but years later "the report got through to Abraham" of Nahor's progeny, including news of Aram.—Ge 22:20-23; 11:27, 31; 24:4, 10.

3. One of the four "sons of Shemer" (Shomer) of the tribe of Asher, and listed among the "heads of the house of the forefathers, select, valiant, mighty men, heads of the chieftains." (1Ch 7: 31, 32, 34, 40) Both Aram and his father were born in Egypt, since his grandfather and great-grandfather were numbered among the offspring of Jacob who 'came into Egypt.'—Ge 46:8, 17.

4. In the *King James Version,* Aram occurs at Matthew 1:3, 4 and at Luke 3:33.—See ARNI; RAM No. 1.

5. The name Aram is used in a geographic sense, by itself and in conjunction with other terms, to refer to regions in which the descendants of Aram (No. 1) were concentrated.

Aram, used alone, basically applies to Syria and is generally so translated. (Jg 10:6; 2Sa 8:6, 12; 15:8; Ho 12:12) It included the region from the Lebanon Mountains across to Mesopotamia and from the Taurus Mountains in the N down to Damascus and beyond in the S.—See SYRIA.

Aram-naharaim (Ps 60:Sup) is generally translated with the Greek word "Mesopotamia," which is understood to refer to "land between rivers." The two rivers were the Euphrates and the Tigris. Stephen speaks of Abraham as living in Mesopotamia while yet down in Ur of the Chaldeans (Ac 7:2), and when sending his servant to seek a wife for Isaac many years later, Abraham told him to go to the city of Nahor in (Upper) Mesopotamia (Aram-naharaim). (Ge 24:2-4, 10) Balaam of Pethor was also from a mountainous region in the northern part of Mesopotamia.—De 23:4; compare Nu 23:7; see MESOPOTAMIA.

Paddan-aram is used particularly with reference to the area around the city of Haran in Upper Mesopotamia.—Ge 25:20; 28:2-7, 10; see PADDAN.

The Aramaeans, Semitic descendants of Aram, were to be found throughout all these areas. Additionally, the name of Uz, one of Aram's four sons, is applied to the area of the Arabian Desert east of the Promised Land and touching on the borders of Edom. (Job 1:1; La 4:21) Aramaic, the language of the Aramaeans, was closely related to Hebrew and in time became an international language of both trade and diplomacy throughout the regions of the Fertile Crescent. —2Ki 18:26; see ARAMAIC.

It was doubtless due to Jacob's 20-year residence in Aram with his Aramaean father-in-law Laban that Deuteronomy 26:5 speaks of him as a "Syrian" (literally, an "Aramaean"). Additionally, Jacob's mother Rebekah was an Aramaean, as were his wives Leah and Rachel. The Israelites were therefore closely related indeed to the Aramaeans.

Aramaean Kingdoms. Aramaean kingdoms begin to be mentioned in the Bible record contemporaneously with the de-velopment of the nation of Israel. Cushanrishathaim, a king from Aram-naharaim (Mesopotamia), subjugated Israel for eight years until Judge Othniel liberated them.—Jg 3:8-10.

Aram-Zobah was an Aramaean kingdom referred to as an enemy of Saul's rule (1117-1078 B.C.E.). (1Sa 14:47) It appears to have been situated to the N of Damascus and exercised dominion N as far as Hamath and E to the Euphrates. When David was fighting Israel's enemies he came into conflict with Hadadezer, powerful king of Aram-Zobah, and defeated him. (2Sa 8:3, 4; 1Ch 18:3; compare Ps 60:Sup.) Subsequent to this, the Aramaean marauder Rezon moved into power at Damascus, and this city soon became the most prominent Aramaean city (1Ki 11:23-25) and "the head of Syria." (Isa 7:8) As such it manifested active hostility toward Israel throughout the entire history of the northern kingdom.—See DAMASCUS.

Aram-maacah is mentioned along with Zobah, Rehob, and Ishtob as among the Aramaean kingdoms from which the Ammonites hired chariots and horsemen to war against David. The king of Aram-maacah joined these mercenary forces, which David's army soon put to flight. (1Ch 19:6-15; 2Sa 10:6-14) The kingdom of Maacah probably lay E of the Jordan, with Mount Hermon on its N side.—Jos 12:5; 13:11.

Geshur was a small Aramaean kingdom to the E of the Jordan and evidently just below Maacah,

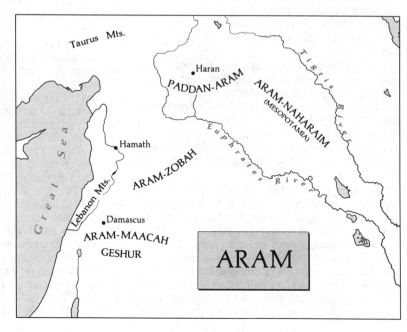

with its S boundaries extending down to the E side of the Sea of Galilee. Like Maacah, it lay within the territory assigned to the tribe of Manasseh.—De 3:14; Jos 13:11; see GESHUR No. 1.

By David's conquest of Aramaean kingdoms he extended the boundaries of his kingdom far to the N so that it reached to the Euphrates River, not far from Haran of Paddan-aram. He thus fulfilled Jehovah's promise concerning the extent of Israel's inheritance in the Promised Land.—De 1:7; 11:24; Jos 1:4.

For further information concerning Israel's relations with Aram, see SYRIA.

ARAMAEAN. See ARAM Nos. 1 and 5.

ARAMAIC (Ar·a·ma′ic). An ancient Semitic language having a close relationship to Hebrew and originally spoken by the Aramaeans. (See ARAM No. 5.) With the passing of time, however, it came to embrace various dialects (some of them viewed as separate languages) and enjoyed wide use, especially in SW Asia. Aramaic was employed particularly from the second millennium B.C.E. to about 500 C.E. It is one of the three languages in which the Bible was originally written. The Hebrew word *'Ara·mith'* occurs five times and is translated "in the Syrian language" or "in the Aramaic language."—2Ki 18:26; Isa 36:11; Da 2:4; Ezr 4:7 (twice).

Biblical Aramaic, formerly called Chaldee, is found in Ezra 4:8 to 6:18 and 7:12-26; Jeremiah 10:11; and Daniel 2:4b to 7:28. Aramaic expressions also appear in other parts of the Bible, but many of the attempts of scholars to identify Aramaic sources for Hebrew words are simply conjectural.

The use of some Aramaic expressions is not surprising, for the Hebrews had close contact with the Aramaeans and with the Aramaic language for a long time. Among the earliest renditions of the Hebrew Scriptures into other languages were the Aramaic Targums, though they were not put into writing until several centuries after the production of the Greek *Septuagint* commenced, about 280 B.C.E.

The Language. Aramaic and Hebrew are both classified as being in the Northwest Semitic family of languages. Though Aramaic differs considerably from Hebrew, it is a cognate language having the same letters in its alphabet with the same names as the Hebrew. Like Hebrew, it is written from right to left, and originally the Aramaic script was consonantal. However, the Aramaic employed in the Bible was later vowel pointed by the Masoretes, just as they vowel pointed

the Hebrew. Aramaic has been influenced by its contact with other languages. Besides containing various Hebrew, Akkadian, and Persian proper names of localities and persons, Biblical Aramaic shows Hebrew influence in religious terms, Akkadian influence particularly in political and financial terms, and Persian influence in such terms as those relating to political and legal matters.

Aramaic, in addition to having the same script as Hebrew, bears a similarity to it in verbal, nominal, and pronominal inflections. The verbs have two states, the imperfect (denoting incompleted action) and the perfect (signifying completed action). Aramaic employs singular, dual, and plural nouns and has two genders, the masculine and the feminine. It differs from other Semitic languages by displaying a preference for the vowel sound *a*, and in other ways, including certain consonantal preferences, such as *d* for *z* and *t* for *sh*.

Basic divisions. Aramaic is generally divided into Western and Eastern groups. However, from a historical standpoint the following four groups have been recognized: Old Aramaic, Official Aramaic, Levantine Aramaic, and Eastern Aramaic. It has been suggested that likely various dialects of Aramaic were spoken around and within the Fertile Crescent and Mesopotamia during the second millennium B.C.E. A difference between early forms of Aramaic and Hebrew may be noted at Genesis 31:47. After Jacob and Laban effected a reconciliation, a heap of stones was set up as a witness between them. Laban called it "Jegarsahadutha" in Aramaic (Syrian), while Jacob called it "Galeed" in Hebrew, both expressions meaning "Witness Heap."

Old Aramaic is a name applied to certain inscriptions discovered in northern Syria and said to date from the tenth to the eighth centuries B.C.E. Gradually, however, a new dialect of Aramaic became the lingua franca or the international auxiliary language during the time of the Assyrian Empire, supplanting Akkadian as the language used for official governmental correspondence with outlying areas of the empire. In view of its use, this standard form of Aramaic is referred to as Official Aramaic. It continued to be employed during the time Babylon was the World Power (625-539 B.C.E.) and thereafter, during the time of the Persian Empire (538-331 B.C.E.). Especially did it then enjoy wide usage, being the official language of government and business over a wide area, as archaeological discoveries attest. It appears in dockets on cuneiform tablets; on ostraca, papyri, seals, coins; in inscriptions on stone, and so forth. These artifacts have been found in such lands as Mesopotamia, Persia, Egypt, Anatolia, northern Arabia; in regions as far N as the Ural Mountains; and to the E as distant as Afghanistan and Kurdistan. The use of Official Aramaic continued during the Hellenistic period (323-30 B.C.E.).

It seems that it is this Official Aramaic that is found in the writings of Ezra, Jeremiah, and Daniel. The Scriptures also give evidence of the fact that Aramaic was a lingua franca of those ancient times. Thus, in the eighth century B.C.E., appointed spokesmen for King Hezekiah of Judah appealed to Assyrian King Sennacherib's representative Rabshakeh, saying: "Speak, please, to your servants in the Syrian [Aramaean, and hence, Aramaic] language, for we are listening; and do not speak to us in the Jews' language in the ears of the people that are on the wall." (Isa 36:11; 2Ki 18:26) The officials of Judah understood Aramaic, or Syrian, but evidently it was not understood by the common people among the Hebrews at that time in Jerusalem.

A number of years after the Jews returned from Babylonian exile Ezra the priest read the book of the Law to Jews assembled in Jerusalem, and various Levites explained it to the people, Nehemiah 8:8 stating: "They continued reading aloud from the book, from the law of the true God, it being expounded, and there being a putting of meaning into it; and they continued giving understanding in the reading." This expounding or interpreting may have involved paraphrasing the Hebrew text into Aramaic, Aramaic possibly having been adopted by the Hebrews when in Babylon. The expounding also, no doubt, involved exposition so that the Jews, even if understanding the Hebrew, would comprehend the deep significance of what was being read.

What Language Did Jesus Speak? On this question there is considerable difference of opinion among scholars. However, concerning languages used in Palestine when Jesus Christ was on earth, Professor G. Ernest Wright states: "Various languages were undoubtedly to be heard on the streets of the major cities. Greek and Aramaic were evidently the common tongues, and most of the urban peoples could probably understand both even in such 'modern' or 'western' cities as Caesarea and Samaria where Greek was the more common. Roman soldiers and officials might be heard conversing in Latin, while orthodox Jews may well have spoken a late variety of Hebrew with one another, a language that we know to have been neither classical Hebrew nor Aramaic, despite its similarities to both." Commenting further, on the language spoken by Jesus Christ, Professor Wright says: "The language spoken by Jesus has been much debated. We have no certain way of knowing whether he could speak Greek or Latin, but in his teaching ministry he regularly used either Aramaic or the highly Aramaized popular Hebrew. When Paul addressed the mob in the Temple, it is said that he spoke Hebrew (Acts 21:40). Scholars generally have taken this to mean Aramaic, but it is quite possible that a popular Hebrew was then the common tongue among the Jews."—*Biblical Archaeology,* 1963, p. 243.

It is possible that Jesus and his early disciples, such as the apostle Peter, at least at times spoke Galilean Aramaic, Peter being told on the night Christ was taken into custody: "Certainly you also are one of them, for, in fact, your dialect gives you away." (Mt 26:73) This may have been said because the apostle was using Galilean Aramaic at the time, though that is not certain, or he may have been speaking a Galilean Hebrew that differed dialectally from that employed in Jerusalem or elsewhere in Judea. Earlier, when Jesus came to Nazareth in Galilee and entered the synagogue there, he read from the prophecy of Isaiah, evidently as written in Hebrew, and then said: "Today this scripture that you just heard is fulfilled." Nothing is said about Jesus' translating this passage into Aramaic. So it is likely that persons present on that occasion could readily understand Biblical Hebrew. (Lu 4:16-21) It may also be noted that Acts 6:1, referring to a time shortly after Pentecost 33 C.E., mentions Greek-speaking Jews and Hebrew-speaking Jews in Jerusalem.

Professor Harris Birkeland (*The Language of Jesus,* Oslo, 1954, pp. 10, 11) points out that Aramaic's being the written language of Palestine when Jesus was on earth does not necessarily mean that it was spoken by the masses. Also, the fact that the Elephantine Papyri belonging to a Jewish colony in Egypt were written in Aramaic does not prove that it was the chief or common tongue in their homeland, for Aramaic was then an international literary language. Of course, the Christian Greek Scriptures contain a number of Aramaisms, Jesus using some Aramaic words, for instance. However, as Birkeland argues, perhaps Jesus ordinarily spoke the popular Hebrew, while occasionally using Aramaic expressions.

While it may not be provable, as Birkeland contends, that the common people were illiterate as far as Aramaic was concerned, it does seem that when Luke, an educated physician, records that Paul spoke to the Jews 'in Hebrew' and when the apostle said the voice from heaven spoke to him 'in Hebrew,' a form of Hebrew was actually meant (though perhaps not the ancient Hebrew) and not Aramaic.—Ac 22:2; 26:14.

Lending further support to the use of a form of Hebrew in Palestine when Jesus Christ was on earth are early indications that the apostle Matthew first wrote his Gospel account in Hebrew. For instance, Eusebius (of the third and fourth centuries C.E.) said that "the evangelist Matthew delivered his Gospel in the Hebrew tongue." (*Patrologia Graeca,* Vol. XXII, col. 941) And Jerome (of the fourth and fifth centuries C.E.) stated in his work *De viris inlustribus* (Concerning Illustrious Men), chapter III: "Matthew, who is also Levi, and who from a publican came to be an apostle, first of all composed a Gospel of Christ in Judaea in the Hebrew language and characters for the benefit of those of the circumcision who had believed. . . . Moreover, the Hebrew itself is preserved to this day in the library at Caesarea, which the martyr Pamphilus so diligently collected." (Translation from the Latin text edited by E. C. Richardson and published in the series "Texte und Untersuchungen zur Geschichte der altchristlichen Literatur," Leipzig, 1896, Vol. 14, pp. 8, 9.) Hence, Jesus Christ as a man on earth could well have used a form of Hebrew and a dialect of Aramaic.—See HEBREW, II.

ARAM-MAACAH. See ARAM No. 5.

ARAM-NAHARAIM. See ARAM No. 5.

ARAM-ZOBAH. See ARAM No. 5.

ARAN (A'ran). A son of Sheik Dishan; descendant of Seir the Horite.—Ge 36:20, 28; 1Ch 1:42.

ARARAT (Ar'a·rat). The name applied to a region and also to a mountain range in what is now eastern Turkey, lying close to the borders of Iran and the U.S.S.R.

Following the Flood, Noah's ark settled on "the mountains of Ararat." (Ge 8:4) In the reign of King Hezekiah, it was to "the land of Ararat" that Sennacherib's sons, Adrammelech and Sharezer, fled after murdering their father. (2Ki 19:37; Isa 37:38) Jeremiah foretold that Ararat would be among "the kingdoms" to come up against Babylon at the time of her destruction, in the sixth century B.C.E. (Jer 51:27) These latter Scriptural references indicate a land N of Assyria. Eusebius, Jerome, and the majority of other early "Christian" writers considered Ararat as equivalent to Armenia, and the Greek *Septuagint* rendering of Isaiah 37:38 and the Latin *Vulgate* reading of 2 Kings 19:37 so represent it. Numerous Assyrian inscriptions from the reigns of Shalmaneser I, Ashurnasirpal II, Shalmaneser III, Tiglath-pileser III, and Sargon II in the ninth and eighth centuries B.C.E. make

reference to Ararat as "Urartu." An inscription of Esar-haddon, another son of Sennacherib and successor to the Assyrian throne, says that he defeated his patricidal brothers' armies at Hanigalbat, in the area of Armenia. On the basis of these inscriptions and the association by Jeremiah of Ararat with the kingdoms of Minni and Ashkenaz, it appears that the land of Ararat was situated in the mountainous region of Lake Van in ancient Armenia, with the headwaters of the Tigris River to the S and the Caucasus Mountains to the N.

The name Ararat is specifically applied to the culminating mountain of this region, and it is the traditional resting-place of Noah's ark. There are two conical peaks about 11 km (7 mi) apart and separated by a deep depression. The higher of the peaks rises some 5,165 m (16,950 ft) above sea level and is covered with perpetual snow for the last 900 m (3,000 ft) up to its summit. The lower peak, to the SE, is 3,914 m (12,840 ft) above sea level. The loftier peak is of particularly difficult ascent and was first ascended by Parrot in 1829. Many place-names in the region recall the Biblical account. Mount Ararat itself is called by the Turks *Aghri Dagh* (Mount of the Ark) and by the Persians *Koh-i-nuh* (Noah's Mountain).—See ARK No. 1.

ARAUNAH (A·rau'nah). The Jebusite owner of the threshing floor purchased by King David for building an altar to Jehovah. This action resulted as the divinely indicated means of ending a scourge provoked by David's numbering of the people.—2Sa 24:16-25; 1Ch 21:15-28.

Araunah apparently offered the place, along with cattle and wood implements for the sacrifice, without charge, but David insisted on paying a price. The record at 2 Samuel 24:24 shows that David purchased the threshing floor and the cattle for 50 silver shekels ($110). However, the account at 1 Chronicles 21:25 speaks of David's paying 600 gold shekels (c. $77,000) for the site. The writer of Second Samuel deals only with the purchase as it relates to the altar location and the materials for the sacrifice then made, and it thus appears that the purchase price referred to by him was restricted to these things. On the other hand, the writer of First Chronicles discusses matters as relating to the temple later built on the site and associates the purchase with that construction. (1Ch 22:1-6; 2Ch 3:1) Since the entire temple area was very large, it appears that the sum of 600 gold shekels applies to the purchase of this large area rather than to the small portion needed for the altar first built by David.

A natural stone scarp still exists today under the Muslim Dome of the Rock occupying part of the original temple site, and this stone may represent the early threshing floor of Araunah.

In the Chronicles record Araunah is called Ornan.—1Ch 21:18-28; 2Ch 3:1.

ARBA (Ar′ba) [Four]. He is called "the father" or "the great man" of the Anakim and appears to have been the founder of Kiriath-arba, later called Hebron. (Jos 14:15; 15:13; 21:11) Some consider Anak to be a name applying to the giant race descended from Arba rather than to be the personal name of Arba's son and thus view Arba as the actual progenitor of the Anakim.—See ANAK; ANAKIM.

ARBATHITE (Ar′bath·ite) [Of (Belonging to) Beth-arabah]. One belonging to the wilderness city of Beth-arabah (Jos 15:61), a city situated near Jericho in the District of the Jordan Valley. (Jos 18:21, 22) One of David's mighty men of war, Abi-albon, or Abiel, was an Arbathite.—2Sa 23:8, 31; 1Ch 11:10, 32.

ARBEL, HOUSE OF (Ar′bel). The house of Arbel ("Beth-arbel," AT, JB, RS) was despoiled at some unspecified time by Shalman. (Ho 10:14) This place is usually linked with Irbid, located about 29 km (18 mi) SE of the Sea of Galilee, hence in Gilead.

ARBITE (Ar′bite). A native of the city of Arab, located near Hebron in the mountainous region of Judah. Paarai, one of David's mighty men, was an Arbite.—2Sa 23:8, 35.

ARCHAEOLOGY. Biblical archaeology is the study of the peoples and events of the Bible through the intriguing record buried in the earth. The archaeologist digs up and analyzes rock, ruined walls and buildings, and shattered cities as well as uncovers pottery, clay tablets, written inscriptions, tombs, and other ancient remains, or artifacts, from which he gleans information. Such studies often improve understanding of the circumstances under which the Bible was written and under which ancient men of faith lived, as well as the languages they, and the peoples around them, employed. They have expanded our knowledge of all the regions touched by the Bible: Palestine, Egypt, Persia, Assyria, Babylonia, Asia Minor, Greece, and Rome.

Biblical archaeology is relatively a new science. Only in 1822 did decipherment of the Rosetta Stone unlock Egyptian hieroglyphics. Assyrian cuneiform was decoded more than 20 years later. Systematic excavations were begun in Assyria in 1843 and in Egypt in 1850.

Some Major Sites and Finds. Archaeology has served to confirm many historical features of the Biblical account with regard to these lands and to substantiate points once held in question by modern critics. Skepticism as regards the Tower of Babel, denials of the existence of a Babylonian king named Belshazzar and of an Assyrian king named Sargon (whose names, up until the nineteenth century C.E., were not found in sources independent of the Bible record), and other adverse criticisms as to Bible data relating to these lands have all been demonstrated to be without foundation. Contrariwise, a wealth of evidence has been unearthed that harmonizes fully with the Scriptural account.

Babylonia. Excavations in and around the ancient city of Babylon have revealed the sites of several ziggurats, or pyramidlike, staged temple-towers, including the ruined temple of Etemenanki inside Babylon's walls. Records and inscriptions found concerning such temples often contain the words, "Its top shall reach the heavens," and King Nebuchadnezzar is recorded as saying: "I raised the summit of the Tower of stages at Etemenanki so that its top rivalled the heavens." One fragment found N of the temple of Marduk in Babylon related the fall of such a ziggurat in these words: "The building of this temple offended the gods. In a night they threw down what had been built. They scattered them abroad, and made strange their speech. The progress they impeded." (*Bible and Spade,* by S. L. Caiger, 1938, p. 29) The ziggurat located at Uruk (Biblical Erech) was found to be built with clay, bricks, and asphalt.—Compare Ge 11:1-9.

Near the Ishtar Gate in Babylon some 300 cuneiform tablets were uncovered relating to the period of King Nebuchadnezzar's reign. Among lists of the names of workers and captives then living in Babylon to whom provisions were given appears that of "Yaukin, king of the land of Yahud," that is, "Jehoiachin, the king of the land of Judah," who was taken to Babylon at the time of Nebuchadnezzar's conquest of Jerusalem in 617 B.C.E. He was released from the house of detention by Awil-Marduk (Evil-merodach), Nebuchadnezzar's successor, and was given a daily allowance of food. (2Ki 25:27-30) Five of Jehoiachin's sons are also mentioned on these tablets. —1Ch 3:17, 18.

Abundant evidence has been found of Babylon's pantheon of gods, including the chief god Marduk, commonly referred to later as Bel, and the god Nebo, both mentioned at Isaiah 46:1, 2. Much of the information on Nebuchadnezzar's own inscriptions deals with his vast building program that made Babylon such a magnificent city. (Compare Da 4:30.) The name of his successor Awil-Marduk (called Evil-merodach at 2Ki 25:27) appears on a vase discovered at Susa (Elam).

Near modern Baghdad excavations in the latter half of the 19th century produced numerous clay tablets and cylinders, including the now famous Nabonidus Chronicle. All objections to the record at Daniel chapter 5 as to Belshazzar's ruling in Babylon at the time of its fall were dispelled by this document, which proved that Belshazzar, eldest son of Nabonidus, was coregent with his father and that in the latter part of his reign Nabonidus entrusted the government of Babylon to his son Belshazzar.

Ur, the ancient home of Abraham (Ge 11:28-31), similarly proved to have been a prominent metropolis with a highly developed civilization. A Sumerian city, it was located on the Euphrates near the Persian Gulf. Excavations there by Sir Leonard Woolley indicate that it was at the height of its power and prestige at the time of Abraham's departure for Canaan (b. 1943 B.C.E.). Its ziggurat temple is the best preserved of those found. The royal tombs of Ur yielded an abundance of gold objects and jewelry of very high artistic caliber, also musical instruments such as the harp. (Compare Ge 4:21.) A small steel (not merely iron) ax was also found. (Compare Ge 4:22.) Here, too, thousands of clay tablets revealed much of the details of life nearly 4,000 years in the past.—See Ur No. 2.

At the site of ancient Sippar on the Euphrates about 32 km (20 mi) from Baghdad, a clay cylinder about King Cyrus the conqueror of Babylon was found. This cylinder tells about the ease with which Cyrus captured the city and also outlines his policy of restoring to their native lands the captive peoples residing in Babylon, thus harmonizing with the Biblical account of Cyrus as the prophesied conqueror of Babylon and of the restoration of the Jews to Palestine during Cyrus' reign. —Isa 44:28; 45:1; 2Ch 36:23.

Assyria. Near Khorsabad, on a northern tributary of the Tigris River, in 1843 the palace of Assyrian King Sargon II, covering some 10 ha (25 acres), was discovered, and subsequent archaeological work there brought this king, mentioned at Isaiah 20:1, out of secular obscurity to a position of historical prominence. (PICTURE, Vol. 1, p. 960) In one of his annals he claims to have captured Samaria (740 B.C.E.). He also records the capture of Ashdod, referred to at Isaiah 20:1. Once considered nonexistent by many prominent scholars, Sargon II is now one of the best known of the kings of Assyria.

Nineveh, Assyria's capital, was the site of excavations that unearthed the immense palace of Sennacherib, containing about 70 rooms, with sculptured slabs lining over 3,000 m (nearly 10,-000 ft) of the walls. One depicted Judean prisoners being led into captivity following the fall of Lachish in 732 B.C.E. (2Ki 18:13-17; 2Ch 32:9; PICTURE, Vol. 1, p. 952) Of even greater interest were the annals of Sennacherib found here at Nineveh, which were recorded on prisms (clay cylinders). On certain prisms Sennacherib describes the Assyrian campaign against Palestine in Hezekiah's reign (732 B.C.E.), but, notably, the boastful monarch makes no claim of having taken the city, thus confirming the Bible account. (See SENNACHERIB.) The account of Sennacherib's assassination at the hands of his sons is also recorded on an inscription of Esar-haddon, Sennacherib's successor, and the assassination is referred to in an inscription of the following king. (2Ki 19:37) In addition to the mention of King Hezekiah by Sennacherib, the names of Judean Kings Ahaz and Manasseh, and the names of Israelite Kings Omri, Jehu, Jehoash, Menahem, and Hoshea, and also Hazael of Damascus, all appear on cuneiform records of various Assyrian emperors.

Persia. Near Behistun, Iran (ancient Persia), King Darius I (521-486 B.C.E.; Ezr 6:1-15) had an immense inscription carved high up on a limestone cliff, describing his unification of the Persian Empire and attributing his success to his god Ahura Mazda. Of primary value is the fact that the inscription was recorded in three languages, Babylonian (Akkadian), Elamite, and old Persian, thus serving as a key for the deciphering of the Assyro-Babylonian cuneiform, till then undeciphered. Thousands of clay tablets and inscriptions in the Babylonian language can now be read as a result of this work.

Shushan, the scene of the events recorded in the book of Esther, was excavated by French archaeologists between 1880 and 1890. (Es 1:2) The royal palace of Xerxes, covering about 1 ha (2.5 acres), was uncovered, revealing the splendor and magnificence of the Persian kings. The finds confirmed the exactitude of details set down by the writer of Esther as relating to the administration of the Persian kingdom and the construction of the palace. The book *The Monuments and the Old Testament,* by I. M. Price (1946, p. 408), comments: "There is no event described in the Old Testament whose structural surroundings can be so vividly and accurately restored from actual

excavations as 'Shushan the Palace.'"—See SHU-
SHAN.

Mari and Nuzi. The ancient royal city of Mari
(Tell Hariri) near the Euphrates River, about
11 km (7 mi) NNW of Abu Kemal in SE Syria, was
the site of excavations from 1933 on. An enormous
palace covering some 6 ha (15 acres) and containing 300 rooms was discovered, and its archives
yielded more than 20,000 clay tablets. The palace
complex included not only the royal apartments
but also administrative offices and a school for
scribes. Great mural paintings or frescoes decorated many of the walls, the bathrooms were
equipped with tubs, and cake molds were found
in the kitchens. The city appears to have been one
of the most outstanding and brilliant of the period
in the early second millennium B.C.E. The texts on
the clay tablets included royal decrees, public no-
tices, accounts, and orders for construction of canals, locks, dams, and other irrigation projects, as
well as correspondence concerning imports, exports, and foreign affairs. Frequent censuses were
taken involving taxation and military enrollment.
Religion was prominent, particularly the worship
of Ishtar, the goddess of fertility, whose temple
was also found. Divination was practiced as in
Babylon by observation of livers, astronomy, and
similar methods. The city was largely destroyed
by Babylonian King Hammurabi. Of particular interest was the appearance of the names of Peleg,
Serug, Nahor, Terah, and Haran, all listed as cities of northern Mesopotamia and reflecting the
names of the relatives of Abraham.—Ge 11:17-32.

Nuzi, an ancient city to the E of the Tigris and
SE of Nineveh, excavated during 1925-1931, yielded an inscribed clay map, the oldest yet discovered, as well as evidence that as early as the 15th
century B.C.E. there was buying and selling on the
installment plan there. Some 20,000 clay tablets, considered to have been written by Hurrian scribes in the Babylonian language, were
unearthed. These contain a wealth of detail regarding the legal jurisprudence at that time, involving such things as adoption, marriage contracts, rights of inheritance, and wills. Certain
aspects show a relatively close parallel to customs
described in the Genesis account concerning the
patriarchs. The practice of a childless couple's
adopting a son, whether freeborn or slave, to care
for them, bury them, and be their heir, shows a
similarity to the statement by Abraham concerning his trusted slave Eliezer at Genesis 15:2. The
selling of birthrights is described, recalling the
case of Jacob and Esau. (Ge 25:29-34) The texts
also show that possession of the family gods, often
small clay figurines, was viewed as similar to

holding a title deed, so that the one possessing the
gods was considered to hold the right to the property or the inheritance thereof. This may illustrate
the situation involving Rachel's taking her father's
teraphim and his great concern for their recovery.
—Ge 31:14-16, 19, 25-35.

Egypt. The closest view given in the Bible of
Egypt centers around Joseph's entry there and the
subsequent arrival and sojourn of the entire family of Jacob in that land. Archaeological finds show
this picture to be an extremely accurate one, and
one that could not reasonably have been thus
presented by a writer living at a much later time
(as some critics have tried to say was the case
with the recorder of that portion of the Genesis
account). As the book *New Light on Hebrew Origins,* by J. G. Duncan (1936, p. 174), states concerning the writer of the account about Joseph:
"He employs the correct title in use and exactly as
it was used at the period referred to, and, where
there is no Hebrew equivalent, he simply adopts
the Egyptian word and transliterates it into Hebrew." The Egyptian names, the position of Joseph
as Potiphar's house manager, the prison houses,
the titles "the chief of the cupbearers" and "the
chief of the bakers," the importance placed on
dreams by the Egyptians, the practice of Egyptian
bakers of carrying baskets of bread on their heads
(Ge 40:1, 2, 16, 17), the position as prime minister
and food administrator accorded Joseph by Pharaoh, the manner of inducting him into office,
the Egyptian detestation of herders of sheep, the
strong influence of magicians in the Egyptian
court, the settling of the sojourning Israelites in
the land of Goshen, the Egyptian burial practices
—all these and many other points described in the
Bible record are clearly substantiated by the archaeological evidence produced in Egypt.—Ge 39:
1–47:27; 50:1-3.

At Karnak (ancient Thebes), on the Nile River, a
vast Egyptian temple contains an inscription on its
S wall confirming the campaign of Egyptian King
Shishak (Sheshonk I) in Palestine, described at
1 Kings 14:25, 26 and 2 Chronicles 12:1-9. The
giant relief depicting his victories shows 156 man-
acled Palestinian prisoners, each representing a
city or village, the name of which is given in
hieroglyphics. Among the names identifiable are
those of Rabbith (Jos 19:20), Taanach, Beth-shean
and Megiddo (where a portion of a stele or inscribed pillar of Shishak has been excavated) (Jos
17:11), Shunem (Jos 19:18), Rehob (Jos 19:28),
Hapharaim (Jos 19:19), Gibeon (Jos 18:25), Beth-
horon (Jos 21:22), Aijalon (Jos 21:24), Socoh (Jos
15:35), and Arad (Jos 12:14). He even lists the
"Field of Abram" as one of his captures, the

earliest reference to Abraham in Egyptian records. Also found in this area was a monument of Merneptah, son of Ramses II, containing a hymn in which the only occurrence of the name Israel in ancient Egyptian texts is to be found.

At Tell el-Amarna, about 270 km (170 mi) S of Cairo, a peasant woman accidentally discovered clay tablets that led to the uncovering of many documents in Akkadian from the royal archives of Amenhotep III and his son Akhenaton. The 379 published tablets comprise correspondence to Pharaoh from the vassal princes of the numerous city-kingdoms of Syria and Palestine, including some from the governor of Urusalim (Jerusalem), and reveal a picture of warring feuds and intrigue completely concordant with the Scriptural description of those times. The "Habiru," about whom numerous complaints are made in these letters, have been related by some to the Hebrews, but the evidence indicates that they were, rather, diverse nomadic peoples occupying a low social status in the society of that period.—See HEBREW, I (The "Habiru").

Elephantine, an island in the Nile to the extreme S of Egypt (near Aswan) bearing this Greek name, was the site of a Jewish colony following the fall of Jerusalem in 607 B.C.E. A large number of documents written in Aramaic, mainly on papyrus, were found here in 1903, bearing dates from the fifth century B.C.E. and the reign of the Medo-Persian Empire. The documents make mention of Sanballat, the governor of Samaria.—Ne 4:1.

Undoubtedly the most valuable finds produced in Egypt have been the papyrus fragments and portions of Bible books, of both the Hebrew and the Greek Scriptures, dating all the way back to the first century B.C.E. Egypt's dry climate and sandy soil made it an unexcelled storehouse for preserving such papyrus documents.—See MANU-SCRIPTS OF THE BIBLE.

Palestine and Syria. Some 600 datable sites have been excavated in these areas. Much of the information obtained is of a general nature, supporting the Bible record on a broad basis instead of specifically relating to certain details or events. As an example, in the past, efforts were made to discredit the Bible's account of the complete desolation of Judah during the Babylonian exile. The excavations, however, collectively substantiate the Bible. As W. F. Albright states: "There is not a single known case where a town of Judah proper was continuously occupied through the exilic period. Just to point the contrast, Bethel, which lay just outside the northern boundary of Judah in pre-exilic times, was not destroyed at that time,

but was continuously occupied down into the latter part of the sixth century."—*The Archaeology of Palestine,* 1971, p. 142.

Beth-shan (Beth-shean), an ancient fortress city that guarded the approach to the Valley of Jezreel from the E, was the site of major excavations that revealed 18 different levels of occupation, requiring digging to a depth of 21 m (70 ft). (DIAGRAM, Vol. 1, p. 959) The Scriptural account shows that

Stele on which Merneptah, son of Ramses II, gloats over conquest of Israel; the only known mention of Israel in ancient Egyptian texts

Beth-shan was not among the towns originally occupied by the invading Israelites and that at the time of Saul it was occupied by the Philistines. (Jos 17:11; Jg 1:27; 1Sa 31:8-12) The excavations in general support this record and indicate a destruction of Beth-shan sometime after the Israelites' defeat near Shiloh. (Jer 7:12) Of particular interest was the discovery of certain Canaanite temples at Beth-shan. First Samuel 31:10 states that the Philistines put King Saul's armor "in the house of the Ashtoreth images, and his corpse they fastened on the wall of Beth-shan," while 1 Chronicles 10:10 says "they put his armor in the house of their god, and his skull they fastened to the house of Dagon." Two of the temples unearthed were of the same time period and one gives evidence of being the temple of Ashtoreth, while the other is thought to be that of Dagon, thus harmonizing with the above texts as to the existence of two temples in Beth-shan.

Ezion-geber was Solomon's seaport city on the Gulf of 'Aqaba. It is possibly the present-day Tell el-Kheleifeh, which was excavated during 1937-1940 and produced evidence of a copper-smelting site, copper slag and bits of copper ore being found on a low mound in that region. However, the original conclusions of archaeologist Nelson Glueck concerning the site were radically revised by him in an article in *The Biblical Archaeologist* (1965, p. 73). His opinion that there had been a blast furnace system of smelting employed there was based on the finding of what were thought to be "flue-holes" in the principal building excavated. He now has come to the conclusion that these holes in the building's walls are the result of "the decay and/or burning of wooden beams laid across the width of the walls for bonding or anchoring purposes." The building, previously thought to be a smelter, is now believed to be a storehouse-granary structure. While it is still believed that metallurgical operations did take place here, they are not now considered to have been of the dimensions previously conjectured. This underscores the fact that the meaning ascribed to archaeological findings is dependent primarily upon the individual interpretation of the archaeologist, which interpretation is by no means infallible. The Bible itself mentions no copper industry at Ezion-geber, describing only the casting of copper items at a site in the Jordan Valley.—1Ki 7:45, 46.

Hazor in Galilee was described as being "the head of all these kingdoms," in Joshua's time. (Jos 11:10) Excavations there showed that the city once covered some 60 ha (150 acres), with a large population, making it one of the major cities of that region. Solomon fortified the city, and the evidence from that period indicates it may have been a chariot city.—1Ki 9:15, 19.

Jericho has been subjected to excavations during three different expeditions (1907-1909; 1930-1936; 1952-1958) and the successive interpretations of the findings demonstrate again the fact that archaeology, like other fields of human science, is not a source of positively stable information. Each of the three expeditions has produced data, but each has arrived at different conclusions as to the history of the city and particularly as to the date of its fall before the Israelite conquerors. At any rate, the combined results may be said to present the general picture set forth in the book *Biblical Archaeology*, by G. E. Wright (1963, p. 78), which states: "The city underwent a terrible destruction or a series of destructions during the second millennium B.C., and remained virtually unoccupied for generations." The destruction was accompanied by intense fire, as is shown by the excavated evidence. —Compare Jos 6:20-26.

In Jerusalem in 1867 an old water tunnel was discovered, running from the fountain of Gihon back into the hill behind. (See GIHON No. 2.) This may illustrate the account of David's capture of the city at 2 Samuel 5:6-10. In 1909-1911 the entire system of tunnels connected with the Gihon spring was cleared. One tunnel, known as the Siloam Tunnel, averaged 1.8 m (6 ft) in height and was cut through solid rock for a distance of some 533 m (1,749 ft) from Gihon to the Pool of Siloam in the Tyropoeon Valley (within the city). It thus seems to be the project of King Hezekiah described at 2 Kings 20:20 and 2 Chronicles 32:30. Of great interest was the ancient inscription found on the tunnel wall in early Hebrew monumental script describing the cutting of the tunnel and its length. This inscription is used for comparison in dating other Hebrew inscriptions found.

Lachish, 44 km (27 mi) WSW of Jerusalem, was a principal fortress protecting the Judean hill country. At Jeremiah 34:7 the prophet tells of Nebuchadnezzar's forces fighting against "Jerusalem and against all the cities of Judah that were left remaining, against Lachish and against Azekah; for they, the fortified cities, were the ones that remained over among the cities of Judah." Excavations at Lachish produced evidence of destruction by fire twice within a period of a few years, believed to represent two attacks by the Babylonians (618-617 and 609-607 B.C.E.), after which it lay uninhabited for a long period.

In the ashes of the second burning were found 21 ostraca (pieces of pottery inscribed with writing), believed to represent correspondence shortly before the destruction of the city in Nebuchadnezzar's final assault. Known as the Lachish Letters, these writings reflect a period of crisis and anxiety and appear to have been written from remaining outposts of Judean troops to Yaosh, a military commander in Lachish. (PICTURE, Vol. 1, p. 325) Letter number IV contains the statement: "May YHWH [that is, Jehovah] let my lord hear even now tidings of good. . . . we are watching for the fire signals of Lachish, according to all the signs which my lord gives, because we do not see Azekah." This passage remarkably expresses the situation described at Jeremiah 34:7, quoted above, and apparently indicates that Azekah had already fallen or at least was failing to send out the fire or smoke signals expected.

Letter number III, written by "Hoshaiah," includes the following: "May YHWH [that is, Jehovah] cause my lord to hear tidings of peace! . . . And it has been reported to your servant saying, 'The commander of the army, Coniah son of Elnathan, has come down in order to go into Egypt and to Hodaviah son of Ahijah and his men he has sent to obtain [supplies] from him.'" This portion could well represent the fact of Judah's turning to Egypt for help, as condemned by the prophets. (Isa 31:1; Jer 46:25, 26) The names Elnathan and Hoshaiah, occurring in the complete text of this letter, are also found at Jeremiah 36:12 and Jeremiah 42:1. Other names appearing in the letters also occur in the book of Jeremiah: Gemariah (36:10), Neriah (32:12), and Jaazaniah (35:3). Whether in any case they represent the same individual or not cannot be said, but the coincidence in itself is notable in view of Jeremiah's being a contemporary of that period.

Of special interest is the frequent use of the Tetragrammaton in these letters, thus manifesting that at that time the Jews had no aversion to the use of the divine name. Also of interest is a clay seal impression found that refers to "Gedaliah, who is over the house." Gedaliah is the name of the governor appointed over Judah by Nebuchadnezzar after Jerusalem's fall, and many consider it likely that the seal impression refers to him.—2Ki 25:22; compare Isa 22:15; 36:3.

Megiddo was a strategic fortress city commanding an important pass to the Valley of Jezreel. It was rebuilt by Solomon and is mentioned with the storage and chariot cities of his reign. (1Ki 9:15-19) Excavations at the site (Tell el-Mutesellim), a 5.3-ha (13 acre) mound, uncovered what some scholars (but not all) think were stables capable of caring for some 450 horses. At first these structures were credited to Solomon's time, but later scholars redated them to a later period, perhaps the time of Ahab.

The Moabite Stone was one of the earliest discoveries of importance in the area E of the Jordan. (PICTURE, Vol. 1, p. 325) Found in 1868 at Dhiban, N of the Arnon Valley, it presents Moabite King Mesha's version of his revolt against Israel. (Compare 2 Ki 1:1; 3:4, 5.) In part the inscription says: "I (am) Mesha, son of Chemosh-[. . .], king of Moab, the Dibonite . . . As for Omri, king of Israel, he humbled Moab many years (lit., days), for Chemosh [the god of Moab] was angry at his land. And his son followed him and he also said, 'I will humble Moab.' In my time he spoke (thus), but I have triumphed over him and over his house, while Israel hath perished for ever! . . . And Chemosh said to me, 'Go, take Nebo from Israel!' So I went by night and fought against it from the break of dawn until noon, taking it and slaying all . . . And I took from there the [vessels] of Yahweh, dragging them before Chemosh." (*Ancient Near Eastern Texts,* edited by J. B. Pritchard, 1974, p. 320) Thus the stone not only mentions the name of King Omri of Israel but also, in the 18th line, contains God's name in the form of the Tetragrammaton.

The Moabite Stone also mentions numerous places referred to in the Bible: Ataroth and Nebo (Nu 32:34, 38); the Arnon, Aroer, Medeba, and Dibon (Jos 13:9); Bamoth-baal, Beth-baal-meon, Jahaz, and Kiriathaim (Jos 13:17-19); Bezer (Jos 20:8); Horonaim (Isa 15:5); Beth-diblathaim and Kerioth. (Jer 48:22, 24) It thus supports the historicity of all these places.

Ras Shamra (ancient Ugarit), on the N Syrian coast opposite the island of Cyprus, has provided information about worship quite similar to Canaan's, including its gods and goddesses, temples, "sacred" prostitutes, rites, sacrifices, and prayers. A room was found between a temple to Baal and another temple devoted to Dagon that contained a library of hundreds of religious texts considered to date from the 15th and early 14th centuries B.C.E. The mythological poetical texts reveal much about the Canaanite divinities El, Baal, and Asherah and the degrading form of idolatry that accompanied their worship. Merrill F. Unger in his book *Archaeology and the Old Testament* (1964, p. 175) comments: "The Ugaritic epic literature has helped to reveal the depth of depravity which characterized Canaanite religion. Being a polytheism of an extremely debased type, Canaanite cultic practice was barbarous and thoroughly licentious." Images of Baal and other gods were also found. (See GODS

AND GODDESSES [Canaanite Deities].) A previously unknown type of alphabetic cuneiform writing (different from the Akkadian cuneiform) distinguished these texts. It follows the same order as Hebrew but adds other letters to make a total of 30. As at Ur, a steel battle-ax was also unearthed.

Samaria, the strongly fortified capital of the northern kingdom of Israel, was built on a hill rising some 90 m (295 ft) above the valley floor. Proof of its strength to resist long sieges, such as those described at 2 Kings 6:24-30 in the case of Syria, and 2 Kings 17:5 in the case of the powerful Assyrian army, is evidenced by the remains of sturdy double walls, at some points forming a bulwark 10 m (33 ft) wide. The stone masonry found on the site, considered as of the time of Kings Omri, Ahab, and Jehu, is of splendid workmanship. What appears to be the palace platform measures about 90 m (295 ft) by about 180 m (590 ft). Large quantities of ivory pieces, plaques, and panels were found in the palace area and may relate to Ahab's house of ivory mentioned at 1 Kings 22:39. (Compare Am 6:4.) At the NW corner of the summit a large cemented pool was found, measuring some 10 m (33 ft) in length and about 5 m (17 ft) in width. It could be "the pool of Samaria," in which Ahab's chariot was washed of his blood.—1Ki 22:38.

Of interest were 63 potsherds with ink inscriptions (ostraca) considered as dating from the eighth century B.C.E. Receipts for shipments of wine and oil to Samaria from other towns show an Israelite system of writing numbers by use of vertical, horizontal, and slanted strokes. A typical receipt reads as follows:

In the tenth year.

To Gaddiyau [probably the steward of the treasury].

From Azah [perhaps the village or district sending the wine or oil].

Abi-ba'al 2

Ahaz 2

Sheba 1

Meriba'al 1

These receipts also reveal a frequent use of the name Baal as part of the names, about 7 names including this name for every 11 containing some form of the name Jehovah, likely indicating the infiltration of Baal worship as described in the Bible account.

The fiery destruction of Sodom and Gomorrah and the existence of pits of bitumen (asphalt) in that region are described in the Bible. (Ge 14:3, 10; 19:12-28) Many scholars believe that the waters of the Dead Sea may have risen in the past and extended the southern end of the sea for a considerable distance, thus covering what may have been the sites of these two cities. Explorations show the area to be a burned-out region of oil and asphalt. Concerning the matter, the book *Light From the Ancient Past,* by Jack Finegan (1959, p. 147), states: "A careful survey of the literary, geological, and archeological evidence points to the conclusion that the infamous 'cities of the valley' (Genesis 19:29) were in the area which now is submerged . . . and that their ruin was accomplished by a great earthquake, probably accompanied by explosions, lightning, ignition of natural gas, and general conflagration."—See also SODOM.

Relating to the Christian Greek Scriptures. The use by Jesus of a denarius coin bearing the head of Tiberius Caesar (Mr 12:15-17) is confirmed by the finding of a silver denarius coin bearing the head of Tiberius and put in circulation about the year 15 C.E. (PICTURE, Vol. 2, p. 544) (Compare Lu 3:1, 2.) The fact that Pontius Pilate was then Roman governor of Judea is also demonstrated by a stone slab found at Caesarea bearing the Latin names *Pontius Pilatus* and *Tiberieum.* —See PILATE; PICTURE, Vol. 2, p. 741.

The Acts of Apostles, which gives clear evidence of having been written by Luke, contains numerous references to cities and their provinces and to officials of different types and with varying titles, holding office at a particular time—a presentation fraught with possibility of error on the part of the writer. (Note also Lu 3:1, 2.) Yet the archaeological evidence produced demonstrates to a remarkable degree Luke's accuracy. Thus, at Acts 14:1-6, Luke places Lystra and Derbe within the territory of Lycaonia but implies that Iconium was in another territory. Roman writers, including Cicero, referred to Iconium as being in Lycaonia. However, a monument discovered in 1910 shows that Iconium was considered to be indeed a city of Phrygia rather than of Lycaonia.

Similarly, an inscription discovered at Delphi confirms that Gallio was proconsul of Achaia, likely in 51-52 C.E. (Ac 18:12) Some 19 inscriptions dating from the second century B.C.E. to the third century C.E. confirm the correctness of Luke's use of the title city rulers (singular, *po·li·tar'khes*) as applying to the officials of Thessalonica (Ac 17:6, 8), five of these inscriptions referring specifically to that city. (See CITY RULERS.) Likewise, the reference to Publius as "the principal man" (*pro'tos*) of Malta (Ac 28:7) employs the exact title to be used, as is shown by its appearance on two Maltese inscriptions, one in Latin and one in Greek. Magical texts as well as the temple of Artemis were found at Ephesus (Ac 19:19, 27); excavations there also unearthed a theater capable of holding some 25,000 people, and inscriptions referring to "the commissioners of festivals and games," like those who intervened on Paul's behalf, and also to a "recorder," like the one who quieted the mob on that occasion.—Ac 19:29-31, 35, 41.

Some of such findings moved Charles Gore to write of Luke's accuracy in *A New Commentary on Holy Scripture:* "It should of course be recognized that modern archæology has almost forced upon critics of St. Luke a verdict of remarkable accuracy in all his allusions to secular facts and events."—Edited by Gore, Goudge, and Guillaume, 1929, p. 210.

Comparative Value of Archaeology. Archaeology has produced beneficial information that has aided in the identification (often tentative) of Biblical sites, has unearthed written documents that have contributed to a better understanding of the original languages in which the Scriptures were written, and has shed light on the living conditions and activities of ancient peoples and rulers referred to in the Bible. Yet, insofar as archaeology relates to the authenticity and reliability of the Bible, as well as to faith in it, its teachings, and its revelation of God's purposes and promises, it must be said that it is a nonessential supplement and an unrequired confirmation of the truth of God's Word. As the apostle Paul expresses it: "Faith is the assured expectation of things hoped for, the evident demonstration of realities though not beheld. By faith we perceive that the systems of things were put in order by God's word, so that what is beheld has come to be out of things that do not appear." (Heb 11:1, 3) "We are walking by faith, not by sight."—2Co 5:7.

This does not mean that Christian faith does not have any basis in what can be seen or that it deals only with intangibles. But it is true that in every period and age there has been ample contemporary evidence surrounding people, as well as within themselves and their own experiences, that could convince them that the Bible is the true source of divine revelation and that it contains nothing that is out of harmony with provable facts. (Ro 1:18-23) The knowledge of the past in the light of archaeological discovery is interesting and appreciated, but not vital. The knowledge of the past in the light of the Bible is, alone, essential and solidly reliable. The Bible, with or without archaeology, gives true meaning to the present and illuminates the future. (Ps 119:105; 2Pe 1:19-21) It is, in reality, a weak faith that must rely on moldering bricks, broken vases, and crumbling walls to bolster it up and serve as a crutch.

Uncertainty underlying conclusions. While archaeological discoveries at times have provided a convenient answer to those who have carped at Bible accounts or criticized the historicity of certain events, and while such finds have helped to disencumber the minds of sincere persons who have been overly impressed by the arguments of such critics, yet archaeology has not silenced Bible critics nor is it a truly sound foundation for basing one's belief in the Bible record. The conclusions drawn from the majority of the excavations made depend mainly upon the deductive and inductive reasoning of the investigators, who, somewhat like detectives, assemble a case for which they argue. Even in modern times, although detectives may uncover and amass an impressive array of circumstantial and material evidence, any case founded purely upon such evidence while lacking in the testimony of creditable witnesses directly relating to the matter in question would, if brought to court, be considered very weak. Decisions based solely on such evidence have resulted in gross error and injustice. How much more so must this be the case when 2,000 or 3,000 years intervene between the investigators and the time of the event.

A similar parallel is drawn by archaeologist R. J. C. Atkinson, who says: "One has only to think how difficult would be the task of future archaeologists if they had to reconstruct the ritual, dogma and doctrine of the Christian Churches from the ruins of the church buildings alone, *without the aid of any written record or inscription.* We thus have the paradoxical situation that archaeology, the only method of investigating man's past in the absence of written records, becomes increasingly less effective as a means of inquiry the more nearly it approaches those aspects of human life which are the more specifically *human.*"—*Stonehenge,* London, 1956, p. 167.

Complicating the matter further is the fact that, in addition to their obvious inability to bring the ancient past into focus with anything more than approximate accuracy, and in spite of their endeavoring to maintain a purely objective viewpoint in considering the evidence they unearth, the archaeologists, like other scientists, are nonetheless subject to human failings and personal leanings and ambitions, which can stimulate fallible reasoning. Pointing up the problem, Professor W. F. Albright comments: "On the other hand, there is danger in seeking new discoveries and novel points of view at the expense of more solid earlier work. This is particularly true in fields like Biblical archaeology and geography, where mastery of tools and of methods of investigation is so arduous that there is always a temptation to neglect sound method, substituting clever combinations and brilliant guesses for slower and more systematic work."—*The Westminster Historical Atlas to the Bible,* edited by G. E. Wright, 1956, p. 9.

Differences in dating.   It is important to realize this when considering the dates offered by archaeologists with regard to their finds. Illustrating this, Merrill F. Unger says: "For example, Garstang dates the fall of Jericho *c.* 1400 B.C. . . . ; Albright subscribes to the date *c.* 1290 B.C. . . . ; Hugues Vincent, the celebrated Palestinian archeologist, holds to the date 1250 B.C. . . . ; while H. H. Rowley views Rameses II as the Pharaoh of the Oppression, and the Exodus as having taken place under his successor Marniptah [Merneptah] about 1225 B.C." (*Archaeology and the Old Testament,* p. 164, ftn. 15) While arguing on behalf of the reliability of modern archaeological process and analysis, Professor Albright acknowledges that "it is still very difficult for the non-specialist to pick his way among the conflicting dates and conclusions of archaeologists."—*The Archaeology of Palestine,* p. 253.

It is true that the radiocarbon clock has been employed, along with other modern methods, for dating the artifacts found. However, that this method is not completely accurate is evidenced in the following statement by G. Ernest Wright in *The Biblical Archaeologist* (1955, p. 46): "It may be noted that the new Carbon 14 method of dating ancient remains has not turned out to be as free from error as had been hoped. . . . Certain runs have produced obviously wrong results, probably for a number of reasons. At the moment, one can depend upon the results without question only when several runs have been made which give virtually identical results and when the date *seems correct from other methods of computation* [italics ours]." More recently, *The New Encyclopædia Britannica* (Macropædia, 1976, Vol. 5, p. 508) stated: "Whatever the cause, . . . it is clear that carbon-14 dates lack the accuracy that traditional historians would like to have."—See CHRONOLOGY (Archaeological Dating).

Relative worth of inscriptions.   Thousands upon thousands of ancient inscriptions have been found and are being interpreted. Albright states: "Written documents form by far the most important single body of material discovered by archaeologists. Hence it is extremely important to gain a clear idea of their character and of our ability to interpret them." (*The Westminster Historical Atlas to the Bible,* p. 11) They may be written on broken pottery, clay tablets, papyrus, or carved in granite rock. Whatever the material, the information they convey must still be weighed and tested as to its reliability and worth. Error or outright falsehood can be and frequently has been set down in stone as well as on paper.—See CHRONOLOGY (Bible Chronology and Secular History); SARGON.

As an illustration, the Bible record states that King Sennacherib of Assyria was killed by his two sons, Adrammelech and Sharezer, and was succeeded to the throne by another son, Esar-haddon. (2Ki 19:36, 37) Yet, a Babylonian chronicle stated that, on the 20th of Tebeth, Sennacherib was killed by his son in a revolt. Both Berossus, Babylonian priest of the third century B.C.E., and Nabonidus, Babylonian king of the sixth century B.C.E., gave the same account, to the effect that Sennacherib was assassinated by only one of his sons. However, in a more recently discovered fragment of the Prism of Esar-haddon, the son who succeeded Sennacherib, Esar-haddon clearly states that his brothers (plural) revolted and killed their father and then took flight. Commenting on this, Philip Biberfeld, in *Universal Jewish History* (1948, Vol. I, p. 27), says: "The Babylonian Chronicle, Nabonid, and Berossus were mistaken; only the Biblical account proved to be correct. It was confirmed in all the minor details by the inscription of Esarhaddon and proved to be more accurate regarding this event of Babylonian-Assyrian history than the Babylonian sources themselves. This is a fact of utmost importance for the evaluation of even contemporary sources not in accord with Biblical tradition."

Problems in deciphering and translating. There is also need for due caution on the part of the Christian as to accepting without question the interpretation made of the many inscriptions found in the diverse ancient languages. In some cases, as with the Rosetta Stone and the Behistun Inscription, the decipherers of the languages have been given considerable insight into a previously unknown language by parallel presentations of that language alongside another known language. Yet, it should not be expected that such helps solve all problems or allow for a full understanding of the language with all its shades of meaning and idiomatic expressions. Even the understanding of the basic Bible languages, Hebrew, Aramaic, and Greek, has progressed considerably in recent times, and these languages are still under study. As to the inspired Word of God, we can rightly expect that the Bible's Author would enable us to obtain the correct understanding of its message through the available translations into the modern languages. This is not the case, however, with the uninspired writings of the pagan nations.

Illustrating this need for caution and also manifesting again that an objective approach to the problems existing in the deciphering of the ancient inscriptions is often not as prominent as one might think, the book *The Secret of the Hittites*, by C. W. Ceram, contains the following information concerning a prominent Assyriologist who worked at decoding the "Hittite" language (1956, pp. 106-109): "His work is absolutely phenomenal —a brilliant intermingling of wild blunders with remarkable perceptions . . . Some of his errors were supported by arguments so cogent that decades of study were necessary to overcome them. His ingenious reasoning was backed by such a wealth of philological learning that winnowing the chaff from the wheat was no easy affair." The writer then describes the strong obstinacy of this scholar about any modification of his findings; after many years he finally did agree to make some changes—only to change the very readings that later proved to be the correct ones! In relating the violent dispute, fraught with personal recriminations, that arose between this scholar and another decipherer of the "Hittite" cuneiform, the author states: "Yet the very fanaticism which brings on such quarrels is a necessary motive force if scholars are to make discoveries." Hence, although time and study have eliminated many errors in the understanding of ancient inscriptions, we do well to realize that further investigation may likely bring additional corrections.

The preeminence of the Bible as the source of reliable knowledge, truthful information, and sure guidance is enhanced by these facts. As a body of written documents, the Bible gives us the clearest picture of man's past, and it has reached us, not by excavation, but through its preservation by its Author, Jehovah God. It is "alive and exerts power" (Heb 4:12) and is "the word of the living and enduring God." "All flesh is like grass, and all its glory is like a blossom of grass; the grass becomes withered, and the flower falls off, but the saying of Jehovah endures forever."—1Pe 1:23-25.

ARCHANGEL. The prefix "arch," meaning "chief" or "principal," implies that there is only one archangel, the chief angel; in the Scriptures, "archangel" is never found in the plural. First Thessalonians 4:16, in speaking of the preeminence of the archangel and the authority of his office, does so in reference to the resurrected Lord Jesus Christ: "The Lord himself will descend from heaven with a commanding call, with an archangel's voice and with God's trumpet, and those who are dead in union with Christ will rise first." It is, therefore, not without significance that the only name directly associated with the word "archangel" is Michael.—Jude 9; see MICHAEL No. 1.

ARCHELAUS (Ar·che·la′us) [Ruler of the People]. Son of Herod the Great by his fourth wife, Malthace. Archelaus became king in Judea while young Jesus was down in Egypt with Joseph and Mary. Rather than face his tyrannical rule on their return, Joseph settled his family outside Archelaus' jurisdiction, up in Nazareth of Galilee.—Mt 2:22, 23.

Archelaus' father Herod the Great willed to him the rulership of Judea, Samaria, and Idumea, which was twice the share given to each of the other two sons, and which included the important cities of Jerusalem, Samaria, Joppa, and Caesarea. After Herod's death, Archelaus endeavored to make his rulership more secure by appearing before Augustus in Rome; in spite of opposers to his claim, including his brother and a delegation of Jews, Archelaus was allowed to retain his power, though Augustus made him, not a king, but an ethnarch, a tributary prince ranking higher than a tetrarch. Matthew, however, rightly refers to him as 'reigning,' for the local army had previously proclaimed him king.—*Jewish Antiquities*, by F. Josephus, XVII, 194, 195 (viii, 2).

Archelaus was a cruel ruler and very unpopular with the Jews. In quelling a riot, he once had 3,000 of them ruthlessly slain in the temple grounds; he twice deposed the high priest; and in addition, his divorce and remarriage were contrary to Jewish law. Complaints from the Jews and Samaritans to Augustus finally resulted in an investigation and Archelaus' banishment in the ninth or tenth year of his reign. Judea thereafter was under Roman governors.—See HEROD Nos. 1 and 2.

ARCHER. A person who uses bow and arrow. The use of the bow and arrow after the Flood enabled man to kill (for food, clothing, and shelter) animals that were too fast and too dangerous to be taken otherwise. With the rise of Nimrod, archers likely were pressed into his service.

In the 20th century B.C.E., Abraham's firstborn son Ishmael "became an archer" to sustain himself in the wilderness. (Ge 21:20) Similarly, Esau, the grandson of Abraham, could handle the bow with skill. (Ge 27:3) Monuments testify that from the earliest times Egypt's principal offensive warriors were archers, and there are also Babylonian sculptures of archers. In the days of Joshua (Jos 24:12) and David (1Ch 12:1, 2), and thereafter, archers were an important part of Israel's army. (2Ch 14:8; 26:14) Archers of the Philistines, Syrians, and Egyptians shot Kings Saul, Ahab, and Josiah respectively.—1Sa 31:1-3; 1Ki 22:34, 35; 2Ch 35: 20, 23.

Reliefs in Nineveh illustrate Assyrian archers in chariots carrying two bows, one long, one short. When shooting one arrow they held extras in the hand, thus increasing the rapidity of their fire. The Assyrian plan of attack seems to have been to overwhelm the enemy under a flood of arrows, and then use the sword and spear in pursuit.

Archer of the royal Persian guard

The Persians have been called the most expert archers in the world. Reliefs from Persepolis and Susa show Median and Persian soldiers equipped with bows and quivers. From the age of 5 until 20, Persian boys were taught archery and riding; their cavalry were experts even when shooting backward. Mobility along with freedom of movement of the archers was the basic plan of Persian strategy in storming the foe under a hail of arrows.

The Western empires of Greece and Rome did not esteem the bow and arrow as highly as did the Eastern nations, though at times archers played a significant role in their victories. This may have been due to the Greek method of drawing the bow to the body, a less effective style, instead of drawing the bow to the cheek or eye as did the Egyptians and Persians. Mercenary Cretans and Asiatics seemed to have supplied the skilled bowmen, while the Greeks and Romans relied on the sword and spear.—See ARMS, ARMOR.

Figurative Usage. Evidently referring to the unjust treatment of Joseph by his brothers, Jacob said of his son Joseph: "Archers [literally, owners of arrows] kept harassing him and shot at him."

(Ge 49:23) Job said of God's seeming animosity toward him: "His archers encircle me." (Job 16:13) The Hebrew word *rav*, here translated 'archer,' comes from *ra·vav'*, meaning "shoot." (Ge 49:23) The Hebrew word *rav* also occurs in Proverbs 26:10, which reads: "As an archer piercing everything is the one hiring someone stupid or the one hiring passersby." This proverb highlights the harm that can be caused when one in a responsible position employs someone not qualified for a particular assignment.

ARCHIPPUS (Ar·chip'pus) [Ruler of the Horse]. In his letter to the Colossian Christians, Paul exhorts Archippus to faithfulness in the ministry, and in his letter to Philemon he affectionately refers to him as a "fellow soldier." (Col 4:17; Phm 2) Both letters, written near the end of Paul's first imprisonment in Rome (c. 60-61 C.E.), indicate that Archippus was then living in or near Colossae in Asia Minor.

ARCHITE (Ar'chite). Although the term could refer to a member of an unidentified Canaanite tribe, it appears more likely that it refers to a well-known family or clan located in the area of Ataroth, SW of Bethel. (Jos 16:2) A town named 'Ein 'Arik to the W of Bethel is suggested by some as the source or the remaining evidence of the name. Hushai, David's faithful counselor, was an Archite.—1Ch 27:33; see HUSHAI.

ARCHITECTURE. The art or science of building. The Bible shows a diversification of dwelling places and living habits early in human history, during the 1,656 years prior to the Flood of Noah's day. Cain, after the murder of Abel, is spoken of as 'taking up residence' in a certain area, and there "he engaged in building a city." (Ge 4:16, 17) Yet, one of his descendants, Jabal, became "the founder of those who dwell in tents and have livestock." Another became a "forger of every sort of tool of copper and iron." (Ge 4:20, 22) The descendants of Cain perished at least by the time of the Flood; however, constructive ability and the use of tools did not perish with them.

The outstanding building work of that pre-Flood period was done by descendants of Seth: the ark constructed by Noah and his sons. While the basic plans and dimensions were provided by God, some architectural ability must doubtless be attributed to Noah as the human director of works. The ark was 300 cubits long, 50 cubits wide, and 30 cubits high (133.5 m × 22.3 m × 13.4 m; 437 ft 6 in. × 72 ft 11 in. × 43 ft 9 in.). It could have had about 0.9 ha (2.2 acres) of floor space. The three floors plus the wide roof span probably required, in addition to the 'compartment' divisions, the use of some wooden columns and beams to support the weight, as well as to give the structure necessary stability. Although the ark was caulked with tar, there would also be need for careful fitting of the timbers to ensure a reasonably watertight construction.—Ge 6:13-16; see ARK No. 1.

Early Post-Flood Construction. In the post-Flood era Nimrod is described as a prominent builder of several cities. (Ge 10:8-12) Another major building project was now put forward, the Tower of Babel, disapproved by God. Here, new materials are mentioned, kiln-baked bricks with bitumen serving as mortar. The tower was intended to be the highest structure up till that time.—Ge 11:3, 4.

Abraham, the forefather of the Israelites, doubtless saw fairly advanced styles of architecture in Ur of the Chaldeans. (Ge 11:31) Excavations there reveal evidences of city streets, two-story houses with brick stairs, and complexes of temples and palaces, considered as dating back to the third millennium B.C.E. Here, too, is found some of the earliest evidence of the use of the corbel vault or the cantilever arch (formed by building the two sides of a wall closer and closer together until the gap between them can be bridged with a row of stones or bricks), as well as of the true curved arch with keystone.

Later, during his stay in Egypt (Ge 12:10), Abraham may have witnessed some of the architectural splendors of that land. The Step Pyramid of King Djoser at Saqqara is supposed to date from the third millennium B.C.E. and is one of the earliest examples remaining of major constructions using cut stone. (PICTURE, Vol. 1, p. 530) The Great Pyramid of Khufu, built somewhat later at Giza, has a huge base of 5.3 ha (13 acres) and was made of some 2,300,000 blocks of limestone, each weighing 2.3 metric tons on the average. It was originally 147 m (482 ft) high. Not only the size but also the precision achieved makes it a project amazing even modern engineers. Several centuries later at Karnak, farther up the Nile, the Egyptians produced the largest known temple built by man. The roof of its great hall was supported by 134 enormous columns, each some 3 m (10 ft) in diameter, decorated with richly colored reliefs.

Israelite Architecture. During the oppression of the Israelites in Egypt, they did considerable building work as slaves under Egyptian taskmasters. (Ex 1:11-14) Later, in the wilderness Jehovah gave them precise instructions for the construction of the tabernacle, with panel frames, socket pedestals, bars, and pillars, which also required considerable architectural ability on their part. (Ex 25:9, 40; 26:15-37; Heb 8:5) While the majority of those who were doing such work (and who had done building in Egypt) undoubtedly died before reaching the Promised Land, a concept of building methods and the use of tools was surely carried over by the survivors. (Compare De 27:5.) The Mosaic Law prescribed at least one requirement for construction. (De 22:8) The Israelites, upon conquering the land, of course, did take over entire cities and villages with their completed constructions, but they also did building themselves. (Nu 32:16; De 6:10, 11; 8:12) At the time of their entry (1473 B.C.E.), Canaan was a land with numerous walled cities and strong fortifications.—Nu 13:28.

While it is true that no striking constructions remain to indicate Israelite originality or ingenuity as to architecture, it does not logically follow that they were lacking in such ability. Unlike the pagan nations, they did not erect huge monuments in honor of political rulers or military heroes. The one temple constructed was at Jerusalem, although apostasy produced other religious sites. Nothing remains of the original temple or of its successor. Among the more impressive ruins uncovered are those of the identical city gates of ancient Megiddo, Hazor, and Gezer, thought to have been built in Solomon's time. (1Ki 9:15) In each case the 20-m-long (66 ft) external walls were made with carefully drafted stones. Within the gate passage there were three successive pairs of jambs or extended piers, thus producing six recessed chambers flanking the passage on either side, in which business might be transacted or from which soldiers could harass any troups attempting to force their way through the gates. (See GATE, GATEWAY.) At Megiddo and at Samaria examples of expert masonry have been found, the stones being carefully chiseled, laid, and joined with fine precision, in some cases so exactly that even a thin knife blade cannot be inserted between the joined stones. Undoubtedly the work on the temple built by Solomon was of the same high quality.—1Ki 5:17; 6:7.

On the basis of archaeological investigation it appears that Israelite houses were generally of very modest construction, some researchers holding that they were quite crude. Yet the evidence on which such opinions are based is very meager. As *The Interpreter's Dictionary of the Bible* (Vol. 1, p. 209) comments: "Modern knowledge of the subject is restricted both by the inattention of ancient writers to matters of architectural interest and by the scanty survival of the buildings themselves, most of which time and succeeding generations of builders have utterly destroyed." (Edited by G. A. Buttrick, 1962) Thus, it is rare to find more than one or two courses of masonry above the foundation of any ruined building in Palestine. It is also logical that the better homes would suffer most at the hands of destroyers and, subsequently, of those seeking building materials.

Ancient Building Materials and Methods. Stone foundations were common from the earliest times. Whereas rough stones might be employed, they were aligned and bonded by the cornerstones, which were carefully smoothed and fitted. (Compare Ps 118:22; Isa 28:16.) Clay mortar or plaster inside Israelite stone houses is mentioned at Leviticus 14:40-48. If the remainder of the house was not completed in stone, sun-dried or kiln-baked bricks were frequently used above the foundation. (Compare Isa 9:10.) Wood was at times interspersed with the bricks. The materials employed depended principally on what was locally available. The lack of wood and stone in Mesopotamia resulted in most constructions' being made of mud brick, whereas in Palestine limestone or other stones were generally abundant. An early method of forming an economical wall was that of the wattle and daub. Stakes were driven into the ground and reeds or flexible branches were interwoven between them horizontally to form a mesh framework upon which clay could be spread. After the clay had been thoroughly dried and hardened by the sun, plaster was applied periodically to preserve the walls from the elements.—See WALLS.

The roof of a building was generally formed by laying long stones or timbers across the supporting walls. Posts or pillars might be introduced to increase the span of the roof, the common "post and lintel" method. Since the corbel vault and the curved arch were known from ancient times, it is probable that in large buildings these were used to hold up such flat roofs as were capable of supporting considerable weight. In these larger buildings one or two rows of pillars were often used; the wood or stone pillars were set in a stone plinth, or base, and it is suggested by some that the pillars in the house of Dagon to which the Philistines brought blind Samson were of this type. In addition to those gathered within the building, some 3,000 people were on the roof observing when Samson dislodged the two main pillars, causing the collapse of the house.—Jg 16:25-30.

The roofs of smaller buildings and domestic dwellings were frequently formed of branches or reeds that were bound together and laid across the beams and then packed and covered with mud or clay, which was then rolled smooth. A slight slope given to the roof allowed the rain to run off. Such roofs are still to be found in the Jordan Valley in present-day dwellings.

The basic type of building in Palestine was of rectangular form; if a dwelling, there was usually a somewhat loose arrangement of small rectangular rooms within. The limited space available within cities, often crowded, determined the size and shape of the buildings. If space allowed, there might be an inner courtyard with all the rooms opening off it and with only one entranceway from the street. The same basic rectangular style was used not only for the domestic house but also for the royal house (palace), the storehouse, the house of assembly (synagogue), the house of God (temple), and the house of the dead (tomb).

Works of the Kings of Judah and Israel. The only particular construction mentioned as occurring during King David's reign appears to be the "house of cedars," built with materials and by workers supplied by Phoenician King Hiram of Tyre (1Ch 14:1; 17:1), although it is recorded that David continued building other houses in Jerusalem. (1Ch 15:1) David also made great preparations for the temple construction to be accomplished by his son Solomon, including the hewing of squared stones, the fashioning of iron nails, and the preparing of copper and of cedar timbers "in great quantity," as well as the setting aside of supplies of gold, silver, precious stones, and mosaic pebbles. (1Ch 22:1-4; 29:1-5) He was also used to provide the divinely inspired "architectural plan" for the entire temple layout and equipment. (1Ch 28:11, 19) The Hebrew word for "architectural plan" (*tav·nith'*) comes from the root *ba·nah'* ("build"; 1Ch 22:11) and is elsewhere rendered "pattern" and "representation."—Ex 25:9; 1Ch 28:18.

Under Solomon, Israelite architecture reached its high point. (2Ch 1:15; Ec 2:4-6) Although the Phoenician workers of King Hiram were employed in the cutting of timbers in Lebanon for the temple construction, the record does not support the view often advanced that the temple at Jerusalem was primarily and essentially the work of Phoenicians. An Israeli-Phoenician named Hiram is mentioned as contributing to the immediate construction, but this was mainly in decorative work and metalwork, done after the building was erected and according to the plans provided by King David. (1Ch 28:19) King Hiram of Tyre acknowledged that there were "skillful men" among the Israelites as well. (1Ki 7:13-40; 2Ch 2:3, 8-16; compare 1 Ch 28:20, 21.) Solomon himself directed the building of the temple structure. (1Ki 6:1-38; 2Ch 3:1-4: 22) Additionally, he built the temple courtyard, the House of the Forest of Lebanon, noteworthy for its 45 pillars of cedarwood and special illumination features, the Porch of Pillars, the Porch of the Throne, as well as his own house and the house for Pharaoh's daughter, all constructed of expensive stones hewn "according to measures." —1Ki 7:1-12.

Other kings prominent in building were Asa (1Ki 15:23), Baasha (1Ki 15:17), Omri (1Ki 16:23, 24), Ahab (1Ki 22:39), Jehoshaphat (2Ch 17:12), Uzziah (2Ch 26:6-10, 15), Jotham (2Ch 27:3, 4), and Hezekiah (2Ki 20:20). The tunnel of Siloam (533 m [1,749 ft] in length), attributed to Hezekiah, and the tunnels found at Lachish, Gibeon, Gezer, and Megiddo were remarkable engineering feats.

Postexilic Building in Palestine. The postexilic period seems to have seen only modest construction among the Jews. However, Herod the Great (first century B.C.E.), and his successors, engaged in great architectural projects, including the reconstruction of the temple at Jerusalem (Mr 13:1, 2; Lu 21:5), the harbor at Caesarea, the great viaduct spanning the central part of Jerusalem, as well as public buildings, theaters, hippodromes, and baths. A most remarkable feat was Herod's development of the fortress on the hill of Masada over 400 m (1,300 ft) above the Dead Sea. Besides the fortifications, Herod built an elegant, three-tiered hanging palace with a terrace and with bathing pools, as well as another palace with a Roman bathhouse having heating pipes in the walls, and a sit-down lavatory with flushing system. He equipped the huge rock fortress with a dozen great cisterns able to hold in all almost 40,000 kl (10,500,000 gal) of water.—PICTURE, Vol. 2, p. 751.

Assyrian, Babylonian, Persian Architecture. As a result of the fall of the northern kingdom of Israel (740 B.C.E.) and the overthrow of the southern kingdom of Judah (607 B.C.E.), the Jewish people became acquainted with the architectural splendors of the Assyrian, Babylonian, and Persian Empires. The palace of Sargon II at Khorsabad was notable for its regularity and use of symmetry, as well as its splendid reliefs, glazed bricks, and enameled tile paintings. Sennacherib's palace at Nineveh was an immense structure of about 70 rooms, with over 3,000 m (nearly 10,000 ft) of wall space lined with sculptured slabs. (2Ki 19:36; compare Jon 3:2, 3.) Sennacherib is also believed to have built the 48-km (30 mi) aqueduct that carried water from the Gomer River to the gardens of Nineveh. At Mari, on the Euphrates in eastern Syria, an enormous 300-room palace complex covered some 6 ha (15 acres). The ruins of ancient Babylon likewise indicate the onetime magnificence of that city with its formidable walls, famous streets, and numerous palaces and temples.

Under Persian rule, Jews in Shushan might have viewed the splendor of the palace of Darius I there, with its interiors beautified by splendidly colored glazed bricks. (PICTURES, Vol. 2, p. 330) At Persepolis the grandeur was perhaps yet more impressive (PICTURES, Vol. 2, p. 329), from the Gate of Xerxes, with its colossal bulls, to the palace and huge audience halls of Darius and Xerxes, including the hall of 100 columns. The Persian columns were more graceful and slender than the famed Ionic columns of the Greeks. The ratio of height to diameter of the columns in the Hall of Xerxes was 12 to 1 as compared to a ratio of 10 to 1 maximum for Corinthian columns, and only 6 to 1 for Egyptian columns. Likewise, the span attained between the columns in Persian buildings was as much as twice that of the Greek buildings, thus creating a greater sense of spaciousness than found in similar ancient structures.

Grecian and Roman Styles and Methods. Greek architecture entered its "golden period" in the seventh century B.C.E. That period lasted down to the fourth century B.C.E. Athens became the site for majestic temples and buildings erected in honor of the Greek gods and goddesses. These buildings included the Parthenon, the Temple of the Wingless Victory, and the Erechtheum; while at Corinth the Temple of Apollo and the vast marketplace (or a·go·ra') were outstanding. The style of architecture is generally designated by the three main orders of beautiful Greek columns developed: the Doric, the Ionic, and the Corinthian.

The Romans were much indebted to the Greeks as to architectural style. Roman architecture was generally more functional than the Greek, while lacking some of its subtle beauty. The Romans also benefited from the Etruscans, who were noted for their true arch formed with wedge-shaped stones. In the sixth century B.C.E. such true arches were used in a most impressive way in the construction of the great sewers of Rome. The Roman architects are to be credited also with the development of the double arch and the dome, both of which they used in producing enormous column-free rotundas and spacious halls. The Greek masons had built majestic structures without the use of mortar or cement because of their surpassing skill and precision in fitting and joining the marble blocks used. Roman masons made use of a volcanic earth combined with lime called pozzolana, a hydraulic cement of great cohesive strength. With pozzolana as mortar, the Romans could extend the span of their arches as well as construct multistoried edifices, including the mammoth four-story Colosseum, built in the first century C.E., with a seating capacity variously estimated to be from 40,000 to 87,000 persons. Among the more valuable Roman constructions were the great military roads and splendid aqueducts built particularly from the third century B.C.E. forward. The apostle Paul made much use of these Roman highways and undoubtedly saw the aqueduct of Emperor Claudius along the Appian Way when traveling to Rome.

Christian Building. Even as the nation of Israel was not noted for architectural splendor or pomp, so too the early Christians of spiritual Israel constructed with modesty. *Unger's Bible Dictionary* (1965, pp. 84, 85) comments: "As early as in the 3rd century buildings erected by them existed, but they were neither substantial nor costly." It was not until the time of Emperor Constantine, when encouragement was given to those so inclined to enter relations with the political state, that nominal Christians began to produce a particular style of architecture, eventually constructing some of the most ornate and pompous edifices known.

Architecture in Prophecy and Figure. There are numerous uses of architectural terms in Biblical prophecies and figures. The restoration prophecies deal to a great extent with the building (or rebuilding) of God's people and their cities. (Isa 58:12; 60:10; 61:4; Eze 28:26; 36:36) Zion is foretold to be built upon stones laid with hard mortar, with sapphire foundations, ruby battlements, and gates of fiery glowing stones. (Isa 54:11, 12) Wisdom is described as building its own house (Pr 9:1) and, along with discernment and knowledge, as being the means for building up a household. (Pr 14:1; 24:3, 4) Jehoiakim is condemned for building his palace in unrighteousness by failing to pay the workers, and the Chaldeans are condemned for building a city with the blood and toil of conquered peoples. (Jer 22:13-15; Hab 2:12, 13) False imagining of peace with God is compared to the building of a plastered partition wall that Jehovah blasts with the windstorm and hail of his rage, tearing it down and revealing its foundations. (Eze 13:10-16) The psalmist assures that unless Jehovah builds the house, the builders labor in vain. (Ps 127:1) Prior to "the great day of Jehovah," those who disregard God will build but will not come to occupy their buildings. (Zep 1:12-14; compare Am 5:11.) By contrast, God's servants are to "build houses and have occupancy" and "use to the full" the work of their hands.—Isa 65:17-23; compare Ec 3:3.

In the Christian Greek Scriptures, the importance of making a cost estimate before beginning construction was referred to by Jesus when he encouraged his hearers to appreciate exactly what is involved in becoming his followers. (Lu 14:28-30) The need for a solid foundation is used in a number of illustrations. (Mt 7:24-27; Lu 6:48, 49; 1Ti 6:17-19; 2Ti 2:19; Heb 11:10) Christ Jesus speaks of founding his congregation on a rock-mass (*pe'tra*) (Mt 16:18), and Jesus himself is shown to be the one foundation, besides which "no man can lay any other"; yet he is "the stone that the builders rejected." (1Co 3:11; Mt 21:42; Ac 4:11; Ps 118:22) Because he is the chief cornerstone, all the other "living stones" of this temple are founded on and aligned with him, with justice as "the measuring line" and righteousness as "the leveling instrument." (Eph 2:20, 21; 1Pe 2:4-8; Isa 28:16, 17) Jesus spoke of the temple of his body as being raised up "in three days," although the literal temple and surrounding buildings at Jerusalem in his day had taken 46 years to build and they still were not finished. (Joh 2:18-22) Paul, as "a wise director of works," admonished concerning the use of high-quality, noncombustible materials in building on Christ as the foundation. (1Co 3:10-17) Love is described as a prime element of building. (1Co 8:1; compare Ps 89:2.) John's vision of the New Jerusalem presents it as a radiant city formed of precious stones with its walls resting on foundation stones inscribed with the names of "the twelve apostles of the Lamb." (Re 21:9-27) God himself is presented as the Great Constructor of all things, hence as not residing in buildings made by men.—Heb 3:4; Ac 7:48-50; 17:24, 25; Isa 66:1.

ARD (Ard). One of the 'seventy souls of the house of Jacob who came into Egypt.' (Ge 46:21, 27) In the Genesis account he is called a son of Benjamin, but in view of Numbers 26:40, it seems likely that the meaning here is "grandson." If this is the case, then he is also probably the same as Addar in 1 Chronicles 8:3.

ARDITES (Ard'ites) [Of (Belonging to) Ard]. A Benjamite family descended from Ard, a son of Bela.—Nu 26:40.

ARDON (Ar'don). One of the sons of Caleb the son of Hezron; of the tribe of Judah.—1Ch 2:18.

ARELI (A·re'li), **ARELITES** (A·re'lites). The seventh-named son of Gad, who was one of those who came into Egypt with Jacob's family in 1728 B.C.E. He became family head of the Arelites, who were included in the wilderness census shortly before entering the Promised Land.—Ge 46:8, 16; Nu 26:17.

AREOPAGUS (Ar·e·op'a·gus) [Hill of Ares; Mars' Hill]. A hill to the NW of the towering Athenian Acropolis, separated from it by a shallow valley. This rather narrow, barren ridge of limestone is 113 m (370 ft) high, and the Acropolis to its SE rises another 43 m (141 ft) higher. The approach to Mars' Hill is gentle from the N; on the S it is abrupt. Crowning this hill at one time were Grecian altars, temple sanctuaries, statues, and the open-air supreme court of the Areopagus. Today all of this is gone, and only a few of the benchlike seats carved in the rock remain.

Greek plaque memorializing Paul's speech on the Areopagus (Ac 17:22-31)

On one of the apostle Paul's visits to Athens, certain Athenians laid hold of him and led him to the Areopagus, saying: "Can we get to know what this new teaching is which is spoken by you? For you are introducing some things that are strange to our ears." (Ac 17:19, 20) In reply Paul carefully laid one solid fact upon another, building up as he went along, a logical, persuasive, and convincing argument. Paul did not complete his speech, for "when they heard of a resurrection of the dead" mockers began to jeer. However, by the time this interruption came, the apostle had succeeded in splitting his audience three ways in their opinions. While some mocked, and some said they would hear more later, others "became believers, among whom also were Dionysius, a judge of the court of the Areopagus, and a woman named Damaris, and others besides them." (Ac 17:22-34) Today a bronze plaque on Mars' Hill commemorating the event contains this speech of the apostle Paul. It cannot be stated for a certainty that Paul spoke on that occasion before the court of the Areopagus, but he did have at least one member of that noted court in his audience.—PICTURE, Vol. 2, p. 746.

ARETAS (A·re'tas) [Virtuous; Excellent]. The last of several Arabian kings of this name controlled Damascus when its governor joined a plot of the Jews to do away with Paul. The apostle Paul escaped in a wicker basket lowered from a window in the city wall.—Ac 9:23-25; 2Co 11:32, 33.

Aretas had given his daughter in marriage to Herod Antipas (see HEROD No. 2), who divorced her to marry Herodias—the adulterous affair that John the Baptizer condemned. (Mt 14:3, 4) Further aggravated by border disputes, Aretas attacked and totally defeated Antipas. Emperor Tiberius then ordered the governor of Syria, Vitellius, to take Aretas dead or alive. Vitellius, himself no friend of Antipas, mobilized his forces, but Tiberius died in 37 C.E., and the campaign against Aretas was called off. Tiberius' successor Caligula reversed this foreign policy, installed Herod Agrippa I in place of Antipas, and permitted Aretas to rule Damascus. A coin of Damascus bearing an inscription of Aretas is dated in this period.

ARGOB (Ar'gob) [Clod of Earth].

1. Possibly one of the men assassinated with King Pekahiah of Israel in about 778 B.C.E., by a usurper named Pekah, who was assisted in the crime by 50 Gileadites.—2Ki 15:23-25.

2. A region of Bashan that was conquered while Israel was still E of the Jordan and that became part of the territory of the tribe of Manasseh. It appears to have been the seat of the king-

dom of Og and is described as having 60 fortified cities besides very many rural towns. (De 3:4, 5, 13, 14) This was "the land of the Rephaim," or land of giants.

Argob lay E of the Sea of Galilee. Although the traditional site for Argob is that of Al-Ledja, a lava-covered area about 32 km (20 mi) S of Damascus, the description in Deuteronomy of an area with rural towns would seem to favor the fertile plain to the W of Al-Ledja probably centered on the region between Nahr al-Ruqad, Nahr al-'Alan, and Nahal Yarmuk. On this broad tableland the cities had no natural defenses and would have need for the 'high walls' mentioned in the Scriptures. There are ruins of such great cities studding the entire territory of Bashan.

In King Solomon's time Argob was part of one of 12 districts placed under deputies responsible for providing food for the royal household.—1Ki 4:7, 13.

ARIDAI (Ar'i·dai). One of Haman's ten sons. —Es 9:9, 10; see HAMAN.

ARIDATHA (A·ri·da'tha). One of Haman's ten sons.—Es 9:8, 10; see HAMAN.

ARIEH (A·ri'eh). Perhaps a man assassinated in Samaria in about 778 B.C.E. together with King Pekahiah of Israel, by usurper Pekah.—2Ki 15:25.

ARIEL (Ar'i·el) [Altar Hearth of God; or, Lion of God].

1. A Moabite whose two sons were killed by Benaiah.—2Sa 23:20; 1Ch 11:22.

2. One of the nine head ones especially used by Ezra in obtaining qualified "ministers for the house of our God." This was in the spring of 468 B.C.E. when about 1,500 Israelite males under Ezra were about to depart from the river Ahava for Jerusalem.—Ezr 8:15-17, 31.

3. A cryptic name applied to Jerusalem in Isaiah 29:1, 2, 7. Jerusalem was the location of God's temple that had within its precincts the sacrificial altar. Because of this the city was, in effect, God's altar hearth. It was also supposed to be the center of Jehovah's pure worship. However, the message in Isaiah 29:1-4 is ominous in content and predicts the destruction due to come to Jerusalem at the hands of the Babylonians in 607 B.C.E., when she would become an "altar hearth" in a different sense: as a city running with shed blood and consumed by fire and filled with the bodies of victims of the fiery destruction. The underlying causes for this calamity are stated in verses 9 to 16. Isaiah 29:7, 8, however, shows that the nations wreaking such destruction on Jerusalem would fail in their ultimate purpose or goal.

ARIMATHEA (Ar·i·ma·the'a) [from Heb., meaning "Height"]. "A city of the Judeans" in the time of Jesus, and the native city of Joseph, the secret disciple who obtained Jesus' corpse for burial. (Lu 23:50-53; Mt 27:57-60; Mr 15:43-46; Joh 19:38-42) The location of Arimathea is generally considered to be at the site of modern Rentis (Rantis), about 35 km (22 mi) NW of Jerusalem and about 26 km (16 mi) E of Joppa (modern Tel Aviv-Yafo).

ARIOCH (Ar'i·och).

1. The king of Ellasar who, in league with Chedorlaomer and two other kings, shared in crushing the rebellion of Sodom, Gomorrah, and their allies and in carrying off Lot and his household. Abraham then overtook the victors, defeated Arioch and his confederates, and rescued Lot. (Ge 14:1-16; see CHEDORLAOMER.) The ancient location of Ellasar is not certain.—See ELLASAR.

2. The chief of Nebuchadnezzar's bodyguard, who was under orders to kill all the wise men of Babylon after they had failed to reveal and interpret the king's dream. Upon learning that Daniel was prepared to reveal the dream and give the interpretation, "Arioch, in a hurry, took Daniel in before the king."—Da 2:12-25.

ARISAI (Ar'i·sai). One of Haman's ten sons. —Es 9:9, 10; see HAMAN.

ARISTARCHUS (Ar·is·tar'chus) [Best (Noblest) Ruler]. One of Paul's close associates, a traveling companion and fellow prisoner, a Macedonian from Thessalonica. (Ac 20:4; 27:2) He is introduced in the account of Paul's third missionary journey; at the height of the Ephesian riot Aristarchus and Gaius were forcibly dragged into the theater. (Ac 19:29) He could have been "the brother" who assisted Paul with the contribution for the Judeans that was collected in Macedonia and Greece.—2Co 8:18-20.

Aristarchus accompanied Paul on the voyage to Rome, but how he secured passage is uncertain, perhaps as a slave for Paul. (Ac 27:2) While in Rome he further assisted and encouraged Paul and for a time shared his prison bonds. Greetings from Aristarchus are conveyed in Paul's letters to the Colossians (4:10) and Philemon (23, 24).

ARISTOBULUS (A·ris·tob'u·lus) [Best (Noblest) Counselor]. An individual, some of whose household in Rome were sent greetings by Paul. —Ro 16:10.

ARK.

1. Noah's ark was the provision by which forefathers of all mankind survived the global Deluge of 2370-2369 B.C.E. (See DELUGE; NOAH No. 1.) Detailed instructions were given to Noah by Jehovah as to its size, shape, design for light and ventilation, and materials to be used for its construction.—Ge 6:14-16.

Design and Size. The ark (Heb., *te·vah'*; Gr., *ki·bo·tos'*) was a rectangular chestlike vessel presumably having square corners and a flat bottom. It needed no rounded bottom or sharp bow to cut rapidly through the water; it required no steering; its only functions were to be watertight and to stay afloat. A vessel so shaped is very stable, cannot be easily capsized, and contains about one third more storage space than ships of conventional design. There was a door provided in the side of the ark for loading and unloading the cargo.

In size the ark was 300 cubits long, 50 cubits wide, and 30 cubits high. Conservatively calculating the cubit as 44.5 cm (17.5 in.) (some think the ancient cubit was nearer 56 or 61 cm), the ark measured 133.5 m by 22.3 m by 13.4 m (437 ft 6 in. × 72 ft 11 in. × 43 ft 9 in.), less than half the length of the ocean liner *Queen Elizabeth 2*. This proportion of length to width (6 to 1) is used by modern naval architects. This gave the ark approximately 40,000 cu m (1,400,000 cu ft) in gross volume. It is estimated that such a vessel would have a displacement nearly equal to that of the mighty 269-m (883 ft) *Titanic* of this 20th century. No cargo vessel of ancient times even slightly resembled the ark in its colossal size. Internally strengthened by adding two floors, the three decks thus provided gave a total of about 8,900 sq m (96,000 sq ft) of space.

"You will make a *tso'har* [roof; or, window] for the ark," Noah was told. (Ge 6:16) Just what this was or how it was constructed is not altogether clear. Some scholars think *tso'har* is related to *light* and so they translate it "window" (*KJ, Mo*), "light" (*AS, JP*), "a place for light" (*Ro*). Others, however, associate *tso'har* with a later Arabic root meaning "back (of the hand)," "back (of a beast)," "deck (of a ship)," that is, the part away from the ground or water, and for this reason translate it "roof." (*AT, RS, JB*) This *tso'har*, Noah was told, was to be completed "to the extent of a cubit upward."—Ge 6:16.

It could be, therefore, that the *tso'har* provided for adequate light and ventilation, not just a single cubit-square "peephole," but an opening a cubit in height near the roof and extending around the four sides to give an opening of nearly 140 sq m (1,500 sq ft). On the other hand, while still allowing an ample opening for ventilation under the roof or elsewhere, the roof could have had slightly angled sides. Regarding this possibility James F. Armstrong wrote in *Vetus Testamentum* (Leiden, 1960, p. 333): "'Unto a cubit upward you shall finish it' is difficult to understand when *sohar* is translated either 'light (= window)' or even '(flat) roof'. If, however, a gable-type roof be postulated, the 'one cubit upward' can refer to the elevation of the crease of the roof above the level of the tops of the walls. In modern architectural terms, the 'one cubit' would be the height of the kingposts between which the ridgepiece is laid. . . . According to the argument that has been presented, the roof of Noah's ark was conceived as having a four per-cent pitch (1 cubit elevation — 25 cubits from wall to ridge), quite adequate to permit the water of the rains to flow off."

Of what this huge ark was to be built was made plain by Jehovah: "Make for yourself an ark out of wood of a resinous tree [literally, trees of gopher]." (Ge 6:14) This resinous wood here prescribed is thought by some to be cypress or a similar tree. In that part of the world what today is called cypress was in abundant supply; it was particularly favored for shipbuilding by the Phoenicians and by Alexander the Great, as it is even down to the present time; and it is especially resistant to water and decay. Doors and posts made of cypress are reported to have lasted 1,100 years. In addition, Noah was told not merely to caulk the seams but to "cover [the ark] inside and outside with tar."—See BITUMEN.

Ample Carrying Capacity. The passenger list of the ark was quite impressive. Besides Noah, his wife, his three sons, and their wives, living creatures "of every sort of flesh, two of each," were to be taken aboard. "Male and female they will be. Of the flying creatures according to their kinds and of the domestic animals according to their kinds, of all moving animals of the ground according to their kinds, two of each will go in there to you to preserve them alive." Of the clean beasts and fowls, seven of each kind were to be taken. A great quantity and variety of food for all these creatures, to last for more than a year, also had to be stowed away.—Ge 6:18-21; 7:2, 3.

The "kinds" of animals selected had reference to the clear-cut and unalterable boundaries or limits set by the Creator, within which boundaries creatures are capable of breeding "according to their kinds." It has been estimated by some that the hundreds of thousands of species of animals today could be reduced to a comparatively few family "kinds"—the horse kind and the cow kind, to mention but two. The breeding boundaries according to "kind" established by Jehovah were not and could not be crossed. With this in mind some investigators have said that, had there been as few as 43 "kinds" of mammals, 74 "kinds" of birds, and 10 "kinds" of reptiles in the ark, they could have produced the variety of species known today. Others have been more liberal in estimating that 72 "kinds" of quadrupeds and less than 200 bird "kinds" were all that were required. That the great variety of animal life known today could have come from inbreeding within so few "kinds" following the Flood is proved by the endless variety of human*kind*—short, tall, fat, thin, with countless variations in the color of hair, eyes, and skin —all of whom sprang from the one family of Noah.

These estimates may seem too restrictive to some, especially since such sources as *The Encyclopedia Americana* indicate that there are upwards of 1,300,000 species of animals. (1977, Vol. 1, pp. 859-873) However, over 60 percent of these are insects. Breaking these figures down further, of the 24,000 amphibians, reptiles, birds, and mammals, 10,000 are birds, 9,000 are reptiles and amphibians, many of which could have survived outside the ark, and only 5,000 are mammals, including whales and porpoises, which would have also remained outside the ark. Other researchers estimate that there are only about 290 species of land mammals larger than sheep and about 1,360 smaller than rats. (*The Deluge Story in Stone,* by B. C. Nelson, 1949, p. 156; *The Flood in the Light of the Bible, Geology, and Archaeology,* by A. M. Rehwinkel, 1957, p. 69) So, even if estimates are based on these expanded figures, the ark could easily have accommodated a pair of all these animals.

Five months after the Deluge began, "the ark came to rest on the mountains of Ararat," not likely, however, atop the uppermost peak (nearly 5,165 m; 16,950 ft), but on suitable terrain where everyone aboard lived comfortably for some months more. Finally, after a year and ten days from the time the Deluge began, the door again was opened and all aboard disembarked.—Ge 7:11; 8:4, 14.

Claims that remains of the ark have been found are as yet unconfirmed.

2. The small chest in which Jochebed concealed her three-month-old "good-looking" baby later named Moses, and which was found by Pharaoh's daughter among the reeds by the bank of the Nile.

This ark or chest (Heb., *te·vah'*) was made of papyrus and was waterproofed with a coating of bitumen and pitch.—Ex 2:2-4, 10, ftn; 6:20.

3. The container made of acacia wood in which the second set of stone tablets of the Law given Moses on Mount Sinai were temporarily kept until the ark of the testimony was constructed some months later. (De 10:1-5) The Hebrew word *'arohn'*, rendered "ark" in Deuteronomy 10:1-5, is elsewhere rendered "coffin" (Ge 50:26) and "chest."—2 Ki 12:9, 10, ftn; 2Ch 24:8, 10, 11.

4. See ARK OF THE COVENANT.

ARKITE (Ark'ite). Descendants of Ham through Canaan and one of the 70 post-Flood families. (Ge 10:17; 1Ch 1:15) They settled along the Mediterranean Coast W of the Lebanon Mountains.

ARK OF THE COVENANT. The sacred chest located in the Most Holy of the tabernacle and, later, in the temple built by Solomon. The Ark was made at Jehovah's command and according to his design.

Bible writers designate the ark of the covenant in more than 20 different ways. The more common of these expressions, "the ark of the covenant [Heb., *'arohn' hab·berith'*; Gr., *ki·bo·tos' tes di·a·the'kes*]" (Jos 3:6; Heb 9:4) and "the ark of the testimony" (Ex 25:22), are not peculiar to any certain writer and are used interchangeably.

Pattern and Design. The first thing Jehovah gave Moses, when instructing him to build the tabernacle, was the pattern and design of the Ark, for indeed it was the central and paramount object of the tabernacle and the whole camp of Israel. The chest itself measured 2.5 cubits long, 1.5 cubits wide, and 1.5 cubits high (c. 111 × 67 × 67 cm; 44 × 26 × 26 in.). It was made of acacia wood, overlaid inside and out with pure gold. An artistic "border of gold" served as a crowning wreath "round about upon it." The second section of the Ark, its cover, was made of solid gold, not just wood overlaid with gold, and was the full length and breadth of the chest. Mounted on this cover were two golden cherubs of hammered workmanship, one at each end of the cover facing each other, with heads bowed and wings extending upward and overspreading the Ark. (Ex 25:10, 11, 17-22; 37:6-9) This cover was also known as the "mercy seat" or "propitiatory cover." —Ex 25:17; Heb 9:5, ftn; see PROPITIATORY COVER.

Long poles were provided for carrying the Ark. They were also made of acacia wood covered with gold and were inserted through two rings of gold on each side of the chest. These poles were not to be removed from their rings; hence there was never a necessity for bearers of the Ark to touch it. There were four feet, "walking feet, feet bent as if for walking," located at the corners to raise the Ark off the floor, but how high is not disclosed. (*Commentary on the Old Testament,* by C. F. Keil and F. Delitzsch, 1973, Vol. 1, The Second Book of Moses, p. 167) The rings may have been mounted immediately above the feet, if not on the feet themselves.—Ex 25:12-16; Nu 4:5, 15; 1Ki 8:8; 1Ch 15:15.

Inauguration and Use. Bezalel and the wise-hearted ones assisting him followed the plans explicitly, constructing the Ark from the materials contributed by the people. (Ex 35:5, 7, 10, 12; 37:1-9) When the tabernacle was completed and set up a year after the Exodus, Moses took the two stone tablets of the Law and put them into the Ark. (Deuteronomy 10:1-5 indicates that a temporary ark made of acacia wood housed the tablets during only the few months' interval from the time Moses received them in the mountain until they were transferred to the Ark made by Bezalel.) Next, Moses inserted the poles in the rings of the Ark, laid the cover on, brought it into the tent, and put up the screen that was to separate the Holy from the Most Holy. Then, as part of the inauguration ceremony, Moses anointed the Ark and all other furnishings with oil. From then on, when the priests disassembled the tabernacle to move camp, the same dividing screen, together with additional sealskins and blue cloth, was used to cover the Ark to prevent the people from looking upon it 'for the least moment of time, lest they die.'—Ex 40:3, 9, 20, 21; Nu 3:30, 31; 4:5, 6, 19, 20; 7:9; De 10:8; 31:9; see TABERNACLE.

The Ark served as a holy archive for the safe-keeping of sacred reminders or testimony, the principal contents being the two tablets of the testimony, or the Ten Commandments. (Ex 25:16) A "golden jar having the manna and the rod of Aaron that budded" were added to the Ark but were later removed sometime before the building of Solomon's temple. (Heb 9:4; Ex 16:32-34; Nu 17:10; 1Ki 8:9; 2Ch 5:10) Just before Moses died, he gave a copy of the "book of the law" to the Levitical priests with instructions that it should be kept, not within, but "at the side of the ark of the covenant of Jehovah your God, . . . as a witness there against you."—De 31:24-26.

Associated with God's presence. The Ark was associated with God's presence throughout its history. Jehovah promised: "I will present myself to you there and speak with you from above the cover, from between the two cherubs that are

upon the ark of the testimony." "In a cloud I shall appear over the cover." (Ex 25:22; Le 16:2) Samuel wrote that Jehovah "is sitting upon the cherubs" (1Sa 4:4); hence the cherubs served as "the representation of the chariot" of Jehovah. (1Ch 28:18) Accordingly, "whenever Moses went into the tent of meeting to speak with [Jehovah], then he would hear the voice conversing with him from above the cover that was upon the ark of the testimony, from between the two cherubs; and he would speak to him." (Nu 7:89) Later, Joshua and High Priest Phinehas also inquired of Jehovah before the Ark. (Jos 7:6-10; Jg 20:27, 28) However, only the high priest actually entered the Most Holy and saw the Ark, one day a year, not to communicate with Jehovah, but in carrying out the Atonement Day ceremony.—Le 16:2, 3, 13, 15, 17; Heb 9:7.

In other ways the presence of Jehovah as represented by the Ark brought blessings to Israel. It was customary when Israel moved camp for the Ark with its overhead cloud to lead the way. (Nu 10:33, 34) So, at the crossing of the Jordan, when the priests carrying the Ark stepped into the river's water, Jehovah stopped its flow, allowing them to pass. (Jos 3:1–4:18) In the line of march around Jericho, the war-equipped forces were followed by seven priests blowing horns, then the Ark, and behind was the rear guard. (Jos 6:3-13) In contrast to the victory at Jericho was the defeat suffered when certain rebels presumptuously pushed ahead in an attempt to take the Promised Land contrary to divine instructions, and when "the ark of Jehovah's covenant and Moses did not move away from the midst of the camp." (Nu 14:44, 45) Even the enemy Philistines recognized the presence of Jehovah when the Ark appeared on the battlefield. In their fright they cried out: "God has come into the camp [of Israel]!" "Woe to us, for such a thing as this never occurred before! Woe to us! Who will save us from the hand of this majestic God? This is the God that was the smiter of Egypt with every sort of slaughter in the wilderness."—1Sa 4:6-8.

Jehovah's presence continued to be demonstrated when the Philistines captured the Ark and took it to Ashdod to sit alongside the image of Dagon. That night, Dagon fell on his face; the next night he again toppled before the ark of Jehovah and his head and the palms of both of his hands were cut off. During the next seven months, as the Ark circulated among the Philistine cities, the people were plagued with piles, and the city of Ekron was plunged into "a death-dealing confusion," until finally the Ark was returned to Israel with proper offering.—1Sa 5:1–6:12.

The fact that the Ark was associated with the presence of Jehovah demanded that due respect and high regard be given the Ark. Hence, when the Ark set out on the move and when it came to rest, Moses proclaimed words of praise to Jehovah. (Nu 10:35, 36) High Priest Eli was so shocked to hear that the Philistines had captured the Ark that he lost his balance and fell over backward, breaking his neck; also his daughter-in-law in the throes of death lamented, "Glory has gone away from Israel into exile, because the ark of the true God has been captured." (1Sa 4:18-22) King Solomon acknowledged that "the places to which the ark of Jehovah has come are something holy." —2Ch 8:11.

Not a magic charm. However, the Ark was not a magic charm. Its presence alone did not guarantee success; Jehovah's blessings depended on the spiritual standing and faithful obedience of those possessing the Ark. Hence, the Israelites under the leadership of Joshua suffered defeat at Ai because of unfaithfulness, despite the presence of the Ark in their camp. (Jos 7:1-6) Similarly, Israel's trusting in the presence of the Ark among the very fighting forces did not prevent the Philistines from killing 30,000 Israelites and capturing the Ark. (1Sa 4:1-11) The return of the Ark from the Philistines was an occasion for great rejoicing, offering of sacrifices, and thanksgiving, yet Jehovah "struck down the people with a great slaughter." Why? "Because they had looked upon the ark of Jehovah" in violation of his command. (1Sa 6:11-21; Nu 4:6, 20) Exactly how many died on that occasion is not certain. The Masoretic text reads: "So he struck down among the people seventy men—fifty thousand men." This ambiguous construction might suggest that "fifty thousand men" is an interpolation. The Syriac *Peshitta* and the Arabic say that "five thousand and seventy men" were struck down. The Targum Jonathan reads: "And he struck down seventy men among the older men of the people, and fifty thousand among the congregation." The Greek *Septuagint* says that "seventy men among them, and fifty thousand of the men" were struck down. Josephus mentions only seventy men as being killed.—*Jewish Antiquities,* VI, 16 (i, 4).

Locations Where the Ark Was Kept. The Ark had no permanent resting-place until the erection of Solomon's temple. With the major conquest of the land completed (c. 1467 B.C.E.), it was moved to Shiloh, where it apparently remained (with the exception of a time when it was at Bethel) until captured by the Philistines. (Jos 18:1; Jg 20:26, 27; 1Sa 3:3; 6:1) Upon its return to Israelite territory it rested successively at Beth-shemesh and Kiriath-jearim, at this latter place for about 70 years.—1Sa 6:11-14; 7:1, 2; 1Ch 13:5, 6.

According to the Masoretic text, 1 Samuel 14:18 indicates that, during a conflict with the Philistines, King Saul had Ahijah the high priest bring the Ark to his campsite. However, the Greek *Septuagint* states that Saul said to Ahijah: "'Bring the ephod near!' (For he carried the ephod in that day before Israel.)."

David's desire to have the Ark brought to Jerusalem was a good one, but the method he first used led to disaster. Instead of having it carried by the poles on the shoulders of the Kohathite Levites as instructed, David let it be placed on a wagon. The bulls caused a near upset, and Uzzah was struck down because he reached out to grab hold of the Ark, contrary to God's law.—2Sa 6:2-11; 1Ch 13:1-11; 15:13; Nu 4:15.

The Ark was finally brought to Jerusalem, properly carried by the Levites (1Ch 15:2, 15), and there it remained in a tent during the remainder of David's reign. (2Sa 6:12-19; 11:11) The priests attempted to take the Ark along when they fled Absalom's rebellion, but David insisted that it remain in Jerusalem, trusting that Jehovah would bring them all back safely to it. (2Sa 15:24, 25, 29; 1Ki 2:26) David desired to build a permanent house for the Ark, but Jehovah postponed such construction until Solomon's reign. (2Sa 7:2-13; 1Ki 8:20, 21; 1Ch 28:2, 6; 2Ch 1:4) On the occasion of the dedication of the temple, the Ark was moved from the tent on Zion into the Most Holy of the temple up on Mount Moriah, where it was placed under the overshadowing wings of two large cherubs. It was the only piece of furniture from the original tabernacle that became part of Solomon's temple.—1Ki 6:19; 8:1-11; 1Ch 22:19; 2Ch 5:2-10; 6:10, 11; see TEMPLE (Solomon's Temple); CHERUB No. 1.

The only post-Solomonic historical reference to the ark of the covenant, nearly 900 years after it was made, is at 2 Chronicles 35:3 where King Josiah, in 642 B.C.E., commanded that it be returned to the temple. How it had come to be removed is not stated. Josiah came to the throne following some very apostate kings, one of whom had put an image in the house of Jehovah, and possibly one of these wicked kings removed the Ark. (2Ch 33:1, 2, 7) On the other hand, Josiah sponsored extensive repairs of the temple, during which time the Ark might have been kept elsewhere for its own protection against damage. (2Ch 34:8—35:19) There is no mention of the Ark's being taken to Babylon. The Ark is not enumerated among the temple articles carried off. Likewise, there is no mention of its being returned and placed in Zerubbabel's rebuilt temple; neither was a replacement made for it. When and under what circumstances the Ark disappeared is unknown. —2Ki 25:13-17; 2Ch 36:18; Ezr 1:7-11; 7:12-19.

Jeremiah foretold a time when the ark of the covenant would be no more, but that it would not be missed and Jehovah's worshipers would experience no hardship because of not having it. Instead 'Jerusalem itself will be called the throne of Jehovah.'—Jer 3:16, 17.

In the symbolic book of Revelation, John says that "the ark of his covenant was seen in his temple sanctuary" in heaven. This ark of the covenant has to do with the new covenant of God with men and the appearing of the Ark was an indication that Jehovah was again ruling by means of his Anointed One.—Re 11:15, 19.

ARM. A limb of the human body. The Hebrew and Greek terms for "arm" (*zeroh′a′*; *bra·khi′on*) are often used figuratively in the Bible to represent the ability to exert strength or power. (Ge 49: 24, ftn; Job 22:8, ftn; compare Lu 1:51.) The "arm" of Jehovah God is immeasurably powerful, able to do marvelous creative works. (Jer 27:5; 32:17) By his "arm" Jehovah also rules (Isa 40:10; Eze 20: 33), saves those in distress (Ps 44:3; Isa 52:10), delivers his people (Ex 6:6; Isa 63:12; Ac 13:17), supports and cares for them (De 33:27; Isa 40:11; Ho 11:3), judges (Isa 51:5), and scatters his enemies (Ps 89:10; Lu 1:51). Breaking the arm represents shattering one's might. (Job 38:15; Ps 10:15; Jer 48:25) Through Jesus Christ, clothed with authority and power and acting as Judge and Executioner, Jehovah manifests His might, represented by His "arm."—Isa 53:1; Joh 12:37, 38.

The arm of flesh, representing human power, is described in the Bible as unreliable and failing the one trusting in it. Jehovah warns his people of the fallacy and disaster of trusting in the human arm. (2Ch 32:8; Jer 17:5) He will break the arm of the wicked, which is described as resting oppressively on their victims.—Job 35:9; 38:15; Ps 10:15.

In King Nebuchadnezzar's dream image, the breasts and arms of silver represent Medo-Persia, the kingdom succeeding Babylon, the head of gold, as world power.—Da 2:32, 39.

ARMAGEDDON. See HAR–MAGEDON.

ARMONI (Ar·mo′ni) [Of the Dwelling Tower; Born in the Dwelling Tower]. One of two sons born to Saul by his concubine Rizpah. To expiate Saul's bloodguilt, seven of his offspring, including Armoni, were given to the Gibeonites, who put them

to death and exposed their corpses on the mountain. Rizpah kept watch, not letting fowl or beast molest them, until David had the bones buried. —2Sa 21:5-14.

ARMOR. See ARMS, ARMOR.

ARMOR-BEARER. A military attendant who carried the armor and weapons of a king or other leader, stood by him in danger, and did his bidding. "Armor-bearer" translates the Hebrew expression *no·se′′ ke·lim′*, literally meaning "one carrying armor or weapons." (1Sa 14:6; compare 1Sa 14:1.) Foes wounded by a prominent warrior might be given the final deathblow by his armor-bearer. (1Sa 14:13) These attendants were selected from among valiant soldiers, and some were evidently very devoted to their commanders. —1Sa 14:6, 7; 31:5.

Mortally wounded Abimelech had the attendant bearing his weapons put him to death so that it might not be said, "It was a woman that killed him." (Jg 9:52-54) David once served as King Saul's armor-bearer (1Sa 16:21); while a later armor-bearer, who refused to put the dying ruler to death, followed Saul in the course of suicide. (1Sa 31:3-6) Armor-bearers also attended Jonathan and Joab (1Sa 14:6-14; 2Sa 18:15; 23:37; 1Ch 11:39) and chief warriors of various ancient nations, such as the Philistine giant Goliath.—1Sa 17:7, 41.

ARMS, ARMOR. Arms and armor are often mentioned in the Bible, but no extensive details on their manufacture and utilization are provided.

While the Hebrew Scriptures in particular tell repeatedly of the use of the literal sword, spear, shield, and other arms, they also consistently emphasize the vital necessity and advantage of trusting in Jehovah. (Ge 15:1; Ps 76:1-3; 115:9-11; 119:114; 144:2) Reliance upon Him was evident in David's words to Goliath: "You are coming to me with a sword and with a spear and with a javelin, but I am coming to you with the name of Jehovah of armies, the God of the battle lines of Israel, whom you have taunted. This day Jehovah will surrender you into my hand . . . And all this congregation will know that neither with sword nor with spear does Jehovah save, because to Jehovah belongs the battle." (1Sa 17:45-47) Dependence upon Jehovah's spirit and not military force is shown to be essential and effective. (Zec 4:6) And in confirming his love for his figurative wife, Zion, Jehovah assured: "Any weapon whatever that will be formed against you will have no success . . . This is the hereditary possession of the servants of Jehovah."—Isa 54:17.

The Hebrew word *keli'* may denote a "weapon," but it can also refer to an "article," "utensil," "instrument," 'implement,' or "vessel." (Jg 9:54; Le 13:49; Eze 4:9; Nu 35:16; Ec 9:18; Le 6:28) In the plural form it can refer to "armor," as well as "goods," "equipment," "luggage," and "baggage." (2Ch 9:24; Ge 31:37; 45:20; 1Sa 10:22; 17:22) One other Hebrew word for "armor" (*ne'sheq*) comes from the root *na·shaq'*, meaning "be armed; be equipped." (1Ki 10:25; 1Ch 12:2; 2Ch 17:17) The Greek word *ho'plon* (weapon) is related to *pa·no·pli'a,* meaning "full armament; complete suit of armor."—Joh 18:3; Lu 11:22; Eph 6:11.

Arms (Offensive). *Sword and dagger.* The Hebrew word *che'rev* is usually rendered "sword," but it may also be rendered 'dagger,' "chisel," and 'knife.' (Ge 3:24; 1Ki 18:28; Ex 20:25; Jos 5:2) In the Hebrew Scriptures the sword is the most frequently mentioned weapon of offense and defense. It had a handle and a metal blade, which might be made of brass, copper, iron, or steel. Swords were employed for cutting (1Sa 17:51; 1Ki 3:24, 25) and thrusting or running through. (1Sa 31:4) Some swords were short, others long, being single- or double-edged. Archaeologists separate daggers from swords by length, the point of differentiation being about 40 cm (16 in.).

Generally the sword was suspended on the left side from the girdle (1Sa 25:13) and was worn in a sheath, a leather case or covering for the sword or the dagger. Second Samuel 20:8 allows for the possibility that Joab deliberately adjusted his sword so that it fell from its sheath and then merely held the weapon in his hand instead of sheathing it once again. Unsuspecting Amasa perhaps thought it had fallen accidentally, and he was unconcerned. That proved fatal.

In the Christian Greek Scriptures, the Greek word *ma'khai·ra* is usually used for the sword (Mt 26:47), though *rhom·phai'a,* denoting a "long sword," is also employed. (Re 6:8) The fact that two swords were available among the disciples on the night of Jesus' betrayal was not unusual for those times (Lu 22:38), and there is evidence that for Galileans in particular it was not uncommon to carry arms. (See *The Jewish War,* by F. Josephus, III, 42 [iii, 2].) Jesus' words at Luke 22:36, "Let the one having no sword sell his outer garment and buy one," would not indicate that his disciples were about to enter into a hazardous life. Rather, he desired to have a sword available among his followers on that night in order to demonstrate clearly that, though they would come into circumstances that could easily provoke armed resistance, he did not intend to resort to the sword but

would give himself up voluntarily in harmony with God's will. Thus, when Peter did react and try to put up armed resistance, lopping off the ear of Malchus, Jesus ordered him: "Return your sword to its place, for all those who take the sword will perish by the sword." (Mt 26:52; Joh 18:10, 11) Certainly, Peter's sword and the other one at hand would have availed little against such a large group of armed men, and by trying to use them, they would undoubtedly have 'perished by the sword.' (Mt 26:47) More important, such attempted delivery of Jesus would have failed, being completely contrary to Jehovah God's purpose. (Mt 26:53, 54) As it was, later that day Jesus could plainly state to Pilate: "If my kingdom were part of this world, my attendants would have fought that I should not be delivered up to the Jews. But, as it is, my kingdom is not from this source."—Joh 18:36.

Spear, lance, javelin, and dart. Weapons used for thrusting or hurling, consisting of a shaft fitted with a sharp point or head. (1Sa 18:11; Jg 5:8; Jos 8:18; Job 41:26) Various kinds were used by all the nations of antiquity. Precise delineation between them, as designated by different Hebrew words, is somewhat uncertain.

In the Hebrew Scriptures, the spear (Heb., *chanith'*) was apparently the largest of these four weapons, having a long wooden shaft and generally a sharp stone or metal head. In importance it ranked second to the sword. The giant Goliath carried a spear with a blade weighing "six hundred shekels of iron" (6.8 kg; 15 lb) and with a wooden shaft "like the beam of loom workers." (1Sa 17:7) Some spears had a metal point at the butt end by which they might be fixed in the ground. Hence, this end, and not just the spearhead, could be used effectively by a warrior. (2Sa 2:19-23) A spear stuck in the earth might denote a king's temporary abode.—1Sa 26:7.

In the Christian Greek Scriptures the spear (Gr., *log'khe*) is mentioned in John 19:34, which says that after Jesus Christ had died, "one of the soldiers jabbed his side with a spear." Since this was a Roman soldier, the Roman pilum was probably used. Such a weapon was about 1.8 m (6 ft) long, with a barbed iron head extending halfway down the length of the wooden shaft.

The lance (Heb., *ro'mach*), a weapon with a long shaft and a sharp point, was used for thrusting. (Nu 25:7, 8) It was a standard weapon of the Hebrews.

The javelin (Heb., *ki·dhohn'*) had a pointed metal head and was usually thrown. It was apparently smaller and lighter than the conventional spear, which would allow for it to be held with outstretched arm. (Jos 8:18-26) The javelin was customarily carried not in the hand but on the back.

The dart (Heb., *mas·sa'*) was evidently a short pointed missile similar to the arrow. (Job 41:26) *She'lach,* the Hebrew word for a missile, comes from the root verb *sha·lach',* meaning "send (out); put out; thrust out." (2Ch 23:10; Ge 8:8, 9; Ex 9:15) The Hebrew word *ziq·qim'* denotes "fiery missiles" and is related to *zi·qohth',* meaning "sparks; fiery arrows."—Pr 26:18; Isa 50:11, ftn.

The Greek *be'los* (missile) comes from the root *bal'lo,* meaning "throw." The apostle Paul used this Greek word when he wrote about "burning missiles" that one is able to quench with the large shield of faith. (Eph 6:16) Among the Romans, darts were made of hollow reeds, and on the lower part, under the point, there was an iron receptacle that could be filled with burning naphtha. The dart was then shot from a slack bow, as projecting it from a taut bow would put out the fire. Endeavoring to extinguish such a missile with water would just increase the flame, and the only way to put it out was by covering the destructive projectile with earth.

Bow and arrow. From early times the bow (Heb., *qe'sheth;* Gr., *to'xon*) was used in hunting and warfare. (Ge 21:20; 27:3; 48:22; Re 6:2) It was a standard weapon among the Israelites (2Ch 26:14, 15), those who fought for Egypt (Jer 46:8, 9), the Assyrians (Isa 37:33), and the Medo-Persians.—Jer 50:14; 51:11; see also ARCHER.

The reference to "a bow of copper" is likely to be understood as meaning a wooden bow mounted with copper. (2Sa 22:35) The expression 'to bend the bow' (literally, 'to tread the bow') refers to stringing the bow. (Ps 7:12; 37:14; Jer 50:14, 29) This might be done by firmly planting the foot against the middle of the bow; or one end of the bow with the string attached might be held to the ground by the foot while the other end was bent to receive the free end of the string.

Arrows (Heb., *chits·tsim'*) were made of reed shafts or light wood, their bases usually feathered. Arrowheads were at first made of flint or bone and later of metal. Sometimes arrows were barbed, were dipped in poison (Job 6:4), or were dressed with combustible material. (Ps 7:13) In the case of an incendiary arrow, oil-soaked tow was placed into holes along the edge of its metal head, to be ignited when the arrow was used.

Thirty arrows were commonly placed in a leather case or quiver. Assyrian reliefs show that the quivers carried on chariots held 50 arrows. —Compare Isa 22:6.

Sling. From ancient times the sling (Heb., *qe'la'*) has been the weapon of shepherds (1Sa 17:40) and warriors. (2Ch 26:14) It was a leather thong or was a band woven of such materials as animal sinews, rushes, or hair. "The hollow of the sling," a widened center part, held the projectile. (1Sa 25:29) One end of the sling might be tied to the hand or wrist while the other was held in the hand, to be freed when the sling was swung. The loaded sling was whirled overhead, perhaps several times, and then one end was suddenly released, sending the missile forward with considerable force and speed. Smooth, round stones were especially desired for slinging, though other projectiles were also used. (1Sa 17:40) Slingers were a regular part of the armies of Judah (2Ch 26:14) and Israel.—2Ki 3:25.

War club, handstave, and battle-ax. The "war club" was evidently a heavy club or mace, sometimes studded with metal. (Pr 25:18) The 'handstave' was a wooden staff, perhaps tipped with a metal point, that was used as a weapon. (Eze 39:9) The battle-ax was a weapon usually having a relatively short wooden or metal handle and a stone or metal head with a sharp blade. There is an allusion to the battle-ax in figurative speech at Psalm 35:3, where Jehovah is asked by David to "draw spear and double ax to meet those pursuing me."

Armor (Defensive). In order to protect his body from the offensive weapons of the enemy, a soldier employed various kinds of shields and personal armor.

Shield. A broad piece of defensive armor used by all ancient nations. It was equipped with an inside handle and was carried by the warrior during battle, usually on the left arm or in the left hand, although during the march it may have been hung from a shoulder strap. Isaiah 22:6 indicates that some may have been provided with a cover that was removed at time of combat. In peacetime, shields were often placed in arsenals. —Ca 4:4.

Shields used in ancient times were often made of wood covered with leather, and such shields could be burned. (Eze 39:9) Whereas wooden and leather shields were in general use, it appears that metal shields were less common, being used especially by leaders, royal guards, or possibly for ceremonial purposes. (2Sa 8:7; 1Ki 14:27, 28) Shields were oiled to make them pliable and moisture resistant, to keep the metal from rusting, or to make them smooth and slippery. (2Sa 1:21) The leather shield was often decked with a heavy center boss (a knob or stud) of metal, which gave added protection.—Job 15:26.

The "large shield" (Heb., *tsin·nah'*) was carried by the heavily armed infantry (2Ch 14:8) and sometimes by a shield bearer. (1Sa 17:7, 41) It was either oval or else rectangular like a door. Apparently a similar "large shield" is designated at Ephesians 6:16 by the Greek word *thy·re·os'* (from *thy'ra,* meaning "door"). The *tsin·nah'* was large enough to cover the entire body. (Ps 5:12) It was on occasion used to set up solid-front battle lines with lances protruding. The large shield is some-

Roman legionnaire with large shield

times mentioned with the lance or spear as a form of reference to weapons in general.—1Ch 12:8, 34; 2Ch 11:12.

The smaller "shield" or "buckler" (Heb., *ma·ghen'*) was customarily carried by archers and is usually associated with light weapons such as the bow. For instance, it was carried by Benjaminite bowmen of Judean King Asa's military force. (2Ch 14:8) The smaller shield was usually round and more common than the large shield, probably being used chiefly in hand-to-hand fighting. That the Hebrew *tsin·nah'* and *ma·ghen'* differed considerably in size seems to be indicated by the gold shields Solomon made, the large shield being overlaid with four times as much gold as the smaller shield, or buckler. (1Ki 10:16, 17; 2Ch 9:15, 16) *Ma·ghen',* like *tsin·nah',* seems to be used as part of a formula for weapons of war.—2Ch 14:8; 17:17; 32:5.

The Hebrew word *she'let,* rendered 'circular shield,' occurs seven times in the Hebrew Scriptures and is evidently similar to the more common *ma·ghen'* (shield), since it is used in conjunction with *ma·ghen'* in The Song of Solomon 4:4.

Helmet. A military headgear designed to protect a fighter during battle and a very basic part of defensive armor. The Hebrew word for "helmet" is *koh·va''* (alternately *qoh·va''*), while the Greek term is *pe·ri·ke·pha·lai'a,* literally meaning "around the head."—1Sa 17:5, 38; Eph 6:17.

Originally, Israelite helmets were probably made of leather. Later these were covered with copper or iron and were worn over woolen, felt, or leather bonnets. Copper helmets were used in Israel as early as the days of King Saul. (1Sa 17:38) While helmets may at first have been reserved for kings and other leaders, later they were in general use, Uzziah furnishing his entire army with them. —2Ch 26:14.

The Philistines possessed metal helmets; Goliath wore one of copper. (1Sa 17:5) Ezekiel mentioned helmets in connection with Persians, Ethiopians, and others.—Eze 27:10; 38:5.

Coat of mail. A coat worn for protection during battle. The coat of mail (Heb., *shir·yohn'* or *shir·yan'*) consisted of a cloth or leather cloak that had hundreds of small adjoining pieces of metal (somewhat like fish scales) attached to its surface. Often it covered the breast, back, and shoulders, though it sometimes reached to the knees or even the ankles.—1Sa 17:5.

Among the Hebrews the coat of mail was frequently made of leather covered with metal scales or plates. The wearer enjoyed considerable protection thereby, but, nonetheless, would be vulnerable where the scales were connected or where the coat of mail adjoined other parts of the armor. Thus, King Ahab was mortally wounded by a bowman who "got to strike the king of Israel between the appendages and the coat of mail." —1Ki 22:34-37.

Girdle. The military girdle of ancient times was a leather belt worn around the waist or hips. It varied in width from 5 to 15 cm (2 to 6 in.) and was often studded with plates of iron, silver, or gold. The warrior's sword was suspended from it, and at times the belt was supported by a shoulder strap. (1Sa 18:4; 2Sa 20:8) Whereas a loosened girdle denoted leisure (1Ki 20:11), girding up the loins or hips indicated readiness for action or battle.—Ex 12:11; 1Ki 18:46; 1Pe 1:13, ftn.

Greaves. Armor consisting of thin plates of metal, covering the leg between the ankle and the knee. The only Biblical reference to them is at 1 Samuel 17:6, where it is shown that the giant Philistine warrior Goliath from Gath had "greaves [Heb., *mits·chath'*] of copper above his feet." The Israelites may also have used greaves to some extent.

Spiritual Armor. Although true Christians do not share in fleshly warfare, they are engaged in a battle and are likened to soldiers. (Php 2:25; 2Ti 2:3; Phm 2) A Christian has a wrestling "against the governments [not made up of flesh-and-blood humans], against the authorities, against the world rulers of this darkness, against the wicked spirit forces in the heavenly places." (Eph 6:12) Since physical weapons and armor would be of no value in a battle against superhuman spirits, Christians must "take up the complete suit of armor from God."—Eph 6:13.

Paul advises Christians to have their "loins girded about with truth." (Eph 6:14) Just as a girdle can provide support and protection for the loins, an unbreakable attachment to divine truth can strengthen a Christian in his determination to remain firm despite trials.

Next, a Christian must put on "the breastplate of righteousness." (Eph 6:14) A literal breastplate served to protect vital organs, especially the heart. The need of righteousness as a protective breastplate for the figurative heart is especially evident because of the heart's sinful inclination.—Ge 8:21; Jer 17:9.

Part of the spiritual armor is to have the feet "shod with the equipment of the good news of peace." (Eph 6:15) The Greek word *he·toi·ma·si'a,* translated "equipment," has the basic meaning "readiness." (See *Int; NIV; TEV.*) A Christian's always being equipped and ready to make known the "good news" to others, and doing so despite hardships, can help him to endure faithfully.

A prominent part of the spiritual armor is "the large shield of faith." Like a large shield covering most of the body, faith in Jehovah God and his ability to fulfill his promises will enable a Christian to "quench all the wicked one's burning missiles." (Eph 6:16; compare Ps 91:4.) Faith will help a Christian withstand attacks by wicked spirits, resist temptations to immorality, shun materialistic desires, and not give in to fear, doubt, or excessive grief.—Ge 39:7-12; Heb 11:15; 13:6; Jas 1:6; 1Th 4:13.

As a helmet protects a soldier's head, so "the helmet of salvation" safeguards the Christian's mental powers from ungodly influences. (Eph 6:17) Having on "as a helmet the hope of salvation" means looking "intently toward the payment of the reward," as Moses did.—1Th 5:8; Heb 11:26.

"The sword of the spirit, that is, God's word" is indispensable to the Christian in warding off false teachings and traditions of men and in teaching the truth and 'overturning strongly entrenched things.'—Eph 6:17; 2Co 10:4, 5.

ARMY. A large body of men organized and trained for warfare on land. The common Hebrew term for "army" (*tsa·va'*) is usually used with reference to human armed forces (Nu 1:3), but it can also denote spirit creatures in the heavens (1Ki 22:19) and physical heavenly bodies. (De 4:19) The Hebrew *cha'yil,* evidently from a root meaning "endure" (Job 20:21), is used to refer to a "military force" and a "combat force" (2Sa 8:9; 1Ch 20:1), but it also means "ability; vital energy; capableness; resources; wealth." (1Ch 9:13; De 33:11; Pr 31:29; Isa 8:4; Eze 28:4) The Hebrew *gedhudh'* denotes a "marauder band" or "troops." (2Sa 22:30; 2Ch 25:9) Of the four Greek terms referring to an army in the Scriptures, three (*stra·ti·a', stra'teu·ma,* and *stra·to'pe·don*) come from the Greek root *stra·tos',* basically referring to an encamped army, as opposed to one formed into battle lines. *Stra·to'pe·don,* containing the element *pe'don* (ground; earth), is appropriately rendered 'encamped army.' (Lu 21:20) The Greek term *pa·rem·bo·le'* (from *pa·ra'* [beside] and *bal'lo* [throw]) literally refers to the distribution or arranging of soldiers in battle order. It can mean "army," "soldiers' quarters," or "camp."—Heb 11:34; Ac 21:34; Re 20:9.

From the time of Abraham, Jehovah's pre-Christian servants engaged in armed warfare. After the Elamite Chedorlaomer and his allies carried off Abraham's nephew Lot and his household,

Abraham mustered his army of "trained men, three hundred and eighteen slaves," and with his neighboring confederates went in pursuit up to Dan, about 200 km (120 mi) NNE. He then divided the forces and attacked by night, a strategy repeatedly employed in Biblical times.—Ge 14:13-16.

Israelite. The nation of Israel, over 400 years later, left Egypt in great haste, but in well-organized "battle formation," possibly like a five-part army composed of a main body with vanguard, rear guard, and two wings. (Ex 6:26; 13:18) The Egyptian army in pursuit consisted of "six hundred chosen chariots and all the other chariots of Egypt." Each chariot usually carried three men, one to manage the horses and two to fight, likely archers, since the bow was the principal offensive weapon of the Egyptians. The cavalry accompanied them. (Ex 14:7, 9, 17) According to Josephus (*Jewish Antiquities*, II, 324 [xv, 3]), the Hebrews were "pursued by 600 chariots along with 50,000 horsemen and heavy infantry to the number of 200,000."—See ADJUTANT.

Soon after the Exodus the Israelites engaged in their first military combat as a freed people. The Amalekites attacked them at Rephidim, in the region of Mount Sinai. At Moses' direction, Joshua quickly assembled a fighting force. The battle lasted the major part of the day, and in spite of their inexperience in the art of warfare, Jehovah gave Israel the victory.—Ex 17:8-14.

About a year after the Exodus, a count was taken of those eligible for service in the army, males 20 years old and upward. The census totaled 603,550. (Nu 1:1-3, 45, 46) A similar count toward the end of the wilderness journey showed that the army strength had dropped slightly to 601,730. (Nu 26:2, 51) The Levites were exempt from army duty, hence not included in these figures but were numbered separately.—Nu 1:47-49; 3:14-39; 26:57, 62.

Exemptions. Besides the tribe of Levi, the following exemptions from military service were granted: (1) the man who "has built a new house and has not inaugurated it"; (2) "the man that has planted a vineyard and not begun to use it"; (3) "the man that has become engaged to a woman and has not taken her"; (4) the one who marries "should not go out into the army, [but] . . . should continue exempt at his house for one year"; (5) "the man that is fearful and fainthearted."—De 20:5-8; 24:5.

Army arrangements after conquest of Canaan. After the general settlement in Canaan there was little need for a large standing army; border skir-

mishes were usually handled by the local tribes involved. When it was necessary to assemble a larger unified fighting force from several tribes, Jehovah raised up Judges to take command. The call to arms was accomplished in different ways: trumpet signals, messengers, or tokens were sent to stir the fighting men to action.—Nu 10:9; Jg 3:27; 6:35; 19:29; 1Sa 11:7.

Warriors appear to have furnished their own weapons: swords, spears, lances, darts, slings, bows, and arrows. The men generally were responsible for their own foodstuffs; hence Jesse sent provisions for his sons in Saul's army. (1Sa 17:17, 18) There is one case, however, when 10 percent of the volunteers were set aside to procure provisions for the rest.—Jg 20:10.

Jehovah's presence in Israel's camp called for sanctity, ceremonial cleanness on the part of the soldiers. (De 23:9-14) As sexual intercourse made a man unclean until the next day, under the Law, both David and Uriah carefully avoided sex relations while on active duty. (Le 15:16-18; 1Sa 21:1-6; 2Sa 11:6-11) The armies of pagan nations often raped the women of conquered cities, but not so the victorious soldiers of Israel. Nor were they permitted for a month to marry a captive woman.—De 21:10-13.

Israel's ultimate victories depended on Jehovah, yet good handling of the army was necessary. This responsibility rested on appointed officers and chiefs over thousands and over hundreds. Priests were assigned to encourage and to give direction and purpose to the campaigns. (Nu 31:6, 14; De 20:2-4, 9) During the days of the Judges, the one whom Jehovah raised up led the army personally into battle. The judge also planned the tactics and strategy. He deployed his forces in various ways: division into units (usually three), attack by surprise, ambush, frontal assault, securing river fords, and so forth.—Jos 8:9-22; 10:9; 11:7; Jg 3:28; 4:13, 14; 7:16; 9:43; 12:5.

Under the monarchy. Not satisfied with the theocratic arrangement under the Judges, the people wanted to be "like all the nations," having a king to go out before them and fight their battles. (1Sa 8:20) Samuel, however, warned them that such a king would not fight single-handed; he would take their sons "and put them as his in his chariots and among his horsemen, and some will have to run before his chariots." (1Sa 8:11, 12; see RUNNERS.) The king was commander in chief, with the chief of the army second in authority.—1Sa 14:50.

The size and strength of Saul's army varied according to the demands. On one occasion he selected 3,000 men, 1,000 of whom were under the command of his son Jonathan. (1Sa 13:2) For another exploit 330,000 were assembled. (1Sa 11:8) But compared with the highly mechanized armies of the Philistines, who, according to the Masoretic text, were capable of mustering 30,000 chariots, 6,000 horsemen, and "people like the grains of sand . . . for multitude," as they did at Michmash, Israel appeared ill equipped. "It happened on the day of battle that not a sword or a spear was found in the hand of any of the people," except Saul and Jonathan.—1Sa 13:5, 22.

During the reign of David the army of Israel was greatly improved, both in size and efficiency. There were well over 300,000 men equipped for war that came to Hebron and turned the kingship of Saul over to David. (1Ch 12:23-38) Non-Israelites also served in David's army.—2Sa 15: 18; 20:7.

David retained many of the older organizational plans of the army, such as holding the position of commander in chief himself, appointing field commanders like Joab, Abner, and Amasa, and having under them the heads over thousands and over hundreds. (2Sa 18:1; 1Ki 2:32; 1Ch 13:1; 18:15) However, David instituted some novel plans of his own. A system of monthly rotation provided 12 groups of 24,000 (a total of 288,000), so that a soldier normally served only one month a year. (1Ch 27:1-15) This does not mean that all 24,000 for one month came from the same tribe, but, rather, each tribe furnished its share of the monthly quota throughout the year.

Cavalry and chariot units. Chariots, mobile firing platforms, were highly prized by the Babylonians, Assyrians, and Egyptians for their speed and maneuverability. They thus became fitting symbols of military power of the leading world empires. Under David, Israel's greatest military commander, the army in its entirety was composed of the foot soldier with his hand weapons —sword, spear, bow, or sling. David must have remembered that Jehovah counseled against relying on the horse for victory (De 17:16; 20:1), that Pharaoh's horses and chariots were "pitched into the sea" by Jehovah (Ex 15:1, 4), and that Jehovah opened the floodgates of heaven on Sisera's "nine hundred war chariots with iron scythes" so that "the torrent of Kishon washed" the enemy away. —Jg 4:3; 5:21.

Therefore, as Joshua hamstrung captured horses and burned enemy chariots, David did the same with horses seized from Hadadezer, king of Zobah. He hamstrung all except a hundred of the many horses captured from the king of Zobah. (Jos

11:6-9; 2Sa 8:4) In a song David explained how his enemies concerned themselves with chariots and horses, "but, as for us, concerning the name of Jehovah our God we shall make mention." "The horse is a deception for salvation." (Ps 20:7; 33:17) As the proverb says: "The horse is something prepared for the day of battle, but salvation belongs to Jehovah."—Pr 21:31.

With the rule of Solomon a new chapter was written in the annals of Israel's army. His reign was comparatively peaceful, yet he multiplied horses and chariots. (See CHARIOT.) For the most part these horses were purchased and imported from Egypt. Whole cities had to be built throughout the territory to accommodate these new military divisions. (1Ki 4:26; 9:19; 10:26, 29; 2Ch 1:14-17) However, Jehovah never blessed this innovation of Solomon, and with his death and the dividing of the kingdom came the decline in Israel's army. As Isaiah later wrote: "Woe to those going down to Egypt for assistance, those who rely on mere horses, and who put their trust in war chariots, because they are numerous, and in steeds, because they are very mighty, but who have not looked to the Holy One of Israel and have not searched for Jehovah himself."—Isa 31:1.

During the divided kingdom. Following the division of the kingdom there was constant hostility between Judah and Israel. (1Ki 12:19, 21) Rehoboam's successor Abijah had only 400,000 men in his army when Jeroboam came against him with 800,000. In spite of being outnumbered two to one, the southern kingdom proved successful "because they leaned upon Jehovah." Israel lost 500,000 men.—2Ch 13:3-18.

In addition to intertribal strife, there was the external antagonism from the pagan nations round about. Israel was obliged to maintain a standing army because of provocative foreign relations with Syria to the north. (2Ki 13:4-7) Judah also had to resist the advances of pagan armies. On one occasion Egypt invaded Judah and took away much booty. (1Ki 14:25-27) At another time Ethiopia came against Judah with an army of 1,000,000 men and 300 chariots. King Asa's forces were only 580,000, but when he "began to call to Jehovah his God," "Jehovah defeated the Ethiopians," and not a single one was left alive.—2Ch 14:8-13.

Again, when Moab, Ammon, and the Ammonim came up against Jehoshaphat, although he had a force numbering 1,160,000, Jehoshaphat "set his face to search for Jehovah," who assured him, "The battle is not yours, but God's." (2Ch 17:12-19; 20:1-3, 15) Military history was made on that occasion, for a chorus of trained voices "went out ahead of the armed men," singing, "Give praise to Jehovah." In confusion the enemy forces destroyed each other.—2Ch 20:21-23.

Roman. The Roman army, estimated to number 300,000 during Augustus' reign, was organized quite differently from those of former empires. The principal part of the Roman military establishment was the legion. It was a large independent unit, a complete army in itself, rather than a specialized portion of a greater force. Sometimes legions fought together, merging their resources and strength under a central command, as when four legions combined under Titus for the siege of Jerusalem, 70 C.E. But usually the legion stood alone with its individual commission of duty. Supplementing the legionnaires were noncitizens from all parts of the empire who made up the *auxilia,* often volunteers from the local district. Auxiliaries, backed up by the legions, were stationed along the borders. Upon honorable discharge one in the *auxilia* was granted Roman citizenship.

The number of legions varied at different times, from 25 or less to as many as 33. Likewise the number of soldiers comprising the legion fluctuated from about 4,000 to 6,000; in the first century the force usually numbered 6,000. For this reason "legion" as used in the Scriptures apparently means an indefinite, large number. (Mt 26:53; Mr 5:9; Lu 8:30) Each legion had its own commander, responsible solely to the emperor, and under him were six tribunes, called chiliarchs (military commanders, *NW*).—Mr 6:21; Joh 18:12; Ac 21: 32–23:22; 25:23; see MILITARY COMMANDER.

The legion was divided into ten cohorts, or bands. Thus the Scriptures speak of "the Italian band" and "the band of Augustus." (Ac 10:1; 27:1; see AUGUSTUS, BAND OF.) When Herod Agrippa died, 44 C.E., there were five cohorts in Caesarea. Further subdivided, the legion had 60 centuries, usually 100 men each, under the leadership of a centurion (army officer, *NW*). These officers were especially valuable, having the responsibility of training soldiers. (Mt 8:5-13; 27:54; Ac 10:1; 21: 32; 22:25, 26; 23:17, 23; 24:23; 27:1, 6, 11, 31, 43; see ARMY OFFICER.) In each legion there were ten officers of special rank who acted as body guardsmen, couriers, and sometimes as executioners. —Mr 6:27.

The Roman legions had their various standards and ensigns bearing images of eagles or some animals; later small statues of the emperor were added. These banners had religious significance, were considered sacred and holy to the point of being worshiped, and were guarded at the cost of human life. It was for such reasons that the Jews violently opposed their presence in Jerusalem.

Those Known as Early Christians. Early Christians refused to serve in the Roman army, in both the legions and *auxilia,* considering such service as wholly incompatible with the teachings of Christianity. Says Justin Martyr, of the second century C.E., in his "Dialogue With Trypho, a Jew" (CX): "We who were filled with war, and mutual slaughter, and every wickedness, have each through the whole earth changed our warlike weapons,—our swords into ploughshares, and our spears into implements of tillage." (*The Ante-Nicene Fathers,* Vol. I, p. 254) In his treatise "The Chaplet, or De Corona" (XI), when discussing "whether warfare is proper at all for Christians," Tertullian (c. 200 C.E.) argued from Scripture the unlawfulness even of a military life itself, concluding, "I banish from us the military life."—*The Ante-Nicene Fathers,* 1957, Vol. III, pp. 99, 100.

"A careful review of all the information available goes to show that, until the time of Marcus Aurelius [121-180 C.E.], no Christian became a soldier; and no soldier, after becoming a Christian, remained in military service." (*The Rise of Christianity,* by E. W. Barnes, 1947, p. 333) "It will be seen presently that the evidence for the existence of a single Christian soldier between 60 and about 165 A.D. is exceedingly slight; . . . up to the reign of Marcus Aurelius at least, no Christian would become a soldier after his baptism." (*The Early Church and the World,* by C. J. Cadoux, 1955, pp. 275, 276) "In the second century, Christianity . . . had affirmed the incompatibility of military service with Christianity." (*A Short History of Rome,* by G. Ferrero and C. Barbagallo, 1919, p. 382) "The behavior of the Christians was very different from that of the Romans. . . . Since Christ had preached peace, they refused to become soldiers." (*Our World Through the Ages,* by N. Platt and M. J. Drummond, 1961, p. 125) "The first Christians thought it was wrong to fight, and would not serve in the army even when the Empire needed soldiers." (*The New World's Foundations in the Old,* by R. and W. M. West, 1929, p. 131) "The Christians . . . shrank from public office and military service." ("Persecution of the Christians in Gaul, A.D. 177," by F. P. G. Guizot in *The Great Events by Famous Historians,* edited by R. Johnson, 1905, Vol. III, p. 246) "While they [the Christians] inculcated the maxims of passive obedience, they refused to take any active part in the civil administration or the military defence of the empire. . . . It was impossible that the Christians, without renouncing a more sacred duty, could assume the character of soldiers, of magistrates, or of princes."—*The Decline and Fall of the Roman Empire,* by Edward Gibbon, Vol. I, p. 416.

Heavenly. Heavenly armies, in the sense of well-organized multitudes, refer not only to the physical stars but more frequently to the mighty hosts of angelic spirit creatures under the supreme command of Jehovah God. (Ge 2:1; Ne 9:6) The expression "Jehovah of armies" occurs 283 times in the Hebrew Scriptures, first at 1 Samuel 1:3, and twice its equivalent is found in the Greek Scriptures. (Ro 9:29; Jas 5:4; see JEHOVAH OF ARMIES.) In discussing the angelic warriors, such military terms are used as "legions," "war chariots," "horsemen," and so forth. (2Ki 2:11, 12; 6:17; Mt 26:53) In size, the camp of Jehovah's invisible armies includes "tens of thousands, thousands over and over again," of war chariots. (Ps 68:17) As a fighting force, they are invincible. "The prince of the army of Jehovah" with drawn sword appeared to Joshua and gave instructions on how Jericho would be captured. (Jos 5:13-15) One angel of these heavenly armies slew 185,000 Assyrians in a single night. (2Ki 19:35) When war broke out in heaven Michael and his angels hurled Satan and his demons down to the vicinity of the earth. (Re 12:7-9, 12) Furthermore, there will be no escape when "the armies . . . in heaven" follow the "King of kings and Lord of lords" as he brings destruction upon "the wild beast and the kings of the earth and their armies." (Re 19:14, 16, 19, 21) At the same time, however, this mighty invisible army of Jehovah gives protection to his faithful servants on earth.—2Ki 6:17; Ps 34:7; 91:11; Da 6:22; Mt 18:10; Ac 12:7-10; Heb 1:13, 14.

See also ARMS, ARMOR; SOLDIER; WAR.

ARMY OFFICER. This translates the Greek terms *he·ka·ton·tar'khes* (or *he·ka·ton'tar·khos*) and *ken·ty·ri'on,* and it designates an officer in command of a hundred soldiers, a centurion. The Roman legion, regardless of its size, was always divided into 60 centuries, each under the command of a centurion. If the legion shrank below 6,000, still one sixtieth, even when less than 100, was under a centurion. These army officers were nominated by tribunes and were approved by higher government authorities. The office of centurion was the highest rank the common soldier could reach, though there were opportunities for some advancement within the ranks of the centurions themselves.

The centurions were keymen and served a most important function in the legion. While they were under the authority of the tribunes and responsible to carry out their orders, the army officer was the real and immediate head of the soldiers. He drilled the soldiers; worked with them; inspected their arms, supplies, and food; regulated their conduct. He was the disciplinarian who supervised scourgings and capital punishment, the one who authorized punishment of his troops. The readiness and efficiency of the Roman army, for the most part, depended more on centurions than on anyone else; they were, generally speaking, the most experienced and valuable men in the Roman army.—See ARMY.

Army officers appear in the Christian Greek Scripture narratives on several occasions. The army officer from Capernaum who sought Jesus' healing power on behalf of his slave was commended by the Master for his exemplary faith. (Mt 8:5-13) The statement of the Jews, "He loves our nation and he himself built the synagogue for us"; the centurion's acknowledgment that "I am not fit to have you come in under my roof"; and Jesus' comment, "Not even in Israel have I found so great a faith," all indicate that the army officer was a Gentile. If he was a Roman, this was all the more remarkable, for Romans were not noted for their compassion toward slaves.—Lu 7:1-9.

An army officer headed the four soldiers who put Jesus to death. (Joh 19:23) This centurion likely had been present when the claim of divine Sonship was discussed before Pilate. (Joh 19:7) Observing this trial and the other circumstances surrounding the impalement, as well as the miraculous phenomena accompanying Jesus' death, "the army officer began to glorify God," saying, "Really this man was righteous," "Certainly this was God's Son." (Lu 23:47; Mt 27:54) Undoubtedly it was of him that Pilate inquired whether Jesus was dead before giving the body over for burial. —Mr 15:44, 45.

Cornelius, a centurion of the Italian band, stationed in Caesarea, was the first uncircumcised Gentile to become a Christian. (Ac 10:1-48) The fact that he had his own house and attendant soldiers indicates that officers of this rank were allowed to live detached from the regular troops. —See CORNELIUS.

Army officers stationed in the Tower of Antonia, together with their soldiers and the military commander, rushed down to the adjoining temple grounds and rescued Paul from a mob, about 56 C.E. (Ac 21:32) Later, Paul escaped scourging on the order of the military commander by disclosing to an attending army officer that he was a Roman citizen. (Ac 22:25, 26) Upon learning of a plot against his life, Paul called an army officer to lead his nephew to the military commander with this report. In turn, two army officers were ordered to ready a force of 470 soldiers, cavalry, and spearmen to ensure Paul's safe conduct out of Jerusalem.—Ac 23:17, 23.

Julius, an army officer of the band of Augustus (see AUGUSTUS, BAND OF), was responsible for Paul's passage from Adramyttium to Rome. He treated Paul with kindness, though at first ignoring the apostle's advice. Eventually, however, this centurion learned to respect Paul's judgment, and he was instrumental in saving the apostle's life. —Ac 27:1, 6, 11, 31, 43.

ARNAN (Ar'nan). A name appearing in a list of King David's descendants. Arnan lived after the return from Babylonian exile.—1Ch 3:1, 21.

ARNI (Ar'ni). A person named in the human ancestry of Jesus Christ. A variant of the Greek equivalent of the Hebrew name Ram; in the Greek *Septuagint,* the Hebrew name Ram is rendered Aram.—Lu 3:33; 1Ch 2:10; see RAM No. 1.

ARNON, TORRENT VALLEY OF (Ar'non). About halfway down the eastern side of the Dead Sea the deep gorge of the Arnon Valley cuts through the high plateau region. This torrent, the Wadi Mujib (Nahal Arnon), is fed by numerous tributaries (Nu 21:14) and, after the Jordan, is the only important stream emptying into the Dead Sea. The sheer red and yellow sandstone cliffs drop down abruptly to flank the sides of the narrow valley with its small perennial stream of limpid waters, replete with fish. Alongside grow willows, oleanders, and other vegetation in abundance. Where the stream leaves the steep chasm walls to enter the flat shore of the Dead Sea its size varies from 12 to 30 m (40 to 100 ft) in width, with a flow of from 0.3 to 1.2 m (1 to 4 ft) in depth.

The formidable canyon, which, at the top, measures some 3 km (2 mi) in width and is nearly 520 m (1,700 ft) deep, was crossed by only a few passages (Isa 16:2) and hence became an obvious natural boundary. At the time of the Israelite conquest it separated the Amorites on the N from the Moabites on the S (Nu 21:13), but Jephthah's

View toward the north across the torrent valley of Arnon

message to the Ammonites shows that the side to the N had once been under Ammonite control and had been invaded by the Amorites prior to Israel's arrival. (Jg 11:12-27) Israel, having skirted the territory of Moab, reached the Arnon, probably at its upper reaches. Attacked by Sihon, the Amorite king, Israel gained the victory and took possession of the land from the Arnon up to the Jabbok. (Nu 21:21-24; De 2:24-36; see JABBOK, TORRENT VALLEY OF.) This first conquest thereafter became the territory of the tribes of Reuben and Gad.—De 3:16; Jos 12:1, 2; 13:8, 9, 15-28.

Because of Jehu's failure to walk strictly according to Jehovah's law, this region was later overrun by the invading forces of Hazael of Syria. (2Ki 10:32, 33) The Arnon is referred to on line 26 of the famed Moabite Stone, King Mesha of Moab there boasting that he had constructed a highway through the valley. Archaeological discoveries give evidence of a number of forts and bridges in the area testifying to the strategic importance of the Arnon. Its name figures in prophecies directed against Moab.—Isa 16:2; Jer 48:20.

AROD (Ar'od), **ARODI** (Ar·o'di), **ARODITES** (Ar'od·ites). Sixth-named son of Gad and one of the souls who came into Egypt with Jacob's family in 1728 B.C.E. He became family head of the Arodites included in the wilderness census of 1473 B.C.E.—Ge 46:8, 16; Nu 26:17.

AROER (A·ro'er) [Juniper Tree].

1. A city located on the N rim of the deep gorge forming the torrent valley of the Arnon. At the time of the conquest by Israel (c. 1474 B.C.E.) it was the southernmost city of the Amorite kingdom. (De 2:36; 4:47, 48; Jos 12:2) Thereafter it passed to the tribe of Reuben, although the tribe of Gad is mentioned as building (probably, repairing) the city. (Nu 32:33, 34; De 3:12; Jos 13:8, 9, 15, 16; 1Ch 5:8) It marked the southern boundary of Israel E of the Jordan and so corresponded to Beer-sheba, a major southern city W of the Jordan.

After some 300 years of Israelite occupation, the Ammonites pressed a claim for the region lying between the Arnon and the Jabbok, but Judge Jephthah refuted their claim by showing that Israel had taken the land, including Aroer, from the Amorites.—Jg 11:13, 22, 26.

This city of Aroer appears to have been the starting point for the census ordered by King David, which thereafter swung N to Dan-jaan and looped over to Tyre and Sidon and then S to Beer-sheba in the Negeb. (2Sa 24:4-8) The mention of "the city that is in the middle of the torrent

valley" coincides with similar references at Deuteronomy 2:36 and Joshua 13:9, 16. This unnamed city is considered by some to correspond to Khirbet el-Medeiyineh, about 11 km (7 mi) SE of Aroer.

During the reign of King Jehu of Israel (c. 904-877 B.C.E.), King Hazael of Syria overran the territories of Gad and Reuben, as far S as Aroer on the Arnon. (2Ki 10:33) Perhaps during this time, Moabite King Mesha fortified the city and built his road by the Arnon, as related on line 26 of the Moabite Stone. At the time of Jeremiah's prophecy against Moab the city was under Moabite control. —Jer 48:19.

The site of the ancient city is identified with Khirbet 'Ara'ir, about 23 km (14 mi) E of the Dead Sea, about 6 km (3.5 mi) SSE of Dibon, and close by the King's Highway, the main N-S route on that side of the Jordan. The ruins contain evidences of an ancient fortress, which, from its vantage point on the edge of the impressive gorge, could likely control the passages over the Arnon.

2. A town of the territory of Gad, described as "in front of Rabbah" (modern 'Amman), the chief city of the Ammonites. (Jos 13:24, 25) It is possibly the Aroer mentioned in the description of Jephthah's conquest over the Ammonites at Judges 11:33. The location of the place is uncertain since the expression "in front of" is not particularly restrictive, though often considered as meaning "to the east of."

3. A town in the southern part of the territory of Judah. After David's victory over the Amalekite raiders he distributed portions of the spoil to the older men of the city. (1Sa 30:26, 28) It is identified with Khirbet 'Ar'arah (Horvat 'Aro'er), about 17 km (11 mi) SE of Beer-sheba, where the ruins of a fort remain. Some scholars believe that it may be the same place as the "Adadah" of Joshua 15:22, the Hebrew letter da'leth (ד) being substituted for rehsh (ר) in both instances.

The reference to "the cities of Aroer" at Isaiah 17:2 could apply to either of the first two cities here considered. The prophecy primarily deals with Damascus, and in view of the Syrian conquest of Israel reaching as far as Aroer on the Arnon, the expression may refer to this southernmost point of their extension of power E of the Jordan.—2Ki 10:33.

AROERITE (A·ro'er·ite) [Of (Belonging to) Aroer]. An inhabitant of one of the cities named Aroer. At 1 Chronicles 11:44 Hotham, the father of two of David's mighty men named Shama and Jeiel, is referred to as an Aroerite. His sons' association with David may place their father's home city in the territory of Judah.—See AROER No. 3.

ARPACHSHAD (Ar·pach'shad). A son of Shem. He was born two years after the Flood, that is, about 2368 B.C.E., and died 438 years later. He was an ancestor of the Hebrews through his grandson Eber. (Ge 10:22, 24; 11:10-13; 1Ch 1:17-27) He is shown to be the father of Shelah, although Luke's account (3:35, 36), by the inclusion of Cainan, apparently would make him Shelah's grandfather; but see CAINAN No. 2.—Ge 10: 24; 11:12; 1Ch 1:24.

ARPAD (Ar'pad). A royal city of N Syria always associated in the Bible with the city of Hamath. Arpad has been identified with Tell Erfad (Tell Rif'at) about 30 km (19 mi) NNW of Aleppo. Situated on the road leading S to Hamath and Damascus, it came under frequent attack from the Assyrians and was eventually conquered by Tiglath-pileser III and later by Sargon II. Thus Sargon's son, Sennacherib, when threatening Jerusalem in 732 B.C.E., had his spokesman Rabshakeh refer to the fate of Arpad as an evidence of the inability of the gods of the nations to resist Assyria's mighty power. (2Ki 18:34; 19:12, 13; Isa 36:19; 37:12, 13) The prophet Isaiah had earlier foretold such boasting. (Isa 10:9) Later Jeremiah prophesied that Hamath and Arpad would become ashamed and disintegrate before "a bad report," evidently concerning the conquests of Babylonian King Nebuchadnezzar.—Jer 49:23.

ARROW. See ARMS, ARMOR.

ARROW SNAKE [Heb., qip·pohz']. A snake evidently so called from its darting and springing on its prey, in the manner of the rattlesnake. The Hebrew root from which the name is derived seems to be related to an Arabic root verb meaning "jump" or "leap." The arrow snake is mentioned in the prophecy of Isaiah (34:15) as one of the creatures to inhabit Edom. This would emphasize the fact that Edom was to become such a desolate ruin that it would become a safe place for the arrow snake to 'make its nest and lay eggs and hatch them and gather them together under its shadow.' Most snakes lay eggs, and this text may refer to the practice of some snakes of coiling around their eggs. Says H. W. Parker's book *Snakes: A Natural History* (1977, p. 55): "The 'brooding' habit and coiled body give a measure of temperature control as well as protection because the mother can cover or uncover her eggs at will as the weather varies and so ensure a more uniform, and probably higher, temperature; at the same time coiling reduces the exposed surfaces."

Samuel Bochart (1599-1667), in his work *Hierozoicon* (Leipzig, 1796, Vol. 3, Part II, Book III,

chap. XI, pp. 194-204), made a detailed study of the Hebrew word qip·pohz' and concluded that it refers to the snake called in Greek a·kon·ti'as and in Latin *jaculus*—the arrow snake. However, modern lexicographers are not in agreement regarding the meaning of this Hebrew word.

ART. Art, as it relates to painting, sculpture, and design, receives relatively little attention in the Bible. Yet man's life began, not in a barren field, but in a garden, a paradise with trees not only "good for food" but also "desirable to one's sight." (Ge 2:9) Man was made to appreciate beauty, and the unsurpassed beauty, artistry, and design manifest in creation—flowers, trees, mountains, valleys, lakes, waterfalls, birds, animals, as well as the human form itself—evoke praise for their divine Creator. (Ps 139:14; Ec 3:11; Ca 2:1-3, 9, 13, 14; 4:1-5, 12-15; 5:11-15; Ro 1:20) Art, as here discussed, implies, basically, the representation of such things by use of various materials and the use of different forms and expression.

Already in Abraham's time the Bible makes mention of gifts of "a gold nose ring," golden bracelets, and other articles of silver and gold, bestowed on Rebekah. (Ge 24:22, 53) The Royal Tombs of Ur, in which city Abraham once lived, have yielded many exquisite ornaments of high artistic skill. However, many of the art objects recovered through archaeological explorations in the lands of Iraq, Israel, Egypt, and adjacent regions bear some relation to the idolatrous pagan religions or the proud political rulers, thus indicating an early perversion of the use of art.

Variety of Materials. Glass appears to have been produced as far back as the second millennium B.C.E. by the Egyptians and perhaps the Phoenicians. Yet, evidently it originated in Mesopotamia, where pieces of well-made glass have been found, believed to date from as early as the third millennium B.C.E. Job (c. 1600 B.C.E.) spoke of glass as being very precious. (Job 28:17) Though opaque, it was used in making animal figurines, perfume boxes, necklaces, and other jewelry. The Romans were among the first to produce transparent glass.—Compare Re 4:6; see GLASS.

The ancient artists worked with a considerable variety of materials, including clay, terra-cotta, wood, bronze or copper, iron, gold, silver, precious and semiprecious gems, glass, ivory, limestone, and marble.—See SEAL.

Hebrew Art. There is little material evidence remaining to present any clear picture of Hebrew art, yet art appreciation is manifest in the Bible record. On coming out of Egypt, the people brought with them gold and silver articles obtained from the Egyptians. (Ex 12:35) They gladly contributed such items for the decoration of the tabernacle in the wilderness. (Ex 35:21-24) The work of producing the tabernacle with its decorations and equipment gave outlet for their artistic ability in woodworking, metalworking, embroidery, and jewelwork, Bezalel and Oholiab particularly taking the lead and instructing. It is notable that credit for their artistic ability is given to Jehovah.—Ex 35:30-35; 36:1, 2.

Prior to the tabernacle work, Aaron had employed artistic ability for a perverse use in using a graving tool to make a molten image of a calf for worship. (Ex 32:3, 4) Moses (or someone assigned by him) also showed such ability, though properly, when making the serpent of copper at a later time. (Nu 21:9) However, the provisions in the Law forbidding the making of images for worship, while not prohibiting all representational art, doubtless exercised a restrictive influence on painting or sculpturing among the Hebrews. (Ex 20:4, 5) In view of the gross idolatry so prevalent in all nations and the widespread use of art to foster such idolatry, it is evident that paintings or carvings of figures, human or animal, would be viewed as suspect by those keeping the Law provisions and by those charged with enforcing it. (De 4:15-19; 7:25, 26) Even the cherubs of the tabernacle were covered over with a cloth when being transported and thus were hidden from the gaze of the populace (Nu 4:5, 6, 19, 20), while those of the later temple were seen only by the high priest on one day a year. (1Ki 6:23-28; Heb 9:6, 7) Additionally, after their entry and establishment in the Promised Land, the basically agricultural life of the Israelites was seldom such that it allowed for the leisure time and funds necessary for extensive artwork.

During the period of the Judges the only artwork indicated was involved in apostate religious practices.—Jg 2:13; 6:25; 8:24-27; 17:3-6; 18:14.

Artwork under the monarchy. While the ancient nation of Israel is not renowned today for its works of art, yet the evidence indicates that, when occasion arose, they were able to produce work of artistic quality that gained wide attention and admiration. The prophet Ezekiel depicts the manner in which Jehovah adorned and beautified Jerusalem so that " 'a name began to go forth among the nations because of your prettiness, for it was perfect because of my splendor that I placed upon you,' is the utterance of the Sovereign Lord Jehovah." (Eze 16:8-14) However, the succeeding verses (15-18, 25) show that such prettiness was put

to a perverted use, as Jerusalem prostituted herself with the surrounding political nations. Jeremiah, too, describes those looking on Jerusalem after her fall to Babylon as saying: "Is this the city of which they used to say, 'It is the perfection of prettiness, an exultation for all the earth'?" (La 2:15; compare Ps 48:2; 50:2; Isa 52:1.) The temple built by Solomon was evidently an artistic work of consummate beauty and is called a "house of holiness and beauty."—Isa 64:11; 60:13.

In dealing with the construction of the temple in King Solomon's time, much comment has been made in reference works about the assumed lack of artistic skill on the part of the Israelites, to the point of giving practically all the credit to the Phoenicians. The record, however, shows that Solomon requested only one Phoenician artisan, aside from the lumbermen employed in King Hiram's own forests of Lebanon and the stone quarriers. (1Ki 5:6, 18; 2Ch 2:7-10) This artisan, also named Hiram, was an Israeli-Phoenician skilled in working with precious metals, weaving, and engraving. Yet, the record refers to Solomon's own skilled men, and King Hiram likewise spoke of these and the skilled men of Solomon's father David. (2Ch 2:13, 14) The architectural plan of the temple and of all its features was delivered to Solomon by David, providing "insight for the entire thing in writing from the hand of Jehovah . . . , even for all the works of the architectural plan." (1Ch 28:11-19) By contrast, unfaithful King Ahaz did become enamored with the pagan altar at Damascus and sent "the design of the altar and its pattern" to priest Urijah to have a copy of it made. —2Ki 16:1-12.

King Solomon also made a great ivory throne, overlaid with gold, of unique design, with figures of lions standing by the armrests and lining the six steps of approach. (1Ki 10:18-20) The extensive use of ivory in the royal palace is indicated at Psalm 45:8. In the northern kingdom of Israel, with its capital at Samaria, ivory carving in furniture, paneling, and art objects was apparently popular in the days of King Ahab and thereafter. (1Ki 22:39; Am 3:12, 15; 6:4) Archaeological excavations turned up large quantities of ivory pieces, plaques, and panels in what is believed to have been the palace area. Inlaid work of gold, lapis lazuli, and glass occur in some pieces. In Megiddo some 400 ivory pieces were found, including beautifully carved panels, ivory inlaid boxes, and gaming boards, estimated as dating from about the 12th century B.C.E.

In a vision, Ezekiel saw carved representations of reptiles, animals, and idols on a wall of the temple area in apostate Jerusalem (Eze 8:10), and symbolic Oholibah (representing unfaithful Jerusalem) is spoken of as seeing images of Chaldeans carved on a wall and painted with vermilion, a bright-red pigment.—Eze 23:14; compare Jer 22:14.

Relationship to Christianity. Paul was a witness of the artistic splendor of Athens, developed around the worship of the Grecian gods and goddesses, and he showed an audience there how illogical it was that humans, owing their life and existence to the true God and Creator, should imagine that "the Divine Being is like gold or silver or stone, like something sculptured by the art and contrivance of man." (Ac 17:29) He thus demonstrated again that artistic beauty, no matter how impressive or attractive, does not of itself recommend any religion as being true worship.—Compare Joh 4:23, 24.

There is no record or existing evidence of artwork among the Christians of the first century C.E. It is only during the second and third centuries C.E. that some paintings and sculptures appear in the catacombs attributed to nominal Christians. After the union of Church and State in the fourth century, however, art began to be given a prominence that in time equaled that of the pagan religions and was often related to or in direct imitation of such religions, in both its symbolisms and its forms. Louis Réau, who held the chair of the History of Art of the Middle Ages at the Sorbonne University of France, demonstrates in his work *Iconographie de l'art chrétien* (Paris, 1955, Vol. I, p. 10) that such paganism has long been recognized by historians of art and that the responsibility for it is to be placed not merely on the artists but on the policies that were followed by the church itself. He points out (p. 50) that instead of really converting the pagans from their old practices and forms of worship, the church chose to respect "the ancestral customs and continue them under another name."

Thus, it is not surprising to find the signs of the zodiac, so prominent in ancient Babylon, displayed on cathedrals such as that of Notre Dame in Paris, where they appear on the left doorway and surround Mary in the huge centrally located rose window. (Compare Isa 47:12-15.) Similarly, a guidebook to the cathedral at Auxerre, also in France, states that in the central entrance to the cathedral, "the sculptor there mixed certain pagan heroes: an Eros [Greek god of love] nude and sleeping . . . a Hercules and a Satyr [one of the Greeks' semihuman demigods]! The register at

the lower right represents the parable of the Prodigal Son."

Similarly at the entrance of Saint Peter's Cathedral in Rome appear not only the figure of Christ and the "Virgin" but also that of Ganymede "carried off by the eagle" to become cupbearer of Zeus, king of the gods, and "Leda [who bore Castor and Pollux] fertilized by the swan" Zeus. Commenting further on such pagan influence, Réau asks: "But what is one to say then of the Final Judgment of the Sistine Chapel, the principal chapel of the Vatican, where one sees the nude Christ of Michelangelo lance the lightning like a thundering Jupiter [the Roman father of the gods] and the Damned cross the Styx [the river over which the Greeks believed the dead were ferried] in Charon's barque?" As he states: "An example that came from so high [that is, approved by the papacy] could not fail to be followed."

As has been seen, art was not given major attention by fleshly Israel and is virtually absent from the record of the early congregation of spiritual Israel of the first century C.E. It is, rather, in the field of literature that they surpassed all other peoples, being used by God to produce a work of superb beauty, not only in form but primarily in content: the Bible. Their inspired writings are "as apples of gold in silver carvings," with crystal-clear truths of such brilliance as to rival the finest gems, and word pictures that convey visions and scenes of a grandeur and loveliness beyond the ability of human artists to portray.—Pr 25:11; 3:13-15; 4:7-9; 8:9, 10.

ARTAXERXES (Ar·ta·xerx′es). A name or title applied in the Bible to two Persian kings.

1. The Persian ruler who caused the building of Jehovah's temple at Jerusalem to be stopped. (Ezr 4:7-24) Between the reigns of Cyrus the Great, who allowed the Jews to return to Jerusalem (537 B.C.E.), and of Darius the Great, who in 520 B.C.E. removed the ban imposed on the temple construction, possibly three kings ruled: Cambyses II, his brother Bardiya (or possibly a Magian known as Gaumata who is said to have pretended to be Bardiya and ruled for seven months), and Nidintu-Bel (who was defeated and killed by Darius after just two months). Cambyses is evidently represented by the "Ahasuerus" mentioned at Ezra 4:6 to whom the first protest was made by the opposers of the temple reconstruction. Therefore, beginning with Ezra 4:7, the ruler referred to as "Artaxerxes" is either Bardiya or Gaumata, whose rule lasted but seven months (522 B.C.E.).

The people of the cities of Samaria wrote a letter against the Jews to this Persian king. (Ezr 4:7)

This was while the Jews were busy building the temple. (Ezr 4:1-3) In order to achieve their goal, the adversaries of the Jews resorted to lies, stating that the Jews were then rebuilding the city of Jerusalem, including its walls. (Ezr 4:11-16) As a result of these false accusations, "the work on the house of God" came to a halt.—Ezr 4:24.

2. Artaxerxes Longimanus, the son of Xerxes I, is the king referred to at Ezra 7:1-28 and Nehemiah 2:1-18; 13:6. Whereas most reference works give his accession year as 465 B.C.E., there is sound reason for placing it in 475 B.C.E.—See PERSIA, PERSIANS (The Reigns of Xerxes and of Artaxerxes).

Artaxerxes Longimanus extended permission to Ezra the priest and also to Nehemiah to make trips to Jerusalem. (Ezr 7:1-7; Ne 2:1, 7, 8) Ancient historians credit him with a generally benign and generous personality. This coincides with his actions during the seventh year of his reign (468 B.C.E.), when Longimanus granted Ezra "all his request" in a decree that provided for silver, gold, and vessels for temple use, as well as provisions of wheat, wine, oil, and salt. (Ezr 7:6, 12-23; 8:25-27) This generous contribution may explain why Artaxerxes is included along with Cyrus and Darius at Ezra 6:14 as one of those whose orders contributed to the 'building and finishing' of the temple, although the actual construction had been completed 47 years previous, in 515 B.C.E. The king's decree even authorized Ezra to appoint magistrates and judges to teach God's law (as well as that of the king) and to use capital punishment against violators where necessary.—Ezr 7:25, 26.

During the 20th year of his reign (455 B.C.E.), Artaxerxes Longimanus granted permission to Nehemiah to return to Jerusalem to rebuild the walls and gates of the city. (Ne 2:1-8) Because this is referred to at Daniel 9:25 as relating to the time of the promised coming of the Messiah, the date of Artaxerxes' 20th year is very important.

Nehemiah 13:6 refers to "the thirty-second year of Artaxerxes," that is, 443 B.C.E., when Nehemiah returned for a time to the court of this king.

ARTEMAS (Ar′te·mas). A companion whom Paul considered sending to Titus in Crete (Tit 3:12), perhaps as a replacement in order that Titus might join Paul in Nicopolis. Since Paul's choice was to be between Artemas and Tychicus, Artemas was evidently well esteemed, as is indicated by Paul's remarks about Tychicus at Ephesians 6:21, 22.

ARTEMIS (Ar′te·mis). A Greek virgin goddess of hunting is known as Artemis; she was identified by the Romans with Diana. Equipped with

bow and arrows, this Artemis is depicted as pursuing game, especially stags. Although the Greeks identified the Ephesian Artemis with their own Artemis, the Artemis of Ephesus, who was worshiped in cities throughout Asia Minor, has little in common with the Greek deity of classical mythology. (Ac 19:27) The Ephesian Artemis was a fertility goddess represented as having multiple breasts, a turreted crown, and a kind of nimbus behind her head. The mummylike lower half of her body was decorated with various symbols and animals.

The Artemis worshiped at Ephesus has been closely connected with prominent goddesses of other peoples, and it has been suggested that they have a common origin. *A Dictionary of the Bible* (Vol. I, p. 605) observes: "Artemis presents such close analogies with the Phrygian Cybele, and with other feminine envisagements of the divine power in Asiatic countries, like the Cappadocian Ma, the Phœnician Astarte or Ashtaroth, the Syrian Atargatis and Mylitta, as to suggest that these

Ephesian Artemis, the fertility goddess; griffins surround the head, and signs of the zodiac appear below a garland around the neck

are all mere varieties of one ultimate religious conception, presenting in different countries certain differences, due to varying development according to local circumstances and national character."—Edited by J. Hastings, 1904.

The ancients ranked the temple of Artemis at Ephesus as one of the seven wonders of the world. It was an imposing structure made of cedar, cypress, white marble, and gold.

For the great festivals held in the month of Artemision (March-April) visitors numbering hundreds of thousands arrived at Ephesus from all of Asia Minor. One feature of the celebration was the religious procession, with the image of Artemis being paraded about the city in a most jubilant manner.

The making of silver shrines of Artemis proved to be a profitable enterprise for Demetrius and other Ephesian silversmiths. Therefore, when the apostle Paul's preaching in Ephesus caused a considerable number of persons to forsake the unclean worship of this goddess, Demetrius stirred up the other craftsmen, telling them that not only did Paul's preaching pose a threat to their financial security but also the danger existed that the worship of the great goddess Artemis would come to nothing. This culminated in a riot that was finally dispersed by the city recorder.—Ac 19:23-41; see EPHESUS.

ARUBBOTH (A·rub'both) [Windows]. A town that served as an administrative center under one of the 12 deputies assigned by King Solomon to provide food for the royal household. The son of Hesed functioned there, having oversight over Socoh and the land of Hepher. (1Ki 4:7, 10) Arubboth is presently identified with modern 'Arraba, situated near Dothan and about 14 km (9 mi) N of Samaria, hence in the territory of Manasseh.

ARUMAH (A·ru'mah) [Height; Exalted Place]. A town in the territory of Ephraim in which Abimelech, the son of Jerubbaal, resided and from which he launched his attack on the Shechemites. (Jg 9:41) It is tentatively identified with Khirbet el-'Ormah (Horvat el-'Urmeh), about 8 km (5 mi) SE of Shechem. Some suggest that it is the same as the Rumah referred to at 2 Kings 23:36.—See RUMAH.

ARVAD (Ar'vad). In Ezekiel's prophetic dirge concerning Tyre reference is made to men from Arvad who served as skilled rowers in Tyre's navy and as valorous warriors in her army. (Eze 27:8, 11) Arvad is identified with the small rocky island today known as Arwad, lying about 3 km (2 mi) off the coast of northern Syria, about 186 km

(116 mi) NNE of Tyre. The inhabitants were descendants of Canaan.—Ge 10:15, 18.

ARVADITE (Ar'vad·ite) [Of (Belonging to) Arvad]. A member of the family descended from Ham through Canaan and that evidently inhabited Arvad, an island just off the northern coast of Syria. (Ge 10:6, 15, 18; 1Ch 1:16) The only other mention of them is Ezekiel's reference to Arvadites as being skilled sailors and valiant soldiers for Tyre.—Eze 27:8, 11.

ARZA (Ar'za). Steward of the household of Elah, king of Israel (c. 952 B.C.E.), in whose house in Tirzah the king was "drinking himself drunk" when assassinated by Zimri.—1Ki 16:9, 10.

ASA (A'sa).

1. The third king of Judah following the division of the nation into two kingdoms. Asa was the son of Abijam (Abijah) and the grandson of Rehoboam. He reigned for 41 years (977-937 B.C.E.).—1Ki 15:8-10.

Asa's Zeal for Pure Worship. Judah and Benjamin had become steeped in apostasy during the 20 years following the split of the nation into two kingdoms. "Like David his forefather," Asa demonstrated a zeal for pure worship and courageously set about cleaning the male temple prostitutes and the idols out of the land. He removed his grandmother, Maacah, from her position as a sort of 'first lady' of the land because of her making "a horrible idol" to the sacred pole, or Asherah, and he burned the religious idol.—1Ki 15:11-13.

The record at 2 Chronicles 14:2-5 states that Asa "removed the foreign altars and the high places and broke up the sacred pillars and cut down the sacred poles." However, 1 Kings 15:14 and 2 Chronicles 15:17 indicate that "the high places he did not remove." It may be, therefore, that the high places referred to in the earlier Chronicles account were those of the adopted pagan worship that infected Judah, while the Kings account refers to high places at which the people engaged in worship of Jehovah. Even after the setting up of the tabernacle and the later establishment of the temple, occasional sacrificing was done to Jehovah on high places, which was acceptable to him under special circumstances, as in the cases of Samuel, David, and Elijah. (1Sa 9:11-19; 1Ch 21:26-30; 1Ki 18:30-39) Nevertheless, the regular approved place for sacrifice was that authorized by Jehovah. (Nu 33:52; De 12:2-14; Jos 22:29) Improper modes of high-place worship may have continued in spite of the removal of the pagan high places, perhaps because the king did not pursue their elimination with the same vigor as he did the removal of the pagan sites. Or Asa may have effected a complete removal of all high places; but if so, such cropped up again in due time and had not been removed by the time of the conclusion of his reign, allowing for their being smashed by his successor Jehoshaphat.

Asa's zeal for right worship brought blessings of peace from Jehovah during the first ten years of his reign. (2Ch 14:1, 6) Later Judah was subjected to attack by a force of a million warriors under Zerah the Ethiopian. Though greatly outnumbered, Asa went out to meet the invasion at Mareshah about 38 km (23 mi) WSW of Jerusalem in the Judean lowlands. His fervent prayer before the battle was joined acknowledged God's power to deliver and pleaded for Jehovah's help, saying: "Upon you we do lean, and in your name we have come against this crowd. O Jehovah, you are our God. Do not let mortal man retain strength against you." Total victory resulted. —2Ch 14:8-15.

Asa is thereafter met by the prophet Azariah, who reminds him: "Jehovah is with you as long as you prove to be with him," and "if you leave him he will leave you." He calls to mind the destructive strife the nation experienced when alienated from Jehovah and urges Asa to continue his activity courageously on behalf of pure worship. (2Ch 15:1-7) Asa's ready response and strengthening of the nation in true service to Jehovah results in a great number of persons from the northern kingdom abandoning that region to join in a grand assembly at Jerusalem in Asa's 15th year of rule (963 B.C.E.), at which assembly a covenant is made declaring the people's determination to seek Jehovah and providing the death penalty for those not keeping this covenant. —2Ch 15:8-15.

Intrigue and Warfare Against Baasha. King Baasha of Israel set out to block the path of any inclining toward a return to Judah by fortifying the frontier city of Ramah, located on the main road to Jerusalem and only a short distance N of that city. Asa, by some process of human reasoning or because of heeding bad counsel, now failed to rely solely on Jehovah and resorted to diplomacy and conspiratorial maneuvering to remove this threat. He took the temple treasures and those from the royal house and sent them as a bribe to King Ben-hadad I of Syria to induce him to divert Baasha's attention through an attack on Israel's northern frontier. Ben-hadad I accepted, and his raid on Israelite cities in the N disrupted Baasha's building work and brought a withdrawal of his forces from Ramah. Asa now conscripted all the available manpower from the entire kingdom of Judah and carried off all Baasha's supplies of building materials, using them to build up the cities of Geba and Mizpah. —1Ki 15:16-22; 2Ch 16:1-6.

For this, Asa was confronted by Hanani the seer, who pointed out Asa's inconsistency in not leaning upon the God who had delivered him from the vast Ethiopian force, reminding Asa that "as regards Jehovah, his eyes are roving about through all the earth to show his strength in behalf of those whose heart is complete toward him." For his foolishness, Asa would now face continued warfare. Resenting correction, Asa unjustly jailed Hanani and showed himself oppressive to others of the people. —2Ch 16:7-11.

The statement at 2 Chronicles 16:1 that Baasha came up against Judah "in the thirty-sixth year of the reign of Asa" has caused some question, since Baasha's rule, beginning in the third year of Asa and lasting only 24 years, had terminated about 10 years prior to Asa's 36th year of rule. (1Ki 15:33) While some suggest a scribal error and believe the reference is to the 16th or the 26th year of Asa's reign, the assumption of such error is not required to harmonize the accounts. Jewish commentators quote the *Seder Olam*, which suggests that the 36th year was reckoned from the existence of the separate kingdom of Judah (997 B.C.E.) and corresponded to the 16th year of Asa (Rehoboam ruling 17 years, Abijah 3 years, and Asa now in his 16th year). (*Soncino Books of the Bible*, London, 1952, ftn on 2Ch 16:1) This was also the view of Archbishop Ussher. So, too, the apparent difference between the statement at 2 Chronicles 15:19 to the effect that, as for "war, it did not occur down to the thirty-fifth [actually, the fifteenth] year of Asa's reign," and the statement at 1 Kings 15:16 to the effect that "warfare itself took place between Asa and Baasha the king of Israel all their days," may be explained in that once conflicts began between the two kings they were thereafter continuous, even as Hanani had foretold. —2Ch 16:9.

Illness and Death. Asa's last three years brought suffering due to an illness of the feet (perhaps gout), and he unwisely sought physical healing over spiritual healing. At his death he was given an honorable burial in his personally prepared tomb in the City of David. —1Ki 15:23, 24; 2Ch 16:12-14.

Despite the lack of wisdom and spiritual insight he manifested at times, Asa's good qualities and freedom from apostasy evidently outweighed his errors, and he is viewed as one of the faithful kings of the line of Judah. (2Ch 15:17) The 41-year reign of Asa touched or covered the reigns of eight kings of Israel: Jeroboam, Nadab, Baasha, Elah, Zimri, Omri, Tibni (who ruled a segment of Israel in opposition to Omri), and Ahab. (1Ki 15:9, 25, 33; 16:8, 15, 16, 21, 23, 29) Upon Asa's death his son Jehoshaphat became king.—1Ki 15:24.

2. A son of the Levite Elkanah and the father of Berechiah, who is listed as dwelling in "the settlements of the Netophathites" following the return from the Babylonian exile.—1Ch 9:16.

ASAHEL (As'a·hel) [God Has Made].

1. A son of David's sister or half sister Zeruiah and the brother of Abishai and Joab; hence, David's nephew. (1Ch 2:15, 16) Honored as among the 30 outstanding warriors under David, Asahel was particularly noted for his fleetness, "like one of the gazelles that are in the open field." (2Sa 2:18; 23:24) This proved to be his undoing. Following the test struggle at the Pool of Gibeon and the subsequent rout of the Israelite forces under Abner, Asahel doggedly pursued the fleeing Abner. After pleading twice with Asahel to desist, the powerful Abner rammed the butt end of his spear through Asahel's abdomen, and Asahel died on the spot. Though Asahel's brother Joab finally called off the Judean forces in response to Abner's remonstrations, Asahel's death caused bitterness within Joab so that at a later opportunity he craftily maneuvered into position to put Abner to death by the sword.—2Sa 2:12-28; 3:22-27.

At 1 Chronicles 27:7 Asahel is listed as a divisional commander of the month-by-month arrangement of troops. Since Asahel died before David became king over all Israel, his mention here may be rather with reference to his house, represented in his son Zebadiah, who is referred to in the text as Asahel's successor. A further suggestion is that given by *The Interpreter's Dictionary of the Bible* (edited by G. A. Buttrick, 1962, Vol. 1, p. 244): "It is possible that we may have here the prototype of the Davidic militia, organized early in the Judean rule of the king, and that this original list has been brought up to date by the inclusion of Zebadiah, son and successor of Asahel in this command."—Compare 1Ch 12.

2. One of the Levites assigned to teach the Law throughout Judah, beginning in the third year of Jehoshaphat's reign (934 B.C.E.).—2Ch 17:7, 8; compare De 33:8-10.

3. A commissioner serving at the temple during Hezekiah's reign (745-717 B.C.E.) in connection with the contributions and tithes.—2Ch 31:13.

4. The father of a certain Jonathan, a contemporary of Ezra.—Ezr 10:15; see JAHZEIAH.

ASAIAH (A·sai'ah) [Jah Has Made].

1. A descendant of Merari, Levi's third son, and a head of a paternal house. He was one of the chief men among the Levites who formed part of the group of 862 chosen to share in bringing up the ark of the covenant to Jerusalem at the time of David's second (and successful) attempt.—1Ch 6:29, 30; 15:4-12.

2. A chieftain of the tribe of Simeon in the days of King Hezekiah (745-717 B.C.E.). He was among those Simeonites who took part in conquering a rich valley in the area of Gedor, till then occupied by Hamites and the Meunim.—1Ch 4:36-41.

3. Called "the king's servant," he was one of a commission of five, headed by Hilkiah, whom King Josiah sent to the prophetess Huldah to inquire of Jehovah about the meaning of the recently discovered book of the Law (in 642 B.C.E.). —2Ki 22:3, 8, 12-14; 2Ch 34:20, 21.

4. The firstborn of the Shilonites (1Ch 9:1-3, 5), listed among those returning from Babylon after the exile. At Nehemiah 11:5 mention is made of Maaseiah as a "Shelanite" descendant of Judah, and because of the similar meaning of the names (Maaseiah meaning "Work of Jehovah") some consider them to be the same and descended from Shelah, the youngest son of Judah by the daughter of Shua the Canaanite.—Ge 38:2, 5; see MAASEIAH No. 17.

ASAPH (A'saph) [He [God] Has Gathered].

1. A son of Levi through Gershom. (1Ch 6:39, 43) During King David's reign (1077-1038 B.C.E.) Asaph was appointed by the Levites as a chief singer and player of cymbals, accompanying the Ark as it was brought up from Obed-edom's home to "the City of David." (1Ch 15:17, 19, 25-29) Thereafter Asaph, along with Heman and Ethan, served before the tabernacle in directing the music and singing. (1Ch 6:31-44) Like Heman and Jeduthun (apparently the same as Ethan), Asaph is called a "visionary," who did "prophesying with the harp."—1Ch 25:1-6; 2Ch 29:30; 35:15.

Asaph's sons continued to form a special group in the orchestral and choral arrangements, taking a prominent part at the time of the temple's inauguration and the bringing up of the Ark from Zion to the temple location (2Ch 5:12); at the time of King Hezekiah's reforms (2Ch 29:13-15); and at the time of the great Passover celebrated during King Josiah's reign. (2Ch 35:15, 16) Some of his descendants were also among the first group returning to Jerusalem from Babylonian exile. —Ezr 2:1, 41; Ne 7:44.

The superscriptions for Psalms 50 and 73 to 83 credit these songs to Asaph. However, it seems likely that the name is there used as referring to the house of which he was paternal head, since some of the psalms (Ps 79, 80) evidently describe events later than Asaph's day.

2. A descendant of Levi's son Kohath. His descendants were gatekeepers in the tabernacle service in King David's time.—1Ch 26:1; Nu 16:1.

3. Among the officials of King Hezekiah (745-717 B.C.E.) is mentioned "Joah the son of Asaph the recorder." (2Ki 18:18, 37; Isa 36:3, 22) While John Kitto's *Cyclopædia of Biblical Literature* (1880, Vol. I, p. 233) applies the term "recorder" to Asaph, most scholars view it as applying to Joah (thus, Joah ben Asaph, the recorder). Since the term "son" is often used in the sense of "descendant," some suggest that this Asaph is the same as No. 1.

4. "The keeper of the park" for King Artaxerxes at the time of Nehemiah's return to Jerusalem (455 B.C.E.). (Ne 2:8) The park was a wooded area, perhaps in Lebanon, which was also under Persian control. The park keeper's Hebrew name may indicate that he was a Jew occupying this official position, even as Nehemiah had served in the relatively important position of the king's cupbearer.—Ne 1:11.

ASAREL (As'a·rel). One of four sons of Jehallelel of the tribe of Judah.—1Ch 4:16.

ASCENSION. The return of Jesus Christ to heaven 40 days after his resurrection.

The scene of Jesus' ascension was the Mount of Olives (Ac 1:9, 12), near the town of Bethany (Lu 24:50), which town lies on the eastern side of the Mount of Olives. Those witnessing the ascension were a limited group, his faithful apostles. (Ac 1:2, 11-13) The record states that "while they were looking on, he was lifted up and a cloud caught him up from their vision." They continued looking into the sky until advised otherwise by the angels, who informed them: "This Jesus who was received up from you into the sky will come thus in the same manner as you have beheld him going into the sky."—Ac 1:9-11.

It is to be noted that the angels referred to the "manner" (Gr., *tro'pos*) not the form (Gr., *mor·phe'*) in which Jesus departed. As the cloud caught him up, he became invisible to human eyes. The Acts account shows that his ascension was without ostentation or fanfare, discerned by only a few faithful followers and that for only the initial part of the ascension. The manner of his ascension was such that it would qualify the apostles to serve as witnesses of that fact, even as they were of Jesus' resurrection. (Ac 1:3) Thus, he did not simply 'disappear' from them, as he did earlier from the two disciples at Emmaus, or as the angel who had appeared to Gideon "vanished from his sight." (Lu 24:31; Jg 6:21, 22) To an extent, his ascension was more like that of the angel who appeared to Manoah and his wife. He had them prepare a sacrifice, and "as the flame ascended from off the altar heavenward, then Jehovah's angel ascended in the flame of the altar while Manoah and his wife were looking on."—Jg 13:20.

Since Acts 1:3-9 shows that Jesus' ascension took place 40 days from the time of his resurrection, there is a time lapse between the events recorded at Luke 24:1-49 as occurring on Jesus' resurrection day and the ascension of Jesus as described in verse 51 of that chapter. It may also be noted that the words "and began to be borne up to heaven," appearing in that verse, are lacking in some ancient manuscripts and are therefore omitted in some modern translations (*NE, AT*). They do appear, however, in the Bodmer Papyrus (P[75]), the Alexandrine Manuscript, the Vatican Manuscript No. 1209, and other ancient manuscripts.

Effect on Disciples. Up until the day of Jesus' ascension it appears that the disciples still thought in terms of an earthly kingdom ruled by him, as is seen by their statement at Acts 1:6. By beginning his ascension in a visible way and allowing his disciples to witness the initial portion of it, Jesus thus made obvious to them that his Kingdom was heavenly and that, different from David who "did not ascend to the heavens," Jesus' position from then onward would be at 'God's right hand,' as Peter boldly testified on the day of Pentecost.—Ac 2:32-36.

Such action likewise should call to their mind Jesus' many previous statements pointing to such a heavenly position and help his disciples to understand these. He had shocked some by saying: "What, therefore, if you should behold the Son of man ascending to where he was before?" (Joh 6:62); and he told the Jews: "You are from the realms below; I am from the realms above." (Joh 8:23) On the night of his final meeting with his apostles, he told them he was 'going his way to the Father to prepare a place for them' (Joh 14:2, 28); while among them on his last night of life as a human, he reported to his Father that he had 'finished the work on earth' assigned to him and prayed, saying: "Glorify me alongside yourself with the glory that I had alongside you before the world was," saying also, "I am coming to you."

(Joh 17:4, 5, 11) When arrested, he gave similar indication before the Sanhedrin. (Mt 26:64) After his resurrection he told Mary Magdalene: "Stop clinging to me. For I have not yet ascended to the Father. But be on your way to my brothers and say to them, 'I am ascending to my Father and your Father and to my God and your God.'" (Joh 20:17) Yet, despite all of this, it is evident that the significance of these statements was brought home to the disciples only at the occasion of the ascension. Later, Stephen was given a vision of Jesus at God's right hand (Ac 7:55, 56), and Paul experienced the effect of Jesus' heavenly glory. —Ac 9:3-5.

The Inauguration of a 'New and Living Way.' While Jesus began his ascent in a physical form, thus being visible to his watching disciples, there is no basis for assuming that he continued to retain a material form after the cloud interposed itself. The apostle Peter states that Jesus died in the flesh but was resurrected "in the spirit." (1Pe 3:18) Paul declares the rule that "flesh and blood cannot inherit God's kingdom." (1Co 15:50; compare also Jesus' statement at Joh 12:23, 24 with 1Co 15:35-45.) Paul likens Jesus' ascent to God's presence in the heavens to the entry of the high priest into the Most Holy compartment of the tabernacle on the Day of Atonement and specifies that on such occasion the high priest carried only the blood (not the flesh) of the sacrificial victims. (Heb 9:7, 11, 12, 24-26) Paul then compares the curtain, which separated the first compartment from the Most Holy compartment, to Christ's flesh. The high priest in passing into the Most Holy, into God's typical presence, did not carry the curtain with him but passed through that barrier and beyond it, so that it was behind him. Thus, Paul states that "we have boldness for the way of entry into the holy place by the blood of Jesus, which he inaugurated for us as a new and living way through the curtain, that is, his flesh."—Heb 9:3, 24; 10:10, 19, 20; compare Joh 6:51; Heb 6:19, 20.

Jesus' ascension to heaven to present the ransoming value of his lifeblood to Jehovah inaugurated "a new and living way" of approach to God in prayer. That it also opened the way to heavenly life harmonizes with Jesus' own statement to the effect that, prior thereto, "no man has ascended into heaven but he that descended from heaven, the Son of man." (Joh 3:13) Thus, neither Enoch nor Elijah inaugurated this way, any more than David had. (Ge 5:24; 2Ki 2:11; Ac 2:34) As Paul states: "The holy spirit makes it plain that the way into the holy place had not yet been made manifest while the first tent was standing."—Heb 9:8; see ELIJAH No. 1; ENOCH No. 2.

Correctness of the Term. Some raise objections to the account of the ascension, saying that it conveys the primitive concept that heaven is "up" from the earth, thus manifesting ignorance of the structure of the universe and of the earth's rotation. However, to satisfy such critics would, in effect, require the virtual elimination of the words "up," "above," and so forth, from human language. Even in this space age, we still read of astronauts making an "ascent" to a "184-mile-high orbit" above the earth (*The New York Times*, June 19, 1983), whereas we know that technically they moved out or away from the earth's surface that distance. Interestingly, the account of the angelic delegation that chorused the announcement of Jesus' birth reports that, when their mission was completed, "the angels . . . *departed* from them into heaven." (Lu 2:15; compare Ac 12:10.) Thus Jesus' ascension, while beginning with an upward movement, from the viewpoint of his disciples, may have thereafter taken any direction required to bring him into his Father's heavenly presence. It was an ascension not only as to direction but, more important, as to the sphere of activity and level of existence in the spirit realm and in the lofty presence of the Most High God, a realm not governed by human dimensions or directions. —Compare Heb 2:7, 9.

Why Essential. Jesus' ascension to the heavenly realm was essential for several reasons or purposes. He had stated that it was necessary for him to 'go his way' in order that he might send God's holy spirit as helper to his disciples. (Joh 16:7-14) The outpouring of that spirit by Jesus on the day of Pentecost was to the disciples an evident demonstration of the fact of Jesus' having reached God's presence and that he had presented the value of his ransom sacrifice to Him. (Ac 2:33, 38) This presentation of the value of his lifeblood also made such ascension vital, for it was not to be made on earth, in the Most Holy of the temple in Jerusalem, but only in "heaven itself . . . before the person of God." (Heb 9:24) It was also made necessary by Jesus' being appointed and glorified as the "great high priest who has passed through the heavens." (Heb 4:14; 5:1-6) Paul explains that "if, now, he were upon earth, he would not be a priest," but that, having "sat down at the right hand of the throne of the Majesty in the heavens," Jesus has now "obtained a more excellent public service, so that he is also the mediator of a correspondingly better covenant." (Heb 8:1-6) Because of this, Christians subject to inherited sin are comforted in knowing they "have a helper with the Father, Jesus Christ, a righteous one."—1Jo 2:1; Ro 8:34; Heb 7:25.

Finally, the ascension was necessary for Jesus' administration of the Kingdom to which he became heir, with "angels and authorities and powers . . . made subject to him." (1Pe 3:22; Php 2:6-11; 1Co 15:25; Heb 10:12, 13; compare Da 7:14.) Having "conquered the world" (Joh 16:33), Jesus took part in fulfilling the prophecy at Psalm 68:18, 'ascending on high and carrying away captives,' the significance of which Paul explains at Ephesians 4:8-12.

ASCENTS. The Hebrew expression *Shir hamma·alohth'*, forming the superscription for 15 psalms (Ps 120-134), is variously translated as "A Song of degrees" (*KJ*), "A gradual canticle" (*Dy*, Ps 119-133), "A Song of the Stairsteps" (*NW* ftn on Ps 120:Sup), "A Song of [or, "for the"] Ascents" (*AT*, *RS*). Four of these psalms are attributed to David and one to Solomon. The exact meaning of the superscription is a subject of discussion.

At one time Jewish tradition (Mishnah, *Middot* 2:5) held that these 15 songs were sung by the Levites in ascending the 15 steps from the Court of Women to the Court of Israel at the temple in Jerusalem, but this view is generally discounted today. Some suggest that the phrase refers to the exalted contents of these psalms, though there seems to be little reason thus to elevate them above the other inspired psalms. Most commentators believe the title derives from the use of these psalms by the Israelite worshipers when traveling or ascending to the lofty city of Jerusalem situated high in the mountains of Judah as they joyfully attended the three great annual festivals there. (De 12:5-7; 16:16; Ps 42:4; Isa 30:29) The word *ma·alah'* is used in a similar way at Ezra 7:9 when referring to the "going up" of the Israelites from Babylon to Jerusalem after the exile. The expressions in Psalm 122:1-4 lend themselves well to this view, while the content of the other psalms of this group is of such varied nature as to leave the matter still uncertain.

ASENAPPAR (As'e·nap·par). This name appears in a portion of the book of Ezra (4:10) recorded in Aramaic and is evidently a clipped rendering of the name of the Assyrian king Ashurbanipal and, like the Persian, which has no letter *l*, substitutes an *r* for the final *l*. The inhabitants of Susa (capital of Elam) were transplanted to Samaria by Asenappar. (Compare 2Ki 17:24-28.) History shows Ashurbanipal to be the only Assyrian king in position to carry out such action as regards the inhabitants of Elam.

Ashurbanipal was the son of Esar-haddon (Ezr 4:2) and grandson of Sennacherib. He was a contemporary of King Manasseh of Judah (716-662 B.C.E.), whose name is found on a prism of Ashurbanipal listing some 20 kings as tributaries of Assyria. (Compare 2Ch 33:10-13.) Under him, Assyria reached its greatest heights. Apparently appointed as crown prince three or four years earlier, Ashurbanipal took the throne of Assyria upon his father's death, while his brother, Shamash-shum-u-kin, was the king of Babylon.

Ashurbanipal quelled an uprising in Egypt, conquering and ravaging the city of Thebes (No-amon; compare Na 3:8-10). Later he was engaged in a lengthy conflict with his brother, the king of Babylon, and after subduing Babylon, destroyed Susa, the capital of Elam. It is this conquest that is the historical basis for relating him to Asenappar of Ezra 4:9, 10.

Ashurbanipal is best known, however, for his literary interests, a unique trait among the formidable Assyrian monarchs. Beginning in 1845 C.E., excavations revealed a great library formed by Ashurbanipal at Nineveh, containing some 22,000 clay tablets and texts. In addition to incantations, prayers, and hymns, the thousands of cuneiform writings include treatises on history, geography, astronomy, mathematical tables, medicine, grammar, as well as business documents involving contracts, sales, and loans. They are viewed as a valuable source of information about Assyria.

ASENATH (As'e·nath). The daughter of the Egyptian priest Potiphera of On, given by Pharaoh to Joseph as his wife. She became the mother of Manasseh and Ephraim.—Ge 41:45, 50-52; 46:20.

ASH.

1. The name of a tree (Heb., *tidh·har'*) that occurs twice in the Hebrew Scriptures, at Isaiah 41:19 and 60:13. In the first text it is included among trees such as the juniper and cypress, which are to flourish in the desert plain under foretold paradisaic conditions, and in the latter text it is included among the same trees as part of the "glory of Lebanon." The identification of this tree is conjectural, but there is some evidence that favors the ash tree.—See *Theologische Literaturzeitung*, Leipzig, 1926, p. 216.

Two varieties of ash, *Fraxinus ornus* and *Fraxinus oxycarpa*, are found along rivers and streams in the mountains of Lebanon and the upper extremity of Palestine, though not throughout Palestine generally. This tree qualifies as part of the "glory of Lebanon," for it is a large tree growing up to 15 m (50 ft) high. It has light-green foliage and ash-colored branchlets. Although of the same family botanically as the olive, the ash differs from the olive in that it sheds its leaves each fall.

2. See ASH CONSTELLATION.

ASHAN (A'shan) [possibly, Smoke]. A city in the Shephelah or lowland region of Judah. Originally assigned to Judah, it was thereafter given to Simeon, because Judah's territory was overly large. (Jos 15:42; 19:7, 9; 1Ch 4:32) From them it passed to the Levite family of the Kohathites. (1Ch 6:54, 59) First Samuel 30:30 refers to "Borashan" as one of the cities in that general region to which David sent spoils after his victory over the Amalekites, and this is thought by some to be the same as Ashan. At Joshua 21:16 the list of cities given to the Kohathites, corresponding to that at 1 Chronicles 6:59, is presented, but "Ain" appears in the Joshua list in place of Ashan. The *Soncino Books of the Bible* (London, 1950), commenting on the text, suggests that the full name of the city may have been Ain-ashan.

Many identify Ashan with Khirbet 'Asan, located about 2.5 km (1.5 mi) NW of modern Beersheba, alongside the Nahal 'Ashan. Yohanan Aharoni suggests identifying Ashan with Tel Bet Mirsham, 25 km (16 mi) NNE of Beer-sheba.

ASHARELAH (Ash·a·re'lah). A son of Asaph serving in the service groups of musicians and singers at the house of Jehovah in the time of David. (1Ch 25:1, 2) It is probable that Jesharelah of verse 14 is a variation of his name.

ASHBEA (Ash·be'a) [Let Me Make One Swear (Take an Oath)]. The house of Ashbea descended from Judah's son Shelah and was noted for its production of fine fabric. (1Ch 4:21) The Targums add that their linen was made for kings and priests.

ASHBEL (Ash'bel), **ASHBELITES** (Ash'belites). Ashbel was a son of Benjamin, listed third at Genesis 46:21, but second at 1 Chronicles 8:1. In 1728 B.C.E. he came into Egypt with Jacob's family. He appears to be called Jediael at 1 Chronicles 7:6, 10. The Ashbelites, his descendants, were registered in the census taken on the desert plains of Moab about 1473 B.C.E.—Nu 26:38.

ASH CONSTELLATION. The fact that the Hebrew words 'Ash and 'A'yish as well as other terms are used in association with sun, stars, and heaven in both cases indicates that they refer to some celestial constellation. (See Job 9:7-9; 38:32, 33.) It is impossible at present to specify which constellation they refer to and hence it is safer to transliterate the name (as in our heading) rather than to translate the Hebrew with specific names

such as "Arcturus" (Gr., *Ar·ktou'ros,* literally meaning "Guardian of the Bear") (*KJ*), or "Bear" (*RS*).

The fact that Job 38:32 refers to Ash "alongside its sons" strengthens the basis for believing that a constellation is involved. Ursa Major (the Great Bear) is the constellation most often suggested, having seven main stars in it that could be "its sons." The important point in the text is, not the precise identification of the constellation, but the question there raised: "Can you conduct them?" Jehovah God thus impresses upon Job the wisdom and power of the Creator, inasmuch as it is utterly impossible for man to govern the movements of these immense stellar bodies.

ASHDOD (Ash'dod). One of the five principal cities of the Philistines under their "axis lords" and evidently the religious center of Philistia with its worship of the false god Dagon. The other cities were Gath, Gaza, Ashkelon, and Ekron. (Jos 13:3) Ashdod is identified with Esdud (Tel Ashdod) about 6 km (3.5 mi) SSE of, and inland from, modern Ashdod on the coast.

It is first mentioned at Joshua 11:22 as the residing place, along with Gaza and Gath, of the remnant of the giantlike Anakim. Due to the eminence on which it was built and its position on the military road running along the coast from Egypt through Palestine, Ashdod occupied a strategic location militarily. At the time of the Israelite conquest it was assigned, along with its suburban villages, to Judah (Jos 15:46, 47); but evidently its residents are included among "the inhabitants of the low plain" who could not be dispossessed "because they had war chariots with iron scythes." —Jg 1:19.

The Philistine cities seem to have been at the peak of their power during the time of King Saul. Before Saul's kingship the Philistines inflicted a severe defeat upon the Israelites at Ebenezer and captured the ark of the covenant, which they then transported to Ashdod and placed in the temple of Dagon, alongside the image of their god. After two humiliations miraculously executed on Dagon's image, the Ashdodites began to experience a plague of piles of such gravity as to create panic among them. A conference of Philistine axis lords brought a transfer of the Ark to the city of Gath, with a resulting extension of the plague there. Within seven months the Ark was on its way back to Israel, accompanied by an offering in gold. —1Sa 5:1–6:18; see PHILISTIA, PHILISTINES.

Although King David administered several defeats to the Philistines, their principal cities evidently remained independent until the time of

King Uzziah (829-778 B.C.E.). Uzziah is described as the maker of "engines of war" (2Ch 26:15), and 2 Chronicles 26:6 tells us that Uzziah "proceeded to go out and fight against the Philistines and break through the wall of Gath and the wall of Jabneh and the wall of Ashdod, after which he built cities in Ashdod territory and among the Philistines."

Evidently the territory of Ashdod did not remain under Judean control, for in later periods inscriptions show Assyrian King Sargon II as deposing the local king Azuri and installing Ahimiti in his place. A revolt caused Sargon to campaign against Philistia, conquering Gath, "Asdudu" (Ashdod), and "Asdudimmu" (Ashdod-by-the-Sea, evidently a separate place located on the seacoast). This may be the campaign referred to at Isaiah 20:1 and a partial fulfillment of the prophecy at Amos 1:8. In the following century Herodotus (II, 157) records that Ashdod (Azotus) was subjected to a siege lasting 29 years laid against the city by Pharaoh Psamtik (Psammetichus).

A stone prism of Sennacherib of Assyria says that "Mitinti from Ashdod" brought him sumptuous gifts and kissed his feet, and it adds concerning King Hezekiah of Judah (745-717 B.C.E.): "His towns which I had plundered, I took away from his country and gave them (over) to Mitinti, king of Ashdod." (*Ancient Near Eastern Texts,* edited by J. B. Pritchard, 1974, pp. 287, 288) Ashdod seems to have been in a weakened state by the time of Jeremiah (after 647 B.C.E.) so that he spoke of "the remnant of Ashdod." (Jer 25:20) Nebuchadnezzar, whose rule began in 624 B.C.E., makes mention of the king of Ashdod as one of the prisoners at the Babylonian court.—Compare Zep 2:4.

In the postexilic period Ashdod was still a focal point of opposition to the Israelites (Ne 4:7), and Nehemiah severely reprimanded those Jews who had married Ashdodite wives, resulting in sons who were "speaking Ashdodite, and there were none of them knowing how to speak Jewish." (Ne 13:23, 24) During the Maccabean period idolatrous Ashdod (called Azotus) came under attack by Judas Maccabaeus about 163 B.C.E. and later by Judas' brother Jonathan about 148 B.C.E., the temple of Dagon being burned down in this second attack.—1 Maccabees 5:68; 10:84.

It is noteworthy that the prophecy of Zechariah pointed to the time when Ashdod would be overtaken by foreigners. Evidently because the native Philistine population and rulership would be no more, the prophetic word was: "An illegitimate son will actually seat himself in Ashdod."—Zec 9:6.

The city was rebuilt by the Romans about the year 55 B.C.E. and was generally known by its Greek name Azotus. Philip the evangelist passed through Ashdod in his preaching tour recorded at Acts 8:40.

ASHDODITE (Ash′dod·ite) [Of (Belonging to) Ashdod]. An inhabitant of the Philistine city of Ashdod. (Jos 13:3) Like the other Philistines, the Ashdodites were descendants of Ham through Mizraim and Casluhim, reaching Canaan apparently from the island of Crete.—Ge 10:6, 13, 14; Am 9:7; see ASHDOD; PHILISTIA, PHILISTINES.

At Nehemiah 13:24 the term "Ashdodite" is also applied to their language. In view of the absence of any record of their speech, it cannot be determined whether they were still speaking the ancient Philistine language or a dialect resulting from centuries of foreign domination.

ASHER (Ash′er) [Happy; Happiness].

1. The eighth son of Jacob and second of two sons through Zilpah, Leah's maidservant. (Ge 35: 26) Thus Asher's only full brother was Gad. Asher's four sons and one daughter are listed at 1 Chronicles 7:30, though his wife is not named. He was not prominent among the 12 sons of Jacob. However, in his father's deathbed prophecy, Asher was promised a life blessed with an abundance of rich foods (Ge 49:20), and the history of his descendants demonstrates the fulfillment of this prediction.

2. The name applies as well to the tribe descended from Asher. A year after the Exodus from Egypt the tribe's adult male descendants numbered 41,500 (Nu 1:41) and, about 39 years later, had increased to 53,400, making it the fifth most populous tribe. (Nu 26:47) In the camp of Israel, Asher occupied a position N of the tabernacle, with the tribes of Dan and Naphtali.—Nu 2:25-30.

Prior to entry into Canaan, Moses' prophetic blessing again predicted a prosperous portion for Asher. The tribe was figuratively to 'dip its foot in oil.' (De 33:24, 25; compare Job 29:6.) Their allotment of territory stretched along the Mediterranean coastal plains from below the town of Dor, S of Mount Carmel, on up to the N boundary of Palestine at Sidon. (Jos 17:7-11; 19:24-31) This included some of the most fertile land in all Israel, where olive trees would provide abundant oil, while other fruits would provide dainties fit to grace a royal table. (Ge 49:20; De 33:24) The territories of Zebulun and Naphtali lay along Asher's E boundary, with Manasseh and Issachar to the S and SE.

Asher is named in Joshua 17:7 as being on the boundary of the tribe of Manasseh. Asher is also referred to in this same account at verse 10, where it clearly refers to the tribal territory of Asher.

ASHERAH. See Sacred Pole.

ASHERITE (Ash'er·ite) [Of (Belonging to) Asher]. A descendant of Asher, Jacob's second son by Leah's maidservant Zilpah (Ge 30:12, 13); a member of the tribe of Asher.—Jg 1:31, 32; see Asher.

ASHES. The term often employed in the Scriptures for the residue from the burning of materials, frequently having symbolic or figurative connotations. The word "ashes" renders two Hebrew words. One ('e'pher; Nu 19:9) is also translated "powder." (Mal 4:3) De'shen, besides denoting "fatty ashes," may also refer to "fatness." (Le 1:16; Isa 55:2) The Greek noun spo·dos' means "ashes" (Mt 11:21), while the verb te·phro'o means "reduce to ashes." (2Pe 2:6) The residue from burning could also be referred to as dust ('a·phar'). —Nu 19:17; 2Ki 23:4.

Each day a Levitical priest removed the fatty ashes (de'shen) resulting from the burning of animal sacrifices upon the altar and took them "out to a clean place outside the camp." (Le 6:9-11) According to Numbers chapter 19, a sound red cow without defect and upon which no yoke had come was also slaughtered and burned outside the camp. The ashes of this "sin offering" were deposited in a clean place outside the camp (Nu 19:9) and thus a portion was available for mixing with water to be sprinkled on unclean persons or things to purify them. (Nu 19:17) The apostle Paul referred to the figurative cleansing of the flesh by "the ashes [Gr., spo·dos'] of a heifer" to highlight the far greater cleansing of "consciences from dead works" possible through "the blood of the Christ."—Heb 9:13, 14.

Jeremiah 31:40 refers to "the low plain of the carcasses and of the fatty ashes [wehad·de'shen]," apparently a part of the valley of the son of Hinnom. Until relatively recent times a mound of ashes near the Kidron Valley was a familiar landmark. It is said to have been about 150 m long, 60 m wide, and 18 m deep (490 × 200 × 60 ft) and is considered by some to relate to the place mentioned by Jeremiah. A part of the valley of the son of Hinnom could have been set aside for the disposal of ashes left after burning sacrifices (Le 4:12), before Josiah made Topheth in the valley unfit for worship. (2Ki 23:10) But animal carcasses and the dead bodies of vile criminals might also have been cast into the valley, and a mound there might even include the ashes of humans once sacrificed in false religious rites.—Jer 32:35.

In Biblical times it was customary to burn captured cities, so that 'reducing a place to ashes' was indicative of its complete destruction, as is shown in the cases of Tyre, Sodom, and Gomorrah.—Eze 28:18; 2Pe 2:6.

Ashes also served as a figure of what was insignificant or valueless, Abraham acknowledging before Jehovah, for instance, "I am dust and ashes." (Ge 18:27; see also Isa 44:20; Job 30:19.) And Job likened the sayings of his false comforters to "proverbs of ashes."—Job 13:12.

It was a practice in Biblical days to sit in ashes or to scatter them upon oneself in symbol of mourning, humiliation, and repentance. (Es 4:1-3; Jer 6:26; 2Sa 13:19) Deep misery and affliction are figuratively linked with the 'eating of ashes' (Ps 102:9), and afflicted Job sat "in among the ashes." —Job 2:8.

Sackcloth and ashes were sometimes associated with fasting, weeping, or sorrow. (Es 4:3; Isa 58:5; Eze 27:30, 31; Da 9:3) A national example of humiliation and repentance is furnished in the case of Nineveh in Jonah's day, even her king covering himself with sackcloth and sitting down in the ashes. (Jon 3:5, 6) Repenting in sackcloth and ashes was a circumstance referred to by Jesus Christ (Mt 11:21), and in answering Jehovah, Job contritely declared: "I do repent in dust and ashes."—Job 42:6.

During the 70-year desolation of Judah, the Jews in Babylon mourned over the desolation of Zion or Jerusalem and its temple. But through Isaiah assurance had been given that under the power of Jehovah's spirit there would be action "to assign to those mourning over Zion, to give them a headdress instead of ashes." Jesus Christ applied the passage of Isaiah 61:1-3 to himself as the Messianic Liberator who would be instrumental in relieving greater spiritual desolation and mourning. (Lu 4:16-21) It was also foretold that the wicked would become like pulverized, powdery ashes to the righteous, for Malachi wrote: "'And you people will certainly tread down the wicked ones, for they will become as powder ['e'pher] under the soles of your feet in the day on which I am acting,' Jehovah of armies has said."—Mal 4:3.

ASH-HEAPS, GATE OF THE. See Gate, Gateway.

ASHHUR (Ash'hur) [possibly, Blackness]. According to the Masoretic text, the son of Hezron, born after his father's death; the great-grandson of Judah. (1Ch 2:4, 5, 24; see Hezron No. 2.) By his two wives he fathered seven sons. (1Ch 4:5-7) He is also said to be the father of Tekoa, which appears to mean that he was the founder of the town by that name.

ASHIMA (A·shi′ma). A deity worshiped by the people from Hamath whom the king of Assyria settled in Samaria after his taking the Israelites into captivity. (2Ki 17:24, 30) Ashima, according to the Babylonian Talmud (*Sanhedrin* 63*b*), was represented as a hairless he-goat, and for this reason some have identified Ashima with Pan, a pastoral god of fertility. Another suggestion is that the name Ashima may be a deliberate alteration of "Asherah" (the Canaanite fertility goddess) to combine it with the Hebrew word *'a·sham'* ("guilt"; Ge 26:10). However, nothing can be stated with any certainty aside from what is contained in the Bible.

ASHKELON (Ash′ke·lon) [possibly, Place of Weighing Out (Paying)]. A seaport on the Mediterranean and one of the five principal Philistine cities. (Jos 13:3) It is identified with 'Asqalan (Tel Ashqelon) located about 19 km (12 mi) NNE of Gaza. The city was situated in a naturally formed rocky amphitheater, the concave part facing toward the Mediterranean. The countryside is fertile, producing apples, figs, and the small onion known as the scallion, which apparently derives its name from that of the Philistine city.

Ashkelon was assigned to the tribe of Judah and was captured by them, but it apparently did not remain subject to them for long. (Jg 1:18, 19) It was a Philistine city in the time of Samson and of Samuel. (Jg 14:19; 1Sa 6:17) David mentions it in his lament over the death of Saul and Jonathan. (2Sa 1:20) In King Uzziah's conquest of Philistine cities, Ashkelon is not listed as among those taken. —2Ch 26:6.

In the prophecy of Amos (c. 804 B.C.E.) prediction was made of defeat for the ruler of Ashkelon. (Am 1:8) Secular history shows that in the succeeding century Tiglath-pileser III of Assyria made *Asqaluna* (Ashkelon) a vassal city. Jeremiah (after 647 B.C.E.) uttered two prophecies involving Ashkelon. While Jeremiah 47:2-7 could have seen some fulfillment when Nebuchadnezzar sacked the city early in his reign (c. 624 B.C.E.), the prophecy at Jeremiah 25:17-20, 28, 29 clearly indicates a fulfillment subsequent to the fall of Jerusalem in 607 B.C.E. Zephaniah's prophecy (written before 648 B.C.E.) also foretold a coming desolation for Ashkelon, along with other Philistine cities, after which the remnant of Judah would eventually occupy "the houses of Ashkelon."

(Zep 2:4-7) Finally, about 518 B.C.E., Zechariah proclaimed doom for Ashkelon in connection with the time of Tyre's desolation (332 B.C.E.).—Zec 9:3-5.

ASHKELONITE (Ash′ke·lon·ite) [Of (Belonging to) Ashkelon]. A resident of the Philistine city of Ashkelon.—Jos 13:3.

ASHKENAZ (Ash′ke·naz).

1. The first named of three sons of Gomer, the son of Japheth.—Ge 10:3; 1Ch 1:6.

In Jewish writings of medieval times (and even thereafter) the term "Ashkenaz" was applied to the Teutonic race, and more specifically to Germany. Thus, even today Jews from Germanic countries are referred to as Ashkenazim in contrast to the Sephardim, Jews from Spain and Portugal.

2. Jeremiah 51:27 mentions a kingdom of Ashkenaz as allying itself with the kingdoms of Ararat and Minni against Babylon at the time of her downfall (539 B.C.E.). Since Ararat is believed to have been located in the region of Lake Van in Armenia, and Minni (referred to as "Mannai" in Assyrian inscriptions) is considered to have been SE of Lake Van, it is likely that the kingdom of Ashkenaz lay near these regions, probably somewhat to the N in the area between the Black Sea and the Caspian Sea.

The name Ashkenaz is considered by archaeologists as equivalent to the Assyrian *Ashguzai*, which term was evidently applied to the ancient Scythians of the Black Sea and Caspian Sea area. Cuneiform tablets record an alliance between this tribe and the Mannai (Minni) in a revolt against Assyria in the seventh century B.C.E.

ASHNAH (Ash′nah).

1. A town of Judah in the Shephelah mentioned among other cities, including Eshtaol and Zorah. (Jos 15:33) A tentative identification is the village of 'Aslin, between Eshtaol and Zorah, near the edge of the Judean coastal plain.

2. A second town of Judah, listed among nine cities and evidently farther to the S than the first Ashnah. (Jos 15:43) The identification is uncertain; a suggested site is Idhna, located about midway between Hebron and Lachish, and about 8 km (5 mi) ESE of Mareshah, which appears in the same list.

ASHPENAZ (Ash′pe·naz). The name of the chief court official in Babylon during Nebuchadnezzar's reign. (Da 1:3) Evidently he headed the corps of eunuchs but was not necessarily himself a eunuch. One of his duties was the training of youths to serve as pages of the monarch.

ASHTAROTH (Ash'ta·roth). A city in the region of Bashan, generally identified today with Tell 'Ashtarah about 32 km (20 mi) E of the Sea of Galilee. The low hill there is surrounded by a well-watered plain. Its name may indicate that it was a center of worship of the goddess Ashtoreth.

Biblical references to it are principally with regard to giant King Og of Bashan, who is spoken of as reigning "in Ashtaroth, in Edrei." (De 1:4; Jos 9:10; 12:4; 13:12) The conquered territory of Og's kingdom was originally assigned to the Machirites of the tribe of Manasseh, but Ashtaroth later passed to the Gershonites as a Levite city. (Jos 13:29-31; 1Ch 6:71) At Joshua 21:27, which corresponds with the account at 1 Chronicles 6:71, the city is called Beeshterah.

The city is referred to in Assyrian inscriptions and in the Amarna Tablets.

ASHTERATHITE (Ash'te·rath·ite) [Of (Belonging to) Ashtaroth]. An inhabitant of Ashtaroth. Only Uzzia, one of David's mighty men, is so designated.—1Ch 11:44.

ASHTEROTH-KARNAIM (Ash'te·roth-kar·na'im). The site of the defeat of the Rephaim by Chedorlaomer, king of Elam. (Ge 14:5) Some have supposed it to be the full name for Ashtaroth and that the addition of "karnaim" (horns) refers to the two horns of the crescent moon symbolizing the goddess Astarte or to twin peaks adjacent to the town. However, it is also suggested that the name means "Ashteroth Near Karnaim" and that it thus refers to the city of Ashtaroth with Karnaim being mentioned as a separate but adjacent town. Karnaim is considered to be located at Sheikh Sa'ad, which lies in the vicinity of the generally accepted site of Ashtaroth (Tell 'Ashtarah).—See ASHTAROTH.

ASHTORETH (Ash'to·reth). A goddess of the Canaanites, considered to be the wife of Baal. Ashtoreth is often represented as a nude female with rudely exaggerated sex organs. The worship of this goddess was widespread among various peoples of antiquity, and the name Ashtoreth was common in one form or another. The Greek name is Astarte. Among the Philistines, Ashtoreth was evidently viewed as a goddess of war, as is indicated by the fact that the armor of defeated King Saul was placed in the temple of the Ashtoreth images. (1Sa 31:10) Chiefly, however, Ashtoreth was apparently a fertility goddess. The most prominent part of her worship consisted of sex orgies in the temples or high places devoted to Baal worship, where male and female prostitutes

served.—See CANAAN, CANAANITE No. 2 (Conquest of Canaan by Israel).

The worship of Ashtoreth possibly existed in Canaan as early as Abraham's time, for one of the cities there was called "Ashteroth-karnaim." (Ge 14:5) Also mentioned in Scripture is the city of Ashtaroth, the dwelling place of the giant King Og of Bashan. Its name would indicate that this city may have been a center of Ashtoreth worship. —De 1:4; Jos 9:10; 12:4.

The singular form 'ash·to'reth (Ashtoreth) first appears in the Bible with reference to King Solomon's apostatizing toward the latter part of his reign. At that time Israelites began worshiping the Ashtoreth of the Sidonians. (1Ki 11:5, 33) The only other occurrence of the singular form is in connection with King Josiah's tearing down the high places that Solomon had built to Ashtoreth and other deities. (2Ki 23:13) The plural 'ash·ta-rohth' ("Ashtoreth images," NW; "Ashtarts," AT) probably refers to the images or manifestations of this pagan goddess.—Jg 2:13; 10:6; 1Sa 7:3, 4.

ASHURBANIPAL. See ASENAPPAR.

ASHURITE (Ash'ur·ite). A people subject to the kingship of Ish-bosheth, Saul's son. At 2 Samuel 2:9 they are listed between Gilead and Jezreel. The Latin *Vulgate* and Syriac *Peshitta* here read "Geshurites," while the Targums say "Asherites." (Compare Jg 1:32.) The name Asshurim is used at Genesis 25:3, but there refers to Arabian descendants of Abraham through Dedan.—See CYPRESS.

ASHVATH (Ash'vath). A man of the tribe of Asher, house of Japhlet.—1Ch 7:33.

ASIA. In the Christian Greek Scriptures the term "Asia" is used as referring to the Roman province occupying the western part of Asia Minor, not to the continent of Asia.

The Roman Province of Asia. The Roman province of Asia included the older countries of Mysia, Lydia, Caria, and, at times, part of Phrygia, as well as the adjacent islands. It was thus bounded by the Aegean Sea and the provinces of Bithynia, Galatia (which embraced part of Phrygia), and Lycia. The precise borders, however, are difficult to define because of repeated shifting.

Initially, the capital was located at Pergamum in Mysia, but during the reign of Augustus it was transferred to Ephesus, farther to the south. In the year 27 B.C.E., the province was made senatorial and was thereafter governed by a proconsul. (Ac 19:38) It was also divided into 9 judicial districts and subdivided into 44 city districts.

Luke, in describing the regions from which the Jews had come to Jerusalem at the time of Pentecost in the year 33 C.E., lists Asia along with the provinces of Cappadocia, Pontus, and Pamphylia. (Ac 2:9, 10; compare 1Pe 1:1.) He there lists Phrygia apart from Asia, as he does again at Acts 16:6. Pliny the Elder, Roman author of the first century C.E., did likewise. (*Natural History,* V, XXVIII, 102) The account at Acts 16:6, 7 states that Paul was "forbidden by the holy spirit to speak the word in the district of Asia" when traveling westward on his second missionary tour (c. 49-52 C.E.). He therefore moved through Phrygia and Galatia northward toward the province of Bithynia, but he was again diverted westward through Mysia to the seaport of Troas, the natural point for embarking to Macedonia. Here Paul received his vision inviting him to "step over into Macedonia and help us." (Ac 16:9) So, whereas Paul actually passed through the northern part of the province of Asia, he did not spend time there until his return trip after completing his work in Macedonia and Achaia. He then spent a short time in Ephesus, preaching in the synagogue and, at his departure, promised to return.—Ac 18:19-21.

During his third journey (c. 52-56 C.E.) Paul spent over two years in Ephesus, with the result that "all those inhabiting the district of Asia heard the word of the Lord, both Jews and Greeks." (Ac 19:1-10, 22) It was evidently at this time (c. 55 C.E.), in Ephesus, that Paul wrote his first letter to the Corinthians, to whom he sent greetings from "the congregations of Asia," thereby indicating good progress. (1Co 16:19) When he wrote his second letter to the Corinthians later from Macedonia, he made reference to the difficulties and grave danger experienced in Asia. (Ac 19:23-41; 2Co 1:8) On his return voyage, not wanting to spend further time in Asia, Paul sailed past Ephesus, touching in at the island of Samos and landing at Miletus in Caria, part of the province of Asia, to which point he invited "the older men" of the Ephesian congregation to come for a meeting with him.—Ac 20:15-18.

When traveling to Rome for his first trial (c. 60/61 C.E.), which resulted from a mob action at Jerusalem instigated by "Jews from Asia" (Ac 21:27, 28; 24:18, 19; compare 6:9), Paul initially embarked on a ship that was going to "places along the coast of the district of Asia," but he then transferred to another ship at Myra in the neighboring province of Lycia.—Ac 27:2-6.

Paul's words at 2 Timothy 1:15, evidently written from Rome about the year 65 C.E., may indicate that the strong persecution then beginning to rage against the Christians on the part of the Roman authorities had now caused many of the Christian 'men of Asia' to shun association with the imprisoned apostle Paul, turning away from Paul at a critical time. The expression "all the men in the district of Asia" does not imply a total turning away of all Christians in Asia, because Paul immediately thereafter commended Onesiphorus, who was evidently a resident of Ephesus.—2Ti 1:16-18; 4:19.

A continuation of Christian faith is also manifest in the Revelation and the seven messages sent by John to seven congregations in prominent cities of

ASIA MINOR
Old Regional Names

BITHYNIA PAPHLAGONIA GALATIAN PONTUS

MYSIA
Troas

GALATIA

LYDIA

ASIAN PHRYGIA GALATIAN PHRYGIA
Antioch
LYCAONIA

CAPPADOCIA

COMMAGENE

Ephesus

CARIA PISIDIA

PAMPHYLIA CILICIA

LYCIA

Antioch

SYRIA

Great Sea

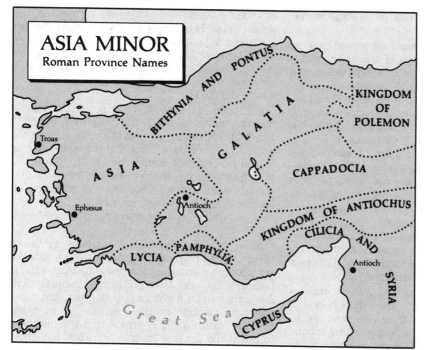

ASIA MINOR
Roman Province Names

BITHYNIA AND PONTUS

GALATIA

ASIA

Troas

Ephesus

Antioch

KINGDOM OF ANTIOCHUS

PAMPHYLIA

LYCIA

CAPPADOCIA

KINGDOM OF POLEMON

CILICIA AND

Antioch

SYRIA

CYPRUS

Great Sea

Asia: Ephesus, Smyrna, Pergamum, Thyatira, Sardis, Philadelphia, and Laodicea, most of these congregations being commended for having endured tribulation. (Re 1:4, 11; 2:2, 3, 9, 10, 13, 19; 3:10) John was then (c. 96 C.E.) on the island of Patmos, a short distance off the coast of the province of Asia. It is generally believed that John's Gospel account and three letters were written in or near Ephesus, subsequent to his release from Patmos.

Other cities of the province of Asia mentioned Scripturally are Colossae, Hieropolis, Adramyttium, and Assos.

ASIEL (As′i·el) [Made by God]. Simeonite forefather of Jehu, a chieftain in the days of King Hezekiah.—1Ch 4:35, 38, 41.

ASNAH (As′nah). The family head of certain Nethinim who returned from Babylonian exile to Jerusalem with Zerubbabel in 537 B.C.E. (Ezr 2:1, 50) They are, however, omitted from a similar list in Nehemiah 7:52.

ASP [Gr., a·spis′]. A name popularly used today for several unrelated poisonous snakes.

The word "asps" appears once in the Holy Bible, at Romans 3:13, where the apostle Paul, speaking of sinners, says: "Poison of asps is behind their lips." Here the apostle is quoting from Psalm 140: 3: "The venom of the horned viper is under their

lips." Therefore, the asps referred to at Romans 3:13 must be horned vipers.—See VIPER, HORNED.

ASPATHA (As·pa′-tha). One of Haman's ten sons.—Es 9:7, 10; see HAMAN.

ASRIEL (As′ri·el). A male descendant of Manasseh who became the family head of the Asrielites. Numbers 26:29-31 indicates that he was the great-grandson of Manasseh through Machir and his son Gilead. According to 1 Chronicles 7:14, Asriel was a son of Manasseh born to him by his Syrian concubine. However, part of an apparent parenthetical statement that follows reads: "She bore Machir the father of Gilead." Hence, as is not uncommon in Biblical genealogies, Asriel may here be termed a "son" of Manasseh only in the sense of being one of his later descendants (through Machir, Manasseh's son by his Syrian concubine). But it is possible that Manasseh had both a direct son and a great-grandson bearing the same name. "The sons of Asriel" were among the descendants of Manasseh to whom Joshua made territorial allotments in the Promised Land. —Jos 17:1-4.

ASRIELITES (As′ri·el·ites) [Of (Belonging to) Asriel]. A Manassite family descended from Asriel.—Nu 26:29, 31.

ASS [Heb., chamohr′; ′a·thohn′, "she-ass"; ′a′yir, "full-grown ass"; Gr. o′nos; o·na′ri·on, "young ass"]. A hard-hoofed animal of the horse family, distinguished from the horse by its smaller size, shorter mane, longer ears, and shorter tail hair, only the end half of the tail having a brush. Since its little, sharp hooves make it more surefooted than the horse, the ass is better adapted to the rough and mountainous terrain so frequently encountered in Palestine. Although the ass' stupidity and stubbornness are proverbial, its intelligence is actually considered to be superior to that of the horse, and it is a patient, long-suffering creature that, like other animals, has often experienced abuse at man's hand.

The ass (*Equus asinus*) has long served man as a beast of burden, a means of transport, and a draft animal, first mention of it being made in the Scriptures in connection with Abraham. (Ge 12: 16; 22:3; Jos 15:18; 2Ch 28:15; Isa 30:24) Evidently from the standpoint of the hard work of burden bearing done by the ass, Jacob likened his son Issachar to this animal. (Ge 49:14) On the other hand, reference is made to the sexual heat of asses in connection with the kingdom of Judah's prostituting herself to the nations.—Eze 23:20.

In one of his visions the prophet Isaiah saw "a war chariot of asses." (Isa 21:7) This would indicate that asses were also used in warfare, probably as pack animals, if not also to carry warriors into the actual fight. In this regard it is of interest that the Greek historian Herodotus (IV, 129) tells of the use of asses by the Persian army.

According to the Law, the ass was an unclean animal. Hence, since all the firstborn belonged to Jehovah and the firstborn of an ass could not be sacrificed, it either had to be redeemed by substituting a sheep in its place or its neck was to be broken.—Ex 13:13; 34:20.

Although unclean, asses were eaten in Samaria because of the severity of the famine during King Ben-hadad's siege of the city, and even the most inedible part, the bony, thinly fleshed head of an ass became, in effect, a luxury food costing 80 silver pieces (if shekels, $176).—2Ki 6:24, 25.

God's law prescribed humane treatment for domestic animals, such as the ass. An ass lying down under its load was to be relieved thereof, and an ass and a bull were not to be yoked together. (Ex 23:5; De 22:10) Being inferior in size and strength and different in nature, the ass would have suffered as a result of such an unequal yoking.

The number of asses the Israelites had must have been very great, in view of the fact that in their campaign against the Midianites alone they took a total of 61,000 asses as spoils of war. (Nu 31:3, 32-34) The frequent mention of this creature in the Scriptures suggests that few households were without one. (De 5:21; 22:4; 1Sa 12:3) This is also borne out by the fact that there was one of these animals for about every six men (not including the slaves and singers) returning with Zerubbabel from Babylonian exile. (Ezr 2:1, 2, 64-67; Ne 7:66-69) The recognition on the part of the ass of its place in relation to its master was employed as an example to rebuke unfaithful Israel, because of her failure to recognize Jehovah.—Isa 1:3.

The ass, at death, was simply dragged uncere-moniously outside the city and thrown on the refuse heap. Thus God's prophet foretold the debasement of proud and faithless Jehoiakim, son of Josiah, king of Judah: "With the burial of a he-ass he will be buried, with a dragging about and a throwing away, out beyond the gates of Jerusalem."—Jer 22:19.

Both men and women, even prominent Israelites, rode asses. (Jos 15:18; Jg 5:10; 10:3, 4; 12:14; 1Sa 25:42) Solomon, the son of David, rode to his anointing to office on his father's she-mule, a hybrid offspring of a male ass. (1Ki 1:33-40) It was therefore most appropriate that Jesus, the one greater than Solomon, fulfilled the prophecy of Zechariah 9:9 by riding, not a horse, but an ass' colt "on which none of mankind ever sat."—Lu 19:30, 35.

Some consider the Gospel accounts to be at variance with respect to the animal Jesus rode on his triumphal entry into Jerusalem. Mark (11:7), Luke (19:35), and John (12:14, 15) indicate that Jesus rode upon a colt or a young ass, but they make no mention of the presence of an older ass. Yet Matthew (21:7) writes that the disciples "brought the ass and its colt, and they put upon these their outer garments, and he seated himself upon them." Jesus obviously did not seat himself on the two animals, but upon the garments that were laid upon the colt. Evidently, since he did not ride the ass, but rather its colt, Mark, Luke, and John do not mention the presence of the parent ass in their accounts.

Wild Ass. The wild ass [Heb., 'a·rohdh'; Aramaic, 'aradh'] is distinguished from the domestic ass, not by its appearance, but by its wild and intractable disposition. This harmonizes completely with the Bible's description of an animal with 'loosened bands,' as it were.—Job 39:5.

The home of the wild ass (*Equus hemionus*) is the desert plain and the salt country, far away from the turmoil of a town. It instinctively avoids places inhabited by man, so "the noises of a stalker it does not hear." Not that the wild ass cannot hear well; it is exceedingly wary because of its keen senses of hearing, sight, and smell. Should a man try to stalk this creature, it would dart off with utmost rapidity. Restlessly wild asses migrate in search of greenery, even exploring mountain areas for pasturage. They feed on every sort of green plant, gnawing even down into the roots. Salt also constitutes a part of their diet. (Job 39:5-8) The preference of the wild ass for free and unrestricted life far from human habitation adds significance to the fact that Nebuchadnezzar's dwelling was with these creatures during his seven years of insanity.—Da 5:21; see ZEBRA.

ASSEMBLY. As the Universal Sovereign, Jehovah God has the right to decree that his servants should assemble and to specify the time and place of assembly. In these ways he acts for their benefit. Assemblies of God's people of ancient times varied as to purpose. Yet they surely contributed to unity, for all in attendance had the opportunity to hear the same things at the same time. Such gatherings resulted in many spiritual benefits and were often occasions of great joy.

Hebrew and Greek Terms. Several Hebrew and Greek words are employed in the Bible to denote a gathering. One that is common in the Hebrew text is *'e·dhah'*. It is from the root *ya·'adh'*, meaning "appoint; designate," and thus indicates a group assembled by appointment. (Compare 2Sa 20:5; Jer 47:7.) *'E·dhah'* is often applied to the community of Israel and is used in the expressions "the assembly" (Le 8:4, 5; Jg 21:10), "assembly of Israel" (Ex 12:3; Nu 32:4; 1Ki 8:5), and "Jehovah's assembly" (Nu 27:17).

The Hebrew word *moh·'edh'* is from the same root as *'e·dhah'* and means "appointed time" or "appointed place." (1Sa 13:8; 20:35) It is used 223 times in the Hebrew Scriptures, as in the expression "the tent of meeting." (Ex 27:21) *Moh·'edh'* is employed in connection with seasonal festivals. (Le 23:2, 4, 37, 44) It appears at Isaiah 33:20, where Zion is called "the town of our festal occasions."

The Hebrew term *miq·ra'*, meaning "convention," comes from the root verb *qa·ra'* (call). It occurs at Isaiah 4:5, which mentions Mount Zion's "convention place." Frequent is the use of this word in the expression "holy convention" (Ex 12:16; Le 23:2, 3); during such a holy convention no work of a secular sort was to be done.

Another Hebrew word used to designate gatherings is *qa·hal'*, related to a verb meaning "call together; congregate." (Ex 35:1; Le 8:4) It is often used to represent a congregation as an organized body. Sometimes *qa·hal'* (congregation) is used in conjunction with *'e·dhah'* (assembly). (Le 4:13; Nu 20:8, 10) Forms of both words appear in the expression "congregation of the assembly of Israel [Heb., *qehal' 'adath-Yis·ra·'el'*]."—Ex 12:6.

Still another is the Hebrew word *'atsa·rah'*, rendered "solemn assembly." This term is used in connection with the Festival of Booths and the Passover.—Le 23:36; De 16:8.

Intimate gatherings of various kinds are designated by the Hebrew word *sohdh*, meaning "confidential talk; intimacy." (Ps 83:3; Job 29:4) It is rendered "intimate group" at Psalm 89:7, which states: "God is to be held in awe among the inti-

mate group of holy ones; he is grand and fear-inspiring over all who are round about him."

The Greek word *ek·kle·si'a* (from *ek*, "out of," and *kle'sis*, "a calling") is usually used in the *Septuagint* to translate the Hebrew word *qa·hal'* (congregation) and is sometimes employed for *'e·dhah'* (assembly), though for the latter the Greek word *sy·na·go·ge'* (meaning "a bringing together," from *syn*, "together," and *a'go*, "bring") is also used. In the Christian Greek Scriptures, *ek·kle·si'a* is generally rendered "congregation." At Acts 7:38 it is used with reference to the congregation of Israel. The Greek word *sy·na·go·ge'* appears at Acts 13:43 ("synagogue assembly") and at James 2:2 ("gathering"). Another Greek word, *pa·ne'gy·ris* (from *pan*, "all," and *a·go·ra'*, designating any kind of assembly) is rendered "general assembly" at Hebrews 12:23.—*NW, KJ, AS.*

The Scriptures have much to say about spiritually upbuilding assemblies, though they also mention assemblies of wicked or unrighteous character. Partisans of rebellious Korah are called "his entire assembly." (Nu 16:5) In prayer to Jehovah, David said, "The very assembly of tyrannical ones have looked for my soul." (Ps 86:14) Also, when the silversmith Demetrius fomented opposition to Paul in Ephesus and a crowd gathered, "some were crying out one thing and others another; for the assembly was in confusion, and the majority of them did not know the reason why they had come together."—Ac 19:24-29, 32.

It is to be noted that order prevailed during gatherings of Jehovah's people; such assemblies were well supported, and they were occasions of spiritual benefit, often times of great rejoicing.

In accord with the divine will, Moses and Aaron assembled all the older men of Israel in Egypt. The words of Jehovah were related, signs were performed, and the people believed. (Ex 4:27-31) Thereafter, as God ordered, the Israelites assembled at the base of Mount Sinai (Horeb), experienced a thrilling spectacle, and witnessed the giving of the Law.—Ex 19:10-19; De 4:9, 10.

While the Israelites were in the wilderness, Jehovah instructed Moses to make two silver trumpets that were to be blown for convening the assembly and for breaking up the camp. If both were sounded, the whole assembly would keep their appointment with Moses; if only one was blown, the chieftains alone would thus be summoned. In the wilderness, the specified place of assembly was "the entrance of the tent of meeting." (Nu 10:1-4; Ex 29:42) Later, it was Jehovah's will that the Israelites assemble regularly at the temple in Jerusalem, gathering there for the three major annual festivals.—Ex 34:23, 24; 2Ch 6:4-6.

Representative Assemblies. At times, the people of Israel were represented in gatherings by "chieftains of the assembly" (Ex 16:22; Nu 4:34; 31:13; 32:2; Jos 9:15, 18; 22:30), or "older men." (Ex 12:21; 17:5; 24:1) When judicial matters required attention, a number of persons might assemble at the city gate. However, whether gathered there or elsewhere, they would not all vote on the case under consideration in a democratic fashion. Instead, theocratically, respected older men would weigh matters in the light of God's law and then announce their decision. (De 16:18; 17:8-13) Similarly, the early Christian congregation was represented in such matters by those placed in positions of responsibility by the holy spirit. (Ac 20:28) In Israel, if the wrongdoing required the death sentence, the whole assembly might execute it.—Le 24:14; Nu 15:32-36; De 21:18-21.

General Assemblies. Occasions of general assembly in Israel included religious festivals, solemn assemblies (2Ch 34:29, 30; Joe 2:15), or events of great national significance; runners sometimes summoned the populace. (1Sa 10:17-19; 2Ch 30:6, 13) The weekly Sabbath, a day of "complete rest, a holy convention" (Le 23:3), was a time to consider God's Word, as in the later synagogues where 'Moses was read aloud on every sabbath.' (Ac 15:21) There was also the new moon observance (Nu 28:11-15), the day of the trumpet blast (Nu 29:1-6), the annual Atonement Day (Le 16), the Passover (commemorating Israel's deliverance from Egypt; Ex 12:14), and, later, the Festival of Purim (commemorating the Jews' deliverance from threatened annihilation in the Persian Empire; Es 9:20-24) as well as the Festival of Dedication (in remembrance of the temple's rededication on Chislev 25, 165 B.C.E.; Joh 10:22, 23). Additionally, there were three annual "seasonal festivals of Jehovah": the Festival of Unfermented Cakes, the Festival of Weeks (later called Pentecost), and the Festival of Booths (Le 23), respecting which festivals God decreed: "On three occasions in the year every male of yours will appear before the face of the true Lord, Jehovah." (Ex 23:14-17) Recognizing the high spiritual value of these festivals, many men saw to it that their entire family attended. (Lu 2:41-45) Also, Moses expressly stated that every seven years, during the Festival of Booths, the men, women, children, and alien residents of Israel should be congregated in the place Jehovah chose "in order that they may listen and in order that they may learn, as they must fear Jehovah your God and take care to carry out all the words of this law." (De 31:10-12) Hence, provision was made for the Israelites to assemble very frequently to consider Jehovah's Word and purposes.—See FESTIVAL.

Following the completion of the temple, Solomon convened a grand assembly in Jerusalem in connection with the dedication of that splendid religious structure. That assembly lasted for many days, and when the people were sent home they were "joyful and feeling good at heart over the goodness that Jehovah had performed toward David and toward Solomon and toward Israel his people."—2Ch 5:1–7:10.

Throngs assembling at the temple during the annual festivals experienced great delight and spiritual benefit, as at the Passover celebration of King Hezekiah's time, when "there came to be great rejoicing in Jerusalem." (2Ch 30:26) In Nehemiah's day an assembly was called that proved to be an occasion of "very great rejoicing." (Ne 8:17) To the people assembled in Jerusalem, Ezra read from the book of the Law of Moses, doing so before "all intelligent enough to listen," and they were attentive. (Ne 8:2, 3) As a result of the instruction then imparted by Ezra and other Levites, all the people rejoiced, "for they had understood the words that had been made known to them." (Ne 8:12) They thereafter commemorated the Festival of Booths, and on the eighth day "there was a solemn assembly, according to the rule."—Ne 8:18; Le 23:33-36.

Synagogues as Assembly Places. While the Jews were exiles in Babylon, or shortly thereafter, synagogues, or buildings that were Jewish places of assembly, came into use. Eventually these were established in various places, large cities having more than one. Primarily, synagogues were schools where the Scriptures were read and taught. They were also places of prayer and for the giving of praise to God. It was customary for Jesus Christ and his disciples to go to them to instruct and encourage persons present. (Mt 4:23; Lu 4:16; Ac 13:14, 15; 17:1, 2; 18:4) Because the Scriptures were regularly read in the synagogues, James was able to say to the Christian governing body in Jerusalem: "From ancient times Moses has had in city after city those who preach him, because he is read aloud in the synagogues on every sabbath." (Ac 15:21) The basic features of worship in the synagogue were carried over into Christian assembly places, where Scripture reading and exposition, encouragement, prayer, and the giving of praise were to be found.—1Co 14:26-33, 40; Col 4:16; see SYNAGOGUE.

Christian Assemblies. On various occasions, large crowds assembled before Jesus Christ, realizing many benefits, as in the case of the Sermon on the Mount. (Mt 5:1–7:29) While these were not like specially arranged assemblies, at times they lasted long enough to make necessary the feeding of the congregated multitudes, a circumstance that Jesus met with the miraculous multiplication of food. (Mt 14:14-21; 15:29-38) Often Christ gathered his disciples and gave them spiritual instruction, and after his death his followers met together, as on the day of Pentecost 33 C.E., when the holy spirit was bestowed upon such assembled ones.—Ac 2:1-4.

It was the custom of early Christians to meet together, generally in small groups. However, sometimes at their gatherings "quite a crowd" would assemble. (Ac 11:26) Jesus' half brother James found it appropriate to give spiritual Israelites counsel against showing favoritism toward the rich at a public gathering (Gr., *sy·na·go·ge'*) of the congregation.—Jas 2:1-9.

Importance of Assembling. The importance of taking full advantage of Jehovah's provisions for assembling to gain spiritual benefits is emphasized in connection with the annual Passover observance. Any male who was clean and was not on a journey but who neglected to keep the Passover was to be cut off in death. (Nu 9:9-14) When King Hezekiah called inhabitants of Judah and Israel to Jerusalem for a Passover celebration, his message was, in part: "You sons of Israel, return to Jehovah . . . do not stiffen your neck as your forefathers did. Give place to Jehovah and come to his sanctuary that he has sanctified to time indefinite and serve Jehovah your God, that his burning anger may turn back from you. . . . Jehovah your God is gracious and merciful, and he will not turn away the face from you if you return to him." (2Ch 30:6-9) Willful failure to attend would certainly have indicated a forsaking of God. And, while such festivals as the Passover are not observed by Christians, Paul fittingly urged them not to abandon regular assemblies of God's people, stating: "Let us consider one another to incite to love and fine works, not forsaking the gathering of ourselves together, as some have the custom, but encouraging one another, and all the more so as you behold the day drawing near."—Heb 10:24, 25; see CONGREGATION.

ASSHUR (As'shur).

1. A son of Shem, named second at Genesis 10:22 and 1 Chronicles 1:17. He was the forefather of the Assyrians, and the same Hebrew word is rendered "Asshur" as well as "Assyria(n)." Either their nation or one of its main cities, Asshur (modern Qal'at Sherqat), is meant at Ezekiel 27:23.

2. The foremost divinity of the Assyrians, their god of military prowess, to whom this warlike people prayed for aid. Asshur was a sort of "deified patriarch," and in venerating him, the Assyrians may actually have worshiped their ancestor, Asshur, the son of Shem. The name Asshur is incorporated in many Assyrian names, such as those of Esar-haddon and Ashurbanipal.

The false god Asshur was believed to be the chief protector of the Assyrians, being represented in their art by the winged sun disk. It was in their god Asshur's name and with his approval (indicated by favorable omens) that Assyrian troops entered battle, carrying his sacred symbol into the fray. Their kings ascribed victories "to the help of Asshur."—See PICTURE, Vol. 2, p. 529; ASSYRIA.

ASSHURIM (As·shu'rim). Descendants of Dedan, son of Jokshan, one of Abraham's sons by Keturah. (Ge 25:1-3) The use in the Hebrew text of the plural ending (*im*) with this name may indicate that Asshurim represents a tribe or people. Specific identification is not possible, but some north Arabian tribe is probably meant. They should not be confused, however, with the Assyrians who were descendants of Shem's son Asshur.

ASSIR (As'sir) [possibly, Prisoner].

1. A Levite born in Egypt who was one of the sons of Korah.—Ex 6:24; 1Ch 6:22.

2. First Chronicles 6:23, 37 appears to indicate a second Assir as a son or descendant of Ebiasaph.

The *King James Version* uses the name Assir at 1 Chronicles 3:17; however, many modern translations (*AS, AT, Mo, NW, Ro, RS*) view the Hebrew word here, not as a proper name, but, rather, as a common adjective descriptive of Jeconiah (Jehoiachin) as a captive or prisoner in Babylon. (2Ki 24:12-15; 25:27-30) The *New World Translation* fittingly reads: "And the sons of Jeconiah as prisoner [*'as·sir'*] were Shealtiel . . ."

ASSOCIATION. The apostle Paul employed the Greek noun *ho·mi·li'a* when warning Christians about the danger of bad "associations." (1Co 15:33) This Greek word is related to the verb *ho·mi·le'o*, meaning "converse." (Ac 20:11) It denotes association or intercourse with another, usually through speech but sometimes through sexual relations. The Greek *Septuagint* used this word to translate the Hebrew for "persuasiveness" in Proverbs 7:21 and for the "marriage due" in Exodus 21:10.

Those who desire God's approval choose as their companions persons who are devoted to righteousness and truth. (2Ti 2:22) They also stop "associating [literally, mixing themselves up]" socially with members of the congregation whose way of life has led to official censure of their disorderly conduct. While continuing to manifest love toward such ones, they make it clear that they do not approve of their disorderly conduct. (2Th 3:6-15) Whereas good associates can be a real aid in one's continuing to walk in harmony with divine wisdom, there is no denying the damaging consequences of bad association. The inspired proverb states: "He that is walking with wise persons will become wise, but he that is having dealings with the stupid ones will fare badly." (Pr 13:20; compare Pr 22:24, 25; 28:7; 29:3.) The Hebrew word ra·ʹah', translated 'have dealings with' in Proverbs 13:20, is also rendered 'associate with' and is related to the Hebrew word reʹa', meaning "fellowman; companion."—Jg 14:20; Le 19:18; Ps 15:3.

That unwholesome companions are indeed hurtful to one's welfare is evident from many Scriptural examples. Jacob's daughter Dinah unwisely chose Canaanite girls as her associates, and this led to her being violated by Shechem, the son of a Hivite chieftain. (Ge 34:1, 2) David's son Amnon listened to the bad counsel of his companion Jehonadab and raped his own half sister Tamar. Thus he incurred the hatred of Absalom, her full brother, who later arranged to have him murdered. (2Sa 13:3-29) Contrary to Jehovah's commands, the Israelites began associating with the Canaanites, formed marriage alliances with them, and adopted their degraded form of worship, resulting in Jehovah's disfavor and abandonment. (De 7:3, 4; Jg 3:5-8) Even Solomon turned from worship of Jehovah when he took worshipers of false gods as wives. (Ne 13:26) It was the influence of Baal-worshiping Jezebel that made Ahab worse than all the Israelite kings prior to his time. (1Ki 21:25) Close association with the royal house of Ahab nearly cost godly Jehoshaphat his life, and the marriage alliance that he had formed with Ahab later almost destroyed the royal house of David.—2Ch 18:1-3, 29-31; 22:10, 11.

The united body of true Christians, though composed of small groups, congregations, or physically isolated individuals, constitutes an "association of brothers," or a brotherhood, designated by the Greek expression a·del·phoʹtes. (1Pe 2:17; 5:9) To remain a part of that brotherhood, true Christians avoid all association with any from their midst who become promoters of false, divisive teachings. (Ro 16:17, 18) The Christian apostle John directed fellow believers never to accept such a false teacher into their homes or to greet him, which would give him an opening for presenting his twisted, corrupt doctrine. Greeting such a person would have indicated a measure of approval and made one a sharer in "his wicked works." (2Jo 10, 11) Despite the overwhelming evidence regarding the certainty of the resurrection from the dead, the apostle Paul knew that association with those who had rejected this Christian teaching would be destructive to faith. That is why he wrote: "Do not be misled. Bad associations spoil useful habits."—1Co 15:12-22, 33; see APOSTASY.

ASSOS (Asʹsos). A seaport town in Mysia on the N shore of the Gulf of Adramyttium, hence within the Roman province of Asia. The site is today known as Behramköy.

On his third missionary tour, the apostle Paul was heading back to Jerusalem and had stopped at Troas. From there he sent Luke and others by boat to Assos, where he planned to join them. The boat had to travel around Cape Baba (Lectum) to get to Assos (on the other side of the promontory from Troas), and this enabled Paul to walk the shorter distance (c. 32 km; 20 mi) on foot and still arrive at Assos in time to board the ship, which then traveled to Mitylene on the island of Lesbos, S of Assos.—Ac 20:6, 13, 14.

ASSYRIA (As·syrʹi·a). The name applied to the country anciently occupying the northern end of the Mesopotamian plain or the extreme northern portion of what is today the modern country of Iraq. Basically, it lay within the triangle formed by the Tigris and Little Zab rivers, these rivers constituting generally its western and southern boundaries, while the mountains of ancient Armenia formed the northern boundary, and the Zagros Mountain range and the land of Media the eastern boundary. It should be noted, however, that these boundaries were quite fluid, Assyria spreading S of the Little Zab when Babylon weakened, but retreating when Assyrian political fortunes were low and those of Babylon were in ascendancy. Such fluctuation was true of the other boundaries and particularly that of the Tigris, as Assyria early extended its influence W of that river. The Assyrian Empire, of course, came to embrace a far larger area.—MAP, Vol. 1, p. 954.

There was a continued close relationship between Assyria and Babylon throughout their history. They were neighboring states jointly occupying a region with no real natural division to serve as a frontier between their territories. The

Carving from the north palace in Nineveh. The king and his queen enjoying a garden party; on the tree in front of the harpist is the head of a conquered king

region of Assyria proper, however, was mostly a highlands area, generally of rugged terrain, with a more invigorating climate than that of Babylonia. The people were more energetic and aggressive than the Babylonians. They are represented in carved reliefs as of strong physique, dark-complexioned, with heavy eyebrows and beard, and prominent nose.

The city of Asshur, located W of the Tigris, is considered to have been the original capital of the region. Thereafter, however, Nineveh became its most prominent capital, while both Calah and Khorsabad were used at times by Assyrian monarchs as capital cities. A trade route to the Mediterranean and to Asia Minor ran along the northern part of Assyria, and other routes branched off into Armenia and the region of Lake Urmia. Much of Assyria's warring was in order to gain or maintain control of such trade routes.

Militarism. Assyria was essentially a military power, and the historical picture left of its exploits is one of great cruelty and rapaciousness. (PICTURES, Vol. 1, p. 958) One of their warrior monarchs, Ashurnasirpal, describes his punishment of several rebellious cities in this way:

"I built a pillar over against his city gate, and I flayed all the chief men who had revolted, and I covered the pillar with their skins; some I walled up within the pillar, some I impaled upon the pillar on stakes, . . . and I cut off the limbs of the officers, of the royal officers who had rebelled. . . . Many captives from among them I burned with

fire, and many I took as living captives. From some I cut off their hands and their fingers, and from others I cut off their noses, their ears, and their fingers(?), of many I put out the eyes. I made one pillar of the living, and another of heads, and I bound their heads to posts (tree trunks) round about the city. Their young men and maidens I burned in the fire . . . Twenty men I captured alive and I immured them in the wall of his palace. . . . The rest of them [their warriors] I consumed with thirst in the desert of the Euphrates."—*Ancient Records of Assyria and Babylonia*, by D. D. Luckenbill, 1926, Vol. I, pp. 145, 147, 153, 162.

Reliefs often show their captives being led by cords attached to hooks that pierced the nose or the lips, or having their eyes put out at the point of a spear. Thus, sadistic torture was a frequent feature of Assyrian warfare, about which they shamelessly boasted and which they carefully recorded. The knowledge of their cruelty doubtless served them to an advantage militarily, striking terror into the hearts of those in their line of attack and often causing resistance to crumble. Assyria's capital, Nineveh, was aptly described by the prophet Nahum as a "lair of lions" and as "the city of bloodshed."—Na 2:11, 12; 3:1.

What sort of religion did the Assyrians practice?

Assyria's religion was largely inherited from Babylon, and although their own national god Asshur was viewed as supreme by the Assyrians, Babylon continued to be viewed by them as the chief religious center. The Assyrian king served as the high priest of Asshur. One seal, found by

A. H. Layard in the ruins of an Assyrian palace and now preserved in the British Museum, represents the god Asshur with three heads. The belief in triads of gods as well as that of a pentad, or five gods, was prominent in Assyrian worship. The chief triad was formed of Aner, representing heaven; Bel, representing the region inhabited by man, animals, and birds; and Ea, representing the terrestrial and subterranean waters. A second triad was composed of Sin, the moon-god; Shamash, the sun-god; and Ramman, god of storm, although his place was often filled by Ishtar, queen of the stars. (Compare 2Ki 23:5, 11.) Then followed the five gods representing five planets. Commenting on the gods forming the trinitarian groups, *Unger's Bible Dictionary* (1965, p. 102) states: "These gods are invoked at times severally in phrases which seem to raise each in turn to a position of supremacy over the others." Their pantheon, however, included innumerable other minor deities, many serving as patrons of towns. Nisroch is mentioned as being worshiped by Sennacherib at the time of his assassination.—Isa 37:37, 38.

The religion practiced in connection with these gods was animistic, that is, the Assyrians believed every object and natural phenomenon to be animated by a spirit. It was somewhat distinguished from other nature worship prevalent in surrounding nations in that war was the truest expression of the national religion. (PICTURE, Vol. 1, p. 956) Thus, Tiglath-pileser I said of his fighting: "My Lord ASHUR urged me on." In his annals, Ashurbanipal says: "By command of ASSUR, SIN, and SHAMAS, the great gods my lords who protected me, into Minni I entered and marched victoriously." (*Records of the Past: Assyrian and Egyptian Monuments,* London, 1875, Vol. V, p. 18; 1877, Vol. IX, p. 43) Sargon regularly invoked Ishtar's help before going to war. The armies marched behind the standards of the gods, apparently wooden or metal symbols on poles. Great importance was attached to omens, ascertained by examination of livers of sacrificed animals, by the flight of birds, or by the position of the planets. The book *Ancient Cities,* by W. B. Wright (1886, p. 25) states: "Fighting was the business of the nation, and the priests were incessant fomenters of war. They were supported largely from the spoils of conquest, of which a fixed percentage was invariably assigned them before others shared, for this race of plunderers was excessively religious."

Culture, Literature, and Laws. The Assyrians built impressive palaces, lining the walls with sculptured slabs portraying with quite powerful realism scenes of war and peace. Human-headed, winged bulls, carved from a single block of limestone weighing as much as 36 metric tons, adorned the entranceways. Their cylinder seals show intricate engraving. (See ARCHAEOLOGY.) Their metal casting indicated considerable knowledge of metallurgy. Their kings built aqueducts and developed systems of irrigation; they produced royal botanical and zoological parks containing plants, trees, and animals from many lands. Their palace buildings often gave evidence of a well-planned drainage system and quite good sanitation.

Of particular interest have been the great libraries built up by certain Assyrian monarchs, containing tens of thousands of cuneiform inscribed clay tablets, prisms, and cylinders setting out major historical events, religious data, and legal and commercial matters. Certain laws dating from one period of Assyrian history, however, illustrate again the harshness so frequently characterizing the nation. Mutilation is provided as punishment for certain crimes. Thus, a slave girl was not allowed to go veiled in public, and for violating such ordinance her ears were to be cut off. The lack of legal protection available for a married woman is evidenced by one law stating: "Leaving aside the penalties relating to a married woman which are inscribed on the tablet, a man may flog his wife, pull out her hair, split and injure her ears. There is no legal guilt (involved) in it."—*Everyday Life in Babylonia and Assyria,* by H. W. F. Saggs, 1965, p. 152.

Biblical and Secular History. The first reference to Assyria in the Bible record is at Genesis 2:14, where the Hiddekel River (the Tigris), originally one of the four heads of the river "out of Eden," is described by Moses in his day as "going to the east of Assyria."—Ge 2:10.

The land derived its name from Shem's son Asshur. (Ge 10:22) It thus appears to have been first populated by Semites shortly after the Flood. However, it was early subjected to infiltration, as Ham's grandson Nimrod entered into Assyria and built "Nineveh and Rehoboth-Ir and Calah and Resen between Nineveh and Calah: this is the great city." (Ge 10:11, 12; compare Mic 5:6.) Whether this was subsequent to the erection of the Tower of Babel and the resulting confusion of tongues is not stated (Ge 11:1-9), although different "tongues" are already mentioned in this tenth chapter of Genesis. (Ge 10:5, 20, 31) Nevertheless, it is established that Nineveh, the capital of Assyria, was developed from Babylon, and secular history harmonizes with this. At a later date, the

Assyrian chariots carrying religious standards into battle

tribes that descended from Abraham's son Ishmael are described as reaching up to Assyria in their nomadic movements.—Ge 25:18.

The period between about 1100 and 900 B.C.E. (following the rule of Tiglath-pileser I) was a period of decline for Assyria, and this has been suggested as a favorable circumstance for the extension of the boundaries of the nation of Israel under the rule of David (1077-1038 B.C.E.) and the further extension of its influence under Solomon's reign (1037-998 B.C.E.). The success of such expansion was, of course, due primarily to God's backing and hence not dependent on Assyrian weakness.—2Sa 8, 10; 1Ki 4:21-24.

Ashurnasirpal II and Shalmaneser III. Assyrian aggression began drawing close to Israel during the rule of Ashurnasirpal II, who was noted for his ruthless warring campaigns and cruelty, already mentioned. Inscriptions show him crossing the Euphrates and overrunning northern Syria and exacting tribute from the cities of Phoenicia. His successor, Shalmaneser III, is the first king who records direct contact with the northern kingdom of Israel. Assyrian records show Shalmaneser advancing to Karkar on the Orontes River, where, he claims, he fought against a coalition of kings. The result of the battle was indecisive. Shalmaneser's Black Obelisk at Nimrud lists Jehu (c. 904-877 B.C.E.) as paying tribute to him and carries a carving in relief possibly depicting Jehu's emissary delivering the tribute to the Assyrian monarch.—See SHALMANESER No. 1.

Adad-nirari III and his successors. After Shamshi-Adad V, the successor of Shalmaneser III, Adad-nirari III came to the Assyrian throne. Inscriptions report his attacking Damascus and receiving tribute from Jehoash of Samaria. Perhaps sometime around the middle of the ninth century B.C.E. (c. 844), the prophet Jonah was sent on a mission to Assyria's capital Nineveh, and as a result of his warning of coming destruction, the entire city, including its king, responded with repentance. (Jon 3:2-6) It may be that the Assyrian king at that time was Adad-nirari III, but this is not certain.

History records that the kings following Adad-nirari III included Shalmaneser IV, Ashur-dan III, and Ashur-nirari V, all sons of Adad-nirari III. This period was one of decline as far as Assyrian aggressiveness is concerned.

Tiglath-pileser III. The first Assyrian king to be mentioned by name in the Bible is Tiglath-pileser III (2Ki 15:29; 16:7, 10), also called "Pul" at 2 Kings 15:19. At 1 Chronicles 5:26 both names are used, and this caused some in the past to view them as separate kings. However, the Babylonian King List A refers to "Pulu," indicating that both names apply to the same individual. The suggestion is made by some that this king was originally known as Pul and that he assumed the name Tiglath-pileser upon ascending to the Assyrian throne.

It was during the reign of Menahem of Israel (c. 790-781 B.C.E.) that Tiglath-pileser III entered the domain of that northern kingdom. Menahem made a payment to him of a thousand silver talents ($6,606,000) and thus obtained the withdrawal of the Assyrian. (2Ki 15:19, 20) Later, however, King Pekah of Israel (c. 778-759 B.C.E.) joined together with King Rezin of Syria against Judean King Ahaz (761-746 B.C.E.). Despite Isaiah's prophecy foretelling the certain elimination of this Syro-Israelite threat through the power of the king of Assyria (Isa 7:1-9, 16, 17; 8:3, 4), Ahaz chose the unwise course of sending a bribe to Tiglath-pileser so that he might attack that combine and thus relieve the pressure upon Judah. The Assyrian monarch responded by capturing a number of cities in the northern part of the kingdom of Israel, as well as the regions of Gilead, Galilee, and Naphtali. Earlier in his reign, Tiglath-pileser had inaugurated the policy of transplanting the populations of conquered areas in order to reduce the possibility of future uprisings, and he now proceeded to deport some of the Israelites. (1Ch 5:6, 26) Additionally, Judah was now in a subservient position toward Assyria, and Ahaz of Judah traveled to Damascus, which had also fallen to the Assyrians, and evidently rendered homage to Tiglath-pileser.—2Ki 15:29; 16:5-10, 18; 2Ch 28:16, 20, 21, compare Isa 7:17-20.

Shalmaneser V. Shalmaneser V succeeded Tiglath-pileser III. Hoshea (c. 758-740 B.C.E.), who usurped the throne of Israel, at first submitted to Assyria's exaction of tribute. Later he conspired with Egypt to free Israel from the Assyrian yoke, and Shalmaneser began a three-year siege of the city of Samaria that eventually brought its fall (740 B.C.E.) and Israel's exile. (2Ki 17:1-6; 18:9-11; Ho 7:11; 8:7-10) Most reference works state that Shalmaneser died before completing the conquest of Samaria and that Sargon II was king by the time the city finally fell.—See, however, SARGON; SHALMANESER No. 2.

Sargon II. Sargon's records speak of the deportation of 27,290 Israelites to locations in the Upper Euphrates and Media. Description is also given of his campaign in Philistia in which he conquered Gath, Ashdod, and Asdudimmu. It was at the time of this campaign that the prophet Isaiah was instructed to warn of the futility of putting trust in Egypt or Ethiopia as a means of protection against the Assyrian aggressor. (Isa 20:1-6) It was perhaps first during Sargon's reign that people from Babylon and Syria were brought into Samaria to repopulate it, the Assyrian king later sending an Israelite priest back from exile to instruct them in "the religion of the God of the land."—2Ki 17:24-28; see SAMARIA No. 2; SAMARITAN.

Sennacherib. Sennacherib, the son of Sargon II, attacked the kingdom of Judah during Hezekiah's 14th year (732 B.C.E.). (2Ki 18:13; Isa 36:1) Hezekiah had rebelled against the Assyrian yoke imposed as a result of the action of his father Ahaz. (2Ki 18:7) Sennacherib reacted by sweeping through Judah, reportedly conquering 46 cities (compare Isa 36:1, 2), and then, from his camp at Lachish, he demanded of Hezekiah a tribute of 30 gold talents (c. $11,560,000) and 300 silver talents (c. $1,982,000). (2Ki 18:14-16; 2Ch 32:1; compare Isa 8:5-8.) Though this sum was paid, Sennacherib sent his spokesmen to demand unconditional surrender of Jerusalem. (2Ki 18:17–19:34; 2Ch 32:2-20) Jehovah's subsequently causing the destruction of 185,000 of his troops in one night obliged the boasting Assyrian to withdraw and return to Nineveh. (2Ki 19:35, 36) There he was later assassinated by two of his sons and replaced on the throne by another son, Esar-haddon. (2Ki 19:37; 2Ch 32:21, 22; Isa 37:36-38) These events, with the exception of the destruction of the Assyrian troops, are also recorded on a prism of Sennacherib and one of Esar-haddon.—PICTURES, Vol. 1, p. 957.

Esar-haddon. During Manasseh's reign (716-662 B.C.E.), Assyrian army chiefs were permitted by Jehovah to take this Judean king captive to Babylon (then under Assyrian control). (2Ch 33:11) Some think this may have been at the time of Esar-haddon's victorious campaign against Egypt. At any rate, *Menasi* (Manasseh) of Judah is named in inscriptions as one of those paying tribute to Esar-haddon. Manasseh was later restored to Jerusalem. (2Ch 33:10-13) It appears from Ezra 4:2 that the transplanting of people from and to the northern kingdom of Israel was still continuing in the days of Esar-haddon, which may explain the period of "sixty-five years" in the prophecy at Isaiah 7:8.—See AHAZ No. 1; ESAR-HADDON.

Ashurbanipal. Prior to Esar-haddon's death he had appointed his son Ashurbanipal as crown prince of Assyria and another son, Shamash-shum-u-kin, as crown prince of Babylonia. Shamash-shum-u-kin later rebelled against his brother, and Ashurbanipal overcame the rebellion and sacked the city of Babylon.

Ashurbanipal brought about the greatest expansion of the empire. He put down an uprising in Egypt and sacked the city of Thebes (No-amon). The boundaries of the Assyrian Empire now embraced the regions of Elam, part of Media up into Ararat, as far W as Cilicia in Asia Minor, through Syria and Israel (but not Jerusalem), and down into Egypt, Arabia, and Babylonia. Apparently he is "the great and honorable Asenappar" referred to at Ezra 4:10.—See ASENAPPAR.

The fall of the empire. The Babylonian Chronicle B.M. (British Museum) 21901 recounts the fall of Nineveh, the capital of Assyria, following a siege carried out by the combined forces of Nabopolassar, the king of Babylon, and of Cyaxares the Mede during the 14th year of Nabopolassar (632 B.C.E.): "The city [they turned] into ruin-hills and hea[ps (of debris)]." (*Ancient Near Eastern Texts*, edited by J. B. Pritchard, 1974, p. 305; brackets and parentheses theirs.) Thus the fierce Assyrian Empire came to an ignominious end.—Isa 10:12, 24-26; 23:13; 30:30-33; 31:8, 9; Na 3:1-19; Zep 2:13.

According to the same chronicle, in the 14th year of Nabopolassar (632 B.C.E.), Ashur-uballit II attempted to continue Assyrian rule from Haran as his capital city. This chronicle states, under the

17th year of Nabopolassar (629 B.C.E.): "In the month Du'uzu, Ashur-uballit, king of Assyria, (and) a large [army of] E[gy]pt [who had come to his aid] crossed the river (Euphrates) and [marched on] to conquer Harran." (*Ancient Near Eastern Texts*, p. 305; brackets and parentheses theirs.) Actually, Ashur-uballit was trying to reconquer it after having been driven out. This record is in harmony with the account relative to the activity of Pharaoh Nechoh recorded at 2 Kings 23:29, which activity resulted in the death of King Josiah of Judah (c. 629 B.C.E.). This text states that "Pharaoh Nechoh the king of Egypt came up to the king of Assyria by the river Euphrates"—evidently to help him. "The king of Assyria" to whom Nechoh came may well have been Ashur-uballit II. Their campaign against Haran did not succeed. The Assyrian Empire had ended.

The title "king of Assyria" was applied to the Persian king (Darius Hystaspis) who dominated the land of Assyria in the time of the rebuilding of the temple at Jerusalem (completed in 515 B.C.E.). —Ezr 6:22.

Assyria in Prophecy. Assyria figured in the prophecy uttered by Balaam about the year 1473 B.C.E. (Nu 24:24) Numerous references to Assyria are found in the prophecies of Isaiah, Jeremiah, Ezekiel, Micah, Nahum, Zephaniah, and Zechariah, while the warning about Assyria's ravaging of the northern kingdom of Israel is interwoven throughout the entire prophecy of Hosea. Frequent condemnation was made of the reliance placed upon such pagan nations by apostate Israel and Judah, often vacillating between Egypt and Assyria, like "a simpleminded dove without heart." (Jer 2:18, 36; La 5:6; Eze 16:26, 28; 23:5-12; Ho 7:11) The disastrous results of such a course were vividly described. (Eze 23:22-27) The humiliation of the Assyrians and the restoration of the exiled Israelites to their homeland were also prophesied. (Isa 11:11-16; 14:25; Jer 50:17, 18; Eze 32:22; Zec 10:10, 11) Finally, the time was even foretold when peaceful relations would exist between the lands of Assyria and Egypt and they would be united with Israel in God's favor and constitute "a blessing in the midst of the earth."—Isa 19:23-25.

Wall panel from Nimrud shows Assyrian soldiers carrying away gods of a conquered city

ASTROLOGERS.

The word *ga·zerin'* occurs only in that part of Daniel written in Aramaic (Da 2:4b–7:28) and has the root meaning "cut out," the reference being thought to point to those who divide the heavens into configurations. (Da 2:34) Some English versions (*Dy, KJ, Le, AS*) translate the original Aramaic word *ga·zerin'* as "soothsayers." (Da 2:27; 4:7 [vs 4, *Dy; Le*]; 5:7, 11) This astrological cult consisted of those "who, from the position of the stars at the hour of birth, by various arts of computation and divining . . . determined the fate of individuals." (*Gesenius's Hebrew and Chaldee Lexicon*, translated by S. P. Tregelles, 1901, pp. 166, 167) Astrology is essentially polytheistic; its birth in the lower Mesopotamian Valley likely dates back to shortly after the Flood when men turned away from the pure worship of Jehovah. The name Chaldean in time became practically synonymous with "astrologer."

In this false science of astrology a different god was believed to rule over each section of the heavens. Every celestial movement and phenomenon, such as the rising and setting of the sun, the equinoxes and solstices, moon phases, eclipses, and meteors, were said to be the doings of these gods. These cosmic movements were therefore regularly noted, elaborate charts and tables of their occurrences were made, and from these, human affairs and terrestrial events were predicted. All matters, both public and private, were believed to be controlled by these gods of the heavens. As a consequence, political or military decisions were not made until the astrologers were called to read and interpret the omens and give their advice. In this way the priestly class grew to have great power and influence over the lives of the people. They claimed supernatural power, insight, and great wisdom. No great temple was erected among the Babylonians that was not equipped with its own celestial observatory.

In the eighth century B.C.E., the prophet Isaiah, in foretelling the destruction of Babylon, challenged the stargazing astrological counselors of that doomed city to save her: "You [Babylon] have grown weary with the multitude of your counselors. Let them stand up, now, and save you, the worshipers of the heavens, the lookers at the stars, those giving out knowledge at the new moons concerning the things that will come upon you."—Isa 47:13.

In the course of history, Daniel and his three companions became captives in this land of the astrologers. Put to the test "as regards every matter of wisdom and understanding," these Hebrews were found by the Babylonian king to be "ten times better than all the magic-practicing priests and the conjurers that were in all his royal realm." (Da 1:20) Daniel was thereafter called "chief of the magic-practicing priests" (Da 4:9), but it is important to note that he never gave up Jehovah's worship to become a stargazing 'divider of the heavens.' For example, Nebuchadnezzar was so infuriated when the astrologers and the rest of "the wise men" failed to reveal his dream that he exclaimed: "Dismembered is what you will be, and into public privies your own houses will be turned." (Da 2:5) Daniel and his companions were included in this sweeping order, but before the execution was carried out, Daniel was brought in before the king, to whom he said: "There exists a God in the heavens who is a Revealer of secrets," but "as for me, it is not through any wisdom that exists in me more than in any others alive that this secret is revealed to me."—Da 2:28, 30.

Who were the Magi that visited the young child Jesus?

Astrologers (Gr., *ma'goi;* "Magi," *AS* ftn, *CC, We;* "Magians," *ED*) brought gifts to the young child Jesus. (Mt 2:1-16) Commenting on who these *ma'goi* were, *The Imperial Bible-Dictionary* (Vol. II, p. 139) says: "According to Herodotus the magi were a tribe of the Medes [I, 101], who professed to interpret dreams, and had the official charge of sacred rites . . . they were, in short, the learned and priestly class, and having, as was supposed, the skill of deriving from books and the observation of the stars a supernatural insight into coming events . . . Later investigations tend rather to make Babylon than Media and Persia the centre of full-blown magianism. 'Originally, the Median priests were not called magi . . . From the Chaldeans, however, they received the name of magi for their priestly caste, and it is thus we are to explain what Herodotus says of the magi being a Median tribe' . . . (J. C. Müller in Herzog's Encl.)."—Edited by P. Fairbairn, London, 1874.

Rightly, then, Justin Martyr, Origen, and Tertullian, when reading Matthew 2:1, thought of *ma'goi* as astrologers. Wrote Tertullian ("On Idolatry," IX): "We know the mutual alliance of magic and astrology. The interpreters of the stars, then, were the first . . . to present Him [Jesus] 'gifts.'" (*The Ante-Nicene Fathers*, 1957, Vol. III, p. 65) The name Magi became current "as a generic term for astrologers in the East."—*The New Funk & Wagnalls Encyclopedia*, 1952, Vol. 22, p. 8076.

So the circumstantial evidence is strong that the *ma'goi* who visited the infant Jesus were astrologers. Thus *The New Testament* translated by C. B. Williams reads "star-gazers," with a footnote in explanation: "This is, students of stars in relation to events on earth." Fittingly, then, modern English translations read "astrologers" at Matthew 2:1.—*AT, NE, NW, Ph.*

How many of these astrologers "from eastern parts" brought "gold and frankincense and myrrh" to the child Jesus is not disclosed; there is no factual basis for the traditional notion that there were three. (Mt 2:1, 11) As astrologers, they were servants of false gods and were, wittingly or unwittingly, led by what appeared to them as a moving "star." They alerted Herod to the fact that the "king of the Jews" had been born, and Herod, in turn, sought to have Jesus killed. The plot, however, failed. Jehovah intervened and proved superior to the demon gods of the astrologers, so instead of returning to Herod, the astrologers headed home another way after being given "divine warning in a dream."—Mt 2:2, 12.

Liver Divination and Astrology. The practice of 'looking into the liver' appears to have been a special aspect of astrology. (Eze 21:21) A clay model of a liver was found in a temple school in Babylon dating back to the time of Hammurabi. One side of it was divided into areas representing "day" and "night." The edge was divided into 16 parts, and corresponding names of the deities of the heavens were given to each section. So, as this brand of divination divided up the heavens in a purely imaginary way, similarly they divided up the liver of their sacrificial victims. When offering these sacrifices they looked at the liver, considering it a miniature reflection of the heavens, in order to see what omens the gods were revealing to them.—See DIVINATION.

Molech and Astrology in Israel. There is evidence to show that astrology was closely allied with the worship of Molech, a god who was sometimes depicted with a bull's head. The bull was worshiped by the Babylonians, Canaanites, Egyptians, and others as a symbol of their deities —Marduk, Molech, Baal, and so forth. The bull was one of the most important signs of the zodiac, Taurus. The sun-god was often represented by bulls, the horns signifying the rays, and the bull's strong reproductive power, the sun's power as "giver of life." The female, the cow, was given equal honor as a symbol of Ishtar or Astarte, as she was variously called. So when Aaron and Jeroboam introduced in Israel such worship of the bull (calf worship) it was indeed a great sin in Jehovah's eyes.—Ex 32:4, 8; De 9:16; 1Ki 12:28-30; 2Ki 10:29.

The apostate ten-tribe kingdom of Israel was denounced for joining this astrology cult, for "they kept leaving all the commandments of Jehovah their God and proceeded to make for themselves molten statues, two calves, and to make a sacred pole, and they began to bow down to all the army of the heavens and to serve Baal; and they continued to make their sons and their daughters pass through the fire and to practice divination and to look for omens."—2Ki 17:16, 17.

In the two-tribe kingdom to the south wicked King Ahaz and his grandson Manasseh both took the lead in worshiping the star gods and in fiendishly offering up their children to be burned alive as sacrifices. (2Ki 16:3, 4; 21:3, 6; 2Ch 28:3, 4; 33:3, 6) Good King Josiah, however, "put out of business the foreign-god priests" who were "making sacrificial smoke to Baal, to the sun and to the moon and to the constellations of the zodiac and to all the army of the heavens," and he tore down the high places and made Topheth unfit for worship so "that no one might make his son or his daughter pass through the fire to Molech." (2Ki 23:5, 10, 24) Jehovah, by his prophets Zephaniah and Jeremiah, denounced them for their astrological practices, as "those who are bowing down upon the roofs to the army of the heavens," and as those "making sworn oaths by Malcam [Molech]."—Zep 1:5; Jer 8:1, 2; 19:13.

Further showing the interconnection of Molech worship, calf worship, and astrology is Stephen's account of the rebellion of the Israelites in the wilderness. When they cried out to Aaron, "Make gods for us to go ahead of us," Jehovah "handed them over to render sacred service to the army of heaven, just as it is written in the book of the prophets, 'It was not to me that you offered victims and sacrifices . . . But it was the tent of Moloch and the star of the god Rephan that you took up.'"—Ac 7:40-43.

Divine Condemnation of Astrology. A great truth is simply stated: "In the beginning God created the heavens and the earth," including the planets of our solar system and the fixed stars in their constellations. (Ge 1:1, 16; Job 9:7-10; Am 5:8) In such grand creation, however, it was not Jehovah's will that man make gods out of these things. He, therefore, strictly forbade his people to worship "a form like anything that is in the heavens above." (Ex 20:3, 4) Astrology in every form was outlawed.—De 18:10-12.

ASYNCRITUS (A·syn'cri·tus) [Without Compare]. A Christian in Rome to whom the apostle Paul sent a greeting in his inspired letter to the Romans written from Corinth about 56 C.E. (Ro

16:14) Further information on Asyncritus is not provided in the Scriptures; however, archaeological evidence in inscriptions and papyri indicates that the name Asyncritus was used to some extent at that time.

ATAD (A'tad) [Bramble]. A place of uncertain location in the region of the Jordan was called "the threshing floor of Atad." There Jacob's funeral cortege stopped for seven days of mourning while en route from Egypt to the cave of the field of Machpelah in Canaan. Atad may have been a person, but the name itself appears to designate a location. The funeral party included Pharaoh's servants as well as the older men of Egypt, and when the Canaanites saw the mourning rites, they exclaimed: "This is a heavy mourning for the Egyptians!" Hence, the place was called Abel-mizraim, meaning "Mourning of the Egyptians."—Ge 50:7-13.

Various translations (for example, *AS, AT, RS*) use "beyond the Jordan" at Genesis 50:10, 11, and some conclude that the threshing floor of Atad was situated E of the Jordan River. This would mean that the procession took, not a direct, but a circuitous route, around the Dead Sea, which it could have done in order to avoid contact with the Philistines. However, the Hebrew expression *be'e-ver*, translated "beyond," can refer to a region either E or W of the Jordan. From Moses' viewpoint in the land of Moab at the time of the completion of the Pentateuch, "beyond the Jordan" could mean W of the river. Yet, all difficulties are overcome by the *New World Translation,* which accurately renders the Hebrew text "in the region of the Jordan" in these verses.

ATARAH (At'a·rah) [Crown]. One of the wives of Jerahmeel of the tribe of Judah and the mother of Onam.—1Ch 2:3-5, 25, 26.

ATAROTH (At'a·roth) [Crowns [that is, circular enclosures]].

1. A town on the E side of the Jordan, among those requested by the tribes of Gad and Reuben as their possession. The section was considered especially suitable for the livestock of these tribes. (Nu 32:1-5) The town was thereafter rebuilt by the Gadites.—Nu 32:34.

The Moabite Stone of King Mesha also mentions this place, in lines 10 and 11 of the inscription. In part it says: "Now the men of Gad had always dwelt in the land of Ataroth, and the king of Israel had built Ataroth for them; but I fought against the town and took it and slew all the people of the town . . . And I brought back from there Arel (or Oriel), its chieftain . . . and I settled there men of

Sharon and men of Maharith."—*Ancient Near Eastern Texts,* edited by J. B. Pritchard, 1974, p. 320.

The location of this site is generally considered to be present-day Khirbet 'Attarus, E of the Dead Sea and some 13 km (8 mi) NW of Dibon (mentioned after Ataroth in Nu 32:3). The ruins are located on the W slope of a mountain bearing the same name and about 750 m (2,500 ft) high. Although this location is within the territory of Reuben, it appears that there was some mutual sharing of tribal territory between Gad and Reuben.

2. A town along the boundary between the territories of Ephraim and Benjamin. (Jos 16:2) It is evidently the same as Ataroth-addar referred to at Joshua 16:5 and 18:13. In this latter verse it is presented as forming part of the N boundary of Benjamin and as located "upon the mountain that is on the south of Lower Beth-horon."

3. A town on the NE boundary of the tribe of Ephraim.—Jos 16:7.

ATAROTH-ADDAR (At'a·roth-ad'dar) [Crowns [that is, circular enclosures] of Addar]. A town in Ephraim. (Jos 16:5; 18:13) Evidently the same as Ataroth in Joshua 16:2.—See ATAROTH No. 2.

ATER (A'ter) [Closed; Impeded].

1. A man of Israel, 98 of whose sons or descendants returned from Babylonian exile with Zerubbabel in 537 B.C.E. (Ezr 2:1, 2, 16; Ne 7:21) They are listed thus: "The sons of Ater, of Hezekiah, ninety-eight," perhaps indicating that they were offspring of Ater, the descendant of a certain Hezekiah (but probably not the Judean king of that name), or that they were Ater's descendants *through* one Hezekiah. It may be a descendant of this Ater who was one of the headmen of the people attesting by seal the "trustworthy arrangement" of Nehemiah's day.—Ne 9:38; 10:1, 17.

2. A family head whose offspring were among the Levitical "sons of the gatekeepers" of the temple who returned from Babylon to Jerusalem with Zerubbabel.—Ezr 2:42; Ne 7:45.

ATHACH (A'thach). A town of Judah mentioned among the places to which David sent portions of the spoil resulting from his victory over the raiding Amalekites.—1Sa 30:26, 30.

ATHAIAH (A·thai'ah). A man of the tribe of Judah, a descendant of Perez, listed with other residents of Jerusalem in Nehemiah's time, after the release from Babylonian exile.—Ne 11:4-6.

ATHALIAH (Ath·a·li′ah).

1. Queen of Judah, daughter of King Ahab of Israel and his wife Jezebel; granddaughter of Omri. (2Ki 8:18, 26) She was the sister of Israel's King Jehoram, and sister or half sister of the other 70 sons of Ahab, all of whom Jehu ordered killed. (2Ki 3:1, 2; 10:1-9) Athaliah was given in a marriage of political expediency to Jehoram, the eldest son of Jehoshaphat of Judah. (2Ki 8:25-27; 2Ch 18:1) She was the mother of Ahaziah, who in time became king of Judah.

Like her mother Jezebel, Athaliah egged on her husband, Jehoram, to do what was bad in Jehovah's eyes during his eight-year reign. (1Ki 21:25; 2Ch 21:4-6) And like her mother, Athaliah wantonly shed the blood of the innocent. When her wicked son Ahaziah died after a one-year reign, she killed off all the others of the royal line, except the infant Jehoash, who had been hidden by the high priest and his wife, who was Jehoash's aunt. Thereupon Athaliah installed herself as queen for six years, c. 905-899 B.C.E. (2Ch 22:11, 12) Her sons robbed Jehovah's temple of the holy things and offered them up to Baal.—2Ch 24:7.

When Jehoash reached seven years of age, God-fearing High Priest Jehoiada brought the lad out of secrecy and crowned him rightful heir to the throne. Hearing the tumult, Athaliah rushed to the temple and, upon seeing what was happening, cried, "Conspiracy! Conspiracy!" High Priest Jehoiada ordered her taken outside the temple grounds to be executed at the horse gate of the palace; she was perhaps the last of Ahab's abominable house. (2Ki 11:1-20; 2Ch 22:1–23:21) How true it proved to be: "Nothing of Jehovah's word will fall unfulfilled to the earth that Jehovah has spoken against the house of Ahab"!—2Ki 10:10, 11; 1Ki 21:20-24.

2. A Benjamite of the house of Jeroham who dwelt in Jerusalem.—1Ch 8:26-28.

3. Father of one who returned to Jerusalem with Ezra in 468 B.C.E.; of the family of Elam. —Ezr 8:1, 7.

ATHARIM (Ath′a·rim).

The Israelites are reported to have traveled "by the way of Atharim" when journeying to the Promised Land from Kadesh-barnea by way of Mount Hor. (Nu 21:1) They were thereupon attacked by the king of Arad in the Negeb region. Atharim may refer to a place or to a particular route.

ATHENS (Ath′ens) [Of (Belonging to) Athena].

The modern capital of Greece, and its most prominent city in ancient times. It is located toward the southern end of the Plain of Attica, about 8 km (5 mi) from the Aegean Sea, being served by its neighboring seaport Piraeus, with which it was connected in pre-Christian times by long, nearly parallel walls. Its geographic location contributed much to its greatness in history. The mountains surrounding the city provided a natural defense, and the mountain passes were sufficiently far away to avoid the possibility of a surprise land attack. It was also far enough from the sea to be safe from an invading fleet, yet its three natural harbors in neighboring Piraeus were readily accessible from the city.

Cultural and Religious Center. Although Athens enjoyed some military fame as the capital of a small empire and as a strong naval power in the fifth century B.C.E., it was distinguished primarily as the center of Greek learning, literature, and art. It became a university city filled with professors, lecturers, and philosophers, being the home of such famous philosophers as Socrates, Plato, and Aristotle. Four schools of philosophy were established there, the Platonic, Peripatetic, Epicurean, and Stoic (Ac 17:18), and these were attended by students from throughout the empire in Roman times.

Athens was also a very religious city, provoking the apostle Paul's comment that Athenians "seem to be more given to the fear of the deities than others are." (Ac 17:22) According to the historian Josephus, the Athenians were 'the most pious of the Greeks.' (*Against Apion,* II, 130 [11]) The State controlled religion and encouraged it by paying for public sacrifices, rites, and processions in honor of the gods. Idols were to be found in temples, in public squares, and on the streets, and people regularly prayed to the gods before engaging in their intellectual feasts or symposiums, political assemblies, and athletic contests. In order not to offend any of the gods, the Athenians even built altars "To an Unknown God," to which fact Paul refers in Acts 17:23. Second-century geographer Pausanias confirms this, explaining that while he was traveling along the road from Phaleron Bay harbor to Athens (perhaps traversed by Paul on his arrival) he noticed "altars of the gods named Unknown, and of heroes."—*Description of Greece, Attica,* I, 4.

Early History. The city grew up around the Acropolis, an oblong hill about 150 m (500 ft) high, which rises sheer on three sides. (PICTURE, Vol. 2, p. 749) During the seventh century B.C.E. it was ruled by a hereditary nobility or aristocracy known as the Eupatridae, who had a monopoly of the political power and also had control of the Areopagus, the chief criminal court at the time. During the early part of the sixth century B.C.E., however, a legislator named Solon made constitutional reforms that improved the lot of the poor and laid the foundation for a democratic government. However, it was democracy for only the free citizens of the land, as a large section of the population was made up of slaves.

Following victories over the Persians in the fifth century B.C.E., Athens became the capital of a small empire, controlling most of the coastal areas around the Aegean Sea and extending its trade and influence from Italy and Sicily in the W to Cyprus and Syria in the E. The city became the cultural leader of the ancient world, enjoying brilliant achievements in literature and art. At this time many beautiful public buildings and temples were erected, including the Parthenon (the temple of Athena) and the Erechtheum, the ruins of which can still be seen atop the Acropolis in modern Athens. The Parthenon was considered the principal architectural monument of ancient pagan religion and was ornamented by a 9-m (30 ft) gold and ivory statue of Athena.

This material beauty, however, did not produce true spiritual uplift for the Athenians, for the gods and goddesses honored by it were themselves depicted in Greek mythology as practicing every immoral and criminal act known to humans. Thus, in Paul's day, the Greek philosopher Apollonius criticized the Athenians for their orgiastic dances at the Festival of Dionysus (Bacchus) and for their enthusiasm for the shedding of human blood at the gladiatorial contests.

The Athenian Empire dissolved after its defeat by the Spartans in the Peloponnesian wars at the end of the fifth century B.C.E., but its conquerors showed consideration to the city on account of its culture and did not totally ruin it. It was conquered by the Romans in 86 B.C.E. and was stripped of its trade and commerce; so, by the time Jesus and the early Christians came on the Palestinian scene, Athens' importance lay primarily in its universities and schools of philosophy.

Paul's Activity in Athens. In about 50 C.E. the apostle Paul visited Athens on his second missionary tour. He had left Silas and Timothy behind in Beroea with instructions to follow as soon as possible. (Ac 17:13-15) While waiting for them, he became irritated at the many false gods of the city and so began to reason with the people, both in the Jewish synagogue and in the marketplace. (Ac 17:16, 17) In recent years this marketplace, or agora, to the NW of the Acropolis has been fully excavated by the American School of Classical Studies. The agora was evidently not only a location for transacting business but also a place to debate and conduct civic affairs. The inquisitive attitude of the Athenians described in the account at Acts 17:18-21 is reflected in the criticism by Demosthenes of his fellow Athenians for their love of moving around the marketplace continually inquiring, "What news?"

While in the marketplace Paul was accosted by Stoic and Epicurean philosophers and was viewed suspiciously as being "a publisher of foreign deities." (Ac 17:18) There were many sorts of religion in the Roman Empire, but Greek and Roman law prohibited the introduction of strange gods and new religious customs, especially when these were in opposition to the native religion. Paul evidently encountered difficulty due to religious intolerance in the Romanized city of Philippi. (Ac 16:19-24) The inhabitants of Athens proved to be more skeptical and tolerant than the Philippians, but they were still evidently concerned about how this new teaching might affect the security of the state. Paul was taken to the Areopagus, but whether he spoke before the court known as the Areopagus cannot be definitely stated. Some say that in Paul's day the court itself was no longer meeting on the hill but in the agora.

Paul's eloquent testimony before these learned men of Athens is a lesson in tact and discernment. He showed that, instead of preaching about a new deity, he was preaching about the very Creator of heaven and earth, and he tactfully made reference to the "Unknown God," whose altar he had seen, and he even quoted from *Phænomena* by Aratus, a Cilician poet, and from *Hymn to Zeus* by Cleanthes. (Ac 17:22-31) Although the majority ridiculed him, some Athenians, including Areopagus Judge Dionysius and a woman named Damaris, became believers.—Ac 17:32-34.

It is possible that Timothy joined Paul at Athens and was then sent back to Thessalonica; but it appears more likely that Paul sent word to him at Beroea to make this trip, thus leaving Paul without companions in Athens. The expression "we" at 1 Thessalonians 3:1, 2 appears to be used in the editorial sense by Paul as applying simply to himself. (Compare 1Th 2:18; 3:6.) If such was the case, then Paul departed alone from Athens, going on to Corinth, where Silas and Timothy eventually rejoined him. (Ac 18:5) It is likely that Paul revisited Athens on his third missionary tour (55 or 56 C.E.), since the record states that he spent three months in Greece at that time.—Ac 20:2, 3.

ATHLAI (Athʹlai). Son of Bebai; one of the Israelites who dismissed their foreign wives after Ezra came to Jerusalem in 468 B.C.E.—Ezr 10: 28, 44.

ATONEMENT.

The English word "atonement" is derived from the expression "at one" and, as applied Biblically, means a covering of sins. In the Hebrew Scriptures terms pertaining to atonement appear many times, especially in the books of Leviticus and Numbers. *Ka·phar'* is the Hebrew word for making atonement, and probably it originally meant "cover," though "wipe off" has also been suggested.

Man's Need for Atonement. Man is in need of sin covering, or atonement, due to inherited sin (1Ki 8:46; Ps 51:5; Ec 7:20; Ro 3:23), responsibility for which rests, not with God, but with man himself. (De 32:4, 5) Adam, who lost everlasting life in human perfection, bequeathed sin and death to his offspring (Ro 5:12), and Adam's descendants therefore came under condemnation to death. If humankind was to regain the opportunity to enjoy everlasting life, then, in harmony with a legal principle that Jehovah later included in the Mosaic Law, namely, that like must go for like, exact atonement would be required for what had been lost by Adam.—De 19:21.

As used in the Bible, "atonement" has the basic thought of "cover" or "exchange," and that which is given in exchange for, or as a "cover" for, another thing must be its duplicate. Thus, anything making satisfaction for something that is lost or forfeited must be "at one" with that other thing, completely covering it as its exact equivalent. There must be no overlapping and no coming short. No imperfect human could provide such a covering or atonement to restore perfect human life to any or all of mankind. (Ps 49:7, 8) To make adequate atonement for what was forfeited by Adam, a sin offering having the precise value of a perfect human life would have to be provided.

Jehovah God instituted an arrangement for atonement among the Israelites that typified a greater atonement provision. It is Jehovah and not man who is to be credited with determining and revealing the means of atonement for covering inherited sin and providing relief from the resulting condemnation to death.

Atonement Sacrifices. As God directed, the Israelites were to offer sacrifices as sin offerings in order to make atonement. (Ex 29: 36; Le 4:20) Of particular significance was the annual Atonement Day, when Israel's high priest offered animal sacrifices and made atonement for himself, for the other Levites, and for the nonpriestly tribes of Israel. (Le 16) Sacrificial animals were to be unblemished, indicating the necessity of perfection on the part of their antitype. Also, that atonement is a costly matter is shown in that the victim's life was given, its blood being shed to make atonement. (Le 17:11) Sin offerings made by the Israelites and the various features of the yearly Day

Modern-day Athens with its prominent hill known as Lycabettus

of Atonement undoubtedly impressed upon their minds the seriousness of their sinful state and their great need of complete atonement. However, animal sacrifices could not completely atone for human sin because beasts are inferior to man, who was given dominion over them.—Ge 1:28; Ps 8:4-8; Heb 10:1-4; see ATONEMENT DAY; OFFERINGS.

Fulfillment in Christ Jesus. The Christian Greek Scriptures plainly link complete atonement for human sins with Jesus Christ. In him the types and shadows of the Mosaic Law find fulfillment, since he is the very One to whom the various animal sacrifices thereof pointed forward. As a perfect, sinless human, Jesus was the sin offering for all of Adam's descendants who eventually are delivered from inherited sin and death. (2Co 5:21) Christ "offered one sacrifice for sins perpetually" (Heb 10:12), and he is unquestionably "the Lamb of God that takes away the sin of the world." (Joh 1:29, 36; 1Co 5:7; Re 5:12; 13:8; compare Isa 53:7.) Forgiveness is dependent on the pouring out of blood (Heb 9:22), and Christians who are walking in the light are assured that "the blood of Jesus [God's] Son cleanses us from all sin."—1Jo 1:7; Heb 9:13, 14; Re 1:5.

Jesus' perfect human life offered in sacrifice is the antitypical sin offering. It is the valuable thing that accomplishes the purchase of mankind, redeeming them from inherited sin and death. (Tit 2:13, 14; Heb 2:9) Christ himself declared: "The Son of man came, not to be ministered to, but to minister and to give his soul a ransom [Gr., *ly'-tron*] in exchange for many." (Mr 10:45; see RANSOM.) His sacrifice atoned exactly for what was forfeited by the sinner Adam, since Jesus was perfect and hence Adam's equal prior to the first man's sin.—1Ti 2:5, 6; Eph 1:7.

Reconciliation made possible. Human sin causes division between God and man, for Jehovah does not approve of sin. The breach between man and his Creator could be healed only by fulfillment of the requisite of a true "covering," or atonement, for such sin. (Isa 59:2; Hab 1:13; Eph 2:3) But Jehovah God has made reconciliation between himself and sinful mankind possible through the perfect man Jesus Christ. Thus, the apostle Paul wrote: "We are also exulting in God through our Lord Jesus Christ, through whom we have now received the reconciliation." (Ro 5:11; see RECONCILIATION.) To come into Jehovah's favor, it is necessary to accept God's provision for reconciliation through Jesus Christ. Only by this means is it possible to come into a position comparable to that of Adam prior to his sin. God's love is dis-

played in making such reconciliation possible. —Ro 5:6-10.

Justice satisfied by propitiation. Still, justice required satisfaction. Man, though created perfect, fell from that state through sin and thus Adam and his offspring came under God's condemnation. Justice and fidelity to principles of righteousness necessitated that God execute the sentence of his law against disobedient Adam. But love moved God to purpose a substitutional arrangement whereby justice would be satisfied, and yet without any violation of justice, repentant offspring of sinner Adam could be forgiven and could achieve peace with God. (Col 1:19-23) Therefore, Jehovah "sent forth his Son as a propitiatory sacrifice for our sins." (1Jo 4:10; Heb 2:17) Propitiation is that which makes propitious, or favorable. Jesus' propitiatory sacrifice removes the reason for God to condemn a human creature and makes possible the extending to him of God's favor and mercy. This propitiation removes the charge of sin and the resulting condemnation to death in the case of spiritual Israel and all others availing themselves of it.—1Jo 2:1, 2; Ro 6:23.

The idea of substitution is prominent in certain Biblical texts relating to atonement. For instance, Paul observed that "Christ died for our sins according to the Scriptures" (1Co 15:3), and that "Christ by purchase released us from the curse of the Law by becoming a curse instead of us [Jews], because it is written: 'Accursed is every man hanged upon a stake.'" (Ga 3:13; De 21:23) Peter commented: "He himself bore our sins in his own body upon the stake, in order that we might be done with sins and live to righteousness. And 'by his stripes you were healed.'" (1Pe 2:24; Isa 53:5) Peter also wrote: "Christ died once for all time concerning sins, a righteous person for unrighteous ones, that he might lead you to God."—1Pe 3:18.

Loving provision calls for response of faith. Love has been exemplified by God and Christ in connection with the provision of complete atonement for inherited human sins. (Joh 3:16; Ro 8:32; 1Jo 3:16) However, to benefit therefrom a person must be truly repentant and he must exercise faith. Jehovah was not pleased with Judah's sacrifices when offered without the proper attitude. (Isa 1:10-17) God sent Christ forth "as an offering for propitiation through faith in his blood." (Ro 3:21-26) Those who in faith accept God's provision for atonement through Jesus Christ can gain salvation; those who spurn it cannot. (Ac 4:12) And, for any who "practice sin willfully after having received the accurate knowledge of the truth, there is no longer any sacrifice for sins left, but there is a certain fearful expectation of judgment." —Heb 10:26-31.

ATONEMENT DAY.

The Day of Atonement (Heb., *yohm hak·kip·pu·rim',* "day of the coverings") was one of propitiation or sin covering, commemorated by Israel on the tenth day of the seventh month of the sacred year, or on Tishri 10. (Tishri corresponds approximately to September-October.) On this day Israel's high priest offered sacrifices as a sin covering for himself, for the other Levites, and for the people. It was also a time for cleansing the tabernacle or the later temples from the polluting effects of sin.

The Atonement Day was a time of holy convention and of fasting, as is indicated by the fact that the people were then to 'afflict their souls.' This was the only fast enjoined under the Mosaic Law. It was also a sabbath, a time to abstain from regular labors.—Le 16:29-31; 23:26-32; Nu 29:7; Ac 27:9.

On only one day a year, on the Atonement Day, was the high priest permitted to enter the Most Holy compartment of the tabernacle or of the temple. (Heb 9:7; Le 16:2, 12, 14, 15) The Jubilee year, when due, began with the Day of Atonement.—Le 25:9.

Moses' brother Aaron was Israel's high priest when this observance was instituted in the wilderness of the Sinai Peninsula in the 16th century B.C.E. What he was instructed to do furnished the pattern for later observances of the Atonement Day. Visualizing the impressive events of the day makes possible a better understanding of what it meant to the Israelites. Undoubtedly they were then moved to greater consciousness of their sinfulness and the need of redemption as well as to a fuller appreciation of Jehovah's abundant mercy in making this arrangement to cover their sins of the past year.

Features of the Atonement Day. Aaron was to come into the holy place with a young bull for a sin offering and a ram for a burnt offering. (Le 16:3) On the Atonement Day he set aside his regular priestly garb, bathed in water, and dressed himself in holy linen garments. (Le 16:4) Lots were next drawn by the high priest over two goats (male kids) that were exactly alike in their sound and unblemished condition, these having been obtained from the assembly of the sons of Israel. (Le 16:5, 7) The high priest drew lots over them to determine which of the two would be sacrificed to Jehovah as a sin offering and which would be released in the wilderness, bearing their sins as the 'goat for Azazel.' (Le 16:8, 9; compare

14:1-7; see AZAZEL.) He then sacrificed the young bull as a sin offering for himself and his house, which included the entire tribe of Levi, of which his household was a part. (Le 16:6, 11) He thereafter took perfumed incense and the fire holder full of burning coals from off the altar and went inside the curtain, entering the Most Holy. The incense was burned in this innermost room, where the ark of the testimony was located, the cloud of the burning incense overspreading the golden Ark cover on which were two cherubs fashioned in gold. (Le 16:12, 13; Ex 25:17-22) This act paved the way for Aaron afterward to reenter the Most Holy safely.

Aaron, returning from the Most Holy, obtained some of the bull's blood, entered this compartment with it, and spattered some of the blood with his finger seven times in front of the Ark cover on the E side. Thus was completed the atonement for the priesthood, which rendered the priests clean and able to mediate between Jehovah and his people.—Le 16:14.

The goat on which the lot fell "for Jehovah" was sacrificed as a sin offering for the people. (Le 16:8-10) The high priest then took the blood of the goat for Jehovah into the Most Holy, using it there to make atonement for the 12 nonpriestly tribes of Israel. In a manner similar to the handling of the bull's blood, the blood of the goat was sprinkled "toward the cover and before the cover" of the Ark.—Le 16:15.

By these means Aaron also made atonement for the holy place and the tent of meeting. Then, taking some of the blood of the bull and of the 'goat for Jehovah,' he made atonement for the altar of burnt offering, putting some of such blood upon the horns of the altar. He was also to "spatter some of the blood upon it with his finger seven times and cleanse it and sanctify it from the uncleannesses of the sons of Israel."—Le 16:16-20.

The high priest now turned his attention to the remaining goat, the one for Azazel. He laid his hands upon its head, confessed over it "all the errors of the sons of Israel and all their revolts in all their sins," put these upon its head, and then sent it away "by the hand of a ready man into the wilderness." Thus, the goat carried the errors of the Israelites into the wilderness, where it disappeared. (Le 16:20-22) Thereafter the man who led the goat away had to wash his garments and bathe his flesh in water before reentering the camp.—Le 16:26.

Aaron now came into the tent of meeting, stripped off the linen garments, bathed, and put on his usual attire. He next rendered up his burnt offering and the people's burnt offering (using the rams mentioned in Le 16:3, 5) and made atonement, and he made the fat of the sin offering smoke upon the altar. (Le 16:23-25) Jehovah God always claimed the fat of a sacrifice for himself, and the Israelites were prohibited from eating it. (Le 3:16, 17; 4:31) The remains of the carcasses of the bull and the goat of the sin offering were taken from the court of the tabernacle to a place outside the camp, where they were burned. The one doing the burning had to wash his garments and bathe his flesh in water, after which he could come into the camp. (Le 16:27, 28) Additional sacrifices of the day are mentioned at Numbers 29:7-11.

Cessation of Legitimate Observance. While adherents of Judaism still celebrate the Day of Atonement, such celebration has little resemblance to that instituted by God, for they have no tabernacle, no altar, no ark of the covenant, there is failure to sacrifice bulls and goats, and there exists no Levitical priesthood. Christians, however, realize that servants of Jehovah are now under no such obligation. (Ro 6:14; Heb 7:18, 19; Eph 2:11-16) Furthermore, the destruction of Jerusalem's temple in 70 C.E. forced the cessation of services of the true Levitical priesthood, and there is now no way to establish who could properly act as such priests. *The Encyclopedia Americana* (1956, Vol. XVII, p. 294) states concerning the Levites: "After the destruction of the temple in the dispersion, they disappeared from history, being merged in the crowd of captives scattered over the Roman world."

Antitypical Fulfillment. When it was suitably observed, the annual Atonement Day, like other features of the Mosaic Law, served as a picture of something far greater. Careful examination of this observance in the light of the apostle Paul's inspired remarks shows that Jesus Christ and his redemptive work in behalf of mankind were typified by Israel's high priest and by the animals used in connection with the ceremony. In his letter to the Hebrews, Paul shows that Jesus Christ is the great antitypical High Priest. (Heb 5:4-10) The apostle also indicates that the high priest's entry into the Most Holy one day a year with the blood of sacrificial animals foreshadowed the entrance of Jesus Christ into heaven itself with his own blood, thus to make atonement for those exercising faith in his sacrifice. Of course, Christ, being sinless, did not have to offer sacrifice for any personal sins, as did Israel's high priest.—Heb 9:11, 12, 24-28.

Aaron sacrificed the bull for the priests and the rest of the tribe of Levi, sprinkling its blood in the Most Holy. (Le 16:11, 14) Christ comparably presented the value of his human blood to God in heaven, where it could be applied to benefit those who would come to rule with him as priests and kings. (Re 14:1-4; 20:6) The goat for Jehovah was also sacrificed and its blood was spattered before the Ark in the Most Holy, this to benefit Israel's nonpriestly tribes. (Le 16:15) Similarly, the one sacrifice of Jesus Christ also benefits mankind aside from priestly spiritual Israel. Two goats were needed, for just one goat could not serve as a sacrifice and still be used to carry away the sins of Israel. Both goats were referred to as one sin offering (Le 16:5) and were treated similarly until the casting of lots over them, which indicates that together they formed one symbol. Not only was Jesus Christ sacrificed but also he carries away the sins of those for whom he died sacrificially.

The apostle Paul demonstrated that, while it was not possible for the blood of bulls and of goats to take away sins, God prepared a body for Jesus (which he showed a willingness to sacrifice when presenting himself for baptism), and according to the divine will, Christ's followers "have been sanctified through the offering of the body of Jesus Christ once for all time." (Heb 10:1-10) As the remains of the bodies of the bull and the goat offered on the Day of Atonement were finally burned outside the camp of Israel, the apostle notes that Christ suffered (being impaled) outside the gate of Jerusalem.—Heb 13:11, 12.

Hence it is evident that, while the Jewish Atonement Day did not produce complete and permanent removal of sin even for Israel, the various features of that annual celebration were typical in character. They foreshadowed the grand atonement made for sins by Jesus Christ, the High Priest whom Christians confess.—Heb 3:1; see ATONEMENT; RANSOM.

ATROTH-BETH-JOAB (At′roth-beth-jo′ab) [Crowns [that is, circular enclosures] of the House of Joab]. A name appearing among "the sons of Salma" in the genealogy of the tribe of Judah. (1Ch 2:54) Some consider this to be the name of a town in Judah, pointing to the inclusion of such names as Kiriath-jearim, Beth-gader, Bethlehem, and others in these genealogies. However, the mere correspondency of a name with that of a town is not a certain indication that the town is referred to, since there are numerous instances of persons and towns bearing the same name. Nevertheless, the form or meaning of certain names in the genealogies does seem to be of a geographic nature rather than a personal one. The solution may rest in the view held by many scholars that it is more precisely to the *inhabitants* of the town that reference is made, rather than to the geographic site itself. Thus, the expression "father of" in certain occurrences is understood to mean the "founder of" or "chief settler of" the particular population dwelling in the place indicated.

It may be noted that the word "father" appears in the original Hebrew at Genesis 4:20, 21 but in some translations is rendered "ancestor" (*AT; JB*) or "founder" (*NW*). Hebrew lexicons include among the possible meanings of the Hebrew term "father" that of "ruler, chief" (*A Hebrew and English Lexicon of the Old Testament,* by Brown, Driver, and Briggs, 1980, p. 3), "forefather, ancestor of tribe, nation . . . of a place . . . founder of a class or station, . . . of a trade . . . founder, chief magistrate of a place." (*Lexicon in Veteris Testamenti Libros,* by L. Koehler and W. Baumgartner, Leiden, 1958, p. 1)—Compare Isa 22:20-22.

ATROTH-SHOPHAN (At'roth-sho'phan) [Crowns [that is, circular enclosures] of Shophan]. A city rebuilt by the tribe of Gad from among those captured from the realms of Kings Sihon and Og.—Nu 32:33, 35.

ATTAI (At'tai) [shortened form of Athaiah].

1. Grandson of Sheshan, a descendant of Judah through Hezron. Sheshan had daughters only, one of whom he gave in marriage to his Egyptian slave Jarha, who fathered Attai. In turn Attai was the father of a certain Nathan.—1Ch 2:25, 34-36.

2. One of the 11 valiant Gadites who crossed the overflowing Jordan to join David's army in the wilderness.—1Ch 12:8, 11-15.

3. Second of the four sons that Rehoboam's favorite wife Maacah, the granddaughter of Absalom, bore to him. Attai was therefore grandson of Solomon and brother of King Abijah (Abijam). —2Ch 11:20, 21.

ATTALIA (At·ta·li'a) [Of (Belonging to) Attalus]. At the close of Paul's first missionary tour he embarked from the seaport town of Attalia on the coast of Pamphylia in Asia Minor, heading for Antioch in Syria, about 500 km (300 mi) distant. —Ac 14:24-26.

Attalia, modern Antalya, was founded by Attalus II, king of Pergamum (159-138 B.C.E.), at the mouth of the Cataractes River. It became the chief port of the province of Pamphylia, serving as an outlet for the rich interior region of SW Phrygia and being the natural point of embarkation from central Asia Minor to Syria and Egypt. Although it was originally the port for the nearby city of Perga, which lies about 13 km (8 mi) inland, Attalia had displaced that city in importance in apostolic times.

ATTITUDES AND GESTURES. The Scriptures richly abound in references to forms of posture and gestures, the descriptions in the Bible being sufficient to show that they were much the same as those practiced in the Middle East today. These Orientals are considerably more demonstrative and less inhibited in the expression of their feelings than are many of the Western peoples. Either accompanied by words or without words, attitudes and gestures carried considerable force and meaning.

Prayer and Homage. *Standing.* Among the Hebrews and many of the other nations mentioned in the Bible, there was no set form of posture for prayer. All the attitudes assumed were highly respectful. Standing was a common posture. Jesus spoke of this position for prayer. (Mr 11:25) Immediately after being baptized, Jesus was evidently standing and praying when the heaven was opened up and the holy spirit in bodily shape like a dove came down upon him, and God's own voice was heard from the heavens. —Lu 3:21, 22.

Kneeling was a common attitude of prayer. Jesus himself knelt in the garden of Gethsemane. (Lu 22:41) In representing the nation of Israel in prayer Solomon knelt at the inauguration of the temple. (1Ki 8:54) While many of the instances in the Bible use the word "knees" in the plural, it may be that at times a person would kneel upon one knee, as is done sometimes by modern Orientals. —Ac 9:40; 20:36; 21:5; Eph 3:14.

Bowing. The Jews, wherever they were found, when worshiping turned their faces toward the city of Jerusalem and its temple. (1Ki 8:42, 44; Da 6:10) In vision Ezekiel saw 25 men with their backs toward the temple of Jehovah, bowing with their faces toward the E. (Eze 8:16) Temples of the sun worshipers were built in such a manner that the entrance was on the W side, making the worshipers face E on entering. But the temple of Jehovah was built with the entrance in the E so that the worshipers of Jehovah there turned their backs on the place of the rising of the sun.

Extending the arms. In the postures of standing and kneeling, the palms of the hands would sometimes be spread out to the heavens, or the hands would be lifted up or extended forward as in supplication. (1Ki 8:22; 2Ch 6:13; Ne 8:6) The face would sometimes be uplifted (Job 22:26), or a person might lift up his eyes toward the heavens. —Mt 14:19; Mr 7:34; Joh 17:1.

Sitting and prostrating. Sitting was another posture employed in prayer, the petitioner evidently kneeling and then sitting back upon his heels. (1Ch 17:16) From this position he could bow his head or rest it on his bosom. Or, as Elijah did, he might crouch to the earth and put his face between his knees. (1Ki 18:42) 'Falling down' or 'falling on one's face' is often the way the Scriptures express a person's prostrating himself. This was usually done by falling on the knees and bowing forward, resting on the hands or, more often, the elbows, with the head touching the ground. (Ge 24:26, 48; Ne 8:6; Nu 16:22, 45; Mt 26:39) In great sorrow or very fervent prayer the petitioner might actually lie on his face with his body outstretched. In cases of extreme distress, the petitioner might wear sackcloth. (1Ch 21:16) False worshipers also bowed down before their idols. (Ex 20:5; Nu 25:2; 2Ki 5:18; Da 3:5-12) Additionally, false worshipers would often kiss their idols.—1Ki 19:18.

Religious gestures toward an object. Job pointed out the danger of letting one's heart be enticed toward some object of reverence such as the sun or the moon to the point of making a worshipful gesture toward it, perhaps placing one's hand to one's mouth in a kiss the way pagan moon worshipers and those giving homage to idols did. Job realized that this was a denial of the true God and would require an accounting for such error.—Job 31:26-28.

Christian postures for prayer. Jesus prayed publicly, in sincerity, as did Paul and others. He also recommended private prayer. (Mt 6:5, 6) But Jesus condemned ostentatiousness in making long prayers for a pretense, a practice into which some of the scribes had fallen. (Mr 12:40; Lu 20:47) However, Christians adopted many of the customs and practices of the Jewish synagogue—ones that God did not disapprove—and the same attitudes and postures of prayer are mentioned in the Christian Greek Scriptures. Nowhere do they give support to a facial or bodily attitude of assumed piety and sanctimoniousness. They do not make any given posture, such as placing the palms together or clasping the hands when offering prayer, essential. In fact, prayers can be made silently and completely without outward manifestation, when the individual is carrying on an assigned duty or is faced with an emergency. (Compare Ne 2:4.) Christians are told to carry on prayer "with every form of prayer and supplication."—Eph 6:18.

Respect, Humility. *Kneeling.* The attitudes and postures of the Orientals in expressing respect for one another and especially when petitioning superiors were much the same as the attitudes assumed in prayer. We find examples of kneeling in supplication before others. This was not in worship of the person but in acknowledgment of that one's position or office, with deep respect. —Mt 17:14; Mr 1:40; 10:17; 2Ki 1:13.

Bowing was more frequently used in greeting others, in approaching them on a matter of business, or in displaying a high degree of respect. Jacob bowed seven times on meeting Esau. (Ge 33:3) Solomon, even though he was king, showed respect to his mother by bowing to her.—1Ki 2:19.

Bowing could also be a symbol of acknowledgment of defeat. (Isa 60:14) Those persons defeated might appear before their conqueror in sackcloth and, additionally, with ropes upon their heads in an appeal for mercy. (1Ki 20:31, 32) Some think that the ropes mentioned were put about their necks to symbolize their captivity and submission.

Although it was a common thing for the Jews to bow before authority to show respect, Mordecai refused to bow before Haman. This was because Haman, as an Agagite, was very likely an Amalekite, concerning whom Jehovah had said that he would completely wipe out their remembrance from under the heavens and that he would have war with Amalek from generation to generation. (Ex 17:14-16) Since bowing down or prostration would have a connotation of peace toward Haman, Mordecai refused to perform this act, because he would have violated God's command in doing so. —Es 3:5.

Prostrating. Joshua prostrated himself before an angel, "as prince of the army of Jehovah," not in worship, but in acknowledgment of the superior office the angel held and of the fact that the angel was obviously sent from Jehovah with a command for him.—Jos 5:14.

When Jesus was on earth, persons would prostrate themselves before him to petition and to do obeisance to him, and he did not reprove them. (Lu 5:12; Joh 9:38) This was because he was the appointed King, the King-Designate, as he himself said: "God's royal majesty has approached" (*ED*); "The kingdom of God has drawn near." (*NW*, Mr 1:15) Jesus was the heir to the throne of David and therefore was rightfully honored as a king.—Mt 21:9; Joh 12:13-15.

However, the apostles of Jesus Christ refused to permit others to prostrate themselves before them. This was because, in the instances described, prostration was done as an attitude of worship, as though the power of the holy spirit in the apostles, which performed the healing and other powerful works, were their own. The apostles realized that the power was from God and that credit for these things should be given to him and all worship should be directed toward Jehovah through Jesus Christ, of whom they were merely the representatives.—Ac 10:25, 26.

In connection with the respect paid to Jesus, the word often used is *pro·sky·ne′o,* a word having the basic meaning "do obeisance," but also translated "worship." (Mt 2:11; Lu 4:8) Jesus was not accepting worship, which belongs to God alone (Mt 4:10), but recognized the act of the one doing obeisance as recognition of the authority given Him by God. The angel whom Jesus Christ sent to bring the Revelation to John expressed the principle that man's worship belongs only to God, when he refused to accept worship from John.—Re 19:10; see OBEISANCE; WORSHIP.

Covering the head was a sign of respect on the part of women. This custom was followed in the Christian congregation. In discussing the principle of Christian headship, the apostle Paul stated: "Every woman that prays or prophesies with her head uncovered shames her head . . . That is why the woman ought to have a sign of authority upon her head because of the angels."—1Co 11:3-10; see HEADSHIP.

Removing one's sandals was a gesture of respect or reverence. Moses was commanded to do this at the burning bush and Joshua in the presence of an angel. (Ex 3:5; Jos 5:15) Since the tabernacle and the temple were holy places, the priests are said to have performed their duties at the sanctuary barefoot. Likewise, the loosening of the laces of another person's sandals or bearing his sandals for him was considered a menial duty and an expression of one's humility and consciousness of insignificance when contrasted with his master. It is still a practice in the Middle East that when one enters a house, his sandals are taken off, sometimes by a servant.—Mt 3:11; Joh 1:27; see SANDAL.

Pouring water on another's hands. Elisha was identified as the minister or servant of Elijah by the expression "[he] poured out water upon the hands of Elijah." This was a service performed particularly after meals. In the Middle East it was not the custom to use knives and forks, but fingers, and the servant would afterward pour water over the hands of his master for washing. (2Ki 3:11) A similar practice was the washing of feet, performed as an act of hospitality, also of respect and, in certain relationships, of humility.—Joh 13:5; Ge 24:32; 43:24; 1Ti 5:10.

Agreement, Sharing Together. *Handshaking* and *striking the palms* of the hands were gestures employed to express agreement, ratification, or confirmation of a contract or bargain. (Ezr 10:19) The Scriptures warn against doing this in guaranteeing security of a loan for another person. (Pr 6:1-3; 17:18; 22:26) Joint participation, or sharing together, was also denoted by a handshake or grasping of another's hand.—2Ki 10:15; Ga 2:9.

Blessing. *Putting hands on head; lifting hands.* Since the Hebrew word *ba·rakh′* has to do with bending the knees and kneeling as well as blessing, it is probable that, when receiving a blessing, persons knelt down and bowed themselves toward the one giving the blessing. Then the one blessing would put his hands on the head of the one being blessed. (Ge 48:13, 14; Mr 10:16) In bestowing a blessing upon a group of people, it was common to lift the hands toward them as the blessing was uttered.—Le 9:22; Lu 24:50.

Swearing. *Raising hand; placing hand under thigh.* In making an oath, it was customary to raise the right hand. God speaks of himself as doing this, symbolically. (De 32:40; Isa 62:8) The angel in Daniel's vision raised both his right hand and his left to heaven to utter an oath. (Da 12:7) Another method of confirming an oath was to place one's hand under the other's thigh (hip), as Abraham's steward did in swearing that he would get a wife for Isaac from Abraham's relatives (Ge 24:2, 9), and as Joseph did for Jacob in swearing not to bury Jacob in Egypt. (Ge 47:29-31) The word "thigh" applies to the upper part of the leg from the hip to the knee, in which the femur is located. According to the Jewish rabbi Rashbam, this method of swearing was used when a superior adjured an inferior, such as a master his servant or a father his son, who also owes him obedience. And according to another Jewish scholar, Abraham Ibn Ezra, it was the custom in those days for a servant to take an oath in this manner, placing his hand under his master's thigh, the latter sitting upon his hand. This signified that the servant was under his master's authority.—*The Soncino Chumash,* edited by A. Cohen, London, 1956, p. 122.

Grief, Shame. *Throwing dust on the head; ripping garments; wearing sackcloth.* Grief was usually accompanied by weeping (Ge 50:1-3; Joh 11:35), often by bowing the head sadly (Isa 58:5), by throwing dust on one's head (Jos 7:6), or by sitting on the ground (Job 2:13; Isa 3:26). Grief was often expressed by the ripping of garments (1Sa 4:12; Job 2:12; see RIPPING OF GARMENTS) and sometimes by putting ashes on the head. (2Sa 13:19) When the Jews were condemned to destruction at the hands of their enemies by the order of King Ahasuerus, "sackcloth and ashes themselves came to be spread out as a couch for many." (Es 4:3) Jehovah warned Jerusalem to gird on sackcloth and wallow in ashes for the trouble coming against her. (Jer 6:26) Micah told those of the Philistine city of Aphrah to "wallow in the very dust."—Mic 1:10.

Cutting off or pulling out hair; beating breast. Cutting off the hair (Job 1:20), pulling some of the hair out of one's own beard (Ezr 9:3), covering the head (2Sa 15:30; Es 6:12), covering the mustache (Eze 24:17; Mic 3:7), and laying one's hands on his own head denoted grief or shame, even to the point of being stunned. (2Sa 13:19; Jer 2:37) Some believe that the latter gesture signified that the heavy hand of God's affliction was resting on the mourner. Isaiah walked about naked and barefoot as a sign of the shame to come upon Egypt and Ethiopia. (Isa 20:2-5) Under the feeling of unusual grief or contrition one might beat the breast in grief (Mt 11:17; Lu 23:27), or slap the thigh for regret, shame, and humiliation or mourning.—Jer 31:19; Eze 21:12.

Anger, Ridicule, Insult, Calling Down Evil. *Wagging the head; slapping another's face.* Generally accompanied by words, various gestures denoted strong expressions of anger, animosity, derision, reproach, contempt, and so forth, toward others. Among them were gestures with the mouth and wagging the head or the hand (2Ki 19:21; Ps 22:7; 44:14; 109:25; Zep 2:15), a slap in the face (Job 16:10; Mt 5:39; Joh 18:22), and pulling out the hair of another's beard (Isa 50:6). Jesus suffered the highest forms of indignity before the Jewish high court by being spit on, slapped, having his face covered, and then being hit with fists and taunted with the words: "Prophesy to us, you Christ. Who is it that struck you?" (Mt 26:67, 68; Mr 14:65) Afterward he was given similar treatment by the soldiers.—Mt 27:30; Mr 15:19; Joh 19:3.

Dust throwing was another form of contempt. Shimei employed this against David along with cursing and throwing stones at him. (2Sa 16:13) As an evidence of the fury of the mob as Paul made his defense before them in Jerusalem, they raised their voices, crying out and throwing their outer garments about and tossing dust into the air.—Ac 22:22, 23.

Clapping the hands might be a gesture merely to command attention, as at Joshua 15:18. More often it was a sign of anger (Nu 24:10), contempt or ridicule (Job 27:23; La 2:15), sorrow (Eze 6:11), or animosity, rejoicing at bad that befell a rival, a hated enemy, or an oppressor; it was sometimes accompanied by stamping of the feet.—Eze 25:6; Na 3:19.

Appointing. *Anointing.* Certain gestures were employed to represent an appointment to office or authority. At the inauguration of the

priesthood, Aaron was anointed with the holy anointing oil. (Le 8:12) Kings were anointed. (1Sa 16:13; 1Ki 1:39) King Cyrus of Persia was not literally anointed by a representative of God but was figuratively spoken of as Jehovah's anointed one because of his appointment to conquer Babylon and to release God's people. (Isa 45:1) Elisha was 'anointed' by being appointed but was never literally anointed with oil. (1Ki 19:16, 19) Jesus was anointed by his Father Jehovah, not with oil, but with holy spirit. (Isa 61:1; Lu 4:18, 21) Through him, his spirit-begotten brothers making up the Christian congregation are anointed. (2Co 1:21; Ac 2:33) This anointing appoints, commissions, and qualifies them as ministers of God. —1Jo 2:20; 2Co 3:5, 6; see ANOINTED, ANOINTING.

The laying on of hands was a method of designating the appointment of a person to an office or a duty, as in the case of the seven men who were appointed by the apostles to care for the food distribution in the congregation at Jerusalem. (Ac 6:6) Timothy was appointed to a particular service by the body of older men in the congregation. (1Ti 4:14) Later he was delegated by the apostle Paul to make appointments of others, which he was admonished to do only after careful consideration. —1Ti 5:22.

The laying on of hands also had other significances, one being the acknowledgment of something, as at Exodus 29:10, 15, where Aaron and his sons acknowledged the sacrifices as being offered in their behalf. Similar meaning is found in Leviticus 4:15.

The laying on of hands was also used to designate certain ones to whom benefits or power would flow, as in Jesus' healing (Lu 4:40) and in the holy spirit's coming upon those upon whom Paul laid his hands. (Ac 19:6) This does not mean that the spirit passed through the hands of Paul, but that as Christ's representative, he was authorized to designate, in harmony with the requirements laid down, who would receive gifts of the spirit. (See also Ac 8:14-19.) That it was not necessary to lay on hands to transmit the gifts of the spirit was shown by the fact that in the case of Cornelius and his household the apostle Peter was merely present when they were given holy spirit and the gift of tongues.—Ac 10:44-46.

Favor. *Standing before a superior.* Favor and recognition were represented by standing before an authority, since permission was required to enter into the presence of a king. (Pr 22:29; Lu 1:19; 21:36) At Revelation 7:9, 15 a great crowd is shown as standing before the throne, indicating that they have favored recognition before God.

To speak of *lifting up another person's head* was, at times, a symbolic way of signifying his being raised or restored to favor.—Ge 40:13, 21; Jer 52:31.

Filling Hands With Power. *The filling of the hands of the priests with power* of the priestly office was represented by Moses when, as mediator, he put the various items to be sacrificed on the hands of Aaron and his sons and waved the offering to and fro before Jehovah. The waving to and fro represented constant presentation before Jehovah.—Le 8:25-27.

Friendship. *Kissing; washing feet; anointing head.* Friendship was expressed by a kiss (Ge 27:26; 2Sa 19:39), and on occasions of greater emotion, falling on the neck in embrace along with kissing and tears. (Ge 33:4; 45:14, 15; 46:29; Lu 15:20; Ac 20:37) There were three gestures that were always considered necessary as marks of hospitality toward a guest: kissing him in greeting, washing his feet, and anointing his head.—Lu 7:44-46.

In the reclining manner of eating that was practiced during the days Jesus was on earth, to *lean on another's bosom* was an attitude of intimate friendship or favor, and this was known as the bosom position. (Joh 13:23, 25) This custom was the basis of the illustrations in Luke 16:22, 23 and John 1:18.

Eating another's bread with him was symbolic of friendship and peace toward him. (Ge 31:54; Ex 2:20; 18:12) To turn thereafter to do him harm was considered the vilest treachery. Of this the traitor Judas was guilty.—Ps 41:9; Joh 13:18.

Innocence, and Denial of Responsibility. *Washing hands.* Innocence in a matter or the act of relieving oneself of responsibility was figuratively demonstrated by one's washing one's hands. (De 21:6) In this way the psalmist declares his innocence at Psalm 73:13; see also Psalm 26:6. Pilate tried to evade his responsibility in connection with the death of Jesus by washing his hands before the crowd, saying: "I am innocent of the blood of this man. You yourselves must see to it."—Mt 27:24.

Shaking out the garments. Disclaiming of further responsibility was shown by Paul when he shook out his garments before the Jews in Corinth to whom he had preached and who opposed him, and then said: "Let your blood be upon your own heads. I am clean. From now on I will go to people of the nations." (Ac 18:6) When Nehemiah shook out his "bosom," that is, the bosom of his garment, he was signifying utter casting out by God.—Ne 5:13.

Shaking dust from feet. Shaking the dirt or the dust off of one's feet likewise indicated disclaiming of responsibility. Jesus instructed his disciples to take this action toward a place or city that would not receive them or hear them.—Mt 10:14; Lu 10:10, 11; Ac 13:51.

Joy. *Clapping hands.* Joy was demonstrated by clapping the hands (2Ki 11:12; Ps 47:1) and by dancing, often accompanied by music. (Jg 11:34; 2Sa 6:14) Shouting and singing at work, particularly during the grape harvest, were expressions of happiness or of grateful joy.—Isa 16:10; Jer 48:33.

Opposition. *Waving the hand* (threateningly) against someone indicated opposition.—Isa 10:32; 19:16.

Lifting up one's own head was the figurative description of an attitude having the significance of taking action, usually to oppose, fight, or oppress.—Jg 8:28; Ps 83:2.

Lifting up the hand against someone in authority indicates rebellion against him.—2Sa 18:28; 20:21.

Licking the dust is symbolic of defeat and destruction.—Ps 72:9; Isa 49:23.

Hand or foot on the back of the neck of one's enemies is a figurative way of describing the defeat of an enemy, his being put to rout and fleeing away, being pursued and caught.—Ge 49:8; Jos 10:24; 2Sa 22:41; Ps 18:40.

Taking Authority or Action. *To stand up or to rise* carried with it the significance of taking authority, power, or action. Kings are spoken of as standing up when they take their kingly authority or begin to exercise it. (Da 8:22, 23; 11:2, 3, 7, 21; 12:1) Jehovah is represented as rising up to carry out judgment of the people. (Ps 76:9; 82:8) Satan is described as standing up against Israel when he incited David to take a census of them.—1Ch 21:1.

Girding up of the loins implies preparation for action. This had reference to the custom in Bible times of binding up one's flowing garments with a belt or girdle in order not to be hampered in connection with doing work, running, and so forth.—Job 40:7; Jer 1:17; Lu 12:37; 1Pe 1:13, ftn.

Miscellaneous. *Lying down at feet.* When Ruth wanted to remind Boaz of his position as repurchaser, she came at night, uncovering his feet and lying down by them. When he awoke, she said to him: "I am Ruth your slave girl, and you must spread out your skirt over your slave girl, for you are a repurchaser." Ruth hereby indicated that she was willing to undergo brother-in-law marriage.—Ru 3:6-9.

Appearance when fasting. 'Afflicting one's soul' most likely referred to fasting and could represent mourning, acknowledgment of sins, repentance, or contrition. (Le 16:29, 31; 2Sa 1:12; Ps 35:13; Joe 1:13, 14) When Jesus was on earth, hypocritical persons put on a sad face, disfiguring their faces in order to make a show of "holiness" by fasting, but Jesus told his disciples that when fasting they should grease their heads and wash their faces so that they would appear normal to men, knowing that the Father looks upon the heart. (Mt 6:16-18) Fasting was sometimes practiced by Christians in order for them to give undivided attention to spiritual matters.—Ac 13:2, 3; see FAST.

Laying hand on eyes of deceased. Jehovah's expression to Jacob, "Joseph will lay his hand upon your eyes" (Ge 46:4), was a way of saying that Joseph would close Jacob's eyes after his death, which was ordinarily a duty of the firstborn son. So it seems that Jehovah here indicated to Jacob that the right of firstborn should go to Joseph. —1Ch 5:2.

Whistling. To "whistle at" something represented astonishment or wonderment. Such was the attitude produced in those viewing the awesome desolation of Judah, and later, the fearsome ruin of Babylon.—Jer 25:9; 50:13; 51:37.

It was the custom of kings or men of authority to *lean on the arm* of a servant or one in an inferior position, as did King Jehoram of Israel. (2Ki 7:2, 17) King Ben-hadad II supported himself on the hand of his servant Naaman as he bowed down at the house of his god Rimmon.—2Ki 5:18.

Illustrative Usage. *Washing another's feet.* Jesus employed one of the Oriental customs in an illustrative way when, giving his disciples a lesson in humility and serving one another, he washed his disciples' feet. Peter spoke up, asking him to wash not only his feet but also his hands and his head. But Jesus replied: "He that has bathed does not need to have more than his feet washed, but is wholly clean." (Joh 13:3-10) Here Jesus was referring to the fact that after one had been to the bath he would, on returning from the bath to his house, need only to wash the dust of the road from his sandaled feet. He used this cleanness as figurative of spiritual cleanness.

Walking. Another illustrative expression is "to walk," meaning to follow a certain course of action, as "Noah walked with the true God." (Ge 6:9; 5:22) Those walking with God followed the life course outlined by God and found his favor. The Christian Greek Scriptures, using this same expression, picture the two contrasting courses of action pursued by one before and after becoming a servant of God. (Eph 2:2, 10; 4:17; 5:2) In a similar man-

ner "running" is used to symbolize a course of action. (1Pe 4:4) God said that the prophets in Judah "ran" though not sent by him, meaning that they took the prophetic course falsely, unauthorized. (Jer 23:21) Paul describes the Christian course in terms of "running." He likens it to a race that a person must run according to the rules in order to win the prize.—1Co 9:24; Ga 2:2; 5:7.

AUGUSTUS (Au·gus'tus) [August One]. This title was given to Gaius Octavius. Later Roman emperors also assumed the title (Ac 25:21, 25), but by itself when used as a name, it refers to Octavius, the first emperor of the Roman Empire.

In September, 31 B.C.E., 13 years after the assassination of his great-uncle Julius Caesar, Octavius emerged the undisputed ruler of the Roman Empire. He declined the titles "king" and "dictator" but accepted the special title "Augustus" bestowed upon him by the Senate, January 16, 27 B.C.E. After the death of Lepidus in 12 B.C.E., Augustus assumed the title "Pontifex Maximus." With his rise in power he made reforms in government, reorganized the army, established the Praetorian Guard (Php 1:13), and built and repaired many temples.

In 2 B.C.E. "a decree went forth from Caesar Augustus for all the inhabited earth to be registered; and all people went traveling to be registered, each one to his own city." (Lu 2:1, 3) This decree resulted in Jesus' being born in Bethlehem in fulfillment of Bible prophecy. (Da 11:20; Mic 5:2) Aside from this registration of the people for taxation and army conscription, appointment of governors in some provinces, and execution of the death penalty, Augustus interfered very little with local government. His policy, which continued after his death, granted the Jewish Sanhedrin sweeping powers. (Joh 18:31) This imperial leniency gave the subjects less provocation to rebel.

Augustus had little choice for a successor. His nephew, two grandsons, a son-in-law, and a stepson all died, leaving only his stepson Tiberius. Augustus died August 17, 14 C.E. (August 19, Julian calendar), the month he had named after himself.

AUGUSTUS, BAND OF. When, as a result of his appeal to Caesar, the apostle Paul was sent to Rome, he was put under the charge of an army officer (centurion) of "the band of Augustus" named Julius. (Ac 27:1) The transmission of Paul and other prisoners to the army officer's charge took place at Caesarea.—Ac 25:13; 26:30–27:1.

It is not possible to identify positively "the band of Augustus" from which Julius came. Because the word "Augustus" here translates the Greek word *Se·ba·ste'*, some have endeavored to identify the band with Samaria, which at that time was called Sebaste, and thus they claim this was a body of soldiers drawn from Samaritan recruits. Josephus does mention "a troop of cavalry known as 'Sebastenians.'" (*The Jewish War*, II, 236 [xii, 5]) However, there does not seem to be much justification for placing such a construction on this term as used by the writer of Acts.

Another view is that the Augustan band refers to the *frumentarii,* a special imperial corps of officers who served as a sort of liaison department of couriers between the emperor and the military establishments in the provinces, and whose members are said to have acted in conducting prisoners. This view, in part at least, seeks support in the *King James Version* rendering of Acts 28:16, which includes a doubtful portion stating that "the centurion delivered the prisoners to the captain of the guard." Those advancing this view presume this "captain of the guard" to be the chief over the *frumentarii.* This phrase, however, does not appear in most modern translations of the verse.

The *Revised Standard Version* calls this band "the Augustan Cohort," as do a number of other translations. The Greek word *spei'ra* (band), when used in a military sense, generally stood for a Roman *manipulus,* a detachment equal to three "centuries," or up to 300 men. However, the term is also used for a larger body of men and, as used in the Greek Scriptures, is believed to represent a Roman "cohort" (the tenth part of a legion, with from about 400 to about 600 men). In addition to the regular Roman legions made up of Roman citizens and divided into cohorts, there were also second-grade troops or *auxilia,* formed of cohorts recruited from among the Roman subjects (not citizens). These were independent infantry units and generally served along the frontiers of the empire. While the cohorts within the regular Roman legions were not given distinctive names, these auxiliary cohorts were often named. Inscriptions have been found of a *Cohors I Augusta* (Lat.) and *Spei'ra Au·gou'ste* (Gr.), though not necessarily identified with the band under discussion.

AUNT. The sister of one's mother or father; the wife of one's uncle. Only in the Hebrew Scriptures is this kinship mentioned. There, sexual intercourse with such a near relative as an aunt is classified as incest and is strictly forbidden under the Mosaic Law.—Le 18:12-14; 20:19, 20.

Concerning Moses' parents, the Masoretic text reads: "Now Amram took Jochebed his father's sister as his wife." (Ex 6:20; Nu 26:59) Such a marriage at that time was permissible, as it oc-

curred over 80 years before the Law was given. —See JOCHEBED.

AUTHORITIES. See SUPERIOR AUTHORITIES.

AVEN (A'ven).

1. Aven appears in the Hebrew Masoretic text at Ezekiel 30:17 and is so rendered in the *King James Version.* Many modern translations here read "On," the city in Egypt called Heliopolis by the Greeks. The Hebrew consonants for Aven are the same as for On, but the vowel pointing differs. Some commentaries suggest that the change in the vowel pointing was a deliberate play on words in order to express contempt for the idolatrous city of On, the center of Egyptian sun worship. —See ON No. 2.

[2, 3: Hurtfulness; Something Hurtful]

2. At Hosea 10:8 Aven appears in the Hebrew text evidently as an abbreviation for Beth-aven. —Compare Ho 4:15; 5:8; 10:5; see BETH-AVEN No. 2.

3. Amos 1:5 refers to the "valley plain of Aven," and this expression from the Hebrew is rendered "Bikath-aven" in *NW, JP,* and *JB.*—See BIKATH-AVEN.

AVENGER OF BLOOD. In Hebrew this expression is *go·'el' had·dam'.* The Hebrew word *go·'el'* (which has been applied to a blood avenger) is a participle of *ga·'al',* meaning "recover; reclaim; buy back; repurchase; redeem." (Ex 15:13; Ps 69:18; Le 25:25; Isa 43:1; Jer 31:11) In Hebrew law the term applied to the nearest male relative, who was under obligation to avenge the blood of one who had been killed. (Nu 35:19) The term *go·'el'* also designated a kinsman with the right to repurchase (or redeem).—Le 25:48, 49; Ru 2:20, ftn; see REPURCHASE, REPURCHASER.

The avenging of blood is based on the mandate regarding the sanctity of blood and human life stated to Noah wherein Jehovah said: "Your blood of your souls shall I ask back . . . from the hand of each one who is his brother, shall I ask back the soul of man. Anyone shedding man's blood, by man will his own blood be shed, for in God's image he made man." (Ge 9:5, 6) A deliberate murderer was to be put to death by "the avenger of blood," and no ransom was to be accepted for such a murderer.—Nu 35:19-21, 31.

Jehovah will see to it that the innocent blood of all his faithful servants is avenged in due time. —De 32:43; Re 6:9-11.

Jehovah's just laws made a clear distinction between willful and accidental killing. For the latter, cities of refuge were lovingly provided for the protection of accidental manslayers from avengers of blood. (Nu 35:6-29; De 19:2-13; Jos 20:2-9) Also, legal courts were established to hear cases involving questions of bloodguilt.—De 17:8, 9; 2Ch 19:10.

AVITH (A'vith). The royal city or home of Hadad, the fourth king of the Edomites, who defeated the Midianites in battle. (Ge 36:35; 1Ch 1:46) A suggested site is Khirbet el-Jiththeh, located in the ancient Edomite territory between Ma'an and Khirbet el-Bastah, about 100 km (62 mi) SSE of the Dead Sea. The mountain of the same name (Jebel el-Jiththeh) rises there to an elevation of 1,332 m (4,370 ft).

AVRÉKH (A·vrekh'). The term of honor and dignity called out before the chariot of Joseph after Pharaoh made him second in the kingdom. (Ge 41:43) If of Hebrew origin, as the ancient translator Aquila conjectured and as supported by the Latin *Vulgate,* it could mean "bow the knee," and is so translated in many versions. (*AS, KJ, Da, Dy, ER, Ro, RS*) However, this view is rejected by many in favor of similar words in other languages. For example, some think it may be a Babylonian or an Assyrian title of a high official, meaning "seer" or "grand vizier." Some turn to the Coptic and say it means "bow the head"; others observe that the Arabs say something similar in commanding their camels to kneel down. The Syriac *Peshitta* reads: "Father and Ruler!" Other investigators believe that it is strictly Egyptian. Origen, a native of Egypt, and Jerome think it means "a native Egyptian," and because of the disregard Egyptians had for foreigners, they reason that it was a public proclamation of naturalization. A similar expression, appearing in a papyrus finding, means 'your commandment is the object of our desire,' that is, 'we are at your service.'—*The Life and Times of Joseph in the Light of Egyptian Lore,* by H. Tomkins, London, 1891, pp. 49, 50.

The exact meaning of this expression has therefore not yet been determined, hence some versions leave it untranslated. (*NW, JP, JB*) This non-Hebrew custom of making public acclamation before an honored one as he rode through town also finds an example in Esther 6:11, when Mordecai was publicly honored at the command of Persian King Ahasuerus.

AVVA (Av'va). A town in northern Syria, under the control of Assyria in the eighth century B.C.E. Apparently the same as Ivvah.—2Ki 17:24; 18:34; 19:13; Isa 37:13; see IVVAH.

AVVIM (Av'vim).

1. Early settlers in that part of the land of Canaan that lay westward toward Gaza. Forty years after the Exodus, Moses told how, for the most part, these Avvim had been dispossessed by the Caphtorim. (De 2:23) Shortly before Joshua's death, in about the middle of the 15th century B.C.E., a remnant of the Avvim still remained. —Jos 13:1, 3.

2. A city of Benjamin, listed between Bethel and Parah at Joshua 18:21-23. It may have been populated by remaining members of the tribe of the Avvim. It is identified with Khirbet Haiyan (Horvat Hayan), about 4 km (2.5 mi) ESE of Bethel (Beitin), according to F.-M. Abel.—*Géographie de la Palestine,* Paris, 1938, Vol. II, p. 257.

AVVITES (Av'vites). Inhabitants of Avva, who were among the peoples whom the Assyrians used to replace exiled Israelites after capturing Samaria in 740 B.C.E. (2Ki 17:24) All these transplanted inhabitants came to be known as Samaritans. The Avvites, though learning the fear of Jehovah to some degree, nevertheless, made and worshiped the gods Nibhaz and Tartak.—2Ki 17:29-33; see AVVA.

AWE. The Hebrew verbs *ya·re"* (Le 19:30; 26:2) and *'a·rats'* (Ps 89:7; Isa 29:23; 47:12) may convey the sense of awe, or reverential fear. The verb *'a·rats'* often signifies trembling in terror, fear, or awe, or causing such trembling.—Isa 8:12; Ps 10:18; see FEAR.

Discernible evidence of Jehovah's presence filled beholders with awe. When assembled at Mount Sinai, the Israelites saw the descent of a dark cloud, accompanied by thunders, lightnings, and the sound of a horn that became louder and louder. The entire mountain shook, and smoke ascended from it. This display of power filled the Israelites with fear; even Moses trembled. The purpose of this manifestation of Jehovah's glory was to instill the Israelites with a wholesome fear so that they would not sin.—Ex 19:9, 16-19; 20:18, 20; Heb 12:21.

Visionary representations of Jehovah's glory had an awe-inspiring impact. The platform of the celestial chariot, above which the prophet Ezekiel saw the glory of Jehovah, sparkled like awesome ice. High above the heads of the living creatures, which were representations of cherubs, this platform was like a translucent expanse, awesome in size and appearance. Through the translucent platform, the representation of what appeared to be a throne of sapphire stone was visible. The seated form on the throne glowed with the yellow brilliance of electrum in a refiner's fire, the whole form also being surrounded by a similar brightness. This vision of Jehovah's glory moved Ezekiel to fall upon his face in worshipful reverence.—Eze 1:15-22, 25-28.

It is Jehovah alone who should be held in such awe, or reverential fear, so that one is moved to worship him. (Ps 89:7; Isa 29:23) Christians are encouraged to "render God sacred service with godly fear and awe [form of Gr. de'os]." (Heb 12:28) God's servants give evidence of this awe by earnestly striving to please him, recognizing that he will call all to account and render judgment without partiality.—1Pe 1:17; Re 14:7.

Individual humans and nations also may at times inspire a certain sense of awe in others, whether by design or otherwise. For example, the Shulammite made such an overpowering impression on King Solomon that he said she was as awesome as military hosts assembled around banners, prepared for battle. In the record of this, in The Song of Solomon 6:4, 10, the Hebrew term 'a·yom' denotes "awesome" or "fear-inspiring." When the nation of the Chaldeans went forth to battle, it was fear-inspiring. (Hab 1:6, 7) And through the prophet Isaiah, Babylon was prophetically called upon to use her spells and sorceries to strike with awe those coming against her, thus saving herself from calamity. But all efforts at preventing the conquest were to fail. (Isa 47:12-15) Babylon was to fall to the armies under the command of Cyrus the Persian.—Isa 44:24–45:2.

Because of the manner in which Jehovah used Moses and dealt with him, Moses exercised great awesomeness (Heb., moh·ra') before the eyes of God's people. (De 34:10, 12; Ex 19:9) Those with faith had a wholesome fear of Moses' authority. They realized that God spoke by means of him. Regarding Jehovah's sanctuary, too, the Israelites were to be in awe. (Le 19:30; 26:2) This meant that they were to manifest a reverent regard for the sanctuary, carrying out worship in the manner that Jehovah directed and conducting themselves in harmony with all of his commands.

AX. A tool with a bladed head on a handle, used for cutting wood or stone; also used as a weapon.

Several Hebrew and Greek words refer to this tool. The Hebrew word gar·zen', found in the Bible and referring to an ax used to chop wood, is also found in the Siloam inscription for an ax used to excavate stone. (De 19:5; Isa 10:15) According to Koehler and Baumgartner's Lexicon in Veteris Testamenti Libros (Leiden, 1958, p. 650), the Hebrew word sa·ghar', occurring in Psalm 35:3, denotes a "double axe." And at 2 Kings 6:5, 6, the Hebrew word bar·zel', literally meaning "iron," has the meaning of "axhead."

At Revelation 20:4, reference is made to heirs of the heavenly kingdom who were "executed with the ax for the witness they bore to Jesus and for speaking about God." Since the ax was at times used by the political state for execution, this must mean that human governments have judged these loyal servants of God as unworthy to live.

AXIS LORDS. The Hebrew word sera·nim' appears to be a Philistine loanword. (Jos 13:3) It has the same consonants as the Hebrew word for "axles" at 1 Kings 7:30. It is a title that is applied to the five lords ruling the Philistine cities of Gaza, Ashkelon, Ashdod, Ekron, and Gath, apparently because of their being in a coalition or alliance. The Philistines, according to Amos 9:7, came to the coast of Canaan from Crete, near the Aegean Sea, so it is thought by some that this is an Aegean word.

The axis lords dominated Philistia as rulers of individual city-states and as a council of coequals with regard to matters of mutual interest. Achish is called king of Gath. (1Sa 21:10; 27:2) Apparently he was not a king in the usual sense but, rather, was a prince. Consequently the title of 'prince' (Heb., sar) is occasionally applied to these rulers. —1Sa 18:30; 29:2-4.

These officials are frequently found cooperating in some cause. They were called together and, in turn, consulted their priests and diviners as to what to do with the captured ark of the covenant after its presence had brought a severe plague of piles, the axis lords themselves being affected. (1Sa 5:9–6:4) They collaborated when their armies would go up against Israel. (1Sa 7:7) In the case of Samson we see them working together to overcome him. (Jg 16:5) They all gathered at the house of the god Dagon at Gaza to celebrate their capture of Samson, at which time the five axis lords then in power were killed.—Jg 16:21-30.

However, the independent city-states under them never united to form one kingdom subject to one ruler. Instead, the five chief cities with their dependent towns functioned somewhat like a confederacy, an axis. When making decisions that affected them all, the axis lords did what was agreed upon by the majority. This is seen in the decision to reject David and his men from the Philistine army, although Achish, the axis lord of Gath, with whom David had dwelt as a refugee from King Saul, was in favor of David's force being accepted to fight with them against Saul.—1Sa 29:2, 6, 7, 9.

Throughout Israel's history, especially until they were subdued by David, they were the determined enemies of Jehovah's people and entered many times into alliance with other nations against Israel, often having Israel under oppressive domination. David reduced their power so that they were no longer a major threat. After David's time, the term "axis lords" is no longer found, but the term "king" is applied to their rulers.—Jer 25:20; Zec 9:5; see PHILISTIA, PHILISTINES.

'AYIN [ע] ('a'yin). The 16th letter of the Hebrew alphabet. The Greek vowel *o'mi·kron* ("o") is derived from 'a'yin; however, the Hebrew letter is not a vowel but a *consonant*. It represents a peculiar guttural sound pronounced at the back of the throat and has no equivalent in English. It is transliterated as '. It appears as the initial letter in each of the verses of Psalm 119:121-128, Hebrew text.

AZALIAH (Az·a·li'ah) [Jehovah Has Proved Himself Distinguished]. Son of Meshullam and father of Shaphan the secretary of the house of Jehovah.—2Ki 22:3; 2Ch 34:8.

AZANIAH (Az·a·ni'ah) [Jah Has Given Ear]. Father of the Levite Jeshua; his descendant, if not he himself, lived in Nehemiah's time.—Ne 10:9.

AZAREL (Az'ar·el) [God Has Helped].
  1. One of the mighty men who joined David at Ziklag.—1Ch 12:1, 6.
  2. Head of the 11th of the 24 divisions of temple singers in David's time; also called Uzziel.—1Ch 25:1, 4, 18.
  3. Son of Jeroham and prince of the tribe of Dan under David's rule.—1Ch 27:22; 28:1.
  4. One of the descendants of Binnui who, at Ezra's urging, sent away their foreign wives and sons.—Ezr 10:19, 38-41, 44.
  5. Father or ancestor of the Amashsai who dwelt in Jerusalem under Governor Nehemiah. He was of the priestly house of Immer.—Ne 11:1, 13.
  6. A musician in the procession headed by Ezra as they walked atop Jerusalem's rebuilt wall at its inauguration. Perhaps the same as No. 5 above. —Ne 12:31, 36.

AZARIAH (Az·a·ri'ah) [Jehovah Has Helped].
  1. A descendant of Judah by Tamar; of the house of Ethan.—1Ch 2:4, 6, 8.
  2. A Levite through Kohath; son of Zephaniah and forefather of the prophet Samuel.—1Ch 6:33, 36.
  3. A descendant of Aaron in the line of Eleazar; son of Ahimaaz.—1Ch 6:9.
  4. One of Solomon's princes. (1Ki 4:2) He is referred to as the son of Priest Zadok; he may be the brother of Ahimaaz.—1Ch 6:8.

  5. Son of Nathan; the prince that Solomon appointed head over the 12 food-supply deputies of the king's household.—1Ki 4:5, 7, 19.
  6. A prophet, son of Oded, who helped arouse Asa in 963 B.C.E. to "search for Jehovah." As a result, the king removed "the disgusting things" from all the land and brought the people into an oath-bound covenant, so that "anyone that would not search for Jehovah the God of Israel should be put to death."—2Ch 15:1-15.
  7, 8. Two of Jehoshaphat's seven sons, listed second and fifth. They were given many gifts and fortified cities by their father, but when their elder brother, Jehoram, became king, these sons were killed. (2Ch 21:1-4) "It seems far-fetched to suppose [as some have] that the name was used twice because the boys were only half brothers or because one had already died in infancy." (*The Interpreter's Dictionary of the Bible,* edited by G. A. Buttrick, 1962, Vol. 1, p. 325) It is unusual for two brothers to have apparently the same name, but in Hebrew there is a slight difference between the two in spelling and pronunciation, 'Azar·yah' ("Jah Has Helped") and 'Azar·ya'hu ("Jehovah Has Helped").
  9. Son of a certain Jehu and father of Helez; of the tribe of Judah, seven generations removed from his Egyptian forefather Jarha.—1Ch 2:3, 34-39.
  10. King of Judah, the youngest son of Jehoram and Athaliah; also called Jehoahaz and Ahaziah. —2Ki 8:25-29; 2Ch 21:17; 22:1, 6; see AHAZIAH No. 2.
  11. Son of Jeroham. One of the five chiefs of hundreds who helped overthrow usurper Athaliah and place Jehoash on the throne of Judah in 898 B.C.E.—2Ch 23:1-15.
  12. Son of Obed. One of the five chiefs of hundreds who helped enthrone Jehoash in place of usurper Athaliah, 898 B.C.E.—2Ch 23:1-15.
  13. King of Judah for 52 years (829-778 B.C.E.). Son of Amaziah and Jecoliah. (2Ki 14:21; 15:1, 2) He is called Uzziah in 2 Kings 15:13.—See UZZIAH No. 3.
  14. A high priest, son of Johanan, descendant of Aaron. (1Ch 6:1-10) When King Uzziah presumptuously attempted to offer incense in the temple, perhaps it was this Azariah who then ordered him out, and when he resisted, Jehovah struck the king with leprosy. (2Ch 26:16-21) Some three decades after Uzziah died, during the first year of Hezekiah's reign (745 B.C.E.), Azariah, still serving as high priest (or another bearing the same name), acknowledged Jehovah's blessing on the king's reforms.—2Ch 31:9, 10, 13.

15. A prince of Ephraim, son of Jehohanan. After defeating Judah in the middle of the eighth century B.C.E., Israel was leading 200,000 captives back when Azariah and other princes of Ephraim effected their release and assisted materially in their return.—2Ch 28:5-15.

16. A descendant of Levi through Kohath whose son Joel helped cleanse the temple at the command of Hezekiah in 745 B.C.E.—2Ch 29:1-12, 15.

17. A descendant of Levi through Merari; son of Jehallelel; one of those sharing in temple cleansing as ordered by Hezekiah.—2Ch 29:1-12, 15.

18. Son of Meraioth; an ancestor of Ezra.—Ezr 7:3.

19. Son of Hilkiah the high priest under Josiah and father of Seraiah (2Ki 22:3, 4; 1Ch 6:13, 14); forefather of Ezra the copyist.—Ezr 7:1.

20. Son of Hoshaiah. (Jer 43:2) He is also called Jezaniah (Jer 40:8; 42:1) and Jaazaniah (2Ki 25:23). Azariah was one of the chiefs of the military forces who supported Gedaliah (Jer 40:7-10); one who requested Jeremiah to pray in their behalf for direction (Jer 42:1-3); and, finally, one of "the presumptuous men" who repudiated Jehovah's answer by the mouth of Jeremiah.—Jer 43:1-3.

21. One of the Hebrew youths taken captive to Babylon in 617 B.C.E., whose name was changed to Abednego, probably meaning "Servant of Nebo [a Babylonian god]." (Da 1:3-7) After a special three-year training course, Azariah and his companions (Daniel, Hananiah, Mishael) were found to be "ten times better than all the magic-practicing priests and the conjurers" of Babylon. (Da 1:5, 14-20) First threatened with death (Da 2:13-18), then promoted to the office of administrator (Da 2:49), Azariah's supreme test of loyalty to Jehovah came when he was thrown into a superheated furnace for refusing to worship the image set up by Nebuchadnezzar. (Da 3:12-30) Indeed a man of faith, he is alluded to by the apostle Paul as one who "stayed the force of fire."—Heb 11:34.

22. One who returned to Jerusalem with Zerubbabel in 537 B.C.E. following exile in Babylon. (Ne 7:6, 7) Called Seraiah at Ezra 2:2.

23. One of the priests who lived in Jerusalem following the exile. (1Ch 9:11) In a parallel list (Ne 11:11) the name is Seraiah. Possibly the same as No. 22 above.

24. Son of Maaseiah the son of Ananiah. Under Nehemiah's oversight, he repaired a section of Jerusalem's wall near his home in 455 B.C.E.—Ne 3:23, 24.

25. One appointed by Nehemiah to walk with Ezra and others in the procession upon the rebuilt wall of Jerusalem at its inauguration; perhaps the same as No. 27.—Ne 12:31-36.

26. One of the 13 Levites who assisted Ezra in explaining the Law as it was read to the people. —Ne 8:7, 8.

27. A priest, or the forefather of one, who in the days of Governor Nehemiah attested by seal to the "trustworthy arrangement."—Ne 9:38; 10:1, 2, 8.

AZAZ (A'zaz) [shortened form of Azariah]. A descendant of Jacob's firstborn son Reuben.—1Ch 5:1, 8.

AZAZEL (A·za'zel) [Goat That Disappears]. The word "Azazel" occurs four times in the Bible, in regulations pertaining to Atonement Day.—Le 16:8, 10, 26.

The etymology of this word is disputed. If we hold to the spelling in the Hebrew Masoretic text, 'aza·'zel' seems to be a combination of two root words meaning "goat" and "disappear." Thus the meaning "Goat That Disappears." According to another derivation, based on the belief that there has been a transposition of two consonants, it means "Strength of God." The Latin *Vulgate* renders the Hebrew word as *capro emissario*, that is, "the emissary goat," or "the scapegoat." And the Greek expression used in the *Septuagint* means "the one carrying away (averting) evil."

Two goats (male kids) were obtained from the assembly of the sons of Israel by the high priest for use on the annual Day of Atonement. By the casting of lots, one goat was designated "for Jehovah," and the other "for Azazel." After a bull had been sacrificed for the high priest and his household (doubtless including all the Levites), the goat for Jehovah was sacrificed as a sin offering. However, the goat for Azazel was preserved alive for a time "before Jehovah to make atonement for it, so as to send it away for Azazel into the wilderness." (Le 16:5, 7-10) Atonement for this live goat issued from the blood of the goat for Jehovah, which had just been killed as a sin offering, the life of the flesh being in the blood. (Le 17:11) The blood value, or life value, of the slain goat was thus transferred to the live goat, or the goat for Azazel. Thus, though it was not killed by the priest, this live goat bore upon it a sin-atoning merit or a value of life. The fact that it was presented before Jehovah evidently indicates that he recognized this transfer of merit or sin-atoning power. A correspondency with this was the prescribed manner of cleansing an Israelite who was healed of leprosy, or of cleansing a house healed of that plague. In this case a living bird was dipped in the blood of a bird that had been killed. The living bird was then permitted to fly away, carrying away sin.—Le 14:1-8, 49-53.

Both goats were to be unblemished, sound, and as much alike as possible. Before the casting of lots over them, both goats stood the chance of being selected as the goat for Jehovah. After sacrificing the goat for Jehovah, the high priest laid his hands upon the head of the living goat and confessed the sins of the people over it. This goat was then sent away, being taken into the wilderness by "a ready man." (Le 16:20-22) The goat for Azazel thus symbolically carried off the people's sins of the past year, disappearing with them into the wilderness.

The two goats were referred to as one sin offering. (Le 16:5) Two were used apparently to add emphasis to what was accomplished by this provision to atone for the sins of the people. The first goat was sacrificed. The second, having the sins of the people confessed over it and being sent far away into the wilderness, added force to the forgiveness that Jehovah grants to repentant ones. Psalm 103:12 gives the assurance: "As far off as the sunrise is from the sunset, so far off from us he has put our transgressions."

As the apostle Paul explained, by Jesus' offering of his own perfect human life as a sacrifice for the sins of mankind, he accomplished far more than had been achieved by "the blood of bulls and of goats." (Heb 10:4, 11, 12) He thus served as "the scapegoat," being the 'carrier of our sicknesses,' the one "pierced for our transgression." (Isa 53:4, 5; Mt 8:17; 1Pe 2:24) He 'carried away' the sins of all who exercise faith in the value of his sacrifice. He demonstrated the provision of God to take sinfulness into complete oblivion. In these ways the goat "for Azazel" pictures the sacrifice of Jesus Christ.

AZAZIAH (Az·a·zi'ah) [Jehovah Has Proved Superior in Strength].

1. One of six harpists in the procession that brought the ark of the covenant to Jerusalem. —1Ch 15:21.

2. Father of Hoshea, the prince of the tribe of Ephraim in David's time.—1Ch 27:16, 20, 22.

3. A Levite, one of the ten commissioners appointed by King Hezekiah to bring in the contributions to Jehovah's house.—2Ch 31:12, 13.

AZBUK (Az'buk). Father of prince Nehemiah, who lived at the same time, but is not the same

individual, as the governor and Bible writer.—Ne 3:16.

AZEKAH (A·ze'kah) [from a root meaning "dig up" [that is, hoe]]. A city in the Shephelah region, guarding the upper reaches of the Valley of Elah. The site is identified as Tell Zakariyeh (Tel 'Azeqa), about 26 km (16 mi) NW of Hebron.

The first mention of the city occurs at Joshua 10:5-11 with regard to the combined attack of five Canaanite kings against Gibeon. Joshua and his army, coming to the relief of Gibeon, chased the Canaanite armies "as far as Azekah and Makkedah," a distance of about 30 km (19 mi). The city was thereafter assigned to the tribe of Judah. —Jos 15:20, 35.

During the reign of King Saul (1117-1078 B.C.E.) the Philistines massed their forces between Socoh and Azekah, putting forth Goliath as their champion. When the Israelites arrived, the two armies faced each other across the Valley of Elah until David's surprise victory over Goliath put the Philistines to flight.—1Sa 17:1-53.

At the division of the nation following Solomon's death (c. 998 B.C.E.), King Rehoboam of Judah fortified Azekah along with Lachish and other strategic cities. (2Ch 11:5-10) Excavations made at Tell Zakariyeh reveal the remains of walls and towers and evidence of a fortified citadel at the location's highest point.

When Nebuchadnezzar's Babylonian troops overran the kingdom of Judah (609-607 B.C.E.), Azekah and Lachish were the last two fortified cities to fall before the overthrow of Jerusalem itself. (Jer 34:6, 7) Apparent confirmation of this was revealed by the discovery of the inscribed ostraca called the Lachish Letters, one of them containing the following message, evidently directed by a military outpost to the military commander at Lachish, which reads in part: "we are watching for the signals of Lachish, according to all the indications which my lord hath given, for we cannot see Azekah." (*Ancient Near Eastern Texts,* edited by J. B. Pritchard, 1974, p. 322) If, as seems to be the case, this letter was written at the time of the Babylonian attack, it would indicate that Azekah had already fallen so that no signals were being received from that fortress.

Following the 70-year period of desolation of the land, Azekah was one of the cities resettled by the returning Jewish exiles.—Ne 11:25, 30.

AZEL (A'zel) [Distinguished Man].

1. A descendant of Saul through Jonathan; he had six sons.—1Ch 8:33-38; 9:43, 44.

2. A place mentioned in Zechariah 14:5 as the point to which the valley would reach as a result

of the prophesied cleavage of the Mount of Olives. It must, therefore, refer to a site near Jerusalem, and there may be an echoing of the name in that of the Wadi Yasul (Nahal Azal), which is an afflux to the Kidron Valley from the Mount of Olives.

AZGAD (Az'gad) [Strong Is Gad]. The head of a paternal house, some of whose members returned to Jerusalem with Zerubbabel in 537 B.C.E. (Ezr 2:12; Ne 7:17), and some with Ezra in 468 B.C.E. (Ezr 8:12) It was probably one of his descendants who attested to the "trustworthy arrangement" negotiated by Nehemiah.—Ne 9:38; 10:1, 14, 15.

AZIEL. See JAAZIEL.

AZIZA (A·zi'za) [Strong One]. One of those who, at Ezra's urging, dismissed their foreign wives and sons.—Ezr 10:27, 44.

AZMAVETH (Az'ma·veth) [Death Is Strong].
1. One of David's valiant men who was a Barhumite (Baharumite). (2Sa 23:31; 1Ch 11:33) Possibly the same as No. 2.
2. The father of Jeziel and Pelet of the tribe of Benjamin, who were among the mighty men that joined David's forces at Ziklag. (1Ch 12:1-3) Possibly the same as No. 1.
3. A son of Adiel who, in the days of King David, was in charge of the king's treasures.—1Ch 27:25.
4. A descendant of, and sixth in line from, Saul through Jonathan.—1Ch 8:33-36; 9:39-42.
5. A town situated within the territory of Benjamin, also called Beth-azmaveth. Exiles from there were among those returning after the exile. (Ezr 2:1, 24; Ne 7:28) At the inauguration of the wall of restored Jerusalem, the town provided some of the singers for the occasion. (Ne 12:29) It is identified with modern Hizmeh (Hizma), about 8 km (5 mi) NNE of Jerusalem, between Geba and Anathoth.

AZMON (Az'mon) [Bone Place]. A place forming part of the southern boundary of the Promised Land, between Hazar-addar and the Torrent Valley of Egypt. (Nu 34:3-5; Jos 15:1-4) A suggested location is that of 'Ain el-Qeseimeh, over 13 km (8 mi) NW of Kadesh-barnea. There is a small spring at this location.

AZNOTH-TABOR (Az'noth-ta'bor). A town or location on the southern boundary of the territory of Naphtali. (Jos 19:32, 34) Khirbet Umm Jebeil (Tel Govel), about 4.5 km (3 mi) N of the summit of Mount Tabor, is suggested as the possible location.

AZOR (A'zor) [from Heb., meaning "One Offering Help"]. A postexilic ancestor of Jesus' adoptive father Joseph.—Mt 1:13, 14, 16.

AZRIEL (Az'ri·el) [God Is My Help].
1. Father of prince Jerimoth, tribe of Naphtali, in David's time.—1Ch 27:19, 22.
2. A household head of the half tribe of Manasseh E of the Jordan, one of the "valiant, mighty fellows" whose descendants were permitted to be taken into exile by the Assyrian king Tiglathpileser III because they had turned to worshiping false gods.—1Ch 5:23-26.
3. Father of Seraiah, who was one of the three sent to arrest Baruch and Jeremiah.—Jer 36:26.

AZRIKAM (Az·ri'kam) [My Help Has Risen Up].
1. One of Azel's six sons, a descendant of King Saul through Jonathan of the tribe of Benjamin.—1Ch 8:33-38; 9:44.
2. "The leader of the household" of wicked King Ahaz of Judah. He was killed by the Ephraimite Zichri when King Pekah of Israel battled Judah.—2Ch 28:6, 7.
3. A Levite of the Merari family whose descendant Shemaiah lived in Jerusalem after the return from exile.—1Ch 9:2, 14; Ne 11:15.
4. The third-listed son of Neariah and a descendant of David.—1Ch 3:1, 23.

AZUBAH (A·zu'bah) [Left Entirely; Abandoned].
1. One of the wives of Caleb the son of Hezron.—1Ch 2:18, 19; see JERIOTH.
2. Daughter of Shilhi and mother of King Jehoshaphat son of Asa.—1Ki 22:41, 42; 2Ch 20:31, 32.

AZZAN (Az'zan) [from a root meaning "strong"]. Father of Paltiel, whom Jehovah chose to represent the tribe of Issachar at the division of the Promised Land.—Nu 34:26, 29.

AZZUR (Az'zur) [One Offering Help].
1. Father of the false prophet Hananiah from Gibeon.—Jer 28:1.
2. Father of Jaazaniah, who was one of the "princes of the people" among the 25 men Ezekiel envisioned "scheming hurtfulness and advising bad counsel" against Jerusalem.—Eze 11:1, 2.
3. One of "the heads of the people" whose descendant, if not he himself, attested by seal to Nehemiah's "trustworthy arrangement."—Ne 10:1, 14, 17; 9:38

B

BAAL (Ba′al) [Owner; Master].

1. The fourth-listed son of Jeiel, a Benjamite. —1Ch 8:29, 30; 9:35, 36.

2. A Reubenite whose son Beerah was among those taken captive by the Assyrian king Tiglath-pileser III.—1Ch 5:5, 6, 26.

3. A Simeonite enclave city within the territory of Judah, apparently the same as Baalath-beer and Ramah of the south (or Negeb).—Compare 1Ch 4:32, 33 and Jos 19:7-9.

4. In the Scriptures, the Hebrew word ba′al is employed with reference to (1) a husband as owner of his wife (Ge 20:3); (2) landowners (Jos 24:11, ftn); (3) "owners of the nations" (Isa 16:8, ftn); (4) "confederates" (literally, "owners [masters] of the covenant") (Ge 14:13, ftn); (5) owners or possessors of tangibles (Ex 21:28, 34; 22:8; 2Ki 1:8, ftn); (6) persons or things having something that is characteristic of their nature, manner, occupation, and the like, for example, an archer (literally, "owner of arrows") (Ge 49:23), a "creditor of the debt" (literally, "owner of a debt of his hand") (De 15:2), "anyone given to anger" (literally, "owner of anger") (Pr 22:24), "judicial antagonist" (literally, "owner of judgment") (Isa 50:8, ftn); (7) Jehovah (Ho 2:16); (8) false gods (Jg 2:11, 13).

The term hab·Ba′al (the Baal) is the designation applied to the false god Baal. The expression hab-Be′a·lim′ (the Baals) refers to the various local deities thought of as owning or possessing and having influence over particular places.

The term "Baal" occurs once in the Christian Greek Scriptures, in Romans 11:4, where it is preceded in the Greek text by the feminine article he. Commenting on the use of the feminine article before "Baal" in the Greek Septuagint and Romans 11:4, John Newton wrote in an essay on Baal worship: "Though he is of the masculine gender in the Hebrew, [hab·Ba′al], the lord, yet Baal is called [he Ba′al], = the lady, in the Septuagint; Hos. ii. 8; Zeph. i. 4; and in the New Testament, Romans xi. 4. At the licentious worship of this androgyne, or two-sexed god, the men on certain occasions wore female garments, whilst the women appeared in male attire, brandishing weapons."—Ancient Pagan and Modern Christian Symbolism, by T. Inman, 1875, p. 119.

At times in Israel's history Jehovah was referred to as "Baal," in the sense of his being the

Owner or Husband of the nation. (Isa 54:5) Also, the Israelites may have improperly associated Jehovah with Baal in their apostasy. The latter appears to be borne out by Hosea's prophecy that the time would come when Israel, after going into and being restored from exile, would repentantly call Jehovah "My husband," and no more "My owner" ("My Baal," AT). The context suggests that the designation "Baal" and its associations with the false god would never again pass the lips of the Israelites. (Ho 2:9-17) The bad connotation that appears to have become attached to the Hebrew word ba′al because of its association with the degraded worship of Baal is thought by some to be the reason the writer of Second Samuel used the names "Ish-bosheth" and "Mephibosheth" (bo′-sheth means shame) instead of "Eshbaal" and "Merib-baal."—2Sa 2:8; 9:6; 1Ch 8:33, 34; see Ish-bosheth.

Baal Worship. Little was known about Baal worship aside from the many Scriptural references to it until excavations at Ugarit (the modern Ras Shamra on the Syrian coast opposite the NE tip of the island of Cyprus) brought to light many religious artifacts and hundreds of clay tablets. Many of these ancient documents, now known as the Ras Shamra texts, are thought to be the liturgies of or words spoken by those participating in the rituals at the religious festivals.

In the Ras Shamra texts, Baal (also called Aliyan [the one who prevails] Baal) is referred to as "Zabul [Prince], Lord of the Earth" and "the Rider of the Clouds." This harmonizes with a representation of Baal, showing him as holding a club or mace in his right hand and a stylized lightning flash with a spearhead in his left. He is also depicted as wearing a helmet with horns, suggesting an intimate connection with the bull, a symbol of fertility.

Normally from late April to September there is hardly any rain in Palestine. In October the rains start and continue throughout winter and into April, resulting in abundant vegetation. The changes of the seasons and the resulting effects were thought to come in cycles because of the never-ending conflicts between the gods. The cessation of the rains and the dying of vegetation were attributed to the triumph of the god Mot (death and aridity) over Baal (rain and fertility), compelling Baal to withdraw into the depths of the earth. The beginning of the rainy season was believed to indicate that Baal had awakened to life. This, it was thought, was made possible by the triumph of Baal's sister Anath over Mot, allowing her brother Baal to return to his throne. The mating of Baal with his wife, presumably Ashtoreth, was believed to ensure fertility for the coming year.

The farming and cattle-raising Canaanites probably thought that their engaging in a prescribed ritual, a sort of sympathetic magic, helped to stimulate their gods to action according to the pattern enacted at their religious festivals and was necessary to ensure productive crops and herds in the coming year and to avert droughts, locust plagues, and so forth. Hence Baal's coming to life again to be enthroned and mated with his consort apparently was celebrated with licentious fertility rites, marked by sexual orgies of unrestrained debauchery.

Undoubtedly each Canaanite city built its Baal sanctuary in honor of its local patron Baal. Priests were appointed to conduct the worship at these sanctuaries and the many shrines on neighboring hilltops known as high places. (Compare 2Ki 17: 32.) Inside the shrines there may have been images or representations of Baal, whereas near the altars outside were to be found stone pillars (likely phallic symbols of Baal), sacred poles representing the goddess Asherah, and incense stands. (Compare 2Ch 34:4-7; see SACRED POLE.) Male and female prostitutes served at the high places, and besides ceremonial prostitution, even child sacrifice was practiced. (Compare 1Ki 14:23, 24; Ho 4:13, 14; Isa 57:5; Jer 7:31; 19:5.) Worship of Baal was also carried out right on the housetops of the people, from where sacrificial smoke to their god was frequently seen to rise.—Jer 32:29.

There are indications that Baal and other gods and goddesses of the Canaanite pantheon were associated in the minds of their worshipers with certain heavenly bodies. For instance, one of the Ras Shamra texts mentions an offering to "Queen Shapash (the Sun) and to the stars," and another alludes to "the army of the sun and the host of the day."

It is, therefore, noteworthy that the Bible makes several references to the heavenly bodies in connection with Baal worship. Describing the wayward course of the kingdom of Israel, the Scriptural record states: "They kept leaving all the commandments of Jehovah . . . , and they began to bow down to all the army of the heavens and to serve Baal." (2Ki 17:16) Concerning the kingdom of Judah, it is noted that right in the temple of

Jehovah there came to be "utensils made for Baal and for the sacred pole and for all the army of the heavens." Also, the people throughout Judah made "sacrificial smoke to Baal, to the sun and to the moon and to the constellations of the zodiac and to all the army of the heavens."—2Ki 23:4, 5; 2Ch 33:3; see also Zep 1:4, 5.

Each locality had its own Baal, and the local Baal was often given a name denoting his being attached to a specific locality. For instance, the Baal of Peor (Baal-peor), who was worshiped by Moabites and Midianites, took his name from Mount Peor. (Nu 25:1-3, 6) The names of these local Baals later came to be transferred through a figure of speech (metonymy) to the localities themselves, as, for example, Baal-hermon, Baal-hazor, Baal-zephon, Bamoth-baal. However, although there were many local Baals, officially, among the Canaanites, it was understood that there was actually just one god Baal.

What effect did Baal worship have on Israel?

Baalism is implied early in the Bible, although apparently it had not reached the level of degradation in the days of the patriarchs that existed when the Israelites entered the land of Canaan. (Compare Ge 15:16; 1Ki 21:26.) The listing of the city of Ashteroth-karnaim, possibly named after Baal's consort Ashtoreth, gives the first suggestion of it. (Ge 14:5) Before the Israelites crossed the Red Sea, the location Baal-zephon could be seen in the wilderness. (Ex 14:2, 9) With respect to the inhabitants of Canaan, specific warnings were given to Moses on Mount Sinai to pull down their altars, shatter their sacred pillars, and cut down their sacred poles. (Ex 34:12-14) Thus all appendages of Baal worship were to be eradicated from the Promised Land.

While the Israelites were camped on the Plains of Moab, King Balak took Balaam up to Bamoth-baal (meaning "High Places of Baal") to see the mighty throng. (Nu 22:41) After proving unsuccessful in bringing a curse directly upon the Israelites, Balaam advised Balak to lure them into idolatry through temptation to commit sexual immorality with the female idol worshipers of Baal of Peor. Thousands of Israelites succumbed to this temptation and lost their lives.—Nu 22:1–25:18; Re 2:14.

Despite this bitter experience and the clear warnings by Moses and Joshua (De 7:25, 26; Jos 24:15, 19, 20), the Israelites, in taking up residence in the land, began to imitate the remaining Canaanites, apparently with a view to ensuring fertility in their cattle and crops. At the same time, they carried on a pretense of worshiping Jehovah. Following the death of Joshua, wholesale apostasy set in. (Jg 2:11-13; 3:5-8) The people kept altars, poles, and other appendages of Baal worship in their fields, and apparently they listened to their Canaanite neighbors as to how they might please the "owner," or Baal, of each piece of land. The Israelites were also ensnared by the immoral practices associated with Baal worship. As a result, Jehovah abandoned them to their enemies.

However, when the people turned back to him, Jehovah mercifully delivered them by raising up judges such as Gideon, whose name was changed to Jerubbaal (meaning, "Let Baal Make a Legal Defense (Contend)"). (Jg 6:25-32; 1Sa 12:9-11) But no permanent reform then took place. (Jg 8:33; 10:6) Baalism continued to be practiced even beyond the days of Samuel, although it is written that, at his urgings, the people put away the Baals and Ashtoreth images and began serving Jehovah alone.—1Sa 7:3, 4.

Although we do not hear of Baalism again until the end of Solomon's reign, it may have lingered on in parts of the kingdom. Many varieties of Baalism were introduced into the country as Solomon married his many heathen wives, and they induced him and their children to serve other gods and goddesses, such as Ashtoreth and Molech, who were associated with Baal worship.—1Ki 11:4, 5, 33; Jer 32:35.

With the split of the kingdom in 997 B.C.E., Jeroboam set up calf worship in the northern kingdom of Israel at Dan and Bethel. The native Baalism and the calf worship were carried on side by side, just as in Judah a semblance of true worship was carried on at Jerusalem as Baalism was also practiced throughout the land.—1Ki 14: 22-24.

A different Baal cult was introduced into Israel in King Ahab's day (c. 940-920 B.C.E.), that of Melkart, the Baal of Tyre. (PICTURE, Vol. 2, p. 532) Ahab formed a marriage alliance with the daughter of the king of Tyre, named Ethbaal (meaning "With Baal"). This resulted in Ethbaal's daughter, Jezebel, importing this more virile cult into Israel, with many priests and at-

tendants. (1Ki 16:31-33) Finally, a famous showdown came at Mount Carmel between Jehovah and Baal.

Likely because Baal, believed to be the owner of the sky, was regarded by his worshipers as the giver of rains and fertility, a drought was ordered by Elijah in the name of Jehovah. (1Ki 17:1) After three years and six months of drought, Baal having proved unable to bring an end to the drought in answer to the many appeals undoubtedly made by his priests and worshipers, Elijah summoned all the people to Mount Carmel to witness the great test as to who is the true God. The test resulted in the humiliation of the Baal worshipers and the slaughter of 450 Baal prophets. Jehovah, and not Baal, then brought rain to end the drought.—1Ki 18:18-46; Jas 5:17.

Ahab's son and successor, Ahaziah, continued to serve Baal. (1Ki 22:51-53) Ahaziah's brother, Jehoram, succeeded him, and it is reported that he removed the sacred pillar of Baal that his father had made, although he persisted in calf worship. —2Ki 3:1-3.

Later (c. 905 B.C.E.) Jehu was anointed king. He avenged the murder of Jehovah's prophets by killing off Jezebel and the house of her husband

Representations of Baal.
Each locality where this god
was worshiped had its own Baal

Ahab. All the worshipers of Baal were then summoned to Samaria under pretense of holding "a solemn assembly for Baal." At Jehu's command all the Baal worshipers were killed. The sacred poles were burned, and the sacred pillar and house of Baal were pulled down, the house being set aside for a public privy. With this it is said that Jehu "annihilated Baal out of Israel." (2Ki 10:18-28) So, at least for the time, Baal worship was suppressed. However, it was on account of such Baalistic religion that Jehovah finally let the ten-tribe kingdom of Israel go into exile.—2Ki 17:16-18.

In Judah, Baalism evidently remained entrenched, despite the efforts of King Asa to remove its appendages. (2Ch 14:2-5) When Ahab married off Athaliah, his daughter by Jezebel, to Jehoram, the seventh Judean king, her wicked influence established Tyrian Baalism among the royal family in Judah. Even reforms at the beginning of the reign of Athaliah's grandson, King Jehoash, and those later by King Hezekiah, did not effect permanent removal of Baal worship. (2Ki 11:18; 18:4) Hezekiah's son Manasseh rebuilt the very high places that his father had destroyed. (2Ki 21:3) While apparently most of the Judean kings were contaminated with Baal worship, Manasseh was excessive in his pursuit of this degraded cult. (2Ki 21:9-11) King Manasseh's later reform and even the extensive purge by his grandson, King Josiah, did not bring about a permanent return to true worship. Punishment by exile and desolation of the land was the result of this thorough contamination with false worship. —2Ch 33:10-17; 2Ki 23:4-27; Jer 32:29.

Jeremiah, carrying on his prophetic work from the days of Josiah to the exile to Babylon, denounced Israel for degrading herself by Baal worship, likening Israel to an adulterous wife who prostituted herself under every luxuriant tree and on every high place, committing adultery with stones and trees, and forgetting Jehovah, "the husbandly owner" of the people. (Jer 2:20-27; 3:9, 14) After the exile to Babylon and the return of the Jews to Palestine, Baalism is not mentioned in the Bible as being practiced by the Israelites.

BAALAH   (Ba′al·ah) [Place of the Mistress].

1. A city on the N border of Judah, also called Kiriath-baal but better known as Kiriath-jearim. It is tentatively identified with Deir el-'Azar (Tel Qiryat Ye'arim), about 13 km (8 mi) WNW of Jerusalem.—Jos 15:9, 10, 60; 18:14; 1Ch 13:6; see KIRIATH-JEARIM.

2. A mountain in the NW corner of Judah, between the towns of Shikkeron and Jabneel,

forming part of the N boundary of Judah's territory. (Jos 15:11) It may possibly be identified with the hill of Mughar just N of the torrent valley of Sorek and 3 km (c. 2 mi) ESE of Jabneel (modern Yavne).

3. A town in the Negeb region of Judah (Jos 15:29), evidently referred to as Balah in Joshua 19:3 and Bilhah in 1 Chronicles 4:29. It was subsequently allotted to the tribe of Simeon as an enclave city. Its specific location is unknown, but evidently it lay to the SE of Beer-sheba.

BAALATH   (Ba′al·ath) [Place of the Mistress]. A border town of the original territory of Dan, mentioned at Joshua 19:44, 45 as being between Gibbethon and Jehud. It is evidently the same place that Solomon later included in his rebuilding program. (2Ch 8:5, 6) Its identification geographically is uncertain; Josephus (*Jewish Antiquities*, VIII, 152 [vi, 1]) refers to it along with Beth-horon as not far from Gezer, another fortified city.—1Ki 9:17, 18.

BAALATH-BEER   (Ba′al·ath-be′er) [Mistress of the Well]. An enclave city of Simeon within the territorial limits of Judah. (Jos 19:1, 8) Also called "Ramah of the south" (or Negeb), it is evidently referred to simply as Baal at 1 Chronicles 4:33 and may be the same as the "Ramoth of the south" at 1 Samuel 30:27. The references to it would place it S of Beer-sheba, well into the Negeb.

BAAL-BERITH   (Ba′al-be′rith) [Owner of the Covenant; once, at Jg 9:46, El-berith, God of a Covenant]. The Baal of Shechem, whom the Israelites began worshiping after the death of Judge Gideon. (Jg 8:33) The designation "Baal-berith" may denote that this particular Baal was believed to watch the keeping of covenants.

A kind of treasury was evidently attached to the house or temple of Baal-berith at Shechem. (Jg 9:4) In connection with the grape harvest, the Shechemites apparently held a festival in honor of Baal-berith, climaxed by a kind of sacrificial meal in the temple of their god. It was in the temple of Baal-berith on the occasion of their eating and drinking and cursing Abimelech, likely under the influence of wine, that Gaal incited the Shechemites to revolt against King Abimelech. (Jg 9:27-29) Later, when threatened by Abimelech, the landowners of the tower of Shechem (Migdal-Shechem, *AT*) sought refuge in the vault of the house of El-berith (Baal-berith), only to perish in the conflagration when Abimelech and his men set the vault on fire.—Jg 9:46-49.

BAALE-JUDAH.   See KIRIATH-JEARIM.

BAAL-GAD (Ba'al-gad) [Owner of Gad (Good Fortune)]. A town in the valley plain of Lebanon at the base of Mount Hermon, on its W side. It is used to describe the most northerly point of Joshua's conquest of the land of Canaan, as compared with the southerly point of Mount Halak in the Negeb. (Jos 11:17; 12:7; 13:5) The exact location is uncertain, but it is generally identified with Hasbaiya in the Wadi et-Teim or a site nearby.

BAAL-HAMON (Ba'al-ha'mon) [Owner of a Crowd (Multitude)]. A place mentioned at Song of Solomon 8:11 as the location of a productive vineyard of King Solomon. No indication is given as to its site. While many view it as a literal location, some suggest that it is used in this poetic writing figuratively to represent the realm over which Solomon ruled and which produced great wealth. —Compare 1Ki 4:20, 21.

BAAL-HANAN (Ba'al-ha'nan) [Baal Has Shown Favor; Baal Is Gracious].

1. Son of Achbor; the seventh of eight kings of Edom who ruled "before any king reigned over the sons of Israel."—Ge 36:31, 38, 39; 1Ch 1:49, 50.

2. The Gederite whom David made chief "over the olive groves and the sycamore trees that were in the Shephelah."—1Ch 27:28, 31.

BAAL-HAZOR (Ba'al-ha'zor) [Owner of the Courtyard (Settlement)]. A place near "Ephraim" (perhaps the city of Ephrain[m] mentioned at 2Ch 13:19; compare Joh 11:54) that served as the site of Absalom's sheepshearing festival in which he maneuvered the death of his brother Amnon. (2Sa 13:23, 28) It is identified with the 1,032-m-high (3,386 ft) mountain Jebel 'Asur (Ba'al Hazor), about 8 km (5 mi) NE of Bethel. From Baal-hazor Absalom fled to the small kingdom of Geshur, E of the Sea of Galilee.

BAAL-HERMON (Ba'al-her'mon) [Owner of Hermon]. This name appears at Judges 3:3 and 1 Chronicles 5:23. In the first instance it describes a point in the region inhabited by the Sidonians and the Hivites who remained unconquered by the Israelites, and it is here referred to as "Mount Baal-hermon." It is usually identified with Mount Hermon itself but may refer to the Anti-Lebanon Range in general or to some portion thereof. At 1 Chronicles 5:23 "Baal-hermon" is used along with Senir and Mount Hermon and the region of Bashan to outline the territory occupied by the half tribe of Manasseh. While it may refer to a town or place near Mount Hermon, it may likewise be a designation for the mountainous region of Hermon.—See HERMON.

BAALIS (Ba'a·lis). King of Ammon, who reportedly sent Ishmael to murder Governor Gedaliah of Judah in 607 B.C.E. The Greek *Septuagint* spells this name "Belisa."—Jer 40:14.

A seal impression bearing the name Ba'alyish'a was discovered in 1984 in the excavations at Tell el-'Umeiri in Jordan. This seal impression was dated paleographically to the latter part of the seventh century B.C.E. The inscription on it, written in ancient Ammonite characters, reads: "Belonging to Milkom'or [or, Milkom'ur], servant of Ba'alyish'a." Ba'alyish'a is possibly the Baalis of the Bible.

BAAL-MEON (Ba'al-me'on) [shortened form of Beth-baal-meon]. A prominent town on the tableland of N Moab assigned to the tribe of Reuben along with Nebo, Kiriathaim, and other towns of the region. (Nu 32:37, 38; 1Ch 5:8) The Reubenites, desiring the region for its good grazing land, evidently rebuilt and renamed the towns. In the earlier list at Numbers 32:3, 4, Baal-meon may be represented by the name "Beon." Joshua thereafter refers to it as Beth-baal-meon, likely the full name of the place.—Jos 13:17.

Baal-meon seems to have been retaken by the Moabites during the reign of King Mesha of Moab, evidently in the latter part of the tenth century B.C.E. The Moabite Stone inscription (line 9) states that Mesha "built [perhaps, fortified] Baal-meon, making a reservoir in it," and on line 30 he refers to it by the fuller name Beth-baal-meon. Additionally, on a piece of inscribed pottery found in Samaria (Ostraca 27 of Samaria) mention is made of a certain "Baala the Baal-meonite."

In the seventh century B.C.E. the prophet Jeremiah issued a divine warning to Moab foretelling the despoiling of the land by Babylon, specifically mentioning certain towns, including Beth-meon (likely Baal-meon). (Jer 48:20-23) Ezekiel includes Baal-meon as one of the Moabite sites to be possessed by the "Orientals" (or, "sons of the East"). (Eze 25:9, 10) Secular history and archaeological investigation confirm the fulfillment of these prophecies.—See MOAB, MOABITES No. 2.

Baal-meon is identified with the ruins of Ma'in, forming a mound of considerable size about 6 km (3.5 mi) WSW of Medeba and 12 km (7 mi) E of the Dead Sea. The plateau on which Ma'in lies is about 800 m (2,600 ft) in elevation.

BAAL OF PEOR (Ba'al of Pe'or). The particular Baal worshiped at Mount Peor by both Moabites and Midianites. (Nu 25:1, 3, 6) It has been suggested that Baal of Peor may actually have been Chemosh, in view of the fact that the latter deity was the chief god of the Moabites. (Nu 21:29) As with Baalism generally, grossly licentious rites were probably connected with the worship of Baal of Peor. The Israelites, while encamped at Shittim on the high plains of Moab, were enticed into immorality and idolatry by the female worshipers of this god.—Nu 25:1-18; De 4:3; Ps 106:28; Ho 9:10; Re 2:14.

Israel's sin in connection with Baal of Peor resulted in Jehovah's sending a death-dealing scourge that killed thousands of Israelites. A question arises as to the number of those actually killed by the scourge in view of a seeming discrepancy between Numbers 25:9 and 1 Corinthians 10:8. Apparently 23,000 were directly killed by the scourge, whereas 1,000 "head ones" or ringleaders were killed by the judges of Israel and then hung up, exposed to public view.—Nu 25:4, 5; see BAAL No. 4.

BAAL-PERAZIM (Ba'al-pe·ra'zim) [Owner of Breakings Through]. The site of a complete victory by King David over the combined forces of the Philistines, sometime after David's conquest of the stronghold of Zion. (2Sa 5:9, 17-21) The record states that, upon hearing of the Philistines' aggressive approach, David and his men "went down to the place hard to approach," while the Philistines were "tramping about in the low plain of Rephaim." Receiving assurance from Jehovah of his support, David attacked, and the Philistines fled, leaving their idols behind. Attributing the victory to Jehovah, David said: "Jehovah has broken through my enemies ahead of me, like a gap made by waters"; and for this reason he "called the name of that place Baal-perazim." The account at 2 Samuel 5:21 says that David and his men 'took the Philistines' abandoned idols away.' The parallel account at 1 Chronicles 14:12 shows the final action taken, stating: "Then David said the word, and so they [the idols] were burned in the fire."

Mount Perazim referred to by Isaiah (28:21) is considered to be the same location. Its use in his prophecy recalls Jehovah's victory through David at Baal-perazim, cited as an example of the strange deed due to be effected, in which, Jehovah declares, he will break in upon his enemies like an overflowing flash flood.

The Low Plain of Rephaim is considered to be the Plain of the Baqa' to the SW of the Temple Mount, which, after sloping downward for about 1.5 km (1 mi), contracts into a narrow valley, the Wadi el Werd (Nahal Refa'im). On this basis, some scholars suggest Baal-perazim to be a site in the vicinity of this valley. However, on the basis of the

parallel with "the low plain near Gibeon" drawn by Isaiah (28:21), some scholars suggest a site to the NW, possibly Sheikh Bedr, about 4 km (2.5 mi) WNW of the Temple Mount. (Jos 15:8, 9) This would be in harmony with the fact that the escape route of the Philistines who were pursued by David was in the direction of Gibeon and Gezer. —2Sa 5:22, 25; 1Ch 14:16.

BAAL-SHALISHAH (Ba'al-shal'i·shah) [Owner of Shalishah]. A place from which a man brought 20 barley loaves of the firstfruits of his harvest and some fresh grain to present to the prophet Elisha. (2Ki 4:42-44) It was a time of famine, and Elisha was at Gilgal. The humble supply proved sufficient for the hundred "sons of the prophets" there, with leftovers.—2Ki 4:38, 43; compare Mt 14:20; Mr 8:8.

Baal-shalishah is considered to have been near Gilgal and probably in "the land of Shalishah," through which Saul passed when searching for his father's she-asses. (1Sa 9:4) There is a reference to Baal-shalishah in the Babylonian Talmud describing it as a place where the fruits ripened especially early. (*Sanhedrin* 12a) A suggested location is that of Kafr Thulth in the foothills of Ephraim, the name Thulth being the precise equivalent in Arabic of the Hebrew Shalishah. Kafr Thulth is located about 46 km (29 mi) NNW of Jerusalem.

BAAL-TAMAR (Ba'al-ta'mar) [Owner of the Palm Tree]. A site near Gibeah where Israelite fighting men drew up in formation against the tribe of Benjamin in a costly battle provoked by a revolting sex crime. Some of Israel's forces were massed at Baal-tamar, while others were placed as an ambush against the Benjamites. (Jg 19:25-28; 20:33) The location of Baal-tamar is uncertain.

BAAL-ZEBUB (Ba'al-ze'bub) [Owner of the Flies]. The Baal worshiped by the Philistines at Ekron. There are indications that it was a common practice among the Hebrews to change the names of false gods to something similar but degrading. Hence, the ending "zebub" may be an alteration of one of the titles of Baal shown in the Ras Shamra texts as "Zebul" ("Prince"). Some scholars, however, suggest that the name was given to the god by his worshipers because of his being viewed as the producer of flies and therefore able to control this common pest of the Middle East. Since the giving of oracles was associated with Baal-zebub, others favor the view that Baal-zebub was a god who was regarded as giving oracles by the flight or buzzing of a fly.—2Ki 1:2.

Ahaziah the king of Israel sent messengers to

inquire of Baal-zebub as to whether he would recover from his serious injury or not. Through his prophet Elijah, Jehovah rebuked Ahaziah, saying: "Is it because there is no God at all in Israel that you are sending to inquire of Baal-zebub the god of Ekron? Therefore, as regards the couch upon which you have gone up, you will not come down off it, because you will positively die."—2Ki 1:2-8; see BEELZEBUB.

BAAL-ZEPHON (Ba'al-ze'phon) [Owner of the North (North Boundary)]. A geographic point used to define or give the situation of the camping site of the Israelites at Pihahiroth prior to their crossing the Red Sea. (Ex 14:2; Nu 33:1-7) Having left Rameses, they first camped at Succoth, then at Etham "at the edge of the wilderness." (Ex 13:20) At this point Jehovah told them to "turn back and encamp before Pihahiroth between Migdol and the sea in view of Baal-zephon." It was here that Pharaoh's charioteers, cavalry, and military forces began to overtake them.—Ex 14:2, 9.

The location of Baal-zephon is uncertain. It was evidently a familiar place at that time. The major factor is, of course, the Israelite's crossing of the Red Sea, the account of which shows that they went through a body of water of considerable depth. Such situation is found only when reaching as far S as the northern end of the Gulf of Suez. On this basis some scholars associate Baal-zephon with the mountains in that region. *A Hebrew and English Lexicon of the Old Testament,* by Brown, Driver, and Briggs (1980, p. 128), says: "near Red Sea in Egypt, prob[ably] Mt. *'Ataka.'* This mountain lies near the head of the Gulf of Suez, a short distance to the SW of the present city of Suez. Others suggest Jebel el Galala, some 40 km (25 mi) or so farther S. Those favoring this site believe that Migdol, mentioned along with Baal-zephon in the accounts, was a watchtower located strategically on Jebel (Mount) 'Ataqah.—See EXODUS; PIHAHIROTH.

BAANA (Ba'a·na).

1. One of the 12 deputies whom Solomon appointed to secure food for the king's household. Baana's assignment was the fifth-listed district, primarily the fertile valleys of Megiddo and Jezreel. Son of Ahilud; possibly the brother of Solomon's recorder Jehoshaphat.—1Ki 4:3, 7, 12.

2. Another of Solomon's 12 food deputies, responsible for the ninth-listed district, in northern Palestine. Son of Hushai, David's companion.—1Ki 4:7, 16; 2Sa 15:32-37.

3. Father of the Zadok who assisted Nehemiah to repair Jerusalem's walls, 455 B.C.E.—Ne 3:3, 4.

BAANAH (Ba'a·nah).

1. A son of Rimmon the Benjamite. He and his brother Rechab were chiefs of marauding bands belonging to Saul's son Ish-bosheth. Baanah and his brother murdered Ish-bosheth while he was taking a siesta, but when they brought his head to David, who had recently been installed as king, he ordered them killed, had their hands and feet cut off, and had them hanged by the pool in Hebron. —2Sa 4:2-12.

2. Father of one of David's mighty men, Heleb the Netophathite.—2Sa 23:29; 1Ch 11:30.

3. One who was possibly a leader of those returning from Babylonian exile with Zerubbabel. —Ezr 2:2; Ne 7:7.

4. One of "the heads of the people" whose descendant, if not he himself, attested to Nehemiah's "trustworthy arrangement." (Ne 9:38; 10:14, 27) He may be the same as No. 3, above.

BAARA (Ba'a·ra). One of the wives of Shaharaim the Benjamite.—1Ch 8:1, 8.

BAASEIAH (Ba·a·se'iah). A descendant of Levi through Gershom; ancestor of temple musician Asaph.—1Ch 6:39, 40, 43.

BAASHA (Ba'a·sha). Third king of the ten-tribe kingdom of Israel; son of Ahijah of the tribe of Issachar and of insignificant background. He usurped the throne by killing his predecessor Nadab, after which he struck down the entire house of Jeroboam, as had been prophesied. (1Ki 15:27-30; 14:10) Baasha, however, continued Jeroboam's calf worship, and extermination was also promised for his own house for this. (1Ki 16:1-4) When he waged war against Judah, Asa induced the king of Syria to harass Baasha from the N. The fortified city of Ramah, which Baasha was building, Asa then razed. (1Ki 15:16-22; 2Ch 16:1-6; see ASA No. 1 [Intrigue and Warfare Against Baasha].) After having ruled from about 975 to 953 B.C.E., Baasha died and was buried in his capital, Tirzah. His son Elah became king in the 26th year of Asa the king of Judah (1Ki 16:8), but in the 27th year of Asa (1Ki 16:15) Zimri rebelled and wiped out Baasha's house, fulfilling Jehovah's decree.

BABEL (Ba'bel) [Confusion]. One of the first cities to be built after the Flood. Here God "confused the language of all the earth." (Ge 11:9) The name is derived from the verb *ba·lal',* meaning "confuse." Local citizens, thinking of their city as God's seat of government, claimed that the name was compounded from *Bab* (Gate) and *ilu* (God), signifying "Gate of God."

The beginning of the kingdom of wicked Nimrod, the "mighty hunter in opposition to Jehovah," was here at Babel, "in the land of Shinar," on the alluvial plain built up by silt from the flooding Euphrates and Tigris rivers. (Ge 10:9, 10) Stones were not available for construction, so the builders made use of the great deposits of clay. "Let us make bricks and bake them with a burning process," they said. Because of an absence of lime, the mortar consisted of bitumen.—Ge 11:3.

Babel's God-defying program centered around construction of a religious tower "with its top in the heavens." It was not built for the worship and praise of Jehovah, but was dedicated to false manmade religion, with a motive of making a "celebrated name" for the builders.—Ge 11:4.

The approximate time of such building may be drawn from the following information: Peleg lived from 2269 to 2030 B.C.E. His name meant "Division," for "in his days the earth [that is, "earth's population"] was divided"; Jehovah "scattered them from there over all the surface of the earth." (Ge 10:25; 11:9) A text of Skarkalisharri, king of Agade (Accad) in patriarchal times, mentions his *restoring* a temple-tower at Babylon, implying that such a structure existed prior to his reign.

BABYLON (Bab'y·lon) [Confusion].

1. The later name given to Babel. This city of renown was located along the Euphrates River on the Plains of Shinar approximately 870 km (540 mi) E of Jerusalem and some 80 km (50 mi) S of Baghdad. The ruins of Babylon extend over a vast area in the form of a triangle. Several mounds are scattered over the area. Tell Babil (Mujelibe), in the northern part of the triangle, preserves the ancient name and is located about 10 km (6 mi) NE of Hilla, Iraq.—See BABYLON No. 2; SHINAR.

The city lay on both sides of the Euphrates River. A double system of walls surrounded Babylon, making it seemingly impregnable.

The inner rampart, constructed of crude bricks, consisted of two walls. The inner wall was 6.5 m (21.5 ft) thick. The outer wall, situated 7 m (23 ft) away, was about 3.5 m (11.5 ft) thick. These walls were buttressed by defense towers, which also served to reinforce the walls structurally. About 20 m (66 ft) outside the outer wall was a quay made of burnt brick set in bitumen. Outside this wall was a moat connected with the Euphrates to the N and S of the city. It provided both water supply and protection against enemy armies. Babylonian documents indicate that eight gates gave access to the interior of the city. So far, four of Babylon's gates have been discovered and excavated.

The outer rampart E of the Euphrates was added by Nebuchadnezzar II (who destroyed Solomon's temple), thus enclosing a large area of the plain to the N, E, and S for the people living nearby to flee to in case of war. This outer rampart also consisted of two walls. The inner wall, made of unbaked bricks, was about 7 m (23 ft) thick and was buttressed with defense towers. Beyond this, about 12 m (40 ft) away, was the outer wall of baked bricks, made in two parts that were interlocked by their towers: one was almost 8 m (26 ft) thick, and the adjoining part was about 3.5 m (11.5 ft) thick.

Nabonidus joined the ends of the outer rampart by constructing a wall along the eastern bank of the river. This wall was about 8.5 m (28 ft) wide and also had towers as well as a quay 3.5 m (11.5 ft) wide.

Herodotus, Greek historian of the fifth century B.C.E., says that the Euphrates River was flanked on either side with a continuous quay, which was separated from the city proper by walls having 25 gateways. According to him, the city walls were about 90 m (295 ft) high, 26.5 m (87 ft) thick, and about 95 km (59 mi) long. However, it appears that Herodotus exaggerated the facts regarding Babylon. Archaeological evidence shows that Babylon was much smaller in size, with the outer rampart much shorter in length and height. No evidence has been found to verify the existence of a quay lining the immediate western bank of the river.

Streets ran through the city from the gates in the massive walls. The Processional Way, the main boulevard, was paved and the walls alongside it were decorated with lions, dragons, and bulls in symbol of the honored gods. (PICTURE, Vol. 2, p. 323) Nebuchadnezzar II repaired and enlarged the old palace and built a summer palace some 2 km (1.5 mi) to the north. He also built a great structure of vaulted archways, tier upon tier, known as the Hanging Gardens of Babylon and famed as a "wonder of the ancient world."

This sprawling metropolis astride the watercourse of the Euphrates was a commercial and industrial center of world trade. More than an important manufacturing center, it was a commercial depot for trade between the peoples of the East and the West, both by land and by sea. Thus her fleet had access to the Persian Gulf and the seas far beyond.

History. Nimrod, who lived in the latter part of the third millennium B.C.E., founded Babylon as the capital of man's first political empire. Construction of this city, however, suddenly came to a halt when confusion in communication occurred.

(Ge 11:9) Later generations of rebuilders came and went. Hammurabi enlarged the city, strengthened it, and made it the capital of the Babylonian Empire under Semitic rule.

Under the control of the Assyrian World Power, Babylon figured in various struggles and revolts. Then with the decline of the second world empire, the Chaldean Nabopolassar founded a new dynasty in Babylon about 645 B.C.E. His son Nebuchadnezzar II, who completed the restoration and brought the city to its greatest glory, boasted, "Is not this Babylon the Great, that I myself have built?" (Da 4:30) In such glory it continued as the capital of the third world power until the night of October 5, 539 B.C.E. (Gregorian calendar), when Babylon fell before the invading Medo-Persian armies under the command of Cyrus the Great.

That fateful night in the city of Babylon, Belshazzar held a banquet with a thousand of his grandees. Nabonidus was not there to see the

ominous writing on the plaster wall: "MENE, MENE, TEKEL and PARSIN." (Da 5:5-28) After suffering defeat at the hands of the Persians, Nabonidus had taken refuge in the city of Borsippa to the SW. But Jehovah's prophet Daniel was on hand in Babylon on that night of October 5, 539 B.C.E., and he made known the significance of what was written on the wall. The men of Cyrus' army were not sleeping in their encampment around Babylon's seemingly impregnable walls. For them it was a night of great activity. In brilliant strategy Cyrus' army engineers diverted the mighty Euphrates River from its course through the city of Babylon. Then down the riverbed the Persians moved, up over the riverbanks, to take the city by surprise through the gates along the quay. Quickly passing through the streets, killing all who resisted, they captured the palace and put Belshazzar to death. It was all over. In one night Babylon had fallen, ending centuries

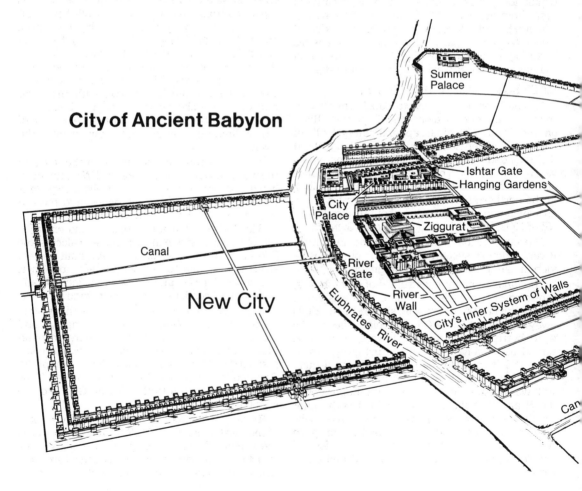

City of Ancient Babylon

Summer Palace

Ishtar Gate

Hanging Gardens

City Palace

Ziggurat

Canal

New City

River Gate

River Wall

Euphrates River

City's Inner System of Walls

Can

of Semitic supremacy; control of Babylon became Aryan, and Jehovah's word of prophecy was fulfilled.—Isa 44:27; 45:1, 2; Jer 50:38; 51:30-32; see PICTURE, Vol. 2, p. 325; CYRUS.

From that memorable date, 539 B.C.E., Babylon's glory began to fade as the city declined. Twice it revolted against the Persian emperor Darius I (Hystaspis), and on the second occasion it was dismantled. A partially restored city rebelled against Xerxes I and was plundered. Alexander the Great intended to make Babylon his capital, but he suddenly died in 323 B.C.E. Nicator conquered the city in 312 B.C.E. and transported much of its material to the banks of the Tigris for use in building his new capital of Seleucia. However, the city and a settlement of Jews remained in early Christian times, giving the apostle Peter reason to visit Babylon, as noted in his letter. (1Pe 5:13) Inscriptions found there show that Babylon's temple of Bel existed as late as 75 C.E. About the

fourth century C.E. the city appears to have passed out of existence. It became nothing more than "piles of stones."—Jer 51:37.

Today nothing remains of Babylon but mounds and ruins, a veritable wasteland. (PICTURE, Vol. 2, p. 324) The book *Archaeology and Old Testament Study* states: "These extensive ruins, of which, despite Koldewey's work, only a small proportion has been excavated, have during past centuries been extensively plundered for building materials. Partly in consequence of this, much of the surface now presents an appearance of such chaotic disorder that it is strongly evocative of the prophecies of Isa. xiii. 19–22 and Jer. l. 39 f., the impression of desolation being further heightened by the aridity which marks a large part of the area of the ruins."—Edited by D. W. Thomas, Oxford, 1967, p. 41.

Religion. Babylon was a most religious place. Evidence from excavations and from ancient texts points to the existence of more than 50 temples. The principal god of the imperial city was Marduk, called Merodach in the Bible. It has been suggested that Nimrod was deified as Marduk, but the opinions of scholars as to identifications of gods with specific humans vary. Triads of deities were also prominent in the Babylonian religion. One of these, made up of two gods and a goddess, was Sin (the moon-god), Shamash (the sun-god), and Ishtar; these were said to be the rulers of the zodiac. And still another triad was composed of the devils Labartu, Labasu, and Akhkhazu. Idolatry was everywhere in evidence. Babylon was indeed "a land of graven images," filthy "dungy idols." —Jer 50:1, 2, 38.

The Babylonians believed in the immortality of the human soul.—*The Religion of Babylonia and Assyria*, by M. Jastrow, Jr., 1898, p. 556.

The Babylonians developed astrology in an effort to discover man's future in the stars. (See ASTROLOGERS.) Magic, sorcery, and astrology played a prominent part in their religion. (Isa 47:12, 13; Da 2:27; 4:7) Many heavenly bodies, for example, planets, were named after Babylonian gods. Divination continued to be a basic component of Babylonian religion in the days of Nebuchadnezzar, who used it to reach decisions.—Eze 21:20-22.

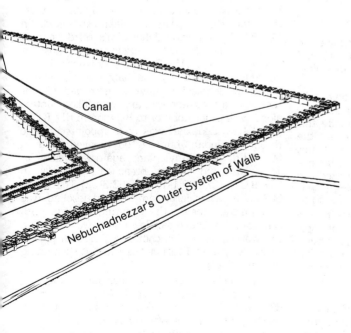

Canal

Nebuchadnezzar's Outer System of Walls

Israel's Age-Old Enemy. The Bible makes many references to Babylon, beginning with the Genesis account of the original city of Babel. (Ge 10:10; 11:1-9) Included in the spoil taken by Achan from Jericho was "an official garment from Shinar." (Jos 7:21) After the fall of the northern kingdom of Israel in 740 B.C.E., people from Babylon and other areas were brought in to replace the captive Israelites. (2Ki 17:24, 30) Hezekiah made the mistake of showing messengers from Babylon the treasures of his house; these same treasures as well as some of Hezekiah's "sons" were later taken to Babylon. (2Ki 20:12-18; 24:12; 25:6, 7) King Manasseh (716-662 B.C.E.) was also taken captive to Babylon, but because he humbled himself, Jehovah restored him to his throne. (2Ch 33:11) King Nebuchadnezzar took the precious utensils of Jehovah's house to Babylon, along with thousands of captives.—2Ki 24:1–25:30; 2Ch 36:6-20.

The Christian Greek Scriptures tell how Jeconiah (Jehoiachin), taken prisoner to Babylon, was a link in the lineage to Jesus. (Mt 1:11, 12, 17) The apostle Peter's first canonical letter was written from Babylon. (1Pe 5:13; see PETER, LETTERS OF.) That "Babylon" was the city on the Euphrates, and not Rome as claimed by some.

See BABYLON THE GREAT.

2. The Babylonian Empire was also referred to by the name of its capital city, Babylon, and was centered in the lower Mesopotamian valley. —MAP, Vol. 2, p. 321.

Sometimes historians subdivide Babylonia, calling the northern part Akkad (Accad) and the southern part Sumer or Chaldea. Originally this territory was designated in the Scriptures as "the land of Shinar." (Ge 10:10; 11:2; see SHINAR.) Later, when dominating rulers made Babylon their capital, this area was known as Babylonia. Because Chaldean dynasties sometimes held sway, it was also called "the land of the Chaldeans." (Jer 24:5; 25:12; Eze 12:13) Some of the ancient cities in Babylonia were Adab, Akkad, Babylon, Borsippa, Erech, Kish, Lagash, Nippur, and Ur. The Babylonian Empire, of course, extended beyond Babylonia, taking in Syria and Palestine down to the border of Egypt.

About the first half of the eighth century B.C.E., an Assyrian king by the name of Tiglath-pileser III (Pul) ruled Babylonia. (2Ki 15:29; 16:7; 1Ch 5:26) Later a Chaldean called Merodach-baladan became the king of Babylon, but after 12 years he was ousted by Sargon II. Sennacherib, in succeeding Sargon II, faced another Babylonian revolt led by Merodach-baladan. After Sennacherib's unsuccessful attempt to capture Jerusalem in

732 B.C.E., Merodach-baladan sent envoys to Hezekiah of Judah possibly to seek support against Assyria. (Isa 39:1, 2; 2Ki 20:12-18) Later Sennacherib drove out Merodach-baladan and crowned himself ruler of Babylon, a position he held until death. His son Esar-haddon rebuilt Babylon. The Babylonians rallied around Nabopolassar and bestowed the kingship on him. With him began the Neo-Babylonian dynasty that was to continue until Belshazzar. That dynasty from Nabopolassar's son Nebuchadnezzar on to Belshazzar is represented in Bible prophecy by the head of gold of Nebuchadnezzar's dream image (Da 2:37-45) and, in a dream-vision of Daniel, by a lion that had the wings of an eagle and the heart of a man.—Da 7:4.

In 632 B.C.E. Assyria was subdued by this new Chaldean dynasty, with the assistance of Median and Scythian allies. In 625 B.C.E., Nabopolassar's eldest son, Nebuchadnezzar (II), defeated Pharaoh Necho of Egypt at the battle of Carchemish, and in the same year he assumed the helm of government. (Jer 46:1, 2) Under Nebuchadnezzar, Babylon was "a golden cup" in the hand of Jehovah to pour out indignation against unfaithful Judah and Jerusalem. (Jer 25:15, 17, 18; 51:7) In 620 B.C.E. he compelled Jehoiakim to pay tribute, but after about three years Jehoiakim revolted. In 618 B.C.E., or during Jehoiakim's third year as tributary ruler, Nebuchadnezzar came against Jerusalem. (2Ki 24:1; 2Ch 36:6) However, before he could be taken by the Babylonians, Jehoiakim died. Jehoiachin, having succeeded his father, quickly surrendered and was taken captive along with other nobility to Babylon in 617 B.C.E. (2Ki 24:12) Zedekiah was next appointed to the throne of Judah, but he too rebelled; and in 609 B.C.E. the Babylonians again laid siege to Jerusalem and finally breached its walls in 607 B.C.E. (2Ki 25:1-10; Jer 52:3-12) That year, 607 B.C.E., when Jerusalem was laid desolate, was a significant one in the counting of time until Jehovah, the Universal Sovereign, would set up the world ruler of his choice in Kingdom power. —See APPOINTED TIMES OF THE NATIONS (Beginning of 'trampling').

One cuneiform tablet has been found referring to a campaign against Egypt in Nebuchadnezzar's 37th year (588 B.C.E.). This may be the occasion when mighty Egypt was brought under Babylonian control, as foretold by the prophet Ezekiel evidently in the year 591 B.C.E. (Eze 29:17-19) Finally, after a 43-year reign, which included both conquest of many nations and a grand building program in Babylonia itself, Nebuchadnezzar II died in October of 582 B.C.E. and was succeeded by Awil-Marduk (Evil-merodach). This new ruler showed kindness to captive King Jehoiachin. (2Ki 25:27-30) Little is known about the reigns of Neriglissar, evidently the successor of Evil-merodach, and of Labashi-Marduk.

More complete historical information is available for Nabonidus and his son Belshazzar, who were evidently ruling as coregents at the time of Babylon's fall.

By now the Medes and Persians under command of Cyrus the Great were on the march to take over control of Babylonia and become the fourth world power. During the night of October 5, 539 B.C.E. (Gregorian calendar), Babylon was seized, and Belshazzar was slain. In the first year of Cyrus, following the conquest of Babylon, he issued his famous decree permitting a group that included 42,360 males, besides many slaves and professional singers, to return to Jerusalem. Some 200 years later, Persian domination of Babylonia came to an end when Alexander the Great captured Babylon in 331 B.C.E. By the middle of the second century B.C.E. the Parthians, under their king Mithradates I, were in control of Babylonia.

Since Jewish communities had been flourishing in this land, Peter the apostle to the Jews went to Babylon, and it was from there that he wrote at least one of his inspired letters. (Ga 2:7-9; 1Pe 5:13) Jewish leaders in these Eastern communities also developed the Babylonian Targum, otherwise known as the Targum of Onkelos, and produced a number of manuscripts of the Hebrew Scriptures. One of the most important of the Eastern or Babylonian line of texts is cataloged as the Codex Babylonicus Petropolitanus of 916 C.E., now in Leningrad, U.S.S.R.

BABYLON THE GREAT.
Among John's visions recorded in the book of Revelation appear pronouncements of judgment against "Babylon the Great," as well as a description of her and of her downfall.—Re 14:8; 16:19; chaps 17, 18; 19:1-3.

In Revelation 17:3-5, Babylon the Great is described as a woman arrayed in purple and scarlet, richly adorned, and sitting upon a scarlet-colored wild beast having seven heads and ten horns. Upon her forehead a name is written, "a mystery: 'Babylon the Great, the mother of the harlots and of the disgusting things of the earth.'" She is also depicted as sitting on "many waters" representing "peoples and crowds and nations and tongues." —Re 17:1-15.

The luxury and the dominion attributed to Babylon the Great do not allow for simply equating her with the literal city of Babylon in Mesopotamia. After ancient Babylon fell to Cyrus the Persian in 539 B.C.E., it lost its position as a dominant world power, its captives, including the Jews, being freed. Although the city continued to exist even beyond the days of the apostles, and hence existed in John's day, it was no longer a city of world importance, and it eventually fell into decay and utter ruin. Thus, Babylon the Great must be viewed as a symbolic city, one of which the literal city of Babylon was the prototype. Because the ancient city gives the mystic city its name, it is helpful to consider briefly the outstanding features of Babylon on the Euphrates, features that provide clues as to the identity of the symbolic city of John's vision.

Characteristics of Ancient Babylon. The founding of the city of Babylon on the Plains of Shinar was concurrent with the attempt at building the Tower of Babel. (Ge 11:2-9) The popular cause to be advanced by the tower and city construction was, not the exaltation of God's name, but that the builders might "make a celebrated name" for themselves. The ziggurat towers uncovered not only in the ruins of ancient Babylon but elsewhere in Mesopotamia would seem to confirm the essentially religious nature of the original tower, whatever its form or style. The decisive action taken by Jehovah God to overthrow the temple construction clearly condemns it as of a false religious origin. Whereas the Hebrew name given the city, Babel, means "Confusion," the Sumerian name (Ka-dingir-ra) and the Akkadian name (Bab-ilu) both mean "Gate of God." Thus the remaining inhabitants of the city altered the form of its name to avoid the original condemnatory sense, but the new or substitute form still identified the city with religion.

The Bible lists Babel first when giving the 'beginning of Nimrod's kingdom.' (Ge 10:8-10) Throughout the Hebrew Scriptures the ancient city of Babylon is featured prominently as the longtime enemy of Jehovah God and his people.

Though Babylon became the capital of a political empire in the seventh and sixth centuries B.C.E., it was outstandingly prominent during its entire history as a religious center from which religious influence radiated in many directions.

Professor Morris Jastrow, Jr., in his work *The Religion of Babylonia and Assyria* (1898, pp. 699-701), says regarding this: "In the ancient world, prior to the rise of Christianity, Egypt, Persia, and Greece felt the influence of the Babylonian religion. . . . In Persia, the Mithra cult reveals the unmistakable influence of Babylonian conceptions; and if it be recalled what a degree of importance the mysteries connected with this cult acquired among the Romans, another link will be added connecting the ramifications of ancient culture with the civilization of the Euphrates Valley." In conclusion he refers to "the profound impression made upon the ancient world by the remarkable manifestations of religious thought in Babylonia and by the religious activity that prevailed in that region."

Babylon's religious influence is traced eastward to India in the book *New Light on the Most Ancient East,* by archaeologist V. Childe (1957, p. 185). Among other points he states: "The swastika and the cross, common on stamps and plaques, were religious or magical symbols as in Babylonia and Elam in the earliest prehistoric period, but preserve that character also in modern India as elsewhere." Thus, ancient Babylon's religious influence spread out to many peoples and nations, much farther and with greater potency and endurance than did her political strength.

Like mystic Babylon, the ancient city of Babylon, in effect, sat on the waters, located, as it was, astride the Euphrates River and having various canals and water-filled moats. (Jer 51:1, 13; Re 17:1, 15) These waters served as a defense to the city, and they provided the thoroughfares upon which ships brought wealth and luxuries from many sources. Notably, the water of the Euphrates is depicted as drying up prior to Babylon the Great's experiencing the wrath of divine judgment.—Re 16:12, 19.

Distinguishing Features of Mystic Babylon.
The symbolic woman bearing the name Babylon the Great is "the great city that has a kingdom over the kings of the earth," a kingdom that allows her, in effect, to sit on "peoples and crowds and nations and tongues." (Re 17:1, 15, 18) A kingdom over other kingdoms and nations is what is defined as an "empire." Babylon the Great places herself above earthly kings, exercising power and influence over them. She rides the symbolic seven-headed beast, beasts being used elsewhere in the Bible as symbols of political world powers. —See BEASTS, SYMBOLIC.

Some scholars assume that Babylon the Great is a political empire, either Babylon or Rome. We have already seen that Babylon as a political empire had long since ceased to exist when John received his prophetic vision. As to Rome, the nature of its political rule does not harmonize with the description of Babylon the Great's course and her methods of dominating. She is a harlot, committing fornication with the kings of the earth,

making them drunk with the wine of her fornication, misleading the nations by her "spiritistic practice." (Re 17:1, 2; 18:3, 23) Rome's dominion, by contrast, was gained and maintained by its ironlike military might and its firm application of Roman law among its provinces and colonies. Recognizing this fact, *The Interpreter's Dictionary of the Bible* says: "It is not sufficient to identify Rome and Babylon. Babylon embraces more than one empire or culture. It is defined rather by dominant idolatries than by geographical or temporal boundaries. Babylon is coextensive with the kingdom of that beast which has corrupted and enslaved mankind, and whom the Lamb must conquer (Rev. 17:14) if mankind is to be freed." —Edited by G. Buttrick, 1962, Vol. 1, p. 338.

The symbol of a harlot or a fornicatrix is used frequently in the Hebrew Scriptures. The nation of Israel was warned against entering into covenant relations with the nations of Canaan because this would lead them to commit "immoral intercourse ["play the harlot," *RS*] with their gods." (Ex 34:12-16) Both Israel and Judah apostatized from the true worship of Jehovah God and were condemned by him as having engaged in harlotry, prostituting themselves to the political nations and their gods. (Isa 1:21; Jer 3:6-10, 13; Eze 16:15-17, 28, 29, 38; Ho 6:10; 7:11; 8:9, 10) It may be noted here that God was not viewing Israel or Judah as mere political entities entering into relations with other political governments. Instead God reprimanded them on the basis of their being in a sacred covenant with him, hence responsible to be a holy people devoted to him and his pure worship.—Jer 2:1-3, 17-21.

A similar usage of this figure is found in the Christian Greek Scriptures. The Christian congregation is likened to a virgin espoused to Christ as her Head and King. (2Co 11:2; Eph 5:22-27) The disciple James warned Christians against committing spiritual adultery through friendship with the world. (Jas 4:4; compare Joh 15:19.) The fornications of Babylon the Great and her "daughters" are of a similar nature and not some unique exception. (The term "daughters" at times is employed in the Bible to refer to the suburbs or surrounding towns of a city or metropolis, as the "dependent towns" [literally, "daughters" in Hebrew] of Samaria and Sodom; see Eze 16:46-48.)

An additional significant factor is that when Babylon the Great goes down under the devastating attack of the ten horns of the symbolic wild beast, her fall is mourned by her companions in fornication, the kings of the earth, and also by the merchants and shippers who dealt with her in supplying luxurious commodities and gorgeous fineries. While these political and commercial representatives survive her desolation, notably no religious representatives are depicted as still on the scene to share in mourning her downfall. (Re 17:16, 17; 18:9-19) The kings of the earth are shown as having judgment executed upon them sometime after mystic Babylon's annihilation, and their destruction comes, not from the "ten horns," but from the sword of the King of kings, the Word of God.—Re 19:1, 2, 11-18.

A further distinguishing characteristic of Babylon the Great is her drunkenness, she being pictured as "drunk with the blood of the holy ones and with the blood of the witnesses of Jesus." (Re 17:4, 6; 18:24; 19:1, 2) She thus is the spiritual counterpart of the ancient city of Babylon, expressing the same enmity toward the true people of God. Significantly, it was to the charge of religious leaders that Jesus laid the responsibility for "all the righteous blood spilled on earth, from the blood of righteous Abel to the blood of Zechariah." While those words were addressed to religious leaders from among Jesus' own race, the Jewish nation, and while persecution against Jesus' followers was particularly intense from that sector for a time, history shows that thereafter the opposition to genuine Christianity came from other sources (the Jews themselves suffering considerable persecution).—Mt 23:29-35.

All the above factors are significant, and they must all be considered in arriving at a true picture of symbolic Babylon the Great and what it represents.

BACA (ba'ca) [Heb., ba·kha']. The plant that played an important role in David's encounter with the Philistines "in the low plain of Rephaim." (2Sa 5:22-25; 1Ch 14:13-16) The only other reference to the plant is at Psalm 84:6: "Passing along through the low plain of the baca bushes, they turn it into a spring itself." This may refer to the same "low plain of Rephaim" where David's fight took place and which plain is believed to be SW of Jerusalem.

The Hebrew word used comes from a root meaning "weep." (Compare Ge 21:16.) It therefore seems to indicate a plant, shrub, or tree that exudes tears of gum or perhaps a milky sap. Its identification is uncertain; the name baca is simply a transliteration of the Hebrew word. There is no apparent foundation for the rabbinic view that relates it to the mulberry tree (as also translated in KJ). Since balsam trees (of which there are several in the different tree families) exude gum or resin, these have been suggested by many

scholars. A balsam tree of the poplar family (Populus euphratica) is recommended by some botanists, primarily because of the ease with which its leaves are stirred by any breeze, producing a rustling sound. However, the Bible does not specify how "the sound of a marching" was produced (whether by means of the leaves, the branches, or some other part of the plant) and simply indicates that it occurred in "the tops" of the plants. It could have been a mere rustling sound that served as a signal, or as suggested by some, it may have been a noise of some volume produced by a rushing wind that served to cover up or even to simulate the sound of a marching army.—2Sa 5:24; 1Ch 14:15.

BACKBITING. This is a rendering of the Greek term ka·ta·la·li·a'. The related verb ka·ta·la·le'o literally means "speak against," doing so without justification and usually in a malicious or hostile manner. (1Pe 2:12; 3:16) The disciple James linked the expression with wrongful judging or condemning, thus conveying the sense of unjustifiably censuring.—Jas 4:11; compare Ps 50:20.

Backbiters, or persons who speak against others maliciously behind their back, are among those against whom Jehovah's wrath is directed, and his Word shows that all who continue as such are deserving of death. (Ro 1:18, 28-30, 32) The apostle Paul expressed grave concern that, in addition to other serious wrongs, he might find members of the congregation at Corinth engaging in backbiting. (2Co 12:20) For God's Word or message to have its full effect on new disciples of Jesus Christ, they must rid themselves of backbiting and all other forms of badness. Only then can the "milk belonging to the word," Scriptural truths suited to their needs, promote growth to salvation.—1Pe 2:1, 2.

BAG. Composed of various types of skins, cloth, and woven materials, bags in ancient times were used to hold grains and food, stone weights, valuables, lumps of gold and silver, and in later periods, minted coins. Bags used for water and wine were usually made from tanned skins of animals. —Jos 9:4; Mt 9:17.

The English word "sack" is derived from the Hebrew saq and, though used in the Bible primarily with reference to sackcloth (Le 11:32), this Hebrew word is also used as today to refer to containers for food and grains. (Ge 42:25, 27, 35) The Hebrew word 'am·ta'chath ("bag," NW; "sack," KJ; derived from a verb meaning "spread out" [Isa 40:22]) is employed in the account concerning the visit of Joseph's brothers to Egypt and appears to be more or less synonymous with *saq,* perhaps describing the form of the bag rather than the material from which it was made.—Ge 42:27, 28; 43:18-23.

When preparing for his encounter with Goliath, David placed five stones in his shepherds' "bag" (Heb., *keli'*), which receptacle is suggested to have been a sort of haversack carried across the shoulder and usually made from undressed skins of animals. (1Sa 17:40, 49) The Hebrew word here used is of very general meaning and more frequently refers simply to a receptacle, vessel, or utensil of earthenware, wood, metal, or skin.—Le 6:28; 11:32, 33; Nu 31:20; 1Ki 10:21.

Syrian army officer Naaman gave greedy Gehazi "two talents of silver in two bags [Heb., *chari·tim'*], with two changes of garments, and gave them to two of his attendants, that they might carry them." Since a talent was equal to about 34 kg (92 lb t), it is evident that such a container (*cha·rit'*) must have been of ample size and strength to hold a talent plus a change of garment and, hence, when filled was about as much as one man could carry. (2Ki 5:23) However, the same word is also used to refer to the "purses" used as articles of luxurious adornment by the haughty daughters of Zion.—Isa 3:16, 22.

There was also the bag (Heb., *kis*) carried by merchants, doubtless much like those that have continued to be used in Oriental lands till recent times. Judging from these later types, they were likely made of woven cotton, of flexible rushes, or of leather. These bags were used by traders, or merchants, for carrying weights required in business transactions where products, grains, or precious metals had to be weighed out. Referring to the *kis,* a warning against fraudulent business practices in the Mosaic Law stated: "You must not come to have in your bag two sorts of weights." (De 25:13) Through his prophet, Jehovah asked: "Can I be morally clean with wicked scales and with a bag of deceptive stone weights?" (Mic 6:11; Pr 16:11) The *kis* could also be used as a "bag" or "purse" for carrying money and valuables.—Pr 1:13, 14; Isa 46:6.

The Hebrew word *tserohr'* is derived from a verb meaning "wrap up" (Ex 12:34) and describes a common form of receptacle tied with a cord or string, either as a "bundle" (Ge 42:35) or as a "bag" with only the neck being drawn together and tied. (Pr 7:20; Ca 1:13) It appears that the money received from the chest of temple contributions was bound into such bundles, doubtless of uniform quantities. (2Ki 12:10) In ancient times, in business transactions involving large sums of money, the pieces were at times weighed and then put in such bundles or bags, the knot thereafter being sealed. If desired, the bag could then pass from one person to another as warranted to contain the stipulated amount. The unbroken seal thus could vouch for the amount of silver, gold, or other metal contained. Job apparently uses such a figure at Job 14:17, saying to God: "Sealed up in a bag is my revolt, and you apply glue over my error." Abigail expressed confidence in Jehovah's protection of David, stating that when an enemy pursued David his soul would "prove to be wrapped up in the bag of life with Jehovah [his] God."—1Sa 25:29.

In the Christian Greek Scriptures reference is made to a "food pouch" (*NW*) or "bag" (*AT, RS*). (Mt 10:10; Lu 9:3) The Greek word *pe'ra* is described in *Vine's Expository Dictionary of Old and New Testament Words* (1981, Vol. 4, p. 196) as "a traveller's leathern bag or pouch for holding provisions."—See FOOD POUCH.

At John 12:6; 13:29 in the *King James Version,* Judas is spoken of as carrying a "bag"; however, most modern translations render the Greek word *glos·so'ko·mon* as "box" or "money box." Originally used to refer to a case for keeping the mouthpiece of a wind instrument, the Greek word came to stand for a small box used for any purpose, including the keeping of money. The translators of the Greek *Septuagint* used this word to refer to the chest mentioned at 2 Chronicles 24:8, 10. For the "purse" (Lu 10:4) or "girdle purses" (Mt 10:9), see PURSE.

BAGGAGE. See LUGGAGE.

BAGPIPE. Although the Aramaic word *sum·pon·yah',* appearing in Daniel 3:5, 10, 15, has been translated "dulcimer" (a stringed instrument) (*KJ, Kx*) and "symphony" (*Dy, Yg*), modern Bible translations generally render the expression as "bagpipe." Koehler and Baumgartner's *Lexicon in Veteris Testamenti Libros* gives the meaning "bagpipe."—Leiden, 1958, p. 1103.

Sum·pon·yah' may have resembled present-day simple Oriental bagpipes. The required airtight bag is made from a goatskin, without the feet, tail, or head, but many times with the hair still covering it. A tube to fill the bag with air is inserted into this bag and so are flutelike pipes that are made from reeds and the tips of cows' horns.

BAHARUMITE (Ba·ha'rum·ite) [Of (Belonging to) Bahurim]. A native of the village of Bahurim. Azmaveth, one of David's mighty men, was from this place and is called both "the Baharumite" at 1 Chronicles 11:33 and "the Bar·humite" at 2 Samuel 23:31. Shimei, the reviler of fleeing King David, was also a Baharumite.—2Sa 19:16; 1Ki 2:8; see BAHURIM.

BAHURIM (Ba·hu′rim) [Chosen]. A village by the Mount of Olives, situated on the N side of an ancient road leading to Jericho and the Jordan. It is generally identified with Ras et-Tmim, 2 km (c. 1 mi) NE of the Temple Mount.

Weeping Paltiel walked after Saul's daughter Michal as far as Bahurim when she was being returned to King David. General Abner's order: "Go, return!" sufficed to turn him back at that point. (2Sa 3:16) Later, David, when abandoning Jerusalem because of his son Absalom's conspiracy, crossed the torrent valley of Kidron, went up "the ascent of the Olives," crossed beyond the summit, and came to Bahurim. (2Sa 15:23, 30; 16:1, 5) Here Shimei, the Benjamite relative of Saul, began walking along the mountainside, cursing David, throwing stones, and tossing dust. (2Sa 16:5-13; 19:15-23) Bahurim was also the point at which Ahimaaz and Jonathan, the sons of Zadok and Abiathar, had to hide in the well of a certain man when they were on their way to deliver a message to King David.—2Sa 15:27; 17:17-20.

BAKBAKKAR (Bak·bak′kar) [possibly, Large Flask]. A Levite who dwelt in Jerusalem after the Babylonian exile.—1Ch 9:3, 14, 15, 34.

BAKBUK (Bak′buk) [Flask]. Forefather of certain Nethinim who returned to Jerusalem with Zerubbabel, 537 B.C.E.—Ezr 2:43, 51; Ne 7:53.

BAKBUKIAH (Bak·bu·ki′ah) [Flask of Jah].

1. A Levite who returned to Jerusalem with Zerubbabel and served as a guard. (Ne 12:1, 9) Possibly the same as No. 2 below.

2. A Levite guard recorded as the head of a paternal house.—Ne 12:23, 25; see No. 1 above.

3. A Levite, possibly of the singers, selected to reside in Jerusalem under Nehemiah.—Ne 11: 17, 18.

BAKE, BAKER. "Bake" means cook (or dry out; harden) by dry heat. The most common Hebrew term for "bake" is ʾa·phahʹ, root of ʾo·phehʹ (baker). (Ge 19:3; 40:2) Another Hebrew word for "bake" (ʾugh; Eze 4:12) is evidently related to ʾu·ghahʹ, meaning "round cake."—Ge 18:6; see CAKE.

In the Hebrew home the baking of bread and cakes was a chief duty of the women, though slaves did the baking in some larger households. Speaking for Jehovah, Samuel told the Israelites, who had requested a human king: "Your daughters he will take for ointment mixers and cooks and bakers." (1Sa 8:13) Yet, men might oversee the work or do some baking themselves, as is indicated by Lot's actions when two angels visited him in Sodom. "He baked unfermented cakes, and they went to eating" the prepared feast.—Ge 19:1-3.

Bread was generally baked in ovens in Bible times. (See OVEN.) Occasionally, however, baking was done by kindling a fire on stones that had been laid together. When they were well heated, the cinders were swept aside and dough was placed on the stones. After a while, the cake was turned and then left on the stones until the bread was thoroughly baked. (Ho 7:8) Travelers might bake coarse bread in a shallow pit filled with hot pebbles, upon which a fire had been built. After the embers were removed, dough was laid on the heated stones, perhaps being turned several times while the bread was baking.—1Ki 19:6.

Grain offerings made by the Israelites were often "something baked in the oven," came "from off the griddle," or were from "out of the deep-fat kettle." (Le 2:4-7) The griddle was a thick pottery plate having depressions (comparable to a modern waffle iron), though iron griddles were also used. —Eze 4:3.

Professional bakers were in business in the cities. While Jeremiah was in custody in the Courtyard of the Guard in Jerusalem during the time of scarcity prior to that city's overthrow in 607 B.C.E., he was given a daily ration of a round loaf of bread "from the street of the bakers," as long as the supply lasted. (Jer 37:21) So, commercial bakers evidently occupied a particular street in Jerusalem. Years later, when Jerusalem's walls were restored under Nehemiah's supervision, "the Tower of the Bake Ovens" was also repaired. (Ne 3:11; 12:38) Just how the tower came to be named is uncertain, but it is possible that it was given its unusual name because the ovens of commercial bakers were located there.

The royal baker was evidently a man of some importance in ancient Egypt. A wall painting from the tomb of Ramses III in the Valley of the Kings at Thebes depicts an Egyptian royal bakery in full operation, showing the kneading of dough with the feet, the making of cakes of bread, and the preparing of the oven. As reported in Genesis, one Egyptian royal baker gained particular notoriety because he sinned against the king and was cast into prison. There he had a dream in which he saw himself carrying three baskets of bread on his head, with fowls eating from the topmost basket.

This "chief of the bakers" was taken out on the third day and "hung up," thus fulfilling Joseph's interpretation: "The three baskets are three days. In three days from now Pharaoh will lift up your head from off you and will certainly hang you upon a stake; and the fowls will certainly eat your flesh from off you."—Ge 40:1-3, 16-22.

BALAAM (Ba′laam) [possibly, One Swallowing Down]. Son of Beor, of the 15th century B.C.E. He lived in the Aramaean town of Pethor in the upper Euphrates Valley and near the Sajur River. Though not an Israelite, Balaam had some knowledge and recognition of Jehovah as the true God, speaking of him on one occasion as "Jehovah my God." (Nu 22:5, 18) This may have been because devout worshipers of Jehovah (Abraham, Lot, and Jacob) formerly lived in the vicinity of Haran, not far from Pethor.—Ge 12:4, 5; 24:10; 28:5; 31: 18, 38.

Balaam turned down the offer of the first delegation from the Moabite king Balak, who brought with them "payments for divination," saying: "Jehovah has refused to let me go with you." (Nu 22:5-14) When "other princes in greater number and more honorable" came (Nu 22:15), and Balaam again sought God's permission to go, Jehovah said: "Get up, go with them. But only the word that I shall speak to you is what you may speak." —Nu 22:16-21; Mic 6:5.

On the way Jehovah's angel three times stood in the road, causing Balaam's ass first to turn into a field, then to squeeze Balaam's foot against a wall, and at last to lie down. Three times Balaam beat the animal, which then miraculously uttered a spoken protest. (Nu 22:22-30) Finally, Balaam himself saw Jehovah's angel, who announced: "I have come out to offer resistance, because your way has been headlong against my will." Yet Jehovah once again allowed Balaam to continue in his chosen course.—Nu 22:31-35.

From start to finish God unalterably disapproved any cursing of Israel, insisting that if Balaam went he would have to bless, not curse. (Jos 24:9, 10) However, God permitted him to go. It was as in the case of Cain, when Jehovah expressed his disapproval but at the same time allowed the individual personal choice, either to abandon his bad way or plunge ahead in his wicked course. (Ge 4:6-8) Balaam, then, like Cain, was headstrong in disregarding Jehovah's will in the matter, and was determined to gain his own selfish objective. In Balaam's case it was greed of reward that blinded him to the wrongness of his way, as Jude writes: 'Balaam rushed into the erroneous course for reward.' The apostle Peter comments: "Balaam, the son of Beor, . . . loved the reward of wrongdoing, but got a reproof for his own violation of what was right. A voiceless beast of burden, making utterance with the voice of a man, hindered the prophet's mad course." —Jude 11; 2Pe 2:15, 16.

Upon reaching Moabite territory and meeting King Balak on the bank of the Arnon, Balaam wasted no time in going to work for these opposers of Jehovah's people the next day. Balaam together with Balak offered up sacrifices, and then Balaam withdrew, hoping to "come upon any unlucky omens" (Nu 23:3; 24:1), but the only message received was a blessing for Israel from Jehovah. The same sacrificial procedure was again followed atop Pisgah, and again there was "no unlucky spell against Jacob," only blessings. Finally, the performance was repeated atop Peor, and again for the third time "God changed the malediction into a benediction."—Nu 22:41–24:9; Ne 13:2.

At this turn of events, "Balak's anger blazed against Balaam," and, clapping his hands in a rage, he exclaimed: "It was to execrate my enemies that I called you, and, look! you have blessed them to the limit these three times. And now run your way off to your place. I had said to myself I was without fail going to honor you, but, look! Jehovah has held you back from honor." (Nu 24:10, 11) Balaam tried to excuse himself, blaming Jehovah for his failure at cursing Israel, saying he was not "able to pass beyond the order of Jehovah," and that 'whatever Jehovah said is what he had to speak.' So with a few more proverbial pronouncements against Israel's enemies, "Balaam got up and went and returned to his place."—Nu 24:12-25.

When it says that Balaam "returned to his place" it does not necessarily mean he actually reached his home back in Pethor. The words themselves do not imply that Balaam left more than the immediate vicinity of Mount Peor. As Cook's *Commentary* observes on Numbers 24:25: *"Returned to his own place* . . . Not to his own land, for he remained amongst the Midianites to plot by new means against the people of God, and to perish in his sin. . . . The phrase, which is of frequent recurrence (cf. *e.g.* Gen. xviii. 33, xxxi. 55; I S. xxvi. 25; 2 S. xix. 39), is idiomatic, meaning merely that Balaam went away whither he would."

Balaam still entertained hope of having that rich reward for which he had come so far and for which he had worked so hard. If he could not curse Israel, he reasoned, perhaps God himself would curse his own people, if only they could be seduced to engage in sex worship of the Baal of Peor. So "Balaam . . . went teaching Balak to put a stumbling block before the sons of Israel, to eat things sacrificed to idols and to commit fornication." (Re 2:14) "By Balaam's word," the daughters of Moab and Midian "served to induce the sons of Israel to commit unfaithfulness toward Jehovah over the affair of Peor, so that the scourge came upon the assembly of Jehovah." (Nu 31:16) The result: 24,000 men of Israel died for their sin. (Nu 25:1-9) Neither Midian nor Balaam escaped divine punishment. Jehovah commanded that all the men, women, and boys of Midian be executed; only virgins were spared. "And they killed Balaam the son of Beor with the sword." (Nu 25:16-18; 31:1-18) As for the Moabites, they were barred from the congregation of Jehovah "to the tenth generation."—De 23:3-6.

BALADAN (Bal′a·dan) [from Akkadian, meaning "God Has Given a Son"]. The father of Merodach-baladan (Isa 39:1; "Berodach-baladan" at 2Ki 20:12). Baladan's son Merodach-baladan was king of Babylon during at least part of the reign of King Hezekiah of Judah (745-717 B.C.E.).

BALAH. See BAALAH No. 3.

BALAK (Ba′lak) [He Has Laid Waste]. Baal-worshiping king of Moab in the 15th century B.C.E.; son of Zippor. Balak's people were frightened and filled with "a sickening dread" when they saw what Israel had done to the Amorites. In league with Midian, Balak sent to the town of Pethor by the Euphrates River for Balaam to come from Mesopotamia and curse Israel with "uncanny power," hoping thereby to gain a military advantage. (Nu 23:21) "Look!" Balak said to Balaam, "[the Israelites] have covered the earth as far as one can see, and they are dwelling right in front of me." At first Balaam declined to go, but after Balak sent a more honorable delegation of princes and raised his offer, the greedy prophet finally accepted, with Jehovah's allowance. Upon coming to the bank of the Arnon, Balak chided him: "Why did you not come to me [at first]? Am I not really and truly able to honor you?"—Nu 22:2-37.

Balak took Balaam to three vantage points from which to view the host of Israel. At each point the same sacrificial procedure was followed; Balak was directed to construct seven altars upon which seven bulls and seven rams were sacrificed. However, at each place, instead of cursing Israel, Balaam blessed them.—Nu 22:41–24:9; Mic 6:5.

At this, "Balak's anger blazed against Balaam." Clapping his hands in a rage, he exclaimed: "It was to execrate my enemies that I called you, and,

look! you have blessed them to the limit these three times. And now run your way off to your place." But before this prophet from Pethor departed, he foretold the Messianic "star" coming through Jacob's seed.—Nu 24:10-17; Jos 24:9, 10; Jg 11:25.

Subsequent events show that Balaam also "went teaching Balak to put a stumbling block before the sons of Israel, to eat things sacrificed to idols and to commit fornication."—Re 2:14; Nu 25:1-18.

BALDNESS. The absence of hair on the head, although not necessarily a total loss of hair. Often baldness occurs in spots or patches, while on other parts of the head the hair grows normally. This kind of hair loss is called pattern baldness and accounts for about 90 percent of all cases. The Bible makes mention of "baldness" (Heb., qor·chah′), "baldness of the crown" (Heb., qa·ra′chath), and "forehead baldness" (Heb., gib·be′ach and gab·ba′chath). (Le 13:41-44; 21:5) The exact cause of baldness is unknown. Heredity is considered the primary contributing factor, while infection, hormone imbalance, aging, nervous disorders, even some medical treatments, and syphilis may be factors.

Baldness is a defect that interferes with personal attractiveness and so among peoples of ancient times was associated with shame, mourning, and distress. (Isa 3:24; 15:2; Jer 47:5; Eze 27:31; Am 8:10; Mic 1:16) However, under the Law of Moses, baldness was not considered as uncleanness. (Le 13:40) The Law given through Moses does not list baldness as a defect that would prevent one from being allowed to serve as priest. In the prophet Ezekiel's vision the command was given that the priests should wear their hair neither loose nor shaved, but clipped.—Eze 44:20.

Jehovah's prophet Elisha was bald. After he had succeeded to the prophetic office of Elijah, he was proceeding uphill from Jericho toward Bethel when he was mocked by a mob of children who cried: "Go up, you baldhead! Go up, you baldhead!" The primary reason for their jeers seems to have been not that Elisha was bald but that they saw a bald man wearing Elijah's familiar official garment. They did not want any successor of Elijah around. He should either keep going his way up to Bethel or ascend in a windstorm to the heavens as the former wearer of that official garment had done. (2Ki 2:11) To answer this challenge of his being Elijah's successor and to teach these young people and their parents proper respect for Jehovah's prophet, Elisha called down evil upon the jeering mob in the name of the God of Elijah. It was a test of his prophetship. Jehovah manifested his approval of Elisha by causing two she-bears to come out of the nearby woods and to tear to pieces 42 of them.—2Ki 2:23, 24.

Some peoples made a practice of artificially imposing baldness by shaving in time of sorrow at the death of a relative or for religious reasons, but the Israelites were forbidden to practice this. (De 14:1) Priests were given a specific command that they should not make themselves bald or shave the extremities of their beards for the dead. (Le 21:5) Israel was commanded that they should not cut the sidelocks or extremity of their beards.—Le 19:27; Jer 9:26; see BEARD.

In Egypt, the men generally shaved their heads, and they looked upon beards as a sign of mourning or slovenliness. For this reason Joseph, when taken out of prison, shaved before being brought into the presence of Pharaoh. (Ge 41:14) However, the Egyptians covered baldness with wigs, and many who shaved their heads and beards wore wigs and tied on false beards. In the Ebers Papyrus, an Egyptian medical treatise from the second millennium B.C.E., there are 11 prescriptions for preventing baldness.

In the Law, one with head leprosy was to shave his head at the beginning of his quarantine period, on the day of purification, and again on the seventh day. (Le 13:33; 14:8, 9) If a Nazirite became defiled, then at the time of establishing his purification he shaved his head. (Nu 6:9) A captive woman whom an Israelite soldier was to take as a wife had to shave her head.—De 21:12.

Nebuchadnezzar's troops experienced temporary baldness during the strenuous and difficult siege of the land city of Tyre. Jehovah said to Ezekiel that "every head was one made bald, and every shoulder was one rubbed bare" as Nebuchadnezzar's military force performed "a great service" in rendering judgment on Tyre. Their heads were made bald by the chafing of helmets and their shoulders from the rubbing of materials (for the construction of towers and fortifications). —Eze 26:7-12; 29:17, 18.

In some places in the days of the apostles, such as in the immoral city of Corinth, women caught committing adultery or fornication were punished by having their hair shaved off. Slave girls had their hair clipped short. Paul apparently draws on this circumstance for illustration, showing that a woman in the Christian congregation who would pray or prophesy with her head uncovered, even though she had her hair as a covering, might as well go the whole way and show her shame in disrespecting God's headship principle by having her hair completely shaved off.—1Co 11:3-10.

BALSAM, BALSAM OF GILEAD. The term "balsam" applies to any of the many plants, shrubs, and trees producing an aromatic and, commonly, oily and resinous substance. There are balsamiferous trees among the fir, spruce, poplar, and other tree families. The balsamic oil is used medicinally (usually containing benzoic or cinnamic acid) and as a perfume.

Balsam plants and trees were always highly prized by the peoples of the Orient. The first mention of "balsam oil" (Heb., bo'sem, be'sem, or ba·sam') occurs at Exodus 25:6 with reference to its use as an ingredient in the holy anointing oil of the tabernacle. (See also Ex 35:8, 28.) The Hebrew word is sometimes translated as "perfumes," "sweet," or "spice," according to the context. (Ex 30:23; Ca 4:10, 14, 16; 5:13; 6:2; 8:14) At Isaiah 3:24 its aromatic fragrance is contrasted with "a musty smell."

The balsam used for the tabernacle service in the wilderness evidently came from outside of Palestine, perhaps from Egypt. During King Solomon's reign the preciousness of balsam oil caused it to be ranked along with the gold and precious stones among the treasures that the queen of Sheba brought as gifts; it was also included in the tribute paid by the kings of many lands to the wise king in Jerusalem. (1Ki 10:2, 10, 25; 2Ch 9:1, 9, 24) It was among the precious things stored in the king's treasure-house that Hezekiah unwisely showed to the emissaries from Babylon. (2Ki 20: 13; 2Ch 32:27; Isa 39:2) It was used in the embalming (though not in the Egyptian way) of King Asa's body. (2Ch 16:14) The English word "embalm" appears to be originally derived from the Hebrew ba·sam'. Esther was massaged with aromatic balsam oil during the final six-month period prior to her appearance before King Ahasuerus. —Es 2:12.

The "balsam [Heb., tsori'] in Gilead" appears to have been of a unique quality and possessed of special medicinal properties. (Jer 8:22; 46:11) This balsam is first mentioned as among the articles carried by the caravan of Ishmaelites from Gilead, E of the Jordan, and to whom Joseph was subsequently sold. (Ge 37:25-28) Jacob later included it in with "the finest products of the land" when sending a gift to Egypt with his returning sons. (Ge 43:11) According to Ezekiel 27:17, the wealthy merchants of Tyre imported it from the kingdom of Judah.

References to the healing virtues of balsam, chiefly as a cure for wounds, are common in ancient literature. All references to such healing properties in the Scriptures are made by Jeremiah. He uses these, however, in a figurative sense, first when lamenting the spiritual breakdown in Judah (Jer 8:14, 15, 21, 22; compare Jas 5:14, 15), then in chiding Egypt as to her vain efforts to avoid defeat by Babylon (Jer 46:11-13), and finally in pronouncing God's judgment of calamity against Babylon.—Jer 51:8-10.

Identification of the specific plants or trees represented by the Hebrew words *bo'sem* and *tsori'* is not definite. The name "balsam of Gilead" has been applied to a shrublike evergreen tree called *Commiphora opobalsamum* (or, *Commiphora gileadensis*). Its greenish-yellow oily resin is gathered by making incisions in the stem and branches, and the little balls of sap that form are later collected. While this particular tree is found chiefly in S Arabia, the Jewish historian Josephus indicates that it was cultivated around Jericho in Solomon's time, and the Greek geographer Strabo records that in Roman times it was also grown beside the Sea of Galilee.

It has been suggested that *tsori'* may refer to the mastic tree (*Pistacia lentiscus*), which produces a pale-yellow fragrant gum called mastic, as well as an oil used for medicinal purposes obtained from the bark, leaves, and berries. The tree is common in Palestine, and its name in Arabic is very similar to the Hebrew *tsori'*.

BAMOTH   (Ba'moth) [High Places]. One of the encampment stages of the nation of Israel on its approach to the land of Canaan. (Nu 21:19, 20) Bamoth is listed as between Nahaliel and "the valley that is in the field of Moab, at the head of Pisgah." It is probably a shortened form of Bamoth-baal.—See BAMOTH-BAAL.

BAMOTH-BAAL   (Ba'moth-ba'al) [High Places of Baal]. A town in Moab to which Balak, the king of Moab, conducted the prophet Balaam so that he might see the camp of Israel and call down a curse upon it. (Nu 22:41) Balak's selection of this location for the enacting of the curse and the accompanying sacrifices may indicate that it was a center for Baal worship, evidently situated in an elevated place. (Nu 23:1-9) Thereafter, Bamoth-baal and other towns "on the tableland" were assigned to the tribe of Reuben as an inheritance. (Jos 13:15, 17) In the latter part of the tenth century B.C.E. King Mesha of Moab states that he rebuilt "Beth-bamoth, for it had been destroyed." (Line 27 of the Moabite Stone) It seems likely that Bamoth, Bamoth-baal, and Beth-bamoth were all names of the same place.—Compare Baal-meon, Beon, Beth-baal-meon in the article on BAAL-MEON.

The description given in the Bible account indicates a place on the plateau region toward the NE corner of the Dead Sea. While the identification is only tentative, a suggested location is that of Khirbet Quweijiya, about 14 km (9 mi) E of the Dead Sea, near the probable location of Mount Nebo.

BAN.   This word is used in certain modern translations (*JB, NE, NW*) to render the Hebrew *che'rem*, also rendered in the *New World Translation* as "thing devoted to destruction." The Hebrew word refers to that which is irrevocably and irredeemably devoted to God and thus separated out for sacred use, but is most frequently used with reference to things thus separated for complete destruction. It can apply to an individual person. (Ex 22:20; *JB* here reads: "Anyone who sacrifices to other gods shall come under the ban ["be devoted to destruction," *NW*]"; Le 27:29) Or it may apply to his possessions (Ezr 10:8); to an animal, to a field, or to any article so devoted to sacred use (Le 27:21, 28); or to an entire city and all things therein.—De 13:15-17; Jos 6:17.

Sacred bans figured in certain prophecies. (Mic 4:13; Zec 14:11) For a complete discussion of the subject, see DEVOTED THING.

BANGLE.   See ANKLET.

BANI   (Ba'ni) [from a root meaning "build"].

1. A Levite in the line of Merari, and ancestor of the Ethan whom David appointed to temple service.—1Ch 6:31, 44, 46.

2. One of David's mighty men, a Gadite.—2Sa 23:36.

3. A descendant of Judah through Perez, whose descendants lived in Jerusalem after the exile. (1Ch 9:3, 4) It is possible that this family head was the same as Nos. 4 and 5 or as 4 and 6 below.

4. A family head whose descendants, over 600 in number, returned to Jerusalem with Zerubbabel. (Ezr 2:1, 10) He is called Binnui at Nehemiah 7:15.—See No. 3 above.

5. A family head, six of whose descendants dismissed their foreign wives and sons in Ezra's time. Not the same as No. 6 below.—Ezr 10:29, 44; see No. 3 above.

6. A family head in Israel who apparently had 12 descendants who dismissed their foreign wives and sons in Ezra's day. Not the same as No. 5 above.—Ezr 10:34, 44; see No. 3 above.

7. A Levite whose son Rehum helped repair Jerusalem's wall in 455 B.C.E. Compare Nos. 8-10, 12 below.—Ne 3:17.

8. A Levite who assisted Ezra with reading and explaining the Law to the people.—Ne 8:7; 9:4, 5; see No. 7 above.

9. The second-listed of two Levites named Bani who were on the platform when public confession of Israel's sins was made in 455 B.C.E.—Ne 9:4.

10. A Levite whose descendant, if not he himself, attested by seal to Nehemiah's "trustworthy arrangement."—Ne 9:38; 10:13.

11. One of "the heads of the people" whose descendant, if not he himself, also attested to the "trustworthy arrangement."—Ne 9:38; 10:14.

12. A Levite descendant of Asaph whose son Uzzi was overseer of the Levites in Jerusalem in the days of Nehemiah.—Ne 11:22; see No. 7 above.

BANK, BANKER. In Jesus' parables of the talents and the minas he referred to bankers and to a bank as giving interest on money deposited with them. (Mt 25:27; Lu 19:23) Much like the English word "bank" (which derives from the Italian word *banca* for bench or counter), the Greek word translated bank, *tra'pe·za*, literally meant a "table" (Mt 15:27), or when associated with financial operations, as with the money changers, it referred to a counter for money.—Mt 21:12; Mr 11:15; Joh 2:15.

The reference to the banker (Gr., *tra·pe·zei'tes*) as accepting deposits and paying interest indicates a larger operation than that generally performed by a money broker (Gr., *ker·ma·ti·stes'*), or money changer (*kol·ly·bi·stes'*), whose main operations were to exchange local money for foreign money and provide coins of lesser value in exchange for ones of greater value, receiving a certain fee for each such service. (See MONEY CHANGER.) Some of these men may also have done banking, accepting deposits and making loans, while in other cases these financial transactions were handled by men of wealth, such as merchants and owners of large estates.

Evidence of such banking activity goes back apparently to the time of Abraham, for the ancient Sumerians of the land of Shinar carried on "a surprisingly complex system of lending, borrowing, holding money on deposit, and providing letters of credit." (*The Encyclopedia Americana*, 1956, Vol. III, p. 152) In Babylon, as later in Greece, the banking activities centered around the religious temples whose sacrosanct position in the minds of the people provided security against assault by thieves.

Inasmuch as the economy of the nation of Israel was fundamentally agricultural, the need for financial enterprises was considerably less than in such commercial centers as Babylon, Tyre, and Sidon. While the taking of any interest on loans made to their fellow Israelites is condemned at Deuteronomy 23:19, this appears to have been primarily in cases of borrowing done by needy and impoverished persons. (Compare Ex 22:25; Le 25:35-37; 2Ki 4:1-7.) Interest was specifically allowable on loans to non-Israelites. (De 23:20) Valuables were often left in the care of some trusted persons for safekeeping (Ex 22:7), while others resorted to burying them in the ground, as did the sluggish slave of Jesus' parable. (Mt 25:25; compare Mt 13:44.) Evidence of this practice is seen in the large quantities of valuables and coins unearthed by both archaeologists and farmers in Bible lands.

Certain ones of the Israelites who returned from Babylon to the land of Judah were condemned for applying harsh banking practices toward their needy brothers, exacting security in the form of their homes, lands, vineyards, and even their children, and charging an interest rate of 12 percent annually (one hundredth part per month). Those debtors who defaulted because of insolvency thus suffered the loss of their properties. (Ne 5:1-11) Such improper action, however, did not place a blanket condemnation on the receiving of interest, as is evidenced by Jesus' later expression of implied approval of the use of capital to obtain increased funds.—See INTEREST.

BAPTISM. The Greek *ba'pti·sma* refers to the process of immersion, including submersion and emergence; it is derived from the verb *ba'pto*, meaning "dip." (Joh 13:26) In the Bible, "to baptize" is the same as "to immerse." In illustration of this, *The Holy Bible, An Improved Edition*, renders Romans 6:3, 4 as follows: "Or, are ye ignorant, that all we who were baptized (immersed) into Christ Jesus were baptized (immersed) into his death? We were buried therefore with him through our baptism (immersion) into his death." (See also *Ro; ED*.) The Greek *Septuagint* uses a form of the same word for "dip" at Exodus 12:22 and Leviticus 4:6. (See *NW* ftns.) When one is immersed in water, one is temporarily "buried" out of sight and then lifted out.

We shall consider four different aspects of baptism, together with related questions: (1) John's baptism, (2) water baptism of Jesus and his followers, (3) baptism into Christ Jesus and into his death, (4) baptism with fire.

John's Baptism. The first human authorized by God to perform water baptism was John the son of Zechariah and Elizabeth. (Lu 1:5-7, 57) The very fact that he was known as "John the Baptist" or "the baptizer" (Mt 3:1; Mr 1:4) implies that baptism or water immersion came to the attention of the people especially through John, and the Scriptures prove that his ministry and baptism came from God; they were not of John's origin. His works were foretold by the angel Gabriel as from God (Lu 1:13-17), and Zechariah prophesied by holy spirit that John would be a prophet of the Most High to make Jehovah's ways ready. (Lu 1:68-79) Jesus confirmed that John's ministry and baptism were from God. (Lu 7:26-28) The disciple Luke records that "God's declaration came to John the son of Zechariah in the wilderness. So he came . . . preaching baptism." (Lu 3:2, 3) The apostle John states of him: "There arose a man that was sent forth as a representative of God: his name was John."—Joh 1:6.

Further understanding of the meaning of John's baptism is gained by comparing various translations of Luke 3:3. John came "preaching baptism in symbol of repentance for forgiveness of sins" (*NW*); "baptism conditioned on repentance" (*CB*); "baptism whereby men repented, to have their sins forgiven" (*Kx*); "baptism in token of repentance for the forgiveness of sins" (*NE*); "Turn away from your sins and be baptized, and God will forgive your sins" (*TEV*). These renderings make plain that the baptism did not wash away their sins, but the repentance and changing of their ways did, and of this, baptism was a symbol.

The baptism performed by John was therefore not a special cleansing from God through his servant John, but a public demonstration and symbol of the individual's repentance over his sins against the Law, which was to lead them to Christ. (Ga 3:24) John thereby prepared a people to "see the saving means of God." (Lu 3:6) His work served to "get ready for Jehovah a prepared people." (Lu 1:16, 17) Such a work had been prophesied by Isaiah and Malachi.—Isa 40:3-5; Mal 4:5, 6.

Some scholars try to read anticipation of John's baptism and the Christian baptism in ancient purification ceremonies under the Law (Ex 29:4; Le 8:6; 14:8, 31, 32; Heb 9:10, ftn) or in individual acts. (Ge 35:2; Ex 19:10) But these instances bear no analogy to the real meaning of baptism. They were washings for ceremonial cleanness. In only one instance is there anything approaching a dipping of the body completely under water. This is in the case of Naaman the leper, and the plunging into water was done *seven* times. (2Ki 5:14) It did not bring him into any special relationship with God, but it merely cured him of leprosy. Besides, Scripturally, proselytes were circumcised, not baptized. To partake of the Passover or engage in worship at the sanctuary one had to be circumcised.—Ex 12:43-49.

Neither are there any grounds for the assertion made by some that John's baptism was probably borrowed from the Jewish sect the Essenes or from the Pharisees. Both of these sects had many requirements for ablutions to be performed often. But Jesus showed such to be mere commandments of men who overstepped the commandments of God by their tradition. (Mr 7:1-9; Lu 11:38-42) John baptized in water because, as he said, he was sent by God to baptize in water. (Joh 1:33) He was not sent by the Essenes or by the Pharisees. His commission was not to make Jewish proselytes but to baptize those who were already members of the Jewish congregation.—Lu 1:16.

John knew that his works were merely a preparing of the way before God's Son and Messiah and would give way to the greater ministry of that One. The reason for John's baptizing was that the Messiah might be made manifest to Israel. (Joh 1:31) According to John 3:26-30, the Messiah's ministry would increase, but John's ministry was to decrease. Those who were baptized by Jesus' disciples during Jesus' earthly ministry and who therefore also became Jesus' disciples were baptized in symbol of repentance in the manner of John's baptism.—Joh 3:25, 26; 4:1, 2.

Jesus' Baptism in Water. The baptism of Jesus himself as performed by John must of necessity have had a meaning and purpose quite different from John's baptism, as Jesus "committed no sin, nor was deception found in his mouth." (1Pe 2:22) So he could not submit to an act symbolizing repentance. Undoubtedly it was for this reason that John objected to baptizing Jesus. But Jesus said: "Let it be, this time, for in that way it is suitable for us to carry out all that is righteous." —Mt 3:13-15.

Luke states that Jesus was praying at the time of his baptism. (Lu 3:21) Further, the writer of the letter to the Hebrews says that when Jesus Christ came "into the world" (that is, not when he was born and could not read and say these words, but when he presented himself for baptism and began his ministry) he was saying, in accord with Psalm 40:6-8 (*LXX*): "Sacrifice and offering you did not want, but you prepared a body for me. . . . Look! I am come (in the roll of the book it is written about me) to do your will, O God." (Heb 10:5-9) Jesus was by birth a member of the Jewish nation, which nation was in a national covenant with God, namely, the Law covenant. (Ex 19:5-8; Ga 4:4) Jesus, by reason of this fact, was therefore already in a covenant relationship with Jehovah God when he thus presented himself to John for baptism.

Jesus was there doing something more than what was required of him under the Law. He was presenting himself to his Father Jehovah to do his Father's "will" with reference to the offering of his own "prepared" body and with regard to doing away with animal sacrifices that were offered according to the Law. The apostle Paul comments: "By the said 'will' we have been sanctified through the offering of the body of Jesus Christ once for all time." (Heb 10:10) The Father's will for Jesus also involved activity in connection with the Kingdom, and for this service too Jesus presented himself. (Lu 4:43; 17:20, 21) Jehovah accepted and acknowledged this presentation of his Son, anointing him with holy spirit and saying: "You are my Son, the beloved; I have approved you."—Mr 1:9-11; Lu 3:21-23; Mt 3:13-17.

Water Baptism of Jesus' Followers. John's baptism was due to be replaced by the baptism commanded by Jesus: "Make disciples of people of all the nations, baptizing them in the name of the Father and of the Son and of the holy spirit." (Mt 28:19) This was the only water baptism having God's approval from Pentecost, 33 C.E., forward. Some years after 33 C.E., Apollos, a zealous man, was teaching correctly about Jesus, but he had an understanding of only John's baptism. On this matter he had to be corrected, as did the disciples whom Paul met at Ephesus. These men in Ephesus had undergone John's baptism, but evidently after its valid performance had ended, since Paul's visit to Ephesus was about 20 years after the termination of the Law covenant. They were then baptized correctly in the name of Jesus and received holy spirit.—Ac 18:24-26; 19:1-7.

That Christian baptism required an understanding of God's Word and an intelligent decision to present oneself to do the revealed will of God was evident when, at Pentecost, 33 C.E., the Jews and proselytes there assembled, who already had a knowledge of the Hebrew Scriptures, heard Peter speak about Jesus the Messiah, with the result that 3,000 "embraced his word heartily" and "were baptized." (Ac 2:41; 3:19–4:4; 10:34-38) Those in Samaria first believed Philip's preaching of the good news, and then they were baptized. (Ac 8:12) The Ethiopian eunuch, a devout Jewish proselyte who, as such, also had knowledge of Jehovah and the Hebrew Scriptures, heard first the explanation of the fulfillment of these scriptures in Christ, accepted it, and then wanted to be baptized. (Ac 8:34-36) Peter explained to Cornelius that "the man that fears [God] and works righteousness is acceptable" (Ac 10:35) and that everyone putting faith in Jesus Christ gets forgiveness of sins through his name. (Ac 10:43;

11:18) All of this is in harmony with Jesus' command to "make disciples . . . teaching them to observe all the things I have commanded you." Those who accept the teaching and who become disciples properly get baptized.—Mt 28:19, 20; Ac 1:8.

At Pentecost, Jews who bore community responsibility for Jesus' death, and who doubtless knew of John's baptism, were "stabbed to the heart" by Peter's preaching and asked: "Brothers, what shall we do?" Peter answered: "Repent, and let each one of you be baptized in the name of Jesus Christ for forgiveness of your sins, and you will receive the free gift of the holy spirit." (Ac 2:37, 38) Notice that Peter pointed out something new to them—that, not repentance and baptism in John's baptism, but repentance and baptism *in the name of Jesus Christ* was necessary for forgiveness of sins. He did not say that baptism itself washed away sins. Peter knew that "the blood of Jesus [God's] Son cleanses us from all sin." (1Jo 1:7) Later, after speaking of Jesus as "the Chief Agent of life," Peter said to Jews at the temple: "Repent, therefore, and turn around so as to get your sins blotted out, that seasons of refreshing may come from the person of Jehovah." (Ac 3:15, 19) Here he instructed them that repenting of their bad deed against Christ and 'turning around,' to recognize him, was what brought forgiveness of sin; he did not at this point mention baptism.

As for the Jews, the Law covenant was abolished on the basis of Christ's death on the torture stake (Col 2:14), and the new covenant became operative at Pentecost, 33 C.E. (Compare Ac 2:4; Heb 2:3, 4.) Nevertheless, God extended special favor to the Jews about three and a half years longer. During this time Jesus' disciples confined their preaching to Jews, Jewish proselytes, and Samaritans. But about 36 C.E. God directed Peter to go to the home of the Gentile Cornelius, a Roman army officer, and by pouring out His holy spirit on Cornelius and his household, showed Peter that Gentiles could now be accepted for water baptism. (Ac 10:34, 35, 44-48) Since God no longer recognized the Law covenant with the circumcised Jews but now recognized only his new covenant mediated by Jesus Christ, natural Jews, whether circumcised or uncircumcised, were not considered by God as being in any special relationship with him. They could not attain to a status with God by observing the Law, which was no longer valid, nor by John's baptism, which had to do with the Law, but were obliged to approach God through faith in his Son and be baptized in water in the name of Jesus Christ in order to have

Jehovah's recognition and favor.—See SEVENTY WEEKS (Covenant in force "for one week").

Consequently, after 36 C.E., all, Jews and Gentiles, have had the same standing in God's eyes. (Ro 11:30-32; 14:12) The people of the Gentile nations, except for those who had been circumcised Jewish proselytes, were not in the Law covenant and had never been a people having a special relationship with God the Father. Now the opportunity was extended to them as individuals to become God's people. Before they could be baptized in water they, therefore, had to come to God as believers in his Son Jesus Christ. Then, according to Christ's example and command, they would properly submit to water baptism.—Mt 3:13-15; 28:18-20.

Such Christian baptism would have a vital effect on their standing before God. After referring to Noah's constructing of the ark in which he and his family were preserved through the Flood, the apostle Peter wrote: "That which corresponds to this is also now saving you, namely, baptism, (not the putting away of the filth of the flesh, but the request made to God for a good conscience,) through the resurrection of Jesus Christ." (1Pe 3: 20, 21) The ark was tangible evidence that Noah had dedicated himself to do God's will and had then faithfully done the work assigned by God. This led to his preservation. In a corresponding way, those who would dedicate themselves to Jehovah on the basis of faith in the resurrected Christ, get baptized in symbol of that, and do God's will for his servants would be saved from the present wicked world. (Ga 1:3, 4) No longer would they be headed for destruction with the rest of the world. They would be saved from this and would be granted a good conscience by God.

No Infant Baptism. In view of the fact that 'hearing the word,' 'embracing the word heartily,' and 'repenting' precede water baptism (Ac 2:14, 22, 38, 41) and that baptism requires the individual to make a solemn decision, it is apparent that one must at least be of age to hear, to believe, and to make this decision. An argument is made by some in favor of infant baptism. They refer to the instances where 'households' were baptized, such as the households of Cornelius, Lydia, the Philippian jailer, Crispus, and Stephanas. (Ac 10:48; 11: 14; 16:15, 32-34; 18:8; 1Co 1:16) They believe that this implies that small babies in those families were also baptized. But, in the case of Cornelius, those who were baptized were those who had heard the word and received the holy spirit, and they spoke in tongues and glorified God; these

things could not apply to infants. (Ac 10:44-46) Lydia was "a worshiper of God, . . . and Jehovah opened her heart wide to pay attention to the things being spoken by Paul." (Ac 16:14) The Philippian jailer had to "believe on the Lord Jesus," and this implies that the others in his family also had to believe in order to be baptized. (Ac 16:31-34) "Crispus the presiding officer of the synagogue became a believer in the Lord, and so did all his household." (Ac 18:8) All of this demonstrates that associated with baptism were such things as hearing, believing, and glorifying God, things infants cannot do. At Samaria when they heard and believed "the good news of the kingdom of God and of the name of Jesus Christ, they proceeded to be baptized." Here the Scriptural record specifies that the ones baptized were, not infants, but "men and women."—Ac 8:12.

The statement made by the apostle Paul to the Corinthians that children were "holy" by reason of a believing parent is no proof that infants were baptized; rather, it implies the opposite. Minor children too young to have the ability to make such a decision would come under a form of merit because of the believing parent, not because of any so-called sacramental baptism, imparting independent merit. If infants could properly be baptized, they would not need to have the merit of the believing parent extended to them.—1Co 7:14.

It is true that Jesus said: "Stop hindering [the young children] from coming to me, for the kingdom of the heavens belongs to suchlike ones." (Mt 19:13-15; Mr 10:13-16) But they were not baptized. Jesus blessed them, and there is nothing to indicate that his laying his hands upon them was a religious ceremony. He further showed that the reason 'the kingdom of God belongs to such' was not because they were baptized but because they were teachable and trusting. Christians are commanded to be "babes as to badness," yet "fullgrown in powers of understanding."—Mt 18:4; Lu 18:16, 17; 1Co 14:20.

The religious historian Augustus Neander wrote of the first-century Christians: "The practice of infant baptism was unknown at this period. . . . That not till so late a period as (at least *certainly* not earlier than) Irenæus [c. 140-203 C.E.], a trace of infant baptism appears, and that it first became recognised as an apostolic tradition in the course of the third century, is evidence rather *against* than *for* the admission of its apostolic origin." —*History of the Planting and Training of the Christian Church by the Apostles*, 1864, p. 162.

Complete Immersion. From the definition of baptism as stated earlier, it is clear that baptism is complete immersion or submersion in water, not a mere pouring or sprinkling. The Bible examples of baptism corroborate this fact. Jesus was baptized in a sizable river, the Jordan, and after being baptized he came "up out of the water." (Mr 1:10; Mt 3:13, 16) John selected a location in the Jordan Valley near Salim to baptize, "because there was a great quantity of water there." (Joh 3:23) The Ethiopian eunuch asked to be baptized when they came to "a body of water." They both "went down into the water." Afterward they came "up out of the water." (Ac 8:36-40) All these instances imply, not a small ankle-deep pool, but a large body of water into and out of which they would have to walk. Further, the fact that baptism was also used to symbolize a burial indicates complete submersion.—Ro 6:4-6; Col 2:12.

Historical sources show that the early Christians baptized by immersion. On this subject the *New Catholic Encyclopedia* (1967, Vol. II, p. 56) states: "It is evident that Baptism in the early Church was by immersion." *Larousse du XXe Siècle*, Paris, 1928, says: "The first Christians received baptism by immersion everywhere where water was found."

Baptism Into Christ Jesus, Into His Death. Jesus knew at the time of his baptism in the Jordan River that he was entering upon a sacrificial course. He knew that his 'prepared body' must be put to death, that he must die in innocence as a perfect human sacrifice with ransoming value for mankind. (Mt 20:28) Jesus understood that he must be plunged into death but that he would be raised out of it on the third day. (Mt 16:21) So he likened his experience to a baptism into death. (Lu 12:50) He explained to his disciples that he was already undergoing this baptism during his ministry. (Mr 10:38, 39) He was baptized *fully* into death when he was plunged into death by being impaled on the torture stake on Nisan 14, 33 C.E. His resurrection by his Father Jehovah God on the third day completed this baptism, which includes a raising up. Jesus' baptism into death is clearly distinct and separate from his water baptism, for he had completely undergone water baptism at the beginning of his ministry, at which time his baptism into death only began.

The faithful apostles of Jesus Christ were baptized in water by John's baptism. (Joh 1:35-37; 4:1) But they had not yet been baptized with holy spirit when Jesus pointed out that they were also to be baptized in a symbolic baptism like his, a baptism into death. (Mr 10:39) So baptism into his death is something apart from water baptism.

Paul expressed himself in his letter to the Christian congregation at Rome, saying: "Do you not know that all of us who were baptized into Christ Jesus were baptized into his death?"—Ro 6:3.

It is Jehovah God who is responsible for the performing of such baptism into Christ Jesus as well as baptism into his death. He anointed Jesus, making him the Christ or Anointed One. (Ac 10:38) Thus God baptized Jesus with the holy spirit in order that, through Jesus, his followers might thereafter be baptized with holy spirit. Therefore, those who become joint heirs with him, with heavenly hopes, have to be "baptized into *Christ* Jesus," that is, into the *Anointed* Jesus who, at the time of his anointing, was also begotten to be a spiritual son of God. They thereby become united to him, their Head, and they become members of the congregation that is the body of Christ.—1Co 12:12, 13, 27; Col 1:18.

The course of these Christian followers who are baptized into Christ Jesus is a course of integrity-keeping under test from the time they are baptized into Christ, a daily facing of death and finally a death of integrity, as described by the apostle Paul when he explained to the Roman Christians: "Therefore we were buried with him through our baptism into his death, in order that, just as Christ was raised up from the dead through the glory of the Father, we also should likewise walk in a newness of life. For if we have become united with him in the likeness of his death, we shall certainly also be united with him in the likeness of his resurrection."—Ro 6:4, 5; 1Co 15:31-49.

Clarifying the matter still further, Paul, in writing to the congregation at Philippi, described his own course as "a sharing in [Christ's] sufferings, submitting myself to a death like his, to see if I may by any means attain to the earlier resurrection from the dead." (Php 3:10, 11) Only the Almighty God the heavenly Father, who is the Baptizer of those who are baptized in union with Jesus Christ and into his death, can complete the baptism. This He does through Christ by raising them up out of death to be united with Jesus Christ in the likeness of his resurrection, which is to heavenly, immortal life.—1Co 15:53, 54.

That a congregation of people can, so to speak, be baptized or immersed into a liberator and leader is illustrated by the apostle Paul when he describes the congregation of Israel as being "baptized into Moses by means of the cloud and of the sea." There they were covered with a protecting cloud and with the walls of water on each side of them, being, symbolically speaking, immersed.

Moses foretold that God would raise up a prophet like himself; Peter applied this prophecy to Jesus Christ.—1Co 10:1, 2; De 18:15-19; Ac 3:19-23.

What is baptism "for the purpose of being dead ones"?

The passage at 1 Corinthians 15:29 is variously rendered by translators: "What shall they do which are baptized for the dead?" (*KJ*); "on behalf of their dead?" (*AT*); "on behalf of the dead?" (*NE*); "for the purpose of being dead ones?" (*NW*)

Many different interpretations have been offered for this verse. The most common interpretation is that Paul was referring to the custom of vicarious baptism in water, that is, baptizing living persons in behalf of dead ones in a substitutionary way in order to benefit the dead. The existence of such a practice in Paul's day cannot be proved, nor would it be in accord with those scriptures that clearly state that "disciples," those who themselves 'embraced the word heartily,' those who personally "believed," were the ones that got baptized.—Mt 28:19; Ac 2:41; 8:12.

A Greek-English Lexicon, by Liddell and Scott, includes "for," "on behalf of," and "for the sake of" among its definitions of the Greek preposition *hy·per'*, which is used with the genitive case in 1 Corinthians 15:29. (Revised by H. Jones, Oxford, 1968, p. 1857) In some settings the expression "for the sake of" is equivalent to "for the purpose of." Already in 1728 Jacob Elsner noted cases from various Greek writers where *hy·per'* with the genitive has final meaning, that is, a meaning expressive of purpose, and he showed that in 1 Corinthians 15:29 this construction has such meaning. (*Observationes Sacræ in Novi Foederis Libros,* Utrecht, Vol. II, pp. 127-131) Consistent with this, in this verse the *New World Translation* renders *hy·per'* as meaning "for the purpose of."

Where an expression can grammatically be translated in more than one way, the correct rendering is one that agrees with the context. In the context, 1 Corinthians 15:3, 4 shows that what is principally under discussion is belief in the death and resurrection of Jesus Christ. The following verses then present evidence of the soundness of that belief (vss 5-11); they discuss the serious implications of denying belief in the resurrection (vss 12-19), the fact that the resurrection of Christ gives assurance that others will be raised from the dead (vss 20-23), and how all of this works toward the unification of all intelligent creation with God (vss 24-28). Verse 29 obviously is an integral part of this discussion. But whose resurrection is at issue in verse 29? Is it the resurrection of the ones whose baptism is referred to there? Or is it that of someone who died before that baptism took place? What do the following verses indicate? Verses 30 to 34 clearly show that the future life prospects of *living* Christians are there being discussed, and verses 35 to 58 state that those were faithful Christians who had the hope of heavenly life.

That agrees with Romans 6:3, which says: "Do you not know that all of us who were baptized into Christ Jesus were baptized into his death?" As this scripture makes plain, that is not a baptism that a Christian undergoes on behalf of someone already dead but is, instead, something that affects the person's own future.

In what sense, then, were those Christians "baptized for the purpose of being dead ones," or "baptized into his death"? They were immersed into a course of life that was to lead them as integrity-keepers to death, as was the case with Christ, and with the hope of a resurrection like his to immortal spirit life. (Ro 6:4, 5; Php 3:10, 11) This was not a baptism that was accomplished quickly, as water immersion is. More than three years after his immersion in water, Jesus spoke of a baptism that was not yet completed in his own case and that was yet future for his disciples. (Mr 10:35-40) Since this baptism leads to resurrection to heavenly life, it must begin with the operation of God's spirit on the person in such a way as to engender that hope, and it must end, not at death, but with realization of the prospect of immortal spirit life by means of the resurrection.—2Co 1:21, 22; 1Co 6:14.

A Person's Place in God's Purpose. It should be noted that the one being baptized in water enters a special relationship as Jehovah's servant, to do His will. The individual does not determine what the will of God is for him, but it is God who makes the decision as to the use of the individual and the placing of such one in the framework of His purposes. For example, in times past, the entire nation of Israel was in special relationship with God; they were Jehovah's property. (Ex 19:5) But only the tribe of Levi was selected to perform the services at the sanctuary, and out of this tribe only Aaron's family constituted the priesthood. (Nu 1:48-51; Ex 28:1; 40:13-15) The kingship came to be established exclusively in the line of David's family by Jehovah God.—2Sa 7:15, 16.

Likewise those who undergo Christian baptism become God's property, his slaves, to employ as he sees fit. (1Co 6:20) An example of God's direction of such matters is found in Revelation, where reference is made to a definite number of persons finally "sealed," namely, 144,000. (Re 7:4-8) Even before such final approval, God's holy spirit serves as a seal that gives those sealed a token in advance of their inheritance, a heavenly one. (Eph 1:13, 14; 2Co 5:1-5) He also told these having such a hope: "God has set the members in the body [of Christ], each one of them, just as he pleased."—1Co 12: 18, 27.

Jesus called attention to another group when he said: "I have other sheep, which are not of this fold; those also I must bring, and they will listen to my voice, and they will become one flock, one shepherd." (Joh 10:16) These are not of the "little flock" (Lu 12:32), but they too must approach Jehovah through Jesus Christ and be baptized in water.

The vision given to the apostle John, as recorded in Revelation, harmonizes with this when, after showing John the 144,000 "sealed" ones, it turns his eyes to "a great crowd, which no man was able to number." These are shown as having "washed their robes and made them white in the blood of the Lamb," indicating faith in the ransom sacrifice of Jesus Christ the Lamb of God. (Re 7:9, 14) They are therefore given favorable recognition, "standing before [God's] throne," but are not those whom God selects to be the "sealed" 144,000. As to this "great crowd," the vision goes on to point out that they serve God day and night and will be protected and will be cared for by him.—Re 7:15-17.

Baptism With Fire. When many Pharisees and Sadducees came out to John the Baptizer, he called them "offspring of vipers." He spoke of the coming One and said: "That one will baptize you people with holy spirit and with fire." (Mt 3:7, 11; Lu 3:16) The baptism with fire is not the same as baptism with holy spirit. The fiery baptism could not be, as some say, the tongues of fire at Pentecost, for the disciples there were not immersed in fire. (Ac 2:3) John told his listeners that there would be a division, there would be a gathering of the wheat, after which the chaff would be burned up with fire that could not be put out. (Mt 3:12) He pointed out that the fire would not be a blessing or a reward but would be because 'the tree did not produce fine fruit.'—Mt 3:10; Lu 3:9.

Using fire as a symbol of destruction, Jesus foretold the execution of the wicked to take place during his presence, saying: "On the day that Lot came out of Sodom it rained fire and sulphur from heaven and destroyed them all. The same way it will be on that day when the Son of man is to be revealed." (Lu 17:29, 30; Mt 13:49, 50) Other instances of fire representing, not a saving force, but a destructive one, are found at 2 Thessalonians 1:8; Jude 7; and 2 Peter 3:7, 10.

BARABBAS (Bar·ab′bas) [Son of the Father; possibly, Son of the Teacher]. The imprisoned criminal guilty of robbery, sedition, and murder whom Pilate set free in place of Jesus. Pilate did this, "wishing to satisfy the crowd" who clamored for the release of Barabbas at the insistence of the chief priests and older men.—Mt 27:15-26; Mr 15:6-15; Lu 23:16-25; Joh 18:39, 40; Ac 3:14.

This unique custom of releasing a prisoner on the eve of the Passover every year finds no basis or precedent in the Hebrew Scriptures, and there is no extrabiblical evidence of it as a Roman practice. It evidently was of Jewish origin, because Pilate said to the Jews: *"You have a custom* that I should release a man to you at the passover." —Joh 18:39.

BARACHEL (Bar′a·chel) [God Has Blessed]. Father of Job's friend Elihu; a Buzite, likely a descendant of Abraham's nephew Buz.—Job 32:2, 6; Ge 22:20, 21.

BARACHIAH (Bar·a·chi′ah) [Jehovah Has Blessed]. Father of the Zechariah who was murdered "between the sanctuary and the altar."—Mt 23:35; Lu 11:50, 51.

As to the words "son of Barachiah," they are not found in Luke's account, and they are omitted from Matthew's account in the Codex Sinaiticus (original scribe). It has been suggested that Jehoiada, the father of a Zechariah who was murdered, may have had two names, as is the case with other persons in the Bible.—Compare Mt 9:9 and Mr 2:14; Mt 10:2, 3.

It is generally understood that Jesus here referred to Zechariah "the son of Jehoiada the priest." (2Ch 24:20-22) This is the most logical conclusion, since Chronicles is listed last in the traditional Jewish canon, thereby making Abel the first and Zechariah the last righteous man recorded in the Hebrew Scriptures as having been murdered. According to 2 Chronicles 24:21, Zechariah was murdered "in the courtyard of Jehovah's house." The altar of burnt offering was in the inner courtyard, outside of and in front of the entrance to the sanctuary. This would correspond with Jesus' location of the incident "between the sanctuary and the altar."

Concerning both Abel and Zechariah a reckoning for the shedding of their blood was foretold. (Ge 4:10; 2Ch 24:22) Also, there is a strong parallel between the circumstances and events in the days of Zechariah the son of Jehoiada and those of the generation living when Jesus spoke these words. As Zechariah was dying he said: "Let Jehovah see to it and ask it back." Very soon his prophetic words began to be fulfilled. A small Syrian force came up, and Jehovah delivered a great military force of Judah into their hand, the princes of Judah being greatly ruined and despoiled. The Syrians executed acts of judgment on Jehoash and left him with many diseases, after which he was murdered by his servants. (2Ch 24:23-25) After describing the bloodguilt of those to whom he was talking, Jesus said: "All these things will come upon this generation." (Mt 23:36) Jesus' prophecy was fulfilled on Jerusalem and Judea in 70-73 C.E.

BARAK (Ba'rak) [Lightning]. Son of Abinoam of Kedesh in the territory of Naphtali. During an early period in the time of the judges the Israelites fell away from true worship, and so for 20 years God permitted them to be oppressed by Jabin, the king of Canaan. They cried out to Jehovah for relief, and it was then that Barak became their God-appointed leader. (Jg 4:1-3) Whereas the Israelites' Canaanite oppressors were heavily armed, "a shield could not be seen, nor a lance, among forty thousand in Israel." (Jg 5:8) However, in Barak's day, Jehovah gave Israel victory over their foes, a triumph that was not forgotten. (Ps 83:9) The two accounts of these matters in Judges (chapter 4, and in the exultant song of Deborah and Barak in chapter 5) complement each other and paint a vivid picture of what occurred at that time.

The prophetess Deborah, who was then judging Israel, spurs Barak to take the initiative in freeing his people. Barak consents, but on the condition that Deborah accompany him. She agrees, though telling Barak that Jehovah will sell Sisera, chief of Jabin's forces, into the hand of a woman.—Jg 4:4-9.

Barak recruits 10,000 men from Naphtali, Zebulun, and other tribes of Israel (Jg 4:6; 5:9-18) and ascends Mount Tabor. Hearing of this, Sisera and his forces, equipped with 900 chariots having iron scythes, advance toward the Israelites along the dry bed of the Kishon (in the Plain of Jezreel). With Barak in the lead, the Israelite army, being only lightly equipped, courageously descends from Mount Tabor, ready for the fray with the fully armored Canaanites. However, the Kishon became an overwhelming torrent, immobilizing the enemy chariots. Indeed, "from heaven did the stars fight, from their orbits they fought against Sisera. The torrent of Kishon washed them away." Barak and his men press their advantage, and the account states: "All the camp of Sisera fell by the edge of the sword. Not as much as one remained."—Jg 5:20-22; 4:10-16.

Sisera himself, having abandoned his chariot and his beleaguered army, flees and finds refuge in the tent of Jael, the wife of Heber, a Kenite who is at peace with Jabin. Jael extends hospitality to Sisera, but while he sleeps, she kills him by driving a tent pin through his temples and into the earth. When Barak comes along, Jael invites him into the tent, where he sees that Jehovah's word has come true; Sisera has actually been sold into the hand of a woman. (Jg 4:17-22; 5:24-27) Thereafter, the hand of the victorious Israelites "went on getting harder and harder against Jabin the king of Canaan, until they had cut off Jabin." Consequently, that area of Israel "had no further disturbance for forty years."—Jg 4:23, 24; 5:31.

Barak is cited as a faithful example among those "who through faith defeated kingdoms in conflict, . . . became valiant in war, routed the armies of foreigners."—Heb 11:32-34.

Barak may be the "Bedan" of 1 Samuel 12:11 (if *LXX* and *Sy* are followed).—See BEDAN No. 1.

BARBARIAN (Bar·bar'ian). The repetition of "bar bar" in the Greek bar'ba·ros conveyed the idea of stammering, babble, or unintelligible speech; hence the term "barbarian" was originally applied by the Greeks to a foreigner, particularly one speaking a different tongue. At that time it did not indicate lack of civilization, refinement, or good manners, nor did it convey any feeling of hostile contempt. "Barbarian" simply distinguished especially non-Greeks from Greeks, much the same as "Gentile" divides off non-Jews from Jews. These non-Greeks did not object or feel insulted because they were called barbarians. Some Jewish writers, including Josephus, recognized themselves as being designated by the term (*Jewish Antiquities,* XIV, 187 [x, 1]; *Against Apion,* I, 58 [11]); Romans called themselves barbarians until they adopted Greek culture. It is in this not unfavorable light, then, that Paul in writing to the Romans used an all-inclusive expression: "Both to Greeks and to Barbarians."—Ro 1:14.

The principal factor separating Greeks from the barbarian world was their language; hence the term had special reference to those who did not speak Greek, as, for example, the inhabitants of Malta who spoke an unrelated tongue. In this instance the *New World Translation* gives meaning to bar'ba·roi by rendering it "foreign-speaking people." (Ac 28:1, 2, 4) Writing on the gift of tongues, Paul twice calls one speaking in an unintelligible tongue bar'ba·ros ("foreigner"). (1Co 14: 11; see also Col 3:11.) Similarly, the Greek *Septuagint* uses bar'ba·ros at Psalm 113:1 (114:1 in Hebrew and English versions) and Ezekiel 21:36 (21:31 in English).

Because the Greeks felt that their language and culture were superior to all others, and because they suffered indignities at the hand of their enemies, the term "barbarian" gradually assumed its common disparaging connotation.

BAR-HUMITE (Bar-hu'mite). A variant reading of Baharumite; a resident of the village of Bahurim.—Compare 2Sa 23:31 and 1Ch 11:33; see BAHURIM; BAHARUMITE.

BARIAH (Ba·ri'ah) [Fugitive; Runaway]. Distant descendant of David through Solomon.—1Ch 3:1, 10, 22.

BAR-JESUS (Bar-Je'sus) [Son of Jesus]. A certain Jew of Paphos on the island of Cyprus in the first century C.E., who was "a sorcerer, a false prophet." (Ac 13:6) He assumed the professional name or title Elymas, meaning "Sorcerer."—See ELYMAS.

It appears that Bar-Jesus held the influential position of court magician and adviser to Sergius Paulus, the Roman proconsul at Paphos. As a "priest" of the divination cult, Bar-Jesus was naturally against Christianity, and wanting to protect his own lucrative position, he was adamant in his opposition to the preaching of Paul and Barnabas. So, when Sergius Paulus "earnestly sought to hear the word of God," Elymas "began opposing them, seeking to turn the proconsul away from the faith."—Ac 13:7, 8.

Thereupon, Paul looked this Satanic sorcerer in the eye and, "filled with holy spirit," responded: "O man full of every sort of fraud and every sort of villainy, you son of the Devil, you enemy of everything righteous, will you not quit distorting the right ways of Jehovah? Well, then, look! Jehovah's hand is upon you, and you will be blind, not seeing the sunlight for a period of time." Instantly Bar-Jesus was struck with blindness. The proconsul, upon witnessing this first recorded miracle of Paul, "was astounded at the teaching of Jehovah," and he immediately accepted the message and "became a believer."—Ac 13:9-12.

BARKOS (Bar'kos). Forefather of some Nethinim who returned to Jerusalem with Zerubbabel.—Ezr 2:43, 53; Ne 7:46, 55.

BARLEY (bar'ley) [Heb., se'o·rah'; Gr., kri'the']. An important cereal of the genus *Hordeum*, widespread in its cultivation from ancient times till now. It was one of the valuable products awaiting the Israelites in the Promised Land, and that region continues to be "a land of wheat and barley" to this day.—De 8:8.

The Hebrew name for barley (se'o·rah') is related to the word for "hair" (se·'ar') and is descriptive of the long slender bristles or awns forming the characteristic beard of the barley head. It is a very hardy plant, better able to withstand drought and adapt to a wider range of climates than any other grain. When mature it stands about 1 m (3 ft) high, with somewhat broader leaves than those of wheat.

The barley harvest figures prominently in the dramatic events of the book of Ruth. Sowing of barley was done in Israel during the month of Bul (October-November) after the early rains had begun to fall and the ground could be plowed. (Isa 28:24, 25) Barley matures more rapidly than wheat (Ex 9:31, 32), and the harvest began in the early spring during the month of Nisan (March-April), commencing in the hot Jordan Valley and continuing into the higher, more temperate sections until it reached the highland plateau region E of the Jordan in the month of Ziv (April-May). Barley harvest thus marked a definite time of the year (Ru 1:22; 2Sa 21:9), and its start corresponded to Passover time, the sheaf waved by the priest on the 16th day of Nisan being of the barley firstfruits.—Le 23:10, 11.

Barley was esteemed as of less value than wheat, just one third that of wheat in John's vision at Revelation 6:6. It was sufficiently common and abundant that it could be used as fodder for Solomon's horses (1Ki 4:28), a purpose that it still serves in modern times. It was ground into flour and made into bread, often in the form of a round cake (2Ki 4:42; Eze 4:12; Joh 6:9, 13), and sometimes mixed with other grains.—Eze 4:9.

Though undoubtedly more frequently used among the poor because of its lower cost, there is nothing to indicate that barley was viewed with disdain among the Israelites, even by those able to afford wheat. Thus, it was included in the provisions suitable for offering to King David's company upon their arrival in Gilead during the time of Absalom's revolt. (2Sa 17:27-29) Solomon provided 20,000 cor measures (4,400 kl; 125,000 bu) of barley, along with a corresponding quantity of wheat, and large amounts of oil and wine to Hiram as supplies for the Tyrian king's servants who were preparing temple materials. (2Ch 2:10, 15) King Jotham of Judah exacted tribute of the king of Ammon that included 10,000 cor measures (2,200 kl; 62,500 bu) of barley. (2Ch 27:5) Men seeking to avoid death at the hands of assassin Ishmael after the fall of Jerusalem assured him they had "hidden treasures in the field, wheat and barley and oil and honey."—Jer 41:8.

Nevertheless, barley was a common and a lowly food, and some commentators suggest that these qualities are represented in the figure of "a round cake of barley bread" that was seen in the Midianite's dream and that symbolized Gideon's humble army.—Jg 7:13, 14.

Hosea paid 15 silver pieces (if shekels, $33) and one and a half homer measures (330 L; 300 dry qt) of barley to buy back the adulterous woman Gomer as his wife (Ho 1:3; 3:1, 2), a price that some commentators consider to total the price of a slave, 30 silver shekels ($66). (Ex 21:32) The "offering of jealousy" required by the Law in the case of a man suspecting his wife of sexual infidelity was to be a tenth of an ephah (2.2 L; 2 dry qt) of barley flour. (Nu 5:14, 15) Barley was also used in measuring, the amount required for sowing a field being the legal means for determining the field's value.—Le 27:16.

BARNABAS (Bar'na·bas) [Son of Comfort]. This prominent figure of first-century Christianity is first introduced to us in the Scriptures by Luke in Acts 4:34-36. There we learn that this devout man was a Levite and a native of the island of Cyprus, but at the time of his being introduced, he was in Jerusalem. Of the many believers who shortly after Pentecost sold their fields and houses and gave the price to the apostles for the advancement of the Christian work, this man was one mentioned by name. His given name was Joseph, but the apostles surnamed him Barnabas, meaning "Son of Comfort." This practice of giving surnames in keeping with one's characteristics was not uncommon.

He was a very warmhearted and generous person, one who did not hesitate to offer both himself and his material possessions willingly for the advancement of the Kingdom interests. He gladly 'came to the aid' of his brothers (Ac 9:27), and in the presence of newly interested persons "he rejoiced and began to encourage them all to continue in the Lord with hearty purpose." Barnabas "was a good man and full of holy spirit and of faith" (Ac 11:23, 24), a prophet and teacher in Antioch. (Ac 13:1) The apostles referred to Barnabas as among their "loved ones" who had "delivered up their souls for the name of our Lord Jesus Christ." (Ac 15:25, 26) Although he was not one of the 12 apostles, he was properly called an apostle (Ac 14:14), for, indeed, he was one "sent out by the holy spirit."—Ac 13:4, 43.

The close association that Barnabas had with Paul, and that extended over the years, had its beginning about three years after Paul's conversion when he wanted to get in touch with the Jerusalem congregation. How Barnabas first got to meet Paul is not revealed. But it was Barnabas who had the privilege of introducing Paul to Peter and to the disciple James.—Ac 9:26, 27; Ga 1:18, 19.

In the meantime a great deal of interest in Christianity had been aroused in Antioch of Syria by certain Greek-speaking Jews from Cyprus and Cyrene. As a result, the governing body at Jerusalem sent Barnabas down to Antioch to encourage and build up these new believers further. The choice of Barnabas for this work was a good one, since he was a Greek-speaking Cypriot. When "a considerable crowd was added to the Lord" in Antioch, Barnabas hastened over to Tarsus and persuaded Paul to come and help out in the ministry. About that time divine warning of a coming famine caused the brothers in Antioch to gather many provisions that, in due time, were sent to the Jerusalem congregation by the hands of Barnabas and Paul.—Ac 11:22-24, 27-30; 12:25.

This relief work accomplished, the two were back in Antioch by about 47 C.E. and from there left on a missionary assignment under the direction of the holy spirit. This took Barnabas and Paul first to Cyprus, where they were instrumental in bringing God's truth to the proconsul Sergius Paulus. From there they traveled through the interior of Asia Minor. At times they were severely persecuted by mobs. Once, when they cured a lame man in Lystra, they had no sooner succeeded in restraining "the crowds from sacrificing to them" (thinking that Barnabas was the god Zeus and Paul, "the one taking the lead in speaking," was Hermes, or Mercury), than the Jews "persuaded the crowds, and they stoned Paul and dragged him outside the city."—Ac 13:1-12; 14:1-20.

In about 49 C.E., Barnabas and Paul took the burning question of circumcision of non-Jews up to the governing body in Jerusalem, and with that settled, they were soon back in Antioch preparing for their next missionary tour. (Ac 15:2-36) However, because they could come to no agreement over taking John Mark along, they each departed for separate territories. Barnabas took his cousin Mark to Cyprus, and Paul took Silas through the districts of Syria and Cilicia. (Ac 15:37-41) Thus ends the record made of Barnabas in the Scriptures, except for brief mention of him in some of Paul's letters.—1Co 9:6; Ga 2:1, 9, 13; Col 4:10.

BARRENNESS. The idea of the inability to bring forth children is conveyed by the Hebrew words 'a·qar' ("barren"; Ge 11:30) and gal·mudh' ("sterile"; Isa 49:21). Also, in Proverbs 30:16, barrenness is literally described as "restraint of the womb." (*NW* ftn) The Greek word for "barren" is *stei'ros*. (Lu 1:7, 36) Barrenness is also spoken of as "deadness of the womb."—Ro 4:19.

Jehovah's original mandate to Adam and Eve, later repeated to Noah's sons, included the command, "Be fruitful and become many." (Ge 1:28; 9:7) Failure on the part of a married woman to bring forth children was therefore viewed in ancient times as a reproach, an affliction, a punishment, one of the greatest misfortunes. "Give me children or otherwise I shall be a dead woman," pleaded Rachel with her husband Jacob.—Ge 30:1.

That Jehovah is capable of making a barren woman fruitful is shown by the words of Jacob to Rachel: "Am I in the place of God, who has held back the fruit of the belly from you?" Finally, we are told, "God remembered Rachel, and God heard and answered her in that he opened her womb. And she became pregnant and brought a son to birth." (Ge 30:2, 22, 23) Other cases demonstrating Jehovah's power to give children to women afflicted with natural barrenness over a long period of time may be cited: Sarah (Ge 11:30; 17:19; 21:1, 2); Rebekah (Ge 25:21); Samson's mother (Jg 13:2, 3); Hannah (1Sa 1:10, 11; 2:5); a Shunammite woman (2Ki 4:14-17); and Elizabeth (Lu 1:7, 36). With Jehovah's blessing, the Israelites during their sojourn in Egypt became so prolific that the Egyptians were alarmed, thinking they would soon be outnumbered. (Ex 1:7-12, 18-21) Jehovah was also given credit for granting conception to Ruth the ancestress of David.—Ru 4:13.

When Jehovah withheld his blessing even the land would become a barren and desolate waste. On the other hand, with divine blessing, the land was capable of bringing forth much fruitage. (Le 26:3-5) Similarly, with Jehovah's rich blessing, it was promised, "neither a woman suffering an abortion nor a barren woman will exist in your land." (Ex 23:26; De 7:13, 14; 28:4, 11; Ps 127:3-5; 128:3) Conversely, Jehovah, on one occasion, "tightly shut up every womb" of Abimelech's house when he contemplated taking Sarah as wife.—Ge 20:17, 18.

Because of the terrible distress foretold to come on first-century Jerusalem, Jesus said "barren women" would be happy, relieved, not having the anguish of seeing their children suffer.—Lu 23:29.

Isaiah and the psalmist prophesied of a barren woman whose reproach and shame are to be forgotten, for she will bring forth many sons, all of them taught by Jehovah. (Ps 113:9; Isa 54:1-15) The apostle Paul applies Isaiah's words to "the free woman," that is, "the Jerusalem above."—Ga 4:26-31.

BARSABBAS (Bar'sab·bas). This may have been a family name or just an added name given to two individuals: *Joseph,* surnamed Justus, who was the rejected candidate for the apostleship vacated by Judas Iscariot; and *Judas,* who accompanied Paul, Barnabas, and Silas from Jerusalem to Antioch in about 49 C.E. There is no evidence that the two men were brothers.—Ac 1:23; 15:22; see JOSEPH No. 11; JUDAS No. 7.

BARTHOLOMEW (Bar·thol'o·mew) [Son of Tolmai]. One of Jesus' 12 apostles, generally thought to be Nathanael. A comparison of the Gospel accounts shows that Matthew and Luke link Bartholomew and Philip together in the same way that John associates the name Nathanael with Philip. (Mt 10:3; Lu 6:14; Joh 1:45, 46) For details on this apostle's activity, see NATHANAEL.

BARTIMAEUS (Bar·ti·mae'us) [Son of Timaeus (Honored)]. A blind beggar whose sight Jesus restored. Bartimaeus and an unidentified companion were sitting outside Jericho when Jesus and a crowd came along. Bartimaeus inquired what the excitement was, and when told, he began shouting: "Son of David, Jesus, have mercy on me!" Others sternly told him to be silent, but he was even more persistent. When Jesus called, he threw off his outer garment, hurried to the Master, and begged for recovery of his sight. Jesus, discerning the man's faith and moved to pity, cured Bartimaeus, who then followed him, glorifying God.—Mr 10:46-52; Mt 20:29-34; Lu 18:35-43.

In reporting this event, Mark and Matthew say it occurred when Jesus was "going out of Jericho," but Luke says it was "as he [Jesus] was getting near to Jericho." (Mt 20:29; Mr 10:46; Lu 18:35) Some have said that these refer to two separate incidents. On this, Joseph P. Free writes: "Archaeology, however, has thrown additional light on this apparent discrepancy. Early in the twentieth century A.D., excavations were made at Jericho by Ernest Sellin of the German Oriental Society (1907-1909). The excavations showed that the Jericho of Jesus' time was a double city . . . The old Jewish city was about a mile away from the Roman city. In the light of this evidence, it is possible that Matthew is speaking of the Jewish city which Christ had left, whereas Luke is speaking of the Roman, at which Christ had not yet arrived. Thus, on His way from the old to the new city, Christ met and healed the blind Bartimaeus." —*Archaeology and Bible History,* 1964, p. 295.

BARUCH (Bar'uch) [Blessed].

1. The scribal secretary of Jeremiah. Baruch was the son of Neriah and brother of Seraiah, Zedekiah's quartermaster who read Jeremiah's scroll alongside the Euphrates.—Jer 32:12; 51: 59-64.

In the fourth year of King Jehoiakim, 625 B.C.E., Baruch began writing in a scroll the prophetic message of Jerusalem's doom, dictated by Jeremiah. In the late fall of the following year, 624 B.C.E., Baruch read the scroll aloud "in the ears of all the people" at the entrance of Jehovah's house. He was then summoned to read it to an assembly of the princes, who, moved by what they heard and fearing the consequences when the word got to the king's ears, urged Baruch and Jeremiah to hide. Jehoiakim, upon hearing the denunciation, burned the scroll piece by piece and commanded that Baruch and Jeremiah be brought before him, "but Jehovah kept them concealed." At Jeremiah's dictation, Baruch then wrote another scroll like the first, but containing "many more words" from the mouth of Jehovah.—Jer 36:1-32.

Sixteen years later, in the tenth year of Zedekiah, only months before Jerusalem was sacked, Baruch took the deeds for the property Jeremiah had purchased from a cousin and put them in an earthenware vessel for preservation and safekeeping.—Jer 32:1, 9-16.

At one point during the writing of the first scroll, when Baruch complained of his weariness, Jehovah warned him: 'Do not keep on seeking great things for yourself.' Nevertheless, because of his faithfulness he was promised preservation and safety 'in all the places to which he might go,' not only during the terrible siege of Jerusalem but also afterwards when the rebellious populace compelled him and Jeremiah to go down to Egypt with them.—Jer 45:1-5; 43:4-7.

2. Son of Zabbai; Baruch "worked with fervor" assisting Nehemiah to rebuild Jerusalem's walls. (Ne 3:20) Possibly the same as No. 3.

3. A priest whose descendant, if not he himself, attested to Nehemiah's "trustworthy arrangement." (Ne 9:38; 10:1, 6, 8) If Baruch himself was the one sealing this agreement, he may have been the same as No. 2.

4. Father or forefather of Maaseiah, who lived in Jerusalem in Nehemiah's time. A descendant of Judah.—Ne 11:4-6.

BARZILLAI (Bar·zil'lai) [Of Iron].

1. A Meholathite whose son Adriel married Saul's daughter Merab.—1Sa 18:19; 2Sa 21:8.

2. A wealthy Gileadite, "a very great man," of the town of Rogelim. Barzillai was one of three who assisted David and his army with supplies of food and bedding during Absalom's rebellion. (2Sa 17:27-29) When David returned to Jerusalem, Barzillai escorted the party to the Jordan, but because of his age ("I am eighty years old today"), he declined David's offer to become part of the royal court, sending Chimham in his place. In saying farewell, David kissed and blessed him. (2Sa 19:31-40) Shortly before dying, David remembered Barzillai and requested Solomon to show kindness toward his sons by arranging for them to 'be among those eating at his table.'—1Ki 2:7.

3. A priest who married a daughter of Barzillai the Gileadite (most likely No. 2) and adopted his father-in-law's name. His descendants, on their return from Babylonian exile, were unable to find their registration in the genealogical records and so were disqualified from the priesthood.—Ezr 2:61, 62; Ne 7:63, 64.

BASEMATH (Bas'e·math) [Perfumed; Balsam Oil; Spicy].

1. A wife of Esau. She was a daughter of Elon the Hittite, therefore either the same person as Adah or her sister. Basemath was "a source of bitterness" to Isaac and Rebekah.—Ge 26:34, 35; 27:46; 28:8; 36:2.

2. Another wife of Esau, possibly the same as Mahalath. She was a daughter of Abraham's son Ishmael, sister of Nebaioth, and therefore Esau's first cousin. Esau took her as wife after seeing his father's great displeasure over his Canaanite wives. She bore his son Reuel.—Ge 28:8, 9; 36:3, 4, 10.

3. A daughter of Solomon and wife of Ahimaaz, one of Solomon's food deputies.—1Ki 4:7, 15.

BASHAN (Ba'shan) [possibly, Fertile (Stoneless) Plain].

A large region E of the Sea of Galilee. The approximate boundaries of Bashan were Mount Hermon on the N, the mountainous region of Mount Hauran (Jebel ed Druz) on the E, Gilead on the S, and the hills bordering the eastern side of the Sea of Galilee on the W.—De 3:3-14; Jos 12:4, 5.

Bashan was located mainly on a high plateau, with an average height of about 600 m (2,000 ft). The land is generally flat, though containing some mountain ridges, and is of volcanic origin with much hard black basalt rock, which provides good retention of moisture. The soil is a mixture of tufa and red-brown earth. Water and melted snow flowing down from Mount Hermon helped to turn the entire region into an excellent agricultural area. The great fertility of this plain made the area a rich granary and provided fine pasture lands. This, in turn, contributed to the production of splendid strains of cattle and sheep. The bulls of Bashan and its male sheep were the subjects of song and poetry and were symbols of richness, strength, and prosperity.—De 32:14; Eze 39:18; Ps 22:12.

The plains of Bashan appear to have been, in the main, treeless, but the mountain ridges were well wooded and contained massive trees, probably oaks (which are still to be found in that area today). In prophecy, these trees are used as symbols of great loftiness. (Isa 2:13; Zec 11:1, 2) Ezekiel 27:5, 6 indicates that the Phoenician boat builders of Tyre used the juniper trees of Senir for their planks and the tall cedars of Lebanon for their masts, but they fashioned their powerful oars from the sturdy trees of Bashan.

Bashan's fertility and productivity are doubtless the reason for its being associated with other productive areas such as Carmel and Lebanon. (Jer 50:19; Isa 33:9) Jeremiah links the heights of Bashan with Lebanon as a vantage point from which to view the calamity due to come upon the land of the Israelites because of their forsaking Jehovah. (Jer 22:20) The mention of the "mountain of God" and the "mountain of peaks" of Bashan, at Psalm 68:15, 16, may refer to the mountainous region of Mount Hauran (Jebel ed Druz). Zalmon (mentioned in Ps 68:14) may have been its highest peak.

The region of Bashan apparently first enters the Bible record at Genesis 14:5 in the reference to the Rephaim (giants) in Ashteroth-karnaim, who were defeated by the invading kings of Abraham's time (before 1933 B.C.E.). At the time of the Israelite invasion (c. 1473 B.C.E.), Og, the king of Bashan and the last remaining one of the giantlike men of that area, was defeated and slain, and the land was occupied by Israel. (Nu 21:33-35; De 3:1-3, 11; Jos 13:12) The tribe of Manasseh received Bashan as its inheritance, although it appears that a southern portion of it was allotted to the tribe of Gad.—Jos 13:29-31; 17:1, 5; 1Ch 5:11, 16, 23.

The principal cities of Bashan were: Ashtaroth (a city of Og and later a Levite city), Edrei (the frontier city where Israel defeated Og), Golan (which also became a Levite city and one of the three cities of refuge E of the Jordan), and Salecah. (De 4:41-43; Jos 9:10; 12:4, 5; 20:8, 9; 1Ch 6:64,

71) In the region of Argob alone there were 60 walled cities, and ruins of ancient towns still dot the entire area today.—De 3:3-5; see ARGOB No. 2.

During Solomon's reign one of the 12 commissariat districts placed under deputies and assigned to provide food for the royal tables included Bashan.—1Ki 4:7, 13.

In the area E of the Jordan, the principal route from N to S, called "the king's road," ran through Bashan at the city of Ashtaroth, and this fact, together with Bashan's great fertility and its proximity to Damascus, made it the goal of military conquest. King Hazael of Damascus captured Bashan during Jehu's reign (c. 904-877 B.C.E.), but it was evidently recovered in the reign of Jehoash (2Ki 10:32, 33; 13:25) or at least by the time of Jeroboam II (c. 844-804 B.C.E.). (2Ki 14:25) Tiglath-pileser III of Assyria overran the whole area in the reign of Pekah (c. 778-759 B.C.E.). —2Ki 15:29; 1Ch 5:26.

In postexilic times Bashan came under Greek control and later became one of the major wheat granaries of the Roman Empire. It was divided into four districts, and with the exception of the NE district called Trachonitis, these districts preserved to some extent original names from the area: the district of Gaulanitis in the W drew its name from Golan, Auranitis in the S from Hauran, and central Batanaea from Bashan. Aside from a reference to Trachonitis (Lu 3:1), Bashan is not mentioned in the Christian Greek Scriptures.—See HAURAN.

BASIN. The Scriptures do not provide a detailed description of basins used in ancient times, though such vessels were commonly earthenware or were made of wood or metal. Some basins served a domestic purpose, like those that were among the provisions brought to David and the people with him when they fled from Absalom. (2Sa 17:27-29) The Hebrew word *saph* is used for a basin of this kind. It is also employed for the basin into which the Israelites in Egypt put the blood of the Passover victim (Ex 12:22) and for the temple basins that Nebuchadnezzar took to Babylon. (Jer 52:19) This word may also be rendered "bowl," and thus Jehovah is represented as saying prophetically: "Here I am making Jerusalem a bowl [*saph*] causing reeling to all the peoples round about."—Zec 12:1, 2.

Sanctuary Use. Basins were also used for sacred purposes in connection with Jehovah's worship at the tabernacle and the later temples. As Jehovah instructed Moses, the tabernacle articles included a large basin that was to be filled with water. It was made of copper, rested on a copper stand, and was placed between the tent of meeting and the altar to provide the high priest and the other priests with water for washing their hands and feet either before entering the tent of meeting or before ministering at the altar. (Ex 30:17-21; 31:9; 40:30, 31) This basin, called a laver in some translations (*AS; AT; KJ; RS*), was made "by the use of the mirrors of the women servants who did organized service at the entrance of the tent of meeting."—Ex 38:8.

According to the Masoretic text, there is no specific instruction given on the transporting of the tabernacle basin. However, the Greek *Septuagint* (which agrees with the ancient Samaritan *Pentateuch*) adds to Numbers 4:14 the words: "And they will take a purple cloth and cover the basin and its stand and put them in a blue skin covering and put [them] upon poles."

The Hebrew word *ki·yohr'* (or *ki·yor'*), meaning "basin" or "laver," is used for the tabernacle basin. (Ex 35:16, ftn) It is also used to refer to the ten basins Solomon had made for temple use, in which things having to do with the burnt offering were rinsed.—2Ch 4:6, 14.

Each of the ten copper basins (lavers, *AT; RS*) Hiram made for temple use could hold "forty bath measures," or about 880 L (230 gal) of water. If these basins were hemispherical in shape this would mean that they had a diameter of perhaps 1.8 m (6 ft). Of course, if they bulged and tapered somewhat toward the top, the measurements would be different, and it must be observed that the Bible does not provide detailed information on their form, though it says that "each basin was four cubits." Each basin was placed on a four-wheeled carriage skillfully made with ornamental work and engravings, five being placed on the right and five on the left side of the house. —1Ki 7:27-39.

Another basin of great size was the large ornamented molten sea that stood upon 12 fashioned bulls and was "placed at the right side, to the east, toward the south" of the house. Stored therein was water the priests used. It was circular, 10 cubits (4.5 m; 14.6 ft) from brim to brim and 5 cubits (2.2 m; 7.3 ft) high.—2Ch 4:2-6, 10.

The Greek *ni·pter'* is used to refer to the "basin," or "washbasin," that Jesus used when he washed the feet of his disciples.—Joh 13:5; compare *Int.*

Bowls. As with other vessels mentioned in the Scriptures, bowls were variously made of clay, wood, or metal. The Hebrew term *miz·raq'* denotes a metal vessel evidently used in connection with sacrifices in worship. (Ex 27:3; Nu 4:14; 7:13; 1Ki 7:50; 2Ch 4:8) Among the larger bowls used at meals was the *tsal·la'chath* ("banquet bowl"; Pr 26:15) and the *se'phel* ("large banquet bowl"; Jg 5:25). *Gul·lah'* is used to denote a "bowl" (Zec 4:2), but it is also rendered "bowl-shaped" and "round" to describe the capitals of the pillars standing before the temple in Solomon's time. (1Ki 7:41) The two Greek terms for bowls are *try'bli·on* and *phi·a'le. Try'bli·on* denotes a relatively deep bowl from which a meal was eaten (Mt 26:23), whereas *phi·a'le* refers to a "bowl" often used for offering liquid sacrifices.—Re 16:2-17.

BASKET. A container made of such materials as palm-leaf fibers, reeds, rushes, rope, twigs, and willows was often used by persons in ancient times for agricultural, domestic, or other purposes. Their baskets varied greatly in shape, size, and construction. There were those with an open weave and others with a close weave. Some had handles and lids, whereas other baskets lacked either or both of these things.

The Scriptures do not provide detailed descriptions of the different kinds of baskets used in antiquity in Bible lands, and various Hebrew and Greek words are used for baskets. The Hebrew word most often employed to denote a basket is *sal.* It is used for the three baskets containing white bread that Pharaoh's chief of the bakers dreamed he was carrying on his head, a dream Joseph rightly interpreted as signifying death for the dreamer. (Ge 40:16-19, 22) *Sal* is also used for the basket in which unfermented bread, cakes, and wafers were placed for use when installing Israel's priesthood, it further being called "the installation basket." (Ex 29:3, 23, 32; Le 8:2, 26, 31) This same Hebrew term was used for the basket containing the unfermented cakes and wafers used ceremonially on the day that one's Naziriteship came to the full. (Nu 6:13, 15, 17, 19) Also, it was into a *sal* that Gideon put the meat he set before Jehovah's angel. (Jg 6:19) While the Scriptures do not describe the *sal,* it seems that this type of basket was of fine weave and, in later times at least, was made of peeled willows or palm leaves. It may have been fairly large and flat, thus being a type convenient for carrying bread, as in the royal baker's prophetic dream. In the British Museum there is a painted wooden model of an Egyptian woman balancing on her head a large flat and open basket filled with food provisions supposedly for the dead.

During the Israelites' bondage in Egypt and their "hard slavery at clay mortar and bricks" (Ex 1:14), they evidently used baskets to carry construction materials, clay for bricks, and bricks themselves. Reflecting on the way in which Jehovah effected the release of Israel from Egyptian slavery, the psalmist Asaph represents God as saying: "His own hands got to be free even from the basket [mid·dudh´]." (Ps 81:4-6) This same Hebrew term (dudh) is applied to a basket for carrying figs. (Jer 24:1, 2) It also denotes a type of cooking pot ("two-handled cooking pot" [1Sa 2:14]; 'round-bottomed pot' [2Ch 35:13]) and "a furnace." —Job 41:20.

The Hebrew te´ne´ was the basket in which the harvest firstfruits were placed for presentation to God, being deposited before the altar of Jehovah. (De 26:2, 4) This basket served as a container for products of the soil and was probably a large, deep receptacle. Moses used the Hebrew term te´ne´ for "basket" when he apprised Israel of the consequences of obedience and of disobedience to Jehovah. He said, "Blessed will be your basket and your kneading trough," if a course of obedience was pursued, but, "Cursed will be your basket and your kneading trough," if Israel was disobedient. —De 28:5, 17.

The Hebrew word keluv´ may denote a basket woven of rushes or leaves. This term is employed for "basket" at Amos 8:1, 2, where the prophet reports that Jehovah caused him to see "a basket of summer fruit." It is also used to refer to "a cage" for birds in Jeremiah 5:27.

One other Hebrew word referring to a kind of basket is kar, rendered "woman's saddle basket" in Genesis 31:34.

After Jesus Christ miraculously multiplied loaves and fishes to feed about 5,000 men, besides women and young children, there were 12 baskets full of surplus fragments. (Mt 14:20; Mr 6:43; Lu 9:17; Joh 6:13) For the type of basket used to gather the leftovers, all four Gospel writers use the Greek word ko´phi·nos. This type may have been a relatively small wicker hand basket in which one could carry provisions on a journey, or, possibly, it had a cord serving as a handle by which the basket could be carried on one's back. Its general capacity may be deduced from the fact that this Greek term is also used for the Boeotian measure of approximately 7.5 L (2 gal).

After Matthew and Mark tell that Jesus fed about 4,000 men, besides women and young children, from the seven loaves and a few little fishes, they show that seven baskets of surplus fragments were collected. But they use a different Greek word, sphy·ris´ (or, spy·ris´); this denotes a large provision basket or hamper. (Mt 15:37; Mr 8:8) Whereas the smaller ko´phi·nos would suffice when one was traveling in Jewish territory and

away from home only a short time, a larger basket would be needed when going on an extended journey through foreign areas. At times this type was quite large, big enough to hold a man. Gospel writers draw a distinction between the ko´phi·nos and sphy·ris´ (NW using "baskets" for the former and "provision baskets" for the latter) when reporting Jesus Christ's later references to his acts of miraculously multiplying food.—Mt 16:9, 10; Mr 8:19, 20.

The sphy·ris´ is the kind of basket in which Paul was lowered to the ground through an opening in the wall of Damascus. (Ac 9:25) In telling the Corinthian Christians about this escape, the apostle used the Greek word sar·ga´ne, which denotes a plaited or "wicker basket" made of rope or entwined twigs. Both of these Greek terms can be used for the same type of basket.—2Co 11:32, 33.

Jesus Christ, after identifying his disciples as "the light of the world," told them: "People light a lamp and set it, not under the measuring basket, but upon the lampstand, and it shines upon all those in the house." Such a "measuring basket" (Gr., mo´di·os) was a dry measure that had a capacity of about 9 L (8 dry qt), but Christ used it illustratively as a covering. Jesus encouraged his disciples not to hide their spiritual light under a figurative "measuring basket." Instead, he admonished them: "Let your light shine before men, that they may see your fine works and give glory to your Father who is in the heavens."—Mt 5:1, 2, 14-16; see also Mr 4:21; Lu 11:33.

BAT [Heb., 'ata·leph´]. A flying mammal that, apart from its large wings of membranous skin, resembles the mouse. The Scriptures classify the bat among the unclean flying creatures that were not to be eaten by the Israelites. (Le 11:19; De 14:18) About 20 different species of bats (Chiroptera) are found in Israel today.

During the daylight hours bats generally roost head downward in dark caves or deserted buildings, then they come forth at dusk to hunt for food during the hours of darkness. Where large numbers of them roost in one place, there is a repulsive, mousy odor. In some caves bat manure has built up into layers of considerable thickness, providing a valuable source of fertilizer. It is doubtless because of the bat's habit of roosting in dark places that the prophet Isaiah speaks of throwing gods of gold and silver to the bats. A place of darkness and uncleanness is all such idols deserve, instead of the places of honor and prominence accorded them by their deceived worshipers.—Isa 2:20.

BATH. A liquid measure amounting to a tenth of a homer (cor) and corresponding to the dry-measure ephah. (Eze 45:10, 11, 14) On the basis of jar fragments bearing the designation "bath" in ancient Hebrew characters, it has been estimated that the bath measure equaled 22 L (5.81 gal).

BATHING. The Hebrew word ra·chats' is rendered either "bathe" or "wash" and applies to the human body and other objects that are cleansed by dipping or by having water poured over them. (Le 16:24; Ge 24:32) However, to describe the washing of clothes when they are pounded under water, Bible writers used the Hebrew word ka·vas', related to the Arabic kabasa (knead; stamp) and the Akkadian kabasu (tread down). We, therefore, read in Leviticus 14:8: "And the one cleansing himself must wash [a form of ka·vas'] his garments and shave off all his hair and bathe [wera·chats'] in water and must be clean."—See also Le 15:5-27; Nu 19:19.

The Greek word for "bath" is lou·tron'.—Tit 3:5.

Physical cleanliness is required of those who worship Jehovah in holiness and purity. This was demonstrated in connection with the tabernacle arrangement and the later temple service. At their installation, High Priest Aaron and his sons bathed before donning the official garments. (Ex 29:4-9; 40:12-15; Le 8:6, 7) To wash their hands and feet, the priests used water from the copper basin in the courtyard of the tabernacle and, later, from the huge molten sea at Solomon's temple. (Ex 30:18-21; 40:30-32; 2Ch 4:2-6) On the Day of Atonement the high priest bathed twice. (Le 16:4, 23, 24) Those who took the goat for Azazel, the remains of the animal sacrifices, and the sacrificial red cow outside the camp had to bathe their flesh and wash their garments before reentering the camp.—Le 16:26-28; Nu 19:2-10.

Ceremonial bathing on the part of the Israelites in general was required for various reasons. Anyone who recovered from leprosy, anyone who contacted things touched by those with "a running discharge," a man who had an emission of semen, a woman after menstruation or hemorrhaging, or anyone having sexual intercourse was "unclean" and had to bathe. (Le 14:8, 9; 15:4-27) One in a tent with, or touching, a human corpse was "unclean" and had to be purified with cleansing water. If anyone refused to comply with this regulation, he "must be cut off from the midst of the congregation, because it is Jehovah's sanctuary that he has defiled." (Nu 19:20) Appropriately, then, washing is used figuratively to denote a clean standing before Jehovah. (Ps 26:6; 73:13; Isa 1:16; Eze 16:9) Bathing with Jehovah's word of truth, symbolized by water, has power to cleanse. —Eph 5:26.

Passing references in the Bible are made to individuals bathing: Pharaoh's daughter in the Nile (Ex 2:5); Ruth before presenting herself to Boaz (Ru 3:3); Bath-sheba unwittingly in the sight of David (2Sa 11:2, 3); David before prostrating himself in the house of Jehovah (2Sa 12:20); prostitutes at a pool in Samaria (1Ki 22:38). Leprous Naaman, at Elisha's command, 'Bathe and be clean,' did so seven times in the Jordan River. (2Ki 5:9-14) It was a custom to bathe newborn babes and also to bathe the bodies of the dead before burial.—Eze 16:4; Ac 9:37.

In the hot climate of the Middle East where people walked dusty roads in open sandals, it was a mark of hospitality and kindness to provide for washing the feet of one's guests. Abraham extended this kindness to angels (Ge 18:1-4); other examples included Lot, Laban, and Abigail. (Ge 19:1, 2; 24:29-32; 1Sa 25:41; Lu 7:38, 44; 1Ti 5:10) Jesus also washed the feet of his disciples. —Joh 13:5-17; see WASHING OF FEET.

The Pharisees washed "their hands up to the elbow," not for hygienic reasons, but strictly because of rabbinic traditions.—Mr 7:1-5; Mt 15:1, 2.

BATH-RABBIM (Bath-rab'bim) [Daughter of the Many]. In The Song of Solomon, the Shulammite maiden's eyes are likened to "the pools in Heshbon, by the gate of Bath-rabbim." (Ca 7:4) Heshbon was a city in the territory of Gad but was assigned to the Levites. (Jos 21:38, 39) While some believe the name Bath-rabbim is the name of a gate of Heshbon facing toward the city of Rabbah (modern 'Amman) to the NE, others suggest that Bath-rabbim (meaning "Daughter of the Many") is used figuratively to mean the populous city of Heshbon itself and that the gate is so called because many people passed in and out of the city or gathered at the gate for assembly. Around the present ruins of the city, evidence remains of ancient pools as well as of a large reservoir. The poetic description gives an apt picture of limpid, serene beauty seen in the shining eyes of the Shulammite, the city gate perhaps representing the forehead.

BATH-SHEBA (Bath-she'ba) [Daughter of Plenty; possibly, Daughter [Born on] the Seventh [Day]]. Daughter of Eliam (Ammiel, 1Ch 3:5); possibly a granddaughter of Ahithophel. (2Sa 11:3; 23:34) First the wife of Uriah the Hittite, one of David's mighty men; later married to David after being involved in one of the blackest episodes of David's life.—2Sa 23:39.

Late one spring day, Bath-sheba was bathing herself, when a neighbor, King David, on the rooftop of his palace, caught sight of this beautiful woman, described as "very good in appearance." Upon learning that her husband was off to war, the passion-aroused king had Bath-sheba brought to the palace, where he had relations with her. "Later she returned to her house," and after some time informed David that she was pregnant. Thereupon David plotted to have Uriah sleep with his wife as a cover-up for the adultery, but when this scheme failed, the king had Uriah killed in battle. As soon as her mourning period was over, Bath-sheba became David's wife and bore the child.—2Sa 11:1-27.

"But the thing . . . appeared bad in the eyes of Jehovah." His prophet Nathan rebuked the king with an illustration in which he represented Bath-sheba as the "one female lamb" of the poor man, Uriah, that the rich man, David, took to entertain a visitor. In great sorrow David repented (Ps 51), but the adulterine child, which remains nameless, died. (See DAVID.) Years later, further distress came to David for his sin, his own concubines being defiled by his son Absalom.—2Sa 11:27–12:23; 16:21, 22.

Bath-sheba found comfort in her repentant husband, repeatedly addressed him as "my lord," as Sarah had done to her husband (1Ki 1:15-21; 1Pe 3:6), and in time she bore him a son named Solomon, whom Jehovah loved and blessed. (2Sa 12:24, 25) She also had three other sons, Shimea, Shobab, and Nathan, the latter being an ancestor of Jesus' mother Mary. Since Joseph descended from Solomon, both of Jesus' earthly parents traced their ancestry to Bath-sheba as well as David.—1Ch 3:5; Mt 1:6, 16; Lu 3:23, 31.

Bath-sheba comes forward in the account again toward the close of David's 40-year reign. David had sworn to her: "Solomon your son is the one that will become king after me." So when Solomon's older half brother Adonijah attempted to usurp the throne just before David's death, Bath-sheba, on the suggestion of the prophet Nathan, reminded David of his oath. Immediately David put Solomon on the throne, and Bath-sheba thus became the queen mother.—1Ki 1:5-37.

After Solomon's throne was firmly established, Bath-sheba appeared before him as an influential intermediary with a request in behalf of Adonijah. Solomon immediately "rose to meet her and bowed down," and ordered that a throne be placed for his mother, "that she might sit at his right." However, her request only revealed Adonijah's

duplicity, so Solomon had him put to death.—1Ki 2:13-25.

BATTERING RAM. An instrument of warfare used by besiegers to breach or break down the gates and walls of a city or fortress. In its simplest form, it was a heavy beam of timber with an iron tip resembling the head of a ram. Perhaps on account of this or because of its butting action when in use, it is designated by the same Hebrew word (*kar*) as the ram.—Eze 4:1, 2; 21:22.

Besiegers would cast up a mound, or siege rampart, against the city walls to serve as an inclined plane on which battering rams and other engines of war might be brought. Towers as high as the city walls might be pushed up the rampart, thus placing attackers on the same level as defenders. The defending soldiers would endeavor to put the battering rams out of action by dropping firebrands on them or by catching them with chains or grapnels.

BAVVAI (Bav'vai). A Levite worker on Nehemiah's wall-rebuilding project in Jerusalem. He was from the district of Keilah; the son of Henadad and possibly a brother of Binnui.—Ne 3:18, 24.

BAZLUTH (Baz'luth), **BAZLITH** (Baz'lith). A family head whose descendants were among the Nethinim returning to Jerusalem with Zerubbabel in 537 B.C.E.—Ezr 2:1, 2, 52; Ne 7:54.

BDELLIUM GUM [Heb., *bedho'lach*]. A fragrant resinous gum resembling myrrh in appearance and sometimes used to adulterate it. (See also MYRRH.) It is obtained from a tree (*Commiphora africana*) found in NW Africa and Arabia and also from a related type in NW India. This is a genus of small trees or bushes with a scrubby, spiny appearance and little foliage, growing in hot sunny places. When the bark is cut, a fragrant, resinous juice, or gum, oozes out. After the gum is removed from the tree it soon hardens, becomes waxlike and transparent, and is similar to a pearl in appearance.

In describing the land of Havilah encircled by the river Pishon (one of the four rivers branching off from the river issuing out of Eden), mention is made of its valuable things: gold, bdellium gum, and onyx stone. (Ge 2:11, 12) At Numbers 11:7 the manna that the Israelites gathered during the wilderness trek is said to have had "the look of bdellium gum." Manna had previously been likened to "hoarfrost upon the earth." (Ex 16:14) This corresponds with the near-white color of bdellium gum. Josephus, in discussing the provision of the

*Assyrian battering ram
and mobile assault tower*

manna, refers to bdellium as a "spicy herb."
—*Jewish Antiquities*, III, 28 (i, 6).

BEADS. Small perforated ornaments made of
such materials as glass, gems, gold, and silver.
They are usually worn as necklaces and have been
found on Egyptian mummies, in Greek and Roman graves, and in Assyrian temple ruins, as well
as at Megiddo, Ashdod, and Beth-shemesh.

Concerning the lovely Shulammite girl of The
Song of Solomon, it is said: "Your cheeks are comely among the hair braids, your neck in a string of
beads." (Ca 1:10) Clearly, then, strings of beads
were among the articles of adornment used by
Hebrew women of ancient times.—See ORNA-
MENTS.

BEALIAH (Be·a·li′ah) [Jah Is Owner]. A Benjamite warrior who joined up with David at Ziklag.
—1Ch 12:1, 2, 5.

BEALOTH (Be·a′loth) [Place of the Mistresses].

1. A city in the extreme S of Judah, referred to
at Joshua 15:24. The location is unknown.

2. A district in the vicinity of Asher under
Baana as Solomon's commissariat. Called Aloth in
the *King James Version*.—1Ki 4:16.

BEAR [Heb., *dov* or *dohv*; Gr., *ar′kos*]. The Syrian brown bear (*Ursus arctus syriacus*) is the
animal formerly encountered in Palestine, and is
still found in N Syria, NW Iran, and S Turkey. It is
most often light brown in color and averages
about 140 kg (310 lb) in weight. Despite seeming
awkwardness, the bear can move with great rapidity even over rough ground, some varieties
attaining a speed of nearly 48 km (30 mi) an hour
for a short distance. Bears are also good swimmers, and most of them can climb.

The idea that bears hug or squeeze their victims
to death is not borne out by the facts. When
engaged in a struggle, the bear strikes with its
huge paws, and its powerful, heavy arms drive the
nonretractile claws deep into the body of its opponent. A single blow may be sufficient to kill an
animal such as a deer. Most appropriately, therefore, the Scriptures allude to the bear's dangerous-
ness in parallel with that of the lion. (Am 5:19; La
3:10) Naturalists, in fact, consider the bear to be
even more dangerous than the large cats. Usually,
however, the bear, like other animals, does not
molest humans but avoids them, although it may
attack when provoked or surprised.

The ferocity of the female bear when its young
are lost is mentioned several times in the Scrip-

tures. (2Sa 17:8; Pr 17:12; Ho 13:8) Bears, on one occasion, served as God's executioners against the delinquent youths who mocked the prophet Elisha.—2Ki 2:24.

Bears subsist on a varied diet, feeding on leaves and roots of plants, fruits, berries, nuts, eggs, insects, fish, rodents, and the like, and have a special fondness for honey. Although there are exceptions, bears seem to prefer a vegetarian diet. Nonetheless, in ancient Israel, when fruits and other nonflesh items of the bear's diet were scarce, herders of sheep and goats had to be on guard against the depredations of bears. In his youth David had to brave the attack of a bear in order to protect his father's flock.—1Sa 17:34-37.

When bears are hungry and get the scent of prey, they are known to make an impatient groaning sound. So the prophet Isaiah describes the Israelites as 'groaning like bears' in expectation of justice and salvation, only to be disappointed repeatedly. (Isa 59:11) An onrushing bear is also fittingly likened to a wicked ruler who harries and oppresses his lowly subjects.—Pr 28:15.

In Daniel's vision of terrible beasts symbolizing world powers of earth, the bear represented the Medo-Persian World Power and its greed for territorial conquest and pillage. (Da 7:5, 17) Rapacious like this, the wild beast out of the sea, having seven heads and ten horns, is seen in John's vision to have feet "as those of a bear." (Re 13:2) The peacefulness among Jehovah's regathered people, under Messiah's rule, is indicated by the prophecy that the bear will feed with the cow.—Isa 11:7.

BEARD.   The hair growing on a man's chin and cheeks, sometimes including that growing on the upper lip. In the Hebrew Scriptures, za·qan' is the word for "beard," while sa·pham', pertaining to the lip, is variously rendered by translators as "beard," "mustache," and "upper lip." In a few instances the word za·qan' refers not to the beard but to the "chin."—Le 13:29, 30; 14:9.

Among many ancient peoples of the East, including the Israelites, a beard was cherished as an evidence of manly dignity. God's law to Israel prohibited the cutting off of the "sidelocks," the hair between the ear and the eye, and the extremity of the beard. (Le 19:27; 21:5) This was doubtless because among some pagans it was a religious practice.

During extreme grief, shame, or humiliation, a man might pluck hairs from his beard, or he might leave the beard or the mustache untended. (Ezr 9:3) It may have been the untended beard of Mephibosheth, son of Jonathan, that indicated to David that Mephibosheth was perhaps telling the

truth when he said that his servant Ziba had slandered him, and that Mephibosheth was actually mourning while David was a refugee from Absalom, contrary to what Ziba had reported. (2Sa 16:3; 19:24-30) The removing of the beard illustrated calamity or great mourning because of calamity.—Isa 7:20; 15:2; Jer 48:37; Eze 5:1.

After the destruction of Jerusalem in 607 B.C.E., men from Shechem, Shiloh, and Samaria expressed their distress by shaving their beards, ripping their garments apart, and cutting themselves. Even though they were bringing offerings to the house of Jehovah, they were bloodless offerings, apparently to be offered at the place where the temple had been. (Jer 41:5) That the practices of these men were not fully in harmony with the law of God is shown by the fact that they made cuts upon themselves, a practice sternly prohibited by the Law.—Le 19:28; 21:5.

The importance of the beard and its being well groomed played a part in the attitude of Achish the king of Gath toward David when the latter disguised his sanity by letting his saliva run down upon his beard. This served to help convince King Achish that David was insane. (1Sa 21:13) Later, when Hanun the king of Ammon grossly insulted David's ambassadors by cutting off half their beards, David sympathetically told his men to stay in Jericho until their beards grew abundantly again. The Ammonites knew that it was a signal insult to David and that they had become foul-smelling in his eyes over the incident, and so they prepared for war.—2Sa 10:4-6; 1Ch 19:1-6.

It was customary for men to wear beards, even before the Law covenant was made. While the Hebrews did not make monuments with figures of themselves, many monuments and inscriptions have been found in Egypt, Mesopotamia, and other Middle Eastern lands, in which the Assyrians, Babylonians, and Canaanites are pictured with beards. Even some representations dated as far back as the third millennium B.C.E. show beards of varying styles. Among the above-named peoples, eunuchs were mainly the ones depicted beardless. The making of eunuchs was not a practice in Israel, however, because the Law excluded eunuchs from the congregation of Israel.—De 23:1.

Since most Semites are pictured as wearing beards, even prior to the time of the Law, it would logically follow that the faithful men of the line of Shem, who continued to speak the language of Eden and who doubtless followed more closely the original customs from the time of their forefather Seth, possessed beards. Consequently, there is good reason to believe that Noah, Enoch, Seth, and Adam likewise were bearded men.

Herodotus (II, 36) says the Egyptians shaved the hair both of the face and of the head. For the men it was a sign of mourning or of slovenliness to let the hair and beard grow. For this reason Joseph, when taken out of prison, shaved before being brought into the presence of Pharaoh. (Ge 41:14) However, false beards as well as wigs were worn by the Egyptians.

Did Jesus, when on earth, wear a beard? Certainly it was a custom strictly held by the Jews. Jesus, born a Jew, "came to be under law" and he fulfilled the Law. (Ga 4:4; Mt 5:17) Like all other Jews, Jesus was dedicated to Jehovah God from his birth, by reason of the Law covenant, and was under obligation to keep the whole Law, including the prohibition on shaving the extremity of the beard. Also, at the time that Jesus was on earth, the Roman custom was beardlessness. Therefore, if Jesus had been beardless, he would have been challenged as being either a eunuch or a Roman. Significantly, a prophecy concerning Jesus' suffering states: "My back I gave to the strikers, and my cheeks to those plucking off the hair."—Isa 50:6.

BEASTS, SYMBOLIC. From time immemorial, mankind has observed the characteristics and habits of animals and has applied them in a figurative or symbolic sense to persons, peoples, governments, and organizations. The Bible makes good use of this effective means of illustration. Examples pertaining to the figurative use of the qualities residing in an animal, or suggested by its characteristics, are listed in the accompanying charts.

Beasts as Symbols of Governments. Certain major world powers of history appear directly in the Biblical record, and all of these, as well as other nations, have used animals as symbols of their governments. In Egypt, the serpent figured prominently, the uraeus, the sacred asp, appearing on the headdress of the Pharaohs. However, Egypt was also represented by the bull, as was Assyria. Medo-Persia used the eagle (the shields of the Medes bore the golden eagle; the Persians bore an eagle fixed to the end of a lance). Athens was designated by the owl; Rome, the eagle; Great Britain is designated by the lion; the United States, the eagle. From the most remote times China has been symbolized by the dragon. Well known are the Russian "bear" and the German "two-headed eagle."

The Wild Beasts of Daniel and of Revelation. That the beasts described in these books represent political kingdoms or governments, exercising rulership and authority, is clearly stated. (Da 7:6, 12, 23; 8:20-22; Re 16:10; 17:3, 9-12) A consideration of the Biblical passages reveals that, while these political 'wild beasts' vary in symbolic form, yet all have certain characteristics in common. All are shown as standing in opposition to God's rule by the Messianic Kingdom over mankind. They are also depicted as in opposition to God's "holy ones," his covenant people, first the Jewish nation, then the Christian congregation. Those specifically named (Medo-Persia and Greece) were major world powers, and the great size attributed to the others or the description of their actions indicates that these too were not minor kingdoms. (It may be noted that subordinate kingdoms are symbolized by horns in some cases.) All the beasts are represented as very aggressive, seeking the dominant position over the nations or peoples within the reach of their power.—Compare Da 7:17, 18, 21; 8:9-11, 23, 24; Re 13:4-7, 15; 17:12-14.

Many commentators endeavor to limit the fulfillment of the visions of the beasts in the book of Daniel so that it does not extend beyond the time when Jesus Christ was on the earth, at which time the Roman Empire was the dominant power. The prophecies themselves, however, make plain that they extend beyond that time. The final forms of the beasts are shown as reaching down to the 'arrival of the definite time for God's holy ones to take possession of the kingdom' in "the appointed time of the end." Then the Messiah destroys such beastly opposition for all time. (Da 7:21-27; 8:19-25; compare also Re 17:13, 14; 19:19, 20.) It may be noted that Christ Jesus expressly foretold that opposition to the Messianic Kingdom would continue into the time of the end, so that his disciples then preaching that Kingdom would be "objects of hatred by all the nations." (Mt 24:3, 9-14) This obviously does not allow for any nation, particularly world powers, to be excluded from possible identification with the final forms or expressions of the symbolic wild beasts.

Daniel's vision of the beasts out of the sea. After Egypt and Assyria had finished their respective periods of dominance, and toward the close of the Babylonian Empire, Jehovah God gave Daniel a vision of "four huge beasts" coming up out of the vast sea. (Da 7:1-3) Isaiah 57:20 likens persons alienated from God to the sea, saying: "But the wicked are like the sea that is being tossed, when it is unable to calm down, the waters of which keep tossing up seaweed and mire."—See also Re 17:15.

Bible commentators regularly link this vision with that of the colossal image in the second chapter of Daniel. As a comparison of chapters 2 and 7 shows, there are definite similarities. The colossal image had four principal parts or sections, to compare with the four beasts. The metals of the image began with the most precious, gold, and became successively inferior, while the beasts began with the majestic lion. In both visions the fourth part, or "kingdom," receives particular consideration, shows the greatest complexity of form, introduces new elements, and continues down till the time when divine judgment is executed upon it for standing in opposition to God's rule.

Briefly the four beasts were: a *lion*, first having eagle's wings, then losing them and taking on human qualities; a *bear* (a less majestic and more ponderous creature than the lion), devouring much flesh; a *leopard* with four wings (adding to its great speed) and four heads; and a fourth *wild beast* not corresponding to any actual animal, unusually strong, with large iron teeth, ten horns, and another horn developing with eyes and "a mouth speaking grandiose things." Much of the chapter relates to the fourth beast and its unusual horn. While each beast was "different from the others," this was especially true of the fourth one.—Da 7:3-8, 11, 12, 15-26.

In the last quarter of the seventh century B.C.E., Babylon became the dominant power in the Middle East. The Babylonian kingdom swiftly extended its domain over Syria and Palestine, overthrowing the kingdom of Judah with its line of Davidic rulers who sat on the glorious throne of Jehovah in Jerusa-

SYMBOLISM OF DESIRABLE THINGS

ANIMAL	CHARACTERISTIC OR QUALITY	SYMBOLISM
Ass	Ability to do hard work	Tribe of Issachar lending itself to labor (Ge 49:14, 15)
Bull	Strength, power (Job 39:9-11)	Power, attribute of "living creature" near Jehovah's throne (Re 4:7)
Bull, young (calf)	Sacrificial animal	Fruit of lips, sacrifices of praise (Ho 14:2; Heb 13:15) Jesus Christ as a sacrifice (Heb 9:11-14)
Dove (turtle-dove)	Lovableness, beauty, innocence	Shulammite girl (Ca 1:15; 5:2) God's servants innocent, not lawbreakers (Mt 10:16)
	Homing quality	Jehovah's people being gathered (Isa 60:8)
Eagle	Farsightedness	Wisdom, attribute of "living creature" near Jehovah's throne (Re 4:7) Discernment, spiritual forevision of God's servants (Mt 24:28; Lu 17:37)
Eagle's wings	Power of flight	Refreshing vigor, endurance (Ps 103:5; Isa 40:31)
	Care, protection	Jehovah's care for Israel (Ex 19:4) and for his "woman" (Re 12:14)
Fish	Some fish clean according to the Law (Le 11:9-12)	People fine, righteous, suitable for the Kingdom (Mt 13:47-50)
Gazelle (and related animals)	Beauty, lovableness	Shepherd lover of the Shulammite (Ca 2:9)
	Speed	Speed of Gadite warriors (1Ch 12:8)
Goat	Sacrificial animal	Jesus Christ as a sacrifice (Heb 9:11-14)
Hen	Protectiveness of young	Jesus' tender care (Mt 23:37; Lu 13:34)
Hind	Swiftness	Tribe of Naphtali swift in battle (Ge 49:21)
	Surefootedness	Stability and guidance of one's steps by Jehovah (2Sa 22:34; Ps 18:33)
	Lovableness	One's own wife (Pr 5:19)
Horned snake (serpent)	Dangerousness	Tribe of Dan, competent rear guard of Israel (Ge 49:17)
Horse (white)	War mount	Righteous warfare (Re 19:11, 16)
Lion	Majesty, courage, destructiveness to enemies	Justice, attribute of "living creature" near Jehovah's throne (Re 4:7) Jesus as royal majesty, King, executor of justice (Ge 49:9; Re 5:5) Jehovah (Isa 31:4; Ho 11:10) Jehovah's people (Mic 5:8)
Serpent	Cautiousness (Ge 3:1)	God's servants cautious (Mt 10:16)
Sheep	Sacrificial animal; meekness, docility, gregariousness	Jesus Christ, "the Lamb of God" (Joh 1:29; Re 5:6; 14:1; 22:3) Jehovah's flock of people (Ps 79:13; Joh 10:7; Heb 13:20) Persons who do good toward Christ's spiritual brothers, and who enter into Kingdom blessings (Mt 25:32-34)
Wolf	Fighter	Tribe of Benjamin, fighter against God's enemies (Ge 49:27)

lem. (1Ch 29:23) It may be observed that, when warning Judah of its impending fall to Babylon, the prophet Jeremiah likened the future conqueror to 'a lion going up out of a thicket.' (Jer 4:5-7; compare 50:17.) After the fall of Jerusalem, Jeremiah said that Babylon's forces had been "swifter than the eagles" in their pursuit of the Judeans. (La 4:19) History shows that Babylon's expansion, at one time reaching as far as Egypt, before long came to a halt, and in the latter part of the empire, Babylon's rulers showed little of the earlier aggressiveness.

Babylon fell to the Medo-Persian kingdom, with its heartland in the hills to the east of the plains of Mesopotamia. The Medo-Persian Empire was quite different from the Semitic Babylonian Empire, being the first Japhetic (or Aryan) power to gain the dominant position in the Middle East. The Jews, though allowed to return to Judah, continued as a subject people under the Medo-Persian yoke. (Ne 9:36, 37) This empire showed an even greater appetite for territory than had the Babylonian, extending its domain from "India to Ethiopia."—Es 1:1.

Medo-Persia's domination was ended by the lightning conquest of the Grecian forces headed by Alexander the Great. In a few short years he built up an empire that embraced parts of Europe, Asia, and Africa. This was the first European-based power to hold such a position. After Alexander's death his generals struggled for control of the empire, four of them eventually gaining the rulership of different sections. Palestine was fought over by the rival Seleucid and Ptolemaic kingdoms.

The Grecian Empire was eventually taken over completely by Rome. The Roman Empire surpassed all the preceding empires not only in the extent of its domain (covering the entire Mediterranean area and in time reaching to the British Isles) but also in the efficiency of its military machine and the firmness of its application of Roman law to the provinces of its far-flung empire. Rome, of course, was the political instrument used to execute the Messiah, Christ Jesus, as well as to persecute the early Christian congregation. The empire extended for nearly a thousand years thereafter in different forms but eventually broke up into various nations, with Britain finally gaining the dominant position.

Historian H. G. Wells makes the following interesting observations on the distinctiveness of the Roman Empire: "Now this new Roman power which arose to dominate the western world in the second and first centuries B.C. was in several respects a different thing from any of the great empires that had hitherto prevailed in the civilised world. It was not at first a monarchy, and it was not the creation of any one great conqueror. . . . It was the first republican empire that escaped extinction and went on to fresh developments. . . . Its population was less strongly Hamitic and Semitic than that of any preceding empire. . . . It was so far a new pattern in history, it was an expanded Aryan republic. . . . It was always changing. It never attained to any fixity. In a sense the [administrative] experiment failed. In a sense the experiment remains unfinished, and Europe and America to-day are still working out the riddles of world-wide statecraft first confronted by the Roman people."—*The Pocket History of the World*, 1943, pp. 149-151.

The ram and the male goat. In the vision Daniel received two years later (Da 8:1), the powers represented by the two symbolic beasts involved are clearly named. The kingdom of Medo-Persia is here pictured as a male sheep (a ram) having two horns, the taller horn coming up afterward. History shows that the Medes first were the stronger, and the Persians thereafter gained the ascendancy, though both peoples remained united in a dual power. A he-goat, moving very fast across the earth, symbolized the world power of Greece. (Da 8:3-8, 20, 21) The prophetic vision shows that the goat's "great horn" located between its eyes, representing the first king, was broken "as soon as it became mighty," and four kingdoms resulted, though of inferior strength. (Da 8:5, 8, 21, 22) The rapid conquest of the Medo-Persian Empire by Alexander has already been commented on, as well as the division of his kingdom among four of his generals.

It is worthy of mention here that the same nation or its rulers may be represented by different animal symbols in different prophecies. Thus, the kings of Assyria and Babylon are represented by lions at Jeremiah 50:17, while at Ezekiel 17:3-17 the rulers of Babylon and Egypt are pictured by great eagles. Ezekiel elsewhere likens Egypt's Pharaoh to a "great sea monster" lying in the Nile canals. (Eze 29:3) Hence the fact that Medo-Persia and Greece are represented by certain symbolisms in Daniel chapter 8 does not eliminate the possibility of their being represented by other symbolisms in the earlier vision (Da 7) nor in subsequent prophecies.

The seven-headed wild beast out of the sea. In the vision had by the apostle John and recorded at Revelation 13, a seven-headed, ten-horned wild beast comes up out of the sea, leopardlike, yet

SYMBOLISM OF THAT WHICH IS BAD AND UNDESIRABLE

ANIMAL	CHARACTERISTIC OR QUALITY	SYMBOLISM
Animals in general	Lack of reasoning	Wicked men (2Pe 2:12; Jude 10)
Ass	Strong sexual desire	Faithless Judah in turning to Assyria and Egypt (Eze 23:20)
Bear	Ferocity	Wicked rulers (Pr 28:15) Medo-Persian World Power (Da 7:5)
Bull	Ferocity	Wicked enemies of David (Ps 22:12)
Camel (female)	Aimless seeking of fulfillment of desire	Israel's unfaithful seeking after pagan nations and their gods (Jer 2:23)
Dog	Viciousness, uncleanness, operating in packs, unsatisfied in sexual desire	Wicked enemies of David (Ps 22:16; 59:6, 14) Sexual pervert (De 23:18; Php 3:2; Re 22:15) Worthless individual (2Sa 16:9) Wicked shepherds of Israel (Isa 56:10, 11) Ancient Jewish view of uncircumcised Gentiles (Mt 15:26, 27) Apostates (2Pe 2:22)
Dove	Easily distracted, unstable, simpleminded	Ten-tribe kingdom of Israel (Ho 7:11)
Dragon	Devouring, crushing, swallowing	Satan the Devil (Re 12:9) King of Babylon (Jer 51:34, ftn)
Eagle	Rapacious, predatory	Kings of Babylon and Egypt (Eze 17:3, 7, 12, 15)
Fish	Some fish unclean according to the Law (Le 11:10-12)	Wicked persons, unsuitable for Kingdom (Mt 13:47-50)
Fox	Craftiness, slyness	Treacherous King Herod Antipas (Lu 13:32)
Goat	Stubbornness, independent disposition, tendency to butt	Persons not friendly toward Christ's spiritual brothers, "cursed" ones going into destruction (Mt 25:32, 41, 46) Grecian World Power (Da 8:5, 21)
Horse	Usefulness in battle (Job 39:19-25) Strong sexual desire	Warfare, war equipment (Ps 33:17; 147:10; Isa 31:1; Jer 4:13) Sex-mad Israelites of Jeremiah's day (Jer 5:8)
Leopard	Speed	Rapidity of Chaldean conquest (Hab 1:8) Grecian World Power (Da 7:6)
Lion	Fierce, rapacious, predatory	Wicked enemies of David (Ps 22:13) Babylonian World Power (Da 7:4) Kings of Assyria and Babylon (Jer 50:17) Devil (1Pe 5:8)
Serpent	Cunning, deceptiveness (2Co 11:3)	Satan the Devil (Re 12:9)
Sheep (male)	Butting	Medo-Persian World Power (Da 8:3, 4, 20)
Sow	Uncleanness	Apostates (2Pe 2:22)
Wolf	Ferocity, rapacity, viciousness, craftiness	False prophets (Mt 7:15) Wicked, false Christians; false teachers (Ac 20:29) Wicked men of the world (Mt 10:16)

with feet of a bear and the mouth of a lion. It is thus a composite form of several of the symbols appearing in Daniel's vision of the four beasts. The dragon, identified at Revelation 12:9 as Satan the Devil, gives the beast its authority and power. (Re 13:1, 2) This beast's seven heads (bearing ten horns) distinguish it from the one-headed beasts of Daniel's vision. Seven (and ten) are commonly acknowledged as Biblical symbols of completeness. (See NUMBER, NUMERAL.) This is corroborated by the extent of this beast's domain, for it exercises authority, not over one nation or a group of nations, but "over every tribe and people and tongue and nation." (Re 13:7, 8; compare 16:13, 14.) Noting these factors, *The Interpreter's Dictionary of the Bible* comments: "The first of these beasts [of Re 13] combines in itself the joint characteristics of the four beasts of Daniel's vision . . . Accordingly, this first beast represents the combined forces of all political rule opposed to God in the world."—Edited by G. Buttrick, 1962, Vol. 1, p. 369.

Two-horned beast. Then John saw a beast out of the earth with two horns like those of a harmless lamb, yet speaking as a dragon, exercising the full authority of the first wild beast, just described. It directs making an image of the globally ruling seven-headed beast, putting all persons under compulsion to accept its "mark."—Re 13:11-17.

It may be recalled that the two-horned ram of Daniel chapter 8 represented a dual power, Medo-Persia. Of course, that power had long

ANIMAL	CHARACTERISTIC OR QUALITY	SYMBOLISM
Worm	Low, weak, insignificant	God's nation Israel (Jacob) weak in itself, strong by Jehovah's power (Isa 41:13-15)
Zebra (female)	Craving sexual satisfaction from any quarter	Israel unfaithfully seeking after pagan nations and their gods (Jer 2:24)

since disappeared by the apostle John's day, and his vision was of things yet future. (Re 1:1) Other dual powers have existed since John's day, but among these the historical association of Britain and the United States is particularly notable and of long duration.

The other notable characteristic of the two-horned beast, its speaking like a dragon, recalls the "mouth speaking grandiose things" on the outstanding horn of the fourth beast of Daniel 7 (vss 8, 20-26); while its 'misleading' earth's inhabitants compares with the deception practiced by the 'fierce king' described at Daniel 8:23-25. —Re 13:11, 14.

The scarlet-colored wild beast. At Revelation 17 the apostle records his vision of a scarlet-colored beast with seven heads and ten horns, mounted by the symbolic woman "Babylon the Great." This beast thus resembles, or is in the image of, the first beast of Revelation 13 but is distinct because of its scarlet color and the fact that no crowns are seen on its ten horns. Beholding the beast, John is told that five of the seven kings represented by the seven heads had already fallen, while one existed at that time, and the seventh was yet to come. The scarlet-colored beast itself is an eighth king but springs from or is a product of the previous seven. The "ten kings" represented by the ten horns exist and exercise authority in association with the scarlet beast for a short time. Warring against the Lamb, Jesus Christ, and those with him, they go down in defeat.—Re 17:3-5, 9-14.

Some scholars would apply this vision to pagan Rome, and the seven heads to seven emperors of Rome, followed by an eighth emperor. They disagree, however, as to which emperors should be included. The Bible itself does not mention more than three Roman emperors by name, with a fourth (Nero) being mentioned under the title of "Caesar." Other scholars understand the "heads" or "kings" to represent world powers, as in the book of Daniel. It is noteworthy that the Bible does name five world powers in the Hebrew Scriptures, namely, Egypt, Assyria, Babylon, Medo-Persia, and Greece, while the Greek Scriptures

name a sixth, Rome, ruling in John's day. While this would leave the seventh 'king' unnamed, the fact that it had not yet appeared when John recorded the Revelation would allow for such anonymity. The eighth king, the symbolic scarlet beast, in some way unites in itself these seven heads while at the same time springing from them.

BEATING. The Mosaic Law provided for punishment by beating. This was with a stick or a rod. The judges were to decide the number of strokes to be given according to the misdeed committed, considering also the motive, circumstances, and so forth. The position was prescribed: "The judge must also have him laid prostrate and given strokes before him by number to correspond with his wicked deed." The punishment was limited to 40 strokes. (De 25:2, 3) The reason given for such limitation was that more than this would disgrace the person in the eyes of his fellow countrymen. This is one of the examples showing that the Law given through Moses allowed for no cruel or unusual punishment. The purpose of the punishment was corrective, not vindictive and vicious as were the punishments meted out by other nations. The one administering the beating would be punished if he exceeded the legal number of strokes. Therefore, the Jews restricted the strokes to 39, so as not to go beyond the limit by mistake and thereby violate the law.—2Co 11:24.

A Hebrew slave owner was permitted to strike his slave man or slave girl with a stick if the slave was disobedient or rebellious. But if the slave died under the beating, the slave owner was to be punished. If the slave lived for a day or two afterward, however, this would be evidence tending to indicate that the slave owner did not have murder in his heart. He had the right to mete out disciplinary punishment, for the slave was "his money." A man would be very unlikely to want to destroy completely his own valuable property, thereby suffering a loss. Also, if the slave died after the passage of a day or more, it might not be certain whether death was from the beating or from some other cause. So if the slave continued alive a day or two, the master would not be punished.—Ex 21:20, 21.

If a man charged his wife with deceptively claiming to be a virgin at the time of marriage and his charge was false, the older men of the city, as judges, were to discipline him and also impose a fine because he brought a bad name upon a virgin of Israel. This discipline might have been the administering of a certain number of strokes.—De 22:13-19.

The Scriptures repeatedly emphasize the value of strokes as a disciplinary measure. Proverbs 20:30 shows that discipline can go very deep, resulting in good to the individual. It reads: "Bruising wounds are what scours away the bad; and strokes, the innermost parts of the belly." The person being disciplined in this way should recognize that he has acted foolishly and should change. (Pr 10:13; 19:29) A really wise person can be corrected by words and will avoid the need of strokes.

Since all mankind are brought forth "with error" and conceived "in sin" (Ps 51:5), the Scriptures counsel that the parental rod of authority must be strictly exercised, sometimes in the form of the literal rod. (Pr 22:15) Thereby the child may be saved from disfavor and death.—Pr 23:13, 14.

It appears that the Jews did not continue to confine themselves to the rod but later used the scourge. (Heb 11:36) This is a more severe punishment than beating with rods, and while it was a legalized punishment during the time Jesus was on earth, it was not based on the Law. (Mt 10:17; 23:34) The Mishnah, which is supposed to be a development of the oral tradition, describes the procedure of scourging:

"They bind his two hands to a pillar on either side, and the minister of the synagogue lays hold on his garments—if they are torn they are torn, if they are utterly rent they are utterly rent—so that he bares his chest. A stone is set down behind him on which the minister of the synagogue stands with a strap of calf-hide in his hand, doubled and re-doubled, and two [other] straps that rise and fall [are fastened] thereto.

"The handpiece of the strap is one handbreadth long and one handbreadth wide; and its end must reach to his navel. He gives him one-third of the stripes in front and two-thirds behind; and he may not strike him when he is standing or when he is sitting, but only when he is bending low, for it is written, *The judge shall cause him to lie down.* And he that smites, smites with his one hand with all his might.

" . . . If he dies under his hand, the scourger is not culpable. But if he gave him one stripe too many and he died, he must escape into exile because of him."

"How many stripes do they inflict on a man? Forty save one, for it is written, *By number forty;* [that is to say,] a number near to forty."—*Makkot* 3:12–14, 10; translated by H. Danby.

An unusual form of scourging was adopted by Gideon toward the 77 princes and older men of Succoth, who refused to give provision to his men when he was chasing after the kings of Midian. He apparently made scourges of the thorns and briers of the wilderness to thresh them. It is said that he put them "through an experience."—Jg 8:7, 14, 16.

Other nations used a more severe form of beating, and they did not limit themselves to 40 strokes. The Israelites in Egypt were beaten by their Egyptian overseers, no doubt very severely. —Ex 5:14, 16; 2:11, 12.

Romans used rods for beating, the outer garments first being stripped off. (Ac 16:22, 23) The Greek word translated 'beat with rods' in Acts 16:22 is *rha·bdi'zo,* related to *rha'bdos* (rod; staff). (Compare 1Co 4:21, *Int.*) Both these Greek words are related to *rha·bdou'khos,* translated 'constable' in Acts 16:35, 38 and literally meaning "rod bearer."—Compare *Int.*

The Romans also used the scourge. The victim was stretched out, apparently having his hands tied to a post with thongs. (Ac 22:25, 29) The number of strokes administered was altogether up to the commander. The punishment of scourging usually preceded impaling. The account says that after Pilate gave in to the Jews' insistent cry for Jesus' impalement, and he released Barabbas to them, "at that time, therefore, Pilate took Jesus and scourged him." (Joh 19:1; Mt 20:19) The Romans used the scourge at times to 'examine' victims in order to obtain confessions or testimony. (Ac 22:24, 25) Two Greek verbs for "scourge" are *ma·sti·go'o* (Mt 10:17) and *ma·sti'zo* (Ac 22:25). Both are related to *ma'stix,* which can mean "scourging" in the literal sense (Ac 22:24; Heb 11:36) and, metaphorically, "grievous disease (sickness)." (Mr 3:10; 5:34) However, to scourge a Roman citizen was illegal. The *Lex Valeria* and the *Lex Porcia,* enacted at various times between 509 and 195 B.C.E., exempted Roman citizens from scourging—the *Lex Valeria,* when the citizen appealed to the people; the *Lex Porcia,* without such appeal.

The most terrible instrument for scourging was known as the *flagellum.* It consisted of a handle into which several cords or leather thongs were fixed. These thongs were weighted with jagged pieces of bone or metal to make the blow more painful and effective. The Greek noun *phra·gel'li·on* ("whip"; Joh 2:15) was drawn from the Latin *flagellum.* The related verb *phra·gel·lo'o* means "whip."—Mt 27:26; Mr 15:15.

Jesus told his disciples that for his name's sake they would be beaten in the synagogues. (Mr

13:9) This prophecy was fulfilled numerous times. Some of the apostles were arrested and brought before the Jewish Sanhedrin and were flogged after they had refused to agree to stop their preaching work. (Ac 5:40) Saul, who afterward became the apostle Paul, was a fierce persecutor of Christians before his conversion, imprisoning them and flogging them in one synagogue after another. (Ac 22:19) The Greek verb used in these accounts (*de'ro*) is related to *der'ma* ('skin'; Heb 11:37, *Int*) and basically means "flay."—Compare Lu 12:47, *Int*.

Paul was flogged with rods in the city of Philippi. He turned this incident against his persecutors, using the opportunity to defend and legally establish the good news that he preached. He had been publicly beaten and thrown into prison, but when the magistrates found out that he was a Roman citizen, they were very fearful, for they not only had flogged a Roman citizen but had done so even before he had been condemned by trial. In this case too, Paul and Silas had been publicly displayed as malefactors. So when the magistrates ordered the jailer to release Paul and Silas, Paul replied: "They flogged us publicly uncondemned, men who are Romans, and threw us into prison; and are they now throwing us out secretly? No, indeed! but let them come themselves and bring us out." The magistrates had to personally acknowledge their error. "So the constables reported these sayings to the civil magistrates. These grew fearful when they heard that the men were Romans. Consequently they came and entreated them and, after bringing them out, they requested them to depart from the city." (Ac 16:22-40) Thereby, the preaching of the good news was vindicated as being no violation of the law, for the magistrates themselves, by taking this action, made it a matter of public record that Paul and Silas had done no wrong. Paul acted in this way because it was his desire 'legally to establish the good news.'—Php 1:7.

Figurative Usage. King Rehoboam compared his intended way of ruling with the rule of his father Solomon by metaphorically referring to the more serious punishment of the scourge as contrasted with whips. (In the Hebrew, the word for "scourges" [*'aq·rab·bim'*] literally means "scorpions" and apparently was a type of whip with knots, or with barbed ends like a scorpion's stinger, or perhaps with knotted or thorny twigs.)—1Ki 12:11-14, ftn.

When Jehovah made a covenant with David for a kingdom, He told David that the throne would be established in his line but that if his dynasty or any of his line of descent should do wrong, Jeho-vah would "reprove him with the rod of men and with the strokes of the sons of Adam." (2Sa 7:14; Ps 89:32) This did take place when Jehovah allowed the kings of the Gentile nations to defeat the kings of Judah, particularly when Nebuchadnezzar, the king of Babylon, removed Zedekiah from the throne in Jerusalem.—Jer 52:1-11.

Jehovah said that the nations the Israelites failed to dispossess would become 'a scourge on their flanks.' (Jos 23:13) Isaiah 10:24-26 shows that, while the Assyrian used the rod to strike Zion unjustly, Jehovah was to brandish "a whip" against the Assyrian. A plague, disease, or calamity sent out from Jehovah as a punishment was referred to as a scourge. (Nu 16:43-50; 25:8, 9; Ps 106:29, 30) Discipline from Jehovah is likened to scourging.—Heb 12:6.

Jesus foretold that at the time of his presence he would appoint "the faithful and discreet slave . . . over all his belongings." God's Son also spoke of an evil slave that would not be alert and anxiously watching for his master's arrival. Such an "evil slave" would say: "My master is delaying." Not only would he eat and drink with the confirmed drunkards but he would go further by beating his fellow slaves and opposing their work of providing the spiritual food at the proper time for God's faithful slaves. This one, in turn, would be punished with the greatest severity and assigned a part with the hypocrites. (Mt 24:45-51; Lu 12:42-46) Jesus went on then to show that one who has greater responsibility and fails to take care of it is more reprehensible than one who does not know or understand his duties so well. Such a one's punishment, the number of "strokes," would be proportionate to his responsibility.—Lu 12: 47, 48.

Isaiah prophesied that the Messiah would bear the sicknesses and pains of those who would exercise faith in him. He said: "Because of his wounds there has been a healing for us." (Isa 53:3-5) Peter applies this prophecy to Jesus Christ, saying: "He himself bore our sins in his own body upon the stake, in order that we might be done with sins and live to righteousness. And 'by his stripes you were healed.'"—1Pe 2:24.

BEAUTIFUL GATE.   See GATE, GATEWAY.

BEBAI   (Be'bai).

1. A household head whose descendants, over 600, returned to Jerusalem with Zerubbabel in 537 B.C.E. (Ezr 2:1, 2, 11; Ne 7:16) Twenty-nine more came with Ezra in 468 B.C.E. (Ezr 8:11) Four of the first group had taken foreign wives, which they put away at the insistence of Ezra.—Ezr 10:28, 44.

2. A prominent man or a representative of the sons of Bebai (No. 1), who attested to Nehemiah's agreement of faithfulness.—Ne 9:38; 10:1, 15.

BECHER   (Be'cher) [Young Male Camel].

1. The second-named son of Benjamin in the list of Jacob's descendants at Genesis chapter 46. (See Ge 46:21; 1Ch 7:6.) Becher is omitted in the genealogical lists at Numbers 26:38 and 1 Chronicles 8:1, 2. His descendants through his nine sons as family heads numbered 20,200 "valiant, mighty men," according to the account recorded at 1 Chronicles 7:8, 9.

2. Family head of Becherites (Bachrites, *KJ*) of the tribe of Ephraim.—Nu 26:35.

BECHERITES   (Be'cher·ites) [Of (Belonging to) Becher]. An Ephraimite family descended from Becher.—Nu 26:35.

BECORATH   (Be·co'rath) [Firstborn]. Ancestor of King Saul; of the tribe of Benjamin.—1Sa 9:1.

BED.   During Bible times, as today, the facilities for sleeping varied in type, style, and structure, according to the people's wealth, status in life, and customs. The bare ground, sometimes cushioned with a pad or pallet, often sufficed for the poor, the herdsman, and the traveler; very costly and ornate furnishings were used by rulers and the rich in their permanent dwellings.

The common Hebrew term for "bed" is *mish-kav'*, from the root *sha·khav'* (lie down). (Ge 49:4; Le 26:6) The usual Greek term is *kli'ne,* from *kli'no* (incline). (Mt 9:2; Lu 9:58, *Int*) Another Greek term for "bed," *koi'te,* which basically denotes a place to lie down (Lu 11:7), is also used to refer to the "marriage bed" (Heb 13:4) and "illicit intercourse" (Ro 13:13); by metonymy it refers to conceiving a child. (Ro 9:10) Other Hebrew terms for places for lying down are *mat·tah'* (couch), *'e'res* (divan), and *ya·tsu·a''* (lounge). The Greek *kra'bat-tos* refers to a cot. (Mr 2:4) Bible writers did not always make a distinction between these various terms and frequently used two or more of them for the same thing, calling a bed a divan (Job 7:13), a bed a cot (Mt 9:6; Mr 2:11), a couch a divan (Ps 6:6), a bed a lounge (Ge 49:4). These were used by those sleeping at night or taking a siesta (2Sa 4:5-7; Job 33:15), by those sick, by ones having intercourse (Ps 41:3; Eze 23:17), and as a resting-place for the dead in a grand tomb (2Ch 16:14). The custom of reclining at a meal required couches. (Es 7:8; Mt 26:20; Lu 22:14) A couch especially designed to carry one about in regal style was called a *litter.*—Ca 3:7-10; see LITTER.

Certain accessories are usually associated with beds, for example, a pillow. Jesus, when crossing the Sea of Galilee, fell asleep "upon a pillow" in the stern of the boat. (Mr 4:38) During the colder season a "woven sheet" or other covering was used (Isa 28:20), but it was common to sleep in everyday garments; hence the Mosaic Law forbade keeping another person's garments after sunset: "It is his only covering. . . . In what will he lie down?"—Ex 22:26, 27.

The Oriental bed was often a simple mat made of straw or rushes, with perhaps quilting or a mattress of some sort for added comfort. When not in use, these were rolled up and stored away. A more permanent arrangement employed a wooden frame or bedstead that elevated the sleeper off the ground or floor. (Mr 4:21) These served as couches or divans upon which to sit during the daytime. The simplest cotlike beds were lightweight, easily picked up and carried about.—Lu 5:18, 19; Joh 5:8; Ac 5:15.

The wealthy had beds draped with elegant decorations of rich embroidery. "With coverlets I have bedecked my divan, with many-colored things, linen of Egypt. I have besprinkled my bed with myrrh, aloes and cinnamon," the seductive prostitute declared. (Pr 7:16, 17) Like the "couches of gold and silver" of a Persian palace, so also "a splendid couch," "a Damascene divan," and "couches of ivory," were described by the prophet as the furnishings of rebellious Israel.—Es 1:6; Am 3:12; 6:4.

Separate bedrooms or inner bedrooms were used by those who could afford large houses. (Ex 8:3; 2Ki 6:12; 11:2) During the hot summer, the cooler rooftops frequently served as sleeping quarters.

Also in a figurative sense, beds, couches, and lounges are referred to in the Scriptures. The state of the dead, for example, is as those lying in a bed. (Job 17:13; Eze 32:25) Jehovah's loyal ones "cry out joyfully on their beds," in contrast with wayward ones who keep howling and scheming what is bad while lying in bed. (Ps 149:5; Ho 7:14; Mic 2:1) Unlike Reuben, who with reckless license had relations with his father Jacob's concubine and in this sense profaned his father's bed (Ge 35:22; 49:4), Christians must not defile the sacred marital arrangement, "the marriage bed," in any way. —Heb 13:4.

BEDAD   (Be'dad). Father of Edomite King Hadad, who ruled in Avith before any king ruled over Israel.—Ge 36:31, 35; 1Ch 1:43, 46.

BEDAN   (Be'dan).

1. Listed with Gideon (Jerubbaal), Jephthah, and Samuel as delivering Israel from enemies. (1Sa 12:11) However, nowhere else in the Bible nor in secular history is mention made of such a Bedan. Regarding this text, C. F. Keil and F. Delitzsch remark: "It is extremely improbable that Samuel should have mentioned a judge here, who had been passed over in the book of Judges on account of his comparative insignificance."—*Commentary on the Old Testament,* 1973, Vol. II, 1 Samuel, p. 118.

Bedan is by some understood to refer to Barak. The context of 1 Samuel 12:11 denotes a major deliverer and recalls the oppression by Sisera and the deliverance that followed, a deliverance in which Jehovah used Barak. Barak is named along with Gideon and Jephthah in Hebrews 11:32. The Greek *Septuagint* and Syriac *Peshitta* read "Barak" at 1 Samuel 12:11. Others believe Bedan refers to Judge Abdon.—See BARAK.

2. A descendant of Manasseh.—1Ch 7:17.

BEDEIAH   (Be·dei'ah). One of the 12 sons of Bani who, at Ezra's urging, sent away their foreign wives and sons.—Ezr 10:10, 11, 34, 35, 44.

BEE   [Heb., *devoh·rah'*]. Biblical references in the main quite evidently relate to wild honeybees. The description of Canaan as "a land flowing with milk and honey" indicates that bees were very numerous in that land from early times. (Ex 3:8) The warm climate and the abundance of flowers continue to make it a land suitable for a large bee population, and beekeeping is very popular there in modern times. Of the more than 20,000 varieties of bees known, the kind most common in Israel today is a dark bee called *Apis mellifica syriaca.*

The honey eaten by Jonathan during one military campaign was found in the woods, the bees' nest likely being in a hollow tree. (1Sa 14:25-27) Wild honeybees of the Jordan Valley provided John the Baptizer with a large proportion of his food. (Mt 3:4) Bees nest not only in trees but also in other hollow cavities, such as clefts of rocks and walls.—De 32:13; Ps 81:16.

The account at Judges 14:5-9 has caused some question. Samson, having slain a lion, returned to find "a swarm of bees in the lion's corpse, and honey." The strong aversion of most bees to dead bodies and carrion is well known. It should be noted, however, that the account states that Samson returned "after a while" or, literally in the Hebrew, "after days," a phrase that can refer to a period of even a year. (Compare 1Sa 1:3 [The expression "from year to year" in the Hebrew is literally "from days to days."]; compare Ne 13:6.) The time elapsed would allow for the scavenger birds or animals and also insects to have consumed much of the flesh and for the burning rays of the sun to desiccate the remainder. That a fair amount of time had passed is also evident from the fact that the swarm of bees not only had formed their nest within the lion's corpse but also had produced a quantity of honey.

The ferocity of attack by a disturbed hive of bees is used to describe the way in which the Amorites chased the Israelite forces out of their mountainous domain. (De 1:44) Comparing enemy nations to a swarm of attacking bees, the psalmist says they were held off only by faith in Jehovah's name.—Ps 118:10-12.

The prophet Isaiah graphically foretold the invasion of the Promised Land by the armies of Egypt and Assyria, likening their troops to swarms of flies and bees for which Jehovah God figuratively whistles so that they come in and settle on the torrent valleys and the clefts of the crags. (Isa 7:18, 19) The 'whistling' does not denote an actual practice among those keeping bees but simply indicates that Jehovah attracts the attention of the aggressive nations to the land of his covenant people.

Two women in the Bible bore the name Deborah (meaning "Bee"), the nursing woman of Rebekah (Ge 35:8) and the prophetess who cooperated with Judge Barak in the defeat of Canaanite King Jabin. —Jg 4:4.

BEELIADA   (Be·e·li'a·da) [Owner Knows]. A son of David born after his coming to Jerusalem. (1Ch 14:3-7) He is called "Eliada" (meaning "God Has Known") at 2 Samuel 5:16 and 1 Chronicles 3:8.

BEELZEBUB   (Be·el'ze·bub) [possibly an alteration of Baal-zebub, meaning "Owner of the Flies," the Baal worshiped by the Philistines at Ekron. Alternately, Beelzeboul and Beezeboul, possibly meaning, "Owner of the Lofty Abode (Habitation)"; or, if a play on the non-Biblical Heb. word *ze'vel* (dung), "Owner of the Dung"]. "Beelzebub" is a designation applied to Satan the prince, or ruler, of the demons. The religious leaders blasphemously accused Jesus Christ of expelling demons by means of Beelzebub.—Mt 10:25; 12:24-29; Mr 3:22-27; Lu 11:15-19; see BAAL-ZEBUB.

BEER, I   (Be'er) [Well]. The Hebrew word *be'er'* usually refers to a well in contrast to a natural spring (Heb., *'a'yin*). It commonly occurs in compound place-names.—Compare BEER-ELIM; BEER-SHEBA.

1. After passing the Arnon on their approach to the Promised Land, the Israelites came to Beer. (Nu 21:13-16) Here a well was dug, apparently by the princely heads of the tribes, using their own staffs, and water sprang up. This event was cause for the poetic song set forth in verses 17, 18.

Due to the part played by the princes in the digging of the well, some suggest that this is the same place as Beer-elim (meaning "Well of the Big Trees"). (Isa 15:8) The location is uncertain, but it is considered likely to have been in the torrent valley called the Wadi Thamad, N of the Arnon and some 56 km (35 mi) E of the Dead Sea. Water is often found here quite easily by scooping out the soil.

2. A place to which Jotham, Gideon's (Jerubbaal's) son, fled after exposing Abimelech's treachery. (Jg 9:3-5, 21) Al-Bira, about 12 km (7.5 mi) N of Beth-shan and SE of Mount Tabor, is suggested by some as the probable location; others connect it with Beeroth. (See BEEROTH.) In view of the absence of any indication of the direction of Jotham's flight from Mount Gerizim, however, the identification is uncertain.

BEER, II. A beverage rather low in alcohol content, brewed by slow fermentation from wheat or other grain. The Hebrew word *so've'*, rendered "wheat beer," may also be translated "liquor."—Isa 1:22, ftn; Ho 4:18, ftn; Na 1:10, ftn.

Cuneiform tablets reveal that the art of brewing beer from grain was practiced in ancient Mesopotamia as early as the third millennium B.C.E. When Abraham first arrived in Egypt he probably found that beer was already a common drink there. At a later date, it is said, Ramses III prized beer so highly that he offered up some 114,000 L (30,000 gal) a year to his gods. Many Philistine beer mugs with their strainer spouts have been found. Those various nations, it seems, had a great variety of beers to suit every taste—sweet beer, dark beer, perfumed beer, sparkling beer, spiced beer—served either hot or cold, watered down or thick and syrupy.—See WINE AND STRONG DRINK.

BEERA (Be·e'ra) [Well]. A family head and descendant of Asher.—1Ch 7:30, 37, 40.

BEERAH (Be·er'ah) [Well]. A Reubenite chieftain taken into exile by Assyrian King Tiglath-pileser III apparently during the reign of Pekah (c. 778-759 B.C.E.).—1Ch 5:6.

BEER-ELIM (Be'er-e'lim) [Well of the Big Trees]. A place named in Isaiah's pronouncement against Moab. (Isa 15:8) The foretold desolation is to cause "howling" clear to Eglaim and to Beer-elim. The location is unknown; many scholars relate it to Beer, mentioned at Numbers 21:16.—See BEER, I, No. 1.

BEERI (Be·e'ri) [Of (Belonging to) Beer or Beeroth].

1. Hittite father of Esau's wife Judith.—Ge 26:34.

2. Father of the prophet Hosea.—Ho 1:1.

BEER-LAHAI-ROI (Be'er-la'hai-roi) [Well of the Living One Who Sees Me]. Hagar, Sarai's Egyptian maidservant, when fleeing from her mistress' wrath followed "the way to Shur," leading through the Negeb down to Egypt. Reaching a certain fountain (Heb., *'a'yin*), however, she was reassured by an angel, instructed to return to her mistress, and told of the birth and future of Ishmael (whose name means "God Hears (Listens)"). Therefore, the well there was called "Beer-lahai-roi," Hagar saying of Jehovah, "You are a God of sight."—Ge 16:7-14.

Later, Isaac was coming from "the way that goes to Beer-lahai-roi" in the Negeb when he caught sight of the camel caravan bringing his future bride, Rebekah. (Ge 24:62, 63) Following Abraham's death, Isaac resided "close by Beer-lahai-roi."—Ge 25:11.

Beer-lahai-roi is stated to have been "between Kadesh and Bered." (Ge 16:14) A Bedouin tradition places it at 'Ain Muweilih, about 19 km (12 mi) NW of 'Ain Qedeis (the probable site of Kadesh-barnea). But the absence of any clear identification of Bered leaves the identification uncertain.

BEEROTH (Be·er'oth) [Wells]. One of four Hivite cities that astutely arranged a covenant with Joshua, the men of the city of Gibeon apparently taking the lead in the matter. (Jos 9:3-17) The city thereafter was included within the inheritance of the tribe of Benjamin. (Jos 18:21, 25) In describing the assassination of Saul's son Ish-bosheth by men from Beeroth, the statement is made that "Beer-oth, too, used to be counted as part of Benjamin." This may indicate that the city lay near the border line of a neighboring tribe, hence the need to specify the tribal territory in which it was situated. (2Sa 4:2-6) Mention is made of the flight of its residents to Gittaim, but the reason is not explained; it may have been due to Philistine raids following their victory over Saul's forces at Mount Gilboa, or it may have taken place after the assassination of Ish-bosheth, the flight being to avoid acts of vengeance in reprisal for that murder. However, following the exile in Babylon, men of Beeroth are listed among those returning to the land of Judah.—Ezr 2:1, 25; Ne 7:29.

Though some suggest Khirbet el Burj or Nabi Samwil to the S, others suggest el Bira, a neighboring town of modern Ramallah, located about 14 km (9 mi) N of Jerusalem and about 8 km (5 mi) NNE of Gibeon, hence, near the border of Ephraim. A spring there provides a fine supply of water. Traces of an old caravansary indicate that it was a stopping place for caravans.

BEEROTH BENE-JAAKAN (Be·er′oth Ben′e-ja′a·kan) [Wells of the Sons of Jaakan]. A place at which the Israelites camped perhaps more than once during their wanderings in the wilderness, the last time being shortly before Aaron's death on Mount Hor. (De 10:6) It is tentatively identified with el-Birein, about 62 km (38 mi) SW of Beersheba and near modern 'Ezuz. There are wells here, and the probable location of Kadesh-barnea is but a few miles south. Nelson Glueck comments: "There is a strikingly large number of antiquity sites in this district." (*Rivers in the Desert*, 1960, p. 97) Beeroth Bene-jaakan is evidently referred to as simply Bene-jaakan at Numbers 33:31.—See BENE-JAAKAN.

BEEROTHITE (Be·er′oth·ite) [Of (Belonging to) Beeroth]. A resident or native of Beeroth. At the time of the Israelites' entry into Canaan its inhabitants were Hivites. The territory was thereafter assigned to Benjamin, and the Hivite residents became "gatherers of wood and drawers of water." (Jos 9:17, 27; 18:21, 25; see BEEROTH.) The assassins of Ish-bosheth, namely, Baanah and Rechab, were "sons of Rimmon the Beerothite, of the sons of Benjamin." (2Sa 4:2, 5, 9) Naharai, one of David's mighty men, is called "the Beerothite" in 2 Samuel 23:37 and "the Berothite" in 1 Chronicles 11:39.

BEER-SHEBA (Be′er-she′ba) [Well of the Oath; or, Well of Seven]. The place of a well and, later, of a city in southern Judah. It lies about midway between the Mediterranean Coast and the southern end of the Dead Sea, about 45 km (28 mi) SW of Hebron, and about the same distance SE of Gaza.

Beer-sheba came to stand for the southernmost point in describing the length of the Promised Land, as expressed in the proverbial phrase "from Dan down to Beer-sheba" (Jg 20:1), or, in a converse direction, "from Beer-sheba to Dan." (1Ch 21:2; 2Ch 30:5) After the division of the nation into two kingdoms, Beer-sheba continued to be used to indicate the southern extremity of the kingdom of Judah in the expressions "from Geba as far as Beer-sheba" (2Ki 23:8) and "from Beersheba to the mountainous region of Ephraim" (where the northern kingdom of Israel began). (2Ch 19:4) In postexilic times the expression was used in a yet more limited form to refer to the area occupied by the repatriated men of Judah, extending from Beer-sheba "clear to the valley of Hinnom."—Ne 11:27, 30.

In reality, there were other towns of the Promised Land that lay to the S of Beer-sheba, even as there were Israelite towns N of Dan. However, both Dan and Beer-sheba were situated at natural frontiers of the land. In the case of Beer-sheba, its position was below the mountains of Judah on the edge of the desert. Additionally, it was one of the principal cities of Judah (along with Jerusalem and Hebron), and this was not only because it had an excellent supply of water as compared with the surrounding region, thus allowing for both farming and grazing of herds and flocks, but also because important roads converged on it from several directions. From Egypt an ancient route led up by the "Way of the Wells" through Kadeshbarnea to Beer-sheba, being joined by another road over which traveled the camel caravans from the "Spice Kingdoms" of the Arabian Peninsula, heading for Philistia or Judah. From Ezion-geber, at the head of the Gulf of 'Aqaba, another route led up through the Arabah and then turned W, climbing the Ascent of Akrabbim to Beer-sheba. At Gaza, in the Philistine Plain, a road branching from the highway led SE to Beer-sheba. And, connecting it with the rest of Judah, a road ran from Beer-sheba to the NE, climbing the plateau up into the mountains of Judah to Jerusalem and points farther N.—Ge 22:19.

The site is first mentioned in connection with Hagar, who wandered with her son Ishmael "in the wilderness of Beer-sheba" when dismissed by Abraham. (Ge 21:14) Expecting her son to die of thirst, she withdrew from Ishmael, but God heard the boy and directed Hagar to a well. (Ge 21:19) This may have been a well dug earlier by Abraham, but at that time still unnamed, in view of the account that follows. Some of the Philistines seized a well in this area by violence, seemingly unknown to Abimelech the king of Gerar. He and Phicol the chief of his army approached Abraham to propose a covenant of peace. When Abraham severely criticized Abimelech for his servants' act of violence in seizing the well, Abimelech avowed his ignorance, concluded a covenant with Abraham, and accepted seven female lambs from him in evidence of Abraham's title to the well. "That is why [Abraham] called that place Beer-sheba, because there both of them had taken an oath." (Ge 21:31) Abraham then planted a tamarisk tree there and called upon "the name of Jehovah the indefinitely lasting God." (Ge 21:33) It was from Beer-sheba that Abraham went to Moriah to offer Isaac as a sacrifice, and he returned there to dwell. —Ge 22:19.

When Abraham died, the Philistines stopped up the wells he had dug, but when Isaac later took up dwelling here he began to reopen them and call them by the names that his father had given them. (Ge 26:18) Opposed by the Philistines, he withdrew from place to place until he found ample room at Rehoboth, and later he went up to Beer-sheba. (Ge 26:22, 23) While Isaac's servants were excavating a well at Beer-sheba, Abimelech, possibly another king of Gerar (by the same name or the same title as the one that had covenanted with Abraham, or perhaps the same one), came with Phicol the chief of his army to Isaac to propose a covenant of peace with him. After feasting and drinking, they arose early the next morning and made sworn statements one to the other. That same day the well produced water, and Isaac called its name Shibah, meaning "Oath; or, Seven" and referring to an oath or statement sworn to by seven things. (Ge 26:31-33; see SHIBAH.) By using "Shibah" (another form of the name Sheba), Isaac apparently was preserving the name Beer-sheba, given to the place by Abraham. The possibility of this being the same well previously dug by Abraham and reexcavated by Isaac's men is shown by Genesis 26:18, previously cited. During the years that Isaac lived here, he blessed Jacob in place of Esau and sent him away to Haran to take a wife from the daughters of Laban, his mother's brother. (Ge 28:1, 2, 10) Later on, Jacob, now known as Israel, offered sacrifices to the God of Isaac at Beer-sheba on his way to join Joseph, his son, in Egypt.—Ge 46:1-5.

In the upwards of 250 years that intervened until Canaan was apportioned to the 12 tribes of Israel, a city had grown up at Beer-sheba (Jos 15:21, 28), which was assigned to the tribe of Simeon as an enclave city in the territory of Judah. (Jos 19:1, 2) Here Samuel's sons officiated as judges. (1Sa 8:1, 2) Elijah, fleeing from Queen Jezebel's wrath, left his attendant at Beer-sheba and headed southward across the Negeb toward Horeb. (1Ki 19:3) Zibiah, the mother of King Jehoash of Judah, came from this place. (2Ki 12:1) Beer-sheba was named as the terminating point of David's registering of the people throughout Israel (2Sa 24:2, 7) and the starting place of Jehoshaphat's reforms in worship. (2Ch 19:4) The references of Amos to Beer-sheba in his day strongly suggest that it was then a place of unclean religious activities (Am 5:5; 8:14), perhaps associated in some way with the idolatrous northern kingdom. Figurines of the goddess Astarte have been excavated there, as in many other parts of Israel. From this time forward, except for the brief mention of the reoccupation of the city and its dependent towns after the Babylonian exile (Ne 11:27), the name disappears from the Bible record.

The city during the period of the kings has been identified with Tell es-Saba' (Tel Be'er Sheva'), 4 km (2.5 mi) E of present-day Be'er Sheva'. Secular writers of the fourth century C.E. describe Beer-sheba as then being a large village or town and a Roman garrison. Today, it retains its position as a crossroads town and an important marketplace. Though the Beer-sheba basin is steppeland, receiving only about 15 to 20 cm (6 to 8 in.) of rainfall a year, the soil is productive, and there are good farms in the area. Several wells are to be found there, the largest of which is nearly 4 m (13 ft) in diameter, the lower part being cut through about 5 m (16 ft) of solid rock.

BEESHTERAH   (Be·esh'te·rah) [possibly, House of Ashtoreth]. A city E of the Jordan, given to the Gershonites of the tribe of Levi. (Jos 21:27) The parallel passage at 1 Chronicles 6:71 indicates it to be the same as Ashtaroth.

BEGGAR, BEGGING.   While the English word "begging" may mean simply to implore or plead, the discussion here deals primarily with begging in the sense of the habitual practice of publicly asking for charity.

The patriarchal arrangement, which the Bible indicates existed prior to and after the global Flood of Noah's day, doubtless served greatly to prevent situations where individuals would find themselves isolated, in dire straits, and dependent upon public charity, and thus it worked against the development of a pauper class. From ancient times hospitality to strangers or travelers seems to have been quite freely practiced; such hospitality is at least reflected in the Biblical accounts, with rare exceptions. (Ge 19:1-3; Ex 2:18-20; Jg 19:15-21) The development of cities contributed to the weakening of the patriarchal arrangement and possibly this, together with a selfish tendency to take undue advantage of the hospitality or charity of others, led to the development of begging among humankind.

Begging, or mendicancy, is apparently of very ancient origin in the lands of the Orient. This makes all the more notable the fact that in the

Hebrew Scriptures there is no indication that begging existed to any degree or that it constituted a particular problem in the nation of Israel from the time of the formation of the nation until it went into exile in Babylon. When moving out of Egypt and their slavery in that land, the Israelites "went asking [a form of the Heb. verb sha·'al'] from the Egyptians articles of silver and articles of gold and mantles. . . . and they stripped the Egyptians." (Ex 12:35, 36) This, however, was in accord with God's command and prophecy, and it was evidently viewed as just compensation for their long years of slave labor and the injustices endured by them at the hands of the Egyptians. (Ex 3:21, 22; compare De 15:12-15.) It set no precedent for the practice of begging.

The Mosaic Law contained forceful legislation on behalf of the poor, which, when observed, removed all cause for begging. (Le 19:9, 10; De 15:7-10; 24:19-21; see GIFTS OF MERCY.) The Hebrew Scriptures strongly express trust in God's providence for those adhering to righteousness, even as David in his old age exclaimed: "I have not seen anyone righteous left entirely, nor his offspring looking for ["begging," KJ; a form of the Heb. biq·qesh'] bread," even though such righteous ones themselves are shown to be openhanded in their generosity. (Ps 37:25, 26; contrast with the experience of apostate Jerusalem at La 1:11; 4:4.) On the other hand, Proverbs 20:4 portrays the lazy man as "begging in reaping time," and Psalm 109:10 describes the execution of punishment on the wicked as obliging "his sons [to] go wandering about; and they must do begging, and they must look for food from their desolate places." In these two latter texts the word "begging" translates the Hebrew sha·'al', which term basically means "ask" or "request" (Ex 3:22; 1Ki 3:11); however, in these two cases the implication is that the asking is done in the active, and perhaps public, manner characterizing begging.

It appears that during the period from the time of the Jews' return from exile (537 B.C.E.) down to the time of Jesus' appearance on the earthly scene, the concept developed among the Jews that the act of giving alms, or gifts of charity, had merit in itself toward salvation. This is evidenced by the statement contained in the Apocryphal book of Ecclesiasticus (3:30) (written in the early part of the second century B.C.E.) that "almsgiving atones for sins." Such view undoubtedly served to encourage begging. (Compare the much-publicized giving denounced by Jesus in Mt 6:2.)

Domination by the foreign powers brought oppression to the Jewish people and doubtless caused considerable disruption of the application of the Mosaic Law concerning ancestral land rights and similar provisions. This, together with false religious philosophies, which failed to inculcate a genuine and principled love of neighbor (Mt 23:23; Lu 10:29-31), also likely shared responsibility for the growth of begging in Palestine. Thus we find a number of references in the Christian Greek Scriptures to beggars in that land.

The blind, the lame, and the diseased figure among the beggars described in the time of Jesus and the apostles. Ophthalmia (a disease of the eyes still common in the Middle East) perhaps caused some of the blindness among these men. (Mr 10:46-49; Lu 16:20, 22; 18:35-43; Joh 9:1-8; Ac 3:2-10) Like beggars today, they often situated themselves along public thoroughfares or near places frequented by crowds, as at the temple. Despite the prominence given to almsgiving, beggars were looked down upon, so that the steward of Jesus' parable said, "I am ashamed to beg."—Lu 16:3.

The two Greek verbs used to refer to mendicancy are related to ai·te'o, meaning "ask."—Mt 7:7.

The Greek word pto·khos', used by Luke (16:20, 22) in recording Jesus' reference to Lazarus as a beggar, describes one who crouches and cringes, and it refers to the very poor, the destitute, the beggars. This same term is used at Matthew 5:3 with regard to those "conscious of their spiritual need ["those who are beggars for the spirit," ftn]" ("poor in spirit," KJ). Concerning the use of pto·khos' in this text, M. R. Vincent's Word Studies in the New Testament (1957, Vol. I, p. 36) says that "it is very graphic and appropriate here, as denoting the utter spiritual destitution, the consciousness of which precedes the entrance into the kingdom of God, and which cannot be relieved by one's own efforts, but only by the free mercy of God."

This same term is also used by Paul at Galatians 4:9 in expressing his concern over those who were "turning back again to the weak and beggarly [pto·kha'] elementary things" formerly practiced. Such things were "beggarly" in comparison with the spiritual riches obtainable through Christ Jesus.

Although Jesus and his apostles showed kindness to beggars, they did not encourage begging; though they gratefully accepted hospitality, they did not beg. Jesus told those who followed him merely to obtain bread that their concern should be, not for "the food that perishes, but for the food that remains for life everlasting." (Joh 6:26, 27) Peter told a lame beggar at the temple: "Silver and gold I do not possess, but what I do have is what I give you," using his spiritual gifts to heal the man. (Ac 3:6) Though at times hungry, homeless, and lacking clothing, the apostles toiled, 'working with their own hands, night and day, so as not to be a burden on others.' (1Co 4:11, 12; 1Th 2:9) The standard among Christians was: "If anyone does not want to work, neither let him eat."—2Th 3:10-12.

BEHEADING.

A mode of capital punishment not prescribed by the Mosaic Law. It was one form of execution that existed in most of the nations. In Israel, when a beheading was performed, it was usually after the individual had been slain and was generally done to bring the person's death before public attention as a reproach or as a public notice of judgment or warning.

Pharaoh 'lifted up the head from off' his chief baker, evidently beheading him. (Ge 40:19) David, after felling Goliath with a stone from his sling, took Goliath's sword and "definitely put him to death" by beheading him before the armies of Israel and the Philistines. This threw great fear into the Philistine army and resulted in a mighty rout. (1Sa 17:51, 52) The Philistines cut Saul's head from his body after his death, then hung his body with that of his sons on the wall of the city of Beth-shan. (1Sa 31:9, 12) Rechab and Baanah, wicked men, killed Saul's son Ish-bosheth and beheaded him in order to take his head to David, thinking they would gain David's favor. For this David had them put to death. (2Sa 4:5-12) In order to save their city, the people of the city of Abel of Beth-maacah acted on the counsel of a wise woman and cut off the head of Sheba the son of Bichri, which they pitched over the wall to Joab. Whether Sheba was killed before beheading is not stated. (2Sa 20:15, 21, 22) The older and distinguished men of Samaria slaughtered the 70 sons of Ahab and sent their heads in baskets to Jehu at Jezreel, where they were displayed in two heaps at the city gate as evidence of the fulfillment of Jehovah's judgment spoken by Elijah.—2Ki 10:6-10; 1Ki 21:20-22.

The Bible records that Herod Antipas had John the Baptizer beheaded in prison at the request of the daughter of Herodias. (Mt 14:8-11; Mr 6:24-28; Lu 9:9) John, in a vision, "saw the souls of those executed with the ax for the witness they bore to Jesus and for speaking about God."—Re 20:4; see CRIME AND PUNISHMENT.

BEHEMOTH

(Be·he′moth). The designation "Behemoth," appearing at Job 40:15, has been variously viewed as (1) a derivative of an Egyp-

tian word for "water ox," (2) a word possibly of Assyrian origin meaning "monster," and (3) an intensified plural of the Hebrew word behe·mah′ (beast; domestic animal) that is understood to denote "great beast" or "huge beast." In the Greek Septuagint the word the·ri′a (wild beasts) translates the Hebrew behe·mohth′. Evidently, though, a single animal is meant, as is indicated by the fact that the description given of Behemoth is not that of several creatures but of only one, generally considered to be the hippopotamus (Hippopotamus amphibius). In fact, a number of Bible translations (AT, La, Ro, NW, JB, RS) use the word "hippopotamus" in the main text or in footnotes to identify the creature referred to by God.

The hippopotamus is a huge, thick-skinned, almost hairless mammal that frequents rivers, lakes, and swamps. It is noted for its short legs, huge jaws, and large head, which is said to weigh up to a ton. So great is the power in its jaw and teeth that one bite can pierce the armor of a crocodile. Full grown it may be 4 to 5 m (12 to 15 ft) long and may weigh up to 3,600 kg (8,000 lb). An amphibious creature, the hippopotamus, in spite of its prodigious size, can move relatively fast both in and out of water. It feeds on soft water plants, grass, reeds, and bushes, each day taking more than 90 kg (200 lb) of greenery into its 150- to 190-L (40 to 50 gal) stomach.

The skin of the hide, especially that of the belly, is extremely tough, hence able to withstand bumping and scraping as the hippopotamus drags its low body over sticks and stones of riverbeds. The nostrils are strategically located at the tip of the snout, and the eyes are high up on the front of the head, enabling the hippopotamus both to breathe and to see while it is almost completely submerged. The ears and valvelike nostrils close when it submerges. Even while sleeping, when the carbon dioxide in the blood reaches a certain level, the animal automatically surfaces for fresh air and then submerges again.

At one time the hippopotamus was found in most of the large lakes and rivers of Africa, but, as a result of man's hunting, it has disappeared from many regions and is said to be unknown N of the cataract at Khartoum, Sudan. In ancient times the hippopotamus may even have frequented the Jordan. In fact, it is reported that tusks and bones of this creature have been found in various parts of Palestine.

The description in the 40th chapter of the book of Job offers a vivid word picture of this huge mammal, Behemoth. It is described as being herbivorous. (Vs 15) The sources of its tremendous power and energy are noted to be in the hips and in the tendons of its belly, that is, the muscles of its back and those of its belly. (Vs 16) The tail of Behemoth is like a cedar. Since the tail of a hippopotamus is fairly short, measuring about 46 to 51 cm (18 to 20 in.), this is likely to be understood as meaning that the animal can set its thick tail rigidly upright or swing it about like a tree. "The sinews of its thighs are interwoven," so that the fiber and tendons of muscles of its thighs are twisted together and braided like powerful cables. (Vs 17) The bones of its legs are as strong as "tubes of copper," thus being able to support the great weight of the body. The bones and ribs are like wrought-iron rods. (Vs 18) The Behemoth's immense consumption of food is alluded to (vs 20), and mention is made of its relaxing under the thorny lotus trees or concealing itself in a swampy place, beneath the shade of the poplars. (Vss 21, 22) Even when a river overflows its banks, this creature does not panic, for it can still keep its head above the level of water and swim against the force of the deluge. (Vs 23) Jehovah asked Job: 'Since Behemoth is so mighty and formidably equipped, would a man have the hardihood to try to confront it before its eyes and try to pierce its nose with a hook?'—Vs 24.

BEHTH [ב]. The second letter in the Hebrew alphabet. The name assigned to the letter means "house."

It has a labial sound similar to the English "b" when a dot is placed in the middle of this Hebrew character to harden the letter's pronunciation. Without the dot it has a softer sound close to "v," as in the word "vine."

In the Hebrew text, the opening word in each of the eight verses of Psalm 119:9-16 begins with this letter, in keeping with the acrostic style of the psalm.—See HEBREW, II.

BEL [from Akkadian, meaning "Owner; Master"]. A Babylonian deity whose shameful fall was foretold to coincide with Babylon's destruction.—Isa 46:1; Jer 50:2; 51:44.

The title Bel was first applied to the god Enlil. Bel was part of the original Sumerian triad of deities, along with Anu and Enki (Ea). When Marduk (Merodach) became the chief god of Babylon, he was also given the name Bel.—See GODS AND GODDESSES (Babylonian Deities).

When one considers the high esteem in which Bel was held, it becomes evident why Jehovah's prophets, under inspiration, made reference to him as one of the deities to be humiliated at Babylon's fall. Almost 200 years before Babylon

fell to the Medes and Persians, Isaiah foretold that Bel would have to bend down and Nebo would have to stoop over in shameful defeat. Their idol images were for the wild beasts to carry off; unable to help themselves, they would be hauled away as luggage on beasts of burden. Bel and Nebo would not escape. "Their own soul," that is, they themselves, would go into captivity. (Isa 46:1, 2; see also Jer 50:2.) Jehovah would force Bel to give up what he had swallowed by means of his worshipers, who attributed their victories to him. Especially would Bel have to give up Jehovah's exiled people and the sacred utensils of His temple. No more would the people of the nations whom Babylon had conquered stream to the worship of Bel or surrender to his worshipers as if to the chief god of the world.—Jer 51:44; see MERODACH.

BELA (Be'la).

1. The firstborn son of Benjamin, and one of Jacob's household that "came to Jacob into Egypt." He became the family head of the Belaites.—Ge 46:8, 21, 26; Nu 26:38; 1Ch 7:6; 8:1-5.

2. The son of Beor and the first-named king of Edom. Long before Israel had a king, Bela reigned in his capital city of Dinhabah.—Ge 36:31, 32; 1Ch 1:43.

3. A son of Azaz of the tribe of Reuben.—1Ch 5:3, 8.

4. A variant, and apparently an earlier name for the city of Zoar; mentioned along with other cities of the plain at Genesis 14:2, 8.—See ZOAR.

BELAITES (Be'la·ites) [Of (Belonging to) Bela]. A family descended from Bela, Benjamin's firstborn.—Nu 26:38.

BELIAL (Be'li·al) [from Heb., meaning "Good for Nothing"; a compound of beli', "not, without," and ya·'al', "be of benefit; be beneficial"]. The quality or state of being useless, base, good for nothing. The Hebrew term beli·ya''al is applied to ideas, words, and counsel (De 15:9; Ps 101:3; Na 1:11), to calamitous circumstances (Ps 41:8), and most frequently, to good-for-nothing men of the lowest sort—for example, men who would induce worship of other gods (De 13:13); those of Benjamin who committed the sex crime at Gibeah (Jg 19:22-27; 20:13); the wicked sons of Eli (1Sa 2:12); insolent Nabal (1Sa 25:17, 25); opposers of God's anointed, David (2Sa 20:1; 22:5; 23:6; Ps 18:4); Rehoboam's unsteady associates (2Ch 13:7); Jezebel's conspirators against Naboth (1Ki 21:10, 13); and men in general who stir up contention (Pr 6:12-14; 16:27; 19:28). Indicating that the enemy power would no longer interfere with the carrying out of true worship by his people in their land, Jehovah declared through his prophet: "No more will any good-for-nothing person pass again through you. In his entirety he will certainly be cut off."—Na 1:15; see also 1Sa 1:16; 10:27; 30:22; Job 34:18.

By the time Bible writing resumed in the first century, "Belial" was used as a name for Satan. So when Paul wrote at 2 Corinthians 6:15 in his series of parallel contrasts, "What harmony is there between Christ and Belial?" the conclusion usually drawn is that "Belial" is Satan. The Syriac *Peshitta* here reads "Satan."

BELL. A hollow metallic vessel. This instrument is usually pear-shaped or cuplike, and gives a dominant musical note when struck.

The first mention of bells in the Bible is in connection with the tabernacle service in the book of Exodus, where the Hebrew word *pa·'amohn'* occurs four times. On the hem of the solid-blue coat of the high priest were attached golden bells alternated with pomegranates of blue, purple, and scarlet material.—Ex 28:33-35; 39:25, 26.

In Zechariah 14:20 the Hebrew word *metsil·lah'* is used to denote the bells attached to the harnesses of horses. It comes from a root meaning "tingle." (1Sa 3:11) The fact that horse bells were to be engraved with the words "Holiness belongs to Jehovah," the same words as found on "the shining plate" attached to the turban of the high priest of Israel, would indicate that everything would be pervaded with an awareness of Jehovah's holiness.—Ex 39:30, 31; compare Zec 14:21.

BELLOWS. A device that can be alternately expanded and contracted, first drawing in air through a valve, then forcibly expelling it out an exit tube. For giving furnaces a forced draft, the bellows are more efficient than mere fanning, or the antiquated lung-powered hollow reeds and blowtubes also used for this purpose. The construction of bellows was simple: A bag mounted on a frame or base was attached to a tube leading to the furnace, which tube may have been of iron, or reed tipped with fire-resistant clay. Hand-operated bellows were useful for small forges; but for large high-temperature furnaces, dual foot-powered bellows were employed, one under each foot of the operator, who pumped down alternately, first one foot and then the other, each time pulling a cord to refill the compressed one. To give these big furnaces a constant draft, two men worked two pairs of bellows. The Hebrew word for bellows is *map·pu'ach,* which comes from the root *na·phach',* meaning "blow." (Ge 2:7) This instru-

ment is specifically mentioned only once in the Scriptures (Jer 6:29), though perhaps alluded to at Isaiah 54:16 and Ezekiel 22:20, 21. In these texts the references are figurative, and the illustrations are drawn from the methods used for refining metals.—See REFINE, REFINER.

BELLY. The front part of the human trunk not enclosed by the ribs, and containing the digestive system and other organs; generally considered synonymous with the abdomen.

Besides being used to denote the general area of the abdomen (Jg 3:21, 22; Pr 13:25), the Hebrew word *be'ten* is used several times in connection with the formation of a child in its mother's body. (Ge 25:23, 24; Job 1:21; Ps 127:3; Ec 11:5; Isa 44:2; Ho 9:11) Children are the fruitage of the womb, located in the belly. However, another Hebrew word, *re'chem* (or *ra'cham*), specifically refers to the womb, as can be noted at Job 31:15: "Did not the One making me in the belly make him, and did not just One proceed to prepare us in the womb?"—See also Ge 49:25; Ps 22:10; Pr 30:16.

The Hebrew *be'ten* (belly) is also used as an architectural term at 1 Kings 7:20, referring to a protuberance, a rounded projection.

In the Christian Greek Scriptures the word *koi·li'a* means a "cavity" and is variously rendered "belly" (1Co 6:13, *Int;* Php 3:19), "womb" (Lu 1:15, 41), "intestines" (Mt 15:17), and "inmost part" (Joh 7:38), according to the context.

"Belly" is used figuratively to denote fleshly appetite, or desire (Ro 16:18; Php 3:19), and as a source of speech or argument. (Job 15:2; 32:19) When in the fish's belly, Jonah compared the inside of the fish to Sheol when he said, "Out of the belly of Sheol I cried for help," because he was as good as dead unless Jehovah would deliver him miraculously.—Jon 2:2; see INTESTINES; WOMB.

BELSHAZZAR (Bel·shaz'zar) [from Akkadian, meaning "Protect His Life"; or, possibly, "[May] Bel Protect the King"]. The firstborn son of Nabonidus, and coregent of Nabonidus in the last years of the Babylonian Empire. He is mentioned in the Bible account only by the prophet Daniel, and for long his position as "king of Babylon" was denied by Bible critics. (Da 5:1, 9; 7:1; 8:1) However, archaeological evidence in the form of ancient texts has since demonstrated the historicity of the Bible account.

At Daniel 5:2, 11, 18, 22, Nebuchadnezzar is referred to as the "father" of Belshazzar, and Belshazzar as Nebuchadnezzar's "son." The book *Nabonidus and Belshazzar* (by R. P. Dougherty, 1929) reasons that it is probable that Belshazzar's mother was Nitocris and that she was a daughter of Nebuchadnezzar (II). If so, Nebuchadnezzar was the grandfather of Belshazzar. (See Ge 28:10, 13 for a comparable use of "father.") However, not all scholars find the evidence for such a relationship completely satisfying. It may be that Nebuchadnezzar was simply the "father" of Belshazzar as to the throne, Nebuchadnezzar being a royal predecessor. In a similar manner, the Assyrians used the expression "son of Omri" to denote a successor of Omri.—See OMRI No. 3.

Does secular history confirm the role of Belshazzar as a ruler of Babylon?

A cuneiform tablet dated as from the accession year of Neriglissar, who followed Awil-Marduk (Evil-merodach) on the Babylonian throne, refers to a certain "Belshazzar, the chief officer of the king," in connection with a money transaction. It is possible, though not proved, that this refers to the Belshazzar of the Bible. In 1924 publication was made of the decipherment of an ancient cuneiform text described as the "Verse Account of Nabonidus," and through it valuable information was brought to light clearly corroborating Belshazzar's kingly position at Babylon and explaining the manner of his becoming coregent with Nabonidus. Concerning Nabonidus' conquest of Tema in his third year of rule, a portion of the text says: "He entrusted the 'Camp' to his oldest (son), the firstborn [Belshazzar], the troops everywhere in the country he ordered under his (command). He let (everything) go, entrusted the kingship to him and, himself, he [Nabonidus] started out for a long journey, the (military) forces of Akkad marching with him; he turned towards Tema (deep) in the west." (*Ancient Near Eastern Texts,* edited by J. Pritchard, 1974, p. 313) Thus, Belshazzar definitely exercised royal authority from Nabonidus' third year on, and this event likely corresponds with Daniel's reference to "the first year of Belshazzar the king of Babylon."—Da 7:1.

In another document, the Nabonidus Chronicle, a statement is found with regard to Nabonidus' seventh, ninth, tenth, and eleventh regnal years. It reads: "The king (was) in Tema (while) the prince, the officers, and his army (were) in Akkad [Babylonia]." (*Assyrian and Babylonian Chronicles,* by A. Grayson, 1975, p. 108) Apparently Nabonidus spent much of his reign away from Babylon, and while not relinquishing his position as supreme ruler, he entrusted administrative authority to his son Belshazzar to act during his

absence. This is evident from a number of texts recovered from the ancient archives proving that Belshazzar exercised royal prerogatives, that he issued orders and commands. Matters handled by Belshazzar in certain documents and orders were those that would normally have been handled by Nabonidus, as supreme ruler, had he been present. However, Belshazzar remained only second ruler of the empire, and thus he could offer to make Daniel only "the third one in the kingdom." —Da 5:16.

It is true that official inscriptions give Belshazzar the title "crown prince," while in the book of Daniel his title is "king." (Da 5:1-30) An archaeological discovery in northern Syria suggests why this may be the case. In 1979, a life-sized statue of a ruler of ancient Gozan was unearthed. On its skirt were two inscriptions, one in Assyrian and the other in Aramaic—the language of the Belshazzar account in Daniel. The two almost identical inscriptions had one outstanding difference. The text in the imperial Assyrian language says that the statue was of "the governor of Gozan." The text in Aramaic, the language of the local people, describes him as "king."

Thus, archaeologist and language scholar Alan Millard writes: "In the light of the Babylonian sources and of the new texts on this statue, it may have been considered quite in order for such unofficial records as the Book of Daniel to call Belshazzar 'king.' He acted as king, his father's agent, although he may not have been legally king. The precise distinction would have been irrelevant and confusing in the story as related in Daniel."—*Biblical Archaeology Review,* May/June 1985, p. 77.

Those who wielded sovereign power in Babylonia were expected to be exemplars in reverencing the gods. There are six cuneiform texts concerning events from the 5th to the 13th year of Nabonidus' reign that demonstrate Belshazzar's

Babylonian temple cylinder that names King Nabonidus and his son Belshazzar

devotion to Babylonian deities. As acting king in Nabonidus' absence, Belshazzar is shown in the documents to have offered gold, silver, and animals to the temples in Erech and Sippar, thereby comporting himself in a manner consistent with his royal position.

The End of Belshazzar's Rule. On the night of October 5, 539 B.C.E. (Gregorian calendar, or October 11, Julian calendar), Belshazzar celebrated a great feast for a thousand of his grandees, as chapter 5 of Daniel relates. (Da 5:1) Babylon was then menaced by the besieging forces of Cyrus the Persian and his ally Darius the Mede. According to Jewish historian Josephus (who, in turn, quotes the Babylonian Berossus), Nabonidus had holed up in Borsippa after having been defeated by the Medo-Persian forces in battle. (*Against Apion,* I, 150-152 [20]) If so, Belshazzar was the acting king in Babylon itself. The holding of a feast when the city was in state of siege is not so unusual when it is remembered that the Babylonians confidently regarded the city's walls as impregnable. Historians Herodotus and Xenophon also state that the city had abundant supplies of necessary items and hence was not concerned with shortages. Herodotus describes the city as in a festive mood on that night, with dancing and enjoyment.

During the feast and under the influence of wine, Belshazzar called for the vessels from the temple of Jerusalem to be brought so that he and his guests and his wives and concubines might drink from them while praising the Babylonian gods. Obviously, this request was due to no shortage of drinking vessels, but, rather, it constituted a deliberate act of contempt by this pagan king in reproach of the God of the Israelites, Jehovah. (Da 5:2-4) He thereby expressed defiance of Jehovah, who had inspired the prophecies foretelling Babylon's downfall. While Belshazzar seemed lighthearted about the siege set by the enemy forces, he was now severely shaken when a hand suddenly appeared and began writing on the palace wall. His knees knocking, he called upon all his wise men to provide an interpretation of the written message, but to no avail. The record shows that the queen now gave him sound counsel, recommending Daniel as the one able to give the interpretation. (Da 5:5-12) Certain scholars consider "the queen" to be, not Belshazzar's wife, but his mother, believed to be Nebuchadnezzar's daughter, Nitocris. Daniel, by inspiration, revealed the meaning of the miraculous message, predicting the fall of Babylon to the Medes and the Persians. Though the aged prophet condemned Belshazzar's blasphemous act in using vessels of Jehovah's worship in praising see-nothing, hear-

nothing, know-nothing gods, Belshazzar held to his offer and proceeded to invest Daniel with the position of third ruler in the doomed kingdom. —Da 5:17-29.

Belshazzar did not live out the night, being killed as the city fell during the night of October 5, 539 B.C.E., when, according to the Nabonidus Chronicle, "the army of Cyrus (II) entered Babylon without a battle." (*Assyrian and Babylonian Chronicles,* pp. 109, 110; see also Da 5:30.) With the death of Belshazzar and the apparent surrender of Nabonidus to Cyrus, the Neo-Babylonian Empire came to a close.—See CYRUS; NABONIDUS.

BELT. See DRESS.

BELTESHAZZAR (Bel·te·shaz'zar) [from Akkadian, meaning "Protect the Life of the King"]. The Babylonian name given to Daniel after he was taken into exile in 617 B.C.E.—not to be confused with Belshazzar. (Da 1:7) The name is evidently a shortened form of an invocation to Bel and hence was selected, as Nebuchadnezzar said, "according to the name of my god." (Da 4:8; 5:12) The purpose was evidently to effect Daniel's naturalization and alienate him from the worship of Jehovah. However, the Babylonians continued to speak of him also by his name Daniel.—Da 4:18, 19; 5:12, 13; see DANIEL No. 2.

BEN [Son].

1. A Levite musician of David's day who accompanied the ark of the covenant to Jerusalem. —1Ch 15:15, 18.

2. The Hebrew prefix *ben* often occurs in names such as Benjamin (meaning "Son of the Right Hand") or Ben-ammi (meaning "Son of My People [that is, relatives]"). It is equivalent to *bar* in Aramaic names such as Barnabas (meaning "Son of Comfort"). (Ac 4:36) It is frequently used also to define relationships other than parental, such as race, "sons of [*beneh'*] Israel," "sons of the Cushites" (2Ch 35:17; Am 9:7); location, "sons of the jurisdictional district" (Ezr 2:1); or condition, "sons of youth," "sons of unrighteousness" (Ps 127:4; Ho 10:9).

BENAIAH (Be·nai'ah) [Jehovah Has Built].

1. Son of a Levitical chief priest named Jehoiada, and father of at least two sons, Ammizabad and Jehoiada. (1Ch 27:5, 6, 34) Benaiah was a mighty warrior of great valor and courage, "distinguished even more than the thirty" mighty men of David's forces, though "to the rank of the three he did not come."—2Sa 23:20-23.

Benaiah demonstrated his prowess in a threefold way: by striking down two of Moab's powerful heroes, by fearlessly descending into a water pit and killing a lion, and by overcoming exceptional odds to slay an Egyptian giant with the victim's own spear. (1Ch 11:22-24) David put this courageous man over his personal bodyguard. (1Ch 11:24, 25) The Cherethites and Pelethites, headed by Benaiah, remained loyal to the king during the rebellions of Absalom and Adonijah. (2Sa 8:18; 15:18; 20:23; 1Ki 1:8, 10, 26; 1Ch 18:17) Additionally, Benaiah was appointed over the third rotating division of the army, a force of 24,000 men. (1Ch 27:5, 6) In David's old age Benaiah and the Cherethites and Pelethites supported the coronation of Solomon. (1Ki 1:32-40) Later, under Solomon's reign Benaiah was assigned to carry out the execution of Adonijah, Joab, and Shimei, and he was also put in command of the army by Solomon. —1Ki 2:24, 25, 28-46; 4:4.

2. One of David's mighty men, commander of the 11th rotational army division; a Pirathonite of the tribe of Ephraim.—2Sa 23:30; 1Ch 11:31; 27:14.

3. A Levite musician who played his stringed instrument accompanying the ark of the covenant when it was brought to Jerusalem and placed in the tent David had prepared for it.—1Ch 15:18, 20; 16:1, 5.

4. A priest who played a trumpet when the Ark was brought to Jerusalem during David's reign. —1Ch 15:24; 16:6.

5. A Levite descendant of Asaph.—2Ch 20:14.

6. A Simeonite, possibly a contemporary of King Hezekiah.—1Ch 4:24, 36-43.

7. A Levite appointed by Hezekiah to help care for the bounteous contributions to Jehovah's house.—2Ch 31:12, 13.

8. Father of Pelatiah, one of the wicked princes seen in Ezekiel's vision.—Eze 11:1, 13.

9, 10, 11, 12. Four men who, at Ezra's admonition, dismissed their foreign wives and sons. These four were descendants of Parosh, Pahath-moab, Bani, and Nebo respectively.—Ezr 10:25, 30, 34, 35, 43, 44.

BEN-AMMI (Ben-am′mi) [Son of My People [that is, relatives]]. Son of Lot by his younger daughter, hence half brother of Moab. Modern findings attest to the common use of the name during this period. Ben-ammi, also called Ammon, was forefather of the Ammonites.—Ge 19:31-38; see AMMON.

BENE-BERAK (Ben′e-be′rak) [Sons of Berak]. A city of Dan identified with Ibn Ibraq (or Kheiri-yeh [Horvat Bene-beraq]), 8 km (5 mi) ESE of Tel Aviv-Yafo (Joppa). (Jos 19:40, 45) The Arabic name Ibn Ibraq corresponds to the Hebrew Bene-berak. In a prism of Sennacherib, that emperor's account of the Assyrian campaign against Hezekiah states that he "besieged Beth-Dagon, Joppa, Banai-Barqa [Bene-berak], Azuru."—*Ancient Near Eastern Texts*, edited by J. Pritchard, 1974, p. 287.

BENE-JAAKAN (Ben′e-ja′a·kan) [Sons of Jaakan]. A station of the Israelites on their journey through the wilderness. (Nu 33:31, 32) Jaakan appears to be the Akan of Genesis 36:27 and 1 Chronicles 1:42 (where the Masoretic text reads "Jaakan"). The account in the book of Numbers states that the Israelites "pulled away from Moseroth and went camping in Bene-jaakan. After that they pulled away from Bene-jaakan and went camping in Hor-haggidgad."

At Deuteronomy 10:6 reference is made to Beeroth Bene-jaakan in connection with "Moserah" (singular of Moseroth), probably indicating that Beeroth Bene-jaakan (meaning "Wells of the Sons of Jaakan") is the same location as Bene-jaakan. However, the account at Deuteronomy lists the direction of Israel's travel in reverse order from the Numbers account, stating that "the sons of Israel pulled away from Beeroth Bene-jaakan for Moserah." In view of the many years spent in the wilderness, it is quite possible that the Israelites passed twice through this region. As *The Pentateuch and Haftorahs* says on this text: "A probable explanation is that the Israelites, after journeying in a southern direction to the land of Edom, had to turn sharply to the north." (Edited by J. Hertz, London, 1972) They may have had to retrace their steps for a short distance and revisit some of the places they had passed through, this time in the reverse order. It is to be noted that the record of Deuteronomy (10:6) refers to Aaron's death immediately after referring to the station of Moserah, whereas the Numbers account (33:31-39) describes the Israelites' travels to Ezion-geber and then NW to Kadesh before dealing with the matter of the death of Aaron. This, together with the long period of years involved, would certainly allow for a measure of backtracking, if such were the case.

Bene-jaakan (Beeroth Bene-jaakan) is usually identified with a site a few miles N of Kadesh-barnea.—See BEEROTH BENE-JAAKAN.

BEN-HADAD (Ben-ha′dad) [Son of Hadad]. The name of three kings of Syria mentioned in the Bible record. Hadad was the storm god worshiped throughout Syria and other nearby regions.

1. The first king of Syria named Ben-hadad in the Biblical account was the son of Tabrimmon and grandson of Hezion. He had entered into a covenant with King Baasha of Israel, but King Asa of Judah, alarmed when Baasha began fortifying Ramah just a few miles N of Jerusalem, bribed Ben-hadad to break his covenant and attack the northern kingdom, thereby forcing Baasha to withdraw. In exchange for the royal treasures of Judah and those from the temple sanctuary, Ben-hadad invaded Israel, overrunning various cities in the territory of Naphtali and in the region of the Sea of Galilee. As expected, Baasha withdrew to his capital in Tirzah. (1Ki 15:16-21; 2Ch 16:1-6) This action took place about 962 B.C.E. (the "thirty-sixth year" at 2 Chronicles 16:1 evidently refers to the 36th year from the division of the kingdom in 997 B.C.E.).—See Asa No. 1.

2. The next mention of a Syrian king named Ben-hadad occurs during the reign of King Ahab of Israel (c. 940-920 B.C.E.). About the fifth year before Ahab's death, "Ben-hadad the king of Syria" led the combined forces of 32 kings, evidently vassals, against Samaria, besieging the city and calling on King Ahab to surrender unconditionally. (1Ki 20:1-6) Ahab called a council of the older men of the land, who advised him to resist. Then, while the Syrian forces were preparing for an assault on the city and while Ben-hadad and the other kings were drinking themselves drunk in the booths they had erected, Ahab, following divine counsel, used strategy to initiate a surprise attack on the Syrian camp, and he successfully routed them.—1Ki 20:7-21.

Accepting his counselors' theory that Jehovah was "a God of mountains" and that therefore the Israelites could be defeated on level land, the following year Ben-hadad led his army to Aphek, a town apparently located E of the Sea of Galilee. (See Aphek No. 5.) The Syrian forces had been reorganized, the 32 kings having been replaced by governors as heads of the troops, evidently because it was thought that the governors would fight more unitedly and obediently and perhaps would also have stronger incentive for winning promotion to higher rank than the more independent kings. Ben-hadad's religious and military theories, however, proved worthless against the Israelite forces who, though vastly outnumbered, were forewarned by a prophet of the attack and had the backing of the King of the universe, Jehovah God. The Syrian forces were cut to pieces, and Ben-hadad fled into Aphek. Ahab, however, let this dangerous enemy go free, with this promise from Ben-hadad: "The cities that my father took from your father I shall return; and streets you will assign to yourself in Damascus the same

as my father assigned in Samaria."—1Ki 20:22-34.

There is considerable difference of opinion as to whether this Ben-hadad is the same Syrian king of Baasha and Asa's day or whether he is instead a son or grandson of that king. For Ben-hadad I (of Asa's time) to be the Ben-hadad of Ahab's and even of Jehoram's time (c. 917-905 B.C.E.) would require a reign of some 45 years or more. This, of course, is not impossible.

However, those who hold that the Syrian king of Ahab's day should be called Ben-hadad II point to the promise made by Ben-hadad to Ahab, quoted above. (1Ki 20:34) On the face of it, this appears to say that Ben-hadad's father had taken cities from Omri, Ahab's father. But if the seizure referred to was that effected by Ben-hadad I during Baasha's rule, that would make Ben-hadad I the father (or perhaps simply the predecessor) of the Ben-hadad II of Ahab's reign. Likewise, Ahab's "father" could possibly refer to a royal predecessor on the throne even though not related by blood as a lineal ancestor.—See Belshazzar.

Nevertheless, the fact that Ben-hadad's promise to Ahab made reference to Samaria would appear to limit the Syrian capture of the Israelite cities to the reign of Omri, since Samaria was built by him and thereafter made Israel's capital. The "streets" assigned apparently were for the establishment of bazaars, or markets, to promote commercial interests.

Whatever the circumstances and time of the capture of the Israelite cities, the Scriptural evidence would seem to point to a different Ben-hadad as ruling by Ahab's time, and hence he may be referred to as Ben-hadad II. It appears that the promise of Ben-hadad to return the cities taken from Israel by his father was not completely fulfilled, for in Ahab's final year of rule this Israelite king formed an alliance with Jehoshaphat in a vain attempt to recover Ramoth-gilead (E of the Jordan) from the Syrians. Ben-hadad II is evidently the anonymous "king of Syria" who ordered his "thirty-two chiefs of the chariots" to concentrate their attack on Ahab in that battle. (1Ki 22:31-37) He must also be the king who sent his leprous army chief Naaman to be cured by Elisha during Jehoram's reign. The Syrian king worshiped the god Rimmon (whose name forms part of that of Tabrimmon, the father of Ben-hadad I).—2Ki 5:1-19.

Despite the healing service rendered his general, Ben-hadad maintained his animosity toward Israel and sent invading parties into Israel. (2Ki 6:8; compare verse 23.) However, Elisha consistently warned the king of Israel in advance as to the route of the invading parties so that Ben-hadad began to suspect the presence of a traitor among his own servants. Learning that Elisha was the one informing the king of Israel about 'the things that Ben-hadad spoke in his inner bedroom,' the Syrian king sent a heavy military force to capture Elisha at Dothan. Elisha, however, caused the troops to be miraculously stricken with a form of blindness, and he led them right into the middle of the Israelite capital, Samaria. This experience, perhaps along with the merciful treatment and release granted the Syrians there, brought a halt to the marauding activity, though it did not eliminate Ben-hadad's aggressive attitude.—2Ki 6:9-23.

Still bent on overthrowing the Israelite kingdom, Ben-hadad later massed his forces and besieged Samaria, provoking famine conditions of the gravest kind. (2Ki 6:24-29) Yet, when Jehovah one evening caused the Syrian camp to hear the sound of a large approaching army, they hastily concluded that Jehoram had hired the Hittites and Egyptians to rescue him, and thereupon they fled back to Syria in the darkness, leaving behind all their equipment and provisions.—2Ki 7:6, 7.

Ben-hadad II was on his sickbed when Elisha traveled to Damascus carrying out the divine commission given to his predecessor Elijah. (1Ki 19:15) Sending 40 camel loads of gifts to the prophet, Ben-hadad inquired as to the possibilities of recovery from his illness. Elisha's answer, delivered to Hazael, showed that the king would die, with Hazael taking the kingship. The following day Hazael caused Ben-hadad's death by suffocation, and then Hazael took the throne as king. —2Ki 8:7-15.

3. The son of Hazael, king of Syria. (2Ki 13:3) Ben-hadad III was evidently associated with his father in the oppression of Israel in the days of Jehoahaz (876-c. 860 B.C.E.) and in the Syrian capture of Israelite cities. Jehovah, however, raised up "a savior" for Israel, apparently in the persons of Jehoahaz' son Jehoash (c. 859-845 B.C.E.) and his successor Jeroboam II (c. 844-804 B.C.E.). (2Ki 13:4, 5) In fulfillment of Elisha's final prophecy, Jehoash recaptured "from the hand of Ben-hadad the son of Hazael the cities that he had taken from the hand of Jehoahaz," defeating the Syrian forces on three occasions. (2Ki 13:19, 23-25) Jeroboam II followed up his father's victories over Syria, returning Israel's boundaries to their former state, thus serving as a savior for Israel. (2Ki 14:23-27) Ben-hadad III is not mentioned in connection with Jeroboam's conquests and may not have been living by that time.

The expression "the dwelling towers of Ben-hadad," used by the prophet Amos (who prophesied during Jeroboam II's reign) to refer to the royal palaces in Damascus (Am 1:3-5; compare 2Ki 16:9), continued to be used in a similar way by Jeremiah some two centuries later.—Jer 49:23-27.

Ben-hadad in Ancient Inscriptions. An inscription of Shalmaneser III, after relating a conflict with the Syrians, states: "Hadadezer (himself) perished. Hazael, a commoner (lit.: son of nobody), seized the throne." (*Ancient Near Eastern Texts,* edited by J. Pritchard, 1974, p. 280) Thus, Ben-hadad II appears to be called "Hadadezer" (Assyrian, *Adad-idri*) by Shalmaneser III.

The Zakir Stele describes a punitive effort launched by "Barhadad, the son of Hazael, king of Aram," at the head of a coalition of Syrian kings against "Zakir, king of Hamat and Lu'ath," thereby adding archaeological testimony to the existence of Ben-hadad III, son of Hazael.—*Ancient Near Eastern Texts,* p. 655.

A stele, known as the Melqart Stele, was found in 1940 about 6 km (3.5 mi) N of Aleppo in northern Syria, and although the inscription is not entirely legible, it reads in part: "A stela set up by Barhadad . . . for his Lord Melqart." (*Ancient Near Eastern Texts,* p. 655) Whether this Barhadad should be identified with Ben-hadad I, II, III, or some other Ben-hadad is uncertain.

BEN-HAIL (Ben-ha'il). One of the five princes sent by Jehoshaphat in the third year of his reign to teach the Law to the inhabitants of Judah. —2Ch 17:7, 9.

BEN-HANAN (Ben-ha'nan) [Son of the One Showing Favor; Son of the Gracious One]. One of the four sons of Shimon; descendant of Judah. —1Ch 4:1, 20.

BENINU (Be·ni'nu). A Levite, or forefather of one, who attested by seal to Nehemiah's "trustworthy arrangement."—Ne 9:38; 10:1, 13.

BENJAMIN (Ben'ja·min) [Son of the Right Hand].

1. Jacob's 12th son and the full brother of Joseph. Benjamin appears to be the only son born to Jacob in the land of Canaan, the other sons being born in Paddan-aram. (Ge 29:31–30:25; 31:18) Rachel gave birth to Benjamin, her second son, while on the way from Bethel to Ephrath (Bethlehem), achieving the difficult childbirth at the cost of her life. While dying, she called this son Benoni, meaning "Son of My Mourning"; but her bereaved husband thereafter named him Benjamin, meaning "Son of the Right Hand."—Ge 35:16-19; 48:7.

From the time of his birth until after his brother Joseph's being sold into slavery in Egypt, nothing further is told us about Benjamin. As Jacob's youngest son by his beloved wife Rachel (Ge 44: 20), Benjamin was obviously the object of great affection by his father, particularly so now that Jacob assumed that Joseph was dead. Jacob was therefore extremely reluctant to let Benjamin go with his brothers to Egypt, doing so only after much persuasion. (Ge 42:36-38; 43:8-14) It should be noted that, although Judah at this time referred to Benjamin as a "boy," Benjamin by now was a young man. The record at Genesis 46:8, 21 presents Benjamin as the father of children at the time of Jacob's taking up residence in Egypt. Nevertheless, he was Jacob's beloved "child of his old age," upon whom the elderly parent leaned in many more ways than one. (Ge 44:20-22, 29-34) Joseph also manifested deep affection for his younger brother.—Ge 43:29-31, 34.

The genealogy of Benjamin's descendants is presented in several places, some apparently more complete than others. Genesis 46:21 lists ten persons as "sons of Benjamin," and the absence of the names of several of these in succeeding lists has led some to suggest that certain sons may have died at an early age or may not have fathered sons who produced family lines. There are evidently some variations in spelling of the names in these lists (compare Ehi, Ahiram, Aharah), and some of those listed at Genesis 46:21 may be merely descendants. (Nu 26:38-40; 1Ch 7:6; 8:1) Objections have been raised to the possibility of Benjamin's having so many sons or even having grandsons by this time, yet it should be kept in mind that the reference to them as among "the souls who came to Jacob into Egypt" does not necessarily require that they had to be born before actual entry into the country. They may have 'come into Egypt' by being born there during the 17 years of Jacob's residence in Egypt prior to his death, even as Joseph's two sons born there are listed among "the souls of the house of Jacob who came into Egypt." (Ge 46:26, 27) By the time of his father's death, Benjamin was apparently in his 40's and hence old enough to have grandchildren.

The parental blessing pronounced upon Benjamin as one of the heads of the 12 tribes of Israel is considered below.—Ge 49:27, 28.

2. The name Benjamin also designates the tribe descended from Jacob's son. At the time of the Exodus from Egypt, it was next to the smallest (after Manasseh) in male population of all the tribes. (Nu 1:36, 37) In the census taken later on the Plains of Moab, the tribe of Benjamin had moved up to seventh place. (Nu 26:41) When encamped in the wilderness, the tribe occupied a place on the W side of the tabernacle, along with the tribes descended from Joseph's sons Manasseh and Ephraim, and this three-tribe division occupied third place in the order of march.—Nu 2:18-24.

Within Canaan, the territory assigned to the tribe of Benjamin lay between that of the tribes of Ephraim and Judah, while the territory of Dan bordered it on the W. Its frontier in the N ran from the Jordan River near Jericho, crossed the mountainous terrain by Bethel and continued westward to a point near Lower Beth-horon; proceeding from there, the western frontier ran down to Kiriath-jearim, then, on the S, turned eastward and passed Jerusalem through the Valley of Hinnom, wound down the rugged eastern slopes to the Jordan again at the N end of the Dead Sea, the Jordan River thus forming its eastern boundary. (Jos 18:11-20; compare Judah's N boundary at Jos 15:5-9 and the S boundary of "the sons of Joseph" at Jos 16:1-3.) From N to S the area measured about 19 km (12 mi) and from E to W about 45 km (28 mi). With the exception of the portion of the Jordan Valley around the Jericho oasis, the territory was hilly and broken, though having some fertile areas on the western slopes. The torrent valleys running westward toward the Philistine plain and eastward toward the Jordan made this section a principal way of approach to the highland region, both for commercial and for military purposes. The warring forces of the Philistines surged up into this area during the early part of Saul's reign, pillaging the Israelites at will from their encampment at Michmash, a short distance N of Saul's home in Gibeah, until Jonathan's exploit at Michmash initiated their rout and flight back down toward the coastal plains.—1Sa 13:16-18; 14:11-16, 23, 31, 46.

Among the prominent cities listed as originally assigned to Benjamin are Jericho, Bethel, Gibeon, Gibeah, and Jerusalem. The conquest of Bethel, however, was effected by the house of Joseph. At a later time Bethel became a prominent city of neighboring Ephraim and a center of idolatrous calf worship. (Jg 1:22; 1Ki 12:28, 29; see BETHEL No. 1.) While Jerusalem was also part of Benjamin's territory, it lay on the border with Judah; and it was this tribe that initially captured and burned the city. (Jg 1:8) Neither Judah nor Benjamin was successful in driving the Jebusites out of Jerusalem's citadel however (Jos 15:63; Jg 1:21), and it was only during King David's reign that complete control was gained and the city made Israel's capital.—2Sa 5:6-9.

During the period of the Judges, the tribe of Benjamin displayed a spirit of obstinacy in refusing to deliver up the perpetrators of a vile act performed in the city of Gibeah. This led to civil war with the other tribes, who were determined not to let the wrong go unpunished, and it resulted in the near extermination of the tribe of Benjamin. (Jg 19-21) Nevertheless, by the method devised by the other tribes for preserving the tribe, Benjamin recovered and grew from about 600 men to nearly 60,000 warriors by the time of David's kingship.—1Ch 7:6-12.

The fighting ability of Benjamin's descendants was pictured in Jacob's deathbed prophecy in which he said of this beloved son: "Benjamin will keep on tearing like a wolf. In the morning he will eat the animal seized and at evening he will divide spoil." (Ge 49:27) Benjamite fighters were noted for their ability with the sling, slinging stones with either the right hand or the left and hitting the mark "to a hairbreadth." (Jg 20:16; 1Ch 12:2) Left-handed Judge Ehud, the slayer of oppressive King Eglon, was of Benjamin. (Jg 3:15-21) It may also be noted that it was "in the morning" of the kingdom of Israel that the tribe of Benjamin, though one "of the smallest of the tribes," provided Israel's first king, Saul the son of Kish, who proved to be a fierce fighter against the Philistines. (1Sa 9:15-17, 21) Likewise "at evening" time, as far as the nation of Israel was concerned, the tribe of Benjamin provided Queen Esther and Prime Minister Mordecai, who served to save the Israelites from annihilation under the Persian Empire.—Es 2:5-7.

Though certain men of the Benjamites supported the outlawed David while he was pursued by King Saul (1Ch 12:1-7, 16-18), when Saul died the majority of the tribe gave Saul's son Ish-bosheth their initial support. (2Sa 2:8-10, 12-16) Thereafter, however, they acknowledged David's kingship and thenceforth remained loyal to the kingdom of Judah, with rare exceptions. A partisan spirit continued among some, such as Shimei and Sheba, resulting in temporary alienation (2Sa 16:5; 20:1-22); but at the time of the division of the nation, in which the neighboring tribe of Ephraim (descended from Benjamin's nephew) became the prominent tribe of the northern kingdom, the tribe of Benjamin faithfully adhered to Judah in recognition of Jehovah's decree.—1Ki 11:31, 32; 12:21; 2Ch 11:1; Ge 49:8-10.

Following the exile in Babylon, the tribes of Benjamin and Judah were most prominent among the restored Israelites in Palestine. (Ezr 4:1; 10:9) Benjamin's loyal association with Judah and Jerusalem doubtless contributed to its position in Ezekiel's vision of the division of the land under the promised kingdom, in which vision the tribe of Benjamin is pictured as located right on the southern border of "the holy contribution," while the tribe of Judah is placed on the northern border. —Eze 48:8, 21-23.

Among the loyal followers of Jesus, "the Lion that is of the tribe of Judah," was the apostle Paul, a Benjamite who proved himself a fierce fighter in the spiritual warfare against false doctrine and practice. (Re 5:5; Ro 11:1; Php 3:5) The tribe of Benjamin is rightly represented among the tribes of spiritual Israel.—Re 7:8.

Ancient letters, found at Mari on the Euphrates River and considered to be of the 18th century B.C.E., make mention of a fierce tribe of nomads called *Binu-jamina*. Regarding this name, *The Illustrated Bible Dictionary* states that some scholars "have sought here the antecedents of the biblical tribe; but the difference in time and origin makes this very uncertain."—Edited by J. Douglas, 1980, Vol. 1, p. 185.

3. A Benjamite, descendant of Jediael through Bilhan.—1Ch 7:6, 10.

4. One of "the sons of Harim" who sent away their foreign wives in Ezra's day. (Ezr 10:31, 32, 44) He may be the same as the Benjamin mentioned at Nehemiah 3:23 and 12:34, but this is uncertain.

BENJAMITES. See BENJAMIN No. 2.

BENO (Be′no). A Levite of David's time, descendant of Merari.—1Ch 24:20, 26, 27.

BEN-ONI (Ben-o′ni) [Son of My Mourning]. The name given by Rachel to her second son as she was dying during the delivery. Jacob changed his name to Benjamin, meaning "Son of the Right Hand."—Ge 35:18; see BENJAMIN No. 1.

BEN-ZOHETH (Ben-zo′heth) [Son of Zoheth]. Listed among the posterity of Judah as the son of Ishi and brother of Zoheth. But since the prefix of his name (Ben-) means "son of," he may have been the son of Zoheth and grandson of Ishi.—1Ch 4:20.

BEON. See BAAL-MEON.

BEOR (Be′or).

1. An Edomite whose son Bela is listed as Edom's first king.—Ge 36:31, 32; 1Ch 1:43.

2. Father of the prophet Balaam.—Nu 22:5; 2Pe 2:15.

BERA (Be'ra). King of Sodom whom Chedorla-omer and his allies defeated in the Low Plain of Siddim. (Ge 14:1-11) Abraham pursued the victors in order to free his nephew Lot, recovered the spoil, and returned it to the king of Sodom rather than keeping it for himself. Abraham did this, he says, in order that the king of Sodom could never boast: "It was I who made Abram rich."—Ge 14:14-24.

BERACAH (Ber'a·cah) [Blessing].

1. One of the mighty men skilled in the use of the bow, from the tribe of Benjamin, who joined up with David at Ziklag. This was at the time David was still under restrictions because of Saul. —1Ch 12:1-3.

2. A low plain in Judah lying between Bethlehem and Hebron. It is presently identified with the Wadi el-'Arrub, and nearby Khirbet Bereikut (Berakhot) seems to preserve evidence of the original name. This valley runs E-W, connecting the hill country of Judah with the wilderness area W of the Salt Sea.

Following the miraculous victory over the combined forces of Ammon, Moab, and Edom, Jehoshaphat congregated the people at this low plain to bless Jehovah, hence the name of the Low Plain of Beracah (meaning "Blessing").—2Ch 20:26.

BERAIAH (Be·ra'iah) [Jah Has Created]. Son of Shimei, and head of a paternal house of Benjamites living in Jerusalem.—1Ch 8:1, 21, 28.

BERECHIAH (Ber·e·chi'ah) [Blessed by Jehovah].

1. The son of Shimea, in the line of descent from Levi through Gershom. Berechiah's son Asaph was the principal leader of the singers appointed by King David, and through him sprang many succeeding generations of temple singers. This Berechiah may have been the same as No. 2. —1Ch 6:39; 15:17; 25:1-9; Ezr 2:41; Ne 7:44.

2. One of the four Levite gatekeepers for the Ark when David was king. He may have been the same as No. 1.—1Ch 15:23, 24.

3. The son of Meshillemoth. (2Ch 28:12) At the time that Ahaz was king of Judah, this southern kingdom suffered a terrible defeat at the hands of the northern kingdom, but when 200,000 were being taken captive to Samaria, Berechiah and three other headmen of Ephraim acted quickly on the counsel of Jehovah's prophet Oded. Not only did they prevent the victors from enslaving their brothers but they also went so far as to clothe and feed the captives as well as assist in their return. —2Ch 28:6-15.

4. A descendant of David through Solomon. —1Ch 3:1, 10, 20.

5. A Levite who lived after the Babylonian exile; the son of Asa.—1Ch 9:16.

6. The son of Meshezabel. Berechiah's son Meshullam worked on the rebuilding of Jerusalem's walls in Nehemiah's time, and his granddaughter married the son of Tobiah.—Ne 3:4, 30; 6:18.

7. The son of the prophet Iddo and the father of the prophet Zechariah.—Zec 1:1, 7.

BERED (Be'red) [Hail].

1. A grandson of Ephraim through Shuthelah. —1Ch 7:20.

2. A place in southern Palestine mentioned in the account of Hagar's fleeing from Sarai. The well of Beer-lahai-roi, at which Hagar stopped, lay in the wilderness between Bered and Kadesh, on the way to Shur. (Ge 16:7, 14) The wilderness of Shur is a region SW of Philistia and on the way to Egypt, which may indicate that Hagar was heading back to her homeland.—Ex 15:22.

BERI (Be'ri). Son of Zophah and family head in the tribe of Asher.—1Ch 7:36, 40.

BERIAH (Be·ri'ah) [With Calamity].

1. The fourth-listed son of Asher who, perhaps with his own two sons Heber and Malchiel, came to Egypt with Jacob's household. (Ge 46:8, 17) He and his two sons are listed as ancestral family heads, his descendants being Beriites.—Nu 26:44, 45; 1Ch 7:30, 31.

2. A son of Ephraim, born after men of Gath had killed his older brothers. Ephraim "called his name Beriah, because it was *with calamity* [Heb., *bera·'ah'*] that she [Beriah's mother] happened to be in his house."—1Ch 7:20-23.

3. One of the five sons of Elpaal and one of the Benjamite family heads who chased away the inhabitants of Gath.—1Ch 8:12, 13.

4. The last-named son of Shimei, a Levite descendant of Gershon. Beriah and his brother Jeush "did not have many sons; so they became a paternal house for one official class."—1Ch 23:6-11.

BERIITES (Be·ri'ites) [Of (Belonging to) Beriah]. An Asherite family descended from Beriah. —Nu 26:44.

BERNICE (Ber·ni'ce) [from a root meaning "conquer"]. Daughter of Herod Agrippa I by his wife Cypros; born about 28 C.E.; sister of Drusilla and Herod Agrippa II. (See HEROD No. 4.) Bernice and her brother Agrippa visited Governor Festus at Caesarea in 58 C.E., where the two of them, at the invitation of Festus, "came with much pompous show and entered into the audience chamber together with military commanders as well as men of eminence in the city." The prisoner Paul was then brought in and allowed to make his powerful and eloquent defense before all these dignitaries.—Ac 25:13, 23; 26:1-30.

Secular history tells of the immoral life of this shameless woman. She was married first to Marcus, son of Alexander Lysimachus. After the death of Marcus she married her uncle Herod, king of Chalcis. By him she had two boys before he died in 48 C.E. She then incestuously lived with her brother until public scandal pressured her into marrying Polemo the king of Cilicia. Soon, however, she deserted him and again became her brother's consort, and it was during this time that she and Agrippa visited Caesarea. Though Bernice attempted to defend the Jews in 66 C.E., she did not hesitate to take an oath of allegiance to the Roman emperor Vespasian. She later became the mistress of Vespasian's son Titus.

BERODACH-BALADAN. See MERODACH-BAL-ADAN.

BEROEA (Be·roe′a). A populous city of the province of Macedonia visited by the apostle Paul during his second missionary journey. (Ac 17:10-14) Modernly called Veroia, it was located in a fertile area at the base of Mount Bermios about 65 km (40 mi) WSW of Thessalonica. It thus lay some 40 km (25 mi) inland from the Aegean Sea.

It was probably about 50 C.E. when Paul and Silas arrived at Beroea after a nighttime departure from Thessalonica made necessary by mob violence. Beroea had a Jewish community and a synagogue in which the two missionaries preached. The readiness of the Beroeans to give ear to their message, and their diligence in examining the Scriptures in search of confirmation of the things learned, earned them the commendation found at Acts 17:11. A number of converts resulted from among these "noble-minded" persons, both Jews and Greeks. Paul's work was cut short, however, by the arrival of fanatical Jews from Thessalonica bent on causing further mob activity. He sailed for Athens, leaving Silas and Timothy behind to care for the new group of believers in Beroea.—Ac 17:12-15.

Paul doubtless passed through or near Beroea on his third missionary journey, which brought him again into Macedonia. Among his companions at that time was Sopater, a Christian from Beroea. —Ac 20:1-4.

BEROTHAH (Be·ro′thah), **BEROTHAI** (Be-ro′thai) [Wells]. In Ezekiel's vision concerning the territorial inheritance of Israel, Berothah is listed as on the northern boundary in the area between Hamath and Damascus. (Eze 47:16) It appears to be the same as Berothai of 2 Samuel 8:8, a city belonging to Hadadezer king of Zobah, from which David carried away "copper in very great quantity." In the parallel record at 1 Chronicles 18:8 the name Cun appears in its place. Berothah (or Berothai) is generally identified with present-day Britel (Bereitan), about 10 km (6 mi) SW of Baalbek in the valley known as the Beqa′, lying between the Lebanon and the Anti-Lebanon mountains.

BEROTHITE. See BEEROTHITE.

BERYL. A translucent or opaque mineral composed of a silicate of aluminum and beryllium. It is harder than quartz and is usually yellow green, but sometimes it is green, yellow, blue, white, pale red, or colorless. Dark-green beryl is classed as emerald, the blue-green is aquamarine, and the rose variety is called morganite. Beryl is found normally in granitic rocks in the form of six-sided crystals. Individual beryl crystals weighing over 25 tons have been discovered.

Beryl was a very popular gemstone in ancient times. The Greeks made fine intaglios from it, and the Romans worked the natural crystals into ear pendants. Beryl (Gr., be′ryl·los) is mentioned once in the Scriptures (NW, NE, RS), it being the eighth foundation of the wall of New Jerusalem.—Re 21:2, 19, 20.

BESAI (Be′sai). Forefather of certain Nethinim who returned to Jerusalem from Babylon, 537 B.C.E.—Ezr 2:1, 2, 43, 49; Ne 7:6, 7, 46, 52.

BESODEIAH (Bes·o·dei′ah) [In the Intimate Group of Jah]. Father of the Meshullam who helped repair "the Gate of the Old City" under Nehemiah's direction.—Ne 3:6.

BESOR, TORRENT VALLEY OF (Be′sor). A torrent valley mentioned only in connection with David's pursuit of the raiding Amalekites who had captured and burned the city of Ziklag. (1Sa 30:1, 10, 21) It is evident that the raiders then headed south toward their home territory in the Negeb, but their precise direction of movement is not stated. Hence, the torrent valley of Besor, the point at which 200 of David's army stopped due to exhaustion, cannot be identified with any certainty. Generally, however, it is considered likely to be connected with the Wadi Ghazzeh (Nahal Besor), a large wadi to the SW of Ziklag that empties into the Mediterranean below Gaza.

David's action, following his victory over the Amalekites, in sharing the spoils with those of his warriors who had remained in the valley guarding the baggage, evidently followed the principle stated earlier by Jehovah at Numbers 31:27, after the Israelite victory over Midian. David, thereafter, kept this practice "set as a regulation and a judicial decision for Israel."—1Sa 30:21-25.

BESTIALITY. Unnatural sexual intercourse of a man or a woman with an animal. The Mosaic Law emphatically condemned this perverted practice, sentencing the guilty person and the beast to death. "Where a man gives his seminal emission to a beast, he should be put to death without fail, and you should kill the beast. And where a woman approaches any beast to have a connection with it, you must kill the woman and the beast."—Le 20:15, 16; 18:23; Ex 22:19; De 27:21.

This prohibition, together with the rest of God's laws governing sex relations, lifted the Israelites to a much higher moral level than their neighbors. In Egypt, bestiality constituted a part of idolatrous animal worship; historians attest to the cohabitation of women with goats, for example. Similar practices were also prevalent among the Canaanites (Le 18:23-30), and reportedly in Rome.

The depraved practice of bestiality is included in the Greek word *por·nei'a* that is rendered "fornication." (See FORNICATION.) Anyone indulging in such filthy practice is morally unclean, and if a member of the Christian congregation was to indulge in such a practice, that one would be subject to disfellowshipping.—Eph 5:3; Col 3:5, 6.

BETAH (Be'tah). A town mentioned along with Berothai in connection with David's defeat of Hadadezer, king of Zobah. (2Sa 8:8) The site is unknown, although the Aramaean kingdom of Zobah is considered to have been to the N of Damascus. In a parallel account of David's victory, 1 Chronicles 18:8 refers to "Tibhath," and some lexicographers consider Tibhath to be the more correct rendering. The Syriac *Peshitta* reads "Tebah" instead of Betah at 2 Samuel 8:8. It is to be noted that simply by an inversion of the first two Hebrew consonants Betah becomes Tebah. Since Betah (or Tibhath) was an Aramaean city, some scholars associate it with Tebah, the son of Nahor.—Ge 22:24; see TIBHATH.

BETEN (Be'ten) [Pistachio Nut]. A city named only at Joshua 19:25; one of the boundary towns of Asher. Its location is not certain, since the sites of several of the other towns mentioned in the list are unknown. However, it is generally identified with Khirbet Ibtin, about 17 km (11 mi) S of Acco and 13 km (8 mi) SE of Haifa, in the southern end of the Plain of Acco.

BETHABARA. See BETHANY No. 2.

BETH-ANATH (Beth-a'nath) [House of Anath]. One of the fortified cities that was assigned to the tribe of Naphtali (Jos 19:38, 39), but from which they did not drive out the Canaanite inhabitants, reducing them instead to forced labor. (Jg 1:33) It is possibly identified with Safed el-Battikh, 24 km (15 mi) ESE of Tyre. The town is mentioned in the lists of various Egyptian rulers of the "New Kingdom" period.

BETH-ANOTH (Beth-a'noth) [House of Answers [that is, to prayers]]. One of the cities assigned to the tribe of Judah in the mountainous region of that tribe's territory. (Jos 15:59) It is presently identified with Khirbet Beit 'Anun, about 6 km (3.5 mi) NNE of Hebron.

BETHANY (Beth'a·ny).

1. A village "about two miles" away from Jerusalem, the measurement used by the Gospel writer at that time being the Roman stadium, with the "fifteen stadia" mentioned by him equaling about 2.8 km (1.7 mi). (Joh 11:18, ftn) It lay on the E slope of the Mount of Olives on an ancient approach to Jerusalem from Jericho and the Jordan. (Mr 10:46; 11:1; Lu 19:29) Today the site is marked by the small village of el-'Azariyeh (El 'Eizariya), an Arabic name meaning "the Place of Lazarus," located 2.5 km (1.5 mi) ESE of the Temple Mount.—PICTURE, Vol. 2, p. 950.

Just as Capernaum was Jesus' home in Galilee (Mr 2:1), Bethany might be called his home in Judea. It was the "certain village" that Jesus visited during his later Judean ministry (approximately October to December, 32 C.E.), the location of the home of Martha, Mary, and Lazarus, who became beloved friends of Jesus. (Lu 10:38) Here Jesus later performed the miracle of Lazarus' resurrection.—Joh 11:1, 38-44.

Six days before Jesus' final Passover (as the weekly Sabbath began, on Nisan 8, 33 C.E.), Jesus arrived at Bethany. (Joh 12:1) Following the Sabbath (that is, at the beginning of Nisan 9) he enjoyed an evening meal in the home of Simon the leper, with Martha, Mary, and Lazarus participating. This was the scene of Mary's anointing him with costly oil, provoking Judas' hypocritical objections and the rebuke administered to him by Jesus. (Mt 26:6-13; Mr 14:3-9; Joh 12:2-8) By this time, too, news had reached Jerusalem that Jesus was in the vicinity, and now that the Sabbath had ended, a great crowd of the Jews flocked out to see him and the resurrected Lazarus. (Joh 12:9) The next day (still on Nisan 9) Jesus made his triumphal ride into Jerusalem, evidently over the Mount of Olives along the path from Bethany. (Mt 21:1-11; Mr 11:1-11; Lu 19:29-38) It was on the way from Bethany to Jerusalem on Nisan 10 that Jesus cursed the barren fig tree, which had completely withered by the time he and his disciples passed it the following day (Nisan 11).—Mr 11:12-14, 19, 20.

During the last four days of his earthly life, Jesus spent the daytime in activity at Jerusalem, but at night he and his disciples would leave the big city to lodge in the unpretentious village of Bethany on the E slope of the Mount of Olives, doubtless at the home of Martha, Mary, and Lazarus.—Mr 11:11; Mt 21:17; Lu 21:37.

Forty days after Jesus' resurrection, when the time came for him to part from his disciples, he led them, not to the temple that was now abandoned by God but, rather, "out as far as Bethany" on the Mount of Olives, where his ascension began.—Lu 24:50-53; Ac 1:9-12.

It is generally believed that the Benjamite city of Ananiah (Ne 11:32) was the ancient site corresponding to the village of Bethany in Jesus' day.

2. Bethany across the Jordan is mentioned but once (Joh 1:28) as the place where John was baptizing and, apparently, where he identified Jesus to his disciples as "the Lamb of God." (Joh 1:35, 36) In the third century Origen substituted the name Bethabara for Bethany, and the *King James Version* follows this rendering; however, the most reliable manuscripts read Bethany. The site of this Bethany beyond or E of the Jordan is unknown. Some, favoring the traditional location for Jesus' baptism, would place it across the Jordan opposite Jericho. However, the record at John 1:29, 35, 43; 2:1 seems to indicate a place no more than a day's journey from Cana of Galilee; while that of John 10:40 and 11:3, 6, 17 may suggest that it lay about two days' journey from the Bethany that was the home of Lazarus. Thus, a site somewhat S of the Sea of Galilee seems the most likely, but no positive identification is possible.

BETH-ARABAH (Beth-ar′a·bah) [House of the Desert Plain]. One of the six cities within Judah's territory described as "in the wilderness." (Jos 15:61) It is used in describing the mutual boundaries of the tribes of Benjamin and Judah. (Jos 15:6) Though listed as within the tribal assignment of Judah, it is thereafter spoken of as pertaining to Benjamin, perhaps indicating the site as an enclave city of the Benjamites. (Jos 18:21, 22) Remaining evidence of the name may be seen in 'Ain el-Gharabah, a spring on the N side of the Wadi el Qilt about 6 km (3.5 mi) ESE of Jericho.

This location would place it in the desert region at the N end of the Dead Sea.

BETH-ARBEL. See ARBEL, HOUSE OF.

BETH-AVEN (Beth-a′ven) [House of Hurtfulness (Something Hurtful)].

1. A town in the territory of the tribe of Benjamin, close by the ancient city of Ai. (Jos 7:2; 18:11, 12) It was in the wilderness, located E of Bethel and W of Michmash, and became involved in an outstanding battle when Saul and Jonathan routed the Philistines from this latter city.—1Sa 13:5; 14:23.

2. In lamenting the idolatrous conditions to which Israel had turned in his time, the prophet Hosea mentions Beth-aven together with Gibeah and Ramah, other prominent cities of Benjamin. (Ho 4:15; 5:8; 10:5, 8) It appears that the prophet applies the name in a derogatory sense to the city of Bethel, which at one time had been a 'house of God' but had now become a 'house of what is hurtful' because of the calf worship instituted there.—1Ki 12:28-30.

BETH-AZMAVETH. See AZMAVETH No. 5.

BETH-BAAL-MEON. See BAAL-MEON.

BETH-BARAH (Beth-bar′ah) [House of Barah]. When Gideon's forces were pursuing the fleeing Midianites, Gideon sent word to the men of Ephraim to capture "the waters as far as Beth-barah and the Jordan" (Jg 7:24), evidently to prevent the enemy from crossing the Jordan. Since the battle took place in the Low Plain of Jezreel (Jg 6:33), this would indicate a site W of the Jordan. The identification is unknown, but a location between the Wadi Far′ah and the Jordan is suggested. A similar tactic was employed by Ehud in the fight against the Moabites when they "got to capture the fords of the Jordan against the Moabites."—Jg 3:27, 28.

BETH-BIRI (Beth-bir′i). A town in the Negeb region of Judah but assigned to the sons of Simeon. (1Ch 4:24, 31) In the parallel list of towns at Joshua 19:6 it appears as Beth-lebaoth, and some suggest that Beth-biri may be a postexilic name for the same place, used by Ezra as the writer of the Chronicles. Evidence of the name may remain in that of Jebel el-Biri, a mountain about 40 km (25 mi) SW of Beer-sheba. On this basis, some propose that Beth-biri was on or near this mountain.—See BETH-LEBAOTH.

BETH-CAR [House of the Ram]. A point mentioned in the account of Israel's defeat of the Philistines at Mizpah. The Israelites pursued the fleeing Philistines "as far as south of Beth-car." (1Sa 7:11) Many relate Beth-car to Beth-haccherem (Jer 6:1; Ne 3:14), identified by some with 'Ain Karim ('En Kerem), about 7 km (4.5 mi) W of the Temple Mount in Jerusalem. Such route, if followed, would have lead the Philistines from Mizpah through the deep Wadi beit Hanina down to the Valley of Sorek, and through it to the Plains of Philistia.—See BETH-HACCHEREM.

BETH-DAGON   (Beth-da'gon) [House of Dagon].

1. A town in the allotment of territory assigned to the tribe of Judah. (Jos 15:21, 41) Although it is listed along with other towns of the Shephelah or lowland region, the suggested location is on the Plains of Philistia at Khirbet Dajun, a short distance SW of modern Beit Dajan (Bet Dagan) and about 10 km (6 mi) SE of Tel Aviv-Yafo. In this regard, it may be noted that other cities of the Philistine plain are listed in subsequent verses. (Jos 15:45-47) This would make it an enclave city within the territory of Dan, as was also apparently the case with Gederah.—Jos 15:36.

2. A town in the territory of Asher, evidently in the eastern part thereof and near its border with Zebulun. (Jos 19:24, 27) Identification is uncertain.

BETH-DIBLATHAIM   (Beth-dib·la·tha'im) [House of Diblathaim]. A city in Moab (Jer 48:22) the location of which is unknown. However, it may be the place called Almon-diblathaim mentioned at Numbers 33:46. A city called Beth-diblathen is mentioned in the inscription of the Moabite Stone as having been built by Mesha, king of Moab.

BETH-EDEN   (Beth-e'den) [House of Eden]. A city or region of Syria referred to at Amos 1:5 in that prophet's message against Damascus. It is now generally associated with the Bit-adini of the Assyrian inscriptions, a region located between the Euphrates and Balikh rivers. Such identification can be acceptable, however, only if "Damas-

Ruins where ancient Bethel was located.
At this city on the roadway that led down to Jerusalem,
Jeroboam established a center for calf worship

cus" in the prophecy is understood to represent the Aramaean (Syrian) kingdoms in general, inasmuch as the kingdom of Bit-adini lay some 480 km (300 mi) to the N of Damascus. Damascus is, indeed, called "the head of Syria" at Isaiah 7:8.

Amos' prediction (likely c. 804 B.C.E.) that "the people of Syria will have to go as exiles to Kir" was apparently fulfilled in the time of the Assyrian monarch Tiglath-pileser III, during the reign of King Ahaz (761-746 B.C.E.).—2Ki 16:9.

"The sons of Eden" mentioned at 2 Kings 19:12 and Isaiah 37:12 may refer to the people of Beth-eden, perhaps the "Eden" of Ezekiel 27:23.—See EDEN No. 2.

BETHEL (Beth'el) [House of God].

1. A prominent city of Israel, more frequently mentioned in the Bible than any other except Jerusalem. It is identified with the ruins by the modern village of Beitin, about 17 km (11 mi) N of Jerusalem. It thus lay on a rocky ridge in the extreme southern part of the mountainous region of Ephraim at about 900 m (3,000 ft) above sea level. The surrounding area today is quite barren, consisting of a stony plateau with sparse vegetation. Yet the existence of several springs there shows that the ancient city had an excellent water supply.

Bethel's position was strategic and contributed greatly to its importance. Situated on the backbone of the central mountain range, it was on the important N-S route that followed the watershed line, running all the way from Shechem southward through Bethel, Jerusalem, Bethlehem, Hebron, and down to Beer-sheba. (Compare Jg 21:19.) Another route connected Bethel with Joppa to the W on the Mediterranean and with Jericho to the E near the Jordan. Bethel was thus a crossroads town, as were Samaria, Jerusalem, Hebron, and Beer-sheba. Additionally, the evidence indicates that the area between Jerusalem and Bethel was a region of dense population, having a greater concentration of towns than any other part of Palestine.

Archaeological excavations at Beitin reveal it to be a site of great antiquity, the suggestion being given that the original settlement dated back to about the 21st century B.C.E. Evidence was also found of a severe destruction and conflagration leaving debris and ashes 1.5 m (c. 5 ft) deep in some places, and this is believed likely to have occurred during the conquest of Canaan by Israel.

Upon Abraham's entry into Canaan, he stopped at Shechem and then moved S "to the mountainous region to the east of Bethel and pitched his tent with Bethel on the west and Ai on the east." (Ge 12:8) After spending some time in Egypt because of a famine in Canaan, Abraham again settled to the E of Bethel, in company with his nephew Lot. Since in both cases Abraham pitched tent to the E of Bethel, it is suggested that the site of his encampment was at Burj Beitin, a short distance SE of Beitin, which has been called "one of the great view-points of Palestine." (*Encyclopædia Biblica*, edited by T. K. Cheyne, London, 1899, Vol. I, col. 552) It may have been from such a vantage point that Abraham invited Lot to select the direction in which he would go upon separating from Abraham, with the result that Lot "raised his eyes and saw the whole District of the Jordan" and decided in favor of that region. (Ge 13:8-11) Jehovah thereafter invited Abraham to view the land in all directions, assuring him that it would be for an inheritance to him and his seed.—Ge 13:14, 15.

Although Moses, in compiling the Genesis account, speaks of the town near which Abraham camped as "Bethel," the subsequent record shows its original Canaanite name to have been "Luz." (See LUZ No. 1.) Jacob spent the night near the city when traveling from Beer-sheba to Haran, and after having a dream of a ladder reaching to the heavens and hearing God's confirmation of the Abrahamic promise, he thereafter set up a pillar and called the name of the place Bethel, although "Luz was the city's name formerly." (Ge 28:10-19) Some 20 years later God spoke to Jacob at Haran, identifying himself as the one who had addressed Jacob at Bethel, and instructed him to return to Canaan.—Ge 31:13.

Following the defilement of Dinah at Shechem and the act of vengeance executed by Jacob's sons against the Shechemites, Jacob received God's instruction to return to Bethel. After eliminating false religious articles from his household and servants, he traveled to Bethel under divine protection, built an altar there, and restated the name he had given the place earlier, calling it El-bethel, meaning "The God of Bethel." Here Rebekah's nursing woman Deborah died and was buried. Here, too, Jehovah confirmed the change of Jacob's name to Israel, restating the Abrahamic promise.—Ge 35:1-16.

Centuries later, upon the entry of the nation of Israel into Canaan (1473 B.C.E.), the name Bethel is again used to refer to the city previously called Luz rather than to the camping site of Abraham and Jacob. In the account of the attack upon Ai, the record indicates that the Canaanite men of Bethel endeavored to support the men of that neighboring city, but to no avail. If not at that point, then at a later time Bethel's king met defeat by Joshua's forces. (Jos 7:2; 8:9, 12, 17; 12:9, 16) Bethel thereafter appears as a boundary city between the territories of the tribes of Ephraim and Benjamin. It is listed as assigned to Benjamin, but the record shows that it was the house of Joseph (of which Ephraim was a part) that effected the conquest of the city. (Jos 16:1, 2; 18:13, 21, 22; Jg 1:22-26) From this point forward the name Luz is no longer applied to the city.

During the period of the Judges, the dwelling place of Deborah the prophetess was located "between Ramah and Bethel in the mountainous region of Ephraim." (Jg 4:4, 5) It appears that, at the time of meting out justice to the tribe of Benjamin for the crime committed by its members, the ark of the covenant had been temporarily transported from Shiloh to Bethel, this latter city being considerably nearer the scene of the conflict centering around Gibeah, about 12 km (7.5 mi) S of Bethel. —Jg 20:1, 18, 26-28; 21:2.

Bethel was on the circuit visited by Samuel as he judged the people annually at that city as well as at Gilgal and Mizpah, and it was still viewed as a place favored for worship. (1Sa 7:16; 10:3) However, from then till the division of the kingdom (997 B.C.E.), Bethel is mentioned only in connection with King Saul's stationing of troops in preparation for combat with the Philistines.—1Sa 13:2.

As a major city of the northern kingdom under Jeroboam, Bethel, once prominent as a place of revelation by the true God, now became renowned as a center of false worship. At Bethel, in the extreme S of the newly formed kingdom of Israel, and at Dan, in the extreme N thereof, Jeroboam set up the golden calves in his effort to dissuade the people of his realm from going to the temple at Jerusalem. (1Ki 12:27-29) With its own religious house and altar, a specially invented festival time, and priests selected from among the non-Levitical tribes, Bethel became a symbol of rank apostasy from true worship. (1Ki 12:31-33) Jehovah God did not delay in expressing his disapproval through a "man of the true God" sent to Bethel to pronounce judgment against the altar used in connection with calf worship. The ripping apart of this altar served as a portent, confirming the sure fulfillment of the prophet's words. After leaving Bethel, however, this "man of the true God" allowed himself to be induced by an old prophet of Bethel to accept and act on a supposed message from an angel in violation of the direct orders from God, with disastrous consequences to himself. Slain by a lion, he was buried at Bethel in the personal burial place of the old prophet who saw in all these events the certainty of the fulfillment of Jehovah's word and thus requested that his own body be buried at death in the same burial site.—1Ki 13:1-32.

King Abijah of Judah temporarily wrested Bethel and other towns from the control of the northern kingdom (2Ch 13:19, 20), but it appears that Bethel had been restored to the northern kingdom at least by the time of King Baasha of Israel, since he endeavored to fortify Ramah, considerably to the S of Bethel. (1Ki 15:17; 2Ch 16:1) Even though King Jehu later eradicated Baal worship from Israel, the golden calves continued undisturbed at Dan and Bethel.—2Ki 10:28, 29.

Despite the prevalence of false worship there, the record shows Bethel as the location of a group of prophets in the time of Elijah and Elisha. Bethel was also the home of the group of jeering boys who mocked Elisha, this costing many of them their lives as a result of divine execution.—2Ki 2:1-3, 23, 24.

The prophets Amos and Hosea, in the late ninth and mid-eighth centuries B.C.E., proclaimed God's condemnation of the religious corruption centered at Bethel. Although Hosea makes direct mention of Bethel (meaning "House of God") only when recalling God's revelation of himself to faithful Jacob there (Ho 12:4), he evidently employs the name "Beth-aven," meaning "House of Hurtfulness (Something Hurtful)," as applying to that city and the effect of its false religious practices. (Ho 4:15; 5:8) He warns that its calf idol served by foreign-god priests will come to be a cause for mourning to idolatrous Israel, its high places will be annihilated, and thorns and thistles will cover its altars; while the people, faced with exile in Assyria, cry out to the mountains, "Cover us!" and to the hills, "Fall over us!" (Ho 10:5-8; compare Lu 23:30; Re 6:16.) The prophet Amos spoke in similar vein, showing that, no matter how frequent the sacrifices offered by the people at Bethel's altars, their pious pilgrimages to that place only constituted the commission of transgression, and warning that Jehovah's burning anger would blaze against them inextinguishably. (Am 3:14; 4:4; 5:5, 6) Angered at this prophesying done by Amos right in Bethel, the apostate priest Amaziah accused Amos of seditious talk and ordered him to 'go back to Judah where he came from' and there do his prophesying: "But at Bethel you must no longer do any further prophesying, for it is the sanctuary of a king and it is the house of a kingdom."—Am 7:10-13.

Bethel continued as an idolatrous sanctuary till the fall of the northern kingdom to Assyria in 740 B.C.E. Thus Jeremiah, over a century later, could refer to it as a warning example to those trusting in false gods to their eventual shame. (Jer 48:13) Even thereafter Bethel continued as a religious center, for the king of Assyria sent one of the exiled priests back to Israel to teach the lion-plagued people "the religion of the God of the land," and this priest settled in Bethel, teaching the people "as to how they ought to fear Jehovah." The results clearly indicate that he was a priest of the golden calf, since "it was of Jehovah that they became fearers, but it was of their own gods that they proved to be worshipers," and things continued on the same false and idolatrous basis initiated by Jeroboam.—2Ki 17:25, 27-33.

In fulfillment of Hosea's prophecy the golden calf of Bethel had been carried off to the king of Assyria (Ho 10:5, 6), but the original altar of Jeroboam was still there in the time of King Josiah of Judah. During or following Josiah's 18th year of rule (642 B.C.E.), he extended his purge of false religion up into Bethel and also to the cities of Samaria. Josiah destroyed the site of idolatrous worship in Bethel, first burning the bones from nearby tombs on the altar, thereby desecrating it in fulfillment of the prophecy given by "the man of the true God" over three centuries earlier. The only grave spared was that of "the man of the true God," in that way sparing also the bones of the old prophet occupying the same grave.—2Ki 22:3; 23:15-18; 1Ki 13:2, 29-32.

Men of Bethel were among the Israelites returning from exile in Babylon (Ezr 2:1, 28; Ne 7:32), and Bethel was resettled by Benjamites. (Ne 11:31) During the Maccabean period it was fortified by Syrian General Bacchides (c. 160 B.C.E.) and was captured later by Roman General Vespasian prior to his becoming emperor of Rome.

2. One of the cities to which David sent gifts following his victory over the Amalekites. (1Sa 30:18, 26, 27) The fact that it is included among "the places where David had walked about, he and his men," seems to indicate that it is the place elsewhere called Bethul or Bethuel, a Simeonite city in the territory of Judah.—1Sa 30:31; Jos 19:1, 4; 1Ch 4:30; see BETHUEL No. 2.

BETH-EMEK (Beth-e′mek) [House of the Low Plain]. A town in the territory of the tribe of Asher. (Jos 19:24, 27) It is presently identified with Tell Mimas (Tel Bet Ha′Emeq), about 8 km (5 mi) NE of Acco. The original name appears to be reflected in that of the nearby Arab village of ′Amqa now abandoned.

BETH-EZEL (Beth-e′zel). A town, evidently in Judah, mentioned only in Micah's prophecy foretelling the disaster due to come upon unfaithful Samaria and Jerusalem. (Mic 1:11) The prophet repeatedly makes a play on words in the use of the names of several towns in this portion of the prophecy, so that in reality he says: "In the house of Aphrah [probably meaning "Dust"] wallow in the very dust. Make your way across, O inhabitress of Shaphir [meaning "Elegant; Polished; Agreeable"], in shameful nudity. The inhabitress of Zaanan has not gone forth. The wailing of Beth-ezel [meaning "House Nearby (Alongside)"] will take from you people its standing place. For the inhabitress of Maroth [from a root meaning "be bitter"] has waited for good, but what is bad has come down from Jehovah to the gate of Jerusalem." (Mic 1:10-12) The prophet's warning, directed to those due to experience the disaster, thus in effect tells them that the wailing will spread to as far as Jerusalem.

Though the identification is only tentative, Beth-ezel has been located at the site of present-day Deir el-′Asal, about 16 km (10 mi) WSW of Hebron.

BETH-GADER (Beth-ga′der) [House of the Stone Wall]. A name appearing in the genealogy of Judah. (1Ch 2:50, 51) The name appears to be more geographic than personal, causing some scholars to regard it as relating to a town in Judah. Beth-gader may possibly be linked with Geder, a town whose king was among those conquered by Joshua in the region W of the Jordan.—Jos 12:13.

BETH-GAMUL (Beth-ga′mul) [House of One Weaned (or, One Receiving Due Treatment)]. A city mentioned in connection with Jehovah's pronouncements against Moab. It is listed together with Dibon and other cities of "the land of level country" of Moab. (Jer 48:21, 23) It is generally identified with Jumaiyil, on the tableland region of Moab about 13 km (8 mi) E of Dibon (Dhiban). This region just N of the Arnon shows evidence of intense cultivation in ancient times.

BETH-GILGAL. See GILGAL No. 1.

BETH-HACCHEREM (Beth-hac·che′rem) [House of the Vineyard]. A place near Jerusalem mentioned by Jeremiah as a place suitable for raising a fire signal to warn of advancing enemy forces out of the N. (Jer 6:1) In postexilic times a district of Judah bore this name, with Malchijah as "prince" over it. (Ne 3:14) Because of the mention of Tekoa together with Beth-haccherem at Jeremiah 6:1, some consider Beth-haccherem to have been situated to the S of Jerusalem, between that city and Tekoa. Jerome, of the fourth century C.E., referred to it at such location under the name of Bethacharma. In harmony with such views, the site of Khirbet Salih (Ramat Rahel), 4.5 km (3 mi) SSW of the Temple Mount, has been proposed. Others, however, do not consider the mention of Tekoa as necessarily indicating a geographic proximity of Beth-haccherem and hold to the site of 'Ain Karim ('En Kerem) (meaning "Spring of the Vineyard") 7.5 km (4.5 mi) WSW of the Temple Mount. This is in a fertile section with olive groves and vineyards, and it lies at the foot of Jebel 'Ali, from which height may be seen the Mount of Olives, part of Jerusalem, and, to the W, the Mediterranean Sea. Large stone mounds found on the summit are suggested by some to have been used for lighting signal fires such as those mentioned by Jeremiah.—See BETH-CAR.

BETH-HARAN (Beth-ha'ran), **BETH-HARAM** (Beth-ha'ram). A city on the eastern side of the Jordan in the territory requested by the tribe of Gad because of its good pastureland. It was either built or rebuilt by the Gadites, and although situated in a low plain, it became one of their fortified cities.—Nu 32:1, 34, 36; Jos 13:27.

The name seems to have continued in that of Tell er-Rameh on the Wadi er-Rameh (Wadi Husban) in the Plains of Moab, but the original site of Beth-haran (Beth-haram) is identified with Tell Iktanu, about 13 km (8 mi) ENE of the point where the Jordan flows into the Dead Sea. The site was near a source of renowned hot springs, which may partly account for King Herod's having built a palace in this area. In the first part of the Common Era, the site of Tell er-Rameh was known as Livias, a name given it by Herod Antipas, and later its name was changed to Julias.

BETH-HOGLAH (Beth-hog'lah). A Benjamite border town situated in the southeastern corner of this tribe's territory and on the boundary between Benjamin and Judah. (Jos 15:1, 6; 18:11, 19, 21) Scholars generally locate Beth-hoglah near 'Ein Hajla, about 8 km (5 mi) SE of Jericho.

BETH-HORON (Beth-ho'ron). Two towns, Upper and Lower Beth-horon, were strategically situated on the ancient route leading from Joppa and the maritime plain up the Valley of Aijalon to Bethel or to Gibeon and Jerusalem. Today the sites are occupied by two modern villages, the upper: Beit 'Ur el Fauqa (Bet Horon 'Elyon) and the lower: Beit 'Ur et Tahta (Bet Horon Tahton). Upper Beth-horon thus lies about 16 km (10 mi) NW of Jerusalem, with Lower Beth-horon 2.5 km (1.5 mi)

WNW of Upper Beth-horon, both sites occupying hilltops.

The building (or founding) of these places is credited originally to Sheerah, a daughter or granddaughter of Ephraim. (1Ch 7:22-24) The towns formed part of the southern boundary of the tribe of Ephraim (Jos 16:3, 5), while the boundary of the tribe of Benjamin is stated to have come to "the mountain that is on the south of Lower Beth-horon." (Jos 18:13, 14) This appears to place both towns fittingly as within the inheritance of Ephraim. Beth-horon, perhaps just one of the towns, thereafter was given to the Levites of the sons of Kohath.—Jos 21:20, 22; 1Ch 6:68.

Situated as they were on a principal route from the maritime plain up into the hill country, these towns frequently saw the passing of warring forces. At the time of the Israelite conquest, Joshua defeated five Amorite kings who had combined to war against Gibeon, "pursuing them by way of the ascent of Beth-horon." Here Jehovah caused great hailstones to strike down many of the Amorites as they fled along "the descent of Beth-horon." (Jos 10:6-12) "The descent of Beth-horon" is considered by some to refer to the descent from Upper Beth-horon to Lower Beth-horon, there being a difference of about 240 m (800 ft) in altitude between the two places.

Later, during King Saul's reign, "the road of Beth-horon" was one of three routes used by pillaging bands of Philistines making raids from Michmash. (1Sa 13:16-18) King Solomon built or fortified both towns, strengthening them with walls, doors, and bar, doubtless considering that they served as a block to invading forces from Egypt or Philistia. (2Ch 8:5) Shishak of Egypt, who invaded Judah during Rehoboam's reign, listed "Beth-horon" as one of the towns claimed as conquered or under his domination. (1Ki 14:25; 2Ch 12:2-9) When King Amaziah of Judah dismissed Ephraimite mercenary troops before engaging in battle with the Edomites, these soldiers from the northern kingdom with its capital in Samaria expressed their hot anger over their dismissal by raiding Judean cities as far as Beth-horon.—2Ch 25:5-13.

BETH-JESHIMOTH (Beth-jesh'i·moth) [House of the Desolations]. The southernmost point to which the encampment of the Israelites reached as they camped on the Plains of Moab before crossing the Jordan into Canaan. (Nu 33:48, 49) The camp reached from Beth-jeshimoth to Abel-shittim, a distance of about 8 km (5 mi) according to the suggested sites for these places. Beth-jeshimoth is presently identified with Tell el-'Azeimeh near the NE corner of the Dead Sea and 19 km (12 mi) SE of Jericho. Nearby is Khirbet Sweimeh, which, as a Roman settlement, was known by the Greek name of Besimoth. A strong spring is also found in the vicinity. Tell el-'Azeimeh is situated on a platform of land overlooking the plains below, and it is in position to guard the exit from one of the torrent valleys leading down from the mountains to the E.

Beth-jeshimoth formed part of the realm of King Sihon of the Amorites and, after the Israelite conquest of that region, was assigned to the tribe of Reuben. (Jos 12:1-3; 13:15-21; compare Jg 11:13-27.) In the time of the prophet Ezekiel, it is included with certain cities of Moab located on the slope of his frontier and described as "the decoration of the land." (Eze 25:8-10) The prophecy indicates that Jehovah would cause these frontier cities to be opened up, exposing Moab to attack by the "Orientals," or "sons of the East," the nomadic tribes living in the Arabian Desert. (Compare Jg 6:3, ftn; 8:10.) If not earlier, Moab likely took over Beth-jeshimoth and other cities of Reuben following the deportation of that tribe to Assyria.—1Ch 5:26.

BETH-LEBAOTH (Beth-le·ba'oth) [House of Lionesses].

A city listed among the places given to the tribe of Simeon as enclave cities within the territory of Judah. (Jos 19:1, 6) It is named between Hazar-susah and Sharuhen, and this indicates a location in the Negeb region, apparently to the W or SW of Beer-sheba. At Joshua 15:32 it evidently appears simply as Lebaoth, while at 1 Chronicles 4:31 Beth-lebaoth is replaced by the name "Beth-biri." This latter name could be a postexilic name for the same location.—See BETH-BIRI.

BETHLEHEM (Beth'le·hem) [House of Bread].

1. A town in the Judean highlands overlooking the principal highway leading from Jerusalem down to Beer-sheba. It is today called Beit Lahm (Bet Lehem), located about 9 km (5.5 mi) SSW of the Temple Mount. Its altitude of some 777 m (2,550 ft) above sea level is about the same elevation as Jerusalem itself. The countryside, though rocky, produces olives, grapes, and various cereals.—Ru 1:22.

The earlier name of Bethlehem evidently was Ephrath (or, Ephrathah). Jacob buried Rachel "on the way to Ephrath, that is to say, Bethlehem." (Ge 35:19; 48:7) Among the early descendants of Jacob's son Judah are mentioned "Salma the father of Bethlehem" (1Ch 2:51, 54) and "Hur the firstborn of Ephrathah the father of Bethlehem." (1Ch 4:4) This expression may point to these men as

Bethlehem, the birthplace of Jesus, as it appears today

forefathers of the Israelites who later occupied Bethlehem. (See EPHRATHAH No. 2.) When the Israelites entered Canaan, Bethlehem fell within the territory of Judah, though it is not specifically mentioned in any list of Judean cities nor is there anything to indicate its size or prominence at that time. Since there was another Bethlehem in the territory of Zebulun (Jos 19:10, 15), the town in Judah was usually distinguished by reference to Ephrath, or by calling it "Bethlehem in Judah." —Jg 17:7-9; 19:1, 2, 18.

Thus Judge Ibzan may have been from Bethlehem in Judah, but the absence of any reference to Judah, or Ephrath, causes many to view him as from Bethlehem in Zebulun. (Jg 12:8-10) Elimelech, his wife Naomi, and their sons were from Bethlehem, and here Naomi returned with Ruth the Moabitess. (Ru 1:1, 2, 19, 22) Boaz was also of Bethlehem, and the remaining events of the book of Ruth involving ancestors of Jesus (Mt 1:5, 6) center around this town and its fields.—Ru 2:4; 4:11.

David the son of "Jesse the Bethlehemite" was born in Bethlehem of Judah, tended his father's sheep in that area, and was later anointed there by Samuel to be Israel's future king. (1Sa 16:1, 4, 13, 18; 17:12, 15, 58; 20:6) Later, as a fugitive, David longed for a drink of water from a cistern at Bethlehem, then the site of a Philistine outpost. (2Sa 23:14, 15; 1Ch 11:16, 17) It may be noted that three wells are still found on the N side of the town. Elhanan, one of David's outstanding warriors, was the son of a man of Bethlehem (2Sa 23:24), as were David's nephews Joab, Abishai, and Asahel. Fleet-footed Asahel was buried there following his being slain by powerful Abner.—2Sa 2:18-23, 32.

Despite its being in a central location, on a major highway, and in a good position militarily (since it was at a high altitude and built on a site commanding a limestone ridge), and although it was David's hometown, Bethlehem was not chosen to be David's capital. It is not until the reign of Solomon's son Rehoboam that Bethlehem is directly mentioned again, when it was included among the cities fortified by that king. (2Ch 11:5, 6) Near Bethlehem the remnant of the people left in Judah after the fall of Jerusalem to Babylon made a stopover before going on down to Egypt. (Jer 41:17) Men of Bethlehem were among those returning from Babylon following the exile.—Ezr 2:21; Ne 7:26.

As noted previously, Bethlehem was not listed among the cities of Judah in the accounts of the tribal divisions. Though Bible books mention it in connection with certain individuals, it does not otherwise seem to have been a prominent town nor did it have a large population—a "village" when Jesus was on earth. (Joh 7:42) Hence the prophet Micah in his Messianic prophecy at Micah 5:2 could refer to Bethlehem Ephrathah as "the one too little to get to be among the thousands of Judah." Yet his prophecy showed that small Bethlehem would have the singular honor of being the town from which the Messiah would come. The Jewish people understood this prophecy to mean that the Messiah or Christ would be born in and proceed from that town (Joh 7:40-42), a belief also expressed by their chief priests and scribes.—Mt 2:3-6.

Thus, though Mary became pregnant in Nazareth of Galilee, she gave birth to Jesus in Bethlehem of Judea, in order to fulfill the divine prophecy. (Lu 1:26-38; 2:4-7) This meant a trip that, on present roads, covers a distance of about 150 km (93 mi) through hilly country.

At the time of the birth, shepherds were living outdoors in the fields and keeping watches at night over their flocks. (Lu 2:8) While sheep may be led out to pasture during the daytime at any season of the year, the fact that the shepherds were living out in the fields and spending the night there with their flocks provides a definite time indication for the period of Jesus' birth. The rainy season for Palestine begins about mid-October, lasting several months. By December, Bethlehem, like Jerusalem, experiences frequent frost at night. Thus the fact that shepherds of Bethlehem were in the fields at night points to a time prior to the start of the rainy season. It is also most unlikely that Caesar Augustus would unnecessarily provoke the Jews by ordering a registration in the wintry and rainy month of December, when traveling is particularly difficult.—Lu 2:1-6; compare Mt 24:20.

The original location of the stable in Bethlehem in which Jesus was born is unknown. Sometime after Jesus' birth when his parents were residing, not in a stable, but in a house, Bethlehem was visited by some Oriental astrologers searching for "the young child." (Mt 2:1-12) Although divine action prevented their visit from bringing death to the child Jesus, the town of Bethlehem and its surrounding territory suffered the loss of all its male children of two years of age and under, murdered at the order of King Herod. (Mt 2:12, 16) At Matthew 2:17, 18 the inspired writer quoted the prophecy at Jeremiah 31:15 as applying to what then occurred.—See RACHEL.

2. A town in the territory of Zebulun. (Jos 19:10, 15) It was probably from this Bethlehem that Judge Ibzan proceeded, and it was in this town

that he was buried, since no mention is made of Ephrath or of Judah in the account. (Jg 12:8-10) Bethlehem of Zebulun has been identified with Beit Lahm (Bet Lehem Ha-Gelilit) about 11 km (7 mi) WNW of Nazareth.

BETHLEHEMITE (Beth'le·hem·ite) [Of (Belonging to) Bethlehem].

An inhabitant of Bethlehem. In three of its four occurrences in the Bible, "Bethlehemite" is applied to Jesse, David's father. —1Sa 16:1, 18; 17:58; 2Sa 21:19.

BETH-MAACAH. See ABEL-BETH-MAACAH.

BETH-MARCABOTH (Beth-mar'ca·both) [House of the Chariots].

One of the enclave cities of Simeon given them within the territory of the tribe of Judah. (Jos 19:1, 5; 1Ch 4:31) In the parallel account of the cities originally assigned to Judah (Jos 15:31), Beth-marcaboth's place is possibly taken by Madmannah. If Beth-marcaboth is the same as Madmannah, then it evidently lay on the main highway leading from Beer-sheba to Jerusalem and locations N, and the name Beth-marcaboth may be a secondary name for Madmannah. The name of the town listed after Beth-marcaboth, Hazar-susah (or Hazar-susim), means "Courtyard (Settlement) of the Mare (or Horses)." Some suggest that both places were depots and stations for horses and chariots, which traveled the ancient routes between Palestine and Egypt. Chariots were also used for war (Jg 1:19), and Beth-marcaboth may have been a fortress city of the Canaanites from which their war chariots could proceed out onto the flatlands in the area of Beer-sheba.—See MADMANNAH No. 2.

BETH-MEON (Beth-me'on) [shortened form of Beth-baal-meon].

A city of Moab mentioned at Jeremiah 48:23, likely the same as Baal-meon or Beth-baal-meon.—See BAAL-MEON.

BETH-MERHAK (Beth-mer'hak) [House Far Away; Distant House].

When King David withdrew from Jerusalem because of the rebellion of his son Absalom, he stopped at Beth-merhak, perhaps the last house of Jerusalem in the direction of the Mount of Olives before crossing the Kidron Valley. (2Sa 15:17, 23) It appears that at this point King David reviewed his forces as they were crossing over the valley, thus indicating that David was not engaged in a wild, panicky flight but, rather, was making an orderly withdrawal from the city.—2Sa 15:18-26.

BETH-MILLO. See MILLO.

BETH-NIMRAH (Beth-nim'rah) [House of the Leopard].

A town assigned to the tribe of Gad on the E side of the Jordan, also called simply Nimrah. (Nu 32:3, 34, 36) It is described as in "the low plain" and as previously forming part of the realm of King Sihon. (Jos 13:27) The ancient name seems to be preserved in modern Tell Nimrin, situated on the S side of the Wadi Nimrin, but the original site is evidently at Tell Bleibil, about 2.5 km (1.5 mi) to the NE, on the N side of the wadi, where investigations show evidence of occupation during the Israelite period followed by abandonment. It thus lay about 19 km (12 mi) ENE of Jericho.

BETH-PAZZEZ (Beth-paz'zez) [House of Smashing].

A boundary town of Issachar. (Jos 19: 17, 21) The location is uncertain, some favoring Kerm el-Hadetheh near the suggested site of En-haddah mentioned along with Beth-pazzez.

BETH-PELET (Beth-pel'et) [House of Escape].

A town in the southern part of Judah's inheritance. (Jos 15:21, 27) It was among the Judean cities reoccupied after the Babylonian exile. (Ne 11:26) The other towns listed with it indicate a location in the vicinity of Beer-sheba, but the identification is uncertain.

BETH-PEOR (Beth-pe'or) [House of Peor].

In the final year of their wilderness journey the nation of Israel was encamped "in the valley in front of Beth-peor." (De 3:29) Beth-peor may have been a town situated on the slopes of Peor. Both the mountain and the town may well have been associated with the worship of "the Baal of Peor." As reported at Numbers 25:1-9, the Israelites became ensnared with the immoral rites involved in such worship.—See BAAL OF PEOR.

It was on the Plains of Moab, in the region of the Jordan, that Moses restated the Law to Israel, and thereafter Moses was buried "in the valley in the land of Moab in front of Beth-peor." Beth-peor thus appears to have been in "the land of Moab," that is, in land the Moabites had occupied, but in the territory more recently controlled by King Sihon of the Amorites, that is, until his defeat by the nation of Israel. (De 4:46; 34:6) It was later assigned to the tribe of Reuben, being mentioned along with "the slopes of Pisgah and Beth-jeshimoth."—Jos 13:15, 20.

These texts all indicate a location near the NE end of the Dead Sea and facing the Plains of Moab. The precise location is uncertain. Nevertheless, Eusebius referred to such a place about six Roman miles (9 km; 5.5 mi) E of Livias (modern Tell er-Rameh). (Onomasticon, 48, 3-5) On this basis some suggest an identification with Khirbet esh-Sheikh-Jayil about 5 km (3 mi) WNW of the traditional site of Mount Nebo. This site is on the slope of a summit that may have been the "Peor" to which Balaam was taken as the final place to do cursing of Israel. If the above location is correct, then "the valley in front of Beth-peor" would likely be the Wadi Husban.—Nu 23:28; De 4:46; see PEOR.

BETHPHAGE
(Beth′pha·ge) [from Heb., probably meaning "House of the Early Figs"]. Bethphage figures in the account of Jesus' approach to Jerusalem and as the point from which he sent out his disciples to obtain the ass upon which he rode during his triumphal entry into Jerusalem, Nisan 9, of the year 33 C.E. (Mt 21:1, 2; Mr 11:1, 2; Lu 19:29, 30) The references show it to be located on the Mount of Olives, near Jerusalem, and also near Bethany. While some consider Bethphage to have been located across the ravine to the SE of Bethany at present-day Abu Dis, the traditional location is between Bethany and Jerusalem at et-Tur, on the SE slope of the Mount of Olives. From this point it is but a short distance to one of the peaks of the Mount of Olives. Descending from there, one would have the city of Jerusalem in full view. —Compare Lu 19:37, 41.

Talmudic references to Bethphage indicate that it was considered as at the limit of the sabbatical zone around the city of Jerusalem.—Babylonian Talmud, *Menahot* 78b; compare Ac 1:12, ftn.

BETH-RAPHA
(Beth-ra′pha) [House of Rapha]. The name appears at 1 Chronicles 4:12 where Eshton is said to have become "father to Beth-rapha." The use of "Beth" (meaning "House") in the name has led many commentators to view it as applying to a family "house" or to a place. Keil and Delitzsch's *Commentary on the Old Testament* (1973, Vol. III, 1 Chronicles, p. 88) observes: "Eshton begat the house (the family) of Rapha, of whom also nothing further is said; for they can be connected neither with the Benjamite Rapha (viii. 2) nor with the children of Rapha (xx. 4, 6, 8)."

BETH-REHOB
(Beth-re′hob) [House of the Public Square (Broad Place)]. Evidently the name of a small Aramaean kingdom, perhaps applied primarily to its principal city. In the account of the attack on Laish by 600 Danites, Laish is described as "in the low plain that belonged to Beth-rehob." (Jg 18:7, 28) Later, in David's time, the Ammonites hired Syrian mercenaries from Beth-rehob in a vain attempt to defend themselves against the Israelite forces. (2Sa 10:6) It was also called simply "Rehob" (2Sa 10:8) and is, therefore, thought to be the same place mentioned among the points reached by the 12 Israelite spies in their prelimi-

nary investigation of the land of Canaan.—Nu 13:21.

Beth-rehob's association with "the low plain" in which Laish (later Dan) was situated and the statement at Numbers 13:21, that Rehob was in the direction of "the entering in of Hamath," likely point to a location in the southern part of the Beqa′ Valley, which lies between the Lebanon and the Anti-Lebanon mountains. The exact location is uncertain.

BETHSAIDA
(Beth·sa′i·da) [from Aramaic, meaning "House of the Hunter (or, Fisherman)"]. The city from which Philip, Andrew, and Peter came (Joh 1:44), although Simon Peter and Andrew seem to have taken residence in Capernaum by the time of Jesus' ministry. (Mt 8:5, 14; Mr 1:21, 29) It was a city "of Galilee." (Joh 12:21) Following the death of John the Baptizer, Jesus withdrew to Bethsaida with his disciples, and at an isolated grassy place in its vicinity, he miraculously provided food for about 5,000 men, besides women and children, who had gathered to hear him. (Lu 9:10-17; compare Mt 14:13-21; Joh 6:10.) Outside Bethsaida, Jesus later restored sight to a blind man. (Mr 8:22) Since these powerful works were done in their neighborhood, the people of Bethsaida in general, along with the population of Chorazin, came in for merited reproach because of their unrepentant attitude.—Lu 10:13.

The identification of "the village" (Mr 8:22, 23) or "city" (Lu 9:10) of Bethsaida has been a subject of some discussion. The Scriptural references point to a place on the N shores of the Sea of Galilee. The name is connected by Josephus with a populous village lying a short distance to the E of the point where the Jordan River enters the Sea of Galilee. This village was rebuilt by Philip the tetrarch and was named Julias in honor of the daughter of Caesar Augustus. (*Jewish Antiquities,* XVIII, 28 [ii, 1]) The ancient ruins of the site of Julias itself are at et-Tell, about 3 km (2 mi) from the sea; however, remains of a smaller fishing settlement are located at el-′Araj right on the shore. Here a natural harbor was used by fishermen up until recent times, so the place geographically fits the meaning of the name Bethsaida.

While accepting this identification as applying to Bethsaida in some of the texts, a number of commentators contend for a second Bethsaida somewhere to the W of the Jordan. This view is due to the understanding, based on statements by Josephus and others, that the territorial limitation of Galilee did not extend E of the Jordan. Josephus himself speaks of Julias as in "lower Gaulanitis,"

Beth-shean, built on this mound, dominated the east entrance to the Valley of Jezreel

the region to the E of the Sea of Galilee. (*The Jewish War*, II, 168 [ix, 1]) Yet Bethsaida is said to be "of Galilee." (Joh 12:21) However, the region of Galilee does not seem to have always been so precisely defined, Josephus even referring to one Judas of Gaulanitis as "a Galilaean." (*Jewish Antiquities*, XVIII, 4 [i, 1]; *The Jewish War*, II, 118 [viii, 1]) It is also quite possible that the city of Bethsaida had some of its population extending as far as the W bank of the Jordan, about 1.5 km (1 mi) distant.

Additionally, since the *King James Version* rendering of Mark 6:45 states that Jesus instructed his apostles "to go [by boat] to the other side before unto Bethsaida," while the parallel passage at John 6:17 gives their destination as Capernaum, some have held that this likewise requires a second Bethsaida on the W side of the Jordan near Capernaum. Modern translations of the text at Mark 6:45, however, allow for the understanding that the apostles began their trip toward Capernaum by first going coastwise "toward Bethsaida" (the point from which they left Jesus evidently being near the site of the miraculous feeding of the 5,000, likely some distance S of Bethsaida and on the opposite side of the sea from Capernaum), and thereafter crossing over the northern end of the sea, heading for the ultimate destination, Capernaum. They landed on the shores of the land of Gennesaret, apparently somewhat S of the city of Capernaum.—Mr 6:53.

Thus, while various locations have been suggested for a second Bethsaida, the Biblical accounts do not require this. It may also be noted that these suggested sites are all near Capernaum and it would be quite unlikely for two cities bearing the name of Bethsaida to be situated only a few miles apart.

BETH-SHEAN (Beth-she'an), **BETH-SHAN.** Initially, a major fortified city of the Canaanites, located at a strategic point commanding the entrance to the Valley of Jezreel from the Jordan Valley. The name is continued in that of Beisan (Bet She'an), while the ancient site is located nearby at Tell el-Husn (Tel Bet She'an). The land in the area of Beth-shean is about 120 m (390 ft) below sea level, and to the E it drops off sharply to a point some 275 m (900 ft) below sea level by the banks of the Jordan River, about 5 km (3 mi) away. Built on a large mound on the rim of this declivity, Beth-shean was in an excellent position militarily. To the W of Beth-shean the flat valley plain, through which the river Jalud (Nahal Harod) courses, is well watered and fertile and steadily rises until it reaches Jezreel some 17 km (11 mi) to the ESE.

Beth-shean was also a junction town on the favored route leading from the Mediterranean

Coast through to the Jordan Valley and on to Damascus and Arabia.

Archaeological excavations at Beth-shean have revealed numerous strata or levels of ancient ruins, the earliest evidently dating back before the time of Abraham. (DIAGRAM, Vol. 1, p. 959) Toward the middle of the second millennium B.C.E., Beth-shean appears to have come under Egyptian domination as a result of Thutmose III's victory at Megiddo. Archaeological evidence indicates that it was an Egyptian outpost throughout the reigns of several Pharaohs.

At the time of the Israelite conquest of Canaan (1473-c. 1467 B.C.E.), Beth-shean was located within the territory allotted to Issachar but was assigned to the tribe of Manasseh for a possession. (Jos 17:11; 1Ch 7:29) The men of Manasseh failed to drive out the Canaanites in Beth-shean and other towns of the valley, presenting as their reason the military advantage exercised by the Canaanites with their war chariots equipped with iron scythes, which reason, however, did not satisfy their commander Joshua. The Canaanites, though not dispossessed, nevertheless were eventually subjugated to the point of rendering forced labor.—Jos 17:12, 13, 16-18; Jg 1:27, 28.

Beth-shean was in the possession of the Philistines at the time of the reign of King Saul, and following Saul's defeat at adjacent Mount Gilboa the Philistine victors placed Saul's armor in "the house of the Ashtoreth images" and his head on the house of Dagon, and hung the dead bodies of Saul and his sons on the wall of Beth-shan (Beth-shean), evidently on the interior side facing the city's public square. Courageous and daring Israelites of Jabesh-gilead, about 20 km (12 mi) away on the other side of the Jordan, retrieved the bodies, perhaps penetrating the city at night in order to do so.—1Sa 31:8-13; 2Sa 21:12; 1Ch 10:8-12.

In harmony with the above account, in the excavations at Tell el-Husn the ruins of two temples were uncovered, one of which is considered to be the temple of Ashtoreth, while the other, farther to the S, is suggested by some to be the temple of Dagon. The temple of Ashtoreth is estimated to have continued in use until about the tenth century B.C.E. Evidence indicates an earlier worship of a Baal god referred to in one stele as "Mekal the master [Baal] of Beth-shan."

The city was eventually conquered by the Israelites, doubtless during the time of David's reign; and during the reign of Solomon, Beth-shean was included in one of the 12 royal supply districts. (1Ki 4:12) Following the division of the kingdom,

Pharaoh Shishak (called Sheshonk by the Egyptians) invaded Palestine during King Rehoboam's fifth year (993 B.C.E.). (1Ki 14:25) A relief on a wall at Karnak in Egypt depicts Shishak's victorious campaign and conquest of numerous towns, including Beth-shean.

By the time of the Maccabees the name of Beth-shean had been changed to Scythopolis, and it is referred to by Jewish historian Josephus as one of the largest cities of the Decapolis. It was the only one of these ten cities lying W of the Jordan.

BETH-SHEMESH (Beth-she'mesh) [House of the Sun]. The name of four cities in the Biblical account.

1. A city located on the northern boundary of Judah, listed between Chesalon and Timnah. (Jos 15:10) It is evidently called Ir-shemesh (meaning "City of the Sun") at Joshua 19:41, where it appears as a boundary town of the tribe of Dan, Judah's neighbor to the north. Judah subsequently bequeathed Beth-shemesh to the Levites as a priestly city.—Jos 21:13, 16; 1Ch 6:59.

Beth-shemesh is identified with Tell er-Rumeileh (Tel Bet Shemesh) just W of the ruins of the Byzantine city near present-day 'Ain Shems, this latter place partly preserving the ancient name. Beth-shemesh thus lay about 26 km (16 mi) W of Jerusalem and was situated on the main road from that city to the Philistine cities of Ashdod and Ashkelon. It was evidently a strategic point militarily as it guarded the upper portion of the torrent valley of Sorek and one of the main approaches from the coastal plains into the Shephelah region and the mountains of Judah. Excavations carried out at the site indicate an ancient history for the city, with considerable evidence of Philistine influence.

When the Philistines, plagued by disease, sent the ark of Jehovah back to Israel, the cows pulling the wagon of their own accord headed for this Levite city of Beth-shemesh. However, the improper action of some of the inhabitants of Beth-shemesh in looking upon the ark of the covenant brought death to 70 of them. (1Sa 6:9-20) The phrase "fifty thousand men" occurring at 1 Samuel 6:19 in the Hebrew is not connected with the "seventy men" by any conjunction, and this is considered by some to indicate an interpolation. Josephus (*Jewish Antiquities,* VI, 16 [i, 4]) in discussing the Biblical account mentions only 70 men as killed, omitting all reference to the 50,000. —See 1Sa 6:19, ftn.

Beth-shemesh was one of the cities connected with King Solomon's administrative arrangement to provide food for the royal table. (1Ki 4:7, 9)

Long, narrow rooms believed to have been used for grain storage have been found there, as well as a huge stone-lined silo some 7 m (23 ft) in diameter and almost 6 m (20 ft) deep. Numerous winepresses and olive presses unearthed indicate that the area was very productive in oil and wine.

King Amaziah (858-830 B.C.E.) unwisely challenged Jehoash of Israel and suffered defeat and capture at Beth-shemesh. (2Ki 14:9-13; 2Ch 25:18-23) During the reign of Ahaz (761-746 B.C.E.) national degradation and infidelity resulted in the loss of Beth-shemesh to the Philistines. (2Ch 28:18, 19) A stamped jar handle bearing the inscription "belonging to Eliakim, steward of Jaukin [a shortened form of the name Jehoiachin]," was excavated at Beth-shemesh and is suggested to relate to the king of that name, perhaps indicating that the kingdom of Judah in time regained control of the city from the Philistines.

2. A fortified city in the territory of Naphtali. (Jos 19:35-39) Though not driven out, the Canaanites residing in this city became subject to forced labor for the Naphtalites. (Jg 1:33) The ancient site remains unidentified.

3. A town of Issachar near the Jordan. (Jos 19:22, 23) While different sites have been suggested, some scholars prefer an identification with el-'Abeidiyeh on the banks of the Jordan about 3 km (2 mi) S of the Sea of Galilee and about 16 km (10 mi) E of Mount Tabor. The ancient name is possibly preserved at nearby Khirbet Shamsawi.

4. A city in Egypt included in Jeremiah's prophecy of coming devastation upon that nation. (Jer 43:13) It is considered to be the same as Heliopolis (meaning "City of the Sun"), located on the NE edge of modern Cairo. It is elsewhere referred to in the Scriptural account by its Egyptian name, On.—See ON No. 2.

BETH-SHEMITE (Beth-she'mite) [Of (Belonging to) Beth-shemesh]. An inhabitant of Beth-shemesh of Judah. The term is applied to Joshua, the owner of the field where the ark of the covenant rested on "a large stone," exposed to view, after being taken there on a Philistine wagon. —1Sa 6:14, 18.

BETH-SHITTAH (Beth-shit'tah) [House of the Acacia [Tree]]. A town mentioned in describing the line of flight followed by the Midianites after their rout in the Low Plain of Jezreel by Judge Gideon. (Jg 7:22) Since the Midianites were heading for the region of the Jordan, Beth-shittah must be located somewhere to the E or SE of the hill of Moreh and the well of Harod, in which

vicinity the battle took place. (Jg 7:1) Shattah (Bet Ha-Shitta), about 4.5 km (3 mi) ESE of modern 'En Harod, is suggested by some as the likely location and one giving evidence of the original name. Others consider it too near to the scene of the battle and recommend a location more to the SE, though offering no definite identification.

BETH-TAPPUAH (Beth-tap'pu·ah) [House of the Apple [Tree]]. A city in the hill country near Hebron and part of Judah's territorial inheritance. (Jos 15:20, 48, 53) Some suggest that it received its name from the Judean named Tappuah (1Ch 2:42, 43); however, it is also possible that Bethtappuah was named after the apple trees that likely once grew there in abundance. It is identified today with modern Taffuh, about 6 km (3.5 mi) WNW of Hebron.

BETHUEL (Be·thu'el).

1. Abraham's nephew, born to his brother Nahor by Milcah. (Ge 22:20, 22) Bethuel became father to Rebekah and Laban. (Ge 22:23; 24:15, 24, 29) He later acknowledged the divine direction that brought Abraham's slave to his home in search of a wife for Isaac, saying, along with Laban, "From Jehovah this thing has issued." (Ge 24:50) He is called a Syrian or an Aramaean, dwelling in the flatland of Aram.—Ge 25:20; 28:2, 5.

2. A comparison of the lists of towns given at Joshua 15:30; 19:4 and 1 Chronicles 4:30 indicates that this town is also called Bethul and Chesil. It was in the southern part of the territory of Judah but was assigned to the tribe of Simeon as an enclave city. It, therefore, appears also to be the "Bethel" referred to at 1 Samuel 30:27 as one of the places to which David sent portions of spoil as a gift. A tentative identification is with Khirbet el-Qaryatein (Tel Qeriyyot), about 19 km (12 mi) S of Hebron; although some prefer Khirbet er-Ras (Horvat Rosh) about 24 km (15 mi) to the W of this site.—See CHESIL.

BETHUL. See BETHUEL No. 2.

BETHZATHA (Beth·za'tha). The name occurs with reference to a pool bearing this name at which Jesus healed a man who had been ill for 38 years. (Joh 5:1-9) In John 5:2, some manuscripts and translations (KJ, NE) read "Bethesda." The pool is described as having five colonnades, in which large numbers of sick, blind, and lame persons congregated, evidently attributing healing powers to the waters, particularly so immediately after the waters were disturbed. The last seven words of verse 3 as found in the King James

Version and verse 4 of this chapter, attributing the disturbing of the waters to an angel, are not found in some of the oldest Greek manuscripts and are viewed as an interpolation. Thus the Bible does not give any indication as to the cause of the water disturbance but merely shows the people's belief in the curative powers of the waters.

The location of the pool is indicated by the evident reference to the "sheepgate" (although in the original Greek the word "gate" must be supplied), which gate is generally held to have been in the north part of Jerusalem. Nehemiah 3:1 shows that this gate was built by the priests, and hence it is assumed to have been an entrance near the temple area. Additionally, the name Bethzatha is associated with the section of ancient Jerusalem called Bezetha, located to the north of the temple area. In Jesus' day this sector lay outside the city walls, but Herod Agrippa I (who died 44 C.E.) added a third northern wall to the city during the rule of Claudius (41-54 C.E.), and this placed Bezetha within the city walls, so that John could properly speak of the pool as being "in Jerusalem," as he had known the city before its destruction in 70 C.E.

In 1888 excavations just to the N of the temple site revealed a double pool divided by a rock partition and embracing an overall area about 46 by 92 m (150 × 300 ft). Evidence of colonnades existed and a faded fresco portraying an angel moving the waters, although the painting may well have been a later addition. The location seems to fit the Biblical description.

BETH-ZUR   [House of the Rock]. A town in the mountainous region of Judah listed between Halhul and Gedor. (Jos 15:58) The name is still preserved at Burj es-Sur, while excavations have shown the actual site of the ancient city to be at Khirbet et-Tubeiqeh (Bet Zur), about 0.5 km (0.3 mi) to the NW. This location is 7.5 km (4.5 mi) N of Hebron, with Gedor about 5 km (3 mi) farther NNW and Halhul 1.5 km (1 mi) to the SSE. It is described as one of the highest ruined towns in Palestine, being situated on a hill 1,007 m (3,304 ft) above sea level. As it was near the highway leading N-S along the ridge of the watershed route and also guarded the routes leading to Mareshah and Libnah in the W, Beth-zur occupied a position of strategic importance.

Following the division of the kingdom, Beth-zur was one of 15 cities rebuilt and fortified by King Rehoboam as a means of protecting Judah and Benjamin against invasion. (2Ch 11:5-12) It was among the cities reinhabited by the Jews returning from the Babylonian exile. (Ne 3:16) During the Maccabean period Beth-zur (then called Bethsura) figured prominently in the Jews' struggle against the Seleucid kings of Syria, the Apocryphal book of First Maccabees describing a signal victory won there by Judas Maccabaeus against the Syrian forces (165 B.C.E.), following which he fortified the city again. (1 Maccabees 4:61; 6:26) In 162 B.C.E. the Syrians besieged the city, and it eventually capitulated because of lack of food supplies. (1 Maccabees 6:30-50) It became a Syrian garrison, and General Bacchides strengthened its fortifications.—1 Maccabees 9:52.

Archaeological excavations at Beth-zur in 1931 and 1957 revealed evidence of strong fortifications. Numerous coins were found dating from the fourth to the second century B.C.E.; these included silver Jewish coins believed to date from the Persian period or about the fourth century B.C.E.

The name Beth-zur appears in a genealogical list of the descendants of Caleb the brother of Jerahmeel at 1 Chronicles 2:45. Maon is there said to be "the father of Beth-zur." Many commentators understand Beth-zur to refer to the town of that name, Maon in such case being the father of those settling there, or perhaps the chief or principal one of the city.

BETONIM   (Bet′o·nim) [Pistachio Nuts]. A city E of the Jordan that Moses gave as "a gift" to the tribe of Gad. (Jos 13:24-27) Betonim is generally held to be the present-day Khirbet Batneh in the mountainous country 21 km (13 mi) W of Rabbah (in Ammon).

BEULAH   (Beu′lah) [Owned as a Wife]. A Hebrew word (*Be′u·lah′*) transliterated as a name at Isaiah 62:4 in some translations (*AS; KJ; Ro*), whereas in others it is rendered "Married" (*AT; RS*), "Espoused" (*Le*), "my wedded wife" (*Mo*), and "Owned as a Wife" (*NW*).

The spiritual woman Zion was to be in a desolate state following the destruction of Jerusalem by the Babylonians and the complete desolation of Judah. However, the restoration prophecy given by Jehovah through Isaiah, one of great import to Jewish exiles in ancient Babylon and to members of spiritual Israel, assured restoration and repopulation of the land, a changed condition. Oncedesolate Zion would no longer be "a woman left entirely," and her land would no longer be desolate, it being promised: "But you yourself will be called My Delight Is in Her [Heb., *Cheph·tsi-vah′*], and your land Owned as a Wife [Heb., *Be′u·lah′*]. For Jehovah will have taken delight in you, and your own land will be owned as a wife." Zion's returning "sons," released from Babylonian exile, would settle in her once again, also 'taking ownership of her as a wife.' The restoration of Zion, or Jerusalem, meant a new condition for her, one that contrasted with her former desolate state. Because of this restored condition, Jehovah, who delights in Zion, declared that she would be called "My Delight Is in Her," and her land, "Owned as a Wife."—Isa 62; compare Isa 54:1, 5, 6; 66:8; Jer 23:5-8; 30:17; Ga 4:26-31.

BEZAI (Be′zai) [shortened form of Bezalel].

1. An Israelite whose descendants numbering over 300 returned to Jerusalem with Zerubbabel in 537 B.C.E.—Ezr 2:17; Ne 7:23.

2. One by this name, or a representative of such a family group, who attested to Nehemiah's "trustworthy arrangement."—Ne 9:38; 10:1, 14, 18.

BEZALEL (Bez′al·el) [Under God's Shadow (Shelter)].

1. Chief artisan and builder of the tabernacle, "the son of Uri the son of Hur of the tribe of Judah." (Ex 31:1, 2; 1Ch 2:20) Jehovah himself appointed Bezalel and promised to "fill him with the spirit of God in wisdom and in understanding and in knowledge and in every kind of craftsmanship, for designing devices, for working in gold and silver and copper, and in working of stones to set them and in working of wood to make products of every kind." (Ex 31:3-5; 35:30-33) These costly materials that Bezalel worked with were supplied by the generous contributions of the "willing-hearted" people, and they proved "more than enough."—Ex 35:4-9, 20-29; 36:3-7.

Bezalel had as his chief assistant Oholiab (Ex 31:6), and there were many "wise-hearted" ones who worked along with them, yet the responsibility of directing the complicated work remained on Bezalel. (Ex 35:10-19, 25, 26, 34; 36:1, 2) This is evident by the interchange of the pronouns "he," referring to Bezalel, and "they," referring to his assistants. (Ex 36-39) The great diversity of Bezalel's skills and the fact that he was filled "with the spirit of God" (Ex 35:31) enabled him to oversee making the tent cloths and their embroidery, gold and copper hooks, the outer coverings of skins, wooden panel frames overlaid with gold, the interior screen (Ex 36), the overlaid ark of the covenant and its cherubs, the table and its utensils, the golden lampstand and incense altar, the prescribed anointing oil and incense (Ex 37), the altar of burnt offering, the copper basin and stand, the courtyard (Ex 38), the ephod and its breastpiece set with precious stones, and the priestly robes (Ex 39). When Solomon came to the throne 475

years later, the tabernacle tent, the ark of the covenant, and the copper altar were still in use. —2Ch 1:1-6.

2. One of the sons of Pahath-moab who dismissed their foreign wives and sons at Ezra's urging.—Ezr 10:30, 44.

BEZEK (Be′zek).

1. The site at which Judah and Simeon defeated 10,000 Canaanite and Perizzite troops under Adoni-bezek. (Jg 1:3-7) Some identify this Bezek with that of 1 Samuel 11:8 (No. 2 below), which is in an extreme northern location in relation to Jerusalem and the territory occupied by Judah and Simeon. Such a view would require the assumption that Adoni-bezek came S to join other Canaanite forces but was met by Judah and Simeon, was chased N to Bezek, and was defeated there. The context, however, seems to indicate a place in the general area of Jerusalem. In view of these circumstances, Bezek, the city of Adoni-bezek, is tentatively located in the Shephelah region at the site of Khirbet Bezka, about 5 km (3 mi) NE of Gezer.

2. The location where Saul assembled the sons of Israel and Judah to fight against the Ammonites who were camped against Jabesh in Gilead. (1Sa 11:8-11) The fact that this place was no more than a night's march from Jabesh substantiates the view that it was located at the modern site of Khirbet Ibziq, 21 km (13 mi) NE of Shechem. A mountain W of Khirbet Ibziq rises 713 m (2,339 ft) above sea level and may have provided a suitable place for Saul to gather his forces.

BEZER (Be′zer).

1. [possibly, Precious Ore]. One of "the sons of Zophah" of the tribe of Asher.—1Ch 7:30, 36, 37.

2. [Unapproachable Place]. A Levite city of refuge, one of the three on the E side of the Jordan, designated primarily for the tribe of Reuben. (De 4:41-43; Jos 20:8; 21:36; 1Ch 6:78) It is spoken of as "on the tableland" and "at Jericho to the east of the Jordan . . . in the wilderness." Bezer is generally identified with modern Umm el-'Amad, located on the plateau region, 19 km (12 mi) S of Rabbah (in Ammon). It is mentioned in the Moabite Stone as being one of the cities captured and fortified by King Mesha of Moab in his revolt against Israel after the death of King Ahab in about 920 B.C.E.—2Ki 3:5.

BIBLE.
The Holy Scriptures, the inspired Word of Jehovah, acknowledged as the greatest book of all times because of its antiquity, its total circulation, the number of languages into which it has

been translated, its surpassing greatness as a literary masterpiece, and its overwhelming importance to all mankind. Independent of all other books, it imitates no other. It stands on its own merits, giving credit to its unique Author. The Bible is also distinguished as having survived more violent controversy than any other book, hated as it is by many enemies.

Name. The English word "Bible" comes through the Latin from the Greek word *bi·bli'a*, meaning "little books." This, in turn, is derived from *bi'blos*, a word that describes the inner part of the papyrus plant out of which a primitive form of paper was made. The Phoenician city of Gebal, famous for its papyrus papermaking, was called by the Greeks "Byblos." (See Jos 13:5, ftn.) In time *bi·bli'a* came to describe various writings, scrolls, books, and eventually the collection of little books that make up the Bible. Jerome called this collection *Bibliotheca Divina*, the Divine Library.

Jesus and writers of the Christian Greek Scriptures referred to the collection of sacred writings as "the Scriptures," or "the holy Scriptures," "the holy writings." (Mt 21:42; Mr 14:49; Lu 24:32; Joh 5:39; Ac 18:24; Ro 1:2; 15:4; 2Ti 3:15, 16) The collection is the written expression of a communicating God, the Word of God, and this is acknowledged in phrases such as "expression of Jehovah's mouth" (De 8:3), "sayings of Jehovah" (Jos 24:27), "commandments of Jehovah" (Ezr 7:11), "law of Jehovah," "reminder of Jehovah," "orders from Jehovah" (Ps 19:7, 8), "word of Jehovah" (Isa 38:4), 'utterance of Jehovah' (Mt 4:4), "Jehovah's word" (1Th 4:15). Repeatedly these writings are spoken of as "sacred pronouncements of God."—Ro 3:2; Ac 7:38; Heb 5:12; 1Pe 4:11.

Divisions. Sixty-six individual books from Genesis to Revelation make up the Bible canon. The choice of these particular books, and the rejection of many others, is evidence that the Divine Author not only inspired their writing but also carefully guarded their collection and preservation within the sacred catalog. (See APOCRYPHA; CANON.) Thirty-nine of the 66 books, making up three quarters of the Bible's contents, are known as the Hebrew Scriptures, all having been initially written in that language with the exception of a few small sections written in Aramaic. (Ezr 4:8–6:18; 7:12-26; Jer 10:11; Da 2:4b–7:28) By combining some of these books, the Jews had a total of only 22 or 24 books, yet these embraced the same material. It also appears to have been their custom to subdivide the Scriptures into three parts—'the law of Moses, the Prophets, and the Psalms.' (Lu 24:44; see HEBREW SCRIPTURES.) The last quarter of

the Bible is known as the Christian Greek Scriptures, so designated because the 27 books comprising this section were written in Greek. The writing, collecting, and arrangement of these books within the Bible's canon also demonstrate Jehovah's supervision from start to finish.—See CHRISTIAN GREEK SCRIPTURES.

Subdividing the Bible into chapters and verses (*KJ* has 1,189 chapters and 31,102 verses) was not done by the original writers, but it was a very useful device added centuries later. The Masoretes divided the Hebrew Scriptures into verses; then in the 13th century of our Common Era chapter divisions were added. Finally, in 1555 Robert Estienne's edition of the Latin *Vulgate* was published as the first complete Bible with the present chapter and verse divisions.

The 66 Bible books all together form but a single work, a complete whole. As the chapter and verse marks are only convenient aids for Bible study and are not intended to detract from the unity of the whole, so also is the sectioning of the Bible, which is done according to the predominant language in which the manuscripts have come down to us. We, therefore, have both the Hebrew and Greek Scriptures, with "Christian" added to the latter to distinguish them from the Greek *Septuagint*, which is the Hebrew portion of the Scriptures translated into Greek.

"Old Testament" and "New Testament." Today it is a common practice to refer to the Scriptures written in Hebrew and Aramaic as the "Old Testament." This is based on the reading in 2 Corinthians 3:14 in the Latin *Vulgate* and the *King James Version*. However, the rendering "old testament" in this text is incorrect. The Greek word *di·a·the'kes* here means "covenant," as it does in the other 32 places where it occurs in the Greek text. Many modern translations correctly read "old covenant." (*NE, RS, JB*) The apostle Paul is not referring to the Hebrew and Aramaic Scriptures in their entirety. Neither does he mean that the inspired Christian writings constitute a "new testament (or, covenant)." The apostle is speaking of the old Law covenant, which was recorded by Moses in the Pentateuch and which makes up only a part of the pre-Christian Scriptures. For this reason he says in the next verse, "whenever Moses is read."

Hence, there is no valid basis for the Hebrew and Aramaic Scriptures to be called the "Old Testament" and for the Christian Greek Scriptures to be called the "New Testament." Jesus Christ himself referred to the collection of sacred writings as "the Scriptures." (Mt 21:42; Mr 14:49; Joh 5:39)

TABLE OF BIBLE BOOKS IN ORDER COMPLETED

(The order in which the Bible books were written and where each stands in relation to the others is approximate; some dates [and places written] are uncertain. The symbol a. means "after"; b., "before"; and c., "circa" or "about.")

Hebrew Scriptures (B.C.E.)

Book	Writer	Date Completed	Time Covered	Place Written
Genesis	Moses	1513	"In the beginning" to 1657	Wilderness
Exodus	Moses	1512	1657-1512	Wilderness
Leviticus	Moses	1512	1 month (1512)	Wilderness
Job	Moses	c. 1473	Over 140 years between 1657 and 1473	Wilderness
Numbers	Moses	1473	1512-1473	Wilderness / Plains of Moab
Deuteronomy	Moses	1473	2 months (1473)	Plains of Moab
Joshua	Joshua	c. 1450	1473-c. 1450	Canaan
Judges	Samuel	c. 1100	c. 1450-c. 1120	Israel
Ruth	Samuel	c. 1090	11 years of Judges' rule	Israel
1 Samuel	Samuel; Gad; Nathan	c. 1078	c. 1180-1078	Israel
2 Samuel	Gad; Nathan	c. 1040	1077-c. 1040	Israel
Song of Solomon	Solomon	c. 1020		Jerusalem
Ecclesiastes	Solomon	b. 1000		Jerusalem
Jonah	Jonah	c. 844		
Joel	Joel	c. 820 (?)		Judah
Amos	Amos	c. 804		Judah
Hosea	Hosea	a. 745	b. 804-a. 745	Samaria (District)
Isaiah	Isaiah	a. 732	c. 778-a. 732	Jerusalem
Micah	Micah	b. 717	c. 777-717	Judah
Proverbs	Solomon; Agur; Lemuel	c. 717		Jerusalem
Zephaniah	Zephaniah	b. 648		Judah
Nahum	Nahum	b. 632		Judah
Habakkuk	Habakkuk	c. 628 (?)		Judah
Lamentations	Jeremiah	607		Nr. Jerusalem
Obadiah	Obadiah	c. 607		
Ezekiel	Ezekiel	c. 591	613-c. 591	Babylon
1 and 2 Kings	Jeremiah	580	c. 1040-580	Judah/Egypt
Jeremiah	Jeremiah	580	647-580	Judah/Egypt
Daniel	Daniel	c. 536	618-c. 536	Babylon
Haggai	Haggai	520	112 days (520)	Jerusalem
Zechariah	Zechariah	518	520-518	Jerusalem
Esther	Mordecai	c. 475	493-c. 475	Shushan, Elam
1 and 2 Chronicles	Ezra	c. 460	After 1 Chronicles 9:44, 1077-537	Jerusalem (?)
Ezra	Ezra	c. 460	537-c. 467	Jerusalem
Psalms	David and others	c. 460		
Nehemiah	Nehemiah	a. 443	456-a. 443	Jerusalem
Malachi	Malachi	a. 443		Jerusalem

The apostle Paul referred to them as "the holy Scriptures," "the Scriptures," and "the holy writings."—Ro 1:2; 15:4; 2Ti 3:15.

Authorship. The accompanying table shows that about 40 human secretaries or scribes were used by the one Author to record the inspired Word of Jehovah. "All Scripture is inspired of God," and this includes the writings in the Christian Greek Scriptures along with "the rest of the Scriptures." (2Ti 3:16; 2Pe 3:15, 16) This expression "inspired of God" translated the Greek phrase the·o'pneu·stos, meaning "God-breathed." By 'breathing' on faithful men, God caused his spirit, or active force, to become operative upon them and directed what he wanted recorded, for, as it is written, "prophecy was at no time brought by man's will, but men spoke from God as they were borne along by holy spirit."—2Pe 1:21; Joh 20:21, 22; see INSPIRATION.

This unseen holy spirit of God is his symbolic "finger." Therefore, when men saw Moses perform supernatural feats they exclaimed: "It is the finger of God!" (Ex 8:18, 19; compare with Jesus' words at Mt 12:22, 28; Lu 11:20.) In a similar display of divine power "God's finger" began the writing of the Bible by carving out the Ten Commandments on stone tablets. (Ex 31:18; De 9:10) It would, therefore, be a simple matter for Jehovah to use men as his scribes even though some were "unlettered and ordinary" in scholastic training (Ac 4:13), and regardless of whether the individual was by trade a shepherd, farmer, tentmaker, fisherman, tax collector, physician, priest, prophet, or king. Jehovah's active force put the thoughts into the writer's mind and, in certain instances, allowed him to express the divine thought in his own words, thus permitting personality and individual traits to show through the writing, yet at the same time maintaining a superb oneness in theme and in purpose throughout. In this way the resultant Bible, reflecting as it does the mind and will of Jehovah, exceeded in wealth and in scope the writings of mere men. The Almighty God saw to it that his written Word of truth was in language easily understood and easily translated into practically any tongue.

No other book took so long to complete as the Bible. In 1513 B.C.E. Moses began Bible writing. Other sacred writings were added to the inspired Scriptures until sometime after 443 B.C.E. when Nehemiah and Malachi completed their books. Then there was a gap in Bible writing for almost 500 years, until the apostle Matthew penned his historic account. Nearly 60 years later John, the last of the apostles, contributed his Gospel and three letters to complete the Bible's canon. So, all together, a period of some 1,610 years was involved in producing the Bible. All the cowriters were Hebrews and, hence, part of that people "entrusted with the sacred pronouncements of God."—Ro 3:2.

The Bible is not an unrelated assortment or collection of heterogeneous fragments from Jewish and Christian literature. Rather, it is an organizational book, highly unified and interconnected in its various segments, which indeed reflect the systematic orderliness of the Creator-Author himself. God's dealings with Israel in giving them a comprehensive law code as well as regulations governing matters even down to small details of camp life—things that were later mirrored in the Davidic kingdom as well as in the congregational arrangement among first-century Christians—reflect and magnify this organizational aspect of the Bible.

Christian Greek Scriptures (C.E.)				
Book	Writer	Date Completed	Time Covered	Place Written
Matthew	Matthew	c. 41	2 B.C.E.–33 C.E.	Palestine
1 Thessalonians	Paul	c. 50		Corinth
2 Thessalonians	Paul	c. 51		Corinth
Galatians	Paul	c. 50-52		Corinth or Syr. Antioch
1 Corinthians	Paul	c. 55		Ephesus
2 Corinthians	Paul	c. 55		Macedonia
Romans	Paul	c. 56		Corinth
Luke	Luke	c. 56-58	3 B.C.E.–33 C.E.	Caesarea
Ephesians	Paul	c. 60-61		Rome
Colossians	Paul	c. 60-61		Rome
Philemon	Paul	c. 60-61		Rome
Philippians	Paul	c. 60-61		Rome
Hebrews	Paul	c. 61		Rome
Acts	Luke	c. 61	33–c. 61 C.E.	Rome
James	James	b. 62		Jerusalem
Mark	Mark	c. 60-65	29-33 C.E.	Rome
1 Timothy	Paul	c. 61-64		Macedonia
Titus	Paul	c. 61-64		Macedonia (?)
1 Peter	Peter	c. 62-64		Babylon
2 Peter	Peter	c. 64		Babylon (?)
2 Timothy	Paul	c. 65		Rome
Jude	Jude	c. 65		Palestine (?)
Revelation	John	c. 96		Patmos
John	John	c. 98	After prologue, 29-33 C.E.	Ephesus, or near
1 John	John	c. 98		Ephesus, or near
2 John	John	c. 98		Ephesus, or near
3 John	John	c. 98		Ephesus, or near

Contents. In contents this Book of Books reveals the past, explains the present, and foretells the future. These are matters that only He who knows the end from the beginning could author. (Isa 46:10) Starting at the beginning by telling of the creation of heaven and earth, the Bible next gives a sweeping account of the events that prepared the earth for man's habitation. Then the truly scientific explanation of the origin of man is revealed—how life comes only from a Life-Giver—facts that only the Creator now in the role of Author could explain. (Ge 1:26-28; 2:7) With the account of why men die, the overriding theme that permeates the whole Bible was introduced. This theme, the vindication of Jehovah's sovereignty and the ultimate fulfillment of his purpose for the earth, by means of his Kingdom under Christ, the promised Seed, was wrapped up in the first prophecy concerning 'the seed of the woman.' (Ge 3:15) More than 2,000 years passed before this promise of a "seed" was again mentioned, God telling Abraham: "By means of your seed all nations of the earth will certainly bless themselves." (Ge 22:18) Over 800 years later, renewed assurance was given to Abraham's descendant King David, and with the passing of more time Jehovah's prophets kept this flame of hope burning brightly. (2Sa 7:12, 16; Isa 9:6, 7) More than 1,000 years after David and 4,000 years after the original prophecy in Eden, the Promised Seed himself appeared, Jesus Christ, the legal heir to "the throne of David his father." (Lu 1:31-33; Ga 3:16) Bruised in death by the earthly seed of the "serpent," this "Son of the Most High" provided the ransom purchase price for the life rights lost to Adam's offspring, thus providing the only means whereby mankind can get everlasting life. He was then raised on high, there to await the appointed time to hurl "the original serpent, the one called Devil and Satan," down to the earth, finally to be destroyed forever. Thus the magnificent theme announced in Genesis and developed and enlarged upon throughout the balance of the Bible is, in the closing chapters of Revelation, brought to a glorious climax as Jehovah's grand purpose by means of his Kingdom is made apparent.—Re 11:15; 12:1-12, 17; 19:11-16; 20:1-3, 7-10; 21:1-5; 22:3-5.

This Kingdom under Christ the Promised Seed is the means by which the vindication of Jehovah's name will be accomplished. Following through on this theme, the Bible magnifies God's personal name to a greater extent than any other book; the name occurs 6,973 times in the Hebrew Scripture portion of the *New World Translation.* That is in addition to the use of the shorter form "Jah" and the scores of instances where it combines to form other names like "Jehoshua," meaning "Jehovah Is Salvation." (See JEHOVAH [Importance of the Name].) We would not know the Creator's name, the great issue raised by the Edenic rebellion involving this name, or God's purpose to sanctify and vindicate that name before all creation if these things were not revealed in the Bible.

In this library of 66 little books the theme of the Kingdom and Jehovah's name are closely interwoven with information on many subjects. Its reference to fields of knowledge such as agriculture, architecture, astronomy, chemistry, commerce, engineering, ethnology, government, hygiene, music, poetry, philology, and tactical warfare is only incidental to development of the theme; not as a treatise. Nevertheless, it contains a veritable treasure-house of information for the archaeologists and paleographers.

As an accurate historical work and one that penetrates the past to great depths, the Bible far surpasses all other books. However, it is of much greater value in the field of prophecy, foretelling as it does the future that only the King of Eternity can reveal with accuracy. The march of world powers down through the centuries, even to the rise and ultimate demise of present-day institutions, was prophetically related in the Bible's long-range prophecies.

God's Word of truth in a very practical way sets men free from ignorance, superstitions, human philosophies, and senseless traditions of men. (Joh 8:32) "The word of God is alive and exerts power." (Heb 4:12) Without the Bible we would not know Jehovah, would not know the wonderful benefits resulting from Christ's ransom sacrifice, and would not understand the requirements that must be met in order to get everlasting life in or under God's righteous Kingdom.

The Bible is a most practical book in other ways too, for it gives sound counsel to Christians on how to live now, how to carry on their ministry, and how to survive this anti-God, pleasure-seeking system of things. Christians are told to "quit being fashioned after this system of things" by making their minds over from worldly thinking, and this they can do by having the same mental attitude of humility "that was also in Christ Jesus" and by stripping off the old personality and putting on the new one. (Ro 12:2; Php 2:5-8; Eph 4:23, 24; Col 3:5-10) This means displaying the fruitage of God's spirit, "love, joy, peace, long-suffering, kindness, goodness, faith, mildness, self-control" —subjects on which so much is written throughout the Bible.—Ga 5:22, 23; Col 3:12-14.

Authenticity. The veracity of the Bible has been assailed from many quarters, but none of these efforts has undermined or weakened its position in the least.

Bible history. Sir Isaac Newton once said: "I find more sure marks of authenticity in the Bible than in any profane history whatsoever." (*Two Apologies,* by R. Watson, London, 1820, p. 57) Its integrity to truth proves sound on any point that might be tested. Its history is accurate and can be relied upon. For example, what it says about the fall of Babylon to the Medes and Persians cannot be successfully contradicted (Jer 51:11, 12, 28; Da 5:28), neither can what it says about people like Babylonian Nebuchadnezzar (Jer 27:20; Da 1:1); Egyptian King Shishak (1Ki 14:25; 2Ch 12:2); Assyrians Tiglath-pileser III and Sennacherib (2Ki 15:29; 16:7; 18:13); the Roman emperors Augustus, Tiberius, and Claudius (Lu 2:1; 3:1; Ac 18:2); Romans such as Pilate, Felix, and Festus (Ac 4:27;

23:26; 24:27); nor what it says about the temple of Artemis at Ephesus and the Areopagus at Athens (Ac 19:35; 17:19-34). What the Bible says about these or any other places, people, or events is historically accurate in every detail.—See AR- CHAEOLOGY.

Races and languages. What the Bible says about races and languages of mankind is also true. All peoples, regardless of stature, culture, color, or language, are members of one human family. The threefold division of the human family into the Japhetic, Hamitic, and Semitic races, all descending from Adam through Noah, cannot be successfully disputed. (Ge 9:18, 19; Ac 17:26) Says Sir Henry Rawlinson: "If we were to be guided by the mere intersection of linguistic paths, and independently of all reference to the Scriptural record, *we should still be led to fix on the plains of Shinar, as the focus from which the various lines had radiated.*"—*The Historical Evidences of the Truth of the Scripture Records,* by G. Rawlinson, 1862, p. 287; Ge 11:2-9.

Practicality. The Bible's teachings, examples, and doctrines are most practical for modern man. The righteous principles and high moral standards contained in this book set it apart as far above all other books. Not only does the Bible answer important questions but it also provides many practical suggestions which, if followed, would do much to raise the physical and mental health of earth's population. The Bible lays down principles of right and wrong that serve as a straightedge for just business dealings (Mt 7:12; Le 19:35, 36; Pr 20:10; 22:22, 23), industriousness (Eph 4:28; Col 3:23; 1Th 4:11, 12; 2Th 3:10-12), clean moral conduct (Ga 5:19-23; 1Th 4:3-8; Ex 20:14-17; Le 20:10-16), upbuilding associations (1Co 15:33; Heb 10:24, 25; Pr 5:3-11; 13:20), good family relationships (Eph 5:21-33; 6:1-4; Col 3:18-21; De 6:4-9; Pr 13:24). As the famous educator William Lyon Phelps once said: "I believe a knowledge of the Bible without a college course is more valuable than a college course without a Bible." (*The New Dictionary of Thoughts,* p. 46) Regarding the Bible, John Quincy Adams wrote: "It is of all books in the world, that which contributes most to make men good, wise, and happy."—*Letters of John Quincy Adams to His Son,* 1849, p. 9.

Scientific accuracy. When it comes to scientific accuracy the Bible is not lacking. Whether describing the progressive order of earth's preparation for human habitation (Ge 1:1-31), speaking of the earth as being spherical and hung on "nothing" (Job 26:7; Isa 40:22), classifying the hare as a cud chewer (Le 11:6), or declaring, "the soul of the flesh is in the blood" (Le 17:11-14), the Bible is scientifically sound.

Cultures and customs. On points relating to cultures and customs, in no regard is the Bible found to be wrong. In political matters, the Bible always speaks of a ruler by the proper title that he bore at the time of the writing. For example, Herod Antipas and Lysanias are referred to as district rulers (tetrarchs), Herod Agrippa (II) as king, and Gallio as proconsul. (Lu 3:1; Ac 25:13; 18:12) Triumphal marches of victorious armies, together with their captives, were common during Roman times. (2Co 2:14) The hospitality shown to strangers, the Oriental way of life, the manner of purchasing property, legal procedures in making contracts, and the practice of circumcision among the Hebrews and other peoples are referred to in the Bible, and in all these details the Bible is accurate.—Ge 18:1-8; 23:7-18; 17:10-14; Jer 9:25, 26.

Candor. Bible writers displayed a candor that is not found among other ancient writers. From the very outset, Moses frankly reported his own sins as well as the sins and errors of his people, a policy followed by the other Hebrew writers. (Ex 14:11, 12; 32:1-6; Nu 14:1-9; 20:9-12; 27:12-14; De 4:21) The sins of great ones such as David and Solomon were not covered over but were reported. (2Sa 11:2-27; 1Ki 11:1-13) Jonah told of his own disobedience. (Jon 1:1-3; 4:1) The other prophets likewise displayed this same straightforward, candid quality. Writers of the Christian Greek Scriptures showed the same regard for truthful reporting as that displayed in the Hebrew Scriptures. Paul tells of his former sinful course in life; Mark's failure to stick to the missionary work; and also the apostle Peter's errors are related. (Ac 22:19, 20; 15:37-39; Ga 2:11-14) Such frank, open reporting builds confidence in the Bible's claim to honesty and truthfulness.

Integrity. Facts testify to the integrity of the Bible. The Bible narrative is inseparably interwoven with the history of the times. It gives straightforward, truthful instruction in the simplest manner. The guileless earnestness and fidelity of its writers, their burning zeal for truth, and their painstaking effort to attain accuracy in details are what we would expect in God's Word of truth. —Joh 17:17.

Prophecy. If there is a single point that alone proves the Bible to be the inspired Word of Jehovah it is the matter of prophecy. There are scores of long-range prophecies in the Bible that have been fulfilled. For a partial listing, see the book *"All Scripture Is Inspired of God and Beneficial,"* pp. 343-346.

Preservation. Today none of the original writings of the Holy Scriptures are known to exist. Jehovah, however, saw to it that copies were made to replace the aging originals. Also, from and after the Babylonian exile, with the growth of many Jewish communities outside Palestine, there was an increasing demand for more copies of the Scriptures. This demand was met by professional copyists who made extraordinary efforts to see that accuracy was attained in their handwritten manuscripts. Ezra was just such a man, "a skilled copyist in the law of Moses, which Jehovah the God of Israel had given."—Ezr 7:6.

For hundreds of years handwritten copies of the Scriptures continued to be made, during which period the Bible was expanded with the addition of the Christian Greek Scriptures. Translations or versions of these Holy Writings also appeared in other languages. Indeed, the Hebrew Scriptures are honored as the first book of note to be translated into another language. Extant today are thousands of these Bible manuscripts and versions.—See MANUSCRIPTS OF THE BIBLE; VERSIONS.

The first printed Bible, the Gutenberg Bible, came off the press in 1456. Today distribution of the Bible (the whole or in part) has reached over two billion copies in upwards of 1,800 languages. But this has not been accomplished without great opposition from many quarters. Indeed, the Bible has had more enemies than any other book; popes and councils even prohibited the reading of the Bible under penalty of excommunication. Thousands of Bible lovers lost their lives, and thousands of copies of the Bible were committed to the flames. One of the victims in the Bible's fight to live was translator William Tyndale, who once declared in a discussion with a cleric: "If God spare my life ere many years, I will cause a boy that driveth the plough shall know more of the Scripture than thou doest."—*Actes and Monuments*, by John Foxe, London, 1563, p. 514.

All credit and thanksgiving for the Bible's survival in view of such violent opposition is due Jehovah, the Preserver of his Word. This fact gives added meaning to the apostle Peter's quotation from the prophet Isaiah: "All flesh is like grass, and all its glory is like a blossom of grass; the grass becomes withered, and the flower falls off, but the saying of Jehovah endures forever." (1Pe 1:24, 25; Isa 40:6-8) We, therefore, do well to pay "attention to it as to a lamp shining in a dark place" in this 20th century. (2Pe 1:19; Ps 119:105) The man whose "delight is in the law of Jehovah, and in his law he reads in an undertone day and night" and who puts in practice the things he reads is the one who prospers and is happy. (Ps 1:1, 2; Jos 1:8) To him Jehovah's laws, reminders, orders, commandments, and judicial decisions contained in the Bible are "sweeter than honey," and the wisdom derived therefrom is "more to be desired than gold, yes, than much refined gold," for it means his very life.—Ps 19:7-10; Pr 3:13, 16-18; see CANON.

BICHRI (Bich'ri). The Benjamite father or forefather of the good-for-nothing fellow named Sheba who rebelled against David. In this action the Bichrites (Berites, *KJ*) supported Sheba.—2Sa 20:1-22.

BICHRITES (Bich'rites). Apparently descendants of the Benjamite Bichri or members of his family. They supported the insurrectionist "Sheba the son of Bichri" in his rebellion against King David.—2Sa 20:1, 2, 14, 15.

BIDKAR (Bid'kar) [possibly, Son of Deker]. Jehu's adjutant who, "according to the word of Jehovah," threw the body of King Jehoram of Israel into the field of Naboth.—2Ki 9:25, 26.

BIGTHA (Big'tha). One of seven court officials sent by King Ahasuerus to bring his queen, Vashti, before him.—Es 1:10, 11; see COURT OFFICIAL.

BIGTHAN (Big'than), **BIGTHANA** (Big·tha'na). One of two doorkeepers in the Persian palace who conspired against the life of King Ahasuerus. Mordecai learned of the plot, Queen Esther revealed it to the king, Bigthan was hanged, and the incident was recorded in the royal archives.—Es 2:21-23; 6:2.

BIG TREE [Heb., *'e·lah'*; *'e·lohn'*], **MASSIVE TREE** [Heb., *'al·lah'*, *'al·lohn'*]. These Hebrew words are variously rendered "oak," "elm," and "teil tree" in the *King James Version*, also "terebinth" in the *American Standard Version*. However, many authorities acknowledge that these words may have been applied in Bible times simply to big trees in general.

At Amos 2:9 the Amorite people were likened to the cedar for height and to "massive trees" for vigor. These "massive trees" were especially abundant in Bashan, E of the Jordan, and are used in comparisons along with the cedars of Lebanon. (Isa 2:13; Zec 11:1, 2) Oars were fashioned from their wood. (Eze 27:6) Deborah was buried under such a tree at Bethel, resulting in the name Allonbacuth, which means "Massive Tree of Weeping." (Ge 35:8) The location of such trees on hills and high places made them popular places of shade under which false worshipers would engage in idolatrous practices.—Ho 4:13.

Doubtless the massive trees of Bashan included the oak. Renowned for their sturdiness and strength, oak trees live to a very great age. Several kinds of oaks continue to grow in Bashan as well as in the lofty parts of the Hauran, Gilead, Galilee, and Lebanon. Some of them are evergreen, while others are deciduous (that is, losing their leaves each fall). Their fruit, the acorn, is set in a cup and is rich in tannin. It is believed that the color for the "coccus scarlet" material used in the sanctuary (Ex 25:4; 26:1) was obtained from a scale insect that infects the branches of a species of oak.—See DYES, DYEING.

A tree considered likely to be among "the big trees" of the Bible is the terebinth, or turpentine tree (*Pistacia palaestina* or *Pistacia atlantica*). (Ge 12:6; 14:13) It is a common tree in Palestine and has a thick trunk and widespreading branches. Some varieties may attain to heights of as much as 15 m (50 ft), providing excellent shade. By making incisions in the bark, one can obtain a perfumed resin from which turpentine is produced.

BIGVAI (Big′vai).

1. Forefather of some 2,000 "sons of Bigvai" who returned to Jerusalem with Zerubbabel in 537 B.C.E. (Ezr 2:1, 2, 14; Ne 7:19) Later, in 468 B.C.E., more of his descendants made the trip with Ezra.—Ezr 8:1, 14.

2. One listed prominently among those returning to Jerusalem from Babylonian exile with Zerubbabel.—Ezr 2:1, 2; Ne 7:7.

3. One by this name, or a representative of the family group mentioned in No. 1, who attested to Nehemiah's "trustworthy arrangement."—Ne 9:38; 10:1, 16.

BIKATH-AVEN (Bik′ath-a′ven) [Valley Plain of Hurtfulness (Something Hurtful)]. A place or valley plain associated with Damascus and Beth-eden in Jehovah's prophecy through Amos foretelling the exile of the people of Syria. (Am 1:5) In the absence of any record of a Syrian city or town by that name, some scholars connect Bikath-aven with the Beqa′ Valley between the Lebanon and the Anti-Lebanon mountains. The predicted cutting-off of the inhabitants of Bikath-aven evidently came about as a result of Assyrian King Tiglath-pileser III's conquest of Syria.—2Ki 16: 9, 10.

BILDAD (Bil′dad). One of Job's three companions, called the Shuhite; a descendant of Shuah, the son of Abraham by Keturah. (Job 2:11; Ge 25:2; 1Ch 1:32) Taking his second-place turn in the three rounds of debate, Bildad usually followed the general theme set by Eliphaz; his speeches were shorter and more biting, though not to the degree of Zophar's. Bildad was the first to accuse Job's children of wrongdoing and of therefore meriting the calamity that befell them. With misguided reasoning he used this illustration: As papyrus and reeds dry up and die without water, likewise "all those forgetting God"—a statement true in itself, but most erroneous in the intimation that it applied to God-fearing Job. (Job 8) Like Eliphaz, Bildad falsely classified Job's afflictions as those coming upon the wicked: "no posterity and no progeny" for poor Job, Bildad implied. (Job 18) With his third speech, a short one in which Bildad argued that man is "a maggot" and "a worm" and hence unclean before God, the words of "comfort" from Job's three companions came to an end. (Job 25) Finally, Bildad, along with the other two, was divinely instructed to offer a burnt sacrifice and to have Job pray in their behalf.—Job 42:7-9.

BILEAM (Bil′e·am) [possibly, One Swallowing Down]. A town assigned to the Levites of the family of Kohath, given to them from the territory of the half tribe of Manasseh located W of the Jordan River. (1Ch 6:70; *LXX*, "Ieblaam") The listing of Levite cities at Joshua 21:11-39 does not include Bileam, but many scholars believe that a scribal error caused Gath-rimmon to be repeated in verse 25 in place of Bileam. Bileam appears to be a variant spelling of Ibleam, this latter form being more frequently used.

BILGAH (Bil′gah) [Brightening].

1. Head of the 15th of the 24 priestly service divisions when David reorganized the sanctuary service.—1Ch 24:1, 3, 14.

2. A priest who returned to Jerusalem with Zerubbabel in 537 B.C.E. (Ne 12:1, 5, 7) In the following generation the head of his paternal house was Shammua.—Ne 12:12, 18, 26.

BILGAI (Bil′gai) [Brightening]. A priest, or forefather of one, who agreed to the covenant Nehemiah arranged.—Ne 10:1, 8.

BILHAH (Bil′hah).

1. One of the maidservants of Laban's household whom he gave to his daughter Rachel to be her maidservant at the time of her marriage to Jacob. (Ge 29:29) That occurred in Paddan-aram, which was in the northern plateau region of Mesopotamia. When, with the passing of time, Rachel proved to be barren, she gave Bilhah to Jacob as a secondary wife, that by means of her maidservant

Rachel might have children, even as Sarah had done. (Ge 16:2) In this way Bilhah had the privilege of becoming the mother of two sons, Dan and Naphtali, whose descendants formed 2 of the 12 tribes of Israel. (Ge 30:3-8; 35:25; 1Ch 7:13) When Jacob returned to the land of Canaan, Bilhah, together with her children, was personally introduced to Jacob's twin brother Esau. After the death of Rachel, the oldest son of Jacob, Reuben, committed fornication with Bilhah.—Ge 35: 22; 49:3, 4.

2. A town belonging to the tribe of Simeon located within the Negeb region of Judah (1Ch 4:29), evidently the same as Baalah in Joshua 15:29.

BILHAN (Bil'han).

1. First-listed son of Sheik Ezer, a Horite.—Ge 36:20, 21, 27; 1Ch 1:42.

2. Son of Jediael, a Benjamite. Bilhan's seven sons were family heads whose descendants on one occasion numbered 17,200 "valiant, mighty men." —1Ch 7:6, 10, 11.

BILLHOOK. This translates the Hebrew word *ma·'atsadh'*, which denotes a tool used for shaping wood, and even iron. (Jer 10:3; Isa 44:12) The root from which this Hebrew term is considered to be drawn has been linked with words in related languages meaning "reap," "cut off." Consequently Koehler and Baumgartner define *ma·'atsadh'* as "billhook." (*Lexicon in Veteris Testamenti Libros*, Leiden, 1958, p. 550) The modern billhook consists of a handle and a blade with a hook-shaped point. However, others understand *ma·'atsadh'* to designate a kind of ax, since this is its meaning in late Hebrew, and suggest that it may refer to an adz.

BILSHAN (Bil'shan). One of the prominent ones who returned to Jerusalem with Zerubbabel, 537 B.C.E.—Ezr 2:2; Ne 7:7.

BIMHAL (Bim'hal). A head of the chieftains in the tribe of Asher.—1Ch 7:30, 33, 40.

BINDING HOUSE OF THE SHEPHERDS.

A place on the road from Jezreel to Samaria where, by a cistern, Jehu met and slew the brothers of King Ahaziah of Judah. (2Ki 10:12-14) Its name apparently indicates a house where the sheep were bound to facilitate the work of shearing. Some versions render *behth-'e'qedh* as "meeting house," indicating an inn where "the shepherds" (*ha·ro·'im'*) met; others simply transliterate the Hebrew name, viewing it as the name of a town. It is generally identified with Beit Qad (Bet Qad) about 6 km (3.5 mi) ENE of modern Jenin. There are several cisterns at this place.

BINEA (Bin'e·a). A descendant of Saul's son Jonathan; of the tribe of Benjamin.—1Ch 8:33-37, 40; 9:39-43.

BINNUI (Bin'nu·i) [shortened form of Benaiah, meaning "Jehovah Has Built"].

1. A forefather in Israel whose descendants, over 600 in number, returned to Jerusalem in 537 B.C.E. (Ne 7:6, 7, 15) He is called Bani at Ezra 2:10.

2. A Levite who returned with Zerubbabel, 537 B.C.E. (Ne 12:1, 8) Apparently it was his son Noadiah who helped care for the additional temple utensils when Ezra delivered them to the temple in Jerusalem in 468 B.C.E.—Ezr 8:33.

3. One of "the sons of Pahath-moab" who, at Ezra's encouragement, sent away their foreign wives and sons.—Ezr 10:30, 44.

4. An Israelite, several of whose "sons" dismissed their foreign wives.—Ezr 10:38, 44.

5. An Israelite who assisted Nehemiah with rebuilding Jerusalem's wall. (Ne 3:24) This son of Henadad may have been the same as No. 6.

6. One of the Levitical sons of Henadad. Possibly the forefather of one who concurred in the "trustworthy arrangement" in the days of Nehemiah; in which case he could be the same as No. 2. (Ne 9:38; 10:1, 9) If, on the other hand, Binnui himself sealed this agreement, instead of one of his descendants, he could have been the same as No. 5. Or he may have simply been another person with that name.

BIRDCATCHER. A person engaged in the capture of birds. (Pr 6:5; Ps 124:7) Among the Hebrews, this seems to have been done primarily by means of traps, snares, or nets, although other means may well have been used, such as bow and arrow, and sling.

After the Flood, birds, properly bled, were made available to man as food. (Ge 9:2-4) Although the Mosaic Law later proscribed the eating of certain kinds, a great variety of birds were counted as "clean" for eating. (De 14:11-20) Birds caught in hunting were to have their blood 'poured out and covered with dust.' (Le 17:13, 14) In addition to use as food (Ne 5:18; 1Ki 4:22, 23), some of the captured birds, specifically young pigeons and turtledoves, could be used in sacrifices (Le 1:14), and birdcatchers probably supplied some of the doves sold at the temple in Jerusalem during the time Jesus was on earth. (Joh 2:14, 16) Some birds of lovely plumage or attractive song were likely sold as pets.—Compare Job 41:5; 1Ki 10:22.

Traps and Snares. Of the Hebrew terms used to designate traps and snares, two (*moh·qesh'* and pach) are considered to relate primarily to those used by birdcatchers. It has been suggested that *moh·qesh'* ("snare"; Am 3:5) denotes a snare that was operated by the birdcatcher (or a team of them), while *pach* (Job 22:10; Ps 91:3) describes a trap that was sprung automatically upon the bird's entry therein. The bird was drawn into the trap by means of bait or a lure. (Pr 7:23) The Hebrew word for "birdcatcher" (*ya·qush'* or *ya·qohsh'*) comes from the root verb *ya·qosh'*, meaning "lay a snare."—Jer 50:24.

The birdcatcher of ancient times had to study the various habits and peculiarities of each kind of bird and employ clever methods of concealment and camouflage in placing traps. (Compare Job 18:10; Ps 64:5, 6; 140:5.) Because of the placement of their eyes on each side of the head, most birds have a wider range of vision than do humans. Also, some birds can discern objects at a distance that would require the use of binoculars by men. Such vision, added to the natural cautiousness of birds, points up the truth of the proverb that "it is for nothing that the net is spread before the eyes of anything owning wings."—Pr 1:17.

Man, unable to foresee the future and limited in his ability to cope with calamity, is likened to "birds that are being taken in a trap [Heb., *bap·pach'*], . . . ensnared at a calamitous time, when it falls upon them suddenly." (Ec 9:12) The righteous are confronted with subtle snares, hidden traps, attractive lures, and bait placed in their path to draw them into the domain of the wicked who seek to bring them to moral and spiritual ruin. (Ps 119:110; 142:3; Ho 9:8) False prophetesses are condemned for "hunting down . . . souls as though they were flying things." (Eze 13:17-23) However, because Jehovah proves to be with his faithful servants, their "soul is like a bird that is escaped from the trap of baiters. The trap is broken, and we ourselves have escaped." (Ps 124:1, 7, 8) The psalmist prayed: "Keep me from the clutches of the trap [*phach*] that they have laid for me and from the snares [*u·mo·qeshohth'*, feminine plural form of *moh·qesh'*] of those practicing what is hurtful. The wicked will fall into their own nets all together, while I, for my part, pass by."—Ps 141:9, 10.

BIRDS. Birds are warm-blooded, feathered vertebrates and are oviparous, that is, egg laying. There are some 300 references to birds in the Bible, with about 30 different varieties being specifically named. Reference is made to their flight, often in escaping their enemies (Ps 11:1; Pr 26:2; 27:8; Isa 31:5; Ho 9:11); their roosting in trees (Ps 104:12; Mt 13:32); their nesting (Ps 84:3; Eze

31:6); their uses, particularly young pigeons and turtledoves, in sacrifice (Le 1:14; 14:4-7, 49-53) and as food (Ne 5:18), including their eggs (Isa 10:14; Lu 11:11, 12); and God's provision and care for them (Mt 6:26; 10:29; compare De 22:6, 7).

Birds were among the earliest living souls on earth, coming into existence on the fifth creative "day" along with the marine creatures. (Ge 1:20-23) Of the general terms used in the Bible that apply to birds, the most frequent Hebrew word is *'ohph*, basically meaning "flying creature" (Ge 1:20), which may include not only birds but also winged insects. (Compare Le 11:13, 21-23.) The Hebrew *tsip·pohr'* also occurs in a large number of texts and is a generic term applying to birds in general. (Ge 7:14) A third Hebrew term, *'a'yit*, is applied solely to the birds of prey.

The following terms are found in the Greek Scriptures: *or'ne·on*, meaning simply "bird" (Re 18:2); *pe·tei·non'* and *pte·nos'*, both literally meaning "flier." (Ro 1:23; 1Co 15:39; compare *Int.*) At Acts 17:18 Athenian philosophers referred to the apostle Paul as a "chatterer." The Greek word here (*sper·mo·lo'gos*) was applied to a bird that picks up seeds, while figuratively it was used of a person who picks up scraps by begging or stealing, or, as in the case cited, one who repeats scraps of knowledge, an idle babbler.

A thoughtful study of birds gives convincing proof of the Biblical teaching that they are of divine creation. While birds and reptiles are both oviparous, reptiles are cold-blooded, often sluggish, whereas birds are warm-blooded and among the most active of all earth's creatures; they also have an unusually rapid heartbeat. The evolutionary view that reptilian scales and fins eventually developed into feathered wings is both fanciful and baseless. The fossils of birds called by scientists *Archaeopteryx* (or, ancient wing) and *Archaeornis* (or, ancient bird), though showing teeth and a long vertebrated tail, also show that they were completely feathered, had feet equipped for perching, and had fully developed wings. No intermediate specimens, exhibiting scales developing into feathers or front legs into wings, exist to give any semblance of support to the evolution theory. As expressed by the apostle Paul, birds are of a distinct "flesh" from others of earth's creatures. —1Co 15:39.

The psalmist called upon the "winged birds" to praise Jehovah (Ps 148:1, 10), and birds do this by their very structure and their complex design. A single bird may have from 1,000 to over 20,000 feathers. Yet each feather is composed of a shaft from which branch out hundreds of barbs forming an inner web, each barb containing several hundred smaller barbules and each barbule having hundreds of barbicels and hooklets. A single six-inch wing feather of a pigeon is thus estimated to contain some hundreds of thousands of barbules and literally millions of barbicels. The aerodynamic principles built into birds' wings and body design surpass in complexity and efficiency that of modern-day aircraft. A bird's hollow bones contribute to its lightness, and thus the skeleton of a frigate bird with a 2-m (7 ft) wingspan may weigh only about 110 g (4 oz). Certain wing bones of large soaring birds even have trusslike supports, like the struts inside airplane wings, within the hollow portions.

At the time of the Flood, Noah introduced into the ark for preservation pairs of birds "according to their kinds." (Ge 6:7, 20; 7:3, 23) There is no certain way of knowing how many different "kinds" of birds then existed, some types of birds having become extinct even in recent times. However, it is of interest to note that the listing of birds according to present-day scientific classification presented in *The New Encyclopædia Britannica* (1985, Vol. 15, pp. 14-106) gives a total of only 221 bird "families," including some that are now extinct or known only in fossil form. There are, of course, thousands of varieties included within these "families."—See ARK No. 1.

Following the global Flood, Noah offered up "clean flying creatures" along with animals as a sacrifice. (Ge 8:18-20) Birds were thereafter made allowable by God for inclusion in man's diet, as long as the blood was not eaten. (Ge 9:1-4; compare Le 7:26; 17:13.) The 'cleanness' of certain birds at that time therefore evidently relates to some divine indication of acceptableness for sacrifice; the Biblical record shows that, as regards their being used as food, none of the birds were designated as "unclean" until the introduction of the Mosaic Law. (Le 11:13-19, 46, 47; 20:25; De 14:11-20) The factors determining which birds were designated ceremonially "unclean" are not expressly stated in the Bible. Thus, while most of those so designated were birds of prey or scavengers, not all of them were. (See HOOPOE.) This prohibition was lifted following the establishment of the new covenant, as God made evident to Peter by a vision.—Ac 10:9-15.

The identification of the birds specifically named in the Bible presents a difficult problem in some cases. Lexicographers generally are guided by the root meaning of the name, since this is usually descriptive, by indications in the context as to the bird's habits and habitat, and by observation of the birds known to be found in the Bible lands. In many cases the names are believed to be onomatopoeic, that is, imitating the sound produced by the bird.

The diverse topography of Palestine, ranging from cool mountain peaks to deep sweltering valleys and from arid deserts to maritime plains, all together near the SE corner of the Mediterranean Sea, makes it a focal point for a great variety of bird types. Mount Hermon, in the N, is snow-capped for much of the year, while the region about 200 km (125 mi) to the S along the lower Jordan Valley and near the Dead Sea is hot and tropical. Each of these zones contains birds peculiar to its own environment, either alpine or tropical, as do also the temperate zones and the desert regions. (Ps 102:6; 104:16, 17) Additionally, Palestine is on one of the major migrational routes followed annually by birds (storks, turtledoves, quail, swifts, swallows, bulbuls, cuckoos, and others) traveling N from Africa in the spring or S from Europe and Asia in the fall. (Ca 2:11, 12; Jer 8:7) Thus it is estimated that about 470 varieties of birds may be found in Palestine at some time during the course of a year. In view of the deterioration of Palestinian forests and vegetation over the centuries, it is likely that in Biblical times the bird population was even greater.

Particularly notable are the great numbers of birds of prey (Heb., *'a'yit*) found in Palestine, including eagles, hawks, falcons, kites, and vultures. Back in Abraham's time, birds of prey tried to descend upon Abraham's sacrifice of certain animals and birds, obliging him to drive them off until the sun began to set. (Ge 15:9-12; compare 2Sa 21:10.) In their search for food these birds rely on their powerful telescopic sight, rather than on their relatively weak sense of smell.

The well-known sight of a cluster of scavenger birds gathered around a carcass often served as the basis for an ominous warning to an enemy (1Sa 17:44, 46), and repeatedly formed part of divinely inspired prophetic warnings to the nation of Israel and its rulers (De 28:26; 1Ki 14:11; 21:24; Jer 7:33; 15:3) as well as to foreign nations. (Isa 18:1, 6; Eze 29:5; 32:4) Thus, the one used by Jehovah to execute judgment is figuratively represented by "a bird of prey." (Isa 46:11) Desolation of a city or land was depicted by its becoming the habitat of certain birds of solitary nature (Isa 13:19-21; compare Re 18:2) or by the disappearance of all bird life. (Jer 4:25-27; 9:10; 12:4; Ho 4:3; Zep 1:3) The proclamation calling all the birds to gather to feast upon the dead bodies of Gog of Magog and his crowd (Eze 39:1-4, 17-21) is paralleled by that recorded in Revelation in which the bodies of national rulers and their armies become food for "all the birds that fly in midheaven" as a result of the executional work of Christ Jesus as King.—Re 19:11-21; contrast this with God's comforting words to his people, at Ho 2:18-20.

Worship of birds as representing the true God was prohibited to the nation of Israel (De 4:15-17) but was prominent among the pagan nations, particularly in Egypt. (Ro 1:23) Hundreds of bird mummies have been found in Egyptian tombs, principally of birds such as the falcon, the vulture, and the ibis, all of which were sacred among the Egyptians. Egyptian hieroglyphics contain some 22 different bird signs.

BIRSHA (Bir'sha). King of Gomorrah whom Chedorlaomer and his allies defeated in the Low Plain of Siddim.—Ge 14:1-11.

BIRTH. The Hebrew word *ya·ladh'* means "give birth; bear; produce; become father to." (Ge 4:1, 2; 16:15; 30:39; 1Ch 1:10) It is related to *ye'ledh* ("child" [Ge 21:8]), *moh·le'dheth* (birth; home; relatives [Ge 31:13, ftn]), and *toh·le·dhohth'* (history; historical origins; begettings; geneology [Ge 2:4, ftn; Mt 1:1, ftn]). The Hebrew term *chil* (or, *chul*), though used primarily with respect to experiencing labor pains, is used in Job 39:1 and Proverbs 25:23 to refer to giving birth. (Compare Isa 26:17, 18; see LABOR PAINS.) The Greek term *gen·na'o* means "become father to; become mother to; bring forth; be born." (Mt 1:2; Lu 1:57; Joh 16:21; Mt 2:1) *Ti'kto* is rendered "give birth to." —Mt 1:21.

There is "a time for birth," Solomon said, and normally in humans it occurs about 280 days after conception. (Ec 3:2) For parents, the day their baby is born is usually one of great rejoicing, though for the individual, according to wise King Solomon, the day of a person's death, if he has a lifetime of good accomplishments behind him and a good name with God, is even better than the day of his birth.—Lu 1:57, 58; Ec 7:1.

From early times midwives assisted in childbirth. Birthstools of some sort were used as an assistance to the mother and as an aid to the midwife in making the delivery. Such may have been two stones or bricks upon which the mother crouched or squatted during parturition. (Ex 1:16) The Hebrew word translated "stool for childbirth" in Exodus ('ov·na'yim) is related to the Hebrew word for "stone" and occurs only one other time in the Bible (Jer 18:3), where it is rendered "potter's wheels." *The International Standard Bible Encyclopedia* states: "The word is used in both places in the dual form, which points, no doubt, to the fact that the potter's wheel was composed of two discs, and suggests that the birth stool was similarly double." (Vol. 1, 1979, p. 516) Ancient hieroglyphics confirm that such childbirth stools were used in Egypt.

Postnatal procedures, most often performed by midwives, are mentioned at Ezekiel 16:4, though in a figurative sense. The umbilical cord was cut and the baby was washed, rubbed with salt, and then wrapped in swaddling bands. The use of salt may have been to dry the skin and make it firm and tight. Wrapping the baby in swaddling bands from head to foot, as was done with Jesus (Lu 2:7), gave the infant an almost mummylike appearance and served to keep the body warm and straight; by passing the bands under the chin and around the top of the head, it is said, the child was trained to breathe through its nostrils. Caring for newborn infants in this way dates far back into antiquity, for Job was familiar with swaddling bands. —Job 38:9.

After the immediate needs of the mother and child were cared for, the baby was presented to the father, or the news of the birth was announced, and the father acknowledged the baby as his. (Jer 20:15) So too when a maidservant as a substitute had a child fathered by the husband of her barren mistress, the offspring was acknowledged as belonging to the mistress. (Ge 16:2) This is evidently what Rachel meant when she requested that her slave girl Bilhah "give birth upon my knees" so that she might "get children from her." (Ge 30:3) It was not that the delivery was literally to be upon the knees of Rachel, but that she might dandle the child on her knees as if it were her very own.—Compare Ge 50:23.

Either when the baby was born or when he was circumcised, eight days later, the infant was named by one of the parents. If there was a difference of opinion, the father's decision on a name was final. (Ge 16:15; 21:3; 29:32-35; 35:18; Lu 1:59-63; 2:21) The baby was ordinarily suckled by the mother (Ge 21:7; Ps 22:9; Isa 49:15; 1Th 2:7), although it appears that other women were sometimes used. (Ex 2:7) Usually the child was not weaned until it was two or three years old or older. Isaac, it seems, was five; and in his case the event called for celebration and feasting.—Ge 21:8; 1Sa 1:22, 23.

Under the Mosaic Law a woman giving birth to a boy was ceremonially unclean for 7 days, with an additional 33 days required for her purification. If the child was a girl, then the mother was considered unclean for 14 days, requiring 66 days more for purification. At the conclusion of the purification period a burnt offering and a sin offering were to be made for her: a young ram and a turtledove or a young pigeon, or two turtledoves or two young pigeons, as the circumstances of the parents allowed. (Le 12:1-8; Lu 2:24) If the son was the firstborn, he had to be redeemed by the payment of five silver shekels ($11).—Nu 18:15, 16; see FIRSTBORN, FIRSTLING.

Many times the Scriptures use terms relating to natural birth in a figurative sense. (Ps 90:2; Pr 27:1; Isa 66:8, 9; Jas 1:15) The severity of labor pangs well describes inescapable suffering coming from other sources. (Ps 48:6; Jer 13:21; Mic 4:9, 10; Ga 4:19; 1Th 5:3) In a spiritual sense, Jesus said that one must be "born from water and spirit" in order to enter the Kingdom. This involves being baptized in water and begotten by God's spirit, thus becoming a son of God with the prospect of sharing in the heavenly Kingdom. (Joh 3:3-8; 2Co 5:17; 1Pe 1:3, 23) Revelation, in symbolic language, describes the 'birth of a son, a male,' in heaven after a period of agonizing pain.—Re 12:1-5.

BIRTHDAY. The day or anniversary of one's birth; in Hebrew, *yohm hul·le′dheth* (Ge 40:20) and in Greek, *ge·ne′si·a* (Mt 14:6; Mr 6:21).

The Hebrews kept records of the year one was born, as the Bible's genealogical and chronological data reveal. (Nu 1:2, 3; Jos 14:10; 2Ch 31:16, 17) The ages of Levites, priests, and kings were not left to guesswork. (Nu 4:3; 8:23-25; 2Ki 11:21; 15:2; 18:2) This was also true in the case of Jesus. —Lu 2:21, 22, 42; 3:23.

According to the Scriptures, the day the baby was born was usually one of rejoicing and thanksgiving on the part of the parents, and rightly so, for "look! Sons are an inheritance from Jehovah; the fruitage of the belly is a reward." (Ps 127:3; Jer 20:15; Lu 1:57, 58) However, there is no indication in the Scriptures that faithful worshipers of Jehovah ever indulged in the pagan practice of annually celebrating birthdays.

The Bible makes direct reference to only two birthday celebrations, those of Pharaoh of Egypt (18th century B.C.E.) and Herod Antipas (1st century C.E.). These two accounts are similar in that both occasions were marked with great feasting and granting of favors; both are remembered for executions, the hanging of Pharaoh's chief baker in the first instance, the beheading of John the Baptizer in the latter.—Ge 40:18-22; 41:13; Mt 14:6-11; Mr 6:21-28.

While the expression "on the day of our king," at Hosea 7:5, may possibly indicate a birthday party for the apostate king of Israel when the princes "sickened themselves . . . because of wine," it could as easily be the anniversary day of his accession to the throne when similar festivities were held.

When Job's sons "held a banquet at the house of each one on his *own day*" it should not be supposed that they were celebrating their birthdays. (Job 1:4) "Day" in this verse translates the Hebrew word *yohm* and refers to a period of time from sunrise to sunset. On the other hand, "birthday" is a compound of the two Hebrew words *yohm* (day) and *hul·le′dheth*. The distinction between "day" and one's birthday may be noted in Genesis 40:20, where both expressions appear: "Now on the third day [*yohm*] it turned out to be Pharaoh's birthday [literally, "the day (*yohm*) of the birth (*hul·le′dheth*) of Pharaoh"]." So it is certain that Job 1:4 does not refer to a birthday, as is unquestionably the case at Genesis 40:20. It would seem that Job's seven sons held a family gathering (possibly a spring or harvest festival) and as the feasting made the week-long circuit, each son hosted the banquet in his own house "on his own day."

With the introduction of Christianity the viewpoint toward birthday celebrations did not change. Jesus inaugurated a binding Memorial, not of his birth, but of his death, saying: "Keep doing this in remembrance of me." (Lu 22:19) If early Christians did not celebrate or memorialize the birthday of their Savior, much less would they celebrate their own day of birth. Historian Augustus Neander writes: "The notion of a *birthday festival* was far from the ideas of the Christians of this period." (*The History of the Christian Religion and Church, During the Three First Centuries*, translated by H. J. Rose, 1848, p. 190) "Origen [a writer of the third century C.E.] . . . insists that 'of all the holy people in the Scriptures, no one is recorded to have kept a feast or held a great banquet on his birthday. It is only sinners (like Pharaoh and Herod) who make great rejoicings over the day on which they were born into this world below.'"—*The Catholic Encyclopedia*, 1913, Vol. X, p. 709.

Clearly, then, the festive celebration of birthdays does not find its origin in either the Hebrew or the Greek Scriptures. Additionally, M'Clintock and Strong's *Cyclopædia* (1882, Vol. I, p. 817) says the Jews "regarded birthday celebrations as parts of idolatrous worship . . . , and this probably on account of the idolatrous rites with which they were observed in honor of those who were regarded as the patron gods of the day on which the party was born."

BIRTHRIGHT

BIRTHRIGHT. The right that naturally belonged to the father's firstborn son. Both the Hebrew and Greek terms for "birthright" (*bekho·rah'; pro·to·to'ki·a*) come from roots having the basic idea of "firstborn."

Under the patriarchal system, upon the death of the father the oldest son became the head of the family, with authority over the others as long as they were in the household. He was responsible to care for the members of his father's household. He also succeeded to the father's position in representing the family before Jehovah. The firstborn generally received the father's special blessing. (Ge 27:4, 36; 48:9, 17, 18) Moreover, he was entitled to two parts of the father's estate; that is, he received twice as much as each of his brothers. Under the Mosaic Law a man with more than one wife could not take the birthright from the oldest son and give it to the son of a specially loved wife. —De 21:15-17.

In patriarchal times the birthright could be transferred by the father to another son for a cause, as in the case of Reuben, who lost his right as firstborn because of fornication with his father's concubine. (1Ch 5:1, 2) The firstborn could sell his birthright to one of his brothers, as did Esau, who despised his birthright and sold it to his brother Jacob in exchange for one meal. (Ge 25:30-34; 27:36; Heb 12:16) There is no record that Jacob asserted his purchased birthright in order to get a double share of Isaac's property (which was movable or personal property, for Isaac owned no land, except the field of Machpelah, in which was a cave for a burial place). Jacob was interested in passing on spiritual things to his family, that is, the promise given to Abraham concerning the seed.—Ge 28:3, 4, 12-15.

With respect to the kings of Israel, the birthright seems to have carried with it the right of succession to the throne. (2Ch 21:1-3) However, Jehovah, as Israel's real King and their God, set aside such right when it suited his purposes, as in the case of Solomon.—1Ch 28:5.

Jesus Christ, as "the firstborn of all creation," always faithful to his Father Jehovah God, has the birthright through which he has been appointed "heir of all things."—Col 1:15; Heb 1:2; see INHERITANCE.

BIRZAITH (Bir'za·ith). A name in the genealogy of Asher of the family of Malchiel. (1Ch 7:30, 31) Because Birzaith is the only name of those listed in 1 Chronicles 7:30, 31 that is not found in the parallel genealogical record of Genesis 46:17, some consider Birzaith to refer to a site around which the descendants of Malchiel settled, or they think it was an area in which Malchiel was a chief inhabitant, even as Shobal is spoken of as "the father of Kiriath-jearim" and Salma as "the father of Bethlehem." (1Ch 2:51, 52) Supposing Birzaith to have been the name of a place, some would identify it with Birzeit, about 21 km (13 mi) NNW of Jerusalem; but, despite the similarity of the names, Birzeit's location near the southern border of Ephraim (instead of in the territory of Asher) does not lend support to such an identification.

BISHLAM (Bish'lam) [possibly, In Peace]. An opposer of the postexilic temple rebuilding who shared in writing a letter of false accusation against the Jews to Persian King Artaxerxes.—Ezr 4:6, 7; see ARTAXERXES No. 1.

BITHIAH (Bi·thi'ah) [from Egyptian, meaning "Queen"]. Daughter of a Pharaoh and wife of Mered of the tribe of Judah.—1Ch 4:1, 18.

BITHYNIA (Bi·thyn'i·a). A Roman province in the northern part of Asia Minor. It was located in what is now NW Turkey, extending eastward from Istanbul along the southern shore of the Black Sea. On Paul's second missionary journey, after he and Silas had been joined by Timothy at Lystra, they endeavored to travel into Bithynia, but "the spirit of Jesus did not permit them." (Ac 16:7) The area is not mentioned as being the scene of apostolic preaching, but there obviously were Christians there when Peter wrote his first canonical letter about 62-64 C.E. (1Pe 1:1) Pliny the Younger, writing from Bithynia to the Roman emperor Trajan while Pliny was special commissioner, makes mention of numerous Christians in the province, stating that at the beginning of the second century Christianity was not confined to the towns only, but had spread into "villages and rural districts too."—*The Letters of Pliny*, X, XCVI, 9.

BITTER GREENS [Heb., *mero·rim'*]. Along with roasted lamb and unleavened bread, the Israelites were to eat bitter greens or herbs on the Passover night (Ex 12:8), and this continued to be the arrangement in all future Passover celebrations. (Nu 9:11) Nothing specific is stated as to the kind or kinds of bitter greens. The bitter greens were apparently intended to remind the Israelites of the bitterness of the experience during the Egyptian bondage.

The same Hebrew term (*mero·rim'*) occurs at Lamentations 3:15 and is usually rendered "bitterness," or "bitter things," though some suggest "bitter herbs (or greens)" as a suitable translation to correspond to the mention of wormwood in the same verse.

THERE is solid evidence that the Bible, the inspired Word of God, has been accurately copied and transmitted down to us. The evidence consists of ancient manuscripts available today—perhaps 6,000 of the entire Hebrew Scriptures or portions of it and some 5,000 of the Christian Scriptures in Greek.

Original Writings

The original Bible writings were handwritten on perishable materials such as papyrus and vellum; none of the originals are known to exist today

Copies—Hebrew or Greek

Soon after the originals were written, manuscript copies began to be produced. The copyists exercised great care to transmit the text accurately; the Masoretes counted even the letters that they copied

Early Translations

To make the Scriptures available in other languages, Bible translation became necessary. There exist today manuscripts of such early versions as the *Septuagint* (a translation of the Hebrew Scriptures into Greek, from the third and second centuries B.C.E.) and Jerome's *Vulgate* (a translation of Hebrew and Greek texts into Latin, originally produced c. 400 C.E.)

Master Texts

By a comparative study of hundreds of existing Bible manuscripts, scholars have prepared master texts. These printed editions of original-language texts suggest the best readings available while drawing attention to variations that may exist in certain manuscripts. Texts of the Hebrew Scriptures with comparative readings in footnotes have been prepared by such scholars as Ginsburg and Kittel. Included among the master texts of the Christian Greek Scriptures are those published by Westcott and Hort as well as by Nestle and Aland

Modern Translations

Bible translators today generally use original-language master texts to produce modern translations

Hebrew Scriptures

Caves at Qumran,
near the northwest
shore of the Dead Sea,
where many ancient Biblical
scrolls were discovered

Section of Dead Sea Scroll of
Isaiah (dated toward the end
of the second century B.C.E.).
When compared with
the Masoretic text of more
than a thousand years later,
only minor differences were
found, mostly in spelling

Portion of the Aleppo Codex.
Notice that a Hebrew letter
has been raised to indicate
that it is the middle letter of
the Psalms. The marginal
Masoretic note draws special
attention to this letter. Early
scribes counted even the
letters that they copied!

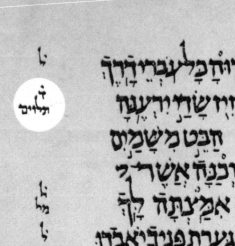

Christian Greek Scriptures

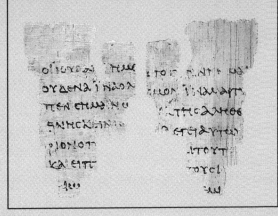

Papyrus Rylands 457 (P⁵²) —both sides of a fragment of the Gospel of John dated to the first half of the second century C.E., only a few decades after the original was written

Sinaitic Manuscript—a vellum codex from the fourth century C.E., containing all of the Christian Greek Scriptures and part of the Greek *Septuagint* translation of the Hebrew Scriptures

St. Catherine's Monastery at Mount Sinai, where the Sinaitic Manuscript was discovered. According to Tischendorf, some leaves of this valuable manuscript were in a wastebasket, waiting to be burned

Comparative study of the thousands of ancient manuscripts provides evidence that the Scriptures have come down to us in reliable form. As Sir Frederic Kenyon said: "The general result of all these discoveries and all this study is to strengthen the proof of the authenticity of the Scriptures, and our conviction that we have in our hands, in substantial integrity, the veritable Word of God."—*The Story of the Bible*, 1937, p. 144.

JEHOVAH—the name of the Sovereign Lord of the universe. It is the name by which he himself chose to be identified. The Tetragrammaton (as the four Hebrew letters of God's name are known) occurs in the Hebrew text of the Bible nearly 7,000 times—far more often than does any descriptive title for God. That name is no mere label. It distinguishes the true God from all other gods, including man-made gods. It is the name that all intelligent creatures should know, honor, and sanctify.

The name Jehovah identifies the Creator of heaven and earth (Ge 2:4), the God and Father of Jesus Christ (Mt 4:10; Joh 20:17), the One who has promised to establish "new heavens and a new earth" in which righteousness will prevail. —Isa 65:17, 25; 2Pe 3:13.

Surprisingly, many Bible translations today do not contain the divine name at all. Why? A superstitious idea arose among the Jews that it was wrong to

יהוה וזהי   𐤉𐤄𐤅𐤄

Various styles in which the divine name was written in Hebrew in times past

pronounce that name. This resulted first in avoiding spoken use of the divine name among the Jews, then in removal of God's personal name from Greek manuscripts of the Holy Scriptures. Eventually, in most translations of the Bible the divine name was completely replaced by expressions such as "Lord" and "God." It is noteworthy that only the most vital name of all—Jehovah—was tampered with; other Bible names were not.

Yet, it is vital for all mankind to know the divine name. (Ro 10:13) This involves much more than just knowing what God's personal name is. It includes knowing also the person represented by the name and living in a way consistent with the purposes connected with that name. It is the responsibility of all who worship the true God to be diligent in making his name known to others, as Jesus did. (Joh 17:6, 26) Jehovah God promises to bless those who know, use, and honor his great name.—Ps 91:14.

Tampering With the Bible. As shown here, the Hebrew manuscript (Aleppo Codex; below, at left) of De 32:3, 6 contains the divine name. The Greek *Septuagint* translation (P. Fouad Inv. 266, in center) of the same passage also contains the divine name in Hebrew characters

But notice that the name does not appear in those verses in the Codex Alexandrinus (above, at right), of the fifth century C.E. The divine name was removed. It was not translated into a Greek equivalent but was replaced with an abbreviated form of the Greek word *Ky′ri·os* (Lord)

Non-Biblical sources point to everyday use of the divine name in ancient times

The Moabite Stone, of the tenth century B.C.E., gives evidence that even pagan nations near Israel knew the name Jehovah

On this fragment of pottery, from Arad in Judah, a letter was written, evidently in the seventh century B.C.E. It begins: "To my lord Eliashib: May Jehovah ask for your peace," and it ends: "He dwells in the house of Jehovah"

In this Lachish Letter, believed to date from the seventh century B.C.E., the name Jehovah, as represented by the Tetragrammaton, is used twice

In 1961 this burial cave was discovered about 35 km (22 mi) southwest of Jerusalem. An inscription on its wall, perhaps from the eighth century B.C.E., declared: "Jehovah is the God of the whole earth"

In these fragments of an early Greek manuscript, God's personal name appears as the Tetragrammaton written in Hebrew characters within the Greek text

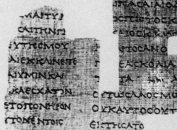

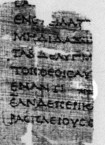

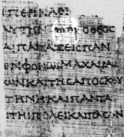

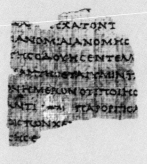

These papyrus fragments of the Greek *Septuagint* (Fouad Inv. 266), from the first century B.C.E., show the Tetragrammaton in portions of Deuteronomy. The use of these four Hebrew letters representing the divine name continued in some copies of the *Septuagint* for centuries thereafter. Thus, in addition to having the Hebrew text of the Scriptures, Jesus Christ and his disciples had the Greek *Septuagint;* both of these contained the divine name. Undoubtedly, then, the original writers of the Christian Greek Scriptures used the divine name, especially when they quoted passages from the Hebrew Scriptures that contained the Tetragrammaton

OVER 4,350 years ago, according to the Bible's historical record, the floodgates of the heavens were opened and a deluge overwhelmed the entire earth. Ungodly, violent humans and all those who were so indifferent that they refused to take note of God's warning were destroyed. The Flood was survived only by righteous Noah and his family, eight persons in all, along with a limited number of each kind of animal life, in a huge ark built at God's direction.—Ge 7:1-24.

The fact that the Flood really occurred is verified by a number of Bible writers. (Isa 54:9; 2Pe 3:5, 6; Heb 11:7) The strongest evidence, however, is the testimony of Jesus Christ himself, who was an eyewitness in the heavens. (Compare Joh 8:58.) He pointedly said: "In the days of Noah, . . . the flood arrived and destroyed them all."—Lu 17:26, 27.

The account of the Flood is far more than a story. Jesus Christ indicated that it has prophetic significance. In his prophecy about "the conclusion of the system of things," he made specific reference to "the days of Noah." He pointed to the Flood as a warning example of a greater destruction to come during "the presence of the Son of man."—Mt 24:3, 37-39.

Could the Ark Have Held All the Animals?

It is true that encyclopedias refer to over a million species of animals. But Noah was instructed to preserve only representatives of every "kind" of land animal and flying creature. Some investigators have said that just 43 "kinds" of mammals, 74 "kinds" of birds, and 10 "kinds" of reptiles could have produced the great variety of species of these creatures that are known today. The ark had about 40,000 cu m (1,400,000 cu ft) of usable space —ample for the passenger list

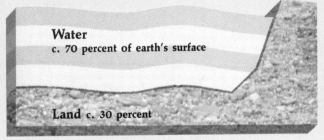

Water c. 70 percent of earth's surface

Land c. 30 percent

Where Did the Floodwaters Go?

Evidently they are right here on earth. Today there is about 1.4 billion cu km (326 million cu mi) of water on the earth. It covers more than 70 percent of the globe's surface. The average depth of the oceans is 4 km (2.5 mi); average elevation of the land is only 0.8 km (0.5 mi) above sea level. If the earth's surface was smoothed out, it would all be covered with water to a depth of 2,400 m (8,000 ft)

Flood Legends

Samples from six continents and the islands
of the sea; hundreds of such legends are known

Destruction by Water
  Divine Cause
    Warning Given
      Humans Spared
        Animals Spared
          Preserved in a Vessel

Australia - Kurnai
Babylon - Berossus' account
Babylon - Gilgamesh epic
Bolivia - Chiriguano
Borneo - Sea Dayak
Burma - Singpho
Canada - Cree
Canada - Montagnais
China - Lolo
Cuba - original natives
East Africa - Masai
Egypt - Book of the Dead
Fiji - Walavu-levu tradition
French Polynesia - Raïatéa
Greece - Lucian's account
Guyana - Macushi
Iceland - Eddas
India - Andaman Islands
India - Bhil
India - Kamar
Iran - Zend-Avesta
Italy - Ovid's poetry
Malay Peninsula - Jakun
Mexico - Codex Chimalpopoca
Mexico - Huichol
New Zealand - Maori
Peru - Indians of Huarochirí
Russia - Vogul
U.S.A. (Alaska) - Kolusches
U.S.A. (Alaska) - Tlingit
U.S.A. (Arizona) - Papago
U.S.A. (Hawaii) - legend of Nu-u
Vanuatu - Melanesians
Vietnam - Bahnar
Wales - Dwyfan/Dwyfach legend

It is of interest that the Chinese
character for "ship" is derived
from the idea of "eight persons
in a vessel." This bears a striking
resemblance to the Bible account
about Noah and his family,
eight persons, who survived the
Flood in an ark (1Pe 3:20)

舟　　VESSEL

＋

八　　EIGHT

＋

口　　MOUTH
　　　(or Persons)

船　　SHIP

Reconstruction of a frozen
mammoth uncovered in Siberia in
1901. After thousands of years,
vegetation was still in its mouth.
Some see in this, as well as in such
other things as marine fossils found
on high mountains, convincing
evidence of a sudden, catastrophic
global flood

ALL mankind descended from the first human pair, Adam and Eve. (Ge 1:28; 3:20; 5:1, 2) After the Flood, earth's new population, including all the races and national groups on earth today, descended from Noah through his three sons and their wives, who were survivors of that global Deluge. Thus, after listing 70 offspring of the sons of Noah, the Genesis account says: "From these the nations were spread about in the earth."—Ge 10:32.

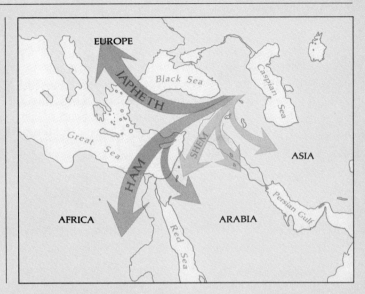

NOAH

Table of the 70 Families After the Flood

JAPHETH
Aryan Branch
of Speech:
Indo-European
(14 families)

GOMER Cimmerians, N of Black Sea
ASHKENAZ SE of Black Sea
RIPHATH Paphlagonians
TOGARMAH Armenians
MAGOG
MADAI Medes, S of Caspian Sea

JAVAN Ionians, Greeks of SE Europe
ELISHAH Near Greece
TARSHISH Pre-Spanish
  in SW Europe
KITTIM Cyprus
DODANIM (RODANIM) Island of
  Rhodes and Aegean Islands

TUBAL Tibareni, in Asia Minor
MESHECH Phrygians
  of Asia Minor
TIRAS Tyrrhenians, of the
  Aegean Islands and Coastlands

HAM
Hamitic Branch
of Speech:
Afro-Asiatic
(30 families)

CUSH Ethiopians in
  E Africa and Arabia
SEBA In E Africa
HAVILAH In SW Arabia
SABTAH In S Arabia
RAAMAH In SW Arabia
SHEBA In SW Arabia
DEDAN In Arabia
SABTECA In S Arabia or Ethiopia
MIZRAIM Egyptians
LUDIM In N Africa

ANAMIM In Egypt
LEHABIM Libyans
NAPHTUHIM In N Egypt
PATHRUSIM In Upper Egypt
CASLUHIM
PHILISTINES Coastal Plain
  of Palestine
CAPHTORIM Cretans
PUT In N Africa
CANAAN W of Jordan River
SIDON Sidonians (Phoenicians)

HETH Hittites
JEBUSITE Around early Jerusalem
AMORITE In Palestine
GIRGASHITE W of Jordan River
HIVITE Central Palestine
ARKITE W of the
  Lebanon Mountains
SINITE
ARVADITE Island off Syrian Coast
ZEMARITE N Phoenician Coast
HAMATHITE N of Palestine

SHEM
Semitic Branch
of Speech:
Asiatic
(26 families)

(With their
descendants
or areas where
they settled)

ELAM SE of Mesopotamia
ASSHUR Assyrians
ARPACHSHAD
SHELAH
EBER In Arabia and Mesopotamia
PELEG
JOKTAN Arabians
ALMODAD
SHELEPH

HAZARMAVETH
JERAH
HADORAM
UZAL
DIKLAH
OBAL
ABIMAEL
SHEBA
OPHIR

HAVILAH
JOBAB
LUD Lydians of Asia Minor
ARAM Aramaeans, Syrians
UZ
HUL Near Armenia
GETHER
MASH Syro-Arabian Desert
  or N Mesopotamia

THE life of Abraham is of great interest to us today. Why? Because it was to him that Jehovah said: "All the families of the ground will certainly bless themselves by means of you." However, for Abraham to enjoy such a role in God's purpose, he had to prove himself to be a man of faith and obedience to God. —Ge 12:1-3; Ac 7:2, 3.

This involved leaving behind his home and relatives in prosperous Ur, never to return. On foot and using primitive transport, he moved some 960 km (600 mi) to Haran. On Nisan 14, 1943 B.C.E., he crossed the Euphrates River and went south. He finally arrived in the heart of Canaan after a journey totaling about 1,650 km (1,025 mi).

At Jehovah's appointed time, among Abraham's descendants, God caused his own Son from the heavens, Jesus, to be born as a human. Through Jesus, the blessing of eternal life was made possible for us.

LOCATIONS ON MAP
With Related Scriptures

Ai	Ge 12:8; 13:3, 4
Beer-sheba	Ge 21:31-33; 22:19
Bethel	Ge 12:8
Damascus	Ge 14:15
Dan	Ge 14:14
Gerar	Ge 20:1-18
Gomorrah	Ge 18:20, 21
Haran	Ge 11:32; 12:4, 5
Hebron	Ge 13:18
Hobah	Ge 14:15, 16
Mamre	Ge 13:18; 18:1-33; 25:9, 10
Moriah	Ge 22:2-18
Negeb	Ge 12:9; 13:1
Shechem	Ge 12:6, 7
Shur	Ge 16:7-12
Sodom	Ge 19:24
Ur	Ge 11:31

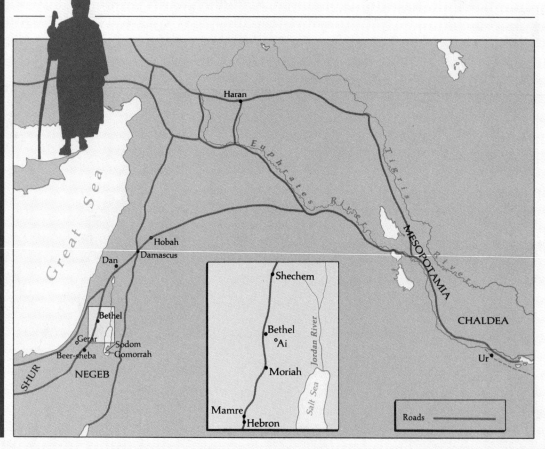

The Euphrates River.
Abraham crossed the
river likely to the
south of here near
Carchemish

Upper Galilee; the land
that Abraham saw as he traveled
south toward Shechem

Mount Gerizim (left) and Mount Ebal
(right) towering over Shechem. In this
valley Jehovah promised Abraham:
"To your seed I am going to give
this land" (Ge 12:6, 7)

Hebron as it appears today. Near here,
Abraham built an altar for worship of
Jehovah (Ge 13:18)

THE land that God gave to ancient Israel includes an extraordinary variety of geographic features. In the north are snowcapped mountains; areas in the south are tropical. Within its borders are productive lowlands, hill country for orchards and the grazing of flocks, as well as areas of desolate wilderness. Here in a relatively small area is a cross section of geographic features of the earth.

Bordering the eastern end of the Mediterranean Sea is a strip of fertile plain. To the east of that is the Shephelah, hilly lowland where vineyards and olive groves flourish. Farther east a mountain range runs the length of the land like a huge backbone. Then the land takes a dramatic plunge into the Rift Valley, which slices the land lengthwise. Through this valley the Jordan River winds its way from the Sea of Galilee down to the Salt Sea. East of the Jordan are fertile hills and grazing lands. Beyond this inviting land, to the east, the Arabian Desert begins.

At its peak, the Promised Land with all its diversity was like the garden of Eden. Israel thus provided a small-scale example of what Paradise under the Kingdom of God will mean for mankind in all parts of the earth.

Headwaters of the Jordan River

Mount Hermon, the tallest in the Palestine area. Its melting snows helped to form dew for the land and water for the Jordan River

Mt. Hermon

Mountains
of
Galilee

BASHAN

T.V. of Yarmuk

Mt. Tabor

Mt. Carmel

Low Plain of Jezreel

GILEAD

Great Sea

T.V. of Jabbok

Mountains
of
Samaria

Jordan River

COASTAL PLAIN

SHEPHELAH

Mt. Nebo

Mountains
of
Judah

Wilderness of Judah

Salt Sea

T.V. of Arnon

NEGEB

The Jordan Valley, through which
the river twists and turns for some
320 km (200 mi) to cover a distance
of 105 km (65 mi) to the Dead Sea

Mount Tabor
rises majestically
above the
Valley of Jezreel

The productive Valley of Jezreel

The Wilderness of Judah. Here David
sought refuge from Saul, and in such a lonely
wilderness the Devil sought to tempt Jesus

Pasturelands in Bashan, east of the Sea
of Galilee—an area noted for its livestock

The Plain of Sharon, where
citrus orchards thrive even now

Northwest shore of the
Sea of Galilee, a view
to the southwest. Note
Mount Tabor in the
background

Salt formations in the Dead Sea,
the saltiest body of water on earth

BITUMEN (bi·tu'men). The same black or brownish mineral asphalt is referred to by three Hebrew words. Two of these describe the difference in hardness: pitch (*ze'pheth*), its liquid form; bitumen (*che·mar'*), its solid state. The third word, tar (*ko'pher*), describes its usage: how it is applied in overlaying woodwork. (See PITCH.) Because of its waterproofing qualities, bitumen's usefulness to man predates the Flood, for Noah, on being instructed to build the ark, was told to "cover it inside and outside with tar."—Ge 6:14.

The papyrus ark in which the baby Moses floated among the Nile reeds was watertight because it had been impregnated with both "bitumen and pitch." (Ex 2:3) The city builders of Babylon learned that bitumen's waterproof characteristics were combined with adhesive qualities that made it a most useful mortar for their kiln-dried bricks.—Ge 11:3.

At one time the Valley of Siddim, located near Sodom and Gomorrah in the Dead Sea area, was noted for its "pits upon pits of bitumen" ("slime-pits," *KJ*). (Ge 14:10) Even today bitumen is occasionally washed ashore, suggesting that Siddim is presently located beneath the waters of the Dead Sea. Bitumen is also a flammable material and is so described by Isaiah, who prophesied that the land of Edom would "become as burning pitch."—Isa 34:9.

BIZIOTHIAH (Biz·i·o·thi'ah). Listed after Beer-sheba as one of the towns in Judah's tribal inheritance in the Negeb region. (Jos 15:21, 28) The location is unknown. The Greek *Septuagint* here reads "their villages" instead of the proper name Biziothiah.—Compare Ne 11:27.

BIZTHA (Biz'tha). One of seven court officials whom King Ahasuerus sent to bring Queen Vashti.—Es 1:10, 11; see COURT OFFICIAL.

BLACK. See COLORS.

BLACK CUMIN. See CUMIN, BLACK CUMIN.

BLACK MULBERRY TREE [Gr., *sy·ka'mi·nos*]. Also called the sycamine, this tree is mentioned but once, in Jesus' statement to the apostles relative to their faith. (Lu 17:5, 6, ftn) The Greek word used was regularly applied to the mulberry tree, and the black mulberry (*Morus nigra*) is commonly cultivated in Israel. It is a sturdy tree growing to a height of about 6 m (20 ft), with large heart-shaped leaves and dark-red or black fruit resembling the blackberry.

BLAMELESSNESS. One Hebrew word rendered "blameless" is *tam*. It is used regarding the exemplary moral standing of Job and concerning the flawless beauty of the Shulammite. (Job 1:1, 8; Ca 5:2; 6:9) By reason of his peaceful, quiet life in tents as contrasted with his brother's wild, adventurous life as a hunter, Jacob was said to be blameless. (Ge 25:27) Another Hebrew word at times rendered "blameless" is *ta·mim'*, having the sense of being "faultless; sound; perfect." (Pr 2:21; 11:5, 20) The Hebrew words *tam* and *ta·mim'* come from the root verb *ta·mam'*, which has the meaning "be complete, completed; come to perfection; come to a finish." (Ps 19:13; 1Ki 6:22; Isa 18:5; Jer 24:10; compare 1Sa 16:11, where the phrase translated "Are these all the boys?" literally means "Are the boys completed?") In the Greek *Septuagint*, the Hebrew word *tam* is sometimes translated *a'mem·ptos*. (Job 1:1, 8; 2:3; 9:20) Forms of this word also appear in the Christian Greek Scriptures and may be defined as "blameless; faultless."—Lu 1:6; Php 3:6; Heb 8:7; see PERFECTION.

When used in describing humans, the term "blameless" must always be viewed as relative, not absolute. Suffering Job drew wrong conclusions about Jehovah, including how the Almighty regarded blameless ones. (Job 9:20-22) Zechariah, the father of John the Baptizer, manifested lack of faith in Jehovah's declaration through the angel Gabriel. (Lu 1:18-20) Still, Job and Zechariah were said to be blameless, for they measured up to what Jehovah expected of humans who, though faithful, were marred by imperfection.—Job 1:1; Lu 1:6.

From the standpoint of his Jewish contemporaries, Paul was blameless before he became a disciple of Jesus Christ. He did what the Law commanded, fulfilling the obligations placed upon him and refraining from what was forbidden. (Php 3:6) But Paul did not then enjoy a blameless standing before Jehovah. He was guilty of grave sin as a persecutor of Christ's brothers and was a blasphemer and an insolent man.—1Ti 1:13, 15.

The Most High takes pleasure in those whose conduct is a reflection of their spiritual soundness, their purity, their blamelessness. (Pr 11:20) So it is vital that Christians live in a manner that is blameless, free from justifiable censure.—Php 2:15; 1Th 5:23.

BLASPHEMY. This is the anglicized form of the Greek word *bla·sphe·mi'a*. The Greek term basically means injurious, defamatory, or abusive speech and was used with reference to such speech whether directed against God or against humans. (Compare Re 16:11; Mt 27:39.) The English word "blasphemy," however, is usually restricted to irreverent or abusive speech against God and sacred things. It is thus the antithesis of words of worship directed to the Divine Being. —See ABUSIVE SPEECH.

In view of the name *Di·a'bo·los* (meaning "Devil" or "Slanderer") given to him, it is evident that the first one guilty of blasphemy was God's original adversary. Though his speech to Eve in Eden was veiled and subtle, it, nevertheless, portrayed the Creator as untruthful. (Ge 3:1-5) Satan has been, therefore, the prime instigator of blasphemy from then till now.—Joh 8:44-49.

The "calling on the name of Jehovah" that started in the time of Enosh during the pre-Flood period must not have been of an upright and proper nature, for Abel long before that had undoubtedly been directing himself to God by the divine name. (Ge 4:26; Heb 11:4) If, as some scholars hold, this calling on God's name was in the sense of misusing it and improperly applying Jehovah's name to humans or to idolatrous objects, then this would constitute a blasphemous act.—See ENOSH, ENOS.

Faithful Job was concerned lest his children had at some time "cursed God in their heart" by sinful thoughts; and, when made to undergo great adversity, Job himself "did not sin or ascribe anything improper to God" in spite of the Adversary's blasphemous attempts to cause him to 'curse God to his very face.' (Job 1:5, 11, 20-22; 2:5-10) Job's three companions, either wittingly or unwittingly, misrepresented God and 'pronounced God wicked,' while insinuating that Job had spoken and acted blasphemously.—Job 15:6, 25; 32:3; 42:7, 8.

Blasphemy Under the Law Covenant. The first three commandments of the "Ten Words," or Ten Commandments, set forth Jehovah God's unique position as Universal Sovereign and his exclusive right to worship, warning also: "You must not take up the name of Jehovah your God in a worthless way, for Jehovah will not leave the one unpunished who takes up his name in a worthless way." (Ex 34:28; 20:1-7) Calling down evil upon God and cursing a chieftain were condemned. (Ex 22:28) Thereafter the first recorded instance of spoken blasphemy was that of a son of mixed parentage who, in a struggle with an Israelite man, "began to abuse the Name and to call down evil upon it." Jehovah decreed the penalty of death by stoning for the offender, and He established this as the due punishment for any future "abuser of Jehovah's name," whether a native Israelite or an alien resident among them.—Le 24:10-16.

Soon afterward the great majority of Israelites became guilty of disrespectful murmuring against Jehovah. As a result, they were sentenced to wander 40 years in the wilderness, and those from 20 years old upward were sentenced to die there. (Nu 14:1-4, 11, 23, 29; De 1:27, 28, 34-39) Their blasphemous attitude brought them to the point of talking of stoning God's faithful servants. (Nu 14: 10) While the abusive speech of Korah, Dathan, and Abiram was actually directed against God's representatives, Moses and Aaron, yet, prior to God's execution of these men and those of their households before their tents, Moses told those observing: "You will then know for certain that these men have *treated Jehovah disrespectfully,*" by disdaining his theocratic appointments.—Nu 16:1-3, 30-35.

Even where there were no spoken expressions against God, one's actions against the laws of God's covenant evidently could amount to "speaking abusively of Jehovah" or a blaspheming of him. Thus, while merciful consideration was given to the unintentional violator of God's law, the individual committing deliberate, willful offenses, whether native Israelite or alien resident, was to be put to death as having spoken abusively of Jehovah and as having despised his word and commandment.—Nu 15:27-31; compare De 31:20; Ne 9:18, 26.

Other acts of blasphemy recorded in the Hebrew Scriptures were those of priest Eli's sons (1Sa 3:12, 13) and that of the pagan Assyrian official Rabshakeh. (2Ki 19:4-6, 22, 23) Innocent Naboth was convicted of blasphemy and put to death on the basis of testimony by false witnesses. (1Ki 21:10-13) In later times, God condemned the false prophets who reassured those disrespectful of Jehovah. (Jer 23:16, 17) Jehovah gave positive warning that his reproachers would be rendered their due reward "into their own bosom." (Isa 65:6, 7; compare Ps 10:13; Isa 8:20-22.) Because of Israel's apostate course, Jehovah's name came under reproach among the nations.—Isa 52:4, 5; Eze 36:20, 21.

In time rabbinic teaching fostered the erroneous view that Leviticus 24:10-23 prohibited as blasphemous the very pronunciation of the name Jehovah. Talmudic tradition also prescribed that when the religious judges heard testimony setting forth blasphemous words supposedly used by the accused, they were to rend their garments, following the example at 2 Kings 18:37; 19:1-4.—*The Jewish Encyclopedia,* 1976, Vol. III, p. 237; compare Mt 26:65.

"Blasphemy" in the Greek Scriptures. The apostle Paul showed the basic meaning of *bla·sphe·mi'a* by using the related Greek verb *bla-*

sphe·me'o at Romans 2:24 when quoting from Isaiah 52:5 and Ezekiel 36:20, 21, cited above.

Blasphemy includes the act of claiming the attributes or prerogatives of God, or ascribing these to another person or thing. (Compare Ac 12:21, 22.) The Jewish religious leaders accused Christ Jesus of blasphemy because he said that the sins of certain persons were forgiven (Mt 9:2, 3; Mr 2:5-7; Lu 5:20, 21), and they tried to stone him as a blasphemer because of his declaring himself to be God's Son. (Joh 10:33-36) When Jesus made a statement to the Sanhedrin concerning God's purpose toward him and the high position to be granted him, the high priest ripped his garments and accused Jesus of blasphemy, for which Jesus was condemned as worthy of death. (Mt 26:63-66; Mr 14:61-64) Having no authority from the Romans to implement the death sentence, the Jewish religious leaders shrewdly changed their accusation of blasphemy to that of sedition when taking Jesus before Pilate.—Joh 18:29–19:16.

Since Jesus was God's Son and direct representative, the things spoken against him may also properly be defined as blasphemy. (Lu 22:65) So, too, since the holy spirit or active force emanates from God and is intimately connected with God's person, Jesus could speak of "blasphemy against the spirit." This is stated to be the unforgivable sin. (Mt 12:31; Mr 3:28, 29; Lu 12:10) Blasphemy is shown to originate within one's heart (Mt 15:19; Mr 7:21, 22); hence the heart condition, manifest in the willfulness involved, must relate to such blasphemy against the spirit. The incident that led to Jesus' statement concerning the unpardonableness of such sin demonstrates that it refers to opposing the operation of God's spirit. This would not be because of deception, human weakness, or imperfection; but the opposition would be willful and deliberate. The Pharisees clearly saw God's spirit at work in Jesus to accomplish good, yet for selfish reasons they attributed this power to Beelzebub, Satan the Devil, thereby blaspheming God's holy spirit.—Mt 12:22-32; compare Heb 6:4-6; 10:26, 27.

Like Jesus, Stephen was martyred on a charge of blasphemy. (Ac 6:11-13; 7:56-58) Paul, as Saul, had been a blasphemer and had tried to force Christians to make "a recantation" (literally, "to blaspheme"). However, upon becoming a disciple himself, he suffered blasphemous contradictions from the Jews, and in Ephesus his teaching was possibly labeled by certain elements as blasphemous against the goddess Artemis. (Ac 13:45; 19:37; 26:11; 1Ti 1:13) By a disfellowshipping, Paul handed Hymenaeus and Alexander "over to

Satan that they may be taught by discipline not to blaspheme." (1Ti 1:20; compare 2Ti 2:16-18.) James showed that the rich, as a class, were prone to "blaspheme the fine name" by which the disciples were called. (Jas 2:6, 7; compare Joh 17:6; Ac 15:14.) In "the last days" blasphemers would abound (2Ti 3:1, 2), as the book of Revelation also foretells by statement and by symbol.—Re 13:1-6; 16:9-11, 21; 17:3.

BLASTUS (Blas'tus). The man in charge of the bedchamber of King Herod Agrippa I. Because of his position of influence, when the people of Tyre and Sidon sued for peace with Herod, they first won Blastus over, perhaps by bribery.—Ac 12:20.

BLEMISH. A physical or moral defect, imperfection; unsoundness; "anything bad."—De 17:1.

The Hebrew word for a physical or moral "defect" is *mum*. (Le 21:17; Job 31:7) The Greek *mo'mos* means "blemish," while the related *a'mo·mos* means "without blemish." (2Pe 2:13; Eph 1:4) Both are related to the root *mo·ma'o·mai*, meaning "find fault with."—2Co 6:3; 8:20.

In contrast with Jehovah, who is 'perfect in his activity ["without blemish (spotless) are his works," *Sy*],' of Israel God said: "They have acted ruinously on their own part; they are not his children, the defect is their own."—De 32:4, 5.

A Levitical priest ministering before the God of perfection, therefore, had to be free from such physical blemishes as blindness, lameness, a slit nose, abnormalities such as an elongated hand, a hunched back, fractured hand, consumptive thinness, eye or skin diseases, a broken hand or foot, and broken or crushed testicles. (Le 21:18-20) Free from such defects, Israel's high priest well represented the Great High Priest Jesus Christ, who is "guileless, undefiled."—Heb 7:26.

Soundness, freedom from blemish, was required of the sacrificial animals under the Mosaic Law. (Ex 12:5; Le 4:3, 28; De 15:21) The same was also true of the sacrifices in connection with the pictorial temple envisioned by Ezekiel. (Eze 43:22, 23) In like manner, Christ, "an unblemished and spotless lamb," "offered himself without blemish to God."—1Pe 1:19; Heb 9:14.

Among persons whose physical appearance is described as having "no defect" were Absalom, the Shulammite girl, and certain sons of Israel in Babylon. (2Sa 14:25; Ca 4:7; Da 1:4) Everyone under the Law was encouraged to watch out for and protect one another, lest they become blemished in any way. "In case a man should cause a defect in his associate, then just as he has done, so it should be done to him. Fracture for fracture, eye for eye, tooth for tooth; the same sort of defect he may cause in the man, that is what should be caused in him." (Le 24:19, 20) The apostle expressed concern over keeping the Christian congregation free from blemishes in a spiritual sense. —Eph 1:4; 5:27; Col 1:22; see also Jude 24.

BLESSING.

A making or pronouncing holy; a request of God for the bestowal of divine favor; bestowing goodness; favor; extolling as holy; glorifying; speaking well of; protecting or guarding from evil; bringing happiness.

The various forms of the Hebrew words generally translated "bless" or "blessing" occur about 400 times in the Scriptures. The verb ba·rakh' is usually rendered "bless." In a few passages the word is rendered "wish . . . well" (1Sa 25:14); "congratulate" (1Ch 18:10); "greet" (2Ki 4:29). The noun form of the Hebrew word is found in the name of the Low Plain of Beracah (meaning "Blessing"), for it was here that Jehoshaphat and his people blessed Jehovah. (2Ch 20:26) A verb of the same form is translated "kneel" or "kneel down."—Ge 24:11; 2Ch 6:13; Ps 95:6.

The Jewish Sopherim, or scribes, emended several passages to read "bless" instead of "curse" (1Ki 21:10, 13; Job 1:5, 11; 2:5, 9), holding the view that it was blasphemous even to note anyone's cursing God.—See NW appendix, p. 1569.

The Greek verb eu·lo·ge'o literally means "speak well of." The term eu·lo·gi'a (literally, blessing) is used in Romans 16:18 in an unfavorable sense, as "complimentary speech" to seduce one's heart.

The Scriptures use "bless" and "blessing" in at least four principal aspects: (1) Jehovah blessing humans; (2) humans blessing Jehovah; (3) humans blessing Christ; (4) humans blessing other humans.

Jehovah Blessing Humans. "The blessing of Jehovah—that is what makes rich, and he adds no pain with it." (Pr 10:22) Jehovah blesses those whom he approves by protecting, prospering, guiding, giving success, and supplying their needs, with a beneficial outcome for them.

Jehovah's goodwill toward his earthly creations was expressed at the time he brought them forth. To the animal kinds created on the fifth day, God's blessing was a pronouncement of his purpose regarding them. (Ge 1:22) God's blessing on Adam and Eve at the end of the sixth day would have enabled them, had they remained obedient, to continue in his favor, because he provided for all their spiritual and material needs.—Ge 1:28; 2:9; 5:2.

After Jehovah had completed his earthly creative work on the six creative days, nothing was lacking for the welfare of his creation. (Ge 1:31) Then God proceeded to rest, or desist from this work, blessing the seventh day, declaring it sacred, holy. Happiness with endless blessing was the prospect set before human creation.—Ge 2:3; Ex 20:11.

When Noah and his family came out of the ark, Jehovah looked with favor on them, blessing them and giving them a statement of his will for them. By doing Jehovah's will, they would prosper with his favor and protection.—Ge 9:1.

Of vital importance to all mankind is the blessing concerning Abraham and his Seed. (Ge 12:3; 18:18; 22:18) Jehovah blessed Abraham and Sarah by miraculously renewing their reproductive powers, enabling them to have a son in their old age. (Ge 17:16; 21:2) He prospered Abraham and used him in a pictorial way to foreshadow greater things. (Ga 4:21-26) Therefore, God's blessing in providing a seed for Abraham has higher significance in the promise that the people of all nations will be blessed by means of the one Isaac foreshadowed, Jesus Christ.—Ga 3:8, 14; Ac 3:25, 26; Heb 6:13-20.

The blessing of Jehovah on a person or a people is contingent upon obedience to him. (Ex 23:25) The sharp contrasts drawn at Deuteronomy chapters 27 and 28 clearly show that Jehovah's curse, resulting in severe punishment, is upon the disobedient ones, whereas his blessing rests upon the obedient ones, producing spiritual prosperity and filling their material needs, making itself evident in their homes, their land, their offspring, their animals, their food supply, their traveling, their every deed. "Blessings are for the head of the righteous one." (Pr 10:6, 7) When Jehovah's people are faithfully obedient, he is pleased to 'open the floodgates of the heavens and actually empty out a blessing until there is no more want.'—Mal 3:10.

Humans Blessing Jehovah. Humans bless Jehovah primarily by praising him. Expressing gratitude, acknowledging Jehovah as the one from whom all blessings flow, speaking well of him on every occasion, and performing acts of adoration and service also bless Jehovah. (Ps 26:12) Preaching the good news is a way of blessing Jehovah, since it praises his name and purposes.—Mt 24:14; Heb 13:15.

Men have blessed Jehovah for delivering his people from oppression (Ex 18:9, 10); for providing their needs (De 8:10); for his dignity, mightiness, rulership, and beauty as Head over all (1Ch 29:10-12, 20); for moving his people to support his worship (2Ch 31:8); in prayer of confession because of his covenant keeping and mercy (Ne 9:5, 31, 32); for giving wisdom and might (Da 2:19-23); for protecting his servants and demonstrating his sovereignty (Da 3:28; 4:34). The book of Psalms constantly blesses Jehovah and calls for all in heaven and earth to praise his name for his many magnificent qualities. Another reason for man's blessing Jehovah is the gift of his Son Jesus Christ.—Ps 16:7; 103:1, 20-22; 145:2, 10; Joh 3:16; compare Ac 2:8-11; Re 7:11, 12; 14:6, 7.

Humans Blessing Christ. Jesus himself is also to be blessed by all. Elizabeth blessed Jesus' mother Mary and the yet unborn fruit of her womb. (Lu 1:42) Jesus' heavenly origin, his coming in Jehovah's name as his Son, his ministry, his sacrifice, his priesthood, his kingship, and his undeserved kindness all justly warrant his being hailed as a blessed one. (Joh 12:13; 2Co 8:9; Heb 1:2; 7:24-26) In fulfillment of Psalm 118:26, the crowd welcomed him as the blessed one of Jehovah on his triumphal entry into Jerusalem. (Mt 21:9) Angelic creatures and earthlings are all to bless him.—Re 5:12, 13.

Humans Blessing Other Humans. In contrast to Jehovah, who always fulfills the blessing He speaks, when a human pronounces a blessing on another human he may not have the ability to fulfill it. In the Bible, man's pronouncement of a blessing often amounts to an appeal for divine blessing, even though not necessarily expressed in a prayer. So while man may be the intended object of such a blessing, the Source is admittedly God himself. Again, man's blessing of other men may often constitute an expression of gratitude, an appreciative acknowledgment of fine qualities or of a job well done.

It is with reference to being able to bless with effectiveness, to have the authority from God to bless or the power to carry out the blessing, that Paul, in arguing the superiority of Melchizedek's priesthood over that of Levi, expresses the principle: "Now without any dispute, the less is blessed by the greater." (Heb 7:7) Melchizedek was a priest of God and a king and could speak for God authoritatively and prophetically in giving Abraham a blessing.—Ge 14:18-20; Heb 7:1-4.

When individuals have done something that contributes to Jehovah's praise, others have seen fit to pronounce a blessing on them. Moses blessed Bezalel and the other workers at their completion of the tabernacle construction. (Ex 39:43) The priests and Levites, as spiritual leaders of Israel, were appointed to bless the people on numerous occasions. (Nu 6:23-27; Le 9:22, 23; De 10:8; 21:5;

1Ch 23:13; 2Ch 30:27) High Priest Eli blessed Samuel's parents for the gift of their child to temple service. (1Sa 2:20, 21) David blessed the people after he had brought the Ark to Jerusalem. (2Sa 6:18; 1Ch 16:2) Solomon wisely followed the same course when he dedicated the temple to Jehovah. (1Ki 8:14, 55) Aged Simeon blessed Jesus' parents. (Lu 2:34) Jesus blessed the children who came to him.—Mr 10:16.

Occasions for Expressing Blessing. In prayer, one praises and thanks God, blessing him, and, in turn, speaks on behalf of those united in faith and those seeking God, blessing them. Saying or asking a blessing upon food before a meal is usually done in prayer. In such prayer thanks and praise are given to Jehovah for his spiritual and material provisions, asking that Jehovah will direct the nourishment to be used for the benefit of those partaking and that the food will strengthen them to serve him. (1Sa 9:13; Mt 14:19; Lu 9:16) In blessing the bread and the wine at the Lord's Evening Meal, praise and thanks are given to God with the request that all partaking may benefit spiritually from the things that these symbolize and may remain in unity and integrity as the body of Christ.—Mt 26:26; 1Co 10:16.

In a patriarchal society a father often blessed his sons shortly before his death. This was a matter of great importance and was highly valued. Thus Isaac blessed Jacob, thinking he was the firstborn Esau. Isaac pronounced favor and prosperity for Jacob ahead of his brother Esau, undoubtedly petitioning Jehovah to carry out the blessing, as Isaac himself was blind and old. (Ge 27:1-4, 23-29; 28:1, 6; Heb 11:20; 12:16, 17) Later Isaac knowingly confirmed and enlarged on the blessing. (Ge 28:1-4) Before dying, Jacob blessed first Joseph's two sons, then his own sons. (Ge 48:9, 20; 49:1-28; Heb 11:21) Similarly, Moses, before his death, blessed the whole nation of Israel. (De 33:1) In all these cases the results prove that they spoke prophetically. In some instances, when pronouncing such blessings, the hand of the one blessing was placed upon the head of the one being blessed.—Ge 48:13, 14.

As a greeting, one's offering a blessing was a wish for the other's welfare. Jacob, on being brought in before Pharaoh, blessed him. (Ge 47:7; see also 1Sa 13:10; 25:14; 1Ki 1:47; 2Ki 10:15.) Blessings might be bestowed at a time of departure. Rebekah, for example, was blessed by her family when leaving home to marry Isaac.—Ge 24:60; see also Ge 28:1; 2Sa 19:39; 1Ki 8:66.

Giving a gift was also associated with blessings. (Ge 33:11; Jos 14:13; 15:18, 19) Understandably the gift itself might come to be called the blessing, "a gift blessing." Gifts might be offered as expressions of well-wishing toward a loved one, in an endeavor to find favor, or as an expression of gratitude.—1Sa 25:27; 30:26.

Blessings can be bestowed in the form of compliments. Boaz blessed Ruth for her lovingkindness. (Ru 3:10) Men volunteering to perform a service in behalf of Jehovah's worship were blessed by observers. (Ne 11:2) Parents are entitled to blessing from their children.—Pr 30:11.

A blessing can consist of favorable or upbuilding speech. Jesus admonished his hearers "to bless those cursing" them. (Lu 6:28) "Keep on blessing those who persecute; be blessing and do not be cursing." (Ro 12:14) This does not mean to praise opposers, but good conduct toward such ones, coupled with kind, considerate, truthful speech that would be beneficial to them if heeded, may result in winning their goodwill. (1Co 4:12; 1Pe 3:9) The manner of speaking must also be considered. (Pr 27:14) To turn someone away from wicked deeds is indeed a blessing, working for that person's best interests and to Jehovah's praise. —Ac 3:26.

Being a Blessing to Others. A person can be a blessing to his fellowman by following a course of obedience to God. The association of such ones whom Jehovah blesses brings blessings to others. Laban was blessed because Jacob kept his flocks. (Ge 30:27, 30) Potiphar's household and field prospered because of Joseph's oversight. (Ge 39:5) The presence of ten righteous citizens could have caused God to spare Sodom. (Ge 18:32) The dedicated servant of God can bring God's favorable consideration to an unbelieving mate and their young children. (1Co 7:14) Jesus said that, in the world's time of greatest tribulation, "on account of the chosen ones those days will be cut short," otherwise "no flesh would be saved." (Mt 24:21, 22; compare Isa 65:8.) To imitate the example of God's blessed ones brings even greater blessings. (Ga 3:9; Heb 13:7; 1Co 11:1; 2Th 3:7) Doing good to Christ's brothers, God's "chosen ones," brings Jehovah's blessings to "the sheep," with the reward of everlasting life.—Mt 25:31-34, 40, 46.

BLINDNESS. The Hebrew and Greek words for "blind" are 'iw·wer' and ty·phlos', both being used in a literal and a figurative sense.—De 27:18; Isa 56:10; Mt 15:30; 23:16.

Blindness appears to have been quite a common affliction in the ancient Middle East. Besides a sizable number of references to it in the Bible, secular writings, such as the Ebers Papyrus from Egypt, frequently refer to the condition, describ-

ing several forms of it and its symptoms, prescribing eyewashes, and naming some of the surgical instruments used. Israel's law of retaliation, requiring soul for soul, *eye* for *eye*, tooth for tooth, hand for hand, foot for foot, not only emphasized the sanctity of life but also impressed strongly upon the Israelites the need for extraordinary care to avoid doing injury to another. It also emphasized the need for people to be sure that any testimony they presented in court was true and accurate, since the person bearing false testimony would suffer the very punishment he would have brought on an innocent person. (Ex 21:23, 24; De 19:18-21; Le 24:19, 20) If a master caused his slave to lose an eye, the master did not have one of his own eyes put out, but the slave was set free. (Ex 21:26) While slaves could be required to work and could be beaten if rebellious, yet the master was thereby kept conscious of the need to refrain from being unduly severe.

It was a common practice of the Assyrians and Babylonians to put out the eyes of those whom they defeated in warfare. Samson was blinded by the Philistines, and King Zedekiah by Nebuchadnezzar. (Jg 16:21; 2Ki 25:7; Jer 39:7) Nahash, the king of the Ammonites, said that he would accept the surrender of the city of Jabesh in Gilead "on the condition of boring out every right eye of yours, and I must put it as a reproach upon all Israel."—1Sa 11:2; see NAHASH No. 1.

The Bible records several cases of blindness from senility or old age, where the eyes were not diseased but were "dim" or "set." Because of it, Isaac was led to bestow the blessing on the deserving one, Jacob. High Priest Eli began to lose his vision sometime before his death at the age of 98 years. Jeroboam's wife schemed to take advantage of the aged prophet Ahijah's blindness, but Jehovah thwarted the plot. (Ge 27:1; 1Sa 3:2; 4:14-18; 1Ki 14:4, 5) However, at the advanced age of 120 years it is reported of Moses that "his eye had not grown dim."—De 34:7.

Jehovah, who made the eye, can also bring about blindness. (Ex 4:11) He warned the nation of Israel that if they rejected his statutes and violated his covenant he would bring upon them burning fever, causing the eyes to fail. (Le 26:15, 16; De 28:28) The wicked men of Sodom and the sorcerer Elymas were struck with blindness. (Ge 19:11; Ac 13:11) Saul of Tarsus was blinded by the brilliance of the light when Jesus appeared to him "as if to one born prematurely." He regained sight when Ananias laid his hands on him, and "there fell from his eyes what looked like scales." (1Co 15:8; Ac 9:3, 8, 9, 12, 17, 18) In a prophetic utterance by the prophet Zechariah, Jehovah points out that the horses of those who come against Jerusalem will be struck with loss of sight (Zec 12:4) and that in the day belonging to Jehovah all the peoples that will actually do military service against Jerusalem will experience a scourge in which their very eyes will "rot away in their sockets."—Zec 14:1, 12.

The blindness that was brought on the military force of the Syrians at the word of Elisha was evidently mental blindness. If the entire army had been struck with physical blindness, they would all have had to be led by hand. But the account simply says that Elisha told them: "This is not the way, and this is not the city. Follow me." On this phenomenon William James in his *Principles of Psychology* (1981, Vol. 1, p. 59) states: "A most interesting effect of cortical disorder is *mental blindness*. This consists not so much in insensibility to optical impressions, as in *inability to understand them*. Psychologically it is interpretable as *loss of associations* between optical sensations and what they signify; and any interruption of the paths between the optic centres and the centres for other ideas ought to bring it about." This was apparently the kind of blindness removed by Jehovah when the Syrian army reached Samaria. (2Ki 6:18-20) Such mental blindness also may have been involved in the case of the men of Sodom, since the account shows that, instead of being distressed at loss of the faculty of sight, they persisted in trying to find the door of Lot's house. —Ge 19:11.

Blindness disqualified a man from serving as a priest at Jehovah's sanctuary. (Le 21:17, 18, 21-23) The sacrifice of an animal that was blind was also unacceptable to Jehovah. (De 15:21; Mal 1:8) But Jehovah's law reflected consideration and sympathy for the blind. The one who put an obstacle in the way of a blind man or misled him was cursed. (Le 19:14; De 27:18) God's righteous servant Job said: "Eyes I became to the blind one." (Job 29:15) Jehovah himself indicates that in time he will do away with blindness.—Isa 35:5.

When Jesus Christ was on earth he miraculously restored the sight of many blind persons. (Mt 11:5; 15:30, 31; 21:14; Lu 7:21, 22) When Jesus was near Jericho he cured blind Bartimaeus and his companion. (Mt 20:29-34; Mr 10:46-52; Lu 18:35-43) On another occasion he healed two blind men at the same time. (Mt 9:27-31) Again he cured a demon-possessed man who was both blind and unable to speak. (Mt 12:22; compare Lu 11:14.) One man's sight was restored gradually. This may have been to enable the man so used to being in darkness to accommodate his eyes to the brilliance of sunlight. (Mr 8:22-26) Another man blind from birth, on having his sight restored, became a believer in Jesus. (Joh 9:1, 35-38) In the latter two cases Jesus used saliva or saliva mixed with clay, but this purported resemblance to folk remedies does not diminish the miraculous aspect of the healings. In the case of the man blind from birth, he was told to go wash in the Pool of Siloam before he received his sight. (Joh 9:7) This was undoubtedly for a test of his faith, just as Naaman was required to bathe in the Jordan River before he was freed from his leprosy.—2Ki 5:10-14.

Figurative Uses. Many times the groping about of the blind serves as an illustration of helplessness. (De 28:29; La 4:14; Isa 59:10; Zep 1:17; Lu 6:39) The Jebusites were so confident that their citadel was impregnable that they taunted David, saying their own feeble blind, weak though they were, could defend the fortress of Zion against Israel.—2Sa 5:6, 8.

Miscarriage of justice through judicial corruption was symbolized by blindness, and many are the exhortations in the Law against bribery, gifts, or prejudice, as such things can blind a judge and prevent the impartial administration of justice. "The bribe blinds clear-sighted men." (Ex 23:8) "The bribe blinds the eyes of wise ones." (De 16:19) A judge, no matter how upright and discerning, may be consciously or even unconsciously affected by a gift from those involved in the case. God's law thoughtfully considers the blinding effect not only of a gift but also of sentiment, as it states: "You must not treat the lowly with partiality, and you must not prefer the person of a great one." (Le 19:15) So, for sentimentality or for popularity with the crowd, a judge was not to render his verdict against the rich merely because they were rich.—Ex 23:2, 3.

Spiritual Blindness. The Bible attributes far greater importance to spiritual sight than to the physical. Jesus used the occasion of healing the man blind from birth to point out the reprehensibility of the Pharisees because they professed to be those with spiritual sight and willfully refused to come out of their blind condition. They were like those who loved darkness rather than light. (Joh 9:39-41; 3:19, 20) The apostle Paul spoke to the Ephesian congregation about having the eyes of their heart enlightened. (Eph 1:16, 18) Jesus points out that those who profess to be Christians but who are not conscious of their spiritual need are blind and naked, not discerning their pitiful, groping condition. (Re 3:17) Just as being in darkness for a long period of time will cause blindness to the natural eyes, the apostle John points out that a Christian who hates his brother is walking aimlessly in a blinding darkness (1Jo 2:11); and Peter warns that one not developing Christian fruitage, the greatest of which is love, is "blind, shutting his eyes to the light." (2Pe 1:5-9) The source of such darkness and spiritual blindness is Satan the Devil, who, transforming himself into an angel of light, actually is "the god of this system of things" and the god of darkness who has blinded the minds of the unbelievers so that they do not discern the good news about the Christ.—Lu 22: 53; 2Co 4:4; 11:14, 15.

BLOOD.   A truly marvelous fluid that circulates in the vascular system of humans and most multicelled animals; in Hebrew, *dam,* and in Greek, *hai'ma.* Blood supplies nourishment and oxygen to all parts of the body, carries away waste products, and plays a major role in safeguarding the body against infection. The chemical makeup of blood is so exceedingly complex that there is a great deal that is still unknown to scientists.

In the Bible, the soul is said to be in the blood because blood is so intimately involved in the life processes. God's Word says: "For the soul of the flesh is in the blood, and I myself have put it upon the altar for you to make atonement for your souls, because it is the blood that makes atonement by the soul in it." (Le 17:11) For like reason, but making the connection even more direct, the Bible says: "The soul of every sort of flesh is its blood." (Le 17:14) Clearly, God's Word treats both life and blood as sacred.

Taking Life.   With Jehovah is the source of life. (Ps 36:9) Man cannot give back a life that he takes. "All the souls—to me they belong," says Jehovah. (Eze 18:4) Therefore, to take life is to take Jehovah's property. Every living thing has a purpose and a place in God's creation. No man has the right to take life except when God permits and in the way that he instructs.

After the Flood, Noah and his sons, the progenitors of all persons alive today, were commanded to show respect for the life, the blood, of fellowmen. (Ge 9:1, 5, 6) Also, God kindly allowed them to add animal flesh to their diet. However, they had to acknowledge that the life of any animal killed for food belonged to God, doing so by pouring its blood out as water on the ground. This was like giving it back to God, not using it for one's own purposes.—De 12:15, 16.

Man was entitled to enjoy the life that God granted him, and anyone who deprived him of that life would be answerable to God. This was shown when God said to the murderer Cain: "Your brother's blood is crying out to me from the ground." (Ge 4:10) Even a person hating his brother, and so wishing him dead, or slandering him or bearing false witness against him, and so endangering his life, would bring guilt upon himself in connection with the blood of his fellowman.—Le 19:16; De 19:18-21; 1Jo 3:15.

Because of God's view of the value of life, the blood of a murdered person is said to defile the earth, and such defilement can be cleansed only by shedding the blood of the murderer. On this basis the Bible authorizes capital punishment for murder, through duly constituted authority. (Nu 35:33; Ge 9:5, 6) In ancient Israel no ransom could be taken to deliver the deliberate murderer from the death penalty.—Nu 35:19-21, 31.

Even in cases where the manslayer could not be found on investigation, the city nearest the site where the body was found was counted bloodguilty. To remove the bloodguilt, the responsible city elders had to perform the procedure required by God, had to disclaim any guilt or knowledge of the murder, and had to pray to God for his mercy. (De 21:1-9) If an accidental manslayer was not seriously concerned over the taking of a life and did not follow God's arrangement for his protection by fleeing to the city of refuge and remaining there, the dead man's nearest of kin was the avenger authorized and obligated to kill him in order to remove bloodguilt from the land.—Nu 35:26, 27; see AVENGER OF BLOOD.

Proper Use of Blood.   There was only one use of blood that God ever approved, namely, for sacrifice. He directed that those under the Mosaic Law offer animal sacrifices to make atonement for sin. (Le 17:10, 11) It was also in harmony with His will that His Son, Jesus Christ, offered up his perfect human life as a sacrifice for sins.—Heb 10:5, 10.

The lifesaving application of Christ's blood was prefigured in a variety of ways in the Hebrew Scriptures. At the time of the first Passover, in Egypt, the blood on the upper part of the doorway and on the doorposts of the Israelite homes protected the firstborn inside from death at the hand of God's angel. (Ex 12:7, 22, 23; 1Co 5:7) The Law covenant, which had a typical sin-removing feature, was validated by the blood of animals. (Ex 24:5-8) The numerous blood sacrifices, particularly those offered on the Day of Atonement, were for typical sin atonement, pointing to the real sin removal by the sacrifice of Christ.—Le 16:11, 15-18.

The legal power that blood has in God's sight as accepted by him for atonement purposes was illustrated by the pouring of blood at the base, or foundation, of the altar and the putting of it on the horns of the altar. The atonement arrangement had its basis, or foundation, in blood, and the power (represented by horns) of the sacrificial arrangement rested in blood.—Le 9:9; Heb 9:22; 1Co 1:18.

Under the Christian arrangement, the sanctity of blood was even more strongly emphasized. No longer was animal blood to be offered, for those animal offerings were only a shadow of the reality, Jesus Christ. (Col 2:17; Heb 10:1-4, 8-10) The high priest in Israel used to take a token portion of the blood into the Most Holy of the earthly sanctuary. (Le 16:14) Jesus Christ as the real High Priest entered into heaven itself, not with his blood, which was poured out on the ground (Joh 19:34), but with the value of his perfect human life as represented by blood. This life right he never forfeited by sin, but he retained it as usable for sin atonement. (Heb 7:26; 8:3; 9:11, 12) For these reasons the blood of Christ cries out for better things than the blood of righteous Abel did. Only the blood of the perfect sacrifice of the Son of God can call for mercy, while the blood of Abel as well as the blood of martyred followers of Christ cries out for vengeance.—Heb 12:24; Re 6:9-11.

To whom does the prohibition on the eating of blood apply?

Noah and his sons were allowed by Jehovah to add animal flesh to their diet after the Flood, but they were strictly commanded not to eat blood. (Ge 9:1, 3, 4) God here set out a regulation that applied, not merely to Noah and his immediate family, but to all mankind from that time on, because all those living since the Flood are descendants of Noah's family.

Concerning the permanence of this prohibition, Joseph Benson noted: "It ought to be observed, that this prohibition of eating blood, given to Noah and all his posterity, and repeated to the Israelites, in a most solemn manner, under the Mosaic dispensation, has never been revoked, but, on the contrary, has been confirmed under the New Testament, Acts xv.; and thereby made of perpetual obligation."—Benson's *Notes*, 1839, Vol. I, p. 43.

Under the Mosaic Law. In the Law covenant made by Jehovah with the nation of Israel, he incorporated the law given to Noah. He made it clear that "bloodguilt" was attached to anyone who ignored the procedure stipulated by God's law even in the killing of an animal. (Le 17:3, 4) The blood of an animal to be used for food was to be poured out on the ground and covered with dust. (Le 17:13, 14) Anyone who ate blood of *any sort* of flesh was to be 'cut off from among his people.' Deliberate violation of this law regarding the sacredness of blood meant being "cut off" in death.—Le 17:10; 7:26, 27; Nu 15:30, 31.

Commenting on Leviticus 17:11, 12, M'Clintock and Strong's *Cyclopædia* (1882, Vol. I, p. 834) says: "This strict injunction not only applied to the Israelites, but even to the strangers residing among them. The penalty assigned to its transgression was the being 'cut off from the people,' by which the punishment of death appears to be intended (comp. Heb. x, 28), although it is difficult to ascertain whether it was inflicted by the sword or by stoning."

At Deuteronomy 14:21 allowance was made for selling to an alien resident or a foreigner an animal that had died of itself or that had been torn by a beast. Thus a distinction was made between the blood of such animals and that of animals that a person slaughtered for food. (Compare Le 17:14-16.) The Israelites, as well as alien residents who took up true worship and came under the Law covenant, were obligated to live up to the lofty requirements of that Law. People of all nations were bound by the requirement at Genesis 9:3, 4, but those under the Law were held by God to a higher standard in adhering to that requirement than were foreigners and alien residents who had not become worshipers of Jehovah.

Under the Christian arrangement. The governing body of the first-century Christian congregation, under the direction of the holy spirit, ruled on the matter of blood. Their decree states: "For the holy spirit and we ourselves have favored adding no further burden to you, except these necessary things, to keep abstaining from things sacrificed to idols and from blood and from things strangled and from fornication. If you carefully keep yourselves from these things, you will prosper. Good health to you!" (Ac 15:22, 28, 29) The prohibition included flesh with the blood in it ("things strangled").

This decree rests, ultimately, on God's command not to eat blood, as given to Noah and his sons and, therefore, to all mankind. In this regard, the following is found in *The Chronology of Antient Kingdoms Amended*, by Sir Isaac Newton (Dublin, 1728, p. 184): "This law [of abstaining from blood] was ancienter than the days of *Moses*, being given to *Noah* and his sons, long before the days of *Abraham*: and therefore when the

Apostles and Elders in the Council at *Jerusalem* declared that the Gentiles were not obliged to be circumcised and keep the law of *Moses,* they excepted this law of *abstaining from blood, and things strangled,* as being an earlier law of God, imposed not on the sons of *Abraham* only, but on all nations, while they lived together in *Shinár* under the dominion of *Noah:* and of the same kind is the law of *abstaining from meats offered to Idols or false Gods, and from fornication."*—Italics his.

Observed since apostolic times. The Jerusalem council sent its decision to the Christian congregations to be observed. (Ac 16:4) About seven years after the Jerusalem council issued the decree, Christians continued to comply with the "decision that they should keep themselves from what is sacrificed to idols as well as from blood and what is strangled and from fornication." (Ac 21:25) And more than a hundred years later, in 177 C.E., in Lyons (now in France), when religious enemies falsely accused Christians of eating children, a woman named Biblis said: "How would such men eat children, when they are not allowed to eat the blood even of irrational animals?"—*The Ecclesiastical History,* by Eusebius, V, I, 26.

Early Christians abstained from eating any sort of blood. In this regard Tertullian (c. 160-230 C.E.) pointed out in his work *Apology* (IX, 13, 14): "Let your error blush before the Christians, for we do not include even animals' blood in our natural diet. We abstain on that account from things strangled or that die of themselves, that we may not in any way be polluted by blood, even if it is buried in the meat. Finally, when you are testing Christians, you offer them sausages full of blood; you are thoroughly well aware, of course, that among them it is forbidden; but you want to make them transgress." Minucius Felix, a Roman lawyer who lived until about 250 C.E., made the same point, writing: "For us it is not permissible either to see or to hear of human slaughter; we have such a shrinking from human blood that at our meals we avoid the blood of animals used for food."—*Octavius,* XXX, 6.

Integrity Involved. From the time that the new covenant was inaugurated over the blood of Jesus Christ, Christians have recognized the life-giving value of this blood through Jehovah's arrangement and through Jesus as the great High Priest who "entered, no, not with the blood of goats and of young bulls, but with his own blood, once for all time into the holy place and obtained an everlasting deliverance for us." Through faith in the blood of Christ, Christians have had their consciences cleansed from dead works so that they may render sacred service to the living God. They are concerned about their physical health, but they are primarily and far more seriously concerned with their spiritual health and their standing before the Creator. They want to maintain their integrity to the living God, not denying the sacrifice of Jesus, not counting it as of no value, and not trampling it underfoot. For they are seeking, not the life that is transitory, but everlasting life.—Heb 9:12, 14, 15; 10:28, 29.

BLOODGUILT. At times the Hebrew word for "blood" (*dam;* plural, *da·mim'*) refers to guilt incurred by the shedding of innocent blood and is thus rendered "bloodguilt."—Ex 22:2, ftn; 1Ki 2: 37, ftn.

"Hands that are shedding innocent blood" have been one of the most detestable things to Jehovah ever since righteous Abel's blood cried out from the ground. (Pr 6:16, 17; Ge 4:10; Ps 5:6) Men also have long been aware of the sacredness of blood; when Noah and his family came out of the ark they were informed of the dire consequences befalling those upon whom there was bloodguilt. —Ge 9:6; 37:21, 22; 42:22.

In due time laws were published, spelling out what constituted crimes worthy of death, and in this way, everyone could avoid doing that which would bring bloodguilt upon his own head. Other legislation was enacted as preventive safeguard to protect people from spilling innocent blood. Parapets had to be built around the edge of the flat-topped houses so people would not fall off. (De 22:8) A man had to provide safeguards to prevent his bull from goring people. (Ex 21:29) If a thief was killed while breaking in at night, there was no bloodguilt; but if he was killed during the daylight, it was a different matter. (Ex 22:2, 3) Cities of refuge were set up to protect the accidental manslayer from the avenger of blood. (Nu 35:25; De 19:9, 10; Jos 20:2, 3; see AVENGER OF BLOOD.) If Ezekiel failed in his duty as a watchman to Israel, the blood of the inhabitants would be upon him. (Eze 3:18, 20; 33:6, 8) With this in mind we find understandable what the apostle Paul meant when he said that he was innocent of bloodguilt. —Ac 18:6; 20:26.

The Bible lists both those that were free of bloodguilt and those that were not free of it, and these well serve as warning examples. There was Saul, who at one time escaped bloodguilt because he refrained from killing David; yet later Saul brought bloodguilt upon his whole household when he foolishly killed off some of the Gibeonites. (1Sa 19:5, 6; 2Sa 21:1) There were others too that in various ways became bloodguilty. (Jg 9:24; 2Sa 1:16; 4:6-12) David, on the other hand, escaped such guilt when he heeded Jehovah's warning sent to him through Abigail. (1Sa 25:24-26, 31, 33) The city of Jerusalem was destroyed in 607 B.C.E. because of gross bloodguilt. (Eze 22:2-4; 23:37, 45) The false religious leaders of Jesus' day could not deny their bloodguiltiness any more than the leaders of Jeremiah's time, for, in both instances, their skirts were crimson red with the blood of Jehovah's faithful ones. (Jer 2:34; Mt 23:35, 36; 27:24, 25; Lu 11:50, 51) The great "harlot" Babylon the Great is so bloodguilty that she is said to be drunk with the blood of Jehovah's people.—Re 17:5, 6; 18:24.

Truly such bloodguilty ones are not worthy of living half their lives, as David said. (Ps 55:23) As David did, all should likewise pray that Jehovah will deliver them both from bloodguiltiness and from the bloodguilty ones. (Ps 51:14; 59:2; 139:19) As the Revelation prophecy foretold, the time will shortly come when a mighty chorus of praise will ascend to Jehovah because the last elements of Babylon the Great will have been destroyed and the blood of all these innocent ones will have been forever avenged.—Re 19:1, 2.

The Christian Greek Scriptures outline three distinct ways in which a Christian could become bloodguilty before God: (1) by bloodshed, murder —this would include those actively or tacitly supporting the activities of a bloodguilty organization (such as Babylon the Great [Re 17:6; 18:2, 4] or other organizations that have shed much innocent blood [Re 16:5, 6; compare Isa 26:20, 21]); (2) by eating or drinking blood in any way (Ac 15:20); and (3) by failing to preach the good news of the Kingdom, thereby withholding the lifesaving information it contains.—Ac 18:6; 20:26, 27; compare Eze 33:6-8.

BLUE. See COLORS.

BOANERGES (Bo·a·ner′ges) [Sons of Thunder]. A Semitic expression found, with its translation, only at Mark 3:17. Jesus gave it as a surname to the sons of Zebedee, James and John, likely reflecting the fiery enthusiasm of these two apostles. (Lu 9:54) Unlike Simon's new name Peter, Boanerges does not appear to have been commonly used.

BOAR [Heb., chazir′]. This animal is mentioned in the Scriptures at Psalm 80:13, where there is allusion to its depredations on unguarded vineyards. It is believed that the wild boar (not to be confused with the male of the domesticated hog,

to which it is related) is meant. This animal (Sus scrofa) is still to be found in the swamps of Palestine.

A large wild boar may weigh some 160 kg (350 lb), measure nearly 1.5 m (5 ft) in length, and may stand 1 m (3 ft) high at the shoulder. The snout of the wild boar is specially suited to rooting for food amid forest undergrowth. The tusks, especially those of the male, constitute a formidable weapon, with which it can easily rip up a horse. This animal is not only dangerous but also destructive, it being said that a group of them can ruin an entire vineyard in one night. Its diet, although basically vegetarian, includes a great variety of foods such as roots, grain, earthworms, snails, small animals, birds' eggs, and the like.

BOAZ, I (Bo′az) [possibly, In Strength]. A landowner of Bethlehem in Judah, "a man mighty in wealth" of about the 14th century B.C.E. (Ru 2:1) Boaz was the son of Salma (Salmon) and Rahab, and he was the father of Obed. (Mt 1:5) He was a link in the family line of the Messiah, the seventh in line of descent from Judah. (1Ch 2:3-11; Lu 3:32, 33) How this very unusual turn of events came about, allowing Boaz to be included in the genealogy of Jesus, is preserved for us in the book of Ruth.

Boaz had a close relative named Elimelech, who, along with his two sons, died leaving no male heirs. Of the widows of the two sons, one, Ruth, stuck by Elimelech's widow Naomi. It was harvesttime, and Ruth was gleaning "by chance" in the field belonging to Boaz. (Ru 2:3) Now Boaz was a true Judean, a devout worshiper of Jehovah. Not only did he greet his harvesters with "Jehovah be with you," but, after observing Ruth's loyalty toward Naomi, he also said to her, "May Jehovah reward the way you act, and may there come to be a perfect wage for you from Jehovah." (Ru 2:4, 12) When Ruth reported these things to her mother-in-law, Naomi exclaimed: "Blessed be he of Jehovah . . . He is one of our repurchasers." (Ru 2:20) Furthermore, when the harvest ended, Naomi explained to Ruth the customary way of bringing this matter to Boaz' attention. As Boaz was sleeping at his threshing floor, he awakened to find Ruth lying down at his uncovered feet, asking that he repurchase Elimelech's estate by levirate marriage. (See BROTHER-IN-LAW MARRIAGE.) Ruth was to be the substitute for Naomi, who was beyond the age of childbearing. Wasting no time, Boaz the next morning summoned another kinsman more closely related, but this person, referred to in the Bible only as So-and-so, refused to comply with the divine arrangement. Boaz, however, was quick to do so and took Ruth as his wife, with the blessing of the townspeople. She bore him a son named Obed, the grandfather of King David.—Ru 3:1–4:17.

Throughout the account, from his first kind greeting to the workers to his acceptance of the responsibility for preserving the family name of Elimelech, Boaz is observed to be an outstanding man—a man of action and authority yet having good self-control, faith, and integrity, being generous and kind, morally chaste, and fully obedient to Jehovah's commandments in all respects.

BOAZ, II (Bo′az) [possibly, In Strength]. The northernmost of the two huge copper pillars erected before the porch of Solomon's glorious temple was named Boaz, possibly meaning "In Strength." The southern pillar was called Jachin, meaning "May [Jehovah] Firmly Establish; [Jehovah] Has Firmly Established." So, putting the two together and reading from right to left as one faced the E would convey the thought 'May [Jehovah] firmly establish [the temple] in strength.'—1Ki 7:15-21; see CAPITAL.

BOCHERU (Bo′che·ru) [His Firstborn; He Is the Firstborn]. A descendant of King Saul and Jonathan; tribe of Benjamin.—1Ch 8:38; 9:39, 44.

BOCHIM (Bo′chim) [Weepers]. A site at which Jehovah's angel addressed the Israelites, reproving them for having disregarded Jehovah's warning against entering into relations with the pagan inhabitants of the land. The weeping that thereafter resulted among the people gave the place its name. (Jg 2:1-5) The site is unknown, but the expression "went up from Gilgal to Bochim" would indicate a location W of Gilgal, Gilgal evidently lying in the low valley of the Jordan.

BODY. The physical structure of a human or an animal. The Hebrew word gewi·yah′ refers to a body, whether alive (Ge 47:18) or dead. (1Sa 31:10; Ps 110:6) The Hebrew neve′lah′ comes from the root verb na·vel′ ("wither"; Ps 1:3) and is variously rendered "dead body," 'carcass,' and "corpse." (Le 5:2; De 14:8; Isa 26:19) Ba·sar′, the Hebrew word for flesh, can represent the whole body. (Compare Ps 16:9; see FLESH.) The usual Greek word for "body" is so′ma (Mt 5:29), but khros, literally "skin," is rendered "body" in Acts 19:12. The Greek word pto′ma, which comes from the root verb pi′pto (fall), refers to a fallen body or "corpse." (Mt 14:12) The different kinds of physical bodies are composed of different kinds of flesh, together with the life-force.—1Co 15:39; Jas 2:26; Ge 7:22; see SOUL.

Spiritual Bodies. While there are physical bodies, visible and palpable, there are also spiritual bodies, invisible to human eyes and entirely beyond human senses. (1Co 15:44) The bodies of spirit persons (God, Christ, the angels) are glorious. "At no time has anyone beheld God." (1Jo 4:12) Man cannot see God and live. (Ex 33:20) When the apostle Paul had only a glimpse of the manifestation of Jesus Christ after Jesus' resurrection, he fell to the ground and was blinded by the brilliance, a miracle being required to restore his sight. (Ac 9:3-5, 17, 18; 26:13, 14) Likewise, angels are far more powerful than men. (2Pe 2:11) They are glorious, brilliant ones and have appeared as such in physical manifestations. (Mt 28:2-4; Lu 2:9) These spirit sons of God have vision strong enough to see and endure the brilliance of the Almighty God.—Lu 1:19.

Because we cannot see God with physical eyes, he uses certain anthropomorphic expressions to help us to understand and appreciate things about himself. The Bible speaks of him as having eyes (Ps 34:15; Heb 4:13); arms (Job 40:9; Joh 12:38); feet (Ps 18:9; Zec 14:4); heart (Ge 8:21; Pr 27:11); hands (Ex 3:20; Ro 10:21); fingers (Ex 31:18; Lu 11:20); nose, nostrils (Eze 8:17; Ex 15:8); and ears (1Sa 8:21; Ps 10:17). It is not to be supposed that he literally possesses these organs in the way that we know them. The apostle John, who had hope of life in heaven, said to fellow heirs of heavenly life: "Beloved ones, now we are children of God, but as yet it has not been made manifest what we shall be. We do know that whenever he is made manifest we shall be like him, because we shall see him just as he is." (1Jo 3:2) It will be a body conformed to the "glorious body" of Jesus Christ (Php 3:21), who is "the image of the invisible God," "the reflection of his glory and the exact representation of his very being." (Col 1:15; Heb 1:3) They will, therefore, receive bodies that are incorruptible, having immortality, as distinguished from angels in general and from mankind, who are mortal. —1Co 15:53; 1Ti 1:17; 6:16; Mr 1:23, 24; Heb 2:14.

Christ's Body of Flesh. At the institution of the Lord's Evening Meal, Jesus offered the unfermented bread to the 11 faithful apostles, saying: "This means my body which is to be given in your behalf." (Lu 22:19) The apostle Peter later said: "He [Jesus] himself bore our sins in his own body upon the stake."—1Pe 2:24; Heb 10:10; see LORD'S EVENING MEAL.

In order for Jesus to be "the last Adam" (1Co 15:45) and to be "a corresponding ransom for all [mankind]," his fleshly body had to be a real human body, no incarnation. (1Ti 2:5, 6; Mt 20: 28) It had to be perfect, for it was to be sacrificed to present to Jehovah God the purchase price. (1Pe 1:18, 19; Heb 9:14) No imperfect human could provide the needed price. (Ps 49:7-9) For this reason Jesus said to his Father when presenting himself for baptism, to begin his sacrificial course: "You prepared a body for me."—Heb 10:5.

The physical body of Jesus Christ was not allowed to decay into dust as did the bodies of Moses and David, men who were used to foreshadow Christ. (De 34:5, 6; Ac 13:35, 36; 2:27, 31) When his disciples went to the tomb early on the first day of the week, Jesus' body had disappeared, and the bandages with which his body had been wrapped were left in the tomb, his body doubtless having been disintegrated without passing through the process of decaying.—Joh 20:2-9; Lu 24:3-6.

After Jesus' resurrection he appeared in different bodies. Mary mistook him for the gardener. (Joh 20:14, 15) He again appeared, entering a room with locked doors, having a body with wound marks. (Joh 20:24-29) Several times he manifested himself and was recognized, not by his appearance, but by his words and actions. (Lu 24:15, 16, 30, 31, 36-45; Mt 28:16-18) Once a miracle performed at his direction opened his disciples' eyes to his identity. (Joh 21:4-7, 12) Jesus, having been resurrected as a spirit (1Pe 3:18), could materialize a body for the occasion as the angels did in past times, when they appeared as messengers. (Ge 18:2; 19:1, 12; Jos 5:13, 14; Jg 13:3, 6; Heb 13:2) During the days before the Flood, the angels that "did not keep their original position but forsook their own proper dwelling place" performed an incarnation and married human wives. That these angelic sons of God were not truly human but had materialized bodies is shown by the fact that the Flood did not destroy these angels, but they dematerialized and returned to the spirit realm.—Jude 6; Ge 6:4; 1Pe 3:19, 20; 2Pe 2:4.

Symbolic Usage. Jesus Christ is spoken of as the Head of "the congregation, which is his body." (Eph 1:22, 23; Col 1:18) This Christian body of people has no divisions racially, nationally, or otherwise, Jews and people of all nations being represented in it. (Ga 3:28; Eph 2:16; 4:4) All are baptized by holy spirit into Christ and into his death. They are, therefore, all baptized into one body. (1Co 12:13) Thus all the body follows the head, dying his kind of death and receiving his kind of resurrection.—Ro 6:3-5; see BAPTISM (Baptism Into Christ Jesus, Into His Death).

The apostle Paul uses the functioning of the human body to illustrate the operation of the Christian congregation, likening the members living on earth at any particular time to a body, with Christ as the invisible Head. (Ro 12:4, 5; 1Co 12) He emphasizes the importance of the place each member occupies, the interdependency, the mutual love and care, and the accomplishment of work. God has set each one in his position in the body, and through the various operations of the holy spirit the body performs what is necessary. The Head, Jesus Christ, as liaison member, supplies the members of the body the things they need through the "joints and ligaments," the means and arrangements for supplying spiritual nourishment as well as communication and coordination, so that "the body" is spiritually well fed and each part is informed of the task to perform. —Col 2:19; Eph 4:16.

Proper Use of One's Body. The Christian should appreciate the body God has given him and should love himself to the extent of caring properly for his body so that he may be able to present it in acceptable, sacred service to God. (Ro 12:1) This requires the use of reason and the maintaining of the body with food and other necessities, as well as physical cleanliness, but other types of care are even more important. These involve spirituality, seeking God's Kingdom and his righteousness, and practicing moral uprightness. (Mt 6:25, 31-33; Col 2:20-23; 3:5) The apostle counsels: "Bodily training is beneficial for a little; but godly devotion is beneficial for all things, as it holds promise of the life now and that which is to come."—1Ti 4:8.

One who is an anointed member of the Christian congregation, the body of Christ, and who commits fornication is taking a member of the Christ away and making that one member of a harlot. Any such Christian committing fornication is bringing in moral defilement and is also "sinning against his own [fleshly] body." He is putting himself in peril of being removed from the body of Christ, the temple organization, and is exposing himself to the danger of loathsome diseases. (1Co 6:13, 15-20; Pr 7:1-27) He may be 'handed over by the congregation to Satan for the destruction of the flesh.'—1Co 5:5.

One who is a member of the body of Christ, as well as other dedicated persons who are associated with these spiritually begotten body members, must avoid not only physical fornication but also spiritual fornication. The Scriptures call one who has friendship with the world an 'adulteress.' (Jas 4:4) Jesus said of his disciples: "They are no part of the world, just as I am no part of the world."

(Joh 17:16) Therefore, Jesus is careful that those who make up the members of his body are clean morally and spiritually. (Eph 5:26, 27) They are said to have their "bodies bathed with clean water." (Heb 10:22) As the apostle Paul says, speaking of husbands: "In this way husbands ought to be loving their wives as their own bodies. He who loves his wife loves himself, for no man ever hated his own flesh; but he feeds and cherishes it, as the Christ also does the congregation, because we are members of his body. 'For this reason a man will leave his father and his mother and he will stick to his wife, and the two will become one flesh.' This sacred secret is great. Now I am speaking with respect to Christ and the congregation."—Eph 5:28-32.

See parts of the body under individual names.

BODYGUARD. See CARIAN BODYGUARD; also GUARD.

BOHAN (Bo′han) [possibly, Thumb].

1. A descendant of Reuben after whom a boundary stone for the territory of Judah was named.—Jos 15:6; 18:17.

2. "The stone of Bohan" served as a boundary marker for the tribes of Benjamin and Judah. (Jos 15:6; 18:17) It lay near the NW corner of the Salt Sea and evidently toward the foot of the plateaulike Low Plain of Achor.

BOIL. Generally, a furuncle, a localized, painful swelling of the skin resulting, not from a previous wound, but from infection caused by bacteria that invade hair follicles or sweat or sebaceous glands; in Hebrew, shechin′. Beginning with a small red swelling, the boil eventually discharges some pus and, subsequently, its hard center core. At times, a number of boils develop in an affected area. A "carbuncle" is more dangerous than a furuncle, covers a larger area, sometimes produces greater pain, and may be attended by such symptoms as headache, fever, and prostration. It is sometimes fatal.

At the time of Jehovah's sixth blow against Egypt, the Egyptians and their beasts were plagued by painful "boils with blisters." (Ex 9:8-11) These may have been severe raised skin eruptions filled with pus, and such blisterlike pustules possibly covered a large area. However, the brief Scriptural description makes definite identification with a specific modern-day disorder impossible.

The Israelites were warned that the consequences of disobedience to God would include his striking them with "the boil of Egypt." It was further said: "Jehovah will strike you with a ma-lignant boil [Heb., bish·chin′ ra‵] upon both knees and both legs, from which you will not be able to be healed, from the sole of your foot to the crown of your head."—De 28:15, 27, 35.

The Law indicated that a healed boil might be the place of development of a leprous eruption or blotch. In some cases, the symptoms were such that the victim was immediately declared unclean and leprous; in others, a seven-day quarantine was imposed. If it was thereafter found that the condition had not spread, it was identified merely as "the inflammation of the boil" and the priest pronounced the person clean.—Le 13:18-23.

Satan struck Job "with a malignant boil [Heb., bish·chin′ ra‵] from the sole of his foot to the crown of his head." (Job 2:7) The specific medical designation of the disease from which Job suffered is uncertain. In agony, Job scraped himself with a fragment of earthenware. (Job 2:8) His flesh was covered with maggots, his skin formed crusts (Job 7:5), his breath was loathsome (Job 19:17), he was racked with pain, and his skin blackened and dropped off (Job 30:17, 30).

King Hezekiah of Judah was afflicted with a boil and "got sick to the point of dying." At Isaiah's suggestion, a cake of pressed dried figs was applied to the boil as a poultice, after which Hezekiah gradually revived. (2Ki 20:1, 7; Isa 38:1, 21) Nonetheless, his recovery was due, not to natural healing alone, but to cure by Jehovah.—2Ki 20:5.

BOND. A thing that confines or restrains from liberty, such as a fetter or chain, a shackle, a manacle; also confinement (when plural); a binding force or influence; a cause of union; a uniting tie. In Bible times various means were employed for restraint of prisoners, including fetters, stocks, shackles, and handcuffs, as well as prison houses.

In the Scriptures the Hebrew word necho′sheth, usually meaning "copper," is frequently translated "fetters of copper" or "copper fetters," because fetters were often made of copper or bronze, although wood and iron were also employed. (2Sa 3:34; 2Ki 25:7) In the British Museum there is a pair of bronze fetters from Nineveh in the form of a bar with a ring at each end. The rings were cut so that they could be hammered together to embrace the ankles after the feet of the prisoner had passed through them. One of the rings is broken off, but, when whole, the fetters may have weighed about 4 kg (9 lb). The Greek word for a "fetter" is pe′de, related to pous (foot).—Lu 8:29.

The Hebrew verb 'a·sar′, meaning "tie; bind; put in bonds" (Jg 16:5; Eze 3:25; 2Ki 23:33), is the root of three other words having to do with bondage.

'E·sur' refers to "fetters" (Jer 37:15), *moh·se·rohth'* to "bands" (Ps 2:3), and *ma·so'reth* to a "bond" (Eze 20:37). The Greek word for a bond is *de·smos'* (Lu 8:29), while *syn'de·smos* refers to a "uniting bond," or "joint-bond."—Eph 4:3, *Int.*

Chains were also used to bind prisoners. Two Hebrew words to denote a chain (*rethu·qah'* and *rat·tohq'*) come from the root *ra·thaq'*, meaning "bind." (Na 3:10) *Ha'ly·sis* is the Greek word for a chain.—Mr 5:3, 4.

Many of the faithful pre-Christian witnesses suffered bonds and imprisonment. (Heb 11:36) Of Jacob's son Joseph in Egypt it is said, "with fetters they afflicted his feet, into irons his soul came." (Ps 105:18) Delilah used seven still-moist sinews and, later, new ropes as bonds in an attempt to bring Samson into captivity to the Philistines, but these he broke easily. Finally, after he lost his strength and was captured, he was bound with two fetters of copper. (Jg 16:6-12, 21) Jeremiah was put in stocks by Pashhur, the temple commissioner, and was imprisoned by the princes of Judah in "the house of fetters."—Jer 20:2, 3; 37:15.

Fettered prisoners painted on the soles of the feet of mummy wrappings. Figuratively, enemies were 'put under foot'

Because of unfaithfulness, Jehovah allowed King Manasseh of Judah to be put in fetters of copper by the king of Assyria. King Nebuchadnezzar led King Zedekiah captive to Babylon, confined by fetters of copper. (2Ki 25:7; 2Ch 33:11; Jer 39:7; 52:11) Jeremiah was released, and his handcuffs were removed by Nebuchadnezzar's chief bodyguard Nebuzaradan.—Jer 40:1, 4.

Jesus was bound by the men who seized him in the garden of Gethsemane and was led to Annas and sent away in the same condition to Caiaphas. After his trial before the Sanhedrin, he was bound at their order and taken to Pilate. (Joh 18:12, 13, 24, 28; Mr 15:1) Saul, before he was converted to Christianity to become the apostle Paul, was hunting out Christians to bring them bound to the Jewish high court. (Ac 9:2, 21) Peter was bound in chains between two soldiers by Herod, according to Roman custom.—Ac 12:6, 7.

During his first imprisonment in Rome, Paul, in several of his letters written from there, mentions being in prison bonds, and he refers to himself as "an ambassador in chains." (Eph 6:20; Php 1:7, 13-17; Col 4:18; Phm 10, 13) However, as the description of his situation in Acts 28:16-31 indicates, he was granted considerable freedom of movement, which allowed for writing, as well as receiving guests and visitors and preaching to them. Paul was set free but later rearrested. During his second imprisonment in Rome, which ended with his execution, Paul was again confined in chains.—Phm 22; 2Ti 1:16; 2:9; 4:6-8.

Metaphoric and Symbolic Uses. The expressions "bonds" and "chains" are often used metaphorically in the Scriptures for imprisonment or some form of confinement. With reference to the Babylonian exile, Zion is prophetically spoken of as being in bonds or as having bands on her neck. (Isa 52:2) Although many exiles did come to have their own houses and considerable freedom, they were not at liberty to return to Zion, or Jerusalem.—Jer 29:4, 5.

God has restricted the disobedient angels in "eternal bonds under dense darkness." (Jude 6) They are also said to be delivered into "pits of dense darkness." (2Pe 2:4) Scriptural evidence shows that they are not denied all freedom of movement, inasmuch as they have been able to get possession of humans and even had access to the heavens until they were cast out by Michael and his angels and hurled down to the earth. (Mr 1:32; Re 12:7-9) Satan the Devil is to be bound with a great chain by the angel having the key of the abyss and hurled into the abyss for a thousand years, after which he is to be loosed for a little while. (Re 20:1-3) Since angels are not creatures of flesh and blood, this chain undoubtedly has reference to some binding force of which we have no knowledge.

The woman whom Jesus healed, who had been bent double through a spirit of weakness for 18 years, Jesus spoke of as bound by Satan. (Lu 13:11, 16) Peter called Simon, who was attempting to buy the gift of holy spirit, "a bond of unrighteousness."—Ac 8:23.

The hands of an immoral woman are likened to fetters, and the man who goes after her is just as one who is "fettered for the discipline of a foolish man."—Ec 7:26; Pr 7:22.

In a favorable sense, Ezekiel speaks of "the bond of the covenant" because of a covenant's binding force. (Eze 20:37) Those in the marriage covenant are viewed as "bound" by it. (Ro 7:2; 1Co 7:27, 39) Love is spoken of as "a perfect bond of union." —Col 3:14.

BONES. Composed of living tissues, bones form a strong framework in the bodies of vertebrates. Too complicated in construction to be fully understood by scientists, man is 'woven together' with a skeleton of more than 200 bones and their connecting sinews. (Job 10:11; Ec 11:5) Pound for pound, bone is stronger than steel, and its construction is comparable to reinforced concrete. In fact, in describing "Behemoth," Jehovah says: "Its bones are tubes of copper; its strong bones are like wrought-iron rods." (Job 40:15, 18) The description aptly fits the hippopotamus, the bones of whose short, powerful legs and heavily built hips support his massive weight of from 2,300 to 3,600 kg (5,000 to 8,000 lb).

The common Hebrew word for "bone" is 'e'tsem (Ge 2:23); a synonym is ge'rem. (Pr 25:15) O·ste'·on is the Greek term.—Joh 19:36.

Eve, the first woman, was formed from a rib taken from Adam. This was appropriate in view of the fact that bones are the body's foundation, are wholly made up of living cells, and are blood-cell producers. Adam could truly say of Eve: "This is at last bone of my bones and flesh of my flesh." She was the closest possible relative of Adam. (Ge 2:22, 23) A like expression is used several times in the Scriptures to denote close kinship.—Ge 29:14; Jg 9:2; 2Sa 5:1; 19:12; 1Ch 11:1.

Faith-Strengthening Attestations. Joseph knew that it would be some time before God would lead Israel up out of Egypt and establish them in Canaan. In faith, as a testimony to Israel, he commanded that his bones be taken up when Israel went out. (Ge 50:25; Heb 11:22) Israel kept this in mind, and Moses followed out the injunction when he led Israel up out of Egypt. (Ex 13:19) Joseph's bones were finally buried in Shechem in the tract that Jacob had bought.—Jos 24:32.

A miracle performed in connection with Elisha (posthumously) was the immediate raising to life of a man whose dead body was thrown into Elisha's burial place and touched his bones. This was proof that it was God's power, not Elisha's, that performed the miracles Elisha had accomplished, and it was a powerful attestation or a seal of God as to the genuineness of his faithful prophet.—2Ki 13:20, 21.

After Jesus' resurrection he appeared to some of his disciples, who thought they were beholding a spirit. To reassure them Jesus said: "Feel me and see, because a spirit does not have flesh and bones just as you behold that I have." (Lu 24:39) Jesus' not saying he was flesh and blood has caused some to say that he had a "spiritualized" body of flesh and bones with no blood. There is no foundation for this argument, for the disciples could see that he had bones and flesh, but no blood was running from his body for him to call to their attention. Jesus thereby provided evidence by the mouth of 11 apostles and others assembled with them on that occasion that he was truly resurrected to life and that the disciples were suffering no hallucination in declaring his resurrection.

Uncleanness. Under the Law given through Moses, a person was religiously unclean for seven days if he touched a corpse, a bone of a man, or a burial place. (Nu 19:16) King Josiah fought false worship by filling with human bones the places where sacred poles of pagan worship had been and burning on the altars the bones from burial places, thus making the altars defiled and unfit for use.—2Ki 23:14, 16, 19; 2Ch 34:5.

Figurative Usage. The Bible in its references to bones highlights how vital they are literally to the physical health of the individual and figuratively to his spiritual health. The bones are the interior supporting framework of the body, and as such are used in the Bible metaphorically to represent one's being, especially as affected by deep feelings and emotions. Thus, the bones of a fearful individual are said to be "filled with dread." (Job 4:14) One's bones can shake because of extreme dejection or be "hot from dryness" because of disease. (Jer 23:9; Job 30:30) The fear of Jehovah is 'a refreshment to the bones.' (Pr 3:8) A good report is said to 'make the bones fat' or fill them with marrow, that is, invigorate the whole body. (Pr 15:30) "Pleasant sayings are . . . a healing to the bones." (Pr 16:24) On the other hand, negative emotions can have a harmful effect on one's organism. "A spirit that is stricken makes the bones dry." (Pr 17:22) A wife that acts shamefully is said to be to her husband "as rottenness in his bones." (Pr 12:4) The harboring of jealousy toward others can also be destructive to a person physically and spiritually, and so "jealousy is rottenness to the bones."—Pr 14:30.

Because of the strong construction of bones, Proverbs 25:15 says concerning the power of patience and kind words to overcome stiff, firm opposition: "By patience a commander is induced, and a mild tongue itself can break a bone."

Prophetic Usage. At the institution of the Passover, Jehovah commanded that the lamb (or goat) be roasted whole and "you must not break a bone in it." (Ex 12:46) This was fulfilled in Jesus Christ, "the Lamb of God," who is the antitypical Passover sacrifice. (Joh 1:29; 1Co 5:7) Jesus died on the torture stake. The soldiers came around to break the legs of those who were impaled that day, as was the custom in order to hasten death. They broke the legs of the two evildoers. However, they found that Jesus had already died, so they did not break his legs, but one jabbed his side with a spear.—Joh 19:31-36; Ps 34:20.

Jehovah gave Ezekiel, in Babylon, a vision in which he likened Israel to dry bones lying in a valley plain. In the vision, as Ezekiel prophesied to the bones, they miraculously came together, and flesh came upon them. Then he prophesied to the wind, and it brought breath into their bodies so that they stood up as a great army. Jehovah explained the vision as applying to Israel who, swallowed up in Babylonian exile, were as people whose hope had perished. (Eze 37:1-11) Similarly, Jeremiah likened the king of Assyria, who took the ten-tribe kingdom into exile, and Nebuchadnezzar king of Babylon, who carried away Judah, to lions devouring God's people and gnawing on their bones. (Jer 50:17) God had permitted this because of Israel's apostasy. But Jehovah was going to remember them and put into them his spirit, which would revive and revitalize them as well as bring them back to be settled in the Promised Land.—Eze 37:12-14.

After Jehovah's destruction of Gog and his hordes who come up in attack against Jehovah's people, there will be continual employment "for seven months" in marking the places of the bones of Gog's crowd and burying them, in order to cleanse the surface of the earth from all uncleanness and defilement.—Eze 39:14-16.

With a reference to bone marrow, Jehovah figuratively describes the rich blessings he will bring to his people when he wipes out death, saying that he will make for them a banquet of "well-oiled dishes filled with marrow."—Isa 25:6.

BOOK. The Hebrew word *se'pher* (book; letter; writing) is associated with the verb *sa·phar'* (count) and the noun *so·pher'* (scribe; copyist). (Ge 5:1; 2Sa 11:15; Isa 29:12; 22:10; Jg 5:14; Ne 13:13) When used with reference to official writings, *se'pher* is variously rendered "written document," "certificate," and "deed." (Es 9:25; Jer 3:8; 32:11) *Bi'blos* is the Greek term for "book"; its diminutive form *bi·bli'on* (literally, little book) is rendered "book," "certificate," and "scroll." (Mr 12:26; Heb 9: 19, *Int;* Mt 19:7; Lu 4:17) The word "Bible" comes from these Greek words.—See BIBLE.

An early "book" might be a tablet or a collection of tablets made of clay, stone, wax, wood covered with wax, metal, ivory, or perhaps even a group of potsherds (ostraca). Handwritten scrolls (rolls) were formed of attached sheets of papyrus, of parchment (skin of animals, such as sheep and goats), or of the finer material vellum, made of the skin of young calves, and, still later, of linen, and linen paper. Finally a book became a collection of consecutive handwritten or printed, folded sheets, strung, sewn, glued, stitched, or otherwise fastened together to form a bound volume.

Scrolls usually had writing on only one side (if leather, the originally hairy side). The writing material was sometimes wound on a stick. The reader would begin reading at one end, holding the scroll in his left hand and winding it around the stick with his right hand (if reading Hebrew; reverse if reading Greek). If the record was lengthy, the roll might be wound on two sticks, with the middle part of the text visible when picked up to read. Hence the word "volume," derived from the Latin word *volumen,* meaning a "roll."

A common size for the sheets that were used in making scrolls was 23 to 28 cm (9 to 11 in.) long and 15 to 23 cm (6 to 9 in.) wide. A number of these sheets were joined together side by side with paste. However, the sheets of the Dead Sea Scroll of Isaiah, of the second century B.C.E., were sewn together with linen thread. The scroll was made of 17 parchment strips averaging 26.2 cm (10.3 in.) in height and varying in width from about 25.2 cm (nearly 10 in.) to 62.8 cm (about 25 in.), totaling 7.3 m (24 ft) in length in its present state of preservation. A common length of scroll in the time of Pliny (probably those on sale commercially) was 20 sheets. An Egyptian papyrus roll chronicling the reign of Ramses II, called the Harris Papyrus, is 40.5 m (133 ft) in length. The Gospel of Mark would have required a roll 5.8 m (19 ft) long; Luke, about 9.5 m (31 ft).

The edges of the roll were trimmed, smoothed with pumice stone, and colored, generally black. Dipping in cedar oil protected the scroll from insects. The writing was usually done on one side of the scroll unless there was more information than could be put on the inside. In that case, some writing might be on the outside, or the reverse side. The visionary scrolls containing judgments that were seen by the prophets Ezekiel and Zechariah and the apostle John had writing on both sides. This indicates that the judgments were great, extensive, and weighty.—Eze 2:10; Zec 5:1-3; Re 5:1.

Important documents were sealed with a lump of clay or wax having the impression of the seal of the writer or maker, and it was attached to the document by strings. The apostle John saw in vision a scroll with seven seals, handed by the one on the throne to the Lamb.—Re 5:1-7.

Earlier scrolls appear to have had up to four columns per page, while later ones generally contained one column. Jeremiah's scroll consisted of "page-columns." As three or four columns were read, King Jehoiakim cut that portion off the scroll and threw it into the fire. (Jer 36:23) The 17 strips of the Dead Sea Scroll of Isaiah contain 54 columns of text, with an average of about 30 lines per column.

The scroll form of book served the Israelites down to the period of the Christian congregation. The records in the ancient national archives of Israel and Judah as well as the inspired writings of Jehovah's prophets, though sometimes called books, were actually in this scroll form.—1Ki 11:41; 14:19; Jer 36:4, 6, 23.

Each synagogue, a development after the Babylonian exile, kept and utilized scrolls of the Sacred Scriptures, and there was public reading from them on every Sabbath. (Ac 15:21) Jesus himself read from that type of scroll, probably one like the Dead Sea Scroll of Isaiah.—Lu 4:15-20.

Codex. It appears that Christians used mainly the roll, or scroll, form of book at least until about the end of the first century C.E. The apostle John wrote the Revelation about 96 C.E., and the book calls itself a scroll at chapter 22, verses 18 and 19. But the scroll form of book was very unwieldy. After the transition of the codex from notebook to book form, the superiority of the codex over the traditional scroll became apparent. For example, a scroll 31.7 m (104 ft) long might be needed to contain the four Gospels, whereas one compact codex could accommodate them all. In addition, the codex was more economical, since it was possible to write on both sides of a page. Furthermore, the lids afforded excellent protection for the contents, and various references could be located quickly without the tedious manipulation of scrolls.

It would be inconvenient, in fact, practically impossible, to make quick reference to certain statements in a large scroll. The indications are that the Christians were quick to adopt the use of the codex, or leaf-book, because they were interested in preaching the good news and they consulted and pointed out many references in the Scriptures in their Bible study and preaching.

As to the fact that the Christians, if they did not invent the leaf-book, took the lead in the use of it, Professor E. J. Goodspeed in his book *Christianity Goes to Press* (1940, pp. 75, 76) says: "There were men in the early church keenly alive to the part publication was playing in the Graeco-Roman world, who, in their zeal to spread the Christian message over that world, seized upon all the techniques of publication, not just the old traditional threadbare ones, but the newest and most progressive ones, and made use of them to the full in their Christian propaganda. In doing this they began the use on any large scale of the leaf-book, now in universal use. Their gospel was not an esoteric, secret mystery, but something to be proclaimed upon the housetops, and they made it their business to carry into effect the old slogan of the prophets, 'Publish good tidings.' The writing of the individual gospels was a great matter, of course, but the collecting of them, together with their publication as a collection, was an altogether different act, and one of almost as much importance as the writing of some of them."—See also *Encyclopædia Britannica*, 1971, Vol. 3, p. 922.

Based on an address by Professor Sanders (published in the *University of Michigan Quarterly Review*, 1938, p. 109), Professor Goodspeed sets forth in his book (p. 71) a table comparing the findings of classical and of Christian works of the second, third, and fourth centuries C.E., as to the number of fragments of roll-books and of codex, or leaf-books, found in each group:

	CLASSICAL		CHRISTIAN	
Century	Roll	Codex	Roll	Codex
II			1?	4
III	291	20	9?	38
IV	26	49	6?	64

Of early Christians as publishers of books, Professor Goodspeed goes on to say (p. 78): "They were not only abreast of their times in such matters, they were in advance of them, and the publishers of the subsequent centuries have followed them." He further states (p. 99): "It was the publication of the Bible that had stimulated the development of the leaf-book for literary purposes in the second century, and it was the publication of the Bible that stimulated the invention of printing."

Professor Goodspeed ventures (p. 81): "The curious remark in II Tim. 4:13 'Bring . . . the books, especially the parchments,' (the Greek words are *biblia, membranas*) makes one wonder whether the biblia does not mean the scrolls of Jewish scripture, and the membranai the newer leaf-books of Christian origin—the gospels and Paul. Professor Sanders' argument strongly suggests that north of the Mediterranean, leaf-books were at first more likely to be made of parchment."

Palimpsests. Because of the cost or scarcity of writing material, it was sometimes reused. Manuscripts were at times partially erased by scraping, sponging, or using various preparations to remove as much as possible of the original. With papyrus, sponging was done if the ink was fairly fresh; otherwise the old writing was crossed out, or the back of the material was used for the writing surface. On some palimpsests, because of atmospheric action, and other conditions, the original writing might appear clearly enough to be deciphered. A number of Bible manuscripts are among these, a notable one of which is the Codex Ephraemi, containing, under what was probably 12th-century writing, a part of the Hebrew and Greek Scriptures in writing thought to be of the 5th century C.E.

Other Books Referred To in the Bible. A number of uninspired books are referred to in the Bible. Some were source material for inspired writers. Some appear to be journals compiled from state records. Among them are the following:

Book of the Wars of Jehovah. Quoted by Moses at Numbers 21:14, 15, this book was undoubtedly a reliable record, or history, of the wars of God's people. It may have begun with Abraham's successful warfare against the four allied kings who captured Lot and his family.—Ge 14:1-16.

Book of Jashar. This book is cited at Joshua 10:12, 13, which passage deals with the appeal of Joshua for the sun and the moon to stand still during his fight with the Amorites, and at 2 Samuel 1:18-27, setting forth a poem, called "The Bow," a dirge over Saul and Jonathan. It is

thought, therefore, that the book was a collection of poems, songs, and other writings. They were undoubtedly of considerable historical interest and were widely circulated among the Hebrews.

Other historical writings. Several other uninspired historical writings are referred to in the books of Kings and Chronicles, one being "the book of the affairs of the days of the kings of Israel." (1Ki 14:19; 2Ki 15:31) "The book of the affairs of the times of the kings of Judah" is its counterpart for the kings of the southern kingdom, starting with Solomon's son Rehoboam. It is referred to 15 times. (1Ki 14:29; 2Ki 24:5) Another record of Solomon's rule is mentioned at 1 Kings 11:41 as "the book of the affairs of Solomon."

In compiling and writing Chronicles after the exile, Ezra refers at least 14 times to other sources, including "the Book of the Kings of Israel," "the account of the affairs of the days of King David," and "the Book of the Kings of Judah and of Israel." (1Ch 9:1; 27:24; 2Ch 16:11; 20:34; 24:27; 27:7; 33:18) Ezra also made reference to books by previous inspired writers. (1Ch 29:29; 2Ch 26:22; 32:32) Ezra notes that other prophets of Jehovah made written records that are not preserved in the inspired Holy Scriptures. (2Ch 9:29; 12:15; 13:22) A "book of the affairs of the times" is mentioned by Nehemiah. (Ne 12:23) Persian governmental records are noted in the Bible. In these were included reports of services rendered to the king, such as Mordecai's disclosure of an assassination plot.—Ezr 4:15; Es 2:23; 6:1, 2; 10:2.

The wise writer of Ecclesiastes warns against the endless procession of books that are a product of worldly reasoning and conflict with godly wisdom, books that do not instill the fear of the true God and the keeping of his commandments. (Ec 12:12, 13) An example of such was found in Ephesus, where spiritism and demonism were rampant. After the preaching of the good news about Christ, the believers brought their books of magic and burned them publicly, the calculation of their price being 50,000 pieces of silver (if denarii, $37,200).—Ac 19:19.

In Exodus 17:14 is Jehovah's command to write his judgment against Amalek in "the book," indicating that the writings of Moses, the first writings known to be inspired, were already under way in 1513 B.C.E.

Some other references to the Bible or parts of it are: "The book of the covenant," apparently containing the legislation set out at Exodus 20:22 to 23:33 (Ex 24:7); and "the roll of the book," the Hebrew Scriptures.—Heb 10:7.

Figurative Use. Several times "book" is used figuratively, as in the expressions "your [God's] book" (Ex 32:32), "book of remembrance" (Mal 3:16), and "book of life" (Php 4:3; Re 3:5; 20:15). It appears that these are all basically the same, that is, they are all God's "book" of remembrance with a view to rewarding with eternal life (in heaven or on earth) the ones whose names are written in it. God's "book" evidently receives names conditionally, since the Scriptures indicate that a person's name can be 'wiped out' of it. (Ex 32:32, 33; Re 3:5) So only if a person continues faithful is his name retained in the book.—See LIFE.

BOOTH. A rooflike shelter constructed of tree branches and leaves, sometimes with a wooden floor elevated off the ground; in Hebrew, *suk·kah′* (*sokh* in La 2:6), and in Greek, *ske·ne′*. (Ac 15:16) During the annual Festival of Booths at Jerusalem, booths were built on housetops, in courtyards, in public squares, even on the temple grounds, and around the roads near Jerusalem. Branches of poplar, olive, and oil trees as well as the leaves of the palm and the fragrant myrtle were used in their construction. This was to remind Israel that Jehovah made them dwell in booths when he brought them up out of Egypt.—Le 23:34, 40-43; Ne 8:15; see FESTIVAL OF BOOTHS.

Booths were also used for a number of practical purposes. Jacob made booths under which to shelter his herd, and he affixed to that place the name Succoth, meaning "Booths." (Ge 33:17) Booths were used by armies in the field, especially by the officers.—1Ki 20:12, 16.

A booth, or hut, was often built in a vineyard or in the center of a field so that the watchman could have shelter from the hot sun as he kept guard against thieves or animals. (Isa 1:8) There the harvesters enjoyed their noonday meals in the shade and saved time otherwise lost by going in from the field. Thickly thatched leaves kept the rain off those beneath. (Isa 4:6) Jonah made himself such a booth so that it might protect him from the sun as he waited to see what would become of Nineveh, against which he had prophesied.—Jon 4:5.

Figurative Uses. Isaiah illustrates the desolated condition of Jerusalem in Jehovah's eyes, likening it to a booth in a vineyard, in contrast to a populous, built-up city. (Isa 1:8) Jehovah pictures himself as dwelling in a booth of clouds when he temporarily descends from heaven to earth. There majestic omnipotence conceals itself, and from there come the crashings of thunder. (Ps 18:9, 11; 2Sa 22:10, 12; Job 36:29) David likens the

place of concealment for those trusting in Jehovah to Jehovah's "booth."—Ps 31:20.

Amos refers to the rebuilding of "the booth of David that is fallen." (Am 9:11) David was promised by Jehovah that David's kingdom would be steadfast to time indefinite. Regarding the overthrow of the kingdom of Judah and its last king Zedekiah of the line of David, Ezekiel was inspired to prophesy: "A ruin, a ruin, a ruin I shall make it. As for this also, it will certainly become no one's until he comes who has the legal right, and I must give it to him." (Eze 21:27) From this time on no king of the line of David occupied "Jehovah's throne" in Jerusalem. (1Ch 29:23) But Peter on the day of Pentecost, 33 C.E., pointed out that Jesus Christ was of David's line and the one of whom God really spoke as being the permanent King. Peter informed the Jews gathered there at Jerusalem that, in their time, Jehovah had raised Jesus up and made him both Lord and Christ. (Ac 2:29-36) Later, the disciple James applied Amos' prophecy as undergoing fulfillment in the gathering of disciples of Christ (Kingdom heirs) from both the Jews and the Gentile nations.—Ac 15:14-18; Ro 8:17.

BOOTHS, FESTIVAL OF. See FESTIVAL OF BOOTHS.

BORASHAN (Bor′a·shan) [possibly, Pit of Smoke]. One of the places that David and his men frequented during his time as a fugitive. (1Sa 30:30, 31) Some scholars consider it to be the same as Ashan (Jos 19:7), a Simeonite enclave city in the southern part of Judah's territory, a short distance NW of Beer-sheba.—See ASHAN.

BORN AGAIN. See SON(S) OF GOD (Christian Sons of God).

BOSOM. See BREAST, BOSOM.

BOSOM POSITION. In an illustration, Jesus spoke of a beggar named Lazarus who was carried at his death to "the bosom position of Abraham," and John refers to Jesus as being in "the bosom position with the Father." (Lu 16:22, 23; Joh 1:18) The expression "bosom position" alludes to one's reclining in front of another person on the same couch at a meal.

Guests reclined on their left side with a pillow supporting their left elbow, leaving the right arm free. Usually three persons occupied each couch, but there could be as many as five. The head of each one would be on or near the breast, or bosom, as it were, of the person behind him. The person with no one at his back was considered in the highest position and the one next to him in the second place of honor. In view of the nearness of the guests to one another, it was the custom that friend be placed next to friend, which made it rather easy to engage in confidential conversation if desired. To be in such a bosom position of another at a banquet was indeed to occupy a special place of favor with that one. So the apostle John, whom Jesus dearly loved, "was reclining in front of Jesus' bosom," and in such a position he "leaned back upon the breast of Jesus" and privately asked him a question at the celebration of the last Passover.—Joh 13:23, 25; 21:20.

For these reasons John, in describing the very special position of favor enjoyed by Jesus, said that he was in "the bosom position" of his Father Jehovah. Likewise, in Jesus' illustration, Lazarus was carried to "the bosom position" of Abraham, denoting that this beggar finally came into a position of special favor with one who was his superior.—See MEAL.

BOTTLE. A container used to hold such things as water, oil, milk, wine, butter, and cheese. Bottles of ancient times varied greatly in size and shape, some of them being leather bags and others narrow-necked containers with stoppers. The Egyptians had ornamented vases that served as bottles, and these were made out of alabaster, bone, bronze, glass, gold, ivory, porcelain, silver, or stone. Glass bottles were in use in ancient Assyria, and earthenware bottles were common in various Bible lands of antiquity. However, the ancients especially used skin bottles.

The common way to make a skin bottle was to kill an animal, cut off its head and feet, and then carefully draw it out of the hide in such a way that it was unnecessary to cut open the creature's belly. The skin would be tanned, and then all openings but one would be sewed up. The neck or perhaps one of the projections for the legs would be left unsewn, and this served as the opening, which could be closed with a plug or a string. The hides of sheep, goats, and sometimes of cattle were used for this purpose, and in some instances, the hair was left on the skins used to hold milk, butter, cheese, and water. However, a more thorough tanning process was required when the skin bottles were to be used for oil and wine. Even in more recent times many skin bottles have been made similarly in the Middle East. When skin water bottles are not tanned, they impart an unpleasant taste to the water kept in them.

When dismissing Hagar, Abraham equipped her with a "skin bottle [Heb., *che'meth*]." (Ge 21:14, 15, 19) The Gibeonites told Joshua: "These are the wine skin-bottles [Heb., *no'·dhohth'*] that we

filled new, and, look! they have burst." (Jos 9:13) Such a thing could happen in time because of pressure built up because of active fermentation of the wine. Elihu said: "Look! My belly is like wine that has no vent; like new *skin bottles* [Heb., *'o·vohth'*] it wants to burst open." (Job 32:19) Generally, however, new wineskins would be able to withstand the internal pressure developed because of active fermentation of the wine. Yet, old wineskins would in time become hard and lose their elasticity, and they were then likely to burst. Hence, Jesus Christ fittingly said: "Neither do people put new wine into old wineskins; but if they do, then the wineskins burst and the wine spills out and the wineskins are ruined. But people put new wine into new wineskins, and both things are preserved."—Mt 9:17.

David, a fugitive beleaguered by foes, referred to the skin bottle figuratively, saying: "Do put my tears in your skin bottle." (Ps 56:8) Thus David requested God, in whom he placed his trust, to put his tears as if in a skin bottle in order to remember them.

Probably skins filled with wine were sometimes hung where they could be smoked in order to protect them from insects or to impart certain desired properties to the wine quickly. On the other hand, when not in use, skin bottles might be hung in a room without a chimney and thus become darkened by smoke from fires built there. These wineskins would soon lose their elasticity and shrivel up. Perhaps with this in mind, the psalmist who was beset with trials said: "For I have become like a skin bottle in the smoke."—Ps 119:83; see POTTER; VESSELS; WINESKINS.

BOTTLE-GOURD PLANT [Heb., *qi·qa·yohn'*]. The Hebrew term represents the plant that Jehovah caused to grow miraculously overnight to provide shade for the prophet Jonah as he sat in a booth awaiting the results of his prophesying against Nineveh. The plant brought great relief to Jonah until Jehovah caused a worm to attack it, resulting in its withering. The prophet was thereby left exposed to the beating rays of the sun. —Jon 4:5-11.

Two plants are commonly suggested as possible translations of the Hebrew *qi·qa·yohn'*. Some Bible translations (*RS*, ftn; *JB*) prefer the "castor-oil plant" (*Ricinus communis*), a perennial plant of rapid growth attaining a height of 3 m (10 ft) or more, and having large leaves. This preference is based on a suggestion made by Jerome that *qi·qa·yohn'* might be the castor-oil tree, as well as on the similarity between the Hebrew word and the Egyptian *kiki*. Other scholars and translators suggest the "gourd" (*AT*) or "bottle-gourd plant" (*NW*). *A Hebrew and English Lexicon of the Old Testament* (by Brown, Driver, and Briggs, 1980, p. 884) suggests the meaning "bottle-gourd," a broad-leafed plant classified botanically as *Cucurbita lagenaria*.

The bottle-gourd plant develops rapidly. Regarding this plant, *Dictionnaire de la Bible* (Vol. 5, col. 1098) states: "It is known that the gourd plant grows very rapidly in hot countries and that it is used for covering with verdure the walls of houses and shelters where it clings like the Virginia creeper, providing a protection against the heat by means of its entwinings and its large leaves. . . . In the symbolic paintings based on the story of Jonah found in the catacombs, it is always this plant that is portrayed." (Edited by F. Vigouroux, Paris, 1912) So a gourd plant that normally grows rapidly was miraculously caused to grow up in one night by Jehovah's power in order to shield Jonah from the hot rays of the sun.

BOUNDARY.

The Hebrew word *gevul'* means "boundary." It may also mean the territory or land enclosed within a border or boundary. Thus, Joshua 13:23 states: "And the boundary [Heb., *gevul'*] of the sons of Reuben came to be the Jordan; and this as a territory [*u·gevul'*] was the inheritance."

Boundaries Set by Jehovah. Prior to the global Flood, God had expelled the first human pair from the garden of Eden, obliging them to live outside of it (Ge 3:23, 24), had banished Cain from the immediate "ground" from which Abel's blood was "crying out" (Ge 4:10, 11), and later had set a limit of "a hundred and twenty years" (Ge 6:3) in which the pre-Flood population could continue dwelling upon the earth before the destruction of the vast majority of them. (Ge 6:13) He decreed that the Flood survivors should "fill the earth," and when an attempt was made to hold back from spreading abroad in the earth, God overruled such action and compelled men to carry out that decree.—Ge 9:1, 19; 11:1-9.

Centuries later, to Abraham and his seed God promised a certain land with definitely stated boundaries. (Ge 15:18-21; Ex 23:31) God permitted the resident Canaanites to continue dwelling in that Promised Land for a foretold period of "four hundred years" more before he would enforce an eviction decree when "the error of the Amorites" came to its completion. (Ge 15:13-16) On the other hand, Jehovah God also decreed that the Israelites should not encroach on the boundaries of the nations of Edom, Moab, and Ammon, anciently descended from relatives of the Israelites' forefathers. (De 2:4, 5, 18, 19) The words of Moses' song

in Deuteronomy 32:8 are to be understood in the light of these facts. That text says: "When the Most High gave the nations an inheritance, when he parted the sons of Adam from one another, he proceeded to fix the boundary of the peoples *with regard for the number of the sons of Israel.*"

It was on the basis of Jehovah's sovereign right to decree such boundaries that Judge Jephthah later defended Israel's right to its God-given land. (Jg 11:12-15, 23-27) However, due to Israel's failure to adhere devotedly to God's commands, Jehovah allowed some of the enemy peoples to remain within Israel's borders (Nu 33:55; Jg 2:20-23), and it was not until King David's reign, some four centuries from the nation's entry into Canaan, that Israel gained dominion over all the territory within the promised boundaries.—2Sa 8:1-15.

Eventually, in accord with his earlier warning pronouncement, Jehovah allowed the pagan nations to overrun the boundaries of the Promised Land and lead Israel into exile, as a punishment upon an apostate people. (De 28:36, 37, 49-53; Jer 25:8-11) By his prophets Isaiah, Jeremiah, Ezekiel, and Daniel, God foretold the rise and fall of the world powers from Babylon forward and the order of their appearance. (Isa 13:1–14:4; 44:28–45:5; Jer 25:12-29; Eze 21:18-27; Da chaps 2, 7, 8, and 11:1–12:4) Though tolerating the existence and domination of the earth by the political nations for an 'appointed season,' Jehovah also foretold their ultimate destruction and the wiping out of the boundaries of their political dominion, this by the Kingdom of the Messiah.—Da 2:44; compare Re 11:17, 18; 19:11-16.

"The Set Limits" of Men's Dwelling. Paul told his Athenian listeners that God "decreed the appointed times and the set limits [Gr., *ho·ro·the·si'as*, literally, "settings of bounds"] of the dwelling of men." (Ac 17:26) A similar thought is expressed in Psalm 74:17 with reference to the Creator: "It was you that set up all the boundaries of the earth; summer and winter—you yourself formed them." The Most High is responsible for the existence of natural boundaries such as rivers, lakes, seas, and mountains, which determine where people live.—Compare Jer 5:22.

Israel's Tribal Boundaries. (MAP, Vol. 1, p. 744) At the time of Israel's conquest of the Promised Land, the tribes of Reuben, Gad, and the half tribe of Manasseh had been granted the right to receive their inheritance of land "from the side of the Jordan toward the sunrising." (Nu 32:1-5, 19, 33-42; 34:14, 15; Jos 13:8-13, 15-32) Following six years of warfare in subduing the Canaanites, the time came for determining the tribal boundaries W of the Jordan for the other nine tribes and the remaining half tribe of Manasseh. Joshua, Eleazar the priest, and one chieftain out of each tribe were appointed by Jehovah to serve as a land committee overseeing the distribution. (Nu 34:13-29; Jos 14:1) The procedure followed was according to God's earlier command to Moses: "According to the great number you should increase one's inheritance, and according to the fewness you should reduce one's inheritance. Each one's inheritance should be given in proportion to his registered ones. Only by the lot should the land be apportioned."—Nu 26:52-56; 33:53, 54.

It thus appears that the distribution of the land among the tribes was governed by two factors: the result of the casting of the lot, and the size of the tribe. The lot may have established only the approximate location of the land inheritance each tribe would have, thus designating an inheritance in one section or another of the land, such as to the N or S, E or W, along the coastal plain, or in the mountainous region. The decision of the lot proceeded from Jehovah and hence would serve to prevent jealousy or quarreling among the tribes. (Pr 16:33) By this means God would also guide matters so that the situation of each tribe would fall in accordance with the inspired deathbed prophecy of the patriarch Jacob recorded at Genesis 49:1-33.

After the casting of the lot had determined the geographic location of a tribe, it would then be necessary to determine the extent of its territory on the basis of the second factor: its proportionate size. "You must apportion the land to yourselves as a possession by lot according to your families. To the populous one you should increase his inheritance, and to the sparse one you should reduce his inheritance. To where the lot will come out for him, there it will become his." (Nu 33:54) The decision of the lot as to the basic geographic location would stand, but adjustment could be made as to the size of the inheritance. Thus, when Judah's territory was found to be too large, its land area was reduced by assigning portions of it to the tribe of Simeon.—Jos 19:9.

The increasing or decreasing of the inheritance does not seem to have been merely on the basis of land area, for the tribe of Dan, though second most populous, received one of the smaller portions as to actual dimensions. Other factors, such as the number of cities, the type of land, and the quality of the soil, may have been considered. —Compare Jos 17:14-18.

When the more precise boundaries of the tribal divisions had been worked out, then the individual family holdings could be assigned, and this ap-

pears to have been done, not by lot, but by the direction of the appointed committee, composed of Eleazar, Joshua, and the chieftains. (Jos 17:3, 4) So, Deuteronomy 19:14 states that "when the *ancestors* will have set the boundaries in your inheritance" they should not be moved back.—See BOUNDARY MARK.

The account of the division of the territory W of the Jordan shows that first the lots for Judah (Jos 15:1-63), Joseph (Ephraim) (Jos 16:1-10), and the half tribe of Manasseh settling W of the Jordan (Jos 17:1-13) were determined, their boundaries and cities being enumerated. After this, there appears to have been an interruption of the dividing of the land, since the camp of Israel is shown to have moved from Gilgal to Shiloh. (Jos 14:6; 18:1) The length of time involved is not stated, but Joshua eventually reprimanded the remaining seven tribes for their dilatory attitude as to settling the rest of the land. (Jos 18:2, 3) Various explanations have been offered as to the cause of this attitude on the part of the seven tribes, some commentators reasoning that the abundance of spoil obtained during the conquest and the relative freedom from any immediate threat of attack by the Canaanites may have caused these tribes to feel no particular urgency about taking possession of the remaining portion of the territory. A reluctance to face up to the problem of dealing with the pockets of strong enemy resistance there may have contributed to this tardiness. (Jos 13:1-7) Also, their knowledge of this portion of the Promised Land may have been considerably more limited than of those sections already allotted.

To expedite the matter, Joshua sent out a delegation of 21 men, 3 from each of the 7 tribes, to "map out the land into seven shares," and after the men had "mapped it out by cities," Joshua drew lots for them in order to obtain Jehovah's decision. (Jos 18:4-10) The individual inheritances allotted are discussed in Joshua 18:11–19:49.

The priestly tribe of Levi was not given a particular region as its allotment but was granted 48 scattered cities and pasture grounds located within the boundaries of other tribes.—Jos 13:14, 33; 21:1-42.

Other Boundaries. By the Law covenant God 'divided Israel off' as his chosen people for 1,545 years (Le 20:26), but by the sacrificial death of his Son he destroyed the figurative "wall in between" that fenced off the Gentile peoples from the Jews, abolishing the Law of commandments. At Ephesians 2:12-16, Paul alluded to the barrier, or wall (soreg), in the temple area. Under penalty of death, Gentiles were prohibited beyond that boundary, such wall serving the apostle as an apt illustration of the division created by the Law covenant.

Under the new covenant mediated by Christ Jesus, a spiritual demarcation, far more impressive than any geographic boundary, was made, separating off the spiritual nation of the Christian congregation from the rest of the world of mankind. (Joh 17:6, 14-19; 1Pe 2:9-11) Jehovah had long before prophesied that he would build Zion with precious gems and make all her boundaries of "delightsome stones," and Jesus quoted from this prophecy applying the succeeding verse to those becoming his disciples. (Isa 54:12, 13; Joh 6:45; compare Re 21:9-11, 18-21.) These spiritual boundaries are to be held inviolate, for God warns that those invading them will meet with destruction.—Compare Isa 54:14, 15; 60:18 with 1Co 3:16, 17.

Conversely, those forming that spiritual nation are required to remain within its confines, recognizing the moral limitations set forth (1Co 5:9-13; 6:9, 10; 1Th 4:3-6) and the spiritual boundaries separating them from false worship and worldly systems (2Co 6:14-18; Jas 4:4; Re 18:4), as well as the regulations governing proper relationships between Christians and "the superior authorities" of the existing governments (Ro 13:1, 5; 1Pe 2:13-16; Ac 4:19, 20; 5:29), between husband and wife (1Co 7:39; 1Pe 3:1, 7), and in many other aspects of life.

Paul also shows there were boundaries governing the territory assigned for ministerial activity. —2Co 10:13-16.

BOUNDARY MARK. When the Israelites occupied Canaan, a plot of land was given to each family, and such holdings were marked off by landmarks, or boundary marks. These are not described in the Bible, but they may have been posts, stones, or even furrows in the ground. The Hebrew word for "boundary mark" (*gevul'*) is the same as that for "boundary" and "territory." (Ge 10:19; 47:21) At least some boundary marks in Palestine bore inscriptions of identification. Elaborate inscriptions do appear on landmarks, or boundary stones, in Egypt and Mesopotamia. For example, an inscribed boundary stone of Nebuchadnezzar I was discovered at Nippur.

Jehovah's law prohibited the moving back of boundary marks. (De 19:14; see also Pr 22:28.) In fact, cursed was the one moving back "the boundary mark of his fellowman." (De 27:17) Since landholders generally were dependent upon the produce of their plots of ground, moving back a boundary mark would mean depriving another person of some of his means of sustenance. Doing this was equivalent to theft and was so viewed in ancient times. (Job 24:2) But there were unscrupulous persons who were guilty of such abuses, and princes of Judah in Hosea's time were likened to those moving back a boundary.—Ho 5:10.

Jehovah is considerate of the widowed and fatherless. Thus it is said that he will tear down the house of the self-exalted, "but he will fix the boundary of the widow." (Pr 15:25) Then, too, Proverbs 23:10, 11 declares: "Do not move back the boundary of long ago, and into the field of fatherless boys do not enter. For their Redeemer is

Boundary stone from Susa featuring symbols of Babylonian gods

strong; he himself will plead their cause with you."

BOW. See ARMS, ARMOR.

BOWELS. See INTESTINES.

BOWING DOWN. See ATTITUDES AND GESTURES.

BOWL. See BASIN; VESSELS.

BOWMAN. See ARCHER; ARMS, ARMOR.

BOY. See CHILD, CHILDREN; SON.

BOZEZ (Bo'zez). One of two rocks, or toothlike crags, associated with Jonathan's victory over the Philistines, recorded at 1 Samuel 14:4-14. Jonathan, looking for a passage to cross over to attack the Philistine outpost, saw the two crags, one on the N facing Michmash (where the Philistines were encamped), the other on the S facing Geba. (1Sa 13:16; 14:5) Between these two cities the Wadi Suweinit (Nahal Mikhmas) descends toward the Jordan and becomes a deep gorge with nearly vertical cliffs somewhat to the E of the cities. The location of the two crags is considered to have been at the point where the wadi makes a sharp bend, though the precise identification of the crags is conjectural.

BOZKATH (Boz'kath) [Swollen Thing [that is, an elevated spot]]. A town in the inheritance of Judah (Jos 15:39); home of King Josiah's maternal grandfather Adaiah. (2Ki 22:1) Listed between Eglon and Lachish, it was apparently in the lowland, or Shephelah region. Its identification is uncertain; some would place it at Dawa'imeh (present-day Amazya), about 19 km (12 mi) W of Hebron.

BOZRAH (Boz'rah) [Unapproachable Place].

1. A prominent city of Edom, the home of the father of Jobab, an Edomite king in the second millennium B.C.E. (Ge 36:31, 33; 1Ch 1:44) Its prominence is evident from the fact that the prophets Isaiah, Jeremiah, and Amos under inspiration referred to it as representative of all Edom, due for desolation.—Isa 34:5, 6; 63:1-4; Jer 49:12, 13, 17, 22; Am 1:11, 12.

Bozrah is identified with modern Buzera, located about 50 km (30 mi) NNE of Petra and situated near the ancient road called the King's Highway. It thus occupied a fairly central position in the Edomite kingdom and guarded the approaches to the copper mines in the Arabah. The ancient ruins at Buzera show Bozrah to have been a fortified city built on a narrow spur jutting out from the Jebel esh-Shera' with deep wadis on either side.

The rendering of Micah 2:12 in the *King James Version* contains the name "Bozrah," but most modern translations view this as referring, not to a town, but to an enclosure or pen for sheep.

2. In prophesying against Moab, Jeremiah 48:24 refers to Bozrah as among cities "of the land of Moab." It is included among other cities of the tableland or "land of level country" (Jer 48:21), and the use of this same Hebrew expression in connection with Bezer (De 4:43) has caused some scholars to view them as likely the same place. —See BEZER No. 2.

BRACELET. A decorative circlet worn on the wrist or lower arm, sometimes forming a complete circle, though in other instances having an opening or clasp. In ancient times bracelets were worn by both men and women, sometimes on just one arm, but occasionally on both. Bracelets of antiquity were made of bronze, glass, iron, silver, and gold and were often highly ornamented, sometimes being studded with jewels.

The Hebrews wore bracelets, and they were in general use from early times in Palestine, where archaeologists have found a number of them, made of various materials, particularly bronze. Abraham's servant gave Rebekah a gold nose ring and also two bracelets (Heb., *tsemi·dim'*) having a weight of ten shekels (114 g; 3.7 oz t) of gold. (Ge 24:22, 30, 47) Among the items taken as war booty from the Midianites were bracelets, which were among the valuable articles the Israelites presented to God.—Nu 31:50.

Through Ezekiel, God represented himself as decking Jerusalem with bracelets and other ornaments. But since she had used such beautiful articles idolatrously and had prostituted herself, Jehovah foretold that he would punish her and would have these things taken from her. (Eze 16:11, 17, 38, 39) Bracelets (Heb., *sheh·rohth'*) were among the things Jehovah said he would take away from the haughty "daughters of Zion." —Isa 3:16, 19.

The armlet or bracelet for the upper arm (Heb., *'ets·'a·dhah'*) was worn by monarchs as one of their insignia of regal authority or sovereign power. The bracelet King Saul of Israel wore upon his arm may have had such significance.—2Sa 1:10; see ORNAMENTS.

BRAMBLE [Heb., *'a·tadh'*]. The Hebrew word is identified as referring to the bramble or the buckthorn (*Rhamnus*) in *A Hebrew and English Lexicon of the Old Testament,* by Brown, Driver, and Briggs (1980, p. 31). The Palestinian buckthorn (*Rhamnus palaestina*) is a straggling bush, growing about 1 to 2 m (3 to 6 ft) high, its twigs lined with sharp, strong prickles. Though frequent in the lower warmer regions of the country, it is also found in mountainous regions, as at Jerusalem. Walter Baumgartner identifies 'a·tadh' as the boxthorn or *Lycium europaeum,* a thorny shrub growing about 1 to 2 m (3 to 6 ft) high, blossoming with small violet flowers and bearing small, round, edible red berries.—*Hebräisches und Aramäisches Lexikon zum Alten Testament,* Leiden, 1967, p. 36; see THORN.

The bramble appears most prominently in the account of Judges 9:8-15 in which the olive tree, the fig tree, and the vine are contrasted with the lowly bramble. As the rest of the chapter makes evident, the valuable plants represent those worthy persons, such as Gideon's 70 sons, who did not seek the position of kingship over their fellow Israelites, while the bramble, useful only for fuel, represents the kingship of Abimelech, the murderer of all, except one, of the other sons of Gideon, his brothers. (Jg 9:1-6, 16-20) Jotham's suggestion that the other figurative trees seek refuge in the shadow of the bramble was doubtless ironic, as the low-growing bramble obviously could not provide shadow for trees, especially the stately cedars mentioned.

The warning was given by Jotham that fire might come out of the bramble "and consume the cedars of Lebanon," perhaps alluding to the ease with which the dry and leafless plant might catch fire during the hot summer months. Psalm 58:9 also refers to the use of brambles for fuel.

The Hebrew word 'a·tadh' also appears as the name of a place at Genesis 50:10.—See BRIER.

BRANCH, SPROUT.

A branch is a smaller division of a main part, such as of a tree, a stream, or a family. In the Bible several Hebrew and Greek words are variously translated "branch," "sprout," "sprig," "shoot," "offshoot," "bough," "frond," "twig," and "treetop." Branches of trees played a part in the worship of Israel. During the Festival of Booths, in the seventh month, Ethanim or Tishri, branches of trees, including palm, olive, myrtle, and poplar, were used in constructing booths in which the people resided for the duration of the festival.—Le 23:40; Ne 8:15.

At Jesus' entry into Jerusalem on Nisan 9, 33 C.E., the crowd that had come to Jerusalem for the Passover and the Festival of Unfermented Cakes greeted him by waving palm branches, hailing him as the king of Israel. (Joh 12:12, 13) Likewise, the "great crowd" of John's vision at Revelation chapter 7 are shown waving palm branches as they attribute salvation to God, who is on the throne, and to the Lamb.—Re 7:9, 10.

Figurative Usage. Jesus was brought up in the small town of Nazareth, probably meaning "Sprout-Town." The apostle Matthew calls attention to Jesus' being called a Nazarene (apparently from the Heb. *ne'tser,* sprout) as a fulfillment of prophecy, alluding to the prophecy at Isaiah 11:1. —Mt 2:23.

The apostle Paul likens the congregation of the Jewish candidates *naturally* in line for the heavenly Kingdom to an olive tree with a definite number of branches attached to the tree trunk. Wild olive branches (people of the nations, Gentiles) were grafted in to replace "broken off" natural branches (Jews) because only a few accepted Christ, the majority failing. Thus the full God-ordained number is completed, in its final state being composed of Jews and Gentiles.—Ro 11:17-24.

"Offshoot" or "bough" and the related terms mentioned above are used in the Scriptures to denote a son or offspring, a descendant. In Jacob's blessings to his sons he calls Joseph an offshoot (Heb., *ben,* "son"). (Ge 49:22, ftn) Destruction leaving neither root nor bough symbolizes the wiping out of the family or of all of a certain kind, or complete destruction beyond possibility of revival.—Mal 4:1; compare Isa 5:24; Ho 9:16.

Jesus Christ is prophetically spoken of in the Hebrew Scriptures as Jehovah's servant "Sprout" (*NW, Le*) or "the Branch" (*KJ, AT*), "the Bud" (*Ro*). (Zec 3:8) At Zechariah 6:12, 13, "the man whose name is Sprout" is described as building the temple of Jehovah and sitting as a priest upon his throne. This can apply to none other than Jesus Christ, since he alone could fill the office of King and Priest under God's arrangement. Jesus Christ is promised as a righteous "sprout" raised up to David. This One will execute righteousness and justice. (Jer 23:5; 33:15; compare Isa 53:2; Re 22:16.) He is also called a twig and a sprout out of Jesse, David's father.—Isa 11:1.

The end of the dynasty of the kings of Babylon was pictured by likening it to "a detested sprout," thrown away and not deserving of a burial.—Isa 14:19.

Just as Jehovah the Creator causes the sprouting growth in garden plants and trees, so "sprout," "bough," and similar terms are associated with prosperity, increase, and blessings from Jehovah. (Isa 4:2; 60:21, 22; Job 29:19) He has promised that "just like foliage ["a branch," *KJ;* "a green leaf," *RS*] the righteous ones will flourish."—Pr 11:28.

BRAND MARK.

Among some pagans brand marks of various designs were burned or inscribed into the flesh of slaves as a sign of ownership.

Jehovah foretold that as slaves to foreign conquerors the haughty women of Judah would come to have "a brand mark [Heb., *ki*] instead of prettiness."—Isa 3:24.

Idol worshipers on occasion had the name, emblem, or image of their idol god reproduced on themselves to display the fact that they were devoted to that god. Deliberate disfigurement of the flesh was prohibited under the Mosaic Law. (Le 19:28) Under the Law the only mark ever put on a slave was the piercing of the ear of one who voluntarily requested slavery to his master "to time indefinite."—De 15:16, 17.

Paul wrote to the Galatians: "I am carrying on my body the brand marks [Gr., *stig'ma·ta*] of a slave of Jesus." (Ga 6:17) Many were the physical abuses administered to Paul's fleshly body because of his Christian service, some of which undoubtedly left him scarred, testifying to the authenticity of his claim as a faithful slave belonging to Jesus Christ. (2Co 11:23-27) These things may have been the marks alluded to. Or he may have had reference to the life he lived as a Christian, displaying the fruitage of the spirit, carrying out the work of his Christian ministry.—See MARK, II.

BRASS. See COPPER, BRASS, BRONZE.

BRAZIER. Generally, a heating device consisting of a panlike receptacle elevated off the ground by means of legs and designed for holding burning coals or charcoal. The Hebrew word rendered "brazier" (*'ach*) is of Egyptian origin, suggesting that the brazier itself was an innovation from Egypt.

It appears that in the better homes the brazier was preferred to a depression in the floor of the house, in which a fire could be built. King Jehoiakim had a brazier, likely one made of metal, in his winter house.—Jer 36:22, 23.

BREAD. A baked food, sometimes leavened, the basic ingredient of which is flour or meal. Bread (Heb., *le'chem;* Gr., *ar'tos*) was a staple in the diet of the Jews and other peoples of antiquity, the art of bread making being common knowledge among the Israelites, Egyptians, Greeks, Romans, and others. Even in modern times in some parts of the Middle East, bread is of chief importance, and other types of food are of secondary significance. At times the Bible seems to use "bread" for food in general, as at Genesis 3:19 and in the model prayer, which contains the request: "Give us today our bread for this day."—Mt 6:11; compare Ec 10:19, ftn.

In making bread, the Hebrews generally used wheat flour or barley flour. Wheat was more expensive, so persons might often have to content themselves with barley bread. Reference is made to barley bread at Judges 7:13; 2 Kings 4:42; and John 6:9, 13. Some flour was rather coarse, being prepared by the use of mortar and pestle. However, "fine flour" was also in use. (Ge 18:6; Le 2:1; 1Ki 4:22) The manna Jehovah God provided for the Israelites during their wilderness trek was ground in hand mills or pounded in a mortar.—Nu 11:8.

It was customary to grind the grain and bake fresh bread daily, and often the bread was unleavened (Heb., *mats·tsah'*). The flour was simply mixed with water, and no leaven was added before the kneading of the dough. In making leavened bread, the general practice was to take a piece of dough retained from a previous baking and use it as a leavening agent by crumbling it into the water prior to the mixing in of the flour. Such a mixture would be kneaded and permitted to stand until it leavened.—Ga 5:9; see CAKE; LEAVEN; LOAF.

Offerings made to Jehovah by the Israelites consisted of some baked things. (Le 2:4-13) It was not permissible to use leaven in offerings made by fire to Jehovah, though certain offerings were not burned on the altar and could contain leaven. (Le 7:13; 23:17) The use of leavened bread was not allowed during the Passover and the Festival of Unfermented Cakes associated with it.—Ex 12:8, 15, 18; see SHOWBREAD.

The prominence of bread in the daily diet of Biblical times is indicated by repeated references to it throughout the Scriptures. For example, Melchizedek "brought out bread and wine" before blessing Abraham. (Ge 14:18) When Abraham sent away Hagar and Ishmael he "took bread and a skin water bottle and gave it to Hagar." (Ge 21:14) Imprisoned Jeremiah was given a daily ration of "a round loaf of bread." (Jer 37:21) On two occasions Jesus Christ miraculously multiplied bread to feed vast crowds. (Mt 14:14-21; 15:32-37) Jesus taught his followers to pray for "bread for the day according to the day's requirement." (Lu 11:3) And the psalmist fittingly identified Jehovah God as the one providing "bread that sustains the very heart of mortal man."—Ps 104:15.

Figurative Use. The term "bread," as used in the Bible, has a number of figurative applications. For instance, Joshua and Caleb told the assembled Israelites that the inhabitants of Canaan "are bread to us," apparently meaning that they could easily be conquered and that the experience would sustain or strengthen Israel. (Nu 14:9) Great sorrow that might be associated with divine disfavor seems to be reflected in Psalm 80:5, where it is said of Israel's Shepherd Jehovah: "You have made them eat the bread of tears." Jehovah is also spoken of as giving his people "bread in the form of distress and water in the form of oppression," evidently referring to conditions they would experience under siege and that would be as common to them as bread and water.—Isa 30:20.

In speaking of those who are so wicked that they "do not sleep unless they do badness," the book of Proverbs says: "They have fed themselves with the bread of wickedness." (Pr 4:14-17) Yes, they seem to sustain themselves on wicked deeds. Of one who may acquire the material provisions for life by deceit or fraud, Proverbs 20:17 states: "Bread gained by falsehood is pleasurable to a man, but afterward his mouth will be filled with gravel." But regarding the good and industrious wife it is said: "The bread of laziness she does not eat."—Pr 31:27.

The Bible also uses "bread" figuratively in a favorable sense. Isaiah 55:2 shows that Jehovah's spiritual provisions are far more important than material things, stating: "Why do you people keep paying out money for what is not bread, and why is your toil for what results in no satisfaction? Listen intently to me, and eat what is good, and let your soul find its exquisite delight in fatness itself."

When instituting the new meal that would commemorate his death (on Nisan 14, 33 C.E.), "Jesus took a loaf and, after saying a blessing, he broke it and, giving it to the disciples, he said: 'Take, eat. This means my body.'" (Mt 26:26) The loaf meant Jesus' own fleshly body "which is to be given in your behalf."—Lu 22:19; 1Co 11:23, 24.

About a year earlier, Jesus Christ had contrasted "bread that comes down from heaven" with the manna eaten by the Israelites in the wilderness and had plainly stated: "I am the bread of life." He showed that he was "the living bread that came down from heaven," adding: "If anyone eats of this bread he will live forever; and, for a fact, the bread that I shall give is my flesh in behalf of the life of the world." (Joh 6:48-51) This 'eating' would have to be done in a figurative way, by exercising faith in the value of Jesus' perfect human sacrifice. (Joh 6:40) Jesus presented the merit of his ransom sacrifice to his Father Jehovah God upon his ascension to heaven. By means of this merit, Christ can give life to all obedient ones of mankind. As foretold under divine inspiration, Jesus was born in Bethlehem, which means "House of Bread" (Mic 5:2; Lu 2:11), and through Jesus Christ life-giving "bread" is provided for all believing mankind.—Joh 6:31-35.

BREAST, BOSOM. The breast is a mammary gland; frequently, however, the term is used with reference simply to the forepart of the human body (male or female) between the neck and the abdomen. Two Hebrew words that denote human breast are *shadh* and *shodh*. (Ca 8:1; Job 24:9) Greek words for breast are *ma·stos'* (Lu 11:27) and *ste'thos.* (Re 15:6) The human breast is used in the Scriptures to denote closeness, intimacy, and favor (Ca 1:13; Joh 13:25; 21:20); maturity (Ca 8:8, 10; Eze 16:7); beauty (Ca 4:5; 7:3, 7, 8); sexual intercourse ("between her breasts" [Ho 2:2]; "breasts were squeezed," 'bosoms pressed' [Eze 23:3, 21]); fertility (Ge 49:25; Ho 9:14); exultation and prosperity (Isa 60:16; 66:11). 'Beating the breasts' or 'tearing out the breasts' signified extreme humiliation, distress, and grief.—Isa 32:12; Eze 23:34; Lu 18:13; 23:48.

A woman hearing Jesus speak cried out: "Happy is the womb that carried you and the breasts that you sucked!" Since it was every woman's desire to have a worthy son, and Jewish women desired the privilege of being the mother of a prophet and particularly the Messiah, it is understandable that this Jewish woman made such a remark. But Jesus' answer, "No, rather, Happy are those hearing the word of God and keeping it!" showed that it was not being close to Jesus in a fleshly way that counted; spirituality was the important thing. This principle precludes any veneration of Mary as the mother of our Lord.—Lu 11:27, 28.

Because of the nearness of Jerusalem's destruction, to be accompanied by the appalling slaughter of its inhabitants, Jesus said: "Look! days are coming in which people will say, 'Happy are the barren women, and the wombs that did not give birth and the breasts that did not nurse!'"—Lu 23:29; compare Jer 16:1-4.

The Hebrew Scriptures, by using a different term, make a distinction between the human breast and the breast of animals, which is anatomically different. In communion sacrifices made by the Israelites the breast (Heb., *cha·zeh'*) of a sacrificial animal was the portion that became the priest's for his food.—Le 7:29-35; 10:14, 15.

Bosom. The word is used in a manner very similar to the usage of breast, although it often has reference to the fold in the upper part of the robe, rather than to the breast itself. The bosom was designated in Hebrew by *cheqh* (1Ki 1:2), *cho'tsen* (Ne 5:13), and the dual form of *dadh* (Eze

23:3); in Greek, *kol'pos*. (Joh 13:23) A dearly beloved or cherished one would be held close to one's bosom (Heb., *chehq*), the way Naomi held Ruth's baby Obed, in acknowledging him as the legal heir of Naomi's dead husband Elimelech. (Ru 4:16) In the custom of reclining at meals, the one in front of the bosom of another was in a position of intimacy with him, generally the favored position. (Joh 13:23) Jesus employed this well-known custom in illustrating Lazarus as being in "the bosom position of Abraham," signifying favor with God. (Lu 16:22, 23) The apostle John described Jesus as being "in the bosom position with the Father," as *the intimate* of Jehovah, the one person who could explain God to a fuller and more thorough extent than any other.—Joh 1:18; see BOSOM POSITION.

The garment worn by Israelites in Bible times was quite voluminous over the chest, so that in its folds a person could place his hands, money, or other articles and could even carry a baby or a young lamb. (Ex 4:6, 7; Nu 11:12; 2Sa 12:3) Jehovah says he will carry his lambs in his bosom, an illustration of his tender love and care for them. (Isa 40:11) The expression "wife of [one's] bosom," as in some translations (*KJ; Ro; RS; AT*), is given clearer meaning when rendered, "wife thou dost cherish in thy bosom" (*Kx*), "your cherished wife." (*NW*) (De 13:6; 28:54) Intercourse is sometimes referred to.—Ge 16:5; 2Sa 12:8.

To "render the reward into their own bosom" or to 'measure out their wages into their own bosom' are understandable expressions when we appreciate that the pockets of garments were not in one's skirts or the lower part of the garment as today. (Isa 65:6, 7; Ps 79:12; Jer 32:18) Similarly, the expressions 'carrying reproach in one's bosom,' 'raking fire together into his bosom,' 'taking a bribe from the bosom' and "a bribe in the bosom" have reference to the use of the upper folds of the garment.—Ps 89:50; Pr 6:27; 17:23; 21:14.

BREASTBAND. A sash or girdle worn by a bride on her wedding day. It marked her status as a married woman. Jehovah as a "husband" to Israel illustrates the sin and extreme disregard of Israel toward him, saying: "Can a virgin forget her ornaments, a bride her breastbands? And yet my own people—they have forgotten me days without number." Israel's God should have been her greatest ornament, but she had forsaken him for other gods.—Jer 2:32; Isa 3:20; compare Isa 49:18.

BREASTPIECE. The sacred embroidered pouch worn by Israel's high priest over his heart whenever he entered the Holy. The breastpiece (Heb., *cho'shen*) was to serve as "a memorial" and was apparently referred to as "the breastpiece of judgment" because of containing the Urim and Thummim by means of which Jehovah's judgments were revealed.—Ex 28:15, 29, 30.

Like the ephod, the breastpiece was made of the finest of materials, gold, blue thread, wool dyed reddish purple, coccus scarlet material, and fine twisted linen. (Ex 28:15) The same fabrics were used in making the ten tent cloths embroidered with cherubs, the curtain separating the Holy from the Most Holy, and the screen for the entrance of the tent, the needed materials having been voluntarily contributed by the Israelites and fashioned into final form either directly by Bezalel and Oholiab or under their direction.—Ex 26:1, 31, 36; 31:2-6; 35:21-29.

The fabric for the breastpiece was evidently a cubit in length and a span in width so it would make a square when folded, thus forming a pouch into which the Urim and Thummim may have been placed. The front of the breastpiece was adorned with 12 precious stones fitted into sockets of gold and arranged in four rows of three stones each. On each stone the name of one of the tribes of Israel was engraved. (Ex 28:15-21, 28; 39:8-14; Le 8:8) The jewels in each row may have been arranged as listed from right to left (as in reading Hebrew). It cannot be stated with any certainty which precious stone corresponded to which tribe. —See the precious stones under their individual headings.

The breastpiece was securely mounted on the ephod in the following manner: Two wreathed chains of pure gold were attached to two gold rings at opposite corners of the upper part of the breastpiece. These chains, in turn, were fastened to the two gold settings on top of the shoulder pieces of the ephod. Two other gold rings were affixed at opposite extremities of the bottom edge of the breastpiece upon the side facing inward toward the ephod. These rings were tied by means of a blue string to the two gold rings at the base of the shoulder pieces of the ephod just above its girdle.—Ex 28:22-28; 39:15-21.

BREASTPLATE. See ARMS, ARMOR.

BREATH. See SPIRIT.

BRIBE. Generally a valuable consideration given with a view to influencing its recipient to act, usually unjustifiably or corruptly, in behalf of the giver. Depending on the context, the Hebrew word for a bribe (*sho'chadh*) may also be rendered "gift" or "present." (Ex 23:8, ftn; 1Ki 15:19; Pr

17:8) The Scriptures indicate that the accepting of bribes led not only to the perversion of justice but even to bloodshed.—De 16:19; 27:25; Eze 22:12.

Accepting bribes was specifically prohibited by God's law to Israel, and Jehovah, as the Supreme Judge, set the perfect example by always rendering impartial decisions and never accepting bribes. (Ex 23:8; 2Ch 19:7) Hence, those who would be guests in Jehovah's tent must imitate him in this respect.—Ps 15:1, 5; see also Isa 33:15, 16.

The Bible contains numerous examples of those who were not free from bribery. Delilah was bribed to betray Samson, each axis lord of the Philistines paying 1,100 silver pieces ($2,422, if the "silver pieces" were shekels). (Jg 16:5) The sons of Samuel the prophet and judge, unlike their father, accepted bribes and perverted judgment. (1Sa 8:3; 12:3) David speaks of those whose right hand, which should have been supporting the cause of right, was full of bribery. (Ps 26:10) Kings Asa and Ahaz bribed the king of Syria and the king of Assyria respectively for military aid. (1Ki 15:18, 19; 2Ki 16:8) The head ones, or princes, of unfaithful Jerusalem proved to be lovers of bribes. (Isa 1:23; 5:23; Mic 3:11) Unlike ordinary prostitutes who receive hire, unfaithful Jerusalem actually bribed others to come to her.—Eze 16:33.

In the first century C.E., Judas Iscariot, in effect, accepted a bribe to betray Jesus Christ (Mt 26:14-16, 47-50), and Governor Felix withheld justice in Paul's case in the hope of receiving a bribe from the apostle.—Ac 24:26, 27.

The expressions "a bribe from the bosom" and "a bribe in the bosom" can be better understood when considering that in Hebrew the word "bosom" may also refer to the fold of a garment above the belt. Therefore, these expressions indicate that the bribe apparently was hidden in the upper fold of the garment and then given in secrecy to another who, in turn, likewise concealed it.—Pr 17:23; 21:14; see GIFTS, PRESENTS.

BRICK. Generally, a building block made of hardened mud or clay. From earliest times brick (Heb., leve·nah') has been widely used in Bible lands. The builders of ancient Babel found no stone in the vicinity of the site they chose for their city and, therefore, utilized bricks instead of stone, and bitumen served as mortar for them. Apparently the bricks were kiln dried, that is, hardened "with a burning process." (Ge 11:3) In ancient Egypt, the enslaved Israelites labored at brickmaking. Their lot was made more difficult by having to gather the straw themselves and still produce the same number of bricks. (Ex 5:7-19) In

the Promised Land, the Israelites continued using bricks in construction work, although it appears that stone was preferred. (Isa 9:10) While abundant in the hills of Palestine, in some sections little good-quality building stone is available. Hence in the lowlands, at cities such as Jericho and Eziongeber, brick was used not only for the city walls but also for dwellings. In modern times in parts of Syria and Palestine, houses have been built partly of hewed stone with the remainder of sun-dried brick, the hewed stone being used for the walls most exposed to winter storms.

In the manufacture of bricks, after foreign substances were removed from the mud or clay, it was generally mixed with finely chopped straw or other vegetable matter. This is borne out by a statement in the Anastasi Papyri, from ancient Egypt, that reads: "There was no one to mould bricks, and there was no straw in the neighbourhood." (Life in Ancient Egypt, by A. Erman, 1894, p. 117) Although bricks made without straw have been found in Egypt, this was evidently an exception and provides no valid basis for concluding that the Israelites resorted to making bricks without straw when forced to obtain it themselves. Experiments conducted in recent years indicate that adding straw to clay makes it easier to work and triples the strength of the bricks produced therefrom.

The mixture of mud or clay and straw was moistened with water, trampled underfoot, and then molded by hand or pressed into a four-sided wooden "brick mold." (Heb., mal·ben'; Na 3:14) The sides of the molds were probably dusted with dry earth so that the molds could be slipped off easily. Often, while the brick was still wet, it was stamped with the mark of the reigning monarch. The bricks were then left to dry in the sun or were kiln dried.

In Babylonia bricks were commonly kiln dried, and such bricks were generally used for city walls and the walls and floors of palaces. Sometimes sun-dried bricks were used in the interiors of buildings or laid with burned bricks in alternate layers several feet thick. In Egypt, Assyria, and Palestine, sun-drying appears to have predominated. Kiln-processed bricks are superior in quality to those dried in the sun. The latter tend to disintegrate when subjected to floods and shrivel under the intense heat of the summer sun. In certain cases, however, sun-dried bricks have proved to be very substantial, such as those at Ezion-geber, which have remained for centuries.—See KILN.

The extensive use of sun-dried brick explains why the sites of certain ancient cities have remained undiscovered for centuries. Mounds of earth much like the surrounding soil were formed by the crumbled bricks of former cities. In Palestine and Syria such mounds frequently contain the ruins of several cities.

Bricks varied considerably in size and shape. In Egypt the rectangular shape was common, and wedge-shaped bricks were used in the construction of arches. Egyptian bricks were approximately 36 to 51 cm (14 to 20 in.) in length, 15 to 23 cm (6 to 9 in.) in width, and 10 to 18 cm (4 to 7 in.) in thickness. In Babylonia, square, oblong, triangular, and wedge-shaped bricks have been found. However, brick of later periods, as that from the time of Nebuchadnezzar, was generally square-shaped, measuring about 30 cm (12 in.) across.

Israel's making sacrificial smoke upon the bricks in Isaiah's time may have reference to the pavement of the place for offering sacrifice or to the roof tiles.—Isa 65:3.

BRIDE-PRICE.   See MARRIAGE.

BRIDLE.
The headgear with which a horse is governed and restrained, consisting of a headstall, a bit, and reins, often with other appurtenances. In Hebrew it is *me'theg* (2Ki 19:28) and *re'sen* (Job 30:11), while in Greek it is *kha·li·nos'*.—Jas 3:3.

"Bridle" is generally used figuratively in the Bible, or in drawing an illustration. The psalmist says: "Do not make yourselves like a horse or mule without understanding, whose spiritedness is to be curbed even by bridle or halter before they will come near to you." (Ps 32:9) Men should not be like unreasoning beasts, unable to guide themselves properly. However, as such brute beasts require correction by whip and bridle, the rod is serviceable for use on the stupid person.—Pr 26:3.

In Revelation "the vine of the earth" is thrown into a winepress and trodden roughly with the shod feet of horses, the blood coming "as high up as the bridles of the horses, for a distance of a thousand six hundred furlongs [296 km; 184 mi]." (Re 14:18-20) So great a depth of blood covering such a distance represents the tremendous scope of the destruction wrought by the angels and reflects the fact that the winepress is big enough to catch all and allow escape for none who make up the symbolic "vine of the earth" at the time of the fullness of its guiltiness.

Jehovah told King Sennacherib of Assyria: "I shall certainly put my hook in your nose and my bridle between your lips, and I shall indeed lead you back by the way by which you have come." (2Ki 19:28; Isa 37:29) Not willingly, but by Jehovah's hand, Sennacherib was forced to forgo any

siege of Jerusalem and to return to Nineveh, where he was later assassinated by his own sons. (2Ki 19:32-37; Isa 37:33-38) Jehovah's putting a bridle in the jaws of enemy peoples indicates their coming under the type of complete control gained over animals by means of a bridle.—Isa 30:28.

Job, lamenting his sorrowful condition in sickness and under ridicule, says of his persecutors: "The bridle they left loose on my account." (Job 30:11) Job's enemies went ahead full speed, unbridled, in complete disrespect and unrestraint, in venting their hostility upon him.

James the half brother of Jesus gives counsel on the proper use of the tongue, likening the control of it to a bridle. If one has self-control through the application of Scriptural principles, and by this can control the tongue, he can control his entire body. (Jas 3:2, 3) A bridle on the tongue itself is necessary for a person professing to be a worshiper of God, or else his form of worship will be futile. —Jas 1:26.

BRIER.
The brier is a plant with a woody stem that is itself thorny or prickly, and the name may refer to numerous plants of this type. Some scholars identify the Hebrew term *bar·qanim'* (briers) with that designated by a cognate noun in Arabic, the *Centaurea scoparius,* a common thistlelike plant with thorny heads. Gideon used *bar·qanim'* in punishing the men of Succoth for their refusal to supply bread to his hungry soldiers during his fight against the Midianites.—Jg 8:6, 7, 16.

The Hebrew word *che'dheq* (brier) has been identified with *Solanum coagulans,* the gray nightshade, a spiny shrub. (*Thesaurus of the Language of the Bible,* edited in part by M. Z. Kaddari, Jerusalem, 1968, Vol. 3, p. 88) Using the term *che'dheq,* Proverbs 15:19 likens the path of the lazy man to a brier hedge, apparently in the sense of his envisioning or imagining difficulties and thorny problems in every possible undertaking, and on that basis excusing himself from moving ahead. The moral decay of the nation of Israel caused the prophet Micah to say of the people that their "best one is like a brier [Heb., *keche'dheq*], their most upright one is worse than a thorn hedge," evidently meaning that even the best among the Israelites was as hurtful to those having dealings with him as is a prickly brier or a thorn hedge to anyone approaching too close. —Mic 7:4.

BROAD BEANS
[Heb., *pohl*]. The Hebrew term corresponds with the Arabic *ful* and is identified with the broad bean, *Vicia faba,* an annual plant extensively cultivated in Syria and Palestine.

This type of bean has been found in Egyptian mummy coffins, indicating the use of it in Egypt from ancient times.

The plant is hardy and erect, reaches a height of about 1 m (3 ft), and produces a sweet perfume when in blossom. The ripe pods are large and thick, and the beans are brown or black in color. Planted after the early rains in the autumn, they are usually harvested in the late spring toward the close of the barley and wheat harvest. The plants are winnowed much like grain. As a food, the green immature pods may be boiled whole as a vegetable, while the ripe beans are often cooked with oil and meat.

When David moved out of Jerusalem and across the Jordan because of Absalom's revolt, his company was greeted in Mahanaim by a delegation voluntarily offering equipment and foodstuffs, including broad beans. (2Sa 17:24-29) Ezekiel was instructed to mix broad beans with lentils and grains to make a coarse bread to be eaten by weight, depicting famine conditions.—Eze 4:9, 10.

BRONZE. See COPPER, BRASS, BRONZE.

BROOCH. A decorative clasp made of metal and having a pin or tongue by which it can be fastened to a person's clothing. In ancient times brooches were worn by both men and women, as among the Greeks and Romans. The Roman brooch or fibula sometimes consisted of a curved piece of metal with a hook at one end and a pin extending from the other end, in safety-pin fashion. Being not only ornamental but also useful, the brooch was often used for such purposes as pinning together two parts of a scarf or cloak. Brooches of antiquity were made of bronze, iron, gold, or silver. Their use in early Palestine has been established by archaeological finds, among these being bow-shaped brooches discovered at Tell en-Nasbeh.

When the Israelites were granted the privilege of contributing toward the construction of the tabernacle, the men and women brought various ornaments including "brooches" or "buckles." (Ex 35:21, 22) These brooches were evidently hooked ornaments of some type, for the same Hebrew word used for them (chach) is rendered "hook" elsewhere. (2Ki 19:28) However, the Scriptures do not describe these brooches.—See ORNAMENTS.

BROOM TREE [Heb., ro'them]. The broom tree (Retama raetam) is in reality a desert shrub of the pea family. The corresponding Arabic name (ratam) aids in identifying the plant and shows the rendering "juniper tree" in the King James Version to be incorrect.

This bush is one of the most abundant plants of the Judean wilderness, the Sinai Peninsula, as well as the rest of Arabia, and is found in ravines, in rocky places, on hillsides, and even in open sand stretches of desert areas, where its roots sink deep to draw up moisture. It grows from about 1 to 4 m (3 to 13 ft) in height, with numerous thin, rodlike branches and narrow, straight leaves. When blossoming, the small clusters of delicate flowers, ranging in color from white to pink, make a lovely sight as they carpet the otherwise barren hillsides. The Hebrew name for the plant (ro'them) evidently comes from a root word meaning "attach," perhaps referring to its ability to hold back sand dunes. According to Pliny, its pliant branches were used for binding.—Natural History, XXIV, XL, 65.

When Elijah fled into the wilderness to escape Jezebel's wrath, the record at 1 Kings 19:4, 5 says, he "sat down under a certain broom tree" and then slept there. While the smaller broom trees would provide very scant shade from the burning sun of the wilderness, one of good size could give welcome relief. This desert bush also served as fuel. The wood of the broom tree makes excellent charcoal, which burns with an intense heat.

Because the roots of the broom tree are bitter and nauseating, some have suggested that the reference by Job (30:4) to these as being used for food by persons starving in barren desolation perhaps refers to an edible parasitic plant (Cynomorium coccineum) that grows like a fungus on these roots. While this may be the case, it is also possible that another variety of this plant existed in Job's day (over 3,000 years ago) rather than just the present white broom tree (Retama raetam) that now grows. Presenting another viewpoint regarding Job 30:4, N. Hareuveni wrote: "Since, unlike the leaves of the saltplant, roots of the broom are totally inedible in any form, it is obvious that Job is speaking of white broom roots made into something that can be sold to earn one's bread. These young men who now scorn Job made embers from the roots of the white broom to sell in the marketplace." (Tree and Shrub in Our Biblical Heritage, Kiryat Ono, Israel, 1984, p. 31) In harmony with this, some suggest that the vowel pointing of the Hebrew word translated "their food" be adjusted so that the Hebrew would read "to warm them."

BROTHER. A male having the same parent or parents as another; in Hebrew, 'ach, and in Greek, a·del·phos'. Full brothers mentioned in the Bible, sons of the same father and the same mother, include Cain and Abel, sons of Adam and Eve (Ge 4:1, 2; 1Jo 3:12); Jacob and Esau, twin sons of

Isaac and Rebekah (Ge 25:24-26); James and John, sons of Zebedee and his wife (Mt 4:21; 27:56; compare Jg 8:19). Moses and Aaron were brothers of Miriam (Nu 26:59); Lazarus was brother to Martha and Mary. (Joh 11:1, 19) "Brothers" also designates half brothers, those with the same father but a different mother, as in the case of Jacob's 12 sons by four different women (Ge 35:22-26; 37:4; 42:3, 4, 13); also, offspring of the same mother but of different fathers, as in the case of Jesus and his brothers, and possibly in that of David's relationship to his sisters.—Mt 13:55; 1Ch 2:13-16; 2Sa 17:25; see "Brothers of Jesus" below.

The term "brother," however, was not limited to the immediate fleshly relationship. Abraham and Laban referred to their nephews Lot and Jacob respectively as brothers. (Ge 11:27; 13:8; 14:14, 16; 29:10, 12, 15; compare Le 10:4.) Fellow members of the same tribe in Israel enjoyed a brotherly relationship (2Sa 19:12, 13; Nu 8:26), and in a still larger sense the entire nation of Israel were brothers, offspring, as they were, of one common father Jacob, and they were united in worship of the same God, Jehovah. (Ex 2:11; De 15:12; Mt 5:47; Ac 3:17, 22; 7:23; Ro 9:3) Even the Edomites, who descended from Abraham through Jacob's twin brother Esau, thereby being related to Israel, were called brothers. (Nu 20:14) The reunited kingdoms of Judah and Israel were referred to as in a "brotherhood" (Heb., 'a·chawah').—Zec 11:14.

"Brother" is also applied to those united in a general cause and having similar aims and purposes. For example, King Hiram of Tyre called King Solomon his brother, not simply because he was an equal in rank and position but also perhaps because of mutual interests in supplying timbers and other things for the temple. (1Ki 9:13; 5:1-12) "Look! How good and how pleasant it is for brothers to dwell together in unity!" David wrote, implying that it is not blood relations alone that make for peace and unity between fleshly brothers. (Ps 133:1) In fact, mutual affection and interest, not common parentage, prompted David to call Jonathan his brother. (2Sa 1:26) Companions having similar natures and dispositions, even when such are bad, are properly called brothers. —Pr 18:9.

In the patriarchal society and under the Mosaic Law, certain privileges and obligations were assumed by fleshly brothers. With the death of the father, the oldest brother, the firstborn, received a double share of the family inheritance and the responsibility of acting as head for the family. A fleshly brother was first in line for the right of repurchase, levirate marriage, and avenging blood. (Le 25:48, 49; De 25:5) Incestuous relations between brother and sister were strictly forbidden by the Mosaic Law.—Le 18:9; De 27:22.

In the Christian congregation members enjoy a common spiritual relationship analogous to that of brothers. Jesus called his disciples brothers. (Mt 25:40; 28:10; Joh 20:17) He strongly emphasized this relationship, saying: "Whoever does the will of my Father . . . , the same is my brother, and sister, and mother." (Mt 12:48-50) Hence blood relatives must be loved less than Christ and left behind on his account if necessary. (Mt 10:37; 19:29; Lu 14:26) Indeed, brother may deliver brother over to death. (Mr 13:12) The term "brother" extends out beyond the immediate associates of Jesus to include the whole congregation of believers (Mt 23:8; Heb 2:17), "the whole association of brothers" "who have the work of witnessing to Jesus." (1Pe 2:17; 5:9; Re 19:10) Such an association of spiritual brothers shows "brotherly love" in its fullest measure.—Ro 12:10; Heb 13:1.

Peter at Pentecost addressed those from faraway lands, including proselytes, all as "brothers." (Ac 2:8-10, 29, 37) Sometimes male Christian believers were distinguished as "brothers" and females as "sisters" (1Co 7:14, 15), but generally "brothers" was the accepted greeting to mixed groups and was not restricted to males. (Ac 1:15; Ro 1:13; 1Th 1:4) The term is used in this sense in all but three of the inspired Christian letters (Titus, 2John, Jude) and in the works of early church writers. The apostles warned against "false brothers" who infiltrated the congregations.—2Co 11:26; Ga 2:4.

Brothers of Jesus. The four Gospels, the Acts of Apostles, and two of Paul's letters mention "the Lord's brothers," "the brother of the Lord," "his brothers," "his sisters," naming four of the "brothers": James, Joseph, Simon, and Judas. (Mt 12:46; 13:55, 56; Mr 3:31; Lu 8:19; Joh 2:12; Ac 1:14; 1Co 9:5; Ga 1:19) The majority of Bible scholars accept the cumulative evidence that Jesus had at least four brothers and two sisters and that all were offspring of Joseph and Mary by natural means after the miraculous birth of Jesus.

The arbitrary notions that these brothers of Jesus were sons of Joseph by a former marriage, or by levirate marriage with Joseph's sister-in-law, must be classified as fictitious, since there is no factual confirmation or even a suggestion to this effect in the Scriptures. The claim that "brother" (a·del·phos') here means "cousin" (a·ne·psi·os') is a theoretical contention, the invention of which is credited to Jerome, and dates back no earlier than 383 C.E. Not only does Jerome fail to cite any support for his newborn hypothesis but in later writings he wavers in his opinions and even expresses misgivings about his "cousin theory." J. B. Lightfoot states that "St Jerome pleaded no traditional authority for his theory, and that therefore the evidence in its favour is to be sought in Scripture alone. I have examined the scriptural evidence, and the . . . combination of difficulties . . . more than counterbalances these secondary arguments in its favour, and in fact must lead to its rejection."—*St. Paul's Epistle to the Galatians,* London, 1874, p. 258.

In the Greek Scriptures where the account involved a nephew or cousin, *a·del·phos'* is not used. Rather, the relationship is explained, as "the son of Paul's sister" or "Mark the cousin [*a·ne·psi·os'*] of Barnabas." (Ac 23:16; Col 4:10) In Luke 21:16, the Greek words *syg·ge·non'* (relatives, such as cousins) and *a·del·phon'* (brothers) both occur, showing that the terms are not used loosely or indiscriminately in the Greek Scriptures.

When, during Jesus' ministry, "his brothers were, in fact, not exercising faith in him," this would certainly rule out their being his brothers in a spiritual sense. (Joh 7:3-5) Jesus contrasted these fleshly brothers with his disciples, who believed in him and who were his spiritual brothers. (Mt 12:46-50; Mr 3:31-35; Lu 8:19-21) This lack of faith on the part of his fleshly brothers prohibits identifying them with apostles of the same names: James, Simon, Judas; they are explicitly distinguished from Jesus' disciples.—Joh 2:12.

The relationship these fleshly brothers of Jesus had with his mother Mary also indicates they were her children rather than more distant relatives. They are usually mentioned in association with her. Statements to the effect that Jesus was Mary's *"firstborn"* (Lu 2:7), and that Joseph "had no intercourse with her *until* she gave birth to a son," also support the view that Joseph and Mary had other children. (Mt 1:25) Even Nazarene neighbors recognized and identified Jesus as "the brother of James and Joseph and Judas and Simon," adding, "And his sisters are here with us, are they not?"—Mr 6:3.

In the light of these scriptures, the question is asked: Why, then, should Jesus just before his death entrust the care of his mother Mary to the apostle John instead of to his fleshly brothers? (Joh 19:26, 27) Manifestly because Jesus' cousin, the apostle John, was a man who had proved his faith, he was the disciple whom Jesus loved so dearly, and this spiritual relationship transcended

that of the flesh; in fact, there is no indication that his fleshly brothers were, as yet, disciples of Jesus.

After Jesus' resurrection his fleshly brothers changed their doubting attitude, for they were present with their mother and the apostles when assembled for prayer after Jesus' ascension. (Ac 1:14) This suggests that they were present also at the outpouring of the holy spirit on the day of Pentecost. Jesus' brother James, who was singled out prominently among the older men of the governing body in Jerusalem, wrote the letter bearing his name. (Ac 12:17; 15:13; 21:18; Ga 1:19; Jas 1:1) Jesus' brother Jude penned the book bearing his name. (Jude 1, 17) Paul indicates that at least some of Jesus' brothers were married.—1Co 9:5.

BROTHER-IN-LAW MARRIAGE.

Known also as levirate marriage; a custom whereby a man would marry his deceased brother's sonless widow in order to produce offspring to carry on his brother's line. The Hebrew verb meaning "perform brother-in-law marriage" is *ya·vam'*, related to the Hebrew terms for "brother-in-law" and "brother's widow."—Ge 38:8; De 25:5, ftn; 25:7.

The law regarding brother-in-law marriage at Deuteronomy 25:5, 6 reads: "In case brothers dwell together and one of them has died without his having a son, the wife of the dead one should not become a strange man's outside. Her brother-in-law should go to her, and he must take her as his wife and perform brother-in-law marriage with her. And it must occur that the firstborn whom she will bear should succeed to the name of his dead brother, that his name may not be wiped out of Israel." This doubtless applied whether the surviving brother was married or not.

Jehovah is the one "to whom every family in heaven and on earth owes its name." (Eph 3:15) He shows concern for the preservation of the family name and line. This principle was followed in patriarchal times and was later incorporated into the Law covenant with Israel. The woman was not to "become a strange man's outside," that is, she should not marry anyone outside the family. When her brother-in-law took her, the firstborn would bear, not the name of the brother-in-law, but that of the deceased man. This does not mean that the child always bore the same given name but that he carried on the family line and the hereditary possession remained in the household of the deceased man.

"In case brothers dwell together" apparently did not mean that they lived in the same house but in the same vicinity. However, the Mishnah (*Yevamot* 2:1, 2) says that it meant not in the same community but at the same time. Of course, living at a great distance would make it difficult for the brother to take care of his own and his brother's inheritance until an heir could do it. But family inheritances were usually in the same area.

An example of brother-in-law marriage in patriarchal times is the case of Judah. He took a wife, Tamar, for Er his firstborn, and when Er proved wicked in Jehovah's eyes, Jehovah put him to death. "In view of that Judah said to Onan [Er's brother]: 'Have relations with your brother's wife and perform brother-in-law marriage with her and raise up offspring for your brother.' But Onan knew that the offspring would not become his; and it occurred that when he did have relations with his brother's wife he wasted his semen on the earth so as not to give offspring to his brother." (Ge 38:8, 9) Because Onan refused to fulfill his obligation in connection with the arrangement of brother-in-law marriage, Jehovah put him to death. Judah then told Tamar to wait until his third son Shelah matured, but Judah did not require Shelah to perform his duty toward Tamar.

In due time, after the death of Judah's wife, Tamar maneuvered events so as to get an heir from her father-in-law. This she did by disguising herself, putting on a shawl and a veil, and seating herself by the road along which she knew Judah would be passing. Judah took her for a harlot and had relations with her. She obtained tokens from him as evidence of their relations, and when the truth came out, Judah did not blame her but declared that she was more righteous than he was. The record states that he did not have further intercourse with her when he learned who she was. Thus Judah himself unwittingly produced an heir to Er through his daughter-in-law. —Ge 38.

Under the Law, in case a brother-in-law did not want to perform his duty, the widow was to take the matter to the older men of the city and inform them of this fact. He was to appear before them and state that he did not want to marry her. At that the widow was to draw off his sandal from his foot and spit in his face. After this the man's "name must be called in Israel 'The house of the one who had his sandal drawn off,'" an expression of reproach toward his household.—De 25:7-10.

The practice of taking off the sandal may have arisen from the fact that when anyone took possession of landed property he did so by treading upon the soil and asserting his right of possession by standing upon it in his sandals. In taking off his sandal and handing it to another, he was renouncing his position and property before the constituted older witnesses at the city gate.—Ru 4:7.

Further light is thrown on the matter in the book of Ruth. A Judean man named Elimelech died, as did his two sons, leaving his widow Naomi and two widowed daughters-in-law. There was a man referred to in the Bible as "So-and-so" who was a close relative of Elimelech, perhaps a brother. This one, being nearest of kin, was the one called the *go·'el'*, or the repurchaser. This one refused to carry out his duty but drew off his sandal and evidently gave it to Boaz, thus leaving Boaz the next nearest of kin with the right of repurchase. Boaz then bought Elimelech's land and thereby took Naomi, but since Naomi was too old for childbearing, the widowed daughter-in-law Ruth was actually the one becoming the wife to Boaz to raise up a child to the name of Elimelech. When the child Obed was born, neighbor ladies said: "A son has been born to Naomi," considering the child the son of Elimelech and Naomi. Boaz and Ruth performed a service to Jehovah, the name given to their son meaning "Servant; One Serving." Jehovah blessed this arrangement, for Obed became the ancestor of David and was, therefore, in the direct lineage of Jesus Christ. —Ru 4.

The right of levirate marriage evidently descended to the nearest male relative as outlined in the law governing inheritance of property, namely, the oldest brother, other brothers according to age, then the paternal uncle, and so forth. (Nu 27:5-11) In the reference made to brother-in-law marriage at Matthew 22:23-28 and Luke 20:27-33, it is indicated that the duty to marry the childless man's widow would pass from one brother to the next in the event of their successive deaths. Another brother evidently could not run ahead of the older brother, who had the prior obligation, unless the older brother refused to exercise it.

BROWN.   See COLORS.

BUILDER, BUILDING. The verb "build" means construct or make by assembling materials. The Hebrew word for "build" is *ba·nah'*. From it comes *bin·yah'* ("house"; Eze 41:13), *bin·yan'* ("building"; Eze 41:12), *miv·neh'* ("structure"; Eze 40:2), and *tav·nith'* ("pattern" [Ex 25:40]; "representation" [De 4:16]; "architectural plan" [1Ch 28:11]). *Oi·ko·do·me'o* is the common Greek verb for "build"; the related noun form *oi·ko·do·me'* means "building."—Mt 16:18; 1Co 3:9.

Jehovah God as Creator of all things is the Builder par excellence. (Heb 3:4; Job 38:4-6) The Logos (Word), who became Jesus Christ, was the Master Worker that He used in creating all things. (Joh 1:1-3; Col 1:13-16; Pr 8:30) Man cannot create but must build with materials already existent. The ability to plan, to manufacture instruments, and to build was planted in man at his creation and was manifested early in human history.—Ge 1:26; 4:20-22.

Cain, the first son of Adam and Eve, is the first man mentioned in the Bible as the builder of a city, giving it the name of his son Enoch. (Ge 4:17) Noah was the builder of an ark, the pattern of which was given to him by Jehovah. (Ge 6:13, 14) Nimrod, "a mighty hunter in opposition to Jehovah," was the builder of several cities, namely, Babel, Erech, Accad, Calneh, as well as Nineveh, Rehoboth-Ir, Calah, and Resen.—Ge 10:9-12.

When the Israelites were in slavery in Egypt they built cities as storage places for Pharaoh, namely, Pithom and Raamses. (Ex 1:11) When they were led by Jehovah into the Promised Land they there found cities that had been built by the Canaanite inhabitants. Many of these cities with their houses were taken and used by the Israelites. —De 6:10, 11.

In the wilderness Moses supervised the building of the tabernacle with all its utensils, the pattern having been divinely provided. (Ex 25:9) Taking the lead in the fabrication and construction were Bezalel and Oholiab, whose abilities were accentuated by God's holy spirit so that the finished work was done exactly as God had commanded Moses.—Ex 25:40; 35:30–36:1.

After David took the city of Jerusalem from the Jebusites, he did considerable building there, including constructing a house for himself. (2Sa 5:9-11) His son Solomon was a builder of renown, the temple of Jehovah being his foremost project. The architectural plans for this temple had been given to David by inspiration. (1Ch 28:11, 12) David had gathered much of the material for the temple building, gold, silver, copper, iron, timbers, stones, and precious stones, contributed by the people and also from David's own funds. (1Ch 22:14-16; 29:2-8) Hiram, king of Tyre, acted toward Solomon as he had toward David by supplying materials, particularly cedar and juniper timbers, as well as many workmen. (1Ki 5:7-10, 18; 2Ch 2:3) King Hiram also sent a man named Hiram (Hiram-abi), son of a Tyrian man and an Israelite woman, a very skilled worker in gold, silver, copper, iron, stones, timbers, and fabrics. —1Ki 7:13, 14; 2Ch 2:13, 14.

Solomon did other extensive building works, including a house for himself as well as the House of the Forest of Lebanon, the Porch of Pillars, and the Porch of the Throne. The building of the temple and other governmental buildings occupied 20 years. (1Ki 6:1; 7:1, 2, 6, 7; 9:10) Following this,

Solomon embarked on a nationwide building program, including Gezer and Lower Beth-horon, Baalath and Tamar (Tadmor) in the wilderness, along with storage cities, chariot cities, and cities for the horsemen. (1Ki 9:17-19) Excavations in Palestine, particularly at Hazor, Megiddo, and Gezer, have uncovered city gates and fortifications that archaeologists attribute to Solomon.

A notable builder among the kings of Israel and Judah was Solomon's son Rehoboam. His works included the rebuilding of Bethlehem, Etam, Tekoa, Beth-zur, Soco, Adullam, Gath, Mareshah, Ziph, Adoraim, Lachish, Azekah, Zorah, Aijalon, and Hebron. Rehoboam also reinforced and provisioned the fortified places. (2Ch 11:5-11) Other builders were King Baasha of Israel, who "began to build Ramah"; King Asa of Judah, building at Geba in Benjamin and Mizpah; Hiel the Bethelite, who forfeited two sons when he rebuilt ruined Jericho—Abiram his firstborn at the laying of its foundation and Segub his youngest at the putting up of the doors—as Joshua had prophesied (1Ki 15:17, 22; 16:34; Jos 6:26); and King Ahab of Israel, who constructed a house of ivory, besides several cities (1Ki 22:39).

King Uzziah of Judah was an extensive builder. (2Ch 26:9, 10) Uzziah displayed evidence of military genius in fortifying Jerusalem with "engines of war, the invention of engineers." (2Ch 26:15) Scenes of wall reliefs depicting Sennacherib's assault on Lachish show special kinds of fortifications on the towers, attributed by archaeologists to Uzziah.

Jotham did a great deal of building. (2Ch 27: 3, 4) And Hezekiah did considerable fortifying of Jerusalem, in connection with which he dug a water tunnel from the spring of Gihon to bring water inside the city. (2Ch 32:2-5, 30) This water tunnel can still be viewed by visitors to Jerusalem.

After the exile, Zerubbabel traveled from Babylon with about 50,000 men and began the rebuilding of the temple of Jehovah in Jerusalem. It was completed by March 6 of 515 B.C.E. Later, in 455 B.C.E., Nehemiah came from Shushan to rebuild the wall of the city.—Ezr 2:1, 2, 64, 65; 6:15; Ne 6:1; 7:1.

King Nebuchadnezzar of Babylon is known mainly for his military exploits. Nonetheless, he was a great builder. At Babylon he built many temples to false gods. He was also a notable builder of public works. His inscriptions concern themselves not with his military exploits but with his building projects, including temples, palaces, streets, embankments, and walls. He made Babylon the wonder city of the ancient world, and in all of Babylonia no building compared with the famous Hanging Gardens that King Nebuchadnezzar built to satisfy the homesick longings of his Median queen. Those gardens were rated as one of the seven wonders of the ancient world.

King Herod the Great rebuilt the second temple of Jehovah at Jerusalem. Because of distrust on the part of the Jews, he was compelled to bring the materials in first, then to raze the second temple piecemeal as he constructed the new one. Due to their distrust and dislike of Herod, the Jews do not consider it the third temple, although it is often designated as such by others. By the year 30 C.E. reconstruction in the temple area had been under way for 46 years (Joh 2:20), and it continued for many more years. Herod also built an artificial harbor city, Caesarea, and he rebuilt Samaria and carried on other vast building projects within Palestine as well as in other lands.

Jesus, when on earth, was in the building trade, being referred to as a "carpenter."—Mr 6:3.

Building materials used in Bible times were earth, wood of various sorts, stone, precious stones, metals, fabrics, plaster, mortar, and bitumen. Whitewash made of lime was also used, as were coloring for decorating wood, and dyes for fabrics. At times bricks were painted or enameled. —See BRICK.

A number of building tools and instruments are mentioned in the Bible, including the ax (De 19:5), hammer (Jg 4:21), forge hammer, anvil, nails (Isa 41:7), saw (Isa 10:15), stone-saw (1Ki 7:9), measuring line or rope (Zec 1:16; 2:1), measuring reed (Eze 40:3; Re 21:15), plummet (Am 7:7, 8; Zec 4:9, 10), leveling instrument (2Ki 21:13; Isa 28:17), wood scraper, compass (Isa 44:13), billhook (Isa 44:12; Jer 10:3), chisel (Ex 20:25), and scales (Isa 40:12).

Figurative Usage. The Christian congregation is considered a house or temple built upon the foundation of the apostles and prophets, with Christ Jesus as the foundation cornerstone. It is called "God's building," "a place for God to inhabit by spirit." (1Co 3:9; Eph 2:20-22) Jesus applied the fulfillment of Psalm 118:22 to himself, as being "the stone" that the Jewish religious leaders and their followers, as "builders," rejected. (Mt 21:42; Lu 20:17; Ac 4:11; 1Pe 2:7) The individual members of the congregation are spoken of as "living stones." (1Pe 2:5) The glorified congregation, also known as the bride of Jesus Christ, is pictured as a city, the New Jerusalem.—Re 21:2, 9-21.

Jesus likened his hearers to two kinds of builders, one of which built his personality and way of life on the rock-mass of obedience to Christ and was, therefore, able to withstand the storms of opposition and tribulation. The other, building on sand, was unable to stand when pressure came. (Mt 7:24-27) Building of Christian personalities in others also is discussed by the apostle Paul, a "director of works." (1Co 3:10-15) On one occasion Jesus said to the Jews: "Break down this temple, and in three days I will raise it up." (Joh 2:19) The Jews thought he was speaking of the temple of Herod and used this against him at his trial, witnesses against him saying: "We heard him say, 'I will throw down this temple that was made with hands and in three days I will build another not made with hands.'" (Mr 14:58) Jesus was using figurative speech, referring to "the temple of his body." He was put to death and on the third day rose again. (Joh 2:21; Mt 16:21; Lu 24:7, 21, 46) He was resurrected by his Father Jehovah God in another body, not one made with hands like the temple of Jerusalem, but a spirit body made (built) by his Father. (Ac 2:24; 1Pe 3:18) This use of building as applied to one's body is not unique, for, speaking of Eve's creation, it was said: "And Jehovah God proceeded to build the rib that he had taken from the man into a woman."—Ge 2:22.

Jesus Christ foretold that in the "last days" people would be involved in building operations and other activities of life, oblivious to the real meaning of the times, just as they were in the days of Lot, and that destruction would come upon them unawares in the midst of these activities.—Lu 17:28-30; see ARCHITECTURE; FORTIFICATIONS.

BUKKI (Buk'ki) [shortened form of Bukkiah].

1. A chieftain from the tribe of Dan whom Jehovah appointed to assist with the tribal division of the Promised Land. Son of Jogli.—Nu 34:16-18, 22.

2. Descendant of Aaron through Eleazar and Phinehas, and ancestor of Ezra. (1Ch 6:4, 5, 50, 51; Ezr 7:1-6) He may have served as high priest sometime during the period of the Judges.

BUKKIAH (Buk·ki'ah) [from a root meaning "flask"]. Son of Heman of the tribe of Levi. Bukkiah was chosen by lot to head the 6th of 24 musician groups that David organized for service at Jehovah's sanctuary. He and his sons and brothers assisting him totaled 12.—1Ch 25:1, 4, 9, 13, 31.

BUL [from a root meaning "yield; produce"]. The eighth lunar month of the sacred calendar of the Israelites corresponding to the second month of the secular calendar. (1Ki 6:37, 38; Ge 7:11) It included part of October and part of November. Following the Babylonian exile, this month was called Marheshvan or Marchesvan, later abbreviated to Heshvan. These postexilic names do not appear in the Bible but are found in the Jewish Talmud, the writings of Josephus, and other works.

Bul came at about the start of the rainy season in the autumn. (De 11:14; Joe 2:23; Jas 5:7) It was a month in which the sowing of barley and wheat went on, and in northern Galilee olives were gathered. The shepherds were now bringing their flocks of sheep back in from the open fields to put them under cover during the winter months of cold and rain.

According to Genesis 7:11 and 8:14, the Flood of Noah's day began on the 17th day of "the second month," and by the same month a lunar year and ten days later the earth had dried off. Concerning this, Josephus (*Jewish Antiquities*, I, 80 [iii, 3]) commented: "This catastrophe happened in the six hundredth year of Noah's rulership, in what was once the second month, called by the Macedonians Dius and by the Hebrews Marsuan, according to the arrangement of the calendar which they followed in Egypt." Therefore, according to Josephus, the second month in Noah's time corresponded to the month Bul, or Marheshvan.

Following the Exodus from Egypt, Bul became the eighth month in the sacred calendar, and it was during this month that Solomon completed the construction of the temple at Jerusalem. (1Ki 6:38) Jeroboam, the founder of the separatist northern kingdom of Israel, arbitrarily made this month a festival month, as part of his plan to divert the people's attention from Jerusalem and its feasts.—1Ki 12:26, 31-33.

BULBUL   (bul'bul) [Heb., 'a·ghur']. The name of a number of types of medium-sized thrushlike birds found in Africa and southern Asia, including Palestine. The bulbul characteristically has a short neck, short wings, and a long tail. While many translations render 'a·ghur' as "crane," Hezekiah's reference to the bird's "chirping" would hardly describe the deep trumpeting sound made by that large bird. (Isa 38:14) *Lexicon in Veteris Testamenti Libros* (by L. Koehler and W. Baumgartner, Leiden, 1958, p. 679) identified 'a·ghur' as the bulbul (*Pycnonotus Reichenovi*). Ludwig Koehler says the Hebrew 'a·ghur' describes a bird that 'ruffles or bristles its feathers' and says concerning the bulbul that "during the pauses (of its song) it lifts . . . from time to time the extended crestlike feathers of the back of the head." (*Kleine Lichter* [German], Zurich, 1945, pp. 38, 39) Unlike the somewhat bellowing sound of the crane, the song of the bulbul is rather flutelike in tone and is described as a combination chirp and warble.

Jeremiah (8:7) evidently refers to the seasonal arrival of migratory birds in his censuring the Israelites for not discerning the time of God's judgment on them.

BULL   [Heb., *shohr* (Ex 21:28), *par* (Ex 29:10), *ba·qar'* (1Ki 7:25), *'agha·lim'* ("young bulls"; Am 6:4), *re'em'* ("wild bull"; Nu 23:22); Aramaic, *tohr* (Da 5:21); Gr., *tau'ros* (Mt 22:4), *bous* (1Co 9:9), *mo'skhos* ("young bull"; Lu 15:23)]. These original-language words for the male of cattle have been variously translated "bull," "bullock," "calf," "ox." In modern English usage "ox" has come to apply especially to a castrated bull, but the original-language words often rendered "ox" and "oxen" in various translations are not to be understood in this restricted sense. Although castration is the method ordinarily employed for breaking bulls for service as draft animals, apparently this was not practiced by the Israelites, for a mutilated animal was unfit for sacrifice. (Le 22:23, 24; De 17:1; compare 1Ki 19:21.) It has, therefore, been suggested that the breed used by the Israelites may have been of a gentle temper.

The male of beef cattle has occupied a prominent place in the religions of many pagan peoples. Whether because of its great strength or its potential as sire of numerous offspring, it has been honored, even worshiped. The Babylonians employed the bull as the symbol of their principal god, Marduk. In Egypt living bulls were venerated as incarnations of a god—Apis at Memphis and Mnevis at Heliopolis. The occurrence of the bull, Taurus, as one of the primary signs of the zodiac offers additional evidence of the important place accorded the bull in pagan religions.

Shortly after the Exodus, even the Israelites, likely because of being contaminated by the religious concepts with which they became acquainted while in Egypt, exchanged Jehovah's glory for "a representation of a bull." (Ps 106:19, 20) Later, the first king of the ten-tribe kingdom, Jeroboam, set up calf worship at Dan and Bethel. (1Ki 12:28, 29) Of course, according to God's law to Israel, no veneration whatsoever, not even in a representative way, was to be given to the bull or any other animal.—Ex 20:4, 5; compare Ex 32:8.

Bulls were offered in sacrifice by the Israelites (Ex 29; Le 22:27; Nu 7; 1Ch 29:21), and at certain times the Law specifically directed that bulls were to be sacrificed. If the high priest committed a sin that brought guiltiness upon the people, he was required to offer a bull, the largest and most valuable sacrificial victim, this undoubtedly in keeping with his responsible position as leader of Israel in true worship. A bull also had to be offered when the entire assembly of Israel made a mistake. (Le 4:3, 13, 14) On Atonement Day a bull was to be offered in behalf of the priestly house of Aaron. (Le 16) In the seventh month of their sacred calendar the Israelites were required to offer more than 70 bulls as burnt offerings. —Nu 29.

The bull was used by the Israelites in the work related to farm operations, for plowing and threshing. (De 22:10; 25:4) The creature was to be treated humanely. The apostle Paul applied to God's Christian servants the principle embodied in the Law with respect to not muzzling a bull while it is threshing, indicating that just as the working bull was entitled to feed on the grain it was threshing, likewise the one sharing spiritual things with others is worthy of receiving material provisions. (Ex 23:4, 12; De 25:4; 1Co 9:7-10) Legislation covered cases of theft of a bull and of damage done to persons and property by an untended bull.—Ex 21:28–22:15.

The bulls sacrificed by the Israelites symbolized the one unblemished offering of Christ as the only adequate sacrifice for the sins of mankind. (Heb 9:12-14) Sacrificial bulls are also representative of another sacrifice, one that delights Jehovah in all times and circumstances, namely, the spontaneous fruitage of lips that, like vigorous young bulls, are used to "make public declaration to his name."—Ps 69:30, 31; Ho 14:2; Heb 13:15.

In Bible symbolism the bull is used to denote power and strength. The molten sea in front of Solomon's temple rested on representations of 12 bulls, in groups of three facing each of the cardinal directions. (2Ch 4:2, 4) The four living creatures seen in vision by the prophet Ezekiel accompanying the chariotlike throne of Jehovah each had four faces, one of which was that of a bull. (Eze 1:10) In the vision of the apostle John, one of the four living creatures around the throne was like a young bull. (Re 4:6, 7) Hence, the bull would fitly represent one of Jehovah's basic attributes, namely, unlimited power.—Ps 62:11; Isa 40:26.

In the Scriptures the bull also figures as a symbol of the aggressive enemies of Jehovah and of his worshipers, who would seek to enslave or destroy God's servants but who would themselves be annihilated at Jehovah's day of vengeance.—Ps 22:12; 68:30; Isa 34:7, 8; Eze 39:18; see CALF; OFFERINGS.

In Scripture, allusion is made to several of the characteristics of the "wild bull" (re'em'): its intractable disposition (Job 39:9-12), its swiftness and invincibility (Nu 23:22; 24:8), the power of its great horns (De 33:17; Ps 22:21; 92:10), and its friskiness in youth (Ps 29:6). Wild bulls are also used to represent the intractable enemies of Jeho-

vah against whom the execution of his judgments is directed.—Isa 34:7.

BUNAH (Bu'nah) [shortened form of Benaiah, meaning "Jehovah Has Built"]. Son of Jerahmeel in the tribe of Judah; brother of Ram through whom the Messianic lineage is traced.—1Ch 2:3, 25.

BUNNI (Bun'ni) [shortened form of Benaiah, meaning "Jehovah Has Built"].

1. A Levite whose descendant was chosen by lot to live in Jerusalem after the wall rebuilding by Nehemiah.—Ne 11:1, 15.

2. A leading Levite in the days of Ezra and Nehemiah who was among those on the platform 'crying out with a loud voice' in repentance to Jehovah.—Ne 9:4.

3. One of "the heads of the people" whose descendant, if not he himself, concurred with the covenant of faithfulness that Nehemiah sponsored.—Ne 10:1, 14, 15.

BURDEN. Something carried; a load, literal or figurative. Various Hebrew and Greek words are used in the Scriptures to denote a "burden" or "load," sometimes relating to material that is carried but often to such figurative things as responsibility, guilt, or a message from God. A burden is generally viewed as a heavy load. Of the various Hebrew roots relating to burdens and loads, one (ka·vedh') basically means "be heavy." (Ge 18:20; compare 1Sa 4:18; Ex 10:14.) Another, the verb na·sa', means "lift; carry" (Ge 45:19; 47:30) and is the root of mas·sa', rendered "burden; load." (2Ch 35:3; Nu 4:15) The verb sa·val', translated "bear burdens" in Genesis 49:15, is related to sab·bal' ("burden bearer" [Ne 4:10]) and se'vel ("burden" [Ne 4:17]; "compulsory service" [1Ki 11:28]).

Chiefs of forced labor were placed over the Israelites in Egypt "for the purpose of oppressing them in their burden-bearing" and compelling them to carry and use such building materials as clay mortar and bricks. (Ex 1:11-14; 2:11) But, Jehovah brought them "out from under the burdens of the Egyptians." (Ex 6:6; Ps 81:6) When the tabernacle and its articles were moved from place to place, the Kohathite, Gershonite, and Merarite Levites had their specific loads to carry. (Nu 4) Later, Solomon came to have 70,000 burden bearers in his large work force. (1Ki 5:15; 2Ch 2:18) Burden bearers were also needed and used when King Josiah repaired the temple (2Ch 34:12, 13) and, years later, when Nehemiah supervised the rebuilding of Jerusalem's wall.—Ne 4:17; see COMPULSORY SERVICE.

Animals were often used to carry loads in ancient times, and the Israelites were told that upon seeing the ass of someone hating them lying down under its load, instead of leaving it, one was "without fail to get it loose." (Ex 23:5) The amount of material an animal can carry is called a load, such as "the load of a pair of mules."—2Ki 5:17.

Figurative Use. The Hebrew word *mas·sa'*, often used for a literal load or a burden, can denote a "weighty message," such as the one King Lemuel's mother gave him in correction. (Pr 31:1) It can also pertain to a pronouncement. (Isa 13:1; 14:28; Eze 12:10; Na 1:1) Usually the pronouncement is one of denunciation for wickedness and thus is like a heavy burden of judgment.

The person faithful to God can throw his figurative burden, or the lot that has been given to him in such things as trials and cares, upon Jehovah. Thus, David declared: "Throw your burden upon Jehovah himself, and he himself will sustain you. Never will he allow the righteous one to totter." (Ps 55:22; compare 1Pe 5:6, 7.) David was also moved to exclaim: "Blessed be Jehovah, who daily carries the load for us, the true God of our salvation."—Ps 68:19.

A "burden" can be a burden of responsibility imposed by Christ. (Re 2:24) The holy spirit and the Christian governing body favored adding no further "burden" to Christians except necessary things, that is, "to keep abstaining from things sacrificed to idols and from blood and from things strangled and from fornication."—Ac 15:28, 29.

In another sense, Paul assured the Corinthians that he would not become a burden to them and was not seeking their possessions but would "most gladly spend and be completely spent" for their souls. (2Co 12:14-18) As an apostle of Christ, Paul justifiably could have been "an expensive burden" on Christians in Thessalonica. However, he did not even eat food from anyone free and could remind them that "by labor and toil night and day we were working so as not to impose an expensive burden upon any one of you," not because of lacking authority to do so, but to serve as an example they could imitate.—2Th 3:7-10.

Jesus denounced the scribes and Pharisees, saying: "They bind up heavy loads and put them upon the shoulders of men, but they themselves are not willing to budge them with their finger." (Mt 23:2, 4) Jesus was evidently referring to minute rules and burdensome traditions that these men laid upon the common people, being unwilling to lift even one small regulation to make things easier for them.—Mt 23:13, 23, 24.

On the other hand, Jesus freed persons spiritually from such oppressive traditions. (Joh 8:31, 32) He invited those who were toiling and loaded down to come to him, to take his yoke upon them, and to become his disciples, for he was mild-tempered and lowly in heart, and they would thus find refreshment for their souls. He said: "My yoke is kindly and my load is light." (Mt 11:28-30) Christ was not harsh or oppressive but kind, and those coming to him would receive proper treatment. Christ's yoke, by comparison with that placed upon the people by religious traditionists, would be a comparatively light one. Jesus may also have meant that those weary of the burden of sin and error should come to him for spiritual refreshment. Carrying Jesus' light "load" evidently involved acquaintance with and the fulfilling of divine requirements, something Jesus did with delight during his earthly life and ministry. (Joh 17:3; 4:34) Paul later likened the Christian career to being on a racecourse and urged fellow believers to unburden themselves, telling them to put off "every weight and the sin that easily entangles us," and to "run with endurance the race that is set before us," while looking intently at "the Chief Agent and Perfecter of our faith, Jesus."—Heb 12:1, 2.

Carrying Others' Burdens. Paul wrote to the Galatians: "Go on carrying the burdens [or, "troublesome things"; literally, "heavy things"] of one another, and thus fulfill the law of the Christ." (Ga 6:2, ftn) Here for "burdens" the apostle used *ba're*, the plural form of *ba'ros*, a Greek word always used to denote something burdensome or heavy. Certainly the sin and hence the burden of a man taking some "false step" (referred to in the preceding verse) would not be light but heavy. However, in verse 5 the apostle states: "For each one will carry his own load," that is, his load of responsibility. For "load" Paul here used the Greek word *phor·ti'on*, signifying something that is to be borne or carried, without any reference to the weight of the thing. So he drew a distinction between "burdens" and "load" in these verses. This would indicate that if a Christian got into spiritual difficulty that was very hard for him to bear, fellow believers would aid him, thus helping to bear another's burden. Such persons would be displaying love and would thus fulfill the law of Christ. (Joh 13:34, 35) This harmonizes with what Paul had just said, as recorded in Galatians 6:1, about endeavoring to restore a man spiritually, something that may be possible through love, kindness, and prayer. (Compare Jas 5:13-16.) Yet, as the apostle proceeded to show, bearing the burdens of one another does not mean carrying another person's load of spiritual responsibility to God. In the same context, Paul makes clear that a person is deceiving his own mind if he thinks that he is something when he is nothing, and the apostle urged the Christian to "prove what his own work is," for "then he will have cause for exultation in regard to himself alone, and not in comparison with the other person." (Ga 6:3, 4; compare 2Co 10:12.) It was then that the apostle observed that "each one will carry his own load" of responsibility before the Supreme Judge, Jehovah God.

BURIAL, BURIAL PLACES.

The interment of the body of a deceased person was an act of considerable importance to people in the Biblical period. Thus, Abraham, the first person directly mentioned in the record as performing a burial, was willing to spend a fair sum of money in order to obtain a suitable place as a burial ground. (See PURCHASE.) The Hittites (sons of Heth), from whom the purchase was made, had their own 'choice' burial places. (Ge 23:3-20) The cave obtained by Abraham became a family burial site, receiving his wife's body and, eventually, his own, and those of Isaac, Rebekah, Leah, and Jacob. (Ge 25:9; 49:29-32) Jacob was seriously concerned that his body not be buried in Egypt but, rather, with his forefathers. (Ge 47:29-31) This necessitated the embalming of his body, which otherwise would have putrefied during the hot journey from Egypt to the cave of Machpelah. (Ge 50:1-3, 13) Joseph expressed a similar desire, and his body was likewise embalmed and placed in a coffin, awaiting the time of the Exodus for transferal. (Ge 50:24-26; Jos 24:32) This desire doubtless related to their sharing the same faith in God's promises and was an expression of their conviction as to the eventual fulfillment of these.—Heb 11:13-22, 39.

Following the model of Abraham, family burial places seem to have been preferred. (2Sa 19:34-37) Gideon, Samson, and Asahel are each spoken of as being buried 'in the burial place of his father.' (Jg 8:32; 16:31; 2Sa 2:32) However, the frequent expression 'to lie down, or be buried, with his forefathers' does not necessarily imply a sharing of the same burial site, for this phrase is used concerning men who were clearly not buried in the same place as their forefathers. (Ge 15:15; De 31:16; 32:50; 1Ki 2:10; Ac 13:36) It must thus refer to their common entrance into Sheol (Hades), the common grave of mankind. Such common grave is called "the house of meeting for everyone living."—Job 30:23.

The act of burying another's body was viewed as an expression of loving-kindness, and the men of Jabesh-gilead risked their lives to effect such a burial for Saul and his sons. (1Sa 31:11-13; 2Sa 2:4-6) To be deprived of burial was considered calamitous (Jer 14:16) and is stated as being a divine means of expressing God's repudiation of persons due to their wrong course. (Jer 8:1, 2; 9:22; 25:32, 33; Isa 14:19, 20; compare Re 11:7-9.) The body was thereby exposed to be consumed as food by animals and carrion-eating birds. (Ps 79:1-3; Jer 16:4) The pathetic picture of Rizpah's refusing to abandon her dead sons' bodies, perhaps for months, until they were finally accorded a burial vividly portrays the importance attached to the matter.—2Sa 21:9-14.

Jehovah's law through Moses even provided for burial of criminals. (De 21:23; compare Jos 8:29.) Ahithophel, though a suicide, received burial. (2Sa 17:23) At the same time that Solomon ordered Joab's execution, he also gave instructions for his burial. (1Ki 2:31) Jehu intended to give wicked Jezebel a burial out of consideration for her being "the daughter of a king," but he was overruled by the fulfillment of Jehovah's prophecy that she should become "as manure upon the face of the field."—2Ki 9:10, 34-37; compare 2Ch 22:8, 9.

Aside from the cases of Jacob and Joseph, burial was evidently effected by the Israelites on the same day of the death. Early interment was necessary because of rapid decomposition in the usually warm climate of Bible lands. Lying Ananias was buried within about three hours of his death. (Ac 5:5-10) Additionally, under the Mosaic Law the dead body was viewed as making those touching it unclean for a seven-day period. Whereas death's being the result of sin and imperfection was doubtless the underlying basis for this judicial decision, it also worked for the prevention of the spread of disease and benefited its observers hygienically. Those failing to observe the purifying procedure prescribed in the Law were subject to the death penalty. (Nu 19:11-20; compare De 21: 22, 23.) Josiah used the bones of idol worshipers to make their religious altars unfit for worship, and he also desecrated their burial places.—2Ki 23:14-16; 2Ch 34:4, 5.

In view of the Biblical attitude toward dead bodies, it is evident that the veneration of the bodies of prominent servants of God was not practiced or countenanced. Moses' body was buried by God himself in an unknown site, and this also made impossible any future pilgrimages to his burial place.—De 34:5, 6; compare Jude 9.

The places selected for burial purposes were varied. Burial in the soil, a common method in the West, though certainly practiced, was not as highly favored in the Middle East. Rebekah's nursing woman Deborah and also, initially at least, King Saul and his sons were buried under large trees. (Ge 35:8; 1Ch 10:12) But natural caves or artificial ones excavated in the soft limestone rock so common in Palestine seem to have been preferred, as in Abraham's case. The burial place was often personally prepared well in advance. (Ge 50:5; Isa 22:16; 2Ch 16:14) The site might be near the person's house, perhaps in a garden (1Sa 25:1; 1Ki 2:34; 2Ki 21:25, 26); the expression "at his house" does not mean within the building, as is shown by a comparison of 2 Chronicles 33:20 and 2 Kings 21:18.

Archaeological investigations give an idea of the type of burial places used in ancient times. Aside from simple earthen graves, in Palestine these could be vaults or chambers cut in the rock, often on hillsides. Elevated places seem to have been preferred. (Jos 24:33; 2Ki 23:16; 2Ch 32:33; Isa 22:16) The chamber might be for a single burial, the body being laid in an excavated place in the floor. Or it might be arranged for multiple burials, with long slots, large enough to accommodate one body each, cut into the sides of the chamber at right angles to the walls. The narrow opening through which the body was inserted was then covered with a stone cut to fit. In other cases a benchlike niche, or shelf, was cut into the rear and side walls (Mr 16:5), or there might be a double row of such shelves, thus increasing the capacity of the burial place. The tomb might even consist of more than one chamber, although the single chamber seems to have been the common type among the Jews. Where the body lay exposed on a shelf, it was, of course, necessary to seal off the entrance against the depredations of wild animals. Thus, the main entrance to the chamber was closed off with a large stone, at times hinged as a door, and occasionally with a circular one set in a track and rolled in front of the entrance. Such circular stones might weigh as much as a ton or more.—Mt 27:60; Mr 16:3, 4.

Simplicity marks the earlier Jewish burial places. They thus contrasted greatly with the pagan tombs, which often had paintings on the walls and other ornamentation. Although Jacob erected a pillar over Rachel's grave, perhaps a single stone (Ge 35:20), this seems to have been simply a marker, not a monument. (1Sa 10:2) A "gravestone" is also mentioned at 2 Kings 23:17 as marking a burial spot. Jesus referred to tombs "not in evidence, so that men walk upon them and do not know it." (Lu 11:44) Because there was ceremonial defilement associated with the dead, burial places of the Jewish people were frequently whitewashed, thereby advising the passersby of their presence. (Mt 23:27) This whitewashing is said to have been done annually, prior to the Passover. —The Mishnah, *Shekalim* 1:1.

Following the death of an individual, the body was generally washed (Ac 9:37) and anointed with aromatic oils and ointments, which, if considered a type of embalming, was not the kind done by the ancient Egyptians. (Compare Mr 14:3-8; Joh 12:3, 7.) The body was then wrapped in cloth, generally linen. (Mt 27:59; Joh 11:44) Spices such as myrrh and aloes were customarily included in with such bandages (Joh 19:39, 40), or the body might be laid in oil and ointment, as was done with King Asa's body. (2Ch 16:14) The great "funeral burning" mentioned in this latter case was evidently a burning of such spices, giving off an aromatic incense. The head might be covered by a separate cloth.—Joh 20:7.

The women who went to Jesus' tomb on the third day to grease his body with spices may have done so because of the hurried circumstances under which Jesus was buried and hence with the purpose of doing a more complete work as a means of preserving the body for a longer period. —Mr 16:1; Lu 23:55, 56.

The body was likely carried to the burial site on a bier, or funeral litter, possibly made of wickerwork, and a considerable procession might accompany it, perhaps including musicians playing mournful music. (Lu 7:12-14; Mt 9:23) Amid weeping, some expression concerning the deceased might be made at the gravesite.—2Sa 3:31-34; 2Ch 35:23-25.

In course of time cemeteries came into existence as the number of dead multiplied. These were customarily outside the city walls. But Judean kings were buried in "the City of David," and those of Israel were buried in the capital city of the northern kingdom. (1Sa 25:1; 1Ki 22:37; 2Ch 9:31; 24:15, 16) In the book *Digging Up Biblical History* (1931, Vol. II, p. 186), J. G. Duncan writes: "As a rule the Hebrews, though they sometimes buried within the city walls, excavated their rock-tombs on a hill-slope near to their city. The presence of rock-tombs on one hill-slope is often a sure indication that the hill opposite or near had had a settlement on it, and, on the other hand, the absence of any indication of burials near a site is a sure proof that that site had not been occupied." The cliffs surrounding Jerusalem abound with burial places. (Compare Isa 22:16.) The reference to "the graveyard of the sons of the people" ("the burial place of the common people," *RS*) in the Valley of Kidron is believed to refer to a graveyard for the poorer class. (Jer 26:23; 2Ki 23:6) Mention is also made of "the potter's field" for the burial of strangers.—Mt 27:7; see AKELDAMA.

Cremation, widely practiced by the later Babylonians, Greeks, and Romans, was rare among the Jews. The corpses of Saul and his sons were burned; the bones, however, were buried.—1Sa 31:8-13; note also Am 6:9, 10.

In the Hebrew Scriptures the words *qe'ver* ("burial place"; Ge 23:4) and *qevu·rah'* ("grave"; Ge 35:20) are distinct in meaning from the Hebrew *she'ohl'*, which refers, not to an individual grave or graves, but to the common grave of mankind, gravedom. Likewise, in the Christian Greek Scriptures the Greek word *ta'phos* ("grave"; Mt 27:61) and the words *mne'ma* ("tomb"; Mr 15:46) and *mne·mei'on* ("memorial tomb"; Lu 23: 55) are distinct from the word *hai'des,* the Greek equivalent of *she'ohl'.*—See HADES; MEMORIAL TOMB; SHEOL.

Burial Places of the Kings or of David. On Pentecost, Peter stated: "David . . . both deceased and was buried and his tomb is among us to this day." (Ac 2:29) This indicates that the burial place of King David was still in existence as of the year 33 C.E.

First Kings 2:10 tells us that David was buried in "the City of David," and apparently this became the customary burial place of later kings of Judah. Twelve of the 20 kings following David are directly mentioned as being buried in the City of David, though not all of these were placed in "the burial places of the kings"—Jehoram, Joash (Jehoash), and Ahaz being specifically mentioned as not buried there. (2Ch 21:16, 20; 24:24, 25; 28:27) Instead of being one common tomb of many chambers, "the burial places of the kings" may have constituted a particular area within the City of David where the memorial tombs of the kings were located. King Asa was buried in a "grand burial place that he had excavated for himself in the City of David" (2Ch 16:14), and Hezekiah is spoken of as being buried "in the ascent to the burial places of the sons of David." (2Ch 32:33) Leprous King Uzziah was buried "with his forefathers, but in the burial field that belonged to the kings, for they said: 'He is a leper.'" This would seem to indicate the placement of his diseased body in the ground rather than in a tomb hewed out of rock.—2Ch 26:23.

Of the other kings of Judah, Manasseh and Amon were evidently buried in a different location, in "the garden of Uzza." (2Ki 21:18, 23, 26) The statement that Amon's son, faithful King Josiah, was buried in "the graveyard of his forefathers" may refer either to the royal tombs in the City of David or to the burial places of Manasseh and Amon. (2Ch 35:23, 24) Three kings died in exile: Jehoahaz (in Egypt), Jehoiachin and Zedekiah (in Babylon). (2Ki 23:34; 25:7, 27-30) Jehoiakim received "the burial of a he-ass," "thrown out to the heat by day and to the frost by night" in fulfillment of Jeremiah's prophecy.—Jer 22:18, 19; 36:30.

Righteous High Priest Jehoiada was accorded the honor of a burial in "the City of David along with the kings," the only person not of the royal line mentioned as having received such distinction.—2Ch 24:15, 16.

The location of these royal burial places has not been determined. On the basis of the reference to "the Burial Places of David" at Nehemiah 3:16 and the mention of "the ascent to the burial places of the sons of David" at 2 Chronicles 32:33, some believe the likely location to have been on the SE hill of the city near the Kidron Valley. A number of what appear to be ancient rock-cut tombs have been found in this area, their entrances being in the form of sunken rectangular shafts. However, no positive identification can be made; any effort at identification was complicated not only by the destruction of the city in the year 70 C.E. and again in 135 C.E. but also by the use of the southern part of the city by the Romans as a stone quarry. Hence, the above-mentioned tombs are in a greatly deteriorated state.

The mausoleum of Queen Helena of Adiabene, located in the N of the modern city of Jerusalem, has acquired the misleading name of the "Tombs of the Kings." It was actually built in the first century C.E. and should not be confused with the royal burial grounds mentioned in the Bible account.

"The Carcasses of Their Kings." At Ezekiel 43:7-9 Jehovah condemned the house of Israel and their kings for defiling his holy name by "their fornication and by the carcasses of their kings at their death" and said, "Now let them remove their fornication and the carcasses of their kings far from me, and I shall certainly reside in the midst of them to time indefinite." Some commentators have taken this to indicate that the Jews were guilty of having made the burial places of certain kings near the temple area. In verse 7, about 20 Hebrew manuscripts and editions and the Targums contain the phrase "at their death," while the Masoretic text reads, instead, "their high places," and the Greek *Septuagint* says "in the midst of them."

Even if the phrase "at their death" is the correct reading here, this seems to be no solid basis for believing that any of the kings of Judah were buried near the temple grounds. Since the dead body of a person was unclean according to the Law, to bury anyone near the temple would be an open affront to God, and such an obvious and gross violation of the temple's sanctity is not even hinted at in the histories of the kings. Those kings not accorded a burial in "the burial places of the kings" or "of the sons of David" are not likely to have been given a more exalted place of burial, such as near the temple but, rather, a less prominent and less honorable place.

A closer consideration of Ezekiel 43:7-9 indicates that the discussion involved idolatry and that, even as the "fornication" is primarily figurative, so too "the carcasses of their kings" represent the dead idols that the house of Israel and their rulers had worshiped. Thus, at Leviticus 26:30 Jehovah warned the Israelites that their disobedience would cause him to "annihilate your sacred high places and cut off your incense stands and lay your own carcasses upon *the carcasses of your dungy idols.*" (Compare Jer 16:18; Eze 6:4-6.) The record shows that such idols were introduced into the temple area. (Eze 8:5-17) It may also be noted that some of these idol gods were designated as kings, the word for "king" being included within the names Molech (1Ki 11:7), Milcom (1Ki 11:5), and Malcam (Jer 49:1). Concerning the idol gods of the northern kingdom, the prophet Amos (5:26) wrote: "And you will certainly carry Sakkuth your king and Kaiwan, your images, the star of your god, whom you made for yourselves." So, there seems to be greater weight for viewing the text as being a condemnation of idolatry rather than of a desecration of the dedicated ground by improper burial of literal rulers.

BURNT OFFERING.   See OFFERINGS.

BUSH   [Heb., *si'ach*]. A low, densely branched shrub or a cluster of shrubs. The Hebrew word *si'ach* occurs only four times, at Genesis 2:5; 21: 15; Job 30:4, 7. Some trees in the Palestine region may properly be designated as bushes, including the dwarf juniper, the thorny lotus, the broom tree; while others are often or usually shrublike in size and appearance, such as the acacia, myrtle, storax, tamarisk, and willow trees.

In the wilderness of Beer-sheba, despairing Hagar threw Ishmael under a bush (Ge 21:15), while Job describes persons living in a waterless region "plucking the salt herb by the bushes" and crying out from among the bushes.—Job 30:4, 7.

The burning bush by which Jehovah's angel attracted Moses' attention and spoke with him is understood to have been some type of thornbush (Heb., *seneh'*). (Ex 3:2-5; De 33:16) In referring to this event, the Christian writers of the Greek Scriptures employed the Greek word *ba'tos*, which means a bramble or any thorny bush. (Mr 12:26; Lu 20:37; Ac 7:30, 35) In Greek the blackberry is called *ba'ton* (derived from *ba'tos*), and hence some lexicographers connect the thorny bush (*seneh'*) with the blackberry bush (*Rubus sanctus*), which is common throughout Syria and much of Palestine. It is not found growing wild in the Sinai Peninsula in modern times, however. For this reason others favor an association with some type of acacia tree, as these thorny, often bushlike trees are very common throughout the Sinai region. However, no certain identification can be made.

BUTTER.   An emulsion principally of fat produced by agitating or churning milk or cream. In Bible times this milk product was unlike that of the modern Western world, for instead of being solid it was in a semifluid state. (Job 20:17) Hence, Koehler and Baumgartner define the Hebrew word *chem·ah'* as sweet, fresh butter, still soft. (*Lexicon in Veteris Testamenti Libros,* Leiden, 1958, p. 308) Franciscus Zorell says that this word refers to "thick, curdled milk." (*Lexicon Hebraicum et Aramaicum Veteris Testamenti,* Rome, 1968, p. 248) The same word is rendered "curdled milk" at Judges 5:25.

"The churning [literally, squeezing] of milk is what brings forth butter." (Pr 30:33) This was done by putting the milk in a skin bottle and kneading it, rocking it upon the knees, or suspending it between poles and swinging it back and forth abruptly until the desired consistency was reached.

Butter, though considered a delicacy, has been eaten and enjoyed since patriarchal times. Abraham included it in the feast he spread for the angelic visitors (Ge 18:8); David's friends came to him with butter and other gifts of sustenance. —2Sa 17:29.

"Butter" at Psalm 55:21 is used figuratively to refer to the pleasant, smooth, oily words of a traitor.

BUZ.

1. Son of Abraham's brother Nahor by his wife Milcah; Rebekah's uncle. (Ge 22:20-23) His descendants were presumably Buzites, Elihu's father being described as such.—Job 32:2, 6; see No. 3 below.

2. A family head and descendant of Jacob's son Gad.—1Ch 5:11, 14.

3. A place in Arabia against which Jeremiah foretells doom. (Jer 25:17, 23) It was presumably inhabited by the descendants of No. 1 above.

BUZI   (Bu'zi) [Of (Belonging to) Buz]. The Levitical and priestly father of the prophet Ezekiel. —Eze 1:3.

BUZITE.   See BUZ No. 1.

C

CAB. A measure that, according to rabbinic sources, was 1/18 ephah (2Ki 6:25), and hence also 1/18 bath measure. (Eze 45:11) If the bath measure is to be viewed as having a capacity of 22 L (5.81 gal; 4.99 dry gal), as archaeological evidence seems to indicate, then the cab measure would have a capacity of 1.22 L (2.58 liquid pt; 2.2 dry pt).

CABBON (Cab'bon). One of the cities of Judah in the Shephelah. (Jos 15:40) The Greek *Septuagint* reads "Chabra" instead of Cabbon, and this has led some to relate the town to Khirbet Hibra 5 km (3 mi) ESE of Lachish. On the basis of the Hebrew name, however, others suggest an identification with Al Qubeiba (Horvat Kefar Lakhish), 5 km (3 mi) SW of Beit Jibrin (Bet Guvrin).

CABUL (Ca'bul).

1. A town assigned to the tribe of Asher as part of its inheritance. (Jos 19:24, 27) It is represented by modern Kabul, situated about 13 km (8 mi) ESE of Acco.

2. The name applied to a Galilean district of 20 cities given by Solomon to King Hiram of Tyre, the gift likely deriving from Solomon's appreciation for Hiram's assistance in his building program. Hiram, however, on inspecting the cities, found them "not just right in his eyes," saying to Solomon: "What sort of cities are these that you have given me, my brother?" Thereafter they came to be called "the Land of Cabul."—1Ki 9:10-13.

According to Josephus, the cities "lay not far from Tyre." (*Jewish Antiquities*, VIII, 142 [v, 3]) Galilee is called by Isaiah (9:1) "Galilee of the nations," and certain scholars consider it probable that the 20 cities were inhabited by a pagan population. It does not seem likely that Solomon would turn them over to a foreign king if they were inhabited by Israelites, and they may indeed have been outside the boundaries actually inhabited by Israel, though still within the limits of the original area promised Israel by God and conquered by Solomon's father David. (Ex 23:31; 2Sa 8:1-15) The propriety of Solomon's action has been questioned because of God's law at Leviticus 25:23, 24. This law may have been regarded as applying only to the region actually occupied by God's covenant people, in which case Solomon's gift would not have been improper. If otherwise, then it would be an additional example of his failure to adhere completely to divine counsel, as in the case of his multiplying horses and also taking many wives from the foreign nations. —Compare De 17:16, 17 with 1Ki 4:26; 11:1-8.

The account does not give the reason for Hiram's lack of satisfaction with the cities. Some suggest that the pagan inhabitants kept them in poor condition; others, that their geographic situation was undesirable. At any rate his displeasure with them resulted in their receiving the name "the Land of Cabul." The meaning of Cabul in this text has been a subject of considerable discussion. Josephus (as above) says that Cabul "in the Phoenician tongue is interpreted to mean 'not pleasing,'" but modern scholars find no other evidence to support this interpretation. Lexicographers generally advance the suggestion that a form of pun is involved, Cabul being used in the sense of the similar-sounding Hebrew phrase *keval'*, meaning "as good as nothing."

In the parallel account of events following the completion of Solomon's building project, 2 Chronicles 8:2 mentions cities "that Hiram had given to Solomon," which cities Solomon rebuilt for use by the Israelites. Whether or not these were the same cities that Solomon had first presented as a gift to Hiram is not stated. If so, then this text would indicate that Hiram rejected the gift. It is also suggested by some that an exchange of gifts of cities was involved, though this is not mentioned in the account at First Kings 9.

CAESAR (Cae'sar). A Roman family name that became a title. In 46 B.C.E., Gaius Julius Caesar was appointed dictator of Rome for ten years, but he was murdered in 44 B.C.E. Caesar was the name of his family (Gaius being his personal name and Julius that of his clan or house). The family name passed to his adopted son and ultimate successor Gaius Julius Caesar Octavianus (Octavian). Octavian established his rulership over the realm in 31 B.C.E., and in 27 B.C.E. he was accorded the title of Augustus by the Roman Senate, becoming known as Caesar Augustus.—Lu 2:1-7.

Thereafter, the next four Roman emperors (Tiberius, Gaius [Caligula], Claudius, and Nero) laid claim to the name on the basis either of actual relationship or of adoption. The family name thus became so closely associated with the position of sovereign ruler that, even after the end of the Caesarean dynasty, the name was retained as a regal title equivalent to that of emperor, producing the later forms kaiser (German) and czar (Russian).

The Caesars ruling during the period covered by the Christian Greek Scriptures, along with their reigns and the major events of the Bible taking place during these, are listed on the accompanying chart. Of these, only three are mentioned by name in the Bible itself: Augustus, Tiberius, and Claudius. For fuller discussion, see articles under their names.

God and Caesar. Jesus' only recorded reference to Caesar is when laying down the principle: "Pay back, therefore, Caesar's things to Caesar, but God's things to God." (Mt 22:17-21; Mr 12:14-17; Lu 20:22-25) The question evoking this statement was with regard to the

Name	Years of Rule	Major Biblical Events During Reign
Augustus (Octavian)	31 B.C.E.– 14 C.E.	Birth of John (the Baptizer); decree of registration, and birth of Jesus at Bethlehem (Lu 2:1); death of Herod the Great
Tiberius	14-37 C.E.	Ministries of both John and Jesus (Lu 3:1); also their deaths. Pentecost of 33 C.E. and initial activity of newly established Christian congregation. The conversion of Saul (Paul)
Gaius (Caligula)	37-41 C.E.	
Claudius	41-54 C.E.	Paul's first two missionary tours and part of third. A major famine; Jews banished from Rome (Ac 11:28; 18:2)
Nero	54-68 C.E.	Paul's first trial in Rome. (Ac 25:21; 26:32) Start of strong official persecution against Christians following the great fire in Rome; likely also Paul's second trial and execution. Beginning of Jewish revolt (66 C.E.)
Galba	68-69 C.E.	
Otho	69 C.E.	
Vitellius	69 C.E.	
Vespasian	69-79 C.E.	Destruction of Jerusalem (70 C.E.)
Titus	79-81 C.E.	
Domitian	81-96 C.E.	Exile of apostle John to Patmos (Re 1:9)
Nerva	96-98 C.E.	
Trajan	98-117 C.E.	Bible canon likely completed during first year of his reign

payment of "head tax" by Jews to the Roman state. It therefore dealt with an established law or regular practice and hence neither the question nor the answer was evidently intended to be restricted to Tiberius, then ruling. (Compare Mt 17:25.) "Caesar" meant, or symbolized, the civil authority, the state, represented by its duly appointed representatives, called "the superior authorities" by Paul and expressed by Peter as "the king" and his "governors."—Ro 13:1-7; Tit 3:1; 1Pe 2:13-17; see SUPERIOR AUTHORITIES.

Caesar's "things" were therefore the payment due for services rendered by the secular government and for which services the government levied taxes or tribute. Despite its imperialistic nature, the Roman state provided numerous services for its subject peoples, including the construction of highways, and a form of mail service, as well as the maintenance of civil order and protection from criminal elements. The people paid for these services by taxes. This is underscored by Jesus' reference to Caesar's coin, called "the head tax coin." —Mt 22:19.

That "Caesar's" authority to exact payment even from Christians could not be allowed to infringe

upon the Christian's service to God was shown by Jesus' statement that 'God's things should be paid back to God.' (Mt 22:21) Jesus' apostles showed that they understood that their duty toward human authorities was limited, or relative, and not absolute, for when later brought before the Jewish high court they firmly declared: "We must obey God as ruler rather than men," that is, when human laws or requirements clashed with those of God.—Ac 5:29.

Jesus' Trial. When Jesus was brought to trial before the Roman governor Pontius Pilate, he was charged by the religious leaders with grave offenses: "subverting [the Jewish] nation and forbidding the paying of taxes to Caesar and saying he himself is Christ a king." (Lu 23:1, 2) This three-pronged charge actually meant they were accusing Jesus of high treason or, as the Romans expressed it, *crimen laesae majestatis* (today called lèse-majesté). Pilate recognized this because later he said, "You brought this man to me as one inciting the people to revolt." (Lu 23:13, 14) In 48 B.C.E., the law called *lex Julia majestatis* had made it an offense to engage in any activity against the sovereign power of Rome. This law was given broad application so that, by Jesus' time, virtually any insult to Caesar or any activity giving an outward appearance of sedition could be the basis for the charge of treason. Tiberius, the Caesar then reigning, was particularly sensitive to criticism or opposition, and his rule was noted for the encouragement of "informers" who would bring accusations against supposed traitors.

Throughout the Roman Empire no king could rule without Caesar's consent. Thus, Pilate, in questioning Jesus, apparently concentrated his interrogation on the issue of Jesus' kingship. (Mt 27:11; Mr 15:2; Lu 23:3; Joh 18:33-37) Pilate endeavored to free Jesus as guiltless, but the Jewish leaders cried out: "If you release this man, you are not a friend of Caesar. Every man making himself a king speaks against Caesar." (Joh 19:12) The term "friend of Caesar" was a title of honor often bestowed on provincial governors; but the Jewish leaders here evidently used it in a general way, implying that Pilate was laying himself open to the charge of condoning high treason. Fear of a jealous emperor was a factor influencing Pilate in pronouncing the death sentence on an innocent man. Meanwhile the priests loudly proclaimed their loyalty to the imperial throne, saying, "We have no king but Caesar," thereby rejecting any theocratic rule. (Joh 19:13-16; compare Isa 9:6, 7; 33:22.) They objected in vain to the title "King of the Jews" that Pilate had placed on Jesus' stake. (Joh 19:19-22) The Romans customarily posted a sign identifying the crime for which a criminal was condemned.

Paul's Appeal and Imprisonment. When the Jewish religious leaders of Thessalonica formed a mob to try to stop the preaching of Paul and Silas, they also trumped up a similar charge of treason against the imperial throne. (Ac 17:1-9) By now Claudius (41-54 C.E.) was ruling as Caesar.—Ac 11:28.

The remainder of the Biblical references to Caesar apply to Nero, who ruled from 54 to 68 C.E., when he committed suicide at about the age of 31. It was to Nero that Paul referred when on trial in Caesarea before Festus, evidently about 58 C.E. Paul denied any guilt due to acts against Caesar and refused to submit to a trial in Jerusalem, saying: "I am standing before the judgment seat of Caesar, where I ought to be judged. . . . I appeal to Caesar!" (Ac 25:1, 6-11) Paul was here exercising his rights as a Roman citizen. Such appeal to Caesar could be made either after the pronouncement of judgment or at any earlier point in the trial. Since Festus gave evidence of not wanting to decide the matter himself and since a trial in Jerusalem held virtually no hope of justice, Paul

made this formal petition to be judged by the highest court of the empire. It appears that in some cases the appeal could be denied, as, for example, in the case of a thief, a pirate, or a seditionist caught in the act. Likely for this reason Festus conferred first with "the assembly of counselors" before admitting the appeal. The subsequent hearing before the visiting Herod Agrippa II was in order that Festus might have clearer information to submit in transmitting Paul's case to "the August One," Nero. (Ac 25:12-27; 26:32; 28: 19) Paul's appeal served a further purpose, that of taking him to Rome, fulfilling an intention expressed earlier. (Ac 19:21; Ro 15:22-28) Jesus' prophetic promise and the angelic message later received both show divine direction in the matter. —Ac 23:11; 27:23, 24.

It was apparently during Paul's first imprisonment in Rome that he wrote his letter to the Philippians (c. 60-61 C.E.). At the letter's close, Paul includes the greetings of the brothers in Rome and "especially those of the household of Caesar." (Php 4:21, 22) The term "household of Caesar" does not necessarily refer to the immediate family of Nero, then reigning, but may apply to those in government service, Caesar's slaves and minor officials. Whether these Christians from Caesar's household were products of Paul's preaching is not stated. If his prison quarters were at all connected with the Praetorian Guard (Php 1:13), this would place him, and the preaching he there did, in the proximity of Nero's palace, hence near many of the household of Caesar. (Ac 28:16, 30, 31) Whatever the manner of his meeting these Christians of Caesar's household, they apparently had special interest in the brothers of Philippi. Since Philippi was a Roman colony with many retired soldiers and government servants, it may be that a number of the Christians there were related to or were friends of those on whose behalf Paul conveyed greetings.

A great fire ravaged Rome in 64 C.E., destroying about a fourth of the city. The rumor circulated that Nero was responsible and, according to Roman historian Tacitus, Nero tried to protect himself by placing the blame on the Christians. (*The Annals*, XV, XLIV) Mass arrests followed, and Christians as well as those suspected of being Christians were tortured, put to death in large numbers, some even being burned alive in public. This appears to have marked the start of a great wave of persecution, not from religious opposers, but from political sources bent on exterminating the Christian congregation. Likely Paul, who evidently was freed after two years of imprisonment in Rome (c. 59-61 C.E.), now experienced his second imprisonment (c. 65 C.E.). It is generally held that he thereafter was put to death at Nero's order.—Compare 2Ti 1:16, 17; 4:6-8.

The Jewish revolt began in 66 C.E., two years before Nero's death, but was not suppressed until 70 C.E. in the reign of Vespasian (69-79 C.E.). The apostle John is thought to have been exiled to the island of Patmos during the rule of Domitian (81-96 C.E.), a harsh opponent of Christianity. —Re 1:9.

CAESAREA (Caes·a·re′a) [Of (Belonging to) Caesar]. An important seaport city built by Herod the Great on the Mediterranean seacoast during the latter part of the first century B.C.E. The original site was previously known as Straton's or Strato's Tower, thought to be so named after a Sidonian ruler. The ancient name has been preserved in the Arabic name Qaisariye (today called Horvat Qesari in Hebrew). It is situated about 40 km (25 mi) S of Mount Carmel and about 87 km (54 mi) NNW of Jerusalem.

The Jewish historian Josephus is the prime source of information about the construction and early history of the city. Herod the Great had received the site along with Samaria and other towns as a gift from Caesar Augustus. After rebuilding Samaria, which he named Sebaste, he turned his attention to the seacoast and proceeded to build a magnificent port and city at Strato's Tower, the construction covering a period of 10 to 12 years, and the time of its dedication coming about the year 10 B.C.E. (according to some scholars). These projects were named by Herod in honor of Caesar Augustus—the city was called Caesarea, whereas its seaport was called Sebastos (Greek for Augustus). The city was most beautiful both in material and in construction, and it contained a temple, a theater, and an amphitheater large enough to accommodate a great crowd of people. An aqueduct supplied Caesarea with fresh water, and a drainage system underneath the city carried water and sewage out to the sea. The major feat, however, was the construction of the city's artificial harbor.

Following the removal of Herod the Great's son Archelaus, Caesarea became the official residence of the Roman procurators who governed Judea. In the Bible account of the Acts of Apostles, the city figures prominently both as a seaport and as a seat of government.

Philip, who had accomplished successful missionary service in Samaria, subsequently engaged in "declaring the good news" in the coastal territory from the city of Ashdod through all the cities on up to Caesarea, about 90 km (56 mi) to the N. (Ac 8:5-8, 40) Shortly thereafter, Paul's conversion took place, and because of a plot against him when he began preaching in Jerusalem, the disciples there took their new brother to the seaport of Caesarea and sent him off to his hometown, Tarsus.—Ac 9:28-30.

As the main headquarters for the Roman military forces, Caesarea was a natural place for the centurion Cornelius to have his residence. The city, though having a substantial number of Jewish residents, is considered to have been mainly of Gentile population. Thus in the year 36 C.E. Peter was divinely directed to a fitting site for witnessing to uncircumcised Cornelius, his relatives, and his intimate friends and for their being baptized as the first uncircumcised Gentiles to be admitted into the Christian congregation.—Ac 10:1-48.

It was to Caesarea that Herod Agrippa I withdrew after his unsuccessful imprisonment of Peter, and here he received the delegations from Tyre and Sidon and shortly thereafter died (44 C.E.), as an expression of God's adverse judgment. (Ac 12:18-23) Paul went through

Caesarea, with a breakwater built by Herod the Great to form an artificial harbor

Caesarea on returning to Palestine when nearing completion of his second and third missionary tours. (Ac 18:21, 22; 21:7, 8) At the time of his second visit, Paul and his companions lodged with Philip the evangelizer, who possibly settled in Caesarea at the close of his earlier preaching tour. Some of the local disciples now accompanied the apostle from that seaport up to Jerusalem, though Paul, while in Caesarea, had been warned by the prophet Agabus of the danger awaiting him.—Ac 21:10-16.

Because of an assassination plot against him in Jerusalem, Paul, under arrest, was later taken to Caesarea under heavy guard and delivered to Governor Felix for trial. (Ac 23:23, 24) The notable contrast between the emotional religious prejudice accompanied by riotous conditions in Jerusalem and the relatively orderly conditions in Caesarea are considered to be evidence of the strong Roman influence in the latter city as well as its position as the chief garrison of Roman troops. Governor Festus, who succeeded Felix, obliged Paul's Jewish opposers in Jerusalem to come down to Caesarea to present their charges against him, at which time Paul appealed to Caesar rather than face trial in Jerusalem. (Ac 25:1-12) While still in Caesarea awaiting transfer to Rome, Paul was able to give a strong witness concerning Christianity before Festus and his royal visitors, King Agrippa II and his sister (and incestuous companion) Bernice. (Ac 25:13, 22-27; 26:1-32) From Caesarea Paul, as prisoner, set sail on the voyage that would eventually take him to Rome.—Ac 27:1, 2.

During the reign of Nero, bitter rivalry broke out between the Jewish and Syrian inhabitants of Caesarea, and incidents there are considered to have served to ignite the flame of revolt that eventually led to the destruction of Jerusalem in 70 C.E.

In 1961 a stone was found in the theater of Caesarea bearing a Latin inscription that includes the name of Pontius Pilate, the first such inscription to be found.

CAESAREA PHILIPPI (Caes·a·re′a Phi·lip′pi) [Caesarea of Philip].

A town situated at the headwaters of the Jordan River, today represented by the small village of Banyas. At an elevation of 350 m (1,150 ft) above sea level, its location is one of great natural beauty. The village is enclosed on three sides by mountains, with the snowcapped peak of Mount Hermon rising majestically to the NE, while to the W extends a lush green plain watered by one of the principal sources of the Jordan springing from a nearby cavern.

The town was the site of a battle between Egypt and the victorious forces of Antiochus III (the Great) (c. 200 B.C.E.). It was then known as Paneas, a name given the town in honor of the pagan god Pan, a fertility deity, who was worshiped there. In the year 20 B.C.E. Caesar Augustus gave Paneas to Herod the Great, who thereafter built a white marble temple in the place, dedicating it to Augustus. Herod's son, Philip the tetrarch, later enlarged and beautified the city in honor of Tiberius Caesar. It was then given the name Caesarea and, to distinguish it from the seaport city of the same name, was called Caesarea Philippi. Still later the city was again enlarged and adorned by Herod Agrippa II, and its name was changed to Neronias, though this name quickly passed into disuse following the death of Nero. Josephus relates that, after the destruction of Jerusalem in 70 C.E., General Titus staged gladiatorial events there, using captive Jews as victims. (*The Jewish War*, VII, 23, 24 [ii, 1]) In course of time the name of the city reverted to its ancient name of Paneas, and in Arabic (which uses no "p") this became Banyas.

It was on the way to "the villages of Caesarea Philippi" that Jesus questioned his disciples: "Who are men saying the Son of man is?" giving rise to the meaningful conversation regarding the Christian congregation's rock-mass foundation and the use of the keys of the Kingdom of the heavens. —Mr 8:27; Mt 16:13-20.

CAGE.

An enclosure used for confining birds or other animals. (Jer 5:27; compare Am 8:1, 2, where the same Hebrew word, *keluv′*, is rendered "basket.") The prophet Ezekiel evidently alluded to King Jehoiachin of Judah under the figure of a lion that was put in a cage (Heb., *su·ghar′*) and transported to the king of Babylon.—Eze 19:9; compare 2Ki 24:12-15.

CAIAPHAS (Ca′ia·phas).

Joseph Caiaphas was the high priest during Jesus' earthly ministry. (Lu 3:2) He was the son-in-law of High Priest Annas (Joh 18:13; see ANNAS) and was appointed to office by the predecessor of Pontius Pilate, Valerius Gratus, about the year 18 C.E., although some say as late as the year 26 C.E. He held the office until about the year 36 C.E., longer than any of his immediate predecessors, this being due to his skillful diplomacy and cooperation with Roman rule. He and Pilate were reportedly good friends. Caiaphas was a Sadducee.—Ac 5:17.

A ringleader in the plot to do away with Jesus, Caiaphas prophesied, though not of his own originality, that Jesus would shortly die for the nation, and to that end he gave his wholehearted support. (Joh 11:49-53; 18:12-14) At Jesus' trial before the Sanhedrin, Caiaphas ripped his garments and said: "He has blasphemed!" (Mt 26:65) When Jesus was before Pilate, Caiaphas was undoubtedly there crying: "Impale him! Impale him!" (Joh 19:6, 11); he was there asking for the release of Barabbas instead of Jesus (Mt 27:20, 21; Mr 15:11); he was there shouting: "We have no king but Caesar" (Joh 19:15); he was also there protesting the sign over Jesus' head: "The King of the Jews" (Joh 19:21).

The death of Jesus did not mark the end of Caiaphas' role as a chief persecutor of infant Christianity. The apostles were next haled before this religious ruler; they were sternly commanded to stop their preaching, were threatened, and were even flogged, but to no avail. "Every day in the temple and from house to house they continued without letup," Caiaphas notwithstanding. (Ac 4:5-7; 5:17, 18, 21, 27, 28, 40, 42) The blood of righteous Stephen was soon added to Jesus' bloodstains on the skirts of Caiaphas, who also armed Saul of Tarsus with letters of introduction so the murderous campaign could be extended to Damascus. (Ac 7:1, 54-60; 9:1, 2) However, not long thereafter Vitellius, a Roman official, removed Caiaphas from office.

CAIN [Something Produced]. The first child born on earth to the original human pair, Adam and Eve.

Following the birth of Cain, Eve said: "I have produced a man with the aid of Jehovah." (Ge 4:1) Did she have in mind that she might be the foretold woman who would produce the seed by means of which deliverance would come? (Ge 3:15) If so, she was greatly mistaken. However, she could validly say that Cain was produced "with the aid of Jehovah" because God had not taken away the reproductive powers of sinful Adam and Eve and because, when passing judgment on her, God had said that she would "bring forth children," though it would be with birth pangs.—Ge 3:16.

Cain became a cultivator of the ground and, "at the expiration of some time," he, as well as his younger brother Abel, brought offerings to present to Jehovah, feeling the need to gain God's favor. Cain's offering of "some fruits of the ground," however, was not 'looked upon with any favor' by God. (Ge 4:2-5; compare Nu 16:15; Am 5:22.) While some point out that Cain's offering is not said to be of the choicest fruits whereas Abel's offering is specified to have been of the "firstlings of his flock, even their fatty pieces," the problem

was not in the quality of produce that Cain offered. As Hebrews 11:4 points out, Cain's offering lacked the motivation of faith that made Abel's sacrifice acceptable. The fact that God did not view Cain's offering with favor may also have been because his offering was bloodless, whereas Abel's represented a life poured out.

The manner in which the distinction between the approved and the disapproved offerings was made is not stated, but it was undoubtedly evident to both Cain and Abel. Jehovah, who reads the heart of man (1Sa 16:7; Ps 139:1-6), knew the wrong attitude of Cain, and His rejection of Cain's sacrifice resulted in that wrong disposition being made clearly manifest. "The works of the flesh" now began to be openly produced by Cain: "enmities, strife, jealousy, fits of anger." (Ga 5:19, 20) Jehovah showed the sullen man that exaltation could be his if he would simply turn to doing good. He could have humbled himself to imitate his brother's approved example, but he chose to ignore God's counsel to get the mastery over the sinful desire that 'lurked at the door,' craving to dominate him. (Ge 4:6, 7; compare Jas 1:14, 15.) This disrespectful course was "the path of Cain." —Jude 11.

Subsequently, Cain said to his brother: "Let us go over into the field." (Ge 4:8) (Though these words are not in the Masoretic text, a number of Hebrew manuscripts have the sign of omission here, while the Samaritan *Pentateuch,* the Greek *Septuagint,* the Syriac *Peshitta,* and Old Latin texts all include these words as spoken by Cain to Abel.) In the field Cain attacked Abel, killing him, and thereby becoming the first human murderer. As such he could be said to have "originated with the wicked one," who is the father of manslayers as well as of the lie. (1Jo 3:12; Joh 8:44) Cain's callous response to Jehovah's inquiry as to Abel's whereabouts was further evidence of his attitude; it was not an expression of repentance or remorse but a lying retort: "I do not know. Am I my brother's guardian?"—Ge 4:9.

God's sentencing of Cain to banishment from the ground evidently meant his eviction from the neighborhood of the garden of Eden, and the curse already upon the earth would be increased in Cain's case, the earth not responding to his cultivation of it. Cain expressed regret over the severity of his punishment and showed anxiety as to the possibility of Abel's murder being avenged upon him, but still no sincere repentance. Jehovah "set up a sign for Cain" to prevent his being killed, but the record does not say that this sign or mark was placed on Cain's person in any way. The "sign" likely consisted of God's solemn decree itself, known and observed by others.—Ge 4:10-15; compare vs 24 where that decree is referred to by Lamech.

Cain went into banishment in "the land of Fugitiveness to the east of Eden," taking with him his wife, an anonymous daughter of Adam and Eve. (Ge 4:16, 17; compare 5:4, also the much later example of Abraham's marriage to his half sister Sarah, Ge 20:12.) Following the birth of his son Enoch, Cain "engaged in building a city," naming it for his son. Such city may have been but a fortified village by present standards, and the record does not state when it was completed. His descendants are listed in part and include men who distinguished themselves in nomadic stock raising, the playing of musical instruments, and the forging of metal tools as well as those who were known for their practice of polygamy and their violence. (Ge 4:17-24) Cain's line ended with the global Flood of Noah's day.

CAINAN (Ca·i′nan).

1. Son of Enos (Enosh); an ancestor of Jesus' earthly mother Mary. (Lu 3:37) Cainan is evidently called Kenan at Genesis 5:9-14 and 1 Chronicles 1:2.

2. One listed in Luke's genealogy of Jesus Christ as the son of Arpachshad. (Lu 3:36) The name Cainan appears in genealogical lists in present copies of the Greek *Septuagint*, such as the Alexandrine Manuscript of the fifth century C.E. (Ge 10:24; 11:12, 13; 1Ch 1:18 but not 1Ch 1:24), although it is not found in extant Hebrew manuscripts of the Hebrew Scriptures. The name Cainan is also missing at Luke 3:36 in two Bible manuscripts (Papyrus Bodmer 14, 15, of c. 200 C.E.; Bezae Codices, of the fifth and sixth centuries C.E.). This omission is in harmony with the Masoretic text at Genesis 10:24; 11:12, 15; and 1 Chronicles 1:18, according to which Shelah, not Cainan, is the son of Arpachshad.—See ARPACHSHAD; GENEALOGY OF JESUS CHRIST (A Problem in Luke's Genealogy of Jesus).

CAKE.

Among the Hebrews and other Oriental peoples of ancient times bread was often baked in the form of flat disks, and it was not uncommon to refer to such bread by the term "cake." However, cakes were of various shapes. For instance, "ring-shaped cakes" (Heb., chal·lohth′) were used at the time of the installing of Israel's priesthood (Ex 29:2, 23), and Tamar prepared "heart-shaped cakes." (Heb., levi·vohth′; 2Sa 13:8, ftn; see LOAF.) Abraham told Sarah to make "round cakes" (Heb., ′u·ghohth′) to feed the materialized angels that visited him.—Ge 18:6; see also Nu 11:8; 1Ki 19:6; Eze 4:12.

Through the prophet Hosea, Jehovah said: "Ephraim himself has become a round cake not turned on the other side." (Ho 7:8) Ephraim (Israel) had mingled with pagan peoples, adopting their ways and also seeking alliances with heathen nations, and consequently was like a cake not turned. It was not uncommon to bake cakes on hot ashes or hot stones. If such cakes were not turned, they might be baked or even burned on one side and not baked at all on the other side.

During Israel's Passover celebration "unfermented cakes" (yeastless, or unleavened, bread; Heb., mats·tsohth′) were to be eaten, and associated with this observance was "the festival of unfermented cakes." (Ex 12:8, 15, 17-20; 13:3-7; 23:15; 34:18; De 16:3, 8, 16) Unfermented ring-shaped cakes moistened with oil or unfermented wafers that were smeared with oil were among the offerings Israel was to make to Jehovah God. (Le 2:4-7, 11, 12) In the law of the communion sacrifice to be presented to Jehovah, provision was also made for offering ring-shaped cakes of leavened bread.—Le 7:13.

After the ark of the covenant had been brought to Jerusalem, David "apportioned to all the people, to the whole crowd of Israel, man as well as woman, to each one a ring-shaped cake [Heb., chal·lath′] of bread and a date cake [Heb., ′esh·par′] and a raisin cake [Heb., ′ashi·shah′], after which all the people went each to his own house." (2Sa 6:19) The raisin cake consisted of compressed dried grapes or raisins. However, it is possible that at least some of the raisin cakes prepared in ancient times were made from raisins and flour.

In Jeremiah's day the people of Judah and Jerusalem engaged in false worship, and the women among them were "kneading flour dough in order to make sacrificial cakes to the 'queen of the heavens.'" (Jer 7:18) Reference is also made to this false deity and "sacrificial cakes" (Heb., kaw·wa·nim′) made for her in Jeremiah 44:19. Just what these sacrificial cakes consisted of is uncertain, but they were evidently put on the altar as an offering.—See QUEEN OF THE HEAVENS.

Other types of cakes mentioned in the Bible are 'cakes of pressed [or dried] figs' (Heb., deve·lim′ [1Sa 30:12; Isa 38:21]), "sweet cake" (Heb., la·shadh′; Nu 11:8), "flat cakes" (Heb., tsap·pi·chith′; Ex 16:31), "round cake" (Heb., tselul′; Jg 7:13), "cakes of raisins" (Heb., tsim·mu·qim′; 1Sa 25:18), and "sprinkled cakes" (Heb., niq·qu·dim′; 1Ki 14:3). The Greek word a′zy·mos means "unfermented; unleavened," and its neuter plural form is used to refer to "unfermented cakes" and "the festival of unfermented cakes."—1Co 5:8; Mr 14:1.

CALAH (Ca'lah). A city founded by Nimrod in Assyria and originally part of "the great city" composed of Nineveh, Calah, Resen, and Rehoboth-Ir, the latter three places apparently being suburbs of Nineveh. (Ge 10:9-12) Calah appears as *Kalhu* on Assyrian cuneiform texts, and during the period of the Assyrian Empire, it became one of the three principal cities of the realm, along with Nineveh and Asshur. Calah was situated at the NE angle of the junction of the Great Zab River with the Tigris, about 35 km (22 mi) SSE of Nineveh. The present modern town now found on the site is called Nimrud, thereby preserving the name of the ancient founder of the city.

In the ninth century B.C.E., Ashurnasirpal II claims to have restored the city from a decayed condition and made it his capital, building massive walls that were fortified with scores of towers, a royal palace, and temples; these included a ziggurat tower some 38 m (125 ft) high. Research indicates that the city covered an area of 358 ha (885 acres) and contained not only palaces, temples, and houses but also gardens and orchards, watered by a canal dug from the Zab River. The banquet provided by Ashurnasirpal at the completion of his new capital is stated to have included all the city's residents plus visiting dignitaries, to a total of 69,574 persons.

When excavated, the ruins of Calah produced some of the finest examples of Assyrian art, including colossal winged, man-headed lions and winged bulls, many huge bas-reliefs that lined the palace walls, and also a rich find of beautifully carved ivory objects. An excellently preserved statue of Ashurnasirpal was uncovered, as well as the stone referred to as the Black Obelisk of Shalmaneser III, which names King Jehu of Israel as paying tribute to Assyria.—See SHALMANESER No. 1.

Finally, Calah suffered desolation along with the other royal cities of the realm with the downfall of the Assyrian Empire.

CALAMUS, CANE [Heb., *qa·neh'*]. The Hebrew *qa·neh'* is the original source of the English word "cane" (as well as of the word "canon"), and *qa·neh'* is often translated as "stalk" (Ge 41:5, 22), 'branch' (Ex 25:31, 32), or "reed" (1Ki 14:15). In certain texts, however, either the context or a modifying word indicates that an aromatic plant is referred to, and *qa·neh'* is thus translated "calamus" (Ex 30:23) and "cane."—Ca 4:14; Isa 43:24.

Among the ingredients used in preparing the holy anointing oil was "sweet calamus," the sweetness referring to its odor, not its taste. (Ex 30:22-25) The Song of Solomon (4:14) includes "cane" among other odoriferous spices. Jehovah through his prophet Isaiah (43:24) reproved the sinful Israelites for 'having bought' (Heb., *qa·ni'tha*) for his temple service no "[sweet] cane" (*qa·neh'*), thereby making a play on words in Hebrew. Jeremiah (6:20) refers to cane received from a "land far away," while Ezekiel (27:3, 19) includes cane among the products for which wealthy Tyre traded.

The English word "calamus" is derived from the Greek *ka'la·mos*, used by the translators of the Greek *Septuagint* to render the Hebrew *qa·neh'*. Like the Hebrew word, *ka'la·mos* also has the basic meaning of reed or cane, whereas the English word "calamus" today is used principally to refer to the sweet flag (*Acorus calamus*) or its aromatic root.

Regarding the sweet cane, or calamus, of the Hebrew Scriptures, many scholars prefer to identify it with an aromatic reed grass of India, such as *Cymbopogon martini*, a perennial grass whose leaves when crushed produce a fragrant oil known as ginger-grass oil. Other varieties of these Indian grasses produce citronella oil and lemongrass oil. The view that one or more of such sweet-scented grasses is represented by the sweet cane, or calamus, is based mainly on Jeremiah's reference to the product as coming from a "land far away," which in this case would be India. Other areas, however, may have been producers of the aromatic cane, or calamus, as is indicated by Ezekiel's prophecy (27:19). Thus, while some kind of aromatic reed or cane is meant, the plant's precise identification remains uncertain.

CALCOL (Cal'col) [Perfected]. One whose wisdom, though great, was exceeded by King Solomon's (1Ki 4:31); possibly the same as the descendant of Judah through Zerah.—1Ch 2:4, 6.

CALEB (Ca'leb) [Dog].

1. Son of Hezron, brother of Jerahmeel and great-grandson of Judah and Tamar (1Ch 2:3-5, 18); also called Chelubai (1Ch 2:9). One of his descendants was Bezalel, the skilled craftsman assigned to oversee the building of the tabernacle. (1Ch 2:19, 20; Ex 35:30) It appears that No. 2 below was his descendant.

2. Son of Jephunneh the Kenizzite of the tribe of Judah, uncle of Othniel, and likely a descendant of No. 1. (Nu 32:12; Jos 15:17; 1Ch 4:13, 15; see OTHNIEL.) When 40 years old, Caleb was one of the

12 spies sent out by Moses on a 40-day preview of the land of Canaan, and upon returning, Caleb together with Joshua stood up against the opposition of all the others to give a favorable report, saying: "Let us go up directly, and we are bound to take possession of it." (Nu 13:6, 30; 14:6-9) Because he had 'followed Jehovah his God fully,' he was the only one of that adult generation besides Joshua and some Levites to enter the Promised Land in 1473 B.C.E. Six years later, when 85 years old, Caleb declared: "Now here Jehovah has preserved me alive, just as he promised, these forty-five years since Jehovah made this promise to Moses when Israel walked in the wilderness, and now here I am today eighty-five years old. Yet I am today as strong as on the day of Moses' sending me out. As my power was then, so my power is now for the war, both to go out and to come in." —Jos 14:6-11.

The city of Hebron (the stronghold called Kiriath-arba, which was held by the giant Anakim) as well as its surrounding territory, including nearby Debir, was assigned to Caleb for his possession. In 1 Samuel 30:13, 14, where it tells about the Amalekites making a raid "upon the south of Caleb," it evidently does not refer to a city by that name but, rather, to this area assigned to Caleb and called by his name; hence the raid was 'upon the south of Caleb's territory.'

Upon receiving this possession, Caleb declared: "Whoever strikes Kiriath-sepher [also called Debir] and does capture it, I shall certainly give him Achsah my daughter as a wife." Othniel his nephew (the first judge of Israel after the death of Joshua) captured the city and won the prize. Caleb then gave his daughter, at her request, the Upper and the Lower Gulloth as a wedding present, in addition to the "piece of land to the south."—Jos 15:13-19; Jg 1:11-15; 3:9-11.

Achsah is listed as the daughter of "Caleb the brother of Jerahmeel" (No. 1 above) who lived about a century and a half before "Caleb the son of Jephunneh." (1Ch 2:42, 49) Some commentators say there was only one Caleb. But the great lapse of time between Judah's grandson Hezron and the settlement of Canaan precludes such a conclusion. Others say that both Calebs must have had daughters by the same name. However, women are mentioned in genealogies only when they have had a major role in the history of God's people. And since there was only one famous Achsah, she must have been the daughter of the second Caleb, the son of Jephunneh. Still other commentators would drop this statement about Achsah from the verse (1Ch 2:49) as a misplaced scribal addition, but they have no textual authority. However, it is more reasonable to think that the original writer intentionally included this abrupt notice in verse 49 for a special purpose, using "daughter" in its wider sense to mean a descendant to call attention to the fact that Achsah was not only the daughter of Caleb the son of Jephunneh but also a direct descendant of Caleb the son of Hezron.

CALEB-EPHRATHAH (Ca'leb-eph'ra·thah). This name appears at 1 Chronicles 2:24 in the Masoretic text as the place of the death of Hezron of the tribe of Judah. (Compare *LXX*.) No further mention is made of it, nor has any identification been made with a geographic site.—See HEZRON No. 2.

CALEBITE (Ca'leb·ite) [Of (Belonging to) Caleb]. A designation identifying foolish Nabal as a descendant of Caleb.—1Sa 25:3.

CALENDAR. A calendar is an orderly system of dividing time into years, months, weeks, and days. Long before man's creation, God provided the basis for such measuring of time. Genesis 1:14, 15 tells us that one of the purposes of the "luminaries in the expanse of the heavens" is that they might serve for "seasons and for days and years." The solar day, the solar year, and the lunar month are thus natural divisions of time, governed respectively by the daily turning of the earth on its axis, by its annual orbit around the sun, and by the monthly phases of the moon in its relation to earth and sun. The division of time into weeks and the division of the day into hours, on the other hand, are arbitrary ones.

From the first man Adam forward, time has been measured in terms of years. Thus, Adam was "a hundred and thirty years" of age when he became father to Seth.—Ge 5:3.

Monthly divisions also came into use. By the time of the Flood we find time divided into months of 30 days, since a period of 5 months is shown to equal 150 days. (Ge 7:11, 24; 8:3, 4) The same record also indicates that Noah divided the year into 12 months.—See YEAR.

Seven-day periods are mentioned at this time and may even have been in regular use since early in human history. (Ge 7:4, 10; 8:10, 12) There is, however, no evidence of a divinely required weekly Sabbath observance by man until God's positive instructions to Israel following their Exodus from Egypt.—See WEEK.

Various calendar systems have been developed by men in the past, and a number continue in use today. Early calendars were mainly lunar calendars, that is, the months of the year were counted by complete cycles of the moon, as, for example, from one new moon to the next new moon. On the average, such lunation takes about 29 days, 12 hours, and 44 minutes. The months were usually counted as of either 29 or 30 days, but in the Bible record the term "month" generally means 30 days.—Compare De 21:13; 34:8; also Re 11:2, 3.

A year of 12 lunar months falls nearly 11 days short of a solar year of 365¼ days. Since the solar year determines the return of the seasons, there was need to adjust the calendar to this solar year, and this resulted in what are called lunisolar, or bound solar, years—that is, years in which the months were lunar but the years were solar. This was done by the addition of a number of days each year or of an additional month during certain years to compensate for the shortness of the 12 lunar months.

Hebrew Calendar. The Israelites used such a lunisolar, or bound solar, calendar. This is evident from the fact that Jehovah God established the beginning of their sacred year with the month Abib in the spring and specified the celebration of certain festivals on fixed dates, festivals that were related to harvest seasons. For these dates to have coincided with the particular harvests, there had to be a calendar arrangement that would synchronize with the seasons by compensating for the difference between the lunar and solar years.—Ex 12:1-14; 23:15, 16; Le 23:4-16.

The Bible does not indicate what method was originally used to determine when additional days or an additional, or intercalary, month should be inserted. It is logical, however, that either the vernal or the autumnal equinox served as a guide to indicate when the seasons were falling behind sufficiently to require calendar adjustment. Though not specifically mentioned in the Bible, a 13th month that was added by the Israelites to accomplish this adjustment was called, in postexilic times, Veadar, or the second Adar.

We do not find record of a definitely fixed or standardized form of Jewish calendar until the fourth century of our Common Era (c. 359 C.E.), when Hillel II specified that the leap years of 13 months should be the 3rd, 6th, 8th, 11th, 14th, 17th, and 19th of each 19 years. Such a 19-year cycle is commonly called the Metonic cycle, after the Greek mathematician Meton (of the fifth century B.C.E.), although there is also evidence that such a cycle was perfected before him by the Babylonians. (See *Babylonian Chronology, 626 B.C.–A.D. 75,* by R. A. Parker and W. H. Dubberstein, 1971, pp. 1, 3, 6.) This cycle takes into account that every 19 years the new and the full moons fall again on the same days of the solar year.

The Jewish months ran from new moon to new moon. (Isa 66:23) Thus, one Hebrew word, *cho'dhesh,* rendered "month" (Ge 7:11) or "new moon"

Calendar Months of the Bible

The Jewish months ran from new moon to new moon. (Isa 66:23) One Hebrew word, *cho'dhesh,* "month" (Ge 7:11), comes from a root meaning "new," while another word for month, *ye'rach,* means "lunation."

MONTHS		WEATHER	CROPS
Sacred	Secular		
1st	7th	Jordan swells from rains, melting snow	Flax harvest. Barley harvest begins
2nd	8th	Dry season begins. Mostly clear skies	Barley harvest. Wheat harvest in low areas
3rd	9th	Summer heat. Clear air	Wheat harvest. Early figs. Some apples
4th	10th	Heat increases. Heavy dews in areas	First grapes. Vegetation and springs dry up
5th	11th	Heat reaches maximum	Grape harvest begins
6th	12th	Heat continues	Harvest of dates and summer figs
7th	1st	Summer ending. Early rains begin	Harvest concluding. Plowing begins
8th	2nd	Light rains	Wheat and barley sown. Olive harvest
9th	3rd	Rain increases. Frost. Mountain snows	Grass developing
10th	4th	Maximum cold. Rainy. Mountain snows	Green lowlands. Grain, flowers developing
11th	5th	Cold weather lessens. Rain continues	Almond trees blossom. Fig trees bud
12th	6th	Frequent thunder and hail	Carob trees blossom. Citrus fruit harvest
13th		An intercalary month was added seven times in 19 years generally as a second Adar (Veadar)	

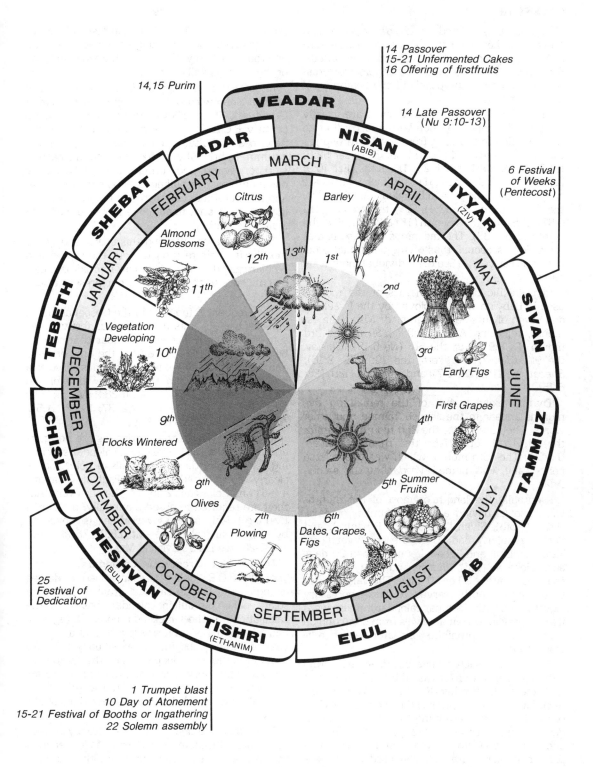

14 Passover
15-21 Unfermented Cakes
16 Offering of firstfruits

14,15 Purim

14 Late Passover
(Nu 9:10-13)

6 Festival
of Weeks
(Pentecost)

VEADAR

ADAR

NISAN
(ABIB)

SHEBAT

MARCH

IYYAR
(ZIV)

FEBRUARY

APRIL

Citrus

Barley

SIVAN

Almond
Blossoms

JANUARY

Wheat

MAY

TEBETH

12th

13th

1st

2nd

11th

JUNE

Vegetation
Developing

10th

3rd

Early Figs

First Grapes

DECEMBER

9th

4th

TAMMUZ

CHISLEV

Flocks Wintered

JULY

8th

5th Summer
Fruits

NOVEMBER

Olives

7th

6th

AB

Plowing

Dates, Grapes,
Figs

AUGUST

25
Festival of
Dedication

HESHVAN
(BUL)

OCTOBER

SEPTEMBER

ELUL

TISHRI
(ETHANIM)

1 Trumpet blast
10 Day of Atonement
15-21 Festival of Booths or Ingathering
22 Solemn assembly

(1Sa 20:27), is related to *cha·dhash'*, meaning "new." Another word for month, *ye'rach*, is rendered "lunar month." (1Ki 6:38) In later periods, fire signals were used or messengers were dispatched to advise the people of the beginning of the new month.

In the Bible the individual months are usually designated simply by numbering according to their position in the year, from the 1st through to the 12th. (Jos 4:19; Nu 9:11; 2Ch 15:10; Jer 52:6; Nu 33:38; Eze 8:1; Le 16:29; 1Ki 12:32; Ezr 10:9; 2Ki 25:1; De 1:3; Jer 52:31) Only four months are named prior to the exile in Babylon, namely, *Abib*, the first month (Ex 13:4); *Ziv*, the second (1Ki 6:37); *Ethanim*, the seventh (1Ki 8:2); and *Bul*, the eighth (1Ki 6:38). The meanings of these names are strictly seasonal, thus giving additional proof of a lunisolar year.—See the individual months by name.

In postexilic times the names of the months used in Babylon were employed by the Israelites, and seven of these are mentioned: *Nisan*, the 1st month, replacing Abib (Es 3:7); *Sivan*, the 3rd month (Es 8:9); *Elul*, the 6th (Ne 6:15); *Chislev*, the 9th (Zec 7:1); *Tebeth*, the 10th (Es 2:16); *Shebat*, the 11th (Zec 1:7); and *Adar*, the 12th (Ezr 6:15).

The postexilic names of the remaining five months appear in the Jewish Talmud and other works. They are *Iyyar*, the 2nd month; *Tammuz*, the 4th; *Ab*, the 5th; *Tishri*, the 7th; and *Heshvan*, the 8th. The 13th month, which was intercalated periodically, was named *Veadar*, or the second Adar.

Eventually the length of most of the months was fixed as having a specific number of days. Nisan (Abib), Sivan, Ab, Tishri (Ethanim), and Shebat regularly had 30 days each; Iyyar (Ziv), Tammuz, Elul, and Tebeth regularly had 29 days each. Heshvan (Bul), Chislev, and Adar, however, could have either 29 or 30 days. The variations in these latter months served to make necessary adjustments with the lunar calendar but also were used to prevent certain festivals from occurring on days viewed as prohibited by later Jewish religious leaders.

Whereas the sacred year began in the spring with the month Abib (or Nisan) by God's decree at the time of the Exodus (Ex 12:2; 13:4), the Bible record indicates that prior to this the Israelites had counted the year as running from fall to fall. God gave recognition to this arrangement so that, in effect, there was a dual system of a sacred and a secular or agricultural calendar used by his people. (Ex 23:16; 34:22; Le 23:34; De 16:13) In postexilic times, Tishri 1, in the last half of the year, marked the beginning of the secular year, and the Jewish New Year, or Rosh Hashanah (head of the year), is still celebrated on that date.

In 1908 the only approximation of an ancient written Hebrew calendar was found at the site of Gezer, and it is believed to be from the tenth century B.C.E. It is an agricultural calendar and describes agricultural activity beginning with the autumn. In brief, it describes two months each of storage, sowing, and spring growth, followed by one month each of pulling up flax, barley harvest, and a general harvest, then two months of pruning the vines and, finally, one month of summer fruit.—Le 26:5.

The chart accompanying this article shows the months in their relation to both the sacred and secular calendars and also their approximate correspondence to the months of our present calendar.

The frequent references in the Gospel accounts and the book of Acts to the various festival seasons show that the Jewish calendar continued to be observed by the Jews during the time of Jesus and the apostles. These festival seasons serve as a guide for determining the relative time of the Biblical events of that day.—Mt 26:2; Mr 14:1; Lu 22:1; Joh 2:13, 23; 5:1; 6:4; 7:2, 37; 10:22; 11:55; Ac 2:1; 12:3, 4; 20:6, 16; 27:9.

It should be noted that Christians are not governed by any sacred or religious calendar specifying certain holy days or festivals, a point that is clearly stated by the apostle Paul at Galatians 4:9-11 and Colossians 2:16, 17. The one event that they are required to observe annually, the Lord's Evening Meal, at Passover time, is governed by the lunar calendar.—Mt 26:2, 26-29; 1Co 11:23-26; see LORD'S EVENING MEAL.

Julian and Gregorian Calendars. In the year 46 B.C.E., Julius Caesar issued a decree changing the Roman calendar from a lunar to a solar year. This Julian calendar, based on the calculations of the Greek astronomer Sosigenes, had 12 months of arbitrary length and a regular year of 365 days beginning on January 1. It also brought in the use of leap years by the addition of an extra day every four years, to compensate for the extra fraction of a day in the length of the tropical year, which has a little less than 365¼ days.

The Julian calendar year was actually a little more than 11 minutes and 14 seconds longer than the true solar year. Thus, by the 16th century a discrepancy of ten full days had accumulated. In

1582 C.E., Pope Gregory XIII introduced a slight revision of the Julian calendar, whereby the leap years every four years were retained but with the exception that only those century years with a number divisible by 400 were to be counted as leap years. By papal bull in 1582, ten days were to be omitted in that year, so that the day after October 4 became October 15. The Gregorian calendar is now in general use in most parts of the world. It is the basis for the historical dates used throughout this publication.

Whereas Christians today customarily use the calendar in effect in their particular land, they are aware that the God of eternity, Jehovah, has his own calendar of events not governed by human systems of reckoning. As his prophet Daniel wrote: "He is changing times and seasons, removing kings and setting up kings, giving wisdom to the wise ones and knowledge to those knowing discernment. He is revealing the deep things and the concealed things, knowing what is in the darkness; and with him the light does dwell." (Da 2:21, 22) So, in his position as Universal Sovereign he stands far above our spinning earth, with its day and night, its lunar cycles, and its solar year. However, in his Word, the Bible, God does helpfully relate his actions and purposes to such measurements of time, thereby allowing his creatures on earth to learn where they stand in relation to his grand calendar of events.—See CHRONOLOGY.

CALF

CALF [Heb., 'e'ghel]. A young bull. Calves were offered in sacrifice (Le 9:2, 3), and on special occasions or under special circumstances a fattened calf was slaughtered and prepared for the table.—Ge 18:7, 8; 1Sa 28:24; Lu 15:23.

'Cutting the calf in two and passing between its parts' alludes to an ancient mode of entering into a solemn obligation or covenant. (Compare Ge 15:9-21.) Doubtless Jeremiah used this expression to stress the sacredness of the covenant into which the Jews had entered before God, and by the terms of which they were obligated to liberate fellow Israelites whom they had enslaved.—Jer 34:17-19.

Illustrative Usage. Unfaithful Israel was corrected like an inexperienced 'calf that had not been trained' to the yoke. (Jer 31:18) Egypt's mercenary soldiers are likened to fattened calves that would prove to be unable to resist the Babylonians and would take to flight. (Jer 46:21, 26) At the time the wicked and presumptuous ones are reduced to dust, the fearers of God's name are shown going forth and pawing the ground like fattened calves released from the stall.—Mal 4:1, 2.

Calf Worship. Calf worship was the first form of idolatry mentioned in the Bible to which the Israelites succumbed after the Exodus from Egypt. While Moses was in the mountain receiving God's law, the people became impatient and approached Aaron with the request that he make a god for them. From the gold earrings contributed by the Israelites, Aaron formed a molten statue of a calf, undoubtedly a young bull. (Ps 106:19, 20) It was regarded as representing Jehovah, and the festival held the following day was designated "a festival to Jehovah." The Israelites sacrificed to the golden calf, bowed before it, ate, drank, and enjoyed themselves in song and dance.—Ex 32:1-8, 18, 19; Ne 9:18.

The molten calf was not necessarily made of solid gold. This is indicated by the fact that Isaiah, when referring to the making of a molten image, mentions that the metalworker overlays it with gold. (Isa 40:19) Hence, the golden calf was perhaps formed of wood and then overlaid with gold. Therefore, when Moses subjected the image to a burning process, the wooden center was reduced to charcoal and the gold layer either entirely or partially melted. Whatever was left was crushed and ground to pieces until it was fine like dust, and this dust, composed of charcoal and gold, Moses scattered upon the surface of the water.—Ex 32: 20; De 9:21.

Idolatrous Egyptian worship, which associated gods with cows, bulls, and other animals, likely had influenced the Israelites to a great extent, causing them to adopt calf worship so soon after being liberated from Egypt. This is confirmed by Stephen's words: "In their hearts they turned back to Egypt, saying to Aaron, 'Make gods for us to go ahead of us. . . . ' So they made a calf in those days and brought up a sacrifice to the idol and began to enjoy themselves in the works of their hands." —Ac 7:39-41.

The first king of the ten-tribe kingdom, Jeroboam, fearing that his subjects would revolt and go back to the house of David if they continued going up to Jerusalem for worship, had two golden calves made. (1Ki 12:26-28) The Bible record does not reveal to what extent Jeroboam's choice of a calf to represent Jehovah was influenced by earlier calf worship in Israel, by what he had observed while in Egypt (1Ki 12:2), or by the religion of the Canaanites and others, who often represented their gods as standing upon an animal, such as a bull.

One of the golden calves Jeroboam set up at the far northern city of Dan, the other at Bethel about 17 km (11 mi) N of Jerusalem. He told his subjects that it was too much for them to go up to Jerusalem for worship and that the calf represented the God who had brought them up out of the land of Egypt. (Compare Ex 32:8.) Since the priests of the tribe of Levi stayed loyal to Jehovah's worship at Jerusalem, Jeroboam appointed his own priests to lead the false worship before the idol calves at Dan and Bethel. (2Ch 11:13-15) He also arranged for a festival similar to the Festival of Booths, but it was celebrated a month later than the festival in Jerusalem.—1Ki 12:28-33; 2Ch 13:8, 9; Le 23:39.

Jehovah condemned this calf worship and, through his prophet Ahijah, foretold calamity for the house of Jeroboam. (1Ki 14:7-12) Nevertheless, calf worship remained entrenched in the ten-tribe kingdom. Even King Jehu, who eradicated Baal worship in Israel, let calf worship remain, likely in order to keep the ten-tribe kingdom distinct from the kingdom of Judah. (2Ki 10:29-31) In the ninth century B.C.E., Jehovah raised up his prophets Amos and Hosea to proclaim His condemnation of calf worship, which included kissing the idol calves, and also to foretell doom for the ten-tribe kingdom. The golden calf of Bethel was to be carried away to the king of Assyria, giving cause for the people as well as the foreign-god priests to mourn. The high places would be annihilated, and thorns and thistles would grow upon the altars that had been used in false worship. (Ho 10:5-8; 13:2; Am 3:14; 4:4; 5:5, 6) Calamity did come when the ten-tribe kingdom fell to Assyria in 740 B.C.E. About a century later, Jeremiah prophesied that the Moabites would be just as ashamed of their god Chemosh as the Israelites had become of their center of idolatrous calf worship, Bethel.—Jer 48:13; see BETHEL No. 1; BULL; COW; IDOL, IDOLATRY (Under the rule of the kings).

CALNEH (Cal′neh).

1. A city founded by Nimrod in the land of Shinar. (Ge 10:10) It thus evidently lay in southern Mesopotamia, but the location is uncertain. Nippur, an ancient Babylonian city about 90 km (56 mi) SE of Babylon, has long been suggested as its site, based on Talmudic tradition and other factors. Some scholars, however, prefer an identification with Kulunu, the early name of a city of some importance near Babylon. A third possibility is a twin city of Kish called Hursagkalama, the latter part of the name (-kalama) supposedly representing Calneh. Some translations (*RS, JB, NE*) render Calneh, not as a place-name, but as the phrase "all of them" so that the text reads, "Babel, Erech, and Accad, *all of them* in the land of Shinar." This, however, requires an adjustment in the vowel pointing of the Masoretic text.

2. A place mentioned by the prophet Amos, along with the cities of Hamath and Gath, when warning the people of Israel and Judah of coming calamity. (Am 6:2) While some commentators consider it to be the same as No. 1 above, most scholars view its association with Hamath and Gath as indicating a location in the region adjacent to the eastern Mediterranean Sea, rather than in Mesopotamia. They suggest an identification with Kullani of the Assyrian inscriptions in

Arabian camel, well suited to desert life

northern Syria (apparently represented today by modern Kullan Köy, about 16 km [10 mi] SE of Arpad), mentioned by Tiglath-pileser III as among the places subjugated during an Assyrian campaign in the west. If this identification is correct, then Calneh here may be the same as Calno of Isaiah 10:9.

CALNO (Cal'no). A city listed in Isaiah's prophecy concerning the boasting of the Assyrians as to their conquests and the futility of trying to withstand their might. (Isa 10:5, 9-11) Most scholars consider Calno to be an alternate spelling of Calneh. (Am 6:2) Calno's mention in connection with Carchemish would harmonize with the identification of Calneh with Kullani of the Assyrian texts, located between Carchemish and Aleppo in northern Syria. Kullani was conquered by Tiglath-pileser III, a contemporary of King Menaham of Israel.

CALVARY. See GOLGOTHA.

CAMEL [Heb., *ga·mal'; be'kher,* 'young male camel' (Isa 60:6); *bikh·rah',* "young she-camel" (Jer 2:23); *kir·ka·rohth',* "swift she-camels" (Isa 66:20); Gr., *ka'me·los*]. An animal that has long served man as a beast of burden and a means of transport, especially in desert regions. There are two varieties of camel, the Bactrian and the Arabian. The Bactrian (*Camelus bactrianus*) has two humps on its back, is stronger than the Arabian, and is able to carry greater loads; the Arabian (*Camelus dromedarius*), thought to be the one generally referred to in the Bible, has only one hump.

The camel's characteristics ideally fit it for life in desert regions, where it fills the place usually assigned the horse or donkey in other lands. This animal's thick hair shields it from desert heat. Its long slitlike nostrils can close at will, a useful precaution against the blowing sand. Its eyes are shielded from blistering sandstorms by heavy eyelids and long eyelashes. The camel's feet are provided with a hardened skin and are padlike, remarkably shaped for walking on soft and yielding sand. Callous pads on which the animal rests protect its chest and knees. These pads are present at birth. The camel's strong teeth enable it to chew practically anything. This creature needs little grain and can subsist on the common plants of the desert, making it an animal quite economical to use.

The camel's hump serves as a sort of portable pantry. Here most of its food reserve is stored in the form of fat. If the camel is required to draw nourishment from its stored-up food supply for too long a time, the skin of the hump, instead of standing up, falls over and hangs like an empty bag on the side of the dorsal ridge. In ancient times, as today, loads were placed on the humps of camels. (Isa 30:6) Mention is also made in Scripture of a "woman's saddle basket of the camel," which undoubtedly was placed on the camel's hump.—Ge 31:34.

Although folklore has it that the camel stores water in its hump, this is not the case. It is generally thought that the camel can get along without water for a prolonged period because of its ability to retain much of the water that it drinks. A contributory factor is the design of the nose, which enables the animal to extract water vapor when exhaling. The camel can tolerate a loss of water of 25 percent of its weight, in contrast to 12 percent for humans. It does not lose moisture by perspiration as rapidly as do other creatures, because its body temperature can vary 6° C. (11° F.) without marked effects. Its blood is unique in that loss of fluid is minimal even when water is in short supply for several days. It can also replace lost body weight by drinking as much as 135 L (35 gal) in ten minutes.

Some camels are known to have traveled at amazing speeds. At 1 Samuel 30:17, an allusion to swift camels may be noted. It was only the 400 young men that rode camels who escaped when David struck down the Amalekite raiders.

According to the Law, the camel was an unclean animal and, therefore, was not used by the Israelites for food. (Le 11:4; De 14:7) However, camel hair was woven into cloth. John the Baptizer wore a garment of this material. (Mt 3:4; Mr 1:6) Even today the cloth made from camel hair is used for making articles of clothing.

Use From Early Times. The first Bible mention of the camel relates to Abraham's temporary residence in Egypt, where he acquired a number of these beasts of burden. (Ge 12:16) When Abraham's faithful servant was sent to Mesopotamia to procure a wife for Isaac, a train of ten camels, with all sorts of gifts, accompanied him. (Ge 24:10) It was to a camel caravan of Ishmaelites bound for Egypt that Joseph was sold by his half brothers.—Ge 37:25-28.

Job is introduced as "the greatest of all the Orientals." His material possessions included 3,000 camels, and following the test of his integrity, Jehovah blessed Job, so much so that he came to possess 6,000 camels and a vast quantity of other livestock.—Job 1:3; 42:12.

In common with other livestock of Egypt, the camels suffered from the plagues God brought upon Pharaoh's domain. (Ex 9:3, 10, 25; 12:29) Whether any camels went with the Israelites on the trek through the wilderness is not indicated in the Bible record, but likely this was the case.

The first reference to camels after Israel's settling in the Promised Land is in connection with their use by invaders. When Midianite hordes and their 'camels without number' spread over the land and impoverished it, a critical situation faced God's people Israel. (Jg 6:5; 7:12) At times, with Jehovah's help, the Israelites defeated their enemies and captured vast numbers of camels, on one occasion 50,000.—1Ch 5:21; 2Ch 14:15.

While outlawed from Saul's court, David and his men warred against the Geshurites, the Girzites, and the Amalekites, striking down all the men and women but taking domestic animals, including camels, as booty. (1Sa 27:8, 9) During the reign of David, a special official, Obil, was in charge of his camels. (1Ch 27:30) The queen of Sheba brought gifts to King Solomon in a camel train, and Ben-hadad II of Syria sent presents to the prophet Elisha loaded upon 40 camels.—1Ki 10:1, 2; 2Ki 8:9.

In foretelling the fall of Babylon, the prophet Isaiah alluded to the conquering armies under the symbol of "a war chariot of camels." (Isa 21:7) According to the Greek historian Herodotus (I, 80), Cyrus did make use of the camel in his military campaigns. When describing the oncoming doom of Rabbah, capital city of the Ammonites, Ezekiel 25:5 says that the city would become "a pasture ground of camels." Also, the faithless house of Israel, in its adulterous course, having illicit relations with pagan nations round about, was likened to a young she-camel in heat, aimlessly running to and fro.—Jer 2:23, 24.

Reminiscent of the plagues that struck the livestock of Egypt, Zechariah foretold a scourge that would come upon the camels and other livestock of the nations who fight against Jehovah's people on earth. (Zec 14:12, 15) After their restoration from exile, God's people are depicted as being covered by a "heaving mass of camels," all bearing tribute. Camels are also mentioned among the beasts of burden bringing the brothers of God's servants to Jerusalem out of all the nations "as a gift to Jehovah." (Isa 60:6; 66:20) It is of interest that, in the first fulfillment of Isaiah's restoration prophecy, there were 435 camels among the livestock of the Jews returning from Babylon in 537 B.C.E.—Ezr 2:67; Ne 7:69.

Illustrative Use. Jesus made reference to the camel in an illustrative way. On one occasion he pointed out that it would be easier for a camel to go through a needle's eye than for a rich man to get into the Kingdom. (Mt 19:24; Mr 10:25; Lu 18:25) A question has arisen as to whether "camel" should not be more correctly rendered "rope" in this instance. In fact, George M. Lamsa's translation uses the word "rope" in the main text, and a footnote on Matthew 19:24 reads: "The Aramaic word *gamla* means *rope* and *camel.*" Also, the Greek words for rope (*ka'mi·los*) and camel (*ka'me·los*) are very similar, and it has been suggested that there was a confusion of the Greek words. It is noteworthy, though, that *A Greek-English Lexicon* (by Liddell and Scott, revised by Jones, London, 1968, p. 872) defines *ka'mi·los* as "rope" but adds that perhaps it was coined as an emendation of the phrase, "It is easier for a camel to go through the eye of a needle than for a rich man to enter into the kingdom of God," thus indicating that *ka'me·los,* rather than *ka'mi·los,* appeared in the original Greek text.

In the oldest extant Greek manuscripts of the Gospel of Matthew (the Sinaitic, the Vatican No. 1209, and the Alexandrine), the word *ka'me·los* appears. Matthew wrote his account of the life of Jesus first in Hebrew and then may have translated it himself into Greek. He knew, therefore, exactly what Jesus said and meant. Hence he knew the proper word, and the word used in the oldest extant Greek manuscripts was *ka'me·los.* There is good reason, therefore, for believing "camel" to be the correct rendering.

By means of this illustration, not meant to be taken literally, Jesus was pointing out that just as it was not possible for a literal camel to go through the eye of a literal needle it was even less possible for a rich man, while continuing to cling to his riches, to enter into the Kingdom of God.—See NEEDLE'S EYE.

In his condemnation of the hypocritical Pharisees, Jesus spoke of their 'straining out the gnat but swallowing the camel.' Those men used to strain out the gnat from their wine, not merely because it was an insect, but because it was ceremonially unclean; yet they figuratively gulped down camels, which were also unclean. While insisting upon compliance with the minutest of the Law's requirements, they entirely overlooked the weightier matters—justice, mercy, and faithfulness.—Mt 23:23, 24.

CAMP. The Hebrew word for "camp" (*ma-chaneh'*) comes from the root verb *cha·nah',* meaning "camp; encamp; pitch camp." (Jg 15:9; Ex 14:2; Ge 33:18) These terms are used with regard to a transitory site of nomadic people (Ge

32:21; 33:18), the temporary and mobile tenting arrangement of the Israelites on their trek through the wilderness (Nu 2:17), or the protective enclosure of an army (2Ki 25:1). The Greek word for "camp" is *pa·rem·bo·le'*.—See ARMY.

Camp of Israel. Israel's Exodus from Egypt was not in tumultuous confusion but in well-ordered "battle formation" befitting "the armies of Jehovah." (Ex 13:18; 12:41; 6:26) Such battle formation was possibly like that of an army consisting of five parts, with a van or forward detachment, a main body, a rear guard, and two wings. At the time, the Israelites were still under patriarchal arrangements, and this would be reflected in assigning tribes and families their places in the order of march. According to such customs, the servants, retainers, and others attached to the family were reckoned as part of the household, and so the "vast mixed company" that left Egypt likely were intermingled with the various tribes, clans, and families.—Ex 12:38; Nu 11:4; De 29:11.

With the establishment of the tabernacle, the camp arrangement was organized according to divine instructions toward the beginning of the second year. The camp center, both in location and in importance, was the tent of Jehovah's presence, the tabernacle, with its surrounding courtyard. Its entrance faced the E, where Moses, Aaron, and the priests encamped. (Nu 3:38) The rest of the Levites (numbering 22,000 males, a month old and up) camped on the three remaining sides: the Kohathites on the S, the Gershonites to the W, and the Merarites on the N. (Nu 3:23, 29, 35, 39) With these latter two groups, certain baggage, wagons, and animals used for transporting the tabernacle and its equipment were associated. Thus those assigned to serve at Jehovah's sanctuary lived near to and surrounding the tabernacle, providing a protective cordon from intrusion by non-Levites, "that no indignation may arise against the assembly."—Nu 1:53; 7:3-9.

Out and beyond the Levitical tents, the 12 tribes camped in a quadrilateral arrangement oriented by the four points of the compass. It appears that the people in general were removed a considerable distance from the tabernacle; some commentators suggest some 900 m (3,000 ft), because there was to be a distance of "about two thousand cubits" between the people and the ark of the covenant when the crossing of the Jordan began. (Jos 3:4) The 12 tribes were divided into four grand divisions, each called by the name of the central tribe of the division. So the three-tribe division to the E of the tabernacle was called Judah, with Issachar on the one side of Judah and

Zebulun on the other side. (Nu 2:3-8) When this arrangement was set up in 1512 B.C.E., this three-tribe division of Judah numbered 186,400 able-bodied males 20 years old and up. (Nu 1:1-3; 2:9) Clockwise to the S was the three-tribe division of Reuben, with Simeon and Gad alongside Reuben, and numbering 151,450 men of war. (Nu 2:10-16) These two divisions on the E and S, together with the Levites, were Jacob's descendants by Leah and her handmaid Zilpah. (Ge 35:23, 26) Incidentally, with both Reuben and the Kohathites camping S of the sanctuary, the physical association between the Reubenite rebels Dathan and Abiram and the Kohathite Korah is explained. (Nu 16:1) Around to the W was the three-tribe division of Ephraim, flanked by Manasseh and Benjamin, all descendants of Rachel, and numbering 108,100 army men. (Nu 2:18-24) Finally, on the N was the three-tribe division of Dan, associated with Asher and Naphtali, and totaling 157,600 fighting men. (Nu 2:25-31) Dan and Naphtali were descendants of Rachel's handmaid Bilhah, but Asher was of Leah's maidservant Zilpah.—Ge 35:25, 26.

The size of this camp of Israel was very great. The above register figures total 603,550 fighting men, in addition to women and children, old folks and handicapped, 22,000 Levites, and "a vast mixed company" of aliens—perhaps all together 3,000,000 or more. (Ex 12:38, 44; Nu 3:21-34, 39) How much area such an encampment would cover is not certain; estimates vary greatly. When the camp was pitched opposite Jericho on the Plains of Moab, it is described as extending "from Beth-jeshimoth to Abel-shittim."—Nu 33:49.

The plan, or layout, of the camp is usually illustrated as being rectangular or square, an arrangement thought to be superior in efficiency and security. Definite camp boundaries are indicated by reference to going outside or entering the camp. (Le 13:46; 16:26, 28; 17:3) And there were 'gates,' or ports of entrance, to the camp. (Ex 32:26, 27) In his description, Josephus mentions that roads were laid out within the camp. (*Jewish Antiquities*, III, 289 [xii, 5]) All of this required engineering and organization if the Israelites were to set up camp quickly on a new location with minimal effort and delay.

"Signs for the house of their fathers" were provided to help a person find his proper place in the camp. (Nu 2:2) Since the Hebrew expression *de'-ghel*, rendered "three-tribe division," also means "banner" (as in Ca 2:4), it is possible that there were tribal markers as well as family ensigns. The Bible gives neither the number nor a description of these signs.

The government of the camp of Jehovah was most efficient. Under the theocratic arrangement, chiefs were appointed over 10's, 50's, 100's, and 1,000's. These were "capable men, fearing God, trustworthy men, hating unjust profit." (Ex 18:21; De 1:15) Under their direction, good supervision and maintenance as well as an equitable judicial system were provided; also through them quick communication with all the people was achieved. Coded trumpet blasts signaled the assembly of just the chieftains of the tribes or of the entire assembly as represented by all the appointed representatives of the congregation.—Nu 1:16; 10:2-4, 7, 8.

An elaborate code of laws regulated every aspect of camp life. The health and purity of the camp were preserved through various sanitary regulations. Lepers, anyone with an infectious disease or a running discharge, and those who had touched a dead body were excluded from the camp until pronounced clean. (Nu 5:2, 3) The dead were buried outside the camp. (Le 10:4, 5) Ashes from the burnt sacrifices, also the carcasses of certain sacrifices, were disposed of outside the camp. (Le 4:11, 12; 6:11; 8:17) Criminals were executed outside (Le 24:14; Nu 15:35, 36), and captives of war and returning warriors were kept outside for a cleansing period.—Nu 31:19.

Movement of this vast camp from one site to another (about 40 such encampments are reviewed by Moses in Numbers 33) was also a marvelous display of organization. As long as the cloud rested over the tabernacle, the camp remained in place. When the cloud moved, the camp moved. "At the order of Jehovah they would encamp, and at the order of Jehovah they would pull away." (Nu 9:15-23) Two hammered silver trumpets communicated these orders of Jehovah to the camp in general. (Nu 10:2, 5, 6) Special fluctuating blasts signaled the breaking up of the camp. The first time this occurred was "the second year [1512 B.C.E.], in the second month, on the twentieth day." With the ark of the covenant in the lead, the first three-tribe division headed by Judah and followed by Issachar, then Zebulun, moved out. They were followed by the Gershonites and Merarites carrying their assigned parts of the tabernacle. Next came the three-tribe division headed by Reuben and followed by Simeon and Gad. After them came the Kohathites with the sanctuary, then the third three-tribe division, of Ephraim, followed by Manasseh and Benjamin. Finally, in the rear guard was the division headed by Dan and accompanied by Asher and Naphtali. Thus the two most numerous and powerful divisions took the positions of forward and rear guard.—Nu 10:11-28.

"So they went marching from the mountain of Jehovah for a journey of three days . . . And Jehovah's cloud was over them." (Nu 10:33, 34) How long a line this cloud-led column of marchers formed is not disclosed, nor the speed or distance covered in a day. With their little children and flocks, they probably traveled slowly. While on this march, which took three days, there was probably no formal camp layout with a setting up of the tabernacle for the temporary overnight encampment; rather, just the adjustments necessary for eating and sleeping.

Military Camps. In connection with warfare, use of the term "camp" varies. It may, for example, denote the headquarters, or base of operations, from which raiding parties sally forth; Gilgal and Shiloh are such examples. (Jos 4:19; 5:10; 9:6; 10:6, 15, 43; 18:9; Jg 21:12) Or "camp" sometimes means the army itself, rather than the place where they pitch their tents at night. (Jos 10:5; 11:4, 5) "Camping against" a city had the meaning of warring against the city, just as 'pitching camp' also indicated preparation for war.—Jg 9:50; 1Sa 11:1; 28:4; 2Ki 25:1.

Several factors influenced the selection of a site for an army encampment. High ground with limited access afforded natural protection and required less guarding than open and vulnerable spots. (1Sa 26:3) The camp had to have access to water. (2Ki 3:9) Joshua defeated a federation of kings camped at the waters of Merom. (Jos 11:5) Gideon's forces camped at the well of Harod (Jg 7:1), and one third of David's army camped at the torrent valley of Besor until their companions returned from the victory.—1Sa 30:9, 10.

A protective enclosure, as around Saul's camp, may have been made of baggage, wagons, and animals. (1Sa 26:5, 7) Armies having chariots may have used them to encircle their camps. More permanent campsites were sometimes protected by trenches and dirt mounds round about. Battles were not usually fought at the campsite, except in cases of surprise attack. (Jos 11:7) Hence extensive entrenchment and strong walled enclosures were not usually built.

Secular histories give glimpses of army camp life among the pagans as it was in Bible days. The Egyptian camp of Ramses II, for example, was fenced with shields. The Assyrian fortified camp was generally circular and strengthened with walls and towers. The tents in Persian camps all faced the E, and their encampments were protected by trenches and embankments. Greek military camps were also circular, with the commanding officer tented in the middle of the camp. When the Roman army pitched camp a sizable ditch was dug around the whole of the new campsite.

CANA

CANA (Ca'na) [probably from Heb. *qa·neh'*, "reed," hence, Place of Reeds]. The hometown of Nathanael. (Joh 21:2) Evidently it was just the third day after Nathanael's introduction to Jesus and his becoming a disciple that Jesus was in Cana and attended a marriage feast, at which his mother and brothers were also present. Here Jesus performed his first miraculous sign, that of changing water into fine wine. From here he and his family and disciples "went down to Capernaum." (Joh 1:43-49; 2:1-12) Later, when again in Cana, Jesus was approached by an attendant of the king, begging him to "come down" to Capernaum to heal his dying son. Without making the trip Jesus performed the cure.—Joh 4:46-54.

The town is called "Cana of Galilee" in each case, evidently to distinguish it from Kanah in Asher. (Jos 19:28) Kafr Kanna, a town 6.5 km (4 mi) NE of Nazareth, is the traditional site of Cana. Springs provide an ample water supply there. However, lexicographers consider the form Kanna to be a very unlikely transition from Cana, particularly because of the doubling of the "n." There is reason to believe that Kafr Kanna's claim to being Cana stems largely from its being easily accessible to pilgrims from Nazareth, causing it to have the favor of church tradition.

The balance of opinion and the weight of evidence favor an identification with Khirbet Qana, about 13 km (8 mi) N of Nazareth. Here the ruins of an ancient village lie on a hill at the edge of the Plain of Asochis, modernly called el-Battuf (Biq-'at Bet Netofa). Reeds are abundant in a nearby marshy plain, making the name Cana very fitting. It is still known in Arabic as Qana el-Jelil, equivalent of Cana of Galilee. Josephus, the Jewish historian of the first century C.E., speaks of residing "at a village of Galilee called Cana" and later makes mention of "the great plain, called the plain of Asochis, in which my quarters lay." (*The Life,* 86 [16]; 207 [41]) This testimony would also favor the location of Cana of Galilee at the site of Khirbet Qana, rather than Kafr Kanna. Although no spring is found at Khirbet Qana, the ruins reveal the remains of ancient cisterns; potsherds (fragments of earthen vessels), and coins believed to date from the first century C.E. have also reportedly been found there.—PICTURE, Vol. 2, p. 738.

In ancient times a road led past Khirbet Qana down to the shores of the Sea of Galilee and along the shoreline to Capernaum, which lay some 206 m (676 ft) below sea level; hence the expression to "come down" to Capernaum. (Joh 4:47) The distance by road was about 40 km (25 mi).

CANAAN

CANAAN (Ca'naan) [Merchant Land; Land of the Tradesman], **CANAANITE** (Ca'naan·ite).

1. The fourth-listed son of Ham and grandson of Noah. (Ge 9:18; 10:6; 1Ch 1:8) He was the progenitor of 11 tribes who eventually inhabited the region along the eastern Mediterranean between Egypt and Syria, thereby giving it the name "the land of Canaan."—Ge 10:15-19; 1Ch 16:18; see No. 2.

Following the incident regarding Noah's drunkenness, Canaan came under Noah's prophetic curse foretelling that Canaan would become the slave of both Shem and Japheth. (Ge 9:20-27) Since the record mentions only that "Ham the father of Canaan saw his father's nakedness and went telling it to his two brothers outside," the question arises as to why Canaan rather than Ham became the object of the curse. Commenting on Genesis 9:24, which states that when Noah awoke from his wine he "got to know what his *youngest son* had done to him," a footnote in Rotherham's translation says: "Undoubtedly Canaan, and not Ham: Shem and Japheth, for their piety, are blessed; Canaan, for some unnamed baseness, is cursed; Ham, for his neglect, is neglected." Similarly, a Jewish publication, *The Pentateuch and Haftorahs,* suggests that the brief narrative "refers to some abominable deed in which Canaan seems to have been implicated." (Edited by J. H. Hertz, London, 1972, p. 34) And, after noting that the Hebrew word translated "son" in verse 24 may mean "grandson," this source states: "The reference is evidently to Canaan." *The Soncino Chumash* also points out that some believe Canaan "indulged a perverted lust upon [Noah]," and that the expression "youngest son" refers to Canaan, who was the youngest son of Ham.—Edited by A. Cohen, London, 1956, p. 47.

These views, of necessity, are conjectural since the Biblical record does not give any details as to Canaan's implication in the offense against Noah. Yet some implication seems definitely intended by the fact that, just before relating the case of Noah's drunkenness, Canaan is abruptly introduced into the account (Ge 9:18) and, in describing Ham's actions, the record refers to him as "Ham the father of Canaan." (Ge 9:22) That the expression "saw his father's nakedness" may indicate some abuse or perversion that involved Canaan, is a reasonable conclusion. For in most instances incest or other sexual sins are meant when the Bible speaks of 'laying bare' or 'seeing the nakedness' of another. (Le 18:6-19; 20:17) So, it is possible that Canaan had committed or attempted to commit some abuse on the unconscious Noah and that Ham, though having knowledge of this, failed either to prevent it or to take disciplinary action against the offender, and compounded the wrong by making known to his brothers Noah's disgrace.

The prophetic element of the curse must also be considered. There is no evidence to indicate that Canaan himself became the slave of Shem or Japheth during his lifetime. But, God's foreknowledge was at work, and since the curse expressed by Noah was divinely inspired, and since God's disfavor is not expressed without just cause, it is likely that Canaan had already manifested a definitely corrupt trait, perhaps of a lustful nature, and that God foresaw the bad results in which this characteristic would eventually culminate among Canaan's descendants. In the earlier case of Cain, Jehovah had noted a wrong heart attitude and had warned Cain of the danger of being overcome by sin (Ge 4:3-7); God also had discerned the unreformable bent toward wickedness on the part of the majority of the pre-Flood population, making their destruction warranted. (Ge 6:5) The most obvious evidence of the justness of the curse placed on Canaan is thus seen in the later history of his descendants, for they built up a particularly sordid record of immorality and depravity, as both Biblical and secular history testify. The curse on Canaan saw its fulfillment some eight centuries after its pronouncement, when Canaan's descendants were subjugated by the Semitic Israelites, later coming under the domination of the Japhetic powers of Medo-Persia, Greece, and Rome.

2. The name Canaan also applies to the race descended from Ham's son and to the land of their residence. Canaan was the earlier and native name of that part of Palestine lying W of the Jordan River (Nu 33:51; 35:10, 14), although the Canaanitish Amorites did invade the land E of the Jordan sometime prior to the Israelite conquest. —Nu 21:13, 26.

Boundaries and Early History. The earliest description of the boundaries of Canaan show it as extending from Sidon in the N down to Gerar near Gaza in the SW and over to Sodom and the neighboring cities in the SE. (Ge 10:19) In Abraham's time, however, it seems that Sodom and the other "cities of the District" were viewed as distinct from Canaan. (Ge 13:12) The later territories of Edom and Moab, inhabited by descendants of Abraham

and Lot, were also apparently considered to be outside of Canaan. (Ge 36:6-8; Ex 15:15) The territory of Canaan as promised to the nation of Israel is outlined in fuller detail at Numbers 34:2-12. It evidently began farther N than Sidon and extended S as far as the "torrent valley of Egypt" and Kadesh-barnea. The Philistines, who were not Canaanites (Ge 10:13, 14), had occupied the coastal region S of the Plain of Sharon, but this, too, had previously been "reckoned" as Canaanite land. (Jos 13:3) Other tribes, such as the Kenites (one family of which is later associated with Midian; Nu 10:29; Jg 1:16) and the Amalekites (descended from Esau; Ge 36:12) had also penetrated the territory.—Ge 15:18-21; Nu 14:45.

Whether the descendants of Canaan migrated to and settled in this land directly after the breakup at Babel (Ge 11:9) or whether they first accompanied the main body of Hamites to Africa and then worked their way back up into the Palestinian region, the Bible does not say. At any rate, by 1943 B.C.E. when Abraham left Haran in Paddan-aram and headed toward that land, the Canaanites were settled there, and Abraham had certain dealings with both Amorites and Hittites. (Ge 11:31; 12:5, 6; 13:7; 14:13; 23:2-20) Abraham received repeated promises from Jehovah God that his seed, or descendants, would inherit the land, and he was instructed to "go about in the land through its length and through its breadth." (Ge 12:7; 13:14-17; 15:7, 13-21; 17:8) On the basis of this promise and out of respect for God's curse, Abraham was careful that his son Isaac's wife should not be a Canaanitess.—Ge 24:1-4.

The relative ease with which Abraham and, later, Isaac and Jacob were able to move about the land with their large herds and flocks indicates that the region was not as yet thickly populated. (Compare Ge 34:21.) Archaeological investigations also give evidence of a rather sparse settlement at that time, with most of the towns located along the coast, in the Dead Sea region, in the Jordan Valley, and on the Plain of Jezreel. Concerning Palestine in the early part of the second millennium B.C.E., W. F. Albright says that the hill country was in the main still unoccupied by sedentary population, so the Biblical tradition is absolutely correct in making the patriarchs wander over the hills of central Palestine and the dry lands of the south, where there was still plenty of room for them. (*Archaeology of Palestine and the Bible,* 1933, pp. 131-133) Canaan was evidently subject to some Elamite (and hence Semitic) influence and domination at this time, as indicated by the Biblical record at Genesis 14:1-7.

Among the towns around which Abraham, Isaac, and Jacob camped were Shechem (Ge 12:6), Bethel and Ai (Ge 12:8), Hebron (Ge 13:18), Gerar (Ge 20:1), and Beer-sheba (Ge 22:19). Though no great animosity seems to have been manifested by the Canaanites toward the Hebrew patriarchs, divine protection nevertheless was the prime factor in their freedom from attack. (Ps 105:12-15) Thus, after the assault by Jacob's sons on the Hivite city of Shechem, it was because "the terror of God" came to be upon the neighboring cities that "they did not chase after the sons of Jacob." —Ge 33:18; 34:2; 35:5.

Secular history indicates that Egypt exercised suzerainty over Canaan for some two centuries prior to the Israelite conquest. During this period, messages (known as the Amarna Tablets), sent by vassal rulers in Syria and Palestine to Pharaohs Amenhotep III and Akhenaton, present a picture of considerable intercity strife and political intrigue in the region. At the time of Israel's arrival at its frontier (1473 B.C.E.), Canaan was a land of numerous city-states or petty kingdoms, though still showing some cohesion according to tribal relations. The spies who had searched out the land nearly 40 years earlier found it to be a land rich in fruitage and found its cities to be well fortified. —Nu 13:21-29; compare De 9:1; Ne 9:25.

Distribution of the Tribes of Canaan. Of the 11 Canaanite tribes (Ge 10:15-19), the Amorites appear to have occupied a principal position in the land. (See AMORITE.) Aside from the land conquered by them E of the Jordan in Bashan and Gilead, the references to the Amorites show that they were strong in the mountainous country of Canaan proper, both in the N and in the S. (Jos 10:5; 11:3; 13:4) Perhaps second in strength were the Hittites, who, though found as far S as Hebron in Abraham's time (Ge 23:19, 20), later seem to have been mainly to the N, in the direction of Syria.—Jos 1:4; Jg 1:23-26; 1Ki 10:29.

Of the other tribes, the Jebusites, the Hivites, and the Girgashites are next most frequently mentioned at the time of the conquest. The Jebusites were evidently centered in the mountainous region around Jerusalem. (Nu 13:29; Jos 18:16, 28) The Hivites were scattered from as far S as Gibeon (Jos 9:3, 7) on up to the base of Mount Hermon in the N. (Jos 11:3) The territory of the Girgashites is not indicated.

The remaining six tribes, the Sidonians, Arvadites, Hamathites, Arkites, Sinites, and the Zemarites, may well be included in the comprehensive term "Canaanites" frequently used in association with the specific names of other tribes, unless the expression is simply used to refer to cities or groups that were of mixed Canaanite population. (Ex 23:23; 34:11; De 7:1; Nu 13:29) All these six tribes seem to have been primarily located N of the region originally conquered by the Israelites and receive no specific mention in the account of the conquest.

Conquest of Canaan by Israel. (MAPS, Vol. 1, pp. 737, 738) In the second year after the Exodus the Israelites had made an initial attempt to penetrate the southern borders of Canaan, but without divine backing, and they were routed by the Canaanites and allied Amalekites. (Nu 14:42-45) Toward the close of the 40-year period of wandering, Israel again moved toward the Canaanites and was attacked by the king of Arad in the Negeb, but this time the Canaanite forces were defeated, and their cities were destroyed. (Nu 21:1-3) Still the Israelites did not follow up this victory with an invasion from the S but circled around to approach from the E. This brought them into conflict with the Amorite kingdoms of Sihon and Og, and the defeat of these kings put all of Bashan and Gilead under Israelite control, including 60 cities "with a high wall, doors and bar" in Bashan alone. (Nu 21:21-35; De 2:26–3:10) The defeat of these powerful kings had a weakening effect on the Canaanite kingdoms W of the Jordan, and the subsequent miraculous crossing of the Jordan dryshod by the Israelite nation caused the Canaanites' hearts to 'begin to melt.' Thus, the Canaanites made no attack upon the Israelite camp at Gilgal during the period of the recovery of many of the Israelite males from circumcision and during the subsequent celebration of the Passover. —Jos 2:9-11; 5:1-11.

Able now to obtain ample water from the Jordan and to draw food supplies from the conquered region E of the Jordan, the Israelites at Gilgal had a good base from which to proceed with the conquest of the land. The nearby outpost city of Jericho, now tightly shut up, was their first target, and its mighty walls fell by Jehovah's power. (Jos 6:1-21) Then the invading forces ascended some 1,000 m (3,300 ft) into the mountainous region N of Jerusalem and, after an initial setback, captured Ai and burned it. (Jos 7:1-5; 8:18-28) While the Canaanite kingdoms throughout the land began to form a massive coalition to repulse the Israelites, certain Hivite cities now sought peace with Israel by means of a subterfuge. This secession of Gibeon and three other neighboring cities evidently was viewed by the other Canaanite kingdoms as an act of treason endangering the unity of the entire 'Canaanite league.' Five Canaanite kings, therefore, united to fight, not against Israel, but against Gibeon, and an all-night march by

Israelite troops under Joshua was undertaken to save the beleaguered city. Joshua's defeat of the five attacking kings was accompanied by a miraculous downpour of huge hailstones and also by God's causing the delay of the setting of the sun. —Jos 9:17, 24, 25; 10:1-27.

The victorious Israelite forces then made a sweep through the entire southern half of Canaan (with the exception of the Plains of Philistia), conquering cities of the Shephelah, the mountainous region, and the Negeb, and then they returned to their base camp at Gilgal by the Jordan. (Jos 10:28-43) Now the Canaanites in the northern sector under the leadership of the king of Hazor began to mass their troops and war chariots, uniting their forces at a rendezvous by the waters of Merom, N of the Sea of Galilee. Joshua's army, however, made a surprise attack on the Canaanite confederacy and put them to flight, thereafter marching on to capture their cities as far N as Baal-gad at the base of Mount Hermon. (Jos 11:1-20) The campaign evidently covered a considerable period of time and was followed by another offensive action in the mountainous region in the S, this attack being directed at the giantlike Anakim and their cities.—Jos 11:21, 22; see ANAKIM.

By now some six years had passed since the start of the fighting. The major conquest of Canaan had been accomplished, and the strength of the Canaanite tribes was broken, thus allowing for the distribution of the land among the Israelite tribes to begin. (See BOUNDARY.) However, a number of regions remained yet to be subdued, including such major sections as the territory of the Philistines, who, though not Canaanites, were nevertheless usurpers of the land promised to the Israelites; the territory of the Geshurites (compare 1Sa 27:8); territory from the area around Sidon on up to Gebal (Byblos); and all the region of Lebanon (Jos 13:2-6). Besides these, there were pockets of resistance scattered throughout the land, some of which were later captured by the inheriting tribes of Israel, while others remained unconquered or were allowed to remain and made to perform forced labor for the Israelites.—Jos 15:13-17; 16:10; 17:11-13, 16-18; Jg 1:17-21, 27-36.

Though so many of the Canaanites survived the major conquest and resisted subjugation, it could still be said that "Jehovah gave Israel all the land that he had sworn to give to their forefathers," that he had given them "rest all around," and that "not a promise failed out of all the good promise that Jehovah had made to the house of Israel; it all came true." (Jos 21:43-45) All around the Israel-ites the enemy peoples were cowed and offered no genuine threat to their security. God had stated earlier that he would drive the Canaanites out "little by little" so that the wild beasts would not multiply in a suddenly desolated land. (Ex 23:29, 30; De 7:22) Despite the superior war equipment of the Canaanites, including war chariots with iron scythes, any failure of the Israelites finally to take certain areas could not be charged to Jehovah's account as a failure on his part to fulfill his promise. (Jos 17:16-18; Jg 4:13) Rather, the record shows that the Israelites' few defeats were due to unfaithfulness on their part.—Nu 14:44, 45; Jos 7:1-12.

Why did Jehovah decree the extermination of the Canaanites?

The historical account shows that the populations of the Canaanite cities conquered by the Israelites were subjected to complete destruction. (Nu 21:1-3, 34, 35; Jos 6:20, 21; 8:21-27; 10:26-40; 11:10-14) This fact has been used by some critics as a means for depicting the Hebrew Scriptures, or "Old Testament," as imbued with a spirit of cruelty and wanton slaughter. The issue involved, however, is clearly that of whether God's sovereignty over the earth and its inhabitants is acknowledged or not. He had deeded over the right of tenure of the land of Canaan to the 'seed of Abraham,' doing so by an oath-bound covenant. (Ge 12:5-7; 15:17-21; compare De 32:8; Ac 17:26.) But more than a mere eviction or dispossessing of the existing tenants of that land was purposed by God. His right to act as "Judge of all the earth" (Ge 18:25) and to decree the sentence of capital punishment upon those found meriting it, as well as his right to implement and enforce the execution of such decree, was also involved.

The justness of God's prophetic curse on Canaan found full confirmation in the conditions that had developed in Canaan by the time of the Israelite conquest. Jehovah had allowed 400 years from Abraham's time for the 'error of the Amorites to come to completion.' (Ge 15:16) The fact that Esau's Hittite wives were "a source of bitterness of spirit to Isaac and Rebekah" to the extent that Rebekah had 'come to abhor her life because of them' is certainly an indication of the badness already manifest among the Canaanites. (Ge 26:34, 35; 27:46) During the centuries that followed, the land of Canaan became saturated with detestable practices of idolatry, immorality, and bloodshed. The Canaanite religion was extraordinarily base and degraded, their "sacred poles" evidently

Steles found at Hazor. The inscription on center stele may symbolize a petition to the moon-god

being phallic symbols, and many of the rites at their "high places" involving gross sexual excesses and depravity. (Ex 23:24; 34:12, 13; Nu 33:52; De 7:5) Incest, sodomy, and bestiality were part of 'the way of the land of Canaan' that made the land unclean and for which error it was due to "vomit its inhabitants out." (Le 18:2-25) Magic, spellbinding, spiritism, and sacrifice of their children by fire were also among the Canaanites' detestable practices.—De 18:9-12.

Baal was the most prominent of the deities worshiped by the Canaanites. (Jg 2:12, 13; compare Jg 6:25-32; 1Ki 16:30-32.) The Canaanite goddesses Ashtoreth (Jg 2:13; 10:6; 1Sa 7:3, 4), Asherah, and Anath are presented in an Egyptian text as both mother-goddesses and as sacred prostitutes who, paradoxically, remain ever-virgin (literally, "the great goddesses who conceive but do not bear"). Their worship apparently was invariably involved with the services of temple prostitutes. These goddesses symbolized the quality not only of sexual lust but also of sadistic violence and warfare. Thus, the goddess Anath is depicted in the Baal Epic from Ugarit as effecting a general slaughter of men and then decorating herself with suspended heads and attaching men's hands to her girdle while she joyfully wades in their blood. The figurines of the goddess Ashtoreth that have been discovered in Palestine are of a nude woman with rudely exaggerated sex organs. Of their phallic worship, archaeologist

W. F. Albright observes that: "At its worst, . . . the erotic aspect of their cult must have sunk to extremely sordid depths of social degradation." —*Archaeology and the Religion of Israel,* 1968, pp. 76, 77; see ASHTORETH; BAAL No. 4.

Added to their other degrading practices was that of child sacrifice. According to Merrill F. Unger: "Excavations in Palestine have uncovered piles of ashes and remains of infant skeletons in cemeteries around heathen altars, pointing to the widespread practice of this cruel abomination." (*Archaeology and the Old Testament,* 1964, p. 279) *Halley's Bible Handbook* (1964, p. 161) says: "Canaanites worshipped, by immoral indulgence, as a religious rite, in the presence of their gods; and then, by murdering their first-born children, as a sacrifice to these same gods. It seems that, in large measure, the land of Canaan had become a sort of Sodom and Gomorrah on a national scale. . . . Did a civilization of such abominable filth and brutality have any right longer to exist? . . . Archaeologists who dig in the ruins of Canaanite cities wonder that God did not destroy them sooner than he did."—PICTURE, Vol. 1, p. 739.

Jehovah had exercised his sovereign right to execute the sentence of death upon the wicked population of the entire planet at the time of the global Flood; he had done so with regard to the entire District of the cities of Sodom and Gomorrah because of 'the loud cry of complaint about them and their very heavy sin' (Ge 18:20; 19:13); he had executed a decree of destruction upon Pharaoh's military forces at the Red Sea; he had also exterminated the households of Korah and other rebels among the Israelites themselves.

However, in these cases, God had employed natural forces to accomplish the destruction. By contrast, Jehovah now assigned to the Israelites the sacred duty of serving as principal executioners of his divine decree, guided by his angelic messenger and backed by God's almighty power. (Ex 23:20-23, 27, 28; De 9:3, 4; 20:15-18; Jos 10:42) The results, nevertheless, were precisely the same to the Canaanites as if God had chosen to destroy them by some phenomenon such as a flood, fiery explosion, or earthquake, and the fact that human agents effected the putting to death of the condemned peoples, however unpleasant their task may seem, cannot alter the rightness of the divinely ordained action. (Jer 48:10) By using this human instrument, pitted against "seven nations more populous and mighty" than they were, Jehovah's power was magnified and his Godship proved.—De 7:1; Le 25:38.

The Canaanites were not ignorant of the powerful evidence that Israel was God's chosen people and instrument. (Jos 2:9-21, 24; 9:24-27) However, with the exception of Rahab and her family and the cities of the Gibeonites, those who came in for destruction neither sought mercy nor availed themselves of the opportunity to flee, but instead they chose to harden themselves in rebellion against Jehovah. He did not force them to bend and give in to his expressed will but, rather, "let their hearts become stubborn so as to declare war against Israel, in order that he might devote them to destruction, that they might come to have no favorable consideration, but in order that he might annihilate them" in execution of his judgment against them.—Jos 11:19, 20.

Joshua wisely "did not remove a word from all that Jehovah had commanded Moses" as to the destruction of the Canaanites. (Jos 11:15) But the Israelite nation failed to follow up his good lead and completely eliminate the source of pollution of the land. The continued presence of the Canaanites among them brought infection into Israel that, in the course of time, undoubtedly contributed toward more deaths (not to mention crime, immorality, and idolatry) than the decreed extermination of all the Canaanites would have produced had it been faithfully effected. (Nu 33:55, 56; Jg 2:1-3, 11-23; Ps 106:34-43) Jehovah had warned the Israelites that his justice and his judgments would not be partial and that for the Israelites to enter into relations with the Canaanites, intermarry with them, practice interfaith, and adopt their religious customs and degenerate practices would mean their inevitably bringing down upon themselves the same decree of annihilation and would result in their also being 'vomited out of the land.'—Ex 23:32, 33; 34:12-17; Le 18:26-30; De 7:2-5, 25, 26.

Judges 3:1, 2 states that Jehovah let some of the Canaanite nations stay "so as by them to test Israel, that is, all those who had not experienced any of the wars of Canaan; it was only in order for the generations of the sons of Israel to have the experience, so as to teach them war, that is, only those who before that had not experienced such things." This does not contradict the earlier statement (Jg 2:20-22) that Jehovah allowed these nations to remain because of Israel's unfaithfulness and in order to "test Israel, whether they will be keepers of Jehovah's way." Rather, it harmonizes with that reason and shows that later generations of Israelites would thereby be faced with the opportunity to demonstrate obedience to God's commands concerning the Canaanites, putting their faith to the test to the point of endangering their lives in war in order to prove obedient.

In view of all of this, it is clear that the opinion held by some Bible critics that the destruction of the Canaanites by Israel is not in harmony with the spirit of the Christian Greek Scriptures does not accord with the facts, as a comparison of such texts as Matthew 3:7-12; 22:1-7; 23:33; 25:41-46; Mark 12:1-9; Luke 19:14, 27; Romans 1:18-32; 2 Thessalonians 1:6-9; 2:3; and Revelation 19:11-21 will demonstrate.

Later History. Following the conquest, the situation between the Canaanites and the Israelites gradually became one of relatively peaceful coexistence, though this was to Israel's detriment. (Jg 3:5, 6; compare Jg 19:11-14.) Syrian, Moabite, and Philistine rulers successively gained temporary domination over the Israelites, but it was not until the time of Jabin, called "the king of Canaan," that the Canaanites regained sufficient power to accomplish a 20-year subjugation of Israel. (Jg 4:2, 3) After Jabin's ultimate defeat by Barak, Israel's difficulties during the prekingdom period came principally from non-Canaanite sources, the Midianites, Ammonites, and Philistines. Likewise during the time of Samuel, of the Canaanite tribes only the Amorites are briefly mentioned. (1Sa 7:14) King David evicted the Jebusites from Jerusalem (2Sa 5:6-9), but his major campaigns were against the Philistines, Ammonites, Moabites, Edomites, Amalekites, and the Syrians. Thus, the Canaanites, though still possessing cities and holding land in Israel's territory (2Sa 24:7, 16-18), had evidently ceased to be a threat militarily. Two Hittite warriors are mentioned among David's fighting force.—1Sa 26:6; 2Sa 23:39.

During his rule Solomon put the remnants of the

Canaanite tribes to forced labor in his many projects (1Ki 9:20, 21), extending his building work even to the far northern Canaanite city of Hamath. (2Ch 8:4) But Canaanite wives later contributed to Solomon's downfall, the loss of much of the kingdom for his heir, and the religious corruption of the nation. (1Ki 11:1, 13, 31-33) From Solomon's reign (1037-998 B.C.E.) down to the rule of Jehoram of Israel (c. 917-905 B.C.E.), only the Hittites appear to have maintained a considerable measure of prominence and strength as a tribe, though evidently located to the N of Israel's territory and adjacent to or in Syria.—1Ki 10:29; 2Ki 7:6.

Intermarriage with Canaanites still was a problem among the returned Israelites after the Babylonian exile (Ezr 9:1, 2), but the Canaanite kingdoms, including those of the Hittites, had evidently disintegrated under the impact of Syrian, Assyrian, and Babylonian aggression. The term "Canaan" came to refer primarily to Phoenicia, as in Isaiah's prophecy concerning Tyre (Isa 23:1, 11, ftn) and in the case of the "Phoenician" (literally, "Canaanite" [Gr., *Kha·na·nai′a*]) woman from the region of Tyre and Sidon who approached Jesus.—Mt 15:22, ftn; compare Mr 7:26.

Commercial and Geopolitical Importance. Canaan formed a land bridge connecting Egypt with Asia and, more particularly, Mesopotamia. Though the economy of the country was basically agricultural, commercial trade was also engaged in, and the seaport cities of Tyre and Sidon became major trade centers with fleets of ships that were renowned throughout the then-known world. (Compare Eze 27.) Thus, as far back as Job's time, the word "Canaanite" had become synonymous with 'tradesman' and is so translated. (Job 41:6; Zep 1:11; note also the reference to Babylon as "the land of Canaan," Eze 17:4, 12.) Canaan thus occupied a very strategic place in the Fertile Crescent and was the target of the great empires of Mesopotamia, Asia Minor, and Africa that were seeking to control military passage and commercial traffic through Canaan's confines. God's placing of his chosen people in this land, therefore, was certain to draw the attention of the nations and have far-reaching effects; in a geographic sense, though more importantly in a religious sense, the Israelites could be said to dwell "in the center of the earth."—Eze 38:12.

Language. Although the Bible record clearly shows the Canaanites to be Hamitic, the majority of reference works speak of them as of Semitic origin. This classification is based on the evidence of a Semitic language spoken by the Canaanites.

The evidence most frequently appealed to is the large number of texts found at Ras Shamra (Ugarit) written in a Semitic language or dialect and considered to date from as far back as the 14th century B.C.E. However, Ugarit apparently did not come within the Biblical boundaries of Canaan. An article by A. F. Rainey in *The Biblical Archaeologist* (1965, p. 105) states that on ethnic, political, and, probably, linguistic bases "it is now clearly a misnomer to call Ugarit a 'Canaanite' city." He gives further evidence to show that "Ugarit and the land of Canaan were separate and distinct political entities." Hence, these tablets provide no clear rule by which to determine the language of the Canaanites.

Many of the Amarna Tablets found in Egypt do proceed from cities in Canaan proper, and these tablets, predating the Israelite conquest, are written mainly in cuneiform Babylonian, a Semitic language. This, however, was the diplomatic language of the entire Middle East at that time, so that it was used even when writing to the Egyptian court. Thus, it is of considerable interest to note the statement in *The Interpreter's Dictionary of the Bible* (edited by G. A. Buttrick, 1962, Vol. 1, p. 495) that "the Amarna Letters contain evidence for the opinion that *non-Semitic ethnic elements* settled in Palestine and Syria at a rather early date, for a number of these letters show *a remarkable influence of non-Semitic tongues.*" (Italics ours.) The facts are that there is still uncertainty as to the *original* language spoken by the first inhabitants of Canaan.

It is true, however, that the Bible account itself appears to show that Abraham and his descendants were able to converse with the people of Canaan without the need of an interpreter, and it may also be noted that, while some place-names of a non-Semitic type were used, most of the towns and cities captured by the Israelites already bore Semitic names. Still, Philistine kings in Abraham's time and also, evidently, David's time, were called "Abimelech" (Ge 20:2; 21:32; Ps 34:Sup), a thoroughly Semitic name (or title), whereas it is nowhere contended that the Philistines were a Semitic race. So, it would appear that the Canaanite tribes, over a period of some centuries from the time of the confusion of tongues at Babel (Ge 11:8, 9), apparently changed over to a Semitic tongue from their original Hamitic language. This may have been because of their close association with the Aramaic-speaking peoples of Syria, as a result of Mesopotamian domination for a period of time, or for other reasons not now apparent. Such a change would be no greater than that of other ancient nations, such as the ancient Persians, who, though of Indo-European (Japhetic) stock, later adopted the Semitic Aramaean language and writing.

"The language of Canaan" referred to at Isaiah 19:18 would by then (eighth century B.C.E.) be the Hebrew language, the principal language of the land.

CANAL.　See NILE CANALS; POOL OF THE CANAL.

CANANAEAN (Ca·na·nae′an) [from Aramaic, meaning "Zealot; Enthusiast"]. A designation distinguishing the apostle Simon from the apostle Simon Peter. (Mt 10:4; Mr 3:18) The term "Cananaean" is thought to be of Aramaic origin and apparently corresponds to the Greek word ze·lo·tes′ meaning "zealot; enthusiast."—Lu 6:15; Ac 1:13.

CANDACE (Can·da′ce). A queen of Ethiopia whose treasurer became a Christian. (Ac 8:27) Instead of being a specific personal name, "Candace," like "Pharaoh" and "Caesar," is considered to be a title. Ancient writers, including Strabo, Pliny the Elder, and Eusebius, used this designation in referring to queens of Ethiopia. Pliny the Elder (c. 23-79 C.E.) wrote that "the town [Meroë, capital of ancient Ethiopia] possesses few buildings. They said that it is ruled by a woman, Candace, a name that has passed on through a succession of queens for many years."—*Natural History,* VI, xxxv, 186.

CANE.　See CALAMUS, CANE.

CANNEH (Can′neh). A place mentioned along with Haran and Eden as being among the traders of ancient Tyre. (Eze 27:23) Its association with Haran and Eden would seem to place it in northern Mesopotamia, along the middle course of the Euphrates River. Some scholars view the name as a contracted form of Calneh.

CANON (of the Bible). Originally the reed (Heb., qa·neh′) served as a rule or measuring device. (Eze 40:3-8; 41:8; 42:16-19) The apostle Paul applied ka·non′ to the "territory" measured out as his assignment, and again to the "rule of conduct" by which Christians were to measure how they acted. (2Co 10:13-16; Ga 6:16) The "Bible canon" came to denote the catalog of inspired books worthy of being used as a straightedge in measuring faith, doctrine, and conduct.—See BIBLE.

The mere writing of a religious book, its preservation for hundreds of years, and its esteem by millions do not prove it is of divine origin or canonical. It must bear credentials of Divine Authorship demonstrating that it was inspired by

God. The apostle Peter states: "Prophecy was at no time brought by man's will, but men spoke from God as they were borne along by holy spirit." (2Pe 1:21) An examination of the Bible canon shows that its contents measure up to this criterion in every respect.

Hebrew Scriptures.　The Bible began with the writings of Moses, 1513 B.C.E. In these are preserved God's commandments and precepts to Adam, Noah, Abraham, Isaac, and Jacob, as well as the regulations of the Law covenant. What is called the *Pentateuch* includes the five books of Genesis, Exodus, Leviticus, Numbers, and Deuteronomy. Job, apparently also written by Moses, fills in history after the death of Joseph (1657 B.C.E.) and before Moses proved himself to be an integrity-keeping servant of God, a time when there was "no one like [Job] in the earth." (Job 1:8; 2:3) Moses also wrote Psalm 90 and, possibly, 91.

That these writings of Moses were of divine origin, inspired of God, canonical, and a safe guideline for pure worship, there can be no doubt, in the light of internal evidence. It was not through Moses' initiative that he became the leader and commander of the Israelites; at first Moses drew back at the suggestion. (Ex 3:10, 11; 4:10-14) Rather, God raised Moses up and invested in him such miraculous powers that even Pharaoh's magic-practicing priests were compelled to acknowledge that what Moses did originated with God. (Ex 4:1-9; 8:16-19) So it was not Moses' personal ambition to be an orator and writer. Rather, in obedience to God's command and with the divine credentials of holy spirit, Moses was moved first to speak and then to write down part of the Bible canon.—Ex 17:14.

Jehovah himself set the precedent for having laws and commandments written down. After speaking to Moses in Mount Sinai, Jehovah "proceeded to give Moses two tablets of the Testimony, tablets of stone written on by God's finger." (Ex 31:18) Later we read, "And Jehovah went on to say to Moses: 'Write down for yourself these words.'" (Ex 34:27) Jehovah, therefore, was the one who communicated with Moses and instructed him to write down and preserve the first five books of the Bible canon. No council of men made them canonical; from their inception they had divine approval.

"As soon as Moses had finished writing the words of this law in a book," he commanded the Levites, saying: "Taking this book of the law, you must place it at the side of the ark of the covenant of Jehovah your God, and it must serve as a witness there against you." (De 31:9, 24-26) It is noteworthy that Israel acknowledged this record of God's dealings and did not deny these facts. Since the contents of the books in many instances were a discredit to the nation generally, the people might well have been expected to reject them if possible, but this never seems to have been an issue.

Like Moses, the priestly class were used by God both to preserve these written commandments and to teach them to the people. When the Ark was brought into Solomon's temple (1027 B.C.E.), nearly 500 years after Moses began writing the Pentateuch, the two stone tablets were still in the Ark (1Ki 8:9), and 385 years after that, when "the very book of the law" was found in the house of Jehovah during Josiah's 18th year (642 B.C.E.), the same high regard for it was still shown. (2Ki 22:3, 8-20) Similarly, there was "great rejoicing" when, after the return from Babylonian exile, Ezra read from the book of the Law during an eight-day assembly.—Ne 8:5-18.

Following Moses' death, the writings of Joshua, Samuel, Gad, and Nathan (Joshua, Judges, Ruth, 1 and 2 Samuel) were added. Kings David and Solomon also made contributions to the growing canon of Holy Writings. Then came the prophets from Jonah to Malachi, each contributing to the Bible canon, each endowed with miraculous prophetic ability from God, each in turn meeting the requirements of true prophets as outlined by Jehovah, namely, they spoke in the name of Jehovah, their prophecy came true, and they turned the people toward God. (De 13:1-3; 18:20-22) When Hananiah and Jeremiah were tested on the last two points (both spoke in Jehovah's name), only the words of Jeremiah came to pass. Thus Jeremiah proved to be Jehovah's prophet.—Jer 28:10-17.

Just as Jehovah inspired men to write, it logically follows that he would direct and watch over the collecting and preserving of these inspired writings in order that mankind would have an enduring canonical straightedge for true worship. According to Jewish tradition, Ezra had a hand in this work after the exiled Jews were resettled in Judah. He was certainly qualified for the work, being one of the inspired Bible writers, a priest, and also "a skilled copyist in the law of Moses." (Ezr 7:1-11) Only the books of Nehemiah and Malachi remained to be added. The canon of the Hebrew Scriptures, therefore, was well fixed by

JEWISH CANON OF THE SCRIPTURES		
The Law	**The Prophets**	**The Writings** (Hagiographa)
1. Genesis	6. Joshua	14. Psalms
2. Exodus	7. Judges	15. Proverbs
3. Leviticus	8. 1, 2 Samuel	16. Job
4. Numbers	9. 1, 2 Kings	17. Song of Solomon
5. Deuteronomy	10. Isaiah	18. Ruth
	11. Jeremiah	19. Lamentations
	12. Ezekiel	20. Ecclesiastes
	13. The Twelve Prophets	21. Esther
	(Hosea, Joel, Amos, Obadiah, Jonah, Micah, Nahum, Habakkuk, Zephaniah, Haggai, Zechariah, Malachi)	22. Daniel
		23. Ezra, Nehemiah
		24. 1, 2 Chronicles

the end of the fifth century B.C.E., containing the same writings that we have today.

The canon of the Hebrew Scriptures was traditionally divided into three sections: the Law, the Prophets, and the Writings, or Hagiographa, contained in 24 books, as shown in the chart. By further combining Ruth with Judges, and Lamentations with Jeremiah, some Jewish authorities counted 22, the same as the number of letters in the Hebrew alphabet. In his prologue to the books of Samuel and Kings, Jerome, though seeming to favor counting 22, said: "Some would include both Ruth and Lamentations among the Hagiographa . . . and thus would get twenty-four books."

The Jewish historian Josephus, in answering opponents in his work *Against Apion* (I, 38-40 [8]) around the year 100 C.E., confirms that by then the canon of the Hebrew Scriptures had been fixed for a long time. He wrote: "We do not possess myriads of inconsistent books, conflicting with each other. Our books, those which are justly accredited, are but two and twenty, and contain the record of all time. Of these, five are the books of Moses, comprising the laws and the traditional history from the birth of man down to the death of the lawgiver. . . . From the death of Moses until Artaxerxes, who succeeded Xerxes as king of Persia, the prophets subsequent to Moses wrote the history of the events of their own times in thirteen books. The remaining four books contain hymns to God and precepts for the conduct of human life."

Canonicity of a book therefore does not rest in whole or in part on whether some council, committee, or community accepts or rejects it. The voice of such noninspired men is valuable only as witness to what God himself has already done through his accredited representatives.

The exact *number* of books in the Hebrew Scriptures is not important (whether a certain two are combined or left separated), nor is the particular order in which they follow one another, since the books remained as separate rolls long after the canon was closed. Ancient catalogs vary in the order the books are listed, as, for example, one listing places Isaiah after the book of Ezekiel. What is most important, however, is *what* books are included. In reality, only those books now in the canon have any solid claim for canonicity. From ancient times efforts to include other writings have been resisted. Two Jewish councils held at Yavne or Jamnia, a little S of Joppa, about 90 and 118 C.E. respectively, when discussing the Hebrew Scriptures, expressly excluded all Apocryphal writings.

Josephus bears witness to this general Jewish opinion of the Apocryphal writings when he says: "From Artaxerxes to our own time the complete history has been written, but has not been deemed worthy of equal credit with the earlier records, because of the failure of the exact succession of the prophets. We have given practical proof of our reverence for our own Scriptures. For, although such long ages have now passed, no one has ventured either to add, or to remove, or to alter a syllable; and it is an instinct with every Jew, from the day of his birth, to regard them as the decrees of God, to abide by them, and, if need be, cheerfully to die for them."—*Against Apion,* I, 41-43 (8).

This long historical position of the Jews toward the Hebrew Scripture canon is very important, in view of what Paul wrote to the Romans. The Jews, the apostle says, "were entrusted with the sacred pronouncements of God," which included writing and protecting the Bible canon.—Ro 3:1, 2.

Acknowledging but by no means establishing the Bible canon that God's holy spirit had authorized were early councils (Laodicea, 367 C.E.; Chalcedon, 451 C.E.) and so-called church fathers who were singularly unanimous in accepting the established Jewish canon and in rejecting the Apocryphal books. Examples of such men include: Justin Martyr, Christian apologist (died c. 165 C.E.); Melito, "bishop" of Sardis (2nd century C.E.); Origen, Biblical scholar (185?-254? C.E.); Hilary, "bishop" of Poitiers (died 367? C.E.); Epiphanius, "bishop" of Constantia (from 367 C.E.); Gregory (257?-332 C.E.); Rufinus of Aquileia, "the learned Translator of Origen" (345?-410 C.E.); Jerome (340?-420 C.E.), Biblical scholar of the Latin church and compiler of the *Vulgate.* In his prologue to the books of Samuel and Kings, after enumerating the 22 books of the Hebrew Scriptures, Jerome says: "Whatever is beyond these must be put in the apocrypha."

The most conclusive testimony on the canonicity of the Hebrew Scriptures is the unimpeachable word of Jesus Christ and the writers of the Christian Greek Scriptures. Though they nowhere give an exact number of books, the unmistakable conclusion drawn from what they said is that the canon of the Hebrew Scriptures did not contain the Apocryphal books.

If there was not a definite collection of Holy Writings known and recognized by them and those to whom they spoke and wrote, they would not have used such expressions as "the Scriptures" (Mt 22:29; Ac 18:24); "the holy Scriptures" (Ro 1:2); "the holy writings" (2Ti 3:15); the "Law," often meaning the whole body of Scripture (Joh 10:34; 12:34; 15:25); "the Law and the Prophets," used as a generic term meaning the entire Hebrew Scriptures and not simply the first and second sections of those Scriptures (Mt 5:17; 7:12; 22:40; Lu 16:16). When Paul referred to "the Law," he quoted from Isaiah.—1Co 14:21; Isa 28:11.

It is most unlikely that the original Greek *Septuagint* contained Apocryphal books. (See APOCRYPHA.) But even if some of these writings of doubtful origin crept into subsequent copies of the *Septuagint* circulated in Jesus' day, neither he nor the writers of the Christian Greek Scriptures quoted from them even though using the *Septuagint;* they never cited as "Scripture" or the product of holy spirit any Apocryphal writing. So, not only do the Apocryphal books lack internal evidence of divine inspiration and attestation by ancient inspired writers of Hebrew Scriptures but they also lack the stamp of approval by Jesus and his divinely accredited apostles. However, Jesus did approve the Hebrew canon, referring to the entire Hebrew Scriptures when he spoke of "all the things written in the *law* of Moses and in the *Prophets* and *Psalms,*" the Psalms being the first and longest book in the section called the Hagiographa or Holy Writings.—Lu 24:44.

Jesus' words at Matthew 23:35 (and at Lu 11:50, 51) are also very significant: "That there may come upon you all the righteous blood spilled on earth, from the blood of righteous Abel to the blood of Zechariah son of Barachiah, whom you murdered between the sanctuary and the altar." Timewise, the prophet Urijah was put to death during the reign of Jehoiakim more than two centuries after Zechariah's murder near the end of Jehoash's reign. (Jer 26:20-23) So if Jesus wanted to cite the whole list of martyrs, why did he not say 'from Abel to *Urijah'*? Evidently it was because the instance concerning Zechariah is found at 2 Chronicles 24:20, 21, and hence near the *end* of the traditional Hebrew canon. So in this sense Jesus' statement did embrace all the murdered witnesses of Jehovah mentioned in the Hebrew Scriptures, from Abel listed in the first book (Genesis) to Zechariah cited in the last book (Chronicles), which, by illustration, would be like our saying "from Genesis to Revelation."

Christian Greek Scriptures. The writing as well as the collecting of the 27 books comprising the canon of the Christian Greek Scriptures was similar to that of the Hebrew Scriptures. Christ "gave gifts in men," yes, "he gave some as apostles, some as prophets, some as evangelizers, some as shepherds and teachers." (Eph 4:8, 11-13) With God's holy spirit on them they set forth sound doctrine for the Christian congregation and, "by way of a reminder," repeated many things already written in the Scriptures.—2Pe 1:12, 13; 3:1; Ro 15:15.

Outside the Scriptures themselves there is evidence that, as early as 90-100 C.E., at least ten of Paul's letters were collected together. It is certain that at an early date Christians were gathering together the inspired Christian writings.

We read that "near the close of the 1st cent., Clement bishop of Rome was acquainted with Paul's letter to the church at Corinth. After him, the letters of both Ignatius bishop of Antioch and Polycarp bishop of Smyrna attest the dissemination of the Pauline letters by the second decade of the 2nd century." (*The International Standard Bible Encyclopedia,* edited by G. W. Bromiley, 1979, Vol. 1, p. 603) These were all early writers —Clement of Rome (30?-100? C.E.), Polycarp (69?-155? C.E.), and Ignatius of Antioch (late 1st and early 2nd centuries C.E.)—who wove in quotations and extracts from various books of the Christian Greek Scriptures, showing their acquaintance with such canonical writings.

Justin Martyr (died c. 165 C.E.) in his "Dialogue With Trypho, a Jew" (XLIX), used the expression "it is written" when quoting from Matthew, in the same way the Gospels themselves do when referring to the Hebrew Scriptures. The same is also true in an earlier anonymous work, "The Epistle of Barnabas" (IV). Justin Martyr in "The First Apology" (LXVI, LXVII) calls the "memoirs of the apostles" "Gospels."—*The Ante-Nicene Fathers,* Vol. I, pp. 220, 139, 185, 186.

Theophilus of Antioch (2nd century C.E.) declared: "Concerning the righteousness which the law enjoined, confirmatory utterances are found both with the prophets and in the Gospels, because they all spoke inspired by one Spirit of God." Theophilus then uses such expressions as 'says the Gospel' (quoting Mt 5:28, 32, 44, 46; 6:3) and "the divine word gives us instructions" (quoting 1Ti 2:2 and Ro 13:7, 8).—*The Ante-Nicene Fathers,* 1962, Vol. II, pp. 114, 115, "Theophilus to Autolycus" (XII, XIII).

By the end of the second century there was no question but that the canon of the Christian Greek Scriptures was closed, and we find such ones as Irenaeus, Clement of Alexandria, and Tertullian recognizing the writings comprising the Christian Scriptures as carrying authority equal to that of the Hebrew Scriptures. Irenaeus in appealing to the Scriptures makes no fewer than 200 quotations from Paul's letters. Clement says he will answer his opponents by "the Scriptures which we believe are valid from their omnipotent authority," that is, "by the law and the prophets, and besides by the blessed Gospel."—*The Ante-Nicene Fathers,* Vol. II, p. 409, "The Stromata, or Miscellanies."

The canonicity of certain individual books of the Christian Greek Scriptures has been disputed by some, but the arguments against them are very weak. For critics to reject, for example, the book of Hebrews simply because it does not bear Paul's name and because it differs slightly in style from his other letters is shallow reasoning. B. F. Westcott observed that "the canonical authority of the Epistle is independent of its Pauline authorship." (*The Epistle to the Hebrews,* 1892, p. lxxi) Objection on the grounds of unnamed writership is far outweighed by the presence of Hebrews in the Chester Beatty Papyrus No. 2 (P^{46}) (dated within 150 years of Paul's death), which contains it along with eight other letters of Paul.

Sometimes the canonicity of small books such as James, Jude, Second and Third John, and Second Peter is questioned on the grounds that these books are quoted very little by early writers. However, they make up all together only one thirty-sixth of the Christian Greek Scriptures and were therefore less likely to be referred to. In this connection it may be observed that Second Peter is quoted by Irenaeus as bearing the same evidence of canonicity as the rest of the Greek Scriptures. The same is true of Second John. (*The Ante-Nicene Fathers,* Vol. I, pp. 551, 557, 341, 443, "Irenæus Against Heresies") Revelation, also rejected by some, was attested to by many early commentators, including Papias, Justin Martyr, Melito, and Irenaeus.

The real test of canonicity, however, is not how

many times or by what nonapostolic writer a certain book has been quoted. The contents of the book itself must give evidence that it is a product of holy spirit. Consequently, it cannot contain superstitions or demonism, nor can it encourage creature worship. It must be in total harmony and complete unity with the rest of the Bible, thus supporting the authorship of Jehovah God. Each book must conform to the divine "pattern of healthful words" and be in harmony with the teachings and activities of Christ Jesus. (2Ti 1:13; 1Co 4:17) The apostles clearly had divine accreditation and they spoke in attestation of such other writers as Luke and James, the half brother of Jesus. By holy spirit the apostles had "discernment of inspired utterances" as to whether such were of God or not. (1Co 12:4, 10) With the death of John, the last apostle, this reliable chain of divinely inspired men came to an end, and so with the Revelation, John's Gospel, and his epistles, the Bible canon closed.

The 66 canonical books of our Bible in their harmonious unity and balance testify to the oneness and completeness of the Bible and recommend it to us as indeed Jehovah's Word of inspired truth, preserved until now against all its enemies. (1Pe 1:25) For a complete listing of the 66 books that make up the entire Bible canon, the writers, when the books were completed, and the time covered by each, see "Table of Bible Books in Order Completed" under BIBLE.—See also individual article for each Bible book.

CAPER BERRY [Heb., *'avi·yoh·nah'*]. The fruit of the caper plant. Some translations of Ecclesiastes 12:5 render the Hebrew term *'avi·yoh·nah'* as "desire" so that the passage is made to read "and desire fails." (*RS;* see also *KJ; Ro.*) However, many modern translators (*AT; JB; JP; NW; NC* [Spanish]) consider that the writer of Ecclesiastes, in this chapter describing the conditions of man in his old age, used a metaphor, as is the case throughout the description, and that *'avi·yoh·nah'* refers to the caper berry (as stimulating desire or appetite). This latter view finds support in the renderings of the Greek *Septuagint,* the Latin *Vulgate,* the Syriac *Peshitta,* and Arabic translations.

The caper plant (*Capparis spinosa*) may reach a height of 1 m (3 ft) but usually spreads over the ground in vinelike fashion. It is abundant in Israel, often growing from clefts in rocks or spreading over walls or ruins much like ivy. The spiny branches bear rich green oval leaves. The plant flowers in May with large white blossoms, purple filaments extending out from their centers.—PICTURE, Vol. 1, p. 543.

The berries of the plant are not used as much as the small young buds. These are pickled and eaten as a condiment to stimulate appetite, a quality for which they have been known from ancient times. Thus the writer of Ecclesiastes apparently says that, when an old man's sense of taste diminishes and his appetite weakens, even the stimulation of the caper berry is unable to awaken his desire for food.

CAPERNAUM (Ca·per'na·um) [from Heb., meaning "Village of Nahum"; or, "Village of Comforting"]. A city of major importance in Jesus' earthly ministry, located on the NW shores of the Sea of Galilee. It had a tax office, where Jesus called Matthew to be his disciple (Mt 9:9), and perhaps a military post, for a centurion resided there. (Mt 8:5) These indications, plus the fact that an attendant of the king, wealthy enough to have slaves, lived there (Joh 4:46-53), all seem to make it likely that Capernaum was of some size and importance and hence worthy of being called "a city of Galilee."—Lu 4:31.

Two principal sites have been suggested as the original location of Capernaum. The ruins of Khan Minyeh (Horvat Minnim), situated on the Sea of Galilee at the NE corner of the Plain of Gennesaret, were viewed by many as the probable location of Capernaum, but excavations there indicate that the ruins are of Arab origin. This leaves Tell Hum (Kefar Nahum), an extensive ruin about 4 km (2.5 mi) farther along the shore to the NE from Khan Minyeh, and almost that same distance SW of the point where the Jordan River enters the Sea of Galilee. The coastal plain here is quite narrow, but in ancient times a road led from the Jordan down past Capernaum and through the Plain of Gennesaret to connect with the great trade route leading from Mesopotamia and Damascus, through Palestine and on to Egypt. A number of springs flow across the Plain of Gennesaret, emptying into the blue waters of the Sea of Galilee, and the large amount of vegetable matter these springs carry draws large numbers of fish, making the area an excellent location for fishermen. —PICTURE, Vol. 2, p. 739.

Early in his ministry, following the marriage at Cana, where his first miracle was performed, Jesus, together with his mother, brothers, and disciples, traveled from Cana down to Capernaum, spending a few days there before going up to Jerusalem for the Passover of the year 30 C.E. —Joh 2:12, 13.

Later, after beginning his great Galilean ministry and while again in Cana, Jesus performed a long-distance miraculous cure of the son of a member of the royal court of Herod Antipas, the sick child being healed in Capernaum though about 26 km (16 mi) away from Cana. (Joh 4:46-54) The news of this miracle evidently spread quickly to the neighboring towns so that, when Jesus moved on from Cana to his hometown of Nazareth, he could say to his listeners in that city that they would likely ask him to do in Nazareth "the things we heard as having happened in Capernaum." (Lu 4:16, 23) Leaving Nazareth, where the people had attempted to kill him, Jesus "took up residence in Capernaum beside the sea in the districts of Zebulun and Naphtali" (Mt 4:13-16; Lu 4:28-31), thereby fulfilling Isaiah's prophecy (9:1, 2) that a great light would be seen in that region by those walking in darkness.

It was possibly along the nearby Plain of Gennesaret, SW of Capernaum, that Jesus again met Peter and Andrew (already his disciples; Joh 1:35-42) and gave them the express invitation to become his active followers in the ministry, doing the same thereafter for James and John. (Mr 1:16-21) Following this, Jesus preached in the synagogue of Capernaum, healing a demonized man in attendance, and from this strategically located city the report of his preaching and miracles "kept going out into every corner of the surrounding country." (Lu 4:31-37; Mr 1:21-28; see SYNAGOGUE.) The home of the fishermen Peter and Andrew was in Capernaum, and here Jesus healed Peter's mother-in-law; after this, the house was besieged by people bringing ill and demon-possessed persons to him for healing.—Mr 1:29-34; Lu 4:38-41.

Following a preaching tour of Galilee, accompanied by the four disciples called from the Capernaum vicinity, Jesus returned to Capernaum, which by now could be called "his own city," the place where he could be said to be "at home." (Mt 9:1; Mr 2:1) Again the crowds flocked around the house, and on this occasion Jesus healed a paralytic who was lowered through an opening in the roof. (Mr 2:2-12) Later, coming upon Matthew in the tax office, Jesus issued the call to him, and Matthew became the fifth disciple to join in the active ministry with Jesus. At Matthew's house in Capernaum Jesus attended a big reception feast at which there were many tax collectors, a group despised by the Pharisees.—Mt 9:9-11; Lu 5:27-30.

After going into Judea and Jerusalem and attending the Passover of 31 C.E., Jesus returned to Galilee, and it seems likely that it was on a mountain in the neighborhood of Capernaum that he chose the 12 to be his apostles and delivered the renowned Sermon on the Mount. (Lu 6:12-49) Entering Capernaum, he was met by Jewish elders acting as intermediaries on behalf of an army officer who had demonstrated love for the Jewish nation, even building a synagogue in the city for them. This Gentile officer's unquestioning faith in Jesus' power to heal a sick slave even from a distance (as he had earlier healed the child of the king's attendant) caused Jesus to marvel and resulted in Jesus' prophecy that persons "from eastern parts and western parts" would recline at the table along with Abraham, Isaac, and Jacob in the Kingdom of the heavens.—Mt 8:5-13; Lu 7:1-10.

Toward the close of his second preaching tour in Galilee and after activity in the country of the Gerasenes (or Gadarenes) SE of the Sea of Galilee, Jesus "crossed back again . . . to the opposite shore," likely to the vicinity of Capernaum. (Mt 8:28; Mr 5:1, 21; Lu 8:26, 40) Among the expectant crowd gathered on the shore, a woman was healed simply by touching Jesus' garment, after which Jesus performed a far greater miracle by bringing to life the deceased daughter of Jairus, a presiding officer of the synagogue. Again, though Jesus gave orders against telling others of this resurrection, "the talk about this spread out into all that region." (Mt 9:18-26; Mr 5:22-43; Lu 8:40-56) Possibly in Capernaum or its vicinity Jesus also healed two blind men as well as a speechless man possessed of a demon.—Mt 9:27-34.

At the close of his third Galilean preaching tour and shortly before the Passover of 32 C.E. (Joh 6:4), Jesus walked on the waters of the Sea of Galilee during a crossing to the shores of Gennesaret near Capernaum. After entering Capernaum, he was located by crowds who had followed him from across the sea. When Jesus gave a discourse designed to correct the basically materialistic interest in him that had been shown by the majority, many of his disciples defected from the ranks of his followers. This left a smaller number of faithful ones. (Mt 14:23-34; Mr 6:53; Joh 6:17-71) It was likely in Capernaum, after having attended the Passover of 32 C.E. in Jerusalem, that Jesus rebuked the Pharisaic traditionalists for criticizing Jesus' disciples while at the same time making God's Word void by their traditions.—Mt 15:1-20; Mr 7:1-23; Joh 7:1.

Finally, it was in Capernaum, sometime prior to the Festival of Booths in the year 32 C.E., when his major activity in Galilee and the northern part of the country was nearing its conclusion, that Jesus miraculously provided money for the temple tax and presented illustrations concerning greatness in the Kingdom of the heavens, strayed sheep, and the settling of difficulties.—Mt 17:24–18:35; Mr 9:33-50; Lu 9:46-50.

Capernaum was included by Jesus with the nearby cities of Chorazin and Bethsaida as one of the places in which most of his powerful works had been performed. (Mt 11:20-24; Lu 10:13-15) Capernaum had been exalted heaven high in a spiritual way by the presence, preaching, and miracles of Jesus, but it would now be abased, as it were, to Hades, here representing the depth of its abasement. Ancient Sodom would have certainly produced ten righteous persons if it had been so highly favored as was Capernaum. Today Capernaum, like Sodom, no longer exists as a city, its ruins at Tell Hum (Kefar Nahum) stretching out for about 1.5 km (1 mi) along the seacoast.

CAPHTOR (Caph'tor), **CAPHTORIM** (Caph'to-rim). Among the descendants of Ham through Mizraim are the Caphtorim. (Ge 10:6, 13, 14; 1Ch 1:12) At some unspecified time prior to the Israelite Exodus from Egypt (1513 B.C.E.), the Caphtorim had taken over land in the SW part of Canaan, dispossessing a people known as the Avvim. (De 2:23) Elsewhere, the name Caphtor (also, Crete, NW) is applied to the "island" or "coastland" (*RS, AT,* others) from which the Philistines migrated to Canaan.—Jer 47:4; Am 9:7.

The identification of Caphtor has been a subject of much discussion. Among the places suggested are the Delta region of Egypt, the southeastern coast of Asia Minor (including Cilicia), Cappadocia, and Crete. The majority of scholars today favor an identification with the island of Crete, lying off the SE coast of Greece. Some would also include neighboring islands and coastlands under the name Caphtor. Caphtor is understood to be represented by the name *Kaptara,* found in the Assyro-Babylonian texts, and by *Kfty(w)* in Egyptian inscriptions. There is evidence indicating that the Egyptians (also descendants of Mizraim) carried on trade with the Cretans from early times, perhaps from a period contemporaneous with Abraham.

Many scholars consider that the reference to "the Caphtorim" at Deuteronomy 2:23 actually applies to the Philistines. However, since the Philistines are shown to have gone forth from among the Casluhim (another branch of Mizraim's descendants), the Philistines could only be called Caphtorim in a geographic (and not a genealogical or racial) sense, that is, in the sense of their having lived in the territory of Caphtor before coming to Canaan. They would then be called Caphtorim in

the same way that the Hebrew Jacob was called a Syrian (or Aramaean). (De 26:5) Otherwise, it must be understood that the Philistines are not meant at Deuteronomy 2:23 and that the national group of the Caphtorim had its own emigrants to Canaan.

CAPITAL. The uppermost section and crowning decoration of a building's column. Massive capitals topped Jachin and Boaz, the pillars that stood in front of Solomon's temple. (2Ch 3:15-17) These capitals and the pillars upon which they rested were made under the direction of the craftsman Hiram at the time of the temple's construction (1034-1027 B.C.E.) and survived over 400 years until Jerusalem was sacked by the Babylonians in 607 B.C.E. (2Ch 4:11-13; Jer 52:17, 22) In every reference to these capitals, except for one, the Hebrew word *ko·the'reth* is used. It comes from the root *ka·thar'* ('surround'; Jg 20:43) and is related to *ke'ther* ("headdress"; Es 1:11). The Hebrew word for "capital" occurring in 2 Chronicles 3:15 (*tse'pheth*) comes from the root verb *tsa·phah',* meaning "overlay."—Ex 25:11.

The pillars themselves were of cast copper, about 1.7 m (5.6 ft) in diameter and 18 cubits (8 m; 26 ft) high. In addition, the capitals were 5 cubits (2.2 m; 7.3 ft) high. (1Ki 7:15, 16) In view of the passages indicating that the capitals were five cubits high, a number of scholars have concluded that the reference to "three cubits" in 2 Kings 25:17 is a scribal error. That is why some Bible translations (for example, *JB, NAB*) have replaced "three cubits" with "five cubits." Since the pillars were hollow, with walls about 7.5 cm (3 in.) thick, it is reasonable to suppose that the capitals were of similar construction and were also cast in clay molds "in the District of the Jordan."—2Ch 4:17; Jer 52:21.

From the limited description of these bowl-shaped capitals, it is impossible to describe their exact appearance or design. Around the bottom part of each there were seven nets of copper network, and from these hung two rows of 100 copper pomegranates each, suspended on copper chains. These were arranged like necklaces around the capitals. (1Ki 7:17, 18, 20, 42; 2Ch 3:16) It appears that on the side of the capital next to the temple, four pomegranates in each chain of 100 were rather obscured from view, for Jeremiah says there "came to be ninety-six, on the sides" (literally, "windward"; "on the outside," *AT;* "being visible," *Mo*). (Jer 52:23) Above these pomegranate decorations there was "lily work" of 4 cubits (1.8 m; 5.8 ft).—1Ki 7:19, 22.

Other capitals that are mentioned in the Bible are Nineveh's "pillar capitals" (Heb., *kaph·toh·rim′*), doomed to be frequented by "pelican and porcupine."—Zep 2:13, 14.

CAPPADOCIA (Cap·pa·do′ci·a). In the days of the apostles, Cappadocia was a large inland region in the eastern part of Asia Minor, with a generally cold climate and rather sparse woodlands. It occupied a plateau having elevations of 900 m (3,000 ft) in much of the region. Though the boundaries fluctuated throughout its history, basically they were Pontus on the N, Galatia and Lycaonia in the W, Cilicia and the Taurus Mountains on the S, and Armenia and the upper Euphrates River on the E. Extensive pasturing of sheep was done, and cattle and fine horses were also abundant. Wheat was the major grain product.

Cappadocia was made part of the Persian Empire under Cyrus and the original region was formed into the two satrapies of Pontus and Cappadocia. During the Seleucid dynasty of Syria, tributary kings were allowed to rule. Roman Emperor Tiberius ended this in 17 C.E., and Cappadocia became a Roman province under the administration of a procurator. Vespasian enlarged the province in 70 C.E., combining it with Armenia, thereby forming a major frontier province in the East. Cappadocia held strategic importance because of the roads traversing the region, one of these running from Tarsus on the Mediterranean, through the gap in the Taurus Range known as the Cilician Gates, across Cappadocia to the province of Pontus, and to ports on the Black Sea.

The natives of Cappadocia were evidently Aryans of Japhetic stock, but Jewish settlements were in evidence by the second century B.C.E. Jews from Cappadocia were present at Jerusalem on Pentecost of 33 C.E. (Ac 2:9) Likely as a result of this, Christianity spread into Cappadocia at an early date, and Cappadocian Christians were among those addressed by Peter in his first letter.—1Pe 1:1.

CAPTAIN OF THE TEMPLE. The officer, second in dignity to the high priest (Ac 4:1), who had charge over the officiating priesthood and the Levites who were organized under lesser captains to guard the temple in Jerusalem and to keep order. (Lu 22:4, 52) There were 24 divisions of the Levites, which divisions served a week at a time in rotation, twice a year. Each division likely also had a captain over it, with several captains of smaller groups.

The captains were men of influence. They conspired with the chief priests in hiring Judas to betray Jesus. They brought their forces along with the priests to arrest Jesus. (Lu 22:3, 4, 52) It was the temple captain who lent official flavor to the arrest of Peter and John in the temple. (Ac 4:1, 3) On a later occasion, after Peter and some of the apostles had been released from prison by an angel, the temple captain went with his officers to bring them before the Sanhedrin in an apparently legal way without violence.—Ac 5:24-26.

CAPTIVE. A person in bondage, exile, confinement, or under restraint, especially one seized and carried off as a result of war. (Nu 21:1) In ancient times the spoils of war often included, besides captured livestock, the populace of conquered cities and territories. (1Ch 5:21; 2Ch 14:14, 15; Am 4:10) On one occasion the ark of the covenant was carried off as booty, with dire consequences to its Philistine captors. (1Sa 4:11–5:12) References to captives date back to patriarchal times; the first mentioned in the Bible is Lot, who was rescued from the forces of Chedorlaomer by Abraham. (Ge 14:14; 31:26; 34:25-29) In a sense Job, although no war casualty, was in a "captive condition" until Jehovah rescued him from his misery.—Job 42:10.

When the Israelites moved in to possess the Promised Land, certain cities, including their populations, were entirely devoted to destruction, as, for example, Jericho, the firstfruits of the conquest. (Jos 6:17, 21) When capturing other cities not devoted to destruction, the Israelites, unlike the pagan nations, were not allowed to rape the women. If they desired a captive woman for a wife, certain requirements had to be met first. —La 5:11; Nu 31:9-19, 26, 27; De 21:10-14.

However, when enemy nations came up against the Israelites, Jehovah sometimes allowed his people to be carried off captive when they had been unfaithful to him. (2Ch 21:16, 17; 28:5, 17; 29:9) The most notable examples of this were in the eighth and seventh centuries B.C.E., when thousands of Israelites were exiled as captives by the Assyrian and Babylonian World Powers. (See CAPTIVITY.) Ahijah and Jeremiah foretold this coming national disaster. (1Ki 14:15; Jer 15:2) Moses too had warned that their sons and daughters would "go off into captivity" as a penalty for disobedience to Jehovah, adding that if they repented, such captives would in time return. (De 28:41; 30:3) Solomon foresaw captivity resulting from unfaithfulness, and he prayed for Jehovah to release the captives if they repented.—1Ki 8:46-52; 2Ch 6:36-39; see also 2Ch 30:9; Ezr 9:7.

The treatment of captives varied a great deal, depending on many circumstances. Sometimes they were permitted to remain in their own land on condition that they pay tribute and not rebel against their new master. (Ge 14:1-4; 2Sa 8:5, 6; 2Ki 17:1-4) A conquered monarch was sometimes permitted to continue reigning as a vassal king, or he might be replaced. (2Ki 23:34; 24:1, 17) In some instances great numbers of captives were put to death, like the 10,000 who were thrown down from a crag so "they, one and all, burst apart." (2Ch 25:12) Some conquerors were very cruel and fiendish in their treatment of captives, hanging them "by just their hand" (La 5:12), cutting off their noses and ears (Eze 23:25), blinding them with red-hot irons or boring out their eyes with spears or daggers (Jg 16:21; 1Sa 11:2; Jer 52:11), or "slitting open the pregnant women" of a captured town. (Am 1:13) The sadistic Assyrians, particularly noted for their extreme cruelty, are depicted in monuments as tying captives down and then skinning them alive.

Captives were often led away to forced labor (2Sa 12:29-31; 1Ch 20:3), taken into slavery, or sold as chattel (1Sa 30:1, 2; 2Ki 5:2; Isa 14:3, 4). Often conquerors delighted in roping captives together around the neck or head (compare Isa 52:2), or binding them in fetters (2Ki 25:7), and leading them off "naked and barefoot, and with buttocks stripped," to their humiliation and shame.—Isa 20:4.

Release and return of the Jewish captives was the happy theme of many prophecies. (Isa 49:24, 25; Jer 29:14; 46:27; Eze 39:28; Ho 6:11; Joe 3:1; Am 9:14; Zep 3:20) The psalmist also looked toward the time when "Jehovah gathers back the captive ones of his people." (Ps 14:7; 53:6; 85:1; 126:1, 4) Many of these prophecies were fulfilled in a miniature way from and after 537 B.C.E., when a remnant of the captives that had come under control of the Persian Empire began streaming back to Jerusalem to rebuild the city and its great temple. (Ezr 2:1; 3:8; 8:35; Ne 1:2, 3; 7:6; 8:17) Certain enemies of Jehovah's people were especially mentioned as destined for captivity themselves, nations such as Babylon (Isa 46:1, 2; Jer 50:1, 2), Egypt (Jer 43:11, 12; Eze 30:17, 18), and Moab (Jer 48:46).

Jesus quotes from Isaiah 61:1, 2, applying it to himself as sent by Jehovah "to preach a release to the captives and a recovery of sight to the blind." (Lu 4:16-21) The apostle Paul draws illustrations from the ancient practice of conquerors' taking captives. (Eph 4:8; 2Co 10:5) In the last book of the Bible the principle is set forth: "If anyone is meant for captivity, he goes away into captivity." —Re 13:10.

CAPTIVITY. In Biblical history a number of different captivities are mentioned. (Nu 21:29; 2Ch 29:9; Isa 46:2; Eze 30:17, 18; Da 11:33; Na 3:10; Re 13:10; see CAPTIVE.) However, "the captivity" generally refers to the great exiling of Jews from the Promised Land in the eighth and seventh centuries B.C.E. by the Assyrian and Babylonian World Powers, and is also called "the Exile" and "the deportation."—Ezr 3:8; 6:21; Mt 1:17; see EXILE.

Jeremiah, Ezekiel, and other prophets warned of this great calamity in statements like these: "Whoever is for the captivity, to the captivity!" "As for you, O Pashhur, and all the inhabitants of your house, you will go into captivity; and to Babylon you will come." "There is this pronouncement against Jerusalem and all the house of Israel . . . 'Into exile, into captivity they will go.'" (Jer 15:2; 20:6; Eze 12:10, 11) Later, concerning the return from Babylonian captivity, Nehemiah (7:6) relates: "These are the sons of the jurisdictional district who came up out of the captivity of the exiled people whom Nebuchadnezzar the king of Babylon had taken into exile and who later returned to Jerusalem and to Judah."—See also Ezr 2:1; 3:8; 8:35; Ne 1:2, 3; 8:17.

Assyria, it seems, was the first to introduce the policy of uprooting and removing the entire populations of captured towns from their homeland and repopulating the territory with captives from other parts of the empire. This deportation policy of Assyria was not enforced against only the Jews, for when Damascus, the capital of Syria, fell under the crushing military onslaught of this second world power, its people were banished to Kir, as foretold by the prophet Amos. (2Ki 16:8, 9; Am 1:5) The practice had a twofold effect: It discouraged the few remaining ones from subversive activity; and the surrounding nations that may have been friendly with those taken captive were less inclined to give aid and assistance to the new foreign element brought in from distant places.

In both the northern ten-tribe kingdom of Israel and the southern two-tribe kingdom of Judah, the root cause leading up to captivity was the same: abandonment of true worship of Jehovah in favor of the worship of false gods. (De 28:15, 62-68; 2Ki 17:7-18; 21:10-15) Jehovah, for his part, continually sent his prophets to warn them both but to no avail. (2Ki 17:13) None of the ten-tribe kingdom of Israel's kings ever made a complete purge of the false worship instituted by that nation's first king, Jeroboam. Judah, her sister kingdom to the S, failed to heed both Jehovah's direct warnings and the example of the captivity into which Israel had fallen. (Jer 3:6-10) The inhabitants of both kingdoms eventually were carried away into exile, each nation in more than one principal deportation.

Beginning of the Exile. During the reign of Israelite King Pekah at Samaria (c. 778-759 B.C.E.), Assyrian King Pul (Tiglath-pileser III) came against Israel, captured a large section in the N, and deported its inhabitants to eastern parts of his empire. (2Ki 15:29) This same monarch also captured territory E of the Jordan and from that area "he took into exile those of the Reubenites and of the Gadites and of the half tribe of Manasseh and brought them to Halah and Habor and Hara and the river Gozan to continue until this day."—1Ch 5:26.

In 742 B.C.E. the Assyrian army under Shalmaneser V besieged Samaria. (2Ki 18:9, 10) When Samaria fell in 740 B.C.E., thus ending the ten-tribe kingdom, its inhabitants were taken into exile "in Halah and in Habor at the river Gozan and in the cities of the Medes." This was because, as the Scriptures say, "they had not listened to the voice of Jehovah their God, but kept overstepping his covenant, even all that Moses the servant of Jehovah had commanded. They neither listened nor performed."—2Ki 18:11, 12; 17:6; see SARGON.

Captives from other widely scattered places were then brought in and settled in the cities of Samaria. "Subsequently the king of Assyria brought people from Babylon and Cuthah and Avva and Hamath and Sepharvaim and had them dwell in the cities of Samaria instead of the sons of Israel; and they began to take possession of Samaria and to dwell in its cities." (2Ki 17:24) This foreign element imported with them their pagan religion; "each different nation came to be a maker of its own god." And because they showed no regard or respect for Jehovah, he "sent lions among them, and they came to be killers among them." The king of Assyria then returned one of the Israelite priests, "and he came to be a teacher of them as to how they ought to fear Jehovah." So, as the account then says, "It was of Jehovah that they became fearers, but it was of their own gods that they proved to be worshipers, according to the religion of the nations from among whom they had led them into exile."—2Ki 17:25-33.

During the century and more that followed the overthrow of the northern kingdom, other notable exiles began. Before Sennacherib's humiliating defeat at God's hand in 732 B.C.E., he attacked various places in Judah. It is claimed by Sennacherib in his annals that he captured 200,150 from towns and fortresses in Judah's territory, though,

judging from the tone of the annals, the number is probably an exaggeration. (2Ki 18:13) His successor Esar-haddon and the Assyrian monarch that followed him, Asenappar (Ashurbanipal), both transported captives to foreign territories.—Ezr 4:2, 10.

In 628 B.C.E., Egypt's Pharaoh Necho put Josiah's son Jehoahaz of the southern kingdom in bonds and carried him captive to Egypt. (2Ch 36:1-5) But it was more than a decade later, in 617 B.C.E., that the first captives from Jerusalem were taken into exile at Babylon. Nebuchadnezzar came against the rebellious city and carried off the upper class of the population, including King Jehoiachin and his mother, and men such as Ezekiel, Daniel, Hananiah, Mishael, and Azariah, together with "the princes and all the valiant, mighty men —ten thousand he was taking into exile—and also every craftsman and builder of bulwarks. No one had been left behind except the lowly class of the people . . . Court officials and the foremost men of the land he led away as exiled people from Jerusalem to Babylon. As for all the valiant men, seven thousand, and the craftsmen and the builders of bulwarks, a thousand, all the mighty men carrying on war, the king of Babylon proceeded to bring them as exiled people to Babylon." He also took much of the treasure from the temple. (2Ki 24:12-16; Es 2:6; Eze 1:1-3; Da 1:2, 6) Jehoiachin's uncle Zedekiah was left behind as a vassal king. A few others of note, including the prophet Jeremiah, also remained in Jerusalem. In view of the large number of captives recorded at 2 Kings 24:14, the figure 3,023 given at Jeremiah 52:28 apparently refers to those of a certain rank, or to those who were family heads—their wives and children, numbering thousands, not being included in the figure.

The final capture of Jerusalem by Nebuchadnezzar was completed in 607 B.C.E., after an 18-month siege. (2Ki 25:1-4) This time the city was emptied of most of its inhabitants. Some of the lowly ones of the land were allowed to remain "as vinedressers and as compulsory laborers" under the governorship of Gedaliah at Mizpah. (Jer 52:16; 40:7-10; 2Ki 25:22) Those taken captive to Babylon included "some of the lowly ones of the people and the rest of the people that were left remaining in the city and the deserters . . . and the rest of the master workmen." The expression "that were left remaining in the city" apparently indicates that great numbers had died from famine, disease, or fire, or else they were slaughtered in the war. (Jer 52:15; 2Ki 25:11) Zedekiah's sons, the princes of Judah, court officials, certain priests, and many other prominent citizens were put to death at the order of the king of Babylon. (2Ki 25:7, 18-21; Jer 52:10, 24-27) All of this could account for the rather low number of those actually listed as exiles that were led off, the number given being only 832, probably heads of households, their wives and children not being counted. —Jer 52:29.

Some two months later, after the assassination of Gedaliah, the rest of the Jews left behind in Judah fled to Egypt, taking Jeremiah and Baruch along with them. (2Ki 25:8-12, 25, 26; Jer 43:5-7) Some of the Jews also may have fled to other nations round about. Probably from among these nations were the 745 captives, as household heads, exiled five years later when Nebuchadnezzar, as Jehovah's symbolic club, dashed to pieces the nations bordering Judah. (Jer 51:20; 52:30) Josephus says that five years after the fall of Jerusalem, Nebuchadnezzar overran Ammon and Moab and then went on down and took vengeance on Egypt.—*Jewish Antiquities*, X, 181, 182 (ix, 7).

The situation with Jerusalem was different from that of other conquered cities such as Samaria, which was reinhabited with imported captives from other parts of the Assyrian Empire. In contrast to the usual policy of the Babylonians toward the cities they conquered, Jerusalem and its vicinity were emptied and left desolate, just as Jehovah had predetermined. Bible critics may question that Judah's once-prosperous land was suddenly made "a desolate waste, without an inhabitant," but there is admittedly no historical evidence, no records from this period, to prove otherwise. (Jer 9:11; 32:43) Archaeologist G. Ernest Wright declares: "The violence visited upon Judah is clear . . . from archaeological surveys which show that city after city ceased to be inhabited at this time, many never to be reoccupied." (*Biblical Archaeology*, 1963, p. 182) William F. Albright agrees: "There is not a single known case where a town of Judah proper was continuously occupied through the exilic period."—*The Archaeology of Palestine*, 1971, p. 142.

Condition of the Exiles. The captivity was regarded in general as a period of oppression and bondage. Jehovah said that, instead of showing mercy to Israel, "upon the old man you [Babylon] made your yoke very heavy." (Isa 47:5, 6) No doubt certain payments (tax, tribute, toll), based on what they were able to produce or earn, were exacted of them the same as was levied on other captives. Also, the very fact that the great temple of Jehovah in Jerusalem had been stripped and destroyed, its priesthood either killed or taken into exile, and its worshipers carried away into captiv-

ity and made subjects to a foreign power, certainly constituted a state of oppression.

However, being exiled to a foreign land was not as bad as being sold into cruel perpetual slavery or being executed in the sadistic manner typical of Assyrian and Babylonian conquests. (Isa 14:4-6; Jer 50:17) The exiled Jews, it seems, enjoyed a certain measure of freedom to move around, and they exercised some degree of internal administration of their affairs. (Ezr 8:1, 16, 17; Eze 1:1; 14:1; 20:1) "To all the exiled people, whom I have caused to go into exile from Jerusalem to Babylon," Jehovah said: "Build houses and inhabit them, and plant gardens and eat their fruitage. Take wives and become father to sons and to daughters; and take wives for your own sons and give your own daughters to husbands, that they may give birth to sons and to daughters; and become many there, and do not become few. Also, seek the peace of the city to which I have caused you to go into exile, and pray in its behalf to Jehovah, for in its peace there will prove to be peace for you yourselves." (Jer 29:4-7) Some of them developed skills in various trades that proved useful after the exile ended. (Ne 3:8, 31, 32) Engaging in commercial enterprises and general merchandising became their specialties. Many Jewish names were found among business records. As a result of such commercial intercourse and social contact with non-Jews, the Hebrew language began to reflect Aramaic influence.

The period of captivity, amounting to 80 years for some, naturally affected community worship of the true God Jehovah. With no temple, no altar, and no organized priesthood, the offering of daily sacrifices was not possible. However, the practice of circumcision, abstention from unclean foods, Sabbath observance, and constancy in prayer were things the faithful could do in spite of the scorn and ridicule of others. Captive Daniel's "serving with constancy" his God was well known by King Darius and others. Even when an interdict was legalized that prohibited under the penalty of death the making of a petition to anyone except the king, "three times in a day [Daniel] was kneeling on his knees and praying and offering praise before his God, as he had been *regularly* doing prior to this." (Da 6:4-23) Such faithfulness in their limited worship helped to prevent these exiles from losing their national identity. They could also profit from the contrast they observed between the pure simplicity of Jehovah's worship and the ostentatious idolatrous materialism of Babylon. No doubt they also benefited from the presence of Jehovah's prophets, Ezekiel and Daniel.—Eze 8:1; Da 1:6; 10:1, 2.

As the local synagogue arrangement developed among the Jews, the need for copies of the Scriptures in the communities of Jewish exiles all over Media, Persia, and Babylonia intensified. Ezra was known as "a skilled copyist in the law of Moses," indicating that copies of Jehovah's Law had been brought from Judah, reproductions of which were made. (Ezr 7:6) Without doubt these precious scrolls of past generations included the book of Psalms, with the probability that Psalm 137, and perhaps also Psalm 126, were composed during or shortly after the captivity. The six so-called Hallel Psalms (113 to 118) were sung at the great Passover feasts following the return of the remnant from Babylon.

Restoration and the Dispersion. Hope of release from the captivity was not to be found in Babylon's policy of no return. Egypt, to whom Israel had once looked for assistance, was in no position militarily or otherwise to help, and the other nations were likewise helpless, if not outright hostile toward the Jews. Only in Jehovah's prophetic promises was there any basis for hope. Moses and Solomon, centuries before, had spoken of restoration that would follow captivity. (De 30:1-5; 1Ki 8:46-53) Other prophets also gave reassurance of a deliverance from exile. (Jer 30: 10; 46:27; Eze 39:25-27; Am 9:13-15; Zep 2:7; 3:20) Isaiah, in the last 18 chapters (49-66) of his prophecy, developed this restoration theme to a sweeping climax. The false prophets, however, proved wrong in predicting an early release, and any who trusted in them were sadly disappointed. —Jer 28:1-17.

Faithful Jeremiah proved to be the one giving the correct length of the desolation of Jerusalem and Judah as 70 years, after which time restoration would come. (Jer 25:11, 12; 29:10-14; 30:3, 18) Concerning this, Daniel, in the first year of Darius the Mede, "discerned by the books the number of the years concerning which the word of Jehovah had occurred to Jeremiah the prophet, for fulfilling the devastations of Jerusalem, namely, seventy years."—Da 9:1, 2.

How many exiles returned to Jerusalem from Babylon in 537 B.C.E.?

Early in 537 B.C.E., Persian King Cyrus II issued a decree permitting the captives to return to Jerusalem and rebuild the temple. (2Ch 36:20, 21; Ezr 1:1-4) Preparations were soon under way. With the direction of Governor Zerubbabel and High Priest Jeshua, "the sons of the Exile" (Ezr 4:1), numbering 42,360 men in addition to 7,537 slaves

and singers, made the trip of about four months. A footnote in the sixth edition of Isaac Leeser's translation of the Bible suggests that the entire number amounted to about 200,000, including women and children. By the seventh month, in the fall, they were settled in their cities. (Ezr 1:5–3:1) Providentially, the royal line of David leading to Christ had been preserved through Jehoiachin (Jeconiah) and Zerubbabel. Also, the lineage of the Levitical high priest continued unbroken through Jehozadak and, in turn, his son Jeshua.—Mt 1:11-16; 1Ch 6:15; Ezr 3:2, 8.

Later, more captives returned to Palestine. In 468 B.C.E., Ezra was accompanied by more than 1,750, which figure apparently includes only adult males. (Ezr 7:1–8:32) A few years later Nehemiah made at least two trips from Babylon to Jerusalem, but how many Jews returned with him is not disclosed.—Ne 2:5, 6, 11; 13:6, 7.

The captivity put an end to the separation of Judah and Israel. The conquerors made no distinction according to tribal origins when deporting the exiles. "The sons of Israel and the sons of Judah are being oppressed together," Jehovah observed. (Jer 50:33) When the first contingent returned in 537 B.C.E., representatives of all the tribes of Israel were among them. Later, at the completion of the temple rebuilding, a sacrifice of 12 male goats was made, "according to the number of the tribes of Israel." (Ezr 6:16, 17) Such reunification after the captivity was indicated in prophecy. For example, Jehovah promised to "bring Israel back." (Jer 50:19) Furthermore, Jehovah said: "I will bring back the captives of Judah and the captives of Israel, and I will build them just as at the start." (Jer 33:7) Ezekiel's vision of the two sticks that were made one (37:15-28) indicated that the two kingdoms would again become one nation. Isaiah foretold that Jesus Christ would become a stumbling stone "to both the houses of Israel," hardly meaning that Jesus, or the 12 whom he sent out during his third tour of Galilee, would have to visit settlements in far-off Media in order to preach to descendants of Israelites from the northern kingdom. (Isa 8:14; Mt 10:5, 6; 1Pe 2:8) The prophetess Anna, in Jerusalem at the time of Jesus' birth, was of the tribe of Asher, which tribe was once numbered with the northern kingdom.—Lu 2:36.

Not all the Jews returned to Jerusalem with Zerubbabel, only "a mere remnant." (Isa 10:21, 22) Among those returning, there were very few who had seen the original temple. Old age prevented many from risking the hardships of the trip. Others who from a physical point of view could have made the trip chose to remain behind. Many, no doubt, had gained a little material success over the years and were satisfied to remain where they were. If the rebuilding of Jehovah's temple did not occupy the first place in their lives, they would not be inclined to make the hazardous trip, with an uncertain future awaiting them. And, of course, those who had proved apostate had no incentive to go back.

This means that as a people, part of the Jews remained scattered and came to be known as the Di·a·spo·ra', or "Dispersion." In the fifth century B.C.E. communities of Jews were found throughout the 127 jurisdictional districts of the Persian Empire. (Es 1:1; 3:8) Even certain descendants of the exiles still found positions high in government office: for example, Mordecai and Esther under the Persian king Ahasuerus (Xerxes I), and Nehemiah as royal cupbearer to Artaxerxes Longimanus. (Es 9:29-31; 10:2, 3; Ne 1:11) Ezra, when compiling Chronicles, wrote that many of those dispersed in various eastern cities "continue until this day" (c. 460 B.C.E.). (1Ch 5:26) With the rise of the Grecian Empire, Jews were brought by Alexander the Great to his new Egyptian city of Alexandria, where they learned to speak Greek. It was there that the translating of the Hebrew Scriptures into Greek to produce the Septuagint was begun in the third century B.C.E. The Syro-Egyptian wars brought about the transferal of many Jews into Asia Minor and into Egypt respectively. Pompey, upon conquering Jerusalem in 63 B.C.E., took Jews to Rome as slaves.

The great dispersion of Jews throughout the Roman Empire was a factor contributing to the rapid spread of Christianity. Jesus Christ limited his own preaching to the soil of Israel, but he commanded his followers to reach out and spread their ministry "to the most distant part of the earth." (Ac 1:8) Jews from different parts of the Roman Empire were in Jerusalem attending the Pentecost festival in 33 C.E., and they heard the spirit-begotten Christians preaching about Jesus in the languages of Parthia, Media, Elam, Mesopotamia, Cappadocia, Pontus, the district of Asia, Phrygia, Pamphylia, Egypt, Libya, Crete, Arabia, and Rome. Thousands, upon returning to their lands, took with them their newly found faith. (Ac 2:1-11) In most of the cities Paul visited he found synagogues where he could readily speak to Jews of the Dispersion. In Lystra, Paul met Timothy, whose mother was a Jewess. Aquila and Priscilla were newly arrived from Rome when Paul got to Corinth, about 50 C.E. (Ac 13:14; 14:1; 16:1; 17:1, 2; 18:1, 2, 7; 19:8) The great numbers of Jews in Babylon made it worth the effort for Peter to go there to carry on his ministry among "those who

are circumcised." (Ga 2:8; 1Pe 5:13) This community of Jews in Babylon continued as the most important center of Judaism for quite some time after the destruction of Jerusalem in 70 C.E.

CARCHEMISH (Car'che·mish). An important trade center situated on the W bank of the upper Euphrates at one of the main fords of that river. A principal trade route ran from Nineveh up to Haran (only about 88 km [55 mi] E of Carchemish), then crossed the Euphrates at Carchemish, and continued on to the Orontes Valley in Lebanon, from which point other routes led to the Mediterranean or S to Palestine and Egypt. Caravans passing through provided revenue in the form of taxes, and the city evidently became quite wealthy.

Because of its strategic position, both commercially and militarily, control of Carchemish was sought by aggressor kingdoms from early times. Pharaoh Thutmose III (of the middle of the second millennium B.C.E.) obtained plunder from it, and Ramses III also records an assault on the city. Ashurnasirpal II (of the ninth century B.C.E.) describes his crossing of the Euphrates on rafts buoyed up with inflated goatskins and claims to have received tribute from the king of Carchemish that included 20 talents of silver, 100 talents of copper, 250 talents of iron, plus gold objects, furniture inlaid with ivory, garments of linen and wool, and other booty.

Carchemish figures in the Biblical account at Isaiah 10:9-11, where Jehovah foretold the Assyrian attack against Israel and Judah. The boastful Assyrian ruler is described as listing Carchemish among the kingdoms that could not withstand his might. This doubtless refers to the Assyrian conquest of the independent kingdom of Carchemish by Sargon II, a contemporary of King Hezekiah. Thereafter Carchemish was ruled by an Assyrian governor.

Then, after the fall of Nineveh, the Assyrian capital, Pharaoh Necho led his army northward to the aid of the Assyrians. King Josiah of Judah unwisely tried to turn the Egyptian forces back at Megiddo and was killed in the attempt (c. 629 B.C.E.). (2Ch 35:20-24) In 625 B.C.E. a decisive battle was fought at Carchemish between the Egyptian and Babylonian armies. Nebuchadnezzar led the Babylonians to a smashing victory over Pharaoh Necho's forces and swept over Syria and Canaan. This battle marked the end of Egyptian imperial strength in these regions. The Bible account at Jeremiah 46:2 is paralleled by that of the Babylonian Chronicles (B.M. 21946), both describing the defeat of the Egyptian army.

Excavations have been made at the site of Carchemish at Jerablus on the border of Turkey and Syria, about 100 km (62 mi) NE of Aleppo (Halab). A large number of documents in the language presently called Hittite were found, and it is believed that Carchemish was dominated for about two centuries during the latter part of the second millennium B.C.E. by the empire whose capital was Hattushash. (See, however, HITTITES.) Also found were reliefs bearing, among other things, the image of a sphinx, as well as the crux ansata symbol, or ankh, indicating strong Egyptian influence.

CARIAN BODYGUARD

(Ca'ri·an). A body of troops that aided Jehoiada in the overthrow of Athaliah and the installation of Jehoash as king of Judah.—2Ki 11:4, 13-16, 19.

Many scholars consider the Carian bodyguard to be another name for the Cherethites, mentioned as serving in the military forces of David and Solomon. In the view of some scholars, the Cherethites also functioned as a special bodyguard for these kings. (2Sa 8:18; 1Ki 1:38; 1Ch 18:17) This connection of the Carian bodyguard with the Cherethites is additionally based on the fact that the Masoretic text says "Carian bodyguard" at 2 Samuel 20:23, while the reading in its margin, as well as in many Hebrew manuscripts, is "Cherethites."

There is an ancient district of Caria in the SW part of Asia Minor. Because Ezekiel 25:16 and Zephaniah 2:5 associate the Cherethites with the Philistines, and because the Greek *Septuagint* rendering of these texts has "Cretans" instead of Cherethites, some believe that this district of Caria was the original homeland of those in the Carian bodyguard.

CARKAS

(Car'kas). One of King Ahasuerus' seven court officials by whom he sent the unheeded demand for Vashti's presence.—Es 1:10-12; see COURT OFFICIAL.

CARMEL

(Car'mel) [Orchard]. The name of both a mountain range and a city. The Hebrew word *kar·mel'* is used to refer to an "orchard."—Isa 16:10; 32:15; Jer 2:7.

1. The Carmel Range is a wedge-shaped spur of the central mountain range of Israel, running out therefrom in a NW direction with its NW headland coming to about 180 m (600 ft) from the Mediterranean Sea. The entire range measures some 50 km (30 mi) in length, stretching from the Mediterranean down to the Plain of Dothan, beyond which lie the hills of Samaria. The range has three distinct sections, the ridges of the NW and

SE being separated by a lower rocky basin or plateau in the center. The NW section, which is located NW of 'Isfiya, has the highest point, some 545 m (1,790 ft) above sea level. It is not certain whether the name Carmel in Bible times applied to the entire range or only to the NW ridge, which is about 21 km (13 mi) long. In modern times the name Mount Carmel (Jebel el-Karmal; Har Karmel) is assigned to this latter part. Jokneam, a royal Canaanite city, lay at the SE end of this upper section, and it is spoken of as being "in Carmel." Megiddo and Taanach, on the E slopes of the SE section, are not so designated.—Jos 12:22.

The land into which Israel moved when they crossed the Jordan may be divided geographically into three basic sections, each running the length of the land from N to S: the Jordan Valley, the hill country, and the coastal plain. The Carmel Range, however, makes a definite break in this general pattern. Interrupting the continuity of the N-S mountain ranges, it produces the well-known Valley of Jezreel, or Esdraelon, which flanks the SE side of the Carmel Range. Similarly, the headland or promontory of Carmel, jutting into the Mediterranean coastal plain, divides it into the Plain of Asher (N of Carmel) and the plains of Sharon and of Philistia (S of Carmel). Immediately N of the Carmel headland, the coastline cuts back sharply to form the Bay of Acco, where modern Haifa now constitutes a major seaport. Carmel formed one of the boundary markers in the territory of the tribe of Asher.—Jos 19:24-26.

Carmel formed a natural roadblock to caravans and armies traveling between Mesopotamia and Egypt. The eastern slopes (facing the Plain of Asher and the Valley of Jezreel) rise very steeply, and from ancient times the Carmel Range has been covered by a thick growth of trees and shrubs, which make passage difficult. There is a narrow strip of land between the foot of the Carmel headland and the sea, but to take this route meant a considerable detour and also placed advancing armies in a vulnerable position. There were mountain passes leading from the Valley of Jezreel across the range by the fortress cities of Jokneam and Taanach, but the pass at Megiddo, between these two, was much easier to traverse and so was more vital. Another principal route, however, ran S from the crossroads town of Megiddo, skirted the remainder of the Carmel Range, and then swung W over to the coast via the Plain of Dothan.

Carmel is often associated with fertile regions such as Lebanon, Sharon, and Bashan. (Isa 35:2; Jer 50:19) King Uzziah, "a lover of agriculture," had farmers and vinedressers in Carmel (2Ch 26:10), and the remains of numerous rock-hewn winepresses and olive presses are found there. The prophets symbolized the disastrous effects of Jehovah's adverse judgment against Israel by the withering up of Carmel's abundant vegetation. (Isa 33:9; Am 1:2; Na 1:4) Its slopes, swept by the sea winds, still contain fruit orchards, olive groves, and vines, and in the spring are carpeted with a magnificent display of flowers. In The Song of Solomon (7:5), the Shulammite maiden's head is likened to Carmel, the simile referring either to the luxuriance of her hair or to the way in which her shapely head rose majestically upon her neck. The majestic appearance of Carmel, particularly the headland that sweeps dramatically upward from the coast, even as Mount Tabor rises impressively in the Valley of Jezreel, was also used to represent the imposing figure of Nebuchadnezzar advancing to the conquest of Egypt.—Jer 46:18.

Carmel was evidently one of the principal places to which people of Samaria fled when seeking refuge. Though by no means the highest of the ranges, its sparse population, its dense forest cover, and also the numerous caves in the soft limestone of its rocky slopes served to hide the refugees. Yet, the prophet Amos showed that such refuge would prove futile to those fleeing from Jehovah's righteous judgment.—Am 9:3.

Historically, Mount Carmel figures primarily in the activities of the prophets Elijah and Elisha. (PICTURE, Vol. 1, p. 950) It was here that Elijah had King Ahab assemble the people to witness the test between Baal, represented by the 450 prophets of Baal, and the true God Jehovah, represented by Elijah. (1Ki 18:19-39) After the test, Elijah had the false prophets brought down to the torrent valley of Kishon, which courses along the eastern foot of Carmel before ending in the Bay of Acco, and there slaughtered them. (1Ki 18:40) From the summit of Carmel, Elijah prayed for the end of the three-and-a-half-year drought, and from there his attendant saw the small cloud that was the precursor of the mighty rainstorm that was to follow. (1Ki 18:42-45; Jas 5:17) From here Elijah ran at least 30 km (19 mi) to Jezreel, by Jehovah's help outpacing Ahab's chariot all the way.—1Ki 18:46.

Elijah's successor, Elisha, after their separation at the Jordan River, traveled from Jericho via Bethel to Carmel. (2Ki 2:15, 23, 25) Elisha was again at Mount Carmel when the woman of Shunem (a short distance N of Jezreel) came seeking his help for her dead child.—2Ki 4:8, 20, 25.

2. A city in the mountainous region of Judah (Jos 15:1, 48, 55), identified by most geographers with Khirbet el-Kirmil (Horvat Karmel) some 11 km (7 mi) SSE of Hebron.

King Saul erected "a monument [Heb., yadh]" at Carmel apparently commemorating his victory over the Amalekites. (1Sa 15:12) Although the Hebrew word yadh appearing in this text is usually translated "hand," it can also refer to a "monument" or standing memorial, as is shown by the use of the accompanying verb phrase "was erecting" in connection with Saul's act and by the fact that years later "Absalom's Monument," or yadh, is specifically called a pillar.—2Sa 18:18.

At the time David was a fugitive from murderous Saul, "Nabal the Carmelite" (though apparently a resident of nearby Maon) grazed his large flocks in Carmel's rolling mountainous pastoral regions. (1Sa 25:2; 30:5; 2Sa 2:2; 3:3) When Nabal refused to repay David's protective forces with deserved provisions, the initiative and tact of Nabal's wife, "Abigail the Carmelitess," served to restrain David from bloodguilt. (1Sa 25:2-35) Abigail later became David's wife.—1Sa 25:36-42; 27:3; 1Ch 3:1.

"Hezro the Carmelite" was among the mighty men of David's military forces.—2Sa 23:8, 35; 1Ch 11:26, 37.

CARMELITE. See CARMEL No. 2.

CARMI (Car'mi) [possibly, Vinedresser].

1. A son of Reuben and the brother of Hanoch, Pallu, and Hezron; forefather of the Carmites. Carmi, with the rest of Jacob's household, came to Egypt.—Ge 46:9; Ex 6:14; Nu 26:6; 1Ch 5:3.

2. Father of Achan; a descendant of Judah and Tamar through Zerah and Zabdi. (Jos 7:1, 18) The designation "sons of Judah" at 1 Chronicles 4:1, where Carmi is listed, evidently is to be understood as including later descendants.—Compare 1Ch 2:4-7.

CARMITES (Car'mites) [Of (Belonging to) Carmi]. A family descended from Carmi, a son of Reuben.—Nu 26:5, 6.

CAROB POD [Gr., ke·ra'ti·on]. In the illustration of the prodigal son, Jesus describes the starving lad as desiring to eat the carob pods that were fed to the pigs. (Lu 15:16) These pods grow on the carob tree (Ceratonia siliqua), an attractive evergreen that grows throughout Palestine as well as in the rest of the Mediterranean area. The tree reaches a height of up to 9 m (30 ft), with small glistening leaves resembling those of the ash. The fruit or pods have a shiny leathery shell of a purplish-brown color and, in harmony with their name in Greek (ke·ra'ti·on, "small horn"), have a curved horn shape. They measure from 15 to 25 cm (6 to 10 in.) in length and about 2.5 cm (1 in.) in width. Inside are several pealike seeds separated from one another by a sweet, sticky, edible pulp. Carob pods are widely used till this day as a food for horses, cattle, and pigs. Grafting of the trees is employed to produce a quality of carob that people also eat.

CARPENTER.

An artisan, craftsman, or worker in wood. The Hebrew term *cha·rash'* is the general designation for a "craftsman," "worker," or "builder," who would use various materials such as wood, metal, or stone. (2Ki 12:11; 2Ch 24:12; Ex 28:11; 1Ch 14:1) The Greek equivalent is *te'kton,* translated "carpenter" in Matthew 13:55 and Mark 6:3.

Noah and his three sons had much carpentry work to do in building the huge ark, according to the pattern given by Jehovah.—Ge 6:14-16.

The carpenter in Israel would be employed in constructing houses and, in later times, structures such as synagogues. Although buildings were for the most part made of stone or earth, some wood was used, for example, in beams and doors. The things constructed by the carpenter in Bible times included furniture, such as tables, stools, and benches. Many implements such as plows and threshing sledges were partly or entirely made of wood. (2Sa 24:22) In the construction of the tabernacle and its furnishings, Bezalel and Oholiab were especially guided by Jehovah God. His spirit accentuated their ability to do the finest work in wood, as well as other materials. (Ex 31:2-11) Skilled workers in wood were brought from Tyre for the building of David's house. (2Sa 5:11) Zerubbabel used carpenters in building the second temple in Jerusalem.—Ezr 3:7.

Jesus was called not only "the carpenter's son" (Mt 13:55) but "the carpenter" as well. (Mr 6:3) Since the Hebrew father usually taught his son his trade, Jesus no doubt learned carpentry from his adoptive father Joseph.

CARPUS

(Car'pus) [Fruit]. A Christian residing at Troas, with whom Paul had left his cloak. Likely Carpus was Paul's host when the apostle visited there.—2Ti 4:13.

CARSHENA

(Car·she'na). The first listed of the seven princes of Media and Persia consulted by Ahasuerus on the matter of Vashti's disobedience. —Es 1:14; see MEMUCAN.

CARVING.

The art of sculpturing wood, stone, metal, and clay. Under the broad aspects of this subject, carving and engraving are terms used interchangeably to translate a number of Hebrew words. However, the most frequently used Hebrew word, *pe'sel,* occurs with reference to carved or engraved images.

The prohibition to Israel against making carved images for the purpose of worshiping them was first stated in the Decalogue (Ex 20:4) and was later repeated. "Cursed is the man who makes a carved image." (De 27:15; 4:16, 23; 5:8) The prophets over and over again pointed out the foolishness of making and worshiping carved idols and they condemned the practice. (Ps 97:7; Isa 42:17; 44:9-20; 45:20; Jer 10:14, 15; Na 1:14; Hab 2:18) For God's covenant people to give reverential regard to carved images in their worship was to divide the exclusive devotion that was due Jehovah. So, whenever Israel fell away from God and worshiped the carvings of their own hands, they understandably lost divine favor.—Jg 18:18, 30, 31; 2Ki 21:7-9; 2Ch 33:7, 22; Eze 8:10.

On the other hand, the carving work done for the tabernacle and the great temple of Solomon was not to be worshiped but was intended for decorative purposes and to convey symbolic meaning. Jehovah himself commanded that these carvings be made, and God placed his spirit on Bezalel and Oholiab, the skilled craftsmen chosen to oversee the tabernacle construction. (Ex 35:30, 31, 34) Objects such as the lampstand, the cherubs on the Ark's cover, the engraving on the jewels of the breastpiece, and the gold plate on the turban of the high priest are some examples of carved objects of gold and precious stones in the tabernacle arrangement. (Ex 25:18, 19, 31-40; 28:2, 21, 36) In Solomon's temple there were cedarwood carvings of cherubs, palm-tree figures, blossoms, and gourd-shaped ornaments, all overlaid with gold. (1Ki 6:18-35; 2Ch 2:7) Similarly, there was a great array of carvings in the pictorial temple envisioned by Ezekiel.—Eze 41:17-20.

Because of the divine condemnation of carved idols and images for worship, it is no surprise that those found in Palestine by archaeologists show pagan origin or influence. Not only did the Israelites abstain from carving monuments of their great leaders but they also refrained from cutting reliefs depicting their military victories. However, reliefs, statues, and other carved replicas from Egypt, Assyria, Babylonia, and Persia shed light on the worship, warfare, and daily life of those ancient people. Some of the more common things that have been found reveal that stone, clay, wood, glass, ivory, precious gems, bone, plaster, shell, metals, and alabaster were used by the carver in making thrones, lions, columns, jewelry, signets and seals, sarcophagi, stone tablets, furniture, wall decorations, and utensils.

CASIPHIA (Ca·si·phi′a) [possibly, Place of Silversmiths]. A "place" evidently situated in Babylonia and apparently near the gathering point of the exiles returning with Ezra to Jerusalem in 468 B.C.E. (Ezr 8:17-20) Other than stating that it was the area from which Ezra recruited Levites and Nethinim while encamped at the river Ahava, the Bible does not precisely identify Casiphia as either a city or a district.

CASLUHIM (Cas·lu′him). A son or people descended from Mizraim, the son of Ham. The Biblical record shows that it was the Casluhim "from among whom the Philistines went forth." (Ge 10:6, 13, 14; 1Ch 1:8, 11, 12) Since other texts speak of the Philistines as coming from Caphtor or Crete (Jer 47:4; Am 9:7), some scholars suggest that the above phrase should be transposed to come after the last-named descendant of Mizraim, Caphtorim. However, there is no need to assume a contradiction in these texts. The record at Genesis (paralleled by that in Chronicles) is genealogical. The other references to the Philistines as proceeding from Caphtor are likely geographic, indicating a migration from the territory of the Caphtorim.

The Casluhim do not appear elsewhere in the Bible and have left no definite mark in secular history. Aside from their descending from Mizraim, whose name was equivalent to Egypt in Bible times, there is no information to show where they settled.

CASSIA [Heb., qid·dah′; qetsi·‘ah′]. Although two Hebrew words are used to refer to this plant in the Bible, the Syriac and Targum versions indicate that they apply to the same tree or a product of it. The cassia bark tree (Cinnamomum cassia) now grows in eastern Asia and is of the same family as the cinnamon tree. It may reach a height of 12 m (40 ft) and has glossy, stiff leaves. The inner bark of the branches (called cassia lignea), when cut, dries and peels off, rolling itself into tubes, which are then sent to market. The cassia bark is coarser and more pungent than cinnamon bark. The buds are used as cloves in preparing food dishes, and the mature flowers, when dried, serve as an aromatic incense.

When the holy anointing oil was prepared at the time of making the tabernacle, cassia was included among the ingredients as one of "the choicest perfumes." (Ex 30:23-25) Cassia was prominent among the products in which the merchants and traders of the city of Tyre dealt. (Eze 27:19) At Psalm 45:8 the word qetsi·‘ah′ is used to describe the garments of the king as giving off delightful fragrance at the time of his marriage. The only other occurrence of this word is as the name of Job's second daughter, Keziah, born after his recovery from illness.—Job 42:14.

CASTLE. The Hebrew word bi·rah′, rendered "castle" or 'fortified place,' occurs only in the books of Daniel, Esther, Chronicles, and Nehemiah, which were completed between about 536 and sometime after 443 B.C.E., following the Babylonian exile.—1Ch 29:1, ftn; 2Ch 17:12; Es 1:2, ftn.

Writing in the language of his day, Ezra records David's calling Solomon's temple a "castle" when he encouraged the people fully to support its construction.—1Ch 29:1, 19.

Nehemiah built a castle or fortress just to the NW of the rebuilt temple, the direction from which the grounds were most vulnerable. (Ne 2:8; 7:2) Evidently this castle was replaced by the Maccabees and rebuilt by Herod the Great, who named it the Tower (Fortress) of Antonia. It was here that Paul was interrogated by the Roman military commander.—Ac 21:31, 32, 37; 22:24; see ANTONIA, TOWER OF.

"Shushan the castle," some 360 km (225 mi) E of Babylon, was a part-time residence of the Persian king. Here Nehemiah worked as a royal cupbearer before leaving for Jerusalem. (Ne 1:1) Here also was the setting of one of Daniel's visions. (Da 8:2) But "Shushan the castle" is best known as the background for the book of Esther. (Es 1:2, 5; 3:15; 8:14) "Shushan the castle," it seems, was not one particular building but was a complex of royal edifices within a fortified area. This is supported by certain details given in the account. "The house of the women," where the virgins were prepared for presentation to Ahasuerus, was located there. (Es 2:3, 8) Before his elevation in the government, Mordecai was daily stationed "in the king's gate" located "in Shushan the castle."—Es 2:5, 21; 3:2-4; see SHUSHAN.

CATERPILLAR [Heb., ga·zam′]. The larval stage of butterflies or moths. The Hebrew word ga·zam′ is thought to be derived from a root meaning "cut." In numbers, caterpillars, like locusts, literally cut or shear away the leaves of vegetation piece by piece, leaf by leaf, until the plant is almost denuded of its greenery. (Joe 1:4; 2:25; Am 4:9) While the traditional view is that the Hebrew term ga·zam′ signifies "locust," the translators of the Septuagint used the Greek word kam′pe, meaning caterpillar. Also, Koehler and Baumgartner favor translating ga·zam′ as caterpillar. (Lexicon in Veteris Testamenti Libros, Leiden, 1958, p. 178) It is thus rendered, at Joel 1:4; 2:25, in the translation by Isaac Leeser and in the *New World Translation;* "palmerworm" in the *King James Version;* "shearer" in *An American Translation.*

Caterpillars are almost exclusively vegetarian. Their appetites are voracious, some caterpillars consuming twice their own weight of greenery in a day. Hence, in large numbers they cause no little damage to vegetation.

CAUDA (Cau′da). An island off the SW coast of Crete passed by the apostle Paul and Luke on the voyage to Rome in about 58 C.E. Having lifted anchor at Fair Havens, their ship hugged the S coast of Crete until, likely after rounding Cape Matala, they were caught and driven by a tempestuous wind that could have forced the boat into the quicksands off the shores of North Africa. However, they came into the shelter of "a certain small island called Cauda" and the island's position evidently broke the force of the wind, providing them smoother waters, likely along its SW shore. This gave the crew sufficient time to hoist in the skiff, undergird the boat, and lower its gear.—Ac 27:13-17.

The Cauda of Luke's narrative is today called Gavdos, an island 11 km (7 mi) long by 5 km (3 mi) broad, lying about 65 km (40 mi) WSW of Fair Havens.

CAVE. An underground hollow or cavern with an opening to the surface. The word "cave" is translated from the Hebrew *me′a·rah′* (Ge 19:30) and the Greek *spe′lai·on.* (Joh 11:38) The Hebrew *chor* or *chohr* denotes a "hole," sometimes big enough for humans to penetrate. (1Sa 14:11; Job 30:6; 2Ki 12:9) Another Hebrew word for "hole" is *mechil·lah′.*—Isa 2:19.

Caves abound in the limestone of Palestine; Mount Carmel and the vicinity of Jerusalem, for example, were undermined with many caves. Accordingly, they are frequently mentioned in Scripture, sometimes in a figurative sense. Some of them were large enough to hold hundreds of persons and were used for permanent dwellings, as at Petra, or they were used as temporary shelters, burial sites, cisterns, stables, or storehouses. Many artifacts have been recovered from these natural shelters.

Caves provided refuge in times of danger. The first mention of such a place concerns Lot and his two daughters living in a cave after leaving Zoar because of fear. (Ge 19:30) At Makkedah five confederate Amorite kings hid from Joshua in a cave that afterward became their common tomb. (Jos 10:16-27) When fleeing from the Philistines in the days of King Saul, some Israelites hid in caves. (1Sa 13:6; 14:11) To escape the wrath of Saul, David took refuge in a cave near Adullam and was there joined by "about four hundred men." (1Sa 22:1, 2) Again pursued by Saul, David concealed himself in a cave in the wilderness of En-gedi, and it was here that David cut off the skirt of Saul's coat when he "came in to ease nature." (1Sa 24:1-15) It may have been David's experiences on these two occasions that prompted him to compose Psalms 57 and 142, as their superscriptions show. After David was made king, the cave of Adullam apparently served as military headquarters during a campaign against the Philistines. (2Sa 23:13; 1Ch 11:15) When wicked Jezebel attempted to kill off all of Jehovah's prophets, Obadiah fed 100 of them who were hiding "in a cave." (1Ki 18:4, 13) Elijah also fled from the anger of Jezebel to a cave at Horeb, and it was there that he received divine instructions to return and anoint Hazael as well as Jehu. (1Ki 19:1-17) So from these examples Paul had ample support for writing that men of faith "wandered about in . . . caves and dens of the earth." (Heb 11:38) Many years later the catacombs of Rome served as underground refuges and meeting places for persecuted Christians.

The dead were often buried in caves. The very rocky soil in much of Palestine made digging graves difficult. The Bible's second mention of a cave is concerning the one of Machpelah at Hebron that Abraham bought and used as a burial site, and where Sarah, Abraham, Isaac, Rebekah, Jacob, and Leah were all buried. (Ge 23:7-20; 25:9, 10; 49:29-32; 50:13) The memorial tomb of Jesus' friend Lazarus "was, in fact, a cave."—Joh 11:38.

Caves often served as excellent storehouses, especially in times of danger. Thus, to protect their crops from Midianite raiders during the days of Gideon, "the sons of Israel made for themselves the underground store places that were in the mountains, and the caves and the places difficult to approach." (Jg 6:2) Similarly, the Dead Sea Scrolls were evidently hidden for safekeeping in caves near the Wadi Qumran, NW of the Dead Sea, where they remained undisturbed for many centuries until their discovery began in 1947.

Figurative Use. Jesus accused the money changers of making the temple "a cave of robbers." (Mt 21:13; Jer 7:11) The prophecies recorded by Isaiah and in Revelation tell that some will try to escape God's judgment, "the dreadfulness of Jehovah," by hiding themselves in "the caves," but according to Ezekiel "the caves" they make their strongholds will furnish no protection from God. —Isa 2:19-21; Re 6:15-17; Eze 33:27.

CEDAR

[Heb., *'e'rez*]. The cedar trees, and particularly those of Lebanon, were renowned in Bible times and are especially prominent in the account of the temple construction by Solomon.

The cedar of Lebanon (*Cedrus libani*) is a majestic tree of massive proportions, with deep, strong roots. Large forests of these cedars once blanketed the mountains of Lebanon, but today only a few small groves remain because of indiscriminate use and the failure to replenish the trees by proper conservation and reseeding. The ravages of war doubtless contributed to this depletion as well. (Isa 14:5-8) However, the remaining trees still present an impressive sight.—Compare Ca 5:15.

The cedars sometimes reach a height of 37 m (120 ft) and the trunk may have a circumference of up to 12 m (40 ft). The long, spreading branches, stretching out horizontally from the trunk, may give a total circumference of as much as 60 to 90 m (200 to 300 ft). The trees are somewhat pyramid-shaped when young but tend to flatten out on top as they mature. The foliage grows in distinct horizontal tiers or layers (instead of interlacing), the boughs bearing round flowerlike sprays of bright-green needles about 1.3 cm (0.5 in.) in length, and tan-colored cones that exude a fragrant resin. The bark is reddish brown in color and quite rough. The trunk becomes gnarled with age.

The wood of the cedar has a warm red tone, is free from knots, and was valued highly for building purposes because of its beauty, fragrance, durability, and resistance to attack by insects. (Ca 1:17; 4:11) The Phoenician shipbuilders used it for their masts. (Eze 27:5) King Hiram of Tyre supplied men and materials for building "a house of cedars" for David in Jerusalem. (2Sa 5:11; 7:2; 2Ch 2:3) Solomon later used cedarwood in the temple, for the beams (1Ki 6:9), for overlaying the altar of incense (1Ki 6:20), and for paneling the interior of the temple in its entirety so that "there was no stone to be seen." (1Ki 6:15-18) "The House of the Forest of Lebanon," constructed later, was probably so named because of its 45 pillars of cedarwood. (1Ki 7:2, 3) Cedar was also used in the Porch of the Throne and in the temple courtyard. —1Ki 7:7-12.

Such extensive use of cedarwood required the labor of thousands of workers in cutting the trees, transporting them to Tyre or Sidon on the Mediterranean seacoast, forming them into rafts, and floating them down the coast, probably to Joppa. They were then hauled overland to Jerusalem. This was worked out by a contract between Solomon and Hiram. (1Ki 5:6-18; 2Ch 2:3-10) Thereafter the flow of lumber continued so that it could be said that Solomon made 'cedarwood like the sycamore tree for quantity' during his reign.—1Ki 10:27; compare Isa 9:9, 10.

Following the exile, cedar timbers from Lebanon were again obtained for reconstruction work on the temple.—Ezr 3:7.

Figurative Use. In the Scriptures the majestic cedar is used figuratively to represent stateliness, loftiness, and strength, either real or apparent. (Eze 31:2-14; Am 2:9; Zec 11:1, 2) Thus, King Jehoash of Israel intended his reply to King Amaziah of Judah to be a withering insult when he compared Amaziah's kingdom to a "thorny weed" while likening his own kingdom to a mighty cedar of Lebanon. (2Ki 14:9; compare Jg 9:15, 20.) The cedar figures dramatically in Ezekiel's riddle (chap 17), wherein the king and princes of Judah are likened to the treetop of a cedar of Lebanon carried off to Babylon. (Eze 17:1-4, 12, 13) Thereafter the Messiah is prophetically pictured as a twig from the very top of the cedar, which Jehovah then plants on a lofty mountain.—Eze 17:22-24; compare Isa 11:1; Jer 23:5; 33:15; Ps 2:6; Re 14:1; Da 4:17.

The cedarwood used in the wilderness by the Israelites was evidently from a type of cedar other than that of Lebanon. The brown-berried cedar (*Juniperus oxycedrus*) and the Phoenician juniper (*Juniperus phoenicia*) have been suggested, both being well known in the Sinai desert region. Certain purification rites required the use of cedarwood, and it may be that, because of its well-known resistance to decay, it was there used to symbolize freedom from corruption or disease. —Le 14:2-7, 49-53; Nu 19:6.

That the cedar served figuratively in an adverse as well as a favorable sense is evident. It became a status symbol among the unfaithful materialistic kings of Judah and symbolized their self-exaltation and false security. (Jer 22:13-15, 23; Isa 2:11-13) Yet, the growth and development of the righteous man is likened to that of the firmly rooted cedar. (Ps 92:12; compare Isa 61:3 with Ps 104:16.) So, while on the one hand Jehovah manifests his power by breaking the mighty cedars of Lebanon and making them 'skip about the mountains like calves' (Ps 29:4-6), on the other hand he foretells the time when he will make the cedar grow even in the wilderness regions (Isa 41:19, 20) and singles it out among the trees as one of the many creations that will praise his lofty name. —Ps 148:9, 13.

CENCHREAE

(Cen'chre·ae). The account at Acts 18:18 relates that in Cenchreae Paul had his hair clipped because he had made a vow, and afterward he apparently sailed from Cenchreae to

Ephesus accompanied by Priscilla and Aquila (in c. 52 C.E.). Writing to Rome about four years later, the apostle referred to "the congregation that is in Cenchreae." Paul's letter to the Romans may have been carried to its destination by Phoebe of the city of Cenchreae.—Ro 16:1, 2.

Cenchreae lay on the Saronic Gulf side of a narrow isthmus about 11 km (7 mi) E of Corinth, and was linked to that city by a chain of military fortifications. Cenchreae was Corinth's port for points E of Greece, while Lechaeum, on the opposite side of the isthmus, served as Corinth's port for Italy and the west. Ruins in the area today include buildings and breakwaters near the present village of Kechriais.

CENSER. See FIRE HOLDER.

CENSUS. See REGISTRATION.

CENTURION. See ARMY OFFICER.

CEPHAS. See PETER.

CHAFF. The thin protective covering or husk on the kernels of cereal grains such as barley and wheat. Though the Biblical references to chaff are figurative, they reflect the threshing practices common in ancient times. After harvesting, this inedible membrane covering of the valuable grain was useless, and hence was an appropriate symbol of something light, worthless, and undesirable, something to be separated from the good and to be disposed of.

First, the threshing operation broke the chaff loose from the kernel. Then by winnowing, the light chaffy part was carried away like dust in the wind. (See WINNOWING.) This well illustrates how Jehovah God both removes the apostates from among his people and also disposes of wicked persons and opposing nations. (Job 21:18; Ps 1:4; 35:5; Isa 17:13; 29:5; 41:15; Ho 13:3) God's Kingdom will crush its enemies into such small particles that they will be easily blown away like the chaff.—Da 2:35.

The worthless chaff was often gathered and burned to prevent it from blowing back and contaminating the piles of grain. Similarly, John the Baptizer foretold the coming burning destruction of the wicked false religionists—the Thresher, Jesus Christ, will gather in the wheat, "but the chaff he will burn up with fire that cannot be put out." —Mt 3:7-12; Lu 3:17; see THRESHING.

CHAINS. See BOND.

CHALCEDONY (chal·ced′o·ny). The modern stone bearing this name is a transparent or translucent cryptocrystalline variety of quartz used for ornaments and gems. It is not quite as hard as pure quartz, and it occurs in masses in the cavities of volcanic rocks. The common kind of chalcedony is partially transparent and figured with milky-white swirls and spots. It appears in many colors, such as white, gray, yellow, blue, and brown.

Chalcedony was a stone commonly used for engraved gems in ancient times. It was named after an old Greek city called Chalcedon (in Asia Minor), which once was a source of the mineral. The only Biblical text referring to this stone states that the third foundation of New Jerusalem's wall was chalcedony (Gr., khal·ke·don′).—Re 21:2, 19; see JEWELS AND PRECIOUS STONES.

CHALDEA (Chal·de′a), **CHALDEAN** (Chal·de′-an). Originally the land and people occupying the southern portion of the Babylonian alluvial plain, the rich delta area of the Tigris and Euphrates rivers. At one time these rivers may have emptied into the Persian Gulf separately, the cities of Eridu and Ur being seaports. But over the years the river silts may have gradually filled in the bay, pushing the coastline to the SE and allowing the Tigris and Euphrates to join together before emptying into the sea. In early times the region's most important city was Ur, the hometown of Abraham, from which he and his family departed at God's command before 1943 B.C.E. (Ge 11:28, 31; 15:7; Ne 9:7; Ac 7:2-4) About 300 years later Satan the Devil caused Chaldean raiders to inflict heavy losses on faithful Job.—Job 1:17.

As the influence of the Chaldeans spread northward, the whole territory of Babylonia became known as "the land of the Chaldeans." Isaiah in his prophecies anticipated this Chaldean rise to power and their subsequent fall. (Isa 13:19; 23:13; 47:1, 5; 48:14, 20) Particularly was this domination manifest during the seventh and sixth centuries B.C.E. when Nabopolassar, a native of Chaldea, and his successors, Nebuchadnezzar II, Evil-merodach (Awil-Marduk), Neriglissar, Labashi-Marduk, Nabonidus, and Belshazzar, ruled the Third World Power, Babylon. (2Ki 24:1, 2; 2Ch 36:17; Ezr 5:12; Jer 21:4, 9; 25:12; 32:4; 43:3; 50:1; Eze 1:3; Hab 1:6) That dynasty came to its end when "Belshazzar the Chaldean king was killed." (Da 5:30) Darius the Mede was "made king over the kingdom of the Chaldeans."—Da 9:1; see BABYLON No. 2.

From early times the Chaldeans were noted for their knowledge of mathematics and astronomy. In the days of Daniel a special cult of prognosticators who considered themselves skilled in the so-called science of divination were called Chaldeans. —Da 2:2, 5, 10; 4:7; 5:7, 11.

CHALK. The only occurrence of the Hebrew word *se'redh* in the Bible is at Isaiah 44:13, and it has reference to the "red chalk" used by wood craftsmen for marking purposes.

CHALKSTONE. Outcroppings of this very soft, easily powdered, sedimentary rock with a high calcium carbonate content are found in various parts of Palestine. Because it is worthless as a building stone and can be so readily crumbled and pulverized, the prophet Isaiah used chalkstone in an effective simile to show what must be done to the idolatrous altars of Israel if forgiveness was to be attained. (Isa 27:9) The Aramaic equivalent of the Hebrew term *gir* (chalk) occurs in Daniel 5:5 and is translated "plaster."—See LIME; PLASTER.

CHAMELEON [Heb., *tin·she'meth*]. The name of this reptile is included among "the swarming creatures" that were "unclean" under the Mosaic Law. (Le 11:29, 30) The name is considered to have been derived from *na·sham'*, a root word meaning "pant." (Compare Isa 42:14.) Koehler and Baumgartner, by a comparison with Arabic, suggest "snorter" as the meaning. (*Lexicon in Veteris Testamenti Libros,* Leiden, 1958, p. 1035) While identification is uncertain, the name may apply to the chameleon. The common *Chamaeleo vulgaris* is frequently found in Egypt and Palestine.

The chameleon is a slow-moving, tree-dwelling lizard noted for its color-changing ability. Color response is primarily determined by temperature, light intensity, and emotional state.

At Leviticus 11:18 the same Hebrew word is applied to the swan as among "unclean" fowl.

CHAMOIS [Heb., *ze'mer*]. A small goatlike antelope characterized by its hook-tipped horns and noted for its agility and surefootedness at dizzying heights. The grown male may measure 80 cm (32 in.) at the shoulder and may weigh over 30 kg (66 lb). The summer coat of the chamois is a tawny color that gets darker with the advent of the winter season. The chamois is listed among the animals suitable for food, according to the requirements of the Law.—De 14:5.

There is uncertainty as to the animal meant by the Hebrew word *ze'mer,* which is variously rendered "chamois" (*KJ, AS, ER, NW, Yg*), "mountain goat" (*La*), "mountain sheep" (*AT, JB, Mo, Ro*), "antelope" (*Le*), and simply transliterated as "zemer" (*Kx*). The Hebrew root from which the word *ze'mer* is derived is thought to be related to the Arabic *zamara* (bounce; flee), suggesting a bouncing, leaping animal, hence likely a kind of gazelle. Some zoologists maintain that the chamois (*Rupi-*

capra rupicapra) was never found in Palestine. However, it may be noted that local varieties of this animal are to be found in the Carpathian and Caucasus mountains, thus allowing for the possibility that at one time a variety of the chamois may have existed in the ranges of Lebanon.

CHARCOAL. A black, brittle, and porous form of carbon, usually the residue of partially burned wood. In ancient times it was made by covering a pile of wood with earth and burning it slowly for several days with only a sufficient amount of air to burn off the gases. This practice left behind a relatively pure form of carbon. It was a time-consuming process requiring careful supervision, but charcoal was a favored fuel when intense, sustained heat without smoke was desired. There is no evidence that natural mineral coal was used in ancient Israel.

Charcoal, in an open fire or in a brazier, was used to warm oneself in cold weather. (Isa 47:14; Jer 36:22; Joh 18:18) Its even heat with an absence of flame and smoke also highly recommended it for cooking. (Joh 21:9) For smelting and refining metals, charcoal was indispensable; without it, reaching and sustaining the great temperatures required to reduce the ores to pure metals was hardly possible. (Isa 44:12; 54:16; see RE-FINE, REFINER.) Much the same as is done today in charging an iron blast furnace, the ore was sandwiched in between layers of charcoal. This practice apparently gave rise to the proverb: Kindness toward an enemy is like coals of fire upon his head; it softens his anger and brings out the good in him. (Pr 25:22; Ro 12:20) The glow of slow-burning charcoal was used by the "wise woman" of Tekoa as an illustration of living posterity.—2Sa 14:1-7.

However, the Hebrew words *ga·che'leth* and *pe·cham'* are not always rendered "charcoal," for they often simply refer to coals, burning coals, or embers. Wood was used as fuel for the tabernacle altar (Le 1:7, 8; 3:5), and on the Day of Atonement "burning coals of fire from off the altar" made the incense overspread the ark of the covenant like a cloud. (Le 16:12, 13) Isaiah described the idolater that makes a god out of part of the same tree with which he builds a fire, the coals of which bake his bread.—Isa 44:14, 15, 19.

In a number of Scripture passages "coals" are used in a somewhat figurative or illustrative sense, indicating any kind of glowing, hot, burning substance. (2Sa 22:9; Job 41:21; Ps 18:8, 12, 13; 140:10; Isa 6:6; Eze 1:13; 10:2; 24:11) The hot "burning coals of the broom trees" were used to represent the retribution upon one with a "tricky tongue."—Ps 120:2-4.

CHARIOT.

A two-wheeled, horse-drawn vehicle, developed primarily for the battlefield rather than for troop movement behind the lines. All four Hebrew terms referring to the chariot (*mer·kav'* [1Ki 4:26]; *mer·ka·vah'* [Ge 41:43]; *re'khev* [1Ki 1:5]; *rekhuv'* [Ps 104:3]) come from the root verb *ra·khav'*, meaning "ride." (Ge 24:61; 1Sa 25:42; 1Ki 18:45) The Greek term is *har'ma*. (Ac 8:28) The chariot provided fast transport in combat, gave soldiers a mobile firing platform, and furnished them with psychological shock power when charging into ranks of foot soldiers. Chariots with many variations of design are widely illustrated on ancient monuments, attesting to both their antiquity and their widespread use.

Basically, the chariot usually consisted of a platform mounted on a single axle, with thigh-high sides; the open back of the car provided quick and easy entrance. The chariot car had a tongue and yoke harnessed to speedy horses. Often chariots were outfitted with auxiliary equipment consisting of quiver and bow cases, shields, and spears. An added menace to foot soldiers was the practice of extending iron scythes from the hubs of the wheels of some war chariots. (Jos 17:16, 18; Jg 1:19) When there was only one charioteer, the reins were held around his waist or hips in battle, leaving his hands free to handle the weapons. Larger and heavier chariots with multiple spans of horses had crews of two, three, or four, with a driver and one or two fighters, and perhaps a shield-man.—Ex 14:7, ftn.

Speed, maneuverability, and stability were prime factors that were improved with continued development. For example, by moving the axle toward the rear, greater maneuverability and stability were achieved. Replacing solid wheels with spoked ones lightened the weight and increased the speed. (1Ki 7:33) The six-spoke wheel became the most common, though some wheels were designed with four, or with eight or more. Using lightweight woods, with only the fittings of leather, bronze, or iron, made chariots light enough that one or two men could carry them over rough terrain or small streams.

War chariots were employed by many of the pagan nations that opposed Israel. At the Red Sea in 1513 B.C.E., Pharaoh's entire army, including his 600 special war chariots "and all the other chariots of Egypt," were destroyed by Jehovah. (Ex 14:6, 7; 15:4, 19; Jos 24:6) When conquering the Promised Land, the Israelites routed the enemy and burned many of their captured chariots. (Jos 11:4-9) Jabin the king of Canaan held the Israelites in bondage for 20 years until Jehovah pinned down and destroyed his fleet of 900 chariots equipped with iron scythes and commanded by Sisera, at the torrent valley of Kishon. (Jg 4:2, 3, 13, 15, 16; 5:28) During the period of Israel's kings, at one time or another, the Philistines, Egyptians, Ethiopians, Syrians, Assyrians, and Babylonians battled against them with large chariot forces, as many as 32,000 chariots on one occasion. (1Sa 13:5; 2Sa 1:6; 1Ch 19:6, 7, 18; 2Ch 12:2, 3; 14:9; 16:8; Isa 37:21, 24) In pronouncements of doom, the prophets sometimes mentioned the chariots in which such nations prided themselves.—Jer 50:37; 51:21; Mic 5:10, 15.

The more level places, such as the Plains of Philistia and the broad Valley of Jezreel, were better suited for chariot warfare than was the hilly country. On one occasion the Syrians boasted that their chariots would overcome Israel if the latter could be lured out of the mountains to fight on the flat land, for, as they thought, "[Israel's] God is a God of mountains." However, the great defeat suffered by the Syrians proved that Jehovah is also "a God of low plains."—1Ki 20:23-30.

In Israel no sizable national chariot force developed until the time of Solomon. This was due in large measure to God's warning that the king was not to multiply horses, as if the nation's security depended on them. This restriction limited the use of chariots, since horses were used to power such vehicles. (De 17:16) When Samuel warned of the burden that human kings would inflict on the people, he told them: "Your sons he will take and put them as his in his chariots." (1Sa 8:11) Absalom and Adonijah, in attempting to usurp the kingship, each had a chariot made for himself, with 50 men to run before it. (2Sa 15:1; 1Ki 1:5) When David defeated the king of Zobah, he preserved 100 chariot horses.—2Sa 8:3, 4; 10:18.

King Solomon, in building up the army of Israel, expanded the number of chariots to 1,400. (1Ki 10:26, 29; 2Ch 1:14, 17) In addition to Jerusalem, other towns known as chariot cities had special facilities for taking care of all this mechanized war equipment.—1Ki 9:19, 22; 2Ch 8:6, 9; 9:25.

After Solomon's death, chariots were common in both the northern and southern kingdoms. The northern kingdom had a "chief of half the chariots," indicating that there were two principal divisions of chariots. (1Ki 16:9) King Jehu was recognized by his furious chariot driving. (2Ki 9:20) Several kings of both Judah and Israel, namely, Ahab, Jehoram, Ahaziah, and Josiah, were fatally wounded in their chariots.—1Ki 22:34-38; 2Ki 9:21, 24, 27; 2Ch 18:33, 34; 35:23, 24.

The prophet Isaiah declared to rebellious Israel: "Woe to those going down to Egypt for assistance, those who rely on mere horses, and who put their trust in war chariots, because they are numerous, and in steeds, because they are very mighty, but who have not looked to the Holy One of Israel and have not searched for Jehovah himself."—Isa 31:1.

The chariot was primarily a war implement, and it was useful in the chase of wild animals. There are also instances where it was used for peaceful purposes. Joseph as a food administrator of Egypt rode in a chariot of honor, second only to that of Pharaoh. In his chariot he rode out to meet his father when Jacob entered Egypt. (Ge 41:43; 46:29) Upon Jacob's death many chariots were in the funeral procession that went from Egypt to Machpelah, the burial place that Abraham had purchased. (Ge 50:7-14) As a means of transportation, chariots were also employed by Kings Rehoboam and Ahab, Naaman the Syrian army chief, and the Ethiopian official who invited the evangelist Philip to ride with him on the road down to Gaza. (1Ki 12:18; 18:44, 45; 2Ki 5:21, 26; Ac 8:28-31, 38) Richly decorated and shaded chariots carried victorious rulers in processions. Sacred chariots and the horses that drew them were dedicated to sun worship by apostate Judean rulers.—2Ki 23:11.

Figurative Use. In a figurative and prophetic sense, chariots are symbols of war just like the bow and sword. (Isa 21:7, 9; Zec 9:10) "The war chariots of God" are said to be "in tens of thousands, thousands over and over again," denoting God's invincible power to destroy his enemies. —Ps 68:17; 2Ki 6:17.

CHARIOT CITIES. Cities of ancient times set apart as places to station chariots, particularly chariots of war. (2Ch 1:14; 9:25) Solomon had such cities.—1Ki 9:17-19; 10:26; 2Ch 8:5, 6.

CHARM, I. The Hebrew word *chen* has the meaning of favor, charm, or elegance, in form and conduct, and it is generally rendered "favor" (Ge 6:8), though in certain instances it is translated "charm." For example, a prostitute may be "attractive with charm" (Na 3:4), but as observed in the Proverbs: "Charm may be false, and prettiness may be vain; but the woman that fears Jehovah is the one that procures praise for herself." Also, "a woman of charm is the one that takes hold of glory." (Pr 31:30; 11:16; see also Pr 5:18, 19.) Divine wisdom and understanding can be a real ornamental charm (Pr 3:21, 22; 4:7-9), as is also

true of proper speech. (Ps 45:2; Pr 22:11) When the Jews returned from exile in Babylon, Zerubbabel was encouraged to press forward with the temple building, being assured that with the laying of the headstone, "there will be shoutings to it: 'How charming! How charming!'"—Zec 4:7.

CHARM, II. The Hebrew word *'it·tim'* is used in Isaiah 19:3 to refer to "charmers" of Egypt. The Hebrew word *che'ver* (rendered 'spell') refers to a magical formula spoken, sung, or written as a spell in order to 'bind' a person. (Ps 58:5; Isa 47:9, 12) "The ornamental humming shells" possessed, and no doubt worn, by the daughters of Zion were evidently charms, the Hebrew word designating them (*lecha·shim'*) being drawn from a root meaning "whisper; charm." (Isa 3:20; compare 2Sa 12:19; Ps 58:5.) Such spiritistic practices were among "the detestable things" that Jehovah forbade his people to indulge in. (De 18:9-11) The ancient Babylonians, Egyptians, and others were notorious for their trust in charms and the casting of spells.—Isa 19:3; 47:9, 12.

Snake Charming. So-called snake charming can be a form of spiritism and is a survival of the ancient cult of serpent worshipers. The charmer is supposed to cast a spell over the serpent, often a hooded cobra, so it appears enchanted with the playing of music, usually on a flute or pipe instrument. Snakes are not deaf or hard of hearing, as some may think, but as Psalm 58:4, 5 implies, they are able to hear the voice of charmers as well as the music. One might think that it is a mere trick of training the snake as one would train an animal or bird, by placing it in a basket with a lid, playing soft music, quickly dropping the lid if any attempt is made to escape, until the snake finally learns to raise itself upright in obedience to the music without trying to escape. While this may be true in some instances, spiritistic forces are often apparently involved in snake charming.

Attesting to the antiquity of this spiritistic practice is its mention in the Bible.—Ps 58:4, 5; Ec 10:11; Isa 3:3; Jer 8:17.

CHEBAR (Che'bar) [from Babylonian, meaning "Great (Canal)"]. A "river" in "the land of the Chaldeans" near which Jews of the community of Tel-abib were exiled. (Eze 1:1-3; 3:15) When speaking of "the *river* Chebar," Ezekiel used the Hebrew term *na·har'* (rendered "river") apparently in its widest sense to include the numerous Babylonian canals that once intersected the fertile area between the lower courses of the Euphrates and Tigris rivers. This usage would be consistent with the corresponding Babylonian word that also describes either a river or a canal. The precise location of the Chebar is unknown.

However, most Biblical geographers connect the "river Chebar" with the Shatt en-Nil, which has been identified with the *naru Kabaru* (or "Grand Canal") mentioned in cuneiform contract tablets found at the city of Nippur, about 85 km (50 mi) SE of Babylon. The Shatt en-Nil branches off the Euphrates above Babylon and runs in a SE direction, passing near Nippur, to rejoin the Euphrates S of Ur, about 240 km (150 mi) below Babylon.

In 613 B.C.E., Tel-abib, near the river Chebar, was the site of the prophet Ezekiel's first recorded vision, the stunning effects of which lasted seven days, and of his being commissioned as "a watchman . . . to the house of Israel." (Eze 1:1–3:21) Similar visions on later occasions reminded the prophet of his experience at Chebar.—Eze 10:15, 20, 22; 43:3.

CHEDORLAOMER (Ched·or·la·o′mer). A king of ancient Elam who, prior to Abraham's entry into the Promised Land in 1943 B.C.E., had extended his power westward to the borders of Egypt. After 12 years of servitude, five kings near the southern end of the Dead Sea rebelled against their eastern overlord. In the 14th year, Chedorlaomer and three allies, Amraphel of Shinar, Arioch from Ellasar, and Tidal of Goiim, came W to put down the rebellion. Beginning in the N and sweeping S, they defeated cities along the trade routes E of the Jordan, and S of the Dead Sea in territory later occupied by the Amalekites. It was then an easy matter to put to flight the five kings that formed the core of the insurrection.

Among Chedorlaomer's captives was Abraham's nephew Lot, who had been living nearby. Abraham, learning of this, quickly set out in hot pursuit with 318 of his armed servants. At Dan they surprised the enemy's far superior forces and, successfully pursuing them as far as Hobah, N of Damascus, recovered Lot and his possessions. —Ge 14:1-17.

The name Chedorlaomer itself has not been found in listings of ancient rulers of Elam, but it is recognized as Elamite. Kudur, a possible variation of *Chedor,* appears in many compound names. Lagamar, bearing a resemblance to *laomer,* was an Elamite deity.

CHEEK. Either side of the face above the jaw and below the eye; in Hebrew *lechi′,* and in Greek *si·a·gon′.* The Bible speaks of striking the cheek, not so much to inflict physical harm, but to chastise, reproach, or insult. Thus Jehovah's prophet Micaiah was struck on the cheek for prophesying

bad consequences against wicked King Ahab of Israel. (1Ki 22:24; 2Ch 18:23) Job was reproachfully struck on the cheeks by those who disrespected and ridiculed him during his trial at Satan's hands.—Job 16:10.

The prophets Isaiah and Micah prophesied relative to the Messiah's being struck on the cheek and the hair being pulled from the cheeks, all significant of the bitter reproach that his enemies would heap upon him. (Isa 50:6; Mic 5:1) This was fulfilled on Jesus Christ by the Jews at his trial before the Sanhedrin and by the Roman soldiers later on, just before he was put to death on the torture stake. (Mt 26:67, 68; Joh 18:22, 23; 19:3) But Jesus did not retaliate in kind or answer with bitter, angry words.

Jesus had given his disciples counsel: "You heard that it was said, 'Eye for eye and tooth for tooth.' However, I say to you: Do not resist him that is wicked; but whoever slaps you on your right cheek, turn the other also to him." (Mt 5:38, 39) Here Jesus was not teaching pacifism or denying the right of self-defense from bodily harm, but he was teaching that a Christian does not need to pay back blow for blow, retaliating, taking vengeance. He was inculcating the principle of avoiding quarrels by not replying or reacting in kind. A slap on the cheek is not intended to injure physically but only to insult or to provoke into a fight. Jesus did not say that if someone strikes a Christian on the jaw, he should get up off the floor and hold the other side of his face for a target. What Jesus was saying was that if anyone tried to provoke a Christian into a fight or argument by either slapping him with an open hand or stinging him with insulting words, it would be wrong to retaliate. This is in harmony with the statements of the apostles, giving further emphasis to this principle.—Ro 12:17-21; 1Pe 3:9.

CHEESE. Job in poetic language figuratively described how he had been formed in his mother's womb, saying to the Grand Creator: "Did you not proceed to pour me out as milk itself and like cheese to curdle me?"—Job 10:10.

Making cheese differed from making butter; the latter was obtained by churning. To make cheese in ancient times, milk was quickly curdled with rennet from an animal's stomach or with juice of certain leaves or roots. After curdling, the whey was drained off, and the fresh curds were eaten.

David was instructed to take "ten portions of milk" to the chief of the 1,000 under whom his brothers served in Saul's army. (1Sa 17:17, 18) The literal reading of the original is "ten cuts of milk," which may have meant "ten fresh-milk cheeses."

The Latin *Vulgate* reads "ten little forms [or, molds] of cheese." During the civil war instigated by Absalom, friends sent David provisions of food, including "curds of cattle," and these too may have been soft cheeses.—2Sa 17:29.

CHEHTH [ח]. The eighth letter in the Hebrew alphabet. This letter is the harshest of the guttural sounds and is similar to the sound of "ch," as in the Scottish word *loch* or the German *ach.* In the Hebrew, in the eighth section of Psalm 119 (vss 57-64) every verse begins with this letter.

In this work it is transliterated as *ch* to denote strong aspiration.

CHELAL (Che'lal) [Perfection]. A former exile of "the sons of Pahath-moab" among those who put away their foreign wives at Ezra's instruction. —Ezr 10:16, 17, 30, 44.

CHELUB (Che'lub) [Basket; Cage].

1. Descendant of Judah; brother of Shuhah and father of Mehir. (1Ch 4:1, 11) The rendering of the name as "Chelub" is based on the Masoretic text and appears in this form in some translations. (*KJ, NW, Ro, AT*) However, he is called "Caleb" in the Greek *Septuagint,* Syriac *Peshitta,* and the Latin *Vulgate* (Clementine recension), and therefore, this form is found in translations by Knox and Lamsa.

2. Father of Ezri, one serving under King David as overseer of those cultivating the fields.—1Ch 27:26.

CHELUBAI. See CALEB No. 1.

CHELUHI (Chel'u·hi). Descendant of Bani; one of those dismissing their foreign wives in the time of Ezra.—Ezr 10:34, 35, 44.

CHEMOSH (Che'mosh). The chief deity of the Moabites, who are referred to as "the people of Chemosh." (Nu 21:29; Jer 48:46) Some scholars identify this deity with the Baal of Peor because of the latter's association with the Moabites. (Nu 25:1-3) At least in cases of extreme stress, if not generally practiced, children were probably sacrificed to Chemosh.—2Ki 3:26, 27.

The black basalt stele, commonly known as the Moabite Stone, erected by King Mesha of Moab to commemorate his revolt against Israel, provides further insight as to how the Moabites viewed their god Chemosh. According to this monument, Chemosh gave the victories in battle, and warfare was undertaken at his command. King Mesha attributed the deliverance from Israelite oppression to Chemosh, and he reasoned that the actual affliction at the hands of Omri the king of Israel was due to the god's anger with his land.

Jephthah referred to Chemosh as the god of the Ammonites. (Jg 11:24) Some scholars question the correctness of Jephthah's statement in view of the fact that Chemosh is elsewhere always associated with the Moabites. However, it must be remembered that the Ammonites worshiped numerous gods. (Jg 10:6) Furthermore, since the Ammonites and the Moabites were neighboring peoples, with a common ancestry through Lot the nephew of Abraham, there is nothing unusual about both nations' worshiping Chemosh.

The worship of Chemosh was evidently introduced into Israel during the reign of Solomon. Undoubtedly under the influence of his Moabite wives, Solomon built a high place to Chemosh "on the mountain that was in front of Jerusalem." (1Ki 11:1, 7, 8, 33) During Josiah's extensive religious reform, over three centuries later, this high place was made unfit for worship.—2Ki 23:13.

The prophet Jeremiah, in foretelling calamity for Moab, indicated that her principal god Chemosh as well as his priests and princes would go into exile. The Moabites would become ashamed of their god because of his impotence, just as the Israelites of the ten-tribe kingdom had become ashamed of Bethel, likely because of its association with calf worship.—Jer 48:7, 13, 46.

CHENAANAH (Che·na'a·nah) [feminine form of Canaan].

1. Father of Zedekiah the false prophet contemporary with Kings Ahab and Jehoshaphat. —1Ki 22:11, 24; 2Ch 18:10, 23.

2. Descendant of Benjamin through Jediael and Bilhan.—1Ch 7:6, 10.

CHENANI (Che·na'ni) [shortened form of Chenaniah]. A Levite making confession to Jehovah prior to the sealing of the "trustworthy arrangement" contracted during Nehemiah's governorship.—Ne 9:3, 4, 38.

CHENANIAH (Chen·a·ni'ah) [probably, Firmly Established by Jehovah].

1. A Levite contemporaneous with King David. "Chenaniah the chief of the Levites in carrying" was an expert, qualified to instruct others concerning the proper handling of the sacred Ark. —1Ch 15:22, 25-27.

2. A Kohathite of the family of Izhar. Chenaniah and his sons had been designated for "the outside business," evidently consisting of service as judges and officers, of whom there were 6,000 at the time of David's numbering the Levites. (1Ch

26:29; 23:1-4, 12) Since the Kohathites carried the utensils of the sanctuary in Moses' day, possibly this Chenaniah is the same as No. 1 above.—Nu 4:4, 5, 15.

CHEPHAR-AMMONI   (Che′phar-am′mo·ni) [Village of the Ammonites]. A city in the tribal inheritance of Benjamin. (Jos 18:21, 24) The location is uncertain; some connect it with Khirbet Kefr 'Ana, a ruined site about 5 km (3 mi) NNE of Bethel.

CHEPHIRAH   (Che·phi′rah) [Village]. A Hivite city (Jos 9:7, 17), and one of the four cities represented by the Gibeonite ambassadors who falsely claimed to be from a distant land and who by means of this trick were able to conclude a covenant with the Israelites under Joshua. (Jos 9:3-27) Chephirah is easily identifiable today with the impressive uninhabited remains at Khirbet Kefireh, 7 km (4.5 mi) WSW of el-Jib (Gibeon) at the summit of what was once a series of armed terraces. This strategic position of Chephirah served to guard against the approach of enemy forces to Gibeon from the west. At the time of the land distribution Chephirah came within Benjamin's inheritance (Jos 18:26), and after the exile it was among those cities resettled.—Ezr 2:1, 25; Ne 7:29.

CHERAN   (Che′ran). A son of Horite Sheik Dishon.—Ge 36:26; 1Ch 1:41.

CHERETHITES   (Cher′e·thites). The name of a people connected with the Philistines. (Eze 25: 16; Zep 2:5) Some Cherethites served with the military forces of Jehovah's chosen nation.—2Sa 8:18; 20:23; 1Ch 18:17.

Certain Hebrew lexicographers believe that *kere·thim′* comes from the root word *ka·rath′* (meaning "cut off") and should be rendered "executioners." The majority of Bible commentators, however, consider the Hebrew term for "Cherethites" (*kere·thim′*) to refer to nationality. But they do acknowledge that *ka·rath′* may be the correct root of *kere·thim′* and that Jehovah, at Ezekiel 25:16, may be making an alliterative play on words when pledging, "I will cut off [*hikh·rat·ti′*] the Cherethites [*kere·thim′*]," or, in effect, 'I will slay the slayers.'

An affinity between the Cherethites and the Philistines seems indicated by their mention together at Ezekiel 25:15-17 and Zephaniah 2:5-7. The Greek *Septuagint* rendering of these verses substitutes the term "Cretans" for "Cherethites," perhaps attempting thereby to link them with the Philistines who came "out of Crete [Caphtor]." (Am

9:7) Because of this and the apparent connection of the Cherethites with "the land of the Philistines" at 1 Samuel 30:14, 16, most scholars conclude that the Cherethites and Philistines were either the same people or two closely associated peoples. Others reason that the Cherethites may have been a principal Philistine tribe.

One suggestion advanced is that, though originally two peoples, the Philistines were either the more powerful of the two or were the earlier arrivals in Canaan and so eventually predominated, giving their name to the section of land called Philistia, although the name Cherethites did not entirely fade out. According to this view, the meaning of the above-cited prophecies of Ezekiel and Zephaniah would be that Jehovah was going to bring vengeance and woe upon all the inhabitants of the cities of Philistia, both the Philistines and the Cherethites, prophecies apparently brought to fulfillment by the Babylonians.

Some of the Cherethites came to be among David's armed forces, and they and the Pelethites (often mentioned with them) may have served as the royal bodyguard under Benaiah. (2Sa 8:18; 20:23; 1Ch 18:17; compare 2Sa 23:22, 23; 1Ch 11:25.) In view of this, scholars often seek to connect them with "the Carian bodyguard" of the time of priest Jehoiada, more than 100 years later. (2Ki 11:4, 19; see CARIAN BODYGUARD.) Though apparently foreign born, the Cherethites of David's day were not mere mercenaries, acting solely out of personal gain (as is often wrongly argued), but they were genuinely devoted to David as Jehovah's anointed. This was amply demonstrated by their faithfully sticking with David when he was forced to evacuate Jerusalem because "the heart of the men of Israel" had come to be with rebel Absalom. (2Sa 15:13, 18) Similarly, the Cherethites later obediently aided in suppressing the revolt of Sheba the Benjamite, and in supporting Solomon, David's choice as Israel's royal successor. —2Sa 20:7; 1Ki 1:38, 39, 44.

CHERITH, TORRENT VALLEY OF   (Che′rith) [Excavated]. A torrent valley E of the Jordan where Elijah concealed himself and was fed by ravens after announcing a coming drought to Israel's King Ahab. (1Ki 17:1-7) The exact location is unknown.

CHERUB.

1. (cher′ub). An angelic creature of high rank having special duties, distinguished from the order of seraphs. The first of the 91 times they are mentioned in the Bible is at Genesis 3:24; after God's driving Adam and Eve out of Eden, cherubs

(Heb., *keru·vim'*) were posted at the E entrance with a flaming blade of a sword "to guard the way to the tree of life." Whether more than two were stationed there is not disclosed.

Representative figures of cherubs were included in the furnishings of the tabernacle set up in the wilderness. Rising above each end of the Ark's cover were two cherubs of hammered gold. They were facing each other and bowing toward the cover in an attitude of worship. Each had two wings that spread upward and screened over the cover in a guarding and protecting manner. (Ex 25:10-21; 37:7-9) Also, the inner covering of tent cloths for the tabernacle and the curtain dividing the Holy from the Most Holy had embroidered cherub figures.—Ex 26:1, 31; 36:8, 35.

These were not grotesque figures fashioned after the monstrous winged images worshiped by pagan nations round about, as some contend. According to the unanimous testimony of ancient Jewish tradition (the Bible is silent on this matter), these cherubs had human form. They were finest works of art, representing angelic creatures of glorious beauty, and were made in every detail "according to . . . the pattern" Moses received from Jehovah himself. (Ex 25:9) The apostle Paul describes them as "glorious cherubs overshadowing the propitiatory cover." (Heb 9:5) These cherubs were associated with the presence of Jehovah: "And I will present myself to you there and speak with you from above the cover, from between the two cherubs that are upon the ark of the testimony." (Ex 25:22; Nu 7:89) Hence, Jehovah was said to be "sitting upon [or, between] the cherubs." (1Sa 4:4; 2Sa 6:2; 2Ki 19:15; 1Ch 13:6; Ps 80:1; 99:1; Isa 37:16) In symbol, the cherubs served as "the representation of the chariot" of Jehovah upon which he rode (1Ch 28:18), and the wings of the cherubs offered both guarding protection and swiftness in travel. So David, in poetic song, described the speed with which Jehovah came to his aid, like one who "came riding upon a cherub and came flying" even "upon the wings of a spirit." —2Sa 22:11; Ps 18:10.

The detailed architectural plans for Solomon's magnificent temple called for two huge cherubs in the Most Holy. They were made of oil-tree wood overlaid with gold, each standing ten cubits (4.5 m; 14.6 ft) high. They both stood facing the E on a N-S line running presumably through the center of the room. Although standing ten cubits apart, one wing of each cherub reached to touch the tip of the other's extended wing in the center of the room, overshadowing the ark of the covenant and its poles, which rested beneath. The outer wings of each cherub touched the N and S walls respectively. Thus the wings of the cherubs spanned the 20-cubit width of the room. (See TEMPLE.) Engraved carvings of cherubs, overlaid with gold, also decorated the walls and doors of the temple. Likewise the sides of the copper water carriages were ornamented with cherubs. (1Ki 6:23-35; 7:29-36; 8:6, 7; 1Ch 28:18; 2Ch 3:7, 10-14; 5:7, 8) In a similar manner, carved cherubs ornamented the walls and doors of the temple that Ezekiel envisioned.—Eze 41:17-20, 23-25.

Ezekiel also relates a number of visions in which symbolic cherubs of unusual description were seen. After speaking of them as "living creatures" (Eze 1:5-28), he later identifies them as "cherubs." (Eze 9:3; 10:1-22; 11:22) In these pictorial visions the cherubs are intimately associated with the glorious personage of Jehovah and constantly attendant upon him.

In his prophetic book Ezekiel was also told to "lift up a dirge concerning the king of Tyre," in which he calls the king a glorious covering cherub that was once "in Eden, the garden of God," but who was stripped of his beauty and made as ashes upon the ground. "This is what the Sovereign Lord Jehovah has said: . . . 'You are the anointed cherub that is covering, and I have set you. On the holy mountain of God you proved to be. In the midst of fiery stones you walked about. You were faultless in your ways from the day of your being created until unrighteousness was found in you. . . . I shall put you as profane out of the mountain of God, and I shall destroy you, O cherub that is covering ["O protecting cherub," *Vg*].'"—Eze 28:11-19.

2. (pronounced ke'rub). A city in Babylonia from which certain exiles returned to Jerusalem in 537 B.C.E.; they were unable to trace their genealogy and therefore could not prove whether they were Israelites.—Ezr 2:59; Ne 7:61.

CHESALON (Ches'a·lon) [(On the) Loin [that is, slope]]. A city mentioned with Mount Jearim and serving to mark part of the N boundary of Judah. (Jos 15:10) It is today commonly identified with Kesla (Kesalon), located about 17 km (11 mi) W of Jerusalem.

CHESED (Che'sed). One of the eight sons Milcah bore to Nahor, the brother of Abraham.—Ge 22:20-22.

CHESIL (Che'sil) [Loin [that is, slope]]. The name of a town appearing in the list of places within the territory of Judah. (Jos 15:21, 30) A comparison of Joshua 15:30 with Joshua 19:4 and 1 Chronicles 4:30 indicates that Chesil may be the same as Bethuel.—See BETHUEL No. 2.

CHESULLOTH   (Che·sul′loth) [Loins, [that is, slopes]]. A boundary city of Issachar (Jos 19:18) and probably the same as Chisloth-tabor. (Jos 19:12) It is generally identified with Iksal (Kislot Tavor), situated at the base of the hills of Nazareth and 3 km (2 mi) SE of that city. Hence it lay in the Plain of Jezreel to the W of Mount Tabor.

CHIDON   (Chi′don). The name of the owner of the threshing floor or the threshing floor itself where Uzzah was struck down by Jehovah when an attempt was made to move the ark of the testimony in an improper manner from Kiriath-jearim to the City of David. The threshing floor was apparently located between these two points and near the house of Obed-edom. (1Ch 13:6-14) Its precise location is unknown. The parallel narrative at 2 Samuel 6:6 says "Nacon," which possibly indicates that one account uses the name of the location of the threshing floor, while the other uses the name of its owner. After the above incident the place came to be called Perez-uzzah, meaning "Rupture Against Uzzah."

CHIEFTAIN.   A man in a ruling position, such as the hereditary head of a tribe or a paternal house. The Hebrew word *na·si″* is variously rendered by Bible translators as "prince," "leader," "ruler," "chieftain." (See LEADER, NOBLE, PRINCE.) The heads of the 12 paternal houses or tribes of Israel were termed "chieftains." (Nu 1:16; Jos 22: 14) The term is also applied to the heads of the 12 clans springing from Ishmael. (Ge 17:20; 25:16) The title was used regarding Kings Solomon and Zedekiah as rulers. (1Ki 11:34; Eze 21:25) The esteem that the Hittites had for Abraham might be indicated by his being called "a chieftain of God," or a mighty chieftain.—Ge 23:6, ftn.

In the days of Moses, the chieftains took the lead in worship and acted as representatives of the people before Moses, the priests, and Jehovah. Moses selected a chieftain from each of the tribes (except the tribe of Levi) to spy out the Promised Land. The bad report of the ten unfaithful spies had a great influence upon the people. (Nu 13:2-16, 25-33) Two hundred and fifty chieftains of the sons of Israel were in the rebellion led by Korah to take over the priesthood from Aaron's house. (Nu 16:2, 10, 17, 35) The chieftains had a share in making a covenant for Israel with the Gibeonites. (Jos 9:15, 18) After Joshua had led Israel into Canaan and had defeated the nations there, the chieftains played a prominent role in dividing up the land. (Nu 34:18; Jos 14:1) Eleazar, the son of Aaron, was appointed as chieftain over the heads of the paternal houses of the tribe of Levi, making him a "chieftain of the chieftains."

(Nu 3:32) King Solomon called all the chieftains of the tribes together to Jerusalem at the time that he had the ark of the covenant brought into the newly built temple.—1Ki 8:1.

The Israelites were to give a chieftain proper respect, never subjecting him to verbal abuse. (Ex 22:28) When the apostle Paul was on trial before the Sanhedrin the high priest Ananias ordered those standing by Paul to strike him on the mouth. Then Paul said to him: "God is going to strike you, you whitewashed wall," not knowing that it was the high priest to whom he was speaking. When this was called to his attention, he said: "Brothers, I did not know he was high priest. For it is written, 'You must not speak injuriously of a ruler of your people.'"—Ac 23:1-5.

Although chieftains were to be respected, they were not above obedience to the law of God. When they sinned against the Law, they were required to meet its regulations regarding such sins. Because of their responsible position and the effect their conduct, example, and influence would have on others, a distinction was made in the individual sin offerings made by them for unintentionally violating a command of God. The high priest was required to offer a young bull, a chieftain was to offer a male goat, and anyone of the rest of the people, either a female goat or a female lamb.—Le 4:3, 22, 23, 27, 28, 32.

Ezekiel's Vision.   Ezekiel speaks prophetically of a chieftain, in Ezekiel chapters 44 to 48. In the vision, he describes an administrative strip of land running from the eastern border at the Jordan River and the Dead Sea to the Western, or Mediterranean, Sea. To the north and south of the strip and running parallel to it were sections of land assigned to Israel's tribes. Located within the strip of land was a section 25,000 cubits (13 km; 8 mi) square, called the contribution, which was itself divided into three sections: The northern section was assigned to the nonpriestly Levites, the middle section contained Jehovah's sanctuary, and the southernmost section contained the city. (See CUBIT; HOLY CONTRIBUTION.) The ruler of the city government evidently was "the chieftain."

It is noteworthy that in the vision the city was separate from the temple, or sanctuary. In addition, "the chieftain" was not a priest, as is indicated by the priests' rendering up the chieftain's "whole burnt offering and his communion sacrifices." (Eze 46:2) So in the fulfillment of Ezekiel's vision, the visionary city evidently would not picture the heavenly government of Jesus Christ and his associate kings and priests. Instead, it would seem to picture an earthly, visible seat of administration under the direction of the heavenly Kingdom. Correspondingly, "the chieftain" would stand for those who are appointed as visible, 'princely' representatives of the heavenly government.—Ps 45:16; Isa 32:1, 2.

CHILD, CHILDREN. Hebrew and Greek terms conveying a variety of helpful details are used to refer to human offspring. The common Hebrew term for a child is ye'ledh. (Ge 21:8) The related yal·dah' refers to a "female child," a "young lady," or a 'girl.' (Joe 3:3; Ge 34:4; Zec 8:5) Both words come from the root ya·ladh', meaning "bring forth; give birth to; bear." Two other Hebrew words for a child ('oh·lel' and 'oh·lal') come from the root verb 'ul, meaning "give suck." (1Sa 22:19; Jer 6:11; Ge 33:13) The usual Hebrew term for a boy or young man is na'ar. (Ge 19:4; Jg 8:20) However, the term is also used with reference to infants like three-month-old Moses. (Ex 2:6; compare 2Sa 12:16.) Hebrew taph (little children; little ones) conveys the basic idea of ones walking "with tripping steps." (Ge 43:8; 45:19; Isa 3:16) Among the Greek terms are te'knon (child), te·kni'on (little child), pai·di'on (young child), and ar'sen (male child). (Mt 10:21; Joh 13:33; Mt 2:8; Re 12:13) The Greek ne'pi·os refers to a "babe" (1Co 13:11), and the Greek bre'phos refers to an "infant." (Lu 1:41) At times the Hebrew and Greek words for "son" are rendered 'child.'—Ge 3:16; Lu 20:34; see SON.

The Creator, Jehovah, arranged for the multiplication of the human race by the birth of children who, in turn, would become adults and, in time, become parents themselves. The procreation mandate is expressed at Genesis 1:28. It is a normal desire of people to have children. The ancient Israelites were especially concerned about bringing forth children because of God's promise to make them a mighty nation and because through them would come the seed of Abraham by means of whom all the families of the earth would bless themselves. (Ge 28:14) Having many children was considered a blessing from God. (Ps 127:3-5; 128:3-6) Sterility was looked on as a reproach.—Ge 30:23.

In Bible times a boy's birth was usually a happier occasion than a girl's, although in the family circle a girl was loved by the parents just as much as the boy. The preference for a boy lay in the fact that it assured a continuance of the family line and name, and it assured the holding of family property. The priority of the male is also indicated by the fact that the purification period under the Law was twice as long for female births. (Le 12:2-5) The firstborn son belonged to Jehovah and was to be redeemed by an offering.—Ex 13:12, 13; Nu 18:15.

Anciently, at birth the infant was first washed with water, then rubbed with salt. (Eze 16:4) This was done to make the skin dry, tight, and firm. Swaddling clothes or cloth bands were tightly wrapped around the infant. (Job 38:9; Lu 2:12) The mother breast-fed it for two and a half or three years, or longer. Under exceptional circumstances, such as a mother's dying or being unable to furnish milk, nurses were employed.

In earlier history names were given to children at birth, either by the father (Ge 5:29; 16:15; 21:3; 35:18) or by the mother (Ge 4:25; 29:32; 1Sa 1:20), but in later times in Israel names were given to the boys at the time of circumcision, which was on the eighth day. (Lu 1:59; 2:21) Sometimes the name of a boy was the same as that of his father, but usually the name had to do with circumstances preceding or accompanying the birth, or it was a name in connection with the name of Jehovah. As time elapsed, certain names became merely traditional and had nothing to do with the original meaning.

Mothers used various methods to transport their young children. At times the child was bundled on the back or carried on the shoulder. Jehovah through Isaiah alludes to mothers clutching their children to their bosom, hoisting them on their shoulders, or carrying them on the flank, just above the hip. (Isa 49:22; 66:12) Also, the words of Moses indicate that children were carried in the bosom.—Nu 11:12.

Boys were mainly cared for by the mother until about five years of age. Of course, the father had the primary responsibility of teaching the child the Scriptures from its infancy, and the mother assisted. (De 6:7; Pr 1:8; Eph 6:4; 2Ti 3:15) As children grew older they were given practical training by the father in agriculture, raising livestock, or a trade such as carpentry. Both Joseph and David were young shepherd lads.—Ge 37:2; 1Sa 16:11.

Girls were under the immediate care of the mother, subject, of course, to the father's jurisdiction. While at home they were taught the domestic arts that would be of value in adult life. Rachel was a shepherdess. (Ge 29:6-9) Young women worked in the fields during the grain harvest (Ru 2:5-9), and the Shulammite girl says that her brothers made her keeper of the vineyards.—Ca 1:6.

Young children in Israel knew the joy of relaxation and amusements, sometimes playing in the marketplace, imitating things they had observed while watching grown-ups.—Mt 11:16, 17; Zec 8:5.

But the well-trained Israelite youths remembered their Creator in the days of their young manhood, and some even served him as ministers. Samuel as a boy was used to minister to Jehovah at the tabernacle. (1Sa 2:11) Jesus was very concerned with the service of his Father when he was only 12 years of age, learning all that he could by talking to the teachers in the temple. (Lu 2:41-49) A little Hebrew girl, who had implicit faith in Jehovah and his prophet Elisha, was the one responsible for directing Naaman to Elisha to be healed of leprosy. (2Ki 5:2, 3) At Psalm 148:12, 13 both boys and girls are commanded to praise Jehovah. Because of their training in the Bible, boys were able to cry out when they saw Jesus at the temple, saying: "Save, we pray, the Son of David!" and Jesus commended them.—Mt 21: 15, 16.

The parents were the ones responsible for the education and training of their children, they themselves being the instructors and guides, both by word and by example. The educational program was as follows: (1) Fear of Jehovah was taught. (Ps 34:11; Pr 9:10) (2) The child was admonished to honor his father and mother. (Ex 20:12; Le 19:3; De 27:16) (3) Discipline or instruction in the Law, its commandments and teachings, and education in the activities and revealed truths of Jehovah were diligently inculcated in the impressionable minds of the young offspring. (De 4:5, 9; 6:7-21; Ps 78:5) (4) Respect for older persons was stressed. (Le 19:32) (5) The importance of obedience was indelibly stamped on the youngster's mind. (Pr 4:1; 19:20; 23:22-25) (6) Stress was put on practical training for adult living, such as teaching girls to do things around the home, or teaching boys the trade of the father or some other trade. (7) Education in reading and writing was given.

After the Babylonian exile, synagogues existed in most cities, and in later times boys were instructed by teachers there. Additionally, religious instruction was given as the parents took their children with them when going to the assemblies that were held for the purpose of worshiping and praising Jehovah. (De 31:12, 13; Ne 12:43) Jesus' parents had taken him up to Jerusalem for the Passover. When on the return trip, they missed him and found him in the temple, "sitting in the midst of the teachers and listening to them and questioning them."—Lu 2:41-50; see EDUCATION.

If an occasion arose where a son became absolutely rebellious and incorrigible after repeated warnings and the necessary discipline, a still sterner measure was taken. The son was brought before the older men of the city, and after testimony from the parents that he was an irreformable offender, the delinquent suffered capital punishment by stoning. Such arrangement evidently had reference to a son beyond the age of what is usually considered a young child, for this one the Scriptures describe as "a glutton and a drunkard." (De 21:18-21) One striking his father or mother, or calling down evil upon his parents, was put to death. The reason for such strong measures was that the nation might clear away what was bad from their midst and so that "all Israel [would] hear and indeed become afraid." Therefore, any tendency in the nation toward juvenile delinquency or disrespect of parental authority would be greatly retarded by the punishment inflicted upon such offenders.—Ex 21:15, 17; Mt 15:4; Mr 7:10.

Great disrespect was shown to God's appointed prophet Elisha by a group of small boys who derided him, crying out: "Go up, you baldhead! Go up, you baldhead!" They wanted Elisha, who was wearing Elijah's familiar garment, either to go on his way up to Bethel or to get off the earth as Elijah was supposed to have done. (2Ki 2:11) They did not want him around. Elisha finally turned and called down evil upon them in the name of Jehovah. "Then two she-bears came out from the woods and went tearing to pieces forty-two children of their number."—2Ki 2:23, 24.

Jesus prophesied that children would rise up against their parents and parents against their children because of the stand that they would take as followers of him. (Mt 10:21; Mr 13:12) The apostle Paul foretold that the major problems marking "the last days" would include children who would be disobedient to parents and an absence of natural affection.—2Ti 3:1-3.

In setting forth the qualifications for overseers and ministerial servants in the Christian congregation, the apostle Paul specified that men selected for these positions were to have "believing children that were not under a charge of debauchery nor unruly," and that they must be in subjection with all seriousness; for, says Paul, "if indeed any man does not know how to preside over his own household, how will he take care of God's congregation?"—Tit 1:6; 1Ti 3:4, 5, 12.

Parental Authority. The authority of the parents, particularly the father in the family, was quite broad in scope. As long as the father was alive and able to manage the household, the sons were subject to him. However, if a son finally set up an independent home, then he became the head of his own household. Children could be sold into temporary bondage by a father for the payment of debts contracted. (Ex 21:7; 2Ki 4:1; Mt 18:25) The father's authority over the daughter was such that he could annul a vow made by the daughter. However, his authority could not be used to forbid his daughter's worship of Jehovah or cause failure to obey Jehovah's commands, for the reason that the father as a member of the nation of Israel was dedicated to God and fully under God's Law. (Nu 30:3-5, 16) Parental authority was also manifest in marriage inasmuch as the parents selected wives for their sons or made arrangements for the marriage. (Ge 21:21; Ex 21:8-11; Jg 14:1-3) A widow or a divorced woman could return to her father's house and again become subject to him.—Ge 38:11.

The inheritance rights came through the father. At the birth of twins, great care was exercised to distinguish the child that came into the world first (Ge 38:28), since the firstborn son received two portions of his father's inheritance, while the other son received only one portion. (De 21:17; Ge 25:1-6) Usually the older son assumed the responsibility of supporting the females in the family after his father had died. A son born through levirate marriage was raised up as the son of the dead man and inherited his property.—De 25:6; Ru 4:10, 17.

Figurative Uses. The words "child" and "children" as used in the Bible have considerable latitude in meaning. The descendants of Israel are referred to as "children in the flesh," also as "children of transgression" by Isaiah because of their rebellious ways against Jehovah. (Ro 9:8; Isa 57:4) In the days of the apostles, wicked persons were classified as "accursed children" and "children of the Devil." (2Pe 2:14; 1Jo 3:10) In contrast, persons exercising faith in Christ and becoming spirit-begotten ones are called "God's children." (Joh 1:12; Ro 8:16) Disciples are often called children.—Joh 13:33; Heb 2:13.

Individuals privileged to receive a resurrection from the dead are spoken of as "children of the resurrection" (Lu 20:36); also those who are joint heirs with Christ are "the children by the promise" (Ro 9:8) or children "of the free woman" (Ga 4:31). All those desiring to attain life in the Kingdom of heaven must display the childlike qualities of humility, receptiveness, and trust. (Mt 18:2-4) Men and women who strive to obey God by manifesting the light of truth in their lives are described as "obedient children" and as "children of light."—1Pe 1:14; Eph 5:8.

Paul counseled the congregation at Corinth as he would children, to "widen out" in affection; prior to this he had encouraged them not to become children in powers of understanding.—2Co 6:13; 1Co 14:20.

CHILDBEARING. A privilege granted exclusively to womankind by the Creator, for which he especially designed and equipped the female. The Edenic mandate given to the first human couple and later repeated to the survivors of the Flood included conceiving and bearing children. (Ge 1:28; 9:7) However, because of sin and disobedience, Jehovah said to Eve, in connection with childbearing: "I shall greatly increase the pain of your pregnancy; in birth pangs you will bring forth children."—Ge 3:16; see BIRTH; LABOR PAINS.

Concerning childbearing and motherhood, the apostle Paul recommended that younger widows, who may be greatly distracted if their motherly instincts are not satisfied, get married and bear children rather than spend their time gadding about as "gossipers and meddlers in other people's affairs." (1Ti 5:11-15) Concerning women in the Christian congregation, Paul said that they "will be kept safe through childbearing, provided they continue in faith and love and sanctification along with soundness of mind."—1Ti 2:15.

CHILEAB (Chil′e·ab). David's second son born in Hebron. His mother Abigail was the former wife of Nabal. (2Sa 3:2, 3) Chileab is called Daniel at 1 Chronicles 3:1.—See DANIEL No. 1.

CHILION (Chil′i·on) [One Failing; One Coming to an End]. A son of Naomi and Elimelech and the brother of Mahlon the husband of Ruth. The family had moved from Bethlehem, in Judah, to Moab to escape a famine that occurred in the time of the Judges. After the death of his father, Chilion married the Moabitess Orpah. Both he and his brother died childless in Moab.—Ru 1:1-5; 4:9, 10.

CHILMAD (Chil′mad). Evidently a place listed among those trading with Tyre in the sale of fine clothing, dyed materials, carpets, and ropes.—Eze 27:2, 23, 24.

CHIMHAM (Chim′ham) [Grown Faint [with longing]]. Presumably a son of Barzillai. When the aged Barzillai declined the invitation to become part of King David's court and recommended that Chimham go in his place, David replied: "With me Chimham will go across [the Jordan], and I myself shall do to him what is good in your eyes; and all that you may choose to lay upon me I shall do for you." (2Sa 19:33, 37-40) Apparently Chimham remained in the royal court, as is indicated by

David's final instructions to Solomon. (1Ki 2:7) Reference is made at Jeremiah 41:17 to "the lodging place of Chimham" near Bethlehem. It is not known whether this refers to the Chimham of David's time or to a later man by the same name. Some commentators say that Chimham may have been given a tract of land for his services to David, or that it was a place where Chimham had built a lodging place for travelers.

CHINNERETH (Chin'ne·reth).

1. A fortified city of Naphtali. (Jos 19:32, 35) It is presently identified with Khirbet el-'Oreimeh (Tel Kinnerot), situated on a mound over 3 km (2 mi) SW of Capernaum, overlooking the NW portion of the Sea of Galilee. Chinnereth appears on the temple walls of Karnak at Thebes, Egypt, in the list of Canaanite cities conquered by Thutmose III (whose reign historians assign to the 16th century B.C.E.).

2. A district or region of Israel attacked by Syrian King Ben-hadad I at the instigation of King Asa of Judah. (c. 962 B.C.E.) (1Ki 15:20; compare 2Ch 16:4.) The expression "all Chinnereth" is usually considered to refer to the fertile Plain of Gennesaret.

3. The early name of the Sea of Galilee. (Nu 34:11) Associating the name with the Hebrew word for harp (*kin·nohr'*), some suggest that it is applied to the lake because of the harp-shaped form of this body of water. The names Sea of Galilee and Sea of Tiberias as well as Gennesaret, probably the Greek form of the name, were used when Jesus was on earth.—Lu 5:1; Joh 6:1.

In addition to being included among the boundaries of the Promised Land (Nu 34:11), the lake formed part of the W boundary of the Amorite kingdom of Og and, following the Israelite conquest, figured in the W boundary of the tribe of Gad. (De 3:16, 17; Jos 13:24-27) The reference to "the desert plains [Heb., *'ara·vah'*] south of Chinnereth" (Jos 11:2) evidently means the section of the Jordan Valley S of the Sea of Galilee, known as the Ghor.—See GALILEE, SEA OF.

CHIOS (Chi'os).

One of the larger islands in the Aegean Sea and separated from the W coast of Asia Minor by a strait 8 km (5 mi) or more wide. The island measures some 50 km (30 mi) in length (N to S) and varies between 13 and 29 km (8 to 18 mi) in breadth (E to W).

Chios is mentioned in the account in Acts 20 concerning Paul's return trip to Jerusalem at the close of his third missionary journey, in about 56 C.E. The ship on which Paul was traveling left Mitylene (Ac 20:14) some 100 km (60 mi) to the NE, probably in the morning, and "arrived opposite Chios" (Ac 20:15), likely by sunset. Then, the following day, the voyage continued to Samos, approximately 100 km (60 mi) farther down the coast.

At the time of Paul's journey Chios was considered a free city-state of the Roman province of Asia, a status it maintained until the reign of Emperor Vespasian (69-79 C.E.). Both the island and its chief city are today called Khios by the Greeks and Scio by the Italians.

CHISLEV (Chis'lev).

The postexilic name of the ninth Jewish lunar month, which fell within November and December. (Ne 1:1; Jer 36:9; Zec 7:1) It corresponded to the third month of the secular calendar.

This was a winter month, a month of cold and rain. So we read that King Jehoiakim was "sitting in the winter house, in the ninth month, with a brazier burning before him." (Jer 36:22) In postexilic Jerusalem, the people who gathered for the assembly ordered by priest Ezra beginning on the 20th day of this month "kept sitting in the open place of the house of the true God, shivering because of the matter and on account of the showers of rain."—Ezr 10:9, 13.

The Festival of Dedication, held in the wintertime at Jerusalem, is mentioned at John 10:22. As shown in the Apocryphal book of 1 Maccabees (4:52-59), this eight-day festival was instituted by Judas Maccabaeus on the 25th day of Chislev in the year 165 B.C.E. to commemorate the rededication of the temple in Jerusalem. This festival is today known as Hanukkah.—See FESTIVAL OF DEDICATION.

CHISLON (Chis'lon) [possibly, Stupid].

A Benjamite of Moses' day whose son Elidad assisted with the division of the Promised Land into inheritance portions.—Nu 34:17, 21.

CHISLOTH-TABOR (Chis'loth-ta'bor) [Loins [that is, slopes] of Tabor].

A city marking Zebulun's boundary and apparently a variant form of Chesulloth. (Jos 19:12, 18) It is usually identified with Iksal (Kislot Tavor), 3 km (2 mi) SE of Nazareth, at the foot of Mount Tabor, which location may account for its name.

CHITLISH (Chit'lish).

A city in the Shephelah in the inheritance of Judah. (Jos 15:33, 40) It is tentatively identified with modern-day Khirbet el-Maghaz (Mishlat Ma'ahaz), 7 km (4.5 mi) SW of Lachish.

CHLOE (Chlo'e) [from a root meaning "green"; probably, First Green Shoot of Plants].

A woman through whose household Paul received reports

concerning the dissensions existing in the Corinthian congregation. (1Co 1:11) Though Paul's letter does not state that Chloe was a Christian residing at Corinth or at Ephesus, where the letter was penned, in view of the apostle's reference to this household by name, evidently at least some members thereof, either family members or slaves, were Christians known to the Corinthians.

CHORAZIN (Cho·ra′zin). A city among those reproached by Jesus and located at the N end of the Sea of Galilee. (Mt 11:21; PICTURE, Vol. 2, p. 739) It is usually identified by scholars with Khirbet Kerazeh (Korazim), only about 3 km (2 mi) NNW of the suggested site of ancient Capernaum (Mt 11:23), the city that Jesus apparently used as a base of operations during his great Galilean ministry of over two years' duration. Jesus pronounced coming "woe" for the Jewish inhabitants of Chorazin who, during that period, were witnesses of "powerful works" that would have moved the pagans of Tyre and Sidon to repentance, and yet who failed to act on Jesus' message. After this, in the fall of 32 C.E., when dispatching the 70 disciples during his later Judean ministry, Jesus inserted a reference to Chorazin's impenitent attitude into his discussion apparently to emphasize that great woe would be experienced by the unresponsive cities against which his disciples were to 'wipe the dust' off their feet.—Lu 10:10-16.

CHRIST. This title from the Greek *Khri·stos′* is equivalent to the Hebrew *Ma·shi′ach,* "Messiah; Anointed One." (Compare Mt 2:4, ftn.) "Christ" is not a mere appellative added to distinguish the Lord Jesus from others of the same name; it is an official title.—See JESUS CHRIST; MESSIAH.

The coming of the Christ, the one whom Jehovah would anoint with his spirit to be the Messianic King, had been foretold centuries before Jesus' birth. (Da 9:25, 26) However, at his birth, Jesus was not yet the Anointed One or Christ. In foretelling his birth, the angel instructed Joseph: "You must call his name Jesus." (Mt 1:21) But when the shepherds near Bethlehem were given the angelic announcement, in anticipation of Jesus' future role they were told: "There was born to you today a Savior, who is Christ the Lord," that is, "who *is to be* Christ the Lord."—Lu 2:11, ftn.

The personal name of Jesus followed by the title Christ may call attention to the person himself and that he is the one who became the Anointed One of Jehovah. This occurred when he reached about 30 years of age, was baptized in water, and was anointed with Jehovah's spirit visibly observed in the form of a dove descending upon him.

(Mt 3:13-17) This is the point Peter made at Pentecost: "God made him both Lord and Christ, this Jesus," evidently recalling the expression he had heard from the lips of Jesus, who first used the term "Jesus Christ." (Ac 2:36-38; Joh 17:3) This expression "Jesus Christ" is also used in the opening and closing words of the Christian Greek Scriptures.—Mt 1:1; Re 22:21.

On the other hand, putting the title ahead of the name and saying "Christ Jesus" instead of "Jesus Christ" places greater emphasis on the office or position held by Jesus. It focuses attention primarily on the office, secondarily on the office holder, as in saying King David or Governor Zerubbabel. It would remind one of the singular official position Jesus holds as the Anointed One of Jehovah, an honored position not shared by others of his followers who are also anointed. Only Jehovah's beloved Son is entitled "Christ Jesus." Paul used this expression in his first inspired letter. (1Th 2:14) Luke also used it, once, at Acts 24:24 (*NW; RS*), when speaking about Paul's bearing witness.

The use of the article "the" with the title ("the Christ") is another way attention is sometimes drawn to the office as held by Jesus. (Mt 16:16; Mr 14:61) The grammatical structure of the sentence, however, may be a factor determining whether the article is used or not, for says W. E. Vine: "Speaking generally, when the title [Christ] is the subject of a sentence it has the article; when it forms part of the predicate the article is absent." —*Vine's Expository Dictionary of Old and New Testament Words,* 1981, Vol. 1, p. 190.

In the Scriptures titles are never multiplied before or after Jesus' name; but if one title precedes the personal name, then any other title is added only after the name. We never find a combination like the *Lord Christ* Jesus or the *King Christ* Jesus, but we do find the *Lord* Jesus *Christ.* The expression "our Savior, Christ Jesus," at 2 Timothy 1:10, in the Greek text has the expression "of us" between "Savior" and "Christ" to identify who the Savior is, in keeping with the expression "Christ Jesus our Savior [literally, "Christ Jesus the Savior of us"]." (Tit 1:4) In the text at 1 Timothy 2:5 mention is made of "a man, Christ Jesus" as the Mediator, but "a man" is not a title. The expression only explains that Christ Jesus was at one time a man on earth.

An exceptional use of the title "Christ" is Paul's reference to Moses rather than Jesus, when he writes: "He [Moses] esteemed the reproach of the Christ [*Khri·stou′,* "Anointed One"] as riches greater than the treasures of Egypt; for he looked intently toward the payment of the reward." (Heb

11:26) Moses was never anointed with any literal oil as were the high priests and kings of Israel. (Ex 30:22-30; Le 8:12; 1Sa 10:1; 16:13) But neither was Jesus nor were his followers, and yet the Scriptures speak of them as having been anointed. (Ac 10:38; 2Co 1:21) In these latter cases their anointing with God's holy spirit served as an appointment by God, or a commission, even though literal anointing oil was not used. So, in a similar sense Moses received a special appointment. Paul, therefore, could say of Moses that he was Jehovah's anointed one, or Christ, the recipient of a commission given to him at the burning bush, which appointment he considered to be greater riches than all the treasures of Egypt.—Ex 3:2–4:17.

The term "Christ" is also used when speaking of the Christian congregation and its relationship to the Lord Jesus Christ. "Now you are Christ's body, and members individually," in a spiritual sense. (1Co 12:27) Those "baptized into Christ Jesus were baptized into his death," with hope of being "joint heirs with Christ" of the heavenly Kingdom. (Ro 6:3-5; 8:17) They share in "the sufferings of the Christ," being "reproached for the name of Christ." (1Pe 4:13, 14; 5:1) A number of times this relationship is described as being "in union with Christ" or "in Christ," and also the reverse expression "Christ in union with you," with its different implications, is used. (Ro 8:1, 2; 16:10; 1Co 15:18; 1Th 4:16; Col 1:27) Weak ones in such association, who should be strong, are called "babes in Christ." (1Co 3:1) In the course of time all things in heaven and on earth are gathered again "in the Christ." —Eph 1:10.

False Christs. In his prophecies on the conclusion of the system of things, Christ warned his followers: "Look out that nobody misleads you; for many will come on the basis of my name, saying, 'I am the Christ,' and will mislead many. For false Christs [Gr., *pseu·do'khri·stoi*] and false prophets will arise and will give great signs and wonders so as to mislead, if possible, even the chosen ones." (Mt 24:4, 5, 24) Such wicked persons who falsely lay claim to the title and office of the Lord Jesus Christ are included in the *an·ti'khri·stos* (Greek for "antichrist") mentioned five times by the apostle John.—1Jo 2:18, 22; 4:3; 2Jo 7; see ANTICHRIST.

Other Uses of the Term "Christ." The *Septuagint* translation of the Hebrew Scriptures uses the same Greek word *khri·stos'* more than 40 times, frequently as a title of anointed priests, kings, and prophets. Aaron the high priest was "the anointed one," commissioned and "appointed in behalf of men over the things pertaining to

God." (Le 4:3, 5, 16; 8:12; Heb 5:1) Expressing his judgment on the house of Eli, Jehovah promised to raise up a faithful priest who would walk before God's anointed one (*khri·stos'*) for all time.—1Sa 2:35.

The kings shared this same honored title because of their relationship to Jehovah in their kingly office. So Samuel spoke of Saul as *khri·stos'* at 1 Samuel 12:3, in the Greek *Septuagint.* "It is unthinkable, on my part," exclaimed David, "to thrust my hand out against [Saul] the anointed [*LXX, khri·ston'*] of Jehovah!" (1Sa 26:11) And David would not allow his nephew Abishai to touch Saul. (1Sa 26:8, 9) David also had the Amalekite slain because that one said he had killed Saul "the anointed [*LXX, khri·ston'*] of Jehovah." (2Sa 1:13-16) This title and commission to be king was also bestowed on David, and thereafter he spoke of himself as Jehovah's "anointed one [*LXX, khri·stoi'*]." (1Sa 16:12, 13; 2Sa 22:51) King Zedekiah, who sat on the throne as an heir of David, was also called "the anointed one [*khri·stos'*] of Jehovah." —La 4:20.

The prophets too were titled Jehovah's anointed ones, as is indicated by the parallelism in Psalm 105:15. Jehovah gave the command to his prophet Elijah: "Elisha . . . you should anoint as prophet in place of you," though the details of the actual anointing are not recorded.—1Ki 19:16.

There are other instances where the Greek *Septuagint* uses *khri·stos'* prophetically. There are ten references to *khri·stos'* in the book of Psalms, the one in Psalm 2:1, 2 being particularly noteworthy: Nations in tumult and kings of the earth massing together "against Jehovah and against his anointed one." The apostles quoted this prophecy and applied the title to the 'holy servant Jesus, whom Jehovah had anointed.' (Ac 4:24-27) A more unusual example is where the term is applied to the Persian king Cyrus. Before his birth, the prophecy of Isaiah (45:1-3) declared: "This is what Jehovah has said to his anointed one [*LXX, khri·stoi'*], to Cyrus, whose right hand I have taken hold of." Cyrus was never literally anointed with holy oil as were the kings of Israel, but as in other instances in the Bible, the expression "anointed one" is a titled form of address given to him because of his commission and appointment from God.—See ANOINTED, ANOINTING.

CHRISTIAN. The Latinized Greek term *Khri·sti·a·nos'*, found only three times in the Christian Greek Scriptures, designates followers of Christ Jesus, the exponents of Christianity.—Ac 11:26; 26:28; 1Pe 4:16.

"It was first in Antioch [Syria] that the disciples were by divine providence called Christians." (Ac 11:26) It is possible, then, that this name was used as early as the year 44 C.E. when the events surrounding this text occurred, although the grammatical structure of this phrase does not necessarily make it so; some think it was a little later. At any rate, by about 58 C.E., in the city of Caesarea, the term was well known and used even by public officials, for at that time King Herod Agrippa II said to Paul: "In a short time you would persuade me to become a Christian."—Ac 26:28.

Bible writers in addressing fellow believers or describing followers of Christ used expressions such as "believers in the Lord," "brothers" and "disciples" (Ac 5:14; 6:3; 15:10), "chosen ones" and "faithful ones" (Col 3:12; 1Ti 4:12), "slaves to God" and "slaves of Christ Jesus" (Ro 6:22; Php 1:1), "holy ones," "congregation of God," and "those who call upon the Lord." (Ac 9:13; 20:28; 1Co 1:2; 2Ti 2:22) These terms with doctrinal meaning were used primarily as internal congregational designations. To outsiders Christianity was referred to as "The Way" (Ac 9:2; 19:9, 23; 22:4), and opponents called it "the sect of the Nazarenes" or just "this sect."—Ac 24:5; 28:22.

It was first in Syrian Antioch that Christ's followers became known as Christians. It is most unlikely that the Jews first styled Jesus' followers "Christians" (Greek) or "Messianists" (Hebrew), for they would not reject Jesus as being the Messiah, or Christ, and then tacitly recognize him as the Anointed One, or Christ, by stamping his followers "Christians." Some think the heathen population may have nicknamed them Christians out of jest or scorn, but the Bible shows that it was a God-given name; they "were *by divine providence* called Christians."—Ac 11:26.

The Greek verb *khre·ma·ti'zo* in this text is generally rendered simply "were called." A check of some 50 translations in several modern languages reveals that only the *New World Translation* and *Young's* indicate that God had anything to do with selecting the name "Christian"; *Young's* reads: "The disciples also were divinely called first in Antioch Christians."

The Greek word *khre·ma·ti'zo* as used in the Christian Greek Scriptures is always associated with something supernatural, oracular, or divine. Strong's *Exhaustive Concordance of the Bible,* in its Greek dictionary (1890, p. 78), defines it as "to utter an oracle . . . i.e. divinely intimate." Edward Robinson's *Greek and English Lexicon* (1885, p. 786) gives the meaning: "Spoken in respect to a divine response, oracle, declaration, to give response, to speak as an oracle, to warn from God." Thayer's *Greek-English Lexicon of the New Testament* (1889, p. 671): "to give a divine command or admonition, to teach from heaven . . . to be divinely commanded, admonished, instructed . . . to be the mouthpiece of divine revelations, to promulge the commands of God." Thomas Scott in his *Explanatory Notes* on this text (1832, Vol. III, p. 419) says: "The word implies that this was done by divine revelation: for it has generally this signification in the New Testament, and is rendered 'warned from God' or 'warned of God,' even when there is no word for GOD in the Greek." Concerning Acts 11:26, Clarke's *Commentary* says: "The word [*khre·ma·ti'sai*] in our common text, which we translate *were called,* signifies in the New Testament, to *appoint, warn,* or *nominate,* by *Divine direction.* In this sense, the word is used, Matt. ii. 12 . . . If, therefore, the name was given by *Divine appointment,* it is most likely that Saul and Barnabas were directed to give it; and that, therefore, the name *Christian* is from God."—See Mt 2:12, 22; Lu 2:26; Ac 10:22; Ro 7:3, *Int;* Heb 8:5; 11:7; 12:25, where this Greek verb occurs.

The Scriptures speak of Jesus Christ as the Bridegroom, the Head and Husband of his anointed followers. (2Co 11:2; Eph 5:23) Appropriately, then, as a wife is happy to take her husband's name, so this "bride" class of Christ was pleased to receive a name identifying its members as belonging to him. In this way observers of these first-century Christians readily recognized them not only by their activity but also by their name as altogether different from the practitioners of Judaism; here was a growing association where there was neither Jew nor Greek but all were one under their Head and Leader, Jesus Christ.—Ga 3:26-28; Col 3:11.

What It Means to Be a Christian. Jesus extended the invitation to be his follower, saying: "If anyone wants to come after me, let him disown himself and pick up his torture stake and continually follow me." (Mt 16:24) Those who are true Christians have full faith that Jesus Christ is God's specially Anointed One and only-begotten Son, the Promised Seed who sacrificed his human life as a ransom, was resurrected and exalted to the right hand of Jehovah, and received authority to subdue his enemies and vindicate Jehovah's name. (Mt 20:28; Lu 24:46; Joh 3:16; Ga 3:16; Php 2:9-11; Heb 10:12, 13) Christians view the Bible as the inspired Word of God, absolute truth, beneficial for teaching and discipling mankind.—Joh 17:17; 2Ti 3:16; 2Pe 1:21.

More is required of true Christians than a mere confession of faith. It is necessary that belief be demonstrated by works. (Ro 10:10; Jas 2:17, 26) Born as sinners, those who become Christians repent, turn around, dedicate their lives to Jehovah, to worship and serve him, and then submit to water baptism. (Mt 28:19; Ac 2:38; 3:19) They must keep themselves clean from fornication, from idolatry, and from eating blood. (Ac 15:20, 29) They strip off old personalities with their fits of anger, obscene talk, lying, stealing, drunkenness, and "things like these," and they bring their lives into accord with Bible principles. (Ga 5:19-21; 1Co 6:9-11; Eph 4:17-24; Col 3:5-10) "Let none of you," wrote Peter to Christians, "suffer as a murderer or a thief or an evildoer or as a busybody in other people's matters." (1Pe 4:15) Christians are to be kind and considerate, mild-tempered and long-suffering, lovingly exercising self-control. (Ga 5:22, 23; Col 3:12-14) They provide and care for their own and love their neighbors as themselves. (1Ti 5:8; Ga 6:10; Mt 22:36-40; Ro 13:8-10) The main identifying quality by which true Christians are recognized is the outstanding love they have toward one another. "By this," Jesus said, "all will know that you are my disciples, if you have love among yourselves." —Joh 13:34, 35; 15:12, 13.

True Christians imitate Jesus' example as the Great Teacher and Faithful Witness of Jehovah. (Joh 18:37; Re 1:5; 3:14) "Go . . . make disciples of people of all the nations" is their Leader's command. (Mt 28:19, 20) In carrying it out, Christians 'witness publicly and from house to house,' urging people everywhere to flee out of Babylon the Great and put their hope and confidence in God's Kingdom. (Ac 5:42; 20:20, 21; Re 18:2-4) This is really good news, but proclaiming such a message brings upon Christians great persecution and suffering, even as was experienced by Jesus Christ. His followers are not above him; it is enough if they are like him. (Mt 10:24, 25; 16:21; 24:9; Joh 15:20; 2Ti 3:12; 1Pe 2:21) If one "suffers as a Christian, let him not feel shame, but let him keep on glorifying God in this name," counseled Peter. (1Pe 4:16) Christians render to "Caesar" what belongs to the superior authorities of this world —honor, respect, tax—but at the same time they remain separate from this world's affairs (Mt 22: 21; Joh 17:16; Ro 13:1-7), and for this the world hates them.—Joh 15:19; 18:36; 1Pe 4:3, 4; Jas 4:4; 1Jo 2:15-17.

It is understandable why people with such high principles of morality and integrity, accompanied by an electrifying message delivered with fiery zeal and outspokenness, quickly gained attention in the first century. Paul's missionary travels, for example, were like a spreading prairie fire that set city after city ablaze—Antioch in Pisidia, Iconium, Lystra, Derbe, and Perga on one trip; Philippi, Thessalonica, Beroea, Athens, and Corinth on another—causing people to stop, think, and take their stand, either accepting or rejecting the good news of God's Kingdom. (Ac 13:14–14:26; 16: 11–18:17) Many thousands abandoned their false religious organizations, wholeheartedly embraced Christianity, and zealously took up the preaching activity in imitation of Christ Jesus and the apostles. This, in turn, made them objects of hatred and persecution, which was instigated chiefly by the false religious leaders and misinformed political rulers. Their leader Jesus Christ, the Prince of Peace, had been put to death on the charge of sedition; now peace-loving Christians were accused of "disturbing our city," 'overturning the inhabited earth,' and being a people 'that everywhere is spoken against.' (Ac 16:20; 17:6; 28: 22) By the time Peter wrote his first letter (c. 62-64 C.E.) it seems that the activity of Christians was well known in places such as "Pontus, Galatia, Cappadocia, Asia, and Bithynia."—1Pe 1:1.

Non-Christian Testimony. Secular writers of the first two centuries also acknowledged the presence and influence of early Christians in their pagan world. For example, Tacitus, a Roman historian born about 55 C.E., tells of the rumor charging that Nero was the one responsible for burning Rome (64 C.E.), and then says: "Therefore, to scotch the rumour, Nero substituted as culprits, and punished with the utmost refinements of cruelty, a class of men, loathed for their vices [as the Romans viewed matters], whom the crowd styled Christians. . . . First, then, the confessed members of the sect were arrested; next, on their disclosures, vast numbers were convicted, not so much on the count of arson as for hatred of the human race. And derision accompanied their end: they were covered with wild beasts' skins and torn to death by dogs; or they were fastened on crosses, and, when daylight failed were burned to serve as lamps by night." (*The Annals*, XV, XLIV) Suetonius, another Roman historian, born toward the end of the first century C.E., relates events that occurred during Nero's reign, saying: "Punishment was inflicted on the Christians, a class of men given to a new and mischievous superstition."—*The Lives of the Caesars* (Nero, XVI, 2).

Flavius Josephus, in his *Jewish Antiquities* (XVIII, 64 [iii, 3]), mentions certain events in the life of Jesus, adding: "And the tribe of the Christians, so called after him, has still to this day [about 93 C.E.] not disappeared." Pliny the Younger, governor of Bithynia in 111 or 112 C.E., faced with the 'Christian problem,' wrote to Emperor Trajan, outlining the methods he was using and asking for advice. "I have asked them in person if they are Christians," wrote Pliny. If they admitted it, they were punished. However, others "denied that they were or ever had been Christians." Put to the test, not only did these offer up pagan sacrifices but they even "reviled the name of Christ: none of which things, I understand, any genuine Christian can be induced to do." In answering this letter, Trajan commended Pliny on the way he had handled the matter: "You have followed the right course of procedure . . . in your examination of the cases of persons charged with being Christians."—*The Letters of Pliny*, X, XCVI, 3, 5; XCVII, 1.

First-century Christianity had no temples, built no altars, used no crucifixes, and sponsored no garbed and betitled ecclesiastics. Early Christians celebrated no state holidays and refused all military service. "A careful review of all the information available goes to show that, until the time of Marcus Aurelius [who ruled 161-180 C.E.], no Christian became a soldier; and no soldier, after becoming a Christian, remained in military service."—*The Rise of Christianity*, by E. Barnes, 1947, p. 333.

Nevertheless, as indicated in Pliny's letter, not all who bore the name Christian were uncompromisingly such when put to the test. Just as had been foretold, the spirit of apostasy was already at work before the apostles fell asleep. (Ac 20:29, 30; 2Pe 2:1-3; 1Jo 2:18, 19, 22) Within a period of less than 300 years, the wheat field of Christianity had been overrun with the weeds of apostate antichrists to the point where wicked Constantine the Great (himself incriminated in the murder of no less than seven close friends and relatives) figured in events that led to the development of a state religion disguised as "Christianity."

CHRISTIAN GREEK SCRIPTURES. So designated to distinguish them from the pre-Christian Greek *Septuagint* translation of the Hebrew Scriptures. It is a common practice to call this latter portion of the Bible the New Testament. —See BIBLE.

There are 27 canonical books that make up the Christian Greek Scriptures. After the death of Jesus, these books were penned under inspiration by eight men: Matthew, Mark, Luke, John, Paul, James, Peter, and Jude. Not all these men followed Jesus during his ministry; in fact, as far as is known for a certainty, only the three apostles

Matthew, John, and Peter did. Mark may have been the "certain young man" who followed Jesus at a distance after he was arrested. (Mr 14:51, 52) At Pentecost, James, Jude, and perhaps Mark were present along with them. (Ac 1:13-15; 2:1) Later the apostle Paul was converted. All these writers became closely associated with the governing body of the first-century congregation in Jerusalem.

In what language were these books originally written? With the exception of the book of Matthew, which was written originally in Hebrew and later translated into Greek, all the other 26 books were written in the common Greek, Koine, the international language of the day.—See MATTHEW, GOOD NEWS ACCORDING TO.

Nor was it a mere coincidence that these inspired Christian men, all of them natural-born Jews (Ro 3:1, 2), had their writings sent out in Greek. These were not private communications but were intended for wide circulation, to be read and studied by all the congregations. (Col 4:16; 1Th 5:27; 2Pe 3:15, 16) The writers were under divine command to spread this good news and teaching to the most distant part of the earth, to places where Hebrew and Latin were not read. (Mt 28:19; Ac 1:8) Even in territories closer to Palestine, there was an increasingly large number of non-Jews coming into the local congregations. Also, when quoting the Hebrew Scriptures, these writers frequently used the Greek *Septuagint*.

The books of the Christian Greek Scriptures, listed according to the approximate year (C.E.) written, are as follows: Matthew, 41; 1 and 2 Thessalonians, 50 and 51; Galatians, 50-52; 1 and 2 Corinthians, 55; Romans, 56; Luke, 56-58; Ephesians, Colossians, Philemon, Philippians, 60-61; Hebrews, Acts, 61; James, before 62; Mark, 60-65; 1 Timothy, Titus, 61-64; 1 Peter, 62-64; 2 Peter, 64; 2 Timothy, Jude, 65; Revelation, 96; John and 1, 2, 3 John, 98. This period of less than 60 years is quite a contrast with the nearly 11 centuries taken to complete the Hebrew Scriptures.

When it came time to combine these books of the Christian Greek Scriptures into a single volume, they were not assembled in the order in which they were written. Rather, they were put in a logical arrangement according to subject matter, which can be classified as (1) the five historical books of the Gospels and Acts, (2) the 21 letters, and (3) the Revelation.

The four Gospels (the word "Gospel" meaning "good news"), written by Matthew, Mark, Luke, and John, give us a fourfold historical account of the life and activity of Jesus, each account being an independent report. The first three of these are sometimes called synoptic (meaning "like view") because they have a relatively similar approach to Jesus' ministry in comparison with John's Gospel, yet each reflects individualism on the part of the writer. John's Gospel fills in certain details omitted by the other three. The Acts of Apostles then follows in logical sequence, carrying the history of the Christian congregation as established at Pentecost on down nearly 30 years after the death of Jesus.

The congregation's inner workings, its problems, its public preaching, its other privileges, and its hopes are dealt with in the 21 letters that follow the historical section. Paul is named as the writer of 13 letters. The letter to the Hebrews is also generally ascribed to Paul. Following these writings is a group of letters, most of which were written to all the congregations in general, by James, Peter, John, and Jude. Lastly, as a delightful climax to the whole Bible, is the Revelation with its preview of profound events of the future.

To what extent did writers of the Christian Greek Scriptures quote from the Hebrew Scriptures?

The writers of the Christian Greek Scriptures quoted the Hebrew Scriptures hundreds of times. In the Christian Greek Scriptures, the *New World Translation* presents as direct quotations 320 passages from the Hebrew Scriptures. According to a listing published by Westcott and Hort, the combined total of quotations and references is some 890. (*The New Testament in the Original Greek,* Graz, 1974, Vol. I, pp. 581-595) Examples are drawn from the Hebrew Scriptures by all the inspired Christian writers. (1Co 10:11) These Christian writers undoubtedly employed the divine name Jehovah when they were quoting from the Hebrew Scriptures. These later writers acknowledge and include the Hebrew Scriptures as inspired of God and beneficial for completely equipping the man of God for every good work. —2Ti 3:16, 17; 2Pe 1:20, 21.

After the death of the apostles, uninspired writers quoted profusely from the Greek Scriptures, even as the inspired Christian Bible writers had quoted from what came before them.

There are available for comparative study more than 13,000 papyrus and vellum manuscripts containing the whole or a part of the Christian Greek Scriptures, dating from the 2nd to the 16th century. Of these, some 5,000 are in Greek, and the remainder in various other languages. More than 2,000 of the ancient copies contain the Gospels, and more than 700, the letters of Paul. While the original writings themselves are not currently extant, copies date back to the second century, which is very close to the time the originals were written. This vast number of manuscripts has enabled Greek scholars in the course of years to produce a highly refined Greek text of the Scriptures, confirming in many respects the dependability and integrity of our present-day translations of the Christian Greek Scriptures.—See MANUSCRIPTS OF THE BIBLE.

This vast mountain of manuscripts caused one scholar to remark: "The great bulk of the words of the New Testament stand out above all discriminative processes of criticism, because they are free from variation, and need only to be transcribed. . . . If comparative trivialities, such as changes of order, the insertion or omission of the article with proper names, and the like, are set aside, the words in our opinion still subject to doubt can hardly amount to more than a thousandth part of the whole New Testament." (*The New Testament in the Original Greek,* Vol. I, p. 561) To this may be added the observation of Jack Finegan: "The close relationship in time between the oldest New Testament manuscripts and the original texts is also nothing less than amazing. . . . For our knowledge of the writings of most of the classical authors we are dependent upon manuscripts the oldest of which belong to a time between the ninth and eleventh centuries A.D. . . . Thus it is that the certainty with which the text of the New Testament is established exceeds that of any other ancient book. The words which the New Testament writers addressed to their world and time have crossed the further miles and centuries to us substantially unchanged in form and certainly undiminished in power."—*Light From the Ancient Past,* 1959, pp. 449, 450.

As an integral part of the written Word of God, the Christian Greek Scriptures are of inestimable value. They contain four accounts of the ministry of God's only-begotten Son, including his origin, his teaching, his example, his sacrificial death, and his resurrection. The historical record of the formation of the Christian congregation and the outpouring of the holy spirit, which enabled it to grow so successfully, as well as details concerning its problems and how they were resolved—all of this is so essential for the operation of the true Christian congregation today. The separate books that were independently written for particular persons or situations, or with a special view and purpose in mind, all merge to form a great unified complete entity with no details lacking. They complement and complete the Bible canon and are presently of universal importance, interest, and concern primarily to spiritual Israel, which is the congregation of God, but, additionally, to all persons who seek the approval of God.

For information on the contents of the 27 books, their writers, the time written, and proof of authenticity, see the individual books by name.

CHRONICLES, THE BOOKS OF.

Two inspired books of the Hebrew Scriptures that were apparently one volume in the original Hebrew canon. The Masoretes regarded them as one single work, and they are reckoned as one book in the counts that regard the Hebrew Scriptures as made up of 22 or 24 books, and as two books in the count that regards the total number of books as 39. The division into two books seemingly originated with the translators of the Greek *Septuagint.* In Hebrew manuscripts the twofold division began in the 15th century. In the Hebrew text, Chronicles appears at the end of the section called Writings. The Hebrew name, *Div·reh′ Hai·ya·mim′,* means "The Affairs of the Days." Jerome suggested the name Chronicon, from which we get Chronicles in the English Bible. A chronicle is a record of happenings in the order in which they occurred. The Greek title (in the *Septuagint*) is *Pa·ra·lei·po·me′non,* meaning "Things Passed Over (Left Untold; Omitted)," that is, from the books of Samuel and Kings. However, it is to be noted that the Chronicles are by no means a mere supplement to those books.

Writer, Time, and Period Covered. The Jewish priest Ezra is recognized, for a number of reasons, as the writer. Jewish tradition has long held to this view. It is also supported by the striking resemblance between the writing style of Chronicles and the style of the book of Ezra. There is repetition at the close of Second Chronicles and at the beginning of Ezra that is virtually word for word. Moreover, the statement of Cyrus' decree found at the end of Second Chronicles is given in full in the book of Ezra, indicating that the writer closed the book of Chronicles with the intention of writing another book (Ezra) that would deal with the decree and its execution more fully. Chronicles was completed about 460 B.C.E. Evidently, only two books of the Hebrew canon were completed after 460 B.C.E., namely, Nehemiah and Malachi.

Aside from the genealogical lists that run from Adam, the Chronicles cover the period from the death of King Saul to the carrying away of exiles to Babylon, with a conclusion telling of Cyrus' decree at the end of the 70-year exile.

Sources. Ezra assumed that his readers were familiar with the books of Kings and therefore did not try to cover the same ground. The material he used, which in some instances reads exactly or nearly like portions of Kings, is included only in order to retain that which, by its relationship, gives meaning to the additional information in Chronicles. It may be that Ezra used the books of Samuel and Kings as well as some other parts of the Bible as sources, but it seems that in most if not all cases, he had access to writings not now known to be in existence. Some of these may have been documents of state from both Israel and Judah, genealogical records, and historical works written by prophets, also documents possessed by tribal or family heads. A portion of the sources used were no doubt the work of professional recorders.—1Ki 4:3.

Ezra names or describes as follows some of the sources he used:

(1) The Book of the Kings of Judah and of Israel (2Ch 16:11; 25:26)

(2) The Book of the Kings of Israel and of Judah (2Ch 27:7; 35:27)

(3) The Book of the Kings of Israel (2Ch 20:34) (The above-listed sources may be the same collection of state documents, with varied ways of stating the title, or could possibly refer to the books of Kings in the Bible.)

(4) The Book of the Kings of Israel (evidently a genealogical work) (1Ch 9:1)

(5) The exposition of the Book of the Kings (2Ch 24:27) (for information on Jehoash of Judah)

(6) The affairs of the kings of Israel (2Ch 33:18) (for information on Manasseh)

(7) The words of Samuel the seer and of Nathan the prophet and of Gad the visionary (1Ch 29:29) (for information on David) (This may be one work, two, or three; or it may refer to Judges and the books of Samuel.)

(8) The words of Nathan the prophet (2Ch 9:29) (for information on Solomon)

(9) The prophecy of Ahijah the Shilonite (2Ch 9:29) (about Solomon)

(10) "Shemaiah . . . wrote" (1Ch 24:6) (about David), and the words of Shemaiah the prophet and of Iddo the visionary by genealogical enrollment (2Ch 12:15) (about Rehoboam) (perhaps two or three sources)

(11) The words of Jehu the son of Hanani, which were inserted in the Book of the Kings of Israel (2Ch 20:34) (about Jehoshaphat)

(12) The rest of the affairs of Uzziah, by Isaiah the son of Amoz the prophet (2Ch 26:22)

(13) The words of (Manasseh's) visionaries (2Ch 33:19)

(14) Dirges (of Jeremiah, and possibly of singers) (2Ch 35:25) (about Josiah)

(15) The exposition of the prophet Iddo (2Ch 13:22) (about Abijah)

(16) The account of the affairs of the days of King David (1Ch 27:24)

(17) The commandment of David and of Gad and of Nathan the prophet (2Ch 29:25) (as enforced by Hezekiah)

(18) The writing of David and of Solomon his son (2Ch 35:4) (as referred to by Josiah)

(19) The commandment of David and of Asaph and of Heman and of Jeduthun the visionary of the king (2Ch 35:15) (referred to in connection with Josiah's acts)

(20) The writing of Elijah to King Jehoram of Judah (2Ch 21:12-15)

(There are also references in Chronicles to writings, particularly genealogies, that may designate other sources used by Ezra.)

It is evident that Ezra was extremely careful, doing meticulous research, going through all the documentary sources accessible to him, evidently investigating every document that would shed light on the subject. He documents his writings not merely as proof of accuracy as to what he has written but also to direct the reader of that time to other sources for more detail. Ezra's painstaking thoroughness should commend the Chronicles as worthy of our utmost confidence in their accuracy and historical authenticity. But, above all, the knowledge that Ezra wrote under inspiration (2Ti 3:16) and the fact that the Chronicles are included in the Hebrew canon, fully accepted by Jesus and the apostles (Lu 24:27, 44), ensure their reliability. Moreover, the Chronicles constitute part of the complete written Word of God, the purity of which he has guarded for the followers of his Son, Jesus Christ. These facts recommend Chronicles highly as a source of faith.

Purpose. Ezra's work was not merely to fill in what was left out by the books of Samuel and Kings; rather, he discerned among the returned exiles the need of such a summary of their national history. The work was undoubtedly prepared for those recently returned from exile, as they would be greatly lacking in knowledge of their sacred history and customs. They needed to know about temple worship and the duties of Levites, and Ezra provided this information. And to the returned exiles few things would have greater interest than their ancestral genealogies, to which Ezra devoted much attention. Israel was functioning again as a nation, in their land, with temple, priesthood, and governor, even though without a king. They would continue as a nation down to the Messiah's coming. They needed the information Chronicles provided for unity and true worship.

Both Samuel and Jeremiah were historical writers, but they were also Levites. Jeremiah was a prophet and a priest. Ezra was a priest. But it is a mistake to say that Jeremiah would be especially interested in the fulfillment of prophecies and not so interested in the matters of temple worship and that Ezra would be especially interested in Levitical work and not so interested in prophecies. Both

HIGHLIGHTS OF FIRST CHRONICLES

Genealogy and details regarding true worship at Jehovah's temple, especially needed following the exile in Babylon

Written perhaps 55 years after Zerubbabel rebuilt the temple, and before Jerusalem's walls were restored

---

Genealogies from Adam onward (1:1–9:44)

Judah's posterity through David and Solomon (vital in identifying the Messiah)

Levi's posterity (needed to identify those who could properly serve at the temple) and their various temple duties

Saul's unfaithfulness results in his death (10:1-14)

Aspects of David's rule as king (11:1–29:30)

Anointed anew as king while at Hebron; captures Zion; later made king over all Israel

Ark of covenant moved improperly, on wagon; Uzzah dies for touching Ark; Ark finally brought to the City of David amid rejoicing

David expresses desire to build a temple for Jehovah; instead, Jehovah makes covenant for royal house to time indefinite with David

Enemies of Israel are defeated on all sides

David is incited by Satan to take a census of Israel; 70,000 die

Extensive preparations made for building of the temple; David organizes the Levites, arranges 24 divisions of priests, also assigns singers, gatekeepers; gives inspired architectural plans to Solomon; David and the people contribute generously

David dies after Solomon begins to sit on "Jehovah's throne"

HIGHLIGHTS OF SECOND CHRONICLES

A vivid summary of history under kings of the royal house of David, highlighting the consequences of obedience to God and of disobedience

Originally part of one scroll with First Chronicles

The kingship of Solomon (1:1–9:31)

His wisdom, prosperity; but unwisely he acquires many horses from Egypt and has as a wife the daughter of Pharaoh

Construction of the temple; Solomon's prayer of dedication

Queen of Sheba visits

Events associated with the reign of other kings of the royal house of David, and their outcome (10:1–36:23)

Following Rehoboam's harsh reply ten tribes break away under Jeroboam and turn to calf worship; Rehoboam also leaves God's law, is abandoned to Shishak of Egypt

Because Abijah leans upon Jehovah, Judah is victorious over army of Israel that relies on superior numbers and worship of golden calves; 500,000 are slain

When Asa relies on Jehovah, a million invading Ethiopians are defeated; Asa foolishly makes alliance with Syria and gets incensed over rebuke from Jehovah's prophet

Jehoshaphat institutes program of education in God's law; unwisely makes marriage alliance with Ahab

Moab, Ammon, Seir invade Judah; Jehoshaphat turns to Jehovah for help; reminded, 'The battle is God's!'

Jehoram (whose wife is daughter of Ahab and Jezebel) acts wickedly, as does his son Ahaziah; then murderous Athaliah, Jehoram's widow, usurps the throne

Jehoash starts out well under High Priest Jehoiada's influence; later becomes apostate and orders stoning of faithful Zechariah

Amaziah begins well, then worships idols of Seir; defeated by Israel, assassinated

Uzziah also begins well; later haughtily attempts to offer incense in temple, is smitten with leprosy

Jotham does right, but people act ruinously

Ahaz turns to Baal worship; nation suffers severely

Hezekiah cleans up temple; Sennacherib invades Judah, taunts Jehovah; Hezekiah relies on Jehovah; 185,000 Assyrians slain by angel

Manasseh practices gross idolatry and sheds much innocent blood; taken captive by Assyrians; repents, is restored by Jehovah to his throne

Amon follows bad example of his father Manasseh; does not humble himself

Josiah conducts zealous religious reform, repairs temple; insists on fighting Pharaoh Necho and is killed

Jehoahaz rules briefly, then is taken captive to Egypt

Jehoiakim acts detestably; son and successor Jehoiachin is taken captive to Babylon

Zedekiah rebels against Babylon's yoke; Jews are carried into exile; land desolate 70 years

Cyrus of Persia issues decree liberating Jews for return to Jerusalem to rebuild the temple

---

of them were servants of God and had concern for his words, his dealings with his people, and every feature of his worship. The fact is that Ezra was inspired by Jehovah to produce the books of Chronicles and Ezra for a special purpose.

The Jews who returned from Babylon in 537 B.C.E. did so, not to establish political independence, but to restore true worship, the first work being to erect the altar and then to rebuild the temple. It was appropriate, therefore, that much be said by Ezra concerning worship and the services of the priesthood and the Levites. Also, the genealogies were important. Ezra 2:59-63 shows that some, including certain sons of the priests, were unable to find their register to establish their genealogy publicly. While in Babylon these genealogies might not have been so important, but now they were the means of regaining possession of the heritage of their fathers. This is one of the reasons for the lists of genealogies compiled by Ezra, which are also of great value to Bible students today.

Thus we see that Ezra in writing Chronicles wished to strengthen his contemporaries in fidelity to Jehovah. He encouraged them to fulfill their covenant duties by focusing on the past history of Israel, and particularly by the use of actual historical examples he emphasized the results of faithful adherence to true worship on the one hand and, on the other hand, the calamity of forsaking the worship of Jehovah God.

Value of the Books. It is a fine thing for our faith and understanding of the Bible that the books of Chronicles were written. Ezra has added much concerning the temple worship and the arrangements of the priests, Levites, doorkeepers, singers, and musicians. He has given us many details that bear on true worship: the bringing of the Ark to Jerusalem by David (1Ch chaps 15, 16); David's preparations for the temple and its service (1Ch chaps 22–29); the fact that the priests stayed with Rehoboam at the time of the secession of the ten tribes (2Ch 11:13-17); the war between Abijah and Jeroboam (2Ch 13); the reforms in favor of true religion under Asa (2Ch chaps 14, 15), Jehoshaphat (2Ch chaps 17, 19, 20), Hezekiah (2Ch chaps 29–31), and Josiah (2Ch chaps 34, 35); Uzziah's being stricken with leprosy for his presumptuousness (2Ch 26:16-21); and Manasseh's repentance (2Ch 33:10-20).

Ezra shows that he is interested not only in priestly affairs but also in the prophets. (2Ch 20: 20; 36:12, 16) He uses the words "prophet," "seer," or "visionary" about 45 times and gives added information on many prophets and persons whose names are not otherwise mentioned in the Scriptures. A few are Iddo, Eliezer the son of Dodavahu, Jahaziel the son of Zechariah, a number of people named Zechariah, and Oded of the time of King Ahaz of Judah.

There is much information in Chronicles that helps to round out our knowledge of the history of Judah, for example, the record of the sickness and burial of Asa and of the bad conduct of Jehoash after Jehoiada the high priest died. Then there are the genealogies that are vital in establishing the lineage of Christ. The books are also of assistance in establishing an accurate chronology. Here we can see the wisdom of Jehovah, the Author of the Bible, in having his servant Ezra write these things to fill in that which is necessary so that believers in the Bible have the most complete and harmonious record of man's history.

CHRONOLOGY.

The English word "chronology" comes from the Greek *khro·no·lo·gi'a* (from *khro'nos,* time, and *le'go,* say or tell), that is, "the computation of time." Chronology makes possible the placing of events in their orderly sequence or association and the assigning of proper dates to particular events.

Jehovah is "the Ancient of Days" and the God of Eternity. (Da 7:9; Ps 90:2; 93:2) That he is an accurate Timekeeper is evident not only from the superb precision manifest in the movements of the stellar bodies but also from the divine record of his acts. In fulfillment of his promises or prophecies, he caused events to occur at the exact time foretold, whether the intervening time was of only a day (Ex 9:5, 6), a year (Ge 17:21; 18:14; 21:1, 2; 2Ki 4:16, 17), decades (Nu 14:34; 2Ch 36:20-23; Da 9:2), centuries (Ge 12:4, 7; 15:13-16; Ex 12: 40, 41; Ga 3:17), or millenniums (Lu 21:24; see APPOINTED TIMES OF THE NATIONS). We are assured that his purposes for the future are certain of execution at the predetermined time, right down to the day and hour designated.—Hab 2:3; Mt 24:36.

God purposed that man, made in his Creator's image and likeness (Ge 1:26), should measure the flow of time. The Bible early states that the "luminaries in the expanse of the heavens" were to serve in making "a division between the day and the night; and . . . as signs and for seasons and for days and years." (Ge 1:14, 15; Ps 104:19) (A discussion of the way in which these divisions have been observed since the beginning of man's history may be found in the articles CALENDAR; DAY; MOON; WEEK; YEAR.) Human reckoning and recording of time periods has continued from Adam's day till the present hour.—Ge 5:1, 3-5.

Eras. Accurate chronology requires that some point in the stream of time be set as the marker from which to count either forward or backward in time units (such as hours, days, months, years). That starting point could be simply the sunrise (for measuring the hours of a day), or a new moon (for measuring the days of a month), or the start of the spring season (for measuring the span of a year). For counting longer periods, men have resorted to the establishing of a particular "era," using some outstanding event as their starting point from which to measure periods of many years. Thus, in nations of Christendom, when a person says that 'today is October 1, 1987 C.E. (Common Era),' he means that 'today is the first day of the tenth month of the one thousand nine hundred and eighty-seventh year counting from what was believed by some to be the time of the birth of Jesus.'

Such use of an era in secular history is of rather late inception. The Greek era, supposedly the earliest secular case of such chronological reckoning, apparently was not put into practice until about the fourth century B.C.E. (Before the Common Era). The Greeks figured time by means of four-year periods called Olympiads, starting from the first Olympiad, calculated as beginning in 776 B.C.E. Additionally, they often identified specific years by referring to the term of office of some particular official. The Romans eventually established an era, reckoning the years from the traditional date of the founding of the city of Rome (753 B.C.E.). They also designated specific years by reference to the names of two consuls holding office in that year. It was not until the sixth century C.E. that a monk named Dionysius Exiguus calculated what is now popularly known as the Christian Era, or, more correctly, the Common Era. Among the Muhammadan (Islamic) peoples the years are dated from the Hegira (Muhammad's flight from Mecca in 622 C.E.). The early Egyptians, Assyrians, and Babylonians, however, give no evidence of having used such an era system consistently over any considerable period of time.

As to the Biblical record, no one era arrangement is expressly set forth as the starting point by which all events are thereafter dated. This of itself does not mean that a timetable did not exist for assigning to past events their specific and correct location in the stream of time. The fact that the Bible writers, when relating particular events, could cite precise figures involving periods of several centuries demonstrates that chronological interest was not lacking among the people of Israel or their ancestors. Thus, Moses could write that "it came about at the end of the four hundred and thirty years [counting here from the time when Abraham crossed the Euphrates on his way to the land of Canaan, at which time, evidently, God validated the covenant with Abraham], it even came about on this very day that all the armies of Jehovah went out of the land of Egypt." (Ex 12: 41; see EXODUS; compare Ga 3:16, 17.) Again, at 1 Kings 6:1, the record states that it was "in the four hundred and eightieth year after the sons of Israel came out from the land of Egypt" that King Solomon began to construct the temple at Jerusalem. Still, neither the validating of the Abrahamic covenant nor the Exodus came to be commonly used as the start of an era in recording other events.

Chronological factors in the Bible, therefore, should not be expected to conform exactly to modern systems whereby all events are mathematically dated in relation to one fixed point in the past, such as the start of the Common Era. More often, events were located in the stream of time in much the same way as people do naturally in everyday life. Just as today one might fix an event by saying it took place "the year after the drought," or "five years after World War II," so the Bible writers related the events they recorded to relatively current time markers.

A definite conclusion cannot be reached for some chronological points, since we do not always know precisely the starting point or time marker used by the Bible writer. Then, too, a writer might use more than one such starting point to date events during the course of treating a certain historical period. This variation in starting points does not imply vagueness or confusion on the part of the writer; we cannot properly judge his methods simply on the basis of our own opinion as to the proper way of recording events based on present-day procedures. And while copyists' errors could be involved in some of the more difficult points, it is not wise to assume these where no

sound evidence exists in the form of variant readings in ancient manuscript copies of the Scriptures. The available evidence convincingly demonstrates the remarkable accuracy and care that distinguished the copying of the Bible books, resulting in the preservation of their internal integrity.—See MANUSCRIPTS OF THE BIBLE; SCRIBE.

Bible Chronology and Secular History. Concern is often expressed over the need to try to "harmonize" or "reconcile" the Biblical account with the chronology found in ancient secular records. Since truth is that which conforms to fact or reality, such coordinating would indeed be vital —*if* the ancient secular records could be demonstrated to be unequivocally exact and consistently reliable, hence a standard of accuracy by which to judge. Since the Biblical chronology has so often been represented by critics as inferior to that of the pagan nations, it is worth while to examine some of the ancient records of nations and peoples whose activities and life touch on and connect with the people and events recorded in the Bible.

The Bible is a historical book, preeminently so among ancient writings. The histories of the ancient Egyptians, Assyrians, Babylonians, Medes, Persians, and others are, in the main, fragmentary; their earlier periods are either obscure or, as presented by them, obviously mythical. Thus, the ancient document known as The Sumerian King List begins: "When kingship was lowered from heaven, kingship was (first) in Eridu. (In) Eridu, A-lulim (became) king and ruled 28,800 years. Alalgar ruled 36,000 years. Two kings (thus) ruled it for 64,800 years. . . . (In) Bad-tibira, En-men-lu-Anna ruled 43,200 years; En-men-gal-Anna ruled 28,800 years; the god Dumu-zi, a shepherd, ruled 36,000 years. Three kings (thus) ruled it for 108,-000 years."—*Ancient Near Eastern Texts*, edited by J. B. Pritchard, 1974, p. 265.

What is known from secular sources of these ancient nations has been laboriously pieced together from bits of information obtained from monuments and tablets or from the later writings of the so-called classical historiographers of the Greek and Roman period. While archaeologists have recovered tens of thousands of clay tablets bearing Assyro-Babylonian cuneiform inscriptions, as well as large numbers of papyrus scrolls from Egypt, the vast majority of these are religious texts or business documents consisting of contracts, bills of sale, deeds, and similar matter. The considerably smaller number of *historical* writings of the pagan nations, preserved either in the form of tablets, cylinders, steles, or monumental inscriptions, consist chiefly of material glorifying their emperors and recounting their military campaigns in grandiose terms.

The Bible, by contrast, gives an unusually coherent and detailed history stretching through some 4,000 years, for not only does it record events with remarkable continuity from man's beginning down to the time of Nehemiah's governorship in the fifth century B.C.E. but also it may be considered as providing a basic coverage of the period between Nehemiah and the time of Jesus and his apostles by means of Daniel's prophecy (history written in advance) at Daniel chapter 11. The Bible presents a graphic and true-to-life account of the nation of Israel from its birth onward, portraying with candor its strength and its weaknesses, its successes and its failures, its right worship and its false worship, its blessings and its adverse judgments and calamities. While this honesty alone does not ensure accurate chronology, it does give sound basis for confidence in the integrity of the Biblical writers and their sincere concern for recording truth.

Detailed records were manifestly available to Bible chroniclers, such as the writers of First and Second Kings and of First and Second Chronicles. This is seen by the lengthy genealogies they were able to compile, amounting to many hundreds of names; also the connected and factual presentation of the reigns of each of the kings of Judah and Israel, including their relations with other nations and with one another. Modern historians still express uncertainty as to the correct positioning of certain Assyrian and Babylonian kings, even some in the later dynasties. But there is no such uncertainty regarding the sequence of the kings of Judah and Israel.

There are references to "the book of the Wars of Jehovah" (Nu 21:14, 15), "the book of the affairs of the days of the kings of Israel" (1Ki 14:19; 2Ki 15:31), "the book of the affairs of the days of the kings of Judah" (1Ki 15:23; 2Ki 24:5), "the book of the affairs of Solomon" (1Ki 11:41), as well as the numerous references to similar annals or official records cited by Ezra and Nehemiah. These show that the information set down was not based upon mere remembrance or oral tradition but was carefully researched and fully documented. Governmental records of other nations are also cited by the Biblical historians, even as some portions of the Bible were written in lands outside of Israel, including Egypt, Babylon, and Persia.—See BOOK; ESTHER, BOOK OF; EZRA, BOOK OF.

A factor that doubtless contributed toward an accurate count of the passage of years, at least to the extent that the Israelites faithfully kept the Mosaic Law, was their observance of sabbatical years and Jubilee years, thereby dividing the time up into 7-year and 50-year periods.—Le 25:2-5, 8-16, 25-31.

Particularly distinguishing the Biblical record from the contemporaneous writings of the pagan nations is the sense of time, not only of the past and the present but also of the future, that runs through its pages. (Da 2:28; 7:22; 8:18, 19; Mr 1:15; Re 22:10) The unique prophetic element made chronological accuracy a matter of far greater importance to the Israelites than to any of the pagan nations because the prophecies often involved specific time periods. As God's Book, the Bible stresses his punctuality in carrying out his word (Eze 12:27, 28; Ga 4:4) and shows that accurate prophecies were proof of his Godship. —Isa 41:21-26; 48:3-7.

True, some of the non-Biblical documents are several centuries older than the oldest manuscript copies of the Bible thus far discovered. Engraved in stone or inscribed in clay, some ancient pagan documents may seem very impressive, but this does not ensure their correctness and their freedom from falsehood. Not the material written on, but the writer, his purpose, his respect for truth, his devotion to righteous principles—these are the important factors that give sound basis for confidence, in chronological as well as other matters. The great age of the secular documents is certainly outweighed by the vastly inferior quality of their contents when compared with the Bible. Because the Bible records were evidently made on perishable materials, such as papyrus and vellum, their continued use and the deteriorating effect of weather conditions in much of Israel (different from the extraordinarily dry climate of Egypt) may well explain the absence of extant original copies today. Yet, because it is Jehovah's inspired Book, the Bible has been carefully copied and preserved in full form until today. (1Pe 1:24, 25) Divine inspiration, by which the Bible historians were able to set down their records, assures the reliability of Bible chronology.—2Pe 1:19-21.

Well illustrating why secular histories do not qualify as the standard of accuracy by which to judge Bible chronology is this statement by archaeological writer C. W. Ceram, commenting on the modern science of historical dating: "Anyone approaching the study of ancient history for the first time must be impressed by the positive way modern historians date events which took place thousands of years ago. In the course of further study this wonder will, if anything, increase. For as we examine the sources of ancient history we see how scanty, inaccurate, or downright false, the records were even at the time they were first written. And poor as they originally were, they are poorer still as they have come down to us: half destroyed by the tooth of time or by the carelessness and rough usage of men." He further describes the framework of chronological history as "a purely hypothetical structure, and one which threatens to come apart at every joint."—*The Secret of the Hittites,* 1956, pp. 133, 134.

This evaluation may seem extreme, but as regards the secular records, it is not without basis. The information that follows will make clear why there is no reason to feel doubt about the accuracy of the Biblical chronology simply because certain secular records are at variance with it. On the contrary, it is only when the secular chronology harmonizes with the Biblical record that a person may rightly feel a measure of confidence in such ancient secular dating. When considering the records of these pagan nations that had relations with the nation of Israel, it should be kept in mind that some of the apparent discrepancies in their records may simply be due to the inability of modern historians to interpret correctly the methods anciently used, similar to their inability to interpret correctly the methods used by the Biblical historians. There is, however, considerable evidence of definite carelessness and inaccuracy or even of deliberate falsification on the part of the pagan historians and chronologers.

Egyptian Chronology. Egyptian history meshes with that of Israel at various points. In this publication we show the date 1728 B.C.E. for Israel's entry into Egypt, and for the Exodus, 215 years later, 1513 B.C.E. Pharaoh Shishak's attack on Jerusalem came during Rehoboam's fifth year in 993 B.C.E.; King So of Egypt was contemporary with Hoshea's reign (c. 758-740 B.C.E.); and Pharaoh Necho's battle resulting in Josiah's death likely came in 629 B.C.E. (1Ki 14:25; 2Ki 17:4; 2Ch 35:20-24) The difference between the above dates and those generally assigned by modern historians amounts to as much as a century or more for the Exodus and then narrows down to about 20 years by Pharaoh Necho's time. The following information shows why we prefer to hold to the chronology based on the Biblical reckoning.

Modern historians rely principally on certain documents in the form of Egyptian king lists or annals. Among these are: the fragmentary Palermo Stone, presenting what are considered to be the first five "dynasties" of Egyptian history; the Turin Papyrus, very fragmentary and giving a list of kings and their reigns from the "Old Kingdom" into the "New Kingdom"; and additional inscrip

tions in stone, likewise fragmentary. These separate lists and other independent inscriptions have been coordinated in chronological order by means of the writings of Manetho, an Egyptian priest of the third century B.C.E. His works, dealing with Egyptian history and religion, arrange the reigns of the Egyptian monarchs into 30 dynasties, an arrangement still used by modern Egyptologists. These sources, together with astronomical calculations, based on Egyptian texts dealing with lunar phases and the rising of the Dog Star (Sothis), have been used to produce a chronological table.

Problems of Egyptian chronology. Uncertainties are multiple. The works of Manetho, used to give order to the fragmentary lists and other inscriptions, are preserved only in the writings of later historians, such as Josephus (first century C.E.), Sextus Julius Africanus (third century C.E., hence over 500 years from Manetho's time), Eusebius (fourth century C.E.), and Syncellus (late eighth or early ninth century C.E.). As stated by W. G. Waddell, their quotations of Manetho's writings are fragmentary and often distorted and hence "it is extremely difficult to reach certainty in regard to what is authentic Manetho and what is spurious or corrupt." After showing that Manetho's source material included some unhistorical traditions and legends that "introduced kings as their heroes, without regard to chronological order," he says: "There were many errors in Manetho's work from the very beginning: all are not due to the perversions of scribes and revisers. Many of the lengths of reigns have been found impossible: in some cases the names and the sequence of kings as given by Manetho have proved untenable in the light of monumental evidence." —*Manetho,* introduction, pp. vii, xvii, xx, xxi, xxv.

The probability that *concurrent* reigns rather than *successive* reigns are responsible for many of Manetho's excessively long periods is shown in the book *Studies in Egyptian Chronology,* by T. Nicklin (Blackburn, Eng., 1928, p. 39): "The Manethonian Dynasties . . . are not lists of rulers over all Egypt, but lists partly of more or less independent princes, partly . . . of princely lines from which later sprang rulers over all Egypt." Professor Waddell (pp. 1-9) observes that "perhaps several Egyptian kings ruled at one and the same time; . . . thus it was not a succession of kings occupying the throne one after the other, but several kings reigning at the same time in different regions. Hence arose the great total number of years."

Since the Bible points to the year 2370 B.C.E. as the date of the global Flood, Egyptian history must have begun after that date. The problems in Egyptian chronology shown above are doubtless responsible for the figures advanced by modern historians who would run Egyptian history all the way back to the year 3000 B.C.E.

Greater confidence is placed by Egyptologists in the ancient inscriptions themselves. Yet, the carefulness, truthfulness, and moral integrity of the Egyptian scribes are by no means above suspicion. As Professor J. A. Wilson states: "A warning should be issued about the precise historical value of Egyptian inscriptions. That was a world of . . . divine myths and miracles." Then after suggesting that the scribes were not above juggling the chronology of events to add praise to the particular monarch in power, he says: "The historian will accept his data at face value, unless there is a clear reason for distrust; but he must be ready to modify his acceptance as soon as new materials put the previous interpretation in a new light."—*The World History of the Jewish People,* 1964, Vol. 1, pp. 280, 281.

Absence of information concerning Israel. This is not surprising, since the Egyptians not only refused to record matters uncomplimentary to themselves but also were not above effacing records of a previous monarch if the information in such records proved distasteful to the then reigning pharaoh. Thus, after the death of Queen Hatshepsut, Thutmose III had her name and representations chiseled out of the monumental reliefs. This practice doubtless explains why there is no known Egyptian record of the 215 years of Israelite residence in Egypt or of their Exodus.

The pharaoh ruling at the time of the Exodus is not named in the Bible; hence, efforts to identify him are based on conjecture. This partly explains why modern historians' calculations of the date of the Exodus vary from 1441 to 1225 B.C.E., a difference of over 200 years.

Assyrian Chronology. From the time of Shalmaneser III (early part of first millennium B.C.E.), Assyrian inscriptions mention contacts with the Israelites, at times naming certain kings of Judah and of Israel. The Assyrian inscriptions include display inscriptions, such as are found on the walls of palaces; royal annals; king lists, such as that from Khorsabad; and the limmu, or eponym, lists.

Assyrian display inscriptions and annals. Albert Olmstead, in his *Assyrian Historiography* (1916, pp. 5, 6), described the Assyrian display inscriptions as follows: "We may . . . use the Display inscription to fill gaps in the Annals [royal chronicles listing events annually], but it has not the slightest authority when it disagrees with its original." After showing that the main purpose of these display inscriptions was not the giving of a connected history of the reign, he adds: "Equally serious is it that they rarely have a chronological order. . . . That they are to be used with caution is obvious."

Of the annals, he says: "We have here a regular chronology, and if errors, intentional or otherwise, can sometimes be found, the relative chronology at least is generally correct. . . . But it would be a great mistake to assume that the annals are always trustworthy. Earlier historians have too generally accepted their statements unless they had definite proof of inaccuracy. In the last few years, there has been discovered a mass of new material which we may use for the criticism of the Sargonide documents. . . . Add to this the references in foreign sources such as Hebrew or Babylonian, and we hardly need internal study to convince us that the annals are far from reliable."

To this may be added the testimony of D. D. Luckenbill: "One soon discovers that the accurate portrayal of events as they took place, year by year during the king's reign, was not the guiding motive of the royal scribes. At times the different campaigns seem to have been shifted about without any apparent reason, but more often it is clear that royal vanity demanded playing fast and loose with historical accuracy."—*Ancient Records of Assyria and Babylonia,* 1926, Vol. I, p. 7.

The royal annals usually went through a series of editions as the king's reign progressed. Later editions presented new events, but they also seem to have juggled the facts and figures of the previous years to suit the king's fancy. Professor Olmstead makes reference to the "cool taking by [Ashurbanipal] of bit after bit of the last two Egyptian campaigns of his father until in the final edition there is nothing that he has not claimed for himself."—*Assyrian Historiography,* p. 7.

Examples of such evident unreliability, deliberate or otherwise, could be multiplied many times over. The compilers of tribute lists were not above listing a vassal king as paying tribute even though other records showed him to be dead at the time. George Smith, after citing an instance where the same tribute list of Esar-haddon is credited to his son Ashurbanipal 13 years later, says that this later list is "most probably a literal copy of the earlier document, without any attempt to ascertain if these kings were still reigning, and if they really paid tribute."—*The Assyrian Eponym Canon,* London, 1875, p. 179.

Eponym (limmu) lists. Despite the above evidence, modern chronologers generally hold that the eponym, or limmu, lists somehow escaped any such corruption so as to be virtually impeccable in their freedom from error. These eponym lists are simply lists of officials' names and ranks or lists of such names accompanied by some brief mention of a warring campaign or other noteworthy event. For example, one section of the eponym list reads:

Bel-harran-bel-usur	(governor) of Guzana	against Damascus
	Shalmaneser	took his seat on the throne
Marduk-bel-usur	(governor) of Amedi	in the land
Mahde	(governor) of Nineveh	against [Samaria]
Assur-ishmeani	(governor) of [Kakzi]	against [Samaria]
Shalmaneser	king of Assyria	against [Samaria]

From this it can be seen that no actual dates are given, but it is considered that each name represents a year, thereby apparently allowing for a year-by-year count. Modern historians endeavor to synchronize Assyrian and Biblical history by means of these eponym lists, particularly for the period from 911 to 649 B.C.E., to which they assign the names or eponyms on the lists. For a pivotal point, they rely on the reference to an eclipse of the sun mentioned in an entry opposite the name of a certain Bur-Sagale, governor of Guzana. The eclipse was in the month of Sivan (May-June) and historians generally fix it as taking place on June 15, 763 B.C.E. The reliability of this date, and the synchronization of Assyrian history with that of Judah and Israel that they based on it, will be discussed later under the heading "Astronomical Calculations."

Because of the extremely reduced amount of information involved in the eponym lists (as compared with the annals and other inscriptions), it is obvious that the means for discovering error is considerably diminished. When apparent contradictions are found between the eponym lists and the annals, such as the placing of a certain campaign in a different year of a king's reign or during a different eponymy, the modern historians usually charge the error to the annals rather than to the eponym lists. Yet, even with regard to the so-called Assyrian synchronistic history, a famous tablet containing a terse account of the relations between Assyria and Babylonia during a period of centuries, no such claim for positive accuracy is made. A. T. Olmstead, after presenting evidence to show that this document is only a copy of an earlier display inscription, says: "So we can consider our document not even a history in the true sense of the word, merely an inscription erected to the glory of Ashur [Assyria's chief god] and of his people . . . When we take this view, we are no longer troubled by the numerous mistakes, even to the order of the kings, which so greatly reduce the value of the document where its testimony is most needed."—*Assyrian Historiography,* p. 32.

It should be clear that such variable arrangement as is apparent in the eponym lists would make it extremely difficult for modern scholars to arrive at an exact chronology, especially when the compilation of data covering several centuries was done by scribes to whom care and historical accuracy apparently meant so little. It is also evident that the modern historians feel justified in adjusting or overruling the count of the Assyrian eponym lists when other factors or evidence make such action advisable.

The information above points to the conclusion that Assyrian historiography either is not correctly understood by modern historians or is of very low caliber. In either case, we do not feel compelled to attempt to coordinate the Biblical chronology with history as presented in the Assyrian records. Therefore, we show only the more definite synchronisms between Assyria and Israel and Judah as indicated in the Bible account.

Babylonian Chronology. Babylon enters the Biblical picture principally from the time of Nebuchadnezzar II onward. The reign of Nebuchadnezzar's father Nabopolassar marked the start of what is called the Neo-Babylonian Empire; it ended with the reigns of Nabonidus and his son Belshazzar and the overthrow of Babylon by Cyrus the Persian. This period is of great interest to Bible scholars since it embraces the time of the Babylonian destruction of Jerusalem and the greater part of the 70-year period of Jewish exile.

Jeremiah 52:28 says that in the seventh year of Nebuchadnezzar (or Nebuchadrezzar) the first group of Jewish exiles was taken to Babylon. In harmony with this, a cuneiform inscription of the Babylonian Chronicle (British Museum 21946) states: "The seventh year: In the month Kislev the king of Akkad mustered his army and marched to Hattu. He encamped against the city of Judah and on the second day of the month Adar he captured the city (and) seized (its) king [Jehoiachin]. A king of his own choice [Zedekiah] he appointed in the city (and) taking the vast tribute he brought it into Babylon." (*Assyrian and Babylonian Chronicles,* by A. K. Grayson, 1975, p. 102; compare 2Ki 24:

1-17; 2Ch 36:5-10.) (PICTURE, Vol. 2, p. 326) For the final 32 years of Nebuchadnezzar's reign, there are no historical records of the chronicle type except a fragmentary inscription of a campaign against Egypt in Nebuchadnezzar's 37th year.

For Awil-Marduk (Evil-merodach, 2Ki 25:27, 28), tablets dated up to his second year of rule have been found. For Neriglissar, considered to be the successor of Awil-Marduk, contract tablets are known dated to his fourth year.

A Babylonian clay tablet is helpful for connecting Babylonian chronology with Biblical chronology. This tablet contains the following astronomical information for the seventh year of Cambyses II son of Cyrus II: "Year 7, Tammuz, night of the 14th, $1\frac{2}{3}$ double hours [three hours and twenty minutes] after night came, a lunar eclipse; visible in its full course; it reached over the northern half disc [of the moon]. Tebet, night of the 14th, two and a half double hours [five hours] at night before morning [in the latter part of the night], the disc of the moon was eclipsed; the whole course visible; over the southern and northern part the eclipse reached." (*Inschriften von Cambyses, König von Babylon*, by J. N. Strassmaier, Leipzig, 1890, No. 400, lines 45-48; *Sternkunde und Sterndienst in Babel*, by F. X. Kugler, Münster, 1907, Vol. I, pp. 70, 71) These two lunar eclipses can be identified with the lunar eclipses that were visible at Babylon on July 16, 523 B.C.E., and on January 10, 522 B.C.E. (Oppolzer's *Canon of Eclipses*, translated by O. Gingerich, 1962, p. 335) Thus, this tablet establishes the seventh year of Cambyses II as beginning in the spring of 523 B.C.E. This is an astronomically confirmed date.

Since the seventh year of Cambyses II began in spring of 523 B.C.E., his first year of rule was 529 B.C.E. and his accession year, and the last year of Cyrus II as king of Babylon, was 530 B.C.E. The latest tablet dated in the reign of Cyrus II is from the 5th month, 23rd day of his 9th year. (*Babylonian Chronology, 626 B.C.–A.D. 75*, by R. Parker and W. Dubberstein, 1971, p. 14) As the ninth year of Cyrus II as king of Babylon was 530 B.C.E., his first year according to that reckoning was 538 B.C.E. and his accession year was 539 B.C.E.

Berossus. In the third century B.C.E. Berossus, a Babylonian priest, wrote a history of Babylon in the Greek language, evidently based on cuneiform records. Of his writings, Professor Olmstead said: "Only the merest fragments, abstracts, or traces, have come down to us. And the most important of these fragments have come down through a tradition almost without parallel. Today we must consult a modern Latin translation of an Armenian translation of the lost Greek original of the Chronicle of Eusebius, who borrowed in part from Alexander Polyhistor who borrowed from Berossus direct, in part from Abydenus who apparently borrowed from Juba who borrowed from Alexander Polyhistor and so from Berossus. To make a worse confusion, Eusebius has in some cases not recognized the fact that Abydenus is only a feeble echo of Polyhistor, and has quoted the accounts of each side by side! And this is not the worst. Although his Polyhistor account is in general to be preferred, Eusebius seems to have used a poor manuscript of that author." (*Assyrian Historiography*, pp. 62, 63) Josephus, Jewish historian of the first century C.E., also claims that he quotes from Berossus. But it seems evident that chronological data supposedly from Berossus could hardly be considered conclusive.

Other factors allowing for differences. Casual students of ancient history often labor under the misconception that the cuneiform tablets (such as may have been used by Berossus) were always written at the same time or shortly after the events recorded on them. But, aside from the many cuneiform business documents that were truly contemporary, the Babylonian historical texts and even many astronomical texts often give evidence of being of a much later period. Thus, according to Assyriologist D. J. Wiseman, one portion of the so-called Babylonian Chronicle, covering the period from the rule of Nabu-nasir to Shamash-shum-u-kin (a period dated by secular historians as from 747-648 B.C.E.), is "a copy made in the twenty-second year of Darius [footnote says: I.e. 500/499 B.C. if Darius I] from an older and damaged text." (*Chronicles of Chaldaean Kings*, London, 1956, p. 1) So, not only was this writing separated from the events recorded on it by anywhere from 150 to 250 years but it was also a copy of a defective earlier document, perhaps an original, perhaps not. Of the Neo-Babylonian Chronicle texts, covering the period from Nabopolassar to Nabonidus, the same author states: "The Neo-Babylonian Chronicle texts are written in a small script of a type which does not of itself allow any precise dating but which can mean that they were written from any time almost contemporary with the events themselves to the end of the Achaemenid rule." This allows for the possibility that they were written as late as the close of the Persian Empire, which occurred in 331 B.C.E. some 200 years after the fall of Babylon. We have already seen that data, including numbers, can easily suffer change and even perversion at the hands of pagan scribes in the course of a few centuries. In view of all these factors it is certainly not wise to insist that the traditional figures for the reigns of the Neo-Babylonian kings be received as definite.

Both the lack of contemporary historical records and the ease with which data could be altered definitely allow for the possibility that one or more of the Neo-Babylonian rulers had a longer reign than the traditional figures show. The fact that no tablets have been discovered that would cover the later years of such reign cannot consistently be used as a strong argument against this possibility. There are cases of kings whose reigns come much farther along in the stream of time and for whom no such confirming tablets have been found. For example, for both Artaxerxes III (Ochus) (who, historians say, ruled for 21 years [358 to 338 B.C.E.]) and Arses (credited with a 2-year rule [337 to 336 B.C.E.]) there is no known contemporary cuneiform evidence to help establish the length of their reigns.

In reality, historians do not know where to place certain Babylonian kings for whom records do exist. Professor A. W. Ahl (*Outline of Persian History*, 1922, p. 84) states: "On the Contract Tablets, found in Borsippa, appear the names of Babylonian kings which do not occur elsewhere. In all probability they belong to the last days of Darius I, extending into the first days of Xerxes I, as Ungnad conjectures." Still, this remains only conjecture.

Persian Chronology. A number of important Biblical events took place during the Persian period: the fall of Babylon, followed by Cyrus' release of the Jews and the end of the 70-year desolation of Judah; the reconstruction of the temple at Jerusalem, completed "in the sixth year of the reign of Darius [I, Persian]"; and the rebuilding of Jerusalem's walls by Nehemiah, according to the decree given in the 20th year of Artaxerxes Longimanus. —2Ch 36:20-23; Ezr 3:8-10; 4:23, 24; 6:14, 15; Ne 2:1, 7, 8.

The date of 539 B.C.E. for the fall of Babylon can be arrived at not only by Ptolemy's canon but by other sources as well. The historian Diodorus, as well as Africanus and Eusebius, shows that Cyrus' first year as king of Persia corresponded to Olympiad 55, year 1 (560/559 B.C.E.), while Cyrus' last year is placed at Olympiad 62, year 2 (531/530 B.C.E.). Cuneiform tablets give Cyrus a rule of nine years over Babylon, which would therefore substantiate the year 539 as the date of his conquest of Babylon.—*Handbook of Biblical Chronology*, by Jack Finegan, 1964, pp. 112, 168-170; *Babylonian Chronology, 626 B.C.–*

A.D. 75, p. 14; see comments above under "Babylonian Chronology," also PERSIA, PERSIANS.

Several inscriptions of Persian kings have come down to us, yet they are not useful for establishing the length of the reigns of Persian kings. For example, a number of dated tablets were found at Persepolis, but the names of the kings are not included.

Astronomical Calculations. The claim is made that "astronomical confirmations can convert a relative chronology [one that merely establishes the sequence of events] into an absolute chronology, specifically, a system of dates related to our calendar." (*The Old Testament World*, by Martin Noth, 1966, p. 272) While the celestial bodies are the means provided by man's Creator for human measurement of time, nevertheless the correlation of astronomical data with human events in the past is subject to various factors and human interpretation allowing for error.

Many of the so-called synchronizations of astronomical data with events or dates of ancient history are based on solar or lunar eclipses. However, any "particular town or city would on the average experience about 40 lunar eclipses and 20 partial solar eclipses in 50 years, [although] only one total solar eclipse in 400 years." (*Encyclopædia Britannica*, 1971, Vol. 7, p. 907) So, only in the case of a *definitely stated total* solar eclipse visible in a *specific area* would there be little reason for doubt in the fixing of a particular historical date by such means. In many cases the material from the ancient cuneiform texts (or other sources) concerning eclipses does not provide such specific information.

An example is the solar eclipse relied upon by historians to correlate Assyrian chronology with Biblical chronology. It is mentioned in the Assyrian eponym lists as taking place in the third month (counting from the spring) during the eponymy of Bur-Sagale. Modern chronologists calculate it to be the eclipse occurring on June 15, 763 B.C.E. Counting back 90 years (or 90 names on the eponym lists) from this date, they arrive at 853 B.C.E. as the date for the battle of Karkar in Shalmaneser III's sixth year. They claim that Shalmaneser lists King Ahab of Israel as in the enemy coalition facing Assyria in that battle, and that 12 years afterward (Shalmaneser's 18th year) the Assyrian king refers to King Jehu of Israel as paying tribute. They then deduce that the year 853 B.C.E. marked the date of Ahab's last year and 841 B.C.E. the start of Jehu's reign. How sound are these calculations?

First, though it is assumed that the solar eclipse was total, the eponym list does not state this. And, whereas most historians today would apply this reference to the eclipse of 763 B.C.E., not all scholars have done so, some preferring the year 809 B.C.E., during which year an eclipse occurred that would have been at least partially visible in Assyria (as was also the case in 857 and 817 B.C.E., etc.). (Oppolzer's *Canon of Eclipses*, charts 17, 19, 21) Though modern historians object to any change from the solar eclipse of 763 B.C.E. on the grounds that it would 'introduce confusion into Assyrian history,' we have already seen that the Assyrians themselves introduced considerable confusion into their own history.

Moreover, the presence of King Ahab at the battle of Karkar is very unlikely. Thus, even if the reigns of Ahaziah and Jehoram (which intervened between Ahab and Jehu) could be reduced to just 12 years (compare 1Ki 22:40, 51; 2Ki 1:2, 17; 3:1), the evidence is against any precise synchronization of the battle of Karkar with Ahab. Shalmaneser's mention of Jehu, therefore, may very well not relate to Jehu's first year of rule. The accusation that the Assyrians juggled the years of their campaigns and credited kings with receiving tribute from persons no longer living might reduce even more the supposed value of the synchronization. The chart "Outstanding Dates During the Period of the Kings of Judah and of Israel," accompanying this article, shows Ahab's death as occurring about 920 B.C.E. with Jehu's kingship counting from about 904 B.C.E.

Ptolemy's canon. Claudius Ptolemy was a Greek astronomer who lived in the second century C.E., or over 600 years after the close of the Neo-Babylonian period. His canon, or list of kings, was connected with a work on astronomy that he produced. Most modern historians accept Ptolemy's information about the Neo-Babylonian kings and the length of their reigns.

Evidently Ptolemy based his historical information on sources dating from the Seleucid period, which began more than 250 years after Cyrus captured Babylon. It thus is not surprising that Ptolemy's figures agree with those of Berossus, a Babylonian priest of the Seleucid period.

Lunar eclipses. These have been used to try to substantiate the dates given for particular years of the Neo-Babylonian kings on the basis of Ptolemy's canon and data in the cuneiform records. But even though Ptolemy may have calculated accurately or recorded the dates of certain eclipses in the past (a modern astronomer found three fifths of Ptolemy's dates correct), this does not prove

that his transmission of historical data is correct, that is, that his correlation of eclipses with the reigns of certain kings is consistently based on true historical fact.

The date of Herod the Great's death provides an illustration of problems that can be encountered in dating by lunar eclipses. Josephus' writings (*Jewish Antiquities*, XVII, 167 [vi, 4]; XVII, 188-214 [viii, 1–ix, 3]) show Herod's death occurring shortly after a lunar eclipse and not long before the start of the Passover season. Many scholars date Herod's death as in 4 B.C.E. and cite as proof the lunar eclipse of March 11 (March 13, Julian calendar) in that year. Because of this reckoning, many modern chronologers place the birth of Jesus as early as 5 B.C.E.

However, that eclipse in 4 B.C.E. was of only 36-percent magnitude and would have attracted the attention of very few people at the early morning hour that it occurred. Two other eclipses took place in 1 B.C.E., either one of which might fit the requirement of an eclipse not long before the Passover. The partial lunar eclipse of December 27 (December 29, Julian calendar) that year was perhaps observable in Jerusalem but probably not as a conspicuous event. According to calculations based on Oppolzer's *Canon of Eclipses* (p. 343), the moon was passing out of the earth's shadow as twilight fell in Jerusalem, and by the time it was dark the moon was again shining full. On the other hand, it is not included in the comprehensive listing by Manfred Kudlek and Erich Mickler. Thus the extent to which that eclipse was visible in Jerusalem or whether it was visible at all is uncertain at this point in history. More striking than either of the above was the late-night lunar eclipse that occurred in the early hours of January 8, 1 B.C.E. (January 10, Julian calendar). This was a total eclipse in which the moon was blacked out for 1 hour 41 minutes. It would have been noticed by anyone who was awake, even if the sky was overcast. So during the years here discussed, more than one eclipse occurred shortly before a Passover. Viewed from the standpoint of information available now, it seems that the one most likely to have been noted was that on January 8, 1 B.C.E. —*Solar and Lunar Eclipses of the Ancient Near East From 3000 B.C. to 0 With Maps*, by M. Kudlek and E. H. Mickler; Neukirchen-Vluyn, Germany; 1971, Vol. I, p. 156.

Not all the texts historians use to date events and periods of ancient history are based on eclipses, however. Astronomical diaries have been found that give the position (in relation to certain stars or constellations) of the moon at its first and last visibility on a specific day in Babylon (for example, "the moon was one cubit in front of the rear foot of the lion"), along with the positions of certain of the planets at these same times. Modern chronologers point out that such a combination of astronomical positions would not be duplicated again in thousands of years. These astronomical diaries contain references to the reigns of certain kings and appear to coincide with the figures given in Ptolemy's canon. While to some this might seem like incontrovertible evidence, there are factors greatly reducing its strength.

The first is that the observations made in Babylon may have contained errors. The Babylonian astronomers showed greatest concern for celestial events or phenomena occurring close to the horizon, at the rising or setting of the moon or of the sun. However, the horizon as viewed from Babylon is frequently obscured by sandstorms. Commenting on these factors, Professor O. Neugebauer states that Ptolemy complained about "the lack of reliable planetary observations [from ancient Babylon]. He [Ptolemy] remarks that the old observations were made with little competence, because they were concerned with appearances and disappearances and with stationary points, phenomena which by their very nature are very difficult to observe."—*The Exact Sciences in Antiquity*, 1957, p. 98.

Second, the fact is that the great majority of the astronomical diaries found were written, not in the time of the Neo-Babylonian or Persian empires, but in the Seleucid period (312-65 B.C.E.), although they contain data relating to those earlier periods. Historians assume that they are copies of earlier documents. Actually *contemporaneous* astronomical texts are lacking by which to establish the full chronology of the Neo-Babylonian and Persian periods (late seventh to late fourth centuries).

Finally, as in the case of Ptolemy, even though the astronomical information (as now interpreted and understood) on the texts discovered is basically accurate, this does not prove that the historical information accompanying it is accurate. Even as Ptolemy used the reigns of ancient kings (as he understood them) simply as a framework in which to place his astronomical data, so too, the writers (or copyists) of the astronomical texts of the Seleucid period may have simply inserted in their astronomical texts what was then the accepted, or "popular," chronology of that time. That accepted, or popular, chronology may well have contained errors at the critical points dealt with earlier in this article. To illustrate, an ancient astronomer (or a scribe) might state that a certain celestial

event took place in the year that, according to our calendar, would be 465 B.C.E., and his statement may prove correct when accurate computations are made to verify it. But he may also state that the year in which the celestial event took place (465 B.C.E.) was the 21st year of King Xerxes and be entirely wrong. Simply stated, accuracy in astronomy does not prove accuracy in history.

Archaeological Dating. Dating methods based on artifacts found in excavations are discussed under the heading ARCHAEOLOGY. Briefly, it may be said that, in the absence of actually dated inscriptions, dating by artifacts such as pottery shards can never be more than comparative. That is, the archaeologist can only say that 'this particular stratum and its contents in *this* mound evidently belong to the same general period as a certain stratum in *that* mound (or before it or after it).' Thus a general chronological sequence is built up, but always subject to correction and change, the changes sometimes amounting to hundreds of years. For example, in 1937 archaeologist Barton assigned "Early Bronze Age" pottery to the period 2500-2000 B.C.E., whereas in the following year W. F. Albright listed the same period as 3200-2200 B.C.E.

Hence, as G. Ernest Wright stated: "In this area we can seldom work with certainties. Instead, it is necessary to construct hypotheses which always possess greater or lesser degrees of probability. The truth in them rests upon their [the archaeologists'] ability to interpret and hold together a variety of disparate data, but new information at any moment may make it necessary to change a given hypothesis, or cause a scholar to express it somewhat differently."—*Shechem, The Biography of a Biblical City*, 1965, foreword p. xvi.

Further illustrating this is a statement in *Chronologies in Old World Archaeology*, edited by Robert Ehrich, printed in 1965 to supersede an earlier work of 1954, and containing a compendium of views on "the floating network of relative chronologies" as expressed by prominent archaeologists. The foreword (p. vii) says: "The purpose of this book is to present, in series, the chronologies of various contiguous areas as they appear in 1964 to the eyes of regional specialists. Despite the new information, the over-all situation is still fluid, and forthcoming data will render some conclusions obsolete, possibly even before this volume appears in print." This may be kept in mind when evaluating the dates archaeologists give for the age of certain cities, such as Jericho, or the period to which they assign the conquest of Palestine by Israel.

Historians of the Classical Period. The term "classical" here applies to the period and culture of the ancient Greeks and Romans. Besides being a source of Greek and Roman history, the writings of certain classical historians are relied on by modern historians to fill in gaps or to confirm certain data in the record of ancient Egypt, Assyria, Babylon, Persia, Syria, and Palestine. Included among ancient Greek historians are: Herodotus (c. 484-425 B.C.E.); Thucydides (c. 471-401 B.C.E.); Xenophon (c. 431-352 B.C.E.); Ctesias (fifth century B.C.E.); and later, Strabo, Diodorus Siculus, and Alexander Polyhistor of the first century B.C.E.; and Plutarch of the first and second centuries C.E. Roman historians include Titus Livius or Livy (59 B.C.E.–17 C.E.); Gnaeus Pompeius Trogus, a contemporary of Livy; Pliny the Elder (23-79 C.E.); and Sextus Julius Africanus (third century C.E.), probably born in Libya. Aside from these, major sources of information are Manetho and Berossus (already discussed); Josephus, a Jewish historian whose writings (though at times contradictory in their present form) are quite helpful for the first century C.E.; and Eusebius, ecclesiastical historian and bishop of Caesarea (c. 260-342 C.E.).

All of these lived after the Assyrian and Neo-Babylonian period and only the first four mentioned lived during the period of the Persian Empire. For the Assyrian and Neo-Babylonian periods, then, none of these writers present information based on personal knowledge, but they record, rather, the traditional views they heard or, in some cases, may have read and copied. The accuracy of their data obviously depends on the accuracy of the sources used.

Not only this, but what we know of their writings is today dependent upon copies of copies, the oldest copy often dating no farther back than the medieval period of the Common Era. We have already seen how the chronologies of Manetho and Berossus were mutilated by copyists. As to the qualifications and reliability of the other ancient historians of the classical period, the following is noteworthy:

Herodotus' approach to history—asking a question, looking for relevant information, and then drawing a conclusion—is spoken of highly. But it is also said that at times "his data were unsatisfactory" and that "he offers a rational explanation side by side with the irrational." It has also been said that he belongs "distinctly to the romantic school" and so was as much a storyteller as a historian. (*The New Encyclopædia Britannica,* 1985 edition, Vol. 5, pp. 881, 882; 1910 edition,

Vol. XIII, p. 383) As to Xenophon, it is said that "objectivity, thoroughness, and research were not for him" and that he adorned his narratives with "fictitious speeches." (*The New Encyclopædia Britannica,* 1987, Vol. 12, p. 796) George Rawlinson accuses Ctesias of deliberately extending the period of the Median monarchy "by the conscious use of a system of duplication." He further states: "Each king, or period, in Herodotus occurs in the list of Ctesias twice—a transparent device, clumsily cloaked by the cheap expedient of a liberal invention of names."—*The Seven Great Monarchies of the Ancient Eastern World,* 1885, Vol. II, p. 85.

Concerning Roman history of the kingly period (preceding the establishment of the Republic), we read that it "stretches back into the regions of pure mythology. It is little more than a collection of fables told with scarcely any attempt at criticism, and with no more regard to chronological sequence than was necessary to make the tale run smoothly or to fill up such gaps as that between the flight of Aeneas from Troy and the supposed year of the foundation of Rome." Even in the period after the establishment of the Republic (c. 509 B.C.E.), historians were still ready to set down popular tradition alongside historical fact without particularly distinguishing between them. "Pedigrees were invented, imaginary consulships [Roman dating was often done by consulships] and fictitious triumphs inserted, and family traditions . . . were formally incorporated with the history of the state." Of the Roman annalists, we are told: "What they found written they copied; the gaps they supplied, where personal experience failed, by imagination."—*The Encyclopædia Britannica,* 1911, Vol. XVI, pp. 820, 821.

Thucydides. Thucydides is widely regarded as an exception to the general rule of inaccuracy and carelessness with which the classical historians are so often charged. Thucydides is noted for his meticulous research. Of him, *The New Encyclopædia Britannica* (1987, Vol. 11, p. 741) says: "His authority is hardly equalled by that of any other historian. He kept to a strict chronological scheme and, where it can be accurately tested by the eclipses that he mentions, it fits closely."

The classical historians must be resorted to at times for necessary information, particularly for the Persian period (as dealt with in the books of Ezra, Nehemiah, and Esther) and on down to apostolic times. Their writings also are an aid in determining the time and events in fulfillment of parts of Daniel's prophetic visions (chaps 7-9, 11), which extend even beyond the apostolic period. However, the information presented earlier shows there is no reason for placing their histories and chronologies on a par with the Bible itself. Where differences appear, one can confidently rely on the Biblical record, set down either by eyewitnesses or by those who, like Luke, "traced all things from the start with accuracy." (Lu 1:1-4) The accurate chronological information in the accounts of Luke and others makes possible the fixing of the dates for principal events of Jesus' life and of the apostolic period.—Mt 2:1, 19-22; Lu 3:1-3, 21-23; and many others.

The Biblical Count of Time. The ancient secular records obviously must all be used with due caution. They are known to have inaccuracies in many matters, and it is most unlikely that their chronologies should somehow have escaped such inaccuracies. By contrast, the Bible has proved true in all fields dealt with, giving by far the most accurate picture of the ancient times it treats. Its chronology is also reliable.—See BIBLE (Authenticity).

When measuring Biblical periods in harmony with modern dating methods, it should be remembered that cardinal and ordinal numbers differ. Cardinal numbers, such as 1, 2, 3, 10, 100, and so forth, have full value. But with ordinal numbers, such as 3rd, 5th, and 22nd, it is necessary to subtract one to obtain the full number. Thus, in the reference to the "eighteenth year of Nebuchadrezzar," the term "eighteenth" is an ordinal number and represents 17 full years plus some days, weeks, or months (whatever time had elapsed from the end of the 17th year).—Jer 52:29.

When counting a number of years from a calendar date in the "B.C.E." period to one in the "C.E." period, it should be kept in mind that from a date such as October 1 of the year 1 B.C.E. to October 1 of the year 1 C.E. is only one year, not two, as can be seen in this diagram:

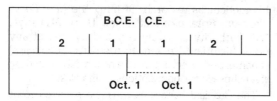

B.C.E.	C.E.
2	1	1	2

Oct. 1   Oct. 1

This is because the year dates are ordinal numbers. Thus, from about October 1 of the year 2 B.C.E. (the approximate time of Jesus' birth) to October 1 of 29 C.E. (the approximate date of Jesus' baptism) is a total of 30 years, that is, one full year plus 3 months in the B.C.E. period and 28

full years plus 9 months in the C.E. period.—Lu 3:21-23.

From Human Creation to the Present. Modern historians are unable to determine any certain date for the beginning of the "historical period" of mankind. Whether they turn to the history of Assyria, Babylon, or Egypt, the chronology becomes increasingly uncertain and unstable as they work their way back through the second millennium B.C.E., and in the third millennium B.C.E. they are faced with confusion and obscurity. By contrast, the Bible provides a connected history that allows for a methodical count back to the beginning of human history, a count that is facilitated by Biblical references to certain large periods of time, such as the 479 full-year period from the Exodus to the start of the temple construction during Solomon's reign.—1Ki 6:1.

To make the count in terms of modern calendar dating, we must use some fixed point or pivotal date with which to commence, that is, a date in history that has sound basis for acceptance and that corresponds with a particular event recorded in the Bible. From this date as a pivotal point we can figure backward or forward and assign calendar dates to many of the events referred to in the Bible.

One such date, harmonizing with both Biblical and secular history, is the year 29 C.E., the early months of which were in the 15th year of Tiberius Caesar, who was named emperor by the Roman Senate on September 15, 14 C.E. (Gregorian calendar). It was in the year 29 C.E. that John the Baptizer began his preaching and also when, perhaps about six months later, he baptized Jesus. —Lu 3:1-3, 21, 23; 1:36.

Another date that can be used as a pivotal point is the year 539 B.C.E., supported by various historical sources as the year for the overthrow of Babylon by Cyrus the Persian. (Secular sources for Cyrus' reign include Diodorus, Africanus, Eusebius, and Ptolemy, as well as the Babylonian tablets.) During Cyrus' first year his decree releasing the Jews from exile was given. And, as considered in the article on CYRUS, it is very probable that the decree was made by the winter of 538 B.C.E. or toward the spring of 537 B.C.E. This would permit the Jews time to make necessary preparations, effect the four-month journey to Jerusalem, and still arrive there by the seventh month (Tishri, or about October 1) of 537 B.C.E.—Ezr 1:1-11; 2:64-70; 3:1.

Using such pivotal dates, we can then relate a very large number of the Bible events to specific calendar dates. The basic framework into which such chronology fits is as follows:

Event	Calendar Date	Time Period Between Events
From the creation of Adam	4026 B.C.E.	
To the start of the Flood	2370 B.C.E.	1,656 years
To the validating of the Abrahamic covenant	1943 B.C.E.	427 years
To the Exodus from Egypt	1513 B.C.E.	430 years
To the start of the temple construction	1034 B.C.E.	479 years
To the division of the kingdom	997 B.C.E.	37 years
To the desolation of Judah	607 B.C.E.	390 years
To the return of the Jews from exile	537 B.C.E.	70 years
To the rebuilding of Jerusalem's walls	455 B.C.E.	82 years
To the baptism of Jesus	29 C.E.	483 years
To the present	1987 C.E.	1,958 years
Total time period from Adam's creation to 1987 C.E.		6,012 years

What, then, is the Biblical basis and, in some cases, the secular history supporting such chronology? We here give further details showing how each of the time periods listed is determined.

From Adam's creation to the Flood. The 1,656 years of this period are set out in Genesis 5:1-29; 7:6, and they may be outlined as shown in the chart at the lower right.

The figures shown for the pre-Flood period are those found in the Masoretic text, on which modern translations of the Hebrew Scriptures are based. These figures differ from those found in the Greek *Septuagint,* but the evidence for accuracy clearly favors the Masoretic text.

Lange's *Commentary on the Holy Scriptures* (Genesis, p. 272, ftn) says: "The internal evidence is shown to be decidedly in favor of the Hebrew from its proportional consistency. The numbers in the LXX evidently follow a plan to which they have been conformed. This does not appear in the Hebrew, and it is greatly in favor of its being an authentic genealogical record. . . . On physiological grounds, too, the Hebrew is to be preferred; since the length of the life does not at all require so late a manhood as those numbers [in the *Septuagint*] would seem to intimate. . . . the added 100 years, in each case, by the Septuagint, shows a design to bring them to some nearer proportional standard, grounded on some supposed physiological no-

tion. . . . To all this must be added the fact that the Hebrew has the best claim to be regarded as the original text, from the well-known scrupulous, and even superstitious, care with which it has been textually preserved."—Translated and edited by P. Schaff, 1976.

While modern historians would extend the period of human habitation on the earth much farther back than 4026 B.C.E., the facts are decidedly against the position they maintain. The thousands of years of "prehistory" they argue for are dependent on speculation, as can be seen from this statement by prominent scientist P. E. Klopsteg, who stated: "Come, now, if you will, on a *speculative* excursion into prehistory. *Assume* the era in which the species sapiens emerged from the genus Homo . . . hasten across the millenniums for which present information depends for the most part on *conjecture* and *interpretation* to the era of the first inscribed records, from which some facts may be gleaned." (Italics ours.)—*Science,* December 30, 1960, p. 1914.

The period of the post-Flood era begins with the year 2369 B.C.E. Whereas some would assign certain pictographic writings to the period 3300 to 2800 B.C.E. (*New Discoveries in Babylonia About Genesis,* by P. J. Wiseman, 1949, p. 36), these are not actually dated documents and their supposed age is based only on archaeological conjecture.

While appeal is sometimes made to datings based on the radiocarbon (C-14) technique, this method of dating has definite limitations. *Science* magazine of December 11, 1959, p. 1630, reported: "What bids to become a classical example of 'C^{14} irresponsibility' is the 6000-year spread of 11 determinations for Jarmo . . . , a prehistoric village in northeastern Iraq, which, on the basis of all archeological evidence, was not occupied for more than 500 consecutive years." There is thus no solid or provable evidence to favor an earlier date than

From Adam's creation to the birth of Seth	130 years
Then to the birth of Enosh	105 years
To the birth of Kenan	90 years
To the birth of Mahalalel	70 years
To the birth of Jared	65 years
To the birth of Enoch	162 years
To the birth of Methuselah	65 years
To the birth of Lamech	187 years
To the birth of Noah	182 years
To the Flood	600 years
Total	1,656 years

2369 B.C.E. for the start of the post-Flood human society.

From 2370 B.C.E. to covenant with Abraham. The chronological structure of this period may be summed up as follows:

From the beginning of the Flood to Arpachshad's birth	2 years
Then to the birth of Shelah	35 years
To the birth of Eber	30 years
To the birth of Peleg	34 years
To the birth of Reu	30 years
To the birth of Serug	32 years
To the birth of Nahor	30 years
To the birth of Terah	29 years
To the death of Terah, when Abraham was 75 years old	205 years
Total	427 years

The basis for these figures is Genesis 11:10 to 12:4. The expression "after the deluge" (Ge 11:10) used in connection with Arpachshad's birth would logically refer to the actual falling of the waters that marked the *start* of the Flood (2370 B.C.E.), rather than simply to the continuance of the waters upon the earth for a period of time thereafter. The Hebrew term for "deluge" also indicates this. —Compare Ge 6:17; 7:4-6, 10-12, 17; 9:11.

The date of the attempt at building the Tower of Babel is not stated in the record. Genesis 10:25 indicates that the division resulting from the confusion of the languages there occurred sometime during 'the days of Peleg.' It does not necessarily follow that this event occurred at Peleg's birth. The expression "in his days" would in fact indicate that the division took place, not at or immediately subsequent to Peleg's birth, but sometime during his life span, which extended from 2269 to 2030 B.C.E. If each post-Flood male parent at the age of 30 were to begin fathering children at the rate of one child every three years, with an average of one male child every six years, and continued this until the age of 90, then in a period of about 180 years from the end of the Flood (that is, by 2189 B.C.E.) the population could have grown to a total of over 4,000 adult males. This conservative number would be ample to fit the circumstances relating to the tower construction and the dispersal of the peoples.

Evidently at the time of Abraham's crossing the Euphrates on his way to the land of Canaan, Jehovah validated with him what has come to be known as the Abrahamic covenant. As Abraham's departure from Haran and his entry into Canaan followed the death of his father Terah, the date of the validating of this covenant is set at 1943 B.C.E. —Ge 11:32; 12:1-5.

From 1943 B.C.E. to the Exodus. Exodus 12: 40, 41 states that "the dwelling of the sons of Israel, who had dwelt in Egypt, was four hundred and thirty years. And it came about at the end of the four hundred and thirty years, it even came about on this very day that all the armies of Jehovah went out of the land of Egypt." Whereas most translations render verse 40 in such a way as to make the 430 years apply entirely to the dwelling in Egypt, the original Hebrew allows for the above translation. Also, at Galatians 3:16, 17, Paul associates that 430-year period with the time between the validating of the Abrahamic covenant and the making of the Law covenant. Evidently when Abraham acted on God's promise, crossing the Euphrates in 1943 B.C.E. on his way to Canaan and actually moving into "the country" to which God directed him, the Abrahamic covenant was validated. (Ge 12:1; 15:18-21) Exactly 430 years after this event, his descendants were delivered from Egypt, in 1513 B.C.E., and in that same year the Law covenant was made with them. Evidence that from early times the period mentioned at Exodus 12:40, 41 was understood to begin counting from the time when the ancestors of the nation made the move to go to Canaan is indicated by the Greek *Septuagint* rendering: "But the dwelling of the sons of Israel which they dwelt in the land of Egypt and in the land of Canaan [was] four hundred and thirty years long."

The period from Abraham's move to Canaan until Jacob's going down into Egypt was 215 years. This figure is derived from the following facts: Twenty-five years passed from Abraham's departure from Haran to the birth of Isaac (Ge 12:4; 21:5); from then to the birth of Jacob was 60 years (Ge 25:26); and Jacob was 130 at the time of his entry into Egypt (Ge 47:9); thus giving a total of 215 years (from 1943 to 1728 B.C.E.). This means that an equal period of 215 years was thereafter spent by the Israelites in Egypt (from 1728 to 1513 B.C.E.). That the Israelites could have multiplied sufficiently in 215 years to have a population including 600,000 "able-bodied men" is demonstrated under the heading EXODUS.—Ex 12:37.

Jehovah told Abram (Abraham): "You may know for sure that your seed will become an alien resident in a land not theirs, and they will have to serve them, and these will certainly afflict them for four hundred years." (Ge 15:13; see also Ac 7:6, 7.) This was stated prior to the birth of the promised heir or "seed," Isaac. In 1932 B.C.E. Ishmael was born to Abram by the Egyptian servant girl Hagar, and in 1918 B.C.E. Isaac was born. (Ge 16:16; 21:5) Counting back 400 years from the Exodus, which marked the end of the 'afflicting' (Ge 15:14), would bring us to 1913 B.C.E., and at that time Isaac was about five years old. It appears that Isaac was weaned then and, already "an alien resident" in a land not his, he now experienced the start of the foretold affliction in the form of Ishmael's "poking fun," Ishmael being about 19. (Ge 21:8, 9) Although in modern times Ishmael's mocking of Abraham's heir might be viewed as inconsequential, such was not the case in patriarchal times. This is evidenced by Sarah's reaction and God's approval of her insistence that Hagar and her son Ishmael be sent away. (Ge 21:10-13) The very fact that this incident was recorded in detail in the divine record also points to its marking the commencement of the prophesied 400-year period of affliction that would not end until the Exodus.—Ga 4:29.

From 1513 B.C.E. to division of kingdom. It was in the "four hundred and eightieth year after the sons of Israel came out from the land of Egypt," in the fourth year of Solomon's reign, that construction began on the temple at Jerusalem. (1Ki 6:1) "Four hundred and eightieth" is an ordinal number representing 479 full years plus some additional time, in this case one month. Counting 479 years from the Exodus (Nisan 1513 B.C.E.) brings us to 1034 B.C.E., with the temple construction beginning in the second month, Ziv (corresponding to part of April and part of May). Since this was the fourth year (another ordinal number) of Solomon's rule, his reign began three full years earlier in 1037 B.C.E. His 40-year rule evidently ran from Nisan 1037 to Nisan 997 B.C.E., with the division of the kingdom taking place in the latter year. The chronological structure for this period would therefore be as shown at the right.

These figures find their basis in texts such as Deuteronomy 2:7; 29:5; Acts 13:21; 2 Samuel 5:4; 1 Kings 11:42, 43; 12:1-20. Some critics call attention to the four periods of 40 years each, occurring in this period, claiming that this is evidence of a 'mere seeking after symmetry' on the part of the Bible writers rather than an accurate chronology. To the contrary, whereas the period

of Israelite wandering before their entry into Canaan was almost exactly 40 years in fulfillment of the divine judgment recorded at Numbers 14: 33, 34 (compare Ex 12:2, 3, 6, 17; De 1:31; 8:2-4; Jos 4:19), the other three periods all may have included fractional figures. Thus, David's reign is shown to have actually lasted for 40½ years, according to 2 Samuel 5:5. If, as seems to have been the practice, regnal years of these kings were counted on a Nisan-to-Nisan basis, this could mean that King Saul's reign lasted only 39½ years, but with the months remaining until the following Nisan being credited to Saul's reign and hence not *officially* included in David's 40 regnal years. Such, at least, was the known practice among Semitic rulers in Mesopotamia, the months intervening between the death of a king and the following Nisan being termed the "accession period" of the succeeding king, but his official first year of rule not beginning to count until the arrival of the month of Nisan.

The length of the period from the entry into Canaan till the end of the period of the Judges is not directly stated, being arrived at only by deduction. That is, by subtracting the 123 years of the known periods (of the wilderness wandering, of Saul and David, and the first three years of Solomon's reign) from the 479 years intervening between the Exodus and Solomon's fourth year, 356 years remain.

The manner in which these 356 years (from Israel's entry into Canaan in 1473 B.C.E. until the start of Saul's reign in 1117 B.C.E.) are to be apportioned is not stated in the Scriptures. Evidently, however, there is considerable overlapping of time periods. Why? Counted in succession, the various periods of oppression, of judgeships, and of peace as listed in the book of Judges would total

Event	Date	Time Period Between Events
From the Exodus to	1513 B.C.E.	
the entry of Israel into Canaan to	1473 B.C.E.	40 years
the close of the period of the Judges and the beginning of Saul's reign to	1117 B.C.E.	356 years
the beginning of David's reign to	1077 B.C.E.	40 years
the beginning of Solomon's reign to	1037 B.C.E.	40 years
the division of the kingdom	997 B.C.E.	40 years
Total years from the Exodus to the division of the kingdom (1513 to 997 B.C.E.)		516 years

410 years. For these periods to fit into the 356-year time period mentioned earlier, some periods must have been concurrent rather than successive, and this is the view of most commentators. The circumstances described in the Bible accounts lend themselves to this explanation. The oppressions involved different areas of the land and affected different tribes. (MAP, Vol. 1, p. 743) Thus the expression "the land had no further disturbance," used after recounting the Israelites' victories over their oppressors, may not in every case embrace the entire area occupied by all 12 tribes but may apply to the portion that the particular oppression primarily affected.—Jg 3:11, 30; 5:31; 8:28; compare Jos 14:13-15.

At Acts chapter 13 the apostle Paul reviewed God's dealings with Israel from the 'choosing of the forefathers' on through the period in Egypt, the Exodus, the wilderness wandering, the conquest of Canaan, and the distribution of the land, and then stated: "All that during about four hundred and fifty years. And after these things he gave them judges until Samuel the prophet." (Ac 13:20) Considerable misunderstanding has resulted from the *King James* rendering of this text, which reads: "And after that he gave unto them judges about the space of four hundred and fifty years, until Samuel the prophet." However, the most ancient manuscripts (including the Sinaitic, Vatican Manuscript No. 1209, and the Alexandrine), as well as most modern translations (such as *JB, Kx,* and others; vss 19, 20, *AS, RS, AT*), all favor the previous translation, which shows the period of the Judges coming *after* the 450 years. Since the period of "about four hundred and fifty years" had its start with God's 'choosing the forefathers' of Israel, it would seem to have begun in the year 1918 B.C.E. with the birth of Isaac, the original "seed" promised to Abraham. It would therefore end about 1467 B.C.E., when the initial conquest of Canaan reached its conclusion, allowing for the distribution to proceed. Inasmuch as the figure is stated to be approximate, a difference of a year or so would not be of consequence.

From 997 B.C.E. to desolation of Jerusalem. A helpful guide to the overall length of this period of the kings is found at Ezekiel 4:1-7 in the mimic siege of Jerusalem that the prophet Ezekiel carried out at God's direction. Ezekiel was to lie on his left side for 390 days to "carry the error of the house of Israel," and on his right side for 40 days to "carry the error of the house of Judah," and each day was shown to stand for a year. The two periods (of 390 years and of 40 years) thus symbolized evidently stood for the length of Jehovah's

forbearance with the two kingdoms in their idolatrous course. The Jewish understanding of this prophecy, as presented in the *Soncino Books of the Bible* (commentary on Ezekiel, pp. 20, 21) is: "The guilt of the Northern Kingdom extended over a period of 390 years ([according to the] Seder Olam [the earliest postexilic chronicle preserved in the Hebrew language], [and Rabbis] Rashi and Ibn Ezra). Abarbanel, quoted by Malbim, reckons the period of Samaria's guilt from the time when the schism took place under Rehoboam . . . until the fall of Jerusalem. . . . The *right* [side, on which Ezekiel lay] indicates the south, i.e. the Kingdom of Judah which lay to the south or right. . . . Judah's corruption lasted forty years beginning soon after Samaria's fall. According to Malbim, the time is reckoned from the thirteenth year of the reign of Josiah . . . when Jeremiah began his ministry. (Jer. i. 2)."—Edited by A. Cohen, London, 1950.

From the division of the kingdom in 997 B.C.E. to the fall of Jerusalem in 607 B.C.E. was 390 years. While it is true that Samaria, the capital of the northern kingdom, had already fallen to Assyria in 740 B.C.E., in Hezekiah's sixth year (2Ki 18:9, 10), it is probable that some of the population fled into the southern kingdom before the Assyrians' advance. (Note also the situation in Judah following the division of the kingdom as described at 2Ch 10:16, 17.) But, more important, the fact that Jehovah God continued to keep the Israelites of the exiled northern kingdom in view, the messages of his prophets continuing to include them long beyond the fall of Samaria, shows that their interests were still represented in the capital city of Jerusalem and that its fall in 607 B.C.E. was an expression of Jehovah's judgment against not Judah alone but the nation of Israel as a whole. (Jer 3:11-22; 11:10-12, 17; Eze 9:9, 10) When the city fell, the hopes of the nation as a whole (with the exception of the few who maintained true faith) suffered collapse.—Eze 37:11-14, 21, 22.

In the chart that follows, this 390-year period is adhered to as a sound chronological guide. A summation of the years listed for all the reigns of the kings of Judah from Rehoboam to Zedekiah gives a total of 393 years. Whereas some Biblical chronologers endeavor to synchronize the data concerning the kings by means of numerous coregencies and "interregnums" on the Judean side, it appears necessary to show only one coregency. This is in the case of Jehoram, who is stated (at least in the Masoretic text and some of the oldest manuscripts of the Bible) to have become king "while Jehoshaphat was king of Judah," thus giving some basis for assuming a coregency. (2Ki 8:16) In this manner the overall period comes within the 390-year limit.

The chart is not intended to be viewed as an absolute chronology but, rather, as a suggested presentation of the reigns of the two kingdoms. The ancient inspired writers were dealing with facts and figures well known to them and to the Jewish people then, and the different chronological viewpoints adopted by the writers at certain points presented no problem. Such is not the case today, and hence we may be satisfied with simply setting out an arrangement that harmonizes reasonably with the Biblical record.

From 607 B.C.E. to return from exile. The length of this period is fixed by God's own decree concerning Judah, that "all this land must become a devastated place, an object of astonishment, and these nations will have to serve the king of Babylon seventy years."—Jer 25:8-11.

The Bible prophecy does not allow for the application of the 70-year period to any time other than that between the desolation of Judah, accompanying Jerusalem's destruction, and the return of the Jewish exiles to their homeland as a result of Cyrus' decree. It clearly specifies that the 70 years would be years of *devastation of the land of Judah*. The prophet Daniel so understood the prophecy, for he states: "I myself, Daniel, discerned by the books the number of the years concerning which the word of Jehovah had occurred to Jeremiah the prophet, for fulfilling the *devastations* of Jerusalem, namely, seventy years." (Da 9:2) After describing the conquest of Jerusalem by Nebuchadnezzar, 2 Chronicles 36:20, 21 states: "Furthermore, he carried off those remaining from the sword captive to Babylon, and they came to be servants to him and his sons until the royalty of Persia began to reign; to fulfill Jehovah's word by the mouth of Jeremiah, *until the land had paid off its sabbaths*. All the days of lying desolated it kept sabbath, to fulfill seventy years."

Jerusalem came under final siege in Zedekiah's 9th year (609 B.C.E.), and the city fell in his 11th year (607 B.C.E.), corresponding to Nebuchadnezzar's 19th year of actual rule (counting from his accession year in 625 B.C.E.). (2Ki 25:1-8) In the fifth month of that year (the month of Ab, corresponding to parts of July and August) the city was set afire, the walls were pulled down, and the majority of the people were led off into exile. However, "some of the lowly people of the land" were allowed to remain, and these did so until the assassination of Gedaliah, Nebuchadnezzar's appointee, whereupon they fled into Egypt, finally leaving Judah completely desolate. (2Ki 25:9-12, 22-26) This was in the seventh month, Ethanim (or Tishri, corresponding to parts of September and October). Hence the count of the 70 years of desolation must have begun about October 1, 607 B.C.E., ending in 537 B.C.E. It was in the seventh month of this latter year that the first repatriated Jews arrived back in Judah, exactly 70 years from the start of the full desolation of the land.—2Ch 36:21-23; Ezr 3:1.

From 537 B.C.E. to conversion of Cornelius. In the second year of the return from exile (536 B.C.E.), the foundation of the temple was relaid in Jerusalem, but the rebuilt temple was not completed until the sixth year of the reign of Darius I (Persian). (Ezr 3:8-10; 6:14, 15) Since Darius did not establish himself in Babylon until defeating the rebel Nebuchadnezzar III in December of 522 and shortly afterward capturing and killing him in Babylon, the year 522 B.C.E. may be viewed as the accession year of King Darius I. His first regnal year, then, began in the spring of 521 B.C.E. (*Babylonian Chronology, 626 B.C.– A.D. 75*, p. 30) Darius' sixth year therefore began April 12, 516 B.C.E., and continued until the end of March of 515 B.C.E. On this basis, Zerubbabel's rebuilding of Jehovah's temple was completed on March 6 of 515 B.C.E.

The next date of major importance is the 20th year of Artaxerxes (Longimanus), the year Nehemiah received permission to go and rebuild Jerusalem. (Ne 2:1, 5-8) The reasons for favoring the date of 455 B.C.E. for this year as against the popular date of 445 B.C.E. are considered in the article PERSIA, PERSIANS. The events of this year that involve the rebuilding of Jerusalem and its walls mark the starting point of the prophecy concerning the "seventy weeks" at Daniel 9:24-27. The weeks there are clearly "weeks of years" (Da 9:24, *RS, AT, Mo*), totaling 490 years. As demonstrated under the heading SEVENTY WEEKS, the prophecy pointed to Jesus' appearance as the Messiah in the year 29 C.E.; his death at "the half of the week" or in the middle of the last week of years, that is, in 33 C.E.; and the end of the period of God's special favor to the Jews in 36 C.E. Thus, the 70 weeks of years closed with the conversion of Cornelius, 490 years from the year 455 B.C.E. —Ac 10:30-33, 44-48; 11:1.

Jesus' appearance as the Messiah came in the precise year foretold, perhaps about six months after John the Baptizer began his preaching in "the fifteenth year of the reign of Tiberius Caesar." (Lu 1:36; 3:1, 2, 21-23) Since the Roman Senate named Tiberius emperor on September 15

OUTSTANDING DATES
During the Period of the Kings of Judah and of Israel

THE TWELVE-TRIBE KINGDOM

	Dates B.C.E.	
SAUL began to rule as king over all 12 tribes (40 years)	1117	
Prophet: Samuel		
High priests: Ahijah, Ahimelech		**NOTE:** This chart is meant to provide a helpful outline of key events in connection with the kings of Judah and of Israel. The Bible record of years that the kings of Judah ruled was allowed to govern when fixing other dates. The dates given for rulership of Judean kings extend from the spring of the stated year to the spring of the following year. Dates for the reigns of kings of the kingdom of Israel were coordinated with those for Judah. There are numerous synchronisms provided in the Bible, and these were taken into account in arriving at these dates.
Birth of David	1107	
Samuel completed book of Judges	c. 1100	
Samuel completed book of Ruth	c. 1090	
Book of 1 Samuel was completed	c. 1078	
DAVID began to rule as king of Judah at Hebron (40)	1077	
Prophets: Nathan, Gad, Zadok		
High priest: Abiathar		
David became king over all Israel; made Jerusalem his capital	1070	
Gad and Nathan completed 2 Samuel	c. 1040	High priests and prophets that are named in the Bible record in connection with the various kings are listed here. But the list is by no means complete. The Aaronic priesthood officiated first at the tabernacle and then at the temple apparently without a break in the line down till the time of the Babylonian exile. And the Bible indicates that, in addition to the prophets that are named, many more served in this sacred office. —1Ki 18:4; 2Ch 36:15, 16.
SOLOMON began to rule as king (40)	1037	
Prophets: Nathan, Ahijah, Iddo		
High priests: Abiathar, Zadok		
Construction of Solomon's temple began	1034	
Temple built by Solomon in Jerusalem was completed	1027	
Solomon wrote Song of Solomon	c. 1020	
Solomon wrote book of Ecclesiastes	b. 1000	

KINGDOM OF JUDAH		KINGDOM OF ISRAEL
REHOBOAM began to rule as king (17 years); nation split into two kingdoms	997	JEROBOAM began to rule as king over the northern 10 tribes, apparently first from Shechem, then from Tirzah (22 years)
Prophets: Shemaiah, Iddo		Prophet: Ahijah
Shishak of Egypt invaded Judah and took treasures from temple in Jerusalem	993	
ABIJAH (ABIJAM) began to rule as king (3)	980	
Prophet: Iddo		
ASA evidently began to rule (41), but his first regnal year counted from 977	978	
Prophets: Azariah, Oded, Hanani		
	c. 976	NADAB began to rule as king (2)
	c. 975	BAASHA assassinated Nadab and then began to rule as king (24)
		Prophet: Jehu (son of Hanani)
Zerah the Ethiopian came against Judah in war	967	
	c. 952	ELAH began to rule as king (2)
	c. 951	ZIMRI, a military chief, assassinated Elah and then ruled as king (7 days)
	c. 951	OMRI, chief of the army, began to rule as king (12)
	c. 951	Tibni became king over part of the people, further dividing the nation
	c. 947	Omri overcame Tibni's opposition and became sole ruler in Israel
	c. 945	Omri bought the mountain of Samaria and built his capital there
	c. 940	AHAB began to rule as king (22)
		Prophets: Elijah, Micaiah

464

KINGDOM OF JUDAH	Dates B.C.E.	KINGDOM OF ISRAEL
JEHOSHAPHAT evidently began to rule (25), but his first regnal year counted from 936 Prophets: Jehu (son of Hanani), Eliezer, Jahaziel High priest: Amariah	937	
	c. 920	AHAZIAH, son of Ahab, 'became king' (2); evidently his father was still living; Ahaziah's years of rulership may count from c. 919 Prophet: Elijah
Jehoram the son of Jehoshaphat became associated in some way with his father in the government	c. 919	
	c. 917	JEHORAM, son of Ahab, began to rule as sole king of Israel (12); but in at least one text the brief reign of his brother Ahaziah, who died sonless, also may have been credited to Jehoram Prophet: Elisha
JEHORAM became official coregent with Jehoshaphat, from which time Jehoram's kingship may be counted (8) Prophet: Elijah	913	
Jehoshaphat died and Jehoram became sole ruler	c. 911	
AHAZIAH, son of Jehoram, began to rule (1), though perhaps anointed to kingship in c. 907 High priest: Jehoiada	c. 906	
ATHALIAH usurped the throne (6)	c. 905	JEHU, a military chief, assassinated Jehoram and then began to rule (28); but it seems that his years of kingship counted from c. 904 Prophet: Elisha
JEHOASH, son of Ahaziah, began to rule as king (40) High priest: Jehoiada	898	
	876	JEHOAHAZ began to rule as king (17)
	c. 862	Jehoash evidently became associated in the kingship with his father, Jehoahaz
	c. 859	JEHOASH, son of Jehoahaz, began to rule as sole king of Israel (16) Prophet: Elisha
AMAZIAH began to rule as king (29)	858	
Jehoash of Israel captured Amaziah, breached the wall of Jerusalem, and took treasures from temple	a. 858	
	c. 844	JEROBOAM II began to rule as king (41) Prophets: Jonah, Hosea, Amos Book of Jonah was written
UZZIAH (AZARIAH) began to rule as king (52) Prophets: Hosea, Joel (?), Isaiah High priest: Azariah (II) Book of Joel was perhaps written	829	
	c. 820	
Uzziah 'became king' in some special sense, possibly now free from domination of Jeroboam II	c. 818	
Book of Amos was written	c. 804	
	c. 803	ZECHARIAH 'began to reign' in some sense, but evidently the kingship was not fully confirmed as his until c. 792 (6 months)
	c. 791	SHALLUM assassinated Zechariah and then ruled as king (1 month)
	c. 791	MENAHEM assassinated Shallum and then began to rule, but it seems that his years of kingship counted from c. 790 (10)
	c. 780	PEKAHIAH began to rule as king (2)
	c. 778	PEKAH assassinated Pekahiah and then began to rule as king (20) Prophet: Oded

KINGDOM OF JUDAH	Dates B.C.E.	KINGDOM OF ISRAEL
JOTHAM began to rule as king (16)	777	
Prophets: Micah, Hosea, Isaiah		
AHAZ evidently began to rule (16), but his first regnal year counted from 761	762	
Prophets: Micah, Hosea, Isaiah		
High priest: Urijah (?)		
Ahaz evidently became tributary to Tiglath-pileser III of Assyria	c. 759	
	c. 758	HOSHEA assassinated Pekah and then 'began to reign' in place of him, but it seems that his control became fully established or possibly he received the backing of the Assyrian monarch Tiglath-pileser III in c. 748 (9 years)
HEZEKIAH evidently began to rule (29), but his first regnal year counted from 745	746	
Prophets: Micah, Hosea, Isaiah		
High priest: Azariah (II or III)		
	a. 745	Book of Hosea was completed
	742	Assyrian army began siege of Samaria
	740	Assyria conquered Samaria, subjugated Israel; northern kingdom came to its end
Sennacherib invaded Judah	732	
Book of Isaiah was completed	a. 732	
Book of Micah was completed	b. 717	
Compiling of Proverbs was completed	c. 717	
MANASSEH began to rule as king (55)	716	
AMON began to rule as king (2)	661	
JOSIAH began to rule as king (31)	659	
Prophets: Zephaniah, Jeremiah, the prophetess Huldah		
High priest: Hilkiah		
Book of Zephaniah was written	b. 648	
Book of Nahum was written	b. 632	
JEHOAHAZ ruled as king (3 months)	628	
JEHOIAKIM began to rule as king, tributary to Egypt (11)	628	
Prophets: Habakkuk (?), Jeremiah		
Book of Habakkuk was perhaps written	c. 628	
Nebuchadnezzar II makes Jehoiakim tributary to Babylon	620	
JEHOIACHIN began to rule as king (3 months 10 days)	618	
Nebuchadnezzar II took Jewish captives and temple treasures to Babylon	617	
ZEDEKIAH began to rule as king (11)	617	
Prophets: Jeremiah, Ezekiel		
High priest: Seraiah		
Nebuchadnezzar II invaded Judah again; siege of Jerusalem began	609	
Walls of Jerusalem were breached on 9th day of 4th month	607	
Jerusalem and temple were burned on 10th day of 5th month	607	
Last Jews abandoned Judah about middle of 7th month	607	
Jeremiah wrote book of Lamentations	607	
Book of Obadiah was written	c. 607	

NOTE: After Samaria was captured, the ten tribes of the kingdom of Israel were taken into exile. But the land was not left desolate, as was the case with Judah following the destruction of Jerusalem in 607 B.C.E. The king of Assyria moved people from Babylon, Cuthah, Avva, Hamath, and Sepharvaim into the cities of Israel to dwell there. Their descendants were still there when the Jews returned to Jerusalem in 537 B.C.E. to rebuild the temple. —2Ki 17:6, 24; Ezr 4:1, 2.

of 14 C.E., his 15th year ran from the latter part of 28 C.E. well into 29 C.E. (See TIBERIUS.) The evidence, then, is that Jesus' baptism and anointing took place in the fall of the year 29 C.E.

Since Jesus was "about thirty years old" at the time of his baptism in 29 C.E. (Lu 3:23), his birth took place 30 years earlier, or about the fall of the year 2 B.C.E. He was born during the reign of Caesar Augustus and the Syrian governorship of Quirinius. (Lu 2:1, 2) Augustus' rule ran from 27 B.C.E. to 14 C.E. The Roman senator P. Sulpicius Quirinius was governor of Syria twice, the first time evidently coming after P. Quintilius Varus, whose term as legate of Syria ended in 4 B.C.E. Some scholars place Quirinius' first governorship in 3-2 B.C.E. (See REGISTRATION.) Herod the Great was then king of Judea, and we have seen that there is evidence pointing to the year 1 B.C.E. as the likely time of his death. Thus, all the available evidence, and particularly the Scriptural references, indicate the fall of 2 B.C.E. for the human birth of God's Son.

The later apostolic period. It is possible to fix approximate dates for a number of the events taking place during this period. The prophecy of a great famine spoken by the Christian prophet Agabus, and the subsequent persecution instigated by Herod Agrippa I, resulting in the apostle James' death and the jailing of Peter, evidently took place in about 44 C.E. (Ac 11:27-30; 12:1-4) Herod Agrippa died that year, and there is evidence that the foretold famine came about the year 46 C.E. This latter date probably marks the time of the relief ministration effected by Paul and Barnabas.—Ac 12:25.

Paul's first visit to Corinth can be dated through the proconsulship of Gallio. (Ac 18:1, 11-18) As explained in the article on GALLIO, this proconsulship appears to have run from the summer of 51 C.E. to the summer of 52 C.E., though some scholars favor 52/53 C.E. Thus, Paul's 18-month activity in Corinth likely began in the autumn of 50 C.E., ending in the spring of 52 C.E. This is further confirmed by the fact that two of Paul's associates in Corinth, Aquila and Priscilla, had recently arrived there from Italy because of Emperor Claudius' edict requiring all Jews to depart from Rome. (Ac 18:2) Paulus Orosius, historian of the fifth century, states that this order was given in Claudius' ninth year, that is, in 49 or early 50 C.E.

The two years Paul spent in prison at Caesarea were during the last two years of the governorship of Felix, Paul thereafter being sent on to Rome by Felix' successor Porcius Festus. (Ac 21:

33; 23:23-35; 24:27) The date of the accession of Festus is somewhat uncertain, since historical evidence does not all point to the same conclusion. However, the year 58 C.E. seems to be the most likely. Paul's subsequent arrival in Rome may be placed between 59 and 61 C.E.

The great fire that ravaged Rome came in July of 64 C.E. and was followed by fierce persecution of Christians, at the instigation of Nero. It is probable that Paul's second imprisonment and his execution took place shortly thereafter. (2Ti 1:16; 4:6, 7) The exiling of John to the isle of Patmos is generally considered to have taken place during the reign of Emperor Domitian. (Re 1:9) The persecution of Christians reached a peak during his rule (81-96 C.E.), particularly in the last three years. The traditional view is that John was released from exile following Domitian's death and died in Ephesus about the close of the first century C.E. Thus, by John's writing his epistles about this time, the Bible canon was completed and the apostolic period came to its close.

CHRYSOLITE (chrys'o·lite). A transparent or translucent, yellow or green semiprecious stone composed of silicates of magnesium and iron. It generally occurs in volcanic rocks (also, in dolomite and some types of limestone) in solid, crystalline, or granular form. "Chrysolite" is from the Greek word *khry·so'li·thos,* meaning "gold stone," and it seems that at least some ancients applied this name to various yellow-colored gems. Fine-quality chrysolite crystals are found in Egypt.

In compliance with Jehovah's instructions, a chrysolite (Heb., *tar·shish'; LXX,* "chrysolite") was placed in the first position in the fourth row on Aaron's "breastpiece of judgment" to represent one of the 12 tribes of Israel. (Ex 28:2, 15, 20, 21; 39:13) Chrysolite was also included among the precious stones that served as a "covering" for the king of Tyre.—Eze 28:12, 13.

When Ezekiel received two separate visions involving four wheels, he noted that the appearance of the wheels was "like the glow of chrysolite." (Eze 1:15-21; 10:9) The Shulammite girl likened the hands of her shepherd lover to "cylinders of gold, filled with chrysolite." Perhaps the gold cylinders designate the fingers and the fillings of chrysolite refer to the fingernails. (Ca 5:14) Similarly, Daniel used chrysolite to describe the body of "a certain man clothed in linen" who came to tell the prophet what would befall his people "in the final part of the days." (Da 10:5, 6, 14) In his vision of New Jerusalem, the apostle John observed that the seventh foundation of the city's wall was chrysolite and engraved upon it was the name of one of "the twelve apostles of the Lamb."—Re 21:2, 10, 14, 20; see JEWELS AND PRECIOUS STONES.

CHRYSOPRASE

(chrys'o·prase). A semiprecious, translucent gemstone, an apple-green variety of chalcedony. The color is caused by a trace of nickel oxide in the mineral. The only Biblical reference to chrysoprase (Gr., *khry·so'pra·sos*) is in Revelation, where it is mentioned as constituting the tenth foundation of the wall of "the holy city, New Jerusalem."—Re 21:2, 20.

CHUB.

An unidentified people included among those allied with Egypt. Chub is listed with Ethiopia, Put, Lud, and "the sons of the land of the covenant" (which may refer to Israelites who fled to Egypt after the murder of Gedaliah in 607 B.C.E.), all of whom are destined to "fall by the very sword." (Eze 30:4, 5) Some think that Chub refers to Libya, and it is so rendered by some translations.—*LXX; RS.*

CHUZA

(Chu'za). Herod Antipas' "man in charge," possibly of the domestic affairs. Chuza's wife Joanna ministered to Jesus.—Lu 8:3; see JOANNA.

CILICIA

(Ci·li'cia). A relatively small and narrow region of SE Asia Minor. On the S lay the Mediterranean Sea, to the W was Pamphylia, on the N the Taurus mountain range separated it from Lycaonia and Cappadocia, and to the E the Amanus (now Nur) Mountains, which form a southern branch of the Taurus Mountains, divided it off from Syria. These, at least, were its boundaries during much of its ancient history.

Basically the region was divided into two natural sections: the western, called Cilicia Tracheia (Cilicia the Rugged) and the eastern, called Cilicia Pedias (Plain Cilicia). Cilicia Tracheia was a wild plateau region of the Taurus Mountains, rich in forest land. Its rugged seacoast, broken by rocky headlands, provided numerous sheltered harbors and inlets. From early times it was a haven for robbers and for pirates, who preyed on the coastal shipping. Cilicia Pedias embraced the broad coastal plain, a well-watered, extremely fertile section. In Roman times this plain was dotted with semiautonomous cities, the most prominent of which was Tarsus, the birthplace of Saul (Paul).—Ac 21:39; 22:3; 23:34.

In addition to wheat, flax, and fruits, Cilicia produced goats' hair, known as *cilicium* in Roman times. Its use in the manufacture of tents may partly account for Paul's early experience as a tentmaker.

Cilicia occupied a strategic position, both militarily and commercially. The principal trade route from Syria passed through the Syrian Gates, a high pass through the Amanus (now Nur) Mountains about 30 km (20 mi) N of Antioch, then traversed Cilicia to Tarsus and ascended the Taurus Mountains to the Cilician Gates, the sharp defiles, or clefts, that give access into central and western Asia Minor.

Under the early Roman Empire, the province was divided, part of the western portion being turned over to the rule of local dynasties, while the rest was evidently administered by neighboring client kingdoms. It was not until the time of Vespasian (72 C.E.) that the eastern and western sections of Cilicia were reunited in a single province. So, during the early part of apostolic times, there was an especially close relationship between Cilicia and Syria, and this seems to be reflected at Acts 15:23, 41 and Galatians 1:21, some researchers suggesting that "Cilicia" in these texts refers to Cilicia Pedias. On the other hand, when Acts 27:5 says that Paul sailed "through the open sea along Cilicia and Pamphylia" on his way to be tried in Rome, "Cilicia" there apparently includes the entire region of eastern and western Cilicia.

Jews from Cilicia were among those disputing with Stephen prior to his death. (Ac 6:9) By about 49 C.E. there were already congregations in Cilicia to which the Christian council in Jerusalem sent a letter. (Ac 15:23) The route for Paul's second and third missionary tours would naturally take him through Cilicia and the Cilician Gates.

CINNAMON

[Heb., *qin·na·mohn'*; Gr., *kin·na'mo·mon*]. The cinnamon tree (*Cinnamomum zeylanicum*) is part of the laurel family, to which both the cassia and the camphor trees belong. It grows best in light, sandy, moist soil and is abundant in Sri Lanka and Java. The Hebrew name is possibly of foreign origin, and the product seems to have been an import into the Promised Land.

The cinnamon grows to a maximum height of about 9 m (30 ft) and has a smooth, ash-colored bark and wide-spreading branches. The lancehead-shaped evergreen leaves are green on top but white on the bottom and measure about 20 to 23 cm (8 to 9 in.) in length and about 5 cm (2 in.) in width. Its small, white or yellowish flowers grow in clusters. The outer bark is almost odorless and of little value. The commercial cinnamon is obtained from the darker inner bark. An aromatic oil is also extracted from the bark.

Cinnamon was used in the preparation of the holy anointing oil as one of "the choicest perfumes." (Ex 30:23) It was sprinkled on beds (Pr 7:17), was figuratively used in describing the beloved Shulammite girl (Ca 4:13, 14), and is included among the products the traveling merchants sell to "Babylon the Great" before her destruction. —Re 18:2, 11-13.

CIRCUMCISION.

The removal of the prepuce, or foreskin, from the male penis. The Hebrew verb *mul* (circumcise) is used in a literal and a figurative sense. The Greek noun *pe·ri·to·me'* (circumcision) literally means "a cutting around." (Joh 7:22) "Uncircumcision" is rendered from the Greek term *a·kro·by·sti'a,* which was used in the Greek *Septuagint* to translate the Hebrew word for "foreskin."—Ro 2:25; Ge 17:11, *LXX.*

Jehovah God made circumcision mandatory for Abraham in 1919 B.C.E., a year before Isaac's birth. God said: "This is my covenant that you men will keep . . . Every male of yours must get circumcised." Every male in Abraham's household of both his descendants and dependents was included, and so Abraham, his 13-year-old son Ishmael, and all his slaves took upon themselves this "sign of the covenant." New slaves brought in also had to be circumcised. From then on, any male of the household, slave or free, was to be circumcised the eighth day after birth. Disregard for this divine requirement was punishable by death.—Ge 17:1, 9-14, 23-27.

Circumcision was practiced in Egypt, as is illustrated in wall paintings and observed in mummies, but it is uncertain when it was first introduced in that country and to what extent it was performed. Some say that Joseph as food administrator introduced it to Egypt. Others cite Herodotus as authority for their claim that Abraham simply borrowed the custom from the Egyptians. Answering these latter claims, W. M. Thomson says: "As to the testimony of Herodotus, who came into Egypt fifteen centuries after, and, with great learning and research, often writes a good deal of nonsense, I refuse utterly to put it in the same category with that of Moses. The great founder of the Jewish commonwealth—the greatest lawgiver on record—born and bred in Egypt, states the facts in relation to the introduction of circumcision among his people. A mere traveller and historian—a foreigner and a Greek—comes along very much later, and makes statements which are partly true, partly erroneous, as Josephus shows in his answer to Apion; and then sceptical authors, more than twenty centuries later than Herodotus, bring up his imperfect statements, and, twisting and expanding them, attempt to prove that Abraham did not receive circumcision from God (as Moses plainly says he did), but from the Egyptians! Not with such weapons can the veracity of Moses be successfully

assailed."—*The Land and the Book,* revised by J. Grande, 1910, p. 593.

Not only did the Egyptians practice circumcision but the Moabites, the Ammonites, and the Edomites also did. (Jer 9:25, 26) Later, the Samaritans that adhered to the requirements set out in the Pentateuch were also circumcised. On the other hand, the Assyrians, the Babylonians, the Greeks, and notably the Philistines did not practice circumcision. The latter in particular, rather than the Canaanites in general, are derogatorily spoken of as "the uncircumcised," and it was from fighting with them that trophies of foreskins were brought.—Jg 14:3; 15:18; 1Sa 14:6; 17:26; 18:25-27; 2Sa 1:20; 1Ch 10:4.

Abraham's descendants through Isaac and Jacob faithfully kept the covenant of circumcision. "Abraham proceeded to circumcise Isaac his son when eight days old, just as God had commanded him." (Ge 21:4; Ac 7:8; Ro 4:9-12) The great-grandsons of Abraham told Shechem and his fellow townsmen: "We cannot possibly . . . give our sister [Dinah] to a man who has a foreskin . . . Only on this condition can we give consent to you, that you *become like us,* by every male of yours getting circumcised." (Ge 34:13-24) Apparently because Moses neglected to circumcise his son, he incurred God's wrath until his wife Zipporah did it for him.—Ex 4:24-26; see ZIPPORAH.

Circumcision Under the Law. Circumcision was made a mandatory requirement of the Mosaic Law. "On the eighth day [after the birth of a male] the flesh of his foreskin will be circumcised." (Le 12:2, 3) So important was it that, if the eighth day fell on the highly regarded Sabbath, circumcision was to be performed anyway. (Joh 7:22, 23) Examples of parents under this Law who faithfully had their children circumcised on the eighth day include the parents of John the Baptizer, Jesus, and Paul. (Lu 1:59; 2:21; Php 3:4, 5) The Law also required aliens to be circumcised before they were allowed to eat the passover.—Ex 12:43-48.

Why did the Law specify that circumcision be done on the eighth day?

Jehovah did not explain, nor was it necessary that he do so. His ways are always right; his reasons, the best. (2Sa 22:31) However, in recent years man has learned some of the physical reasons why the eighth day was a good time to circumcise. Normal amounts of the blood-clotting element called vitamin K are not found in the blood until the *fifth* to the *seventh* day after birth. Another clotting factor known as prothrombin is present in amounts only about 30 percent of normal on the third day but on the eighth day is higher than at any other time in the child's life —as much as 110 percent of normal. So, following Jehovah's instructions would help to avoid the danger of hemorrhage. As Dr. S. I. McMillen observes: "From a consideration of vitamin K and prothrombin determinations the perfect day to perform a circumcision is the *eighth* day . . . [the] day picked by the Creator of vitamin K."—*None of These Diseases*, 1986, p. 21.

Circumcision was usually, though not always, performed by the head of the house. In later times an official designated and trained for this operation was used. By the first century it appears to have become the custom to name the boy when he was circumcised.—Lu 1:59, 60; 2:21.

During the 40-year wilderness wandering, circumcision of the baby boys was not performed. So after crossing the Jordan, Joshua had all those males circumcised with flint knives at Gilgal, and Jehovah protected them until they recuperated. —Jos 5:2-9; see REPROACH.

After the Exile. Two centuries after the Jews returned from Babylon, Greek influence began to dominate the Middle East, and many peoples abandoned circumcision. But when Syrian King Antiochus IV (Epiphanes) proscribed circumcision, he found Jewish mothers willing to die rather than deny their sons the "sign of the covenant." (Ge 17:11) Years later Roman Emperor Hadrian got the same results when forbidding the Jews to circumcise their boys. Some Jewish athletes, however, who desired to participate in Hellenistic games (in which runners wore no clothing) endeavored to become "uncircumcised" by an operation aimed at restoring some semblance of a foreskin in an effort to avoid scorn and ridicule. Paul may have alluded to such a practice when he counseled Christians: "Was any man called circumcised? Let him not become uncircumcised." (1Co 7:18) The Greek verb here rendered "become uncircumcised" (*e·pi·spa′o·mai*) literally means "draw upon," evidently referring to drawing the prepuce forward in order to become as if uncircumcised.—Compare *Int*.

Not Required of Christians. After Jehovah showed his acceptance of Gentiles into the Christian congregation, and since many from the nations were responding to the preaching of the good news, a decision had to be made by the governing body at Jerusalem on the question, Is it necessary for Gentile Christians to get circumcised

in the flesh? The conclusion of the matter: The "necessary things" for Gentiles and Jews alike did not include circumcision.—Ac 15:6-29.

Paul circumcised Timothy shortly after the decree was issued, not as a matter of faith, but to avoid prejudicing Jews to whom they were going to preach. (Ac 16:1-3; 1Co 9:20) The apostle dealt with the subject in several letters. (Ro 2:25-29; Ga 2:11-14; 5:2-6; 6:12-15; Col 2:11; 3:11) "We are those with the *real circumcision* [of the heart], who are rendering sacred service by God's spirit," Paul wrote Gentile Christians at Philippi. (Php 3:3) And to those in Corinth he wrote: "Circumcision does not mean a thing, and uncircumcision means not a thing, but observance of God's commandments does."—1Co 7:19.

Figurative Usage. "Circumcision" is used figuratively in a number of ways. After planting a tree in the Promised Land, for example, it was said to "continue uncircumcised" for three years; its fruit was considered its "foreskin" and was not to be eaten. (Le 19:23) Moses said to Jehovah: "Look! I am uncircumcised in lips, so how will Pharaoh ever listen to me?" (Ex 6:12, 30) In a figurative way "uncircumcised ones" describes with repulsive contempt those worthy only of burial in a common place with slain ones of the lowest sort. —Eze 32:18-32.

Circumcision of the heart was a divine requirement of even the Israelites who were already circumcised in the flesh. Moses told Israel: "You must circumcise the foreskin of your hearts and not harden your necks any longer." "Jehovah your God will have to circumcise your heart and the heart of your offspring, that you may love Jehovah your God with all your heart and all your soul for the sake of your life." (De 10:16; 30:6) Jeremiah reminded that wayward nation in his day of the same thing. (Jer 4:4) 'Circumcision of the heart' means getting rid of anything in one's thinking, affections, or motives that is displeasing and unclean in Jehovah's eyes and that makes the heart unresponsive. Similarly, ears that are not sensitive or responsive are spoken of as "uncircumcised."—Jer 6:10; Ac 7:51.

CISTERN. An artificial underground cavity usually used for the storage of water. Cisterns, unlike wells that are dug down to tap natural underground water, are usually designed to catch and retain rainfall or the runoff from springs. Not open like pools, they are usually covered over at the top. The Hebrew word *bohr*, rendered "cistern," is also translated "waterpit," especially when it appears to be empty of water (Ge 37:20-29; 2Sa 23:20), as "prison hole" when used for that purpose (Ge 40:15), and as "pit" when it refers to or is in parallel with "Sheol" (Ps 30:3; Pr 1:12; Eze 31:14, 16).

Cisterns were vital in the Promised Land. Frequently they were the only means of maintaining a sufficient water supply, because wells and springs were not plentiful in the mountainous country and, where found, often dried up toward the end of summer. Man-made water cisterns even permitted villages to spring up in places where the water supply was otherwise too scant, such as in the Negeb. Assuringly, Jehovah promised his people that they would find cisterns already dug when they entered the Promised Land. (De 6:10, 11; Ne 9:25) King Uzziah is mentioned as hewing out "many cisterns" throughout all Judah. (2Ch 26:1, 10) From upper Galilee down to the Negeb, cisterns numbered literally in the thousands, and many of them have been discovered, practically honeycombing parts of the terrain. It seemed the desirable thing for each household to have its own cistern, even among the Moabites. According to the Moabite Stone, King Mesha, of the tenth century B.C.E., declared: "There was no cistern inside the town at Qarhoh, so I said to all the people, 'Let each of you make a cistern for himself in his house!'" (*Ancient Near Eastern Texts,* edited by J. Pritchard, 1974, p. 320) Sennacherib attempted to entice the inhabitants of Jerusalem by promising that if they capitulated to him, they would "drink each one the water of his own cistern."—2Ki 18:31; Isa 36:16.

Cisterns were most commonly hewed out of rock. If the rock was solid and without cracks, there was little problem with leakage, but in the porous limestone that covered much of Palestine, it was necessary to waterproof the inside walls with plaster. Cisterns dug in earth were lined with brick or stone and then plastered to give them solid walls. These cisterns were commonly pear-shaped, wider at the bottom and narrowing at the top; sometimes the mouth was only a foot or two across. When natural caves were modified or enlarged to serve as cisterns, pillars of native rock were allowed to support the roof, or as in some of those discovered in the Negeb, arches were built inside the cistern to serve the same purpose. Channels in the hillside directed the runoff from rainfall into the underground reservoir.

Ecclesiastes 12:6 refers to "the waterwheel for the cistern," but usually the water was drawn up by means of jars suspended with ropes. Occasional breakage of such jars accounts for the pottery fragments that are found in the bottom of most cisterns. The primitive custom of throwing soil into a cistern that had stagnant or polluted water in order to settle the scum no doubt explains in part why many are partially filled with dirt. Coverings over the openings guarded to some extent against contamination of the water and prevented persons or animals from falling in, although a dead body that might accidentally fall in did not make the waters ceremonially unclean; the one removing the dead body, however, was unclean. (Ex 21:33; Le 11:35, 36) Additionally, the cover on a cistern aided in keeping the water cool and reduced loss from evaporation. (Jer 6:7) Some large cisterns had several openings from which the water was drawn. In cisterns of great size and depth, stairs led down into them as much as 30 m (100 ft) or more.

Other Uses. There are a few instances where cisterns were used for purposes other than water storage. In dry locations, and if sealed against moisture, rats, and insects, they were fine storage areas for grain, being also easily camouflaged against thievery; some cisterns found in terrain where there is no natural source of water were apparently built especially as granaries. Empty cisterns were sometimes employed as prisons. (Zec 9:11) Joseph's brothers threw him into such a waterpit (Ge 37:20-24), and later he found himself in a prison hole (literally, "cistern") down in Egypt. (Ge 40:15, ftn; 41:14) The tenth plague on Egypt reached "to the firstborn of the captive who was in the prison hole [literally, "the house of the cistern"]." (Ex 12:29) Jeremiah was imprisoned in "the house of the cistern" and later thrown into a miry pit. (Jer 37:16; 38:6-13) Once when the Israelites were fleeing from the Philistines, some hid themselves in the cisterns (waterpits), and on another occasion, Asa's large cistern became a burial tomb for 70 bodies. (1Sa 13:6; Jer 41:4-9) Because of their permanent nature, some cisterns served as geographic markers.—1Sa 19:22; 2Sa 3:26; 2Ki 10:14.

Figurative Usage. In two noteworthy passages, "cistern" is used figuratively. Jehovah says that people who have forsaken him to look to other sources for protection and help have actually left "the source of living water, in order to hew out for themselves cisterns, broken cisterns, that cannot contain the water." (Jer 2:13, 18) Solomon, admonishing marital fidelity, said: "Drink water out of your own cistern."—Pr 5:15.

CITIES OF REFUGE.
Jehovah's law on the sanctity of blood was very explicit. The shedding of human blood polluted the land in which the sons of Israel lived, in the midst of which Jehovah was residing, and it could be atoned for only by

the blood of the one shedding it. (Ge 9:5, 6; Nu 35:33, 34) So, in the case of a murderer, the blood of his victim was avenged and the law of 'life for life' was satisfied when the murderer was put to death "without fail" by the avenger of blood. (Ex 21:23; Nu 35:21) But what about the unintentional manslayer, the one, for example, who killed his brother when the axhead accidentally flew off while he was chopping wood? (De 19:4, 5) For such unfortunate ones Jehovah lovingly provided cities of refuge, six in number, where the accidental shedder of blood could find protection and asylum from the avenger of blood.—Nu 35:6-32; Jos 20:2-9.

Locations. Before his death, Moses appointed three of these cities E of the Jordan. The first, *Bezer,* in the S on the tableland of the territory that belonged to the tribe of Reuben, was E of the northern end of the Dead Sea; the second, *Ramoth,* in Gilead, belonged to the tribe of Gad and was in about the middle of the eastern section of the land occupied by Israel; the third, *Golan,* in Bashan, was to the N in the territory of Manasseh. (De 4:43; Jos 21:27, 36, 38) After the Israelites crossed over to the W side of the Jordan, Joshua designated three more cities of refuge: *Hebron,* to the S in Judah's territory; *Shechem,* in the central mountainous region of Ephraim; and to the N, *Kedesh,* in the territory of Naphtali, which was later known as the region of Galilee. (Jos 21:13, 21, 32) All these cities were Levite cities and one, Hebron, was a priestly city. Additionally, because of being set aside as cities of refuge, they received a sacred status.—Jos 20:7.

Legal Procedure. Upon reaching a city of refuge, the fugitive was to state his case to the older men at the city gate and was to be received hospitably. To prevent willful murderers from taking cover under this provision, the fleeing one, after en-

tering the city of refuge, had to stand trial at the city gates in the city having jurisdiction where the killing occurred, in order to prove his innocence. If found innocent, he was returned to the city of refuge. However, his safety could be guaranteed only if he remained in the city the rest of his life or until the death of the high priest. No ransom could be accepted to alter these terms. (Nu 35:22-29, 32; Jos 20:4-6) Even Jehovah's sacred altar provided no protection for murderers, as was illustrated in the case of Joab.—Ex 21:14; 1Ki 1:50; 2:28-34; see AVENGER OF BLOOD.

How different, then, Jehovah's arrangement for the protection of unintentional manslayers was from the sanctuaries provided by ancient pagan nations and by Christendom's churches down through the ages! Whereas the latter sanctuaries offered shelter for criminals along with the innocent, Israel's cities of refuge gave protection only to the unintentional manslayer and then only under restrictions, and thus respect for the sanctity of life was promoted.

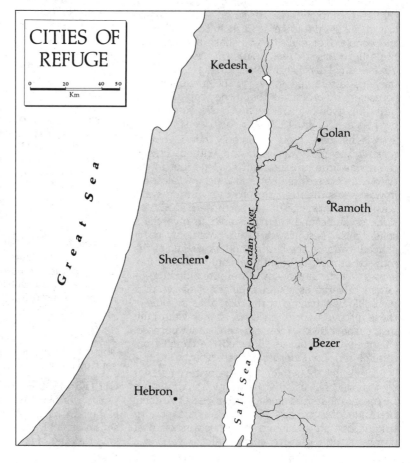

CITIES OF REFUGE

0   20   40   50
        Km

Kedesh

Golan

Great Sea

Ramoth

Jordan River

Shechem

Salt Sea

Bezer

Hebron

CITIZEN, CITIZENSHIP. A citizen is a native-born or naturalized inhabitant of a city or state who is entitled to certain rights and privileges denied others, and who, in turn, assumes the responsibilities attached to such rights by the authorities granting the citizenship. In the Bible the terms "citizen" and "citizenship" occur only in the Christian Greek Scriptures. The Greek words *po·li′tes* (citizen), *po·li·tei′a* (rights as a citizen; citizenship; state), *po·li′teu·ma* (citizenship; life as citizens), *syn·po·li′tes* (fellow citizen), and *po·li·teu′o·mai* (behave as a citizen) are all related to *po′lis,* meaning "city."

In the Hebrew Scriptures, though the terms "citizen" and "citizenship" are not found, the concept of citizen and noncitizen is there in terms such as "native" and "alien resident." (Le 24:22) Under the Mosaic Law arrangement, the congregation was in reality the commonwealth into which aliens could, with certain restrictions, be admitted, there to enjoy many benefits common to the natural-born Israelites. Naturalization, it might be said, came when a male alien resident became circumcised, thus granting him the opportunity of fully entering into the greater privileges in Jehovah's worship, even to the extent of participating in the annual Passover festival.—Ex 12:43-49; Nu 9:14; see ALIEN RESIDENT; FOREIGNER.

Roman Citizenship. Roman citizenship secured for a person special rights and immunities recognized and honored throughout the empire. For example, it was illegal to torture or scourge a Roman citizen for the purpose of extracting a confession from him, these forms of punishment being considered very servile and fit only for slaves. At Jerusalem, Roman soldiers rescued Paul from a Jewish mob. Paul did not at first identify himself as a Roman citizen, but when he was about to be scourged, he said to an army officer standing by: "Is it lawful for you men to scourge a man that is a Roman and uncondemned?" "Well," the account continues, "when the army officer heard this, he went to the military commander and made report, saying: 'What are you intending to do? Why, this man is a Roman.'" When the truth of the matter was learned, immediately "the men that were about to examine him with torture withdrew from him; and the military commander became afraid on ascertaining that he was a Roman and that he had bound him."—Ac 21:27-39; 22:25-29; see also Ac 16:37-40.

Another advantage and privilege enjoyed under Roman citizenship was the right to appeal the decision of a provincial governor to the emperor of Rome. In the case of capital offense, a Roman citizen had the right to be sent to Rome for trial before the emperor himself. So it was, when arguing his case before Festus, that Paul declared: "I am standing before the judgment seat of Caesar, where I ought to be judged. . . . no man can hand me over to [the Jews] as a favor. I appeal to Caesar!" (Ac 25:10-12) Once the right of appeal to Rome was requested, it could not be withdrawn. So after reviewing Paul's case, King Agrippa II said to Festus: "This man could have been released if he had not appealed to Caesar."—Ac 26:32.

Roman citizenship could be obtained in a number of ways. Sometimes the emperors extended this special favor to whole cities or districts, or to individuals, for services rendered. It was also possible at times to purchase citizenship outright for a sum of money, this being the case with the military commander Claudius Lysias, who told Paul: "I purchased these rights as a citizen for a large sum of money." However, Paul countered Claudius Lysias' response of having purchased citizenship rights, saying, "But I was even born in them."—Ac 22:28.

Spiritual Citizenship. In his letters Paul also refers to spiritual citizenship. He describes uncircumcised Gentiles who became spiritual Israelites as those who were at one time without Christ, alienated from Israel and strangers to the covenants, without hope, without God, but who are "now in union with Christ Jesus." "Certainly, therefore," he continues in this vein of thought, "you are no longer strangers and alien residents, but you are fellow citizens of the holy ones." (Eph 2:12, 13, 19) It was especially significant when Paul wrote to the Christians at Philippi, one of those cities granted Roman citizenship, where ten years earlier his Roman citizenship had been trampled on: "As for us, our citizenship exists in the heavens." (Php 3:20) In his same letter he exhorted fellow believers to "behave in a manner worthy of the good news." The Greek word rendered "behave" (*po·li·teu′o·mai*) literally means "behave as a citizen."—Php 1:27; compare *Int.*

CITY. A compact, settled area, greater in size, population, or importance than a town or village. The Hebrew word *'ir,* translated "city," occurs nearly 1,100 times in the Scriptures. Sometimes the word *qir·yah′* (town) is used as a synonym or in a parallelism—for example, "After this you will be called City [*'ir*] of Righteousness, Faithful Town [*qir·yah′*]," or "How is it that the city [*'ir*] of praise has not been abandoned, the town [*qir·yath′*] of exultation?"—Isa 1:26; Jer 49:25.

"Settlements" (Heb., *chatse·rim′*), "dependent towns" (Heb., *ba·noth′*), and "villages" (Heb., *kepha·rim'*), also mentioned in the Hebrew Scriptures, were distinguished from "cities" and "towns" in that they were not walled-in communities but were associated with the open country. (1Sa 6:18) If located in the suburbs or immediate vicinity of a fortified city or town, these communities were described as "dependent towns," literally "daughters" of the walled-in city. (Nu 21:25; see DEPENDENT TOWNS.) The Law of Moses also made a legal distinction between the walled cities and towns, and the unwalled settlements and villages. If a person living in an unwalled settlement sold his house, he always retained the right to buy it back, but if unable to, it was returned to him during the year of Jubilee. When, on the other hand, a house in a walled city was sold, the seller had to repurchase it during the coming year or the property remained irrevocably that of the purchaser, except in the case of Levite cities. (Le 25:29-34) The same distinction is maintained in the Christian Greek Scriptures, where *po'lis* usually denotes a walled "city" and *ko'me* usually refers to an unwalled "village." The Greek word *ko·mo'po·lis* in Mark 1:38 may be rendered 'village town' or 'village city.' (Compare *Int.*) John called Bethlehem "the village where David used to be," and Luke (aware that Rehoboam had fortified the village) spoke of it as a city.—Joh 7:42; Lu 2:4; 2Ch 11:5, 6.

The first city builder was Cain, who named the city after his son Enoch. (Ge 4:17) If there were other cities before the Flood, their names disappeared along with them in the Deluge in 2370 B.C.E. After the Flood, the cities of Babel, Erech, Accad, and Calneh in the land of Shinar formed the initial nucleus of Nimrod's kingdom. He then expanded this by building Nineveh, Rehoboth-Ir, Calah, and Resen (collectively described as "the great city") to the N in the Mesopotamian Valley. (Ge 10:10-12) On the other hand, the patriarchs Abraham, Isaac, and Jacob built no cities but lived as alien residents in tents even when visiting towns and villages in Canaan and Egypt. (Heb 11:9) However, much later the spies who entered Canaan reported that there were many strongly fortified cities in the land.—Nu 13:28; De 9:1.

Purpose in Building. People began to build cities for a number of reasons: for protection, industry, commerce, and religion. Judging from the number and size of the temples uncovered by archaeologists, religion was undoubtedly one of the principal motivations behind the construction of many ancient cities. The city of Babel with its religious tower is one example. "Come on!" said its

builders to one another, "Let us build ourselves a city and also a tower with its top in the heavens, and let us make a celebrated name for ourselves, for fear we may be scattered over all the surface of the earth." (Ge 11:4-9) The danger of enslavement to warlike individuals bent on conquest was another compelling reason for fearful people to band together into cities. They invariably fenced in and walled up these cities, and they closed the gateways at night and in times of danger.—Jos 2:5; 2Ch 26:6.

City dwellers often worked at agriculture and livestock raising, which activities were carried on beyond the walls of the city; the typical farmer still resided inside the city rather than on his farm. Others engaged in handicraft industries. The cities served as storage depots, trade centers, and markets for distribution. Cities like Tyre, Sidon, and Joppa came to be primarily shipping and exchange centers between the traffic of the sea-lanes and the overland caravans.—Eze 27.

Many cities began as simple villages, grew to the size of a town or the status of a city, and sometimes became great city-states controlling the lives of hundreds of thousands of people. With such growth, government and judicial power became concentrated in the hands of a few political and military leaders, and quite often the overriding power dictating the urban way of life resided in a hierarchy of priestly despots. It was, therefore, a striking contrast when Israelite cities began to appear on the world stage, the rule of which was in the hands of theocratically appointed administrators bound by duty to enforce God-given constitutional laws. Jehovah was that nation's King, Lawgiver, and Judge, and when his visible representatives faithfully carried out their duties, the people rejoiced.—Isa 33:22; Ezr 7:25, 26; Pr 29:2.

Selection of Sites. Selecting the location for a city depended on several factors. Since defense was generally of prime importance, ancient cities were usually placed on high elevations. Though this exposed them to open view, they were difficult to reach. (Mt 5:14) Coastal cities and those along the banks of rivers were exceptions. In addition to the natural barriers, often massive walls or a complex of walls and towers and, in some instances, moats were built around the city. (2Ki 9:17; Ne 3:1–4:23; 6:1-15; Da 9:25) As cities grew, it was sometimes necessary to extend the walls to include greater perimeters. Entrances through the walls were secured with strong gates that could withstand prolonged siege. (See FORTIFICATIONS; GATE, GATEWAY; WALLS.) Outside and beyond the walls were the fields, pasture grounds, and suburbs that were often undefended during attack.—Nu 35:1-8; Jos 21:41, 42.

A good nearby water supply was absolutely essential and not to be overlooked when selecting a site for a city. For this reason it was counted ideal when cities had springs or wells enclosed within their limits. In certain instances, notably Megiddo, Gibeon, and Jerusalem, there were underground water tunnels and conduits to bring water inside the walls from sources outside. (2Sa 5:8; 2Ki 20:20; 2Ch 32:30) Reservoirs and cisterns were often constructed for catching and holding water during the wet season for use at a later time. In some instances the terrain was honeycombed with cisterns, as each household endeavored to have its own supply of water.—2Ch 26:10.

Common aims and purposes in building ancient cities led to great similarities in their design and layout. And, since centuries of passing time have made little change, certain cities today are very much as they were two or three millenniums ago. On entering the gates, one found himself in a large open place, the city's marketplace, the public square, where all kinds of selling and buying were carried on, and where contracts were made and sealed before witnesses. (Ge 23:10-18; 2Ki 7:1; Na 2:4) Here was the public forum where news was received and passed on (Ne 8:1, 3; Jer 17:19), where the elders held court (Ru 4:1-10), and where the traveler might spend the night if perchance private hospitality was not extended to him. (Jg 19:15-21) Sometimes other accommodations were available in the city for the visitor. —Jos 2:1; Jg 16:1; Lu 2:4-7; 10:35; see INN.

Certain cities were built to serve special functions, as, for example, Pithom and Raamses, built by Israelite slave labor as storage places for Pharaoh (Ex 1:11), also Solomon's storage cities, chariot cities, and cities for his horsemen (1Ki 9:17-19), as well as Jehoshaphat's storage cities. (2Ch 17:12) Forty-eight cities were set aside for the Levites —13 were for the priests, and 6 were refuge cities for the unintentional manslayer.—Nu 35:6-8; Jos 21:19, 41, 42; see CHARIOT CITIES; CITIES OF REFUGE; PRIESTS' CITIES.

The size of many ancient cities can be figured from the remains of their walls, but population figures cannot be estimated with any degree of certainty. Regarding Nineveh, we are told that it was a very large metropolis: "Nineveh the great city, in which there exist more than one hundred and twenty thousand men who do not at all know the difference between their right hand and their left."—Jon 4:11; 3:3.

The name given to cities mentioned in the Bible usually had meaning and purpose—locality, character, ancestry of the inhabitants, even prophetic significance is disclosed by many of their names. (Ge 11:9; 21:31; Jg 18:29) Sometimes to distinguish one city from another of the same name, the tribal location was added, as in the case of "Bethlehem in Judah," for there was also a Bethlehem in Zebulun. (Jg 17:7; Jos 19:10, 15) Enclave cities were those belonging to one tribe that lay in the territory of another tribe.—Jos 16:9; see ENCLAVE CITIES.

Figurative Use. In the Hebrew Scriptures, cities are used figuratively. (Pr 21:22; Jer 1:18) We find Jesus employing cities in his illustrations (Mt 12:25; Lu 19:17, 19), and Paul likewise in a figure of speech. (Heb 11:10, 16; 12:22; 13:14) In Revelation cities are used to illustrate a number of things: "the holy city" trampled by the nations (Re 11:2), "the great city" called Sodom and Egypt in a spiritual sense (Re 11:8), the "great city, Babylon" (Re 18:10-21; 17:18), and "the holy city, New Jerusalem, coming down out of heaven from God and prepared as a bride adorned for her husband." —Re 21:2-27; 22:14, 19; 3:12.

CITY OF DAVID.   See DAVID, CITY OF.

CITY RECORDER.

In the municipal government of the free cities in Asia Minor under the Roman Empire, the city recorder (Gr., *gram·ma·teus'*) was the most important public officer. He was apparently elected to office by the people and functioned as the leading member of the municipal government. We might compare him in some respects to a modern-day mayor, as some translations render the term. Consequently, he was very influential in city affairs, and his dignified office was held in esteem by the people to a greater degree than is implied by the word "clerk" or "town clerk," as used in several Bible translations at Acts 19:35, where *gram·ma·teus'* appears in a setting and connotation differing from its usual usage as applied to the Jewish scribes. The influence the city recorder wielded is shown by the manner in which this official in Ephesus quieted the mob that gathered against Paul and his companions.—Ac 19:35-41.

The city recorder had direct access to the proconsul of the province and served as the liaison between the city government and Rome's provincial administration of which Ephesus was one of the centers. This enabled the recorder to act as a buffer between the power of the Roman authorities and the people of the city. In the Asian cities, the city recorder was held accountable by the

Roman authority for maintaining law and order within his jurisdiction. This accounts, in part at least, for the concern expressed by the city recorder when the people of Ephesus had been stirred up by the Ephesian silversmiths over the preaching done by the apostle Paul. It was a disorderly mob, an illegal assembly in the theater. There was the liability of a charge of sedition, as the city recorder pointed out to the people. He feared that the Romans would hold him personally responsible.

CITY RULERS. Civic magistrates (Gr., *po·li·tar'khai*) before whom Jason and other Christians were dragged by an angry mob in Thessalonica. (Ac 17:5-8) Regarding the use of the Greek term, G. Ernest Wright says: "An inscription on this gate [the Vardar Gate from Thessalonica], now in the British Museum, mentions some city officials called 'politarchs'. A number of other inscriptions contain the same word. In Acts 17:6 this term is also used as the name of the officials before whom Christians were dragged during the riot caused by Paul's preaching. The word is otherwise unknown in extant Greek literature and the archaeological information is a confirmation of the accuracy of Luke's narrative at this point."—*Biblical Archaeology*, 1963, p. 260; see ARCHAEOLOGY (Relating to the Christian Greek Scriptures).

CLAN. A large social group having a common inheritance, and resembling a tribe in magnitude.

In all three instances where the Hebrew word *'um·mah'* occurs, it refers to a large group of non-Israelites and is translated "clan." Descendants of Ishmael's 12 sons, for example, are described as "clans" early in the history of that ethnic group. (Ge 25:16) The same is true of the descendants of Midian. (Nu 25:15) The term is also found in Hebrew poetry at Psalm 117:1, where it appears in a parallelism with "nations."

The Hebrew word *she'vet*, which is usually rendered "tribe," is translated "clan" at Numbers 18:2. This is an exceptional instance to show the distinction the Hebrew text makes, for in this verse the two words *mat·teh'* and *she'vet* appear, both of which are normally rendered "tribe."

CLAUDIA (Clau'di·a). A Christian woman at Rome whose greetings Paul included in his second letter to Timothy.—2Ti 4:21.

CLAUDIUS (Clau'di·us). Fourth emperor of Rome; son of Drusus the brother of Tiberius, and uncle of Caligula, whom he followed to the throne in 41 C.E. Claudius was not very strong physically or in willpower, and though he was interested in history, writing, and other academic pursuits, his predecessors thought him mentally incompetent to handle the reins of power and therefore favored others as successors. However, during the tumult following Caligula's assassination, the Praetorian Guard prevailed and had Claudius proclaimed Emperor. One of his supporters in this power struggle was Herod Agrippa I, whom Claudius rewarded by confirming his kingship and by adding Judea and Samaria to his domains. Claudius also managed to win the favor of the Senate. His fourth wife reportedly poisoned him with mushrooms in 54 C.E., in the 14th year of his reign. Nero then came to power.

"A great famine . . . upon the entire inhabited earth" was foretold by the prophet Agabus, "which, for that matter, did take place in the time of Claudius." This precipitated "a relief ministration" on the part of the Christians in Antioch for their brothers in Jerusalem and Judea. (Ac 11:27-30) Such a famine in Palestine in the reign of Claudius is called by Josephus (*Jewish Antiquities*, XX, 49-53 [ii, 5]; XX, 101 [v, 2]) the "great famine," and is dated about 46 C.E.

"Claudius . . . ordered all the Jews to depart from Rome," issuing his decree in 49 or early 50 C.E., in the ninth year of his reign. The Roman biographer and historian Suetonius corroborates Claudius' banishment of the Jews from Rome. (*Claudius*, XXV, 4) As a consequence of this expulsion order, two Christian Jews, Aquila and Priscilla, left Rome for Corinth, where not long after their arrival they met the apostle Paul upon his reaching there probably in the fall of the year 50 C.E. (Ac 18:1-3) Toward the beginning of his reign, Claudius had been favorably disposed toward the Jews, even ordering toleration in their behalf and granting them various freedoms throughout the empire. It appears, however, that numerous Jews in Rome were rather riotous, resulting in Claudius' expelling them from the city.

CLAUDIUS LYSIAS (Clau'di·us Lys'i·as). Military commander of the Roman garrison at Jerusalem when the apostle Paul last visited there, about 56 C.E. As a military commander (chiliarch), Claudius Lysias had 1,000 men under his command. His Greek name Lysias suggests that he was a Greek by birth. He acquired Roman citizenship for a large sum of money probably during the reign of Claudius, at which time, as was customary among those procuring citizenship, he adopted the name of the ruling emperor. (Ac 22:28; 23:26) According to the Roman historian Dio Cassius, early in the reign of Emperor Claudius, Roman citizenship was often sold for large sums.—*Dio's Roman History*, LX, 17, 5, 6.

Claudius Lysias figures in the account of Acts because of his dealings with the apostle Paul. He and the soldiers and army officers with him rescued Paul from death at the hands of a rioting mob. Taking hold of Paul, Claudius Lysias directed that the apostle be bound, and when, because of the tumult, he was unable to ascertain through inquiry the nature of the accusation against him, he commanded that the apostle be brought to the soldiers' quarters located in the Tower of Antonia. —Ac 21:30-34.

Claudius Lysias mistakenly concluded that Paul was the Egyptian who had previously stirred up sedition and led the 4,000 "dagger men" into the wilderness. But, upon learning otherwise, he granted the apostle's request to address the crowd from the steps, likely those of the fortress. When violence started anew immediately after Paul's mentioning his commission to go to the nations, Claudius Lysias ordered that he be brought inside the soldiers' quarters and closely examined under scourging.—Ac 21:35-40; 22:21-24.

On receiving report that Paul was a Roman citizen and then making personal inquiry, Claudius Lysias became afraid because of having violated the rights of a Roman by having him bound. (Ac 22:25-29) His acceptance of Paul's claim to Roman citizenship on the basis of the apostle's own statement can be better understood when considering that there was little likelihood of a person's falsely claiming Roman citizenship rights, as such would render the one doing so liable to capital punishment. Says the historian Suetonius: The emperor "forbade men of foreign birth to use the Roman names so far as those of the clans were concerned. Those who usurped the privileges of Roman citizenship he executed in the Esquiline field."—*The Lives of the Caesars,* Claudius XXV, 3.

Still desiring to arrive at the truth concerning the accusation against Paul, Claudius Lysias commanded the Sanhedrin to assemble. On that occasion Paul's introducing the subject of the resurrection resulted in such dissension among the members of the Sanhedrin that Claudius Lysias, fearing that Paul would be pulled to pieces by them, ordered soldiers to snatch the apostle out of their midst.—Ac 22:30; 23:6-10.

Later, upon learning from Paul's own nephew of a Jewish plot to kill the apostle, Claudius Lysias summoned two of his army officers and commanded them to get ready 200 soldiers, 70 horsemen, and 200 spearmen to leave for Caesarea at about 9:00 p.m. in order to take Paul to Governor Felix. (Ac 23:16-24) In compliance with Roman law, he also sent a statement of the case to Governor Felix. This letter, however, was not altogether factual. Although acknowledging Paul's innocence, Claudius Lysias gave the impression that he had rescued Paul because of having learned that the apostle was a Roman, whereas in reality he had violated Paul's citizenship rights by having him bound and even ordering that he be examined under scourings.—Ac 23:25-30.

As to the disciple Luke's knowledge of the letter's contents, it may be that the letter itself was read at the time Paul's case was heard. The apostle may even have received a copy of it after Paul's appeal to Caesar.

CLAY. A fine-grained, natural earthy material that is soft and pliable when wet but hard when dry, particularly if dried by fire. It is largely made up of hydrous aluminum silicates. The Hebrew word *cho'mer* is used to denote the "clay" of a potter (Isa 41:25), the "clay" under a seal (Job 38:14), the "clay" of the streets (Isa 10:6), the "mortar" between bricks (Ge 11:3), and, metaphorically, man as "clay" in the hands of his Former, Jehovah God (Isa 45:9; compare Job 10:9). In the Christian Greek Scriptures *pe·los'* signifies potter's "clay" (Ro 9:21) and the moist "clay" Jesus used to cure a blind man (Joh 9:6, 11, 14, 15; see also BLINDNESS), while *ke·ra·mi·kos'* describes vessels made of potter's "clay."—Re 2:27.

In the lowlands of Israel there is an abundance of clay, and in Bible times it was used for making pottery and bricks. (Jer 18:4, 6; Ex 1:14; Na 3:14; see POTTER.) Due to its ability to receive an impression when moist and retain the same when dry, it was useful for making clay tablets and seal impressions on documents and letters. Clay was employed in sealing pottery used for wine or for the safekeeping of valuable records, such as the deed to Jeremiah's property. (Jer 32:14) The preservation of the Dead Sea Scrolls was due in large measure to the clay jars in which they were found.

The earthy nature of clay is alluded to in expressions such as "the clay of the streets," 'man is made of clay,' or man is 'brought down to the clay.' (Job 10:9; 30:19; 33:6; Isa 10:6) Another metaphoric significance attached to the saying that man is made of clay is the fact that Jehovah is the Potter. (Isa 29:16; 45:9; 64:8; Ro 9:21) Clay, even when baked hard, is not a strong material, and a mixture of iron and clay is worthless. (Da 2:33-35, 41-43, 45) Clay affords little or no protection. (Job 4:19; 13:12; Isa 41:25) Being a very common commodity, its commercial value is rather insignificant.—Job 27:16.

CLEAN, CLEANNESS.

A number of Hebrew and Greek words describe that which is clean and pure as well as the act of purification, that is, restoring to a condition without blemish, spotless, free from anything that soils, adulterates, or corrupts. These words describe not only physical cleanliness but, more often, moral or spiritual cleanness. Often physical and ceremonial cleanness overlap. The Hebrew verb ta·her' (be clean; cleanse) usually refers to ceremonial or moral cleanness. A Hebrew synonym of ta·her' is ba·rar', which, in its various forms, means "clean out; select; keep clean; show oneself clean; cleanse." (Eze 20:38; Ec 3:18; Ps 18:26; Jer 4:11) The Greek word ka·tha·ros', meaning "clean; pure," is used in a physical, moral, and religious sense. (Mt 23:26; Mt 5:8; Tit 1:15) "Uncleanness" is rendered from the Hebrew ta·me'' and the Greek a·ka·thar·si'a. —Le 5:2; Mt 23:27; Ga 5:19.

Physical Cleanness. Their personal habits made the nation of Israel a comparatively healthy people, notwithstanding their nomadic wanderings in the wilderness for 40 years. God's laws governing their camp life, including the diagnosis and treatment of diseases, were unquestionably responsible for this. The importance of clean water was emphasized under this arrangement. Not all animals were classified as clean for food. (See ANIMALS.) Precautionary regulations governed the handling and disposal of dead bodies. Quarantines acted as barriers against the spread of contagious diseases. Sewage disposal by burying excreta was a sanitation requirement far in advance of the times. (De 23:12-14) The requirements of frequent bathing and the washing of clothes were also beneficial provisions in that nation's code of laws.

The Scriptures often use physical cleanness as a symbol or representation of spiritual cleanness. For example, mention is made of "bright, clean, fine linen," and it is said to represent "the righteous acts of the holy ones." (Re 19:8) Jesus also drew upon a principle of physical cleanness when pointing out the spiritual uncleanness and hypocrisy of the Pharisees. Their deceitful conduct was likened to cleaning the outside of a cup or dish without doing the same thing to the inside. (Mt 23:25, 26) Jesus used a similar illustration during the last Passover meal when talking to his disciples with Judas Iscariot present. Even though they had bathed and had their feet washed by the Master, and were therefore "wholly clean" physically, yet spiritually speaking, "Not all of you are clean," Jesus said.—Joh 13:1-11.

The Bible lists some 70 causes of physical uncleanness and ceremonial defilement. Among these are: contact with dead bodies (Le 11:32-40; Nu 19:11-19); contact with unclean persons or things (Le 15:4-12, 20-24; Nu 19:22); leprosy (Le 13:1-59); physical discharges of the sex organs, including emission of semen during sexual intercourse (Le 15:1-3, 16-19, 32, 33); childbirth (Le 12:1-5); eating the flesh of unclean birds, fish, or animals (Le 11:41-47). The priests were especially obligated to be physically as well as ceremonially clean when serving before Jehovah. (Ex 30:17-21; Le 21:1-7; 22:2-8) In a special sense the land could be polluted by acts of murder and idolatry.—Nu 35:33, 34; Eze 22:2-4; 36:25.

Ceremonial Cleanness. This was observed among the Israelites under the penalty of death. "You must keep the sons of Israel separate from their uncleanness, that they may not die in their uncleanness for their defiling of my tabernacle, which is in their midst." (Le 15:31) Cleansing was usually performed by the use of water and ashes of a red cow, and the ceremony was administered in behalf of persons, places, and things. (Nu 19:2-9) Three of the most common causes of uncleanness involving persons are enumerated at Numbers 5:2: "[1] every leprous person and [2] everyone having a running discharge and [3] everyone unclean by a deceased soul."

Leprosy. This was the most loathsome of all diseases and required severe measures of control, including prolonged isolation with careful and repeated examination to determine when a cure had been effected. (Le 13:1-46; De 24:8) It, therefore, required a great deal of faith for the unclean leper to say to Jesus: "Lord, if you just want to, you can make me clean." Jesus not only wanted to but he also showed he had the ability to cure this loathsome disease by commanding: "Be made clean." Jesus then told this restored man: "Go, show yourself to the priest, and offer the gift that Moses appointed."—Mt 8:2-4; Mr 1:40-44; see LEPROSY.

Originally, under the prescribed regulations of the Law, before a cured victim of leprosy could return to normal living, an elaborate two-part ceremony was necessary, the first part involving the use of water, cedarwood, coccus scarlet material, hyssop, and two birds. These things were supplied by the recovered leper when he presented himself to the priest outside the camp of Israel. One of the birds was then killed over running water, and its blood was caught in an earthenware vessel. The cedar, scarlet material, hyssop, and the living bird were dipped in the blood; the cured leper was spattered seven times by the priest with the blood, and the live bird was turned loose. Upon being pronounced clean, the man shaved, bathed, washed his garments, and entered the camp, but he was required to dwell seven days outside his tent. On the seventh day he again shaved off all his hair, including his eyebrows. The next day he brought two rams and a female lamb, less than a year old, together with a little flour and oil, as a guilt offering, sin offering, burnt offering, and grain offering. The guilt offering consisting of one ram and the oil was first presented as a wave offering before Jehovah by the priest, who then killed the ram; he put some of its blood on the lobe of the right ear, the right thumb, and the right big toe of the one being cleansed. Similarly, some of the oil was then placed on top of the blood in the three above-mentioned places; some of the oil was also sprinkled seven times before Jehovah, and the balance of it was put on the head of the one being cleansed. The priest then offered up the sin, burnt, and grain sacrifices, making atonement and pronouncing the cured leper clean. If, because of circumstances, the candidate was very poor, he could substitute two turtledoves or two young pigeons for the lamb and one of the rams used as the sin and the burnt offerings.—Le 14:1-32.

Discharges. There were laws governing both the natural and diseased discharges from the bodies of both sexes, that is, discharges from the sex organs. If a man had an involuntary emission of semen during the night, he was to bathe and wash his garments and remain unclean until the following evening. A woman was to count seven days as the period of uncleanness for her regular menstruation.

However, if a woman had an irregular, abnormal, or prolonged flow, then she was to count also seven days after it stopped. So also the male was to count seven days after a running discharge had stopped. (Such diseased condition of his urinary system is not to be confused with his normal expulsion of semen.) Anything that the man or woman might touch or sit on (beds, chairs, saddles, garments, and so forth) during their state of uncleanness was itself made unclean, and in turn, anyone touching these articles or the unclean person himself was required to bathe, wash his garments, and remain unclean until evening time. In addition to bathing and washing their garments, both the male and female on the eighth day were to bring two turtledoves or two young pigeons to the tent of meeting, and the priest was to offer them, one as a sin offering and the other as a burnt sacrifice, to make atonement for the cleansed person.—Le 15:1-17, 19-33.

When a man and his wife had intercourse in which there was an emission of semen, they were required to bathe and were unclean until evening. (Le 15:16-18) If inadvertently a wife's flow began during intercourse, then the husband was unclean seven days, the same as his wife. (Le 15:24) If they deliberately showed contempt for God's law and had sexual relations while she was menstruating, the penalty of death was imposed on the male and the female. (Le 20:18) For the above reasons, when ceremonial cleanness was required, as, for example, when men were sanctified for a military expedition, they were obliged to refrain from having intercourse with their wives.—1Sa 21:4, 5; 2Sa 11:8-11.

Giving birth also meant a period of uncleanness for the mother. If the baby was a boy, she was unclean for seven days, the same as during her menstrual period. The eighth day the child was circumcised, but for another 33 days the mother was unclean with regard to touching anything holy or coming into the sanctuary, though she did not make unclean everything she touched. If the baby was a girl, this 40-day period was doubled: 14 days plus 66 days. Thus, from birth, the Law distinguished between male and female, assigning to the latter a subordinate position. In either case, at the end of the period of purification she was to bring a ram less than a year old for a burnt offering and a young pigeon or a turtledove for a sin offering. If the parents were too poor to afford a ram, as was the case with Mary and Joseph, then two doves or two pigeons served for the cleansing sacrifices.—Le 12:1-8; Lu 2:22-24.

Why did the Mosaic Law say that sexual intercourse and childbirth made a person "unclean"?

The question arises: Why were such normal, proper things as menstruation, sexual intercourse between married persons, and childbirth viewed in the Law as making one "unclean"? For one thing, it raised the most intimate relations of marriage to the level of sanctity, teaching both mates self-control, a high regard for the reproductive organs, and respect for the sacredness of life and blood. The hygienic benefits that accrued from scrupulous observance of these regulations have also been commented on. But there is yet another aspect of the matter.

In the beginning God created the sex impulses and generative powers in the first man and woman and commanded them to cohabit and bring forth children. It was therefore no sin for the perfect pair to have sexual intercourse. However, when Adam and Eve disobeyed God, not in the matter of sex relations, but in eating the forbidden fruit, drastic changes took place. Suddenly their guilty sin-stricken consciences made them aware of their nakedness, and they immediately covered their genital organs from God's sight. (Ge 3:7, 10, 11) From then on, men could not carry out the procreative mandate in perfection, but, instead, the hereditary blemish of sin and the penalty of death would be transmitted from the parents to children. Even the most upright and God-fearing parents produce sin-infected children.—Ps 51:5.

The Law's requirements pertaining to the functions of the reproductive organs taught men and women self-discipline, restraint of passions, and respect for God's means of propagation. The Law's regulations forcefully reminded creatures of their sinful state; these were not merely health measures to ensure cleanliness or prophylactic safeguards against the spread of diseases. As a reminder of man's inherited sinfulness, it was fitting that both the male and the female with genital discharges due to normal functions of their bodies observe a period of uncleanness. If suffering abnormal prolonged discharges because of defective conditions, a more extensive period of uncleanness was demanded; and in the end, as also when a mother gave birth, in addition to bathing, a *sin offering* was necessary, so that God's priest might make atonement in behalf of the person. Jesus' mother Mary thus confessed to her hereditary sinfulness, acknowledging that she was not sinless, immaculate, by offering a sin-atoning sacrifice after giving birth to her firstborn.—Lu 2:22-24.

Dead bodies. Under the Mosaic Law governing dead bodies, there were different degrees of uncleanness: Touching a dead beast made one unclean for only the day; touching a dead man resulted in uncleanness for a week. In the first instance a person was required only to wash his garments, or in case he ate an animal that had died of itself or had been torn by a wild beast, then he had to bathe in addition to washing his garments. (Le 5:2; 11:8, 24, 27, 31, 39, 40; 17:15) The same injunction was imposed upon the priests, with the further command that if while in an unclean state they ate anything holy, they were to be put to death.—Le 22:3-8.

For persons who touched a human corpse a more involved purification ceremony was necessary. For this purpose ashes were prepared by slaughtering a red cow outside the camp. The priest spattered some of its blood seven times toward the tent of meeting. The whole cow (skin, flesh, blood, dung) was then burned, and the cedarwood, hyssop, and coccus scarlet material were cast into the blaze. The ashes were kept and used "for the water for cleansing," which on the third and seventh days was sprinkled for purification on the one touching the human corpse. At the end of the seven days he was to wash his garments and bathe, and he was then pronounced clean.—Nu 19:1-13.

Under this statute all persons who were in the house or tent when death occurred, as well as the dwelling itself and all open vessels, were made unclean. Touching even a bone of a dead man on the battlefield or touching any burial place, or sepulcher, likewise made one unclean. This is why in Jesus' day it was customary to whitewash the graves a month before Passover in order to safeguard people against inadvertently stumbling upon a grave and thus becoming disqualified to partake of the feast. (Nu 19:14-19; Mt 23:27; Lu 11:44) The occurrence of human death in the presence or alongside of one under a Nazirite vow canceled out the time he had already spent under the vow, and it necessitated the offering of a sacrifice.—Nu 6:8-12; see NAZIRITE; SAMSON.

Under the Law covenant, *places* and *things* that were contaminated had to be cleansed. If a murder was committed by an unknown assailant, it was first determined by measurement which was the city nearest to the crime. The elders of that city then had to take a young unworked cow (as a substitute for the murderer) and break its neck in a torrent valley running with water, and over the animal they had to cleanse themselves symbolically of any responsibility by washing their hands in innocence, pleading that the charge of guilt be not laid to their account.—De 21:1-9.

Garments and vessels that came in contact with dead bodies or that were polluted in other ways had to be cleansed according to prescribed formulas. (Le 11:32-35; 15:11, 12) The development of leprosy in a garment or in the walls of a house was a much more serious matter, for if it could not be contained and seemed to spread, it was necessary to destroy the garment or tear down the house completely.—Le 13:47-59; 14:33-53.

Spoils of war had to be cleansed before they could be brought in. Combustible articles were washed with water, but metal objects had to pass through the fire.—Nu 31:21-24.

Christian Cleanness. Christians are not under the Law and its cleansing requirements, even though such Law and its customs were still in force in the days when Jesus was on earth. (Joh 11:55) The Law had "a shadow of the good things to come"; 'the reality belongs to Christ.' (Heb 10:1; Col 2:17) Hence, Paul wrote concerning these purification matters: "Yes, nearly all things are cleansed with blood according to the Law [Moses sprinkled the book, the people, the tent, and the vessels with blood], and unless blood is poured out no forgiveness takes place. Therefore it was necessary that the typical representations of the things in the heavens should be cleansed by these means." "For if the blood of goats and of bulls and the ashes of a heifer sprinkled on those who have been defiled sanctifies to the extent of cleanness of the flesh, how much more will the blood of the Christ, who through an everlasting spirit offered himself without blemish to God, cleanse our consciences from dead works that we may render sacred service to the living God?"—Heb 9:19-23, 13, 14.

So it is the blood of the Lord Jesus Christ that cleanses Christians from all sin and unrighteousness. (1Jo 1:7, 9) Christ "loved the congregation and delivered up himself for it, that he might sanctify it, cleansing it with the bath of water by means of the word" in order for it to be spotless, holy, and without blemish, "a people peculiarly his own, zealous for fine works." (Eph 5:25-27; Tit 2:14) Every member of this Christian congregation, therefore, should not "become forgetful of his cleansing from his sins of long ago" but should continue to manifest the fruitage of God's spirit (2Pe 1:5-9), remembering that "every one bearing fruit he [God] cleans, that it may bear more fruit." —Joh 15:2, 3.

Christians must, therefore, maintain a high standard of physical, moral, and spiritual cleanness, guarding against "every defilement of flesh and spirit." (2Co 7:1) In view of what Jesus said, that it is 'not what enters a man but what comes forth from him that defiles,' these beneficiaries of the cleansing blood of Christ place the greater emphasis on spiritual cleanliness. They maintain "a clean heart" and "a clean conscience" before God. (Mr 7:15; 1Ti 1:5; 3:9; 2Ti 1:3) To such ones with a clean conscience "all things are clean," in contrast with faithless persons who are defiled in conscience, to whom "nothing is clean." (Tit 1:15) Those who want to remain clean and pure in heart heed the counsel of Isaiah 52:11, which says: "Touch nothing unclean; . . . keep yourselves clean, you who are carrying the utensils of Jehovah." (Ps 24:4; Mt 5:8) Doing this, their "hands" in a figurative sense are cleansed (Jas 4:8), and God deals with them as clean persons.—2Sa 22:27; Ps 18:26; see also Da 11:35; 12:10.

On one occasion the apostle Paul, though no longer under the Law, observed the Law's requirements by ceremonially cleansing himself at the temple. Was this inconsistent on his part? Paul did not fight against the Law or its procedures; he merely showed that obedience to it was not divinely required for Christians. Where its procedures did not violate new Christian truths, there was no real objection to doing what God had prescribed under the Law. Paul took the action he did so that he might not needlessly hinder the Jews from listening to the good news about Jesus Christ. (Ac 21:24, 26; 1Co 9:20) In a similar vein the apostle also argued that food in itself may be clean, but if his eating of it stumbled his brother, then he would refrain from eating. (Ro 14:14, 15, 20, 21; 1Co 8:13) In all of this, Paul showed a great concern for the salvation of others and did everything in his power to bring this about. He therefore could say: "I am clean from the blood of all men."—Ac 20:26; 18:6.

CLEMENT (Clem'ent). A faithful Christian who fought side by side with the apostle Paul, presumably at Philippi, for the sake of "the good news." (Php 4:3) The name Clement was quite common and therefore provides no valid basis for connecting him with Clement of Rome, as is done by Origen.

CLEOPAS (Cle'o·pas) [possibly a contraction of Cleopatros, meaning "Renowned Father"]. One of the two disciples, neither of whom were apostles, who traveled to Emmaus on Jesus' resurrection day. When Jesus joined them as a stranger and asked what they were debating, Cleopas replied: "Are you dwelling as an alien by yourself in Jerusalem and so do not know the things that have occurred in her in these days?" After Jesus explained many scriptures to them and then identified himself, Cleopas and his companion, instead of staying overnight in Emmaus, hastened back to Jerusalem and reported these things to the others. (Lu 24:13-35) This Greek name Cleopas should not be confused with the Aramaic name Clopas.—Joh 19:25.

CLOPAS (Clo'pas). The husband of one of the Marys that stood beside Jesus as he hung on the torture stake. (Joh 19:25) Presumably he was the husband of "the other Mary," and father of the apostle James the Less and of his brother Joses. (Mt 27:56; 28:1; Mr 15:40; 16:1; Lu 24:10) It is quite probable and generally recognized that Clopas was the same person that was called Alphaeus. (Mt 10:3; Mr 3:18; Lu 6:15; Ac 1:13) The two names may be variations in the pronunciation of the Aramaic root, or the same individual may have had two names that were used interchangeably, a practice not uncommon at the time. That Clopas was a brother of Joseph, the adoptive father of Jesus, is a conjecture based entirely on tradition.

CLOTH.

A fabric made by weaving. While little is known about the spinning and weaving processes used by the Israelites, it is evident that they were well acquainted with these crafts. In Egypt, archaeologists have unearthed wall paintings with illustrations of women weaving and spinning, showing the kind of loom that was used. An Egyptian model of a weaving shop with a horizontal loom was found near Girga, Upper Egypt.—See WEAVING.

The robe of fine white linen worn by the Aaronic high priest was to be woven in checkerwork, evidence that the Israelites were well acquainted with the art, being able to weave patterns into their fabrics.—Ex 28:39.

In the construction of the tabernacle, Bezalel and Oholiab were experts whose ability was increased and sharpened by God's holy spirit, so that they could do the required work exactly according to the pattern given by Jehovah. (Ex 35:30-35) Also, there were women with fine ability in this direction, spinning thread from flax and from wool. (Ex 35:25, 26) In making the fabric for the ephod of Aaron the high priest, the workmen "beat plates of gold to thin sheets, and . . . cut out threads to work in among the blue thread and the wool dyed reddish purple and the coccus scarlet material and the fine linen, as the work of an embroiderer."—Ex 39:2, 3.

The Christian Greek Scriptures mention fabrics made of camel hair and of silk. (Mt 3:4; Re 18:12) It is not known whether the Hebrews used cotton. Cotton is mentioned at Esther 1:6 as being used in the Persian palace at Shushan. Cotton was known in India, probably at least as early as 800 B.C.E., and the historian Pliny says that it was used in Egypt. It is grown today in Israel. However, certain materials not native to Israel could be obtained by the Hebrews from traveling merchants from both East and West passing through Israel.

Linen was woven from flax, which has much longer fibers than cotton and is easier to spin but is harder to dye. Linen was a cherished item in the wardrobes of kings and high officials. Joseph was clothed with "garments of fine linen" when he was made a ruler in Egypt. (Ge 41:42) Also, Mordecai went out from before the Persian king in royal apparel of blue and linen. (Es 8:15) Women valued clothing made of linen.—Pr 31:22.

Other materials used for garments were skins, leather, and hair. Tents were made of skins or of the hair of goats. (Ex 26:7, 14) Samples of wool felt have been found. At 1 Samuel 19:13, a net of goats' hair is mentioned.

Colors. The people of Bible lands were able to make fabrics in a variety of colors. In describing the curtains for the tabernacle and the garments in connection with the sanctuary, the Bible mentions blue, scarlet, and reddish purple. (Ex 26:1; 28:31, 33) A wide variety of shades and colors could be produced by using these three colors of dye on fabrics of originally different colors and shades. Joseph was given a striped garment by his father Jacob. (Ge 37:3, 32) David's daughter Tamar wore a striped robe, "for that was the way the daughters of the king, the virgins, used to dress with sleeveless coats." (2Sa 13:18) By using different colors in the warp from those in the woof, a variegated pattern could be produced.—See DYES, DYEING.

The Tabernacle. In the construction of the tabernacle, ten "tent cloths" (Heb., yeri·ʹoth) of fine twisted linen and wool, embroidered with cherubs, constituted the immediate covering of the panel frames, so the priests serving inside the tabernacle could see the cherubs between the parts of those panel frames. (Ex 26:1, 2) Goat's-hair cloth formed the next covering. (Ex 26:7, 8) It served as a fine protection for the embroidered linen. The curtains or screens hanging at the entrances of the Holy and Most Holy compartments were also of linen and wool, the screen of the Most Holy being embroidered with cherubs. (Ex 26:31-37) The linen tent cloths were 4 cubits (1.8 m; 5.8 ft) wide and 28 cubits (12.5 m; 40.8 ft) long. The N and S sides of the courtyard were 100 cubits (44.5 m; 146 ft).—Ex 27:9-11.

Cloths of blue and of coccus scarlet material and of wool dyed reddish purple were used to cover the ark of the covenant, the table of showbread, the lampstand, the altar of incense, the altar of burnt offering, and the other utensils of the ministry when the tabernacle was moved from one location to another. (The color or colors for each item were specified.)—Nu 4:4-14.

Other Uses. Cloth bands were used as swaddling bands for newborn babies. (Lu 2:7) The Jews also had the custom of preparing bodies for burial by binding them with bandages of clean linen along with spices (not an embalming process such as the Egyptians practiced). (Joh 19:40; Mt 27:59) After Jesus' resurrection John and Peter found the bandages and the cloth that had been upon Jesus rolled up separately lying in the tomb. (Joh

20:5-7) When Lazarus was resurrected he came out of the tomb with his countenance still bound up with the cloth that had been placed over his head at burial—apparently a long piece of linen fabric.—Joh 11:44.

Money was sometimes kept wrapped in a cloth. This was the way the wicked slave referred to in one of Jesus' illustrations kept his mina instead of investing it. (Lu 19:20) Money was often carried in the voluminous folds of the bosom of the garment, probably wrapped in such cloths.

God's law to the people of Israel commanded: "You must not wear mixed stuff of wool and linen together." (De 22:11; see also Le 19:19.) Regarding this, the *Encyclopaedia Judaica* (Jerusalem, 1973, Vol. 14, col. 1213) remarked: "The clothing of the priests was notably exempt from the prohibition of *sha'atnez* [a garment of two sorts of thread, *NW*]. Exodus 28:6, 8, 15 and 39:29 prescribe that various pieces be made of linen and colored wool interwoven. . . . This suggests that the general prohibition was grounded on the taboo character of such a mixture, pertaining exclusively to the realm of the sacred."

Figurative Usage.   Because of the cleanness and purity of white linen, it is used in the Scriptures to symbolize righteousness. The garments next to the high priest's body, namely the drawers, robe, and turban, as well as the drawers, robes, and headgears for the underpriests, were made of fine, white linen. (Ex 28:39-42; compare Job 29:14.) The bride of the Lamb is arrayed in bright, clean, fine linen, for "the fine linen stands for the righteous acts of the holy ones." (Re 19:8) The armies following Jesus Christ in heaven are represented as being clothed in white, clean, fine linen. (Re 19:14) Babylon the Great, which has been rich in the traffic of merchandise including fine linen, also has put on an appearance of righteousness, being "clothed with fine linen," while at the same time carrying on the activities of a harlot.—Re 18:3, 16; see COTTON; DRESS.

CLOTHING.   See DRESS.

CLOUD.
A visible mass of particles, usually water or ice, suspended high in the air. The principal Hebrew word for "cloud" is *'a·nan'*, the majority of its occurrences referring to the pillar of "cloud" that led the Israelites through the desert wilderness. (Ex 13:21) A "film of dust," "clouds," "cloudy skies," and the "skies" are denoted by forms of the Hebrew *sha'chaq*, from a root meaning "pound fine; rub away." (Isa 40:15; Ps 36:5; Jer 51:9; Ps 89:37; Ps 18:42; Job 14:19) The Greek words denoting a "cloud" are *ne'phos* and *ne-*

phe'le, whereas *gno'phos* refers to a "dark cloud." —Heb 12:1; Mt 17:5; Heb 12:18.

In Israel, from mid-June until mid-September, the skies are generally clear, with the exception of dust clouds, which appear especially toward the end of the dry season, because of the hot E wind from the desert. Also, particularly in August, there are occasional cirrostratus clouds from the W that do not bring rain. Even these are welcomed by the inhabitants, for they afford some shadow and thus slight relief from the heat. (Isa 25:5; compare Job 7:2.) In September or October clouds begin to appear more frequently on the western horizon, forming over the Mediterranean, although it is often mid-October before the rainy season really begins. But during the summer there is, in some sections of the country, a mist cloud in the mornings that vanishes soon with the rising of the sun.—Ho 6:4.

During the rainy season, a storm can come up very quickly, starting with a very small cloud in the W. (1Ki 18:44, 45) The hopes of the farmer would be raised by a cloud rising in western parts. (Lu 12:54) However, one hesitating to reap because of looking at the uncertain clouds would lose out. This fact is used as an admonition to God's servants to go ahead with their work under all conditions.—Ec 11:4.

The wisdom and mightiness of Jehovah God the Creator are represented in his control over the clouds. He speaks of them as "water jars" that tip over and empty their contents on the earth. He says: "Who can exactly number the clouds in wisdom, or the water jars of heaven—who can tip them over?" (Job 38:37) He describes the process of evaporation and condensation, saying: "He draws up the drops of water; they filter as rain for his mist, so that the clouds trickle, they drip upon mankind abundantly. Indeed, who can understand the cloud layers, the crashings from his booth?"—Job 36:27-29.

Illustrative Usage.   Jehovah, whom no man can see and yet live, symbolizes his presence by a cloud. At Mount Sinai, at the time of giving the Law to Israel, a dark cloud covered the mountain; out of the cloud came lightnings and thunder, the blare of a trumpet, and a loud voice. (Ex 19:16-19; 24:15; Heb 12:18, 19) Jehovah told Moses that he appeared in this manner in order that he might speak to Moses and that, on hearing it, the people might put faith in Moses as God's representative. —Ex 19:9.

Jehovah sent an angel in a cloud as "his own personal messenger" to lead Israel out of Egypt and through the wilderness. (Isa 63:9) By means of the angel, Jehovah representatively looked out of the cloud to throw the camp of the Egyptians into confusion. (Ex 13:21, 22; 14:19, 24, 25) Jehovah also used the cloud to baptize them as a nation into Moses, the waters being at the sides of them and the cloud above and behind. Thus they were "baptized into Moses by means of the cloud and of the sea."—1Co 10:2; see also Nu 14:14.

When the tabernacle was set up in the wilderness, the cloud resided over it and "Jehovah's glory filled the tabernacle," so that Moses was unable to enter. (Ex 40:34, 35; compare 1Ki 8:10-12; Re 15:8.) After this the cloud stood over the Most Holy, in which was the ark of the covenant, and the cloud became a pillar of fire at night. Doubtless this cloud was visible from any part of the camp, marking the camp's center. When it rose, Israel prepared to break camp. When it moved, they followed its direction to the next camping place, although the exact site to set up the camp may have been selected with the help of Hobab, who had a good knowledge of the land, including watering places and other features necessary to a camp of such tremendous proportions. —Ex 40:34-38; Nu 10:29-32.

Inside the Most Holy, over the ark of the covenant, was a cloud that was very brilliant, the only light to illuminate that compartment. (Le 16:2) In post-Biblical Hebrew, it was called the Shechinah. When the high priest went into the Most Holy on Atonement Day with the blood of animals, he was symbolically standing in the presence of Jehovah. At other times, when he did not go into the Most Holy but stood before the curtain to present a matter of importance to Jehovah for his answer, he was considered as standing before Jehovah. —Nu 27:21.

In one instance Jehovah's own voice was heard out of a bright cloud, expressing approval of his only-begotten Son. This was the brilliant cloud overshadowing Jesus and his three apostles Peter, James, and John on the mount of the transfiguration.—Mt 17:5.

When Jesus ascended into heaven, according to the record, "a cloud caught him up from their vision." (Ac 1:9) The disciples did not see Jesus riding away on a cloud, but rather, the cloud obscured their vision of him. This helps us to understand Jesus' words concerning his presence: "They will see the Son of man coming in a cloud with power and great glory," and Revelation's statement: "He is coming with the clouds, and every eye will see him." (Lu 21:27; Mt 24:30; Re 1:7) In past cases clouds represented invisible presence; but observers could "see" the meaning

with their mental "eyes." In this case the physical occurrences that are visible would cause the one looking to "see" or realize that Christ is invisibly present.—See also Mt 24; Mr 13; Re 14:14.

When Jesus came to earth, with all the identifications of the Messiah, the Jews selfishly refused to acknowledge him because they demanded as a proof of his Messiahship that he literally fulfill the vision at Daniel 7:13, 14, where the Son of man is shown coming with the clouds of the heavens before the Ancient of Days, Jehovah God, to receive his kingdom. They confused his presence in Kingdom power with his first coming. He told them that no such sign would be given them.—Lu 11:29.

Favor. "Clouds" have a good connotation toward those who please God. Proverbs 16:15 says that the king's goodwill is "like the cloud of spring rain." A cloud's effect of covering or hiding from visibility is used to describe Jehovah's action toward the sins of his people, wiping their transgressions out "just as with a cloud." (Isa 44:22) Conversely, he blocks the approach of those who are rebellious as with a cloud mass, that their prayer may not pass through.—La 3:44.

Transitoriness, unreliableness. The misty morning clouds that quickly vanish away are used figuratively for the fickle, short-lived lovingkindness of Ephraim and Judah toward God, as well as for the short-livedness Ephraim would experience for turning to false worship.—Ho 6:4; 13:3.

The man who boasts about giving, but who never does so, is as disappointing as a cloud with no rain. (Pr 25:14) Those who are professed Christians but who carry on immorality, practicing corruption and contaminating the congregation, are likened, in their avid following of fleshly desires, to waterless clouds tossed by winds.—Jude 12; see MIST.

CNIDUS (Cni'dus). A city situated on the Resadiye Peninsula, which extends out from the SW corner of Asia Minor into the Aegean Sea, between the islands of Rhodes and Cos.

Though Cnidus is not named on either occasion, the apostle Paul likely passed the city when returning from his second missionary journey, in about 52 C.E. (Ac 18:21, 22), and again toward the close of his third trip, in about 56 C.E., when his ship came to Rhodes and Cos. (Ac 21:1) However, it is specifically mentioned in Acts 27 in connection with Paul's voyage in about 58 C.E. to appear before Emperor Nero in Rome. Leaving Myra, the ship on which Paul and other prisoners were traveling came to Cnidus. (Ac 27:5-7) With favorable winds this trip of about 240 km (150 mi) might be only a day's voyage, but the adverse wind mentioned in the account explains why "quite a number of days" were involved for that particular run. The "boat from Alexandria" on which they were sailing was a grain boat, perhaps one of many that regularly brought agricultural products from Egypt to Rome and which may have ordinarily sailed on a more direct route from Alexandria across the Mediterranean Sea to Rome. (Ac 27:38) However, the strong wind mentioned in verses 4 and 7 may have obliged this boat to alter course and put in at Myra. A large, unwieldy craft loaded with grain would make slow progress against the wind and, understandably, would finally arrive at Cnidus "with difficulty." Recent excavations in the area have revealed much about this site. *The Interpreter's Dictionary of the Bible*, Supplementary Volume, p. 169, describes the locality: "A low and narrow isthmus . . . joins the main body of the Cnidian peninsula to a high point of land sheltering in its lee on either side of the isthmus two fine harbors. The larger harbor on the S must have been the commercial harbor where west- or north-bound ships such as Paul's (Acts 27:7) could wait for unfavorable weather to abate before continuing their journey beyond the windy cape. On the banks of the harbors were moorings; warehouses . . . , market places; small theaters; and a temple of Dionysus."—Edited by K. Crim, 1976.

After referring to the arrival at Cnidus, the record states that "because the wind did not let us get on, we sailed under the shelter of Crete at Salmone." (Ac 27:7) It seems that they could not "get on" with their proposed route of crossing the Aegean Sea past the southern tip of Greece and then on to Rome, being forced by the adverse winds to take a southerly route to Crete and to sail under lee of its shores. As Acts 27:9 shows, it was the fall of the year, and those in charge of the vessel doubtless felt the urgency to make as much progress as possible before seasonal conditions made sailing even more hazardous.

COAL(S). See CHARCOAL.

COAT OF MAIL. See ARMS, ARMOR.

COBRA [Heb., *pe'then*]. An extremely poisonous snake of Asia and Africa. The cobra mentioned in six passages of the Bible is undoubtedly the Egyptian cobra or asp (*Naja haje*), one commonly used in snake charming, both in Bible times and today. Like the common cobra of India and the Asiatic king cobra, the Egyptian cobra inflates its neck when angered.

The cobra strikes with a forward sweep of its raised body accompanied by a sharp hiss. When biting, the cobra's jaw grasps the object tenaciously and then begins a peculiar chewing motion to assure that ample poison enters the wound. Because of this and the extreme toxicity of the venom, cobras are among the most dangerous of all creatures.

The Israelites were well acquainted with this snake, not only while they were in Egypt but also during their wandering through the wilderness. Moses, in addressing the Israelites in the wilderness, referred to the cobra's venom, "the cruel poison of cobras." (De 32:33) The term "cruel" aptly describes the effect of the cobra's venom. Concerning its effect Findlay Russell, M.D., in his book *Snake Venom Poisoning* (1980, p. 362), says that symptoms begin with drooping eyelids, and this may be followed by difficulty in breathing, paralysis of the eyes, the tongue, and the throat and may possibly include even convulsions and cardiac arrest.

The cobra's poison acts on the nerves, causes a paralysis of the respiratory system, and is frequently fatal to man, unless antivenom is promptly given. Zophar speaks of "the gall of cobras" and "the venom of cobras."—Job 20:14, 16.

The psalmist, using figurative speech, links the deadly cobra with the lion and says concerning those who have made Jehovah their trust: "Upon the young lion and the cobra you will tread; you will trample down the maned young lion and the big snake." (Ps 91:13) Isaiah, in speaking of the regathering of Jehovah's people, prophesies of changed conditions for them, describing a time when "the sucking child will certainly play upon the hole of the cobra; and upon the light aperture of a poisonous snake will a weaned child actually put his own hand."—Isa 11:8, 11, 12.

How can a cobra "listen to the voice of charmers"?

The Bible refers to the cobra's ear and alludes to the cobra's ability to "listen to the voice of charmers." (Ps 58:4, 5) Since snakes lack surface ear openings and appeared to naturalists to be indifferent to sound, many have assumed that these reptiles are deaf. Commenting on this error, *The New Encyclopædia Britannica* (1987, Vol. 27, p. 159) states: "This supposition is incorrect; snakes are sensitive to some airborne sound waves and are able to receive them through a mechanism that serves as a substitute for the tympanic membrane. . . . Moreover, while the sensitivity of most snakes to the middle of the low-tone range is below that of most other types of ears, it is not seriously so. In a few snakes, however, the sensitivity is about as keen as in the majority of lizards with conventional types of ear openings and middle-ear mechanisms."

COCCUS. See DYES, DYEING.

COCK
[Gr., a·lek'tor]. A rooster or male chicken. Due to the widespread domestication of the chicken (*Gallus domesticus*), the jaunty figure of the cock is a generally familiar sight. It has bright-colored plumage, long tail feathers arched over its back, and a red wavy fleshlike comb topping its head, with two similar appendages hanging beneath the beak and throat.

The cock is not mentioned in the Hebrew Scriptures and appears in the Christian Greek Scriptures only in connection with its crowing. (See COCKCROWING.) The most frequent references relate to Jesus' prophecy concerning Peter's denials of him, fulfilled on the night prior to Jesus' death and recounted by all four writers of the Gospel accounts.—Mt 26:34, 74, 75; Mr 14:30, 72; Lu 22:34, 60, 61; Joh 13:38; 18:27.

While the Jewish Mishnah (*Bava Kamma* 7:7) contains a prohibition against the keeping of domestic fowl by the Jews, because of the probability of their causing ceremonial defilement, rabbinic sources indicate that they were kept as much by the Jews as by the Romans. An onyx seal bearing the figure of a cock was found near Mizpah and contains the inscription "belonging to Jaazaniah, servant of the king." If, as some suggest, this Jaazaniah (Jezaniah) is the one mentioned at 2 Kings 25:23 and Jeremiah 40:8, this would indicate the keeping of cocks in Israel back in the seventh century B.C.E. The figure of a cock has also been found on a shard of a cooking pot excavated at ancient Gibeon.

Both the hen, with its chicks, and the egg are used by Jesus in his illustrations, indicating that the domestic fowl was well known to his listeners. —Mt 23:37; Lu 11:12; 13:34; see HEN, II.

COCKCROWING.
This was the name given to the third watch period of the night, according to the Greek and Roman division. (Mr 13:35) It corresponded to the time from about midnight to about three o'clock in the morning.

There has been some discussion of the subject of cockcrowing (Gr., a·lek·to·ro·pho·ni'a) owing to Jesus' reference to it in connection with his prediction of Peter's denying him on three occasions. (Mt 26:34, 74, 75; Mr 14:30, 72; Lu 22:34; Joh 13:38)

On the basis of statements made in the Jewish Mishnah (*Bava Kamma* 7:7), some argue that cocks were not bred in Jerusalem, since they caused ceremonial uncleanness by their scratching up the ground. They say that the cockcrowing mentioned by Jesus actually refers to the Roman *gallicinium*, a time signal said to be made with bugles by the Roman guard stationed on the ramparts of the Tower of Antonia in Jerusalem that sounded out at the close of the third night watch.

However, Jewish Talmudic references indicate that cocks were bred in Jerusalem in those times. (For example, see The Mishnah, *Eduyyot* 6:1.) Further indication is that Jesus, when mourning over the city of Jerusalem, chose the simile of a 'mother hen's gathering her chicks under her wings' to express the desire he had held toward it. (Mt 23:37) His choice of illustrations was always such as would readily be appreciated by his listeners. So, in his statement to Peter, there seems to be no good reason for assuming that Jesus meant anything other than a literal cockcrowing.

Others point out an apparent contradiction in the four accounts, since Matthew, Luke, and John mention only one cockcrowing, while Mark quotes Jesus as saying: "Truly I say to you, You today, yes, this night, before a cock crows twice, even you will disown me three times." He repeats this statement in relating what happened later.—Mr 14:30, 72.

This is evidently a matter of one writer giving a more detailed account than the others rather than being a contradiction. The incident involves Peter, and since Mark was his close companion over a period of time and doubtless wrote his Gospel account with Peter's aid or on the basis of his testimony, it is reasonable that Mark's account would be the more detailed one. (At other times Matthew gave the more detailed description of certain events, as seen by a comparison of Mt 8:28 with Mr 5:2 and Lu 8:27, and of Mt 20:30 with Mr 10:46 and Lu 18:35.) So, while Mark quoted Jesus' statement concerning the two cockcrowings, the other three writers mentioned only the second and last one, which provoked Peter's giving way to tears; but by this they did not deny that there was an earlier cockcrowing.

It is generally agreed that cockcrowing has long been and still is a time indicator in the lands to the E of the Mediterranean, and that there is an early cockcrowing around midnight and a later one toward the dawning; while some indicate an additional one between these two. Concerning John 13:38, Clarke's *Commentary* says: "The Jews, and some other nations, divided the cock-crowing into the *first,* the *second,* and the *third* times." While it may not be possible now to assign specific times to these periodic cockcrowings, it is sufficient to know that they existed and that before two such cockcrowings Peter's three denials took place.

COCKROACH [Heb., *cha·sil'*]. There is uncertainty as to the particular insect referred to by the Hebrew word *cha·sil',* considered to be derived from a root meaning "devour." (Compare De 28: 38.) It has been variously rendered "caterpillar," "cricket," "stripper," "shearer," "locust," "grasshopper," and "cockroach." (Compare Isa 33:4 and Joe 1:4 in *AS, AT, JB, Le,* and *NW.*) According to the Hebrew and Aramaic lexicon by Koehler and Baumgartner (p. 319), the noxious insect designated by the Hebrew word *cha·sil'* is different from the locust (*'ar·beh'*) and is probably the cockroach (*Periplaneta furcata* and *Blatta orientalis*).

The cockroach has long, strong legs, enabling it to run with amazing speed. It is, in fact, one of the fastest of insect runners. This insect has a flat face and a short head, equipped with long, threadlike antennae, or feelers, and gives the appearance of looking slightly downward. Its compact-shaped body enables the cockroach to slip into narrow openings. Most of the species are somberly colored in black or brown and have a flattened, slippery body covered with a shiny casing. Disliking bright light, cockroaches usually come out only at night to feed.

The prophet Joel foretold a devastating onslaught by a horde of insects that would desolate the land, mentioning the *cha·sil'* last, as the insect that consumes whatever has been left behind by the others. (Joe 1:4) Later, the prophet tells of the time when there will be blessings and forgiveness. The invader will be turned back and compensation made for what the *cha·sil'* and the other members of God's "great military force" have eaten. (Joe 2:25) With respect to such a divinely sent plague of insects, including the *cha·sil',* Solomon prayed that Jehovah would forgive his people if they repented of their sins. (1Ki 8:37-40; 2Ch 6:28-31) The *cha·sil'* also figured in the devastation Jehovah brought upon Egypt during the plague of locusts. —Ps 78:46.

In chapter 33 of Isaiah, the prophet takes note of the terrifying days of the Assyrian aggression. King Sennacherib's army had been ravaging cities, and Isaiah asks for God's favor, recalling that Jehovah had risen up against nations before. He assures the people that the Almighty will smite the enemy, forcing them to leave behind great spoil, which would be collected by the Israelites. Just as the *cha·sil'* spread over a land, moving to

and fro without molestation, gathering in whatever is in their way, consuming everything—thus God's people would gather in the spoils of the Assyrian army. (Isa 33:1-4) This would be a very striking figure of speech in a land that knew such devastation by hordes of *cha·sil'.*

CODEX.   See BOOK.

COLHOZEH (Col·ho'zeh) [Every Visionary; or, He Is Visioning All].

1. An Israelite whose son Shallun assisted in repairing Jerusalem's wall in Nehemiah's day. —Ne 3:15.

2. Son of Hazaiah of the tribe of Judah. (Ne 11:4, 5) Perhaps the same as No. 1.

COLLECTION.   Paul, while in Ephesus about 55 C.E., wrote to the Corinthians: "Now concerning the collection that is for the holy ones, just as I gave orders to the congregations of Galatia, do that way also yourselves." (1Co 16:1, 2) The Greek word *lo·gi'a* ("collection") was in use at least from the third century B.C.E. It occurs only in these two verses of the Bible.

Matthew 17:24 describes "men *collecting* the two drachmas tax," but here a different word (*lam·ba'no*) is used, which conveys the idea of "receiving." (Compare *Int.*) Likewise, the expression "collect tithes" in Hebrews 7:5 stems from another word (*a·po·de·ka·to'o*) altogether different from *lo·gi'a.*

However, Paul's choice of words does give an indication that the collection was likely money and not food or clothing, and when he says *"the* collection," it indicates a special collection and one already known to the Corinthians. Paul's instructions were only about the manner in which the collection was to be made. It was to be in a private manner at each one's "own house," on a voluntary basis as each "may be prospering," the same as was being done in "the congregations of Galatia." —1Co 16:1, 2.

Paul was giving "orders," not in the sense of arbitrary, compulsory commands, but as one taking the lead and supervising the whole affair, which involved several congregations. (1Co 16:1) He and others had carefully planned this project. In addition to being concerned about the spiritual needs of the congregations, Paul always had the physical needs of poor Christians in mind, and it appears that this collection was especially in behalf of the Judean Christians who were hard pressed at the time. (Ga 2:10) Elsewhere Paul referred to this collection by expressions such as "a contribution to the poor of the holy ones in

Jerusalem" (Ro 15:26), "the ministry . . . for the holy ones" (2Co 9:1), "your bountiful gift previously promised," "this public service" (2Co 9:5, 12), "gifts of mercy" (Ac 24:17). Such loving concern for the needs of fellow Christians was one of the identifying marks of first-century Christianity.—Joh 13:35; see CONTRIBUTION.

COLONNADE OF SOLOMON.

According to the writings of Josephus, this colonnade was originally built by Solomon on an artificial embankment on the E side of the temple. The colonnade existing in the first century C.E., however, is ascribed to Herod's rebuilding work. (*Jewish Antiquities*, VIII, 95-98 [iii, 9]; XX, 219-221 [ix, 7]; *The Jewish War*, I, 401 [xxi, 1]; V, 184-189 [v, 1]) At the Festival of Dedication in the wintertime of 32 C.E., Jesus was confronted by the Jews in the colonnade of Solomon with the demand that he identify himself as the Christ. (Joh 10:22-24) After Jesus' ascension into the heavens, his disciples continued to frequent this area, evidently to preach to the Jews there.—Ac 3:11; 5:12; PICTURE, Vol. 2, p. 745.

COLORS.

Bible words and expressions denoting color do not use the scores of precise terms found in modern color charts. Bible writers conveyed ideas of color by drawing on the subject under consideration, or by comparing unfamiliar objects with well-known things. (Ex 16:31; Re 1:14) The appearance of such common things as blood, snow, certain birds, fire, precious stones, and so forth, were used as color references. (2Ki 3:22; Ps 51:7; Ca 5:11; Mt 16:2, 3; Re 9:17) Colors were also employed with figurative meaning, and definite ideas were sometimes associated with specific colors.

Black is mentioned in describing hair (Le 13:31; Mt 5:36), horses (Zec 6:2, 6), skin (Job 30:30), and the sun (Re 6:12). At Revelation 6:5, 6, the black horse represents famine. The Scriptures also mention "black marble" and "black paint."—Es 1:6; Jer 4:30.

Blue describes dyed materials in various forms, such as thread, string, cloth, and apparel. (Ex 26:4, 31, 36; 39:22; Nu 4:7) A blue string was to be put above the fringed edges of every Israelite's garment. (Nu 15:38, 39) *Hyacinth blue* is one of the beautiful colors decorating the breastplates mentioned at Revelation 9:17.

Brown is found only in a description of sheep. —Ge 30:32, 33, 35, 40.

Crimson was one of the colors of costly dyed material. (2Ch 2:7, 14; 3:14; Na 2:3) Sins are also likened to the deep color of crimson.—Isa 1:18.

Fiery colored symbolically describes the appearance of the great dragon, Satan the Devil. (Re 12:3) A horse of this color symbolizes warfare between nations, as depicted at Revelation 6:4.

Gray is usually employed with reference to the hair of aging persons. (Ge 42:38; Le 19:32; Pr 20:29) Costly wool was sometimes *reddish gray*. —Eze 27:18.

Green is frequently found in the Scriptures, but seldom refers strictly to color. Rather, it brings to mind the freshness and vigor of growing vegetation, or it denotes a healthy and prosperous condition of things. (Ge 1:30; 9:3; Ex 10:15; 2Ki 19:26; Re 8:7) *Yellowish green* is used with reference to the color of such things as leprous spots in cloth and in stone-and-mortar houses or in describing refined gold.—Le 13:49; 14:37; Ps 68:13.

Purple and *reddish purple* are often referred to in the Scriptures, although there are no distinctions drawn between the many varieties of purple shades produced by the different dyes or dye methods used. (Ex 25:4; Nu 4:13; Eze 27:7, 16; Da 5:7, 29; Mr 15:17, 20; Lu 16:19; Re 17:4) Because of its costliness, this color often was associated with or symbolized riches, honor, and royal majesty.

Red, fire red, and *yellowish red* are terms used to describe various articles, such as hair (Ge 25:25), dyed ram skins (Ex 25:5), animals (Nu 19:2; Jg 5:10; Zec 1:8), clothing (Isa 63:2), and the evening sky (Mt 16:2, 3). The Hebrew word for "red" (*'a·dhom'*) comes from *dam*, meaning "blood."—Ge 25:30; 9:6.

Scarlet, a red of brilliant hue, is found in references to cord or thread, cloth and apparel; also to sin. (Ge 38:28, 30; Nu 4:8; Jos 2:18; Jer 4:30; Mt 27:28; Isa 1:18) "The wild beast" described at Revelation 17 is scarlet colored (vs 3), distinguishing it from "the wild beast" of chapter 13. The harlot sitting on the scarlet-colored beast is arrayed in purple and scarlet. (Re 17:3-5) The vision thus pictorially symbolizes the royal claims of the "beast" and the luxury and royalty enjoyed by the woman riding it.

Vermilion (Jer 22:14; Eze 23:14) has reference to a reddish type of paint made from oxides of iron or of lead. It seems to have been first introduced by the Phoenicians, who imported it from natural deposits found in North Africa. At a later time similar deposits in the Middle East were developed.

White is the color most often mentioned in the Scriptures. Besides its descriptive use, it also serves as a symbol of righteousness and spiritual cleanness. (Re 3:4; 7:9, 13, 14) The white horse, as portrayed at Revelation 6:2 and 19:11, symbolizes clean, righteous warfare under Jesus Christ's direction.

White garments were worn by the poor and also by those of superior rank. Where their attire is mentioned, angels are usually depicted as being clothed in white. (Mr 16:5; Joh 20:12; Re 19:14) A few of the other things described as white are hair (Le 13:3; Mt 5:36), flesh (Le 13:16), fields of grain ready for harvest (Joh 4:35), and God's throne of righteous judgment (Re 20:11). Jesus likened the scribes and Pharisees to whitewashed graves. (Mt 23:27) He drew this illustration from the custom of whitewashing the graves in the vicinity of Jerusalem before the Passover to protect people who were coming to celebrate the Passover from becoming unclean by touching them. Degrees of whiteness are distinguished in the Bible, as, for example, reddish white (Le 13:19, 24) and dull white.—Le 13:39.

Yellow and *sulphur yellow* are also mentioned. —Le 13:30, 32, 36; Re 9:17.

Mixed colors. Besides the more specific colors, there are a number of expressions in the Bible that describe objects having rather indefinite colors or having a mixture of colors—for example: color patched (Ge 30:32, 33), glowing colors (Isa 63:1), many colored (Jer 12:9), parti-colored (Zec 6:3, 7), ruddy (1Sa 16:12; Ca 5:10), speckled (Zec 6:3, 6), spotty (Ge 31:10, 12), striped (Ge 37:3; 2Sa 13:19), swarthy (Ca 1:6), two-colored (Eze 27:24), of varied colors (Eze 16:16), having color variety (Eze 17:3), and in various colors (Eze 27:7, 16, 24). —See DYES, DYEING.

Christ's Cloak. The color of the cloak with which Jesus Christ was clothed on the day of his execution has caused some persons to argue that a discrepancy exists in the Bible record with reference to this garment. Matthew said that the soldiers "draped him with a *scarlet* cloak" (Mt 27:28), while Mark and John say that it was purple. (Mr 15:17; Joh 19:2) However, instead of being a discrepancy, such a variation in describing the garment's color merely gives evidence of the individuality of the Gospel writers and the fact that they were not in collusion. Matthew described the cloak as it appeared to him, that is, according to his evaluation of color, and he emphasized the garment's red hue. John and Mark subdued the red tint, calling it purple. "Purple" can be applied to any color having components of both blue and red. So, Mark and John agree with Matthew that the garment was red to some extent. Of course, background and light reflection could have given it different casts. A body of water varies in color at

different times, depending upon the particular color of the sky and the reflection of light at a given time. So, when such factors are considered, it is seen that the Gospel writers were not in conflict in describing the color of the cloak that mocking Roman soldiers clothed Christ with on the last day of his human life.

COLOSSAE (Co·los'sae) [possibly, Colossal]. A city of SW Asia Minor. In the apostle Paul's day Colossae was in the Roman province of Asia, though it formed part of the ancient region of Phrygia. The site is uninhabited at present. It lay near the upper end of the Lycus River valley, about 18 km (11 mi) ESE of Laodicea (near modern Denizli). The Lycus River valley is narrow in the region of Colossae, walled in by great cliffs, but broadens out as it progresses to the NW and the junction of the Lycus with the Maeander (Menderes) River. Through this valley passed the main road leading from Ephesus and the Aegean Coast to the E as far as the Euphrates. A road branched off from there to Sardis and Pergamum to the NW. During the Roman period, however, the road system was changed, and Laodicea and neighboring Hierapolis (Col 4:13) came to surpass Colossae in importance. Nevertheless, Colossae continued to be known as a textile center, noted for its fine wool of unusual hue, called *colossinus*. It lay on the edge of the lonely steppe country, where flocks of sheep were pastured. To the S some 5 km (3 mi), Honaz Dagi (Mt. Cadmus) rises 2,750 m (9,020 ft), its snows feeding streams that flowed past Colossae.

Phrygians were present in Jerusalem on the day of Pentecost, 33 C.E., perhaps some of them being from Colossae. (Ac 2:10) Although Colossae was on the principal E-W route, most scholars believe that Paul followed a more northerly route on his third missionary tour, which took him by land to Ephesus. (Ac 18:22, 23; 19:1) His letter to the Colossians indicates that he had not visited Colossae and that the congregation there was the fruitage of the work of Epaphras, whom Paul describes as representing him and his coworkers by faithfully ministering to the believers in Colossae. (Col 1:7, 8; 2:1; 4:12) Paul, however, knew several Christians of Colossae. He names Onesimus, Archippus, Philemon, and Apphia.—Col 4:9, 17; Phm 1, 2, 10-12.

Added to the original Phrygian population of Colossae were Greek and Jewish elements. (Compare Col 3:11.) The early Phrygians displayed a strong tendency toward spiritistic fanaticism, the Greeks indulged in much speculation and in philosophical arguments, and the Jews were advocates of the Mosaic Law and its dietary and sabbath requirements. All these attitudes were dealt with in Paul's counsel to the Colossian congregation. —Col 2:4, 8, 16, 18, 20-23.

COLOSSIANS, LETTER TO THE. The inspired letter of the apostle Paul to Christians in Colossae. As usually placed in modern English versions of the Bible, it is the 12th book of the Christian Greek Scriptures. Paul identifies himself as the writer of this inspired letter by opening it with the words: "Paul, an apostle of Christ Jesus through God's will, and Timothy our brother to the holy ones and faithful brothers in union with Christ at Colossae." (Col 1:1, 2) The apostle's writership is also established by the final greeting, written in his own hand.—Col 4:18.

There is quite a similarity between Colossians and Ephesians, another of Paul's letters. While this may be due to the closeness in the time of composition and the possibility that similar circumstances prevailed in each of these cities, such correspondency would also mean that if Paul is accepted as the writer of Ephesians, he must also be acknowledged as the writer of Colossians. (For example, compare Col 1:24-29 with Eph 3:1-7; Col 2:13, 14 with Eph 2:1-5, 13-16; Col 2:19 with Eph 4:16; Col 3:8-10, 12, 13 with Eph 4:20-25, 31, 32; Col 3:18-25; 4:1 with Eph 5:21-23; 6:1-9.) Furthermore, the inclusion of the letter to the Colossians with other letters of Paul in the Chester Beatty Papyrus No. 2 (P46, of about 200 C.E.) clearly shows that the early Christians viewed Colossians as one of Paul's inspired writings.

Two factors apparently motivated Paul to write his letter to the Colossians. For one thing, Epaphras had brought the apostle a report of the congregation's spiritual state. Some of the information caused concern; but there was good news too, for Paul said Epaphras "disclosed to us your love in a spiritual way." (Col 1:7, 8) Though there were problems in the congregation, the situation was not critical and there was also much to commend. Then, too, Philemon's slave Onesimus was returning to his master in Colossae. So Paul took advantage of this circumstance by sending his letter to the congregation there by means of Onesimus and his companion Tychicus.—Col 4:7-9.

Place and Date of Composition. Where Paul was when he wrote to the Colossians is not directly stated. Some have suggested Ephesus. However, the letter indicates that the apostle was in prison (Col 1:24; 4:10, 18), and there is no Scriptural account of his being incarcerated in Ephesus. The comments Paul makes at Colossians 4:2-4, 11 seem to be most compatible with the apostle's circumstances during his first imprisonment in

---

HIGHLIGHTS OF COLOSSIANS

A letter emphasizing appreciation for the God-given position of Christ as the means to counteract wrong views and practices

Written by Paul toward the end of his first imprisonment in Rome

---

Appreciation for the position of Christ (1:1–2:12)

Commendation for faith in connection with Christ and for love for all the holy ones with whom they share the heavenly hope

Preeminent position given to Christ: He is the image of God, the firstborn of all creation, the one through whom all other things were created, the head of the congregation, the firstborn from the dead

Through Christ reconciliation to God is effected

Concealed in Christ are all the treasures of true wisdom and knowledge

Go on walking in union with him; do not let anyone take you off as his prey through human philosophy

Mosaic Law has been taken out of the way by God through Christ (2:13-23)

God figuratively nailed the Law covenant to the torture stake on which Christ died

Requirements of Law were a shadow; the reality belongs to the Christ

Let no man deprive you of the prize by inducing you to follow commands and teachings of men instead of holding fast to Christ as the head

Put on the new personality, submitting to Christ's authority (3:1-17)

Keep mind on things above, not on things on the earth

Deaden unclean desires of the flesh; put away wrong attitudes and speech

Clothe selves with compassion, kindness, lowliness of mind, mildness, long-suffering, love

Let the peace of Christ control in hearts

Do everything in the name of the Lord Jesus, thanking God through him

Relationships with others should be influenced by appreciation for God and Christ (3:18-4:18)

Wives, husbands, children, slaves, masters to fulfill responsibilities not as men pleasers but with fear of Jehovah, recognizing that Christ in heaven is our Master

Persevere in prayer; walk in wisdom

Personal greetings to fellow servants of the Lord

Rome (c. 59-61 C.E.). True, Paul was in prison at Caesarea (Ac 23:33-35), and Felix ordered that the apostle have some relaxation of custody. (Ac 24:23) But evidently this was not as great as the freedom Paul had during his first imprisonment in Rome, when he remained for two years in his own hired house and was able to preach the Kingdom of God to those who visited him there.—Ac 28:16, 23, 30, 31.

Another factor that seems to point to the letter's composition in Rome is that Onesimus was present at the place where Paul wrote it and was going to accompany Tychicus in delivering it to Colossae. Certainly Rome, with its teeming population, would be a very likely refuge for a fugitive slave. The letter to the Colossians was evidently written toward the end of Paul's first imprisonment in Rome, or about 60-61 C.E., when he also composed the letter to Philemon. Tychicus and Onesimus delivered not only the letter to the Colossians but also the apostle's letter to Philemon. (Phm 10-12) Since Paul, in his letter to Philemon, expresses hope (vs 22) of being released, it may be concluded that, like Philemon, the letter to the Colossians was written toward the end of Paul's first imprisonment in Rome.

False Views Countered. A deceptive philosophy was being fostered by false teachers in Colossae. Emphasis was being placed on the observance of the Mosaic Law. The practice of asceticism was also being urged. The apostle warned Colossian Christians to look out, so that someone would not carry them off "as his prey through the philosophy and empty deception according to the tradition of men, according to the elementary things of the world and not according to Christ." (Col 2:8) Paul also urged his fellow believers to let no one judge them in eating and drinking "or in respect of a festival or of an observance of the new moon or of a sabbath; for those things are a shadow of the things to come, but the reality belongs to the Christ." (Col 2:16, 17) The apostle recognized mock humility for what it was and scored asceticism, saying: "Those very things are, indeed, possessed of an appearance of wisdom in a self-imposed form of worship and mock humility, a severe treatment of the body; but they are of no value in combating the satisfying of the flesh."—Col 2:20-23.

Paul placed emphasis on the God-given position of superiority Christ enjoys. (Col 1:13-20) This truth would counteract paganistic philosophy, Jewish tradition, and another practice, "a form of worship of the angels." (Col 2:18) The Scriptures do not say whether those involved in it pretended to carry on the form of worship angels were supposed to practice, thought they were emulating the reverential attitude of angels, or were actually worshiping those spirit creatures.

COMMANDER.   See MILITARY COMMANDER.

COMMANDER'S STAFF.   A long rod serving as a symbol of a commander's right to issue orders. The expression "commander's staff" appears four times in the *New World Translation,* translating the participle *mecho·qeq',* which is from the Hebrew root *cha·qaq',* meaning "inscribe" or "engrave" and hence "decree" or "enact." (Isa 30:8; Eze 4:1; Pr 8:27; Isa 10:1) In ancient times, laws that were enacted were inscribed or engraved on stone or metal tablets. The same Hebrew word can apply to a commander who issues decrees, a "statute-giver." (De 33:21) Without peer among legislators is Jehovah, the supreme "Statute-giver."—Isa 33:22.

When a commander was seated, his long staff would often rest upon the ground and lie back against the fold of his robe, between his knees. This fact lends meaning to Jacob's deathbed blessing of Judah: "The scepter will not turn aside from Judah, neither the commander's staff from between his feet, until Shiloh comes." (Ge 49:10) Here the Hebrew word *mecho·qeq'* has been rendered "lawgiver" in some translations (*KJ; Yg*), but its other meaning, "commander's staff" (*NW; Ro*), is more appropriate in this case and has the support of modern lexicographers. (*Lexicon in Veteris Testamenti Libros,* by Koehler and Baumgartner, Leiden, 1958, p. 328; *A Hebrew and English Lexicon of the Old Testament,* by Brown, Driver, and Briggs, 1980, p. 349) That an object and not a person is evidently intended at Genesis 49:10 is the understanding conveyed in various translations, which have renderings such as "ruler's staff" (*AS; RS*), "staff of sway" (*Mo*), and "staff" (*AT*). A staff of some type, a "commander's staff," also nicely parallels the "scepter" and goes with the phrase "from between his feet" appearing in the same verse. Similar usage is found at Numbers 21:17, 18, where a well is said to be excavated "with a commander's staff, with their own staffs," though a possible reading there is, "with a commander, with their rulers." At Genesis 49:10 an alternate reading for "neither the commander's staff" is "neither a commander."

Since a scepter is a staff or rod, some might conclude that there is no difference between "the scepter" and "the commander's staff" of Genesis 49:10. However, it appears that Jacob intended to make a distinction between them. Parallel terms are often employed in poetic expressions. Though they are similar, upon closer examination one term is seen to convey to the mind a thought that is slightly different from what the other conveys, and that frequently enhances one's understanding of what has been said. Jacob seems to have used such a device in blessing his sons. For example, he stated that Dan would "prove to be a *serpent* by the roadside, a *horned snake* at the wayside" (Ge 49:17), using these parallel expressions in a good sense to indicate that Dan would be a peril to the foes of Israel.

God himself is identified as saying: "Judah is my commander's staff." (Ps 60:7; 108:8) While holding the commander's staff indicates that the possessor would be a leader with the power to command, a scepter in a monarch's hand signifies his possession of regal sovereignty or prerogative as a royal ruler. (Ps 45:6) Therefore, the use of the terms "scepter" and "commander's staff" at Genesis 49:10 evidently indicates that significant authority and power would reside with the tribe of Judah. But that more than tribal authority and dominance were involved is clear since Shiloh, to whom "the obedience of the peoples will belong," was to come from the tribe of Judah. That circumstance betokens royal authority and power over the people. When Judah's descendant David became the king of Israel, the scepter and commander's staff proved to be in the possession of the tribe of Judah, and these would not depart from it until the coming of Shiloh, the Messiah. (2Sa 7:8-16) God has indeed given the Shiloh to come, Jesus Christ, a descendant of Judah and David, as "a leader and commander to the national groups." (Isa 55:4) It was foretold that the Messianic Ruler would exercise dominance and power over the nations and peoples. (Ps 2:8, 9; Da 7:13, 14) Hence, he not only holds "the scepter," or royal sovereignty, but also possesses "the commander's staff," having the power to command.—See SHILOH No. 1.

COMMUNICATION.

Information and ideas were transmitted from person to person in a variety of ways in Bible lands of antiquity. To a great extent, ordinary local and foreign news was communicated by word of mouth. (2Sa 3:17, 19; Job 37:20) Travelers, who often journeyed with caravans, related news from distant places when they stopped for food, water, and other provisions at cities or points along the caravan routes. In its unique position with relation to Asia, Africa, and Europe, the land of Palestine was traversed by caravans traveling to and from distant points. So its residents could readily acquire information regarding significant events in foreign lands. News, both national and foreign, could often be obtained in the city marketplace.

Short-range communication was sometimes achieved through the use of audible or visual signals or by word of mouth. (Jos 8:18, 19; 1Sa 20:20-22, 35-39) After Israel departed from Egypt, Moses was instructed to make two silver trumpets for communication purposes. Blasts on these trumpets by the Aaronic priests signaled such things as the convening of the assembly, the gathering of chieftains, the orderly breaking up of camp, or a call for war against an enemy. (Nu 10:1-10) The blowing of a horn by Gideon served as a signal to his men to begin the victorious battle against Midian.—Jg 7:18-22; see HORN; TRUMPET.

Oral or written messages sent out by officials would frequently be carried by runners. (2Sa 18:19-32) Runners carrying letters from King Hezekiah went throughout Israel and Judah summoning the people to Jerusalem for a Passover celebration. (2Ch 30:6-12) Couriers in the service of Persian King Ahasuerus rode speedy posthorses and in that way circulated the royal counterdecree that foiled Haman's scheme to annihilate the Jews in the Persian Empire. (Es 8:10-17) Written letters and documents were used by most governments of antiquity for effective administration. Depending upon time and place, these were usually written on such materials as clay tablets, papyrus, and animal skins. Archaeologists have found many ancient governmental communications or business documents. Royal decrees were proclaimed by heralds. (Da 3:4-6) Of course, messengers were also used by persons other than rulers.—See COURIER; HERALD; MESSENGER.

Communication within a country or over some greater distance came to depend greatly on roads or highways. There were good roads in early Israel and Judah, and they were kept in serviceable condition. Later, the Romans constructed fine roads leading from Rome to all parts of the Empire, these facilitating official communication and the movement of troops. When Jesus Christ was on earth, people traveled over such roads in great numbers. Christians, especially Paul and his fellow missionaries, enjoyed their use when journeying to Asia Minor and Europe to establish and revisit Christian congregations.

Official communications, along with general news, were also carried by ships that sailed the Mediterranean Sea, putting in at various ports. The Roman government used ships on some occasions (usually in summer) to carry official messages, but it seems that the bulk of such communication was transmitted on the overland routes. These were more dependable.

An official postal service was developed by the Romans, but it was used only for governmental communications. The people in general had to depend upon acquaintances to deliver their letters. When the circumcision issue was resolved by the governing body in Jerusalem and a letter was sent out as a means of communication, it was delivered in a direct personal way. (Ac 15:22-31) That was also the case with such inspired letters as the one Paul sent to Christians in Colossae, it being carried by Tychicus and Onesimus.—Col 4:7-9; see LETTERS.

Jehovah is a communicative God and has recognized the need for his people to have written communication. He himself was responsible for the composition of the Ten Commandments on stone tablets. (Ex 31:18) By means of divine inspiration a number of faithful Hebrew men (commencing with Moses in 1513 B.C.E.) were moved to write down Jehovah's communications.

COMPASS.
An instrument used by a carpenter or another craftsman to mark or inscribe a circle or an arc on wood or some other material. The only Biblical reference to a compass is at Isaiah 44:13. There the idolatrous wood-carver is said to use the measuring line, red chalk, and a wood scraper to fashion an idol. And, "with a compass he keeps tracing it out [evidently to make sure it is well proportioned], and gradually he makes it like the representation of a man, like the beauty of mankind, to sit in a house." The Hebrew word for "compass" (mechu·ghah') is related to chugh (circle).—Pr 8:27; Isa 40:22.

COMPASSION.
A sympathetic awareness of another's suffering or adversity coupled with a desire to alleviate it. One of the Hebrew words conveying the sense of compassion is the verb cha·mal', which means "feel (show or have) compassion; spare." (Ex 2:6; Mal 3:17; Jer 50:14) The Greek verb oi·ktei'ro means "show compassion," while the noun oi·ktir·mos' describes the inner feeling of compassion, or tender mercy. (Ro 9:15; 12:1; 2Co 1:3; Php 2:1; Col 3:12; Heb 10:28) The Greek word splag'khna (intestines) may have the sense of tender compassions.—1Jo 3:17.

The most outstanding example of compassion is Jehovah himself. This is well illustrated in his dealings with the Israelites. He not only keenly felt for them during their distresses in Egypt but finally rescued them out of the hands of their oppressors and lovingly cared for them in the wilderness. (Isa 63:7-9) Despite their repeated

lapses into unfaithfulness when settled in the Promised Land, he again and again delivered them out of the hands of their enemies, responding to their cries for aid.—Jg 2:11-19.

Eventually, however, the Israelites reached a point beyond the possibility of repentance. They practiced idolatry on a large scale, bringing idols right into Jehovah's sanctuary and defiling it. The people continued to mock the prophets and to despise Jehovah's word. No longer could the Most High be compassionate toward them. So he abandoned them into the hands of King Nebuchadnezzar, fulfilling the judgment announced beforehand through the prophets.—2Ch 36:15-17; Jer 13:14; 21:7; Eze 5:11; 8:17, 18.

When Not to Be Shown. In imitation of Jehovah, all who have truly come to know him strive to be compassionate. (Eph 4:32–5:1) There are, however, times when compassion is out of place. In the case of persons who persist in sin and set themselves deliberately against Jehovah's righteous ways, it would be wrong to shield them compassionately from the penalty that their course deserves.—De 13:6-11; Heb 10:28.

Yielding to pressure to show compassion when it is contrary to God's will can have serious consequences. This is revealed in what happened to King Saul. The time had come for the execution of divine judgment against the Amalekites, the first people to stage an unprovoked attack on the Israelites after their departure from Egypt. Saul was commanded not to have compassion on them. Giving in to the pressure of his subjects, he did not follow through completely on Jehovah's command. Therefore, Jehovah rejected Saul from being king. (1Sa 15:2-24) A person's cultivating deep appreciation for the rightness of Jehovah's ways and putting loyalty to Him foremost can prevent his erring, as did Saul, and losing divine approval.

COMPENSATION.
An equivalent given or received for services, loss, or injury. The Hebrew verb rendered "make compensation" (sha·lem') is related to sha·lohm', meaning "peace." (Ex 21:36; 1Ki 5:12) Thus the verb implies a restoration of peace through payment or restitution. Under the Law given to Israel through Moses, compensation was demanded where there was injury or loss in any field of human relations. Compensation also had to be made for work done or services rendered. Hired laborers, whether Israelites, alien residents, or others, were to be paid their wages on the same day.—Le 19:13; De 24:14, 15.

Injuries to Persons. One who injured another in a quarrel by striking him was required to make compensation to him for time lost from work, until the person was completely healed. —Ex 21:18, 19.

If, in the process of a fight between men, a pregnant woman was injured or her child(ren) 'came out,' but no fatal accident occurred, the guilty man was to have damages imposed on him by the owner of the woman. (In case the husband made an exorbitant claim, the judges would fix the sum to be paid.)—Ex 21:22.

If a bull was in the habit of goring and its owner had been warned of this fact but did not keep the animal under guard, then, in the event that it gored a slave to death, the slave's master was to receive a 30-shekel ($66) compensation from the bull's owner. This applied to foreign slaves, not Hebrews, according to Jewish commentators. If the bull gored a free person, the owner was to die. However, if, in the eyes of the judges, circumstances or other factors allowed for a more lenient penalty, a ransom could be imposed on him. In such a case the owner of the goring bull had to pay whatever amount the judges imposed. Additionally, the owner suffered the loss of the bull, which was stoned to death. Its flesh could not be eaten. (Ex 21:28-32) This law also evidently applied in the case of other animals able to inflict mortal wounds.

If a man seduced an unengaged virgin, he had to take her as his wife; or if the father flatly refused to give her to him, he had to pay her father the purchase price for virgins (50 shekels; $110), the usual bride-price, because her diminished value as a bride would now have to be compensated for.—Ex 22:16, 17; De 22:28, 29.

Slander. A man falsely charging his wife with deceptively claiming to be a virgin at the time of marriage was required to pay her father double the price for virgins (2 × 50 shekels; $220) for bringing a bad name upon a virgin of Israel. —De 22:13-19.

A form of compensation was also involved in the case of a man falsely charging his wife with unfaithfulness. If the charge had been true, she would have suffered the wasting away of her reproductive organs, losing the privilege of childbearing, whereas, when she was found innocent, her husband was required to make her pregnant. Thus she could be blessed with a child. —Nu 5:11-15, 22, 28.

Stealing. Stealing was deterred by the Law. Concerning a thief, it read: "He is to make compensation without fail. If he has nothing, then he must be sold for the things he stole. If there should be unmistakably found in his hand what was stolen, from bull to ass and to sheep, alive, he is to

make double compensation." This included money or other articles as well as animals. If the thief had slaughtered the stolen animal or had sold it, then he would have to make heavier compensation, namely, for a bull five of the herd, and for a sheep four of the flock. (Ex 22:1, 3, 4, 7) This law had the effect of protecting and recompensing the victim and made the thief work to pay for his crime, rather than sit in a jail as an economic burden to the community, with the victim uncompensated for his loss.

Injuries and Property Damages. A man who killed another's animal was required to pay for it. (Le 24:18, 21) When one bull killed another, the live one was sold, and the price of both it and the dead animal was equally divided between the owners. However, if the bull was known to be a vicious one, the owner compensated the other by giving the other a live bull and taking the dead and, consequently, much less valuable one.—Ex 21:35, 36.

The best of one's own field or vineyard was to be given up as compensation for the damage done by an animal's trespassing and grazing on another's field. If one started a fire that got into another person's field and caused damage, the owner had to be compensated equally. The heavier judgment for damage by the trespassing animal was because animals are easier to control than fire, also because the grazing animal was receiving gain unjustly like a thief; therefore, more than equal compensation was required.—Ex 22:5, 6.

Bailments. When items or goods were left with another for safekeeping and during this time were stolen, the thief, if found, had to make the usual double compensation. Money and articles left with a person did not have to be given special care but were to be kept in a safe place. In the case of a domestic animal kept for another, the one keeping the animal (bailee) was to exercise the same care that he did for his own flock. Such bailees were usually paid for food the animals needed, and sometimes they were probably paid also for the extra trouble of keeping the animals. If an animal died of itself, was torn by a wild beast, or was taken by a band of marauders, the bailee was free from blame. The loss was beyond his control. This might happen to his own animals, but if it was stolen (by someone whom the bailee could have prevented, or through his negligence), the bailee was responsible and was required to make compensation.—Ex 22:7-13; see Ge 31:38-42.

A man who borrowed an animal from another person for his own use had to compensate for any damages incurred. (Ex 22:14) If its owner was with it, no compensation was required, on the principle that the individual would be watching his own property. If it was a hired item, the owner would stand the loss because he supposedly would consider the risk in setting a hiring price.—Ex 22:15.

COMPULSORY SERVICE. The Hebrew word for "compulsory service" is *se'vel*, which has to do with a literal or a figurative load, an enforced burden, or burdensome labor. It can apply to corvée, that is, unpaid or partially unpaid work that an authority imposes on certain people, such as residents of a particular area.

The psalmist, in reflecting on the deliverance of Israel from Egyptian bondage, represented Jehovah as saying: "I turned aside his shoulder even from the burden [or compulsory service]." (Ps 81:6; Ex 1:11) King Solomon conscripted men for forced labor for various building projects and placed foremen over them. (1Ki 5:13; 9:15, 23) When Solomon observed that the young man Jeroboam was a hard worker, "he proceeded to make him overseer over all the compulsory service of the house of Joseph," that is, over the men conscripted from the tribes of Ephraim and Manasseh.—1Ki 11:26-28.

Related to the Hebrew word *se'vel* is *sab·bal'*, meaning "burden bearer." After taking a census of the men who were alien residents in Israel, Solomon put them in service, and 70,000 of their number became burden bearers. (2Ch 2:2, 17, 18) Many years later King Josiah repaired the temple, and "the burden bearers" were among those doing the work.—2Ch 34:12, 13.

The Hebrew word *tsa·va'*, which often applies to military service or service in war, also means "compulsory labor," that is, to pay off debt or guilt. Thus Jerusalem was to be told that her "military service" had been fulfilled and her error had been paid off. (Isa 40:1, 2, ftn) When under test, distressed and pain-racked Job likened life to hard, fatiguing service or "compulsory labor," asking: "Is there not a compulsory labor for mortal man on earth, and are not his days like the days of a hired laborer?" (Job 7:1) With similar sentiment, he later said to God: "You will make your vexation with me greater; hardship after hardship is with me," or "one shift of compulsory labor after another is with me." (Job 10:17, ftn) Job evidently felt that God was adding to his affliction by bringing one new hardship after another upon him. Job also likened the time that the dead spend in Sheol to compulsory labor, a burden that is enforced; yet he expressed hope in a resurrection.—Job 14:14.

CONANIAH (Con·a·ni'ah) [Jehovah Has Firmly Established].

1. The Levite in charge of the contributions for temple service during Hezekiah's reign.—2Ch 31:4, 12, 13.

2. A Levite chief among those generously contributing sheep, goats, and cattle for the great Passover celebration held in the 18th year of Josiah's reign.—2Ch 35:9, 19.

CONCUBINE. Among the Hebrews a concubine occupied a position in the nature of a secondary wife and was sometimes spoken of as a wife. It appears that concubines were slave girls, one of three kinds: (1) a Hebrew girl sold by her father (Ex 21:7-9), (2) a foreign slave girl purchased, or (3) a foreign girl captured in warfare (De 21:10-14). Some were the slave girls or handmaids of the free wife, as in the cases of Sarah, Leah, and Rachel.—Ge 16:3, 4; 30:3-13; Jg 8:31; 9:18.

Concubinage was in existence before the Law covenant and was recognized and regulated by the Law, which protected the rights of both wives and concubines. (Ex 21:7-11; De 21:14-17) Concubines did not have all the rights in the household that the regular wife had, and a man might have a plurality of wives along with concubines. (1Ki 11:3; 2Ch 11:21) In cases where the wife was barren, she sometimes gave her handmaid to the husband as a concubine, and the child born of the concubine would then be considered as the child of the free wife, her mistress. (Ge 16:2; 30:3) Sons of concubines were legitimate and could inherit. —Ge 49:16-21; compare Ge 30:3-12.

Since by Oriental custom the wives and concubines of a king could only become those of his legal successor, Absalom, who demonstrated the greatest disrespect for David, tried to strengthen his efforts to get the kingship by having relations with the ten concubines of his father David. (2Sa 16:21, 22) After King Solomon was enthroned, Adonijah, an older brother of Solomon, who had already made an attempt for the kingship, approached Solomon's mother, Bath-sheba, saying: "You yourself well know that the kingship was to have become mine," and then asked her to request of Solomon, Abishag the Shunammite, who appears to have been viewed as a wife or a concubine of David. Solomon angrily answered: "Request also for him the kingship," and then he ordered that Adonijah be put to death, indicating that he construed Adonijah's request as an effort to get the kingdom.—1Ki 1:5-7; 2:13-25.

God did not see fit to restore the original standard of monogamy as he had established it in the garden of Eden until the appearance of Jesus Christ, but he did protect the concubine by legislation. Concubinage logically worked toward a more rapid increase of the population in Israel. —Mt 19:5, 6; 1Co 7:2; 1Ti 3:2; see MARRIAGE (Polygamy).

Figurative Use. The apostle Paul likens Jehovah to the husband of a free wife, the "Jerusalem above," who is the "mother" of spirit-begotten Christians, as Abraham was husband to Sarah. He compares the relationship of Jehovah to the nation of Israel represented by its capital city Jerusalem to that of a husband and a concubine. Through the Law covenant Jehovah was 'married' to Jerusalem as a "servant girl," a 'concubine,' analogous to the relationship of Abraham to the slave girl and concubine Hagar.—Ga 4:22-29; compare Isa 54:1-6.

CONGREGATION.
A group of people gathered together for a particular purpose or activity. The Hebrew word usually rendered "congregation" in the *New World Translation* is *qa·hal'*, which is from a root meaning "call together; congregate." (Nu 20:8; De 4:10) It is frequently used for an organized body, being found in the expressions "congregation of Israel" (Le 16:17; Jos 8:35; 1Ki 8:14), "congregation of the true God" (Ne 13:1), "congregation of Jehovah" (De 23:2, 3; Mic 2:5), and "Jehovah's congregation" (Nu 20:4; 1Ch 28:8). *Qa·hal'* designates various kinds of human gatherings, as for religious purposes (De 9:10; 18:16; 1Ki 8:65; Ps 22:25; 107:32), for dealing with civil affairs (1Ki 12:3), and for warfare (1Sa 17:47; Eze 16:40). In the book of Ecclesiastes, Solomon is identified as "the congregator" (Heb., *qo·he'leth*). (Ec 1:1, 12) As the king, he congregated or assembled the people to the worship of Jehovah, one notable instance being when he gathered his subjects to the newly constructed temple in Jerusalem.—1Ki 8:1-5; 2Ch 5:2-6.

In the Christian Greek Scriptures the Greek word rendered "congregation" is *ek·kle·si'a*, from which the English word "ecclesia" is derived. *Ek·kle·si'a* comes from two Greek words, *ek*, meaning "out," and *ka·le'o*, meaning "call." Hence, it pertains to a group of persons called out or called together, either officially or unofficially. It is the word used with reference to the congregation of Israel at Acts 7:38 and is also employed for the "assembly" stirred up by the silversmith Demetrius against Paul and his associates in Ephesus. (Ac 19:23, 24, 29, 32, 41) Most often, however, it is used with reference to the Christian congregation. It is applied to the Christian congregation in general (1Co 12:28); to a congregation in some city such as

Jerusalem (Ac 8:1), Antioch (Ac 13:1), or Corinth (2Co 1:1); or to a specific group meeting in someone's home (Ro 16:5; Phm 2). Accordingly, individual Christian congregations or "congregations of God" are also mentioned. (Ac 15:41; 1Co 11:16) Some English versions use "church" in texts pertaining to the Christian congregation, as at 1 Corinthians 16:19. (*AS; KJ*) Since many persons think of a church as a building for religious services rather than a congregation engaging in worship, the rendering "church" can be misleading.

The Greek word *ek·kle·si'a* is employed in the *Septuagint* at times to translate the Hebrew word *qa·hal'*, as at Psalm 22:22 (21:23, *LXX*).—Compare *NW* ftn.

The Congregation of Israel. From the time of Moses onward, the nation of Israel was referred to as a congregation. Jehovah arranged for the congregation to be ruled, not democratically by the people, but theocratically, by God himself. To that end the nation was taken into the Law covenant. (Ex 19:3-9; 24:6-8) As Moses was the mediator of that covenant, it could be said: "Moses laid as a command upon us a law, a possession of the congregation of Jacob." (De 33:4) Jehovah was their Judge, Statute-Giver, and King. (Isa 33:22) Thus, the nation was a congregation of God and could be referred to as "the congregation of Jehovah" and "Jehovah's congregation."—Nu 16:3; 1Ch 28:8.

At times, the Hebrew word *qa·hal'* (congregation) is used in conjunction with the Hebrew word *'e·dhah'* (assembly). (Le 4:13; Nu 20:8, 10) *'E·dhah'* is from a root meaning "appoint," thus signifying a group assembled by appointment, and is frequently applied to the community of Israel, as in the expression "assembly of Israel." (Ex 12:3) In the nation of Israel those who actually constituted the Hebrew population made up the congregation (*qa·hal'*; Nu 15:15), whereas the assembly (*'e·dhah'*) seems to have embraced both the Israelites and alien residents associated with them. (Ex 12:19) So membership in the congregation, in an extended general application, seems to have included circumcised alien residents.—Nu 15:14-16.

However, there were exceptions as to membership in "the congregation of Jehovah." No castrated man or one "having his male member cut off" could enter it; illegitimate sons, male Ammonites, and male Moabites were barred therefrom "even to the tenth generation." But sons born to Edomites and Egyptians "as the third generation" could "come for themselves into the congregation of Jehovah." (De 23:1-8) The exclusion "to the tenth generation" of the sons of one who was illegitimate upheld Jehovah's law against adultery. (Ex 20:14) And though the sexually mutilated were excluded from "the congregation of Jehovah," such ones could draw comfort from words recorded by Isaiah, as found at Isaiah 56:1-7. Of course, individuals excluded from "the congregation of Jehovah" in ancient Israel had the possibility of coming under provisions and blessings Jehovah made for people of the nations in general.—Ge 22:15-18.

Persons who were members of the congregation of Israel were shown mercy if they sinned by mistake. But they were cut off in death for doing something wrong deliberately. (Nu 15:27-31) For instance, an individual would be cut off from the congregation, and from life itself, for refusing to purify himself when he was ceremonially unclean, for eating some of the flesh of the communion sacrifice while in that condition, for partaking of fat of offerings or blood, or for eating holy things while unclean. (Nu 19:20; Le 7:21-27; 17:10, 14; 22:3) Persons were also cut off for working on the Sabbath day (Ex 31:14), for giving their offspring to Molech, for turning to spirit mediums and professional foretellers of events, for certain kinds of sexual immorality, and for not 'afflicting' themselves on the annual Atonement Day.—Le 20:1-6, 17, 18; 23:27-30; see also Ex 30:31-33; Le 17:3, 4, 8, 9; 18:29; 19:5-8.

While individuals made up the congregation of Israel, the nation itself was comprised of tribes, families, and households. The incident involving Achan seems to show this organizational arrangement, for in this case Israel came forward, first tribe by tribe, then family by family, next household by household, and finally able-bodied man by able-bodied man, until Achan was picked as the wrongdoer.—Jos 7:10-19.

In Israel responsible representatives often acted in behalf of the people. (Ezr 10:14) Thus, "chieftains of the tribes" made presentations after the setting up of the tabernacle. (Nu 7:1-11) Also, representatively attesting by seal the "trustworthy arrangement" of Nehemiah's day were priests, Levites, and "the heads of the people." (Ne 9:38–10:27) During Israel's wilderness trek, there were "chieftains of the assembly, summoned ones of the meeting, men of fame," 250 of whom joined Korah, Dathan, Abiram, and On in congregating themselves against Moses and Aaron. (Nu 16:1-3) In keeping with divine direction, Moses selected 70 of the older men of Israel who were officers to help him carry "the load of the people" that he was unable to bear alone. (Nu 11:16, 17, 24, 25) Leviticus 4:15 mentions "the older men of the assembly," and it appears that the representatives of the people were the nation's older men, its heads, its judges, and its officers.—Nu 1:4, 16; Jos 23:2; 24:1.

In the wilderness, two silver trumpets were used to convene the assembly and to break up the camp. The assembly would keep their appointment with Moses at the entrance of the tent of meeting if blasts were blown on both of these trumpets. If just one was sounded, "the chieftains as heads of the thousands of Israel" would put in an appearance there. (Nu 10:1-4) Sometimes kings convened gatherings (1Ki 8:5; 2Ch 20:4, 5), Hezekiah using runners to summon the people to Jerusalem for the grand Passover celebration of his day.—2Ch 30:1, 2, 10-13.

In later times, considerable power was wielded by the judicial body known as the Sanhedrin, composed of 71 members—the high priest and 70 other principal men of the nation, "the assembly of older men."—Mt 26:59; Lu 22:66.

During the Jews' Babylonian exile, or shortly thereafter, synagogues came into general use as buildings where the Jews congregated. In time, synagogues were established in various places; Jesus imparted instruction at the synagogue in Nazareth, for example. (Lu 4:16-21) Synagogues were actually schools where the Scriptures were read and taught, and they were places of prayer and for the giving of praise to God.—Ac 15:21; see SYNAGOGUE.

The congregation of Israel was in a unique position. Moses reminded them: "You are a holy people to Jehovah your God. It is you Jehovah your God has chosen to become his people, a special property, out of all the peoples that are on the surface of the ground." (De 7:6) But the Jewish congregation ceased to be the congregation of God, being cast off because of rejecting his Son.—Ac 4:24-28; 13:23-29; Mt 21:43; 23:37, 38; Lu 19:41-44.

The Christian Congregation of God. Prior to the rejection of the Jewish nation and the end of its position as the congregation of God, Jesus Christ identified himself as the "rock-mass" upon which he would build what he termed "my congregation." (Mt 16:18) This is as Peter, to whom he spoke, understood matters, for the apostle later identified Jesus as the figurative "stone" that was rejected by men but was "chosen, precious, with God" and as the "foundation cornerstone" on which a person could rest his faith without disappointment. (1Pe 2:4-6; Ps 118:22; Isa 28:16) Paul also definitely identified Jesus Christ as the foundation upon which the Christian congregation is built. (Eph 2:19-22; 1Co 3:11) And, belonging to

Jehovah as it does, it is appropriately referred to as "the congregation of God."—Ac 20:28; Ga 1:13.

This Christian congregation (Gr., *ek·kle·si'a*), founded on Christ, also has him as its head. Thus it is stated: "He [God] also subjected all things under his feet, and made him head over all things to the congregation, which is his body, the fullness of him who fills up all things in all."—Eph 1:22, 23; see also Col 1:18.

The Christian congregation of God took the place of the congregation of Israel at Pentecost of 33 C.E., when holy spirit was poured out on Jesus' followers in Jerusalem. The first prospective members of that congregation were chosen shortly after Jesus' baptism, at the beginning of his ministry on earth. (Ac 2:1-4; Joh 1:35-43) From among his early followers Jesus selected 12 apostles (Lu 6:12-16), and later he chose Saul of Tarsus, who became "an apostle to the nations." (Ac 9:1-19; Ro 11:13) The 12 faithful apostles of the Lamb Jesus Christ, including Matthias who replaced Judas, constitute secondary foundations of the Christian congregation.—Ac 1:23-26; Re 21:1, 2, 14.

This congregation is referred to as "the congregation of the firstborn who have been enrolled in the heavens," the full number of which, under Christ the head, is 144,000. (Heb 12:23; Re 7:4) These called-out ones are "bought from among mankind" to carry out a special work here on earth and then to be with Christ in heaven as his bride. As there were requirements for membership in the Hebrew congregation of God, so there are requisites for membership in the Christian "congregation of God." Those making it up are spiritual virgins who keep following the Lamb, Jesus Christ, no matter where he goes, "and no falsehood was found in their mouths; they are without blemish."—Re 14:1-5.

The members of the Christian congregation of God are selected by Jehovah. (Ro 8:30; 2Th 2:13) The first members thereof were called out from the rejected Jewish congregation, which had not accepted God's Son as their Messiah. However, beginning with Cornelius in 36 C.E., members of the Christian congregation were also called out from the nations in general, so that Paul could say: "There is neither Jew nor Greek, there is neither slave nor freeman, there is neither male nor female; for you are all one person in union with Christ Jesus." (Ga 3:28; Ac 10:34, 35; Ro 10:12; Eph 2:11-16) Whereas the Law covenant mediated by Moses and under which the congregation of Israel was regulated was fulfilled by Christ and was taken out of the way by Jehovah God (Mt

5:17; 2Co 3:14; Col 2:13, 14), members of the Christian congregation of God partake of the benefits of the new covenant mediated by the Greater Moses, Jesus Christ. (Mt 26:28; Heb 12:22-24; Ac 3:19-23) Also, while the priests and kings of Israel were anointed with oil (Ex 30:22-30; 2Ki 9:6), those chosen by God to be members of the Christian congregation are anointed with holy spirit (2Co 1:21, 22; 1Jo 2:20) and are adopted by Jehovah God as his sons.—Eph 1:5.

Basically the Hebrew congregation was composed of natural Israelites. Persons comprising the anointed Christian congregation of God are spiritual Israelites, forming the tribes of spiritual Israel. (Re 7:4-8) Inasmuch as the majority of the natural Israelites rejected Jesus Christ, "not all who spring from Israel are really 'Israel,'" that is, spiritual Israel. (Ro 9:6-9) And, regarding the Christian congregation of God comprised of spiritual Jews, Paul stated: "He is not a Jew who is one on the outside, nor is circumcision that which is on the outside upon the flesh. But he is a Jew who is one on the inside, and his circumcision is that of the heart by spirit."—Ro 2:28, 29.

Usually when the Christian Greek Scriptures mention "the congregation" in a general sense, reference is being made to the 144,000 members thereof, the anointed followers of Christ exclusive of Jesus himself. (Eph 5:32; Heb 12:23, 24) However, the inspired application of David's words recorded at Psalm 22:22 to Jesus Christ at Hebrews 2:12 shows that the term "congregation" can be applied to include the head thereof, Jesus Christ. Partly quoting David, the writer to the Hebrews stated: "For both he who is sanctifying and those who are being sanctified all stem from one, and for this cause he [Jesus Christ] is not ashamed to call them 'brothers,' as he says: 'I will declare your name to my brothers; in the middle of the congregation I will praise you with song.'" (Heb 2:11, 12) Like David, who was a member of the congregation of Israel in the middle of which he praised Jehovah, Jesus Christ can, in this instance, be viewed as one of the spiritual congregation, the others in it being called his "brothers." (Compare Mt 25:39, 40.) David belonged to the Israelite congregation of Jehovah God, and Jesus Christ was also a member of it while on earth, preaching amidst its members. A remnant of that congregation became part of Jesus' congregation.

Organization of the Christian Congregation. While Christian congregations of God were established in various places, they did not function independently of one another. Instead, they all recognized the authority of the Christian governing body at Jerusalem. This governing body was comprised of the apostles and older men of the Jerusalem congregation, there being no rival bodies elsewhere seeking to supervise the congregation. It was to the faithful Christian governing body of the first century C.E. that the issue of circumcision was submitted for consideration. When the governing body made its decision, as directed by the holy spirit, that decision was accepted and became binding upon all Christian congregations, these willingly submitting to it. —Ac 15:22-31.

The Christian body in Jerusalem sent out traveling representatives. Thus, Paul and others delivered the governing body's decision just mentioned, it being stated: "Now as they traveled on through the cities they would deliver to those there for observance the decrees that had been decided upon by the apostles and older men who were in Jerusalem." Concerning the effects produced, it is said: "Therefore, indeed, the congregations continued to be made firm in the faith and to increase in number from day to day." (Ac 16:4, 5) Earlier, when the apostles in Jerusalem "heard that Samaria had accepted the word of God, they dispatched Peter and John to them; and these went down and prayed for them to get holy spirit."—Ac 8:14, 15.

The individual congregations adhered closely to the direction of the Christian governing body, which supervised the appointment of older men. (Tit 1:1, 5) So it was that, as directed by the Christian governing body under the influence of the holy spirit, overseers as well as assistants, ministerial servants, were appointed for each congregation. The men placed in these positions of trust and responsibility had to meet specific qualifications. (1Ti 3:1-13; Tit 1:5-9) Traveling representatives of the governing body, such as Paul, followed Christ and set a fine example to be imitated. (1Co 11:1; Php 4:9) In fact, all of those in the position of spiritual shepherds were to become "examples to the flock" (1Pe 5:2, 3), were to show loving concern for individuals within the congregation (1Th 2:5-12), and were to be of real assistance to those spiritually sick.—Ga 6:1; Jas 5:13-16; see OLDER MAN; OVERSEER; MINISTER.

Hence, just as Jehovah organized the congregation of Israel under older men, heads, judges, and officers (Jos 23:2), He saw to the supervision of the Christian congregation by having older men appointed to positions of trust therein. (Ac 14:23) And, as responsible men sometimes acted representatively for the entire congregation of Israel, as in judicial matters (De 16:18), God arranged for each individual Christian congregation to be similarly represented in such matters by responsible men placed in positions of authority by the holy spirit. (Ac 20:28; 1Co 5:1-5) However, should difficulties develop between members of the Christian congregation of God, the words of Jesus Christ recorded at Matthew 18:15-17 (spoken before the Jewish congregation of God had been rejected by Jehovah and thus initially applicable to it) served as a basis for settling or handling such problems.

Jehovah God has set the members in the spiritual "body" of Christ "just as he pleased." And Paul stated: "God has set the respective ones in the congregation, first, apostles; second, prophets; third, teachers; then powerful works; then gifts of healings; helpful services, abilities to direct, different tongues." Not all performed the same functions, but all were needed by the Christian congregation. (1Co 12:12-31) Paul explained that the supplying of apostles, prophets, evangelizers, shepherds, and teachers for the Christian congregation was "with a view to the readjustment of the holy ones, for ministerial work, for the building up of the body of the Christ, until we all attain to the oneness in the faith and in the accurate knowledge of the Son of God, to a full-grown man, to the measure of stature that belongs to the fullness of the Christ."—Eph 4:11-16.

The congregation of Israel was provided with the laws of God and was made to appreciate that "not by bread alone does man live but by every expression of Jehovah's mouth does man live." (De 8:1-3) Jesus Christ also recognized that man could not live on bread alone "but on every utterance coming forth through Jehovah's mouth." (Mt 4:1-4) Hence, adequate provision has been made for the Christian congregation to have needed spiritual food, Christ himself mentioning the "slave" through whom such food is dispensed to Christian "domestics." Jesus, as part of his prophecy concerning his own presence and "the conclusion of the system of things," showed that, on arriving, the "master" would appoint this "faithful and discreet slave" "over all his belongings."—Mt 24:3, 45-47.

Gatherings for the worship of Jehovah and a consideration of his law were important in the congregation of Israel. (De 31:12; Ne 8:1-8) Similarly, meetings for the worship of Jehovah and a study of the Scriptures are an essential feature of the Christian congregation of God, the writer to the Hebrews admonishing the recipients of his letter not to be forsaking such gathering of themselves together. (Heb 10:24, 25) Activities in the synagogues of later Jewish history included the reading and teaching of the Scriptures, the offering of prayers, and the giving of praise to God. Such features were carried over into places of Christian assembly, though without the ritualistic accretions that had eventually developed in synagogue services. In the synagogue no sacerdotal class was set apart, sharing in Scripture reading and exposition being open to any devout male Jew. Comparably, no clergy-laity or similar division existed within the early Christian congregation. Of course, neither therein nor in the synagogue did the women teach or exercise authority over the men.—1Ti 2:11, 12.

The maintaining of proper order at meetings of the Christian congregation of God harmonized with the fact that Jehovah, who made provision for the congregational arrangement among Christ's followers, is a "God, not of disorder, but of peace." This orderliness also worked to the great spiritual benefit of all in attendance.—1Co 14:26-35, 40; see ASSEMBLY.

CONIAH.   See JEHOIACHIN.

CONJURER   (con'jur·er). The Hebrew word 'ash·shaph' (Aramaic, 'a·shaph'; rendered "astrologers," KJ) is properly defined "conjurer, necromancer, enchanter." (A Hebrew and English Lexicon of the Old Testament, by Brown, Driver, and Briggs, 1980, pp. 80, 1083; Lexicon in Veteris Testamenti Libros, by Koehler and Baumgartner, Leiden, 1958, pp. 95, 1055) To conjure means "to swear together" by oath or invocation, as when one solemnly calls up or calls upon so-called spirits of the dead. A necromancer literally means "a diviner of the dead, one who attempts to foretell and control future events through communication with the dead."

Any manner of purported communication with the dead was condemned by God. "And in case they should say to you people: 'Apply to the spiritistic mediums or to those having a spirit of prediction who are chirping and making utterances in low tones,' is it not to its God that any people should apply? Should there be application to dead persons in behalf of living persons?" (Isa 8:19) Though outlawed in Israel, the "mistress of spirit mediumship in En-dor" whom unfaithful King Saul visited was one who contacted the demons as a conjurer of the dead.—1Sa 28:7; Le 20:27.

Conjurers flourished particularly among the Babylonians. Daniel and his three companions who had been taken captive to Babylon, after being given a special three-year schooling in the tongue of the Chaldeans, proved to be "ten times better [in wisdom and understanding] than all the magic-practicing priests and the conjurers" in the realm.—Da 1:3-20.

About eight years later, Nebuchadnezzar called in all branches of diviners, not the conjurers alone, and demanded that they first reveal a certain dream he had had and then give the interpretation. (Da 2:1-3, 27) The king was suspicious of them, for he said: "It is a lying and wrong word that you have agreed to say before me." He also was well aware of their stalling for time, hoping that circumstances would change. So, in order that he might have some guarantee that his wise men were able to give a true interpretation to his awesome vision, Nebuchadnezzar insisted that they first tell him the dream. "Tell me the very dream," the king declared, "and I shall know that you can show me the very interpretation of it." (Da 2:4-9) When the conjurers and their fellow diviners failed to come up with the answer, the king angrily ordered that all the wise men of Babylon be destroyed. However, Daniel learned of the king's edict (which would have included Daniel and his companions), so after "the secret was revealed" to him by God, Daniel hastened to tell the king, disclaiming any credit for himself, for as he said, "it is not through any wisdom that exists in me more than in any others alive that this secret is revealed to me."—Da 2:19-30.

Decades later Belshazzar was shocked by 'handwriting on the wall' that he could not read. After "calling out loudly to bring in the conjurers, the Chaldeans and the astrologers," the king made a most generous offer: "Any man that will read this writing and show me its very interpretation, with purple he will be clothed, with a necklace of gold about his neck, and as the third one in the kingdom he will rule." (Da 5:5-7) These conjurers, along with the rest of the spiritistic diviners, failed, and again Daniel's God Jehovah gave the interpretation.—Da 5:8-29.

CONSCIENCE.   The word is translated from the Greek sy·nei'de·sis, which is drawn from syn (with) and ei'de·sis (knowledge) and thus means co-knowledge, or knowledge with oneself. Conscience is a capacity to look at oneself and render judgment about oneself, bear witness to oneself. The apostle Paul expresses the operation of his conscience in this manner: "My conscience bears witness with me in holy spirit."—Ro 9:1.

Conscience is inherent in man, having been made part of him by God. It is an inward realization or sense of right and wrong that excuses or accuses one. Hence, conscience judges. It also can be trained by the thoughts and acts, convictions and rules that are implanted in a person's mind by study and experience. Based on these things, it makes a comparison with the course of action being taken or contemplated. Then it sounds a warning when the rules and the course conflict, unless the conscience is "seared," made unfeeling by continued violations of its warnings. Conscience can be a moral safety device, in that it imparts pleasure and inflicts pain for one's own good and bad conduct.

From the very start, man has had a conscience. Adam and Eve manifested this as soon as they broke God's law and hid themselves. (Ge 3:7) In Romans 2:14, 15 we read: "For whenever people of the nations that do not have law do by nature the things of the law, these people, although not having law, are a law to themselves. They are the very ones who demonstrate the matter of the law to be written in their hearts, while their conscience is bearing witness with them and, between their own thoughts, they are being accused or even excused." Thus it can be seen that conscience has not been wiped out even among non-Christians. This is because all mankind descended from Adam and Eve, in whom conscience was inherent. Many laws of the nations are in harmony with a Christian's conscience, yet such nations and lawmakers may not have been influenced by Christianity at all. The laws were according to the leadings of their own consciences. All persons have the faculty of conscience, and it is to this that the life course and preaching of Christians appeal. —2Co 4:2.

Conscience must be enlightened; if not, it can mislead. It is an unsafe guide if it has not been trained in right standards, according to the truth. Its development can be wrongly influenced by local environment, customs, worship, and habits. It might judge matters as being right or wrong by these incorrect standards or values. An example of this is shown in John 16:2, where Jesus foretold that men would even kill God's servants, thinking that they were doing Him a service. Saul (later Paul the apostle) actually went out with murderous intent against Christ's disciples, believing he was zealously serving God. (Ac 9:1; Ga 1:13-16) The Jews were seriously misled into fighting against God because of lack of appreciation of God's Word. (Ro 10:2, 3; Ho 4:1-3; Ac 5:39, 40) Only a conscience properly trained by God's Word can correctly assess and set matters of life thoroughly straight. (2Ti 3:16; Heb 4:12) A Christian must have a stable, right standard—God's standard.

Good Conscience. One must approach Jehovah with a cleansed conscience. (Heb 10:22) A Christian must constantly strive for an honest conscience in all things. (Heb 13:18) When Paul stated: "I am exercising myself continually to have a consciousness of committing no offense against God and men" (Ac 24:16), he meant that he continually steered and corrected his course of life according to God's Word and Christ's teachings, for he knew that in the final analysis God, and not his own conscience, would be his ultimate judge. (1Co 4:4) Following a Bible-trained conscience may result in persecution, but Peter comfortingly counsels: "For if someone, because of conscience toward God, bears up under grievous things and suffers unjustly, this is an agreeable thing." (1Pe 2:19) A Christian must "hold a good conscience" in the face of opposition.—1Pe 3:16.

The Law with its animal sacrifices could not so perfect a person as regards his conscience that he could consider himself free from guilt; however, through the application of Christ's ransom to those having faith, a person's conscience can be cleansed. (Heb 9:9, 14) Peter indicates that those who receive salvation have to have this good, clean, right conscience.—1Pe 3:21.

Consideration for Consciences of Others. In view of the fact that in order to make proper evaluations a conscience must be fully and accurately trained in God's Word, an untrained conscience may be weak. That is, it may be easily and unwisely suppressed, or the person may become offended by the actions or words of others, even in instances where no wrongdoing may exist. Paul gave examples of this in connection with eating, drinking, and the judging of certain days as above others. (Ro 14:1-23; 1Co 8:1-13) The Christian with knowledge and whose conscience is trained is commanded to give consideration and allowance to the one with a weak conscience, not using all his freedom or insisting on all his personal "rights" or always doing just as he pleases. (Ro 15:1) One who wounds the weak conscience of a fellow Christian is "sinning against Christ." (1Co 8:12) On the other hand, Paul implies that while he would not want to do something by which the weak brother would be offended, thereby causing him to judge Paul, the weak one should likewise consider his brother, striving for maturity by getting more knowledge and training so that his conscience will not be easily offended, causing him to view others wrongly.—1Co 10:29, 30; Ro 14:10.

Bad Conscience. The conscience can be so abused that it no longer is clean and sensitive. When that happens it cannot sound out warnings or give safe guidance. (Tit 1:15) Man's conduct is then controlled by fear of exposure and punishment rather than by a good conscience. (Ro 13:5) Paul's reference to a conscience that is marked as with a branding iron indicates that it would be like seared flesh that is covered over with scar tissue and void of nerve endings and, therefore, without sense of feeling. (1Ti 4:2) Persons with such a conscience cannot sense right or wrong. They do not appreciate the freedom God grants them and, rebelling, become slaves to a bad conscience. It is easy to defile one's conscience. A Christian's aim should be as shown in Acts 23:1: "Brothers, I have behaved before God with a perfectly clear conscience down to this day."

CONSTABLE.

An official attendant assigned to escort a Roman magistrate in public and to execute his instructions. The Greek term *rhabdou'khos* literally means "rod bearer." (Ac 16: 35, 38; compare *Int.*) The Roman term was *lictor*, and as a mark of office and a symbol of the magistrate's authority the lictor in a Roman colony carried the fasces. This consisted of a bundle of elm or birch rods bound around the handle of an ax, with the blade of the ax projecting from the side of the bundle.

Some of the duties of the Roman constables were policelike in their nature, but they differed from modern-day policemen in that the constables were attached strictly to the magistrate, with the responsibility of being in constant attendance upon him. They were not directly subject to the call of the people but only to the orders of their magistrate.

When the magistrate appeared in public his constables announced his approach, cleared his passage through the crowd, and saw to it that he received the respect due his rank. They mounted guard at his house. They delivered magisterial messages, ordered offenders before the magistrate, and seized lawbreakers, sometimes scourging them.

The constables were technically nominated for one year, but in actuality they often served longer. The majority of them were freedmen. Roman constables were exempted from military service and were given a salary for their service.

Since Philippi was a Roman colony, it was governed by imperial civil magistrates, and these were the ones who gave the command to beat Paul and Silas with rods. The next day, the civil magistrates sent the constables with orders to release Paul and Silas. However, Paul refused to accept relief from the constables but demanded that their superiors, the civil magistrates, acknowledge the wrong done.—Ac 16:19-40; see MAGISTRATE.

CONTRIBUTION.

The gift, money, or assistance given by a person or persons to another or others. The Hebrew *teru·mah'* means "contribution; sacred portion; heave offering." (Ex 25:2, ftn; 29:27, ftn) It comes from the verb *rum*, which literally means "be high; be exalted; lift up" (Job 22:12; 1Sa 2:1; Ge 14:22) and which, in the causative form, may mean "cause to lift up [as a contribution]," hence "contribute."—Le 22:15.

A contribution may or may not involve material giving. Paul thanked God because of the contribution the Philippian Christians made to the good news. In addition to their personal part in spreading the good news, they had materially assisted Paul and probably others, thus loyally supporting the preaching of the good news in this way too. —Php 1:3-5; 4:16-18.

The Israelites were privileged to make contributions for erecting and equipping structures for true worship. They donated materials for the tabernacle and its furnishings (Ex 25:1-9; 35:4-9), "a voluntary offering to Jehovah" that had to be halted because the things given "proved to be enough for all the work to be done, and more than enough." (Ex 35:20-29; 36:3-7) King David's contributions for the construction of the prospective temple included his "special property" of gold and silver, to the amount of more than $1,202,000,000. In turn, the princes and the chiefs of the people happily contributed over $1,993,000,000, in gold and silver, besides copper, iron, and stones.—1Ch 29:1-9.

Some contributions were required under the Law. When Moses took a census of the Israelites, each male 20 years old and upward was to give a ransom for his soul, "a half shekel [probably $1.10] by the shekel of the holy place." It was "Jehovah's contribution" in order to make atonement for their souls and "in behalf of the service of the tent of meeting." (Ex 30:11-16) According to the Jewish historian Josephus (*The Jewish War*, VII, 218 [vi, 6]), this "sacred tax" was thereafter paid annually.—2Ch 24:6-10; Mt 17:24; see TAXATION.

For the support of the Levites, the priestly tribe, God provided that the Israelites contribute "tenth parts" of the land's produce. The Levites, in turn, contributed a tenth part to the high priest, to support him and his family. (Nu 18:26-28; see TITHE.) Jehovah gave Aaron the high priest custody of the contributions the Israelites made to God, allowing him and his sons to partake of their offerings and of the oil, wine, grain, and first ripe fruits of the land that the people gave to Jehovah, as well as granting them portions of animal sacrifices. A tax from the spoils of war was given to the high priest as "Jehovah's contribution," and a portion of the spoils likewise went to the Levites.—Nu 31:1, 2, 28-30.

The Israelites made various offerings and sacrifices to Jehovah, some of which were specifically required by the Law. Others, however, were entirely voluntary, such as thanksgiving and vow offerings.—Le 7:15, 16; see OFFERINGS.

In the days of King Jehoash, a chest was placed at the gate of the house of Jehovah to receive contributions for extensive repair work on the temple. The princes and the people then rejoiced to bring in "the sacred tax," with which it was possible to make the house of God strong, and to make temple utensils.—2Ch 24:4-14.

Non-Israelites also contributed to true worship. When Ezra and the Jewish remnant left Babylon for Jerusalem in 468 B.C.E., they carried with them silver, gold, and utensils, a contribution to the house of God made by King Artaxerxes of Persia, his counselors, his princes, and the Israelites in Babylon. These valuable articles were entrusted to the care of selected men during the journey.—Ezr 7:12-20; 8:24-30.

In performing the ministry, Jesus Christ and his apostles accepted material aid that was contributed. (Lu 8:1-3) Christians in Macedonia and Achaia especially showed eagerness to assist their needy brothers, being "pleased to share up their things by a contribution to the poor of the holy ones in Jerusalem," evidently by contributing money. —Ro 15:26; see COLLECTION.

At Romans 15:26 and 2 Corinthians 9:13, the Greek word for "contribution" (koi·no·ni'a) may be viewed as meaning literally "sharing." This same Greek word is used at Hebrews 13:16: "Do not forget the doing of good and the *sharing of things with others,* for with such sacrifices God is well pleased."

Many Jews and proselytes from other places who had become Christians during the time of Pentecost, 33 C.E., apparently remained for a time in Jerusalem in order to learn more about the faith. So that none might come to want, they contributed their belongings voluntarily; "they had all things in common." (Ac 4:32-37; compare Ac 5:1-4.) Later on, the Jerusalem congregation made a daily distribution of food to needy widows. (Ac 6:1-3) Paul gave instructions as to the use of contributed funds in caring for widows who were truly worthy of help.—1Ti 5:9, 10; see RELIEF.

There was no compulsion to make contributions in the early Christian congregation. In this regard, Paul wrote: "Let each one do just as he has resolved in his heart, not grudgingly or under compulsion, for God loves a cheerful giver."—2Co 9:7.

The size of a contribution does not necessarily give a true picture of the giver's generosity. Once Jesus Christ watched as persons deposited money in the temple's treasury chests. Rich individuals dropped in many coins, but Jesus was impressed with the wholehearted generosity of a needy widow who dropped in only two small coins of very little value, saying: "This widow, although poor, dropped in more than they all did. For all these dropped in gifts out of their surplus, but this woman out of her want dropped in all the means of living she had." (Lu 21:1-4; Mr 12:41-44) When it came to making contributions to aid poor fellow believers, Paul observed: "If the readiness is there first, it is especially acceptable according to what a person has, not according to what a person does not have."—2Co 8:12.

Although no one can actually enrich Jehovah, who owns all things (1Ch 29:14-17), contributing is a privilege that affords the worshiper opportunity to display his love for Jehovah. Contributions given, not for publicity or for selfish motives but with the proper attitude and to advance true worship, bring happiness, along with God's blessing. (Ac 20:35; Mt 6:1-4; Pr 3:9, 10) A person can assure himself of a share in this happiness by setting aside something from his material belongings regularly for the support of true worship and the aid of deserving ones.—1Co 16:1, 2.

Jehovah furnishes the best example of giving, for he has bestowed upon humanity "life and breath and all things" (Ac 17:25), he has given his only-begotten Son for mankind (Joh 3:16), and he enriches Christians for every sort of generosity (2Co 9:10-15). Indeed, "every good gift and every perfect present is from above, for it comes down from the Father of the celestial lights."—Jas 1:17; see GIFTS, PRESENTS.

See also HOLY CONTRIBUTION.

CONVENTION. A gathering or meeting together of people for a specific purpose; an assembly. In the Scriptures the term "convention" is a translation of the Hebrew word miq·ra', meaning "a calling together," or "convening; convoking." An alternate rendering of this Hebrew word is "convocation." Bearing out its basic meaning is its use at Numbers 10:2 to convey the thought of convening the assembly of Israel.—Compare Isa 1:13, ftn.

The "holy conventions" were scheduled as follows: (1) Every Sabbath (Le 23:3); (2) the first and seventh days of the Festival of Unfermented Cakes during Nisan, the first month (March-April) (Nu 28:18, 25; Le 23:6-8); (3) the Festival of Weeks or Festival of Harvest, later known as Pentecost, held in the third month, Sivan (May-June) (Le

23:15-21); (4) the first and tenth days of the seventh month, Ethanim or Tishri (September-October), the latter day being the Day of Atonement (Le 23:23-27; Nu 29:1, 7); (5) the first day of the Festival of Booths, which began on the 15th day of the seventh month, Ethanim or Tishri, also the day after that seven-day festival.—Le 23:33-36.

A unique feature of all of these "holy conventions" was that during them the people were to do no laborious work. For instance, the first and seventh days of the Festival of Unfermented Cakes were "holy conventions," concerning which Jehovah stated: "No work is to be done on them. Only what every soul needs to eat, that alone may be done for you." (Ex 12:15, 16) However, during "holy conventions" the priests were busy offering sacrifices to Jehovah (Le 23:37, 38), certainly no violation of any command against doing normal daily work. These occasions were not periods of idleness for the people in general either but were times of great spiritual benefit. On the weekly Sabbath day, the people met together for public worship and instruction. They were then edified by the public reading and explanation of God's written Word, as in the later synagogues. (Ac 15:21) Therefore, while the people did not do laborious work during the Sabbath day or the other "holy conventions," they would then devote themselves to prayer and meditation on the Creator and his purposes.—See ASSEMBLY.

CONVERSION. See REPENTANCE (Conversion —A Turning Back).

COOKING, COOKING UTENSILS. The preparing of food by boiling, roasting, or baking was usually considered the duty of the women in the Hebrew household, but on certain occasions meals were prepared by men. (Ge 18:6-8; 27:3-9, 14, 30, 31; 1Sa 8:13; 2Sa 13:8) When living in tents, the Hebrews probably did most of their cooking outdoors. When settled in Canaan, living in stone houses, they did some cooking in the home, particularly during inclement weather. (Jg 6:19; 2Sa 13:7-11) The bulk of the cooking done was for the evening meal, the major meal of the day. (Lu 14:12; Re 3:20) Nothing could be cooked on the regular Sabbath day, for the Law forbade even the lighting of a fire.—Ex 35:3.

The Hebrews used various utensils and pieces of equipment in preparing food. There was the hand mill, operated by the women of the household. (De 24:6; Mt 24:41; see MILL.) For spices or smaller quantities of grain, the mortar and pestle sufficed. (Nu 11:8; see MORTAR, I.) Bread dough was mixed in a kneading trough (Ex 12:34) and baked on a hearth or in an oven.—Ex 8:3; 1Ch 9:31.

Forks were employed at the tabernacle and, later on, at the temple. (Ex 27:3; 2Ch 4:16) Mention is made of a three-pronged fork used by the priests. (1Sa 2:12-14) Household cooks may have used a similar fork to take meat out of a pot. They had knives of various kinds to cut up meat for cooking. There is no Scriptural indication that they used knives and forks when eating.

Vessels designed for cooking were generally made of earthenware, although some of them were of copper, such being particularly mentioned in connection with the sanctuary. (Le 6:28) Among household cooking utensils were pots, round containers, varying considerably in size. Bronze cooking pots that stood on legs are depicted in Egyptian tomb paintings, and it is possible that the complaining Israelites in the wilderness had such vessels in mind when they spoke of "sitting by the pots of meat" in Egypt. (Ex 16:3) The Hebrew word translated "pots" in this passage is the one generally used to designate the wide-mouthed pot, which might be used for washing (Ps 60:8) or for cooking. (2Ki 4:38-41; Eze 24:3-5) These came in varied sizes, from the average-sized one about 30 cm (12 in.) in diameter on up to very large ones. Early specimens of this relatively shallow type of pot lacked handles, but during the time of the divided kingdom in Israel a two-handled variety came into use.

Narrow-mouthed cooking pots having one or two handles have been found. They were of more-or-less spherical shape, from about 10 to 36 cm (4 to 14 in.) in diameter.

The Israelites also possessed deep-fat kettles or deep pans and also griddles. Grain offerings were frequently prepared in these. (Le 2:5, 7; 7:9; 1Ch 23:29) Examples of earthenware griddles have been discovered at Gezer. These had small depressions, comparable to the waffle iron of today. Iron griddles were also in use.—Eze 4:1-3.

The Scriptures sometimes use cooking pots in a figurative sense. Jerusalem, which was due to be destroyed in 607 B.C.E., was likened to a wide-mouthed cooking pot, with its inhabitants as the flesh in it.—Eze 11:1-12; 24:6-14; see VESSELS.

COPPER, BRASS, BRONZE. Copper (Heb., necho'sheth; Gr., khal·kos') was a soft metal, easily beaten and shaped into many forms. There is no evidence that the ancients had a secret method for hardening pure copper by tempering, but they knew how to harden the cutting edge of tools simply by cold hammering. When alloyed with other metals, hardness is greatly increased. One such alloy is bronze, copper containing tin (ancient findings having from 2 to 18 percent tin). Brass in the modern sense of an alloy of copper and zinc was unknown in Biblical days. However, as used in the *King James Version,* "brass" in its older definition can include any alloy of copper.

The Hebrew word *chash·man·nim',* translated "bronzeware things" (*NW*) and "bronze" (*RS*), is found only once in the Bible. (Ps 68:31) This Hebrew word is of uncertain meaning and has been variously rendered as "ambassadors" (*JB, La*), "envoys" (*NIV*), "nobles" (vs 32, *JP*), "princes" (*AS, KJ*), and "tribute" (*NE*).

Copper in the free state was not plentiful; metal-bearing ores consisting of oxides, carbonates, or sulfides had to be smelted to release the metallic copper. Copper mines have been located in the Wadi Arabah, that arid part of the Rift Valley that extends S from the Dead Sea to the Gulf of 'Aqaba at the eastern head of the Red Sea. (Job 28:2-4) The mountains of the Promised Land contained copper. (De 8:9) Solomon made castings of copper items near Succoth. (1Ki 7:14-46; 2Ch 4:1-18) Copper was found in abundance on Cyprus. The Bible also speaks of Javan, Tubal, and Meshech as sources of copper.—Eze 27:13.

Copper and its alloys had many varied and practical uses. It being one of the oldest metals known, Tubal-cain prior to the Noachian Flood forged tools out of copper. (Ge 4:22) Household and sanctuary utensils included pots, basins, pans, shovels, and forks. (Ex 38:3; Le 6:28; Jer 52:18) Copper was used for doors, gates, pillars, and musical instruments (2Ki 25:13; 1Ch 15:19; Ps 107:16; Isa 45:2); armor, shields, weapons, and fetters (1Sa 17:5, 6, 38; 2Sa 22:35; 2Ki 25:7; 2Ch 12:10). The metal was used in the making of idols. (Re 9:20) Copper coins were in circulation during Jesus' earthly ministry. (Mt 10:9) The Scriptures also speak of copper in a figurative or symbolic sense.—Le 26:19; Job 6:12; Isa 48:4; 60:17; Jer 1:18; Eze 1:7; Da 2:32; Re 1:15; 2:18.

At 1 Corinthians 13:1, the Greek word *khal·kos'* is translated "[piece of] brass" and may be understood to refer to a gong.

See also METALWORKER; MINE, MINING; MOLTEN SEA; REFINE, REFINER.

COPPER SERPENT.
The copper figure or representation of a serpent made by Moses during Israel's trek in the wilderness. Near the border of Edom the people showed a rebellious spirit, complaining about the miraculously provided manna and the water supply. Jehovah therefore punished them by sending poisonous serpents among them,

and many persons died from serpent bites. After the people showed repentance and Moses interceded for them, Jehovah told him to make a figure in the form of a serpent and to place it upon a signal pole. Moses complied, and "it did occur that if a serpent had bitten a man and he gazed at the copper serpent, he then kept alive."—Nu 21:4-9; 1Co 10:9.

The Scriptures do not identify the type of venomous serpent Jehovah sent among the people. The Hebrew expression for "poisonous serpents" (*han·necha·shim' has·sera·phim'*) at Numbers 21:6 can denote "fiery serpents," perhaps from the burning or inflammation-causing effect of their poison.

The Israelites kept the copper serpent and later improperly began to worship it, making sacrificial smoke to it. Hence, as part of his religious reforms, Judean King Hezekiah (745-717 B.C.E.) had the more than 700-year-old copper serpent crushed to pieces because the people had made an idol of it. According to the Hebrew text, the account at 2 Kings 18:4 literally reads, "he (one) began to call it Nehushtan." Some translations leave the word "Nehushtan" untranslated. (*AT; Ro; RS*) In Koehler and Baumgartner's lexicon, suggested meanings of the Hebrew term *nechush·tan'* are "bronze serpent" and "serpent-idol of bronze." (*Hebräisches und Aramäisches Lexikon zum Alten Testament,* Leiden, 1983, p. 653) The *New World Translation* appropriately says that the copper serpent "used to be called the *copper serpent-idol.*"

Jesus Christ made clear the prophetic meaning of the wilderness event involving the copper serpent when he told Nicodemus: "Moreover, no man has ascended into heaven but he that descended from heaven, the Son of man. And just as Moses lifted up the serpent in the wilderness, so the Son of man must be lifted up, that everyone believing in him may have everlasting life." (Joh 3:13-15) Like the copper serpent that Moses placed on a pole in the wilderness, the Son of God was impaled or fastened on a stake, thus appearing to many as an evildoer and a sinner, like a snake, being in the position of one cursed. (De 21:22, 23; Ga 3:13; 1Pe 2:24) In the wilderness a person who had been bitten by one of the poisonous serpents that Jehovah sent among the Israelites evidently had to gaze at the copper serpent in faith. Similarly, to gain everlasting life through Christ, it is necessary to exercise faith in him.

COPYIST.
Biblically speaking, the term "copyist" applies to a transcriber, or a person who made copies of written material, specifically of the Scriptures. The Hebrew word rendered "copyist" is

so·pher', which has to do with counting and re-cording. It has various meanings. It can denote a scribe (Jg 5:14) or a secretary. (Jer 36:32; Eze 9:2, 3) A scribe is either a public writer penning compositions dictated by various persons, a secretary, a copyist, or a teacher of the Law. However, the term "copyist" is especially apropos when applied to individuals who worked at copying the Law and other portions of the Holy Scriptures. Particularly identified as copyists are Shaphan, a certain Zadok, and the priest Ezra.—Jer 36:10; Ne 13:13; 12:26, 36.

The priest Ezra, who went from Babylon to Jerusalem with the Jewish remnant in the seventh year of Persian King Artaxerxes (468 B.C.E.), is identified as "a skilled copyist in the law of Moses" and as "a copyist of the words of the commandments of Jehovah and of his regulations toward Israel." (Ezr 7:6, 7, 11) In his time the Jewish scribes first became prominent as a group of Scripture copyists. Thousands of Jews had remained in Babylon, and others had been scattered about because of migrations and for business purposes. Local assembly halls known as synagogues sprang up in various places, and for these, copyists had to make handwritten copies of Biblical manuscripts. They did so with great care.—See SCRIBE.

It was Ezra, the skillful priestly copyist, who read "the book of the law of Moses" to a congregation in restored Jerusalem. Competent explanation and instruction given by Ezra and his assistants on that occasion led to "great rejoicing" and rich blessings for the assembled people.—Ne 8.

The psalmist, his heart "astir with a goodly matter" concerning God's Messianic King, said: "May my tongue be the stylus of a skilled copyist." (Ps 45:1-5) His wish was that his tongue prove to be eloquent, a match for the exalted theme of his composition, which was inspired of God. Thus, the psalmist desired that his tongue function efficiently, like a stylus in the hand of a trained and skillful copyist, one with ability.

COR. A dry measure and also one used for measuring oil. The cor corresponded to the homer and contained ten bath measures. (1Ki 4:22; 5:11; 2Ch 2:10; Eze 45:14) With the bath measure reckoned at 22 L (5.81 gal), the cor measure equals 220 L (58.1 gal).

CORAL. The limestone deposits of certain sea organisms called polyps. Living in colonies, these tiny warm-water creatures take the calcium salts from the sea and build out of them beautifully branched, shrublike structures that are as hard as stone. In time the formations of some types of coral may amount to great coral reefs and the foundations of coral islands. There are different colors of coral, varieties of white, black, and red, the latter being the most costly and most desired in ancient times. (Compare La 4:7.) Tyre at one time was noted for her trade in coral, which was harvested from the Mediterranean, the Red Sea, and the Indian Ocean. (Eze 27:16) Out of the raw coral, craftsmen artistically fashioned various ornaments that were highly prized.

Because of the esteemed value of coral, the Bible makes several interesting comparisons. Knowledge and wisdom certainly outrate the value of coral. (Job 28:18; Pr 3:15; 8:11; 20:15) The same is true of a capable wife; "her value is far more than that of corals."—Pr 31:10.

CORBAN (cor'ban). As explained at Mark 7:11, "corban" is "a gift dedicated to God." The Greek word there rendered "corban" is kor·ban', the equivalent of the Hebrew word qor·ban', meaning an offering. Qor·ban' is used in Leviticus and Numbers and applies both to offerings containing blood and to those that are bloodless. (Le 1:2, 3; 2:1; Nu 5:15; 6:14, 21) This Hebrew word is also employed at Ezekiel 20:28 and 40:43. Akin to the Greek word kor·ban' is kor·ba·nas', appearing at Matthew 27:6, where the chief priests are reported to have said that it would not be lawful to take the betrayal money Judas had thrown into the temple and drop these silver pieces into "the sacred treasury [a form of kor·ba·nas']," because they were "the price of blood."

By the time of Jesus Christ's ministry on earth, a condemnable practice had developed in connection with gifts dedicated to God. In regard to this, Jesus denounced the Pharisees as hypocrites because they put their own tradition ahead of God's law. Professing to safeguard for God what had been declared "corban," they set aside the divine requirement to honor one's parents. (Mt 15:3-6) A person might simply say, 'Be it corban,' or, 'It is corban,' regarding his property or some part of it. Pharisees at that time taught that once a person declared his possessions to be "corban," or a gift dedicated to God, he could not use these to satisfy the needs of his parents, however needy they might be, though he could make use of such possessions himself until his own death if he chose to do so. Thus, although these Pharisees professed to honor God, their hearts were not in accord with his righteous requirements.—Mr 7:9-13.

The historian Josephus associated "corban" with persons, stating: "Those who describe themselves as 'Corban' to God—meaning what Greeks would call 'a gift'—when desirous to be relieved of this obligation must pay down to the priests a fixed sum." (*Jewish Antiquities,* IV, 73 [iv, 4]) However, the term "corban" was more generally used for property dedicated as a gift to God.

CORD, ROPE. Several Hebrew words and one Greek word are used in the Scriptures to denote thread, string, cord, and rope of various kinds. Most often employed is the Hebrew word *che'vel.* *Che'vel* is used both literally and figuratively to denote cord and rope. (2Sa 17:13; Ec 12:6; Ho 11:4) It can, among other things, signify a measuring "line" (2Sa 8:2) and thus is sometimes employed as a topographical term for a measured area, an "allotment" (Jos 17:5, 14; 19:9), or a "region."—De 3:4, 13, 14.

The only Greek word used in the Scriptures to signify rope is *skhoi·ni'on,* which is applied to a cord or rope and may denote a rope made of reeds or rushes. In righteous indignation, "after making a whip of ropes," Jesus Christ "drove all those with the sheep and cattle out of the temple," evidently using the whip of ropes, not on the men, but on the animals.—Joh 2:13-17.

Some cords and ropes of ancient times were made from flax, others from hemp fiber, the fiber of ramie, or that of the date palm. Strong, thick rope made of palm-tree bark fiber was discovered at Ezion-geber. Rushes and reeds of various kinds were also evidently used, and among the materials employed by the Egyptians were twisted leather strips that made a powerful rope. The fibers of ramie (*Boehmeria nivea,* an Asiatic plant of the nettle family) made a very strong rope, quite useful for fishnets.

Cords were sometimes used as articles of attire. For instance, Judah seems to have carried his seal ring on a "cord." (Heb., *pa·thil'* [Ge 38:18, 25]) "Wreathed chains, in ropework, [of pure gold]" were put through the two rings at the extremities of the breastpiece worn by Israel's high priest. (Ex 39:15-18) Palace articles of Persian King Ahasuerus included "linen, fine cotton and blue held fast in ropes of fine fabric."—Es 1:6.

"Tent cords" (from Heb., *meh·thar'*) were used to fasten tents. (Isa 54:2; Ex 39:40) There were wagon "cords" (Heb., *'avoth'* [Isa 5:18]) and cords used for "bowstrings." (Heb., *yetha·rim'* [Job 30: 11; Ps 11:2]) Ropes and cords were also used to bind captives. (Jg 15:13-15; Eze 3:25) Ropes served as tackling for ships. (Isa 33:23) Rahab was told to tie a "cord [from Heb. *tiq·wah'*] of scarlet thread [Heb., *chut*]" in the window so that she and her household might be spared during the destruction of Jericho.—Jos 2:18-21.

Figurative Usage. The congregator said: "A threefold cord cannot quickly be torn in two." (Ec 4:12) By untwisting a cord made up of three strands, each strand alone can quickly be broken. But if they are plaited, the resulting "threefold cord" cannot easily be torn in two. Similarly, God's servants entwined with one another, as it were, in unity of view and purpose have greater spiritual strength, such as is needed to cope with opposition. The congregator also urged remembering the Creator in youth, "before the silver cord is removed" (Ec 12:1, 6), "the silver cord" apparently meaning the spinal cord, the severing of which results in death.

David, referring to a time when a violent death appeared imminent and it seemed certain that Sheol awaited him, said "the ropes of death encircled me" and "the very ropes of Sheol surrounded me." Apparently, he felt as if ropes had been cast around him and were pulling him down into the grave, drawing him into death and Sheol.—Ps 18:4, 5.

Isaiah said: "Woe to those drawing error with ropes of untruth, and as with wagon cords sin," perhaps to indicate their attachment to error and sin in a way similar to that in which animals are bound with ropes, or by cords, to wagons they draw behind them.—Isa 5:18.

In an act evidently symbolic of abject subjection and humiliation, defeated Syrians "girded sackcloth upon their loins, with ropes upon their heads, and came in to the king of Israel," seeking Ahab's indulgence toward Syrian King Ben-hadad II. Each may have worn a rope as a band around his head or his neck.—1Ki 20:31-34.

As pagan rulers and nations who did not want to become vassals of the Israelites gathered together against God and his anointed one in ancient times, so Messianic prophecy foretold that kings of the earth and high officials would mass together as one "against Jehovah and against his anointed one, saying: 'Let us tear their bands apart and cast their cords away from us!'" Any restrictions imposed by Jehovah and his Anointed One would be opposed by the rulers and nations. However, their efforts to tear apart such bands and cast away such cords were to be futile.—Ps 2:1-9.

Tent cords torn in two and thus no longer able to hold a tent erect are used figuratively in a description of desolation. (Jer 10:20) But there is prophetic assurance of just the opposite, restoration and Jehovah's favor, in the words: "Behold Zion, the town of our festal occasions! Your own eyes will see Jerusalem an undisturbed abiding place, a tent that no one will pack up. Never will its tent pins be pulled out, and none of its ropes will be torn in two."—Isa 33:20.

CORIANDER SEED   [Heb., *gadh*]. The manna eaten by the Israelites in the wilderness was said to be "white like coriander seed" (Ex 16:31), evidently resembling it not only in color but also in general appearance.—Nu 11:7.

The coriander (*Coriandrum sativum*) is an annual plant of the carrot or parsley family, growing about 40 to 50 cm (16 to 20 in.) high, with parsley-like leaves and pink or white flower clusters. The fruit consists of globular seeds of a grayish-white color and is 1 to 3 mm (0.04 to 0.12 in.) across. The seeds contain an aromatic oil having a pleasant flavor and are used as a spice, as well as medicinally for minor stomach ailments.

Coriander seed was used in Egypt from ancient times and so was undoubtedly well known to the Israelites before the Exodus. It grows wild in that country as well as in the Palestine area.

CORINTH   (Cor'inth). One of the oldest and most prominent cities of ancient Greece, located about 5 km (3 mi) SW of the modern city. The importance of Corinth resulted in large degree from its strategic location at the western end of the isthmus, or narrow neck of land, connecting the central or mainland part of Greece with the southern peninsula, the Peloponnesus. All land traffic, commercial or otherwise, going N and S had to pass Corinth in traversing the isthmus, which at its narrowest point measures only about 6 km (3.5 mi) across. But international maritime traffic was drawn to Corinth as well, for navigators generally preferred to make use of this isthmus between the Gulf of Corinth and the Saronic Gulf rather than risk the long and dangerous voyage around the storm-swept capes at the southern end of the peninsula. Thus, ships from Italy, Sicily, and Spain sailed across the Ionian Sea, through the Gulf of Corinth, and docked at the deep-water harbor of Lechaeum, the western port city tied in with Corinth by two continuous walls. Ships from Asia Minor, Syria, and Egypt came through the Aegean Sea and anchored at the eastern port facilities of Cenchreae or perhaps at the smaller port of Schoenus. (Ro 16:1) Merchandise from large vessels was unloaded at one harbor and transported the few miles overland to the other, there to be transshipped. Smaller vessels, with their cargo aboard, were hauled across the isthmus by means of some kind of shipway called the *di'ol·kos* (literally, "haul-across"). With good reason the isthmus of Corinth was known as the bridge of the sea.

History.   Corinth was already flourishing in the seventh century B.C.E. when the Isthmian Games, celebrated every two years and drawn on by the apostle Paul for some of his most striking illustrations, were established at the isthmian temple of Poseidon (the Greek god of the sea and counterpart of the Roman Neptune). (1Co 9:24-27) From the fourth century B.C.E. onward Corinth was generally under Macedonian domination until its liberation by the Romans in 196 B.C.E. As an independent city-state it joined other cities in the Achaean League, became involved in opposition to Rome, and was destroyed by Roman consul L. Mummius in 146 B.C.E.; its men were slaughtered, and its women and children were sold into slavery. For a century it lay relatively desolate until Julius Caesar, in 44 B.C.E. (some say 46 B.C.E.), refounded the city as a Roman colony, Colonia Laus Julia Corinthiensis. Achaia, as the Romans called Greece apart from Macedonia, became a Roman senatorial province during the reign of Caesar Augustus, and Corinth was made the capital.

Industry and Buildings.   The city of Corinth at which Paul arrived about the year 50 C.E., therefore, was a bustling crossroads of commerce and a political center. The tolls levied on the cargoes flowing across the isthmus contributed much to Corinth's wealth, but it was also an industrial center, famous for its pottery and bronzeware. The city itself was built on two terraces, one about 30 m (100 ft) above the other. At its center was the spacious agora or marketplace, lined with colonnades and public buildings. Rows of shops opened out onto the marketplace, some of the remains discovered giving evidence of shops used for the sale of meat and other foodstuffs, as well as wine. The word *macellum* was applied to one shop in an inscription. This term is the Latin equivalent of the Greek *ma·kel·lon,* used by Paul in referring to the "meat market" at 1 Corinthians 10:25. Another inscription found on a step read "Lucius, the butcher."

Near the center of the agora, excavations revealed an elevated outdoor speakers' stand called the bema, or rostra, extending out from the terrace that divided the upper and lower levels of the agora. Built of white and blue marble and richly decorated with delicate carvings, the stand had two waiting rooms alongside with mosaic floors and marble benches. The bema is believed to be "the judgment seat" where Jews opposed to the Christian message brought Paul for a hearing before Proconsul Gallio. (Ac 18:12-16) An inscription found at Delphi, a city on the N side of the Bay of

Corinth, bears the name of Gallio and indicates that he was proconsul.—See GALLIO.

To the NW of the marketplace stood two theaters, one capable of holding some 18,000 persons. Corinthian Christians could well appreciate Paul's reference to the apostles' being "a theatrical spectacle to the world." (1Co 4:9) In a plaza near the theater, archaeologists found an inscription mentioning a certain Erastus who bore the Latin title of *aedile*, translated by some as "commissioner of public works." This Erastus could be "the city steward" of the same name mentioned by Paul when writing to the Romans from Corinth. (Ro 16:23) The Greek term used by Paul for "steward" (*oi·ko·no′mos*) means, basically, "a house administrator or manager."—Compare Ga 4:2, ftn and *Int;* see ERASTUS No. 2.

Religion and Culture. Notable as Corinth was as a seat of governmental authority and as the leading commercial city of Greece, in the minds of many persons the city symbolized licentiousness and wanton luxury, so much so that the expression "to Corinthianize" came into use as meaning "to practice immorality." This sensuality was a product of Corinthian worship, particularly of the goddess Aphrodite (counterpart of the Roman Venus, the Phoenician and Canaanite Astarte, and the Babylonian Ishtar). A temple dedicated to her worship sat on top of the Acrocorinthus, a steep, rocky hill towering 513 m (1,683 ft) above the agora. (PICTURE, Vol. 2, p. 336) Paul had good reason for giving the Corinthian Christians strong counsel and warning regarding moral conduct. (1Co 6:9–7:11; 2Co 12:21) Corinth, of course, had temples to many other gods and goddesses. At the temple of Asklepios, the god of healing, archaeologists have found flesh-colored terracotta representations of parts of the human body. These were left at the temple as votive offerings by worshipers, each offering representing the particular afflicted member (hand, foot, eye, and so forth) of the worshiper.

Besides the Greeks, there was a considerable segment of Italians who were descended from the earlier colonizers. Many of the Corinthian disciples bore Latin names, such as Justus, Tertius, Quartus, Gaius, Crispus, Fortunatus, and Achaicus. (Ac 18:7; Ro 16:22, 23; 1Co 1:14; 16:17) A large number of Jews had settled there and established a synagogue, drawing some Greek adherents. (Ac 18:4) The presence of Jews in Corinth is indicated by a Greek inscription on a marble lintel found near the gate toward Lechaeum. The inscription, which reads "[*Sy·na·*]*go·ge′ He·br*[*ai′on*]," means "Synagogue of the Hebrews." There was also a constant flow of travelers and merchants, besides those seeking pleasure at this entertainment and athletic center. Doubtless this contributed to a more broad-minded attitude than that prevailing in other cities visited by the apostle, including Athens, the center of Greek culture. Paul received a vision assuring him that Corinth contained many righteously disposed persons, and so he spent a year and six months at this strategic meeting place of the East and the West. (Ac 18:9-11) During this time he likely wrote his two letters to the Thessalonians.

Christian Congregation. Paul's associates in tentmaking and fellow Christians, Aquila and Priscilla, went with him when he finally sailed from the eastern port of Cenchreae heading across the Aegean Sea to Ephesus in Asia Minor. (Ac 18:18, 19) Eloquent Apollos, on the other hand, followed up Paul's activity, watering the seeds sown in Corinth. (Ac 18:24-28; 19:1; 1Co 3:6) Paul showed deep concern for the congregation he had formed in Corinth, dispatching Titus to represent him there on two visits, as well as writing his two weighty letters to the Corinthian congregation. (2Co 7:6, 7, 13; 8:6, 16, 17; 12:17, 18) Unable to make a planned stopover visit with them in transit to Macedonia (2Co 1:15, 16, 23), Paul, nevertheless, did spend three months in Greece later on, probably in 55-56 C.E., and spent part of the time in Corinth, writing his letter to the Romans from there.—Ac 20:2, 3; Ro 16:1, 23; 1Co 1:14.

CORINTHIANS, LETTERS TO THE.

Two inspired canonical letters written by the apostle Paul to the Christians in Greece during the first century C.E. The letters stand in seventh and eighth places, respectively, in most English versions of the Christian Greek Scriptures. Paul identifies himself as the writer of both letters, addressing First Corinthians to "the congregation of God that is in Corinth," and Second Corinthians to "the congregation of God that is in Corinth, together with all the holy ones who are in all of Achaia." —1Co 1:1, 2; 2Co 1:1.

That Paul did indeed write First and Second Corinthians cannot be seriously questioned. In addition to the apostle's own testimony, the authenticity and general acceptance of both letters are attested by external testimony. The two letters are ascribed to Paul and quoted by writers of the first to the third centuries. Also, what is known as "The Canon of Athanasius" (367 C.E.) lists, among "fourteen letters of Paul the apostle," "two to the Corinthians." This list is the first example of the catalog of books of the Christian Greek Scriptures as we have them today, preceding by 30 years the list published by the Council, or Synod, of Carthage, Africa, in 397 C.E.

Paul's Ministry in Corinth. Paul arrived in Corinth about 50 C.E. Initially he gave a talk in the synagogue every Sabbath "and would persuade Jews and Greeks." (Ac 18:1-4) However, after encountering opposition and abusive speech among those in the synagogue, the apostle turned his attention to "people of the nations," the Gentiles in Corinth. Paul's meetings with them were transferred to a house next door to the synagogue, and many "began to believe and be baptized." Told by the Lord in a vision, "I have many people in this city," the apostle remained there for a year and six months "teaching among them the word of God." (Ac 18:5-11) Because Paul had been instrumental in establishing a Christian congregation in Corinth, he could say to them: "Though you may have ten thousand tutors in Christ, you certainly do not have many fathers; for in Christ Jesus I have become your father through the good news." —1Co 4:15.

Gross immorality was practiced in Corinth, and in time it even affected the Christian congregation in that city. Paul found it necessary to rebuke the congregation in a letter because among them arose a case of "such fornication as is not even among the nations," for a certain man had taken his father's wife. (1Co 5:1-5) Using an illustration they could appreciate, he also encouraged them to faithfulness. He knew that they were acquainted with the athletic contests at the Isthmian Games held near Corinth. So he wrote: "Do you not know that the runners in a race all run, but only one receives the prize? Run in such a way that you may attain it. Moreover, every man taking part in a contest exercises self-control in all things. Now they, of course, do it that they may get a corruptible crown, but we an incorruptible one."—1Co 9: 24, 25.

First Corinthians. During his third missionary tour Paul spent some time in Ephesus. (Ac 19:1) Probably during the last year of his stay there, the apostle received disturbing news about

---

HIGHLIGHTS OF FIRST CORINTHIANS

A letter sent by Paul to the congregation in Corinth after he had received shocking reports about dissensions and immorality and in response to an inquiry about marriage

Written from Ephesus, about 55 C.E.

Exhortation to unity (1:1–4:21)

Following men results in divisions

God's view of what is wise and what is foolish is what counts

Boast not in men but in Jehovah, who supplies all things through Christ

Be mature, spiritual persons, appreciating that God causes spiritual growth and that Christ is the foundation on which Christian personalities are built

Let no one get puffed up, thinking he is better than fellow Christians

Keeping the congregation morally clean (5:1–6:20)

Disfellowship any who become fornicators, greedy persons, idolaters, revilers, drunkards, or extortioners

Better to be defrauded than to take a fellow Christian to court before unbelievers

Moral uncleanness defiles God's temple, prevents one from entering the Kingdom

Counsel regarding marriage and singleness (7:1-40)

Sexual due to be rendered, but with consideration

Marriage is better than singleness for persons inflamed with passion

Married Christian not to depart from unbelieving mate; may eventually help mate to gain salvation

Not necessary to change one's status when becoming a Christian

Marriage brings increased anxiety; singleness can be advantageous to one desiring to serve the Lord without distraction

Consideration for the spiritual welfare of others (8:1–10:33)

Do not stumble others by eating foods that were offered to idols

To avoid hindering any from accepting the good news, Paul did not exercise his right to receive material help

Take to heart the warning examples from Israel's wilderness experience—to benefit self and so as not to be a cause of stumbling to others

Though lawful, not all things build up

Congregational order (11:1–14:40)

Respect Christian headship; women's use of head covering

Show respect for the Lord's Evening Meal

Use the gifts of the spirit with appreciation for their source and their purpose

Love is the surpassing way

Maintain orderliness in congregation meetings

Certainty of the resurrection hope (15:1–16:24)

Christ's resurrection a guarantee

Anointed Christians must die in order to be raised to immortality and incorruption

Your labor is not in vain in connection with the Lord; stand firm in the faith

conditions in the Corinthian congregation. Paul had been told "by those of the house of Chloe" that dissensions existed among the Corinthians. (1Co 1:11) Stephanas, Fortunatus, and Achaicus had also come from Corinth and may have provided some information about the situation there. (1Co 16:17, 18) Also, Paul had received a letter of inquiry from the Christian congregation in Corinth. (1Co 7:1) Hence, out of deep regard for the spiritual welfare of his fellow believers there, Paul wrote this first letter to the Christian congregation in Corinth, about 55 C.E. That Ephesus was the place of composition is made certain by Paul's words recorded at 1 Corinthians 16:8: "But I am *remaining* in Ephesus until the festival of Pentecost."

In the introduction to First Corinthians Paul mentions an associate, Sosthenes, who may have penned the letter as dictated by Paul. This is likely, since toward its conclusion we read: "Here is my greeting, Paul's, in my own hand."—1Co 1:1; 16:21.

Second Corinthians. Paul wrote his second letter to the Corinthians probably during the late summer or early autumn of 55 C.E. The apostle had written the first letter in Ephesus, where he probably stayed as planned, until Pentecost of that year, or longer. (1Co 16:8) Paul then departed for Troas, where he was disappointed in not meeting Titus, who had been sent to Corinth to assist in the collection for the holy ones in Judea. So Paul proceeded to Macedonia, where Titus joined him with a report on the Corinthians' reaction to his first letter. (2Co 2:12, 13; 7:5-7) Paul then wrote the second letter to them from Macedonia, evidently dispatching it by the hand of Titus. Then, after a few months, his efforts to visit Corinth materialized. So Paul actually visited the Corinthians twice. After his first visit, at which time he established the congregation, he made a plan for a second visit, which failed. But "the third time" that he planned or got "ready" he was successful, for he was able to see them again in about 56 C.E. (2Co

HIGHLIGHTS OF SECOND CORINTHIANS

A follow-up letter regarding action taken to keep the congregation clean, to stir up desire to help brothers in Judea, and to counteract the influence of false apostles

Written by Paul in 55 C.E., a few months before he arrived in Corinth on his second and final visit

---

Paul's loving concern and the position of Paul and of Timothy in relation to their brothers (1:1–7:16)

Tribulation Paul and Timothy have experienced as Christians has brought them near death, but God's deliverance of them can comfort others

Have conducted selves with holiness and godly sincerity; not masters over the faith of others but fellow workers for their joy

First letter was written out of love and with many tears; now the man who formerly was immoral should be forgiven and comforted

Paul and his associates are qualified by God as ministers of the new covenant; the Corinthians are their letter of recommendation, written on the hearts of these ministers

In carrying out this ministry, they do not adulterate God's word but preach Christ as Lord; such good news is veiled only among those blinded by the god of this system of things

Though in earthly tents, Paul and Timothy as well as Corinthians share the hope of everlasting heavenly dwellings; but each one must be made manifest before the judgment seat of Christ

Anyone in union with Christ is a new creation; all of such share in ministry of reconciliation; all, as ambassadors, urge, "Become reconciled to God"

Paul and associates are recommended as God's ministers by what they have endured in their ministry, by giving evidence of God's spirit in their lives

With widened hearts they appeal to their brothers to widen out in their affections, to avoid becoming unevenly yoked with unbelievers, to cleanse themselves of every defilement of flesh and spirit

Paul's great comfort at report of their fine response to counsel in first letter

Encouragement to help brothers experiencing adversity in Judea (8:1–9:15)

Macedonians, though very poor, begged to have a share

Christ became poor so the Corinthians (and others) could become rich

Corinthians commended for their readiness to share

Let each one do as he has resolved in his heart; God loves a cheerful giver

Arguments to offset the influence of false apostles (10:1–13:14)

Answers to opposers as to Paul's being "weak," 'in territory belonging to them,' "inferior," "unskilled in speech," "unreasonable," and their claim that he proved he is not an apostle like them when he humbled himself to do secular work

Paul equal in genealogy; superior in record of persecution and hardship endured for Christ, in loving concern for congregations, in visions, in signs of apostleship

Keep testing whether you are in the faith

*Cormorant; a bird not to be
eaten according to the Mosaic Law*

1:15; 12:14; 13:1) During this second visit in Corinth he wrote his letter to the Romans.

Reasons for writing. Titus brought Paul a favorable report. The first letter to the Corinthians had awakened in them sadness in a godly way, repentance, earnestness, a desire to clear themselves, indignation, fear, and a righting of the wrong. Paul responded in his second letter commending them for their favorable reception and application of counsel, urging them to "kindly forgive and comfort" the repentant man they had evidently expelled from the congregation. (2Co 7:8-12; 2:1-11; compare 1Co 5:1-5.) Paul also wanted to encourage them to proceed further with the relief work for their needy fellow believers in Judea. (2Co 8:1-15) Then, too, there were persons in the congregation who continued to challenge Paul's position and authority as an apostle, making it necessary for him to defend his apostolic position; really, it was not for himself, but "it was for God," that is, to save the congregation that belonged to God, that Paul spoke very strongly in his letter and 'boasted' of his credentials as an apostle.—2Co 5:12, 13; 10:7-12; 11:16-20, 30-33; 12:11-13.

Light on Scriptures Previously Written.
Paul fortified his arguments by use of the Hebrew Scriptures in his inspired letters to the Corinthians. When exposing the foolishness of worldly wisdom as displayed by the false apostles, he proved the importance of getting the superior wisdom of God. This he did by pointing out what the psalmist had said to a generation centuries before, that "the thoughts of men . . . are as an

exhalation" (Ps 94:11; 1Co 3:20), and by asking what Isaiah had asked the rebellious Jews: "Who has taken the proportions of the spirit of Jehovah, and who . . . can make him know anything?" (Isa 40:13; 1Co 2:16) Paul proved that the Christian minister has a right to receive material aid by showing that Deuteronomy 25:4, "You must not muzzle a bull while it is threshing," really was written primarily for the ministers' sakes. (1Co 9:9, 10) He demonstrated that God had long ago promised a resurrection, by calling on the statements at Isaiah 25:8 and Hosea 13:14, about the swallowing up of death. (1Co 15:54, 55) Additionally, he shed much light on the Lord's Evening Meal by his detailed discussion of Jesus' words spoken at the time He established the observance.—Lu 22:19, 20; 1Co 11:23-34.

Paul demonstrated what God's attitude had always been as to spiritual cleanness by quoting from or alluding to Deuteronomy 17:7; Leviticus 26:11, 12; Isaiah 43:6; 52:11; and Hosea 1:10. (1Co 5:13; 2Co 6:14-18) He showed that the matter of material giving had not been overlooked by God's servants in the past and that the generous Christian is viewed favorably by Jehovah. (Ps 112:9; 2Co 9:9) And he indicated that the principle in the Law of establishing every matter at the mouth of two or three witnesses applies in the Christian congregation. (De 19:15; 2Co 13:1) These and other references to scriptures written beforehand illustrate these texts and clarify their application for us.

CORMORANT [Heb., *sha·lakh'*]. A large webfooted water bird that catches fish by diving. This bird appears only in the list of unclean birds under the Mosaic Law, a list that prohibits the eating of birds most of which basically are birds of prey and carrion eaters. (Le 11:17; De 14:17) The translators of the Greek *Septuagint* understood the bird to be the *ka·tar·ra'ktes,* the Greek name for cormorant, while the Latin *Vulgate* uses *mergulus* (the "diver") to indicate the bird. The cormorant (*Phalacrocorax*) is quite common in Palestine, particularly along the Mediterranean Coast and also in certain inland waters such as the Sea of Galilee. The cormorant is related to birds of the pelican family. Usually long bodied and dark colored, the cormorant is swift and agile in the water, swimming under water mainly by use of its webbed feet. Its sharp, hooked beak makes it a good fisher, and from ancient times cormorants have been trained by fishermen in the Orient and parts of India to catch fish for their owners, a band being placed fairly loosely around the bird's throat to prevent it from swallowing anything but very small fish.

CORNELIUS (Cor·ne′li·us). An army officer (centurion, *KJ*) in command of 100 soldiers of the Italian band. (See ARMY OFFICER.) Stationed at Caesarea, he had his own house. His Roman name suggests that he may have belonged to a noble family in the imperial city. He was "a devout man" who "made many gifts of mercy to the people and made supplication to God continually," "a man righteous and fearing God and well reported by the whole nation of the Jews." It was to this man that an angel appeared in a vision in the fall of 36 C.E., saying: "Your prayers and gifts of mercy have ascended as a remembrance before God." The angel also told Cornelius to send to Joppa for Peter.—Ac 10:1-22.

When Peter arrived, Cornelius, in the presence of "his relatives and intimate friends," said to the apostle: "We are all present before God to hear all the things you have been commanded by Jehovah to say." (Ac 10:24, 33) "While Peter was yet speaking . . . the holy spirit fell upon all those hearing the word." Thus this group of which Cornelius is named as the most notable became the first uncircumcised Gentiles or non-Jews to receive "the free gift of the holy spirit." (Ac 10:44, 45) Water baptism immediately followed. Nothing more is known of the life and activity of Cornelius after this.

Why was the conversion of Cornelius a particularly noteworthy event?

Cornelius was not a proselyte member of the Jewish community as some contend, even though he was acquainted with the writings of the prophets, gave gifts of mercy to the Jews, feared God, prayed continually, and used the name Jehovah. The Scriptures prove conclusively that this army officer was an uncircumcised Gentile in the fullest sense. If Cornelius had been a proselyte, Peter would not have said it was unlawful for him, a Jew, to associate with this "man of another race," in view of what was written in the Law concerning an alien resident. (Le 19:33, 34; Ac 10:28) If he had been a proselyte, the six other Jews with Peter would not have been "amazed" at seeing the holy spirit poured out "upon people of the nations." (Ac 10:45; 11:12) If he had been a proselyte, why

did "supporters of circumcision" contend with Peter over this matter?—Ac 11:2.

In reality, Cornelius was the firstfruits of the uncircumcised non-Jews to become a Christian, showing that by this time it was not necessary for Gentiles to become Jewish proselytes like the Ethiopian eunuch before being accepted into the Christian congregation. "For a certainty," Peter exclaimed on that historic occasion, "I perceive that God is not partial, but in every nation the man that fears him and works righteousness is acceptable to him." (Ac 10:34, 35) As Peter was the first to open up The Way to the Jews at Pentecost, so in this instance he was the first to bring good news of salvation to the uncircumcised Gentiles. James also agreed that it was "the first time" that God turned his attention to "the nations."—Ac 15:7, 14.

CORNER GATE. See GATE, GATEWAY.

CORNERSTONE. A stone placed at an angle or corner of a building where two walls meet, of great importance in joining and binding them together. Usually cut as rectangular blocks, cornerstones are customarily laid endways and sideways alternately from the foundation to the top or roof of a structure. Thus, at an angle or corner, the side of one stone appears below or above the end of the next stone.

The principal cornerstone was the foundation cornerstone, a particularly strong one generally being chosen for public buildings and city walls. The foundation cornerstone would be used as a guide as other stones were put in place, a plummet being dropped to it to align them. Every other stone had to conform to the foundation cornerstone for the building to be properly constructed. Sometimes, foundation cornerstones were quite massive. The foundation cornerstone also served to bind the parts of a structure together.

Another important cornerstone was "the head of the corner" (Ps 118:22), this expression apparently referring to the topmost and hence the crowning stone of a structure. By means of it the two walls meeting at the corner would be held together at the top so that they would not fall apart and the structure collapse.

Joy and the praising of Jehovah marked the laying of the temple's foundation in Zerubbabel's day. (Ezr 3:10, 11) Also, it was foretold that when Zerubbabel would "bring forth the headstone" there would be shoutings to it of "How charming! How charming!" (Zec 4:6, 7) However, sorrow and devastation were in store for Babylon, Jehovah foretelling: "People will not take from you a stone for a corner or a stone for foundations, because desolate wastes to time indefinite are what you will become."—Jer 51:26.

Figurative and Symbolic Use. Concerning the founding of the earth, God asked Job: "Who laid its cornerstone?" The earth, on which man resides and has erected many buildings, was thus likened to a gigantic edifice, a building with a cornerstone. The laying of it, which could be ascribed to no man, for mankind had not yet been created, made the heavenly "sons of God" shout in applause.—Job 38:4-7.

Some translations use "cornerstone(s)" to render a Hebrew word (*pin·nah'*), which carries the basic thought of "corner" but is also used metaphorically for a chief as a 'corner' of defense or support, hence for a keyman. Thus, at Isaiah 19:13 certain translations use "cornerstone(s)" (*RS; AT; AS*), whereas others use "chiefs" (*Le*) and "leaders" (*Mo*), agreeing basically with the *New World Translation* rendering "keymen." (See also Jg 20:2; 1Sa 14:38; Zec 10:4, where the Hebrew is literally "the corner tower(s)," these being pictorial of important or vital men, or chiefs.) Such an application of 'corner' to a keyman seems significant in view of the symbolic application of "cornerstone" in Messianic prophecy.

Jesus Christ is Scripturally spoken of as the "foundation cornerstone" of the Christian congregation, which is likened to a spiritual house. Through Isaiah, Jehovah foretold that He would lay in Zion as a foundation "a stone, a tried stone, the precious corner of a sure foundation." (Isa 28:16) Peter quoted and applied to Jesus Christ this prophecy regarding the "foundation cornerstone" on which individual anointed Christians are built up as "living stones," to become a spiritual house or temple for Jehovah. (1Pe 2:4-6) Similarly, Paul showed that members of the Christian congregation had been built up "upon the foundation of the apostles and prophets, while Christ Jesus himself is the foundation cornerstone," in union with whom the whole building harmoniously joined together "is growing into a holy temple for Jehovah," a place for Him to inhabit by spirit. —Eph 2:19-22.

Psalm 118:22 discloses that the stone rejected by the builders would become "the head of the corner" (Heb., *ro'sh pin·nah'*). Jesus quoted and applied this prophecy to himself as "the chief cornerstone" (Gr., *ke·pha·le' go·ni'as*, head of the corner). (Mt 21:42; Mr 12:10, 11; Lu 20:17) Just as the topmost stone of a building is conspicuous, so Jesus Christ is the crowning stone of the Christian congregation of anointed ones, which is likened to

a spiritual temple. Peter also applied Psalm 118:22 to Christ, showing that he was "the stone" rejected by men but chosen by God to become "the head of the corner."—Ac 4:8-12; see also 1Pe 2:4-7.

COS. The capital city at the NE end of an island bearing the same name. It is located off the SW coast of Asia Minor. Its advantageous position gave Cos high commercial and naval importance at an early date.

Though the apostle Paul apparently sailed past this city when traveling from Ephesus to Caesarea at the conclusion of his second missionary journey in about 52 C.E. (Ac 18:21, 22), it was not until the close of his third tour, about four years later, that the island received mention by name in Acts. After Paul 'tore himself away' from the Ephesian overseers to whom he had spoken at Miletus (Ac 20:17, 36-38), the ship that he and Luke boarded "ran with a straight course," that is, it sailed before the wind, without tacking, and under fair winds, until it "came to Cos," a journey of some 75 km (47 mi) down the coast. It has been estimated by some commentators that, with the Aegean's usual prevailing NW winds, such a distance could be covered in about six hours, allowing, as Luke indicates, for Paul's ship to arrive at Cos on the same day as that of departure from Miletus. It seems likely that this ship spent the night anchored off the E coast of Cos and arrived at Rhodes "the next day," after departing in the morning on the journey of some 120 km (75 mi).—Ac 21:1.

The island of Cos is reputed to have long been a Jewish center in the Aegean. It was a free Roman state in the province of Asia and, according to Tacitus, was granted immunity from taxation by Claudius in 53 C.E.

COSAM (Co'sam). A descendant of David's son Nathan; son of Elmadam and father of Addi; and ancestor of Jesus' mother Mary.—Lu 3:28.

COSMETICS. Substances or treatments applied to the face or other parts of the human body to alter one's appearance, to beautify, or to promote attractiveness. Such preparations can be applied to the skin, the nails, or the hair. The English word "cosmetic" is derived from the Greek word *ko·sme·ti·kos'*, which means "skilled in decorating."

There were ointment makers and mixers among the Israelites (Ex 30:25; 1Sa 8:13; Ne 3:8), and ointments (often scented) were widely used, perhaps more so than other cosmetics. When applied to the skin or the hair in a hot, dry climate, ointments would help to cope with dryness. Perfumed oils were in use, a sinful woman once anointing Jesus Christ's feet with such oil. (Lu

7:37, 38) Also, a few days before Jesus' death, Mary, the sister of Lazarus, "came with an alabaster case of perfumed oil, genuine nard, very expensive," and anointed him.—Mr 14:3; Joh 12:3; Mt 26:6, 7; see OINTMENT AND PERFUMES.

When Jehu came to Jezreel, Jezebel, in addition to attending to her coiffure or doing her head up beautifully, "proceeded to paint her eyes with black paint." (2Ki 9:30) At least some women in Israel, like those in other Middle Eastern lands of antiquity, used eye paint. (Eze 23:40) Eye paint was often black, which color would contrast with the white of the eye and tend to make the eyes look larger. (Jer 4:30) Scriptural references to eye painting do not associate the practice with faithful women of Israel in general, though one of Job's daughters was named Keren-happuch, which possibly means "Horn of the Black (Eye) Paint [that is, a receptacle for makeup]."—Job 42:14.

Modest and tasteful use of cosmetics and articles of adornment is not Scripturally condemned. However, Paul and Peter admonished Christian women to adorn themselves "with modesty and soundness of mind, . . . in the way that befits women professing to reverence God," and to let their adornment be "the secret person of the heart in the incorruptible apparel of the quiet and mild spirit, which is of great value in the eyes of God." (1Ti 2:9, 10; 1Pe 3:3, 4) And, in the inspired appraisal of the good wife, it is fittingly stated: "Charm may be false, and prettiness may be vain; but the woman that fears Jehovah is the one that procures praise for herself."—Pr 31:30.

COTTON.

A white seed fiber produced by certain plants and used to make fabric. The Hebrew word *kar·pas'* corresponds to the Sanskrit word *karpasa* and the Greek *kar'pa·sos*, which may refer to either fine cotton or fine linen. Many modern translations favor the rendering "cotton" at Esther 1:6. It is there mentioned as among the materials used for decorating the palace courtyard during King Ahasuerus' seven-day banquet at Shushan. The growing of cotton in Persia and in India extends far back into ancient times. While linen seems to have been more widely used in Egypt and Palestine, evidence for the use of cotton there also exists from the first millennium B.C.E. on.

The cotton plant of the Bible account is thought to have been the type classified as *Gossypium herbaceum.* The bush grows to a height of about 1.5 m (5 ft), blossoms with yellow or sometimes pink flowers, and following the drying up of the flowers, produces the cotton bolls or seed capsules. When ripe, the bolls split open, allowing the fluffy cotton to push out. After the cotton has been collected, the seeds must be picked out, or combed out, by passing the cotton through a gin. The cotton fibers are then ready for final processing and for weaving. Some scholars suggest that the "white fabrics" of the loom workers of Egypt mentioned at Isaiah 19:9 were probably of cotton. —See CLOTH.

COUNSEL, COUNSELOR.

One who gives advice is a counselor. Counsel is the advice that he gives.

Of the numerous Hebrew and Aramaic words used in the Scriptures to express the idea of "counsel," the Hebrew noun *'e·tsah'* and the related verb *ya·'ats'* appear most often. Though usually rendered "counsel," *'e·tsah'* has also been translated "scheme." (Isa 8:10) In the Christian Greek Scriptures, the concept of "counsel" or "advice" as a noun is expressed by *bou·le'* and *sym·bou'li·on. Bou·le'* is also rendered "design" (Lu 23:51), "scheme" (Ac 5:38), "express will" (Ac 13:36), and "determination" (Ac 27:42).

So the term "counsel" may also signify "will," "purpose," "determination," "design," as when Jehovah declares: "My own counsel will stand." (Isa 46:10) It is the "counsels of the hearts," namely, the plans, designs, purposes, or determinations, of the deep inner self that will be exposed when the Lord Jesus Christ comes to render judgment. (1Co 4:5) At Ephesians 1:11, the phrase "according to the way his will counsels" (literally, "according to the counsel of the will of him") may be understood to mean "according to the purpose, or determination, that is an expression of God's will." The apostle Paul said that he was free of bloodguilt because he did not hold back from teaching "all the counsel of God" ("the whole of God's purpose," *JB;* "the whole will of God," *NIV*), that is, everything that is essential for salvation.—Ac 20:27.

Men known for their wisdom were valued highly as royal counselors or advisers. (See 2Sa 16:23.) Because of their position, they were on occasion offered bribes so that they would use their influence in a corrupt way. When the enemies of the Jews hired counselors, they may have done so by bribing Persians who served in that capacity. —Ezr 4:5.

No one human is the depository of all knowledge. Therefore, the person who heeds sound counsel is wise. (Pr 12:15) For one to reject the good counsel of experienced advisers, as did King Rehoboam, is the height of folly.—1Ki 12:8.

Jehovah is the possessor of wisdom in the absolute sense. He alone needs no one to counsel him. (Isa 40:13; Ro 11:34) His Son is able to act as "Wonderful Counselor," providing guidance and direction, because he received and followed counsel from his Father and has God's spirit. (Isa 9:6; 11:2; Joh 5:19, 30) This emphasizes that if counsel is to be beneficial, it must take Jehovah into consideration. Any advice that stands in opposition to the Most High is valueless. It is no counsel at all. —Pr 19:21; 21:30.

COURAGE.

The quality of being strong, bold, daring, valiant. Courage is the opposite of fear, timidity, and cowardice.—Mr 6:49, 50; 2Ti 1:7.

The Hebrew verb most frequently expressing the sense of being courageous is cha·zaq'. It basically signifies "be strong." (2Sa 13:28; 2Ch 19:11; Eze 3:14) Often cha·zaq' is used together with 'a·mats', which also means "be strong." Both verbs are found in the expressions "Be courageous and strong" (Jos 10:25) and "Be courageous, and may your heart be strong."—Ps 31:24.

The idea of weakening or enfeebling is expressed by the Hebrew term ra·phah', which at times may mean to 'lose courage' (Jer 49:24) or 'show oneself discouraged.' (Pr 24:10) When rendered "drop down," as in the phrase "May your hands not drop down," it has the meaning "lose courage, become too weak to act."—Zep 3:16; Isa 13:7; Eze 7:17.

In Greek, the state of being bold or courageous is expressed by the verbs thar·re'o (2Co 5:8) and thar·se'o. (Mt 9:2) The verb tol·ma'o is variously rendered "dare" (Jude 9), 'have courage' (Mr 12: 34), "venture" (Ro 15:18), 'act bold' (2Co 11:21), the emphasis being on the manifestation of courage or boldness in an undertaking.

God's servants have always needed courage to remain faithful to the Most High. Thus, when the Israelites were ready to cross into the Promised Land, Moses told them: "Be courageous and strong," and he repeated that same admonition to his appointed successor Joshua. (De 31:6, 7) Fortifying those words of Moses, Jehovah himself later told Joshua, "Be courageous and strong . . . Only be courageous and very strong." (Jos 1:6, 7, 9) To be supplied with the needed courage, the nation had to listen to, learn, and obey the law of Jehovah. (De 31:9-12) Similarly, to become courageous and strong, Joshua was told to read God's law regularly and to take care to apply it.—Jos 1:8.

The Scriptures contain many express commands to take courage and they also show how one can gain it. (Ps 31:24) The association of fellow worshipers can be a great aid. (Ac 28:15) At Psalm 27:14 David, himself a man of courage, said: "Be courageous and let your heart be strong." In the preceding verses of Psalm 27, he reveals what helped him to be courageous: Relying upon Jeho-

vah as "the stronghold" of his life (vs 1), past experiences with how Jehovah dealt with his adversaries (vss 2, 3), appreciation for Jehovah's temple of worship (vs 4), trusting in Jehovah's protection and in his help and deliverance (vss 5-10), continued instruction in the principles of God's righteous way (vs 11), and the qualities of faith and hope (vss 13, 14).

The Christian needs courage to remain uncontaminated by the attitudes and actions of a world at enmity with Jehovah God and to remain faithful to Him despite having to face the world's hatred. Jesus Christ told his disciples: "In the world you are having tribulation, but take courage! I have conquered the world." (Joh 16:33) Never did the Son of God yield to the world's influence, but he triumphed over the world by not becoming like it in any respect. The sterling example of Jesus Christ as a conqueror and the outcome of his flawless course can fill one with the needed courage to imitate him in remaining separate from and undefiled by the world.—Joh 17:16.

COURIER.

A man especially selected from the royal bodyguard to deliver royal decrees and other urgent correspondence from a king to distant areas of his realm. The speed of delivery by couriers (Heb., ra·tsim'; literally, runners) was of prime importance. From early times such men were referred to as "runners." They are called this at 2 Chronicles 30:6, 10; Jeremiah 51:31.

In the Persian Empire fast horses were used, along with relay stations, or posts, where fresh couriers and horses waited to carry important messages on their way. (Es 3:13-15; 8:10, 14) They rushed messages to their destinations night and day and in all kinds of weather. In the Roman Empire there were stations placed every few kilometers for the couriers where 40 horses were constantly kept. Roman couriers could travel about 160 km (100 mi) a day, a considerable speed in those times. With this system of post-horses, royal messages could be dispatched to the ends of an empire in a relatively short period of time.

COURT, JUDICIAL.

Jehovah God as the Creator of the universe has the supreme sovereignty. As acknowledged by the ancient nation of Israel, so he is to the universe, namely, Judge, Statute-Giver, and King. (Isa 33:22) The family head Abraham acknowledged him as "Judge of all the earth." (Ge 18:25) Jehovah portrays himself as Supreme Judge in a legal case against Israel (Mic 6:2), also in a legal case in behalf of his people against the nations. (Isa 34:8) He calls on his people as witnesses in a case involving a challenge

of his Godship by the worshipers of false gods.
—Isa 43:9-12.

Patriarchal Society. After the Flood, Noah emerged as the family head or patriarch, and God made a covenant with him and his sons as representatives of the human race. (Ge 9:12-16) Noah also received basic laws in addition to what God had stated previously. (Ge 9:3-6) As patriarch, Noah made decisions that affected not only his immediate household but also his married sons and their offspring.—Ge 9:20-27.

The family head was judge of the family, which included the slaves and all those living under the household of the family head, just as Jehovah God is the great family Head and Judge. (Ge 38:24) Disputes between families were settled between family heads when it was possible to settle them peaceably.

Jacob acted as judge for those in his household when Laban brought accusations that his teraphim had been stolen by someone in Jacob's camp. Jacob said: "Whoever it is with whom you may find your gods, let him not live." (Ge 31:32) However, Jacob did not know that Rachel had taken them, and Laban did not find them, so Rachel was not accused. When Joseph's brothers had sold him into Egypt and presented Joseph's blood-soaked garment to make it appear that he had been killed by a wild beast, Jacob sat in judgment, examined the evidence, and made a judicial decision: "Joseph is surely torn to pieces!" (Ge 37:33) Judah sat in judgment when he found that Tamar was pregnant, sentencing her to be put to death. But when he found that she had maneuvered him into performing that which he legally should have caused his son Shelah to perform, he pronounced Tamar more righteous than himself.—Ge 38:24-26.

Among the worshipers of the true God, Jehovah was always acknowledged as the Supreme Judge. The family head as judge was reckoned as accountable to God, who himself sat in judgment in the cases of Adam and Eve (Ge 3:8-24); of Cain (Ge 4:9-15); of humankind at the time of the Flood (Ge 6:1-3, 11-13, 17-21); of the builders of the Tower of Babel (Ge 11:1-9); of Sodom and Gomorrah (Ge 18:20-33); and of Abimelech (Ge 20:3-7).

Under the Law. With the Exodus of the Israelites from Egypt, Moses as Jehovah's representative became judge. At first he was trying to handle all the cases, which were so numerous that he was busy from morning to evening. On the counsel of Jethro he appointed capable men as chiefs of thousands, of hundreds, of fifties, and of tens. (Ex 18:13-26) It does not appear that this meant that there was one specially appointed judge for every seven or eight able-bodied males. Rather, the nation was organized with chiefs authorized to handle smaller cases whenever necessary. But anything unusually complicated or difficult, or a matter of national importance, was to be brought to Moses or to the sanctuary before the priests.

These hard matters for judgment included the following: Where the husband was suspicious of the chastity of his wife (Nu 5:11-31), a case of bloodshed where there was a dispute (De 17:8, 9), and certain cases where revolt was charged against a man but where the evidence was unclear or suspicious (De 19:15-20). The priests would officiate in a case of unsolved murder.—De 21:1-9.

There were no regular provisions for appeal from the lower courts to the higher, but if the chiefs of tens could not decide a case they could refer it to the chiefs of fifties, and so on, or directly to the sanctuary or to Moses.—Ex 18:26; De 1:17; 17:8-11.

The men selected as judges were to be capable, trustworthy men, fearing Jehovah, hating unjust profit. (Ex 18:21) They were generally family heads or heads of tribes, older men of the city in which they acted as judges. The Levites, who were set aside by Jehovah as special instructors in the Law, served prominently also as judges.—De 1:15.

Many are the admonitions against the perversion of judgment, taking of bribes, or partiality. (Ex 23:6-8; De 1:16, 17; 16:19; Pr 17:23; 24:23; 28:21; 29:4) A poor man was not to be favored merely because he was poor, nor was the rich man to be given advantage over the poor. (Le 19:15) The rights of the alien resident were to be regarded, and they were not to be treated unjustly. The judges were not to oppress such ones, nor widows and orphans, who seemed to have no protector, for Jehovah was their fatherly Judge and Protector. (Le 19:33, 34; Ex 22:21; 23:9; De 10:18; 24:17, 18; 27:19; Ps 68:5) Accordingly, the alien residents were required to respect the law of the land. (Le 18:26) But these statutes and counsels from Jehovah came to be disregarded by the princes and judges in Israel, such disregard being one of the causes for God's adverse judgment of the nation. —Isa 1:23; Eze 22:12; 1Sa 8:3; Ps 26:10; Am 5:12.

Since the judges were to be upright men, judging according to Jehovah's law, they represented Jehovah. Therefore, standing before the judges was considered as standing before Jehovah. (De 1:17; 19:17; Jos 7:19; 2Ch 19:6) The term "assembly" or "congregation" in most cases means the general assembly of the people, but in speaking of taking cases for judgment before the assembly or congregation the Bible refers to the representative members thereof, the judges, as at Numbers 35:12, 24, 25 and Matthew 18:17.

The local court was situated at the gate of a city. (De 16:18; 21:19; 22:15, 24; 25:7; Ru 4:1) By "gate" is meant the open space inside the city near the gate. The gates were places where the Law was read to the congregated people and where ordinances were proclaimed. (Ne 8:1-3) At the gate it was easy to acquire witnesses to a civil matter, such as property sales, and so forth, as most persons would go in and out of the gate during the day. Also, the publicity that would be afforded any trial at the gate would tend to influence the judges toward care and justice in the trial proceedings and in their decisions. Evidently there was a place provided near the gate where the judges could comfortably preside. (Job 29:7) Samuel traveled in a circuit of Bethel, Gilgal, and Mizpah and "judged Israel at all these places," as well as at Ramah, where his house was located. —1Sa 7:16, 17.

The judges were to be treated with respect, inasmuch as they stood in a position representing Jehovah. (Ex 22:28; Ac 23:3-5) When a decision was handed down by the priests, by the Levites at the sanctuary, or by the judge who was acting in those days (for example, Moses or Samuel), it was binding, and anyone who refused to abide by the decision was put to death.—De 17:8-13.

If a man was sentenced to receive a beating with rods, he was to be laid prostrate before the judge and beaten in his presence. (De 25:2) Justice was administered speedily. The only instances where a person was held for a time was when a matter was difficult and the judgment had to be received from Jehovah. Then the accused was held in custody until the decision was received. (Le 24:12; Nu 15:34) The Law did not provide for imprisonment. Only later on, as the nation deteriorated, and also during the time of Gentile domination, was imprisonment practiced.—2Ch 18:25, 26; Jer 20:2; 29:26; Ezr 7:26; Ac 5:19; 12:3, 4.

During the Period of the Kings. After the kingdom was established in Israel the cases of the most difficult nature were taken either to the king or to the sanctuary. The Law, at Deuteronomy 17:18, 19, required the king, upon taking his throne, to write out for himself a copy of the Law and to read in it daily, so that he would be properly qualified to judge difficult cases. David was maneuvered by the prophet Nathan into sitting in

judgment in his own case in the matter of Bathsheba and Uriah the Hittite. (2Sa 12:1-6) Joab shrewdly sent a Tekoite woman to present a case to David in behalf of Absalom. (2Sa 14:1-21) Before his death David appointed 6,000 qualified Levites to act as officers and judges in Israel. (1Ch 23:4) King Solomon was renowned for his wisdom in judging. A case that brought him widespread fame was the maternity case of two prostitutes. (1Ki 3:16-28) Jehoshaphat conducted a religious reform in Judah and strengthened the judicial arrangement.—2Ch 19:5-11.

Who were members of the Jewish Sanhedrin?

The Sanhedrin was the Jewish high court. It was located in Jerusalem. Seventy-one members constituted this high court called the Great Sanhedrin. In the time of Jesus' earthly ministry the 71 members included the high priest and others who had held the office of high priest (a number of such might be living at one time, for the office had become an appointive one under Roman rule). It also included members of the high priestly families, older men, the heads of the tribes and families, and scribes, men versed in the Law. (Ac 4:5, 6) These men were members of the sects of the Pharisees and the Sadducees.—Ac 23:6.

The head and president of the Sanhedrin was the high priest, who called the assembly together. (Ac 5:17, 21, 27; 7:1; 22:5; 23:2) Caiaphas the high priest presided at the trial of Jesus, although Jesus was first brought for questioning before Annas. (Mt 26:3, 57; Mr 14:53, 55, 60, 63; 15:1; Lu 22:54; Joh 18:12, 13, 19-24) Ananias was the high priest presiding over the Sanhedrin at the time of Paul's trial.—Ac 23:2.

According to the Talmud (Tosefta, *Sanhedrin* 7:1), the Sanhedrin sat from the time of the offering of the daily morning sacrifice until the evening sacrifice. It did not sit in judgment on the Sabbath or on feast days. In capital cases the Sanhedrin held trial during the daytime, and the verdict had to be reached during the daytime. If it was a verdict of conviction, it had to be issued on the following day. Therefore, trials could not be held on the eve of a Sabbath or on the eve of a festival day. However, this procedure was ignored in the case of Jesus' trial.

The Mishnah (*Sanhedrin* 4:3) states: "The Sanhedrin was arranged like the half of a round threshing-floor so that they all might see one another. Before them stood the two scribes of the judges, one to the right and one to the left, and they wrote down the words of them that favoured acquittal and the words of them that favoured conviction."—Translated by H. Danby.

According to Jewish tradition the Sanhedrin was set up by Moses (Nu 11:16-25) and reorganized by Ezra immediately after the return from the exile. But there is no historical evidence to support the idea that 70 older men sat as a single court to hear cases in those early times. Rather, the Sanhedrin seems to have come into existence during the time of Greek rule in Palestine. In the time of Jesus' earthly ministry the Roman government allowed the Sanhedrin a great measure of independence, granting it civil and administrative authority. It had officers at its disposal as well as the power of arrest and imprisonment. (Mt 26:47; Ac 4:1-3; 9:1, 2) Its religious authority was recognized even among the Jews of the Dispersion. (See Ac 9:1, 2.) However, under the Roman rule the Sanhedrin in time evidently lost the legal authority to execute the death penalty, unless they got the permission of the Roman governor (procurator). (Joh 18:31) After the destruction of Jerusalem in 70 C.E., the Sanhedrin was abolished.

In Jerusalem there were, in addition, lower courts composed of 23 members each. According to the Mishnah (*Sanhedrin* 1:6), these smaller courts were also located in other cities of sufficient size throughout Palestine. The full number of judges comprising the court did not sit on every case. The number varied according to the seriousness of the matter to be judged and the difficulty in reaching a verdict. Additionally, there was the village court consisting of three men, and a court consisting of seven older men of the village.

The synagogues, which were used primarily for education, were also used to some extent as places for local courts, at times referred to as 'local Sanhedrins,' having the power to inflict the penalties of scourging and excommunication.—Mt 10:17, ftn; 23:34; Mr 13:9; Lu 21:12; Joh 9:22; 12:42; 16:2; see ILLUSTRATIONS (Some of Jesus Christ's prominent illustrations [21]).

The Christian Congregation. The Christian congregation, while having no secular authority as a court, may take action against disorderly members who require spiritual discipline, and it can even expel them from the congregation. Therefore, the apostle Paul tells the congregation that they, that is, the representative members thereof, those having oversight, must judge those inside the organization. (1Co 5:12, 13) In writing to congregations and to overseers both Paul and Peter point out that the elders should keep a close watch on the congregation's spiritual condition and should assist and admonish anyone who is taking an unwise or wrong step. (2Ti 4:2; 1Pe 5:1, 2; compare Ga 6:1.) Those who are causing divisions or sects are to be warned a first and a second time before congregational action is taken. (Tit 3:10, 11) But insistent practicers of sin are to be removed, expelled from the congregation. This constitutes discipline, showing to the offenders that their course of sin cannot be tolerated in the congregation. (1Ti 1:20) Paul instructs those men in the congregation having the responsibility to act as judges to gather together to hear such a matter. (1Co 5:1-5; 6:1-5) They are to accept the accusation as true only when there are two or three witnesses, weighing the evidence without prejudgment, doing nothing according to a biased leaning.—1Ti 5:19, 21.

Jesus commanded his disciples that if one sinned against another, efforts should first be made to settle the matter personally between themselves. If these efforts failed and the issue was of a serious nature, they should take it to the congregation for settlement (that is, to those appointed to responsible positions in governing the congregation). Paul later admonished Christians to settle difficulties in this manner and not to be taking one another before worldly courts.—Mt 18:15-17; 1Co 6:1-8; see LEGAL CASE.

COURT OFFICIAL. The Hebrew word *sa·ris'*, translated "court official" (1Ki 22:9), can also be rendered "eunuch" (Es 2:3; Isa 56:3) and 'officer' (Ge 40:2, 7). At Genesis 37:36 (*KJ*) it is translated "officer," and a marginal note states: "But the word doth signify not only eunuchs, but also chamberlains, courtiers, and officers." The Greek word *eu·nou'khos,* rendered "eunuch," can refer either to a court official (Ac 8:27) or to a person who is deprived of the ability to procreate.—Mt 19:12.

It is generally thought that court officials were the men in charge of the private chambers or apartments of a palace or mansion, as was Blastus, chamberlain of King Herod. (Ac 12:20) (However, the Greek expression *e·pi' tou koi·to'nos*, the one "in charge of the bedchamber," is used here.) But the duties of officials of the king's court varied greatly. Bigthan and Teresh were Medo-Persian court officials who were trusted servants, their duty seemingly being to guard the door of King Ahasuerus' private apartment. (Es 2:21) Others ministered to the person of the king. (Es 1:10, 11) The Bible identifies some court officials as being men who held military offices. (2Ki 25:19) A "principal court official" in Babylon had the responsibility to appoint a guardian over Daniel, Hananiah,

Mishael, and Azariah after they arrived in Babylon when Nebuchadnezzar took King Jehoiachin and certain of the Jews to Babylon in 617 B.C.E. —Da 1:3, 7, 11.

It appears that not all court officials were eunuchs in the literal sense, that is, emasculated men. Literal eunuchs were often in charge of the women's quarters, or harem of a king. But the duties of officers such as chief cupbearer (a high position) and baker would not necessarily give rise to the requirement of emasculation for that office, although they could have been eunuchs who rose to those positions. (Ge 40:2) In Pharaoh's court, Potiphar, a court official and chief of the bodyguard, was a married man. (Ge 39:1) The Ethiopian "eunuch" baptized by Philip the evangelizer was a man in power, over all the treasure of Queen Candace. He was a proselyte of the Jewish religion, a worshiper of Jehovah, under the Law. He could not have been a literal eunuch, for no castrated man could come into the congregation of Israel and no others aside from Jews and proselytes were baptized prior to Cornelius' conversion. (Ac 8:26-38; 10:24, 34, 35, 44-47; De 23:1) David called together his court officials (who would logically not be literal eunuchs in view of the Jewish attitude and the Law), along with the princes and mighty men, to inform them that his son Solomon was designated to build the temple of Jehovah. —1Ch 28:1-6; see CUPBEARER; STEWARD.

COUSIN.

The child of one's aunt or uncle. The only occurrence of the Greek word *a·ne·psi·os'* (cousin) is at Colossians 4:10, where Paul calls Mark "the cousin of Barnabas." The Greek term means primarily "first cousin," but in a wider sense, any cousin. *A·ne·psi·os'* also occurs in the *Septuagint* at Numbers 36:11 (plural), but the Hebrew expression in the Masoretic text is rendered literally "sons of their father's brothers."

The *King James Version* calls Elizabeth Mary's cousin (*syg·ge·nis'*) at Luke 1:36. This Greek word is considered a peculiar form of the word *syg·ge·nes'*, which is rendered "relative" in modern versions. (Lu 2:44; 21:16; Ac 10:24; *CC, ED, NW*) *Syg·ge·nes'* occurs five times in the *Septuagint,* again meaning "relatives" in general rather than the modern restricted designation "cousin."—Le 18:14; 20:20; 25:45; 2Sa 3:39; Eze 22:6; *LXX.*

Though no word for cousin is found in the Hebrew Scriptures, this relationship is there indicated by expressions such as "the sons of . . . Aaron's uncle," "the son of his uncle." (Le 10:4; 25:49) Marriages to cousins are reported: Jacob and Rachel, and the daughters of Zelophehad. (Ge 28:2; 29:10-12; Nu 36:11) Such marriages to cousins were not included in the Mosaic prohibitions against incest. (Le 18:8-16) Today civil laws are at variance on this matter; some states and nations allow cousins to marry, others forbid it.

COVENANT.

An agreement between two or more persons to do or refrain from doing some act; a compact; a contract. The Hebrew word *berith',* whose etymology is uncertain, appears over 280 times in the Hebrew Scriptures; more than 80 of these occurrences are in the five books of Moses. That its basic meaning is "covenant," comparable to our modern legal word "contract," is seen from cuneiform tablets found in 1927 at Qatna, an ancient non-Israelite city SE of Hamath. "The contents of the two tablets [of 15 found] are simple. Tablet A contains a list of names . . . Tablet B is a ration list . . . List A is thus a *compact* in which the men in question . . . agree to enter someone's service or to carry out certain obligations. List B, written by the same scribe, then illustrates the nature of the *compact;* the men were to receive specified rations in return for their services. . . . the Israelite concept of *berith,* 'covenant,' was a central theme in Yahwist theology. Here we have the first published extra-biblical occurrence of the word from early times—not later than the first third of the fourteenth century B.C."—*Bulletin of the American Schools of Oriental Research,* February 1951, p. 22.

In some translations of the Christian Greek Scriptures the word *di·a·the'ke* is variously rendered "covenant," "will," "testament" (*testamentum,* Vg). However, M'Clintock and Strong's *Cyclopædia* (1891) says, under "Covenant": "There seems, however, to be no necessity for the introduction of a new word [other than "covenant"] conveying a new idea. The Sept[uagint] having rendered [*berith'*] (which never means *will* or *testament,* but always *covenant* or *agreement*) by [*di·a·the'ke*] consistently throughout the O.T., the N.T. writers, in adopting that word, may naturally be supposed to intend to convey to their readers, most of them familiar with the Greek O.T., the same idea. Moreover, in the majority of cases, the same thing which has been called a 'covenant' (*berith'*) in the O.T. is referred to in the N.T. (e.g. 2Cor. iii, 14; Heb. vii, ix; Rev. xi, 19); while in the same context the same word and thing in the Greek are in the English [in *KJ*] sometimes represented by 'covenant,' and sometimes by 'testament' (Heb. vii, 22; viii, 8-13; ix, 15)."—See also *NW* appendix, pp. 1584, 1585.

Repeatedly in the book of Hebrews (Heb 7:22; 8:6, 8, 9, 10; 9:4, 15, 16, 17, 20) the writer uses the word *di·a·the'ke* with undeniable reference to a *covenant* in the old Hebrew sense, even quoting from Jeremiah 31:31-34 and referring to "the ark of the covenant." In translating these verses of Jeremiah, the Greek *Septuagint* uses *di·a·the′ke* for the ancient Hebrew *berith′*, meaning "covenant." Also, Hebrews 9:20 quotes from Exodus 24:6-8, where a covenant is unmistakably spoken of.

Application of the Word. Covenants always involved two or more parties. They could be *unilateral* (where the party on one side was solely responsible to carry out the terms) or *bilateral* (where parties on both sides had terms to carry out). Besides the covenants in which God is a party, the Bible records the making of covenants between men, and between tribes, nations, or groups of persons. To break a covenant was a grievous sin.—Eze 17:11-20; Ro 1:31, 32.

The term "covenant" is applied to a sure ordinance, such as that concerning the showbread (Le 24:8), or to God's creation governed by his laws, as the unchangeable succession of day and night (Jer 33:20); it is also used figuratively, as in the expression "covenant with Death." (Isa 28:18) Jehovah also speaks of a covenant in connection with the wild beasts. (Ho 2:18) The marriage compact is called a covenant. (Mal 2:14) The expression "owners (masters) of the covenant" has the sense of "confederates," as at Genesis 14:13.

In effect, any promise made by Jehovah is a covenant; it is certain to be carried out; it can be relied on with confidence for its fulfillment. (Heb 6:18) A covenant is in force as long as the terms of it are operative and the obligation to perform rests on one or both parties. The results or the blessings brought about by the covenant may continue, even forever.

Methods of Ratifying a Covenant. God was often invoked as a witness. (Ge 31:50; 1Sa 20:8; Eze 17:13, 19) An oath was sworn. (Ge 31:53; 2Ki 11:4; Ps 110:4; Heb 7:21) Men at times arranged a sign or witness, such as a gift (Ge 21:30), a pillar or heap of stones (Ge 31:44-54), or the naming of a place (Ge 21:31). Jehovah used a rainbow in one instance. (Ge 9:12-16) One method was to kill and divide animals, the covenanting parties passing between the pieces; from this custom came the standard Hebrew idiom 'cut a covenant.' (Ge 15:9-11, 17, 18, ftn; Jer 34:18, ftn, 19) At times festivities accompanied the making of alliances. (Ge 26:28, 30) A communion meal might be participated in, as in conjunction with the making of the Law covenant. (Ob 7; Ex 24:5, 11) The superior party might present to the other some article of his dress or arms. (1Sa 18:3, 4) Some pagan nations followed the custom of drinking one another's blood or blood mixed with wine (in violation of God's prohibition to all persons, at Genesis 9:4, and to Israel under the Law), and the covenanters uttered the strongest curses on the party who should later violate the covenant.

The Bible uses the expression "covenant of salt" to denote the permanence and immutability of a covenant. (Nu 18:19; 2Ch 13:5; Le 2:13) Among ancient peoples it was a sign of friendship to eat salt together and denoted enduring fidelity and loyalty; the eating of salt with communion sacrifices symbolized perpetual loyalty.

Written Instruments. The Ten Commandments were written on stone by "God's finger" (Ex 31:18; 32:16); Jeremiah wrote a deed, affixed a seal, and took witnesses (Jer 32:9-15); clay tablets of ancient peoples have been found, setting forth the terms of contracts. Often these were sealed within clay envelopes.

The Edenic Promise. Jehovah God, at Genesis 3:15, stated his purpose prophetically in the garden of Eden in the presence of Adam, Eve, and the "serpent."

As to the identity of those involved in this promise and prophecy: The vision given to the apostle John, at Revelation 12:9, informs us that the "serpent" is Satan the Devil. Evidence indicates that the "seed" of the "woman," long looked for by righteous men, is to be identified with the "seed" of Abraham, Jesus Christ. (Ga 3:16; Mt 1:1) The "seed" was to be bruised in the heel by the serpent. Jesus Christ was put to death, a wound that proved not to be permanent, however, for God raised Jesus out of death. But the "seed" is, in turn, to bruise the serpent's head, defeating him permanently.

Who is the "woman" involved in the covenant? Certainly not Eve, who had become God's enemy. In order to defeat, "bring to nothing," the *spirit* creature Satan the Devil, the "seed" would have to be, not human, but spirit. (Heb 2:14) Jesus at birth was a human Son of God, but at the time of Jesus' baptism God acknowledged him as His Son, sending holy spirit down upon him. Jesus here became the *spirit-begotten* Son of God. (Mt 3:13-17; Joh 3:3-5) Later, at his resurrection, he was "made alive in the *spirit.*" (1Pe 3:18) Who, then, was the "mother," not of the human babe Jesus but of the spirit-begotten Son of God? The apostle Paul says that Abraham, Sarah, Isaac, Hagar, and Ishmael figured in a symbolic drama, in which Isaac represented those who had heavenly hopes, including Paul himself. Paul then states that their "mother" is "the Jerusalem above." Jesus Christ calls these his "brothers," indicating they have the same mother. (Heb 2:11) This provides a basis for identifying the "woman" of Genesis 3:15 with "the Jerusalem above."—Ga 4:21-29.

The terms of the promise imply a lapse of time during which the "serpent" would bring forth a "seed" and enmity would develop between the two 'seeds.' Some 6,000 years have passed since the statement of the promise. Just prior to Christ's Thousand Year Reign the "serpent" will be hurled into the abyss of inactivity, and following the end of the thousand years he will be annihilated forever.—Re 20:1-3, 7-10; Ro 16:20.

Covenant With Noah. Jehovah God made a covenant with Noah, who represented his family, with regard to His purpose to preserve human and animal life while destroying the wicked world of that day. (Ge 6:17-21; 2Pe 3:6) Noah had begun to have sons after he was 500 years old. (Ge 5:32) At the time God revealed this purpose to Noah, his sons were grown and married. Noah, on his part, was to build the ark and take in his wife, his sons, and his sons' wives, as well as animals and food; Jehovah was to preserve flesh on earth, both of man and animals. Noah's obediently keeping the terms of the covenant resulted in Jehovah's preservation of human and animal life. The covenant was completely fulfilled in 2369 B.C.E., after the Flood, when men and animals were again able to live on the ground and to reproduce their kind. —Ge 8:15-17.

Rainbow Covenant. The rainbow covenant was made between Jehovah God and all flesh (human and animal), as represented by Noah and his family, in 2369 B.C.E., in the mountains of Ararat. Jehovah stated that he would never again destroy all flesh by means of a flood. The rainbow was then given as a sign of the covenant, which endures as long as mankind lives on earth, that is, forever.—Ge 9:8-17; Ps 37:29.

Covenant With Abraham. The covenant with Abraham apparently went into effect when Abram (Abraham) crossed the Euphrates on his way to Canaan. The Law covenant was made 430 years later. (Ga 3:17) Jehovah had spoken to Abraham when he was living in Mesopotamia, in Ur of the Chaldeans, telling him to travel to the country that God would show him. (Ac 7:2, 3; Ge 11:31; 12:1-3) Exodus 12:40, 41 (*LXX*) tells us that at the end of 430 years of dwelling in Egypt and in the land of Canaan, "on this very day" Israel, who had been in slavery in Egypt, went out. The day they were delivered from Egypt was Nisan 14, 1513 B.C.E., the date of the Passover. (Ex 12:2, 6, 7) This would seem to indicate that Abraham

crossed the Euphrates River on his way to Canaan on Nisan 14, 1943 B.C.E., and evidently that is when the Abrahamic covenant took effect. God appeared to Abraham again after he had traveled into Canaan as far as Shechem and enlarged on the promise, saying, "To your *seed* I am going to give this land," thereby giving an indication of the connection of this covenant with the promise in Eden, and revealing that the "seed" would take a human course, that is, would run through a human line of descent. (Ge 12:4-7) Other enlargements by Jehovah were later expressed, as recorded at Genesis 13:14-17; 15:18; 17:2-8, 19; 22:15-18.

The covenant promises were passed on to Abraham's posterity through Isaac (Ge 26:2-4) and Jacob. (Ge 28:13-15; 35:11, 12) The apostle Paul says that Christ (as primary one) and those in union with Christ are the real "seed."—Ga 3:16, 28, 29.

God revealed the purpose and accomplishments of the Abrahamic covenant, saying that through Abraham the seed of promise would come; this seed would possess the gate of his enemies; Abraham's seed through Isaac would number many, uncountable to man at that time; Abraham's name would be made great; the seed would possess the Promised Land; all families of the earth would bless themselves by means of the seed. (See above texts from Genesis.) There was a literal fulfillment of these things, which was typical of the greater fulfillment through Christ. Paul gives additional information as to the symbolic and prophetic nature of the terms of this covenant when he says that Abraham, Sarah, Isaac, Hagar, and Ishmael enacted a symbolic drama.—Ga 4:21-31.

The Abrahamic covenant is "a covenant to time indefinite." Its terms require that it extend on until the destruction of all God's enemies and the blessing of the families of the earth have been accomplished.—Ge 17:7; 1Co 15:23-26.

In discussing the Abrahamic and the Law covenants, Paul stated the principle that "there is no mediator where only one person is concerned," and then he added that "God is only one." (Ga 3:20; see MEDIATOR.) Jehovah made the covenant with Abraham unilaterally. It was in reality a promise, and Jehovah set forth no conditions that Abraham must meet in order for the promise to be fulfilled. (Ga 3:18) Thus, no mediator was needed. On the other hand, the Law covenant was bilateral. It was made between Jehovah and the nation of Israel, with Moses as mediator. The Israelites agreed to the terms of the covenant, making a sacred promise to obey the Law. (Ex 24:3-8) This latter covenant did not invalidate the Abrahamic covenant.—Ga 3:17, 19.

Covenant of Circumcision. The covenant of circumcision was made in 1919 B.C.E., when Abraham was 99 years old. Jehovah made the covenant with Abraham and his natural seed; all males of the household, including slaves, were to be circumcised; anyone refusing was to be cut off from his people. (Ge 17:9-14) Later, God stated that the alien resident who desired to eat the passover (one who wished to become a worshiper of Jehovah with Israel) would have to circumcise the males of his household. (Ex 12:48, 49) Circumcision served as a seal of the righteousness Abraham had by faith while in the uncircumcised state, and it was a physical sign of the covenant relationship of Abraham's descendants through Jacob, with Jehovah. (Ro 4:11, 12) God recognized circumcision until the ending of the Law covenant, in 33 C.E. (Ro 2:25-28; 1Co 7:19; Ac 15) Even though physical circumcision was carried on under the Law, Jehovah repeatedly showed that he was more concerned with its symbolic significance, counseling Israel to 'circumcise the foreskin of their hearts.'—De 10:16; Le 26:41; Jer 9:26; Ac 7:51.

Law Covenant. The Law covenant between Jehovah and the nation of natural Israel was made in the third month after their leaving Egypt, in 1513 B.C.E. (Ex 19:1) It was a national covenant. One born a natural Israelite was, by birth, in the Law covenant and was thus in this special relationship with Jehovah. The Law was in the form of a code, arranged in an orderly way, its statutes grouped together. The Law, transmitted through angels by the hand of a mediator, Moses, was made operative by a sacrifice of animals (in the place of Moses, the mediator, or "covenanter") at Mount Sinai. (Ga 3:19; Heb 2:2; 9:16-20) At that time Moses sprinkled half the blood of the sacrificed animals on the altar, then he read the book of the covenant to the people, who agreed to be obedient. Afterward he sprinkled the blood upon the book and upon the people. (Ex 24:3-8) Under the Law, a priesthood was established in the house of Aaron, of the family of Kohath of the tribe of Levi. (Nu 3:1-3, 10) The high priesthood passed by descent from Aaron to his sons, Eleazar succeeding Aaron, Phinehas succeeding Eleazar, and so forth.—Nu 20:25-28; Jos 24:33; Jg 20:27, 28.

The terms of the Law covenant were that if the Israelites kept the covenant they would be a people for the name of Jehovah, a kingdom of priests and a holy nation, with His blessing (Ex 19:5, 6; De 28:1-14); if they violated the covenant, they would be cursed. (De 28:15-68) Its purposes were: to make transgressions manifest (Ga 3:19); to lead the Jews to Christ (Ga 3:24); to serve for a shadow of the good things to come (Heb 10:1; Col 2:17); to protect the Jews from false, pagan religion and preserve the true worship of Jehovah; to protect the line of the seed of promise. Added to the covenant with Abraham (Ga 3:17-19), it organized the natural seed-nation of Abraham through Isaac and Jacob.

The Law covenant extended benefits to others not of natural Israel, for they could become proselytes, getting circumcised, and could receive many of the Law's benefits.—Ex 12:48, 49.

How did the Law covenant become "obsolete"?

However, the Law covenant became in a sense "obsolete" when God announced by means of the prophet Jeremiah that there would be a new covenant. (Jer 31:31-34; Heb 8:13) In 33 C.E. the Law covenant was canceled on the basis of Christ's death on the torture stake (Col 2:14), the new covenant replacing it.—Heb 7:12; 9:15; Ac 2:1-4.

Covenant With the Tribe of Levi. Jehovah made a covenant with the tribe of Levi, that the entire tribe should be set aside to constitute the tabernacle service organization, including the priesthood. This occurred in the wilderness of Sinai, in 1512 B.C.E. (Ex 40:2, 12-16; Mal 2:4) Aaron and his sons, of the family of Kohath, were to be priests, the remaining families of Levi taking care of other duties, such as setting up the tabernacle, moving it, and other matters. (Nu 3:6-13; chap 4) Later, they served likewise at the temple. (1Ch 23) The installation services for the priesthood were carried out Nisan 1-7, 1512 B.C.E., and they began serving on Nisan 8. (Le chaps 8, 9) The Levites had no inheritance in the land, but received tithes from the other tribes, and had enclave cities in which to dwell. (Nu 18:23, 24; Jos 21:41) On account of Phinehas' zeal for exclusive devotion to Jehovah, God made a covenant of peace with him, a covenant for the priesthood to time indefinite for him and his offspring. (Nu 25:10-13) The covenant with Levi continued in operation until the ending of the Law covenant. —Heb 7:12.

Covenant With Israel at Moab. Just before Israel entered the Promised Land, in 1473 B.C.E., Jehovah made a covenant with natural Israel at Moab. (De 29:1; 1:3) Much of the Law was here restated and explained by Moses. The purpose of the covenant was to encourage faithfulness to Jehovah and to make adjustments and set forth certain laws necessary for the Israelites as they changed from a life of wandering to a settled life in the land. (De 5:1, 2, 32, 33; 6:1; compare Le 17:3-5 with De 12:15, 21.) This covenant ended with the abolition of the Law covenant, for it was an integral part of the Law.

Covenant With King David. The covenant with David was made at some time during David's reign in Jerusalem (1070-1038 B.C.E.), the parties being Jehovah and David as representative of his family. (2Sa 7:11-16) The terms of this covenant were that a son from David's line would possess the throne forever, and that this son would build a house for Jehovah's name. God's purpose in this covenant was to provide a kingly dynasty for the Jews; to give Jesus, as David's heir, the legal right to the throne of David, "Jehovah's throne" (1Ch 29:23; Lu 1:32); and to provide identification for Jesus as the Messiah. (Eze 21:25-27; Mt 1:6-16; Lu 3:23-31) This covenant included no priesthood; the Levitical priesthood served in conjunction with kings of David's line; priesthood and kingship were strictly separate under the Law. Since Jehovah acknowledges this kingship and works through it forever, the covenant has everlasting duration.—Isa 9:7; 2Pe 1:11.

Covenant to Be a Priest Like Melchizedek. This covenant is expressed at Psalm 110:4, and the writer of the Bible book of Hebrews applies it to Christ at Hebrews 7:1-3, 15-17. It is a covenant made by Jehovah with Jesus Christ alone. Jesus apparently referred to it when making a covenant for a kingdom with his followers. (Lu 22:29) By Jehovah's oath Jesus Christ, the heavenly Son of God, would be a priest according to the manner of Melchizedek. Melchizedek was king and priest of God on earth. Jesus Christ would hold both offices of King and High Priest, not on earth, but in heaven. He was installed permanently into office after his ascension to heaven. (Heb 6:20; 7:26, 28; 8:1) The covenant is forever in operation, since Jesus will act under Jehovah's direction as King and High Priest forever.—Heb 7:3.

New Covenant. Jehovah foretold the new covenant by the prophet Jeremiah in the seventh century B.C.E., stating that it would not be like the Law covenant, which Israel broke. (Jer 31:31-34) On the night before his death, Nisan 14, 33 C.E., when he established the celebration of the Lord's Evening Meal, Jesus Christ announced the new covenant, to be validated by his sacrifice. (Lu 22:20) On the 50th day from his resurrection and 10 days after he had ascended to his Father, he poured out the holy spirit, which he had received from Jehovah, on his disciples gathered in an upper room in Jerusalem.—Ac 2:1-4, 17, 33; 2Co 3:6, 8, 9; Heb 2:3, 4.

The parties to the new covenant are Jehovah, on one side, and "the Israel of God," the spirit-begotten ones in union with Christ, making up his congregation or body, on the other side. (Heb 8:10; 12:22-24; Ga 6:15, 16; 3:26-28; Ro 2:28, 29) The new covenant is made operative by the shed blood (the sacrifice of the human life) of Jesus Christ, the value of which was presented to Jehovah after Jesus' ascension to heaven. (Mt 26:28) When one is selected by God for the heavenly calling (Heb 3:1), God brings that one into His covenant over Christ's sacrifice. (Ps 50:5; Heb 9:14, 15, 26) Jesus Christ is the Mediator of the new covenant (Heb 8:6; 9:15) and is the primary Seed of Abraham. (Ga 3:16) By means of Jesus' mediatorship of the new covenant, he assists those in the covenant to become part of the *real* seed of Abraham (Heb 2:16; Ga 3:29) through forgiveness of their sins. Jehovah declares them righteous.—Ro 5:1, 2; 8:33; Heb 10:16, 17.

These spirit-begotten, anointed brothers of Christ become underpriests of the High Priest, "a royal priesthood." (1Pe 2:9; Re 5:9, 10; 20:6) These do a priestly work, a "public service" (Php 2:17), and are called "ministers of a new covenant." (2Co 3:6) These called ones must follow Christ's steps closely, faithfully, until laying down their lives in death; Jehovah will then make them a kingdom of priests, making them sharers in divine nature, and will reward them with immortality and incorruption as joint heirs in the heavens with Christ. (1Pe 2:21; Ro 6:3, 4; 1Co 15:53; 1Pe 1:4; 2Pe 1:4) The purpose of the covenant is to take out a people for Jehovah's name as a part of Abraham's "seed." (Ac 15:14) They become the "bride" of Christ, and are the body of persons whom Christ takes into a covenant for the Kingdom, to rule with Him. (Joh 3:29; 2Co 11:2; Re 21:9; Lu 22:29; Re 1:4-6; 5:9, 10; 20:6) The purpose of the new covenant requires that it continue in operation until all of the "Israel of God" are resurrected to immortality in the heavens.

Jesus' Covenant With His Followers. On the night of Nisan 14, 33 C.E., after celebrating the Lord's Evening Meal Jesus made this covenant with his faithful apostles. To the 11 faithful apostles he promised that they would sit on thrones. (Lu 22:28-30; compare 2Ti 2:12.) Later, he showed that this promise extended to all spirit-begotten 'conquerors.' (Re 3:21; see also Re 1:4-6; 5:9, 10;

20:6.) On the day of Pentecost he inaugurated this covenant toward them by the anointing with holy spirit of those disciples present in the upper room in Jerusalem. (Ac 2:1-4, 33) Those who would stick with him through trials, dying his kind of death (Php 3:10; Col 1:24), would reign with him, sharing his Kingdom rule. The covenant remains operative between Jesus Christ and these associate kings forever.—Re 22:5.

Various Other Covenants. (a) Joshua and the chieftains of Israel with the inhabitants of the city of Gibeon to let them live. Though they were cursed Canaanites, whom the Israelites were to destroy, yet a covenant was considered so binding that the Gibeonites were allowed to live, but the curse was carried out by making them gatherers of wood and drawers of water for the assembly of Israel. (Jos 9:15, 16, 23-27) (b) Joshua with Israel to serve Jehovah. (Jos 24:25, 26) (c) The older men of Gilead with Jephthah at Mizpah to make him head over the inhabitants of Gilead if Jehovah gave him victory over the Ammonites. (Jg 11: 8-11) (d) Between Jonathan and David. (1Sa 18:3; 23:18) (e) Jehoiada the priest with the chiefs of the Carian bodyguard and of the runners. (2Ki 11:4; 2Ch 23:1-3) (f) Israel with Jehovah to put away foreign wives. (Ezr 10:3) (g) Jehovah to give his servant as a covenant of (for) the people. (Isa 42:6; 49:8) (h) David with all the older men of Israel, at Hebron. (1Ch 11:3) (i) A covenant of the people, during Asa's reign, to search for Jehovah with all their heart and soul. (2Ch 15:12) (j) Josiah with Jehovah to keep Jehovah's commandments, according to the Law. (2Ch 34:31) (k) The "braggarts" who ruled Jerusalem were erroneously thinking they were safe in "a covenant with Death."—Isa 28:14, 15, 18.

COVETOUSNESS. See GREED.

COW
[Heb., pa·rah'; 'e'leph (De 7:13); 'egh·lah', young cow]. The cow filled an important role in the economy of the Israelites. Besides serving as a draft animal, the cow was valued for its production of milk, from which other common items of diet were prepared, including cheese, butter, and buttermilk. (Nu 19:2; Isa 7:21, 22) Also, the hide could be used in making a variety of leather goods.

Young cows, or heifers, were at times sacrificed. (Ge 15:9; 1Sa 6:14; 16:2) The ashes of an entire red cow, burned outside the camp, came to be an ingredient in Israel's "water for cleansing." (Nu 19:2, 6, 9) In the case of an unsolved murder, the representative older men of the town nearest the slain one were required to kill a young cow in an uncultivated torrent valley and then wash their hands over the carcass while testifying to their innocence of the crime.—De 21:1-9.

In the Scriptures numerous illustrative uses of the cow or heifer may be noted. The seven fat-fleshed and seven thin-fleshed cows of Pharaoh's dream were explained as referring to seven years of plenty to be followed by seven years of famine. (Ge 41:26, 27) Samson spoke of his betrothed as his young cow with which the 30 groomsmen had plowed in order to arrive at the solution to his riddle.—Jg 14:11, 12, 18.

The luxury-loving women despoilers dwelling in Samaria are referred to as "cows of Bashan." (Am 3:15; 4:1) Ephraim is likened to "a trained heifer loving to thresh." (Ho 10:11) This comparison takes on added meaning when considering that the animals doing the threshing were not muzzled and, therefore, could eat of the grain, thus receiving direct and immediate benefits from their labor. (De 25:4) Because of becoming fat as a result of God's blessing, Israel "kicked," rebelled against Jehovah (De 32:12-15), and is, therefore, appropriately referred to as a stubborn cow, one that is unwilling to bear the yoke. (Ho 4:16) Egypt is compared to a pretty heifer that would come to disaster at the hand of the Babylonians. (Jer 46: 20, 21, 26) The Babylonians, in their pillaging 'God's inheritance,' Judah, are likened to a frisky heifer pawing in the tender grass.—Jer 50:11.

In prophecy the peaceful conditions that result from the reign of the Messiah, Christ Jesus, are appropriately represented by amicable relations between the relatively harmless cow and the rapacious bear.—Isa 11:7; see BULL; CALF.

COZBI
(Coz'bi). Daughter of Zur, a Midianite chieftain. At the time 24,000 Israelites died for immorality in connection with Baal of Peor, Cozbi, along with the Simeonite Zimri who had brought her into his tent, was killed by having her genital parts pierced through by Phinehas. (Nu 25:1, 6-9, 15, 18) Shortly afterward Cozbi's father was also killed.—Nu 31:7.

COZEBA
(Co·ze'ba) [probably, Liar]. A site in Judah where descendants of Shelah the son of Judah resided. (1Ch 4:21, 22) Most scholars consider Cozeba to be the same as Achzib ("Chezib" in some versions) mentioned at Genesis 38:5 and Joshua 15:44, and on this basis it is tentatively identified with Tell el-Beida (Horvat Lavnin), 5 km (3 mi) WSW of Adullam. The men of Cozeba are apparently included in the expression "they were the potters."—1Ch 4:23; see ACHZIB No. 1.

CRAFTSMAN. One skilled in a manual trade or art. The Hebrew word *cha·rash'* is most frequently translated by the general term "craftsman," but when it occurs along with some particular material, the phrase is rendered more specifically, for example, "wood-and-metal worker" (De 27:15), "workers in wood and workers in stone" (2Sa 5:11), "carver of iron," "wood carver" (Isa 44:12, 13), also as "smith" (1Sa 13:19), and "manufacturers." (Isa 45:16) Further illustrating the many specialties that come under the designation "craftsmanship" is the description of Bezalel who, along with Oholiab, was a worker with metals, precious stones, and wood and was a weaver and dyer, skilled "in every sort of craftsmanship." —Ex 35:30-35; see also 2Ki 12:11, 12.

Many crafts, such as toolmaking, carpentry, brickmaking, spinning, weaving, textile finishing, and making pottery and jewelry, were at one time simple household duties performed by ordinary men or women. Settled communal living, however, brought about specialization. Even before the Flood certain men were known as specialized craftsmen. (Ge 4:21, 22) Nebuchadnezzar took the craftsmen along with the princes and military engineers from Jerusalem captive to Babylon in 617 B.C.E. (2Ki 24:14, 16; Jer 24:1; 29:2) In some towns craftsmen of a particular trade lived together in the same section, where they eventually associated together in guilds and became known by their occupation and exercised great influence in the affairs of the town. (Ne 3:8, 31, 32; 11:35; Jer 37:21; Ac 19:24-41) Details of how these specialized craftsmen carried on their work are not too well preserved, except the writing and artwork that come from Egypt and that vividly describe and illustrate the various craftsmen at work.

The prohibition against idolatry incorporated into the Law of Moses kept the Jews from much of the then-common art of making figurines and the like as objects of devotion. (Ex 20:4; De 4:15-18; 27:15) Indeed, image worship and the development of art and carving grew side by side in nations such as Assyria and Babylonia. (Ps 115:2, 4-8; Isa 40:19, 20; 44:11-20; 46:1, 6, 7; Jer 10:2-5) Demetrius and his fellow craftsmen (or, artisans; Gr., *te·khni'tai*) in Ephesus made a living by manufacturing silver shrines of Artemis.—Ac 19:24-27.

For detailed considerations of the various crafts themselves, see individual subjects such as BRICK; CARPENTER; CARVING; DYES, DYEING; EMBROIDERY; MASON; METALWORKER; POTTER; SPINNING; TANNER; and WEAVING.

CRAG. See ROCK.

CREATION. The act of creating, or causing the existence of, someone or something. It can also refer to that which has been created or brought into existence. The Hebrew *ba·ra'* and the Greek *kti'zo*, both meaning "create," are used exclusively with reference to divine creation.

Throughout the Scriptures Jehovah God is identified as the Creator. He is "the Creator of the heavens, . . . the Former of the earth and the Maker of it." (Isa 45:18) He is "the Former of the mountains and the Creator of the wind" (Am 4:13) and is "the One who made the heaven and the earth and the sea and all the things in them." (Ac 4:24; 14:15; 17:24) "God . . . created all things." (Eph 3:9) Jesus Christ recognized Jehovah as the One who created humans, making them male and female. (Mt 19:4; Mr 10:6) Hence, Jehovah is fittingly and uniquely called "the Creator."—Isa 40:28.

It is because of God's will that all things "existed and were created." (Re 4:11) Jehovah, who has existed for all time, was alone before creation had a beginning.—Ps 90:1, 2; 1Ti 1:17.

While Jehovah, who is a Spirit (Joh 4:24; 2Co 3:17), has always existed, that is not true of the matter of which the universe is made. Hence, when creating the literal heavens and earth, Jehovah did not use preexistent material. This is clear from Genesis 1:1, which says: "In the beginning God created the heavens and the earth." If matter had always existed, it would have been inappropriate to use the term "beginning" with reference to material things. However, after creating the earth, God did form "from the ground every wild beast of the field and every flying creature of the heavens." (Ge 2:19) He also formed man "out of dust from the ground," blowing into his nostrils the breath of life so that the man became a living soul.—Ge 2:7.

Appropriately Psalm 33:6 says: "By the word of Jehovah the heavens themselves were made, and by the spirit of his mouth all their army." While the earth was yet "formless and waste," with "darkness upon the surface of the watery deep," it was God's active force that was moving to and fro over the surface of the waters. (Ge 1:2) Thus, God used his active force, or "spirit" (Heb., *ru'ach*), to accomplish his creative purpose. The things he has created testify not only to his power but also to his Godship. (Jer 10:12; Ro 1:19, 20) And, as Jehovah "is a God, not of disorder, but of peace" (1Co 14:33), his creative work is marked with orderliness rather than chaos or chance. Jehovah reminded Job that He had taken specific steps in founding the earth and barricading the sea and indicated that there exist "statutes of the heavens." (Job 38:1, 4-11, 31-33) Furthermore, God's creative and other works are perfect.—De 32:4; Ec 3:14.

Jehovah's first creation was his "only-begotten Son" (Joh 3:16), "the beginning of the creation by God." (Re 3:14) This one, "the firstborn of all creation," was used by Jehovah in creating all other things, those in the heavens and those upon the earth, "the things visible and the things invisible." (Col 1:15-17) John's inspired testimony concerning this Son, the Word, is that "all things came into existence through him, and apart from him not even one thing came into existence," and the apostle identifies the Word as Jesus Christ, who had become flesh. (Joh 1:1-4, 10, 14, 17) As wisdom personified, this One is represented as saying, "Jehovah himself produced me as the beginning of his way," and he tells of his association with God the Creator as Jehovah's "master worker." (Pr 8:12, 22-31) In view of the close association of Jehovah and his only-begotten Son in creative activity and because that Son is "the image of the invisible God" (Col 1:15; 2Co 4:4), it was evidently to His only-begotten Son and master worker that Jehovah spoke in saying, "Let us make man in our image."—Ge 1:26.

After creating his only-begotten Son, Jehovah used him in bringing the heavenly angels into existence. This preceded the founding of the earth, as Jehovah revealed when questioning Job and asking him: "Where did you happen to be when I founded the earth . . . when the morning stars joyfully cried out together, and all the sons of God began shouting in applause?" (Job 38:4-7) It was after the creation of these heavenly spirit creatures that the material heavens and earth and all elements were made, or brought into existence. And, since Jehovah is the one primarily responsible for all this creative work, it is ascribed to him. —Ne 9:6; Ps 136:1, 5-9.

The Scriptures, in stating, "In the beginning God created the heavens and the earth" (Ge 1:1), leave matters indefinite as to time. This use of the term "beginning" is therefore unassailable, regardless of the age scientists may seek to attach to the earthly globe and to the various planets and other heavenly bodies. The actual time of creation of the material heavens and earth may have been billions of years ago.

Further Creative Activities Involving Earth. Genesis chapter 1 through chapter 2, verse 3, after telling about the creation of the material heavens and earth (Ge 1:1, 2), provides an outline of further creative activities on the earth. Chapter 2 of Genesis, from verse 5 onward, is a parallel account that takes up at a point in the third "day," after dry land appeared but before land plants were created. It supplies details not furnished in the broad outline found in Genesis chapter 1. The inspired Record tells of six creative periods called "days," and of a seventh period or "seventh day" in which time God desisted from earthly creative works and proceeded to rest. (Ge 2:1-3) While the Genesis account of creative activity relating to the earth does not set forth detailed botanical and zoological distinctions such as those current today, the terms employed therein adequately cover the major divisions of life and show that these were created and made so that they reproduce only according to their respective "kinds."—Ge 1:11, 12, 21, 24, 25; see KIND.

The following chart sets forth God's creative activities during the six "days" outlined in Genesis.

EARTHLY CREATIVE WORKS OF JEHOVAH		
Day No.	Creative Works	Texts
1	Light; division between day and night	Ge 1:3-5
2	Expanse, a division between waters beneath the expanse and waters above it	Ge 1:6-8
3	Dry land; vegetation	Ge 1:9-13
4	Heavenly luminaries become discernible from earth	Ge 1:14-19
5	Aquatic souls and flying creatures	Ge 1:20-23
6	Land animals; man	Ge 1:24-31

Genesis 1:1, 2 relates to a time before the six "days" outlined above. When these "days" commenced, the sun, moon, and stars were already in existence, their creation being referred to at Genesis 1:1. However, prior to these six "days" of creative activity "the earth proved to be formless and waste and there was darkness upon the surface of the watery deep." (Ge 1:2) Apparently, a swaddling band of cloud layers still enveloped the earth, preventing light from reaching its surface.

When God said on Day One, "Let light come to be," diffused light evidently penetrated the cloud layers even though the sources of that light could not yet be discerned from the earth's surface. It seems that this was a gradual process, as is indicated by translator J. W. Watts: "And gradually light came into existence." (Ge 1:3, *A Distinctive Translation of Genesis*) God brought about a division between the light and the darkness, calling the light Day and the darkness Night. This indicates that the earth was rotating on its axis as it revolved around the sun, so that its hemispheres, eastern and western, could enjoy periods of light and darkness.—Ge 1:3, 4.

On Day Two God made an expanse by causing a division to occur "between the waters and the waters." Some waters remained on the earth, but a great amount of water was raised high above the surface of the earth, and in between these two there came to be an expanse. God called the expanse Heaven, but this was with relation to the earth, as the waters suspended above the expanse are not said to have enclosed stars or other bodies of the outer heavens.—Ge 1:6-8; see EXPANSE.

On Day Three by God's miracle-working power the waters on the earth were brought together and dry land appeared, God calling it Earth. It was also on this day that, through no chance factors or evolutionary processes, God acted to superimpose the life principle upon atoms of matter, so that grass, vegetation, and fruit trees were brought into existence. Each of these three general divisions was capable of reproducing according to its "kind."—Ge 1:9-13.

The divine will concerning luminaries was accomplished on Day Four, it being stated: "God proceeded to make the two great luminaries, the greater luminary for dominating the day and the lesser luminary for dominating the night, and also the stars. Thus God put them in the expanse of the heavens to shine upon the earth, and to dominate by day and by night and to make a division between the light and the darkness." (Ge 1:16-18) In view of the description of these luminaries, the greater luminary was quite apparently the sun and the lesser luminary the moon, though the sun and moon are not specifically named in the Bible until after its account of the Flood of Noah's day. —Ge 15:12; 37:9.

Previously, on the first "day," the expression "Let light come to be" was used. The Hebrew word there used for "light" is 'ohr, meaning light in a general sense. But on the fourth "day," the Hebrew word changes to ma·'ohr', which refers to a luminary or source of light. (Ge 1:14) So, on the first "day" diffused light evidently penetrated the swaddling bands, but the sources of that light could not have been seen by an earthly observer. Now, on the fourth "day," things evidently changed.

It is also noteworthy that at Genesis 1:16 the Hebrew verb ba·ra', meaning "create," is not used. Instead, the Hebrew verb 'a·sah', meaning "make," is employed. Since the sun, moon, and stars are included in "the heavens" mentioned in Genesis 1:1, they were created long before Day Four. On the fourth day God proceeded to "make" these celestial bodies occupy a new relationship toward earth's surface and the expanse above it. When it is said, "God put them in the expanse of the heavens to shine upon the earth," this would indicate that they now became discernible from the surface of the earth, as though they were in the expanse. Also, the luminaries were to "serve as signs and for seasons and for days and years," thus later providing guidance for man in various ways.—Ge 1:14.

Day Five was marked by the creation of the first nonhuman souls on earth. Not just *one* creature purposed by God to evolve into other forms, but literally *swarms* of living souls were then brought forth by divine power. It is stated: "God proceeded to create the great sea monsters and every living soul that moves about, which the waters swarmed forth according to their kinds, and every winged flying creature according to its kind." Pleased with what He had produced, God blessed them and, in effect, told them to "become many," which was possible, for these creatures of many different family kinds were divinely endowed with the ability to reproduce "according to their kinds."—Ge 1:20-23.

On Day Six "God proceeded to make the wild beast of the earth according to its kind and the domestic animal according to its kind and every moving animal of the ground according to its kind," such work being good, as were all of God's previous creative works.—Ge 1:24, 25.

Toward the end of the sixth day of creative activity, God brought into existence an entirely new kind of creature, superior to the animals even though lower than the angels. This was man, created in God's image and after his likeness. While Genesis 1:27 briefly states concerning humankind "male and female he [God] created them," the parallel account at Genesis 2:7-9 shows that Jehovah God formed man out of the dust of the ground, blew into his nostrils the breath of life, and the man came to be a living soul, for whom a paradise home and food were provided. In this case Jehovah used the elements of the earth in creative work and then, having formed man, He created the female of humankind using one of Adam's ribs as a base. (Ge 2:18-25) With the creation of the woman, man was complete as a "kind."—Ge 5:1, 2.

God then blessed mankind, telling the first man and his wife: "Be fruitful and become many and fill the earth and subdue it, and have in subjection the fish of the sea and the flying creatures of the heavens and every living creature that is moving upon the earth." (Ge 1:28; compare Ps 8:4-8.) For humankind and other earthly creatures, God made adequate provision [*continued on page 545*]

Events in Jacob's Life

JACOB was favored by God because he demonstrated deep appreciation for sacred things. (Heb 12:16, 17) Jehovah assured Jacob that his offspring would inherit the land promised to Abraham, and he added: "By means of your seed all the families of the ground will certainly bless themselves."—Ge 28:4, 10-15.

Though he was blessed with material wealth and 12 sons, Jacob's life was not without difficulties. Yet Jacob never lost his faith in Jehovah and the reliability of his word. Even on his deathbed, he expressed faith in the Messianic promise. (Ge 49:10) Among Jacob's offspring was born Jesus Christ, through whom God will eternally bless mankind.

LOCATIONS ON MAP
With Related Scriptures

Beer-sheba	Ge 28:10
Bethel	Ge 28:11-19; 35:6-15
Bethlehem	Ge 35:16-20
Dothan	Ge 37:13, 17-36
Egypt	Ge 46:5-7, 28-30; 48:1–49:33
Haran	Ge 29:4–31:18
Mahanaim	Ge 32:1, 2
Mamre	Ge 35:27
Penuel	Ge 32:24-32
Shechem	Ge 33:18–34:31
Succoth	Ge 33:17

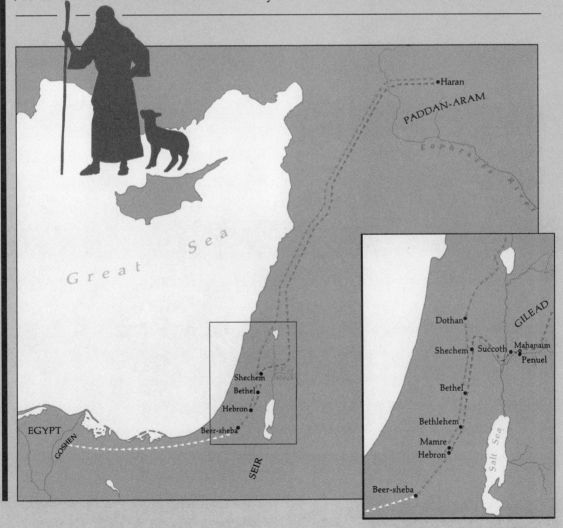

Beitin, near the ruins of ancient Bethel. At Bethel, Jacob was twice told by God that he was heir to the Abrahamic covenant (Ge 28:13-19; 35:6-13)

Ruins of ancient Shechem. Here, association by Jacob's daughter with Canaanite girls led to her being violated (Ge 34:1, 2)

Step Pyramid at Saqqara, Egypt; evidently it existed in Jacob's day. Jacob spent the last 17 years of his life in Egypt

BECAUSE of Israel's repeated contact with Egypt, the Bible contains many details regarding that land. By events in Egypt, Jehovah's own name was magnified in a wonderful way.

Egypt was a land where many gods were worshiped. Certain animals were viewed as gods; others were considered to be sacred to specific ones of the Egyptian gods. Is it any wonder that Moses said that if Israel was to offer animal sacrifices to Jehovah in Egypt, this would bring violence at the hands of the people? (Ex 8:26) We can understand, too, why, when the hearts of Israel in the wilderness turned back to Egypt, they would use a molten statue of a calf in what they referred to as "a festival to Jehovah."—Ex 32:1-5.

Another prominent feature of Egyptian worship was belief in an afterlife. This belief found expression in the practice of embalming the dead and in the erection of huge tombs to honor them.

Despite the fact that Moses was "instructed in all the wisdom of the Egyptians," the commandments regarding worship of Jehovah recorded by him were in no way tainted by Egyptian beliefs. (Ac 7:22) What he wrote was not of human origin but was divinely inspired.

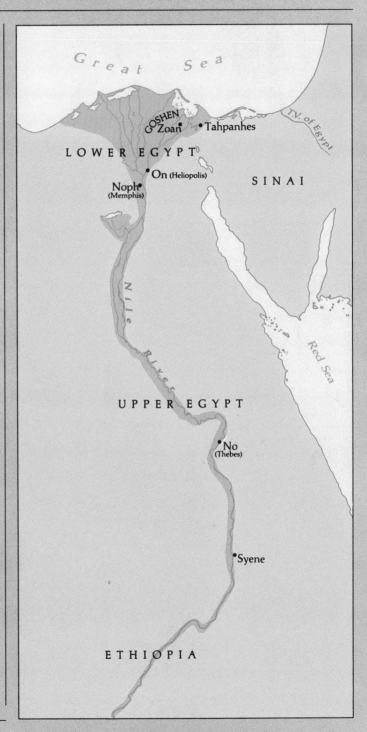

Statue representing Amenhotep III towers 21 m (70 ft) high near Thebes. Such statues were doubtless meant to overawe the people

Large stele that enumerates the building work of Tutankhamen; but King Horemheb later had the inscription changed to credit himself for the work. Such dishonesty was not uncommon in ancient Egyptian records

A triad showing Ramses II between the god Amon and the goddess Mut. Pharaoh was viewed as a god, the living Horus

Pharaoh Taharqa bowing before Horus, whose incarnation he professed to be. Animals were prominent in the religion of Egypt

Below: Impressive temple columns at Luxor. *Lower right:* An avenue of sphinxes leading to the temple of Amon-Ra at Luxor

The sky-goddess Nut surrounded by the signs of the zodiac. Astrology, which came from Babylon, became an element of Egyptian religion

A portion of the "Book of the Dead" (below), which was placed with a mummy; it contained written spells intended to be recited by the deceased for protection and to guide him in the judgment in the afterlife

Egypt depended on the narrow fertile valley along the Nile River. (This fertile area is in green on the map on page 531.) In the background can be seen the abrupt change from vegetation to desert

A pharaoh in his chariot. Such chariots were part of the military equipment of Egypt and were even sold to other nations

On the walls of the temple of Amon-Ra at Karnak, Seti I recorded his military triumphs; captives are shown being seized by their hair. As would be expected, victories were proudly recorded on Egyptian monuments

EVENTS during the period of over two centuries that the forefathers of the nation of Israel were in Egypt are an important part of the Bible record.

Jacob's son Joseph was sold into slavery and taken to Egypt. (Ge 37:28, 36) Some years later, because of divine intervention, he came to the attention of Pharaoh and, as food administrator, was granted authority second only to Pharaoh himself. (Ge 41:38-45) But in time there arose over Egypt a new king who did not respect the memory of Joseph and who imposed tyrannical slavery on the offspring of Jacob (Israel). (Ex 1:8-14) Secular Egyptian history is completely silent about all of this, including Joseph's prominent position. Is that surprising?

This lack of any mention of Joseph's prominence and of Israel's bondage comes as no surprise to those who are acquainted with the records on the monuments of ancient Egypt. It was common for later rulers or religious scribes to remove names from earlier monuments, either because they considered these to be undesirable or to enhance their own prominence. For example, King Horemheb changed inscriptions to credit himself for building work done by Tutankhamen. The Cairo Museum in Egypt and the Oriental Institute at the University of Chicago contain numerous examples of such dishonesty.

In contrast, the Bible record bears every indication of authenticity. It is very unlikely that any nation would claim that its origin is to be traced to slaves in a foreign country if that was not true. The Bible account regarding these events contains a wealth of detail of Egyptian life that could only have been conveyed by one who lived there. Further, the Passover is celebrated annually by the Jews down to this day, a celebration that the Bible reports began while their forefathers were in Egypt and as a result of what occurred there. Any claim that the true account regarding these matters has perished and that the only record in existence is false defies all reason.

Sun-dried bricks being made with straw in Egypt, as in the time of Israel's slavery there (Ex 1:14; 5:7)

JEHOVAH instructed Moses to appear before Pharaoh and, speaking in Jehovah's name, to say: "Send my people away." (Ex 5:1) Pharaoh refused. He did not want to lose a nation of slaves. More than that, Pharaoh did not know, or recognize, Jehovah as the true God. (Ex 5:2) Pharaoh worshiped the gods of Egypt and even considered himself to be a god! Thus the issue was pressed to the fore: Who is the true God? By means of ten plagues Jehovah executed judgment "on all the gods of Egypt," resulting in Israel's release and giving evidence that Jehovah is the living and true God.—Ex 12:12.

As a group, Israel departed from Rameses in Egypt on Nisan 15, 1513 B.C.E. As the throng moved to the east they were undoubtedly joined by others from Goshen. After they reached Etham, Jehovah ordered them to "turn back and encamp before Pihahiroth . . . by the sea." To the Egyptians, it appeared that the people were lost. (Ex 13:20; 14:1-3) They seemed to be trapped between the Red Sea and the mountains. With the Egyptian war chariots behind them, there appeared to be no way out! It was under these circumstances that Jehovah delivered Israel and destroyed Pharaoh and his army. (Ex 14:13-31) Thus, Jehovah demonstrated his great power and caused what he did for Israel to be talked about "in all the earth."—Ex 9:16; Jos 2:10; 9:9.

LOCATIONS ON MAP
With Related Scriptures

Etham	Ex 13:20; Nu 33:6
Goshen	Ge 47:27; Ex 8:22
Memphis (?)	Ex 12:30-32
Migdol	Ex 14:2; Nu 33:7
Pihahiroth	Ex 14:2, 9
Rameses	Ex 12:37
Red Sea	Ex 14:9, 16, 21-30
Succoth	Ex 12:37; 13:20

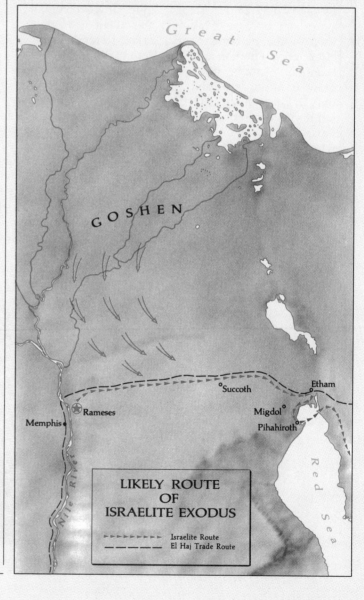

LIKELY ROUTE OF ISRAELITE EXODUS

▶ ▶ ▶ ▶ Israelite Route
— — — — El Haj Trade Route

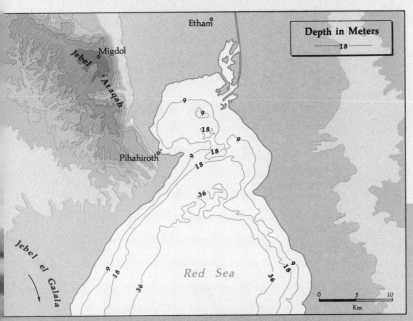

Depth in Meters
—18—

Etham

Migdol

Jebel 'Atagah

Pihahiroth

9
9
18
9
18
9
18
36

Jebel el Galala

Red Sea

9
18
36
9
18
36

0   5   10
Km

Present-day topography of the bottom of the Red Sea where Israel evidently crossed. Some dredging has been done to deepen the channel, but the seabed descends gradually from either shore. From shore to shore, the distance here is about 10 km (6 mi)

View across the Red Sea at the likely location where Jehovah split apart the waters so that Israel could go through on dry land

The Tabernacle

AT Jehovah's direction, the tabernacle was first set up in 1512 B.C.E. in the wilderness at Mount Sinai. It was the center for true worship for Israel; it was also at the center of the Israelite camp. The apostle Paul explains that the tabernacle was a prophetic illustration of "the greater and more perfect tent," God's great place of worship.—Heb 9:9, 11.

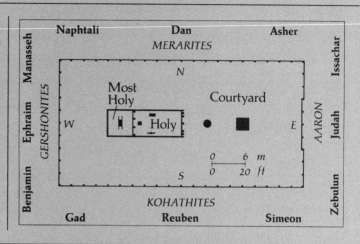

The high priest foreshadowed Jesus Christ (Heb 4:14; 9:11)

The high priest sprinkling blood of animal sacrifices in front of the ark of the covenant. This foreshadowed Jesus' presenting the value of his perfect human sacrifice in heaven, before the presence of God (Heb 9:13, 14, 24)

Animal sacrifices commanded by God pointed forward to the sacrificial death of Jesus Christ as a ransom for mankind (Mt 20:28; Heb 10:5-10)

AFTER their deliverance from Egypt, Israel wandered for 40 years in the Wilderness of Sinai, much of the time far away from well-traveled trade routes. It was a "great and fear-inspiring wilderness, with poisonous serpents and scorpions and with thirsty ground that has no water." (De 8:15) Why were they made to undergo this ordeal?

At Mount Sinai (the likely location of which is shown below), Jehovah assembled the Israelites after their departure from Egypt, gave them his laws through Moses, and organized them into a nation. After that they could have entered the Promised Land within a short time, but they did not. Why? Despite all that Jehovah had done for them, they failed to exercise faith and they rebelled against Moses, whom God had appointed to lead them. Choosing to believe a bad report about Canaan, the Israelites longed to be taken back to Egypt! (Nu 14:1-4) This brought Jehovah's swift judgment: Forty years would pass before the nation would enter the Promised Land. By then, the faithless members of that generation would have died off.

The wilderness experience of Israel is a powerful warning to Christians today to avoid the snare of lack of faith.—Heb 3:7-12.

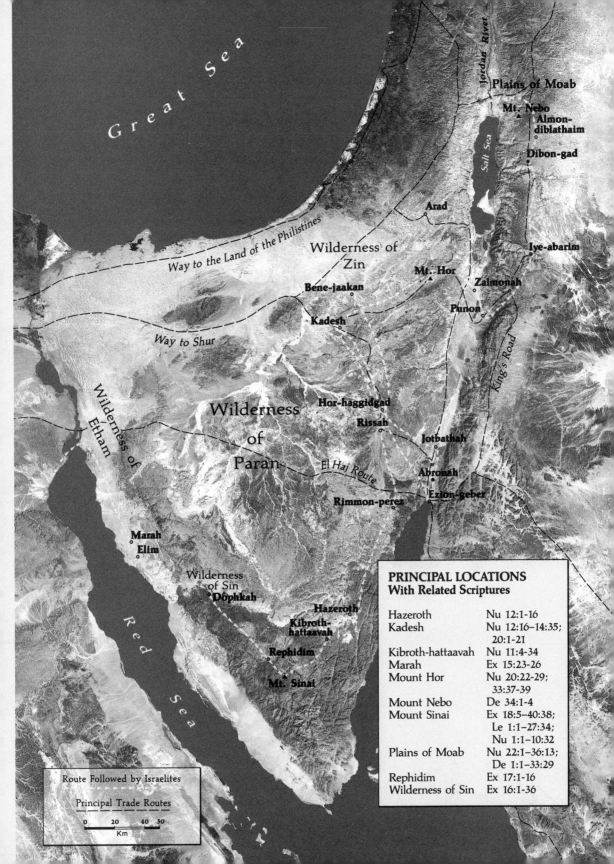

Great Sea

Jordan River

Plains of Moab

Mt. Nebo

Almon-diblathaim

Salt Sea

Dibon-gad

Arad

Way to the Land of the Philistines

Wilderness of Zin

Iye-abarim

Mt. Hor

Zalmonah

Bene-jaakan

Punon

Kadesh

Way to Shur

King's Road

Hor-haggidgad

Wilderness

Rissah

of

Jotbathah

Paran

El Haj Route

Abronah

Ezion-geber

Rimmon-perez

Wilderness of Etham

Marah

Elim

Wilderness of Sin

Dophkah

Hazeroth

Red Sea

Kibroth-hattaavah

Rephidim

Mt. Sinai

PRINCIPAL LOCATIONS
With Related Scriptures

Hazeroth	Nu 12:1-16
Kadesh	Nu 12:16–14:35; 20:1-21
Kibroth-hattaavah	Nu 11:4-34
Marah	Ex 15:23-26
Mount Hor	Nu 20:22-29; 33:37-39
Mount Nebo	De 34:1-4
Mount Sinai	Ex 18:5–40:38; Le 1:1–27:34; Nu 1:1–10:32
Plains of Moab	Nu 22:1–36:13; De 1:1–33:29
Rephidim	Ex 17:1-16
Wilderness of Sin	Ex 16:1-36

Route Followed by Israelites

Principal Trade Routes

0 20 40 50
Km

Oases were few
and far between
in this land that
was described
as having
"no water"

It was a "great
and fear-inspiring
wilderness" through
which Israel wan-
dered for 40 years

The head of the Gulf of
'Aqaba. The Israelites camped
here after being denied permission
to pass through Edom

Plants of the Bible

OLIVE, almond, caper berry, date palm—these are just a few of the nearly one hundred plants and trees mentioned in the Scriptures. Our knowing something about the plants of the Bible provides helpful background, shedding light on the meaning of certain Biblical statements.

Consider as an example the olive tree—one of the most valuable plants in Bible times (see picture at right). This beautiful tree, often twisted, gnarled, and knotty, is quite hardy, frequently living for centuries. It receives early mention in the Scriptures. Following the Flood, a dove returned to Noah in the ark "and, look! there was an olive leaf freshly plucked in its bill." This indicated to Noah that the floodwaters had receded. —Ge 8:11.

The Bible psalmist alluded to some characteristics of the olive tree when he promised those fearing Jehovah: "Your sons will be like slips of olive trees all around your table." (Ps 128:1-3) Cuttings, or slips, cut from a grown olive tree are often used for starting new trees. In addition, aged olive trees may send up shoots from their roots, thereby perpetuating themselves. Like such shoots, sons would surround a father, contributing their part to the happiness of the family.

The evergreen olive tree was especially appreciated for its oil. Olive oil was a basic food in the Israelite diet and was widely used as a cosmetic and as a fuel, and it was an important trade commodity. It was applied to bruises and wounds to soften and soothe them. (Lu 10:33, 34) Applied to the head, olive oil is likewise soothing and refreshing. Thus, older men of the Christian congregation are admonished to pray over a spiritually sick person, figuratively "greasing him with oil in the name of Jehovah"—applying God's Word to soothe, correct, and comfort him. —Jas 5:13-15.

Mallow

Black Cumin

Caper Blossom

The mandrake, of the potato family,
bears a yellowish fruit about the size of a plum

The Shulammite likened her
shepherd lover's locks to date clusters

The almond tree is one of the earliest
fruit-bearing trees to bloom in Israel.
Its nutty fruit is a delicacy

The papyrus, a large aquatic
plant from which paper was made

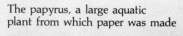

Flax plant, which is
used in making linen

One of the many balsam
plants that produces an aromatic oil

[*continued from page 528*] by giving them "all green vegetation for food." Reporting on the results of such creative work, the inspired Record states: "After that God saw everything he had made and, look! it was very good." (Ge 1:29-31) The sixth day having come to its successful conclusion and God having completed this creative work, "he proceeded to rest on the seventh day from all his work that he had made."—Ge 2:1-3.

Concluding the review of accomplishments on each of the six days of creative activity is the statement, "And there came to be evening and there came to be morning," a first, second, third day, and so forth. (Ge 1:5, 8, 13, 19, 23, 31) Since the length of each creative day exceeded 24 hours (as will be discussed later), this expression does not apply to literal night and day but is figurative. During the evening period things would be indistinct; but in the morning they would become clearly discernible. During the "evening," or beginning, of each creative period, or "day," God's purpose for that day, though fully known to him, would be indistinct to any angelic observers. However, when the "morning" arrived there would be full light as to what God had purposed for that day, it having been accomplished by that time.—Compare Pr 4:18.

Length of Creative Days. The Bible does not specify the length of each of the creative periods. Yet all six of them have ended, it being said with respect to the sixth day (as in the case of each of the preceding five days): "And there came to be evening and there came to be morning, a sixth day." (Ge 1:31) However, this statement is not made regarding the seventh day, on which God proceeded to rest, indicating that it continued. (Ge 2:1-3) Also, more than 4,000 years after the seventh day, or God's rest day, commenced, Paul indicated that it was still in progress. At Hebrews 4:1-11 he referred to the earlier words of David (Ps 95:7, 8, 11) and to Genesis 2:2 and urged: "Let us therefore do our utmost to enter into that rest." By the apostle's time, the seventh day had been continuing for thousands of years and had not yet ended. The Thousand Year Reign of Jesus Christ, who is Scripturally identified as "Lord of the sabbath" (Mt 12:8), is evidently part of the great sabbath, God's rest day. (Re 20:1-6) This would indicate the passing of thousands of years from the commencement of God's rest day to its end. The week of days set forth at Genesis 1:3 to 2:3, the last of which is a sabbath, seems to parallel the week into which the Israelites divided their time, observing a sabbath on the seventh day thereof, in keeping with the divine will. (Ex 20:

8-11) And, since the seventh day has been continuing for thousands of years, it may reasonably be concluded that each of the six creative periods, or days, was at least thousands of years in length.

That a day can be longer than 24 hours is indicated by Genesis 2:4, which speaks of *all* the creative periods as *one* "day." Also indicative of this is Peter's inspired observation that "one day is with Jehovah as a thousand years and a thousand years as one day." (2Pe 3:8) Ascribing not just 24 hours but a longer period of time, thousands of years, to each of the creative days better harmonizes with the evidence found in the earth itself.

Created Things Preceded Man's Inventions. Thousands of years before many of man's inventions appeared on the scene, Jehovah had provided his creations with their own versions of them. For example, the flight of birds preceded by millenniums the development of airplanes. The chambered nautilus and the cuttlefish use flotation tanks to descend and ascend in the ocean as submarines do. Octopus and squid employ jet propulsion. Bats and dolphins are experts with sonar. Several reptiles and sea birds have their own built-in "desalination plants" that enable them to drink seawater.

By ingeniously designed nests and their use of water, termites air-condition their homes. Microscopic plants, insects, fish, and trees use their own form of "antifreeze." Small fractions of temperature change are sensed by the built-in thermometers of some snakes, mosquitoes, mallee birds, and brush turkeys. Hornets, wasps, and yellow jackets make paper.

Thomas Edison is credited with inventing the electric light bulb, but its loss of energy through heat is a drawback. Jehovah's creations —sponges, fungi, bacteria, glowworms, insects, fish—produce cold light and in many colors.

Many migrating birds not only have compasses in their heads but they also have biological clocks. Some microscopic bacteria have rotary motors that they can run forward or in reverse.

It is not without good reason that Psalm 104:24 says: "How many your works are, O Jehovah! All of them in wisdom you have made. The earth is full of your productions."

Some persons seek to associate the Biblical account of creation with mythological pagan accounts, such as the well-known Babylonian Creation Epic. Actually, there were various creation stories in ancient Babylon, but the one that has become well known is a myth having to do with

Marduk, Babylon's national god. Briefly, the story tells of the existence of the goddess Tiamat and the god Apsu, who became the parents of other deities. The activities of these gods became so distressing to Apsu that he determined to destroy them. However, Apsu was killed by one of these gods, Ea, and when Tiamat sought to avenge Apsu, she was killed by Ea's son Marduk, who then split her body, using half of it to form the sky and using the other half in connection with the earth's establishment. Marduk's subsequent acts included creating mankind (with Ea's aid), using the blood of another god, Kingu, the director of Tiamat's hosts.

Did the Bible borrow from Babylonian creation stories?

In his book, P. J. Wiseman points out that, when the Babylonian creation tablets were first discovered, some scholars expected further discovery and research to show that there was a correspondency between them and the Genesis account of creation. Some thought that it would become apparent that the Genesis account was borrowed from the Babylonian. However, further discovery and research have merely made apparent the great gulf between the two accounts. They do not parallel each other. Wiseman quotes *The Babylonian Legends of the Creation and the Fight Between Bel and the Dragon,* issued by the Trustees of the British Museum, who hold that "the fundamental conceptions of the Babylonian and Hebrew accounts are essentially different." He himself observes: "It is more than a pity that many theologians, instead of keeping abreast of modern archaeological research, continue to repeat the now disproved theory of Hebrew 'borrowings' from Babylonian sources."—*Creation Revealed in Six Days,* London, 1949, p. 58.

While some have pointed to what seemed to them to have been similarities between the Babylonian epic and the Genesis account of creation, it is readily apparent from the preceding consideration of the Biblical creation narrative and the foregoing epitome of the Babylonian myth that they are not really similar. Therefore, a detailed analysis of them side by side is unnecessary. However, in considering seeming similarities and differences (such as the order of events) in these accounts, Professor George A. Barton observed: "A more important difference lies in the religious conceptions of the two. The Babylonian poem is mythological and polytheistic. Its conception of

deity is by no means exalted. Its gods love and hate, they scheme and plot, fight and destroy. Marduk, the champion, conquers only after a fierce struggle, which taxes his powers to the utmost. Genesis, on the other hand, reflects the most exalted monotheism. God is so thoroughly the master of all the elements of the universe, that they obey his slightest word. He controls all without effort. He speaks and it is done. Granting, as most scholars do, that there is a connection between the two narratives, there is no better measure of the inspiration of the Biblical account than to put it side by side with the Babylonian. As we read the chapter in Genesis today, it still reveals to us the majesty and power of the one God, and creates in the modern man, as it did in the ancient Hebrew, a worshipful attitude toward the Creator."—*Archaeology and the Bible,* 1949, pp. 297, 298.

Regarding ancient creation myths in general, it has been stated: "No myth has yet been found which explicitly refers to the creation of the universe, and those concerned with the organization of the universe and its cultural processes, the creation of man and the establishment of civilization are marked by polytheism and the struggles of deities for supremacy in marked contrast to the Heb. monotheism of Gn. 1-2."—*New Bible Dictionary,* edited by J. Douglas, 1985, p. 247.

"A New Creation." After the sixth creative period, or "day," Jehovah ceased from earthly creative activity. (Ge 2:2) But he has accomplished grand things in a spiritual way. For example, the apostle Paul wrote: "If anyone is in union with Christ, he is a new creation." (2Co 5:17) To be "in" or "in union with" Christ here means to enjoy a oneness with him as a member of his body, his bride. (Joh 17:21; 1Co 12:27) For this relationship to come into existence, Jehovah God draws the individual to his Son and begets such a one with holy spirit. As a spirit-begotten son of God, he is "a new creation," with the prospect of sharing with Jesus Christ in the heavenly Kingdom.—Joh 3:3-8; 6:4.

Re-Creation. To his apostles Jesus also spoke of a "re-creation" and associated it with the time "when the Son of man sits down upon his glorious throne." (Mt 19:28; Lu 22:28-30) The Greek word translated "re-creation" is *pa·lin·ge·ne·si'a,* which is composed of elements that mean "again; anew; once more" and "birth; origin." Philo used the term with reference to the reconstitution of the world after the Flood. Josephus used it regarding the reestablishment of Israel after the exile. The

Theological Dictionary of the New Testament, edited by G. Kittel, says that the use of *pa·lin·ge·ne·si'a* at Matthew 19:28 "is in full agreement with that of Philo and Josephus." (Translated by G. Bromiley, 1964, Vol. I, p. 688) So the reference is not to a new creation but to a regeneration, or a renewal, by means of which Jehovah's purpose for the earth is fully accomplished.—See TRIBE ("Judging the Twelve Tribes of Israel").

Great blessings under Kingdom rule are assured to obedient mankind, "the creation" that will be "set free from enslavement to corruption and have the glorious freedom of the children of God." (Ro 8:19-21; see SON[S] OF GOD [Glorious Freedom of the Children of God].) In the system of things promised and created by God "righteousness is to dwell." (2Pe 3:13) The certainty of its establishment is emphasized by John's apocalyptic vision and his statement: "I *saw* a new heaven and a new earth."—Re 21:1-5.

CREEPING THING.

The verbal root of the Hebrew term *re'mes* means "creep" or "move about." (Ge 1:21, 28, ftn) Koehler and Baumgartner's Hebrew and Aramaic lexicon suggests that the term indicates a rather aimless movement. (*Lexicon in Veteris Testamenti Libros,* Leiden, 1958, p. 895; compare Hab 1:14.) The noun *re'-mes* appears to embrace a broad variety of living creatures and, in its usage in the different texts, generally distinguishes such "moving animals" from the wild and domestic beasts, the birds, and the fish. (Ge 1:24, 25; 6:7, 20; 7:14, 23; 8:17, 19; 9:3; Eze 8:10; 38:20) This would allow for its including reptiles and other forms of animal life not within those other more prominent categories. It can apply not only to land creatures but also to aquatic creatures.—Ps 104:25.

Among wise King Solomon's 3,000 proverbs were some about "the beasts and about the flying creatures and about the moving things and about the fishes." (1Ki 4:33; compare Pr 30:19, 24-28.) Hosea 2:18 describes a covenant made with the wild beast, flying creature, and the creeping thing of the ground; and Psalm 148:10 includes them among the creatures serving to their Creator's praise.

The Greek *her·pe·ton'* corresponds closely to the Hebrew *re'mes,* being used frequently with reference to reptiles. It is used with regard to the vision Peter had at Joppa (Ac 10:12; 11:6), by Paul in discussing man's idolatry (Ro 1:23), and by James as to creatures being tamable by man. —Jas 3:7.

CRESCENS

(Cres'cens) [from Lat., meaning "Growing; Increasing"]. One mentioned by Paul in his second letter to Timothy as having gone to Galatia.—2Ti 4:10.

CRETE, CRETANS.

The fifth-largest island of the Mediterranean, and its inhabitants. The island measures about 250 km (155 mi) long and varies in breadth from 13 to 56 km (8 to 35 mi). Crete lies at the southern end of the Aegean Sea about 100 km (62 mi) SE of Greece. Mountains, some covered with snow during part of the year, run the full length of the narrow island. Near the center of Crete, Mount Ida rises 2,456 m (8,058 ft) above sea level. The N coast has some good harbors, but the southern coastline is more regular and along much of it the mountains drop off steeply to the sea. So, the S coast provides few favorable sites for harbors, as indicated in the account of Paul's voyage to Rome, considered later.

Crete is generally accepted to be the "Caphtor" referred to in the Hebrew Scriptures, and hence the place from which the Philistines migrated to Canaan. (Jer 47:4; Am 9:7) Some

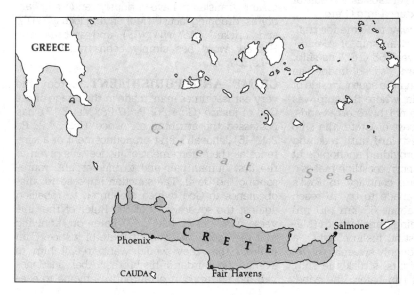

GREECE

Great Sea

Phoenix · C R E T E · Salmone

CAUDA · Fair Havens

scholars also connect the "Cherethites" with the Cretans; the Greek *Septuagint* reads "Cretans" instead of "Cherethites" at both Ezekiel 25:15-17 and Zephaniah 2:5-7. (See CHERETHITES.) If the identification of Caphtor with Crete is accepted, as seems reasonable, then the early inhabitants of the island were descendants of Mizraim, whose name is Biblically equivalent to Egypt.—Ge 10: 13, 14.

The civilization the Cretans developed was very distinctive from those of Mesopotamia and Egypt but equally resplendent. The Cretan religion placed emphasis on the female element, with a mother goddess receiving greatest prominence. As with other fertility religions, the serpent is regularly present in the representations of the goddess, either held in her hands or coiled around her body. A minor male deity is usually associated with her, perhaps in the mother-son relationship frequently found in this type of cult. At Knossos a marble cross was found, the cross likewise being an ancient sex symbol. The ancient civilization disappeared from view toward the last centuries of the second millennium. During the first millennium B.C.E. Crete came finally under Greek domination. By the second century B.C.E. the island had become a center and hideout for pirates who preyed on Mediterranean shipping. Then, in 67 B.C.E. Pompey subdued Crete, and it was made a Roman province together with Cyrene in North Africa.

Paul's Activity There.   Cretan Jews or proselytes were among those in Jerusalem on Pentecost of 33 C.E. (Ac 2:5, 11) Perhaps as a result of this, Christianity was introduced into Crete.

The apostle Paul, on his way to Rome for trial, passed by Crete aboard a grain ship of Alexandria, about the fall of the year 58 C.E. The ship, with 276 persons on board, "sailed under the shelter of Crete," that is along the southern side of the island, the leeward side, where the ship was protected from the adverse northwesterly winds. From Salmone on the E coast of Crete, the ship worked its way slowly westward until reaching Fair Havens, a small bay providing anchorage at a point just before the southern coastline makes a sharp turn to the N. Here, contrary to Paul's counsel, the decision was made to try to reach Phoenix, another harbor about 65 km (40 mi) farther up the coast. Rounding Cape Littinos (Matala), the ship "began coasting inshore" when a tempestuous ENE wind, suddenly sweeping down from the mountainous heights, struck the ship, forcing it to heave to and run before the wind.

From here the boat was driven past the island of Cauda, about 65 km (40 mi) from Fair Havens. —Ac 27:6-16, 37, 38.

The evidence is that, following his two years of imprisonment in Rome, Paul visited Crete and engaged in Christian activity there during the final period of his ministry. On departing, he assigned Titus to remain in Crete to correct certain conditions among the congregations, making appointments of older men "in city after city." (Tit 1:5) Later, when discussing congregational problems in a letter to Titus, Paul quoted the words of a Cretan prophet to the effect that "Cretans are always liars, injurious wild beasts, unemployed gluttons." (Tit 1:10-12) These words are thought to proceed from Epimenides, a Cretan poet of the sixth century B.C.E. This estimate of the ancient Cretans was shared by the Greeks, among whom the name Cretan became synonymous with liar.

CRICKET   [Heb., *char·gol'*]. A kind of leaping insect related to the grasshopper, though differing from the latter in that it has prominent feelers at the tip of its abdomen. Both the house cricket and the field cricket are to be found in Bible lands. Sole mention is made of this insect at Leviticus 11:22, where it is listed as being clean for food.

A number of Bible translations (*KJ; Yg*) render the Hebrew term *char·gol'* as "beetle," the most typical species of which creep rather than jump. But it is generally agreed that the Hebrew word refers to a kind of leaping insect, as indicated by its being listed along with the locust. There is uncertainty, though, as to the exact leaping insect meant. Translators have variously rendered *char·gol'* as "dropping locust" (*Mo*), "flying locust" (*AT*), and "cricket" (*AS; NW; RS*); and at times the Hebrew word has simply been transliterated. —*Le; Da; JB*.

CRIME AND PUNISHMENT.   From the very earliest times man, made in the image of the God of justice (Ge 1:26; Ps 37:28; Mal 2:17), has possessed the attribute of justice. (Isa 58:2; Ro 2:13-15) Jehovah's first pronouncement of a sentence as the enforcement of justice was given to the first human pair and to the serpent, representing the Devil. The sanction imposed for disobedience to God, which amounted to rebellion against the sovereignty of the Ruler of the universe, was death. (Ge 2:17) Later on, knowing that men possessed the attribute of justice, Cain realized that they would want to kill him to avenge the murder of his brother Abel. But Jehovah did not appoint or authorize anyone to execute Cain, reserving the administration of retribution to himself. This he carried out by cutting off Cain's line at the Flood. (Ge 4:14, 15) About 700 years before the Flood, Enoch declared God's coming execution against those who had committed ungodly deeds.—Ge 5:21-24; Jude 14, 15.

After the Flood. After the Flood, God issued further laws, among them being the first authorization to man to execute the penalty for murder. (Ge 9:3-6) Later Jehovah stated concerning Abraham: "For I have become acquainted with him in order that he may command his sons and his household after him so that they shall keep Jehovah's way to do righteousness and judgment." (Ge 18:19) This shows that patriarchal society was under the laws of God, with which they were familiar.

Jehovah revealed his view of adultery and the punishment for it when telling Abimelech that he was as good as dead for taking Sarah with intentions of making her his wife (although Abimelech did not know that she belonged to Abraham). (Ge 20:2-7) Judah decreed the death penalty for Tamar for harlotry.—Ge 38:24.

God's Law for Israel. When Israel was organized as a nation, God became their King, Legislator, and Judge. (Isa 33:22) He gave them the "Ten Words," or "Ten Commandments," as they are often called, setting forth the principles upon which the body of about 600 other laws was based. He began the "Ten Words" with the statement: "I am Jehovah your God, who have brought you out of the land of Egypt." (Ex 20:2) This serves as the primary reason for obedience to the entire Law. Disobedience was not only a violation of the law of the Head of government but also an offense against the Head of religion, their God, and blasphemy of God was lèse-majesté, treason.

Under the Law, the same principles applied as had governed patriarchal society. The Law, however, was more detailed and covered the whole scope of man's activities. The entire Law, which is set forth in the Pentateuch, was of such a *high standard of morality* that no man could attempt to follow the complete Law without finding that he was convicted by it as being a sinner, imperfect. "The commandment is holy and righteous and good," and "the Law is spiritual," says the apostle Paul. "It was added to make transgressions manifest." (Ro 7:12, 14; Ga 3:19) It was the whole law of God for Israel, laying down the principles and official decisions of Jehovah, not just a mere gathering of a set of cases that might arise or that had already arisen.

The sanctions under the Law, therefore, would help to show sin to be "far more sinful." (Ro 7:13) The law of talion, requiring like for like, set out a standard of exact justice. The Law served for the peace and tranquillity of the nation, preserved the nation when Israel obeyed it, and protected the individual against the wrongdoer, compensating him when his property was stolen or destroyed.

The Ten Commandments, as stated at Exodus 20 and Deuteronomy 5, do not expressly state the sanction for every violation. However, these penalties are definitely stated in other places. For a violation of the first seven commandments, the penalty was death. The punishment for stealing was restitution and compensation to the one whose property had been stolen; for false witness, retribution. The last commandment, against covetousness or wrong desire, carried with it no sanction enforceable by the judges. It transcended man-made laws in that it made every man his own spiritual policeman and got at the root, or source, of the violation of all the commandments. If wrong desire was indulged, it would eventually manifest itself in a violation of one of the other nine commandments.

Major crimes under the Law. *Capital crimes.* Under the Law the death penalty was prescribed for (1) blasphemy (Le 24:14, 16, 23); (2) worship of any god other than Jehovah, idolatry in any form (Le 20:2; De 13:6, 10, 13-15; 17:2-7; Nu 25:1-9); (3) witchcraft, spiritism (Ex 22:18; Le 20:27); (4) false prophecy (De 13:5; 18:20); (5) Sabbath breaking (Nu 15:32-36; Ex 31:14; 35:2); (6) murder (Nu 35:30, 31); (7) adultery (Le 20:10; De 22:22); (8) woman marrying with false claim of being a virgin (De 22:21); (9) intercourse with engaged girl (De 22:23-27); (10) incest (Le 18:6-17, 29; 20:11, 12, 14); (11) sodomy (Le 18:22; 20:13); (12) bestiality (Le 18:23; 20:15, 16); (13) kidnapping (Ex 21:16; De 24:7); (14) striking or reviling a parent (Ex 21:15, 17); (15) bearing false witness, in a case where the penalty for the one testified against would be death (De 19:16-21); (16) coming near to the tabernacle if not authorized (Nu 17:13; 18:7).

In many instances the penalty named is 'cutting off,' usually executed by stoning. Besides this being prescribed for willful sin and abusive, disrespectful speech against Jehovah (Nu 15:30, 31), many other things are named that bear this penalty. Some of them are: failure to be circumcised (Ge 17:14; Ex 4:24); willful neglect of the Passover (Nu 9:13); neglect of Atonement Day (Le

23:29, 30); making or using the holy anointing oil for ordinary purposes (Ex 30:31-33, 38); eating blood (Le 17:10, 14); eating a sacrifice in an unclean condition (Le 7:20, 21; 22:3, 4, 9); eating leavened bread during the Festival of Unfermented Cakes (Ex 12:15, 19); offering a sacrifice in any place other than at the tabernacle (Le 17:8, 9); eating of communion offering on the third day from the day of sacrifice (Le 19:7, 8); neglect of purification (Nu 19:13-20); touching holy things illegally (Nu 4:15, 18, 20); intercourse with menstruating woman (Le 20:18); eating fat of sacrifices.—Le 7:25; see CUTTING OFF.

Punishments imposed by the Law. Punishments under the Law given by Jehovah through Moses served to keep the land clean from defilement in God's sight; those who practiced detestable things were cleaned out from among the people. Also, the punishments deterred crime and maintained respect for the sanctity of life, for the law of the land, for the Lawgiver, God, and for one's fellowman. And, when obeyed, the Law preserved the nation from economic failure and from moral decay with its subsequent loathsome diseases and physical deterioration.

There were no barbarous punishments prescribed by the Law. No man could be punished for another's wrongs. The principles were clearly set forth. The judges were granted latitude, considering each case on its own merits, examining the circumstances, as well as the motives and the attitudes of those accused. Justice had to be strictly rendered. (Heb 2:2) A willful murderer could not escape the death penalty by any payment of money. (Nu 35:31) If a man was an accidental manslayer, he could flee to one of the cities of refuge provided. Confined within the boundary of the city, he was forced to realize that life is sacred and that even accidental killing could not be taken lightly, but required some compensation. Yet, working productively in the city of refuge, he was not a financial burden on the community.—Nu 35:26-28.

The sanctions for offenses were designed to give relief and compensation to the victim of a thief or of one who damaged his property. If the thief could not pay the stipulated amount, he could be sold as a slave, either to the victim or to someone else, thus reimbursing the victim and making the criminal work for his upkeep, so that the state would not have him on its hands, as is the case where imprisonment is practiced. These laws were just and served toward the rehabilitation of the criminal.—Ex 22:1-6.

Under the Law, the death sentence was carried out by stoning. (Le 20:2, 27) The sword was occasionally used, especially where a large number were to be executed. (Ex 32:27; 1Ki 2:25, 31, 32, 34) If a city turned apostate, all in the city were to be devoted to destruction by the sword. (De 13:15) At Exodus 19:13, death by the spear, lance, or possibly the arrow, is alluded to. (See Nu 25:7, 8.) Beheading is mentioned, although it may be that execution was carried out by another means and the corpse beheaded. (2Sa 20:21, 22; 2Ki 10:6-8) For the more detestable crimes the Law prescribed burning and hanging. (Le 20:14; 21:9; Jos 7:25; Nu 25:4, 5; De 21:22, 23) These sentences were carried out only after a person had been first put to death, as the cited scriptures plainly state.

Captives of war were usually executed by the sword if they were persons devoted to destruction by God's command. (1Sa 15:2, 3, 33) Others who surrendered were put to forced labor. (De 20:10, 11) Older translations of the passage at 2 Samuel 12:31 make it appear that David tortured the inhabitants of Rabbah of Ammon, but modern translations indicate that he merely put them to forced labor.—See NW; AT; Mo.

Precipitation, that is, throwing one off a cliff or high place, was not enjoined by law, but King Amaziah of Judah inflicted this punishment on 10,000 men of Seir. (2Ch 25:12) The people of Nazareth attempted to do this to Jesus.—Lu 4:29.

Strict justice was enforced by the law of talion or retaliation, like for like, where injuries were deliberately inflicted. (De 19:21) There is at least one recorded instance of the execution of this penalty. (Jg 1:6, 7) But the judges had to determine on the basis of the evidence whether the crime was deliberate or was due to negligence or accident, and so forth. An exception to the law of retaliation was the law dealing with a situation in which a woman tried to help her husband in a fight by grabbing hold of the privates of the other man. In this case, instead of her reproductive organs being destroyed, her hand was to be amputated. (De 25:11, 12) This law demonstrates God's regard for the reproductive organs. Also, since the woman was owned by a husband, this law mercifully took into consideration the right of the husband to have children by his wife.

The Mishnah mentions four methods of inflicting the death penalty: stoning, burning, beheading, and strangling. But these latter three methods were never authorized nor commanded under the Law. The methods prescribed in the Mishnah are part of the traditions that were added, overstepping the commandment of God. (Mt 15:3, 9) An example of the barbarous practices to which it led the Jews is their method of executing the penalty of burning. "The ordinance of them that are to be burnt [is this]: they set him in dung up to his knees and put a towel of coarse stuff within one of soft stuff and wrapt it around his neck; one [witness] pulled one end towards him and the other pulled one end towards him until he opened his mouth; a wick [according to the Gemara (52a) it was a strip of lead] was kindled and thrown into his mouth, and it went down to his stomach and burnt his entrails."—*Sanhedrin* 7:2; translated by H. Danby.

Since man has been governed by law from the beginning, either by divine law or by the law of conscience divinely implanted, it has been true that the closer men held to true worship, the more reasonable and humane were the punishments administered by their laws, and the farther away they strayed, the more corrupt their sense of justice became. This becomes evident when the laws of ancient nations are compared with those of Israel.

Egyptian. Little is known about the punishments imposed by the Egyptians. They administered beatings (Ex 5:14, 16), drowning (Ex 1:22), beheading and afterward hanging on a stake (Ge 40:19, 22), and execution by the sword, as well as imprisonment.—Ge 39:20.

Assyrian. Punishments under the Assyrian Empire were very severe. They included death, mutilation (as by cutting off ears, nose, lips, or by castration), impalement upon a stake, deprivation of burial, strokes of the rod, payment of a certain weight of lead, and royal corvée (forced labor). Under Assyrian law a murderer was handed over to the next of kin of the one murdered, and according to his choice, he could put the murderer to death or take his property. This could lead to blood feuds, for there was little control of the matter, and no cities of refuge were provided, as in Israel. The punishment for adultery was left to the husband. He could put his wife to death, mutilate her, punish her as he saw fit, or let her go free. As he did to the wife, he was required to do also to the adulterous man. Many prisoners of war were flayed (skinned) alive, blinded, or had their tongues torn out; they were impaled, burned, and put to death in other ways.

Babylonian. Hammurabi's code (so called, but not a code as defined by lawyers today), admittedly based on earlier legislation, is a collection of decisions or "casebooks" on clay tablets, copied later (perhaps in a different style of writing) on a stele placed in the temple of Marduk in Babylon. Copies were probably placed in other cities. This stele, carried later to Susa by a conqueror, was discovered there in 1902.

Was Hammurabi's code an "ancestor" of the Mosaic Law?

Unlike the Mosaic Law, it does not seek to establish principles. Rather, its object appears to be to help the judges to decide certain cases by giving them precedents or altering previous decisions to show what ought to be done in future cases. For example, it does not set forth a sanction for murder, because there was already a recognized punishment for that, and doubtless for other common crimes. Hammurabi was not attempting to cover the whole scope of law. Each of the rules of the "code" starts off with the formula: 'If a man does thus and so.' Because it relates to specific instances, rather than laying down principles, it merely tells what judgment must be given to fit a certain simple set of facts. It is based mainly on laws already in existence, merely particularizing to fit certain difficult situations current in Babylonian civilization at the time.

In no way does Hammurabi's code prove to be an ancestor of the Mosaic Law. For example, there existed in Hammurabi's code a "sympathetic" punishment. One of the rules states: "If [a builder] has caused the son of the owner of the house to die [because the house is faulty and collapses], one shall put to death the son of that builder." God's law through Moses, to the contrary, stated: "Fathers should not be put to death on account of children, and children should not be put to death on account of fathers." (De 24:16) The penalty for theft of valuables was generally not restitution, as in the Mosaic Law, but death. In certain cases of theft, restitution up to 30-fold was required. If the man was unable to pay, he was to be put to death. Nebuchadnezzar employed dismemberment, also he used punishment by fire, as in the case of the three young Hebrew men whom he threw alive into a superheated furnace.—Da 2:5; 3:19, 21, 29; Jer 29:22.

Persian. Under Darius the Mede, Daniel was sentenced to the lions' pit, and his false accusers suffered retribution when they, their sons, and their wives died by this means. (Da 6:24) Later on, King Artaxerxes of Persia instructed Ezra that he could execute judgment upon everyone not a doer of the law of Ezra's God or of the king, "whether for death or for banishment, or for money fine or for imprisonment." (Ezr 7:26) Ahasuerus used a stake 50 cubits (22 m; 73 ft) high to hang Haman. Ahasuerus also hanged the two doorkeepers who had conspired against his life. —Es 7:9, 10; 2:21-23.

A few tablets have been found that contain the laws laid down by Darius I of Persia. In them the punishment prescribed for the man who attacked another with a weapon and injured or killed him was lashing with a whip, from 5 up to 200 stripes. Impalement was the punishment sometimes administered. According to Greek writers on Persian laws, offenses against the state, the king, his family, or his property usually carried the death penalty. These punishments were often horrible. For ordinary crimes there is not much information, but mutilation of the hands or feet or blinding appears to have been common punishment.

Other Nations in the Palestine Area. Aside from Israel, the other nations in and around the Promised Land used imprisonment and bonds, mutilation, blinding, killing captives of war by the sword, ripping up pregnant women, and dashing their little ones to death against a wall or a stone. —Jg 1:7; 16:21; 1Sa 11:1, 2; 2Ki 8:12.

Roman. Besides execution by the sword, which included beheading (Mt 14:10), among the more common punishments were: beating; scourging with a whip that was sometimes knotted with bones or heavy pieces of metal, or that had hooks at the ends; hanging; throwing one off of a high rock; drowning; exposure to wild beasts in the arena; forcing one into gladiatorial contests; and burning. Prisoners were often confined in stocks (Ac 16:24) or chained to a soldier guard. (Ac 12:6; 28:20) The *Lex Valeria* and the *Lex Porcia* exempted Roman citizens from scourging —the *Lex Valeria,* when the citizen appealed to the people; the *Lex Porcia,* without such appeal.

Greek. Greek punishments were in many cases the same as those imposed by the Romans. Precipitation off a cliff or into a deep cavern, beating to death, drowning, poisoning, and death by the sword were inflicted on criminals.

For further details, see crimes and punishments under individual names.

CRIMSON. See COLORS.

CRISPUS (Cris'pus) [from Lat., meaning "Curled"]. The presiding officer of the synagogue at Corinth whom the apostle Paul personally baptized and whose entire household became Christians.—Ac 18:8; 1Co 1:14.

CROCODILE. See LEVIATHAN.

CROSS. See TORTURE STAKE.

CROWN. A headgear, simple or ornate, worn by persons of distinction, such as kings, queens, other rulers, priests, and individuals to be specially honored or rewarded. After the Flood, crowns came to be used as symbols of authority, dignity, power, honor, and reward.

The early form of the crown was evidently that of the diadem (Heb., *ne'zer*), a simple band that was probably first used to hold back the long hair of the wearer. However, it was adopted as a royal headdress even among peoples wearing short hair. Such fillets are represented in sculptures of Egypt, Nineveh, and Persepolis. Distinctions were drawn as to honored ones in later times by the use of diadems of various colors and types of weaving or design. Some of these bands were about 5 cm (2 in.) wide and were made of linen, silk, and even silver and gold. Sometimes the diadem was worn over a cap. There were also radiated diadems (having points all around the band running out from it like rays), and there were those set with precious stones.

The Hebrew word *ne'zer,* in addition to meaning "diadem" (2Ch 23:11), can pertain to a thing singled out, separated, or dedicated, as in the case of the chief priest who had upon him "the sign of dedication, the anointing oil of his God." (Le 21:10-12; compare De 33:16, ftn.) In view of this basic meaning, the *New World Translation* appropriately renders *ne'zer* at times as "sign of dedication," with reference to the plate of gold worn by Israel's high priest upon his turban. On this gold plate were inscribed the words "Holiness belongs to Jehovah."—Ex 29:6; 39:30, ftn; Le 8:9.

Diadems as symbols of royalty were worn by Hebrew kings, such as Saul. (2Sa 1:10) However, the main Hebrew word denoting a crown in the usual sense and generally rendered "crown" is *'ata·rah',* from *'a·tar',* meaning "surround." (Compare Ps 5:12.) It does not necessarily signify a diadem. The crown (*'ata·rah'*) David took as a prize of war from the Ammonites at Rabbah originally was kept on the head of the idol Malcam. This crown's form is not revealed, but it was "a talent of gold in weight [c. 34 kg; 92 lb t], and in it there were precious stones." "It came to be on David's head," he possibly placing this heavy crown on his head only briefly, perhaps to signify his triumph over the false deity.—1Ch 20:2; see MOLECH.

Some crowns were made of refined gold (Ps 21:3); others additionally were studded with precious stones. (2Sa 12:30) At times, several bands, or diadems, were combined, and this seems to have been the usual nature of "a grand crown." (Job 31:36) The expression "grand crown" at Zechariah 6:14 is, literally, "crowns" in Hebrew, but it is accompanied by a verb in the singular number. Hence, it appears to be in the plural number of excellence or grandeur.

Concerning unfaithful Zedekiah, the last of Judah's kings, Jehovah decreed: "Remove the turban, and lift off the crown." This may relate to a kingly turban, over which a golden crown was worn. (Compare Ps 21:3; Isa 62:3.) Both of these symbols of active royal power were removed, and God's decree indicated that active rulership on "Jehovah's throne" (1Ch 29:23) would be held in abeyance until the coming of God's Messianic King.—Eze 21:25-27; Ge 49:10.

A "royal headdress" of the Persian Empire is mentioned at Esther 1:11; 2:17; 6:6-10. The Hebrew word for "headdress" in this account (ke'ther) comes from ka·thar' (surround). (Compare Jg 20:43.) The Bible does not describe the Persian "royal headdress," though the Persian monarch himself ordinarily wore one consisting of a stiff cap, perhaps of cloth or of felt, that had a blue-and-white band around it, the band actually being a diadem.

When Upper and Lower Egypt were united under one monarch, the Egyptian royal headdress became a combination crown. The crown of Lower Egypt (a flat red cap with a high point in the back and a projection with a curled end jutting out diagonally toward the front) was superimposed upon that of Upper Egypt (a round, high, white cap tapering to a knob). Usually the uraeus (the Egyptians' sacred asp) appears at the front of the crown. The royal headdress of the Assyrian king, which has been described as a high miter, was often adorned with such figures as flowers and was arranged in bands of silk or linen. It was a sort of conical cap somewhat similar to a modern fez, though higher. Greek and Roman crowns were simpler; sometimes they were radiated diadems or they were in the form of wreaths.

Jehovah spoke of men putting bracelets upon the hands of Oholah and Oholibah and "beautiful crowns" on their heads. (Eze 23:36, 42) In recent centuries, Arab women of distinction and wealth have worn (around dome-shaped caps) crowns that were jeweled gold circlets. A similar type of headdress may have been worn by certain women of antiquity.

The Greek word ste'pha·nos is rendered "crown." Roman soldiers, in mockery of Christ's royal status and probably also to add to his agony, braided a crown of thorns and placed it on Jesus' head. (Mt 27:29; Mr 15:17; Joh 19:2) There have been various suggestions as to the plant used. However, the Gospel writers do not name the plant.

Crowns of a wreath or a garland of flowers were used in connection with athletic events. (2Ti 2:5) Winners in Grecian games were given crowns or wreaths that were usually made of the leaves of trees and were adorned with flowers. For instance, in the Pythian Games the victors received a crown made of laurel; winners in the Olympian Games got crowns of wild olive leaves; and victors in the Isthmian Games (held near Corinth) were given crowns made of the pine.

The English word "crown" is also applied, among other things, to the top of the head. It is used in that sense in the Scriptures as well.—Ge 49:26; De 28:35; Ps 68:21.

Figurative Use. A capable wife is considered to be "a crown to her owner," because her good conduct brings honor to her husband, raising him in the estimation of others. (Pr 12:4) The symbolic woman Zion was to become "a crown of beauty" in Jehovah's hand, possibly denoting that she was the product of his workmanship being held up in the hand, as it were, so that others could view her with admiration.—Isa 62:1-3.

Paul's ministry and that of his traveling companions resulted in the forming of a Christian congregation in Thessalonica, which Paul rejoiced in as a "crown of exultation," it being one of the uppermost causes of joy to him.—1Th 2:19, 20; compare Php 4:1.

Gray-headedness is like a glorious "crown of beauty when it is found in the way of righteousness," a life spent in fear of Jehovah being beautiful from his viewpoint and meriting respect by all humans as a good example. (Pr 16:31; see Le 19:32.) Wisdom, like a crown, exalts and wins respect for its possessor. (Pr 4:7-9) Jesus Christ, who had been made "a little lower than angels," was "crowned with glory and honor [as a heavenly spirit creature exalted far above the angels] for having suffered death." (Heb 2:5-9; Php 2:5-11) In heaven, Jesus' anointed followers receive as a reward for faithfulness "the unfadable crown of glory," an "incorruptible one." (1Pe 5:4; 1Co 9:24-27; 2Ti 4:7, 8; Re 2:10) But unfaithfulness that results in one's loss of Kingdom interests on earth also means his loss of the heavenly crown.

Hence, the glorified Jesus Christ admonished: "Keep on holding fast what you have, that no one may take your crown."—Re 3:11.

In the Christian Greek Scriptures, the Greek word *di·a'de·ma* is rendered "diadem" by modern translations. It is always used as a symbol of kingly dignity, whether real or merely claimed. The "great fiery-colored dragon" (Satan the Devil) has a diadem upon each of its seven heads. (Re 12:3, 9) A diadem adorns each of the ten horns of the symbolic seven-headed "wild beast" that ascends out of "the sea." (Re 13:1) The one called Faithful and True, namely, Jesus Christ, has upon his head "many diadems," his being from Jehovah, the rightful Source of authority and power. (Re 19:11-13; 12:5, 10) Also at Revelation 6:2 and 14:14, Jesus Christ is pictured as wearing a crown (*ste'pha·nos*).

CRYSTAL. As used in the Bible, crystal denotes a clear, transparent mineral, probably the variety of quartz presently called rock crystal. Rock crystal is quartz in its purest form, composed of silicon and oxygen. It is found in its characteristic six-sided form in nearly all kinds of rock and is colorless, clear, and glassy in appearance. Rock crystal is much harder than other common minerals, and it is sometimes cut for gemstones.

The comparative worth of "rock crystal" (Heb., *ga·vish'*) in Job's day may be suggested by his appraisal of it along with coral and pearls, and yet he considered them all to be of less value than wisdom. (Job 28:18) Revelation uses clear, brilliant, pure crystal (Gr., *kry'stal·los*) to describe "a glassy sea like crystal," the radiance of the holy city, New Jerusalem, as "a jasper stone shining crystal-clear," and "a river of water of life, clear as crystal."—Re 4:6; 21:11; 22:1.

CUBIT. A linear measure roughly corresponding to the distance from the elbow to the tip of the middle finger. (De 3:11) There are indications that the Israelites commonly used a cubit of about 44.5 cm (17.5 in.), and calculations in this publication are figured accordingly. The Siloam Inscription, for instance, gives 1,200 cubits as the length of the water tunnel built by King Hezekiah. According to modern measurements, this tunnel is 533 m (1,749 ft) long. Thus, when taken at face value, these figures yield a cubit of 44.4 cm (17.49 in.). Also, numerous buildings and enclosures excavated in Palestine can be measured in whole numbers of this unit, giving further basis for reckoning the cubit at about 44.5 cm (17.5 in.).

Evidently the Israelites also used a larger cubit that was one handbreadth (7.4 cm; 2.9 in.) longer than the "common" cubit. This larger cubit of about 51.8 cm (20.4 in.) figured in the measurements of Ezekiel's visionary temple. (Eze 40:5) There may also have been a short cubit of about 38 cm (15 in.), measured from the elbow to the knuckles of the clenched hand.—Jg 3:16, ftn.

CUCKOO [Heb., plural, *bar·bu·rim'*]. In the Bible, this name occurs only once at 1 Kings 4:23, where the list of daily provisions of food for Solomon's court includes "cuckoos [*bar·bu·rim'*]." (*JB; NW*) While other versions (*KJ, RS*) here read "fowl," *bar·bu·rim'* seems to refer to a specific kind of bird rather than being simply a general term. Though some have identified it with the capon, the guinea hen, or the goose, lexicographer W. Baumgartner (*Hebräisches und Aramäisches Lexikon zum Alten Testament*, Leiden, 1967, p. 147) suggests the "cuckoo," and this seems to be indicated by the Arabic name for that bird, *abu burbur*.

The common cuckoo (*Cuculus canorus*) and the great spotted cuckoo (*Clamator glandarius*) both pass through Palestine on their northern migration, arriving in early March. The cuckoo is a moderate-sized bird, resembling a small hawk, with a slightly curved, sharp, pointed beak. Usually cuckoos have inconspicuous colors such as light gray or light brown to reddish-brown or black. The underparts are often whitish with narrow black bars.

While some consider the cuckoo to be a rather small bird to be used on Solomon's menu, it may be noted that even plucked sparrows were anciently sold in Middle Eastern markets. (Mt 10:29) Additionally, these cuckoos were "fattened" ones, and concerning such *The American Cyclopædia* says: "In autumn they are fat and esteemed as food; the ancients were very partial to them, and their flesh was supposed to have valuable medicinal properties." (1883, Vol. V, p. 557) The Romans are known to have eaten stuffed cuckoos, and cuckoos are said to be considered a delicacy even till this day in Italy and Greece.

The cuckoo is neither a carrion eater nor a bird of prey, but a valuable consumer of insects. It was legally "clean" and fit for use on Solomon's royal table. While "the cuckow" is included in the *King James Version* as among the unclean birds, at Leviticus 11:16 and Deuteronomy 14:15, this translation (of the Hebrew *sha'chaph*) is no longer considered acceptable.—See GULL.

CUCUMBER [Heb., *qish·shu·'ah'*]. Among the foods of Egypt for which the complaining Israelites and mixed crowd expressed great longing were the cucumbers, along with watermelons, leeks, onions, and garlic. (Nu 11:5) Some scholars, viewing the cucumber as too ordinary a food to provoke such longing, suggest the muskmelon (*Cucumis melo*) as a likely identification. However, the evidence from cognate languages, as well as that from early translations, points to the cucumber.

The cucumber grows as a long, trailing vine bearing yellow or whitish flowers. The fruit of the common cucumber (*Cucumis sativus*) has a smooth, green to blue-green rind, and greenish-white seedy pulp inside. The well-watered banks of the Nile and the dew-moistened land of Palestine, combined with the heat of the sun, provide ideal growing conditions for the plant extensively cultivated in these countries.

It was customary to erect a booth or hut in vegetable gardens or in vineyards as a shelter for the watchman who guarded the products of the fields against thieves and marauding animals. If like those used in recent times, the hut was a rather frail structure formed of four upright poles driven into the earth, with crosspieces to connect them. Branches were used to form the roof and sides, these sometimes being wattled (that is, the twigs and slender branches were interwoven), while the main joints of the structure were tied together with withes (flexible twigs used as rope). Once the growing season ends, these huts are deserted, and as the autumn winds and rain begin, they may sag or even collapse. Thus, in the midst of desolation, Zion is graphically depicted as "left remaining like a booth in a vineyard, like a lookout hut in a field of cucumbers."—Isa 1:8.

Pillars, poles, or other devices were also placed in the cultivated fields to scare off the animals, and to such a mute inanimate "scarecrow of a cucumber field" the prophet Jeremiah likened the images made by the idolatrous nations.—Jer 10:5.

CUD. The food brought up from the digestive system of an animal to be chewed again. Under the Mosaic Law, animals that chewed the cud and in addition had split or cleft hooves were considered clean for eating. "Clean," cud-chewing animals included the stag, gazelle, roebuck, antelope, chamois, domestic and wild cattle, sheep, and goats. This classification excluded the camel, rock badger, and hare or rabbit, for though they chewed the cud, their hooves were not split. (Le 11:1-8, 26; De 14:4-8) Some commentators claim that clawless, cud-chewing animals are usually cleaner in their eating habits and that their twice-chewed food is digested more thoroughly, so that if poisonous plants are eaten, much of the poison is neutralized or removed by the complex chemistry involved in the longer digestive process.

The process of cud chewing is one of the interesting marvels of creation. The majority of cud-chewing animals have three or four compartments in their stomach and generally cycle their food in a similar pattern. Most of the food they eat passes only partially chewed into the first cavity, and from there into the second, where it is softened and shaped into round cuds. When the animal has stopped grazing and is resting, muscular contraction forces the cuds back into the mouth for rechewing and further mixing with saliva. When swallowed the second time, the food goes through the first and second compartments into the third, and finally it goes into the fourth to complete digestion.

Why does the Bible classify the hare as a cud chewer?

The Scriptural reference to the hare as a cud chewer has frequently been doubted by some critics of the Bible. (Le 11:4, 6; De 14:7) It should not be overlooked, however, that the modern, scientific classification of what constitutes chewing of the cud provides no basis for judging what the Bible says, as such classification did not exist in the time of Moses. Even in the 18th century, English poet William Cowper, who had at length observed his domestic rabbits, commented that they "chewed the cud all day till evening." Linnaeus, famed naturalist of the same century, believed that rabbits chewed the cud. But it remained for others to supply more scientific data. Frenchman Morot discovered in 1882 that rabbits reingest up to 90 percent of their daily intake. Concerning the hare, Ivan T. Sanderson in a recent publication remarks: "One of the most extraordinary [habits], to our way of thinking, is their method of digestion. This is not unique to Leporids [hares, rabbits] and is now known to occur in many Rodents. When fresh green food, as opposed to desiccated [dried] winter forage, is available, the animals gobble it up voraciously and then excrete it around their home lairs in a semi-digested form. After some time this is then re-eaten, and the process may be repeated more than once. In the Common Rabbit, it appears that

only the fully grown adults indulge this practice."
—*Living Mammals of the World,* 1955, p. 114.

Certain British scientists of this century made close observations of the rabbits' habits under careful controls, and the results they obtained were published in the *Proceedings of the Zoological Society of London,* 1940, Vol. 110, pp. 159-163. Briefly this is the way the hare reingests its food: If a rabbit eats a breakfast of fresh food, it passes through the stomach into the small intestine, leaving behind in the cardiac end of the stomach some 40 or 50 grams of pellets that were already present when the fresh food was eaten. From the small intestine the morning meal enters the caecum or blind end of the large intestine and there remains for a period of time. During the day the pellets descend, and in the intestines the bacterial protein in them is digested. When they reach the large intestine they bypass the material in the caecum and go on into the colon where the excess moisture is absorbed to produce the familiar dry beans or droppings that are cast away. This phase of the cycle completed, the material stored in the dead end of the caecum next enters the colon, but instead of having all the moisture absorbed it reaches the anus in a rather soft condition. It is in pellet form with each coated with a tough layer of mucus to prevent them from sticking together. Now when these pellets reach the anus, instead of being cast away, the rabbit doubles up and takes them into the mouth and stores them away in the cardiac end of the stomach until another meal has been eaten. In this way the special rhythmic cycle is completed and most of the food has passed a second time through the digestive tract.

Dr. Waldo L. Schmitt, Head Curator, Department of Zoology of the Smithsonian Institution, Washington, D.C., in commenting on these findings, wrote: "There seems to be no reason to doubt the authenticity of the reports of various workers that rabbits customarily store semi-digested food in the caecum and that this is later reingested and passes a second time through the digestive tract." He also observed that here is an explanation for "the phenomenally large caecum of rabbits as compared with most other mammals."—*Awake!,* April 22, 1951, pp. 27, 28.

CUMIN [Heb., *kam·mon',* Gr., *ky'mi·non*], **BLACK CUMIN** [Heb., *qe'tsach*]. The cumin plant (*Cuminum cyminum*) is of the carrot or parsley family, growing about 0.3 m to 0.6 m (1 to 2 ft) high, with long, slender leaves and umbels (bouquetlike clusters) of small pink or white flowers growing at the ends of the upward-rising branch-

es. The plant is best known for its pungently aromatic seeds, used in Middle Eastern and other countries as a spice for flavoring bread, cakes, stews, and even liquors. Caraway seeds, which the cumin seeds resemble in flavor and appearance, have since become more commonly used than cumin because of being milder and of greater nutritive value.

Mentioned along with the cumin at Isaiah 28: 25, 27 is the plant described by the Hebrew word *qe'tsach.* It has been variously identified by translators as "fitches" (*KJ*), "fennel" (*Mo*), and "dill" (*AT; RS*); but "black cumin" (*JP; NW*) seems to be favored by the context and also by the corresponding name in Arabic (*qazha*). Despite its English name, black cumin (*Nigella sativa*) is not classified botanically with the cumin plant, and though known as "the nutmeg flower," it likewise differs from the cultivated nutmeg. It is of the Ranunculaceae (buttercup) family, grows to about the same height as the cumin, has similar feathery leaves, but blossoms with individual, attractive flowers with white to blue petals. The seed vessels have interior compartments, and the tiny black seeds, smaller than the cumin, are acrid as well as aromatic and are used on foods as a rather peppery seasoning. It was a favorite spice of the ancient Greeks and Romans.—Picture, Vol. 1, p. 543.

Though neither the cumin nor the black cumin is widely cultivated in the region of Palestine today, in Bible times they both were more popular there. Jehovah through the prophet Isaiah describes the Israelite farmer's scattering seeds broadcast over the plowed land, while giving greater care to the sowing of the more valuable grains, such as wheat, millet, and barley. He likewise shows that after harvesting, the threshing of the seeds of the cumin and black cumin plants was not done with heavy wheels or rollers of threshing instruments, but was accomplished by beating the seed capsules with a staff or, for the stouter pods of the black cumin, a rod so the small tender seeds would not be damaged. Coming, as it does, after Jehovah's exhortation to the people of Israel to cease scoffing in view of the imminent extermination facing the northern kingdom, this illustration apparently was given to show that the people had the option either of responding to the disciplinary beating by Jehovah's rod or of being subjected to severe and incessant threshing as under the crushing weight of a heavy rollered wagon.—Isa 28:22-29.

Under the Mosaic Law, the Israelites were to

pay the tithe or tenth "of all the produce of your seed," which would seem to include all cultivated crops. (De 14:22; Le 27:30) In Jesus' day the Pharisees were scrupulously careful to pay the tenth of such small products as mint, dill, and cumin (all marketable commodities), but they were guilty of passing over the more serious obligations.—Mt 23:23; compare Lu 11:42.

CUN. One of the cities of King Hadadezer of Zobah from which David took large amounts of copper, later used in the temple construction. (1Ch 18:8) In the parallel account at 2 Samuel 8:8 the name Berothai appears in its place and may refer to the same place. Others suggest that Kuna at Ras Ba'albek, 43 km (27 mi) NE of Bereitan, the suggested location of Berothai, is possibly to be identified with the Biblical Cun.—See BEROTHAH, BEROTHAI.

CUP. See VESSELS.

CUPBEARER. An official of the royal court who served wine or other drinks to the king. (Ge 40:1, 2, 11; Ne 1:11; 2:1) The duties of the chief cupbearer sometimes included testing wine by tasting it before giving it to the king. This was because the possibility always existed that an attempt might be made on the king's life by poisoning his wine.

Thorough trustworthiness was a chief qualification for the office, since the life of the king was at stake. The position was one of the most honorable in the court. The chief cupbearer was often present at royal conferences and discussions. Being in a close and usually confidential relationship with the king, he often had considerable influence with the monarch. It was Pharaoh's cupbearer who recommended Joseph. (Ge 41:9-13) King Artaxerxes of Persia had a high regard for his cupbearer, Nehemiah. (Ne 2:6-8) When Nehemiah traveled to Jerusalem, Artaxerxes provided him with a military escort.—Ne 2:9.

The fact that cupbearers are often present in ancient illustrations indicates the importance of their position. The queen of Sheba was greatly impressed by Solomon's "drinking service and their attire."—2Ch 9:4.

CURSE. The desiring, threatening, or pronouncing of evil upon someone or something is the basic idea of a number of Hebrew and Greek words in the Bible that are translated by the word "curse" or similar expressions.

The first curse employed was, logically, at the time of the Edenic rebellion and was directed by God against the instigator of the rebellion through the agent that one employed, the serpent. (Ge 3:14, 15) This curse was to end in his destruction. At the same time the ground was cursed on Adam's account, resulting in its producing thorns and thistles but *not* in its destruction. (Ge 3:17, 18; 5:29) The curse that Jehovah placed on Cain condemned him to a fugitive life. —Ge 4:11, 12.

Following the Flood, the first curse pronounced by a human was that which Noah directed against Canaan, son of Ham, condemning him to slave for Shem and Japheth, a curse that saw its major realization some eight centuries later with the conquest of Canaan by the Semite nation of Israel. (Ge 9:25-27) Thus the Gibeonites, descendants of Canaan, were told by Joshua that they were a "cursed people," in view of which they were assigned to a slave's position.—Jos 9:23.

Such cursing, therefore, should not be confused with profanity, nor does it necessarily imply violent anger, as is evident from the case of the Gibeonites. In the above texts the Hebrew word 'a·rar' is used. This word is found 18 times in the formal declaration of pronouncements at Deuteronomy 27:15-26; 28:16-19, and also in solemn pronouncements, such as those at Exodus 22:28; Jeremiah 11:3; 17:5; and 48:10. The related noun me'e·rah' occurs five times. (De 28:20; Pr 3:33; 28:27; Mal 2:2; 3:9) The Bible usage of these words indicates a solemn pronouncement or a prediction of evil and, when made by God or by an authorized person, has a prophetic value and force. Joshua's curse made against any man who, in the future, might rebuild devastated Jericho was fulfilled many centuries later. (Jos 6:26; 1Ki 16:34) King Balak's requests for Balaam to curse Israel, however, were disapproved by Jehovah, and He caused blessings to be pronounced instead.—Nu 22:6–24:25; see EXECRATION.

'A·lah', another Hebrew word rendered "oath" as well as "curse," implies an oath that carries with it a curse as its penalty for violation of the oath, or because of the oath's proving to be false. —Ge 24:41, ftn; Nu 5:21, 23, 27; De 29:19-21; 2Ch 34:24; 1Ki 8:31, 32; see OATH.

In the Greek Scriptures the two basic words translated "curse" are a·ra' and a·na'the·ma, along with related words such as ka·ta'ra, e·pi·ka·ta'ra·tos, ka·ta·ra'o·mai, ka·ta'the·ma, and ka·ta·the·ma·ti'zo.

The word a·ra' has the meaning of an imprecation or a prayer calling down evil from a divine source. John uses the related e·pa'ra·tos in writing that the Pharisees viewed the common people who listened to Jesus as "accursed people" who did not know the Law. (Joh 7:49) By contrast, Paul showed that all the Jews needed to be redeemed from the curse of the Law covenant by Christ's becoming a curse for them through his death on the torture stake. (Ga 3:10, 13) At Galatians 3:10 Paul used e·pi·ka·ta'ra·tos to translate the Hebrew word 'a·rar' (the first word considered in this article), as found at Deuteronomy 27:26. In verse 13 he used the same word to translate the Hebrew word qela·lah' (something accursed; malediction), as found at Deuteronomy 21:23. —See MALEDICTION.

A form of the word ka·ta·ra'o·mai is used to describe Jesus' action in cursing the "goat" class (Mt 25:41), and also in instructing his followers to "bless those cursing you." (Lu 6:28) Paul and James used forms of the same word in giving like counsel at Romans 12:14 and James 3:9. Paul used the word ka·ta'ra in likening Christians who fall away after having partaken of holy spirit to the "ground" that is unresponsive to rain and that produces only thorns and thistles (Heb 6:7, 8), while Peter uses the same word to describe as "accursed" those who are covetous, who "have eyes full of adultery" and entice unsteady souls. —2Pe 2:14.

The word a·na'the·ma literally means that which is "laid up" and originally applied to votive offerings laid up or set apart as sacred in a temple. (See Lu 21:5, where a related word is used.) In the Greek Scriptures the Bible writers use a·na'the·ma to apply to that which is accursed or subject to becoming accursed and, therefore, set apart as evil or execrated. Thus Paul wrote to the Galatians (1:8) that they should consider as "accursed" anyone (even angels) who declared to them as good news something contrary to that which they had received. Those who had "no affection for the Lord" were due to come under a similar designation. (1Co 16:22) In his anguish over his fellow Israelites who had not accepted Christ, Paul said that he could even wish that he himself were "separated as the cursed one from the Christ" in their behalf. (Ro 9:3) In other cases a·na'the·ma is evidently used to refer to the declaring of an oath that, if not carried out or if proved false, was intended to result in a curse, as in the case of the 40 men who formed the oath-bound conspiracy to kill Paul. (Ac 23:12-15, 21) The words ka·ta·the·ma·ti'zo and a·na·the·ma·ti'zo are used in connection with Peter's denial of Christ. (Mt 26:74; Mr 14:71) In effect, Peter was

here saying that he wished he 'might be cursed or set apart as evil if he knew the man.'

At Revelation 22:3 the promise is made concerning the New Jerusalem that "no more will there be any curse [ka·ta'the·ma]." This appears to serve as a contrast with earthly Jerusalem, which did come under God's curse. It is likewise in sharp contrast to the cursed condition that results to the symbolic city Babylon the Great as a result of God's judicial decree against her. The "anathema" pronounced against her is evident from the command given at Revelation 18:4-8.—See also 2Co 6:17.

In the Greek Septuagint the translators generally used a·na'the·ma to render the Hebrew che'-rem.—See DEVOTED THING.

CUSH.

1. The first-named son of Ham and father of six sons: Seba, Havilah, Sabtah, Raamah, Sabteca, and Nimrod. (Ge 10:6-8; 1Ch 1:8-10) Cush and his named descendants are included among those from whom "the nations were spread about in the earth after the deluge." (Ge 10:32) Thus, while no details are given concerning Cush as an individual in the Genesis account, his name is used throughout the Hebrew Scriptures as representing his descendants and the land or regions that they settled, as described in No. 2.

It may here be noted, however, that Cush is very evidently a principal progenitor (perhaps along with Put) of the dark-complexioned branch of the human family (Jer 13:23), as is indicated by the areas of settlement of certain of his descendants. This disproves the theory advanced by those who incorrectly endeavor to apply to the Negro peoples the curse pronounced on Canaan, for Canaan, the brother of Cush, did not produce any Negro descendants but, rather, was the forefather of the various Canaanite tribes of Palestine. (Ge 9:24, 25; 10:6) There is, therefore, no Scriptural connection whatsoever between the dark complexion of certain descendants of Cush and the curse pronounced on Canaan.

2. Aside from the genealogical accounts at Genesis chapter 10 and 1 Chronicles chapter 1, and the use of the name in the superscription of Psalm 7, considered in No. 3, the name Cush is employed in all other texts to refer to the progeny of that son of Ham and the place of their habitation.

The name of Cush is associated through his son Nimrod with Babel and the kingdom that Nimrod forged in post-Flood times. (Ge 10:8-12) Some connect Cush's name with the ancient city of Kish, revealed by excavations in lower Mesopotamia near Babylon, and said to be the city from which emperors of the third millennium B.C.E. in Babylonia assumed the title of "king of the world." "The Sumerian King List," an ancient record, though highly legendary, contains the statement: "After the Flood had swept over (the earth) (and) when kingship was lowered (again) from heaven, kingship was (first) in Kish." (*Ancient Near Eastern Texts,* edited by J. Pritchard, 1974, p. 265) Referring to this ancient city, Professor Albright comments: "Unless Kish is the prototype of the Cush of Gen. 10:8, as is quite possible, it is not mentioned in the Bible. Nimrod was in any case probably considered as the first ruler of Kish." (Young's *Analytical Concordance to the Bible,* Supplement on "Recent Discoveries in Bible Lands," by W. Albright, 1955, p. 14) Thus, although Babylonia later came fully under Semitic domination, there seems to be some historical evidence that harmonizes with the Biblical record of Cushite rule in that area at an early time.

The "Land of Cush." The "land of Cush" referred to at Genesis 2:13 as the land originally encircled by the river Gihon, one of the four heads of the "river issuing out of Eden," is of uncertain location. (Ge 2:10) The translators of the *Septuagint* rendered the Hebrew word for "Cush" by the Greek name Ethiopia in this text. The name Cush did become more or less synonymous with ancient Ethiopia at an early time, yet it cannot arbitrarily be said that such is necessarily the case at Genesis 2:13. Josephus, following the rendering of the *Septuagint,* associated the Gihon River with the Nile. (*Jewish Antiquities,* I, 39 [i, 3]) However, the Gihon's having had a common source with the Euphrates and the Tigris rivers certainly does not seem to allow for such identification, unless the global Deluge is assumed to have brought about extreme changes in the topography of the area.

The term "Cush" at Genesis 2:13 is, therefore, connected by some scholars with the Kassu or Kassites of the Assyrian inscriptions, a people of uncertain origin inhabiting the plateau region of central Asia. An article by P. English in the *Journal of Near Eastern Studies* (1959, Vol. XVIII, pp. 49-53) presents evidence of a Negro population in ancient times in the region of the SE corner of the Black Sea and later in the Caucasus region farther N. It suggests a relationship between the names of the regions of Abkhazia and Khazaria, inhabited by such tribes, and the Biblical Cush. There is, of course, the possibility that

the reference to Cush at Genesis 2:13 could apply to some segment of the Cushite family that did not migrate southward with the main body of Cushites but settled in the region of Asia Minor described above.

Still others suggest that the "land of Cush" encircled by the Gihon was on the Arabian Peninsula, since the name "Cushan" is used to parallel "the land of Midian" at Habakkuk 3:7, Midian being located generally in the vicinity of the Gulf of 'Aqaba. It is possibly with reference to such an Arabian "Cush" that Moses' Midianite wife Zipporah is called a "Cushite."—Ex 18:1-5; Nu 12:1.

After the Tower of Babel. Following the breakup at Babel because of the confusion of language, the main body of Cush's descendants appear to have migrated southward. Whether they reached Africa by first going into the Arabian Peninsula and then crossing over the narrow strait known as Bab al-Mandab or whether they settled initially in Africa and then crossed over into Arabia is uncertain, although the basic association of "Cush" with Africa might favor the latter migratory movement. The name of Cush's son Seba is associated with E Africa, while those of Havilah, Sabtah, Raamah, and Sabteca are generally associated with regions on the Arabian Peninsula. (See individual articles under names of sons.) It is of note that, while the names of these sons appear to have been perpetuated by tribes descended from them, this does not seem to be the case with the name of Nimrod, his name appearing in ancient history solely as that of an individual. This may indicate that Nimrod remained childless.

Though Cushites were to be found in Arabia, the name Cush as used in the Bible in most cases clearly refers to a region in Africa, and where the relationship is obvious, translators simply render "Cush" as "Ethiopia." It is regularly associated with Egypt (Isa 20:3-5; 43:3; Jer 46:7-9) and also with Libya. (2Ch 12:2, 3; Da 11:43; Na 3:9) Isaiah 11:11 presents the ancient geographic designations for the regional divisions running southward from the Nile Delta: "Egypt" (or "Mizraim," here, Lower Egypt), "Pathros" (Upper Egypt), and "Cush" (Nubia-Ethiopia). Ezekiel 29:10 speaks of the devastation of Egypt "from Migdol to Syene and to the boundary of Ethiopia [Cush]." Thus, Cush or ancient Ethiopia appears to have been beyond Syene (modern Aswan) and, according to archaeological evidence, continued S perhaps as far as modern Khartoum. Cush thus embraced a more extensive and generally more southern area than that included in present-day Ethiopia. "The rivers of Ethiopia [Cush]" are suggested to have been the Blue and White Nile rivers, which have their junction at Khartoum, and also the Atbara River, which joins the Nile S of the fifth cataract. —Zep 3:10.

"The Arabs that were by the side of the Ethiopians [Ku·shim′]" (2Ch 21:16) possibly were those Arab tribes occupying the SW coast of the Arabian Peninsula and thus facing Africa across the Red Sea.

Much of the land of Cush was evidently arid desert country. "The region of the rivers of Ethiopia" is described as "the land of the whirring insects with wings" (Isa 18:1), perhaps referring to the locusts that swarm in Ethiopia and Egypt; however, some suggest the mosquitoes, and others point out that the Hebrew word for "whirring" (tsela·tsal′) resembles in sound the name given to the tsetse fly (tsaltsalya) by the Galla tribes (a Hamitic people living in modern Ethiopia). Ivory, ebony, gold, precious stones, iron, and aromatics were products of the land, and Biblical mention is made of "the merchants of Ethiopia" (Isa 45:14) and "the topaz of Cush."—Job 28:19.

Later History. Cush, or Ethiopia, had come under Egyptian domination by about the time of the Exodus of Israel from Egypt, and it continued thus for some 500 years. A viceroy administering this domain under the Egyptian Pharaoh was known by the title "King's Son of Kush." Evidently toward the close of the second millennium B.C.E., Ethiopia freed itself from Egypt's control. The Ethiopian capital was thereafter located first at Napata, near the fourth cataract, and later at Meroë, about 210 km (130 mi) NNE of Khartoum.

Ethiopian warriors formed part of Pharaoh Shishak's forces that attacked Judah in the fifth year of Rehoboam (993 B.C.E.). (2Ch 12:2, 3) Following King Asa's tenth year, or about 967 B.C.E., the Ethiopian Zerah marched against Judah with a million men but suffered complete defeat at Mareshah.—2Ch 14:1, 9-15; 16:8.

Secular history shows that in the latter part of the eighth century B.C.E. Ethiopia conquered Egypt and dominated it for some 60 years. This was during the "Twenty-fifth (Ethiopian) Dynasty," which included among its rulers King Taharqa, called Tirhakah in the Bible. This king came up against the forces of Sennacherib during their invasion of Judah (732 B.C.E.) but, according to the Assyrian inscriptions, was defeated at Elteke(h).—2Ki 19:9; Isa 37:8, 9.

Assyrian Emperors Esar-haddon and Ashurbanipal invaded Egypt during their respective reigns, and the destruction of Thebes in Upper Egypt (called No-amon at Na 3:8-10) by Ashurbanipal (c. 684 B.C.E.) completely subjugated Egypt and also ended Ethiopian dominance of the Nile valley. This fulfilled the prophecy uttered about a half century earlier by the prophet Isaiah. —Isa 20:3-6.

At the battle of Carchemish in 625 B.C.E., Ethiopian forces formed part of Pharaoh Necho's army, which suffered defeat there at the hands of Nebuchadnezzar. (Jer 46:2, 9) Nebuchadnezzar's later invasion of Egypt (possibly 588 B.C.E.) would cause "severe pains" in Cush and "drive self-confident Ethiopia [Cush] into trembling." —Eze 29:19; 30:4-9.

Persian King Cambyses II (529-522 B.C.E.) conquered Egypt during the days of Pharaoh Psamtik III, and this opened the way for bringing Ethiopia under Persian control; thus, Ahasuerus (Xerxes I) could be spoken of as ruling "from India to Ethiopia [Cush]." (Es 1:1; 8:9) Confirming this, Xerxes states in an inscription: "These are the countries—in addition to Persia—over which I am king . . . India . . . (and) Kush."—*Ancient Near Eastern Texts,* p. 316.

Judean exiles were foretold to return to their homeland from faraway lands, including Cush. (Isa 11:11, 12; compare Zep 3:10.) In Daniel's prophecy of "the time of the end," the aggressive "king of the north" is described as having Ethiopia and Libya "at his steps," that is, responsive to his direction. (Da 11:40-43) Ethiopia (Cush) also has a place in the wicked battle forces of "Gog of the land of Magog" in his stormlike assault upon Jehovah's regathered ones "in the final part of the years." (Eze 38:2-5, 8) Yet the psalmist favorably foretells that Cush will be counted among those bringing gifts to God.—Ps 68:29-32.

3. The superscription of Psalm 7 states that the psalm is "concerning the words of Cush the Benjaminite." No other mention is made of this person. If the psalm relates to the early period of David's history, the reference might be to some opposer of David in Saul's court; if to a later period, the name might be used to refer enigmatically to Shimei the Benjaminite who cursed David.—2Sa 16:5-8.

CUSHAN (Cu′shan). Cushan appears at Habakkuk 3:7 as paralleling "the land of Midian" and hence evidently is another name for Midian or relates to a neighboring country. As shown in the article CUSH (No. 2), some descendants of Cush appear to have settled on the Arabian Peninsula;

and the name *Kusi* or *Kushim* was anciently used to describe certain Arabic peoples of that region.

CUSHAN-RISHATHAIM (Cu'shan-rish·a-tha'im) [possibly, Cushite (Ethiopian) of the Double Wickedness].

A king of Mesopotamia from whose domination Othniel liberated the Israelites after eight years of servitude. He is also called "the king of Syria." (Jg 3:7-11) Some view the second half ("rishathaim") of this composite name as the name of a place or region, while others translate it to mean "Double Wickedness." "Cushan" is used at Habakkuk 3:7 to parallel Midian; however, it is stated that King Cushan-rishathaim was from Mesopotamia (Heb., *'Aram' na·hara'yim;* compare Ge 24:10, where the same term is used to describe the location of the city of Nahor in Syria). A list of Pharaoh Ramses III mentions a district in northern Syria called Qusanaruma, and this is suggested by some scholars to have been the possible seat of this king's domain. Cushan-rishathaim was Israel's first major oppressor during the period of the Judges.

CUSHI (Cush'i) [Cushite, Ethiopian].

1. Father of the prophet Zephaniah.—Zep 1:1.

2. Forefather of Jeremiah's secretary, Baruch Jehudi.—Jer 36:14.

CUSHITE (Cush'ite) [Of (Belonging to) Cush (Ethiopia)].

The term "Cushite" may refer to inhabitants of the land of Cush in Africa or it may in some instances apply to people residing on the Arabian Peninsula. The latter identification evidently applies to Moses' wife Zipporah. (Ex 18:1-5; Nu 12:1) Zipporah was a Kenite whose ancestry cannot be determined. (Ge 15:18, 19; Jg 4:11) The expression at 2 Chronicles 21:16 "by the side of the Ethiopians [Cushites]" as applying to certain Arabs may also mean "under the control of the Ethiopians," and this might indicate one basis for applying the name "Cushite" to persons not descended from Cush. Several of Cush's sons are believed to have settled on the Arabian Peninsula.—See HAVILAH No. 3; SABTAH.

Basically, however, "Cushite" refers to Africans residing in the region anciently called Ethiopia. In addition to "Zerah the Ethiopian [Cushite]" and "Tirhakah the king of Ethiopia" (2Ch 14:9; 2Ki 19:9), other Cushites mentioned in the Bible are Ebed-melech (Jer 38:7-12; 39:16-18), the Ethiopian eunuch who became a convert to Christianity, and the queen he served, Candace. (Ac 8:26, 27) General Joab selected an unnamed Cushite runner (called Cushi in *KJ*) rather than an Israelite to

deliver the news to David of his son Absalom's defeat and death.—2Sa 18:19-32; see CUSH No. 2.

CUSTODY.

The care and keeping of anything; the detaining of a person by virtue of lawful process or authority; actual imprisonment.

The Biblical law most clearly explaining the responsibilities of a custodian is outlined at Exodus 22:10-13, involving animals entrusted to another. This law, undoubtedly based on an earlier patriarchal law (Ge 31:39), states: "In case a man should give his fellow . . . any domestic animal to keep, and it does die or get maimed or gets led off while nobody is looking, . . . the other is not to make compensation. But if they should for a fact be stolen from him, he is to make compensation to their owner. If it should for a fact be torn by a wild beast, he is to bring it as evidence. For something torn by a wild beast he is not to make compensation."—Compare Ge 31:39.

When a shepherd or herdsman said he would keep or guard a flock or herd, he was indicating legal acceptance of the custody of these animals. He was guaranteeing the owner that they would be fed and not stolen, or else compensation would be paid. However, his responsibility was not absolute, for the above law absolved the guardian of liability in the case of an occurrence beyond normal human control, such as attack by wild beasts. To be relieved of the responsibility of custody, though, he had to submit evidence to the owner, as, for example, the torn carcass. The owner, on examination of such evidence, was bound to return a verdict of innocence on the part of the custodian.

The same principle applied in general to any entrusted property, even in family relationships, for example, the oldest brother was considered the legal guardian of his younger brothers and sisters. Hence, we can understand the concern that Reuben as an eldest son had for Joseph's life, as recorded at Genesis 37:18-30, when the other brothers spoke of killing him. "He said: 'Let us not strike his soul fatally.' . . . 'Do not spill blood. . . . do not lay a violent hand upon him.' His purpose was to deliver him out of their hand in order to return him to his father." And when Reuben discovered Joseph's absence, his anxiety was so extreme that "he ripped his garments apart" and exclaimed: "The child is gone! And I—where am I really to go?" He knew that he could be held accountable for the loss of Joseph. To escape responsibility, the brothers shrewdly fabricated evidence to the effect that Joseph had been killed by a wild beast. This they did by soaking Joseph's striped garment in goat's blood. They then submitted this evidence to Jacob, their father and patriarchal judge, who absolved Reuben of any responsibility because, on the basis of Joseph's blood-soaked garment that his brothers presented as evidence, Jacob concluded that Joseph had been killed.—Ge 37:31-33.

At Galatians 3:19-25, a spiritual application of the terms "guarded" and "custody" is made. Paul says that the Law made transgressions manifest and that "the Scripture delivered up all things together to the custody of sin." But he continues: "However, before the faith arrived, we were being guarded under law, being delivered up together into custody, looking to the faith that was destined to be revealed." He thereby emphasized how natural Israel was in spiritual custody, being guarded or kept by the Law, until the faith toward Christ arrived.

Custody as used by the Bible in some instances means the detention of a person. An example is the half Israelite who abused Jehovah's name while in the camp of Israel. After he transgressed the Law, the account states: "Then they committed him into custody till there should be a distinct declaration to them according to the saying of Jehovah." (Le 24:10-16, 23) As a rule Israel did not commit criminals into any extended custody, because they were required to execute justice swiftly. (Jos 7:20, 22-25) However, in this case, as well as the case of the Sabbath breaker at Numbers 15:32-36, a clarification of the law was being awaited; but as soon as Jehovah's saying on the matter was clear, the sentence was immediately executed. Similarly, Peter and the other apostles were committed into custody, though unjustly, pending trial before the Sanhedrin on the following day. (Ac 4:3; 5:17, 18) The Scriptures also take note of the fact that Jeremiah was unjustly put in custody, not merely being held for trial but actually imprisoned.—Jer 37:21.

CUTH, CUTHAH

(Cu'thah). Both "Cuth" and "Cuthah" refer to the same original home of a people moved by the king of Assyria to the cities of Samaria after Israel's exiling in 740 B.C.E. (2Ki 17:23, 24, 30) The deportees from Cuthah and other locations were, however, plagued with man-killing lions and, on appealing to the Assyrian king for aid, were supplied with a priest formerly of the northern kingdom of Israel. Since the worship practiced in Israel had long been disapproved by God (1Ki 13:33, 34; 16:31-33), this priest's services failed to produce genuine worshipers of Jehovah, so that "it was of their own

gods that [the colonists] proved to be worshipers," those from Cuthah continuing to serve their god Nergal. The race formed by the intermarrying of the 'people of Cuthah' and other nations with the remaining Israelites came to be generally called "Samaritan." According to Josephus, these were "called Chuthaioi (Cuthim) in the Hebrew tongue, and Samareitai (Samaritans) by the Greeks." (Jewish Antiquities, IX, 290 [xiv, 3]) The designation "Cuthim" was apparently used because of the predominance of people from Cuthah among the original settlers.—2Ki 17:24-41.

The discovery of contract tablets at Tell Ibrahim (Imam Ibrahim), about 50 km (30 mi) NE of Babylon, containing the name Kutu (the Akkadian equivalent of Cuth), has led most geographers to identify Tell Ibrahim with the Biblical Cuthah. The indications are that Cuthah was at one time among the more important cities in the Babylonian Empire and was also probably quite extensive, as the mound marking it today is some 18 m (60 ft) high and 3 km (2 mi) in circumference. What is believed to have been the site of an ancient temple dedicated to Nergal is pointed out amid these ruins in accord with the Biblical statement that "the men of Cuth" were devotees of that god.—2Ki 17:29, 30.

CUTTING OFF.

In Israel, when used regarding a punishment for violation of the Law, it meant a cutting off in death. Some rabbinic scholars believe that it merely constituted expulsion from the congregation of Israel, though they differ widely in opinion.

By examining the Scripture texts naming the offenses for which this punishment is prescribed, it can be determined that it has reference to the death penalty, executed either by the authorities in Israel or by God himself. The crimes for which cutting off are prescribed are those of a most serious nature. They include disrespect of Jehovah (Israel's God and King), idolatry, child sacrifice, spiritism, desecration of sacred things, and such disgusting practices as incest, bestiality, and sodomy. In some instances the death penalty is specifically mentioned in connection with the offense for which 'cutting off' is decreed as the sanction.—Ex 31:14; Le 7:27; 18:6, 22, 23, 29; 20:3-6; 22:3, 4, 9; 23:28-30; Nu 4:15, 18, 20; 15:30, 31; see also Ex 30:31-33, 38.

The writer of the letter to the Hebrews evidently had in mind the statement at Numbers 15:30: "The soul that does something deliberately . . . that soul must be cut off from among his people," when he said: "Any man that has disregarded the law of Moses dies without compassion, upon the testimony of two or three." (Heb 10:28) Jesus used the expression in setting out the punishment for the symbolic "goats": "These will depart into everlasting cutting-off [Gr., *ko'la·sin;* literally, "lopping off; pruning"], but the righteous ones into everlasting life." (Mt 25:46) Here the contrast is between life and death.

CUTTINGS. The making of cuttings upon the flesh or scratching the arms, hands, and face in times of mourning was evidently a common practice among the ancients. (Jer 47:5; 48:37) This may have been done with a view to pacifying or propitiating the deities believed to preside over the dead. With reference to this practice among the Scythians upon the death of their king, the Greek historian Herodotus (IV, 71) wrote: "They cut off a part of their ears, shave their heads, make cuts round their arms, tear their foreheads and noses, and pierce their left hands with arrows."

Inflicting lacerations upon the flesh, however, was not limited to mourning rites. In the hope of having their god answer their appeals, the prophets of Baal cut themselves "according to their custom with daggers and with lances, until they caused blood to flow out upon them." (1Ki 18:28) Similar rites were engaged in by other ancient peoples. For example, Herodotus (II, 61) mentions that during the festival of Isis, the Carians residing in Egypt cut their foreheads with knives.

God's Law specifically forbade the making of cuttings upon the flesh for the dead. (Le 19:28; 21:5; De 14:1) The reason for this was that Israel was a holy people to Jehovah, a special property. (De 14:2) As such, Israel was to remain free from all idolatrous practices. Then, too, such extreme displays of mourning accompanied by self-inflicted lacerations upon the flesh were most inappropriate for a people who were fully aware of the actual condition of the dead as well as the resurrection hope. (Da 12:13; Heb 11:19) Also, the prohibition against self-mutilation would have impressed upon the Israelites proper respect for God's creation, the human body.

Apparently, though, the Israelites on occasion disregarded God's law with respect to making cuttings upon their flesh.—Jer 41:5; compare Mic 5:1.

CYMBALS. In Bible times, a percussion instrument similar to modern cymbals, used to accompany the harp, trumpet, and other instruments. (2Sa 6:5; 1Ch 15:28; 2Ch 5:12, 13) The two Hebrew words for cymbals (*tsel·tselim'* and *metsil·ta'yim*) come from the root *tsa·lal'*, meaning "tingle; quiver." (1Sa 3:11; Hab 3:16) According to 1 Chronicles 15:19, the cymbals for Jehovah's temple were made of copper, but beyond this there is no further Scriptural description. A pair of cymbals have been found in an ancient Egyptian tomb that may be somewhat representative of Biblical cymbals. They are about 14 cm (5.5 in.) in diameter with handles in the center, and they were made of copper alloyed with a slight amount of silver.

Psalm 150:5 indicates that more than one type of cymbal may have been known in Israel. The first occurrence of the term in this text describes "cymbals of melodious sound," while the second reference is to "clashing cymbals." Because each stanza of verses 3 and 4 of this song refers to one or more different musical instruments, the two stanzas of verse 5 could quite consistently be referring first to smaller, tinkling, well-tuned cymbals and, second, to cymbals of a larger diameter producing louder, deeper-toned sounds, when clashed together in heavy strokes.

The figure of "a clashing cymbal" is used by the apostle Paul to illustrate the shallowness of one's speaking in tongues, if the motive of love is lacking. (1Co 13:1) However, other references to cymbals, in addition to those already mentioned, are in connection with the worship of Jehovah. (1Ch 13:8; 16:5, 42; 25:1, 6; 2Ch 29:25; Ezr 3:10; Ne 12:27) Whenever temple service was involved, trained Levites were the instrumentalists. (1Ch 16:4, 5, 42) While some scholars are inclined to believe that cymbals were strictly a Levitical and even a priestly instrument, Psalm 150:1, 5 may indicate a more general usage: "Praise Jah, you people! . . . Praise him with the cymbals."

CYPRESS [Heb., *te'ash·shur'*]. An evergreen tree of the cone-bearing family. Cypress is included along with other trees as forming part of the "glory of Lebanon," and this is indicative of the place where it grew and also suggests a tree of desirable qualities or impressive appearance. The "box tree" referred to in the *King James Version* is not a likely translation since, according to some scholars, the box tree does not grow in Palestine, and in Syria it is only a small shrub. (*Unger's Bible Dictionary*, 1965, p. 1134; *The Interpreter's Dictionary of the Bible*, edited by G. Buttrick, 1962, Vol. 2, p. 292) The cypress is considered by many to be the tree probably referred to by this Hebrew word at Isaiah 41:19; 60:13.—See Moffatt's translation; *A Dictionary of*

Life in Bible Times, by W. Corswant, Suffolk, 1960, p. 55; The Interpreter's Dictionary of the Bible, Vol. 1, p. 459; Vol. 2, p. 292; Lexicon in Veteris Testamenti Libros, by L. Koehler and W. Baumgartner, Leiden, 1958, p. 1017.

The cypress (Cupressus sempervirens) has dark-green foliage and branches that extend upward somewhat like those of the Lombardy poplar. It has an average height of 9 to 15 m (30 to 50 ft) but at times may grow as high as 24 m (80 ft). It is commonly cultivated throughout Palestine; some specimens have been found growing wild in Gilead, Edom, and on the slopes of Mount Lebanon. The wood has a rich reddish hue, is fragrant, and is of great durability. It was possibly employed by the Phoenicians, Cretans, and Greeks in shipbuilding (Eze 27:6), and it is suggested by some that the "resinous tree" from which Noah obtained wood for the ark was the cypress tree.—Ge 6:14; see RESINOUS TREE.

At Isaiah 41:19 Jehovah promises to cause trees growing normally in fertile lands to thrive in desert areas as well, and in a prophecy concerning Zion's future exaltation and prosperity, it is foretold that the cypress, along with the ash and the juniper, will be used to beautify the place of God's sanctuary.—Isa 60:13.

At Ezekiel 27:6, the expression "in cypress wood" is in agreement with the Targums. However, the Hebrew is bath-'ashu·rim' and means "the daughter of the Ashurites." A number of scholars have concluded that these two Hebrew words should read as one word, bith·'ash·shu·rim', meaning "in cypress wood."

CYPRUS (Cy'prus). An island in the NE corner of the Mediterranean Sea, situated about 70 km (43 mi) from the coast of Cilicia in Asia Minor and about 100 km (62 mi) from the Syrian coast. Cyprus is the third-largest island of the Mediterranean, coming after Sicily and Sardinia. The main body of Cyprus is about 160 km (100 mi) long, but a narrow arm of land extends out at the NE corner about another 72 km (45 mi). The island is 97 km (60 mi) across at its broadest point. The SW section is mountainous, with one peak (Mount Olympus, or Troodos) rising to 1,951 m (6,401 ft). Another mountain range runs along the northern coast, and between these two ranges lies the central plain. Winter caps the mountain peaks with snow, while summer brings hot, dry weather to the plains. From ancient times the island was famous for its rich copper resources, and the name of the island became synonymous with this metal. (The English word "copper" is derived from the Greek Ky'pros.)

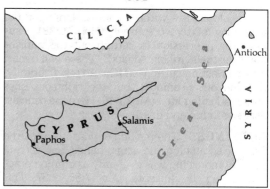

Historical evidence points principally to Cyprus as the "Kittim" of the Hebrew Scriptures. (Isa 23:1, 12; Da 11:30) The island was renowned not only for its copper but also for its fine timber, particularly cypress wood, which was apparently exported to Tyre on the Phoenician coast for use in shipbuilding.—Eze 27:2, 6.

Because of its associations with the Biblical Kittim, it is to be expected that the original population of Cyprus would show some connection with Greece. (See Ge 10:4; Javan is the progenitor of the Ionians or early Greeks.) And, as is shown in the article KITTIM, this connection did exist.

The kings of the city-states of Cyprus were under Greek rule following Alexander the Great's victory at the Battle of Issus in 333 B.C.E. After Alexander's death, the Ptolemaic dynasty of Egypt took control, and Cyprus remained for the most part within the Egyptian realm until 58 B.C.E., when it was annexed by Rome. Though not specifically listed, it is likely that Jews from Cyprus were present in Jerusalem at the feast of Pentecost in 33 C.E. The Levite Joseph, better known as Barnabas, was born in Cyprus.—Ac 4:36.

Christianity. As a result of the persecution of Christians that followed the martyrdom of Stephen, the disciples were dispersed, and some of them went to Cyprus, where they witnessed to the resident Jews. Certain Cypriot Christians went to the city of Antioch, opposite Cyprus on the Syrian coast, and preached with much success among people who, like themselves, were Greek speaking. (Ac 11:19, 20) When Paul and Barnabas, accompanied by John Mark, were sent out from Antioch on their first missionary tour (c. 47-48 C.E.), their initial territory was in Barnabas' home island, Cyprus. Arriving at the important commercial city of Salamis, on the E coast of Cyprus, they found more than one synagogue, indicating a Jewish population of some size. After publishing God's word here, they traveled across the entire island to Paphos on the W coast, then the Roman provincial capital. Here the encounter with the interested proconsul, Sergius Paulus, and with the opposing sorcerer, Elymas (Bar-Jesus), took place.—Ac 13:1-12.

Historian Luke's reference to a proconsul on Cyprus is accurate. Cyprus had been transferred to the control of the Roman Senate in 22 B.C.E., and hence the appointed governor of the island thereafter bore the title, not of legate, but of proconsul, a deputy governor acting as the Senate's representative.

From the port of Paphos, Paul and his companions sailed to Pamphylia on the Asia Minor coast. (Ac 13:13) About two years later Barnabas returned to his homeland with John Mark to do further discipling work, while Paul set out on his second missionary journey through Asia Minor (c. 49 C.E.). (Ac 15:36-41) At the close of Paul's third tour (c. 56 C.E.), when sailing from Patara on the SW coast of Asia Minor en route to Phoenicia, the apostle passed within sight of Cyprus but "left it behind on the left side," evidently passing the SW end of the island as the ship headed for Tyre. (Ac 21:1-3) Not long thereafter, on arriving in Jerusalem, Paul was entertained at the home of Mnason, who, like Barnabas, was a native of Cyprus. (Ac 21:15, 16) On Paul's voyage to Rome his ship sailed "under the shelter of Cyprus, because the winds were contrary." Since the prevailing winds at that time of year are from the W and NW, which would work against crossing the open sea, this evidently caused the ship to sail around the E end of Cyprus and then along the coast of Asia Minor, where land breezes would help it along on its westward course.—Ac 27:4, 5, 9, 12.

CYRENE (Cy·re′ne), CYRENIAN (Cy·re′ni·an).

Cyrene was the original ancient capital of the district of Cyrenaica on the N coast of Africa, nearly opposite the island of Crete. It was situated some 16 km (10 mi) inland and lay on a plateau 550 m (1,800 ft) above the Mediterranean Sea. Ancient Cyrene is today a mass of uninhabited remains near modern Shahhat (formerly Cirene) in Libya.

Cyrene was apparently first settled by the Greeks in the seventh century B.C.E. and came to be considered one of their greatest colonies. By 96 B.C.E. Cyrene was under Roman political control, and in 67 B.C.E. the district of Cyrenaica and the island of Crete were united to form a single province.

Simon of Cyrene (perhaps a Hellenistic Jew), who was pressed into assisting in the carrying of Jesus' torture stake, is called "a native" of that city. (Mt 27:32; Mr 15:21; Lu 23:26) It may be that, though born in Cyrene, Simon later settled in Palestine. On the basis of Acts 6:9 concerning the "Cyrenians" that disputed with Stephen, many scholars believe that there were sufficient numbers of Jews from Cyrene regularly residing in Palestine for them to have established their own synagogue in Jerusalem.

On the other hand, Simon, "a native of Cyrene," may have been among the other foreigners who crowded into Jerusalem at Passover time. In a similar manner, 51 days later, a large number of "reverent men, from every nation," including some from "the parts of Libya, which is toward Cyrene," were in attendance at the Jewish Festival of Pentecost. (Ac 2:5, 10, 41) Some of these latter ones were likely among the "about three thousand souls" that were baptized after the outpouring of the holy spirit and Peter's subsequent discourse, and they may have thereafter carried the message of Christianity back to their homeland.

Christianity. A few years later, after Cornelius had become a Christian, men from Cyrene assisted in spearheading the introduction of "the good news of the Lord Jesus" at Syrian Antioch among those referred to (by most Greek texts of Ac 11:20) as *Hel·le·ni·stas′*. Since this same Greek word is translated "Greek-speaking Jews" (*AT, NW*) at Acts 6:1, some have concluded that those preached to in Syrian Antioch must also have been circumcised Jews or proselytes who spoke the Greek tongue. However, while the preaching to Greek-speaking Jews and proselytes had been going on since the day of Pentecost 33 C.E., the conversion of the large numbers at Antioch appears to have been something new and unusual, since Barnabas was dispatched to that city likely to investigate as well as encourage the work there. (Ac 11:22, 23) Also indicating that this was a change in discipling procedures is the fact that the work done by the Cyrenians and their coworkers seems to be set off in contrast to the preaching among the "Jews only" done by others who had traveled to Antioch. (Ac 11:19, 20) In view of this and also the fact that a number of reliable ancient Greek manuscripts use the word *Hel′le·nas* (meaning "Greeks"; see Ac 16:3) instead of *Hel·le·ni·stas′*, most modern translators refer to those converted with the assistance of the men from Cyrene as "Greeks" (*AS, AT, Da, Fn, JB, Mo, RS*), though others prefer "heathen" (*CK*) or

"Gentiles" (*TEV, NE*), which terms would indicate that the ones at Antioch were not adherents to the Jewish religion. However, some scholars acknowledge the possibility that these at Antioch may have been *both* Jews and Gentiles familiar with the Greek language, and so they describe them with the expression "Greek-speaking people." (*NW*) "Lucius of Cyrene" was listed among the teachers and prophets in this Antioch congregation when Paul started on his first missionary tour in about 47 C.E.—Ac 11:20; 13:1.

CYRUS (Cy'rus). The founder of the Persian Empire and the conqueror of Babylon; called "Cyrus the Great," thereby distinguishing him from Cyrus I, his grandfather.

Following his conquest of the Babylonian Empire, Cyrus is represented in the cuneiform document known as the Cyrus Cylinder as saying: "I am Cyrus, king of the world, great king, legitimate king, king of Babylon, king of Sumer and Akkad, king of the four rims (of the earth), son of Cambyses (*Ka-am-bu-zi-ia*), great king, king of Anshan, grandson of Cyrus [I], . . . descendant of Teispes . . . of a family (which) always (exercised) kingship." (*Ancient Near Eastern Texts,* edited by J. Pritchard, 1974, p. 316) Cyrus is thus shown to be of the royal line of the kings of Anshan, a city or district of rather uncertain location, placed by some in the mountains to the N of Elam but generally thought to have been to the E of Elam. This line of kings is called the Achaemenian line after Achaemenes the father of Teispes.

The early history of Cyrus II is somewhat obscure, depending largely upon rather fanciful accounts by Herodotus (Greek historian of the fifth century B.C.E.) and Xenophon (another Greek writer of about a half century later). However, both present Cyrus as the son of the Persian ruler Cambyses by his wife Mandane, the daughter of Astyages, king of the Medes. (*Herodotus,* I, 107, 108; Xenophon's *Cyropaedia,* I, ii, 1) This blood relationship of Cyrus with the Medes is denied by Ctesias, another Greek historian of the same period, who claims instead that Cyrus became Astyages' son-in-law by marrying his daughter Amytis.

Cyrus succeeded his father Cambyses I to the throne of Anshan, which was then under the suzerainty of the Median king Astyages. Diodorus (first century B.C.E.) places the start of Cyrus' reign in the first year of the 55th Olympiad, or 560/559 B.C.E. Herodotus relates that Cyrus revolted against the Median rulership and, because of the defection of Astyages' troops, was able to gain an easy victory and capture the capital of the Medes, Ecbatana. According to the Nabonidus Chronicle, King Ishtumegu (Astyages) "called up his troops and marched against Cyrus, king of Anshan, in order to me[et him in battle]. The army of Ishtumegu revolted against him and in fetters they de[livered him] to Cyrus." (*Ancient Near Eastern Texts,* p. 305) Cyrus was able to gain the loyalty of the Medes, and thus Medes and Persians thereafter fought unitedly under his leadership. In the following years Cyrus moved to establish his control over the western sector of the Median Empire, advancing all the way to the eastern border of the Lydian Empire at the Halys River in Asia Minor.

Next, Cyrus defeated wealthy King Croesus of Lydia and captured Sardis. He then subdued the Ionian cities and placed all Asia Minor within the realm of the Persian Empire. Thus, in a matter of a few years, Cyrus had become the major rival of Babylon and its king, Nabonidus.

Conquest of Babylon. Cyrus now girded for a confrontation with mighty Babylon, and from this point forward, in particular, he figured in the fulfillment of Bible prophecy. In Isaiah's inspired restoration prophecy concerning Jerusalem and its temple, this Persian ruler had been named as the one appointed by Jehovah God to effect the overthrow of Babylon and the release of the Jews who would be exiled there. (Isa 44:26–45:7) Although this prophecy had been recorded well over one and a half centuries before Cyrus' rise to power and though the desolation of Judah evidently took place before Cyrus was even born, still Jehovah declared that Cyrus would act as His "shepherd" on behalf of the Jewish people. (Isa 44:28; compare Ro 4:17.) By virtue of this advance appointment, Cyrus was called Jehovah's "anointed one" (a form of the Hebrew *ma·shi'ach,* messiah, and the Greek *khri·stos',* christ). (Isa 45:1) God's 'calling him by his name' (Isa 45:4) at that early date does not imply that He gave Cyrus his name at birth, but means that Jehovah foreknew that such a man by that name would arise and that Jehovah's call to him would be, not anonymous, but direct, specific, by name.

Thus, unknown to King Cyrus, who was likely a pagan devotee of Zoroastrianism, Jehovah God had been figuratively 'taking Cyrus' right hand' to lead or strengthen him, girding him and preparing and smoothing the way for his accomplishing the divine purpose: the conquest of Babylon. (Isa 45:1, 2, 5) As the One "telling from the beginning the finale, and from long ago the things that have not been done," Almighty God had shaped the circumstances in human affairs for fully carrying out his counsel. He had called Cyrus "from the sunrising," from Persia (to the E of Babylon), where Cyrus' favorite capital of Pasargadae was built, and Cyrus was to be like "a bird of prey" in swiftly pouncing upon Babylon. (Isa 46:10, 11) It is of note that, according to *The Encyclopædia Britannica* (1910, Vol. X, p. 454), "the Persians bore an eagle fixed to the end of a lance, and the sun, as their divinity, was also represented upon their standards, which . . . were guarded with the greatest jealousy by the bravest men of the army."

How did Cyrus divert the water of the Euphrates?

The Bible prophecies relating to Cyrus' conquest of Babylon foretold that its rivers would be dried up and its gates left unshut, that there would be a sudden invasion of the city and a lack of resistance on the part of Babylon's soldiers. (Isa 44:27; 45:1, 2; Jer 50:35-38; 51:30-32) Herodotus describes a deep, wide moat encompassing Babylon, relating that numerous bronze (or copper) gates provided entrance through the interior walls along the Euphrates River, which bisected the city. Laying siege to the city, according to Herodotus (I, 191, 192), Cyrus went "drawing off the river by a canal into the lake [the artificial lake said to have been made earlier by Queen Nitocris], which was till now a marsh, he made the stream to sink till its former channel could be forded. When this happened, the Persians who were posted with this intent made their way into Babylon by the channel of the Euphrates, which had now sunk about to the height of the middle of a man's thigh. Now if the Babylonians had known beforehand or learnt what Cyrus was planning, they would have suffered the Persians to enter the city and brought them to a miserable end; for then they would have shut all the gates that opened on the river and themselves mounted up on to the walls that ran along the river banks, and so caught their enemies as in a trap. But as it was, the Persians were upon them unawares, and by reason of the great size of the city—so say those who dwell there—those in the outer parts of it were overcome, yet the dwellers in the middle part knew nothing of it; all this time they were dancing and making merry at a festival . . . till they learnt the truth but too well. [Compare Da 5:1-4, 30; Jer 50:24; 51:31, 32.] Thus was Babylon then for the first time taken."

Xenophon's account differs somewhat as to details but contains the same basic elements as that of Herodotus. Xenophon describes Cyrus as deeming it nearly impossible to storm Babylon's mighty walls and then goes on to relate his laying siege to the city, diverting the waters of the Euphrates into trenches and, while the city was in festival celebration, sending his forces up the riverbed past the city walls. The troops under the command of Gobryas and Gadatas caught the guards unawares and gained entrance through the very gates of the palace. In one night "the city was taken and the king slain," and the Babylonian soldiers occupying the various citadels surrendered the following morning.—*Cyropaedia*, VII, v, 33; compare Jer 51:30.

Jewish historian Josephus records an account of Cyrus' conquest written by the Babylonian priest Berossus (of the third century B.C.E.) as follows: "In the seventeenth year of his [Nabonidus'] reign Cyrus advanced from Persia with a large army, and, after subjugating the rest of the kingdom, marched upon Babylonia. Apprised of his coming, Nabonnedus [Nabonidus] led his army to meet him, fought and was defeated, whereupon he fled with a few followers and shut himself up in the town of Borsippa [the twin city of Babylon]. Cyrus took Babylon, and after giving orders to raze the outer walls of the city, because it presented a very redoubtable and formidable appearance, proceeded to Borsippa to besiege Nabonnedus. The latter surrendering, without waiting for investment, was humanely treated by Cyrus, who dismissed him from Babylonia, but gave him Carmania for his residence. There Nabonnedus spent the remainder of his life, and there he died." (*Against Apion*, I, 150-153 [20]) This account is distinct from the others primarily because of the statements made concerning Nabonidus' actions and Cyrus' dealings with him. However, it harmonizes with the Biblical account that Belshazzar, rather than Nabonidus, was the king who was slain on the night of Babylon's fall.—See BELSHAZZAR.

The cuneiform tablets found by archaeologists, though not giving details concerning the exact manner of the conquest, do confirm the sudden fall of Babylon to Cyrus. According to the Nabonidus Chronicle, in what proved to be the final year of Nabonidus' reign (539 B.C.E.) in the month of Tishri (September-October), Cyrus attacked the Babylonian forces at Opis and defeated them. The inscription continues: "The 14th day, Sippar was seized without battle. Nabonidus fled. The 16th day, Gobryas (*Ugbaru*), the governor of Gutium and the army of Cyrus entered Babylon without battle. Afterwards Nabonidus was arrested in Babylon when he returned . . . In the month of Arahshamnu [Marchesvan (October-November)], the 3rd day, Cyrus entered Babylon." (*Ancient Near Eastern Texts,* p. 306) By means of this inscription, the date of Babylon's fall can be fixed as Tishri 16, 539 B.C.E., with Cyrus' entry 17 days later, occurring on Marchesvan 3.

Aryan world domination begins. By this victory Cyrus brought to an end the domination of Mesopotamia and the Middle East by Semitic rulers and produced the first dominant world power of Aryan origin. The Cyrus Cylinder, a cuneiform document historians consider to have been written for publication in Babylon, is strongly religious, and in it Cyrus is represented as ascribing the credit for his victory to Marduk, the chief god of Babylon, saying: "He [Marduk] scanned and looked (through) all the countries, searching for a righteous ruler willing to lead him . . . (in the annual procession). (Then) he pronounced the name of Cyrus (*Ku-ra-as*), king of Anshan, declared him (lit.: pronounced [his] name) to be-(come) the ruler of all the world. . . . Marduk, the great lord, a protector of his people/worshipers, beheld with pleasure his (i.e. Cyrus') good deeds and his upright mind (lit.: heart) (and therefore) ordered him to march against his city Babylon (Ká.dingir.ra). He made him set out on the road to Babylon (DIN.TIR^{ki}) going at his side like a real friend. His widespread troops—their number, like that of the water of a river, could not be established—strolled along, their weapons packed away. Without any battle, he made him enter his town Babylon (Su.an.na), sparing Babylon (Ká-dingir.ra^{ki}) any calamity."—*Ancient Near Eastern Texts,* p. 315.

Why does the Cyrus Cylinder explain Babylon's fall in a manner different from the Bible?

Despite this pagan interpretation of events, the Bible shows that, on making his proclamation authorizing the exiled Jews to return to Jerusalem and rebuild the temple there, Cyrus acknowledged: "All the kingdoms of the earth Jehovah the God of the heavens has given me, and he himself has commissioned me to build him a house in Jerusalem, which is in Judah." (Ezr 1:1, 2) This, of course, does not mean that Cyrus became a Jewish convert but simply that he knew the Biblical facts regarding his victory. In view of the high

administrative position in which Daniel was placed, both before and after the fall of Babylon (Da 5:29; 6:1-3, 28), it would be most unusual if Cyrus were not informed of the prophecies that Jehovah's prophets had recorded and spoken, including Isaiah's prophecy containing Cyrus' very name. As regards the Cyrus Cylinder, already quoted, it is acknowledged that others aside from the king may have had a hand in the preparation of this cuneiform document. The book *Biblical Archaeology* by G. Ernest Wright (1963, p. 203) speaks of "the king, or the bureau which framed the document" (compare the similar case with Darius at Da 6:6-9), while Dr. Emil G. Kraeling (*Rand McNally Bible Atlas,* 1966, p. 328) calls the Cyrus Cylinder "a propaganda document composed by the Babylonian priests." It may, indeed, have been drawn up under the influence of the Babylonian clergy (*Ancient Near Eastern Texts,* p. 315, ftn. 1), thereby serving their purpose of explaining away the utter failure of Marduk (also known as Bel) and the other Babylonian gods to save the city, going even to the extent of attributing to Marduk the very things that Jehovah had done.—Compare Isa 46:1, 2; 47:11-15.

Cyrus' Decree for the Return of the Exiles. By his decreeing the end of the Jewish exile, Cyrus fulfilled his commission as Jehovah's 'anointed shepherd' for Israel. (2Ch 36:22, 23; Ezr 1:1-4) The proclamation was made "in the first year of Cyrus the king of Persia," meaning his first year as ruler toward conquered Babylon. The Bible record at Daniel 9:1 refers to "the first year of Darius," and this may have intervened between the fall of Babylon and "the first year of Cyrus" over Babylon. If it did, this would mean that the writer was perhaps viewing Cyrus' first year as having begun late in the year 538 B.C.E. However, if Darius' rule over Babylon were to be viewed as that of a viceroy, so that his reign ran concurrent with that of Cyrus, Babylonian custom would place Cyrus' first *regnal* year as running from Nisan of 538 to Nisan of 537 B.C.E.

In view of the Bible record, Cyrus' decree freeing the Jews to return to Jerusalem likely was made late in the year 538 or early in 537 B.C.E. This would allow time for the Jewish exiles to prepare to move out of Babylon and make the long trek to Judah and Jerusalem (a trip that could take about four months according to Ezr 7:9) and yet be settled "in their cities" in Judah by "the seventh month" (Tishri) of the year 537 B.C.E. (Ezr 3:1, 6) This marked the end of the prophesied 70 years of Judah's desolation that began in the same month, Tishri, of 607 B.C.E. —2Ki 25:22-26; 2Ch 36:20, 21.

Cyrus' cooperation with the Jews was in notable contrast with their treatment by earlier pagan rulers. He restored the precious temple utensils that Nebuchadnezzar II had carried off to Babylon, gave royal permission for them to import cedar timbers from Lebanon, and authorized the outlay of funds from the king's house to cover construction expenses. (Ezr 1:7-11; 3:7; 6:3-5) According to the Cyrus Cylinder (PICTURE, Vol. 2, p. 332), the Persian ruler followed a generally humane and tolerant policy toward the conquered peoples of his domain. The inscription quotes him as saying: "I returned to [certain previously named] sacred cities on the other side of the Tigris, the sanctuaries of which have been ruins for a long time, the images which (used) to live therein and established for them permanent sanctuaries. I (also) gathered all their (former) inhabitants and returned (to them) their habitations."—*Ancient Near Eastern Texts,* p. 316.

Aside from the royal proclamation quoted in Ezra 1:1-4, the Biblical record speaks of another document by Cyrus, a "memorandum," which was filed away in the house of the records at Ecbatana in Media and was discovered there during the reign of Darius the Persian. (Ezr 5:13-17; 6:1-5) Concerning this second document, Professor G. Ernest Wright says, "[it] is explicitly entitled a *dikrona,* an official Aramaic term for a memorandum which recorded an oral decision of the king or other official and which initiated administrative action. It was never intended for publication but solely for the eye of the proper official, following which it was filed away in government archives."—*Biblical Archaeology,* p. 203.

Death and Prophetic Significance. Cyrus is believed to have fallen in battle in 530 B.C.E., though the details are somewhat obscure. Prior to his death, his son Cambyses II evidently became coregent with him, succeeding to the Persian throne as sole ruler when his father died.

The prophecies concerning the sudden fall of symbolic Babylon the Great as set forth in the book of Revelation parallel in major respects the description of Cyrus' conquest of the literal city of Babylon. (Compare Re 16:12; 18:7, 8 with Isa 44:27, 28; 47:8, 9.) The king at the head of the mighty military forces described immediately after the account of symbolic Babylon's fall, however, is no earthly king but the heavenly "Word of God," Jehovah's true anointed Shepherd, Christ Jesus.—Re 19:1-3, 11-16.

D

DABBESHETH (Dab'be·sheth) [Hump]. A town of Zebulun. (Jos 19:11) Its precise location is unknown; however, the site of Tell esh-Shammam (Tel Shem), about 5 km (3 mi) E of Jokneam on the Plain of Jezreel, appears to fit the Biblical context.

DABERATH (Dab'e·rath) [Pasture]. A city mentioned in the boundary list of Zebulun (Jos 19:10, 12) but regarded as belonging to the neighboring tribe of Issachar when later apportioned with its pasture ground to Levites of the family of Gershon. (Jos 21:27, 28; 1Ch 6:71, 72) Daberath is not included in the list of sites assigned to Issachar, but many geographers think it is likely represented by Rabbith at Joshua 19:20, a view that finds support in the text of Vatican Manuscript No. 1209.—See RABBITH.

Daberath is identified today with ruins at Khirbet Dabura (Horvat Devora), near the village of Dabburiya on the NW edge of Mount Tabor.

DAGGER. See ARMS, ARMOR.

DAGGER MEN. The "dagger men" were members of a fanatical political Jewish faction existing in the first century C.E. that engaged in organized political killings. When the Jews rioted against Paul at Jerusalem during his last visit there, the military commander Claudius Lysias suspected the apostle of being the Egyptian who had previously stirred up sedition and had led the 4,000 "dagger men" into the wilderness.—Ac 21:30-38; 23:26, 27.

The Greek expression translated "dagger men" literally means "men of the Sicarii." The Greek word for "Sicarii" (*si·ka'ri·oi*) comes from the Latin *sicarii,* which, in turn, is derived from *sica* (dagger).

According to the Jewish historian Josephus, especially during the festivals, the "dagger men," or Sicarii, with daggers concealed under their garments, mingled among the crowds at Jerusalem and stabbed their enemies in broad daylight. Then, to avoid suspicion, they joined those expressing indignation about the killings. Josephus further indicates that the Sicarii took a leading part in the revolt against Rome. In 66 C.E., a band of Sicarii, under the command of Eleazar, son of Jairus, seized and massacred the Roman garrison at Masada. This band of fanatical patriots continued their defiance of Rome until 73 C.E., in which year the defenses of Masada were breached. The Romans, however, did not have to make an assault on the fortress itself. In order to avoid being captured, the Sicarii had carried out a systematic suicidal massacre of 960 men, women, and children. Only two women and five children, who had hidden in a cave, survived.

DAGON (Da'gon). A god of the Philistines. The existence of cities called "Beth-dagon" (likely named after the god Dagon) in the territories of Judah and Asher suggests that the worship of this deity was well established in Canaan at the time of Israel's conquest of the Promised Land. (Jos 15:41; 19:27) It is believed that the Philistines adopted Dagon worship from the Canaanites.

There is no agreement as to the derivation of the name Dagon. Some scholars associate it with the Hebrew word *dagh* (fish), while others favor linking the name with the Hebrew word *da·ghan'* (grain). At 1 Samuel 5:4 it is stated concerning the fallen Dagon, "Only the fish part [literally, "Only Dagon"] had been left upon him," his head and the palms of his hands having been cut off. The Hebrew word literally meaning "Dagon" in this text has been variously rendered "body" (*NIV, TEV*), "Dagon's body" (*NE*), and "Dagon himself" (*Ro*) by some translators, while others have translated it as "fish portion" (*Le*), "fish-stump" (*Da*), "fishy part" (*Yg*), or "fish part" (*NW*).

Dagon at times figures in the Biblical narratives. By bracing himself against the two middle supporting pillars, Samson caused the collapse of a house at Gaza used for Dagon worship, killing the Philistines who had assembled there. (Jg 16:21-30) At the house of Dagon in Ashdod, the Philistines deposited the sacred ark of Jehovah as a war trophy. Twice the image of Dagon fell on its face before the Ark. The second time the idol itself was broken. Perhaps in order not to defile the place where the pieces of their god had lain, the priests and others entering the temple of Dagon at Ashdod were careful not to tread upon the threshold. (1Sa 5:2-5) By experiencing the painful effects of piles and the ruining of their

land by jerboas, the Philistines came to recognize that the hand of the God of Israel had been hard against them and their god Dagon. (1Sa 5:6, 7; 6:5) When King Saul was discovered among the slain at Gilboa, the Philistines cut off his head. After informing the houses of their idols as well as the people back home, they fastened Saul's skull to the house of Dagon.—1Sa 31:8-10; 1Ch 10:8-10.

It may be that the Philistines carried idols of their god Dagon into battle.—2Sa 5:21.

DALETH [ד] (*da'leth*). The fourth letter of the Hebrew alphabet. There is considerable similarity between the letters *da'leth* [ד] and *rehsh* [ר], allowing for possible scribal errors in copying. This may account for various differences in spelling, such as that of the "Rodanim" at 1 Chronicles 1:7 and the "Dodanim" at Genesis 10:4.

In the Hebrew, this fourth letter is used as the initial letter in the first word of each of the eight verses of Psalm 119:25-32.—See HEBREW, II.

DALMANUTHA (Dal·ma·nu'tha). An area to which Jesus retired by boat with his disciples after the miraculous feeding of 4,000 men near the Sea of Galilee. (Mr 8:1-10) Though various sites have been suggested for Dalmanutha, the name is not referred to in other Biblical or non-Biblical sources, so its exact location remains unknown. Some scholars feel Dalmanutha may be a scribal alteration, since the parallel narrative at Matthew 15:29-39 has "Magadan" and certain ancient manuscripts of Mark's account also use "Magadan" or "Magdala" instead of Dalmanutha. However, since the best Greek manuscripts do have Dalmanutha, instead of considering the term to be a textual error, it seems best to preserve the reading Dalmanutha. Possibly Dalmanutha was simply another name for Magadan, or it may have been a nearby area the name of which, though little used or not widely known, has nevertheless been preserved for us in Mark's Gospel.

DALMATIA (Dal·ma'tia). An area in the mountainous region E of the Adriatic Sea in what is today Yugoslavia. After 9 C.E. it was considered the southernmost of two districts comprising the Roman province of Illyricum, though apparently Dalmatia was often used interchangeably with Illyricum as the name of the province. Paul's companion Titus departed for Dalmatia sometime prior to the apostle's execution, assumed to be about 65 C.E. (2Ti 4:6-10) In the same verse in which Demas is said to have "forsaken" Paul, Titus is mentioned as going there. However, while there are no definite statements as to the purpose of Titus' mission to Dalmatia, it appears he left with Paul's approval. Since Paul, when nearing the completion of his third missionary tour about nine years earlier, had said his circuit extended as far N as Illyricum (Ro 15:19), some scholars reason that Titus was at this time being dispatched to that region to regulate its congregational affairs and engage in missionary activities. If so, he would be acting in a capacity similar to the one he exercised in Crete. (Tit 1:5) In his letter to Titus, Paul had asked him to leave Crete (Tit 3:12), and it seems likely that Titus was with the apostle until his assignment to Dalmatia.

DALPHON (Dal'phon). One of Haman's ten sons.—Es 9:7, 10; see HAMAN.

DAMARIS (Dam'a·ris). A woman who heard Paul's defense at the Athenian Areopagus (Mars' Hill) and became a believer. (Ac 17:33, 34) Damaris possibly was not a Greek, in view of the fact that in Athenian society women normally remained in seclusion. Since Damaris is the only woman named, she may have been of some prominence. There is no valid basis for concluding that she was married to Dionysius, simply because the two are mentioned together.

DAMASCENES (Dam·a·scenes') [Of (Belonging to) Damascus]. The inhabitants of Damascus. (2Co 11:32) Paul used the term when recounting his narrow escape from that city about 20 years after it occurred, as narrated in Acts 9:23-25.

DAMASCUS (Da·mas'cus). An ancient and important city of Syria. Damascus (present-day esh-Sham, or Dimasq) lies at the foot of the Anti-Lebanon Range, with the nearby Arabian-Syrian Desert stretching out before it to the E. (Ca 7:4) To the SW of the city, snowcapped Mount Hermon rises 2,814 m (9,232 ft), marking the southern end of the Anti-Lebanon Range.

The slopes behind Damascus to the W are quite barren, but the cool waters of the Barada River (the Abanah of 2Ki 5:12) come rushing through a gorge in the mountains and flow onto the plain where the city is situated. Thereafter irrigation creates a luxuriant oasis some 16 km (10 mi) wide and 48 km (30 mi) long. This abundant water supply made Damascus a key point on the ancient military and trade routes between the lands of the eastern Mediterranean, the countries of Mesopotamia, and the Orient. Also serving to channel traffic by Damascus are the Lebanon and Anti-Lebanon ranges, since these act as a natural barrier to caravan traffic moving toward or from the Mediterranean seaboard.

Near the city there is a break in the mountain range, and from ancient times, a major highway led through this pass, swung SW to the Jordan River at a point just S of the Hula Basin, then went down along the W side of the Sea of Galilee through the Plains of Megiddo toward the seacoast, and continued S through Philistia and on to Egypt. This was the road over which marched the armies of Egypt, Assyria, Babylon, and Persia. Another prominent route, commonly called the King's Highway (compare Nu 21:22), ran due S from Damascus, following the edge of the plateau E of the Jordan on down to the Red Sea and the Arabian Peninsula. In yet another direction, caravans heading for Mesopotamia first went from Damascus to Tadmor and from there to the Euphrates region. Another route led north to Hamath, Aleppo, and Carchemish.

The plain on which Damascus is situated is a plateau region some 700 m (2,300 ft) above sea level, and the city enjoys a pleasant climate, with average temperatures varying from about 7° C. (45° F.) in winter to 29° C. (84° F.) in summer. The very fertile land produces fine orchards of olives, figs, and apricots, as well as rich grainfields. The city's prosperity, however, came primarily from the commercial traffic and also because it was a natural trading center for nomadic tribes. Damascus is called a "merchant" of Tyre by the prophet Ezekiel, evidently trading wine from the neighboring city of Helbon and reddish-gray wool in exchange for Tyre's exports of manufactured articles. (Eze 27:18) The "streets" that Ben-hadad II offered to be assigned to Ahab in Damascus were evidently for the establishment of bazaars, or markets, to promote Ahab's commercial interests in that Syrian capital.—1Ki 20:34.

History. The initial history of Damascus is unknown. Josephus (*Jewish Antiquities,* I, 145 [vi, 4]) presents the traditional Jewish view that it was founded by Uz, the son of Aram and grandson of Shem, though there are indications of a more southerly position for the descendants of Uz. (Ge 10:21-23; see Uz No. 4.) Abraham likely passed by or through Damascus on his way to the Promised Land. Eliezer, the servant of childless Abraham, was "a man of Damascus." (Ge 15:2) To a place N of Damascus called Hobah, Abraham pursued the invading kings to recover his captive nephew Lot.—Ge 14:1-16.

Opposes Israel. Damascus thereafter disappears from the Biblical account for nearly a thousand years, and when it reappears it is generally as an opponent of the nation of Israel. By then it was the center of one of the many Aramaean kingdoms of Syria. When David fought and defeated the king of Zobah, "Syria of Damascus" came to help the losers. David defeated them as well, stationed garrisons in the Damascene kingdom, and made Damascus tributary to Israel. (2Sa 8:3-6; 1Ch 18:5, 6) During Solomon's reign, however, a fugitive named Rezon from the Aramaean kingdom of Zobah gained control of Damascus, setting himself up as king. His hatred for Israel was vented in acts of aggression.—1Ki 11:23-25.

King Ben-hadad I of Damascus, after first making a covenant with Baasha of the northern kingdom of Israel, sold out to Asa of Judah (977-937 B.C.E.) and invaded his former ally's territory. (1Ki 15:18-20; 2Ch 16:2-4) At the head of a coalition of 32 allied kings, his successor Ben-hadad II made two invasions of the northern kingdom of Israel, suffering defeat both times. (1Ki 20:1, 16-22, 26-34) Though captured on the second attempt, he was released by King Ahab (c. 940-920 B.C.E.) and later, at the battle of Ramoth-gilead, directed his chariot forces against the combined forces of Judah and Israel, defeating them and causing Ahab's death. (1Ki 22:29-37) During the reign of Jehoram of Israel (c. 917-905 B.C.E.), Ben-hadad II mounted a final attempt to capture Samaria but was miraculously routed.—2Ki 6:24; 7:6, 7.

Fulfilling the commission given to his predecessor Elijah, the prophet Elisha went to Damascus and told Hazael he would replace Ben-hadad II as king of Syria. (1Ki 19:15; 2Ki 8:7-13) Prior to Ben-hadad's death, Damascus had been the focal point of Syrian resistance to the expansion of the Assyrian Empire, which was bent on dominating the lands bordering the Mediterranean. As a key junction point on the main route from Mesopotamia to the Mediterranean, Damascus was a principal target. At the head of a coalition of neighboring kingdoms, Damascus resisted with some success a series of attacks by Shalmaneser III of Assyria. One of Shalmaneser's inscriptions records the seizure of the Syrian throne by Hazael. After one major conflict, Shalmaneser bottled up Hazael in Damascus, besieging the city, but was unable to take it.

As king of Damascus, Hazael continued an aggressive policy toward Israel. (2Ki 10:32) Extending Damascene power as far as the Philistine city of Gath, he even invaded Judah, intimidating King Jehoash (898-859 B.C.E.) so that the Judean king paid a huge tribute to spare Jerusalem from Syrian attack. (2Ki 12:17, 18; 13:3, 22; 2Ch 24:23, 24) Under Hazael's successor, Ben-hadad III, the yoke of Damascus was loosened from Israel's territory as Jehoash of Israel (c. 859-845 B.C.E.) inflicted three defeats on Syria. (2Ki 13:24, 25) Then Jeroboam II of Israel (c. 844-804 B.C.E.) pushed deep into Syria as far as "the entering in of Hamath," and "restored Damascus and Hamath to Judah in Israel." (2Ki 14:23-28) This is generally understood to mean the making of these kingdoms tributary, similar to their position under David and Solomon.—1Ki 4:21.

Jehovah's judgments on Damascus. A century later, however, Damascus is shown again in its position as "the head of Syria." (Isa 7:8) During the reign of King Ahaz of Judah (761-746 B.C.E.), Rezin of Damascus, in league with Pekah of Israel, swept through Judah to Elath on the Gulf of 'Aqaba. This so frightened King Ahaz that he sent a bribe to Tiglath-pileser III of Assyria, asking him to divert Syrian pressure from Judah. With alacrity, the Assyrian attacked Damascus, captured it, put Rezin to death, and exiled many of the Damascenes. (2Ki 16:5-9; 2Ch 28:5, 16) Thereby Jehovah's prophecies through Isaiah and Amos were fulfilled (Isa 8:4; 10:5, 8, 9; Am 1:3-5), yet Ahaz, on going to Damascus to meet (and likely pay homage to) Tiglath-pileser, senselessly had a copy made of the Damascene altar for false worship he saw there, and later he sacrificed upon it to "the gods of Damascus."—2Ki 16:10-13; 2Ch 28:23.

Damascus never constituted a threat to Israel thereafter. Though weak militarily, the city evidently regained commercial strength, as is indicated by Ezekiel's prophecy. (Eze 27:18) But Damascus, once so highly praised, was also foretold by Jeremiah to suffer distress as a result of the bad report coming from Hamath and Arpad in northern Syria, a report likely relating to the harsh conquest of the Aramaean kingdoms by the advancing Babylonian armies of Nebuchadnezzar. (Jer 49:23-27) Damascus, the jewel of the desert, would not escape the effects of that conquest. Still later Damascus is included in an adverse pronouncement through Jehovah's prophet Zechariah, whose prophecy was written in 518 B.C.E. The prophecy likely found fulfillment in the time of Alexander the Great, who occupied Syria and Phoenicia following his victory at the Battle of Issus in 333 B.C.E.—Zec 9:1-4.

During the Seleucid period, Damascus was replaced by Antioch as the Syrian provincial capital. King Aretas III of the Arabic Nabataean kingdom captured the city in 85 B.C.E. Rome conquered all of Syria in 64-63 B.C.E., and Damascus continued as a Roman city until 33 C.E. It was listed by Pliny (Roman historian of the first century C.E.) as one of the original ten cities of the Decapolis.

In the first century C.E. When Saul of Tarsus headed for Damascus in his campaign of persecuting Christians, the city had a number of Jewish synagogues. (Ac 9:1, 2) It evidently then formed part of the domain of Nabataean King Aretas IV and was ruled by an appointed governor. (2Co 11:32, 33) After his conversion, blinded Saul was led to a home on the street called Straight. (See STRAIGHT.) Paul (Saul) preached for a time in the synagogues of Damascus, but a murder plot made necessary his escape by night through an opening in the city wall.—Ac 9:11, 17-25; 26:20; Ga 1:16, 17.

DAN [Judge].

1. The 5th of Jacob's 12 sons; born in Paddan-aram. (Ge 35:25, 26) Dan was the firstborn of his mother Bilhah, the maidservant of her barren mistress Rachel, who substituted for her as a secondary wife to Jacob. It was for this reason that Rachel quickly adopted the boy and called his name Dan, saying: "God has acted as my judge . . . so that he gave me a son." (Ge 30:6) The name of Dan's full brother was Naphtali. By the time Jacob moved down into Egypt, taking along the whole household, Dan himself had a son named Hushim (called Shuham at Nu 26:42). (Ge 46:7, 23, 26) Seventeen years later, when dying Jacob called his sons to his bedside, Dan had full legal status along with the other 11 as family heads of the 12 tribes of Israel. In blessing him, Jacob said: "Dan will judge his people as one of the tribes of Israel. Let Dan prove to be a serpent by the roadside, a horned snake at the wayside, that bites the heels of the horse so that its rider falls backward. I shall indeed wait for salvation from you, O Jehovah."—Ge 49:16-18.

2. One of the tribes of Israel, named after the 5th son of Jacob. Dan's son Hushim was also called Shuham, and the Shuhamites were the only family enrolled for Dan. (Nu 26:42) When entering Egypt, Dan had only this one son, yet some two centuries later after coming out of slavery, the tribe numbered 62,700 men 20 years old and upward. (Ge 46:23; Nu 1:1, 38, 39) It was the second most populous tribe as to men of battle age. In the wilderness Dan's tribe, with Ahiezer

as chieftain, was assigned to camp on the N of the tabernacle alongside the tribes of Asher and Naphtali. On the move the tribe marched in the highly important position as rear guard, a compliment to their courage, loyalty, and dependability. —Nu 2:25-31; 10:25.

When the Promised Land was divided up, with chieftain Bukki the son of Jogli representing Dan, as matters turned out, this tribe got one of the smallest territories, despite the fact that it was still the second largest in number. Its lot, however, the seventh, fell on very desirable soil, bordering the tribes of Judah, Ephraim, and Benjamin, a land extending from the fertile valleys of the Shephelah to the seacoast plains of the Mediterranean. But because of not driving out the squatter nations, as Jehovah had commanded, Dan suffered severely. (Nu 26:43; 34:22; Jos 19:40-46; Jg 1:34) It was for such reason that part of the tribe moved to the northern extremity of Palestine and took over the city of Leshem, or Laish, and called it "Dan." (Jos 19:47, 48; Jg 18:11-31) In the course of this exploit the Danites robbed a man named Micah of his carved image and set it up as their own god, notwithstanding that members of Dan had been chosen years earlier to stand for the maledictions from Mount Ebal, which included, "Cursed is the man who makes a carved image or a molten statue, a thing detestable to Jehovah." (De 27:13-15) Dan was conspicuously absent from giving support to Judge Barak against the forces of Sisera.—Jg 5:17.

In Bible history certain individuals of the tribe of Dan distinguished themselves. There was Oholiab, son of Ahisamach, who was given divine wisdom to assist Bezalel; he was a man highly skilled in embroidering and weaving costly materials for the tabernacle furnishings. (Ex 31:1-6; 35:34, 35; 38:22, 23) Samson the faithful servant of Jehovah as judge of Israel for 20 years proved true both Jacob's deathbed prophecy ("Dan will judge his people") and Moses' prediction ("Dan is a lion cub"). (Ge 49:16; De 33:22; Jg 13:2, 24, 25; 15:20) When David became king, 28,600 Danites were numbered among his loyal troops. Later, Azarel the son of Jeroham is mentioned as chief prince of the tribe. (1Ch 12:35; 27:22) The mother of the "skillful man" that the king of Tyre sent to assist Solomon in building the temple was of the tribe of Dan.—2Ch 2:13, 14.

3. A city in the extreme N of Palestine. Prior to its capture by the tribe of Dan, it was called Leshem or Laish by the pagan inhabitants. (Jos

19:47; Jg 18:7, 27) The Danites rebuilt the destroyed city and called it "Dan by the name of their father, Dan." (Jg 18:28, 29) However, the city is mentioned some four centuries earlier by the name of Dan in the account of Abraham's pursuit of Chedorlaomer and his allies all the way "up to Dan." (Ge 14:14) There is nothing to argue against the existence of this name, Dan, as applying to the indicated area in the time of Abraham. The correspondence of this early name to that of the forefather of the tribe of Dan may have been coincidental or even divinely directed.

The name Dan again appears in the Pentateuch at Deuteronomy 34:1, where it is included among the extremities of the territory seen by Moses in his final view of the Promised Land from his position on Mount Nebo. Since Dan is located at the base of the Anti-Lebanon mountains (and not far from Mount Hermon), this may mean that Moses' view reached up to that range. The use of the name Dan here could correspond to its usage in the case of Abraham or could be the result of Joshua's recording the final portion of the book, which includes events following Moses' death.

Dan lay in "the low plain that belonged to Beth-rehob," and this area, N of the waters of Merom and just below Lebanon, was a fertile and very desirable region, well watered. (Jg 18:28) The site has been identified with Tell el-Qadi (Tel Dan), which Arabic name means "Mound of the Judge," thus preserving the meaning of the Hebrew "Dan." Two springs there join to form the Nahr el-Leddan, which is the most abundant in water of the streams that combine a few miles

away to form the Jordan. The city was on a high mound near the southern foot of Mount Hermon and overlooked the spacious Hula Basin. Its position was also strategic, as it lay on the important trade route between Tyre and Damascus.

Dan became synonymous with the extreme N of Israel as shown by the frequent expression "from Dan to Beer-sheba." (Jg 20:1; 1Sa 3:20; 2Sa 3:10; 1Ki 4:25; 2Ch 30:5) There were, in actuality, other towns farther N than Dan, even as there were several towns farther S than Beer-sheba, but apparently Dan was a city of major importance in the N as Beer-sheba was in the S. Because of its position it was logically among the first to suffer when the land was attacked from the N, as in the invasion by Syrian Ben-hadad. (1Ki 15:20; 2Ch 16:4) This is doubtless reflected in Jeremiah's prophetic expressions at Jeremiah 4:15; 8:16. Following the division of the kingdom, Jeroboam set up golden calves at Dan and at Bethel in his effort to divert his subjects from the temple in Jerusalem.—1Ki 12:28-30; 2Ki 10:29.

DANCING. The rhythmic performance of bodily movements, usually accompanied by music, ranging anywhere from a slow tempo to a violent frenzy. Dancing is an outward expression of one's emotions and attitudes, often those of joy and ecstasy, rarely of hatred and revenge (as exhibited in war dances). The emotions and feelings displayed in the dance are heightened by appropriately colored costumes or symbolic accessories.

The art of dancing is of very ancient origin, and from earliest times it has been used by almost all

Ruins of the city of Dan near the headwaters of the Jordan. Here in the far north Jeroboam established a second center for calf worship when ten tribes broke away from Judah

races as a medium of emotional expression, particularly in worship. In the Hebrew Scriptures several expressions occur that are translated "dancing," "circle dances," "dancing around," and "skipping about." The Hebrew verb *chul*, which basically means "whirl; turn," is also rendered "dance." (Jg 21:21; compare Jer 30:23; La 4:6.) Two nouns meaning "dance; circle dance" are drawn from this verb, namely *ma·chohl'* (Jer 31:4; Ps 150:4) and *mecho·lah'.*—Ca 6:13; Jg 21:21.

Victory and Festive Dances. Dancers expressed their heartfelt praise and thanksgiving to Jehovah after Israel witnessed the faith-inspiring demonstration of Jehovah's power in destroying the Egyptians. So, as the men joined Moses in singing a victory song, Miriam led the women in dances to the accompaniment of tambourines. (Ex 15:1, 20, 21) Another victory dance motivated by deep religious feelings was that of Jephthah's daughter, who came out to join her father in praising Jehovah for having given the Ammonites into his hands. (Jg 11:34) The women of Israel, dancing to the music of lutes and tambourines, welcomed Saul and David back after Jehovah's victory over the Philistines. (1Sa 18:6, 7; 21:11; 29:5) Dancing was a part of certain annual festivals in connection with the worship of Jehovah. (Jg 21:19-21, 23) The Psalms also endorse dancing as a means of honoring and praising Jehovah. "Praise Jah, you people! . . . Let them praise his name with dancing. With the tambourine and the harp let them make melody to him." "Praise him with the tambourine and the circle dance."—Ps 149:1, 3; 150:4.

It was a great occasion when the ark of the covenant finally arrived in Jerusalem, especially for King David, who gave way to his emotions in a most vigorous dance. "And David was dancing around before Jehovah with all his power, . . . leaping and dancing around before Jehovah." (2Sa 6:14-17) In the parallel passage David is described as "skipping about."—1Ch 15:29.

Dancing also had a religious significance among the people of the pagan nations. The processions of ancient Babylon and other nations were usually of a religious nature, and often processional dances were staged as part of the event. The dances in Greece usually acted out some legend connected with their gods, who were themselves depicted as dancing. Fertility dances were designed to stimulate the sexual passions of both participants and observers. The Canaanites performed circle dances around their idols and sacred poles honoring the fertility forces of nature. The worship of Baal was associated with wild, unrestrained dances. In Elijah's time there was such a display by the priests of Baal who, in the course of the demonic dance, lacerated themselves with knives as they kept "limping around" the altar. (1Ki 18:26-29) Other translations say they "performed a limping dance" (*AT*), "danced in halting wise" (*JP*), "performed their hobbling dance" (*JB*). On making the golden calf, the Israelites also indulged in a form of pagan dancing before their idol, thus meriting Jehovah's condemnation.—Ex 32:6, 17-19.

Other Bible Mention of Dancing. In Israel, dancing was performed mostly in groups, particularly by women. When men joined in the dance, they were in separate companies; apparently there was no mingling of the sexes in their dances. The dances were both processional and circular (Jg 21:21; 2Sa 6:14-16), but these styles did not make the dances akin to the pagan processional or circle dances. The motives and objectives behind the dances themselves, the announced purpose of the dances, the movements of the dancing bodies, and the ideas such movements convey to observers are the important things to consider and compare in determining resemblance in dance patterns.

In the Christian Greek Scriptures the word *or·khe'o·mai* is translated "dance." According to W. E. Vine it "probably originally signified to lift up, as of the feet; hence, to leap with regularity of motion." (*An Expository Dictionary of New Testament Words*, 1962, Vol. 1, p. 266) Herod was so pleased with Salome's dancing at his birthday party that he granted her request and had John the Baptizer beheaded. (Mt 14:6-11; Mr 6:21-28; see SALOME No. 2.) Jesus Christ likened his generation to the young children he observed playing games and dancing in the marketplace. (Mt 11:16-19; Lu 7:31-35) In Jesus' illustration of the prodigal son, however, a different Greek word is used, *kho·ros'*, from which the English word "chorus" is drawn. This Greek word has reference to a company of dancers, evidently a dancing troupe hired as entertainment for such a festive occasion. —Lu 15:25.

DANIEL (Dan'i·el) [My Judge Is God].

1. David's second son, born to him at Hebron by Abigail. (1Ch 3:1) He is called Chileab at 2 Samuel 3:3. With the slaying of the firstborn, Amnon, he could feel in line for the kingship after David, but no mention is made of a usurpation, suggesting either that he respected the God-given appointment of Solomon or that he died before his father.

2. An outstanding prophet of Jehovah of the tribe of Judah. The writer of the book bearing his name. Very little is known of his early life, but he tells of being taken to Babylon, likely as a teenage prince, along with other royal offspring and nobles. (Da 1:3-6) This was in Jehoiakim's third year (as tributary king to Babylon), which third year started in the spring of 618 B.C.E. (Da 1:1) With Jehoiakim's inglorious death, Jehoiachin, his son, ruled for a few months before surrendering. Early in 617 B.C.E., Jehoiachin and other "foremost men," also young Daniel (2Ki 24:15), were taken into captivity by Nebuchadnezzar.

Under Babylonian Rule. While many of the exiles were located by the river Chebar outside the city of Babylon, Daniel and his three companions were selected to receive special training in the writing and the tongue of the Chaldeans to equip them for governmental service. In accord with custom, they were given Babylonian names, Daniel's being Belteshazzar, according to the name of Nebuchadnezzar's god. (Da 1:7; 4:8; see BELTESHAZZAR.) Not wishing to pollute himself with the foods allotted, which might include some prohibited by the Mosaic Law or defiled by pagan rituals, he made request that their diet be limited to vegetables and water. Jehovah God gave them "knowledge and insight in all writing and wisdom; and Daniel himself had understanding in all sorts of visions and dreams." (Da 1:17) Examined by the king at the end of three years, they were found to be "ten times better than all the magic-practicing priests and the conjurers that were in all his royal realm."—Da 1:20.

Daniel continued in court service until the fall of Babylon. At Daniel chapter 1, verse 19, it is stated that his three companions also "continued to stand before the king" (of Babylon). Whether they lived to hold this position until Babylon's fall is not stated, but Daniel did; and after this he was in the Persian court until at least the third year of Cyrus.—Da 10:1.

Nebuchadnezzar's dreams. In Nebuchadnezzar's second year (probably dating from Jerusalem's overthrow in 607 B.C.E.), he has a dream that 'agitates his spirit.' All the wise men being unable to reveal it, Daniel comes before the king and not only tells him the dream, by divine revelation, but interprets it, thereby saving himself and the other wise men from execution. This prompts Nebuchadnezzar to make Daniel "ruler over all the jurisdictional district of Babylon and the chief prefect over all the wise men." (Da 2:48) His three companions receive high positions outside the court, while Daniel serves in the court of the king.

Just why Daniel was not also involved in the issue of integrity encountered by his companions, Shadrach, Meshach, and Abednego, when commanded to worship the golden image set up in the Plain of Dura, is not certain. (Da 3) The Bible is silent on the matter. Daniel's previous course as well as his later loyalty to God even in danger of death, as described in chapter 6, provides full assurance that, if present, and whatever the circumstances, Daniel did not compromise by bowing before the image. Also, Jehovah's Word expresses his approval of Daniel as wholly devoted, listing him alongside Noah and Job.—Eze 14:14, 20; Mt 24:15; Heb 11:32, 33.

Later Daniel interpreted Nebuchadnezzar's dream, regarding the immense tree that was cut down and then allowed to sprout again, as representing the great Babylonian monarch himself (in the prophecy's first fulfillment). (Da 4:20-22) Nebuchadnezzar would be insane for seven years and then would regain his sanity and his kingdom. Nebuchadnezzar confirmed the fulfillment of the divinely sent dream upon himself, for he saw fit to publicize the occurrence throughout the realm.—Da 4:1, 2.

Visions. During the first and third years of Belshazzar, Daniel received two visions (Da chaps 7, 8) in which various animals represented successive world powers, leading to the time when these would be forcefully broken up and the heavenly rulership would be given to "someone like a son of man." (Da 7:11-14) Whether Daniel was actually in Shushan when he received the vision recorded in chapter 8, or saw himself there in vision, is not certain. It appears that for many years after Nebuchadnezzar's death Daniel was used little, if at all, as counselor, so that the queen (likely the queen mother) found it necessary to bring him to Belshazzar's attention when none of the wise men were able to interpret the ominous handwriting on the palace wall at the time of Belshazzar's riotous and blasphemous feast. As promised, "they heralded concerning [Daniel] that he was to become the third ruler in the kingdom," Nabonidus being first ruler and his son Belshazzar being second. That same night the city fell to the Medes and Persians, and Belshazzar was slain. —Da 5:1, 10-31.

Under Medo-Persian Rule. During the reign of Darius the Mede, Daniel was one of the three high officials appointed over the 120 satraps who were to rule the kingdom. Excelling greatly in governmental service because of divine favor, Daniel was about to be elevated over all the kingdom when envy and jealousy caused the other officials to scheme for his execution. The law that they induced the king to enact would have to be in connection with Daniel's worship of God, as they could find no fault with him otherwise. The king acted reluctantly to carry out the law, which, according to custom, could not be changed, but he did cast Daniel into the pit of the lions. For Daniel's firm integrity and faith, Jehovah sent His angel to deliver him from the lions' mouths. Darius then executed justice on the conspirators, having them destroyed by the same lions.—Da 6.

In the first year of Darius, Daniel discerned the nearness of the end of the 70 years of desolation of Jerusalem, according to the writings of Jeremiah. (Jer 25:11, 12) Humbly Daniel acknowledged the sins of his people and prayed that Jehovah would cause His face to shine upon the desolated sanctuary in Jerusalem. (Da 9:1, 2, 17) He was favored with a revelation through Gabriel, who gave him the prophecy of the 70 weeks, pinpointing the year of Messiah's arrival. Daniel happily lived to see the return of the Jews under Zerubbabel in 537 B.C.E., but it is not stated that he accompanied them. During the third year of Cyrus (536 B.C.E.), Daniel was given a vision by an angel who, in his mission to visit Daniel, had to contend with the prince of Persia. The angel spoke to reveal what was to "befall [Daniel's] people in the final part of the days, because it is a vision yet for the days to come." (Da 10:14) Starting with the kings of Persia, he recorded history in advance. The prophecy revealed that the world scene would come to be dominated by two main opposing political powers, termed "the king of the north" and "the king of the south," which situation would prevail until the standing up of Michael, with a great time of distress to follow.—Da chaps 11, 12.

Daniel may not have lived much beyond the third year of Cyrus. If he was a teenager at the time of being brought to Babylon in 617 B.C.E., he would be almost 100 years old when he received that vision recorded in chapters 10 through 12. The angel's statement to Daniel, "As for you yourself, go toward the end; and you will rest, but you will stand up for your lot at the end of the days," seems to imply that his life was nearing its close, with assurance of a resurrection for him.—Da 12:13.

Daniel's Writership. Daniel is referred to by Christ (Mt 24:15) and alluded to at Hebrews 11: 33. It cannot be demonstrated successfully by the critics that one or more later writers of Maccabean times had to do with the writing of all or parts of the canonical book of Daniel. However, three additions called "The Song of the Three Holy Children," "Susanna and the Elders," and "The Destruction of Bel and the Dragon" are Apocryphal and are by a later hand. These and other writings that claim Daniel as the writer or that set forth unusual feats or teachings by him are more in the realm of fable, revolving around the great fame of Daniel, and are not reliable. —See APOCRYPHA; also DANIEL, BOOK OF.

3. A priest of the Levite house of Ithamar who accompanied Ezra to Jerusalem in 468 B.C.E. (Ezr 8:2) Possibly the same priest or his descendant signed the confession contract during Nehemiah's governorship (Ne 10:6), but he was not the same person as the prophet Daniel, who was of the tribe of Judah.—Da 1:6.

DANIEL, BOOK OF.

A prophetic book placed in the English Bible among the major prophets, immediately after Ezekiel. This is the order followed in the Greek *Septuagint* and in the Latin *Vulgate*. In the Hebrew canon, Daniel is placed in the "Writings" or "Hagiographa."

Writer. That Daniel was the writer is made evident by the book itself. It reports: "In the first year of Belshazzar the king of Babylon, Daniel himself beheld a dream and visions of his head upon his bed. At that time he wrote down the dream itself. The complete account of the matters he told." (Da 7:1) His being the writer is also apparent from the fact that chapters 7 through 12 are written in the first person.

Chapters 1 through 6 are written in the third person, but this does not argue against Daniel's writership. He took the position of an observer who was reporting what was happening to himself and others. Another Bible writer, Jeremiah, does this frequently. (See Jer 20:1-6; 21:1-3; and chaps 26, 36.) Again, Jeremiah writes in the first person.—Jer 1, 13, 15, 18; see DANIEL No. 2.

Setting and Time of Writing. The setting of the book is in Babylon, with one of its visions in Shushan by the river Ulai. Whether Daniel was in Shushan in reality or in a visionary way is not clear. The writing was completed in about 536 B.C.E., and the book covers the period from 618 to about 536 B.C.E.—Da 8:1, 2.

Authenticity. Some critics question the authenticity of Daniel, assuming the position taken by a third-century heathen philosopher and enemy of Christianity, Porphyry, who contended that the book of Daniel was forged by a Palestinian

HIGHLIGHTS OF DANIEL

Prophecies concerning the rise and fall of human governments from ancient Babylon until God's Kingdom crushes all of them and takes over world rulership

Written by Daniel, who was in Babylon from 617 B.C.E. until after the Jewish exiles returned to Jerusalem in 537 B.C.E.

Daniel and three companions when exiles in Babylon demonstrate integrity to Jehovah

While being prepared for service in Nebuchadnezzar's court, they abstain from his wine and delicacies; God favors them with knowledge and insight (1:1-21)

Shadrach, Meshach, and Abednego refuse to join in worshiping Nebuchadnezzar's giant image; they firmly tell the angry king that they will not worship his gods; he has them bound and thrown into superheated furnace; angel delivers them without injury (3:1-30)

Jealous officials scheme against Daniel; despite an interdict forbidding it, he continues to pray to his God and does not try to conceal that fact; is thrown into lions' pit; angel delivers him uninjured (6:1-28)

Prophetic dreams and visions point to God's Kingdom in the hands of his Messiah

Immense image that is crushed by stone cut without hands out of a mountain; the image depicts the succession of world powers starting with Babylon and ending with all of them being crushed and replaced by the Kingdom of God (2:1-49)

Immense tree that is cut down and banded for seven times; initially fulfilled when the king goes insane and lives like a beast for seven years, until he recognizes that the Most High is Ruler in the kingdom of mankind and that He gives rulership to the one He chooses (4:1-37)

Handwriting appears on the wall when Belshazzar uses vessels from Jehovah's temple to toast his idol gods; Daniel is called, fearlessly rebukes the king, explains the writing, telling him that his kingdom has been given to the Medes and the Persians (5:1-31)

March of world powers depicted by lion, bear, leopard, fearsome beast with ten horns, as well as a small horn from the head of the latter beast; then the Ancient of Days gives rulership over all peoples to one like a son of man (7:1-28)

Ram, male goat, and small horn represent world powers to succeed Babylon; small horn defies Prince of the army of the heavens, then is broken without a hand (8:1-27)

Seventy weeks (of years); after 7 + 62 weeks Messiah is to appear and thereafter be cut off; covenant (Abrahamic) to be kept in force for Jews exclusively for one week (9:1-27)

Struggle between king of the north and king of the south, the standing up of Michael as deliverer, and events that follow this (10:1–12:13)

Jew of the time of Antiochus Epiphanes. This forger, he theorized, took past events and made them appear to be prophecies. The genuineness of the book of Daniel was not seriously questioned, however, from that day until the early part of the 18th century. Jesus Christ's own acceptance of Daniel's prophecy is an even more significant evidence of its authenticity.—Mt 24:15; Da 11:31.

Historical. Several manuscripts of parts of the book of Daniel were found in the Dead Sea caves. The earliest manuscript dates from the first half of the first century B.C.E.; the book of Daniel was an accepted part of the Scriptures in that time and was so well known to the Jews that many copies had already been made of it. That it was recognized as a canonical book of that time is supported by the writer of the Apocryphal, but historical, book of First Maccabees (2:59, 60), who made reference to Daniel's deliverance from the den of lions, and that of the three Hebrews from the fiery furnace.

We have also the testimony of the Jewish historian Josephus, who states that the prophecies of Daniel were shown to Alexander the Great when he entered Jerusalem. This occurred in about 332 B.C.E., more than 150 years before the Maccabean period. Josephus says of the event: "When the book of Daniel was shown to him, in which he had declared that one of the Greeks would destroy the empire of the Persians, he believed himself to be the one indicated." (*Jewish Antiquities,* XI, 337 [viii, 5]) History also recounts that Alexander bestowed great favors on the Jews, and this is believed to have been because of what Daniel said about him in prophecy.

Language. Daniel 1:1–2:4a and 8:1–12:13 are written in Hebrew, while Daniel 2:4b–7:28 is written in Aramaic. Regarding the vocabulary used in the Aramaic portion of Daniel, *The International Standard Bible Encyclopedia* (Vol. 1, p. 860) says: "When the Aramaic vocabulary of Daniel is examined, nine-tenths of it can be attested immediately from West Semitic inscriptions, or papyri from the 5th cent. B.C. or earlier. The remaining words have been found in sources such as Nabatean or Palmyrene Aramaic, which are later than the 5th cent. B.C. While it is at least theoretically possible that this small balance of vocabulary suddenly originated after the 5th cent. B.C., it is equally possible to argue from a fifth-century B.C. written form to an earlier oral one. By far the most probable explanation, however, is that the missing tenth represents nothing more serious than a gap in our current knowledge of the linguistic situation, which we may confidently expect to be filled in process of time." —Edited by G. Bromiley, 1979.

There are some so-called Persian words in Daniel, but in view of the frequent dealings that the Jews had with Babylonians, Medes, Persians, and others, this is not unusual. Furthermore, most of the foreign names used by Daniel are names of officials, articles of clothing, legal terms, and such, for which the Hebrew or Aramaic of the time apparently had no equally suitable terms. Daniel was writing for his people who were for the most part in Babylonia, and many were scattered in other places at this time. Therefore, he wrote in language that would be understandable to them.

Doctrinal. Some critics object because Daniel alludes to the resurrection. (Da 12:13) They assume that this is a doctrine that was developed later or was taken from a pagan belief, but the reference in Daniel is in agreement with the rest of the Hebrew Scriptures, which contains statements of belief in a resurrection. (Job 14:13, 15; Ps 16:10) Also, there are actual instances of resurrection. (1Ki 17:21, 22; 2Ki 4:22-37; 13:20, 21) And on no less authority than the apostle Paul we have the statement that Abraham had faith in the raising up of the dead (Heb 11:17-19) and also that other faithful servants of God of ancient times looked forward to the resurrection. (Heb 11:13, 35-40; Ro 4:16, 17) Jesus himself said: "But that the dead are raised up even Moses disclosed, in the account about the thornbush, when he calls Jehovah 'the God of Abraham and God of Isaac and God of Jacob.'"—Lu 20:37.

Those who claim that the book is not really prophetic but was written after the events occurred would have to move up the time of writing of the book beyond the days of Jesus' ministry on earth, for the ninth chapter admittedly contains a prophecy concerning the Messiah's appearance and sacrifice. (Da 9:25-27) Also, the prophecy continues on and recounts the history of the kingdoms that would rule right down to "the time of the end," when they will be destroyed by the Kingdom of God in the hands of his Messiah.—Da 7:9-14, 25-27; 2:44; 11:35, 40.

Value of the Book. Daniel is outstanding in his recording of prophetic time periods: The 69 weeks (of years) from the decree to rebuild Jerusalem to the coming of the Messiah; the events to take place within the 70th week, and the destruc-tion of Jerusalem to follow soon afterward (Da 9:24-27); the "seven times," which Jesus called "the appointed times of the nations" and indicated were still running at the time that he was on earth, with their conclusion at a much later date (Da 4:25; Lu 21:24); the periods of 1,290, 1,335, and 2,300 days; and "an appointed time, appointed times and a half." All of these time prophecies are vital to an understanding of God's dealings with his people.—Da 12:7, 11, 12; 8:14; see APPOINTED TIMES OF THE NATIONS; SEVENTY WEEKS.

Daniel also gives details concerning the rise and fall of world powers from the time of ancient Babylon right on down till the time when the Kingdom of God crushes them out of existence forever. The prophecy directs attention to the Kingdom of God, in the hands of his appointed King and his associate "holy ones," as the government that will endure forever, for the blessing of all who serve God.—Da 2:44; 7:13, 14, 27.

The angel's inspired interpretation of the prophecy regarding the beasts as representing world powers (Da 7:3-7, 17, 23; 8:20, 21) is of great assistance in understanding the symbolism of the beasts in Revelation.—Re 13:1-18; see BEASTS, SYMBOLIC.

Daniel's record of the deliverance of his three companions from the fiery furnace for refusing to bow down before Nebuchadnezzar's great golden image (Da 3) is an account of the legal establishment of the right of Jehovah's worshipers to give Him exclusive devotion, in the realm of the first world power during the "Gentile times." It also helps Christians to discern that their subjection to the superior authorities, as mentioned at Romans 13:1, is relative, in harmony also with the actions of the apostles in Acts 4:19, 20 and 5:29. It strengthens Christians as to their position of neutrality as regards the affairs of the nations, revealing that their neutrality may bring them into difficulty, but whether God delivers them at the time, or even permits them to be killed for their integrity, the Christian position is that they will worship and serve Jehovah God alone.—Da 3:16-18.

DANITES.   See DAN No. 2.

DAN-JAAN   (Dan-ja'an). A place mentioned only once, on the route followed by Joab when taking the census ordered by David. (2Sa 24:1-6) The description seems to place its location in the extreme N of Israel, since it is stated that they went "on to Dan-jaan and went around to Sidon." The fact that Beer-sheba is mentioned in the following verse (2Sa 24:7) calls to mind the common expression "from Beer-sheba to Dan," used by David in instructing Joab about the census. (1Ch 21:2) Dan-jaan may therefore refer to the city of Dan or possibly a suburb of that northern city.—Compare Jg 18:28, 29, where Dan and Sidon are also mentioned jointly; see also DAN No. 3.

DANNAH (Dan'nah). A city situated in the mountainous region of Judah. (Jos 15:49) Its exact location is unknown today.

DARA (Da'ra), **DARDA** (Dar'da). A descendant of Judah through Zerah (1Ch 2:4, 6); his wisdom, though great, was not equal to Solomon's.—1Ki 4:31; see MAHOL.

DARIC. A Persian gold coin weighing 8.4 g (0.27 oz t) and hence presently evaluated at $94.50. The obverse side of a daric that was coined for two centuries from the latter part of the sixth century B.C.E. onward depicts a king in a half-kneeling position, with a spear in his right hand and a bow in his left. The reverse side shows the oblong punch impression made when the coin was stamped. At 1 Chronicles 29:7 one of the figures for temple contributions during David's reign is stated in terms of darics, although the Persian daric was unknown in David's time. Evidently the writer of Chronicles converted the original figure into terms then current and familiar to his readers.—Ezr 8:27.

Gold daric

DARIUS (Da·ri'us). In the Biblical record, the name is applied to three kings, one a Mede, the other two Persians. Some consider it possible that "Darius" may have been used, at least in the case of Darius the Mede, as a title or throne name rather than a personal name.

1. Darius the Mede, successor to the kingdom of the Chaldean king Belshazzar following the conquest of Babylon by the forces of Cyrus the Persian, at which time Darius was about 62 years of age. (Da 5:30, 31) He is further identified as "the son of Ahasuerus of the seed of the Medes." —Da 9:1.

Exercising his administrative capacity, Darius appointed 120 satraps to serve throughout the realm, and he also appointed three high officials who, acting on behalf of the king's interests, had jurisdiction over the satraps. The prime concern of the arrangement may well have been financial, as the collecting of revenues and tributes for the royal coffers was one of the chief duties of satraps. (Compare Ezr 4:13.) One member of the triumvirate of high officials assigned was Daniel, who so distinguished himself over the other officials and satraps that Darius contemplated making him prime minister. Evidently because of envy, though perhaps also because of resentment of the restraint against corruption and graft that Daniel's integrity doubtless produced, the other two high officials, in league with the satraps, devised a legal trap. Appearing as a throng before the king, they presented for the king's signature an edict, ostensibly favored by the entire body of all ranking government officials (Daniel not being mentioned, however). It would prohibit the making of "a petition to any god or man" other than Darius for 30 days. The proposed penalty was that the violator would be thrown into the lions' pit. The decree had all the appearances of serving to establish Darius, a foreigner, firmly in his newly received position as king of the realm and of being an expression of loyalty and support on the part of the government officials advocating it. —Da 6:1-3, 6-8.

Darius signed the decree and soon was faced with the result, one that should have revealed to him the hidden purpose of the edict. For continuing prayer to Jehovah God, Daniel, as the edict's first violator (compare Ac 5:29), was thrown into the lions' pit despite Darius' sincere efforts to find a way of circumventing the unchangeable statute. Darius expressed trust in the power of Daniel's God to preserve him and, after a sleepless night and fasting, hurried to the lions' pit and rejoiced to find Daniel still alive and unharmed. The king then not only had Daniel's accusers and their families thrown into the lions' pit as retributive justice but also had a proclamation made throughout the realm that "in every dominion of my kingdom, people are to be quaking and fearing before the God of Daniel."—Da 6:9-27.

Historical records show that, from ancient times, Mesopotamian kings were viewed as divine and had worship offered to them. Many commentators consider that the restriction on the making of 'petitions' set forth in Darius' edict was entirely with regard to petitions of a religious nature, not applying to requests of a general kind. The existence of a "lions' pit" in Babylon is in conformity with the testimony of ancient inscriptions that show that Oriental rulers frequently had menageries of wild animals. The *Soncino Books of the Bible* (Daniel, Ezra and Nehemiah, p. 49) in commenting on this states: "The Persians are known to have inherited from the Assyrian kings the practice of keeping these animals in their zoological gardens."—Edited by A. Cohen, London, 1951.

After chapter 6 of Daniel the only further mention of Darius is with regard to an event in his "first year" of rule. It was during that year that Daniel "discerned" the 70-year limit on the desolation of Judah and received the revelation concerning the 70 prophetic weeks and Messiah's coming. (Da 9:1, 2, 24-27) The angel who brought Daniel the vision depicting the strivings of "the king of the north" and "the king of the south" also revealed that he had earlier acted as an angelic strengthener and fortress during Darius the Mede's first year. (Da 11:1, 6) Commentators generally have understood that the angel rendered this service to Darius, but it seems more likely that such assistance was given to Michael, who is mentioned in the previous verse (Da 10:21) as contending alongside this particular angelic messenger. Thus there was angelic cooperation and collaboration in contending with the demon 'prince of Persia' who endeavored to thwart the fulfillment of Jehovah's purposes.—Da 10:13, 14.

Identification of Darius the Mede. No reference to "Darius the Mede" has as yet been found in any non-Biblical inscription, nor is he mentioned by ancient secular historians prior to Josephus (Jewish historian of the first century C.E.). This has served as the basis or pretext for many critics to label Darius the Mede as a fictitious personage.

Some scholars present Cambyses (II) as being made "King of Babylon" by his father Cyrus soon after the conquest of Babylon. While Cambyses evidently did represent his father annually at the "New Year's" festival at Babylon, he seems to have resided at Sippar during the rest of the time. Research based on study of cuneiform texts indicates that Cambyses evidently did not assume

the title "King of Babylon" until Nisan 1 of the year 530 B.C.E., being made coregent with Cyrus, who was then setting out on the campaign that resulted in his death. Efforts to associate Darius with Cyrus' son Cambyses II do not agree with Darius' being "about sixty-two years old" at the time of Babylon's fall.—Da 5:31.

The view that Darius might be another name for Cyrus himself does not harmonize with Darius' being a "Mede" and "of the seed of the Medes," this latter expression pointing to his father, Ahasuerus, as Median. Cyrus is definitely called "Persian," and while his mother may have been Median as some historians claim, his father, according to the Cyrus Cylinder, was Cambyses I, a Persian. —Da 9:1; 6:28.

Others would identify Darius with a supposed "uncle" of Cyrus, presented by Greek historian Xenophon as "Cyaxares, the son of Astyages." Xenophon relates that Cyaxares succeeded to the throne of Astyages, the Median king, but that Cyaxares later gave both his daughter and all of Media to his nephew Cyrus. (*Cyropaedia*, I, v, 2; VIII, v, 19) Both Herodotus and Ctesias (Greek historians more or less contemporaneous with Xenophon) give accounts contradicting that of Xenophon, however, and Herodotus (I, 109) claims that Astyages died sonless. The Nabonidus Chronicle shows Cyrus gaining kingship over the Medes through the capture of Astyages. Additionally, this identification of Darius with Cyaxares II would require the assumption that Astyages was known also as Ahasuerus, since Darius the Mede was "the son of Ahasuerus." (Da 9:1) So this view is lacking in confirmation.

Who really was Darius the Mede?

More recently, a number of reference works have favored an identification of Darius with Gubaru (commonly identified with the Gobryas mentioned in Xenophon's *Cyropaedia*), who became governor of Babylon after the Medo-Persian conquest of that city. Basically the evidence they present is as follows:

The ancient cuneiform text known as the Nabonidus Chronicle, in recounting the fall of Babylon, says that *Ugbaru* "the governor of Gutium and the army of Cyrus entered Babylon without battle." Then, after relating Cyrus' entry into the city 17 days later, the inscription states that *Gubaru*, "his governor, installed (sub-) governors in Babylon." (*Ancient Near Eastern Texts*, edited by J. Pritchard, 1974, p. 306; compare *Darius the*

Mede, by J. C. Whitcomb, 1959, p. 17.) Note that the names *"Ugbaru"* and *"Gubaru"* are not the same. While they appear to be similar, in the cuneiform style of writing the sign for the first syllable of Ugbaru's name is quite different from that for Gubaru. The Chronicle states that Ugbaru, the governor of Gutium, died within a few weeks of the conquest. Other cuneiform texts show that Gubaru continued living and served for 14 years as governor not only of the city of Babylon but of the entire region of Babylonia as well as of the "Region beyond the River," which included Syria, Phoenicia, and Palestine down to the Egyptian frontier. Thus Gubaru was ruler over a region that extended the full length of the Fertile Crescent, basically the same area as that of the Babylonian Empire. Darius the Mede, it will be remembered, is spoken of as being "made king over the kingdom of the Chaldeans" (Da 5:31; 9:1), but not as "the king of Persia," the regular form for referring to King Cyrus. (Da 10:1; Ezr 1:1, 2; 3:7; 4:3) So the region ruled by Gubaru would at least appear to be the same as that ruled by Darius.

Since Gubaru is nowhere called "Darius," the suggestion is made that "Darius" was his title or throne name. W. F. Albright states: "It seems to me highly probable that Gobryas [Gubaru] did actually assume the royal dignity, along with the name 'Darius,' perhaps an old Iranian royal title, while Cyrus was absent on an Eastern campaign." (*Journal of Biblical Literature,* 1921, Vol. XL, p. 112, ftn. 19) In answer to the objection that the cuneiform tablets nowhere speak of Gubaru as "king," those advocating Gubaru's identification with King Darius point to the fact that the title of king is likewise not applied to Belshazzar in the cuneiform tablets, yet the cuneiform document known as the "Persian Verse Account of Nabonidus" definitely states that Nabonidus "entrusted the kingship" to his son.

Along this line, Professor Whitcomb points out that, according to the Nabonidus Chronicle, *Gubaru,* as Cyrus' district-governor, "appointed . . . (district-governors) in Babylon," even as Daniel 6:1, 2 shows that Darius "set up over the kingdom one hundred and twenty satraps." Whitcomb therefore holds that Gubaru, as a governor over governors, was likely addressed as king by his subordinates. (*Darius the Mede,* pp. 31-33) And, referring to the extensive region over which Gubaru (Gobryas) exercised dominion, A. T. Olmstead says: "Over this whole vast stretch of fertile country, Gobryas [Gubaru] ruled almost as an independent monarch."—*History of the Persian Empire,* 1948, p. 56.

In harmony with the above, some scholars consider it likely that Darius the Mede was in reality a viceroy who ruled over the kingdom of the Chaldeans but as a subordinate of Cyrus, the supreme monarch of the Persian Empire. A. T. Olmstead observes: "In his dealings with his Babylonian subjects, Cyrus was 'king of Babylon, king of lands.' By thus insisting that the ancient line of monarchs remained unbroken, he flattered their vanity, won their loyalty . . . But it was Gobryas the satrap who represented the royal authority after the king's departure." (*History of the Persian Empire,* p. 71) Those who hold that the Biblical Darius was indeed such a vicegerent point to the fact that Darius is stated to have *"received* the kingdom" and that he was *"made* king over the kingdom of the Chaldeans" as evidence that he was indeed subordinate to a superior monarch.—Da 5:31; 9:1; compare 7:27, where "the Supreme One," Jehovah God, *gives* the Kingdom to "the holy ones."

While in many respects the information available concerning Gubaru appears to parallel that regarding Darius, and while Darius may have been a viceroy under Cyrus, still such identification cannot be considered conclusive. The historical records do not tell us Gubaru's nationality nor his parentage to show thereby that he was a "Mede" and "the son of Ahasuerus." They do not show that he had kingly authority to the extent of being able to make a proclamation or edict of the nature described at Daniel 6:6-9. Additionally, the Bible record appears to indicate that Darius' rule over Babylon was not of long duration and that Cyrus thereafter took over the kingship of Babylon, though it is possible that they ruled concurrently and that Daniel made special mention of only the year that Darius came to prominence in Babylon. (Da 6:28; 9:1; 2Ch 36:20-23) Gubaru continued in his position for 14 years.

Why historical identification is uncertain. The truth of the Bible account is, of course, not dependent upon confirmation by secular sources. The numerous cases where individuals or events recorded in the Bible, once rejected as 'unhistorical' by critics, have eventually been demonstrated beyond denial to be historical should protect the student of God's Word against giving undue weight to adverse criticism. (See BELSHAZZAR; SARGON.) The hundreds of thousands of cuneiform tablets unearthed in the Middle East still present a very imperfect history with various gaps and blanks. As for other sources, the ancient secular historians, copies of whose writings have survived (though often in fragmentary form), were few in number, the majority of them Greek, and they were separated from the events in the book of Daniel by one, two, or more centuries.

A far more cogent reason, however, for the lack of information concerning Darius in the Babylonian records is provided by the book of Daniel itself. It shows that Darius assigned Daniel to a high position in the government, much to the distaste of the other high officials. Their plot against Daniel was abortive, and Darius executed Daniel's accusers and their families, likely incurring the animosity of the remaining officials by doing so. Darius' proclamation ordering all in the kingdom to 'fear before the God of Daniel' inevitably must have caused deep dissatisfaction and resentment among the powerful Babylonian clergy. Since the scribes were assuredly under the direction of the aforementioned elements, it would not be in the least strange if the records were subsequently altered and evidence concerning him eliminated. Similar actions are known to have been taken in the history of those times.

The dual form of the Medo-Persian rule presented in the Bible must therefore be given its proper weight. (Da 5:28; 8:3, 4, 20) Though secular history accords overwhelming prominence to Cyrus and the Persians, the Bible record shows that the Medes continued in an apparent partnership arrangement with the Persians, and the laws continued to be those of "the Medes and the Persians." (Da 6:8; Es 1:19) The Medes played a major part in the overthrow of Babylon. (Isa 13:17-19) Note, too, that Jeremiah (51:11) foretold that "the kings [plural] of the Medes" would be among Babylon's attackers. Darius may well have been one of these kings.

2. Darius Hystaspis, also called Darius the Great or Darius I (Persian). He is viewed as one of the outstanding rulers of the Persian Empire. Darius describes himself as "son of Hystaspes, an Achaemenid, a Persian, son of a Persian, an Aryan, of Aryan seed." (*History of the Persian Empire*, pp. 122, 123) He thus claimed royal descent from the same ancestor as Cyrus the Great, though being of a different family branch from Cyrus.

Following the death of Cambyses II in 522 B.C.E. while he was returning from Egypt, the Persian throne was occupied for a short time by his brother Bardiya (or possibly by a Magian named Gaumata). Darius, with the aid of six other Persian nobles, slew the occupant of the throne and gained it for himself. Darius' version of this is set forth in three languages in the immense inscription that he had carved on sheer cliffs at Behistun, facing a plain through which ran the principal caravan route from Baghdad to Tehran. According to the inscription, Gaumata was a usurper, posing as Cambyses' brother who had been put to death. Most modern scholars accept this account (which is laced with repeated assurances by Darius that "it is true and not lies") as basically factual, while some believe that Darius was a "monumental liar" and that the evidence indicates him to be the actual usurper. Whatever the case, Darius was faced with an empire in revolt upon assuming the kingship and is considered to have spent the next two years subduing the insurrectionary elements throughout the realm. Egypt, which had thrown off the Persian yoke, was reconquered by Darius about 519-518 B.C.E. Thereafter he extended the imperial borders into India in the E and into Thrace and Macedonia in the W. He is noted as well for his efficient reorganization of the administrative structure throughout the empire, for the formation of an imperial law code, called the Ordinance of Good Regulations, and for having reopened the canal connecting the Nile River of Egypt with the Red Sea.

It is particularly with regard to the rebuilding of the temple at Jerusalem that Darius Hystaspis figures in the Bible record. The temple foundation was laid in 536 B.C.E., but rebuilding work came under ban in 522 B.C.E. and "continued stopped until the second year of the reign of Darius" (520 B.C.E.). (Ezr 4:4, 5, 24) During this year the prophets Haggai and Zechariah stirred up the Jews to renew the construction, and the work got under way again. (Ezr 5:1, 2; Hag 1:1, 14, 15; Zec 1:1) This provoked an inquiry and the sending of a letter to Persian King Darius by Tattenai, the governor representing the imperial interests in the region W of the Euphrates, and other officials. The letter advised him of the construction work, set forth the Jews' claim for the legality of the project, and requested an investigation in the royal archives to see if there existed written evidence to substantiate that claim. (Ezr 5:3-17) The Jewish declaration that contrasted the actions of the Chaldean Nebuchadnezzar, as the destroyer of the temple, with the Persian Cyrus, as the one authorizing its reconstruction, should have had an appropriate and felicitous effect on Darius since, in the first years of his reign, he had to overcome two revolts by rebels each taking the name

Nebuchadnezzar (called Nebuchadnezzar III and Nebuchadnezzar IV by historians), claiming to be sons of Nabonidus, and endeavoring to make Babylon independent of the Persian Empire.

The official search of records in the archives at Ecbatana, the ancient Median capital, uncovered the document by Cyrus. Darius thereupon sent orders to Governor Tattenai that he and the other officials should not only refrain from interfering with the temple work but also provide building funds from "the royal treasury of the tax beyond the River," as well as animals and other necessary supplies for the sacrificial offerings. Anyone violating the king's order was to be impaled on a stake and his house "turned into a public privy." —Ezr 6:1-12.

With this official cooperation and with continued prophetic encouragement (Zec 7:1; 8:1-9, 20-23), the temple work went on to successful completion "by the third day of the lunar month Adar, that is, in the sixth year of the reign of Darius" (Ezr 6:13-15; by March 6 of 515 B.C.E.). Since Darius' inscriptions show him to be a devoted worshiper of Ahura Mazda, it is evident that his action, though serving Jehovah God's purpose and doubtless having His direction, was basically taken out of respect for the irrevocable nature of the Medo-Persian laws and in harmony with a policy of tolerance by Darius' government, evidence for which tolerance is found in some of his inscriptions.

Later Campaigns in Greece. Toward the turn of the century, various Greek cities of Ionia revolted against Persian domination, and though their revolt was quelled, Darius determined to punish Athens and Eretria for their having rendered aid to the rebellious cities. This led to a Persian invasion of Greece, resulting, however, in defeat of Darius' forces at the battle of Marathon in 490 B.C.E. Though Darius made careful preparations for a further Grecian campaign, he was unable to carry it out before his death in 486 B.C.E. He was succeeded by his son Xerxes.

3. Nehemiah 12:22 mentions the recording of Levitical heads of paternal houses "in the days of Eliashib, Joiada and Johanan and Jaddua . . . down till the kingship of Darius the Persian." Since Eliashib was high priest at the time of Nehemiah's return to Jerusalem (Ne 3:1) and since by the time of Nehemiah's second visit to that city (following the 32nd year of Artaxerxes [443 B.C.E.]) Joiada had a married son (Ne 13:28), it is likely that the "Darius" mentioned was Darius Ochus (also called Nothus), who ruled from 423 to 405 B.C.E.

A letter found among the Elephantine Papyri, reckoned as dating from the last years of the fifth century B.C.E., makes reference to "Johanan" as high priest at Jerusalem at that time.

DARKON (Dar′kon). One whose descendants were represented among "the sons of the servants of Solomon" returning with Zerubbabel from Babylonian exile.—Ezr 2:1, 2, 55, 56; Ne 7:6, 7, 57, 58.

DATE. The fruit of the date palm (*Phoenix dactylifera*), a tree common to Palestine. Dates are oval shaped, fleshy, sweet tasting, and produce one seed.

In the Bible account, dates are mentioned only indirectly. For example, the Shulammite maiden describes the dark locks of her shepherd lover's hair as being like "date clusters" ("bushy," *KJ*; Heb., *tal·tal·lim′*; 'date-panicles,' *Lexicon in Veteris Testamenti Libros*, by L. Koehler and W. Baumgartner, Leiden, 1958, p. 1030). Solomon likens her stature to a palm tree and her breasts to "date clusters" ("clusters of grapes," *KJ*) and to "fruit stalks of dates" (Heb., *san·sin·nim′*; see *Lexicon in Veteris Testamenti Libros*, p. 662).—Ca 5:11; 7:7, 8; see PALM TREE.

DATHAN (Da′than). Son of Eliab of the tribe of Reuben and the brother of Abiram and Nemuel. Dathan and Abiram supported the Levite Korah in his rebellion against the authority of Moses and Aaron and, in effect, challenged Jehovah's promises by referring to Egypt as the "land flowing with milk and honey." Because of their rebellion, Dathan and Abiram as well as their households perished when the ground swallowed them up.—Nu 16:1-35; 26:7-11; De 11:6; Ps 106:17; see ABIRAM No. 1.

DAUGHTER. A female offspring; in Hebrew, *bath*, and in Greek, *thy·ga′ter*. (Ge 5:4; Mt 14:6; Ac 21:9) The birth of daughters in the household in Biblical times was not as great an occasion as was the arrival of sons; their position was less honored than that of boys, and their names have not been recorded as often. (1Ch 2:34, 35) Yet most parents dearly loved their daughters and protected their interests. When grieving parents interceded, Jesus healed a Phoenician woman's daughter, and he raised the daughter of Jairus from the dead.—Mt 15:22-28; Lu 8:41, 42, 49-56.

In the patriarchal society, daughters had certain rights, responsibilities, and also limitations. They were assigned various chores. Priests' daughters ate from the priestly portions of sacrifices. (Ge 24:16, 19, 20; 29:6-9; Le 10:14) A daughter was the property of her father until he gave her in marriage (Jos 15:16, 17; 1Sa 18:17, 19, 27), and as such she could even be used as security or sold into slavery, though not to a foreigner. (Ex 21:7-10; Ne 5:2-5) Until she was married, her vows were subject to her father's annulment. (Nu 30:3-5) A father could not lawfully make her a prostitute, and if she were violated, he could collect damages. (Ex 22:16, 17; Le 19:29; De 22: 28, 29) There are instances where fathers offered their virgin daughters to depraved mobs in order to protect their guests. (Ge 19:6-8; Jg 19:22-24) Daughters were sometimes given an inheritance along with their brothers, but in the case of the five daughters of Zelophehad whose father died without sons, they received the entire inheritance of their forefathers, on the condition that they marry sons of Manasseh so that the property would remain in the same tribe. (Nu 36:1-12; Jos 15:19; Job 42:15) If a daughter was divorced or widowed, she could come back into her father's household.—Ge 38:11; Le 22:13.

"Daughter"—is it always an immediate female offspring?

The term "daughter" was applied to relationships other than one's immediate progeny. For example, under certain circumstances the term referred to a sister (Ge 34:8, 17), an adopted daughter (Es 2:7, 15), a daughter-in-law (Jg 12:9; Ru 1:11-13), a granddaughter (1Ki 15:2, 10, where the Hebrew word for daughter, *bath*, is rendered "granddaughter" in *Mo, NW;* see 2Ch 13:1, 2), and a descendant.—Ge 27:46; Lu 1:5; 13:16.

Aside from these direct relatives, the term "daughter" was applied to women in general (Ge 6:2, 4; 30:13; Pr 31:29); women of a particular land, people or city (Ge 24:37; Jg 11:40; 21:21); and female worshipers of false gods (Mal 2:11). It was used as a general address of kindness by one with authority or by an older person to a younger woman. (Ru 3:10, 11; Mr 5:34) Forms of the word *bath* are also used when referring to "branches" of a tree (Ge 49:22) and "dependent towns" of a larger city. (Nu 21:25; Jos 17:11; Jer 49:2) The term for "daughter," in its many senses, occurs over 600 times in the Bible.

DAUGHTER-IN-LAW. The wife of one's son. The same Hebrew (*kal·lah'*) and Greek (*nym'phe*) words translated "daughter-in-law" are also rendered "bride" in certain instances.

—Ca 4:8-12; Isa 61:10; Jer 7:34; Joh 3:29; Re 18:23; 21:2, 9; 22:17.

Since the father himself in patriarchal times usually arranged for the marriage of his son, his daughter-in-law was largely his own choice. (Ge 24) She was welcomed into his household, and when it moved she moved with it. (Ge 11:31) The Mosaic Law prohibited a man from having relations with his daughter-in-law under the penalty of death.—Le 18:15; 20:12; Eze 22:11.

Dispositions of daughters-in-law and their attitudes toward in-laws varied a great deal. Ruth, for example, proved a most loyal and devoted companion to her mother-in-law Naomi, more so than Orpah, saying, "Your people will be my people, and your God my God. Where you die I shall die." (Ru 1:6-17, 22; 4:14, 15) Esau's Hittite wives were most disconcerting to their in-laws Isaac and Rebekah. (Ge 26:34; 27:46) Christ Jesus foretold that the Kingdom message would separate daughters-in-law from mothers-in-law.—Lu 12:53.

DAVID (Da'vid) [probably, Beloved]. In the *New World Translation* the name occurs 1,079 times in the Hebrew Scriptures, including 75 times in superscriptions of 73 psalms, and 59 times in the Christian Greek Scriptures. Of all Hebrew Scripture personages, only Moses and Abraham are mentioned more frequently by Christian Bible writers. In the 1,138 places where the name David occurs, reference is to but one individual, the second king of Israel, or the one of whom David, at times, served as a pictorial type: "Jesus Christ, son of David."—Mt 1:1.

This shepherd, musician, poet, soldier, statesman, prophet, and king stands out in the Hebrew Scriptures in great prominence. Here was a fierce fighter on the battlefield who showed endurance under hardships, a leader and commander strong and unwavering in courage, yet humble enough to acknowledge his mistakes and repent of his gross sins, a man capable of tender compassion and mercy, a lover of truth and righteousness, and above all, one with implicit trust and confidence in his God Jehovah.

David, a descendant of Boaz and Ruth, had an ancestry running back through Perez to Judah. (Ru 4:18-22; Mt 1:3-6) This youngest of Jesse's eight sons also had two sisters or half sisters. (1Sa 16:10, 11; 17:12; 1Ch 2:16) One of David's brothers evidently died without having children and was thus dropped from later genealogical records. (1Ch 2:13-16) The name of David's mother is not given. Some have suggested that Nahash was his mother, but it is more probable that Nahash was the father of David's half sisters.—2Sa 17:25; see NAHASH No. 2.

Bethlehem, located about 9 km (5.5 mi) SSW of Jerusalem, was David's hometown, the town where his forefathers Jesse, Obed, and Boaz had lived, and which was sometimes called "David's city" (Lu 2:4, 11; Joh 7:42), not to be confused with "the City of David," that is, Zion in Jerusalem.—2Sa 5:7.

As a Youth. We first meet up with David as he is tending his father's sheep in a field near Bethlehem, reminding us that it was also in a field near Bethlehem where shepherds more than a millennium later were overawed at being chosen to hear Jehovah's angel announcing the birth of Jesus. (Lu 2:8-14) Samuel, sent by God to the house of Jesse to anoint one of his sons to be the future king, turns down David's seven older brothers, saying, "Jehovah has not chosen these." Finally David is fetched from the field. There is an atmosphere of suspense when he enters—"ruddy, a young man with beautiful eyes and handsome in appearance"—for until now no one knows why Samuel has come. "Get up," Samuel is commanded by Jehovah, "anoint him, for this is he!" This is the one of whom Jehovah says, "I have found David the son of Jesse, a man agreeable to my heart, who will do all the things I desire."—1Sa 16:1-13; 13:14; Ac 13:22.

David's years spent as a shepherd lad had a profound influence on the rest of his life. Outdoor life prepared him to live as a fugitive when, in later life, he fled the wrath of Saul. He also acquired skill in throwing slingstones, and he developed endurance, courage, and a willingness to pursue and rescue sheep separated from the flock, not hesitating to kill a bear or a lion when necessary.—1Sa 17:34-36.

But for all of his valor as a warrior, David will also be remembered as one skilled on the harp and as a composer of song, abilities he perhaps acquired during the long hours spent tending the sheep. David also had a reputation for developing new musical instruments. (2Ch 7:6; 29:26, 27; Am 6:5) David's love for Jehovah raised his lyrics far above the common level of simple entertainment and made them classical masterpieces dedicated to the worship and praise of Jehovah. The superscriptions of no less than 73 psalms indicate that David was their composer, but still other psalms are elsewhere attributed to David. (Compare Ps 2:1 with Ac 4:25; Ps 95:7, 8 with Heb

4:7.) Some, for example Psalms 8, 19, 23, 29, quite likely reflect David's experiences as a shepherd.

All this training while caring for sheep prepared David for the greater role of shepherding Jehovah's people, as it is written: "[Jehovah] chose David his servant and took him from the pens of the flock. From following the females giving suck he brought him in to be a shepherd over Jacob his people and over Israel his inheritance." (Ps 78:70, 71; 2Sa 7:8) However, when David first left his father's sheep it was not to take over the kingship. Instead, he served as the court musician upon the recommendation of an adviser of Saul, who described David not only as "skilled at playing" but also as "a valiant, mighty man and a man of war and an intelligent speaker and a well-formed man, and Jehovah is with him." (1Sa 16:18) So David became the harpist to troubled Saul, as well as his armor-bearer.—1Sa 16:19-23.

Later, for reasons not disclosed, David returns to his father's house for an indeterminate period. Upon bringing provisions to his brothers in Saul's army, which at the time is in a standoff position with the Philistines, he is incensed at seeing and hearing Goliath reproach Jehovah. "Who is this uncircumcised Philistine that he has to taunt the battle lines of the living God?" David asks. (1Sa 17:26) "Jehovah," he adds, "who delivered me from the paw of the lion and from the paw of the bear, he it is who will deliver me from the hand of this Philistine." (1Sa 17:37) Granted permission, the killer of the lion and the bear approaches Goliath with the words: "I am coming to you with the name of Jehovah of armies, the God of the battle lines of Israel, whom you have taunted." Suddenly David hurls the stone in his sling and brings the enemy champion down. Then with Goliath's own sword David decapitates him, and he returns to camp with the trophies of war, the giant's head and sword.—1Sa 17:45-54; PICTURE, Vol. 1, p. 745.

It is noteworthy that the *Septuagint,* as it appears in the fourth-century Greek manuscript Vatican 1209, omits 1 Samuel 17:55 through the word "down" in 18:6a. Hence *Moffatt* marks all except the last of these verses in double brackets, calling them "either editorial additions or later interpolations." However, there is evidence favoring the reading of the Masoretic text.—See SAMUEL, BOOKS OF (Sections Missing in the Greek *Septuagint*).

As a Fugitive. (MAP, Vol. 1, p. 746) These fast-moving events catapulted David from the obscurity of the wilderness to public notice before the eyes of all Israel. Placed over the men of war, David was greeted with dancing and rejoicing when he returned from a victorious expedition against the Philistines, the popular song of the day being, "Saul has struck down his thousands, and David his tens of thousands." (1Sa 18:5-7) "All Israel and Judah were lovers of David," and Saul's own son Jonathan concluded with him a lifelong covenant of mutual love and friendship, the benefits of which extended to Jonathan's son Mephibosheth and grandson Mica.—1Sa 18:1-4, 16; 20:1-42; 23:18; 2Sa 9:1-13.

This popularity stirred up envy in Saul, who kept "looking suspiciously at David from that day forward." Twice when David was playing as in former times, Saul hurled a spear with the intent of pinning David to the wall, and both times Jehovah delivered him. Saul had promised to give his daughter to whoever killed Goliath, but now he was reluctant to give her to David. Finally Saul agreed to the marriage of a second daughter, provided David brought him "a hundred foreskins of the Philistines," an unreasonable demand that Saul calculated would mean David's death. Courageous David, however, doubled the dowry, presented Saul with 200 foreskins, and was married to Michal. So now two of Saul's children had lovingly entered covenants with David, circumstances that made Saul hate him all the more. (1Sa 18:9-29) When David was again playing before Saul, the king for the third time sought to pin him to the wall. Under the cover of night David fled, to see Saul again only under different and indeed strange circumstances.—1Sa 19:10.

For the next several years David lived as a fugitive, constantly in flight from place to place, relentlessly pursued by an obstinate and wicked king bent on killing him. David first took refuge with the prophet Samuel in Ramah (1Sa 19:18-24), but when this ceased to be a hiding place he headed for the Philistine city of Gath, stopping on the way to see High Priest Ahimelech in Nob, where he obtained Goliath's sword. (1Sa 21:1-9; 22:9-23; Mt 12:3, 4) However, it was only by disguising his sanity, making childish cross marks on the gate and letting saliva run down his beard, that he was able to escape from Gath. (1Sa 21:10-15) Based on this experience, David composed Psalms 34 and 56. He then fled to the cave of Adullam, where his family and about 400 unfortunate and distressed men joined him. Psalm 57 or 142, or both, may commemorate his stay in this cave. David kept on the move—from there to Mizpeh in Moab and then back to the forest of Hereth in Judah. (1Sa 22:1-5) When

living in Keilah, he learned that Saul was preparing to attack, whereupon he and his men, now numbering about 600, departed for the Wilderness of Ziph. Saul continued the chase from one place to another, from the Wilderness of Ziph at Horesh to the Wilderness of Maon. When Saul was about to seize his prey, word came of a Philistine raid, so for a period of time Saul abandoned the chase, allowing the fugitive to escape to En-gedi. (1Sa 23:1-29) Beautiful Psalms praising Jehovah for providing miraculous deliverance (Ps 18, 59, 63, 70) were born out of similar experiences.

At En-gedi, Saul entered a cave to ease nature. David, who had been hiding there in the back of the cave, crept up and cut off the skirt of Saul's garment but spared his life, saying that it was unthinkable on his part to harm the king, "for he is the anointed of Jehovah."—1Sa 24:1-22.

Following Samuel's death. After Samuel's death, David, still in a state of exile, took up dwelling in the Wilderness of Paran. (See PARAN.) He and his men extended kindness to Nabal, a wealthy stock raiser whose work was in Carmel, to the S of Hebron, only to be rebuffed by this ingrate. Quick thinking on the part of Nabal's wife Abigail stayed David's hand from exterminating the males of the household, but Nabal was stricken by Jehovah and died. Thereupon David married the widow, so that now, in addition to Ahinoam from Jezreel, David had yet another wife, Abigail of Carmel; during David's long absence, Saul had given Michal to another man.—1Sa 25:1-44; 27:3.

For the second time David took refuge in the Wilderness of Ziph, and again the hunt was on. David likened Saul and his 3,000 men to those searching "for a single flea, just as one chases a partridge upon the mountains." One night David and Abishai crept into the sleeping camp of Saul and made off with his spear and water jug. Abishai wanted to kill Saul, but David spared Saul's life the second time, saying that, from Jehovah's viewpoint, it was unthinkable for him to thrust out his hand against God's anointed one. (1Sa 26:1-25) This occasion was the last time David saw his adversary.

David settled at Ziklag in Philistine territory, out of Saul's reach for a period of 16 months. A number of mighty men deserted Saul's forces and joined the exiles at Ziklag, enabling David to raid towns of Israel's enemies on the S, thus securing Judah's boundaries and strengthening his future position as king. (1Sa 27:1-12; 1Ch 12:1-7, 19-22) When the Philistines were preparing to assault

Saul's forces, King Achish, thinking David was "a stench among his people Israel," invited him to go along. However, the other axis lords rejected David as a security risk. (1Sa 29:1-11) In the battle that culminated on Mount Gilboa, Saul and three of his sons, including Jonathan, died.—1Sa 31:1-7.

Meanwhile, the Amalekites robbed and burned out Ziklag, carrying off all the women and children. Immediately David's forces pursued, overtook the marauders, and recovered their wives and children and all the goods. (1Sa 30:1-31) Three days later an Amalekite brought the diadem and bracelet of Saul, deceitfully boasting that he had put the wounded king to death and hoping to receive a reward. Even though he lied in the matter, David ordered him killed for claiming to have "put the anointed of Jehovah to death."—2Sa 1:1-16; 1Sa 31:4, 5.

As King. (MAP, Vol. 1, p. 746) The tragic news of Saul's death grieved David very much. He was not so concerned that his archenemy was dead as he was that the anointed one of Jehovah had fallen. In lamentation, David composed a dirge entitled "The Bow." In it he bewails how his worst enemy and his best friend had fallen together in battle—"Saul and Jonathan, the lovable ones and the pleasant ones during their life, and in their death they were not separated."—2Sa 1:17-27.

David now moved to Hebron, where the older men of Judah anointed him as king over their tribe in 1077 B.C.E., when he was 30 years old. Saul's son Ish-bosheth was made king of the other tribes. About two years later, however, Ish-bosheth was assassinated, his assailants bringing his head to David hoping to receive a reward, but they too were put to death like the pretended killer of Saul. (2Sa 2:1-4, 8-10; 4:5-12) This paved the way for the tribes who had till then supported Saul's son to join Judah, and in time, a force numbering 340,822 rallied and made David king of all Israel.—2Sa 5:1-3; 1Ch 11:1-3; 12:23-40.

Rule at Jerusalem. David ruled at Hebron seven and a half years before moving his capital, at Jehovah's direction, to the captured Jebusite stronghold, Jerusalem. There he built the City of David on Zion and continued to rule another 33 years. (2Sa 5:4-10; 1Ch 11:4-9; 2Ch 6:6) While living at Hebron, King David took more wives, had Michal returned, and fathered a number of sons and daughters. (2Sa 3:2-5, 13-16; 1Ch 3:1-4) After moving to Jerusalem, David acquired still more wives and concubines who, in turn, bore him more children.—2Sa 5:13-16; 1Ch 3:5-9; 14:3-7.

When the Philistines heard that David was king of all Israel, they came up to overthrow him. As in the past (1Sa 23:2, 4, 10-12; 30:8), David inquired of Jehovah whether he should go against them. "Go up," was the answer, and Jehovah burst upon the enemy with such overpowering destruction that David called the place Baal-perazim, meaning "Owner of Breakings Through." In a return encounter Jehovah's strategy shifted, and he ordered David to circle around and strike the Philistines from the rear.—2Sa 5:17-25; 1Ch 14:8-17.

David attempted to bring the ark of the covenant to Jerusalem, but this failed when Uzzah touched it and was struck down. (2Sa 6:2-10; 1Ch 13:1-14) Some three months later, with careful preparations, including sanctifying the priests and Levites and making sure the Ark was carried on their shoulders instead of being placed on a wagon as at first, it was brought to Jerusalem. David, simply clad, showed his joy and enthusiasm on this great occasion by "leaping and dancing around before Jehovah." But his wife Michal chided David, saying he acted "just as one of the empty-headed men." For this unjustified complaint Michal "came to have no child down to the day of her death."—2Sa 6:11-23; 1Ch 15:1-29.

David also arranged for expanded worship of Jehovah at the Ark's new location by assigning gatekeepers and musicians and seeing that there were "burnt offerings . . . constantly morning and evening." (1Ch 16:1-6, 37-43) In addition, David thought of building a temple-palace of cedar to house the Ark, to replace its tent. But David was not permitted to build the house, for God said: "Blood in great quantity you have spilled, and great wars you have waged. You will not build a house to my name, for a great deal of blood you have spilled on the earth before me." (1Ch 22:8; 28:3) However, Jehovah made a covenant with him promising that the kingship would everlastingly remain in his family, and in connection with this covenant God assured him that his son Solomon, whose name is from a root meaning "peace," would build the temple.—2Sa 7:1-16, 25-29; 1Ch 17:1-27; 2Ch 6:7-9; Ps 89:3, 4, 35, 36.

It was therefore in line with this kingdom covenant that Jehovah permitted David to expand his territorial rule from the river of Egypt to the Euphrates, securing his borders, maintaining peace with the king of Tyre, battling and conquering opponents on all sides—Philistines, Syrians, Moabites, Edomites, Amalekites, and Ammonites. (2Sa 8:1-14; 10:6-19; 1Ki 5:3; 1Ch 13:5; 14:1, 2; 18:1–20:8) These God-given victories made David a most powerful ruler. (1Ch 14:17) However, David was always conscious that this position was not his by conquest or inheritance but that it was from Jehovah, who had placed him on the throne of this typical theocracy. —1Ch 10:14; 29:10-13.

Sins bring calamity. During the continued campaign against the Ammonites, one of the saddest episodes of David's life occurred. It all began when the king, upon observing from his rooftop beautiful Bath-sheba bathing herself, entertained wrong desires. (Jas 1:14, 15) After learning that her husband Uriah was off to war, David had the woman brought to his palace, where he had relations with her. In time the king was notified that she was pregnant. No doubt fearing that Bath-

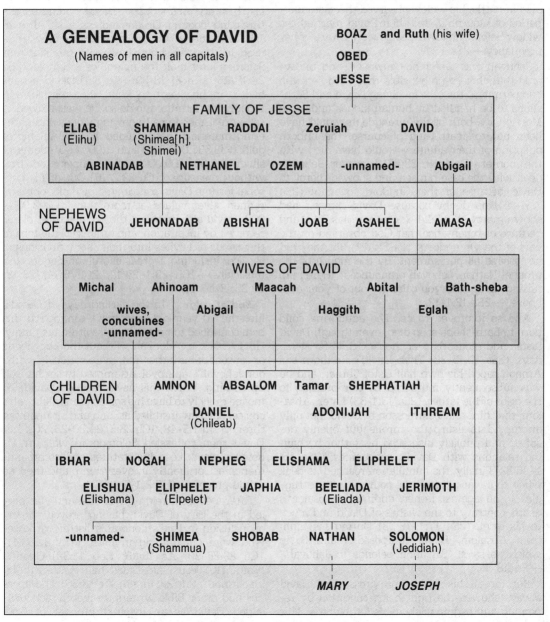

A GENEALOGY OF DAVID

(Names of men in all capitals)

BOAZ   and Ruth (his wife)

OBED

JESSE

FAMILY OF JESSE

| ELIAB (Elihu) | SHAMMAH (Shimea[h], Shimei) | RADDAI | Zeruiah | DAVID |
| ABINADAB | NETHANEL | OZEM | -unnamed- | Abigail |

NEPHEWS OF DAVID

JEHONADAB   ABISHAI   JOAB   ASAHEL   AMASA

WIVES OF DAVID

Michal   Ahinoam   Maacah   Abital   Bath-sheba

wives, concubines -unnamed-   Abigail   Haggith   Eglah

CHILDREN OF DAVID

AMNON   ABSALOM   Tamar   SHEPHATIAH

DANIEL (Chileab)   ADONIJAH   ITHREAM

IBHAR   NOGAH   NEPHEG   ELISHAMA   ELIPHELET

ELISHUA (Elishama)   ELIPHELET (Elpelet)   JAPHIA   BEELIADA (Eliada)   JERIMOTH

-unnamed-   SHIMEA (Shammua)   SHOBAB   NATHAN   SOLOMON (Jedidiah)

MARY   *JOSEPH*

sheba would be publicly exposed and put to death for immoral conduct, David quickly sent word to the army that Uriah should report to him in Jerusalem, with the hope that Uriah would spend the night with his wife. But even though David got him drunk, Uriah refused to sleep with Bath-sheba. In desperation, David sent him back to the army with secret instructions to the commander Joab to have Uriah put in the front lines, where he would surely be killed. The scheme worked. Uriah died in battle, his widow observed the customary period of mourning, and then David married the widow before the townspeople were aware of her pregnancy.—2Sa 11:1-27.

Jehovah was watching, however, and uncovered the whole reprehensible matter. If Jehovah had permitted the case involving David and Bath-sheba to be handled by human judges under the Mosaic Law, both of the wrongdoers would have been put to death, and of course, the unborn offspring of their adultery would have died with the mother. (De 5:18; 22:22) However, Jehovah dealt with the case himself and showed mercy to David because of the Kingdom covenant (2Sa 7:11-16), no doubt because David himself had shown mercy (1Sa 24:4-7; compare Jas 2:13) and because of repentance that God observed on the part of the wrongdoers. (Ps 51:1-4) But they did not escape all punishment. By the mouth of the prophet Nathan, Jehovah pronounced: "Here I am raising up against you calamity out of your own house."—2Sa 12:1-12.

And so it proved to be. The adulterine child born to Bath-sheba soon died, even though David fasted and mourned over the sick child for seven days. (2Sa 12:15-23) Then David's firstborn son Amnon raped his own half sister Tamar, and he was subsequently murdered by her brother, to the grief of his father. (2Sa 13:1-33) Later, Absalom, the third and beloved son of David, not only attempted to usurp the throne but openly despised and publicly disgraced his father by having relations with David's concubines. (2Sa 15:1–16:22) Finally, the humiliation reached its peak when civil war plunged the country into a struggle of son against father, ending in Absalom's death, contrary to the wishes of David and much to his grief. (2Sa 17:1–18:33) During his flight from Absalom, David composed Psalm 3, in which he says, "Salvation belongs to Jehovah." —Ps 3:8.

But for all his faults and gross sins, David always showed the right heart condition by repenting and begging Jehovah's forgiveness. This was demonstrated in the affair involving Bath-sheba, after which David wrote Psalm 51, stating, "With error I was brought forth . . . in sin my mother conceived me." (Ps 51:5) Another instance when David humbly confessed his sins was when Satan incited him to take a census of the men qualified for the military forces.—2Sa 24:1-17; 1Ch 21:1-17; 27:24; see REGISTRATION.

Purchase of temple site. When the pestilence that resulted from the king's error in this last instance was stopped, David purchased the threshing floor of Ornan and, as a sacrifice to Jehovah, offered up the cattle with the sledge used for the threshing. It was on this site that Solomon later built the magnificent temple. (2Sa 24:18-25; 1Ch 21:18-30; 2Ch 3:1) David always had it in his heart to build that temple, and though not permitted to do so, he was allowed to set a great task force to hewing stones and gathering materials that included 100,000 talents of gold ($38,535,000,000) and 1,000,000 talents of silver ($6,606,000,000), and copper and iron without measure. (1Ch 22:2-16) Out of his personal fortune David contributed gold of Ophir and refined silver valued at more than $1,202,000,-000. David also provided the architectural plans, received by inspiration, and organized the tens of thousands of Levites into their many divisions of service, including a great chorus of singers and musicians.—1Ch 23:1–29:19; 2Ch 8:14; 23:18; 29:25; Ezr 3:10.

End of reign. In the closing days of David's life, the 70-year-old king, now confined to his bed, continued to reap calamity within his family. His fourth son, Adonijah, without the knowledge or consent of his father and, more seriously, without Jehovah's approval, attempted to set himself up as king. When this news reached David, he moved quickly to have his son Solomon, Jehovah's choice, officially installed as king and sit upon the throne. (1Ki 1:5-48; 1Ch 28:5; 29:20-25; 2Ch 1:8) David then counseled Solomon to walk in Jehovah's ways, keep his statutes and commandments, act prudently in everything, and then he would prosper.—1Ki 2:1-9.

After a 40-year reign David died and was buried in the City of David, having proved worthy of inclusion in Paul's honorable list of witnesses who were outstanding in faith. (1Ki 2:10, 11; 1Ch 29:26-30; Ac 13:36; Heb 11:32) Quoting Psalm 110, Jesus said David had written it "by inspiration." (Mt 22:43, 44; Mr 12:36) The apostles and other Bible writers frequently acknowledged David as an inspired prophet of God.

—Compare Ps 16:8 with Ac 2:25; Ps 32:1, 2 with Ro 4:6-8; Ps 41:9 with Joh 13:18; Ps 69:22, 23 with Ro 11:9, 10; Ps 69:25 and 109:8 with Ac 1:20.

Pictorial. The prophets often referred to David and his royal house, sometimes in connection with the last kings of Israel who sat on "the throne of David" (Jer 13:13; 22:2, 30; 29:16; 36: 30) and sometimes in a prophetic sense. (Jer 17:25; 22:4; Am 9:11; Zec 12:7-12) In certain Messianic prophecies attention is focused on Jehovah's kingdom covenant with David. For example, Isaiah says that the one called "Wonderful Counselor, Mighty God, Eternal Father, Prince of Peace" will be firmly established on "the throne of David" to time indefinite. (Isa 9:6, 7; compare also 16:5.) Jeremiah likens Messiah to "a righteous sprout" whom Jehovah "will raise up to David." (Jer 23:5, 6; 33:15-17) Through Ezekiel, Jehovah speaks of the Messianic Shepherd as "my servant David."—Eze 34:23, 24; 37:24, 25.

In telling Mary that she would have a son called Jesus, the angel declared that "Jehovah God will give him the throne of David his father." (Lu 1:32) "Jesus Christ, son of David," was both the legal and the natural heir to the throne of David. (Mt 1:1, 17; Lu 3:23-31) Paul said that Jesus was the offspring of David according to the flesh. (Ro 1:3; 2Ti 2:8) The common people also identified Jesus as the "Son of David." (Mt 9:27; 12:23; 15:22; 21:9, 15; Mr 10:47, 48; Lu 18:38, 39) It was important to establish this, for, as the Pharisees admitted, Messiah would be David's son. (Mt 22: 42) The resurrected Jesus himself also bore witness, saying: "I, Jesus, . . . am the root and the offspring of David."—Re 22:16; also Re 3:7; 5:5.

DAVID, CITY OF.

The name given to "the stronghold of Zion" after its capture from the Jebusites. (2Sa 5:6-9) This section is understood to be the spur or ridge that runs S from Mount Moriah. It thus lay S of the site of the temple later built by Solomon. Today it is a narrow southern plateau considerably lower than Mount Moriah. Extensive quarrying was carried out in this area, especially during the reign of Emperor Hadrian and the construction of the Roman city Aelia Capitolina around 135 C.E. So, evidently in ancient times its height was more comparable to Mount Moriah, though still beneath the elevation of the temple site.—PICTURES, Vol. 1, p. 747, and Vol. 2, p. 947.

This site was very suitable for a "stronghold," since it was protected by deep valleys on three sides, on the W the Tyropoeon Valley, and on the E the Kidron Valley, which joins the Valley of Hinnom at the southern end of the spur. (1Ch 11:7) The city required major protection only from the N, and here the ridge became even narrower, making an attack extremely difficult. The northern boundary of this "City of David" has not yet been definitely established, though some scholars recommend as likely the above-mentioned narrow place. Over the centuries, debris has filled in the valleys to a great extent, making the strategic location and strength of this site less notable. The total area of the ancient City of David is estimated to have been 4 to 6 ha (10 to 15 acres).

In the Kidron Valley near the foot of the eastern flank of the spur on which the stronghold sat, there is a spring called Gihon. (1Ki 1:33) Archaeological excavations indicate that in ancient times a tunnel or shaft was cut through the rock, making access to the spring possible without leaving the city walls. It has been suggested that it was by climbing up this shaft that Joab and his men were able to penetrate the stronghold and take it. —2Sa 5:8; 1Ch 11:5, 6.

The name "City of David" resulted from David's making his royal residence there, after ruling for seven and a half years in Hebron. Here, with contributions from Hiram of Tyre, David's "house of cedars" was built. (2Sa 5:5, 9, 11; 7:2) David had the ark of the covenant brought from the house of Obed-edom up to the City of David, his wife, Michal, being able to see the procession approach from a window of David's house. (2Sa 6:10-16; 1Ch 15:1, 29) Upon his death, the king was buried in the city, a custom followed with many other monarchs of the Davidic line.—1Ki 2:10.

From Solomon's Reign Onward. Solomon transferred the Ark to the newly constructed temple on the more spacious plateau to the N of the City of David. The expression that they 'brought up the ark out of the City of David' shows that the temple area lay on higher ground, Mount Moriah being higher than the southern spur. (1Ki 8:1) After his marriage to Pharaoh's daughter, Solomon had placed her in the City of David. (1Ki 3:1) But, upon the completion of a new residence closer to the temple area, he removed her from the City of David because it was viewed as holy, the Ark having been stationed there. (1Ki 9:24; 2Ch 8:11) Solomon did further building work in the City of David, and Hezekiah did repair work there in preparation for Assyrian Sennacherib's attack. (1Ki 11:27; 2Ch 32:5)

Hezekiah also diverted the waters of the Gihon spring, bringing them over to the W side of the City of David, evidently by means of the rock-cut tunnel that has been discovered connecting that spring with the Pool of Siloam on the SW slope of the spur. (2Ch 32:30) His son and successor, Manasseh, built an outer wall along the eastern slope facing the Kidron Valley.—2Ch 33:14.

From the above texts it is evident that, although Jerusalem's area expanded in course of time, the City of David remained a distinct sector. This held true even after the return from Babylonian exile, certain features of the city being mentioned in connection with the work crews repairing the city walls. (Ne 3:15, 16) "The Stairway of the City of David" apparently led down from the southern extremity of the city. (Ne 12:37) Excavations here have revealed portions of such a stairway, and a flight of steps roughly cut in the rock still leads down from the hill at this point.

In the Christian Greek Scriptures the term "David's city" is applied to Bethlehem, the birthplace of David and of Jesus.—Lu 2:4, 11; Joh 7:42; see JERUSALEM.

DAY. Jehovah God introduced this fundamental division of time on the first "day" of the period during which he prepared the earth for mankind, when diffused light evidently penetrated the swaddling bands, thus causing the moisture-covered earth to experience its first day and night as it rotated on its axis through the light of the sun. "God brought about a division between the light and the darkness. And God began calling the light Day, but the darkness he called Night." (Ge 1:4, 5) Here the word "Day" refers to the daylight hours in contrast with the nighttime. However, the record thereafter goes on to use the word "day" to refer to other units of time of varying length. In both the Hebrew and the Greek Scriptures, the word "day" (Heb., *yohm;* Gr., *he·me′ra*) is used in a literal and in a figurative or even symbolic sense.

A *solar day,* the fundamental unit of time, is established by one complete rotation of the earth on its axis, as from the time the sun leaves a meridian, the highest point it attains at midday, until it returns to it. This solar or civil day is currently divided into two periods of 12 hours each. The forenoon period is indicated by the Latin *ante meridiem* (a.m.) and the afternoon period by the Latin *post meridiem* (p.m.). However, in Bible times various other methods were used for dividing the day.

The Hebrews began their day in the evening, after sunset, and ended it the next day at sunset. The day, therefore, ran from evening to evening. "From evening to evening you should observe your sabbath." (Le 23:32) This follows the pattern of Jehovah's creative days, as indicated at Genesis 1:5: "There came to be evening and there came to be morning, a first day."—Compare Da 8:14.

The Hebrews were not the only ones who reckoned a day from evening to evening; the Phoenicians, Numidians, and Athenians also did so. The Babylonians, on the other hand, counted the day from sunrise to sunrise; while the Egyptians and the Romans reckoned it from midnight to midnight (as is commonly done today).

Although the Hebrews officially began their day in the evening, they sometimes spoke of it as if beginning in the morning. For example, Leviticus 7:15 says: "The flesh of the thanksgiving sacrifice of his communion sacrifices is to be eaten on the day of his offering. He must not save up any of it until morning." This usage was doubtless simply a matter of convenience of expression, to indicate overnight.

As mentioned in the creation account, the *daylight period* is also called day. (Ge 1:5; 8:22) In the Bible it is divided up into natural periods: the morning twilight or morning darkness, just before the day's beginning (Ps 119:147; 1Sa 30:17); the rising of the sun or dawning (Job 3:9); the morning (Ge 24:54); noon or midday (De 28:29; 1Ki 18:27; Isa 16:3; Ac 22:6); the time of the sunset, marking the day's close (Ge 15:12; Jos 8:29); and the evening twilight or evening darkness (2Ki 7:5, 7). The times for making certain offerings or the burning of incense by the priests were also time periods known to the people.—1Ki 18:29, 36; Lu 1:10.

What is the time "between the two evenings"?

With reference to the slaying of the Passover lamb on Nisan 14, the Scriptures speak of "the two evenings." (Ex 12:6) While Jewish tradition tends to present this as the time from noon (when the sun begins to decline) on until sundown, it appears that the correct meaning is that the first evening corresponds with the setting of the sun, and the second evening with the time when the sun's reflected light or afterglow ends and darkness falls. (De 16:6; Ps 104:19, 20) This understanding was also that offered by the Spanish rabbi Aben-Ezra (1092-1167), as well as by the Samaritans and the Karaite Jews. It is the view presented by such scholars as Michaelis, Rosenmueller, Gesenius, Maurer, Kalisch, Knobel, and Keil.

There is no indication that the Hebrews used hours in dividing up the day prior to the Babylonian exile. The word "hour" found at Daniel 3:6, 15; 4:19, 33; 5:5 in the *King James Version* is translated from the Aramaic word *sha·'ah'*, which, literally, means "a look" and is more correctly translated a "moment." The use of hours by the Jews, however, did come into regular practice following the exile. As to "the shadow of the steps" referred to at Isaiah 38:8 and 2 Kings 20:8-11, this may possibly refer to a sundial method of keeping time, whereby shadows were projected by the sun on a series of steps.—See SUN (Shadow That Went Ten Steps Back).

The early Babylonians used the sexagesimal system based on a mathematical scale of 60. From this system we get our time division whereby the day is partitioned into 24 hours (as well as into two periods of 12 hours each), and each hour into 60 minutes of 60 seconds each.

In the days of Jesus' earthly ministry, the practice of dividing the daylight period into hours was common. Thus, at John 11:9 Jesus said: "There are twelve hours of daylight, are there not?" These were generally counted from sunrise to sunset, or from about 6:00 a.m. to 6:00 p.m. So, "the third hour" would be about 9:00 a.m., and it was at this time that the holy spirit was poured out at Pentecost. (Mt 20:3; Ac 2:15) When Jesus, tired out from a journey, was sitting at Jacob's fountain it was about "the sixth hour," or noon, which was also the time when Peter became very hungry at Joppa. (Joh 4:6; Ac 10:9, 10) It was also about noon when darkness fell over all the earth until "the ninth hour," or about 3:00 p.m., when Jesus expired on the torture stake. (Mt 27:45, 46; Lu 23:44, 46) This ninth hour was also called "the hour of prayer." (Ac 3:1; 10:3, 4, 30) So, "the seventh hour" would be about 1:00 p.m. and "the eleventh hour," about 5:00 p.m. (Joh 4:52; Mt 20:6-12) The night was also divided into hours at that time.—Ac 23:23; see NIGHT.

There are times when the Hebrews used 'day and night' to mean only a *portion of a solar day* of 24 hours. For example, 1 Kings 12:5, 12 tells of Rehoboam's asking Jeroboam and the Israelites to "go away for three days" and then return to him. That he did not mean three full 24-hour days but, rather, a portion of each of three days is seen by the fact that the people came back to him "on the third day." At Matthew 12:40 the same meaning is given to the "three days and three nights" of Jesus' stay in Sheol. As the record shows, he was raised to life on "the third day." The Jewish priests clearly understood this to be the meaning of Jesus' words, since, in their effort to block his resurrection, they quoted Jesus as saying: "After three days I am to be raised up," and then they requested Pilate to issue a command for "the grave to be made secure until the third day."—Mt 27:62-66; 28:1-6; note other examples in Ge 42: 17, 18; Es 4:16; 5:1.

No names were used by the Hebrews for the days of the week, except for the seventh day, called the Sabbath. (See SABBATH DAY.) Reference was made to the various days by their numerical order. In the days of Jesus and his apostles, the day preceding the Sabbath was called the Preparation. (Mt 28:1; Ac 20:7; Mr 15:42; Joh 19:31; see WEEK.) The practice of naming the days after the names of the planets and other heavenly bodies was pagan. The Romans named the days after the Sun, Moon, Mars, Mercury, Jupiter, Venus, and Saturn, but in northern Europe, four of these names were later changed into the Germanic equivalents of the Roman gods whom the days represented.

Sometimes the word "day" is used to indicate a *measure of distance,* as in the expressions "a day's journey" and "a sabbath day's journey." —Nu 11:31; Ac 1:12; see WEIGHTS AND MEASURES.

In *prophecy* a day is at times used to stand for one year. This can be noted at Ezekiel 4:6: "You must lie upon your right side in the second case, and you must carry the error of the house of Judah forty days. A day for a year, a day for a year, is what I have given you."—See also Nu 14:34.

Certain specific numbers of days given in connection with prophecies are: three and a half days (Re 11:9); 10 days (Re 2:10); 40 days (Eze 4:6); 390 days (Eze 4:5); 1,260 days (Re 11:3; 12:6); 1,290 days (Da 12:11); 1,335 days (Da 12:12); and 2,300 days (Da 8:14).

The term "day(s)" is also used with reference to a *time period contemporaneous with a particular person,* as for example, "the days of Noah" and "the days of Lot."—Lu 17:26-30; Isa 1:1.

Other cases where the word "day" is used in a flexible or figurative sense are: "the day of God's creating Adam" (Ge 5:1), "the day of Jehovah" (Zep 1:7), the "day of fury" (Zep 1:15), "the day of salvation" (2Co 6:2), "the day of judgment" (2Pe

3:7), "the great day of God the Almighty" (Re 16:14), and others.

This flexible use of the word "day" to express units of time of varying length is clearly evident in the Genesis account of creation. Therein is set forth a week of six *creative days* followed by a seventh day of rest. The week assigned for observance by the Jews under the Law covenant given them by God was a miniature copy of that creative week. (Ex 20:8-11) In the Scriptural record the account of each of the six creative days concludes with the statement: "And there came to be evening and there came to be morning" a first, second, third, fourth, fifth, and sixth day. (Ge 1:5, 8, 13, 19, 23, 31) The seventh day, however, does not have this ending, indicating that this period, during which God has been resting from his creative works toward the earth, continued on. At Hebrews 4:1-10 the apostle Paul indicated that God's rest day was still continuing in his generation, and that was more than 4,000 years after that seventh-day rest period began. This makes it evident that each creative day, or work period, was at least thousands of years in length. As *A Religious Encyclopædia* (Vol. I, p. 613) observes: "The days of creation were creative days, stages in the process, but not days of twenty-four hours each."—Edited by P. Schaff, 1894.

The entire period of the six time units or creative "days" dedicated to the preparation of planet Earth is summed up in one all-embracing "day" at Genesis 2:4: "This is a history of the heavens and the earth in the time of their being created, in the *day* that Jehovah God made earth and heaven."

Man's situation does not compare with that of the Creator, who does not reside within our solar system and who is not affected by its various cycles and orbits. Of God, who is from time indefinite to time indefinite, the psalmist says: "For a thousand years are in your eyes but as yesterday when it is past, and as a watch during the night." (Ps 90:2, 4) Correspondingly, the apostle Peter writes that "one day is with Jehovah as a thousand years and a thousand years as one day." (2Pe 3:8) For man, a 1,000-year period represents some 365,242 individual time units of day and night, but to the Creator it can be just one unbroken time period in which he begins the carrying out of some purposeful activity and brings it on to its successful conclusion, much as a man begins a task in the morning and concludes it by the day's end.

Jehovah is the Originator of our universe in which time, space, motion, mass, and energy

have all been proved to be inescapably interrelated. He controls them all according to his purpose, and in dealing with his creatures on earth he makes definite time appointments for his own actions toward them, right down to the "day and hour." (Mt 24:36; Ga 4:4) He keeps such appointments with the utmost punctuality.

DAY OF JEHOVAH. The special period of time, not 24 hours, when Jehovah actively manifests himself against his enemies and in behalf of his people. With divine judgment executed against the wicked, Jehovah comes off victorious over his opposers during this "day." It is also a time of salvation and deliverance for the righteous, the day in which Jehovah himself is highly exalted as the Supreme One. Thus, in a double way it is uniquely and exclusively Jehovah's great day.

This day is detailed in the Scriptures as a time of battle, a great and fear-inspiring day of darkness and burning anger, a day of fury, distress, anguish, desolation, and alarm. "What, then, will the day of Jehovah mean to you people?" God asked wayward Israel by the mouth of his prophet Amos. This: "It will be darkness, and no light, just as when a man flees because of the lion, and the bear actually meets him; and as when he went into the house and supported his hand against the wall, and the serpent bit him." (Am 5:18-20) Isaiah was told: "Look! The day of Jehovah itself is coming, cruel both with fury and with burning anger." (Isa 13:9) "That day is a day of fury, a day of distress and of anguish, a day of storm and of desolation, a day of darkness and of gloominess, a day of clouds and of thick gloom." (Zep 1:15) During such a time of trouble, one's money is absolutely worthless. "Into the streets they will throw their very silver . . . Neither their silver nor their gold will be able to deliver them in the day of Jehovah's fury."—Eze 7:19; Zep 1:18.

A sense of urgency is attached to the day of Jehovah by the prophets, who repeatedly warned of its nearness. "The great day of Jehovah is near. It is near, and there is a hurrying of it very much." (Zep 1:14) "Alas for the day; because the day of Jehovah is near." "Let all the inhabitants of the land get agitated; for the day of Jehovah is coming, for it is near!"—Joe 1:15; 2:1, 2.

Times of Destructive Judgment. From certain features of the prophecies, and in view of subsequent events, it appears that the expression, "the day of Jehovah," at least in a miniature way, referred to different times of destructive judgment that occurred long ago at the hands of the

Most High. For example, Isaiah envisioned what would befall unfaithful Judah and Jerusalem on "the day belonging to Jehovah of armies," which was coming "upon everyone self-exalted and lofty" among them. (Isa 2:11-17) Ezekiel addressed himself to the unfaithful prophets of Israel, warning that they would in no way serve to fortify their cities "in order to stand in the battle in the day of Jehovah." (Eze 13:5) By the mouth of his prophet Zephaniah, Jehovah foretold how he was about to stretch out his hand against Judah and Jerusalem, giving special attention so that not even the princes or the sons of the king would escape. (Zep 1:4-8) As the facts show, that "day of Jehovah" came upon the inhabitants of Jerusalem in 607 B.C.E.

In that distressing time of trouble upon Judah and Jerusalem, her neighboring nations such as Edom showed their hatred for Jehovah and his people, causing the prophet Obadiah (vss 1, 15) to prophesy against them: "For the day of Jehovah against all the nations is near. In the way that you have done, it will be done to you." Similarly, "the day of Jehovah" and all the fiery destruction embraced within that expression befell Babylon and Egypt just as foretold.—Isa 13:1, 6; Jer 46:1, 2, 10.

Later, through the prophet Malachi, another "great and fear-inspiring day of Jehovah" was foretold, and it was said that it would be preceded by the coming of "Elijah the prophet." (Mal 4:5, 6) The original Elijah had lived some 500 years before that prophecy was uttered, but in the first century C.E. Jesus indicated that John the Baptizer was the foretold counterpart of Elijah. (Mt 11:12-14; Mr 9:11-13) So at that time a "day of Jehovah" was near at hand. At Pentecost of 33 C.E., Peter explained that what was occurring was the fulfillment of Joel's prophecy (Joe 2:28-32) concerning the outpouring of God's spirit and that this too was due to happen before "the great and illustrious day of Jehovah." (Ac 2:16-21) That "day of Jehovah" came in 70 C.E., when, in fulfillment of his Word, Jehovah caused the armies of Rome to execute divine judgment upon the nation that had rejected the Son of God and defiantly shouted: "We have no king but Caesar."—Joh 19:15; Da 9:24-27.

However, the Scriptures point forward to yet another "day of Jehovah." After the restoration of the Jews to Jerusalem following the Babylonian exile, Jehovah caused his prophet Zechariah (14:1-3) to foretell "a day . . . belonging to Jehovah" when he would gather not merely one nation but "all the nations against Jerusalem," at the climax of which day "Jehovah will certainly go forth and war against those nations," bringing them to their end. The apostle Paul, under inspiration, associated the coming "day of Jehovah" with the presence of Christ. (2Th 2:1, 2) And Peter spoke of it in connection with the establishment of 'new heavens and a new earth in which righteousness is to dwell.'—2Pe 3:10-13.

Security and safety during the great day of Jehovah should concern everyone. After asking, "Who can hold up under it?" Joel says, "Jehovah will be a refuge for his people." (Joe 2:11; 3:16) The invitation is graciously extended to all, but few avail themselves of this provision of refuge by following Zephaniah's counsel: "Before the statute gives birth to anything, before the day has passed by just like chaff, before there comes upon you people the burning anger of Jehovah, before there comes upon you the day of Jehovah's anger, seek Jehovah, all you meek ones of the earth, who have practiced His own judicial decision. Seek righteousness, seek meekness. Probably you may be concealed in the day of Jehovah's anger."—Zep 2:2, 3.

DEAD SEA. See SALT SEA.

DEAFNESS. Partial or complete inability to hear, often caused by disease, accident, or loud noise, either intense and sudden or prolonged. In some cases persons are born deaf. Another cause of deafness mentioned in the Bible is demon possession. (Mr 9:25-29) The root of the Hebrew term *che·resh'* ('deaf one'; Isa 35:5) refers to either deafness on the part of the object or silence on the part of the subject and is variously rendered "be [or become] deaf" and "keep silent." —Ps 28:1; 35:22, ftn; 50:3, ftn; Mic 7:16.

Jehovah, the Creator of the ear (Pr 20:12), required his people to show consideration for the deaf. The Israelites were not to ridicule or call down evil upon deaf persons, for the deaf could not defend themselves against statements they could not hear.—Le 19:14; compare Ps 38:13, 14.

The words at Exodus 4:11, where Jehovah refers to himself as 'appointing the deaf,' do not mean that he is responsible for all cases of deafness. However, Jehovah can cause a person to become literally deaf, unable to speak, or blind for a particular reason or purpose. The father of John the Baptizer was temporarily made speechless because of not believing. (Lu 1:18-22, 62-64) God can also "appoint" persons to be spiritually deaf by allowing them to remain in that state if they so choose.—Compare Isa 6:9, 10.

Jesus Christ, during his ministry, demonstrated miraculous curative powers by restoring the hearing of physically deaf individuals on several occasions. (Mt 11:5; Mr 7:32-37; Lu 7:22) This makes certain that under his rulership over the earth all afflictions, including deafness, will be eliminated.

The psalmist compared the wicked, who refuse to listen to direction, to a cobra that makes itself deaf to the voice of charmers. (Ps 58:3-5) Similarly, in Isaiah's day, the Israelites, although having ears, were as though deaf because of being slow to listen and respond to Jehovah's word. (Isa 42:18-20; 43:8) However, after the foretold restoration from exile, God's people would cease to be deaf spiritually. They would hear the word of Jehovah, that is, pay attention to it. (Isa 29:18; 35:5) Jesus Christ, while on earth, opened many ears of understanding, enabling the cured ones to act upon what they heard.—Mt 13:16, 23.

DEATH. The cessation of all functions of life, hence, the opposite of life. (De 30:15, 19) In the Bible the same original-language words for "death" or "dying" are applied to humans, animals, and plants. (Ec 3:19; 9:5; Joh 12:24; Jude 12; Re 16:3) However, for humans and animals the Bible shows the vital function of the blood in maintaining life, stating that "the soul of the flesh is in the blood." (Le 17:11, 14; Ge 4:8-11; 9:3, 4) Both humans and animals are spoken of as 'expiring,' that is, 'breathing out' the breath of life (Heb., *nish·math' chai·yim'*). (Ge 7:21, 22; compare Ge 2:7.) And the Scriptures show that death in humans and animals follows the loss of the spirit (active force) of life (Heb., *ru'ach chai·yim'*). —Ge 6:17, ftn; 7:15, 22; Ec 3:19; see SPIRIT.

From the Biblical viewpoint, what is death?

It is of interest to note the correspondency of these Biblical points with what is known scientifically of the death process. In humans, for example, when the heart stops beating, the blood ceases to circulate nourishment and oxygen (obtained by breathing) to the billions of body cells. However, *The World Book Encyclopedia* (1987, Vol. 5, p. 52b) pointed out: "A person whose heart and lungs stop working may be considered *clinically dead,* but somatic death may not yet have occurred. The individual cells of the body continue to live for several minutes. The person may be revived if the heart and lungs start working again

and give the cells the oxygen they need. After about three minutes, the brain cells—which are most sensitive to a lack of oxygen—begin to die. The person is soon dead beyond any possibility of revival. Gradually, other cells of the body also die. The last ones to perish are the bone, hair, and skin cells, which may continue to grow for several hours." Thus while the vital importance of breathing and of the blood in maintaining the active life-force (*ru'ach chai·yim'*) in the body cells is evident, at the same time it is also clear that it is not the cessation of breathing or of heartbeat alone but the disappearance of the life-force or spirit from the body cells that brings death as referred to in the Scriptures.—Ps 104:29; 146:4; Ec 8:8.

Cause of Death in Humans. The first reference to death in the Scriptures occurs at Genesis 2:16, 17 in God's command to the first man concerning the eating from the tree of the knowledge of good and bad, violation of which command would result in death. (See *NW* ftn.) However, death among animals as a natural process was evidently already in effect, since they are passed over completely in the Biblical presentation of the introduction of death into the human family. (Compare 2Pe 2:12.) The gravity of God's warning about the death penalty for disobedience would therefore be understandable to his human son, Adam. Adam's disobedience to his Creator brought death to him. (Ge 3:19; Jas 1:14, 15) Thereafter, Adam's sin and its consequence, death, spread to all men.—Ro 5:12; 6:23.

Certain texts are, at times, brought forth as supposed evidence that physical death was intended as a natural eventuality for humans, even as for the animals; for example, the references to man's life span as being 'seventy or eighty years' (Ps 90:10) and the apostle's statement that "it is reserved for men to die once for all time, but after this a judgment." (Heb 9:27) Nevertheless, all such texts were written *after* the introduction of death among mankind, and are applied to imperfect, sinful humans. The tremendous longevity of the men living prior to the Flood must at least be considered as reflecting a remarkable potential in the human body, surpassing that found in any animal even under the most ideal conditions. (Ge 5:1-31) The Bible unmistakably relates the entrance of death into the human family to Adam's sin, as already shown.

Alienated from God by sin, mankind in general is said to be in "enslavement to corruption." (Ro 8:21) This enslavement is due to the workings of sin in their bodies, bringing forth its corrupting fruit, and all persons not obedient to God are under the rule of sin as its slaves "with death in view." (Ro 6:12, 16, 19-21) Satan is stated to have "the means to cause death." (Heb 2:14, 15) He is called "a manslayer" (Joh 8:44), not necessarily because he kills directly but because he does so by deceit and seduction to sin, by inducing or stimulating wrongdoing that leads to corruption and death (2Co 11:3), and also by fathering murderous attitudes in the minds and hearts of men. (Joh 8:40-44, 59; 13:2; compare Jas 3:14-16; 4:1, 2.) Death is therefore presented, not as the friend of man, but as man's "enemy." (1Co 15:26) It is generally those in extreme or unbearable pain who are shown as desiring death.—Job 3:21, 22; 7:15; Re 9:6.

Condition of Human Dead. The dead are shown to be "conscious of nothing at all" and the death state to be one of complete inactivity. (Ec 9:5, 10; Ps 146:4) Those dying are described as going into "the dust of death" (Ps 22:15), becoming "impotent in death." (Pr 2:18; Isa 26:14) In death there is no mention of God or any praising of him. (Ps 6:5; Isa 38:18, 19) In both the Hebrew and the Greek Scriptures, death is likened to sleep, a fitting comparison not only because of the unconscious condition of the dead but also because of the hope of an awakening through the resurrection. (Ps 13:3; Joh 11:11-14) The resurrected Jesus is spoken of as "the firstfruits of those who have fallen asleep in death."—1Co 15:20, 21; see HADES; SHEOL.

Whereas the ancient Egyptians and other peoples of pagan nations, and particularly the Grecian philosophers, were strong in their belief in the deathlessness of the human soul, both the Hebrew Scriptures and the Christian Greek Scriptures speak of the soul (Heb., ne'phesh; Gr., psykhe') as dying (Jg 16:30; Eze 18:4, 20; Re 16:3), needing deliverance from death (Jos 2:13; Ps 33:19; 56:13; 116:8; Jas 5:20), or as in the Messianic prophecy concerning Jesus Christ, being "poured out . . . to the very death" (Isa 53:12; compare Mt 26:38). The prophet Ezekiel condemns those who connived "to put to death the souls that ought not to die" and "to preserve alive the souls that ought not to live."—Eze 13:19; see SOUL.

Thus, *The Interpreter's Bible* (Vol. II, p. 1015), commenting on 1 Samuel 25:29, observes that "the idea of man as consisting of body and soul which are separated at death is not Hebrew but Greek." (Edited by G. Buttrick, 1953) Similarly, Edmond Jacob, Professor of Old Testament at the

University of Strasbourg, points out that, since in the Hebrew Scriptures one's life is directly related with the soul (Heb., ne'phesh), "it is natural that death should sometimes be represented as the disappearance of this nephesh (Gen. 35:18; I Kings 17:21; Jer. 15:9; Jonah 4:3). The 'departure' of the nephesh must be viewed as a figure of speech, for it does not continue to exist independently of the body, but dies with it (Num. 31:19; Judg. 16:30; Ezek. 13:19). No biblical text authorizes the statement that the 'soul' is separated from the body at the moment of death."—*The Interpreter's Dictionary of the Bible,* edited by G. Buttrick, 1962, Vol. 1, p. 802.

Redemption From Condemnation of Death. Psalm 68:20 states: "To Jehovah the Sovereign Lord belong the ways out from death." By means of the sacrifice of his human life, Christ Jesus became God's "Chief Agent" of life and salvation (Ac 3:15; Heb 2:10), and through him the abolishing of death is assured. (2Ti 1:10) By suffering death, Jesus 'tasted death for every man' and provided "a corresponding ransom for all." (Heb 2:9; 1Ti 2:6) By means of Jesus' "one act of justification," a cancellation of the condemnation of death that sin brings now became possible, so that men of all sorts might enjoy "a declaring of them righteous for life." (Ro 5:15, 16, 18, 19; Heb 9:27, 28; see DECLARE RIGHTEOUS; RANSOM.) Thus, concerning Jesus' true followers, it could be said that they had, in effect, "passed over from death to life." (Joh 5:24) Those disobeying the Son and not exercising love, however, 'remain in death' and under God's condemnation. (1Jo 3:14; Joh 3:36) Those who want to be free from condemnation and free from "the law of sin and of death" must be guided by God's spirit and produce its fruits, for "the minding of the [sinful] flesh means death."—Ro 8:1-6; Col 1:21-23.

Jesus' sacrificial course, terminating in his death and resurrection, was likened by him to baptism. (Mr 10:38, 39; Lu 12:50; compare Eph 4:9, 10.) The apostle Paul showed that Jesus' anointed followers also would go through a similar baptism into death, their resurrection to heavenly glory ensuing. (Ro 6:3-5; Php 3:10, 11) In expressing his earnest desire to take up heavenly life, Paul showed that it was not death itself that was wanted by spirit-begotten Christians, nor to lie "naked" in death, but the 'putting on' of a heavenly body in order to be at "home with the Lord." (2Co 5:1-8; compare 2Pe 1:13-15.) In the meantime, death "is at work" in them, while, by their ministry, they bring a message of life to those to whom they minister.—2Co 4:10-14; Pr

18:21; see Baptism (Baptism Into Christ Jesus, Into His Death).

Those who benefit from that ministry include the great crowd that have the prospect of surviving the great tribulation and enjoying eternal life on a paradise earth. Because of their faith in the sin-atoning value of Jesus' sacrifice, they, too, come to have a clean standing before God.—1Jo 2:2; Re 7:9, 14.

Jesus speaks of himself as having "the keys of death and of Hades" (Re 1:18), and he uses these in releasing those held by death. (Joh 5:28, 29; Re 20:13) Jehovah God's release of Jesus from Hades serves as a "guarantee to all men" of God's future day of judgment or reckoning and provides assurance that there will be a resurrection of those in Hades. (Ac 17:31; 1Co 15:20, 21) Those inheriting God's Kingdom in immortality are described as triumphing over death in their resurrection, so that its "sting" is overcome.—1Co 15:50, 54-56; compare Ho 13:14; Re 20:6.

The Destruction of Death. At Isaiah 25:8 the prophetic promise is made that God "will actually swallow up death forever, and the Sovereign Lord Jehovah will certainly wipe the tears from all faces." The sting producing death is sin (1Co 15:56), and thus all having sin and its accompanying imperfection have death working in their bodies. (Ro 7:13, 23, 24) The abolition of death, therefore, would require the abolition of that which produces death: sin. By the removal of the last trace of sin from obedient mankind, the authority of death will be abolished and death itself will be destroyed, and this is to be accomplished during the reign of Christ. (1Co 15:24-26) Thereby death, brought upon the human race by Adam's transgression, "will be no more." (Ro 5:12; Re 21:3, 4) Its destruction is figuratively likened to its being hurled into a "lake of fire."—Re 20:14; see Lake of Fire.

Second Death. "The lake of fire" into which death, Hades, the symbolic "wild beast" and "the false prophet," Satan, his demons, and the persistent practicers of wickedness on earth are cast is shown to mean "the second death." (Re 20:10, 14, 15; 21:8; Mt 25:41) Initially death resulted from and was passed on to mankind as a result of Adam's transgression; hence "the second death" must be distinct from this inherited death. It is evident from the cited texts that there is no release possible from "the second death." The situation of those in "the second death" corresponds to the outcome warned of in such texts as Hebrews 6:4-8; 10:26, 27; and Matthew 12:32.

On the other hand, those represented as gaining "the crown of life" and having part in "the first resurrection" are free from any possibility of harm by the second death. (Re 2:10, 11) These, who are to reign with Christ, receive immortality (deathlessness) and incorruption and hence are beyond the "authority" of the second death.—1Co 15:50-54; Re 20:6; compare Joh 8:51.

Illustrative Use. Death is personified as a "king" ruling over mankind from the time of Adam (Ro 5:14), along with the rule of King Sin. (Ro 6:12) Thus, these kings are spoken of as exercising their "law" over those subject to their dominion. (Ro 8:2) With Christ's coming and the provision of the ransom, undeserved kindness began exercising a superior kingship over those accepting God's gift, "with everlasting life in view."—Ro 5:15-17, 21.

Though men, disregarding God's purposes, may try to make their own pact or covenant with King Death, it will fail. (Isa 28:15, 18) Like a horseman riding behind war and famine, death is pictured as bringing mass mortality to earth's inhabitants.—Re 6:8; compare Jer 9:21, 22.

Those spiritually sick or distressed are described as "arriving at the gates of death" (Ps 107:17-20; compare Job 38:17; Ps 9:13), and those passing through such "gates" enter the figurative "house of meeting for everyone living" (Job 30:23; compare 2Sa 12:21-23), with its "interior rooms" (Pr 7:27) and a capacity for victims that is never completely filled. (Hab 2:5) Those going into Sheol are like sheep shepherded by death.—Ps 49:14.

"The pangs of death." At Acts 2:24 the apostle Peter spoke of Jesus as being 'loosed from the pangs of death, for it was not possible for him to continue to be held fast by it.' The Greek word (o·din') here translated "pangs" is elsewhere used to mean the pains of childbirth (1Th 5:3) but may also mean travail, pain, calamity, or distress generally. (Mt 24:8) Additionally, it was used by the translators of the Greek *Septuagint* in rendering the Hebrew word *che'vel* in texts where the evident meaning is "rope." (2Sa 22:6; Ps 18:4, 5) A related Hebrew word means "birth pangs," leading some commentators and lexicographers to suggest that the Greek term (o·din') used by Luke at Acts 2:24 also had this double meaning, at least in Hellenistic Greek of apostolic times. Thus some translations render the phrase in this verse as "the bands [or bonds] of death." (*NC* [Spanish]; *Segond, Ostervald* [French]) In numerous texts the danger of death is represented as reaching out to snare the threatened one (Pr 13:14; 14:27)

with ropes that encircle him and bring him down into "the distressing circumstances of Sheol." (Ps 116:3) Whereas other texts, already considered, show that there is no consciousness in death, and it is obvious that Jesus was not in any literal pain while dead, nonetheless death is presented as a bitter and distressing experience (1Sa 15:32; Ps 55:4; Ec 7:26) not only in the pain usually preceding it (Ps 73:4, 5) but in the loss of all activity and freedom that its paralyzing grip brings. So, it may be that it is in this sense that Jesus' resurrection 'loosed' him from "the pangs of death," freeing him from its distressing grip.

Change in spiritual state or condition. The death state is used to illustrate the spiritually dead condition of the world in general, so Jesus could speak of 'the dead burying the dead,' and the apostle Paul could refer to the woman living for sensual gratification as "dead though she is living." (Lu 9:60; 1Ti 5:6; Eph 2:1) And since physical death discharges one from any debts or obligations existing up to that time (Ro 6:7), a Christian's being freed or liberated from sin (Ro 6:2, 11) and from the condemnation of the Mosaic Law (Ro 7:2-6) is also likened to death, such one having 'died' to his former situation and obligations. The one figuratively dying in such a way, of course, is still alive physically and is now free to follow Christ as a slave to righteousness.—Ro 6:18-20; Ga 5:1.

The use of death to represent a change in one's state or condition throws light on prophetic visions, such as that in the book of Ezekiel wherein God's people in exile in Babylon are likened to dried-out bones and to persons dead and buried. (Eze 37:1-12) They were to "come to life" again and be settled on their own soil once more. (Eze 37:13, 14) Comparable illustrations are found at Revelation 11:3, 7-12 and Luke 16:19-31.

DEBIR (De′bir) [Innermost; Hindmost].

1. The king of Eglon, one of four petty kingdoms allied with the king of Jerusalem to attack the city of Gibeon for making peace with Joshua. (Jos 10:1-5) Gibeon's surrender to Joshua caused fear, since it likely weakened any united front against Israel (Jos 9:1, 2) and at the same time apparently gave Joshua greater mobility between northern and southern parts of the Promised Land, allowing for conquest of the land section by section. Gibeon's siege brought Joshua's army to its rescue, and aided by miracles, Joshua routed the Canaanite military, forcing Debir and the other kings to take refuge in a cave. Here they were trapped until later executed.—Jos 10:6-27.

2. A royal Canaanite city (Jos 10:38, 39), also known as Kiriath-sepher and Kiriath-sannah. (Jos 15:15, 49; Jg 1:11) It was in the inheritance of Judah but became a Levitical city of the Kohathites.—Jos 21:9, 15; 1Ch 6:54, 58.

There are apparently two accounts of Israel's first conquest of Debir as part of Joshua's military operations. The first account simply states that Debir's population was annihilated. (Jos 10:38, 39) The second, Joshua 11:21-23, is likely a recapitulation of the same conquest (since verse 18 refers to the 'many days when Joshua waged war with all these kings'), while supplying the additional information that Joshua "cut off the Anakim . . . from Debir" and other cities. This supplementary material may have been included to show that even the tall Anakim, who had struck such fear in the hearts of Israel's spies more than 40 years earlier (Nu 13:28, 31-33; De 9:2), had not proved invulnerable.

Nevertheless, it appears that the Anakim reestablished themselves in the city of Debir, perhaps coming in from the Philistine coast (Jos 11:22) while Israel was temporarily at its Gilgal camp or was warring in the N. (Jos 10:43–11:15) Though Joshua's initial campaigns had served to subdue the unified resistance of enemy forces in the land of Canaan, rapidly demolishing all major strongholds, apparently this type of warfare did not allow for the establishing of garrisons to hold the sites of all the destroyed cities. So, a second conquest or "mopping up" operation was effected at Debir by Othniel, who, because of distinguishing himself in the city's conquest, was given Achsah, the daughter of veteran warrior Caleb, as a wife. —Jos 15:13-19; Jg 1:11-15.

It cannot be ascertained precisely when in Israel's history this second conquest occurred. The book of Judges opens with the phrase *"after* the death of Joshua," and the account of Caleb's taking of Debir follows thereafter. (Jg 1:11-15) This, according to some, would make Judah's conquest of Debir subsequent to Joshua's death and would mean that the similar account found at Joshua 15:13-19 was a later addition to the book bearing Joshua's name. However, others view Judges 1:1 as only a formal introduction to connect it with the book of Joshua, arguing that Caleb would hardly wait for years until Joshua died before driving the Anakim from his promised possession. Hence, they consider the Judges account to be a restatement of that in Joshua.

Various suggestions have been put forth by Biblical scholars regarding the location of Debir in the mountainous region of Judah. In the past it was identified with Tell Beit Mirsim, about 20 km (12 mi) WSW of Hebron. However, now it is identified with Khirbet Rabud, about 13 km (8 mi) SW of Hebron.

Debir's ancient name, Kiriath-sepher (Jos 15: 15; Jg 1:11), means "Town of the Book." This has led some to conjecture that Debir was the center of Canaanite religious and legal learning and a place where public registers were kept.

3. A site "at the low plain of Achor" appearing in Judah's boundary list. (Jos 15:7) Though its exact location is not now known, some geographers believe the name has survived in Thogheret ed-Debr, SW of Jericho.

4. A location on the boundary of Gad in Gilead. (Jos 13:26) This Debir is usually considered to be the same as Lo-debar, where the home of Machir (who hosted Mephibosheth and, later, David) was located. (2Sa 9:4-6; 17:27-29) Some tentatively identify Debir in Gad with Umm ed-Dabar, 16 km (10 mi) S of the Sea of Galilee.

DEBORAH   (Deb'o·rah) [Bee].

1. Rebekah's nurse. When Rebekah left the household of her father Bethuel to move to Palestine and marry Isaac, Deborah accompanied her. (Ge 24:59) After years of service in Isaac's household, Deborah came to be in Jacob's household, perhaps after the death of Rebekah. Evidently some 125 years after Rebekah's marriage to Isaac, Deborah died and was buried under a big tree at Bethel. The name given to the tree (Allon-bacuth, meaning "Massive Tree of Weeping") indicates how beloved she had become to Jacob and his family.—Ge 35:8.

2. A prophetess in Israel; the wife of Lappidoth. (Jg 4:4) There is no evidence that Lappidoth and Barak were the same person, as some suggest. The association of Deborah and Barak was purely because of their common interest in liberating Israel from Canaanite oppression. Deborah dwelt under a palm tree located in the mountainous region of Ephraim between Ramah and Bethel; "the sons of Israel would go up to her for judgment."—Jg 4:5.

Jehovah used Deborah to summon Barak from Kedesh-naphtali and inform him of God's purpose to use 10,000 men in defeating the huge army of Canaanite King Jabin under his army chief Sisera. Barak had Jehovah's promise that He would give the enemy into his hand. But in addition, as he gathered the troops and led them to Mount Tabor, he insisted on the presence of Deborah as God's

representative, even though Deborah was a woman. Deborah proved willing to leave her place of greater security and to join Barak. However, she prophesied that "the beautifying thing" of the victory would go to a woman. These words were fulfilled when the woman Jael put Sisera to death. —Jg 4:6-10, 17-22.

Deborah and Barak joined in singing a song on the day of victory. Part of the song is written in the first person, indicating that Deborah was its composer, in part, if not in its entirety. (Jg 5:7) It was a custom for the women to celebrate victories with song and dance. (Ex 15:20, 21; Jg 11:34; 1Sa 18:6, 7; Ps 68:11) The song gives all credit and praise to Jehovah for the victory in behalf of his people. It adds considerably to the narrative that precedes it, and to get a full picture the two must be viewed side by side. After describing Jehovah's might and majesty and recalling the condition of Israel prior to Barak's fight, it commends the tribes who responded to the call and inquires about others who did not. It graphically adds details concerning the battle and the rout of the Canaanites, the courageous act of Jael in killing Sisera, and the disappointment of Sisera's mother, who waited in vain for spoils and slaves of Israel to be brought back after the expected victory of her son Sisera.—Jg 5.

DEBT, DEBTOR.   A debt refers to that which is owed, an obligation to pay or render something. In ancient Israel, debts were incurred primarily because of financial reverses. For an Israelite to become a debtor was a misfortune; the borrower, in effect, became the lender's servant. (Pr 22:7) God's people were therefore commanded to be generous and unselfish in lending to needy fellow Israelites, not seeking to profit from their adversity by charging them interest. (Ex 22:25; De 15:7, 8; Ps 37:26; 112:5) But foreigners could be required to pay interest. (De 23:20) Jewish commentators understand this provision to apply to business loans, not to cases of need. Ordinarily foreigners were in Israel only temporarily, often as merchants, and could reasonably be expected to pay interest, especially since they would also be lending to others on interest.

At times a third party would assume responsibility, or go surety, for a debtor. This practice is repeatedly warned against in the book of Proverbs (6:1-3; 11:15; 17:18; 22:26), since the one going surety would be the loser in case of the debtor's default.

The first-century Christian view of debts is expressed at Romans 13:8: "Do not you people be owing anybody a single thing, except to love one another."

Law Protected Creditors and Debtors. Under the Mosaic Law, even a thief was required to pay off the debt he incurred through his wrongdoing. If unable to do so, he was to be sold into slavery. (Ex 22:1, 3) Thus the victim was certain of being compensated for his loss.

Faithful Israelites recognized that meeting their debts was a divine requirement. (Ps 37:21) So the creditor could rest assured of receiving repayment. An Israelite with no material assets could sell himself or his children into slavery to care for his debts.—Ex 21:7; Le 25:39; compare 2Ki 4:1-7.

On the other hand, the Law also protected the debtor. The creditor could not enter the house of the debtor and seize a pledge but had to wait outside until the debtor brought it to him. (De 24:10, 11) Neither the garment of a widow nor necessities, such as a hand mill or the upper grindstone thereof, could be seized as a pledge. (De 24:6, 17) Since it was common for the poor to have only one outer garment (mantle), in which they also slept, this garment, if taken as a pledge, had to be returned by the creditor at sunset.—Ex 22:26, 27; De 24:12, 13.

According to Deuteronomy 15:1-3, it appears that during the Sabbath year (every seventh year) a creditor could not press a fellow Israelite for payment of a debt. Unlike the Sabbath-keeping Israelite who realized virtually no return from his land, the foreigner continued to have an income from his nonagricultural work. Reasonably, therefore, he could be pressed for payment of a debt during the Sabbath year. At the approach of the Sabbath year, some Israelites, knowing that they would not be able to press matters, may have refrained from lending to their needy brothers. But the Law condemned such selfishness.—De 15:9.

During the Jubilee year (every 50th year) Hebrew slaves were set free; all hereditary possessions, with the exception of houses in walled cities not formerly belonging to Levites, were returned to their original owners. This arrangement prevented Israelite families from sinking into hopeless debt and poverty. Even one who mismanaged his assets could not permanently lose his inheritance for his family.—Le 25:10-41.

Strict adherence to God's law would have resulted in a stable economy free from great national and internal debts. The Israelites were assured: "For Jehovah your God will indeed bless you just as he has promised you, and you will certainly lend on pledge to many nations, whereas you yourself will not borrow."—De 15:6.

Abuses. As Israel lapsed into a course of unfaithfulness, needy debtors were among those that suffered. The fact that debtors joined themselves to David while he was outlawed suggests that they were hard pressed by their creditors. (1Sa 22:2) Lending on interest to fellow Israelites appears to have become common. (Isa 24:2) Through his prophet Amos, Jehovah condemned Israel for selling "someone poor for the price of a pair of sandals." (Am 2:6) And by means of Ezekiel, He denounced the Israelites for charging interest and fraudulently profiting from their companions.—Eze 22:12.

After the return from Babylonian exile, a deplorable situation developed among the Jews because of their failure to obey God's law about making interest-free loans to needy fellow Israelites. In the time of Nehemiah, many Jews had been forced to put up their houses, fields, and even their sons and daughters as security. However, after Nehemiah's exhortation to rectify matters, the creditors agreed to make restoration to their debtors and to lend without interest.—Ne 5:1-13.

Jesus' Illustrations. In the first century C.E., the relationship of creditors and debtors was very familiar to the Jews, and Jesus at times drew on this for his illustrations. He emphasized the need to be forgiving by telling about a wicked slave who, although having been released from a 60,000,000-denarius (c. $40,000,000) debt, had a fellow slave thrown into prison for a 100-denarius (c. $70) debt. (Mt 18:23-33) The illustration of two debtors, one of whom was forgiven a 500-denarius (c. $350) debt and the other a 50-denarius (c. $35) debt, highlighted the principle: "He who is forgiven little, loves little." (Lu 7:41-47) Wise use of "unrighteous" (material) riches to make friends with God is illustrated by the unrighteous steward who, when about to lose his position, shrewdly used his authority to make friends with the debtors of his master by reducing their debts.—Lu 16:1-9.

Other Debts. In the Scriptures, the words "debt" and "debtor" are also used with reference to obligations other than those accrued by borrowing. The wage due a worker is counted as a "debt." (Ro 4:4) Sinners are "debtors" to those against whom they have transgressed and therefore must seek their forgiveness. God's forgiveness of "debts" depends on whether a person has forgiven his personal "debtors." (Mt 6:12, 14, 15;

Lu 13:4) In view of his obligation to preach "the good news," the apostle Paul spoke of himself as a "debtor" to all persons. (Ro 1:14, 15) Gentile believers were, in effect, "debtors" to the Jewish Christians at Jerusalem because of having benefited spiritually from them. Therefore, it was only proper that they assist their poor Jewish brothers materially.—Ro 15:26, 27.

DECALOGUE.   See TEN WORDS.

DECAPOLIS   (De·cap'o·lis) [Ten-City Region].
A league or confederation of ten cities (from Greek *de'ka,* meaning "ten," and *po'lis,* "city"). The name also applied to the region in which most of these cities were centered.—Mt 4:25.

Following the conquest by Alexander the Great in about 332 B.C.E., Greek colonies developed in Syria and Palestine, apparently settled by veterans from Alexander's armies who were thereafter followed by Greek-speaking immigrants. In many cases these colonies grew on the sites of earlier Jewish towns, while in others they were built on fresh sites, particularly E of the Jordan River. They flourished during the rule of the Seleucids of Syria and the Ptolemies of Egypt, but the rise of the Maccabean-Jewish state (starting c. 168 B.C.E.) greatly jeopardized their relatively independent position. While the populations of these cities doubtless included many Jews, still these cities were centers of Greek culture and organization and hence were very much out of step with the Maccabean aims. When Pompey conquered and reorganized Palestine in 63 B.C.E., these Hellenistic cities were given Roman protection and a favored status. They were allowed to mint their own coins and, to a great extent, to exercise self-government, although they still owed allegiance to Rome and to the Syrian provincial government and were required to pay taxes and provide men for military service.

Formation of the League.   Likely sometime between Pompey's conquest and the death of Herod the Great (c. 1 B.C.E.) ten of these Hellenistic cities formed themselves into the loose federation known as the Decapolis. The motive underlying this union seems to have been a mutual interest in close trade relations and also defense against either anti-Hellenistic forces within Palestine or aggressive nomadic tribes in the desert regions to the E. The term "Decapolis" first appears in the Christian Greek Scriptures and in the writings of Josephus and Pliny the Elder (both of the first century C.E.). Pliny, while acknowledging that some difference of opinion already existed, listed the following cities as among the original ten: Damascus, Philadelphia, Raphana, Scythopolis, Gadara, Hippo (Hippos), Dion, Pella,

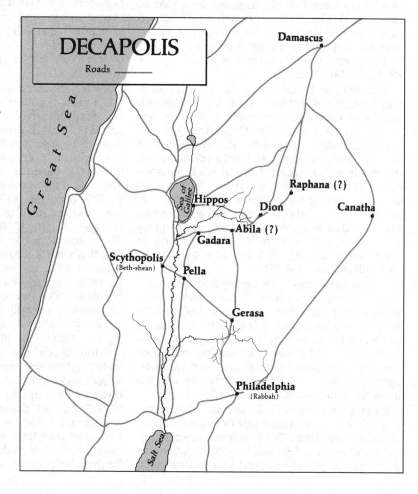

DECAPOLIS

Roads _____

Damascus

Great Sea

Sea of Galilee

Hippos

Raphana (?)

Dion

Canatha

Abila (?)

Gadara

Scythopolis
(Beth-shean)

Pella

Gerasa

Philadelphia
(Rabbah)

Salt Sea

Galasa (Gerasa), and Canatha. (*Natural History,* V, XVI, 74) Of these, only Scythopolis (Beth-shean) lay W of the Jordan; because of the strategic position of the Valley of Esdraelon, it served as an important link with the Mediterranean Coast and seaports. Damascus, far to the N in Syria, was evidently included because of its importance as a trade center. Philadelphia (ancient Rabbah, modern 'Amman) was the southernmost of the ten cities, only about 40 km (25 mi) NE of the northern end of the Dead Sea. The remainder of the cities were in the fertile region of Gilead or neighboring Bashan. Most of them are believed to have been on or near the main roads of that region. Canatha is likely the Kenath of Numbers 32:42.

In the second century C.E., Ptolemy names 18 cities as in the "Decapolis," which may indicate that the name came to be used in a general way and that the number of cities varied. Some scholars would put Abila, listed by Ptolemy, in place of Raphana as among the original ten. It seems evident, at any rate, that the Decapolis region did not have precisely defined boundaries and that the authority of the cities of the Decapolis did not embrace all the intervening territory but applied only within the district of each particular city.

Jesus' Ministry and the Decapolis.   While people from the Decapolis were among the crowds that flocked to hear Jesus' teaching in Galilee (Mt 4:25), there is no specific mention of his having devoted time to any of its Hellenistic cities. Jesus did enter the region of Decapolis during his Galilean ministry when he crossed the Sea of Galilee and entered the country of the Gerasenes (or Gadarenes according to Mt 8:28). (Mr 5:1) But here, after he had cast out demons and permitted them to enter a herd of swine, resulting in the herd's destruction, the people from the nearby city and countryside urged Jesus to 'get out of their districts.' He complied, but the man he had freed from demon possession obeyed Jesus' instruction to go witness to his relatives, and he proclaimed Jesus' healing works in the Decapolis. (Mr 5:2-20) Some scholars believe the herd of swine there was a further evidence of the non-Jewish influence prevalent in that region.

After the Passover of 32 C.E., and upon returning from a trip to the regions of Tyre and Sidon in Phoenicia, Jesus came "to the sea of Galilee up through the midst of the regions of Decapolis." (Mr 7:31) Somewhere in this region he healed a deaf man having a speech impediment and later miraculously fed a crowd of 4,000.—Mr 7:32–8:9.

Later History.   According to Eusebius, prior to the destruction of Jerusalem in 70 C.E., Christians of Judea fled to the Decapolitan city of Pella in the mountainous region of Gilead, thereby giving heed to Jesus' prophetic warning.—Lu 21:20, 21; *The Ecclesiastical History,* III, V, 3.

By no means alone among the cities of Palestine in their Hellenistic leanings, the cities of the Decapolis reflected the most powerful expression of Greek influence. They are believed to have reached their peak during the second century C.E., and in the following century the league began to break up. Evidence of the strong Greek influence, as well as the wealth of the Decapolitan cities, can be seen in the impressive remains of theaters, amphitheaters, temples, baths, aqueducts, and other structures at Gerasa (modern Jarash) as well as at other cities.

DECLARE RIGHTEOUS.

The Hebrew verb *tsa·dheq'* (related to *tse'dheq,* meaning "righteousness") at times is rendered "declare righteous" and "pronounce righteous." (Ex 23:7; De 25:1) This Biblical expression is also rendered as "justify," and the noun forms are translated "justification." The original words (*di·kai·o'o* [verb], *di·kai'o·ma* and *di·kai'o·sis* [nouns]) in the Christian Greek Scriptures, where the fullest explanation of the matter is found, basically carry the idea of absolving or clearing of any charge, holding as guiltless, and hence acquitting, or pronouncing and treating as righteous.—See W. Bauer's *Greek-English Lexicon of the New Testament* (revised by F. W. Gingrich and F. Danker), 1979, pp. 197, 198; also *A Greek-English Lexicon,* by H. Liddell and R. Scott (revised by H. Jones), Oxford, 1968, p. 429.

Thus the apostle Paul speaks of God as being "proved righteous [form of *di·kai·o'o*]" in His words and winning when being judged by detractors. (Ro 3:4) Jesus said that "wisdom is proved righteous by its works" and that, when rendering an account on Judgment Day, men would be "declared righteous [form of *di·kai·o'o*]" or condemned by their words. (Mt 11:19; 12:36, 37) Jesus said that the humble tax collector who prayed repentantly in the temple "went down to his home proved more righteous" than the boastful Pharisee praying at the same time. (Lu 18:9-14; 16:15) The apostle Paul states that the person who dies is "acquitted [form of *di·kai·o'o*] from his sin," having paid the penalty of death. —Ro 6:7, 23.

However, in addition to such usages, these Greek words are used in a special sense as referring to an act of God whereby one is accounted guiltless (Ac 13:38, 39; Ro 8:33) and also to God's act in declaring a person perfect in integrity and judged worthy of the right to life, as will be seen.

In Pre-Christian Times. Originally, Adam was perfect, a righteous man, a human "son of God." (Lu 3:38) He was righteous by virtue of God's creation of him and was declared "very good" by his Creator. (Ge 1:31) But he failed to maintain integrity before God and lost righteousness for himself and for his future offspring.—Ge 3:17-19; Ro 5:12.

Nevertheless, from among his descendants there came men of faith who "walked with the true God," such as Noah, Enoch, and Job. (Ge 5:22; 6:9; 7:1; Job 1:1, 8; 2:3) Of Abraham, it is stated that he exercised faith in God and was "declared righteous"; also, it is written that Rahab of Jericho manifested her faith by her works and so was "declared righteous," her life being spared when the city of Jericho was destroyed. (Jas 2:21-23, 25) It may be noted that in James' epistle (as cited) and also in Paul's letter to the Romans (4:3-5, 9-11), in which he quotes Genesis 15:6, it is stated that Abraham's faith was "counted to him as righteousness." Understanding of this expression is aided by considering the sense of the Greek verb lo·gi′zo·mai, "count," here used.

How "counted" righteous. This Greek verb lo·gi′zo·mai was used regularly in ancient times for numerical calculations or computations such as in accounting, being used when referring both to something that was entered on the debit side of an account and also to something entered on the credit side thereof. In the Bible it is used to mean "reckon, credit, count, or take into account." Thus 1 Corinthians 13:5 says that love "does not keep account [form of lo·gi′zo·mai] of the injury" (compare 2Ti 4:16); and the psalmist David is quoted as saying: "Happy is the man whose sin Jehovah will by no means take into account." (Ro 4:8) Paul showed to those who looked at things according to their face value the need to make a proper evaluation of matters, to look at both sides of the ledger, as it were. (2Co 10:2, 7, 10-12) At the same time, Paul was concerned that "no one should put to [his] credit [form of lo·gi′zo·mai]" more than was correct as regards his ministry. —2Co 12:6, 7.

The word lo·gi′zo·mai may also mean "esteem, appraise, count, rate, or reckon (with a group, class, or type)." (1Co 4:1) Thus Jesus said that he would be "reckoned [form of lo·gi′zo·mai] with lawless ones," that is, counted or classed as in among them or as if one of them. (Lu 22:37) In his letter to the Romans, the apostle says that in the case of the uncircumcised person keeping the Law, his "uncircumcision will be counted as circumcision," that is, estimated or looked upon as if it were circumcision. (Ro 2:26) In a similar sense, Christians were urged to 'reckon themselves to be dead as regards sin but alive as regards God by Christ Jesus.' (Ro 6:11) And anointed Christians from among the Gentiles, though not fleshly descendants of Abraham, were "counted as the seed" of Abraham.—Ro 9:8.

How could Abraham be declared righteous before the death of Christ?

So, also, Abraham's faith, combined with works, was "counted [reckoned, credited, or attributed] to him as righteousness." (Ro 4:20-22) This, of course, does not mean that he and other faithful men of pre-Christian times were perfect or free from sin; yet, by virtue of their exercise of faith in God's promise concerning the "seed" and because they were striving to follow God's commands, they were not classed as unrighteous with no standing before God, like the rest of the world of mankind. (Ge 3:15; Ps 119:2, 3) Jehovah lovingly accounted them guiltless, when compared with the world of mankind alienated from God. (Ps 32:1, 2; Eph 2:12) Thus, God could, by reason of their faith, have dealings with such imperfect men and bless them, doing so while still remaining true to his own perfect standards of justice. (Ps 36:10) However, such ones recognized their need for redemption from sin and were awaiting God's due time to provide it.—Ps 49:7-9; Heb 9:26.

Christ Jesus' "One Act of Justification." The Scriptures show that Jesus Christ when on earth was actually perfect in human organism (1Pe 1:18, 19) and that he maintained his perfection by continuing to retain and strengthen his integrity under test. This was in accord with God's purpose to make the Chief Agent of salvation "perfect through sufferings." (Heb 2:10) That is, Jesus was perfected as to obedience and integrity keeping and was perfected for his position as God's High Priest of salvation, as Paul shows at Hebrews 5:7-10. Finishing his earthly course free from flaw in any sense of the word, Jesus was acknowledged by God as justified. He was thus the only man who, through test, stood firmly and positively just, or righteous before God *on his own merit.* By this "one act of justification [form of *di·kai'o·ma*]," that is, by Jesus' proving himself perfectly righteous through his entire flawless course, including his sacrifice, he provided the basis for declaring righteous those persons having faith in Christ.—Ro 5:17-19; 3:25, 26; 4:25.

In the Christian Congregation. With the coming of God's Son as the promised Redeemer, a new factor existed upon which God could base his dealings with his human servants. The followers of Jesus Christ who are called to be his spiritual brothers, with the prospect of being joint heirs with him in the heavenly Kingdom (Ro 8:17), are first declared righteous by God on the basis of their faith in Jesus Christ. (Ro 3:24, 28) This is a judicial act of Jehovah God; therefore before him as the Supreme Judge no one can "file accusation" against his chosen ones. (Ro 8:33, 34) Why does God take this action toward them?

First, it is because Jehovah is perfect and holy (Isa 6:3); hence, in harmony with his holiness, those whom he accepts as his sons must be perfect. (De 32:4, 5) Jesus Christ, God's chief Son, showed himself perfect, "loyal, guileless, undefiled, separated from the sinners." (Heb 7:26) His followers, however, are taken from among the sons of Adam, who, because of sin, fathered an imperfect, sinful family. (Ro 5:12; 1Co 15:22) Thus, as John 1:12, 13 shows, Jesus' followers were not, to begin with, sons of God. By his undeserved kindness, Jehovah God arranged a process of "adoption" through which he accepts such favored ones and brings them into a spiritual relationship as part of his family of sons. (Ro 8:15, 16; 1Jo 3:1) Consequently, God lays the basis for their entry into or their adoption to sonship by declaring them righteous through the merit of Christ's ransom sacrifice in which they exercise faith, acquitting them of all guilt due to sin. (Ro 5:1, 2, 8-11; compare Joh 1:12.) They are, therefore, "counted," or credited, as being completely righteous persons, all their sins being forgiven and not charged against them.—Ro 4:6-8; 8:1, 2; Heb 10:12, 14.

This declaring of such Christians righteous, therefore, goes much farther than in the case of Abraham (and other pre-Christian servants of Jehovah), previously discussed. Indicating the scope of Abraham's justification, the disciple James wrote: "The scripture was fulfilled which says: 'Abraham put faith in Jehovah, and it was counted to him as righteousness,' and he came to be called 'Jehovah's friend.'" (Jas 2:20-23) So, because of his faith, Abraham was declared righteous *as a friend of God,* not as a son of God because of being "born again" with heavenly life

in view. (Joh 3:13) The Scriptural record makes clear that prior to Christ's coming neither such sonship nor such a heavenly hope had been opened up to men.—Joh 1:12, 17, 18; 2Ti 1:10; 1Pe 1:3; 1Jo 3:1.

It can be seen that, though enjoying the status of righteous persons before God, these Christians do not possess actual or literal perfection in the flesh. (1Jo 1:8; 2:1) In view of the prospect of heavenly life for these followers of Christ, such literal perfection in fleshly organism now is not actually needed. (1Co 15:42-44, 50; Heb 3:1; 1Pe 1:3, 4) However, by their being declared righteous, having righteousness "counted," or credited, to them, God's requirements of justice are satisfied, and he brings the adopted ones into the "new covenant" validated by the blood of Jesus Christ. (Lu 22:20; Mt 26:28) These adopted spiritual sons in the new covenant that is made with spiritual Israel are 'baptized into Christ's death,' eventually dying a death like his.—Ro 6:3-5; Php 3:10, 11.

Although Jehovah forgives their sins of fleshly weakness and imperfection, nevertheless, a conflict exists in these Christians, as illustrated in Paul's letter to the Romans (7:21-25). It is between the law of their renewed mind (Ro 12:2; Eph 4:23), or "God's law," and "sin's law" that is in their members. This is because their fleshly bodies are not perfected, even though they are counted righteous and their sins are forgiven. This conflict contributes to the test of their integrity toward God. They can win this conflict by the help of God's spirit and with the assistance of their merciful High Priest, Christ Jesus. (Ro 7:25; Heb 2:17, 18) To win, however, they must constantly exercise faith in Christ's ransom sacrifice and follow him, thus maintaining their righteousness in God's eyes. (Compare Re 22:11.) Thereby they 'make their calling and choosing sure' for themselves. (2Pe 1:10; Ro 5:1, 9; 8:23-34; Tit 3:6, 7) If, on the other hand, they take up the *practice* of sin, falling away from the faith, they lose their favored standing before God as righteous persons because they "impale the Son of God afresh for themselves and expose him to public shame." (Heb 6:4-8) Such ones face destruction. (Heb 10:26-31, 38, 39) Thus, Jesus spoke of the sin that has no forgiveness, and the apostle John distinguished between the sin that "does not incur death" and the sin that "does incur death."—Mt 12:31, 32; 1Jo 5:16, 17.

Jesus Christ, after maintaining his faithfulness until death, was "made alive in the spirit," given immortality and incorruption. (1Pe 3:18; 1Co 15: 42, 45; 1Ti 6:16) He was thus "declared [or pronounced] righteous in spirit" (1Ti 3:16; Ro 1:2-4) and sat down at the right hand of God in the heavens. (Heb 8:1; Php 2:9-11) The faithful footstep followers of Christ await a resurrection like his (Ro 6:5), looking forward to becoming recipients of "divine nature."—2Pe 1:4.

Other Righteous Ones. In one of Jesus' illustrations, or parables, relating to the time of his coming in Kingdom glory, persons likened to sheep are designated as "righteous ones." (Mt 25:31-46) It is notable, however, that in this illustration these "righteous ones" are presented as separate and distinct from those whom Christ calls "my brothers." (Mt 25:34, 37, 40, 46; compare Heb 2:10, 11.) Because these sheeplike ones render assistance to Christ's spiritual "brothers," thus demonstrating faith in Christ himself, they are blessed by God and are called "righteous ones." Like Abraham, they are accounted, or declared, righteous as friends of God. (Jas 2:23) This righteous standing will mean survival for them when the "goats" depart "into everlasting cutting-off."—Mt 25:46.

A parallel situation may be noted in the vision recorded at Revelation 7:3-17. Here, a "great crowd" of indefinite number are shown as distinct from the 144,000 'sealed ones.' (Compare Eph 1:13, 14; 2Co 5:1.) That this "great crowd" enjoys a righteous standing before God is indicated by the fact that they are described as having "washed their robes and made them white in the blood of the Lamb."—Re 7:14.

The "great crowd," who survive the "great tribulation," are not yet declared righteous *for life* —that is, as worthy of the right to everlasting life on earth. They need to continue partaking of the "fountains of waters of life," as guided by the Lamb, Christ Jesus. They will need to do this during the Millennial Reign of Christ. (Re 7:17; 22:1, 2) If they prove loyal to Jehovah through a final test at the end of the thousand years, they will have their names permanently retained in God's book of life, Jehovah thus declaring, or acknowledging, that they finally are righteous in the complete sense.—Re 20:7, 8; see LIFE (Trees of Life).

God Proved Righteous in All His Acts. It can be seen that in his dealings with imperfect humans, God never violates his own standards of righteousness and justice. He does not declare sinful persons righteous on their own merit, thereby overlooking or condoning sin. (Ps 143:

1, 2) As the apostle Paul explains: "All have sinned and fall short of the glory of God, and it is as a free gift that they are being declared righteous by his undeserved kindness through the release by the ransom paid by Christ Jesus. God set him forth as an offering for propitiation through faith in his blood. This was in order to exhibit his own righteousness, because he was forgiving the sins that occurred in the past while God was exercising forbearance; so as to exhibit his own righteousness in this present season, that he might be righteous even when declaring righteous the man that has faith in Jesus." (Ro 3:23-26) Thus God, through undeserved kindness, has provided a legal arrangement on the basis of Christ's sacrifice by which he can be completely just and righteous in forgiving the sins of those exercising faith.

Attempts at Proving Oneself Righteous. Since God alone can declare a man righteous, attempts to prove oneself righteous on the basis of one's own merit or by acceptance of the judgment of others as to one's righteousness are of no value. Job was reproved because, though not charging God with any wrong, he was "declaring his own soul righteous rather than God." (Job 32:1, 2) The man versed in the Law who questioned Jesus about the way to everlasting life was indirectly reproved by Jesus for his attempt to prove himself righteous. (Lu 10:25-37) Jesus condemned the Pharisees for seeking to declare themselves righteous before men. (Lu 16:15) The apostle Paul, in particular, showed that, because of the imperfect, sinful state of all mankind, none could be declared righteous through trying to establish their own righteousness by works of the Mosaic Law. (Ro 3:19-24; Ga 3:10-12) Instead, he stressed faith in Christ Jesus as the true basis for such declaration of righteousness. (Ro 10:3, 4) The inspired letter of James complements Paul's statement by showing that such faith must be made to live, not by works of Law, but by works of faith, as in the cases of Abraham and Rahab. —Jas 2:24, 26.

Certain men, falsely claiming to be apostles, unjustly challenged the apostleship and Christian works of Paul, seeking thereby to draw away the Corinthian congregation to themselves. (2Co 11: 12, 13) Paul, knowing that he was faithfully carrying out a stewardship for Christ, stated that he was not concerned with the judgment of men who, wholly unauthorized, sat in effect as a "human tribunal" to judge him. He did not even rely on his own judgment of himself, but he looked to Jehovah as his Examiner. (1Co 4:1-4) Thus the principle is set forth that reliance cannot be put in the judgment of men as to one's righteousness or lack of it, unless their judgment is backed up by God's Word. The person must look into God's Word and let it examine him. (Heb 4:12) However, where the backing of God's Word is evident, a person being reproved by a Christian brother, especially by an elder in the congregation, would not properly turn aside such reproof by trying to prove himself righteous. (Pr 12:1; Heb 12:11; 13:17) And anyone in a position of responsibility who sits in judgment of a matter or a dispute would be condemned by God if he pronounced "the wicked one righteous in consideration of a bribe."—Isa 5:23; Jas 2:8, 9.

DEDAN (De'dan).

1. A Cushite in the line of Raamah. (Ge 10:7; 1Ch 1:9) His posterity apparently settled part of Arabia.

2. A descendant of Abraham through Jokshan. (Ge 25:3; 1Ch 1:32) The Dedanites descending from Jokshan apparently settled S and SE of the Promised Land in the same general vicinity to which Abraham sent all his offspring through Keturah.—Ge 25:6.

Since both families of Dedanites (those of Raamah and of Jokshan) evidently settled in sections of Arabia, there is some question as to which Dedan is meant when the name occurs in later Biblical writings. However, the connection that is sometimes made with other Semitic peoples such as Edom, Tema, and Buz indicates Dedan through Jokshan. For example, Dedan is listed as at one extremity of Edom, whose land was due to be ravaged. (Eze 25:13) Dedan, in "the desert plain," is also told to flee before the invading forces. The Dedanite caravans are to seek quarters in the woods, while Tema, through whose territory they apparently make their flight, is called on to provide food and drink for the fugitives' sustenance. (Isa 21:11-15; Jer 49:8) Like Edom, Dedan would also ultimately be forced to taste of the cup of the wine of Jehovah's rage.—Jer 25:15, 21, 23.

Scholars link Dedan with the oasis of el-Ula, about 120 km (75 mi) SW of Taima.

Other references to Dedan give no indications as to whether a Hamitic or a Semitic people is meant. For instance, Dedan is named at Ezekiel 27:15, 20 as a trader with Tyre. Dedan also views with selfish interest the planned plundering of God's people by Gog of Magog.—Eze 38:13.

DEDICATION. A separation or setting apart

for a sacred purpose. The Hebrew verb *na·zar'* (dedicate) has the basic meaning "keep separate; be separated; withdraw." (Le 15:31; 22:2; Eze 14:7; compare Ho 9:10, ftn.) The related Hebrew word *ne'zer* refers to the sign or symbol of holy dedication worn as a crown upon the sanctified head of a high priest or on the head of an anointed king; it also referred to Naziriteship.—Nu 6:4-6; compare Ge 49:26, ftn.

At Aaron's installation as high priest, a turban made of fine linen was placed on his head. Fastened with a string of blue thread on the front of this turban for all to see was the holy "sign of dedication [*ne'zer*]," a shining plate of pure gold engraved as a seal with the words, in Hebrew, "Holiness belongs to Jehovah." The holy anointing oil was next poured upon the high priest in the installation ceremony. (Ex 29:6, 7; 39:30, 31, ftn; Le 8:9, 12) Consistently the high priest had to be careful to avoid doing anything that would profane the sanctuary, "because the sign of dedication, the anointing oil of his God, is upon him."—Le 21:12.

Similarly, the word *ne'zer* had reference to the "diadem," an official headpiece worn by the anointed kings of Israel as a symbol of their holy office.—2Sa 1:10; 2Ki 11:12; 2Ch 23:11; Ps 89:39; 132:18; Pr 27:24.

When a person took the Nazirite vow to Jehovah he was not to cut his hair or shave his beard as long as the vow was upon him. So his long hair became a crowning sign of his Naziriteship (*ne'zer*). (Nu 6:4-21) In personifying Jerusalem as one who had broken her sacred vows of holiness to Jehovah, the prophet Jeremiah exclaimed: "Shear off your uncut hair [or "dedicated hair"; *niz·rekh'*, a form of *ne'zer*] and throw it away." (Jer 7:29) By another prophet, Jehovah describes how wayward Israel "went in to Baal of Peor, and they proceeded to dedicate themselves [*wai·yin·na·zeru'*, a form of the verb *na·zar'*] to the shameful thing."—Ho 9:10.

In the Christian Greek Scriptures reference is made to certain dedicated things. The winter "festival of dedication" (*en·kai'ni·a*) is mentioned in connection with Jesus' earthly ministry. (Joh 10:22; see FESTIVAL OF DEDICATION.) This Greek word *en·kai'ni·a* has the same root as *en·kai·ni'zo*, which at Hebrews 9:18 is rendered "dedicate" by certain translations (*AS, KJ, Dy, Sp*), but "inaugurate" by others. (*CC, Mo, NE, NW, We*) Similarly, at Hebrews 10:20 some translate it "dedicate" (*AS, Dy, Sp*), others, "inaugurate." (*CC, Mo, NW*) Jesus called attention to the traditional teachings of the Pharisees in regard to "corban," that is, a gift dedicated to God. (Mr 7:11; Mt 15:5; see CORBAN.) Jesus also warned that the time was coming when Herod's temple, together with its "fine stones and dedicated things [a·na·the′ma·sin]," would be thrown down.—Lu 21:5, 6.

DEED. A written agreement duly signed and sometimes sealed, containing the legal terms for the accomplishment of an intended purpose; the documented instrument for the transfer of real estate. The Bible's only use of the Hebrew word *se′pher* in this particular sense concerns Jeremiah's purchase of a field from his cousin Hanamel. —Jer 32:6-15.

The details surrounding the drawing up of this deed are interesting. The money for the purchase, "seven shekels and ten silver pieces," was weighed out in the presence of witnesses. (Jer 32:9) If this stipulation of 'seven and ten' is assumed to be a legal form meaning 17 silver shekels (c. $37), it would be a reasonable price, considering the time and circumstances under which the property was sold. It was a time of war and famine (not many months before Jerusalem was captured by Nebuchadnezzar).

When the money was paid, two deeds, presumably identical, were drafted 'according to the judicial commandment and legal regulations.' One of these was known as "the deed of purchase, the one sealed," and the other was called "the one left open." (Jer 32:11) Only the first one is said to have been signed by witnesses, the whole transaction taking place "before the eyes of all the Jews who were sitting in the Courtyard of the Guard." (Jer 32:12) Both deeds were then placed in an earthenware jar for safekeeping.—Jer 32:14.

The custom of making duplicate deeds but sealing only one was very practical. Leaving one copy open permitted it to be referred to by the interested parties. If it was ever damaged, or its authenticity called into question, or if there was suspicion that it had been altered, then the sealed copy could be presented to the city judges who, after examining the seal, would break it open and make a comparison of the two copies.

DEFECT. See BLEMISH.

DEKER (De′ker) [Piercing]. Father of one of Solomon's 12 deputies. Deker's son provided food for Solomon and his household one month out of the year apparently from the region of southern Dan.—1Ki 4:7, 9.

DELAIAH (De·la′iah) [Jehovah Has Drawn Up [in deliverance]].

1. An Aaronic priest of David's time designated by lot as the head of the 23rd priestly division. —1Ch 24:1, 5, 18.

2. Son of Shemaiah; one of the princes in the court of King Jehoiakim who heard Baruch read the book written by Jeremiah and thereafter apparently made report to the king. Then, at the time the roll was read before Jehoiakim, Delaiah and two other princes vainly pleaded with the king not to burn it.—Jer 36:11-26.

3. The forefather of certain ones that came to Jerusalem with Zerubbabel in 537 B.C.E. but who were unable to prove that they were Israelites. —Ezr 2:1, 59, 60; Ne 7:61, 62.

4. Son of Mehetabel and the father of the Shemaiah who was hired by Sanballat and Tobiah to intimidate Nehemiah the governor.—Ne 6:10-13.

5. One of Elioenai's seven sons; descendant of David through Solomon and Zerubbabel.—1Ch 3:10, 24.

DELILAH (De·li′lah) [possibly, Dangling]. A woman living in the torrent valley of Sorek. Delilah is introduced into the Bible account toward the final part of Samson's 20-year judgeship as the object of his love.—Jg 16:31.

The axis lords of the Philistines, anxious to destroy Samson, each offered Delilah 1,100 pieces of silver (if shekels, $2,422) to find out for them wherein Samson's great power lay. She cooperated by questioning Samson as to what would render him powerless. Each time Samson answered, she notified the Philistines and hid in her house Philistine warriors who were ready to take advantage of Samson in the event he lost his strength. After three misleading answers by Samson, Delilah continued to pester him and "pressured him with her words all the time and kept urging him, [so that] his soul got to be impatient to the point of dying." Then he told her of his Naziriteship and that no razor had ever touched his head. Certain of having the truth this time, she sent for the Philistine axis lords, and they came to bring her the money. While Samson slept upon her knees, an attendant cut off the seven braids of his hair. Upon awakening, Samson found that this time his divinely provided power was not there. The hiding Philistines grabbed hold of him, blinded him, and took him prisoner. (Jg 16:4-21) Delilah is mentioned no more in the Bible account.

The Bible does not say that sexual relationship took place between Delilah and Samson or that she was a prostitute. The prostitute mentioned at Judges 16:1, 2 is not the same as Delilah. This prostitute lived at Gaza, whereas Delilah lived in the torrent valley of Sorek. Also, the following evidence indicates Delilah possibly was an Israelitess, not a Philistine: When the axis lords presented their proposal it was based on an extravagant sum of money and not on patriotic sentiment.—Jg 16:5.

DELUGE.

The catastrophic destruction of men and animals by an overwhelming flood in the days of Noah, 2370 B.C.E. This greatest cataclysm in all human history was sent by Jehovah because wicked men had filled the earth with violence. The survival of righteous Noah and his family, eight souls in all, together with selected animals, was by means of a huge ark, or chest.—Ge 6:9–9:19; 1Pe 3:20; see ARK No. 1; NOAH No. 1.

Extent of the Deluge. This was no local flash flood or cloudburst. In fact, the Greek word used in the Bible to refer to the Flood, or Deluge, is *ka·ta·kly·smos'*, a cataclysm. (Lu 17:27, ftn) Local floods come and go in a matter of days; this one lasted over a year, the greater portion of which was required for the water to subside. How unreasonable to believe that Noah spent perhaps 50 or 60 years building a huge vessel of approximately 40,000 cu m (1,400,000 cu ft) for the survival of his family and a few animals through a mere local flood! If only a comparatively small area was affected, why the need of bringing into the ark specimens of "every living creature of every sort of flesh" in order to "preserve offspring alive on the surface of the entire earth"? (Ge 6:19; 7:3) Definitely this was a global deluge, the like of which had never occurred before nor has since. "The waters overwhelmed the earth so greatly that all the tall mountains that were under the whole heavens came to be covered. Up to 15 cubits [c. 6.5 m; 22 ft] the waters overwhelmed them and the mountains became covered." (Ge 7:19, 20) "The end of all flesh has come before me," Jehovah said, hence "I will wipe every existing thing that I have made off the surface of the ground." And it was just so. "Everything in which the breath of the force of life was active in its nostrils, namely, all that were on the dry ground, died . . . only Noah and those who were with him in the ark kept on surviving."—Ge 6:13; 7:4, 22, 23.

Timing of the Deluge. The Deluge did not come suddenly without warning. Years of time were spent building the ark, time that Noah the "preacher of righteousness" also used in warning that wicked generation. (2Pe 2:5) Finally the time limit was up "in the six hundredth year of Noah's life, in the second month, on the seventeenth day of the month." The "male and female of every sort of flesh" had been brought into the ark with Noah's family, as well as a sufficient food supply for all, and "after that Jehovah shut the door."

Then "the floodgates of the heavens were opened." (Ge 7:11, 16) There was an incessant torrential downpour for "forty days and forty nights"; "the waters continued overwhelming the earth" a hundred and fifty days. (Ge 7:4, 12, 24) Five months after the downpour began, the ark "came to rest on the mountains of Ararat." (Ge 8:4) It was nearly two and a half months later before "the tops of the mountains appeared" (Ge 8:5), another three months before Noah removed the ark's covering to see that the earth had practically drained (Ge 8:13), and nearly two months later when the door was opened and the survivors set foot on dry ground once again.—Ge 8:14-18.

Noah and his family entered the ark in the 600th year of Noah's life, the 2nd month (October-November), the 17th day. (Ge 7:11) One year later (a year consisting of 360 days) was the 17th day, 2nd month, 601st year. Ten days after that would be the 27th day of the 2nd month, when they came out; a total of 370 days, or parts of 371 separate days, spent in the ark. (Ge 8:13, 14) In the log that Noah kept, it appears he used months of 30 days each, 12 of them equaling 360 days. In this way he avoided all the complicated fractions involved had he used strictly lunar months consisting of slightly more than $29\frac{1}{2}$ days. That such calculations were used in the account is evident from the fact that a five-month period consisted of 150 days.—Ge 7:11, 24; 8:3, 4.

The Floodwaters. It has been said that if all the moisture in the atmosphere were suddenly released as rain it would not amount to even a couple of inches if spread over the earth's surface. So from what source was this vast deluge of Noah's day? According to the Genesis account, God said to Noah: "Here I [Jehovah] am bringing the deluge [or, "heavenly ocean"; Heb., *mab·bul'*] of waters upon the earth." (Ge 6:17, ftn) Describing what happened, the next chapter says: "All the springs of the vast watery deep were broken open and the floodgates of the heavens were opened." (Ge 7:11) So overwhelming was the Deluge that "all the tall mountains that were under the whole heavens came to be covered."—Ge 7:19.

Where did this "heavenly ocean" come from? The Genesis account of creation tells how on the second "day" Jehovah made an expanse about the earth, and this expanse (called "Heaven") formed a division between the waters below it, that is, the oceans, and the waters above it. (Ge 1:6-8) The waters suspended above the expanse evidently remained there from the second "day" of creation until the Flood. This is what the apostle Peter was talking about when he recounted that there "were heavens from of old and an earth standing compactly out of water and in the midst of water by the word of God." Those "heavens" and the waters above and beneath them were the means that God's word called into operation, and "by those means the world of that time suffered destruction when it was deluged with water." (2Pe 3:5, 6) Various explanations have been offered as to how the water was held aloft until the Flood and as to the processes that resulted in its falling. But these are only speculative. The Bible says simply that God made the expanse with waters above it and that he brought the Deluge. His almighty power could easily accomplish it.

Since, as the Genesis account says, "all the tall mountains" were covered with water, where is all that water now? Evidently it is right here on the earth. It is believed that there was a time when the oceans were smaller and the continents were larger than they are now, as is evidenced by river channels extending far out under the oceans. It should also be noted that scientists have stated that mountains in the past were much lower than at present, and some mountains have even been pushed up from under the seas. As to the present situation, it is said that "there is ten times as much water by volume in the ocean as there is land above sea level. Dump all this land evenly into the sea, and water would cover the entire earth, one and one-half miles deep." (*National Geographic*, January 1945, p. 105) So, after the floodwaters fell, but before the raising of mountains and the lowering of seabeds and before the buildup of polar ice caps, there was more than enough water to cover "all the tall mountains," as the inspired record says.—Ge 7:19.

Effect on the Earth. With the Deluge great changes came, for example, the life span of humans dropped very rapidly. Some have suggested that prior to the Flood the waters above the expanse shielded out some of the harmful radiation and that, with the waters gone, cosmic radiation genetically harmful to man increased. However, the Bible is silent on the matter. Incidentally, any change in radiation would have altered the rate of formation of radioactive carbon-14 to such an extent as to invalidate all radiocarbon dates prior to the Flood.

With the sudden opening of the 'springs of the watery deep' and "the floodgates of the heavens," untold billions of tons of water deluged the earth. (Ge 7:11) This may have caused tremendous changes in earth's surface. The earth's crust is relatively thin (estimated at between 30 km [20 mi] and 160 km [100 mi] thick), stretched over a rather plastic mass thousands of kilometers in diameter. Hence, under the added weight of the water, there was likely a great shifting in the crust. In time new mountains evidently were thrust upward, old mountains rose to new heights, shallow sea basins were deepened, and new shorelines were established, with the result that now about 70 percent of the surface is covered with water. This shifting in the earth's crust may account for many geologic phenomena, such as the raising of old coastlines to new heights. It has been estimated by some that water pressures alone were equal to "2 tons per square inch," sufficient to fossilize fauna and flora quickly.—See *The Biblical Flood and the Ice Epoch,* by D. Patten, 1966, p. 62.

What evidence proves that there truly was a global deluge?

Other possible evidence of a drastic change: Remains of mammoths and rhinoceroses have been found in different parts of the earth. Some of these were found in Siberian cliffs; others were preserved in Siberian and Alaskan ice. (PICTURE, Vol. 1, p. 328) In fact, some were found with food undigested in their stomachs or still unchewed in their teeth, indicating that they died suddenly. It is estimated, from the trade in ivory tusks, that bones of tens of thousands of such mammoths have been found. The fossil remains of many other animals, such as lions, tigers, bears, and elk, have been found in common strata, which may indicate that all of these were destroyed simultaneously. Some have pointed to such finds as definite physical proof of a rapid change in climate and sudden destruction caused by a universal flood. Others, however, favor explanations for the death of these animals that do not involve an earth-wide catastrophe. Proof that the Flood occurred is not dependent on such fossils and frozen animal remains.

Flood Legends. Such a cataclysm as the Deluge, which washed the whole world of that time out of existence, would never be forgotten by the survivors. They would talk about it to their children and their children's children. For 500 years after the Deluge, Shem lived on to relate the event to many generations. He died only ten years before the birth of Jacob. Moses preserved the true account in Genesis. Sometime after the

Flood, when God-defying people built the Tower of Babel, Jehovah confused their language and scattered them "over all the surface of the earth." (Ge 11:9) It was only natural that these people took with them stories of the Flood and passed them on from father to son. The fact that there are not merely a few but perhaps hundreds of different stories about that great Deluge, and that such stories are found among the traditions of many primitive races the world over, is a strong proof that all these people had a common origin and that their early forefathers shared that Flood experience in common.—CHART, Vol. 1, p. 328.

These folklore accounts of the Deluge agree with some major features of the Biblical account: (1) a place of refuge for a few survivors, (2) an otherwise global destruction of life by water, and (3) a seed of mankind preserved. The Egyptians, the Greeks, the Chinese, the Druids of Britain, the Polynesians, the Eskimos and Greenlanders, the Africans, the Hindus, and the American Indians —all of these have their Flood stories. *The International Standard Bible Encyclopedia* (Vol. 2, p. 319) states: "Flood stories have been discovered among nearly all nations and tribes. Though most common on the Asian mainland and the islands immediately south of it and on the North American continent, they have been found on all the continents. Totals of the number of stories known run as high as about 270 . . . The universality of the flood accounts is usually taken as evidence for the universal destruction of humanity by a flood and the spread of the human race from one locale and even from one family. Though the traditions may not all refer to the same flood, apparently the vast majority do. The assertion that many of these flood stories came from contacts with missionaries will not stand up because most of them were gathered by anthropologists not interested in vindicating the Bible, and they are filled with fanciful and pagan elements evidently the result of transmission for extended periods of time in a pagan society. Moreover, some of the ancient accounts were written by people very much in opposition to the Hebrew-Christian tradition." —Edited by G. Bromiley, 1982.

In times past, certain primitive people (in Australia, Egypt, Fiji, Society Islands, Peru, Mexico, and other places) preserved a possible remnant of these traditions about the Flood by observing in November a 'Feast of Ancestors' or a 'Festival of the Dead.' Such customs reflected a memory of the destruction caused by the Deluge. According to the book *Life and Work at the Great Pyramid,* the festival in Mexico was held on the 17th of November because they "had a tradition that at that time the world had been previously destroyed; and they dreaded lest a similar catastrophe would, at the end of a cycle, annihilate the human race." (By Professor C. Piazzi Smyth, Edinburgh, 1867, Vol. II, pp. 390, 391) Notes the book *The Worship of the Dead:* "This festival [of the dead] is . . . held by all on or about the very day on which, according to the Mosaic account, the Deluge took place, viz., *the seventeenth day of the second month*—the month nearly corresponding with our November." (By J. Garnier, London, 1904, p. 4) Interestingly, the Bible reports that the Flood began "in the second month, on the seventeenth day of the month." (Ge 7:11) That "second month" corresponds to the latter part of October and the first part of November on our calendar.

Scriptural Confirmation. Stronger evidence of the historicalness of the Deluge than the pagan traditions of primitive people is the endorsement other Bible writers gave under inspiration. The only other place where the same Hebrew word (*mab·bul'*, deluge) occurs outside the Genesis account is in David's melody where he describes Jehovah as seated "upon the deluge." (Ps 29:10) However, other writers make reference to and confirm the Genesis account, as, for example, Isaiah. (Isa 54:9) Ezekiel also endorses the historicity of Noah. (Eze 14:14, 18, 20) Peter draws heavily upon the Deluge account in his letters. (1Pe 3:20; 2Pe 2:5; 3:5, 6) Paul testifies to the great faith Noah displayed in constructing the ark for the survival of his household. (Heb 11:7) Luke lists Noah in the lineage of Messiah's forebears. —Lu 3:36.

Even more significant is what Jesus said about the days of the Deluge, as recorded by both Luke and Matthew. Far more than just a simple endorsement of the veracity of the Deluge account, Jesus' words show the pictorial and prophetic significance of those ancient events. In answer to the disciples' question, "What will be the sign of your presence and of the conclusion of the system of things?" Jesus said, among other things: "For just as the days of Noah were, so the presence of the Son of man will be. For as they were in those days before the flood, eating and drinking, men marrying and women being given in marriage, until the day that Noah entered into the ark; and they took no note until the flood came and swept them all away, so the presence of the Son of man will be." (Mt 24:3, 37-39; Lu 17:26, 27) There is, therefore, abundant evidence from the inspired Holy Scriptures themselves to support the authenticity and genuineness of the Deluge account. It does not rest on mere traditions of men, on the folklore of primitive people, or on geologic and archaeological findings.

DEMAS (De′mas) [possibly a shortened form of "Demetrius," meaning "Of (Belonging to) Demeter"]. A onetime fellow worker of the apostle Paul. Demas was in Rome with the apostle during his first imprisonment there, his greetings being included in letters to the Colossians and to Philemon. (Col 4:14; Phm 24) When Paul wrote to Timothy during his second imprisonment, Demas had forsaken the apostle and departed to Thessalonica, perhaps his hometown.—2Ti 4:10.

The exact nature of Demas' forsaking Paul 'because of his love for the present system of things' is not disclosed. The apostle does not say Demas became an apostate or opposer. Perhaps Demas' love for material things and worldly pleasures became stronger than that for spiritual things. Fear of martyrdom with Paul may have caused Demas to seek a safer place and thus preserve his life in the then-existing system of things. In any event, when conditions became unfavorable, Demas failed to use his marvelous opportunity to strengthen his brother Paul.

DEMETRIUS (De·me′tri·us) [Of (Belonging to) Demeter [Greek goddess of agriculture]].

1. A silversmith of the city of Ephesus in Asia Minor who stirred up a riot against the apostle Paul and his companions at the close of Paul's stay of between two and three years in Ephesus (c. 53-55 C.E.), in the course of his third missionary journey. Paul's preaching had been blessed with success, many turning from the practice of magic and burning their books. Demetrius, who conducted a flourishing business of making silver shrines of the goddess Artemis, becoming alarmed at the prospect of loss of income through Paul's success in making disciples of Christ, roused the craftsmen and others. With a twofold argument of threatened loss of business and the danger of disrepute to the temple of Artemis, he succeeded in causing the entire city to be thrown into confusion.

After about two hours the city recorder managed to quell the disturbance; he pointed out that if Demetrius and the craftsmen had a charge against Paul and his companions, there were courts to handle the matter legally but that this disorderly demonstration made the city liable to a charge of sedition by the Roman government. The crowd then quieted down, releasing Paul's

fellow workers and leaving the theater, the scene of the disgraceful riot. Shortly afterward Paul set forth for Macedonia.—Ac 19:18, 19, 23-41; 20:1.

2. A Christian mentioned favorably by the apostle John in a letter to Gaius, about 98 C.E. Demetrius may have delivered the letter to Gaius. John's recommendation of Demetrius may have been to encourage hospitality on the part of Gaius, as it seems to have been a custom of the congregations to assist in providing food and lodging for the faithful brothers who traveled in behalf of the good news.—3Jo 1, 12.

DEMON. An invisible, wicked, spirit creature having superhuman powers. The common Greek word for demon (dai′mon) occurs only once in the Christian Greek Scriptures, in Matthew 8:31; elsewhere the word dai·mo′ni·on appears. Pneu′ma, the Greek word for "spirit," at times is applied to wicked spirits, or demons. (Mt 8:16) It also occurs qualified by terms such as "wicked," "unclean," "speechless," and "deaf."—Lu 7:21; Mt 10:1; Mr 9: 17, 25; see SPIRIT (Spirit Persons).

The demons as such were not created by God. The first to make himself one was Satan the Devil (see SATAN), who became the ruler of other angelic sons of God who also made themselves demons. (Mt 12:24, 26) In Noah's day disobedient angels materialized, married women, fathered a hybrid generation known as Nephilim (see NEPHILIM), and then dematerialized when the Flood came. (Ge 6:1-4) However, upon returning to the spirit realm, they did not regain their lofty original position, for Jude 6 says: "The angels that did not keep their original position but forsook their own proper dwelling place he has reserved with eternal bonds under dense darkness for the judgment of the great day." (1Pe 3:19, 20) So it is in this condition of dense spiritual darkness that they must now confine their operations. (2Pe 2:4) Though evidently restrained from materializing, they still have great power and influence over the minds and lives of men, even having the ability to enter into and possess humans and animals, and the facts show that they also use inanimate things such as houses, fetishes, and charms.—Mt 12:43-45; Lu 8:27-33; see DEMON POSSESSION.

The purpose of all such demonic activity is to turn people against Jehovah and the pure worship of God. Jehovah's law, therefore, strictly forbade demonism in any form. (De 18:10-12) However, wayward Israel went so far astray as to sacrifice their sons and daughters to the demons. (Ps 106:37; De 32:17; 2Ch 11:15) When Jesus was on earth demon influence was very prevalent, and some of his greatest miracles consisted of expelling wicked spirits from victimized persons. (Mt 8:31, 32; 9:33, 34; Mr 1:39; 7:26-30; Lu 8:2; 13:32) Jesus gave this same power to his 12 apostles and to the 70 that he sent out, so that in the name of Jesus they too could cast out the demons.—Mt 10:8; Mr 3:14, 15; 6:13; Lu 9:1; 10:17.

Demon influence in human affairs is no less manifest today. It is still true that "the things which the nations sacrifice they sacrifice to demons." (1Co 10:20) In the last book of the Bible, the "revelation by Jesus Christ, which God gave him, to show his slaves the things that must shortly take place," prophetic warning is given concerning accelerated demon activity on the earth. (Re 1:1) "Down the great dragon was hurled, the original serpent, the one called Devil and Satan, who is misleading the entire inhabited earth; he was hurled down to the earth, and his angels [*demons*] were hurled down with him. On this account . . . woe for the earth and for the sea, because the Devil has come down to you, having great anger, knowing he has a short period of time." (Re 12:9, 12) Unclean, froglike expressions "are, in fact, expressions inspired by *demons* and perform signs, and they go forth to the kings of the entire inhabited earth, to gather them together to the war of the great day of God the Almighty."—Re 16:13, 14.

Christians must, therefore, put up a hard fight against these unseen wicked spirits. James, in arguing that belief alone is not sufficient, says: "You believe there is one God, do you? You are doing quite well. And yet the demons believe and shudder." (Jas 2:19) "In later periods of time," warned Paul, "some will fall away from the faith, paying attention to misleading inspired utterances and teachings of demons." (1Ti 4:1) One cannot eat of Jehovah's table and at the same time feed from the table of demons. (1Co 10:21) The faithful, therefore, must put up a hard fight against the Devil and his demons, "against the world rulers of this darkness, against the wicked spirit forces in the heavenly places."—Eph 6:12.

To the Greeks to whom Paul preached, what were demons?

This use of the word "demon" is narrow and specific compared with the notions of ancient philosophers and the way the word was used in classical Greek. In this regard the *Theological Dictionary of the New Testament,* edited by

G. Kittel (Vol. II, p. 8) remarks: "The meaning of the adj[ective *dai·mo'ni·os*] brings out most clearly the distinctive features of the G[ree]k conception of demons, for it denotes that which lies outwith human capacity and is thus to be attributed to the intervention of higher powers, whether for good or evil. [*To dai·mo'ni·on*] in pre-Christian writers can be used in the sense of the 'divine.'" (Translated and edited by G. Bromiley, 1971) When speaking controversially with Paul, some Epicurean and Stoic philosophers concluded: "He seems to be a publisher of foreign deities [Gr., *dai·mo·ni'on*]."—Ac 17:18.

When speaking to the Athenians, Paul used a compound of the Greek word *dai'mon,* saying: "You seem to be more given to the fear of the deities [Gr., *dei·si·dai·mo·ne·ste'rous;* Latin *Vulgate,* 'more superstitious'] than others are." (Ac 17:22) Commenting on this compound word, F. F. Bruce remarks: "The context must decide whether this word is used in its better or worse sense. It was, in fact, as vague as 'religious' in Eng[lish], and here we may best translate 'very religious'. But AV 'superstitious' is not entirely wrong; to Paul their religion was mostly superstition, as it also was, though on other grounds, to the Epicureans."—*The Acts of the Apostles,* 1970, p. 335.

When speaking to King Herod Agrippa II, Festus said that the Jews had certain disputes with Paul concerning their "worship of the deity [Gr., *dei·si·dai·mo·ni'as;* Latin *Vulgate,* 'superstition']." (Ac 25:19) It was noted by F. F. Bruce that this Greek word "might be less politely rendered 'superstition' (as in AV). The corresponding adjective appears with the same ambiguity in [Acts] 17: 22."—*Commentary on the Book of the Acts,* 1971, p. 483.

See GOAT-SHAPED DEMON.

DEMON POSSESSION. The captive control and influence of a person by an invisible wicked spirit. In Bible times demonized persons were afflicted in various ways: some were unable to speak, some were blind, some acted insane, and some possessed superhuman strength. All were woefully mistreated by these invisible bullies. (Mt 9:32; 12:22; 17:15; Mr 5:3-5; Lu 8:29; 9:42; 11: 14; Ac 19:16) Men, women, and children were their victims. (Mt 15:22; Mr 5:2) Sometimes the agony was compounded when many demons gained possession of a person at the same time. (Lu 8:2, 30) When the demon was expelled, the person returned to a normal, sane state of mind.

There is a difference between demon possession and ordinary physical sickness and disease, for Jesus cured both types of disorder.—Mt 8:16; 17:18; Mr 1:32, 34.

Some of Jesus' greatest miracles involved the setting of possessed persons free from captivity to the demons. They were powerless against him. But not everyone was happy with his demon-expelling work. The Pharisees accused him of being in league with the ruler of the demons, Beelzebub, whereas in reality, as Jesus pointed out, they themselves were the offspring of the Devil. (Mt 9:34; 12:24; Mr 3:22; Lu 11:15; Joh 7:20; 8:44, 48-52) Jesus knew the source of the power that gave him mastery over the demons, and he openly confessed that it was Jehovah's spirit. (Mt 12:28; Lu 8:39; 11:20) The demons themselves recognized Jesus' identity and addressed him as the "Son of God," "the Holy One of God," and "Jesus, Son of the Most High God." (Mt 8:29; Mr 1:24; 3:11; 5:7; Lu 4:34, 41; Ac 19:15; Jas 2:19) However, at no time would Jesus allow them to witness in his behalf. (Mr 3:12) On the other hand, a man who was set free from the power of the demons was encouraged to publish to his relatives 'all the things Jehovah had done for him.'—Mr 5:18-20.

Jesus also gave authority over the demons to his 12 apostles, and later to the 70 that he sent out, so that in the name of Jesus they too were able to cure the demon-possessed. (Mt 10:8; Mr 3:15; 6:13; Lu 9:1; 10:17) Even one not an immediate associate of Jesus or his apostles was able to exorcise a demon on the basis of Jesus' name. (Mr 9:38-40; Lu 9:49, 50) After the death of Jesus, the apostles continued to have this power. Paul ordered "a demon of divination" out of a slave girl, much to the anger of her money-loving owners. (Ac 16:16-19) But when certain impostors, the seven sons of priest Sceva, attempted to cast out a demon in the name of "Jesus whom Paul preaches," the demon-possessed man seized and severely mauled the seven of them and stripped them naked.—Ac 19:13-16.

Often the wild and uncontrolled conduct of mentally unbalanced persons is due to possession by these invisible minions of Satan. Sometimes it is reported that spirit mediums have cast these demons out; this calls to mind what Jesus said: "Many will say to me in that day, 'Lord, Lord, did we not . . . expel demons in your name?' And yet then I will confess to them: I never knew you!" (Mt 7:22, 23) Compelling reasons, then, for heeding the counsel, "Be watchful," and, "Put on the complete suit of armor from God that you may be able to stand firm against the machinations of the Devil" and his demons.—1Pe 5:8; Eph 6:11.

DENARIUS. A Roman silver coin that weighed about 3.85 g (0.124 oz t) and hence would have a modern value of 74 cents. It bore a likeness of the head of Caesar and was "the head tax coin" exacted by the Romans from the Jews. (Mt 22:19-21) In the days of Jesus' earthly ministry, agricultural laborers commonly received a denarius for a 12-hour workday. (Mt 20:2) Hence, Revelation 6:6 depicts an extreme condition in stating that a quart of wheat or three quarts of barley would cost a denarius (a full day's wage).

If the costly nard that Mary, Lazarus' sister, used in greasing Jesus Christ had been sold for 300 denarii (nearly a year's wages), likely this would have meant that a sizable amount of money would have gone into the money box kept by Judas Iscariot. Little wonder that dishonest Judas Iscariot raised strong objections, since he would be unable to embezzle even a fraction of this large sum.—Joh 12:3-6; 13:29; Mr 14:3-11.

Two sides of a Roman denarius

The neighborly Samaritan of Jesus' illustration spent two denarii (two days' wages) to help an unknown stranger, and he declared himself willing to care for additional expenses in his behalf. (Lu 10:33-35) By contrast, in one of Jesus' illustrations emphasizing the need of being forgiving, a slave whose debt of 60,000,000 denarii had been canceled was unwilling to pardon the 100-denarius debt of a fellow slave.—Mt 18: 24-33.

DEPENDENT TOWNS. Small towns in the neighborhood of a larger town or city. The capital or primary city of a district was the metropolis, or "mother" city, as at 1 Chronicles 18:1: "Gath and its dependent towns" (literally, "Gath and her daughters"). Tyre is called the "daughter" of Sidon, a city evidently older than Tyre, which seems to have been originally a colony of Sidon. (Isa 23:8, 12; Ge 10:19; Jos 11:8) The towns of Judah were dependent on Jerusalem. (Ps 48:11; 97:8; La 3:51) Other "mother" cities with dependent towns were Samaria and Sodom (Eze 16:53), Rabbah of Ammon (Jer 49:3), Kenath (Nu 32:42), Ekron (Jos 15:45), Ashdod and Gaza (Jos 15:47), Beth-shean, Ibleam, Dor, En-dor, Taanach, and Megiddo (Jos 17:11).

The "daughter" towns either originated from or were politically, economically, and sometimes religiously dependent on the "mother" city. In some cases the dependent towns were unwalled or less fortified, and in times of siege the inhabitants would seek safety in the "mother" city.—Jer 4:5; 8:14.

The ancient city of Jerusalem as the "mother" of the dependent towns of Judah is used symbolically to picture "heavenly Jerusalem," Jehovah's Messianic Kingdom through Jesus Christ, in which those seeking righteousness will find refuge in "the day of Jehovah against all the nations."—Heb 12:22, 28; Ob 15, 17; Ps 48:11-13; Joe 2:32.

Babylon the Great is pictured in Revelation, chapter 17, as a prostitute woman and as a city, with daughters. These are organizations springing from the mother organization. Dependent on her, they will fall to destruction with her.—See CITY.

DEPUTY. The Hebrew participle translated "deputy" (*nits·tsav'*) has the basic meaning of one "stationed," 'put in position,' or "set" by appointment to fulfill a duty. (1Sa 22:9; Ex 7:15; Ru 2:5) During the reign of Solomon (1037-998 B.C.E.), 12 deputies were appointed to high-ranking administrative positions. Each was responsible for providing food and other supplies for the royal household one month during the year, on a rotational basis.—1Ki 4:7.

In lieu of a general tax for the support of the government, foodstuffs were taken from the produce of the land. The deputies were therefore overseers of production, harvesting, storage, and delivery of the monthly quotas, which amounted to a considerable tonnage. (1Ki 4:22, 23) These deputies may also have served as civil administrators in their assigned territories, in addition to their work of supervising the commissary supplies.

There was equity in this system, for it appears that the districts were set up with due consideration to population and productivity of the land, rather than according to the fixed tribal boundaries. Nine of the administrative districts were located W of the Jordan; the other three, E. Since the listing of the districts is not in any sequence according to location, they may be listed according to the monthly order in which each deputy furnished his supplies.

The personal names of only seven deputies are given in the Masoretic text; the other five are listed only as "son of" so-and-so. (1Ki 4:8-19) Some translations (*AS; AT;* 3Ki, *Dy; Ro; RS*) simply prefix "Ben" (meaning "son of") to the father's name, as "Ben-hur," "Ben-deker," "Ben-hesed," "Ben-abinadab," "Ben-geber." So that all ran smoothly, with no shortages, the 12 deputies were placed under the supervision of one of Solomon's leading princes, "Azariah the son of Nathan."—1Ki 4:5.

"Princely deputies" also served as foremen and overseers of the labor force engaged in construction during Solomon's reign. It seems that the two accounts of these deputies in First Kings and Second Chronicles differed only in methods of classification, the first listing 3,300 plus 550 for a total of 3,850 (1Ki 5:16; 9:23), and the second giving 3,600 plus 250, which also totals 3,850. (2Ch 2:18; 8:10) Scholars (Ewald, Keil, Michaelis) suggest that the Chronicles figures distinguish between the 3,600 non-Israelite and the 250 Israelite deputies, whereas in Kings the distinction in deputies is between 3,300 subordinate foremen and 550 chief supervisors, this latter figure including 300 non-Israelites.

During the rule of Jehoshaphat, king of Judah (936-c. 911 B.C.E.), "a deputy was king" in Edom, which, at the time, was under Judean control. (1Ki 22:47) This indicates that a vicegerent had been appointed or approved to act in the place of the king.

"Deputy rulers" (Heb., *segha·nim'*, always used in the plural) occurs 17 times in the Bible, as, for example, at Ezra 9:2; Nehemiah 2:16; Isaiah 41:25; Jeremiah 51:23; and Ezekiel 23:6. It meant subordinate rulers or petty officials, as distinguished from nobles, princes, and governors. Some translators render it "deputies."—*Mo, Ro.*

DERBE (Der'be). A 'city of Lycaonia' in Asia Minor, personally visited two times, or perhaps three, by the apostle Paul.

Probably sometime prior to the winter of

47-48 C.E., during his first missionary journey, Paul arrived at Derbe after a severe stoning at nearby Lystra. At Derbe, he and Barnabas 'declared the good news' and made "quite a few disciples," including, possibly, "Gaius of Derbe," who is later mentioned as a traveling companion of the apostle. While secular history indicates that after 41 C.E. Derbe was the easternmost city of the *political* province of Galatia, Luke's description of it in this account as a 'city of Lycaonia' is apparently in a regional or ethnographic sense. (Ac 14:6, 19-21; 20:4) A number of months later, after the Jerusalem council concerning circumcision (c. 49 C.E.), and while on his second tour, Paul returned to Derbe. (Ac 15:36; 16:1) Though not singled out by name, Derbe may also have been a stop on Paul's third tour when he strengthened the disciples in "the country of Galatia." (Ac 18:23) There is no record of Paul's meeting physical resistance at Derbe, and he makes no mention of the city many years later when recounting his sufferings at other places in its vicinity.—2Ti 3:11.

Derbe is possibly identified with Kerti Hüyük 21 km (13 mi) NNE of Karaman (ancient Laranda) and about 100 km (62 mi) SE of Konya (ancient Iconium). As to whether Derbe was included in Paul's letter addressed "to the congregations of Galatia," see GALATIANS, LETTER TO THE.—Ga 1:2.

DESERT.   See WILDERNESS.

DESTRUCTION.   The act of destroying, ruining, or annihilating. Destruction usually refers to the physical end of an object or a living creature. (2Ki 21:3; Jer 18:7; Da 2:12, 14, 18) It may also refer to spiritual ruin.—1Co 3:17; see TEMPLE (The Anointed Christians—A Spiritual Temple).

A Hebrew word commonly translated "destroy" is *'a·vadh'*. (Le 23:30; Ps 21:8, 10) It has the basic meaning "be lost," or "perish," and corresponds to the Greek term *a·pol'ly·mi*. (Ex 10:7; 1Sa 9:20; Mr 3:6; 4:38; Lu 15:4) The noun form of *'a·vadh'* is *avad·dohn'*, meaning "destruction." (Job 26:6, ftn; see ABADDON; APOLLYON.) The Hebrew term *cha·ram'* means "devote to destruction," or place under a sacred ban, that is, restrict from common or profane use.—Ex 22:20, ftn; see DEVOTED THING.

At times, Jehovah has found it necessary to execute judgment upon those meriting destruction in order to uphold his name and his standards of righteousness. As a result of the wicked conduct of the people in Noah's day, Jehovah executed a judgment of destruction when he caused a global flood to destroy the world of that time. (2Pe 3:5, 6) Similarly, because of the 'loud cry of complaint about Sodom and Gomorrah' and their 'heavy sin,' Jehovah destroyed the cities and their inhabitants. (Ge 18:20; 19:13, 24, 25) In addition to natural forces, Jehovah at times used human agents to accomplish a sentence of destruction. In the case of the wicked nations of Canaan, Jehovah used his people Israel as principal executioners of his condemnatory decree. —De 9:1, 3, 4; 20:15-18.

Jehovah justly destroys deliberate lawbreakers, liars, and those showing hostility to his servants. (Le 23:30; Ps 5:6; 143:12) He acts against false religion and its idols. (Nu 33:52; De 12:2, 3) Jehovah even took destructive action against his people Israel when they proved disobedient to his covenant.—De 8:19, 20; 28:63; Jer 31:28.

Will all persons who were destroyed by God in times past be dead forever?

The Bible indicates that not all destruction is eternal. This is demonstrated by the fact that the Hebrew word *'avad·dohn'* (destruction) is used twice to parallel "Sheol." (Job 26:6; Pr 15:11) The prophet Zephaniah spoke of the destruction of Assyria, whereas Ezekiel said that the Assyrians would go down to Sheol. (Zep 2:13; Eze 32:21, 22) When speaking of the destruction of the rebels Dathan and Abiram, Moses wrote that they went down "alive into Sheol." (Nu 16:31, 33) Since Sheol in the Bible denotes the common grave of mankind from which there will be a resurrection, it is evident that not all destruction—not even all destruction at the hand of God—is necessarily eternal.

This is also illustrated by what happened to the cities of Sodom and Gomorrah and their inhabitants. Jude indicated that these cities were everlastingly destroyed. (Jude 7; compare 2Pe 2:6.) However, Jesus' words recorded in Matthew 10:15 show that at least some of the inhabitants of Sodom and Gomorrah will receive a resurrection. —See JUDGMENT DAY.

Everlasting Destruction.   The Bible does not indicate that all the dead will be resurrected. Jesus implied this when he spoke of "those who have been counted worthy of gaining that system of things and the resurrection from the dead." (Lu 20:35) The possiblity of eternal destruction for some is also indicated by Jesus' words at Matthew 10:28: "Do not become fearful of those who kill the body but cannot kill the soul; but rather be in fear of him that can destroy both soul and body in Gehenna." Regarding this text, *The New International Dictionary of New Testament Theology* (edited by C. Brown, 1978, Vol. 3, p. 304) states: "Matt. 10:28 teaches not the potential immortality of the soul but the irreversibility of divine judgment on the unrepentant." Also, Bauer's *Greek-English Lexicon of the New Testament* (revised by F. W. Gingrich and F. Danker, 1979, p. 95) gives the meaning "eternal death" with reference to the Greek phrase in Matthew 10:28 translated "destroy both soul and body in Gehenna." Thus, being consigned to Gehenna refers to utter destruction from which no resurrection is possible. —See GEHENNA.

The possibility of eternal destruction is particularly an issue during the conclusion of the system of things. When Jesus was asked by his disciples what would be 'the sign of his presence and of the conclusion of the system of things,' he included as part of his answer the parable of the sheep and the goats. (Mt 24:3; 25:31-46) Concerning "the goats" it was foretold that the heavenly King would say: "Be on your way from me, you who have been cursed, into the everlasting fire prepared for the Devil and his angels," and Jesus added, "These will depart into everlasting cutting-off." Clearly the attitude and actions of some individuals will result in their permanent destruction.

However, Jehovah "does not desire any to be destroyed but desires all to attain to repentance." (2Pe 3:9; compare Eze 18:23, 32.) In fact, Jehovah loved humans so much that he provided the ransom sacrifice of his own Son, Jesus Christ. (Joh 3:16; compare Jas 4:12.) Despite this loving provision, the majority refuse to follow "the road leading off into life," but they remain on "the road leading off into destruction."—Mt 7:13, 14.

The Bible indicates that a number of things, individuals, and organizations are to be everlastingly destroyed. Jesus referred to Judas as "the son of destruction." (Joh 17:12) Judas' deliberate betrayal of the Son of God made him subject to eternal destruction. The same is true of those who blaspheme the holy spirit. They are guilty of "everlasting sin" and are forgiven neither "in this system of things nor in that to come." (Mr 3:28, 29; Mt 12:32; see BLASPHEMY.) Permanent destruction also awaits those who by choice "do not know God and those who do not obey the good news." (2Th 1:8, 9) The composite apostate "man of lawlessness" is also termed "the son of destruc-

tion." (2Th 2:3; see MAN OF LAWLESSNESS.) A judgment of eternal destruction has been determined for Satan, his demons, the symbolic "wild beast" and "false prophet," and even death and Hades. (Mt 25:41; Re 20:10, 14, 15; 21:8) All of these are consigned to "the lake of fire," that is, they are everlastingly destroyed.—See LAKE OF FIRE.

Fire was used in Bible times as the most thorough means of destruction. Hence, Jesus used fire to illustrate the complete destruction of the wicked.—Mt 13:40-42, 49, 50; see FIRE.

DETESTABLE THING. The word *ta·ʼav'* (detest) and the related *toh·ʻe·vah'* (detestable thing) occur some 140 times in the Hebrew Scriptures. Their usage in the Bible indicates strong aversion to or rejection of things or persons on the basis of their violating certain principles or not meeting definite standards held by the one so viewing them.

Thus at Genesis 43:32 we read that it was "a detestable thing" ("abomination," *KJ*; "abhorrent," *AT*) for Egyptians to eat with Hebrews, and at Genesis 46:34 that "every herder of sheep is a detestable thing ["abomination," *KJ*; "abhorrent," *AT*] to Egypt." According to G. Rawlinson, this aversion was based on the Egyptian contempt for foreigners in general and for herdsmen in particular. Again, at Exodus 8:25-27, we find Moses, fully aware of the Egyptians' adoration of certain animals (and particularly of the cow) as sacred, insisting that Pharaoh allow the Israelites to withdraw into the wilderness to make their sacrifices because these would be "a thing detestable to the Egyptians." (*Egypt and Babylon From Sacred and Profane Sources*, 1885, p. 182) Such Egyptian standards, of course, were not divinely set or approved by Jehovah God.—See ABHORRENT THING.

God's own declared standards, principles, and requirements are shown to be the proper basis for detestation. (Le 18:1-5; De 23:7) Thus, Psalm 14:1 says: "The senseless one has said in his heart: 'There is no Jehovah.' They have acted ruinously, they have acted detestably [a form of *ta·ʼav'*] in their dealing. There is no one doing good." Examination of the texts using the Hebrew words *ta·ʼav'* and *toh·ʻe·vah'*, therefore, gives insight into God's mind on matters. It also shows why there is a marked contrast or open conflict between the position or mental attitude of those who follow God's Word and those ignoring or rejecting it in preference to their own standards or those of others.—Pr 29:27.

Among the Canaanites. Before Israel's entry into Canaan, Jehovah made plain to them the practices and customs of the peoples of Canaan that were detestable to him, and these they were to detest. (Le 18:26-30) Outstanding was their practice of idolatry. God said: "The graven images of their gods you should burn in the fire. You must not desire the silver and the gold upon them, nor indeed take it for yourself, for fear you may be ensnared by it; for it is a thing detestable [*thoh·'avath'*] to Jehovah your God. And you must not bring a detestable thing [*thoh·'e·vah'*] into your house and actually become a thing devoted to destruction like it. You should thoroughly loathe it and absolutely detest it [*wetha·'ev' tetha·'aven'nu*], because it is something devoted to destruction." (De 7:25, 26) Any Israelite guilty of making images for religious worship was to be accursed. (De 27:15) Regardless of the craftsmanship they reflected, such images were to be morally repugnant to God's people.—Eze 7:20; compare Isa 44:18-20.

Other practices of the Canaanites to be detested by Israel were: spiritism with its seances, casting of spells, fortune-telling (De 18:9-12), offering children up in fire to their gods (De 12:31; Jer 32:35; 2Ki 16:3), incest, sodomy, and bestiality. (Le 18:6, 22-30; 20:13) Doubtless the morally repugnant practice of sodomy was the reason for the severity of the rule declaring the wearing of apparel of the opposite sex to be "detestable." (De 22:5) The Canaanites also practiced "sacred" prostitution by male and female temple prostitutes, but Jehovah prohibited the bringing of "the hire of a harlot or the price of a dog" into his house, "because they are something detestable."—De 23:17, 18; 1Ki 14:24.

On the basis of these and other "abominable" or "detestable" practices, Jehovah God ordered Israel to devote the Canaanites to destruction so that no contamination by false religion would result. (De 20:17, 18) Any Israelite practicing the same things or advocating such apostasy was to receive precisely the same penalty.—De 13:12-15; 17:2-7; Ezr 9:1, 11-14.

Israel Infected. In the rest of the Hebrew Scriptures, *ta·'av'* and *toh·'e·vah'* are used to describe commercial cheating or fraud (De 25:13-16; Pr 11:1; 20:10, 23), lying (Ps 5:6; 119:163; Pr 12:19, 22), adultery (Eze 33:26), robbery, greed, oppression of the poor (Eze 18:10-13), pride, shedding of innocent blood, hurtful scheming, bearing false witness, and causing contention among brothers; all such are termed "detestable"

by God.—Pr 3:32; 6:16-19; 11:20; 15:26; 24:9; 26:24-26.

The practice of these things also makes a person's worship unacceptable to God, causing the sacrifices and even the prayers of that person to be "detestable" to God. (Pr 15:8, 9; 21:27; 28:9) For this reason Jehovah later called the apostate Israelites' sacrifices, incense, as well as new moon and Sabbath celebrations, "detestable." (Isa 1:11-17) He asked them: "Can there be stealing, murdering and committing adultery and swearing falsely and making sacrificial smoke to Baal and walking after other gods whom you had not known, and must you come and stand before me in this house upon which my name has been called, and must you say, 'We shall certainly be delivered,' in the face of doing all these detestable things ["abominations," *KJ*]? Has this house upon which my name has been called become a mere cave of robbers in your eyes?" (Jer 7:9-11) They came to be past shame or humiliation for their detestable acts.—Jer 6:15; 8:12.

Even though Israel's leaders, the kings and the priests, were guilty of these acts or condoned them (1Ki 21:25, 26; 2Ki 21:2-12; 2Ch 28:1, 3; 33:2-6; 36:8, 14; Eze 8:6-17; 43:7, 8), God's faithful prophets were ordered to cause the people to know Jehovah's detestation of their rebellious course and warn them of the consequences. (Eze 16:2, 51, 52; 20:4; 22:2; 23:36) The people were urged to reject such detestable practices and return to God's statutes and standards of conduct. (Eze 14:6) To continue practicing what God detests could only lead to eventual desolation and destruction. (Jer 44:4, 22; Eze 6:11; 7:3-9; 11:21; 12:16; 33:29) After the exile some would become ashamed of their bad ways, and Jehovah would give them "a new spirit."—Eze 6:9; 11:18-21; 36:31.

Job's experience shows that those who uphold God's standards may be mocked (Job 30:9, 10) and rejected by former acquaintances (Job 19:19; Ps 88:8), because such ones "have hated a reprover, and a speaker of perfect things they detest." (Am 5:10) "It is something detestable to the stupid ones to turn away from bad." (Pr 13:19) But God detests those who twist his standards so as to pronounce "the wicked one righteous" and "the righteous one wicked." (Pr 17:15) He promises a complete reversal of circumstances in the future for his servants who are thus detested.—Isa 49:7; compare Mt 5:10-12; 1Pe 3:16; 4:1-5; see DISGUSTING THING, LOATHSOME THING.

DEUEL (Deu'el) [God's Knowledge; God Knows]. One whose son Eliasaph served as the chieftain of the tribe of Gad during Israel's wilderness wanderings. (Nu 1:14; 7:42, 47; 10:20) In the Masoretic text and the Syriac *Peshitta*, he is called "Reuel" at Numbers 2:14. This may be due to a scribal error, since the Hebrew letters for "D" and "R" are very similar and the name "Deuel" does, in fact, appear at Numbers 2:14 in the Samaritan *Pentateuch*, the Latin *Vulgate*, and over a hundred Hebrew manuscripts.

DEUTERONOMY. The Hebrew name of this fifth book of the Pentateuch is *Deva·rim'* (Words), drawn from the opening phrase in the Hebrew text. The name "Deuteronomy" comes from the *Septuagint* Greek title *Deu·te·ro·no'mi·on,* literally meaning "Second Law; Repetition of the Law." This comes from the Greek rendering of a Hebrew phrase in Deuteronomy 17:18, *mish·neh' hat·toh·rah',* correctly rendered 'copy of the law.'

The authenticity of Deuteronomy as a book of the Bible canon and the writership of Moses are well established by the fact that Deuteronomy has always been considered by the Jews as a part of the Law of Moses. The evidence for the authenticity of Deuteronomy is, in general, the same as that for the other four books of the Pentateuch. (See PENTATEUCH; also books under individual names.) Jesus is the foremost authority for the authenticity of Deuteronomy, quoting from it

HIGHLIGHTS OF DEUTERONOMY

Discourses explaining portions of the Law and exhorting Israel to love and obey Jehovah in the land that they were about to enter

Written by Moses just before Israel entered the Promised Land in 1473 B.C.E.

___

Exhortation to remember what Jehovah has done and to serve only him (1:1–4:49)

Moses recalls the sending out of spies, the faithless and rebellious response to their report, Jehovah's oath that that generation would die in the wilderness

Israel was not to molest the sons of Esau (descended from Jacob's brother) or Moab and Ammon (offspring of Abraham's nephew Lot); but Jehovah gave Israel the land held by Amorite Kings Sihon and Og, E of the Jordan

Moses begs Jehovah to let him cross the Jordan; instead, Jehovah tells him to commission and strengthen Joshua to lead the nation

Moses reminds nation of Jehovah's burning anger regarding Baal of Peor; must not forget what they witnessed in Horeb, never make a carved image for worship; Jehovah, the only true God, exacts exclusive devotion

Admonition to love Jehovah and to obey all of his commandments (5:1–26:19)

Moses recounts giving of the Law at Horeb, restates the Ten Words, urges Israel to do just as Jehovah commanded

Must love Jehovah with all one's heart, soul, and vital force; God's commands to be kept constantly before them; should explain to their sons the reason for Jehovah's regulations

Seven nations to be destroyed out of the land, along with their altars and images; no marriage alliances with them

Should not forget how God dealt with them in the wilderness so as to make them know that man lives not by bread alone but by every expression of Jehovah's mouth

Must remember how they provoked Jehovah by making molten calf; now should fear, serve, and cling to him; keep the whole commandment

Regulations to be obeyed in Promised Land: Wipe out false religion of Canaan; worship at the place that Jehovah chooses; do not eat blood; put apostates to death; eat clean food; give tenth of produce to Jehovah; show consideration for the poor; keep annual festivals; pursue justice; shun spiritism; listen to the one Jehovah raises up as prophet; respect boundary marks; keep land clean from bloodguilt; show compassion; keep clean from sexual immorality; give the firstfruits of the land to Jehovah; prove holy to Jehovah

Blessings for obeying Jehovah, curses for disobedience (27:1–28:68)

After nation crosses the Jordan, the Law is to be written on great stones

Cursings for disobedience to be pronounced on Mount Ebal

Blessings for obedience to all of Jehovah's commands to be pronounced on Mount Gerizim

Covenant made on Plains of Moab (29:1–30:20)

Recounts Jehovah's care in Egypt and during Israel's 40 years in the wilderness; warns against stubborn disobedience

Foretells Jehovah's mercy for those repenting

Sets before them choice between life and death; urges them to choose life by loving Jehovah, listening to his voice, and sticking to him

Transfer of leadership to Joshua, and Moses' final blessings (31:1–34:12)

Joshua is commissioned to lead Israel

Moses teaches Israel a song that will be a witness against them when they forsake Jehovah

Moses blesses the tribes of Israel, then he dies on Mount Nebo

three times in turning away the temptations of Satan the Devil. (Mt 4:1-11; De 6:13, 16; 8:3) Also, Jesus answered the question as to what was the greatest and first commandment by quoting from Deuteronomy 6:5. (Mr 12:30) And Paul quotes from Deuteronomy 30:12-14; 32:35, 36.—Ro 10:6-8; Heb 10:30.

The time covered by the book of Deuteronomy is somewhat over two months in the year 1473 B.C.E. It was written on the Plains of Moab and consists of four discourses, a song, and a blessing by Moses as Israel camped on Canaan's borders prior to entering the land.—De 1:3; Jos 1:11; 4:19.

Purpose. Despite the meaning of the name Deuteronomy, this book is not a second law nor a repetition of the entire Law but, rather, an explanation of it, as Deuteronomy 1:5 says. It exhorts Israel to faithfulness to Jehovah, using the generation of the 40 years' wandering as an example to avoid. Moses explains and elaborates on some of the essential points of the Law and the principles therein, with a view to the altered circumstances of Israel when they would be settled permanently in the land. He adjusts some of the laws accordingly and gives further regulations concerning the administration of government in their settled condition in the Promised Land.

In exhorting them and calling on them to enter into this renewed covenant with Jehovah through Moses, the book of Deuteronomy places the emphasis strikingly on knowledge, teaching, and instruction. The words "teach," "teaching," and "taught" occur much more often in Deuteronomy than in Exodus, Leviticus, or Numbers. Moses explained that Jehovah was teaching Israel by feeding them with manna. (De 8:3) He told the Israelites to place Jehovah's law, figuratively speaking, as frontlets between their eyes and on the doorposts of their houses and on their gates. (6:8, 9) He commanded them to inculcate his law in their sons. (6:6, 7) Instructions were given to read the Law every seventh year, during the time of the (annual) Festival of Booths. (31:10-13) Special instructions were given for the king that Israel might have in the future. He was to write a copy of the Law for himself and read in it every day. (17:18-20) Each time Israel went out to battle, the priests were to admonish the people to faith and courage and to assure them of victory, for Jehovah their God was marching with them. (20:1-4) When they should enter the Promised Land, they were to divide the tribes into two groups, with one group on Mount Ebal and the other on Mount Gerizim, and then they were to have God's Law read to them.—27:11-26; compare Jos 8:33-35.

Love Highlighted. Love, kindness, and consideration are also highlighted in Deuteronomy. The word "love" itself, either as a noun or as a form of the verb, occurs more than five times as often in Deuteronomy as in Exodus, Leviticus, and Numbers combined. Here we also have the greatest commandment, to which Jesus referred (Mt 22:36, 37), uniquely stated: "You must love Jehovah your God with all your heart and all your soul and all your vital force." (De 6:5; see also 10:12; 11:13.) Jehovah repeatedly expresses his love for Israel. (7:7-9; 23:5; 33:3) The very tone of Deuteronomy highlights Jehovah's love for his people: "If only they would develop this heart of theirs to fear me and to keep all my commandments always, in order that it might go well with them and their sons to time indefinite!" (5:29) In fact, we find such expressions as "that it may go well with you" and "that you may keep alive" time and again in Deuteronomy.—4:40; 5:16; 6:3; 22:7; 30:19, 20.

Even though warfare was ahead of Israel in taking the land, Jehovah did not overlook loving consideration. Victory was not so important or urgent that ruthless demands were to be made. An engaged man was exempt. (De 20:7) Exemption was made for a newly married man, so that he could cherish his wife and she have her husband for at least a full year. (24:5) If a man planted a vineyard and had not eaten the fruit of it or built a house and had not inaugurated it, he was excused from warfare so that he might enjoy the fruits of his labors.—20:5, 6.

Explicit details were given with respect to waging war and taking the land of Canaan. The fearful were to be sent home, lest they make the hearts of their brothers also weak. (De 20:8) The cities of the specified nations of Canaan whose wickedness had come to the full were to be devoted to destruction without fail, but the cities not of these specified nations were to be given the alternative of surrender or destruction. If they surrendered, they were to be put to forced labor, but the Law required that even slaves be treated with kindness, and its commandments protected the women from being molested even in cities taken in war. In cases of cities that refused to surrender, all the males were put to death, only the little children and the women who had not had relations with men being spared. (20:10-18; compare Nu 31:17, 18.) In building siegeworks around a city, the Israelites were not permitted to cut down fruit trees.—De 20:19, 20.

Animals were also given loving consideration in the book of Deuteronomy. The Israelites were prohibited from taking a bird sitting on a nest, for it was the protective instinct for her offspring that made her vulnerable. She was allowed to escape, but the young could be claimed by the Israelites for themselves. The mother was thus free to raise more young. (De 22:6, 7) The farmer was not permitted to hitch an ass with a bull, to prevent hardship on the weaker animal. (22:10) The bull was not to be muzzled while threshing the grain so that he would not be tormented with hunger while grain was so close at hand and he was exerting his energy in work to thresh it.—25:4.

In family and social life consideration was shown. The firstborn son was to receive the double portion, regardless of whether he was the son of the favorite wife or not. (De 21:15-17) Brother-in-law marriage was stated as a law for the first time, and penalties were outlined in order to give it force. (25:5-10) Honest weights and measures were mandated. (25:13-16) The value of life was stressed by the command to build a parapet around the roof of a house. (22:8) Consideration even for the wrongdoer that was to be given strokes was indicated by the Law that limited the strokes to 40. (25:1-3) All these regulations gave more detail to the Law, while also showing great consideration. At the same time there was more strictness.

Warnings and Laws. Deuteronomy is filled with warnings against false worship and unfaithfulness as well as instructions on how to deal with it so that pure worship might be preserved. The exhortation to holiness was an outstanding thing in Deuteronomy. The Israelites were admonished not to intermarry with the nations round about, because this would present a threat to pure worship and loyalty to Jehovah. (De 7:3, 4) They were warned against materialism and self-righteousness. (8:11-18; 9:4-6) Strong laws were made regarding apostasy. They were to watch themselves so that they would not turn to other gods. (11:16, 17) They were warned against false prophets. Instructions were given in two places as to how to identify a false prophet and how he should be dealt with. (13:1-5; 18:20-22) Even if a member of one's own family should become apostate, the family was not to have pity but was to share in stoning such a one to death.—13:6-11.

Cities of Israel that turned apostate were to be devoted to destruction, and nothing was to be

preserved for personal benefit by anyone. The city was never to be rebuilt. (De 13:12-17) Delinquents whose parents could not control them were to be stoned to death.—21:18-21.

Holiness and freedom from bloodguilt were emphasized by the law concerning the way to handle an unsolved murder. (De 21:1-9) Indicative of the zeal for pure worship, Deuteronomy contained regulations as to who could become a member of Jehovah's congregation and when. No illegitimate son to the tenth generation, no Moabite or Ammonite to time indefinite, and no eunuch could be admitted. However, Egyptians and Edomites of the third generation could become members of the congregation.—23:1-8.

Deuteronomy outlines the judicial arrangement for Israel when settled in the Promised Land. It sets forth the qualifications for judges and the arrangement of courts in the city gates, with the sanctuary as the supreme court of the land, whose judgments were to be followed by all Israel.—De 16:18–17:13.

Deuteronomy emphasizes Jehovah's position as the unique God (De 6:4), Israel's position as his unique people (4:7, 8), and the establishment of one central place of worship (12:4-7). It foretells the one who would be raised up as a prophet like Moses and who would speak in Jehovah's name, one to whom all must be subject.—18:18, 19.

DEVIL. This descriptive name was given to Satan because he is the chief and foremost slanderer and false accuser of Jehovah, his good word, and his holy name. The Greek *di·aʹbo·los* means "slanderer." (Compare Lu 16:1, where the related verb *di·a·balʹlo* occurs.)—See SATAN.

Down through the centuries the Devil has demonstrated that he is the arch-opposer of both God and man. He disputed with Michael over the body of Moses (Jude 9); showed he has power to ensnare others (1Ti 3:7; 2Ti 2:26); used people such as the false religious leaders, Judas Iscariot, and Bar-Jesus as his children (Joh 8:44; 13:2; Ac 13:6, 10); oppressed persons beyond the cure of the physicians (Ac 10:38); had righteous ones thrown into prison (Re 2:10); and even had the means to cause untimely death (Heb 2:14). Christians are, therefore, admonished not to give this Slanderer of God an opening by continuing in a provoked state. (Eph 4:27) "Keep your senses, be watchful," Peter warns. "Your adversary, the Devil, walks about like a roaring lion, seeking to devour someone."—1Pe 5:8.

There are other instances in the original text of the Christian Greek Scriptures where the word di·a'bo·los occurs but does not refer to Satan, so the word is properly rendered "slanderer." For example, in referring to Judas, Jesus said to the 12, "One of you is a slanderer" (Joh 6:70); women in the congregation were cautioned not to be slanderous (1Ti 3:11; Tit 2:3); that "men will be . . . slanderers" is one of the evidences of "the last days."—2Ti 3:1-5.

Jehovah's law to the nation of Israel forbade them to slander one another. (Le 19:16) The tenor of the entire Bible is against such misuse of the tongue.—2Sa 19:27; Ps 15:3; 101:5; Pr 11:13; 20:19; 30:10; Jer 6:28; 9:4.

DEVOTED THING.

In his dealings with the nation of Israel, Jehovah God decreed that certain things, persons, or even entire cities be placed under a sacred ban, thereby restricting them from any common or profane use. Koehler and Baumgartner define che'rem as a "thing or person devoted (to destruction or sacred use a[nd] therefore secluded from profane use)," and the causative form of the verb cha·ram' as "banish (by banning . . . seclude from society a[nd] life, devote to destruction)." (Lexicon in Veteris Testamenti Libros, Leiden, 1958, p. 334) Such devoted things in a sense, therefore, became "taboo" for the Israelites. The related word in Arabic retains a similar meaning till this day. To the Arab Muslims, the sacred territory of Mecca and Medina is considered haram; and the harim of a sheik has long been forbidden ground to all persons other than the master of the harem or his eunuchs.

It was in the declaration of the Law that sacred banning was first expressed. At Exodus 22:20 we read: "One who sacrifices to any gods but Jehovah alone is to be devoted to destruction [a form of cha·ram']." This decree was applied impartially against the Israelites themselves, as in the case of the idolatry carried on at Shittim that resulted in the death of some 24,000 of the nation. (Nu 25:1-9) The possession of a thing devoted to destruction could also make the possessor subject to such ban. Thus, concerning the religious images of the nations of Canaan, God warned the Israelites: "You must not bring a detestable thing [image] into your house and actually become a thing devoted to destruction [che'rem] like it. You should thoroughly loathe it and absolutely detest it, because it is something devoted to destruction."—De 7:25, 26.

The sacred ban did not always mean destruction. Articles, animals, and even fields could be devoted to Jehovah and thus become holy items for sacred use by the priesthood or in temple service. However, persons who came under sacred ban were to be put to death without fail. No devoted thing was redeemable at any price, and this was a major distinction between a devoted thing and something otherwise sanctified.—Le 27:21, 28, 29; compare with verses 19, 27, 30, 31; Nu 18:14; Jos 6:18, 19, 24; Eze 44:29; Ezr 10:8.

Canaanites. It was in the conquest of Canaan that this sacred banning reached its greatest prominence. Prior to the official entry into the land, when the Canaanite king of Arad attacked Israel down in the Negeb, Jehovah approved the Israelites' vow to devote the cities of his kingdom to destruction. (Nu 21:1-3) Following their attacks on Israel, the kingdoms of Sihon and Og, E of the Jordan, next came under ban, resulting in the destruction of all persons in their cities and the preservation of only the domestic animals and other spoil. (De 2:31-35; 3:1-7) Later, on the Plains of Moab, just before the crossing of the Jordan by the Israelites, Jehovah reemphasized the vital need for clean worship and the avoidance of all corrupting influences. He decreed that seven nations in the Promised Land were to be placed under sacred ban and that their idolatrous populations were to be devoted to destruction by the Israelites, who were to act as his executioners. (De 7:1-6, 16, 22-26) Only faraway cities not of these nations were to be given the option of seeking peace; but those nations designated by God as devoted to destruction were to be annihilated, "in order that they may not teach you to do according to all their detestable things, which they have done to their gods, and you may indeed sin against Jehovah your God." (De 20:10-18) The sparing of any of them would lead inevitably to infection and contamination by their false religions. Their extermination could serve to preserve the lives of the Israelites themselves; but, of greater importance, it would maintain the purity of the worship of the Universal Sovereign, Jehovah God. The same ban was to apply to any apostatizing member of their families or to the future inhabitants of any of the Israelite cities that might be established in the Promised Land. —De 13:6-17.

West of the Jordan, Jericho was the first city devoted to destruction, with nothing being preserved except the metal articles for temple use. Because of her faith, Rahab and her family were granted exemption from the ban. In spite of Joshua's strong warning that failure to observe the ban could result in the whole nation's being devoted to destruction, Achan took some of the banned articles and thus made himself "a thing devoted to destruction." Only his death relieved the entire nation from coming under the same ban.—Jos 6:17-19; 7:10-15, 24-26.

Gibeonites. Thereafter, numerous cities were devoted to destruction. (Jos 8:26, 27; 10:28-42; 11:11, 12) Concerning such cities, the record states: "There proved to be no city that made peace with the sons of Israel but the Hivites inhabiting Gibeon. All the others they took by war. For it proved to be Jehovah's course to let their hearts become stubborn so as to declare war against Israel, in order that he might devote them to destruction, that they might come to have no favorable consideration, but in order that he might annihilate them, just as Jehovah had commanded Moses."—Jos 11:19, 20.

Assyrian Failure. The Assyrian Sennacherib boasted that no god had been able to save the nations whom his forefathers had devoted to destruction. (2Ch 32:14) Assyria's false gods, however, were unable to make effective such a ban on Jerusalem, and the true God Jehovah proved Sennacherib's threat to be impotent. Nevertheless, the very land of Judah, because of the stubbornness and rebellion of the people, did eventually become a land devoted by God to destruction, and it suffered devastation at the hands of Nebuchadnezzar. (Jer 25:1-11; Isa 43:28) Babylon thereafter came in for a devoting to destruction in the full sense of the expression.—Jer 50:21-27; 51:1-3; compare Re 18:2-8.

Other Mention. After Israel settled in the land, the Israelites residing in Jabesh-gilead came under ban for failing to support a united action against the tribe of Benjamin in punishment for its wickedness. (Jg 21:8-12) King Saul failed to carry out completely the terms of a ban on Amalek and its king, offering the pretext that the things preserved were to be offered in sacrifice to Jehovah. He was told that "to obey is better than a sacrifice" and that the kingship would now be given to another. (1Sa 15:1-23) King Ahab was guilty of a similar action with regard to the Syrian Ben-hadad II. (1Ki 20:42) The inhabitants of Mount Seir were devoted to destruction by the Ammonites and Moabites.—2Ch 20:22, 23.

Sacred bans figure in a number of prophecies. Malachi 4:5, 6 foretells the work of "Elijah the prophet before the coming of the great and fear-inspiring day of Jehovah," in order that Jehovah "may not come and actually strike the earth with a devoting of it to destruction." (Compare Mt 24:21, 22.) Daniel 11:44 describes the symbolic "king of the north" going forth in great rage "to annihilate and to devote many to destruction." Jehovah, because of his indignation, is described as devoting "all the nations" to destruction. (Isa 34:2; compare Re 19:15-21.) The triumphant "daughter of Zion" is said to devote, by a ban, the unjust profit and the resources of the enemy peoples to "the true Lord of the whole earth." (Mic 4:13) It is foretold that Jerusalem, delivered from all her enemies, will be inhabited and that henceforth there will occur "no more any banning to destruction."—Zec 14:11; compare Re 22:3.

These scriptures all serve to emphasize the divine statement at Deuteronomy 7:9, 10: "And you well know that Jehovah your God is the true God, the faithful God, keeping covenant and loving-kindness in the case of those who love him and those who keep his commandments to a thousand generations, but repaying to his face the one who hates him by destroying him. He will not hesitate toward the one who hates him; he will repay him to his face." God's Son, who gave his life as a ransom, declared: "He that exercises faith in the Son has everlasting life; he that disobeys the Son will not see life, but the wrath of God remains upon him." (Joh 3:36) The cursed "goats" of the prophetic parable at Matthew 25:31-46 are clearly such persons upon whom the wrath of God remains and who are therefore devoted to everlasting destruction.

In the *Septuagint* the word *che'rem* is generally translated by the Greek *a·na'the·ma.*—See CURSE; VOW.

DEVOTION. See EXCLUSIVE DEVOTION; GODLY DEVOTION.

DEW. Small drops of water produced by the condensation of moisture in the air, of water vapor arising from the ground, and of moisture exuded by plants. The Hebrew word for "dew," *tal,* also signifies "light rain." (Pr 3:20) Dew becomes silvery-white, icy hoarfrost when the lower air strata drop in temperature to 0° C. (32° F.). Jehovah is responsible for the dewdrops and is said to scatter the hoarfrost "just like ashes."—Ps 147:16; Job 38:28.

Dew forms when night air laden with water vapor cools, depositing the vapor, condensed to liquid form, on cooler objects. It also develops when warm watery vapor rising from the ground comes in contact with the cooling air. The Bible explains that early in earth's history, before it rained on earth, "a mist [vapor] would go up from the earth and it watered the entire surface of the ground." (Ge 2:6 and ftn) Dew is also produced when moisture from vegetation evaporates into the air. A plant continues to draw water that has been absorbed by its roots until a balance is obtained between the temperature at the tip of the leaves and that at the plant's roots. The great amount of dew thus produced by some trees can often be heard dripping from them at night. Most morning dew seems to have this source. Job said, "My root is opened for the waters, and dew itself will stay overnight upon my bough."—Job 29:19.

In Israel there is normally little if any rain from mid-April to mid-October. However, dew forms and waters the vegetation during these months. *The Geography of the Bible* by D. Baly (1974, p. 45) says: "The value of the dew was well appreciated by the Israelites, . . . for it swells the grapes during the drought of summer." Isaiah refers to the "dew in the heat of [grape] harvest." (Isa 18:4, 5) After this came the "autumn," or "early," rains. (Joe 2:23; Jas 5:7) Night dews in certain areas are so heavy that trees and other plants thereby obtain more than enough moisture to compensate for loss through evaporation during the day. Hence, nocturnal dews may well account for a bountiful harvest where drought and starvation would otherwise prevail.

The importance of dew is emphasized by the discovery that when plants have wilted from the heat, they have recovered more rapidly when moisture condensed on their leaves at night than they did when the ground was watered. They absorbed so much moisture that they functioned normally during the succeeding day without any watering of the ground. The amount of water absorbed from dew and later excreted through the roots into the soil for storage sometimes equaled the plant's entire weight.

During Israel's 40-year wilderness trek, the divinely provided manna regularly descended with the dew, remaining upon the earth after the dew's evaporation. (Ex 16:13-18; Nu 11:9) By two signs involving dew, Gideon obtained proof of divine support before going forth to fight the Midianites. First, he kept a fleece of wool exposed on a threshing floor overnight, the dew developing only on the fleece while the earth was dry. In the second test, matters were reversed. It is not revealed whether this was the rainless season when dew could be expected.—Jg 6:36–7:1.

Figurative Use. Dew is Scripturally associated with blessing, fertility, and abundance. (Ge 27:28; De 33:13, 28; Zec 8:12) A return to Jeho-

vah would result in blessing, God saying: "I shall become like the dew to Israel." (Ho 14:1, 5) Through Micah, God foretold that "the remaining ones of Jacob" would "become in the midst of many peoples like dew from Jehovah, like copious showers upon vegetation," foretelling that the remnant of spiritual Jacob (Israel) would be a blessing from God to the people.—Mic 5:7.

Conversely, lack or the withholding of dew is associated with a disfavored condition. (Ge 27:39; Hag 1:10) When God withheld dew and rain from the land of Israel in the days of King Ahab and Elijah, famine resulted.—1Ki 17:1; Lu 4:25.

Morning clouds and dew in Israel vanished rapidly in the sun's heat. What little loving-kindness there was in Ephraim (Israel) and Judah had vanished similarly. (Ho 6:4) And because of wrongdoing, the inhabitants of Ephraim (Israel) would be taken into exile, becoming "like the dew that early goes away."—Ho 13:1-3, 16.

Dewdrops are quiet and numerous. Perhaps to denote stealthiness or a multitude as numerous as dewdrops, Hushai told Absalom: "We ourselves will be upon [David] just as the dew falls upon the ground." (2Sa 17:12) Jehovah's King has his "company of young men just like dewdrops," perhaps as to number.—Ps 110:3.

Dew is also gentle and refreshing. It is aptly applied to Moses' farewell prophetic song. (De 32:2) A king's goodwill is likened to the refreshing effect of dew on vegetation. (Pr 19:12) The loving unity prevailing among God's people is refreshing "like the dew of Hermon that is descending upon the mountains of Zion." Mount Hermon's forest-covered and perpetually snow-streaked heights caused night vapors to arise that could be carried so far by cold air currents coming down over Hermon from the N that these vapors could condense upon Zion's mountains many miles to the south.—Ps 133:1-3; PICTURE, Vol. 1, p. 332.

DIADEM. See CROWN.

DIAMOND. A brilliant precious stone, the hardest natural mineral yet discovered and among the most valuable of gems. Although diamonds are generally colorless, some have such tints as yellow, green, red, brown, blue, and black. Most uncut diamonds are eight-sided transparent or translucent crystals and are composed of nearly pure carbon. Diamonds are thought to have been formed long ago when the earth's carbon was subjected to great pressure and heat. Early diamonds were found in streambeds, but in modern times they are usually mined from rock formations deep in the earth.

The Hebrew word *sha·mir'* (translated "diamond" twice, "emery stone" once in *NW*) is evidently related to the Akkadian word *ashmur,* meaning "emery." Some suggest that *sha·mir'* may apply to a very hard mineral loosely identified by the general term "adamant" (from Gr. *a·da'mas,* meaning "unconquerable"), which may refer to diamond or to a number of very hard substances, such as corundum and emery.

Jehovah referred to the use of diamonds for scratching or engraving hard materials when he said: "The sin of Judah is written down with an iron stylus. With a diamond point it is engraved on the tablet of their heart, and on the horns of their altars." (Jer 17:1, 2) The house of Israel also became obstinate and hardhearted. Therefore, Jehovah said to Ezekiel: "Look! I have made your face exactly as hard as their faces and your forehead exactly as hard as their foreheads. Like a diamond, harder than flint, I have made your forehead." (Eze 3:7-9) Similarly, because of the Jews' stubbornness, Jehovah declared through Zechariah: "Their heart they set as an emery stone [Heb., *sha·mir'*] to keep from obeying the law and the words that Jehovah of armies sent by his spirit, by means of the former prophets." —Zec 7:12; see JEWELS AND PRECIOUS STONES.

DIBLAH (Dib'lah). A site mentioned by Ezekiel (6:14) when recording Jehovah's prophecy of the desolation to come upon the land of Israel as recompense for its idolatrous worship. Any ancient location by this name is unknown, and most modern scholars, therefore, hold that "Diblah" is a copyist's error for "Riblah," the initial Hebrew letter for "R" (ר) being easily mistaken for the Hebrew letter for "D" (ד). If this is the case, it may be identified with the Biblical Riblah (ruins near modern Ribleh) at the Orontes River, "in the land of Hamath" (2Ki 23:33), and "the wilderness toward Diblah [Riblah]" could have reference to the gravelly unbroken plain of the Syrian Desert that lies to the S and SE of Riblah. Some translators, however, render Ezekiel's words to read "from the wilderness to Riblah." (*RS*) According to such rendering, the meaning might be that Jehovah's judgment would extend from "the wilderness," the Promised Land's traditional southern boundary (Ex 23:31), to the region of "Hamath" (represented by Riblah) far to the north. (1Ki 8:65) Ezekiel's use of such a phrase would then be the equivalent of the better known "from Dan down to Beer-sheba."—Jg 20:1; see RIBLAH No. 2.

DIBLAIM (Dib·la'im) [Two Cakes of Pressed Figs]. Parent of Hosea's wife Gomer.—Ho 1:2, 3.

DIBON (Di'bon).

1. A city E of the Dead Sea, wrested from the Moabites by Sihon the Amorite but later taken from him by Israel at the time of the Israelite entry into the land under Moses.—Nu 21:25-30.

Ancient Dibon is today identified with Dhiban, 5 km (3 mi) N of the Arnon, 21 km (13 mi) E of the Dead Sea. It has been the site of recent intensive archaeological investigations and has achieved some fame as the scene of the discovery of the famous Moabite Stone in 1868. Statements on this stele, set up by Mesha, the king of Moab, have been interpreted by some to identify Dibon as his capital city (including Qarhah) and as "the chief city of Moab" at one time.

Soon after the initial Israelite conquest of this area, the tribe of Gad lived there and "proceeded to build [or, rebuild] Dibon," apparently giving it the lengthened name of Dibon-gad, a location listed as one of the nation's camping sites. (Nu 32:34; 33:45, 46) However, Dibon was considered part of the inheritance of Reuben. (Nu 32:2, 3; Jos 13:8, 9, 15-17) Dibon probably suffered under the revival of Moabite power during the reign of King Eglon, until it gained relief as a result of Judge Ehud's victory. (Jg 3:12-30) Mesha, king of Moab, revolted against Israelite domination many centuries later, "as soon as Ahab died," according to the Bible account at 2 Kings 3:4, 5. The Bible does not say precisely how long this uprising lasted, and it is possible that, as Mesha boasts on the Moabite Stone, he managed to annex several Israelite cities to "Qarhah" at that time. Nevertheless, unlike Mesha's propagandistic inscription, the Scriptural record makes it clear that Moab was soundly defeated when its forces entered into battle against the combined armies of Israel, Judah, and Edom.—2Ki 3:4-27.

Less than 200 years later Dibon was once more known as a Moabite city, and against it Isaiah (15:2) uttered a pronouncement of doom. The inhabitants of the region are therefore spoken of prophetically as going "up to The House and to Dibon, to the high places," mourning the desolation of Moab.

Certain scholars have theorized that Isaiah alluded to the threatening Assyrian menace as causing the "weeping" at "the high places" near Dibon; however, there is no record of an Assyrian devastation of that region. When Jehovah's servant Jeremiah prophesied about a hundred years later that Dibon would "get down from glory, and sit down in thirst" (Jer 48:18), Isaiah's earlier prophecy had apparently not yet been fulfilled. Therefore the later prophet was evidently presenting anew a similar message and thereby making the prediction of doom on Moab doubly certain. Sometime after the fall of Jerusalem in 607 B.C.E., when Nebuchadnezzar thoroughly devastated Moab, he may have left Dibon's citizens, not only 'thirsting' for the luxuries of its previous glory but also forsaken as humbled captives, literally thirsting for water and other common necessities.—Jer 25:9, 17-21.

The finding of large stores of remarkably preserved grain at Dibon, which grain is considered to date back to sometime in the latter half of the first millennium B.C.E., seems to confirm the view of some that the Dibon region, even today an agriculturally productive area, may have at one time been a breadbasket of Palestine.

Some commentators consider Dibon to be the same as Dimon mentioned in Isaiah 15:9.—See DIMON.

2. A location in Judah (Ne 11:25), thought by some to be the same as Dimonah.—Jos 15:22; see DIMONAH.

DIBON-GAD.   See DIBON No. 1.

DIBRI   (Dib'ri) [probably, Wordy]. An Israelite of the tribe of Dan whose daughter Shelomith married an Egyptian. Shortly after the Exodus from Egypt, the son of this union was stoned to death for abusing Jehovah's name.—Le 24: 10-16, 23.

DIDRACHMA.   A Greek silver coin having the value of two drachmas, or $1.31 according to modern values. The Jews paid a yearly temple tax of two drachmas, or a didrachma.—Mt 17: 24, ftn.

DIKLAH   (Dik'lah). A descendant of Shem through Joktan. (Ge 10:21, 26, 27; 1Ch 1:17, 20, 21) Some scholars believe his tribe settled in southern Arabia. This, however, cannot be determined with any certainty.

DILEAN   (Di'le·an). A Judean city in the Shephelah. (Jos 15:20, 33, 38) Though its exact location is uncertain, some geographers place it at Tell en-Najileh (Tel Nagila), about 10 km (6 mi) SW of Lachish.

DILL   [Gr., a'ne·thon]. Modern lexicographers agree that the plant referred to by the Greek term a'ne·thon is the dill (Anethum graveolens) rather than the anise (Gr., an'ne·son), as in older translations (KJ, Dy). The dill is more commonly cultivated than the anise in the Palestine region today, and evidence indicates that it was cultivated from ancient times in the Middle East, as well as by the Greeks and Romans. Dill was among the plants the hypocritical Pharisees punctiliously tithed, while failing to observe the weightier matters of the Law. (Mt 23:23) The Jewish Mishnah (Ma'aserot 4:5) prescribed that not only the seeds but also the plant and pods were subject to tithe.

The plant is weedlike in growth, resembles anise, and attains a height of about 0.5 m (2 ft) with finely cut, clear green leaves and sprays of small yellow flowers. It is cultivated for its aromatic seeds, which are much valued for flavoring foods and also medicinally for treatment of stomach ailments.

DIMNAH   (Dim'nah). Evidently the same as Rimmon (Jos 19:13) and Rimmono (1Ch 6:77), a city on the E border of Zebulun's territory given to the Merarite Levites. (Jos 21:34, 35) Dimnah is commonly identified with modern Rummana (Rimmon) about 10 km (6 mi) N of Nazareth.

DIMON   (Di'mon). A site mentioned in Isaiah's pronouncement of doom upon Moab; the slaughter of the Moabites causes the waters of Dimon to become "full of blood."—Isa 15:9.

Some commentators consider Dimon to be another form of Dibon (mentioned in verse 2 of the prophecy), Dimon being used to provide an alliteration, or play on the sound, of the Hebrew word for "blood" (dam), thus "Dimon . . . full of dam." In favor of such a view is the fact that the Dead Sea Scrolls read "Dibon" instead of "Dimon" here in verse 9, and Jerome's statement that in his day (c. 347-420 C.E.) the two names were used interchangeably.

Others, however, consider it improbable that the name of Dibon would be presented in two different ways within the brief pronouncement, and they also note that no other place in the pronouncement receives double mention. They further point out that Dibon did not stand by any large "waters," it being a considerable distance from the nearest wadi, the Arnon. They suggest, therefore, that Dimon may be a scribal alteration of Madmen, mentioned in Jeremiah's condemnation of Moab (Jer 48:2), and usually identified with Dimna, about 4 km (2.5 mi) WNW of Rabbath-Moab, on a height dominating the waters of the 'Ain el-Megheisil to the SE.

Both views are conjectural, the latter having in

its favor identification with a site associated with waters, which the context seems to require.

DIMONAH (Di·mo'nah). A southern city of Judah near the border of Edom. (Jos 15:21, 22) It is suggested by some to be the same as "Dibon" mentioned at Nehemiah 11:25, but its exact location remains uncertain.

DINAH (Di'nah) [Judged [that is, acquitted; vindicated]]. Daughter of Jacob by Leah. Dinah may have been about six years of age when Jacob returned to Canaan and settled at Succoth, she having been born at Haran when her father was residing there.—Ge 30:21, 22, 25; 31:41.

At the time Jacob and his family were tenting outside the city of Shechem, young Dinah unwisely made it a practice to visit the Canaanite girls there. On one of these visits she was violated by Shechem the son of the Hivite chieftain Hamor. Shechem fell in love with her, and Dinah remained in his home until avenged by her full brothers Simeon and Levi. (Ge 34:1-31) Some contend that Dinah must have been just a child when she was violated. However, it must be borne in mind that before coming to Shechem, Jacob built a house and booths at Succoth, indicating that he resided there for some time. (Ge 33:17) At Shechem he bought a tract of land and apparently became established there for a while. All of this, together with the fact that Shechem fell in love with Dinah, the "young woman," would argue that Dinah, though still young, was not a mere child at the time of her association with Shechem.—Ge 33:18, 19; 34:12.

Years later, Dinah, with the rest of Jacob's household, came into Egypt at the invitation of Joseph.—Ge 46:7, 15.

DINHABAH (Din'ha·bah). The city of Bela, king of Edom. (Ge 36:32; 1Ch 1:43) Its present-day location is unknown.

DIONYSIUS (Di·o·nys'i·us) [Of (Belonging to) Dionysus [the god of wine]]. An Areopagite, or judge of the Athenian Areopagus, who heard Paul's defense and became a Christian.—Ac 17: 34; see AREOPAGUS.

DIOTREPHES (Di·ot're·phes) [Fed by Zeus]. A man mentioned by the apostle John in his letter to Gaius. In addition to being ambitious, proud, disrespectful of apostolic authority, rebellious, and inhospitable, Diotrephes tried to hinder those desiring to show hospitality to the brothers and to expel these from the congregation.—3Jo 9, 10.

DIPHATH (Di'phath). A descendant of Noah through Japheth and Gomer; called Riphath in the Latin *Vulgate*, the Greek *Septuagint*, and about 30 Hebrew manuscripts, as well as at Genesis 10:3. (1Ch 1:4-6, ftn) The spelling "Diphath" found in the Masoretic text at 1 Chronicles 1:6 may have arisen through a copyist's error, since the Hebrew letters for "R" (ר) and "D" (ד) look very much alike.

DIRGE. A composition, lyrical or musical, expressing deep sorrow, such as the grief occasioned by the death of a friend or loved one; an elegy. In the *New World Translation* the rendering "dirge" usually is from the Hebrew word *qi·nah'*, which denotes a mournful composition, an elegy, or a lamentation.

The Hebrew term *shig·ga·yohn'* in the superscription of Psalm 7 is also translated "dirge" and may denote a highly emotional song with rapid changes of rhythm. (*NW* ftn) A plural form of the Hebrew word appears in Habakkuk 3:1, where it is rendered "dirges." Because of their nature, dirges are associated with moaning and wailing (Eze 2:10), and at least some of them were written down and preserved. Second Chronicles 35:25 reports that Jeremiah chanted over deceased King Josiah and indicates that there once existed a collection of dirges (Heb., *qi·nohth'*), for it is there stated: "All the male singers and female singers keep talking about Josiah in their dirges down till today; and they have them set as a regulation over Israel, and there they are written among the dirges."

Dirges are linked with mourning, as when Jehovah told unfaithful Israel: "I will turn your festivals into mourning and all your songs into a dirge." (Am 8:10) Hence, taking up a dirge signified intoning an elegy, or mournful composition, perhaps one denoting rejection by Jehovah or contrasting earlier favorable circumstances with a later unhappy situation. (Jer 7:29; Eze 19:1-14) A dirge would be chanted, often by women.—Eze 27:32; Jer 9:20.

Some dirges were of the historical type, being composed after an event, such as the death of a cherished acquaintance. An example of this kind is the dirge David chanted in sorrow over Saul and Jonathan, who had fallen in death upon Mount Gilboa during warfare with the Philistines. (2Sa 1:17-27; 1Sa 31:8) King David also chanted over Abner after that one's burial. (2Sa 3:31-34) While dirges relating to a person's death may have been composed partly to afford some consolation to survivors, among faithful servants of

God these were not for the purpose of glorifying the deceased.—Ec 9:5, 10.

The book of Lamentations is a dirge written by Jeremiah after the destruction of Jerusalem at Babylonian hands in 607 B.C.E. While it expresses grief over that desolation, it also reflects faith and hope in Jehovah; and the fifth chapter opens with an appeal to God to remember his people who had become "mere orphans without a father."—La 3:22-27; 5:1-3; see LAMENTATIONS, BOOK OF.

Some Biblically recorded dirges are prophetic and graphically portray coming calamity, sometimes as though it had already been accomplished. Prophetic dirges were raised up against Tyre and its king (Eze 26:17; 27:1, 2; 28:11-19), as well as against Pharaoh and Egypt. (Eze 32:2-16) The raising up of a dirge over Judah and Jerusalem is mentioned in connection with their desolation.—Jer 9:9-11.

DISCHARGE, RUNNING.

A Biblical expression applicable to conditions of the genital organs of men and women. (Le 15:2, 19, 25; Nu 5:2, 3; 2Sa 3:29) In the case of men, it related to an unhealthy state, in which there was a flow of matter from the genital organ or the organ was obstructed by such matter. (Le 15:2, 3) No male offspring of Aaron was permitted to eat of "the holy things" while unclean because of a running discharge.—Le 22:4.

The expression "running discharge" sometimes applied to a woman's regular, normal menstrual flow. (Le 15:19-24) Yet it was also used to designate a diseased, extended, and thus abnormal, flow of blood. (Le 15:25-30) In the latter sense, it applied to the chronic "flow of blood" from which one woman suffered for 12 years before Jesus Christ cured her.—Mt 9:20-22.

According to the Law, a person having a running discharge was unclean, made articles and persons he or she touched unclean, and so forth. After a *diseased* discharge ceased, the individual took specified steps for purification.—Le 15; see CLEAN, CLEANNESS.

DISCIPLE.

A taught one, a learner, a pupil. The Hebrew word for a disciple (*lim·mudh'*) basically refers to one who learns, is taught, or is trained. (Compare Isa 8:16, ftn.) The related word *mal·madh'* denotes a "goad" used to train cattle. (Jg 3:31; compare Ho 10:11.) The Greek word *ma·the·tes'* (disciple) primarily denotes one who directs his mind to something.

In the Greek Scriptures we read of disciples of Jesus, of John the Baptizer, of the Pharisees, and of Moses. (Mt 9:14; Lu 5:33; Joh 9:28) Jesus' first disciples came from among the disciples of John. (Joh 1:35-42) The 12 chosen as apostles are called disciples at Matthew 10:1 and 11:1. In a wide sense the word "disciple" applied to those believing Jesus' teaching, at least one of such being a secret disciple. (Lu 6:17; Joh 19:38) However, in the Gospel accounts it usually applies to the body of intimate followers of Jesus who traveled with him on his preaching tours and who were taught and instructed by him. The principal application of the term is to all those who not only believe Christ's teachings but also follow them closely. They must be taught to "observe all the things" Jesus commands.—Mt 28:19, 20.

Jesus' purpose in teaching his disciples was to make them like himself, preachers and teachers of the good news of the Kingdom. "A pupil is not above his teacher, but everyone that is perfectly instructed will be like his teacher," Jesus said. (Lu 6:40) The effectiveness of Christ's teaching was proved by subsequent history. His disciples continued in the work he had taught them and made disciples throughout the Roman Empire, in Asia, Europe, and Africa, before the close of the first century. This was their principal work, in accord with Jesus Christ's command at Matthew 28: 19, 20.

That Christians to this very day are obligated to make disciples of the people of the nations is made clear by the closing words of Jesus' command: "And, look! I am with you all the days until the conclusion of the system of things." They are not making disciples for themselves, as those taught are really disciples of Jesus Christ, for it is the teaching, not of men, but of Christ, that they follow. For this reason the disciples were by divine providence called Christians. (Ac 11:26) Similarly, the prophet Isaiah had disciples but not for himself. Isaiah's disciples knew Jehovah's law, and with them the testimony of the law resided. —Isa 8:16.

Being a disciple of Jesus is not the taking of a course of ease in life. Jesus did not please himself, but he followed a path that involved the greatest resistance from the Devil and his agents. (Ro 15:3) He said that his disciples must love him more than their closest relatives on earth and even more than their own souls. They must love their Christian fellow disciples. They must bear spiritual fruitage. A person who wants to be a disciple of Jesus has to take up his torture stake and follow the path that Christ traveled. In doing this, he will have to "say good-bye to all his belongings," but he will receive many more valuable things now, with persecutions, and with everlasting life to come.—Lu 14:26, 27, 33; Joh 13:35; 15:8; Mr 10:29, 30; see CHRISTIAN.

DISCIPLINE. The Hebrew noun *mu·sar'* and the verb form *ya·sar'* convey the sense of "discipline," "chastisement," "correction," "exhortation." In the Greek *Septuagint* and in the Christian Greek Scriptures, the corresponding noun *pai·dei'a* and the verb *pai·deu'o* have basically the same significance. Drawn from *pais,* meaning "child," *pai·dei'a* primarily relates to what is needed in bringing up children—discipline, instruction, education, correction, chastisement.

Sources and Objective. In expression of his love, Jehovah provides discipline for his people. (Pr 3:11, 12) He gives them instruction that corrects wrong viewpoints and that molds their mental faculties and course of conduct. For the Israelites during the time of Moses, the discipline included their witnessing manifestations of God's greatness. There were displays of matchless power when Jehovah executed judgment on all the gods of Egypt, liberated his people, and destroyed the Egyptian army in the Red Sea. There were fearsome judgments executed upon disobedient Israelites. And there was miraculous provision of food and water coupled with lessons in the importance of taking to heart and applying *everything* that Jehovah says. All this discipline served to humble them and to impress upon them the need for a proper fear of Jehovah, to be shown by faith and obedience.—De 8:3-5; 11:2-7.

Often Jehovah's discipline comes through his representatives, duly constituted authorities. An Israelite who falsely accused his wife of not being a virgin at the time of marriage was to be disciplined by the elders who served as judges. (De 22:13-19) Parents represent Jehovah when they properly discipline their offspring. And children are to respond to such discipline as an expression of parental love, designed to promote their lasting welfare. (Pr 1:8; 4:1, 13; 6:20-23; 13:1, 24; 15:5; 22:15; 23:13, 14; Eph 6:4) In the Christian congregation, God's Word is used by elders to provide discipline—admonition, correction, reproof. (2Ti 3:16) The object of discipline from Jehovah administered to Christians in cases of wrongdoing is to recover them from a fall into sin and to prevent their sharing in the condemnatory judgment to be expressed against the ungodly world. (1Co 11:32) As head of the Christian congregation, Jesus Christ, in expression of his affection, sees to it that needed discipline is provided.—Re 3:14, 19.

A severe form of discipline is expulsion from the congregation. The apostle Paul resorted to this when handing Alexander and Hymenaeus "over to Satan." (1Ti 1:20) Cut off from the congregation, they were again part of the world under Satan's control.—1Co 5:5, 11-13.

What Jehovah may permit to come upon his servants in the form of persecution can serve as discipline, or training, producing the desirable fruit of righteousness, to be enjoyed in peace after the trial is over. (Heb 12:4-11) Even the Son of God was equipped to be a compassionate and sympathetic high priest by reason of the suffering that his Father allowed him to undergo.—Heb 4:15.

Results From Heeding and From Ignoring. The wicked, the fools, or the morally worthless ones show their hatred of Jehovah's discipline by rejecting it completely. (Ps 50:16, 17; Pr 1:7) The bad results that come from such foolishness constitutes further discipline, often severe chastisement. As the proverb puts it: "The discipline of the foolish ones is foolishness." (Pr 16:22) They may bring upon themselves poverty, disgrace, sickness, and even untimely death. The history of the Israelites illustrates how great the loss can be. They paid no attention to the discipline in the form of reproof and correction expressed through the prophets. They were heedless of the discipline in the form of Jehovah's withholding his protection and blessing. Finally, they experienced the severe discipline announced beforehand—conquest and exile.—Jer 2:30; 5:3; 7:28; 17:23; 32:33; Ho 7:12-16; 10:10; Zep 3:2.

By contrast, acceptance of discipline, coupled with a wholesome fear of Jehovah, makes one wise, able to use knowledge aright, and thus helps one to avoid much pain and suffering. When acted upon, discipline received appreciatively can contribute to a lengthening of one's present life and holds promise of an abiding future. Rightly, then, discipline should be highly esteemed.—Pr 8:10, 33-35; 10:17.

DISEASES AND TREATMENT. The Scriptures frequently refer to illness, an unhealthy condition of the body or the mind, also to spiritual sickness, or the state of being figuratively diseased. While the Bible was not written primarily as a book of instruction on medical or other forms of treatment for various maladies, the information it presents on such matters is scientifically accurate. Significantly, it shows how to overcome spiritual sickness.

Disease is a consequence of the imperfection resulting in death that was passed on to the human race by the sinner Adam. (Ge 3:17-19; Ro 5:12) Yet, Jehovah directly "touched Pharaoh and his household with great plagues because of Sarai, Abram's wife." (Ge 12:17) God was responsible for the "boils with blisters" that broke out on man and beast during the sixth blow he inflicted upon ancient Egypt. (Ex 9:8-11) He struck presumptuous Miriam with leprosy (Nu 12:9-15), dealt a blow to the illegitimate child of David and Bathsheba so that it took sick and eventually died (2Sa 12:15-18), and "gave a pestilence in Israel" in David's day (2Sa 24:15). All these acts of God were in upholding his name and law, and for the protection, liberation, or fatherly disciplining of his chosen people.

However, by Jehovah's permission, Satan "struck Job with a malignant boil from the sole of his foot to the crown of his head." (Job 2:6, 7) This allowed Job to stand as an example for God's people in the matter of keeping integrity. Job was later healed by God, and his life was extended 140 years for his faithfulness. (Job 42:10, 16) Demons were sometimes responsible for infirmities, as in the case of a demon-possessed blind and speechless man cured by Jesus Christ. (Mt 12:22) But the Scriptures differentiate between normal maladies and those caused by demon possession.—Mt 4:24; Mr 1:32-34; Ac 5:16; see DEMON POSSESSION.

Failure to obey God's Word, as in matters involving sexual morality, can lead to illness and even death. (Pr 7:21-27) The Israelites were warned that if they disobeyed Jehovah, he would strike them with various diseases.—De 28:58-61.

The Bible mentions a number of diseases and afflictions. For example, the Israelites, if disobedient, would suffer with such disorders as tuberculosis, boils, piles, eczema, and madness. (De 28: 22, 27, 28, 35) The Law furnished information on diagnosing and handling cases of leprosy. (Le chaps 13, 14) A descendant of Aaron who had ringworm was barred from performing priestly functions, and an animal with it was unacceptable for sacrifice. (Le 21:17, 20; 22:22) Jesus Christ, by God's power, cured congenital blindness (Joh 9:1-7), deafness (Lu 7:22), dropsy (Lu 14:1-4), leprosy (Lu 5:12, 13), epilepsy, paralysis, and other diseases and infirmities (Mt 4:23, 24). On Malta, Paul healed the father of Publius, who was "distressed with fever and dysentery."—Ac 28:1-8.

Present-day researchers sometimes endeavor to be more specific than the Bible in describing the symptoms and the maladies it mentions, but often their views vary considerably. However, since the Bible is the inspired Word of God, when its writers named a disease they were accurate. Yet at times they left afflictions unnamed. For instance, the Bible does not name the sicknesses that took the lives of the two boys thereafter restored to life by Jehovah through Elijah and Elisha. (1Ki 17:17-24; 2Ki 4:17-37) It does not reveal the nature of "the sickness with which [Elisha] was to die" (2Ki 13:14, 20) or disclose the illness that resulted in the death of Lazarus.—Joh 11:1-4.

Treatment in Ancient Times. Physicians, practitioners of medicine or various healing arts, were common in ancient Israel and other Biblical lands. In Egypt "the physicians embalmed Israel," deceased Jacob. (Ge 50:1-3) The disciple Luke is called "the beloved physician." (Col 4:14) Mark tells us of a woman who was "subject to a flow of blood twelve years" and who "had been put to many pains by many physicians and had spent all her resources and had not been benefited but, rather, had got worse."—Mr 5:25-29.

Hebrew physicians apparently used some herbs and perhaps certain dietetic remedies. 'Balsam of Gilead,' a scented oil obtained from plants in ancient Gilead, was sometimes applied to wounds, perhaps to serve antiseptic purposes or to produce a soothing effect and lessen pain. (Jer 46:11; 51:8) The use of some leaves for medicinal purposes seems to be indicated. (Eze 47:12; Re 22:1, 2) Apparently poultices were used. (2Ki 20:7; Isa 38:21) Oil was sometimes applied to soften wounds and bruises (Isa 1:6), both oil and wine at times being applied to wounds. (Lu 10:34) Moderate drinking of wine was occasionally recommended for its cheering effect and for its medicinal properties.—Pr 31:6; 1Ti 5:23.

Medicine and surgery were practiced by the ancient Egyptians, about whom the historian Herodotus wrote (II, 84): "The practice of medicine is so divided among them, that each physician is a healer of one disease and no more. All the country is full of physicians, some of the eye, some of the teeth, some of what pertains to the belly, and some of the hidden diseases."

In Egypt surgical techniques included cauterization to control hemorrhage, and elevating a fragment of bone that might be pressing against a person's brain in cases of skull fracture. Splints were used for broken bones, some mummies even having been discovered with splints made of tree bark fastened with bandages. (Compare Eze 30: 20, 21.) That early Babylon had some surgeons is indicated in the Code of Hammurabi, which set certain fees of physicians and made references to "a bronze operating knife."

Dentistry was practiced in Phoenicia. One specimen of dental work found involved the use of fine gold wire to bind together six teeth in the lower jaw. In another, a gold wire prosthesis served to "bridge in" teeth taken from another person.

Influence of Magic and of False Religion. Concerning Egypt's physicians and their remedies, *The International Standard Bible Encyclopaedia* (Vol. IV, p. 2393) states: "From the ancient medical papyri which have been preserved, the largest of which is the Papyrus Ebers, we know that the medical knowledge of these physicians was purely empirical, largely magical and wholly unscientific. In spite of their ample opportunities they knew next to nothing of human anatomy, their descriptions of diseases are hopelessly crude, and three-fourths of the hundreds of prescriptions in the papyri are wholly inert. Even their art of embalming was so imperfect that few of their mummies would have remained in any other climate than that of Egypt."—Edited by J. Orr, 1960.

French physician and scholar Georges Roux (in his book *Ancient Iraq,* 1964, pp. 305-309) states: "The diagnosis and prognosis of Mesopotamian physicians were a mixture of superstition and accurate observation." There were trained professional physicians who believed that most diseases had a supernatural origin but who also considered other causes, such as contagion, food, and drink. The physician sometimes referred patients to a diviner, the *baru*-priest, who sought to uncover the concealed sin responsible for a malady. Or, the physician sent the sufferer to the *ashipu*-priest, who employed incantations and magical rites to exorcise demons. Roux observes: "The physicians of Mesopotamia, like her astronomers, founded their art upon metaphysical doctrines and thereby closed the door to a fruitful quest for rational explanations."

The Babylonians regarded Ea as the principal god of healing. As a protection against evil spirits, they wore objects such as amulets and charms. The Greeks thought Hygeia was the goddess guarding health, and physicians in ancient Greece drew inspiration from Asclepius (Asklepios, Aesculapius). The Romans associated certain deities with the curing of particular afflictions. For example, for heart pains there was Angina, and for

fevers, Febris. Interestingly, a staff with a single snake wound around it was a symbol associated with the Greek god Asclepius. (PICTURE, Vol. 2, p. 530) The somewhat similar caduceus, a winged staff with intertwined serpents, which is a medical emblem, is a copy of the staff shown in Roman art as being carried by the god Mercury.

Concerning ancient pathological concepts in general, *The Interpreter's Dictionary of the Bible* (Vol. 1, p. 847) states: "Among primitive races, disease was either regarded as the result of hostile magic gaining a hold upon a person, or else its incidence was ascribed to the violation of a taboo. In either event a background of magic, sorcery, and witchcraft was presupposed where cases of intractable sickness were encountered, and such remedial measures as were undertaken inevitably involved the shaman, or medicine man. It was his function to divine the supernatural cause of the disease, and attempt to banish it by the use of spells, charms, drugs, and incantations."—Edited by G. Buttrick, 1962.

The Scriptures show that Satan afflicted Job (Job 2:7) and that demon possession has occasionally been linked with disease. (Mt 17:14-18) So the ancient pagans had a basis for associating at least some illness with demon possession. But, unlike them, never did faithful Hebrew priests and physicians resort to magic in an attempt to effect cures. (De 18:9-13) No magical incantations were uttered by Jesus Christ or his true followers, even when expelling demons in effecting cures. Upon embracing Christianity, onetime practicers of magic abandoned such demonistic activities, and certainly a Christian physician would neither employ occultism nor send a patient to a practicer of magic.—Ac 19:18, 19.

Accuracy of Scriptural Concepts. Regarding Hippocrates, a Greek physician of the fifth and fourth centuries B.C.E. who has become known as "the father of modern medicine," it is said: "He had no connection with the temple hospitals of his time, which were controlled by the priests of Asclepius, the god of healing." (*The World Book Encyclopedia,* 1987, Vol. 9, p. 227) Hippocrates was virtually contemporaneous with Malachi, but much that the Bible says about diseases was written by Moses about a thousand years earlier. Yet, significantly, it has been said: "The best informed medical researchers now doing the best work are arriving at the conclusion that the Bible is a very accurate scientific book. . . . The facts of life, diagnosis, treatment, and preventive medicine as given in the Bible are far more advanced and reliable than the theories of Hippocrates, many still unproven, and some found to be grossly inaccurate."—Dr. H. O. Philips, in a letter to *The AMA* [American Medical Association] *News,* published in its issue of July 10, 1967.

Concerning the Christian physician Luke, who wrote a Gospel and the book of Acts, Dr. C. Truman Davis stated: "Where medical description is given, it is meticulously accurate. Luke uses a total of twenty-three Greek technical words found in Hippocrates, Galen and other medical writings of the period."—*Arizona Medicine,* March 1966, "Medicine and the Bible," p. 177.

Health benefits often resulted from observance of the Law. For instance, it required that at a military encampment human excrement be covered over (De 23:9-14), thus providing considerable protection from fly-borne infectious diseases such as dysentery and typhoid fever. Contamination of food and water was guarded against, the Law specifying that anything upon which an "unclean" creature fell in its death was rendered unclean and requiring that certain measures be taken, including the smashing of an earthenware vessel thus contaminated.—Le 11:32-38.

Significantly, it has been stated: "Prophylactic considerations were basic to this legislation, which when followed would go far toward preventing the incidence of food-borne polioencephalitis, the enteric fevers, food poisoning, and the parasitic worms. Insistence on the safeguarding of a clean supply of water was the most effective means of forestalling the rise and dissemination of diseases such as amoebiasis, the fevers of the enteric group, cholera, bilharziasis, and spirochetal jaundice. These prophylactic measures, which constitute a fundamental part of any system of public health, were of particular importance for the welfare of a nation living under primitive conditions in a subtropical region of the earth." —*The Interpreter's Dictionary of the Bible,* edited by G. Buttrick, 1962, Vol. 2, pp. 544, 545.

In his book *The Bible and Modern Medicine,* A. Rendle Short, M.D., pointed out that public sanitary law existed, if at all, only in elementary form among nations that surrounded ancient Israel, and stated: "It is the more surprising therefore that in a book like the Bible, alleged to be unscientific, there should be a sanitary code at all, and equally surprising that a nation just escaped from slavery, frequently overrun by enemies and carried away into captivity from time to time,

should have on its statute books so wise and reasonable a code of rules of health. This has been recognized by good authorities, even those with no great interest in the religious aspect of the Bible."—London, 1953, p. 37.

According to the Law, the hare and the pig were among animals the Israelites were not permitted to eat. (Le 11:4-8) Regarding this, Dr. Short states: "True, we eat the pig, the rabbit and the hare, but these animals are liable to parasitic infections and are safe only if the food is well cooked. The pig is an unclean feeder, and harbours two worms, trichina and a tape worm, which may be passed on to man. The danger is minimal under present conditions in this country, but it would have been far otherwise in Palestine of old, and such food was better avoided."—*The Bible and Modern Medicine,* pp. 40, 41.

Adherence to Jehovah's righteous requirements as to sexual morality also had a good effect on the Israelites spiritually, mentally, and physically. (Ex 20:14; Le 18) Healthful benefits are similarly enjoyed by Christians who maintain moral cleanness. (Mt 5:27, 28; 1Co 6:9-11; Re 21:8) Observing the Bible's high moral standards affords protection from sexually transmitted diseases.

Paul recommended that Timothy take a little wine for the sake of his stomach and his frequent cases of sickness. (1Ti 5:23) That wine has medicinal properties is confirmed by present-day research. Dr. Salvatore P. Lucia, Professor of Medicine, University of California School of Medicine, has stated: "Wine is widely used in the treatment of diseases of the digestive system. . . . The tannin content and the mildly antiseptic properties of wine make it valuable in the treatment of intestinal colic, mucous colitis, spastic constipation, diarrhea and many infectious diseases of the gastrointestinal tract." (*Wine as Food and Medicine,* 1954, p. 58) Of course, Paul suggested that Timothy "use a little wine," not much wine, and the Bible condemns drunkenness.—Pr 23:20; see DRUNKENNESS.

The Scriptures recognize the psychosomatic principle, though only in relatively recent times have medical researchers in general become aware that there is some connection between pathological conditions in the body and a person's emotional state. Proverbs 17:22 states: "A heart that is joyful does good as a curer, but a spirit that is stricken makes the bones dry." Such emotions as envy, fear, greed, hate, and selfish ambition

are injurious, whereas good and sometimes remedial effects are produced through cultivating and
displaying love, joy, peace, long-suffering, kindness, goodness, faith, mildness, and self-control,
the fruitage of God's spirit. (Ga 5:22, 23) The
Scriptures do not, of course, classify all illness as
psychosomatic, nor do they rule out as objection-
able all consulting of and treatment by physicians. Paul called the faithful Christian Luke "the
beloved physician."—Col 4:14.

Quarantine. According to the Law, a person
who had or was suspected of having a communi-
cable disease was quarantined, that is, kept away
from others or isolated for a time. Seven-day
periods of quarantine were imposed in tests for
leprosy in the case of persons, garments, and
other items, or houses. (Le 13:1-59; 14:38, 46)
Also, a person was rendered unclean for seven
days as a result of touching a human corpse. (Nu
19:11-13) Though the Scriptures do not say that
the latter regulation was given for health reasons,
some protection was thus afforded other individuals if the corpse was that of a person who had
died of an infectious disease.

Figurative Application. Judah and Jerusalem became spiritually sick because of their sinfulness. (Isa 1:1, 4-6) Although Jerusalem's religious leaders tried vainly to heal the breakdown
of the people, falsely saying there was peace (Jer
6:13, 14), they were unable to avert the city's
destruction in 607 B.C.E. But Jehovah promised to
effect the recuperation of Zion, or Jerusalem (Jer
30:12-17; 33:6-9), a healing realized with the
return of the Jewish remnant to their homeland
in 537 B.C.E.

Jesus Christ recognized the spiritually sick state
of sinners and sought to turn them to Jehovah for
spiritual healing. Hence, when criticized for eating and drinking with tax collectors and sinners,
Jesus said: "Those who are healthy do not need a
physician, but those who are ailing do. I have
come to call, not righteous persons, but sinners to
repentance."—Lu 5:29-32.

Treatment of spiritual sickness experienced by
a member of the Christian congregation is considered at James 5:13-20. The context, which contrasts being sick with being in good spirits, shows
that James was dealing, not with physical illness,
but with spiritual sickness. Concerning remedial
steps and their effectiveness, James wrote: "Is
there anyone [spiritually] sick among you? Let
him call the older men [the elders] of the congregation to him, and let them pray over him [so he
can hear the prayer and show he agrees by say-

ing "Amen"], greasing him with oil [encouraging
him with comforting, soothing instruction from
God's Word, to restore him to unity with the
congregation (Ps 133:1, 2; 141:5)] in the name of
Jehovah [with faithfulness to God and according
to His purpose]. And the prayer of faith [offered
by the older men on behalf of the spiritually ailing
person] will make the indisposed one [spiritually]
well, and Jehovah will raise him up [as out of
despondency and a feeling of being abandoned by
God, Jehovah strengthening him to go in the way
of truth and righteousness (Php 4:13)]. Also, if he
has committed sins, it will be forgiven him [by
Jehovah (Ps 32:5; 103:10-14), if the individual
responds favorably to the prayers and the reproof, correction, and exhortation from Jehovah's
Word given to him by the older men, and he
repentantly turns around and goes in the right
way (Ps 119:9-16)]."

Coping With Illness. Sickness is a calamity
that may befall a person even if he is materially
rich. (Ec 5:16, 17; compare Mt 16:26.) Some individuals have delicious food in abundance but are
unable to enjoy it because of some stomach or
bowel disorder. (Ec 6:1, 2) Jesus Christ's spiritual
brothers were also spoken of as being physically
sick at times. (Mt 25:39, 40) Physical sickness was
experienced by such Christians as Epaphroditus,
Timothy, and Trophimus (Php 2:25-30; 1Ti 5:23;
2Ti 4:20), but the Bible reports no miraculous
apostolic healing of these Christian men.

Nevertheless, when one of God's servants is
physically ill, it is proper for him to pray to
Jehovah for the fortitude needed to bear his malady and for spiritual strength to maintain integrity during this period of weakness in the flesh.
"Jehovah himself will sustain [such a person]
upon a divan of illness."—Ps 41:1-3; see also 1Ki
8:37-40.

However, if a person were to take blood into his
body for the treatment of disease, this would
violate the law of God.—Ge 9:3, 4; Ac 15:28, 29;
see BLOOD.

Jehovah can remove sicknesses. (Ex 15:26; 23:
25; De 7:15) Isaiah wrote of a time when "no
resident will say: 'I am sick'" (Isa 33:24) and
about spiritual healing of the blind, deaf, lame,
and speechless, these prophecies also giving
promise of physical cure. (Isa 35:5, 6) Jesus
Christ, when on earth, accomplished both physical and spiritual healing of ailing ones by fulfilling
the Messianic prophecy, "He himself took our
sicknesses and carried our diseases." (Mt 8:14-17;
Isa 53:4) The basis for these cures was the

sacrifice of his human life, which would be the climax of the course he had been following ever since God's spirit came upon him at the Jordan River in 29 C.E. Christians thus have a basis for hope and abundant proof that through the resurrected Jesus Christ and by means of God's Kingdom, obedient mankind will receive, not merely temporary treatment of disease, but permanent release from sin, disease, and death traceable to Adam. For this all praise is due Jehovah, identified by David as the one "who is healing all your maladies."—Ps 103:1-3; Re 21:1-5.

DISFELLOWSHIPPING.   See EXPELLING.

DISGUSTING THING, also LOATHSOME THING.

The Hebrew nouns *she'qets* (loathsome thing) and *shiq·quts'* (disgusting thing) come from the root *sha·qats'*, used in the sense of "loathe" (Le 11:11, 13) and, in the causative form, 'make loathsome.' (Le 11:43; 20:25) These Hebrew terms refer to that which is repugnant from the standpoint of Jehovah's true worship. They are commonly rendered by such words as "abominate," "abominable," or "abomination" in many translations. This has resulted in the well-known expression "abomination of desolation." (Da 11:31; 12:11, *KJ*) The Gospel writers Matthew and Mark used the Greek *bde'lyg·ma* to translate the Hebrew *shiq·quts'* (plural, *shiq·qu·tsim'*). (Da 9:27; Mt 24:15; Mr 13:14) This Greek term basically implies that which causes disgust.—See DETESTABLE THING.

The Mosaic Law prohibited the eating of certain creatures, declaring them "unclean" for that purpose (as well as for sacrificing). Therefore, *in these respects* such a creature was to be viewed as a "loathsome thing" and any person eating one (or using it for sacrifice) would make himself "loathsome," since he would thereby be showing contempt for God's commands. (Le 7:21; 11:10-13, 20-23, 41, 42; 20:25; Isa 66:17) That the proscribed animals were not to be loathed in a general way, however, can be seen from other texts. For example, though "unclean" for food or sacrifice, the ass was regularly used by the Israelites for transportation and for bearing burdens (Ex 23:4, 5; Mt 21:2-5); King David had herds of camels, and camel hair was used for clothing (1Ch 27:30, 31; Mt 3:4); and the eagle was used as a fitting metaphor and simile to represent God's protective care of Israel during the Exodus. (Ex 19:4; De 32:9-12) With the removal of the Law covenant, the injunction to view any of such creatures as "loathsome" for food ended.—Ac 10:9-15; 1Ti 4:1-5; see ANIMALS.

Whereas the Hebrew *she'qets* is used exclusively with regard to "unclean" animals, the word *shiq·quts'* is used principally with respect to idols and idolatrous practices. At the time of the Exodus, Jehovah instructed the Israelites to throw away "the disgusting things" and "the dungy idols of Egypt," but individuals failed to obey, thereby profaning God's name. (Eze 20:6-9) On its way to the Promised Land, Israel passed among pagan nations and saw "their disgusting things and their dungy idols, wood and stone, silver and gold." They were commanded to "thoroughly loathe" such religious imagery as "something devoted to destruction," refusing to bring it into their residences. (De 29:16-18; 7:26) The false gods and goddesses of these nations, including Milcom, or Molech, as well as Chemosh and Ashtoreth, were themselves 'disgusting things.' (1Ki 11:5, 7; 2Ki 23:13) When Israel practiced such idolatry, it too became repugnant in God's eyes, and the later defilement of the temple with idolatrous objects brought God's fury upon that nation, finally resulting in its desolation. (Jer 32:34, 35; Eze 7:20-22; Ho 9:10) By thus "ministering to wood and stone," they were engaging in "immoral intercourse," spiritual fornication, cutting themselves off from communication with God.—Eze 20:30-32; compare Jer 13:27.

Only by vigorous and courageous action to rid the land of idolatry did certain kings bring periods of blessing to the nation. (2Ki 23:24; 2Ch 15:8-15) God made clear that only by a thorough cleansing of themselves from such practices could the Israelites assure their restoration from the coming captivity and enjoy reinstatement as his people. (Eze 11:17-21) In a similar prophecy, the references to David as being the king of this cleansed people and their "one shepherd" and "chieftain to time indefinite" clearly point to a greater fulfillment on the nation of spiritual Israel, the Christian congregation, under the anointed Heir to David's throne, Christ Jesus.—Eze 37:21-25; compare Lu 1:32; Joh 10:16.

At Nahum 3:6, the prophecy against Assyria's capital, Nineveh, foretells the end of her political and international prostitutions and that Jehovah would "throw disgusting things [Heb., *shiq·qu·tsim'*]" on her. Such disgusting things evidently refer, not to idolatrous objects, but to things generally unclean or repulsive, as dirt and filth, thereby making the rapacious city despicable in the eyes of all. (Na 3:4-7) The bloodstained and disgusting things to be removed from the teeth of the Philistine (Zec 9:6, 7) likely relate to the pagan practice of eating sacrificial animals along with their blood.—Compare Eze 33:25.

While the Jewish people, and particularly their religious leaders in Jesus' days on earth, were evidently scrupulous in avoiding anything connected with literal idols, they were, nevertheless, guilty of disgusting practices of self-idolatry, disobedience, hypocrisy, greed, and falsehood, and Jesus said that, like their forefathers, they had turned the temple into "a cave of robbers." (Mt 23:1-15, 23-28; Lu 16:14, 15; compare Mt 21:13 and Jer 7:11, 30.) This bad condition and heart attitude led to their monumental act of rebellion in rejecting God's own Son, and Jesus showed that this would bring certain destruction upon them.—Mt 21:33-41; Lu 19:41-44.

'Disgusting Things Leading to Desolation.' Daniel's prophecy foretold "disgusting things" associated with desolation. (Da 9:27) The popular view has generally followed early Jewish tradition in applying this expression to the profanation of Jehovah's temple at Jerusalem in the year 168 B.C.E. by Syrian King Antiochus IV (Epiphanes). Attempting to stamp out the worship of Jehovah, Antiochus built an altar over the great altar of Jehovah and sacrificed upon this a pig to the Olympian Zeus (Jupiter). An expression like that of Daniel (associating disgusting things with desolation) appears in the Apocryphal book of 1 Maccabees (1:54) as applying to this event.

But this was only the Jewish interpretation of matters, not an inspired revelation. Christ Jesus showed this view to be in error when he gave the warning to his disciples: "Therefore, when you catch sight of the disgusting thing that causes desolation, as spoken of through Daniel the prophet, standing in a holy place, (let the reader use discernment,) then let those in Judea begin fleeing to the mountains." (Mt 24:15, 16) These words show that "the disgusting thing that causes desolation" was not then past but future.

The pagan desecration of the temple altar by Antiochus, however disgusting in God's sight, did not result in desolation—for Jerusalem, for the temple, or for the Jewish nation. But 33 years after Jesus' death, Christians did "catch sight of the disgusting thing that causes desolation . . . standing in a holy place." (Mt 24:15) In 66 C.E. pagan Roman armies surrounded "the holy city" Jerusalem, now the center of Jewish revolt against Rome. Thus, the 'causing of desolation' by the disgusting thing was imminent, and so this was the final signal for discerning Christians to

'flee to the mountains.' (Mt 4:5; 27:53; 24:15, 16; Lu 19:43, 44; 21:20-22) Following their flight, the desolation of the city and nation occurred, Jerusalem being destroyed in the year 70 C.E., and the last Jewish stronghold, Masada, falling to the Romans in 73 C.E.—Compare Da 9:25-27.

Additional prophecies of a disgusting thing. It should be noted, however, that Daniel 11:31-35 and 12:9, 11 connect a 'disgusting thing causing desolation' with "the time of the end." It is reasonable that the development of this latter expression of 'the disgusting thing causing desolation' in the time of the end should follow the general pattern of that in the first century C.E., though not being restricted to the land of Israel.

Jerusalem's desolation in 70 C.E. brought the end of the "holy place," Jerusalem, "the holy city." (Mt 27:53) However, the Scriptures direct our attention to a "heavenly Jerusalem," the Messianic Kingdom, which is represented on earth by anointed Christians. (Heb 12:22) There are also others that falsely claim to represent that Kingdom, and Revelation chapter 17 shows that their religious field of operations will be desolated by the "ten horns" (kings) of a symbolic "wild beast."

Disgusting Things of Babylon the Great. In the prophetic vision of Revelation 17, the symbolic immoral woman, Babylon the Great, is depicted. She is called "the mother of the harlots and of the disgusting things of the earth." She holds a golden cup 'full of the disgusting things of her fornication with the kings of the earth.' Though she curries the favor of the earthly kingdoms, sitting on top of a symbolic wild beast composed of such kingdoms, the time comes when this "beast" refuses to carry her, turns on her, and completely desolates her.—See BABYLON THE GREAT.

Any possibility that persons continuing in the practice of a "disgusting thing" might gain entrance into the "New Jerusalem," the Lamb's chaste "bride" class, is ruled out at Revelation 21:9, 10, 27.

DISHAN (Di'shan) [possibly, Antelope]. A Seirite, a sheik of the Horite in the land of Edom. (Ge 36:20, 21; 1Ch 1:38) Genesis 36:28 says the sons of "Dishan" were Uz and Aran, while 1 Chronicles 1:42 in the Hebrew Masoretic text, Greek *Septuagint,* and Syriac *Peshitta* refers to "Dishon" as their progenitor. This difference in vocalization, apparently the result of a copyist's error, is resolved in many English translations (*AS, KJ, JB, Le, NW, Ro, Yg*) by using the same rendering in both texts, as does the Clementine recension of the Latin *Vulgate.*

DISHON (Di'shon) [possibly, Antelope]. The name of one or possibly two different men in the genealogies recorded at Genesis 36:20-28 and 1 Chronicles 1:38-42.

At Genesis 36:20, 21 (also vss 29, 30) seven "sons of Seir the Horite" are listed as sheiks, namely, Lotan, Shobal, Zibeon, Anah, Dishon, Ezer, and Dishan. Then, in verses 22 to 28, each of the seven sheiks is listed with his sons. At verse 25 one of the sons of Anah is named Dishon. Some believe that this Dishon is a grandson of Seir and a nephew of Sheik Dishon, considering that the seven sheiks were all "sons" of Seir in the strict sense of the word, that is, of the same generation.

Others, however, believe the account to present the seven sheiks merely as *descendants* of Seir, not of the same generation, hence "sons" in the broad sense of the word. So they suggest that the Dishon of verse 25 is the same as Sheik Dishon (Ge 36:21, 26) and not his nephew. According to this view, although actually the son of Sheik Anah, Dishon is named with the other six sheiks not because of being their brother but because of being their equal in the sense of being a sheik.

DISTAFF. A stick from which the prepared, loosely wound fibers of flax, wool, or other materials were drawn and then attached to the spindle to make thread.—Pr 31:19; see SPINNING.

DISTRICT. The word "district" denotes an administrative unit, a region around a city, or a region within certain boundaries.

When Nehemiah organized the rebuilding of the wall of Jerusalem, he assigned portions to the leaders, or 'princes,' and inhabitants of certain 'districts.' These districts were named after their principal city, and some (Jerusalem, Beth-zur, Keilah) were double. (Ne 3:9, 12, 14-18) They were evidently subdivisions of the Persian "jurisdictional district," or "province," of Judah. (Ne 1:3; KJ, RS) The Hebrew word to designate these districts (*pe'lekh*) is said to be derived from the Akkadian word *pilku*, perhaps indicating that they were instituted by the Babylonians after the fall of Jerusalem.—See JURISDICTIONAL DISTRICT.

The Hebrew term *kik·kar'* conveys the idea of something round. It is used to denote a "round loaf" of bread (Ex 29:23), a "circular lid" of lead (Zec 5:7), a "talent" of gold or silver (Ex 25:39; 1Ki 20:39), and a roughly circular "district" or "basin." —Ge 13:10, ftn; Ne 12:28.

In the Christian Greek Scriptures, the word *ho'ri·on* (always plural) literally denotes the "boundaries" or "frontiers" of a geographic area, but it may also denote that which is enclosed, namely a "district" or "region." (Ac 13:50; Mt 19:1; 2:16; 15:22) The term *me·ris'*, used to refer to the "district" of Macedonia in Acts 16:12, literally denotes a "part."—Compare *Int;* Ac 8:21.

DISTRICT OF THE JORDAN. The roughly circular basin, or oval-shaped area, into which the Jordan River flows. This includes the lower part of the Jordan Valley, as can be seen by the mention of "the District of the Jordan" in connection with Solomon's copper-casting activities between Succoth and Zarethan. (1Ki 7:46; 2Ch 4:17; compare 2Sa 18:23.) However, "the District" also appears to extend down to the southern end of the Dead Sea where "the cities of the District" evidently were located. (Ge 13:10-12) Thus it not only took in the valley plain of Jericho but reached as far as Zoar, the city to which Lot and his daughters fled.—Ge 19:17-25; De 34:3.

Research conducted at the southern extremity of the Dead Sea indicates that a large portion of land below the tongue of land called the Lisan has become covered by the waters of the Sea. Many scholars believe that "the cities of the District" lie submerged in this region. It was once "well-watered" and like "the garden of Jehovah." (Ge 13:10) This was true not only of the region N of the Dead Sea, where today only the Plains of Moab and the oasis of Jericho retain considerable fertility, but also of the southern part of the District. Even today the plain that lies beside the Lisan is described as a "prolonged oasis" where barley, wheat, dates, and vines can be cultivated. The delta region of the Zered River, which flows into the southern end of the Dead Sea, is also called a "rich oasis."

DIVAN. See BED.

DIVINATION. Divination embraces generally the whole scope of gaining secret knowledge, especially about future events, through the aid of spiritistic occult powers. (See SPIRITISM.) For consideration of specialized aspects of divination, see ASTROLOGERS; CONJURER; FORETELLER OF EVENTS; MAGIC AND SORCERY.

Practitioners of divination believe that superhuman gods reveal the future to those trained to read and interpret certain signs and omens, which, they say, are communicated in various ways: By celestial phenomena (the position and movement of stars and planets, eclipses, meteors), by terrestrial physical forces (wind, storms, fire), by behavior of creatures (howling of dogs, flight of birds, movement of snakes), by patterns of tea leaves in cups, by oil configurations on water, by the direction falling arrows take, by the appearance of body parts of sacrificed animals (liver, lungs, entrails), by the lines in the palm of the hand, by the casting of lots, and by the "spirits" of the dead.

Certain fields of divination have been given specific names. For example, augury, popular with the Romans, is a study of omens, portents, or chance phenomena; palmistry predicts the future from lines on the inside of the hand; hepatoscopy inspects the liver; haruspication inspects entrails; belomancy with arrows; rhabdomancy uses the divining rod; oneiromancy is divination by dreams; necromancy is a purported inquiring of the dead. Crystal gazing and oracular divination are still other forms.

Origin. The birthplace of divination was Babylonia, the land of the Chaldeans, and from there these occult practices spread around the earth with the migration of mankind. (Ge 11:8, 9) Of the portion of Ashurbanipal's library that has been unearthed, one fourth, it is said, contains omen tablets that purport to interpret all the peculiarities observed in the heavens and on earth, as well as all the incidental and accidental occurrences of everyday life. King Nebuchadnezzar's decision to attack Jerusalem was made only after resorting to divination, concerning which it is written: "He has shaken the arrows. He has asked by means of the teraphim; he has looked into the liver. In his right hand the divination proved to be for Jerusalem."—Eze 21:21, 22.

Looking into the liver in quest of omens was based on the belief that all vitality, emotion, and affection were centered in this organ. One sixth of man's blood is in the liver. The variations in its lobes, ducts, appendages, veins, ridges, and markings were interpreted as signs, or omens, from the gods. (See ASTROLOGERS.) A large number of clay models of livers have been found, the oldest being from Babylon, containing omens and texts in cuneiform used by diviners. (PICTURE, Vol. 2, p. 324) Ancient Assyrian priests were called *baru,* meaning "inspector" or "he who sees," because of the prominent part liver inspecting played in their fortune-telling religion.

Condemned by Bible. All the various forms of divination, regardless of the name by which they are called, stand in sharp contrast with, and

open defiance of, the Holy Bible. Jehovah through Moses sternly and repeatedly warned Israel not to take up these divination practices of the other nations, saying: "There should not be found in you anyone who makes his son or his daughter pass through the fire, anyone who employs divination, a practicer of magic or anyone who looks for omens or a sorcerer, or one who binds others with a spell or anyone who consults a spirit medium or a professional foreteller of events or anyone who inquires of the dead. For everybody doing these things is something detestable to Jehovah, and on account of these detestable things Jehovah your God is driving them away from before you." (De 18:9-12; Le 19:26, 31) Even if their prophetic signs and portents came true, practicers of divination were not exempted from condemnation. (De 13:1-5; Jer 23:32; Zec 10:2) The Bible's extreme hostility toward diviners is shown in its decree that all such were to be put to death without fail.—Ex 22:18; Le 20:27.

But despite these repeated commandments, apostates flouted Jehovah—not just commoners like the woman of En-dor, but mighty kings like Saul and Manasseh, and Queen Jezebel. (1Sa 28:7, 8; 2Ki 9:22; 21:1-6; 2Ch 33:1-6) Though good King Josiah cleaned out the divination practitioners in his day, it was not enough to save Judah from being destroyed, as her sister kingdom Israel had been. (2Ki 17:12-18; 23:24-27) Jehovah, however, in his loving-kindness, first sent his prophets to warn them regarding their disgusting practices, the same as his prophets warned the mother of all divination, Babylon.—Isa 3:1-3; 8:19, 20; 44:24, 25; 47:9-15; Jer 14:14; 27:9; 29:8; Eze 13:6-9, 23; Mic 3:6-12; Zec 10:2.

Divination was also very prevalent in the days of Jesus' apostles. On the island of Cyprus, a sorcerer by the name of Bar-Jesus was struck with blindness because of his interference with the apostle Paul's preaching; and in Macedonia, Paul cast a demon of divination out of a bothersome girl, much to the consternation of her masters, who made much gain by her occult power of prediction. (Ac 13:6-11; 16:16-19) However, others, like Simon of Samaria, voluntarily gave up their practice of magical arts, and at Ephesus there were so many who burned their books of divination that the value of them totaled 50,000 pieces of silver (if denarii, $37,200).—Ac 8:9-13; 19:19.

Man's natural desire to know the future is satisfied when he worships and serves his Grand

Creator, for through God's channel of communication He lovingly reveals ahead of time what it is good for man to know. (Am 3:7) However, when men turn away from Jehovah and become alienated from the only One who knows the end from the beginning, they easily fall victim to spiritistic demon influence. Saul is such a striking example, one who at first looked to Jehovah for knowledge of future events but who, after being cut off from all contact with God because of his unfaithfulness, turned to the demons as a substitute for divine guidance.—1Sa 28:6, 7; 1Ch 10:13, 14.

A sharp distinction, therefore, exists between revealed truth from God and information obtained by divination. Those who turn to the latter are often seized in violent convulsions by invisible demonic powers, sometimes working themselves into a frenzy by weird music and certain drugs. No such physical or mental distortions are experienced by true servants of Jehovah when moved by holy spirit to speak. (Ac 6:15; 2Pe 1:21) God's prophets in a sense of duty spoke freely without payment; the pagan diviners plied their trade for selfish personal gain.

Nowhere in the Bible is any form of divination given a good connotation. Many times in the same condemnatory texts spiritistic practices of divination are spoken of together with adultery and fornication. (2Ki 9:22; Na 3:4; Mal 3:5; Ga 5:19, 20; Re 9:21; 21:8; 22:15) In God's eyes divination is comparable to the sin of rebellion. (1Sa 15:23) It is, therefore, unscriptural to speak of Jehovah's communication with his servants as a manifestation of "good" divination.

Jehovah frustrates diviners. Jehovah's unlimited power compared with the very restricted power displayed by magic-working diviners is dramatized in the case of Moses and Aaron before Pharaoh. When Aaron's rod became a snake, the Egyptian magicians seemed to duplicate the feat. But what a rebuff the latter suffered when Aaron's rod swallowed up those of the sorcerers! Seemingly Egypt's priests turned water to blood and caused frogs to come up over the land. But when Jehovah caused the dust to become gnats, the sorcerers with their secret arts had to admit it was by "the finger of God."—Ex 7:8-12, 19-22; 8:5-11, 16-19; 9:11.

Wicked Haman had "someone [evidently an astrologer] cast Pur, that is, the Lot, . . . from day to day and from month to month," in order to determine the most favorable time to have Jehovah's people exterminated. (Es 3:7-9) Regarding this text, one commentary says: "In resorting to this method of ascertaining the most auspicious day for putting his atrocious scheme into execution, Haman acted as the kings and nobles of Persia have always done, never engaging in any enterprise without consulting the astrologers, and being satisfied as to the lucky hour." (*Commentary on the Whole Bible*, by Jamieson, Fausset, and Brown) Based on this divination, Haman immediately set in motion his wicked scheme. However, Jehovah's power to deliver his people was again demonstrated, and Haman, who trusted in divination, was hanged on the very stake he had prepared for Mordecai.—Es 9:24, 25.

Another example of Jehovah's superior power over the occult forces is the instance when the Moabites came "with the payments for divination in their hands" to hire Balaam the Mesopotamian diviner to curse Israel. (Nu 22:7) Although Balaam sought "to come upon any unlucky omens," Jehovah caused him to utter only blessings. In one of his proverbial utterances Balaam, under the compelling power of Jehovah, admitted: "There is no unlucky spell against Jacob, nor any divination against Israel."—Nu chaps 23, 24.

"Spirit of Python." In Philippi, Macedonia, Paul met a servant girl who was possessed by "a demon of divination," literally, "a spirit of python" (Gr., *pneu′ma py′tho·na;* Ac 16:16). "Python" was the name of the mythical snake that guarded the temple and oracle of Delphi, Greece. The word *py′thon* came to refer to a person who could foretell the future and also to the spirit that spoke through that one. Although later used to denote a ventriloquist, here in Acts it is used to describe a demon who enabled a young girl to practice the art of prediction.

DIVINE. That which belongs to God or pertains to him, that which is godlike or heavenly.

In some places in the Hebrew Scriptures, the words *'El* (the singular form of the word "God") and *'Elo·him′* (the plural form of excellence of the word "God") are used one after the other. Thus at Joshua 22:22 and Psalm 50:1 the Hebrew text reads *'El 'Elo·him′ Yehwah′.* While some translations (*Ro;* Ps 49:1, *BC* [Spanish]) simply transliterate the first two words of this phrase, others render them as "the God of gods" (*AT, JB, La, VM* [Spanish]) or, somewhat more accurately, "The Mighty One, God" (*AS, Mo, RS*), and "Divine One, God" (*NW*).—See GOD.

In the Christian Greek Scriptures, certain words derived from *the·os′* (god) appear and relate to that which is divine. The related words *thei′os, thei·o'tes,* and *the·o'tes* occur at Acts 17:29, Romans 1:20, Colossians 2:9, and 2 Peter 1:3, 4.

At Acts 17:29, Paul, when in Athens, showed that it is illogical for humans to imagine that "the Divine Being [*to thei'on,* form of *thei'os*] is like gold or silver or stone." Many translators here use terms such as "the Godhead," "the Deity," or "the divinity" (*KJ, AS, Dy, ED, JB, RS*), while E. J. Goodspeed's translation says "the divine nature." According to *The International Standard Bible Encyclopedia,* the expression *to thei'on* "is derived from the adjective *theios,* meaning 'pertaining to God,' 'divine.'" (Edited by G. Bromiley, 1979, Vol. 1, p. 913) Liddell and Scott's *Greek-English Lexicon* gives as the meaning "the Divinity." (Revised by H. Jones, Oxford, 1968, pp. 787, 788) So the phrase *to thei'on* can be understood to refer to a person or to a quality. Obviously, then, the context must guide the translator in his choice of words. Here at Acts 17:29, the context clearly shows that the person of God is being described, and so the expression is appropriately rendered "Divine Being" in the *New World Translation.* —Compare *NIV.*

At Romans 1:20 the apostle refers to the undeniable visible evidence of God's "invisible qualities," particularly his "eternal power and *Godship* [*Thei·o'tes*]." Other translations read "Godhead" or "deity" (*KJ, NE, RS, JB*), conveying to many the idea of personality, the state of being a person. However, according to Liddell and Scott's *Greek-English Lexicon,* the Greek word *thei·o'tes* means "divine nature, divinity." (P. 788) So there is a basis for rendering *thei·o'tes* as referring to the quality of being a god, not the person of God, and this is supported by the context. The apostle is discussing things that are discernible in the physical creation. For example, while the creation does not reveal the name of God, it does give evidence of his "eternal power"—needed to create and sustain the universe. The physical creation also displays his "Godship," the fact that the Creator truly is God and is worthy of our worship.

Then, at Colossians 2:9 the apostle Paul says that in Christ "all the fullness of the *divine quality* [form of *the·o'tes*] dwells bodily." Here, again, some translations read "Godhead" or "deity," which Trinitarians interpret to mean that God personally dwells in Christ. (*KJ, NE, RS, NAB*) However, Liddell and Scott's *Greek-English Lexicon* defines *the·o'tes* in basically the same way it does *thei·o'tes,* as meaning "divinity, divine nature." (P. 792) The Syriac *Peshitta* and the Latin *Vulgate* render this word as "divinity." Thus, here

too, there is a solid basis for rendering *thei·o'tes* as referring to quality, not personality.

A consideration of the context of Colossians 2:9 clearly shows that having "divinity," or "divine nature," does not make Christ the same as God the Almighty. In the preceding chapter, Paul says: "God saw good for all fullness to dwell in him." (Col 1:19) Thus, all fullness dwells in Christ because it "pleased the Father" (*KJ, Dy*), because it was "by God's own choice." (*NE*) So the fullness of "divinity" that dwells in Christ is his as a result of a decision made by the Father. Further showing that having such "fullness" does not make Christ the same person as Almighty God is the fact that Paul later speaks of Christ as being "seated at the right hand of God."—Col 3:1.

Considering the immediate context of Colossians 2:9, it is noted that in verse 8, Christians are warned against being misled by those who advocate philosophy and human tradition. They are also told that "carefully concealed in [Christ] are all the treasures of wisdom and of knowledge," and they are urged to "go on walking in union with him, rooted and being built up in him and being stabilized in the faith." (Col 2:3, 6, 7) In addition, verses 13 to 15 explain that they are made alive through faith, being released from the Law covenant. Paul's argument, therefore, is that Christians do not need the Law (which was removed by means of Christ) or human philosophy and tradition. They have all they need, a precious "fullness," in Christ.—Col 2:10-12.

Finally, at 2 Peter 1:3, 4 the apostle shows that by virtue of "the precious and very grand promises" extended to faithful anointed Christians, they "may become sharers in divine nature, having escaped from the corruption that is in the world through lust." Elsewhere in the Scriptures, Christians are referred to as 'sharing' with Christ in his sufferings, in a death like his, and in a resurrection like his to immortality as spirit creatures, becoming joint heirs with him in the heavenly Kingdom. (1Co 15:50-54; Php 3:10, 11; 1Pe 5:1; 2Pe 1:2-4; Re 20:6) Thus it is evident that the sharing of Christians in "divine nature" is a sharing with Christ in his glory.

The verb form "to divine" generally means to employ divination, a practice directly condemned by Jehovah God.—De 18:10-12; see DIVINATION.

DIVORCE. Legal dissolution of the marital union. Hence the severance of the marriage bond between a husband and a wife. Various original-language terms for "divorce" literally mean "send away" (De 22:19, ftn), "release" or "loose off" (Mt

1:19, *Int;* 19:3, ftn), "drive out; cast out" (Le 22:13, ftn), and "cut off."—Compare De 24:1, 3, where the expression "a certificate of divorce" literally means "a book of cutting off."

When Jehovah united Adam and Eve in wedlock, he made no provision for divorce. Jesus Christ made this clear when answering the Pharisees' question: "Is it lawful for a man to divorce his wife on every sort of ground?" Christ showed that God purposed for man to leave his father and his mother and stick to his wife, the two becoming one flesh. Then Jesus added: "So that they are no longer two, but one flesh. Therefore, what God has yoked together let no man put apart." (Mt 19:3-6; compare Ge 2:22-24.) The Pharisees next asked: "Why, then, did Moses prescribe giving a certificate of dismissal and divorcing her?" In reply, Christ said: "Moses, out of regard for your hardheartedness, made the concession to you of divorcing your wives, but such has not been the case from the beginning."—Mt 19:7, 8.

Though divorce was allowed among the Israelites on various grounds as a concession, Jehovah God regulated it in his Law given to Israel through Moses. Deuteronomy 24:1 reads: "In case a man takes a woman and does make her his possession as a wife, it must also occur that if she should find no favor in his eyes because he has found something indecent on her part, he must also write out a certificate of divorce for her and put it in her hand and dismiss her from his house." Just what "something indecent" (literally, "the nakedness of a thing") was is not specifically stated. That it was not adultery is indicated by the fact that God's law given to Israel decreed that those guilty of adultery be put to death, not merely be divorced. (De 22:22-24) Doubtless, originally the 'indecency' that would have given a Hebrew husband some basis for divorcing his wife involved serious matters, perhaps the wife's showing gross disrespect for the husband or bringing shame on the household. Since the Law specified that "you must love your fellow as yourself," it is not reasonable to assume that petty faults could be used with impunity as excuses for divorcing a wife.—Le 19:18.

In the days of Malachi many Jewish husbands were dealing treacherously with their wives, divorcing them on all kinds of grounds, ridding themselves of the wives of their youth, possibly in order to marry younger, pagan women. Instead of upholding God's law, the priests allowed this, and Jehovah was greatly displeased. (Mal 2:10-16) That Jewish men were using many

grounds for divorce when Jesus Christ was on earth is indicated by the question the Pharisees put to Jesus: "Is it lawful for a man to divorce his wife on *every sort* of ground?"—Mt 19:3.

Among the Israelites a man customarily paid a dowry for the woman who became his wife, and she was considered his possession. While enjoying many blessings and privileges, hers was the subordinate role in the marital union. Her position is further shown by Deuteronomy 24:1-4, which pointed out that the husband might divorce his wife but said nothing about the wife's divorcing her husband. Being considered his property, she could not divorce him. In secular history, the first recorded instance of a woman in Israel trying to divorce her husband was when King Herod's sister Salome sent her husband, the governor of Idumea, a bill of divorce dissolving their marriage. (*Jewish Antiquities,* XV, 259 [vii, 10]) That such divorce action by women had begun to crop up when Jesus was on earth or that he foresaw its development may be indicated by Christ's words: "If ever a woman, after divorcing her husband, marries another, she commits adultery."—Mr 10:12.

Certificate of Divorce. It should not be concluded from the later abuses that the original Mosaic divorce concession made it easy for an Israelite husband to divorce his wife. In order to do so, he had to take formal steps. It was necessary to write a document, to "write out a certificate of divorce for her." The divorcing husband had to "put it in her hand and dismiss her from his house." (De 24:1) While the Scriptures do not provide additional details on this procedure, this legal step apparently involved consultation with duly authorized men, who might first endeavor to effect a reconciliation. The time involved in preparing the certificate and legally implementing the divorce would afford the divorcing husband opportunity to reconsider his decision. There would have to be a basis for the divorce, and when the regulation was properly applied, this would logically serve as a deterrent to rash action in obtaining divorces. Then, too, the wife's rights and interests were thus protected. The Scriptures do not disclose the contents of the "certificate of divorce."

Remarriage of Divorced Mates. Deuteronomy 24:1-4 also stipulated that the divorced woman "must go out of his house and go and become another man's," meaning that she was eligible for remarriage. It was also stated: "If the latter man has come to hate her and has written out a certificate of divorce for her and put it in her hand and dismissed her from his house, or in case the latter man who took her as his wife should die, the first owner of her who dismissed her will not be allowed to take her back again to become his wife after she has been defiled; for that is something detestable before Jehovah, and you must not lead the land that Jehovah your God is giving you as an inheritance into sin." The former husband was barred from taking the divorced wife back, perhaps in order to prevent the possibility of any scheming between him and this remarried wife to force her divorce from her second husband or to cause his death, thereby allowing for remarriage with her previous husband. If her former marriage mate took her back, it would be an unclean thing in God's eyes; the first husband would make himself look foolish because he had dismissed her as a woman in whom he had found "something indecent" and then, after she had been lawfully joined to another man and used as his wife, he took her back once again.

Doubtless the very fact that the original husband could not remarry his divorced wife after she became another man's, even if that man divorced her or died, made the husband contemplating divorce action think seriously before acting to end the marriage. (Jer 3:1) However, nothing was said that would prohibit him from remarrying his divorced wife *if she had not remarried* after the legal severance of their marriage tie.

Sending Away Pagan Wives. Before the Israelites entered the Promised Land, they were told to form no marriage alliances with its pagan inhabitants. (De 7:3, 4) Nonetheless, in the days of Ezra, the Jews had taken foreign wives, and in prayer to God, Ezra acknowledged their guiltiness in this matter. In response to his urging and in acknowledgment of their error, the men of Israel who had taken foreign wives sent them away "along with sons."—Ezr 9:10–10:44.

However, Christians, coming from all different nations (Mt 28:19), were not to divorce mates who were not worshipers of Jehovah, nor was it even desirable for them to separate from such marriage partners, as Paul's inspired counsel shows. (1Co 7:10-28) Yet, when it came to contracting a new marriage, Christians were counseled to marry "only in the Lord."—1Co 7:39.

Joseph's Contemplated Divorce. While Mary was promised in marriage to Joseph, but before they were united, she was found to be pregnant by holy spirit, and the account states: "However,

Joseph her husband, because he was righteous and did not want to make her a public spectacle, intended to divorce her secretly." (Mt 1:18, 19) Since engagement was such a binding arrangement among the Jews at that time, the word "divorce" is properly used here.

If an engaged girl submitted to having relations with another man, she was stoned to death the same as an adulteress. (De 22:22-29) In cases that might result in stoning an individual to death, two witnesses were required in order to establish the person's guilt. (De 17:6, 7) Obviously, Joseph had no witnesses against Mary. Mary was pregnant, but Joseph did not understand the matter thoroughly until Jehovah's angel gave him the explanation. (Mt 1:20, 21) Whether the 'secret divorce' he contemplated would have included the giving of a certificate of divorce or not is not stated; but it is likely that Joseph was going to act in accord with the principles set out at Deuteronomy 24:1-4, possibly giving her the divorce in front of just two witnesses so the matter would be settled legally without bringing undue shame on her. While Matthew does not give every detail regarding the procedure Joseph intended to follow, he does indicate that Joseph wanted to deal mercifully with Mary. Joseph is not considered an unrighteous man for this, but rather, it was "because he was *righteous* and did not want to make her a public spectacle" that he "intended to divorce her secretly."—Mt 1:19.

Circumstances Barring Divorce in Israel. According to God's law given to Israel, there were conditions in which divorce was impossible. It might occur that a man took a wife, had relations with her, and then came to hate her. He might falsely state that she was not a virgin when he married her, thus improperly charging her with notorious deeds and bringing a bad name upon her. When the girl's parents produced evidence that their daughter had been a virgin at the time of her marriage, the men of the city would have to discipline the false accuser. They would fine him a hundred silver shekels ($220), giving these to the girl's father, and she would continue to be the man's wife, it being stated: "He will not be allowed to divorce her all his days." (De 22:13-19) Also, if it was discovered that a man seized a virgin who was not engaged and had relations with her, it was stipulated: "The man who lay down with her must also give the girl's father fifty silver shekels [$110], and she will become his wife due to the fact that he humiliated her. He will not be allowed to divorce her all his days." —De 22:28, 29.

What is the only Scriptural basis for divorce among Christians?

Jesus Christ, in his Sermon on the Mount, stated: "Moreover it was said, 'Whoever divorces his wife, let him give her a certificate of divorce.' However, I say to you that everyone divorcing his wife, except on account of fornication, makes her a subject for adultery, and whoever marries a divorced woman commits adultery." (Mt 5:31, 32) Also, after telling the Pharisees that the Mosaic concession of divorcing their wives was not the arrangement that had prevailed "from the beginning," Jesus said: "I say to you that whoever divorces his wife, except on the ground of fornication, and marries another commits adultery." (Mt 19:8, 9) Today, generally, distinction is made between "fornicators" and "adulterers." According to modern usage, those guilty of fornication are unmarried persons who willingly have sexual relations with someone of the opposite sex. Adulterers are married persons who willingly have sexual relations with a member of the opposite sex who is not their legal marriage mate. As shown in the article FORNICATION, however, the term "fornication" is a rendering of the Greek word *por·nei'a* and includes all forms of illicit sexual relations outside of Scriptural marriage. Hence, Jesus' words at Matthew 5:32 and 19:9 mean that the only divorce ground that actually severs the marriage bond is *por·nei'a* on the part of one's marriage mate. The follower of Christ may avail himself of that divorce provision if that is his desire, and such a divorce would free him to marry an eligible Christian.—1Co 7:39.

Sexually immoral acts committed by a married person with someone of the same sex (homosexuality) are filthy and disgusting. Unrepentant persons of this type will not inherit God's Kingdom. And, of course, bestiality is Scripturally condemned. (Le 18:22, 23; Ro 1:24-27; 1Co 6:9, 10) These grossly filthy acts come under the broad designation *por·nei'a*. It is also noteworthy that, under the Mosaic Law, homosexuality and bestiality carried the death penalty, freeing the innocent mate for remarriage.—Le 20:13, 15, 16.

Jesus Christ pointed out that "everyone that keeps on looking at a woman so as to have a passion for her has already committed adultery with her in his heart." (Mt 5:28) But Jesus did not say that what was in the heart, but not carried into action, furnished a basis for divorce. Christ's words show that the heart should be kept clean and one should not entertain improper thoughts and desires.—Php 4:8; Jas 1:14, 15.

The Jews' rabbinic law laid emphasis on the married person's duty to perform the marital act and allowed a husband to divorce his wife if she was unable to produce children. However, the Scriptures do not give Christians the right to divorce their mates for such a reason. Barrenness for many years did not cause Abraham to divorce Sarah, Isaac to divorce Rebekah, Jacob to divorce Rachel, or the priest Zechariah to divorce Elizabeth.—Ge 11:30; 17:17; 25:19-26; 29:31; 30:1, 2, 22-25; Lu 1:5-7, 18, 24, 57.

Nothing is said in the Scriptures that would permit a Christian to divorce a marriage partner because that one was physically unable to perform the marital act, or had gone insane or contracted an incurable or loathsome disease. The love that Christians are to show would call, not for divorce, but for merciful treatment of such a mate. (Eph 5:28-31) Nor does the Bible grant Christians the right to divorce their marriage mates because of difference in religion; it shows instead that by remaining with an unbelieving mate the Christian may win that individual over to the true faith.—1Co 7:12-16; 1Pe 3:1-7.

In his Sermon on the Mount, Jesus said that "everyone divorcing his wife, except on account of fornication, makes her a subject for adultery, and whoever marries a divorced woman commits adultery." (Mt 5:32) By this, Christ showed that if a husband divorces his wife for reasons other than her "fornication" (*por·nei'a*), he exposes her to adultery in the future. That is so because the unadulterous wife is not properly disunited from her husband by such a divorce and is not free to marry another man and have sexual relations with another husband. When Christ said that whoever "marries a divorced woman commits adultery," he was referring to a woman divorced on grounds other than "on account of fornication" (*por·nei'a*). Such a woman, though divorced legally, would not be divorced Scripturally.

Mark, like Matthew (Mt 19:3-9), recorded Jesus' statements to the Pharisees regarding divorce and quoted Christ as saying: "Whoever divorces his wife and marries another commits adultery against her, and if ever a woman, after divorcing her husband, marries another, she commits adultery." (Mr 10:11, 12) A similar statement is made at Luke 16:18, which reads: "Everyone that divorces his wife and marries another commits adultery, and he that marries a woman divorced from a husband commits adultery." Taken alone, these verses seem to forbid all divorce by Christ's followers, or at least to indicate that a divorced individual would not be entitled to remarry except after the death of the divorced marriage partner. However, Jesus' words as recorded by Mark and Luke must be understood in the light of the more complete statement recorded by Matthew. He includes the phrase "except on the ground of fornication" (Mt 19:9; see also Mt 5:32), showing that what Mark and Luke wrote in quoting Jesus on divorce applies if the ground for procuring the divorce is anything other than "fornication" (*por·nei'a*) committed by the unfaithful marriage partner.

A person is not Scripturally obligated to divorce an adulterous though repentant marriage partner, however. The Christian husband or wife may extend mercy in such a case, even as Hosea seems to have taken back his adulterous wife Gomer and as Jehovah extended mercy to repentant Israel that had been guilty of spiritual adultery.—Ho 3.

God's original standard restored. It is clear that Jesus Christ's statement pointed to a return to the high standard for marriage originally set by Jehovah God, and it showed that those who would become Jesus' disciples would have to adhere to that high standard. Though the concessions provided by the Mosaic Law were still in effect, those who would be true disciples of Jesus, doing the will of his Father and 'doing' or putting into effect the sayings of Jesus (Mt 7:21-29), would no longer avail themselves of such concessions to exercise "hardheartedness" toward their marriage mates. (Mt 19:8) As genuine disciples, they would not violate the original divine principles governing marriage by divorcing their mates on any grounds other than the one Jesus specified, namely "fornication" (*por·nei'a*).

A single person who commits fornication with a prostitute makes himself "one body" with that person. Similarly, the adulterer makes himself "one body," not with his legal wife, but with the immoral person with whom he has sexual relations. The adulterer thus sins not only against his own personal flesh but also against his legal wife who until then has been "one flesh" with him. (1Co 6:16-18) For that reason adultery provides a true basis for breaking the marital bond in accord with divine principles, and where such ground exists, a divorce obtained brings about the formal and final dissolution of the legal marriage union, freeing the innocent partner to remarry with honor.—Heb 13:4.

Figurative Divorce. The marriage relationship is used symbolically in the Scriptures. (Isa 54:1, 5, 6; 62:1-6) Reference is also made to symbolic divorcing, or the sending away of a wife.—Jer 3:8.

The kingdom of Judah was overthrown and Jerusalem was destroyed in 607 B.C.E., the inhabitants of the land being taken into Babylonian exile. Years earlier Jehovah had said prophetically to Jews who would then be in exile: "Where, then, is the divorce certificate of the mother of you people, whom I sent away?" (Isa 50:1) Their "mother," or national organization, had been put away with just cause, not because Jehovah broke his covenant and started divorce proceedings, but because of her wrongdoing against the Law covenant. But a remnant of Israelites repented and prayed for a renewal of Jehovah's husbandly relationship with them in their homeland. Jehovah, for his own name's sake, restored his people to their homeland as promised, in 537 B.C.E., at the end of the 70-year desolation.—Ps 137:1-9; see MARRIAGE.

DIZAHAB (Di'za·hab) [possibly, Place of Gold]. A site, E of the Jordan River, where Israel was camped at the time Moses delivered his farewell address. Its exact location is unknown today.—De 1:1.

DODAI. See DODO No. 2.

DODANIM (Do'da·nim). At Genesis 10:4 this name appears as the fourth-listed son of Javan. The Greek *Septuagint* and the Samaritan *Pentateuch* here read "Rodanim." "Rodanim" is also found in the Hebrew Masoretic text at 1 Chronicles 1:7, although many Hebrew manuscripts, as well as the Syriac *Peshitta* and the Latin *Vulgate,* there read "Dodanim."—See RODANIM.

DODAVAHU (Dod·av'a·hu) [possibly, Beloved of Jehovah]. A man from Maresha whose son Eliezer prophesied disaster for the ships of Jehoshaphat that were built in partnership with wicked King Ahaziah of Israel.—2Ch 20:36, 37.

DODO (Do'do) [from a root meaning "beloved"].

1. An ancestor, probably the grandfather, of Judge Tola of the tribe of Issachar.—Jg 10:1.

2. A descendant of Benjamin through Ahohi. Dodo's son Eleazar was one of David's three mighty men. (2Sa 23:9; 1Ch 11:12) Dodai (an alternate form of Dodo) served, perhaps in a representative sense through his son Eleazar, as

chief of the army division of the second month. —1Ch 27:4.

3. A resident of Bethlehem whose son Elhanan was one of David's mighty men.—2Sa 23:24; 1Ch 11:26.

DOEG (Do'eg) [possibly, Anxious; In Fright]. An Edomite serving as King Saul's principal shepherd, a responsible position of oversight. (1Sa 21:7; 22:9) Doeg evidently was a proselyte. Because of being "detained before Jehovah" at Nob, possibly on account of a vow, some uncleanness, or suspected leprosy, Doeg witnessed High Priest Ahimelech's providing David with showbread and the sword of Goliath. Later, when Saul, in addressing his servants, voiced the opinion that they were conspiring against him, Doeg revealed what he had seen at Nob. After summoning the high priest as well as the other priests of Nob and then questioning Ahimelech, Saul ordered the runners to put the priests to death. When these refused, Doeg, at Saul's command, unhesitatingly killed a total of 85 priests. After this wicked act, Doeg devoted Nob to destruction, slaughtering all of its inhabitants, young and old, as well as the livestock.—1Sa 22:6-20.

As indicated by the superscription of Psalm 52, David wrote concerning Doeg: "Adversities your tongue schemes up, sharpened like a razor, working deceitfully. You have loved what is bad more than what is good, falsehood more than speaking righteousness. You have loved all devouring words, O you deceitful tongue."—Ps 52:2-4.

DOG [Heb., ke'lev; Gr., ky'on; ky·na'ri·on, 'little dog' (Mt 15:26)]. To the Israelites this animal was ceremonially unclean, and it is therefore unlikely that they gave any thought to the training of dogs. (Le 11:27; Isa 66:3) Although sheep and shepherds are often mentioned in the Bible, only Job, a non-Israelite, speaks of "the dogs of my flock."—Job 30:1.

Dogs (*Canis familiaris*), like carrion birds, were scavengers, particularly in the cities. The Law directed throwing to the dogs flesh that had been torn by a wild beast. (Ex 22:31) At times Jehovah's judgment against his enemies was that their dead bodies would be eaten or their blood licked up by scavenger dogs. Because of the course of gross unfaithfulness followed by Kings Jeroboam, Baasha, and Ahab, any who belonged to their respective households and who died in the city were to be devoured by dogs. (1Ki 14:11; 16:4; 21:24) In fulfillment of Jehovah's word, the dogs licked up Ahab's blood, and the flesh of his wife Jezebel became food for the dogs. (1Ki 21:19; 22:38; 21:23; 2Ki 9:10, 35, 36) Indicating that dogs would lick up the blood of the foes of Jehovah's people, the psalmist wrote: "That the tongue of your dogs may have its portion from the enemies." (Ps 68:23) It was foretold that dogs would share in the ruin that would come upon unfaithful Jerusalem and Judah. Dead bodies the dogs would drag away, mutilating, devouring, and licking up blood.—Jer 15:3.

Illustrative Use. The dog's repulsive habit of disgorging food it has gulped down and then returning to eat it again later is used to illustrate the course of those abandoning the way of righteousness and returning to their former state of defilement. (2Pe 2:20-22; Pr 26:11) Morally unclean persons are called dogs. God's law to Israel stated: "You must not bring the hire of a harlot or the price of a dog ["male prostitute," *AT;* "likely a pederast; one who practices anal intercourse, especially with a boy," *NW,* ftn] into the house of Jehovah your God for any vow, because they are something detestable to Jehovah your God, even both of them." (De 23:18) All those who, like scavenger dogs of the streets, practice disgusting things, such as sodomy, lesbianism, viciousness, and cruelty, are debarred from access to New Jerusalem.—Re 22:15; see also Php 3:2.

Further indication of the contempt in which these wild, scavenging dogs were held are the following examples: "Am I a dog?" bellowed Goliath to David, because the latter came to him with a staff. (1Sa 17:43) "After whom are you chasing? After a dead dog?" asked David of King Saul, thus showing that he was insignificant and could do no more harm to Saul than a dead dog. (1Sa 24:14) Similarly, Mephibosheth, the son of Jonathan, in speaking to King David, referred to himself as "the dead dog," the lowest condition possible. (2Sa 9:8; see also 2Sa 3:8; 16:9; 2Ki 8:13.) The prophet Isaiah compared God's professed spiritual watchmen to speechless, slumbering dogs full of soulful desire, completely ineffectual in the case of danger. (Isa 56:10, 11) The enemies of Jehovah's servants were likened to dogs, and so were the Gentiles. (Ps 22:16, 20; 59:6, 14; Mt 15:26, 27; see SYROPHOENICIAN.) Jesus Christ compared persons having no appreciation for spiritual things to dogs, saying: "Do not give what is holy to dogs." —Mt 7:6.

In the light of the unfavorable figurative sense attached to the dog, the very low state of the Lazarus of Jesus' illustration is clearly reflected in the words, "Dogs would come and lick his ulcers."

(Lu 16:21) However, even the despised dog is better off than a dead lion, for the living dog is conscious, whereas the dead lion, the regal beast, is conscious of nothing at all.—Ec 9:4, 5.

The dog's manner of lapping water while at the same time keeping its eyes open to surrounding conditions was referred to when God prescribed a test for the volunteers of Gideon's army. Only those who were alert, lapping up water from their hands, "just as a dog laps," were to be chosen for the fight against Midian.—Jg 7:5.

DOORKEEPER. See GATEKEEPER.

DOORWAY.
The "entrance" (Heb., *pe'tach;* Ge 19:11) of a room, a house, or some other building consisting of: (1) the "upper part of the doorway" (Heb., *mash·qohph';* Ex 12:7), that is, the lintel, a horizontal beam of wood or stone spanning the door-opening at the top and carrying the weight of the structure above the door; (2) the two upright "doorposts" (Heb., *mezu·zohth';* Ex 12:7, ftn), one on each side of the doorway, on which the lintel rests; (3) the door (Heb., *de'leth;* Gr., *thy'ra*) itself; (4) the "threshold" (Heb., *saph* [Jg 19:27]) lying beneath the door.

The *lintel* and *doorposts* of the entrances of Israelite houses in Egypt were obediently splashed with the blood of the Passover victim as a sign for God's angel to pass over such homes and not destroy their firstborn. (Ex 12:7, 22, 23) According to the Law, if a slave (male or female) desired to remain permanently in his master's service, the master brought the slave up against the door or the doorpost and pierced his ear through with an awl. (Ex 21:5, 6; De 15:16, 17) The Hebrew word for doorpost (*mezu·zah'*) has come to be applied to a small container called a mezuzah. It is nailed to the doorpost by Orthodox Jews and contains a parchment bearing the words of Deuteronomy 6:4-9; 11:13-21.—See MEZUZAH.

The *door* was generally made of wood, and many of them turned on pivots fitted into sockets in the lintel and the threshold. (Pr 26:14) Door pivots were often wooden, but the Egyptians sometimes fastened to a door's lower and upper ends metal hinges having projections that fitted into sockets, these doors thus pivoting in that way. Sockets for the doors of the temple built by Solomon were of gold.—1Ki 7:48, 50.

Doors of average homes were small and not ornate. But the entrance of Solomon's temple had two, two-leaved juniper-wood doors, and there were two doors made of oil-tree wood leading to the Most Holy, all these doors having carved representations of cherubs, palm trees, and blossoms, overlaid with gold. (1Ki 6:31-35) Large doors having folding sections or leaves were also used elsewhere. For instance, Jehovah saw to it that Babylon's copper "two-leaved doors" were opened to King Cyrus.—Isa 45:1, 2.

For the *threshold* generally wood or stone was used. However, the thresholds of "the house of Jehovah" built by Solomon were covered with gold.—2Ch 3:1, 7.

Doors of houses or gates were sometimes fastened by means of bars or crossbeams of wood or iron (Isa 45:2; De 3:5; 2Ch 8:5; 14:7), usually affixed in a way that allowed them to be slid into sockets in gateposts or doorposts. City gates sometimes had both bars and bolts. (Ne 3:3; 7:3) The bolt may have been a rod or shaft that could be moved into a socket in the threshold inside the gate. Some city gates had locks (De 33:25), as did the doors of houses.—2Sa 13:17, 18; Lu 11:7; see GATE, GATEWAY; LOCK.

Metal door knockers were used to some extent, but the Bible does not specifically say the Hebrews employed them. To rouse the occupants of a house, one knocked on the door of the house or of the gateway.—Ca 5:2; Ac 12:13.

Figurative Use. Jesus Christ encouraged persistence, saying: "Keep on knocking, and it will be opened to you." (Mt 7:7) At Revelation 3:20, Christ states that he is "standing at the door and knocking," with spiritual fellowship and benefit assured to the one opening the door and receiving him.

If the Shulammite girl had been unsteady in love and virtue, like a door turning on its pivots, her brothers determined to "block her up with a cedar plank," thus barring the "door" shut and preventing its swinging open to anyone unwholesome.—Ca 8:8, 9.

Leviathan, with its double jaw, is represented as having "doors" in its face. (Job 41:1, 13, 14) The congregator observed that in the case of the aged man "the doors onto the street have been closed," perhaps to show that the two doors of the mouth no longer open very much or at all to give expression of what is in the house of the body.—Ec 12:1, 4.

Jesus Christ recommended vigorous exertion to gain salvation, "to get in through the narrow door." (Lu 13:23, 24; Php 3:13, 14; compare Mt 7:13, 14.) On another occasion he likened himself to the door of a figurative sheepfold, Jesus being the right kind of shepherd who leads his "little flock" into a relationship with Jehovah on the basis of the new covenant sealed with Jesus' own blood. (Lu 12:32; Joh 10:7-11) Jesus' likening himself to such a door harmonizes with the fact that through him, by virtue of his ransom sacrifice, sheeplike persons can approach God, be saved, and gain life.—Joh 14:6.

Jehovah was responsible for opening to the nations "the door to faith." (Ac 14:27) Paul remained at Ephesus for a time because "a large door that leads to activity" in declaring the good news had been opened to him there.—1Co 16:8, 9; Ac 19:1-20; compare 2Co 2:12, 13; Col 4:3, 4.

In vision, John saw "an opened door in heaven," which enabled him to see future things and enter, as it were, into the presence of Jehovah.—Re 4:1-3.

DOPHKAH (Doph′kah) [possibly, Driven; Shoved]. The first stopping place for the Israelites after leaving the Wilderness of Sin on their way to the Promised Land. (Nu 33:12, 13) The Bible does not indicate its exact geographic location. However, many scholars associate Dophkah with the Egyptian *mafqat,* a district named for the turquoise mined since ancient times around Sarabit el-Khadim, about 34 km (21 mi) E of modern-day Abu Zanima on the Sinai Peninsula.

DOR. One of the Palestinian cities that allied with Canaanite King Jabin of Hazor to fight against Joshua (Jos 11:1, 2) and was summarily defeated. (Jos 11:12; 12:23) Though Dor and its dependent towns actually lay in Asher's territory, these were given to the tribe of Manasseh, who proved unable to dispossess the inhabitants remaining there. (Jos 17:11-13; 1Ch 7:29) Later the territory of Dor, overseen by one of Solomon's sons-in-law, provided food one month out of the year for the king's household.—1Ki 4:11.

The city of Dor is usually identified with Khirbet el-Burj (Tel Dor), 13 km (8 mi) N of Caesarea, on the long narrow coastal plain stretching along the Mediterranean Sea. This location on the coastal plain has caused some discussion as to the meaning of the frequently used phrase "the mountain ridges [from the Heb. *na·phah′*] of Dor." (Jos 11:2) Some scholars believe this refers to the cliffs that line much of the coast in this region, thus associating the Hebrew *na·phah′* with the Arabic term *nafnaf,* meaning "cliff, precipice." Others believe it may indicate the hilly slopes that begin 3 km (2 mi) inland from Dor and culminate in the heights of Mount Carmel.

DORCAS (Dor′cas) [Gazelle]. A Christian woman in the Joppa congregation abounding in "good deeds and gifts of mercy," evidently including the making of inner and outer garments for needy widows. (Ac 9:36, 39) "Dorcas" corresponds to the Aramaic "Tabitha," both names meaning "Gazelle." Possibly Dorcas was known by both names, as it was not uncommon then for Jews, especially those living in a seaport such as Joppa with its mixed population of Jews and Gentiles, to have a Hebrew name as well as a Greek or Latin name. Or, Luke may have translated the name for the benefit of Gentile readers. Dorcas is the only woman mentioned in the Scriptures as having the feminine form of the word "disciple" applied to her. This, however, does not mean that she held a special position in the congregation, for all Christians were actually disciples of Jesus Christ. (Mt 28:19, 20) Though her death in 36 C.E. caused much weeping among the widows who had apparently benefited greatly from her kindness, the fact that no mention is made of sorrow on the part of a husband suggests that Dorcas was unmarried at the time.

At her death the disciples at Joppa prepared her for burial and, on learning that Peter was in Lydda, about 18 km (11 mi) SE of Joppa, sent for him. Undoubtedly they had heard about Peter's healing the paralytic Aeneas there, and this may have given them a basis for reasoning that the apostle might resurrect Dorcas. On the other hand, they may have turned to Peter simply for consolation.—Ac 9:32-38.

Following a procedure similar to that used by Jesus in resurrecting Jairus' daughter (Mr 5:38-41; Lu 8:51-55), Peter, after dismissing everyone from the upper chamber, prayed and then said: "Tabitha, rise!" Dorcas opened her eyes, sat up, and took Peter's hand to rise. This is the first reported resurrection performed by an apostle, resulting in many becoming believers throughout Joppa.—Ac 9:39-42.

DOTHAN (Do′than). A city figuring in two Biblical narratives. Dothan is today identified with Tell Dothan (Tel Dotan), situated on a hill in a small basinlike plain lying between the hills of Samaria and the Carmel Range, 16 km (10 mi) NNE of Samaria.—PICTURE, Vol. 1, p. 950.

Young Joseph found his brothers and their flocks "at Dothan." It is thought likely that they were to the N of that city, on the pasture ground through which ran the road that connected Gilead (E of the Jordan) with the Mediterranean seacoast and Egypt. This may have been the route traveled by the "caravan of Ishmaelites" who purchased Joseph.—Ge 37:17-36.

Centuries later the king of Syria dispatched a heavy military force to Dothan to arrest Elisha. Here the prophet's fearful attendant had his eyes miraculously opened to see the fiery war equipment of God in "the mountainous region . . . all around Elisha," that is, either on the same hill where Dothan stood or on the nearby hills to the E, S, and W of Dothan. (2Ki 6:11-17) The Syrians, in encircling the city, may have also posted themselves in these surrounding hills, from which they then 'came down' when Elisha went out of the city to meet them. The enemy forces were rendered harmless, however, when miraculously struck with a type of blindness, Jehovah perhaps using the angelic forces in accomplishing this. —2Ki 6:18, 19; compare Ge 19:1, 10, 11.

DOVE [Heb., yoh·nah'; Gr., pe·ri·ste·ra']. The dove is one of the first two birds specifically named in the Bible, Noah having sent out a dove three times after the Flood to determine the drainage of the waters. (Ge 8:8-12) The Hebrew name yoh·nah' is thought to derive from the word 'a·nah', meaning "mourn," and evidently is in imitation of the mournful cooing sound made by the dove. (Isa 38:14; 59:11, 12; Eze 7:16; Na 2:7) While "dove" and "pigeon" are often used interchangeably in English, both birds being classed as of the family Columbidae, the term "dove" is usually restricted to the smaller varieties generally living wild and regularly migrating. Since the distinction in English between dove and pigeon is quite indefinite, translators usually render yoh·nah' as "dove" except when it occurs in association with "turtledove" (as in all cases relating to sacrifices), in which texts it is generally translated "pigeon."—See PIGEON; TURTLEDOVE.

Varieties and Description. The most common varieties of doves found in Israel are the rock dove (Columba livia), the ring dove (Columba palumbus; also called the wood pigeon), and the stock dove (Columba oenas). Ring doves are found particularly in the forests of Gilead and Carmel. The stock dove settles chiefly around Jericho and on the eastern side of the Jordan, while the rock dove breeds on the coastlands, along the gorges of the Jordan Valley and the highlands to the west. Doves characteristically have a plump, full-breasted body, a graceful neck, a small rounded head with rather slender bill, and short legs. The feathers are very compact, giving the bird a rather sleek look. The doves are frequently of a blue-gray color, while some have an iridescent sheen on parts of the plumage, causing it to take on a metallic appearance in the golden sunlight. This may be alluded to at Psalm 68:13, although the reference there to "the wings of a dove covered with silver and its pinions with yellowish-green gold" is thought by some to refer to some richly wrought piece of art taken as spoil.

The dove has a soft, gentle appearance and disposition, earning for it the description 'the sheep of the bird world.' Thus the name Jonah (Yoh·nah') was and is a popular name for Jewish boys. (Jon 1:1) The birds are notable for their devotion to their mates and their affection, and in courtship they bring their heads together and each bird takes the other's beak in its own much like a lover's kiss. "My dove" was thus an apt term of endearment used by the Shulammite maiden's shepherd lover. (Ca 5:2; 6:9) The maiden's eyes were likened to the soft gentle eyes of a dove (Ca 1:15; 4:1), while she likened the shepherd's eyes to blue-gray doves bathing in pools of milk, by this lovely simile evidently representing the darker iris surrounded by the gleaming white of the eye. (Ca 5:12) Doves are fond of bathing, preferring to nest near a source of water.

A timid bird, trembling when frightened (Ho 11:11), the dove in its wild state often nests in valleys (Eze 7:16), while the rock dove makes its nest on ledges and in holes of cliffs and rocky gorges. (Ca 2:14; Jer 48:28) When domesticated, they fly back to the dovecotes prepared for them, the white undersides of the wings of a large flock of doves giving the appearance of a moving cloud. (Isa 60:8) Dovecotes, some of considerable size, have been excavated in Israel.

The dove has strong wings, is able to fly long distances in search of food, and is swift enough to elude most of its enemies. (Ps 55:6-8) Yet doves are quite trusting of humans and are rather easily entrapped or snared with a net. Thus, apostate Ephraim, foolishly placing its confidence first in Egypt and then in Assyria, was likened to a "simpleminded dove," due to be caught in a net. (Ho 7:11, 12) Jesus, in warning his disciples against wolflike opposers, counseled them to be not only "innocent as doves" but also "cautious as serpents."—Mt 10:16.

At the time of Jesus' baptism and subsequent anointing by God's holy spirit, that holy spirit was caused to appear "in bodily shape like a dove," its visible descent upon Jesus perhaps being similar to the fluttering descent of the dove as it approaches its perch. (Lu 3:22; Mt 3:16; Mr 1:10; Joh 1:32-34) It was an apt symbol, in view of its characteristic innocence.—Mt 10:16.

Doves were used for sacrificial purposes, as is indicated by their being sold by those pursuing commercial activities at the temple in Jerusalem, although the term "doves [Gr., *pe·ri·ste·ras'*]" may here indicate the "turtledoves" or "young pigeons" mentioned in the Mosaic Law.—Mr 11:15; Joh 2:14-16.

DOVE'S DUNG.
The description of the siege of Samaria by Syrian King Ben-hadad relates that the famine created became so severe that "an ass's head got to be worth eighty silver pieces, and the fourth of a cab measure of dove's dung was worth five silver pieces." (2Ki 6:24, 25) The cost of an ass's head was approximately $176 (if the "silver pieces" were shekels) and "the fourth of a cab measure [0.3 L; 0.55 dry pt] of dove's dung" was worth about $11. This indicates that, because of the scarcity of food, such a thing as the bony, thinly fleshed ass's head became an expensive food item (although the ass was an unclean animal according to the Mosaic Law), and even dove's dung was very costly. The reference to dove's dung has occasioned considerable discussion as to whether the term is literal and as to the use to which it was put by the buyer.

Arguments have been advanced that the term "dove's dung" may have been applied to a certain plant. However, there is no evidence that the plants referred to by those favoring this view were ever known by the name dove's dung or that such plants would be accessible to the people bottled up in Samaria by the siege.

Those who acknowledge a literal meaning of the expression are, in turn, divided as to the use made of the substance. Some point out that dove's dung has long been used as a fertilizer by people in the Middle East in the cultivation of melons, but it seems reasonable that persons bordering on death by starvation would be concerned with food for immediate consumption rather than with a crop that would not be available for perhaps several months.

Many prefer the view that the dove's dung was actually used for food, pointing out that the subject is that of famine and the terrible extremes to which humans are driven by the pangs of hunger. Though purposely extreme and cruel in order to create a weakening fear, the threat by Sennacherib's officer, Rabshakeh, that a siege by Assyria would cause the people of Jerusalem to have to "eat their own excrement and drink their own urine" may have had some basis in fact. (2Ki 18:27) While the thought of using literal dung for human consumption is extremely repulsive, that in itself is no basis for rejecting this view. The fact that the hunger was so great in Samaria that women would boil and eat their own children indicates that they had reached the point of consuming anything available. (2Ki 6:26-29) While some point out that dung would have little value as a nutrient, this factor alone would not disprove the possibility of its being purchased for food, for starving persons are frequently irrational, eating anything to deaden the pangs of hunger.

Perhaps an even more likely suggestion is that of certain rabbins who hold that the dung was used for fuel. There is some Biblical parallel in this, since the prophet Ezekiel was instructed to picture the equally dire siege conditions due to come upon Jerusalem by cooking his food with dung as the fuel. (Eze 4:12-17) Dried cattle dung, called cow chips by some, serves as a common fuel in many parts of the earth till this day. If this view should be correct, then the account might simply be stating the cost of the food (in this case an ass's head) and the cost of the fuel for cooking it. The succeeding verses indicate that the people were as yet not eating the flesh raw.

DRACHMA.
A Greek silver coin still in use in the first century C.E. (Lu 15:8, 9) The Attic drachma bore the head of the goddess Athena on one side and an owl on the other side. By the time of Jesus' earthly ministry, the drachma probably had depreciated to about 3.4 g (0.109 oz t) and hence would be presently evaluated at 65 cents. In the first century C.E. the Greeks equated the drachma with the denarius, but the Roman government officially reckoned the value of the drachma at three fourths of a denarius. The Jews paid an annual temple tax of two drachmas (a didrachma).—Mt 17:24.

The Greek silver drachma is not to be confused with the gold "drachma" (*dar·ke·mohn'*) of the Hebrew Scriptures, a coin generally equated with the Persian daric (8.4 g; 0.27 oz t; $94.50 according to modern values).—Ezr 2:69; Ne 7:70-72.

DRAGNET.
A net that was dragged along the bottom of a body of water to catch fish. (Eze 26:5, 14; 47:10) In ancient Egypt, dragnets were made of flax cords and were equipped with lead weights at the bottom and wooden floats at the top. Likely those used by the Israelites were similar.

The methods of dragnet fishing used anciently were probably much like those employed in the Middle East in more recent times. The dragnet was let down from boats in such a way as to surround a school of fish, and the long ropes attached to the opposite ends of the net were taken ashore, where several men on each rope gradually pulled the net as a semicircle to the beach. (Mt 13:47, 48) Another method was to draw the net together in a narrowing circle. Fishermen then dived into the water and pulled a portion of the weighted edge under the rest of the net, thus forming a bottom. After this, the net was drawn into a boat or boats. (Lu 5:6, 7) Sometimes the net was first dragged into shallower water before being emptied.—Compare Joh 21:8, 11.

In the Scriptures, the dragnet is used figuratively with reference to the gathering of prospective members of "the kingdom of the heavens." (Mt 13:47, 48) It is also used to depict the heart of an immoral woman (Ec 7:26) as well as schemes to ensnare others. (Mic 7:2) Also, military conquest is likened to fishing with a dragnet.—Hab 1:15-17.

DRAGON.
From the Greek dra'kon, depicting a terrifying monster, a serpentlike devourer. It occurs 13 times in the Bible but only in the highly symbolic book of Revelation, and it represents Satan the Devil. He is the "great fiery-colored dragon, with seven heads and ten horns," having a tail that draws "a third of the stars of heaven" after him, these first being induced to materialize as humans before the Flood and then becoming demons. (Re 12:3, 4; Jude 6) Together with these demons, Satan the Dragon is cast out of heaven down to the vicinity of the earth. "So down the great dragon was hurled, the original serpent, the one called Devil and Satan." (Re 12:7-9) In this debased state he persecutes the remnant of God's "woman," those having "the work of bearing witness."—Re 12:13-17.

Dragonlike Satan is also the one that gives power and great authority to the symbolic wild beast having seven heads and ten horns, and in turn, he is worshiped by the peoples of "all the earth." (Re 13:2-4) John in vision also sees that the croaking froglike "expressions inspired by demons," which go out to "the kings of the entire inhabited earth," come from the mouth of the Dragon, or Satan, as well as out of the mouths of "the wild beast" and "the false prophet." The effect this has is to gather these rulers and their supporters "to the war of the great day of God the Almighty . . . to the place that is called in Hebrew Har–Magedon [Armageddon]." (Re 16:13-16) Following this greatest of all wars, the "angel" that comes down from heaven will seize "the dragon, the original serpent, who is the Devil and Satan," and will bind him and abyss him for a thousand years.—Re 20:1-3; see SATAN.

DREAD.
This is the usual rendering for the Hebrew noun pa'chadh (verb pha·chadh'), having the basic sense of that which causes quivering. (Compare Mic 7:17.) A form of the word quts has been translated "feel a sickening dread" (Ex 1:12; Nu 22:3; Isa 7:16), and this term often conveys the sense of "abhorrence." (See ABHORRENT THING.) The expression "dread during the nights" refers to what may cause dread, or intense fear, during the night, such as surprise assault by robbers or attack by large beasts of prey.—Ca 3:8.

Jacob referred to the Almighty as "the Dread of Isaac," the one that Isaac viewed with reverential awe, fearing to displease Him. That Jacob shared the viewpoint of his father Isaac is shown by his making an oath "by the Dread of his father Isaac."—Ge 31:42, 53.

A wholesome dread of Jehovah, reflected in a desire to shun what He disapproves, is vital if a person is to remain his servant. This dread made it possible for Job to be blameless and upright. (Job 1:1; 23:15; 31:23) And it enabled the psalmist to persevere in a divinely favored course despite the persecution by princes. (Ps 119:120, 161) Jehoshaphat encouraged appointed judges to have this proper dread so that they would be impartial in rendering just decisions.—2Ch 19:5-7.

Jehovah is the Protector and Sustainer of his people. So there is no reason for one to be in dread of men, manifesting intense fear of what they might do, and so yield to their improper demands. (Ps 27:1; 78:53; 91:2-5; Isa 12:2) But this does not mean that servants of God will never suffer in the present system of things. At times they do find themselves in a pitiable, disadvantaged position. Not discerning that such ones are still the objects of Jehovah's care, faithless persons may abandon them in dread, not wanting to share their seemingly hopeless lot. (Ps 31:11) But Jehovah will not forsake them.—Ps 27:10; 94:14.

It is because of having no dread of God that the wicked continue in their evil ways. (Ps 36:1-4) But they will not escape the dread that comes from the calamity befalling them on account of their ignoring godly wisdom.—Pr 1:26, 27.

When Jehovah withdrew his protection from the unfaithful Israelites, they experienced dread day and night, being uncertain of their very lives. There was no escape from disaster. (De 28:66, 67; Isa 24:17-20; 33:14; Jer 30:5; La 3:47) This kind of dread would not be experienced by those acting in harmony with godly wisdom, those always having reverential awe of the Creator.—Pr 1:33; 3:24, 25; 28:14.

Manifestations of Jehovah's matchless power, backing, or favor may cause observers to be in dread. (2Ch 17:10; Ps 53:5; 105:38; Isa 19:16, 17; Jer 33:9) For example, the Israelites, with divine help, gained remarkable and truly fear-inspiring victories over their enemies (De 11:25; 1Ch 14:17; 2Ch 14:12-14; 20:29), and during the time of Mordecai and Esther the unexpected turn of events in favor of the Jews caused their enemies to be in dread. (Es 8:17; 9:2, 3) Also the evidence of divinely inspired courage and strength may bring about a wholesome dread and an obedient response. Thus, when King Saul forcefully appealed to the Israelites to join in the defense of Jabesh-gilead, they were filled with "the dread of Jehovah" and responded "as one man."—1Sa 11:7.

Because Jehovah had foretold the fall of Babylon by the hand of Cyrus, the Israelites had no reason to be in dread of that world-shaking event. For them it had to be a liberation from the dread of Babylonian rage. The makers of idols, however, were bound to feel dread, as all the deities manufactured by human hands would prove to be of no assistance in saving Babylon.—Isa 44:8-11, 24-28; 51:12, 13.

DREAM.
The thoughts or mental images a person has while asleep. The Scriptures refer to dreams from God (Nu 12:6), natural dreams (Job 20:8), and false dreams (Jer 29:8, 9) such as those that involve divination.—Zec 10:2.

Dreams From God. Dreams from God were received by Jehovah's servants and by persons not devoted to him. (1Ki 3:5; Jg 7:13, 14) Some furnished warnings that protected his servants, and others gave them guidance. Thus, in a dream God warned Abimelech the king of Gerar not to touch Sarah, with the result that she remained undefiled. (Ge 20) Complying with "divine warning in a dream," the astrologers who visited Jesus did not return to murderous Herod. (Mt 2:11, 12) In response to angelic instruction in dreams, Joseph took Mary as his wife and also fled with Jesus and Mary into Egypt. Later dreams from God led Joseph to return from Egypt with them and settle in Nazareth in order to fulfill the proph-

ecy, "He will be called a Nazarene."—Mt 1:18-25; 2:13-15, 19-23.

Some dreams from God gave his servants assurance of divine favor or helped them to understand how Jehovah was aiding them. When God was about to conclude a covenant with Abram (Abraham), a deep sleep and great darkness fell upon the patriarch, and Jehovah then apparently spoke to him in a dream. (Ge 15:12-16) At Luz (Bethel) God caused Jacob to have a dream in which he saw a ladder reaching from earth to heaven, thus denoting communication with heaven. Angels ascended and descended on it, a representation of Jehovah was stationed above it, and God pronounced a blessing on Jacob. (Ge 28:10-19; compare Joh 1:51.) It was also by means of a dream that God, years later, showed his approval of Jacob and gave him angelic instruction to return to his homeland.—Ge 31:11-13.

As a youth, Jacob's son Joseph had dreams that indicated he had divine favor, these dreams also being prophetic. In one, he and his brothers were binding sheaves in the field. Joseph's sheaf stood erect, and those of his brothers encircled it and bowed down to it. In another dream, the sun, moon, and 11 stars bowed down to him. (Ge 37:5-11) Both of these dreams were fulfilled when Jacob and his household moved to Egypt during a severe famine. To obtain food, they all became dependent upon Joseph, then Egypt's food administrator.—Ge 42:1-3, 5-9.

Some dreams from God experienced by persons not worshiping him were also prophetic. In Egypt, while Joseph was imprisoned with Pharaoh's chief of the cupbearers and chief of the bakers, these men had dreams that God enabled Joseph to explain as meaning that in three days the chief of the cupbearers would be restored to his position, whereas the chief of the bakers would be executed. These events occurred three days later, on Pharaoh's birthday. In time these dreams served the purpose of bringing Joseph to Pharaoh's attention as a man having God's spirit.—Ge 40.

Warning and the prophetic element were combined in two dreams that Pharaoh of Joseph's day had in one night. In the first, he saw seven fat-fleshed cows devoured by seven poor, thin-fleshed cows. In Pharaoh's second dream, seven full and good ears of grain came up on one stalk, only to be swallowed up by seven shriveled, thin, wind-scorched ears of grain. Joseph, ascribing the interpretation to God, correctly explained that both dreams pointed to seven years of plenty to be followed by seven of famine. (Ge 41) It was God's direction to save many from starvation and particularly to preserve the life of Abraham's descendants, to fulfill his promises to Abraham. —Ge 45:5-8.

Babylonian King Nebuchadnezzar also had two prophetic dreams from God. One was of a metallic image with a head of gold, breast and arms of silver, belly and thighs of copper, legs of iron, and feet of iron and clay. A stone cut out without hands struck and crushed its feet and then pulverized the rest of the image. Daniel identified Nebuchadnezzar as "the head of gold" and explained that a succession of human kingdoms would follow that of Babylon. Ultimately, God himself would set up a Kingdom that would "never be brought to ruin."—Da 2:29-45.

In another dream from God, Nebuchadnezzar beheld a great tree that was chopped down, its remaining rootstock being restrained with "a banding of iron and of copper" until "seven times" passed over it. In keeping with Daniel's explanation, boasting Nebuchadnezzar (symbolized by the tree that was cut down) went mad, remaining in that state until seven times, or years, passed. Thereafter he acknowledged God's supremacy, and his sanity having returned, he was reestablished in his kingship.—Da 4; see APPOINTED TIMES OF THE NATIONS.

Daniel himself had a dream from Jehovah in which he beheld four huge beasts coming up out of the sea, these creatures representing human governments. (Da 7:1, 3, 17; see BEASTS, SYMBOLIC.) Daniel also saw the Ancient of Days, from whom "someone like a son of man" received lasting "rulership and dignity and kingdom."—Da 7:13, 14.

Joel foretold that the outpouring of God's spirit would be followed by such manifestations as prophesying and the dreaming of inspired dreams. (Joe 2:28) It was on the day of Pentecost in the year 33 C.E. that some 120 disciples of Jesus Christ received the holy spirit and began speaking in various tongues "about the magnificent things of God." (Ac 2:1-18) Later, other believers, including the former persecutor Saul (Paul), received the holy spirit and were empowered with miraculous gifts. (Ac 8:17-19; 9:17; 10:44-46) While in Troas, Paul had a night vision or dream that provided guidance as to where he and his associates were to preach "the good news." (Ac 16:9, 10) Other disciples doubtless also had dreams under the influence of God's spirit, fulfilling the words of Joel's prophecy.

When Jesus Christ stood on trial before Pontius Pilate, the Roman governor's wife sent him this message respecting Jesus: "Have nothing to do with that righteous man, for I suffered a lot today in a dream because of him." (Mt 27:19) Evidently of divine origin, the dream should have warned Pilate that Christ's case was one of extreme importance.

Natural Dreams. Natural dreams may be stimulated by certain thoughts or emotions, sensations or daily activities (anxiety, one's physical condition, his occupation, and so forth). (Ec 5:3) These dreams are of no great significance. (Ps 73:20) A hungry person may dream of eating and a thirsty one of drinking, but they awake unsatisfied. Comparable delusion was in store for all the nations "waging war against Mount Zion."—Isa 29:7, 8.

Concerning the pagan view of dreams, it is stated: "Babylonians had such trust in dreams that on the eve of important decisions they slept in temples, hoping for counsel. Greeks desiring health instruction slept in shrines of Aesculapius, and Romans in temples of Serapis. Egyptians prepared elaborate books for dream interpretation." (Harper's Bible Dictionary, edited by M. and J. L. Miller, 1961, p. 141) But such practices did not exist among faithful Hebrews and early Christians. The Scriptures warn against looking for omens, whether in natural dreams or in various incidents.—De 18:10-12; see DIVINATION.

False Dreams. False dreams are Biblically condemned. According to the Law, a false dreamer who urged the committing of idolatry was to be put to death. (De 13:1-5) God might sometimes speak to his true prophets by means of dreams (Nu 12:6), but he was against "the prophets of false dreams," who led his people away from true worship. (Jer 23:25-32; 27:9, 10) Practicers of divination were described as speaking "valueless dreams."—Zec 10:2.

The Bible speaks of dreams in a figurative sense in describing the ungodly defilers of the flesh who slipped into the Christian congregation. Jude warned fellow believers against such men "indulging in dreams," these persons apparently dreaming (imagining) that they could with impunity violate God's Word and defile flesh in the congregation. This was a mistake, for they would inescapably receive adverse judgment from the Supreme Judge, Jehovah.—Jude 8; 1Co 6:9, 10, 18-20.

DREGS. Suspended particles that precipitate and settle to the bottom when wine is allowed to stand undisturbed. In the Scriptures the term occurs five times, always in the plural (Heb., *shema·rim'*). It is generally rendered "lees" by Bible translators. Keeping a good wine "on the dregs" for a long time to age fully gives it clarity, strength, and mellowness. (Isa 25:6) On the other hand, when a wine that is bad to start with because of a poor quality of grape is left to congeal on the dregs, it does not improve in taste or smell, facts to which the prophets refer in illustrations. (Jer 48:11; Zep 1:12) Also, in a figure of speech the psalmist says that "all the wicked ones of the earth" will be compelled to drain the cup of Jehovah's anger, drinking the dregs and all, down to the last bitter drop.—Ps 75:8; compare Eze 23:32-34; see WINE AND STRONG DRINK.

DRESS.

DRESS. Apart from mention, with some description, of various articles of clothing in the Bible, there is little historical information as to the dress worn by the Hebrews—far less than that of the Egyptians and the Assyrians. The reason is that the nation of Israel did not erect monuments or make inscriptions lauding their military victors, with figures of themselves from which we could get an idea as to their style of dress. Numerous Egyptian and Assyrian bas-reliefs, and those of other nations, illustrate the dress of their own peoples, and several show captives of different nationalities. Some of those depicted are believed to be Hebrews, but this cannot be proved. It seems reasonable, however, that some of the clothing worn today by people in the Bible lands may be roughly similar to what was worn centuries ago, since the same purposes are served and since some customs have remained unchanged for centuries. On the other hand, archaeological evidence seems to show that the Hebrews used color in their dress to a greater extent than do the modern Arab Bedouin. Additionally, the dress worn by modern-day Jews and by other people in those lands has often been greatly influenced by religion and by Greek, Roman, and Western customs, so that we can at best get only a general idea by comparison.

Materials. The very earliest clothing material was the fig leaf, Adam and Eve sewing fig leaves together to make loin coverings. (Ge 3:7) Later, Jehovah made them long garments of skin. (Ge 3:21) "A hair garment" was used by Elijah and by Elisha as an "official garment" of their prophetic ministry. Elijah also wore a belt of leather. John the Baptizer dressed similarly. (2Ki 1:8; 2:13; Heb 11:37; Mt 3:4) Sackcloth, usually made of hair (Re 6:12), was worn by mourners.

(Es 4:1; Ps 69:10, 11; Re 11:3) Linen and wool were the principal fabrics. (Le 13:47-59; Pr 31:13) The coarser fabrics of the poor were made of goat hair and camel hair, although they also used wool. Linen was a more expensive material. Cotton may also have been used. In only one place in the Bible is it certain that silk is mentioned, it being listed as an article of Babylon the Great's commerce. (Re 18:12) Garments were of various colors, variegated, and striped, and some were embroidered. (Jg 5:30) Varieties of weave existed. The high priest's white linen robe was woven "in checkerwork." (Ex 28:39) The Israelites who were not priests might wear a garment of linen and another of wool but were forbidden by God's law to wear a garment of two sorts of thread, mixed. —Le 19:19; De 22:11; see CLOTH; DYES, DYEING.

Garments. The general term for garment most often used in the Hebrew Scriptures is *be'-ghedh*. Other terms were used, sometimes in a general way, but they also appear in places as applying to specific articles of clothing.

Inner garments. There seems to have been an innermost garment in the form of a loincloth, or perhaps drawers, worn next to the skin, for the exposure of absolute nakedness was shameful. The priests were required to wear linen drawers (Heb., *mikh·na·sa'yim*) to prevent indecent exposure when they served at the altar. Pagan priests sometimes served naked, a thing disgusting to Jehovah.—Ex 28:42, 43.

The *sa·dhin'* (Heb.) was an undergarment worn by both men and women. (Isa 3:23) Some think that one form of this inner article of clothing was in the nature of a wraparound garment. It would be worn without outer garments by workmen in fields or by fishermen, carpenters, hewers of wood, drawers of water, and so forth. When worn beneath outer clothing, the style of it appears to have been shirtlike, reaching to or below the knees, having sleeves and worn with or without a sash. It was made of wool or linen.

The Hebrew *kut·to'neth*, a type of robe, seems to correspond to the Greek *khi·ton'*. Both terms are most widely used to refer to a tunic or shirtlike article of apparel, long- or half-sleeved, reaching to the knees or to the ankles. It was the indoor costume for family life and familiar outdoor surroundings. In some styles of the *kut·to'neth*, or *khi·ton'*, the fabric may have been draped over one shoulder, leaving the other bare, and was white or of varied colors. The longer style might be slit in each side from the hem up about 30 cm (1 ft) for freedom of walking. Some were of linen but probably more often of wool, especially among the poor. This garment was also worn by both men and women, a woman's robe likely being longer.

Kut·to'neth is the word used for the robe of the high priest and the underpriests. (Ex 28:39, 40) The word is also used for Joseph's long striped shirtlike garment (Ge 37:3) and for Tamar's striped robe, which she ripped apart in grief and humiliation. (2Sa 13:18) Jesus' inner garment (khi·ton'), over which the soldiers cast lots, was woven in one piece without a seam. (Joh 19:23, 24) The kut·to'neth, or khi·ton', could be worn with a sash, as in the case of the priests, or without; likely, in most cases, a sash was used. Probably different styles of it were worn, depending on the activity of the wearer. One engaged in work or physical activity would reasonably wear a shorter version of the garment, for more liberty of movement. Jude's illustration, at verse 23, is appropriate, for the khi·ton' would be in contact with the flesh.

Outer garments. The me'il', a sleeveless coat often open at the front, was worn on top of the kut·to'neth or white linen robe of the high priest. (Le 8:7) The me'il' was not restricted to the priesthood, however, but was a common item of apparel. Samuel, Saul, David, as well as Job and his three companions are among those mentioned as wearing sleeveless coats. (1Sa 2:19; 15:27; 18:4; 24:4; 1Ch 15:27; Job 1:20; 2:12) In each case it is quite clear that it refers to an upper or secondary garment worn over another one. The Septuagint often renders me'il' in Greek as sto·le' and hi·ma'ti·on, terms denoting an upper garment. This article of dress was often longer than the kut·to'neth. The sal·mah' (Heb.) may also have been a form of outer garment.

The sto·le', as referred to in the Christian Greek Scriptures, was a stately robe reaching down to the feet. Jesus criticized the scribes for loving to wear this type of robe in public places to attract attention and to impress people with their importance. (Lu 20:46) The angel at Jesus' tomb was wearing this form of clothing. (Mr 16:5) It was this robe, "the best," that was put on the prodigal son at his return. (Lu 15:22) And the martyred servants of God in John's vision are clothed with the sto·le' (Re 6:11), as are also the members of the "great crowd."—Re 7:9, 13, 14.

E·sthes' (Gr.) usually had reference to a robe or garment that was ornate, splendid. Angels appeared in such attire. (Lu 24:4; see also Jas 2:2, 3.) Herod clothed Jesus in such a robe in mockery. (Lu 23:11) After Jesus was scourged at Pilate's orders, the soldiers put on him a scarlet cloak (khla·mys') (Mt 27:28, 31), or hi·ma'ti·on. (Joh 19:2, 5) This was apparently a cloak or robe worn by kings, magistrates, military officers, and so forth.

The sim·lah' (Heb.), "mantle," was the outermost garment worn by the majority. It was

Articles of Israelite dress

Simlah   Me'il   Kuttoneth

also the largest and heaviest, made of wool, linen, or goat hair, and perhaps, in some cases, of sheepskin or goatskin. The mantle was often the garment that was ripped to express grief. (Ge 37:34; 44:13; Jos 7:6) It seems to have been a large rectangular piece of material, usually placed on the left shoulder, brought up under the right arm from behind, drawn across the chest and thrown back over the left shoulder again, leaving the right arm free. In bad weather it was drawn around the body more closely, over both arms, and even covering the head. It was occasionally in the form of a large square piece of material with slits for the arms. The mantle, comparable in some respects to our shawl, could be used as a covering (Ge 9:23), as bed clothing (Ex 22:27; De 22:17), and to bind or wrap up articles.—Ex 12: 34; Jg 8:25; 1Sa 21:9.

The *sim·lah'* was worn by both men and women, the woman's being distinguishable from the man's, perhaps in size, color, and decoration such as embroidery. God commanded that a woman should not wear a man's garment, nor a man a woman's mantle; this command doubtless being given in order to prevent sex abuses.—De 22:5.

A poor man might have only one mantle, but the well-to-do had several changes. (Ex 22:27; De 10:18; Ge 45:22) Because it was the poor person's covering during the chilly nights, it was forbidden to take a widow's garment as a pledge or to keep the garment of a poor man overnight, the mantle here being referred to primarily.—De 24: 13, 17.

The Greek *hi·ma'ti·on,* "outer garment," probably corresponds largely to the mantle (*sim·lah'*) of the Hebrew Scriptures. In some cases it appears to have been a loose robe, but more often it was a rectangular piece of material. It was easily put on and thrown off. Usually it was taken off when its owner was working nearby. (Mt 24:18; Mr 10:50; Joh 13:4; Ac 7:58) Jesus spoke of this piece of apparel when he said: "From him that takes away your outer garment [*hi·ma'ti·on*], do not withhold even the undergarment [*khi·to'na*]." (Lu 6:29) He may refer here to a forcible or illegal removal of garments, the outer garment naturally being first to be pulled off. At Matthew 5:40, he reverses the order. There he is discussing legal action, in which the judges might first award the complainant the *khi·ton',* the inner garment, which was of less value.

That *hi·ma'ti·on* and *khi·ton'* may have been used at times interchangeably to mean "garment" is indicated in the accounts of Jesus' trial by Matthew and Mark. The high priest ripped his clothing to demonstrate forcibly his sanctimoniously assumed horror and indignation. Matthew uses the word *hi·ma'ti·on* here, while Mark uses *khi·ton'.* (Mt 26:65; Mr 14:63) Or it is possible that in his fervor he ripped one garment, then another.

The *phe·lo'nes* (Gr.), which Paul asked Timothy to bring to him in prison, was likely a traveling cloak for protection against cold or stormy weather. It was not a religious or ecclesiastical vestment.—2Ti 4:13.

The *'ad·de'reth* (Heb.) was the official garment of one such as a prophet or a king. (2Ki 2:8; Jon 3:6) The prophet's official garment was likely made of camel or goat hair. (2Ki 1:8; Mt 3:4; Mr 1:6; compare Ge 25:25.) Elijah appointed Elisha as his successor by throwing his official garment upon him, and Elisha took up this garment after Elijah ascended to the heavens in a windstorm. (1Ki 19:19; 2Ki 2:13) It was an official garment from Shinar that Achan took from the "devoted" city of Jericho, in violation of Jehovah's command.—Jos 7:1, 21.

The Greek word *en'dy·ma* is used with reference to a wedding garment (Mt 22:11, 12), to the clothing of the angel at Jesus' tomb (Mt 28:3), to John the Baptizer's camel-hair clothing, and to garments in general.—Mt 3:4; 6:25, 28; Lu 12:23.

Veil. The woman's "headdress" or "veil" that the apostle Paul speaks of in connection with the symbol of woman's subjection to headship is *pe·ri·bo'lai·on* (Gr.), something that is thrown around, a wrap. (1Co 11:15) It is different from the face veil, or covering, worn by Moses when his face shone so that the Israelites could not look upon it. (Ex 34:33-35; 2Co 3:13) Rebekah put on a headcloth when meeting Isaac, her espoused, to denote her subjection. (Ge 24:65) The Hebrew word *tsa·'iph',* used here, is translated "shawl" (*NW*) and "veil" (*AT, RS*) at Genesis 38:14, 19.

Sash, belt, or girdle. A sash was often worn over the inner or the outer garments. When one engaged in some form of physical activity or work, he would 'gird up his loins' by wearing a sash, often pulling the ends of the garment up between his legs and tucking these ends under the sash so that he would have freedom of movement. (1Ki 18:46; 2Ki 4:29; 9:1) The high priest wore a woven sash over his linen robe, and when wearing the ephod, a girdle of the same material was worn to hold the back and front parts of the apronlike ephod close to the waist. (Ex 28:4, 8, 39; 39:29) A belt or girdle was a commonly worn item because of its additional convenience for holding sheathed daggers or swords, money, the inkhorn of the secretary, and so forth.—Jg 3:16; 2Sa 20:8; Eze 9:3.

Since those engaged in some form of work, and servants or slaves, wore a sash or girdle, it came to be symbolic of service or of one ministering to others. Jesus' expression "let your loins be girded" figuratively describes readiness for spiritual activity on the part of God's servants. (Lu 12:35) Jesus laid aside his outer garments and girded himself with a towel. He then ministered to the apostles by washing their feet, thus teaching them, by example, to serve their brothers. The angels seen in vision by John had golden girdles, signifying a most precious service.—Joh 13:1-16; Re 15:6.

Elijah wore a belt (Heb., *'e·zohr'*) of leather "girded about his loins," as did John the Baptizer (*zo'ne* being the Gr. word for John's girdle).—2Ki 1:8; Mt 3:4.

Fringes and tassels. God commanded the Israelites to make fringed edges on the skirts of their garments, with a blue string above the fringe. This seems to have been peculiar to Israelite dress and provided a visual reminder that they were set aside as a people holy to Jehovah. It would keep before their eyes the fact that they should obey Jehovah's commandments. (Nu 15:38-41) Tassels were also to be put on the four extremities of their clothing; possibly this had reference to the four corners of the mantle. (De 22:12) The hem of the high priest's blue sleeveless coat was fringed with alternate golden bells and pomegranates of cloth material.—Ex 28: 33, 34.

Pins. Where a robe or a sash needed fastening, the Hebrews may have used a toggle pin. Specimens found in the Middle East are pointed on one end and had a hole like a needle's eye at the middle, into which a cord was tied. The garment would be fastened by inserting the pin into it and then winding the cord around the pin's protruding ends. It appears that about the tenth century B.C.E. a form of safety pin somewhat resembling our modern safety pin may have been introduced into ancient Israel.

Right and Wrong View of Dress. Jehovah's people are told not to be unduly anxious about having sufficient clothing. (Mt 6:25-32) The Christian woman is warned not to let expensive, showy dress or style be the thing she seeks but, rather, to let her clothing be modest, yet well arranged, showing soundness of mind. She should, therefore, give attention to her dress but should put the primary stress on the apparel of a quiet and mild spirit. (1Ti 2:9; 1Pe 3:3-5) Yet, the wise writer of Proverbs describes a good wife as seeing that her family is well clothed, industriously making garments with her own hands.—Pr 31:13, 21, 24.

On the other hand, many women of Bible times used their attire as a means of gaining their selfish objectives. It was a custom for women of pagan cities, when about to be captured by the enemy, to put on their finest apparel in order to attract soldiers who might take them as wives. But, in case a captive woman was taken by an Israelite soldier, she was required to set aside her items of dress, some of which might be connected with pagan religion, before he could marry her. —De 21:10-13.

After Israel had fallen into many idolatrous and immoral practices, Jehovah condemned the women of the nation who haughtily garbed and decorated themselves in order to attract men, even men of other nations, and who decked themselves with the ornaments of false religion.—Isa 3:16-23; compare Pr 7:10.

Figurative Usage. Jehovah portrays Jerusalem as once figuratively attired by him in beautiful garments. But she trusted in her prettiness and consorted with the pagan nations, decking herself out to be attractive, as a prostitute.—Eze 16:10-14; see also Eze 23:26, 27; Jer 4:30, 31.

Clothing is used symbolically in many Bible passages. Jehovah portrays himself as clothed with dignity, splendor, eminence, light, righteousness, zeal, and vengeance. (Ps 93:1; 104:1, 2; Isa 59:17) He is said to clothe his people in garments of righteousness and salvation. (Ps 132:9; Isa 61:10) His enemies will be clothed with shame and humiliation. (Ps 35:26) Paul commands Christians to strip off the old personality and to clothe themselves with the new personality, some of the features of which are the tender affections of compassion, kindness, lowliness of mind, long-suffering, and, especially, love.—Col 3:9-14.

Many other symbolic references are made to clothing. Just as a uniform or special attire identifies one as belonging to a certain organization or supporting a certain movement, so clothing, as used symbolically in the Bible, indicates the identification of a person by the stand he takes and his activities in harmony with it, as in the case of Jesus' illustration of the marriage garment. (Mt 22:11, 12; see HEADDRESS; SANDAL.) At Revelation

16:14, 15, the Lord Jesus Christ warns against falling asleep spiritually and being stripped of one's identity as a faithful witness of the true God. This could be disastrous on the eve of "the war of the great day of God the Almighty."

DRINK OFFERING. See OFFERINGS.

DRUNKENNESS.

The condition of being intoxicated because of excessive drinking of alcoholic beverages. A drunkard is a person who habitually overindulges in strong drink to the point of drunkenness.

Intoxicating drinks in ancient Biblical lands included wine made from grapes (De 32:14) and alcoholic beverages prepared from other fruits such as the pomegranate (Ca 8:2) or from grains. (Isa 1:22) Moderate use of wine and other strong drinks is acceptable to Jehovah, who provides "wine that makes the heart of mortal man rejoice."—Ps 104:14, 15; see BEER, II; WINE AND STRONG DRINK.

Condemned in the Bible. Use of strong drink to the point of drunkenness is strongly censured in the Bible. The wise writer of Proverbs paints a vivid and scientifically accurate picture of the effects of drinking alcoholic beverages to excess. He warns: "Who has woe? Who has uneasiness? Who has contentions? Who has concern? Who has wounds for no reason? Who has dullness of eyes? Those staying a long time with the wine, those coming in to search out mixed wine. Do not look at wine when it exhibits a red color, when it gives off its sparkle in the cup [when the wine looks unduly attractive, sparkling], when it goes with a slickness [when it slides down the throat too easily]. At its end it bites just like a serpent, and it secretes poison just like a viper [it can make one sick physically (for example, causing cirrhosis of the liver) and mentally (producing delirium tremens), and it can actually kill]. Your own eyes will see strange things [the alcohol acts on the control centers of the brain, repressing them; attitudes normally repressed come to the fore; hallucinations appear; gaps in memory are filled by the individual's telling fantastic experiences in a most plausible way; the person exhibits uninhibited behavior], and your own heart will speak perverse things [thoughts and desires normally suppressed will be expressed]."—Pr 23:29-33; Ho 4:11; Mt 15:18, 19.

The drunkard's personal experience is described as the writer continues: "And you will certainly become like one lying down in the heart of the sea [experiencing the confusion of one drowning, finally passing into unconsciousness], even like one lying down at the top of a mast [as the rocking of the ship is greatest at this point, the drunkard's life is in danger from accident, stroke, a fight, and so forth]. 'They have struck me, but I did not become sick; they have smitten me, but I did not know it [says the drunkard, as if talking to himself; he was insensible to what was actually going on and to the punishment that the experience has inflicted on him]. When shall I wake up? I shall seek it yet some more [he must now sleep off the effects of overindulgence, but he is enslaved by the drink and looks forward to drinking more when he is able].'" He will come to poverty, by spending excessive amounts for liquor and also by becoming unreliable and rendering himself unable to work.—Pr 23:20, 21, 34, 35.

Prohibited in the Christian Congregation. The drunkard is prone to boisterousness or rough, unrestrained noisiness and to ridiculous actions, bringing reproach. (Pr 20:1; Ps 107:27; Isa 19:14) Consequently, the practice of drunkenness is not to be tolerated in the Christian congregation. God's attitude toward drunkenness was revealed in his Law to Israel. A son who was stubborn and rebellious, who was a glutton and a drunkard, was to be stoned to death. (De 21:18-21) Similarly, the Bible commands that unrepentant or habitual drunkards are to be expelled from the Christian congregation. (1Co 5:11-13) "The works of the flesh" include "drunken bouts, revelries," which things the nations in general practice. A Christian, having been cleansed from such practices but thereafter returning to them and proving unrepentant, would be prevented from entering God's Kingdom. (1Co 6:9-11) He is to cease spending his time working out the will of the nations by engaging in their excesses with wine and their drinking matches. (1Pe 4:3) He must devote himself to producing the fruits of God's spirit.—Ga 5:19-24.

Moderation and soundness of mind are therefore among the requirements for Christian overseers (1Ti 3:1-3; Tit 1:7); ministerial servants (1Ti 3:8); aged men and women (Tit 2:2, 3); young men and women (Tit 2:4-8); children (especially those of overseers).—Tit 1:6.

In discussing the Lord's Evening Meal, the apostle Paul reproved the Corinthian Christians for certain abuses. There were those who brought their own food and drink to the congregation's meeting place. Though overindulging in food and drink, they refused to share of their abundance and thus shamed their needy brothers. Hence, when it came time for the observance of the Lord's Evening Meal, some were not in a fit condition to partake because of excesses, while others were hungry. That is why Paul said: "One is hungry but another is intoxicated."—1Co 11: 20-22.

As shown in the Law, it is not fitting to indulge in alcoholic beverages just before engaging in religious service. The priests of Israel were commanded that they must drink no wine or intoxicating liquor while engaging in their official duties, lest they should die.—Le 10:8-11.

Why does the Bible tell about such men as Noah and Lot getting intoxicated?

Several instances of drunkenness are mentioned in the Bible when such incidents throw light on some important matter. Thus it relates that, after the Flood, Noah planted a vineyard, "began drinking of the wine and became intoxicated." This happening is recorded in the Scriptures to show how Noah's curse on Canaan came to be uttered. (Ge 9:20-27) In another case, on two different nights, Lot's two daughters gave him so much wine that he became drunk and they had sexual relations with him. (Ge 19:30-38) This account enlightens us on the origin of the nations of Moab and Ammon and their relationship to Israel. Lot was evidently drunk enough to lose control of his good sense but not dead drunk, that is, not too drunk to have sexual relations. Since God's Word so strongly condemns drunkenness, we can be sure that these righteous men were not habitual in drinking to excess, were not drunkards. But the candor of the Bible is here illustrated, in its not sparing the truth when relating events involving Bible personages for our enlightenment. Some other cases of drunkenness are recorded at 1 Samuel 25:36-38; 2 Samuel 11:13; 1 Kings 20:15-21.

A False Supposition. When the holy spirit was poured out upon Christ's disciples on Pentecost of 33 C.E., they spoke in different languages and some said: "They are full of sweet wine." But Peter explained: "These people are, in fact, not drunk, as you suppose, for it is the third hour of the day," or about 9:00 a.m., counting from sunrise (about 6:00 a.m.). (Ac 2:1-4, 13-15) These observers of Pentecost had the scroll of Isaiah's prophecy, where it is written: "Woe to those who are getting up early in the morning that they may seek just intoxicating liquor." (Isa 5:11) Actually, it was not customary to have a feast or banquet at that early hour, and it was unrealistic to think that 120 people would all be drunk together at that time of morning. Paul expresses the custom when he says: "Those who get drunk are usually drunk at night."—1Th 5:7.

Figurative Drunkenness. The leaders of the ten-tribe kingdom, with Ephraim as its dominant tribe, were spiritually drunk with "wine." For one thing, they doted on political independence and alliances with the enemies of the kingdom of Judah, whose kings sat on "Jehovah's throne." (1Ch 29:23) They doubtless had their literal drunken bouts as well. These men were in a covenant with Jehovah God but were violating it in an arrogant, drunken way and reproaching him.—Isa 28:1-4.

Similarly, the priests and leaders of Judah became figuratively drunk. As religious guides, they added traditions of men; they saw and spoke false things about God's holy nation. They looked to Assyria for help instead of to God. (Isa 29:1, 9-14; 2Ki 16:5-9) As foretold, drunken Israel was carried off by Assyria in 740 B.C.E. Later, apostate Judah was forced to drink the cup of Jehovah's rage and was sent reeling into exile to Babylon in 607 B.C.E. (Isa 51:17-23) Because of Babylon's harsh treatment of God's people, Babylon ("the king of Sheshach") drank the same cup 68 years later.—Jer 25:15-29.

Symbolic "Babylon the Great" is depicted in the Bible as a drunken prostitute, having in her hand a golden cup "full of disgusting things and the unclean things of her fornication." Earth's inhabitants have been made drunk with "the wine of her fornication." She herself is "drunk with the blood of the holy ones and with the blood of the witnesses of Jesus." Her debauchery will result in her everlasting destruction.—Re 17:1-6, 16; 14:8; 18:8; see BABYLON THE GREAT.

DRUSILLA (Dru·sil'la). The third and youngest daughter of Herod Agrippa I, born about 38 C.E.; sister of Agrippa II, Bernice, and Mariamne III. Her mother's name was Cypros. Before she was six years old, her marriage to prince Epiphanes of Commagene was arranged, but it never materialized because of the refusal of the groom-to-be to embrace Judaism. A Syrian king, Azizus of Emesa, met the terms of circumcision, and Drusilla became his bride at the age of 14. Aggravated by his cruelty and nettled by the envy of her less attractive sister Bernice, Drusilla was easily induced to divorce Azizus, contrary to

Jewish law, and marry Governor Felix about 54 C.E. Perhaps she was present when prisoner Paul "talked about righteousness and self-control and the judgment to come," which proved to be most disquieting subjects for Governor Felix. After two years, when Felix turned the governorship over to Festus, he left Paul in chains "to gain favor with the Jews," which some think was done to please his youthful wife "who was a Jewess." (Ac 24:24-27) Drusilla's son by Felix was another Agrippa, reportedly killed in the great eruption of Mount Vesuvius in 79 C.E.

DUKE.

A man who is appointed, installed, invested as a prince or principal one. Five Midianite chieftains, "dukes of Sihon," called "kings of Midian" at Numbers 31:8, were killed when Israel took vengeance on the Midianites for the affair of the Baal of Peor. (Jos 13:21) The leaders of the enemies of God's people are called "dukes" ("princes," *AT; KJ; RS*) at Psalm 83:11. The Hebrew term *na·sikh'* (duke) appears also at Ezekiel 32:30.

A Messianic prophecy states that, when the enemies of God's people come against them, "seven shepherds, yes, eight dukes of mankind ["princes of men," *KJ*, margin; *RS*]" will be raised up. Seven representing completeness, the "eight dukes" would evidently mean that a considerable number of capable men appointed under the Messiah would be taking the lead among Jehovah's people.—Mic 5:5.

DUMAH (Du'mah).

1. The sixth in the list of Ishmael's 12 sons. By the marriage of his sister Mahalath, Dumah became the brother-in-law to his half cousin Esau. Dumah also became a chieftain and head of a clan, or nation, in fulfillment of Jehovah's promise to Abraham.—Ge 17:20; 25:14-16; 28:9; 1Ch 1:30.

The Ishmaelite Dumah evidently gave his name to a region in N Arabia about midway between the Promised Land and S Babylonia. The name continues in that of the oasis Dumat al-Ghandal (now known as Al-Jawf). Assyrian King Sennacherib mentions an *Adummatu*, which was "situated in the desert." Esar-haddon says that an Adumu was conquered by his father Sennacherib.

2. A city listed among those assigned to the tribe of Judah after the conquest of the land by Joshua. (Jos 15:52) It was in the mountainous region and is identified with Khirbet Domeh ed-Deir (Duma), about 15 km (9 mi) SW of Hebron.

3. At Isaiah 21:11 a pronouncement is made against "Dumah." However, mention is immediately made of "Seir," and this may indicate that the message is directed against Edom. (Ge 32:3) The Greek *Septuagint* at Isaiah 21:11 says "Idumea" (the land of the Edomites) rather than "Dumah."

DUNG.

The excrement of humans, birds, and beasts is represented by various words in Biblical languages. In the Scriptures, dung often has figurative associations.

A "private place" or "privy" was at the service of Israel's soldiers outside their army camps, and they were to cover their excrement. (De 23:12-14) This preserved the army's cleanness before Jehovah and also helped to prevent the spread of fly-borne infectious diseases.

One of Jerusalem's gates was the "Gate of the Ash-heaps," usually called "the Dung Gate." (Ne 2:13; 3:13, 14; 12:31) It was situated a thousand cubits (445 m; 1,458 ft) to the E of the Valley Gate and hence to the S of Mount Zion. This gate was probably so named because of the refuse heaped up in the Valley of Hinnom located below it and to which it led; the city's garbage was possibly taken out through this gate.

Some of the nomadic peoples may have used dung as fuel. Ezekiel, enacting a scene prophetic of Jerusalem's siege, objected when God commanded him to use human excrement for fuel in baking bread. God kindly permitted him to use cattle manure instead. (Eze 4:12-17) This seems to indicate that it was not the normal practice in Israel.

Dung was used as manure to fertilize the soil. Straw and dung seem to have been mixed in "a manure place," the straw possibly being trodden into it by animals. (Isa 25:10) A way to fertilize a fig tree was to "dig around it and put on manure." —Lu 13:8.

Generally, dung was considered to be offensive refuse, something for disposal. Expressive of its offensiveness and also giving force to the thought of removal were Jehovah's words concerning the wayward house of Israel's King Jeroboam: "I shall indeed make a clean sweep behind the house of Jeroboam, just as one clears away the dung until it is disposed of."—1Ki 14:10.

Turning a man's house into a public privy was the greatest insult and a punishment. (Ezr 6:11; Da 2:5; 3:29) During the test of godship atop Mount Carmel, Elijah taunted the prophets of unresponsive Baal by saying: "He must be concerned with a matter, and he has excrement and has to go to the privy." (1Ki 18:27) Jehu later had the house of Baal pulled down, and "they kept it set aside for privies."—2Ki 10:27.

Dung or manure is also employed as a simile to denote an ignominious end of an individual or a nation. (2Ki 9:36, 37; Ps 83:10; Jer 8:1, 2; 9:22; 16:4) God foretold that during his controversy with the nations those slain by Jehovah would not be bewailed, gathered up, or buried, but they would become "as manure on the surface of the ground."—Jer 25:31-33; compare Zep 1:14-18.

According to the Law, no sin offering, the blood of which was brought into the sanctuary to make atonement, was to be eaten by the priest. Its carcass and its dung were to be burned in a clean place outside the camp. (Le 4:11, 12; 6:30; 16:27) This was because none of the animal was to be put to any other use or allowed to decay. It was "clean," that is, sanctified to Jehovah and therefore had to be burned in a clean place.—Compare Heb 13:11-13.

Paul, who highly esteemed spiritual things and greatly valued his hope in Christ, declared: "On account of him I have taken the loss of all things and I consider them as a lot of refuse, that I may gain Christ and be found in union with him." (Php 3:8, 9) The Greek word here rendered "refuse" (sky'ba·lon) denotes either excrement or the things left from a feast and thrown away from the table. Even if the apostle had the latter meaning in mind, his evaluation of "all things" as "refuse" emphasizes the high value he placed on gaining and being found in union with Christ. —See DOVE'S DUNG.

Regarding the expression "dungy idols," see IDOL, IDOLATRY (Viewpoint of God's Servants Toward Idolatry).

DUNGEON. A dark, small room, usually underground, used as a prison. The Hebrew word for "dungeon" (mas·ger') comes from a root meaning "shut; close." (Ge 19:6; Jg 3:23) David felt as though he were in a dungeon at the time he was hiding in a cave as an outlaw refugee from King Saul. His circumstances looked very dark, his life was constantly in danger, traps were in his pathway, and there was no other place to flee. He prayed to Jehovah for liberation. (Ps 142:7) Isaiah uses the term symbolically in two places: (1) In connection with Jehovah's giving attention to "the army of the height" (possibly meaning the disobedient angels) and "the kings of the ground," the prophet states that they will "be shut up in the dungeon" and given attention "after an abundance of days," perhaps alluding to the temporary release of the disobedient angels. (Isa 24:21, 22;

compare Re 20:1-3.) (2) At Isaiah 42:7, the prophet refers to the dungeon when foretelling a liberation from spiritual darkness and imprisonment. The aged Simeon, under inspiration, applied the latter prophecy to those to whom Jesus Christ would bring the light of truth.—Lu 2:25-32; see PRISON.

DURA (Du'ra). The plain where Nebuchadnezzar set up a gold image.—Da 3:1.

It is Biblically described as being "in the jurisdictional district of Babylon," and so apparently was relatively near that city. For this reason, some scholars today accept Tulul Dura, 10 km (6 mi) SE of Babylon, as the most likely of the many proposed sites. The ruins of a dried-brick mound measuring 14 m (46 ft) square were discovered here and have been conjectured by some to be the base of Nebuchadnezzar's image. Nevertheless, the Akkadian term duru, meaning "circuit," "wall," or "walled place," appears frequently in Mesopotamian place-names, making any positive identification impossible at this time.

DUST. Fine particles of matter, light enough to be raised and borne easily by currents of air. Strong winds passing over dry desert regions, common to Bible lands, often produce violent dust storms that are considered by some to be more dreadful than storms encountered at sea. Volcanic eruptions, fires, and agricultural activities are among common causes of mineral dust. Vegetable matter produces dust in the form of pollen, molds, plant fiber, and seed parts. Animals also indirectly produce dust, resulting from dried dung, fine hair, and bacteria. The most common Biblical word for dust is the Hebrew 'a·phar', which may also denote "dry earth" and "clay mortar."—Ge 26:15; Le 14:41, 42.

Although some may consider dust to be a nuisance, it is a provision of the Creator that is essential to mankind's existence and comfort. It is an important factor in the condensation of moisture in the form of rain, fog, or mist, which are vital to plant growth. Moreover, without the light-scattering property of atmospheric dust, the eyes of earth's creatures would be exposed to the unbearable glare of the sun's direct rays, and the familiar phenomenon of dusk and beautifully colored sunsets would cease to occur.

The Creator used "dust from the ground" when he formed the first man (Ge 2:7; 1Co 15:47, 48), and when Adam was sentenced for disobeying God's law, Jehovah decreed: "To dust you will return." (Ge 3:19) God also pronounced a curse of great prophetic significance when saying to the serpent in Eden: "Upon your belly you will go and dust is what you will eat [or, bite] all the days of your life."—Ge 3:14.

Frailty, Mortality, and Lowliness. In view of man's fall from perfection, dust is sometimes used figuratively for mankind's frailty. God shows mercy to those fearing him, "remembering that we are dust." (Ps 103:13, 14; Ge 18:27) It is also symbolic of the mortality of humans, for at death "back to their dust they go." (Ps 104:29; Ec 3:19, 20; 12:1, 7) Since man returns to the dust at death, the grave is sometimes figuratively called "the dust." (Ps 22:29; 30:9) The dust of the ground can denote a lowly condition. Jehovah is "a Raiser of a lowly one from the dust."—1Sa 2:8; Ps 113:7.

Representing Numerousness. In the Scriptures the numerousness of people or the inability of humans to state their number is indicated by comparing them to dust particles. Thus, God promised Abram (Abraham): "I will constitute your seed like the dust particles of the earth." (Ge 13:14, 16) Jehovah also made a similar promise to Jacob. (Ge 28:10, 13, 14) Concerning the Israelites during their wilderness trek, Balaam asked: "Who has numbered the dust particles of Jacob, and who has counted the fourth part of Israel?" (Nu 23:10) Jehovah had greatly increased Abraham's offspring through Isaac and Jacob. Jehovah's bountiful provision of quail for his covenant people in the wilderness is indicated by the statement that "he proceeded to make sustenance rain upon them just like dust, even winged flying creatures just like the sand grains of the seas."—Ps 78:27; Ex 16:11-18; Nu 11:31, 32.

Use in God's Judgment of Nations. Because of the nations' relative insignificance from God's standpoint, he accounts them "as the film of dust on the scales." (Isa 40:15) Jehovah's fear-inspiring power was manifested in connection with his blows against one such nation, Egypt. When the third blow was to begin, in keeping with God's command to Moses, "Aaron stretched out his hand with his rod and struck the dust of the earth, and the gnats came to be on man and beast." When this occurred throughout Egypt, the magic-practicing priests, unable to duplicate this miracle, had to admit: "It is the finger of God!" —Ex 8:16-19.

The Israelites, too, were told that if they failed to keep God's commandments, they could expect various maledictions, one of these being drought, for it was stated: "Jehovah will give powder and dust as the rain of your land. From the heavens it will come down upon you until you have been annihilated."—De 28:15, 24.

Symbolic of Lamentation and Debasement. To symbolize their mournful lamentation over Jerusalem's destruction by the Babylonians in 607 B.C.E., the older men of the city are represented as sitting on the earth in silence, having "brought up dust upon their head." (La 2:10) Many years earlier, through Isaiah, Jehovah prophetically called upon Babylon to come down off her throne, saying: "Come down and sit down in the dust, O virgin daughter of Babylon. Sit down on the earth where there is no throne, O daughter of the Chaldeans." (Isa 47:1) Babylon was reduced to this low state in 539 B.C.E., at her conquest by the Medes and Persians. And, because of the destruction of symbolic Babylon the Great, ship captains, voyagers, sailors, and all those making a living by the sea are depicted as throwing dust upon their heads and bemoaning her devastation.—Re 18:17-19.

Other Uses. Dust is also Scripturally linked with repentance. When Job made a retraction for talking without understanding in arguing his case before God, he said: "I do repent in dust and ashes."—Job 42:1, 3, 6.

Causing foes to "lick the dust" means vanquishing them, effecting their complete subjection. (Ps 72:9; Mic 7:16, 17) Tossing dust into the air or throwing it at a person was a way of registering strong disapproval of him. It is a custom in parts of Asia to demand justice against a criminal by throwing dust on him. Unjustifiably enraged by certain words of Paul, a crowd in Jerusalem showed their animosity toward him by "tossing dust into the air." Through their emotional demonstration and their words, they made their disapproval of Paul clear to the military commander. (Ac 22:22-24) Similarly, Shimei manifested disapproval of David's kingship by "walking abreast of him that he might call down evil; and he kept throwing stones while abreast of him, and he threw a lot of dust."—2Sa 16:5-13.

Jesus Christ instructed his disciples that when anyone failed to receive them or listen to their words, they were to shake or wipe the dust off their feet upon leaving that house or that city. This practice served "for a witness against them," implying that Jesus' followers were peacefully departing and leaving that house or that city to the consequences that would come from God. —Mt 10:11-15; Lu 9:5; 10:10-12; Ac 13:50, 51.

DYES, DYEING. The art of imparting particular hues and tints to thread, fabric, and other materials by employing coloring matter was known and practiced before the days of Abraham and is probably as old as the art of weaving. The Israelites used such goods as blue thread, coccus scarlet material, and wool dyed reddish purple for the tabernacle and for priestly garments. (Ex chaps 25-28, 35, 38, 39) Dyeing, more of a domestic activity in earlier times, eventually became quite a commercial enterprise in various

Murex shells; the animal inside was the source of highly prized purple dye

places. The early Egyptians were noted for their particularly brilliant dyed goods (Eze 27:7), and after Egypt's decline, Tyre and other Phoenician cities became important dye centers.

Ancient Processes. Dyeing processes varied from place to place. Sometimes the thread was dyed, whereas in other cases the dye was applied to finished cloth. It seems that thread was bathed in dye twice, being squeezed after its removal from the vat the second time so that the valued dye could be retained. The thread was thereafter laid out so that it could dry.

Each material had to be treated in a different way. Sometimes, though rarely, the coloring matter had a natural affinity for the fiber being dyed. But when that was not so, it was necessary to treat the material first with a mordant, a sub-

stance having an attraction for both the fiber and the dye. To serve as a mordant, a substance must at least have an attraction for the coloring matter, so that it will combine with it to form a colored compound that is insoluble. Discoveries show that the Egyptians employed mordants in dyeing processes. For instance, red, yellow, and blue were three of the colors they used, and it is said that such dyes could not have been fixed without using oxides of arsenic, iron, and tin as mordants.

Evidently, animal skins were first tanned and then dyed. Even recently in Syria, ram skins have been tanned in sumac and then the dye has been applied. After the dye dried, the skins were rubbed with oil and then polished. Shoes and other leather items used by the Bedouin have thus been dyed red and may well remind one of the "ram skins dyed red" used for the tabernacle. —Ex 25:5.

Interesting in connection with dyed materials is a building inscription of Assyrian King Tiglath-pileser III. After telling of his military campaigns against Palestine and Syria, he states that he received tribute from a certain Hiram of Tyre and other rulers. The listed articles include "linen garments with multicolored trimmings, . . . blue-dyed wool, purple-dyed wool, . . . also lambs whose stretched hides were dyed purple, (and) wild birds whose spread-out wings were dyed blue."—*Ancient Near Eastern Texts,* edited by J. Pritchard, 1974, pp. 282, 283.

Sources of Dyes. Dyes were acquired from various sources. In Palestine, yellow dyes were obtained from almond leaves and ground pomegranate rind, though the Phoenicians also used turmeric and safflower. The Hebrews could obtain black dye from the bark of the pomegranate tree and red from the roots of the madder plant (*Rubia tinctorum*). Indigo plants (*Indigofera tinctoria*) that were probably brought into Palestine from Egypt or Syria could be used for blue dye. Part of one method used to impart purple hues to wool consisted of steeping the wool in grape juice overnight and sprinkling powdered madder on it.

Coccus scarlet and crimson dyes had as their source the oldest dyestuff known, a parasitic homopterous insect of the family Coccidae (the *Coccus ilicis*). Because the living female, about the size of a cherry pit, resembles a berry, the Greeks applied to it their word *kok'kos,* meaning "berry." The Arab name for the insect is *qirmiz* or *kermez,* from which the English word "crimson" is derived. This insect is found throughout the Middle East. Only its eggs contain the purplish-red dyestuff, rich in kermesic acid. Toward the end of April, the wingless female, filled with eggs, attaches herself by means of her proboscis to the twigs, and sometimes to the leaves, of the kermes oak (*Quercus coccifera*). The grubs, or kermes, are gathered and dried, and the valued dye is obtained by boiling them in water. This is the red dye that was used extensively for the appurtenances of the tabernacle and for the garments worn by Israel's high priest.

Purple dye was obtained from shellfish or mollusks such as the *Murex trunculus* and *Murex brandaris.* In the neck of these creatures there is a small gland containing but a single drop of fluid called the flower. Initially it has the appearance and consistency of cream, but upon exposure to air and light it gradually changes to a deep violet or reddish purple. These shellfish are found along the shores of the Mediterranean Sea, and the shades of color acquired from them vary according to their location. The larger specimens were broken open individually, and the precious fluid

was carefully removed from them, whereas the smaller ones were crushed in mortars. Since the amount of fluid acquired from each shellfish was quite small, accumulating a considerable amount was a costly process. Hence, this dye was expensive, and garments dyed purple became the mark of wealthy persons or those in high station. (Es 8:15; Lu 16:19) Another shellfish (the cerulean mussel) has been suggested as the source of a blue dye.

Ancient Tyre became famous for a purple or deep-crimson dye known as Tyrian or Imperial purple. Though the Tyrians are said to have employed a method of double-dyeing, the exact formula used to obtain this color is unknown. The coloring matter was evidently obtained from the *Murex* and *Purpura* mollusks, piles of emptied shells of the *Murex trunculus* having been found along the shore of Tyre and in the vicinity of Sidon. The Phoenician city of Tyre is depicted by Jehovah as having wool dyed reddish purple and other colorful materials, as well as carrying on trading in such articles.—Eze 27:2, 7, 24; see COLORS.

E

EAGLE [Heb., *ne'sher;* Aramaic, *neshar';* Gr., *a·e·tos'*]. A large bird of prey. Some believe that the Hebrew name derives from a root word meaning "tear in pieces or lacerate." Others view it as onomatopoeic (that is, a name whose very sound suggests the thing meant) and believe that *ne'sher* represents a "rushing sound," or "gleaming flash," hence a bird that dives after its prey, plummeting downward with a rushing sound and like flashing light through the air. In either case, the Hebrew term well describes the eagle, whose lightning plunge from great heights causes a whining sound as the air rushes through its widespread pinions (the outer wing feathers). A bird of prey and a drinker of blood (Job 39:27, 30), the eagle was included among those birds listed as "unclean" by the Mosaic Law.—Le 11:13; De 14:12.

Palestinian Varieties. Among the eagles to be found in Israel today are the imperial eagle (*Aquila heliaca*), the golden eagle (*Aquila chrysaëtos*), and the short-toed eagle (*Circaëtus gallicus*). The golden eagle, named thus because of

the golden sheen on its head and nape, is an impressive dark-brown bird that measures about 1 m (3 ft) in length, with a total wingspan of about 2 m (6.5 ft). Eagles characteristically have a rather broad head with a projecting ridge above the eyes; a short, powerful, hooked beak; sturdy legs; and sharp, powerful talons.

'Carried on wings of eagles'—what basis is there for such a figure of speech?

The Sinai region is called "eagle country," where the birds soar and glide on their strong, broad wings. So, the liberated Israelites gathered at Mount Sinai could well appreciate the aptness of the picture conveyed by God's words, that he had carried them out of Egypt "on wings of eagles." (Ex 19:4; compare Re 12:14.) Nearly 40 years later Moses could compare Jehovah's leading of Israel through the wilderness to that of an eagle that "stirs up its nest, hovers over its fledglings, spreads out its wings, takes them, carries them on its pinions." (De 32:9-12) When the young eaglets reach the time to begin flying, the parent eagle stirs them up, fluttering and flapping its own wings to convey the idea to its young, and then edges or lures them out of the nest so that they try out their wings.

Though some have doubted that the eagle ever actually carries the young on its back, a guide in Scotland is reported by Sir W. B. Thomas as testifying concerning the golden eagle that "the parent birds, after urging, and sometimes shoving the youngster into the air, will swoop underneath and rest the struggler for a moment on their wings and back." (*The Yeoman's England*, London, 1934, p. 135) An observer in the United States is quoted in the *Bulletin* of the Smithsonian Institution (1937, No. 167, p. 302) as saying: "The mother started from the nest in the crags, and roughly handling the young one, she allowed him to drop, I should say, about ninety feet; then she would swoop down under him, wings spread, and he would alight on her back. She would soar to the top of the range with him and repeat the process. . . . My father and I watched this, spellbound, for over an hour." G. R. Driver, commenting on these statements, says: "The picture [at Deuteronomy 32:11] then is not a mere flight of fancy but is based on actual fact."—*Palestine Exploration Quarterly*, London, 1958, pp. 56, 57.

Lofty Nest and Farsightedness. The nest-building habits of the eagle are emphasized in God's questioning of Job at Job 39:27-30. The nest or aerie may be in a high tree or on the crag of a cliff or rocky canyon. Over the years the nest may grow to be as much as 2 m (6.5 ft) high, that of some eagles coming to weigh as much as a ton! The apparent security and inaccessibility of the eagle's nest were also used figuratively by the prophets in their messages against the lofty kingdom of Edom in the rugged mountains of the Arabah.—Jer 49:16; Ob 3, 4.

The farsightedness of the eagle, mentioned at Job 39:29, is borne out by Rutherford Platt in his book *The River of Life* (1956, pp. 215, 216), which also shows the unusual design of the eye of the eagle, testifying to the Creator's wisdom. The book says:

"We find the championship eyes of the whole animal kingdom . . . [in] the eyes of the eagle, the vulture, and the hawk. So keen are they that they can look down from a thousand feet in the air and spot a rabbit or a grouse half hidden in the grass.

"Sharp eyesight of the hunter eye is caused by the reflection of the object falling on a dense clump of pointed, cone-shaped cells. This tiny spot in the back of the eyeball absorbs light rays from the object through thousands of points, in a special manner which summons up a clear image in the mind. For almost all hunters, such as the skunk, the cougar, and ourselves, the single spot of cones is enough; we look straight ahead and approach directly the object of our gaze. But not so the eagle or the hawk, which, having fixed the rabbit in the grass with its sharp focusing cones, may then approach by a long, slanting dive. This causes the image of the target to move across the back of the eyeball on a curved path. Such a path is precisely plotted for the eagle eye so that instead of a clump of cones the diving bird has a curved path of cones. As the eagle zooms down, the rabbit in the grass is thus held in constant focus."—Compare Jer 49:22.

Flight Abilities. The eagle's swiftness is highlighted in many texts. (2Sa 1:23; Jer 4:13; La 4:19; Hab 1:8) There are reports of eagles surpassing a speed of 130 km/hr (80 mph). Solomon warned that wealth "makes wings for itself" like those of a skyward-bound eagle (Pr 23:4, 5), while Job mourned the swiftness of life's passing, comparing it to the speed of an eagle in search of prey. (Job 9:25, 26) Yet those trusting in Jehovah receive power to go on, as if mounting up on the seemingly tireless wing of the soaring eagle. —Isa 40:31.

Modern scientists have wondered at "the way of an eagle in the heavens," as did the writer of Proverbs 30:19. Clarence D. Cone, Jr., relates the manner in which observation of the majestic and almost effortless soaring of eagles, hawks, and vultures "has helped to lead the way to the discovery of a fundamental mechanism of meteorology." He shows the manner in which such large birds utilize to the full the dynamic power of the great "bubbles" of heated air that float up from the land because of the heat of the sun and the way in which the "slotted" wing tips of the eagle are so designed aerodynamically that they eliminate air drag on the wing.—*Scientific American*, April 1962, pp. 131, 138.

Figurative Usage. This powerful bird of prey was a frequent symbol used by the prophets to represent the warring forces of enemy nations in their sudden and often unexpected attacks. (De 28:49-51; Jer 48:40; 49:22; Ho 8:1) The Babylonian and Egyptian rulers were characterized as eagles. (Eze 17:3, 7) It is notable that in many ancient nations, including Assyria, Persia, and Rome, the figure of the eagle was regularly used on the royal scepters, standards, and steles, even as it has been used in modern times by Germany, the United States, and others.

Some have questioned the use of the word "eagles" at Matthew 24:28 and Luke 17:37, holding that the texts must refer instead to vultures, gathered around a carcass. However, although the eagle is not primarily a carrion eater, as is the vulture, it does feed on such dead bodies at times. (*Palestine Exploration Quarterly*, 1955, p. 9) So too the eagle, though usually a solitary hunter, unlike the gregarious vulture, is known to hunt in pairs occasionally; and the book *The Animal Kingdom* (Vol. II, p. 965) reports an instance in which "a number of them launched a mass attack upon a prong-horned antelope." (Edited by F. Drimmer, 1954) Jesus' prophecy mentioned above was given in connection with his promised "presence." Hence, it would not apply merely to the desolation in 70 C.E. of the Jewish nation by the Roman armies, who had their standards emblazoned with the figures of eagles.

Eagles are used in Revelation to represent creatures attending God's throne and announcing the judgment messages of God for those on earth, doubtless to indicate swiftness and farsightedness.—Re 4:7; 8:13; compare Eze 1:10; 10:14.

Another text that many scholars view as applying to the vulture rather than to the eagle is Micah 1:16, which speaks of Israel's figuratively 'broadening out its baldness like that of the eagle.' The eagle's head is well feathered; even the North American bald eagle is referred to as "bald" only because its white head feathers give it the appearance of baldness from a distance. The griffon vulture (*Gyps fulvus*), still to be seen in Israel, has only some soft white down on its head, and the neck is sparsely feathered. If the text applies to it, this would indicate that the Hebrew *ne'sher* has broader application than to the eagle only. It may be noted that the griffon vulture, while not classed by ornithologists as of the same "species" or "genus" as the eagle, is counted as of the same "family" (Accipitridae). Some, however, believe Micah 1:16 has reference to the molting that the eagle undergoes, although this is said to be a gradual and rather inconspicuous process. This molting process, bringing some reduction of activity and strength and followed by a renewal of normal life, may be what the psalmist meant by one's youth "renewing

itself just like that of an eagle." (Ps 103:5) Others see in this a reference to the relatively long life of the eagle, some having been known to reach an age of 80 years.

The name Aquila (Ac 18:2) is Latin for eagle.

EAR. The organ for hearing, designed and created by Jehovah God. (Ps 94:9; Pr 20:12) The ear consists of three parts: the outer ear, the middle ear, and the inner ear. The middle ear is a small chamber that begins with the eardrum and leads to the maze of passageways that constitute the inner ear. Besides its function in connection with hearing, the inner ear also possesses organs having to do with balance and motion. The use of two ears greatly helps a person to locate the source and direction of sounds.

The human ear detects sounds within the range of about 20 to 20,000 cycles per second. The ears of many animals are sensitive to tones of higher pitch that are inaudible to the human ear. The range of sound energy perceived by the human ear is remarkable. The loudest sound that the ear can tolerate without danger is two million million times as powerful as the least perceptible sound. The human ear has the maximum sensitivity that it is practical to possess, for if the ears were any keener they would respond to the unceasing molecular motions of the air particles themselves.

Since the Maker of the ear can hear, the Bible speaks of him as possessing ears, symbolically. (Nu 11:18; Ps 116:1, 2) By this symbolism Jehovah pictures himself as having ears open to the prayers, petitions, and cries of the righteous. (Ps 10:17; 18:6; 34:15; 130:2; Isa 59:1; 1Pe 3:12) While he hears the murmurings of complainers and the wicked speech of his enemies (Nu 11:1; 2Ki 19:28), he refuses to hear their distress calls when execution of judgment catches up with them. (Eze 8:18) Although idol images may have ears carved or engraved on them, they, of course, cannot hear and are powerless to receive or answer the prayers of their worshipers.—Ps 115:6.

Figurative Use. In the Bible the word "ear" is used very forcefully in a figurative sense as representing the complete process of hearing. The term is used with respect to the faculty of hearing and then weighing the truthfulness and value of what is spoken. (Job 12:11; 34:3) The way the expression "give ear" or 'incline one's ear' is used indicates that it means to pay attention with a view to acting on that which is heard. (Ps 78:1; 86:6; Isa 51:4) To 'have the ears opened' means that the individual receives understanding or enlightenment on a matter. (Isa 50:5) The expression 'uncover the ear' may originate from the fact that, in Oriental lands, a person would partially remove the headdress in order to hear more clearly. This expression, as well as the phrase 'disclose to the ear,' refers to the giving of information in private or the revealing of a secret or something not previously known.—1Sa 9:15; 20:2, 12, 13; 2Sa 7:27.

An 'awakened ear' is one that is made attentive. (Isa 50:4) Such an ear may belong to a person who has formerly been among the ones "deaf [spiritually] though they have [literal] ears." (Isa 43:8) The righteous man is described in the Bible as listening to God but stopping up his ear to wickedness. (Isa 33:15) Similarly, the Greek word for "listen" may have the sense of 'giving attention to, understanding, and acting upon,' as when Jesus Christ said: "My sheep listen to my voice," and, "a stranger they will by no means follow but will flee from him, because they do not know the voice of strangers."—Joh 10:27, 5.

On the other hand, the ears of the rebellious ones are said to be "heavy" (KJ) or "unresponsive," and they 'hear with annoyance.' (Isa 6:10; Mt 13:15; Ac 28:27) Such wicked ones are likened to the cobra that stops up its ears, refusing to listen to the voice of the charmer.—Ps 58:4.

Jehovah, through his servants, spoke of the stubborn, disobedient Israelites as having 'uncircumcised ears.' (Jer 6:10; Ac 7:51) They are as though stopped up with something that impedes hearing. They are ears that have not been opened by Jehovah, who gives ears of understanding and obedience to those who seek him but allows the spiritual hearing of the disobedient ones to become dulled. (De 29:4; Ro 11:8) The apostle Paul foretold a time when some professing to be Christians would apostatize from the true faith, not wanting to hear the truth of God's Word, but desiring to have their ears "tickled" by things pleasing to them, and would therefore listen to false teachers. (2Ti 4:3, 4; 1Ti 4:1) Also, one's ears may "tingle" because of hearing startling news, especially news of calamity.—1Sa 3:11; 2Ki 21:12; Jer 19:3.

When Saul of Tarsus was blinded by a supernatural light, did the men with him hear the voice that Saul heard?

An example where literal hearing of a sound and hearing with understanding are contrasted is found in the account of the conversion of Saul of Tarsus and his own recounting of it later. (Ac 9:3-8; 22:6-11) The account at Acts 9:7 says that the men with Saul heard "a voice" (KJ) or "the sound of a voice." (NW) Yet, as recorded at Acts 22:9, Paul (Saul) says that the men with him did not hear the voice. When what was said in the two verses is properly understood, there is no contradiction. The Greek word for "voice" (pho·ne') at Acts 9:7 is in the genitive case (pho·nes') and gives, in this verse, the sense of hearing of a voice—hearing the sound but not understanding. At Acts 22:9 pho·ne' is in the accusative case (pho·nen'): the men "did not hear the voice" —they heard the sound of a voice but did not get the words, the meaning; they did not understand what Jesus was saying to Saul, as Saul did. (Ac 9:4) This knowledge of the Bible's use of the idea of 'hearing' in both senses helps to clear up what would otherwise seem to be discrepancies.

At the installation of the priesthood in Israel, Moses was commanded to take some of the blood of the ram of the installation and put it on the lobe of the right ear of Aaron and of each of his sons, as well as on the right hand and right foot, indicating that what they listened to, the work they did, and the way they walked should be directly affected by what was there taking place. (Le 8:22-24) Similarly, in the case of the cleansed leper, the Law said that the priest was to put some of the blood of the ram offered as a guilt offering, as well as some of the oil offered, on the lobe of the leper's right ear. (Le 14:14, 17, 25, 28) An arrangement of comparable nature was found in the provision made for the man who wished to continue in slavery to his master to time indefinite. In such case the slave was to be brought to the doorpost, and his master was to pierce his ear through with an awl. This prominent mark, being made on the organ for hearing, evidently represented the slave's desire to continue in obedient attention to his master.—Ex 21:5, 6.

Regarding man's great need to hear God, in the sense of giving close attention and obedience to his words as the Bible directs, rather than to see God as some demand, R. C. Dentan remarks: "In the Bible, the key word for man's response to God is 'hearing' rather than 'seeing' . . . For the mystery religions the highest religious experience was that of 'seeing' the god; but for the Bible, where the basic religious attitude is obedience to the divine word, the emphasis is on 'hearing' his voice. The most important formula of Israel's religion begins characteristically:

'Hear, O Israel.' 'He who is of God' is not the mystic who has seen a vision, but one who 'hears the words of God' (John 8:47)."—*The Interpreter's Dictionary of the Bible,* edited by G. Buttrick, 1962, Vol. 2, p. 1; see DEAFNESS.

EARDROP. See EARRING.

EARRING. A ring or other ornament worn on the ear for purposes of adornment. The Hebrews do not appear to have had a specific word for "earring," for one of the words they applied to this ornament (*ne'zem*) can be used for either a nose ring or an earring. (Pr 11:22; Ex 32:2) The context in which *ne'zem* appears in the Scriptures sometimes, though not always, makes it possible to determine whether an earring or a nose ring is meant. Probably in many cases earrings and nose rings varied little in shape. The Hebrew word *'a·ghil'* is also used to designate an earring and relates to a circular ornament.—Nu 31:50; Eze 16:12.

In many nations of antiquity men, women, and children all wore earrings. That they were worn by men of many lands is evident from representations of foreigners on Egyptian monuments. However, in Egypt it seems that it was not customary for men to wear earrings, and it is uncertain whether Israelite men customarily wore them or not. Earrings were worn by the Midianites, from whom the Israelites took them as part of the spoils of war. (Nu 31:1, 2, 50) When Aaron was about to make the golden calf in the wilderness, he instructed the Israelites: "Tear off the gold earrings that are in the ears of your wives, of your sons and of your daughters and bring them to me."—Ex 32:1-4.

Common with Egyptian women were earrings consisting of large golden hoops, some being 4 to 5 cm (1.5 to 2 in.) in diameter, though others were even larger and were made of as many as six individual rings soldered together. Silver earrings were found at Thebes, some of them being merely studs. At times Egyptian earrings, like those of the Assyrians, were quite elaborately designed; some of them were cross-shaped. It was customary to attach the earring by passing the ring itself or a hook through a hole that had been pierced in one's earlobe.

In ancient Egypt, persons of high station sometimes wore golden ear ornaments having the form of an asp, the body of which was studded with precious stones. Middle Eastern earrings at times consisted of rings to which jewels of some sort were attached as pendants. Some were

called "eardrops" (Heb., *neti·phohth'*, from *na·taph'* [meaning "drip" or "drop"]). This term evidently relates to a drop-shaped ornament or pendant. "Eardrops" could have been pearls or spherical beads of silver or gold, but they are not described in the Bible. (Jg 8:26) They were among the things Jehovah said he would take away from the haughty "daughters of Zion."—Isa 3:16, 19.

Faithful Hebrews and Christians did not wear earrings as amulets, though others of ancient times did so. While the Bible does not specifically say that "the earrings" possessed by Jacob's household had been viewed as amulets, Jacob buried both "the foreign gods" and "the earrings" of his household under the big tree near Shechem. (Ge 35:2-4) "The ornamental humming shells" possessed by the haughty "daughters of Zion" were charms of some type that may have been suspended from necklaces or worn on the ears.—Isa 3:20.

When Israel was granted the privilege of making contributions for the tabernacle, willing-hearted persons donated various articles, including earrings. (Ex 35:20-22) Centuries later, Jehovah told Jerusalem that, among other things, he had shown her love by placing earrings on her ears. (Eze 16:1, 2, 12) And Solomon used a gold earring illustratively when he said: "An earring of gold, and an ornament of special gold, is a wise reprover upon the hearing ear."—Pr 25:1, 12.

EARTH. The fifth-largest planet of the solar system and the third in order of position from the sun. It is an oblate spheroid, being slightly flattened at the poles. Satellite observations have indicated other slight irregularities in the shape of the earth. Its mass is approximately 5.98×10^{24} kg (13.18×10^{24} lb). Its area is about 510,-000,000 sq km (197,000,000 sq mi). Earth's measurements are (approximately): circumference at the equator, just over 40,000 km (24,900 mi); diameter at the equator, 12,750 km (7,920 mi). Oceans and seas cover approximately 71 percent of its surface, leaving about 149,000,000 sq km (57,500,000 sq mi) of land surface.

The earth rotates on its axis, bringing about day and night. (Ge 1:4, 5) A solar day or an apparent day is a period of 24 hours, the time taken for an observer at any one point on the earth to be again in the same position relative to the sun. The tropical year, which concerns the return of the seasons, the interval between two consecutive returns of the sun to the vernal equinox, is 365 days, 5 hours, 48 minutes, and 46 seconds, on the average. This figure is the one used in solar-year calendar reckoning, and its fractional nature has caused much difficulty in accurate calendar making.

The axis of the earth tilts 23° 27′ away from a perpendicular to the earth's orbit. The gyroscopic effect of rotation holds the earth's axis in basically the same direction relative to the stars regardless of its location in its orbit around the sun. This tilt of the axis brings about the seasons.

The earth's atmosphere, composed principally of nitrogen, oxygen, water vapor, and other gases, extends over 960 km (600 mi) above the earth's surface. Beyond this is what is termed "outer space."

Bible Terms and Significance.   In the Hebrew Scriptures, the word used for earth as a planet is *'e'rets*. *'E'rets* refers to (1) earth, as opposed to heaven, or sky (Ge 1:2); (2) land, country, territory (Ge 10:10); (3) ground, surface of the ground (Ge 1:26); (4) people of all the globe (Ge 18:25).

The word *'adha·mah'* is translated "ground," "soil," or "land." *'Adha·mah'* refers to (1) ground as tilled, yielding sustenance (Ge 3:23); (2) piece of ground, landed property (Ge 47:18); (3) earth as material substance, soil, dirt (Jer 14:4; 1Sa 4:12); (4) ground as earth's visible surface (Ge 1:25); (5) land, territory, country (Le 20:24); (6) whole earth, inhabited earth (Ge 12:3). *'Adha·mah'* seems to be related etymologically to the word *'a·dham'*, the first man Adam having been made from the dust of the ground.—Ge 2:7.

In the Greek Scriptures, *ge* denotes earth as arable land or soil. (Mt 13:5, 8) It is used to designate the material from which Adam was made, the earth (1Co 15:47); the earthly globe (Mt 5:18, 35; 6:19); earth as a habitation for human creatures and animals (Lu 21:35; Ac 1:8; 8:33; 10:12; 11:6; 17:26); land, country, territory (Lu 4:25; Joh 3:22); ground (Mt 10:29; Mr 4:26); land, shore, as contrasted with seas or waters. (Joh 21:8, 9, 11; Mr 4:1).

Oi·kou·me'ne, translated "world" in the *King James Version*, denotes "inhabited earth."—Mt 24:14; Lu 2:1; Ac 17:6; Re 12:9.

In each case of all the above senses in which these words are used, the form of the word in the original language, and more particularly the setting or context, determine which sense is meant.

The Hebrews divided the earth into four quarters or regions corresponding to the four points of the compass. In the Hebrew Scriptures the words "before" and "in front of" designate and are translated "east" (Ge 12:8); "behind" may mean "west" (Isa 9:12); "the right side" may denote "south" (1Sa 23:24); and "the left" may be translated "north" (Job 23:8, 9; compare *Ro*). East was also (in Heb.) sometimes called the sunrising, as for example, at Joshua 4:19. West (in Heb.) was the setting of the sun. (2Ch 32:30) Also, physical characteristics were used. Being almost the total western boundary of Palestine, the "Sea" (the Mediterranean) was sometimes used for west. —Nu 34:6.

Creation.   The planet's coming into existence is recounted in the Bible with the simple statement: "In the beginning God created the heavens and the earth." (Ge 1:1) Just how long ago the starry heavens and the earth were created is not stated in the Bible. Therefore, there is no basis for Bible scholars to take issue with scientific calculations of the age of the planet. Scientists estimate the age of some rocks as being three and a half billion years, and the earth itself as being about four to four and a half billion or more years.

As to time, the Scriptures are more definite about the six creative days of the Genesis account. These days have to do, not with the creation of earth's matter or material, but with the arranging and preparing of it for man's habitation.

The Bible does not reveal whether God created life on any of the other planets in the universe. However, astronomers today have not found proof that life exists on any of these planets and, in fact, know of no planet besides the earth that is at present capable of supporting the life of fleshly creatures.

Purpose.   Like all other created things, the earth was brought into existence because of Jehovah's will ("pleasure," *KJ*). (Re 4:11) It was created to remain forever. (Ps 78:69; 104:5; 119: 90; Ec 1:4) God speaks of himself as a God of purpose and declares that his purposes are certain to come to fruition. (Isa 46:10; 55:11) He made his purpose for the earth very clear when he said to the first human pair: "Be fruitful and become many and fill the earth and subdue it, and have in subjection the fish of the sea and the flying creatures of the heavens and every living creature that is moving upon the earth." (Ge 1:28) There were no flaws in earth or the things on it. Having created all necessary things, Jehovah saw that they were "very good" and "proceeded to rest" or desist from other earthly creative works.—Ge 1:31–2:2.

Man's habitation on earth is also permanent. When God gave man the law regarding the tree of the knowledge of good and bad, he implied that man could live on earth forever. (Ge 2:17) We are assured by Jehovah's own words that "all the days the earth continues, seed sowing and harvest, and cold and heat, and summer and winter, and day and night, will never cease" (Ge 8:22) and that he will never destroy all flesh again by a flood. (Ge 9:12-16) Jehovah says that he did not make the earth for nothing but, rather, that he has given it to men as a home and that death will eventually be done away with. God's purpose, therefore, is for the earth to be the habitation of man in perfection and happiness with eternal life.—Ps 37:11; 115:16; Isa 45:18; Re 21:3, 4.

That this is the purpose of Jehovah God, sacred to him and not to be thwarted, is indicated when the Bible says: "And by the seventh day God came to the completion of his work that he had made . . . And God proceeded to bless the seventh day and make it sacred, because on it he has been resting from all his work that God has created for the purpose of making." (Ge 2:2, 3) The seventh, or rest, day is not shown in the Genesis account as ending, as in the case of the other six days. The apostle Paul explained that the rest day of God had been continuous right through Israelite history down to his own time and had not yet ended. (Heb 3:7-11; 4:3-9) God says the seventh day was set aside as sacred to him. He would carry out his purpose toward the earth; it would be fully accomplished during that day, with no necessity of further creative works toward the earth during that time.

The Bible's Harmony With Scientific Facts. The Bible, at Job 26:7, speaks of God as "hanging the earth upon nothing." Science says that the earth remains in its orbit in space primarily because of the interaction of gravity and centrifugal force. These forces, of course, are invisible. Therefore the earth, like other heavenly bodies, is suspended in space as if hanging on nothing. Speaking from Jehovah's viewpoint, the prophet Isaiah wrote under inspiration: "There is One who is dwelling above the circle of the earth, the dwellers in which are as grasshoppers." (Isa 40: 22) The Bible says: "He [God] has described a circle upon the face of the waters." (Job 26:10) The waters are limited by his decree to their proper place. They do not come up and inundate the land; neither do they fly off into space. (Job

38:8-11) From the viewpoint of Jehovah, the earth's face, or the surface of the waters, would, of course, have a circular form, just as the edge of the moon presents a circular appearance to us. Before land surfaces appeared, the surface of the entire globe was one circular (spherical) mass of surging waters.—Ge 1:2.

Bible writers often speak from the standpoint of the observer on the earth, or from his particular position geographically, as we often naturally do today. For example, the Bible mentions "the sunrising." (Nu 2:3; 34:15) Some have seized upon this as an opportunity to discredit the Bible as scientifically inaccurate, claiming that the Hebrews viewed earth as the center of things, with the sun revolving around it. But the Bible writers nowhere expressed such a belief. These same critics overlook the fact that they themselves use the identical expression and that it is in all of their almanacs. It is common to hear someone say, 'it is sunrise,' or 'the sun has set,' or 'the sun traveled across the sky.' The Bible also speaks of "the extremity of the earth" (Ps 46:9), "the ends of the earth" (Ps 22:27), "the four extremities of the earth" (Isa 11:12), "the four corners of the earth," and "the four winds of the earth" (Re 7:1). These expressions cannot be taken to prove that the Hebrews understood the earth to be square. The number four is often used to denote that which is fully rounded out, as it were, just as we have four directions and sometimes employ the expressions "to the ends of the earth," "to the four corners of the earth," in the sense of embracing all the earth.—Compare Eze 1:15-17; Lu 13:29.

Figurative and Symbolic Expressions. The earth is spoken of figuratively in several instances. It is likened to a building, at Job 38:4-6, when Jehovah asks Job questions concerning earth's creation and Jehovah's management of it that Job obviously cannot answer. Jehovah also uses a figurative expression describing the result of earth's rotation. He says: "[The earth] transforms itself like clay under a seal." (Job 38:14) In Bible times some seals for "signing" documents were in the form of a roller engraved with the writer's emblem. It was rolled over the soft clay document or clay envelope, leaving behind it an impression in the clay. In similar manner, at the arrival of dawn, the portion of the earth coming from the blackness of night begins to show itself to have form and color as the sunlight moves progressively across its face. The heavens, the location of Jehovah's throne, being higher than the earth, the earth is, figuratively, his footstool. (Ps 103:11; Isa 55:9; 66:1; Mt 5:35; Ac 7:49)

Those who are in Sheol, or Hades, the common grave of mankind, are regarded as being under the earth.—Re 5:3.

The apostle Peter compares the literal heavens and earth (2Pe 3:5) with the symbolic heavens and earth (2Pe 3:7). "The heavens" of verse 7 do not mean Jehovah's own dwelling place, the place of his throne in the heavens. Jehovah's heavens cannot be shaken. Neither is "the earth" in the same verse the literal planet earth, for Jehovah says that he has established the earth firmly. (Ps 78:69; 119:90) Yet, God says that he will shake both the heavens and the earth (Hag 2:21; Heb 12:26), that the heavens and earth will flee away before him, and that new heavens and a new earth will be established. (2Pe 3:13; Re 20:11; 21:1) It is evident that "heavens" is symbolic and that "earth" here has symbolic reference to a society of people living on the earth, just as at Psalm 96:1.—See HEAVEN (New heavens and new earth).

Earth is also symbolically used to denote the firmer, more stable elements of mankind. The restless, unstable elements of mankind are illustrated by the characteristic restlessness of the sea.—Isa 57:20; Jas 1:6; Jude 13; compare Re 12:16; 20:11; 21:1.

John 3:31 contrasts one that comes from above as being higher than one who comes from the earth (ge). The Greek word e·pi'gei·os, "earthly," is used to denote earthly, physical things, especially as contrasted with heavenly things, and as being lower and of coarser material. Man is made of earth's material. (2Co 5:1; compare 1Co 15:46-49.) Nevertheless, he can please God by living a "spiritual" life, a life directed by God's Word and spirit. (1Co 2:12, 15, 16; Heb 12:9) Because of mankind's fall into sin and their tendency toward material things to the neglect or exclusion of spiritual things (Ge 8:21; 1Co 2:14), "earthly" can have an undesirable connotation, meaning "corrupt," or "in opposition to the spirit." —Php 3:19; Jas 3:15.

EARTHQUAKE.

A sudden tremor or a shaking of the earth's surface as a result of forces at work within the globe. The Hebrew noun ra'ash refers not only to the "quaking" of the earth, or an "earthquake" (1Ki 19:11; Am 1:1), but also to the "tremors" caused by a tramping army (Isa 9: 5, ftn), the "rattling" of war chariots or a javelin (Jer 47:3; Job 41:29), and the "pounding" of horses (Job 39:24). The Greek sei·smos' (earthquake) denotes a quaking, shaking, or trembling.—Mt 27:54; compare Mt 27:51; 28:4; Re 6:13.

Shakings and tremblings of the earth occurred throughout Biblical history, at times as a result of natural geologic forces (Zec 14:5) and sometimes as direct acts of God for judicial purposes or for purposes involving his servants. The geology of the area explains Israel's past history of seismic activity, which still is not finished.

The temple area of Jerusalem is situated on a line of structural weakness within the earth. The Mosque of el-Aqsa, located in the temple area (not the Dome of the Rock, which is a shrine), has been repeatedly damaged by earthquake activity.

A tremendous earthquake, apparently coupled with volcanic action, provided an awe-inspiring setting for the inauguration of the Law covenant at Sinai. (Ex 19:18; Ps 68:8) Jehovah had a direct hand in this display of power, for he spoke out of the mountain by means of an angel.—Ex 19:19; Ga 3:19; Heb 12:18-21.

At times the fear-inspiring force of earthquakes has been an evidence of Jehovah's hand in judging violations of his law. (Na 1:3-6) An earthquake was the executional method used by Jehovah against the rebellious Dathan, Abiram, and the household of Korah; the earth opened its mouth and swallowed them down alive into Sheol. (Nu 16:27, 32, 33) Elijah experienced a quaking of the earth before Jehovah spoke to correct his viewpoint and to send him back to further service assignments. (1Ki 19:11-18) Earthquakes have been a miraculous aid to Jehovah's people, as when Jonathan and his armor-bearer courageously attacked a Philistine outpost. Jehovah backed up their faith in him by bringing about an earthquake that threw the entire camp of the Philistines into confusion, so that these killed off one another and were thoroughly routed.—1Sa 14:6, 10, 12, 15, 16, 20, 23.

On the day of Jesus' death, about three o'clock in the afternoon, an earthquake took place, splitting rock-masses open, causing the memorial tombs to be opened, and causing dead bodies to be thrown from their graves. The curtain of the sanctuary in the temple rebuilt by Herod was torn in two, from top to bottom. Prior to this, darkness had fallen over the land. Some think that volcanic action was involved, for often volcanoes belch out smoke and dust that blacken the sky. But there is no real evidence that there was any volcanic action connected with this earthquake. (Mt 27:45, 51-54; Lu 23:44, 45) Another earthquake occurred on the day of Jesus' resurrection, when an angel descended from heaven and rolled away the stone from in front of his tomb. (Mt 28:1, 2) The apostle Paul and his companion Silas, while in prison at Philippi, had their prayers and songs of praise answered by a great earthquake that opened the prison doors and loosened the bonds of the prisoners. This led to the conversion of the jailer and his household. —Ac 16:25-34.

Jesus foretold earthquakes in significant number and intensity as a feature of the sign of his presence. (Mt 24:3, 7, 8; Lu 21:11) Since 1914 C.E., there has been an increase in the number of earthquakes, resulting in much distress. With data obtained from the National Geophysical Data Center in Boulder, Colorado, supplemented by a number of standard reference works, a tabulation was made in 1984 that included only earthquakes that measured 7.5 or more on the Richter scale, or that resulted in destruction of five million dollars (U.S.) or more in property, or that caused 100 or more deaths. It was calculated that there had been 856 of such earthquakes during the 2,000 years before 1914. The same tabulation showed that in *just 69 years* following 1914 there were 605 of such quakes. These statistics are a means of indicating the extent of suffering from earthquakes during this period of history.

Figurative and Symbolic Uses. Earthquakes are often used figuratively in the Scriptures to describe the shaking and overthrow of nations and kingdoms. Ancient Babylon trusted in false gods such as Nebo and Marduk, which in the people's imaginations filled their heavens. They also relied greatly on the strength of their mighty military force, but God said in pronouncement against Babylon: "I shall cause heaven itself to become agitated, and the earth will rock out of its place at the fury of Jehovah of armies." (Isa 13:13) As far as Babylon was concerned, it must have been a great shock when her empire fell and her territory ceased to belong to her as the third world power and she became merely a province in the Persian Empire.—Da 5:30, 31.

Elsewhere, David describes Jehovah as fighting for him as by means of an earthquake. (2Sa 22:8; Ps 18:7) Jehovah speaks of rocking the heavens and the earth, the sea and the dry ground, of rocking all nations in behalf of his people, with the result that the desirable things of all the nations would come in and he would fill his house with glory.—Hag 2:6, 7.

The apostle Paul uses as an illustration the awe-inspiring display at Sinai, comparing it with the greater and more awesome assemblage of the Christian congregation of the firstborn before God and his Son as Mediator at the heavenly Mount Zion. He goes on to follow through with the illustration of the earthquake that took place at Sinai and gives a symbolic application, encouraging Christians to continue serving in courage and faith, realizing that the Kingdom and those who hold on to it will be able to remain standing while all other things of the symbolic heavens and earth are shaken to pieces.—Heb 12:18-29.

The greatest earthquake of all yet to come is a symbolic one, described in connection with the seventh of the symbolic seven final plagues of Revelation. It is pictured as wrecking, not one or two cities, as some of the most violent earthquakes have done, but "the cities of the nations." John's account of this cataclysm reads: "A great earthquake occurred such as had not occurred since men came to be on the earth, so extensive an earthquake, so great. And the great city [Babylon the Great] split into three parts, and the cities of the nations fell."—Re 16:18, 19.

EAST. This expression is translated from the Hebrew *miz·rach'*, meaning literally "sunrising" (De 3:27; 1Ch 4:39), and from *qe'dhem*, meaning "before," "in front of." (Eze 48:2) It was the practice of the Hebrews to face the rising sun when determining direction, which meant that E was in front of them, W was behind, N on the left hand, and S on the right hand.

Sometimes *qe'dhem* was used to mean a generally eastward direction, as at Genesis 11:2. At other times it meant the "east" in relation to something else, as at Numbers 34:11, where the expression "east of Ain" is used. At still other times it referred to the area that lay E and NE of Israel. This included the lands of Moab and Ammon, the Arabian Desert, Babylonia, Persia, Assyria, and Armenia.

The various peoples living in the lands referred to by the word "east" were spoken of as "sons of the East." Job was called the greatest of all the "Orientals," or "sons of the East." (Job 1:3) He lived in this eastern area. When Jacob went to Mesopotamia to get a wife, he went, we are told, to the land of "the Orientals," or "sons of the East." (Ge 29:1) The people to the E of Israel were also called "sons of the East," or "Easterners," as at Judges 6:3; 8:10.

In Palestine the E wind was a hot wind that blew in from desert lands to the E and was destructive to vegetation. (Eze 19:12) This is the basis for the expression "fill [one's] belly with the east wind."—Job 15:2.

The tabernacle, the temples of Solomon and Zerubbabel, and the second temple as rebuilt by Herod all faced the E. (Nu 3:38) Ezekiel's visionary temple faced eastward. (Eze 47:1) The coming of Jehovah and Christ to the temple would therefore be expected from the E.

At Isaiah 46:11, Cyrus, the Persian king, is spoken of as coming from "the east" (*KJ*), or "the sunrising" (*NW*). The reports foretold as coming from "the east" (*KJ*) are, literally, out of "the sunrising," or *miz·rach'*. (Da 11:44) In the book of Revelation back-reference is made to Darius and Cyrus as prophetic of "the kings from the rising of the sun," in connection with the drying up of the symbolic Euphrates in the time of Babylon the Great's judgment.—Re 16:12, 19.

The astrologers that came to see Jesus at the time of his birth came from the direction of Babylon, from "eastern parts." (Mt 2:1) When they said that they saw his star "in the east [Gr., *a·na·to·lei'*, literally, "rising"]," as some Bible translations state, they did not mean that it was E of where their land was but that they saw it from the East or when they were in the East. —Mt 2:2, ftn.

EASTERN SEA.   See SALT SEA.

EAST GATE.   See GATE, GATEWAY.

EBAL   (E'bal). The third-named son of the Horite sheik Shobal descended from Seir. (Ge 36:20, 23; 1Ch 1:40) The Horites dwelt in Seir before being dispossessed and annihilated by the sons of Esau.—De 2:12.

EBAL, MOUNT   (E'bal). A mountain now identified as Jebel Eslamiyeh (Har 'Eval), situated in the district of Samaria. Mount Ebal is opposite Mount Gerizim, these mountains being separated by a beautiful, narrow valley, the Vale of Shechem (Nablus Valley), in which nestles the city of Nablus, not far from ancient Shechem. Only its lower slopes sustain such vegetation as vines and olive trees, the higher elevations being quite barren and rocky. Like other mountains in Samaria, Ebal consists of a limestone core with an outer shell of chalk. It stands to the NE of Mount Gerizim and rises to a peak of over 900 m (3,000 ft) above the level of the Mediterranean. Mounts Ebal and Gerizim are situated to the W of the Jordan River.—De 11:29, 30.

Looking N from the summit of Ebal, one can see the greater part of the land of Galilee and also Mount Hermon. The heights in the vicinity of

A view from Mt. Gerizim across toward Mt. Ebal

Jerusalem can be seen to the S, and the Plain of Sharon and the Mediterranean to the W. To the E it is possible to see as far as the Hauran across the Jordan. Abram (Abraham) once camped in the valley between these two mountains, near the big trees of Moreh.—Ge 12:6.

Moses told the Israelites that when Jehovah brought them into the land that they were going to possess, they "must also give the blessing upon Mount Gerizim and the malediction upon Mount Ebal." (De 11:29, 30) He also instructed that great uncut stones be selected, whitewashed with lime, and set on Mount Ebal. An altar was to be erected there, upon which sacrifices were to be presented to Jehovah. Moses also said, "You must write on the stones all the words of this law, making them quite clear."—De 27:1-8.

After Israel crossed the Jordan, the tribes of Reuben, Gad, Asher, Zebulun, Dan, and Naphtali were to "stand for the malediction on Mount Ebal," and the other tribes were to "stand to bless the people on Mount Gerizim." At that time the blessings to be enjoyed by those obeying God's law, as well as the curses or maledictions to be experienced by those breaking his law, would be recited. (De 27:12-14) When the curses for disobedience were pronounced, all the people were to say "Amen!" that is, "So be it!" to show they agreed that practicers of wickedness merited condemnation.—De 27:15-26.

After Israel's victory at Ai, Joshua complied with Moses' instructions, building an altar to Jehovah in Mount Ebal. Upon stones (perhaps, but not necessarily, those of the altar itself) he wrote "a copy of the law of Moses that he had written before the sons of Israel." Then, in front of the congregation of Israel (including the alien residents) assembled as Moses had directed, Joshua "read aloud all the words of the law, the blessing and the malediction, according to all that is written in the book of the law." Half the congregation stood in front of Mount Ebal and the other half in front of Mount Gerizim, the ark of the covenant and the Levites being between the two groups. (Jos 8:30-35) The slopes of Mount Ebal in relation to the slopes of Mount Gerizim provided excellent acoustics for this occasion. Notably, too, these things occurred approximately in the heart of the land of promise and in the vicinity where Jehovah promised the land to Israel's forefather Abram (Abraham). —Ge 12:6, 7.

Jewish tradition holds that the Levites, standing between Mounts Ebal and Gerizim, faced Mount Gerizim when pronouncing a blessing, to which the people assembled there answered "Amen!" Then it is said that they turned to face Mount Ebal and pronounced one of the curses, to which those assembled on that side said "Amen!" The Scriptures, however, do not outline the exact procedure followed on that notable occasion.

At Deuteronomy 27:4 it is said that the stones were to be set up in Mount "Gerizim" according to the Samaritan *Pentateuch*. However, the reading is "Ebal" according to the Masoretic text, the Latin *Vulgate*, the Syriac *Peshitta*, and the Greek *Septuagint*. Joshua 8:30-32 indicates that it was on Mount Ebal that Joshua set up the stones on which "a copy of the law of Moses" was written. —See GERIZIM, MOUNT.

EBED   (E'bed) [Servant; or, shortened form of Obadiah, meaning "Servant of Jehovah"].

1. Father of Gaal, the one who led the landowners of Shechem in an unsuccessful rebellion against Abimelech.—Jg 9:26, 29, 39-41.

2. Son of Jonathan. Ebed, accompanied by 50 males of the paternal house of Adin, returned with Ezra to Jerusalem from Babylon.—Ezr 8:6.

EBED-MELECH   (E'bed-mel'ech) [Servant of the King]. An Ethiopian eunuch in the house of King Zedekiah who, by his course of action, demonstrated that he was in full agreement with the work of Jehovah's prophet Jeremiah. When the princes of Judah falsely charged Jeremiah with sedition, Zedekiah surrendered the prophet into their hands. These princes then took Jeremiah and threw him into the miry cistern of Malchijah in the Courtyard of the Guard, there to die without food. (Jer 38:4-6) Courageously, notwithstanding the danger in which it placed him because of the prevailing bitter hatred for Jeremiah and his message, Ebed-melech publicly approached the king seated in the Gate of Benjamin and there presented an appeal in behalf of Jeremiah. Zedekiah responded favorably. Then Ebed-melech, at the king's command, took 30 men to the cistern and let down ropes with worn-out rags and pieces of cloth for Jeremiah to place under his armpits in order to bring him up out of the cistern. (Jer 38:7-13) Likely Zedekiah directed Ebed-melech to take 30 men along, not that so many men were needed to get Jeremiah out of the cistern, but in order to effect a successful deliverance despite any possible interference on the part of the princes or the priests. Because of this righteous act toward God's prophet, Ebed-melech was assured by Jehovah, through Jeremiah, that he would not perish during the Babylonian siege but would be furnished an escape. —Jer 39:15-18; see EUNUCH.

EBENEZER (Eb·en·e′zer) [Stone of Help].

1. A site near which Israel was twice defeated by the Philistines, resulting not only in the death of 34,000 Israelites, including Hophni and Phinehas, but also in enemy capture of the ark of the covenant. News of this latter event precipitated the death of Eli the priest. (1Sa 4:1-11, 17, 18; 5:1) Scholars tentatively place Ebenezer at Majdel Yaba, 4 km (2.5 mi) SE of Aphek in the Plain of Sharon (where the Philistines were encamped).

2. The name given to a stone erected by Samuel more than 20 years after the events mentioned in the preceding chapter, likely to commemorate Israel's victory over the Philistines by God's help. (1Sa 7:2, 12) Although its exact location is today unknown, it was apparently a number of miles SE of No. 1 above, "between Mizpah and Jeshanah."

EBER (E′ber) [from a root meaning "pass over (cross)"; or, "other side [that is, the opposite side]"]. In addition to being the personal name of five different men in the Bible, "Eber" is used at Numbers 24:24 as either indicating the Hebrew race or else as referring to a region. The Greek *Septuagint,* the Syriac *Peshitta,* and the Latin *Vulgate* here render "Eber" as "the Hebrews." However, "Eber" may in this case be referring to the land or people on the 'other side' of the Euphrates (in addition to Assyria, mentioned in the same verse). In Hebrew the expression for "beyond the River" (Heb., *′e′ver han·na·har′*) is used at times to refer to the region W of the Euphrates. (Ne 2:7, 9; 3:7) At 1 Kings 4:24 the same Hebrew expression is translated "this side of the River" (*NW*) or "west of the Euphrates." (*RS*) The corresponding Aramaic expression is used to designate generally the region of Syria and Palestine.—Ezr 4:10, 11, 16, 17, 20; 5:3, 6; 6:6, 13.

1. A forefather of Abraham; the son of Shelah and the father of Peleg and Joktan as well as of other children. In the days of his son Peleg, whom Eber outlived by about 191 years, "the earth was divided." This may have reference to Jehovah's confusing the language of those who were building Babel and its tower under the direction of Nimrod.—Ge 10:25; 11:14-19, 26.

Genesis 10:21 refers to "Shem, the forefather of all the sons of Eber ["ancestor of all the Hebrews," *AT, Mo*], the brother of Japheth the oldest." Evidently Eber is here listed in close relation to Shem because of the Biblical importance attached to Eber's descendants, particularly from Abraham forward. The text, therefore, does not restrict Shem's descendants to just the Hebrews, as the succeeding verses make clear. Eber's descendants through Joktan appear to have settled in Arabia, while those through Peleg are associated with Mesopotamia.

2. A Gadite listed along with other 'heads of the house of their forefathers.'—1Ch 5:13, 15.

3. A Benjamite identified as a son of Elpaal. —1Ch 8:12, 28.

4. A Benjamite headman listed among the sons of Shashak.—1Ch 8:22-25.

5. A Levite priest; the head of the paternal house of Amok. Evidently Eber was a contemporary of High Priest Joiakim, Governor Nehemiah, and Ezra the priest and scribe.—Ne 12:12, 20, 26.

EBEZ (E′bez). A town in Issachar's territory. (Jos 19:17, 20) Its location is not known.

EBIASAPH.   See ABIASAPH.

EBONY [Heb., *ho·venim′*]. The term is believed to apply to the wood from the *Diospyros ebenum* or similar types of the same genus of trees. The tree grows tall, with simple leaves and bell-shaped flowers. The outer wood is soft and white, but the inner heartwood, which reaches a maximum diameter of about 0.5 m (2 ft), is very hard, close grained, durable, and black or dark brown in color. It takes a very high polish. These qualities make it very desirable for fine furniture, ornamental articles, and for inlay work with ivory. It was also used by the pagans in making idols for worship.

Ebony is mentioned only once in the Bible, at Ezekiel 27:15, where it is presented as an item of commerce. It is suggested that the ebony and ivory there mentioned were brought out of India or Sri Lanka, perhaps across the Arabian Sea and up the Red Sea and then overland, or else from Nubia in NE Africa. It was highly appreciated by the ancient Egyptians, and products of it have been found in Egyptian tombs.

EBRON (E′bron). The name of a boundary city apportioned to Asher. (Jos 19:24, 28) Since many Hebrew manuscripts here read "Abdon," most scholars generally consider "Ebron" to be an erroneous spelling of that name.—See ABDON No. 5.

ECBATANA

ECBATANA (Ec·bat'a·na). The capital city of ancient Media, from about 700 B.C.E. Persian King Cyrus II took it from Median King Astyages, after which the Medes and Persians joined forces under Cyrus. Ecbatana is Scripturally identified as a place that was in the jurisdictional district of Media in the days of Persian King Darius I (Hystaspis).—Ezr 6:1, 2.

"Ecbatana" is the English rendering of this city's name at Ezra 6:2. This form of the name corresponds to the reading of the Latin *Vulgate* and is also found in the Greek text of the Apocryphal writings that came to be included in the *Septuagint.* The Masoretic text and the Syriac *Peshitta,* however, give the name as "Achmetha." Early Greek writers seem to have applied the name Ecbatana to several places. However, there is general agreement among scholars today that the Ecbatana captured by Cyrus (and thus that mentioned at Ezr 6:2) is the modern city of Hamadan, an important commercial center of Iran situated at the foot of Mount Alwand approximately 290 km (180 mi) WSW of Tehran. Just as ancient Ecbatana was a significant city along the chief route leading from Mesopotamia to points farther E, so modern Hamadan is traversed by various roads, such as that running from Baghdad to Tehran.

When certain Persian-appointed officials questioned the legality of the Jews' temple-rebuilding work in Zerubbabel's day, these opposers sent a letter to King Darius I of Persia requesting confirmation of Cyrus' decree authorizing the reconstruction. (Ezr 5:1-17) Darius had an investigation made, and Cyrus' decree was found in Ecbatana, thus establishing the legality of the temple-rebuilding work. In fact, Darius put through an order so that the Jews' work might go on without hindrance, and their opposers were even ordered to provide them with needed materials, which "they did promptly." The temple was finally completed "by the third day of the lunar month Adar, that is, in the sixth year of the reign of Darius the king," or near the spring of 515 B.C.E.—Ezr 6:6-15.

ECCLESIASTES.

ECCLESIASTES. The Hebrew name *Qo·he'-leth* (meaning "Congregator; Assembler; Convener; Convoker") fittingly describes the role of the king in the theocratic government that Israel enjoyed. (Ec 1:1, 12) It was the responsibility of the ruler to hold the dedicated people of God together in faithfulness to their true King and God. (1Ki 8:1-5, 41-43, 66) For that reason, whether a king was good or bad for the nation was determined by whether he led the nation in the worship of Jehovah or not. (2Ki 16:1-4; 18:1-6) The congregator, who was Solomon, had already done much congregating of Israel and their companions, the temporary residents, to the temple. In this book he sought to congregate God's people away from the vain and fruitless works of this world to the works worthy of the God to whom they as a nation were dedicated. The name used in our English Bibles is taken from the translation of *Qo·he'leth* in the Greek *Septuagint,* namely, *Ek·kle·si·a·stes'* (Ecclesiastes), meaning "a member of an ecclesia (congregation; assembly)."

Writer. There was only one "son of David," namely, Solomon, who was "king over *Israel* in Jerusalem" (Ec 1:1, 12), for kings after Solomon did not reign over all Israel. Solomon was the king so well known for his surpassing wisdom. (Ec 1:16; 1Ki 4:29-34) He was a builder. (Ec 2:4-6; 1Ki 6:1; 7:1-8) He was a composer of proverbs. (Ec 12:9; 1Ki 4:32) Solomon was renowned for his wealth. (Ec 2:4-9; 1Ki 9:17-19; 10:4-10, 14-29) Since the book mentions the building program of Solomon, it must have been written after that time but before he "began to do what was bad in the eyes of Jehovah." (1Ki 11:6) The book was therefore written before 1000 B.C.E., in Jerusalem. That Solomon would be one of the best qualified men to write the book is supported by the fact that he was not only the richest but probably one of the best informed kings of his day; his sailors and tradesmen as well as visiting dignitaries would bring news and knowledge of people of other lands.—1Ki 9:26-28; 10:23-25, 28, 29.

Authenticity. *Qo·he'leth,* or Ecclesiastes, is accepted as canonical by both the Jewish and the Christian churches. It is in agreement with other portions of the Bible that treat the same subjects. For example, it agrees with Genesis on man's being made up of a body composed of the dust of the ground and having the spirit or life-force from God and the breath that sustains it. (Ec 3:20, 21; 12:7; Ge 2:7; 7:22; Isa 42:5) It affirms the Bible teaching that man was created upright but willfully chose to disobey God. (Ec 7:29; Ge 1:31; 3:17; De 32:4, 5) It acknowledges God as the Creator. (Ec 12:1; Ge 1:1) It concurs with the rest of the Bible as to the state of the dead. (Ec 9:5, 10; Ge 3:19; Ps 6:5; 115:17; Joh 11:11-14; Ro 6:23) It strongly advocates the worship and the fear of God. It uses the expression *ha·'Elo·him',* "the true God," 32 times. The equivalent for the name Jehovah is found in the Syriac *Peshitta* and Jewish Targum of the book at Ecclesiastes 2:24. While some claim that the book contradicts itself, this is only because they do not see that the book many times sets forth the common view as opposed to the view that reflects divine wisdom. (Compare Ec 1:18; 7:11, 12.) So one must read with a view to getting the sense and must keep in mind the theme of the book.

HIGHLIGHTS OF ECCLESIASTES

A vivid description of works that are vain and those that are worth while

Written by Solomon in the latter part of his kingship, after he had engaged in the numerous pursuits that he describes

A life devoted to vain pursuits is empty

To a natural man all is vanity; one generation is replaced by another, and even natural cycles are repetitious and wearisome (1:1-11)

Increased human wisdom can result in increased pain; what is crooked in this system cannot be made straight (1:12-18)

Devoting oneself to pleasure-seeking through materialism is like striving after the wind (2:1-11, 26)

Wisdom is better than folly, but both the wise and the stupid ones die and are forgotten (2:12-16)

Working hard all one's life only to leave everything to a man who may not appreciate it—this is calamitous (2:17-23)

Events in earthly life often occur in cycles, many of which are beyond human control (3:1-9)

In the present system, all (both man and beast) eventually die (3:18-22)

Many acts of oppression take place, with no hope from a human standpoint (4:1-3)

Hard work and proficiency because of rivalry or simply to accumulate wealth is vanity, and the lazy person is stupid (4:4-8)

The life of a ruler can also be vain (4:13-16)

Accumulating riches will not bring contentment, but it may rob the owner of his sleep; and when he dies he will leave them all behind (5:9-17)

Though a person has many possessions, circumstances —perhaps illness or an unfulfilled longing—may prevent him from finding contentment (6:1-12)

In the present system, the same eventuality awaits both righteous and wicked—all die; so, some give free rein to badness (9:2, 3)

Wisdom is not always appreciated when it comes from a needy man (9:13-18)

Indulging in foolishness gives one a bad reputation; when such incompetent ones are in positions of authority, it is hazardous for them and hard on others (10:1-19)

Youth and the prime of life are vanity; the duration of youthful vigor is so uncertain (11:10)

If a person has not been guided in life by constant remembrance of the Creator, everything is vanity! (12:8)

Things that are worth while and that give meaning to one's life

Enjoy the fruits of your work, recognizing these as a gift from God (2:24, 25; 5:18-20)

The works of God are all pretty; before mankind he has set the prospect of life to time indefinite (3:10-13)

The general pattern of human life that exists according to God's permission or purpose cannot be changed by man; so wait on God to act as Judge in his appointed time (3:14-17; 5:8)

A person who works with a partner is better off than a loner (4:9-12)

Proper fear of God should move us to listen carefully to what he requires of us and to fulfill any vow we make to him (5:1-7)

Appreciate the importance of a good name and the brevity of our present life in which to acquire it, the benefit of patience, the superior value of wisdom, and the need to submit humbly to what God permits (7:1-15)

Avoid going to extremes but be guided by fear of God; do not get overly concerned about what other people say; shun the snare of a prostitute (7:16-29)

Be law abiding; even though men dominate others to their injury and human justice is lax, do not let it spoil your enjoyment of life; remember, it will turn out well with those who fear the true God; do not expect to fathom all the reasons for what God does and permits to occur (8:1-17; 10:20)

The righteous ones and the wise ones are in the hand of the true God—they will not lose their reward; but in death a person knows nothing and can do nothing, so use your life now in a manner that God will approve; enjoy it in wholesome ways while you have it (9:1, 4-12)

Seize appropriate opportunities to be generous, to accomplish good; do not let uncertainties of life stifle your activity (11:1-8)

Young man, enjoy your youth, but do not forget that you are accountable to God for your actions; remember your Grand Creator while you are young, before the weakness and decrepitude of old age come, before life ends (11:9; 12:1-7)

The most beneficial writings are those that reflect the wisdom of the "one shepherd," Jehovah God (12:9-12)

Fear the true God and keep his commandments; he sees everything that we do, and he will bring our works into judgment (12:13, 14)

EDEN (E'den) [Pleasure].

1. A region in which the Creator planted a gardenlike park as the original home of the first human pair. The statement that the garden was "in Eden, toward the east," apparently indicates that the garden occupied only a portion of the region called Eden. (Ge 2:8) However, the garden is thereafter called "the garden of Eden" (Ge 2:15) and, in later texts, is spoken of as "Eden, the garden of God" (Eze 28:13), and as "the garden of Jehovah."—Isa 51:3.

The *Septuagint* rendered the Hebrew word for "garden" (*gan*) by the Greek word *pa·ra'dei·sos*. To this fact we owe our association of the English word "paradise" with the garden of Eden.

Genesis 2:15 states that "God proceeded to take the man and settle him in the garden of Eden." While this might appear to indicate that man's creation took place outside the garden, it may simply refer to God's 'taking' man in the sense of his forming and creating him from the earthly elements, then assigning him to reside initially in the garden in which he came to life. The cultivation and care of the garden was man's work assignment. Eden's trees and plants included all those providing scenic beauty as well as those providing food in wide variety. (Ge 2:9, 15) This fact alone would indicate that the garden covered an area of considerable size.

There was a great variety of animal life in the garden. God brought before Adam "all the domestic animals and . . . flying creatures of the heavens and . . . every wild beast of the field," the naming of which was given to Adam as one of his earliest tasks. (Ge 2:19, 20) Eden's soil was watered by the waters of the river "issuing out of Eden." (Ge 2:10) In view of man's nakedness it may be assumed that the climate was very mild and agreeable.—Ge 2:25.

What was the forbidden fruit in Eden?

Eden's fruit trees were all there for man to eat from "to satisfaction." (Ge 2:16) But one tree, that "of the knowledge of good and bad," was placed off limits for the human pair. Eve quoted Jehovah's prohibition given to her husband as including even the 'touching' of the tree, with the penalty of death to result from disrespect for and violation of the divine law. (Ge 2:17; 3:3) Traditional teachings have attempted to explain the prohibited fruit in a variety of ways: as a symbol of sexual intercourse, represented by an "apple"; as standing for the mere cognizance of right and

wrong; and as the knowledge attained upon reaching maturity and also through experience, which knowledge can be put to a good or a bad use. Yet, in view of the Creator's command to "be fruitful and become many and fill the earth" (Ge 1:28), sexual intercourse must be rejected as being what the tree's fruit represented, for in what other way could procreation and multiplication have been effected? The mere ability to recognize right and wrong most certainly cannot be meant, for obedience to God's command required of sinless man that he be able to exercise such moral discrimination. Nor could the knowledge attained upon reaching maturity be meant, for it would not be sin on man's part to reach this state, nor would his Creator logically obligate him to remain in an immature state.

As to the genus of the tree, the Scriptural record is silent. But it becomes apparent that the tree of the knowledge of good and bad symbolized the divine right or prerogative, which man's Creator retains, to designate to his creatures what is "good" and what is "bad," thereafter properly requiring the practice of that which is declared good and the abstention from that which is pronounced bad in order to remain approved by God as Sovereign Ruler. (See TREES.) Both the prohibition and the subsequent pronouncement of the sentence passed upon the disobedient pair emphasize the fact that it was the *act of disobedience* in eating the prohibited fruit that constituted the original sin.—Ge 3:3.

While some modern critics may balk at the very simplicity of the Edenic account, it should be obvious that the actual circumstances made a simple test most fitting. The life of the newly created man and woman was simple, not complicated and encumbered with all the complex problems, predicaments, and perplexity that disobedience to God has since brought to the human race. Nonetheless, for all its simplicity, the test succinctly and admirably expresses the universal truth of God's sovereignty as well as man's dependence upon God and his duty toward God. And it must be said that, while simple, the account of Eden's events presents matters on an infinitely higher level than those theories that would place man's start, not in a garden, but in a cave, representing him as both crudely ignorant and without moral sense. The simplicity of the test in Eden illustrates the principle stated millenniums later by God's Son, that "the person faithful in what is least is faithful also in much, and the person unrighteous in what is least is unrighteous also in much."—Lu 16:10.

Eden's having this proscribed tree within it, however, was clearly not intended to serve as a thorn in the flesh of the human pair, nor was it so designated in order to raise an issue, or to serve as the subject for debate. If Adam and Eve had acknowledged God's will in the matter and had respected his instructions, their garden home would have continued unmarred as a place of pleasure and delight. The record shows that the issue and debate over the tree, along with the temptation to violate God's ordinance, were thrust upon mankind by God's Adversary. (Ge 3:1-6; compare Re 12:9.) Adam and Eve's exercise of their will, as free moral agents, in rebellion against God's rightful sovereignty led to their loss of Paradise and the blessedness of its confines. Of even graver consequence, they lost the opportunity to partake of another of Eden's trees, this one representing the right to life everlasting. Thus the account says that Jehovah "drove the man out and posted at the east of the garden of Eden the cherubs and the flaming blade of a sword that was turning itself continually to guard the way to the tree of life."—Ge 3:22-24.

Location of Eden. The original site of the garden of Eden is conjectural. The principal means of identifying its geographic location is the Bible's description of the river "issuing out of Eden," which thereafter divided into four "heads," producing the rivers named as the Euphrates, Hiddekel, Pishon, and Gihon. (Ge 2:10-14) The Euphrates (Heb., *Perath'*) is well known, and "Hiddekel" is the name used for the Tigris in ancient inscriptions. (Compare also Da 10:4.) The other two rivers, the Pishon and the Gihon, however, are unidentified.—See CUSH No. 2; HAVILAH No. 1.

Some, such as Calvin and Delitzsch, have argued in favor of Eden's situation somewhere near the head of the Persian Gulf in Lower Mesopotamia, approximately at the place where the Tigris and the Euphrates draw near together. They associated the Pishon and Gihon with canals between these streams. However, this would make these rivers tributaries, rather than branches dividing off from an original source. The Hebrew text points, rather, to a location in the mountainous region N of the Mesopotamian plains, the area where the Euphrates and Tigris rivers have their present sources. Thus *The Anchor Bible* (1964), in its notes on Genesis 2:10, states: "In Heb[rew] the mouth of the river is called 'end' (Josh xv 5, xviii 19); hence the plural of *ro's* 'head' must refer here to the upper course. . . .

This latter usage is well attested for the Akk[adian] cognate *resu.*" The fact that the Euphrates and Tigris rivers do not now proceed from a single source, as well as the impossibility of definitely determining the identification of the Pishon and Gihon rivers, is possibly explained by the effects of the Noachian Flood, which undoubtedly altered considerably the topographical features of the earth, filling in the courses of some rivers and creating others.

The traditional location for the garden of Eden has long been suggested to have been a mountainous area some 225 km (140 mi) SW of Mount Ararat and a few kilometers S of Lake Van, in the eastern part of modern Turkey. That Eden may have been surrounded by some natural barrier, such as mountains, could be suggested by the fact that cherubs are stated to have been stationed only at the E of the garden, from which point Adam and Eve made their exit.—Ge 3:24.

After Adam's banishment from the paradisaic garden, with no one to "cultivate it and to take care of it," it may be assumed that it merely grew up in natural profusion with only the animals to inhabit its confines until it was obliterated by the surging waters of the Flood, its location lost to man except for the divine record of its existence. —Ge 2:15.

2. A place mentioned along with Haran and Canneh as a principal trading center with Tyre, specializing in fine garments, carpets, and rope. (Eze 27:23, 24) It is suggested to be an abbreviated form of the name Beth-eden referred to at Amos 1:5. "The sons of Eden" are included among other inhabitants of places that were vanquished by the Assyrian forces (2Ki 19:12; Isa 37:12), and some consider this Eden (Beth-eden) to be the small district of Bit-adini along the middle course of the Euphrates River.—See BETH-EDEN.

3. One of the Levites who responded to King Hezekiah's call for reform; thereafter assigned to work under Kore, "the gatekeeper to the east," in the distribution of the holy contributions among the priestly divisions.—2Ch 29:12; 31:14, 15.

EDER (E'der).

1. A descendant of Beriah of the tribe of Benjamin who dwelt in Jerusalem.—1Ch 8:1, 15, 16, 28.

2. A descendant of Mushi of the Levitical family of Merari, assigned to priestly service during the time of David.—1Ch 23:21, 23-25; 24:30.

3. A city in the southern part of Judah. (Jos 15:21) Since the Hebrew consonants of the name Eder with the last two transposed are the same as the Hebrew consonants of Arad, and since the *Septuagint* (Vatican Manuscript No. 1209) has "Ara" instead of "Eder" in this text, most scholars consider Eder to be identical with Arad (Tel 'Arad), about 28 km (17 mi) E of Beer-sheba.

4. [Drove]. A tower near which Jacob (Israel) pitched his tent sometime after the death of Rachel. Although its exact location is not known, it was apparently located some place between Bethlehem and Hebron. The name Eder indicates it provided shelter for shepherds and served as a watchtower from which they could oversee their flocks. (Ge 35:19, 21, 27) While Jacob was tenting here, his son Reuben 'profaned Jacob's lounge,' having relations with Jacob's concubine Bilhah. —Ge 35:22; 49:3, 4.

The same Hebrew expression here translated "tower of Eder" (*migh·dal-'eʹdher*) is used by Micah (4:8) when referring to the "tower of the drove." This expression may allude to the name of Jacob's camping site and is used in connection with the restoration of Jehovah's "limping" people. (Mic 4:7) With "Zion" restored, they would be watched over as from a lookout "tower" and thereby be guarded from further danger. Such an illustration is consistent with other similes in Micah's prophecy; he referred to the Messiah as one who would do "shepherding" (Mic 5:2-4) and Jehovah's people as "the flock of [God's] inheritance."—Mic 7:14.

EDOM (Eʹdom) [Red], **EDOMITES** (Eʹdomites). Edom was the secondary name or byname given to Esau, Jacob's twin brother. (Ge 36:1) It was applied to him because of his selling his birthright for the *red* stew. (Ge 25:30-34) Coincidentally, Esau at birth had had a very red color (Ge 25:25), and a similar color prevailed in parts of the land he and his descendants later inhabited.

Seir and Edom. Sometime during Jacob's 20-year stay in Haran, Esau (Edom) had begun to establish himself in the land of Seir, "the field of Edom." (Ge 32:3) Thus, even before the death of his father (Ge 35:29), Esau was apparently beginning to fulfill Isaac's prophetic blessing, directing his attention away from the fertile soils around Hebron and, doubtless, beginning to 'live by his sword,' along with the 400 men under his command. (Ge 27:39, 40; 32:6, 8) The record indicates, however, that he still maintained resi-

dence or a base camp in the Hebron area, not transferring definitely to the mountainous region of Seir until after his father's death (1738 B.C.E.). By then his family had grown and his possessions were great.—Ge 36:6-8.

The land of Seir had previously been the domain of Horites (Ge 14:6; 36:20-30), but Esau's sons dispossessed the Horite sheiks and took over the region. (De 2:12) Thereafter the land became known as the land of Edom, though the older name of Seir still continued to be in use.—Nu 24:18.

Geographic Description. The territory of Edom extended about 160 km (100 mi) from its frontier with Moab in the N, formed by the torrent valley of Zered, down to Elath (Eloth) on the Gulf of 'Aqaba in the S. (De 2:1-8, 13, 14; 1Ki 9:26) To the E, the Edomite domain apparently extended out to the edge of the Arabian Desert, while to the W it reached across the Arabah to the Wilderness of Zin and embraced the Negeb highlands region stretching from the SW corner of the Salt Sea on down to Kadesh-barnea. The western portion of Edom therefore came to form the SE boundary of Judah's territory.—Jos 15:1; compare Nu 34:3.

The true heartland of the Edomite territory, however, evidently lay E of the Arabah, for here the high mountain range, with some points reaching an altitude of 1,700 m (5,600 ft), receives some rainfall. This is because the land W of the Arabah, the Negeb, is considerably lower, allowing the remnants of Mediterranean storm clouds to pass over and reach the higher mountains of Edom, where they release some of their remaining moisture. Thus, archaeological investigations show a string of ancient settlements and fortresses along a narrow tongue of arable land on the highest part of the long mountainous tableland, or plateau, but these run out as one proceeds S toward the Gulf of 'Aqaba. Modern Tafileh, about 30 km (19 mi) S of the Dead (Salt) Sea, has large olive groves, though this is due in great measure to the flow of water from eight fine springs, only about 28 cm (11 in.) of rainfall being deposited annually.

Though fertile land was in short supply, this rugged mountainous region held valuable deposits of copper and iron; mining and smelting were carried on around modern Feinan, some 48 km (30 mi) S of the Dead Sea. Evidence can also be seen of the existence of ancient pine forests of considerable size.

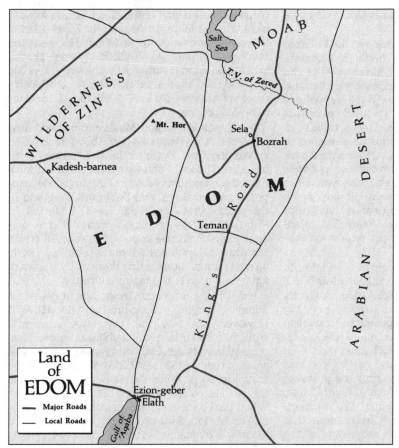

Land
of
EDOM

—— Major Roads

—— Local Roads

contributed greatly to Edom's wealth. Weary desert travelers also may have paid for food and lodging upon reaching Edom.

The steep escarpment, or wall of the plateau, that faced the Arabah gave the main stronghold of Edom excellent protection from that direction. The deep canyon of the torrent valley of Zered impeded invasion from Moab. (Note, however, Am 2:1.) A chain of fortresses faced the desert to the more vulnerable E, providing defense against Midianite and other nomadic tribes. Additionally, the clefts that cut into the mountains and plateaus are generally walled in by unscalable red sandstone cliffs forming forbidding gorges. With good reason Jehovah's prophecy through Jeremiah speaks of the Edomites as confidently "residing in the retreats of the crag, holding the height of the hill," and like an eagle in its nest.—Jer 49:7, 16.

In harmony with the above, Moses, upon sending messengers to the king of Edom, spoke of the Israelite position at Kadesh-barnea as "at the extremity of your territory," and when requesting permission for peaceful passage through Edomite territory, Moses referred to their fields, vineyards, and wells.—Nu 20:14-17.

Strategic Position. Moses requested permission for Israel to travel over "the king's road" through Edom. (Nu 20:17) This road, generally called the King's Highway, may have run from the Gulf of 'Aqaba on up to Damascus in Syria, following the edge of the high plateaus lining the E side of the Arabah when traversing Edom. Along it were to be found the major cities of Edom. (Ge 36:33) A route also led to the E from the Negeb through Ma'an on the edge of the Arabian Desert and connected there with another route running N and S. Over these roads passed rich cargoes from Egypt, Arabia, Syria, and Mesopotamia. Tolls collected from camel or donkey caravans traversing the roads likely

The People of Edom. The Edomites as descendants of Esau were basically a Semitic race, but with a strong Hamitic strain. This was because two of Esau's wives were from Hamitic Canaanite stock (Hittite and Hivite); only one wife named was part Semitic, through Abraham's son Ishmael. (Ge 36:2, 3) If, as some scholars hold, the name Horite means simply "cave dweller," Esau's Hivite wife Oholibamah, the daughter of Anah, may have come from the Horite dwellers of Seir. (Compare Ge 36:2, 20, 24, 25.) At any rate, the Edomites, like Lot's descendants the Moabites and the Ammonites (note Da 11:41), were related to the Israelites, and originally they also practiced circumcision. (Jer 9:25, 26; compare Eze 32:29.) Jehovah referred to them as Israel's "brothers," and Edomite land rights were to be held inviolable by the Israelites advancing through the wilderness, since Jehovah had granted Edom's descendants Mount Seir as a holding.—De 2:1-8.

Originally formed into sheikdoms, the Edomite tribes later were organized under a kingdom. The royal line of succession indicates that the kings came from different tribes or sheikdoms, hence not taking the throne on a hereditary family basis. (Ge 36:15-19, 31-43) Some critics have viewed the reference at Genesis 36:31 to the Edomite rulers as "the kings who reigned in the land of Edom before any king reigned over the sons of Israel" as an anachronism or as a later insertion. This is not the case, however, since Moses, the recorder of Genesis, already knew God's clear promise to Jacob (Israel) that "kings will come out of your loins." (Ge 35:11) Moses himself foretold that Israel would eventually have a king.—De 28:36.

The Greek *Septuagint* contains an addition to Job 42:17 that would identify Job with Jobab, the Edomite king of Genesis 36:33. Job, however, was from the land of Uz, a name given originally to an Aramaean tribe and repeated in Aramaean Nahor's lineage. (Job 1:1; compare Ge 10:23; 22:20, 21.) Lamentations 4:21 does speak of Edom as 'dwelling in the land of Uz,' but this text, written many centuries after the probable time of Job's life, does not equate Uz with Edom, especially since, at Jeremiah 25:20, 21, "the kings of the land of Uz" are distinct from Edom. The text may rather indicate an extension of the Edomite domain.—See Uz No. 4.

On the other hand, it seems definite that one of the three "companions" who visited and criticized Job in his diseased state was an Edomite, namely, Eliphaz the Temanite. (Job 2:11; compare Ge 36:11, 34.) Teman is presented as a center of Edomite wisdom at Jeremiah 49:7, the regular Edomite contact and communication with travelers from the Orient perhaps contributing to their reputation for wisdom.

From Exodus to Close of Judean History. The destruction of Pharaoh's forces and Israel's miraculous deliverance at the Red Sea had repercussions in Edom, as in all the region in and around Canaan. (Ex 15:14, 15) In the wilderness of the Sinai Peninsula, Israel's first armed opposition came from a far-ranging Edomite tribe, the Amalekites, a source of trouble for Israel throughout their history. (Ex 17:8-16; compare Ge 36:12, 16; see AMALEK, AMALEKITES.) At the close of the period of wandering, Moses' respectful request for safe conduct over the King's Highway through Edom was rejected, and the un-

named Edomite king marshaled a strong force to block any Israelite intrusion. (Nu 20:14-21) So, following Aaron's death at Mount Hor near the border of Edom (Nu 20:22-29), Israel skirted Edom's heartland, camped by the torrent valley of Zered, and thereafter traveled N past Moab's eastern frontier.—Nu 21:4, 10-13; Jg 11:18; compare De 2:26-29.

In the poetic blessing Moses pronounced over Israel before his death, he described Jehovah God as 'coming from Sinai,' as having "flashed forth from Seir [Edom]," and as having 'beamed forth from the mountains of Paran.' A similar description occurs in Barak and Deborah's song and in the prophecy of Habakkuk. (De 33:2; Jg 5:4, 5; Hab 3:3, 4) This prophetic portrayal thus evidently sets forth the arena, or theater, in which Jehovah had manifested himself to his newly formed nation, illuminating them as by flashes of light shining over the mountain peaks.

Israel had been commanded not to detest an Edomite, "for he is your brother." (De 23:7, 8) However, not only the aggressive Amalekite tribe, but Edom as a whole followed a course of opposition to Israel. Saul successfully waged war against them. (1Sa 14:47, 48) Yet, Saul had an Edomite, Doeg, as head over his shepherds, and this man acted as informer to Saul against David. When Saul's men were averse to attacking the priests of Nob, Saul used Doeg to accomplish a wholesale massacre.—1Sa 21:7; 22:9-18.

David, as king, won a major victory over the Edomites in the Valley of Salt. (2Sa 8:13; see SALT, VALLEY OF.) While the action provoking the battle is not stated, Edomite aggression was doubtless responsible, perhaps because the Edomites' thought that David's campaigns into Syria had left the southern part of his kingdom vulnerable to invasion. At 1 Chronicles 18:12 and in the superscription of Psalm 60, Abishai and Joab respectively are described as effecting the conquest of the Edomites. Since David was commander in chief and Joab was his principal general, while Abishai was a divisional commander under Joab, it can be seen how the accounts could differ in crediting the victory, depending upon the viewpoint taken, even as is the case in modern times. Similarly the difference in figures in these texts is likely due to the narrator's particular view of the different aspects or campaigns of the war. (Compare 1Ki 11:15, 16.) At any rate, David stationed garrisons of Israelite troops throughout Edom, and Edom's remaining population became subject to Israel. (2Sa 8:14; 1Ch

18:13) The "yoke" of Jacob now rested heavily on the neck of Edom (Esau).—Ge 27:40; compare Nu 24:18.

Solomon, who married Edomite women (1Ki 11:1), made use of Israelite control over the Edomite coastal cities on the Red Sea, Eloth (Elath) and Ezion-geber, for developing a shipping enterprise. (1Ki 9:26; 2Ch 8:17, 18) Edom's depleted male population was unable to lift off the Israelite yoke, though an escapee of royal blood, Hadad, did lead a resistance movement of some sort.—1Ki 11:14-22.

Whether this situation prevailed continuously for a full century after David's initial conquest cannot be said. The attack by "the sons of Ammon, and Moab and the mountainous region of Seir [Edom]" (2Ch 20:1, 2, 10, 22) may have taken place before the combined assault by Judean, Israelite, and Edomite forces against Moab. (2Ki 3:5-9; see MOAB, MOABITES.) Edom apparently formed part of each triple alliance, fighting first on one side and then on the other. It is also stated that at some point in Jehoshaphat's reign Edom had no king; the land was ruled by a deputy, who evidently was answerable to the Judean throne, so Judah's access to the Gulf of 'Aqaba and its port or ports was unobstructed. (1Ki 22:47, 48) With regard to the campaign against Moab, the predicted flooding of the previously dry torrent valley where the allied armies camped may have resulted from a desert thunderstorm on the higher plateau. Such storms in modern times can send torrents of water rushing down the wadis toward the Arabah. Or the water may have appeared by purely miraculous means. —2Ki 3:16-23.

Edom revolted and threw off the Judean yoke in the reign of Jehoshaphat's son Jehoram and reestablished its independent monarchy. Although Jehoram won a military victory in an encounter with them, the Edomites remained in revolt. (2Ki 8:20-22; 2Ch 21:8-10) In the first half of Amaziah's reign (858-830 B.C.E.), the Valley of Salt was again the scene of military disaster for Edom, and Amaziah seized the major Edomite city of Sela, being ensnared, however, by worship of Edom's impotent false gods. (2Ki 14:7; 2Ch 25:11-20) His son, Uzziah (Azariah), restored Elath to Judean control.—2Ki 14:21, 22.

Syria, in an offensive action against Judah during Ahaz' reign (761-746 B.C.E.), put the Red Sea port of Elath back into Edom's hands. (2Ki 16:5, 6) The Edomites, evidently free from Judah's dominion, joined other nations, including Assyria, in raids against Judah.—2Ch 28:16-20; compare Ps 83:4-8.

No written records have been found from Edomite sources. Secular records of other nations, however, make mention of them. An Egyptian papyrus thought to be of the second millennium B.C.E. refers to Bedouin tribes from Edom entering the Delta region in search of pasturage for their cattle. Pharaohs Merneptah and Ramses III claimed dominion over Edom, as did the Assyrian monarch Adad-nirari III. Sometime after this latter king, Tiglath-pileser III (a contemporary of Ahaz) boasts of receiving tribute from "Kaushmalaku of Edom," while Esar-haddon, Sennacherib's successor, lists "Qaushgabri" as an Edomite vassal king.—*Ancient Near Eastern Texts,* edited by J. Pritchard, 1974, pp. 282, 291.

Edom in Prophecy. As early as King Uzziah's rule, the prophets Joel and Amos pronounced Jehovah's positive condemnation of Edom for its unrelenting fury expressed against Israel by the unmerciful use of the sword. (Am 1:6, 11, 12) Edom, by its vicious opposition to Jehovah's covenant people, had forfeited its title to the land it had held by divine warrant. (Joe 3:19; Am 9:11, 12) The Edomites sealed their doom when the Babylonians conquered Judah and Jerusalem in 607 B.C.E. Edomite hatred was clearly revealed as they urged on the devastators of Jerusalem (Ps 137:7), rejoiced at Judah's tragedy, and in their enmity and desire for revenge even turned over Judean escapees for slaughter by the Babylonians. They joined other neighboring peoples in plundering the land, and they planned to take over the abandoned country of Judah and of Israel, speaking boastfully against Jehovah. For this, Jehovah directed his prophets Jeremiah, Ezekiel, and Obadiah to assure Edom that its rejoicing would be short-lived and the treatment meted out to Judah would also become Edom's portion. (La 4:21, 22; Eze 25:12-14; 35:1-15; 36:3-5; Ob 1-16) As the prophet Isaiah had earlier foretold, the sword-wielding Edomites would come under Jehovah's own sword of justice and judgment, all classes, great and small, becoming like sacrificial animals devoted to destruction.—Isa 34:5-8.

Edom was to become like Sodom and Gomorrah, uninhabited for all time. (Jer 49:7-22; compare Isa 34:9-15.) Meriting Jehovah's hatred, Edom would be called "the territory of wickedness" and "the people whom Jehovah has denounced to time indefinite." (Mal 1:1-5) Edom thus evidently stands as symbolic of the hard-set enemies of God's covenant people at Isaiah 63:1-6, where the divine Warrior with bloodstained garments who has trod the winepress of God's vengeance appropriately is described as coming from Edom (meaning "Red") and from Edom's most prominent city Bozrah (possibly used here as a play on the Hebrew word *batsir'*, meaning "grape gathering").—Compare Re 14:14-20; 19:11-16.

Later History and Disappearance. The king of Edom was warned by means of Jehovah's prophet Jeremiah to bring his neck under the yoke of Nebuchadnezzar, the king of Babylon. (Jer 27:1-7) What the Edomites actually did in this regard is not recorded. However, after the destruction of Jerusalem in 607 B.C.E., some Judean exiles found temporary refuge in Edom. Then, after the departure of the Babylonian armies, these refugees returned to their land and finally fled down to Egypt. (Jer 40:11, 12; 43:5-7) Soon the time for Edom to drink deeply from the cup of Jehovah's wrath arrived. (Jer 25:15-17, 21) This occurred about the middle of the sixth century B.C.E., under the Babylonian king Nabonidus. According to C. J. Gadd, a scholar of Babylonian history and literature, the troops of Nabonidus that conquered Edom and Tema included Jewish soldiers. Commenting on this, John Lindsay wrote: "Thus, in part at least, the words of the prophet found a fulfilment when he wrote of Yahweh saying 'I will lay my vengeance upon Edom *by the hand of my people Israel*' (Ezek. 25.14). We have also a partial fulfilment of the words of Obadiah who said that Edom's 'allies', 'confederates', 'trusted friends' would 'deceive', 'prevail against' and 'set a trap under' them. Here we may see a reference to the Babylonians who, although in the days of Nebuchadrezzar were willing to allow them a share in Judah's loss, under Nabonidus curbed once and for all the commercial and mercantile ambitions of Edom (cf. Obad. 1 and 7)."—*Palestine Exploration Quarterly*, London, 1976, p. 39.

The book of Malachi, written some 100 years after the campaign into Edom by Nabonidus, relates that God had already made Edom's "mountains a desolated waste and his inheritance for the jackals of the wilderness." (Mal 1:3) The Edomites were hoping to return and rebuild their devastated places, but they would not be successful.—Mal 1:4.

By the fourth century B.C.E. the Nabataeans were inhabiting the Edomite territory, and the Edomites were never able to return. Instead, they found themselves in the Negeb to the S of Judah. The Edomites moved as far N as Hebron, and eventually the southern part of Judah became known as Idumea. According to Josephus, John Hyrcanus I subjugated them sometime between 130 and 120 B.C.E. and compelled them to accept Judaism. (*Jewish Antiquities*, XIII, 257, 258 [ix, 1]; XV, 253, 254 [vii, 9]) Thereafter they were gradually absorbed by the Jews, and following the Roman destruction of Jerusalem in 70 C.E., they ceased to exist as a people.—Ob 10, 18; see IDUMEA.

EDREI (Ed're·i).

1. A royal city of Og, king of Bashan. (Jos 12:4; 13:12) After defeating Sihon the Amorite, the Israelite forces under Moses' direction "went up," that is, went northward, until they encountered Og's military force in "the battle of Edrei," at what was apparently Bashan's southern frontier. Though Og was the last of the giantlike Rephaim and may have presented a formidable army, the Israelites, advised by Jehovah to be fearless, wiped out Og, his sons, and people, taking possession of his territory. (Nu 21:33-35; De 3:1-10) The city was later granted to Manasseh as part of its inheritance. (Jos 13:31) Edrei is generally identified with the present-day city of Der'a about 50 km (31 mi) ESE of the southern end of the Sea of Galilee, near the Yarmuk. Ruins there include a partially excavated subterranean city, cut in the rock beneath the ground-level city.

2. A fortified city of Naphtali. (Jos 19:32, 35, 37) It has been associated with modern Tell Khureibeh, about 7 km (4 mi) NNW of Hazor.

EDUCATION. The imparting or acquisition of knowledge and skill. Education is accomplished through (1) explanation and repetition; (2) discipline, training administered in love (Pr 1:7; Heb 12:5, 6); (3) personal observation (Ps 19:1-3; Ec 1:12-14); (4) reproof and rebuke (Ps 141:5; Pr 9:8; 17:10).

Jehovah God is the great Educator and Instructor, of whom there is no equal. (Job 36:22; Ps 71:17; Isa 30:20) God's earthly son Adam was created with the ability to speak a language. (Ge 2:19, 20, 23) He received instruction about creation (Ge chaps 1, 2) and God's requirements for him.—Ge 1:28-30; 2:15-17.

In Patriarchal Society. Throughout the entire Bible the family is the basic unit for imparting education. In earliest society the father was the head of the family and of the household, which might even be a large community, such as that of Abraham. The family head was responsible for the education of his household. (Ge 18:19) The good training manifested by Joseph indicates that Isaac and Jacob followed their father Abraham in teaching their children. (Ge 39:4, 6, 22; 41:40, 41) Job of the land of Uz, a distant relative of Abraham, displayed acquaintance with the scientific understanding and industrial developments of his day, and he was given a lesson in natural history by Jehovah.—Job 9:1, 9; chaps 28, 38-41.

At the same time there was considerable knowledge in Egypt of astronomy, mathematics, geometry, architecture, construction, and other arts and sciences. Moses, besides getting an education in the worship of Jehovah from his mother (Ex 2:7-10), was "instructed in all the wisdom of the Egyptians. In fact, he was powerful in his words and deeds." (Ac 7:22) The Israelites, though they had been slaves in Egypt, were able to read and write and to teach their children. Just before entering the Promised Land, they were instructed to write the commands of God upon the doorposts of their houses and on their gates, figuratively so, and they were to teach their children God's law. This was, of course, in the Hebrew language.—De 6:6-9; compare De 27:3; Jos 8:32.

Education Under the Law Before the Exile. Parents were still the primary educators, responsible for the instruction of their children. (Ex 12:26, 27; De 4:9; 6:7, 20, 21; 11:19-21) The spiritual, moral, and mental education from childhood up was regarded by the Jews from the very beginning of their history as one of the principal duties of parents. Samson's father, Manoah, prayed for guidance in the manner in which his son should be trained. (Jg 13:8) The father was the chief instructor, but the mother also taught, especially encouraging the child to follow the father's instruction and discipline. (Pr 1:8; 4:1; 31:26, 27) The parents realized that right training in youth would safeguard right conduct in later years.—Pr 22:6.

The children were to regard their parents with the greatest respect. The rod of parental authority was firmly exercised. (Pr 22:15) It was to be used in love, but discipline was severe for the disobedient child, the rod at times being literal. (Pr 13:24; 23:13, 14) A child who cursed or struck his parents could be put to death. (Le 20:9; Ex 21:15) An incurably rebellious older son was to be stoned. (De 21:18-21) In fact, the first commandment with a promise was the fifth of the Ten Commandments: "Honor your father and your mother, . . . in order that your days may prove long and it may go well with you on the ground that Jehovah your God is giving you." —De 5:16; Eph 6:2, 3.

The education given by parents was to be regular and constant, at home, at work, or when traveling, and it was to be not only verbal and disciplinary but also by example, for God's law was to direct parents in all their activities of life. Going to the festivals at Jerusalem three times a year provided education in geography, and at the same time it acquainted the child with his countrymen from all over the land of Israel.—De 16:16.

Along with the religious education would come education for the young men in following their father's secular occupation or learning a trade. Bezalel and Oholiab, expert craftsmen, were qualified by God's spirit to teach others during construction of the tabernacle in the wilderness. (Ex 35:34) The young women in a household would learn the wifely duties, and these prospective wives were trained to have great respect for their husbands, as Sarah had given the example. (Ge 18:12; 1Pe 3:5, 6) The good wife had many abilities, accomplishments, and responsibilities, as described in Proverbs, chapter 31.

It appears that both boys and girls received training in music. There were female musicians and singers. (Jg 11:34) Among the Levite males there were composers of songs and poetry, musicians, and singers.—Ps 87:Sup; 88:Sup; 1Ch 25.

God also set aside the entire tribe of Levi as a religious educational body. The priesthood was inaugurated in 1512 B.C.E. One of its chief functions was the education of the people in God's law. Moses the Levite as mediator was, of course, an instructor of the people in the law of God (Ex 18:16, 20; 24:12), and the priests, together with the nonpriestly Levites, were charged with the responsibility of seeing that the people understood all the regulations spoken by Jehovah through Moses. (Le 10:11; 14:57; De 17:10, 11; 2Ch 15:3; 35:3) The Levites were to read the Law to the people. This was done publicly for all the people at the time of the Festival of Booths in the Sabbath year, and here there was no segregation according to age or sex, but all the people, old and young, including the alien resident within the gates and all who could understand, would be gathered together to hear the reading. (De 31:9-13) King Jehoshaphat, in the third year of his reign, instituted a teaching campaign in

Judah, sending the princes, priests, and Levites in a circuit throughout Judah to instruct the people in God's law.—2Ch 17:9.

A considerable portion of the Hebrew Scriptures consists of poetry, which, from an educational viewpoint, is an effective memory aid. Hebrew poetry was not expressed in rhyme but in parallelism of thought, thought rhythm. Powerful metaphors were also used; these were based on natural creation, things familiar to all, even to children. Alphabetic acrostics, in which the letters beginning the verses are arranged in alphabetic order, were employed. (Ps 25, 34, 37, 111, 112, 119; Pr 31:10-31; La 1-4) Sometimes several verses would begin with the same letter; for example, in the 119th Psalm eight lines begin with the Hebrew letter 'a'leph, eight with behth, and so forth, to complete 176 lines for the 22 letters of the Hebrew alphabet.

After the Restoration. After the return from Babylon and the rebuilding of the temple, the greatest need was the education of the people in true worship. The scribe Ezra was a well-educated man and a Bible copyist. (Ezr 7:1, 6) Ezra compiled many records, and he copied and had a share in arranging the canon of the Hebrew Scriptures. Further, he undertook a general education of the nation of Israel in God's law. In doing this, he was carrying out his duties as a Levitical priest. (Ezr 7:11, 12, 25) He organized the priests and Levites who had returned from Babylon, in order to carry out an educational program in restoration of true worship for the repatriated Israelites and their children. (Ne 8:4-9) The Hebrew copyists, or scribes (Sopherim), were men educated in the Law, and although not all of these were Levites, they came to be most prominent in the instruction of the people. As time went on, however, they brought in many traditions and corrupted the true teaching of God's Word.—See SCRIBE.

Education in the First Century C.E. Parents continued as the primary ones responsible for the education of their children, especially their earlier education. (2Ti 1:5; 3:14, 15) We read about Jesus that he was brought up in Nazareth by his adoptive father and his mother and that he continued growing and getting stronger, being filled with wisdom. At the age of 12 he amazed the teachers at the temple by his understanding and his answers. (Lu 2:41, 46-52) The scribes continued to be the chief educators publicly and in the schools that had been set up in the synagogues. (See SYNAGOGUE.) Physi-

cal science was taught as well as the Law and the rabbinic teachings that had been added to the Law. Parents were required also to teach their children a trade.

Jesus was the teacher *par excellence*. Even among his contemporaries he was acknowledged as a teacher of exceptional influence and popularity. His disciples used to call him "Rabbi," which means "Teacher" or "Instructor." (Mr 9:5; see RABBI.) His opponents on occasion even acknowledged his fine speaking, and at one time officers who were sent by the Pharisees to arrest him, when asked why they returned empty-handed, replied: "Never has another man spoken like this."—Joh 7:46; Lu 20:39, 40; Mr 12:32, 34.

First of all, as he said, Jesus did not speak of his own initiative but came in his Father's name and spoke the things that he had learned from his Father. (Joh 5:19, 30, 43; 6:38; 10:25) He was an intimate of Jehovah God, being his only-begotten Son from the heavens, and as such he was the very best teacher concerning the qualities, works, and purposes of his Father. (Mt 11:27) He had the next most vital qualification of a good teacher in that he loved those whom he taught. (Mr 10:21; Joh 13:1, 34; 15:9, 12) Few teachers have loved their disciples so much that they were willing to give their lives for them, as Jesus did. (Joh 15:13) He had an understanding of the minds of his listeners. (Joh 2:25) He had deep discernment. (Lu 6:8) He had no selfish interests at heart in his teaching, for he was sinless and without guile. (Heb 7:26) He did not teach with the philosophical words of the scribes but used illustrations involving everyday things. For this reason his teachings are still understandable today. His instruction was full of illustrations.—See ILLUSTRATIONS.

Jesus' teaching included reproof and discipline. (Mr 8:33) He taught by example as well as by word; thus he personally carried out a vigorous campaign of preaching and teaching. His speech was with an authority that none of the scribes could match; accompanying this was God's holy spirit, which gave his teachings the stamp of heavenly backing, so that he could, with authority and power, command the demons to come out of those who were possessed by them. (Mr 1:27; Lu 4:36) He was bold and fearless in denouncing false teachers who would hinder others from hearing his teachings.—Mt 23.

Education and the Christian Congregation. Jesus' disciples followed his footsteps in Christian educational work and had success similar to his.

They not only *preached* the good news of God's Kingdom everywhere but also *taught* those who would listen. (Ac 2:42) They, like Jesus, were bold and spoke with authority. (Ac 4:13, 19, 20; 5:29) God's spirit empowered them and gave evidence of divine approval of their teaching. They taught in the temple, in synagogues, and from house to house. (Ac 5:16, 21; 13:14-16; 20:20) They met with fellow Christians for teaching and inciting one another to love and fine works.—Ac 20:7, 8; Heb 10:24, 25.

The apostle Paul described the different offices and activities in the congregation that were filled by mature men, among them being teachers. He showed that the purpose of all these activities was education, with a view to the training of the holy ones, for ministerial work, for the building up of the body of the Christ. (Eph 4:11-16) A regular program of education in God's Word was carried on by the congregation, as outlined in 1 Corinthians chapter 14. All the members of the Christian congregation, even the women, were to be teachers; they were to make disciples of the people of the world. (Ac 18:26; Heb 5:12; Ro 12:7) But within the congregation itself mature men were appointed to oversight, as, for example, Timothy and Titus. (1Ti 2:12) Such men had to be those qualified to teach the congregation and to correct things that may have got out of line. They were to use extraordinary care to ensure that their teaching was accurate and healthful.—1Ti 4:16; 2Ti 4:2, 3; Tit 2:1.

On the subject of physical education the Bible has little to say, except that the apostle Paul counsels: "For bodily training is beneficial for a little; but godly devotion is beneficial for all things, as it holds promise of the life now and that which is to come." (1Ti 4:8) Physical activity is required, however, in energetic preaching and teaching, which is encouraged. Jesus did a great deal of walking. So did his disciples; Paul's ministry, for example, included much travel, which in that time meant much walking.

The Bible gives limited comment on education of a secular nature. It warns Christians not to involve themselves in philosophies of men nor to take time to delve into foolish and unprofitable questions. It strongly counsels against mental intercourse with those who do not believe God and his Word. (1Ti 6:20, 21; 1Co 2:13; 3:18-20; Col 2:8; Tit 3:9; 1:14; 2Ti 2:16; Ro 16:17) Christians recognized that they were obligated before God to provide properly for their families. Often some form of education and training was re-quired to equip them for such secular occupation. (1Ti 5:8) But from the history of early Christianity we find that, primarily, they were interested in any legitimate method for getting "the good news" preached, in Bible education for themselves and all who would hear them. (1Co 9:16) As Professor E. J. Goodspeed says, in *Christianity Goes to Press,* (1940, p. 111):

"The Christians from the moment they awoke to the possibilities of publication in spreading their gospel over the world availed themselves of them to the full, not only publishing new books but searching out old ones for publication, and this genius for publication has never forsaken them. It is a mistake to suppose that it began with the discovery of printing; it was a characteristic of Christian attitudes from A.D. 70 on, gathering strength as the great fruitfulness of the method emerged. Even the barbarian invasions and the Dark Ages could not quench it. And it is all an evidence of the tremendous dynamic which informed the whole of early Christian life, which sought not only by deed and word but by all the most advanced techniques of publication to carry the gospel, in its fulness and without reserve, to all mankind."—See SCHOOL; TUTOR.

EGLAH (Eg'lah) [Young Cow; Heifer]. The mother of King David's sixth son Ithream, born to him in Hebron.—2Sa 3:5; 1Ch 3:3.

EGLAIM (Eg·la'im). Evidently one of the geographic extremities of Moab that, according to Isaiah 15:1, 8, was due to 'howl' over that nation's despoiling. The exact location of the ancient site is uncertain. However, the name Eglaim and a similar name, Agallim, mentioned by Eusebius (*Onomasticon,* 36, 19-21) as about 12 km (7.5 mi) S of Rabbath-Moab, may be preserved at Rujm el-Jilimeh in that area or at Khirbet Jeljul, a location dating from Nabataean-Roman times, 7 km (4 mi) farther south. Yohanan Aharoni suggests identifying it with Mazra', an oasis NE of the Lisan Peninsula.

EGLATH-SHELISHIYAH (Eg'lath-she·li'-shi·yah) [probably, Third Eglath]. A term used by Isaiah (15:5) and Jeremiah (48:34) in their pronouncements of doom against Moab, apparently referring to a site in that nation. Some hold that there were three towns in one vicinity with the same name, and that the third ("the third Eglath," *AT*) is here the target of the prophets' utterances. A precise identification of such sites has never been made.

Many scholars, however, are of the opinion that the Hebrew (*'egh·lath' sheli·shi·yah'*) should not be transliterated as a proper noun. They view it as a symbolic expression and would translate it as "a heifer of three years old." (*Dy, JP*; see *KJ, Ro.*) In this case, the prophets might be likening vanquished Moab to a sturdy, young, though full-grown, cow, but from which are heard only pitiful 'cries' of anguish.

EGLON   (Eg'lon) [Little Calf].

1. A king of Moab in the days of the Judges, who oppressed Israel for 18 years, "because they did what was bad in Jehovah's eyes." (Jg 3:12-25) Eglon was head of the confederacy of Moab, Ammon, and Amalek in their assault upon Israel. His downfall came when left-handed Ehud, after presenting the customary tribute, said: "I have a secret word for you, O king." In the privacy of his cool chamber atop the flat roof of his palace, Eglon, after dismissing his attendants, rose up from his throne to receive what Ehud said was "a word of God." Thereupon Ehud thrust into Eglon's very fat belly a double-edged sword so that "the handle kept going in also after the blade," and "the fecal matter began to come out." Concerning Judges 3:22, Clarke's *Commentary* says: "Either the contents of the bowels issued through the wound, or he had an evacuation in the natural way through the *fright* and *anguish.*"

2. A royal Canaanite city whose king joined a confederacy against Gibeon when that city made peace with Joshua and Israel. Joshua slew the five kings involved, hung them on stakes, and later conquered Eglon, devoting its inhabitants to destruction. (Jos 10:1-5, 22-27, 34, 35; 12:12) It was thereafter included in the territory of the tribe of Judah. (Jos 15:39) The original site is believed to be found at Tell el-Hesi, about 25 km (16 mi) ENE of Gaza, and about 11 km (7 mi) W of the site of Lachish, and thus near the edge of the Plains of Philistia. The ancient name, however, is preserved at the ruins of Khirbet 'Ajlan, a few miles distant.

EGYPT, EGYPTIAN.   Egypt and its inhabitants are referred to over 700 times in the Bible. In the Hebrew Scriptures, Egypt is usually designated by the name Mizraim (*Mits·ra'yim*) (compare Ge 50:11), evidently pointing to the prominence or predominance of the descendants of that son of Ham in the region. (Ge 10:6) The name *Misr* is applied to Egypt even today by Arabs. In certain psalms it is called "the land of Ham."—Ps 105:23, 27; 106:21, 22.

Boundaries and Geography.   (MAP, Vol. 1, p. 531) In ancient and modern times, Egypt has owed its existence to the Nile River, with its fertile valley stretching like a long, narrow green ribbon through the parched desert regions of northeastern Africa. "Lower Egypt" comprised the broad Delta region where the Nile waters fan out before emptying into the Mediterranean Sea, at one time through at least five separate branches, today by only two. From the point where the Nile's waters diverge (in the region of modern Cairo) to the seacoast is about 160 km (100 mi). The site of ancient Heliopolis (Biblical On) is found a short distance N of Cairo, while a few miles S of Cairo lies Memphis (usually called Noph in the Bible). (Ge 46:20; Jer 46:19; Ho 9:6) To the S of Memphis began the region of "Upper Egypt," extending up the valley all the way to the first cataract of the Nile at Aswan (ancient Syene), a distance of some 960 km (600 mi). Many scholars, however, consider it more logical to refer to the northern part of this section as "Middle Egypt." In this entire region (of Middle and Upper Egypt) the flat Nile Valley rarely exceeds 19 km (12 mi) in width, and it is bounded on both sides by limestone and sandstone cliffs, which form the edge of the desert proper.

Beyond the first cataract lay ancient Ethiopia, so that Egypt is said to have reached "from Migdol [a site evidently in NE Egypt] to Syene and to the boundary of Ethiopia." (Eze 29:10) While the Hebrew term *Mits·ra'yim* is regularly used to stand for the entire land of Egypt, many scholars believe that in some cases it represents Lower Egypt, and perhaps Middle Egypt, with Upper Egypt being designated by "Pathros." The reference to 'Egypt [Mizraim], Pathros, and Cush' at Isaiah 11:11 is paralleled by a similar geographic lineup in an inscription of Assyrian King Esar-haddon, who lists within his empire the regions of 'Musur, Paturisi, and Kusu.'—*Ancient Near Eastern Texts*, edited by J. Pritchard, 1974, p. 290.

Bounded by the Mediterranean Sea on the N and the first cataract of the Nile and Nubia-Ethiopia on the S, Egypt was hemmed in by the Libyan Desert (part of the Sahara) on the W and the Red Sea Desert on the E. Thus, for the most part, it was quite insulated against outside influence and was protected from invasion. The isthmus of Sinai on the NE, however, formed a bridge with the Asiatic continent (1Sa 15:7; 27:8); and over this land bridge came commercial caravans (Ge 37:25), migrants, and, in time, invading armies. "The torrent valley of Egypt," usually identified with Wadi el-'Arish in the Sinai Peninsula, evidently marked the NE extremity of Egypt's established domain. (2Ki 24:7) Beyond this lay Canaan. (Ge 15:18; Jos 15:4) In the desert to the W of the Nile, there were at least five oases that came to form part of the Egyptian kingdom. The large Faiyum oasis, about 72 km (45 mi) SW of ancient Memphis, received water from the Nile by means of a channel.

Economy dependent on Nile. Whereas today the desert regions lining the Nile Valley provide little or no vegetation to sustain animal life, the evidence is that in ancient times the wadis, or torrent valleys, contained many game animals hunted by the Egyptians. Still, rain was evidently scant and today is negligible (Cairo receiving perhaps 5 cm [2 in.] annually). Thus life in Egypt depended on the waters of the Nile.

The Nile's sources take their rise in the mountains of Ethiopia and neighboring lands. Here seasonal rainfall was sufficient to swell the river's flow, causing it to flood its banks in Egypt each year during the months of July to September. (Compare Am 8:8; 9:5.) This not only provided water for irrigation canals and basins but also deposited valuable silt to enrich the soil. So fertile was the Nile Valley, and also the Delta, that the well-watered region of Sodom and Gomorrah viewed by Lot was likened to "the garden of Jehovah, like the land of Egypt." (Ge 13:10) However, the amount of inundation was variable; when low, production was poor and famine resulted. (Ge 41:29-31) The complete failure of the Nile inundations would represent a disaster of the first order, converting the country into a barren wasteland.—Isa 19:5-7; Eze 29:10-12.

Products. Agriculturally rich, Egypt's main crops were barley, wheat, spelt (a type of wheat), and flax (from which fine linen was made and exported to many lands). (Ex 9:31, 32; Pr 7:16) There were vineyards and date, fig, and pomegranate trees; vegetable gardens provided a good variety of products, including cucumbers, watermelons, leeks, onions, and garlic. (Ge 40:9-11; Nu 11:5; 20:5) The allusion to 'irrigating the land with one's foot' (De 11:10) is understood by some scholars to refer to the use of a foot-powered waterwheel. It might also refer to use of the foot to open and to close channels through which irrigation water flowed.

When famine hit neighboring lands, people often made their way down to fruitful Egypt, as did Abraham early in the second millennium B.C.E. (Ge 12:10) In time Egypt came to be a granary for much of the Mediterranean area. The ship out of Alexandria, Egypt, that the apostle Paul boarded at Myra in the first century C.E. was a grain ship on its way to Italy.—Ac 27:5, 6, 38.

Another important export of Egypt was papyrus, the reedy plant that grew in the abundant marshes of the Delta (Ex 2:3; compare Job 8:11) and that was used for making writing material. Lacking in forests, however, Egypt was obliged to import lumber from Phoenicia, especially cedar from port cities such as Tyre, where Egypt's many-colored linens were prized. (Eze 27:7) Egyptian temples and monuments were built of granite and some softer stones, such as limestone, supplies of which were abundant in the hills flanking the Nile Valley. Ordinary homes and even palaces were made of mud brick (the common material for construction of all buildings in Mesopotamia). Egyptian mines in the hills along the Red Sea (as well as over in the Sinai Peninsula) produced gold and copper; bronze products made from this copper were also exported.—Ge 13:1, 2; Ps 68:31.

Stock raising played an important part in the Egyptian economy; Abraham acquired sheep and cattle while there, as well as such beasts of burden as asses and camels. (Ge 12:16; Ex 9:3) Horses are mentioned during the period of Joseph's administration in Egypt (1737-1657 B.C.E.) and are generally considered to have been introduced from Asia. (Ge 47:17; 50:9) These may have first been obtained by trade or by capture during Egyptian raids into lands to the NE. By Solomon's time, Egyptian horses were sufficient in number and esteemed highly enough to be an important item (along with Egyptian chariots) on the world market.—1Ki 10:28, 29.

Birds of prey and scavenger birds, such as vultures, kites, eagles, and falcons, as well as many water birds, including the ibis and the crane, were numerous. The Nile abounded with fish (Isa 19:8), and hippopotamuses and crocodiles were common. (Compare symbolic language of Eze 29:2-5.) The desert regions were inhabited by jackals, wolves, hyenas, and lions as well as various types of snakes and other reptiles.

The People. The people of Egypt were Hamites, evidently descended primarily from Ham's son Mizraim. (Ge 10:6) After the dispersal at Babel (Ge 11:8, 9), many of Mizraim's descendants, such as the Ludim, Anamim, Lehabim,

Naphtuhim, and Pathrusim, may have migrated to N Africa. (Ge 10:6, 13, 14) As already noted, Pathros (singular form of Pathrusim) is associated with Upper Egypt, and there is some evidence for placing the Naphtuhim in the Delta region of Egypt.

Supporting the view that there was a rather composite population formed of different family tribes is the fact that the country from great antiquity was divided into numerous sections (later called nomes) and that these divisions continued to exist and formed part of the governmental structure after the country was unified under one principal ruler, in fact, until the end of the empire. There were generally 42 nomes recognized, 20 in Lower Egypt and 22 in Upper Egypt. The continued distinction made between Upper and Lower Egypt throughout Egypt's history, though perhaps relating to geographic differences, may also point to an original tribal division. When the central government weakened, the country tended to split into these two major sections or even approach disintegration into numerous petty kingdoms in the various nomes.

On the basis of ancient paintings and also mummified bodies, the early Egyptians are described as generally small-statured, slender, and while not Negroid, dark-complexioned. Considerable variety, however, is evident in ancient paintings and sculptures.

Language. Modern scholars incline to class the Egyptian language by such terms as "Semito-Hamitic." While the language was basically Hamitic, it is claimed that there are many analogous points in its grammar and that of the Semitic tongues, as well as some similarities in the vocabulary. Despite such apparent connections, it is acknowledged that "Egyptian differs from all the Semitic tongues a good deal more than any one of them differs from any other, and at least until its relationship to the African languages is more closely defined, Egyptian must certainly be classified as standing outside the Semitic group." (*Egyptian Grammar*, by A. Gardiner, London, 1957, p. 3) When hiding his identity from his brothers, Joseph spoke to them through an Egyptian interpreter.—Ge 42:23.

There are, at any rate, a number of factors making it extremely difficult to draw definite conclusions as to the earliest forms of language used in Egypt. One of these is the Egyptian system of writing. The ancient inscriptions use pictographic signs (representations of animals,

birds, plants, or other objects) along with certain geometric forms, a system of writing called hieroglyphics by the Greeks. While certain signs came to represent syllables, these were used only to supplement the hieroglyphics and never replaced them. Furthermore, the precise sounds expressed by those syllables are not known today. Some help is obtained from the references to Egypt in certain cuneiform writings as early as the middle of the second millennium B.C.E. Greek transcriptions of Egyptian names and of other words dating from about the sixth century C.E., and Aramaic transcriptions beginning about a century later, likewise give some idea of the spelling of the Egyptian words transcribed. But the reconstruction of the phonology, or sound system, of ancient Egyptian is still based primarily on Coptic, the form of Egyptian spoken from the third century C.E. onward. So, the original structure of the ancient vocabulary in its earliest form, particularly before the period of the Israelite sojourn in Egypt, can only be approximated. For example, see No, No-AMON.

Additionally, knowledge of other ancient Hamitic languages in Africa is very limited today, thereby making it difficult to determine the relationship of Egyptian to them. No inscriptions of non-Egyptian African languages are known earlier than the start of the Common Era. The facts support the Biblical account of the confusion of language, and it seems evident that the early Egyptians, as descendants of Ham through Mizraim, spoke a language separate and distinct from the Semitic tongues.

Hieroglyphic writing was used especially for inscriptions on monuments and wall paintings, where the symbols were executed in great detail. While it continued to be used down to the start of the Common Era, particularly for religious texts, a less cumbersome writing that used more simplified, cursive forms was developed at an early date by scribes writing with ink on leather and papyrus. Called hieratic, it was followed by an even more cursive form called demotic, particularly from what is styled the "Twenty-sixth Dynasty" (seventh and sixth centuries B.C.E.) onward. Deciphering of Egyptian texts was not accomplished until after the discovery of the Rosetta Stone in 1799. This inscription, now in the British Museum, contains a decree honoring Ptolemy V (Epiphanes) and dates from 196 B.C.E. The writing is in Egyptian hieroglyphic, demotic, and Greek, and the Greek text became the key making decipherment of Egyptian possible.

Religion. Egypt was an ultrareligious land, rife with polytheism. Every city and town had its own local deity, bearing the title "Lord of the City." A list found in the tomb of Thutmose III contains the names of some 740 gods. (Ex 12:12) Frequently the god was represented as married to a goddess who bore him a son, "thus forming a divine triad or trinity in which the father, moreover, was not always the chief, contenting himself on occasion with the role of prince consort, while the principal deity of the locality remained the goddess." (*New Larousse Encyclopedia of Mythology*, 1968, p. 10) Each of the chief gods dwelt in a temple that was not open to the public. The god was worshiped by the priests who awoke him each morning with a hymn, bathed him, dressed him, "fed" him, and rendered him other services. (Contrast Ps 121:3, 4; Isa 40:28.) In this the priests were apparently regarded as acting as the representatives of the Pharaoh, who was believed to be a living god himself, the son of the god Ra. This situation certainly emphasizes the courage shown by Moses and Aaron in going before Pharaoh to present him with the decree of the true God and adds

Statue symbolizing
Amon's protection of Pharaoh

significance to Pharaoh's disdainful response, "Who is Jehovah, so that I should obey his voice?" —Ex 5:2.

Despite the great mass of archaeological material unearthed in Egypt in the form of temples, statues, religious paintings, and writings, relatively few facts are known about the actual religious *beliefs* of the Egyptians. Religious texts present a very spotty and fragmentary picture, generally omitting as much as or more than they include. Much of the understanding of the nature of their gods and practices is based on deduction or on data provided by Greek writers such as Herodotus and Plutarch.

The lack of unity of belief is apparent, however, as regional differences continued throughout Egyptian history and resulted in a maze of legends and myths, often contradictory. The god Ra, for example, was known under 75 different names and forms. Only a few, relatively speaking, of the hundreds of deities seem to have received worship on a truly national basis. Most popular among these was the trinity or triad of Osiris, Isis (his wife), and Horus (his son). Then there were the "cosmic" gods headed by Ra, the sun-god, and including gods of the moon, sky, air, earth, the river Nile, and so forth. At Thebes (Biblical No) the god Amon was most prominent and in time was accorded the title "king of the gods" under the name Amon-Ra. (Jer 46:25) At festival times (Jer 46:17), the gods were paraded through the city streets. When, for example, the idol image of Ra was carried by his priests in religious procession, the people made it a point to be on hand, expecting to get merit thereby. Considering their mere presence as a fulfillment of their religious obligation, the Egyptians felt that Ra, in turn, was obligated to continue to prosper them. They looked to him only for material blessings and prosperity, never asking for anything spiritual. There are numerous correspondencies between the principal gods of Egypt and those of Babylon, the evidence favoring Babylon as the source and Egypt as the receiver or perpetuator. —See GODS AND GODDESSES.

This polytheistic worship had no beneficial or uplifting effect on the Egyptians. As is observed by the *Encyclopædia Britannica* (1959, Vol. 8, p. 53): "Marvellous mysteries, occultly harbouring deep truths, are assigned to them by the classical and modern imagination. They had mysteries, of course, like the Ashantis or Ibos [African tribes]. It is a mistake, however, to think that these mysteries enshrined truth, and that there was an occult 'faith' behind them." In reality, the available evidence shows that magic and primitive superstition were basic elements of the Egyptian worship. (Ge 41:8) Religious magic was employed to prevent disease; spiritism was prominent, with many "charmers," "spirit mediums," and "professional foretellers of events." (Isa 19:3) Beads, amulets, and "good-luck" charms were worn, and magic spells were written on scraps of papyrus and tied around the neck. (Compare De 18:10, 11.) When Moses and Aaron performed miraculous acts by divine power, the priestly magicians and sorcerers of Pharaoh's courts made a show of duplicating such acts through magical arts until forced to admit failure.—Ex 7:11, 22; 8:7, 18, 19.

Animal worship. This superstitious worship led the Egyptians to practice a most degrading idolatry that embraced the worship of animals. (Compare Ro 1:22, 23.) Many of the most prominent gods were regularly depicted as having a human body with the head of an animal or bird. Thus the god Horus was represented with a falcon's head; Thoth with the head of an ibis or else that of an ape. In some cases the god was considered to be actually incarnate in the body of the animal, as in the case of the Apis bulls. The living Apis bull, viewed as the incarnation of the god Osiris, was kept in a temple and at death received an elaborate funeral and burial. The belief that some animals, such as cats, baboons, crocodiles, jackals, and various birds, were sacred by virtue of their association with certain gods resulted in the Egyptians' mummifying literally

Jehovah's plague of pestilence on the livestock of Egypt disgraced their god Apis, represented by a bull

hundreds of thousands of such creatures, burying them in special cemeteries.

Why did Moses insist that Israel's sacrifices would be "detestable to the Egyptians"?

The fact that so many different animals were venerated in one part of Egypt or another is doubtless what gave force and persuasiveness to Moses' insistence that Israel be allowed to go into the wilderness to make their sacrifices, saying to Pharaoh: "Suppose we would sacrifice a thing detestable to the Egyptians before their eyes; would they not stone us?" (Ex 8:26, 27) It appears that most of the sacrifices Israel later did make would have been highly offensive to the Egyptians. (In Egypt the sun-god Ra was at times represented as a calf born of the celestial cow.) On the other hand, as shown under Gods and Goddesses, by the Ten Plagues on Egypt, Jehovah executed judgments "on all the gods of Egypt," bringing great humiliation upon them while making his own name known throughout the land.—Ex 12:12.

The nation of Israel did not completely escape contamination with such false worship during its two centuries of sojourning in Egypt (Jos 24:14), and this was doubtless, to a considerable extent, at the root of the wrong attitudes displayed early in the Exodus journey. Though Jehovah instructed the Israelites to throw away "the dungy idols of Egypt," they failed to do so. (Eze 20:7, 8; 23:3, 4, 8) The making of a golden calf for worship in the wilderness likely reflects the Egyptian animal worship that had infected some Israelites. (Ex 32:1-8; Ac 7:39-41) Just before Israel entered the Promised Land, Jehovah again gave explicit warning against any association of animal forms or of any of the "cosmic" bodies in Israel's worship of Him. (De 4:15-20) Yet, animal worship surfaced again centuries later when Jeroboam, who had recently returned from Egypt, made two golden calves for worship when he gained kingship in the northern kingdom of Israel. (1Ki 12:2, 28, 29) It is noteworthy that the inspired Scriptures recorded by Moses are entirely free from any corruption by such Egyptian idolatry and superstition.

Spiritual and moral qualities lacking. Some scholars suggest that whatever concept of sin was manifest in certain Egyptian religious texts was the later result of Semitic influence. Yet, confession of sin was always in a negative sense, as the *Encyclopædia Britannica* (1959, Vol. 8, p. 56) comments: "When [the Egyptian] confessed he did not say 'I am guilty'; he said 'I am not guilty.' His confession was negative, and the *onus probandi* [the burden of proof] lay on his judges, who, according to the funerary papyri, always gave the verdict in his favour—or at any rate it was hoped and expected that they would do so." (Contrast Ps 51:1-5.) Ancient Egypt's religion appears to have been mainly a matter of ceremonies and spells, designed to achieve certain desired results through the providence of one or more of their numerous gods.

Though the claim is made that a form of monotheism existed during the reigns of Pharaohs Amenhotep III and Amenhotep IV (Akhenaton), when the worship of the sun-god Aton became nearly exclusive, it was not a true monotheism. The Pharaoh himself continued to be worshiped as a god. And even in this period there was no

Giant Sphinx seems to be standing guard in front of pyramids at Giza

ethical quality to the Egyptian religious texts, the hymns to the sun-god Aton merely praising him for his life-giving heat but remaining barren of any expression of praise or appreciation for any spiritual or moral qualities. Any suggestion that the monotheism of Moses' writings derived from Egyptian influence is therefore completely without foundation.

Beliefs about the dead. Strikingly prominent in Egyptian religion was the concern for the dead and the preoccupation with ensuring one's welfare and happiness after the "change" of death. The belief in reincarnation or the transmigration of the soul was an all-pervading doctrine. The soul was believed to be immortal; nevertheless, it was believed that the human body must also be preserved so that the soul might return and use it on occasion. Because of this belief, the Egyptians embalmed their dead. The tomb in which the mummified body was placed was considered the deceased's "home." The pyramids were colossal residences for the royal dead. The necessities and luxuries of life, including jewelry, clothing, furniture, and supplies of food, were stored away in the tombs for future use by the deceased, along with written spells and charms (such as the "Book of the Dead") to provide the departed with protection from evil spirits. (PICTURE, Vol. 1, p. 533) However, these spells did not even protect them from the human tomb robbers who eventually ransacked virtually every major tomb.

While the bodies of Jacob and Joseph were embalmed, in Jacob's case this was doubtless largely for the purpose of preservation until his body could be transferred to a burial place in the Promised Land as an expression of their faith. Particularly in Joseph's case, the embalming may have been done by the Egyptians as an expression

Gigantic statues at Abu Simbel, all honoring Ramses II

Circumcision was a regular practice among the Egyptians from ancient times, and the Bible lists them with other circumcised peoples. —Jer 9:25, 26.

Education seems to have consisted primarily of schools for the scribes, run by the priests. Besides being expert in Egyptian writing, royal scribes also were thoroughly familiar with Aramaic cuneiform; already in the middle of the second millennium B.C.E. subject rulers in Syria and Palestine regularly communicated with the Egyptian capital in Aramaic. Egyptian mathematics was sufficiently well developed to allow for the stupendous construction feats mentioned previously, and some knowledge of geometric and algebraic principles is evident. It may be noted that "Moses was instructed in all the wisdom of the Egyptians." (Ac 7:22) While there was much false wisdom in Egypt, some knowledge of practical value was also available.

Government and law were centered on the king or Pharaoh, regarded as a god in human form. He ruled the land through subordinates, or ministers, and through feudal chiefs, whose power in times of royal weakness rivaled that of the king. Perhaps these latter chieftains were indeed viewed by those under their domain as virtual kings, thus accounting for the Biblical mention of "the kings [plural] of Egypt" when referring to specific times. (2Ki 7:6; Jer 46:25) After the Egyptian conquest of Nubia-Ethiopia to the S, that region was governed by a viceroy called "the king's son of Cush," and there is evidence of an Egyptian viceroy in Phoenicia as well.

No actual code of law is known from Egypt; laws existed but evidently they were simply by royal decree, like those of Pharaoh concerning the Israelites' brickmaking labor and the order to drown all newborn Israelite male babies. (Ex

of respect and honor.—Ge 47:29-31; 50:2-14, 24-26.

Egyptian Life and Culture. Scholars have long presented Egypt as the 'most ancient civilization' and as the source of many of mankind's earliest inventions and progress. More recently, however, the accumulated evidence has pointed to Mesopotamia as the so-called cradle of civilization. Certain Egyptian architectural methods, the use of the wheel, perhaps the basic principles of their pictographic writing, and particularly the fundamental features of Egyptian religion are all thought to have had a Mesopotamian origin. This, of course, is in accord with the Bible record of the dispersion of peoples following the Flood.

The best known achievements in Egyptian *architecture* are the pyramids constructed at Giza by Pharaohs Khufu (Cheops), Khafre, and Menkure of what is styled the "Fourth Dynasty." The largest, that of Khufu, has a base covering about 5.3 ha (13 acres), with a peak some 137 m (450 ft) high (the equivalent of a modern 40-story building). It is calculated that 2,300,000 blocks of stone, averaging 2.3 metric tons each, were used. The blocks were shaped so carefully that they fitted within a few millimeters. Colossal temples were also built; one at Karnak, in Thebes (Biblical No; Jer 46:25; Eze 30:14-16), was the largest columnar structure ever constructed by man.

1:8-22; 5:6-18; compare Ge 41:44.) Taxes were imposed on all crops of landowners, and this seems to have had its beginning in Joseph's day, when all land, except that of the priests, came to be property of the Pharaoh. (Ge 47:20-26) Taxes included not only portions of the produce or livestock but also labor for government projects and for military service. Punishment for crimes included cutting off the nose, exile to labor in the mines, beating with rods, imprisonment, and death, often by beheading.—Ge 39:20; 40:1-3, 16-22.

Marriage customs permitted polygamy and brother-and-sister marriages, this latter practice being known in some places in Egypt up until the second century C.E. Certain Pharaohs are known to have married their sisters, apparently because no other women were considered sacred enough to mate with such a "living god." The Law given Israel after they had left Egypt forbade incestuous marriage, saying, "The way the land of Egypt does . . . you must not do; [nor] the way the land of Canaan does."—Le 18:3, 6-16.

Ancient Egyptian knowledge of *medicine* has often been presented as quite scientific and advanced. While some knowledge of anatomy is evident and certain simple surgical methods were developed and cataloged, much ignorance is also revealed. Thus, while an Egyptian papyrus text speaks of the heart as being connected by vessels to every part of the body, the same text presents the vessels as carrying, not blood, but air, water, semen, and mucus. Not only was there a fundamental misunderstanding of the functions of the living body, but the medical texts are heavily dosed with magic and superstition; magical spells and incantations make up a major portion of the information. Remedies not only included beneficial herbs and plants but also prescribed such ingredients as the blood of mice, urine, or the excrement of flies, which, together with the spells, were "calculated to drive the possessing demon out of the man's body in sheer disgust." (*History of Mankind,* by J. Hawkes and Sir Leonard Woolley, 1963, Vol. I, p. 695) Such lack of understanding may have contributed to some of the 'fearsome diseases of Egypt,' likely including elephantiasis, dysentery, smallpox, bubonic plague, ophthalmia, and other ailments; Israel could gain protection from them by faithful obedience. (De 7:15; compare De 28:27, 58-60; Am 4:10.) The hygienic measures imposed on the Israelites following the Exodus are in dramatic contrast to many of the practices described in the Egyptian texts.—Le 11:32-40; see DISEASES AND TREATMENT.

Egyptian *trades* embraced the usual range: pottery making, weaving, metalworking, the making of jewelry and religious charms, and many other skills. (Isa 19:1, 9, 10) Already by about the middle of the second millennium B.C.E., Egypt was a center of glass manufacturing.—Compare Job 28:17.

Transportation within the country centered on the Nile River. The prevailing winds out of the N aided the sailing vessels in going upstream, while those boats traveling from the S were carried downstream by the current. Besides this main "highway," there were canals and a few roads, leading, for example, up into Canaan.

International trade was carried on with other African countries by caravans and by ships on the Red Sea, while large Egyptian galleys carried cargoes and passengers to many ports of the eastern Mediterranean Sea.

Egyptian *dress* was simple. The men during much of early history wore merely a kind of apron, gathered in pleats at the front; later only the humbler classes left the upper part of the body bare. Women wore a long close-fitting chemise with shoulder straps, the garment often being made of fine linen. It was customary to go barefoot, a possible factor in the prevalence of certain diseases.

Egyptian paintings show the men with their hair cut short or shaved, and as clean shaven. (Ge 41:14) The use of cosmetics was common among the women.

Egyptian *homes* varied from the simple huts of the poor to the spacious villas of the wealthy, with their surrounding gardens, orchards, and ponds. Since Potiphar served as an official of Pharaoh, his home was likely a fine villa. (Ge 39:1, 4-6) *Furniture* varied from simple stools to elaborate chairs and couches. Homes of some size were generally built around open courtyards. (Compare Ex 8:3, 13.) Kneading of dough and cooking of food were often done in the courtyard. *Food* for most Egyptians was likely barley bread, vegetables, fish (both abundant and cheap; Nu 11:5), and beer, the common drink. Those who could afford it added various meats to their diet. —Ex 16:3.

Egyptian *military* men handled the standard weapons of the time: bow and arrow, spear or lance, mace, ax, and dagger. Horse-drawn chariots played a major role in their warfare. Though body armor seems to have been little used in earlier times, it later came into use as also did helmets, often plumed. Thus, Jeremiah's prophecy (46:2-4) gives an accurate description of the Egyptian military in the seventh century B.C.E. Much of the army seems to have been formed of conscripts from among the people; in later times mercenary troops from other nations were regularly employed.—Jer 46:7-9.

History. Egyptian history from secular sources is very uncertain, especially for the earlier periods.—See CHRONOLOGY (Egyptian Chronology).

Abraham's visit. Sometime after the Flood (2370-2369 B.C.E.) and the subsequent split-up of the peoples at Babel, Hamites occupied Egypt. By the time (sometime between 1943 B.C.E. and 1932 B.C.E.) that famine forced Abraham (Abram) to leave Canaan and go down to Egypt, a kingdom was functioning under a Pharaoh (unnamed in the Bible).—Ge 12:4, 14, 15; 16:16.

Egypt was apparently receptive to strangers, and no animosity appears to have been shown to nomadic Abraham, a tent dweller. Yet Abraham's fear of being murdered because of his beautiful wife was evidently founded on fact and indicates a low state of morality in Egypt. (Ge 12:11-13) The plagues brought on Pharaoh because of his taking Sarah into his house were effective and resulted in Abraham's being ordered to leave the country; when he left he took not only his wife but also increased possessions. (Ge 12:15-20; 13:1, 2) Perhaps Sarah's maidservant Hagar was obtained during Abraham's stay in Egypt. (Ge 16:1) Hagar became the mother of Abraham's son Ishmael (1932 B.C.E.), and on growing up, Ishmael married a woman from his mother's native land, Egypt. (Ge 16:3, 4, 15, 16; 21:21) Thus, the Ishmaelites as a race were originally predominantly Egyptian, and their range of camping sites at times took them near Egypt's border.—Ge 25:13-18.

A second famine again made Egypt a place for seeking relief, but now (sometime after 1843 B.C.E., the year of Abraham's death) Jehovah instructed Isaac to reject any idea of a move into that land.—Ge 26:1, 2.

Joseph in Egypt. Then, nearly two centuries after Abraham's sojourn in Egypt, Jacob's young son Joseph was sold to a Midianite-Ishmaelite caravan and resold in Egypt to an official of Pharaoh's court (1750 B.C.E.). (Ge 37:25-28, 36) As Joseph later explained to his brothers, this was permitted by God to prepare the way for the preservation of Jacob's family during a period of extreme famine. (Ge 45:5-8) The report of the major events of Joseph's life presents a picture of Egypt that is undeniably accurate. (See JOSEPH No. 1.) The titles of officials, customs, dress, use of magic, and many other details described can be corroborated by data obtained from Egyptian monuments, pictures, and writings. The investiture of Joseph as viceroy of Egypt (Ge 41:42), for example, follows the procedure depicted in Egyptian inscriptions and murals.—Ge chaps 45-47.

The Egyptian distaste for eating with Hebrews, as at the meal Joseph provided for his brothers, may have been due to religious or racial pride and prejudice, or it may have been tied in with their detestation of shepherds. (Ge 43:31, 32; 46:31-34) This latter attitude, in turn, quite possibly was simply due to an Egyptian caste system, in which shepherds seem to have been near the bottom; or it could have been that since the land available for cultivation was limited, there was a strong dislike for those seeking pasture for flocks.

"Hyksos Period." Many commentators place Joseph's entry into Egypt and that of his father and family in what is popularly known as the Hyksos Period. However, as Merrill Unger comments (*Archaeology and the Old Testament,* 1964, p. 134): "Unfortunately, [this period] is one of great obscurity in Egypt, and the Hyksos conquest is very imperfectly understood."

Some scholars assign the Hyksos to the "Thirteenth to the Seventeenth Dynasties" with a 200-year rule; others confine them to the "Fifteenth and Sixteenth Dynasties" during a century and a half or only one century. The name Hyksos has been interpreted by some as meaning "Shepherd Kings," by others, "Rulers of Foreign Countries." Conjectures as to their race or nationality have been even more varied, with Indo-Europeans from the Caucasus or even in Central Asia, Hittites, Syrian-Palestinian rulers (Canaanites or Amorites), and Arabian tribes all being suggested.

Some archaeologists depict the "Hyksos conquest" of Egypt as northern hordes sweeping through Palestine and Egypt in swift chariots, while others refer to it as a creeping conquest, that is, a gradual infiltration of migrating nomads or seminomads who either slowly took over control of the country piecemeal or by a swift coup d'état put themselves at the head of the existing government. In the book *The World of the Past* (Part V, 1963, p. 444) archaeologist Jacquetta Hawkes states: "It is no longer thought that the Hyksos rulers . . . represent the invasion of a conquering horde of Asiatics. The name seems to mean Rulers of the Uplands, and they were wandering groups of Semites who had long come to Egypt for trade and other peaceful purposes." While this may represent the present popular view, it still leaves the difficult problem of explaining how such "wandering groups" could take over the land of Egypt, especially since the "Twelfth Dynasty," prior to this period, is considered to have brought the country to a peak of power.

As *The Encyclopedia Americana* (1956, Vol. 14, p. 595) says: "The only detailed account of them [the Hyksos] in any ancient writer is an unreliable passage of a lost work of Manetho, cited by Josephus in his rejoinder to Apion." Statements attributed by Josephus to Manetho are the source of the name Hyksos. Interestingly, Josephus, claiming to quote Manetho verbatim, presents Manetho's account as directly connecting the Hyksos with the Israelites. Josephus, it seems, accepts this connection but argues vehemently against many of the details of the account. He seems to prefer the rendering of Hyksos as "captive shepherds" rather than "king-shepherds." Manetho, according to Josephus, presents the Hyksos as conquering Egypt without a battle, destroying cities and "the temples of the gods," and causing slaughter and havoc. They are represented as settling in the Delta region. Finally the Egyptians are said to have risen up, fought a long and terrible war, with 480,000 men, besieged the Hyksos at their chief city, Avaris, and then, strangely, reached an agreement allowing them to leave the country unharmed with their families and possessions, whereupon they went to Judea and built Jerusalem.—*Against Apion*, I, 73-105 (14-16); 223-232 (25, 26).

In the contemporary writings the names of these rulers were preceded by titles such as "Good God," "Son of Re'," or *Hik-khoswet*, "Ruler of Foreign Lands." The term "Hyksos" is evidently derived from this latter title. Egyptian documents immediately following their rule called them Asiatics. Regarding this period of Egyptian history, C. E. DeVries noted: "In attempting to correlate secular history with the biblical data, some scholars have tried to equate the expulsion of the Hyksos from Egypt with the Israelite Exodus, but the chronology rules out this identification, and other factors as well make this hypoth-

esis untenable. . . . The origin of the Hyksos is uncertain; they came from somewhere in Asia and bore Semitic names for the most part."—*The International Standard Bible Encyclopedia*, edited by G. Bromiley, 1982, Vol. 2, p. 787.

Since Joseph's elevation to power and the benefits it brought Israel were by divine providence, there is no need to seek some other reason in the form of friendly "Shepherd Kings." (Ge 45:7-9) But it is possible that Manetho's account, actually the foundation of the "Hyksos" idea, simply represents a garbled tradition, one that developed from earlier Egyptian efforts to explain away what took place in their land during the Israelite sojourn in Egypt. The tremendous effect on the country produced by Joseph's ascension to the position of acting ruler (Ge 41:39-46; 45:26); the profound change his administration brought, resulting in the Egyptians' sale of their land and even of themselves to Pharaoh (Ge 47:13-20); the 20-percent tax they thereafter paid from their produce (Ge 47:21-26); the 215 years of Israelite residence in Goshen, with their eventually exceeding the native population in number and strength, according to Pharaoh's statement (Ex 1:7-10, 12, 20); the Ten Plagues and the devastation they wrought not only on the Egyptian economy but even more so on their religious beliefs and the prestige of their priesthood (Ex 10:7; 11:1-3; 12:12, 13); the Exodus of Israel following the death of all Egypt's firstborn and then the destruction of the cream of Egypt's military forces at the Red Sea (Ex 12:2-38; 14:1-28)—all these things certainly would require some attempted explanation by the Egyptian official element.

It should never be forgotten that the recording of history in Egypt, as in many Middle Eastern lands, was inseparably connected with the priesthood, under whose tutelage the scribes were trained. It would be most unusual if some propagandistic explanation were not invented to account for the utter failure of the Egyptian gods to prevent the disaster Jehovah God brought upon Egypt and its people. History, even recent history, records many occasions when such propaganda so grossly perverted the facts that the oppressed were presented as the oppressors, and the innocent victims were presented as the dangerous and cruel aggressors. Manetho's account (over a thousand years after the Exodus), if preserved with some degree of correctness by Josephus, may possibly represent the distorted traditions handed down by succeeding generations of Egyptians to account for the basic elements of the true account, in the Bible, concerning Israel in Egypt.—See EXODUS (Authenticity of the Exodus Account).

Israel's slavery. Since the Bible does not name the Pharaoh who initiated the oppression upon the Israelites (Ex 1:8-22) nor the Pharaoh before whom Moses and Aaron appeared and in whose reign the Exodus took place (Ex 2:23; 5:1), and since these events have either been deliberately omitted from Egyptian records or the records have been destroyed, it is not possible to assign these events to any specific dynasty nor to the reign of any particular Pharaoh of secular history. Ramses (Rameses) II (of the "Nineteenth Dynasty") is often suggested as the Pharaoh of the oppression on the basis of the reference to the building of the cities of Pithom and Raamses by the Israelite laborers. (Ex 1:11) It is held that these cities were built during the reign of Ramses II. In *Archaeology and the Old Testament* (p. 149) Merrill Unger comments: "But in the light of Raamses II's notorious practice of taking credit for achievements accomplished by his predecessors, these sites were most certainly merely rebuilt or enlarged by him." Actually the name "Rameses" seems to have applied to an entire district already in the time of Joseph.—Ge 47:11.

By means of God's deliverance through Moses, the nation of Israel was freed from "the house of slaves" and "the iron furnace," as Egypt continued to be called by Bible writers. (Ex 13:3; De 4:20; Jer 11:4; Mic 6:4) Forty years later Israel began the conquest of Canaan. There has been an effort to connect this Biblical event with the situation described in what are known as the Amarna Tablets, found at Tell el-Amarna on the Nile, about 270 km (170 mi) S of Cairo. The 379 tablets are letters by various Canaanite and Syrian rulers (including those of Hebron, Jerusalem, and Lachish), many containing complaints to the ruling Pharaoh (generally Akhenaton) about the incursions and depredations of the "Habiru" (*'apiru*). While some scholars have tried to identify the "Habiru" with the Hebrews, or Israelites, the contents of the letters themselves do not allow for this. They show the Habiru to be merely raiders, at times allied with certain Canaanite rulers in an intercity and intraregional rivalry. Among the towns menaced by the Habiru was Byblos in northern Lebanon, far beyond the range of the Israelite attacks. Also, they do not present a picture comparing with the major battles and victories of the Israelite conquest of Canaan after the Exodus.—See HEBREW, I (The "Habiru").

Israel's sojourn in Egypt was indelibly engraved on the nation's memory, and their miraculous release from that land was regularly recalled as an outstanding proof of Jehovah's Godship. (Ex 19:4; Le 22:32, 33; De 4:32-36; 2Ki 17:36; Heb 11:23-29) Thus the expression, "I am Jehovah your God from the land of Egypt." (Ho 13:4; compare Le 11:45.) No single circumstance or event surpassed this until their release from Babylon gave them further proof of Jehovah's power to deliver. (Jer 16:14, 15) Their experience in Egypt was written into the Law given them (Ex 20:2, 3; De 5:12-15); it was the basis for the Passover festival (Ex 12:1-27; De 16:1-3); it guided them in their dealings with alien residents (Ex 22:21; Le 19:33, 34) and with poor persons who sold themselves into bondage (Le 25:39-43, 55; De 15:12-15); it provided a legal basis for the selection and sanctification of the tribe of Levi for sanctuary service (Nu 3:11-13). On the basis of Israel's alien residence in Egypt, Egyptians who met certain requirements could be accepted into the congregation of Israel. (De 23:7, 8) The kingdoms of Canaan and peoples of neighboring lands experienced awe and fear because of the reports they heard of God's power demonstrated against Egypt, paving the way for Israel's conquest (Ex 18:1, 10, 11; De 7:17-20; Jos 2:10, 11; 9:9) and being remembered for centuries thereafter. (1Sa 4:7, 8) Throughout their history, the whole nation of Israel sang about these events in their songs.—Ps 78:43-51; Ps 105 and 106; 136:10-15.

After Israel's conquest of Canaan. Not until the reign of Pharaoh Merneptah, son of Ramses II (in the latter part of the "Nineteenth Dynasty"), is there a direct Egyptian mention made of Israel; in fact, this is the only direct mention of them as a people thus far found in ancient Egyptian records. In a victory stele, Merneptah boasts of defeats inflicted on various cities of Canaan and then claims: "Israel is laid waste, his seed is not." Though apparently only an idle boast, this would seem to be evidence that Israel was then established in Canaan. If so, and if the reading of the text is accurate, then it would appear that the Israelite conquest of Canaan (1473 B.C.E.) took place sometime between the reign of Akhenaton (to whom a large portion of the Amarna Letters were written) and that of Merneptah (whose rules Egyptologists place in the "Eighteenth and Nineteenth Dynasties" respectively).

No contact of Israel with Egypt is reported during the period of the Judges or during the reigns of Saul and David, aside from mention of combat between one of David's warriors and an Egyptian "of extraordinary size." (2Sa 23:21) By the reign of Solomon (1037-998 B.C.E.), relations between the two nations were such that Solomon could make a marriage alliance with Pharaoh, taking his daughter as wife. (1Ki 3:1) Just when this unidentified Pharaoh had conquered Gezer, which he now gave to his daughter as a farewell wedding gift, or dowry, is not stated. (1Ki 9:16) Solomon also carried on business operations with Egypt, dealing in horses and Egyptian-made chariots.—2Ch 1:16, 17.

Egypt, however, was a haven for certain enemies of the kings of Jerusalem. Hadad the Edomite escaped to Egypt following David's devastation of Edom. Though a Semite, Hadad was honored by Pharaoh with a home, food, and land; he married into royalty, and his offspring, Genubath, was treated as a son of Pharaoh. (1Ki 11:14-22) Later Jeroboam, who became king of the northern kingdom of Israel after Solomon's death, likewise took refuge for a time in Egypt in the reign of Shishak.—1Ki 11:40.

Shishak (known as Sheshonk I from Egyptian records) had founded a Libyan dynasty of Pharaohs (the "Twenty-second Dynasty"), with its capital at Bubastis in the eastern Delta region. In the fifth year of the reign of Solomon's son Rehoboam (993 B.C.E.), Shishak invaded Judah with a powerful force of chariots, cavalry, and foot soldiers including Libyans and Ethiopians; he captured many cities and even threatened Jerusalem. Because of Jehovah's mercy, Jerusalem was not devastated, but its great wealth was handed over to Shishak. (1Ki 14:25, 26; 2Ch 12:2-9) A relief on a temple wall at Karnak depicts Shishak's campaign and lists numerous cities in Israel and Judah as having been captured.

Zerah the Ethiopian, who led a million Ethiopian and Libyan troops against King Asa of Judah (967 B.C.E.), likely initiated his march from Egypt. His forces, gathered in the valley of Zephathah SW of Jerusalem, met utter defeat.—2Ch 14:9-13; 16:8.

Judah and Israel enjoyed respite from Egyptian attack for another two centuries. Egypt appears to have experienced considerable internal disturbance during this period, with certain dynasties ruling contemporaneously. Meanwhile, Assyria came to the fore as the dominant world power. Hoshea, last king of the ten-tribe kingdom of Israel (c. 758-740 B.C.E.), became a vassal of Assyria and then tried to break the Assyrian

yoke by conspiring with King So of Egypt. The effort failed, and the Israelite northern kingdom soon fell to Assyria.—2Ki 17:4.

Egypt seems to have come under considerable domination by Nubian-Ethiopian elements by this time, the "Twenty-fifth Dynasty" being classed as Ethiopian. Assyrian King Sennacherib's loud-talking official, Rabshakeh, told the people of the city of Jerusalem that to trust in Egypt for help was to trust in a "crushed reed." (2Ki 18:19-21, 24) King Tirhakah of Ethiopia, who marched up into Canaan at this time (732 B.C.E.) and temporarily diverted the Assyrian's attention and force, is generally associated with the Ethiopian ruler of Egypt, Pharaoh Taharqa. (2Ki 19:8-10) This seems to be substantiated by Isaiah's earlier prophecy (Isa 7:18, 19) that Jehovah would "whistle for the flies that are at the extremity of the Nile canals of Egypt and for the bees that are in the land of Assyria," thereby resulting in a clash of the two powers in the land of Judah and subjecting that land to double pressure. As Franz Delitzsch observed: "The emblems also correspond to the nature of the two countries: the fly to [marshy] Egypt with its swarms of insects . . . and the bee to the more mountainous and woody Assyria."—*Commentary on the Old Testament,* 1973, Vol. VII, Isaiah, p. 223.

Isaiah apparently foretells the unsettled state of affairs existing in Egypt during the latter part of the eighth and the early part of the seventh century B.C.E. in his pronouncement against Egypt. (Isa 19) He describes civil war and disintegration, with fighting of "city against city, kingdom against kingdom" in Egypt. (Isa 19:2, 13, 14) Modern historians find evidence for contemporaneous dynasties ruling in different sections of the country at that time. The vaunted "wisdom" of Egypt with her 'valueless gods and charmers' did not protect her from being delivered up into "the hand of a hard master."—Isa 19:3, 4.

Assyrian invasion. Assyrian King Esarhaddon (a contemporary of Judean King Manasseh [716-662 B.C.E.]) invaded Egypt, conquered Memphis in Lower Egypt, and sent many into exile. The ruling Pharaoh at the time was evidently still Taharqa (Tirhakah).

Ashurbanipal, Assyria's last king, renewed the assault and sacked the city of Thebes (Biblical No-amon) in Upper Egypt, where Egypt's greatest temple treasures were located. Again, the Bible shows Ethiopian, Libyan, and other African elements as being involved.—Na 3:8-10.

Assyrian garrisons were later pulled back from Egypt, and the country began to recover some of its earlier prosperity and power. When Assyria fell to the Medes and Babylonians, Egypt had gained sufficient strength (with the support of mercenary troops) to come up to the aid of the Assyrian king. Pharaoh Nechoh (II) led the Egyptian forces but, on the way, was confronted by the Judean army of King Josiah at Megiddo and, against his wishes, was forced to engage in battle; he defeated Judah and caused the death of Josiah. (2Ki 23:29; 2Ch 35:20-24) Three months later (in 628 B.C.E.) Nechoh removed Josiah's son and successor Jehoahaz from the Judean throne and replaced him with his brother Eliakim (renamed Jehoiakim), carrying Jehoahaz captive to Egypt. (2Ki 23:31-35; 2Ch 36:1-4; compare Eze 19:1-4.) Judah was now tributary to Egypt, paying an initial sum equivalent to almost $1,046,-000. It was during this period that the prophet Urijah made his vain flight to Egypt.—Jer 26:21-23.

Defeat by Nebuchadnezzar. But Egypt's bid to reestablish Egyptian control in Syria and Palestine was short-lived; Egypt was doomed to drink the bitter cup of defeat, according to Jehovah's prophecy already pronounced by Jeremiah (25:17-19). Egypt's downfall began with its decisive defeat at Carchemish on the Euphrates River by the Babylonians under Nebuchadnezzar as crown prince in 625 B.C.E., an event described at Jeremiah 46:2-10 as well as in a Babylonian chronicle.

Nebuchadnezzar, now king of Babylon, next took over Syria and Palestine, and Judah became a vassal state of Babylon. (2Ki 24:1) Egypt made one last attempt to remain a power in Asia. A military force of Pharaoh (his name is not mentioned in the Bible) came out of Egypt in answer to King Zedekiah's request for military support in his revolt against Babylon in 609-607 B.C.E. Producing only a temporary lifting of the Babylonian siege, Egypt's troops were forced to withdraw, and Jerusalem was left to destruction.—Jer 37:5-7; Eze 17:15-18.

Despite vigorous warning by Jeremiah (Jer 42:7-22), the remnant of Judah's population fled to Egypt as a sanctuary, evidently joining Jews already in that land. (Jer 24:1, 8-10) Places specifically mentioned where they took up dwelling are Tahpanhes, apparently a fortress city in the Delta region (Jer 43:7-9); Migdol (Nu 33:7, 8); and Noph, considered to be the same as Memphis, an early capital in Lower Egypt (Jer 44:1;

Eze 30:13). Thus, "the language of Canaan" (evidently Hebrew) was now being spoken in Egypt by these refugees. (Isa 19:18) Foolishly they renewed in Egypt the very idolatrous practices that had brought Jehovah's judgment against Judah. (Jer 44:2-25) But the fulfillment of Jehovah's prophecies caught up with the Israelite refugees when Nebuchadnezzar marched against Egypt and conquered the land.—Jer 43:8-13; 46:13-26.

One Babylonian text, dated to Nebuchadnezzar's 37th year (588 B.C.E.), has been found that mentions a campaign against Egypt. Whether it relates to the original conquest or merely to a subsequent military action cannot be said. At any rate, Nebuchadnezzar received Egypt's wealth as his pay for military service rendered in Jehovah's execution of judgment against Tyre, an opposer of God's people.—Eze 29:18-20; 30:10-12.

At Ezekiel 29:1-16 a desolation of Egypt is foretold, due to last 40 years. This may have come after Nebuchadnezzar's conquest of Egypt. While some commentaries refer to the reign of Amasis (Ahmose) II, the successor of Hophra, as exceedingly prosperous during more than 40 years, they do so primarily on the testimony of Herodotus, who visited Egypt over a hundred years later. But as the *Encyclopædia Britannica* (1959, Vol. 8, p. 62) comments on Herodotus' history of this period (the "Saitic Period"): "His statements prove not entirely reliable when they can be checked by the scanty native evidence." The Bible *Commentary* by F. C. Cook, after noting that Herodotus even fails to mention Nebuchadnezzar's attack on Egypt, says: "It is notorious that Herodotus, while he faithfully recorded all that he heard and saw in Egypt, was indebted for his information on past history to the Egyptian priests, whose tales he adopted with blind credulity. . . . The whole story [by Herodotus] of Apries [Hophra] and Amasis is mixed with so much that is inconsistent and legendary that we may very well hesitate to adopt it as authentic history. It is by no means strange that the priests should endeavour to disguise the national dishonour of having been subjected to a foreign yoke." (Note B., p. 132) Hence, while secular history provides no clear evidence of the prophecy's fulfillment, we may be confident of the accuracy of the Bible record.

Under Persian domination. Egypt later supported Babylon against the rising power of Medo-Persia. But by 525 B.C.E., the land was subjugated by Cambyses II, son of Cyrus the Great, and thereby came under Persian imperial rule. (Isa 43:3) While many Jews doubtless left Egypt to return to their homeland (Isa 11:11-16; Ho 11:11; Zec 10:10, 11), others remained in Egypt. Thus, there was a Jewish colony in Elephantine (Egyptian, *Yeb*), an island in the Nile near Aswan, some 690 km (430 mi) S of Cairo. A valuable find of papyri reveals conditions prevailing there during the fifth century B.C.E., about the time when Ezra and Nehemiah were active in Jerusalem. These documents, in Aramaic, contain the name of Sanballat of Samaria (Ne 4:1, 2) and of Johanan the high priest. (Ne 12:22) Of interest is an official order issued during the reign of Darius II (423-405 B.C.E.) that "the festival of unfermented cakes" (Ex 12:17; 13:3, 6, 7) be celebrated by the colony. Also notable is the frequent use of the name *Yahu,* a form of the name Jehovah (or Yahweh; compare Isa 19:18), although there is considerable evidence, too, of definite infiltration of pagan worship.

Under Greek and Roman rule.   Egypt continued under Persian rule until the conquest by Alexander the Great in 332 B.C.E., supposedly liberating Egypt from the Persian yoke but ending for all time the rule by native Pharaohs. Mighty Egypt had indeed become "a lowly kingdom."—Eze 29:14, 15.

During Alexander's reign the city of Alexandria was founded, and after his death the country was ruled by the Ptolemies. In 312 B.C.E., Ptolemy I captured Jerusalem, and Judah became a province of Ptolemaic Egypt until 198 B.C.E. Then, in the long struggle with the Seleucid Empire in Syria, Egypt finally lost control of Palestine when Syrian King Antiochus III defeated the army of Ptolemy V. Thereafter Egypt gradually came more and more under the influence of Rome. In 31 B.C.E., in the decisive battle of Actium, Cleopatra deserted the fleet of her Roman lover Mark Antony, who was defeated by Octavius, grandnephew of Julius Caesar. Octavius proceeded to the conquest of Egypt in 30 B.C.E., and Egypt became a Roman province. It was to this Roman province that Joseph and Mary fled with the young child Jesus to escape Herod's murderous decree, returning after the death of Herod, so that the words of Hosea, "out of Egypt I called my son," were fulfilled.—Mt 2:13-15; Ho 11:1; compare Ex 4:22, 23.

The "Egyptian" seditionist with whom the military commander at Jerusalem confused Paul is possibly the same one mentioned by Josephus. (*The Jewish War,* II, 254-263 [xiii, 3-5]) His in-surrection is stated to have taken place during the reign of Nero and the procuratorship of Felix in Judea, circumstances fitting the account at Acts 21:37-39; 23:23, 24.

The second destruction of Jerusalem, by the Romans in 70 C.E., resulted in a further fulfillment of Deuteronomy 28:68, as many surviving Jews were sent to Egypt as slaves.—*The Jewish War,* VI, 418 (ix, 2).

Other Prophetic and Symbolic References. A large number of the references to Egypt are in pronouncements of judgment, couched in symbolic language. (Eze 29:1-7; 32:1-32) To the Israelites, Egypt represented military strength and power through political alliance, so that dependence on Egypt became symbolic of dependence on human power instead of on Jehovah. (Isa 31:1-3) But, at Isaiah 30:1-7, Jehovah showed that Egypt's might was more in appearance than in fact, calling her "Rahab—they are for sitting still ["Rahab-do-nothing," *JB*]." (Compare Ps 87:4; Isa 51:9, 10.) Along with the many condemnations, however, there were promises that many out of "Egypt" would come to know Jehovah, to the extent that it would be said: "Blessed be my people, Egypt."—Isa 19:19-25; 45:14.

Egypt is mentioned as part of the realm of the symbolic "king of the south." (Da 11:5, 8, 42, 43) At Revelation 11:8 unfaithful Jerusalem, where the Lord Jesus Christ was impaled, is "in a spiritual sense" called Egypt. This is appropriate when we consider that unfaithful Jerusalem religiously oppressed and enslaved the Jews. Also, the first Passover victims were slain in Egypt, while the antitypical Passover Lamb, Jesus Christ, was killed at Jerusalem.—Joh 1:29, 36; 1Co 5:7; 1Pe 1:19.

Valuable Papyrus Finds. The unusually dry soil of Egypt has made possible the survival of papyrus manuscripts, which, in more moist conditions, would have been destroyed. Since the latter part of the 19th century, many papyri have been discovered there, including a considerable number of Biblical papyri, such as the Chester Beatty collection. These provide especially important links between the original writings of the Holy Scriptures and the later vellum manuscript copies.

EGYPT, TORRENT VALLEY OF.   A long wadi (or ravine) marking the God-ordained SW boundary of the Promised Land, that is, "the land of Canaan." (Nu 34:2, 5; 1Ki 8:65; Isa 27:12) While this torrent valley was not actually in

Egypt, that nation's domain apparently extended, at least in certain periods, up to that point. (2Ki 24:7) The abbreviated expression "the torrent valley," used in defining the borders of the land of Israel in Ezekiel's vision, apparently refers to this same ravine.—Eze 47:19; 48:28.

The torrent valley of Egypt is usually identified with Wadi el-'Arish, which starts over 200 km (125 mi) inland on the Sinai Peninsula, near Jebel et-Tih. It runs N until meeting the Mediterranean Sea at the town of el-'Arish (Rhinocolura), about 145 km (90 mi) E of Port Said. In the summer it is nothing more than a dry bed. During the rainy season, however, when numerous tributaries pour into it, the Wadi el-'Arish becomes a swollen torrent that tears at its banks, even uprooting trees and sweeping them down its turbulent course. This might allow for its identification as "the *river* of Egypt" in the boundary listing of the Promised Land at Genesis 15:18.—See, however, SHIHOR.

EHI. See AHIRAM.

EHUD (E'hud).

1. A descendant of Jediael of the tribe of Benjamin, through Bilhan; a valiant, mighty man. —1Ch 7:6, 10, 11.

2. Son of Gera of the tribe of Benjamin (Jg 3:15), Ehud was chosen by God to deliver the nation from an 18-year bondage to King Eglon of Moab, an oppression God permitted because "they did what was bad in Jehovah's eyes."—Jg 3:12-14.

When the Israelites began to call to Jehovah for aid, God raised up "a savior" in the person of Ehud. In time, the Israelites sent tribute to Eglon by means of Ehud, who had made a two-edged sword for himself, "its length being a cubit [Heb., go'medh]," actually a linear measurement about which there is uncertainty in this particular case. Some believe it was a short cubit of about 38 cm (15 in.). Ehud was a left-handed man, or, literally, "a man closed (impeded) of his right hand." But this does not mean that Ehud was crippled, as such Hebrew phraseology is used in connection with 700 Benjamite warriors, who are not likely to have had a physical defect but were "left-handed" and evidently ambidextrous. (Jg 3:15, 16, ftn; 20:16; compare 1Ch 12:2.) The Bible does not specifically say Ehud was ambidextrous, though that is possible. Nevertheless, being left-handed, he girded the sword underneath his garment upon his right thigh.

After presentation of the tribute, Ehud sent the tribute bearers away but turned back at the quarries of Gilgal. Ehud then came to Eglon as the Moabite king sat in his roof chamber, and he said to him: "A word of God I have for you." Interested, Eglon arose from his throne. At that, Ehud "thrust in his left hand and took the sword off his right thigh," plunging it into obese Eglon's belly, with the result that "the handle kept going in also after the blade so that the fat closed in over the blade." A right-handed man would likely draw his sword from his left side, across his body. So it is not probable that Eglon would expect Ehud to draw a sword from the right thigh, using his left hand. The enemy ruler now dead, Ehud escaped through the air hole, after closing and locking the doors of the roof chamber behind him. When Eglon's servants finally opened the doors, they discovered that "their lord was fallen to the earth dead!"—Jg 3:15-25.

Ehud, having escaped to the mountainous region of Ephraim, marshaled an army of Israelites, saying to them: "Follow me, because Jehovah has given your enemies, the Moabites, into your hand." After capturing the fords of the Jordan, the Israelites cut off the Moabites' retreat to their homeland. Doubtless already greatly demoralized by their king's death, 10,000 Moabites were struck down by the Israelites, "every one robust and every one a valiant man; and not a single one escaped." Moab having been subdued under Israel's hand and Ehud's leadership, "the land had no further disturbance for eighty years." —Jg 3:26-30.

Ehud is not specifically called "Judge Ehud"; rather he is referred to as "a savior." (Jg 3:15) But Othniel was called both "a savior" and a "judge" (Jg 3:9, 10), and the period was the time of the Judges. So Ehud was apparently considered not only "a savior" but also a judge.

3. A name that appears among the descendants of Benjamin at 1 Chronicles 8:1, 6.

EKER (E'ker) [Member [of the family]]. A son of Ram, Jerahmeel's firstborn, of the tribe of Judah.—1Ch 2:4, 5, 9, 25, 27.

EKRON (Ek'ron). A leading Philistine city, apparently the northernmost seat of one of their five axis lords. (Jos 13:3) Its exact position is uncertain, but it is generally identified with Khirbet el-Muqanna' (Tel Miqne), about 18 km (11 mi) E of Ashdod. Recent excavation there has unearthed the largest city of its period and gives it current preference as the site of Ekron.

Ekron's history is one of constantly changing domination. Joshua's conquest did not include

Ekron. It was not until later that the Judeans captured it. (Jos 13:2, 3; Jg 1:18) In the initial division of the Promised Land, Ekron was on the border between Judah and Dan but within the tribe of Judah. (Jos 15:1, 11, 45, 46; 19:40-43) By the time the Philistines captured the ark of the covenant, Ekron was back in their possession. The presence of the Ark caused "a death-dealing confusion" to break out in this city, and it was from Ekron that the Ark was finally sent back to the Jews. (1Sa 5:10-12; 6:16, 17) After another period under Israelite control, the Philistines apparently again had Ekron at the time David slew Goliath. (1Sa 7:14; 17:52) It was in the early tenth century B.C.E. that Pharaoh Shishak of Egypt claimed to have taken Ekron. Some two centuries later, according to Sennacherib's annals, Ekron's King Padi was loyal to the Assyrians.

EL. See GOD.

ELA (E′la) [possibly, God]. Father of Shimei, one of Solomon's 12 deputies who provided food for the king and his household.—1Ki 4:7, 18.

ELAH (E′lah).
[1-5: related to Heb. *'El*, "God"]

 1. An Edomite sheik who likely occupied the village of Elath.—Ge 36:40, 41, 43; 1Ch 1:52; see ELATH, ELOTH; TIMNA No. 3.

 2. A son of Caleb the spy; father of Kenaz of the tribe of Judah.—1Ch 4:15.

 3. Fourth king of the northern ten-tribe kingdom of Israel. Elah came to the throne in about 952 B.C.E. on the death of his father Baasha and ruled in Tirzah for parts of two years. (1Ki 16:8) While Elah was drunk, Zimri, the chief over half the chariots, put him to death to get the kingship for himself and then went on to wipe out all of Baasha's house, fulfilling Jehovah's prophecy.—1Ki 16:1-14.

 4. Father of King Hoshea, the last monarch of the northern kingdom.—2Ki 15:30; 17:1; 18:1, 9.

 5. A descendant of Benjamin who lived in Jerusalem.—1Ch 9:3, 7, 8.

What was the setting in which David faced Goliath?

---

 6. [Big Tree]. A low plain, or valley, perhaps named for an outstandingly large tree located therein. "The low plain of Elah" was the site of the encounter between the Israelites and the Philistines, championed by Goliath. (1Sa 17:2, 19; 21:9) It is usually associated with the fertile Wadi es-Sant, one of the principal wadis extending from the Philistine plains through the Shephelah into the mountainous regions of Judah, passing between the suggested locations of Azekah and Socoh. (1Sa 17:1) It thus lay about 25 km (15 mi) SW of Jerusalem. The well-watered plain is about half a kilometer (0.25 mi) wide and quite level. The opposing forces faced each other across this valley, each side having a strong position on a mountainside, the Philistines perhaps to the S and the Israelites to the N or NE. Through the low plain ran "the torrent valley," probably the dry streambed still found there. (1Sa 17:40) Perhaps the delay of "forty days" spent by the two armies was due in part to the weak position in which either side would place itself in having to cross over this torrent valley and then go up against the enemy force on the opposing mountainside. (1Sa 17:16) David selected five smooth stones from the torrent valley when crossing over to face Goliath. After David's victory, the routed Philistine army fled down the valley to the Philistine plain and the cities of Gath and Ekron. —1Sa 17:52.

ELAM (E′lam).

 1. One of the five sons of Shem from whom descended "families, according to their tongues, in their lands, according to their nations." (Ge 10:22, 31; 1Ch 1:17) The names of Elam's sons are not specified; his name, however, designates both a people and a region on the SE border of Mesopotamia.

 Historically, the name Elam applied to an area in what is now called Khuzestan in SW Iran. It included the fertile plain on the eastern side of the lower Tigris Valley, watered by the Karun and Karkheh rivers, and evidently extended into the mountainous regions bordering this plain on the N and E, although these two boundaries are the least certain. A region called Anshan is believed to have been situated in these mountainous regions and is represented in inscriptions as forming a part of Elam from an early period. Elam, located at the extreme eastern end of the Fertile Crescent, was, therefore, in somewhat of a frontier position, being one of the regions where territory populated and generally dominated by Semitic races confronted or merged with races descended from Noah's other sons, principally the Japhetic line.

 The land of Elam was called *elamtu* by the Assyrians and Babylonians and Elymais by the classical Greek writers, who also at times referred to it as "Susiana" after the city of Susa, or Shushan, at one time evidently the capital of Elam. Under the Persian Empire, Susa (Shushan) was a royal city. (Ne 1:1; Es 1:2) It was situated on the trade routes leading off to the SE and also up into the Iranian plateau. Efforts to gain control of these routes made Elam the object of frequent invasion by Assyrian and Babylonian rulers.

Language. In discussing Elam, reference works generally claim that the writer of Genesis listed Elam under Shem only on a political or a geographic basis since, they say, the people of Elam were not Semitic. This view they base on the claim that the language of the Elamites was not Semitic. Investigation, however, reveals that the earliest inscriptions found in the geographic region designated Elam are "mere lists of objects pictorially jotted down on clay-tablets with the numbers of each beside them, indicated by a simple system of strokes, circles and semicircles . . . their contents at this time are purely economic or administrative." (*Semitic Writing*, by G. R. Driver, London, 1976, pp. 2, 3) These inscriptions could reasonably be called "Elamite" only as meaning that they were found *in the territory* of Elam.

The weight of the argument of those opposing the inclusion of Elam among the Semitic peoples, therefore, rests principally upon later inscriptions in cuneiform, regarded as dating considerably within the second millennium B.C.E., as well as on the Behistun monument (of the sixth century B.C.E.), which contains parallel texts in Old Persian, Akkadian, and "Elamite." The cuneiform inscriptions attributed to the Elamites are said to be in an agglutinative language (one in which root words are joined together to form compounds, thereby distinguished from inflectional languages). Philologists have not been able successfully to relate this "Elamite" language to any other known tongue.

In evaluating the above information, it should be remembered that the geographic region in which the descendants of Elam eventually concentrated may well have been occupied by other peoples prior to or even during such Elamite residence there, just as the early non-Semitic Sumerians resided in Babylonia. The *Encyclopædia Britannica* (1959, Vol. 8, p. 118) states: "The whole country [designated Elam] was occupied by a variety of tribes, speaking agglutinative dialects for the most part, *though the western*

districts were occupied by Semites."—Italics ours; MAP and CHART, Vol. 1, p. 329.

That the cuneiform inscriptions found in the region of Elam would not of themselves prove that the true Elamites were originally non-Semitic can be seen from the many ancient historical examples that can be cited of peoples adopting a tongue other than their own because of domination or infiltration by foreign elements. There are likewise examples of ancient peoples simultaneously employing another language along with their own for commercial and international uses, even as Aramaic became a lingua franca used by many peoples. The "Hittites" of Karatepe wrote bilingual inscriptions (evidently in the eighth century B.C.E.) in "Hittite" hieroglyphic script and in old Phoenician. Some 30,000 clay tablets of the time of Persian King Darius I were found at Persepolis, a royal Persian city. They were mainly in the language termed "Elamite." Yet Persepolis would not be called an Elamite city.

Further showing that it is unwise to view the table of nations at Genesis chapter 10 as purely geographic, and not actually genealogical, is the evidence in the form of sculptures carved for Elamite kings and dated by archaeologists as far back as the time of Sargon I (whose rule they assign to the latter part of the third millennium). These sculptures not only present the form of typical Akkadian (*Semitic* Assyro-Babylonian) figures but also bear Akkadian inscriptions. —*The Illustrated Bible Dictionary*, edited by J. D. Douglas, 1980, Vol. 1, p. 433.

History. The first Biblical mention of Elam as a country, or nation, is in the time of Abraham (2018-1843 B.C.E.) when Chedorlaomer "king of Elam" marched with an alliance of kings against a Canaanite coalition of kings in the Dead Sea region. (Ge 14:1-3) Chedorlaomer is indicated as the leader of the alliance and as having held suzerainty over the Canaanite kings, upon whom he now inflicted punishment. (Ge 14:4-17) Such a campaign, requiring a round-trip journey of perhaps 3,200 km (2,000 mi), was not unusual for Mesopotamian kings even in that ancient time. Secular history confirms that in the early part of the second millennium B.C.E. there was such a period of Elamite dominance in the Mesopotamian region. An Elamite official named Kudur-Mabuk who successfully occupied the prominent city of Larsa (along the Euphrates north of Ur) appointed his son Warad-Sin as king there. Noteworthy is the fact that Warad-Sin and

Rim-Sin (Warad-Sin's brother who succeeded him as king) are both Semitic names, further substantiating a Semitic element in Elam.

This period of Elamite power in Babylonia was upset and terminated by Hammurabi, and it was not until the latter part of the second millennium B.C.E. that Elam was able to conquer Babylon and again establish control for a period of some centuries. It is believed that it was during this time that a stele bearing the famous Code of Hammurabi was taken from Babylonia to Susa, where modern archaeologists discovered it.

Elam again was reduced to a subordinate position by Nebuchadnezzar I (not the Nebuchadnezzar who, several centuries later, destroyed Jerusalem), but it continued to be a frequent participant in the power struggle between Assyria and Babylon until finally Assyrian Emperors Sennacherib and Ashurbanipal (Asenappar) defeated the Elamite forces, transplanting some of the people to the cities of Samaria. (Ezr 4:8-10) Also, Israelite captives were sent into exile in Elam. (Isa 11:11) Inscriptions of the Assyrian emperors vividly describe this subjugation of Elam.

Following the downfall of the Assyrian Empire, Elam appears to have come under Japhetic (Aryan) control. The Medes and Persians are thought to have spread into the Iranian plateau region several centuries earlier, and under Cyaxares, the Medes fought with the Babylonians in overthrowing the Assyrian capital of Nineveh. Daniel 8:2 seems to indicate that Elam thereafter became a Babylonian district. Whatever the immediate effects on Elam from the Assyrian collapse, the Persians evidently succeeded in taking from Elam the region called Anshan, as Persian rulers Teispes, Cyrus I, Cambyses, and Cyrus II were all respectively called by the title "King of Anshan." While some consider such conquest of Anshan to be in fulfillment of Jeremiah's prophecy concerning Elam (Jer 49:34-39), most scholars place the conquest of Anshan by Teispes many years prior to the pronouncement of that prophecy made in about 617 B.C.E.

Isaiah's warning at Isaiah 22:4-6 foretold that Elamite archers would be among those attacking Judah and Jerusalem. The Elamites were also prophesied to unite with Media in despoiling Babylon (539 B.C.E.), Media by that time being under the rule of the Persian Cyrus II, "King of Anshan." (Isa 21:2) Elamites thus contributed toward the release of Israel from exile, yet having aligned themselves at various times with

enemies of God's people, Elam along with the other nations would, in due time, be made to drink of the cup of God's wrath and go down into Sheol.—Jer 25:17, 25-29; Eze 32:24.

On the day of Pentecost, 33 C.E., Elamites were among the thousands hearing the message spoken by the disciples in the language then currently spoken in Elam. (Ac 2:8, 9) As a nation and people, however, they have since ceased to exist, even as foretold at Jeremiah 49:34-39.

2. A Levite gatekeeper during David's reign and a son of Meshelemiah of the family of the Korahites.—1Ch 25:1; 26:1-3.

3. A son of Shashak and a headman of the tribe of Benjamin.—1Ch 8:24, 25, 28.

4. Progenitor of an Israelite family of whom 1,254 descendants returned from Babylon with Zerubbabel (Ezr 2:1, 2, 7; Ne 7:12) and a later contingent of 71 males accompanied Ezra. (Ezr 8:7) Some of his descendants were among those agreeing to put away their foreign wives (Ezr 10:19, 26), and a representative of the family signed the covenant in Nehemiah's time.—Ne 10:1, 14.

5. One designated as "the other Elam," also a family head with the same number, 1,254 descendants, accompanying Zerubbabel's company to Judah.—Ezr 2:31; Ne 7:34.

6. A Levite present at the inauguration of the wall of Jerusalem by Nehemiah.—Ne 12:27, 42.

ELAMITES.   See ELAM No. 1.

ELASAH   (El·a'sah) [God Has Made]. The son of Shaphan who, with Gemariah, was sent by Zedekiah to Nebuchadnezzar in Babylon. The prophet Jeremiah on that occasion sent his letter to the exiles in Babylon by the hand of Elasah and of Gemariah.—Jer 29:1-3.

ELATH   (E'lath) [possibly, Ram; or, Place of the Ram], **ELOTH** (E'loth [plural]). A site first mentioned in Moses' recapitulation of the Israelites' 40-year trek through the wilderness. (De 2:8) Elath is mentioned along with Ezion-geber and lay on "the shore of the Red Sea in the land of Edom." (1Ki 9:26) This points to a location on the NE arm or branch of the Red Sea known as the Gulf of 'Aqaba. Scholars basically agree with Jerome, of the fourth and fifth centuries C.E., who identified Elath with the city then known as Aila, associated with the Nabataeans. This would place Elath at or near the present-day Arab city of 'Aqaba situated at the NE corner of the gulf (the modern Jewish city called Elat being at the NW corner).

Elath was part of the Edomite domain when the Israelites passed through the region on their way to Canaan. Seals bearing the Edomite name of "Qos'anal, servant of the king," dated by archaeologists as from the seventh century B.C.E. have been found in the Elath area.

Evidently as a result of David's conquest of Edom, Elath and neighboring Ezion-geber came under Judean control (2Sa 8:13, 14), and they are mentioned in connection with Solomon's ship-building activities. (1Ki 9:26; 2Ch 8:17) The fact that Ezion-geber is referred to as "by Eloth" may indicate that Elath (Eloth) was the more prominent of the two sites, at least at that time.

Control of Elath evidently reverted to Edom during the reign of Jehoram of Judah. (2Ki 8:20-22) In the following century the city was restored to Judah and rebuilt by King Uzziah (Azariah). (2Ki 14:21, 22; 2Ch 26:1, 2) Then, during the rule of Ahaz (761-746 B.C.E.), it was wrested from Judah by the Syrians and was reoccupied by the Edomites, thereafter never returning to the Judeans. (2Ki 16:6) The Masoretic text here reads "Syria" or "Aram" (Heb., 'Aram') instead of "Edom" ('Edhohm'). Most current scholars, however, accept the latter reading, in the margin, believing that a scribe confused the Hebrew letter da'leth (ד) with the similar-shaped letter rehsh (ר).

Essentially an oasis, Elath was a stopping point on the caravan route leading from S Arabia to Egypt, Canaan, or Damascus. Along with Ezion-geber, it was also located at the gateway for the "ships of Tarshish" that plied the waters to and from Arabia, East Africa, and possibly India. (1Ki 10:22; 9:26, 27) Aramaic writings, such as wine receipts from the period of the Persian Empire, have been found in the area, also remnants of high-quality pottery of Grecian style, perhaps intended for transshipment to Arabia.

EL-BERITH. See BAAL-BERITH.

EL-BETHEL (El-beth'el) [The God of Bethel]. The name given by Jacob to the spot where he erected an altar in obedience to God's command. (Ge 35:1, 7) Certain scholars consider "The God of Bethel" to be an unlikely name for a location, and note that in the Greek *Septuagint,* Latin *Vulgate,* Syriac *Peshitta,* and Arabic versions the initial "El" was omitted. However, it should be remembered that the area around Bethel was full of meaning for Jacob. It was in this area over 20 years earlier that God revealed himself to Jacob

in a dream, promising to protect him. At that time the patriarch was moved to respond, "Truly Jehovah is in this place." (Ge 28:10-22) Since this was the case, when later naming the altar site, Jacob was saying in effect, 'God is in Bethel.' —Compare Ge 33:20.

ELDAAH (El·da'ah) [possibly, God's Knowledge; God Knows]. A son of Midian the fourth-named son of Abraham by Keturah.—Ge 25:1, 2, 4; 1Ch 1:33.

ELDAD (El'dad) [possibly, God Has Loved]. One of the 70 older men selected by Moses to assist him in carrying the load of the people. Because of murmuring on the part of the mixed crowd and also the Israelites about the manna and not having meat to eat, Moses voiced the feeling that the load was too heavy for him alone. Therefore Jehovah directed Moses to gather 70 older men and take them to the tent of meeting. Two of these older men, Eldad and Medad, however, did not go to the tent of meeting but, undoubtedly for a valid reason, remained in the camp. Jehovah then proceeded to take some of the spirit that was upon Moses and put it upon the older men; these, in turn, began to prophesy. The spirit also settled down upon Eldad and Medad, and they began to act as prophets in the camp. This was reported to Moses, and when Joshua, feeling jealous for Moses, requested that he restrain them, Moses replied: "No, I wish that all of Jehovah's people were prophets, because Jehovah would put his spirit upon them!"—Nu 11:13-29.

ELDER. See OLDER MAN.

ELEAD (E'le·ad) [God Has Borne Witness]. Likely, son of Ephraim who was killed along with his brother Ezer by the men of Gath "because they came down to take their livestock."—1Ch 7:20, 21; see EPHRAIM No. 1.

ELEADAH (E·le·a'dah) [God Has Decked Himself]. One of Ephraim's descendants.—1Ch 7:20.

ELEALEH (E·le·a'leh). A site regularly mentioned with Heshbon and located in the pastoral country E of the Jordan. The tribe of Reuben "built" (or rebuilt) the city soon after its conquest. (Nu 32:3-5, 37) Centuries later, when it was under Moab's control, Isaiah and Jeremiah prophesied that Elealeh was due to "cry out" at that nation's collapse. (Isa 15:4; 16:9; Jer 48:34) It is usually thought to be located on a hill at el-'Al, about 3 km (2 mi) NE of Heshbon.

ELEASAH (El·e·a′sah) [God Has Made].

1. Son of Helez and father of Sismai, a descendant of Judah through Jerahmeel. Jarha, an Egyptian slave who married the daughter of his master Sheshan, was one of the forefathers of Eleasah.—1Ch 2:33, 34, 39, 40.

2. A descendant of Jonathan the son of King Saul.—1Ch 8:33-37; 9:39-43.

3. A priest of "the sons of Pashhur" among those heeding Ezra's exhortation to dismiss their foreign wives.—Ezr 2:36, 38; 10:22, 44.

ELEAZAR (El·e·a′zar) [God Has Helped].

1. The third-named son of High Priest Aaron by his wife Elisheba. Eleazar was of the family of Kohath the son of Levi. (Ex 6:16, 18, 20, 23; Nu 3:2) Aaron and his sons, Nadab, Abihu, Eleazar, and Ithamar, constituted the priesthood of Israel at the time of its installation by Moses.—Le 8.

In the second year after leaving Egypt, when the tabernacle had been set up, Eleazar is mentioned as being chief of the Levites. (Nu 1:1; 3:32) He must have been at least 30 years of age at the time, inasmuch as he was performing priestly duties.—Nu 4:3.

Eleazar was one of those above 20 years of age who had left Egypt and who also entered the Promised Land. Being of the tribe of Levi, he was not included in God's condemnation expressed against the other 12 tribes, that none of them from 20 years old upward would enter the Promised Land, with the exception of Joshua and Caleb. Levi had no representative among the 12 spies, 10 of whom brought back bad reports, and the Levites apparently were not included in the faithless, rebellious murmuring against Jehovah. —Nu 13:4-16; 14:26-30.

Shortly after the dedication of the tabernacle and the consecration of Aaron and his sons for the priesthood (Le 8), Nadab and Abihu offered up illegitimate fire to Jehovah and were killed by fire proceeding from Jehovah. (Le 10:1, 2; Nu 3:2-4) Aaron, with his two faithful sons Eleazar and Ithamar, continued to carry on the priesthood. With the division of duties in the care of the sanctuary, Eleazar had oversight of the tabernacle with its utensils, constant grain offering, oil, and incense. (Nu 4:16) At Jehovah's command Eleazar took up the copper fire holders that Korah and the others associated with him (none of whom were priests) had used to offer up incense to Jehovah in a desire to take over priestly duties. These were made into thin metal plates with which the altar was overlaid. (Nu 16:37-40)

Eleazar officiated at the sin offering of the red heifer that provided the ashes for cleansing from certain uncleannesses.—Nu 19:2, 3; Heb 9:13.

After the Israelites went to war to punish the Midianites for the affair of Peor, Eleazar was on hand to aid in dividing the spoils taken from the Midianites and to declare God's statute regarding the things taken.—Nu 31:6, 21-41.

Phinehas, Eleazar's son by one of the daughters of Putiel, was rewarded by Jehovah with a covenant of peace for his zealous action in behalf of pure worship at the time Israel sinned in connection with the Baal of Peor. This may be considered as added to the covenant for the priesthood Jehovah had made with the tribe of Levi.—Nu 25:1-13; Ex 6:25.

Becomes High Priest. In the 40th year of the wilderness journey, upon Aaron's death at the age of 123 years, Eleazar, then about 70 years of age, became high priest. (Nu 33:37-39) Eleazar, therefore, was the first high priest of Israel to officiate in the Promised Land when they entered about eight months later. (Nu 20:25-28; De 10:6; Jos 4:19) It was before Eleazar that Joshua was to stand to be appointed as Moses' successor, and Eleazar was to continue to give support to Joshua in the appointment and to transmit to him Jehovah's decisions on questions of importance according to the judgment of the Urim and the Thummim. (Nu 27:18-23) Eleazar also worked together with Joshua in the distribution of the Promised Land after the conquest of Canaan. —Jos 14:1; 21:1-3.

Head of Major Priestly House. The time of Eleazar's death is not stated in the Scriptures with exactness, but it seems to have been near the time of the death of Joshua. Eleazar was succeeded by his son Phinehas. (Jos 24:29, 30, 33; Jg 20:27, 28) Eleazar manifested the trait of zeal for Jehovah's true worship and conducted the priesthood with honor all his days. Jewish tradition holds that during the time the tabernacle was in Shiloh, there were 16 courses of priests, 8 in the family of Eleazar and 8 in that of his brother Ithamar. However, in David's time there were more chief men in the family of Eleazar than of Ithamar. Therefore David made 16 priestly divisions of the house of Eleazar and 8 of the house of Ithamar, making a total of 24 divisions that served in turn later at the temple. —1Ch 24:1-4.

2. The son of Abinadab who was sanctified to guard the sacred Ark that was brought to the

house of his father in the city of Kiriath-jearim, after its return by the Philistines.—1Sa 7:1, 2.

3. Son of Dodo the Ahohite; one of David's three outstanding mighty men. At Pas-dammim, during a military campaign with David, Eleazar distinguished himself by taking his stand in a field full of barley and single-handedly striking down the Philistines, "so that Jehovah saved with a great salvation."—1Ch 11:12-14; 2Sa 23:9, 10.

4. Son of Mahli the Merarite of the tribe of Levi. Eleazar did not have any sons but had only daughters. Therefore, the sons of Kish, their cousins, took them as wives.—1Ch 23:21, 22.

5. Son of a certain Phinehas, mentioned as assisting Meremoth the priest when, on the fourth day of Ezra's arrival in Jerusalem, the silver and the gold and the utensils for temple use were weighed out.—Ezr 8:29, 32, 33.

6. A descendant of Parosh among those having taken foreign wives but who followed through on Ezra's exhortation to dismiss them. —Ezr 10:25, 44.

7. A Levite priest in the procession arranged by Nehemiah at the inauguration of the rebuilt wall of Jerusalem.—Ne 12:42.

8. An ancestor of Jesus' adoptive father Joseph.—Mt 1:15.

ELECTRUM. The shining alloy of gold and silver, which, when heated in the furnace, has a quivering beauty and glowing yellow brilliance all its own.—Eze 1:4, 27; 8:2.

ELHANAN (El·ha′nan) [God Has Shown Favor; God Has Been Gracious].

1. The son of Jair who, in war with the Philistines, struck down Lahmi the brother of Goliath the Gittite. (1Ch 20:5) In 2 Samuel 21:19 Elhanan is identified as "the son of Jaare-oregim the Bethlehemite," and it is said that he struck down Goliath. However, it is many scholars think that the original reading of 2 Samuel 21:19 corresponded to 1 Chronicles 20:5, the differences in the two texts having arisen through scribal error.—See JAARE-OREGIM; LAHMI.

2. Son of Dodo of Bethlehem; one of David's mighty men.—2Sa 23:24; 1Ch 11:26.

ELI, I (E′li) [Ascended; Gone Up]. A high priest of Israel; evidently a descendant of Aaron's fourth-named son Ithamar. (Compare 2Sa 8:17; 1Ki 2:27; 1Ch 24:3; Ex 6:23.) As high priest, Eli judged Israel for 40 years. Samuel began to be a prophet during his lifetime. (1Sa 4:18; 3:10-13, 19-21) Eli's day was one character-

ized by spiritual famine in Israel, for "word from Jehovah had become rare in those days; there was no vision being spread abroad."—1Sa 3:1.

The first glimpse of Eli is given in chapter 1 of First Samuel. Eli is seated outside by the doorpost of the tabernacle and is rebuking righteous Hannah, whom he judges to be drunk, when actually she has been praying extendedly before Jehovah there in front of the tabernacle. Upon Hannah's reply that she is not drunk but has spoken out of the abundance of her concern and vexation, Eli dismisses her in peace. Jehovah answers Hannah's prayer, and she gives birth to a son whom she names Samuel. As soon as he is weaned she, in keeping with her vow, turns him over for service at the tabernacle.—1Sa 1:9-18, 20, 24, 28; 2:11, 18.

Lax in Disciplining Sons. As a father and high priest in Israel, Eli is lax in applying Jehovah's discipline. His two sons, Hophni and Phinehas, serve as officiating priests, but they are "good-for-nothing men," only interested in satisfying their bellies and unclean sexual desires. They are not content with the portion of the sacrifice assigned to them by God's law, and even serve themselves ahead of Jehovah by having an attendant demand raw meat from the offerer before making the fat smoke upon the altar. Eli's greedy, sensual sons use their position at the tent of meeting to carry on vice and theft at the expense of Jehovah's pure worship. Even when his corrupt sons have immoral intercourse with the women who serve at the entrance of the tabernacle, Eli does not oust them from office but merely rebukes them mildly. Eli keeps honoring his sons more than Jehovah.—1Sa 2:12-17, 22-25, 29.

In the course of time a prophet of God comes with a dire message of warning: The power and influence of the house of Eli is to be chopped off, so that there will not come to be an old man in his house. His corrupt sons are appointed to die in one day. (1Sa 2:27-36) Through none other than the young boy Samuel, Jehovah reaffirms the adverse judgment upon the house of Eli. (1Sa 3:11-14) Samuel is afraid to relate the message, but does so at Eli's request. Eli then meekly submits, saying: "It is Jehovah. What is good in his eyes let him do."—1Sa 3:15-18.

Jehovah Judges His House. Retribution comes according to God's word. Israel loses about 4,000 men in battle with the Philistines. The Israelites decide to get the Ark from Shiloh and to bring it into the camp, thinking that this will result in deliverance from their enemies. But the

Philistines step up their battle efforts. Thirty thousand Israelites are slain. The Ark is captured. Hophni and Phinehas, who are there with the Ark, die. A man from Benjamin hurries from the battle lines to bring the report to Eli. Blind and feeble, 98-year-old Eli is sitting on a seat by the roadside, his heart atremble concerning the Ark. Upon hearing that the Ark has been captured, Eli falls over backward and dies of a broken neck.—1Sa 4:2-18.

Further retribution against the house of Eli came at the hands of King Saul, who ruthlessly ordered the murder of the priests of Nob, the descendants of Eli through Phinehas' son Ahitub. (1Sa 14:3; 22:11, 18) Only Abiathar, a son of Ahimelech, escaped the massacre and continued serving as priest throughout David's reign. (1Sa 22:20; 2Sa 19:11) However, Abiathar was removed as priest by Solomon for having offered help to the rebellious conspirator Adonijah. (1Ki 1:7; 2:26, 27) Thus the judgment of Jehovah on Eli's house was fulfilled, and his descendants were ousted from the high-priestly office for all time.—1Sa 3:13, 14.

ELI, II (E'li). As Jesus was dying on the torture stake, about the ninth hour, or about 3:00 p.m., he called out: *"E'li, E'li, la'ma sa·bach·tha'ni?"* ("My God, my God, why have you forsaken me?") (Mt 27:46; Mr 15:34) Bystanders thought that he was calling for Elijah. Perhaps they misunderstood Jesus' words because his speech was indistinct as a result of his intense suffering or because his dialect differed from theirs. (Mt 27:47; Mr 15:35) In calling out to his heavenly Father, acknowledging him as his God, Jesus fulfilled Psalm 22:1.

ELIAB (E·li'ab) [My God Is Father].

1. Son of Helon of the tribe of Zebulun; one of the 12 chieftains designated by Jehovah to aid Moses and Aaron in numbering the sons of Israel for the army. (Nu 1:1-4, 9, 16) Eliab was over the army of his tribe, which was a part of the three-tribe division of the camp of Judah. (Nu 2:3, 7; 10:14-16) In addition to sharing in the group presentation made by the chieftains after the setting up of the tabernacle, chieftain Eliab thereafter presented his own offering on the third day for the inauguration of the altar.—Nu 7:1-3, 10, 11, 24-29.

2. Son of Pallu of the tribe of Reuben; father of Nemuel. Eliab's other sons, Dathan and Abiram, supported Korah in his rebellion against Moses and were swallowed up along with their house-

holds by the miraculous opening up of the earth. —Nu 16:1, 12; 26:8-10; De 11:6.

3. A Levite of the family of Kohathites and an ancestor of Samuel the prophet. (1Ch 6:22, 27, 28, 33, 34) His name is given as Eliel at 1 Chronicles 6:34 and as Elihu at 1 Samuel 1:1.

4. The firstborn of King David's father Jesse. (1Sa 17:13; 1Ch 2:13) Eliab's appearance and the height of his stature so impressed Samuel that he concluded this one was God's choice for the kingship. Jehovah, though, had rejected Eliab and selected David.—1Sa 16:6-12.

Eliab, Abinadab, and Shammah, the three oldest sons of Jesse, were in Saul's army at the time the Philistine champion Goliath directed his challenge to the men of Israel. Shortly before Goliath again came up from the battle lines of the Philistines to taunt Israel, David, having been sent by his father, arrived on the scene with provisions of food for his three brothers. Angered greatly by David's making inquiry among the Israelite warriors about the reward to be received by the one striking down Goliath, Eliab lashed out against David, suggesting that he was negligent in caring for his shepherding duties and accusing him of being presumptuous and having a bad heart. (This account about David's errand and Eliab's anger is omitted by the Vatican Manuscript No. 1209.)—1Sa 17:13, 17, 26-28.

Much later David's son Jerimoth, it seems, married Abihail the daughter of Eliab.—2Ch 11:18.

5. One of the Gadites who attached themselves to David while he was still under restriction because of King Saul. The Gadites are described as "valiant, mighty men," with the least one being equal to a hundred, and the greatest to a thousand.—1Ch 12:1, 8, 9, 14.

6. A Levite musician of the second division who assisted with the music when King David had the ark of Jehovah moved to Jerusalem from the house of Obed-edom.—1Ch 15:18, 20, 25; 16:5.

ELIADA (E·li'a·da) [God Has Known].

1. A son of David born at Jerusalem. (2Sa 5:13-16; 1Ch 3:5-8) Called Beeliada at 1 Chronicles 14:7.

2. Father of a resister of Solomon named Rezon.—1Ki 11:23.

3. A Benjamite army officer commanding 200,000 bowmen during Jehoshaphat's reign. —2Ch 17:12, 17.

ELIAHBA (E·li′ah·ba) [possibly, My God Hides Himself]. A Shaalbonite; one of David's mighty men.—2Sa 23:32; 1Ch 11:33.

ELIAKIM (E·li′a·kim) [My God Raises Up].

1. Son of Hilkiah; chief administrator of the affairs of the house of Hezekiah the king of Judah at the time the Assyrian king Sennacherib invaded Judah in 732 B.C.E.

While Shebna was still "over the house," the prophet Isaiah foretold that he would be ripped from this position and be replaced by Eliakim, whom Jehovah calls "my servant." The transfer was to be made by clothing Eliakim with Shebna's official robe and sash. Also, "the key of the house of David" was to be placed upon Eliakim's shoulder, suggesting that he would be entrusted with the oversight of the king's chambers and the authority to decide who might be accepted into the service of the king.—Isa 22:15-24.

Acting in this official capacity, Eliakim, Shebna the secretary, and Joah, apparently the recorder, came out to speak with Rabshakeh, who had come to Jerusalem with a heavy military force to demand the surrender of the city. Then, with garments ripped apart, the three of them reported the words of Sennacherib's spokesmen to King Hezekiah, who, in turn, proceeded to send Eliakim, Shebna, and the older men of the priests to Isaiah to make inquiry of Jehovah.—Isa 36:11, 22; 37:1, 2; 2Ki 18:17, 18, 26, 36, 37; 19:1, 2.

2. King of Judah (628-618 B.C.E.) whom Pharaoh Nechoh placed upon the throne, changing his name to Jehoiakim. Eliakim was King Josiah's son.—2Ki 23:34; see JEHOIAKIM.

3. One of the Levite priests with the trumpets who was in the procession arranged by Nehemiah at the inauguration of the rebuilt wall of Jerusalem.—Ne 12:31, 41.

4. An ancestor of Jesus' adoptive father Joseph.—Mt 1:13.

5. An ancestor of Jesus' earthly mother Mary.—Lu 3:30.

ELIAM (E·li′am) [God of the People].

1. Father of Bath-sheba. (2Sa 11:3) Called Ammiel at 1 Chronicles 3:5.

2. One of David's mighty men; son of Ahithophel. (2Sa 23:34) He may possibly have been the same as No. 1 above, which would make Bath-sheba the granddaughter of Ahithophel.

ELIASAPH (E·li′a·saph) [God Has Added (Increased)].

1. Son of Deuel (or Reuel) of the tribe of Gad; one of the 12 chieftains whom Jehovah selected to assist Moses and Aaron in taking the sum of the males for the army. (Nu 1:1-4, 14; 2:14) Eliasaph was over the army of his tribe, which was a part of the three-tribe division of the camp of Reuben. (Nu 2:10-15; 10:18-20) Besides sharing in the group presentation made by the chieftains after the setting up of the tabernacle, Eliasaph thereafter presented his own offering on the sixth day for the inauguration of the altar.—Nu 7:1, 2, 10, 42-47.

2. Son of Lael and chieftain of the paternal house of the Gershonites. Under the direction of Eliasaph, the Gershonites transported the tent coverings and the screen of the tabernacle entrance, the screen of the courtyard entrance and the hangings of the courtyard as well as the tent cords.—Nu 3:21-26.

ELIASHIB (E·li′a·shib) [My God Returns (Brings Back)].

1. A Levite from the sons of Aaron to whom the lot of the 11th priestly division fell in the time of David.—1Ch 24:1, 5, 6, 12.

2. Father of a certain Jehohanan.—Ezr 10:6.

3. A Levite temple singer among those dismissing their foreign wives in the time of Ezra.—Ezr 10:16, 17, 23, 24, 44.

4. Descendant of Zattu also among the men sending their foreign wives away.—Ezr 10:16, 17, 27, 44.

5. Descendant of Bani likewise among those putting their foreign wives away.—Ezr 10:16, 17, 34, 36, 44.

6. Grandson of Jeshua, who returned with Zerubbabel from Babylonian exile. Eliashib was high priest in the days of Nehemiah and shared with the other priests in rebuilding the Sheep Gate of the wall of Jerusalem. (Ne 12:1, 10; 3:1) During Nehemiah's absence Eliashib himself defiled the temple by making a dining hall in the courtyard of the temple for his relative Tobiah the Ammonite. But Nehemiah, upon his return, threw out Tobiah's furniture and had the dining halls cleansed. Nehemiah also chased away one of the sons of Joiada the son of Eliashib because of his being married to a daughter of Sanballat the Horonite.—Ne 13:4, 5, 7-9, 28.

7. Son of Elioenai, a descendant of King David.—1Ch 3:1, 5, 10, 24.

ELIATHAH (E·li′a·thah) [My God Has Come]. A son of Heman who, during the rule of King David, was designated by lot to be a musician in the 20th service group at the house of Jehovah.—1Ch 25:1, 4-6, 9, 27.

ELIDAD (E·li′dad) [My God Has Loved]. A Benjamite chieftain, the son of Chislon; he was appointed at Jehovah's command to have a direct part in dividing the Promised Land among the Israelites.—Nu 34:17, 18, 21, 29.

ELIEHO-ENAI (El′ie·ho-e′nai) [Toward Jehovah Are My Eyes].

1. A gatekeeper of the Korahites appointed by David; the seventh son of Meshelemiah of the tribe of Levi.—1Ch 26:1-3.

2. The son of Zerahiah who, accompanied by 200 males of the paternal house of Pahath-moab, returned from Babylon to Jerusalem with Ezra. —Ezr 8:1, 4.

ELIEL (E′li·el) [My God Is God].

1. One of the heads of the half tribe of Manasseh. Like the other heads, Eliel was a valiant, mighty fellow, a man of fame.—1Ch 5:24.

2. A Levite of the family of the Kohathites and an ancestor of the prophet Samuel. (1Ch 6:33, 34) He evidently is called Elihu in 1 Samuel 1:1 and Eliab in 1 Chronicles 6:27.

3. A descendant of Shimei of the tribe of Benjamin.—1Ch 8:1, 20, 21.

4. A descendant of Shashak of the tribe of Benjamin.—1Ch 8:1, 22, 25.

5. A Mahavite, one of David's mighty men. —1Ch 11:26, 46.

6. Another of David's mighty men.—1Ch 11: 26, 47.

7. A Gadite, one of the swift, courageous, mighty men who separated themselves to David's side while he was still under restrictions because of King Saul. The least of these Gadites is described as equal to a hundred, and the greatest to a thousand.—1Ch 12:1, 8, 11, 14.

8. Son of Hebron; one of the Levite heads selected by David to bring the Ark to Jerusalem. —1Ch 15:9, 11, 12.

9. A Levite commissioner at the side of Conaniah, who was in charge of "the contribution and the tenth and the holy things" in the days of King Hezekiah.—2Ch 31:11-13.

ELIENAI (E·li·e′nai) [shortened form of Elieho-enai]. A descendant of Shimei of the tribe of Benjamin who dwelt in Jerusalem.—1Ch 8:1, 20, 21, 28.

ELIEZER (E·li·e′zer) [My God Is Helper].

1. A man of Damascus and the apparent heir of childless Abraham. Abraham referred to him as "a son of my household." (Ge 15:2, 3) Archaeological discoveries, such as the tablets from Nuzi, shed light on why Abraham considered Eliezer his heir. Often childless couples adopted a son who would then care for them in old age and arrange for their burial at death, thereupon inheriting the property. It was stipulated, however, that, in the event a son was born to them after the adoption, the real son would become the principal heir.

Likely Eliezer was the one spoken of as Abraham's oldest servant and manager of his household, who was sent by Abraham to Nahor's household in upper Mesopotamia to bring back a wife for Isaac. Like his master Abraham, Eliezer looked to Jehovah for guidance and recognized His leading.—Ge 24:2, 4, 12-14, 56.

2. The younger of Moses' two sons, so named by Moses because God had been his helper in delivering Moses from Pharaoh's sword. (Ex 18:4) Eliezer had only one son, Rehabiah, through whom came many descendants. In David's day one of these, Shelomoth, along with his brothers, was appointed over all the things made holy. —1Ch 23:17; 26:25, 26, 28.

3. A son of Becher and a descendant of Benjamin.—1Ch 7:6, 8.

4. One of the seven priests loudly sounding the trumpets before the ark of Jehovah when David had it brought up to Jerusalem from the house of Obed-edom.—1Ch 15:24.

5. Son of Zichri and leader of the tribe of Reuben during David's reign.—1Ch 27:16.

6. Son of Dodavahu of Maresha; a prophet who foretold that Jehovah would break down King Jehoshaphat's works as regards his shipbuilding partnership with wicked King Ahaziah. —2Ch 20:35-37; 1Ki 22:48.

7. One of the head ones of the exiles who returned to Jerusalem with Ezra.—Ezr 8:16.

8. A priest of "the sons of Jeshua" among those following through on Ezra's exhortation and promising to send their foreign wives away. —Ezr 10:18, 19.

9. A Levite among the men dismissing their foreign wives, following Ezra's exhortation.—Ezr 10:23, 44.

10. A descendant of Harim among those heeding Ezra's words to dismiss their foreign wives.—Ezr 10:31, 44.

11. An ancestor of Jesus' earthly mother Mary.—Lu 3:29.

ELIHOREPH (El·i·hor'eph) [possibly, God of Winter]. A son of Shisha who, along with his brother Ahijah, served as a secretary for King Solomon.—1Ki 4:1-3.

ELIHU (E·li'hu) [My God Is He].

1. "The son of Barachel the Buzite of the family of Ram." As a descendant of Buz, Elihu was evidently a distant relative of Abraham. (Job 32:1, 2, 6; Ge 22:20, 21) Likely Elihu listened carefully to the entire debate between Job and his three would-be comforters. But, out of due respect for their age, he remained silent until all had finished speaking. Though modern critics have labeled Elihu as loquacious, saying that his speeches were long-winded, the statements of Elihu were not those of an impertinent young man. He fully appreciated that wisdom was not the exclusive possession of those advanced in years, but that God's spirit made one truly wise. Elihu, therefore, leaned heavily on God's spirit. He was thus able to discern correctly that Job had failed to appreciate that the vindication of Jehovah God is far more important than the vindication of any man and that Job's three friends had actually pronounced God wicked. —Job 32:2-9, 18.

Elihu was impartial, not bestowing a flattering title on anyone. He recognized that he, like Job, was made of clay and that the Almighty was his Creator. Elihu had no intention of terrifying Job but spoke to him as a true friend, addressing Job by name, something that was not done by Eliphaz, Bildad, or Zophar.—Job 32:21, 22; 33:6.

In every respect Elihu exalted the position of the true God: The Almighty is just, rewarding the individual according to his conduct. He judges without partiality and is fully aware of the course taken by men. God hears the outcry of the afflicted. He is a Teacher who makes men wiser than the animal creation. Only untruth does God not hear, and so Elihu encouraged Job to wait for Him. Furthermore, Elihu assured Job that God was with him and that He would not preserve the wicked alive, but that those serving Him "will finish their days in what is good." (Job 36:11) Job was then admonished to magnify the activity of God, the great Provider, who gives food in abundance. Elihu called Job's attention to the great things done by God and His control of natural forces, encouraging Job to show himself "attentive to the wonderful works of God." (Job 37:14) Elihu concluded on a lofty plane, saying concerning the Almighty: "He is exalted in power, and justice and abundance of righteousness he will

not belittle. Therefore let men fear him."—Job 37:23, 24; chaps 34-37.

Only by God's spirit was it possible for Elihu to evaluate matters correctly and to speak the words having a fulfillment upon Job when he was restored: "Let him off from going down into the pit! I have found a ransom! Let his flesh become fresher than in youth; let him return to the days of his youthful vigor."—Job 33:24, 25.

2. An ancestor of the prophet Samuel; the son of Tohu. (1Sa 1:1) Elihu is evidently also called Eliab and Eliel.—1Ch 6:27, 34.

3. Thought to be King David's oldest brother Eliab; became the prince of the tribe of Judah. —1Ch 27:18, 22; compare 1Sa 16:6; see ELIAB No. 4.

4. One of the seven heads of the thousands who belonged to Manasseh and who deserted to David at Ziklag.—1Ch 12:20.

5. A Korahite of the family of Obed-edom who was a gatekeeper at the house of God, appointed during David's reign.—1Ch 26:1, 4, 7, 8.

ELIJAH (E·li'jah) [My God Is Jehovah].

1. One of the foremost prophets of Israel. Evidently his home was in Tishbeh, thought by some to be a village in the land of Gilead, E of the Jordan River. (1Ki 17:1) He started his long career as prophet in Israel during the reign of King Ahab, who began to rule about 940 B.C.E., and continued during the reign of Ahab's son Ahaziah (began c. 919 B.C.E.). (1Ki 22:51) The last time he is mentioned as serving as a prophet (this time for Judah) is toward the end of the eight-year reign of King Jehoram of Judah, which rule started in 913 B.C.E.—2Ch 21:12-15; 2Ki 8:16.

Through Elijah, Jehovah provided a pillar of strength for true worship in a time when Israel's spiritual and moral condition had fallen to an alarmingly low state. King Ahab the son of Omri had continued the calf worship established by Jeroboam, but worse, he had married Jezebel the daughter of the Sidonian king Ethbaal. Under her influence, Ahab added greatly to his sins beyond all Israel's previous kings by introducing Baal worship on a grand scale. Baal priests and prophets multiplied, and corruption reached an extreme state. Jezebel's hatred of Jehovah caused persecution and slaughter of the prophets; they were driven into hiding in caves.—1Ki 16:30-33; 18:13.

Fed by Ravens. Elijah first appears in the record when he is sent by Jehovah to announce chastisement upon Israel for their sins. His first reported words are: "As Jehovah the God of Israel before whom I do stand is living." Elijah points out that Jehovah the living God of Israel has decreed that no rain or dew will occur for a period of years, except at Elijah's word. This time period proves to be three years and six months. (1Ki 17:1; Jas 5:17) After this announcement Jehovah directs Elijah to the torrent valley of Cherith to the E of the Jordan in the territory of the tribe of Gad. Here, miraculously, ravens bring food to him. He gets water from the torrent valley, which in due time dries up because of the drought. Jehovah continues to guide him, sending him outside the territory of Israel to Zarephath, a Phoenician town dependent upon Sidon at that time. Here, near the city of Sidon, where King Ahab's father-in-law Ethbaal is ruling (1Ki 16:31), Elijah meets a widow preparing a final meal for herself and her son with their very last bit of flour and oil. Elijah requests a cake, with the promise of Jehovah's provision for her during the drought. Because she recognizes him as a man of God, she complies and is blessed. (Compare Mt 10:41, 42.) During Elijah's stay in her home her son dies. Elijah prays to God, who brings him to life, the first recorded resurrection and the third of Elijah's eight miracles.—1Ki 17.

How did Elijah impress upon Israel that Jehovah is indeed the true God?

In the meantime Ahab has looked everywhere in a fruitless search for Elijah, doubtless to put him to death. (1Ki 18:10) Eventually God instructs Elijah to show himself to Ahab. Elijah encounters Ahab and requests a meeting with the 450 prophets of Baal and the 400 prophets of the sacred pole (Asherah). Ahab gathers the prophets to Mount Carmel, not far from the Mediterranean Sea. (PICTURE, Vol. 1, p. 950) Elijah now, before the people, proposes a test to prove who is the true God to be followed. The one that answers by consuming a bull sacrificed to him is to be acknowledged by all. Fair enough, the people agree. Baal is first called on, but in vain. There is no fire, no proof that Baal is a living god, although his prophets keep praying to him, yes, even cutting themselves according to their ritual. They limp about the altar under a burning sun for the greater part of the day while Elijah mercilessly mocks them, increasing their frenzy. —1Ki 18:18-29.

Now it is Elijah's turn. Using 12 stones, he mends an altar that was torn down, probably at Jezebel's instance. Then he has the people soak the offering and the altar in water three times; even the trench around the altar, circumscribing an area perhaps 32 m (103 ft) square, is filled with water. (1Ki 18:30-35) About the time of the daily evening grain offering, Elijah prays once to Jehovah, who sends fire from the heavens to consume not just the offering but also the wood, the stones of the altar, and the water in the trench. (1Ki 18:36-38) The people, seeing this, fall upon their faces and say: "Jehovah is the true God! Jehovah is the true God!" Then Elijah has all the 450 prophets of Baal slaughtered at the torrent valley of Kishon. Answering Elijah's prayer, Jehovah breaks the drought by a downpour of rain. By Jehovah's power Elijah then runs ahead of Ahab's chariot, perhaps as much as 30 km (19 mi), to Jezreel.—1Ki 18:39-46.

Flees From Jezebel. On being informed of the death of her Baal prophets, Queen Jezebel vows to have Elijah put to death. In fear Elijah flees some 150 km (95 mi) southwestward to Beer-sheba, to the W of the lower Dead Sea. (MAP, Vol. 1, p. 949) Leaving his attendant there, he goes still farther into the wilderness, praying to die. Here the angel of Jehovah appears to him, to prepare him for a long journey to "the mountain of the true God," Horeb. Sustained for the 40-day journey by what he eats then, he covers a distance of over 300 km (190 mi). At Horeb, Jehovah speaks to him after an awe-inspiring display of power in a wind, an earthquake, and a fire. Jehovah is not in these manifestations; he is not a nature god, or just natural forces that are personified. These natural forces are merely expressions of his active force, not Jehovah himself. The Almighty shows Elijah that he still has work to do as a prophet. Jehovah corrects Elijah's thought that he is the lone worshiper of the true God in Israel by showing that there are 7,000 who have not bowed to Baal. He sends Elijah back to his assignment, naming three persons who are to be anointed, or commissioned, to do a work for Jehovah: Hazael as king over Syria, Jehu as king over Israel, and his own successor Elisha.—1Ki 19:1-18.

Appoints Elisha as Successor. Elijah next travels toward the hometown of Elisha, Abel-meholah. Finding Elisha plowing a field, Elijah throws his official garment over him, indicating an appointing, or anointing. Elisha follows Elijah closely from that time on as his attendant. He is doubtless with Elijah when another occasion arises to prophesy against Ahab. The greedy Baal-worshiping king has illegally seized a vineyard, the hereditary possession of Naboth the Jezreelite, by allowing his wife Jezebel to use false charges, false witnesses, and unrighteous judges to have Naboth murdered. Elijah meets Ahab at the vineyard and tells Ahab that his blood will be licked up by the dogs at the same place where they had licked up the blood of Naboth. He also announces a similar fate for Jezebel.—1Ki 19:19; 21:1-26.

About three years later Ahab dies in battle. His war chariot is washed by the pool of Samaria, and the dogs lick up his blood. Jezebel's execution, however, awaits a time perhaps 15 years later. Ahab was succeeded by his son Ahaziah. This king follows in his wicked father's footsteps, for when he is injured in an accident he turns to the false god Baal-zebub, the god of Ekron, to inquire regarding the outcome of his sickness. Elijah sends him Jehovah's word that because of this he will positively die. When Ahaziah sends in succession three groups to get Elijah, each group composed of a chief with 50 men, the prophet calls down fire from the heavens to annihilate the first two groups, but on the plea of the third chief, he goes back with him to pronounce the judgment against Ahaziah in person.—1Ki 22:1, 37, 38; 2Ki 1:1-17.

Elisha Succeeds Him. In harmony with Elijah's action in appointing Elisha years earlier, the time comes when Elijah must transfer the mantle of this prophetic office to Elisha, who has been well trained. This takes place during the rule of Ahaziah's successor, his brother Jehoram of Israel. At that time Elijah goes to Bethel, from there to Jericho and down to the Jordan, Elisha sticking close to him all the way. There Elisha is rewarded for his faithfulness by seeing a fiery war chariot and fiery horses and Elijah ascending in a windstorm to the heavens. Elisha takes up Elijah's official garment that had fallen off him, and "two parts" (like a firstborn son's portion) in Elijah's spirit, a spirit of courage and of being "absolutely jealous for Jehovah the God of armies," come on him.—2Ki 2:1-13; 1Ki 19:10, 14; compare De 21:17.

Elijah does not die at this time, nor does he go into the invisible spirit realm, but he is transferred to another prophetic assignment. (Joh 3:13) This is shown by the fact that Elisha does not hold any period of mourning for his master. A number of years after his ascension in the windstorm Elijah is still alive and active as a prophet, this time to the king of Judah. Because

of the wicked course taken by King Jehoram of Judah, Elijah writes him a letter expressing Jehovah's condemnation, which is fulfilled shortly thereafter.—2Ch 21:12-15; see HEAVEN (Ascension to Heaven).

Miracles. Eight miracles are credited to Elijah in the Bible account. They are: (1) shutting off rain from heaven, (2) keeping the flour and oil supply of the widow of Zarephath renewed, (3) resurrecting the widow's son, (4) having fire fall from heaven in answer to prayer, (5) having rain break the drought in answer to prayer, (6) calling down fire on King Ahaziah's captain and his 50 men, (7) calling down fire on a second captain and his 50, and (8) parting the Jordan River by smiting it with his official garment. His ascension to the heavens was also miraculous, but it was the direct act of God, not something initiated by a prayer or proclamation made by Elijah.

Elijah was a powerful advocate of the true worship of Jehovah. He did a tremendous destructive work against Baalism in Israel; the work begun by him was carried on by Elisha, and the execution of Jezebel and the destruction of unclean Sidonian Baalism were accomplished by Jehu. In Elijah's day 7,000, including Obadiah, Ahab's household manager, were found to be faithful to Jehovah; Elijah doubtless strengthened some of them greatly. Elijah appointed Elisha as his successor, but the anointing of Hazael and that of Jehu were left for Elisha to carry out.

The apostle Paul undoubtedly refers to Elijah when he speaks of "Samuel and the other prophets, who through faith . . . effected righteousness . . . Women received their dead by resurrection." He is therefore among the "cloud" of faithful witnesses of old. (Heb 11:32-35; 12:1) The disciple James points to Elijah as proof of the efficacy of prayers of "a man with feelings like ours," who righteously serves God.—Jas 5:16-18.

Work Prophetic of Things to Come. About 450 years after Elijah's time, Malachi prophesied that Elijah the prophet would appear "before the coming of the great and fear-inspiring day of Jehovah." (Mal 4:5, 6) The Jews of Jesus' day were in expectation of Elijah's coming to fulfill this prophecy. (Mt 17:10) Some thought that Jesus was Elijah. (Mt 16:14) John the Baptizer, who wore a hair garment and a leather girdle around his loins as did Elijah, denied that he actually was Elijah in person. (2Ki 1:8; Mt 3:4; Joh 1:21) The angel had not told John's father Zechariah that

John would be Elijah, but that he would have "Elijah's spirit and power . . . to get ready for Jehovah a prepared people." (Lu 1:17) Jesus indicated that John did that work but was not recognized by the Jews. (Mt 17:11-13) After John's death a visionary appearance of Elijah along with Moses occurred at Jesus' transfiguration, indicating that there was something yet to take place as represented by the work that Elijah had done. —Mr 9:1-8.

2. A son of the Benjamite Jeroham; an inhabitant of Jerusalem and the head of his house. —1Ch 8:1, 27, 28.

3. A Levite priest of "the sons of Harim" (1Ch 24:8; Ezr 2:1, 2, 39) among those complying with Ezra's admonition to dismiss their foreign wives. —Ezr 10:21, 44.

4. A descendant of Elam among those following through on Ezra's exhortation to dismiss their foreign wives.—Ezr 10:26, 44.

ELIKA (E·li'ka). One of David's mighty men, evidently from the town of Harod.—2Sa 23:25.

ELIM (E'lim) [Big Trees]. The second encampment location of the Israelites after crossing the Red Sea. (Ex 15:27; 16:1; Nu 33:9, 10) Although its exact location is not certain, it is traditionally identified with Wadi Gharandel on the Sinai Peninsula, about 88 km (55 mi) SSE of Suez. Like the Biblical Elim, which had "twelve springs of water and seventy palm trees," this modern site is well known as a watering place with vegetation and palms.

ELIMELECH (E·lim'e·lech) [My God Is King]. A man of Bethlehem who, along with his wife Naomi and their two sons Mahlon and Chilion, left Judah because of a famine in the days of the Judges and took up alien residence in Moab, where he died.—Ru 1:1-3.

ELIOENAI (Eli·o·e'nai) [shortened form of Elieho-enai].

1. A son of Neariah and a descendant of King Solomon. Elioenai was the father of Hodaviah, Eliashib, Pelaiah, Akkub, Johanan, Delaiah, and Anani.—1Ch 3:10, 23, 24.

2. A chieftain of the tribe of Simeon.—1Ch 4:24, 36-38.

3. A son of Becher and a descendant of Benjamin.—1Ch 7:6, 8.

4. A priest of "the sons of Pashhur" among those heeding Ezra's exhortation to send their foreign wives away.—Ezr 2:36, 38; 10:18, 19, 22.

5. A descendant of Zattu. Elioenai was among those dismissing their foreign wives in Ezra's time.—Ezr 10:27, 44.

6. One of the priests with trumpets who were in the procession arranged for by Nehemiah at the inauguration of the wall of Jerusalem.—Ne 12:27, 31, 40, 41.

ELIPHAL (E·li'phal) [possibly, My God Has Arbitrated]. The son of Ur listed among the mighty men of David's military forces. Eliphal may be the Eliphelet of 2 Samuel 23:34.—1Ch 11:26, 35.

ELIPHAZ (El'i·phaz).

1. Firstborn son of Esau, by his Canaanite wife Adah. Six or seven of Eliphaz' sons, including Teman, Omar, and Amalek, became sheiks of Edomite tribes.—Ge 36:4, 10-12, 15, 16; 1Ch 1:35, 36; see SHEIK.

2. One of Job's three companions. (Job 2:11) A Temanite, he was likely a descendant of No. 1 above, therefore a descendant of Abraham and distantly related to Job. He and his posterity boasted of their wisdom. (Jer 49:7) Of the three "comforters," Eliphaz stands out as the most important and influential, suggesting that he may also have been the oldest. He speaks first in the three rounds of the debate, and his speeches are longer.

Eliphaz' reasoning in his first speech went like this: "Who that is innocent has ever perished? And where have the upright ever been effaced?" Hence, the conclusion he draws is that Job must have done something wicked to receive God's punishment. (Job chaps 4, 5) In his second upbraiding Eliphaz ridicules Job's wisdom: "Will a wise person himself answer with windy knowledge, or will he fill his belly with the east wind? . . . What do you actually know that we do not know?" "Over the Almighty," Eliphaz implies, Job "tries to show himself superior." Concluding his second smear of Job's virtues, the Edomite paints righteous Job as an apostate, living in tents of bribery, a man full of deceit. (Job 15) Finally Eliphaz torments Job for the third time, falsely accusing him of all sorts of crimes—extortion, withholding water and bread from the needy, and oppressing widows and orphans.—Job 22.

Following Eliphaz' second tirade Job answers well: "All of you are troublesome comforters! Is there an end to windy words?" (Job 16:2, 3) At the conclusion of the debates Jehovah himself addresses Eliphaz: "My anger has grown hot against you and your two companions, for you men have not spoken concerning me what is truthful as has my servant Job." Eliphaz is told that they should offer up a sacrifice and that Job will then pray in their behalf.—Job 42:7-9.

ELIPHELEHU (E·liph′e·le·hu) [possibly, May God Make Him Distinct]. A Levite musician of the second division who acted as one of the directors in playing the harp at the time the sacred Ark was transferred from the house of Obed-edom to Jerusalem.—1Ch 15:17, 18, 21.

ELIPHELET (E·liph′e·let) [My God Is Escape; God of Escape].

1. Son of Ahasbai; one of David's mighty men. (2Sa 23:34) Eliphelet possibly is the Eliphal of 1 Chronicles 11:35.

2. A son born to David in Jerusalem (1Ch 3:5, 6), also called Elpelet at 1 Chronicles 14:5.

3. The last-named son of David to be born in Jerusalem. (2Sa 5:16; 1Ch 3:8; 14:7) Commentators who do not view the repetition of the name in the Chronicles account to be a scribal error suggest that this second Eliphelet was born after the death of the first son by that name.

4. The third son of Eshek, a descendant of King Saul.—1Ch 8:33, 39.

5. A descendant of Adonikam who returned to Jerusalem from Babylon with Ezra.—Ezr 8:1, 13.

6. A man listed among those having taken foreign wives but who, in compliance with Ezra's exhortation, sent them away.—Ezr 10:33, 44.

ELISHA (E·li′sha) [God Is Salvation]. The son of Shaphat and a prophet of Jehovah in the tenth and ninth centuries B.C.E.; successor to the prophet Elijah. Elijah was directed by Jehovah to anoint Elisha from Abel-meholah. Finding Elisha plowing, Elijah threw his official garment over him, designating an appointment. (1Ki 19: 16) Elisha was plowing behind 12 spans of bulls, "and he with the twelfth." It is of interest that in the 19th century William Thomson in *The Land and the Book* (1887, p. 144) reported that it was a custom among the Arabs to work together with their small plows, and one sower could easily sow all that they plowed in a day. Elisha, in the rear of the group, would be able to stop without disrupting the work of the rest. The fact that he sacrificed a span of the bulls and used the implements as fuel speaks for Elisha's promptness, decisiveness, and appreciativeness for Jehovah's call. After preparing a meal, Elisha immediately left to follow Elijah.—1Ki 19:19-21.

For perhaps six years Elisha served as Elijah's attendant. Elijah served as head prophet, and Elisha worked closely with him, being known as the one who "poured out water upon the hands of Elijah" when Elijah washed his hands.—2Ki 2:3-5; 3:11.

Elisha, from the time he joined Elijah, did prophetic work in Israel during the reigns of Kings Ahab, Ahaziah, Jehoram, Jehu, and on into the reign of Jehoash. Ruling at this time in Judah were Jehoshaphat, Jehoram, Ahaziah, Athaliah, Jehoash, and, likely, Amaziah. Elisha enjoyed about 60 years of ministry by himself after Elijah's departure.—MAP, Vol. 1, p. 949.

The record of Elisha's prophetic activity in Second Kings does not appear to be altogether in chronological order. For example, in chapter 5, Gehazi is struck with leprosy, which would exclude him from normal society. Yet, in chapter 8, he is speaking in a friendly way to Jehoram of Israel. Also, the death of King Jehoash of Israel is recorded in chapter 13, but this is followed by a record of his last interview with Elisha. (2Ki 13:12-21) In some parts of the account the works and miracles of Elisha seem to be grouped according to their nature or likeness, for example: (1) those that were for the good of the prophets and private persons (2Ki 4:1–6:7), then (2) those that had to do with the nation and the king.—2Ki 6:8–7:20.

Succeeds Elijah. Elisha's activity as successor to Elijah commences about 917 B.C.E. or shortly thereafter, at the time of Elijah's ascension in a windstorm to the heavens. (2Ki 1:17; 2:1, 11, 12) Before Elijah leaves, Elisha asks him for "two parts in [his] spirit," that is, a double part, which was due the firstborn son. This position he occupies because of his official appointment as Elijah's successor at the time that Elijah threw his official garment over him. (2Ki 2:9) Elijah, realizing that this is not his to give, tells Elisha that, if he sees Elijah when taken from him, his desire will be granted. Jehovah confirms this by permitting Elisha to see Elijah ascend in a windstorm to the heavens. As Elijah departs, his rough mantle, his official garment, falls from him. Elisha picks it up, thereby identifying himself as Elijah's successor. At the shore of the Jordan River, Jehovah shows that he is with Elisha when he miraculously divides the Jordan waters as Elisha strikes them with the garment. —2Ki 2:9-15.

Crossing the Jordan, Elisha returns to the group of the sons of the prophets at Jericho. Further establishing Elisha as the head of God's company of prophets is his healing of the water supply of the city of Jericho, which has been bad and has been causing miscarriages. Going to the source of the water, he throws salt from a small new bowl into it, and "the water continues healed down to this day."—2Ki 2:19-22.

From Jericho, Elisha climbs to Bethel, about 900 m (3,000 ft) above sea level, where he had previously visited a group of the sons of the prophets in company with Elijah. (2Ki 2:3) On the way, a band of juvenile delinquents comes out and shows great disrespect both to him and his office as prophet. "Go up, you baldhead! Go up, you baldhead!" they jeer. They mean for him either to keep on going up to Bethel or to get off the earth just as his predecessor was supposed to have done. (2Ki 2:11) To teach these boys and their parents respect for the prophet of Jehovah, he turns and calls down evil upon them in Jehovah's name. Suddenly two she-bears come out from the woods and tear to pieces 42 of their number.—2Ki 2:23, 24.

King Jehoram of Israel, King Jehoshaphat of Judah, and the king of Edom become trapped in a waterless wilderness during an expedition to put down a revolt by King Mesha of Moab (who erected what has been called the Moabite Stone). King Jehoshaphat calls for a prophet of God. Not for Jehoram's benefit, but out of respect for Jehoshaphat, who is in Jehovah's favor, Elisha calls for a stringed instrument player, that under the influence of music he may receive inspiration from Jehovah. (Compare 1Sa 10:5, 6.) Elisha has the people dig ditches. The next morning they are full of water. As the early morning sun shines upon the water in the ditches it appears to the Moabites to be blood. Thinking that Israel and their allies have been slaughtered in confused fighting among themselves, the Moabites rush in to carry away the booty. But to their surprise Israel rises up and defeats them. (2Ki 3:4-27) This event takes place between 917 and 913 B.C.E.

A series of miracles of a domestic nature now appear in Elisha's record. A widow of one of the former sons of the prophets is in dire need. Elisha miraculously multiplies her meager oil supply and saves her sons from being taken into slavery to her creditor. (2Ki 4:1-7) This miracle is parallel to the second miracle of Elijah, where he multiplied the flour and oil of the widow of Zarephath. —1Ki 17:8-16.

At Shunem in the Valley of Jezreel a prominent woman shows unusual hospitality to Elisha because she recognizes him as "a holy man of God," even providing a room for him as he frequently passes by her home. For her kindness Elisha promises her a son, though her husband at that time is old. True to his promise, a son is born about a year later, but he dies while still a child. Elisha now performs his first resurrection, bringing the boy back to life as Elijah similarly raised the son of the widow in Zarephath. (2Ki 4:8-37; 1Ki 17:17-24) For her kindness to a prophet of God, she is richly rewarded.—Compare Mt 10:41.

Elisha returns to Gilgal, N of Bethel in the mountains, to the sons of the prophets there. A famine is on. As a stew is being prepared someone unwittingly puts in some poisonous gourds. Immediately upon tasting the stew, they shout: "There is death in the pot, O man of the true God." Since it would not do to waste food during the famine, Elisha calls for some flour, putting it into the pot and making the stew edible so that "nothing injurious [proves] to be in the pot."—2Ki 4:38-41.

During the critical times of the famine, a faithful remnant of Israelite worshipers who have not bent down to Baal appreciate the efforts of Jehovah's prophets and supply material food to them. When a man brings 20 barley loaves and some grain, Elisha gives orders that this small supply be fed to all. But there are 100 men of "the sons of the prophets" to be fed. Despite the doubts of the one doing the serving, all eat to satisfaction, after which there are leftovers.—2Ki 4:42-44; compare Mr 6:35-44.

Heals Naaman. During his reign, King Ben-hadad II of Syria sends his highly respected army chief Naaman, a leper, to the king of Israel to be healed of his leprosy. This valiant man had, although leprous, saved Syria. Evidently the leprous condition of Naaman does not bar him from holding such a high office in Syria, whereas it would have removed him from holding such office in Israel. (Le 13:46) King Ben-hadad's action in sending Naaman comes about because of the testimony of a young Israelite girl who is a captive and who is serving in the house of Naaman. This young girl trusts in Jehovah and tells her mistress of Jehovah's prophet Elisha of Israel. The king of Israel feels sure that Ben-hadad is picking a fight with him, for, as he says: "Am I God, to put to death and to preserve alive?" Elisha, hearing of the king's distress, tells the king, "Let him come, please, to me that he may know that there exists a prophet in Israel."—2Ki 5:1-8.

Elisha does not come out to see Naaman, but he sends instructions through his attendant for Naaman to bathe seven times in the Jordan River. At first this enrages Naaman, but finally he humbles himself to perform the simple procedure and becomes clean. Naaman returns to Elisha and vows that from now on he will serve Jehovah the God of Israel faithfully. He takes back with him some Israelite soil, "the load of a pair of mules," upon which he will sacrifice to Jehovah, without doubt looking toward the temple of Jerusalem. As an officer of the king of Syria he will carry on his work, which includes going with the king into the house of the false god Rimmon. As the king is supported by him he will have to bow with the king, but he says he will no longer worship Rimmon. He will be performing, not a religious duty, but only his duty in service of the king. He offers Elisha a gift, which is refused. This harmonizes with the principle that the miracle is by Jehovah's power, not his, and he will not profit from the office Jehovah has given him.—2Ki 5:9-19; compare Mt 10:8.

Elisha's attendant Gehazi, greedy for selfish gain, overtakes Naaman and asks for some of the gifts that Elisha refused. Lyingly he tries to conceal the matter from Elisha. As a due punishment, Elisha tells him, "the leprosy of Naaman will stick to you and your offspring to time indefinite."—2Ki 5:20-27.

It becomes necessary for the sons of the prophets with whom Elisha is associated to move to more spacious quarters. They are at the Jordan River cutting beams for their new housing. One of the prophets is using a borrowed ax, and the axhead comes off and falls into the water. Elisha, apparently concerned that no reproach come upon the prophets, throws a piece of wood into the water where the axhead had fallen, and the axhead floats to the top. Jehovah thereby proves that he is backing up his prophets.—2Ki 6:1-7.

Israel Delivered From Syria. During the reign of King Jehoram of Israel, Syria plans a surprise attack upon Israel. More than once maneuvers of Ben-hadad II are frustrated by Elisha, who reveals to King Jehoram every move of the Syrians. At first Ben-hadad thinks that there is a traitor in his own camp. But when he finds out the real source of his difficulty, he sends a military force to Dothan, surrounding it with horses and war chariots to get Elisha. (PICTURE, Vol. 1, p. 950) Elisha's attendant is struck with fear, but Elisha prays to God to open the attendant's eyes, "and, look! the mountainous region [is] full of

horses and war chariots of fire all around Elisha." Now, as the Syrian hosts close in, Elisha prays for the opposite kind of miracle, "Please, strike this nation with blindness." Elisha says to the Syrians, "Follow me," but he does not have to lead them by the hand, indicating that it is mental rather than physical blindness. They do not recognize Elisha, whom they came to take, nor do they know where he is taking them.—2Ki 6:8-19.

With what sort of blindness did Jehovah strike the Syrians who tried to seize Elisha?

As to this form of blindness, William James, in his *Principles of Psychology* (1981, Vol. 1, p. 59), states: "A most interesting effect of cortical disorder is *mental blindness*. This consists not so much in insensibility to optical impressions, as in *inability to understand them.* Psychologically it is interpretable as *loss of associations* between optical sensations and what they signify; and any interruption of the paths between the optic centres and the centres for other ideas ought to bring it about."

Bringing the Syrians to Samaria, Elisha prays that Jehovah open their eyes, and the Syrians find themselves right in the middle of Samaria before King Jehoram himself. Elisha manifests faith in Jehovah's power and shows complete lack of vindictiveness when he prevents the king of Israel from killing the Syrians, for, says he, they are like captives of war. He instructs the king to feed them, and they are feasted and sent home. The result is: "Not once did the marauding bands of the Syrians come again into the land of Israel."—2Ki 6:20-23.

However, later on, Ben-hadad II invades, not with sporadic marauding forays, but in force and lays siege to Samaria. The siege is so severe that at least one case is reported to the king in which a woman eats her own son. As the offspring of Ahab, the "son of a murderer," King Jehoram swears to kill Elisha. But the rash oath is not carried out. Arriving at the prophet's house with his adjutant, Jehoram states that he has lost all hope of aid from Jehovah. Elisha assures the king that food supplies will be abundant the next day. The king's adjutant scoffs at this prediction, causing Elisha to tell him: "Here you are seeing it with your own eyes, but from it you will not eat." By a noise that Jehovah causes to be heard in the camp of the Syrians, they are led to believe that a great army of combined nations is advancing against them, and they flee, leaving the camp intact with all its food supplies. When the king finds out about the desertion of the Syrians, he puts the adjutant in charge of guarding the gate of Samaria, and there he is trampled to death when the starving crowd of Israelites rush out to plunder the camp. He sees the food but does not eat from it.—2Ki 6:24–7:20.

Hazael, Jehu, Named as Kings. Our attention now swings to Damascus in Syria, where King Ben-hadad II lies near death. The king's envoy Hazael meets Elisha and inquires if his master will revive. Jehovah's spirit becomes operative and enables Elisha to see a bitter picture, saddening to Elisha: Hazael as supplanter of Ben-hadad will in time mete out unspeakable injury to Israel, although it is a just punishment from Jehovah for their sins. He tells Hazael to say to Ben-hadad: "'You will positively revive,' and Jehovah has shown me that he will positively die." Hazael reports the first part in words but the second part by actions, suffocating the king under a wet coverlet and taking the throne of Syria. —2Ki 8:7-15.

There is yet an unfinished work of Elijah for Elisha to carry out, namely, the anointing of Jehu as God's executioner against the wicked house of Ahab. (2Ki 9:1-10) He carries it out over 18 years after Jehovah gave the command to Elijah. Elisha gets to see the fulfillment of the prophecies at 1 Kings 19:15-17 and 21:21-24.

At the time of Jehu's anointing, Jehoram rules in Israel and Ahaziah his nephew rules in Judah. The Syrian Hazael afflicts Israel greatly during his rule, wounding Jehoram in battle at Ramoth-gilead. (2Ki 9:15) Jehu wastes no time in carrying out his commission to wipe out the evil house of Ahab, letting no survivor remain. (2Ki 10:11) He goes first after King Jehoram of Israel, who is recuperating in Jezreel. In fulfillment of Elijah's prophecy, Jehoram is met outside the city and put to death and thrown into the tract of the field of Naboth the Jezreelite. (2Ki 9:16, 21-26) Entering Jezreel, Jehu kills wicked Jezebel, mother of Jehoram of Israel and grandmother of Ahaziah of Judah. Jehu would have her buried, but Jehovah sees to it that the dogs eat up her fleshy parts just as his prophet Elijah had foretold, so that she can have no tomb to memorialize her. (2Ki 9:30-37) Ahab's 70 sons are beheaded. Ahaziah, Ahab's grandson, is killed (2Ki 10:1-9; 9:27, 28), and 42 brothers of Ahaziah are slaughtered by Jehu's executional sword.—2Ki 10:12-14; 1Ki 21:17-24.

Baal Worship Destroyed. Continuing his ride up to Samaria the capital city, Jehu meets Jehonadab, who fully supports his execution of Baal worship, and the two ride on to Samaria to see the final stroke that will wipe Baalism entirely from Israel. Through strategy Jehu has all the Baal worshipers gather to the house of Baal and put on their garments of identification. The house is filled from end to end, and no worshipers of Jehovah are among them. Jehu gives the command, and his men slaughter every Baal worshiper, tearing down their sacred pillars and pulling down Baal's house, setting the area aside for privies.—2Ki 10:15-27.

Elisha, therefore, completes the work started by Elijah. Baal worship is annihilated out of Israel. Elisha does not experience being carried in a windstorm to the heavens to be taken to another location before his death, as was Elijah. During the reign of King Jehoash of Israel, Elisha dies a natural death. While he is on his deathbed, trouble appears for Israel again from Syria. King Jehoash approaches Elisha and makes an apparent appeal for military help against the Syrians when he addresses Elisha with the words: "My father, my father, the war chariot of Israel and his horsemen!" Upon Elisha's request, Jehoash strikes the earth with his arrows. But as he does this with lack of real zeal, only three times, Elisha tells him that as a consequence he will be granted only three victories over Syria. This is fulfilled. —2Ki 13:14-19, 25.

Work Accomplished. Through God's spirit upon Elisha, he had performed 15 miracles up to this point. But even after his death he is used by Jehovah for a 16th miracle. Elisha had been faithful till death, approved by God. The record relates that after Elisha's burial another man was being buried when a marauding band of Moabites caused the burial party to throw the man into Elisha's burial place and flee. Upon touching Elisha's bones, the dead man came to life and stood upon his feet.—2Ki 13:20, 21.

Jesus calls Elisha a prophet at Luke 4:27, and he is undoubtedly alluded to along with Elijah at Hebrews 11:35, both having performed resurrections. Elijah had come into his prophetic work at a time when Israel was steeped in Baal worship, and this required zeal for true worship. He accomplished a great work in turning the hearts of many back to Jehovah. Elisha took up where Elijah left off, and while his ministry itself was more peaceable, he saw to it that the work started by Elijah was thoroughly carried out, and he lived to see it done. He is credited with 16 miracles as compared with Elijah's 8. Like Elijah, he showed great zeal for Jehovah's name and true worship. He manifested patience, love, and kindness and yet was very firm when Jehovah's name was involved; he did not hesitate to express God's judgment against the wicked. He earned for himself a place among the "so great a cloud of witnesses" mentioned at Hebrews 12:1.

Since the work that Elijah did was prophetic of things to come in the time of Jesus' earthly ministry, and also at a later time, it is reasonable to assume the same thing regarding Elisha's work, since he actually completed the work Elijah began, carrying out his unfinished commission.

ELISHAH

(E·li′shah). Son of Javan and a family head from whom "the population of the isles of the nations was spread about." (Ge 10:4, 5; 1Ch 1:7) The only other Biblical mention of Elishah is in the dirge pronounced against Tyre, where the name appears as that of a land or region trading with Tyre. Tyre is represented as a figurative ship, outfitted by many nations, with "the islands of Elishah" providing the "blue thread and wool dyed reddish purple" for the ship's deck covering (perhaps a type of awning to protect from sun and rain).—Eze 27:1-7.

First-century Jewish historian Josephus applied the name of Halisas (Elishah) to the Halisaens (Aeolians), one of the parent branches of the Greek peoples. (*Jewish Antiquities,* I, 127 [vi, 1]) By Ezekiel's time the name Aeolis had come to designate only a portion of the W coast of Asia Minor. A similarity to the name of Elishah is noted in the district of Elis on the NW coast of the Peloponnesus (the southern peninsula of Greece). The Greeks are also known to have established colonies in southern Italy and on the island of Sicily, and the Aramaic Targum in commenting on Ezekiel 27:7 identifies Elishah as "the province of Italy." Any of these locations would fit the account in Ezekiel in the sense of being regions productive of the purple dye so highly prized, but nothing conclusive can be stated as to their definite connection with Elishah, except that the weight of evidence points in the direction of Greece rather than North Africa or Cyprus. It is also reasonable that the descendants of Elishah may not have remained fixed but that over the centuries the region of their settling may have altered or expanded and that the name of Elishah may thus have applied to different areas at different times.

ELISHAMA

(E·lish′a·ma) [My God Has Heard (Listened)].

1. Son of Ammihud of the tribe of Ephraim; grandfather of Joshua. (Nu 1:10; 2:18; 1Ch 7:26, 27) Elishama was one of the 12 chieftains designated by Jehovah to assist Moses and Aaron in registering the sons of Israel for the army. He was also over the army of his tribe. (Nu 1:1-4, 17; 2:18; 10:22) Besides sharing in the group presentation made by the chieftains after the setting up of the tabernacle, Elishama thereafter presented his own offering on the seventh day for the inauguration of the altar.—Nu 7:1, 2, 5, 10, 11, 48-53.

2. Son of Jekamiah of the tribe of Judah.—1Ch 2:3, 41.

3. A son born to David in Jerusalem. This Elishama is listed as Elishua in 2 Samuel 5:15, in 1 Chronicles 14:5, and in two Hebrew manuscripts at 1 Chronicles 3:6. Elishua is generally considered to be the correct name, as the name Elishama appears again in 1 Chronicles 3:8 and therefore could easily have crept into verse 6 through a scribal error. However, since the Hebrew Masoretic text, the Greek *Septuagint,* the Syriac *Peshitta,* and the Latin *Vulgate* read "Elishama" at 1 Chronicles 3:6, this form of the name has been retained in the *New World Translation* as well as other translations.

4. Another son born to David in Jerusalem. —2Sa 5:16; 1Ch 3:8; 14:7.

5. A priest in the days of King Jehoshaphat who, with other Levites and princes, "kept going around through all the cities of Judah and teaching among the people."—2Ch 17:1, 7-9.

6. A secretary in the court of King Jehoiakim. —Jer 36:12, 20, 21.

7. Grandfather of Ishmael the assassin of the Jewish governor Gedaliah.—2Ki 25:25; Jer 41:1-3.

ELISHAPHAT

(E·li·sha′phat) [My God Has Judged]. One of the chiefs of hundreds whom Jehoiada the priest took into a covenant and who was among those afterward sent throughout Judah to collect the Levites and the heads of the paternal houses of Israel. (2Ch 23:1, 2) Elishaphat gave his support to Jehoiada in securing the kingship for Jehoash the rightful heir to the throne and in deposing the usurper Athaliah.

ELISHEBA

(E·li′she·ba) [My God Is Plenty; God of Plenty]. The daughter of Amminadab and the wife of Moses' brother Aaron. Elisheba bore Nadab, Abihu, Eleazar, and Ithamar to Aaron.

Her brother Nahshon was the chieftain of the sons of Judah.—Ex 6:23; Nu 2:3.

ELISHUA (E·li′shu·a) [God Is Salvation]. One of the sons born to King David in Jerusalem. (2Sa 5:15; 1Ch 14:5) Elishua is called Elishama at 1 Chronicles 3:6.—See ELISHAMA No. 3.

ELIUD (E·li′ud) [from Heb., meaning "My God Is Dignity; God of Dignity"]. An ancestor of Jesus' adoptive father Joseph.—Mt 1:15, 16.

ELIZABETH (E·liz′a·beth) [Gr., *E·lei·sa′bet* from Heb., *'E·li·she′va'*, meaning "My God Is Plenty; God of Plenty"]. The God-fearing wife of the priest Zechariah and the mother of John the Baptizer. Elizabeth herself was of the priestly family of Aaron the Levite. Both she and her husband were well along in years when the angel Gabriel appeared to Zechariah in the Holy of the temple and announced that Elizabeth would give birth to a son who was to be called John. Upon becoming pregnant, Elizabeth kept herself secluded for five months. In the sixth month of her pregnancy she was visited by her relative Mary. On that occasion the unborn John leaped in his mother's womb, and Elizabeth, filled with holy spirit, blessed Mary and the fruit of her womb, calling her "the mother of my Lord."—Lu 1:5-7, 11-13, 24, 39-43.

ELIZAPHAN (E·li·za′phan), **ELZAPHAN** (El·za′phan) [(My) God Has Concealed (Treasured Up)].

1. The son of Aaron's uncle Uzziel, who, along with his brother Mishael, at Moses' direction, carried the bodies of Nadab and Abihu outside the camp. (Ex 6:22; Le 10:4; Nu 3:30) Elizaphan was the ancestral head of a Levitical family, members of which are specifically mentioned in the Bible as serving during the reigns of David and Hezekiah.—1Ch 15:8; 2Ch 29:13.

2. The son of Parnach and the chieftain of the sons of Zebulun who was among those appointed at Jehovah's direction to divide the Promised Land into inheritance portions.—Nu 34:25.

ELIZUR (E·li′zur) [My God Is a Rock]. Son of Shedeur of the tribe of Reuben; one of the 12 chieftains who assisted Moses and Aaron in numbering the sons of Israel. (Nu 1:1-3, 5, 17; 2:10; 10:18) In addition to sharing in the group presentation made by the chieftains after the setting up of the tabernacle, Elizur presented his own offering on the fourth day for the inauguration of the altar.—Nu 7:1, 2, 10, 30-35.

ELKANAH (El·ka′nah) [God Has Produced].

1. A Levite, a son of the rebellious Korah; he and his brothers, Assir and Abiasaph, did not share the fate of their father. (Ex 6:24; Nu 26:11) He is possibly the Elkanah mentioned in 1 Chronicles 6:23.

2. The second of four Levite Kohathites named Elkanah and listed in Chronicles. He is identified as the father of Amasai and Ahimoth, and he appears to have been the son of Joel.—1Ch 6:25, 36.

3. The third of the above Levites; seemingly the son of Mahath.—1Ch 6:26, 35.

4. The son of Jeroham and the father of Samuel the prophet, as well as of other sons and daughters. Elkanah was a resident of Ramah of the mountainous region of Ephraim. Hence he is called an Ephraimite, although genealogically he was a Levite. (1Sa 1:1; 1Ch 6:27, 33, 34) It was Elkanah's practice to go from year to year to Shiloh "to prostrate himself and to sacrifice to Jehovah." He had two wives, Hannah and Peninnah. Although Hannah continued barren, Elkanah loved her and tried to console her for being barren. Later, in answer to Hannah's prayer, Jehovah blessed them with the birth of Samuel and still later with three sons and two daughters. —1Sa 1:2, 3, 5, 8, 19; 2:21.

5. A Levite ancestor of a certain Berechiah. —1Ch 9:16.

6. One of the Korahites who were apparently residing in the territory of Benjamin and who "came to David at Ziklag while he was still under restrictions because of Saul."—1Ch 12:1, 2, 6.

7. One of the gatekeepers for the Ark at the time David had it transferred to Jerusalem from the house of Obed-edom; possibly the same as No. 6.—1Ch 15:23, 25.

8. An official who occupied a position next to King Ahaz of Judah and who was slain by Zichri, a mighty man of Ephraim, when Pekah the king of Israel invaded Judah.—2Ch 28:6, 7.

ELKOSHITE (El′kosh·ite) [Of (Belonging to) Elkosh]. A resident of Elkosh. "Elkoshite" is applied only to the prophet Nahum. (Na 1:1) Some would place Elkosh in Galilee. However, Nahum may have been in Judah at the time he wrote the book bearing his name. (Na 1:15) If so, this would make the suggested identity with Judean site Beit Jibrin (Bet Guvrin), about 6 km (3.5 mi) NE of Lachish, the most likely proposal. The identification, however, remains tentative.

ELLASAR (El·la'sar). A kingdom or city over which Arioch reigned in the time of Abraham and Lot. (Ge 14:1) King Arioch of Ellasar joined forces with Kings Amraphel of Shinar, Chedorlaomer of Elam, and Tidal of Goiim in warring against the kings of the rebelling city-states (Sodom, Gomorrah, Admah, Zeboiim, and Bela, or Zoar) at the Low Plain of Siddim, or the Salt Sea. The rebels were defeated, and Lot, then dwelling at Sodom, was taken captive and carried off toward the N. However, Abram (Abraham), with Mamre, Aner, and Eshcol as his confederates, overtook the four kings' combined forces at Dan. There he put them to flight, rescuing Lot and the people and recovering the goods.—Ge 14:1-16, 24.

Positive identification of ancient Ellasar with a known present-day site still poses a problem for researchers.

ELMADAM (El·ma'dam). An ancestor of Jesus' earthly mother Mary.—Lu 3:28.

ELNAAM (El'na·am) [God Is Pleasantness; God of Pleasantness]. The father of Jeribai and Joshaviah, two mighty men of David's military forces.—1Ch 11:46.

ELNATHAN (El·na'than) [God Has Given].

1. The father of King Jehoiachin's mother Nehushta. (2Ki 24:8) Likely he is the Elnathan identified as "the son of Achbor" whom King Jehoiakim sent down to Egypt to bring back the prophet Urijah. (Jer 26:22, 23) Interestingly, one of the Lachish Letters dating from this period mentions the name Elnathan, saying: "The commander of the host, Coniah son of Elnathan, hath come down in order to go into Egypt."—*Ancient New Eastern Texts*, edited by J. Pritchard, 1974, p. 322.

2, 3, 4. Three men bearing the name Elnathan are mentioned in the book of Ezra. Two are designated as "head ones" and the other as an instructor. At the river Ahava, before making the trip to Jerusalem, Ezra gave them a command to appeal to Iddo and the Nethinim at Casiphia to provide from their number ministers for the house of God, to which the Levites and the Nethinim responded.—Ezr 8:15-20.

ELOHIM. See GOD.

ELON (E'lon) [probably, Big Tree].

1. A Hittite whose daughter became "a source of bitterness" to Isaac and Rebekah as the wife of their son Esau.—Ge 26:34, 35; 27:46; 28:8; 36:2.

2. The second of Zebulun's three sons. He was one included among the members of his grandfather Jacob's household who went into Egypt. He was also the family head of the Elonites.—Ge 46:14; Nu 26:26.

3. A Zebulunite judge of Israel. After a judgeship of ten years they buried him in Aijalon in the territory of Zebulun.—Jg 12:11, 12.

4. A town of the tribe of Dan, listed between Ithlah and Timnah. (Jos 19:42, 43) Identification of its location is uncertain.

ELON-BETH-HANAN (E'lon-beth-ha'nan) [probably, Big Tree of the House of Hanan]. A city mentioned at 1 Kings 4:9 as forming part of one of Solomon's commissariat districts. Some scholars suggest that possibly it is the same as Elon. —See ELON No. 4.

ELONITES (E'lon·ites). [Of (Belonging to) Elon]. A family descended from Zebulun's son Elon.—Nu 26:26.

ELOTH. See ELATH, ELOTH.

ELPAAL (El·pa'al) [God of Activity; God Has Performed]. A descendant of Benjamin; a son of Shaharaim by his wife Hushim.—1Ch 8:1, 8, 11, 12.

EL-PARAN (El-pa'ran) [Big Tree of Paran]. Apparently the southernmost point reached by Chedorlaomer and his allies in their invasion of Canaan. (Ge 14:5, 6) Its description as "at the wilderness" or, "on the border of the wilderness" (*RS*), appears to place it on the eastern edge of "the wilderness of Paran." (Ge 21:21) Some scholars consider El-paran to be an ancient name for Elath.

ELPELET. See ELIPHELET No. 2.

ELTEKE(H) (El'te·ke[h]). A city of Dan (Jos 19:44) given, with its pasture ground, to the Kohathite Levites. (Jos 21:20, 23) On the Taylor Prism, Assyrian King Sennacherib (a contemporary of Hezekiah, 745-717 B.C.E.) boasts that he "besieged, captured, and sacked Eltekeh [Assyrian, *Altaqu*]" after defeating Egyptian and Ethiopian forces "upon the plain of Eltekeh."

Most scholars formerly placed Eltekeh at Khirbet el-Muqanna' (Tel Miqne), 36 km (22 mi) W of Jerusalem. However, as a result of recent excavations, that site has since been connected with Biblical Ekron. Thus, while no certain identification is now possible, some tentatively locate Eltekeh at Tell esh-Shallaf (Tel Shalaf), 18 km (11 mi) NE of Ashdod.

ELTEKON (El'te·kon). A city in the mountainous region of Judah. (Jos 15:20, 48, 59) Though Eltekon's exact location is presently unknown, some tentatively identify it with Khirbet ed-Deir, about 10 km (6 mi) W of Bethlehem.

ELTOLAD (El·to'lad). A city located in the southern part of the territory of the tribe of Judah, toward the border of Edom (Jos 15:21, 30), also called Tolad in 1 Chronicles 4:29. Eltolad was one of the Judean cities allotted to the Simeonites as their inheritance. (Jos 19:1, 4) As 1 Chronicles 4:24-31 shows, these were the Simeonites' cities down till David reigned.

ELUL (E'lul). The postexilic name of the 6th Jewish lunar month of the sacred calendar, but the 12th of the secular calendar, corresponding to part of August and part of September. The meaning of the name is uncertain.

In this closing month of the summer season, the dates were ripe, as was the principal crop of figs. The general vintage was under way, and by the month's end the new wine was flowing.—Le 26:5; Nu 13:23; Jer 8:13.

It was in the month of Elul that Nehemiah completed the 52-day project of reconstructing Jerusalem's walls. (Ne 6:15) In the other Scriptural references the month Elul is mentioned only as the sixth month.—1Ch 27:9; Eze 8:1; Hag 1:1, 15.

The tables prepared by Parker and Dubberstein, in *Babylonian Chronology, 626 B.C.–A.D. 75* (1971, pp. 27-47), show that the month Elul was used intermittently by the Babylonians as an intercalary month along with the month Adar.

ELUZAI (E·lu'zai) [God Is My Strength]. One of the ambidextrous Benjamite mighty men who joined David at Ziklag while he was still under restrictions because of King Saul.—1Ch 12:1-5.

ELYMAS (El'y·mas) [Sorcerer]. The professional name or title of "a certain man, a sorcerer, a false prophet," named Bar-Jesus, a Jew who lived on the island of Cyprus in the first century C.E. (Ac 13:6-8) When Luke says "sorcerer . . . is the way his name is translated," the reference is to the assumed name Elymas, not Bar-Jesus. It was not uncommon for Jews of the time to indulge in magical arts and sorcery, nor, when living in Greek society, to assume a Greek name. —Ac 8:9-11; 19:17-19; see BAR-JESUS.

ELZABAD (El·za'bad) [God Has Endowed].

1. One of the swift and courageous mighty men of the tribe of Gad who joined themselves to David in the wilderness while he was still under restriction because of King Saul. The least of these Gadites is described as equal to a hundred and the greatest to a thousand.—1Ch 12:1, 8, 12, 14.

2. A Levite of the family of Korahites; a son of Shemaiah and a grandson of Obed-edom. A capable man, Elzabad served in the division of the gatekeepers in King David's day.—1Ch 26:1, 4, 7, 12, 15, 19.

ELZAPHAN.   See ELIZAPHAN, ELZAPHAN.

EMBALMING. The process of treating a dead body (human or animal) with substances such as aromatic oils in order to preserve it from decay. If this art was not originated by the Egyptians, it was at least practiced by them in very early times. The dead body of a human or an animal that has been preserved through ancient Egyptian or other embalming methods is called a mummy. The embalming of humans was practiced not only by the Egyptians but also by such ancient peoples as the Assyrians, Persians, and Scythians.

Embalming of Jacob and Joseph. There are only two cases specifically called embalming in the Bible and both of these took place in Egypt. It was there that Jacob died, and after relating Joseph's expression of sorrow over his father's demise, the inspired Record states: "After that Joseph commanded his servants, the physicians, to embalm his father. So the physicians embalmed Israel, and they took fully forty days for him, for this many days they customarily take for the embalming, and the Egyptians continued to shed tears for him seventy days." (Ge 50:2, 3) Joseph died at the age of 110 years, "and they had him embalmed, and he was put in a coffin in Egypt." (Ge 50:26) In Jacob's case the principal purpose apparently was preservation until his burial in the Promised Land. Joseph's prominence may have been the reason in his case.—Ge 49:29-32; 50:13, 24, 25; Ex 13:18, 19; Jos 24:32.

According to Herodotus, Egyptian embalming methods included soaking the corpse in natron for *seventy* days. Yet, when Jacob was embalmed by Egyptian physicians at a much earlier time, the Bible says "they took fully *forty* days for him, for this many days they customarily take for the embalming, and the Egyptians continued to shed tears for him seventy days." (Ge 50:3) Scholars have made various efforts to reconcile Genesis 50:3 with the words of Herodotus. For one thing, the 40 days may not have included the time of the body's immersion in natron. However, it is quite possible that Herodotus simply erred in saying the dead body was placed in natron for 70 days. The later Greek historian Diodorus Siculus (of the first century B.C.E.) said that the Egyptian embalming process lasted over 30 days. (*Diodorus of Sicily,* I, 91, 5, 6) Of course, there may have been Egyptian embalming procedures that neither of these historians discussed, and it is possible that different time periods were involved in the embalming processes at various points in history.

Burial of Hebrews and Christians. The poor condition of human remains found in Palestinian tombs indicates that it was not the general Hebrew custom to embalm the dead (at least for long preservation in the manner of the Egyptians) and that early followers of Christ there did not embalm their deceased ones in an effort to preserve their bodies indefinitely. Faithful Hebrews and true Christians realized that the soul, whether that of a human or of an animal, dies and that the body returns to dust. (Ec 3:18-20; Eze 18:4) The fact that the Scriptures make such limited reference to embalming seems to be added proof that it was not a general practice among Hebrews and early Christians.

The Scriptures, in telling about the burial of King Asa, state: "They laid him in the bed that had been filled with balsam oil and different sorts of ointment mixed in an ointment of special make. Further, they made an extraordinarily great funeral burning for him." This was not cremation of the king, but a burning of spices. (2Ch 16:13, 14) And, if this use of an ointment may be considered a form of embalming at all, it was not the type practiced by the Egyptians.

When Jesus Christ died, Nicodemus brought "a roll of myrrh and aloes, about a hundred pounds of it," and it is stated: "So they took the body of Jesus and bound it up with bandages with the spices, just the way the Jews have the custom of preparing for burial." (Joh 19:39, 40) However, this was not specifically called embalming, and it was not like embalming processes practiced by the Egyptians. It was the customary manner of preparing a body for burial, doubtless being similar to the way that Lazarus was prepared for interment. His case shows that the Jewish custom did not involve an elaborate embalming process designed to preserve the body for a long time, for when Jesus said, "Take the stone away," Martha said: "Lord, by now he must smell, for it is four days." She would not have expected that condition to exist if Lazarus had actually been embalmed. Lazarus' feet and hands were bound with wrappings and "his countenance was bound about with a cloth," but the intention evidently had not been that of preserving his body from putrefaction.—Joh 11:39, 44; see BURIAL, BURIAL PLACES.

EMBROIDERY. The ancient art of using a needle to stitch threads or other materials of various colors or kinds into fabric of some sort or leather to produce raised ornamentation. Interweaving of patterns and figures in cloth by means of needlework is first mentioned Biblically in connection with Israel's tabernacle. Jehovah filled the tabernacle workmen Bezalel and Oholiab with wisdom of heart to do, among other things, all the work of an embroiderer, distinguished from the work of a weaver.—Ex 35:30-35; 38:21-23.

In keeping with divine instructions, cherubs were skillfully embroidered on the tabernacle tent cloths, these figures being visible from within the Holy and the Most Holy. (Ex 26:1; 36:8) Cherubs were also embroidered on the curtain that separated these tabernacle compartments. —Ex 26:31-33; 36:35.

To make the ephod worn by the high priest, plates of gold were beaten into thin sheets, from which were cut threads "to work in among the blue thread and the wool dyed reddish purple and the coccus scarlet material and the fine linen, as the work of an embroiderer." (Ex 39:2, 3; 28:6) Similarly, "workmanship of an embroiderer" went into making the high priest's "breastpiece of judgment."—Ex 28:15; 39:8.

The victory song of Barak and Deborah represents Sisera's mother as expecting him to return from battling Israel with spoils that included embroidered garments. (Jg 5:1, 28, 30) In love, Jehovah had figuratively clothed Jerusalem with a costly "embroidered garment." But her idolatrous inhabitants had evidently used literal embroidered garments to cover the images of a male with which she is represented as prostituting herself. (Eze 16:1, 2, 10, 13, 17, 18) Jehovah also foretold through Ezekiel that, at wealthy Tyre's downfall at Babylonian hands, dethroned "chieftains of the sea" would "strip off their own embroidered garments."—Eze 26:2, 7, 15, 16.

EMEK-KEZIZ (E'mek-ke'ziz) [Low Plain of Cutting Off]. A Benjamite city. (Jos 18:21) The exact location of Emek-keziz is today unknown. The meaning of its name and its mention along with Jericho, Beth-hoglah, and Beth-arabah in the Jordan Valley may indicate a location in that vicinity.

EMERALD. A precious, brilliant, transparent gemstone that is a variety of beryl. Emerald is composed of aluminum and glucinium silicate and a small amount of chromium that imparts the green color to the stone. It is slightly harder than quartz and is usually found in nodular form or in distinct six-sided crystals.

Emeralds were known to the early Egyptians, who obtained them from Upper Egypt. They were probably among the valuable articles received from the Egyptians just prior to Israel's departure from Egypt. (Ex 12:35, 36) Later, an emerald (Heb., *ba·re'qeth*) was placed as the third stone in the first row of stones on the high priest's "breastpiece of judgment." (Ex 28:2, 15, 17, 21; 39:10) The king of Tyre is depicted as wearing a covering of "every precious stone," including the emerald, in the prophetic dirge delivered by Ezekiel.—Eze 28:12, 13.

The apostle John, in his vision of Jehovah's heavenly throne, used the emerald to describe the rainbow that was "round about the throne." (Re 4:1-3) When John saw "the holy city, New Jerusalem," he observed that "the foundations of the city's wall were adorned with every sort of precious stone," the fourth being emerald (Gr., *sma'ra·gdos*).—Re 21:2, 10, 19.

EMIM (E'mim) [Frightful Things]. A tribe or people that dwelt in the territory E of the Dead Sea. They are described as being great, numerous, and tall "like the Anakim." (De 2:10) This comparison with the sons of Anak indicates that the Emim were giantlike in stature and fierce, for Moses stated to Israel: "You yourself have heard it said, 'Who can make a firm stand before the sons of Anak?'" (De 9:2) The origin of the Emim cannot definitely be established, although some think that they were a branch of the Rephaim.

During the time of Abraham, the Elamite king Chedorlaomer defeated the Emim in Shaveh-kiriathaim. (Ge 14:5) The Emim apparently continued to dwell in their land E of the Dead Sea for some time after this, as the Bible speaks of them as finally being dispossessed by the Moabites. The Moabites also used the name Emim to refer to the Rephaim.—De 2:11.

EMMAUS (Em·ma'us). The village toward which Cleopas and a fellow disciple were journeying when they were joined by the materialized Jesus Christ on the day of his resurrection. It

was not, however, until after they reached Emmaus and Jesus "was reclining with them at the meal" that they recognized him. Following Jesus' subsequent disappearance the two disciples returned to Jerusalem that same evening. (Lu 24:13-33) Luke says that the village was 'sixty stadia' (7.5 Roman miles [11 km; 7 mi]) from Jerusalem.

However, the present location of Emmaus is uncertain, at least half a dozen different sites having been proposed. Most prominent among these is 'Imwas on the road to Tel Aviv-Yafo. But 'Imwas is about 175 stadia (32 km; 20 mi) WNW of that city, almost three times as far as Luke mentions. Another oft-proposed site, Qalunyah, located on the main road to Tel Aviv-Yafo and accepted by some as the Ammaous referred to by Josephus, is about 35 stadia (6.5 km; 4 mi) from Jerusalem and so is too close to fit Luke's record. Some, therefore, prefer to identify Emmaus with El-Qubeiba, on a more northerly Roman road than the other suggested sites. Here remains have been found believed to date back to the Greek Scripture period. The location, about 60 stadia (11 km; 7 mi) NW of Jerusalem, lends support to the view that this may be the Biblical city. Nonetheless, any final identification is impossible at this time.

ENAIM (E·na'im) [probably, Two Fountains; Two Springs]. A site near which Tamar, disguised as a prostitute, cohabited with Judah, resulting in the birth of Perez and Zerah. (Ge 38:14-16, 21, 29, 30) Enaim was apparently situated between Adullam and Timnah. (Ge 38:12) While considered by some geographers to be the same as Enam in the Shephelah (Jos 15:34), its exact location is today unknown.

ENAM (E'nam) [related to 'a'yin, "fountain; spring"]. A city in the Shephelah of Judah. (Jos 15:33, 34) Although Enam's exact location is today unknown, some geographers consider it to be the same as Enaim mentioned at Genesis 38:14, 21.

ENAN (E'nan) [related to 'a'yin, "fountain; spring"]. The father of Ahira the chieftain of the tribe of Naphtali in Moses' day.—Nu 1:15; 2:29; 7:78, 83; 10:27.

ENCLAVE CITIES. Cities of a particular people or tribe that are enclosed within the territory of a different tribe. Modern-day examples of enclaves include West Berlin, surrounded by the territory of East Germany, and the property given to the United Nations, totally enclosed within

New York City. A part of ancient Jerusalem remained a Jebusite enclave within Israel's territory for four centuries until David finally captured it.—Jos 15:63; Jg 1:21; 19:11, 12; 2Sa 5:6-9.

In the division of the Promised Land among the 12 tribes, there were cities within the general territory of one tribe that were held by another tribe. According to Joshua 16:9, "the sons of Ephraim had enclave [or, "separated; isolated"] cities in the midst of the inheritance of the sons of Manasseh" (*NW*, ftn), that is, "towns set apart for the Ephraimites inside the inheritance of the sons of Manasseh." (*JB*; see also Jos 17:8, 9.) Some of the sons of Manasseh resided in towns within the boundaries of Issachar and Asher. —Jos 17:11; 1Ch 7:29.

Simeon's inheritance consisted of cities that were located within Judah's territory, because the latter's allotment "proved to be too large for them." (Jos 19:1-9; MAPS, Vol. 1 pp. 744, 947) The 48 cities administered by the Levites, including the 6 cities of refuge, were all enclaves in the territory of other tribes. (Jos 21:3-41) In this manner Jacob's deathbed prophecy concerning Simeon and Levi was fulfilled, that 'they shall have a portion in Jacob, but will be scattered in Israel.'—Ge 49:7.

END. See TIME OF THE END.

EN-DOR [possibly, Fountain (Spring) of the Generation]. A plains city located in the territory of Issachar but assigned to Manasseh. The Canaanites there were not entirely dispossessed but came under forced labor. (Jos 17:11-13) En-dor is usually identified with Khirbet Safsafeh (Horvat Zafzafot), about 11 km (7 mi) SE of Nazareth.

At Psalm 83:9, 10, En-dor is connected with Jehovah's victory over Sisera. While not mentioned in the battle account at Judges chapters 4 and 5, it evidently lay only a few miles S of Mount Tabor, from which Barak's army descended. (Jg 4:6, 12) It was also in the general region of Taanach and Megiddo and the torrent valley of Kishon, where Sisera's forces were miraculously disrupted. (Jos 17:11; Jg 5:19) So, some feature of the battle evidently extended as far as En-dor, and the psalmist, well acquainted with the historical and geographic details, could speak of En-dor as the place where many of the fleeing Canaanites were annihilated.

En-dor is best known as the place where King Saul went to consult a "mistress of spirit mediumship" shortly before Israel's defeat at the hands of the Philistines.—1Sa 28:7; 31:1-13.

ENDURANCE. The Greek verb *hy·po·me'no,* literally meaning "remain or stay under," is rendered 'remain behind' in Luke 2:43 and Acts 17:14. It also came to have the sense "stand one's ground; persevere; remain steadfast," and is thus translated 'endure.' (Mt 24:13) The noun *hy·po·mo·ne'* usually denotes courageous, steadfast, or patient "endurance" that does not lose hope in the face of obstacles, persecutions, trials, or temptations.

Why Needed. Among the things Christians may have to face are indifference on the part of others, reproach, misrepresentation, intense hostility, hatred by close family members, mistreatment, imprisonment, and even death. (Mt 5:10-12; 10:16-22; 24:9, 10, 39; Mr 13:9, 12, 13; Re 13:10) This calls for endurance. Without this essential quality, a person simply could not come into possession of eternal life. (Ro 2:7; Heb 10:36; Re 14:12) This is because what counts is the finish, not how well a person may have started in the course of Christian discipleship. As Jesus Christ expressed it: "He that has endured to the end is the one that will be saved." (Mt 24:13) "By endurance on your part you will acquire your souls."—Lu 21:19.

Persons who quickly accept "the word of God," but only on a surface level, lack endurance. They soon give up under tribulation or persecution, losing out on God's approval and blessing. But those who develop deep appreciation for "the word of God" endure steadfastly. They "bear fruit with endurance," faithfully continuing to proclaim God's message despite hardship, suffering, and discouragement.—Lu 8:11, 13, 15.

How Maintained. Contemplating the fine example set by God's servants—the pre-Christian prophets, Job, the apostles Paul and John, and many more—and noting the outcome of their faithful course can be a great stimulus in maintaining endurance when one is experiencing suffering. (2Co 6:3-10; 12:12; 2Th 1:4; 2Ti 3:10-12; Jas 5:10, 11; Re 1:9) Especially should the flawless endurance of Jesus Christ be kept prominently in view.—Heb 12:2, 3; 1Pe 2:19-24.

It is also important never to lose sight of the Christian hope, eternal life in a sinless state. Not even death at the hands of persecutors can nullify this hope. (Ro 5:4, 5; 1Th 1:3; Re 2:10) The suffering of the present will pale into insignificance when compared with the fulfillment of that grand hope. (Ro 8:18-25) Against the backdrop of eternity, any suffering, though intense at the time, is "momentary and light." (2Co 4:16-18)

A person's remembering the temporary nature of trials and holding fast to the Christian hope can prevent his giving in to despair and becoming unfaithful to Jehovah God.

Endurance in the Christian way is not dependent on personal strength. It is the Most High who, by means of his spirit and the comfort from the Scriptures, sustains and fortifies his servants. He "supplies endurance" to those who rely fully on him, and so Christians rightly pray for his help, including the wisdom needed to deal with a particular trial. (Ro 15:4, 5; Jas 1:5) Jehovah will never permit anyone's being submitted to a trial that would be impossible for him to bear. If a person looks to Him for aid, not losing faith but trusting completely in Jehovah, the Almighty will make the way out so that he is able to endure.—1Co 10:13; 2Co 4:9.

There is no limit to the strength on which Christians can draw when undergoing suffering. The apostle Paul's prayer for the Colossians was that they be "made powerful with all power to the extent of [God's] glorious might so as to endure fully and be long-suffering with joy." (Col 1:11) An example of this "glorious might" in operation is the resurrection of Jesus Christ from the dead and his exaltation to the right hand of the Father.—Eph 1:19-21.

Jehovah God and his Son want all to succeed. This is evident from the encouragement regarding endurance that Jesus Christ gave to members of Christian congregations at Ephesus, Smyrna, Pergamum, Thyatira, Sardis, Philadelphia, and Laodicea.—Re 2:1-3, 8-10, 12, 13, 18, 19; 3:4, 5, 7, 10, 11, 14, 19-21.

Proper View of Trials. Knowing that a person's eternal future depends on endurance and that he can be confident of assistance from on high, Christians should not dread trials and tribulations, resenting them or giving in to complaint, self-pity, or bitterness. The apostle Paul admonished: "Exult while in tribulations, since we know that tribulation produces endurance." (Ro 5:3) Trials borne patiently and steadfastly with divine help reveal that a Christian possesses the needed quality of endurance—something that was not known in actuality and by experience before the tribulation began.

Endurance should be allowed to have "its work complete" by letting the trial run its full course without any attempts to use unscriptural means to bring it to a swift end. Then, faith will be tested and refined, and its sustaining power will be revealed. Areas of weakness may be exposed, putting the Christian in a position to see defects and to make needed improvements. The molding effect of trials endured faithfully can make a person more patient, sympathetic, compassionate, kind, and loving when dealing with fellow humans. Thus, by permitting endurance to "have its work complete," a person will not be "lacking in anything" that Jehovah God looks for in his approved servants.—Jas 1:2-4.

EN-EGLAIM (En-eg′la·im) [Fountain (Spring) of Two Calves]. In a symbolic vision given to Ezekiel the salt-laden waters of the Dead Sea were to be "healed" and fishers were to stand on its shores from En-gedi up to En-eglaim. (Eze 47:8-10) The name itself indicates a place by a spring. Most scholars connect En-eglaim with ′Ain Feshka, near the NW end of the Dead Sea. ′Ain Feshka and, some 29 km (18 mi) to the S, ′Ain Jidi (which perpetuates the name of En-gedi) constitute the two major oases on the Dead Sea's western shore. On the other hand, others suggest a site on the SE shore of the Dead Sea, near Zoar. On the basis of ancient written documents, which refer to the district of ′Agaltain, Y. Yadin concludes that "it is clear that 'the district of ′Agaltain' is the south-eastern sector of the Dead Sea . . . If there is a connection between ′Agaltain and En-eglaim in Ezekiel's prophecy on the Dead Sea (Ezek. 47:10: 'and it shall come to pass that the fishers shall stand upon it from En-gedi even unto En-eglaim')—the interpretation of this passage should be that the Sea will be healed from coast to coast—a very vivid and clear picture. There is no need to look for En-eglaim on the west coast (it was recently suggested to identify it with Ain-Feshkha), an identification that narrows the prophetic vision to the western shore alone."—*Israel Exploration Journal,* Jerusalem, 1962, Vol. 12, pp. 250, 251.

ENEMY. The Hebrew term ′oh·yev′ and the Greek ekh·thros′ refer to one who is hostile or one who hates. (Ex 23:22; Mt 5:43) The first record of enmity in the universe is the action of the "serpent," later identified in the Bible as Satan the Devil (Re 12:9), when he approached Eve with a challenge as to God's truthfulness. (Ge 3:4, 5) Jesus Christ described this spirit creature as a manslayer, also as "a liar and the father of the lie."—Joh 8:44; see SATAN.

Enemies of God. Since that time Satan has been the chief enemy of God. (Mt 13:25, 39) He has exercised influence over mankind, and they have yielded to that influence, so that "the whole world is lying in the power of the wicked one." (1Jo 5:19) This world is therefore the enemy of God. (Jas 4:4) Yet God has been long-suffering with his enemies and merciful to those from among them who desired to serve him. He has provided a means of reconciliation for such ones through the sacrifice of Jesus Christ. (Ro 5:10; Col 1:21, 22) He has constituted those who are in union with Christ "ambassadors" to a hostile world, with the ministry of reconciliation.—2Co 5:18-21.

On the other hand, there are many who become God's hard-set enemies, including Satan and the wicked demons, who gather the nations in opposition to God (Re 16:13-16); the apostate "man of lawlessness," who sets himself in opposition to God (2Th 2:3, 4); "Babylon the Great," whose "sins have massed together clear up to heaven" (Re 17:5; 18:5); "the wild beast" out of the sea, which gets its power and authority from Satan the dragon (Re 13:1, 2, 6); the two-horned "wild beast," which promotes worship of that sea "beast" (Re 13:11, 12); the "scarlet-colored wild beast" that is "full of blasphemous names" (Re 17:3); and those who persist in supporting them (Re 19:17-21). These God will destroy.—De 32: 41; Isa 59:18; Re 20:10.

Enemies of Christ. The enemies of God are also the enemies of Christ. (Joh 8:42-47; Mt 10: 40) When on earth Jesus Christ suffered much at the hands of the enemies of God. Nevertheless, he did not repay them in kind; he did not seek to work injury to them. (1Pe 2:21-23) He even healed one man in the crowd that came out with clubs and swords to seize him.—Lu 22:49-51; Joh 18:10, 11.

However, after his resurrection he "sat down at the right hand of God, from then on awaiting until his enemies should be placed as a stool for his feet." (Heb 10:12, 13; Lu 20:41-43) This prophecy was recorded at Psalm 110, stating Jehovah's command to his Son: "Go subduing in the midst of your enemies." (Ps 110:2) These enemies of Jehovah and of his "anointed one" are shown to be composed of "nations," "national groups," "kings of the earth," and "high officials." (Ps 2:1-9) At Revelation 19:11-21 the one called "Faithful and True," "The Word of God," and "King of kings and Lord of lords" is described as leading the armies of heaven against his enemies. His enemies are here described as "the wild beast and the kings of the earth and their armies," and the "false prophet," all of whom Christ annihilates.

Enemies of Mankind. Those who are enemies of God are at the same time enemies of mankind because they fight against man's recon-

ciliation with God and God's purposes toward the human family. They oppose the proclamation of the truth and are therefore against the interests of all men, just as were those who persecuted the early Christians.—1Th 2:15.

Additionally, because of the entry of sin into the world through Adam, death spread to all men, and it has been, as the Bible calls it, mankind's "enemy." (1Co 15:26; Ro 5:12) Death cannot be overcome by man's efforts. (Ps 89:48) Only Jehovah God through Jesus Christ will do away with this enemy of man.—1Co 15:24-26; Isa 25:8.

The Christian's Fight. The apostle Paul described the warfare of the Christian, saying: "We have a wrestling not against blood and flesh, but against the governments, against the authorities, against the world rulers of this darkness, against the wicked spirit forces in the heavenly places." (Eph 6:12; compare 2Co 10:4.) Therefore the Christian's fight is not against men. It is against wicked spirits who try to turn them away from God. Conversely, Jesus Christ explained to his followers that the world would hate and even kill them (Mt 10:22; 24:9; Joh 16:2) and that in some cases a man's enemies would be those of his own household.—Mt 10:36.

What is to be the Christian's attitude toward fellow humans who make themselves his enemies? Jesus counseled: "Continue to love your enemies, to do good to those hating you." (Lu 6:27, 28) He explained: "You heard that it was said [not in the Bible, but in tradition], 'You must love your neighbor and hate your enemy.' However, I say to you: Continue to love your enemies and to pray for those persecuting you." (Mt 5:43, 44) And, doubtless referring to Proverbs 25:21, the apostle Paul admonishes: "If your enemy is hungry, feed him." (Ro 12:20) This principle was enunciated by the Law, which read: "Should you come upon your enemy's bull or his ass going astray, you are to return it without fail to him. Should you see the ass of someone who hates you lying down under its load, then you must refrain from leaving him. *With him* you are without fail to get it loose."—Ex 23:4, 5.

Because Jehovah's servants follow these fine principles, the result has been that many former enemies have become softened in heart toward them and also toward God himself. This is in harmony with Proverbs 16:7: "When Jehovah takes pleasure in the ways of a man he causes even his enemies themselves to be at peace with him." (Compare Ro 12:17, 18, 21; 1Pe 2:19, 20;

3:9.) An outstanding example of mercy toward an enemy is the treatment accorded by Jesus Christ to Saul of Tarsus (who became the apostle Paul).—Ac 9:1-16; 1Ti 1:13; compare Col 1:21, 22.

Jehovah God says: "Vengeance is mine, and retribution." (De 32:35; Ro 12:19; Heb 10:30) Therefore the servant of God does not take vengeance into his own hands; neither does he wish for calamity on his enemies for personal satisfaction, remembering the wise counsel: "When your enemy falls, do not rejoice; and when he is caused to stumble, may your heart not be joyful." (Pr 24:17) Under the Law, in instances where there might be a question as to whether a manslaying was deliberate or accidental, any previous enmity, hatred, or striking of a man with enmity was a factor that weighed heavily against the accused.—Nu 35:20-25.

There are many "enemies" to be overcome by the Christian during his life course, aside from literal personal opposition. There is grave danger in capitulating to these "enemies," for, if submitted to, they will bring one into the position of an enemy of God. Says the apostle: "The *minding of the flesh* means enmity with God, for it is not under subjection to the law of God, nor, in fact, can it be." (Ro 8:7; Ga 5:17) The Scriptures describe a conflict that goes on within the Christian because of two inimical forces: (1) "the law of God," which Paul spoke of as the law now governing his mind, and also as "the law of that spirit which gives life in union with Christ Jesus," and (2) *"sin's law"* that is in [one's] members," or "the *law of sin and of death."* (Ro 7:22-25; 8:2) The apostle Peter, in similar vein, admonishes Christians to "keep abstaining from *fleshly desires,* which are the very ones that carry on a conflict against the soul." (1Pe 2:11) James the half brother of Jesus concurs, speaking of *"cravings for sensual pleasure* that carry on a conflict in your members." (Jas 4:1) One must recognize these things as enemies in order to stand firm against them.

ENGAGEMENT.
The mutual promise for a future marriage. Among the Hebrews the negotiations involved usually depended on the parents of the couple, particularly the fathers. (Ge 24:1-4; 38:6; 21:21) The young man's wishes in the matter were often considered. (Jg 14:2) In the case of girls who inherited the ancestral property because their father had died without sons, they could become wives to whomever it was fit in their eyes, as long as they married

within their tribe. (Nu 36:6) In the case of Isaac, it was really Jehovah who selected his bride. (Ge 24:50, 51) The selection of the bride and the proposal, usually by the parents or father of the groom, was followed by the espousal, or betrothal. This was a formal proceeding, handled by the parents on the part of the bride and often by a friend or legal representative on the part of the bridegroom.—Ge 24:1-4; Joh 3:29.

A prominent feature of the engagement was the *mo'har,* the bride-price. This term *mo'har* occurs three times in the Bible. (Ge 34:12; Ex 22:16, 17; 1Sa 18:25) The bride-price was usually paid to the parents. In Rebekah's case, Abraham's servant gave "choice things" to her mother and to her brother Laban, who took the leading part in making the arrangements. (Ge 24:53) The *mo'har* could also be in the form of service. (Ge 29:15-30; Jos 15:16) Exodus 22:16, 17 shows that the *mo'har* was paid to the father of a seduced girl as indemnity for the offense committed, even if the father refused to give her in marriage. The bride was occasionally given a present by her father as "a parting gift," and sometimes, as in the case of Rebekah, the bride was presented with gifts at betrothal.—1Ki 9:16; Jos 15:17-19; Ge 24:53.

The Hebrews viewed an engaged couple as bound and as if already married, though cohabitation did not take place until the formalities of the wedding were completed.—Ge 19:8, 14; Jg 14:15, 16, 20.

Among the Jews the engagement was regarded as so binding that if the marriage should not take place because of a change of mind on the part of the bridegroom or for some justifiable reason, the young woman could not be married to another until she was freed by due process of law, that is, by a bill of divorce. (Mt 1:19) If the engaged girl committed fornication with another man during the time of her engagement to her bridegroom, she was judged an adulteress and sentenced to death. (De 22:23, 24) Even if a man had relations with a slave girl designated for another man but not yet redeemed, or freed, both parties were guilty and were punished. However, they were not to be put to death because she had not been set free.—Le 19:20-22.

The engaged man was exempt from military duty.—De 20:7.

With respect to the age of engagement, no restrictions are pronounced in the Bible. In Middle Eastern lands today marriage often takes place after the bride reaches the age of 16 and occasionally when she is younger. Talmudists forbade marriage in the case of a male who was under 13 years and one day, and in the case of a female who was under 12 years and one day.

There generally was not a prolonged interval of years between engagement and marriage, although there could be times when an interval was needed so that the groom might pay the stipulated price or render the desired service. In the case of Jacob, the period of engagement was seven years, during which he served for Rachel but was given Leah. Then he waited one week longer before receiving Rachel, although he continued to serve Laban seven years more for her.—Ge 29:20-28.

The Christian should consider his word of promise as binding, and in the case of a marriage engagement he should follow the principle expressed by Jesus: "Just let your word *Yes* mean Yes, your *No,* No; for what is in excess of these is from the wicked one" (Mt 5:37), and by James: "But let your *Yes* mean Yes, and your *No,* No, so that you do not fall under judgment."—Jas 5:12.

The Bride of Christ. Jesus Christ is espoused to a bride, the Christian congregation, which is his body. (Eph 1:22, 23) At Pentecost, 33 C.E., the first members of the "bride" received the holy spirit with its miraculous gift of tongues. This was similar to gifts of betrothal, constituting for the spiritual bride of Christ "a token in advance of [their] inheritance, for the purpose of releasing by a ransom God's own possession, to his glorious praise." (Eph 1:13, 14) The apostle Paul spoke of those whom he had introduced to the truth about Christ and who had become Christians as promised in marriage, and he exhorted them to maintain cleanness as a chaste virgin to the Christ. (2Co 11:2, 3) Those engaged to, or promised to, the Christ are, while on earth, considered to be engaged and are invited to the evening meal of the Lamb's marriage.—Re 19:9.

EN-GANNIM (En-gan′nim) [Fountain (or, Spring) of Gardens].

1. A Judean city in the Shephelah, or lowland, mentioned in the same group as Adullam at Joshua 15:33-35. Its site is possibly at modern Beit Jimal about 2.5 km (1.5 mi) S of Beth-shemesh, or a site nearby. Umm Jina, which lies about 1 km (0.5 mi) W of Beth-shemesh, has been suggested by some as the site, but it is less probable, because no fountain is found there.

2. A city located in the tribe of Issachar's inheritance. (Jos 19:17, 21) It may be the city that Josephus called Ginae. Today it is identified with Jenin, a village on the S edge of the valley plain of Megiddo, or Jezreel, lying about 18 km (11 mi) SE of Megiddo and 8 km (5 mi) NE of Dothan, on the main road from Jerusalem to Nazareth. Jenin is surrounded by orchards and gardens and has a spring, which characteristics would harmonize with the meaning of the name En-gannim.

En-gannim, with its pasture ground, was allotted to the sons of Gershon as a Levite city. (Jos 21:27-29) In 1 Chronicles 6:73 it is evidently called Anem.

EN-GEDI (En-ge′di) [Fountain (Spring) of the Kid]. The name of a city and the surrounding wilderness in the territory of Judah. (Jos 15:62; 1Sa 24:1) The city is usually identified with Tell Jurn (Tel Goren), near the modern settlement of ʽEn Gedi, about 37 km (23 mi) SSE of Jerusalem on the shore of the Dead Sea.

The Shulammite maiden alluded to the fruitfulness of the region, referring to "a cluster of henna . . . among the vineyards of En-gedi." (Ca 1:14) This, however, only partly describes the rich plant life that flourishes there even today. En-gedi's particular location in the depression of the region of the Dead Sea is conducive to the growth of semitropical vegetation, palms and balsam, plus a variety of fruits, making En-gedi an oasis that stands out from the nearby severely desolate Wilderness of Judah.—See JUDAH, WILDERNESS OF.

Not only this abundant growth but also the inaccessibility of the region made En-gedi an ideal hideout for David when he was being pursued by King Saul. Thus the Bible speaks of certain "places difficult to approach at En-gedi." (1Sa 23:29) Modern-day visitors have similarly depicted the dangerous and precipitous rocky passes in that area. The hostility of parts of the terrain is also indicated by the reference to "the bare rocks of the mountain goats." (1Sa 24:2) Some scholars consider this a proper name, "Rocks of the Wild Goats" (*AT, JB, RS*), referring to some particular locality where goats were likely to congregate, as they do even in modern times in the En-gedi region. However, others view this term as simply a descriptive phrase for the region's goat-inhabited, rough, conical mountains and ridges. The rocks of En-gedi are honeycombed with roomy caves. David and his men may have hidden in one of these. (1Sa 24:3) Some suggest that "the stone sheepfolds" where Saul stopped may refer to these caves, with a rough wall built in front to give weather protection.—1Sa 24:2-10.

The united forces of Ammon, Moab, and the mountainous region of Seir came against Judah in the days of King Jehoshaphat by way of "Hazazon-tamar, that is to say, En-gedi." (2Ch 20:2; see HAZAZON-TAMAR.) In Ezekiel's vision of the "healed" seawater, fishers were prophesied to station themselves "from En-gedi even up to En-eglaim."—Eze 47:8-10.

ENGRAVING. The art of cutting designs or letters into materials such as wood (1Ki 6:29, 32), metal (Ex 39:30), or stone (Zec 3:9). The earliest allusion to engraving in Scripture may be the reference to Judah's seal ring. (Ge 38:18) Engraving was commonly done with pointed tools of iron or even with diamond points. (Jer 17:1) But the Ten Commandments were engraved on stone by God's "finger."—Ex 31:18; 32:16; 34:1; 2Co 3:7.

Each of the two onyx stones on the shoulder pieces of the high priest's ephod was engraved with the names of six different tribes of Israel, and each of the 12 precious stones that adorned his breastpiece was engraved with the name of one of the tribes. The holy sign of dedication, the shining gold plate on the high priest's turban, was engraved with the words: "Holiness belongs to Jehovah." Filled with God's spirit, Bezalel, along with Oholiab, was qualified to do this specialized engraving work as well as to train others. —Ex 35:30-35; 28:9-12; 39:6-14, 30.

EN-HADDAH (En-had'dah) [Sharp (Fierce) Fountain (Spring)]. A city of Issachar, likely near En-gannim. (Jos 19:17, 21) It is generally identified with el-Hadetheh (Tel 'En Hadda), 9 km (5.5 mi) E of Mount Tabor.

EN-HAKKORE (En-hak·kor'e) [Fountain (or, Spring) of the One Calling]. A spring at Lehi. (Jg 15:19) It received its name when Samson, who was thirsty after he had struck down a thousand men, "began to call on Jehovah" for water and the spring was miraculously provided. —Jg 15:14-18.

EN-HAZOR (En-ha'zor) [Fountain (Spring) of Hazor]. A fortified city of the tribe of Naphtali. (Jos 19:32, 35, 37) Some identify it with Khirbet Hazireh, 16 km (10 mi) W of Kedesh.

EN-MISHPAT (En-mish'pat) [Fountain (or, Spring) of Judgment]. Another name for Kadesh. —Ge 14:7; see KADESH, KADESH-BARNEA.

ENOCH (E'noch) [One Trained Up; Inaugurated [that is, dedicated, initiated]].

1. Son of Cain and father of Irad. Enoch was born in the land of Fugitiveness after Cain had killed his brother Abel.—Ge 4:17, 18.

2. The son born to Jared at the age of 162; the seventh man in the genealogical line from Adam. In addition to Methuselah, who was born to him when he was 65 years old, Enoch had other sons and daughters. Enoch was one of the "so great a cloud of witnesses" who were outstanding examples of faith in ancient times. "Enoch kept walking with the true God." (Ge 5:18, 21-24; Heb 11:5; 12:1) As a prophet of Jehovah, he foretold God's coming with His holy myriads to execute judgment against the ungodly. (Jude 14, 15) Likely persecution was brought against him because of his prophesying. However, God did not permit the opposers to kill Enoch. Instead, Jehovah "took him," that is, cut short his life at the age of 365, an age far below that of most of his contemporaries. Enoch was "transferred so as not to see death," which may mean that God put him in a prophetic trance and then terminated Enoch's life while he was in the trance so that he did not experience the *pangs* of death. (Ge 5:24; Heb 11:5, 13) However, he was not taken to heaven, in view of Jesus' clear statement at John 3:13. It appears that, as in the case of Moses' body, Jehovah disposed of Enoch's body, for "he was nowhere to be found."—De 34:5, 6; Jude 9.

Enoch is not the writer of the "Book of Enoch." This is an uninspired, apocryphal book written many centuries later, probably sometime during the second and first centuries B.C.E.

3. The first city mentioned in the Bible. Cain built this city in the land of Fugitiveness to the E of Eden, calling it by the name of his son Enoch. —Ge 4:17.

ENOSH (E'nosh), **ENOS** (E'nos) [Mortal Man]. The son of Seth, born to him at the age of 105. Enosh was 90 years old when he became father to Kenan, and he lived a total of 905 years. (Ge 5:6-11) His name is also listed in the genealogies at 1 Chronicles 1:1 and Luke 3:38. In his day "a start was made of calling on the name of Jehovah." (Ge 4:26) This was evidently not a calling on Jehovah in faith and pure worship as Abel had done more than 105 years before Enosh's birth. Some Hebrew scholars contend that the text should read "began profanely," or "then profanation began." With reference to Enosh's day the Jerusalem Targum says: "That was the generation in whose days they began to err, and to make themselves idols, and surnamed their idols by the name of the Word of the Lord." Men may have applied Jehovah's name to themselves or to other men through whom they pretended to approach God in worship; or else they applied his name to idol objects.

EN-RIMMON (En-rim′mon) [Fountain (or, Spring) of the Pomegranate Tree]. A city of Judah mentioned after the exile as being inhabited by the sons of Judah. (Ne 11:25, 29) Its name is a combination of Ain and Rimmon, mentioned at Joshua 15:32 and 19:7 and 1 Chronicles 4:32. Today it is generally considered identifiable with Khirbet Umm er-Ramamin, about 15 km (9 mi) to the N of Beer-sheba.

EN-ROGEL (En-ro′gel) [Fountain (Spring) of Rogel (Foot)]. A spring or well near Jerusalem that marked the boundary between Judah and Benjamin. (Jos 15:7; 18:16) David's spies Jonathan and Ahimaaz waited at En-rogel for intelligence concerning Absalom's rebellion. (2Sa 17: 17) Near here David's other rebellious son Adonijah later held a feast to enlist support for his usurpation of the throne.—1Ki 1:9.

It is generally agreed that En-rogel corresponds to the modern Bir Ayyub, or Job's well. It is located S of the SE corner of Jerusalem's wall, at the foot of the western bank of the Kidron Valley about 100 m (330 ft) S of the junction with the Valley of Hinnom. The well reaches an underground stream or spring, which, after a rain, sometimes flows so abundantly that it raises the level of water to the surface.

EN-SHEMESH (En-she′mesh) [Fountain (or, Spring) of the Sun]. A site on the boundary between the territorial inheritances of Benjamin and Judah. (Jos 15:1, 7; 18:11, 17) It is generally identified with ʽAin el-Hod, about 3 km (2 mi) E of the Temple Mount in Jerusalem, the last spring found on the Jerusalem-Jericho road before reaching the Jordan Valley.

EN-TAPPUAH (En-Tap′pu·ah) [Fountain (or, Spring) of the Apple (Tree)]. A spring by the city of Tappuah, used as a point of definition of the boundary between the inheritance of the tribe of Manasseh and that of Ephraim. (Jos 17:7) The name may have also been used for the city of Tappuah itself. (Jos 17:8) Some identify En-Tappuah with a spring near the city of Yasuf, to the S of which lies Tell Sheikh Abu Zarad, the suggested location of Tappuah.

ENVY. A feeling of resentment and displeasure toward others by reason of their belongings, prosperity, advantages, position, or reputation.

Envious persons want what others have and may feel that those possessing what is coveted are not entitled to it. While the Hebrew word qin·ʽah′, depending on the context, may refer to zeal, ardor, insistence on exclusive devotion, or jealousy and envying (2Ki 19:31; Ps 79:5; Nu 25:11; 5:14; Job 5:2), the Greek phtho′nos consistently has a negative connotation and denotes envy. —Ro 1:29.

One of the bad inclinations of sinful man is the tendency to envy. (Jas 4:5) It is an expression of hatred. Because the Philistines envied Isaac's prosperity, they maliciously stopped up the wells upon which he depended for watering his flocks and herds. Finally, their king requested that Isaac leave the area. (Ge 26:14-16, 27) In the case of Korah, Dathan, and Abiram, envy of the dignity and honorable position enjoyed by Moses and Aaron caused them to launch a vicious verbal attack. (Nu 16:1-3; Ps 106:16-18) The favorable response of the people to Jesus filled the chief priests and many Jewish elders with envy. Their envy reached a climax when they handed the Son of God over to Pilate in order to have the death sentence imposed.—Mt 27:1, 2, 18; Mr 15:10.

Advocating teachings that are not in line with those of Jesus Christ produces envy. The first concern of the person teaching them is, not the glory of God, but the promotion of his own doctrine. The resulting envy may find expression in efforts to misrepresent and malign true Christians, undermining their labors and wholesome influence. (1Ti 6:3, 4) The apostle Paul had to contend with persons who were wrongly motivated, preaching Christ out of envy. Their intent was to discredit Paul's reputation and apostolic authority, of which they were envious. They tried to discourage and dishearten the imprisoned apostle. At his expense, they sought to build themselves up in order to further their selfish aims.—Php 1:15-17.

Danger of Yielding to Envy. People who gain their ends by fraud and violence may for a time enjoy prosperity, security, and good health. Even the death of wicked ones may be peaceful, not accompanied by great anguish. When a servant of God looks at his possibly less favorable circumstances, he may allow envy of the circumstances of wicked ones to erode his appreciation of the value of doing the divine will, as did the psalmist Asaph. (Ps 73:2-14) That is why the Scriptures repeatedly set out sound reasons for neither envying bad men nor adopting their ways: Practicers of unrighteousness are as transitory as grass that quickly dries up under the intense heat of the sun. (Ps 37:1, 2) Regardless of the prosperity of those who gain their objectives by violence, they are detestable to Jehovah and under his curse. (Pr 3:31-33) Theirs is a life without a future.—Pr 23:17, 18; 24:1, 19, 20.

The pathetic lot of the envious person is set forth in the inspired proverb: "A man of envious [literally, "bad; evil"] eye is bestirring himself after valuable things, but he does not know that want itself will come upon him." (Pr 28:22) The person with an envious eye is actually heading for want. While struggling to raise himself to the level of those he envies, he degrades himself morally, sacrificing right principles. Even if he succeeds in acquiring riches, these are but temporary and must be left behind at death. Thus he has struggled or 'bestirred himself' for nothing. Jesus included "an envious [literally, "wicked"] eye" among the wicked things that issue forth from within a man and defile him.—Mr 7:22, 23.

Envy is a despicable work of the flesh that stands in the way of one's inheriting God's Kingdom. (Ga 5:19-21) All who persist in it are "deserving of death." (Ro 1:29, 32) With the help of God's spirit, however, the tendency to envy can be resisted.—Ga 5:16-18, 25, 26; Tit 3:3-5; 1Pe 2:1.

EPAENETUS (E·pae′ne·tus) [Praised; Commended]. A Christian in the congregation at Rome whom Paul mentions by name and to whom he sends personal greetings. (Ro 16:5) Epaenetus is called "a firstfruits of Asia." Possibly he was contacted personally by Paul, since the household of Stephanus is similarly referred to as "the firstfruits of Achaia," and Paul baptized this household.—1Co 1:16; 16:15.

EPAPHRAS (Ep′a·phras) [a contraction of Epaphroditus]. A faithful minister of Christ who, by preaching the good news, acquainted the Colossians with the undeserved kindness of God and thus very likely was instrumental in establishing the congregation at Colossae. At the time of Paul's first imprisonment, Epaphras came to Rome, bringing an encouraging report in regard to the love and steadfastness of the Colossian congregation. (Col 1:4-8) Evidently he remained in Rome, at least for a time, since Paul, in writing his letter to the Colossians, includes Epaphras' greetings and assures them that this slave of Jesus Christ always exerts himself "in your behalf in his prayers, that you may finally stand complete and with firm conviction in all the will

of God." As testified by Paul, this beloved fellow slave also put forth great effort in behalf of the brothers in Laodicea and Hierapolis. (Col 4:12, 13) Then, too, in writing to Philemon, Paul conveys the greetings of Epaphras and refers to him as "my fellow captive in union with Christ." (Phm 23) Epaphras is not to be confused with Epaphroditus from Philippi.

EPAPHRODITUS (E·paph·ro·di′tus) [from a root meaning "foam up"]. A trustworthy member of the congregation at Philippi, Macedonia, who was sent with a gift to Paul, then a prisoner at Rome (c. 59-61 C.E.). (Php 2:25; 4:18) While in Rome, Epaphroditus "fell sick nearly to the point of death; but God had mercy on him." News of his sickness reached the Philippians and they, perhaps, anxiously made inquiry. Since Epaphroditus was longing to see the Philippians and was distressed that they had learned about his illness, Paul considered it advisable to send Epaphroditus back quickly upon his recovery and entrusted him with his letter to the Philippian congregation. Paul encouraged the brothers to give Epaphroditus "the customary welcome in the Lord" and to "keep holding men of that sort dear." For it had been on account of the Lord's work that Epaphroditus had exposed himself to danger, coming quite near to death. (Php 2: 25-30) Epaphroditus is not to be confused with the Epaphras from Colossae.

EPHAH, I (e′phah). A dry measure equal to ten omers (Ex 16:36) or to one tenth of a homer. The ephah corresponded to the liquid bath measure and is therefore reckoned at 22 L (20 dry qt). (Eze 45:11) In the Scriptures, "ephah" is used with reference to an amount of flour (Le 5:11), barley (Ru 2:17), roasted grain (1Sa 17:17), and wheat (Eze 45:13). The term also refers to the container used for measuring an ephah. (Le 19: 36; Am 8:5) Zechariah 5:6-11 tells of an ephah measure that was covered with a circular lid of lead, in which the woman "Wickedness" was confined.

EPHAH, II (E′phah) [possibly, Obscurity].

1. A son of Midian and a grandson of Abraham and Keturah. (Ge 25:1, 2, 4; 1Ch 1:32, 33) Ephah's descendants apparently had camels in great numbers.—Isa 60:6.

2. Caleb's concubine who bore him three sons, Haran, Moza, and Gazez.—1Ch 2:46.

3. Son of Jahdai of the tribe of Judah.—1Ch 2:3, 47.

EPHAI (E′phai) [Flying Creature]. A Netophathite (Jer 40:8) of the tribe of Judah (1Ch 2:50-54) whose sons were among the chiefs of the military forces who were not taken into Babylonian exile in 607 B.C.E. Ephai's sons and other chiefs of the military forces and their men came to Gedaliah at Mizpah and he, in turn, swore to them that it would go well with them. (Jer 40:7-9) Apparently Ishmael murdered the sons of Ephai when he killed Gedaliah.—Jer 41:3.

EPHER (E′pher) [Young One [of the stags]].

1. The second-named son of Midian; a grandson of Abraham by his wife Keturah.—Ge 25:2, 4; 1Ch 1:33.

2. A man of the tribe of Judah; the third-named son of Ezrah.—1Ch 4:1, 17.

3. One of the seven heads of the half tribe of Manasseh. These family heads are described as valiant, mighty men. Their descendants were unfaithful to God, and therefore Jehovah allowed the king of Assyria to take them into exile.—1Ch 5:23-26.

EPHES-DAMMIM (E′phes-dam′mim). The camping site of the Philistines between Socoh and Azekah, from which point Goliath strode out to mock the battle lines of Israel. (1Sa 17:1, 4-10) Ephes-dammim is apparently the same as Pas-dammim, mentioned at 1 Chronicles 11:13. Its location today is uncertain.

EPHESIANS, LETTER TO THE. A book of the Christian Greek Scriptures, written about 60-61 C.E. by the apostle Paul during his imprisonment in Rome. (Eph 1:1; 3:1; 4:1; 6:20) It was carried to the congregation at Ephesus by Tychicus (Eph 6:21, 22), whom Paul also used to deliver a letter to the Colossians. (Col 4:7-9) Since the letter to the Colossians was written about the same time that Paul wrote to the Ephesian Christians, there are a number of similarities between Ephesians and Colossians. According to Charles Smith Lewis, "out of 155 verses in Eph[esians], 78 are found in Col[ossians] in varying degrees of identity." (*The International Standard Bible Encyclopaedia*, edited by J. Orr, 1960, Vol. II, p. 959) No doubt the conditions in Colossae were somewhat similar to those in Ephesus, and Paul found it good to give the same kind of counsel.

Why Appropriate to Ephesian Christians. A Chester Beatty papyrus (P⁴⁶) as well as the original readings of Vatican Manuscript No. 1209 and the Sinaitic Manuscript omits the words "in Ephesus" in chapter 1, verse 1. However, the words are found in other manuscripts and in all ancient versions. Moreover, early church writers accepted it as the letter to the Ephesians. Though some have thought this letter to be the one mentioned as sent to Laodicea (Col 4:16), it must be noted that no old manuscripts contain the words "to Laodicea," and Ephesus is the only city ever mentioned here in any of the manuscripts of this letter.

Counsel on materialism. Furthermore, an examination of the contents of the letter to the Ephesians indicates that Paul had the Christians in Ephesus in mind; and his counsel was especially fitting, in view of the circumstances prevailing in Ephesus, the most important city in the Roman province of Asia. For instance, Ephesus was known to be a fabulously wealthy city, and the tendency would be to view worldly riches as the most important thing. But in his letter Paul stresses the true riches—"the riches of his undeserved kindness," "the glorious riches" that God holds as an inheritance for the holy ones, "the surpassing riches of his undeserved kindness," "the unfathomable riches of the Christ," and "the riches of his [God's] glory." (Eph 1:7, 18; 2:7; 3:8, 16) Such would help the Ephesian Christians to get a proper view of riches.

Eliminating immorality. Ephesus was also a city noted for its licentiousness and loose conduct, its gross immorality. Consequently, Paul the apostle dwelt on this emphatically as one of the traits of the old personality and said that Christians need to strip off that old personality and put on "the new personality." The loose moral condition in Ephesus would provoke much conversation among the citizens about sexual vice, not in order to condemn it, but to revel in it; and Christians, Paul counsels, are not to be like such people, taking delight in discussing fornication and telling obscene jokes.—Eph 4:20-24; 5:3-5.

Contrasting temples. Paul's illustration of a spiritual temple was also most fitting for the Christian congregation living in the shadow of the awe-inspiring pagan temple of Artemis, which was regarded as one of the seven wonders of the ancient world. Whereas "the whole district of Asia and the inhabited earth" paid worship to Artemis and highly esteemed the famed temple at Ephesus, anointed Christians constitute "a holy temple," in which Jehovah dwells by his spirit. —Ac 19:27; Eph 2:21.

By reason of the fact that the temple of Artemis was a sanctuary, crimes were encouraged and the criminal population of Ephesus increased. No one within a certain area around its walls might be arrested for any crime whatever. The result was that a village of thieves, murderers, and the like grew up around the temple. Paul's words about stealing, along with malicious bitterness, screaming, and injuriousness, were therefore not out of place.—Eph 4:25-32.

Practice of demonism. Ephesus was the center of all kinds of demonism. In fact, the city was known around the world for its many forms of magic. The demons, then, were especially active at Ephesus, and no doubt to offset the influence of magic and sorcery and to help righthearted Ephesians break free from these demonic practices, Paul performed miracles by God's spirit; these even included the expelling of wicked spirits.—Ac 19:11, 12.

Indicating how saturated Ephesus was with magic and how fitting Paul's counsel was about fighting wicked spirits are the following points:

"The Ephesian letters" were famous the world over. "They seem to have consisted of certain combinations of letters or words, which, by being pronounced with certain intonations of voice, were believed to be effectual in expelling diseases, or evil spirits; or which, by being written on parchment and worn, were supposed to operate as *amulets,* or charms, to guard from evil spirits, or from danger. Thus Plutarch (Sympos. 7) says, 'the magicians compel those who are possessed with a demon to recite and pronounce *the Ephesian letters,* in a certain order, by themselves.'" —*Notes, Explanatory and Practical, on the Acts of the Apostles,* by A. Barnes, 1858, p. 264.

Inscriptions uncovered at the ruins of Ephesus indicate the gross darkness in which the Ephesians lived mentally and why the apostle Paul wrote Christians in that city to "no longer go on walking just as the nations also walk in the unprofitableness of their minds, while they are in darkness mentally." (Eph 4:17, 18) The inscriptions on walls and buildings indicate that the populace would govern their lives by superstitions, divination, and the searching for omens.

Because of Paul's preaching, the miraculous works he performed, and the defeat of the exorcising Jews, quite a number of Ephesians became Christians. No doubt many of these persons had

---

HIGHLIGHTS OF EPHESIANS

A letter focusing attention on an administration that results in peace and unity with God through Jesus Christ

While he was a prisoner in Rome, Paul wrote this letter to the congregation in Ephesus, a port city on the W coast of Asia Minor

God's purpose to bring about peace and unity through Jesus Christ

Expressing great undeserved kindness, God foreordained that some humans would be adopted as his sons through Jesus Christ (1:1-7)

God purposed an administration (a way of managing his household affairs) by which he would unite with himself through Christ those chosen to be in the heavens and those who would live on earth (1:8-14)

Paul prays that the Ephesians may truly understand and appreciate the wonderful provision that God made for them through Christ (1:15-23; 3:14-21)

Those granted lofty assignments in connection with Christ were formerly dead in sin; their salvation is God's gift, not a payment for works (2:1-10)

By means of Christ, the Law was abolished and the basis was laid for Jews and Gentiles to become one body, members of the household of God, a temple for God to inhabit by spirit (2:11–3:7)

God's dealings with the congregation reveal, even to those in heavenly places, the diversity of his wisdom (3:8-13)

Unifying factors provided by God: one spiritual body making up the congregation, one holy spirit, one hope, one Lord Jesus Christ, one faith, one baptism, one God and Father (4:1-6)

Gifts in men provided by Christ help all to oneness in the faith; the entire body, under his headship, functions harmoniously because of speaking truth and manifesting love (4:7-16)

Put on the new personality, in harmony with Christ's teaching and example

Not the nations but Christ is the example to follow; doing so requires a new personality (4:17-32)

Imitate God; manifest the kind of love that Christ did (5:1, 2)

Shun immoral speech and conduct; walk as children of light (5:3-14)

Buy out the time; use it to praise Jehovah (5:15-20)

With deep respect for Christ, manifest proper subjection to husbands, parents, masters; show loving consideration to those in your charge (5:21–6:9)

Gird on the complete suit of spiritual armor in order to stand firm against the crafty acts of the Devil

We have a wrestling against wicked spirit forces; divine help can enable us to resist these disrupters of peace and unity (6:10-13)

Spiritual armor from God provides full protection; use it well and pray earnestly, including all the holy ones in your supplications (6:14-24)

indulged in some form of magical practices, for the Bible account says: "Quite a number of those who practiced magical arts brought their books together and burned them up before everybody. And they calculated together the prices of them and found them worth fifty thousand pieces of silver [if denarii, $37,200]." (Ac 19:19) In view of such prevalence of magic at Ephesus and the practice of many forms of demonism, it was most appropriate that Paul gave the Ephesian Christians fine counsel about fighting against wicked spirit forces by putting on "the complete suit of armor from God." No doubt some of those who broke free from the practice of magic would be harassed by demons, and Paul's counsel would help them to resist the wicked spirits. It is to be noted that the destruction of these books relating to demonism was one of the first things that those early Christians did, setting a pattern for those today who wish to break free from demon influence or harassment.—Eph 6:11, 12.

Christ's role. Because of the glorious hope set before them as joint heirs with Christ, it is most fitting that Paul also wrote the Ephesian Christians that Christ has been raised "far above every government and authority and power and lordship and every name named, not only in this system of things, but also in that to come." (Eph 1:21) In this letter Paul reaches heights of grandeur in describing the exalted position of Jesus Christ and the gift of the undeserved kindness of God with love, wisdom, and mercy toward those brought into unity with them. The description of the manner in which all things in heaven and on earth will be unified under Christ and the bringing of both Jews and Gentiles into the congregation as "one man" is the fullest explanation found in the Bible of the "sacred secret" of God, revealed in the good news about the Christ.

EPHESUS (Eph'e·sus). Anciently, a wealthy and important religious and commercial center on the W coast of Asia Minor, nearly opposite the island of Samos. Ephesus was built on the slopes and at the base of several hills, chief of which were Mount Pion and Mount Koressos. This port lay astride the main trade route from Rome to the East. Its location near the mouth of the Cayster River, with access to the river basins of the Gediz (ancient Hermus) and the Menderes (ancient Maeander), placed the city at the junction of overland trade routes in Asia Minor. Roads linked Ephesus with the chief cities of the district of Asia.

The writings of the first-century Roman author Pliny the Elder and the ancient Greek geographer Strabo have given rise to the view that at one time a gulf of the Aegean Sea extended as far as Ephesus but that the coastline gradually moved seaward, for now the ruins of the city are several kilometers inland. However, excavator J. T. Wood, on the basis of his findings at Ephesus, concluded that the city anciently lay 6.5 km (4 mi) from the Aegean Sea. If this is correct, then in Paul's time ships must have come up the mouth of the Cayster River to an inland harbor that was kept navigable by constant dredging. Over the centuries, though, the harbor and the mouth of the river have become filled with silt deposited by the Cayster.

Temple of Artemis. The most outstanding edifice of the city was the temple of Artemis, ranked by the ancients as one of the seven wonders of the world. The temple existing in the first century C.E., when the apostle Paul visited Ephesus, had been rebuilt according to the plan of an earlier Ionic temple said to have been set on fire by Herostratus in 356 B.C.E.

According to excavations of the site in the latter half of the 19th century, the temple was erected on a platform measuring about 73 m (240 ft) in width and 127 m (418 ft) in length. The temple itself was approximately 50 m (164 ft) wide and 105 m (343 ft) long. It contained 100 marble columns, each standing almost 17 m (55 ft) high. The columns measured 1.8 m (6 ft) in diameter at the base and at least some of them were sculptured to a height of about 6 m (20 ft). The temple's inner sanctuary measured about 21 m (70 ft) in width and 32 m (105 ft) in length. The altar contained therein was approximately 6 m (20 ft) square, and the image of Artemis may have stood directly behind this altar.

The fragments that have been found indicate that brilliant color and sculpture adorned the temple. Large white marble tiles covered the roof. Instead of mortar, gold is reputed to have been used between the joints of the marble blocks.

Stadium; Theater. About 1.5 km (1 mi) to the SW of the temple of Artemis was a stadium that had been rebuilt under Nero (54-68 C.E.). This was probably the site for athletic contests and possibly also gladiatorial combats. If the apostle Paul's statement in 1 Corinthians 15:32 about fighting with wild beasts at Ephesus is to

Relief showing men fighting wild beasts, possibly in the stadium in Ephesus

be understood literally, perhaps he had to defend himself against wild beasts in this stadium.

The theater where the Ephesians rioted at the instigation of Demetrius was less than 800 m (0.5 mi) S of the stadium. This theater was situated within the hollow of Mt. Pion. (Ac 19:23-41) Its facade was decorated with pillars, niches, and fine statuary. The marble seats for the spectators were arranged in a half circle of 66 rows; these, it has been estimated, afforded room for about 25,000 persons. The acoustic properties of the theater were excellent. Even today, a word spoken in a low voice at the location of the stage can be heard at the top seats.—PICTURE, Vol. 2, p. 748.

In front of the theater was a wide marble-paved road that ran directly to the harbor. This street was nearly 0.5 km (0.3 mi) long and about 11 m (36 ft) wide. Colonnades 4.5 m (15 ft) deep lined both sides of this street, and behind these were shops and other buildings. A monumental gateway occupied each end of the street.

Paul's Ministry in Ephesus. It was to Ephesus, crossroads of the ancient world, that the apostle Paul, accompanied by Aquila and Priscilla, came, probably in 52 C.E. Paul immediately went to the Jewish synagogue to preach. However, although being requested to remain longer, the apostle left Ephesus, stating that he would return if it should be Jehovah's will. (Ac 18:18-21) Aquila and Priscilla, who remained in Ephesus, met Apollos, a Jew from Alexandria, Egypt, who was acquainted only with John's baptism, and they "expounded the way of God more correctly to him."—Ac 18:24-26.

When Paul returned to Ephesus, likely by the winter of 52/53 C.E., he found several men who had been baptized with John's baptism. Upon his clarifying the matter of baptism to them, they were rebaptized. (Ac 19:1-7) This time Paul taught in the Jewish synagogue for three months. But when opposition arose, he moved to the school auditorium of Tyrannus with those who had become believers; there he discoursed daily for two years. (Ac 19:8-10) In addition, Paul preached extensively from house to house.—Ac 20:20, 21.

Paul's preaching, attended by miraculous healings and the expelling of demons, caused many Ephesians to become believers. Also, the unsuccessful attempt at exorcising by the seven sons of a certain Jewish chief priest named Sceva stirred up much interest. Former practitioners of magical arts publicly burned their books, which had a combined value of 50,000 silver pieces (if denarii, $37,200). (Ac 19:11-20) Ephesus was so renowned for magical arts that Greek and Roman writers referred to books, or rolls, of magical formulas and incantations as "Ephesian writings."

Since many Ephesians had forsaken the worship of Artemis, the silversmith Demetrius pointed out to fellow craftsmen that Paul's preaching was a threat to their occupation and also endangered the worship of Artemis. Enraged silversmiths shouted: "Great is Artemis of the Ephesians!" The city was thrown into an uproar, climaxed by a two-hour riot at a theater capable of holding some 25,000 spectators.—Ac 19:23-41.

After this, Paul left Ephesus. Later, from Miletus he sent for the older men of the congregation at Ephesus, reviewed his own ministry in the district of Asia, and gave them instructions on caring for their duties. (Ac 20:1, 17-38) His reference on that occasion to "three years" spent at Ephesus should evidently be regarded as a round number.—Ac 20:31; compare Ac 19:8, 10.

With the passing of years, the Christians at

Ephesus endured much. However, some did lose the love they had at first.—Re 2:1-6; see ARTEMIS; DEMETRIUS No. 1; EPHESIANS, LETTER TO THE.

EPHLAL (Eph′lal) [possibly, Arbitrator]. The son of Zabad of the family of Jerahmeel and the father of Obed. Ephlal was a descendant of Perez, a son of Judah by Tamar. His great-great-grandfather was Jarha, an Egyptian servant in Sheshan's household. Jarha was given Sheshan's daughter as wife.—1Ch 2:4, 5, 9, 25, 34-37.

EPHOD, I (eph′od). A priestly vestment. The special ephod to be worn by the high priest is described in detail in God's instructions to Moses. (PICTURE, Vol. 1, p. 539) It was apparently an apronlike garment, made of "gold, blue thread and wool dyed reddish purple, coccus scarlet material and fine twisted linen, the work of an embroiderer." It consisted of front and back parts, these being joined together. A girdle of the same material was "upon" it, perhaps fastened to the ephod, holding it close around the waist. In gold settings on the shoulder pieces were two onyx stones, each engraved with the names of six of the sons of Israel. From the gold settings of these stones hung the breastpiece, by chains of gold having the workmanship of a rope. From the bottom corners of the breastpiece blue string ran through gold rings that were fastened to the lower extremity of the shoulder pieces of the ephod just above the girdle. The ephod apparently reached a little below the waist, perhaps not down to the knees.—Ex 28:6-14, 22-28.

The ephod was worn by the high priest over the blue sleeveless coat, called the "coat of the ephod," which, in turn, was atop the linen robe. (Ex 29:5) This ephod was not worn on all occasions. When it was necessary to inquire of Jehovah about a matter of importance to the nation, the high priest wore the ephod and the breastpiece containing the Urim and the Thummim. (Nu 27:21; 1Sa 28:6; Ezr 2:63) On the annual Day of Atonement, after presenting the sin offerings, the high priest would wash and change garments, taking off the pure white garments and apparently putting on his beautiful garments, including the ephod, before offering up the burnt offerings.—Le 16:23-25.

The ephod that Abiathar the priest carried from the sanctuary at Nob to David's camp was likely the ephod of the high priest, since Doeg had killed Abiathar's father, High Priest Ahimelech, and the underpriests with him. (1Sa 22:16-20; 23:6) David had Abiathar bring the ephod near so that he could inquire of Jehovah as to what course of action to take.—1Sa 23:9-12; 30:7, 8.

Ephods of the Underpriests. The underpriests also wore ephods, although the high priest's ephod is the only one specifically mentioned and described in Jehovah's instructions for making the priestly garments. Only "robes," "sashes," "headgears," and "drawers" were specified for Aaron's sons, who served as underpriests under Aaron. (Ex 28:40-43) The wearing of an ephod by underpriests seems to have been a later practice. Samuel, though not an underpriest, wore an ephod when he as a young boy ministered to Jehovah at the sanctuary (1Sa 2:18), as did the 85 priests slain by Doeg at King Saul's command. (1Sa 22:18) These ephods may have denoted the priestly position of the wearers instead of being something prescribed by the Law to be used when performing their official duties. The underpriest's ephod was probably like the high priest's in shape but was made of plain white cloth, not embroidered, and the linen of which it was made may not have been of the quality of the high priest's ephod. The Hebrew word for "linen" used in describing the ephod worn by young Samuel and the 85 priests is *badh,* while *shesh,* "fine linen," is the word used for the high priest's ephod.—Ex 28:6; 1Sa 2:18; 22:18.

When the ark of the covenant was being brought up to Jerusalem to be placed on Mount Zion near his own house, David, dressed in a sleeveless coat of fine fabric, wore over this garment an ephod of linen as he danced before Jehovah celebrating this joyous event.—2Sa 6:14; 1Ch 15:27.

The Ephod Made by Gideon. After Gideon's defeat of the Midianites he used gold taken as booty to make an ephod. (Jg 8:26, 27) Some have objected to this statement on the ground that the 1,700 shekels (19.4 kg; 52 lb t) of gold would be far more than required for an ephod. An attempted explanation has been offered, that Gideon also made a golden image. But the word "ephod" does not signify an image. Gideon was a man of faith in God. He would not do what Jeroboam later did when he led the ten tribes into the worship of calf images. Gideon had shown his disposition toward Jehovah's worship when he was given opportunity to set up a ruling dynasty over Israel. He turned the offer down, saying: "Jehovah is the one who will rule over you." (Jg 8:22, 23) [*Continued on page 753*]

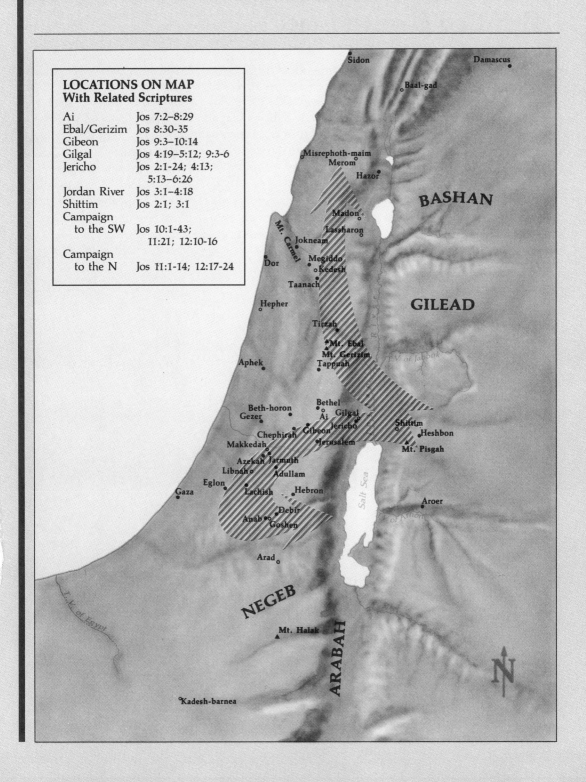

LOCATIONS ON MAP
With Related Scriptures

Ai	Jos 7:2–8:29
Ebal/Gerizim	Jos 8:30-35
Gibeon	Jos 9:3–10:14
Gilgal	Jos 4:19–5:12; 9:3-6
Jericho	Jos 2:1-24; 4:13;
	5:13–6:26
Jordan River	Jos 3:1–4:18
Shittim	Jos 2:1; 3:1
Campaign to the SW	Jos 10:1-43;
	11:21; 12:10-16
Campaign to the N	Jos 11:1-14; 12:17-24

Sidon
Damascus
Baal-gad
Misrephoth-maim
Merom
Hazor
BASHAN
Madon
Lassharon
Mt. Carmel
Jokneam
Dor
Megiddo
Kedesh
GILEAD
Taanach
Hepher
Tirzah
Mt. Ebal
Mt. Gerizim
Aphek
Tappuah
V. of Jabbok
Bethel
Beth-horon
Ai
Gilgal
Gezer
Jericho
Shittim
Chephirah
Gibeon
Heshbon
Makkedah
Jerusalem
Mt. Pisgah
Azekah
Jarmuth
Libnah
Adullam
Eglon
Gaza
Lachish
Hebron
Aroer
Anab
Debir
Goshen
Salt Sea
Arad
NEGEB
ARABAH
Mt. Halak
Kadesh-barnea
L. of Egypt
N

Nations Occupying the Land That God Gave to Israel

WHEN Jehovah gave Israel the land that he had promised to Abraham, morally debased nations were occupying it. The Bible candidly reports that God decreed the destruction of those wicked nations, and he appointed the Israelites to be the executioners. (De 7:2) Many persons have criticized that action. Others humbly acknowledge that it is hardly appropriate for imperfect humans to set themselves up as judges of God. (Compare Eze 18:29.) Their desire is to understand God's ways. What do they learn?

This record clearly demonstrates that all people are accountable to mankind's Creator, Jehovah God, whether they profess to believe in him or not. It shows that God is patient but does not shut his eyes to wrongdoing. (Ge 15:16) It makes clear that Jehovah leaves the responsibility for young children on the shoulders of their parents; he does not relieve the parents of this

and thus allow them to feel that their actions affect only themselves. (De 30:19; Jos 10:40) It also shows that all who will turn from their bad way and worship Jehovah can be spared from destruction.—Jos 6:25; 9:3–10:11.

The Bible clearly identifies the wicked practices in which the inhabitants of Canaan indulged. *Halley's Bible Handbook* (1964, p. 161) concludes: "Archaeologists who dig in the ruins of Canaanite cities wonder that God did not destroy them sooner than he did." The lesson is clear: Jehovah does not forever tolerate wickedness.

Why They Were Destroyed

Moral degradation. (Le 18:3-25)

Spiritistic practices. (De 18:9-12)

Debasing idolatry. (Ex 23:23, 24; 34:11-16; De 7:1-5; 1Ki 21:26)

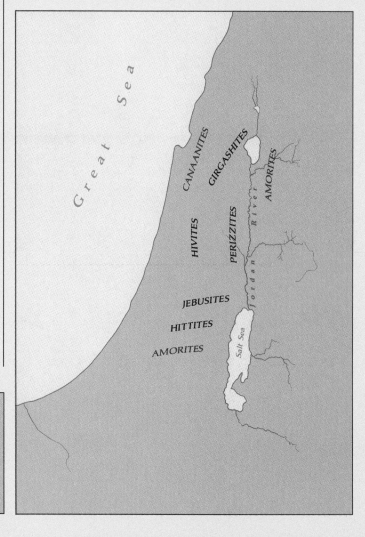

Steles of Tanit and Baal,
with a statue of Tanit
(the counterpart of Ashtoreth);
unearthed in a cemetery near
Carthage (Tunisia, North Africa)

Cemetery where the
bones of thousands of
children sacrificed to
the goddess Tanit
were found. It was
the seafaring
Phoenicians
(Canaanites) who
brought these
murderous religious
rites here. The tragic
site stands as a
monument to the
depravity of the
Canaanites

THE land that God gave to Israel was indeed a good land. When Moses sent spies ahead of the nation to explore the Promised Land and to obtain samples of its produce, they brought back figs, pomegranates, and a cluster of grapes that was so large that two men carried it between them on a bar! Though they drew back in fear because of lack of faith, they did report: The land "is indeed flowing with milk and honey."—Nu 13:23, 27.

Just before they finally entered the land, Jehovah's spokesman assured the people: "Jehovah your God is bringing you into a good land, a land of torrent valleys of water, springs and watery deeps issuing forth in the valley plain and in the mountainous region, a land of wheat and barley and vines and figs and pomegranates, a land of oil olives and honey . . . in which you will lack nothing, a land the stones of which are iron and out of the mountains of which you will mine copper." (De 8:7-9) To this day, the land continues to yield abundantly.

The beauty and splendor of that ancient land of promise is of keen interest to us today. Why? Because Messianic prophecies use the abundance with which Jehovah blessed ancient Israel to illustrate what God will do for all mankind under the rule of Jesus Christ, the "Prince of Peace."—Isa 9:6; Ps 67:4-7; 72:16.

It was a land flowing with milk . . .

. . . and a place that abundantly produced wild honey

It was a well-watered land

They found it to be a land of wheat . . .

. . . and from its fields
they harvested barley

Its vineyards yielded
an abundance of grapes
—and from these, wine
to gladden their hearts

The fig tree, valued for its delicious fruit,
became a symbol of peaceful, prosperous conditions

Pomegranates were the
source of a refreshing drink

Olive trees yielded
oil—ample from
a single tree for a
whole family

THE book of Judges is a thrilling record of the exploits of men of faith who were raised up by Jehovah to deliver Israel from oppression. The oppressors came from various directions; the areas where the Judges were active were not always the same. But, regardless of how powerful the enemy was, when Israel humbly repented of their bad practices and truly trusted in Jehovah, the Judge would deliver them. This Bible book gives a foregleam of the greater deliverance that God will provide for his servants by means of his Son.

Judges and Their Exploits	
Abdon	Jg 12:13-15
Barak	Jg 4:1–5:31
Ehud	Jg 3:12-30
Elon	Jg 12:11, 12
Gideon	Jg 6:1–8:35
Ibzan	Jg 12:8-10
Jair	Jg 10:3-5
Jephthah	Jg 10:6–12:7
Othniel	Jg 3:7-11
Samson	Jg 13:1–16:31
Shamgar	Jg 3:31
Tola	Jg 10:1, 2

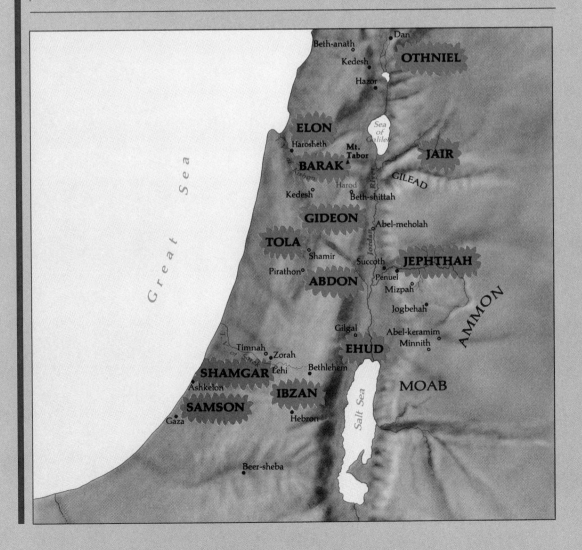

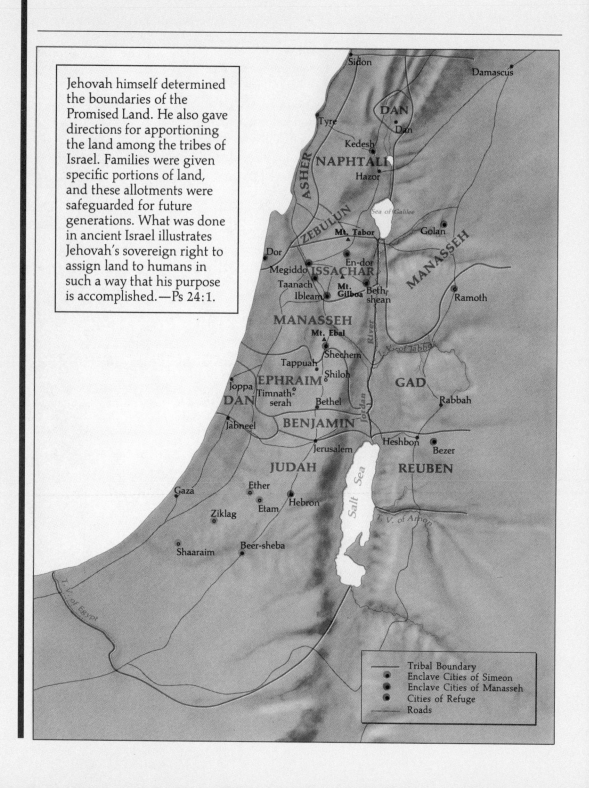

Jehovah himself determined the boundaries of the Promised Land. He also gave directions for apportioning the land among the tribes of Israel. Families were given specific portions of land, and these allotments were safeguarded for future generations. What was done in ancient Israel illustrates Jehovah's sovereign right to assign land to humans in such a way that his purpose is accomplished.—Ps 24:1.

Sidon

Damascus

DAN

Tyre

Dan

Kedesh

NAPHTALI

Hazor

ASHER

ZEBULUN

Sea of Galilee

Mt. Tabor

Golan

Dor

MANASSEH

En-dor

Megiddo

ISSACHAR

Taanach

Mt.

Beth-

Ramoth

Ibleam

Gilboa

shean

MANASSEH

Mt. Ebal

River

T. V. of Jabbok

Shechem

Tappuah

Shiloh

Joppa

EPHRAIM

GAD

Timnath-

DAN

serah

Bethel

Rabbah

Jordan

Jabneel

BENJAMIN

Heshbon

Jerusalem

Bezer

JUDAH

REUBEN

Salt Sea

Gaza

Ether

Etam

Hebron

Ziklag

T. V. of Arnon

Beer-sheba

Shaaraim

T. V. of Egypt

	Tribal Boundary
●	Enclave Cities of Simeon
●	Enclave Cities of Manasseh
●	Cities of Refuge
	Roads

DAVID the son of Jesse was an outstanding musician, poet, warrior, and statesman. But David's prominence in Scripture is primarily due to his relationship with God. Jehovah called him "a man agreeable to my heart."—Ac 13:22; 1Sa 13:14.

God selected David as future king of Israel when he was but a shepherd youth. Soon thereafter, with full reliance on Jehovah, David courageously confronted and slew the Philistine giant Goliath, as depicted at the right. However, King Saul became jealous of David's mounting popularity, and David was forced to take up the life of a fugitive. During this trialsome period David composed many heartfelt psalms, which bring comfort to Bible readers even today.

When finally established as king, David shared in historic events in the nation's history: Israel's boundaries were pushed to their promised limits. The ark of the covenant was brought to Jerusalem. Plans were drawn up for a glorious temple of Jehovah. Highly significant, too, was God's covenant promise to David to raise up a permanent ruler in his royal line. (2Sa 7:12-16) This covenant points the way to the earth-wide rule by Jesus Christ.—Ro 1:3; Lu 1:32.

LOCATIONS ON MAP
With Related Scriptures

Adullam	1Sa 22:1-5
Bethlehem	1Sa 16:1-13, 18, 19
Carmel	1Sa 25:2-42
Elah	
(Low Plain)	1Sa 17:2-52
En-gedi	1Sa 24:1-22
Gath	1Sa 17:4, 52; 21:10-15;
	27:2-4
Gibeah	1Sa 22:6-18
Horesh	1Sa 23:15-18
Jerusalem	1Sa 17:54
Keilah	1Sa 23:1-13
Maon	1Sa 23:24-28; 25:2
Moab	1Sa 22:3, 4
Nob	1Sa 21:1-9; 22:18, 19
Paran	
(Wilderness)	1Sa 25:1
Ramah	1Sa 19:18-24; 28:3
Ziklag	1Sa 27:5–28:2; 30:1-8,
	26; 2Sa 1:1-16
Ziph	
(Wilderness)	1Sa 23:14, 15, 19-24;
	26:1-25

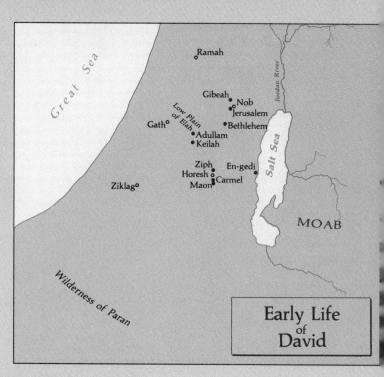

Early Life of David

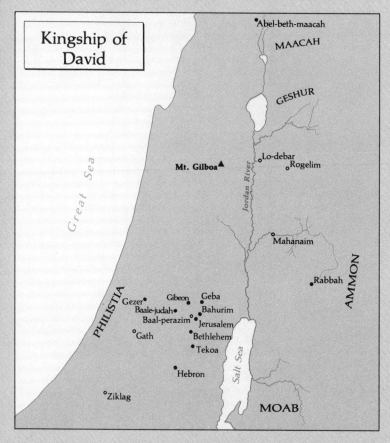

Kingship of David

LOCATIONS ON MAP
With Related Scriptures

Abel-beth-maacah	2Sa 20:14-22
Ammon	2Sa 10:1-14; 12:26-31
Baale-judah	2Sa 6:2-4
Baal-perazim	1Ch 14:8-12
Bahurim	2Sa 3:13-16; 16:5-13
Bethlehem	1Ch 11:16-19
Gath	1Ch 18:1; 20:5-8
Geba	2Sa 5:22-25
Geshur	2Sa 3:3; 13:37, 38
Gezer	2Sa 5:22-25
Gibeon	2Sa 2:12-17; 20:8-10
Gilboa (Mt.)	1Ch 10:1-6
Hebron	2Sa 2:1-4, 11; 3:2-5, 12,
	20-27, 32; 4:8-12;
	5:1-5; 15:7-10;
	1Ch 12:23-40
Jerusalem	2Sa 5:5-10, 13-16;
	11:1–12:14; 15:13-17;
	1Ch 15:1–17:27;
	21:16-28
Lo-debar	2Sa 9:1-5
Maacah	2Sa 10:6-8
Mahanaim	2Sa 2:8-10; 17:24-29
Moab	1Ch 18:2
Rabbah	2Sa 11:1, 14-25; 12:26-31
Rogelim	2Sa 19:31, 32
Tekoa	2Sa 14:1-4
Ziklag	2Sa 1:1-16

Wilderness of Judah. Hiding in
caves and crevices in such areas,
David eluded King Saul

A street in old Hebron, the city
where David was anointed as king
by the men of Judah

City of David (to the south of the
Temple Mount) as it appears today;
from here David ruled as king for
33 years

Solomon's Reign

THE reign of King Solomon gives us a prophetic glimpse of the future. During his royal rule Israel reached its pinnacle of wealth and glory. Solomon was both a wise king and a master organizer. He built a magnificent temple to Jehovah, various government buildings, and a royal palace, as depicted below. He established administrative districts that, on a rotational basis, provided the royal household with a variety of food, regardless of the season.

Solomon's rule was a time of genuine peace and security. This well foreshadows the peaceful reign of the Messiah, who "will have subjects from sea to sea and from the River (Euphrates) to the ends of the earth."—Ps 72:8.

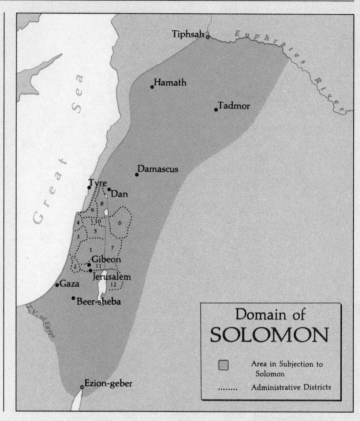

Domain of
SOLOMON

Area in Subjection to Solomon

.... Administrative Districts

During Solomon's reign, Judah and Israel dwelt in security—figuratively speaking, everyone under his own vine and under his own fig tree (1Ki 4:25)

Even rulers of other lands came to hear his wisdom (1Ki 4:34; 10:1)

Solomon built a temple for Jehovah after Israel had settled in the Promised Land and had come into possession of the city upon which Jehovah later put his name. The architect was Jehovah himself. Solomon's father, David, had received "the architectural plan of everything . . . by inspiration." (1Ch 28:11, 12) More than 180,000 men worked for seven and a half years to construct the temple, completing it in 1027 B.C.E. (1Ki 5:13-16; 6:1, 38) The temple, like the tabernacle before it, represented the "true tent," the spiritual temple of Jehovah.—Heb 8:1-5; 9:2-10, 23.

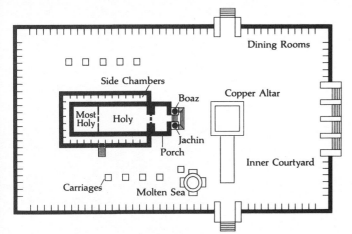

Dining Rooms

Side Chambers

Boaz

Most Holy | Holy

Copper Altar

Jachin

Porch

Inner Courtyard

Carriages

Molten Sea

Ground plan (left) of the temple and of the inner courtyard. An inside view of the temple (below) gives some idea of the beauty of this magnificent structure. The inside walls were made of cedar engraved with carvings of cherubs, palm trees, and blossoms; the walls and ceiling were overlaid with gold and studded with gems

ANCIENT Jerusalem was the place where Jehovah chose to put his name. (2Ch 6:6) It served as both the center of pure worship and the seat of government for Israel. Kings ruling from Jerusalem were said to sit 'on Jehovah's throne.'—1Ch 29:23.

King David wrested the stronghold of Mount Zion from the Jebusites and made it his capital. Solomon enlarged the city and built it up to the peak of its grandeur, constructing a magnificent temple as well as an impressive complex of governmental buildings on Mount Moriah and its slopes. Jerusalem was a city closely associated with Jehovah's name.

This helps us to appreciate why Jerusalem is given such prominence in Bible prophecy. It serves as a fitting symbol of Jehovah's own heavenly organization and his Messianic Kingdom in the hands of Jesus Christ.

Numbers on the Map

(1) The Temple. (2) Great Courtyard. (3) Porch of the Throne. (4) Porch of Pillars. (5) House of the Forest of Lebanon. (6) Solomon's Palace. (7) House of Pharaoh's Daughter. (8) Staircase to the Temple Courtyard. (9) David's Palace. (10) Tent for Ark. (11) Water Gate. (12) Fountain Gate. (13) Western Gate. (14) Sheep Gate. (15) Inspection Gate. (16) Horse Gate.

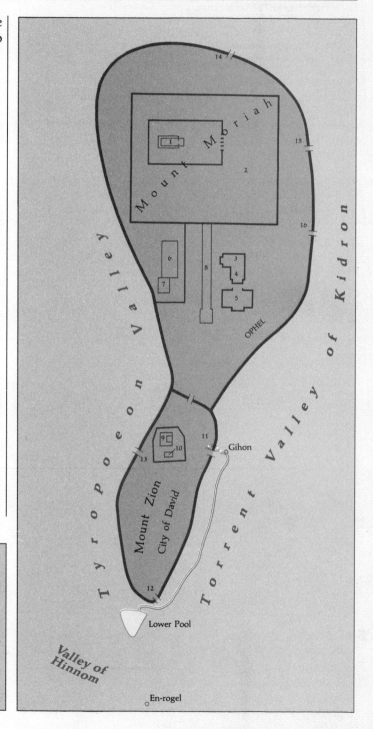

[*Continued from page 736*] It may well be that much of the gold was used to *pay* for the jewels, and so forth, that possibly were used in the ephod. As to the cost of Gideon's ephod, it may well have been of the value stated ($218,365 at modern rates), especially if precious gems were used to decorate it.

In spite of Gideon's good intentions to commemorate the victory Jehovah had given Israel and to honor God, the ephod "served as a snare to Gideon and to his household," because the Israelites committed spiritual immorality by worshiping it. (Jg 8:27) However, the Bible does not say that Gideon himself worshiped it; on the contrary, he is specifically named by the apostle Paul as one of the 'great cloud' of faithful pre-Christian witnesses of Jehovah.—Heb 11:32; 12:1.

Idolatrous Use. An instance of the use of an ephod in idolatrous worship is found at Judges chapters 17 and 18. The ephod, made by an Ephraimite, was first used by one of his own sons acting as priest before a carved image, then by a Levite descendant of Moses who, though not of the priestly family of Aaron, acted as priest. Eventually the ephod and image fell into the hands of men of the tribe of Dan, among whom the Levite and his sons after him continued in this idolatrous capacity in the city of Dan all the days that the house of God was located at Shiloh.

EPHOD, II (E'phod). The father of Hanniel, who was the chieftain of the tribe of Manasseh appointed at Jehovah's command as one responsible for dividing the land of Canaan into inheritance portions.—Nu 34:16, 18, 23, 29.

EPHPHATHA (eph'pha·tha). A Semitic expression meaning "be opened." It was used by Jesus at the time he healed a deaf man with a speech impediment.—Mr 7:32-34.

EPHRAIM (E'phra·im) [Doubly Fruitful].

1. Son of Joseph by his wife Asenath, the daughter of Potiphera the priest of On. Ephraim, the younger brother of Manasseh, was born in Egypt before the seven-year famine began. The name Ephraim was given to him by his father "because, to quote [Joseph], 'God has made me fruitful in the land of my wretchedness.'"—Ge 41:50-52.

On his deathbed, Jacob, in effect, adopted his grandsons Ephraim and Manasseh and appointed them to be the equals of his direct sons. (Ge 48:5) Their father Joseph, who received the right as firstborn among Jacob's sons, received two parts of his father's inheritance by means of the tribal inheritance of Ephraim and Manasseh. (1Ch 5:1; compare Ge 48:21, 22; De 21:17; Jos 14:4.) In blessing Ephraim and Manasseh, the patriarch Jacob gave the preference to Ephraim and prophetically indicated that he would become the greater.—Ge 48:13-20.

First Chronicles 7:20-27 provides a genealogical listing of Ephraim's sons and later descendants, concluding with Joshua, who led the Israelites into the Promised Land. Ezer and Elead, who were likely sons of Ephraim, were slain by the men of Gath. Sometime after the death of these sons, Ephraim fathered Beriah.

2. The name Ephraim is also applied to the tribe that descended from him. About a year after the Exodus from Egypt, Ephraim's 40,500 fighting men from 20 years old upward outnumbered Manasseh's able-bodied men by 8,300. (Nu 1:1-3, 32-35) However, at the end of the 40 years' wandering in the wilderness, the registered males of Ephraim numbered only 32,500, or 20,200 less than those of Manasseh. (Nu 26:34, 37) Nevertheless, Ephraim was foretold to become the greater. Moses, when blessing the Israelites, prophetically spoke of "the tens of thousands of Ephraim," but of "the thousands of Manasseh."—De 33:17.

In the wilderness, the Ephraimites, with Elishama serving as chieftain, were assigned to camp on the W side of the tabernacle, along with the tribes of Manasseh and Benjamin. This three-tribe division was third in the order of march. —Nu 2:18-24.

Tribal Territory. The territory assigned to the tribe of Ephraim occupied a central portion of Canaan, W of the Jordan. The tribe also had enclave cities in Manasseh's territory. On the N, Ephraim was bounded by Manasseh, and on the S, by Benjamin and Dan. (Jos 16:1-9) This region, although mountainous and hilly, is blessed with rich and fertile soil and, in ancient times, was heavily wooded. (Jos 17:15, 17, 18) The chieftain Kemuel served as the divinely appointed representative of Ephraim in dividing the Promised Land into inheritance portions.—Nu 34:18, 24.

At Shiloh, in Ephraim, the tabernacle was set up. (Jos 18:1) Besides Shechem, a city of refuge, a number of other Levite cities were also located in the territory of Ephraim. (Jos 21:20-22; 1Ch 6:66-69) From one of these Levite cities, Gezer, the Ephraimites did not drive out the Canaanites,

but they subjected them to slavish forced labor.
—Jos 16:10; Jg 1:29.

Ephraim From Joshua to David. The territory of Ephraim was the scene of numerous notable events. At Shechem, Moses' successor, the Ephraimite Joshua, congregated the tribes of Israel and appealed to them to serve Jehovah faithfully. (Jos 24:1, 14, 15) Also, here at Shechem, Joseph's bones were finally buried, and both Joshua and Aaron's son Eleazar were buried in the mountainous region of Ephraim. (Jos 24:29-33) Later, Benjamite Judge Ehud assembled the Israelites in the mountainous region of Ephraim to fight against the Moabites. (Jg 3:26-30) After Ehud's death the prophetess Deborah, from her residence in the mountainous region of Ephraim, sent for Barak as the one designated by Jehovah to deliver Israel from the oppression of King Jabin. In the victory song of Barak and Deborah, Ephraim is the first tribe to be mentioned. (Jg 4:1-7; 5:14) At a later time, Tola of the tribe of Issachar judged Israel for 23 years while dwelling at Shamir in the mountainous region of Ephraim. (Jg 10:1, 2) The prophet Samuel of the tribe of Levi was born at Ramah in the mountainous region of Ephraim, and it was there that he, as an adult, established his home. —1Sa 1:1, 2, 19, 20; 7:15-17.

Pride and an extreme desire for prominence caused severe difficulty to the Ephraimites in their relationship to the other tribes. As early as the time of the judges this trait manifested itself. For example, the Ephraimites tried to pick a quarrel with Gideon for not having called them earlier in the fight against Midian. However, Gideon's tactfulness on that occasion averted a clash. (Jg 8:1-3) Later, although having previously turned down an opportunity to assist Jephthah, the Ephraimites felt slighted when he did not call them to fight against the Ammonites. They warred with Jephthah and experienced a humiliating defeat; thousands were killed at the fords of the Jordan, where they were identified as Ephraimites because of their pronunciation of the password "Shibboleth" as "Sibboleth."—Jg 12:1-6; see also 2Ch 25:10.

After the death of King Saul, among those who came to Hebron to turn the kingship over to David there were 20,800 men of Ephraim.—1Ch 12:23, 30.

Dominant Tribe of the Northern Kingdom. From the time the kingdom was divided during the reign of Rehoboam, Ephraim, as the most prominent and influential tribe of the northern kingdom, made a bad name for itself. (Ho 13:1)

The first king, the Ephraimite Jeroboam, established calf worship at Dan and Bethel. (1Ki 11:26; 12:25-30) This plunge into idolatry was never reversed.

As the dominant tribe of the northern kingdom, Ephraim came to stand for the entire ten-tribe kingdom. (2Ch 25:7; Jer 7:15) Therefore the prophets Hosea and Isaiah directed their strong denunciations against Ephraim. Hosea condemned Ephraim for mingling with the nations, learning their works, and serving their idols. He compared Ephraim to a round cake not turned over, baked or even burned on the bottom but not done on the top. (Ho 7:8; compare Ps 106: 35, 36; Ho 4:17; 12:14.) Although having been sapped of strength by strangers, Ephraim, rather than returning to Jehovah, appealed to Egypt for help and made a covenant with Assyria. Thus Ephraim was like a simpleminded dove that would not escape being trapped in a net.—Ho 7:9-12; 8:9; compare 2Ki 17:4; Ho 12:1.

The prophet Isaiah addressed himself to the 'proud drunkards of Ephraim.' Their independence from the kingdom of Judah and their alliances with Syria and other nations had affected them like intoxicating liquor. However, disaster would befall them.—Isa 7:1, 2, 5-9, 17; 9:9-12; 17:3; 28:1-3.

Jehovah's prophets also foretold, however, that the spirit of jealousy and hostility existing between Ephraim (the ten-tribe kingdom) and Judah (the two-tribe kingdom) would cease. (Isa 11:13; Jer 31:6) Judah and Ephraim would become united, and Ephraim would be restored to divine favor.—Jer 31:18-20; 50:19; Eze 37:16-19; Zec 10:7.

Whereas the tribe of Ephraim built up a bad record, individuals within that tribe followed the right course. During the reign of Judah's King Asa, for example, many Ephraimites deserted to him when they saw that Jehovah was with him. (2Ch 15:9) Later, Ephraimites were also present in Jerusalem for the Passover celebration in the first year of Hezekiah's reign and afterward shared in destroying appendages of idolatry. (2Ch 30:18; 31:1) However, when Hezekiah sent out the invitation for the Israelites from the N to come to the Passover, his runners were mocked and derided by many in Ephraim, Manasseh, and Zebulun. Pride kept these from humbling themselves and coming down to Jerusalem for the Passover.—2Ch 30:10, 11.

3. A city generally considered to be the same as the Ephrain captured by Abijah the king of

Judah from Jeroboam the king of Israel. (2Ch 13:19) In the first century C.E., when the religious leaders took counsel to kill him, Jesus Christ, with his disciples, went to Ephraim in the country near the wilderness. (Joh 11:53, 54) The site commonly suggested for this city is the village of et-Taiyiba, about 6 km (3.5 mi) ENE of Bethel and 3 km (2 mi) ESE of the suggested location of Baal-hazor. (2Sa 13:23) According to the Jewish historian Josephus, the Roman general Vespasian conquered Ephraim during his march against Jerusalem.—*The Jewish War,* IV, 551 (ix, 9).

4. "The forest of Ephraim" was an area on the E side of the Jordan where the army of King David fought with that of his rebellious son Absalom. (2Sa 18:6-8) The actual site of the forest of Ephraim in the land of Gilead is unknown, but it was probably in the vicinity of Mahanaim. —2Sa 17:22, 24, 26.

EPHRAIM, GATE OF.   See GATE, GATEWAY.

EPHRAIMITES.   See EPHRAIM No. 2.

EPHRAIN   (E′phra·in). A city taken by King Abijah of Judah in his battle against Jeroboam of Israel. (2Ch 13:19) It was evidently in the territory of the tribe of Ephraim and appears to be the same as the city of Ephraim mentioned at 2 Samuel 13:23 and also at John 11:54.—See EPHRAIM No. 3.

EPHRATH   [Fruitfulness]. A contraction of Ephrathah.

EPHRATHAH   (Eph′ra·thah) [Fruitfulness].

1. The wife of Caleb (Chelubai) son of Hezron of the tribe of Judah. She married Caleb while they were in bondage in Egypt, after the death of his wife Azubah. Ephrathah became the mother of Hur and in time the great-grandmother of Bezalel, the skilled craftsman so famous in the building of the tabernacle.—1Ch 2:9, 19, 50; 4:4; Ex 35:30-35.

2. Evidently the earlier name of Bethlehem or a name applied to the area around it. The names of Bethlehem and Ephrathah are used jointly in several texts. The account of Rachel's death relates that she was buried "on the way to Ephrath [Ephrathah], that is to say, Bethlehem." (Ge 35: 16, 19; 48:7) Members of Elimelech's family are called "Ephrathites from Bethlehem," and it was to Bethlehem that his widow Naomi returned out of Moab. (Ru 1:2, 19) The blessing pronounced on Boaz at the time of his marriage to Ruth was that

he might prove his "worth in Ephrathah and make a notable name in Bethlehem." (Ru 4:11) And finally, in the prophecy concerning the Messiah's birth, the names are combined as "Bethlehem Ephrathah." (Mic 5:2) In view of this it appears that the reference to Ephrathah in Psalm 132:6, which deals with David's concern for the ark of the covenant, also applies to this hometown of David.—See BETHLEHEM No. 1.

EPHRATHITE   (Eph′rath·ite).

1. An inhabitant of Bethlehem, or Ephrathah. —Ru 1:2; 1Sa 17:12.

2. In Hebrew the same term is applied to a member of the tribe of Ephraim (Jg 12:5; 1Ki 11:26) or to one residing in Ephraim, as in the genealogy of the Levite Elkanah. (1Sa 1:1) The *King James Version* renders the Hebrew term as "Ephrathite" in two of these texts.

EPHRON   (E′phron).

1. [from a root meaning "young one [of the stags]"]. A Hittite son of Zohar who owned a field in Machpelah in front of Mamre, that is, in Hebron. Abraham purchased this field from Ephron, together with the cave located on it, as a burial place for his wife Sarah. (Ge 23:3-20) Abraham paid 400 silver shekels (c. $880) for this family burial plot, yet generations thereafter it was still referred to as "the field of Ephron."—Ge 25:9; 49:29, 30; 50:13.

2. [Place of Dust]. A mountain ridge situated between Nephtoah and Kiriath-jearim. (Jos 15:9) It lay on the northern boundary of the tribe of Judah.

3. "Ephron" appears at 2 Chronicles 13:19 in the Masoretic text as well as in the Greek *Septuagint* and some other versions; however, the marginal reading of the Masoretic text gives "Ephrain."—See EPHRAIN.

EPICUREANS   (Ep·i·cu·re′ans). The followers of the Greek philosopher Epicurus (341-270 B.C.E.).

The philosophy originated by Epicurus flourished for seven centuries. It centered around the idea that the pleasure of the individual was the sole or chief good in life. Hence, Epicurus advocated living in such a way as to derive the greatest amount of pleasure possible during one's lifetime, yet doing so moderately in order to avoid the suffering incurred by overindulgence in such pleasure. The emphasis was placed on pleasures of the mind rather than on physical pleasures. Therefore, according to Epicurus, with *whom* a person eats is of greater importance than *what* is eaten. Unnecessary and, especially, artificially produced desires were to be suppressed. Since learning, culture, and civilization as well as social and political involvements could give rise to desires that are difficult to satisfy and thus result in disturbing one's peace of mind, they were discouraged. Knowledge was sought only to rid oneself of religious fears and superstitions, the two primary fears to be eliminated being fear of the gods and of death. Viewing marriage and what attends it as a threat to one's peace of mind, Epicurus lived a celibate life but did not impose this restriction on his followers.

The philosophy was characterized by a complete absence of principle. Lawbreaking was counseled against simply because of the shame associated with detection and the punishment it might bring. Living in fear of being found out or punished would take away from pleasure, and this made even secret wrongdoing inadvisable. To the Epicureans, virtue in itself had no value and was beneficial only when it served as a means to gain happiness. Reciprocity was recommended, not because it was right and noble, but because it paid off. Friendships rested on the same selfish basis, that is, the pleasure resulting to the possessor. While the pursuit of pleasure formed the focal point of the philosophy, paradoxically Epicurus referred to life as a "bitter gift."

The Epicureans believed in the existence of gods, but that they, just like everything else, were made of atoms, though of finer texture. It was thought that the gods were too far away from the earth to have any interest in what man was doing; so it did not do any good to pray or to sacrifice to them. The gods, they believed, did not create the universe, nor did they inflict punishment or bestow blessings on anyone, but they were supremely happy, and this was the goal to strive for during one's life. However, the Epicureans contended that the gods were in no position to aid anyone in this, that life came into existence by accident in a mechanical universe, and that death ends everything, liberating the individual from the nightmare of life. Although it was believed that man has a soul, the soul was thought to be composed of atoms that dissolve at the death of the body, just as water spills out of a pitcher that breaks.

In the light of the foregoing, it can well be appreciated why Epicurean philosophers were among those who took to conversing controver-sially with Paul in the marketplace at Athens and who said: "What is it this chatterer would like to tell?" "He seems to be a publisher of foreign deities." (Ac 17:17, 18) The philosophy of the Epicureans, with its idea of "let us eat and drink, for tomorrow we are to die," denied the resurrection hope taught by Christians in their ministry. —1Co 15:32.

EPILEPSY. A chronic disease of the central nervous system manifested in convulsions or in impairment or loss of consciousness, and perhaps both. This disorder is linked with abnormal activity of the brain. A severely convulsive epileptic fit accompanied by unconsciousness is called *grand mal,* whereas the mild form, attacks of which are of very brief duration, is termed *petit mal,* these being two principal types of epilepsy. An epileptic is a person afflicted with epilepsy.

On the day following the transfiguration, Jesus Christ healed an epileptic that his disciples had been unable to cure. (Mt 17:14-20) From his childhood this boy had a "speechless and deaf spirit" that, among other things, periodically threw him into convulsions; these were accompanied by foaming at the mouth. Jesus rebuked the demon, it came out, and the boy was thus healed.—Mr 9:14-29; Lu 9:37-43.

Though demon activity was associated with epileptic symptoms in this particular case, epilepsy normally has natural causes, and the Scriptures do not imply that it is generally caused by demon possession. Rather, Matthew (4:24) reports that people brought Jesus ailing ones including "demon-possessed *and* epileptic" persons, drawing a distinction between these two types of individuals cured by Christ.

The English term "epilepsy" is derived from the Greek word *e·pi·le·psi'a,* meaning literally "seizure." However, *e·pi·le·psi'a* is not used in the Bible. Rather, for this disorder Matthew (4:24; 17:15) employed forms of the Greek word *se·le·ni·a'zo·mai,* meaning, literally, "be moonstruck." Whereas the *King James Version* uses "lunatick," certain modern translations employ "epileptic(s)" at Matthew 4:24; 17:15.—*AS; NW; RS.*

Interestingly, *The International Standard Bible Encyclopaedia* states: "The original meaning of the term *seleniazomai,* 'moon-struck,' is connected with the popular belief, widespread and of strange persistency, that the moon, in certain of its phases, is injurious to human beings, esp[e-cially] in the case of diseases of a periodic or remittent character. There are no data by which to determine whether, in the N[ew] T[estament] times, this particular word represented a living and active belief or had passed into the state of usage in which the original metaphor disappears, and the word simply indicates the fact signified without reference to the idea embodied in the etymology. We still use the word 'lunatic' to signify a person mentally diseased, although we have long since ceased to believe in the moon's influence in such cases."—Edited by J. Orr, 1960, Vol. III, p. 1941.

Matthew's use of forms of *se·le·ni·a′zo·mai* does not mean that he held any superstitious views associating such a disease with certain phases of the moon. Evidently, he was merely employing the Greek term that was then commonly used to denote an epileptic. Also, the symptoms Matthew, Mark, and Luke describe as present in the boy's case are certainly those associated with epilepsy.

ER [Awaken; Rouse Up].

1. Judah's firstborn son by his Canaanite wife. His father took Tamar as a wife for him, but, because Er proved to be wicked in the eyes of God, Jehovah put him to death before he was able to father any offspring.—Ge 38:1-7; 46:12.

2. A son of Shelah the third son of Judah by his Canaanite wife.—Ge 38:2-5; 1Ch 4:21.

3. An ancestor of Jesus Christ; the son of Jesus (Jose[s]) and the father of Elmadam.—Lu 3:28.

ERAN (E′ran) [One Awakened; One Roused Up], **ERANITES** (E′ran·ites). Eran was the son of Ephraim's son Shuthelah and the forefather of the Eranites.—Nu 26:35, 36.

ERASTUS (E·ras′tus) [Beloved; Lovely].

1. A Christian who ministered to Paul on his third missionary tour and whom Paul sent from Asia to Macedonia along with Timothy. (Ac 19:22) Likely he is the Erastus who remained in Corinth at the time Paul wrote his second letter to Timothy.—2Ti 4:20.

2. The city steward of Corinth whose greetings Paul includes in his letter to the Romans. (Ro 16:23) During excavations in Corinth in 1929 Professor T. L. Shear discovered a pavement with an inscription, in Latin, that reads: "Erastus, procurator [and] aedile, laid this pavement at his own expense." Although it is not known whether this is the Erastus mentioned by Paul, the pavement is believed to have existed in the first century C.E. It has been suggested that the city steward was also Paul's traveling companion (see No. 1, above). However, since it would have been difficult for Erastus to accompany Paul and at the same time care for his duties as city steward, those who favor this identification generally conclude that Erastus held this official position at an earlier time and therefore Paul refers to him by this title.

ERECH (E′rech). One of the four cities constituting "the beginning of [Nimrod's] kingdom" in the land of Shinar. (Ge 10:10) Erech is today represented by a cluster of mounds at the site called Warka by the Arabs and known as Uruk to the ancient Akkadians of Mesopotamia. It is situated about 177 km (110 mi) SE of Babylon on the W bank of the old bed of the Euphrates (the Shatt-ek-Kar), or some 6 km (3.5 mi) E of the present course of that river. An ancient ziggurat has been uncovered there, along with many mounds and coffins that seem to indicate that Erech was once a burial ground of the Assyrian kings.

Inhabitants of Erech ("Archevites," *KJ*) were among those peoples transported to Samaria by Assyrian Emperor Asenappar.—Ezr 4:9, 10.

ERI (E′ri) [One Awakened; One Roused Up], **ERITES** (E′rites). The fifth-named son of Gad and forefather of the Erites.—Ge 46:16; Nu 26:16.

ESAR-HADDON (E′sar-had′don) [from Assyrian, meaning "Asshur Gives a Brother"]. A younger son and successor of Sennacherib, king of Assyria. In one of his inscriptions Esar-haddon confirms the Scriptural account of his father's death (Isa 37:37, 38), saying: "A firm determination 'fell upon' my brothers. They forsook the gods and turned to their deeds of violence, plotting evil. . . . To gain the kingship they slew Sennacherib, their father."—*Ancient Records of Assyria and Babylonia,* by D. Luckenbill, 1927, Vol. II, pp. 200, 201.

Esar-haddon states that, prior to his father's death, he had already been selected as heir apparent, and he seems to have served as viceroy at Babylon before becoming king of Assyria. Following his father's assassination, Esar-haddon tells of pursuing the murderers to Armenia ("the land of Ararat," 2Ki 19:37), where he defeated them. His official reign is considered to have lasted 12 years.

Early in his reign Esar-haddon began the restoration of Babylon, which Sennacherib had destroyed. The temple of Esagila was restored and, of the city itself, Esar-haddon says: "Babylon . . . I built anew, I enlarged, I raised aloft, I made magnificent." —*Ancient Records of Assyria and Babylonia,* Vol. II, p. 244.

His records recount military operations against the *Gimirrai* or Cimmerians, believed to be the descendants of Gomer. (Compare Ge 10:2; Eze 38:6.) He also sacked the city of Sidon, setting up a new city on a nearby site, which he named Kar-Esarhaddon. In one of his inscriptions he lists some 20 vassal kings, including Manasseh of Judah (*Menasi* king of *Yaudi*).

The record at 2 Chronicles 33:10-13 shows that Manasseh was captured by "the chiefs of the army that belonged to the king of Assyria" and taken to Babylon. In the past some have thought that this reference to Babylon was in error, considering Nineveh to be the place to which Manasseh would be taken. However, as has been seen, Esar-

Assyrian King Esar-haddon, who did much of the repopulating of Samaria with foreigners

haddon, whose inscriptions show him to have been contemporaneous with Manasseh, had rebuilt Babylon and is said to have been "much less interested than any other Assyrian king in the embellishment of his capital, Nineveh." (*The Interpreter's Dictionary of the Bible,* edited by G. Buttrick, 1962, Vol. 2, p. 125) If it was during Esar-haddon's reign that Manasseh was captured, there would be nothing incongruous about his being taken to Babylon, about whose restoration Esar-haddon so proudly boasted. It may be noted, however, that Esar-haddon's son Ashurbanipal also makes reference to Manasseh as tributary during his reign.

The "Sixty-Five Years." At the time of the rebuilding of the temple at Jerusalem some of the non-Israelite inhabitants of the land referred to their having been brought to Samaria by "Esar-haddon the king of Assyria." (Ezr 4:2) That the Assyrian transplantation of people to and from Samaria continued until his reign is viewed by some as a clue to the understanding of the period of "sixty-five years" mentioned at Isaiah 7:8 with regard to the desolation of Ephraim (with its capital at Samaria). The interval extending from the reign of Tiglath-pileser III (who initiated the deportation of people from the northern kingdom of Israel shortly after Isaiah's prophecy) to that of Esar-haddon would allow for such a 65-year period until the complete 'shattering to pieces' of Ephraim "so as not to be a people."

Conquest of Egypt. The outstanding military accomplishment of Esar-haddon was the conquest of Egypt, overcoming the Egyptian army under Ethiopian ruler Tirhakah (mentioned as "the king of Ethiopia" at 2Ki 19:9) and taking the city of Memphis. Esar-haddon thus added to his many titles that of "King of the kings of Egypt."

Although Esar-haddon organized Egypt into districts and placed Assyrian governors over the princes of these districts, within a couple of years revolt developed. The Assyrian king set out on a second campaign to crush the rebellion, but he died at Haran while on the way. In his inscriptions Esar-haddon had said: "I am powerful, I am all powerful, I am a hero, I am gigantic, I am colossal." (*Ancient Records of Assyria and Babylonia,* Vol. II, p. 226) Yet, like all other imperfect humans, he was shown to be but an enslaved subject of the rule of Kings Sin and Death, who now claimed him.—Compare Ps 146:3, 4; Ec 9:4; Ro 5:21.

Before his death Esar-haddon had made arrangements to ensure a smooth succession to the throne by proclaiming his son Ashurbanipal crown prince, while assigning another son, Shamash-shum-u-kin, to be king of Babylon. Thus, upon Esar-haddon's death, Ashurbanipal became Assyria's next monarch.

ESAU (E'sau) [Hairy]. The firstborn of Isaac and Rebekah; the twin brother of Jacob and the forefather of the Edomites. He was given the name Esau because of his unusual hairy appearance at birth, but he got the name Edom (meaning "Red") from the *red* lentil stew for which he sold his birthright.—Ge 25:25, 26, 30.

Even before the birth of the twins in 1858 B.C.E., when Isaac was 60 years of age, the infants struggled in their mother's womb. Answering Rebekah's inquiry concerning the meaning of this, Jehovah revealed to her that two national groups would be separated from her inward parts and that the older would serve the younger.—Ge 25:22, 23.

Disdain for Spiritual Matters. Esau became a skilled and adventurous hunter, "a wild man." Unlike his brother, "blameless" Jacob, Esau was fleshly-minded and materialistic. (Ge 25:27) But Isaac loved Esau, "because it meant game in his mouth."—Ge 25:28.

One day Esau, tired and hungry, came along from the field while Jacob was boiling up some stew. In response to Esau's request, "Quick, please, give me a swallow of the red—the red there," Jacob asked him to sell his birthright. Having no appreciation for sacred things, namely, the promise of Jehovah to Abraham respecting the seed through whom all nations of the earth would bless themselves, Esau impetuously, by sworn oath, sold his birthright to Jacob for one meal of lentil stew and bread. By thus despising the birthright, viewing it as of little value, Esau showed a complete lack of faith. He perhaps wanted no part in suffering the fulfillment of God's word concerning Abraham's seed: "Your seed will become an alien resident in a land not theirs, and they will have to serve them, and these will certainly afflict them for four hundred years."—Ge 15:13; 25:29-34; Heb 12:16.

At the age of 40, Esau made his own arrangements for marriage. By choice he became a polygamist, and unlike his father Isaac, who had let his father Abraham arrange for a wife from the worshipers of Jehovah, Esau took two pagan Hittite women, Judith (Oholibamah?) and Basemath (Adah?), as wives. These women proved to be a source of bitterness of spirit to both Isaac and Rebekah.—Ge 26:34, 35; 36:2; 24:1-4, 50, 51; see BASEMATH No. 1; JUDITH.

Bestowal of Jacob's Blessing. When Isaac was advanced in years he desired to give his blessing to his older son Esau. First Isaac directed Esau to hunt some venison and to make a tasty dish for him. This Esau proceeded to do with a view to receiving the blessing as firstborn, though he actually was no longer entitled to that blessing by reason of his having sold his birthright. Thus, he was willing to break his oathbound covenant made at the sale of the birthright. Knowing what Jehovah had said to her before the birth of her twins, Rebekah intervened, advising Jacob to present himself before his father as Esau and thus procure the blessing that was rightfully his. When presenting himself before his blind father, Jacob was dressed in Esau's garments, with the skins of kids on his hands and on the hairless part of his neck. Hence, Isaac did not recognize him.—Ge 25:23; 27:1-23.

No sooner had Isaac finished blessing Jacob than Esau came in from the hunt and proceeded to prepare a tasty dish for his father. On coming in before his father to receive the blessing dishonestly and learning that Isaac had blessed Jacob, "Esau began to cry out in an extremely loud and bitter manner." Earnestly, but with selfish motive, he sought a blessing from his father, but even his breaking out in tears did not change Isaac's mind and cause him to retract the blessing that he had pronounced upon Jacob. Likely Isaac recognized Jehovah's leading in the matter. He then proceeded to say to Esau: "Behold, away from the fertile soils of the earth your dwelling will be found, and away from the dew of the heavens above. And by your sword you will live, and your brother you will serve. But it will certainly occur that, when you grow restless, you will indeed break his yoke off your neck."—Ge 25:33; 27:30-40; Heb 12:17.

Esau knew that Jacob was entitled to the blessing because he had legally acquired the birthright. (Archaeological testimony confirms that among ancient peoples of the Middle East the practice existed of exchanging a birthright for something material. For example, a text from Nuzi tells of one brother's receiving three sheep in exchange for his share of the inheritance.) But Esau, like Cain, harbored animosity toward his brother Jacob and was waiting for an opportunity to put him to death. Therefore, Rebekah, on learning of this, advised Jacob to run away to her brother Laban at Haran. When seeking Isaac's consent in this matter, she kindly chose not to reveal to Isaac the murderous intention of Esau but voiced her feelings as to how she would be affected if Esau ever took a wife like the daughters of Heth. Isaac then called Jacob, blessed him, and directed him to go to Paddan-aram to Rebekah's relatives to obtain a wife. When Esau saw this, he was prompted to take a third wife, Mahalath (Basemath?) the daughter of Abraham's son Ishmael.—Ge 27:41–28:9; 36:3; see BASEMATH No. 2.

Later Events. Sometime during the 20 years that Jacob was away, Esau began to establish interests in Seir, the field of Edom. (Ge 32:3; Jos 24:4) It appears that it was years later that he made the complete move, taking his family and all of his possessions to Seir. (Ge 36:6-8) When Jacob returned to Canaan, he became quite alarmed upon receiving word from the messengers he had sent that Esau, along with 400 men, was on his way to meet him. Esau's reason for coming with a band of 400 men may have been to impress his brother with his superior strength or possibly to show that he was a mighty chieftain. Jacob, after praying to Jehovah, sent ahead a generous gift of more than 550 head of livestock. On seeing Esau, Jacob, in humility, "proceeded to bow down to the earth seven times until he got near to his brother." Esau then went running to meet him, embraced Jacob, fell upon his neck, and kissed him. Both of them burst into tears. Esau at first refused to accept Jacob's gift of livestock, saying: "I have a great many, my brother. Let continue yours what is yours." However, at Jacob's urging, Esau finally accepted the gift. He then offered to accompany Jacob, but his brother tactfully declined this as well as Esau's later proposal to place some of his men at Jacob's disposal, likely for protection. Esau and his men then departed and returned to Seir. The Bible record mentions that, about 23 years later, at the death of Isaac, Esau and Jacob buried their father.—Ge 32:6, 7, 10-15; 33:1-3, 8, 9, 11-16; 35:29.

Divine Principles Illustrated. The personality of Esau clearly shows that the choosing of Jacob as a forefather of the promised Seed was no arbitrary choice or unreasonable favoritism on the part of Jehovah God. Esau's lack of appreciation for spiritual things, coupled with his strong tendency toward satisfying fleshly desires, made Esau unfit to be in the direct line of the promised Seed. Hence, Jehovah's words, through his prophet Malachi: "But I loved Jacob, and Esau I have hated." Esau is excluded from among the faithful cloud of witnesses listed in Hebrews, chapter 11, when Paul says: "By faith Abraham . . . dwelt in tents with Isaac and Jacob, the heirs with him of the very same promise."—Mal 1:2, 3; Heb 11:8, 9; 12:1.

Jehovah's selection of Jacob over Esau shows that God's choosing does not depend on man's dictates. The apostle Paul uses this incident as an illustration of the fact that the true children of Abraham are not necessarily those of fleshly descent, nor those who depend on their own works, but those of the faith of Abraham.—Ro 9:6-12.

Esau is set forth as a warning example to Christians so that they will not be guilty, as was Esau the materialist, of lack of appreciation for sacred or spiritual things.—Heb 12:16; see EDOM, EDOMITES.

ESDRAELON.   See JEZREEL, JEZREELITE.

ESEK   (E'sek) [Contention]. A well of fresh water dug by Isaac's servants in the torrent valley of Gerar. (Ge 26:20) The Philistine shepherds of that area, however, claimed the well as theirs, and the resultant "quarreling" between the two parties gave the site its name. (Ge 26:12-20) Its exact location is today unknown.

ESHAN   (E'shan) [possibly, One Supporting Himself [On]]. A city in the mountainous region of Judah. (Jos 15:20, 48, 52) Though its exact location is unknown, the Greek *Septuagint* (Vatican MS. 1209) rendering of "Soma" has led some scholars to identify it with Khirbet Sam'a (Horvat 'esh-Sham'ah), about 15 km (9 mi) SSW of Jerusalem.

ESHBAAL.   See ISH-BOSHETH.

ESHBAN   (Esh'ban). The second-named son of Sheik Dishon; a descendant of Seir the Horite. The Horites were the inhabitants of the land of Seir before the sons of Esau dispossessed and annihilated them.—Ge 36:20, 26; 1Ch 1:38, 41; De 2:12.

ESHCOL   (Esh'col) [Cluster [of Grapes]].

1. A brother of Aner and Mamre the Amorite. (Ge 14:13) Eshcol and his brothers were confederates of Abraham in defeating a league of Eastern kings.—Ge 14:14, 24; see ANER No. 1.

2. A wadi or torrent valley, probably located a short distance N of Hebron. It was from this valley that the Israelite spies carried off a large cluster of grapes, and the vineyards in this area are still noted for the high quality of their grapes. (Nu 13:23, 24; 32:9; De 1:24) The name possibly resulted from this event during the spying trip.

ESHEK   (E'shek) [possibly, Acting Violently]. A descendant of King Saul. The Scriptural record mentions that this Benjamite had three sons and that the sons of his firstborn, Ulam, "came to be valiant, mighty men, bending the bow, and having many sons and grandsons, a hundred and fifty."—1Ch 8:1, 33, 39, 40.

ESHTAOL (Esh′ta·ol) [possibly, Place of Making Inquiry [of God]]. A city in the Shephelah, assigned to Judah. (Jos 15:20, 33) It was later listed as a town on Dan's border. (Jos 19:40, 41) Judge Samson was first impelled by Jehovah's spirit in this vicinity, and upon his death he was buried there. (Jg 13:25; 16:31) The 5 Danites spying out Laish and the 600 who subsequently captured it departed from Eshtaol and Zorah. —Jg 18:1, 2, 7, 11, 27.

Scholars generally identify Eshtaol with the partially occupied present-day site of Eshwa′ (Eshta′ol). It stands on a platform of rock about 21 km (13 mi) W of Jerusalem.

ESHTAOLITES (Esh′ta·ol·ites) [Of (Belonging to) Eshtaol]. The Judean inhabitants of Eshtaol who sprang from Shobal through the families of Kiriath-jearim.—1Ch 2:53.

ESHTEMOA (Esh·te·mo′a), **ESHTEMOH** (Esh′-te·moh) [possibly, Place of Listening [that is, for God's word]].

1. Son of Ishbah or, possibly, a Judean town many of whose inhabitants descended from Ishbah.—1Ch 4:17.

2. A Maacathite and descendant of Hodiah. —1Ch 4:19.

3. A town in the mountainous region of Judah, also called Eshtemoh. Though originally assigned to Judah, it was thereafter allotted, along with its pasture grounds, to the Levites. (Jos 15:50; 21:14; 1Ch 6:57) It corresponds to the modern village of es Samu′ (Eshtemoa′), situated about 15 km (9 mi) SSW of Hebron. Perhaps the same as No. 1.

Eshtemoa was one of the places frequented by David as a fugitive, and after his victory over the marauding Amalekites, he sent a gift from the spoils to friends there.—1Sa 30:26-28.

ESHTON (Esh′ton). Son of Mehir; descendant of Chelub of the tribe of Judah.—1Ch 4:1, 11, 12.

ESLI (Es′li). A postexilic ancestor of Christ; the son of Naggai and the father of Nahum.—Lu 3:25.

ESTHER (Es′ther). A Jewish orphan girl of the tribe of Benjamin whose Hebrew name was Hadassah (meaning "Myrtle"); a descendant from among those deported from Jerusalem along with King Jehoiachin (Jeconiah) in 617 B.C.E. (Es 2:5-7) She was the daughter of Abihail, the uncle of Mordecai. (Es 2:15) Her guardian was her older cousin Mordecai, one of "the king's servants that were in the king's gate" of the palace at Shushan during the reign of the Persian king Ahasuerus (Xerxes I, in the fifth century B.C.E.). (Es 2:7; 3:2) After Ahasuerus had deposed his queen Vashti for disobedience, he commanded the gathering of all the beautiful virgins for a period of special massage and beauty care, so that the king might select one to replace Vashti as queen. Esther was among those taken to the king's house and entrusted to the care of Hegai the guardian of the women. At Mordecai's direction, she kept secret the fact that she was a Jewess. (Es 2:8, 10) Esther was selected as queen in the seventh year of Ahasuerus' reign. (Es 2:16, 17) All along, she kept in touch with Mordecai, following his counsel. She spoke in Mordecai's name to the king when Mordecai uncovered a plot against the king.—Es 2:20, 22.

In the 12th year of Ahasuerus, Haman the Agagite, who was prime minister, planned the annihilation of all the Jews in the 127 jurisdictional districts in the empire. He received authorization from the king to issue a decree to carry this out. (Es 3:7-13) Acting on the information and advice of Mordecai, Esther revealed to the king the wicked intent of Haman's plot. Haman's reaction added to the king's rage, and Haman was hanged. (Es 4:7–7:10) The king, at Esther's request, issued a second decree authorizing the Jews to fight for their lives on the day set for their slaughter. (Es 8:3-14) Because of the king's edict and for fear of Mordecai, who replaced Haman as prime minister, the governors and officials of the empire helped the Jews to gain a complete victory over their enemies. (Es 9) Mordecai's instructions, confirmed by Esther, commanded the Jews to celebrate the Festival of Purim annually, a custom kept down to this day. —Es 9:20, 21, 29.

While the book of Esther does not mention the name of God, it is evident from the actions of Mordecai and Esther that they were both faithful servants of the true God Jehovah. Esther displayed the qualities of one trusting in God's law. She was "pretty in form and beautiful in appearance" (Es 2:7), but more important is the fact that she manifested the adornment of "the secret person of the heart in the incorruptible apparel of the quiet and mild spirit." (1Pe 3:4) Thus she gained favor before Hegai, the guardian of the women, as well as before the king himself. She did not count showy adornment the important thing and, accordingly, "did not request anything except what Hegai . . . proceeded to mention." (Es 2:15) She showed great tact and self-control. She was submissive to her husband Ahasuerus, approaching him in a tactful and respectful way when her life and the lives of her people were in danger. She kept silent when it was wise to do so but spoke boldly and fearlessly when it was necessary and at the right time. (Es 2:10; 7:3-6) She accepted counsel from her mature cousin Mordecai, even when following it endangered her life. (Es 4:12-16) Her love and loyalty toward her people the Jews, who were also God's covenant people, were demonstrated when she acted in their behalf.—See MORDECAI No. 2.

ESTHER, BOOK OF.

A book of the Hebrew Scriptures, the title of which is taken from the name of its principal character, although some copies of the Latin *Vulgate* call it "Ahasuerus" after the Persian king who figures prominently in the account. The Jews call it *Meghil·lath' 'Es·ter'* or simply the *Meghil·lah'*, meaning "roll; scroll,"

because for them it constitutes in itself a very highly regarded roll.

The Book's Writer. The Scriptures do not say who wrote the book of Esther. Some scholars credit the book to Ezra, but the weight of evidence points to Mordecai. Mordecai was in position to know all the minute facts that are related in the narrative about the personal concerns of himself and Esther, the doings of the members of Haman's family, and particularly what went on in Shushan the castle. After his promotion to the prime ministership of the Persian government he would have access to the official documents mentioned in the account, and just as Daniel, Ezra, and Nehemiah held official positions in the government of Persia during other periods and wrote Bible books describing the relation of the Jews to that world power, so Mordecai, with Jehovah's blessing, was the most likely one to write the book of Esther.

Historical Circumstances. The account sets the time for its events during the reign of the Ahasuerus who ruled while the Persian Empire

---

HIGHLIGHTS OF ESTHER

A vivid account of how Esther, with guidance from her older cousin Mordecai, was used by God to deliver the Jews from extermination

Written evidently by Mordecai, and apparently covering 493–c. 475 B.C.E.

Esther becomes queen in Shushan

When King Ahasuerus (evidently Xerxes I) calls for Queen Vashti during a royal banquet, so he can show off her loveliness, she persistently refuses to come; the king removes her as queen (1:1-22)

Esther is chosen above all the other beautiful virgins in the realm and is made queen; at Mordecai's direction, she does not reveal that she is a Jewess (2:1-20)

Haman conspires to have the Jews exterminated, but the tables are turned

Haman the Agagite is exalted by the king above all the other princes, but Mordecai refuses to bow to him (3:1-4)

Enraged over Mordecai's refusal, Haman schemes to annihilate all the Jews in the empire; the king is induced to agree, the date is set, and the decree is issued (3:5-15)

Mordecai instructs Esther to appeal personally to the king, though her life may be endangered by appearing before him uninvited (4:1-17)

Esther is received favorably by the king; she invites the king and Haman to a banquet; then she requests that they return for another banquet the next day (5:1-8)

Haman's joy is marred, however, because Mordecai again refuses to bow to him, so Haman puts up a very tall stake and plans to urge the king to hang Mordecai on it before the banquet the next day (5:9-14)

That night, when the king is sleepless, he has records read to him, and he learns that Mordecai has not been rewarded for reporting a scheme to assassinate the king; when Haman arrives in the morning, the king asks him what should be done to honor a man in whom the king takes delight; thinking he is the man, Haman offers lavish suggestions; then Haman himself is commanded to confer that honor publicly on Mordecai (6:1-13; 2:21-23)

At the banquet that day, Esther makes known to the king that Haman has sold her and her people to be destroyed; furious, the king orders Haman to be hung on the stake he put up for Mordecai (6:14–7:10)

Mordecai is promoted, and the Jews are delivered

Mordecai is given the king's signet ring that was taken from Haman (8:1, 2)

With the king's approval, a decree is issued permitting the Jews to defend themselves and to annihilate their enemies on the day that had been set for their own destruction; many thousands of the Jews' enemies are slaughtered (8:3–9:19)

It is decreed that this deliverance be commemorated each year (9:20-32)

Mordecai comes to be second to the king and works for the good of his people (10:1-3)

extended from India to Ethiopia and included 127 provinces or jurisdictional districts. (Es 1:1) These facts and its inclusion in the canon by Ezra confine its coverage to the period of the reign of one of the following three kings known to secular history: Darius I the Persian, Xerxes I, and Artaxerxes Longimanus. However, both Darius I and Artaxerxes Longimanus are known to have favored the Jews before the 12th year of their respective reigns, which does not fit the Ahasuerus of the book, as he apparently was not well acquainted with the Jews and their religion, nor was he inclined to favor them. Therefore, the Ahasuerus of the book of Esther is believed to be Xerxes I, son of the Persian king Darius the Great. Some translations (*AT, Mo*) even substitute "Xerxes" for "Ahasuerus" in the text.

In the book of Esther the regnal years of this king apparently are counted from the coregency with his father Darius the Great. Because the first events related in the book of Esther occurred in the third year of his reign and the rest of the account covers the remainder of his reign, the book evidently covers the period from 493 B.C.E. to about 475 B.C.E.—See PERSIA, PERSIANS (The Reigns of Xerxes and of Artaxerxes).

The book of Esther was committed to writing sometime after the 12th year of Xerxes and evidently by the end of Xerxes' reign (c. 475 B.C.E.). The book's vivid style of writing suggests that the writer was an eyewitness. Moreover, the strong implication that the writer had access to governmental documents (Es 10:2) makes it most likely that the book was written in Shushan in the province of Elam, which was then part of Persia. Its Persian and Chaldean words mixed in with Hebrew fit the above-mentioned time of writing as well as the land of Persia for the place of writing.

Ezra could have brought the book from Babylon to Jerusalem in 468 B.C.E., for the Great Synagogue of Jerusalem had it in the canon before its period ended about 300 B.C.E.

Authenticity and Canonicity. Canonical authority for the book of Esther is doubted by some because it is not quoted or alluded to in the Christian Greek Scriptures. But this is no conclusive objection, for the same circumstance exists with other books of well-established canonicity, such as Ezra and Ecclesiastes. Melito of Sardis, Gregory of Nazianzus, and Athanasius are among those who omitted it from their lists of canonical books. However, Jerome, Augustine, and Origen refer to the book by name. It is in the

Chester Beatty collection, the books of Ezekiel, Daniel, and Esther being found in one codex, which was likely compiled in the first half of the third century C.E. It does not appear that its authority was ever doubted by the Jews or by early Christians as a whole. In their Bibles the Jews most often place it among the Hagiographa (the Writings) between Ecclesiastes and Daniel.

Apocryphal additions were later inserted into the book. Some scholars date their origin at approximately 100 B.C.E., about 300 years after the canon of the Hebrew Scriptures was fixed, according to the traditional view.

The book of Esther is accused of exaggeration in its mention of a banquet lasting 180 days in the third year of the reign of Ahasuerus. (Es 1:3, 4) However, it has been expressed that such a long feast may have been held to accommodate the numerous officials from the many provinces who could not, because of their duties, have been there for all of it and all at the same time. Actually, the text does not say the banquet lasted that long, but that the king showed them the riches and glory of his kingdom for 180 days. A banquet is mentioned at 1:3 and 1:5. It may be that two banquets are not meant, but that the seven-day banquet for all in the castle at the end of the great assembly is the one referred to in verse 3.—*Commentary on the Old Testament,* by C. Keil and F. Delitzsch, 1973, Vol. III, Esther, pp. 322-324.

In view of the absence of any direct mention of God in the book, some charge that the book is irreligious. Nevertheless, it tells of fasting and a "cry for aid" on the part of the Jews, implying prayer. (Es 4:3, 16; 9:31) Also, there is indication of God's maneuvering of events in the sleeplessness of the king at the opportune time (6:1) and possible allusion to divine purpose in Esther's attaining to the queenship. (4:14) Furthermore, the fact that Mordecai strictly refused to bow before God's enemy Haman, who as an Agagite may have been a royal Amalekite, is evidence that Jehovah was worshiped by Mordecai.—3:1-6; Ex 17:14.

Evidence of history and archaeology. Historical and archaeological findings have added their voice in confirming the authenticity of the book of Esther. A few examples will suffice. The way Persians honored a man is described authentically. (Es 6:8) White and blue (or violet) were the royal Persian colors. At Esther 8:15 we read that Mordecai wore "royal apparel of blue and linen" and a cloak of reddish purple.

Esther "took her stand in the inner courtyard of the king's house opposite the king's house, while the king was sitting on his royal throne in the royal house opposite the entrance of the house. And it came about that, as soon as the king saw Esther the queen standing in the courtyard, she gained favor in his eyes." (Es 5:1, 2) Excavations have revealed that the detail of the description is exact. A corridor led from the House of the Women to the inner court, and at the side of the court opposite the corridor was the hall, or throne room, of the palace. The throne was placed in the center of the farther wall, and from this vantage point the king could look over the screen that intervened and could see the queen waiting for an audience. Further details in the book show an intimate knowledge on the part of the writer with the palace. It is evident that objections to the book on the grounds of its being unhistorical and inaccurate as to Persian manners and customs are unfounded.

Very strong evidence for the book's authenticity is the Festival of Purim, or Lots, commemorated by the Jews down to this day; on this anniversary the entire book is read in their synagogues. A cuneiform inscription evidently from Borsippa is said to refer to a Persian official by the name of *Mardukâ* (Mordecai?) who was at Susa (Shushan) at the end of the reign of Darius I or the beginning of the reign of Xerxes I.—*Zeitschrift für die alttestamentliche Wissenschaft,* 1940/41, Vol. 58, pp. 243, 244; 1942/43, Vol. 59, p. 219.

The book of Esther is in complete accord with the rest of the Scriptures and complements the accounts of Ezra and Nehemiah by telling what took place with the exiled people of God in Persia. As with all Scripture, it was written to provide encouragement, comfort, and instruction for us. —Ro 15:4.

ETAM (E'tam) [Place of Birds of Prey].

1. A settlement of Simeonites within the territory of Judah. (1Ch 4:24, 32) Its location is uncertain, although some connect it with Tell 'Eitum (Tel 'Aitun), centrally located in Judah's territory about 44 km (27 mi) W of En-gedi and the same distance SW of Jerusalem.

2. The crag Etam, where Samson lived after burning the Philistines' fields. From this crag, 3,000 men of Judah took him, willingly bound, back to the Philistines. (Jg 15:8-13) Whereas no positive identification for the crag Etam is possible, a connection with the town (No. 3 below) cannot be altogether eliminated. However, just 4 km (2.5 mi) ESE of the suggested site of Sam-

son's hometown Zorah (Jg 13:2) is 'Araq Isma'in, an isolated crag with a lofty cavern affording a broad view of the Shephelah below. Appropriate to the meaning of the name, this may possibly be the site of the crag Etam.

3. A town of Judah located probably at Khirbet el-Khokh, on a hill about 2.5 km (1.5 mi) SW of Bethlehem. Apparently Etam and Bethlehem had been settled by close relatives. (1Ch 4:3, 4; see ATROTH-BETH-JOAB.) According to Josephus, King Solomon often took a morning chariot ride from Jerusalem those 13 km (8 mi) out to Etam, where there were gardens and streams. (*Jewish Antiquities,* VIII, 186 [vii, 3]) The town was rebuilt and fortified by Solomon's successor Rehoboam. (2Ch 11:5, 6) According to the Talmud, an aqueduct linked Jerusalem with a spring to the W of Etam.—Babylonian Talmud, *Yoma* 31a; Palestinian (Jerusalem) Talmud, *Yoma* 41a.

ETHAM (E'tham). The second campsite listed by Moses in Israel's march out of Egypt. (Ex 13:20; Nu 33:3-7) It was at Etham, "on the edge of the wilderness," that the Israelites made a change in their direction, 'turning back' toward Pihahiroth, where the crossing of the sea took place. (Nu 33:7, 8) This would indicate that Etham could have been the point of exit from Egypt had not the Israelites been divinely directed to alter their course.

This turning back caused Pharaoh to reason that the Israelites were 'wandering in confusion in the wilderness' and provided him with an incentive to pursue them. This led to God's execution of judgment on the Egyptians at the Red Sea.—Ex 14:1-4.

Some scholars endeavor to place Etham at the eastern end of the Wadi Tumilat, N of the Bitter Lakes. However, this is because they connect the Hebrew Etham (*'E·tham'*) with the Old Egyptian word for fortress (*htm*). Even if such connection were correct, there were a number of places to which that Egyptian name was applied. Since Etham was not on the northern route out of Egypt, which would have led "by the way of the land of the Philistines" (Ex 13:17), it can only be said to have been at some point N of the Red Sea and evidently at the border of the wilderness region forming the NW part of the Sinai Peninsula.

A comparison of Numbers 33:8 with Exodus 15:22 would seem to indicate that the wilderness region by Etham corresponds to "the wilderness of Shur." Or, if the names are not interchangeable, then, depending upon which region was the larger, the wilderness of Etham may have included that of Shur or else was itself a part of the wilderness of Shur.—See SHUR.

ETHAN (E'than) [Enduring; Everflowing].

1. One of four men whose wisdom, though great, was exceeded by Solomon's. (1Ki 4:31) This Ethan may be the writer of Psalm 89, for the superscription identifies Ethan the Ezrahite as its writer. In 1 Chronicles 2:6, Ethan, Heman, Calcol, and Dara are all spoken of as sons of Zerah of the tribe of Judah and possibly are the same as the men mentioned in First Kings. Ethan is referred to as the father of Azariah.—1Ch 2:8; see EZRAHITE.

2. The father of Adaiah and the son of Zimmah, a Levite of the family of Gershom.—1Ch 6:41-43.

3. A son of Kishi (1Ch 6:44) or Kushaiah (1Ch 15:17), a Levite of the family of Merari. Ethan was a singer and a cymbalist. (1Ch 15:19) Because of his close association with Heman it has been suggested that Ethan is the Jeduthun who was appointed by David to serve before the tabernacle at Gibeon and that his name was changed from Ethan to Jeduthun after his appointment. (Compare 1Ch 15:17, 19 with 1Ch 16:39-41 and 25:1.)—See JEDUTHUN No. 1.

ETHANIM (Eth'a·nim) [probably, Enduring [Streams]; Everflowing [Streams]]. This was the seventh lunar month of the sacred calendar of the Israelites, but the first of the secular calendar. (1Ki 8:2) It corresponded to part of September and part of October. Following the Babylonian exile it was called Tishri, a name that does not appear in the Bible record but that is found in postexilic writings.

In speaking of the festival that began on the 15th day of this month (or around the first part of October), the historian Josephus writes: "On the fifteenth of this same month, at which the turning-point to the winter season is now reached, Moses bids each family to fix up tents, apprehensive of the cold and as a protection against the year's inclemency."—*Jewish Antiquities*, III, 244 (x, 4).

Start of Agricultural Year. Whereas Abib (or Nisan) became the first month of the year in the sacred Jewish calendar following the Exodus from Egypt, Ethanim continued to be viewed as the first month in a secular or agricultural sense. With this month, almost all the harvesting had been completed, marking the conclusion of the agricultural year. The early rains that thereafter fell softened the ground for the plowing that would follow and that would denote the initiation of new agricultural operations. Jehovah referred to Ethanim as the turning point of the year when speaking of the festival of ingathering as being "at the outgoing of the year" and "at the turn of the year." (Ex 23:16; 34:22) It is also notable that it was not in the month of Abib but in this month of Ethanim that the Jubilee year began.—Le 25:8-12.

The later name applied to the month, Tishri, means "Beginning of the Year," and Tishri 1 is still observed by the Jews as their New Year's Day or Rosh Hashanah ("Head of the Year").

Festival Month. Ethanim was also a month of festivals. The first day was the "day of the trumpet blast." (Le 23:24; Nu 29:1) Since each new moon was normally announced with a trumpet blast, this day likely was one of additional or extensive trumpeting. (Nu 10:10) On the 10th of Ethanim the annual Day of Atonement was observed. (Le 16:29, 30; 23:27; Nu 29:7) From the 15th to the 21st occurred the Festival of Booths, or Festival of Ingathering, followed on the 22nd day by a solemn assembly. (Le 23:34-36) Thus, a large part of the month of Ethanim was taken up by these festival seasons.

Events Occurring in Ethanim. Since the Bible, from its first book onward, presents chronological data, and since the first mention of years of life is in connection with the life of Adam, it would seem that the ancient use of the month called Ethanim as the initial month of the year would give some basis for believing that Adam's start of life was in this month. (Ge 5:1-5) It was on the first day of the first month (later called Ethanim) that Noah, after having already spent over ten months within the ark, removed the ark's covering and observed that the floodwaters had drained off the ground. (Ge 8:13) Over 1,300 years later Solomon inaugurated the completed temple at Jerusalem in Ethanim. (1Ki 8:2; 2Ch 5:3) After Jerusalem's destruction in 607 B.C.E., the killing of Governor Gedaliah and the subsequent flight to Egypt of the remaining Israelites in the month of Ethanim marked the full desolation of Judah. (2Ki 25:25, 26; Jer 41:1, 2) These events were involved in the reasons for "the fast of the seventh month" mentioned at Zechariah 8:19. Seventy years later, by this very same month, the released Israelite exiles had returned from Babylon to begin the rebuilding of the temple in Jerusalem.—Ezr 3:1, 6.

The evidence also indicates that Jesus' birth, as well as his baptism and anointing, took place during this month.—See JESUS CHRIST.

ETHBAAL (Eth·ba'al) [With Baal]. King of the Sidonians, the father of Jezebel the wife of King Ahab. (1Ki 16:31) By giving his daughter in marriage to Ahab, Ethbaal entered into a political alliance with him. Ethbaal is evidently the Ithobalus mentioned in Josephus' quotation of historian Menander as being the priest of the goddess Astarte (Ashtoreth). This priest got the kingship by murdering Phelles, a descendant of Hiram the king of Tyre with whom Solomon had had dealings in connection with the building of the temple. Ethbaal is said to have ruled for 32 of the 48 years of his life. (*Against Apion*, I, 123 [18]) Indicative of the commercial expansion carried on during his reign is Menander's reference to Ethbaal's building Auza in Libya. Menander also mentions that a one-year drought occurred during Ethbaal's reign.—*Jewish Antiquities*, VIII, 324 (xiii, 2).

ETHER (E'ther). A city of the Shephelah in the territory of Judah, but allotted to Simeon. (Jos 15:33, 42; 19:1-9) Today it is generally identified with Khirbet el-'Ater (Tel 'Eter), about 1.5 km (1 mi) NW of Beit Jibrin (Eleutheropolis; Bet Guvrin). The account at Joshua 19:7 is nearly parallel with that of 1 Chronicles 4:32, and in this latter text Ether appears to be referred to as Tochen.

Some reference works consider that there were two Ethers, that at Joshua 15:42 being located between Libnah and Mareshah (at Khirbet el-'Ater, above mentioned), and the other, referred to at Joshua 19:7, being situated near Ziklag to the S. While the other towns referred to in Joshua 19:7 are all in the S and many of those at Joshua 15:42 are more to the N, it may be noted, nevertheless, that in both texts the town of Ashan is mentioned, so that any clear division becomes difficult.

ETHIOPIA (E·thi·o'pi·a) [Gr., *Ai·thi·o·pi'a*, "Region of Burnt Faces"], **ETHIOPIAN** (E·thi·o'pi·an). Ethiopia was the name applied by the ancient Greeks to the region of Africa S of Egypt. It thus corresponded generally with the Hebrew "Cush," which embraced primarily the present Sudan and the northern part of modern Ethiopia. In Egyptian texts this region was likewise known by the name Keesh. When the *Septuagint* translation was made, the translators used the Greek "Ethiopia" to render the Hebrew "Cush" in all but three passages. (Ge 10:6-8; 1Ch 1:8-10; Eze 30:5) The *King James Version* follows this rendering in all cases except Isaiah 11:11, where it uses "Cush" instead of "Ethiopia"; the *Revised Standard Version* likewise follows the *Septuagint* except at Genesis 2:13 and Ezekiel 38:5. Some translations (*NW, JB*) prefer Cush in yet other texts where the identification with ancient Ethiopia is not made certain by the context. The name Cush can also apply to peoples of Arabia. —See CUSH No. 2; CUSHITE.

The area originally designated by the name Ethiopia now consists of semiarid plains in the N, savannas and plateau land in the central region, and tropical rain forest toward the S. Onetime capitals of ancient Ethiopia were Napata and Meroë. Meroë was the seat of a kingdom in which the right of kingship was carried through the female line rather than the male. The queen mother was thus the one from whom her kingly son derived his right to the throne, and at times she may have been the virtual ruler of the land. The name Candace is mentioned by Greek and Latin writers as a title used by several such Ethiopian queens, evidently including the one referred to at Acts 8:27.

In what sense was the Ethiopian to whom Philip preached a eunuch?

The Ethiopian eunuch who was 'over the treasures' of Queen Candace, and to whom Philip preached, was obviously a circumcised Jewish proselyte. (Ac 8:27-39) He was thus not viewed as a Gentile and hence did not precede Cornelius as the first uncircumcised Gentile convert to Christianity. (Ac 10) For the Ethiopian to engage in worship at the temple in Jerusalem he must have been converted to the Jewish religion and circumcised. (Ex 12:48, 49; Le 24:22) In view of the Mosaic Law, which forbade the entry of castrated persons into the congregation of Israel (De 23:1), it is evident that the Ethiopian was not a eunuch in a fleshly sense. The Hebrew word for "eunuch" (*sa·ris'*) in a broad or special sense also meant an officer, as at Genesis 39:1, where an officer of Pharaoh, Potiphar, a married man, is called a *sa·ris'*. Had the Ethiopian officer been an actual eunuch, he would not have been a proselyte, and if not a proselyte, Philip would not have baptized him, since the good news had not yet begun to be extended to the uncircumcised Gentiles.

Ethiopia (Cush) is one of the lands among which the Jewish exiles were scattered after the Babylonian conquest of Judah. (Isa 11:11) Hence, this Ethiopian official may have had association with Jewish persons in his area or perhaps in Egypt, where many Jews resided. His copy of the scroll of Isaiah was likely a copy of the Greek *Septuagint,* originally made in Alexandria, Egypt. Since the Ethiopian kingdom had become partly Hellenized from the time of Ptolemy II (308-246 B.C.E.), this official's being able to read the Greek language would not be unusual. His becoming a Jewish proselyte and his subsequent conversion to Christianity were in fulfillment of Psalm 68:31.

Ethiopian Language.   The original language of Ethiopia is undetermined; by the close of the eighth century B.C.E. Egyptian hieroglyphic writing was being used for official Ethiopian inscriptions. A native language and script called Meroitic is known from the century prior to the start of the Common Era and for some centuries thereafter. The language called Ethiopic was the vernacular language during the Common Era up until the 14th century. It is of Semitic origin as is the present-day language of modern Ethiopia called Amharic.

ETH-KAZIN   (Eth-ka′zin). A site marking the boundary of Zebulun. (Jos 19:10, 13) Though its exact location is today unknown, some tentatively identify it with modern Kafr Kanna about 20 km (12 mi) W of the Sea of Galilee.

ETHNAN   (Eth′nan) [Hire, Gift]. A son of Ashhur by his wife Helah. Ethnan was of the tribe of Judah and of the family of Hezron.—1Ch 2:3-5, 9, 24; 4:5, 7.

ETHNI   (Eth′ni) [Hire, Gift]. A descendant of Levi through his son Gershom; the son of Zerah and the forefather of the musician Asaph.—1Ch 6:39-43.

EUBULUS   (Eu·bu′lus) [probably, Good Counsel]. One of the Christian brothers who was in Rome at the time of the apostle Paul's last imprisonment and who is mentioned as sending greetings to Timothy.—2Ti 4:21.

EUNICE   (Eu′nice) [from a root meaning "conquer"]. A believing Jewess, the daughter of Lois. She was the wife of an unbelieving Greek and the mother of Timothy. (Ac 16:1) It is very likely that the apostle Paul met Eunice at Lystra in Asia Minor on his first missionary tour and that then, as a result of his preaching, she and her mother

Lois became Christians. (Ac 14:4-18) The faith of Eunice was "without any hypocrisy." (2Ti 1:5) Although married to a pagan husband, she was exemplary in teaching her son Timothy "the holy writings" from his "infancy," and when she became a Christian, she doubtless instructed him accordingly. (2Ti 3:15) Since Eunice's husband was a Greek, Timothy's parents had not had him circumcised.—Ac 16:3.

EUNUCH.   The Hebrew word *sa·ris′* and the Greek word *eu·nou′khos* apply, when used in a literal sense, to a human male who has been castrated. Such were appointed in royal courts as attendants, or caretakers, of the queen, the harem, and the women. (Es 2:3, 12-15; 4:4-6, 9) Because of their closeness to the king's household, eunuchs of ability often rose to high rank. In a broad sense the term also denoted any official assigned to duties in the court of the king, not indicating that these men were literal eunuchs.

Under the Law covenant, a eunuch was not allowed to become part of the congregation of God's people. (De 23:1) There is, accordingly, no indication that any of the Israelites or alien residents among them were made eunuchs for service in the palace of Israelite kings. Under the Law, slaves were to be circumcised, not castrated. However, it was the custom of Eastern pagan nations to make eunuchs out of some of the children taken captive in war.

The court official who was in charge of the treasury of the queen of Ethiopia and to whom Philip preached is called a eunuch. He was a proselyte to the Jewish religion who had come to Jerusalem to worship God. But since a castrated person was not accepted into the congregation of Israel under the Law, the term *eu·nou′khos* would apply here not literally but in its sense of "court official." (Ac 8:26-39; De 23:1) Ebed-melech, the Ethiopian who rescued the prophet Jeremiah from imprisonment in a cistern, was a eunuch in the court of King Zedekiah. It would appear that the term here, too, applies in the frequent sense of officer. Ebed-melech seems to have been a man of authority. He appealed directly to King Zedekiah in Jeremiah's behalf and was given command over 30 men for the rescue operation. —Jer 38:7-13.

Jehovah comfortingly foretold the time when eunuchs would be accepted by him as his servants and, if obedient, would have a name better than sons and daughters. With the abolition of the Law by Jesus Christ, all persons exercising faith, regardless of their former status or condition, could become spiritual sons of God. Fleshly distinctions were removed.—Isa 56:4, 5; Joh 1:12; 1Co 7:24; 2Co 5:16.

Jesus Christ spoke of three classes of eunuchs at Matthew 19:12, saying: "For there are eunuchs that were born such from their mother's womb, and there are eunuchs that were made eunuchs by men, and there are eunuchs that have made themselves eunuchs on account of the kingdom of the heavens. Let him that can make room for it make room for it." Those who are said to have "made themselves eunuchs" because of the kingdom are those who exercise self-control so as to apply themselves to the service of God. The apostle Paul recommends this as the "better" course for Christians who do not become "inflamed with passion." These, he said, could serve the Lord more constantly "without distraction." (1Co 7:9, 29-38) Such "eunuchs" are not persons who have physically castrated themselves or have been emasculated; instead, these persons voluntarily remain in a state of singleness. No vow of celibacy is recommended by the Bible, and "forbidding to marry" is condemned as one of the marks of the apostasy. In fact, some of the apostles were married men.—1Ti 4:1-3; 1Co 9:5; Mt 8:14; Mr 1:30; Lu 4:38; see COURT OFFICIAL.

EUODIA (Eu·o′di·a) [Good Way; Prospering]. A woman in the Christian congregation at Philippi who had fought side by side with the apostle Paul and others "in the good news." Euodia was apparently having some difficulty in resolving a problem that had arisen between her and Syntyche, and Paul admonished these two Christian women "to be of the same mind in the Lord."—Php 4:2, 3.

EUPHRATES (Eu·phra′tes). The longest and most important river of SW Asia, called the Firat Nehri in Turkish, a name closely resembling the Hebrew *Perath′* and the Old Persian *Ufratu*. It is first mentioned at Genesis 2:14 as one of the four rivers once having had their source in Eden.

Boundary of Israel's Assigned Territory. In God's statement to Abraham he covenanted to give Abraham's seed the land "from the river of Egypt to the great river, the river Euphrates." (Ge 15:18) This promise was restated to the nation of Israel. (Ex 23:31; De 1:7, 8; 11:24; Jos 1:4) First Chronicles 5:9 states that certain descendants of Reuben in the period prior to David's reign extended their dwelling "as far as where one enters the wilderness at the river Euphrates." However, since the Euphrates is

some 800 km (500 mi) distant, when traveling "east of Gilead" (1Ch 5:10), this may mean simply that the Reubenites extended their territory E of Gilead into the edge of the Syrian Desert, which desert continues over to the Euphrates. (*RS* reads, "as far as the entrance of the desert this side of the Euphrates"; *JB*, "to the beginning of the desert that ends at the river Euphrates.") It thus appears that Jehovah's promise was first fully realized during the reigns of David and Solomon when the boundaries of Israel's dominion extended to include the Aramaean kingdom of Zobah and thus reached to the banks of the Euphrates, evidently along the section traversing northern Syria. (2Sa 8:3; 1Ki 4:21; 1Ch 18:3-8; 2Ch 9:26) Because of its preeminence, it was often designated simply as "the River."—Jos 24:2, 15; Ps 72:8.

Sources and Course. Some 2,700 km (1,700 mi) in length, the Euphrates has two principal sources. One, known as the Kara Su, takes its rise in NE Turkey about 100 km (60 mi) from the SE corner of the Black Sea. The other, the Murat Nehri, has its headwaters originating about midway between Lake Van and Mount Ararat. Approximately halfway between the two rivers lies the valley of the Araks River, thought by some to be related to the Gihon River of Genesis 2:13. The courses of the Kara Su and the Murat Nehri run fairly parallel in a westerly direction until they unite near the city of Keban, at an elevation of about 610 m (2,000 ft) above sea level.

From this point on, the combined streams form the Euphrates proper. Having already traversed some 640 km (400 mi) of mountainous terrain from the initial headwaters of the Murat Nehri, the river now turns southward for a distance of some 480 km (300 mi), during which its flow is broken by various cataracts and rapids, until it finally emerges on the Syrian plain at a point N of the site of ancient Carchemish (modern Jerablus).

Ford at Carchemish. Carchemish guarded the principal fording place used by armies or caravans crossing from N Mesopotamia into N Syria. Carchemish was a major fortress city that later came under Assyrian control. (Isa 10:5-9) Pharaoh Nechoh took the city about 629 B.C.E., engaging Josiah's army at Megiddo and killing that Judean king while on the way there. (2Ki 23:29; 2Ch 35:20-24) Between three and four years later (625 B.C.E.) Nebuchadnezzar's troops crossed the Euphrates and defeated the Egyptians at Carchemish, initiating the complete decline of any domination by Egypt in Syria-Palestine.—Jer 46:2, 6, 10; 2Ki 24:7.

From Carchemish to the Persian Gulf. The Euphrates by Carchemish is only about 160 km (100 mi) from the Mediterranean Sea; however, the river thereafter makes a turn and takes a SE course, heading for the Persian Gulf, over 1,100 km (680 mi) distant. The "middle" section of the Euphrates reaches from Carchemish down to the city of Hit, in the region of bitumen pits, its flow being strengthened by the waters of the Balikh and Khabur rivers. Below Hit the river courses through the fertile Mesopotamian plain, and some 80 km (50 mi) below Hit, in the neighborhood of Baghdad, it draws within 40 km (25 mi) of the Tigris River. In this lower section of the Euphrates, the river dissipates itself in the extensive marshes and in the ruined canals, and its flow becomes sluggish.

The Euphrates and the Tigris finally unite near Basra, and from this junction to the Persian Gulf the stream is known as the Shatt-al-Arab. According to Pliny and other ancient historians, the Euphrates originally had its outlet into the sea separate from that of the Tigris. (*Natural History*, VI, XXVI, 128-131) It is generally believed that the silt deposited by the two rivers has built up the delta region at the head of the Persian Gulf and that the original coastline extended much farther N, perhaps reaching as far as the ancient city of Ur of the Chaldeans, Abraham's early home.

The Euphrates' waters reach their lowest point in September and then steadily rise until May, when their normal crest is reached. Because of the melting snows, spring floods occur. The annual overflowing of both the Euphrates and the Tigris doubtless is the basis for Isaiah's description of Babylonia as "the wilderness of the sea." (Isa 21:1, 2) This flooding was controlled in ancient times by dikes and sluices that diverted the waters into irrigation canals and into catch basins. These canals formed an irrigation network between the Euphrates and the Tigris that ensured productiveness for most of lower Babylonia. Over the centuries the canals generally have become blocked up and clogged, with resultant agricultural deterioration; the accumulation of salts in the soil because of the irrigation waters also contributed to the gradual ruin of the once-fertile valley.

Major Cities. Along the Euphrates' banks lay many ancient cities, including Ur, Erech, Kish, and Babylon. The river's course has apparently shifted somewhat to the W so that most of the ancient sites now lie several miles to the E of it.

The great city of Babylon was originally built so that it straddled the Euphrates, and the river's waters were used to form a broad deep moat encircling the city and also to form a network of canals within the city walls. At the time of Babylon's fall in 539 B.C.E., Cyrus diverted the waters of the Euphrates so that his troops could march through the riverbed into the unsuspecting city. Thus, the waters of the Euphrates were 'dried up.' (Isa 44:27, 28; 45:1) In symbol, the same thing is prophesied to result from the outpouring of the sixth angel's "bowl" on "the great river Euphrates," as described at Revelation 16:12. The following chapter describes the destruction of symbolic "Babylon the Great," which is said to 'sit on many waters,' these representing "peoples and crowds and nations and tongues."—Re 17:1, 5, 15-18.

A Frontier; Visited by Jeremiah. As the Euphrates River served as the northern frontier of the disputed region of Palestine and Syria, over which Egypt and Babylon fought, so in the time of the Persian Empire it served to divide the East from the West, as indicated by the expression "beyond the River." (Ezr 4:10, 11; 5:3; 6:6; Ne 2:7) In time the Euphrates also formed the eastern boundary of the Roman Empire.

The text at Jeremiah 13:1-7 has been the subject of some discussion inasmuch as a trip by Jeremiah from Jerusalem to the river Euphrates, even at its nearest point some distance S of Carchemish, would represent a trip of over 500 km (300 mi) each way, and the text indicates that he possibly made the trip twice (though the intervening time is not stated). A translation by the Jewish Publication Society here simply transliterates the Hebrew word as "Perath," and some suggest that the reference is not to the Euphrates but to the town of Parah (Jos 18:23), near Anathoth, a few miles from Jerusalem. However, the repetition of the name *Perath'* (Euphrates) four times in the account evidently shows that the place named had a significant relation to the prophetic picture being enacted, whereas the obscure village of Parah would hardly seem to give particular significance to the event. Though some point out that the Hebrew word *na·har'* (river) is not used in connection with *Perath'* in this text, it may be noted that it is likewise lacking at Jeremiah 51:63, yet the reference there obviously is to the Euphrates River. Hence, there seems to be no good reason for assuming that the account at

Jeremiah 13:1-7 refers to anything other than the Euphrates River.

It is quite possible that Jeremiah's hiding of the belt near the river took place at least in the general region of the crossing of the Euphrates by the Babylonian armies under Nebuchadnezzar in their march that eventually led to the desolation of Judah and Jerusalem. At any rate, the trip, or possibly two trips, to the Euphrates by Jeremiah certainly should have given impressive weight to the warning message this action was to convey to the spiritually corrupt people of the kingdom of Judah.—Compare Jer 2:18, 19.

EUROAQUILO (Eu·ro·aq′ui·lo). The violent northeasterly gale that swept down upon the ship in which Paul was sailing en route from Fair Havens to Phoenix, a harbor on the southern coast of Crete. (Ac 27:14) That wind, known to Maltese mariners as the gregale, is the most violent wind on the Mediterranean and would be extremely dangerous to a ship with large sails, which could easily capsize during such a storm. For this reason, when the boat could not keep its head against the wind, the sailors, being in fear of running aground on the quicksands off the northern coast of Africa, "lowered the gear and thus were driven along." (Ac 27:15-17) The five types of gregale recognized by meteorologists are produced by low-pressure areas over Libya or the Gulf of Gabes, which induce strong air currents from Greece. Translations of the Bible based on the Received Text, such as the *King James Version,* call the wind "Euroclydon" (from *eu′ros* [southeast or east wind] and *kly′don* [a surge of the sea]). However, the word *Eu·ra·ky′lon,* translated "Euroaquilo" (from Latin *eu·rus* [east (or southeast) wind] and *aquilo* [north wind]), is found in some of the best manuscripts. "Euroaquilo" is a better rendering, as it indicates the wind to be from the ENE.

EUTYCHUS (Eu′ty·chus) [Fortunate; Successful]. A young man in Troas who is the last person reported in the Scriptures to have been miraculously restored to life. Upon Paul's visit to Troas on his third missionary tour, he prolonged his discourse to the brothers until midnight. Overcome by tiredness and possibly by the heat of the many lamps and the crowded condition in the upper chamber, Eutychus fell into deep sleep and tumbled down from a third-story window. The physician Luke, the writer of Acts and apparently an eyewitness of what happened, reports that Eutychus was not merely unconscious but "was picked up dead." Following a procedure similar to that of Elisha in resurrecting the Shunammite's son, Paul threw himself upon Eutychus and embraced him. Paul's words, "Stop raising a clamor, for his soul is in him," indicated that life had been restored to Eutychus.—Ac 20:7-12; see also 2Ki 4:34.

EVANGELIZER. A preacher of the gospel or good news; a messenger of good. The Greek *eu·ag·ge·li·stes′* (evangelizer) is closely related to the word *eu·ag·ge′li·on,* "good news" or "gospel." (See GOOD NEWS; also Na 1:15, ftn; Mt 4:23, ftn.) Jehovah is the Great Evangelizer, or Bringer of good news. After Adam's fall into sin it was good news to learn, at Genesis 3:15, that there would be a seed to crush the serpent's head. It gave hope to humankind. (Ro 8:20) Enlarging on the promise of the seed to Abraham, Jehovah declared good news to him. (Ga 3:8; Ge 12:1-3) In Isaiah 52:7 it was prophesied that there would be one "bringing good news" with regard to the restoration of the Jews from Babylon. This text is quoted by the apostle Paul in reference to the evangelizing work of Christians. (Ro 10:15) The angel Gabriel was an evangelizer in announcing the good news of the coming birth of John the Baptizer to Zechariah and of Jesus to Mary. An angel was an evangelizer to the shepherds at the time of Jesus' birth. (Lu 1:18-38; 2:10) John the Baptizer was an evangelizer, for it is recorded that he "continued declaring good news to the people." (Lu 3:18) All the disciples of Jesus took part in the public ministry of declaring the good news and were therefore evangelizers.—Ac 8:4.

Special Missionary Evangelizers. While all Christians are commissioned to be evangelizers, the word is used in a special way at Ephesians 4:8, 11, 12, where Paul describes "the gifts in men" that Christ gave to the congregation when he ascended on high: "And he gave some as apostles, some as prophets, some as evangelizers, some as shepherds and teachers, . . . for the building up of the body of the Christ." The specific work of such evangelizers was that of missionaries. Often these would open new fields where the good news had not been previously preached. Evangelizers precede shepherds and teachers in the listing at Ephesians 4:11, because after the good news has been preached and disciples have been made, the shepherds and teachers do a further building work from that point.

Philip is one mentioned especially as an evangelizer. He pioneered the work after Pentecost in the city of Samaria with great success. Philip was directed by an angel to preach the good news about Christ to the Ethiopian eunuch, whom he baptized. Then Philip was led away by the spirit to preach in Ashdod and all the cities on the way to Caesarea. (Ac 8:5, 12, 14, 26-40) Paul did much evangelizing. (2Co 10:13-16) Timothy was an evangelizer, or missionary, and Paul laid special emphasis on evangelizing in giving his parting exhortation to Timothy: "You, though, keep your senses in all things, suffer evil, do the work of an evangelizer, fully accomplish your ministry." Timothy, who engaged with other Christians in preaching the good news, was also carrying on shepherding and teaching work as an overseer in Ephesus.—2Ti 4:5; 1Ti 1:3.

Evangelizing in the "Time of the End." The most extensive evangelizing yet undertaken must be carried out in the "time of the end," according to the express statement of Jesus at Matthew 24:14: "This good news of the kingdom will be preached in all the inhabited earth . . . and then the end will come." In the present time the nations have their economic, political, and medical missionaries and the like. But Christians are under command to preach about God's Kingdom and make disciples of Jesus Christ. (2Ti 4:2; 1Co 9:16; 1Pe 1:12, 25; 4:17) The angel flying in midheaven with the everlasting good news makes the proclamation: "Fear God and give him glory, because the hour of the judgment by him has arrived, and so worship the One who made the heaven and the earth and sea and fountains of waters." (Re 14:6, 7) This is the good news that the Christian evangelizer, or missionary, is to carry. Just as the Bible describes some persons such as Philip the evangelizer as missionaries, or evangelizers, in a special sense, some Christians today may do missionary work in a special sense, even going to other countries to preach. (Ac 21:8) Nevertheless, all Christians are commissioned and obligated to be evangelizers wherever they are, in that they preach the good news to all sorts of men.—Ro 10:9, 10.

EVE [Living One; apparently related to the Heb. verb cha·yah', "live"]. The first woman and the last reported of God's earthly creative works.

Jehovah the Creator knew that it was not good for the man to continue by himself. However, before proceeding to create the woman, God brought various beasts of the earth and flying creatures to the man. Adam named these but found no helper among them. It was then that Jehovah had a deep sleep fall upon Adam, removed a rib from his side, and after having closed up the flesh, built the rib that he had taken from the man into a woman. No doubt knowing by direct revelation from God his Creator and Father how the woman came into existence, Adam was pleased to accept her as his wife, saying: "This is at last bone of my bones and flesh of my flesh," even as was apparent to his very senses. As his complement Adam called his wife 'ish·shah' (woman, or, literally, female man), "because from man this one was taken." (Ge 2:18-23) Thereupon God pronounced his fatherly blessing upon both of them: "Be fruitful and become many and fill the earth and subdue it." They were also to have the animal creation in subjection. (Ge 1:28) As a work of God's hands, the woman was perfectly suited for being a complement to her husband Adam and also being a mother.

Deception and Disobedience. Then came a day when the woman, while not in the company of her husband, found herself near the tree of the knowledge of good and bad. There a cautious, lowly serpent, used as a visible mouthpiece by an invisible spirit, in seeming innocence asked: "Is it really so that God said you must not eat from every tree of the garden?" The woman replied correctly, doubtless having been instructed accordingly by her husbandly head, who was one flesh with her. But when the serpent contradicted God and stated that violating God's command would result in being like God, knowing good and bad, the woman began to look upon the tree from a different viewpoint. Why, "the tree was good for food and . . . something to be longed for to the eyes, yes, the tree was desirable to look upon." Moreover, the serpent had said she would be like God if she ate. (Compare 1Jo 2:16.) Completely deceived by the serpent and with a strong desire for the prospects tied up with eating the forbidden fruit, she became a transgressor of God's law. (1Ti 2:14) As such, she now approached her husband and induced him to join her in disobedience to God. Adam listened to his wife's voice. —Ge 3:1-6.

The immediate effect of their transgression was shame. Hence they used fig leaves to make loin coverings for themselves. Both Adam and his wife went into hiding in between the trees of the garden when they heard the voice of Jehovah. Upon being directly questioned by God as to what she had done, the woman stated that she had eaten because of being deceived by the serpent. In pronouncing sentence upon her, Jehovah indicated that pregnancy and the giving of birth to offspring would be attended by increased pain; she would crave for her husband, and he would dominate her.—Ge 3:7-13, 16.

After their violation of God's law, Adam is reported to have named his wife Eve, "because she had to become the mother of everyone living." (Ge 3:20) Before driving Adam and Eve out of the garden of Eden to face the hardships of a cursed ground, Jehovah extended undeserved kindness to them by providing both of them with long garments of skin.—Ge 3:21.

Was Eve correct in saying that she produced her son Cain "with the aid of Jehovah"?

At the birth of her first son Cain, outside Paradise, Eve exclaimed: "I have produced a man with the aid of Jehovah." (Ge 4:1) Eve is the first one reported to have used God's name, indicating that the name Jehovah was known to the very first humans. Later she gave birth to Abel as well as to other sons and daughters. When Adam was 130 years old, Eve gave birth to a son whom she called Seth, saying: "God has appointed another seed in place of Abel, because Cain killed him." She could properly express herself as she did at the births of both Cain and Seth, since God had given her and Adam their reproductive powers, and because of God's unmerited kindness in not putting her to death immediately when she transgressed His command, she had been able to give birth. With the birth of Seth the Genesis record concerning Eve comes to a close.—Ge 4:25; 5:3, 4.

An Actual Personage. That Eve actually lived and was not a fictional character is testified to by Christ Jesus himself. In being questioned by the Pharisees concerning divorce, Jesus directed attention to the Genesis account with reference to the creation of male and female. (Mt 19:3-6) Additionally, there are Paul's words to the Corinthians, expressing fear that their minds might be corrupted somehow, "as the serpent seduced Eve by its cunning." (2Co 11:3) Then, in discussing woman's proper place in the Christian congregation, Paul presents as a reason for not permitting "a woman to teach, or to exercise authority over a man," the fact that Adam was formed first, and he was not deceived, "but the woman was thoroughly deceived and came to be in transgression."—1Ti 2:12-14.

EVI (E'vi). One of the five Midianite kings or chieftains who were put to death at the time Israel's army fought under Moses in executing Jehovah's vengeance upon Midian for seducing Israel to attach itself to the Baal of Peor. These Midianite kings were dukes, allies, or vassals of Sihon king of the Amorites. Their territory was given to the tribe of Reuben.—Nu 25:17, 18; 31:8; Jos 13:15, 21.

EVIL. That which results in pain, sorrow, or distress. In order to convey the correct thought in English, the very comprehensive Hebrew word *ra'* is variously translated as "bad," "gloomy," "ugly," "evil," "calamitous," "malignant," "ungenerous," and "envious," depending upon the context. (Ge 2:9; 40:7; 41:3; Ex 33:4; De 6:22; 28:35; Pr 23:6; 28:22) The Greek word *ka·kos'* may be defined as that which is (1) morally evil and (2) destructive; among the ways it has been translated are: "bad," "evil," "hurtful," "injurious," "wrong." (Ro 7:19; 12:17; Col 3:5; Tit 1:12; Heb 5:14) The Hebrew verb *qa·lal'* means "call down evil upon."—See MALEDICTION.

As first used in the Scriptures, the word *ra'* is the very antithesis of good. Adam was commanded not to eat of the tree of the knowledge of good and bad (*ra'*) and was also warned of the consequences for disobedience. Hence, it is evident that God sets the standard as to what is good and what is bad; it is not within man's prerogative to do so apart from God. Although Adam transgressed God's express law, this transgression is not chargeable to Jehovah, "for with evil things [form of *ka·kos'*] God cannot be tried nor does he himself try anyone. But each one is tried by being drawn out and enticed by his own desire."—Jas 1:13, 14; Ge 2:16, 17; 3:17-19.

The Meaning of Jehovah's Bringing Evil. Rightly, Jehovah brought evil or calamity upon Adam for his disobedience. Hence, in the Scriptures, Jehovah is referred to as the Creator of evil or calamity. (Isa 45:7; compare *KJ*.) His enforcing of the penalty for sin, namely, death, has proved to be an evil, or a calamity, for mankind. So, then, evil is not always synonymous with wrongdoing. Examples of evils or calamities created by Jehovah are the Flood of Noah's day and the Ten Plagues visited upon Egypt. But these evils were not wrongs. Rather, the rightful administration of justice against wrongdoers was involved in both cases. However, at times Jehovah, in his mercy, has refrained from bringing the intended calamity or evil in execution of his righteous judgment because of the repentance on the part of those concerned. (Jon 3:10) Additionally, in having a warning given, Jehovah has undeservedly provided opportunities for the practicers of bad to change their course and thus to keep living.—Eze 33:11.

Avoidance of Evil. Since Jehovah determines the standard of right and wrong, it behooves the individual to acquaint himself with that standard fully in order to be able to discern what course must be followed. (Heb 5:14) The love of money is one of those evil, or injurious, things to be avoided. (1Ti 6:10) It is unwise to be anxious about material things, for, as Jesus said, "sufficient for each day is its own badness [*ka-ki'a*]," that is, the trouble, or affliction, associated with the day. (Mt 6:34) In putting on the new personality, "hurtful desire" is included among the things to be eliminated. (Col 3:5) As the Devil tempted Jesus with evil, so Christians find that evil thoughts crop up or are presented to them. But to avoid being drawn into sin when this happens, the Christian should follow Jesus' example and dismiss such evil immediately. (Jas 1:13-15; Mt 4:1-11; Php 4:8) Although, because of human imperfection, a Christian finds himself in constant conflict with the fallen flesh, as did Paul, and may do the bad that he does not wish to practice, he must not give in to the flesh but must keep up the fight against it. (Ro 7:21; 8:8) The danger of failing to live up to God's righteous requirements is clearly seen in what Jesus stated concerning the evil slave. The severest punishment is to be meted out to that slave for his failure to care for the responsibilities entrusted to him and for going even to the point of beating his fellow slaves.—Mt 24:48-51.

Christian Suffering of Evil. The Scriptures do not authorize the Christian to bring evil upon others, or to retaliate in kind. The Bible's counsel is: "Return evil for evil to no one." "Do not avenge yourselves . . . 'Vengeance is mine; I will repay, says Jehovah.'" "Do not let yourself be conquered by the evil, but keep conquering the evil with the good." (Ro 12:17, 19, 21) Moreover, in giving relative subjection to the governments ruling over them, servants of God should never be found to be practicers of what is bad, for such governments, through their rulers who have a measure of God-given conscience to a lesser or greater degree, act against badness according to the law of the land and rightfully exercise their authority to punish wrongdoers. (Ro 13:3, 4) For any misuse of their authority they will be accountable to the Supreme Judge. By suffering evil for righteousness' sake, the Christian shares in the privilege of having a part in the glorifying of God's holy name.—1Pe 4:16.

EVIL-MERODACH (E'vil-mer'o·dach) [from Babylonian, meaning "Worshiper of Marduk"]. The Babylonian king who succeeded Nebuchadnezzar to the throne in 581 B.C.E. In the year of his becoming king, Evil-merodach extended kindness to Jehoiachin the king of Judah by releasing him from the house of detention. That was in the 37th year of Jehoiachin's exile in Babylon. Evil-merodach granted him a position of favor above all the other kings who were in captivity in Babylon. (2Ki 25:27-30; Jer 52:31-34) Josephus claims that Evil-merodach viewed Jehoiachin as one of his most intimate friends.

There is also archaeological testimony concerning Evil-merodach (Awil-Marduk, Amil-Marduk). For example, an inscription on a vase found near Susa reads: "Palace of Amil-Marduk, King of Babylon, son of Nebuchadnezzar, King of Babylon." (*Mémoires de la mission archéologique de Susiane,* by V. Scheil, Paris, 1913, Vol. XIV) Berossus, quoted by Josephus, attributes to him a reign of two years. Josephus himself assigns him 18 years. Supposedly slain as the result of a plot, Evil-merodach was replaced by Neriglissar (Nergal-sharezer). Reliable confirmation of these details is lacking.

EXCLUSIVE DEVOTION. This expression has reference to the fact that Jehovah does not tolerate any rivalry, the worship of any other gods. The Hebrew word *qan·na'* is used only of God; it means "exacting exclusive devotion; jealous."—Ex 20:5, ftn; see JEALOUS, JEALOUSY.

God will not transfer to another the honor due himself. (Isa 42:8) To depart from exclusive devotion to him would incur the heat of His zealous anger. (De 4:24; 5:9; 6:15) Israel was regarded as being married to Jehovah. As a husband, Jehovah claimed exclusive devotion, loyalty, fidelity from Israel. He would be zealous, full of ardor in her behalf, in her defense. (Eze 36:5) Conversely, disobedience, going after other gods, would be adultery, thereby meriting Jehovah's righteous anger and his jealousy for his own name.—De 32:16, 21; Eze 16:38, 42.

What is the exclusive devotion that Jehovah requires from his servants?

The word "exclusive" is from the Latin *exclusus,* meaning "altogether shut out." Devotion means strong attachment and ardent love. Exclusive devotion, therefore, means keeping others out of, or excluded from, God's position in our hearts and actions. Everyone and everything else stays outside this honored position that only he can hold.

Jehovah God Tolerates No Rivalry. Exclusive devotion is demanded by Jehovah in the second of the "Ten Words" or Ten Commandments written by the finger of God: "I am Jehovah your God . . . You must never have any other gods against my face [or, "any other gods in defiance of me"]. . . . because I Jehovah your God am a God exacting exclusive devotion." (De 5:6-9) At Exodus 34:14 the French *Drioux Version* (1884) says: "God wants to be loved uniquely," that is, in a class by himself, singularly. Jesus supported this view when he spoke to a Jew who tried to test him. (Mt 22:37) Jehovah was both God and King of Israel, Head of religion and of State. Therefore, for an Israelite to break the first and second commandments by serving other gods meant that he was committing lèse-majesté, or treason, the highest of crimes, meriting the heaviest punishment. On one occasion Israel was engaging in the worship of a false god as well as practicing immorality and, because of Jehovah's full insistence on exclusive devotion, was about to be exterminated. But because Phinehas, Aaron's grandson, took swift action in "tolerating no rivalry" toward Jehovah, Israel was saved.—Nu 25:11.

Jehovah's purpose in restoring his people after the Babylonian exile was for his name's sake. (Eze 39:25-28) At Exodus 34:14, Fenton's translation reads: "The EVER-LIVING is jealous of HIS NAME." Since he is jealous of his name or exclusively devoted to it, he did not tolerate any rivalry by the name of any other god among his people.

Master and Slave Relationship. Exclusive devotion also suggests the relation between master and slave. Jehovah as Creator is Owner and Master. He is God by reason of his creatorship; it is his right to receive exclusive devotion from his created subjects, and they must do his will. The right-minded person, on learning about Jehovah and appreciating his relationship with God, will voluntarily render exclusive devotion from the heart, which is what Jehovah desires. Mere formal devotion or worship he hates. (Mt 15:8, 9) This relationship and the freewill devotion that Jehovah desires were illustrated in the Mosaic Law. A Hebrew slave was let go free in his seventh year of servitude. "But if the slave should insistently say, 'I really love my master, my wife and my sons; I do not want to go out as one set free,' then his master must bring him near to the true God and must bring him up against the door or the doorpost; and his master must pierce his ear through with an awl, and he must be his slave to time indefinite." (Ex 21:2, 5, 6) Paul spoke to non-Jews in the Thessalonian congregation about the voluntary shift of devotion made when they became Christians. They ceased being slaves to idols and began "to slave for a living and true God."—1Th 1:9.

Jesus' Exclusive Devotion to God. As shown in Philippians 2:5-8, both when he was in heaven and when he was on earth, Jesus appreciated the exclusive position of his Father and rendered him exclusive devotion. Jesus pointed out that the most important commandment in the Law demanded wholehearted love of God. (Mt 22:37) Moreover, Jesus manifested exclusive devotion to Jehovah's name and emphasized the fact that his disciples should have the same attitude. In the prayer he taught his disciples, he started off with the words, "Our Father in the heavens, let your name be sanctified." (Mt 6:9) This devotion in Jesus was coupled with burning zeal, as manifested at his cleansing of the temple, where he fulfilled the prophecy, "The zeal for your house will eat me up." (Joh 2:17; Ps 69:9) Nowhere is Jesus' exclusive devotion to his Father exemplified more than in what is written of him at 1 Corinthians 15:24-28, where it says that, after his heavenly Kingdom rule puts down all other authority and all enemies, he turns over the Kingdom to the Father and subjects himself to Him so that "God may be all things to everyone."

EXECRATION. A severe or even violent denunciation of that which is viewed as detestable and worthy of cursing. The Hebrew verb (*qa·vav'*, execrate) appears in the account of King Balak's futile efforts to get the prophet Balaam to execrate the nation of Israel and thus present that nation before God as worthy of his curse. (Nu 22:11, 17; 23:11, 13, 25, 27; 24:10) An imprecation, that is, an invocation of evil from a divine source, is not always stated but may be implied. —See CURSE; MALEDICTION.

EXECUTION, EXECUTIONER. For laws, commandments, and commissions to have vitality and worth, they must be legally enforced. Execution usually has to do with enforcing the penalties, especially the death penalty, imposed for violation of laws. Supreme Law not only has a Lawgiver, it also has a Law Enforcer: "Jehovah is our Judge, Jehovah is our Statute-giver, Jehovah is our King." "One there is that is lawgiver and judge." (Isa 33:22; Jas 4:12) So Jehovah himself is an executioner of judgment and vengeance upon violators of His law.—Ex 12:12; De 10:17, 18; Eze 25:11-17; 2Th 1:6-9; Jude 14, 15.

Jehovah also delegated certain power of execution to others. For example: "Your blood of your souls shall I ask back. . . . From the hand of each one who is his brother, shall I ask back the soul of man. Anyone shedding man's blood, by man will his own blood be shed, for in God's image he made man." (Ge 9:5, 6) In this regard certain responsibilities as executioner fell upon "the avenger of blood." (Nu 35:19; see AVENGER OF BLOOD.) Depending upon the circumstances, the authority as executioner was sometimes invested in the priests of Israel (Nu 5:15-31) or in the entire congregation, with the eyewitnesses taking the lead in executing an offender. (Le 24:14-16; De 17:2-7) The power of execution was also in the hands of the judges and kings or someone whom they appointed.—Jg 8:20, 21; 2Sa 1:15; 1Ch 14:16; 2Ki 9:6-9; 10:24-28; Jer 21:12; 22:3.

Ancient rulers were surrounded by trusted bodyguards to whom execution of their master's edicts could be entrusted. Potiphar was one who held this position. (Ge 37:36; 41:12) It was one of Herod's body guardsmen who beheaded John the Baptizer.—Mr 6:27.

Execution of the death penalty in Israel was either by stoning or by the sword. (Le 20:2; 2Sa 1:15) Jehovah's Messianic King, the Lord Jesus Christ, and other loyal heavenly associates of his are legal executioners, authorized as such by "the Judge of all the earth."—Ge 18:25; Ps 149:6-9; Re 12:7-9; 19:11-16; 20:1-3.

EXILE. Expulsion from one's own native land or home by authoritative decree; literally in Hebrew, "a departing." Cain, who killed his brother Abel, was cursed in banishment from the ground to become a wanderer and a fugitive in the earth. He had been a farmer, but the ground thereafter would not respond to his cultivation.—Ge 4:2, 3, 11-14.

Israel was told that Jehovah would lead the nation away into exile if they became unfaithful to the covenant he made with them through Moses. (De 28:36, 37, 64; 29:28) So God was really the Authority who decreed the exile of his people in several instances, although he allowed the armies of other nations to be his instruments.

These occasions are: (1) Israel's exile by the hand of the Assyrians (2Ki 15:29; 18:9-12); (2) Judah's exile in Babylon (2Ki 25:8-11, 21); (3) the Jewish exile at the hands of the Romans (Lu 21:20-24).

Israel. Tiglath-pileser III took inhabitants of Naphtali into exile in Assyria before Israelite King Pekah's rule ended in about 758 B.C.E. Reubenites, Gadites, and those from the eastern half tribe of Manasseh were also carried off by the king of Assyria, apparently at the same time. (1Ch 5:4-6, 26) Shalmaneser V later besieged Samaria, and after three years, in 740 B.C.E., either he or his successor, Sargon II, deported great numbers of the inhabitants and "brought people from Babylon and Cuthah and Avva and Hamath and Sepharvaim and had them dwell in the cities of Samaria instead of the sons of Israel." —2Ki 17:5, 6, 24.

Judah. In 617 B.C.E., King Nebuchadnezzar took the royal court and the foremost men of Judah into exile at Babylon. (2Ki 24:11-16) About ten years later, in 607 B.C.E., at the fall of Jerusalem to Babylon, Nebuzaradan, the chief of the Babylonian bodyguard, took most of the remaining ones and deserters of the Jews with him to Babylon, from which exile only a mere remnant returned 70 years later.—2Ki 25:11; Jer 39:9; Isa 10:21, 22; see CAPTIVITY.

After the fall of Babylon many Jews did not return to their homeland, and the dispersion therefore continued. In the time of Ahasuerus (Xerxes I, king of Persia, who ruled from India to Ethiopia, over 127 jurisdictional districts), Haman, in making an indictment of them, said: "There is one certain people scattered and separated among the peoples in all the jurisdictional districts of your realm."—Es 1:1; 3:8.

In the First Century C.E. In the first century C.E. there were settlements of Jews in Thessalonica, Athens, Corinth, Ephesus, Rome, and Babylon, as well as in other cities. (Ac 17:1, 16, 17; 18:1, 4, 19) Many Jews lived in Babylon, where Peter preached. (1Pe 5:13) Josephus records that "a great number" of Jews were in Babylonia in the first century B.C.E. (*Jewish Antiquities*, XV, 14 [ii, 2]) In 49 or early 50 C.E. the Roman emperor Claudius banished all the Jews from Rome. This also affected Jews who had become Christians, among them Aquila and Priscilla (Prisca), whom Paul met in Corinth about 50 C.E., shortly after the edict by Claudius. (Ac 18:2) They accompanied Paul to Ephesus, and at the time he wrote from Corinth to fellow Christians in Rome (c. 56 C.E.), they were evidently back in Rome, for Claudius had died and Nero was then ruling. Many of the other Jews had also moved back to Rome.—Ac 18:18, 19; Ro 16:3, 7, 11.

In fulfillment of Jesus' prophecy at Luke 21:24, the Roman army under Titus, in 70 C.E., surrounded Jerusalem, which was then crowded with Jews from many lands assembled for the Festival of Unfermented Cakes. The Romans besieged and finally destroyed the city; 1,100,000 Jews perished and 97,000 were taken captive, to be scattered among the nations.

EXODUS. The deliverance of the nation of Israel from bondage to Egypt. Jehovah spoke to Abraham (before 1933 B.C.E.), after promising that Abraham's seed would inherit the land, and said: "You may know for sure that your seed will become an alien resident in a land not theirs, and they will have to serve them, and these will certainly afflict them for four hundred years. But the nation that they will serve I am judging, and after that they will go out with many goods. . . . But in the fourth generation they will return here, because the error of the Amorites has not yet come to completion."—Ge 15:13-16.

It is clear that the beginning of the 400-year period of affliction had to await the appearance of the promised "seed." While Abraham had earlier visited Egypt during a time of famine in Canaan and had experienced some difficulties with the Pharaoh there, he was then childless. (Ge 12:10-20) Not long after God's statement about the 400 years of affliction, when Abraham was 86 years old (in the year 1932 B.C.E.), his Egyptian slave girl and concubine bore him a son, Ishmael. But it was 14 years later (1918 B.C.E.) that Abraham's free wife Sarah bore him a son, Isaac, and God designated this son as the one by means of whom the promised Seed would result. Still, God's time had not yet arrived for giving Abraham or his seed the land of Canaan, and so they were, as foretold, 'alien residents in a land not theirs.'—Ge 16:15, 16; 21:2-5; Heb 11:13.

Time of the Exodus. When, therefore, did the 400 years of affliction begin, and when did it end? Jewish tradition reckons the count from Isaac's birth. But the actual evidence of *affliction* first came on the day that Isaac was weaned. Evidence points to 1913 B.C.E., when Isaac was about 5 years old and Ishmael about 19, as the date of the start of affliction. It was then that Ishmael "the one born in the manner of flesh began persecuting the one born in the manner of spirit." (Ga 4:29) Ishmael, who was part Egyp-

tian, in jealousy and hatred, began "poking fun" at Isaac, the young child, this amounting to much more than a mere children's quarrel. (Ge 21:9) Other translations describe Ishmael's action as "mocking." (*Yg; Ro,* ftn) The affliction of Abraham's seed continued on during Isaac's life. While Jehovah blessed Isaac as a grown man, he was nevertheless persecuted by the inhabitants of Canaan and forced to move from place to place because of the difficulties they brought against him. (Ge 26:19-24, 27) Eventually, during the later years of the life of Isaac's son Jacob, the foretold "seed" came into Egypt to reside. In time they came into a state of slavery.

By what internal evidence does the Bible fix the date of Israel's Exodus from Egypt?

The 400-year period of affliction thus ran from 1913 B.C.E. until 1513 B.C.E. It was also a period of grace, or of divine toleration, allowed the Canaanites, a principal tribe of whom were Amorites. By this latter date their error would come to completion; they would clearly merit complete ejection from the land. As the preliminary step toward such ejection, God would turn his attention to his people in Egypt, setting them free from bondage and starting them on the way back to the Promised Land.—Ge 15:13-16.

The 430-year period. Another line of calculation is provided in the statement at Exodus 12:40, 41: "And the dwelling of the sons of Israel, who had dwelt in Egypt, was four hundred and thirty years. And it came about at the end of the four hundred and thirty years, it even came about on this very day that all the armies of Jehovah went out of the land of Egypt." The footnote on Exodus 12:40 says regarding the expression "who had dwelt": "In Heb[rew] this verb is pl[ural]. The relative pronoun *'asher'*, 'who,' can apply to the 'sons of Israel' rather than to the 'dwelling.'" The Greek *Septuagint* renders verse 40: "But the dwelling of the sons of Israel which they dwelt in the land of Egypt and in the land of Canaan [was] four hundred and thirty years long." The Samaritan *Pentateuch* reads: ". . . in the land of Canaan and in the land of Egypt." All these renderings indicate that the 430-year period covers a longer period of time than the dwelling of the Israelites in Egypt.

The apostle Paul shows that this 430-year period (at Ex 12:40) began at the time of the validation of the Abrahamic covenant and ended with the Exodus. Paul says: "Further, I say this: As to the [Abrahamic] covenant previously validated by God, the Law that has come into being four hundred and thirty years later [in the same year as the Exodus] does not invalidate it, so as to abolish the promise. . . . whereas God has kindly given it to Abraham through a promise."—Ga 3:16-18.

How long was it, then, from the validation of the Abrahamic covenant until the Israelites moved into Egypt? At Genesis 12:4, 5 we find that Abraham was 75 years old when he left Haran and crossed the Euphrates on his way to Canaan, at which time the Abrahamic covenant, the promise previously made to him in Ur of the Chaldeans, took effect. Then, from the genealogical references at Genesis 12:4; 21:5; 25:26; and Jacob's statement at Genesis 47:9, it can be seen that 215 years elapsed between the validation of the Abrahamic covenant and the move of Jacob with his family into Egypt. This would show that the Israelites actually lived in Egypt 215 years (1728-1513 B.C.E.). The figure harmonizes with other chronological data.

From Exodus to temple building. Two other chronological statements harmonize with and substantiate this viewpoint. Solomon began the building of the temple in his fourth year of kingship (1034 B.C.E.), and this is stated at 1 Kings 6:1 to be "the four hundred and eightieth year" from the time of the Exodus (1513 B.C.E.).

'About 450 years.' Then there is Paul's speech to an audience in Antioch of Pisidia recorded at Acts 13:17-20 in which he refers to a period of "about four hundred and fifty years." His discussion of Israelite history begins with the time God "chose our forefathers," that is, from the time that Isaac was actually born to be the seed of promise (1918 B.C.E.). (Isaac's birth definitely settled the question, which had been in doubt because of Sarah's barrenness, as to whom God would recognize as the seed.) From this starting point Paul then goes on to recount God's acts in behalf of his chosen nation down to the time when God "gave them judges until Samuel the prophet." The period of "about four hundred and fifty years," therefore, evidently extends from Isaac's birth in 1918 B.C.E. down to the year 1467 B.C.E., or 46 years after the Exodus of 1513 B.C.E. (40 years being spent in the wilderness wandering and 6 years in conquering the land of Canaan). (De 2:7; Nu 9:1; 13:1, 2, 6; Jos 14:6, 7, 10) This makes a total number that clearly fits the apostle's round figure of "about

four hundred and fifty years." Both these chronological references therefore support the year 1513 B.C.E. as the year of the Exodus and harmonize as well with the Bible chronology concerning the kings and judges of Israel.—See Chronology (From 1943 B.C.E. to the Exodus).

Other views. This date for the Exodus, 1513 B.C.E., and consequently the Israelite invasion of Canaan and the fall of Jericho in 1473 B.C.E., 40 years after the Exodus, has been considered far too early by some critics, who would place these events as late as the 14th or even the 13th century B.C.E. However, while some archaeologists place the fall of Jericho down in the 13th century B.C.E., they do so, not on the basis of any ancient historical documents or testimony to that effect, but on the basis of pottery finds. Such calculation of time periods by pottery is obviously very speculative, and this is demonstrated by the research at Jericho. The findings there have produced contradictory conclusions and datings on the part of the archaeologists.—See Archaeology (Differences in dating); Chronology (Archaeological Dating).

Similarly with the Egyptologists, the differences among them in dating the dynasties of Egypt have amounted to centuries, making their dates unusable for any specific period. For this reason it is impossible to name with confidence the particular Pharaoh of the Exodus, some saying it was Thutmose III, others Amenhotep II, Ramses II, and so forth, but on very shaky foundations in each case.

Authenticity of the Exodus Account. An objection against the Exodus account has been that the Pharaohs of Egypt did not make any record of the Exodus. However, this is not unusual, for kings of more modern times have recorded only their victories and not their defeats and have often tried to erase anything historical that is contrary to their personal or nationalistic image or to the ideology they are trying to inculcate in their people. Even in recent times rulers have tried to obliterate the works and reputations of their predecessors. Anything regarded as embarrassing or distasteful was left out of Egyptian inscriptions or effaced as soon as possible. An example is the chiseling away by her successor, Thutmose III, of the name and representation of Queen Hatshepsut on a stone monumental record uncovered at Deir al-Bahri in Egypt.—See *Archaeology and Bible History,* by J. P. Free, 1964, p. 98 and photograph opposite p. 94.

Manetho, an Egyptian priest who evidently hated the Jews, wrote in the Greek language about 280 B.C.E. The Jewish historian Josephus quotes Manetho as saying that the ancestors of the Jews "entered Egypt in their myriads and subdued the inhabitants," and then Josephus says that Manetho "goes on to admit that they were afterwards driven out of the country, occupied what is now Judaea, founded Jerusalem, and built the temple."—*Against Apion,* I, 228 (26).

While Manetho's account is in general very unhistorical, the significant fact is that he mentions the Jews as being in Egypt and as going out, and in further writings, according to Josephus, he identifies Moses with Osarsiph, an Egyptian priest, indicating that, even though Egyptian monuments do not record the fact, the Jews *were* in Egypt and *Moses* was their leader. Josephus speaks of another Egyptian historian, Chaeremon, who says that Joseph and Moses were driven out of Egypt at the same time; also Josephus mentions a Lysimachus who tells a similar story.—*Against Apion,* I, 228, 238 (26); 288, 290 (32); 299 (33); 304-311 (34).

The Number Involved in the Exodus. At Exodus 12:37, the round number of 600,000 "able-bodied men on foot" besides "little ones" is given. In the actual census taken about a year after the Exodus, as recorded at Numbers 1:2, 3, 45, 46, they numbered 603,550 males from 20 years old upward besides the Levites (Nu 2:32, 33), of whom there were 22,000 males from a month old upward. (Nu 3:39) The Hebrew term *geva·rim'* (able-bodied men) does not include women. (Compare Jer 30:6.) "Little ones" is from the Hebrew *taph* and refers to one walking with tripping steps. (Compare Isa 3:16.) Most of these "little ones" would have had to be carried or at least could not have marched the full length of the journey.

"In the fourth generation." We must remember that Jehovah told Abraham that in the fourth generation his descendants would return to Canaan. (Ge 15:16) In the entire 430 years from the time when the Abrahamic covenant took effect to the Exodus there were more than four generations, even considering the long life spans that they enjoyed during that time, according to the record. But it was only 215 years that the Israelites were *actually in Egypt.* The 'four generations' following their entering Egypt can be calculated in this way, using as an example just one tribe of Israel, the tribe of Levi:

(1) Levi, (2) Kohath, (3) Amram, and (4) Moses. —Ex 6:16, 18, 20.

The number coming up out of Egypt, namely, 600,000 able-bodied men besides women and children, would mean that there could have been more than three million persons. This, though disputed by some, is not at all unreasonable. For, while there were only four generations from Levi to Eleazar or from Levi to Moses, when viewed from the standpoint of the life span of these long-lived men, each of these men could have seen several generations or several sets of children born during his lifetime. Even at the present time a man 60 or 70 years old often has grandchildren and may even have great-grandchildren (thus four generations living contemporaneously).

Extraordinary increase. The account reports: "And the sons of Israel became fruitful and began to swarm; and they kept on multiplying and growing mightier at a very extraordinary rate, so that the land got to be filled with them." (Ex 1:7) In fact, they became so many that the king of Egypt said: "Look! The people of the sons of Israel are more numerous and mightier than we are." "But the more they would oppress them, the more they would multiply and the more they kept spreading abroad, so that they felt a sickening dread as a result of the sons of Israel." (Ex 1:9, 12) Also, when we realize that polygamy, with concubinage, was practiced and that some Israelites married Egyptian women, it becomes evident how the increase to the point of having an adult male population of 600,000 could have occurred.

Seventy souls of Jacob's immediate household went down into Egypt or were born there shortly thereafter. (Ge 46) If we exclude Jacob himself, his 12 sons, his daughter Dinah, his granddaughter Serah, the three sons of Levi, and possibly others from the number of family heads who began to multiply in Egypt, we might be left with only 50 of the 70. (Levi's sons are excluded inasmuch as the Levites were not numbered among the later 603,550 figure.) Starting, then, with the very conservative figure of 50 family heads and taking into consideration the Bible's statement that "the sons of Israel became fruitful and began to swarm; and they kept on multiplying and growing mightier *at a very extraordinary rate,* so that the land got to be filled with them" (Ex 1:7), we can easily demonstrate how 600,000 men of military age, between 20 and 50 years old, could be living at the time of the Exodus. Consider the following:

In view of the large families then and the desire of the Israelites to have children to fulfill God's promise, it is not unreasonable in our calculation to count each male family head as bringing forth ten children (about half being boys), on the average, during the period of life between 20 and 40 years of age. For conservativeness, we might view each of the original 50 who became family heads as not beginning to father children until 25 years after their entry into Egypt. And, since death or other circumstances could prevent some male children from ever becoming productive children, or could interrupt their child-producing before their reaching the limit of 40 years we have set, we might also reduce by 20 percent the number of males born who became fathers. Put simply, this means that in a 20-year period only 200 sons, instead of 250, born to the 50 original family heads we have designated would produce families of their own.

Pharaoh's decree. Still another factor might be considered: Pharaoh's decree to destroy all the male children at birth. This decree seems to have been rather ineffective and of short duration. Aaron was born some three years before Moses (or in 1597 B.C.E.), and apparently no such decree was then in force. The Bible definitely states that Pharaoh's decree was not very successful. The Hebrew women Shiphrah and Puah, who likely were the heads of the midwife profession, over the other midwives, did not carry out the king's order. They apparently did not instruct the midwives under them as ordered. The result was: "The people kept growing more numerous and becoming very mighty." Pharaoh then commanded all his people to throw every newborn Israelite son into the river Nile. (Ex 1:15-22) But it does not seem that the Egyptian populace hated the Hebrews to this extent. Even Pharaoh's own daughter rescued Moses. Again, Pharaoh may have soon come to the conclusion that he would lose valuable slaves if his decree continued in effect. We know that, later on, the Pharaoh of the Exodus refused to let the Hebrews go for the very reason that he valued them as slave laborers.

However, to make our figure yet more conservative we may reduce by nearly one third the number of boys surviving during a five-year period to represent the possible effects of Pharaoh's unsuccessful edict.

A calculation. Even making all these allowances, the population would still increase in an accelerated manner, and that with God's bless-

ing. The number of children born during each five-year period from and after 1563 B.C.E. (that is, 50 years before the Exodus) up to 1533 (or 20 years before the Exodus) would be as follows:

INCREASE OF MALE POPULATION	
B.C.E.	**Sons Born**
from 1563 to 1558	47,350
from 1558 to 1553	62,300
from 1553 to 1548	81,800
from 1548 to 1543	103,750
from 1543 to 1538	133,200
from 1538 to 1533	172,250
Total	600,650*

*Theoretical male population from the age of 20 to 50 years at time of Exodus (1513 B.C.E.)

It may be noted that even a slight adjustment in the method of computation, for example, increasing by one the number of sons born on the average to each male parent, would send this figure up to over a million.

How significant was the number of people that left Egypt under Moses?

Besides the 600,000 able-bodied men mentioned in the Bible, there were a great number of older men, an even greater number of women and children, and "a vast mixed company" of non-Israelites. (Ex 12:38) So the total population was possibly over three million persons going up out of Egypt. It is not surprising that the Egyptian royalty hated to let such a large slave body go. They thereby lost a valuable economic asset.

That there was a fearful number of fighting men the Bible record attests: "Moab became very frightened at the people, because they were many; and Moab began to feel a sickening dread of the sons of Israel." (Nu 22:3) The fear on the part of the Moabites was, of course, based partly on the fact that Jehovah had worked such wonders for Israel but was also because of their great number, which could not be said of a mere few thousand people. The population figures of the Israelites actually changed very little during the wilderness journey because so many died in the wilderness as a result of unfaithfulness.—Nu 26: 2-4, 51.

In the census shortly after the Exodus the Levites were counted separately, and those from a month old upward numbered 22,000. (Nu 3:39) The question may arise as to why among all the other 12 tribes there were only 22,273 *firstborn* males from a month old upward. (Nu 3:43) This can easily be understood when the fact is appreciated that family heads were not counted, that because of polygamy a man might have many sons but only one firstborn, and that it was the firstborn son of the man and not of the woman that was counted.

Issues Involved. According to God's promise to Abraham, His due time had arrived for Him to deliver the nation of Israel from "the iron furnace" of Egypt. Jehovah considered Israel as his firstborn son by virtue of the promise to Abraham. When Jacob went down to Egypt with his household, he went down voluntarily but his descendants later became slaves. As a nation, they were dear to Jehovah as a firstborn son, and Jehovah had the legal right to deliver them from Egypt without the payment of a price.—De 4:20; 14:1, 2; Ex 4:22; 19:5, 6.

Opposing Jehovah's purpose, Pharaoh did not want to lose the great nation of slave workers. Moreover, when approached by Moses with the request in Jehovah's name to send the Israelites away that they might celebrate a festival to Him in the wilderness, Pharaoh answered: "Who is Jehovah, so that I should obey his voice to send Israel away? I do not know Jehovah at all." (Ex 5:2) Pharaoh considered himself to be a god and did not *recognize* Jehovah's authority, although he had undoubtedly heard the Hebrews use the name many times before. From the beginning Jehovah's people had known his name; Abraham had even addressed God as Jehovah.—Ge 2:4; 15:2.

The issue here raised by Pharaoh's attitude and actions brought up the question of Godship. It was now necessary for Jehovah God to exalt himself above the gods of Egypt, including Pharaoh, who was revered as a god. He did this by bringing Ten Plagues upon Egypt, which resulted in Israel's release. (See GODS and GODDESSES [The Ten Plagues].) At the time of the last plague, the death of the firstborn, the Israelites were commanded to be prepared at the Passover meal to march out of Egypt. Although they went out in haste, being urged on by the Egyptians, who said, "We are all as good as dead!" they did not go out empty-handed. (Ex 12:33) They took their herds and flocks, their flour dough before it was fermented, and their kneading troughs. Besides this, the Egyptians granted to Israel what they asked for, giving them articles of silver and articles of gold and garments. Incidentally, this was not robbing the Egyptians. They had no right to enslave Israel, so they owed the people wages. —Ex 12:34-38.

Along with Israel went out "a vast mixed company." (Ex 12:38) These were all worshipers of Jehovah, for they had to be prepared to leave with Israel while the Egyptians were burying their dead. They had observed the Passover, otherwise they would have been busy with Egypt's mourning and burial rites. To a certain extent this company may have been made up of those who were in some way related by marriage to the Israelites. For example, many Israelite men married Egyptian women, and Israelite women married Egyptian men. A case in point is the person who was put to death in the wilderness for abusing Jehovah's name. He was the son of an Egyptian man and his mother was Shelomith of the tribe of Dan. (Le 24:10, 11) It may also be noted that Jehovah gave permanent instructions concerning the requirements for alien residents and slaves to eat the Passover when Israel would come into the Promised Land.—Ex 12:25, 43-49.

Route of the Exodus. The Israelites must have been in various locations when they started the march out of Egypt, not all initially in one compact body. Some may have merged with the main body of marchers as they went along. Rameses, either the city or a district of that name, was the starting point, the first lap of the journey being to Succoth. (Ex 12:37) Some scholars suggest that, while Moses began the march from Rameses, the Israelites came from all over the land of Goshen and met at Succoth as a rendezvous.—MAP, Vol. 1, p. 536.

The Israelites had left Egypt in haste, urged on by the Egyptians; nevertheless, they were by no means unorganized: "But it was in battle formation that the sons of Israel went up out of the land of Egypt," that is, possibly like an army in five parts, with vanguard, rear guard, main body, and two wings. Besides the able leadership of Moses, Jehovah made manifest his own leadership, at least as early as the encampment at Etham, by providing a pillar of cloud to lead them in the daytime, which became a pillar of fire to give them light at night.—Ex 13:18-22.

By the shortest route it would have been a land journey of about 400 km (250 mi) from the vicinity N of Memphis on up to, say, Lachish in the Promised Land. But that route would have taken the Israelites along the Mediterranean seacoast and along by the land of the Philistines. In former times their forefathers Abraham and Isaac had had difficulties with the Philistines. God, knowing that they might be disheartened by a Philistine attack, inasmuch as they were unacquainted with warfare and also because they had their families and flocks with them, commanded that Israel turn about and encamp before Pihahiroth between Migdol and the sea in view of Baal-zephon. Here they encamped by the sea.—Ex 14:1, 2.

The exact route followed by the Israelites from Rameses to the Red Sea cannot be traced with certainty today, since the sites mentioned in the account cannot be definitely located. Most reference works prefer to show them as crossing through what is known as the Wadi Tumilat in the Delta region of Egypt. This route, however, is predicated principally on the identification of Rameses with a site in the NE corner of the Delta region. But as Professor of Egyptology John A. Wilson states: "Unfortunately, scholars do not agree upon the precise location of Rameses. The Pharaohs named Ramses, particularly Ramses II, were generous in naming towns after themselves. Further, references to this city have been excavated in Delta towns which can make no serious claim to being the location."—*The Interpreter's Dictionary of the Bible,* edited by G. Buttrick, 1962, Vol. 4, p. 9.

Various places have been suggested, have held popularity for a time, and then have been rejected in favor of another possibility. The site of Tanis (modern San el-Hagar) a few kilometers S of the Mediterranean coastal city of Port Said is popular, but so also is Qantir, about 24 km (15 mi) farther S. As to the first site, Tanis, it may be noted that one Egyptian text lists Tanis and (Per-)Rameses as separate places, not the same, and that at least part of the material unearthed at Tanis gives evidence of having come from other places. Thus, John A. Wilson further states that "there is no guarantee that inscriptions bearing the name Rameses were originally at home there." Regarding both Tanis and Qantir, it may be said that the inscriptions relating to Ramses II found in these places would only show an association with that Pharaoh, but do not prove that either site is the Biblical Raamses built by the Israelites as a storage place prior even to Moses' birth. (Ex 1:11) As is shown in the article RAAMSES, RAMESES, the view that Ramses II is the Pharaoh of the Exodus has little evidence in its favor.

The route through the Wadi Tumilat has also been favored because of the popular modern theory that the crossing of the Red Sea did not actually take place at the Red Sea but at a site to the N thereof. Some scholars even advocated a crossing at or near Lake Serbonis along the Mediterranean shore, so that after exiting from the Wadi Tumilat the Israelites turned N in the direction of the coast. This view directly contradicts the specific statement in the Bible that God himself led the Israelites away from the route that would go to the land of the Philistines. (Ex 13:17, 18) Others also favor a route through the Wadi Tumilat but argue for a "sea" crossing in the Bitter Lakes region N of Suez.

Red Sea, not 'sea of reeds.' This latter view is based on the argument that the Hebrew *yam-suph'* (translated "Red Sea") literally means "sea of rushes, or, reeds, bulrushes," and that therefore the Israelites crossed, not the arm of the Red Sea known as the Gulf of Suez, but a sea of reeds, a swampy place such as the Bitter Lakes region. In so holding, however, they do not agree with the translators of the ancient Greek *Septuagint,* who translated *yam-suph'* with the Greek name *e·ry·thra' tha'las·sa,* meaning, literally, *"Red* Sea." But, far more important, both Luke, who was the writer of Acts (quoting Stephen), and the apostle Paul used this same Greek name when relating the events of the Exodus.—Ac 7:36; Heb 11:29; see RED SEA.

Furthermore, there would have been no great miracle if a mere marsh had been crossed, and the Egyptians could not have been "swallowed up" in the Red Sea as "the surging waters proceeded to cover them" so that they went down "into the depths like a stone." (Heb 11:29; Ex 15:5) Not only was this stupendous miracle referred to later on by Moses and Joshua but the apostle Paul said that the Israelites got baptized into Moses by means of the cloud and the sea. That indicated that they were completely surrounded by water, the sea being on both sides and the cloud above and behind them. (1Co 10:1, 2) This would indicate, too, that the body of water was much deeper than anything that could be waded in.

The route of the Exodus depends largely on two factors: where the Egyptian capital was at the time, and the identification of the body of water where the crossing occurred. Since the inspired Christian Greek Scriptures use the expression "Red Sea," there is every reason to believe that it was that body of water that Israel crossed. As for the Egyptian capital, the most likely site is Memphis, the principal seat of government during most of Egypt's history. (See MEMPHIS.) If this was the case, then the starting point of the Exodus march must have been sufficiently near Memphis for Moses to have been called before Pharaoh after midnight on Passover night and then to have reached Rameses in time to begin the march toward Succoth before the 14th day of Nisan ended. (Ex 12:29-31, 37, 41, 42) The oldest Jewish tradition, recorded by Josephus, is to the effect that the march began a short distance N of Memphis.—*Jewish Antiquities*, II, 315 (xv, 1).

A route through the Wadi Tumilat would be so far to the N of Memphis as to make the above circumstances impracticable. For this reason, many earlier commentators have suggested one of the well-known "pilgrim" routes through Egypt, such as the el Haj route leading from Cairo across to Clysma at the head of the Gulf of Suez.

Where was the Red Sea parted to allow Israel to cross over?

It should be noted that, after reaching the second stage of their journey, Etham "at the edge of the wilderness," God ordered Moses to "turn back and encamp before Pihahiroth . . . by the sea." This maneuver would cause Pharaoh to believe the Israelites were "wandering in confusion." (Ex 13:20; 14:1-3) Scholars favoring the el Haj route as the likely one point out that the Hebrew verb for "turn back" is emphatic and does not mean merely to "divert" or "turn aside," but has more the sense of returning or at least of a marked detour. They suggest that, upon reaching a point N of the head of the Gulf of Suez, the Israelites reversed their line of march and went around to the E side of Jebel 'Ataqah, a mountain range bordering the W side of the Gulf. A large host, such as the Israelites were, would find no effective way for swift exit from such a position if pursued from the N, and hence they would be bottled up with the sea blocking their way.

Jewish tradition of the first century C.E. conveys such a picture. (See PIHAHIROTH.) But, more importantly, such a situation fits the general picture portrayed in the Bible itself, whereas the popular views of many scholars do not. (Ex 14:9-16) It seems evident that the crossing must have been far enough from the head of the Gulf (or western arm of the Red Sea) that Pharaoh's forces would not have been able simply to circle

the end of the Gulf and easily come upon the Israelites on the other side.—Ex 14:22, 23.

Pharaoh had changed his mind about the release of the Israelites as soon as he learned of their departure. Certainly the loss of such a slave nation meant a heavy economic blow to Egypt. It would not be difficult for his chariots to overtake this entire nation on the move, particularly in view of their 'turning back.' Now, encouraged by the thought that Israel was wandering in confusion in the wilderness, he went after them with confidence. With a crack force of 600 chosen chariots, all the other chariots of Egypt mounted with warriors, his cavalrymen, and all his military forces, he came upon Israel at Pihahiroth. —Ex 14:3-9.

Strategically the position of the Israelites looked very bad. They were evidently hemmed in between the sea and the mountains, with the Egyptians blocking the way back. In their apparently trapped position, fear struck the hearts of the Israelites and they began to complain against Moses. Now God stepped in to protect Israel by moving the cloud from the front to the rear. On one side, toward the Egyptians, it was darkness; on the other it kept lighting up the night for Israel. While the cloud held back the Egyptians from attacking, at Jehovah's command Moses lifted his rod, and the seawaters split apart, leaving the dry seabed as a path for Israel.—Ex 14:10-21.

Width and depth of place of crossing. Since Israel crossed the sea in one night, it could hardly be assumed that the waters parted in a narrow channel. Rather, the channel may have been a kilometer or more in width. Though in fairly close marching formation, such a group, along with what wagons they had, their baggage, and their cattle, even when rather closely ranked, would occupy an area of perhaps 8 sq km (3 sq mi) or more. It appears, therefore, that the sea-opening allowed the Israelites to cross on a fairly wide front. If there was about a 1.5-km (1 mi) front, then the depth of the Israelite column would probably be about 5 km (3 mi) or more. If it was about a 2.5-km (1.5 mi) front, the depth might be about 3 km (2 mi) or more. It would take such a column several hours to get into the seabed and travel across it. While they did not go in panic, but maintained their battle formation, they would no doubt move with considerable haste.

Had it not been for the cloud, the Egyptians would have easily overtaken and slaughtered many. (Ex 15:9) When the Israelites had gone into the sea and the cloud behind them had moved ahead to reveal this fact to the Egyptians, they pursued. Here, again, is emphasized the necessity of considerable breadth and length of dry seabed, for Pharaoh's military force was great. Bent on destruction and recapture of their former slaves, the entire force went well into the seabed. Then, during the morning watch, which ran from about 2:00 to 6:00 a.m., Jehovah looked out from the cloud and began to throw the camp of the Egyptians into confusion, taking the wheels off their chariots.—Ex 14:24.

The Israelites, by the approaching of morning, got safely across on the eastern shore of the Red Sea. Then Moses was commanded to stretch his hand out so that the waters would come back over the Egyptians. At this "the sea began to come back to its normal condition," and the Egyptians fled from encountering it. This also would indicate that the waters had opened up widely, for a narrow channel would have immediately overwhelmed them. The Egyptians fled from the enclosing walls of water toward the western bank, but the waters kept converging until their depth completely covered all the war chariots and the cavalrymen belonging to Pharaoh's military forces; not so much as one of them was let remain.

It is obvious that such an overwhelming inundation would be impossible in a marsh. Moreover, in a shallow marsh dead bodies would not wash up on the shore, as actually took place, so that "Israel got to see the Egyptians dead on the seashore."—Ex 14:22-31; MAP and PICTURE, Vol. 1, p. 537.

Waters "congealed." According to the Bible description, the surging waters were congealed to let Israel pass through. (Ex 15:8) This word "congealed" is used in the *American Standard Version*, the *King James Version*, and translations by J. N. Darby, I. Leeser, R. Knox, and J. Rotherham. As defined in *Webster's Third New International Dictionary* (1981), congeal means "to change from a fluid to a solid state by or as if by cold . . . : freeze . . . : to make (a liquid) viscid or of a consistency like jelly: curdle, coagulate." The Hebrew word here translated "congealed" is used in Job 10:10 with regard to curdling milk. Therefore, it does not of necessity mean that the walls of water were frozen solid, but that the consistency of the congealed substance may have been like gelatin or curds. Nothing visible was holding back the waters of the Red Sea on each side of the

Israelites, hence the water had the appearance of being congealed, stiffened, curdled, or thickened so that it could remain standing like a wall on each side and not collapse in an inundation upon the Israelites, to their destruction. This was how they looked to Moses when a strong E wind divided the waters and dried up the basin so that it was not miry, nor frozen, but was easily traversable by the multitude.

The pathway opened in the sea was wide enough that the Israelites, numbering possibly three million, could all cross to the eastern banks by morning. Then the congealed waters began to be released and to move in from either side, surging and overwhelming the Egyptians as Israel stood on the eastern bank contemplating Jehovah's unparalleled deliverance of an entire nation from a world power. They realized the literal fulfillment of Moses' words: "The Egyptians whom you do see today you will not see again, no, never again."—Ex 14:13.

So by a spectacular display of power Jehovah exalted his name and delivered Israel. Safe on the E shore of the Red Sea, Moses led the sons of Israel in a song, while his sister Miriam, the prophetess, took a tambourine in her hand and led all the women with tambourines and in dances, responding in song to the men. (Ex 15:1, 20, 21) A complete separation of Israel from their foes had been effected. When they went out from Egypt they were not allowed to suffer harm from man or beast; no dog even snarled at the Israelites or moved its tongue against them. (Ex 11:7) While the Exodus narrative does not mention that Pharaoh personally went into the sea with his military forces and was destroyed, Psalm 136:15 does state that Jehovah "shook off Pharaoh and his military force into the Red Sea."

Typical of Later Events. In bringing Israel up out of Egypt as promised to Abraham, God looked upon the nation of Israel as his son, just as he had told Pharaoh, 'Israel is my firstborn.' (Ex 4:22) Later on, Jehovah said: "When Israel was a boy, then I loved him, and out of Egypt I called my son." (Ho 11:1) This back-reference to the Exodus was also a prophecy that had a fulfillment in the days of Herod when Joseph and Mary returned from Egypt with Jesus after the death of Herod and settled in Nazareth. The historian Matthew applies the prophecy of Hosea to this occurrence, saying of Joseph: "He stayed there until the decease of Herod, for that to be fulfilled which was spoken by Jehovah through his prophet, saying: 'Out of Egypt I called my son.'"—Mt 2:15.

The apostle Paul lists the Exodus among those things that he says went on befalling Israel as examples or types. (1Co 10:1, 2, 11) It therefore appears to be symbolic of something greater. Natural Israel is used in the Bible as symbolic of spiritual Israel, the Israel of God. (Ga 6:15, 16) Also, Moses spoke of the prophet to come who would be like him. (De 18:18, 19) The Jews looked for this one to be a great leader and deliverer. The apostle Peter identifies Jesus Christ as the Greater Moses. (Ac 3:19-23) The deliverance of Israel at the Red Sea and the destruction of the Egyptian army, therefore, must have significance in the deliverance of spiritual Israel from their enemies of symbolic Egypt by a great miracle at the hands of Jesus Christ. And just as the work God performed at the Red Sea resulted in the exaltation of his name, the fulfillment of those typical events in a much larger reality would bring greater and far more extensive fame to the name of Jehovah.—Ex 15:1.

EXODUS, BOOK OF. The second scroll of the Pentateuch, also referred to as the Second Book of Moses. It came to be known in Hebrew as *Shemohth'*, "Names," from its opening phrase, *We'el'leh shemohth'*, "Now these are the names." "Exodus" is the Latinized form of the Greek; this means "Going Forth; Departure," that is, of the Israelites out of Egypt.

This book is an obvious continuation of Genesis, beginning with the expression "Now" (literally, "And") and then relisting the names of the sons of Jacob that are taken from the more complete record at Genesis 46:8-27. Exodus was written in 1512 B.C.E., a year after the Israelites departed from Egypt and camped in the wilderness of Sinai. The book covers a period of 145

HIGHLIGHTS OF EXODUS

The record of how Jehovah delivered Israel from oppressive slavery in Egypt and organized them into a theocratic nation

Written by Moses in 1512 B.C.E., about a year after Israel departed from Egypt

Israel experiences tyrannical slavery in Egypt (1:1–3:1)

By royal decree the Israelites are made to slave under tyranny; death at the time of birth is decreed for all their male offspring

Moses is adopted by Pharaoh's daughter and so is spared from death, but he is taught by his own mother

Moses kills an oppressive Egyptian, flees to Midian, becomes shepherd there

Jehovah delivers Israel by the hand of Moses (3:2–15:21)

Moses is commissioned at burning bush as deliverer, to speak and act in the name of Jehovah

Returns to Egypt; with Aaron, he appears before Pharaoh, telling him that Jehovah has said to send Israel away to worship Him in the wilderness; Pharaoh refuses and increases oppression

Jehovah renews promise to deliver Israel and to give them the land of Canaan, thus deepening their appreciation for his name Jehovah

Ten Plagues, announced by Moses and Aaron, come upon Egypt; after the first three, only the Egyptians are plagued; during the tenth, all the firstborn males, both of Egyptians and of their animals, die, while Israel celebrates the Passover

Using a pillar of cloud by day and a pillar of fire by night, Jehovah leads Israel out of Egypt; he opens the Red Sea to permit them to cross over on dry land, then drowns Pharaoh and his army when they try to cross the seabed in pursuit

Jehovah organizes Israel as a theocratic nation (15:22–40:38)

Provision of drinkable water, as well as meat and manna, is made for Israel in the wilderness; in connection with provision of manna, Sabbath is instituted

At Jethro's suggestion, Moses selects qualified men to serve as chiefs, helping with the work of judging

At Mount Sinai, Jehovah invites the nation to enter into covenant relationship with him; they voluntarily agree; Jehovah gives fear-inspiring display of his glory

Ten Commandments and other laws given through Moses set out Jehovah's requirements for Israel

Law covenant made over blood of sacrificial animals; the people say, "All that Jehovah has spoken we are willing to do and be obedient"

Instructions are given by God on building the tabernacle and its furniture, as well as on making garments for the priests and on installing the priesthood

While Moses is on Mount Sinai, the people turn to worshiping a golden calf; Moses breaks the stone tablets given him by God; Levites prove loyal; about 3,000 idolaters are slain

Moses sees manifestation of Jehovah's glory, hears God declare His name

With voluntary offerings of materials, the tabernacle and its furnishings are built; the tabernacle is set up on Nisan 1, 1512 B.C.E., and Jehovah manifests his approval

years, from Joseph's death in 1657 B.C.E. to the construction of the tabernacle in 1512 B.C.E.

Writership. Moses' writership of Exodus has never been questioned by the Jews. Egyptian expressions used are indicative of a writer contemporary with the times, and not of a Jew born later.

Accuracy, Truthfulness. On the part of the writer of Exodus "an intimate acquaintance with Ancient Egypt may be discerned. The position of the Egyptians with respect to foreigners—their separation from them, yet their allowance of them in their country, their special hatred of *shepherds*, the suspicion of strangers from Palestine as *spies*—their internal government, its settled character, the power of the King, the influence of the Priests, the great works, the employment of foreigners in their construction, the use of bricks, . . . and of bricks with straw in them, . . . the taskmasters, the embalming of dead bodies, the consequent importation of spices, . . . the violent mournings, . . . the fighting with horses and chariots . . .—these are a few out of the many points which might be noted marking an intimate knowledge of Egyptian manners and customs on the part of the author of the Pentateuch."—*The Historical Evidences of the Truth of the Scripture Records,* by George Rawlinson, 1862, pp. 290, 291.

The account of Pharaoh's daughter bathing in the Nile has been disputed (Ex 2:5), but Herodotus (II, 35) says (as ancient monuments also show) that in ancient Egypt the women were under no restraint. Also, the Egyptians believed a sovereign virtue existed in the Nile waters. At times Pharaoh went out to the river evidently for purposes of worship. It was here that he was met at least twice by Moses during the Ten Plagues. —Ex 7:15; 8:20.

As to absence of Egyptian monumental evidence of the Israelites' sojourn in Egypt, this is not surprising, in view of the fact that a study of the monuments there reveals that the Egyptians did not record matters uncomplimentary to themselves. However, an even more powerful testimony than stone monumental evidence is the living monument of the observance of the Passover by the Jews, who have commemorated the Exodus in this way throughout their entire history.

There is strong ground for accepting the historical accuracy and the general narrative as given in Exodus. According to Westcott and Hort, Jesus and the writers of the Christian Greek Scriptures quote or refer to Exodus more than 100 times. The integrity of the writer Moses attests to the book's authenticity. He points out with the greatest candor his own weaknesses, his hesitancy, and his mistakes, not attributing anything of the miracles, leadership, and organization to his own prowess, though he was acknowledged as great by the Egyptians and, in the main, much respected by Israel.—Ex 11:3; 3:10-12; 4:10-16.

The divine hand is revealed in Israel's sojourn in Egypt and their Exodus. A better place could hardly be found for Israel's rapid growth to a mighty nation. Had they remained in Canaan, they would have been subjected to much warfare with the Canaanite inhabitants, while in the territory of the first world power during the time of its zenith they were protected by its might. They lived in the best part of the land, which contributed to their health and fertility, as well as to their intellectual growth to some extent.

But their situation in Egypt was not ideal for moral and spiritual growth; neither was it suitable for their being made a nation under theocratic rule, with a sacrificing and teaching priesthood. Furthermore, God's promise to give Abraham's seed the land of Canaan had to be fulfilled, and God's time for it had come. Israel was to be constituted a great nation, with Jehovah as its King. The book of Exodus relates Jehovah's accomplishment of this purpose.—Ex 15:13-21.

Dead Sea Scrolls. Among the manuscripts found at the Dead Sea, 15 contain fragments of the book of Exodus. One fragment (4QEx^f) has been dated as from about 250 B.C.E. Two of the fragments, believed to date from the second or third century B.C.E., were written in ancient Hebrew characters that were in use before the Babylonian exile.

EXORCISM. See DEMON POSSESSION; SPIRITISM.

EXPANSE. Concerning the second creative period, or "day," Genesis 1:6-8 states: "And God went on to say: 'Let an expanse [Heb., *ra·qi'a'*] come to be in between the waters and let a dividing occur between the waters and the waters.' Then God proceeded to make the expanse and to make a division between the waters that should be beneath the expanse and the waters that should be above the expanse. And it came to be so. And God began to call the expanse Heaven." Later the record speaks of luminaries appearing in "the expanse of the heavens," and still later of flying creatures flying over the earth "upon the face of the expanse of the heavens." —Ge 1:14, 15, 17, 20.

The Greek *Septuagint* used the word *ste·re′o-ma* (meaning "a firm and solid structure") to translate the Hebrew *ra·qi′a′*, and the Latin *Vulgate* used the Latin term *firmamentum*, which also conveys the idea of something solid and firm. The *King James Version,* the *Revised Standard Version,* and many others follow suit in translating *ra·qi′a′* by the word "firmament." However, in its marginal reading the *King James Version* gives the alternate reading "expansion," and the *American Standard Version* gives "expanse" in its footnote. Other translations support such rendering—"expanse" (*Ro; Fn; Yg; An; NW*); *"expansión"* (*VM* [Spanish]); *"étendue* [extent or expanse]" (*Segond; Ostervald* [French]).

Some endeavor to show that the ancient Hebrew concept of the universe included the idea of a solid vault arched over the earth, with sluice holes through which rain could enter and with the stars fixed within this solid vault, diagrams of such concept appearing in Bible dictionaries and some Bible translations. Commenting on this attitude, *The International Standard Bible Encyclopaedia* states: "But this assumption is in reality based more upon the ideas prevalent in Europe during the Dark Ages than upon any actual statements in the O[ld] T[estament]."—Edited by J. Orr, 1960, Vol. I, p. 314.

While it is true that the root word (*ra·qa″*) from which *ra·qi′a′* is drawn is regularly used in the sense of "beating out" something solid, whether by hand, by foot, or by any instrument (compare Ex 39:3; Eze 6:11), in some cases it is not sound reasoning to rule out a figurative use of the word. Thus at Job 37:18 Elihu asks concerning God: "With him can you beat out [*tar·qi′a′*] the skies hard like a molten mirror?" That the literal beating out of some solid celestial vault is not meant can be seen from the fact that the word "skies" here comes from a word (*sha′chaq*) also rendered "film of dust" or "clouds" (Isa 40:15; Ps 18:11), and in view of the nebulous quality of that which is 'beaten out,' it is clear that the Bible writer is only *figuratively* comparing the skies to a metal mirror whose burnished face gives off a bright reflection.—Compare Da 12:3.

So, too, with the "expanse" produced on the second creative "day," no solid substance is described as being beaten out but, rather, the creation of an open space, or division, between the waters covering the earth and other waters above the earth. It thus describes the formation of the atmospheric expanse surrounding the earth and indicates that at one time there was no clear division or open space but that the entire globe was previously enveloped in water vapor. This also accords with scientific reasoning on the early stages of the planet's formation and the view that at one time all of earth's water existed in the form of atmospheric vapor because of the extreme heat of the earth's surface at that point.

That the Hebrew writers of the Bible did not conceive of the sky as originally formed of burnished metal is evident from the warning given through Moses to Israel that, in the event of their disobedience to God, "Your skies that are over your head must also *become* copper, and the earth that is beneath you iron," thus metaphorically describing the effects of intense heat and severe drought upon the skies and land of Israel. —De 28:23, 24.

Similarly, it is obvious that the ancient Hebrews held no pagan concept as to the existence of literal "windows" in the arch of the sky through which earth's rain descended. Very accurately and scientifically the writer of Job quotes Elihu in describing the process by which rain clouds are formed when he states, at Job 36:27, 28: "For he draws up the drops of water; they filter as rain for his mist, so that the clouds [*shecha·qim′*] trickle, they drip upon mankind abundantly." Likewise, the expression "floodgates [*'arub·both′*] of the heavens" clearly manifests a figurative expression.—Compare Ge 7:11; 2Ki 7:1, 2, 19; Mal 3:10; see also Pr 3:20; Isa 5:6; 45:8; Jer 10:13.

In his vision of heavenly arrangements, Ezekiel describes "the likeness of an expanse like the sparkle of awesome ice" over the heads of the four living creatures. The account is filled with figurative expressions.—Eze 1:22-26; 10:1.

Though the formation of the expanse, or atmosphere, surrounding earth did not involve a 'beating out' of something as solid as some metallic substance, yet it should be remembered that the gaseous mixture forming earth's atmosphere is just as real as land and water and has weight in itself (in addition to carrying water and innumerable particles of solid materials, such as dust). The weight of all the air surrounding earth is estimated at more than 5,200,000,000,000,000 metric tons. (*The World Book Encyclopedia,* 1987, Vol. 1, p. 156) Air pressure at sea level runs about 1 kg per sq cm (15 lb per sq in.). It also exercises resistance so that most meteors hitting the immense jacket of air surrounding the earth are burned up by the friction created by the atmosphere. Thus the force implied in the Hebrew word ra·qi'a' is certainly in harmony with the known facts.

In the Psalms "the expanse," along with "the heavens," is said to tell of God's works and praise. —Ps 19:1.

EXPELLING.

The judicial excommunication, or disfellowshipping, of delinquents from membership and association in a community or organization. With religious societies it is a principle and a right inherent in them and is analogous to the powers of capital punishment, banishment, and exclusion from membership that are exercised by political and municipal bodies. In the congregation of God it is exercised to maintain the purity of the organization doctrinally and morally. The exercise of this power is necessary to the continued existence of the organization and particularly so the Christian congregation. The congregation must remain clean and maintain God's favor in order to be used by him and to represent him. Otherwise, God would expel or cut off the entire congregation.—Re 2:5; 1Co 5:5, 6.

Jehovah's Action. Jehovah God took expelling, or disfellowshipping, action in numerous instances. He sentenced Adam to death and drove him and his wife Eve out of the garden of Eden. (Ge 3:19, 23, 24) Cain was banished and became a wanderer and a fugitive in the earth. (Ge 4:11, 14, 16) The angels that sinned were thrown into Tartarus, a condition of dense darkness in which they are reserved for judgment. (2Pe 2:4) Twenty-three thousand fornicators were cut off from Israel in one day. (1Co 10:8) Achan was put to death at Jehovah's command for stealing that which was devoted to Jehovah. (Jos 7:15, 20, 21, 25) Korah the Levite along with Dathan and Abiram of the tribe of Reuben were cut off for rebellion, and Miriam was stricken with leprosy and eventually might have died in that condition if Moses had not pleaded for her. As it was, she was expelled from the camp of Israel under quarantine seven days.—Nu 16:27, 32, 33, 35; 12:10, 13-15.

Under the Mosaic Law. For serious or deliberate violations of God's law given through Moses a person could be cut off, that is, put to death. (Le 7:27; Nu 15:30, 31) Apostasy, idolatry, adultery, eating blood, and murder were among the offenses carrying this penalty.—De 13:12-18; Le 20:10; 17:14; Nu 35:31.

Under the Law, for the penalty of cutting off to be carried out, evidence had to be established at the mouth of at least two witnesses. (De 19:15) These witnesses were required to be the first to stone the guilty one. (De 17:7) This would demonstrate their zeal for God's law and the purity of the congregation of Israel and would also be a deterrent to false, careless, or hasty testimony.

The Sanhedrin and synagogues. During Jesus' earthly ministry the synagogues served as courts for trying violators of Jewish law. The Sanhedrin was the highest court. Under Roman rule the Jews did not have the latitude of authority that they had enjoyed under theocratic government. Even when the Sanhedrin judged someone deserving of death, they could not always administer the death penalty, because of restrictions by the Romans. The Jewish synagogues had a system of excommunication, or disfellowshipping, that had three steps or three names. The first step was the penalty of nid·duy', which was for a relatively short time, initially only 30 days. A person under this penalty was prohibited from enjoying certain privileges. He could go to the temple, but there he was restricted in certain ways, and all besides his own family were commanded to stay at a distance of 4 cubits (c. 2 m; 6 ft) from him. The second step was che'rem, meaning something devoted to God or banned. This was a more severe judgment. The offender could not teach or be taught in the company of others, nor could he perform any commercial transactions beyond purchasing the necessities of life. However, he was not altogether cast out of the Jewish organization, and there was a chance for him to come back. Finally, there was sham·mat·ta', an entire cutting off from the congregation. Some believe the last two forms of excommunication were undistinguishable from each other.

One who was cast out as wicked, cut off entirely, would be considered worthy of death, though the Jews might not have the authority to execute such a one. Nevertheless, the form of cutting off they did employ was a very powerful weapon in the Jewish community. Jesus foretold that his followers would be expelled from the synagogues. (Joh 16:2) Fear of being expelled, or "unchurched," kept some of the Jews, even the rulers, from confessing Jesus. (Joh 9:22, ftn; 12: 42) An example of such action by the synagogue was the case of the healed blind man who spoke favorably of Jesus.—Joh 9:34.

During the time of his earthly ministry, Jesus gave instructions as to the procedure to follow if a serious sin was committed against a person and yet the sin was of such a nature that, if properly settled, it did not need to involve the Jewish congregation. (Mt 18:15-17) He encouraged earnest effort to help the wrongdoer, while also safeguarding that congregation against persistent sinners. The only congregation of God in existence then was the congregation of Israel. 'Speaking to the congregation' did not mean that the entire nation or even all the Jews in a given community sat in judgment on the offender. There were older men of the Jews that were charged with this responsibility. (Mt 5:22) Offenders who refused to listen even to these responsible ones were to be viewed "just as a man of the nations and as a tax collector," association with whom was shunned by the Jews.—Compare Ac 10:28.

Christian Congregation. Based on the principles of the Hebrew Scriptures, the Christian Greek Scriptures by command and precedent authorize expulsion, or disfellowshipping, from the Christian congregation. By exercising this God-given authority, the congregation keeps itself clean and in good standing before God. The apostle Paul, with the authority vested in him, ordered the expulsion of an incestuous fornicator who had taken his father's wife. (1Co 5:5, 11, 13) He also exercised disfellowshipping authority against Hymenaeus and Alexander. (1Ti 1:19, 20) Diotrephes, however, was apparently trying to exercise disfellowshipping action wrongly. —3Jo 9, 10.

Some of the offenses that could merit disfellowshipping from the Christian congregation are fornication, adultery, homosexuality, greed, extortion, thievery, lying, drunkenness, reviling, spiritism, murder, idolatry, apostasy, and the causing of divisions in the congregation. (1Co 5:9-13; 6:9, 10; Tit 3:10, 11; Re 21:8) Mercifully, one promoting a sect is warned a first and a second time before such disfellowshipping action is taken against him. In the Christian congregation, the principle enunciated in the Law applies, namely, that two or three witnesses must establish evidence against the accused one. (1Ti 5:19) Those who have been convicted of a practice of sin are reproved Scripturally before the "onlookers," for example, those who testified concerning the sinful conduct, so that they too may all have a healthy fear of such sin.—1Ti 5:20; see RE-PROOF.

The Christian congregation is also admonished by Scripture to stop socializing with those who are disorderly and not walking correctly but who are not deemed deserving of complete expulsion. Paul wrote the Thessalonian congregation concerning such: "Stop associating with him, that he may become ashamed. And yet do not be considering him as an enemy, but continue admonishing him as a brother."—2Th 3:6, 11, 13-15.

However, regarding any who were Christians but later repudiated the Christian congregation or were expelled from it, the apostle Paul commanded: "Quit mixing in company with" such a one; and the apostle John wrote: "Never receive him into your homes or say a greeting to him." —1Co 5:11; 2Jo 9, 10.

Those who have been expelled may be received back into the congregation if they manifest sincere repentance. (2Co 2:5-8) This also is a protection to the congregation, preventing it from being overreached by Satan in swinging from condoning wrongdoing to the other extreme, becoming harsh and unforgiving.—2Co 2:10, 11.

For expelling of demons, see DEMON POSSESSION; SPIRITISM.

EXTINGUISHERS. *Mezam·me′reth,* the Hebrew word variously translated "snuffers" (*AS*), "knives" (*JB*), and "extinguishers" (*NW*), is derived from a root (*za·mar′*) meaning "trim; prune." Hence some believe that scissorlike utensils designed for trimming the lampwicks are meant. However, all that is definitely known about these utensils is that they were made of gold or copper and were used in connection with the services at the temple.—1Ki 7:50; 2Ki 12:13; 25:14; 2Ch 4:22; Jer 52:18.

EXTORTION. The act or practice of taking or obtaining anything from an unwilling or reluctant person by illegal use of fear, whether by force, threats, or any other undue exercise of power. The basic sense of the Greek word rendered 'extortioner' (*har′pax*) is "snatcher." (1Co 5: 10, *Int*) The Bible repeatedly warns against any seeking of unjust gain, particularly on the part of those in responsible or official positions.—Ex 18: 21; Pr 1:19; 15:27.

Nevertheless, under Roman rule over Palestine, Jewish tax collectors were often guilty of extortion. Their position provided them with wide opportunities to enrich themselves unjustly (and undoubtedly their Roman masters also) at the expense of the people. In an illustration Jesus may have alluded to this when he spoke of a self-righteous Pharisee praying alongside a tax collector and commending himself to God as not being an extortioner. (Lu 18:11) The tax collectors who came to John the Baptizer asking what to do were counseled: "Do not demand anything more than the tax rate."—Lu 3:13.

When Zacchaeus, a rich chief tax collector, was entertaining Jesus as a guest in his home, he repented and turned from his bad course, saying: "Whatever I extorted from anyone by false accusation I am restoring fourfold." (Lu 19:2, 8; see ACCUSATION.) The Law, however, required in such cases of repentance and admission of guilt that only 120 percent be restored to the defrauded one.—Le 6:2-5.

Extortion is listed in the Christian Greek Scriptures along with fornication, adultery, idolatry, greediness, thievery, drunkenness, reviling, and homosexuality as things that will prevent the one who makes a practice of them from entering the Kingdom of God. The apostle Paul, writing to the congregation at Corinth, said that formerly some of them had done such things, but were now washed clean. Therefore, although they could not avoid some contact with these kinds of persons in the world, they must quit associating with any of such ones claiming to be a "brother," and they must remove them from the congregation.—1Co 5:9-11; 6:9-11.

The Christian attitude toward paying extortion in the form of a bribe is illustrated in the apostle Paul's case. The Roman governor Felix attempted to extort money from Paul by prolonging Paul's detention in prison for two years. Of this, Paul was aware, but he offered Felix nothing. Eventually Felix was succeeded in office by Governor Festus.—Ac 24:26, 27.

EYE. The organ of sight, a highly efficient, self-adjusting "camera" that transmits impulses to the brain, where the object focused on the eye's retina is interpreted as sight. The Hebrew 'a'yin and the Greek o·phthal·mos' are both used in literal and figurative senses. The Hebrew term is also used to denote a "fountain" or 'spring.' (Ge 24:13; Ex 15:27) The possession of two eyes, as in the human body, provides stereoscopic vision. The loss of sight is a tremendous handicap because sight is probably the most important channel of communication to the mind.

The eye is one of the most beautiful parts of the body. (Ca 1:15; 4:9; 7:4) So disfiguring and detrimental was an eye affliction that one could not serve as a priest under the Law covenant if he was blind or diseased in either eye. (Le 21: 18, 20) In Israel, under the Law, the man who

knocked out the eye of his slave had to let the slave go free. (Ex 21:26) In order to humiliate and to shatter the power of their enemies, some ancient nations followed the cruel practice of blinding prominent men among the captured enemy. —Jg 16:21; 1Sa 11:2; 2Ki 25:7.

The structure of the eye reveals marvelous design on the part of its Maker, and the process by which the brain interprets what is transmitted through the eye is far from being understood by scientists. All of this points to its Designer's intelligence. Jehovah God himself testifies to his creatorship of the eye, saying: "The One forming the eye, can he not look?"—Ps 94:9; Pr 20:12.

Jehovah's Eyes. God helps humans to understand and appreciate things about himself by likening them to things that we see and know well. Thus he speaks figuratively of his "eyes" being on his people, evidently indicating his watchfulness and loving care for them. The apostle Peter says: "The eyes of Jehovah are upon the righteous ones." (1Pe 3:12) God emphasizes this care and sensitiveness for their welfare when he speaks of his servants as "the pupil" of his eye, metaphorically representing their preciousness in his sight and his quickness to act in their behalf when touched by the enemy.—De 32:10; Ps 17:8.

Describing God's observation of the actions of all men, Jeremiah wrote that His "eyes are opened upon all the ways of the sons of men, in order to give to each one according to his ways." (Jer 32:19) Of Jehovah's omniscience and his purpose to exercise justice toward all, the apostle Paul wrote: "There is not a creation that is not manifest to his sight, but all things are naked and openly exposed to the eyes of him with whom we have an accounting." (Heb 4:13; 2Ch 16:9; Ps 66:7; Pr 15:3) Of the searching quality of God's examination of men, the psalmist says: "His own eyes behold, his own beaming eyes examine the sons of men."—Ps 11:4.

Jehovah's ability to know a person's characteristics and tendencies or his genetic makeup even while he is being formed in the womb, as was the case with Jacob and Esau (Ge 25:21-23; Ro 9:10-13), is indicated by the psalmist David's words: "Your eyes saw even the embryo of me, and in your book all its parts were down in writing, as regards the days when they were formed and there was not yet one among them." —Ps 139:15, 16.

Illustrative Usage. The human eye is an important channel of communication to the mind, strongly influencing the emotions and actions. Satan tempted Eve by causing her to desire something seen with her eyes. (Ge 3:6) He attempted to induce Jesus to sin by reaching out improperly for things seen with his eyes. (Lu 4:5-7) And the apostle John tells us that "the desire of the eyes" is one of the things originating with this world, which is passing away. (1Jo 2:16, 17) Many of the emotions are likewise expressed by the eyes, and so the Scriptures use the expressions "lofty [haughty] eyes" (Pr 6:17); "lustrous eyes" (of the bad, seductive woman—Pr 6:25); "eyes full of adultery" (2Pe 2:14); the "ungenerous eye" (Pr 23:6); the "envious eye" (Pr 28:22); the 'eye that is wicked' ('evil eye,' *KJ*); the latter does not refer to any magical quality of the eye, but to an eye with bad intent, the opposite of an eye that is "kindly."—Mt 20:15; Pr 22:9.

Gestures by means of the eyes are very expressive of the individual's feelings. They may show pity or lack of it (De 19:13); they may 'wink' or 'blink' in derision, or in scheming insincerity. (Ps 35:19; Pr 6:13; 16:30) One who does not want to observe or who does not desire to carry out an act for another may be spoken of as shutting or hiding his eyes. (Mt 13:15; Pr 28:27) The stupid one is said to have his eyes "at the extremity of the earth," wandering here and there without any fixed object, his thoughts being everywhere except where they ought to be. (Pr 17:24) Even a person's health, vigor, or state of happiness is manifested by the appearance of his eyes. (1Sa 14:27-29; De 34:7; Job 17:7; Ps 6:7; 88:9) King Jehoshaphat addressed Jehovah: "Our eyes are toward you."—2Ch 20:12.

In certain contexts the "eyes" refer to a person's judgment (Ge 19:14; Pr 12:15; Mt 21:42), presence (Ge 23:11), knowledge (Nu 15:24), attention (Ge 44:21; Lu 4:20), or sympathy (Pr 28:27). The Hebrew word *'a'yin* (eye) can also refer to the appearance of something, as the "visible surface" of the earth (Ex 10:5, ftn), the "look" of manna and electrum (Nu 11:7, ftn; Eze 1:4), the "sparkle" of wine (Pr 23:31), the "likeness" of an expanse (Eze 1:22), and the "sight" of copper (Da 10:6).—Compare Zec 5:6, ftn.

Seeing God; Jesus. Spirit creatures, angels, are able to behold the brilliance of Jehovah (Mt 18:10; Lu 1:19), an experience that no human eyes could endure, for Jehovah himself told Moses: "No man may see me and yet live." (Ex 33:20) John said: "No man has seen God at any time." (Joh 1:18) Therefore, when Jesus told his disciple Philip: "He that has seen me has seen the Father also" (Joh 14:9), and when the apostle

John said: "He that does bad has not seen God" (3Jo 11), obviously they were speaking of seeing God, not with one's physical eyes, but with what the apostle Paul described as 'the eyes of the heart.' (Eph 1:18) Those who see with the eyes of the heart are those who have really come to *know* God, appreciating his qualities, and that is why John could say: "He that does not love has not come to know God, because God is love." —1Jo 4:8.

So, too, in view of the fact that Jesus said 'the world would behold him no more' (Joh 14:19), the statement at Revelation 1:7: "Every eye will see him [Jesus Christ]," must have reference, not to the literal eye, but, rather, to the effect upon the mind of human observers of the evidences that they can see with their literal eyes when he goes forth to destroy his enemies. The Bible plainly indicates, however, that those whom God calls to heavenly life with Christ will literally see God, which requires for them resurrection in a heavenly spiritual body.—1Pe 1:4; 1Co 15:50-54; compare 1Pe 3:18.

Spiritual Sight. The spiritual eye as well as the physical eye is a gift of God. (Pr 20:12) He promises to heal spiritual eyes as well as physical ones and to remove all causes for tears. (Isa 35:5; Re 21:4) One cannot understand God's purposes without the gift of spiritual eyesight. On the other hand, Jehovah hides his truth from the eyes of those who are stubborn or rebellious, letting "their eyes become darkened." (Ro 11:8-10; Lu 19:42) "They have [literal] eyes, but they cannot see [spiritually]."—Jer 5:21; Isa 59:10.

Jesus also pointed out that one's spiritual vision must be kept sharp and in focus. He said: "The lamp of the body is the eye. If, then, your eye is simple [sincere; all one way; in focus; generous], your whole body will be bright; but if your eye is wicked, your whole body will be dark. If in reality the light that is in you is darkness, how great that darkness is!" (Mt 6:22, 23) Jesus further counsels that a person should not presume to offer to extract a mere "straw" from his brother's eye to help him to render more acceptable judgments, when one's own ability to render proper judgment is impaired by a "rafter."—Mt 7:3-5.

The apostle John saw the throne of God and in conjunction with it four living creatures full of eyes in front and behind. (Re 4:6, 8) Creatures with such equipment could be continually on the watch, able to see all things. They would be fully aware of what was taking place here on earth and would take note of God in all things and observe all his indications of what he wanted done. (Compare Ps 123:2; also Eze 1:18; 10:12.) Jehovah counsels his servants not to let his sayings 'get away from their eyes.'—Pr 4:20, 21; Lu 10:23; see BLINDNESS.

See NEEDLE'S EYE.

EYESALVE. A substance meant to be applied to the eyes for its healing properties; used in a figurative sense in the Bible. The spiritually blind Christians in the Laodicean congregation were urged to buy 'eyesalve, to rub in their eyes that they may see.' (Re 3:17, 18) The Greek word for eyesalve (kol·lou′ri·on) literally means a roll or cake of coarse bread, suggesting that the salve was likely made up into small cakes or rolls. As Laodicea was famous for its medical school and probably also produced the eye medicine known as Phrygian powder, the recommendation to buy eyesalve would have been very meaningful to the Christians there.

EZBAI (Ez′bai). The father of Naarai, one of the mighty men of King David's military forces. —1Ch 11:26, 37.

EZBON (Ez′bon).

1. A son of Gad and the grandson of Jacob. (Ge 46:16) The parallel account in Numbers 26:16 lists Ozni the forefather of the Oznites instead of Ezbon, suggesting that both names apply to the same person.

2. A son of Bela and a descendant of Benjamin. Ezbon is called one of the "heads of the house of their forefathers, valiant, mighty men." —1Ch 7:6, 7.

EZEKIEL (E·ze′ki·el) [God Strengthens]. The son of Buzi, a priest. He was among the captives taken to Babylon by Nebuchadnezzar along with Jehoiachin in 617 B.C.E. His first visions of God came to him in "the thirtieth year, in the fourth month, on the fifth day of the month," in the "fifth year of the exile of King Jehoiachin." He prophesied to the Jews living by the river Chebar, which some modern scholars believe to be one of the great Babylonian canals. "The thirtieth year" seems to have reference to Ezekiel's age. He began his duties as a prophet at this time. —Eze 1:1-3.

Being of a priestly family, he was undoubtedly well acquainted with the temple, its arrangement, and all the activities carried out therein and was well versed in the Law. Likely Ezekiel was also well acquainted with Jeremiah and his prophecies, because Jeremiah was a prophet in Jerusalem during Ezekiel's youth. Then, too, Ezekiel had enjoyed the advantage of living in Judah during part of the reign of righteous King Josiah, who destroyed the Baal altars and the graven images, set about to repair the temple, and intensified his reformation in behalf of pure worship in Judah when the book of the Law (apparently an original written by Moses) was found in the temple.—2Ch 34.

Before Babylon destroyed Jerusalem, in what strategic locations did Jehovah have his prophets?

Ezekiel's prophetic life was contemporaneous with Jeremiah and Daniel. Jeremiah served as God's prophet to the Jews in Jerusalem and Judah, coming in contact with the corrupt Judean kings. Daniel, who was in the court of Babylon and later of Medo-Persia, was given prophecies concerning the succession of world powers and their defeat at the hands of the Kingdom of God. Ezekiel served among the Jewish people and their headmen in Babylonia and continued the work of the prophets there. So, while the Jews in Jerusalem had the benefit of the temple with its high priest and the priestly prophet Jeremiah, those in Babylon were not forsaken by Jehovah. Ezekiel was God's prophet to them, and while not performing sacrificial services, he was there as a counselor and instructor in God's law.

There was also a close relationship between the prophetic work of Jeremiah and Ezekiel, both of them refuting and striving to dispel from the minds of the Jews in Jerusalem and in Babylonia the idea that God was going to bring an early end to Babylonian domination and that Jerusalem would not fall. Jeremiah actually sent a letter to the captives in the land of Babylonia, telling them to settle down and be at peace in Babylon because a 70-year period must pass before they would be delivered. Doubtless Ezekiel got to hear the words of this letter. Also, he may have heard the reading of the book that Jeremiah later sent foretelling the downfall of Babylon.—Jer 29; 51:59-64.

Prophesied to an "Obstinate" People. The captives in Babylonia were in a better position before Jehovah than the Jews remaining in Judah, as illustrated by the baskets of good and bad figs that Jeremiah saw. (Jer 24) But even so,

Ezekiel had no easy task set before him, because the captive Israelites were also a part of the rebellious house. As Ezekiel was told, it was among "obstinate ones and things pricking you and it is among scorpions that you are dwelling." (Eze 2:6) At Jehovah's command he took up dwelling among the exiles at Tel-abib by the river Chebar. (Eze 3:4, 15) Although the Jews were exiles, they were living in their own houses. (Jer 29:5) They were able to continue organized, at least to an extent, religiously. The older men of Judah were able to visit Ezekiel several times. (Eze 8:1; 14:1; 20:1) Even when the time came for the restoration at the end of the 70 years, many of these Jews did not want to leave Babylon.

One of the reasons for the lack of desire to return on the part of at least some of the Jews in Babylon may have been materialism. The archives of a great business house, "Murashu and Sons," were uncovered by an American expedition at the site of a Euphrates canal near Nippur, which some scholars believe was near Chebar. Inscriptions found there contain a number of Jewish names, which indicates that the Israelites had become quite well established and that a good many of them had become involved in the commercial activities of Babylon.

Death of Wife. Ezekiel says that he received his commission by the river Chebar in the fifth year of the exile of King Jehoiachin (or in 613 B.C.E.). He prophesied for at least 22 years to about 591 B.C.E., his last dated prophecy being in the 27th year of the exile. (Eze 29:17) Ezekiel was apparently happily married. Then Jehovah told him: "Son of man, here I am taking away from you the thing desirable to your eyes by a blow." (Eze 24:16) His wife may have been unfaithful to him or to Jehovah, but whatever the reason for her death, Ezekiel was commanded not to weep, but to sigh without words. Ezekiel was told to wear his headdress and not to adopt any signs or evidences of mourning. This was all really for the purpose of a sign to the Israelites there in Babylonian captivity that Jehovah would profane his sanctuary in which the Israelites took such pride, and that, contrary to their hopes, Jerusalem would be destroyed.—Eze 24:17-27.

"A Watchman." In a manner similar to that of Isaiah, Ezekiel received his commission to prophesy. He was given an awe-inspiring vision of Jehovah on his throne attended by living creatures having four faces and wings, accompanied by wheels within wheels, which moved along with the living creatures. Jehovah then spoke, addressing Ezekiel as a "son of man," to remind the prophet that he was but an earthling man. (Eze chaps 1, 2; compare Isa 6.) He was sent as a watchman to the house of Israel to warn them of their wicked way. Though they would be very hardhearted, nonetheless the warning was necessary so that they would know that Jehovah had had a prophet in the midst of them. Even though they would refuse to listen, if he failed to warn them with the words Jehovah gave him, he would be held responsible for their lives—he would be bloodguilty.—Eze 3:7, 17, 18; 2:4, 5; 33:2-9.

Tableaux and Illustrations. Ezekiel frequently prophesied by means of tableaux, performance of symbolic actions, as well as by visions, allegories, or parables. A most outstanding tableau was the 390- and 40-day picture of the siege of Jerusalem, which contains an important time prophecy. It required obedience, patience, and much faith to carry out this pictorial warning to a faithless, ridiculing people. During the siege of Jerusalem, Ezekiel turned prophetic attention to the pagan nations that hated Israel and would take part in and rejoice in Israel's downfall; he described the punishment Jehovah would bring upon them. Subsequent to the fall of Jerusalem the tone of Ezekiel's prophesying was changed. After a strong condemnation of Israel's greedy shepherds and of Seir, he directed his prophetic activities toward building faith in the promise of God that Israel would be revived, regathered, and united, and that the glorious shepherdship of Jehovah's "servant David" would bless them to time indefinite under a covenant of peace. (Eze 37) Ezekiel then gives a detailed description of the rebuilt temple, "blueprinted" for him by Jehovah. This visionary temple was prophetic of something in the far-distant future, for no such temple was ever actually constructed.—Eze 40-48.

Similarities to the Work of Jesus Christ. There are similarities in the work done by Ezekiel and by Jesus. Both Ezekiel and Jesus had to go up against an indifferent, hardhearted people with a message of condemnation, which included a message of hope for those who would turn from their wicked course. Ezekiel was told that people would come and hear his words, but their hearts would not respond. (Eze 33:30-32) Likewise, many crowds came out to hear Jesus talk, but few responded appreciatively to his teachings. Ezekiel preached to captives in Babylonia. Jesus stated his commission to preach release to the captives; (Lu 4:18) he plainly explained to the Jews that they were in spiritual bondage and needed release, which he was sent to provide. (Joh 8:31-36) Like Ezekiel, he never acted as a reprover of the Jews with his own words, but he spoke what Jehovah told him to say.—Joh 5:19, 30.

Ezekiel's Hope. Ezekiel was faithful to God, carrying out every command given, even though his job was difficult. He is among those of the prophets who endured through faith and who were "reaching out for a better place, that is, one belonging to heaven." (Heb 11:16) While not of the class that makes up the Kingdom of heaven (Mt 11:11), Ezekiel looked forward to the time of the establishment of Messiah's Kingdom and will in due time receive, by resurrection, fulfillment of the promise of God and the blessing of Messianic rule. (Heb 11:39, 40) Ezekiel was outstanding in energy, courage, obedience, and zeal for the worship of God.

EZEKIEL, BOOK OF.

This remarkable book bears the name of the prophet who wrote it. Ezekiel the son of Buzi, a priest, may have completed writing the book in Babylonia in about the year 591 B.C.E. It covers a period of approximately 22 years, from 613 to about 591 B.C.E.—Eze 1:1-3; 29:17.

The book of Ezekiel is distinguished by visions, similes, and allegories, or parables, and especially by performance of symbolic actions, as when Ezekiel was told by God to engrave a sketch of Jerusalem on a brick and then to stage a mock siege against it as a sign to Israel. (Eze 4:1-17) Other symbolic actions were the joining of two sticks, representing the two houses of Israel (37:15-23), and Ezekiel's digging a hole in a wall and going out with his luggage, representing the captivity of Jerusalem. (12:3-13) The illustration of Oholah and Oholibah is one of the vivid allegories of the book. (Chap 23) Another notable feature of the book of Ezekiel is the meticulous care Ezekiel took to date his prophecies, giving not only the year of King Jehoiachin's exile but also the month and day of the month.—1:1, 2; 29:1; 30:20; 31:1; 32:1; 40:1.

Authenticity. Proof of the book's authenticity is to be found in the fulfillment of its prophecies. (For examples see AMMONITES; EDOM, EDOMITES; TYRE.) Further attesting to the authenticity of this book is archaeology. The noted American archaeologist W. F. Albright wrote: "Archaeological data have . . . demonstrated the substantial originality of the Books of Jeremiah and Ezekiel, Ezra and Nehemiah, beyond doubt; they have confirmed the traditional picture of events, as well as their order."—*The Bible After Twenty Years of Archeology* (*1932-1952*), 1954, p. 547.

The authenticity of the book of Ezekiel is supported by its harmony with the other books of the Bible. Although it is not quoted or cited directly by any of the writers of the Christian Greek Scriptures, allusions to some of its statements and similar expressions are, nevertheless, frequent. Ezekiel and Jesus speak of the drying up of a moist tree. (Eze 17:24; Lu 23:31) Ezekiel and Jesus both speak of a judgment of people as sheep and goats. (Eze 34:17; Mt 25:32, 33) The book of Revelation uses many illustrations similar to those in Ezekiel.—Compare Eze 1:28 with Re 4:3; Eze 10:3, 4 with Re 15:8; Eze 12:25 with Re 10:6; Eze 37:10 with Re 11:11.

It is to be noted that among the Chester Beatty Greek Biblical papyri is one codex containing, among other portions of the Bible, Ezekiel, Daniel, and Esther. These are all found in one codex, probably consisting originally of 118 leaves. It is a copy written by two scribes, likely in the first half of the third century, indicating the substantial soundness of the book of Ezekiel as it has come down to us.

Since Jeremiah and Ezekiel were contemporaries, their prophecies have many things in common. (Compare Eze 18:2 with Jer 31:29; Eze 24:3 with Jer 1:13; Eze 34:2 with Jer 23:1.) Daniel and Ezekiel, also contemporaries, have similarities of expression in their writings. Ezekiel, while bound by cords, prophesied about the kingdom of Judah and designated "a day for a year," each day of the prophecy corresponding to a year in the fulfillment. (Eze 4:4-8) Daniel spoke of a banded tree stump, a prophecy concerning the Kingdom, and specified the time period until removal of the bands. (Da 4:23) Another time prophecy of Daniel was the 70 weeks in connection with the coming of Messiah the Leader, also using a day to symbolize a year in the fulfillment. —Da 9:24-27.

Arrangement of Material. For the most part, Ezekiel's prophecies and visions are arranged chronologically as well as topically. The four verses of chapter 29:17-20 are placed out of their chronological order (compare Eze 29:1; 30: 20), but topically they belong here with the prophecy against Egypt. Up until the tenth month of the ninth year of the first exile, the central point around which Ezekiel's prophecies revolved was the complete fall and desolation of Jerusalem, with only brief references to the restoration. Such is the tenor of the first 24 chapters.

HIGHLIGHTS OF EZEKIEL

Prophecies regarding the destruction of Jerusalem by Babylon and the restoration of a faithful remnant. A central theme is that people "will have to know that I am Jehovah"

Written in Babylon—most of it during the six years before Jerusalem was destroyed in 607 B.C.E., and some of it as late as about 591 B.C.E.

Jehovah commissions Ezekiel (then an exile in Babylonia) as watchman (1:1–3:27)

Given awe-inspiring vision of Jehovah's glory, along with cherubs having four faces and accompanied by wheels having rims full of eyes

Serious responsibility as watchman

Warning prophecies against unfaithful Judah and Jerusalem (4:1–24:27)

Ezekiel is directed to enact Jerusalem's coming siege by lying before an engraved brick for 390 days on his left side and 40 days on his right, while subsisting on meager amounts of food and water

The land, including sites used for idolatry, to be desolated; unfaithful people to perish, with a remnant to survive; neither gold nor silver of value in providing escape

Because idolatrous practices are carried on in temple precincts, Jehovah determines to express his rage, showing no compassion; only those marked by secretary clothed with linen to be spared

Flight of King Zedekiah and people illustrated by Ezekiel's carrying out luggage through an opening dug in a wall

Jehovah's judgment against false prophets and prophetesses

Eagle-vine riddle indicates bitter consequences because people turn to Egypt for help

Judgment of Jehovah to be according to individual action and not, as wrongly claimed, merely for sins of fathers

Wicked Zedekiah's crown to be removed, and royal rule in David's line to cease until coming of the One having the legal right

Unfaithful Samaria and Jerusalem represented as two prostitutes, Oholah and Oholibah; Jerusalem to receive severe treatment from her former lovers

Besieged Jerusalem compared to heated cooking pot, and the inhabitants to meat inside

Prophecies against surrounding nations, a number of which Jehovah foresees as rejoicing over Jerusalem's downfall (25:1–32:32)

Ammon, Moab, Edom, and Philistia to be desolated

Tyre to be besieged by Nebuchadnezzar and, in time, to become a desolated site; destruction likened to the sinking of a fine ship with its cargo; Tyrian dynasty to end because of arrogance and treachery

Egypt to be plundered by Nebuchadnezzar in payment for his services as executioner of divine judgment against Tyre; Pharaoh and his crowd compared to a cedar that would be cut down

Prophecies of deliverance and restoration of God's people (33:1–48:35)

Jehovah to regather his people, his sheep, and raise up his servant David as a shepherd over them

Whereas Edom is to be desolated, the land of Israel is to flourish like the garden of Eden

As exiles in Babylon, the Israelites resemble dry, lifeless bones, but they are to be raised to life

The union of two sticks, one representing Joseph and the other Judah, illustrates the bringing back of the exiled people into a unity under God's servant David

Jehovah's restored people to come under Gog's attack, but Jehovah promises to protect them and destroy Gog's forces

Ezekiel is given vision of a temple and its features; a stream flows from the temple to the Dead Sea, where waters are healed and a fishing industry develops; trees along the stream's banks yield edible fruit and leaves for healing

Land assignments are outlined; the city "Jehovah Himself Is There" is described

During the siege of Jerusalem, the prophet turned his attention mainly to pronouncing woes upon the pagan nations foreseen by Jehovah God as rejoicing over the downfall of Jerusalem. After arrival of the news that Jerusalem had fallen, the prophet sounds the glorious note of restoration, which is a dominant theme throughout the remainder of the book.—33:20, 21.

The book of Ezekiel reveals that Babylon's false religion had been introduced into the precincts of Jehovah's temple, particularly in the form of worshiping the Babylonian god Tammuz. (Eze 8:13, 14) Besides such detestable false worship at Jehovah's temple itself, the apostate Jews filled the land of Judah with violence. It comes as no surprise, therefore, that in his vision Ezekiel hears the call for Jehovah's executioners to come with their weapons for smashing and to stand beside the altar in the inner courtyard of the temple. Jehovah then gives them orders to go through the midst of unfaithful Jerusalem and kill off everybody not marked as a worshiper of Jehovah: "Old man, young man and virgin and little child and women you should kill off—to a ruination. But to any man upon whom there is the mark do not go near, and from my sanctuary you should start." (9:6) Ezekiel reports that Jehovah's executioners started by killing first the 70 elderly men who were worshiping idolatrous carvings on the wall in a chamber in the inner courtyard. All the women who were sitting at the gate, weeping for the Babylonish god Tammuz, and the sun-worshiping apostates at the temple porch were also killed. (8:7–9:8) The vision of Ezekiel was but a preview of what was about to befall Jerusalem when Jehovah would make her drink the cup of wine of His rage out of His hand by means of His executional servant, King Nebuchadnezzar (Nebuchadrezzar), and his armies. —Jer 25:9, 15-18.

Ezekiel's prophecies of restoration must have been of comfort to the exiled Jews. In the 25th year of his exile (593 B.C.E.) Ezekiel had a remarkable vision of a new temple of Jehovah, the pattern of which came from Jehovah God himself, and of an adjacent city called Jehovah-Shammah, meaning "Jehovah Himself Is There." (Eze 40:1–48:35) In the midst of a land of pagan idolatry, it strengthened hope in the repentant Jewish exiles of again worshiping the true God, Jehovah, at his temple.

Ezekiel's prophecy emphasizes the theme of the Bible, the vindication of Jehovah's name by the Messianic Kingdom. It points out that while God would permit a long period of vacancy on the throne of David, God had not abandoned his covenant with David for a kingdom. The Kingdom would be given to the One who had the legal right. Ezekiel thereby pointed the Jews, as did Daniel, to the hope of the Messiah. (Eze 21:27; 37:22, 24, 25) Jehovah caused Ezekiel to say more than 60 times that people 'will have to know that I am Jehovah.' Ezekiel magnifies the memorial name of God by using the expression "Sovereign Lord Jehovah" 217 times.—Eze 2:4, ftn.

EZEM (E'zem). A Judean site given to the tribe of Simeon as an enclave city. (Jos 15:21, 29; 19:1, 3; 1Ch 4:24, 28, 29) Some scholars identify it with Umm el-'Azem, about 25 km (16 mi) SSE of Beer-sheba.

EZER (E'zer).

1. [possibly, Store Up]. One of the Horite sheiks in the land of Seir. (Ge 36:20, 21, 30) The Horites were later dispossessed and annihilated by the sons of Esau. (De 2:22) The name Ezer in this case possibly means "Store Up," because of a difference in the spelling in the original Hebrew. At 1 Chronicles 1:38 it has been misprinted "Ezar" in many modern editions of the *King*

James Version, although it was correct in the edition of 1611 as well as other early editions. [2-6: Help]

2. Likely a son of Ephraim who was killed along with his brother Elead by the men of Gath "because they came down to take their livestock." —1Ch 7:20, 21.

3. A son of Hur of the tribe of Judah, and "the father" of Hushah. Hushah was either a person or a town of Judah.—1Ch 4:1, 4; see HUSHAH.

4. The chief one of the 11 valiant Gadites who separated themselves to David in the wilderness while he was still under restriction because of Saul. Being the head, Ezer was evidently the greatest and therefore 'equal to a thousand.' —1Ch 12:1, 8, 9, 14.

5. The son of Jeshua, a prince of Mizpah, who shared in repairing a section of the wall of Jerusalem under Nehemiah in 455 B.C.E.—Ne 3:19.

6. One of the priests in the procession arranged by Nehemiah at the inauguration of the rebuilt wall of Jerusalem in 455 B.C.E.—Ne 12: 31, 41, 42.

EZION-GEBER (E'zi·on-ge'ber). A place first mentioned as an Israelite campsite toward the close of the nation's 40 years in the wilderness. The next campsite was at Kadesh in the wilderness of Zin. (Nu 33:35, 36) From Kadesh the request was made to the king of Edom for authorization to pass through his land, but this was denied. (Nu 20:14-22) As Moses later recounted: "So we passed on away from our brothers, the sons of Esau, who are dwelling in Seir, from the way of the Arabah, from Elath and from Ezion-geber." (De 2:8) Both Elath (Eloth) and Ezion-geber are shown elsewhere to have been situated on the Red Sea, evidently at the head of the Gulf of 'Aqaba, the NE arm of the Red Sea.—1Ki 9:26; 2Ch 8:17.

In harmony with Deuteronomy 2:8, the earlier account at Numbers 21:4 describes the Israelites as "trekking from Mount Hor [where Aaron died] by the way of the Red Sea to go around the land of Edom." Some scholars suggest that the Israelites, after leaving Mount Hor, traveled to the southern end of the Dead Sea and went up the torrent valley of Zered (the boundary between Edom and Moab). Many commentators, however, hold that the foregoing texts require a more circuitous route in avoidance of Edom's heartland, a route that led them back "by the way of the Red Sea" and hence to the region of Ezion-geber. They suggest that the route followed took the Israelites S toward the Gulf of 'Aqaba, and that, upon reaching a point N of Ezion-geber, they likely turned to the NE through the Wadi Yatm, thereby skirting the southern extremity of Edom's southern mountain range.

During Solomon's Reign. The next mention of Ezion-geber comes over 400 years later, in the reign of Solomon (1037-998 B.C.E.). At this location on the gulf, Solomon had a fleet of ships constructed and launched, manned by a Phoenician-Judean crew. Phoenician King Hiram of Tyre, also very active in the shipping business, cooperated with Solomon in this enterprise. (1Ki 9:26-28; 10:11) About a century later, King Jehoshaphat (936-c. 911 B.C.E.) endeavored to revive this shipping industry based at Ezion-geber, but he failed, as Jehovah had foretold, his ships being wrecked.—1Ki 22:48, 49; 2Ch 20:36, 37.

It may be noted that both in Solomon's case and in that of Jehoshaphat some of the ships were intended to go not only to Ophir but also to Tarshish. (2Ch 9:21; 20:36, 37) Since the evidence is strong that Tarshish was in Spain, some have doubted that ships sailing from Ezion-geber could have made such a trip in ancient times. As to this, see the article TARSHISH No. 4, where the possibility of the existence of a Nile–Red Sea canal is presented. Such a canal might also explain how King Hiram could send not only men but "ships" to Ezion-geber and Eloth (Elath) for Solomon's use. (2Ch 8:17, 18) On the other hand, it has also been suggested that these ships may have been sent to a point on the Philistine coast, dismantled, and transported overland to the Gulf of 'Aqaba, where they were reconstructed. Those holding this view point out that the Crusaders later used a similar method. Whether by some Nile–Red Sea canal or by an overland route, it seems likely that at least timber was supplied from forest lands elsewhere, since the region around Ezion-geber has palm groves but no trees suitable for ship construction.

Location. Just where ancient Ezion-geber stood cannot be determined with certainty. Most scholars accept Tell el-Kheleifeh ('Ezyon Gever), some 500 m (1,600 ft) from the Gulf of 'Aqaba and over 3 km (2 mi) NW of the modern village of 'Aqaba, as the most likely possibility. Excavations there have uncovered five major periods of occupation, the oldest conjectured to date back to Solomon's time. However, the archaeologists found nothing that they would date beyond that period, hence nothing dating back to the time of the Exodus. For this reason some conclude that the Ezion-geber of Moses' day was either at another point, or that, because the native buildings were simple structures of mud brick, the early settlement has dissolved into the earth, leaving no trace behind.

Storage depot. The excavators at Tell el-Kheleifeh found the remains of a massive city gate and also a structure that was confidently declared to have been the center of a large copper-mining and smelting industry; they attributed its operation to King Solomon. More recently it was acknowledged that this identification was incorrect, and although some copper smelting was evidently done in that area, archaeologists now hold that the building was undoubtedly a storage depot. Such a fortified depot would be convenient at this point where important sea and land trade routes intersected, to house the gold, precious stones, and algum wood from Ophir till their being transported by caravans to their point of destination. (1Ki 9:26; 10:11, 12) For further details on this site, see ARCHAEOLOGY (Palestine and Syria).

EZNITE. See JOSHEB-BASSHEBETH.

EZRA (Ez'ra) [Help].

1. An Aaronic priest, a descendant of Eleazar and Phinehas, a scholar, an expert copyist and teacher of the Law, skilled in both Hebrew and Aramaic. Ezra had genuine zeal for pure worship and "prepared his heart to consult the law of Jehovah and to do it and to teach in Israel regulation and justice." (Ezr 7:1-6, 10) In addition to writing the book bearing his name, Ezra apparently wrote the two books of Chronicles, and Jewish tradition credits him with beginning the compiling and cataloging of the books of the Hebrew Scriptures. Moreover, Ezra was an outstanding researcher, citing about 20 sources of information in the two books of Chronicles. Since many of the Jews were scattered far and wide in Ezra's day, it necessitated the making of many copies of the Hebrew Scriptures, and likely Ezra pioneered this work.

No details of Ezra's early life are given in the Bible. He lived in Babylon. He was from a family of high priests but was not of the particular branch that held the high priesthood immediately after the return from exile in 537 B.C.E. The last of Ezra's ancestors to hold that office was Seraiah, who was high priest in the days of King Zedekiah of Judah. This Seraiah had been put to death by Nebuchadnezzar at the capture of Jerusalem in 607 B.C.E. (Ezr 7:1, 6; 2Ki 25:18, 21) In

Babylon the Jews retained respect for the priesthood, and therefore, the priestly families maintained their identity. Moreover, the Jewish community organization, with the older men as heads, continued functioning. (Eze 20:1) Ezra's family likely was interested in seeing that Ezra was equipped with a knowledge of God's law, as was Ezra himself. Accordingly he was well educated.

If, as some scholars believe, a man could not become a scribe until reaching the age of 30, Ezra may have been more than 30 years old in 468 B.C.E. when he went to Jerusalem. He undoubtedly lived during the rule of Ahasuerus, in the time of Mordecai and Esther, at the time the decree went out to exterminate the Jews throughout the Persian Empire. There were many Jews living in Babylon, so this national crisis must have made an indelible imprint on Ezra, strengthening him in faith in Jehovah's care for and deliverance of his people and serving as training, maturing him in judgment and competence to accomplish the tremendous task later set before him.—Es 1:1; 3:7, 12, 13; 8:9; 9:1.

To Jerusalem. It was in 468 B.C.E., 69 years after the return of the faithful Jewish remnant from Babylon under the leadership of Zerubbabel, that the Persian king Artaxerxes Longimanus granted to Ezra "all his request" with respect to going to Jerusalem and advancing pure worship there. According to the king's official letter, those Israelites who of their own free will desired to go with Ezra to Jerusalem were to do so.—Ezr 7:1, 6, 12, 13.

Even in Ezra's day, why did Jews who left Babylon need strong faith?

Many of the Jews had become prosperous in Babylon, and the prospects offered in Jerusalem were not attractive from a material viewpoint. Jerusalem was sparsely settled. The fine start made by the Jews under Zerubbabel seems to have deteriorated. One commentator, Dean Stanley, says: "Jerusalem itself was thinly inhabited, and seemed to have stopped short in the career which, under the first settlers, had been opening before it. . . . It is certain that, whether from the original weakness of the rising settlement, or from some fresh inroad of the surrounding tribes, of which we have no distinct notice, the walls of Jerusalem were still unfinished; huge gaps left in them where the gates had been burnt and not repaired; the sides of its rocky hills

cumbered with their ruins; the Temple, though completed, still with its furniture scanty and its ornaments inadequate." (*Ezra and Nehemiah: Their Lives and Times,* by George Rawlinson, London, 1890, pp. 21, 22) So to return to Jerusalem meant loss of position, disruption of ties, the denial of a more or less comfortable way of life, and the building of a new life in a distant land under circumstances that were trying, difficult, and possibly dangerous, not to mention a long and hazardous journey, since many hostile Arab tribes and other enemies might be encountered. It called for zeal for true worship, faith in Jehovah, and courage to make the move. Only some 1,500 men and their families were found willing and able to go, perhaps 6,000 or so in all. Ezra had a difficult task as their leader. But Ezra's past course of life had prepared him, and he strengthened himself according to Jehovah's hand upon him.—Ezr 7:10, 28; 8:1-14.

Jehovah God provided much-needed material aid, for the financial condition in Jerusalem was not good and the wealth of those traveling with Ezra was limited. King Artaxerxes and his seven counselors were moved to make a voluntary contribution to be used for buying sacrificial animals and their grain and drink offerings. Furthermore, Ezra was authorized to receive contributions for this purpose in the jurisdictional district of Babylon. If there was any surplus of funds, Ezra and those with him could determine how this might best be used. The vessels for temple service were to be delivered in full to Jerusalem. If needed, additional funds could be obtained from the king's treasury. The treasurers beyond the River were informed that Ezra could request of them silver, wheat, wine, and oil up to a certain amount, and salt without limit, and that his request should be granted promptly. Moreover, the priests and temple workers were exempted from taxation. Additionally, Ezra was empowered to appoint magistrates and judges, and judgment was to be executed upon anyone not obeying God's law and the law of the king, "whether for death or for banishment, or for money fine or for imprisonment."—Ezr 7:11-26.

Recognizing Jehovah's direction in this, Ezra immediately followed through on his commission. He collected the Israelites at the banks of the river Ahava, where he made a three-day inspection of the people. Here he found that, although some priests were among their ranks, not one of the nonpriestly Levites had volunteered, and they were very much needed for service at the temple. Ezra here demonstrated his qualifications as a leader. Undaunted by the situation, he immediately sent a formal embassy to the Jews at Casiphia. These responded well, providing 38 Levites and 220 Nethinim. With their families, this no doubt swelled Ezra's entourage to more than 7,000.—Ezr 7:27, 28; 8:15-20.

Ezra then proclaimed a fast in order to seek from Jehovah the right way. Even though his caravan would be carrying great riches, Ezra did not want to bring the least shadow on Jehovah's name by requesting an escort after he had expressed to the king his full faith in Jehovah's protection for his servants. After entreating God, he called in 12 from among the chiefs of the priests, carefully weighed out to them the contribution, which, according to modern-day values, was evidently worth more than $43,000,000, and entrusted it to them.—Ezr 8:21-30.

The hand of Jehovah did prove to be with Ezra and those with him, protecting them from "the enemy in the way," so that they arrived safely in Jerusalem. (Ezr 8:22) He had no difficulty in getting recognition by the priests and Levites serving at the temple, to whom he turned over the valuables he had brought.—Ezr 8:31-34.

Urges Israel to Dismiss Foreign Wives. After offering sacrifices at the temple, Ezra learned from the princes that many of the people, the priests, and the Levites who had been living in the land had taken foreign wives. Upon hearing this, Ezra ripped his garment and his sleeveless coat apart, pulled out some of the hair of his head and his beard, and kept sitting stunned until the evening grain offering. Then, falling upon his knees and spreading out his palms to Jehovah, he, in the presence of assembled Israelites, made public confession of the sins of his people, starting with the days of their forefathers.—Ezr 8:35–10:1.

Afterward, Shecaniah, speaking in behalf of the people, recommended that they conclude a covenant with Jehovah to dismiss their foreign wives and the children born to them, and then he said to Ezra: "Get up, for the matter devolves upon you, and we are with you. Be strong and act." Accordingly, Ezra had the people take an oath, and word was sent out for all the former exiles to come together at Jerusalem within three days to straighten out this wrong. On that occasion Ezra exhorted those assembled to make confession to Jehovah and to separate themselves from their foreign wives. However, because of

the great number of people involved in this transgression, it was not possible to care for everything right then and there, but gradually, in a period of about three months, the uncleanness was cleared out.—Ezr 10:2-17.

With Nehemiah. Whether Ezra remained in Jerusalem or returned to Babylon is not certain. But the bad circumstances into which the city came, with the corruption that had infected the priesthood, seem to indicate that he was absent. It may be that he was called upon by Nehemiah to return after the rebuilding of Jerusalem's walls. We find, at any rate, that he appears on the scene again, where he is shown reading the Law to the congregated people and instructing them. On the second day of that assembly the heads of the people hold a special meeting with Ezra to gain insight into the Law. The Festival of Booths is held with rejoicing. After the eight-day observance, Tishri 24 is appointed as a day of abstinence and confession of their sins, with prayer. Under the strong leadership and direction of Ezra and Nehemiah, "a trustworthy arrangement" is made, not by word of mouth this time, but in writing, attested to by seal of the princes, Levites, and priests.—Ne 8:1-9, 13-18; chap 9.

Writing. The Bible books of Chronicles as well as the book bearing Ezra's name give evidence that Ezra was an indefatigable researcher, with discernment in deciding between various readings of the copies of the Law existing then. He exhibited unusual zeal in searching the official documents of his nation, and it is evidently due to his efforts that we have the accurate record Chronicles gives us. We must remember, however, that he had God's spirit of inspiration and that God guided him with a view to preserving a great portion of Israel's history for our benefit.

Ezra's zeal for righteousness, his prayerful reliance upon Jehovah, his faithfulness in teaching God's law to Israel, and his diligence in advancing true worship make him, as one of the "so great a cloud of witnesses," a fine example worthy of imitation.—Heb 12:1.

2. A priest who returned with Zerubbabel from Babylon to Jerusalem in 537 B.C.E.—Ne 12:1, 13.

EZRA, BOOK OF. A record showing how Jehovah fulfilled his promises to restore Israel from exile in Babylon and reestablish true worship in Jerusalem. Included are the imperial orders to restore Jehovah's worship among the Jews after the 70-year desolation of Jerusalem and the account of the work done, despite obstacles, to achieve this. Ezra stuck closely to the above purpose throughout the book. This is apparently the reason for the omissions of what went on during certain lapses of time, such as between chapters 6 and 7 of the book, for the writer was not trying to give a complete historical account of the times.

Writer. Ezra, as a priest, scholar, skilled copyist, and man who had "prepared his heart . . . to teach in Israel regulation and justice" and to correct the things wanting in the worship of Jehovah that was carried on among the repatriated Israelites, was eminently qualified to write the book bearing his name. The royal power granted to him by the king of Persia would give him added reason and authority to do the research necessary, and it would be logical for such a man to write a record of this important segment of his nation's history. (Ezr 7:6, 10, 25, 26) The book is honest, therefore, in its use of the first person for the writer from chapter 7, verse 27, through chapter 9. Most scholars are in agreement that the book of Ezra carries on the history at the point where the Chronicles leave off, as a comparison of 2 Chronicles 36:22, 23 with Ezra 1:1-3 will show. This again points to Ezra as the writer. Jewish tradition likewise assigns the writership to Ezra.

Authenticity. The book of Ezra is included in the Hebrew canon. Originally it was combined with Nehemiah to form one scroll. The Babylonian Talmud (*Bava Batra* 14*b*) follows this tradition, but since the 16th century, printed Hebrew Bibles mark a division, although they count the two books as one in the total number of the books of the Hebrew Scriptures. The *Douay Version* uses the designations First and Second Esdras, following the Greek form of spelling. It notes, however, that the second book is also known as Nehemiah. There is an apocryphal book in Greek called Ezra III. This is composed of passages from Second Chronicles, Ezra, and Nehemiah as well as certain popular legends; also there is the book falsely called Ezra IV.

The greater portion of Ezra was written in Hebrew. But a sizable portion is in Aramaic, since Ezra copied from the public records and official documents. These include the copies of letters sent to the Persian kings by officials "beyond the [Euphrates] River" and the royal replies and decrees imposing commands on these officials. Also, Ezra supplied a brief connecting history linking these documents. Aramaic was the diplomatic language and that used in international commerce of Ezra's day. The Aramaic portions are found in chapters 4 to 7. Some of Ezra's information was copied from Jewish archives,

HIGHLIGHTS OF EZRA

The rebuilding of the temple in Jerusalem and the restoration of true worship there after the Babylonian exile

Covers a period of some 70 years following the return of the Jews from exile in Babylon

---

Cyrus issues liberation decree, and a remnant of Jewish exiles return to Jerusalem (in 537 B.C.E.) to rebuild the temple (1:1–3:6)

Rebuilding of the temple (3:7–6:22)

Foundation laid in second year of the return from exile

Enemies repeatedly interfere with temple rebuilding and finally succeed in having the work stopped until the prophets Zechariah and Haggai, in the second year of Darius I (520 B.C.E.), encourage the people to resume construction

An official investigation of Persian records in Babylon and Ecbatana reveals that the temple rebuilding was authorized by Cyrus, so Darius I decrees that the work continue without hindrance, stipulating the death penalty for violators

In the sixth year of Darius I (515 B.C.E.), temple construction is completed, after which the building is inaugurated and the Passover observed

Ezra goes to Jerusalem (in 468 B.C.E.) with gifts for the temple and to appoint judges (7:1–8:36)

Permission for the trip granted by Persian monarch Artaxerxes (Longimanus)

Ezra and about 1,500 men, besides 258 Levites and Nethinim from Casiphia, depart from a point of assembly at the river Ahava with gold, silver, and utensils for the temple; they arrive in Jerusalem over three and a half months later

Cleansing of Israel, including the priesthood (9:1–10:44)

Learning of the defilement from marriage to foreign women, Ezra makes public confession in prayer to Jehovah

Shecaniah acknowledges sin and proposes the making of a covenant to put away foreign wives and their offspring

All former exiles are commanded to assemble at Jerusalem; a decision is then made to have princes investigate the individual cases of defilement progressively

Priests, Levites, and the rest of the men follow through in dismissing foreign wives and sons

and this part is, of course, in Hebrew. These facts also strengthen the argument for the authenticity of Ezra's account.

Ezra 7:23-26 records that the Persian government approved the Law of Moses as applicable to the Jews and that the Persians thus had a hand in restoring true worship. Ezra's references to the Persian kings put them in their accurate order. Today the majority of scholars accept the accuracy of the book, *The New Westminster Dictionary of the Bible* frankly saying that "there is no doubt about the reliability of the historical contents." (Edited by H. Snyder, 1970, p. 291) The record in the book is, therefore, dependable, and Ezra was a historical person.

Time and Setting. The book of Ezra was written about 460 B.C.E., along with the books of Chronicles. Ezra begins by relating the decree of Cyrus for the restoration of the Jews from Babylon. It was in the first year of Cyrus that this Persian king issued a restoration proclamation. (Ezr 1:1) Judah and Jerusalem had been left desolate of inhabitants, in the autumn of 607 B.C.E., when those left by Nebuchadnezzar moved to Egypt. The 70th year of Jerusalem's desolation, the last enforced sabbath on the land, would end in the autumn of 537 B.C.E. Cyrus' decree must have been issued late in 538 B.C.E. or early in 537 for two reasons. The desolation had to last until the 70th year ended, and the released Israelites would not be expected to travel in the winter rainy season, as would have been the case if the decree had been made a few months earlier. Likely it was issued in the early spring of 537 B.C.E. in order to give the Jews a chance to travel during the dry season, arrive in Jerusalem, and set up the altar on the first day of the seventh month (Tishri) of the year 537 B.C.E., September 29 according to the Gregorian calendar.—Ezr 3:2-6.

After describing the Passover and the Festival of Unfermented Cakes that were held after the temple was completed in 515 B.C.E., Ezra passes over the subsequent period of time until the seventh year of the reign of Artaxerxes, the king of Persia, 468 B.C.E., when Ezra personally comes into the picture. Ezra uses the first person from chapter 7, verse 27, to chapter 9 but changes to the third person in chapter 10, putting himself in the background to concentrate on the activities of princes, the priests, the Levites, and the rest of those who had been repatriated, especially dealing with correcting the situation of the ones who had married foreign wives.

EZRAH   (Ez'rah) [Help]. A name appearing in a list of Judah's descendants. Jether, Mered, Epher, and Jalon are identified as the sons of Ezrah.—1Ch 4:1, 17.

EZRAHITE   (Ez'ra·hite) [Native]. A designation applied to Ethan (1Ki 4:31; Ps 89:Sup) and Heman (Ps 88:Sup), both of them famous for their wisdom. Ethan and Heman are identified at 1 Chronicles 2:3-6 as descendants of Judah through Zerah. Thus the designation "Ezrahite" apparently is another word for "Zerahite." (Nu 26:20) The Targum of Jonathan interprets "Ezrahite" as "son of Zerah."

EZRI   (Ez'ri) [My Help]. Son of Chelub and overseer of the cultivators of the king's fields during David's reign.—1Ch 27:26.

F

FABLE.   A false story, fiction, myth, an invention, falsehood; from the Greek *my'thos*. *My'thos* is found at 1 Timothy 1:4; 4:7; 2 Timothy 4:4; Titus 1:14; 2 Peter 1:16.

My'thos is the opposite of *a·le'thei·a*, "truth," signifying the manifested, veritable essence of a matter. At Galatians 2:5 "the truth of the good news" contrasts the true teaching of the gospel with perversions of it. The apostles warned Christians against the danger of being turned away from the truth to false stories, as these had no basis in fact but were the imaginations of men. Judaism was filled with such false stories, the traditions of the elders making up the so-called oral law that came to be incorporated into the Talmud. Judaism, the leading opponent of Christianity in the first century, had been greatly influenced by pagan philosophies and teachings.

As an example of one of these false stories, consider this from the Palestinian (Jerusalem) Talmud: "R. Samuel b. Nahman in the name of R. Jonathan said: The tables [on which Moses received the Ten Commandments] were six hand-breadths long and three wide: and Moses was holding two hand-breadths, and God two, so that there were two hand-breadths interval between their fingers; and when the Israelites were adoring the calf, God sought to snatch the tables away from Moses' hands; but Moses' hands were so powerful that he snatched them from Him." The story continues that then "the letters flew off" the tablets; as a result, since "the writing was sustaining them," the tablets "became too heavy for Moses' hands, and fell, and were broken." —*Ta'anit,* V, pp. 116, 117, translated by A. W. Greenup.

The Apocryphal writings abound in false, imaginary stories, such as the one about Daniel's killing a great dragon with a mixture of pitch, fat, and hair (Addition to Daniel 14:22-26, *Dy*), and another about Tobias' getting curative and demon-exorcising powers out of the heart, gall, and liver of a monstrous fish.—Tobias 6:2-9, 19, *Dy*.

Christians to Reject Fables. At 1 Timothy 1:4, Paul instructs Christians not to pay attention to false stories. These can get Christians involved in research of no real benefit and can turn their minds away from the truth. Some of these false stories are the kind told by old women whose lives have been spent in worldly practices. They violate God's holy, righteous standards. (1Ti 4:6, 7; Tit 1:14) The apostle Peter, at 2 Peter 1:16, makes reference to false stories (which are not only fictitious but also artfully and cunningly devised in order possibly to turn a Christian aside) and contrasts these with the true, factual account of the transfiguration, of which he was an eyewitness. (Mr 9:2) Paul, at 2 Timothy 4:3, 4, foretold that at a future time people would willingly turn aside to false stories in preference to the truth.

FABRIC. See CLOTH; COTTON; LINEN.

FACE. The Hebrew and Greek words for "face" (Heb., *pa·neh'*; Gr., *pro'so·pon*) are used in varied senses, even as is true of the English word.

The literal face, the front part of the head, is often meant. (Ge 50:1; Mt 6:16, 17; Jas 1:23) Similarly, the front or forepart of anything may be meant. (Ex 26:9; 2Sa 10:9; Eze 2:9, 10, where the Hebrew term for "face" is translated "forefront," or "front.") Or the reference may be to the surface (Isa 14:21; Job 38:30; Ac 17:26) or outward appearance of a thing.—Lu 12:56; Jas 1:11.

Attitude or Position. The expressions of one's countenance are an important index of one's frame of mind and feelings. Therefore "face" is often used to describe the attitude of God and man under various circumstances or to denote one's position as viewed by God or others. Some frequent usages are here presented:

'Seeking the face' meant to seek audience before another, as before God or before an earthly ruler, imploring favorable attention or help. (Ps 24:6; 27:8, 9; 105:4; Pr 29:26; Ho 5:15) The Hebrews spoke of *'lifting up another's face,'* thereby meaning 'showing consideration for' such one.—1Sa 25:35; see IMPARTIALITY.

To *'soften another's face'* indicates an allaying of his anger or a gaining of his favor and goodwill.—Ex 32:11; Ps 119:58.

'Making one's face to shine' toward another expresses favor (Nu 6:25; compare Ps 80:7), and *'setting a person before one's face'* denotes favorable attention.—Ps 41:12; compare Ps 140:13.

"Face to face" may denote intimate association or communication. Thus, Moses was privileged to have such a close relationship with God and be used so powerfully by God that he is referred to as a prophet "whom Jehovah knew face to face." (De 34:10-12) While it is said that Moses beheld "the appearance of Jehovah" and that Jehovah spoke to him "mouth to mouth," yet Moses never saw Jehovah's face literally. Rather, as the context shows, it was God's speaking through angelic spokesmen to Moses in open, verbal communication (instead of by visions or dreams) that gave the basis for such expression. (Nu 12:6-8; Ex 33:20; Ac 7:35, 38; Ga 3:19; compare Ge 32:24-30; Ho 12:3, 4.) Moses recalled to Israel that God spoke "face to face" with them, since they heard the loud voice at Sinai, though none of them actually saw Jehovah.—De 5:4; 4:11-15; Heb 12:19.

By contrast, Jesus, in his prehuman existence, had personally been with the Father, and he pointed out that angels, spirit sons of God, also behold "the face" of God, serving in his heavenly courts. (Joh 1:18; 8:57, 58; Mt 18:10; compare Lu 1:19.) So, too, those called to be joint heirs with Christ in the heavens, in due time, see Jehovah God.—1Jo 3:1-3.

Comparing the understanding of God's purpose had by the early Christian congregation with the fuller understanding to be had upon receiving their heavenly reward, and then coming to comprehend the divine purpose in its entirety as prophecy is fulfilled, the apostle Paul said: "For at present we see in hazy outline by means of a metal mirror, but then it will be face to face."—1Co 13:12; compare 2Co 3:18; 4:6.

To say or do anything *'to one's face'* indicates directness, an open confrontation (De 7:10; Job 21:31) and, in an unfavorable sense, may imply audacity and disrespect. (Job 1:11; Isa 65:3) A related expression is *'the rebuke of the face.'*—Ps 80:16.

To *'set or direct one's face'* has the sense of looking toward some goal, purpose, or desire (Ge 31:21; 1Ki 2:15; 2Ki 12:17), and it carries the thought of strong intention and determination. (2Ch 20:3; Da 11:16-19; Lu 9:51-53) Daniel 'set his face to Jehovah' in that he earnestly sought Him, looking to him for help. (Da 9:3; compare 2Co 1:11.) Strong determination is often reflected in the countenance by the firm set of the lips and jaw, as well as the steadiness of the gaze. Isaiah 'set his face like a flint' in his determination not to let enemy attempts turn him from his assigned ministry. (Isa 50:7) Rebellious Judeans "made their faces harder than a crag" in their obstinacy and refusal to accept correction. (Jer 5:3) On the other hand, Jehovah's 'setting his face against' the violators of his righteous law meant their being rejected and condemned, resulting in calamity or death.—Le 17:10; 20:3-6; Jer 21:10; compare 1Pe 3:12.

To *'conceal the face'* has a variety of meanings, depending on the circumstance. Jehovah God's concealing his face often signifies a withdrawal of his favor or his sustaining power. This may be as a consequence of the disobedience of the individual or body of persons involved, such as the nation of Israel. (Job 34:29; Ps 30:5-8; Isa 54:8; 59:2) In some cases it may denote that Jehovah refrains from revealing himself by action or reply, awaiting his own due time. (Ps 13:1-3) David's request, "Conceal your face from my sins," petitioned God to pardon or set aside such transgressions.—Ps 51:9; compare Ps 10:11.

The concealing, or covering, of the face by a human or an angel may express humility or reverential fear and respect. (Ex 3:6; 1Ki 19:13; Isa 6:2) It may also be a sign of mourning. (2Sa 19:4) By contrast, Eliphaz falsely intimated that Job's prosperity had made him arrogant, so that, in effect, he was 'covering his face with his fattiness.' (Job 15:27) As in Haman's case, for another to cover one's face could represent shamefulness and possibly doom.—Es 7:8; compare Ps 44:15; Jer 51:51.

'Turning the face away' may display insulting indifference or contempt. (2Ch 29:6; Jer 2:27; 32:33) God manifests his disdain for those who reject his counsel by showing them "the back, and not the face," in their day of disaster.—Jer 18:17.

To *'spit in the face'* of another was a particularly significant act of reproach or humiliation.—Nu 12:14; De 25:9; Isa 50:6; Mt 26:67.

One's Person or Presence. Since the face is the most distinctive part of a person, identifying him more than any other feature of the body as well as being most expressive of his personality, the word "face" at times was used metonymically for one's own person or self. See, for example, 2 Samuel 7:9; 17:11; and Acts 3:19, where the expressions "before you" (in the phrase "from before you"), "your own person," and "person" come from the original Hebrew or Greek words for "your face" or "face." In other cases the face may refer to the person's presence, as at Acts 3:13.

"The showbread" of the tabernacle is literally called the bread of faces in Hebrew (Ex 25:30), that is, it was the bread of Jehovah's presence. This expression emphasized his closeness to the people as represented in the sanctuary.

Other Usages and Terms. The Greek term for "face" (*pro·so·pon*) at times denotes the "outward appearance" a person presents, by reason of wealth or poverty, high rank or lowly position, and similar things.—Mt 22:16; 2Co 5:12; Ga 2:6.

The Hebrew word *'aph* (nose; nostrils) sometimes refers to the *region* of the nose and is thus rendered "face," usually in the context of bowing. (Ge 3:19; 19:1; 48:12) The Hebrew *'a·yin* (eye) is used in speaking of Jehovah as appearing to his people, figuratively, "face to face."—Nu 14:14, ftn.

FAIR HAVENS [Fine Harbors]. A harbor near the city of Lasea identified with the bay on the S coast of Crete that still bears the same name in modern Greek, Kaloi Limniones. (Ac 27:7, 8) This bay is located about 8 km (5 mi) E of Cape Matala (Akra Lithinon), the southernmost point of Crete.

In about 58 C.E. the apostle Paul, as a prisoner, was sailing from Myra (on the southern coast of Asia Minor) via Cnidus en route to Rome. The more direct way from Cnidus to Rome would have been to the N of Crete. But evidently adverse winds, probably from the NW, forced the mariners to take a southerly course from Cnidus to Crete and then sail under the shelter of the island's S coast, finally reaching Fair Havens with difficulty.—Ac 27:5-8.

When consideration was given to leaving Fair Havens "considerable time had passed," perhaps

*Fair Havens, Crete, where the ship
taking Paul as prisoner to Rome stopped*

in waiting there for the wind to abate or because
of the slow and difficult journey. It was already
past the Atonement Day fast (late September or
early October), and hence navigation was hazardous.—Ac 27:9.

Paul, who had often been in dangers at sea and
had personally experienced at least three previous shipwrecks (2Co 11:25, 26), wisely recommended that the boat winter at Fair Havens.
(Whether his advice was inspired on this occasion is not revealed in the account.) However,
the army officer, evidently in control of matters,
heeded the advice of the pilot and the shipowner
instead. Fair Havens was an "inconvenient" harbor for wintering; so the majority advised leaving there, and the mariners set sail for Phoenix
farther down the coast. The softly blowing S
wind was deceptive. Soon thereafter the ship was
seized by a tempestuous wind and finally was
wrecked on the coast of Malta, about 900 km
(560 mi) to the W.—Ac 27:9-15, 39-41; 28:1.

Regarding this account in Acts, James Smith
writes: "It is interesting to observe how each
addition to our knowledge of the scene of the
narrative confirms its authenticity and accuracy.
It now appears, from Mr. Brown's observations
and the late surveys, that Fair Havens is so well
protected by islands, that though not equal to
Lutro [thought to be Phoenix], it must be a very
fair winter harbour; and that considering the
suddenness, the frequency, and the violence with
which gales of northerly wind spring up, and the
certainty that, if such a gale sprang up in the
passage from Fair Havens to Lutro, the ship must
be driven off to sea, the prudence of the advice
given by the master and owner was extremely questionable, and that the advice given by
St. Paul may probably be supported even on
nautical grounds."—*The Voyage and Shipwreck
of St. Paul*, London, 1866, p. 85, ftn.

FAITH.   The word "faith" is translated from
the Greek *pi′stis*, primarily conveying the
thought of confidence, trust, firm persuasion. Depending on the context, the Greek word may also
be understood to mean "faithfulness" or "fidelity."
—1Th 3:7; Tit 2:10.

The Scriptures tell us: "Faith is the assured
expectation of things hoped for, the evident demonstration of realities though not beheld." (Heb
11:1) "Assured expectation" translates the Greek

word *hy·po'sta·sis*. This term is common in ancient papyrus business documents. It conveys the idea of something that underlies visible conditions and guarantees a future possession. In view of this, Moulton and Milligan suggest the rendering: "Faith is the *title deed* of things hoped for." (*Vocabulary of the Greek Testament,* 1963, p. 660) The Greek word *e'leg·khos,* rendered "evident demonstration," conveys the idea of bringing forth evidence that demonstrates something, particularly something contrary to what appears to be the case. Thereby this evidence makes clear what has not been discerned before and so refutes what has only appeared to be the case. "The evident demonstration," or evidence for conviction, is so positive or powerful that faith is said to be it.

Faith is, therefore, the basis for hope and the evidence for conviction concerning unseen realities. The entire body of truths delivered by Jesus Christ and his inspired disciples constitutes the true Christian "faith." (Joh 18:37; Ga 1:7-9; Ac 6:7; 1Ti 5:8) Christian faith is based on the complete Word of God, including the Hebrew Scriptures, to which Jesus and the writers of the Christian Greek Scriptures frequently referred in support of their statements.

Faith is based on concrete evidence. The visible creative works testify to the existence of an invisible Creator. (Ro 1:20) The actual occurrences taking place during the ministry and earthly life of Jesus Christ identify him as the Son of God. (Mt 27:54; see JESUS CHRIST.) God's record of providing for his earthly creatures serves as a valid basis for believing that he will surely provide for his servants, and his record as a Giver and Restorer of life lends ample evidence to the credibility of the resurrection hope. (Mt 6:26, 30, 33; Ac 17:31; 1Co 15:3-8, 20, 21) Furthermore, the reliability of God's Word and the accurate fulfillment of its prophecies instill confidence in the realization of *all* of His promises. (Jos 23:14) Thus, in these many ways, "faith follows the thing heard."—Ro 10:17; compare Joh 4:7-30, 39-42; Ac 14:8-10.

So faith is not credulity. The person who may ridicule faith usually has faith himself in tried and trusted friends. The scientist has faith in the principles of his branch of science. He bases new experiments on past discoveries and looks for new discoveries on the basis of those things already established as true. Likewise, the farmer prepares his soil and sows the seed, expecting, as in previous years, that the seed will sprout and

that the plants will grow as they receive the needed moisture and sunshine. Therefore faith in the stability of the natural laws governing the universe actually constitutes a foundation for man's plans and activities. Such stability is alluded to by the wise writer of Ecclesiastes: "The sun also has flashed forth, and the sun has set, and it is coming panting to its place where it is going to flash forth. The wind is going to the south, and it is circling around to the north. Round and round it is continually circling, and right back to its circlings the wind is returning. All the winter torrents are going forth to the sea, yet the sea itself is not full. To the place where the winter torrents are going forth, there they are returning so as to go forth."—Ec 1:5-7.

In the Hebrew Scriptures, the word *'a·man'* and other words closely related convey the sense of trustworthiness, faithfulness, steadiness, steadfastness, being firmly established, long-lasting. (Ex 17:12; De 28:59; 1Sa 2:35; 2Sa 7:16; Ps 37:3) One related noun (*'emeth'*) usually denotes "truth," but also "faithfulness" or "trustworthiness." (2Ch 15:3, ftn; 2Sa 15:20; compare Ne 7:2, ftn.) The familiar term "Amen" (Heb., *'a·men'*) also comes from *'a·man'.*—See AMEN.

Ancient Examples of Faith. Each one of the "so great a cloud of witnesses" mentioned by Paul (Heb 12:1) had a valid basis for faith. For example, Abel certainly knew about God's promise concerning a "seed" that would bruise "the serpent" in the head. And he saw tangible evidences of the fulfillment of the sentence Jehovah pronounced upon his parents in Eden. Outside Eden, Adam and his family ate bread in the sweat of their face because the ground was cursed and, therefore, produced thorns and thistles. Likely Abel observed that Eve's craving was for her husband and that Adam dominated his wife. Undoubtedly his mother commented about the pain attending her pregnancy. Then, too, the entrance to the garden of Eden was being guarded by cherubs and the flaming blade of a sword. (Ge 3:14-19, 24) All of this constituted an "evident demonstration," giving Abel the assurance that deliverance would come through the 'seed of promise.' Therefore, prompted by faith, he "offered God a sacrifice," one that proved to be of greater worth than that of Cain.—Heb 11:1, 4.

Abraham had a firm basis for faith in a resurrection, for he and Sarah had experienced the miraculous restoration of their reproductive powers, which was, in a sense, comparable to a resurrection, allowing Abraham's family line to continue through Sarah. Isaac was born as the result of this miracle. When told to offer up Isaac, Abraham had faith that God would resurrect his son. He based such faith on God's promise: "It is by means of Isaac that what will be called your seed will be."—Ge 21:12; Heb 11:11, 12, 17-19.

Evidence for genuine conviction was also involved in the case of those who came to or who were brought to Jesus to be healed. Even if not eyewitnesses personally, they at least had heard about Jesus' powerful works. Then, on the basis of what they saw or heard, they concluded that Jesus could heal them also. Moreover, they were acquainted with God's Word and thus were familiar with the miracles performed by the prophets in times past. Upon hearing Jesus, some concluded that he was "The Prophet," and others that he was "the Christ." In view of this, it was most fitting for Jesus on occasion to say to those who were healed, "Your faith has made you well." Had those persons not exercised faith in Jesus, they would not have approached him in the first place and, therefore, would not have received healing for themselves.—Joh 7:40, 41; Mt 9:22; Lu 17:19.

Likewise, the great faith of the army officer who entreated Jesus in behalf of his manservant rested on evidence, on the basis of which he concluded that Jesus' merely 'saying the word' would result in the healing of his manservant. (Mt 8:5-10, 13) However, we note that Jesus healed *all* who came to him, not requiring faith greater or less according to their disease, nor failing to heal any of these with the excuse that he could not do it because their faith was not strong enough. Jesus performed these healings as a witness, to establish faith. In his home territory, where much unfaithfulness was expressed, he chose not to perform many powerful works, not because of inability, but because the people refused to listen and were unworthy.—Mt 13:58.

Christian Faith. To be acceptable to God, it is now necessary for one to exercise faith in Jesus Christ, and this makes possible a righteous standing with God. (Ga 2:16) Those lacking such faith are rejected by Jehovah.—Joh 3:36; compare Heb 11:6.

Faith is not the possession of all persons, as it is a fruit of God's spirit. (2Th 3:2; Ga 5:22) And a Christian's faith is not static, but it grows. (2Th 1:3) Hence, the request of Jesus' disciples, "Give us more faith," was very appropriate, and he did provide them the foundation for increased faith.

He supplied them with greater evidence and understanding on which to base their faith.—Lu 17:5.

The entire life course of a Christian is actually governed by faith, enabling him to overcome mountainlike obstacles that would hinder his service to God. (2Co 5:7; Mt 21:21, 22) Additionally, there must be works consistent with and in display of faith, but works of the Mosaic Law are not required. (Jas 2:21-26; Ro 3:20) Trials can strengthen faith. Faith serves as a protective shield in the Christian's spiritual warfare, helping him to overcome the Devil and be a conqueror of the world.—1Pe 1:6, 7; Eph 6:16; 1Pe 5:9; 1Jo 5:4.

But faith cannot be taken for granted, because lack of faith is 'the sin that so easily entangles one.' To maintain a firm faith requires putting up a hard fight for it, resisting men who could plunge one into immorality, combating the works of the flesh, avoiding the snare of materialism, shunning faith-destroying philosophies and traditions of men, and, above all, looking "intently at the Chief Agent and Perfecter of our faith, Jesus." —Heb 12:1, 2; Jude 3, 4; Ga 5:19-21; 1Ti 6:9, 10; Col 2:8.

FAITHFUL AND DISCREET SLAVE.

When answering the apostles' question concerning his future presence and the conclusion of the existing system of things, Jesus Christ included a parable, or illustration, dealing with a "faithful and discreet slave" and an "evil slave." The faithful slave's master appointed him over his domestics, or household servants, to provide them their food. If approved at his master's coming (evidently from some trip), the slave would be rewarded by being placed over the master's entire property.—Mt 24:3, 45-51.

In the parallel illustration at Luke 12:42-48, the slave is called a steward, that is, a house manager or administrator, one placed over servants, though he is himself a servant. Such a position was often filled in ancient times by a faithful slave. (Compare Ge 24:2; also the case of Joseph at Ge 39:1-6.) In Jesus' illustration the steward is first assigned only to the supervision and timely dispensation of the food supplies to the master's body of attendants, or servants, and later, because of his faithful and discreet handling of this ministry, his assignment is widened out to embrace supervision of all the master's holdings. Regarding the identification of the "master" (Gr., *ky'ri·os,* also rendered "lord"), Jesus had already shown that he himself occupied such a position toward his disciples, and they addressed him as such on occasion. (Mt 10:24, 25; 18:21; 24:42; Joh 13:6, 13) The question remains concerning the application of the figure of the faithful and discreet slave, or steward, and what his dispensing food to the domestics represents.

Commentators often view this as a general exhortation to any and all who have individual positions of responsibility in the Christian congregation. The requirement of faithfulness in discharging responsibility clearly applies to all such. (Compare Mt 25:14-30; Tit 1:7-9.) Yet, the impossibility of each and every one of these individuals being placed over "all" his master's belongings at the same time, the time of the master's arrival, is obvious. This, however, does not require that the "slave" prefigure only one particular person who would be so privileged. The Scriptures contain examples of the use of a singular noun to refer to a collective group, as when Jehovah addressed the collective group of the Israelite nation and told them: "You are my witnesses [*plural*], . . . even my servant [*singular*] whom I have chosen." (Isa 43:10) Similarly, the figure of the unfaithful "evil slave" could apply to a collective group in the same way that "the antichrist" is shown to be a class made up of individual antichrists.—1Jo 2:18; 2Jo 7.

Those forming the Christian congregation are referred to by the apostle Paul as "members of the household of God" (Eph 2:19; 1Ti 3:15), and the same apostle shows that 'faithful stewardship' among such household members involved the dispensing of spiritual truths on which those becoming believers would 'feed.' (1Co 3:2, 5; 4:1, 2; compare Mt 4:4.) Whereas this was a prime responsibility of those appointed as 'shepherds' of the flock (1Pe 5:1-3), the apostle Peter shows that such stewardship of the divine truths was actually committed to all the 'chosen ones,' all the spirit-anointed ones, of the Christian congregation. (1Pe 1:1, 2; 4:10, 11) Thus the entire anointed Christian congregation was to serve in a united stewardship, dispensing such truths. At the same time the individual members making up such composite body, or the "domestics" making up the "house" of God (Mt 24:45; Heb 3:6; Eph 2:19), would also be *recipients* of the "food" dispensed. (Heb 5:11-14; compare 1Co 12:12, 19-27.) Expanded responsibility would result from faithfulness maintained until the master's promised 'arrival.'—Mt 24:46, 47; Lu 12:43, 44.

FALCON [Heb., *nets*]. Modern lexicographers believe the Hebrew term *nets* applies to falcons, though some consider it to embrace also hawks, which are very similar to the falcons though classified by ornithologists as in a separate "family" grouping. (The Greek *Septuagint* and the Latin *Vulgate* render *nets* as "hawk.") As a predator, eating snakes, lizards, small mammals, and other birds, "the falcon according to its kind" ("the hawk in its several species," *AT*) was among those birds decreed "unclean" in the Mosaic Law.—Le 11:16; De 14:15.

Some falcons vie with the swift as the fastest fliers of the bird family, observers crediting one falcon with a diving speed of 290 km/hr (180 mph). Among the falcons found in Palestine is the peregrine falcon (*Falco peregrinus*), a fairly common passage migrant. There are also the somewhat larger lanner falcons (*Falco biamircus*), once abundant in the cliffs and rocky gorges from Mount Hermon to the Dead Sea area. Saker falcons (*Falco cherrug*) are occasionally seen in the western Negev.

The smaller common kestrel (*Falco tinnunculus*), about 36 cm (14 in.) long, is also a member of the same genus as the falcon. It is abundant the year round throughout Palestine's agricultural settlements and gardens; it even nests on larger buildings in the cities.

Job 39:26 describes the falcon's 'soaring up and spreading its wings to the south wind,' and this is understood by some to refer to a southward migration ("spreads his wings to travel south," *JB*), which would be true of the lesser kestrel of the falcon family and, to some extent, of the peregrine falcon. Others, however, believe that the text describes the bird as turning into the oncoming wind and, by the power of its wings, flying into it, ascending higher and higher. Falcons are said to "rise to a great height, always endeavoring to outsoar any bird of which they may be in pursuit" in order to be able to plummet down with fierce velocity upon the prey below, and in doing so they often "avail themselves of the wind, and by flying against it are borne aloft like a kite." (*Funk and Wagnalls New Standard Encyclopedia,* 1931, Vol. XI, pp. 329, 330) Similarly the kestrel is sometimes called the windhover "because it *hovers* (stays in one place) in the air while it hunts. This bird faces into the wind and beats its wings while watching the ground for prey."—*The World Book Encyclopedia,* 1987, Vol. 11, p. 237.

The falcon held a very prominent place in the religion of Egypt. It became the symbol of Horus, the falcon-headed god of Egypt, who, together with Isis and Osiris, formed the principal trinity or "holy family" among Egypt's gods and goddesses. The falcon symbol was always used in writing the title of the Pharaohs, and in some cases, these rulers were considered to be incarnations of Horus. Of the hundreds of mummified birds found in Egypt, the falcon, particularly the kestrel, is among the most numerous. Herodotus said that anyone killing a falcon in Egypt, even though accidentally, was put to death.

FALSE PROPHET. See PROPHET.

FAMILY. The Hebrew term *mish·pa·chah'* (family), in addition to referring to a household, also means, by extension, a tribe, people, or nation. The Greek word *pa·tri·a'* also is broad in its scope. Jehovah God is the originator of the family arrangement. He is the Father of his heavenly family and the one to whom 'all the families on earth owe their name.' (Eph 3:14, 15) This is so because Jehovah established the first human family, and by this means he purposed that the earth be filled. Additionally, He permitted Adam, though a sinner, to have a family and have children "in his likeness, in his image." (Ge 5:3) In the Bible, Jehovah has since made clear that He accords great importance to the divinely granted power of procreation, the means by which a man can carry on his name and family line in the earth.—Ge 38:8-10; De 25:5, 6, 11, 12.

Structure and Conservation of Family. In ancient Hebrew society the family was the basic unit. The family was a small government; the father as head was responsible to God, and the mother was the subordinate manager over the children in the household. (Ac 2:29; Heb 7:4) The family was, in a small way, a reflection of the grand family of God. God is represented in the Bible as a husband, with the "Jerusalem above" as the mother of his children.—Ga 4:26; compare Isa 54:5.

The family in patriarchal times may be compared in some respects to the modern corporation. There were some things owned by family members as personal. But, for the most part, the property was held in common, with the father managing its disposal. A wrong committed by a member of the family was considered as a wrong against the family itself, especially its head. It brought reproach on him, and he was responsible, as the judge of the household, to take the necessary action on the matter.—Ge 31:32, 34; Le 21:9; De 22:21; Jos 7:16-25.

Monogamy was the original standard Jehovah set for the family. Although polygamy was later practiced, polygamy was always against the original principle that God laid down. However, he tolerated it until his due time to restore his original standard, which he has done in the Christian congregation. (1Ti 3:2; Ro 7:2, 3) Under the Law covenant he recognized the existence of polygamy and regulated it so that the family unit was still kept intact and operative. But it was Jehovah himself who said: "That is why a man will leave his father and his mother and he must stick to his wife and they must become one flesh." And it was his Son who quoted these words and went on to say: "So that they are no longer two, but one flesh. Therefore, what God has yoked together let no man put apart." (Ge 2:24; Mt 19:4-6) The record indicates that Adam had only one wife, who became "the mother of everyone living." (Ge 3:20) Noah's three sons, who began the repopulation of the earth after the global Flood, were all sons of one father and one mother, and each son passed through the Flood with but one wife.—Ge 8:18; 9:1; 1Pe 3:20.

Under the Law Covenant. In giving the Ten Commandments to Israel, God gave attention to the integrity of the family unit. "Honor your father and your mother" is the fifth commandment, the first commandment with a promise. (De 5:16; Eph 6:2) A child rebellious against his parents was as one rebellious against the governmental arrangement established by God as well as against God himself. If he struck or cursed his father or mother, or if he proved to be incorrigibly unmanageable, he was to be put to death. (Ex 21:15, 17; Le 20:9; De 21:18-21) Children were to have proper fear of their parents, and a child who treated his father or mother with contempt was cursed.—Le 19:3; De 27:16.

The seventh commandment, "You must not commit adultery," outlawed any sexual union of a married person with another outside the marriage bond. (Ex 20:14) All children were to be family born. An illegitimate son was not recognized, nor were his descendants allowed to become members of the congregation of Israel even to the tenth generation.—De 23:2.

While the seventh commandment, in forbidding adultery, served to safeguard the family unit, the tenth commandment, by forbidding wrong desires, further protected the integrity of one's own family as well as the other man's house and family. The things most common to family life were protected by this commandment, namely, house, wife, servants, animals, and other property.—Ex 20:17.

Under the Law a careful record of genealogies was kept. Family integrity was even more greatly emphasized by the matter of ancestral land inheritance. Genealogies were especially important in the family line of Judah and, later on, in the lineage of Judah's descendant David. Because of the promise that the Messiah the King would come through these families, the record of family relationship was zealously guarded. And even though polygamy was not abolished by the Law, the family integrity was protected and its genealogy was kept intact by strict laws governing polygamy. In no way was looseness or promiscuity legally tolerated. Sons born of polygamy or concubinage were legitimate, full-fledged sons of the father.—See CONCUBINE.

The Law specifically prohibited marriage alliances with the seven Canaanite nations that were to be ousted from the land. (De 7:1-4) Because of failing to observe this command, the nation of Israel was ensnared in the worship of false gods and finally brought into captivity by their enemies. Solomon is an outstanding example of one who sinned in this respect. (Ne 13:26) Ezra and Nehemiah undertook energetic reforms among those of the repatriated Israelites who were contaminating their families and Israel itself by marriage to foreign wives.—Ezr 9:1, 2; 10:11; Ne 13:23-27.

When God sent his only-begotten Son to earth he caused him to be born into a human family. He provided that he have a God-fearing adoptive father and a loving mother. Jesus as a child was subject to his parents and respected and obeyed them. (Lu 2:40, 51) Even when he was dying on the torture stake he showed respect and loving care for his mother, who was apparently then a widow, when he said to her: "Woman, see! Your son!" and to the disciple whom he loved: "See! Your mother!" thereby evidently directing this disciple to care for her in his own home.—Joh 19:26, 27.

How does the Bible indicate the importance of the family in the Christian congregation?

In the Christian congregation the family is recognized as the basic unit of Christian society.

Much space is devoted in the Christian Greek Scriptures to instructions regarding family relationship. Again the man is dignified with the headship of the family, the wife being in subjection to her husband, managing the household under his general oversight. (1Co 11:3; 1Ti 2:11-15; 5:14) Likening Jesus to the husband and family head over his congregational 'wife,' Paul admonishes husbands to exercise headship in love, and he counsels wives to respect and subject themselves to their husbands. (Eph 5:21-33) Children are commanded to obey their parents, and fathers particularly are charged with the responsibility of bringing up the children in the discipline and mental-regulating of Jehovah. —Eph 6:1-4.

The man used as an overseer in the Christian congregation, if married, must exhibit high standards as a family head, presiding properly and having his children in subjection, these not being unruly or charged with debauchery, for, asks Paul: "If indeed any man does not know how to preside over his own household, how will he take care of God's congregation?" the congregation being similar to a family. (1Ti 3:2-5; Tit 1:6) Wives are exhorted to love their husbands and children, to be workers at home, and to subject themselves to their own husbands.—Tit 2:4, 5.

Jesus foretold that opposition to God's truth would split families. (Mt 10:32-37; Lu 12:51-53) But the apostle Paul strongly admonished believers against breaking up the marriage relationship, appealing on the basis of the welfare of the unbelieving mate as well as of the children. He stressed the great value of the family relationship when he pointed out that God views the young children as holy, even though the unbelieving mate has not been cleansed from his sins by faith in Christ. The unbeliever may, in fact, be practicing some of the same things that Paul says some Christians had practiced before accepting the good news about the Christ. (1Co 7:10-16; 6:9-11) The apostle also guards the unity of the Christian family by giving instructions to husbands and wives regarding the rendering of marriage dues.—1Co 7:3-5.

Association in family relationships proved to be a blessing to many in connection with Christianity, "for, wife, how do you know but that you will save your husband? Or, husband, how do you know but that you will save your wife?" (1Co 7:16) This is also evidenced by the contents of the apostle Paul's greetings to several households. Some believers were privileged to use the family home as a place for the congregation to meet. (Ro 16:1-15) The Christian missionary Philip was a family man, having four faithful Christian daughters. He was blessed by being able to entertain the apostle Paul and his fellow workers for a time in his home in Caesarea. (Ac 21:8-10) The Christian congregation itself is termed "God's household." Its principal member and head is Jesus Christ, and this "household" recognizes him as the Seed by means of whom all the families of the earth will bless themselves.—1Ti 3:15; Eph 2:19; Col 1:17, 18; Ge 22:18; 28:14.

The inspired Scriptures have foretold a vicious attack on the family institution with a consequent breaking down of morality and of human society outside the Christian congregation. Paul classifies among demon-inspired doctrines in "later periods of time" that of "forbidding to marry." He foretells for "the last days" a condition in which disobedience to parents, disloyalty, and absence of "natural affection" would be rife, even among those "having a form of godly devotion." He warns Christians to turn away from such ones.—1Ti 4:1-3; 2Ti 3:1-5.

Babylon the Great, the enemy of God's "woman" (Ge 3:15; Ga 4:27) and of Christ's "bride" (Re 21:9), is a great "harlot" organization, committing fornication with the kings of the earth. Being "the mother of the harlots and of the disgusting things of the earth" indicates that her "daughters" are harlots, also that she causes great disregard for Jehovah God's institutions and commandments, including his requirements that contribute to family integrity. (Re 17:1-6) She has made efforts to induce others to harlotry and has succeeded in producing many 'harlot' daughters, with attempts being made to prevent Christ from having a clean "bride." Nevertheless, his "bride" comes through victorious, clean, righteous, worthy of being in Jehovah's "family" as the "wife" of Jesus Christ, to the blessing and rejoicing of all the universe.—2Co 11:2, 3; Re 19:2, 6-8; see MARRIAGE and other family relationships under their respective names.

FAMINE.
An extreme food shortage; also, a scarcity of hearing the words of Jehovah, that is, a spiritual famine. (Am 8:11) Famine is one of the plagues to come upon symbolic Babylon the Great.—Re 18:8.

Causes and Effects of Famines. Drought, destructive hailstorms (Ex 9:23-25), pests, scorching and mildew of crops, as well as war,

were among the common causes of famine in Bible times. (Am 4:7-10; Hag 2:17) Locusts, sometimes coming in huge hordes, were especially devastating to crops. (Ex 10:15) Sometimes the problem was not lack of rain, but rain at the wrong season, as during the wheat or barley harvest.—Compare Le 26:4; 1Sa 12:17, 18.

Temporary hunger is a natural sensation, but prolonged hunger, as by famine, is very detrimental to mental and physical health. Marked lethargy sets in, the emotions are dulled, and there is mental apathy. The mind is dominated by a desire for food. (Compare Ex 16:3.) Moral standards fall. (Compare Isa 8:21.) Actual starvation may have a dehumanizing effect, resulting in theft, murder, and even cannibalism. Famine is often accompanied by sickness and epidemics because of the weakened condition of those affected.—Compare De 32:24.

Ancient Famines. The first truly historical famine is the one that forced Abram (Abraham) to leave Canaan and take up alien residence in Egypt. (Ge 12:10) In Isaac's day another famine occurred, but Jehovah told him not to go to Egypt. (Ge 26:1, 2) The seven-year famine that came upon Egypt while Joseph served as prime minister and food administrator evidently reached far beyond the boundaries of Egypt, for "people of all the earth came to Egypt to buy [food] from Joseph."—Ge 41:54-57.

While the Egyptian inscriptions scrupulously avoid any reference to Israel's sojourn in Egypt, there are ancient Egyptian texts that describe periods of famine due to insufficient rising of the Nile River. One text describes a period of seven years of low Nile risings and the resulting famine. According to the account, certain portions of land were granted to the priesthood when relief from the famine came. Although the question is raised as to whether the document is "a priestly forgery of some late period, justifying their claim to territorial privileges," at least we see reflected a tradition of a period of seven lean years.—*Ancient Near Eastern Texts*, edited by J. Pritchard, 1974, p. 31.

Before Israel entered the Promised Land, Jehovah, through Moses, assured them that they would have an abundance of food if they continued serving Him in faithfulness. (De 28:11, 12) However, famine would be one of the fearful results to come upon Israel for unfaithfulness. (De 28:23, 38-42) A famine in the days of the Judges prompted Naomi's husband Elimelech of Bethlehem to reside with his family as an alien in

Moab. (Ru 1:1, 2) Jehovah brought a three-year famine upon the land of Israel in David's day because of bloodguilt resting on the house of Saul in connection with the Gibeonites. (2Sa 21:1-6) A three-and-a-half-year drought resulting in severe famine came upon unfaithful Israel in answer to Elijah's prayer. (Jas 5:17; 1Ki 17) In addition to general famines in Elisha's day, there was the famine produced by the Syrian siege of Samaria, during which one case of cannibalism was reported.—2Ki 4:38; 8:1; 6:24-29.

Although God's prophets warned that apostasy would bring death by famine, pestilence, and the sword, the unfaithful Judeans preferred to listen to their false prophets, who assured them that no such calamity would come. (Jer 14:11-18; Eze 5:12-17) Yet the words of God's prophets proved true. So severe was the famine in Jerusalem during the siege by the Babylonians (609-607 B.C.E.) that women boiled and ate their own children.—La 4:1-10; 5:10; 2Ki 25:1-3; Jer 52:4-6; compare De 28:51-53.

Through the prophet Joel, Jehovah forewarned Israel of a tremendous plague of insects that would devastate the land and bring about severe famine prior to the coming of "the day of Jehovah."—Joe 1.

Centuries later, food shortages were foretold by Jesus as being among the characteristics marking the conclusion of "the system of things." (Mt 24:3, 7; compare Re 6:5, 6.) As announced in advance by Agabus, a Christian prophet, a great famine did occur in the time of Emperor Claudius (41-54 C.E.). (Ac 11:28) A few years earlier, in the year 42 C.E., a severe famine had hit Egypt, where many Jews resided. And "great necessity" came on the land of Judah and Jerusalem when the Roman armies under General Titus besieged Jerusalem and finally destroyed it in 70 C.E. (Lu 21:23) Josephus recounts the terrible starvation conditions in the city, in which people resorted to the eating of leather, grass, and hay, and in one instance, a mother even roasted and ate her son. (*The Jewish War*, VI, 193-213 [iii, 3, 4]) When foretelling such food shortages, however, Jesus indicated that he had in mind not only events preceding Jerusalem's destruction but also what would occur when the time arrived for the Son of man to return in the glory of his Kingdom.—Lu 21:11, 27, 31; compare Re 6:5, 6.

Freedom From Famine. Christ Jesus gives assurance that the prayer of faithful servants for their daily bread would be answered by God and that those putting God's Kingdom first would be cared for. (Mt 6:11, 33; compare Ps 33:19; 37:19,

25.) However, because of opposition and persecution, Jesus showed that his servants might suffer hunger at times. (Mt 25:35, 37, 40) The apostle Paul in particular recounts his suffering both hunger and thirst many times while engaged in the ministry under difficult circumstances. (1Co 4:11-13; 2Co 11:27; Php 4:12) Yet he expressed confidence that physical hunger would never be able to separate God's faithful servants from the sustaining strength of God's love.—Ro 8:35, 38, 39; contrast Lu 6:25.

Those who have a proper hunger and thirst for righteousness and truth will always be spiritually filled. (Mt 5:6; Joh 6:35) This includes those of the "great crowd" who have hope of surviving "the great tribulation" and of whom it is written that "they will hunger no more nor thirst anymore." (Re 7:9, 13-17) And under the rule of God's Kingdom there will also come to be an abundance to satisfy the physical hunger of all mankind.—Ps 72:16; Isa 25:6.

FARMING. See AGRICULTURE.

FARMING IMPLEMENTS. Although the Bible mentions various agricultural operations, the implements that were used to cultivate the land are not described in detail. However, the pictures of farm implements on Egyptian monuments as well as actual specimens found in Egypt and Palestine supplement the Bible record to some extent. Moreover, there is great similarity between the simple farming implements still used in parts of Egypt and Palestine.

Forks used for winnowing (Isa 30:24; Jer 15:7), as in more recent times, were probably made of wood and had several curved prongs.

The *harrow* is not referred to in the Bible, but the agricultural operation of harrowing is mentioned as being distinct from plowing. (Job 39:10; Isa 28:24; Ho 10:11) Pulverizing and smoothing the soil constitute the chief function of the modern harrow, though it is also used for mulching, covering seed, and removing weeds. Anciently, perhaps a weighted-down board or a rough log was dragged over the plowed soil to break up the clods and level the ground.

Hoes were employed for clearing land of weeds and probably also for breaking up clods of earth. Certain prophetic passages specifically mention the use of hoes in the vineyard.—Isa 5:5, 6; 7:23-25.

Mattocks were probably used for grubbing and for loosening the soil. They were among the tools that the Israelites in Saul's day had to take to the

Philistines to get sharpened. (1Sa 13:20, 21) Bronze and iron mattocks, somewhat resembling the modern grub hoe, have been found.

The simple wooden *plow* still used in some parts of the Bible lands has undergone little change over the centuries, as a comparison of representations of plows on ancient monuments and even clay tablets clearly shows. The plow was neither equipped with wheels nor designed to turn a furrow; it merely scratched the surface of the soil to a depth of about 8 or 10 cm (3 or 4 in.). Except for the metal plowshare, it was made of wood. (Compare 1Sa 13:20; 1Ki 19:19, 21; Isa 2:4.) A stick, to which the plowshare was attached, constituted the larger part of the plow. The copper and bronze plowshares (actually plowpoints) that have been found in excavations in Israel are generally dented considerably from use.—See PLOWING.

Pruning shears are specifically mentioned in the Bible with reference to pruning the vine. (Isa 18:5) Since the Scriptures refer to converting spears into pruning shears and, by contrast, pruning shears into lances, this tool perhaps consisted of a sharp knifelike blade fastened to a handle and may have been similar to a sickle. —Isa 2:4; Joe 3:10.

Sickles were used mainly for reaping standing grain, though the Bible also speaks of thrusting in the sickle to harvest the vine. (Joe 3:13; Re 14:18) The sickles that have been found in Israel are slightly curved. Some specimens consist of notched flint chips that were pieced together and set with bitumen into a frame of either wood or bone. Iron sickle blades have also been found, and these were fastened to a handle by means of rivets, a tang, or a socket.

The *threshing sledge* was designed to separate the kernels from the ears of grain. The implement used in ancient times likely resembled the two types still employed in some parts of the Bible lands today. One consists of wooden planks joined together and bent back at the front. Its underside is equipped with sharp stones or knives. (Compare 1Ch 21:23; Job 41:30; Isa 41:15.) The driver stands on the sledge to weight it down. The other type has a seat for the driver and consists of a low-built, four-cornered wagon frame. Two or three parallel revolving rollers equipped with iron strips are fitted into this frame.—Compare Isa 28:27, 28.

Winnowing shovels, probably made of wood, were used for tossing threshed grain into the air so that the wind would blow the straw and chaff away.—Mt 3:12.

FAST. Abstinence from all food for a limited period. Rightly motivated fasts were to show godly sorrow and repentance concerning past sins. (1Sa 7:6; Joe 2:12-15; Jon 3:5) They were also fitting in the face of great danger, when in sore need of divine guidance, while enduring tests and meeting temptations, or when studying, meditating, or concentrating on God's purposes. (2Ch 20:3; Ezr 8:21; Es 4:3, 16; Mt 4:1, 2) Fasting was, not a self-inflicted form of punishment, but a humbling of oneself before Jehovah. (Ezr 8:21; 9:5; compare 1Ki 21:27-29.) Jesus fasted 40 days, as did Moses and Elijah, both of whom appeared in a visionary way with Jesus at his transfiguration.—Mt 17:1-9; Ex 34:28; De 9:9; 1Ki 19:7, 8.

The Mosaic Law does not use the term "fast," but in connection with the Day of Atonement it does command, "You must afflict your souls." (Le 16:29-31; 23:27; Nu 29:7) This is generally understood to mean fasting, and this view is supported by Isaiah 58:3, 5 and Psalm 35:13.

Isaiah chapter 58 deals with a time when the sins of the Jews were heavy; yet they did not sincerely repent, though they made a pretense of worshiping Jehovah, giving him lip service and performing religious acts or practices for show. Fasting was one such practice, and they thought it should gain them divine notice and favor. This failing, they asked in apparent bewilderment: "For what reason did we fast and you did not see, and did we afflict our soul and you would take no note?" Jehovah told them why. Even during the fast, while asking for his righteous judgments and acting as if they carried on righteousness itself, they were pursuing their own pleasure and business, indulging in strife, oppression, and violence; they showed none of the godly sorrow and repentance associated with sincere fasts. Their fast was not such as to make their voice heard in heaven, though their showy wailings were noisy indeed. Jehovah denounced the hypocritical act they put on: "Should the fast that I choose become like this, as a day for earthling man to afflict his soul? For bowing down his head just like a rush, and that he should spread out mere sackcloth and ashes as his couch? Is it this that you call a fast and a day acceptable to Jehovah?" —Isa 58:1-5.

To be acceptable, the fast must be accompanied by a correction of past sins. Through his prophet Isaiah, Jehovah made known what he considered to be a real fast, saying: "Is not this the fast that I choose? To loosen the fetters of wickedness, to release the bands of the yoke bar, and to send away the crushed ones free, and that you people should tear in two every yoke bar? Is it not the dividing of your bread out to the hungry one, and that you should bring the afflicted, homeless people into your house? That, in case you should see someone naked, you must cover him, and that you should not hide yourself from your own flesh?"—Isa 58:6, 7.

Four Annual Fasts of the Jews. The Jews established many fasts, and at one time had four annual ones, evidently to mark the calamitous events associated with Jerusalem's siege and desolation in the seventh century B.C.E. (Zec 8:19) The four annual fasts were: (1) "The fast of the fourth month" apparently commemorated the breaching of Jerusalem's walls by the Babylonians on Tammuz 9, 607 B.C.E. (2Ki 25:2-4; Jer 52:5-7) (2) It was in the fifth Jewish month Ab that the temple was destroyed, and evidently "the fast of the fifth month" was held as a reminder of this event. (2Ki 25:8, 9; Jer 52:12, 13) (3) "The fast of the seventh month" was apparently held as a sad remembrance of Gedaliah's death or of the complete desolation of the land following Gedaliah's assassination when the remaining Jews, out of fear of the Babylonians, went down into Egypt. (2Ki 25:22-26) (4) "The fast of the tenth month" may have been associated with the exiled Jews already in Babylon receiving the sad news that Jerusalem had fallen (compare Eze 33:21), or it may have commemorated the commencement of Nebuchadnezzar's successful siege against Jerusalem on the tenth day of that month, in 609 B.C.E.—2Ki 25:1; Jer 39:1; 52:4.

When certain Jews asked: "Shall I weep in the fifth month, practicing an abstinence, the way I have done these O how many years?" by means of Zechariah, Jehovah answered: "When you fasted . . . for seventy years, did you really fast to me, even me?" God showed that a real fast to him would have been accompanied by obedience and that what he required was truthfulness, judgment, peace, and a sincere heart. Then, instead of fasting mournfully and looking back into the past, they would be able to exult and rejoice in festal seasons with the blessings of restoration of true worship and ingathering of others to Jehovah's service.—Zec 7:3-7; 8:16, 19, 23.

Christian Counsel on Fasting. When Jesus was on earth he gave instruction to his disciples: "When you are fasting, stop becoming sad-faced like the hypocrites, for they disfigure their faces

that they may appear to men to be fasting. Truly I say to you, They are having their reward in full. But you, when fasting, grease your head and wash your face, that you may appear to be fasting, not to men, but to your Father who is in secrecy; then your Father who is looking on in secrecy will repay you." (Mt 6:16-18) He alluded here to the insincere fasting of the Pharisees, which he mentioned in an illustration on another occasion. (Lu 18:9-14) It was customary for the Pharisees to fast twice a week, on the second and fifth days of the week.—Lu 18:12.

A person's merely abstaining from food in a formalistic manner is described by Paul as subjecting oneself to decrees, "Do not handle, nor taste, nor touch," and he says that "those very things are, indeed, possessed of an appearance of wisdom in a self-imposed form of worship and mock humility, a severe treatment of the body; but they are of no value in combating the satisfying of the flesh."—Col 2:20-23.

Fasting has been enjoined on their members by some religious sects of Christendom, but the Bible itself gives no command to Christians to fast. When Jesus was talking to his disciples about fasting, as above (Mt 6:16-18), he and his disciples were still under the Mosaic Law and observed the Day of Atonement and its fast.

The text about fasting at Matthew 17:21, appearing in the *King James Version,* is not contained in some of the most important ancient manuscripts. Likewise, although the *King James Version* mentions fasting at Mark 9:29, Acts 10:30, and 1 Corinthians 7:5, according to such manuscripts these texts do not contain any references to fasting.

Some have taken Matthew 9:15 as a command for Christians to fast. In reality, Jesus was merely making a statement of what was going to happen when he died. While Jesus was with his disciples on earth, it was not appropriate for them to fast. When he died, they did mourn and fast. But they had no cause for mournful fasting after his resurrection and especially after the marvelous outpouring of holy spirit. (Mr 2:18-20; Lu 5:33-35) Certainly Christians were not under obligation to fast on the anniversary of the Lord's death, for the apostle Paul, correcting abuses in connection with the eating of supper at the congregation's meeting place before the observance of the Lord's Evening Meal, said: "Certainly you do have houses for eating and drinking, do you not? . . . Consequently, my brothers, when you come together to eat it [the Lord's Evening Meal], wait for one another. If anyone is hungry, *let him eat at home,* that you may not come together for judgment."—1Co 11:22, 33, 34.

While not fasting as a religious requirement, the early Christians did fast on special occasions. When Barnabas and Paul were sent on a special missionary assignment into Asia Minor, there was fasting as well as praying. Also, there was the offering of prayer "with fastings" when elders were appointed in a new congregation. (Ac 13: 2, 3; 14:23) Hence, Christians are neither under command to fast nor prohibited from doing so. —Ro 14:5, 6.

FAT. The English word "fat" is used to translate various Hebrew words that describe not only the substance called fat but also that which is full-fleshed and plump. These terms may also be used in a figurative sense to express that which is rich or fertile (just as in the English expression "fat of the land") or to convey the idea of insensibility or dullness of mind and heart.

Che'lev is ordinarily used to refer to the substance "fat," either of animals (Le 3:3) or of men (Jg 3:22). The "suet," or hard fat about the kidneys or loins, in the burnt offerings is also expressed by another word, *pe'dher.* (Le 1:8, 12; 8:20) *Che'lev* first appears at Genesis 4:4 in connection with Abel's sacrifice to Jehovah of "fatty pieces" from the firstlings of his flock. Most references to *che'lev* thereafter simply relate to sacrificing. *Che'lev* is also used metaphorically for the *best* or *richest part of anything.* For instance, at Genesis 45:18, Pharaoh tells Joseph that his family is welcome to eat "the fat part of the land." Thus, too, Numbers 18:12 reads: "All the best [*che'lev*] of the oil and all the best [*che'lev*] of the new wine and the grain . . . I have given them to you."—See Ps 81:16; 147:14.

The Law Regarding Fat. In the third chapter of Leviticus, Jehovah gave the Israelites instructions concerning the use of fat in communion sacrifices. When offering cattle or goats, they were to make the fat around the loins and intestines and that over the kidneys, as well as the fatty appendage upon the liver, smoke upon the altar. In the case of sheep, the entire fatty tail likewise was to be offered. (The sheep of Syria, Palestine, Arabia, and Egypt have fat tails, often weighing 5 kg [11 lbs] or more.) The Law specifically said, "All the fat belongs to Jehovah . . . You must not eat any fat or any blood at all."—Le 3:3-17.

Fat would burn fiercely and would be quite thoroughly consumed upon the altar. Any fat offered on the altar was not to be left over until the next morning; it was likely to corrupt and become offensive, something very unseemly for any part of the sacred offerings.—Ex 23:18.

Not incumbent on Christians. After the Flood, when permission was given to Noah and his family to add flesh to their diet, nothing was stated regarding fat. (Ge 9:3, 4) However, the eating of blood was prohibited. This was more than 850 years before the Law covenant, with its prohibitions against the eating of both blood and fat, was made with Israel. In the first century C.E. the governing body of the Christian congregation confirmed the prohibition against blood as remaining in force for Christians. (Ac 15:20, 28, 29) As in the case with Noah and his family, however, nothing was stated concerning the eating of fat by Christians. Thus, the law against eating fat was given only to the nation of Israel.

Reason for the law. Under the Law covenant, both the blood and fat were looked upon as exclusively Jehovah's. The blood contains the life, which only Jehovah can give; therefore it belongs to him. (Le 17:11, 14) The fat was viewed as the richest part of the flesh of the animal. The offering of the fat of the animal would evidently be in recognition of the fact that the best parts belong to Jehovah, who provides abundantly, and it would demonstrate the desire of the worshiper to offer the best to God. Because it was symbolic of the Israelites' devotion of their best to Jehovah, it was said to smoke upon the altar as "food" and for "a restful odor" to him. (Le 3:11, 16) To eat fat, therefore, was an illegal appropriation of what was sanctified to God, an invasion of the rights of Jehovah. Eating fat would incur the death penalty. Unlike blood, however, fat could be used for other purposes, at least in the case of an animal that died of itself or was killed by another beast.—Le 7:23-25.

Extent of the law's application. Because of this latter text, many commentators have sought to limit the prohibition of Leviticus 3:17 only to the fat of those kinds of animals that were acceptable for offering in sacrifice, such as bulls, sheep, and goats. Rabbinic Jewish teaching is divided on this subject. However, the injunction on fat at Leviticus 3:17 is linked with the one regarding the eating of blood, a law that clearly included the blood of *all* animals. (Compare Le 17:13; De 12:15, 16.) It seems more consistent, therefore, that the law on fat should also have embraced the fat of all animals, including those killed for the Israelites' common use.

The view that the prohibition applied to all fat is not controverted by the text at Deuteronomy 32:14, which speaks of Jehovah as giving Israel "fat of rams" to eat. This is a figurative expression referring to the best of the flock, or as *The Jerusalem Bible* renders the phrase, "rich food of the pastures." (See also *Da* ftn and *Kx.*) This poetic sense is indicated by later portions of the same verse referring to "the *kidney fat* of wheat" and "the *blood* of the grape." So, too, with Nehemiah 8:10, where the people are commanded, "Go, eat the fatty things," we are not to conclude that they literally consumed whole fat. "Fatty things" refers to rich portions, things not skinny or dry, but luscious, including tasty items prepared with vegetable oils. Thus, Knox' translation here reads "regale yourselves with rich meat," while Moffatt's translation says "eat the dainty pieces."

The Mosaic Law restriction did not prevent the feeding or fattening of sheep or cattle for the table. We read of the "fattened young bull" slaughtered for the prodigal son. (Lu 15:23) Solomon's food included "fattened cuckoos" and cattle. (1Ki 4:23) The Hebrew *'e·ghel-mar·beq'*, translated "fattened calf," occurs at 1 Samuel 28:24; *me'ach* and *meri''* refer to a 'well-fed animal' or a 'fatling.' (Isa 5:17; Eze 39:18) However, this does not mean that this 'fattening' was for the purpose of producing suet or layers of fat; rather, the sense again is that the animals became full-fleshed ("beefy"), not skinny.—Compare Ge 41:18, 19.

Other Hebrew Terms. Among the Hebrew terms used to describe anything in a "fat" condition are those derived from the root verb *sha·men'*. While meaning "grow fat" (De 32:15; Jer 5:28), it also conveys the thought of being "robust." *Sha·men'* appears at Isaiah 6:10, where the *King James Version* reads "make the heart of this people fat," that is, unresponsive and dull, as if their hearts were enveloped in fat. Judges 3:29 describes certain Moabites as "every one robust [*sha·men'*, literally, "fat"] and every one a valiant man." The related *she'men* is usually translated "oil."

'Thriving' may be the thought behind the verb *da·shen'*, also used literally to mean "grow fat." If that is the case, *da·shen'* (and the related *de'·shen*) would imply prosperity, fertility, or abundance. Jehovah told Israel that he would bring them to a land "which flows with milk and honey, and they will certainly eat and be satisfied

and grow fat [*wedha·shen'*]." (De 31:20) We are told that those who are generous, diligent, and reliant on Jehovah "will be made fat," that is, prosper abundantly. (Pr 11:25; 13:4; 28:25) At Proverbs 15:30 good news is said to 'make the bones fat,' or fill them with marrow—in other words, the whole body is invigorated. The noun *de'shen* also reflects this idea of affluence, as at Psalm 36:8, where the sons of men are said to "drink their fill of the fatness [*mid·de'shen;* "abundance," *RS*]" of God's house.—Compare Jer 31:14.

The noun *de'shen* is also rendered "ashes" by many translators, as when referring to the wastes from the tabernacle's altar of sacrifice. (Le 1:16; 4:12; 6:10, 11, *KJ, JB, RS*) To other scholars, however, "ashes" does not fully reflect the original-language root. They, therefore, prefer such terms as "fat-ashes" (*Ro*), or "fatty ashes" (*NW*), reasoning that the term indicates that the hot fat from the sacrifices soaked the burnt firewood below.

The idea of being well fed and healthy is expressed by the word *ba·ri''*. It is translated "plump" (Eze 34:3, 20) and "healthful" (Hab 1:16), though it may also be rendered as "fat" in describing men, cattle, and grain.—Ge 41:2, 7; Jg 3:17.

FATHER. The Hebrew word *'av*, translated "father," is a mimetic (imitative) word taken from the first and simplest sounds of infant lips. The Hebrew *'av* and the Greek *pa·ter'* are both used in various senses: as begetter, or progenitor, of an individual (Pr 23:22; Zec 13:3; Lu 1:67), the head of a household or ancestral family (Ge 24:40; Ex 6:14), an ancestor (Ge 28:13; Joh 8:53), a founder of a nation (Mt 3:9), a founder of a class or profession (Ge 4:20, 21), a protector (Job 29:16; Ps 68:5), the source of something (Job 38:28), and a term of respect (2Ki 5:13; Ac 7:2).

Jehovah God as Creator is called Father. (Isa 64:8; compare Ac 17:28, 29.) He is also the Father of spirit-begotten Christians, the Aramaic term *'Ab·ba'* being used as an expression of respect and of close filial relationship. (Ro 8:15; see ABBA.) All who express faith with a hope of everlasting life can address God as Father. (Mt 6:9) Jesus Christ, the Messiah, because of being God's Chief Agent of life, was prophetically called Eternal Father. (Isa 9:6) Also, anyone who has imitators and followers, or those who exhibit his qualities, is regarded as a father to them. (Mt 5:44, 45; Ro 4:11, 12) In this sense the Devil is spoken of as a father.—Joh 8:44; compare Ge 3:15.

Applying "father" to men as a formalistic or religious *title* was forbidden by Jesus. (Mt 23:9) Because of Paul's bringing the good news to certain Christians and nourishing them spiritually he was like a father to them, but in no scripture is "father" applied to him as a religious *title*. (1Co 4:14, 15) Paul likened himself to both a father *and a mother* in his relation to the Thessalonian Christians. (1Th 2:7, 11) Whereas reference is made at Luke 16:24, 30 to "father Abraham," this is basically in the sense of fleshly ancestry.

Father's Authority and Responsibilities.
As described in the Bible, the father was the head of the household, being guardian, protector, the one making final decisions, and the judge of the family group. (1Co 11:3; Ge 31:32) Among the patriarchs and in Israel before the selection of the Levitical priesthood, the father took the lead in representing his family in worship as a priest. (Ge 12:8; Job 1:5; Ex 19:22) The father had authority over his household until his death. If the son married and set up an independent household, then he became head over it, although due respect was still shown toward the father. When a daughter married, she came under the headship of her husband. (Nu 30:3-8) In Bible times the father usually arranged for the marriage of his children. If he came into dire financial straits, he could sell his daughter into slavery, with certain restrictions for her protection.—Ex 21:7.

Fatherly Concern for the Family Members.
As God's representative, the father is responsible to see that God's principles are taught to his household. (Ge 18:19; Eph 6:4; De 6:6, 7) His teaching and disciplinary duties also include personal instructions and commands, which the mother assists in carrying out. (Pr 1:8; 6:20) The God-fearing father has great love for his children and exhorts and consoles them with great tenderness. (1Th 2:11; Ho 11:3) So that they might walk in the right way, he disciplines, corrects, and reproves them. (Heb 12:9; Pr 3:12) He finds pleasure in his sons, and especially does he rejoice when they display wisdom. (Pr 10:1) On the other hand, he is deeply grieved and vexed by a course of stupidity on the part of his children. (Pr 17:21, 25) He is to be compassionate and merciful. (Mal 3:17; Ps 103:13) He is to be considerate of their needs and requests. (Mt 7:9-11) A pattern for human fathers is provided in the many descriptions of God's love and care for his people.

Genealogical Use of Father's Name.
Ancestry of a man was customarily traced back through the father, not through the mother. Thus, whereas there seems to be sound reason for believing that Luke presents Jesus' genealogy through his mother (an exception to the general rule), Luke does not list her. Apparently he lists her husband Joseph as the son of Heli, evidently Mary's father. This would not be improper in the least, since Joseph would be Heli's son-in-law. —See GENEALOGY OF JESUS CHRIST.

In the absence of family names (surnames), a man was regularly distinguished by being referred to as the son of "So-and-so." For example, Isaac was called "the son of Abraham." (Ge 25:19) Many Hebrew names included the Hebrew *ben* or Aramaic *bar*, "son," followed by the name of the father as a surname, such as "Ben-hur" (1Ki 4:8, *RS;* "the son of Hur," *NW*) and "Simon Bar-jonah," or "Simon son of Jonah."—Mt 16:17, *KJ, NW*.

FATHER-IN-LAW.
In the Hebrew Scriptures, the word *cham* designates the husband's father (Ge 38:13, 25; 1Sa 4:19, 21), and its feminine form, *cha·mohth′,* the husband's mother (the wife's mother-in-law).—Ru 1:14; Mic 7:6.

The Hebrew verb *cha·than′* means "form a marriage alliance." (De 7:3; 1Sa 18:20-27; 1Ki 3:1; 2Ch 18:1) The father-in-law on the bride's side, the wife's father, is designated by a masculine participial form of *cha·than′*. Its feminine participial form refers to mother-in-law.—De 27:23.

Because an engaged couple were considered as bound although the couple had not yet come together in marriage, the woman was spoken of as the man's wife. (Jg 14:20) Therefore, the man was called "son-in-law" (a noun drawn from *cha·than′* being used) regardless of whether the marriage alliance had been fully consummated (Jg 19:5; 1Sa 22:14; Ne 6:18; 13:28) or was only contemplated, as in the case of Lot's "sons-in-law." (Ge 19:12, 14; compare Jg 15:6.) Lot's daughters were only betrothed; otherwise they would most likely have been with their husbands and not living in their father's house. That the two men were only prospective, not actual, sons-in-law (engaged to Lot's daughters but not as yet married to them) is indicated by the Hebrew, which allows for the rendering: "[Lot's] sons-in-law who *were to take* [or, were intending to take] his daughters."—Ge 19:14, *NW; Ro;* compare *JB; Mo; RS*.

In the Christian Greek Scriptures, *pen·the·ros'* is translated "father-in-law" (Joh 18:13); the feminine form, *pen·the·ra'*, is rendered "mother-in-law."—Mt 8:14; 10:35; Mr 1:30; Lu 4:38; 12:53; see DAUGHTER-IN-LAW.

FATHERLESS BOY.

With no man in the house to support them and to protect their interests, the fatherless boy, or orphan, and the widow might more easily become subject to oppression and difficulties. Their welfare was, therefore, provided for under the Law, which ensured justice for the fatherless boy, the widow, and the alien resident and also included provisions for their sustenance. (Ex 22:22-24; De 24:17) Gleanings left in the field, on the olive tree, and in the vineyard were available to these poor ones. (De 24:19-21) A special invitation was extended to them to participate in the bounteous yearly Festival of Ingathering (Festival of Booths), during which they could enjoy the feasting that accompanied the celebration. (De 16:9-14) Every third year the special tithe that the Israelites normally ate at Jerusalem was deposited within the gates of their home cities. From this tithe the fatherless boy was legally entitled to a portion.—De 14:28, 29; 26:12, 13.

How important is loving concern for orphans among God's servants?

Since it was easy to lose sight of these bereaved and defenseless ones, Jehovah used the expression "fatherless boy" in describing the degree of Israel's righteousness or of its deviation therefrom. When the nation was enjoying good spiritual health, the fatherless boy was cared for. When justice became perverted in the land, the fatherless boy was sure to be neglected, and this was a symptom of national decay. (Ps 82:3; 94:6; Isa 1:17, 23; Jer 7:5-7; 22:3; Eze 22:7; Zec 7:9-11; Mal 3:5) Jehovah's curse was on those who oppressed the fatherless boy. (De 27:19; Isa 10:1, 2) Jehovah describes himself as the Redeemer (Pr 23:10, 11), Helper (Ps 10:14), and Father (Ps 68:5) of such ones. He is the One executing judgment in their behalf (De 10:17, 18), showing them mercy (Ho 14:3), giving them relief (Ps 146:9), and preserving them alive.—Jer 49:11.

One of the identifying marks of real Christianity is its consideration for those bereaved by loss of husband or parents. The disciple James writes to Christians: "The form of worship that is clean and undefiled from the standpoint of our God and Father is this: to look after orphans and widows in their tribulation, and to keep oneself without spot from the world."—Jas 1:27.

The Greek word for orphan (*or·pha·nos'*) is used in a figurative sense in John 14:18 and is variously rendered "desolate" (*AS*), "forlorn" (*Mo*), "friendless" (*AT*), and "bereaved" (*NW; Yg*).

FATHER'S HOUSE.

The Hebrew expression *behth 'av* (plural, *behth 'a·vohth'*) could refer (1) to a dwelling place (De 22:21); (2) to the household of one's father at his place of dwelling (Ge 31:30; 38:11); (3) to those making up the household itself, even in a location away from the ancestral home (Ge 46:31; Jg 9:18); or (4), as variously translated, to a "father's house," "chief house," "ancestral house," "paternal house," which, in some cases, took in several families. For example, at the time of numbering the Israelites in the wilderness, four families were regarded as making up the paternal house of Kohath. (Nu 3:19, 30; see also Ex 6:14; Nu 26:20-22; Jos 7:17.) Several paternal houses constituted a tribe (such as the tribe of Levi, made up of the paternal houses of Gershon, Kohath, and Merari).

The terms "paternal house," or "fathers' house," "house of our father," and so forth, were not always limited to the above usages, however. (For a broader use of "paternal house" see Nu 17:2, 6, where a paternal house is a tribe.)

As the population of Israel increased and as various areas of the Promised Land became settled, paternal houses also increased in number. The priests were organized by David into 24 divisions of service according to their paternal houses, 16 divisions for Eleazar and 8 for Ithamar. The 24 headmen were called "heads for their paternal houses." (1Ch 24:4-6) The rest of the Levites were selected for certain duties by lot, without regard to any priority of age of the heads of their paternal houses.—1Ch 24:20-31.

Each Israelite paternal house was represented by its hereditary head in connection with official tribal business and the administration of justice. (Ne 7:70, 71; 11:13) At the celebration of the Passover in Jerusalem in King Josiah's time, the people apparently entered the court of the temple by their paternal houses to offer their sacrifices. The Levites, by their divisions based on paternal houses, received the sacrifices of the people and prepared them.—2Ch 35:4, 5, 12.

Jesus Christ promised his followers that he was going his way to prepare a place for them in his 'Father's house,' by which he had reference to the heavenly dwelling place of Jehovah.—Joh 14:2; see FAMILY.

FATHOM. A unit for measuring the depth of water. The fathom is commonly viewed as being four cubits (c. 1.8 m; 6 ft) and approximately corresponds to the distance between the fingertips of a man's two hands when his arms are stretched in opposite directions. Appropriately, the Greek word for "fathom" (or·gui·a′) comes from a root meaning "stretch out; reach."—Ac 27:28, ftn.

FAULT, FAULTFINDING. A fault is a neglect, failing, defect, an error, imperfection; it can mean failure to do what is right; also, responsibility for failure or for wrongdoing. (Ex 5:16; Ps 50:20; Mt 18:15) Biblically, a fault often refers to an occasion of blame or a particular cause for disapproval.

Faultfinding. The expression "find fault" occurs in both the Hebrew and Christian Greek Scriptures. In Hebrew it renders the verb *riv*, meaning "contend" in a physical, verbal, or legal-judicial sense. Thus, it is rendered 'quarrel,' 'contend,' and 'conduct a legal case' (Ge 26:20; De 33:7; 1Sa 24:15), as well as "find fault."—Ne 5:7; 13:11, 17, 25; Ps 103:9; see QUARREL.

The Greek word *ai·ti′a*, occurring in the expression "find fault," is also translated "cause," "charge," and "ground." (Ac 13:28; 25:18; Mt 19:3) Pilate, after examining Jesus Christ on the charges brought by the Jews, found no evidence of guilt and announced to the Jews three times: "I find no fault in him." (Joh 18:38; 19:4, 6) "Find fault" also renders the Greek *mem′pho·mai*, meaning "blame; lay blame."—Ro 9:19; Heb 8:8.

Jehovah's Dealings With Faulty Mankind. That which Jehovah God makes is perfect, faultless (Heb., *ta·mim′*, referring to something sound, perfect, faultless), as are all his words and acts. (De 32:4, ftn) For this reason and because of his almightiness, he can say, as in correcting Job: "Should there be any contending of a faultfinder [literally, one who chastises, corrects, disciplines] with the Almighty?" (Job 40:1, 2) The apostle Paul points out that God has the right to deal with his creatures as He pleases, just as a potter makes the kinds of vessels he desires to produce. God tolerates "vessels of wrath" for a purpose, just as he did Pharaoh, while he has mercy on "vessels of mercy," and we cannot rightly question God's action in this.—Ro 9:14-24.

On the other hand, man's ways and productions are often faulty. Sin and error are the legacy all men have inherited from Adam. (Ro 5:12;

Ps 51:5) But Jehovah, himself faultless, "well knows the formation of us, remembering that we are dust," and is merciful. (Ps 103:13, 14) He regarded faithful, obedient Noah as "faultless among his contemporaries." (Ge 6:9) He commanded Abraham, "Walk before me and prove yourself faultless." (Ge 17:1) Although both these men were imperfect and died, they were viewed as faultless by Jehovah, who "sees what the heart is." (1Sa 16:7; compare 2Ki 20:3; 2Ch 16:9.) He commanded Israel: "You should prove yourself faultless with Jehovah your God." (De 18:13; 2Sa 22:24) He provided his faultless Son (Heb 7:26) as a ransom sacrifice, and on this basis He can call those exercising faith and obedience "righteous," or faultless, while at the same time maintaining his position as the righteous and faultless Judge.—Ro 3:25, 26; see INTEGRITY; PERFECTION.

The Law Covenant. The apostle Paul says that the Law is "spiritual" and "fine" (Ro 7:14; 1Ti 1:8) and, after discussing its tenth commandment, states that "the Law is holy, and the commandment is holy and righteous and good." (Ro 7:7-12) Why, then, does he also say: "If that first covenant had been faultless [or, blameless], no place would have been sought for a second"? (Heb 8:7) Paul goes on to explain: "He [Jehovah, through Jeremiah] does find fault with [or, blame] the people." (Heb 8:8, 9; compare Jer 31:31, 32.) In another place he shows that there was an incapability on the part of the Law, while it was "weak through the flesh." (Ro 8:3) Also, he logically demonstrates that perfection could not come through the Levitical priesthood, which, along with the law by which it operated, had to be changed; that "the Law made nothing perfect"; and that its gifts and sacrifices were "not able to make the man doing sacred service perfect as respects his conscience."—Heb 7:11, 12, 19; 9:9.

Dealing With One Another's Faults. The Bible counsels us to "continue putting up with one another and forgiving one another freely if anyone has a cause for complaint against another." (Col 3:13) If all our faults were held against us, we would all be condemned. Many faults can be overlooked; surely a Christian should not be anxious to make public the faults of his brothers. The Scriptures say of a wicked person: "You sit and speak against your own brother, against the son of your mother you give away a fault."—Ps 50:16, 20.

However, Jesus Christ instructed his disciples what to do in the case of certain serious sins. As the first step, he counseled: "If your brother commits a sin, go lay bare his fault [literally, "reprove him"] between you and him alone. If he listens to you, you have gained your brother." Jesus then proceeds to outline the steps to take if this first effort fails.—Mt 18:15-17; see also Ga 6:1.

A Faultless Ministry. The apostle Paul, highly grateful and appreciative of the glorious treasure of the ministry, exercised care to glorify this ministry by watching closely every feature of his life and conduct. He said in his letter to the congregation at Corinth: "In no way are we giving any cause for stumbling, that our ministry might not be found fault with." (2Co 6:3) Men who were challenging Paul's apostleship had associated with the congregation there and had indulged in much faultfinding and slander against Paul in order to belittle him and to destroy his apostolic authority over the congregation. Realizing this and knowing also the danger of faultfinding and trouble where money matters are concerned, he assured the congregation that he was sending Titus and another trustworthy brother appointed by the congregations to handle the contributions. "Thus," wrote Paul, "we are avoiding having any man find fault with us in connection with this liberal contribution to be administered by us."—2Co 8:16-21.

FEAR. As commonly used, fear means an expectation of harm or pain, generally a painful emotion characterized by alarm, dread, disquiet. However, fear may also mean a calm recognition or consideration of whatever may injure or damage, such recognition causing one to exercise reasoned caution and intelligent foresight.

What is the fear of Jehovah that we should have?

The Bible shows that there is a proper fear and an improper fear. Thus, fear may be wholesome and cause the individual to proceed with due caution in the face of danger, thereby averting disaster, or it may be morbid, destroying hope and weakening a person's nervous stamina, even to the point of bringing about death. The fear of God is healthful; it is an awe and a profound reverence for the Creator and a wholesome dread of displeasing him. This fear of incurring his displeasure is a result of appreciation of his loving-kindness and goodness together with the realization that he is the Supreme Judge and the

Almighty, who has the power to inflict punishment or death upon those who disobey him. —See AWE; DREAD.

The proper fear of Jehovah God is essential to those who would serve him. This profound fear of Jehovah is "the beginning of wisdom" (Ps 111: 10), "the start of wisdom." (Pr 9:10) It is not a morbid fear that tears down; "the fear of Jehovah is pure." (Ps 19:9) This fear is defined thus at Proverbs 8:13: "The fear of Jehovah means the hating of bad." It will prevent one from following a bad course, for "in the fear of Jehovah one turns away from bad."—Pr 16:6.

Adam and Eve failed to exercise a proper, healthful fear of God and therefore they disobeyed him. This produced in them a painful fear or terror, which caused them to hide from God's presence. Adam said: "Your voice I heard in the garden, but I was afraid." (Ge 3:10) Adam's son Cain felt a similar fear after murdering his brother Abel, and this fear may have been a contributing factor in his deciding to build a city.—Ge 4:13-17.

At Hebrews 12:28 Christians are instructed to have godly fear: "Let us continue to have undeserved kindness, through which we may acceptably render God sacred service with godly fear and awe." An angel in midheaven, having everlasting good news to declare, opened his declaration with the words: "Fear God and give him glory." (Re 14:6, 7) Jesus contrasted the wholesome fear of God with fear of man, saying, as recorded at Matthew 10:28: "Do not become fearful of those who kill the body but cannot kill the soul; but rather be in fear of him that can destroy both soul and body in Gehenna." At Revelation 2:10 he also counsels Christians: "Do not be afraid of the things you are about to suffer." Real love for Jehovah expels the cowardly fear of man that leads to compromise.

Proper fear does, however, include due respect for secular authority, because the Christian knows that just punishment from the authority for a crime would be an indirect expression of God's anger.—Ro 13:3-7.

Jesus predicted that at "the conclusion of the system of things" a climate of fear would cover the earth. He said that there would be "fearful sights" and that men would "become faint out of fear and expectation of the things coming upon the inhabited earth." (Lu 21:11, 26) While people in general would be affected in this way, servants of God should follow the principle expressed at Isaiah 8:12: "The object of their fear you men must not fear." The apostle Paul explains: "For God gave us not a spirit of cowardice, but that of power and of love and of soundness of mind."—2Ti 1:7.

The wise man, after making a careful study of mankind as well as man's occupations and calamitous experiences, said: "The conclusion of the matter, everything having been heard, is: Fear the true God and keep his commandments. For this is the whole obligation of man."—Ec 12:13.

Animals Toward Humans. At Genesis 9:2 the word "fear" is used in connection with the animal creation. God told Noah and his sons: "A fear of you and a terror of you will continue upon every living creature of the earth." During the year that Noah and his family were inside the ark, the animals and birds penned up therein had a fear of these humans that helped to restrain them. Accordingly, when they emerged from the ark after the Flood, Jehovah gave Noah assurance that this fear would continue. This is supported by human experience. Dr. George G. Goodwin, Associate Curator of Mammals, The American Museum of Natural History, said: "Normally, a leopard will not attack a man. If provoked or wounded, however, the animal will turn on human beings and fight." Similarly, if given the opportunity, poisonous snakes known for aggressiveness, such as the mamba and king cobra, prefer, as a rule, cautiously to glide away from the presence of man rather than attack. Though man has mistreated and turned some animals into vicious creatures, it is generally true that this restraining fear still applies. This is in harmony with God's statement at Genesis 1:26-28, that the animal creation was to be subject to man from the time of his creation.

FEAST. See FESTIVAL; MEAL.

FELIX (Fe′lix) [from Lat., Happy]. The procurator of the Roman province of Judea who held Paul prisoner for two years after Paul's last visit to Jerusalem, in about 56 C.E. Tacitus indicates that Felix served jointly with Cumanus in the office of procurator for a number of years and thereafter as the sole procurator of Judea. (*The Annals*, XII, 54) Josephus makes no mention of Felix's serving concurrently with Cumanus, and for that reason most scholars say that Felix began to serve as procurator in 52 C.E. (*Jewish Antiquities*, XX, 137 [vii, 1]; *The Jewish War*, II, 247, 248 [xii, 8]) Nevertheless, on the basis of Felix's years of service, Paul could say to him:

"This nation has had you as judge for many years."—Ac 24:10.

Secular historians say that Felix was once a slave, that his given name was Antonius, that Emperor Claudius granted him and his brother Pallas their freedom, and that he was a cruel and immoral official. Tacitus described him as one who "practised every kind of cruelty and lust, wielding the power of king with all the instincts of a slave." (*The Histories*, V, IX) He is reported to have engineered the killing of High Priest Jonathan. Suetonius says that Felix became the husband of three queens. (*The Lives of the Caesars*, Claudius, XXVIII) Such description agrees with what we learn of Felix in the Bible.

Following Paul's arrest, Claudius Lysias, the Roman military commander, fearing for the safety of his prisoner if allowed to remain in Jerusalem, hustled the apostle down to Caesarea under heavy guard, "commanding the accusers to speak against him" before Felix. (Ac 23:23-30) Five days later High Priest Ananias, a certain Tertullus, and others came down from Jerusalem with preposterous charges against Paul. Felix presided at the trial, deferring judgment. He ordered that Paul be kept, but with some relaxation of custody, and that none of Paul's people be forbidden to wait upon him.

Felix later "sent for Paul and listened to him on the belief in Christ Jesus." It was on this occasion, possibly with Felix's wife Drusilla present, that Paul "talked about righteousness and self-control and the judgment to come." On hearing these things "Felix became frightened" and told the apostle: "For the present go your way, but when I get an opportune time I shall send for you again." Frequently, during a two-year period, Felix sent for and conversed with Paul, futilely hoping that the apostle would give him money as a bribe for his release.—Ac 24:24-27.

The administration by Felix was highly resented by the Jews. Perhaps in 58 C.E. "Felix was succeeded by Porcius Festus; and because Felix desired to gain favor with the Jews, he left Paul bound." (Ac 24:27) However, this gesture on the part of Felix did not soothe the wounds he had inflicted on the Jews; nor did it prevent them from sending a delegation to Rome to press their case against him. His escaping punishment after recall to Rome is accredited only to the favored position and influence his brother Pallas had with Nero.

FERMENT. See LEAVEN.

FESTIVAL

FESTIVAL. Festivals formed an integral part of the true worship of God, being prescribed by Jehovah for his chosen people Israel by the hand of Moses. The Hebrew word *chagh,* which is translated "festival," possibly comes from a verb that denotes circularity of motion or form, dancing around in circles, and hence, celebrating a periodic festival or feast. *Moh·'edh',* also rendered "festival," basically refers to a set time or place of assembly.—1Sa 20:35; 2Sa 20:5.

The festivals, and similar special days, might be outlined as follows:

FESTIVALS IN ISRAEL

BEFORE THE EXILE

ANNUAL FESTIVALS

1. Passover, Abib (Nisan) 14
2. Unfermented Cakes, Abib (Nisan) 15-21
3. Weeks, or Pentecost, Sivan 6
4. Trumpet Blast, Ethanim (Tishri) 1
5. Day of Atonement, Ethanim (Tishri) 10
6. Booths, Ethanim (Tishri) 15-21, with a solemn assembly on the 2nd

PERIODIC FESTIVALS

1. Weekly Sabbath
2. New Moon
3. Sabbath year (every 7th year)
4. Jubilee year (every 50th year)

AFTER THE EXILE

1. Festival of Dedication, Chislev 25
2. Festival of Purim, Adar 14, 15

The Three Great Festivals. The three primary "seasonal festivals," sometimes called pilgrimage festivals because of the assembling of all males at Jerusalem, occurred at appointed times and were designated by the Hebrew word *moh·'edh'.* (Le 23:2, 4) But the word often used when referring exclusively to the three great festivals is *chagh,* which connotes not only a periodic occurrence but also a time of great rejoicing. These three great festivals are:

(1) The Festival of Unfermented Cakes (Ex 23:15). This festival began the day after the Passover and ran from Abib (Nisan) 15th through the 21st. Passover was on Nisan 14 and was really a day of observance to itself, but since it was so closely connected in time with the Festival of Unfermented Cakes, the two were often spoken of together as the Passover.—Mt 26:17; Mr 14:12; Lu 22:7.

(2) The Festival of Weeks or (as called later) Pentecost, celebrated on the 50th day from Nisan 16, that is, on Sivan 6.—Ex 23:16a; 34:22a.

(3) The Festival of Booths (Tabernacles) or Ingathering. This took place in the seventh month, Ethanim (Tishri) 15th through the 21st, with a solemn assembly on the 22nd.—Le 23:34-36.

The time, the place, and the way they were to be conducted were all fixed by Jehovah. As the expression "seasonal festivals of Jehovah" implies, they were associated with various seasons of the sacred calendar year—the early spring, the late spring, and the fall. How significant this was, because at these times the firstfruits of the field and vineyards brought great joy and happiness to the inhabitants of the Promised Land, and recognition was thereby given to Jehovah as the generous Provider of all good things!

Observances Common to These Festivals. The Law covenant required that all males appear "before Jehovah your God in the place that he will choose" every year, during each of the three great annual festivals. (De 16:16) The place eventually chosen for a festival center was Jerusalem. No specific penalty for individual nonattendance was stated, with the exception of the Passover; failure to attend it brought the penalty of death. (Nu 9:9-13) Nonetheless, neglect of any of God's laws, including his festivals and sabbaths, would bring national judgment and distress. (De 28:58-62) The Passover itself had to be observed on Nisan 14 or, in certain circumstances, one month later.

Although women were not under obligation, as were the males, to make the annual festival journeys, yet there are examples of festival attendance by women such as Hannah the mother of Samuel (1Sa 1:7) and Mary the mother of Jesus. (Lu 2:41) Israelite women who loved Jehovah attended such festivals whenever possible. In fact, not only did Jesus' parents attend regularly but their relatives and acquaintances went along with them.—Lu 2:44.

Jehovah promised, "Nobody will desire your land while you are going up to see the face of Jehovah your God three times in the year." (Ex 34:24) Even though no men were left to guard the cities and the land, it proved true that no foreign nation ever came up to take the land of the Jews during their festivals prior to the destruction of Jerusalem in 70 C.E. However, in 66 C.E., which was after the rejection of Christ by the Jewish nation, Cestius Gallus slew 50 persons at Lydda during the Festival of Tabernacles.

None of the male attenders were to come empty-handed; they were to bring a gift "in proportion to the blessing of Jehovah your God that he has given you." (De 16:16, 17) Also, at Jerusalem the 'second' tenth part (in contrast with that given to maintain the Levites [Nu 18: 26, 27]) of the current year's grain, wine, and oil, as well as the firstborn of the herd and the flock were to be eaten; these were to be shared with the Levites. However, in case the journey to the festival place was too far, the Law provided that such goods could be turned into money; then this money could be used to buy food and drink for use while at the sanctuary. (De 14:22-27) These occasions were opportunities for demonstrating allegiance to Jehovah and were to be celebrated with joy; the alien resident, the fatherless boy, and the widow were to be included. (De 16:11, 14) This was providing, of course, that the males among such alien residents were circumcised worshipers of Jehovah. (Ex 12:48, 49) Special sacrifices were always offered in addition to the daily offerings, and while the burnt offerings and the communion sacrifices were made, trumpets were blown.—Nu 10:10.

Just before the building of the temple the priesthood was reorganized by King David, who arranged for the immense staff of hundreds of Aaronic priests to be divided into 24 divisions, along with Levitical assistants. (1Ch 24) Each division of trained workers later served twice each year at the temple, a week at a time, the necessary arrangements being made by the head of the paternal house. Second Chronicles 5:11 indicates that the 24 divisions of priests all served together at the dedication of the temple, which took place during the Festival of Booths, or Tabernacles. (1Ki 8:2; Le 23:34) Alfred Edersheim says that on festival days any priest was welcome to come up and assist in the temple service, but during the Festival of Tabernacles (Booths) all 24 divisions were required to be in attendance.—*The Temple*, 1874, p. 66.

During these festival occasions a tremendous amount of work fell to the priests, the Levites, and the Nethinim serving with them. An example of the work they did is indicated in the description of the Festival of Unfermented Cakes held by King Hezekiah after he had cleansed the temple, which celebration, on this occasion, was extended for another seven days. The account states that Hezekiah himself contributed for sacrifice 1,000 bulls and 7,000 sheep and that the princes contributed 1,000 bulls and 10,000 sheep. —2Ch 30:21-24.

Certain days of these festivals were solemn assemblies or holy conventions; these were sabbaths, and similar to the weekly Sabbaths, they required a complete cessation of ordinary business. No secular work at all was to be done. An exception to the regular Sabbath arrangement was that work such as the preparing of food, unlawful on the weekly Sabbath days, was permitted in connection with the preparation for the festival observances. (Ex 12:16) A distinction exists in this respect between "holy conventions" of the festivals and the regular weekly Sabbaths (and the Sabbath on the tenth day of the seventh month, the Day of Atonement, a time of fasting), on which days no work whatsoever was allowed, not even the lighting of a fire "in any of your dwelling places."—Compare Leviticus 23: 3, 26-32 with verses 7, 8, 21, 24, 25, 35, 36 and with Exodus 35:2, 3.

Importance of Festivals in Life of Israel. Festivals played a very important part in the national life of the Israelites. While they were still in Egyptian bondage, Moses told Pharaoh that the reason for demanding that the Israelites and their livestock be allowed to leave Egypt was that "we have a festival to Jehovah." (Ex 10:9) The Law covenant incorporated many detailed instructions regarding the observance of festivals. (Ex 34:18-24; Le 23:1-44; De 16:1-17) In keeping with God's commands, the festivals helped all the attenders to keep their minds on the word of God and not to become so involved in their personal affairs that they would forget the more important spiritual aspect of their daily life. These festivals also reminded them that they were a people for Jehovah's name. Traveling to and from the festive gatherings would naturally give much opportunity to talk about the goodness of their God and the blessings they were daily and seasonally enjoying. The festivals afforded time and opportunity for meditation, association, and the discussion of Jehovah's law. They broadened knowledge of the God-given land, increased understanding and neighbor love among the Israelites, and promoted unity and clean worship. The festivals were occasions of happiness. The minds of the attenders were filled with God's thoughts and ways, and all who participated in sincerity received a rich spiritual blessing. Consider, for example, the blessing to thousands who attended the Festival of Pentecost at Jerusalem in 33 C.E. —Ac 2:1-47.

The festivals symbolized happiness to the Jews. Before the exile in Babylon, by which time the nation in general had lost sight of the true spiritual purpose of the festivals, the prophets Hosea and Amos linked the coming foretold desolation of Jerusalem with the cessation of these joyous and happy observances, or the turning of them into occasions of mourning. (Ho 2:11; Am 8:10) After Jerusalem's fall Jeremiah lamented that "the ways of Zion are mourning, because there are none coming to the festival." Festival and Sabbath were now "forgotten." (La 1:4; 2:6) Isaiah described in advance the happy condition of the returned exiles from Babylon in 537 B.C.E., saying: "You people will come to have a song like that in the night that one sanctifies oneself for a festival." (Isa 30:29) However, it was not long after their restoration to their God-given land that they again corrupted Jehovah's festivals, so that, through the prophet Malachi, God warned the priests that the dung of their festivals would be scattered upon their faces.—Mal 2:1-3.

The writers of the Christian Greek Scriptures make several references and allusions to the festivals, sometimes giving them a happy, symbolic, and prophetic application to Christians. However, the keeping of these festivals in a literal way was not enjoined upon Christians.—Col 2:16, 17; see the festivals under individual names.

FESTIVAL OF BOOTHS.

Known also as the Festival of Tabernacles, or of Ingathering, or it is called "the festival of Jehovah" at Leviticus 23:39. The instructions on its observance are found at Leviticus 23:34-43, Numbers 29:12-38, and Deuteronomy 16:13-15. The festival occupied the days of Ethanim 15-21, with a solemn assembly on the 22nd. Ethanim (Tishri; September-October) was originally the first month of the Jewish calendar, but after the Exodus from Egypt it became the seventh month of the sacred year, since Abib (Nisan; March-April), formerly the seventh month, was made the first month. (Ex 12:2) The Festival of Booths celebrated the ingathering of the fruits of the ground, "the produce of the land," which included grain, oil, and wine. (Le 23:39) It is referred to as "the festival of ingathering at the turn of the year." The holy convention on the eighth day marked a solemn close to the year's cycle of festivals.—Ex 34:22; Le 23:34-38.

The Festival of Booths actually marked the end of the major part of the agricultural year for Israel. It was, therefore, a time of rejoicing and thanksgiving for all the blessings Jehovah had given in the fruitage of all their crops. Also, since the Day of Atonement had been observed just five days earlier, the people would have a sense of peace with Jehovah. While only the males were obligated to attend, whole families came. They were required to dwell in booths (Heb., suk·kohth') for the seven days of the festival. Usually each family occupied one booth. (Ex 34: 23; Le 23:42) These were erected in the courts of the houses, on the roofs of the dwellings, in the courts of the temple, in the public squares, and on roads within a Sabbath-day's journey of the city. The Israelites were to use "the fruit of splendid trees," palm fronds, boughs of branchy trees and of poplars. (Le 23:40) In the days of Ezra, olive and oil-tree leaves, myrtle (very fragrant), and palm leaves, as well as the branches of other trees, were used to build these temporary structures. The fact that all, rich and poor alike, would dwell in booths, even eating their meals in them during the seven days, and that the booths were all made of the same materials, which had been taken from the hills and valleys of the country, would emphasize the equality of all in relation to the festival.—Ne 8:14-16.

On the day before the festival, Ethanim 14, most of the celebrators, if not all of them, had arrived in Jerusalem. The 14th was the day of preparation, unless that day happened to be a weekly Sabbath day, in which case preparations could be made earlier. Everyone was busily occupied in constructing the booths, in purification, in caring for the offerings each one had brought, as well as in joyful fellowship. The city of Jerusalem and its surroundings provided a unique and picturesque appearance, with the booths located all over the town and in the roads and gardens around Jerusalem. Adding to the festive atmosphere was the colorful beauty of the fruits and the leaves, along with the fragrance of the myrtles. Everyone was in anticipation, awaiting the sound of the trumpet blast from the elevated location of the temple in the early autumn evening, announcing the advent of the festival.

During this festival the number of sacrifices offered was greater than at any other festival of the year. The national sacrifice, starting with 13 bulls on the first day and diminishing one each day, totaled 70 bulls sacrificed, besides 119 lambs, rams, and goats, in addition to the grain and wine offerings. During the week, thousands of individual offerings would also be made by the attenders. (Nu 29:12-34, 39) On the eighth day, on which no laborious work could be done, a bull, a ram, and seven male lambs a year old were presented as a burnt offering, along with grain and drink offerings, as well as a goat as a sin offering.—Nu 29:35-38.

In Sabbath years the Law was read to all the people during the festival. (De 31:10-13) It is likely that the first of the 24 divisions of priests established by David began to serve at the temple after the Festival of Booths, inasmuch as the temple built by Solomon was inaugurated at the time of this festival in 1027 B.C.E.—1Ki 6:37, 38; 1Ch 24:1-18; 2Ch 5:3; 7:7-10.

The distinguishing mark of the Festival of Booths, the primary nature of it, was joyful thanksgiving. Jehovah's desire was that his people should rejoice in him. "You must rejoice before Jehovah your God." (Le 23:40) It was a festival of thanksgiving for the ingathering—not only for the grain but also for the oil and the wine, which contributed much to the enjoyment of life. During this festival, the Israelites could meditate in their hearts upon the fact that their prosperity and the abundance of fine things did not come through their own power. No, it was the care of Jehovah their God for them that brought them into this prosperity. They were to think deeply upon these things, for fear, as Moses had said, that "your heart may indeed be lifted up and you may indeed forget Jehovah your God, who brought you out of the land of Egypt, out of the house of slaves." Moses also declared: "And you must remember Jehovah your God, because he is the giver of power to you to make wealth; in order to carry out his covenant that he swore to your forefathers, as at this day."—De 8:14, 18.

Israel was commanded to live for one week in booths, "in order that your generations may know that it was in the booths that I made the sons of Israel to dwell when I was bringing them out of the land of Egypt. I am Jehovah your God." (Le 23:42, 43) They could recall with joy and thankfulness God's care for them in the wilderness when they were provided shelter by Jehovah, 'who caused them to walk through the great and fear-inspiring wilderness, with poisonous serpents and scorpions and with thirsty ground that has no water; who brought forth water for them out of the flinty rock; who fed them with manna in the wilderness, which their fathers had not known.' (De 8:15, 16) This would give them reason to rejoice over God's continually increasing care and bounty toward them.

Features Added Later. A custom that came to be practiced later, possibly alluded to in the Christian Greek Scriptures (Joh 7:37, 38) but not in the Hebrew Scriptures, was the drawing of water from the Pool of Siloam and pouring it, along with wine, on the altar at the time of the morning sacrifice. According to most scholars, this occurred on seven days of the festival but not on the eighth. The priest would go to the Pool of Siloam with a golden pitcher (except on the opening day of the festival, a sabbath, when the water was taken from a golden vessel in the temple, to which it had been carried from Siloam on the preceding day). He would time himself so as to return from Siloam with the water just as the priests in the temple were ready to lay the pieces of the sacrifice on the altar. As he entered the Court of the Priests by the Water Gate he was announced by a threefold blast from the priests' trumpets. The water was then poured out into a basin leading to the base of the altar, at the same time that wine was being poured into a basin. Then the temple music accompanied the singing of the Hallel (Psalms 113-118), during which time the worshipers waved their palm branches toward the altar. This ceremony may have reminded the joyful celebrators of Isaiah's prophetic words: "With exultation you people will be certain to draw water out of the springs of salvation."—Isa 12:3.

Another ceremony somewhat similar was that each day of the seven days of the festival the priests, in procession, would walk around the altar, singing, "Ah, now, Jehovah, do save, please! Ah, now, Jehovah, do grant success, please!" (Ps 118:25) On the seventh day, however, they made the circuit seven times.

According to rabbinic sources, there was also another outstanding feature of this festival that, like the bringing in of the water of Siloam, was carried out in the time when Jesus was on earth. This ceremony began at the close of the 15th of Tishri, the first day of the festival, actually in the beginning of the 16th, the festival's second day, and was carried on for the five succeeding nights. Preparations were made in the Court of Women. Four great golden lampstands stood in the court, each having four golden bowls. Four youths of priestly descent would climb ladders with large pitchers of oil, filling the 16 bowls. The old clothing of the priests was used as wicks for the lamps. Jewish writers say these lamps made a brilliant light that could be seen at a considerable distance, lighting up the courts of the houses in Jerusalem. Certain men, including some of the elders, danced with flaming torches in their hands and sang songs of praise, accompanied by musical instruments.

An interesting sidelight is that Jeroboam, who broke away from Solomon's son Rehoboam and became king over the ten northern tribes, carried on (in the *eighth* month, not the *seventh*) an imitation of the Festival of Booths, apparently to hold the tribes away from Jerusalem. But, of course, the sacrifices were made to the golden calves that he had set up contrary to Jehovah's command.—1Ki 12:31-33.

Jesus probably alluded to the spiritual significance of the Festival of Booths and perhaps to the ceremony with the water of Siloam when "on the last day, the great day of the festival, Jesus was standing up and he cried out, saying: 'If anyone is thirsty, let him come to me and drink. He that puts faith in me, just as the Scripture has said, "Out from his inmost part streams of living water will flow."'" (Joh 7:37, 38) Also, he may have alluded to the lighting up of Jerusalem by the lamps and torches in the temple area at the festival when he said a little later to the Jews: "I am the light of the world. He that follows me will by no means walk in darkness, but will possess the light of life." (Joh 8:12) Shortly after his discussion with the Jews, Jesus may have connected Siloam with the festival and its lights when he encountered a man who had been born blind. After stating to his disciples, "I am the world's light," he spit on the ground and made a clay with the saliva, put this clay upon the man's eyes and said to him: "Go wash in the pool of Siloam."—Joh 9:1-7.

The waving of palm branches by the people at this festival reminds us also of the crowds that waved palm branches during Jesus' entry into Jerusalem just before his death, although this did not occur at the time of the Festival of Booths, but, rather, prior to the Passover. (Joh 12:12, 13) Again, the apostle John, who saw in vision 144,-000 of God's slaves sealed in their foreheads, tells us: "After these things I saw, and look! a great crowd, which no man was able to number, out of all nations and tribes and peoples and tongues, standing before the throne and before the Lamb, dressed in white robes; and there were palm branches in their hands. And they keep on crying with a loud voice, saying: 'Salvation we owe to our God, who is seated on the throne, and to the Lamb.'"—Re 7:1-10.

Certainly the Festival of Booths was a fitting conclusion to the major part of the agricultural year and to the cycle of festivals for the year. Everything connected with it breathes joy, bountiful blessings from Jehovah's hand, refreshment, and life.

FESTIVAL OF DEDICATION.

The observance of the Festival of Dedication (Heb., *chanukkah'*) commemorates the recovery of Jewish independence from Syro-Grecian domination and the rededication to Jehovah of the temple at Jerusalem, which had been desecrated by Antiochus IV Epiphanes, who called himself *The·os' E·pi·pha·nes'* ("God Manifest"). He built an altar on top of the great altar on which the daily burnt offering had formerly been presented. (1 Maccabees 1:54-59, *AT*) On this occasion (Chislev 25, 168 B.C.E.), to show his hatred and contempt for Jehovah, the God of the Jews, and to defile His temple to the utmost, Antiochus sacrificed swine on the altar and had the broth he had made from some of its flesh sprinkled all over the temple. He also burned the temple gates, pulled down the priests' chambers, and carried away the golden altar as well as the table of showbread and the golden lampstand. Later, the temple of Zerubbabel was rededicated to the pagan god Zeus of Olympus.

Two years later Judas Maccabaeus recaptured the city and the temple. The sanctuary was desolate; weeds were growing in the temple courts. Judas tore down the old defiled altar and built a new altar of unhewn stones. Judas had temple vessels made and he brought the altar of incense, the table of showbread, and the lampstand into the temple. After the temple was purged of defilement the rededication took place on Chislev 25, 165 B.C.E., exactly three years to the day after Antiochus had made his sacrifice on the altar in worship of the pagan god. The daily or continual burnt offerings were renewed.—1 Maccabees 4:36-54; 2 Maccabees 10:1-9, *AT*.

Festival Customs. The very nature of the festival made it a time of great rejoicing. There is some resemblance to the Festival of Booths in the manner of its observance. The celebration lasted eight days from Chislev 25 onward. (1 Maccabees 4:59) There was a great blaze of light in the courts of the temple, and all private dwellings were lighted up with decorative lamps. The Talmud refers to it as the "Feast of Illumination." Later on, some had the practice of displaying eight lamps on the first night and reducing the number on each night by one, others starting with one and increasing to eight. The lamps were placed near doors leading to the street not only so that they would illuminate the house within but also so that all on the outside would see the light. Accompanying the lighting of the lamps was the singing of songs extolling God the Deliverer of Israel. Josephus says about the initiation of the festival: "So much pleasure did they find in the renewal of their customs and in unexpectedly obtaining the right to have their own service after so long a time, that they made a law that their descendants should celebrate the restoration of the temple service for eight days. And from that time to the present we observe this festival, which we call the festival of Lights, giving this name to it, I think, from the fact that the right to worship appeared to us at a time when we hardly dared hope for it." (*Jewish Antiquities,* XII, 324, 325 [vii, 7]) Laborious work was allowed, as it was not considered a sabbath.

There were two former temple dedications, that of the first temple by Solomon and of the second built by Zerubbabel, that were solemnly celebrated after the building work was completed. But there was no anniversary festival in commemoration afterward, as there was of this rededication of the second temple by Judas Maccabaeus. Unlike the three great festivals, which all males were obligated to attend at Jerusalem, the Festival of Dedication could be celebrated in their various cities, as was the case with the Festival of Purim. (Ex 23:14-17; Es 9:18-32) Throughout the land they assembled in their synagogues with singing and jubilation, carrying branches of trees, while the synagogues and the private homes were illuminated by the many lights. The Jews celebrate this festival to the present day.

Significance for Christians. Jesus visited the temple at the time of the Festival of Dedication during the last winter of his ministry, in 32 C.E. The account reads: "At that time the festival of dedication took place in Jerusalem. It was wintertime, and Jesus was walking in the temple in the colonnade of Solomon." (Joh 10:22, 23) Chislev, the ninth month, corresponds to November-December. It was, of course, common knowledge among the Jews that this festival occurred during wintertime. Consequently, the mention of winter here may have reference to the state of the weather rather than the season as a reason for Jesus' choice of a sheltered place for his teaching, in "the colonnade of Solomon." This covered colonnade was on the E side of the outer court of the Gentiles, where many people would gather.—Ac 3:11; 5:12.

There is no direct statement in the inspired Scriptures that Jehovah gave Judas victory and directed his repair of the temple, its refurnishing, the making of utensils, and finally its rededication. Yet, for the prophecies regarding Jesus and his ministry to be fulfilled and for the Levitical sacrifices to continue until the great sacrifice of God's Son would be accomplished, the temple

had to be standing and its services in operation at the time of the Messiah's appearance. (Joh 2:17; Da 9:27) Jehovah had used men of foreign nations, such as Cyrus, to carry out certain purposes as regards His worship. (Isa 45:1) How much more readily might he use a man of his dedicated people, the Jews.

Whatever may be the case, the temple services were observed during the ministry of Jesus Christ. Zerubbabel's temple had been rebuilt (replaced) more elaborately by Herod. For this reason and because of their dislike of Herod, the Jews usually make mention of only two temples, Solomon's and Zerubbabel's. Neither in the words of Jesus nor in any of the writings of his disciples do we find any condemnation of the Festival of Dedication. It is not, however, enjoined on Christians in the new covenant.—Col 2:16; Ga 4:10, 11; Heb 8:6.

FESTIVAL OF NEW MOON. God's command to Israel was that at each new moon, which marked the beginning of the lunar months of the Jewish calendar, trumpets were to be blown over their burnt offerings and communion sacrifices. (Nu 10:10) Special sacrifices were to be offered on these days besides the continual daily sacrifice. The new-moon offering was to consist of a burnt offering of two bulls, one ram, and seven year-old male lambs, with corresponding grain and wine offerings, as well as one kid of the goats for a sin offering.—Nu 28:11-15.

This is all that was commanded concerning its observance in the Pentateuch, but the new-moon observance grew in time to become an important national festival. At Isaiah 1:13, 14 it is placed alongside Sabbaths and festal seasons. In the time of the later prophets, at least, on new-moon days the people did not engage in commercial enterprise, as is indicated at Amos 8:5. This was more than the Scriptures required for new-moon days. Even so, as the last two cited scriptures show, the Jews' observance of the new moon had by that time become a mere formalism, hated in Jehovah's eyes.

The day of the new moon was a day specially regarded for gathering together and feasting. This is seen from Saul's reasoning when David did not appear at Saul's table on the day of the new moon. Saul said to himself: "Something has happened so that he is not clean, for he has not been cleansed." (1Sa 20:5, 18, 24, 26) While certain forms of work could be done on this day that could not be done on the Sabbath, it was viewed as a day for the consideration of spiritual matters. The people would gather in convention (Isa 1:13; 66:23; Ps 81:3; Eze 46:3) or visit the prophets or men of God.—2Ki 4:23.

The observance of the day of the new moon did not involve worship of the moon, as was practiced by some pagan nations, nor did it have any connection with astrology.—Jg 8:21; 2Ki 23:5; Job 31:26-28.

Isaiah wrote about a future time when all flesh would gather to bow down before Jehovah on new-moon days. (Isa 66:23) In Ezekiel's prophecy, during the time of exile in Babylon, when he was given a vision of a temple, Jehovah said to him: "As regards the gate of the inner courtyard that is facing east, it should continue shut for the six workdays, and on the sabbath day it should be opened, and on the day of the new moon it should be opened. And the people of the land must bow down at the entrance of that gate on the sabbaths and on the new moons, before Jehovah."—Eze 46:1, 3.

The Jews today celebrate the new moon with many detailed ceremonies and give it much importance. Christians, however, are shown that they are under no obligation to observe a new moon or a sabbath, which are only part of a shadow of the things to come, the reality being found in Jesus Christ. The festivals of natural Israel have a symbolic significance and a fulfillment in many blessings through God's Son.—Col 2:16, 17.

FESTIVAL OF SABBATH. See SABBATH DAY.

FESTIVAL OF TRUMPET BLAST. This festival occurred on the first day (or the new moon) of the seventh month, Ethanim (Tishri). It was the beginning of the secular year for the Jews. It stood apart from the Festival of the New Moon in the other 11 months as being more important. The command states additionally concerning the Festival of Trumpet Blast that it should be set aside as a day of holy convention, on which no sort of laborious work was to be done.

The festival receives its name from the command: "There should occur for you a complete rest, a memorial by the trumpet blast." "It should prove to be a day of the trumpet blast for you." On this day the sacrifices of one young bull, one ram, and seven sound male lambs a year old, together with a grain offering of fine flour moistened with oil, as well as one male kid of the goats

as a sin offering were presented. This was in addition to the constant daily offerings as well as the sacrifices that were specially given on new-moon days.—Le 23:24; Nu 29:1-6.

This festival, of course, would be an important one, not only because the month it initiated saw the beginning of a new agricultural and labor year but also because the Day of Atonement fell on the 10th day of this month and the Festival of Booths began on the 15th. The completion of the major part of the ingathering of crops of the outgoing year would take place in this month. The crops gathered during this month would include grapes for wine, which makes the heart of man rejoice, and olives, which, among other things, supplied food as well as oil for light and for use in connection with many of the grain offerings. (Ps 104:15) Truly this festival marked the start of a month for thankfulness to Jehovah.

FESTIVAL OF UNFERMENTED CAKES. This festival began Nisan 15, the day after Passover, and continued for seven days through Nisan 21. (See PASSOVER.) Its name is derived from the unfermented cakes (Heb., mats·tsohth'), the only bread allowed during the seven days of the festival. Unleavened bread is kneaded with water but without yeast. It has to be hurriedly prepared if fermentation is to be prevented.

The first day of the Festival of Unfermented Cakes was a solemn assembly, also a sabbath. On the second day, Nisan 16, a sheaf of the firstfruits of the barley harvest, the first crop to ripen in Palestine, was brought to the priest. Prior to this festival no new grain, bread, or roasted grain from the new harvest could be eaten. The priest offered such firstfruits to Jehovah symbolically by waving a sheaf of the grain to and fro, while a sound ram in its first year was offered as a burnt offering along with a grain offering moistened with oil and a drink offering. (Le 23:6-14) There was no command to burn any of the grain or its flour on the altar, as was practiced later by the priests. Not only was there a public or national firstfruit offering but provision was also made for each family and every individual who had a possession in Israel to offer thanksgiving sacrifices during this festive occasion.—Ex 23:19; De 26:1, 2; see FIRSTFRUITS.

Significance. The eating of unfermented cakes at this time was in harmony with the instructions Moses received from Jehovah, as recorded at Exodus 12:14-20, which includes the strict injunction, at verse 19: "Seven days no sourdough is to be found in your houses." In

Deuteronomy 16:3 the unfermented cakes are called "the bread of affliction," and they were a yearly reminder to the Jews of their hurried departure from the land of Egypt (when they did not have time to leaven their dough [Ex 12:34]). They thus recalled the state of affliction and bondage from which Israel had been delivered, even as Jehovah himself said, "that you may remember the day of your coming out of the land of Egypt all the days of your life." The realization of their present freedom as a nation and their acknowledgment of Jehovah as their Deliverer set a fitting background for the first of the three great annual festivals of the Israelites.—De 16:16.

Preexilic Observances. There are three accounts recorded in the Scriptures of the keeping of the Festival of Unfermented Cakes following the Israelites' entry into the Promised Land and prior to their Babylonian exile. But the fact that no other observances are mentioned should not be taken to mean that such were not held. Rather, in the first account, there is a general reference to all the festivals and Solomon's arrangements to observe them.—2Ch 8:12, 13.

In the other two instances the circumstances are outstanding. One is the revival of the observance of the Festival of Unfermented Cakes, after a time of neglect. This revival was during the first year of faithful King Hezekiah's reign. Interestingly, in this case there was not enough time to prepare for the annual festival on Nisan 15, because the work of cleaning and repairing the temple took until Nisan 16. So, advantage was taken of the Law to celebrate the festival during the second month. (2Ch 29:17; 30:13, 21, 22; Nu 9:10, 11) It was such a joyous occasion and resulted in such a religious revival that the celebration of seven days proved to be just too short, and so another seven days were set aside. (2Ch 30:23) King Hezekiah and his princes contributed generously, giving 2,000 bulls and 17,000 sheep to supply food for the multitudes attending.

The festival observance was the start of a great campaign against false religion, and in many cities this was carried out before the worshipers returned to their homes. (2Ch 30:24; 31:1) The keeping of this Festival of Unfermented Cakes brought about Jehovah's blessing as well as freedom from demon worship, and it is a fine example of the beneficial effects that the keeping of these festivals had upon the Israelites.

The last recorded account of preexilic observance of the Festival of Unfermented Cakes was its celebration during the reign of King Josiah when he made a courageous effort to restore the pure worship of Jehovah in Judah.—2Ch 35:1-19.

Although these are the only observances specifically mentioned, prior to the kings the faithful judges and priests of Israel were doubtless concerned with keeping the festivals. Later, both David and Solomon made extensive arrangements to keep the priesthood functioning properly, and other kings of Judah must have seen to it that the festivals were regularly observed. Also, the Festival of Unfermented Cakes was kept quite regularly in postexilic times.

Postexilic Observance. Following the Jews' release from Babylon and their return to the Promised Land, the temple at Jerusalem was rebuilt and completed under the vigorous encouragement given by Jehovah's prophets Haggai and Zechariah. (Ezr 5:1, 2) In 515 B.C.E. the rebuilt house of Jehovah was inaugurated with great joy and with all the appropriate sacrifices attending the Festival of Unfermented Cakes. The record at Ezra 6:22 states: "And they went on to hold the festival of unfermented cakes seven days with rejoicing."

The book of Malachi shows that in time, notwithstanding the zealous start toward restoration of true worship when the exiles returned from Babylon, the priests became careless, proud, and self-righteous. The temple service became a mockery, even though the festivals were kept in a formalistic way. (Mal 1:6-8, 12-14; 2:1-3; 3:8-10) Jesus found the scribes and Pharisees scrupulously keeping the details of the Law, besides their added traditions. They zealously observed the festivals, including the Festival of Unfermented Cakes, but Jesus condemned them, for, because of their hypocrisy, they had lost sight of the real significance of these fine arrangements of Jehovah for their blessing.—Mt 15:1-9; 23:23, 24; Lu 19:45, 46.

Prophetic Significance. Jesus Christ gave the interpretation as to the symbolic significance of ferment, or leaven, as recorded at Matthew 16:6, 11, 12, when he warned his disciples: "Keep your eyes open and watch out for the leaven of the Pharisees and Sadducees." When his disciples reasoned incorrectly among themselves as to what he meant, he spoke plainly: "'How is it you do not discern that I did not talk to you about loaves? But watch out for the leaven of the Pharisees and Sadducees.' Then they grasped that he said to watch out . . . for the teaching of the

Pharisees and Sadducees." Also, Luke reports that Jesus stated specifically on another occasion: "Watch out for the leaven of the Pharisees, which is hypocrisy."—Lu 12:1.

The apostle Paul applies a similar significance to leaven in connection with the Festival of Unfermented Cakes when he describes the course that Christians should take. At 1 Corinthians 5:6-8, he gives this counsel to his Christian brothers: "Do you not know that a little leaven ferments the whole lump? Clear away the old leaven, that you may be a new lump, according as you are free from ferment. For, indeed, Christ our passover has been sacrificed. Consequently let us keep the festival, not with old leaven, neither with leaven of badness and wickedness, but with unfermented cakes of sincerity and truth."

On Nisan 16, the second day of the Festival of Unfermented Cakes, the high priest waved the firstfruits of the barley harvest, which was the first crop of the year, or what might be called the *first* of the firstfruits of the land. (Le 23:10, 11) It is significant that Jesus Christ was resurrected on this very day, Nisan 16, in the year 33 C.E. The apostle compares Christ with others who are resurrected, saying: "However, now Christ has been raised up from the dead, the firstfruits of those who have fallen asleep in death. . . . But each one in his own rank: Christ the firstfruits, afterward those who belong to the Christ during his presence." Christ is also called "the firstborn among many brothers."—1Co 15:20-23; Ro 8:29.

FESTIVAL OF WEEKS. See PENTECOST.

FESTUS
(Fes'tus) [from Lat., Festal; Joyful]. Governor of the Roman province of Judea after the recall of Felix to Rome. (Ac 24:27) The year of this change in governors is not definitely known; the only sources of information are the Bible and Josephus, and neither sheds light on the appointment by Nero. There are two schools of critics, one arguing for the arrival of Porcius Festus in Judea as early as 54 C.E., the other as late as 61. Historians tend to favor a time between 58 and 61 C.E. The year 58 C.E., as given by Young's *Analytical Concordance to the Bible* (p. 342), seems to be the most likely date of Festus' accession as governor of Judea.

Three days after Festus arrived in Caesarea he journeyed to Jerusalem, evidently to familiarize himself with the problems of the people he was to govern. Paul was in Caesarea, left over as a prisoner from the administration of Felix. The Jewish chief priests and principal men wasted no time in requesting that he be brought to Jerusalem, as they hoped to ambush him and kill him on the way. Instead, Festus decided on a retrial for Paul and ordered the accusers to appear before his judgment seat in Caesarea. After the "trial" Festus was convinced of Paul's innocence and later confessed to King Agrippa II: "I perceived he had committed nothing deserving of death." (Ac 25:25) Earlier, "desiring to gain favor with the Jews," Festus had asked if Paul would volunteer to go to Jerusalem for trial. (Ac 25:9) Paul, however, replied: "No man can hand me over to them as a favor. I appeal to Caesar!"—Ac 25:11.

Now Festus was faced with a new problem. In explaining to Agrippa that he had this prisoner to send to Rome, yet had no charges to lay against him, Festus observed: "It seems unreasonable to me to send a prisoner and not also to signify the charges against him." (Ac 25:27) Agrippa offered to hear Paul himself with a view to resolving the problem. In his defense, Paul made such an eloquent and stirring speech that Festus was moved to exclaim: "You are going mad, Paul! Great learning is driving you into madness!" (Ac 26:24) Paul then turned to Agrippa with a strong appeal, eliciting Agrippa's remark: "In a short time you would persuade me to become a Christian." (Ac 26:28) Later Agrippa said to Festus: "This man could have been released if he had not appealed to Caesar." This decision was entirely providential, for the Lord beforehand had disclosed to Paul: "Be of good courage! . . . you must also bear witness in Rome."—Ac 23:11; 26:32.

In comparison with the oppressive administration of Felix, that of Festus is rated as being generally favorable. He suppressed the terrorist bandits known as the Assassins, or *Sicarii* (dagger men), and in other ways tried to uphold Roman law. One ruling of Festus, however, was reversed on appeal to Rome. Agrippa built his dining room overlooking the sacred temple area, whereupon the Jews constructed a wall to obstruct the view. Festus ordered that the wall be removed on the grounds that it blocked out the view of the soldiers, but when the case was appealed to Rome the wall was allowed to stand. Festus died in office and was succeeded by Albinus.

FETTERS. See BOND.

FEVER.
An abnormal elevation in the temperature of the body. Fever can be an indicator of the presence of disease. Though high fever may

result in loss of weight, body fluids, and salt, accompanied by headaches and other discomfort, the fever itself is frequently part of the body's fight against infection. However, when an outstanding symptom of a disease is a high fever, the name of the disease may indicate this, as in the case of scarlet fever, yellow fever, and dengue fever.

Malaria is one of the most common febrile diseases (that is, diseases accompanied by fever) in the Middle East. Dysentery is another febrile disease, one specifically mentioned in the Bible. (Ac 28:8) This ailment is characterized by severe inflammation of the colon, at times producing evacuation of blood and mucus. At Leviticus 26: 16 the Hebrew word qad·da'chath is translated "burning fever"; at Matthew 8:14 the Greek verb py·res'so means "be sick with fever," or, literally, "burn with fever."

While the Law with its provisions was primarily for Israel's spiritual benefit and to maintain its separateness from the pagan nations, an examination of the dietary and sanitary regulations of the Law reveals that it had a beneficial secondary effect in protecting the nation against the causes and spread of many diseases, including certain infectious febrile diseases.

(1) The diet of the Hebrews did not normally include a great deal of meat, but when a family wanted to slaughter a domestic animal for meat, they took the animal to the sanctuary (unless, after they entered the Promised Land, the family lived too far away). (Le 17:3-5; De 12:20-27) They ate the meat after the priest offered some of it on the altar and received his portion. Some communion sacrifices were to be eaten on the same day. Others could not be eaten after the second day, but the flesh was to be burned with fire. Considering Palestine's warm climate and the lack of refrigeration, these requirements safeguarded the Israelites against febrile illnesses that can result from toxins that are produced when certain organisms multiply rapidly on meat that is not kept under refrigeration. Such diseases include Staphylococcus aureus and Salmonella. (2) The flesh of certain prohibited animals, such as pigs, hares, carrion-eating animals and birds, rodents, and certain water animals and fish, is known to be a possible contributory factor in various diseases that are often accompanied by fever. (Le 11:1-31) (3) The sanitary regulations helped safeguard the cooking utensils and also the drinking-water supply from contamination, a source of typhoid and other febrile

diseases. (Le 11:32-38) (4) Anyone either touching the body of an animal that died of itself or eating some of it had to cleanse himself, thus safeguarding against the spread of organisms identified with certain febrile diseases. (Le 11:39, 40) (5) The laws commanding the covering of fecal waste by each individual, also the covering of blood with dust, protected against febrile diseases such as hepatitis. (Le 17:13; De 23:12, 13) (6) The moral laws would practically eliminate all sexually transmitted disease, which disease can affect all organs of the body and is frequently accompanied by fever. (Le 19:20, 22, 23) (7) The quarantine laws worked to prevent the spread of infectious diseases.—Le 13; Nu 19:11, 12, 16; 31:19.

Jehovah warned Israel that if they went contrary to his commandments, they would undergo exhaustion from hunger, a contributory factor in many febrile diseases; they would be afflicted with tuberculosis and burning fever, inflammation and feverish heat; they would suffer boils, skin eruptions (sicknesses that are often accompanied by fever), and blindness. (Le 26:14-16; De 28:22, 27) All of this came to fulfillment after Israel's repeated rebellions against Jehovah and their violations of his laws.—Eze 4:16, 17; 33:10.

When Jesus Christ was on earth many persons sick with fevers were healed by him. One case was that of the mother-in-law of the apostle Simon Peter. (Mt 8:14, 15; Mr 1:29-31) Luke, apparently because he was a physician, draws attention to the degree of fever in that case, classifying it as "a high fever." (Lu 4:38) On one occasion Jesus, in Cana, healed the son of an attendant to King Herod Antipas, although the feverish boy who was dying was about 40 km (25 mi) away in Capernaum. As a result, the man and his entire household became believers.—Joh 4:46-54.

The apostle Paul used the God-given power of healing, one of the miraculous gifts through Jesus Christ to certain members of the early Christian congregation (1Co 12:7-9, 11, 30), to cure the father of Publius, the principal man and a landowner of the island of Malta, who was distressed with fever and dysentery. On learning of this, the island's natives came to Paul, and he healed many of their various sicknesses.—Ac 28:7-9.

FIELD. The Hebrew word sa·dheh', which is most frequently rendered "field," may denote a hunting ground, a tract of land used for pasturage or farming, an uncultivated wooded area, a mountaintop, or even a region occupied by a certain people, for example, "the field of Moab"; the term is also used in contrast with "city." (Ge 27:5; 31:4; 37:5-7; Jg 9:32, 36; 1Sa 14:25; Nu 21:20; De 28:3) The Greek term *a·gros'* refers to a cultivated "field" (Mt 13:24), the "country" as opposed to the city (Mr 16:12), and, in the plural, the "countryside" (Mr 5:14).

Moreover, the combined tracts of several individual owners might be viewed jointly as "the field," as is seen from the account of Ruth. In going out to "the field," Ruth by chance "lighted on the tract of the field belonging to Boaz," indicating that Boaz owned only a section of the area. (Ru 2:2, 3) While vineyards and gardens were apparently enclosed, the indications are that fields were not. (Nu 22:24; Ca 4:12) The Law commanded that no one move the boundary marks of his fellowman, indicating that this was relatively easy to do. (De 19:14) According to the Law, unwalled settlements were accounted as part of the field of the country.—Le 25:31.

Fires could easily spread from one field to another, and care had to be exercised to keep domestic animals in check so that they would not wander into someone else's field. (Ex 22:5, 6) At Isaiah 28:25 spelt is said to be sown as a boundary. Perhaps by planting this inferior grade of wheat around the outer edges of their fields, farmers could, to some extent, protect their more valuable crops, such as wheat and barley, from cattle that might enter the edges of the field.

Likely it was possible to go through the field by means of footpaths, and these could also have served to separate one tract of land from another, for it is most improbable that Jesus and his disciples would have walked right through a field of grain, trampling some of the grain as they went along. If they had done this, the Pharisees undoubtedly would have taken issue on this point also. (Lu 6:1-5) It may have been with reference to such paths that Jesus, in his illustration about the sower, mentioned the seeds that fell alongside the road.—Mt 13:4.

FIELD OF BLOOD. See AKELDAMA.

FIERY SNAKE. The Hebrew noun *sa·raph'*, in its plural form, is translated "seraphs" in Isaiah 6:2, 6 and literally means "fiery one," or "burning one." It is also used in conjunction with the general Hebrew term for serpent (*na·chash'*) and has been translated "poisonous," perhaps referring to the burning and inflaming effect of the venom. (De 8:15) It is first mentioned at the time of God's

inflicting punishment on the rebellious Israelites by sending "poisonous serpents [*necha·shim' sera·phim'*]" among them. After Moses' intercession, Jehovah instructed him to make "a fiery snake" and place it on a signal pole. If those bitten would look at it, they would be healed and would live. Moses formed the snake of copper. (Nu 21:6-9; 1Co 10:9) Jesus gave prophetic significance to this by stating: "Just as Moses lifted up the serpent in the wilderness, so the Son of man must be lifted up, that everyone believing in him may have everlasting life."—Joh 3:14, 15.

At Isaiah 14:29 and 30:6 "a flying fiery snake" is mentioned in God's judgment against Philistia and in the description of the wilderness area to the S of Judah. The expression "flying" is considered by some to refer to the rapid darting or lightninglike striking through the air done by venomous snakes when attacking.

FIG [Heb., *te'e·nah'*; Gr., *sy·ke', sy'kon*]. Along with the olive and the vine, the fig tree (*Ficus carica*) is one of the most prominent plants of the Bible, receiving mention in more than 50 texts. (Jg 9:8-13; Hab 3:17) The fig is native to SW Asia, Israel, Syria, and Egypt and is noted for its remarkable longevity. While the tree will grow wild, to produce good fruitage it needs cultivation. (Lu 13:6-9) It is quite adaptable to various kinds of soil, even doing well in rocky soil. It may reach a height of about 9 m (30 ft), with a trunk diameter of about 0.6 m (2 ft), and it has widespreading branches. While it is primarily appreciated for its fruit, it is also highly valued for its good shade. (Joh 1:48-50) The leaves are large, measuring as much as 20 cm (8 in.) or more in width. The first mention of the fig is in regard to the sewing together of its leaves for use as loin coverings by Adam and Eve. (Ge 3:7) In some parts of the Middle East, fig leaves are still sewed together and used for wrapping fruit and for other purposes.—See SYCAMORE.

Early and Late Crops. There are, basically, two crops of figs produced annually by the trees: the first ripe figs, or early figs (Heb., *bik·ku·rah'*), which mature in June or early July (Isa 28:4; Jer 24:2; Ho 9:10), and the later figs, which grow on the new wood and make up the main crop, generally maturing from August onward. The early figs may be easily shaken from the tree when ripe, and they are prized for their delicate flavor.—Na 3:12.

About February, the first fruit buds appear on the branches from the previous season, and these precede the leaves by about two months, since the leaves do not usually appear until the final part of April or in May. (Mt 24:32) At Song of Solomon 2:13 the first signs of maturity in the new green figs (Heb., *pagh*) are mentioned in connection with the flowering of the grapevines, which flowering begins about April. Hence, by the time the tree is in full leaf it should also be bearing fruit. The fig tree that Jesus Christ cursed seems to have been abnormally early with its leaves, inasmuch as it was then Nisan 10 of the year 33 C.E. Its appearance gave basis for hoping it might also be unseasonably early in producing fruit suitable for eating, and the record at Mark 11:12-14 indicates that Jesus approached the tree with that thought in mind even though "it was not the season of figs," that is, the time for the fruit to be gathered. The tree's having nothing but leaves showed it was not going to produce any crop and was, therefore, deceptive in its appearance. Jesus cursed it as unproductive, causing it to wither.—Compare Mt 7:19; 21:43; Lu 13:6-9.

Food and Medicinal Use. Figs were a staple source of food in Bible times and continue to be such in several Middle Eastern countries. They were formed into "cakes of pressed figs" (Heb., *deve·lim'*), which were convenient for carrying. (1Sa 25:18; 30:12; 1Ch 12:40) Such a cake was used as a medicinal poultice for King Hezekiah's boil, and cakes of this type are still employed in this manner today in the Middle East.—2Ki 20:7.

Figurative and Prophetic Use. The fig and the vine are mentioned jointly in many texts, and Jesus' words at Luke 13:6 show that fig trees were often planted in vineyards. (2Ki 18:31; Joe 2:22) The expression 'sitting under one's own vine and fig tree' symbolized peaceful, prosperous, secure conditions.—1Ki 4:25; Mic 4:4; Zec 3:10.

In view of this prominence of the fig tree in the life of the people, it is understandable why it was so frequently used in prophecy. Because of its importance to the nation's food supply the utter failure of the fig crop would be calamitous. Thus, the fig tree received special mention when destruction, or ruination, was foretold for the land. —Jer 5:17; 8:13; Ho 2:12; Joe 1:7, 12; Am 4:9; Hab 3:17.

The nation of Israel itself was likened by Jehovah to two kinds of figs. (Jer 24:1-10) To illustrate how false prophets could be recognized by their bad fruits, Jesus cited the impossibility of getting "figs from thistles." (Mt 7:15, 16; compare Jas

3:12.) The fig tree's 'putting forth its leaves' toward the middle of the spring season was used by Jesus as a well-known time indicator. (Mt 24:32-34) Finally, the ease with which the 'unripe fig' (Gr., *o'lyn·thos*) is shaken to the ground by high winds is used as a simile by the writer of Revelation.—Re 6:13.

FIG-MULBERRY TREE [Gr., *sy·ko·mo·re'a*]. When short-statured Zacchaeus wanted to get a better look at Christ Jesus he "climbed a figmulberry tree." (Lu 19:4) The Greek name indicates a fig tree (Gr., *sy·ke'*) with leaves like those of the mulberry (Gr., *mo·re'a*). The two trees are of the same family, and the fig-mulberry mentioned in Luke 19:4 appears to be the same as "the sycamore" (*Ficus sycomorus*) of the Hebrew Scriptures.—1Ki 10:27; see SYCAMORE.

FILL HAND WITH POWER. The Hebrew expression *mil·le'' yadh*, translated "consecrate" in many versions, literally means "fill the hand" and is used with reference to putting full power in the hands of those who are to serve in a priestly office. At their installation as priests of Jehovah, Aaron and his sons had their hands filled with power to serve in that capacity. (Ex 28:41; 29:9, 29, 33, 35; Le 8:33; 16:32; 21:10; Nu 3:3) To symbolize this, the ram of installation was killed and cut up, and parts of it together with certain baked items from the basket of unfermented cakes were put by Moses upon the palms of Aaron and his sons, who then waved the offering before Jehovah. Finally the things waved were made to smoke upon the altar on top of the burnt offering.—Ex 29:19-25; Le 8:22-28; see ANOINTED, ANOINTING; INSTALLATION; PRIEST.

Others, too, filled the hands of their priests with power. Idolatrous Micah empowered first a son and then an unfaithful Levite to be priests for his "house of gods." (Jg 17:5, 12) Later, King Jeroboam, in instituting calf worship in Israel, installed his own priests from the people in general; the Aaronic priests and the Levites remained loyal to Jehovah's worship centered at Jerusalem and were, evidently for this reason, driven out of the ten-tribe kingdom.—1Ki 12:31; 13:33; 2Ch 13:9.

FINGER. As an instrument of the hand and arm, the finger has a great deal to do with the direction and finer details of the work done by an individual. Because they form part of the hand, in the Bible the fingers are sometimes used synonymously with "hand." The two words, "fingers"

and "hands," are used in parallel statements in describing the making of idols.—Isa 2:8.

Figuratively, God is spoken of as accomplishing work with his "finger(s)," such as writing the Ten Commandments on stone tablets (Ex 31:18; De 9:10), performing miracles (Ex 8:18, 19), and creating the heavens (Ps 8:3). That God's "fingers" employed in creative activity have reference to his holy spirit, or active force, is indicated by the Genesis account of creation, where it is said that God's active force (ru'ach, "spirit") moved over the surface of the waters. (Ge 1:2) However, the Christian Greek Scriptures give the key to sure understanding of this symbolic usage, Matthew's account explaining that Jesus expelled demons by 'God's holy spirit' and Luke's telling us that it was by "God's finger."—Mt 12:28; Lu 11:20.

Gestures are particularly expressive among Orientals; a small motion often has weighty significance. The Bible portrays the good-for-nothing man as "making indications with his fingers." (Pr 6:12, 13) Israelites would have to remove from their midst such things as "the poking out of the finger" (possibly in scorn or false accusation) along with the speaking of what was hurtful, if they would obtain God's favor. (Isa 58:9-11) Because the fingers are prominently before a person's eyes and are vital in carrying out one's purposes, God's people were figuratively to 'tie his commandments upon their fingers' as a constant reminder and guide in everything they did.—Pr 7:2, 3; compare Ps 144:1.

When a delegation asked King Rehoboam for a lighter load of service than his father Solomon had laid upon them, the king was advised by his young attendants to respond that 'his little finger would be thicker than his father's hips'; this metaphor meant that he would put a much heavier burden on them. (1Ki 12:4, 10, 11) The Hebrew word used here for "little finger" comes from a root meaning "be small, little, least."

Jesus Christ used a similar figure of speech in illustrating the harsh, arrogant domination the scribes and Pharisees exercised. Showing the complete unwillingness of these religious leaders to help the burdened people in the least, Jesus said that 'they bound heavy loads on men's shoulders but were themselves not willing to budge them with their finger.' (Mt 23:2-4) In another metaphor Jesus depicted "the rich man" as desiring to get Lazarus to do even the least thing for him (bring only water on "the tip of his finger"), this request being designed to get Laza-

rus away from his favored position with Abraham.—Lu 16:22, 24.

One of the Rephaim who fought against Israel was a man of extraordinary size, a genetic freak, having his fingers and toes in sixes, 24 in all.—2Sa 21:20; 1Ch 20:6.

FINGERBREADTH. A linear measurement, the smallest mentioned in the Bible. A fingerbreadth equaled ¼ handbreadth or ¹⁄₂₄ cubit (1.85 cm; 0.72 in.). At Jeremiah 52:21 the thickness of the copper used for the pillars Jachin and Boaz is given as four fingerbreadths (7.4 cm; 2.9 in.).—1Ki 7:15, 21.

FIRE. As today, so also in Bible times fire played an important role in man's life. The refining, forging, and casting of metals, along with the preparing of food and the heating of homes, as well as the offering of sacrifices and the burning of incense, are among the things specifically mentioned in the Bible as requiring the use of fire. However, because of the destructiveness of uncontrolled fire, it is described as one of the four things that have not said: "Enough!" (Pr 30:15, 16) For the same reason James compared the tongue when used wrongly to a fire.—Jas 3:5-8; compare Pr 16:27.

The first man and woman were acquainted with fire, for Jehovah, upon expelling them from the garden of Eden, posted at the E of the garden "the cherubs and the flaming blade of a sword that was turning itself continually." (Ge 3:24) Cain and Abel may have brought their offerings to Jehovah before the cherubs and, though it is not directly stated in the Scriptures, likely they used fire in presenting them, or they may have expected fire to come from the cherubs to consume the sacrifices. (Ge 4:3, 4) Tubal-cain, in forging tools of copper and iron, must have employed the heat of intense fires, especially since the melting of iron requires a temperature of 1,535° C. (2,795° F.). (Ge 4:22) After the Flood, bricks were baked with "a burning process," although some were merely sun dried. (Ge 11:3) In view of the difficulty faced in kindling a fire anew, it was evidently a frequent practice to transfer fire from one place to another.—Ge 22:6; Isa 30:14.

In Connection With God's Purposes. Jehovah's angel appeared to Moses in a flame of fire in a burning thornbush that was not consumed. (Ex 3:2) A pillar of fire by night guided the Israelites through the wilderness, which pillar later rested over the tabernacle, signifying Jehovah's presence. (Ex 13:21; 40:38) The manifestation of Jehovah's glory in fire at the giving of the Law to Israel caused Mount Sinai to smoke.—Ex 19:18; 24:17.

As relates to the tabernacle and the temple.
Fire figured in the worship carried on at the tabernacle and then later at the temple. Each morning and between the two evenings, the high priest was to burn incense on the altar of incense. (Ex 30:7, 8) God's law required that the fire on the altar of burnt offering be kept burning continually. (Le 6:12, 13) The traditional Jewish view that the altar fire was originally kindled miraculously by God, though widely accepted, is not actually supported by the Scriptures. According to Jehovah's initial instructions to Moses, the sons of Aaron were to "put fire on the altar and set wood in order on the fire" before placing the sacrifice on the altar. (Le 1:7, 8) It was *after* the installation of the Aaronic priesthood, and therefore after the installation sacrifices had been offered, that fire from Jehovah, probably proceeding from the cloud over the tabernacle, consumed the offering then upon the altar. In view of this, the miraculous fire manifested itself, not in kindling the wood on the altar, but in "consuming the burnt offering and the fatty pieces upon the altar." The fire that then continued to burn on the altar, of course, was likely a result of the mixture of the fire from God and the fire already on the altar. (Le 8:14–9:24) Likewise, miraculous fire from Jehovah consumed the sacrifices right after Solomon's prayer at the dedication of the temple.—2Ch 7:1; see also Jg 6:21; 1Ki 18:21-39; 1Ch 21:26 for other examples of Jehovah's use of miraculous fire when accepting the offerings of his servants.

Legal provisions, and use in executions.
The Mosaic Law prohibited lighting a fire on the Sabbath. (Ex 35:3) According to the Law, if a fire got out of hand and caused a conflagration in the field of another, the one starting the fire had to make compensation. (Ex 22:6) Garments or articles of skin in which a plague of leprosy developed and persisted were to be burned. (Le 13:53-58) In the case of certain violations of God's law, the individuals were stoned to death and then their bodies were burned with fire. (Le 20:14; 21:9; Jos 7:15, 25) If an Israelite city turned to apostasy, its inhabitants were to be struck down with the sword, and the city and its spoil were to be burned in the fire.—De 13:12-16.

In carrying out war operations against their enemies, the Israelites consigned certain cities to the fire. (Nu 31:10; Jos 6:24; 11:11-13) Also, the graven images and sacred poles were burned. (De 7:5, 25; 12:3) In taking spoil, the Israelites passed metals through the fire, in effect sterilizing them.—Nu 31:22, 23.

On numerous occasions Jehovah used literal fire in executing his judgments against wrongdoers. (Nu 11:1; 16:35; 2Ki 1:10-12; Jude 7) At the destruction of apostate Judah and Jerusalem by the Babylonians in 607 B.C.E., Jehovah's anger was figuratively poured out "just like fire." This expression of anger was accompanied by literal fire. (2Ki 25:9; La 2:3, 4) John the Baptizer warned the religious leaders of his day of a baptism with fire, which came upon Jerusalem in 70 C.E., when the Roman armies destroyed the city and burned its temple.—Mt 3:7-12.

Use by Opposers of God's Will. Fire was also used by opposers of God's will in threats, cruel executions, and sacrifices. Angered Ephraimites threatened Jephthah: "Your very house we shall burn over you with fire." Similarly, Samson's 30 Philistine groomsmen threatened to burn his betrothed and her father's house if she did not get Samson to tell her the solution to a riddle and then advise them accordingly. After Samson sent 300 foxes with lighted torches into the standing grain of the pagan Philistines, the Philistines did burn her and her father with fire. (Jg 12:1; 14:15; 15:4-6) Satan the Devil employed fire "from the heavens" by God's permission in the special test allowed on Job.—Job 1:12, 16.

The nations residing in Canaan actually burned their children in the fire as an offering to their false gods. Although specifically commanded by Jehovah not to do this, a violation of this command calling for the death penalty, apostate Israelites sacrificed their own children in the Valley of Hinnom. (Le 20:2-5; De 12:31; 2Ch 28:1-3; Jer 7:31; 19:5) However, faithful King Josiah put an end to this gruesome practice by making Topheth in the Valley of Hinnom unfit for worship.—2Ki 23:10; see MOLECH.

Figurative Usage. Fire or expressions having the thought of burning, or flaming, are figuratively associated with love (Ca 8:6), passion (Ro 1:27; 1Co 7:9), anger and judgment (Zep 2:2; Mal 4:1), or strong emotion (Lu 24:32; 2Co 11:29). When Jeremiah wanted to refrain from speaking Jehovah's word, he found this impossible, for it proved to be like a burning fire shut up in his bones. (Jer 20:9) The Scriptures refer to Jehovah as a consuming fire because of his cleanness, purity, and insistence on exclusive devotion, as well as the fact that he annihilates those who set themselves in opposition to him. (De 4:24; 9:3) His ardor and rage burn like fire, and his "tongue" and word are like a fire. (Ps 79:5; 89:46; Isa 30:27; Jer 23:29) Moreover, Jehovah makes his angelic ministers a devouring fire, and by the fire of his zeal "the earth" will be devoured.—Ps 104:1, 4; Zep 3:8; see also Da 7:9, 10.

Testing, refining, purging. "The messenger of the covenant" is compared to a refiner's fire, a fire used in purifying gold and silver. Hence, Jehovah's fiery testing of "the sons of Levi" by the messenger of the covenant brings about their cleansing. (Mal 3:1-3; see REFINE, REFINER.) A test by fire also reveals the quality of a material, as pointed out by the apostle Paul when emphasizing the importance of building on Jesus Christ with fire-resistant materials.—1Co 3:10-15.

Fire and salt were associated with the sacrifices offered at the temple. (Le 2:9, 13; Eze 43:24) Salt represented freedom from corruption and was a symbol of enduring loyalty, as found in the expression "covenant of salt." (2Ch 13:5) Of what, then, is the fire symbolic?

The apostle Peter refers to trials or sufferings as a "fire" that proves the quality of the Christian's faith. (1Pe 1:6, 7) Later, he likens suffering for righteousness to a burning when he tells his fellow Christians: "Do not be puzzled at the burning among you, which is happening to you for a trial, . . . you are sharers in the sufferings of the Christ, that you may rejoice and be overjoyed also during the revelation of his glory." (1Pe 4:12, 13) That such suffering for righteousness has a beneficial effect is pointed out by the apostle Paul when he says: "Tribulation produces endurance." (Ro 5:3) A person who faithfully and successfully passes through a difficult "burning" trial is stronger and more solidly established as a result of his endurance.—Ac 14:22; Ro 12:12.

Destruction. In Bible times the most thorough means of destruction in use was fire. (Jos 6:24; De 13:16) Hence Jesus at times used the term "fire" in an illustrative way to denote the complete destruction of the wicked. (Mt 13:40-42, 49, 50; compare Isa 66:24; Mt 25: 41.) On one occasion Jesus warned his disciples against letting their hand, foot, or eye stumble them so that they would be pitched into Gehenna. Then he went on to say: "Everyone must be salted with fire." He must have meant that "everyone" who did what he had just warned against would be salted with the "fire" of Ge-

henna, or eternal destruction.—Mr 9:43-49; see GEHENNA.

Peter wrote that "the heavens and the earth that are now are stored up for fire." From the context and in the light of other scriptures, it is evident that this is not a literal fire but signifies everlasting destruction. As the Flood of Noah's day did not destroy the literal heavens and earth, but only the ungodly persons, so also the revelation of Jesus Christ with his powerful angels in a flaming fire will result in permanent destruction only for the ungodly and the wicked system of things of which they are a part.—2Pe 3:5-7, 10-13; 2Th 1:6-10; compare Isa 66:15, 16, 22, 24.

Further examples of the use of fire to represent eternal destruction are found in Revelation and Ezekiel. There we are told that "the ten horns" and "the wild beast" will turn upon Babylon the Great and burn her with fire. (Re 17:16, 17) The attack of Gog and his hordes against God's people arouses Jehovah's anger, and fire and sulfur will rain down upon them. The remaining war implements of the attackers will be used to light fires for seven years. (Eze 38:19, 22; 39:6, 9, 10) Those nations who become rebellious when Satan is released at the end of the Thousand Year Reign of Christ will be devoured by fire, and the Devil and all those not written in the book of life will be cast into the lake of fire, representing the second death.—Re 20:7-10, 15; 21:8; see HINNOM, VALLEY OF; LAKE OF FIRE.

FIRE HOLDER. Fire holders were used in various ways in connection with the service at the sanctuary. There were gold fire holders that apparently served as containers for holding the pieces of burnt lampwick removed from the lamps on the golden lampstand. (Ex 25:38; 37: 23; Nu 4:9) The copper fire holders of the altar of burnt offering evidently served as ashpans or utensils for removing coals from the fire. (Ex 27:3; 38:3) Additionally, fire holders were used to burn incense. (Le 10:1) Each morning and between the two evenings, the high priest made perfumed incense smoke upon the golden altar of incense.—Ex 30:7, 8.

The fire holders as well as the other utensils used with the lampstand and with the altar of burnt offering had to be covered when the Israelites broke camp and the tabernacle was transported to another location during their journeys. —Nu 4:9, 14.

Solomon made fire holders of gold and silver for the temple, the plans of which had been given to David by inspiration. Possibly these were of more ornate form than those used in the tabernacle in the wilderness. (1Ki 7:48-50; 1Ch 28:11-19; 2Ch 4:19-22) Mention is made of genuine gold and silver fire holders being taken from the temple at the time of the Babylonian exile. —2Ki 25:15; Jer 52:19.

At Hebrews 9:4 reference is made to an object that, along with the ark of the covenant, pertained to or was associated with the Most Holy. In Greek it is called *thy·mi·a·te'ri·on.* That word refers to something connected with the burning of incense. Was it the altar of incense? Some translations present the matter that way, and the use of the word by Philo and Josephus with reference to the altar of incense is cited in support. (*NIV, NE, JB, RS*) Of course, it is well known that the altar of incense was not actually in the Most Holy. (Ex 30:1, 6) But it was immediately outside the curtain, or "toward the innermost room," as 1 Kings 6:22 puts it. (Compare Ex 40:3-5.) On the other hand, *thy·mi·a·te'ri·on* can properly be rendered "censer," and a censer was actually taken into the Most Holy by the high priest on Atonement Day. (Le 16:12, 13) In the Greek *Septuagint,* the word *thy·mi·a·te'ri·on* is always used with reference to the censer (2Ch 26:19; Eze 8:11, *LXX*), though a different word is used at Leviticus 16:12 when describing events of Atonement Day. The Jewish Mishnah, however, indicates that a special golden censer came to be used on Atonement Day. (*Yoma* 4:4; 5:1; 7:4) So, with good reason, some translators prefer to render *thy·mi·a·te'ri·on* as "censer."—*NW, CC, Dy, Yg, Da, Kx.*

Misuses. Aaron's sons Nadab and Abihu used their fire holders to offer illegitimate fire before Jehovah and lost their lives as a result. (Le 10:1, 2) Likewise the rebellious 250 men headed by Korah were consumed by fire when they presented their copper fire holders before Jehovah. (Nu 16:16-19, 35, 39) King Uzziah was smitten with leprosy while using a censer illegally. (2Ch 26:18, 19) The 70 older men of Israel seen in Ezekiel's vision were using censers to offer incense to idols.—Eze 8:10, 11; see INCENSE.

FIRSTBORN, FIRSTLING.

The firstborn is primarily the oldest son of a father (rather than the firstborn of the mother), the beginning of the father's generative power (De 21:17); also, the initial male offspring of animals, at times designated as "firstlings."—Ge 4:4.

From earliest times the firstborn son held an honored position in the family and was the one who succeeded to the headship of the household.

He inherited a double portion of the father's property. (De 21:17) Reuben was seated by Joseph at a meal according to his right as firstborn. (Ge 43:33) But the Bible does not always honor the firstborn by listing sons according to birth. The first place is often given to the most prominent or faithful of the sons rather than to the firstborn.—Ge 6:10; 1Ch 1:28; compare Ge 11: 26, 32; 12:4; see BIRTHRIGHT; INHERITANCE.

The firstborn came into considerable prominence at the time that Jehovah delivered his people from slavery in Egypt. Among the Egyptians, the firstborn were dedicated as sacred to the sun-god Amon-Ra, the supposed preserver of all the firstborn. The tenth plague that Jehovah brought upon the Egyptians served to discredit this god and showed up his inability to protect the firstborn. By obeying God's instructions concerning the slaying of a lamb and the splashing of its blood on the doorposts and upper part of the doorway of their houses, the Israelites did not lose their firstborn in death, whereas all the firstborn of the Egyptians, of both man and beast, were slain. (Ex 12:21-23, 28, 29) Evidently the firstborn son of each household is meant in most cases and not the head of the household, even though he may have been a firstborn. Pharaoh himself was probably a firstborn and yet his life was not taken. However, it may be that not every Egyptian household had a literal firstborn son (the married couple being childless or the firstborn son having already died), and in view of the statement at Exodus 12:30, "there was not a house where there was not one dead," the destruction could have included the chief one in the house occupying the *position* of firstborn.

Since the firstborn sons among the Israelites were those in line to become the heads of the various households, they represented the entire nation. Jehovah, in fact, referred to the whole nation as his "firstborn," it being his firstborn nation because of the Abrahamic covenant. (Ex 4:22) In view of his having preserved their lives, Jehovah commanded that "every male firstborn that opens each womb among the sons of Israel, among men and beasts," be sanctified to him. (Ex 13:2) Thus, the firstborn sons were devoted to God.

Later Jehovah took the male Levites, evidently aside from the 300 Levite firstborn (compare Nu 3:21, 22, 27, 28, 33, 34 with 3:39), in place of the firstborn sons of Israel, from those one month old and upward. A ransom price of five shekels ($11) had to be paid to Aaron and his sons for each of the 273 in excess of the Levites. Also, Jehovah took the domestic animals of the Levites in place of the firstborn domestic animals of the other tribes. (Nu 3:40-48) From that time forward, a firstborn son was to be presented to Jehovah at the tabernacle or temple after the period of the mother's uncleanness and be redeemed by the payment of the estimated value for those from a month up to five years old, "five silver shekels by the shekel of the holy place."—Le 12:1-3; 27:6; Nu 18:15, 16.

The firstborn males of clean animals, such as the bull, lamb, or goat, were not to be redeemed. Such a bull was not to be worked, nor was the lamb to be sheared. Instead, they were to be presented to Jehovah as a sacrifice at the tabernacle or temple on the eighth day after birth. (Ex 22:30; Nu 18:17; De 15:19, 20) If, however, the animal had a bad defect, it was not to be sacrificed to Jehovah but was to be eaten at one's place of dwelling.—De 15:21-23.

The firstborn of an ass, an unclean animal, could not be presented as a sacrifice and, therefore, was to be redeemed, or bought back, by substituting a sheep in its place. Otherwise, its neck was to be broken, since it belonged to Jehovah and was not to be used by man. (Ex 13:12, 13; 34:19, 20) However, Leviticus 27:27 reads: "If it is among the unclean beasts and he must redeem it according to the estimated value, he must then give a fifth of it in addition to it. But if it should not be bought back, it must then be sold according to the estimated value." Some commentators view this text as a modification of the regulation concerning the redeeming of an ass. Apparently, though, Leviticus 27:27 deals with a different matter. Instead of referring to an unclean animal, such as an ass, the words "if it is among the unclean beasts" may denote an animal that was unclean in the sense of being unfit for sacrifice because of being blemished.

Why does Jehovah refer to "David my servant" as firstborn, when David was not a firstborn son?

In Psalm 89 Jehovah refers to "David my servant" and reviews the covenant for the kingdom that was made with him. In the midst of this is the statement: "I myself shall place him as firstborn, the most high of the kings of the earth." (Ps 89:20, 27) David was not a firstborn son. (1Ch 2:13-15) So it seems that Jehovah was referring

prophetically to the one foreshadowed by David, God's own "firstborn" Son in heaven upon whom He confers kingship more exalted than that of any human ruler.—Compare Eze 34:24, where Messiah is spoken of as "my servant David."

Jesus Christ is shown to be "the firstborn of all creation" as well as "the firstborn from the dead" —not merely most distinguished in relation to those created or those resurrected but the first one actually created and the first raised from the dead to endless life. (Col 1:15, 18; Re 1:5; 3:14) On earth he was the firstborn child of Mary and was presented at the temple in accordance with Jehovah's law. (Lu 2:7, 22, 23) The apostle Paul speaks of the followers of Jesus Christ who have been enrolled in the heavens as "the congregation of the firstborn," the first ones accepted by God as sons on the basis of their faith in Jesus' sacrifice and the first of Christ's followers to be resurrected with no need to die again.—Heb 12:23.

At Job 18:13 the expression "firstborn of death" is used to denote the most deadly of diseases.

FIRSTFRUITS.

The earliest fruits of a season; the first results or products of anything. The Hebrew word re·shith′ (from a root meaning "head") is used in the sense of first part, point of departure, or "beginning" (De 11:12; Ge 1:1; 10:10); the "best" (Ex 23:19, ftn); and "firstfruits" (Le 2:12). "First ripe fruits" is rendered from the Hebrew bik·ku·rim′, which is used especially with regard to grain and fruit. (Na 3:12) The Greek term for firstfruits (a·par·khe′) comes from a root having the basic meaning "primacy."

Jehovah required of the nation of Israel that the firstfruits be offered to him, whether it be of man, animal, or the fruitage of the ground. (Ex 22:29, 30; 23:19; Pr 3:9) Devoting the firstfruits to Jehovah would be an evidence of the Israelites' appreciation for Jehovah's blessing and for their land and its harvest. It would be an expression of thankfulness to the Giver of "every good gift." —De 8:6-10; Jas 1:17.

Jehovah commanded the nation, representatively, to offer firstfruits to him, especially at the time of the Festival of Unfermented Cakes. Then, on Nisan 16, at the sanctuary the high priest waved before Jehovah some of the firstfruits of the grain harvest, a sheaf of barley, which was the first crop of the year based on the sacred calendar. (Le 23:5-12) Again, at Pentecost, on the 50th day after the sheaf of barley was waved, the firstfruits of the wheat harvest in the form of two leavened loaves made of fine flour were presented as a wave offering.—Le 23:15-17; see FESTIVAL.

Besides these grain offerings by the high priest on behalf of the nation, the Israelites were required to bring the firstfruits of all their produce as offerings. Every firstborn male of man and beast was sanctified to Jehovah, being either offered or redeemed. (See FIRSTBORN, FIRSTLING.) The firstfruits of coarse meal were to be offered in the form of ring-shaped cakes. (Nu 15:20, 21) Fruitage of the soil was also put in baskets and taken by the Israelites to the sanctuary (De 26:1, 2), where they then recited certain words recorded at Deuteronomy 26:3-10. The words were actually an outline of the nation's history from their entering into Egypt to their deliverance and their being brought into the Promised Land.

It is said that the custom arose whereby each locality would send a representative with the firstfruits contributed by the inhabitants of the district in order that not all would have to undergo the inconvenience of going up to Jerusalem each time that the firstfruits were ripe. The quantity of these firstfruits to be offered was not fixed by the Law; it apparently was left to the generosity and appreciative spirit of the giver. However, the choicest portions, the best of the firstfruits, were to be offered.—Nu 18:12; Ex 23:19; 34:26.

In the case of a newly planted tree, for the first three years it was considered impure as though uncircumcised. In the fourth year all its fruit became holy to Jehovah. Then, in the fifth year, the owner could gather in its fruit for himself. —Le 19:23-25.

Contributions of firstfruits to Jehovah by the 12 non-Levitical tribes of Israel were used by the priests and Levites, since they received no inheritance in the land. (Nu 18:8-13) The faithful offering of the firstfruits brought pleasure to Jehovah and a blessing to all parties involved. (Eze 44:30) A failure to bring them would be counted by God as robbing him of his due and would bring his displeasure. (Mal 3:8) In Israel's history at times this practice was neglected, being restored in certain periods by rulers zealous for true worship. In King Hezekiah's reformation work, he held an extended celebration of the Festival of the Unfermented Cakes, and on this occasion Hezekiah instructed the people to fulfill their duty with respect to the contribution of firstfruits and tithes. Cheerfully the people responded by bringing in great quantities of the firstfruits of the grain, new wine, oil, honey, and all the produce of the field, from the third month to the seventh. (2Ch 30:21, 23; 31:4-7) After the restoration from Babylon, Nehemiah led the people in taking an oath to walk in Jehovah's law, including the bringing to him of firstfruits of every sort.—Ne 10:29, 34-37; see OFFERINGS.

Figurative and Symbolic Use. Jesus Christ was spiritually begotten at the time of his baptism and was resurrected from the dead to life in the spirit on Nisan 16, 33 C.E., the day of the year on which the firstfruits of the first grain crop were presented before Jehovah at the sanctuary. He is, therefore, called the firstfruits, being actually the *first* firstfruits to God. (1Co 15:20, 23; 1Pe 3:18) The faithful followers of Jesus Christ, his spiritual brothers, are also a firstfruits to God, but not the primary firstfruits, being similar to the second grain crop, the wheat, which was presented to Jehovah on the day of Pentecost. They number 144,000 and are called the ones "bought from among mankind as firstfruits to God and to the Lamb" and "certain firstfruits of his creatures."—Re 14:1-4; Jas 1:18.

The apostle Paul also speaks of the faithful Jewish remnant who became the first Christians as being "firstfruits." (Ro 11:16) The Christian Epaenetus is called "a firstfruits of Asia for Christ" (Ro 16:5), and the household of Stephanas "the firstfruits of Achaia."—1Co 16:15.

Since the anointed Christians are begotten by the spirit as sons of God with the hope of resurrection to immortality in the heavens, they are said during their lifetime on earth to "have the firstfruits, namely, the spirit . . . while we are earnestly waiting for adoption as sons, the release from our bodies by ransom." (Ro 8:23, 24) Paul says that he and fellow Christians with hopes of life in the spirit have "the token of what is to come, that is, the spirit," which he also says is "a token in advance of our inheritance."—2Co 5:5; Eph 1:13, 14.

FISH. These and other water animals were brought into existence by God on the fifth creative day. (Ge 1:20-23) Although not authorized to use fish for food until after the Flood, man was from the beginning to have these creatures in subjection. (Ge 1:28; 9:2, 3) But instead of exercising proper dominion over the animals, some men became "empty-headed" in their reasonings and came to venerate the creation. (Ro 1:20-23) For example, the Babylonian Ea, a god of the waters, was depicted as a man covered with a body that was part fish; the Syrian Atargatis was a fish goddess; and in Egypt certain kinds of fish were viewed as sacred and were even mummified. Such fish worship was, of course, prohibited in God's law to Israel.—De 4:15-18.

It was most appropriate that Jesus Christ, "the Son of man" (Mt 17:22), who was to have even the fish in subjection, on two occasions demonstrated his power by filling the nets of his apostles with miraculous catches of fish. (Ps 8:4-8; Heb 2:5-9; Lu 5:4-7; Joh 21:6) Faced with the paying of the temple tax, Jesus also exercised his dominion when he instructed Peter: "Go to the sea, cast a fishhook, and take the first fish coming up and, when you open its mouth, you will find a stater coin. Take that and give it to them for me and you."—Mt 17:24-27.

Fish as Food. Fish, a highly nutritious and easily digestible food, evidently was an important item in the diet of the Egyptians as well as of the enslaved Hebrews, for in the wilderness the mixed crowd and the sons of Israel longed for the fish they used to eat in Egypt. (Nu 11:5) The Egyptian economy therefore suffered heavily when the fish in the Nile died as a result of Jehovah's turning Egypt's waters into blood. —Ex 7:20, 21.

Fish continued to be an important food to the Israelites once they were established in the Promised Land. One of the gates of Jerusalem was called the "Fish Gate," suggesting that a fish market was located there or nearby. (2Ch 33:14) In a later period, as mentioned by Nehemiah, the Tyrians sold fish at Jerusalem even on the Sabbath.—Ne 13:16.

Commonly prepared by broiling or salting and drying, fish was often eaten along with bread. Likely the fish used by Jesus in miraculously feeding 5,000 men and later 4,000 men, besides women and children, was dried and salted. (Mt 14:17-21; 15:34-38) After his resurrection Jesus ate some broiled fish to prove to his apostles that they were not seeing a spirit, and on another occasion he prepared a breakfast of bread and fish cooked over a charcoal fire.—Lu 24:36-43; Joh 21:9-12.

Fish of Israel. Fish are plentiful in the inland waters of Palestine, with the exception of the Dead Sea. Among the varieties encountered there are bream, carp, perch, and the unusual mouth-breeding fish such as *Chromis simonis*. The male of *Chromis simonis* takes the eggs, about 200 in number, into his mouth, and the young remain there for several weeks after being hatched.

Certain kinds of fish live even in the salt springs near the Dead Sea, but these soon die if placed in water from the sea itself. The reason for this has been ascribed to the presence of a large percentage of magnesium chloride in the Dead Sea. The swift current of the Jordan, particularly at flood stage, sweeps many fish into the Dead Sea, where stupefied fish become food for birds of prey or where their dead bodies are washed up on the shore and eaten by carrion birds. In sharp contrast with this, the prophet Ezekiel, in vision, saw issuing forth from Jehovah's temple a stream that healed the waters of the Dead Sea, giving rise to a flourishing fishing industry.—Eze 47:1, 8-10.

Clean and Unclean. Although King Solomon's wisdom embraced the field of natural history, including a knowledge of fish (1Ki 4:33), not once is a specific kind of fish named in the Scriptures. However, the Law did make a distinction between clean and unclean water animals. Only water animals having fins and scales were ceremonially clean for food; this ruled out such creatures as catfish, eels, lampreys, rays, sharks, and the crustacea, many of which live on sewage and decaying matter and often are contaminated by the bacteria that cause typhoid and paratyphoid fevers. (Le 11:9-12) Israelite fishermen therefore had to separate the fine fish from those unsuitable for food, a point highlighted in Jesus' illustration of the dragnet.—Mt 13:47, 48.

The Fish That Swallowed Jonah. In spite of the fact that the Son of God himself testified to the truthfulness of the account about Jonah's being swallowed by a "huge fish," this incident is frequently cited with a view to discrediting the reliability of the Scriptural record. (Mt 12:40) Of course, it should be remembered that the Bible simply states that "Jehovah appointed a great fish to swallow Jonah," the kind of fish not being named. (Jon 1:17) There definitely are sea creatures capable of swallowing a man, among them being the white shark and the sperm whale. —See Walker's *Mammals of the World*, revised by R. Nowak and J. Paradiso, 1983, Vol. II, p. 901; *Australian Zoological Handbook*, The Fishes of Australia, by G. P. Whitley, Sydney, 1940, Part 1 —The Sharks, p. 125.

Figurative Usage. In the Scriptures men are at times likened to fish. The congregator compared men to fish from the standpoint of their "being ensnared at a calamitous time" like fish in a net. (Ec 9:12) Jesus Christ constituted his followers as fishers of men, and he likened righteous persons to fine fish and the wicked to unsuitable fish that are thrown away.—Mr 1:17; Mt 13:47-50; see HUNTING AND FISHING.

FISH GATE. See GATE, GATEWAY.

FISHING. See HUNTING AND FISHING.

FLATTERY. The act of pleasing by artful commendation; adulation; false, insincere, or excessive praise. It is usually done to gratify the self-love or vanity of the one flattered and is therefore damaging to him. Its motive is to gain favor or material benefits from another, to create a feeling of obligation toward the flatterer or to bring glory to him. Often it is designed to lead the other person into a trap. (Pr 29:5) The use of flattery is not evidence of the wisdom from above; it is of this world, being characterized by selfishness, the making of partial distinctions, and hypocrisy. (Jas 3:17) Insincerity, lying, adulating or glorifying men, and playing on the vanity of others are all displeasing to God.—2Co 1:12; Ga 1:10; Eph 4:25; Col 3:9; Re 21:8.

A contrast of the Christian course with that of flattery is found in the apostle's words at 1 Thessalonians 2:3-6: "For the exhortation we give does not arise from error or from uncleanness or with deceit, but, just as we have been proved by God as fit to be entrusted with the good news, so we speak, as pleasing, not men, but God, who makes proof of our hearts. In fact, at no time have we turned up either with flattering speech, (just as you know) or with a false front for covetousness, God is witness! Neither have we been seeking glory from men, no, either from you or from others, though we could be an expensive burden as apostles of Christ."

While the use of flattery may appear to be the gainful course, the Bible points out that "he that is reproving a man will afterward find more favor than he will that is flattering with his tongue." (Pr 28:23) When a person employs flattery to gain advantage over another person, it is the opposite of love. A hater may resort to flattery but will eventually have his deceptiveness roll back on him like a stone.—Pr 26:24-28.

Flattery employs smooth talk in order to beguile its victim. The expressions "flattery," "smooth tongue (lip, or words)" (Ps 5:9; 12:2, 3; Da 11:32), "smoothness" (Pr 7:21; Da 11:34, ftn), and "double-faced" (Eze 12:24, ftn) are translations of the Hebrew root word cha·laq' or related words. In every Bible instance cited, the motive of the smooth talker is bad.

An example of the disastrous result of accepting flattery and the praise of men is Herod Agrippa I, who was flatteringly praised by the crowd as speaking with "a god's voice." Because he accepted the flattery and did not give the glory to God, he was struck by God's angel and died. (Ac 12:21-23) On the other hand, Barnabas and Paul quickly prevented a crowd from deifying them. (Ac 14:11-15) Also, when a Jewish ruler attempted application of the flattering title "Good Teacher" to Jesus Christ, Jesus instantly corrected him, saying: "Why do you call me good? Nobody is good, except one, God."—Lu 18:18, 19; compare Job 32:21, 22.

FLAX [Heb., pe'sheth, pish·tah'; Gr., li'non]. A plant that has been cultivated from ancient times, the fibers of which were, as now, commonly made into linen. Flax (Linum usitatissimum) may grow from 0.3 to 1.2 m (1 to 4 ft) in height. The slender stalk of the plant, with its pale-green linear leaves, branches out only at the top. Each branch or branchlet terminates in a deep- or pale-blue (rarely white), five-petal flower.—PICTURE, Vol. 1, p. 544.

When the flax had "flower buds" it was ready for harvesting (Ex 9:31), which was done by pulling or hoeing it up. The flax was then dried. Likely the stalks of flax on the roof of Rahab's house at Jericho had been laid there for this purpose.—Jos 2:6.

The method employed by the Hebrews in processing flax probably corresponded to the description given by Pliny the Elder of the first century C.E. in his Natural History (XIX, III, 17, 18) and to the ancient pictorial representation preserved at Beni Hasan in Egypt. After the seedpods had been removed, the stalks of flax were completely submerged in water and weighted down with stones to prevent them from floating. As the flax soaked in water, the woody part rotted, freeing the fibers. After the exterior part, or rind, of the stalks became loose, the stalks were taken out of the water and were repeatedly turned over in the sun until completely dry. The flax was thereafter beaten with mallets on stone slabs, and the fibers were separated and cleansed by combing. The inferior fibers next to the rind were used for lampwicks (see Isa 42:3; 43:17; Mt 12:20), whereas the interior fibers, whiter and of a finer quality, were made into yarn that was polished by striking it again and again on a hard stone.

Low ground and alluvial soil, so characteristic of Egypt, are said to be especially suited for the cultivation of flax. In the ancient world this country was famous for its fine linen. Thus the divinely sent plague of hail, which ruined the flax and the barley, was a severe blow to the economy of

Egypt. (Ex 9:23, 31) Later, the pronouncement against Egypt, recorded by Isaiah (19:9), included "the workers in carded flax" among those who would become ashamed.—See LINEN.

FLEA [Heb., *par·'osh'*]. A very small wingless parasitic insect. Fleas are usually reddish brown and have short front and middle legs but long hind legs. The flea's strong and spiny legs as well as its flat sides enable it to move with ease and rapidity between the hairs or feathers of its host. The short rearward-pointing hairs covering this insect's oval-shaped body not only permit the flea to move forward readily but also make it more difficult for the victim to remove it. The flea's small head is equipped with a beak that is used to pierce the skin of its victim, causing the blood to flow. Its leaping ability is phenomenal. Although less than 0.3 cm (⅛ in.) long, the flea that lives on humans can jump more than 30 cm (1 ft) horizontally and nearly 20 cm (8 in.) vertically. The Biblical variety of flea is probably that called *Pulex irritans*.

In Scripture the flea is mentioned only twice. When David was being pursued by King Saul, he questioned the king: "After whom are you chasing? . . . After a single flea?" By comparing himself to a flea, David emphasized his littleness in comparison with Saul, thus showing that it was hardly worth while for the king to chase after him. (1Sa 24:14) First Samuel 26:20 conveys a similar thought, but in the Greek *Septuagint* the words "a single flea" read "my soul."

FLESH. The Hebrew *ba·sar'* and the Greek *sarx* primarily refer to the soft substance of a physical body, whether of man, beast, bird, or fish; more specifically, the parts composed chiefly of muscle and fat. The Bible points out that the flesh of the various kinds of living things differs. (1Co 15:39) This has been found to be the case by researchers; they have noted that the chemical composition and cellular structure of the flesh of mankind, beasts, birds, and fish vary greatly.

Jehovah God the Creator is responsible for the existence of all flesh and for its life. He is referred to in the Bible as "Jehovah the God of the spirits [including the life-force] of all sorts of flesh." (Nu 27:16; compare Ge 6:17.) He states that the soul (life) of the fleshly creature is in the blood. (Le 17:11-14) Originally, vegetation and fruit, and not flesh, were given man as his diet. But after the Flood, God added animal flesh, commanding, however, that "flesh with its soul—its blood —you must not eat."—Ge 9:3, 4.

Cannibalism, the eating of human flesh, naturally repugnant to the human mind, was abhorred by God and his ancient covenant people Israel. (De 28:53-57; 2Ki 6:28-30) Neither could they eat the flesh of an animal torn by a wild beast, or one that died of itself. These would be detestable, besides not being properly drained of blood.—Ex 22:31; Le 17:15, 16; De 14:21.

God commanded that, before eating the flesh of an animal, his people were to pour out its blood on the ground and cover it with dust, being careful not to eat the blood, on pain of death. (De 12:23-25; Le 7:27) The governing body of the early Christian congregation restated this prohibition, forbidding the eating of animals strangled or not drained of blood. They additionally forbade eating meat as part of a communion offering to idols, a common practice among pagans in those days. (Ac 15:19, 20, 28, 29) The eating of flesh by Christians is proper, but the apostle Paul pointed out that flesh is not absolutely essential to man as food when he said that if his eating of meat was a source of stumbling to other Christians, he would "never again eat flesh at all."—Ro 14:21; 1Co 8:13.

The fleshly body given to man was to be regarded as inviolate and not to be deliberately mistreated or mutilated, either by the person himself or by another.—Le 19:28; De 14:1; Ex 21:12-27.

Kinship. Kinship is expressed by the term "flesh." Eve bore the closest possible kinship to Adam in that she was, as he said, "bone of my bones and flesh of my flesh." (Ge 2:23; see also Ge 29:14; 37:27; 2Sa 5:1.) The close relationship of man and wife is forcefully stated: "They must become one flesh." (Ge 2:24; Mt 19:5, 6) Paul calls Jesus one "who sprang from the seed of David according to the flesh."—Ro 1:3; compare 9:3.

The Person, Humankind, Fleshly Creation. An extension of the idea that flesh composes the visible, tangible parts of the body is the use of the word "flesh" to refer in a general way to the whole body. (Le 17:14; 1Ki 21:27; 2Ki 4:34) It is also used to refer to the person, or individual, as a human of flesh. (Ro 7:18; Col 2:1, 5) All humankind, especially from the viewpoint of God the Spirit, are described as "flesh" (Ge 6:12; Isa 66:16; Lu 3:6), and at times the animal creation is included. (Ge 7:16, 21) The Bible often makes a contrast of flesh with God the Spirit, emphasizing particularly the relative insignificance of man. (Ge 6:3; 2Ch 32:8; Ps 56:4) Jehovah in his superior position nevertheless recognizes and accordingly takes this fact into account in dealing with mankind with surpassing loving-kindness and merciful long-suffering.—Ps 78:39; compare Ps 103:13-15; 1Pe 1:24, 25.

The word "flesh" may also refer to a part of the body, particularly the male genital organ. Leviticus 15:2 states: "In case any man has a running discharge occur from his genital organ [literally, "his flesh"], his discharge is unclean."—Compare Ge 17:11; Ex 28:42; Eph 2:11; Col 2:13.

Spiritual Bodies. The apostle Paul declares that "if there is a physical body, there is also a spiritual one." (1Co 15:44) This is corroborated by the apostle Peter when he tells persons of fleshly, human nature, called to be joint heirs with Christ, that they are to become partakers of "divine nature," namely, spirit life in the invisible heavens. (2Pe 1:4) This requires a change in organism, for "flesh and blood cannot inherit God's kingdom, neither does corruption inherit incorruption."—1Co 15:50-54.

Jesus Christ's Fleshly Body. Jesus, who was "the Word" of God, "out of heaven," divested himself of spirit nature and "became flesh." (Joh 1:1; 1Co 15:47; Php 2:5-8; Joh 1:14; 1Ti 3:16) That in being born as a human he was no spirit and that he did not merely assume a fleshly body, as angels had done in the past (Ge 18:1-3; 19:1; Jos 5:13-15), is attested to by the apostle John, who says that one is antichrist who denies that Jesus Christ came "in the flesh." (1Jo 4:2, 3) In order to provide the ransom for mankind and thereby to help those who would be his associates in the heavenly calling, the Word *became* flesh, being born all human, no incarnation. The Bible tells us this: "Since the 'young children' are sharers of blood and flesh, he also similarly partook of the same things." (Heb 2:14-16) His earthly sojourn was spoken of as "the days of his flesh." (Heb 5:7) "The bread that I shall give is my flesh in behalf of the life of the world," Jesus said. He went on to state that those hoping to remain in union with him must 'eat his flesh and drink his blood.' Not appreciating the spiritual, symbolic significance of his words, some construed the statement as cannibalistic and were shocked.—Joh 6:50-60.

During Jesus' earthly ministry, although he knew that he would be put to death as the ransom sacrifice, his flesh 'rested in hope.' This was because of his knowledge that his Father would resurrect him, that his sacrifice would successfully serve the ransom purpose, and that his flesh would not see corruption. (Ac 2:26, 31)

Jehovah God evidently disposed of Jesus' fleshly body in his own way (possibly disintegrating it into the atoms of which it was constituted). (Lu 24:2, 3, 22, 23; Joh 20:2) Jesus did not take back his fleshly body and thereby cancel out the ransom for which it was given. The apostle Peter testifies that Christ went into heaven, the realm of spirits, not flesh, "he being put to death in the flesh, but being made alive in the spirit." (1Pe 3:18) Before his ascension to heaven Christ, as a mighty, immortal spirit person, did materialize various fleshly bodies to suit the occasion, for the purpose of giving to his disciples visible, palpable evidence of his resurrection.—Joh 20:13-17, 25-27; 21:1, 4; Lu 24:15, 16.

In Paul's letter to the Hebrews the curtain in the sanctuary before the Most Holy, which represented heaven itself, is shown to have been symbolic, representing Jesus' flesh, for before he sacrificed his fleshly body, the way to life in heaven was not open.—Heb 9:24; 10:19, 20.

Man in His Imperfection. "Flesh" is often used in the Bible to represent man in his imperfect state, 'conceived in sin' as an offspring of rebellious Adam. (Ps 51:5; Ro 5:12; Eph 2:3) In humans who are trying to serve God, 'the spirit [impelling force emanating from the figurative heart] is eager, but the flesh is weak.' (Mt 26:41) Within these servants of God there is a constant conflict; God's holy spirit is a force for righteousness, but the sinful flesh continually wars against the spirit's influence and exerts pressure to induce the individual to perform the works of the flesh. (Ro 7:18-20; Ga 5:17) The works of sinful flesh are contrasted with the fruitage of the spirit, at Galatians 5:19-23.

The apostle Paul also tells us that the Law given through Moses to Israel was "weak through the flesh," the imperfect flesh of those who were under the Law. The Law under which the Aaronic priesthood served was spiritual, from God, but by it fleshly persons "sold under sin" were condemned, instead of being pronounced righteous. (Ro 8:3; 7:14; Heb 7:28) The high priests of the fleshly line of Aaron assigned by the Law were not able to offer an adequate sacrifice for sin. —Heb 7:11-14, 23; 10:1-4.

In saying that "flesh . . . is not under subjection to the law of God, nor, in fact, can it be," the apostle Paul is not saying that flesh in itself must of necessity be corrupt. He tells us that Jesus Christ, although partaking of blood and flesh, becoming "like his 'brothers,'" was "guileless, undefiled, separated from the sinners," "tested in all respects like ourselves, but without sin." (Ro 8:7; Heb 2:14, 17; 4:15; 7:26) Jehovah proved that human flesh can be sinless. "God, by sending his own Son in the likeness of sinful flesh and concerning sin, condemned sin in the flesh." (Ro 8:3) Eventually, through the provision of Christ's sacrifice, all who exercise faith will become perfect, and God's righteous laws will then be kept perfectly by mankind.—Re 21:4.

One of the temptations that influenced Eve to sin was "the desire of the flesh." The Devil used it against Christ but failed. (1Jo 2:16; Ge 3:6; Lu 4:1-4) Jesus' followers, by permitting God's spirit to operate freely in their lives and by Jehovah's undeserved kindness, defeat the sinful flesh. —Ga 5:16, 22-26; Ro 8:1-4.

No Fight With Those of Flesh. It is not fleshly reasoning, but Jehovah's spirit, that reveals God's purposes to men of faith and that guides them. (Mt 16:17; 1Co 2:9, 14; Eph 3:5) Accordingly, Christians do not carry on their Christian warfare "according to [the] flesh," and they do not have a fight with persons of flesh and blood; neither do they use fleshly weapons against anyone. Their fight is against "wicked spirit forces in the heavenly places." (2Co 10:3, 4; Eph 6:12) They trust, not in the 'arm of flesh,' but in Jehovah the Spirit. (Jer 17:5; 2Co 3:17) They are striving, with God's help, to cleanse themselves of "every defilement of flesh and spirit," and God views and judges them, not according to what they are in the flesh, as man often does, but according to what they are spiritually.—1Co 4:3-5; 2Co 5:16, 17; 7:1; 1Pe 4:6; see DECLARE RIGHTEOUS; SOUL; SPIRIT.

FLINT. An extremely hard stone, harder than steel, so hard that when two pieces are struck together a fire can be started from the spark. The Bible makes reference to flint when, in figures of speech, it emphasizes such qualities as hardness, durability, and resistance to opposition.—Isa 5:28; 50:7; Eze 3:9.

Flint is found in limestone and chalk deposits in Israel and in the northern Sinai Peninsula. It is quite brittle and fractures with a glossy surface. Its chips have very sharp edges, a characteristic that man was quick to recognize and put to use. From very early times knives, axheads, chisels, spearheads, arrowheads, and other tools and weapons have been fashioned out of this rock. It was with a flint that the wife of Moses circumcised her son; when the nation of Israel reached Gilgal similar surgery was successfully performed by the use of knives made of flint. (Ex 4:25; Jos 4:19; 5:2, 3, 8, 9) Jehovah brought water out of flinty rock for his people in the wilderness.—De 8:15; Ps 114:8.

FLOGGING. See BEATING.

FLOOD. See DELUGE.

FLOUR. See MILL.

FLUTE. A musical instrument of the woodwind class. Although there is some dispute as to which modern musical instrument corresponds to the Hebrew *cha·lil'* and its Greek equivalent *au·los'*, many modern translations render the words as "flute," in harmony with the identification given by lexicographers. (1Sa 10:5; 1Co 14:7, AT, JB, NW, RS) The Hebrew root word from which *cha·lil'* is believed to have been derived signifies "pierce" (Isa 51:9; 53:5), and it may refer to a process used to make a simple flute, namely, to drill out the center of a section of reed, cane, or even bone or ivory and then to perforate it at suitable intervals. Egyptian inscriptions indicate that a variety of flutelike instruments existed in that country. One type was held in an oblique position, with the mouth against the side of the instrument; they also developed a double flute, with the mouth at the end of the two pipes.

The Greek *au·los'* appears to have been used also as a general designation that included instruments of two types: those utilizing a reed in the mouthpiece, as well as simple flutelike pipes. *Cha·lil'* may also have come to be a general term for all woodwinds, but in modern Hebrew the name is applied only to the flute, and traditional Jewish belief is that the *cha·lil'* of Scripture was the flute.

The flute was one of the most popular of all musical instruments, being played at joyous times such as banquets and weddings (Isa 5:12; 30:29; 1Ki 1:40), a custom imitated by children in public places. (Mt 11:16, 17) It was also played at times of sadness. Professional mourners were often accompanied by flutists playing mournful tunes.—Mt 9:23, 24.

FLY [Heb., *zevuv'*, flies]. A two-winged insect of the genus *Musca* that usually lays its eggs in decayed or waste matter. The tiny hairs covering the fly's body and legs as well as the pads of sticky hairs on each foot carry bacteria—millions of them in the case of a single housefly.

"Dead flies are what cause the oil of the ointment maker to stink, to bubble forth," wrote the congregator. The putrefaction of dead flies would cause the oil to give off an offensive odor as well as to ferment, ruining it, just as a little foolishness would damage the reputation of one known for his wisdom and glory.—Ec 10:1.

Isaiah speaks of Jehovah's whistling for the flies at the extremity of the Nile canals of Egypt and for the bees of the land of Assyria so that these might settle down upon the precipitous torrent valleys, the clefts of the crags, the thorn thickets, and all the watering places of Judah. This is evidently to be understood in a figurative sense, the flies denoting Egypt's armies and the bees the armies of the Assyrians.—Isa 7:18, 19.

The name of the god venerated by the Philistines at Ekron, "Baal-zebub," means "Owner of the Flies." This has given rise to the thought that his worshipers may have regarded him as being able to control these insects. Since the giving of oracles was associated with Baal-zebub, others have suggested that the name may denote that this god gave oracles by means of the flight or buzzing of a fly.—2Ki 1:2, 6; see BAAL-ZEBUB; GADFLY.

FLYING CREATURES.   See BIRDS.

FOOD.
Hebrew and Greek terms rendered "food" have various literal meanings, such as "thing eaten," "nourishment," "bread," and "meat, or flesh."

After creating Adam and Eve, God said: "Here I have given to you all vegetation bearing seed which is on the surface of the whole earth and every tree on which there is the fruit of a tree bearing seed. To you let it serve as food." He further stated that to all the animal creation he had given "all green vegetation for food." To Adam he also said: "From every tree of the garden you may eat to satisfaction," adding a prohibition on one tree, the tree of the knowledge of good and bad.—Ge 1:29, 30; 2:16, 17.

From that time until the Flood, the Bible gives no indication that man included the flesh of animals in his diet. True, a distinction was made between clean and unclean animals, but this evidently was with regard to animals used for sacrificial purposes.—Ge 7:2.

When Noah was commanded to take the animals into the ark, Jehovah told him: "As for you, take for yourself every sort of food that is eaten; and you must gather it to yourself, and it must serve as food for you and for them," again seemingly having reference to food from the vegetable kingdom for the humans and the animals taken into the ark. (Ge 6:21) After the Flood, Jehovah allowed man to add flesh to his diet, saying:

"Every moving animal that is alive may serve as food for you. As in the case of green vegetation, I do give it all to you. Only flesh with its soul—its blood—you must not eat."—Ge 9:3, 4.

Cereals.   Cereals constituted the basic food of the people of Bible lands, as is evident from the fact that in both Hebrew and Greek the expression "eat a meal" literally means "eat bread." (Ge 43:31, 32) Barley and wheat were the chief cereals; other cereals mentioned are millet and spelt, a form of wheat. (Jg 7:13; Isa 28:25; Eze 4:9; Joh 6:9, 13) Besides being used for bread, ordinary flour was made into a sort of porridge. Grain was often eaten roasted, either by taking a bunch of the grain ears together and holding them over a fire or by roasting them in a pan. (Ru 2:14; 2Sa 17:28) It was made into bread, usually with the grain ground coarsely. However, in some of the bread and cakes a finer flour was used. (Ge 18:6; Ex 29:2) One method of baking was to spread the dough on hot rocks or on a flat surface of rocks on which a fire had been built. Ferment or leaven was often used, while some bread was baked unfermented. (Le 7:13; 1Ki 19:6) Ovens were also employed, in which the lumps of dough were flattened on a stone within. Cakes were sometimes prepared in a pan, on a griddle, or in a deep-fat kettle. The fat used was oil, probably olive oil.—Le 2:4, 5, 7; 1Ch 9:31; see BAKE, BAKER.

Vegetables.   Beans and lentils were included in the diet, being made into a stew such as the lentil stew that Jacob made and for which Esau sold his birthright. (Ge 25:34) Sometimes meat or oil was used with the stew. Flour might be made from beans or could be a mixture of grain cereals, beans, and lentils. (Eze 4:9) Cucumbers of a variety that is more tasty than the Western variety constituted a refreshing food. When water was scarce or bad, these could be eaten to provide a substitute for water. Cucumbers were eaten raw, with or without salt, and were sometimes stuffed and cooked. The Israelites looked back with longing for the cucumbers, the watermelons, the leeks, the onions, and the garlic that they ate in Egypt. (Nu 11:4, 5) These foods were also produced in Palestine.

Job mentions "marshmallow," the juice of which he describes as tasteless. (Job 6:6) He also speaks of those in destitute circumstances as eating the salt herb and the roots of broom trees. —Job 30:4.

The Mishnah (*Pesahim* 2:6) mentions endive and chicory as the bitter greens used at the Passover.—Ex 12:8.

Fruits and Nuts. The olive was an outstanding article of food in Palestine. The tree may take ten years or longer to begin producing good harvests, but its great longevity makes it very fruitful. The fruits of the olive tree may have been eaten as today, after being soaked in brine. Olives also provided oil for cooking such items as stews and oiled cakes. The Bible mentions "well-oiled dishes."—Isa 25:6.

Figs were another important item of diet. (De 8:8) Once spotted on a tree, early figs were often eaten immediately. (Isa 28:4) Late figs were dried in the sun and pressed in molds, forming cakes of figs. (1Sa 25:18; 1Ch 12:40) Used as a poultice, they had healing properties. (Isa 38:21) Besides the common fig tree, a tree known as the sycamore (fig-mulberry) also produced edible figs. (1Ch 27:28; Am 7:14) Other fruits were the date, the pomegranate, and the apple.—Ca 5:11; Joe 1:12; Hag 2:19; see APPLE.

Among the nuts eaten in Palestine, the Bible mentions almonds and pistachio nuts.—Ge 43:11; Jer 1:11.

Grapes are one of the most abundant foods in Palestine. When the Israelites spied out the land of Canaan they brought back a great cluster of grapes, carried on a bar between two men. (Nu 13:23) Grapes were eaten in their natural state and also dried (Nu 6:3) and pressed into cakes. (1Sa 25:18; 1Ch 12:40) As today, undoubtedly the young leaves were eaten as a green vegetable; the older leaves were fed to sheep and goats.

The pods of the carob tree were usually fed to animals, although they may have been used for human consumption in time of need. The hungry prodigal son in Jesus' illustration expressed the desire to feed on them.—Lu 15:16; see CAROB POD.

Spices and Honey. Spices prominently used for seasoning were mint, dill, cumin, rue, and mustard leaves. (Mt 23:23; 13:31; Lu 11:42) Salt was the chief article of seasoning, also having preservative properties. Thus, "a covenant of salt" was a sure covenant, not to be violated. (Nu 18:19; 2Ch 13:5) Additionally, the Mishnah (*Shabbat* 6:5) mentions pepper. The caper berry was used as an appetizer.—Ec 12:5.

Honey was considered a choice food that brightened the eyes with energy. (1Sa 14:27-29; Ps 19:10; Pr 16:24) The manna tasted like flat cakes with honey. (Ex 16:31) John the Baptizer ate honey along with insect locusts.—Mt 3:4.

Flesh as Food. God told Noah after the Flood that, along with vegetation, he could use for food every moving animal that is alive. (Ge 9:3, 4) But

under the Law, the Israelites were restricted to eating what were defined as clean animals. These are listed in Leviticus, chapter 11, and Deuteronomy, chapter 14. The common people did not ordinarily eat much meat. But occasionally a goat or a lamb would be slaughtered for a communion sacrifice or in honor of a guest. (Le 3:6, 7, 12; 2Sa 12:4; Lu 15:29, 30) Among the more well-to-do, beef cattle were slaughtered. (Ge 18:7; Pr 15:17; Lu 15:23) Some of the game animals, such as the stag, gazelle, roebuck, wild goat, antelope, wild bull, and chamois, were eaten, and the meat was roasted or boiled. (Ge 25:28; De 12:15; 14:4, 5) The eating of blood was strictly forbidden, as was the eating of fat.—Le 7:25-27.

Fowl were also eaten. The Israelites were miraculously furnished with quail in the wilderness. (Nu 11:31-33) Pigeons, turtledoves, partridge, and sparrows were among the clean fowl. (1Sa 26:20; Mt 10:29) Additionally, eggs were an item of food.—Isa 10:14; Lu 11:11, 12.

Among the edible insects was the locust, which, with honey, formed the food of John the Baptizer. (Mt 3:4) Today locusts are eaten by some Arabs. After having the head, legs, and wings removed, the locusts are dropped into meal and fried in oil or butter.

Fish were obtainable from the Mediterranean and also from the Sea of Galilee. Several of the apostles of Jesus Christ were fishermen, and Jesus, on at least one occasion, after his resurrection, prepared some fish over a charcoal fire for his disciples. (Joh 21:9) Fish were also dried, providing convenient food for travelers. The fish of Jesus' two miracles of feeding multitudes were probably dried fish. (Mt 15:34; Mr 6:38) One of the gates of Jerusalem was named the Fish Gate, probably indicating that there was a fish market at or near it. (Ne 3:3) In the days of Nehemiah, the Tyrians carried on a fish trade in Jerusalem. —Ne 13:16.

Dairy Products and Beverages. Also important as food were milk and milk products, using milk of cows, goats, or sheep. (1Sa 17:18) Milk was normally kept in skin bottles. (Jg 4:19) It would sour quickly. The Hebrew word *chem-'ah'*, translated "butter," can also mean "curdled milk." Cheese was also a well-known item. In fact, the Tyropoeon (Cheesemakers') Valley ran along the W side of the very early city of Jerusalem.—Jg 5:25; 2Sa 17:29; Job 10:10; see CHEESE.

The making of wine was one of the principal uses of the grape. Wine was sometimes spiced and also mixed. (Pr 9:2, 5; Ca 8:2; Isa 5:22) The grape gathering took place in the fall. In a warm climate the juice would not long be free from ferment. Several months intervened between grape harvest and Passover time. At Passover it became the custom for family groups to drink several cups of wine, which, by that time, would be fermented. Hence, in celebrating the Passover of 33 C.E., Jesus drank real red wine, some of which he offered to his disciples in introducing the Lord's Evening Meal. (Mr 14:23-25) It was also fermented wine that Jesus produced at a wedding feast. (Joh 2:9, 10) Wine was used for medicinal purposes as well. (1Ti 5:23) Vinegar derived from grape wine, pure or mixed with spices or fruit juices, was also used. (Nu 6:3; Ru 2:14) Another drink was wheat beer, and a refreshing drink was made from pomegranate juice.—Ca 8:2; Isa 1:22; Ho 4:18.

Manna. Manna was the basic food for the Israelites in the wilderness. It is described at Numbers 11:7, 8 as being like coriander seed, having the appearance of bdellium gum. It was ground in hand mills or pounded in a mortar and boiled or made into cakes tasting like an oiled sweet cake. It is spoken of as "the very bread of powerful ones."—Ps 78:24, 25; see MANNA.

Eating Together. In Bible times the eating of food together indicated a bond of fellowship. (Ge 31:54; 2Sa 9:7, 10, 11, 13; see MEAL.) To refuse to eat food with someone was an indication of anger or other contrary feeling or attitude. (1Sa 20:34; Ac 11:2, 3; Ga 2:11, 12) Food was often used as a gift, to gain or to ensure the goodwill of another, since the acceptance of a gift was considered to obligate the receiver to observe peaceful relations.—Ge 33:8-16; 1Sa 9: 6-8; 25:18, 19; 1Ki 14:1-3.

Christian Viewpoint. Christians are not under the restriction of the Law as to clean and unclean foods. They are required to abstain from blood and things that are strangled, that is, things from which the blood has not properly been drained. (Ac 15:19, 20, 28, 29) But aside from this Bible injunction, they are not to make the eating or the abstaining from certain kinds of food an issue or try to govern another person's conscience by their own conscience as regards the eating of food. They are warned, however, against eating food as an offering to idols and against stumbling another person by insisting on exercising their Christian freedom in the matter of eating food. (1Co 8; 10:23-33) Christians should not put the matter of food or its handling

ahead of the Kingdom and its spiritual interests. —Ro 14:17; Heb 13:9.

Spiritual Food. Jesus delighted to do the will of his Father and spoke of it as food to him. (Joh 4:32, 34) He foretold that he would appoint "the faithful and discreet slave" to give (spiritual) food at the proper time to his disciples. (Mt 24:44-47; see FAITHFUL AND DISCREET SLAVE.) Just as Moses had told the Israelites: "Not by bread alone does man live but by every expression of Jehovah's mouth does man live" (De 8:3), Jesus encouraged his followers to seek, not the material food, but the food that remains for life everlasting. (Joh 6:26, 27; compare Hab 3:17, 18.) He said not to be anxious about food and drink, for "the soul is worth more than food."—Mt 6:25; Lu 12:22, 23.

The apostle Paul spoke of the elementary things of Christian doctrine as being "milk" and the deeper knowledge as being "solid food." (Heb 5:12-14; 6:1, 2; 1Co 3:1-3) Peter, too, spoke of nourishing spiritual growth with "unadulterated milk belonging to the word." (1Pe 2:2) Jesus called himself "the bread of life," superior to the manna provided in the wilderness, and he pointed out that he had a supply that would prevent the eater from ever getting hungry. (Joh 6:32-35) He shocked some of his followers who lacked spiritual-mindedness when he likened his flesh and blood to food and drink (upon which they could "feed" by faith in his ransom sacrifice) for everlasting life.—Joh 6:54-60.

Jehovah promises a time when he will provide an abundance of both spiritual and material food for his faithful people earth wide, with no famine to threaten them.—Ps 72:16; 85:12; Isa 25:6; see COOKING, COOKING UTENSILS; FAMINE; and items of food under their individual headings.

FOOD POUCH. A bag, usually made of leather, carried over the shoulder by travelers, shepherds, farmers, and others. It was used for food, clothing, and other provisions, but it was not the same as the smaller girdle purse used for gold, silver, and copper coins. (Mt 10:9; Mr 6:8) David's "shepherds' bag" was doubtless such a food pouch. (1Sa 17:40) Jesus Christ, when sending out first the 12 apostles and then the 70 disciples to preach in Israel, told them not to carry food pouches. (Mt 10:5, 9, 10; Lu 9:3; 10: 1, 4) Jehovah would care for their needs through the hands of fellow Israelites, among whom hospitality was a custom. Just before his death Jesus indicated that circumstances would change as a result of official opposition, so he told his disciples to take along both purse and food pouch. Nevertheless, they were to seek first God's Kingdom instead of being anxious about material needs; thus they would give evidence that they depended upon Jehovah God to care for them in the ministry.—Lu 22:35, 36; Mt 6:25-34.

FOOL. Rather than denoting a person who is lacking in mental ability, the word "fool," as used in the Bible, generally refers to an individual who spurns reason and follows a morally insensible course out of harmony with God's righteous standards. Various Hebrew terms denoting such a one are *kesil'* ('stupid one'; Pr 1:22), *'ewil'* ("foolish one"; Pr 12:15), *na·val'* ('senseless one'; Pr 17:7), and *lets* ("ridiculer"; Pr 13:1). The Greek *a'phron* refers to an "unreasonable one" (Lu 12: 20), *a·no'e·tos* to one "senseless" (Ga 3:1), and *mo·ros'* to a 'fool' or "foolish" one (Mt 23:17; 25:2).

The course of the man Nabal illustrates the way of a fool (1Sa 25) as does that of people who know the true God and then worship created things. (Ro 1:20-25) Isaiah said a fool, or senseless person, will speak "mere senselessness, and his very heart will work at what is hurtful, to work at apostasy and to speak against Jehovah what is wayward, to cause the soul of the hungry one to go empty, and he causes even the thirsty one to go without drink itself." (Isa 32:6) The fool despises wisdom and discipline. (Pr 1:7) Instead of heeding counsel, the fool continues walking in a way he considers "right in his own eyes." (Pr 12:15) He is quick to take offense and bursts out in disputing. (Ec 7:9; Pr 20:3) He says in his heart (his actions indicating what his lips may not say in so many words): "There is no Jehovah."—Ps 14:1.

Jesus Christ rightly referred to the scribes and Pharisees as "fools and blind ones," that is, persons lacking wisdom and being morally worthless, for they had distorted the truth by manmade traditions and followed a hypocritical course. Moreover, Jesus backed up the correctness of this designation by illustrating their lack of discernment. (Mt 23:15-22; 15:3) However, the individual wrongly calling a brother a "despicable fool," judging and condemning his brother as being morally worthless, would make himself liable to Gehenna.—Mt 5:22; Ro 14:10-12; Mt 7:1, 2.

The foolish man who built his house upon the sand and the rich man whose land was producing well, and who therefore planned to expand his storage facilities and then really enjoy life, are examples of Jesus' fine illustrations from daily life highlighting the foolishness of neglecting spiritual things and thereby missing out on the real blessing. Moreover, failing to "keep on the watch" in a spiritual way is folly, as is emphasized by Jesus' illustration of the five foolish virgins who, in going out to meet the bridegroom, took no oil with them for their lamps. —Mt 7:24-27; Lu 12:16-21; Mt 25:1-13.

To become truly wise, a person must become a fool in the eyes of the world, "for the wisdom of this world is foolishness with God." It is not the worldly wise but those looked down upon as persons without knowledge, fools, whom Jehovah has chosen to represent him. This has resulted in making the foolishness of this world even more apparent. Furthermore, this removes all reason for boasting on the part of the favored individual. Instead, all glory goes rightfully to the Source of wisdom, Jehovah.—1Co 3:18, 19; 1:18-31.

Answering a fool in harmony with or "according to his foolishness" in the sense of resorting to his degrading methods of argument puts the one so doing in agreement with the fool's unsound reasonings or ways. In order not to become like the fool in this respect, we are counseled by the proverb: "Do not answer anyone stupid according to his foolishness." On the other hand, Proverbs 26:4, 5 shows that answering him "according to his foolishness" in the sense of analyzing his contentions, exposing them as being ridiculous, and showing that his own arguments lead to entirely different conclusions from those he has drawn can be beneficial.

FOOT. The Hebrew *re'ghel* and the Greek *pous* basically refer to the lowest part of the leg, the body part upon which a person or an animal stands. Both terms are used literally and figuratively.

In ancient times, as in many parts of the earth today, the feet were the main means of transportation. Some of the common people went barefoot, but sandals consisting of little more than a sole were commonly worn. (See SANDAL.) On entering a house, a person removed his sandals. An essential, virtually obligatory mark of hospitality was to wash the feet of a guest; the service was performed either by the householder or by a servant, or at least water was provided for the purpose.—Ge 18:4; 24:32; 1Sa 25:41; Lu 7:37, 38, 44.

Since the sandals were removed when one was on holy ground, the priests when performing duties in the tabernacle or the temple undoubtedly served barefoot. (Ex 3:5; Jos 5:15) No sandals were included in the instructions for making the priests' garments.—Ex chap 28; see ATTITUDES AND GESTURES.

Christ Washes Disciples' Feet. Jesus Christ gave his disciples a lesson in humility and service to one another when he, their Master, washed their feet. (Joh 13:5-14; compare 1Ti 5:9, 10.) On this occasion Jesus said: "He that has bathed does not need to have more than his feet washed, but is wholly clean," doubtless referring to the fact that even if a person was bathed, his feet would get dusty even in a short walk and would frequently need washing. In the days of Jesus' earthly ministry, the priests and Levites on guard duty at the temple, after immersing themselves early in the morning, were not required to bathe again that day, except to wash their hands and feet. (See also Ex 30:19-21.) By saying, "you men are clean, but not all [referring to Judas]," Jesus apparently gave his actions on this occasion an additional spiritual significance. (Joh 13:10, 11) At Ephesians 5:25, 26 Jesus is shown as cleansing the Christian congregation with "the bath of water by means of the word" of truth. Logically, Jesus' faithful followers were likewise to show humble concern not only for the physical needs of their brothers but even more so for their spiritual needs. Thereby they would help one another to keep clean from the daily temptations and entanglements that might contaminate a Christian while walking in this world.—Heb 10:22; Ga 6:1; Heb 12:13; see WASHING OF FEET.

"Walking." The words "foot" and "feet" are frequently used to denote a person's inclination or the course he takes, good or bad. (Ps 119:59, 101; Pr 1:16; 4:26; 5:5; 19:2; Ro 3:15) The word "walk" is used with similar significance, as in the statement, "Noah walked with the true God," meaning that he took a course in harmony with God's will and commandments. (Ge 6:9; compare Eph 2:1, 2.) God directs the feet of his faithful servants in the right path, figuratively, showing them the way to go so as not to stumble to a spiritual fall or be ensnared in evil, and sometimes even safeguarding them against capture by the enemy. (1Sa 2:9; Ps 25:15; 119:105; 121:3; Lu 1:78, 79) On the other hand, he will cause the wicked to lose their footing and go down in defeat. (De 32:35; Ps 9:15) Jehovah warns against associating in a course with bad persons, or going in a bad path. (Pr 1:10, 15; 4:27) He advises a person to guard his feet when going to the house of God. The person should draw near with a sincere heart to hear and to learn.—Ec 5:1.

Other Figurative Uses. Other figurative expressions are 'resting-place for the sole of the foot,' that is, a place of residence or possession (Ge 8:9; De 28:65); "a footbreadth," to indicate the smallest parcel of land one could possess (Ac 7:5; De 2:5; compare Jos 1:3); 'lift up the foot,' to take or initiate a course of action (Ge 41:44); "make your foot rare at the house of your fellowman," not taking undue advantage of his hospitality (Pr 25:17); 'walking barefoot,' in humiliation or mourning (captives often being led barefoot) (Isa 20:2); 'laying something at the feet of' a person, as a gift or offering (Ac 5:1, 2); 'falling at one's feet,' in obeisance (Mr 5:22); 'putting under the feet,' in subjection (1Co 15:27; Heb 2:8); 'bruising or treading under feet,' in victory (Mal 4:3; Ro 16:20); 'putting feet upon the neck of an enemy,' as a symbol of subduing or conquering him (Jos 10:24); 'washing the foot in blood,' in execution of enemies (Ps 68:22, 23); 'covering the feet,' easing nature (literally, 'keeping the feet hidden'; Jg 3:24; 1Sa 24:3). The phrase "dipping his foot in oil" was used prophetically in foretelling the fat, or abundant, portion that the tribe of Asher would have among the other tribes of Israel. (De 33:24) Ruth uncovered the feet of Boaz and lay down at his feet as a notification for him to take legal action in the matter of brother-in-law marriage.—Ru 3:4, 7, 8.

"Comely" feet. Jehovah has special regard for the feet of those proclaiming the good news of the Kingdom, calling them "comely." (Isa 52:7; Ro 10:15) The Christian must have his feet shod with "the equipment of the good news of peace" so that he can properly carry the good news. (Eph 6:15) Jesus instructed his disciples that when those in a house or a city refused to take them in or listen to their words, they should shake the dust off their feet, thereby showing that they left the unreceptive house or city to the consequences that were due to come from a higher source, from heaven.—Mt 10:14.

'Cut off your foot.' Jesus spoke of 'cutting off one's foot,' not literally but in a figurative sense, when he said: "If, then, your hand or your foot is making you stumble, cut it off and throw it away from you." He meant that, instead of letting a body member such as a hand or a foot cause its owner to commit unforgivable sin, he should deaden such body member as completely as if it were severed from the body.—Mt 18:8; Mr 9:45; compare Col 3:5.

In the Christian "body." The apostle Paul, likening the Christian congregation to a human body, highlights the interdependence of the members thereof when he says: "If the foot should say: 'Because I am not a hand, I am no part of the body,' it is not for this reason no part of the body."—1Co 12:15.

God's Footstool. Jehovah pictures himself in his sovereign position as sitting on a heavenly throne with the earth as his footstool. (Isa 66:1) He says to Zion that he will beautify the place of his sanctuary, and he adds: "I shall glorify the very place of my feet."—Isa 60:13, 14; see HEEL; TOE.

FOOTSTOOL.

A low stool, designed to serve as a rest or a support for the feet when the individual is seated. The Hebrew word *ke'vesh* appears only once in the Scriptures and is used with reference to the gold footstool of King Solomon's throne. (2Ch 9:18) The Hebrew expression *hadhom' ragh·la'yim* (literally, "stool of the feet") occurs six times and is used figuratively to refer to the temple (1Ch 28:2; Ps 99:5; 132:7; La 2:1), to the earth (Isa 66:1), and to the enemies to be crushed by Messiah's rule (Ps 110:1). James reproves those practicing class distinctions in the congregation, using the illustration of a poor man who was told: "Take that seat there under my footstool." (Jas 2:3) All other occurrences of the word "footstool" in the Christian Greek Scriptures are quotations from or references to the Hebrew Scriptures.—Mt 5:35; Ac 7:49; "stool for your [or, his] feet" in Lu 20:43; Ac 2:35; Heb 1:13; 10:13.

FORCED LABOR.

The use of "forced labor" (Heb., *mas*) was evidently quite common in Bible times, with conquered peoples frequently being constituted slaves. (De 20:11; Jos 16:10; 17:13; Es 10:1; Isa 31:8; La 1:1) As slavish forced laborers, the Israelites, under the immediate oversight of Egyptian chiefs who tyrannized over them, engaged in building the storage places of Pithom and Raamses. (Ex 1:11-14) Then, upon entering the Promised Land, instead of following through on Jehovah's command to drive out all the Canaanite inhabitants of the land and devote them to destruction, the Israelites forced them into task work, slavish labor. This had the bad effect of luring Israel into the worship of false gods. (Jos 16:10; Jg 1:28; 2:3, 11, 12) King Solomon continued levying the descendants of these Canaanites, that is, of the Amorites, Hittites, Perizzites, Hivites, and Jebusites, for slavish forced labor. —1Ki 9:20, 21.

At times, Israelite workers were drafted to meet an emergency or to complete a special project that could not be delayed indefinitely. Issachar, according to the words of his dying father Jacob, was to be subjected as a tribe to this type of forced labor. (Ge 49:15) Solomon conscripted 30,000 men of Israel for his temple-building operations. Nevertheless, these were not constituted slaves, for they served in shifts of 10,000 a month in Lebanon and thus were able to spend two months at home and a month at the work. But it appears that considerable resentment built up against the conscripting of Israelites for forced labor. When Rehoboam did not agree to lighten the heavy yoke Israel bore under the rulership of Solomon and subsequently sent Adoram (Hadoram, Adoniram) to them, the Israelites stoned Adoram, who must have been quite advanced in years then, since in David's time he had begun to serve as overseer of those conscripted for work.—2Sa 20:24; 1Ki 4:6; 5:13, 14; 12:14, 18; 2Ch 10:18.

Laziness could easily get an Israelite into debt and in time force him to sell his inheritance and also himself into slavery. Hence the proverb: "The slack hand will come to be for forced labor." —Pr 12:24.

See COMPULSORY SERVICE.

FOREHEAD.

The part of the face above the eyes. One Hebrew expression rendered 'forehead' (De 14:1) and the Greek word for "forehead" (*me'to·pon*) literally mean "between the eyes." As a very prominent and readily seen feature of an individual, the forehead was, in ancient times, a place for marking slaves so that all could see to what master they belonged. Also, the devotees of certain pagan gods were thus marked. Even today some follow the practice of putting religious marks on the forehead, so that all others can be aware of their devotion to their religious beliefs.

Mark in the Forehead. Bearing a mark in the "forehead" is similarly used in a figurative way in the Bible to signify that one is a slave to the true God or to another. At Revelation 7:2-4, reference is made to angelic sealing of 144,000 persons in their foreheads. (See SEAL.) In another part of the vision of Revelation, the 144,000 are represented as having the name of the Lamb, Jesus Christ, and the name of his Father written on their foreheads. As the bride of the Lamb, they would properly take his name. (Re 14:1; 22:3, 4) Since the Hebrew language is twice mentioned in the book of Revelation (9:11; 16:16) and since the apostle John was a Hebrew, it may have been the sacred Tetragrammaton that was written on the foreheads of the 144,000, identifying them as Jehovah's servants and witnesses.

As described at Ezekiel 9:3-6, a class of persons are marked in their forehead for protection from destruction by God's executional forces, not being marked by angels in this instance, nor with a "seal," but by a man who has "a secretary's inkhorn." Pictured as "sighing and groaning over all the detestable things that are being done," these, when 'marked,' show themselves to be slaves and devotees of Jehovah; their actions, practices, and personalities evidently give evidence of this before all, as if written 'on their foreheads.'

In branding slaves for the world political "wild beast" (see BEASTS, SYMBOLIC [The seven-headed wild beast out of the sea]), a symbolic mark is put on the foreheads or the right hands of persons, even by compulsion, as depicted at Revelation 13:16, 17. Those receiving that mark identify themselves as being against God and are due to receive his anger in undiluted form.—Re 14:9-11; see MARK, II.

Israel's High Priest. In Israel the high priest's turban had on its front, over the priest's forehead, a gold plate, "the holy sign of dedication," upon which were inscribed "with the engravings of a seal" the words "Holiness belongs to Jehovah." (Ex 28:36-38; 39:30) As Israel's chief representative of Jehovah's worship, it was fitting that the high priest keep his office holy, and this inscription would also serve as a reminder to all Israel of the need of constant holiness in the service of Jehovah. It also served as a suitable picture of the great High Priest, Jesus Christ, and his being dedicated by Jehovah to this priestly service that upholds God's holiness.—Heb 7:26.

Babylon the Great. Conversely, the symbolic great harlot has the name "Babylon the Great" on her forehead. Ancient Babylon long represented that which was unholy and in opposition to God.—Re 17:1-6; see BABYLON THE GREAT.

Other Uses of Term. Another figurative use of the word "forehead" is found at Isaiah 48:4, where Jehovah stated that Israel's forehead was copper, evidently because her stubbornness and rebelliousness were so great. At Jeremiah 3:3, the brazen and shameless apostasy of unfaithful Jerusalem is metaphorically described as "the forehead of a wife committing prostitution." Also,

at Ezekiel 3:7-9, God told Ezekiel, who prophesied to hardheaded (literally, "strong of forehead"), hardhearted Israelites, that he had made the prophet's forehead "like a diamond," in that he had given him the resolution, determination, and boldness to deliver God's message to them.

When King Uzziah presumptuously and illegally usurped a priest's duties in attempting to offer incense upon the altar of incense in the temple of Jehovah, his sin and Jehovah's judgment were plainly and immediately made manifest by leprosy flashing up in his forehead.—2Ch 26:16, 19, 20.

FOREIGNER. A person of non-Israelite extraction, a Gentile; in Hebrew, *nokh·ri'* or *ben·ne·kar'*, literally, "son of a foreign (country)." (De 14:21; Ex 12:43, ftn) The foreigners among the Hebrews consisted of hired laborers, merchants, captives taken in war, Canaanites not executed or expelled from the Promised Land, and various kinds of transients.—Jos 17:12, 13; Jg 1:21; 2Sa 12:29-31; 1Ki 7:13; Ne 13:16.

Although foreigners' rights were limited by the Law covenant, they were to be treated with justice and fairness and were to receive hospitality as long as they did not flagrantly disobey the laws of the land. The foreigner, by virtue of his having no real ties with Israel, was distinct from the circumcised proselyte who had come into membership in the congregation of Israel by completely accepting Law covenant responsibilities. Similarly, the foreigner was different from the settler who had taken up semipermanent residence in the Promised Land and who, therefore, not only came under certain legal restrictions but also enjoyed certain rights and privileges.—See ALIEN RESIDENT.

During the time that the Israelites were alien residents in Canaan and in Egypt, many non-Israelites composed part of the households of the sons of Jacob and their descendants. This came about through the hiring of servants who lived with the family and through the purchasing of slaves, who, by the terms of the covenant with Abraham, had to be circumcised. (Ge 17:9-14) Some involved in mixed marriages, along with their offspring, were included in the vast mixed company that accompanied the Israelites in the Exodus.—Ex 12:38; Le 24:10; Nu 11:4.

After Israel settled in the Promised Land, foreigners, such as the Canaanites who were not driven out, had to be dealt with. (Jg 2:2, 3) Merchants and craftsmen also began to travel into the land of Israel. (Eze 27:3, 17; 2Sa 5:11; 1Ki 5:6-18) Likely hired laborers accumulated as the Israelites grew more prosperous in developing the Promised Land. (Compare De 8:11-13; Le 22:10.) Foreigners began to be attached to the Israelite armies, and in doing so, they developed an esteem for their Hebrew leaders and a respect for the Israelite religion, as in the cases of the Gittites, the Cherethites, and the Pelethites. —2Sa 15:18-21.

Provisions of the Law Covenant. In the Law covenant Jehovah provided basic legislation to regulate dealings with foreigners and to protect the Israelite commonwealth and the integrity of its citizens and dependents economically as well as religiously and politically. The Israelites were not to have any fellowship, especially religiously, with the foreigners (Ex 23:23-25; De 7:16-26; Jos 23:6, 7), and they were not to conclude any covenants with them or their gods. (Ex 34:12-15; 23:32; De 7:2) Time and again Jehovah stressed the absolute need not to bow down to the gods of the foreigners (Ex 20:3-7; 23:31-33; 34:14), nor were they even to inquire into, or interest themselves in, their religious practices. —De 12:29-31.

Marriage alliances with foreigners were prohibited, primarily because of the danger of corruption of pure worship. (Ex 34:16; De 7:3, 24; Jos 23:12, 13) All inhabitants of cities of the seven Canaanite nations were to be destroyed. (De 20:15-18) But in the capture of a city not of the seven proscribed Canaanite nations, an Israelite soldier could take a virgin from the city as a wife after she had undergone a period of purification. In such cases no actual alliance would be formed with a foreign tribe or family, her parents having been slain when her city was taken.—De 21:10-14; Nu 31:17, 18; De 20:14.

An additional restriction was that no uncircumcised foreigner could eat of the Passover. (Ex 12:43) It appears, however, that foreigners could offer sacrifices through the priestly arrangement, provided the offering itself conformed to divine standards. (Le 22:25) Of course, such persons could never come into the sanctuary (Eze 44:9), but they could come to Jerusalem and 'pray toward God's house,' and they would likely not do so empty-handed, that is, without an accompanying sacrificial offering.—1Ki 8:41-43.

In governmental matters, the foreigner had no political status and could never become a king. (De 17:15) Though the Israelite, the alien resident, and settler in the land could take advantage of the sanctuary provided for the unintentional manslayer in the cities of refuge, there is no mention of such provision for the foreigner.—Nu 35:15; Jos 20:9.

Although Israelites were forbidden to eat an animal that had died without the blood being drained, it could legally be sold to a foreigner. (De 14:21) During Sabbath years the Israelite could not be pressed for payment of debts, but the foreigner was not under this arrangement and could be pressed for payment. (De 15:1-3) Although a fellow Israelite was not to be charged interest, the foreigner could be so charged.—De 23:20.

Source of Difficulty. During Joshua's time and the period of the Judges that followed, many foreigners were in the land and were a source of constant difficulty. (Jos 23:12, 13) The Canaanite foreigners who remained after the Israelite conquest became subject to slavish forced labor (Jos 16:10; 17:13; Jg 1:21, 27-35), but because the Israelites did not drive them from the land and eradicate their worship as Jehovah had commanded (Jg 2:1, 2), the Canaanites in general continued to practice their idolatrous and degraded religions. As a result the Israelites were continually being led into false worship (Ps 106:34-39), particularly the worship of the Baals and the Ashtoreth images. (Jg 2:11-13) These Canaanitish foreigners continued to be found in Israel down through David's time to the reign of Solomon, when they were still being put to forced labor on the temple and Solomon's other building projects.—1Ki 9:20, 21; see FORCED LABOR.

Contrary to divine command, Solomon took many foreign wives, who gradually turned his heart away from the pure worship of Jehovah to that of foreign gods. (1Ki 11:1-8) Intrusion of false religion at the highest governmental level had fatal repercussions. It resulted in the splitting of the nation and eventual exile in Babylon as successive kings, both of Judah and of Israel, led the people into false worship. This culminated in the fulfillment on the nation of the maledictions that were foretold as inescapable sanctions for violations of the Law.—1Ki 11:9-11; 2Ki 15:27, 28; 17:1, 2; 23:36, 37; 24:18, 19; De 28:15-68.

Following restoration of a faithful remnant of Israelites from the exile in Babylon, many Israelites took foreign wives for themselves. (Ezr 9:1, 2; Ne 13:23-25) This wrong course necessitated vigorous purges of foreign wives and their sons under the direction of Ezra and Nehemiah. (Ezr 10:2-4, 10-19, 44; Ne 13:1-3, 27-30) Action was also taken against other foreigners guilty of improprieties.—Ne 13:7, 8, 16-21.

The conquering Babylonians had dealt very harshly with the Jews at the time of the destruction of Jerusalem. (La 2:5-12, 19-22) After the liberation, the Jews were in constant conflict with the foreigners around them in the Promised Land, especially being harassed by the Greek rulers of Syria. In the Jews' efforts to maintain their restored worship, they had to resist the fierce persecutions of Antiochus IV Epiphanes as he attempted to Hellenize the Jews. Throughout the postexilic centuries the Israelites were in a constant struggle for independence, which created a zeal for Judaism and, on the part of some, an intensely nationalistic spirit. These factors, coupled with the fear of mongrelizing their race through intermarriage with foreigners, likely contributed to the departure from the liberal spirit clearly evident in the Hebrew Scriptures respecting foreigners.—Compare 1Ki 8:41-43; 2Ch 6:32, 33; Isa 56:6, 7.

During the First Century C.E. Particularly through the influence of their religious leaders, there developed the aloofness and rigid exclusiveness that existed among the Jews in the first century C.E. Evidence of this attitude is seen in the disdain they showed for the Samaritans, a people of mixed descent from Israelites and foreigners. As a rule the Jews 'had no dealings with the Samaritans,' not even wanting to ask for so much as a drink of water from them. (Joh 4:9) Jesus, however, made clear the wrongness of such an extreme view.—Lu 10:29-37.

The establishment of the new covenant on the basis of Christ's ransom sacrifice brought to an end the legal separation between Jew and Gentile. (Eph 2:11-16) Yet, even after Pentecost of 33 C.E., the early disciples were slow to grasp this fact. The common or standard Jewish view was expressed by Peter to the Gentile Cornelius: "You well know how unlawful it is for a Jew to join himself to or approach a man of another race." (Ac 10:28) John 18:28 shows that entry into a Gentile home was viewed by the Jews as an act that brought ceremonial defilement. While the Law given through Moses made no specific injunction against such minor association, this view was common among the Jews and particularly among their religious leaders. It took some time for the early Jewish Christians to free themselves of the restrictions imposed by prevailing attitudes and recognize the fact emphasized by the apostle Paul that, for those having the 'new

Christian personality,' there is "neither Greek nor Jew, circumcision nor uncircumcision, foreigner, Scythian, slave, freeman, but Christ is all things and in all."—Ga 2:11-14; Col 3:10, 11.

The Greek word for "foreigner" is *bar'ba·ros,* basically referring to one who did not speak Greek.—See BARBARIAN.

FOREKNOWLEDGE, FOREORDINATION.
Foreknowledge means knowledge of a thing before it happens or exists; also called prescience. In the Bible it relates primarily, though not exclusively, to Jehovah God the Creator and his purposes. Foreordination means the ordaining, decreeing, or determining of something beforehand; or the quality or state of being foreordained.

Original-Language Words. The words generally translated as "foreknow," "foreknowledge," and "foreordain" are found in the Christian Greek Scriptures, although the same basic ideas are expressed in the Hebrew Scriptures.

"Foreknowledge" translates the Greek *pro'gno·sis* (from *pro,* before, and *gno'sis,* knowledge). (Ac 2:23; 1Pe 1:2) The related verb *pro·gi·no'sko* is used in two cases with regard to humans: in Paul's statement that certain Jews were "previously acquainted" with him (knew him beforehand), and in Peter's reference to the "advance knowledge" had by those addressed in his second letter. (Ac 26:4, 5; 2Pe 3:17) In this latter case it is obvious that such foreknowledge was not infinite; that is, it did not mean that those Christians knew *all* the details of time, place, and circumstance about the future events and conditions Peter had discussed. But they did have a *general* outline of what to expect, received as a result of God's inspiration of Peter and of other contributors to the Bible.

"Foreordain" translates the Greek *pro·o·ri'zo* (from *pro,* before, and *ho·ri'zo,* mark out or set the bounds). (The English word "horizon" transliterates the Greek word *ho·ri'zon,* meaning the "bounding" or "limiting.") Illustrating the sense of the Greek verb *ho·ri'zo* is Jesus Christ's statement that, as "the Son of man," he was "going his way according to what [was] marked out [*ho·ri·sme'non*]." Paul said that God had "decreed [marked out, *ho·ri'sas*] the appointed times and the set limits of the dwelling of men." (Lu 22:22; Ac 17:26) The same verb is used of human determination, as when the disciples "determined [*ho·ri'san*]" to send relief to their needy brothers. (Ac 11:29) However, specific references to *foreordaining* in the Christian Greek Scriptures are applied only to God.

Factors to Recognize. To understand the matter of foreknowledge and foreordination as relating to God, certain factors necessarily must be recognized.

First, God's ability to foreknow and foreordain is clearly stated in the Bible. Jehovah himself sets forth as proof of his Godship this ability to foreknow and foreordain events of salvation and deliverance, as well as acts of judgment and punishment, and then to bring such events to fulfillment. His chosen people are witnesses of these facts. (Isa 44:6-9; 48:3-8) Such divine foreknowledge and foreordination form the basis for all true prophecy. (Isa 42:9; Jer 50:45; Am 3:7, 8) God challenges the nations opposing his people to furnish proof of the godship they claim for their mighty ones and their idol-gods, calling on them to do so by foretelling similar acts of salvation or judgment and then bringing them to pass. Their impotence in this respect demonstrates their idols to be 'mere wind and unreality.'—Isa 41:1-10, 21-29; 43:9-15; 45:20, 21.

A second factor to be considered is the free moral agency of God's intelligent creatures. The Scriptures show that God extends to such creatures the privilege and responsibility of free choice, of exercising free moral agency (De 30:19, 20; Jos 24:15), thereby making them accountable for their acts. (Ge 2:16, 17; 3:11-19; Ro 14:10-12; Heb 4:13) They are thus not mere automatons, or robots. Man could not truly have been created in "God's image" if he were not a free moral agent. (Ge 1:26, 27; see FREEDOM.) Logically, there should be no conflict between God's foreknowledge (as well as his foreordaining) and the free moral agency of his intelligent creatures.

A third factor that must be considered, one sometimes overlooked, is that of God's moral standards and qualities, including his justice, honesty, impartiality, love, mercy, and kindness. Any understanding of God's use of the powers of foreknowledge and foreordination must therefore harmonize with not only some of these factors but with all of them. Clearly, whatever God foreknows must inevitably come to pass, so that God is able to call "things that are not as though they were."—Ro 4:17.

Does God know in advance everything that people will do?

The question then arises: Is his exercise of foreknowledge infinite, without limit? Does he foresee and foreknow all future actions of all his creatures, spirit and human? And does he foreordain such actions or even predestinate what shall be the final destiny of all his creatures, even doing so before they have come into existence?

Or, is God's exercise of foreknowledge selective and discretionary, so that whatever he chooses to foresee and foreknow, he does, but what he does not choose to foresee or foreknow, he does not? And, instead of preceding their existence, does God's determination of his creatures' eternal destiny await his judgment of their course of life and of their proved attitude under test? The answers to these questions must necessarily come from the Scriptures themselves and the information they provide concerning God's actions and dealings with his creatures, including what has been revealed through his Son, Christ Jesus.—1Co 2:16.

Predestinarian view. The view that God's exercise of his foreknowledge is infinite and that he does foreordain the course and destiny of all individuals is known as predestinarianism. Its advocates reason that God's divinity and perfection require that he be omniscient (all-knowing), not only respecting the past and present but also regarding the future. According to this concept, for him not to foreknow all matters in their minutest detail would evidence imperfection. Examples such as the case of Isaac's twin sons, Esau and Jacob, are presented as evidence of God's foreordaining creatures before their birth (Ro 9:10-13); and texts such as Ephesians 1:4, 5 are cited as evidence that God foreknew and foreordained the future of all his creatures even before the start of creation.

To be correct, this view would, of course, have to harmonize with all the factors previously mentioned, including the Scriptural presentation of God's qualities, standards, and purposes, as well as his righteous ways in dealing with his creatures. (Re 15:3, 4) We may properly consider, then, the implications of such a predestinarian view.

This concept would mean that, prior to creating angels or earthling man, God exercised his powers of foreknowledge and foresaw and foreknew all that would result from such creation, including the rebellion of one of his spirit sons, the subsequent rebellion of the first human pair in Eden (Ge 3:1-6; Joh 8:44), and all the bad consequences of such rebellion down to and beyond this present day. This would necessarily mean that all the wickedness that history has recorded (the crime and immorality, oppression and resultant suffering, lying and hypocrisy, false worship and idolatry) once existed, before creation's beginning, only in the mind of God, in the form of his foreknowledge of the future in all of its minutest details.

If the Creator of mankind had indeed exercised his power to foreknow all that history has seen since man's creation, then the full weight of all the wickedness thereafter resulting was deliberately set in motion by God when he spoke the words: "Let us make man." (Ge 1:26) These facts bring into question the reasonableness and consistency of the predestinarian concept; particularly so, since the disciple James shows that disorder and other vile things do not originate from God's heavenly presence but are "earthly, animal, demonic" in source.—Jas 3:14-18.

Infinite exercise of foreknowledge? The argument that God's not foreknowing all future events and circumstances in full detail would evidence imperfection on his part is, in reality, an arbitrary view of perfection. Perfection, correctly defined, does not demand such an absolute, all-embracing extension, inasmuch as the perfection of anything actually depends upon its measuring up completely to the standards of excellence set by one qualified to judge its merits. (See PERFECTION.) Ultimately, God's own will and good pleasure, not human opinions or concepts, are the deciding factors as to whether anything is perfect.—De 32:4; 2Sa 22:31; Isa 46:10.

To illustrate this, God's almightiness is undeniably perfect and is infinite in capacity. (1Ch 29:11, 12; Job 36:22; 37:23) Yet his perfection in strength does not require him to use his power to the full extent of his omnipotence in any or in all cases. Clearly he has not done so; if he had, not merely certain ancient cities and some nations would have been destroyed, but the earth and all in it would have been obliterated long ago by God's executions of judgment, accompanied by mighty expressions of disapproval and wrath, as at the Flood and on other occasions. (Ge 6:5-8; 19:23-25, 29; compare Ex 9:13-16; Jer 30:23, 24.) God's exercise of his might is therefore not simply an unleashing of limitless power but is constantly governed by his purpose and, where merited, tempered by his mercy.—Ne 9:31; Ps 78:38, 39; Jer 30:11; La 3:22; Eze 20:17.

Similarly, if, in certain respects, God chooses to exercise his infinite ability of foreknowledge in a selective way and to the degree that pleases him, then assuredly no human or angel can rightly say: "What are you doing?" (Job 9:12; Isa 45:9; Da 4:35) It is therefore not a question of ability, what God *can* foresee, foreknow, and foreordain, for "with God all things are possible." (Mt 19:26) The question is what God *sees fit* to foresee, foreknow, and foreordain, for "everything that he delighted to do he has done."—Ps 115:3.

Selective exercise of foreknowledge. The alternative to predestinarianism, the selective or discretionary exercise of God's powers of foreknowledge, would have to harmonize with God's own righteous standards and be consistent with what he reveals of himself in his Word. In contrast with the theory of predestinarianism, a number of texts point to an examination by God of a situation then current and a decision made on the basis of such examination.

Thus, at Genesis 11:5-8 God is described as directing his attention earthward, surveying the situation at Babel, and, at that time, determining the action to be taken to break up the unrighteous project there. After wickedness developed at Sodom and Gomorrah, Jehovah advised Abraham of his decision to investigate (by means of his angels) to "see whether they act altogether according to the outcry over it that has come to me, and, if not, *I can get to know it.*" (Ge 18:20-22; 19:1) God spoke of 'becoming acquainted with Abraham,' and after Abraham went to the point of attempting to sacrifice Isaac, Jehovah said, "For *now I do know* that you are God-fearing in that you have not withheld your son, your only one, from me."—Ge 18:19; 22:11, 12; compare Ne 9:7, 8; Ga 4:9.

Selective foreknowledge means that God could choose *not* to foreknow indiscriminately all the future acts of his creatures. This would mean that, rather than all history from creation onward being a mere rerun of what had already been foreseen and foreordained, God could with all sincerity set before the first human pair the prospect of everlasting life in an earth free from wickedness. His instructions to his first human son and daughter to act as his perfect and sinless agents in filling the earth with their offspring and making it a paradise, as well as exercising control over the animal creation, could thus be expressed as the grant of a truly loving privilege and as his genuine desire toward them—not merely as the giving of a commission that, on their part, was foredoomed to failure. God's arranging for a test by means of "the tree of the knowledge of good and bad" and his creation of "the tree of life" in the garden of Eden also would not be meaningless or cynical acts, made so by his foreknowing that the human pair would sin and never be able to eat of "the tree of life."—Ge 1:28; 2:7-9, 15-17; 3:22-24.

To offer something very desirable to another person on conditions known beforehand to be unreachable is recognized as both hypocritical and cruel. The prospect of everlasting life is presented in God's Word as a goal for all persons, one possible to attain. After urging his listeners to 'keep on asking and seeking' good things from God, Jesus pointed out that a father does not give a stone or a serpent to his child that asks for bread or a fish. Showing his Father's view of disappointing the legitimate hopes of a person, Jesus then said: "Therefore, if you, although being wicked, know how to give good gifts to your children, how much more so will your Father who is in the heavens give good things to those asking him?"—Mt 7:7-11.

Thus, the invitations and opportunities to receive benefits and everlasting blessings set before all men by God are bona fide. (Mt 21:22; Jas 1:5, 6) He can in all sincerity urge men to 'turn back from transgression and keep living,' as he did with the people of Israel. (Eze 18:23, 30-32; compare Jer 29:11, 12.) Logically, he could not do this if he foreknew that they were individually destined to die in wickedness. (Compare Ac 17:30, 31; 1Ti 2:3, 4.) As Jehovah told Israel: "Nor said I to the seed of Jacob, 'Seek me simply for nothing, you people.' I am Jehovah, speaking what is righteous, telling what is upright. . . . Turn to me and be saved, all you at the ends of the earth."—Isa 45:19-22.

In a similar vein, the apostle Peter writes: "Jehovah is not slow respecting his promise [of the coming day of reckoning], as some people consider slowness, but he is patient with you because he does not desire any to be destroyed but desires all to attain to repentance." (2Pe 3:9) If God already foreknew and foreordained millenniums in advance precisely which individuals would receive eternal salvation and which individuals would receive eternal destruction, it may well be asked how meaningful such 'patience' of God could be and how genuine his desire could be that 'all attain to repentance.' The inspired apostle John wrote that "God is love," and the apostle Paul states that love "hopes all things." (1Jo 4:8; 1Co 13:4, 7) It is in harmony with this outstanding, divine quality that God should exer-

cise a genuinely open, kindly attitude toward all persons, he being desirous of their gaining salvation, until they prove themselves unworthy, beyond hope. (Compare 2Pe 3:9; Heb 6:4-12.) Thus, the apostle Paul speaks of "the kindly quality of God [that] is trying to lead you to repentance." —Ro 2:4-6.

Finally if, by God's foreknowledge, the opportunity to receive the benefits of Christ Jesus' ransom sacrifice were already irrevocably sealed off from some, perhaps for millions of individuals, even before their birth, so that such ones could never prove worthy, it could not truly be said that the ransom was made available to all men. (2Co 5:14, 15; 1Ti 2:5, 6; Heb 2:9) The impartiality of God is clearly no mere figure of speech. "In every nation the man that fears [God] and works righteousness is acceptable to him." (Ac 10:34, 35; De 10:17; Ro 2:11) The option is actually and genuinely open to all men "to seek God, if they might grope for him and really find him, although, in fact, he is not far off from each one of us." (Ac 17:26, 27) There is no empty hope or hollow promise set forth, therefore, in the divine exhortation at the end of the book of Revelation inviting: "Let anyone hearing say: 'Come!' And let anyone thirsting come; let anyone that wishes take life's water free."—Re 22:17.

The Things Foreknown and Foreordained. Throughout the Bible record, God's exercise of foreknowledge and foreordination is consistently tied in with his own purposes and will. "To purpose" means to set something before oneself as an aim or an object to be attained. (The Greek word pro'the·sis, translated "purpose," means, literally, "something placed or set forth before.") Since God's purposes are certain of accomplishment, he can foreknow the results, the ultimate realization of his purposes, and can foreordain them as well as the steps he may see fit to take to accomplish them. (Isa 14:24-27) Thus, Jehovah is spoken of as 'forming' or 'fashioning' (from the Hebrew ya·tsar', related to the word for "potter" [Jer 18:4]) his purpose concerning future events or actions. (2Ki 19:25; Isa 46:11; compare Isa 45:9-13, 18.) As the Great Potter, God "operates all things according to the way his will counsels," in harmony with his purpose (Eph 1:11), and "makes all his works cooperate together" for the good of those loving him. (Ro 8:28) It is, therefore, specifically in connection with his own foreordained purposes that God tells "from the beginning the finale, and from long ago the things that have not been done."—Isa 46:9-13.

When God created the first human pair they were perfect, and God could look upon the result of all his creative work and find it "very good." (Ge 1:26, 31; De 32:4) Instead of distrustfully concerning himself with what the human pair's future actions would be, the record says that he "proceeded to rest." (Ge 2:2) He could do so since, by virtue of his almightiness and his supreme wisdom, no future action, circumstance, or contingency could possibly present an insurmountable obstacle or an irremediable problem to block the realization of his sovereign purpose. (2Ch 20:6; Isa 14:27; Da 4:35) There is, therefore, no Scriptural basis for the argument of predestinarianism that for God to refrain from exercising his powers of foreknowledge in this way would jeopardize God's purposes, making them "always liable to be broken through want of foresight, and [that] he must be continually putting his system to rights, as it gets out of order, through the contingence of the actions of moral agents." Nor would this selective exercise of foresight give his creatures the power to "break [God's] measures, make him continually to change his mind, subject him to vexation, and bring him into confusion," as predestinarians claim. (M'Clintock and Strong's *Cyclopædia*, 1894, Vol. VIII, p. 556) If even God's earthly servants have no real need to be "anxious about the next day," it follows that their Creator, to whom mighty nations are as "a drop from a bucket," neither had nor has such anxiety.—Mt 6:34; Isa 40:15.

Concerning classes of persons. Cases are also presented in which God did foreknow the course that certain *groups, nations,* or the *majority of mankind* would take, and thus he foretold the basic course of their future actions and foreordained what corresponding action he would take regarding them. However, such foreknowledge or foreordination does not deprive the individuals within such collective groups or divisions of mankind of exercising free choice as to the particular course they will follow. This can be seen from the following examples:

Prior to the Flood of Noah's day, Jehovah announced his purpose to bring about this act of destruction, resulting in loss of human as well as animal life. The Biblical account shows, however, that such divine determination was made after the conditions developed that called for such action, including violence and other badness. Additionally, God, who is able to "know the heart of the sons of mankind," made examination and found that "every inclination of the thoughts of [mankind's] heart was only bad all the time."

(2Ch 6:30; Ge 6:5) Yet *individuals,* Noah and his family, gained God's favor and escaped destruction.—Ge 6:7, 8; 7:1.

Similarly, although God gave the nation of Israel the opportunity to become "a kingdom of priests and a holy nation" by keeping his covenant, yet some 40 years later, when the nation was at the borders of the Promised Land, Jehovah foretold that they would break his covenant and, as a nation, would be forsaken by him. This foreknowledge was not without prior basis, however, as national insubordination and rebellion already had been revealed. Hence, God said: "For I well know their inclination that they are developing today before I bring them into the land about which I have sworn." (Ex 19:6; De 31: 16-18, 21; Ps 81:10-13) The results to which such manifest inclination would now lead in the way of increased wickedness could be foreknown by God without its making him responsible for such conditions, even as one's foreknowing that a certain structure built of inferior materials and with shoddy workmanship will deteriorate does not make that one responsible for such deterioration. The divine rule governs that 'what is sown is what will be reaped.' (Ga 6:7-9; compare Ho 10:12, 13.) Certain prophets delivered prophetic warnings of God's foreordained expressions of judgment, all of which had basis in already existing conditions and heart attitudes. (Ps 7:8, 9; Pr 11:19; Jer 11:20) Here again, however, individuals could and did respond to God's counsel, reproof, and warnings and so merited his favor. —Jer 21:8, 9; Eze 33:1-20.

God's Son, who also could read the hearts of men (Mt 9:4; Mr 2:8; Joh 2:24, 25), was divinely endowed with powers of foreknowledge and foretold future conditions, events, and expressions of divine judgment. He foretold the judgment of Gehenna for the scribes and Pharisees as a class (Mt 23:15, 33) but did not say thereby that each individual Pharisee or scribe was foredoomed to destruction, as the case of the apostle Paul shows. (Ac 26:4, 5) Jesus predicted woes for unrepentant Jerusalem and other cities, but he did not indicate that his Father had foreordained that each individual of those cities should so suffer. (Mt 11:20-23; Lu 19:41-44; 21:20, 21) He also foreknew what mankind's inclination and heart attitude would lead to and foretold the conditions that would have developed among mankind by the time of "the conclusion of the system of things," as well as the outworkings of God's own purposes. (Mt 24:3, 7-14, 21, 22) Jesus' apostles likewise declared prophecies manifesting God's foreknowledge of certain classes, such as the "antichrist" (1Jo 2:18, 19; 2Jo 7), and also the end to which such classes are foreordained. —2Th 2:3-12; 2Pe 2:1-3; Jude 4.

Concerning individuals. In addition to foreknowledge concerning classes, certain individuals are specifically involved in divine forecasts. These include Esau and Jacob (mentioned earlier), the Pharaoh of the Exodus, Samson, Solomon, Josiah, Jeremiah, Cyrus, John the Baptizer, Judas Iscariot, and God's own Son Jesus.

In the cases of Samson, Jeremiah, and John the Baptizer, Jehovah exercised foreknowledge prior to their birth. This foreknowledge, however, did not specify what their final destiny would be. Rather, on the basis of such foreknowledge, Jehovah foreordained that Samson should live according to the Nazirite vow and should initiate the deliverance of Israel from the Philistines, that Jeremiah should serve as a prophet, and that John the Baptizer should do a preparatory work as a forerunner of the Messiah. (Jg 13:3-5; Jer 1:5; Lu 1:13-17) While highly favored by such privileges, this did not guarantee their gaining eternal salvation or even that they would remain faithful until death (although all three did). Thus, Jehovah foretold that one of David's many sons would be named Solomon and he foreordained that Solomon would be used to build the temple. (2Sa 7:12, 13; 1Ki 6:12; 1Ch 22:6-19) However, though favored in this way and even privileged to write certain books of the Holy Scriptures, Solomon nevertheless fell into apostasy in his later years.—1Ki 11:4, 9-11.

Likewise with Esau and Jacob, God's foreknowledge did not fix their eternal destinies but, rather, determined, or foreordained, which of the national groups descending from the two sons would gain a dominant position over the other. (Ge 25:23-26) This foreseen dominance also pointed to the gaining of the right of the firstborn by Jacob, a right that brought along with it the privilege of being in the line of descent through which the Abrahamic "seed" would come. (Ge 27:29; 28:13, 14) By this means Jehovah God made clear that his choice of individuals for certain uses is not bound by the usual customs or procedures conforming to men's expectations. Nor are divinely assigned privileges to be dispensed solely on the basis of works, which might allow a person to feel he has 'earned the right' to such privileges and that they are 'owed to him.' The apostle Paul stressed this point in showing

why God, by undeserved kindness, could grant to the Gentile nations privileges once seemingly reserved for Israel.—Ro 9:1-6, 10-13, 30-32.

Paul's quotations concerning Jehovah's 'love for Jacob [Israel] and his hatred for Esau [Edom]' comes from Malachi 1:2, 3, written long after Jacob and Esau's time. So the Bible does not necessarily say that Jehovah held such opinion of the twins before their birth. It is a scientifically established fact that much of a child's general disposition and temperament is determined at the time of conception because of the genetic factors contributed by each parent. That God can see such factors is self-evident; David speaks of Jehovah as seeing "even the embryo of me." (Ps 139:14-16; see also Ec 11:5.) To what extent such divine insight affected Jehovah's foreordination concerning the two boys cannot be said, but at any rate, his choice of Jacob over Esau did not of itself doom Esau or his descendants, the Edomites, to destruction. Even individuals from among the accursed Canaanites gained the privilege of association with God's covenant people and received blessings. (Ge 9:25-27; Jos 9:27; see CANAAN, CANAANITE No. 2.) The "change of mind" that Esau earnestly sought with tears, however, was only an unsuccessful attempt to change his father Isaac's decision that the firstborn's special blessing should remain entirely with Jacob. Hence, this indicated no repentance before God on Esau's part as to his materialistic attitude. —Ge 27:32-34; Heb 12:16, 17.

Jehovah's prophecy concerning Josiah called for some descendant of David to be so named, and it foretold his acting against false worship in the city of Bethel. (1Ki 13:1, 2) Over three centuries later a king so named fulfilled this prophecy. (2Ki 22:1; 23:15, 16) On the other hand, he failed to heed "the words of Necho from the mouth of God," and this led to his being killed. (2Ch 35:20-24) Hence, while foreknown by God and foreordained to do a particular work, Josiah was still a free moral agent able to choose to heed or disregard advice.

Similarly, Jehovah foretold nearly two centuries beforehand that he would use a conqueror named Cyrus to effect the release of the Jews from Babylon. (Isa 44:26-28; 45:1-6) But the Persian to whom that name eventually was given in fulfillment of divine prophecy is not stated in the Bible to have become a genuine worshiper of Jehovah, and secular history shows him continuing his worship of false gods.

These cases of foreknowledge prior to the individual's birth thus do not conflict with God's revealed qualities and announced standards. Nor is there any indication that God coerced the individuals to act against their own will. In the cases of Pharaoh, Judas Iscariot, and God's own Son, there is no evidence that Jehovah's foreknowledge was exercised prior to the person's coming into existence. Within these individual cases certain principles are illustrated, bearing on God's foreknowledge and foreordination.

One such principle is God's testing of individuals by causing or allowing certain circumstances or events, or by causing such individuals to hear his inspired messages, the result being that they are obliged to exercise their free choice to make a decision and thus reveal a definite heart attitude, read by Jehovah. (Pr 15:11; 1Pe 1:6, 7; Heb 4:12, 13) According to the way the individuals respond, God can also mold them in the course they have selected of their own volition. (1Ch 28:9; Ps 33:13-15; 139:1-4, 23, 24) Thus, "the heart of earthling man" first inclines toward a certain way before Jehovah does the directing of the steps of such a one. (Pr 16:9; Ps 51:10) Under testing, one's heart condition can become fixed, either hardened in unrighteousness and rebellion or made firm in unbreakable devotion to Jehovah God and the doing of his will. (Job 2:3-10; Jer 18:11, 12; Ro 2:4-11; Heb 3:7-10, 12-15) Having reached such a point of his own choice, the end result of the individual's course can now be foreknown and foretold with no injustice and no violation of man's free moral agency.—Compare Job 34:10-12.

The case of faithful Abraham, already discussed, illustrates these principles. A contrasting case is that of the unresponsive Pharaoh of the Exodus. Jehovah foreknew that Pharaoh would refuse permission for the Israelites to leave "except by a strong hand" (Ex 3:19, 20), and he foreordained the plague resulting in the death of the firstborn. (Ex 4:22, 23) The apostle Paul's discussion of God's dealings with Pharaoh is often incorrectly understood to mean that God arbitrarily hardens the heart of individuals according to his foreordained purpose, without regard for the individual's prior inclination, or heart attitude. (Ro 9:14-18) Likewise, according to many translations, God advised Moses that he would "harden [Pharaoh's] heart." (Ex 4:21; compare Ex 9:12; 10:1, 27.) However, some translations render the Hebrew account to read that Jehovah "let [Pharaoh's] heart wax bold" (Ro); "let [Pharaoh's] heart become obstinate." (NW) In

support of such rendering, the appendix to Rotherham's translation shows that in Hebrew the *occasion* or *permission* of an event is often presented as if it were the *cause* of the event, and that "even *positive commands* are occasionally to be accepted as meaning no more than *permission.*" Thus at Exodus 1:17 the original Hebrew text literally says that the midwives "caused the male children to live," whereas in reality they *permitted* them to live by refraining from putting them to death. After quoting Hebrew scholars M. M. Kalisch, H. F. W. Gesenius, and B. Davies in support, Rotherham states that the Hebrew sense of the texts involving Pharaoh is that "God permitted Pharaoh to harden his own heart—spared him—gave him the opportunity, the occasion, of working out the wickedness that was in him. That is all."—*The Emphasised Bible*, appendix, p. 919; compare Isa 10:5-7.

Corroborating this understanding is the fact that the record definitely shows that Pharaoh himself "hardened his heart." (Ex 8:15, 32, *KJ*; "made his heart unresponsive," *NW*) He thus exercised his own will and followed his own stubborn inclination, the results of which inclination Jehovah accurately foresaw and predicted. The repeated opportunities given him by Jehovah obliged Pharaoh to make decisions, and in doing so he became hardened in his attitude. (Compare Ec 8:11, 12.) As the apostle Paul shows by quoting Exodus 9:16, Jehovah allowed the matter to develop in this way to the full length of ten plagues in order to make manifest his own power and cause his name to be made known earth wide.—Ro 9:17, 18.

Did God predestine Judas to betray Jesus in order to fulfill prophecy?

The traitorous course of Judas Iscariot fulfilled divine prophecy and demonstrated Jehovah's foreknowledge as well as that of his Son. (Ps 41:9; 55:12, 13; 109:8; Ac 1:16-20) Yet it cannot be said that God foreordained or predestinated Judas himself to such a course. The prophecies foretold that some intimate acquaintance of Jesus would be his betrayer, but they did not specify which of those sharing such acquaintance it would be. Again, Bible principles rule against God's having foreordained Judas' actions. The divine standard stated by the apostle is: "Never lay your hands hastily upon any man; neither be a sharer in the sins of others; preserve yourself chaste." (1Ti 5:22; compare 3:6.) Evidencing his concern that the selection of his 12 apostles be wisely and properly made, Jesus spent the night in prayer to his Father before making known his decision. (Lu 6:12-16) If Judas were already divinely foreordained to be a traitor, this would result in inconsistency in God's direction and guidance and, according to the rule, would make him a sharer in the sins that one committed.

Thus, it seems evident that at the time of his being selected as an apostle, Judas' heart presented no definite evidence of a treasonous attitude. He allowed a 'poisonous root to spring up' and defile him, resulting in his deviation and in his accepting, not God's direction, but the Devil's leading in a course of thievery and treachery. (Heb 12:14, 15; Joh 13:2; Ac 1:24, 25; Jas 1:14, 15; see JUDAS No. 4.) By the time such deviation reached a certain point, Jesus himself could read Judas' heart and foretell his betrayal.—Joh 13: 10, 11.

True, in the account at John 6:64, on the occasion of some disciples stumbling over certain teachings of Jesus, we read that "from the beginning ["from the outset," JB] Jesus knew who were the ones not believing and who was the one that would betray him." While the word "beginning" (Gr., ar·khe′) is used at 2 Peter 3:4 to refer to the start of creation, it can also refer to other times. (Lu 1:2; Joh 15:27) For example, when the apostle Peter spoke of the holy spirit falling on Gentiles "just as it did also upon us in the beginning," he obviously was not referring to the beginning of his discipleship or apostleship but to an important point in his ministry, the day of Pentecost, 33 C.E., "the beginning" of the outpouring of the holy spirit for a certain purpose. (Ac 11:15; 2:1-4) It is therefore interesting to note this comment on John 6:64 in Lange's Commentary on the Holy Scriptures (p. 227): "Beginning . . . means not, metaphysically from the beginning of all things, . . . nor from the beginning of His [Jesus'] acquaintance with each one, . . . nor from the beginning of His collecting the disciples around Him, or the beginning of His Messianic ministry, . . . but from the first secret germs of unbelief [that produced the stumbling of some disciples]. So also He knew His betrayer from the beginning."—Translated and edited by P. Schaff, 1976; compare 1Jo 3:8, 11, 12.

Foreordination of the Messiah. Jehovah God foreknew and foretold the Messiah's sufferings, the death he would undergo, and his subsequent resurrection. (Ac 2:22, 23, 30, 31; 3:18; 1Pe 1:10, 11) The realization of things determined by God's exercise of such foreknowledge depended in part upon God's own exercise of power and in part upon the actions of men. (Ac 4:27, 28) Such men, however, willingly allowed themselves to be overreached by God's Adversary, Satan the Devil. (Joh 8:42-44; Ac 7:51-54) Hence, even as Christians in Paul's day were "not ignorant of [Satan's] designs," God foresaw the wicked desires and methods the Devil would devise against Jesus Christ, God's Anointed One. (2Co 2:11) Obviously, God's power could also thwart or even block any attacks or attempts upon the Messiah that did not conform to the manner or time prophesied.—Compare Mt 16:21; Lu 4:28-30; 9:51; Joh 7:1, 6-8; 8:59.

The apostle Peter's statement that Christ, as the sacrificial Lamb of God, was "foreknown before the founding [form of Greek ka·ta·bo·le′] of the world [ko′smou]" is construed by advocates of predestinarianism to mean that God exercised such foreknowledge before mankind's creation. (1Pe 1:19, 20) The Greek word ka·ta·bo·le′, translated "founding," literally means "a throwing down" and can refer to the 'conceiving of seed,' as at Hebrews 11:11. While there was "the founding" of a world of mankind when God created the first human pair, as is shown at Hebrews 4:3, 4, that pair thereafter forfeited their position as children of God. (Ge 3:22-24; Ro 5:12) Yet, by God's undeserved kindness, they were allowed to conceive seed and produce offspring, one of whom is specifically shown in the Bible to have gained God's favor and placed himself in position for redemption and salvation, namely, Abel. (Ge 4:1, 2; Heb 11:4) It is noteworthy that at Luke 11:49-51 Jesus refers to "the blood of all the prophets spilled from the founding of the world" and parallels this with the words "from the blood of Abel down to the blood of Zechariah." Thus, Abel is connected by Jesus with "the founding of the world."

The Messiah, or Christ, was to be the promised Seed through whom all righteous persons of all the families of the earth would be blessed. (Ga 3:8, 14) The first mention of such "seed" came after the rebellion in Eden had already been initiated, but prior to the birth of Abel. (Ge 3:15) This was some 4,000 years before the revelation of "the sacred secret" was made by the clear identification of that Messianic "seed." Hence, it was, indeed, "kept in silence for long-lasting times."—Ro 16:25-27; Eph 1:8-10; 3:4-11.

In his due time Jehovah God assigned his own firstborn Son to fulfill the prophesied role of the "seed" and become the Messiah. There is nothing to show that that Son was "predestined" to such a role even before his creation or before rebellion broke out in Eden. God's eventual selection of him as the one charged with fulfilling the prophecies likewise was not made without prior basis. The period of intimate association between God and his Son previous to the Son's being sent to earth undoubtedly resulted in Jehovah's 'knowing' his Son to an extent that He could be certain of his Son's faithful fulfillment of the prophetic promises and pictures.—Compare Ro 15:5; Php 2:5-8; Mt 11:27; Joh 10:14, 15; see JESUS CHRIST (Tested and Perfected).

Foreordination of the 'called and chosen.' There remain those texts that deal with the Christian "called ones," or "chosen ones." (Jude 1; Mt 24:24) They are described as "chosen according to the foreknowledge of God" (1Pe 1:1, 2), 'chosen before the founding of the world,' 'foreordained to the adoption as sons of God' (Eph 1:3-5, 11), 'selected from the beginning for salvation and called to this very destiny' (2Th 2:13, 14). The understanding of these texts depends upon whether they refer to the foreordination of certain individual persons or whether they describe the foreordination of a class of persons, namely, the Christian congregation, the "one body" (1Co 10:17) of those who will be joint heirs with Christ Jesus in his heavenly Kingdom.—Eph 1:22, 23; 2:19-22; Heb 3:1, 5, 6.

If these words apply to specific individuals as foreordained to eternal salvation, then it follows that those individuals could never prove unfaithful or fail in their calling, for God's foreknowledge of them could not prove inaccurate and his foreordination of them to a certain destiny could never miscarry or be thwarted. Yet the same apostles who were inspired to write the foregoing words showed that some who were "bought" and "sanctified" by the blood of Christ's ransom sacrifice and who had "tasted the heavenly free gift" and "become partakers of holy spirit . . . and powers of the coming system of things" would fall away beyond repentance and bring destruction upon themselves. (2Pe 2:1, 2, 20-22; Heb 6:4-6; 10:26-29) The apostles unitedly urged those to whom they wrote: "Do your utmost to make the calling and choosing of you sure for yourselves; for *if you keep on doing these things* you will by no means ever fail"; also, "Keep working out your own salvation with fear and trembling." (2Pe 1:10, 11; Php 2:12-16) Paul, who was "called to be an apostle of Jesus Christ" (1Co

1:1), obviously did not consider himself individually predestinated to eternal salvation, since he speaks of his strenuous efforts in striving to attain "the goal for the prize of the upward call of God" (Php 3:8-15) and his concern lest he himself should "become disapproved somehow."—1Co 9:27.

Similarly, "the crown of life" offered such ones is granted subject to their faithfulness under trial until death. (Re 2:10, 23; Jas 1:12) Their crowns of kingship with God's Son can be lost. (Re 3:11) The apostle Paul expressed confidence that "the crown of righteousness" was "reserved" for him, but he only did so when he was certain that he was nearing the end of his course, having "run [it] to the finish."—2Ti 4:6-8.

On the other hand, viewed as applying to a class, to the Christian congregation, or "holy nation" of called ones as a whole (1Pe 2:9), the texts previously cited would mean that God foreknew and foreordained that such a class (but not the specific individuals forming it) would be produced. Also, these scriptures would mean that he prescribed, or foreordained, the 'pattern' to which all those in due time called to be members thereof would have to conform, all of this according to his purpose. (Ro 8:28-30; Eph 1:3-12; 2Ti 1:9, 10) He also foreordained the works such ones would be expected to carry out and their being tested because of the sufferings the world would bring upon them.—Eph 2:10; 1Th 3:3, 4.

As to those texts referring to 'names being written in the book of life,' see NAME.

Fatalism and Predestinarianism. Among the pagan peoples of ancient times, including the Greeks and Romans, one's fate, particularly the length of the individual's life, was often considered to be determined beforehand for all individuals by the gods. Grecian mythology represented the control of men's destiny by three goddesses: *Clotho* (spinner), who spun the thread of life; *Lachesis* (disposer of lots), who determined the length of life; and *Atropos* (inflexible), who cut life off when the time expired. A similar triad was found among the Roman deities.

According to Jewish historian Josephus (first century C.E.), the Pharisees endeavored to harmonize the idea of fate with their belief in God and with the free moral agency granted to man. (*The Jewish War*, II, 162, 163 [viii, 14]; *Jewish Antiquities*, XVIII, 13, 14 [i, 3]) *The New Schaff-Herzog Encyclopedia of Religious Knowledge* says: "Previous to Augustine [of the fourth and fifth centuries C.E.] there was no serious development in Christianity of a theory of predestination." Before Augustine, earlier so-called "Church Fathers" such as Justin, Origen, and Irenaeus "know nothing of unconditional predestination; they teach free will." (Hastings' *Encyclopædia of Religion and Ethics,* 1919, Vol. X, p. 231) In their refutation of Gnosticism, they are described as regularly expressing their belief in the free moral agency of man as "the distinguishing characteristic of human personality, the basis of moral responsibility, a divine gift whereby man might choose that which was well-pleasing to God," and as speaking of "the autonomy of man and the counsel of God who constraineth not."—*The New Schaff-Herzog Encyclopedia of Religious Knowledge,* edited by S. Jackson, 1957, Vol. IX, pp. 192, 193.

FORERUNNER. One who goes in advance to prepare for the coming of another. This might include scouting and spying, clearing the way, proclaiming and giving notice of another's approach, or showing the way for others to follow. The forerunner is usually, but not always, of less importance than the person who follows.

It was the Oriental custom that runners go before the royal chariot to prepare and announce the king's coming and to assist him generally. (1Sa 8:11) Absalom and Adonijah, in imitation of such regal dignity and to add prestige and seeming sanction to their respective rebellions, placed 50 runners before their personal chariots.—2Sa 15:1; 1Ki 1:5; see RUNNERS.

John the Baptizer was in reality the forerunner of Christ, in fulfillment of Isaiah 40:3 and Malachi 3:1 and 4:5, 6: "Someone is calling out in the wilderness: 'Clear up the way of Jehovah . . . Make the highway . . . straight.'" "I am sending my messenger, and he must clear up a way before me." John's advance proclamation, therefore, aroused people to expect, look for, and wait for Jesus, that, in turn, they might listen to him, honor him, and follow him. (Mt 3:1-12; 11:7, 10, 14; Mr 9:11-13; Lu 1:13-17, 76; Joh 1:35-37) In a similar manner, messengers were sent out in advance of Jesus, and these went into a village of the Samaritans "to make preparation for him." —Lu 9:52.

Jesus himself, however, is the one referred to in the only passage of Scripture using the word "forerunner." (Heb 6:19, 20) He was not a forerunner in the sense of being inferior to those who followed after him. Rather, he was the first to enter heavenly glory, opening and preparing the way for the heavenly congregation of his footstep followers. (Joh 14:2, 3) Hence, they have boldness of approach to God through the way their Forerunner inaugurated.—Heb 10:19-22.

FORESKIN. See CIRCUMCISION.

FOREST. The Hebrew term for a wooded tract is *ya'ar,* rendered "woods" (De 19:5; 1Sa 14:25) and "forest." (Jos 17:15) At one time the land of Palestine had abundant forests with trees of many types. The Scriptural references to forests and woodlands and to the use of wood materials make it evident that trees were then much more common there than at present, despite the reforestation efforts in recent years. (2Ch 27:4; Jg 9:48, 49) This is also made certain from the description of wild animal life, showing that the forests were able to provide adequate cover and habitation for bears (2Ki 2:23, 24), lions (1Sa 17:34; 1Ch 11:22), and other forms of animal life (Eze 34:25).

But deforestation of large areas has come about because of the devastation of war, the extensive use of timber with no accompanying effort to replenish the forests, and uncontrolled grazing in which the young shoots of new trees have been eaten by goats and other animals. Denis Baly, in his book *The Geography of the Bible* (1974, pp. 77, 115, 116), speaks of centuries of neglect, which has resulted in the disappearance of many woodlands and the loss of as much as 2 m (6.5 ft) of fertile soil, leaving much of the land rocky and barren.

Certain forests are specifically mentioned in the Bible. The forests of Lebanon, now reduced to a few small groves, were outstanding for their splendid tree growth (1Ki 5:2-10, 13-18; 2Ki 19: 23), with great quantities of cedar, juniper, cypress, and other trees. The "forest of Ephraim" (perhaps "forest of Mahanaim"), in which Absalom met disaster, may have been located E of the Jordan River near Mahanaim, and appears to have been of considerable density. (2Sa 18:6, ftn, 8, 17) "The forest of Hereth" was in Judah. (1Sa 22:5) Additionally, the region of Gilead was famous for its woodlands and balsam trees, while Bashan to the N was noted for its "massive trees," apparently including the oak. (Isa 2:13; Zec 11:2) In the days of David and Solomon, sycamore trees grew in abundance in the Shephelah lowland. (1Ki 10:27; 1Ch 27:28; 2Ch 1:15; 9:27) The Jordan Valley had a thick growth of tamarisks and willows, where lions lurked.—Jer 12:5; Zec 11:3.

Symbolic Use. Even as trees are used to symbolize individual persons and rulers, so the Bible uses forests symbolically for peoples or nations and their rulers. The wickedness of apostate Judah was like a flame to burn up her people (Isa 9:18); Jehovah's anger would burn up the southern kingdom (Judah) with an inextinguishable flame. (Eze 20:46-48) Similar prophecies are given against pagan nations, enemies of God's people. The Assyrian warriors would be cut down and thinned out like trees of a forest.—Ps 83:14, 15; Jer 46:22, 23; Isa 10:19, 34.

FORETELLER OF EVENTS.

An individual claiming ability to forecast what will take place in the future, among whom the Bible names magic-practicing priests, spiritistic diviners, astrologers, and others. (See DIVINATION; SPIRITISM.) The Hebrew word *yid·de'o·ni'*, rendered "professional foreteller of events," comes from the root *ya·dha'* (know) and implies knowledge hidden to the ordinary person. It often appears in conjunction with *'ohv*, meaning "spirit medium." (De 18:11) Some individuals possessed occult powers by virtue of contact with the demons, the wicked angelic enemies of God under Satan the Devil, who is the ruler of the demons. (Lu 11:14-20) In ancient times various methods were employed by these prognosticators in obtaining their messages of prediction: stargazing (Isa 47:13), examination of the liver and other viscera of sacrificed animal victims (Eze 21:21), interpretation of omens (2Ki 21:6), consultation with the so-called spirits of the dead, and so forth.—De 18:11.

The lives of the Egyptians, like the lives of the Babylonians, were regulated to a large extent by their fortune-tellers. (Isa 19:3) On the other hand, God's true servants never looked to such persons for information. When the Law was given to Israel shortly after their release from bondage in Egypt, they were strictly forbidden to consult "professional foretellers of events." (Le 19:31) Having "immoral intercourse" with them would result in being cut off (in death) from among God's people. And as to the one practicing the art, the law went on to say: "As for a man or woman in whom there proves to be a mediumistic spirit or spirit of prediction, they should be put to death without fail." (Le 20:6, 27) Nearly 40 years later, when poised to enter the Promised Land and to drive out its inhabitants, Israel was reminded: "You must not learn to do according to the detestable things of those nations. There should not be found in you . . . anyone who

consults a spirit medium or a professional foreteller of events or anyone who inquires of the dead."—De 18:9-11.

More than 350 years later, Israel's first king, Saul, removed all the foretellers of events from the land, but before his death he had fallen so far away from Jehovah that he personally sought out "a mistress of spirit mediumship in En-dor" to foretell his future. At first she was afraid to practice her art, but at Saul's insistence that she "bring up Samuel," she conjured up a vision. She described its form as 'an old man wearing a sleeveless coat.' Saul was convinced that it was the prophet Samuel. (1Sa 28:3, 7-19) But it could not actually have been Samuel, for he was dead, and the dead "are conscious of nothing at all." (Ec 9:5) Samuel, when alive, would certainly have had nothing to do with a spirit medium, and Jehovah God and his holy angels would give such a one no cooperation. God himself told his people: "In case they should say to you people: 'Apply to the spiritistic mediums or to those having a spirit of prediction who are chirping and making utterances in low tones,' is it not to its God that any people should apply? Should there be application to dead persons in behalf of living persons? To the law and to the attestation!" Jehovah goes on to say: "Surely they will keep saying what is according to this statement that will have no light of dawn."—Isa 8:19, 20.

Nearly 400 years after Saul's reign, King Manasseh of Judah "did on a large scale what was bad in Jehovah's eyes, to offend him," including the consulting of professional foretellers of events, who flourished under his rule. (2Ki 21:6; 2Ch 33:6) All of these had to be cleaned out of the land by Manasseh's grandson, righteous King Josiah.—2Ki 23:24.

The only mention in the Christian Greek Scriptures of demonic predicting of the future is the instance in which the apostle Paul, in the city of Philippi, freed "a certain servant girl with a spirit, a demon of divination." She had furnished her masters with much gain "by practicing the art of prediction." Manifesting the fact that such practice is truly demonic and diametrically opposed to God, the masters of the girl from whom the demon was cast out caused Paul much trouble in Philippi, bringing Paul and his companion Silas before the magistrates, who gave the command to beat them and then threw them into jail.—Ac 16:12, 16-24.

FORGIVENESS.

The act of pardoning an offender; ceasing to feel resentment toward him because of his offense and giving up all claim to recompense. The Hebrew verb *sa·lach'* (forgive) is used only with regard to God's pardoning a sinner. The Greek term *a·phi'e·mi* literally means "let go off."—See PARDON.

According to God's law given to the nation of Israel, in order for a person who had sinned against God or against his fellowman to have his sins forgiven, he first had to rectify the wrong as the Law prescribed and then, in most cases, present a blood offering to Jehovah. (Le 5:5-6:7) Hence, the principle stated by Paul: "Yes, nearly all things are cleansed with blood according to the Law, and unless blood is poured out no forgiveness takes place." (Heb 9:22) Actually, though, the blood of animal sacrifices could not take away sins and give the individual a perfectly clean conscience. (Heb 10:1-4; 9:9, 13, 14) By contrast, the foretold new covenant made possible true forgiveness, based on Jesus Christ's ransom sacrifice. (Jer 31:33, 34; Mt 26:28; 1Co 11:25; Eph 1:7) Even while on earth, Jesus, by healing a paralytic, demonstrated that he had authority to forgive sins.—Mt 9:2-7.

Jehovah forgives "in a large way," as is indicated by Jesus' illustrations of the prodigal son and of the king who forgave a slave a debt of 10,000 talents (60,000,000 denarii, or c. $40,000,000), whereas that slave was unwilling to forgive a fellow slave a debt of but a hundred denarii (c. $70). (Isa 55:7; Lu 15:11-32; Mt 18:23-35) Nevertheless, Jehovah's forgiveness is not prompted by sentimentality, for he does not leave notorious acts unpunished. (Ps 99:8) Joshua warned Israel that Jehovah would not forgive apostasy on their part.—Jos 24:19, 20; compare Isa 2:6-9.

God has a required way for seeking and receiving his forgiveness. A person must acknowledge his sin, recognize that it is an offense against God, confess it unqualifiedly, have a deep heartfelt sorrow for the wrong done, and have a determination to turn from such a course or practice. (Ps 32:5; 51:4; 1Jo 1:8, 9; 2Co 7:8-11) He must do what he can to right the wrong or damage done. (Mt 5:23, 24) Then he must pray to God, asking for forgiveness on the basis of Christ's ransom sacrifice.—Eph 1:7; see REPENTANCE.

Moreover, forgiving others for personal offenses, regardless of the number of times involved, is a Christian requirement. (Lu 17:3, 4; Eph 4:32; Col 3:13) God's forgiveness is not extended toward those who refuse to forgive others. (Mt 6:14, 15) However, even when serious wrongdoing leads to expulsion of "the wicked

man" from the Christian congregation, that person may in due time be accorded forgiveness if he proves that he is truly repentant. At that time all in the congregation can confirm their love for him. (1Co 5:13; 2Co 2:6-11) However, Christians are not required to forgive those who practice malicious, willful sin with no repentance. Such become God's enemies.—Heb 10:26-31; Ps 139:21, 22.

It is proper to pray for God's forgiveness in behalf of others, even for an entire congregation. Moses did so respecting the nation of Israel, confessing their national sin and asking forgiveness, and he was favorably heard by Jehovah. (Nu 14:19, 20) Also, Solomon, at the dedication of the temple, prayed that Jehovah might forgive his people when they sinned and then turned back from their wrong course. (1Ki 8:30, 33-40, 46-52) Ezra acted representatively in confessing publicly the sins of the repatriated Jews. His heartfelt prayer and exhortation had the result that the people took action in order to receive Jehovah's forgiveness. (Ezr 9:13-10:4, 10-19, 44) James encouraged the spiritually sick one to call for the older men of the congregation to pray over him, and "if he has committed sins, it will be forgiven him." (Jas 5:14-16) However, there is "a sin that does incur death," sin against the holy spirit, a deliberate practice of sin for which there is no forgiveness. A Christian should not pray for those sinning in this way.—1Jo 5:16; Mt 12:31; Heb 10:26, 27; see SIN, I; SPIRIT.

FORNICATION. Illicit sex relations outside of Scriptural marriage. The Hebrew verb *za·nah'* and its related forms convey the idea of harlotry, immoral intercourse, fornication, or prostitution. (Ge 38:24; Ex 34:16; Ho 1:2; Le 19:29) The Greek word translated "fornication" is *por·nei'a*. Regarding the meanings of *por·nei'a*, B. F. Westcott in his book *Saint Paul's Epistle to the Ephesians* (1906, p. 76) says: "This is a general term for all unlawful intercourse, (I) adultery: Hos. ii. 2, 4 (LXX.); Matt. v. 32; xix. 9; (2) unlawful marriage, I Cor. v. I; (3) fornication, the common sense as here [Eph 5:3]." Bauer's *Greek-English Lexicon of the New Testament* (revised by F. W. Gingrich and F. Danker, 1979, p. 693) defines *por·nei'a* as *"prostitution, unchastity, fornication,* of every kind of unlawful sexual intercourse." *Porneia* is understood to involve the grossly immoral use of the genital organ(s) of at least one human; also there must have been two or more parties (including another consenting human or a beast), whether of the same sex or the opposite sex.

(Jude 7) The unlawful act of a rapist is fornication, but, of course, that does not make the person who is forcibly raped also a fornicator.

When God performed the first human marriage he said: "That is why a man will leave his father and his mother and he must stick to his wife and they must become one flesh." (Ge 2:24) Here the standard set for man and woman was monogamy, and promiscuous sex relationship was ruled out. Also, no divorce and remarriage to another was anticipated.—See DIVORCE.

In patriarchal society God's faithful servants hated fornication, whether between single, engaged, or married persons, and it was considered a sin against God.—Ge 34:1, 2, 6, 7, 31; 38:24-26; 39:7-9.

Under the Law. Under the Mosaic Law, a man committing fornication with an unengaged girl was required to marry the girl and to pay her father the purchase price for brides (50 silver shekels; $110), and he could not divorce her all his days. Even if her father refused to give him the girl in marriage, the man had to pay the purchase price to the father. (Ex 22:16, 17; De 22:28, 29) However, if the girl was engaged, the man was to be stoned to death. If the girl screamed when she was attacked, she was not to be punished, but if the engaged girl failed to scream (thereby indicating consent), she was also put to death.—De 22:23-27.

The sanctity of marriage was emphasized by the law that punished with death a girl who married under the false pretense of being a virgin, having committed fornication secretly. If her husband falsely charged her with such a crime, it was regarded as bringing great reproach on her father's house. For his slanderous action, the man was to be "disciplined" by the judges, perhaps by beating, and fined 100 silver shekels ($220), the money then being given to the father. (De 22:13-21) Prostitution of a priest's daughter brought disgrace on his sacred office. She was to be killed, then burned as something detestable. (Le 21:9; see also Le 19:29.) Fornication between married persons (adultery) was a violation of the seventh commandment and merited the death penalty for both parties.—Ex 20:14; De 5:18; 22:22.

If a man committed fornication with a servant girl who had been designated for another man, but who had not been redeemed or freed, punishment was to take place, but they were not to be put to death. (Le 19:20-22) Evidently this was because the woman was not yet free and in full control of her actions, as a free engaged girl would be. The redemption price had not yet been paid, or at least not fully paid, and she was still a bondservant to her master.

When the mercenary prophet Balaam could not bring a curse upon Israel by divination, he found a way to bring them under God's displeasure by appealing to wrong desire for sexual relations. By means of the women of Moab he seduced the Israelites into practicing the filthy phallic worship of the Baal of Peor, for which 24,000 of the sons of Israel died.—Nu 25:1-9; 1Co 10:8 (likely 1,000 heads of the people were killed and hung on stakes [Nu 25:4] and the rest were destroyed by the sword or the plague).

Forbidden to Christians. Jesus Christ restored God's original standard of monogamy (Mt 5:32; 19:9) and showed the wickedness of fornication by classing it with murder, thievery, wicked reasoning, false testimony, and blasphemy. He pointed out that these come from within a man, from his heart, and defile him. (Mt 15:19, 20; Mr 7:21-23) Later, the governing body of the Christian congregation, comprised of the apostles and older men in Jerusalem, wrote to Christians in about 49 C.E., warning them against fornication, and placing it alongside idolatry and the eating of blood.—Ac 15:20, 29; 21:25.

The apostle Paul points out that fornication is one of the works of the flesh, the opposite of the fruitage of the spirit of God, and warns that the practice of fleshly works will prevent an individual from inheriting the Kingdom. (Ga 5:19-21) He counsels that the Christian should deaden his body "as respects fornication." (Col 3:5) In fact, he warns that it should not even be a topic of conversation among Christians, who should be holy. Similarly, the Israelites were not to mention the names of the pagan gods—not that they would fail to warn their children about these gods, but they would not mention them with any esteem.—Eph 5:3; Ex 23:13.

Fornication is an offense for which an individual may be expelled (disfellowshipped) from the Christian congregation. (1Co 5:9-13; Heb 12:15, 16) The apostle explains that a Christian committing fornication sins against his own body, using reproductive members for a perverted purpose. He is greatly affected spiritually in an adverse way, brings defilement into God's congregation, and lays himself open to the danger of deadly sexually transmitted diseases. (1Co 6:18, 19) He encroaches on the rights of his Christian brothers (1Th 4:3-7) by (1) bringing uncleanness and disgraceful folly, with reproach, into the congregation (Heb 12:15, 16), (2) depriving the one with whom he commits fornication of a clean moral standing and, if that one is single, of being clean when entering into marriage, (3) depriving his own family of a clean moral record, as well as (4) wronging the parents, husband, or fiancé of the one with whom he commits fornication. He disregards, not man, whose laws may or may not condone fornication, but God, who will exact punishment for his sin.—1Th 4:8.

Symbolic Use. Jehovah God spoke of the nation of Israel in covenant relationship to him as "a wife." (Isa 54:5, 6) When the nation became unfaithful to him, ignoring him and turning to other nations such as Egypt and Assyria for help and entering into alliances with them, Israel was like an unfaithful wife, an adulteress, a prostitute, one carrying on fornication promiscuously. (Eze 16:15, 25-29) Likewise, if Christians in a dedicated relationship to God, or professing such a relationship, are unfaithful by engaging in false worship or by being friends of the world, they are called adulteresses.—Jas 4:4.

Concerning the symbolic meaning of por·nei′a in certain texts, F. Zorell (*Lexicon Graecum Novi Testamenti,* Paris, 1961, col. 1106) says: "Apostasy from the true faith, committed either entirely or partially, defection from the one true God Jahve to foreign gods [4Ki 9:22; Jer 3:2, 9; Ho 6:10 etc.; for God's union with his people was considered like a kind of spiritual matrimony]: Re 14:8; 17:2, 4; 18:3; 19:2."—Brackets his; 4Ki in the Greek *Septuagint* corresponds to 2Ki in the Masoretic text.

Babylon the Great, described in the Bible book of Revelation as a harlot, is a symbol of something religious. Her various sects, "Christian" and pagan, have claimed to be organizations of true worship. But she has consorted with the rulers of this world for power and material gain, and with her "the kings of the earth committed fornication." Her unclean, filthy course of fornication has been detestable in God's sight and has caused great bloodshed and distress in the earth. (Re 17:1-6; 18:3) For her course she will suffer the judgment of God on those practicing fornication, namely, destruction.—Re 17:16; 18:8, 9.

FORTIFICATIONS.

The Hebrew term for "fortification" has the basic sense of a place that is impenetrable, inaccessible. (Compare Zec 11:2, ftn.) Fortifications of a town were costly and difficult and required an adequate defense force,

so not all towns were fortified. The larger cities were usually walled cities; the smaller towns in that area, known as dependent towns, were unwalled. (Jos 15:45, 47; 17:11) Inhabitants of these towns could flee to the walled city in the event of an invasion by the enemy. Fortified cities thus served as a refuge for the people in the area. Cities were also fortified when they were strategically located to protect highways, water sources, routes to supply bases, and communication lines.

The strength and height of the fortifications of many cities in the Promised Land were such that the unfaithful spies sent by Moses to spy out Canaan reported that "the fortified cities are very great" and "fortified to the heavens." From their faithless viewpoint the cities looked impregnable. —Nu 13:28; De 1:28.

Cities in Bible lands generally covered an area of but a few acres. Some, however, were much larger. The capital cities of Egypt, Assyria, Babylonia, Persia, and Rome were exceptionally large. Babylon was one of the most strongly defended cities in Bible times. Not only did it have unusually strong walls but it was situated on a river that provided a fine moat for defense as well as a water supply. Babylon felt she could hold her captives forever. (Isa 14:16, 17) But the city was taken in one night by the strategy of Cyrus the Persian, who diverted the Euphrates so that his forces could enter the city through gates in the walls along the quays.—Da 5:30.

Three essentials were required for a fortified city: (1) walls to act as a barrier to the enemy, (2) weapons so that the defending forces could retaliate to repel the attackers, and (3) an adequate water supply. Foodstuffs could be stored during times of peace; but a constant, accessible source of water was essential for a city to withstand a siege of any length.

Moats and Ramparts. Some cities were surrounded by a moat filled with water, especially if a river or lake was nearby. Babylon on the Euphrates was a notable example, as was also No-amon (Thebes) on the Nile canals. (Na 3:8) Where there were no nearby bodies of water, a dry moat was often constructed. Jerusalem was rebuilt with a moat.—Da 9:25.

Rising from the side of the moat was a "rampart" built from the earth dug up when the moat was excavated. (2Sa 20:15) This rampart sometimes was covered with a stone facing and formed a glacis, or incline, sloping up to the wall built on top of the rampart. The moat discovered by archaeologists on the western defenses of the city of Hazor was 80 m (262 ft) wide at the top, 40 m (131 ft) across the bottom, and about 15 m (50 ft) deep. The rampart rising from the moat was an additional 15 m (50 ft). This made the top of the rampart nearly 30 m (100 ft) high, measuring from the bottom of the moat. On top of this stood the city wall.—Compare Ps 122:7.

This rampart was, of course, very difficult to ascend, especially with battering rams, for which reason the attackers built a ramp, or "siege rampart," up which the battering rams were moved. (2Sa 20:15; see BATTERING RAM.) The moat was so wide that it greatly weakened the archery fire of the attacking army, and shooting from the bottom of the moat accomplished little. On the other hand, the builders of the ramps for their battering rams were under constant fire from the city walls, being subjected to a rain of arrows, stones, and sometimes firebrands. Of course, not all cities had moats or sloping ramparts, some basing their defense entirely on vertical walls.

The Walls.   After the moat and rampart, the wall was the next feature of the defenses. Some walls and towers provided fortified positions for soldiers and rooms for storage as well as ladders to the top. The wall was made up of large stones, brick, and earth. Some of the stones were enormous in size. Earlier walls were mostly made of stones without mortar. Later on, mortar was often used between the stones. Mortar was made by treading clay with the feet and mixing it with water, as in making bricks. Otherwise it would crack and weaken the defensive wall.—Compare Eze 13:9-16; Na 3:14.

The wall system often consisted of a high inner wall and a lower outer wall. A dry moat was sometimes constructed between these walls. Along the outer wall were bastions, round or square in shape. They were crenellated (indented with battlements) so that the archers could shoot through the embrasures and at the same time receive some protection against enemy arrows and rock slingers. Bastions extended out from the wall so that the archers not only could command the area in front of them but could also shoot to the right or to the left at the flanks of the enemy forces that might be trying to scale or breach the wall.

The inner wall was heavier and thicker. After the invention of the heavy battering rams, especially like those used by the Assyrians, much stronger, thicker walls were built to withstand the devastations of this instrument. A stone wall at Tell en-Nasbeh (Mizpah?) was found to average 4 m (13 ft) in thickness, and it is estimated to have been 12 m (39 ft) high. The top of the wall was crenellated, as were nearly all city walls.

Towers and Gates.   Towers were built into the inner walls (in addition to bastions or towers in the outer walls). They were higher than the wall, protruding from the wall sometimes as much as 3 m (10 ft). They were equipped with crenellations on top and sometimes with openings below the crenellations, for the convenience of archers and stone throwers. The fact that the towers protruded from the wall and were never placed farther than two bowshots apart, but were usually much closer, enabled the defenders to command all the area along the wall. Also, a balcony at the tower's top had openings in the floor so that archery fire, stones, and firebrands could be directed straight down at the invaders below. These towers are mentioned many times in the Scriptures. (Ne 3:1; Jer 31:38; Zec 14:10) Towers served also as posts for watchmen, who could see the enemy approaching from a distance.—Isa 21:8, 9.

Usually the citadel was built on the highest elevation in the city. It had a tower fortress and its own walls, less massive than the walls surrounding the city. The citadel was the last stronghold of refuge and resistance. When the soldiers of the enemy breached the city walls, they would have to fight through the streets of the city to reach the tower. Such a tower was the one at Thebez, which Abimelech attacked after capturing the city and where a woman broke his skull by pitching an upper millstone upon his head.—Jg 9:50-54.

Besides these city towers, other towers (Heb., *migh·dal′*; plural, *migh·da·lim′*) were built in isolated places. These were constructed as "police stations" to protect wells or other water sources, highways, frontiers, communication lines, or supply lines. King Uzziah of Judah is noted for building towers in Jerusalem as well as in the wilderness; these apparently were erected to protect the cisterns that he built for watering his livestock. (2Ch 26:9, 10) Several of such towers have been found in the Negeb.

The weakest part of the defenses of a city were its gates; therefore the gates were the most hotly defended points in the walls. Only as many gates were constructed as necessary for the traffic of the inhabitants in and out of the city during peacetime. Gates were made of wood or of wood and metal, sometimes being metal covered to resist fire. In archaeological diggings the gateways are often found to be charred, indicating that fire was used in an attempt to burn the gates down.—See GATE, GATEWAY.

Some of the kings of Judah noted for their construction of fortifications were Solomon, who built "fortified cities with walls, doors and bar"; Asa, who put up cities with "walls around and towers, double doors and bars"; and Uzziah, who built "towers in the wilderness" and "engines of war" in Jerusalem.—2Ch 8:3-5; 14:2, 6, 7; 26: 9-15.

Fortifications of the Besieging Army. At times the besieging army built fortifications of its own around its camp. This protected the camp from sorties on the part of those besieged or from attacks by outside allies of the city. These fortified camps might be round or oval in shape and surrounded by a wall, which was often crenellated and had crenellated towers. For these fortifications, they would cut down the trees, sometimes for miles around the city. Jehovah's law directed the Israelites not to cut down fruit trees for this purpose.—De 20:19, 20.

Fortifications With Pointed Stakes. When foretelling the destruction of Jerusalem, Jesus Christ indicated that her enemies would build around her "a fortification with pointed stakes," or, "palisade." (Lu 19:43, *Int*) The historian Josephus confirms the accurate fulfillment of this prophecy. Titus argued in favor of building a fortification to keep the Jews from leaving the city, in order to bring about their surrender or, if this did not materialize, to make it easier to take the city because of the resultant famine. His arguments won out, and the army was organized to undertake the project. The legions and lesser divisions of the army competed with one another to finish the task; individually the men were spurred on by a desire to please their superiors. To provide materials for the construction of this fortification, the countryside about Jerusalem within a distance of about 16 km (10 mi) was denuded of its trees. Amazingly, according to Josephus, the over 7-km-long (4.5 mi) fortification was completed in just three days, an undertaking that ordinarily would have required a number of months. Outside the wall of this fortification, 13 places for garrisons were constructed, and their combined circumference amounted to about 2 km (1 mi).—*The Jewish War*, V, 491-511, 523 (xii, 1, 2, 4).

Archaeological Discoveries. Following up the building operations of his father David, King Solomon was outstanding for his construction

works. Besides building the magnificent temple of Jehovah at Jerusalem, he strengthened Jerusalem's walls and built extensive fortifications at Hazor, Megiddo, and Gezer. Archaeologists were guided in their excavation of these fortifications by the Bible's statement at 1 Kings 9:15: "Now this is the account of those conscripted for forced labor that King Solomon levied to build the house of Jehovah and his own house and the Mound and the wall of Jerusalem and Hazor and Megiddo and Gezer." They found that the gates of these three last-named cities were all built to a single unique plan, each being 17 m (56 ft) wide, with an entrance flanked on both sides by square towers and leading into a vestibule 20 m (66 ft) long, with three chambers on each side. They were somewhat similar to the description of the gates of Ezekiel's visionary temple.—Eze 40:5-16.

Immediately above walls built by Solomon at Megiddo and Hazor, other walls were constructed, possibly by Ahab. These were more thickly and strongly built, doubtless because of the heavy Assyrian battering rams in use during that later period.

The source of water for Megiddo was a well in a natural cave at the western foot of the mound on which the city was built. To get water into the city, they sent a vertical shaft 30 m (98 ft) deep, 22 m (72 ft) of this distance through solid rock; this brought them to the level of the well. From this level they cut a horizontal tunnel with a slight gradient for a distance of 67 m (220 ft) to the well. The slight slope from the well to the bottom of the shaft allowed the water to flow into the city by gravity. The well was sealed from the outside by a thick wall.

Even greater engineering skill was required when Hezekiah sealed up the course of the water flowing from Gihon and cut a channel of some 533 m (1,749 ft) to bring water into Jerusalem, thereby enabling the city to withstand a long siege.—2Ch 32:30.

Often cisterns, both public and individual, were built inside a city to supply the city with water during times of siege. On the monument (now located in the Louvre of Paris) erected at Dibon, in Moab, by Mesha the king of Moab, we find the inscription: "I also built its gates and I built its towers and I built the king's house, and I made both of its reservoirs for water inside the town. And there was no cistern inside the town even at the acropolis, so I said to all the people, 'Let each of you make a cistern for himself in his house.'"

Symbolic Uses. Since the towers in the wilderness were the safest places of refuge for miles around, we can see the appropriateness of Proverbs 18:10: "The name of Jehovah is a strong tower. Into it the righteous runs and is given protection." Also significant are the expressions in Psalm 48: "In [Zion's] dwelling towers God himself has become known as a secure height. March around Zion, you people, and go about it, count its towers. Set your hearts upon its rampart. Inspect its dwelling towers, in order that you may recount it to the future generation." (Compare Heb 12:22.) This would be especially meaningful to Jews who would look up at the great stronghold of Jerusalem situated on an elevation higher than nearly any other major capital city in human history, with its mighty walls of defense. Through the prophet Zechariah, Jehovah speaks of himself as "a wall of fire all around" Jerusalem. This gives his people encouraging assurance that, while walls of stone can be broken down, Jehovah himself is really the defense of his servants.—Ps 48:3, 11-13; Zec 2:4, 5.

FORTUNATUS (For·tu·na′tus) [from Lat., Fortunate; Prosperous]. One of the mature members of the congregation in Corinth who, together with Stephanas and Achaicus, visited Paul at Ephesus. (1Co 16:8, 17, 18) From these men Paul may have learned of the disturbing conditions about which he wrote, and they were possibly the ones who delivered Paul's first canonical letter to the Corinthians.—1Co 1:11; 5:1; 11:18.

FOUNDATION. The base, or substructure, on which a building is erected and which serves to distribute the weight of the superstructure equally over the ground. Since the strength and permanence of a building depend largely on the strength of its foundation, great care must be exercised in laying the foundation. Good foundations were vital in Palestine to withstand not only heavy rains, winds, and floods but also earthquakes, as this region is an earthquake area. A number of Hebrew terms rendered "foundation" come from the root ya·sadh′, meaning "found; lay the foundation; solidly fix." (Isa 23:13; 51:13; Ps 24:2) The Greek term is the·me′li·os, used in a literal sense in Acts 16:26.

The Master Builder Jehovah, in answering Job out of the windstorm, compared the literal earth to a building. (Job 38:4-7) Though the earth hangs upon nothing, it has, as it were, durable foundations that will not be made to totter, for the unchangeable laws governing the universe hold it firmly in place, and God's purpose toward the earth has remained unchanged. (Job 26:7; 38:33; Ps 104:5; Mal 3:6) On the other hand, injustice and disobedience to God's law in effect tear down the foundations that give stability to the land, causing the foundations of the figurative earth (the people and their established systems) to totter.—Ps 82; 11:3; Pr 29:4.

The laying of the foundations of the earth is not to be confused with "the founding [Gr., ka·ta·bo·les′] of the world." From Jesus' words at Luke 11:48-51, it is evident that Abel lived at the founding of the world, which has reference to mankind. The planet Earth's foundations had long previously been laid.—See ABEL No. 1; WORLD.

The laying of a foundation was apparently a time for joy. At the 'founding of the earth' the angels shouted in applause. Also, great rejoicing attended the laying of the foundation of Zerubbabel's temple, although those who had seen the glory of the former temple gave way to weeping. —Job 38:4, 6, 7; Ezr 3:10-13.

As Solomon had used large, costly hewn stones for the foundation of the temple, so a foundation that is precious to God is laid for the "spiritual house" in which Jesus' anointed followers are "living stones." Jesus himself is the foundation cornerstone; upon the foundation of the apostles and Christian prophets the rest of the holy ones are built up into "a place for God to inhabit by spirit." All the "stones" making up this spiritual house are selected by Jehovah.—1Pe 2:4-6; Eph 2:19-22; see CORNERSTONE.

Most appropriately, the 12 symbolic foundation stones of the New Jerusalem, bearing the names of the 12 apostles of the Lamb, are precious stones. (Re 21:14, 19, 20) The New Jerusalem described in Revelation is made up of the 144,000 who are betrothed to the bridegroom. The "heavenly Jerusalem" mentioned at Hebrews 12:22 comprises 144,001, this "one" being the bridegroom King. It is the city with real foundations that Abraham awaited. (Heb 11:10) Thus, the Bible books of Hebrews and Revelation show a close identity between the "heavenly Jerusalem" and the New Jerusalem.

Jesus, who had in his prehuman existence worked alongside his Father as a Master Worker at the laying of earth's foundations, fully appreciated the value of a solid foundation, as is seen from his illustration of the discreet man who went down deep and laid the foundation for his house on a rock-mass, whereas the foolish man built his house upon the sand and suffered severe loss. (Pr 8:29, 30; Mt 7:24-27; Lu 6:47-49) Likewise, in comparing the task of making Christians to a building work, Paul stressed the importance of building with noncombustible materials on Jesus Christ as the foundation, so as not to experience loss.—1Co 3:10-15.

Paul also compared certain primary Bible teachings to a foundation, and he encouraged the Hebrews not to become static upon having learned the primary doctrine about the Christ but to press on to maturity.—Heb 6:1, 2; see EARTH; HOUSE.

FOUNTAIN GATE. See GATE, GATEWAY.

FOUNTAIN OF THE BIG SNAKE.
The Hebrew expression carries the thought of a fountain, spring, or well of a land or sea monster, and it is variously translated as: "dragon well" (KJ, Le); "Serpent's Well" (AT); "snake-fountain" (Ro); "Fountain of the Big Snake" (NW). The Greek Septuagint, however, reads "Fountain of the Fig Trees."

This water source was located along the route Nehemiah took on his first inspection of Jerusalem's broken-down walls. (Ne 2:12, 13) Since this name is not found again in the Scriptures, the fountain or well, if elsewhere referred to, must be under a different designation. En-rogel is commonly suggested as its alternate name. This could well be, for though En-rogel is a considerable distance down the Kidron Valley, the account simply says that Nehemiah passed "in front of the Fountain," and this could mean by the corner of the wall facing En-rogel and within sight of, but still some distance from, the fountain.—See EN-ROGEL.

FOUNTAIN, SPRING.
Generally, a natural source of water (Ex 15:27), in contrast to wells and cisterns that were usually dug (Ge 26:15); also used with reference to a source of something other than water. Two Hebrew terms for "fountain; spring" are 'a'yin (literally, eye) and the related ma·'yan'. The corresponding Greek term is pe·ge'. Since springs were cleared and deepened at times, this may explain why "fountain" and "well" are sometimes used interchangeably for the same water source.—Ge 16:7, 14; 24:11, 13; Joh 4:6, 12; see CISTERN; WELL.

Moses described the Promised Land to the Israelites as a land of "springs and watery deeps issuing forth in the valley plain and in the mountainous region." (De 8:7) Springs are plentiful in Palestine, with an average of six or seven for approximately every 100 sq km (40 sq mi). Because the mountains of Judah and Ephraim are mainly composed of porous rock, the winter rains readily filter down to a great depth. The waters finally reach a waterproof layer, run along it, and then reappear as springs on the western side of the Jordan Valley and the western bank of the Dead Sea, some even flowing into the Dead Sea underground. Many of the springs that empty directly into the Dead Sea and the lower waters of the Jordan have a high temperature. West of the mountain range the waters emerge as springs along the eastern part of the long seacoast lowlands, though some of the water finds its way underground to the Mediterranean. Some springs, such as those surrounding Jerusalem and Hebron, gush up at or near the very crest of the highlands of Palestine. The numerous springs resulting from the melting snows on the Lebanon and Hermon ranges provide the headwaters of the Litany, the Jordan, and the rivers of Damascus.

The importance of springs, or fountains, becomes apparent from the frequence of town names beginning with "En," meaning "spring," "fountain." (Jos 15:62; 17:11; 1Ki 1:9; see AIN.) Towns and villages were often built near springs, as most of Palestine's "rivers" are actually torrent valleys that dry up in the summer months. For defensive purposes cities were generally built on elevated sites, and therefore, the springs were often outside the city walls in the valley below. This made the protection of the water supply vitally important. Conduits were constructed to convey the water from its source right into the city. King Hezekiah built such a conduit to bring the waters of Gihon to the City of David. (2Ki 20:20; 2Ch 32:30) At other times concealed passages or tunnels led to the source of water, ensuring an ample supply of water for the inhabitants of the city even when faced with siege. On the occasion of the Assyrian invasion of Judah, Hezekiah stopped up the fountains outside Jerusalem in order to leave the invaders without a water supply.—2Ch 32:2-4; see FORTIFICATIONS; HEZEKIAH No. 1 (Building and Engineering Works).

Figurative Use. Jehovah established "the fountains of the watery deep." (Pr 8:28; Ge 7:11) He is also identified as the Fountain or Source of life, the Source of living water, and the Source of Israel. (Ps 36:9; Jer 2:13; Ps 68:26) His Son Jesus Christ gives water that becomes in the receiver "a fountain of water bubbling up to impart everlasting life." (Joh 4:14) Joel prophetically foretold that after the nations receive a winepress treatment in the Low Plain of Jehoshaphat, a refreshing spring will go forth from Jehovah's house. —Joe 3:12, 13, 18.

In emphasizing the importance of using the tongue aright, James asks Christians, who should offer the water of life: "A fountain does not cause the sweet and the bitter to bubble out of the same opening, does it?"—Jas 3:11.

Jesus dried up the "fountain of blood" of a woman who had suffered a flow of blood for 12 years, healing her. (Mr 5:25-29) "Water source," or "fountain," is an expression also used with reference to a source of sexual satisfaction.—Pr 5:18.

FOUR. See NUMBER, NUMERAL.

FOWL. Although the English word "fowl" is mainly used today to refer to a large or edible bird, the Hebrew term (*'ohph*), derived from the verb "fly," applied to all winged or flying creatures. (Ge 1:20-22) G. R. Driver said that *'ohph* "seems to represent the rhythmical beating of wings on the air and its displacement thereby." (*Palestine Exploration Quarterly*, London, 1955, p. 5) The term not only embraced all the birds (Ge 9:10; Le 1:14; 7:26), including quail (Ps 78: 27; compare Ex 16:13) and also carrion-eating birds (1Sa 17:44, 46; 2Sa 21:10), but could be applied as well to the winged insects, which are included among the "swarming [Heb, *she'rets*]" winged creatures.—Le 11:20-23; De 14:19; see SWARMING THING.

The expression "fatted fowl" at 1 Kings 4:23 in *KJ* and *RS* is considered under CUCKOO.

FOX [Heb., *shu·'al'*; Gr., *a·lo'pex*]. A doglike animal distinguished by its pointed face, its large, erect, triangular ears, and its bushy tail. The fox is well known for its craftiness, and perhaps with reference to this characteristic Jesus Christ spoke of King Herod as "that fox." (Lu 13:32) To elude its enemies, the fox depends more on cunning than swiftness, although for a short distance the animal has been reported to attain a speed of over 70 km/hr (43 mph).

The present-day natives of Syria and Palestine do not always differentiate between the jackal and the fox, and many scholars believe that the Hebrew designation *shu·'al'* probably includes both the fox (*Vulpes vulpes*) and the jackal (*Canis aureus*). A number of Bible translators have rendered *shu·'al'* as "jackal" in some of its occurrences.

Jesus Christ, in forewarning a man desirous of following him, called attention to the fact that foxes had dens, whereas the Son of man had no place to lay his head. (Mt 8:20; Lu 9:58) Unless foxes use a natural crevice or the deserted or usurped burrow of another animal, they commonly burrow holes in the ground to form their dens.

According to naturalists, the fox is not really as much of a poultry thief as he is purported to be. The animal's diet includes insects, rodents and other small animals, birds, carrion, grass, and fruits. (Ca 2:15) The 18th-century naturalist F. Hasselquist reported that in the neighborhood of Bethlehem and elsewhere steps had to be taken to guard against the inroads of foxes upon the vineyards when the grapes were ripe. (*Voyages and Travels in the Levant*, London, 1766, p. 184) Many feel that the jackal is meant at Psalm 63:10, where reference is made to foxes as having a portion of those slain. The rendering "foxes" is, however, not inappropriate when considering that foxes also feed on carrion.

The Scriptures allude to foxes dwelling in desolate areas, even ruins, away from human habitation. (La 5:18; Eze 13:4) They also tell of Samson's using 300 foxes to burn the grain, vineyards, and olive groves of the Philistines (Jg 15:4, 5) and of Tobiah the Ammonite's ridicule that 'a mere fox could break down the wall of Jerusalem' that was being rebuilt by the repatriated Jews.—Ne 4:3.

FRANKINCENSE. A product of incense trees and bushes of certain species belonging to the genus *Boswellia*, which are related to the turpentine, or terebinth, tree and also to trees producing balsam and myrrh. They are native to parts of Africa and Asia. The Hebrew term for frankincense (*levoh·nah'* or *levo·nah'*) comes from a root meaning "be white" and is evidently drawn from its milky color. The Greek *li'ba·nos* is derived from the Hebrew.

The Song of Solomon mentions "the hill of frankincense," apparently in a figurative way, but may indicate the cultivation of incense trees in Solomon's royal parks. (Ca 4:6, 12-16; Ec 2:5) Frankincense was a principal item carried by the caravans of Oriental traders who traveled the spice routes out of S Arabia up to Gaza near the Mediterranean and to Damascus. Scriptural references indicated it was imported in this way into Palestine from Sheba.—Isa 60:6; Jer 6:20.

Frankincense is obtained by making successive

incisions in the bark or by peeling off the bark at intervals, causing a white juice (after several incisions it is spotted with yellow or red) to flow and form into tears of about 2.5 cm (1 in.) in length. When gathered, the frankincense consists of a fragrant gum resin in small chunks, or beads, that have a bitter taste and produce an aromatic odor when burned.—Ca 3:6.

Aside from the references in The Song of Solomon, frankincense is regularly mentioned in the Hebrew Scriptures in connection with worship. (Compare 2Co 2:14-16.) It was an ingredient of the holy incense used at the sanctuary (Ex 30:34-38) and was used on grain offerings (Le 2:1, 2, 15, 16; 6:15; Jer 17:26; 41:4, 5) and on each row of the showbread of the sanctuary (Le 24:7). But it was not to be included on sin offerings (Le 5:11) or on the "grain offering of jealousy." (Nu 5:15) This was doubtless because the latter offerings had to do with sin, or error, and were not offered up as a sacrifice of praise or thanksgiving to Jehovah.

Frankincense is mentioned as being stored in the rebuilt temple buildings, following the return from Babylonian exile. (1Ch 9:29; Ne 13:5, 9) The Oriental astrologers who visited the child Jesus brought frankincense with them (Mt 2:11), and it is mentioned as one of the items of commerce sold to Babylon the Great before her destruction. (Re 18:8-13) The Greek term for the heavenly incense vessel, at Revelation 8:3, 5, is li·ba·no·tos' and is derived from the Hebrew word for "frankincense."

The prophet Isaiah records Jehovah's displeasure and disapproval of gifts and the use of frankincense when offered by those who reject his Word.—Isa 66:3.

FRAUD.

The intentional use of deception, trickery, or perversion of truth for the purpose of inducing another to part with some valuable thing belonging to him or to give up a legal right. The Hebrew term rendered "defraud" ('a·shaq'; Le 6:2) has the basic sense of misusing one's strength, power, or authority over others. It is thus also rendered 'oppress.' (Ec 4:1; Isa 52:4) The Greek verb a·po·ste·re'o means "deprive; defraud; despoil." (1Co 7:5; Mr 10:19; 1Ti 6:5) The Greek noun do'los ("fraud"; Ac 13:10) is also rendered "deceit."—Mr 7:22.

Fraud, as dealt with in the Bible, is generally associated with business relationships. Dishonest business dealings are forbidden by God's law. The Israelites were to deal honestly with one another. The hired laborer was specifically protected by the Law. (Le 19:13; De 24:14; compare Jas 5:4.) Jesus Christ included the injunction against fraud among the "commandments" of God. (Mr 10:19) Under the Law covenant, if a man defrauded his associate and later repented and brought the matter to light, confessing it, he was required to restore the full amount plus one fifth of it to the person injured, as well as to offer a guilt offering to Jehovah.—Le 6:1-7.

False forms of religion likewise are considered fraudulent in the Scriptures. Paul's sharp denunciation of Elymas the sorcerer resulted in Elymas' being struck with blindness because of the fraud and villainy he had practiced by "distorting the right ways of Jehovah." (Ac 13:8-11) Paul also corrected Christians in Corinth who were taking one another to court, stating that they were wronging and defrauding their brothers by this action of going to court before unrighteous men and not before the holy ones in the congregation. They should rather suffer being defrauded than to take such matters before men of the world. —1Co 6:1-8.

The Bible frequently warns against fraud and fraudulent practices and denounces them, also pointing out that God will judge defrauders and will deliver his people from such ones.—Ps 62: 10; 72:4; 103:6; Pr 14:31; 22:16; 28:16; Mic 2: 1, 2; Mal 3:5.

FREEDMAN, FREEMAN.

During Roman rule, one who was emancipated from slavery was called a "freedman" (Gr., a·pe·leu'the·ros), whereas a "freeman" (Gr., e·leu'the·ros) was free from birth, possessing full citizenship rights, as did the apostle Paul.—Ac 22:28.

Formal emancipation granted the freedman Roman citizenship, but such former slave was not eligible for political office, although his descendants were, in the second or at least the third generation. Informal emancipation, however, gave merely practical freedom to the individual, not civic rights.—See CITIZEN, CITIZENSHIP.

Since the freedman was viewed as belonging to the family of his former master, a mutual obligation rested upon the two parties. The freedman either remained in the home and in the employ of his former master or received a farm and capital to get started in making his own living. The patron buried his freedman, when deceased, in the family tomb, took charge of any surviving minor children, and inherited the property if there were no heirs. On the other hand, if the patron suffered financial reverses, his freedman was required by law to care for him. But the rights of a former master in relation to his freedman could not be passed on to his heirs.

It has been suggested that those who belonged to the "Synagogue of the Freedmen [literally, Libertines]" were Jews who had been taken captive by the Romans and then later were emancipated. Another view is that these persons were freed slaves who had become Jewish proselytes. The reading in the Armenian Version presents these persons as "Libyans," that is, persons from Libya.—Ac 6:9.

As indicated by the Scriptures, although a Christian may be a slave to an earthly master, he is actually Christ's *freedman*, liberated from bondage to sin and death. But having been bought with a price, Jesus' precious blood, a Christian who is a *freeman* in a physical sense is a slave of God and of Jesus Christ, obligated to obey their commands. This indicates that for humans freedom is always relative, never absolute. Therefore, from God's viewpoint, in the Christian congregation there is no difference between slave and freeman. Moreover, the freedom possessed by a Christian does not entitle him to use this as a blind for badness.—1Co 7:22, 23; Ga 3:28; Heb 2:14, 15; 1Pe 1:18, 19; 2:16.

FREEDOM.

Since Jehovah God is the Almighty, the Sovereign Ruler of the universe, and the Creator of all things, he alone has absolute, unlimited freedom. (Ge 17:1; Jer 10:7, 10; Da 4:34, 35; Re 4:11) All others must move and act within the limitations of ability given them and subject themselves to his universal laws. (Isa 45:9; Ro 9:20, 21) For example, consider gravity, and the laws governing chemical reactions, influence of the sun, and growth; the moral laws; the rights and actions of others that influence one's freedom. The freedom of all of God's creatures is therefore a relative freedom.

There is a distinction between limited freedom and bondage. Freedom within God-given limitations brings happiness; bondage to creatures, to imperfection, to weaknesses, or to wrong ideologies brings oppression and unhappiness. Freedom is also to be differentiated from self-determination, that is, ignoring God's laws and determining for oneself what is right and what is wrong. Such leads to encroachments on the rights of others and causes trouble, as can be seen from the effects of the independent, self-willed spirit introduced to Adam and Eve by the Serpent in Eden. (Ge 3:4, 6, 11-19) True freedom is bounded by law, God's law, which allows full expression of the individual in a proper, upbuilding, and beneficial way, and which recognizes the rights of others, contributing to happiness for all.—Ps 144:15; Lu 11:28; Jas 1:25.

The God of Freedom. Jehovah is the God of freedom. He freed the nation of Israel from bondage in Egypt. He told them that as long as they obeyed his commandments they would have freedom from want. (De 15:4, 5) David spoke of "freedom from care" within the dwelling towers of Jerusalem. (Ps 122:6, 7) However, the Law provided that in case a man became poor he could sell himself into slavery so as to provide the necessities for himself and his family. But freedom was granted by the Law to this Hebrew in the seventh year of his servitude. (Ex 21:2) In the Jubilee (occurring every 50th year), liberty was proclaimed in the land to all its inhabitants. Every Hebrew slave was freed, and each man was returned to his land inheritance.—Le 25:10-19.

The Freedom That Comes Through Christ. The apostle Paul spoke of the need of humankind to be set free from "enslavement to corruption." (Ro 8:21) Jesus Christ told Jews who had believed in him: "If you remain in my word, you are really my disciples, and you will know the truth, and the truth will set you free." To those who thought they had freedom just because they were Abraham's fleshly descendants, he pointed out that they were slaves of sin, and he said: "Therefore if the Son sets you free, you will be actually free." —Joh 8:31-36; compare Ro 6:18, 22.

The Christian Greek Scriptures speak of the followers of Christ as being free. Paul showed that they were "children, not of a servant girl, but of the free woman" (Ga 4:31), whom he refers to as being "the Jerusalem above." (Ga 4:26) He then exhorts: "For such freedom [or, "With her freedom," ftn] Christ set us free. Therefore stand fast, and do not let yourselves be confined again in a yoke of slavery." (Ga 5:1) At that time certain men falsely claiming to be Christian had associated themselves with the Galatian congregations. They were making an effort to induce the Galatian Christians to give up their freedom in Christ by trying to gain righteousness by works of the Law, instead of by faith in Christ. Paul warned that they would thereby fall away from Christ's undeserved kindness.—Ga 5:2-6; 6:12, 13.

The freedom that the early Christians enjoyed from bondage to sin and death and from fear ("For God gave us not a spirit of cowardice, but that of power and of love and of soundness of mind") was exemplified in the outspokenness and freeness of speech of the apostles in proclaiming the good news. (2Ti 1:7; Ac 4:13; Php 1:18-20) They recognized this freeness of speech about the Christ to be a valuable possession, one that must be developed, guarded, and maintained in order to receive God's approval. It was also a suitable subject of prayer.—1Ti 3:13; Heb 3:6; Eph 6:18-20.

Proper Use of Christian Freedom. The inspired Christian writers, appreciating God's purpose in extending undeserved kindness through Christ ("You were, of course, called for freedom, brothers"), repeatedly counseled Christians to guard their freedom and not to take license or wrongful advantage of that freedom as an opportunity to indulge in works of the flesh (Ga 5:13) or as a blind for badness. (1Pe 2:16) James spoke of 'peering into the perfect law that belongs to freedom' and pointed out that the one who was not a forgetful hearer, but persisted as a *doer*, would be happy.—Jas 1:25.

The apostle Paul enjoyed the freedom he had gained through Christ but refrained from using his freedom to please himself or from exercising it to the point of hurting others. In his letter to the congregation at Corinth, he showed that he would not injure another person's conscience by doing something that he had the Scriptural freedom to do but that might be questioned by another with less knowledge, whose conscience might be offended by Paul's acts. He cites as an example the eating of meat offered before an idol prior to being put in the market to be sold. Eating such meat might cause one with a weak conscience to criticize Paul's proper freedom of action and thereby to act as a judge of Paul, which would be wrong. Therefore, Paul said: "Why should it be that my freedom is judged by another person's conscience? If I am partaking with thanks, why am I to be spoken of abusively over that for which I give thanks?" Nonetheless, the apostle was determined to exercise his freedom in an upbuilding, not a detrimental, way.—1Co 10:23-33.

The Christian's Fight and Mankind's Hope. Paul shows that there is a danger to the Christian's freedom in that, whereas "the law of that spirit which gives life in union with Christ Jesus has set you free from the law of sin and of death" (Ro 8:1, 2), the law of sin and of death working in the Christian's body fights to bring one into bondage again. Therefore the Christian must set his mind on the things of the spirit in order to win.—Ro 7:21-25; 8:5-8.

After outlining the Christian conflict, Paul goes on to speak of the joint heirs with Christ as "sons of God." Then he refers to others of mankind as "the creation" and presents the marvelous purpose of God "that the creation itself also will be set free from enslavement to corruption and have the glorious freedom of the children of God."—Ro 8:12-21.

Figurative Use. When Job, in his suffering, wished to find release in death, he likened death to a freedom for those afflicted. He evidently alludes to the hard lives of slaves, saying: "[In death] the slave is set free from his master." —Job 3:19; compare verses 21 and 22.

FREE WOMAN.
A woman who is not in slavery. This term is used with reference to Abraham's wife Sarah and "the Jerusalem above." From the time that Jehovah God liberated the Israelites from Egyptian bondage and gave them the Law at Mount Sinai till the termination of the Law covenant in 33 C.E., Jehovah treated the nation of Israel as a secondary wife. (Jer 3:14; 31:31, 32) However, the Law did not give the nation of Israel the status of a free woman, for it showed the Israelites up as under subjection to sin, hence slaves. Most appropriately, therefore, Paul compared the enslaved Jerusalem of his day with the servant girl Hagar, Abraham's concubine, and Jerusalem's "children," or citizens, with Hagar's son Ishmael. In contrast, God's original wife, the Jerusalem above, has, like Sarah, always been a free woman, and her children are likewise free. To become a free child of the Jerusalem above, having "her freedom," it is necessary to be set free by the Son of God from the bondage of sin.—Ga 4:22–5:1 and ftn on 5:1; Joh 8:34-36.

FRIEND.
The Bible describes a true friend as a person who sticks closer than a brother, is constant in his loyalty and friendliness, comes to the aid of his companion in distress, and gives counsel to him in faithfulness. (Pr 18:24; 17:17; 27:6, 9) On the other hand, those who are rich and those who give presents have many friends who are interested only in the selfish benefits derived from the friendship. (Pr 14:20; 19:4, 6, 7) Appropriately Jesus Christ counseled not to invite to an evening meal friends who can repay, but to invite persons who cannot repay. (Lu 14:12-14) Jesus himself set the example in this regard by helping spiritually those looked down upon. For this he was labeled "a friend of tax collectors and sinners." (Mt 11:19) But Jesus indicated that only those obeying his commands

were his real friends. He demonstrated his love for them by surrendering his soul in their behalf and encouraged them to love one another likewise.—Joh 15:12-14.

First-century Christians referred to fellow believers in general as "friends." (3Jo 14) Yet this does not rule out one's being closer to some in the Christian congregation than to others, either because of family relationships, closer association by reason of circumstances, similar backgrounds or interests, simple compatibility of personalities, or because of fine Christian qualities that one has discerned by experiencing association with them. There were certain qualities in Peter, James, and John that caused Jesus to associate these disciples with him in many privileges, such as having them witness the transfiguration scene. In this Jesus may have been looking to the future as to the things he had in mind for these three men, the things he knew he would use them to do in his service.—Mr 9:1-10; 14:32, 33; Lu 8:51.

While, like Jesus, the Christian manifests love toward mankind in general, rightly he accords the kind of love that goes with friendship only to those who are friends of God. The propriety of this is emphasized by the question put to King Jehoshaphat: "Is it to the wicked that help is to be given, and is it for those hating Jehovah that you should have love?" (2Ch 19:2) Persons desiring to be friends of the world make themselves enemies of God.—Jas 4:4.

The most outstanding human friendship recorded in the Hebrew Scriptures was that of David and Jonathan. Although Jonathan was the natural heir to the throne of his father Saul, he did not hate David and come to view him as a rival, but he recognized that Jehovah's favor was on David. So "Jonathan's very soul became bound up with the soul of David, and Jonathan began to love him as his own soul." (1Sa 18:1) After Jonathan's death in battle, David greatly lamented the loss of his friend, saying: "I am distressed over you, my brother Jonathan, very pleasant you were to me. More wonderful was your love to me than the love from women." (2Sa 1:26) This friendship was possible because both David and Jonathan placed loyalty to Jehovah God above everything else.

In sharp contrast, because of the moral corruption in his day the prophet Micah was obliged to warn: "Do not put your trust in a confidential friend." (Mic 7:5) Jesus also indicated that even onetime friends of his followers would turn against them and have them delivered up to be put to death.—Lu 21:16; see LOVE.

Friend of God. Among the divine blessings bestowed upon Abraham was the privilege and honor of being called "Jehovah's friend [or, lover]." This was by reason of Abraham's outstanding faith, which he demonstrated to the greatest degree possible in his willingness to offer up his son Isaac as a sacrifice.—Isa 41:8, ftn; 2Ch 20:7; Jas 2:21-23; see DECLARE RIGHTEOUS.

By proper use of "unrighteous riches" it is possible to make friends with Jehovah God and his Son, who can receive one into "the everlasting dwelling places," as pointed out by Jesus Christ in his illustration about the unrighteous steward. (Lu 16:1-13) Jesus did, in fact, call his disciples his friends, and they were therefore also the friends of his Father. (Joh 15:13-15; 14:21) The requirements for being a guest in Jehovah's tent as one of his friends are outlined in Psalm 15:1-5.

In contrast, friendship with the world constitutes enmity with God. (Jas 4:4; 1Jo 2:15-17) Mankind as a whole is alienated from and at enmity with God. However, reconciliation is possible, but only through Jesus Christ and the ministry of reconciliation with which God has entrusted his Son's ambassadors. Ultimately life everlasting will be the exclusive possession of the friends of God.—2Co 5:18-20; Re 21:3, 4; Ps 37:29.

Friend (Companion) of the King. In using this expression, the Bible does not indicate that it had more than the usual connotation of one who is friendly or a companion. Neither does it directly describe the specific functions of the friend of the king as an official title. However, based on the customs of other lands, it may be that the expression designated a court official who was a confidant, a personal friend, and a companion to a king and who at times executed confidential orders.—Ge 26:26.

Among Solomon's court dignitaries, listed at 1 Kings 4:1-6, are two sons of Nathan. One is mentioned as being "over the deputies," whereas the other, Zabud, is called "the friend of the king." In the reign of Solomon's father, King David, Hushai the Archite is spoken of as having this relationship to King David, being called "David's companion." At David's request, Hushai returned to Jerusalem to frustrate the counsel of Ahithophel when Absalom conspired to usurp the throne.—2Sa 15:32-37; 16:16-19.

Among the old Egyptian kings, there were several ranks of king's "friends." The title did not indicate anything exclusive but was merely an honorary designation for officials whose real duties were indicated by other titles. 'Friends to the king' were also frequently mentioned in connection with the Grecian Empire. There the king conferred with a definite body of these friends before making decisions on important matters. The office existed in Persia, Arabia, and Ethiopia.

Friend of the Bridegroom. In times past, a man of the bridegroom's close acquaintances acted as a legal representative of the bridegroom and took the primary responsibility in making arrangements for the marriage. He would sometimes arrange the espousal with the parents of the bride, delivering the bride-price to the father and gifts to the bride. He was viewed as bringing together the bride and groom. The bridal procession would arrive at the house of the bridegroom's father or at the bridegroom's house, where the marriage feast was celebrated. There the bridegroom and bride would come together. At the feast, on hearing the bridegroom speak to the bride, the friend of the bridegroom was happy, feeling that his duty was successfully concluded.—Joh 3:29.

John the Baptizer, who prepared the way for the Messiah, introduced the first members of the "bride" to Jesus Christ, to whom she was espoused. (2Co 11:2; Eph 5:22-27; Re 21:2, 9) John could therefore say: "You yourselves bear me witness that I said, I am not the Christ, but, I have been sent forth in advance of that one. He that has the bride is the bridegroom. However, the friend of the bridegroom, when he stands and hears him, has a great deal of joy on account of the voice of the bridegroom. Therefore this joy of mine has been made full." Just as the friend of the bridegroom had accomplished his objective at this point and was no longer a principal figure, so John said of himself in relation to Jesus Christ: "That one must go on increasing, but I must go on decreasing."—Joh 3:27-30.

"Friends of the bridegroom" are mentioned at Matthew 9:15. Here reference is made to other friends who joined in the marriage procession and who were invited to the marriage feast.

FROG [Heb., *tsephar·de·aʹ*; Gr., *ba·traʹkhos*]. A tailless amphibian with smooth skin and long, muscular hind legs ideally suited for leaping. In the Hebrew Scriptures frogs are mentioned solely in connection with the second blow Jehovah visited upon Egypt (Ex 8:1-14; Ps 78:45; 105:30), which, like the other plagues, was a judgment on the deities worshiped in that land. (Ex 12:12) The frog was sacred to Heqt, an Egyptian goddess depicted with the head of this creature.

At Revelation 16:13 "unclean inspired expres-

sions" are likened to frogs. This is appropriate, inasmuch as frogs were unclean for food according to the Mosaic Law.—Le 11:12.

FRONTLET BAND. A band worn on the forehead.

Although the Israelites were told that they should 'tie God's law as a sign upon their hand' and have it as a 'frontlet band between their eyes,' this evidently did not refer to the literal wearing of Scripture texts. (De 6:6-8; 11:18) True, they were instructed to wear a literal fringe upon their garments as a reminder of God's commandments. (Nu 15:38-40) However, the evidence that the "sign" and "frontlet band" were to be figurative can be seen from God's instructions to the Israelites concerning their commemoration of his deliverance of them. This commemoration was also to serve "as a sign upon your hand and as a memorial between your eyes" and "as a frontlet band between your eyes."—Ex 13:9, 14-16.

In what sense were Israelites to wear God's law as a frontlet band between their eyes?

It appears that Jehovah meant that the Law should be kept as distinctly in view and should be as carefully attended to as if it were written on a tablet between their eyes, and as if it were a sign upon their hands, so that, wherever they looked and whatever they did, they could not fail to have the Law before them. However, the Jews, sometime after their return from Babylon, developed a formalistic religion based on traditions of men (Mt 15:3, 9), in which they gave this law a literal application. Strips of parchment were used, on which four passages of Scripture were written, namely Exodus 13:1-10, 11-16; Deuteronomy 6:4-9; 11:13-21. At least in later times, the parchment was rolled up in small cases of calfskin and fastened to the forehead and the left arm. Male Jews wore these during morning prayer, except on festival days and the Sabbath.

Jesus Christ condemned the hypocrisy of the scribes and Pharisees, who, in order to impress others with their righteousness, broadened the scripture-containing cases that they wore as safeguards. (Mt 23:2, 5) The Greek word *phy·la·kteʹri·on*, "phylactery," which applies to such a scripture-containing case, means primarily an outpost, fortification, or safeguard. These were worn, therefore, as a safeguard, amulet, or charm.

However, the Bible counsels that the thing to guard is, not beautiful or pious outward appearance, but the heart. (Mt 23:27, 28; Pr 4:23) It stresses that what will greatly benefit a person is, not the wearing of written Scripture texts on the body, but the safeguarding of practical wisdom and thinking ability and the acquiring of understanding.—Pr 3:21, 22; 4:7-9.

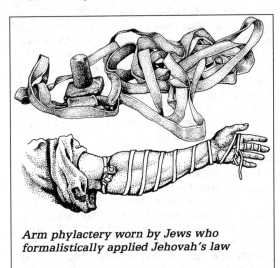

Arm phylactery worn by Jews who formalistically applied Jehovah's law

FUEL. Literally, "food" for fire. (Isa 9:5, 19; Eze 15:4) Charcoal (Isa 47:14; Joh 18:18), sticks (Jer 7:18), rushes (Job 41:20), thorns (Ec 7:6), wood (Jos 9:27; Isa 44:14-16), as well as vines (Eze 15:6), are among the fuels specifically mentioned in the Bible. Additionally, olive oil was a fuel commonly used in lamps. (Ex 27:20; Mt 25:3, 4) Wood, in its natural state or in the form of charcoal, was likely the main fuel of the Israelites. For heating purposes charcoal was commonly burned in a brazier. (Jer 36:22) At other times it was burned without a container, as was undoubtedly the case when Jesus Christ, after his resurrection, prepared breakfast over a charcoal fire.—Joh 21:9, 10; see CHARCOAL.

To depict the severity of Jerusalem's siege, Ezekiel was instructed to use human excrement for fuel, but when he objected, Jehovah permitted him to use cakes of cattle dung instead. (Eze 4:8, 12-15) Although dried cattle dung is today used by some persons in the Middle East because of the scarcity of wood, this does not necessarily mean that the Israelites ordinarily used it, especially since ancient Palestine was more heavily wooded than it is now.

FUGITIVENESS, LAND OF. A land "east of Eden," in which the condemned murderer Cain took up residence. (Ge 4:16) The Hebrew word *nohdh* (fugitiveness) is derived from the root word *nudh*, a form of which is rendered "fugitive" in verses 12 and 14. The location of the land is unknown.

FUNERAL. See BURIAL, BURIAL PLACES.

FURLONG. The Greek word (*sta'di·on*) thus translated denotes a linear measure equal to 185 m (625 Roman ft; 606.75 English ft) or ⅛ Roman mile. (The Roman mile equals 1,479.5 m; 4,854 ft.) (Re 14:20; 21:16) This is the approximate length of both the Attic and the Roman stadium. This is different from the modern furlong of 201 m (660 ft). At 1 Corinthians 9:24 the term *sta'di·on* (stadium) is rendered "race," the length of the Greek racecourse being one stadium. The stadium of the Olympic course, however, was actually 192 m (630 ft).

FURNACE. A structure designed principally for (1) smelting ores, (2) melting previously smelted metals for casting or heating them for forging, and (3) firing pottery and other ceramic items. Furnaces in Bible times were constructed of brick or stone. Circular copper furnaces believed to date from the period of the Judges were found at Tell Qasileh on the northern outskirts of Tel Aviv-Yafo and at Tell Jemmeh (Tel Gamma), S of Gaza. These furnaces were equipped with large mud-brick flues designed to lead air into the fire chamber. Clay crucibles containing copper were set on top of the stone tiles that were placed on the ashes of the fire inside the furnace.

Daniel's three faithful Hebrew companions were thrown into a fiery furnace by Nebuchadnezzar for refusing to bow down before the golden image the king had erected. (Da 3) Whether this was a special furnace constructed for such purpose or whether it was a furnace normally used for other common purposes, the record does not state.

The term "furnace" may also be used to refer to an "oven" for baking bread.—Ho 7:4; Le 2:4.

Figuratively, Egypt, which confined Israel in a harsh yoke of slavery, is compared to an iron furnace. (De 4:20) Also, the outpouring of God's anger upon the house of Israel is likened to the liquefying of metal in a furnace. (Eze 22:18-22) For other uses of the word for comparative or illustrative purposes, see Proverbs 17:3; 27:21; Psalm 12:6 ("smelting furnace").—See KILN; OVEN; REFINE, REFINER.

G

GAAL (Ga'al) [possibly, Abhorring; Abhorred]. The son of Ebed who, along with his brothers, came to Shechem and gained the confidence of the landowners there. (Jg 9:26) These landowners had previously strengthened the hand of Abimelech to kill the sons of Jerubbaal (Gideon) and then proceeded to make him king over them. (Jg 9:1-6) Apparently Abimelech constituted Zebul as resident prince of Shechem, while he himself personally lived in Arumah. In time, a bad spirit developed between Abimelech and the landowners of Shechem. So Gaal and his brothers now incited the city to revolt against Abimelech. When Zebul heard of this, he at once sent word to Abimelech, with a recommendation on how to cope with the situation that was developing. Gaal and those with him were defeated in the ensuing battle with King Abimelech and fled back to the city. Finally Zebul drove Gaal and his brothers out of Shechem.—Jg 9:22-41.

GAASH (Ga'ash) [possibly, Shaking; Shaken]. The name of a hill in the mountainous region of Ephraim, S of Timnath-heres (or Timnath-serah). (Jos 24:30; Jg 2:9) The torrent valleys of Gaash, mentioned in 2 Samuel 23:30 and 1 Chronicles 11:32, apparently refer to ravines in the vicinity of that hill.

GABBAI (Gab·ba'i). A Benjamite jurisdictional district head whose name appears in a listing of those residing in Jerusalem in Nehemiah's day.—Ne 11:3, 7, 8.

GABBATHA. See STONE PAVEMENT.

GABRIEL (Ga'bri·el) [Able-Bodied One of God]. The only holy angel other than Michael named in the Bible; the only materialized angel to give his name. Twice Gabriel appeared to Daniel: first, near the Ulai River "in the third year of the kingship of Belshazzar" to explain Daniel's vision of the he-goat and the ram (Da 8:1, 15-26); and second, "in the first year of Darius" the Mede, to deliver the prophecy concerning the "seventy weeks." (Da 9:1, 20-27) To Zechariah the priest, Gabriel brought the good news that he and his aging wife Elizabeth would have a son, John (the Baptizer). (Lu 1:11-20) To Mary, the virgin girl betrothed to Joseph, Gabriel declared: "Good day, highly favored one, Jehovah

is with you." He then told her that she would give birth to a son, Jesus—he "will be called Son of the Most High; and Jehovah God will give him the throne of David his father, . . . and there will be no end of his kingdom."—Lu 1:26-38.

From the Bible record it is learned that Gabriel is a high-ranking angelic creature in close association with the heavenly court, one "who stands near before God"; that he was one "sent forth" by God to deliver special messages to servants of Jehovah here on earth (Lu 1:19, 26); that his personal envisioned or materialized form was, true to the meaning of his name, "like an able-bodied man."—Da 8:15.

GAD [Good Fortune].

1. Son of Jacob by Leah's maidservant Zilpah, who also bore Gad's younger brother Asher. At his birth in Paddan-aram about 1770 B.C.E., Leah exclaimed: "With good fortune!"; hence the name Gad. (Ge 30:9-13; 35:26) Gad accompanied his brothers on two trips to Egypt to get grain from Joseph. (Ge 42:3; 43:15) He was about 42 years old when he and his family moved to Egypt along with his father Jacob in 1728 B.C.E. (Ge 46:6, 7, 16) Seventeen years later, when Jacob was about to die, he blessed his 12 sons, saying of Gad: "As for Gad, a marauder band will raid him, but he will raid the extreme rear."—Ge 49:1, 2, 19.

2. The tribe that sprang from the seven sons of Gad. The tribe's warriors numbered 45,650 in the second year after the Exodus from Egypt. (Ge 46:16; Nu 1:1-3, 24, 25) Gad was in the three-tribe division with Reuben and Simeon. Their campsite was to the S of the tabernacle. (Nu 2:10-16) When on the march Judah's division was first, followed by the Levites of the families of Gershon and Merari carrying the tabernacle, and after them came the division of which Gad was a part. Eliasaph son of Deuel was chieftain of their army. (Nu 10:14-20) At the end of the wilderness journey, the fighting men of Gad numbered but 40,500, a decrease of 5,150.—Nu 26:15-18.

Territory. The men of the tribe of Gad followed the occupation of their fathers as raisers of livestock. (Ge 46:32) For this reason they requested as their allotment of territory the cattle country E of the Jordan. Moses responded by assigning this territory to Gad, Reuben, and half the tribe of Manasseh, who also possessed much livestock. However, Moses stipulated that this was on the condition that these tribes would assist the others in subduing the territory W of the Jordan. To this they readily agreed, and after constructing stone pens for their livestock and cities for their little ones, they supplied their quota of fighters to cross the Jordan for the conquest of the land. (Nu 32:1-36; Jos 4:12, 13) Gad's territory had been occupied by the Amorites, whom the Israelites had defeated under Moses' leadership.—Nu 32:33; De 2:31-36; 3: 8-20.

The country occupied by Gad was comprised of the lowlands along most of the Jordan River's E bank, S almost to the Dead Sea, and N to near the Sea of Chinnereth. Gad's territory also took in the higher tablelands, including the torrent valley of Jabbok. A large part of Gilead was therefore in Gad's allotment. (De 3:12, 13) Gad was bordered on the N by Manasseh and on the S by Reuben. —Jos 13:24-28.

After the conquest of the land, Joshua gave Gad a share in the spoil and sent them back. Gad then joined with Reuben and Manasseh in constructing a great altar by the Jordan. The other tribes were alarmed at this but were calmed when it was explained that the altar was built as a witness that they, like the tribes W of the Jordan, would engage exclusively in the worship of Jehovah. The altar was to provide assurance that there was no division between the tribes E and W of the Jordan.—Jos 22:1-34.

All these things were in harmony with Jacob's blessing of Gad: "As for Gad, a marauder band will raid him, but he will raid the extreme rear." (Ge 49:19) The tribe was not afraid to have one side (the E) of their boundary open to marauder bands. They did not choose to live on the eastern highlands just to get out of fighting for the land of Canaan. Jacob's parting words to Gad were as a command to strike back confidently at marauders attacking him and violating his borders. Moreover, the Gadites raided the raiders, making these turn about in flight, and then the Gadites would pursue their extreme rear.

Moses also spoke of Gad's good qualities when he said: "Blessed is the one widening the borders of Gad. As a lion he must reside, and he must tear the arm, yes, the crown of the head. And he will pick out the first part for himself, for there the allotment of a statute-giver is reserved. And the heads of the people will gather themselves

together. The righteousness of Jehovah will he certainly execute and his judicial decisions with Israel."—De 33:20, 21.

Ramoth of Gilead, in Gad's territory, was one of the cities of refuge appointed by Moses. (De 4:41-43) Other Levite cities in their territory were Mahanaim, Heshbon, and Jazer. (Jos 21:38, 39) The city of Dibon, where the famous Moabite Stone was found in 1868 C.E., was one of several cities rebuilt by the Gadites when they took over the territory.—Nu 32:1-5, 34, 35.

Gad Gave David Support. When David was under restrictions because of Saul, several army heads of the sons of Gad crossed the Jordan River at flood stage to come to his side at Ziklag in Judah. They are described as "valiant, mighty men, army men for the war, keeping the large shield and the lance ready, whose faces were the faces of lions, and they were like the gazelles upon the mountains for speed. . . . The least one was equal to a hundred, and the greatest to a thousand." (1Ch 12:1, 8-15) In the fight with the Hagrites and their allies, it is said of them (along with Reuben and Manasseh): "It was to God that they called for aid in the war, and he let himself be entreated in their favor because they trusted in him." As a result, an enormous number of captives and much livestock fell into their hands. —1Ch 5:18-22.

Followed Jeroboam. With the division of the kingdom, the tribe of Gad supported the northern faction under Jeroboam. Years later, in Jehu's day, when "Jehovah started to cut off Israel piece by piece," Gad in its exposed position on the eastern frontier became part of the battleground between the northern kingdom of Israel and Syria. (2Ki 10:32, 33) Finally, Tiglath-pileser III, king of Assyria, overran Gad and carried off the inhabitants captive. This allowed the Ammonites to take possession of this territory.—2Ki 15:29; 1Ch 5:26; Jer 49:1.

In Ezekiel's prophetic vision of the division of the land, the portion assigned to Gad is in the extreme S. (Eze 48:27, 28) In the listing of the tribes of Israel in Revelation chapter 7, Gad is named third.

3. A prophet and visionary. He advised David, when he was dwelling in "the inaccessible place" in the cave of Adullam as a fugitive from Saul, to return to Judah. (1Sa 22:1-5) When David presumptuously took a census toward the latter part of his reign, Jehovah by means of Gad gave David three alternative punishments. Gad later advised David to build an altar for Jehovah on the threshing floor of Araunah (Ornan). (2Sa 24:10-19; 1Ch 21:9-19) Gad was partially responsible for the organization of the musicians for the sanctuary. (2Ch 29:25) Nathan and Gad are generally credited with completing First Samuel and writing all of Second Samuel.—1Ch 29:29.

GADARENES (Gad·a·renes') [Of (Belonging to) Gadara]. The name applied to the inhabitants of an area where Christ Jesus expelled demons from two men. According to what is considered to be the best available manuscript evidence, Matthew originally used "country of the Gadarenes," whereas Mark and Luke, in relating this event, employed "country of the Gerasenes." —Mt 8:28; Mr 5:1; Lu 8:26.

Both countries are shown to lie on "the other side," that is, the E side, of the Sea of Galilee. The designation "country of the Gadarenes" possibly applied to the district radiating from the city of Gadara (modern Umm Qeis), situated about 10 km (6 mi) SE of the Sea of Galilee. Coins of Gadara often depict a ship, suggesting that its territory may have extended as far as the Sea of Galilee and therefore could have included at least a part of "the country of the Gerasenes," to the E of that body of water. Scholars favoring this view link "the country of the Gerasenes" with the region around Kursi, a town near the E coast of the Sea of Galilee and about 19 km (12 mi) N of Gadara. However, others believe that "the country of the Gerasenes" may denote the large district centered at the city of Gerasa (Jarash) about 55 km (34 mi) SSE of the Sea of Galilee and suggest that it extended to the E of that lake and embraced "the country of the Gadarenes." In either case, Matthew's account would in no way conflict with that of Mark and Luke.

Near an unnamed city in the country of the Gadarenes, Jesus Christ met two unusually fierce demon-possessed men. These had their dwelling among the tombs, that is, rock-cut tombs or natural caves used as such. Jesus, in expelling the demons, permitted them to take possession of a large herd of swine that subsequently rushed over a precipice and drowned in the Sea of Galilee. This so disturbed the local inhabitants that they entreated Jesus to depart from the area.—Mt 8:28-34.

While Matthew mentions two men, Mark (5:2) and Luke (8:27) center attention on only one, doubtless because his case was more outstanding. Possibly he was more violent and had suffered much longer under demon control than the

other man; yet afterward perhaps he alone wanted to accompany the Son of God. Jesus did not allow him to do so, directing him instead to make known what God had done in his behalf.

This differed from Jesus' usual instructions not to have his miracles advertised. Instead of seeking showy publicity and having people reach conclusions on the basis of sensational reports, Jesus apparently wanted others to decide on solid evidence that he was indeed the Christ. This also fulfilled the prophetic words spoken through Isaiah: "He will not wrangle, nor cry aloud, nor will anyone hear his voice in the broad ways." (Mt 12:15-21; Isa 42:1-4) However, the exception in the case of the former demoniac was appropriate. He could bear witness among people with whom the Son of God would have only limited contact, particularly in view of Jesus' being requested to leave. The man's presence would provide testimony about Jesus' power to work good, counteracting any unfavorable report that might be circulated over the loss of the herd of swine. —Mr 5:1-20; Lu 8:26-39; see SWINE.

GADDI (Gad'di) [possibly from a root meaning "good fortune"]. Son of Susi of the tribe of Manasseh; one of the 12 chieftains Moses sent out from the wilderness of Paran to spy out the land of Canaan.—Nu 13:2, 3, 11.

GADDIEL (Gad'di·el) [Good Fortune of [from] God]. Son of Sodi of the tribe of Zebulun; one of the 12 chieftains sent out by Moses from the wilderness of Paran to spy out the land of Canaan.—Nu 13:2, 3, 10.

GADFLY [Heb., 'a·rov']. There is some uncertainty as to the particular insect designated by the original Hebrew word appearing in the Scriptures with reference to the fourth plague upon Egypt, the first from which the Israelites in Goshen were spared. (Ex 8:21, 22, 24, 29, 31; Ps 78:45; 105:31) 'A·rov' has been variously rendered "gadfly" (JB, NW, Ro), "beetle" (Yg), "flies" (AS, KJ, RS), "gnats" (AT), and "dog fly" (LXX).

The English designation "gadfly" includes the various kinds of horseflies and botflies. Female horseflies pierce the skin of animals as well as man and then suck their blood. In the larval stage botflies live as parasites in the bodies of animals and man; those that infest humans are found in the tropics. A plague of gadflies would, therefore, have brought great suffering to the Egyptians and their livestock and, in certain cases, even death.

GADI (Ga'di) [from a root meaning "good fortune"]. Father of Israel's King Menahem.—2Ki 15:14, 17.

GADITES. See GAD No. 2.

GAHAM (Ga'ham). A son of Abraham's brother Nahor by his concubine Reumah.—Ge 22:23, 24.

GAHAR (Ga'har). A Nethinim family head, some of whose descendants returned with Zerubbabel from Babylonian exile in 537 B.C.E. —Ezr 2:1, 2, 43, 47; Ne 7:49.

GAIUS (Ga'ius) [from a root meaning "land"].

1. A Macedonian who accompanied the apostle Paul on his third missionary tour and who, along with Aristarchus, was forcibly taken into the theater at Ephesus during the riot instigated by the silversmith Demetrius.—Ac 19:29.

2. A Christian from Derbe in Asia Minor who is listed along with six others as accompanying the apostle Paul on his last missionary tour. Gaius and these others evidently separated from Paul and then went on to Troas, on the W coast of Asia Minor, where they waited for him. (Ac 20:4, 5) This Gaius may be the same as No. 1, since Aristarchus is also mentioned in the account. If so, this would likely mean that Gaius was of Macedonian birth (or descent) but had been residing in Derbe.

3. A Christian of Corinth whom Paul personally baptized. When Paul wrote his letter to the Romans, apparently this Gaius was his host as well as that of the congregation. This would indicate that the meetings of the Corinthian congregation were held in Gaius' home.—1Co 1:14; Ro 16:23.

4. A Christian to whom the apostle John wrote his third inspired letter and whom he commended for walking in the truth and, with reference to his hospitality, for his faithful work and his love.—3Jo 1, 3-6.

GALAL (Ga'lal) [Rolling; Rolled Away].

1. A Levite who returned from Babylonian exile.—1Ch 9:14, 15.

2. A Levite referred to as "son of Jeduthun." —1Ch 9:14, 16; Ne 11:17.

GALATIA (Ga·la'ti·a). The Roman province that occupied the central portion of what is now known as Asia Minor. It was bounded by other Roman provinces—in part by Cappadocia on the E, Bithynia and Pontus on the N, Asia on the W, and Pamphylia on the S. (1Pe 1:1) This central

plateau region lay between the Taurus Mountains on the S and the mountains of Paphlagonia on the N. In its north-central portion was the city of Ancyra, now called Ankara, the capital of Turkey. And through this area flowed the middle segment of the Halys River (the modern Kizil Irmak) and the upper Sangarius River (Sakarya), both of which empty into the Black Sea. The history of this region (400 and more years, from the third century B.C.E. forward) shows there were many changes in the boundaries and political affiliations of this strategic area.

It appears that around 278-277 B.C.E. large numbers of Indo-European people known as Celts, or Galli, from Gaul, whom the Greeks called *Ga·la'tai* (hence the name given this region), moved across the Bosporus and settled there. They brought with them their wives and children and apparently avoided intermarrying with the people already there, in this way perpetuating their racial characteristics for centuries. Their last king, Amyntas, died in 25 B.C.E., and it was during his reign as a puppet of the Roman Empire and thereafter that the area designated as Galatia was enlarged to include portions of Lycaonia, Pisidia, Paphlagonia, Pontus, and Phrygia. This then was the expanded Galatia that the apostle Paul and other evangelizing Christians of the first century C.E. visited and in which they found persons eager to be organized into Christian congregations.—Ac 18:23; 1Co 16:1.

Both Paul and Peter addressed letters to Christian congregations located in the province of Galatia. (Ga 1:1, 2; 1Pe 1:1) Whether these were the same congregations established by Paul and Barnabas is not stated. On that swing through Galatia, Paul and Barnabas visited such Galatian cities as Pisidian Antioch, Iconium, Lystra, and Derbe (Ac 13:14, 51; 14:1, 5, 6), and when they returned to the brothers in Antioch of Syria they related how in these and other places God "had opened to the nations the door to faith." (Ac 14:27) One experience they had in Lystra was most unusual. Paul had cured a crippled man who had never walked in his life, and suddenly the crowds began crying out in their native Lycaonian tongue: "The gods have become like humans and have come down to us!" Barnabas they called Zeus and Paul they thought to be Hermes. It was almost more than Paul and Barnabas could do to prevent the excited crowds from offering sacrifices to them as if they were gods.—Ac 14:8-18.

The seeds of Christianity sown among the Galatians bore good fruitage. It was from among them that disciples like Timothy and Gaius came. (Ac 16:1; 20:4) Paul gave instructions to the Galatian congregations as to the manner of laying aside contributions for the Lord's poor and needy ones.—1Co 16:1, 2; Ga 2:10.

GALATIANS, LETTER TO THE.

The inspired letter written in Greek, by Paul an apostle, "to the congregations of Galatia."—Ga 1:1, 2.

Writership. The opening sentence names Paul as the writer of this book. (Ga 1:1) Also, his name is used again in the text, and he refers to himself in the first person. (5:2) A portion of the letter, in the way of an autobiography, speaks of Paul's conversion and some of his other experiences. The references to his affliction in the flesh (4:13, 15) are in harmony with expressions seemingly relating to this affliction in other Bible books. (2Co 12:7; Ac 23:1-5) Paul's other letters were usually written by a secretary, but this one, he says, was written with his "own hand." (Ga 6:11) In his other writings, almost without exception, he sends the greetings of himself and those with him, but in this letter he does not. Had the writer of the letter to the Galatians been an impostor, he would very likely have named a secretary and would have sent some greetings, as Paul usually did. Thus the writer's form of address and his honest direct style vouch for the letter's authenticity. It would not reasonably be fabricated this way.

The letter is not usually contested as being a letter of Paul's except by those who attempt to discredit Paul's writership of all the letters commonly attributed to him. Among evidences from outside the Bible supporting Paul's writership, there is a quotation that Irenaeus (c. 180 C.E.) makes from Galatians and ascribes to Paul.

To Whom Addressed. The question of which congregations were included in the address "the congregations of Galatia" (Ga 1:2) has long been a controversy. In support of the contention that these were unnamed congregations in the northern part of the province of Galatia, it is argued that the people living in this area were ethnically Galatians, whereas those of the S were not. However, Paul in his writings usually gives official Roman names to the provinces, and the province of Galatia in his time included the southern Lycaonian cities of Iconium, Lystra, and Derbe as well as the Pisidian city of Antioch. In all these cities Paul had organized Christian congregations on his first evangelizing tour when he was accompa-

nied by Barnabas. That the congregations in the cities of Iconium, Lystra, Derbe, and Pisidian Antioch were addressed agrees with the way the letter mentions Barnabas, as one apparently known by those to whom Paul was writing. (2:1, 9, 13) There is no indication elsewhere in the Scriptures that Barnabas was known to Christians in the northern part of Galatia or that Paul even made any trips through that territory.

Paul's exclamation, "O senseless Galatians," is no evidence that he had in mind only a certain ethnic people who sprang exclusively from Gallic stock in the northern part of Galatia. (Ga 3:1) Rather, Paul was rebuking certain ones in the congregations there for allowing themselves to be influenced by an element of Judaizers among them, Jews who were attempting to establish their own righteousness through the Mosaic arrangement in place of the 'righteousness due to faith' provided by the new covenant. (2:15–3:14; 4:9, 10) Racially, "the congregations of Galatia" (1:2) to whom Paul wrote were a mixture of Jews and non-Jews, the latter being both circumcised proselytes and non-circumcised Gentiles, and no doubt some were of Celtic descent. (Ac 13:14, 43; 16:1; Ga 5:2) All together, they were addressed as Galatian Christians because the area in which they lived was called Galatia. The whole tenor of the letter is that Paul was writing to those with whom he was well acquainted in the southern part of this Roman province, not to total strangers in the northern sector, which he apparently never visited.

Time of Writing. The period covered by the book is of an undetermined length, but the time of writing has been set between approximately 50 and 52 C.E. It is implied in Galatians 4:13, that Paul made at least two visits to the Galatians before he wrote the letter. Chapters 13 and 14 of the Acts of Apostles describe a visit of Paul and Barnabas to the southern Galatian cities that took place about 47 to 48 C.E. Then, after the conference regarding circumcision in Jerusalem, about 49 C.E., Paul, with Silas, went back to Derbe and Lystra in Galatia and to other cities where Paul and Barnabas had "published the word of Jehovah" (Ac 15:36–16:1) on the first tour. It was evidently after this, while Paul was at another point on his second missionary tour, or else back at his home base, Syrian Antioch, that he received word that prompted him to write to "the congregations of Galatia."

If it was during his year-and-a-half stay in Corinth (Ac 18:1, 11) that Paul wrote this letter, then the time of writing was likely between the autumn of 50 and the spring of 52 C.E., the same general period during which he wrote his canonical letters to the Thessalonians.

If the writing was done during his brief stop in Ephesus or after he got back to Antioch in Syria and "passed some time there" (Ac 18:22, 23), it would have been about 52 C.E. Ephesus is an unlikely place for writing, though, both because of his short stay there and because if Paul had been so close when he heard of the deflection in Galatia, it is to be expected that he would have personally visited the brothers or explained in his letter why it was not possible for him to do so at the time.

What his letter says about the Galatians "being so quickly removed from the One who called [them]" (Ga 1:6) may indicate that the writing of the letter was done soon after Paul had paid a visit to the Galatians. But even if the writing had not taken place until 52 C.E. in Syrian Antioch, it would still have been relatively soon for such a deflection to occur.

Canonicity. Early evidence of the book's canonicity is found in the Muratorian Fragment and in the writings of Irenaeus, Clement of Alexandria, Tertullian, and Origen. These men referred to it by name along with most or all of the other 26 books of the Christian Greek Scriptures. It is mentioned by name in the shortened canon of Marcion and even alluded to by Celsus, who was an enemy of Christianity. All the outstanding lists of the books in the canon of the inspired Scriptures, up to at least the time of the Third Council of Carthage, in 397 C.E., included the book of Galatians. We have it preserved today, along with eight of Paul's other inspired letters, in the Chester Beatty Papyrus No. 2 (P46), a manuscript assigned to about 200 C.E. This gives proof that the early Christians accepted the book of Galatians as one of Paul's letters. Other ancient manuscripts, such as the Sinaitic, Alexandrine, Vatican No. 1209, Codex Ephraemi rescriptus, and Codex Bezae, as well as the Syriac *Peshitta*, likewise include the book of Galatians. Also, it harmonizes completely with Paul's other

---

HIGHLIGHTS OF GALATIANS

A letter emphasizing appreciation for the freedom that true Christians have through Jesus Christ

Written a year or perhaps several years after the Galatians had been informed about the decision of the governing body that circumcision is not required of Christians

Paul defends his apostleship

Paul's apostleship was not of human origin but was by appointment from Jesus Christ and the Father; he did not consult with the apostles in Jerusalem before beginning to declare the good news; not until three years later did he briefly visit Cephas and James (1:1, 13-24)

The good news he proclaimed was received, not from men, but by revelation from Jesus Christ (1:10-12)

By reason of a revelation, Paul, with Barnabas and Titus, went to Jerusalem regarding the circumcision issue; he learned nothing new from James, Peter, and John, but they recognized that he had been empowered for an apostleship to the nations (2:1-10)

At Antioch, when Peter wrongly separated himself from non-Jewish believers in fear of certain visiting brothers from Jerusalem, Paul reproved him (2:11-14)

A person is declared righteous only through faith in Christ, not works of law

If a person could be declared righteous by works of law, Christ's death would have been unnecessary (2:15-21)

Galatians received God's spirit because of their responding in faith to the good news, not because of works of law (3:1-5)

True sons of Abraham are those who have faith like his (3:6-9, 26-29)

Because of being unable to keep the Law perfectly, those seeking to prove themselves righteous by works of the Law are under a curse (3:10-14)

The Law did not invalidate the promise associated with the Abrahamic covenant, but it served to make transgressions manifest and acted as a tutor leading to Christ (3:15-25)

Stand fast in Christian freedom

Jesus Christ, by his death, released those under law, making it possible for them to become sons of God (4:1-7)

Returning to an arrangement of observing days, months, seasons, and years would mean going back into slavery and coming into a position like that of Ishmael, the son of the servant girl Hagar; with his mother he was dismissed from Abraham's household (4:8-31)

Having been liberated from sin and no longer being bound by the Law, they were to resist anyone who would induce them to accept a yoke of slavery (1:6-9; 5:1-12; 6:12-16)

Do not abuse your freedom but yield to the influence of God's spirit, manifesting its fruitage in your life and shunning the works of the flesh (5:13-26)

Readjust in a spirit of mildness anyone taking a false step; but all are individually obligated to carry their own load of responsibility (6:1-5)

writings and with the rest of the Scriptures from which it frequently quotes.

Circumstances Relating to the Letter. The letter reflects many traits of the people of Galatia in Paul's time. Gallic Celts from the N had overrun the region in the third century B.C.E., and therefore Celtic influence was strong in the land. The Celts, or Gauls, were considered a fierce, barbarous people, it having been said that they offered their prisoners of war as human sacrifices. They have also been described in Roman literature as a very emotional, superstitious people, given to much ritual, and this religious trait would likely influence them away from a form of worship so lacking in ritual as Christianity.

Even so, the congregations in Galatia may have included many who formerly had been like this as pagans, as well as many converts from Judaism who had not entirely rid themselves of scrupulously keeping the ceremonies and other obligations of the Mosaic Law. The fickle, inconstant nature attributed to the Galatians of Celtic descent could explain how at one time some in the Galatian congregations were zealous for God's truth and a short time later became an easy prey for opponents of the truth who were sticklers for observance of the Law and who insisted that circumcision and other requirements of the Law were necessary for salvation.

The Judaizers, as such enemies of the truth might be called, apparently kept the circumcision issue alive even after the apostles and other elders in Jerusalem had dealt with the matter. Perhaps, too, some of the Galatian Christians were succumbing to the low moral standards of the populace, as may be inferred from the message of the letter from chapter 5, verse 13, to the end. At any rate, when word of their deflection reached the apostle, he was moved to write this letter of straightforward counsel and strong encouragement. It is evident that his immediate purpose in writing was to confirm his apostleship, counteract the false teachings of the Judaizers, and strengthen the brothers in the Galatian congregations.

The Judaizers were crafty and insincere. (Ac 15:1; Ga 2:4) Claiming to represent the congregation in Jerusalem, these false teachers opposed Paul and discredited his position as an apostle. They wanted the Christians to get circumcised, not seeking the Galatians' best interests, but so that the Judaizers could bring about an appearance of things that would conciliate the Jews and keep them from opposing so violently. The Judaizers did not want to suffer persecution for Christ.—Ga 6:12, 13.

To accomplish their objective, they claimed that Paul's commission came to him secondhand, that it was only from some men prominent in the Christian congregation—not from Christ Jesus himself. (Ga 1:11, 12, 15-20) They wanted the Galatians to follow them (4:17), and in order to nullify Paul's influence, they had to paint him first as no apostle. Apparently they claimed that when Paul felt it expedient, he preached circumcision. (1:10; 5:11) They were trying to make a sort of fusion religion of Christianity and Judaism, not denying Christ outright but arguing that circumcision would profit the Galatians, that it would advance them in Christianity, and that, furthermore, by this they would be sons of Abraham, to whom the covenant of circumcision was originally given.—3:7.

Paul thoroughly refuted the contentions of these false Christians and built up the Galatian brothers so that they could stand firm in Christ. It is encouraging to note that the Galatian congregations did remain true to Christ and stood as pillars of the truth. The apostle Paul visited them on his third missionary tour (Ac 18:23), and the apostle Peter addressed his first letter to the Galatians, among others.—1Pe 1:1.

GALBANUM (gal′ba·num). A yellowish or brownish gum resin procured from certain Asian plants of the carrot, or parsley, family. There is uncertainty as to the precise kind of plant providing the galbanum used by the Israelites.

The milky fluid that hardens into galbanum exudes from the plant stem naturally or its flow is induced by means of an incision. Galbanum was one of the ingredients of the incense specified for exclusive use at the sanctuary. (Ex 30:34-38) When burned alone it is said to give off an offensive odor, but when combined with other aromatic substances, galbanum increases their fragrance and makes the fragrance last longer.

GALEED (Gal′e·ed) [Witness Heap]. The place in the mountainous region of Gilead E of the Jordan where the patriarchs Jacob and Laban concluded a covenant. (Ge 31:43-48) The later name of this region, "Gilead," was probably drawn from "Galeed," the name originally given to the spot where this event occurred about 1761 B.C.E.

In obedience to divine direction, and without giving notice, Jacob left Paddan-aram and the service of Laban, who was both his uncle and his father-in-law. (Ge 28:2) With all his belongings, and with his wives and children, Jacob crossed the Euphrates River and headed for the land of Canaan. After three days Laban, accompanied by his "brothers," went in pursuit for the distance of a seven days' journey, finally overtaking Jacob's caravan in the mountains of Gilead N of the torrent valley of Jabbok.—Ge 31:17-25.

Peaceably settling the points over which they had disputed, Jacob and Laban concluded a covenant with each other. In this connection, Jacob set up a stone pillar and directed his "brothers" to make a heap of stones, perhaps in the form of a table, upon which the covenant meal was eaten. Thereupon, Laban called the place after this heap, giving it the Aramaic (Syrian) name "Jegar-sahadutha," but which Jacob called "Galeed," the Hebrew equivalent. Laban said: "This heap [Heb., gal] is a witness [Heb., 'edh] between me and you today." (Ge 31:44-48) The heap of stones (and the stone pillar) served as a witness to all passersby. It was as verse 49 says, "The Watchtower [Heb., mits·pah']," testifying that Jacob and Laban had agreed to preserve the peace between and within their respective families. (Ge 31:50-53) On later occasions stones were used in a similar fashion as silent witnesses.—Jos 4:4-7; 24:25-27.

GALILEE (Gal'i·lee) [Region; Circuit [from a root meaning "roll; roll away"]], **GALILEAN** (Gal·i·le'an). The first mention of Galilee in the Bible identifies it as a district in the mountainous region of Naphtali, where the city of refuge Kedesh was located. (Jos 20:7) If not earlier, at least by Isaiah's time, Galilee included the territory of Zebulun. Perhaps many non-Israelites lived in Galilee; whence the expression "Galilee of the nations." (Isa 9:1) Some scholars think that the 20 cities of Galilee that King Solomon offered to Hiram the king of Tyre were probably inhabited by pagans. (1Ki 9:10-13; see CABUL No. 2.) The Assyrian king Tiglath-pileser III conquered Galilee during the reign of the Israelite king Pekah (in the eighth century B.C.E.).—2Ki 15:29.

Boundaries. (MAP, Vol. 2, p. 738) Over the years, the territorial boundaries of Galilee did not remain constant. Their greatest extent seems to have been about 100 by 50 km (60 by 30 mi) and embraced the ancient territories of the tribes of Asher, Issachar, Naphtali, and Zebulun. However, during the time of Jesus Christ's earthly ministry, Galilee, while under the jurisdiction of Herod Antipas (Lu 3:1), extended only about 40 km (25 mi) from E to W and about 60 km (37 mi) from N to S.

To the S lay Samaria, Galilee's southern boundary extending from the foot of Mount Carmel along the Plain of Jezreel (Esdraelon) toward Scythopolis (Beth-shean) and then to the Jordan. According to Josephus, the Jordan River, with the Sea of Galilee and Lake Hula (now mostly drained), constituted the eastern boundary, but there may have been areas where that boundary was not so precise. The territory of Tyre, reaching below the ancient city of Kedesh (Kedasa, Cydassa), bounded Galilee on the N. (The Jewish War, III, 35-40 [iii, 1]; II, 459 [xviii, 1]; IV, 104, 105 [ii, 3]) To the W lay the territory of Ptolemais (Acco) and Mount Carmel.

This northerly Roman province of Palestine W of the Jordan was further divided into Upper and Lower Galilee. The boundary between the two Galilees extended from Tiberias on the W bank of the Sea of Galilee to a point in the vicinity of Ptolemais.—The Jewish War, III, 35 (iii, 1).

Geographic Characteristics. In the first century C.E., before the war with Rome, Galilee was densely populated and enjoyed great prosperity. A thriving fishing industry existed at the Sea of Galilee. Other occupations included weaving, stonecutting, shipbuilding, and pottery manufacture. The Jewish historian Josephus claimed there were 204 cities and villages in Galilee, the smallest of these numbering over 15,000 inhabitants. If this testimony is not an exaggeration, as many believe it to be, this would mean that Galilee had a population of about three million. —The Life, 235 (45); The Jewish War, III, 43 (iii, 2).

Galilee was blessed with abundant springs and fertile soil. So the chief occupation of the Galileans apparently was agriculture. Today many different kinds of vegetables, as well as wheat, barley, figs, millet, indigo, olives, rice, sugarcane, oranges, pears, and apricots, are cultivated. Anciently, Galilee was heavily wooded. Among the varieties of trees still found there are cedar, cypress, fir, oak, oleander, palm, pine, sycamore, and walnut.

Both the climate and the geographic features of Galilee are marked by great contrast. The highlands are cool, the seacoast enjoys a mild temperature, and the Jordan Valley is hot. The altitude of Lower Galilee plunges to about 210 m (689 ft) below sea level in the vicinity of the Sea of Galilee and reaches its highest point at Mount Tabor, with an elevation of 562 m (1,844 ft). (PICTURE, Vol. 1, p. 334) However, the hills and mountains of Upper Galilee range from 460 m (1,500 ft) to 1,208 m (3,963 ft) in height.

People of Galilee.

People of Galilee. As a group, the Jews of Galilee differed from those of Judea. According to the testimony of rabbis of ancient times, the Galileans valued reputation, whereas the Judeans placed greater emphasis on money than on a good name. The Galileans generally were not such sticklers for tradition as were the Judeans. In the Talmud (*Megillah* 75a), the former are, in fact, charged with neglecting tradition. In this regard it may be noted that Pharisees and scribes from Jerusalem, not from Galilee, were the ones who took issue with the failure of Jesus' disciples to observe the traditional washing of hands.—Mr 7:1, 5.

Since the Sanhedrin and the temple were in Jerusalem, doubtless a greater concentration of teachers of the Law was to be found there; hence the Jewish proverb: "Go north [to Galilee] for riches, go south [to Judea] for wisdom." But this does not mean that the Galileans were steeped in ignorance. Throughout the cities and villages of Galilee there were teachers of the Law as well as synagogues. The latter were, in effect, educational centers. (Lu 5:17) However, the chief priests and Pharisees at Jerusalem evidently considered themselves superior to the common Galileans and viewed them as ignorant of the Law. For example, when Nicodemus spoke up in defense of Jesus Christ, the Pharisees retorted: "You are not also out of Galilee, are you? Search and see that no prophet is to be raised up out of Galilee." (Joh 7:45-52) Thus they ignored the fulfillment of Isaiah's prophecy concerning Messiah's preaching.—Isa 9:1, 2; Mt 4:13-17.

Some ascribe the distinct Galilean accent to foreign influence. It is not at all unusual that the Galileans were easily recognized by their speech (Mt 26:73), especially since the region of Samaria separated Galilee from Judea. Even today, in many parts of the earth, people are readily identified by their regional accent. Also, among the tribes of Israel pronunciation differences existed centuries previously. A striking example of this is the inability of the Ephraimites in Jephthah's day to pronounce the password "Shibboleth" correctly.—Jg 12:5, 6.

Jesus' ministry in Galilee.

Jesus' ministry in Galilee. Galilee was the scene for many outstanding events in Jesus' earthly life. The Galilean cities of Bethsaida, Cana, Capernaum, Chorazin, Nain, and Nazareth, as well as the regions of Magadan, are specifically mentioned in connection with his activity. (Mt 11:20-23; 15:39; Lu 4:16; 7:11; Joh 2:11; see BETHSAIDA.) Most of his earthly life Jesus spent at the Galilean city of Nazareth. (Mt 2:21-23; Lu 2:51, 52) At a marriage feast in Cana, he performed his first miracle by turning water into the best of wine. (Joh 2:1-11) After the arrest of John the Baptizer, Jesus withdrew from Judea to Galilee and began proclaiming: "Repent, you people, for the kingdom of the heavens has drawn near." (Mt 4:12-17) As Jesus traveled throughout Galilee, he taught in the various synagogues. In the course of time he came to his hometown, Nazareth, where, on the Sabbath day, he read his commission from Isaiah chapter 61. Although those in the synagogue were at first favorably impressed, when Jesus compared them to the Israelites in the days of the prophets Elijah and Elisha, the synagogue audience became enraged, and they were ready to kill him.—Lu 4:14-30.

Afterward Jesus went to Capernaum, "a city of Galilee," and established this as his home. Evidently near Capernaum he called Andrew, Peter, James, and John to be fishers of men. (Lu 4:31; Mt 4:13-22) Accompanied by these four disciples, Jesus began a major preaching tour of Galilee. In the course of his activities of teaching and performing powerful works, Jesus called Matthew from the tax office at Capernaum to be his follower. (Mt 4:23-25; 9:1-9) Later, at a mountain near Capernaum, he chose the 12 apostles. All of them, with the possible exception of Judas Iscariot, were Galileans. Also near Capernaum, Jesus delivered the Sermon on the Mount. (Lu 6:12-49; 7:1) At the Galilean city of Nain, he resurrected the only son of a widow. (Lu 7:11-17) In a later preaching tour, Jesus revisited Nazareth but was again rejected. (Mt 13:54-58) At Capernaum, around Passover time of 32 C.E., during what was apparently his final intensive coverage of Galilean territory, many disciples, stumbled by Jesus' words about 'eating his flesh and drinking his blood,' forsook the Son of God.—Joh 6:22-71.

Although the synoptic Gospels tell mainly of Jesus' ministry in Galilee, the Son of God did not ignore Judea, as some have wrongly concluded. It is noteworthy that the initial interest the Galileans showed in Jesus was aroused by what they saw him do in Jerusalem. (Joh 4:45) However, probably more space is devoted to Jesus' activity in Galilee because the Galileans responded more readily than did the Judeans. This is confirmed by the fact that the first disciples to receive God's holy spirit were Galileans, some 120 in number. (Ac 1:15; 2:1-7) The control and influence of the Jewish religious leaders must not have been as strong among the Galileans as among the Judeans. (Compare Lu 11:52; Joh 7:47-52; 12:42, 43.) Some suggest that the crowd that clamored for Jesus' death was mainly composed of Judeans (Mt 27:20-23), whereas those who had previously hailed Jesus as king were perhaps primarily Galileans. (Mt 21:6-11) The presence of many Galileans and other non-Judeans during the Passover period may also have contributed to the fear of the leaders of Jerusalem to seize Jesus in broad daylight 'lest an uproar occur.'—Mt 26:3-5.

GALILEE, SEA OF.

A freshwater inland lake in N Palestine that has also been called the Sea of Chinnereth (Nu 34:11), the Lake of Gennesaret (Lu 5:1), and the Sea of Tiberias (Joh 6:1). (The Greek word translated "sea" may also mean "lake.")—MAP, Vol. 2, p. 740; PICTURES, Vol. 1, p. 336, and Vol. 2, p. 740.

Size and Topography of Area. The Sea of Galilee lies an average of 210 m (700 ft) below the level of the Mediterranean Sea and is a part of the Rift Valley of the Jordan. Its greatest water depth is about 48 m (157 ft). From N to S, this body of water has an approximate length of 21 km (13 mi), with a maximum width of about 12 km (7.5 mi). Depending upon the season, the clear waters of the Sea of Galilee vary from green to blue in color, and the average water temperature ranges from 14° C. (57° F.) in February to 30° C. (86° F.) in August. This lake is fed primarily by the Jordan River.

The bed of the Sea of Galilee resembles a huge basin. Rising from its shores on the E side are steep limestone mountains overlaid with lava, reaching an elevation of about 610 m (2,000 ft). But on the W the mountains rise less abruptly. Hills and mountains practically surround the Sea of Galilee, except for the plains around the Jordan, that is, the points where the river enters the lake at the N end and where it renews its course at the SW. The area to the N is occupied by a mass of large basalt boulders. Not far S of the city of Tiberias on the W shore, there are hot sulfur springs that have long been famous for their medicinal properties. One of the seven springs there has a temperature of 58° C. (136° F.).

Climate. The warm climate around the Sea of Galilee is conducive to the growth of tropical plants, including the lotus thorn, palms, and indigo plants. Tortoises, turtles, crayfish, and sandhoppers are found along the shores of the lake. Bird life and fish are abundant. In the 19th century, naturalist H. B. Tristram observed: "The density of the shoals of fish in the Sea of Galilee can scarcely be conceived by those who have not witnessed them. Frequently these shoals cover an acre or more of the surface and the fish, as they slowly move along in masses, are so crowded, with their back fins just appearing on the level of the water, that the appearance at a little distance is that of a violent shower of rain pattering on the surface."—*The Natural History of the Bible*, 1889, p. 285.

Sudden storms, such as the one experienced by Jesus Christ and his disciples, are not uncommon. (Mt 8:24; 14:24) Because of the low elevation of the Sea of Galilee, the air temperature is much warmer there than in the surrounding plateaus and mountains. This results in atmospheric disturbances. Also, strong winds rush down the Jordan Valley from snowcapped Mount Hermon, not far to the N.

In the first century C.E., the shores of this lake were well populated. But today, of the nine cities mentioned by Josephus as being on the Sea of Galilee, only Tiberias remains.

Jesus' Ministry in Area. This body of water figured prominently in Jesus' earthly ministry. A number of times the Son of God spoke from a boat to great crowds assembled on its wide, pebbly shore. (Mr 3:9; 4:1; Lu 5:1-3) On one of these occasions he caused some of his disciples to have a miraculous catch of fish and called Peter, Andrew, James, and John to be "fishers of men." (Mt 4:18-22; Lu 5:4-11) In the vicinity of the Sea of Galilee, Jesus performed many powerful works. He healed the sick, expelled demons (Mr 3:7-12), calmed the wind and the sea (Mr 4:35-41), and walked on the water (Joh 6:16-21); once, he miraculously fed more than 5,000 people, and at another time he fed more than 4,000, each time with only a few loaves of bread and several fish. (Mt 14:14-21; 15:29, 34-38) Rightly Jesus condemned three cities in that area, Chorazin, Bethsaida, and Capernaum, for remaining unresponsive despite the many powerful works their inhabitants had witnessed.—Mt 11:20-24.

After his resurrection from the dead, Jesus appeared to some of his disciples by the Sea of Galilee and caused them to have a second miraculous catch of fish. He then stressed the importance of feeding his sheep.—Joh 21:1, 4-19.

GALL.

A fluid produced by the liver and stored in the gallbladder, a small pear-shaped sac that rests on the underside of the right portion of the liver. The gallbladder can hold at one time about one and a half ounces of gall, or bile. It is an extremely bitter yellow or greenish fluid used by the body in digestion. Gall came to be associated with that which is bitter or poisonous, and the word is so used in the Bible.—Ac 8:23.

Describing his painful, bitter experience, Job figuratively speaks of his gallbladder as being poured out to the earth. (Job 16:1, 13) Later, Zophar, in figurative language, accusingly insinuates that Job has acted wickedly and that his "food" will be within him like "the gall [or poison] of cobras." He warns that a weapon will pass "through his gall[bladder]." (Job 20:1, 14, 25) The Hebrew word translated "gall" is related to the word for "bitter."—De 32:32; Job 13:26.

The Greek word for gall is *kho·le'*.—See POISONOUS PLANT.

GALLEY. A long, low, narrow ship powered by one or more tiers of oars and used mainly for naval warfare.

Isaiah represents the inhabitants of Jerusalem as saying: "There the Majestic One, Jehovah, will be for us a place of rivers, of wide canals. On it no galley fleet [literally, fleet of ships of oar] will go, and no majestic ship will pass over it. For Jehovah is our Judge, Jehovah is our Statute-giver, Jehovah is our King; he himself will save us." (Isa 33:21, 22) Jerusalem had no great rivers or canals as defenses against attack. Yet, just as rivers and canals protected cities such as Babylon and No-amon (Na 3:8), Jehovah would protect Jerusalem. So powerful would these "rivers" of God's salvation be that strong enemy forces, symbolized by a fleet of hostile galleys or a majestic ship, would be wrecked in the mighty "waters" if they came up against Jerusalem. Jehovah thereby assured Jerusalem, in a figurative way, of her security under the defense he himself, ruling as her King, would provide for her salvation.

GALLIM (Gal'lim) [Heaps]. The home of Palti, to whom Saul gave his daughter Michal as his wife after David was outlawed. (1Sa 25:44) It is possibly the same as the Gallim whose inhabitants, centuries later, cried out in lamentation over the approaching Assyrian army under Sennacherib. (Isa 10:24, 30) Some scholars place Gallim at Khirbet Kakul (Horvat Ka'kul), about 4.5 km (3 mi) NNE of the Temple Mount.

GALLIO (Gal'li·o). The proconsul of Achaia, before whose judgment seat the Jews accused Paul of leading men into another persuasion in worshiping God. Gallio dismissed the case on the basis that it did not involve a violation of Roman law. Thereupon, the crowd went to beating Sosthenes the presiding officer of the synagogue, but

Gallio chose not to concern himself with this either.—Ac 18:12-17.

According to secular sources, Gallio was born at Cordova, Spain, about the beginning of the first century C.E. He was the son of the rhetorician Seneca and the older brother of Seneca the philosopher. Gallio's original name was Lucius Annaeus Novatus. But, upon being adopted by the rhetorician Lucius Junius Gallio, he assumed the name of his adopter.

An inscription from Delphi helps in dating Gallio's term as proconsul of Achaia. (Ac 18:12) Only fragmentary, the inscription's text has had to be reconstructed, but it definitely contains the name of "[Lucius Ju]nius Gallio, . . . proconsul." Historians are generally agreed that the text is a letter from Emperor Claudius Caesar and that the number 26 found in it refers to Claudius' having received the imperial acclamation for the 26th time. (It was Claudius who restored Achaia to the position of a separate province responsible to the senate and hence having a proconsul.) It is likely that this letter was written in the first half of 52 C.E., for other inscriptions indicate that Claudius was acclaimed emperor for the 27th time before August 1, 52 C.E. A Carian inscription and an inscription on the aqueduct called the Aqua Claudia at Rome place Claudius' 26th and 27th imperial acclamations within the year of his 12th period of tribunician power. This 12th tribunician period corresponded to January 25, 52 C.E., through January 24, 53 C.E. Gallio's proconsulship of Achaia (an office that usually ran for a year, starting with the beginning of summer) therefore appears to have run from the summer of 51 C.E. to the summer of 52 C.E., though some scholars favor 52-53 C.E.

Portion of an inscription
bearing the name Gallio (ΓΑΛΛΙΩ)

GAMALIEL (Ga·ma′li·el) [possibly, Reward (Due Treatment) of God].

1. The son of Pedahzur of the tribe of Manasseh, and the chieftain of his tribe. (Nu 1:10, 16) Gamaliel was one of the 12 chieftains designated by Jehovah to aid Moses and Aaron in numbering the sons of Israel, from 20 years old upward, for the army. (Nu 1:1-4, 10) He was over the army of his tribe, which was a part of the three-tribe division of the camp of Ephraim. (Nu 2:18, 20; 10:23) After the setting up of the tabernacle, the chieftains made their presentations, directed by Jehovah to be used for carrying on the service of the tent of meeting. Gamaliel also presented an offering on the eighth day for the inauguration of the altar. —Nu 7:1-5, 10, 11, 54-59.

2. A member of the Sanhedrin, a Pharisee, and a Law teacher, at whose feet the apostle Paul had been instructed according to the strictness of the ancestral Law. (Ac 5:34; 22:3) Gamaliel is generally regarded as identical with Gamaliel the Elder. Gamaliel the Elder was greatly esteemed, being the first one to have the title of "Rabban" bestowed upon him. This honorary title was even higher than that of "Rabbi." Concerning him the Mishnah (*Sotah* 9:15) says: "When Rabban Gamaliel the Elder died, the glory of the Law ceased and purity and abstinence died." (Translated by H. Danby) Gamaliel evidently was broad-minded and not fanatical in his views, as is reflected by the counsel he gave on the occasion that Peter and the other apostles were brought before the Sanhedrin. By citing examples from the past, Gamaliel illustrated the wisdom of not interfering with the work of the apostles and then added: "If this scheme or this work is from men, it will be overthrown; but if it is from God, you will not be able to overthrow them . . . you may perhaps be found fighters actually against God."—Ac 5:34-39.

GAMES. Early in man's history an interest in diversion and entertainment became manifest. Jubal, in the seventh generation from Adam, is said to be "the founder of all those who handle the harp and the pipe." (Ge 4:21) In course of time, at least in the post-Flood period, games were also developed.

Egypt and Mesopotamia. In widely scattered locations of Egypt, Palestine, and Mesopotamia, archaeologists have unearthed various forms of gaming boards, chessmen, dice, and other game pieces, some of which date back to times before Abraham. A relief from an Egyptian temple gate portrays Ramses III playing a game similar to checkers with one of his concubines. Most games used dice or throw sticks to determine the moves.

Egyptian paintings, in addition to depicting dancing and instrument playing, show scenes of Egyptian girls playing with balls, juggling several at a time. Other youthful games, such as a kind of tug-of-war, involved team play. Marbles were also popular.

Game board from Ur

Israel. No direct reference is made in the Bible to games among the Hebrews, but there are scattered indications of certain forms of recreation in addition to music, singing, dancing, and conversation. Zechariah 8:5 tells of children playing in the public squares, and the singing and dancing of boys are mentioned at Job 21:11, 12. In Jesus' time children played at imitating happy and sad occasions. (Mt 11:16, 17) Excavations in Palestine have produced children's toys such as rattles, whistles, and miniature pots and chariots. Job 41:5 may indicate the keeping of tame birds. It appears likely that target shooting with arrows as well as with slings was practiced. (1Sa 20:20-22, 35-40; Jg 20:16) However, competitive games as such do not appear to have been in practice among the Jews until the Hellenic period.

Riddles and guessing games were popular in Israel, as is illustrated by the riddle Samson propounded to the Philistines.—Jg 14:12-14.

Greece. At about the time that Isaiah began to prophesy in Judah, the Greeks began their famous Olympic athletic contests in honor of

Zeus, in the year 776 B.C.E. While the games at Olympia remained the most famous, three other Greek towns became important centers of the contests. On the Isthmus near Corinth were held the Isthmian Games, consecrated as sacred to Poseidon. Delphi featured the Pythian Games, while the Nemean Games, also in honor of Zeus, were held near Nemea.

The Olympic Games were celebrated every four years and were of profound religious significance. Religious sacrifices and the worship of the Olympic fire were prominent features of the festival. The Isthmian Games near Corinth were held every two years.

The basic program in all the contests included foot racing, wrestling, boxing, discus and javelin throwing, chariot racing, and other events. Participants took a vow to keep the rigid ten-month training schedule, which occupied most of their time. The training schedule was strictly supervised by judges who lived with the participants. The trainees often performed under conditions more difficult than the actual contest, runners training with weights on their feet and boxers training while wearing heavy uniforms. Years were often spent in developing the needed qualities for becoming a victor at the games. The prize consisted of a simple garland, or crown of leaves, wild olive being used at the Olympian Games, pine leaves at the Isthmian Games, laurel at the Pythian Games, and wild celery at the Nemean contests. The prize was often displayed at the finish line alongside the umpire, inspiring participants in the footraces to exert themselves to the utmost as they kept their eye on the prize. Failure to keep the rules, however, resulted in disqualification. The games were the topic of conversation by all before, during, and after the event. Victorious athletes were eulogized, idolized, lavished with gifts, and feted. Corinth gave the winning athletes a life pension.

Rome. The Roman games differed greatly from the Greek games, having as their prime features gladiatorial fighting and other exhibitions of extreme brutality. The gladiatorial contests originally began in the third century B.C.E. as a religious service at funerals and may have had close relationship with ancient pagan rites whereby worshipers lacerated themselves, allowing blood to flow in honor of their gods or in honor of their dead. (1Ki 18:28; compare the prohibition of such practices to Israel at Le 19:28.) The Roman games were later dedicated to the god Saturn. Nothing exceeded them for sheer

brutality and callousness. Emperor Trajan once staged games featuring 10,000 gladiators, most of whom fought to the death before the end of the spectacle. Even some senators, some "noble" women, and one emperor, Commodus, entered the gladiatorial arena. From Nero's time onward large numbers of Christians were slaughtered in these events.

Pagan Games Introduced Into Palestine. During the reign of Antiochus Epiphanes in the second century B.C.E., Hellenizing Jews introduced Greek culture and athletic contests into Israel, and a gymnasium was set up in Jerusalem, according to the first chapter of the Apocryphal book of First Maccabees. It is stated at 2 Maccabees 4:12-15 that even the priests neglected their duties to engage in the games. Others, however, strongly objected to such adoption of pagan customs.

In the first century B.C.E., Herod the Great built a theater at Jerusalem, an amphitheater in the plain, also a theater and amphitheater at Caesarea, and he instituted the celebration of games every five years in honor of Caesar. In addition to wrestling, chariot racing, and other contests, he introduced features from the Roman games, arranging fights between wild animals or pitting men condemned to death against such beasts. According to Josephus, all of this resulted in an abortive conspiracy by offended Jews to assassinate Herod.—*Jewish Antiquities*, XV, 267-291 (viii, 1-4); XV, 331-341 (ix, 6).

The Christian Viewpoint. Tertullian, who was a writer of the second and third centuries C.E., set forth the position of early Christians toward the entertainment common among the Romans by saying that Christians "have nothing to do, in speech, sight or hearing, with the madness of the circus, the shamelessness of the theatre, the savagery of the arena, the vanity of the gymnasium." He added: "Why should we offend you, if we assume the existence of other pleasures? . . . we reject what pleases you; what pleases us gives you no delight." (*Apology*, XXXVIII, 4, 5) With regard to bodily training or discipline as a whole, the apostle Paul sums up the Christian attitude in his counsel to Timothy at 1 Timothy 4:7-10.

Illustrative Use. Features of some of the games were aptly used by Paul and Peter to illustrate points of teaching. In contrast with the prize sought by contestants in Greek games, the crown for which an anointed Christian strives was shown to be, not a fading garland of leaves, but the reward of immortal life. (1Pe 1:3, 4; 5:4) He was to run with the determination of winning the prize and must keep his eyes fixed on it; looking back would be disastrous. (1Co 9:24; Php 3:13, 14) He should contend according to the rules of a moral life so as not to become disqualified. (2Ti 2:5) Self-control, self-discipline, and training are all essential. (1Co 9:25; 1Pe 5:10) The Christian's efforts were to be well aimed, with victory in mind, just as the well-trained boxer's blows count without wasted energy; though the objects of the Christian's blows were, not some other human, but things, including those within himself, that could lead him to failure. (1Co 9:26, 27; 1Ti 6:12) All hindering weights and the entangling sin of lack of faith were to be put off, even as the contestants in the races stripped themselves of cumbersome clothing. The Christian runner was to be prepared for a race requiring endurance, not a short burst of speed.—Heb 12:1, 2.

It is to be noted that at Hebrews 12:1 Paul speaks of a great "cloud of witnesses [Gr., *mar·ty'ron*] surrounding us." That he is not referring to a mere crowd of observers is made clear by the contents of the preceding chapter to which Paul refers by saying, "So, then, . . . " Hence, Paul is encouraging Christians to move onward in the race by pointing, not to mere onlookers, but to the fine example of others who were also runners, and particularly. urging Christians to look intently at the one who had already come off the victor and who was now their Judge, Christ Jesus.

The illustration at 1 Corinthians 4:9 may be drawn from the Roman contests, with Paul and his fellow apostles here likened to those in the last event on the bill at the arena—for the most gory event was usually saved till last, and those reserved for it were certain of death. Hebrews 10:32, 33 may similarly have the Roman games as its background. (See THEATER.) Actually, Paul himself may have been exposed to the perils of the Roman games in view of his reference at 1 Corinthians 15:32 to 'fighting wild beasts at Ephesus.' Some view it as unlikely that a Roman citizen would be put before wild beasts in the arena, and they suggest that this expression is used figuratively to refer to beastlike opposers in Ephesus. However, Paul's statement at 2 Corinthians 1:8-10 concerning the very grave danger experienced in the district of Asia, where Ephesus was located, and of God's rescuing him from "such a great thing as death" would certainly fit an experience with literal wild beasts in the arena much more aptly than it would the human opposition Paul encountered at Ephesus. (Ac 19:23-41) It may thus have been one of the several "near-deaths" Paul underwent in his ministry.—2Co 11:23; see AMUSEMENTS.

GAMUL (Ga'mul) [possibly, One Weaned (or, One Receiving Due Treatment)]. An Aaronic priest in David's time who was chosen by lot to act as chief of the 22nd priestly division in connection with the service at the sanctuary.—1Ch 24:1-3, 5, 17.

GANGRENE. The death of the tissues in a part of the body, such as a toe or a foot, as a result of obstructed blood circulation. In *dry gangrene,* where the arteries are blocked or occluded (as, for example, in arteriosclerosis), the affected part turns black and dry and loses all feeling. *Wet gangrene* usually affects very small blood vessels —the capillaries and small veins. In *gas gangrene,* bacteria present in the dead or dying tissue may form bubbles under the skin, leading to a rapid sloughing off of tissues. Because bacteria are usually associated with gangrene, the resulting infection often promotes rapid spread of cell death. If the bacteria spread to the bloodstream, the condition becomes even more critical, resulting in death unless appropriate treatment is administered promptly.

The apostle Paul uses the word figuratively of the teaching of false doctrine and of "empty speeches that violate what is holy." He stresses the danger that such speech brings to the entire congregation, saying: "For they will advance to more and more ungodliness, and their word will spread like gangrene." He then cites examples: "Hymenaeus and Philetus are of that number. These very men have deviated from the truth, saying that the resurrection has already occurred; and they are subverting the faith of some." (2Ti 2:16-18) In view of Paul's earlier symbolism, picturing the congregation as a body with many members—feet, hands, and so forth (1Co 12)—his figurative use of gangrene, with its danger to the human body, gives strong emphasis to the importance of eliminating false doctrine and ungodly speech from the Christian congregation.

GARDEN. The Hebrew term *gan* and the Greek term *ke'pos* refer to a cultivated area of land, often irrigated. Gardens of Bible times were usually areas enclosed by a hedge of thorns or by a wall of stone or mud, perhaps with thorns along the top.—Ca 4:12.

Generally speaking, the gardens spoken of in the Bible are quite different from the ordinary gardens of the West. Many of them were more in the nature of a park with various kinds of trees, including fruit and nut trees (Ec 2:5; Am 9:14; Ca 6:11), as well as spice plants and flowers. (Ca 6:2) They were well watered by streams or by means of irrigation, and they often had winding paths. Smaller gardens may have been cultivated by individual families. King Ahab wanted Naboth's vineyard, he claimed, for a vegetable garden. —1Ki 21:2.

The above-mentioned parklike gardens would usually be outside the city, except in the case of gardens of kings or very rich men. The King's Garden, near the place where Zedekiah and his men tried to escape from Jerusalem during the Chaldean siege, was probably situated just outside the SE wall of that city. (2Ki 25:4; Ne 3:15) Josephus speaks also of a place called Etan, which he locates 13 to 16 km (8 to 10 mi) from Jerusalem and which he describes as "delightful for, and abounding in, parks and flowing streams", where, so he claims, Solomon was accustomed to ride in his chariot. (*Jewish Antiquities,* VIII, 186 [vii, 3]) The garden in which King Ahasuerus held a great seven-day banquet in Shushan, during the third year of his reign, must have been a large and beautiful one.—Es 1:1-5.

In Babylon. The Hanging Gardens of Babylon constituted one of the seven wonders of the ancient world. King Nebuchadnezzar built them to please his wife, a Median princess, who had come from a hilly country and, upset at the flatness of Babylonia, sighed for her native mountains. It is said that Nebuchadnezzar built arches progressively higher, like steps, and overlaid this mountain of masonry with sufficient soil to nourish the largest trees. At the top he built a reservoir, supplied from the Euphrates by a screw-type water lift.

In Egypt. While in Egypt, the Israelites had cultivated what seem to have been smaller vegetable gardens. Deuteronomy 11:10 says they irrigated these with the foot, possibly either by foot-powered waterwheels or by conducting irrigation water by means of channels, opening and resealing the mud walls of the channels with the foot to water the various parts of the garden.

Gethsemane. The garden of Gethsemane on the Mount of Olives, just across the Kidron Valley from Jerusalem, was a favorite spot with Jesus Christ, where he could find solitude with his disciples. It was to this garden that Jesus retired with his disciples after eating his last Passover

and instituting the Lord's Evening Meal. There he withdrew a short distance from his disciples and prayed fervently, being ministered to by an angel. The traitor Judas, knowing of Jesus' custom, led a mob to Gethsemane, where he betrayed Jesus with a kiss.—Mt 26:36, 46-49; Lu 22:39-48; Joh 18:1, 2.

Burial Places. At times gardens were used as burial places. Manasseh and his son Amon were buried in the garden of Uzza. (2Ki 21:18, 25, 26) It was in a garden, in a new memorial tomb, that Jesus was buried. (Joh 19:41, 42) The Israelites fell into the bad practice of sacrificing to pagan gods in the gardens, seating themselves among the burial places and eating loathsome things in their observance of false religion, for which Jehovah declared that he would render judgment.—Isa 65:2-5; 66:16, 17.

Garden of Eden. The most celebrated garden of history is the garden of Eden. It seems to have been an enclosed area, bounded, no doubt, by natural barriers. The garden, located "in Eden, toward the east," had an entrance on its eastern side. It was here that cherubs were stationed with the flaming blade of a sword, after Adam's sin, to block man's access to the tree of life in the middle of the garden. (Ge 2:8; 3:24) The garden was well watered by a river flowing from it and parting to become the headwaters of four large rivers. This parklike "paradise of pleasure" (Ge 2:8, *Dy*) contained every tree desirable to one's sight and good for food, as well as other vegetation, and was the habitat of animals and birds. Adam was to cultivate it and to keep it and eventually to expand it earth wide as he carried out God's command to "subdue" the earth. It was a sanctuary, a place where God representatively walked and communicated with Adam and Eve; it was a perfect home for them.—Ge 2:9, 10, 15-18, 21, 22; 1:28; 3:8-19; see PARADISE.

Although the Bible does not state how long the cherubs remained to guard the way of the tree of life, it may have been that such an arrangement existed until the Flood, 1,656 years after the creation of Adam. Untended by Adam, who with Eve had been driven out for their disobedience in eating from the forbidden tree of the knowledge of good and bad, the garden likely suffered deterioration. At any rate, it would at the latest have been obliterated by means of the Flood.—See EDEN No. 1.

The beauty of the garden of Eden was recalled centuries after the Flood when Lot viewed the whole District of the Jordan, observing "that all of it was a well-watered region . . . like the garden of Jehovah." (Ge 13:10) Jehovah kept his eyes on the Promised Land, preserving it as an inheritance for Israel. Moses contrasts it with Egypt, where the Israelites had to do irrigating as in a vegetable garden, describing the Promised Land as a land watered by "the rain of the heavens." —De 11:10-12.

Figurative Uses. In a warning to Judah through Joel, Jehovah tells of "a people numerous and mighty" who will devastate the land, converting it from a state "like the garden of Eden" into a wilderness. (Joe 2:2, 3) By contrast, those who do Jehovah's will and enjoy his good pleasure are likened to a well-watered garden. (Isa 58:8-11) Such was to be the situation of Jehovah's covenant people restored from Babylonian exile.—Isa 51:3, 11; Jer 31:10-12.

At Ezekiel 28:12-14 "the king of Tyre" is spoken of as having been in the garden of Eden and on "the holy mountain of God." By the slopes of Mount Lebanon with its famous cedars, the king, decked in gorgeous robes and royal splendor, had been as in a garden of Eden and on a mountain of God.

The shepherd lover in The Song of Solomon likens his Shulammite girl companion to a garden with all its pleasantness, beauty, delight, and fine fruitage.—Ca 4:12-16.

GAREB (Ga′reb) [Scabby].

1. One of David's mighty men, an Ithrite of the tribe of Judah.—2Sa 23:8, 38; 1Ch 2:4, 5, 18, 19, 50, 53; 11:26, 40.

2. A hill mentioned in a restoration prophecy written by Jeremiah (31:39), evidently indicating the western limits of the rebuilt city of Jerusalem. Its precise location is unknown.

GARLAND. An ornamental wreath worn on the head. The Hebrew term tsephi·rah′ (garland) was used symbolically in a prophecy of Jehovah's judgment on Samaria, the capital city of Ephraim, that is, the ten-tribe kingdom of Israel. Samaria was at that time full of political "drunkards," drunk over the northern kingdom's independence from Judah and over its political alliances with Syria and other enemies of Jehovah's kingdom in Judah. (See Isa 7:3-9.) Just as drunkards would wear garlands of flowers on their heads during their wine bouts, so Samaria wore the garland of this political power. It was a decoration of beauty but was a fading blossom that would disappear. Then Jehovah would become for the remaining ones of his people as a crown of decoration and as a garland (or "diadem" according to several translations) of beauty.—Isa 28:1-5.

The same Hebrew word appears at Ezekiel 7:7, 10. Translators, however, are uncertain as to the sense or application of the word in this case. A similar Aramaic word means "morning," and Lamsa's translation of the Syriac Peshitta here reads "dawn," rather than garland, or diadem. Some translators (AS, AT, RS) link the word with a cognate Arabic noun and render it as "doom." Still others, on the belief that the root meaning of the Hebrew word is "to go round," translate it as "turn," in the sense of a turn of events.—JB; JP; "circle," Ro.

In the Christian Greek Scriptures, the plural form of the Greek word stem′ma, "garland," appears at Acts 14:13. As there related, the priest of Zeus at Lystra brought bulls and garlands to the city gates to offer sacrifices, because the people supposed that Paul and Barnabas were gods. They may have intended to put garlands on the heads of Paul and Barnabas, as was sometimes done to idols, or on themselves and the sacrificial animals. Such garlands were generally made up of foliage supposed to be pleasing to the god worshiped.—Ac 14:8-18; see CROWN.

GARLIC [Heb., shu·mim′]. A bulbous perennial plant (Allium sativum), the strong-scented, pungent-tasting bulb of which is composed of up to 20 smaller bulbs, or cloves. The flower stalk of garlic, bearing tiny bulblets and sterile flowers, at times may attain a height of 0.3 m (1 ft) or more.

The indications are that garlic was extensively cultivated in ancient Egypt. In the wilderness the mixed crowd and the Israelites longed for the garlic they used to eat there. (Nu 11:4, 5) The Greek historian Herodotus (II, 125) tells of an inscription that listed garlic as one of the foods provided for the laborers on a certain pyramid. Garlic is still widely used by the inhabitants of Mediterranean areas. In the Mishnah (Nedarim 3:10), the Jews referred to themselves as garlic-eaters. Garlic has been used medicinally as a digestive stimulant, as an antibiotic, and as an antispasmodic.

GARMENT. See DRESS; OFFICIAL GARMENT; RIPPING OF GARMENTS.

GARMITE (Gar′mite) [Of (Belonging to) Gerem (Bone)]. This designation is linked with Keilah, a name appearing in a listing of Judah's descendants.—1Ch 4:19.

GARNER. See STOREHOUSE.

GARRISON.

The Hebrew term *netsiv'* may denote a rather permanent contingent of soldiers stationed at a military installation. The related Hebrew word *mats·tsav'* (outpost) carries a similar idea.—1Sa 13:23; 14:1, 4, 6, 11, 12, 15; 2Sa 23:14.

The Philistines had garrisons in Israelite territory during the reigns of Saul and David. (1Sa 10:5; 13:3, 4; 1Ch 11:16) After David defeated Syria and Edom, he maintained garrisons in their territory to prevent rebellion. (2Sa 8:6, 14; 1Ch 18:13) For the peace and security of the land, Jehoshaphat installed garrisons in Judah and in the cities of Ephraim that Asa had captured. (2Ch 17:1, 2) The presence of such a military body did much to maintain order and protect royal interests in territories where the native inhabitants were likely to rebel.

A Roman garrison was maintained at Jerusalem during the first century C.E. Their quarters were in the high Tower of Antonia adjoining the temple grounds. When a crowd of Jews dragged Paul outside the temple and sought to kill him, soldiers of the garrison were able to come down quickly enough to rescue him. (Ac 21:31, 32) During Jewish festival seasons, extra troops were brought in to strengthen this garrison.—See ANTONIA, TOWER OF.

GATAM

(Ga'tam). The fourth-named son of Esau's firstborn Eliphaz. Gatam became one of the sheiks of the sons of Esau.—Ge 36:10, 11, 15, 16; 1Ch 1:36.

GATE, GATEWAY.

The Bible speaks of several different kinds of gates: (1) gates of the camp (Ex 32:26, 27), (2) gates of the city (Jer 37:13), (3) gate of the courtyard of the tabernacle (Ex 38:18), (4) "gates of the Castle that belongs to the house" (Ne 2:8), (5) temple gates (Ac 3:10), and (6) gate of a house (Ac 12:13, 14).

Construction. Cities usually had as few gates as possible; some cities had only one gate, since these were the vulnerable points of their fortifications. Where there were inner and outer walls, there were, of course, gates in each wall. Early gateways were L shaped to hinder the enemy's entry. Later, after the chariot was introduced (c. 18th century B.C.E.), city gates had a straight, direct entrance. In some uncovered ruins the city gate is composed of an entrance flanked by square towers leading into a vestibule about some 15 to 20 m (49 to 66 ft) long. The passage through the vestibule was flanked by as many as six pilasters, which narrowed the passageway at three places. In some cases there may have been two or three sets of doors for these deep gates. Small rooms inside the vestibule walls were used as guard chambers. In Ezekiel's visionary temple, the gates were provided with guard chambers. (Eze 40:6, 7, 10, 20, 21, 28, 29, 32-36) Some gates had a roof over the vestibule, and some were multistoried, as is evidenced by the stairways found inside.—Compare 2Sa 18:24, 33.

Ancient fortress cities have been uncovered revealing small posterns, or side gates. These were sometimes at the bottom of the rampart and provided easy access for the inhabitants of the city during peacetime. In time of siege they apparently were used as sortie gates through which the defenders could sally forth to attack besiegers and at the same time receive covering fire from their comrades on the walls.

The doors of the gates of a city were usually of wood sheathed with metal plating; otherwise they could be set on fire by the enemy. Some may have been made of iron, as was the case in the days of the apostles. (Ac 12:10) Babylon's gateways are said to have had doors of copper and bars of iron. (Isa 45:2; compare Ps 107:2, 16.) Some gates were apparently locked with wooden bars. (Na 3:13) In Solomon's day, in the region of Argob, in Bashan, there were "sixty large cities with wall and copper bar." (1Ki 4:13) Some towns in Syria have been found with massive stone doors of single slabs about 3 m (10 ft) high, turning on pivots above and below. Samson's feat of picking up the doors of the gate of Gaza along with its two side posts and bar and carrying them to the top of "the mountain that is in front of Hebron" was, in view of these factors, no mean accomplishment. It was done, of course, through the energizing power of Jehovah's spirit.—Jg 16:3.

Function. The "gates" of a city could refer to the city itself, since much of the official business took place at the gates and transactions were recorded there (De 16:11, 14, ftn; Ru 4:10; Ps 87:2; 122:2); and in the capital, business was often carried out at the gateway of the palace grounds. (Es 3:2, 3; 5:9, 13; 6:10, 12) Where the gates, the entrances, of the city were desolate, the glory was also gone. (Isa 3:26; 14:31; Jer 14:2; La 1:4) The gates were the points where the besiegers made the strongest effort to break through. Once controlling them, they would have access to the city. And so, to 'get possession of the gates' of the city meant to take the city. (Ge 22:17; 24:60) When the wall of Jerusalem was broken through, the princes of the Babylonian king directed the further subjection of the city from a position at one of the city gates.—Jer 39:2, 3.

Gates were the centers of public assembly and public life. Broad places, such as the public square before the Water Gate in Jerusalem, were usually provided near the gates. (Ne 8:1) The gates were the city's news centers not only because of the arrival of travelers and merchants but also because nearly all the workmen, especially those working in the fields, went in and out of the gate every day. So the gate was the place for meeting others. (Ru 4:1; 2Sa 15:2) The markets were located there, some of the gates of Jerusalem being named evidently for the commodities sold there (for example, the Fish Gate). —Ne 3:3.

At the city gates the older men of the city sat in judgment. (De 16:18; 21:18-20; 22:15; 25:7) Even kings at times held audiences or sat in judgment there. (2Sa 19:8; 1Ki 22:10; Jer 38:7) Because the judges, the prominent men of the city, the merchants, the businessmen, and a goodly number of people were usually at the gate, prophets often went there to make proclamations. Their messages delivered there would spread much faster. (1Ki 22:10; Jer 17:19) Other important announcements and official proclamations were also made there. (2Ch 32:6-8) It was in the public square before the Water Gate that Ezra read the Law. (Ne 8:1-3) Wisdom is pictured as crying out at the entrances of the gates for all in the city to become aware of its counsel. (Pr 1:20, 21; 8:1-3) Inasmuch as the gate was a news center, the good or bad works of the city's inhabitants would become known there.—Pr 31:31.

It seems to have been a heathen practice to make sacrifices at the gates of a city. (Ac 14:13) This bad practice developed in Judah but was corrected by King Josiah.—2Ki 23:8.

Those found worthy of death by the judges were taken outside the city gates to be executed. (1Ki 21:10-13; Ac 7:58) The carcasses of the sacrificial animals that were offered for sin atonement on the Day of Atonement were taken outside the city and burned. (Le 16:27, 28) Therefore Jesus Christ, the sin offering for the atonement of mankind, was put to death outside the gate of Jerusalem.—Heb 13:11, 12.

Because of the important usages of the city's gateway, it was a high honor to sit down with the older men of the land in the gates. (Job 29:7; Pr 31:23) Such a position was no place for a foolish one. (Pr 24:7) When David was persecuted, he considered it a serious thing for those sitting in the gates to become concerned about him, especially in an unfavorable way. (Ps 69:12) To 'crush the afflicted one in the gate' had reference to judicial corruption, since legal cases were handled there. (Job 5:4; Pr 22:22; Am 5:12) To 'hate a reprover in the gate' meant to hate the judge who corrected or condemned one. (Am 5:10) Those who 'laid bait for the one reproving in the gate' were ones who by bribes or other pressures tried to cause the judges to pervert judgment or who sought to ensnare a prophet who might stand in the gate to reprove them. —Isa 29:19-21.

Wilderness Camp Gates. The 'gates' of the camp of Israel were the ways of entrance. No doubt they were well guarded. The tabernacle was in the camp's center, with the Levites camping in close proximity to it; and the 12 tribes, three on a side, were at a greater distance. This arrangement afforded ample protection for the camp.—Ex 32:26, 27; Nu 3; see GATEKEEPER.

Gates of Jerusalem. In dealing with the gates of Jerusalem, it is well to remember that, from the time of its capture by David, the city developed and expanded, so that several walls or added portions of walls were built. We shall concern ourselves here mainly with the gates mentioned in the book of Nehemiah, which gives us the most complete description or listing. The gates named in Nehemiah's record are gates that had been in the wall that was built prior to the eighth century B.C.E. and in the wall surrounding "the second quarter." (2Ki 22:14; 2Ch 34:22; Zep 1:10) "The second quarter" was a northern part of the city bounded on the W and part of the N by Hezekiah's wall (2Ch 32:5) and joined by Manasseh's wall, which continued on the NE and E. (2Ch 33:14) This was N of the earlier city and wall, but apparently it did not extend as far W as the earlier wall.

Nehemiah's wall. In his account of the reconstruction of the wall of the city (Ne 3), Nehemiah begins at the Sheep Gate and proceeds in a counterclockwise direction. We shall follow this procedure in our listing below, inserting the gates not mentioned in the reconstruction account but named in the description of the inauguration procession (Ne 12), along with gates spoken of in other scriptures, some of which are merely other names for those in Nehemiah's record.

Sheep Gate.

The Sheep Gate was rebuilt by Eliashib the high priest and associate priests. (Ne 3:1, 32; 12:39) This fact would indicate that it was near the temple area. Its location was probably in the wall of the second quarter, the part built by Manasseh (see "Fish Gate" below), at or near the NE corner of the city. This gate may have been so named because through it were brought sheep and goats for sacrifice or perhaps for a market that was located nearby. "The sheepgate" mentioned at John 5:2 is likely this Sheep Gate or a later gate corresponding to it, for it was located in the same vicinity, near the pool of Bethzatha.

Fish Gate.

Hezekiah apparently built a part of the wall around the second quarter as far as the Fish Gate. (2Ch 32:5; 33:14) In Nehemiah's reconstruction and procession accounts, the Fish Gate is placed W of the Sheep Gate, perhaps near the N end of the Tyropoeon Valley. (Ne 3:3; 12:39) It is mentioned in conjunction with the second quarter at Zephaniah 1:10. The name may be due to the gate's nearness to the fish market where the Tyrians sold fish.—Ne 13:16.

Gate of the Old City.

The Gate of the Old City was located on the NW side of the city between the Fish Gate and the Gate of Ephraim. (Ne 3:6; 12:39) In Hebrew, the gate is called simply "Gate of the Old," the word "city" being supplied by some translators. It is suggested that the name was derived from its having been the main N entrance to the old city. It may have been at the junction of the Broad Wall (that formed a N boundary of the old city) and the S end of the W wall of the second quarter. Some think that this gate is identical with "the First Gate" mentioned by Zechariah. He seemingly refers to the E-W limits of the city in saying "from [1] the Gate of Benjamin all the way to the place of [2] the First Gate, all the way to [3] the Corner Gate," and to the N-S limits in saying "from the Tower of Hananel all the way to the press vats of the king." (Zec 14:10) Others would connect the Gate of the Old City with "the Middle Gate" mentioned at Jeremiah 39:3. Some term this Gate of the Old City the "Mishneh Gate" and locate it in the W wall of the second quarter.

Gate of Ephraim.

The Gate of Ephraim was located in the Broad Wall 400 cubits (178 m; 583 ft) E of the Corner Gate. (2Ki 14:13; 2Ch 25:23) It was an exit N in the direction of the territory of Ephraim. It, too, has been identified by some researchers with the Middle Gate (Jer 39:3), by others with the First Gate. (Zec 14:10)

It is thought to be (or correspond to) the Gennath or Garden Gate spoken of by the Jewish historian Josephus. (*The Jewish War,* V, 146 [iv, 2]) Near the Gate of Ephraim there was a public square in which the people made booths to celebrate the Festival of Booths in Nehemiah's time. (Ne 8:16) This gate is not named in Nehemiah's reconstruction text, evidently because it did not need extensive repairs.

Corner Gate.

This gate was evidently located in the NW angle of the city wall, W of the Gate of Ephraim. (2Ki 14:13; 2Ch 25:23) It was on the E side of the Valley of Hinnom, apparently in the W wall of the old city at the point where it joined the Broad Wall. Uzziah built a tower by this gate; whether or not it was the Tower of the Bake Ovens is not stated. (2Ch 26:9) Both Jeremiah and Zechariah appear to refer to the Corner Gate as being on the western edge of the city.—Jer 31:38; Zec 14:10.

There is no other gate described as existing in the W wall from the Corner Gate to the Valley Gate in the SW wall, this no doubt being because of the steep slope of the Valley of Hinnom, making any other gate impractical. The Corner Gate does not appear in Nehemiah's accounts; again the reason may be that it did not need extensive repairs. The account does speak of repairing the Tower of the Bake Ovens, which seems to have been a part of, or near, the Corner Gate.—Ne 3:11.

Valley Gate.

In the SW part of the city wall, the Valley Gate led to the Valley of Hinnom. The "gate of the Essenes" mentioned by Josephus may have been located here or nearby. (*The Jewish War,* V, 145 [iv, 2]) Uzziah, in his city-fortification program, built a tower by this gate. (2Ch 26:9) It was from the Valley Gate that Nehemiah went out for his inspection of the damaged wall, riding eastward through the Valley of Hinnom and then up the Kidron Valley, finally reentering the city by the same gate. (Ne 2:13-15) Although not named as such, the Valley Gate appears to be the point at which the inauguration procession started, one group marching counterclockwise around the walls past the Gate of the Ash-heaps and the other clockwise past the Corner Gate and the Tower of the Bake Ovens.—Ne 12:31-40.

Gate of the Ash-heaps.

This gate is also known as the Gate of the Potsherds and is usually called the Dung Gate. (Ne 2:13; 12:31) Nehemiah's description seems to place it 1,000 cubits (445 m; 1,458 ft) E of the Valley Gate. (Ne 3:13,

14) It was at the SE corner of the city wall and led to the Valley of Hinnom near the point where it joined the Tyropoeon Valley. (Jer 19:2) It was from this gate that Topheth in the Valley of Hinnom was reached by those idolatrously burning their children in the fire to Baal. (Jer 19:1-6) It was also the gate through which Jeremiah led some of the older men and priests of Israel and proclaimed calamity to Jerusalem, breaking an earthenware flask to illustrate God's breaking of

the people for their serving of other gods.—Jer 19:1-3, 10, 11.

The name "Gate of the Potsherds" may have been given because fragments of pottery were thrown near there as refuse, or because fragments of pottery were ground there, the dust from which was used to make cement for plastering cisterns (as has been done in more recent times near a pool at the SW corner of the city). Also, there may have been a potter's industry

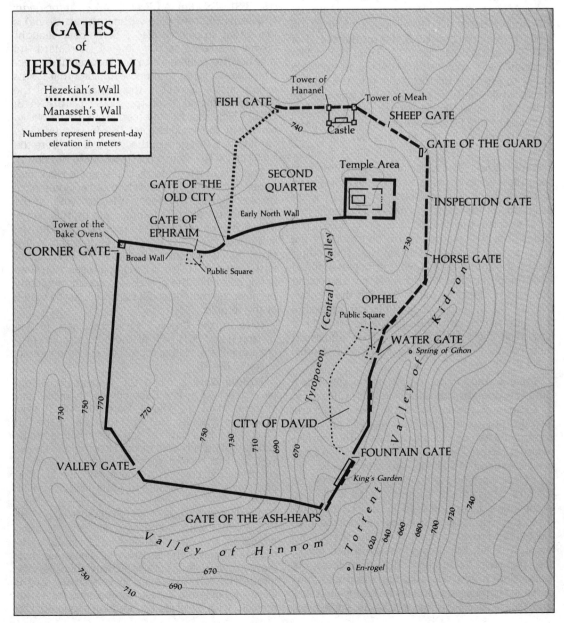

GATES of JERUSALEM

Hezekiah's Wall
Manasseh's Wall

Numbers represent present-day elevation in meters

near this gate, for there was clay nearby in the Valley of Hinnom as well as a water supply at the mouth of the Tyropoeon Valley and at the spring called En-rogel. (Compare Jer 18:2; 19:1, 2.) "The potter's field" (Mt 27:7, 8) has, since the fourth century C.E., been traditionally considered to be located on the S side of the Valley of Hinnom.

Fountain Gate. This gate was so called because of its giving access to a spring or fountain nearby, perhaps En-rogel, which was below the junction of the Kidron Valley and the Valley of Hinnom. Probably the gate was at the S tip of the E hill of the city (that is, at the southern end of "the City of David"). (Ne 2:14; 3:15; 12:37) The Fountain Gate would afford convenient exit and access to En-rogel for those living in the City of David, while the Gate of the Ash-heaps, not far to the SW, would also lead out toward En-rogel and would likely be a better exit for the residents of the Tyropoeon Valley and the SW hill of the city.

Water Gate. The name of this gate may have been derived from its proximity or at least its access to the spring of Gihon about midway up the E side of the city. This gate was near Ophel, not far from the temple area. (Ne 3:26) The Water Gate was where one of the groups of the inauguration procession left the wall, proceeding from there to the temple, where they assembled with the other group, apparently not traversing that part of the city wall to the E of the temple. (Ne 12:37-40) There was a public square before this gate where all the people gathered to hear Ezra read the Law and where they afterward built booths to celebrate the Festival of Booths. —Ne 8:1-3, 16.

Horse Gate. Repair work above the Horse Gate was done by the priests, which implies that its location was near the temple. (Ne 3:28) Some have held that the Horse Gate was one providing communication between two parts of the temple-palace quarter. They reach this conclusion from the account of Athaliah's execution, which reports that, on being led out of the temple by the soldiers, "she came to the entry of the horse gate of the king's house." (2Ch 23:15; 2Ki 11:16) However, this was likely an entry just to the precincts of the royal palace and not the Horse Gate through which the horses passed in and out of the city itself. Nehemiah definitely includes the Horse Gate in his reconstruction description, indicating that it was a gate in the city wall. It was probably located SE of the temple area. (Ne 3:28;

Jer 31:40) The Horse Gate is omitted in the inauguration procession account, evidently because the two parts of the procession left off at the Water Gate and the Gate of the Guard, respectively, and did not walk over the section of the wall E of the temple, where the Horse Gate and the Inspection Gate were located.—Ne 12:37-40.

Inspection Gate. Some call the Inspection (Heb., *ham·miph·qadh'*) Gate the Muster Gate. (Ne 3:31, *RS; Ro*) At Ezekiel 43:21 *miph·qadh'* (the same Hebrew word without the article *ha*) is translated "appointed place." Some have thought it was the same as the Gate of the Guard. Its mention by Nehemiah in his reconstruction account would seem to support the idea that it was a gate in the E wall of the city in front of the temple area and N of the Horse Gate. (Ne 3:27-31) Nehemiah's statement that there was a corner in the wall beyond the Inspection Gate would place this gate in the E wall, S of where the wall turned (likely in a northwestward direction).

The account tells us that the repair work was done "in front of the Inspection Gate." Some have understood this to refer to a repair work on the city wall in front of a temple gate by this name. This does not seem to be the correct view, for the same expression is used respecting the Water Gate, which is acknowledged to have been a gate *in* the city wall. (Ne 3:26, 31) The Inspection Gate is not named in the procession account evidently because the marchers did not traverse the wall E of the temple.

Gate of the Guard. From this gate (called "prison gate," *KJ*) part of the inauguration procession left the wall and proceeded to the temple. —Ne 12:39, 40.

Middle Gate. When the wall of Jerusalem was breached by the Babylonians, their military officers sat in the Middle Gate. (Jer 39:3) Most likely this was identical with the Gate of the Old City, since this gate, at the convergence of the Broad Wall, the N wall of the old city, and the W wall of the second quarter, was a central or commanding position. However, opinions differ, and some favor the Gate of Ephraim or the Fish Gate.

Gate of Benjamin. Some identify the Gate of Benjamin with the Sheep Gate. This location would fit the circumstances of Jeremiah's attempted exit to the territory of Benjamin, evidently toward Anathoth, which lay NE of Jerusalem. (Jer 37:11-13) Zedekiah was sitting in the Gate of Benjamin when approached by Ebed-melech with a plea in Jeremiah's behalf. (Jer

38:7, 8) It is reasonable that the king would be near the point of greatest concern during the Babylonian siege. The Sheep Gate on the N of the city would be the most seriously threatened by the attacking Babylonians. However, some believe that the Gate of Benjamin was the Inspection Gate.

Other gates mentioned. When King Zedekiah fled from the Babylonians, he went out "by the way of the gate between the double wall that is by the king's garden." (Jer 52:7, 8; 39:4) There is much uncertainty as to the identity of "the double wall." However, from present knowledge, either the Gate of the Ash-heaps or the Fountain Gate might fit the circumstances described in the Scriptures, both of these being near the king's garden.—2Ki 25:5.

At 2 Kings 23:8 reference is made to "the high places of the gates that were at the entrance of the gate of Joshua, the chief of the city, which was at the left as a person came into the gate of the city." Here "gate of Joshua" is not the name of a city gate but evidently is a gate within the city walls leading to the governor's residence, which was at the left as a person entered the city gate.

Temple Gates. *East Gate.* Nehemiah's reconstruction account tells us that the keeper of the East Gate shared in the repair work. (Ne 3:29) Thus the East Gate is not designated as a gate in Jerusalem's wall, as some have thought. The East Gate may have been approximately in line with the Inspection Gate in the city wall. This gate is evidently the one mentioned in 1 Chronicles 9:18 as "the king's gate to the east," being the gate where the king went into or came out from the temple.

Gate of the Foundation. A temple gate, the location of which is uncertain.—2Ki 11:6; 2Ch 23:5.

"Upper gate of the house of Jehovah." This may have been a gate leading to the inner court, possibly "the new gate of Jehovah," where Jeremiah was tried; also where Jeremiah's secretary Baruch read the scroll before the people. (Jer 26:10; 36:10) Jeremiah may have called it "the new gate" because it had not been so anciently built as the others; possibly it was "the upper gate of the house of Jehovah" built by King Jotham.—2Ki 15:32, 35; 2Ch 27:3.

"Upper Gate of Benjamin, which was in the house of Jehovah." Probably a gate leading to the inner court, on the N side of the temple. —Jer 20:2; compare Eze 8:3; 9:2.

Beautiful Gate. A doorway of the temple re-built by Herod the Great, the site of Peter's healing of the man who was lame from his mother's womb. (Ac 3:1-10) There is a tradition that identifies this gate with the existing Golden Gate in the city wall, but it may be that the Beautiful Gate was an inner gate of the temple area, corresponding possibly to the ancient "East Gate." Some say that it may have been one of the gates E of the temple building itself, opening upon the Court of Women, a gate described by Josephus as being 50 cubits (22 m; 73 ft) in height and having doors of Corinthian brass.

Other gates mentioned are "the gate behind the runners" and "the gate of the runners." These are temple gates, the location of which is uncertain.—2Ki 11:6, 19.

The Jewish Mishnah (*Middot* 1:3), speaking of the temple rebuilt by King Herod the Great, mentions only five gates to the Temple Mount, that is, in the wall surrounding the entire square of the temple area. These were: the two Huldah Gates on the S, the Kiponus Gate on the W, the Tadi (Todi) Gate on the N, and the Eastern Gate, on which was portrayed the Palace of Shushan. Josephus, on the other hand, refers to four gates on the W. (*Jewish Antiquities,* XV, 410 [xi, 5]) These four gates have now been identified by archaeological investigation. From S to N, they are: the gate that leads over Robinson's Arch to steps going down into the Tyropoeon Valley; the Barclay Gate at street level; the gate leading over Wilson's Arch, supporting a bridge over the Tyropoeon Valley; and the Warren Gate, also at street level. The Kiponus Gate may be identified with either the Barclay Gate or the gate over Wilson's Arch.

The Mishnah additionally states that there were seven gates to the court immediately surrounding the temple.—*Middot* 1:4; see TEMPLE.

Figurative Uses. "The gates of righteousness" and "the gate of Jehovah," into which the righteous enter, are spoken of at Psalm 118:19, 20.—Compare Mt 7:13, 14.

When a person died he was referred to as having entered "the gates of death." (Ps 9:13; 107:18) He went into the common grave for mankind and so entered the gates of Sheol-Hades. (Isa 38:10; Mt 16:18) Since Jesus Christ has the keys of death and of Hades (Re 1:18), his congregation has had the assurance that death and Hades would not hold them forever in bondage. The apostle Paul showed that all of these die, going into death and Hades, as did Christ whom God loosed from the pangs of death and did not leave in Hades. (Ac 2:24, 31) Because of the resurrection, death and Hades do not have final victory over Christ's congregation.—1Co 15:29, 36-38, 54-57.

Because God's people when restored to Zion would reestablish pure worship there, her gates would be called Praise. Zion's gates would be open constantly to bring in the resources of the nations, without fear of being taken under control by the enemy.—Isa 60:11, 18.

Ezekiel was given a vision of a city to be called "Jehovah Himself Is There," having 12 gates named according to the 12 tribes of Israel. (Eze 48:30-35) He also reports a detailed vision of a temple with its various gates.—Eze 40-44.

The holy city "New Jerusalem" is pictured as having 12 gates of pearl, with an angel stationed at each gate, evidently as a guard. These gates are constantly open, for no night exists to occasion closing them. The glory and honor of the nations are brought in through the city gates. Even though open, no entrance can be effected by those practicing wicked, unclean, or disgusting things. Only those maintaining cleanness as overcomers or conquerors, those who become kings and priests with Christ, gain entry past the angelic attendants. (Re 21:2, 12, 21-27; 22:14, 15; 2:7; 20:4, 6) The peoples of the nations of earth who walk in the city's light are blessed.

GATEKEEPER.

In ancient times gatekeepers, also called doorkeepers, served at various places, such as city gates, temple gates, even at the gateways or doorways of homes. Gatekeepers of city gates were appointed to see that the gates were closed at night, and they acted as watchmen at the gate. Other watchmen might be posted as lookouts on top of the gate or in a tower where they could get a broad view and could announce those approaching the city. They cooperated with the gatekeeper. (2Sa 18:24, 26) It was a very responsible position, inasmuch as the safety of the city depended on the gatekeeper to a considerable degree and he was an instrument of communication between those outside the city and those inside. (2Ki 7:10, 11) The doorkeepers of King Ahasuerus, two of whom plotted to assassinate him, were also called court officials.—Es 2:21-23; 6:2.

In the Temple. Shortly before his death, King David thoroughly organized the Levites and temple workers, including the gatekeepers, of whom there were 4,000. In their divisions they would come in for seven days at a time. They were responsible to guard Jehovah's house and see that the doors were opened and closed at the proper times. (1Ch 9:23-27; 23:1-6) Besides guard duty, some took care of the contributions brought in by the people for use at the temple. (2Ki 12:9; 22:4) At a later time, when Jehoiada the high priest anointed Jehoash as king, special guards were assigned to the gates of the temple to protect young Jehoash from the usurper, Queen Athaliah. (2Ki 11:4-8) When King Josiah destroyed idolatrous worship, the doorkeepers assisted in removing from the temple the utensils that had been used in the worship of Baal. These were then burned up outside the city. —2Ki 23:4.

When Jesus Christ was on earth, priests and Levites were assigned as doorkeepers and watchmen in the temple rebuilt by Herod. These were required to be on the alert, for the overseer or officer of the Temple Mount would make his rounds, appearing at unannounced times, and it was necessary for the watchman to remain awake at his post constantly in order not to be caught off guard. There was another officer who was in charge of the casting of lots for the temple services. When he came and knocked on the door, it was necessary for the guard to be awake to open it for him. He, too, might catch the guard asleep. On this matter of wakefulness, the Mishnah (*Middot* 1:2) says: "The officer of the Temple Mount used to go round to every watch with lighted torches before him, and if any watch did not stand up and say, to him, 'O officer of the Temple Mount, peace be to thee!' and it was manifest that he was asleep, he would beat him with his staff, and he had the right to burn his raiment."—Translated by H. Danby; see also Re 16:15.

These gatekeepers and guards were posted at their stations in order to safeguard the temple from robbery and to keep out all unclean persons and all intruders who had no proper business there.

In Homes. In the days of the apostles, some homes employed doorkeepers. At the house of Mary the mother of John Mark, a servant girl named Rhoda answered Peter's knock when he returned from prison after being released by an angel. (Ac 12:12-14) The girl who was employed as a doorkeeper at the home of the high priest asked Peter whether he was one of Christ's disciples.—Joh 18:17.

Shepherds. Shepherds in Bible times used to keep their flocks of sheep in a sheepfold, or sheepcote, during the night. These sheepfolds consisted of a low stone wall with a gateway. The flocks of one man or sometimes of several would be kept in the fold during the night with a doorkeeper to keep watch and to protect them. Jesus apparently drew on this custom for illustration when he mentioned a doorkeeper in speaking of himself not only as the shepherd of God's sheep but also as the door through which the sheep could enter.—Joh 10:1-9.

Christians. Jesus emphasized the need for Christians to keep alert and on the watch concerning his coming as Jehovah's executioner. He likened the Christian to the doorkeeper who was commanded by his master to keep on the watch and look for him on his return from traveling abroad.—Mr 13:33-37; see GATE, GATEWAY; GUARD.

GATH [Winepress].

A city of the Philistine axis lords. (1Sa 6:17, 18) Situated as it was, to the E of the Plain of Philistia, Gath figured prominently in the Israelite-Philistine seesaw domination of the area. Gath was the birthplace of Goliath and other giant warriors, and it was occupied by the Anakim at the time that Israel crossed the Jordan into the Promised Land. (Jos 11:22; 1Sa 17:4; 2Sa 21:15-22; 1Ch 20:4-8) The residents of Gath were called Gittites.—Jos 13:3.

Joshua's conquest of the Promised Land did not include the territory occupied by the Philistines. This was to be accomplished later. Nevertheless, when Jehovah instructed Joshua to assign the territory to the tribes, Judah's assignment included the territory in which Gath was located. —Jos 13:2, 3; 15:1, 5, 12.

At unstated times both the Ephraimites and the Benjamites skirmished with the Gittites, as incidentally noted in the genealogies.—1Ch 7:20, 21; 8:13.

In Samuel's day the captured ark of the covenant was brought to Gath, with disastrous consequences to the city's inhabitants. (1Sa 5:8, 9) Shortly thereafter, Israel subdued the Philistines, and certain cities that the Philistines had taken from Israel "kept coming back to Israel from Ekron to Gath." (1Sa 7:14) Later, when David slew the Gittite giant Goliath, Israel pursued the Philistines as far as Ekron and Gath.—1Sa 17:23, 48-53.

After this, when David was forced to flee from Saul, he took refuge in Gath. When the servants of Achish the king of Gath began to say: "Is not this David the king of the land?" David became afraid and feigned insanity in order to escape. (1Sa 21:10-15) David composed two psalms re-

calling this experience in Gath. (Ps 34:Sup; 56:Sup) On David's next visit to Gath, however, he came, not as a lone fugitive, but as the leader of 600 warriors and their families. No doubt anxious to secure David's support against Saul, Achish granted him and his men safe residence in the town of Ziklag until Saul was killed 16 months later, after which David moved to Hebron. (1Sa 27:2–28:2; 29:1-11; 2Sa 1:1; 2:1-3) In his dirge over Saul and Jonathan, David noted that the news of Saul's death would cause rejoicing and exultation in the Philistine cities of Gath and Ashkelon.—2Sa 1:20.

During David's reign, Gath and its dependent towns came into Israelite hands. (1Ch 18:1) Some men from Gath became loyal supporters of David, and when David fled from Absalom, there were 600 Gittites among those who went with him. (2Sa 15:18) But during Solomon's rule Achish was still referred to as king of Gath. (1Ki 2:39-41) Evidently Achish was a vassal prince and not a king in the usual sense. (See AXIS LORDS.) Solomon's successor Rehoboam rebuilt and fortified Gath.—2Ch 11:5-8.

King Hazael of Syria captured Gath from King Jehoash of Judah sometime after Jehoash's 23rd year (876 B.C.E.). (2Ki 12:6, 17) The Philistines must have regained control of the city later, for Uzziah recaptured it in his campaign against them. (2Ch 26:3, 6) The prophets Amos and, afterward, Micah refer to Gath as a foreign city. (Am 6:2; Mic 1:10) Following the Assyrian king Sargon's boast of conquering it not long after 740 B.C.E., there are no further historical references to Gath, and later Biblical mention of Philistine cities does not include it.—Zep 2:4; Jer 25:17, 20; Zec 9:5, 6.

The exact location of Gath is unknown. Although several sites have been proposed, archaeological excavations at most of these sites did not fit the historical description of the city of Gath. Some scholars now favor Tell es-Safi (Tel Zafit), 18.5 km (11.5 mi) ESE of Ashdod. Yohanan Aharoni states: "Since there remains no suitable tell in this more southerly region, we should reconsider an earlier proposal to equate Gath with Tell es-Safi. This is a large and outstanding site with a contemporary lower city spread out at its feet in which an abundance of Philistine pottery was discovered. Its position at the point where the Wadi es-Sant (the Valley of Elah) enters the western Shephelah corresponds nicely with the account of David's victory over Goliath the Gittite. Their fight took place farther east between Sochoh and Azekah (1 Sam. 17.1), and afterwards the Israelites pursued the Philistines 'as far as Gath . . . and the gates of Ekron, so that the wounded Philistines fell on the way from Shaaraim as far as Gath and Ekron' (vs. 52)." —*The Land of the Bible,* translated and edited by A. Rainey, 1979, p. 271.

GATH-HEPHER (Gath-he'pher) [Winepress of Hepher (Digging)].

A border city of Zebulun (Jos 19:10, 13) and home of the prophet Jonah. (2Ki 14:25) It is usually identified with Khirbet ez-Zurra' (Tel Gat Hefer), about 4 km (2.5 mi) NNE of Nazareth and just W of Meshhed (Mashhad), the traditional site of Jonah's tomb. Surface explorations at Khirbet ez-Zurra' appear to corroborate the Biblical statements that the site was occupied at both time periods in the aforementioned accounts.

GATH-RIMMON (Gath-rim'mon)[Winepress by the Pomegranate Tree].

1. A city of Dan (Jos 19:40, 41, 45) assigned to the Kohathite Levites. (Jos 21:20, 23, 24) First Chronicles 6:66-70 appears to make Gath-rimmon an *Ephraimite* city. However, on the basis of the parallel account at Joshua 21:23, 24, Hebrew scholars believe that, because of scribal error, a portion of the text has accidentally dropped out and been lost. So, they suggest inserting the following (corresponding to Jos 21:23) before 1 Chronicles 6:69: "And from the tribe of Dan, Elteke and its pasture ground, Gibbethon and its pasture ground . . . " This could have been the original reading. However, not to be overlooked is the possibility that Gath-rimmon was a Danite enclave city located within Ephraim's territory.

Gath-rimmon is usually identified with Tell Jerisheh (Tel Gerisa), about 8 km (5 mi) NE of modern Tel Aviv-Yafo.

2. A city of Manasseh, given to the Kohathite Levites. (Jos 21:20, 25) Since the similar account at 1 Chronicles 6:70 has "Bileam," many scholars believe this latter name originally appeared in place of Gath-rimmon at Joshua 21:25.—See IB-LEAM.

GAZA (Ga'za).

1. An ancient city listed in the earliest Canaanite boundary description. (Ge 10:19) Aside from some 20 Scriptural references to Gaza, ancient Egyptian records and inscriptions of Ramses II, Thutmose III, and Seti I mention the city. Gaza was apparently the most southwesterly city assigned to the tribe of Judah. (Jos 15:20, 47; Jg

6:3, 4) Its inhabitants were called Gazites.—Jos 13:3; Jg 16:2.

Some would identify Gaza with Tell el-'Ajul (Tel Bet 'Eglayim), but this has not been confirmed by archaeological diggings there. Generally, the ancient city is linked with modern Gaza (Ghazzeh; 'Azza), located about 80 km (50 mi) WSW of Jerusalem. Although separated from the Mediterranean Sea by about 5 km (3 mi) of rolling sand dunes, Gaza lies in a well-watered region known for its olive groves, fruit and sycamore trees, grapevines, and grain. Agriculture likely contributed to the prosperity of ancient Gaza. But its importance stemmed primarily from its location on the main road linking Egypt with Palestine. This made Gaza a "gateway" both for caravans and military traffic.

Occupied by Philistines. Sometime before Israel's Exodus from Egypt in 1513 B.C.E., the Hamitic Caphtorim (Ge 10:6, 13, 14) dispossessed "the Avvim, who were dwelling in settlements as far as Gaza." (De 2:23) When the Israelites entered the Promised Land, Gaza itself was a Philistine city and its inhabitants included some of the Anakim. Although Israel's war operations under Joshua extended as far as Gaza, the city apparently was not taken. It remained a Philistine city, and some of the Anakim continued to live there. (Jos 10:41; 11:22; 13:2, 3) Assigned to Judah, Gaza was afterward conquered by this tribe, but the Judeans did not retain control over the city. (Jos 15:20, 47; Jg 1:18) In Samson's day Gaza was again a fortified city of the Philistines, with a "house" used for Dagon worship that could accommodate about 3,000 persons, if not more, on its roof.

While Samson was at Gaza on one occasion, he "rose at midnight and grabbed hold of the doors of the city gate and the two side posts and pulled them out along with the bar and put them upon his shoulders and went carrying them up to the top of the mountain that is in front of [that faces] Hebron." (Jg 16:1-3) Hebron was a distance of some 60 km (37 mi) from Gaza. The exact location of the mountain facing Hebron is uncertain. For Samson to carry the gates and sideposts any distance, and up a mountain at that, was clearly a manifestation of miraculous power made possible only by Jehovah's spirit.

Later, Samson caused the collapse of the aforementioned house used for Dagon worship, this resulting in his own death and that of the Philistines who had assembled there.—Jg 16:21-30.

Gaza apparently continued to be a Philistine

city throughout the period of the Judges (1Sa 6:17) and during the rule of Israel's kings. King Solomon held dominion as far as Gaza in the SW, but evidently the Philistines were still there. —1Ki 4:21, 24.

Under Assyrian and Babylonian Rule. Toward the close of the ninth century B.C.E., through his prophet Amos, Jehovah stated that he would send "a fire" onto the walls of Gaza, this in retribution for its taking exiles to hand over to the Edomites. (Am 1:6, 7) Although the "exiles" are not specifically identified as Hebrews, likely the allusion is to captives taken by the Philistines in raids on Judah.—Compare 2Ch 21:16, 17; Joe 3:4-6.

Not long thereafter, about the middle of the eighth century B.C.E., Gaza began to experience the "fire" of war. According to Assyrian annals, Tiglath-pileser III conquered Gaza, but its king, Hanno, fled to Egypt. (*Ancient Near Eastern Texts,* edited by J. Pritchard, 1974, p. 283) Apparently Hanno was soon able to return to Gaza, for Sargon II claims to have defeated both him and the Egyptian army under Sib'e allied with him. Sargon II claims to have personally captured Hanno and taken him away in fetters.—*Ancient Near Eastern Texts,* p. 285.

From this time onward, Gaza appears to have been generally loyal to Assyria. Hence, it may be that King Hezekiah's striking down the Philistines as far as Gaza was a phase of his revolt against Assyria. (2Ki 18:1, 7, 8) After this revolt, King Sennacherib launched his campaign against Judah and, according to his annals, gave captured Judean towns to Mitinti the king of Ashdod, Padi the king of Ekron (who had been imprisoned at Jerusalem), and Sillibel the king of Gaza.—*Ancient Near Eastern Texts,* pp. 287, 288.

In the time of Jeremiah, Egypt's army struck down Gaza. (Jer 47:1) Before this event, Jehovah's utterance against the Philistines indicated that calamity from the N awaited them: "Baldness must come to Gaza." (Jer 47:2-5; see also Jer 25:17, 20.) As suggested by other passages in Jeremiah (1:14; 46:20), the "waters" from "the north" mentioned at Jeremiah 47:2 evidently denote the Babylonian armies. King Nebuchadnezzar of Babylon did, in fact, gain control over this area (2Ki 24:1, 7), and the king of Gaza is mentioned in Babylonian inscriptions. (*Ancient Near Eastern Texts,* p. 308) Consequently, the words "before Pharaoh proceeded to strike down Gaza" (Jer 47:1) appear simply to identify the time when the utterance of Jehovah regarding the

Philistines came to Jeremiah. They would not necessarily be directly related to the coming expression of judgment "from the north" thereafter discussed.

Destroyed. The prophet Zephaniah, a contemporary of Jeremiah, sounded a like judgment from Jehovah for Gaza: "An abandoned city is what she will become." (Zep 2:4) And Zechariah's prophecy, recorded after Babylon's fall, pointed to future calamities: "[Gaza] will also feel very severe pains." (Zec 9:5) History confirms the fulfillment of the foretold calamities. In the latter half of the fourth century B.C.E., Alexander the Great, after a five-month siege (two months, according to *Jewish Antiquities,* XI, 325 [viii, 4]), took Gaza. Many of its inhabitants were slain and the survivors were sold into slavery. Over 200 years later, the Jew Alexander Jannaeus, after a year's siege, completely devastated the city. —*Jewish Antiquities,* XIII, 364 (xiii, 3).

Although the Roman governor of Syria, Gabinius, ordered the rebuilding of Gaza, this was likely done on a new site. (*Jewish Antiquities,* XIV, 87, 88 [v, 3]) Some scholars think that at Acts 8:26 the Greek word *e're·mos* (desolate [place]) refers to the old, abandoned Gaza (*AT,* for example, reads: "The town is now deserted"). Others understand *e're·mos* to refer to the road leading to the city, hence the rendering "this is a desert road."—*NW;* compare *JB, NE, RS.*

2. A city with dependent towns located in Ephraim's territory. (1Ch 7:28) Its exact location is unknown. Gaza may be a site in the vicinity of ancient Ai, if not perhaps identical with that city itself. The reading "Ayyah" found in numerous Bible translations has the support of many Hebrew manuscripts. However, there is also evidence for "Gaza" in other Hebrew manuscripts, as well as in the Targums.

GAZELLE [Heb., *tsevi'; tsevi·yah'* (female gazelle); *tsa·va''; tseva·'ah'* (female gazelle); Gr., *dor·kas'*]. Any of a variety of swift and graceful small antelope. The *Gazella dorcas,* encountered in Arabia, Egypt, Palestine, and Syria, likely was familiar to the ancient Hebrews. This animal is about 1 m (3.5 ft) long and stands approximately 0.6 m (2 ft) high at the shoulder. Both male and female have lyre-shaped, ringed horns that may measure as much as 0.3 m (1 ft) in length. The general coloration of this gazelle is pale fawn, with dark and light stripes on the face and with white underparts and hindquarters. The hair is short and smooth. Another variety of gazelle with which the Israelites may have been acquainted is the somewhat larger, darker, fawn-colored *Gazella arabica*.—PICTURE, Vol. 2, p. 955.

The speed of the gazelle, which ranks among the fastest of mammals, is alluded to in Scripture. (Ca 2:17; 8:14) The swiftness of Joab's brother Asahel and of certain Gadites was likened to that of the gazelle. (2Sa 2:18; 1Ch 12:8) Babylon's fall was foretold to cause her foreign supporters and hangers-on to flee like a gazelle to their respective lands. (Isa 13:14) This creature is also cited as an example of acting quickly so as to avoid being ensnared.—Pr 6:5.

Probably with reference to its beauty and gracefulness, the gazelle figures in certain vivid descriptions contained in The Song of Solomon (2:9; 4:5; 7:3). The gazelle is also mentioned in the oath under which the Shulammite placed the daughters of Jerusalem, in effect obligating them by all that is beautiful and graceful.—Ca 2:7; 3:5.

By the terms of the Law given through Moses, the gazelle could be used for food. (De 12:15, 22; 14:4, 5; 15:22) It constituted one of the regularly provided meats for Solomon's sumptuous table. —1Ki 4:22, 23.

GAZEZ (Ga′zez) [Shearer]. First Chronicles 2: 46 says Caleb's concubine Ephah gave birth to Haran, Moza, and Gazez, and then it states that Haran "became father to Gazez." Hence, there may have been two men named Gazez: (1) a son of Caleb, and (2) a grandson of Caleb. But if the expression, "As for Haran, he became father to Gazez," is simply a clarification identifying the Gazez mentioned initially as, not Caleb's son, but his grandson, this would mean there was only one Gazez, namely, the son of Haran and grandson of Caleb.

GAZITES (Ga′zites) [Of (Belonging to) Gaza]. Inhabitants of Gaza, the word applying in both of its occurrences to Philistines.—Jos 13:2, 3; Jg 16:1, 2; see GAZA No. 1.

GAZZAM (Gaz′zam) [possibly, Caterpillar [that is, a cutter]]. Forefather of some Nethinim who returned from Babylonian exile with Zerubbabel. —Ezr 2:1, 2, 43, 48; Ne 7:46, 51.

GEBA (Ge′ba) [Hill]. A city of Benjamin given to the Kohathites; one of the 13 priestly cities. (Jos 18:21, 24; 21:17, 19; 1Ch 6:54, 60) Geba apparently was situated by the northern boundary of the kingdom of Judah, whence the expression "from Geba as far as Beer-sheba." (2Ki 23:8) The ancient city is usually identified with the

village of Jaba′, almost 9 km (5.5 mi) NNE of the Temple Mount in Jerusalem. A steep valley separates this site from the suggested location of ancient Michmash. In the valley there are two hills with steep rocky sides. These perhaps correspond to the 'toothlike crags' Bozez and Seneh, one "facing Michmash," the other "facing Geba." —1Sa 14:4, 5.

Geba was one of the cities that figured in King Saul's campaign against the Philistines. Evidently at the direction of his father Saul, Jonathan struck down the Philistine "garrison" at Geba. (1Sa 13:3, 4) In retaliation, the Philistines assembled a mighty force at Michmash, whereupon many Israelites fearfully went into hiding, some even fleeing across the Jordan. (1Sa 13:5-7) Later, Jonathan made his way from Geba to the Philistine outpost, undoubtedly stationed at the edge of "the ravine pass of Michmash." On his hands and feet, Jonathan ascended the steep passage to the outpost and, with the cooperation of his armor-bearer, struck down about 20 Philistines.—1Sa 14:6-14; compare 1Sa 13:16, 23.

Years later, Asa fortified Geba with stones and timbers of Ramah. (1Ki 15:22; 2Ch 16:6) At a time not specified in the Bible, certain inhabitants of Geba were taken into exile at Manahath. (1Ch 8:6) On its way toward Jerusalem, the Assyrian army under Sennacherib apparently passed through Geba. (Isa 10:24, 28-32) Among the Jews coming back from Babylonian exile were 'sons of Geba'; the city itself was also reoccupied after the return. (Ezr 2:1, 26; Ne 7:6, 30; 11:31; 12:29) Alluding to the exaltation of rebuilt Jerusalem, the prophet Zechariah spoke of the hilly and mountainous land that lies between Geba and Rimmon as becoming low like the Arabah.—Zec 14:10; see GIBEAH No. 2.

GEBAL (Ge′bal) [possibly, Territory; Border], **GEBALITES** (Ge′bal·ites).

1. Gebal, a Phoenician city on the Mediterranean seacoast, is identified with modern Jebeil, about 28 km (17 mi) NNE of Beirut. Historians consider Gebal, the Byblos of the Greeks, to be one of the oldest cities of the Middle East.—See Jos 13:5, ftn.

Jehovah included "the land of the Gebalites" among those regions yet to be taken by Israel in Joshua's day. (Jos 13:1-5) Critics have picked on this as an inconsistency, since the city of Gebal was far N of Israel (c. 100 km [60 mi] N of Dan) and apparently never came under Israelite domination. Certain scholars have suggested that the Hebrew text may be damaged at this verse and consider that the account anciently read "the land adjoining Lebanon," or 'as far as the border of the Gebalites.' However, it should also be observed that Jehovah's promises in Joshua 13:2-7 were *conditional*. Thus Israel may never have gained Gebal because of its own disobedience. —Compare Jos 23:12, 13.

Gebalites helped Solomon in the 11th century B.C.E. with the preparation of the materials for the temple construction. (1Ki 5:18) Jehovah lists the "old men of Gebal" among those who assisted in maintaining ancient Tyre's commercial might and glory.—Eze 27:9.

2. A different Gebal is listed with Ammon and Amalek in Psalm 83:7, and thus apparently lay S or E of the Dead Sea. Although its exact location is unknown, some scholars place it in the vicinity of Petra, about 100 km (60 mi) NNE of the Gulf of 'Aqaba.

GEBER (Ge'ber) [Able-Bodied Man]. One of Solomon's 12 deputies who had the responsibility of providing food for the king and his household one month out of the year. Geber is identified as the son of Uri, and it is probable that his son also served as a deputy.—1Ki 4:7, 13, 19.

GEBIM (Ge'bim) [Ditches]. A site the inhabitants of which sought shelter from the advancing Assyrian army when it moved against Zion, evidently in the days of Hezekiah. (Isa 10:24, 31; compare chaps 36, 37.) Its exact location is not known.

GECKO [Heb., *'ana·qah'; sema·mith'*]. A small, usually thick-bodied lizard with tiny scales covering its body. The eyes are relatively large, catlike, and the gecko's toes are comparatively broad. Found in warm climates, the geckos live in the woods, among rocks, in trees, and sometimes in human dwellings. Six kinds of these nocturnal lizards are found in Palestine.

The "gecko fanfoot" (*Hemidactylus turcicus*) of Leviticus 11:29, 30 is listed as "unclean" for the Israelites. At Proverbs 30:28, "the gecko lizard" (Heb., *sema·mith'*) is spoken of as taking "hold with its own hands" and making its way into the king's palace. Regarding the gecko's toes, *The International Wildlife Encyclopedia* says: "They have numerous microscopic hooks that catch in the slightest irregularities, even those in the surface of glass, and so a gecko can cling to all but the most highly polished surfaces. The hooks are directed backwards and downwards and to disengage them the toe must be lifted upwards from the tip. As a result, a gecko running up a

tree or a wall or along a ceiling must curl and uncurl its toes at each step with a speed faster than the eye can follow. Some of the hooks are so small the high power of a microscope is needed to see them, yet a single toe armed with numbers of these incredibly small hooks can support several times the weight of a gecko's body."—Edited by M. and R. Burton, 1969, Vol. 7, pp. 856, 857.

GEDALIAH (Ged·a·li'ah) [Jehovah Is Great].

1. A Levite singer who, in David's time, was designated by lot to be in charge of the second of the 24 service groups of 12 musicians each.—1Ch 25:3, 9, 31.

2. Grandfather of the prophet Zephaniah and possibly a descendant of King Hezekiah.—Zep 1:1.

3. Son of Pashhur; one of the princes in Jerusalem who accused Jeremiah before King Zedekiah of weakening the fighting men and all the people and urged that Jeremiah be put to death for this. Upon being given a free hand by the king, these princes threw Jeremiah into a miry cistern.—Jer 38:1-6.

4. "The son of Ahikam the son of Shaphan." After the destruction of Jerusalem in 607 B.C.E., King Nebuchadnezzar appointed Gedaliah as governor over the Jews who had been left remaining in the land of Judah. Gedaliah established his residence at Mizpah, and here the prophet Jeremiah took up dwelling. Then the Judean military chiefs who had escaped capture, upon hearing that Gedaliah had been appointed as governor, came with their men to him at Mizpah. Gedaliah assured them, under oath, that it would go well with them as long as they continued serving the king of Babylon, and he encouraged them to gather wine, oil, and summer fruits. Even the Jews who were dispersed in Moab, Ammon, Edom, and other places continued coming to Gedaliah.

All of this was evidently not to the liking of Baalis the king of Ammon, who was successful in enlisting the cooperation of Ishmael in an assassination plot against Governor Gedaliah. Learning of this, Johanan and the other chiefs of the military forces advised the governor accordingly, but he did not believe them. Johanan even approached Gedaliah in private and offered to thwart the scheme by killing Ishmael. But Gedaliah would not hear of it, thinking that falsehood was being spoken about Ishmael. So when Ishmael, along with ten other men, came to Mizpah, Gedaliah took no precautions. He proceeded to eat with them; and while they were eating, Ishmael and the men with him rose up and killed Gedaliah as well as all the Jews and Chaldeans who were with Gedaliah.—2Ki 25:22-25; Jer 39: 14; 40:5–41:3.

5. One of the priests in Ezra's time among those who had taken foreign wives and who promised to send them away.—Ezr 10:18, 19.

GEDER (Ge′der) [Stone Wall]. A town in Canaan; its king was one of 31 conquered by Joshua. (Jos 12:13) Joshua 12:7, 8 shows it as being on the W side of the Jordan, and its being mentioned next to Debir may place it in the Shephelah region. It may be the same as the Beth-gader at 1 Chronicles 2:51. But its exact location is uncertain. In David's time, a man called Baal-hanan the Gederite was in charge of David's olive groves and sycamore trees in the Shephelah, and it is thought that he may have come from either Geder or Gederah.—1Ch 27:28.

GEDERAH (Ge·de′rah) [Stone Pen].

1. A city in the Shephelah assigned to Judah. (Jos 15:20, 33, 36) Gederah is usually identified with Jedireh (Gedera), about 7 km (4.5 mi) NW of the suggested site of Eshtaol. Some of the inhabitants of this city were known for their pottery. —1Ch 4:23.

2. Apparently the name of a site in Benjamin's territory, the home of "Jozabad the Gederathite." (1Ch 12:1, 2, 4) Some geographers tentatively identify it with Judeira, about 1.5 km (1 mi) NE of Gibeon.

GEDERATHITE (Ge·de′rath·ite) [Of (Belonging to) Gederah]. A designation applied to Jozabad, an ambidextrous Benjamite warrior associated with David, and apparently identifying him as being from Gederah of Benjamin.—1Ch 12:1-4; see GEDERAH No. 2.

GEDERITE (Ge·de′rite) [Of (Belonging to) Geder]. A term applied to Baal-hanan (1Ch 27: 28) and believed to derive from the name of his native city, either Geder (Jos 12:13) or Gederah. —Jos 15:36.

GEDEROTH (Ge·de′roth) [Stone Pens]. A city in the Shephelah assigned to Judah (Jos 15:20, 33, 41) and one of the places taken by the Philistines during the reign of King Ahaz (761-746 B.C.E.). (2Ch 28:18, 19) Some geographers locate Gederoth at Katrah, an abandoned village on a mound within modern Gedera, about 13 km (8 mi) ENE of Ashdod, though others say this is too far W to be in the Shephelah.

GEDEROTHAIM (Ged·e·ro·tha′im) A name that means "Two Stone Pens." It appears among cities of Judah in the Shephelah, but its location is today unknown. (Jos 15:20, 33, 36) Instead of Gederothaim, the Greek *Septuagint* reads "and her sheepfolds," that is, 'the sheepfolds' of the previously listed site, Gederah. This reading would drop the total number of cities in the list from 15 to the stated 14. (Jos 15:33-36) Since such an expression would be unusual in such lists, some suggest that the text could be rendered "Gederah *or* Gederothaim" rather than "Gederah *and* Gederothaim."

GEDOR (Ge′dor) [Stone Wall].

1. The son of Jeiel of the town of Gibeon. A member of the tribe of Benjamin, he was a great-uncle of King Saul.—1Ch 8:29-31; 9:35-39.

2. A son of Penuel of the tribe of Judah.—1Ch 4:4.

3. A son of Jered also of the tribe of Judah. —1Ch 4:18.

4. A town in the mountainous region of Judah. (Jos 15:48, 58) It is identified with Khirbet Jedur about 12 km (7.5 mi) N of Hebron. It may also be referred to at 1 Chronicles 4:18. The mention, in the same verse, of Soco and Zanoah, both of which appear elsewhere as names of towns, is thought by some to indicate that Gedor is likely also a town of which Jered was the founder, or "father."

5. A town that is mentioned in connection with activities of the Simeonites. (1Ch 4:24, 39) The Greek *Septuagint* here reads "Gerar."—See GERAR.

6. A place in Benjamin. (1Ch 12:1, 2, 7) A suggested location is Khirbet el-Gudeira, about 16 km (10 mi) NW of Jerusalem.

GE-HARASHIM (Ge-har′a·shim) [Valley of Craftsmen]. A valley named for the community of craftsmen living there. (1Ch 4:14) The community was 'fathered,' or founded, by Joab, though evidently not the Joab of David's time. It was settled by Benjamites after the Babylonian exile. (Ne 11:31, 35) Some geographers tentatively locate it at Wadi esh-Shellal, a broad valley located a few miles SE of Tel Aviv-Yafo; others prefer the identification with Sarafand el-Kharab to the SW of the former.

GEHAZI (Ge·ha′zi). An attendant of Elisha the prophet.

When Elisha wondered what could be done for a hospitable Shunammite woman, it was Gehazi who called to his master's attention that she was childless and that her husband was old. Accordingly, Elisha told her that she would be rewarded with a son. Years later the miraculously given boy became ill and died. The Shunammite thereupon came riding to see Elisha at Mount Carmel and took hold of his feet. On seeing this, Gehazi tried to push her away but was admonished to let her alone. After she finished speaking, Elisha at once sent Gehazi ahead to the boy, while Elisha and the woman followed. On their way there Gehazi met them, bringing back the report that, although he had placed Elisha's staff on the boy's face, "the boy did not wake up." However, shortly after arriving, Elisha resurrected the Shunammite's son.—2Ki 4:12-37.

Later, because a seven-year famine was due to come, Elisha recommended that the Shunammite and her household take up alien residence wherever possible. After the famine, she returned from Philistia to Israel and approached the king with a plea to have her house and field restored to her. It so happened that at this time Gehazi was relating to the king how Elisha had resurrected this woman's son. On hearing the Shunammite's own account of this, the king instructed that everything be returned to her, including all that her field had produced during her absence.—2Ki 8:1-6.

Greed for selfish gain proved to be the downfall of Gehazi. This was in connection with the healing of Naaman the Syrian. Though Elisha had refused to accept a gift from Naaman for the healing of his leprosy (2Ki 5:14-16), Gehazi coveted a gift and reasoned that it was only proper to receive this. Therefore, he ran after Naaman and, in the name of Elisha, asked for a talent of silver (worth $6,606) and two changes of garments, on the pretense that this was for two young men of the sons of the prophets who had just arrived from the mountainous region of Ephraim. Naaman gladly gave him not just one but two talents of silver, as well as the two changes of garments, and had two of his attendants carry the gift for Gehazi. At Ophel, Gehazi took the gift from the hands of the attendants, dismissed them, deposited the gift in his house, and then presented himself empty-handed before Elisha, even denying that he had gone anywhere when asked: "Where did you come from, Gehazi?" As a result, Gehazi was stricken with leprosy. So his greed, coupled with his deceptiveness, cost Gehazi his privilege of continuing to serve as Elisha's attendant, besides bringing leprosy on himself and his offspring.—2Ki 5:20-27.

GEHENNA

GEHENNA (Ge·hen'na) [Gr. form of the Heb. *Geh Hin·nom'*, "Valley of Hinnom"]. This name appears 12 times in the Christian Greek Scriptures, and whereas many translators take the liberty to render it by the word "hell," a number of modern translations transliterate the word from the Greek *ge'en·na*.—Mt 5:22, *Ro, Mo, ED, NW, BC* (Spanish), *NC* (Spanish), also the footnotes of *Da* and *RS*.

The deep, narrow Valley of Hinnom, later known by this Greek name, lay to the S and SW of ancient Jerusalem and is the modern-day Wadi er-Rababi (Ge Ben Hinnom). (Jos 15:8; 18:16; Jer 19:2, 6; see HINNOM, VALLEY OF.) Judean Kings Ahaz and Manasseh engaged in idolatrous worship there, which included the making of human sacrifices by fire to Baal. (2Ch 28:1, 3; 33:1, 6; Jer 7:31, 32; 32:35) Later, to prevent such activities there in the future, faithful King Josiah had the place of idolatrous worship polluted, particularly the section called Topheth.—2Ki 23:10.

No Symbol of Everlasting Torment. Jesus Christ associated fire with Gehenna (Mt 5:22; 18:9; Mr 9:47, 48), as did the disciple James, the only Biblical writer besides Matthew, Mark, and Luke to use the word. (Jas 3:6) Some commentators endeavor to link such fiery characteristic of Gehenna with the burning of human sacrifices that was carried on prior to Josiah's reign and, on this basis, hold that Gehenna was used by Jesus as a symbol of everlasting torment. However, since Jehovah God expressed repugnance for such practice, saying that it was "a thing that I had not commanded and that had not come up into my heart" (Jer 7:31; 32:35), it seems most unlikely that God's Son, in discussing divine judgment, would make such idolatrous practice the basis for the symbolic meaning of Gehenna. It may be noted that God prophetically decreed that the Valley of Hinnom would serve as a place for mass disposal of dead bodies rather than for the torture of live victims. (Jer 7:32, 33; 19:2, 6, 7, 10, 11) Thus, at Jeremiah 31:40 the reference to "the low plain of the carcasses and of the fatty ashes" is generally accepted as designating the Valley of Hinnom, and a gate known as "the Gate of the Ash-heaps" evidently opened out onto the eastern extremity of the valley at its juncture with the ravine of the Kidron. (Ne 3:13, 14) It seems obvious that such "carcasses" and "fatty ashes" are not related to the human sacrifices made there under Ahaz and Manasseh, since any bodies so offered would doubtless be viewed by the idolaters as "sacred" and would not be left lying in the valley.

Therefore, the Biblical evidence concerning Gehenna generally parallels the traditional view presented by rabbinic and other sources. That view is that the Valley of Hinnom was used as a place for the disposal of waste matter from the city of Jerusalem. (At Mt 5:30 *Ph* renders *ge'enna* as "rubbish heap.") Concerning "Gehinnom," the Jewish commentator David Kimhi (1160-1235?), in his comment on Psalm 27:13, gives the following historical information: "And it is a place in the land adjoining Jerusalem, and it is a loathsome place, and they throw there unclean things and carcasses. Also there was a continual fire there to burn the unclean things and the bones of the carcasses. Hence, the judgment of the wicked ones is called parabolically Gehinnom."

Symbolic of Complete Destruction. It is evident that Jesus used Gehenna as representative of utter destruction resulting from adverse judgment by God, hence with no resurrection to life as a soul being possible. (Mt 10:28; Lu 12:4, 5) The scribes and Pharisees as a wicked class were denounced as 'subjects for Gehenna.' (Mt 23:13-15, 33) To avoid such destruction, Jesus' followers were to get rid of anything causing spiritual stumbling, the 'cutting off of a hand or foot' and the 'tearing out of an eye' figuratively representing their deadening of these body members with reference to sin.—Mt 18:9; Mr 9:43-47; Col 3:5; compare Mt 5:27-30.

Jesus also apparently alluded to Isaiah 66:24 in describing Gehenna as a place "where their maggot does not die and the fire is not put out." (Mr 9:47, 48) That the symbolic picture here is not one of torture but, rather, of complete destruction is evident from the fact that the Isaiah text dealt, not with persons who were alive, but with "the *carcasses* of the men that were transgressing" against God. If, as the available evidence indicates, the Valley of Hinnom was a place for the disposal of garbage and carcasses, fire, perhaps increased in intensity by the addition of sulfur (compare Isa 30:33), would be the only suitable means to eliminate such refuse. Where the fire did not reach, worms, or maggots, would breed, consuming anything not destroyed by the fire. On this basis, Jesus' words would mean that the destructive effect of God's adverse judgment would not cease until complete destruction was attained.

Figurative Use. The disciple James' use of the word "Gehenna" shows that an unruly tongue is itself a world of unrighteousness and that one's whole round of living can be affected by fiery words that defile the speaker's body. The tongue of such a one, "full of death-dealing poison" and so giving evidence of a bad heart condition, can cause the user to be sentenced by God to go to the symbolic Gehenna.—Jas 3:6, 8; compare Mt 12:37; Ps 5:9; 140:3; Ro 3:13.

The Biblical use of Gehenna as a symbol corresponds to that of "the lake of fire" in the book of Revelation.—Re 20:14, 15; see LAKE OF FIRE.

GELILOTH (Gel·i'loth) [Regions; Circuits; from a root meaning "roll; roll away"]. A site listed in connection with the boundary of Benjamin. (Jos 18:17) Geliloth's location, described as "in front of the ascent of Adummim," matches that of Gilgal (Jos 15:7), for which reason some scholars consider it a variant name for the Gilgal near Jericho. Others suggest that Geliloth is a site or small region in the vicinity of Tal'at ed-Damm (Ma'ale Adummim) in the Wadi el Qilt SW of Jericho. —See ADUMMIM; GILGAL No. 1.

GEMALLI (Ge·mal'li) [possibly, Weaned (or, Receiving Due Treatment); or, Camel Owner]. A Danite whose son Ammiel represented his tribe as one of the spies sent into Canaan.—Nu 13: 12, 16.

GEMARIAH (Gem·a·ri'ah) [Jehovah Has Perfected (Completed)].

1. "The son of Shaphan the copyist"; one of the princes during the reign of Jehoiakim (628-618 B.C.E.). Gemariah had his own dining room in the upper courtyard of the temple, and it was here that Baruch read aloud the words of the book dictated to him by the prophet Jeremiah. Micaiah the son of Gemariah heard the initial reading of the book and then reported the word of Jehovah to the princes who, in turn, sent for Baruch to have the book read to them. Upon hearing the words of the book, they advised that Baruch and Jeremiah conceal themselves. Later, when the roll was read to King Jehoiakim, Gemariah was one of the princes who pleaded with the king not to burn the roll.—Jer 36:10-25.

A lump of clay at one time fastened to a document and stamped with a seal was recently found in Jerusalem. The inscription on it read: "Belonging to Gemariah [Heb., *Gemar·ya'hu*], son of Shaphan." This bulla is said to be from about the seventh century B.C.E., and its owner is assumed to be the Gemariah mentioned in Jeremiah chapter 36.

2. "The son of Hilkiah, whom Zedekiah the king of Judah sent to Babylon to Nebuchadnez-

zar." On this occasion Jeremiah sent a letter by the hand of Gemariah and of Elasah to the exiled Jews who had been taken to Babylon with Jehoiachin (Jeconiah) in 617 B.C.E.—Jer 29:1-3.

GENEALOGY. An account of human family pedigrees of ancestors or relatives. Jehovah God is the great Genealogist or Keeper of records of creation, beginnings, birth, and descent. He is "the Father, to whom every family in heaven and on earth owes its name." (Eph 3:14, 15) His Word the Bible contains an accurate record of genealogies that play an important part in his purpose.

Man has an inborn desire to know his ancestry and to keep his family name alive. Many ancient nations kept extensive genealogical records, particularly of the lines of their priests and kings. The Egyptians kept such registers, as did the Arabs. Cuneiform tablets have been found of the genealogies of kings of Babylon and Assyria. More recent examples are the genealogical lists of the Greeks, the Celts, the Saxons, and the Romans.

The Hebrew verb for registering legitimate descent is *ya·chas'*, rendered 'be enrolled genealogically' (1Ch 5:17); the related noun is *ya'chas,* translated "genealogical enrollment." (Ne 7:5) The Greek term *ge·ne·a·lo·gi'a* occurs in 1 Timothy 1:4 and Titus 3:9 with reference to personal pedigrees, or "genealogies."

The apostle Matthew opens his Gospel account with the introduction: "The book of the history [*ge·ne'se·os,* form of *ge'ne·sis*] of Jesus Christ, son of David, son of Abraham." (Mt 1:1) The Greek word *ge'ne·sis* means, literally, "line of descent; origin." This Greek term is used by the *Septuagint* to translate the Hebrew *toh·le·dhohth',* which has the same basic meaning, and evidently denotes "history" in its numerous occurrences in the book of Genesis.—Compare Ge 2:4, ftn.

Matthew, of course, gives more than a genealogy of Christ. He goes on to relate the history of Jesus' human birth, ministry, death, and resurrection. This practice was not uncommon then, for the earliest Greek histories had a genealogical framework. In those ancient times a history revolved around those persons contained in or introduced by its genealogy. Thus the genealogy was an important part of the history, in many cases forming the introduction to it.—See 1Ch 1-9.

At the judgment in Eden, God gave the promise of the "woman's" Seed that was to crush the Serpent's head. (Ge 3:15) This may have given rise to the idea of the Seed's having a human line of descent, although not until Abraham was told that his Seed would be the means for blessing all nations was it specifically stated that the line of the Seed would travel an earthly course. (Ge 22:17, 18) This made the family genealogy of Abraham's line of surpassing importance. The Bible is the sole record not only of Abraham's origins but also of those of all the nations descending from Noah's sons Shem, Ham, and Japheth.—Ge 10:32.

As E. J. Hamlin comments in *The Interpreter's Dictionary of the Bible,* the Genesis table of nations is "unique in ancient literature. . . . Such preoccupation with history cannot be found in any other sacred literature of the world."—Edited by G. Buttrick, 1962, Vol. 3, p. 515.

Purpose of Genealogical Records. Over and above the natural inclination of man to keep a record of birth and relationships, genealogy was important to chronology, particularly in the earliest part of mankind's history. But more than that, because of God's promises, prophecies, and dealings, a record of certain lines of descent became essential.

Following the Flood, Noah's blessing pointed out that Shem's descendants would be divinely favored. (Ge 9:26, 27) Later, God revealed to Abraham that what would be called his "seed" would be through Isaac. (Ge 17:19; Ro 9:7) It became obvious, therefore, that the identification of this Seed would require a very careful record of genealogy. Thus, in course of time, the line of Judah, the tribe that was promised leadership (Ge 49:10), and particularly the family of David, the kingly line, would be painstakingly registered. (2Sa 7:12-16) This record would provide the genealogy of the Messiah, the Seed, the line of extraordinary importance.—Joh 7:42.

The next most carefully guarded genealogy was that of the tribe of Levi, with special emphasis on the priestly family of Aaron.—Ex 28:1-3; Nu 3:5-10.

Additionally, under the Law, genealogical records were essential in order to establish tribal relationships for the division of the land and for determining family relationship for individual land inheritances. They served the necessary purpose of identifying the nearest of kin as the *go·'el',* the one qualified to act in brother-in-law marriage (De 25:5, 6), in repurchasing his relative (Le 25:47-49), and as avenger of blood upon a manslayer (Nu 35:19). Also, the Law covenant prohibited marriage within certain degrees of consanguinity or affinity, which necessitated a knowledge of genealogical relationships.—Le 18: 6-18.

The strictness with which the Israelites held to these genealogies is illustrated in the situation that arose after the return from Babylon, when some, supposedly of priestly descent, were unable to find their register. Nehemiah directed that they not eat of the most holy things provided for the priesthood until they could establish their genealogy publicly. (Ne 7:63-65) Nehemiah's registry of the people included the Nethinim, for they, although not Israelites, were officially a group devoted to temple service.—Ne 7:46-56.

As to chronology, in most instances genealogical lists are by no means intended to supply full data. Nevertheless, they are often an aid to chronology in that they provide a check on certain points of chronology or fill in important details. Neither can the genealogical lists usually be taken as supplying the index of population growth, for in many cases certain intermediate links are left out where they are not necessary to the particular genealogy cited. And since genealogies do not usually contain the names of women, the names of the wives and concubines that a man may have had are not listed; likewise not all of his sons from these wives may be named; even some of the sons of the primary wife may occasionally be left out.

From Adam to the Flood. The Bible gives evidence of the existence of lists of family relationships from man's beginning. At the birth of Adam's son Seth, Eve said: "God has appointed another seed in place of Abel, because Cain killed him." (Ge 4:25) Representatives of the line begun by Seth survived the Flood.—Ge 5:3-29, 32; 8:18; 1Pe 3:19, 20.

From the Flood to Abraham. The line of Noah's son Shem, who received Noah's blessing, brought forth Abram (Abraham), "Jehovah's friend." (Jas 2:23) This genealogy, along with the above-mentioned pre-Flood one, constitutes the sole means for establishing the chronology of man's history down to Abraham. In the pre-Flood list the record runs through the line of Seth, and in the post-Flood list, through Shem. It consistently states the time from a man's birth to the birth of his son. (Ge 11:10-24, 32; 12:4) There are no other extensive genealogical lists covering this historical period—an indication that these lists serve the double purpose of genealogy and chronology. In a few other instances the placing of specific events in the stream of time is accom-

plished by the use of genealogical information. —See CHRONOLOGY (From 2370 B.C.E. to covenant with Abraham).

From Abraham to Christ. By God's own intervention, Abraham and Sarah had a son, Isaac, through whom the "seed" of promise was to come. (Ge 21:1-7; Heb 11:11, 12) From Isaac's son Jacob (Israel) came the original 12 tribes. (Ge 35:22-26; Nu 1:20-50) Judah was to be the kingly tribe, this being narrowed down later to the family of David. Levi's descendants became the priestly tribe, the priesthood itself being restricted to Aaron's line. In order to establish his legal right to the throne, Jesus Christ the King had to be identifiable as of David's family and of the line of Judah. But because his priesthood was, by oath of God, according to the manner of Melchizedek, it did not require the Levitical descent.—Ps 110:1, 4; Heb 7:11-14.

Other Prominent Genealogical Lists. In addition to the line of descent from Adam to Jesus Christ and extensive genealogies of Jacob's 12 sons, there are genealogical registers of the beginnings of the peoples related to Israel. These include the brothers of Abraham (Ge 11:27-29; 22:20-24); the sons of Ishmael (Ge 25:13-18); Moab and Ammon, who were the sons of Abraham's nephew Lot (Ge 19:33-38); the sons of Abraham by Keturah, from whom came Midian and other tribes (Ge 25:1-4); and the posterity of Esau (Edom) (Ge 36:1-19, 40-43).

These nations are important because of their kinship to God's chosen people Israel. Both Isaac and Jacob obtained wives from the family of Abraham's brother. (Ge 22:20-23; 24:4, 67; 28:1-4; 29:21-28) God assigned territories bordering Israel to the nations of Moab, Ammon, and Edom, and Israel was told not to encroach upon the land inheritance of these peoples or interfere with them.—De 2:4, 5, 9, 19.

Official Archives. It appears that in Israel, besides the registers kept by families themselves, national records were kept of genealogies. At Genesis, chapter 46, we find the listing of those born to Jacob's household down to the time of Jacob's entry into Egypt and evidently on to the time of his death. A genealogy, primarily of the descendants of Levi and seemingly copied from an earlier register, appears at Exodus 6:14-25. The nation's first census was taken in the wilderness of Sinai in 1512 B.C.E., the second year of their coming out of Egypt, at which time they had their descent acknowledged "as regards their families in the house of their fathers." (Nu 1:1,

18; see also Nu 3.) The only other divinely authorized national census of Israel on record prior to the exile is the one taken about 39 years later, on the Plains of Moab.—Nu 26.

Apart from the genealogies recorded in Moses' writings, there are such lists by other official chroniclers, including Samuel, who was the writer of Judges, Ruth, and part of First Samuel; Ezra, who wrote First and Second Chronicles and the book of Ezra; and Nehemiah, the writer of the book bearing his name. There is also evidence within these writings of other keepers of genealogy: Iddo (2Ch 12:15) and Zerubbabel, who evidently directed that genealogical enrollment be made among the repatriated Israelites. (Ezr 2) During the reign of righteous King Jotham, there was a genealogical listing of the tribes of Israel living in the land of Gilead.—1Ch 5:1-17.

These genealogies were carefully preserved down to the start of the Common Era. This is proved by the fact that each family of Israel was able to go back to the city of its father's house to be registered in response to Caesar Augustus' decree shortly before Jesus' birth. (Lu 2:1-5) Also, John the Baptizer's father Zechariah is noted as of the priestly division of Abijah and John's mother Elizabeth as from the daughters of Aaron. (Lu 1:5) Anna the prophetess is spoken of as "of Asher's tribe." (Lu 2:36) And, of course, the extensive listings of Jesus' forefathers at Matthew, chapter 1, and Luke, chapter 3, make it clear that such records were kept in the public archives, available for examination.

The historian Josephus gives testimony to the existence of Jewish official genealogical registers when he says: "My family is no ignoble one, tracing its descent far back to priestly ancestors. . . . Not only, however, were my ancestors priests, but they belonged to the first of the twenty-four courses—a peculiar distinction—and to the most eminent of its constituent clans." Then, after pointing out that his mother was descended from Asamonaeus, he concludes: "With such a pedigree, which I cite as I find it recorded in the public registers, I can take leave of the would-be detractors of my family."—*The Life*, 1, 2, 6 (1).

The official genealogies of the Jews were destroyed, not by King Herod the Great, as Africanus maintained in the early third century, but evidently by the Romans at the destruction of Jerusalem in 70 C.E. (*Against Apion*, by F. Josephus, I, 30-38 [7]; *The Jewish War*, II, 426-428 [xvii 6]; VI, 354 [vi, 3]) Since that time the Jews have been unable to establish their descent in even the two most important lines, David and Levi.

Identification of Relationships. In determining relationships, often the context or a comparison of parallel lists or of texts from different parts of the Bible is necessary. For example, "son" may actually mean a grandson or merely a descendant. (Mt 1:1) Again, a list of names may appear to be a register of brothers, the sons of one man. On closer observation and by comparison with other texts, however, it may prove to be the register of a genealogical line, naming some sons and also some grandsons or later descendants. Genesis 46:21 evidently lists both sons and grandsons of Benjamin as "sons," as can be seen by a comparison with Numbers 26:38-40.

The above situation is found even in the genealogies of some major families. For example, 1 Chronicles 6:22-24 lists ten "sons of Kohath." But in the 18th verse, and at Exodus 6:18, we find only four sons attributed to Kohath. And examination of the context shows that the listing of "sons of Kohath" at 1 Chronicles 6:22-24 is in reality part of a genealogy of *families* of the line of Kohath who had representative members present for appointment by David to certain temple duties.

Conversely, "father" may mean "grandfather" or even royal predecessor. (Da 5:11, 18) In many places, such as at Deuteronomy 26:5; 1 Kings 15:11, 24; and 2 Kings 15:38, the Hebrew word 'av (father) is also used in the sense of "ancestor," or "forefather." Similarly, the Hebrew words 'em (mother) and *bath* (daughter) are used occasionally for "grandmother" and "granddaughter" respectively.—1Ki 15:10, 13.

Cities and plural names. In some lists a man may be said to be "the father" of a certain city, as at 1 Chronicles 2:50-54, where, for example, Salma is called "the father of Bethlehem" and Shobal "the father of Kiriath-jearim." Evidently the cities of Bethlehem and Kiriath-jearim were either founded by these men or populated by their descendants. The same list reads further: "The sons of Salma were Bethlehem and the Netophathites, Atroth-beth-joab and half of the Manahathites, the Zorites." (1Ch 2:54) Here Netophathites, Manahathites, and Zorites were evidently families.

At Genesis 10:13, 14, the names of Mizraim's descendants have what appear to be plural forms. It has been suggested that they represent the names of families or tribes rather than individuals. However, it should be borne in mind that other names in dual form, such as Ephraim, Appaim, Diblaim, and also the above-named Mizraim, son of Ham, each refer to one individual.—Ge 41:52; 1Ch 2:30, 31; Ho 1:3; 2Ch 28:12.

Abbreviated lists. Often the Bible writers greatly abbreviated a genealogical list, evidently naming only family heads of the more prominent houses, important personages, or persons most important to the particular history being considered. At times, descent from a certain remote ancestor was apparently all that the chronicler was concerned with showing; therefore he could leave out many intermediate names.

One example of such an abridgment is found in Ezra's own genealogy. (Ezr 7:1-5) He records his descent from Aaron the high priest, but in a parallel listing at 1 Chronicles 6:3-14, several names appear in verses 7 to 10 that are dropped at Ezra 7:3. Likely Ezra did this to avoid unnecessary repetition and to shorten the long list of names. Still, the list was perfectly adequate to prove his priestly descent. Ezra says that he is "the son" of Seraiah, meaning that he was his descendant, for he must have been Seraiah's great-grandson, or possibly his great-great-grandson. Seraiah was high priest and was killed by Nebuchadnezzar at the time of the exile to Babylon (607 B.C.E.), his son Jehozadak being taken into exile. (2Ki 25:18-21; 1Ch 6:14, 15) Joshua (Jeshua) the high priest, who returned 70 years later with Zerubbabel, was Seraiah's grandson. (Ezr 5:2; Hag 1:1) Ezra traveled to Jerusalem 69 years after that, which circumstance would make it impossible for Ezra to be Seraiah's actual son and Jehozadak's brother.

Another thing that we learn from comparing genealogies here is that Ezra, though descended from Aaron through Seraiah, was evidently not from *that* line of Seraiah in which the office of high priest was hereditary, namely, from Jehozadak. The high-priestly line from Seraiah ran through Joshua (Jeshua), Joiakim, and Eliashib, the latter being high priest during the governorship of Nehemiah. Ezra, then, achieved his objective with his abridged genealogy, supplying just sufficient names to prove his position in the lineage of Aaron.—Ne 3:1; 12:10.

Some Reasons for Variations in Lists. A son who died childless was often not named; in some cases the man may have had a daughter but no son, and the inheritance may have been transmitted through a daughter who, in marriage, went under another family head in the same tribe. (Nu 36:7, 8) At times the genealogy may merge a less prominent family under another family head so that such minor family is not listed. Therefore childlessness, transmission of inheritance through women, perhaps adoption, or failure to establish a separate ancestral house caused names to be dropped out of some of the genealogical lists, while new houses formed might add new names to the lists. It is obvious, therefore, that the names in a later genealogy might differ at many points from those in an earlier listing.

A number of family heads may appear in what seems to be a list of brothers but which may actually include nephews, as in Jacob's "adoption" of Joseph's sons, Jacob saying: "Ephraim and Manasseh will become mine like Reuben and Simeon." (Ge 48:5) Later, therefore, Ephraim and Manasseh are counted alongside their uncles as tribal heads.—Nu 2:18-21; Jos 17:17.

Nehemiah, chapter 10, presents a number of names attesting by seal "a trustworthy arrangement" to perform God's commandments. (Ne 9:38) In these lists, the names given are not necessarily those of the individuals entering into the agreements, but they may refer to the houses involved, the ancestral head being named. (Compare Ezr 10:16.) This may be indicated by the fact that many of the names listed are the same as those listed as returning with Zerubbabel from Babylon some 80 years earlier. So, while those present may in some cases have had the same name as the ancestral head, they may have been merely representatives of the ancestral houses listed by those names.

Repetition of names. Quite often in a genealogical list there is a recurrence of the same name. The use of the same name for a later descendant was no doubt a method that made it easier for that person to identify his line of descent, although, of course, sometimes there were persons of the same name in separate family lines. Some of the many instances of such recurrences of names in the same ancestral line are: Zadok (1Ch 6:8, 12), Azariah (1Ch 6:9, 13, 14), and Elkanah.—1Ch 6:34-36.

In a number of cases, the names appearing in parallel lists differ. This may be because certain persons had more than one name, as, for example, Jacob, who was also called "Israel." (Ge 32: 28) Then, too, there might be a slight alteration in spelling of a name, at times even giving the name a different meaning. Some examples are: Abram (meaning "Father Is High (Exalted)") and Abraham (meaning "Father of a Crowd (Multitude)"), Sarai (possibly, "Contentious") and Sarah ("Princess"). The prophet Samuel's ancestor Elihu appears to be also called Eliab and Eliel.—1Sa 1:1; 1Ch 6:27, 34.

In the Christian Greek Scriptures, surnames were occasionally used, as with Simon Peter, who was called Cephas, from the Aramaic equivalent of the Greek name for Peter (Lu 6:14; Joh 1:42); also there was John Mark. (Ac 12:12) A name might be given to a person because of some characteristic trait. Simon "the Cananaean" (also called "the zealous one") distinguishes this apostle from Simon Peter. (Mt 10:4; Lu 6:15) In some instances a differentiation is made by expressions such as "James the son of Alphaeus," distinguishing him from James the son of Zebedee and brother of John the apostle. (Mt 10:2, 3) The city, district, or country from which one came might be added, such as Joseph of Arimathea and Judas the Galilean. (Mr 15:43; Ac 5:37) Judas Iscariot is thought possibly to mean Judas "Man From Kerioth." (Mt 10:4) The same methods were employed in the Hebrew Scriptures. (Ge 25:20; 1Sa 17:4, 58) The name of one's brother might be given to clarify identity. (Joh 1:40) Women with the same name were similarly distinguished by also naming the father, mother, brother, sister, husband, or son.—Ge 11:29; 28:9; 36:39; Joh 19:25; Ac 1:14; 12:12.

In both the Hebrew Scriptures and Christian Greek Scriptures, a family name or a title may be used, the identification of the person being determined by his individual name or else by the time and historical events with which the person was connected. For example, Abimelech was evidently either a personal name or a title of three Philistine kings, comparable to "Pharaoh" among the Egyptians. (Ge 20:2; 26:26; 40:2; Ex 1:22; 3:10) The Abimelech or the Pharaoh under discussion would therefore be identified by the time and circumstances. Herod was a family name; Caesar was a family name that became a title. In referring to one of the Herods, the speaker (if there was a danger of ambiguity) could designate the one meant by using his personal name only, such as Agrippa, or by combining the personal name or additional title with Herod, such as, Herod Antipas, Herod Agrippa—and the Caesars similarly, as Caesar Augustus, Tiberius Caesar.—Lu 2:1; 3:1; Ac 25:13.

Names of Women. Women were named in the genealogical registers occasionally when there was a historical reason to do so. At Genesis 11:29, 30, Sarai (Sarah) is mentioned, evidently

for the reason that the promised Seed was to come through her, not through another wife of Abraham. Milcah may have been named in the same passage because she was the grandmother of Rebekah, Isaac's wife, thereby showing Rebekah's lineage as being from Abraham's relatives, since Isaac was not to have a wife from the other nations. (Ge 22:20-23; 24:2-4) At Genesis 25:1, the name of Abraham's later wife Keturah is given. This shows that Abraham married again after Sarah died and that his reproductive powers were still alive more than 40 years after their miraculous renewal by Jehovah. (Ro 4:19; Ge 24:67; 25:20) Also, it reveals the relationship of Midian and other Arabian tribes to Israel.

Leah, Rachel, and Jacob's concubines, together with the sons they bore, are named. (Ge 35:21-26) This helps us to understand God's later dealings with these sons. For similar reasons we find the names of other women in the genealogical registers. When an inheritance was transmitted through them, their names might be included. (Nu 26:33) Of course, Tamar, Rahab, and Ruth are outstanding. In each case, there is something remarkable about the manner in which these women came to be in the line of ancestry of the Messiah, Jesus Christ. (Ge 38; Ru 1:3-5; 4:13-15; Mt 1:1-5) Among other instances of the mention of women in the genealogical lists are 1 Chronicles 2:35, 48, 49; 3:1-3, 5.

Genealogy and Generations. In some genealogies we find the names of a man and his descendants listed down to great-great-grandsons. These could be counted, from one viewpoint, as four or five generations. However, the man first named might live to see all these generations of descendants. So from his viewpoint a "generation" could mean the time from his birth until his death, or until the most remote descendant whom the man lived to see. If this kind of "generation" is referred to, it would, of course, involve a much longer period of time than in the case of the previous viewpoint mentioned.

To illustrate: Adam lived 930 years, having sons and daughters. During that time he saw at least eight generations of his descendants. Yet his own life span overlapped or linked with that of Lamech, Noah's father. Thus, from this viewpoint, the Flood occurred in the third generation of human history.—Ge 5:3-32.

We find in the Bible a few cases of the latter method of reckoning. Jehovah promised Abraham that his seed would become an alien resident in a land not theirs and that they would return to Canaan "in the fourth generation." (Ge 15:13, 16) The census at Numbers, chapters 1-3, indicates that there must have been many father-to-son generations during the 215-year stay in Egypt, the total number of men 20 years old and upward shortly after the Exodus being 603,550 (aside from the tribe of Levi). But the 'four generations' of Genesis 15:16, counting from the time of the entry into Egypt until the Exodus, might be reckoned as follows: (1) Levi, (2) Kohath, (3) Amram, (4) Moses. (Ex 6:16, 18, 20) These persons averaged well over a hundred years in individual life span. Each one of these four "generations" thus saw numerous descendants, possibly down to great-great-grandchildren or farther, allowing 20 or sometimes even 30 years from father to the birth of his first son. This would explain how 'four generations' could see such a large population come into being by the time of the Exodus.—See EXODUS.

Another problem for Bible scholars concerns the same census. At Numbers 3:27, 28, it is stated that four families sprang from Kohath, totaling, at the time of the Exodus, the high number of 8,600 males (8,300, some MSS of *LXX*) from a month old upward. Thus it would appear that Moses had, at this time, thousands of brothers, male cousins, and nephews. Some have concluded from this that Moses was not the son of Amram the son of Kohath but of another Amram, with several generations between, so as to allow sufficient time for the development of such a large male population in just four Kohathite families by the time of the Israelites' Exodus from Egypt.

But the problem may be resolved in two ways. First, not all of a man's sons were always named, as illustrated earlier. Therefore, it is possible that Kohath, Amram, and Amram's four named sons had more sons than those specifically listed. Second, even though Levi, Kohath, Amram, and Moses represent four generations from the viewpoint of their four lifetimes, each could have seen several generations during his lifetime. Thus, even though we allow 60 years each between the births of Levi and Kohath, Kohath and Amram, and Amram and Moses, many generations could have been born within each 60-year period. Moses could have seen great-great-grandnephews, and possibly even their children, by the time of the Exodus. Hence the total of 8,600 (or, possibly, 8,300) would not necessitate another Amram between Amram the son of Kohath and Moses.

A question arises in connection with the line of the promised Seed, the Messiah, in the genealogy from Nahshon, who was chieftain of the tribe of Judah after the Exodus. At Ruth 4:20-22, Jesse is the fifth link from Nahshon to David. The period of time from the Exodus to David is about 400 years. This would mean that the average age of each of these forefathers of David was possibly 100 years (as was Abraham) at the time of his son's birth. This would not be impossible and may have been the case. These sons listed in the book of Ruth would not have had to be firstborn sons, even as David was not the firstborn but was the youngest of several sons of Jesse. Also, Jehovah may have brought the line of the Seed through this almost miraculous course so that it could be seen in retrospect that He had all along been directing the affairs of the promised Seed, as He had definitely done in the cases of Isaac and Jacob.

Again, it may be that there were intentional omissions of names in this 400-year portion of the Messianic genealogy, which is recorded also at 1 Chronicles 2:11-15; Matthew 1:4-6; and Luke 3:31, 32. But the fact that all the lists agree in this section of the genealogy may mean that no names were left out. Nevertheless, even though the chroniclers compiling these lists did leave out certain names not considered important or necessary for their purpose, it would present no problem, for the assumption that several additional generations intervened would do no violence to other Biblical statements or chronology.

Bible Genealogy Is Reliable. The careful, sincere student of Bible genealogy will not accuse the Bible chroniclers of carelessness, inaccuracy, or exaggeration in an effort to glorify their nation, a tribe, or an individual. It must be kept in mind that those including genealogies in their writings (Ezra and Nehemiah, for example) referred to the national archive and drew their material from the official sources available to them. (See CHRONICLES, THE BOOKS OF.) They found there the information that filled their need. They used these lists to prove satisfactorily to all whatever needed to be proved *then*. Evidently their genealogical listings were fully accepted by those living at that time, persons having access to the facts and the records. Consequently, we must recognize the situation with which they were dealing. Ezra and Nehemiah were dealing with these matters in times of reorganization, and the genealogies they compiled were essential to the functioning of things vital to the nation's existence.

Such genealogical lists were bound to vary from period to period; new names would be added and others would be dropped; often only the more important family heads would be named in those lists dealing with the more remote past. In some cases less important names might appear on certain lists because of being of current interest. The sources employed in some cases may have given only partial lists. Some portions may have been missing, or the chronicler himself may have skipped over sections because they were not necessary for his purpose. And they are not necessary for our purpose today.

In a few instances, copyists' errors may have crept into the text, particularly in the spelling of names. But these do not present problems that have any significant bearing on lineages necessary to our understanding of the Bible; nor do they affect Christianity's foundation.

A careful examination of the Bible will eliminate the false idea sometimes advanced that the ancient genealogies in Genesis, chapters 5 and 11, and in other Bible books contain imaginary, or fictitious, names to suit some scheme of the chronicler. These chroniclers were dedicated servants of Jehovah, not nationalists; they were concerned with Jehovah's name and dealings with his people. Furthermore, not only did other Bible writers refer to many of these individuals as real persons but so did Jesus Christ. (Isa 54:9; Eze 14:14, 20; Mt 24:38; Joh 8:56; Ro 5:14; 1Co 15:22, 45; 1Ti 2:13, 14; Heb 11:4, 5, 7, 31; Jas 2:25; Jude 14) To contradict all this testimony would be accusing the God of truth of lying, or of needing some artifice or expedient to promote belief in his Word. It would also deny the Bible's inspiration.

As the apostle states, "All Scripture is inspired of God and beneficial for teaching, for reproving, for setting things straight, for disciplining in righteousness, that the man

of God may be fully competent, completely equipped for every good work." (2Ti 3:16, 17) Therefore, we may rely fully on the genealogies recorded in the Bible. They provided vital statistics not only for the time they were written but also for us today. By them we have full genealogical assurance that Jesus Christ is the promised, long-awaited Seed of Abraham. We are aided greatly in establishing chronology back to Adam, something found in no other source. We know that God "made out of one man every nation of men, to dwell upon the entire surface of the earth." (Ac 17:26) We see that truly "when the Most High gave the nations an inheritance, when he parted the sons of Adam from one another, he

BIBLE LISTS OF JESUS' GENEALOGY			
Genesis and Ruth	1 Chronicles Chaps 1, 2, 3	Matthew Chap 1	Luke Chap 3
Adam	Adam		Adam
Seth	Seth		Seth
Enosh	Enosh		Enosh
Kenan	Kenan		Cainan
Mahalalel	Mahalalel		Mahalaleel
Jared	Jared		Jared
Enoch	Enoch		Enoch
Methuselah	Methuselah		Methuselah
Lamech	Lamech		Lamech
Noah	Noah		Noah
Shem	Shem		Shem
Arpachshad	Arpachshad		Arpachshad
			Cainan
Shelah	Shelah		Shelah
Eber	Eber		Eber
Peleg	Peleg		Peleg
Reu	Reu		Reu
Serug	Serug		Serug
Nahor	Nahor		Nahor
Terah	Terah		Terah
Abram (Abraham)	Abraham	Abraham	Abraham
Isaac	Isaac	Isaac	Isaac
Jacob (Israel)	Jacob	Jacob	Jacob
Judah (and Tamar)	Judah	Judah (and Tamar)	Judah
Perez	Perez	Perez	Perez
Hezron	Hezron	Hezron	Hezron
Ram	Ram	Ram	Arni (Ram?)
Amminadab	Amminadab	Amminadab	Amminadab
Nahshon	Nahshon	Nahshon	Nahshon
Salmon	Salmon (Salma, 1Ch 2:11)	Salmon (and Rahab)	Salmon
Boaz (and Ruth)	Boaz	Boaz (and Ruth)	Boaz
Obed	Obed	Obed	Obed
Jesse	Jesse	Jesse	Jesse
David	David	David (and Bath-sheba)	David

LISTS OF JESUS' GENEALOGY (cont'd)

1 Chronicles Chaps 1, 2, 3	Matthew Chap 1	Luke Chap 3
Solomon	Solomon	Nathan[1]
Rehoboam	Rehoboam	Mattatha
Abijah	Abijah	Menna
Asa	Asa	Melea
Jehoshaphat	Jehoshaphat	Eliakim
Jehoram	Jehoram	Jonam
Ahaziah		Joseph
Jehoash		Judas
Amaziah		Symeon
		Levi
Azariah (Uzziah)	Uzziah (Azariah)	Matthat
Jotham	Jotham	Jorim
Ahaz	Ahaz	Eliezer
Hezekiah	Hezekiah	Jesus
Manasseh	Manasseh	Er
Amon	Amon	Elmadam
Josiah	Josiah	Cosam
Jehoiakim		Addi
Jeconiah (Jehoiachin)	Jeconiah	Melchi
		Neri
Shealtiel (Pedaiah)[2]	Shealtiel	Shealtiel[3]
Zerubbabel[4]	Zerubbabel	Zerubbabel
		Rhesa
	Abiud	Joanan
		Joda
	Eliakim	Josech
		Semein
	Azor	Mattathias
		Maath
	Zadok	Naggai
		Esli
	Achim	Nahum
		Amos
	Eliud	Mattathias
		Joseph
	Eleazar	Jannai
		Melchi
	Matthan	Levi
		Matthat
	Jacob	Heli (father of Mary)
	Joseph	Joseph (Heli's son-in-law)
	Jesus (foster son)	Jesus (Mary's son)

[1] At Nathan, Luke begins reckoning the genealogy through Jesus' maternal line, while Matthew continues with the paternal line.

[2] Zerubbabel evidently was the natural son of Pedaiah and the legal son of Shealtiel by brother-in-law marriage; or he was brought up by Shealtiel after his father Pedaiah's death and became legally recognized as the son of Shealtiel.—1Ch 3:17-19; Ezr 3:2; Lu 3:27.

[3] Shealtiel the son of Jeconiah possibly was the son-in-law of Neri.—1Ch 3:17; Lu 3:27.

[4] The lines meet in Shealtiel and Zerubbabel, afterward diverging. This divergence could have been through two different descendants of Zerubbabel, or Rhesa or Abiud could have been a son-in-law.

proceeded to fix the boundary of the peoples with regard for the number of the sons of Israel" (De 32:8), and we understand how the nations are related.

By knowing the origin of mankind, that Adam was originally a "son of God" and that we all descended from Adam (Lu 3:38), we can clearly understand the statement: "Just as through one man sin entered into the world and death through sin, and thus death spread to all men because they had all sinned." (Ro 5:12) Also, such knowledge makes understandable how Jesus Christ can be "the last Adam" and the "Eternal Father" and how it can be that "just as in Adam all are dying, so also in the Christ all will be made alive." (Isa 9:6; 1Co 15:22, 45) We can better understand God's purpose to bring obedient men back into the relationship of "children of God." (Ro 8:20, 21) We observe that Jehovah's loving-kindness is expressed toward those loving him and keeping his commandments "to a thousand generations." (De 7:9) We observe his trueness as the covenant-keeping God and his careful preservation of a historical record on which we can safely build our faith. Genealogy, as well as other features of the Bible, proves God to be the great Recorder and Preserver of history.—See GENEALOGY OF JESUS CHRIST.

Paul's Counsel Regarding Genealogies. The apostle Paul, writing about 61-64 C.E., told Timothy not to pay attention to "false stories and to genealogies, which end up in nothing, but which furnish questions for research rather than a dispensing of anything by God in connection with faith." (1Ti 1:4) The force of this warning is more appreciated when we know of the extremes to which the Jews later went in researching genealogies and how minutely they investigated any possible discrepancy. The Babylonian Talmud (*Pesahim* 62b) makes the statement that "between 'Azel' and 'Azel' [1 Chronicles 8:38–9:44, a genealogical portion of the Bible] they were laden with four hundred camels of exegetical interpretations!"—*Hebrew-English Edition of the Babylonian Talmud,* translated by H. Freedman, London, 1967.

To engage in studying and discussing such matters was pointless, and it was even more so at the time Paul wrote to Timothy. It was no longer vital to have the genealogical records maintained to prove one's ancestry, since God did not now recognize any distinction between Jew and Gentile in the Christian congregation. (Ga 3:28) And the genealogical records had already established the descent of Christ through the line of David. Also, it would not be long after Paul wrote this admonition that Jerusalem would be destroyed, and along with it the Jewish records. God did not preserve them. Accordingly, Paul was anxious that Timothy and the congregations should not be sidetracked into spending time in research and in controversy over matters of personal pedigree, which contributed nothing to Christian faith. The genealogy furnished by the Bible is sufficient to prove Christ's Messiahship, the genealogical matter of prime importance to Christians. The other Biblical genealogies stand as a testimony to the authenticity of the Scriptural record, manifesting clearly that it is a genuinely historical account.

GENEALOGY OF JESUS CHRIST.

In the first chapter of Matthew we find the genealogy of Jesus running from Abraham forward. At Luke chapter 3 is a genealogy back to "Adam, son of God." Jesus' genealogy is the only one given in the Christian Greek Scriptures. Part of his genealogy appears at 1 Chronicles chapters 1 to 3, running from Adam through Solomon and Zerubbabel. The books of Genesis and Ruth combined give the line from Adam to David.

The latter three lists (Genesis/Ruth, 1 Chronicles, and Luke) agree fully from Adam to Arpachshad, with minor differences as to certain names, such as Kenan, which is "Cainan" at Luke 3:37. The Chronicles and Genesis/Ruth lists agree down to David, while another "Cainan" is found in Luke's account between Arpachshad and Shelah.—Lu 3:35, 36.

From Solomon to Zerubbabel, the Chronicles record and Matthew agree in the main, Matthew omitting some names. These differences and differences in Luke's account from David to Jesus will be discussed later.

Under GENEALOGY, we have shown that besides many private family records, the Jews kept public records of genealogies and that the chroniclers, such as Ezra, had access to these when compiling their lists; also, that the public registers existed in the first century evidently up until 70 C.E. The matter of the descent of the Messiah from Abraham, and through David, was of prime importance to them. So we can be confident that both Matthew and Luke consulted these genealogical tables.

Reliability of the Gospel Genealogies.

The question arises: Why does Matthew leave out some names that are contained in the listings of the other chroniclers? First of all, to prove one's genealogy it was not necessary to name every link in the line of descent. For example, Ezra, in proving his priestly lineage, at Ezra 7:1-5, omitted several names contained in the listing of the priestly line at 1 Chronicles 6:1-15. Obviously it was not essential to name all these ancestors to satisfy the Jews as to his priestly lineage. Similarly with Matthew: He doubtless used the public register and copied from it, if not every name, the ones necessary to prove the descent of Jesus from Abraham and David. He also had access to the Hebrew Scriptures, which he could consult alongside the official public records.—Compare Ru 4:12, 18-22 and Mt 1:3-6.

The lists made by both Matthew and Luke were comprised of names publicly recognized by the Jews of that time as authentic. The scribes and Pharisees as well as the Sadducees were bitter enemies of Christianity, and they would have used any possible argument to discredit Jesus, but it is noteworthy that they never challenged these genealogies. If either Matthew's or Luke's genealogy of Jesus had been in error, what an opportunity it would have been for these opponents to prove it then and there! For until 70 C.E. they evidently had ready access to the public genealogical registers and the Scriptures.

The same is true regarding the first-century pagan enemies of Christianity, many of whom were, like those Jews, learned men who would readily have pointed to any evidence that these lists of Matthew and Luke were unauthentic and contradictory. But there is no record that the early pagan enemies attacked Christians on this point.

Also, both Matthew and Luke achieved their objective, and that was all they needed to do. To prove that Jesus was descended from Abraham and David, it was not necessary to make a *new* genealogy. All they had to do was copy from the public tables that the nation fully accepted regarding the lineage of David and of the priesthood and all other matters requiring proof of one's descent. (See Lu 1:5; 2:3-5; Ro 11:1.) Even if there was an omission in these tables, it did not detract from what these Gospel writers intended and indeed accomplished, namely, presenting legally and publicly recognized proof of the genealogy of Jesus the Messiah.

Problems in Matthew's Genealogy of Jesus.

Matthew divides the genealogy from Abraham to Jesus into three sections of 14 generations each. (Mt 1:17) This division may have been made as a memory aid. However, in counting the names we find that they total 41, rather than 42. One suggestion as to how they may be counted is as follows: By taking Abraham to David, 14 names, then using David as the starting name for the second 14, with Josiah as the last; finally, by heading the third series of 14 names with Jeconiah (Jehoiachin) and ending with Jesus. Notice that Matthew repeats the name David as the last of the first 14 names and as the first of the next 14. Then he repeats the expression "the deportation to Babylon," which he links with Josiah and his sons.—Mt 1:17.

As stated earlier, Matthew may have copied his list *exactly* from the public register that he used, or he may have purposely left out some links with a view to aiding memory. However, a suggestion as to the omission here of three kings of David's line between Jehoram and Uzziah (Azariah) is that Jehoram married wicked Athaliah of the house of Ahab, the daughter of Jezebel, thereby bringing this God-condemned strain into the line of the kings of Judah. (1Ki 21:20-26; 2Ki 8:25-27) Naming Jehoram as first in the wicked alliance, Matthew omits the names of the next three kings to the fourth generation, Ahaziah, Jehoash, and Amaziah, the fruits of the alliance.—Compare Mt 1:8 with 1Ch 3:10-12.

Matthew indicates that Zerubbabel is the son of Shealtiel (Mt 1:12), and this coincides with other references. (Ezr 3:2; Ne 12:1; Hag 1:14; Lu 3:27) However, at 1 Chronicles 3:19 Zerubbabel is referred to as the son of Pedaiah. Evidently Zerubbabel was the natural son of Pedaiah and the legal son of Shealtiel by reason of brother-in-law marriage; or possibly, after Zerubbabel's father Pedaiah died, Zerubbabel was brought up by Shealtiel as his son and therefore became legally recognized as the son of Shealtiel.

A Problem in Luke's Genealogy of Jesus. Available manuscript copies of Luke list a second "Cainan," between Arpachshad (Arphaxad) and Shelah. (Lu 3:35, 36; compare Ge 10:24; 11:12; 1Ch 1:18, 24.) Most scholars take this to be a copyist's error. In the Hebrew Scriptures, "Cainan" is not found in this relative position in the genealogical listings in the Hebrew or the Samaritan texts, nor is it in any of the Targums or versions except the Greek *Septuagint.* And it does not seem that it was even in the earlier copies of the *Septuagint,* because Josephus, who usually follows the *Septuagint,* lists Seles (Shelah) next as the son of Arphaxades (Arpachshad). (*Jewish Antiquities,* I, 146 [vi, 4]) Early

writers Irenaeus, Africanus, Eusebius, and Jerome rejected the second "Cainan" in copies of Luke's account as an interpolation.—See CAINAN No. 2.

Why do the genealogies of Jesus Christ as given by Matthew and by Luke differ?

The difference in nearly all the names in Luke's genealogy of Jesus as compared with Matthew's is quickly resolved in the fact that Luke traced the line through David's son Nathan, instead of Solomon as did Matthew. (Lu 3:31; Mt 1:6, 7) Luke evidently follows the ancestry of Mary, thus showing Jesus' natural descent from David, while Matthew shows Jesus' legal right to the throne of David by descent from Solomon through Joseph, who was legally Jesus' father. Both Matthew and Luke signify that Joseph was not Jesus' actual father but only his adoptive father, giving him legal right. Matthew departs from the style used throughout his genealogy when he comes to Jesus, saying: "Jacob became father to Joseph the husband of Mary, of whom Jesus was born, who is called Christ." (Mt 1:16) Notice that he does not say 'Joseph became father to Jesus' but that he was "the husband of Mary, of whom Jesus was born." Luke is even more pointed when, after showing earlier that Jesus was actually the Son of God by Mary (Lu 1:32-35), he says: "Jesus . . . being the son, as the opinion was, of Joseph, son of Heli."—Lu 3:23.

Since Jesus was not the *natural* son of Joseph but was the Son of God, Luke's genealogy of Jesus would prove that he was, by human birth, a son of David through his natural mother Mary. Regarding the genealogies of Jesus given by Matthew and by Luke, Frederic Louis Godet wrote: "This study of the text in detail leads us in this way to admit—1. That the genealogical register of Luke is that of Heli, the grandfather of Jesus; 2. That, this affiliation of Jesus by Heli being expressly opposed to His affiliation by Joseph, the document which he has preserved for us can be nothing else in his view than the genealogy of Jesus through Mary. But why does not Luke name Mary, and why pass immediately from Jesus to His grandfather? Ancient sentiment did not comport with the mention of the mother as the genealogical link. Among the Greeks a man was the son of his father, not of his mother; and among the Jews the adage was: 'Genus matris non vocatur genus ["The descendant of the mother is not called (her) descendant"]' ('Baba bathra,' 110, a)."—*Commentary on Luke,* 1981, p. 129.

Actually each genealogy (Matthew's table and Luke's) shows descent from David, through Solomon and through Nathan. (Mt 1:6; Lu 3:31) In examining the lists of Matthew and Luke, we find that after diverging at Solomon and Nathan, they come together again in two persons, Shealtiel and Zerubbabel. This can be explained in the following way: Shealtiel was the son of Jeconiah; perhaps by marriage to the daughter of Neri he became Neri's son-in-law, thus being called the "son of Neri." It is possible as well that Neri had no sons, so that Shealtiel was counted as his "son" for that reason also. Zerubbabel, who was likely the actual son of Pedaiah, was legally *reckoned* as the son of Shealtiel, as stated earlier.—Compare Mt 1:12; Lu 3:27; 1Ch 3:17-19.

Then the accounts indicate that Zerubbabel had two sons, Rhesa and Abiud, the lines diverging again at this point. (These could have been, not actual sons, but descendants, or one, at least, could have been a son-in-law. Compare 1Ch 3:19.) (Lu 3:27; Mt 1:13) Both Matthew's and Luke's genealogies of Jesus vary here from that found in 1 Chronicles chapter 3. This may be because a number of names were purposely left out by Matthew and possibly also by Luke. But the fact should be kept in mind that such differences in the genealogical lists of Matthew and Luke are very likely those already present in the genealogical registers then in use and fully accepted by the Jews and were not changes made by Matthew and Luke.

We may conclude, therefore, that the two lists of Matthew and Luke fuse together the two truths, namely, (1) that Jesus was actually the Son of God and the *natural* heir to the Kingdom by miraculous birth through the virgin girl Mary, of David's line, and (2) that Jesus was also the *legal* heir in the male line of descent from David and Solomon through his adoptive father Joseph. (Lu 1:32, 35; Ro 1:1-4) If there was any accusation made by hostile Jews that Jesus' birth was illegitimate, the fact that Joseph, aware of the circumstances, married Mary and gave her the protection of his good name and royal lineage refutes such slander.

GENERATION.
A generation commonly refers to all persons who were born about the same time. (Ex 1:6; Mt 11:16) Associated with this is the meaning "contemporaries." At Genesis 6:9 it is stated concerning Noah: "He proved himself faultless among his contemporaries [literally, generations]." When used with reference to family relationships, a generation can refer to a group of descendants, as sons and daughters or grandsons and granddaughters.—Job 42:16.

The term can be used as a measure of time with reference to past or future ages. The generations of mankind descended from the sinner Adam have been transitory, as contrasted with the earth, which abides forever. (Ec 1:4; Ps 104:5) But the expressions "unnumbered generations" and "a thousand generations" refer to that which is to time indefinite. (1Ch 16:15; Isa 51:8) The command to the Jews that the celebration of the Passover was to be observed "throughout your generations" denoted continual performance to a time then indefinite. (Ex 12:14) God stated to Moses that Jehovah was his name as a memorial "to time indefinite," "to generation after generation," which implies forever. (Ex 3:15) The apostle Paul tells us that God is to be given glory "to all generations forever and ever." —Eph 3:21.

A generation may mean a *class* of persons, that is, those characterized by certain qualities or conditions. The Bible speaks of "the generation of the righteous one" (Ps 14:5; 24:6; 112:2) and "a generation crooked and twisted," "a generation of perverseness." (De 32:5, 20; Pr 30:11-14) Jesus Christ, when on earth, spoke similarly of the people of the Jewish nation of that day, and the apostle Paul applied such terms to the world of his day in general, which was alienated from God.—Mt 12:39; 16:4; 17:17; Mr 8:38; Php 2:14, 15.

One Hebrew word for "generation" is *dohr,* corresponding to the Aramaic *dar.* (Da 4:3, 34) *Dohr* comes from a root verb meaning "stack in a circle" or "move around" (Eze 24:5; Ps 84:10) and thus has a basic underlying meaning of "circle." The related word *dur* means "ball." (Isa 22:18) The Greek equivalent is *ge·ne·a',* from a root meaning "be born."

Another Hebrew word, *toh·le·dhohth',* is occasionally rendered "generations" or "genealogy" (Nu 3:1; Ru 4:18), also "descendants" or "families" (1Ch 5:7; 7:2, 4, 9) and "history" or "origins." —Ge 2:4; 5:1; 6:9; compare AS, AT, KJ, Dy, NW, RS, and other translations.

Length. When the term "generation" is used with reference to the people living at a particular time, the exact length of that time cannot be stated, except that the time would fall within reasonable limits. These limits would be determined by the life span of the people of that time or of that population. The life span of the ten generations from Adam to Noah averaged more than 850 years each. (Ge 5:5-31; 9:29) But after Noah, man's life span dropped off sharply. Abraham, for example, lived only 175 years. (Ge 25:7) Today, much as it was in the time of Moses, people living under favorable conditions may reach 70 or 80 years of age. Moses wrote: "In themselves the days of our years are seventy years; and if because of special mightiness they are eighty years, yet their insistence is on trouble and hurtful things; for it must quickly pass by, and away we fly." (Ps 90:10) Some few may live longer, but Moses stated the general rule. Moses himself, who lived 120 years, was an exception, as were his brother Aaron (123 years), Joshua (110 years), and some others whose strength and vitality were unusual.—De 34:7; Nu 33:39; Jos 24:29.

"This Generation" of Christ's Prophecies. When Bible prophecy speaks of "this generation," it is necessary to consider the context to determine what generation is meant. Jesus Christ, when denouncing the Jewish religious leaders, concluded by saying: "Truly I say to you, All these things will come upon this generation." History recounts that about 37 years later (in 70 C.E.) that contemporary generation personally experienced the destruction of Jerusalem, as foretold.—Mt 23:36.

Later that same day, Jesus again used practically the same words, saying: "Truly I say to you that this generation will by no means pass away until all these things occur." (Mt 24:34) In this instance, Jesus was answering a question regarding the desolation of Jerusalem and its temple as well as regarding the sign of his presence and of the conclusion of the system of things. Before his reference to "this generation," however, he had focused his remarks specifically on his "coming on the clouds of heaven with power and great glory" and the nearness of the Kingdom of God. Immediately afterward, he continued with references to his "presence." (Mt 24:30, 37, 39; Lu 21:27, 31) Jesus was using the word "generation" with reference to humans whose lives would in some way be associated with the foretold events.—Mt 24.

The people of this 20th-century generation living since 1914 have experienced these many terrifying events concurrently and in concentrated measure—international wars, great earthquakes, terrible pestilences, widespread famine, persecution of Christians, and other conditions that Jesus outlined in Matthew chapter 24, Mark chapter 13, and Luke chapter 21.

GENEROSITY. That noble and warmhearted readiness to bless others by freely giving out of an open hand, unstintingly. The Hebrew word *na·dhiv'*, rendered "generous" in Isaiah 32:8, is also rendered "willing" and 'noble.' (Ps 51:12; Nu 21:18, ftn) The Greek noun *ha·plo'tes* ("generosity" [2Co 8:2; 9:11]; "liberality" [Ro 12:8]; "sincerity" [Eph 6:5]) has the basic meaning "simplicity." (2Co 11:3, *Int*) Jehovah himself is the personification of generosity, the One who fully supplies all the needs of his obedient creatures "according to his will." (1Jo 5:14; Php 4:19) Every good gift and perfect present is from him, including such an intangible gift as wisdom.—Jas 1:5, 17.

Moses urged his fellow Israelites to cultivate this divine quality of generosity, even when making a loan on pledge. "You must not harden your heart or be closefisted toward your poor brother. For you should generously open your hand to him . . . You should by all means give to him, and your heart should not be stingy in your giving to him . . . That is why I am commanding you, saying, 'You should generously open up your hand to your afflicted and poor brother in your land.'"—De 15:7-11.

Says the proverb: "The generous soul [literally, the soul with a blessing gift] will itself be made fat [prosperous], and the one freely watering others will himself also be freely watered." (Pr 11:25) Jesus Christ expressed it this way: "There is more happiness in giving than there is in receiving." (Ac 20:35) Again he said: "Practice giving, and people will give to you. They will pour into your laps a fine measure, pressed down, shaken together and overflowing. For with the measure that you are measuring out, they will measure out to you in return."—Lu 6:38.

In the Christian Congregation. The apostle Paul also stated this proverbial truth in yet another way: "He that sows sparingly will also reap sparingly; and he that sows bountifully will also reap bountifully." Since this is so, the apostle reasons, "let each one do just as he has resolved in his heart, not grudgingly or under compulsion, for God loves a cheerful giver." (2Co 9:6, 7) Paul continues by pointing to Jehovah's great example of generosity not only in abundantly supplying seed for the sower and bread for food but also in enriching the Corinthian brothers "for every sort of generosity," that they might be generous toward others. Such gestures of generosity, Paul declared, resulted in "an expression of thanks to God."—2Co 9:8-13.

Paul, encouraging this same godly generosity, wrote the Romans (12:8): "He that distributes, let him do it with liberality." To the Hebrews (13:16) he wrote: "Moreover, do not forget the doing of good and the sharing of things with others, for with such sacrifices God is well pleased." The congregations in Macedonia were outstanding examples of generous giving. The fact that they had even joyfully gone "beyond their actual ability," contributing out of their poverty, made "the riches of their generosity abound."—2Co 8:1-4.

Let it be noted that these scriptures on generosity and liberality are not in conflict or out of balance with others that condemn ingrates, sluggards, and lazy persons. For example, the lazy one who will not plow in cold weather deserves nothing when begging in harvesttime; he that refuses to work is not entitled to the generosity of others. (Pr 20:4; 2Th 3:10) Widows were not to be put on the list for relief unless they qualified. (1Ti 5:9, 10) The contributions made by the congregations throughout Galatia, Macedonia, and Achaia were not for the needy ones among pagan worshipers in general but for "the holy ones" that were in need.—1Co 16:1; 2Co 9:1, 2.

GENESIS, BOOK OF.

The first book of the Pentateuch (Greek for "five rolls" or "fivefold volume"). "Genesis" (meaning "Origin; Birth") is the name given to the first of these books by the Greek *Septuagint,* whereas its Hebrew title *Bere'·shith'* (In the Beginning) is taken from the first word in its opening sentence.

When and Where Written. The book of Genesis was evidently part of the one original writing (the Torah), and it was possibly completed by Moses in the wilderness of Sinai in the year 1513 B.C.E. After Genesis 1:1, 2 (relating to the creation of the heavens and the earth), the book evidently covers a span of thousands of years involved in the preparation of the earth for human habitation (see CREATION; DAY), and thereafter it covers the period from man's creation on down to the year 1657 B.C.E., when Joseph died. —See CHRONOLOGY (From Human Creation to the Present).

Writership. The objection once raised by some skeptics that writing was not known in Moses' day is today generally discounted. In his book *New Discoveries in Babylonia About Genesis* (1949, p. 35), P. J. Wiseman points out that archaeological research gives ample proof that "the art of writing began in the earliest historical times known to man." Virtually all modern scholars acknowledge the existence of writing long before the time of Moses (in the second millennium B.C.E.). Expressions such as that found in Exodus 17:14, *"Write* this as a memorial in the book," substantiate the fact that writing was in common use in Moses' day. Adam must have had the ability to devise a form of writing, God having given him, as a perfect man, a language, with the ability to handle it perfectly, even to the extent of composing poetry.—Ge 2:19, 23.

From where did Moses get the information he included in Genesis?

All the information contained in the book of Genesis relates to events that took place prior to Moses' birth. It could have been received directly by divine revelation. It is obvious that someone had to receive the information relating to the events prior to man's creation in that way, whether Moses or someone prior to him. (Ge 1:1-27; 2:7, 8) This information and the remaining details, however, could have been transmitted to Moses by means of oral tradition. Because of the long life span of men of that period, the information could have been passed from Adam to Moses through just five human links, namely, Methuselah, Shem, Isaac, Levi, and Amram. A third possibility is that Moses obtained much of the information for Genesis from already existing writings or documents. As far back as the 18th century, the Dutch scholar Campegius Vitringa held this view, basing his conclusion upon the frequent occurrence in Genesis (ten times) of the expression (in *KJ*) "these are the generations of," and once "this is the book of the generations of." (Ge 2:4; 5:1; 6:9; 10:1; 11:10, 27; 25:12, 19; 36:1, 9; 37:2) In this expression the Hebrew word for "generations" is *toh·le·dhohth',* and it is better rendered "histories" or "origins." For example, *"generations* of the heavens and of the earth" would hardly be fitting, whereas *"history* of the heavens and the earth" is meaningful. (Ge 2:4) In harmony with this, the German *Elberfelder,* the French *Crampon,* and the Spanish *Bover-Cantera* all use the term "history," as does the *New World Translation.* There is no doubt that even as men today are interested in an accurate historical record, so they have been from the start.

For these reasons, Vitringa and others since have understood each use of *toh·le·dhohth'* in Genesis to refer to an already existing written historical document that Moses had in his possession and that he relied upon for the majority of the information recorded in Genesis. They believe that the persons named in direct connection with such 'histories' (Adam, Noah, Noah's sons, Shem, Terah, Ishmael, Isaac, Esau, and Jacob) were either the writers or original possessors of those written documents. This, of course, would still leave unexplained how all such documents came to be in the possession of Moses. It also leaves unexplained why documents obtained from men who were not distinguished as faithful worshipers of Jehovah (such as Ishmael and Esau) should be the source of much of the information used. It is entirely possible that the expression "This is the history of" is simply an introductory phrase serving conveniently to divide off the various sections of the long overall history. Compare Matthew's use of a similar expression to introduce his Gospel account.—Mt 1:1; see WRITING.

No definite conclusion can be arrived at, therefore, as to the immediate source from which Moses obtained the information he recorded. Rather than just by one of the methods discussed, the information may have been received by all three, some through direct revelation, some through oral transmission, some by written records. The important point is that Jehovah God guided the prophet Moses so that he wrote by divine inspiration.—2Pe 1:21.

The material was to serve as an inspired guide to future generations. It was to be read to the people on frequent occasions (De 31:10-12; 2Ki 23:2, 3; Ne 8:2, 3, 18), and Israel's kings were to take instructions from it.—De 17:18, 19.

The "Documentary Theory" of Critics. A theory has been set forth by some Bible critics that Genesis is not the work of one writer or compiler, namely, Moses, but rather that it represents the work of several writers, some of these living long after Moses' time. On the basis of supposed differences of style and word usage, they have advanced the so-called documentary theory. According to this theory, there were three sources, which they call "J" (Jahwist), "E" (Elohist), and "P" (Priest Codex). Because of a double mention of a certain event or because of similarity of accounts in different parts of Genesis, some would add still further sources to the list, going so far in dissecting the book of Genesis as to claim that there were up to 14 independent sources. They contend that these various sources or writers held different views and theologies yet that, nevertheless, Genesis as an amalgamated product of these sources somehow forms a connected whole. There are many absurdities to

which they go to support their theories, a few of which may be mentioned.

The original basis for the documentary theory was the use of different titles for God; the critics claim that this indicates different writers. The unreasonableness of such a view, however, can be seen in that in just one small portion of Genesis we find the following titles: "the Most High God" ('El 'El·yohn', Ge 14:18); "Producer of heaven and earth" (14:19); "Sovereign Lord" ('Adho·nai', 15:2); "God of sight" (16:13); "God Almighty" ('El Shad·dai', 17:1); "God" ('Elo·him', 17:3); "the true God" (ha·'Elo·him', 17:18); "the Judge of all the earth" (18:25). Trying to use this as a basis for attributing each of these sections to a different writer produces insurmountable difficulties and becomes absurd. Rather, the truth is that the different titles applied to God in Genesis are used because of their meaning, revealing Jehovah in his different attributes, in his various works, and in his dealings with his people.

Other examples are: Because of the use of the word ba·ra', "created," Genesis 1:1 is said to be written by the source called "P." Yet we find the same word at Genesis 6:7 in the source supposed to be "J." The expression "land of Canaan" appearing in several texts (among which are Ge 12:5; 13:12a; 16:3; 17:8) is said to be a peculiarity of the writer known as "P," and therefore these critics hold that "P" wrote these passages. But in chapters 42, 44, 47, and 50, we find the same expression in the writings attributed by the same critics to "J" and "E." Thus, while the critics claim that their theories are needed to account for supposed inconsistencies in Genesis, examination shows that the theories themselves are riddled with inconsistencies.

If the material attributed to each theoretical source is extricated portion by portion, and sentence by sentence, from the Genesis account and then reassembled, the result is a number of accounts each one of which by itself is illogical and incoherent. If we were to believe that these various sources were used and put together by a later compiler, we would be forced to believe that these incoherent accounts, before being amalgamated, were accepted as historical and were used for centuries by the nation of Israel. But what writer, especially a historian, would even construct such disconnected narratives, and if he did, what nation would accept them as a history of its people?

Illustrating the unreasonableness of the advocates of the "documentary theory" is this statement by Egyptologist K. A. Kitchen: "In Pentateuchal criticism it has long been customary to divide the whole into separate documents or 'hands'. . . . But the practice of Old Testament criticism in attributing these characteristics to different 'hands' or documents becomes a manifest absurdity when applied to other ancient Oriental writings that display precisely similar phenomena." He then cites an example from an Egyptian biography that might, using the

HIGHLIGHTS OF GENESIS

A record of God's creating and preparing the earth for human habitation, of mankind's role in God's purpose, and of God's dealings with men of faith during some 2,300 years of early human history

Covers the period from the beginning of the physical creation down to the death of Joseph in Egypt (1657 B.C.E.)

Creation of physical heavens and earth, and the preparation of the earth for human habitation (1:1–2:25)

Sin and death enter world; "seed" foretold as deliverer (3:1–5:5)

Serpent deceives woman; she and Adam partake of forbidden fruit

Serpent, woman, and Adam sentenced; woman's seed to crush serpent

Cain, firstborn son of Adam and Eve, murders his brother Abel

In fulfillment of God's judgment, Adam dies at 930 years of age

Wicked angels and men ruin earth; God brings global Flood (5:6–11:9)

Noah is born in line of Adam's son Seth; in his day disobedient angels marry women and father the Nephilim, who indulge in violence

Jehovah decrees destruction by a deluge but instructs Noah to build an ark for the preservation of his family and basic animal kinds

Floodwaters overwhelm the whole earth; all humans, flying creatures, and land animals outside ark perish

After the Flood, Jehovah prohibits eating blood, authorizes death penalty for murder, and establishes rainbow covenant, promising never to bring another deluge

During the second generation born after the Flood, people begin to build a tower, defying God's purpose for them to spread abroad; Jehovah confuses their language, scattering them

Jehovah's dealings with Abraham (11:10–25:26)

Shem's descendant Abram leaves Ur in obedience to God's call

In Canaan, Abram is promised that his seed will receive the land

Lot separates from his uncle Abram, settles near Sodom, is taken captive, and afterward is freed by Abram; Melchizedek blesses Abram

Abram takes Hagar as concubine, and she gives birth to Ishmael

Jehovah changes Abram's name to Abraham, and Sarai's name to Sarah; covenant of circumcision is established

Jehovah's angel informs Abraham that Sarah will bear a son—Isaac

Told of judgment upon Sodom, Abraham pleads for the righteous

Angels urge Lot and his family to leave Sodom; Lot's wife perishes for disobedience

Isaac is born; Ishmael's taunts at Isaac's weaning lead to dismissal

In obedience to Jehovah, Abraham attempts to sacrifice Isaac, and he receives assurance respecting the covenant promises

After Sarah's death, Abraham arranges to get a wife for Isaac

Isaac's wife Rebekah gives birth to Esau and Jacob

Jacob (Israel) and his 12 sons; to Egypt for the preservation of life (25:27–50:26)

After Jacob had bought the birthright from Esau for a meal and later, at Rebekah's urging, procured the blessing Isaac intended for Esau, Jacob departs for Paddan-aram, seeking a wife

Rebekah's brother Laban tricks Jacob into marrying Leah; then Jacob marries Rachel; by Leah and Rachel and their two maidservants, Jacob has 11 sons and a daughter Dinah before leaving Paddan-aram with his family

Jacob wrestles with an angel, and his thigh joint is put out of place; he desperately clings to the angel in order to receive a blessing, and his name is changed to Israel

After a peaceful meeting with Esau, Jacob resides at Succoth and then at Shechem, where Dinah is violated

Rachel dies when giving birth to Jacob's 12th son, Benjamin

Out of hatred for Joseph, Rachel's firstborn, his half brothers sell him; he becomes a slave to Potiphar in Egypt

Imprisoned on false charges, Joseph comes into circumstances that bring his ability to interpret dreams to Pharaoh's attention

Joseph interprets Pharaoh's dreams regarding a famine and is made second ruler in Egypt

Famine in Canaan forces Jacob's sons to go to Egypt for food; in time Joseph reveals himself to his half brothers

Jacob and his household move to Egypt; Joseph cares for them

Jacob dies in Egypt after pronouncing prophetic blessings on Joseph's sons, Ephraim and Manasseh, and on his own 12 sons

theoretical methods employed by the critics of Genesis, be attributed to different "hands" but which work the evidence shows "was conceived, composed, written, and carved within months, weeks, or even less. There can be no 'hands' behind its style, which merely varies with the subjects in view and the question of fitting treatment." (*The New Bible Dictionary,* edited by J. Douglas, 1980, p. 349) The weakness of the critics' theories actually gives added strength to the evidence that only one man, Moses, recorded the connected, coherent account found in Genesis as inspired by God.

The Historical Character of Genesis. Genesis is the only source known to humans that provides a logical, coherent history of things back to the beginning. Without its factual history of the first man and woman, we would be left with the fanciful stories or allegorical explanations of man's beginning that are found in the creation accounts of pagan nations. A comparison of the book of Genesis with the pagan creation accounts clearly demonstrates the superiority of the Bible account.

Thus, the principal Babylonian myth says that the god Marduk, the chief god of Babylon, killed the goddess Tiamat, then took her corpse and "split her like a shellfish into two parts: Half of her he set up and ceiled it as sky." So the earth and its sky came into existence. As to the creation of human life, this myth states that the gods caught the god Kingu and they "imposed on him his guilt and severed his blood (vessels). Out of his blood they fashioned mankind." (*Ancient Near Eastern Texts,* edited by James Pritchard, 1974, pp. 67, 68) Egyptian creation myths likewise involve the activities of several gods, but they disagree as to which city's god (that of Memphis or that of Thebes) was the one who conceived the creation. One Egyptian myth relates that the sun-god Ra created mankind from his tears. Greek myths parallel those of the Babylonians. Ancient Chinese records are mostly calendars and chronological calculations or records of merely local or temporary interest.

Not one of such ancient sources furnishes us with the history, genealogy, and chronology that the book of Genesis provides. The writings of the ancient nations in general show uncertainty and confusion as to who their national founders were. The definiteness and detail with which Israel's early history is presented is strikingly different. In reality we should not expect it to be otherwise, in view of God's purpose toward his people. The Bible tells us that the nation of Israel was directly governed by God and that he dealt with their forefathers, especially Abraham, Isaac, and Jacob. Then he used Moses in a very special way, through him giving Israel the Law that established them as a nation. Israel's history is in recorded form not only for Israel's benefit but also for the benefit of all who will learn of the ways and dealings of the true God and serve him.

In answering those who would reject many portions of Genesis as fables or folklore, Wilhelm Möller says: "I do not think that it can be made plausible, that in any race fables and myths came in the course of time more and more to be accepted as actual facts, so that perchance we should now be willing to accept as historical truths the stories of the Nibelungenlied or Red Riding Hood. But this, according to the critics, must have been the case in Israel." (*The International Standard Bible Encyclopaedia,* edited by J. Orr, 1960, Vol. II, p. 1209) He goes on to point out that the prophets accepted the account of the destruction of Sodom and Gomorrah as correct (Isa 1:9; Am 4:11) and that they accepted Abraham, Isaac, Jacob, and Joseph as real persons. (Isa 29:22; Mic 7:20) Not only this, but in the Christian Greek Scriptures, Abraham is mentioned in many places, even by Jesus Christ at Matthew 22:32, in connection with the argument about the resurrection. If Abraham, Isaac, and Jacob had not really lived, Jesus would have used another illustration.—Mt 22:31-33.

Value of the Book. Genesis tells us how the universe came into being. In a matter-of-fact way it describes the wonders of creation, without making these overshadow the main purpose of the book. It is thus unlike the pagan creation stories that make these marvels the main thing and go to absurdities and obvious untruths to stress them. Genesis tells about the work of creation, and it shows God's purpose in creating man, the relationship of man to God, and the relationship of man to the animals. It gives us the reason for death and trouble experienced by mankind and the hope of deliverance. It points out that all humans descended from the one man Adam, who sinned and lost life for his posterity; it thereby enables us to understand how the ransom sacrifice of one man, Jesus Christ, could atone for the sins of mankind. Genesis enables us to see how the issue of the rightfulness of God's sovereignty was raised by the symbolic serpent, Satan the Devil. It gives the sure hope of destruction of Satan and of relief for mankind. It recounts the origin of Babylon and thus of all false religion in the post-Flood earth, thereby aiding in the identification of Babylon the Great in the book of Revelation.—See BABYLON THE GREAT.

Jesus said that if anyone serves God, that one must worship Him with spirit and truth. (Joh 4:24) The Genesis account sets forth the truth of man's beginnings and of God's dealings with him. Since everything recorded in Genesis is true and not mythical, we are able to know the truth about man's history. We can see that up to the time of the Flood men certainly knew the truth of the Biblical account about Eden, for the garden was there and cherubs were there with the flaming sword at its gate. (Ge 3:24) But those who wanted to go the way of their own desires ignored the facts that were before them. Noah, however, served God according to the way that man was originally created to serve him, according to *true* history. Although, following the Flood, Nimrod set up rebellion against God at the Tower of Babel, the patriarchs through the line of Shem continued to hold to the true way of life. When it was God's time to organize Israel into a nation and give them the Law, it did not come to them like something completely unknown, a revolutionary change in their way of life. No, for in the patriarchal society they had done many of the things that are found in the Law. As M'Clintock and Strong's *Cyclopædia* (1881, Vol. III, p. 782), declares: "This theocracy cannot have entered into history without preparatory events. The facts which led to the introduction of the theocracy are contained in the accounts of Genesis."

This, in turn, prepared the way for the Messiah and the introduction of Christianity. When Jesus Christ arrived, those who had been living according to the Law to the best of their ability were soon able to identify him. He did not appear suddenly and announce himself to be a great savior and leader without any background or historical credentials. The background that had been furnished right from Genesis on down enabled the honesthearted ones to recognize and follow him. Therefore a strong organization of Jewish Christians could be established as a nucleus, prepared to bring a convincing gospel message to the nations. The forefathers of the pagan nations had led them away from the truth. They were "alienated from the state of Israel and strangers to the covenants of the promise, and . . . had no hope and were without God in the world." (Eph 2:12) Therefore, they had to learn the principles of God from the beginning before they could become Christians.

Genesis, then, provides a valuable basis for understanding all the other books of the Bible and is essential to Christianity. It sets the theme for the Bible, namely, the vindication of Jehovah's sovereignty and the ultimate fulfillment of his purpose for the earth, by means of his Kingdom under the promised Seed. In addition to the very first and basic prophecy at Genesis 3:15, Genesis has within it numerous other prophecies, a great many of which have been fulfilled since its composition.

GENNESARET (Gen·nes'a·ret).

1. A small, somewhat triangular plain bordering on the NW shore of the Sea of Galilee and measuring about 5 by 2.5 km (3 by 1.5 mi). In this region, Jesus Christ performed works of miraculous healing. (Mt 14:34-36; Mr 6:53-56; PICTURE, Vol. 2, p. 739) According to the Jewish historian Josephus, this plain was a beautiful, fruitful, and well-watered region, where walnut, palm, and olive trees thrived, and where figs and grapes were available for ten months out of the year.—*The Jewish War*, III, 516-521 (x, 8).

2. "The lake of Gennesaret" was another name for the Sea of Galilee. (Lu 5:1) Some scholars believe that Gennesaret is probably the Greek form for the early Hebrew name Chinnereth. —Nu 34:11; see GALILEE, SEA OF.

GENTILES. See NATIONS.

GENTILE TIMES. See APPOINTED TIMES OF THE NATIONS.

GENTLENESS. A mildness of disposition or manner, thus the opposite of roughness or harshness. Gentleness is closely related to humility and meekness.

Gentleness is a requisite for a servant of God, particularly one in a responsible position of oversight. The apostle Paul stated that "a slave of the Lord does not need to fight, but needs to be gentle [Gr., e'pi·on] toward all." (2Ti 2:24) The gentle person is not loud, noisy, or immoderate. Moses, the man of the true God, though not in every instance manifesting the proper disposition, "was by far the meekest of all the men who were upon the surface of the ground." (Nu 12:3; Ps 90:Sup) His speech on one occasion was said to be like "gentle rains upon grass."—De 32:2.

At 1 Thessalonians 2:7 Paul described himself and his companions as becoming "gentle in the midst of you [the Thessalonians], as when a nursing mother cherishes her own children." This was because they had real love for those whom they taught, as well as concern for their spiritual growth. (1Th 2:8) The word e'pi·oi (translated "gentle") is found in Textus Receptus, Tischendorf, Merk, and some manuscripts. According to W. E. Vine, e'pi·os "was frequently used by Greek writers as characterizing a nurse with trying children or a teacher with refractory scholars, or of parents toward their children. In I Thess. 2:7, the Apostle uses it of the conduct of himself and his fellow-missionaries towards the converts at Thessalonica."—Vine's Expository Dictionary of Old and New Testament Words, 1981, Vol. 2, p. 145.

However, at 1 Thessalonians 2:7, the Westcott and Hort Greek text and certain manuscripts read ne'pi·oi, "babes." Regarding this, The New International Dictionary of New Testament Theology remarked: "There are two readings of 1 Thess. 2:7: (a) epioi (we were gentle in your company); (b) nepioi (babes). The preceding word ends with n, and it seems likely that this n has been doubled by mistake in copying. Moreover the interpretation of the second reading leads to difficulties. For in v. 7b it is not himself but the Thessalonians whom Paul likens to 'children'; he and his colleagues were like a nurse (trophos)."—Edited by C. Brown, 1975, Vol. 1, p. 282.

Not Weakness. Gentleness does not denote weakness. It requires strength of disposition to be gentle with others and to pacify them or to spare their feelings, especially when one is under provocation. At 2 Samuel 18:5 David, a man of war, because of fatherly love, commanded Joab to deal gently with his rebellious son Absalom. The Hebrew word here ('at) has reference to a going softly or a gentle motion. The apostle Paul, although gentle, was not a weakling, as testified to by his ability to speak very strongly when the need arose, for example, when he wrote his first and second letters to the Christian congregation in Corinth.

A Unifying Force. It is pleasant and conducive to peace when one speaks and acts with gentleness. Such a person is approachable, not forbidding, and his manner tends toward the spiritual upbuilding of others. Harshness, roughness, boisterousness, and vulgarity are divisive and drive others away. But gentleness attracts and unifies. Jehovah is spoken of as collecting together his lambs and as carrying them in his bosom (referring to the voluminous folds of the upper part of the garment, in which lambs were sometimes carried by shepherds). (Isa 40:11) His

Son Jesus Christ said to Jerusalem: "How often I wanted to gather your children together, the way a hen gathers her chicks together under her wings!" "But," he added, "you people did not want it." (Mt 23:37) Therefore, they received harsh treatment at the hands of the Roman army when their city was desolated in 70 C.E.

False Gentleness. Gentleness in tone or manner, such as being soft-spoken, does not always prove true gentleness. It is a quality that, to be thoroughly genuine, must come from the heart. While Job, God's servant, was suffering at the hands of Satan in a test of his integrity to God, he was verbally attacked by three companions. They charged Job with secret sin, wickedness, and stubbornness, intimating also that he was apostate and that his sons had met death at God's hands because of their wickedness. Yet one of the three, Eliphaz, said to Job: "Are the consolations of God not enough for you, or a word spoken gently with you?" (Job 15:11) Thus, some of their speech at least may have been in a soft tone, yet it was harsh in content, hence not truly gentle.

GENUBATH (Ge·nu'bath). Son of Edomite prince Hadad. When the army chief Joab occupied Moab during the reign of David, Hadad fled to Egypt. There he gained the favor of Pharaoh, whose sister-in-law he was given as a wife. By her, Hadad fathered Genubath, who was raised with the sons of Pharaoh.—1Ki 11:14-20.

GERA (Ge'ra) [possibly, Alien Resident].

1. Son of Benjamin's firstborn Bela. (1Ch 8: 1, 3) The designation "sons" at Genesis 46:21, where Gera is listed, apparently includes grandsons.

2. Evidently another descendant of Bela the Benjamite; possibly identical with the Gera mentioned in 1 Chronicles 8:7.—1Ch 8:5.

3. Father of Benjamite Judge Ehud.—Jg 3:15.

4. Father of the Benjamite Shimei who called down evil upon David.—2Sa 16:5; 19:16, 18; 1Ki 2:8.

GERAH (ge'rah). A weight corresponding to $\frac{1}{20}$ shekel and equivalent to 0.57 g (0.01835 oz t). —Ex 30:13; Le 27:25; Nu 3:47; 18:16; Eze 45:12.

GERAR (Ge'rar). A site near Gaza mentioned in the earliest record of the boundaries of Canaanite territory. (Ge 10:19) In the past Gerar was commonly linked with Tell Jemmeh (Tel Gamma), about 12 km (7.5 mi) S of modern Gaza. But currently it is identified by numerous geographers with Tell Abu Hureirah (Tel Haror), located in the foothills of the mountains of Judea, about 19 km (12 mi) SE of modern Gaza. Many earthenware fragments believed to date from the time of the patriarchs have been found at the site. Abraham and, later, Isaac resided for a time as aliens at Gerar and dealt with its king Abimelech (possibly two different rulers that bore this name or official title).—Ge 20:1-18; 21:22-34; 26:1-31; see ABIMELECH Nos. 1 and 2.

After Jehovah brought about the defeat of the impressive army of Zerah the Ethiopian, King Asa's forces pursued the fleeing enemy as far as Gerar. Thereafter the Judeans struck and plundered "all the cities round about Gerar" (probably because of their being allied with the Ethiopians); "even the tents with livestock they struck so that they took captive flocks in great number and camels."—2Ch 14:8-15.

Some scholars suggest altering 1 Chronicles 4:39, 40 to read "Gerar" (as does *LXX*) instead of "Gedor." This passage connects Gedor with a region originally inhabited by the Hamites and having good pasturage, and this description would fit the Biblical references to the area around Gerar.

GERAR, TORRENT VALLEY OF.

In recent years it has been suggested that the torrent valley of Gerar corresponds to the Wadi esh-Shari'ah (Nahal Gerar), running about 0.5 km (0.3 mi) S of Tell Abu Hureirah (Tel Haror), the probable site of ancient Gerar. The general area around the torrent valley of Gerar was ideal for pastoral life. Apparently water could readily be found by digging pits in the torrent bed. (Ge 26:17-19) The patriarch Abraham resided temporarily as an alien in this region. (Ge 20:1, 2) Later, in a time of famine, Isaac returned to the area. Here he engaged in agriculture and raised flocks and herds. (Ge 26:1, 6, 12-14) In the torrent valley itself Isaac's servants dug two wells that provoked quarrels with the covetous shepherds of Gerar.—Ge 26:17-22.

GERASENES

(Ger'a·senes) [Of (Belonging to) Gerasa]. In "the country of the Gerasenes," of which at least a portion lay E of the Sea of Galilee, Jesus Christ healed two demon-possessed men. (Mr 5:1-20; Lu 8:26-39; compare Mt 8:28-34.) The exact limits of this region are today unknown, and the identification is uncertain. Some scholars would link "the country of the Gerasenes" with the area around Khersa on the E shore of the Sea of Galilee. Others suggest that

the designation may apply to the large district radiating from the city of Gerasa (Jarash).—See GADARENES.

GERIZIM, MOUNT

(Ger'i·zim). Mount Gerizim, now known as Jebel et Tur (Har Gerizim), together with Mount Ebal to the NE, is situated in the heart of the district of Samaria. Standing opposite each other, these mountains are the most eminent ones of the region and guard a significant E-W pass. Between the two mountains is a fertile valley, the Valley of Shechem, in which present-day Nablus is situated. Shechem, a strong and important city of Canaan before the Israelites entered the Promised Land, stood at the eastern end of the valley, about 1.5 km (1 mi) SE of Nablus. The strategic location of Mounts Gerizim and Ebal gave them military and political significance, the area also being one of religious importance.—PICTURE, Vol. 1, p. 331.

Mount Gerizim's summit rises over 850 m (2,800 ft) above the Mediterranean Sea. Though approximately 60 m (200 ft) lower than Mount Ebal, Gerizim offers an excellent view of surrounding territory. From it one can see to the N the snowy peak of Mount Hermon, to the E the fertile valley of the Jordan, to the S the mountains in the territory of Ephraim, and to the W the Plain of Sharon and the blue Mediterranean.

Abram (Abraham) once camped "near the big trees of Moreh" between Mounts Gerizim and Ebal, and there he received Jehovah's promise: "To your seed I am going to give this land." (Ge 12:6, 7) Jacob also camped in this vicinity.—Ge 33:18.

In harmony with instructions given by Moses, the tribes of Israel assembled at Mounts Gerizim and Ebal under Joshua's direction shortly after their conquest of Ai. There the people heard the reading of the blessings they would receive if they obeyed Jehovah and the maledictions that awaited them if they disobeyed him. The tribes of Simeon, Levi, Judah, Issachar, Joseph, and Benjamin stood in front of Mount Gerizim. The Levites and the ark of the covenant were situated in the valley, and the other six tribes stood in front of Mount Ebal. (De 11:29, 30; 27:11-13; Jos 8:28-35) Apparently the tribes stationed in front of Mount Gerizim responded to the blessings read in their direction, whereas the other tribes responded to the curses read in the direction of Mount Ebal. While it has been suggested that the blessings were read toward Mount Gerizim because of its greater beauty and fertility in contrast with rocky, largely barren Mount Ebal, the

Bible does not furnish any information on this matter. The Law was read aloud "in front of all the congregation of Israel, together with the women and the little ones and the alien residents who walked in their midst." (Jos 8:35) This vast throng could hear the words from positions in front of either mountain. This was probably due, at least in part, to the excellent acoustics of the area.—See EBAL, MOUNT.

In the days of Israel's Judges, Gideon's son Jotham addressed the landowners of Shechem while standing "on the top of Mount Gerizim." (Jg 9:7) Even today a ledge about halfway up the mountain is called Jotham's pulpit, but it is merely a traditional site.

Samaritan Temple. A Samaritan temple rivaling the one in Jerusalem was constructed on Mount Gerizim perhaps in the fourth century B.C.E. and was destroyed in 128 B.C.E. According to tradition, it was desolated by John Hyrcanus. (*Jewish Antiquities,* XI, 310, 311, 324 [viii, 2, 4]; XIII, 254-256 [ix, 1]; *The Jewish War,* I, 63 [ii, 6]) Even up to modern times the Samaritans have celebrated festivals such as the Passover on Mount Gerizim, at what they believe to be the site of the ancient temple. It was evidently with reference to Mount Gerizim that the Samaritan woman told Jesus Christ: "Our forefathers worshiped in this mountain; but you people say that in Jerusalem is the place where persons ought to worship."—Joh 4:5, 19, 20.

As depicted on ancient coins discovered at Nablus, a temple of Zeus once stood on the NE part of Mount Gerizim, with an approach calculated to have had 1,500 steps. A church was built on the summit of the mountain in the fifth century C.E., and another was constructed by the Byzantine emperor Justinian. It is suggested that ruins now found there are of Justinian's time.

GERSHOM (Ger'shom) [An Alien Resident There].

1. The first-listed son of Levi the son of Jacob. He was the father of Libni and Shimei. (1Ch 6:16, 17, 20, 43, 62, 71) He is also called Gershon.—Ge 46:11; Ex 6:16, 17; Nu 3:17, 18; 1Ch 6:1; 23:6.

2. The firstborn son of Moses by Zipporah; born in Midian. (Ex 2:21, 22; 1Ch 23:14-16) Moses' father-in-law Jethro came to Moses in the wilderness, bringing with him Moses' wife Zipporah and their two sons, Gershom and Eliezer. (Ex 18:2-4) The priestly service of Gershom's descendant Jonathan on behalf of the Danites was illegal, because, although he was a Levite, he was not of Aaron's family.—Jg 18:30.

3. Head of the paternal house of Phinehas who accompanied Ezra from Babylon.—Ezr 8:1, 2.

GERSHON (Ger'shon) [An Alien Resident There]. The first listed of Levi's three sons. Gershon's descendants were called Gershonites and "sons of Gershon." (Ex 6:16; Nu 3:17, 21; 7:7; 26:57; Jos 21:6, 27; 1Ch 6:1; 23:6) He is also called Gershom. (1Ch 6:16, 17, 20, 43, 62, 71; 15:7) Gershon's sons were Libni (evidently called Ladan at 1Ch 23:7; 26:21) and Shimei.—Ex 6:17; Nu 3:18; 1Ch 6:17, 20.

GERSHONITES (Ger'shon·ites) [Of (Belonging to) Gershon]. The descendants of Gershon, or Gershom—the first named of the three sons of Levi—through his two sons Libni and Shimei. (1Ch 6:1, 16, 17) The Gershonites constituted one of the three great divisions of the Levites. At the first census in the wilderness, they numbered 7,500 males from a month old and upward. Those from 30 to 50 years of age who served at the tabernacle numbered 2,630 males. (Nu 3:21, 22; 4:38-41) The service of the Gershonites in the wilderness included caring for the tabernacle (the tent of meeting), its various coverings, the screen of the entrance of the tabernacle, the hangings of the courtyard, the screen of the courtyard entrance, and the tent cords. (Nu 3:23-26; 4:21-28; Ex 26:1, 7, 14, 36; 27:9, 16) In the camp in the wilderness, their place was on the W side of the tabernacle. Behind them, at a distance from the tabernacle, camped the three-tribe division of Ephraim. (Nu 3:23; 2:18) When the chieftains of Israel presented 6 covered wagons and 12 bulls for tabernacle service, Moses gave 2 wagons and 4 bulls to the sons of Gershon. (Nu 7:1-7) When moving camp, the Gershonites marched with the Merarites between the leading three-tribe division of Judah and the three-tribe division of Reuben.—Nu 10:14-20.

The Gershonites were allotted 13 cities with pasture grounds in the territories of Manasseh, Issachar, Asher, and Naphtali. Kedesh, in Galilee, and Golan, in Bashan, allotted to them, were two of the nation's six cities of refuge. (Jos 21:27-33) When David reorganized the Levites, responsibility in connection with singing and the treasury were duties given to some of the Gershonites. (1Ch 6:31, 32, 39-43; 23:4-11; 26:21, 22) Gershonites were among the Levites who engaged in the work of cleansing the temple in the days of King Hezekiah.—2Ch 29:12-17.

GESHAN (Ge'shan). The third-named son of Jahdai of the tribe of Judah. Geshan is listed among the descendants of Caleb.—1Ch 2:47.

GESHEM (Ge'shem) [possibly, Downpour; Pouring Rain]. An Arabian, who, along with Sanballat and Tobiah, opposed Nehemiah in the rebuilding of Jerusalem's wall. These enemies first derided Nehemiah and his coworkers. (Ne 2:19) Then they conspired and plotted against Nehemiah, to no avail. (Ne 6:1-4) Finally, Sanballat sent a letter to Nehemiah, quoting Geshem's accusation that Nehemiah and the Jews were scheming to rebel and that Nehemiah was becoming a king to them. In this, too, these enemies failed. (Ne 6:5-7) Sanballat's quoting of Geshem in the letter seems to indicate that he was a man of influence. It may be noted that relations between the Persian court and the Arab tribes were reportedly good following Persia's invasion of Egypt.

A dialect form of Geshem, the name Gashm, is mentioned in an inscription found in ancient Dedan, in the northern part of Arabia. The name Geshem appears in an Aramaic inscription on a silver bowl found in Egypt. The text reads: "That-which Qainu bar Gesem [Geshem], king of Qedar, brought-in-offering to [the goddess] han-'Ilat."—*Journal of Near Eastern Studies,* 1956, Vol. XV, p. 2.

GESHUR (Gesh'ur).

1. An Aramaean kingdom bordering on the Argob region of Bashan, E of the Jordan River. Its northerly neighbor was Maacath. Although Israel's early conquests extended as far as Geshur, the region itself was not taken. (De 3:14; Jos 12:1, 4, 5; 13:13) It was to Geshur, the realm of his maternal grandfather Talmai, that Absalom fled after murdering his half brother Amnon. There he continued in banishment for three years, until he was brought back to Jerusalem by Joab. (2Sa 3:2, 3; 13:28-38; 14:23; 15:8) At a later period Geshur and Syria annexed many Israelite cities E of the Jordan.—1Ch 2:23.

2. Domain of the Geshurites in southern Palestine, near Philistine territory. (Jos 13:2; 1Sa 27:7-11) With reference to this area, the form "Geshur" is not specifically employed.

GESHURITES (Gesh'ur·ites) [Of (Belonging to) Geshur].

1. The inhabitants of Geshur, a territory E of the Jordan.—De 3:14; Jos 12:4, 5; 13:11, 13.

2. A people of southern Palestine residing in the vicinity of Philistine territory. (Jos 13:2) While outlawed by King Saul, David made raids on the Geshurites and other peoples dwelling in that general area.—1Sa 27:7-11.

GESTURES. See ATTITUDES AND GESTURES.

GETHER (Ge'ther). A descendant of Aram, son of Shem. (Ge 10:22, 23; 1Ch 1:17) Nothing certain is known concerning Gether's descendants.

GETHSEMANE (Geth·sem'a·ne) [Oil Press]. Probably a garden of olive trees that was equipped with a press for squeezing oil from olives. Gethsemane was located E of Jerusalem, across the Kidron Valley (Joh 18:1), on or near the Mount of Olives. (Lu 22:39) Here Jesus Christ often met with his disciples. (Joh 18:2) On Passover night of 33 C.E., he, with his faithful disciples, retired to this garden to pray. Found and betrayed by Judas Iscariot, Jesus was there seized by an armed mob.—Mt 26:36-56; Mr 14:32-52; Lu 22:39-53; Joh 18:1-12.

The exact location of the garden of Gethsemane cannot be determined, because (according to the testimony of Josephus) all the trees around Jerusalem were cut down during the Roman siege in 70 C.E. (*The Jewish War,* VI, 5-8 [i, 1]) One tradition identifies Gethsemane with the garden that was enclosed by the Franciscans in 1848. It measures about 46 by 43 m (150 by 140 ft) and is located at the foot of the Mount of Olives, at the fork of the road on its W slope. Eight olive trees in that garden have been there for centuries.

GEUEL (Geu'el) [possibly, Eminence of God]. Son of Machi of the tribe of Gad; one of the 12 chieftains sent out by Moses from the wilderness of Paran to spy out the land of Canaan.—Nu 13:2, 3, 15, 16.

GEZER (Ge'zer) [Piece; Part]. A royal city on the inland side of the Palestinian coastal plain. Gezer is first mentioned when its king unsuccessfully tried to save Lachish from the Israelite army under Joshua. (Jos 10:33; 12:7, 8, 12) Gezer was assigned as a boundary site to the Ephraimites (Jos 16:3; 1Ch 7:28), but they did not entirely dispossess the Canaanite inhabitants. (Jos 16:10; Jg 1:29) Gezer was also appointed to the Kohathites as a Levite city.—Jos 21:20, 21; 1Ch 6:66, 67.

The city was associated with the Philistines in David's time, as when he broke their power "from Geba to as far as Gezer." (2Sa 5:25; 1Ch 14:16) Also, Sibbecai the Hushathite distinguished himself during the defeat of the Philistines at Gezer by striking down Sippai, a descendant of the Rephaim. (1Ch 20:4) Egypt's Pharaoh later came against Gezer for some unstated reason. After

View from the Temple Mount toward the traditional location of Gethsemane

connected Egypt with Mesopotamia for trade and military purposes. Tell Jezer's elevated position on a ridge of the Shephelah allowed it to command use of both of these roads.

Archaeological digging first began at this tell early in the 20th century. Since then it has become one of the most thoroughly excavated and explored sites in Palestine. Among the finds there are the "Solomonic gate and casemate wall," built upon a layer of destruction debris that some conjecture to be the result of Pharaoh's burning of Gezer. Its architecture is considered to be so similar to that found in structures at Hazor and Megiddo as to indicate that all three were built from the same plans. Earlier strata show Philistine pottery in abundance. Perhaps the most famous find to come out of Tell Jezer, however, is the Gezer "calendar," a plaque containing what appear to be a schoolboy's memory exercises. It has proved to be of value by informing modern researchers of ancient Israel's agricultural seasons and providing a glimpse into the Hebrew script and language of Solomon's day.

GIAH (Gi′ah) [Bursting Forth; Gushing]. A site near "the hill of Ammah" mentioned in describing the pursuit of Abner by Joab and Abishai. (2Sa 2:24) The context suggests to some that Giah was E of Gibeon in Benjamin's territory. Certain scholars have proposed sites based on textual emendation, but Giah's exact location remains unknown.—See AMMAH.

GIANT. The Bible gives accounts of men of extraordinary size. There was Og, king of Bashan, one of the Rephaim, whose bier was nine cubits (4 m; 13.1 ft) in length and four cubits (1.8 m; 5.8 ft) in width. (De 3:11) Goliath of Gath, whom David killed, was six cubits and a span (2.9 m; 9.5 ft) in height. Indicative of Goliath's size and strength was the weight of his armor. His copper coat of mail weighed 5,000 shekels (57 kg; 126 lb); the iron blade of his spear weighed 600 shekels (6.8 kg; 15 lb).—1Sa 17:4-7.

burning the city and killing its Canaanite population, he gave it as a dowry to Solomon's wife. Solomon rebuilt and possibly fortified the city. —1Ki 9:15-17.

Gezer also finds frequent mention in secular records. On the walls of the temple at Karnak, Thutmose III recorded the capture of Gezer. The city later played a prominent role in the Amarna Tablets, being mentioned by name at least nine times. Pharaoh Merneptah boasted on his stele that he 'seized Gezer.'

Scholars consider ancient Gezer to be modern Tell Jezer (Abu Shusheh; Tel Gezer), located about midway on the route between Jerusalem and Tel Aviv-Yafo (Joppa). It thus lay near another great highway that has for millenniums

Besides Goliath, there were other unusually large men of the Rephaim, among them being Ishbi-benob, the weight of whose spear was 300 shekels of copper (3.4 kg; 7.5 lb) (2Sa 21:16); Saph, or Sippai (2Sa 21:18; 1Ch 20:4); Lahmi, Goliath's brother, "the shaft of whose spear was like the beam of loom workers" (1Ch 20:5); and a man of extraordinary size whose fingers and toes were in sixes, totaling 24 (2Sa 21:20).

The faithless spies reported to the Israelites that in Canaan they "saw the Nephilim, the sons of Anak, who are from the Nephilim; so that we became in our own eyes like grasshoppers, and the same way we became in their eyes." (Nu 13:33) These men of extraordinary size, called the sons of Anak (probably meaning "Long-Necked [that is, of tall stature]"), were not actually Nephilim, as reported, but were only unusually tall men, for the Nephilim, the offspring of angels and women (Ge 6:4), perished in the Flood.

GIBBAR (Gib′bar) [Superior; Mighty; Overwhelming]. Possibly the name of a family head, 95 of whose "sons" (descendants) returned with Zerubbabel from Babylonian exile in 537 B.C.E. (Ezr 2:1, 2, 20) However, in the parallel passage of Nehemiah 7:25, Gibeon is listed instead of Gibbar. Hence "the sons of Gibbar [Gibeon], ninety-five," may have reference to the descendants of the former inhabitants of Gibeon, inasmuch as other place-names appear in Ezra 2:21-34, for example, "the sons of Bethlehem."

GIBBETHON (Gib′be·thon) [Back; Mound]. A city originally assigned to the tribe of Dan (Jos 19:40, 41, 44) but later given to the Kohathites as a Levite city. (Jos 21:20, 23) Centuries later, Gibbethon was in the hands of the Philistines, and it was while Israel's King Nadab was attempting to wrest the city from them that the conspirator Baasha assassinated him. (1Ki 15:27) Gibbethon was under Philistine control some 24 years later when Omri, army chief of Israel, encamped against it. Acclaimed as king by the Israelite camp there, Omri broke off the siege of Gibbethon to attack the rival Israelite king Zimri. —1Ki 16:15-18.

Gibbethon is generally identified with Tell el-Melat (Tel Malot), about 9 km (5.5 mi) N of the suggested site of the Philistine city of Ekron.

GIBEA (Gib′e·a) [Hill]. A descendant of Caleb of the tribe of Judah (1Ch 2:42, 49); or, possibly, the city of Gibeah (Jos 15:57), "fathered," or founded, by one of Caleb's offspring, Sheva.—See GIBEAH No. 1.

GIBEAH (Gib′e·ah) [Hill].

1. A city in the mountainous region of Judah. (Jos 15:1, 48, 57) Some scholars link it with present-day El Jab′a, about 12 km (7.5 mi) WSW of Bethlehem. Others, however, believe that ancient Gibeah was located somewhere in the region SE of Hebron, since it is listed among other cities in that general area. (Jos 15:55-57) This city (or No. 2) may have been the home of Maacah (Micaiah) the mother of the Judean king Abijam (Abijah).—2Ch 13:1, 2; 1Ki 15:1, 2.

2. A city in the territory of Benjamin (Jos 18:28), also called "Gibeah of Benjamin" (1Sa 13:2), "Gibeah of the sons of Benjamin" (2Sa 23:29), and "Gibeah of Saul" (2Sa 21:6). It was apparently situated near the main road between Jebus (Jerusalem) and Ramah. (Jg 19:11-15) Because of its position on one of the heights of Palestine's central mountain ridge, Gibeah served well as a lookout point in time of war. (1Sa 14:16) Scholars generally identify this city with Tell el-Ful (Giv′at Sha′ul), located about 5 km (3 mi) N of the Temple Mount in Jerusalem.

The Hebrew spellings of Geba (masculine form of the word meaning "Hill") and Gibeah (feminine form of the term meaning "Hill") are almost identical. Many believe that this has resulted in scribal errors in the Masoretic text and therefore recommend changing certain scriptures to read "Geba" instead of "Gibeah," and vice versa. On this, one commentary, with reference to First Samuel chapters 13 and 14, observes: "But commentators are much at variance as to where the substitutions should be made (e.g. Smith reads Geba for Gibeah throughout; Kennedy reads Geba for Gibeah in [chapter 13] verse 2, Gibeah for Geba in verse 3, and Geba for Gibeah in xiv. 2); and it is not impossible to understand the progress of the campaign without such alterations." (*Soncino Books of the Bible*, edited by A. Cohen, London, 1951, Samuel, p. 69) At Judges 20:10, 33 the context suggests that "Gibeah" is intended, and therefore many translators depart here from the reading of the Masoretic text and employ "Gibeah" rather than "Geba."

In the period of the Judges, the city of Gibeah figured in an incident that led to the near extermination of the entire tribe of Benjamin. An old man invited an Ephraimite Levite and his concubine to stay with him for the night. Soon good-for-nothing men of Gibeah surrounded the house, demanding that the Levite be turned over to them so that they might have intercourse with him. After the Levite gave his concubine into their hands, they so abused her all night that she died in the morning. (This shocking sin may be alluded to at Ho 9:9 and 10:9.) Since the tribe of Benjamin shielded the guilty men of Gibeah, the other tribes warred against Benjamin. They twice sustained severe losses before finally defeating the Benjamites and consigning Gibeah to the fire. (Jg 19:15–20:48) (Some link the Biblical record concerning the destruction of Gibeah with the archaeological evidence uncovered at Tell el-Ful indicating that the city was burned.)

Gibeah was the home of Israel's first king, Saul (1Sa 10:26; 15:34), and apparently also of Ittai (Ithai), one of David's mighty men (2Sa 23:8, 29; 1Ch 11:26, 31), as well as of Ahi-ezer and Joash, two warriors who joined themselves to David at Ziklag. (1Ch 12:1-3) Gibeah evidently also served as the first capital of the Israelite kingdom under Saul. At Gibeah, messengers from Jabesh (Jabesh-gilead) appealed for aid when faced with an Ammonite siege, and from here King Saul immediately summoned Israel for war to meet this threat. (1Sa 11:1-7) Later, Saul's war operations against the Philistines were launched in the vicinity of Gibeah. (1Sa 13:2-4, 15; 14:2, 16) Also, on two occasions men of Ziph made report to Saul at Gibeah concerning the hideout of outlawed David.—1Sa 23:19; 26:1.

During the reign of David, seven of Saul's sons and grandsons were put to death at Gibeah ("Gibeon," according to Aquila, Symmachus, and *LXX*) because of the bloodguilt that had come upon the house of Saul on account of his having put many Gibeonites to death. And Saul's widowed concubine kept watch over the dead men so that scavenger birds and animals would not feed on their bodies.—2Sa 21:1-10.

In the eighth century B.C.E., through the prophet Isaiah, Jehovah prophetically spoke of Gibeah as having fled from the Assyrian army that was en route to Jerusalem. (Isa 10:24, 29-32) And by means of Hosea, God prophetically portrays a situation that makes it appear as though the northern ten-tribe kingdom had already been conquered, with the enemy threatening Gibeah and Ramah in Benjamin (in the southern kingdom of Judah).—Ho 5:8-10.

GIBEATH-HAARALOTH (Gib'e·ath-ha-ar'a·loth) [Hill of the Foreskins]. The place where all the Israelite males born in the wilderness were circumcised after crossing the Jordan. Gibeath-haaraloth was near the city of Jericho and came to be called Gilgal.—Jos 5:3-10; see GILGAL No. 1.

GIBEATHITE (Gib'e·ath·ite) [Of (Belonging to) Gibeah]. An inhabitant of 'Gibeah of Benjamin' (1Ch 12:1-3); the term is applied to Shemaah, whose "sons" served in David's army.

GIBEON (Gib'e·on) [Hill Place], GIBEONITES (Gib'e·on·ites). The city of Gibeon is today linked with el-Jib, about 9.5 km (6 mi) NNW of the Temple Mount in Jerusalem. Numerous earthenware jar handles bearing the name Gibeon in ancient Hebrew characters have been found there. Located on a hill that rises some 60 m (200 ft) above the surrounding plain, the ancient site covers about 6.5 ha (16 acres).

The site has in recent years been the scene of archaeological diggings. Excavators cleared a 51-m (167 ft) tunnel cut through solid rock. This tunnel was anciently lighted by means of lamps placed in niches at regular intervals along its walls. With its 93 rock-cut steps, the tunnel led from just within Gibeon to a man-made cave-reservoir fed by a spring about 25 m (82 ft) below the city wall. This ensured the Gibeonites a safe water supply even in time of siege. Excavators also uncovered a round, rock-cut pit, or pool, having a diameter of 11.3 m (37 ft). A circular stairway, with steps measuring about 1.5 m (5 ft) wide, leads downward in a clockwise direction around the edge of the pit. From the bottom of the pit, at a depth of 10.8 m (35.4 ft), the steps continue for 13.6 m (44.6 ft) through a tunneled stairwell leading to a water chamber. Whether this pit, or pool, is to be identified with the Biblical "pool of Gibeon" is uncertain.—2Sa 2:13.

Dealings With Joshua. In Joshua's time Gibeon was inhabited by Hivites, one of the seven Canaanite nations in line for destruction. (De 7:1, 2; Jos 9:3-7) The Gibeonites were also called Amorites, as this designation appears at times to have been applied generally to all the Canaanites. (2Sa 21:2; compare Ge 10:15-18; 15:16.) Unlike the other Canaanites, the Gibeonites realized that despite their military strength and the greatness of their city, resistance would fail because Jehovah was fighting for Israel. Therefore, after the destruction of Jericho and Ai, the men of Gibeon, apparently also representing the three other Hivite cities of Chephirah, Beeroth, and Kiriath-jearim (Jos 9:17), sent a delegation to Joshua at Gilgal to sue for peace. The Gibeonite ambassadors—dressed in worn-out garments and sandals and having burst, skin wine-bottles, worn-out sacks, and dry, crumbly bread—represented themselves as being from a distant land, hence not in the way of Israel's conquests. They acknowledged Jehovah's hand in what had earlier befallen Egypt and the Amorite kings Sihon and Og. But wisely they did not mention what had happened to Jericho and Ai, as such news could not have reached their "very distant land" before the supposed departure. Israel's representatives examined and accepted the evidence and covenanted with them to let them live.—Jos 9:3-15.

Shortly thereafter, the ruse was uncovered. But the covenant remained in force; breaking it would have called Israel's trustworthiness into question and brought Jehovah's name into contempt among the other nations. When Joshua confronted the Gibeonites about their craftiness, they again acknowledged Jehovah's dealing with Israel and then placed themselves at his mercy, saying: "Now here we are, in your hand. Just as it is good and right in your eyes to do to us, do." They were then constituted gatherers of wood and drawers of water for the assembly and for Jehovah's altar.—Jos 9:16-27.

Although Joshua and the other chieftains had been tricked into making a covenant with the Gibeonites, this was evidently in harmony with Jehovah's will. (Jos 11:19) Proof of this is seen in the fact that when five Amorite kings sought to destroy the Gibeonites, Jehovah blessed Israel's rescue operation; he even hurled down great hailstones upon the foe and miraculously extended the daylight for battle. (Jos 10:1-14) Also, both in seeking a covenant of peace with Israel and in appealing to Joshua for help when threatened, the Gibeonites manifested faith in Jehovah's ability to fulfill his word and to effect deliverance, something for which Rahab of Jericho was commended and that resulted in the preservation of her life and that of her household. Moreover, the Gibeonites had a wholesome fear of Israel's God. —Compare Jos 2:9-14; 9:9-11, 24; 10:6; Heb 11:31.

Under Israel's Control. Gibeon afterward came to be one of the cities in the territory of Benjamin assigned to the Aaronic priests. (Jos 18:21, 25; 21:17-19) The Benjamite Jeiel apparently 'fathered,' or founded, a house there. (1Ch 8:29; 9:35) One of David's mighty men, Ishmaiah, was a Gibeonite (1Ch 12:1, 4), and the false prophet Hananiah, a contemporary of Jeremiah, was from Gibeon.—Jer 28:1.

In the 11th century B.C.E., Gibeon and its vicinity witnessed a conflict between the army of Ish-bosheth under the command of Abner and

Modern-day Gibeon. The ancient Gibeonites realized that Jehovah was fighting for Israel, so they sued for peace

that of David under the leadership of Joab. Initially, doubtless to settle the issue as to who should be king over all Israel, a combat with 12 men from each side was staged. But this decided nothing, for each warrior transfixed his opponent with the sword so that all 24 perished. Thereafter, fierce fighting erupted, with Abner losing 18 times as many men as Joab. All together there were 380 casualties, including Joab's brother Asahel, killed by Abner. (2Sa 2:12-31) In revenge over Asahel, Joab later murdered Abner. (2Sa 3:27, 30) Sometime after this, near the great stone in Gibeon, Joab also killed his own cousin, Amasa, a nephew of David, whom David had appointed army chieftain.—2Sa 20:8-10.

Throughout the centuries, the original Gibeonites continued to exist as a people, although King Saul schemed to destroy them. The Gibeonites, however, patiently waited on Jehovah to reveal the injustice. This he did by means of a three-year famine in David's reign. Upon inquiring of Jehovah and learning that bloodguilt was involved, David interviewed the Gibeonites to ascertain what should be done to make atonement. The Gibeonites rightly answered that it was not "a matter of silver or gold," because, according to the Law, no ransom could be accepted for a murderer. (Nu 35:30, 31) They also recognized that they could not put a man to death without legal authorization. Therefore, not until David's further questioning did they request that seven "sons" of Saul be handed over to them. The fact that bloodguilt was upon both Saul and his household suggests that, although Saul probably took the lead in the murderous action, the "sons" of Saul may directly or indirectly have shared in it. (2Sa 21:1-9) In that event this would not be a case of sons dying for the sins of their fathers (De 24:16) but would involve the administration of retributive justice in harmony with the law "soul will be for soul."—De 19:21.

During David's lifetime, the tabernacle was moved to Gibeon. (1Ch 16:39; 21:29, 30) It was there that Solomon offered sacrifices early in his reign. Also at Gibeon Jehovah appeared to him in a dream, inviting him to request anything that he might desire.—1Ki 3:4, 5; 9:1, 2; 2Ch 1:3, 6, 13.

Years later, the prophet Isaiah (28:21, 22), in foretelling Jehovah's strange deed and unusual work of rising up against his own people, parallels this with what happened in the Low Plain of Gibeon. Likely the allusion is to David's God-given victory over the Philistines (1Ch 14:16), if not also to the much earlier defeat of the Amorite league in the time of Joshua. (Jos 10:5, 6, 10-14) The prophecy had a fulfillment in 607 B.C.E., when Jehovah allowed the Babylonians to destroy Jerusalem and its temple.

At Mizpah, not long after the foretold destruction, Ishmael murdered Gedaliah, the governor appointed by Nebuchadnezzar the king of Babylon. The assassin and his men also took the remaining people of Mizpah captive. But Johanan, with his men, overtook Ishmael by the abundant waters in Gibeon and recovered the captives.—Jer 41:2, 3, 10-16.

Men of Gibeon were among those returning from Babylonian exile in 537 B.C.E., and certain ones later shared in repairing Jerusalem's wall. —Ne 3:7; 7:6, 7, 25.

GIDDALTI (Gid·dal'ti) [I Have Made Great]. A son of Heman; a Levite singer who in David's time was designated by lot to serve as the head of the 22nd of the 24 service groups of 12 musicians each.—1Ch 25:1, 4, 29.

GIDDEL (Gid'del) [Made Great].

1. An ancestor of a family of Nethinim temple slaves who were among those who returned with Zerubbabel from Babylonian exile in 537 B.C.E. —Ezr 2:1, 2, 43, 47; Ne 7:49.

2. The paternal head of one of the families of "the sons of the servants of Solomon" who are listed among those who returned to Jerusalem and Judah in 537 B.C.E.—Ezr 2:1, 2, 55, 56; Ne 7:58.

GIDEON (Gid'e·on) [Cutter Down; One Who Cuts Off]. One of Israel's outstanding judges; the son of Joash of the family of Abi-ezer of the tribe of Manasseh. Gideon resided at Ophrah, a town evidently W of the Jordan. The tribal division to which he belonged was the most insignificant in Manasseh, and he was "the smallest in [his] father's house."—Jg 6:11, 15.

Gideon lived in a very turbulent time of Israel's history. Because of their unfaithfulness to Jehovah, the Israelites were not enjoying the fruits of their labor. For a number of years, neighboring pagan nations, especially the Midianites, had invaded Israel at harvesttime with hordes "as numerous as the locusts." The hand of Midian proved to be so heavy upon them for seven years that the Israelites made underground storage places for themselves in order to conceal their food supplies from the invaders.—Jg 6:1-6.

Called to Serve as a Deliverer. To avoid discovery by the Midianites, Gideon was threshing grain, not out in the open, but in a winepress, when an angel appeared to him, saying: "Jehovah is with you, you valiant, mighty one." This prompted Gideon to ask how this could be true, in view of the Midianite oppression of the nation. When told that he would be the one to deliver Israel, Gideon modestly spoke of his own insignificance. But he was assured that Jehovah would prove to be with him. Therefore Gideon asked for a sign so that he might know that the messenger was really Jehovah's angel. He brought a gift of meat, unfermented cakes, and broth, and at the angel's direction he placed the items on a big rock and poured out the broth. The angel touched the meat and unfermented cakes with his staff, and fire began to ascend out of the rock and to consume the offering, whereupon the angel vanished.—Jg 6:11-22.

That very night Jehovah put Gideon to the test by commanding him to tear down his father's altar to the god Baal, to cut down the sacred pole alongside it, to build an altar to Jehovah, and then to offer his father's young bull of seven years (evidently a bull that was considered sacred to Baal) upon it, using as firewood the sacred pole. With due caution, Gideon did so at night with the aid of ten servants. When the men of the city got up in the morning and saw what had happened and then learned that Gideon was responsible, they clamored for his life. Joash, though, did not deliver up his son to them but retorted to the effect that Baal should make his own defense. Joash then gave his son Gideon the name Jerubbaal (meaning "Let Baal Make a Legal Defense (Contend)"), saying: "Let Baal make a legal defense in his own behalf, because someone has pulled down his altar."—Jg 6:25-32.

Victory Over Midian. After this, when the Midianites, together with the Amalekites and the Easterners, again invaded Israel and encamped in the Valley of Jezreel, Jehovah's spirit enveloped Gideon. Calling together the Abi-ezrites for battle, Gideon sent messengers throughout Manasseh and to Asher, Zebulun, and Naphtali, urging men to join him. Gideon, desiring further evidence that Jehovah was with him, requested that a fleece exposed at night on the threshing floor be wet with dew the next morning but that the floor be dry. When Jehovah granted him this miracle, Gideon cautiously wanted to establish by yet a second sign that Jehovah was with him, and therefore he requested and received a

miracle with the circumstances reversed.—Jg 6: 33-40.

Thirty-two thousand fighting men rallied around Gideon in response to his call. They encamped at the well of Harod south of the Midianite camp at the hill of Moreh in the low plain. The Israelites' 32,000 were outnumbered more than four to one by the invaders, who had a force of about 135,000. (Jg 8:10) But Jehovah indicated that there were too many men with Gideon, in the sense that if God were to give Midian into their hand, they might conclude it was their own valor that resulted in salvation. At God's direction, Gideon told those who were afraid and trembling to retire. Twenty-two thousand departed, but still there were too many men. Next, Jehovah instructed Gideon to lead the remaining 10,000 men down to the water to be tested. A few, merely 300, scooped water to the mouth by hand, and these were separated to one side. The others, who bent down upon their knees to drink, were not to be used. The 300, by their method of drinking, manifested alertness, concern for the fight for true worship in Jehovah's name. By means of this small band of 300, Jehovah promised to save Israel.—Jg 7:1-7.

Gideon with his attendant Purah proceeded to scout the enemy camp at night. There Gideon overheard a man relating a dream to his companion. His companion, in turn, interpreted the dream to mean that Midian and all the camp would be given into Gideon's hand. Strengthened by what he had heard, Gideon returned to the camp of Israel, organized the 300 into three bands in order to enable him to approach the camp of Midian from three sides, and gave each man a horn and a large jar, inside of which was placed a torch.—Jg 7:9-16.

With his band of 100, Gideon arrived at the edge of the Midianite camp right after they had posted the sentries for the middle night watch. Then, in keeping with Gideon's instructions, his men did exactly what he did. The stillness of the night was shattered by the blowing of 300 horns, the smashing of 300 large water jars, and the resounding of 300 war cries; at the same time, the sky was lit up with 300 torches. Confusion seized the enemy camp. The invaders began shouting and fleeing, and "Jehovah proceeded to set the sword of each one against the other in all the camp; and the camp kept up their flight as far as Beth-shittah, on to Zererah, as far as the outskirts of Abel-meholah by Tabbath."—Jg 7:17-22.

In the meantime, the men of Naphtali, Asher, and Manasseh were called together to chase after Midian. Moreover, messengers were sent to Ephraim to head off the fleeing Midianites. The Ephraimites followed through, capturing the waters as far as Beth-barah and the Jordan. They also captured and killed the two Midianite princes Oreb and Zeeb. On meeting up with Gideon, though, the Ephraimites "vehemently tried to pick a quarrel with him," as he had not called them to help at the beginning. However, Gideon, by modestly pointing out that what he had done was nothing in comparison with what they had done in capturing Oreb and Zeeb, calmed their spirit and thereby averted a clash. —Jg 7:23–8:3.

Crossing the Jordan, Gideon and the 300 men with him, though tired, continued pursuing Zebah and Zalmunna, the kings of Midian, and the men with them. On his way, he requested food from the men of Succoth, but the princes of Succoth refused to lend aid, saying: "Are the palms of Zebah and of Zalmunna already in your hand so that bread has to be given to your army?" The men of Penuel likewise refused to honor Gideon's request.—Jg 8:4-9.

Arriving at Karkor where the invaders, reduced to about 15,000 men, were encamped, Gideon struck the camp while the enemy was off guard. Zebah and Zalmunna took to flight. Gideon immediately went in pursuit and captured them. Furthermore, "he drove all the camp into trembling."—Jg 8:10-12.

While returning from the fight, Gideon captured a young man from Succoth and ascertained from him the names of the princes and older men of the city. In keeping with what he had said earlier when they did not comply with his request for food, Gideon put the older men of Succoth through an experience with thorns and briers. Also, as he had forewarned, Gideon pulled down the tower of Penuel and killed the men of that city for their failure to cooperate in providing food for his men.—Jg 8:13-17.

After this, Gideon directed his firstborn son Jether to slay Zebah and Zalmunna, as they had killed Gideon's brothers, the sons of his mother. Being a young man, Jether was afraid to put the Midianite kings to death. Therefore, Gideon, being challenged by Zebah and Zalmunna to do so himself, executed them.—Jg 8:18-21.

The Ephod Made. Grateful Israelites asked Gideon to establish his family as a ruling dynasty. However Gideon appreciated that Jehovah was Israel's rightful King and therefore did not go along with their request. He then suggested that they contribute the gold jewelry they had acquired as spoils of war, the nose rings alone amounting to 1,700 shekels in gold ($218,365). Gideon then made an ephod from the spoils contributed, exhibiting it in Ophrah. But all Israel began to have 'immoral intercourse' with the ephod, it even becoming a snare to Gideon and his household. Thus, though his action was doubtless properly motivated, the ephod diverted attention from the true sanctuary assigned by Jehovah—the tabernacle. Gideon's efforts miscarried, producing a result contrary to what he had intended.—Jg 8:22-27; see EPHOD, I.

Dies as an Approved Witness. So complete was the deliverance Jehovah brought about through Gideon that there was no further disturbance during the 40 years of his judgeship. Gideon came to have many wives, by whom he had 70 sons. After Gideon's death at a good old age, Israel again fell victim to Baal worship. Furthermore, Abimelech the son of Gideon by his concubine, a woman of Shechem, killed Gideon's other sons. Only Jotham, the youngest, escaped.—Jg 8:28–9:5; see ABIMELECH No. 4; OPHRAH No. 3.

Gideon's faith, in the face of great odds, entitled him to be mentioned as one of the "so great a cloud of witnesses." (Heb 11:32; 12:1) Additionally, his modesty was exemplary, and this was coupled with caution. Apparently Gideon's cautiousness was wholesome and is not to be viewed as springing from a lack of faith on his part, as he was never once censured for being cautious. Furthermore, as indicated by Psalm 83, the defeat of Midian in Gideon's day provides a prophetic pattern of the coming destruction of all of Jehovah's opposers, resulting in the complete vindication of his holy name.—Compare Isa 9:4; 10:26.

GIDEONI (Gid·e·o′ni) [Cutter Down; One Who Cuts Off]. Father of Abidan the chieftain of the tribe of Benjamin in the time of Moses.—Nu 1:11, 16.

GIDOM (Gi′dom) [Cutting Down; Cutting Off]. A site mentioned in Judges 20:45. Following a gross sex crime by Benjamites, the other Israelite tribes pursued the Benjamites as far as this point. Its exact location is unknown.

GIFTS, PRESENTS. From earliest times the giving of presents played an important role in daily life. Abraham's aged servant gave gifts of jewelry to Rebekah after seeing evidence that Jehovah had assigned her as a wife for Isaac. (Ge 24:13-22) Then, upon receiving the approval of Laban and Bethuel for the marriage, Abraham's servant gave additional gifts to Rebekah and also "choice things to her brother and to her mother." (Ge 24:50-53) Later, Abraham turned all his possessions over to Isaac, but he gave gifts to the sons of his concubines and sent them away.—Ge 25:5, 6; compare 2Ch 21:3.

It may have been a practice in patriarchal times to give gifts to those who had suffered adversity. When Jehovah turned back the captive condition of Job, his brothers, sisters, and former acquaintances not only came to comfort him but each one gave him "a piece of money and each one a gold ring."—Job 42:10, 11.

Gifts Given to Open the Way for Benefits. Gifts were often given with a view to gaining something desirable. Jacob got ready an impressive gift of livestock for Esau in order to find favor in the eyes of his brother. (Ge 32:13-18; 33:8) Jacob's insistence that Esau accept this gift can be better understood when considering that, according to Eastern custom, refusing to accept a gift denoted that favor would not be granted. (Ge 33:10) Also, to gain the goodwill of the harsh-speaking food administrator of Egypt (who was actually their own brother Joseph), the sons of Jacob followed through on their father's recommendation to take along a gift of the finest products of the land. (Ge 42:30; 43:11, 25, 26) King Asa sent a present of silver and gold to Ben-hadad in order to induce him to break his covenant with Baasha, the king of Israel.—1Ki 15: 18, 19.

Regarding the benefits to the giver, the proverb says: "A man's gift will make a large opening for him, and it will lead him even before great people." (Pr 18:16) A gift can subdue anger, but it will not allay the rage of an able-bodied man against one who commits adultery with his wife, regardless of how great a present is offered by the adulterer.—Pr 21:14; 6:32-35.

Gifts to Kings, Prophets, and Others. The indications are that it was customary for those going to see a king to bring gifts. "Good-for-nothing men" who had no respect for Saul are singled out as not bringing any gift to him. Solomon especially was given gifts in great abundance by those coming from distant lands to hear his wisdom. The astrologers who came to see "the one born king of the Jews" were simply following this custom when they presented gifts to the young child Jesus. (1Sa 10:27; 1Ki 10:10, 24, 25; Mt 2:1, 2, 11; see also 2Ki 20:12; 2Ch 17:5.) Similarly, at times those going to inquire of a prophet took a gift along. (1Sa 9:7; 2Ki 8:8, 9)

But God's prophets did not expect or seek a gift for their services, as is evident from Elisha's refusal to accept "a blessing gift" at Naaman's hand.—2Ki 5:15, 16.

Gifts were often given to reward those successfully completing a certain task. (2Sa 18:11; Da 2:6, 48; 5:16, 17, 29) According to the Law, an emancipated slave was not to be sent away empty-handed but was to receive a gift, something from the flock, the threshing floor, and the oil and winepress. (De 15:13, 14) Also, occasions of great rejoicing might be attended by the giving of presents.—Es 9:20-22; compare Re 11:10.

In Connection With the Sanctuary. God took the Levites as a gift for the house of Aaron, as those given to Jehovah to carry on the service of the sanctuary. (Nu 18:6, 7) Also, the Gibeonites and others who were made servants at the sanctuary were called Nethinim, meaning "Given Ones." (Jos 9:27; 1Ch 9:2; Ezr 8:20) Furthermore, the contributions for carrying on the service of the sanctuary and also the sacrifices are referred to as gifts.—Ex 28:38; Le 23:37, 38; Nu 18:29; Mt 5:23, 24; Lu 21:1.

By reason of his creatorship, Jehovah owns everything. Therefore, in giving material things for the furtherance of true worship, the giver is merely returning a portion of what he originally received from God.—Ps 50:10; 1Ch 29:14.

Admonition Concerning Gifts. Since gifts in the form of bribes can destroy the heart and pervert justice, the Scriptures admonish the hating of such gifts. Those who chase after gifts are condemned. (De 16:19, 20; Ec 7:7; Pr 15:27; Isa 1:23; see BRIBE.) Moreover, the "man boasting himself about a gift in falsehood," not doing according to his boasting, is compared to vaporous clouds and a wind without any downpour. (Pr 25:14) The giver of gifts may have many companions, but his giving cannot ensure lasting friendship.—Pr 19:6.

The Christian Greek Scriptures strongly censure certain practices in connection with the giving of gifts. Jesus condemned the scribes and Pharisees for overstepping the commandment to honor father and mother. According to them, if a person declared that his material things were a gift dedicated to God, he was free of obligation to use them to aid his parents, though he could personally continue to use them. (Mt 15:1-6; see CORBAN.) There is no merit in giving because one expects something in return. (Lu 6:30-36; 14:12-14) To be pleasing to Jehovah, giving must be done unselfishly and without showy display. —Mt 6:2-4; 1Co 13:3.

Christian Giving. Early Christians made gifts, or contributions, in behalf of their needy brothers. (Ro 15:26; 1Co 16:1, 2) However, all such gifts were voluntary, as is indicated by Paul's words: "Let each one do just as he has resolved in his heart, not grudgingly or under compulsion, for God loves a cheerful giver." (2Co 9:7) Additionally, they aided those who devoted themselves fully to the Christian ministry, as did the apostle Paul. However, though very much appreciating the gifts sent to him by his brothers, Paul did not seek a gift.—Php 4:15-17.

Christians can give things more valuable than material presents. They can give of their time and abilities to edify and build others up mentally and spiritually, which brings greater happiness. The greatest gift that one can offer to another is an understanding of God's Word, for this can lead the receiver to everlasting life.—Joh 6:26, 27; 17:3; Ac 20:35; 2Co 12:15; Re 22:17; see GIFTS OF MERCY.

GIFTS FROM GOD.
The gifts God gives to men are an expression of his undeserved kindness. The very word *kha'ri·sma* (literally, gracious gift), appearing 17 times in the Christian Greek Scriptures, implies a gift involving "undeserved kindness" (*kha'ris*) on God's part. (Ro 6: 23, ftn; 1Co 12:4; 2Ti 1:6; 1Pe 4:10) It is, therefore, only proper that the gifts received from Jehovah be used for the benefit of fellowmen and to the glory of God the giver. (1Pe 4:10, 11) These gifts are not for the selfish profit of the receiver. Since such a person has "received free," he is under obligation to "give free."—Mt 10:8.

"Every good gift and every perfect present is from above." (Jas 1:17) Jehovah is generous in giving, allowing both the righteous and the wicked to benefit from the sunshine and the rain. In fact, he "gives to all persons life and breath and all things." God's gifts, including food and drink and seeing good from one's hard work, are for man's enjoyment. (Mt 5:45; Ac 17:24, 25; Ec 3:12, 13; 5:19; 1Ti 6:17) Both singleness and marriage are gifts from God, to be enjoyed within the limits of his requirements. Since the single person is freer to devote himself to Jehovah's service without distraction, singleness is the better of the two gifts.—Pr 18:22; Mt 19:11, 12; 1Co 7:7, 17, 32-38; Heb 13:4.

God's Gift Through Jesus' Sacrifice. Jehovah's undeserved kindness in providing his Son as a ransom sacrifice is a priceless gift, and those exercising faith in Jesus Christ's sacrifice can thereby gain the gift of everlasting life. (Ro 6:23; Joh 3:16) God's "indescribable free gift" evidently includes all the goodness and loving-kindness that God extends to his people through Jesus Christ.—2Co 9:15; compare Ro 5:15-17.

Holy Spirit. God imparts his spirit as a gift to his people, enabling them to avoid the degrading works of the flesh and to cultivate instead the fruitage of the spirit, namely, love, joy, peace, long-suffering, kindness, goodness, faith, mildness, and self-control. (Ac 2:38; Ro 8:2-10; Ga 5:16-25) Jehovah's spirit is a sure guide and supplies power beyond that which is normal, helping the Christian to fulfill his God-given assignments regardless of the pressures brought against him. (Joh 16:13; 2Co 4:7-10) Jesus assured his disciples that God's spirit would teach them all things, would bring back to their minds the things he had taught them, and would help them to make a defense even before rulers.—Joh 14:26; Mr 13:9-11.

Wisdom and Knowledge. True wisdom and knowledge are gifts from God. Jehovah actually invites his servants to pray for wisdom and knowledge, as Solomon did. (Jas 1:5; 2Ch 1:8-12) Nevertheless, to gain knowledge, effort in studying what God has made available by the gift of his Word is required. (Pr 2:1-6; 2Ti 2:15; 3:15) But a study of God's Word in itself does not guarantee receiving the gifts of knowledge and wisdom. True knowledge and wisdom are available only through Jesus Christ and with the help of God's spirit.—1Co 2:10-16; Col 2:3.

Godly wisdom serves as a protection and a guide in the ways of life. (Ec 7:12; Pr 4:5-7) The wisdom that stems from God is distinctly different from worldly wisdom, which is foolishness from Jehovah's standpoint and also harmful in that it leaves God out of account. (1Co 1:18-21) "But the wisdom from above is first of all chaste, then peaceable, reasonable, ready to obey, full of mercy and good fruits, not making partial distinctions, not hypocritical."—Jas 3:17.

Accurate knowledge of Jehovah's will helps its possessor to "make sure of the more important things," to avoid stumbling others, and "to walk worthily of Jehovah to the end of fully pleasing him." (Php 1:9-11; Col 1:9, 10) Furthermore, knowledge is one of the things helping the Christian to be active and productive in his service to God. (2Pe 1:5-8) This gift from God involves more than a mere acquaintance with facts. It embraces understanding of those facts and knowing how to use them in giving "an answer to each one."—Col 4:6.

Gifts of Service and "Gifts in Men." Assignments of service in God's earthly arrangement, or organization, are really gifts from Jehovah. (Nu 18:7; Ro 12:6-8; Eph 3:2, 7) Those favored with assignments of service by God's undeserved kindness are also called *"gifts in men,"* and Jesus Christ, as God's representative and head of the congregation, has given these to the congregation in order that its members individually might be built up and attain maturity. (Eph 4:8, 11, 12) In order to discharge his responsibilities faithfully to the blessing of others, the one having the gift must continue to cultivate it, never neglecting it. (1Ti 4:14; 2Ti 1:6) With the help of Jehovah, anyone, by putting forth determined efforts to make full use of his capabilities and to surmount the obstacles that may present themselves, can cultivate the ability to perform any divinely assigned service.—Php 4:13.

Gifts of the Spirit. In the first century C.E. miraculous gifts attended the baptism with holy spirit. These served as signs that God was no longer using the Jewish congregation in his service but that his approval rested on the Christian congregation established by his Son. (Heb 2:2-4) On the day of Pentecost, miraculous gifts accompanied the outpouring of the holy spirit, and in each case mentioned thereafter in the Scriptures where the miraculous gifts of the spirit were transmitted, at least one of the 12 apostles or Paul, who was directly chosen by Jesus, was present. (Ac 2:1, 4, 14; 8:9-20; 10:44-46; 19:6) Evidently, with the death of the apostles, the transmittal of the gifts of the spirit ended, and the miraculous gifts of the spirit ceased altogether as those who had received these gifts passed off the earthly scene.

Performing apparently miraculous works would not in itself prove divine authorization, nor would the inability of God's servants to perform miracles with the help of God's spirit cast doubt on the fact that they were being used by him. (Mt 7:21-23) Not every first-century Christian could perform powerful works, heal, speak in tongues, and translate. Paul, and doubtless some others, had by God's undeserved kindness been granted a number of these gifts of the spirit. However, these miraculous gifts marked the infancy of the Christian congregation and were foretold to cease. In fact, even Jesus indicated that his followers would be identified, not by their performance of powerful works, but by

their love for one another.—1Co 12:29, 30; 13:2, 8-13; Joh 13:35.

Paul enumerates nine different manifestations or operations of the spirit: (1) speech of wisdom, (2) speech of knowledge, (3) faith, (4) gifts of healings, (5) powerful works, (6) prophesying, (7) discernment of inspired utterances, (8) different tongues, and (9) interpretation of tongues. All these gifts of the spirit served a beneficial purpose that not only contributed to the numerical growth of the congregation but also resulted in its spiritual upbuilding.—1Co 12:7-11; 14:24-26.

"Speech of wisdom." Although wisdom can be acquired through study, application, and experience, the "speech of wisdom" here mentioned apparently was a miraculous ability to *apply knowledge in a successful way* to solve problems arising in the congregation. (1Co 12:8) It was "according to the wisdom given him" that Paul wrote letters that became part of God's inspired Word. (2Pe 3:15, 16) This gift also appears to have been manifest in the individual's ability to make a defense that opposers were unable to resist or to dispute.—Ac 6:9, 10.

"Speech of knowledge" and "faith." All in the first-century Christian congregation had basic knowledge concerning Jehovah and his Son as well as God's will and his requirements for life. Therefore, "speech of knowledge" was something above and beyond the knowledge shared by Christians in general; it was miraculous knowledge. Likewise "faith" as a gift of the spirit was evidently a miraculous faith that helped the individual to overcome mountainlike obstacles that would otherwise hinder service to God.—1Co 12:8, 9; 13:2.

"Healings." The gift of healing was manifest in the ability to cure diseases completely, regardless of the nature of the affliction. (Ac 5:15, 16; 9:33, 34; 28:8, 9) Prior to Pentecost, healing had been done by Jesus and his disciples. Whereas some persons healed did manifest obvious faith, the afflicted one was not required to make an expression of faith in order to be cured. (Compare Joh 5:5-9, 13.) Jesus, on one occasion, attributed his disciples' inability to cure an epileptic, not to the lack of faith of the one seeking a cure for his son, but to the little faith of his disciples. (Mt 17:14-16, 18-20) Not once do the Scriptures cite an instance where Jesus or his apostles were unable to heal others on account of the lack of faith of those seeking a cure. Furthermore, instead of using the gift of healing in curing

Timothy of his stomach trouble or attributing his frequent cases of sickness to his lack of faith, the apostle Paul recommended that Timothy use a little wine for the sake of his stomach.—1Ti 5:23; see FAITH; HEALING.

"Powerful works." Powerful works included raising dead persons, expelling demons, and even striking opposers with blindness. (1Co 12: 10) The manifestation of such powerful works resulted in adding believers to the congregation. —Ac 9:40, 42; 13:8-12; 19:11, 12, 20.

"Prophesying." Prophesying was a greater gift than speaking in tongues, as it built up the congregation. Moreover, unbelievers were helped thereby to recognize that God was really among the Christians. (1Co 14:3-5, 24, 25) All in the Christian congregation spoke about the fulfillment of the prophecies recorded in God's Word. (Ac 2:17, 18) However, the particular ones having the miraculous gift of prophesying were able to foretell future events, as did Agabus.—Ac 11:27, 28; see PROPHECY; PROPHET (Prophets in the Christian Greek Scriptures).

"Discernment of inspired utterances." Discernment of inspired utterances evidently involved the ability to discern whether an inspired expression originated with God or not. (1Co 12: 10) This gift would prevent its possessor from being deceived and turned away from the truth and would protect the congregation from false prophets.—1Jo 4:1; compare 2Co 11:3, 4.

"Tongues." The miraculous gift of tongues attended the outpouring of God's spirit at Pentecost, 33 C.E. The approximately 120 disciples assembled in an upper room (possibly near the temple) were thereby enabled to speak about "the magnificent things of God" in the native tongues of the Jews and proselytes who had come to Jerusalem from faraway places for the observance of the festival. This fulfillment of Joel's prophecy proved that God was using the new Christian congregation and no longer the Jewish congregation. In order to receive the free gift of the holy spirit, the Jews and proselytes had to repent and be baptized in Jesus' name. —Ac 1:13-15; 2:1-47.

The gift of tongues proved very helpful to first-century Christians in preaching to those who spoke other languages. It was actually a sign to unbelievers. However, Paul, in writing to the Christian congregation at Corinth, directed that when meeting together, not all should speak in tongues, as strangers and unbelievers entering and not understanding would conclude that they were mad. He also recommended that the speaking in tongues "be limited to two or three at the most, and in turns." However, if no one could translate, then the person speaking in a tongue was to remain silent in the congregation, speaking to himself and to God. (1Co 14:22-33) If no translating took place, his speaking in a tongue would not result in upbuilding others, for no one would listen to his speech because it would be meaningless to those unable to understand it. —1Co 14:2, 4.

If the person speaking in a tongue was unable to translate, then he did not understand what he himself was saying nor would others who were not familiar with that tongue, or language. Hence, Paul encouraged those having the gift of tongues to pray that they might also translate and thereby edify all listeners. From the foregoing, it can readily be seen why Paul, under inspiration, ranked speaking in tongues as a lesser gift and pointed out that in a congregation he would rather speak five words with his mind (understanding) than 10,000 words in a tongue.—1Co 14:11, 13-19.

"Interpretation of tongues." The gift of interpretation of tongues was manifest in a person's being able to translate a language unknown to the one having this gift. (1Co 12:10) This gift really enhanced the gift of speaking in tongues, since the entire congregation would be built up by hearing the translation.—1Co 14:5.

Other Operations of the Spirit. When mentioning some of the operations of the spirit in conjunction with the placement of the individual members of Christ's body, Paul states: "God has set the respective ones in the congregation, first, apostles; second, prophets; third, teachers; then powerful works; then gifts of healings; helpful services, abilities to direct, different tongues." (1Co 12:27, 28) "Helpful services" may have included the organized arrangements for aiding needy brothers materially, such as the distributing of food to needy widows, for which seven men "full of spirit and wisdom" were appointed in the Jerusalem congregation. (Ac 6:1-6) "Abilities to direct" were needed in order to follow through on the commission outlined by Jesus to make disciples. (Mt 28:19, 20) The missionary work as well as the establishing of new congregations and then guiding the activities of these congregations required skillful direction. In this regard it is noteworthy that Paul, with reference to his part in God's building program, speaks of himself as "a wise director of works."—1Co 3:10.

Control of the Gifts of the Spirit. Apparently those having the gifts of the spirit were in a position to use them only when Jehovah's spirit came to be operative upon them to exercise the gift. For example, at Caesarea although Paul stayed in the home of Philip, who "had four daughters, virgins, that prophesied," it was not one of these daughters but Agabus, a prophet who had come from Judea, who foretold Paul's arrest. (Ac 21:8-11) At a meeting of the congregation, a prophet could receive a revelation while another prophet was speaking; but those having the gifts of the spirit had control over these when God's spirit enveloped them, that is, they could refrain from speaking until opportunity was afforded. Therefore, prophesying, speaking in tongues, and translating could be done in an orderly way in the congregation, for the edification of all.—1Co 14:26-33.

GIFTS OF MERCY.

These are things given to one in need to relieve his situation. While "gifts of mercy" (in some translations, "alms" or "acts of charity") are not directly referred to as such in the Hebrew Scriptures, the Law gave specific directions to the Israelites about their obligations toward the poor. They were to be, not closefisted, but generous in dealing with their needy brothers.—De 15:7-10.

Provisions for the Poor in Israel. The Law permitted an individual to go into the vineyard and the grainfield of another and there eat of the produce to satisfaction; but none of it was to be carried away. (De 23:24, 25) In harvesting their crops, the Israelites were not to reap the edges of their fields completely nor to glean their fields, olive trees, and vineyards, for the gleanings were for the alien resident, the fatherless boy, and the widow.—Le 19:9, 10; De 24:19-21.

Every third year the Israelites were to bring out the entire tenth part of their produce in that year and deposit it inside their gates for the sustenance of the Levites, alien residents, orphans, and widows.—De 14:28, 29; see TITHE.

Every 7th year and every 50th or Jubilee year, the land was to lie fallow, to enjoy a complete sabbath of rest, and there was no regular harvest ingathering of crops. Then whatever grew of itself was to serve as food for the poor, although landowners, their slaves, and their hired laborers were also entitled to eat of it. Evidently, though, the Israelites in general drew on their stored-up food supplies during the Sabbath year.—Ex 23: 10, 11; Le 25:1-7, 11, 12, 20-22.

The principles relative to Israel's obligations

toward the poor as enunciated in the Law are repeated in other parts of the Hebrew Scriptures. (Job 31:16-22; Ps 37:21; 112:9; Pr 19:17; Ec 11: 1, 2) Those acting with consideration toward the lowly one are pronounced happy and are assured of blessing. (Ps 41:1, 2; Pr 22:9) In Isaiah's day, unfaithful Israelites were called upon to divide their bread with the hungry, to bring the homeless into their houses, and to clothe the naked—a course that would result in divine favor. (Isa 58:6, 7) Concerning a righteous man, Jehovah said through Ezekiel: "To the hungry one he would give his own bread and the naked one he would cover with a garment."—Eze 18:7-9.

Actually, there should have been no poor persons among the Israelites, for Jehovah promised to bless his people. But the absence of poverty was contingent on obedience to the Law. Therefore, because of human imperfection and disobedience to God's law, the Israelites would always have the poor in their midst. (De 15:4, 5, 11) Nevertheless, begging was evidently a rarity in ancient Israel, because one of the calamities said to come upon the wicked one was that his sons would be forced to beg.—Ps 109:10; compare Ps 37:25; see POOR.

Improper Views of Giving. In time, the giving of gifts of mercy came to be viewed by the Jews not only as meritorious in itself but also as possessing power to atone for sins. Proverbs 11:4, which says: "Valuable things will be of no benefit on the day of fury, but righteousness itself will deliver from death," came to be expounded as meaning, in harmony with Talmudic conception: "Water will quench blazing fire; so doth almsgiving make atonement for sins." (*The Jewish Encyclopedia*, 1976, Vol. I, p. 435) Apparently, when Jesus Christ was on earth, giving was done by some with much showy display, causing him to speak out against such a practice in the Sermon on the Mount.—Mt 6:2-4.

Christian Gifts of Mercy. Those of Jesus' "little flock" were encouraged to "sell the things belonging to [them] and give gifts of mercy." (Lu 12:32, 33) To the rich young ruler Jesus gave like counsel, adding, "and come be my follower." (Mt 19:16-22; Lu 18:18-23; see also Joh 13:29.) Jesus placed the emphasis on giving "as gifts of mercy the things that are inside." He may thereby have had reference to the qualities of the heart, in view of his stress on justice and love immediately afterward.—Lu 11:39-42.

Organized relief measures. As a result of the addition of about 3,000 Jews and proselytes to the Christian congregation on the day of Pentecost and the continued increase in numbers shortly thereafter, an unusual situation arose among the Christians, calling for a temporary pooling of financial resources. This was to help those who had come to the festival from distant lands to stay longer than they had originally intended so that they could learn more about their new faith. Therefore, those having possessions sold them and turned over the proceeds of the sale to the apostles for distribution to those in need. "All those who became believers were together in having all things in common." But the entire arrangement was voluntary, as is evident from Peter's question to Ananias: "As long as it remained with you did it not remain yours, and after it was sold did it not continue in your control?"—Ac 2:41-47; 4:4, 34, 35; 5:4.

It appears that in time the extent of these relief measures diminished, but food was still distributed to needy widows in the congregation. In connection with this, the Greek-speaking Jews began to murmur against the Hebrew-speaking Jews, "because their widows were being overlooked in the daily distribution." To remedy the situation, the apostles recommended that the congregation select seven qualified men "full of spirit and wisdom" to distribute the food. The men selected were placed before the apostles who, after prayer, appointed them. Their work doubtless entailed the handling of funds, making purchases, and keeping certain records in the distribution of the food supplies. (Ac 6:1-6) When Paul wrote his first letter to Timothy, there was still an arrangement in operation for the care of widows, as is evident from his instructions to Timothy as to those qualifying for such financial assistance.—1Ti 5:3-16.

In addition to caring for widows, the first-century congregation organized relief measures in behalf of other needy believers. Again, such organized giving, though directed by the congregation's appointed men, was completely voluntary.—Ac 11:28-30; Ro 15:25-27; 1Co 16:1-3; 2Co 9:5, 7; see RELIEF.

Relative importance of material giving. In the Christian Greek Scriptures encouragement is given to be hospitable and share with others, but in addition, providing for the members of one's own family and aiding needy brothers are shown to be Christian requirements. (Ro 12:13; 1Ti 5:4, 8; Jas 2:15, 16; 1Jo 3:17, 18) Sincere concern for the poor characterizes true religion. (Jas 1:27; 2:1-4) In fact, as indicated by Jesus, the doing of good toward "the least of these [his] brothers"

distinguishes "the sheep" from "the goats." (Mt 25:31-46) However, instead of being merely acts of humanitarianism, the aid given by the "sheep" is prompted by their recognition of the position of Christ's followers.—Mt 10:40-42.

For giving to result in real happiness to the giver, it must be done without grumbling and not grudgingly or under compulsion. "God loves a cheerful giver." (2Co 9:7; Ac 20:35; 1Pe 4:9) Then, too, material gifts of mercy are not sufficient in themselves to gain everlasting life and were not given prime importance by Jesus Christ.—Joh 17:3; 12:1-8.

GIHON (Gi′hon) [Bursting Forth; Gushing].

1. One of the four rivers that branched out from the river issuing out of Eden, described as "encircling the entire land of Cush." (Ge 2:10, 13) It is not possible to identify this river today with any degree of certainty. It does not seem likely, at least from a geographic standpoint, that the "land of Cush" referred to here represents Ethiopia, as it frequently does in later accounts. It could refer to the land occupied by Cush prior to the scattering that occurred after the language confusion at Babel. (Ge 11:9) Some would connect the Gihon with the Araxes River (modern Araks River), which takes its rise in the mountains to the NW of Lake Van and has its outlet in the Caspian Sea. Some lexicographers associate the "land of Cush" of Genesis 2:13 with the Kassites (Akkadian, *kassu*), a people of the plateau of central Asia mentioned in ancient cuneiform inscriptions but whose history remains quite obscure. (*Lexicon in Veteris Testamenti Libros,* by L. Koehler and W. Baumgartner, Leiden, 1958, p. 429; *A Hebrew and English Lexicon of the Old Testament,* by Brown, Driver, and Briggs, 1980, p. 469) In another direction, it may be noted that certain Arabians on the Arabian Peninsula were called *Kusi* or *Kushim,* as is indicated by Habakkuk 3:7, where Cushan is made parallel to Midian, evidently as the same place or as a neighboring land. Thus there are various possibilities, but because of apparent topographical changes in the earth's surface as a result of the global Deluge, no positive conclusion can be reached.—See CUSH No. 2.

2. A spring today called Ha Gihon having its fountainhead in a natural cave in the Kidron Valley a short distance E of the upper end of the section of Jerusalem anciently called "the City of David." (2Ch 32:30) It was a principal source of water for the city in ancient times, there being only two springs in the vicinity. The name Gihon is particularly appropriate for this spring inas-

much as it 'gushes forth' intermittently, as much as four or five times a day following a rainy winter, less frequently in the dry season.

The spring of Gihon is generally believed to have been involved in the method employed by General Joab in penetrating the nearly impregnable Jebusite stronghold at Jerusalem, making possible its capture by David. (1Ch 11:6) Although the translation of the Hebrew text at 2 Samuel 5:8 presents certain problems, the usual rendering indicates the presence of a "water tunnel," referred to by David when promoting the attack on the city. In 1867 C.E., Charles Warren discovered a water channel running back from the cave in which the spring of Gihon rises and, after a distance of some 20 m (66 ft), ending in a pool or reservoir. A vertical shaft cut in the rock above this pool extended upward 11 m (36 ft), and at the top of the shaft there was a place where persons could stand and let down containers by rope to draw water from the pool below. A sloping passageway led back nearly 39 m (128 ft) from the shaft up into the interior of the city. By this means it is believed that the Jebusites maintained access to their water source even when unable to venture outside the city walls because of enemy attack. Although the spring of Gihon is not directly mentioned in the account, it is suggested that Joab and his men daringly gained entrance to the city through this water tunnel.

The Spring of Gihon, a principal source of water for ancient Jerusalem

Gihon was thereafter the site at which Solomon was anointed king at David's command. The ensuing noisy procession as the people joyously followed Solomon back to the city, while not visible from the spring called En-rogel about 700 m (2,300 ft) away from Gihon, could easily be heard by presumptuous Adonijah and his guests as they banqueted at En-rogel.—1Ki 1:9, 10, 33-41.

Archaeological excavations also revealed an old surface canal leading from the spring of Gihon southward along the slope of "the City of David."

This canal terminated in a pool at the base of the spur on which the ancient city was first located —at the spur's southern end, toward the junction of the Tyropoeon Valley with the Kidron Valley. The canal was constructed with a minimal decline or rate of fall, resulting in a very gentle flow of water. This canal is probably the one referred to by Isaiah's prophecy in the time of King Ahaz (761-746 B.C.E.), its 'gently-going waters' being contrasted with the violent flood of invading Assyrians that Isaiah foretold would eventually attack Judah.—Isa 8:5-8.

When Assyrian attack became imminent in Hezekiah's reign (732 B.C.E.), King Hezekiah took measures to ensure that Jerusalem's supply of water would not fall into the hands of the enemy. (2Ch 32:2-4) However, possibly with reference to another time, the record at 2 Chronicles 32:30 shows that he shut off the flow of the Gihon through its previous channel and diverted the waters to the western side of "the City of David," well within Jerusalem's fortifications. Evidence of the manner in which this was accomplished came to light in 1880 C.E. when an inscription was found carved in the wall of a water tunnel terminating in what is presently known as the Pool of Siloam on the W side of the old "City of David." The inscription, in early Hebrew script regarded as dating from the eighth century B.C.E., described the excavation of the tunnel through solid rock by the two teams of men working toward each other from opposite ends. When the tunnel was completely cleared in 1910, it was found to measure some 533 m (1,749 ft), with an average height of 1.8 m (6 ft) and at times narrowing to a width of only 0.5 m (20 in.). It seems evident that this remarkable engineering feat is the result of Hezekiah's measures to protect and maintain Jerusalem's water supply originating in the Gihon.

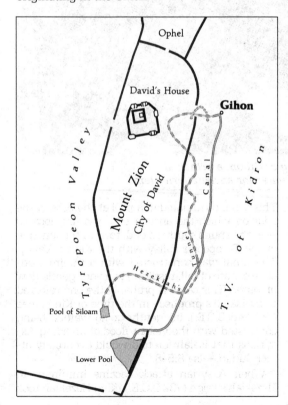

Ophel

David's House

Gihon

Tyropoeon Valley

Mount Zion

City of David

Canal

Kidron

Hezekiah's Tunnel

T. V. of

Pool of Siloam

Lower Pool

King Manasseh, son of Hezekiah, extended Jerusalem's fortifications during his reign (716-662 B.C.E.), building an outer wall for "the City of David" to "the west of Gihon," hence not enclosing the spring of Gihon within its limits. —2Ch 32:33; 33:14.

The Gihon's waters continue to flow today through the "Siloam Tunnel," credited to Hezekiah.

GILALAI (Gil′a·lai). One of the Levite musicians in the procession arranged by Nehemiah at the inauguration of the rebuilt wall of Jerusalem in 455 B.C.E.—Ne 12:27, 31, 36.

GILBOA (Gil·bo′a) [possibly, Hill Country]. A mountain traditionally identified with Jebel Fuqu′ah, a crescent-shaped ridge of limestone hills lying E of the Plain of Jezreel and WSW of Beth-shean. Ravines divide the range into several plateaus. Much of it is barren rock, with rugged channels in the northern and western parts, where chalk has been eroded. But wheat and barley are cultivated on the gradual western slopes. Also, pastureland, as well as fig and olive trees, can be found there. The northern side is the steepest and highest, rising to about 520 m (1,700 ft) above sea level.

Because of its strategic location E of the fertile Plain of Jezreel between the torrent valley of Kishon and the Jordan Valley, Gilboa figured in at least two major battles. At "the well of Harod," commonly linked with the spring located on the NW spur of Gilboa, Gideon and his men encamped. (Jg 7:1) Later, King Saul gathered his forces to Gilboa and there suffered defeat at the hands of the Philistines. There too, three of his sons, Jonathan, Abinadab, and Malchi-shua, were slain and Saul himself committed suicide. —1Sa 28:4; 31:1-4, 8; 2Sa 1:4-10, 21; 1Ch 10:1-8.

GILEAD (Gil′e·ad) [probably derived from Galeed, meaning "Witness Heap"].—Ge 31:47, 48.

1. Son of Machir and grandson of Manasseh; forefather of the Iezerites and the Helekites. —Nu 26:29, 30; 27:1; Jos 17:1, 3; 1Ch 2:21, 23; 7:14-17.

2. A Gadite listed in the genealogy of Abihail. —1Ch 5:11-14.

3. Jephthah's father.—Jg 11:1, 2.

4. A geographic term that is variously employed in the Bible. In a strict sense, Gilead denoted the domelike mountainous region E of the Jordan River that extended N and S of the

JUST 120 years after Saul became the first king of Israel, the nation was torn in two. Why? Because of the apostasy of King Solomon. Desiring to please his foreign wives, Solomon allowed rank idolatry to infiltrate the nation, building 'high places' to false gods. This interfaith was abhorrent to Jehovah. Yet, loyal to his covenant with David, God did not cut short the Davidic dynasty. Rather, he decreed the ripping away of part of the nation.—1Ki 11:7-13.

This occurred in 997 B.C.E. when the actions of Solomon's headstrong son Rehoboam incited ten tribes to rebel and form a kingdom largely in the northern part of the land but also including Simeonite enclave cities scattered throughout Judah. Only the tribes of Benjamin and Levi remained loyal to the southern kingdom in Judah.

Jeroboam, the first king of the northern kingdom, feared he would lose the allegiance of his people if they continued worshiping at Jerusalem, so he instituted a religion of his own. He placed golden calves at Dan far to the north and at Bethel just 17 km (11 mi) north of Jerusalem. He also installed his own priesthood and arranged for his own 'holy days.'—1Ki 12:26-33.

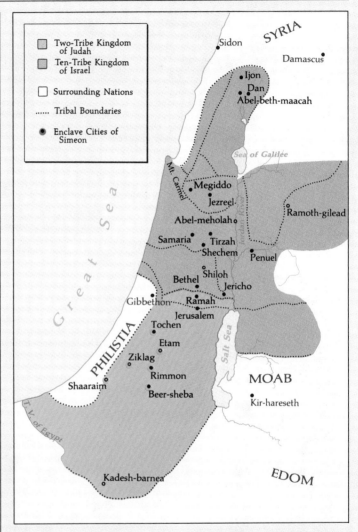

Legend:
- Two-Tribe Kingdom of Judah
- Ten-Tribe Kingdom of Israel
- Surrounding Nations
- ...... Tribal Boundaries
- • Enclave Cities of Simeon

Map labels: Sidon, SYRIA, Damascus, Ijon, Dan, Abel-beth-maacah, Sea of Galilee, Mt. Carmel, Megiddo, Jezreel, Ramoth-gilead, Abel-meholah, Samaria, Tirzah, Shechem, Penuel, Shiloh, Bethel, Jericho, Gibbethon, Ramah, Jerusalem, Tochen, Etam, Ziklag, Rimmon, Shaaraim, Beer-sheba, MOAB, Kir-hareseth, Great Sea, Salt Sea, T. V. of Egypt, PHILISTIA, Kadesh-barnea, EDOM

Israel thus became a land divided both politically and religiously, a land vulnerable to foreign aggression and wracked by civil war. Cut off from Jehovah's pure worship, the ten-tribe kingdom sank deep into moral and spiritual corruption. Yet, Jehovah continued to send his prophets to urge them to repent.

PRINCIPAL LOCATIONS
With Related Scriptures

Bethel	1Ki 12:28, 29
Carmel (Mt.)	1Ki 18:19-40
Dan	2Ki 10:29
Jerusalem	2Ch 11:1
Jezreel	2Ki 9:30-37
Samaria	1Ki 16:23, 24
Shechem	1Ki 12:1, 25
Tirzah	1Ki 15:33
Enclave cities	Jos 19:1-8

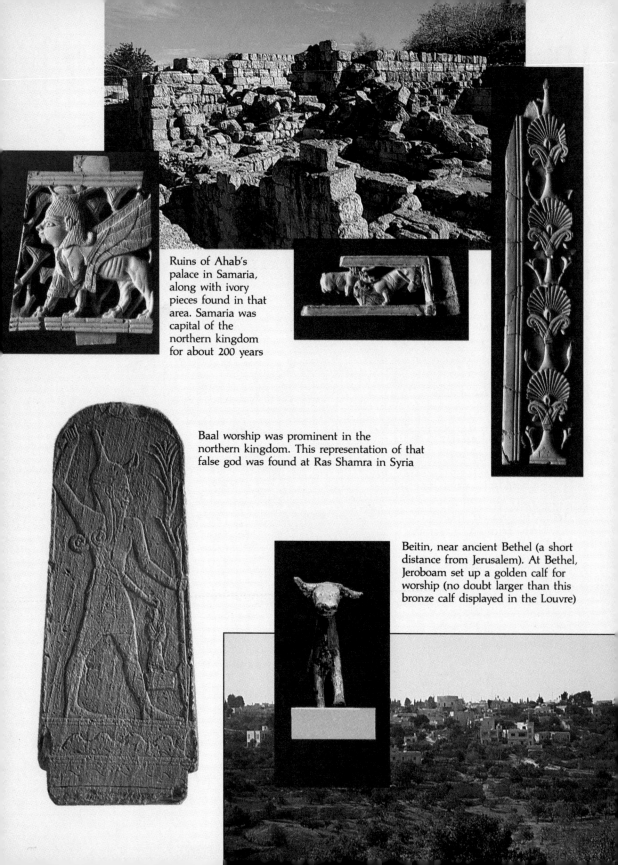

Ruins of Ahab's palace in Samaria, along with ivory pieces found in that area. Samaria was capital of the northern kingdom for about 200 years

Baal worship was prominent in the northern kingdom. This representation of that false god was found at Ras Shamra in Syria

Beitin, near ancient Bethel (a short distance from Jerusalem). At Bethel, Jeroboam set up a golden calf for worship (no doubt larger than this bronze calf displayed in the Louvre)

ELIJAH was a prophet who called for a test of godship at Mount Carmel. The northern kingdom was being corrupted by Baal worship. But Elijah courageously challenged 450 prophets of Baal to prove that Baal was the true God. Frantic hours of prayer on their part yielded nothing. Then Elijah laid out his sacrifice, drenched it repeatedly with water, and prayed to Jehovah. When fire promptly fell from heaven, devoured the sacrifice, and licked up the water, the people exclaimed: "Jehovah is the true God!" At that, Elijah ordered that the prophets of Baal be slaughtered.—1Ki 18:18-40.

Nevertheless, Elijah grew fearful when he learned that Queen Jezebel was plotting to kill him. He fled some 150 km (95 mi) to Beersheba and then traveled another 300 km (190 mi) to Mount Sinai. Jehovah did not reject Elijah for his temporary lapse of courage but assured him that there was further prophetic work for him to do.—1Ki 19:1-18.

Elisha was Elijah's successor. When Elisha was surrounded by Syrian war chariots, he had faith to realize that it was really the Syrian armies that were surrounded —by a host of angelic chariots!—2Ki 6:15-17.

LOCATIONS ON MAP
With Related Scriptures

Abel-meholah	1Ki 19:16
Beer-sheba	1Ki 19:3
Bethel	2Ki 2:1-3, 23, 24
Carmel (Mt.)	1Ki 18:19-40
Damascus	2Ki 8:7-15
Dothan	2Ki 6:13-18
Ekron	2Ki 1:2-4
Gilgal	2Ki 4:38-41
Jericho	2Ki 2:4, 5, 19-22
Jezreel	1Ki 18:45, 46; 21:1, 17-26
Jordan River	2Ki 2:6-14
Kishon (T.V.)	1Ki 18:40
Ramoth-gilead	2Ki 9:1-10
Samaria	2Ki 5:1-27; 6:19-23; 7:1-20
Shunem	2Ki 4:8-37
Sidon	1Ki 17:8, 9
Zarephath	1Ki 17:9-24

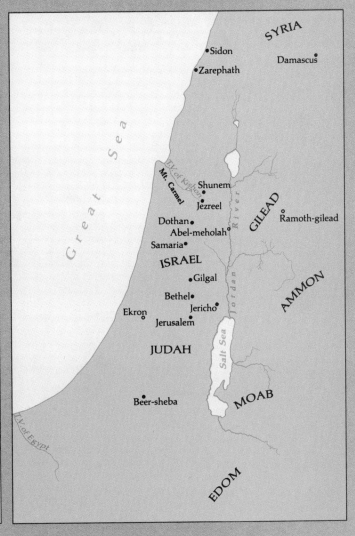

Mount Carmel, site of the fire
test proving that not Baal but
Jehovah is the true God
(1Ki 18:21-39)

Mount Sinai area. Elijah fled
from the wrath of Jezebel
some 450 km (285 mi) to this
region (1Ki 19:1-18)

Ruins of Dothan. Here
Elisha and his attendant
miraculously saw that,
although they were
surrounded by a Syrian
military force, the
mountainous region was
full of angelic war chariots
of fire sent by Jehovah
(2Ki 6:13-17)

AROUND Israel were enemy nations that were intent on seizing its inheritance. Would Israel be swallowed up? As long as Israel remained faithful, it had the decisive edge. "Jehovah himself was fighting for Israel." —Jos 10:14.

This was graphically demonstrated during the rule of King Jehoshaphat (936- c. 911 B.C.E.). The combined forces of Ammon, Moab, and Mount Seir came against Judah. Jehoshaphat appealed to Jehovah: "Here they are . . . coming in to drive us out from your possession that you caused us to possess. O our God, will you not execute judgment upon them?" Indeed He would! Judah was assured: "The battle is not yours, but God's." Jehovah confused the enemy, causing them to slaughter one another.—2Ch 20:1-23.

Finally, after centuries of fighting for Israel, Jehovah allowed enemy nations to conquer it. In 740 B.C.E. the Assyrians brought the ten-tribe kingdom to an end "because the sons of Israel had sinned against Jehovah." (2Ki 17:7-18) Then in 607 B.C.E., for its disobedience the two-tribe kingdom was destroyed by the Babylonians. (2Ki 21:10-15; 22: 16, 17) This period of Israel's history emphasizes the importance of obeying Jehovah.

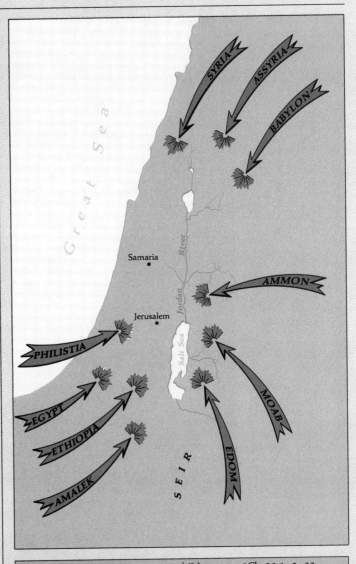

ENEMY NATIONS With Related Scriptures		Edom	2Ch 20:1, 2, 22; 28:17; Ob 1, 12-14
		Egypt	1Ki 14:25, 26; 2Ch 36:2-4
Amalek	Ps 83:2-4, 7		
Ammon	2Ch 20:1-3, 10, 11; 2Ki 24:2	Ethiopia	2Ch 14:9-13
		Moab	Ps 83:2-4, 6
Assyria	2Ki 15:19, 20, 29; 17:1-6; 18:13-35	Philistia	1Sa 17:1-10; 31:1-7; 2Sa 5:17-25
Babylon	2Ki 24:1, 12-17; 25:1-21	Syria	1Ki 20:1-6, 26; 2Ki 12:17, 18; 16:5-9

Assyrian soldiers taking
Jews from Lachish into exile

Egyptian inscription boasting
over the conquest of Judean
cities by Pharaoh Shishak

Babylonian record
of Nebuchadnezzar's
invasion of Judah

The Moabites lived in rugged territory east of the Dead Sea. On the Moabite Stone (left), King Mesha boasts about his god Chemosh and refers to Jehovah with great disrespect

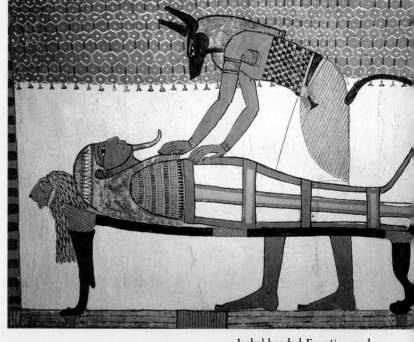

Jackal-headed Egyptian god preparing a mummy. The gods of Egypt included mere men, birds, and animals

Phoenicians, who occupied this land along the east coast of the Mediterranean, worshiped gods such as the one shown here standing on a lion

DWELLING in its God-given land, the nation of Israel found itself surrounded by nations that worshiped false gods. The Israelites had come out of Egypt, where animals were deified. To the east and southeast of them now lay Ammon, Moab, and Edom—distant relatives of the Israelites but idol worshipers. The polytheistic Philistines occupied the coastal plain to the west. North of Israel along the coast were the Phoenicians, whose religious practices included sodomy, bestiality, and child sacrifice. And the religion of the Syrians featured nude representations of goddesses whose gestures emphasized their sexuality. To continue to be acceptable to Jehovah, Israel had to keep separate from the nations around them.

As a safeguard to Israel, Jehovah gave them the Mosaic Law, which constituted a 'wall of separation' to keep them apart from the surrounding nations. (Eph 2:14) They were not to form alliances with such nations, to intermarry with them, or to imitate their religious practices. (2Ch 16:7; 2Ki 17:13-15) To the extent that Israel obeyed these laws, they remained a holy people.

Yet, individuals from surrounding nations were not barred from worshiping the true God. They could abandon their idolatrous ways and become worshipers of Jehovah. "God is not partial." (Ac 10:34) While he was keeping Israel separate, Jehovah was working out his purpose for the eventual blessing of people of all nations. —Ge 22:18.

SURROUNDING NATIONS With Related Scriptures	
Ammon	Jg 10:6-9; 1Ki 11:5
Edom	2Ch 25:14, 15
Moab	Nu 22:4-7; 25:1-3; 2Ki 3:26, 27
Philistia	Jg 10:6; 16:23; 2Ki 1:2
Phoenicia	1Ki 11:1, 2, 5; 16:30, 31
Syria	Jg 10:6; 2Ch 28:20-23

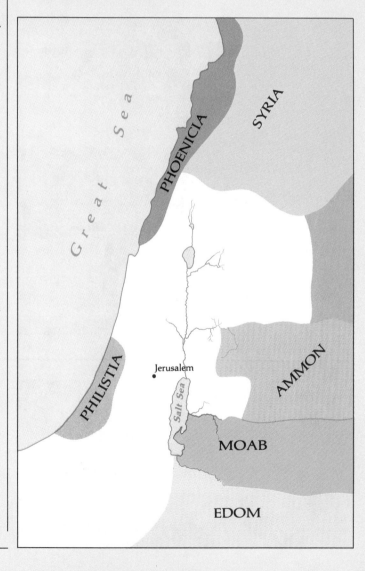

But in sharp contrast to this, "Gilead" was censured for failing to join Barak in the fight against Sisera. (Jg 5:17) Similarly, at a later period the men of Succoth and Penuel, two cities in Gilead, refused to assist Gideon and his men with food supplies while the latter were pursuing the Midianites.—Jg 8:4-9.

After the death of Judge Jair from Gilead, Israel reverted to idolatry, and 18 years of severe Ammonite oppression followed. Faced with this menace, the men of Gilead abandoned false worship and appealed to Gileadite Jephthah to be their commander in the fight against Ammon. Subsequently the Ammonites were subdued. —Jg 10:3, 5-10; 11:4-11, 32, 33.

Years later, though, Gilead continued to have difficulty with the Ammonites. (Am 1:13) Shortly after Saul had been anointed as Israel's first king, Nahash the Ammonite laid siege to Jabesh-gilead and would accept the surrender of this city only on the condition that the men allow their right eyes to be bored out. Upon learning this, Saul quickly rallied an army of 330,000 men and defeated the Ammonites. (1Sa 11:1-11) Gilead then seems to have entered a period of relative security that continued even after Saul's death, as is suggested by the fact that Abner chose the Gileadite city of Mahanaim as the place to make Saul's son Ish-bosheth king. (2Sa 2:8, 9) However, sometime during David's reign trouble with the Ammonites broke out anew. Gilead and its vicinity became the scene of the battles that finally resulted in the complete subjugation of Ammon.—2Sa 10:6-19; 11:1; 12:26-31.

Later, during Absalom's rebellion, King David fled to Gilead and, at Mahanaim, was kindly and hospitably received, particularly by the aged Barzillai. (2Sa 17:27-29; 19:32) Evidently in Gilead the forces of David and of Absalom met in battle. The signal defeat of Absalom paved the way for David to leave Gilead and return to his throne.—2Sa 17:24; 18:6-8.

Not long after the ten-tribe kingdom was established (997 B.C.E.), the Syrians annexed territory from Gilead. Ramoth-gilead, the Gadite city of refuge in eastern Gilead, was in the possession of the Syrians in the time of King Ahab and the Gileadite prophet Elijah. (1Ki 17:1; 22:3) Then, during the reigns of King Jehu and his son Jehoahaz, Gilead lost even more territory and was subjected to a severe threshing experience at the hands of the Syrian kings Hazael and his son Ben-hadad III. (2Ki 10:32-34; 13:1, 3, 7; Am 1: 3, 4) However, Jehoash the son of Jehoahaz defeated the Syrians three times and recovered the cities Israel had lost to the Syrians during his father's reign.—2Ki 13:25.

Finally, in the days of Israelite King Pekah (c. 778-758 B.C.E.), the Assyrian king Tiglath-pileser III carried the inhabitants of Gilead into exile. (2Ki 15:29) Apparently the Ammonites were quick to take advantage of this situation and began to occupy the territory of Gilead. (Ps 83:4-8; Jer 49:1-5) However, through his prophets, Jehovah gave the assurance that in time the Israelites would again be restored to this region. —Jer 50:19; Mic 7:14; Zec 10:10.

5. "A town" mentioned by Hosea as being filled with untruth, bloodshed, and practicers of what is harmful. (Ho 6:8; compare 12:11.) Since Gilead is not identified as a city elsewhere in Scripture, some think that either Jabesh-gilead or Ramoth-gilead is meant. Others suggest that this refers to the entire region E of the Jordan.

GILGAL   (Gil′gal) [Rolling; Rolling Away].

1. A city "on the eastern border of Jericho." (Jos 4:19) Near Gilgal's "quarries," Moabite King Eglon, the oppressor of Israel in the time of Ehud, evidently had his residence.—Jg 3:12-26.

In the past, most geographers favored Khirbet en-Nitleh as the possible location of Gilgal. However, particularly since 1931, Khirbet El Mafjir has been suggested. Its position, 2 km (c. 1 mi) NE of ancient Jericho (Tell es-Sultan; Tel Yeriho), corresponds more closely to early literary references (such as those of Josephus and Eusebius) about the distance from Jericho to Gilgal. Then, too, archaeological excavation at Khirbet en-Nitleh has provided no evidence of pre-Common Era habitation. On the other hand, superficial explorations in the vicinity of Khirbet El Mafjir have yielded earthenware fragments that indicate the presence of some kind of settlement centuries before the Common Era. Although this site does not lie due E of ancient Jericho, the Biblical designation "eastern border of Jericho" may include the NE.

Gilgal was the site of Israel's first encampment after crossing the Jordan in Abib (Nisan) of 1473 B.C.E. Here, in commemoration of Jehovah's drying up the waters of the Jordan to permit Israel to cross, Joshua set up the 12 stones taken from the middle of the riverbed. (Jos 4:8, 19-24) At Gilgal all the Israelite males born in the wilderness were circumcised, Jehovah afterward saying that he "rolled away the reproach of Egypt from off [them]." [*Continued on page 961*]

torrent valley of Jabbok. (Jos 12:2) In the N it was bounded by Bashan; in the S, by the tableland N of the torrent valley of Arnon; and in the E, by the territory of Ammon. (De 2:36, 37; 3:8-10) However, at times "Gilead" or "the land of Gilead"

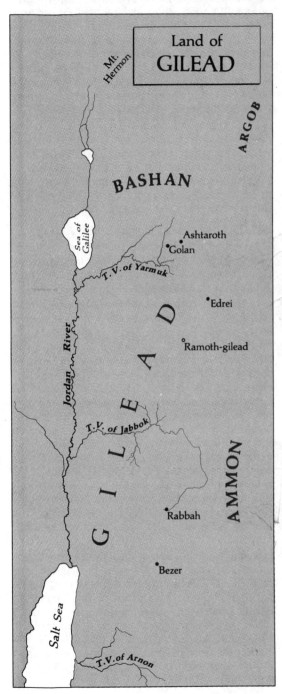

applied generally to the entire Israelite territory E of the Jordan, including Bashan and the tableland N of the Arnon.—Jos 22:9; Jg 20:1, 2; 2Sa 2:9; 2Ki 10:32, 33; see GALEED.

Evidently Gilead was thought of as consisting of two parts. Though simply called Gilead at Numbers 32:40, the territory assigned to the half tribe of Manasseh is more specifically referred to as "the rest of Gilead" (De 3:13) or the "half of Gilead." (Jos 13:31) Similarly, in a more definite sense, the combined territory of Gad and Reuben S of the area given to the half tribe of Manasseh was called "half of the mountainous region of Gilead." (De 3:12) Yet this same area is, on occasion, also called simply Gilead, as is the portion thereof assigned to Gad (where the city of refuge Ramoth was located).—Nu 32:29; Jos 13:24, 25; 21:38.

From at least 210 m (690 ft) below sea level at the Jordan Valley, Gilead rises to an elevation of over 1,000 m (3,300 ft). Blessed with abundant rainfall in winter and heavy dews in summer, as well as many springs, this fertile region anciently supported great forests and was well known for its healing balsam. (Jer 8:22; 46:11; see BALSAM, BALSAM OF GILEAD.) Its rolling plateaus were ideal for raising livestock and cultivating cereals. Also, grapes thrived in Gilead.—Nu 21:22; 32:1.

Historical Events in Gilead.   Shortly before the Israelites entered the Promised Land, the Amorite king Sihon controlled the section of Gilead S of the torrent valley of Jabbok, whereas Og the king of Bashan ruled over the part to the N. (Jos 12:1-4) Under the leadership of Moses, the Israelites defeated both of these kings, and the tribes of Gad and Reuben, because of their numerous livestock, requested that this region be given to them as an inheritance. (Nu 21:21-24, 33-35; 32:1-5) Their request was granted on the condition that the fighting men of both tribes cross the Jordan and assist in the conquest of the Promised Land. (Nu 32:20-24, 28-30) This they agreed to do, and immediately they rebuilt cities for their families, whom they would leave behind. (Nu 32:25-27, 31-38) The half tribe of Manasseh also received an inheritance E of the Jordan.—Nu 32:33, 39, 40.

Upon returning to their inheritance in Gilead, the men of Reuben, Gad, and the half tribe of Manasseh built an altar as a memorial of faithfulness to Jehovah. (Jos 22:9, 10, 26-29) Later, they shared in the united tribal action against the Benjamites for shielding the wrongdoers of Gibeah from being brought to justice. (Jg 20:1-48)

JUST 120 years after Saul became the first king of Israel, the nation was torn in two. Why? Because of the apostasy of King Solomon. Desiring to please his foreign wives, Solomon allowed rank idolatry to infiltrate the nation, building 'high places' to false gods. This interfaith was abhorrent to Jehovah. Yet, loyal to his covenant with David, God did not cut short the Davidic dynasty. Rather, he decreed the ripping away of part of the nation.—1Ki 11:7-13.

This occurred in 997 B.C.E. when the actions of Solomon's headstrong son Rehoboam incited ten tribes to rebel and form a kingdom largely in the northern part of the land but also including Simeonite enclave cities scattered throughout Judah. Only the tribes of Benjamin and Levi remained loyal to the southern kingdom in Judah.

Jeroboam, the first king of the northern kingdom, feared he would lose the allegiance of his people if they continued worshiping at Jerusalem, so he instituted a religion of his own. He placed golden calves at Dan far to the north and at Bethel just 17 km (11 mi) north of Jerusalem. He also installed his own priesthood and arranged for his own 'holy days.'—1Ki 12:26-33.

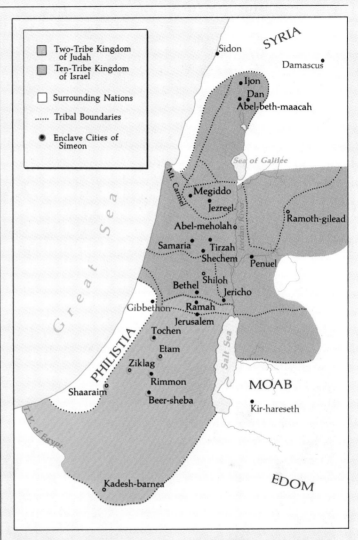

Israel thus became a land divided both politically and religiously, a land vulnerable to foreign aggression and wracked by civil war. Cut off from Jehovah's pure worship, the ten-tribe kingdom sank deep into moral and spiritual corruption. Yet, Jehovah continued to send his prophets to urge them to repent.

PRINCIPAL LOCATIONS
With Related Scriptures

Bethel	1Ki 12:28, 29
Carmel (Mt.)	1Ki 18:19-40
Dan	2Ki 10:29
Jerusalem	2Ch 11:1
Jezreel	2Ki 9:30-37
Samaria	1Ki 16:23, 24
Shechem	1Ki 12:1, 25
Tirzah	1Ki 15:33
Enclave cities	Jos 19:1-8

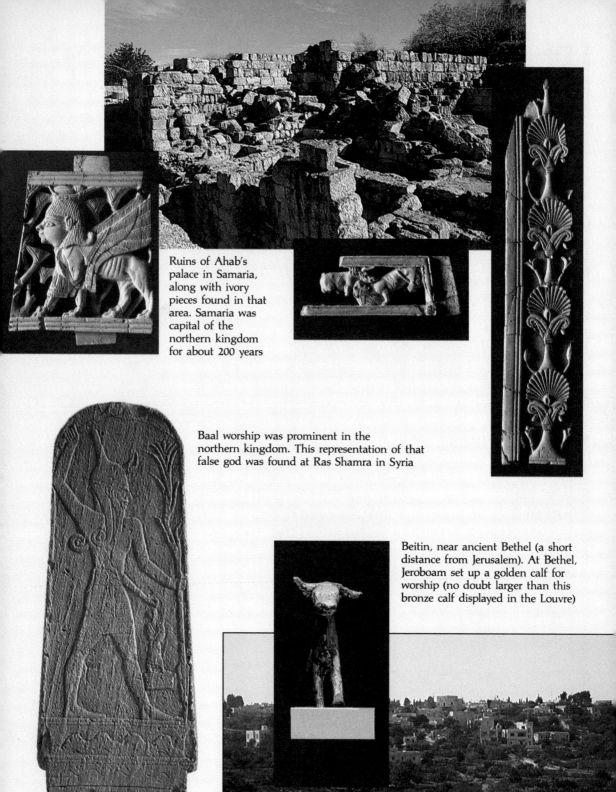

Ruins of Ahab's palace in Samaria, along with ivory pieces found in that area. Samaria was capital of the northern kingdom for about 200 years

Baal worship was prominent in the northern kingdom. This representation of that false god was found at Ras Shamra in Syria

Beitin, near ancient Bethel (a short distance from Jerusalem). At Bethel, Jeroboam set up a golden calf for worship (no doubt larger than this bronze calf displayed in the Louvre)

ELIJAH was a prophet who called for a test of godship at Mount Carmel. The northern kingdom was being corrupted by Baal worship. But Elijah courageously challenged 450 prophets of Baal to prove that Baal was the true God. Frantic hours of prayer on their part yielded nothing. Then Elijah laid out his sacrifice, drenched it repeatedly with water, and prayed to Jehovah. When fire promptly fell from heaven, devoured the sacrifice, and licked up the water, the people exclaimed: "Jehovah is the true God!" At that, Elijah ordered that the prophets of Baal be slaughtered.—1Ki 18:18-40.

Nevertheless, Elijah grew fearful when he learned that Queen Jezebel was plotting to kill him. He fled some 150 km (95 mi) to Beer-sheba and then traveled another 300 km (190 mi) to Mount Sinai. Jehovah did not reject Elijah for his temporary lapse of courage but assured him that there was further prophetic work for him to do.—1Ki 19:1-18.

Elisha was Elijah's successor. When Elisha was surrounded by Syrian war chariots, he had faith to realize that it was really the Syrian armies that were surrounded —by a host of angelic chariots!—2Ki 6:15-17.

LOCATIONS ON MAP
With Related Scriptures

Abel-meholah	1Ki 19:16
Beer-sheba	1Ki 19:3
Bethel	2Ki 2:1-3, 23, 24
Carmel (Mt.)	1Ki 18:19-40
Damascus	2Ki 8:7-15
Dothan	2Ki 6:13-18
Ekron	2Ki 1:2-4
Gilgal	2Ki 4:38-41
Jericho	2Ki 2:4, 5, 19-22
Jezreel	1Ki 18:45, 46; 21:1, 17-26
Jordan River	2Ki 2:6-14
Kishon (T.V.)	1Ki 18:40
Ramoth-gilead	2Ki 9:1-10
Samaria	2Ki 5:1-27; 6:19-23; 7:1-20
Shunem	2Ki 4:8-37
Sidon	1Ki 17:8, 9
Zarephath	1Ki 17:9-24

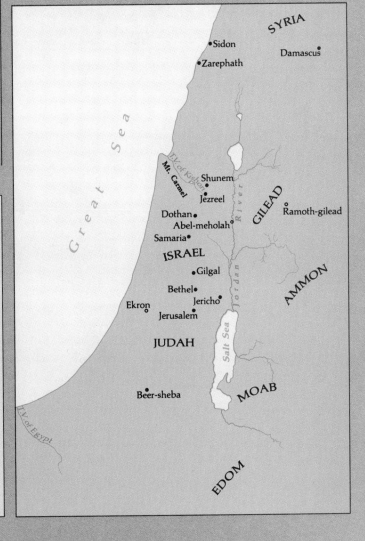

Mount Carmel, site of the fire test proving that not Baal but Jehovah is the true God (1Ki 18:21-39)

Mount Sinai area. Elijah fled from the wrath of Jezebel some 450 km (285 mi) to this region (1Ki 19:1-18)

Ruins of Dothan. Here Elisha and his attendant miraculously saw that, although they were surrounded by a Syrian military force, the mountainous region was full of angelic war chariots of fire sent by Jehovah (2Ki 6:13-17)

AROUND Israel were enemy nations that were intent on seizing its inheritance. Would Israel be swallowed up? As long as Israel remained faithful, it had the decisive edge. "Jehovah himself was fighting for Israel." —Jos 10:14.

This was graphically demonstrated during the rule of King Jehoshaphat (936-c. 911 B.C.E.). The combined forces of Ammon, Moab, and Mount Seir came against Judah. Jehoshaphat appealed to Jehovah: "Here they are . . . coming in to drive us out from your possession that you caused us to possess. O our God, will you not execute judgment upon them?" Indeed He would! Judah was assured: "The battle is not yours, but God's." Jehovah confused the enemy, causing them to slaughter one another.—2Ch 20:1-23.

Finally, after centuries of fighting for Israel, Jehovah allowed enemy nations to conquer it. In 740 B.C.E. the Assyrians brought the ten-tribe kingdom to an end "because the sons of Israel had sinned against Jehovah." (2Ki 17:7-18) Then in 607 B.C.E., for its disobedience the two-tribe kingdom was destroyed by the Babylonians. (2Ki 21:10-15; 22:16, 17) This period of Israel's history emphasizes the importance of obeying Jehovah.

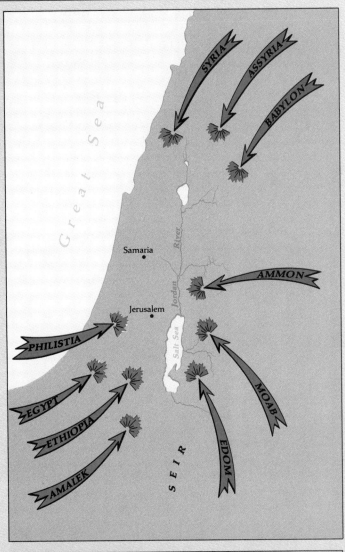

ENEMY NATIONS With Related Scriptures		Edom	2Ch 20:1, 2, 22; 28:17; Ob 1, 12-14
		Egypt	1Ki 14:25, 26; 2Ch 36:2-4
Amalek	Ps 83:2-4, 7	Ethiopia	2Ch 14:9-13
Ammon	2Ch 20:1-3, 10, 11; 2Ki 24:2	Moab	Ps 83:2-4, 6
Assyria	2Ki 15:19, 20, 29; 17:1-6; 18:13-35	Philistia	1Sa 17:1-10; 31:1-7; 2Sa 5:17-25
Babylon	2Ki 24:1, 12-17; 25:1-21	Syria	1Ki 20:1-6, 26; 2Ki 12:17, 18; 16:5-9

Assyrian soldiers taking
Jews from Lachish into exile

Egyptian inscription boasting
over the conquest of Judean
cities by Pharaoh Shishak

Babylonian record
of Nebuchadnezzar's
invasion of Judah

Megiddo

STRATEGICALLY located and dominating major trade and military routes, Megiddo was a focus of international interest in Bible times. The valley plain at its feet became the site of many decisive battles. Therefore, the book of Revelation fittingly names the coming "war of the great day of God the Almighty" Har–Magedon (from Heb., meaning "Mountain of Megiddo"). However, it is not at literal Megiddo that this war will be fought. It will involve "the kings of the entire inhabited earth." (Re 16:14, 16) This time no human ruler will be victor. It will be the Kingdom of God that will prove triumphant over all of them, vindicating Jehovah God, the Almighty, as Universal Sovereign.

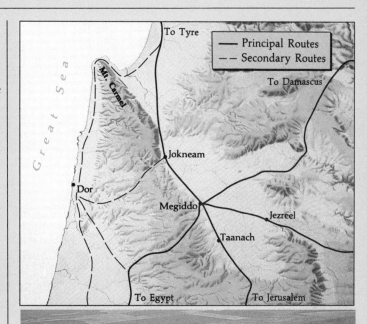

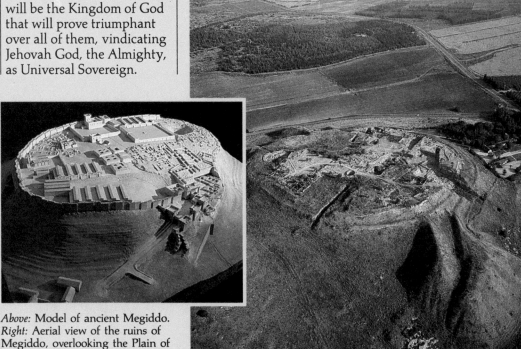

Above: Model of ancient Megiddo.
Right: Aerial view of the ruins of Megiddo, overlooking the Plain of Esdraelon

ASSYRIA was an empire whose record was dominated by military conquest, frequently coupled with sadistic treatment of captives. One of the foremost influences in Assyrian life was religious, and war was viewed as a true expression of their religion. Historian W. B. Wright reports: "Fighting was the business of the nation, and the priests were incessant fomenters of war. They were supported largely from the spoils of conquest, of which a fixed percentage was invariably assigned them before others shared, for this race of plunderers was excessively religious."—*Ancient Cities*, 1886, p. 25.

Both the Bible and secular history report repeated contacts between Israel and Assyria. In time Israel was forced to pay tribute to the king of Assyria. Then in 740 B.C.E., Samaria, the capital of the northern kingdom, was conquered, and thereafter thousands were sent into exile. The fact that Jehovah allowed this to occur reflects the low level to which apostate Israel had sunk. But when Sennacherib attempted to add Jerusalem to his list of conquests, an angel of Jehovah annihilated 185,000 of Assyria's troops in one night. (Isa 36:1–37:38) As Jehovah's prophets foretold, Assyria in time became a desolate ruin, and Babylon succeeded it on the world scene.—Isa 23:13; Zep 2:13.

PROMINENT CITIES

Nineveh: Primary capital of the empire, made architecturally magnificent by Sennacherib but a "city of bloodshed."—Na 3:1

Calah: Later known as Nimrud; chosen by Ashurnasirpal II as his royal city and military capital

Khorsabad: A secondary capital, built by Sargon II but deserted soon after he died

Asshur: Ancient religious capital of the empire; Sennacherib listed 34 temples there

Babylon: Commercial and administrative center of southern Mesopotamia

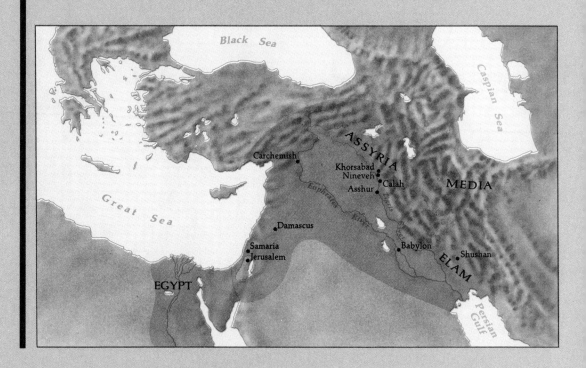

Painting by archaeologist A. H. Layard depicting
the grandeur of the palace of Ashurnasirpal II

This huge winged bull with
a human head once adorned
the palace of Sargon II

From a palace wall in Nimrud.
Lion hunting was a sport of Assyrian
kings; Nineveh itself was referred to
as "the lair of lions" (Na 2:11)

Assyrian monarch with an attendant and a
protective spirit; displayed in the British Museum.
Religion played a key role in Assyria's politics

Assyrian king surrounded by
symbols of his gods. The helmet
with horns is said to represent
Asshur; the winged disk in this
case stands for the sun-god
Shamash; the crescent is the
emblem of the moon-god Sin;
the forked line is the thunderbolt
of Adad; and the star signifies
Ishtar

Assyrian king shown
rushing into battle with
his god flying ahead of
him and also shooting
arrows. Displayed in the
British Museum

Sennacherib's representative taunts Jehovah and demands Jerusalem's capitulation

Sennacherib's annals in which he boasts about his invasion of Judah but makes no mention of the calamity that befell his troops

Assyrian brutality as depicted on their palace walls; captives being tortured, impaled, and flayed alive

True to Bible prophecy, Nineveh (the mound of Kuyunjik in the foreground) became "a city laid waste." (Na 2:10) The Gadd Chronicle (above) relates details of the Babylonian sacking of the once great city

ARCHAEOLOGY is of interest to Bible students. Why? Because in many instances the findings of archaeologists have helped to improve our understanding of life in Bible times and of the original languages in which the Scriptures were written.

At times archaeological finds have even silenced those who criticized the accuracy of certain events or statements made in the Bible. For example, was there a Babylonian king named Belshazzar and an Assyrian king named Sargon? Up until the last century, these names were known only from the Bible record. (Isa 20:1; Da 5:1) But the 19th-century discoveries of Sargon's palace at Khorsabad and the now famous Nabonidus Chronicle upheld the historicity of these rulers.

This does not mean that proof of the Bible's authenticity depends on the discoveries of archaeology. Hebrew archaeologist Yohanan Aharoni noted: "When it comes to historical or historio-geographical interpretation, the archaeologist steps out of the realm of the exact sciences, and he must rely upon value judgements and hypotheses to arrive at a comprehensive historical picture." Thus, when evaluating their finds, archaeologists have at times disagreed with the Bible.

Should this cast doubt on the Bible's authenticity? Not at all. A faith that depends only on the interpretation of archaeological finds is a shaky one indeed. Proof that the Bible is divinely inspired is found within the Bible itself, and not in archaeology.

Mound containing the ruins of Beth-shean

Principal portion excavated

Byzantine/Arab

Hellenistic/Roman

Israelite

Philistine/Israelite

Egyptian

A deep sounding showed a total of 18 levels of occupation, dating back to Canaanite times

Tell el-Husn (Tel Bet She'an)

An inscription that reads: "Hither were brought the bones of Uzziah, king of Judah. Not to be opened." This marked the place of reburial of the king's bones, evidently in about the first century C.E.

The Gezer calendar, believed to be from the tenth century B.C.E., is one of the oldest examples of ancient Hebrew script

Sargon II, whose existence was long doubted by critics, has become well known to archaeologists

On a wall of the tunnel connecting the Spring of Gihon to the Pool of Siloam (apparently built by King Hezekiah) was found the inscription shown here that describes how the work was accomplished

[*Continued from page 944*] The site was then given the name "Gilgal," meaning "Rolling; Rolling Away," to serve as a reminder of this. (Jos 5:8, 9) Later, disguised Gibeonites from the hill country to the W came down to the Jordan Valley and approached Joshua at Gilgal, entering into a covenant with Israel. (Jos 9:3-15) When the Gibeonites afterward came under attack, Joshua's army made an all-night march from Gilgal up to their city to rout the league of five Amorite kings. (Jos 10:1-15) The distribution of the land of Canaan proceeded initially from Gilgal (Jos 14: 6-17:18) and was completed from Shiloh.—Jos 18:1-21:42.

Jehovah's angel is reported to have gone "from Gilgal to Bochim." (Jg 2:1) This may allude to the angelic appearance near Gilgal shortly after Israel had crossed the Jordan (Jos 5:10-14) and therefore suggests that the same angel appeared at Bochim.

It is uncertain whether it was Gilgal near the Jordan or No. 2 below that was included on Samuel's annual circuit. (1Sa 7:15, 16) There he offered sacrifices after Saul's anointing (1Sa 10: 1, 8) and, along with the people, renewed Saul's kingship.—1Sa 11:14, 15.

While Philistine forces were massing up in the hill country around Michmash, King Saul was down in the Jordan Valley at Gilgal. Fearful that the enemy would sweep down upon him, Saul presumptuously offered up a burnt sacrifice. (1Sa 13:4-15) It was also at Gilgal that Saul was told of Jehovah's rejection of him as king because of his failure to obey Jehovah's command to devote all the Amalekites and their flocks and herds to destruction.—1Sa 15:12-28.

After Absalom's revolt failed, the men of Judah came to Gilgal to conduct David across the Jordan.—2Sa 19:15, 40.

Through the prophet Micah, Jehovah reminded his people of his blessings upon them. "From Shittim . . . to Gilgal" he had blocked the Moabite effort to corrupt them, had brought Israel across the Jordan, and had rolled away the reproach of Egypt. But Israel failed to discern these "righteous acts of Jehovah."—Mic 6:5; Nu 25:1.

Gilgal may possibly be also known as Geliloth. —See GELILOTH.

The postexilic Beth-gilgal may be the same as the Gilgal near Jericho or No. 2.—Ne 12:28, 29.

2. Although some view it otherwise, the Gilgal mentioned in connection with Elijah and Elisha is evidently not the same as No. 1. Before being taken up to the heavens in a windstorm, Elijah, accompanied by Elisha, went from Gilgal down to Bethel and then to Jericho. (2Ki 2:1-5) This route suggests a location near Bethel. Also, their going "down" implies that this Gilgal was in a mountainous region. The Gilgal in the Jordan Valley would not fit this description. Hence this Gilgal is usually linked with Jil Jiliya, a large village atop a hill about 11 km (7 mi) N of Bethel. Elisha later rendered harmless a poisonous stew there. (2Ki 4:38-41) Perhaps this or still another Gilgal is the one described at Deuteronomy 11: 29, 30 as having Mount Gerizim and Mount Ebal in front of it.

In later periods this city (or perhaps No. 1) evidently became a center of false worship. (Ho 4:15; 9:15; 12:11) Foreseeing the subsequent exile of the northern kingdom, Jehovah, by his prophet Amos, scornfully tells the irreformable Israelites to be "frequent in committing transgression" at Gilgal, also foretelling exile for its inhabitants.—Am 4:4; 5:5.

3. A site W of the Jordan mentioned in a list of Israelite conquests under Joshua. (Jos 12:7, 8, 23) Some believe that the text may contain a scribal error, hence prefer the Greek *Septuagint* reading of "Galilee," as in *Revised Standard Version.*

GILOH (Gi'loh). A city in the mountainous region of Judah (Jos 15:48, 51) and the home of the traitor "Ahithophel the Gilonite." (2Sa 15:12; 23:34) Though its exact location is unknown, some geographers tentatively identify Giloh with Khirbet Jala, about 10 km (6 mi) NNW of Hebron.

GILONITE (Gi'lon·ite) [Of (Belonging to) Giloh]. An inhabitant of Giloh. This term is applied to Ahithophel, David's counselor.—Jos 15:51; 2Sa 15:12; 23:34.

GIMEL [ג] (gi'mel). The third letter in the Hebrew alphabet. It is the softest of the palatal letters except for *yohdh* [י] and corresponds generally to the English "g" when it has within it the point (daghesh lene); but without this point it is pronounced softer, more down in the throat. (See HEBREW, II.) In the Hebrew, this is the first letter in the opening word in each of the eight verses of Psalm 119:17-24.

GIMZO (Gim'zo). A city of Judah that, with its dependent towns, was captured by the Philistines during the reign of Ahaz. (2Ch 28:18, 19) It is usually identified with Gimzu, a village about 23 km (14 mi) SE of modern Tel Aviv-Yafo.

GINATH (Gi'nath). Father of Tibni the unsuccessful rival of Omri for the kingship over the ten-tribe kingdom of Israel.—1Ki 16:21, 22.

GINNETHOI (Gin′ne·thoi). One of the heads of the priests who returned from Babylon with Zerubbabel in 537 B.C.E. (Ne 12:1, 4, 7); he may be the same as Ginnethon at Nehemiah 12:16.

GINNETHON (Gin′ne·thon).

1. A paternal house of priests headed by a certain Meshullam during Nehemiah's governorship.—Ne 12:12, 16, 26.

2. One of the priests or the forefather of one, who attested by seal the "trustworthy arrangement" contracted during Nehemiah's governorship.—Ne 9:38; 10:1, 6, 8.

GIRDLE. See ARMS, ARMOR; DRESS.

GIRGASHITE(S) (Gir′ga·shite[s]). A people descended from Ham through Canaan. (Ge 10:6, 15, 16; 1Ch 1:8, 13, 14) The Girgashites resided W of the Jordan. Although powerful, they and six other Canaanite nations suffered defeat, for Jehovah delivered them into the hands of his people. (De 7:1, 2; Jos 3:10; 24:11) This fulfilled God's promise made to Abraham centuries earlier. (Ge 15:13-21; Ne 9:7, 8) The names "Girgash" and "Ben-Girgash," found in the Ugaritic literature, have been cited as indirect confirmation of the Girgashites' existence.

GIRZITES (Gir′zites). A people who were among the victims of a raid that David and his 600 men made during their 16-month stay with the Philistines. David took much livestock as spoil but did not preserve any of the Girzites alive. Probably nomads, the Girzites lived in the territory S of Judah in the general direction of Egypt. —1Sa 27:2, 7-9.

GISHPA (Gish′pa). An overseer of the Nethinim temple slaves in Nehemiah's day.—Ne 11:21.

GITTAIM (Git′ta·im) [Two Winepresses]. The site to which (for unstated reasons) the Beerothites fled. (2Sa 4:1-3) Benjamites settled Gittaim after the exile. (Ne 11:31, 33) The exact location is unknown; some suggest an identification with a place called Gamteti in the Amarna Tablets, likely in the vicinity of modern Ramleh.—See BEEROTH.

GITTITE (Git′tite) [Of (Belonging to) Gath]. A term often applied to an inhabitant or native of the Philistine city of Gath. (Jos 13:2, 3) Giant Goliath was a Gittite. (2Sa 21:19; 1Ch 20:5) Gittites, including Ittai (called "a foreigner" and "an exile" from his home), faithfully stuck with David during his flight at the time of Absalom's rebellion.—2Sa 15:13, 18-22; 18:2; see GATH; ITTAI No. 1.

The term "Gittite," however, is also applied to Obed-edom, in whose home the ark of the covenant temporarily rested. (2Sa 6:10, 11; 1Ch 13: 13) Some scholars believe he similarly was from Philistine Gath. It seems more likely, however, that Obed-edom was a Levite and may have been called a Gittite because he came from the Levite city of Gath-rimmon.—Jos 21:20, 23, 24; see OBED-EDOM No. 1.

GITTITH (Git′tith). A musical expression of uncertain meaning, appearing in the superscriptions of Psalms 8, 81, and 84. The term seems to be derived from the Hebrew word *gath,* which is also the name of a town located on the border of Judah and Philistia. Some have suggested that "Gittith" denotes a tune associated with vintage songs, since *gath* refers to a winepress. The Greek *Septuagint* and the Latin *Vulgate,* therefore, render "Gittith" as "winepresses."

GIZONITE (Gi′zo·nite) [Of (Belonging to) Gimzo]. A designation referring either to the family or to the place of origin of Hashem, whose "sons" were among the mighty men of David's military forces.—1Ch 11:26, 34.

GLASS. A mixture of special sand (silica) with traces of other elements such as boron, phosphorus, and lead. These ingredients are melted together at a temperature of about 1650° C. (3000° F.). The newly formed glass, when cooled, is noncrystalline, smooth, extremely hard, and quite brittle. Volcanic heat has produced a form of glass called obsidian, and lightning, when striking sand, sometimes fuses it into long, slender tubes of glass known as fulgurites.

In Egypt have been found glass beads that archaeologists believe were made some 4,000 years ago, about the time Abraham was born. Job, who lived in the 17th century before the Common Era, names glass alongside gold for preciousness when he says: "Gold and glass cannot be compared to [wisdom]."—Job 28:17.

The apostle John, in describing his visions, makes mention of "clear glass" and "transparent glass" (Re 21:18, 21); also of "a glassy sea like crystal."—Re 4:6.

GLEANING. The process of gathering whatever portion of a certain crop the harvesters had intentionally or unintentionally left behind. God's law to Israel specifically directed his people not to reap the edges of their fields completely, not to go over the boughs of the olive tree after having harvested the crop by beating the tree, nor to gather the leftovers of their vineyards. Even if a sheaf of grain was inadvertently left in the field, this was not to be retrieved. Gleaning was the God-given right of the poor in the land, the afflicted one, the alien resident, the fatherless boy, and the widow.—Le 19:9, 10; De 24:19-21.

The account of Ruth provides an outstanding example of the application of this loving provision of God's law. Although having the right to glean, Ruth asked the one in charge of the harvesters for permission to do so, and this may have been the general practice of the gleaners. Ruth was treated kindly, Boaz even instructing his harvesters to pull out some of the ears from the bundles and leave them behind for her to glean. While this made it easier for Ruth, nevertheless it required effort on her part. She kept right on busily gleaning behind Boaz' harvesters from morning to evening, sitting down in the house only a little while and taking time out to eat.—Ru 2:5-7, 14-17.

It is evident that this fine arrangement for the poor of the land, while encouraging generosity, unselfishness, and reliance on Jehovah's blessing, in no way fostered laziness. It throws light on David's statement: "I have not seen anyone righteous left entirely, nor his offspring looking for bread." (Ps 37:25) By availing themselves of the provision made for them by the Law, even the poor, by virtue of their hard work, would not go hungry, and neither they nor their children would have to beg for bread.

Figurative and Illustrative Uses. When the Ephraimites accused Gideon of not calling them to the fight at the start of the battle against Midian, Gideon said: "Are not the gleanings of Ephraim better than the grape gathering of Abiezer [the house to which Gideon belonged]?" He interpreted his illustration by pointing out that Ephraim's part (though it followed the initial battle) in capturing Midian's princes Oreb and Zeeb was far greater than all that Gideon himself had done. (Jg 8:1-3; 6:11) The Scriptures also refer to the slaying of remaining ones in warfare, after the main portion of the conflict was over, as "a gleaning." (Jg 20:44, 45) The ones left over after Jehovah's execution of judgment are likened to "the gleaning when the grape gathering has come to an end," and Micah speaks of the remnant of God's inheritance in the midst of the morally corrupt people as "the gleaning of a grape gathering."—Isa 24:13; Mic 7:1-8, 18; compare Jer 6:9; 49:9, 10.

GLEDE [Heb., *dai·yah'*]. The Hebrew name for this bird occurs in the list of unclean birds at Deuteronomy 14:13 but does not appear in the corresponding list at Leviticus 11:14. Four Hebrew manuscripts, and also the Samaritan *Pentateuch* and the Greek *Septuagint,* omit *dai·yah'* at Deuteronomy 14:13. Some scholars believe that it may be a scribal correction originally placed in the margin but which eventually was introduced into the text itself. However, the plural form (*dai·yohth'*) appears at Isaiah 34:15 as describing birds gathered at the ruins of Edom following its desolation.

The identification of this bird is uncertain. It is suggested that the Hebrew name is derived from the verb meaning "pounce" or "come darting." "Glede" is a suitable translation, since it is a term variously applied to any of several birds of prey, though especially to the red kite (*Milvus milvus*). Most modern scholars relate the Hebrew *dai·yah'* to the kite, there being more than one variety of this bird found in Palestine.—See KITE.

GLORY.　　In the Hebrew Scriptures, the word most often translated "glory" is *ka·vohdh',* which basically has the sense of "heaviness." (Compare Na 2:9, where *ka·vohdh'* is rendered "heavy amount," and 1Sa 4:18, where the related adjective *ka·vedh'* is rendered "heavy.") Thus, glory may refer to anything that makes a person or a thing seem weighty or impressive, such as material wealth (Ps 49:16), position, or reputation. (Ge 45:13) The Greek equivalent of *ka·vohdh'* is *do'xa,* which originally meant "opinion; reputation," but in the Christian Greek Scriptures came to mean "glory." Among its senses are repute or "honor" (Lu 14:10), splendor (Lu 2:9; 1Co 15:40), and that which brings honor to its owner or maker (1Co 11:7).

Often the Scriptures mention glory in connection with Jehovah God. As to its meaning in these cases the *Theological Dictionary of the New Testament,* edited by G. Kittel, explains: "If in relation to man [*ka·vohdh'*] denotes that which makes him impressive and demands recognition, whether in terms of material possessions or striking [dignity or importance], in relation to God it implies that which makes God impressive to man." (Translated by G. Bromiley, 1971, Vol. II, p. 238) So glory may refer to an impressive evidence of God's almighty power. Thus, the visible heavenly bodies are "declaring the glory of God." (Ps 19:1) On Mount Sinai, "Jehovah's glory" was evidenced by such fearsome manifestations as "a devouring fire."—Ex 24:16-18; compare 16:7, 10; 40:34.

Concerning Jesus' first miracle, the Bible says that "he made his glory manifest." (Joh 2:11)

Glory here refers to an impressive evidence of miraculous power identifying Jesus as the promised Messiah. (Compare Joh 11:40-44.) On another occasion, Jesus prayed: "Father, glorify me alongside yourself with the glory that I had alongside you before the world was." (Joh 17:5) Jesus used the term here to refer to the exalted state that he enjoyed in heaven before coming to earth. In answer to that prayer, Jehovah "glorified his Servant, Jesus," by resurrecting him and bringing him back into heaven. (Ac 3:13-15) At Jesus' transfiguration the apostles who were present "saw his glory." (Lu 9:29-32) This has to do with the regal "magnificence" that Jesus was to receive at his "presence" in Kingdom power. —2Pe 1:16.

God's servants are admonished to "do all things for God's glory." (1Co 10:31) God's glory is made manifest through the honor or praise that is given him. One's conduct can cause others to 'give glory to God.' (Mt 5:16; 1Pe 2:12) Christians who truly respond to Jehovah's direction are "transformed . . . from glory to glory," continually making progress in reflecting God's glory. (2Co 3:18) On the other hand, we should beware of seeking glory from men, as did some in the first century. (Joh 12:42, 43) Both Jesus and the apostle Paul set a fine example in not seeking or accepting glory from men.—Joh 5:41; 8:50; 1Th 2:5, 6.

GLUTTON.

A selfish, greedy person given to excessive indulgence, especially voracious eating. Gluttony in any form is diametrically opposed to Bible precepts and principles.

Under the Mosaic Law, parents of an incorrigible son who was a glutton and a drunkard were to bring him to the older men of the city, who would have him stoned to death. (De 21:18-21) As a warning to others, the Proverbs condemned even association with gluttons: "One having companionship with gluttons humiliates his father." "Do not come to be among heavy drinkers of wine, among those who are gluttonous eaters of flesh. For a drunkard and a glutton will come to poverty, and drowsiness will clothe one with mere rags." (Pr 28:7; 23:20, 21) The Hebrew term here used for "glutton" and 'gluttonous eater' is zoh·lel'. The basic sense of the word is possibly "be lavish," that is, wasteful, prodigal. —Compare De 21:20, ftn.

In an effort to discredit Jesus Christ, one of the charges of slander hurled at him by his opponents was: "Look! A man gluttonous and given to

drinking wine." Jesus simply refuted the false charge by saying, "Wisdom is proved righteous by its works" or "by all its children." (Mt 11:19; Lu 7:34, 35) In other words, Jesus was saying, 'Look at my righteous works and conduct and you will know the charge is false.'

Gluttony certainly has no place in the Christian congregation, and the apostle Paul wanted to make sure it would not creep in. So, when leaving Titus in Crete to look after the young Christian organization there, he reminded Titus what one of Crete's own prophets (thought to have been Epimenides, a Cretan poet of the sixth century B.C.E.), had said: "Cretans are always liars, injurious wild beasts, unemployed gluttons [literally, bellies]." Therefore, the overseers whom Titus would appoint, Paul said, should be men free of all such accusations, men who were not drunkards or greedy and who had good self-control. —Tit 1:5-12.

Although not listed separately as a 'work of the flesh,' gluttony often accompanies drunken bouts and revelries, and it is certainly included in the comprehensive expression "things like these," the practicers of which "will not inherit God's kingdom." (Ga 5:19, 21) Moderation in eating habits, as in all other activities, is a Christian virtue. —1Ti 3:2, 11.

GNAT

[Heb., ken, plural, kin·nim'; Gr., ko'nops]. Any of a variety of small two-winged insects, many of which are bloodsuckers. The Hebrew word kin·nim' (or, kin·nam'), when used with reference to the third plague visited upon Egypt (Ex 8:16-18; Ps 105:31), has been variously rendered "gnats" (NW, Ro, RS), "mosquitoes" (AT), and "lice" (KJ); "sand flies" and "fleas" have been given as alternate readings.—AS (Ex 8:16, ftn).

At Isaiah 51:6 the Hebrew term ken is translated "gnat" (NW) and "gnats" (RS; AS, ftn). Ken here is evidently the singular form of kin·nim' (or, kin·nam') and not another Hebrew word of the same form meaning "the right manner, this manner, thus"; the word preceding it in the text, kemoh', by itself means "like" or "in like manner."

The only other reference to the gnat in Scripture is in Jesus' denunciation of the scribes and Pharisees for straining out the gnat but gulping down the camel. The Jewish religious leaders were sticklers for little things, filtering their beverages so as not to contract ceremonial defilement by swallowing a gnat. (Le 11:21-24) However, their disregarding the weightier matters of the Law was comparable to swallowing a camel, likewise a ceremonially unclean animal.—Le 11:4; Mt 23:23, 24.

GOAD. An agricultural implement consisting of a rod approximately 2.5 m (8 ft) in length and chiefly used for driving and guiding bulls when plowing. One end of the rod is equipped with a sharp metal point to prick the animal, and a broad chisellike blade affixed to the other end is used for removing dirt and clay from the plowshare or for clearing it of roots and thorns.

"A cattle goad" was used by Shamgar in killing 600 Philistines. (Jg 3:31) The Hebrew word here rendered "goad" (mal·madh´) comes from the root la·madh´ (learn; teach).

The Bible record mentions that when the Philistines had the upper hand on the Israelites during Saul's reign, the Israelites were not permitted to have smiths and therefore were forced to go down to the Philistines to get their farming implements sharpened and to have their cattle goads (apparently the metal points) fixed fast. —1Sa 13:19-21.

The goad is compared to the words of a wise person, words that move the listener to advance in harmony with the wisdom heard. (Ec 12:11) The figurative expression "kicking against the goads" is drawn from the action of a stubborn bull that resists the prickings of the goad by kicking against it, resulting in injury to himself. The expression, therefore, denotes resisting or rebelling against rightful authority or a condition that cannot be altered, doing so to one's own injury. This is exactly what Saul did before becoming a Christian, by fighting against the followers of Jesus Christ, who had the backing of Jehovah God.—Ac 26:14; compare Ac 5:38, 39.

GOAH (Go´ah). A site, now unknown, named with the hill of Gareb in Jeremiah's prophecy concerning the rebuilding and extending of Jerusalem.—Jer 31:38, 39.

GOAT. A cud-chewing mammal with hollow horns and usually long, relatively straight hair. A number of Hebrew and Greek terms are used to refer to male and female goats and their offspring. The common Hebrew term for "goat" is 'ez. (Le 3:12) Another Hebrew term for goat (sa·ir´) literally means "hairy." (Compare Ge 27:11, where a word of the same form and from the same root is rendered "hairy.") The male leader of a flock of goats was denoted by the Hebrew term 'at·tudh´, rendered 'he-goat.' (Nu 7:17; compare Jer 50:8, ftn.) The term was used figuratively to refer to rulers or leaders and has been rendered "goatlike leaders." (Isa 14:9; Zec 10:3) The ordinary Greek word for "goat" is tra´gos. —Heb 9:12, 13.

The Syrian goat (Capra hircus mambrica), distinguished by its long, drooping ears and its backward-curving horns, is the predominant breed of Palestine. Usually these goats are black; speckled ones are exceptional. (Ge 30:32, 35) He-goats were one of the items of Tyre's trade. —Eze 27:21.

In Bible times, some of the goat herds may have been quite large. Nabal, for example, had 1,000 goats. (1Sa 25:2, 3) Jacob's gift to Esau included 200 she-goats and 20 he-goats. (Ge 32:13, 14) And the Arabs brought 7,700 he-goats to King Jehoshaphat of Judah.—2Ch 17:11.

To the Hebrews the goat was very valuable. (Pr 27:26) It provided them with milk, from which butter and cheese could be made. (Pr 27:27) Its flesh, particularly that of the kid, was eaten. (Ge 27:9; De 14:4; Jg 6:19; 13:15; Lu 15:29) And for the Passover, either a male sheep or a year-old male goat could be used. (Ex 12:5) Goat's hair, made into fabric, was employed in various ways. (Nu 31:20) "The tents of Kedar" may have been made from black goat's hair (Ca 1:5), and goat's hair was used in the construction of the tabernacle. (Ex 26:7; 35:26) Goatskins were made into bottles (see Ge 21:15) and were also used for clothing, as by certain persecuted pre-Christian witnesses of Jehovah.—Heb 11:37.

The Mosaic Law prohibited eating the fat of a goat offered as a sacrifice (Le 7:23-25), and it also prohibited boiling a kid in its mother's milk.—Ex 23:19; 34:26; De 14:21; see MILK.

The goat served as a sacrificial animal, being presented as a burnt offering (Le 1:10; 22:18, 19), a communion sacrifice (Le 3:6, 12), a sin offering (Ezr 8:35), and a guilt offering (Le 5:6). Every firstborn of the goats was to be sacrificed, but not until it was at least eight days old. (Le 22:27; Nu 18:17) A female goat in its first year (or, a female lamb) was the prescribed sin offering for a person not a priest or a chieftain. (Le 4:28, 32) At certain times goats were sacrificed as sin offerings for the nation of Israel as a whole. (Le 23:19; Nu 28:11, 15, 16, 22, 26-30; 29:1-39; 2Ch 29:20-24; Ezr 6:17) A young male goat served as the sin offering for a chieftain. (Le 4:22-26) On the Day of Atonement, two goats were used. One was sacrificed as a sin offering for the 12 non-Levite tribes, and the other was designated for "Azazel" and was sent away into the wilderness. (Le 16:1-27; see ATONEMENT DAY; AZAZEL.) Of course, those goats that were offered in sacrifice could not actually take away sins, but they merely pictured the real sin-atoning sacrifice of Jesus Christ.—Heb 9:11-14; 10:3, 4.

Figurative and Prophetic Usage. The hair of the Shulammite girl was compared to a drove of goats, perhaps alluding to the glistening sheen of black hair or to the luxuriant abundance of the girl's tresses. (Ca 4:1; 6:5) Israel's small army, when compared with that of the Syrians, was likened to "two tiny flocks of goats." (1Ki 20:27) Goats were used to represent people, often those in opposition to Jehovah. (Isa 34:6, 7; compare Jer 51:40; Eze 34:17; Zec 10:3.) In Jesus' illustration of the sheep and the goats, the goats represent those persons who refuse to do good to the least of his brothers.—Mt 25:31-46.

The he-goat of Daniel's prophecy represented the Grecian (or Greco-Macedonian) World Power. (Da 8:5-8, 21) Concerning this *The Imperial Bible-Dictionary* (edited by P. Fairbairn, London, 1874, Vol. I, p. 664) observes: "It is interesting to know that this [the goat] was the recognized symbol of their nation by the Macedonians themselves. Monuments are still extant in which this symbol occurs, as one of the pilasters of Persepolis, where a goat is depicted with one immense horn on his forehead, and a Persian holding the horn, by which is intended the subjection of Macedon by Persia" (something accomplished by the Persians toward the close of the sixth century B.C.E.).

Mountain Goat, Wild Goat. The Hebrew designation *ye'e·lim'*, rendered "mountain goats" (*NW*) and "wild goats" (*KJ*), is generally understood to refer to the Nubian ibex (*Capra ibex nubiana*), a mountain-dwelling wild goat with large, heavily ridged, backward-curving horns. This animal is at home in the high mountains (Ps 104:18), where it negotiates jagged crags and narrow mountain ledges with graceful ease. During the period of gestation these goats seek out places not easily found by man. This may be alluded to at Job 39:1, where the question raised points up the fact that these creatures are quite independent of man, the birth of their young taking place unobserved by man.

The account at 1 Samuel chapter 24 tells of Saul's pursuing David into the rocky area of En-gedi (meaning "Fountain (Spring) of the Kid") on the western side of the Dead Sea. The pursuers looked for David and his men upon "the bare rocks of the mountain goats" (1Sa 24:2), suggesting that mountain goats inhabited this region.

Even in recent times the ibex has been seen there.

The feminine Hebrew form *ya·'alah'* is employed in the passage at Proverbs 5:18, 19. Here the wife of one's youth is compared to "a charming mountain goat," the allusion possibly being to the grace of this animal.

At Deuteronomy 14:4, 5, where the reference is to animals acceptable for food, the Hebrew word *'aq·qoh'* has been translated "wild goat." (*AS, KJ, NW, RS*) Many scholars believe that *'aq·qoh'* may designate the same animal as *ye'e·lim'*, that is, the Nubian ibex.

GOAT-SHAPED DEMON.

The Hebrew *sa·'ir'* (literally, hairy) refers to a goat or kid of the goats. (Le 16:18; Nu 7:16) However, in four texts (Le 17:7; 2Ch 11:15; Isa 13:21; 34:14) the word is generally considered by translators as having a sense beyond its ordinary meaning of "goat" or "kid."

At both Leviticus 17:7 and 2 Chronicles 11:15 it is clear that the term (*se'i·rim'*, plural) is used in referring to things to which worship and sacrifice are given, and this in connection with false religion. The translators of the Greek *Septuagint* and Latin *Vulgate*, therefore, rendered the Hebrew word as "the senseless things" (*LXX*) and "the demons" (*Vg*). Modern translators and lexicographers in general adopt the same view in these two texts, using "demons" (*Ro*), "satyrs" (*RS, AT, JB, JP*), or "goat-shaped demons" (*NW;* see also Koehler and Baumgartner's *Lexicon in Veteris Testamenti Libros,* Leiden, 1958, p. 926, and *A Hebrew and English Lexicon of the Old Testament* by Brown, Driver, and Briggs, 1980, p. 972), exceptions being the translation by Robert Young, which renders the term literally as "goat(s)," and the *American Standard Version,* which uses "he-goats."

Joshua's words at Joshua 24:14 show that the Israelites had been affected to some extent by the false worship of Egypt during their sojourn there, while Ezekiel indicates that such pagan practices continued to plague them long afterward. (Eze 23:8, 21) For this reason some scholars consider that the divine decree issued in the wilderness to prevent the Israelites from making "sacrifices to the goat-shaped demons" (Le 17:1-7) and Jeroboam's establishing priests "for the high places and for the goat-shaped demons and for the calves that he had made" (2Ch 11:15) indicate there was some form of goat worship among the Israelites such as was prominent in Egypt, particularly in Lower Egypt. Herodotus

(II, 46) claims that from such Egyptian worship the Greeks derived their belief in Pan and also in the satyrs, woodland gods of a lustful nature, who were eventually depicted as having horns, a goat's tail, and goat's legs. Some suggest that such half-animal form of these pagan gods is the source of the practice of picturing Satan with tail,

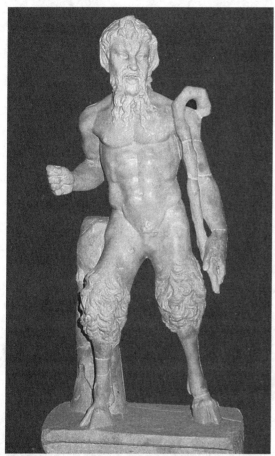

According to Herodotus, the Greek belief in Pan, a god with goatlike features, may have been influenced by Egyptian goat worship

horns, and cloven feet, a custom prevalent among professed Christians in the Dark Ages.

Just what such "hairy ones" (*se'i·rim'*) actually were, however, is not stated. While some consider them to be literal goats or idols in the form of goats, this does not necessarily seem to be indicated; nor do other scriptures provide evidence of that nature. The term used may simply indicate that *in the minds of those worshiping them*

such false gods were conceived of as being goatlike in shape or hairy in appearance. Or, the use of "goats" in these references may be merely a means of expressing contempt for all idolatrous objects in general, even as the word for idols in numerous texts is drawn from a term originally meaning "dung pellets," not denoting, however, that the idols were literally made of dung.—Le 26:30; De 29:17.

The sense of *sa·'ir'* and *se'i·rim'* in the other two texts (Isa 13:21; 34:14) is not as generally agreed upon as being connected with false worship. In these passages the desolate ruins of Babylon and of Edom are depicted as inhabited by wild creatures, including the *se'i·rim'*. Some translations render the term in its ordinary sense as "goat(s)" (*Yg*) or "wild goat(s)" (*AS*), while *Rotherham*, though using "demons" at Leviticus and Second Chronicles, prefers "shaggy creature(s)" in Isaiah. Those preferring such renderings in these texts point out that the word appears among other creatures known to be literal beasts or fowl. Objecting to the rendering of *sa·'ir'* as "satyr" at Isaiah 34:14, G. R. Driver (*Palestine Exploration Quarterly*, London, 1959, p. 57) points out that the satyr was nowhere used in mythology as a symbol of desolation but, rather, of lasciviousness and revelry; in favor of considering the *sa·'ir'* to be a literal goat, he shows that goats flourish in bleak spots and that wild goats are reported to be common at the S end of the Dead Sea, and thus in the direction of desolated Edom, against whom Isaiah's prophecy (34:14) is spoken.

Those favoring a translation in Isaiah such as is indicated by the Leviticus and Second Chronicles texts show that the *Septuagint* translation uses "demons" for *se'i·rim'* in Isaiah and that John uses the same language as that of the *Septuagint* (Isa 13:21) when describing desolated Babylon the Great as the habitat of unclean birds and "demons." (Re 18:2) Of course, whether the apostle John here actually quoted from the *Septuagint* cannot be definitely stated. It is also to be noted that the *Septuagint* uses not only "demons" for *se'i·rim'* but also "monsters" and "satyrs" at Isaiah 13:21, 22, whereas modern translations render the same Hebrew words as "ostriches" and "jackals" or "hyenas" (*Da, Mo, RS, NW*).

Thus, the matter is not one allowing for absolute certainty. Isaiah may have injected into his list of literal animals and birds references to demons, not meaning that such demons actually materialized in the form of goats but, rather, that the minds of the pagans around those places would imaginatively people the desolate sites with such demon inhabitants. History shows that the people of Syria and Arabia have long associated monstrous creatures with similar ruins, and the *jinn* of the Arabs are depicted as having monstrous hairy forms. On the other hand, the *se'i·rim'* occupying the desolate ruins of Edom and Babylon may well have been real animals, shaggy-haired and perhaps of such appearance as to cause observers to think of demons.

GOB. A site where David's men twice struck down giant warriors of the Philistines' forces. (2Sa 21:18, 19) The parallel narrative at 1 Chronicles 20:4 lists the place of the first encounter as "Gezer" ("Gath" in some copies of the Greek *Septuagint* and the Syriac *Peshitta*), while leaving the place of the second encounter unnamed. (1Ch 20:5) Both accounts, however, show that a third confrontation took place at "Gath" (2Sa 21:20; 1Ch 20:6), and therefore many scholars have assumed that "Gob" is a scribal error for "Gath." To others, however, it seems unlikely that such an oversight would occur *twice* in consecutive verses, and they conclude that Gob may simply have been the name of a now unidentified site near Gezer.

GOD. Anything that is worshiped can be termed a god, inasmuch as the worshiper attributes to it might greater than his own and venerates it. A person can even let his belly be a god. (Ro 16:18; Php 3:18, 19) The Bible makes mention of many gods (Ps 86:8; 1Co 8:5, 6), but it shows that the gods of the nations are valueless gods. —Ps 96:5; see GODS AND GODDESSES.

Hebrew Terms. Among the Hebrew words that are translated "God" is *'El,* probably meaning "Mighty One; Strong One." (Ge 14:18) It is used with reference to Jehovah, to other gods, and to men. It is also used extensively in the makeup of proper names, such as Elisha (meaning "God Is Salvation") and Michael ("Who Is Like God?"). In some places *'El* appears with the definite article (*ha·'El',* literally, "the God") with reference to Jehovah, thereby distinguishing him from other gods.—Ge 46:3; 2Sa 22:31; see *NW* appendix, p. 1567.

At Isaiah 9:6 Jesus Christ is prophetically called *'El Gib·bohr',* "Mighty God" (not *'El Shad·dai'* [God Almighty], which is applied to Jehovah at Genesis 17:1).

The plural form, *'e·lim',* is used when referring to other gods, such as at Exodus 15:11 ("gods"). It

is also used as the plural of majesty and excellence, as in Psalm 89:6: "Who can resemble Jehovah among the sons of God [*bi·beneh' 'E·lim'*]?" That the plural form is used to denote a single individual here and in a number of other places is supported by the translation of *'E·lim'* by the singular form *The·os'* in the Greek *Septuagint;* likewise by *Deus* in the Latin *Vulgate.*

The Hebrew word *'elo·him'* (gods) appears to be from a root meaning "be strong." *'Elo·him'* is the plural of *'eloh'ah* (god). Sometimes this plural refers to a number of gods (Ge 31:30, 32; 35:2), but more often it is used as a plural of majesty, dignity, or excellence. *'Elo·him'* is used in the Scriptures with reference to Jehovah himself, to angels, to idol gods (singular and plural), and to men.

When applying to Jehovah, *'Elo·him'* is used as a plural of majesty, dignity, or excellence. (Ge 1:1) Regarding this, Aaron Ember wrote: "That the language of the O[ld] T[estament] has entirely given up the idea of plurality in . . . [*'Elo·him'*] (as applied to the God of Israel) is especially shown by the fact that it is almost invariably construed with a singular verbal predicate, and takes a singular adjectival attribute. . . . [*'Elo·him'*] must rather be explained as an *intensive plural,* denoting *greatness* and *majesty,* being equal to The Great God."—*The American Journal of Semitic Languages and Literatures,* Vol. XXI, 1905, p. 208.

The title *'Elo·him'* draws attention to Jehovah's strength as the Creator. It appears 35 times by itself in the account of creation, and every time the verb describing what he said and did is in the singular number. (Ge 1:1–2:4) In him resides the sum and substance of infinite forces.

At Psalm 8:5, the angels are also referred to as *'elo·him',* as is confirmed by Paul's quotation of the passage at Hebrews 2:6-8. They are called *beneh' ha·'Elo·him',* "sons of God" (*KJ*); "sons of the true God" (*NW*), at Genesis 6:2, 4; Job 1:6; 2:1. *Lexicon in Veteris Testamenti Libros,* by Koehler and Baumgartner (1958), page 134, says: "(individual) divine beings, gods." And page 51 says: "the (single) gods," and it cites Genesis 6:2; Job 1:6; 2:1; 38:7. Hence, at Psalm 8:5 *'elo·him'* is rendered "angels" (*LXX*); "godlike ones" (*NW*).

The word *'elo·him'* is also used when referring to idol gods. Sometimes this plural form means simply "gods." (Ex 12:12; 20:23) At other times it is the plural of excellence and only one god (or goddess) is referred to. However, these gods were clearly not trinities.—1Sa 5:7b (Dagon);

1Ki 11:5 ("goddess" Ashtoreth); Da 1:2b (Marduk).

At Psalm 82:1, 6, 'elo·him' is used of men, human judges in Israel. Jesus quoted from this Psalm at John 10:34, 35. They were gods in their capacity as representatives of and spokesmen for Jehovah. Similarly Moses was told that he was to serve as "God" to Aaron and to Pharaoh.—Ex 4: 16, ftn; 7:1.

In many places in the Scriptures 'Elo·him' is also found preceded by the definite article ha. (Ge 5:22) Concerning the use of ha·'Elo·him', F. Zorell says: "In the Holy Scriptures especially the one true God, Jahve, is designated by this word; . . . 'Jahve is the [one true] God' De 4:35; 4:39; Jos 22:34; 2Sa 7:28; 1Ki 8:60 etc."—Lexicon Hebraicum Veteris Testamenti, Rome, 1984, p. 54; brackets his.

The Greek Term. The usual Greek equivalent of 'El and 'Elo·him' in the Septuagint translation and the word for "God" or "god" in the Christian Greek Scriptures is the·os'.

The True God Jehovah. The true God is not a nameless God. His name is Jehovah. (De 6:4; Ps 83:18) He is God by reason of his creatorship. (Ge 1:1; Re 4:11) The true God is real (Joh 7:28), a person (Ac 3:19; Heb 9:24), and not lifeless natural law operating without a living lawgiver, not blind force working through a series of accidents to develop one thing or another. The 1956 edition of The Encyclopedia Americana (Vol. XII, p. 743) commented under the heading "God": "In the Christian, Mohammedan, and Jewish sense, the Supreme Being, the First Cause, and in a general sense, as considered nowadays throughout the civilized world, a spiritual being, self-existent, eternal and absolutely free and all-powerful, distinct from the matter which he has created in many forms, and which he conserves and controls. There does not seem to have been a period of history where mankind was without belief in a supernatural author and governor of the universe."

Proofs of the existence of "the living God." The fact of the existence of God is proved by the order, power, and complexity of creation, macroscopic and microscopic, and through his dealings with his people throughout history. In looking into what might be called the Book of Divine Creation, scientists learn much. One can learn from a book only if intelligent thought and preparation have been put into the book by its author.

In contrast to the lifeless gods of the nations, Jehovah is "the living God." (Jer 10:10; 2Co 6:16) Everywhere there is testimony to his activity and his greatness. "The heavens are declaring the glory of God; and of the work of his hands the expanse is telling." (Ps 19:1) Men have no reason or excuse for denying God, because "what may be known about God is manifest among them, for God made it manifest to them. For his invisible qualities are clearly seen from the world's creation onward, because they are perceived by the things made, even his eternal power and Godship, so that they are inexcusable."—Ro 1:18-20.

Jehovah God is described in the Bible as living from time indefinite to time indefinite, forever (Ps 90:2, 4; Re 10:6), and as being the King of eternity, incorruptible, invisible, the only true God. (1Ti 1:17) There existed no god before him. —Isa 43:10, 11.

Infinite, but approachable. The true God is infinite and beyond the mind of man fully to fathom. The creature could never hope to become equal to his Creator or understand all the workings of His mind. (Ro 11:33-36) But He can be found and approached, and He supplies his worshiper with all that is necessary for the worshiper's welfare and happiness. (Ac 17:26, 27; Ps 145:16) He is ever at the zenith of his ability and willingness to give good gifts and presents to his creatures, as it is written: "Every good gift and every perfect present is from above, for it comes down from the Father of the celestial lights, and with him there is not a variation of the turning of the shadow." (Jas 1:17) Jehovah always acts within his own righteous arrangements, doing all things on a legal basis. (Ro 3:4, 23-26) For this reason all of his creatures can have complete confidence in him, knowing that he always abides by the principles he establishes. He does not change (Mal 3:6), and there is no "variation" with him in the application of his principles. There is no partiality with him (De 10:17, 18; Ro 2:11), and it is impossible for him to lie.—Nu 23:16, 19; Tit 1:1, 2; Heb 6:17, 18.

His attributes. The true God is not omnipresent, for he is spoken of as having a location. (1Ki 8:49; Joh 16:28; Heb 9:24) His throne is in heaven. (Isa 66:1) He is all-powerful, being the Almighty God. (Ge 17:1; Re 16:14) "All things are naked and openly exposed to the eyes of him," and he is "the One telling from the beginning the finale." (Heb 4:13; Isa 46:10, 11; 1Sa 2:3) His power and knowledge extend everywhere, reaching every part of the universe.—2Ch 16:9; Ps 139:7-12; Am 9:2-4.

The true God is spirit, not flesh (Joh 4:24; 2Co 3:17), though he sometimes likens his attributes of sight, power, and so forth, to human faculties. Thus he speaks figuratively of his "arm" (Ex 6:6), his "eyes," and his "ears" (Ps 34:15), and he points out that, since he is the Creator of human eyes and ears, he certainly can see and hear.—Ps 94:9.

Some of God's primary attributes are love (1Jo 4:8), wisdom (Pr 2:6; Ro 11:33), justice (De 32:4; Lu 18:7, 8), and power (Job 37:23; Lu 1:35). He is a God of order and of peace. (1Co 14:33) He is completely holy, clean and pure (Isa 6:3; Hab 1:13; Re 4:8); happy (1Ti 1:11); and merciful (Ex 34:6; Lu 6:36). Many other qualities of his personality are described in the Scriptures.

His position. Jehovah is the Supreme Sovereign of the universe, the King eternal. (Ps 68:20; Da 4:25, 35; Ac 4:24; 1Ti 1:17) The position of his throne is the ultimate for superiority. (Eze 1:4-28; Da 7:9-14; Re 4:1-8) He is the Majesty (Heb 1:3; 8:1), the Majestic God, the Majestic One. (1Sa 4:8; Isa 33:21) He is the Source of all life.—Job 33:4; Ps 36:9; Ac 17:24, 25.

His righteousness and glory. The true God is a righteous God. (Ps 7:9) He is the glorious God. (Ps 29:3; Ac 7:2) He enjoys eminence above all (De 33:26), being clothed with eminence and strength (Ps 93:1; 68:34) and with dignity and splendor. (Ps 104:1; 1Ch 16:27; Job 37:22; Ps 8:1) "His activity is dignity and splendor themselves." (Ps 111:3) There is glory of splendor in his Kingship.—Ps 145:11, 12.

His purpose. God has a purpose that he will work out and that cannot be thwarted. (Isa 46: 10; 55:8-11) His purpose, as expressed at Ephesians 1:9, 10, is "to gather all things together again in the Christ, the things in the heavens and the things on the earth." By means of Christ all intelligent creation will be brought into full harmony with God. (Compare Mt 6:9, 10.) None existed before Jehovah; therefore he has seniority over all. (Isa 44:6) He, being the Creator, existed before any other gods, and 'none will exist after him,' because the nations will never produce a real, live god that is able to prophesy. (Isa 43:10; 46:9, 10) As the Alpha and the Omega (Re 22:13), he is the one and only Almighty God; he will bring to a successful conclusion the issue over Godship, being forever vindicated as the only Almighty God. (Re 1:8; 21:5, 6) He never forgets or forsakes his purposes or covenants, which makes him a God of dependability and loyalty.—Ps 105:8.

A communicative God. Having great love for his creatures, God provides ample opportunity for them to know him and his purposes. His own voice has been heard by men on earth on three occasions. (Mt 3:17; 17:5; Joh 12:28) He has communicated through angels (Lu 2:9-12; Ac 7:52, 53) and through men to whom he gave directions and revelations, such as Moses, and especially through his Son, Jesus Christ. (Heb 1:1, 2; Re 1:1) His written Word is his communication to his people, enabling them to be completely equipped as his servants and ministers, and directing them on the way to life.—2Pe 1:19-21; 2Ti 3:16, 17; Joh 17:3.

Contrasted with the gods of the nations. The true God, the Creator of the glorious heavenly bodies, has glory and brilliance beyond the ability of fleshly sight to endure, for "no man may see [God] and yet live." (Ex 33:20) Only the angels, spirit creatures, have vision that can behold his face in a literal sense. (Mt 18:10; Lu 1:19) Nevertheless, he does not expose men to such an experience. In loving-kindness he enables men to see his fine qualities through his Word, including the revelation of himself by means of his Son, Christ Jesus.—Mt 11:27; Joh 1:18; 14:9.

God gives us an idea of the effect of his presence in the book of Revelation. The apostle John had a vision that approximated seeing God, in the sense that it revealed the effect of beholding him on his throne. God was not like a man in appearance, for he has not revealed any figure of his to man, as John himself said later: "No man has seen God at any time." (Joh 1:18) Rather, God was shown to be like highly polished gems, precious, glowing, beautiful, that attract the eye and win delighted admiration. He was "in appearance, like a jasper stone and a precious red-colored stone, and round about the throne there [was] a rainbow like an emerald in appearance." (Re 4:3) Thus, he is lovely in appearance and pleasant to look at, causing one to lose oneself in wonderment. About his throne there is further glory and an atmosphere of calmness, serenity; the appearance of a perfect rainbow of emerald indicates that, reminding one of the enjoyable quieting calm that follows a storm.—Compare Ge 9:12-16.

How different the true God is, therefore, from the gods of the nations, who are often depicted as being grotesque, angry, fierce, implacable, merciless, whimsical as to their favors and disfavors, horrifying and fiendish, and ready to torture earthly creatures in some kind of inferno.

"A God exacting exclusive devotion." "Even though there are those who are called 'gods,' whether in heaven or on earth, just as there are many 'gods' and many 'lords,' there is actually to us one God the Father." (1Co 8:5, 6) Jehovah is the Almighty God, the only true God, and he rightfully exacts exclusive devotion. (Ex 20:5) His servants must keep others out of, or excluded from, his proper place in their hearts and actions. He requires his worshipers to worship him with spirit and truth. (Joh 4:24) They should stand in reverent awe of him alone.—Isa 8:13; Heb 12: 28, 29.

Among other mighty ones called "gods" in the Bible is Jesus Christ, who is "the only-begotten god." But he himself plainly said: "It is Jehovah your God you must worship, and it is to him alone you must render sacred service." (Joh 1:18; Lu 4:8; De 10:20) The angels are "godlike ones," but one of them stopped John from worshiping him, saying: "Be careful! Do not do that! . . . Worship God." (Ps 8:5; Heb 2:7; Re 19:10) Mighty men among the Hebrews were called "gods" (Ps 82:1-7); but no man was purposed by God to receive worship. When Cornelius began to do obeisance to Peter, that apostle stopped him with the words, "Rise; I myself am also a man." (Ac 10:25, 26) Certainly the false gods invented and fashioned by men down through the centuries since the rebellion in Eden are not to be worshiped. The Mosaic Law warns strongly against turning from Jehovah to them. (Ex 20:3-5) Jehovah the true God will not forever tolerate rivalry from false, worthless gods.—Jer 10:10, 11.

After Christ's Millennial Reign, during which he brings to nothing all authority and power that is in opposition to God, he hands over the Kingdom to his God and Father, who will then become "all things to everyone." (Ro 8:33; 1Co 15:23-28) Eventually, all those living will acknowledge God's sovereignty and will praise his name continually.—Ps 150; Php 2:9-11; Re 21:22-27; see JEHOVAH.

GODLY DEVOTION.
Reverence, worship, and service to God, with loyalty to his universal sovereignty. The Scriptures use the Greek word *eu·se'bei·a* and related adjective, adverb, and verb forms. The noun as used in the Bible may be translated literally as "well-reverencing" and applies to reverence or devotion toward that which is genuinely holy and righteous. (Compare 2Pe 1: 6, *Int.*) The antonym of "godly devotion" is "ungodliness" or "irreverence" (Gr., *a·se'bei·a*).

In *Christian Words*, Nigel Turner wrote: *"Euse-beia* occurs occasionally in a sense which suggests personal religious devotion in the contemporary inscriptions . . . but its more general meaning in the popular Greek of the Roman period was 'loyalty.' . . . For Christians *eusebeia* is the highest kind of *devotion* to God." (1981, p. 111) The Bible's use of the expression "godly devotion" refers to devotion with loyalty to Jehovah God personally.

The related adjective *eu·se·bes'*, meaning "devout; of godly devotion," occurs in Acts 10:2, 7; 2 Peter 2:9. According to John A. H. Tittmann, *eu·se·bes'* "expresses that reverence for the Deity which shows itself in actions, especially in the worship of God; . . . he is [*eu·se·bes'*] who shows that piety by acting."—*Remarks on the Synonyms of the New Testament*, Edinburgh, 1833, Vol. I, pp. 253, 254.

The verb *eu·se·be'o* is used at 1 Timothy 5:4 with regard to the conduct of children or grandchildren toward their widowed mothers or grandmothers. *A Greek and English Lexicon of the New Testament*, by Edward Robinson (1885, p. 307), states that *eu·se·be'o* can have the meaning of being pious toward anyone. For this reason some translations of this passage read: "They are to learn first of all to do their duty to their own families." (*JB;* compare *The New English Bible* and *The Bible in Basic English.*) But God is the Establisher of the family arrangement (Eph 3:14, 15), and the Bible likens the household of God to the family unit. Therefore, reverence, or godly devotion, in family relationships in the Christian household would actually be reverence to God and obedience to God's commands regarding the family and proper conduct of its members. The rendering of this text, "If any widow has children or grandchildren, let these learn first to practice godly devotion in their own household" (*NW*), is in harmony with this understanding.

The 'Sacred Secret of Godly Devotion.' The prime example of godly devotion is Jesus Christ. The apostle Paul wrote to Timothy: "Indeed, the sacred secret of this godly devotion is admittedly great: 'He was made manifest in flesh, was declared righteous in spirit, appeared to angels, was preached about among nations, was believed upon in the world, was received up in glory.'" (1Ti 3:16) Adam, the perfect man, had not set the perfect example of godly devotion. None of his children, born imperfect, could do so. Who would be able to do this? The coming of God's Son to earth and his integrity-keeping course gave the answer, revealing the solution to the sacred secret. He is the one to whom Timothy should look for the perfect example of conduct manifesting godly devotion.—1Ti 3:15.

Jesus Christ was the one man to manifest godly devotion perfectly, in every sense, proving that man in the flesh can maintain such devotion. Under severe trials, right down to the end of his earthly course Jesus was "loyal, guileless, undefiled, separated from the sinners." (Heb 7:26) No flaw could be found in his integrity, to accuse him before God. He said, before his death: "I have conquered the world," also, "The ruler of the world is coming. And he has no hold on me." (Joh 16:33; 14:30) No unrighteousness could be found in him. He could rightly say to his enemies: "Who of you convicts me of sin?" (Joh 8:46) The solution to "the sacred secret of this godly devotion" is so great and means so much to mankind that it is to be proclaimed worldwide. Jesus Christ himself is the basis upon which Christian godly devotion and conduct in the congregation are patterned.

Training, With Contentment, Is Essential. Strenuous training is necessary on the part of the Christian in order to achieve full godly devotion. It entails the enduring of opposition and persecution. (2Ti 3:12) A person's aim, or objective, in training himself is not to achieve selfish materialistic gain. But there is gain to the one who is content with his lot, who continues in godly devotion along with self-sufficiency. "It holds promise of the life now," namely, spiritual health, satisfaction, happiness, and a purpose in living. It also holds promise of the life that "is to come." —1Ti 4:7, 8; 6:6-8; compare Pr 3:7, 8; 4:20-22.

Though persecution and hardship may come upon the person having godly devotion, he need not fear, for "Jehovah knows how to deliver people of godly devotion out of trial." (2Pe 2:9) The apostle Peter counsels Christians to add to their endurance godly devotion. (2Pe 1:5, 6) He admonishes them to be persons identified by "holy acts of conduct and deeds of godly devotion" in order to survive the judgment of Jehovah's day. —2Pe 3:7, 10, 11; 1Pe 4:18.

The Power of Godly Devotion. A person professing godly devotion must recognize its power to change his personality and must be true and genuine in following godliness. (1Ti 6:11; Eph 4:20-24) He must recognize that God's Word is His expression of the way of godly devotion, and so he must conform to its precepts. (Tit 1:1; 2Pe 1:3) Since godly devotion is toward God personally, his Word and spirit will bring one to know Jehovah personally, intimately, and to become more like him—to be an imitator or copier of him. (Eph 5:1) Such a person will reflect more and more the fine qualities of Jehovah God.—2Co 3:18.

If anyone who professes to serve God relies on his own ideas instead of adhering to the Bible and if his teaching does not 'accord with godly devotion,' thus failing to reflect the teacher's devotion to God, he becomes "mentally diseased." (1Ti 6:3, 4) The apostle Paul warned his younger fellow minister Timothy about ungodly ones who professed devotion to God. He cautioned Timothy to handle the Word of the truth aright, shunning empty speeches that violate what is holy, that Timothy might not be turned from the way of godly devotion. He then pointed out that there would be those who would practice all sorts of wickedness, hypocritically having a form of godly devotion but proving false to its power. (2Ti 2:15, 16; 3:1-5) Jude likewise shows that such ones would have no genuine reverence for God or devotion to him, no respect or appreciation for his undeserved kindness. They would be persons using godliness for materialistic or sensual gain. Their hypocrisy is revealed in their practice of acts of loose conduct.—Jude 4.

What is "the mystery of this lawlessness" to which Paul refers?

Herein lies another mystery, diametrically opposed to Jehovah's "sacred secret." It is "the mystery of this lawlessness." This was a mystery to true Christians because in the apostle Paul's day the identity of "the man of lawlessness" had not taken form in a definitely established and clearly identifiable class. Even after that "man" would take form, his identity would continue to be mysterious to most persons because his wickedness would be practiced under the guise and in the name of godly devotion. It would, in fact, be an apostasy from true godly devotion. Paul said that "the mystery of this lawlessness" was already at work in his day, because there was a lawless influence in the Christian congregation that would eventually result in producing this apostate class. Finally, this one would be done away with by Jesus Christ at the manifestation of his presence. This apostate, Satan-operated "man" would lift himself up "over everyone who is called 'god' or an object of reverence" (Gr., se′ba-sma). Thus this great opposer of God as a Satanic instrument would be extremely deceptive and would bring destruction to those following its practices. The effectiveness of "the man of lawlessness" would lie in the fact that his wickedness would be cloaked in a hypocritical godly devotion.—2Th 2:3-12; compare Mt 7:15, 21-23.

GOD OF GOOD LUCK, GOD OF DESTINY.
The apostate Jews in the time of Isaiah were involved in worshiping "the god of Good Luck" (Heb., *gadh*) and "the god of Destiny" (Heb., *meni'*). The worshipers of these deities set a table of food and drink before them. Jehovah said to such worshipers that he would destine them to slaughter by the sword.—Isa 65:11, 12.

The Assyrians and Babylonians frequently prepared food and drink for their gods. People in Haran made vows and hoped to be accepted by the "Lord of Luck." In his comment on Isaiah 65:11, Jerome wrote that "in all cities, and especially in Egypt and Alexandria, there was an ancient idolatrous custom, that on the last day of the final month of their year they would spread a table covered with various kinds of foods, and a cup mixed with sweet wine, ensuring good luck for the fertility either of the past or the coming year."—*Corpus Christianorum, Series Latina, LXXIII A, S. Hieronymi presbyteri opera, Pars. 1, 2A,* Tyrnholt, 1963, p. 754.

GODS AND GODDESSES.
The deities that have been and still are worshiped by the nations are human creations, the products of imperfect, "empty-headed" men, who "turned the glory of the incorruptible God into something like the image of corruptible man and of birds and four-footed creatures and creeping things." (Ro 1:21-23) It is, therefore, not surprising to note that these deities mirror the very characteristics and weaknesses of their imperfect worshipers. One Hebrew term used to refer to idols or false gods literally means "valueless thing" or "worthless thing."—Le 19:4; Isa 2:20.

The Bible refers to Satan the Devil as "the god of this system of things." (2Co 4:4) That Satan is the "god" there referred to is clearly indicated later in verse 4 where it says that this god "has blinded the minds of the unbelievers." At Revelation 12:9 he is said to be "misleading the entire inhabited earth." Satan's control over the present system of things, including its governments, was indicated when he offered Jesus "all the kingdoms of the world" in exchange for "an act of worship."—Mt 4:8, 9.

The worshipful adoration that men direct toward their idol-gods actually goes "to demons, and not to God." (1Co 10:20; Ps 106:36, 37) Jehovah God requires exclusive devotion. (Isa 42:8) The one who worships an idol-god denies the true God and thus serves the interests of Jehovah's chief Adversary, Satan, and his demons.

Although the Bible makes reference to a number of gods and goddesses of ancient peoples, it is not always possible to identify such gods specifically.

Origin of Gods and Goddesses. The striking similarity readily observable when comparing the gods and goddesses of ancient peoples can hardly be attributed to chance. Concerning this, J. Garnier writes: "Not merely Egyptians, Chaldeans, Phœnicians, Greeks and Romans, but also the Hindus, the Buddhists of China and of Thibet, the Goths, Anglo-Saxons, Druids, Mexicans and Peruvians, the Aborigines of Australia, and even the savages of the South Sea Islands, must have all derived their religious ideas from a common source and a common centre. Everywhere we find the most startling coincidences in rites, ceremonies, customs, traditions, and in the names and relations of their respective gods and goddesses."—*The Worship of the Dead,* London, 1904, p. 3.

The evidence of Scripture points to the land of Shinar as the post-Flood birthplace of false religious concepts. Undoubtedly under the direction of Nimrod, "a mighty hunter in opposition to Jehovah," the building of the city of Babel and its tower, likely a ziggurat to be used for false worship, began. This building project was undertaken, not to bring honor to Jehovah God, but for the self-glorification of the builders, who desired to make "a celebrated name" for themselves. Also, it was in direct opposition to God's purpose, which was for mankind to spread about in the earth. The Almighty frustrated the plans of these builders by confusing their language. No longer being able to understand one another, they gradually left off building the city and were scattered. (Ge 10:8-10; 11:2-9) However, Nimrod apparently remained at Babel and expanded his dominion, founding the first Babylonian Empire.—Ge 10: 11, 12.

As for the scattered people, wherever they went they carried their false religion with them, to be practiced under new terms and in their new language and new locations. The people were scattered in the days of Peleg, who was born about a century after the Deluge and died at the age of 239. Since both Noah and his son Shem outlived Peleg, the dispersal took place at a time when the facts about earlier events, such as the Flood, were known. (Ge 9:28; 10:25; 11:10-19) This knowledge undoubtedly lingered in some form in the memory of the dispersed people. Indicative of this is the fact that the mythologies of the ancients echo various parts of the Biblical record, but in a distorted, polytheistic form. The legends depict certain gods as serpent slayers; also, the religions of many ancient peoples included the worship of a god placed in the role of a benefactor who dies a violent death on earth and then is restored to life. This may suggest that such a god was actually a deified human wrongly viewed as being the 'promised seed.' (Compare Ge 3:15.) The myths tell of the love affairs had by gods and earthly women and of the heroic deeds of their hybrid offspring. (Compare Ge 6:1, 2, 4; Jude 6.) There is hardly a nation on the earth that does not have a legend concerning a global flood, and traces of the tower-building account are likewise to be found in the legends of mankind.

Babylonian Deities. After the death of Nimrod, the Babylonians reasonably would have been inclined to hold him in high regard as the founder and builder and first king of their city and as the organizer of the original Babylonian Empire. Tradition has it that Nimrod died a violent death. Since the god Marduk (Merodach) was regarded as the founder of Babylon, it has been suggested by some that Marduk represents the deified Nimrod. However, the opinions of scholars as to the identification of deities with specific humans are quite varied.

With the passage of time, the gods of the first Babylonian Empire began to multiply. The pantheon came to have a number of triads of gods, or deities. One such triad was composed of Anu (the god of the sky), Enlil (the god of the earth, air, and storm), and Ea (the god presiding over the waters). Another triad was that of the moon-god Sin, the sun-god Shamash, and the fertility goddess Ishtar, the lover or consort of Tammuz. (PICTURE, Vol. 2, p. 529) The Babylonians even had triads of devils, such as the triad of Labartu, Labasu, and Akhkhazu. The worship of heavenly bodies became prominent (Isa 47:13), and various planets came to be associated with certain deities. The planet Jupiter was identified with the chief god of Babylon, Marduk; Venus with Ishtar, a goddess of love and fertility; Saturn with Ninurta, a god of war and hunting and patron of agriculture; Mercury with Nebo, a god of wisdom and agriculture; Mars with Nergal, a

god of war and pestilence and lord of the underworld.

The cities of ancient Babylonia came to have their own special guardian deities, somewhat like "patron saints." In Ur it was Sin; in Eridu, Ea; in Nippur, Enlil; in Cutha, Nergal; in Borsippa, Nebo, and in the city of Babylon, Marduk (Merodach). At the time that Hammurabi made Babylon the capital of Babylonia, the importance of the city's favorite god Marduk was, of course, enhanced. Finally Marduk was given the attribute of earlier gods and displaced them in the Babylonian myths. In later periods his proper name "Marduk" was supplanted by the title "Belu" ("Owner"), so that finally he was commonly spoken of as Bel. His wife was called Belit ("Mistress," *par excellence*).—See BEL; NEBO No. 4.

The picture portrayed of the gods and goddesses in ancient Babylonian texts is but a reflection of sinful mortal man. These accounts say that the deities were born, loved, had families, fought, and even died, as did Tammuz. Terrified by the Deluge, they are said to have 'crouched like dogs.' The deities were also portrayed as being greedy, frequently eating to the point of gluttony, and drinking to the point of intoxication. They had furious tempers and were vindictive and suspicious of one another. Bitter hatreds existed among them. To illustrate: Tiamat, bent on destroying the other gods, was overcome by Marduk, who split her into two halves, forming the sky with one half and using the other half in connection with the establishment of the earth. Eresh-Kigal, the goddess of the underworld, instructed Namtaru, the god of pestilence, to imprison her sister Ishtar and afflict her with 60 miseries.—See NERGAL.

The above gives some indication of the environment that faithful Abraham left behind when he went out from the Chaldean city of Ur, which was then steeped in Babylonian idolatry. (Ge 11:31; 12:1; Jos 24:2, 14, 15) Centuries later, it was into Babylon, "a land of graven images" and filthy "dungy idols," that thousands of Jewish captives were thrust.—Jer 50:1, 2, 38; 2Ki chap 25.

Assyrian Deities. Generally speaking, the Assyrian gods and goddesses are identical with the Babylonian deities. However, one deity, Asshur, the chief god, seems to have been peculiar to the Assyrian pantheon. Since Assyria takes its name from Asshur, it has been suggested that this god is actually Shem's son named Asshur, deified by false worshipers.—Ge 10:21, 22.

Unlike the Babylonian Marduk, who was also worshiped in Assyria but whose seat of worship always remained in the city of Babylon, Asshur's seat of worship changed as the kings of Assyria took up official residence in other cities. Also, sanctuaries to Asshur were built in various parts of Assyria. A military standard was Asshur's primary symbol, and this was carried right into the thick of the battle. The winged circle, or disk, from which the figure of a bearded man often emerges, represented the god Asshur. At times the human figure is shown as holding a bow or in the act of shooting an arrow. Another representation of Asshur suggests a triad concept. In addition to the central figure emerging from the circle, two human heads are shown on top of the wings, one on either side of the central figure. —See PICTURE, Vol. 2, p. 529; ASSYRIA; NISROCH.

It was among such Assyrians that exiles of the northern ten-tribe kingdom found themselves following Samaria's fall in 740 B.C.E. (2Ki 17:1-6) Later, the prophet Nahum foretold the fall of Nineveh (capital of Assyria) and its gods, which destruction came in 632 B.C.E.—Na 1:1, 14.

Egyptian Deities. The gods and goddesses worshiped by the Egyptians give evidence of an underlying Babylonian heritage. There were triads of deities and even triple triads, or "enneads." One of the popular triads consisted of Osiris, his consort Isis, and their son Horus.—PICTURE, Vol. 2, p. 529.

Osiris was the most popular of the Egyptian gods and was regarded as the son of the earth-god Geb and the sky-goddess Nut. It was said that Osiris became the husband of Isis and reigned as king over Egypt. The mythological accounts tell of Osiris' being murdered by his brother Set and then being restored to life, becoming the judge and king of the dead. The relationship of Osiris and Isis and their respective characteristics strikingly correspond to the relationship and characteristics of the Babylonian Tammuz and Ishtar. Hence, numerous scholars consider them to be identical.

Mother-and-son worship was also very popular in Egypt. Isis is often portrayed with the infant Horus on her knees. This representation is so much like that of the Madonna and child that certain ones in Christendom have at times venerated it in ignorance. (PICTURE, Vol. 2, p. 529) With respect to the god Horus, there is evidence of the distortion of the Edenic promise concerning the seed that would bruise the serpent in the head. (Ge 3:15) At times Horus is depicted as trampling

crocodiles and grasping snakes and scorpions. According to one account, when Horus proceeded to avenge the death of his father Osiris, Set, who had murdered Osiris, changed himself into a serpent.

On Egyptian sculptures and paintings the sacred symbol, the crux ansata, occurs very frequently. This so-called sign of life looks like the letter "T" with an oval handle on top and probably represented the male and female organs of reproduction combined. The Egyptian deities are often depicted as holding the crux ansata.—PICTURE, Vol. 2, p. 530.

Many were the creatures venerated as sacred by the Egyptians. These included the bull, the cat, the cow, the crocodile, the falcon, the frog, the hippopotamus, the ibis, the jackal, the lion, the ram, the scarab, the scorpion, the serpent, the vulture, and the wolf. However, some of these were sacred in one part of Egypt and not in another, this, at times, even resulting in the outbreak of civil wars. Not only were animals sacred to certain gods, but some of them were even viewed as incarnations of a god or goddess. The Apis bull, for instance, was regarded as the very incarnation of the god Osiris and also an emanation of the god Ptah.

According to Herodotus (II, 65-67), a person killing a sacred animal deliberately was put to death; if the killing of the animal was by accident, the priests stipulated a fine. However, one killing an ibis or a hawk, whether intentionally or not, was put to death, usually at the hands of an enraged mob. When a cat died, all in the household shaved their eyebrows, whereas at the death of a dog they shaved their entire body. Sacred animals were mummified and given elaborate burials. Among the mummified animals that have been found are the bull, the cat, the crocodile, and the falcon, to mention but a few.

The mythological accounts portray the Egyptian deities as having human weaknesses and imperfections. They were said to have experienced anguish and fright and repeatedly found themselves in peril. The god Osiris was slain. Horus, in childhood, was said to have suffered from internal pains, headaches, and dysentery and to have died from a scorpion's sting, but then was said to have been restored to life. Isis was believed to have suffered from abscess of the breast. With advancing years, it was taught, the strength of the sun-god Ra waned and saliva dripped from his mouth. His very life was in jeopardy after being bitten by a magical serpent formed by Isis, although he recovered as a result of Isis' words of magic. Sekhmet, a goddess representing the destructive power of the sun, was depicted as being bloodthirsty. She took such delight in killing men that Ra was said to have feared for the future of the human race. To save humankind from extermination, Ra distributed 7,000 jugs of a beer and pomegranate mixture over the battlefield. Thinking it to be human blood, Sekhmet drank it ardently until too intoxicated to continue her slaughter. Nephthys was said to have got her brother Osiris, the husband of her sister Isis, drunk and then had relations with him. The sun-gods Tem and Horus were portrayed as masturbators.

Interestingly, when Pharaoh constituted Joseph second ruler of the land of Egypt, Joseph was thus elevated over the worshipers of Egypt's false gods.—Ge 41:37-44.

The Ten Plagues. By means of the plagues he visited upon the Egyptians, Jehovah humiliated and executed judgment upon their gods. (Ex 12:12; Nu 33:4; PICTURES, Vol. 2, p. 530) The first plague, the turning of the Nile and all the waters of Egypt into blood, brought disgrace to the Nile-god Hapi. The death of the fish in the Nile was also a blow to Egypt's religion, for certain kinds of fish were actually venerated and even mummified. (Ex 7:19-21) The frog, regarded as a symbol of fertility and the Egyptian concept of resurrection, was considered sacred to the frog-goddess Heqt. Hence, the plague of frogs brought disgrace to this goddess. (Ex 8:5-14) The third plague saw the magic-practicing priests acknowledging defeat when they proved to be unable by means of their secret arts to turn dust into gnats. (Ex 8:16-19) The god Thoth was credited with the invention of magic or secret arts, but even this god could not help the magic-practicing priests to duplicate the third plague.

The line of demarcation between the Egyptians and the worshipers of the true God came to be sharply drawn from the fourth plague onward. While swarms of gadflies invaded the homes of the Egyptians, the Israelites in the land of Goshen were not affected. (Ex 8:23, 24) The next plague, the pestilence upon the livestock, humiliated such deities as the cow-goddess Hathor, Apis, and the sky-goddess Nut, who was conceived of as a cow having the stars affixed to her belly. (Ex 9:1-6) The plague of boils brought disgrace to the gods and goddesses regarded as possessing healing abilities, such as Thoth, Isis, and Ptah. (Ex 9:8-11) The severe hailstorm put to

shame the gods who were considered to have control of the natural elements; for example, Reshpu, who, it appears, was believed to control lightning, and Thoth, who was said to have power over the rain and thunder. (Ex 9:22-26) The locust plague spelled defeat for the gods thought to ensure a bountiful harvest, one of these being the fertility god Min, who was viewed as a protector of the crops. (Ex 10:12-15) Among the deities disgraced by the plague of darkness were sun-gods, such as Ra and Horus, and also Thoth the god of the moon and believed to be the systematizer of sun, moon, and stars.—Ex 10: 21-23.

The death of the firstborn resulted in the greatest humiliation for the Egyptian gods and goddesses. (Ex 12:12) The rulers of Egypt actually styled themselves as gods, the sons of Ra, or Amon-Ra. It was claimed that Ra, or Amon-Ra, had intercourse with the queen. The son born was, therefore, viewed as a god incarnate and was dedicated to Ra, or Amon-Ra, at his temple. Hence, the death of Pharaoh's firstborn, in effect, actually meant the death of a god. (Ex 12:29) This in itself would have been a severe blow to Egypt's religion, and the complete impotence of all the deities was manifested in their being unable to save the firstborn of the Egyptians from death.—See AMON No. 4.

Canaanite Deities. Extrabiblical sources indicate that the god El was considered to be the creator and sovereign. Although El seems to have been somewhat remote from earthly affairs, he is repeatedly shown as being approached by the other deities with requests. El is depicted as a rebellious son that dethroned and castrated his own father, and also as a bloody tyrant, a murderer, and an adulterer. In the Ras Shamra texts El is referred to as "father bull" and is represented as having gray hair and a gray beard. His consort was Asherah, who is referred to as the progenitress of the gods, whereas El is placed in the role of progenitor of the gods.

Most prominent of the Canaanite gods, however, was the fertility god Baal, a deity of the sky and of rain and storm. (Jg 2:12, 13) In the Ras Shamra texts, Baal is often called the son of Dagon, though El is also spoken of as his father. Baal's sister Anath is shown referring to El as her father and he, in turn, calls her his daughter. Hence, Baal probably was regarded as the son of El, though he may also have been viewed as El's grandson. In the mythological accounts Baal is depicted as assaulting and triumphing over

Yamm, the god who presided over the water and who seems to have been El's favorite or beloved son. But Baal is slain in his conflict with Mot, who was viewed as a son of El and the god of death and aridity. Thus, Canaan, like Babylon, had its god who died a violent death and thereafter was restored to life.—See BAAL No. 4.

Anath, Asherah, and Ashtoreth are the principal goddesses mentioned in the Ras Shamra texts. However, there appears to have been a considerable overlapping in the roles of these goddesses. In Syria, where the Ras Shamra texts were found, Anath may have been viewed as Baal's wife, since she, though repeatedly referred to as "maiden," is shown as having intercourse with Baal. But the Scriptural record mentions only Ashtoreth and the sacred pole, or Asherah, in connection with Baal. Hence, at times Asherah and then again Ashtoreth may have been regarded as wives of Baal.—Jg 2:13; 3:7; 10:6; 1Sa 7:4; 12:10; 1Ki 18:19; see ASHTORETH; SACRED PILLAR; SACRED POLE.

The references to Anath in the Ras Shamra texts give some indication of the degraded conception of the deities that the Canaanites undoubtedly shared with the Syrians. Anath is described as the fairest among Baal's sisters, but as having an extremely violent temper. She is depicted as threatening to smash the skull of her father, El, and cause his gray hair to flow with blood and his gray beard with gore if he did not comply with her wishes. On another occasion Anath is shown going on a killing spree. She attached heads to her back, and hands to her girdle, and she plunged knee-deep in the blood and hip-deep in the gore of valiant ones. Her delight in such bloodshed is reflected in the words: "Her liver swells with laughter, her heart fills up with joy."—*Ancient Near Eastern Texts,* edited by J. Pritchard, 1974, pp. 136, 137, 142, 152.

The extremely base and degraded nature of Canaanite worship underscores the justness of God's executing a decree of destruction upon the inhabitants of the land. (Le 18; De 9:3, 4) However, because the Israelites failed to carry out that divine decree completely, they eventually became ensnared by the degenerate practices associated with the worship of Canaanite gods. —Ps 106:34-43; see also CANAAN, CANAANITE No. 2.

Deities of Medo-Persia. The indications are that the kings of the Medo-Persian Empire were Zoroastrians. While it cannot be proved or dis-

proved that Cyrus the Great adhered to the teachings of Zoroaster, from the time of Darius I the inscriptions of the monarchs repeatedly refer to Ahura Mazda, the principal deity of Zoroastrianism. Darius I referred to Ahura Mazda as the creator of heaven, earth, and man, and he looked to this god as the one who had bestowed upon him wisdom, physical skillfulness, and the kingdom.

A characteristic feature of Zoroastrianism is dualism, that is, the belief in two independent divine beings, one good and the other evil. Ahura Mazda was viewed as the creator of all good things, whereas Angra Mainyu was regarded as the creator of all that is evil. It was thought that the latter could bring about earthquakes, storms, disease, and death as well as stir up unrest and war. Lesser spirits were believed to assist these two gods in carrying out their functions.

The symbol of the god Ahura Mazda was much like the representation of the Assyrian Asshur, namely, a winged circle, from which, at times, a bearded man with the vertical tail of a bird emerges.

Ahura Mazda may have figured in a triad. This is suggested by the fact that Artaxerxes Mnemon invoked the protection of Ahura Mazda, Anahita (a goddess of water and of fertility), and Mithra (a god of light), and he attributed his reconstruction of the Hall of Columns at Susa to the grace of these three deities.

A number of scholars have linked Anahita with the Babylonian Ishtar. Observes E. O. James in his book *The Cult of the Mother-Goddess* (1959, p. 94): "She was worshipped as 'the Great Goddess whose name is Lady', the 'all-powerful immaculate one', purifying 'the seed of males and the womb and the milk of females'. . . . She was, in fact, the Iranian counterpart of the Syrian Anat, the Babylonian Inanna-Ishtar, the Hittite goddess of Comana, and the Greek Aphrodite."

According to the Greek historian Herodotus (I, 131), the Persians also worshiped the natural elements and heavenly bodies. He writes: "As to the usages of the Persians, I know them to be these. It is not their custom to make and set up statues and temples and altars, but those who make such they deem foolish, as I suppose, because they never believed the gods, as do the Greeks, to be in the likeness of men; but they call the whole circle of heaven Zeus, and to him they offer sacrifice on the highest peaks of the mountains; they sacrifice also to the sun and moon and earth and fire and water and winds. These are the only gods to whom they have ever sacrificed from the beginning; they have learnt later, to sacrifice to the 'heavenly' Aphrodite, from the Assyrians and Arabians. She is called by the Assyrians Mylitta, by the Arabians Alilat, by the Persians Mitra."

The Zend-Avesta, the sacred Zoroastrian writings, actually contain prayers to fire, to water, and to planets as well as to the light of the sun, moon, and stars. Fire is even referred to as the son of Ahura Mazda.

Although he may have been a Zoroastrian, King Cyrus was named in Bible prophecy as the one appointed by Jehovah to overthrow Babylon and bring about the release of the Jewish captives. (Isa 44:26–45:7; compare Pr 21:1.) Following Babylon's destruction in 539 B.C.E., the Israelites came under the control of the Zoroastrian Medo-Persians.

Grecian Deities. An examination of the gods and goddesses of ancient Greece reveals the traces of Babylonian influence. Observed Oxford University Professor George Rawlinson: "The striking resemblance of the Chaldæan system to that of the Classical Mythology seems worthy of particular attention. This resemblance is too general, and too close in some respects, to allow of the supposition that mere accident has produced the coincidence. In the Pantheons of Greece and Rome, and in that of Chaldæa, the same general grouping is to be recognized; the same genealogical succession is not unfrequently to be traced; and in some cases even the familiar names and titles of classical divinities admit of the most curious illustration and explanation from Chaldæan sources. We can scarcely doubt but that, in some way or other, there was a communication of beliefs—a passage in very early times, from the shores of the Persian Gulf to the lands washed by the Mediterranean, of mythological notions and ideas."—*The Seven Great Monarchies of the Ancient Eastern World*, 1885, Vol. I, pp. 71, 72.

A distortion of God's statement concerning the seed of promise may possibly be noted in the mythological accounts that tell of the god Apollo's killing the serpent Python, and of the infant Hercules' (the son of Zeus and an earthly woman, Alcmene) strangling two serpents. The familiar theme of a god who dies and then is restored to life again confronts us. Annually the violent death of Adonis and his return to life were commemorated; it was principally the women who bewailed his death and who carried images of his body as in funeral procession and later tossed them into the sea or springs. Another deity whose violent death and restoration to life were celebrated by the Greeks was Dionysus, or Bacchus; he, like Adonis, has been identified with the Babylonian Tammuz.

The mythological accounts make the Grecian gods and goddesses appear much like men and women. Although the gods were thought to be of much greater size and to exceed men in beauty and strength, their bodies were depicted as human bodies. Since their veins supposedly flowed with "ichor," rather than blood, the bodies of the deities were considered to be incorruptible. Nevertheless, it was believed that men, by means of their weapons, could actually inflict painful wounds upon the gods. However, it was said that the wounds always healed and that the gods remained youthful.

For the most part, the deities of the Greeks are depicted as being very immoral and as having human weaknesses. They quarreled among themselves, fought against one another, and even conspired against one another. Zeus, the supreme god of the Greeks, is said to have dethroned his own father Cronus. Earlier, Cronus himself had deposed and even castrated his father Uranus. Both Uranus and Cronus are depicted as cruel fathers. Uranus immediately concealed in the earth the offspring borne to him by his wife Gaea, not even permitting them to see the light. Cronus, on the other hand, swallowed the children borne to him by Rhea. Among the detestable practices attributed to certain deities are adultery, fornication, incest, rape, lying, thievery, drunkenness, and murder. Those who incurred the disfavor of a god or goddess are depicted as being punished in a most cruel manner. For example, the satyr Marsyas, who challenged the god Apollo to a musical contest, was attached by the latter to a tree trunk and skinned alive. The goddess Artemis is said to have changed the hunter Actaeon into a stag and then caused his own hounds to devour him, this because he had seen her nakedness.

Of course, some claimed that these mythological accounts were merely the imaginations of the poets. But on this, Augustine of the fourth century C.E. wrote: "For whereas it is said in their defence, that these tales of their gods were not true, but merely poetical inventions, and false fictions, why this doth make it more abominable, if you respect the purity of your religion: and if you observe the malice of the devil, what more cunning or more deceitful craftiness can there be? For when an honest and worthy ruler of a country is slandered, is not the slander so much more wicked and unpardonable, as this party's life that is slandered is clearer and sounder from touch of any such matter?" (*The City of God,* Book II, chap IX) However, the popularity of the poetical accounts as enacted on the Greek stage indicates that the majority did not regard them as slander, but were in harmony with them. The immorality of the gods served to justify man's wrongdoing, and this found favor with the people.—See GREECE, GREEKS (Greek Religion).

The apostle Paul's ministry brought him in contact with worshipers of the Grecian gods Zeus and Hermes. (Ac 14:12, 13) The Athenians expressed their fear of the deities by building many temples and altars. (Ac 17:22-29) The gross sexual immorality that was a part of Grecian worship even affected the Christian congregation in Corinth, the apostle Paul finding it necessary to rebuke that congregation.—1Co chap 5.

Roman Deities. The religion of the Romans was greatly influenced by the Etruscans, a people generally thought to have come from Asia Minor. The practice of divination definitely links the religion of the Etruscans to that of the Babylonians. For example, the models of clay livers used for divination found in Mesopotamia resemble the bronze model of a liver found at Piacenza in the region of Emilia-Romagna, Italy. So, when the Romans adopted the Etruscan deities they were, in effect, receiving a Babylonian heritage. (See ASTROLOGERS.) The Roman triad of Jupiter (the supreme god, a god of the sky and light), Juno (the consort of Jupiter regarded as presiding over matters of particular concern to women), and Minerva (a goddess presiding over all handicrafts) corresponds to the Etruscan Tinia, Uni, and Menrva.

In the course of time, the prominent Greek gods found their way into the Roman pantheon, although they were known by different names. Also, deities of still other lands were adopted by the Romans, including the Persian Mithras (whose birthday was celebrated on December 25) and the Phrygian fertility goddess Cybele and the Egyptian Isis, both of whom have been identified with the Babylonian Ishtar. Then, too, the Roman emperors themselves were deified.

Saturn was worshiped for bringing a golden age to Rome. The Saturnalia, originally a one-day festival in his honor, was later expanded into a seven-day celebration in the latter half of December. The event was marked by great revelry. Gifts, such as waxen fruits and candles, were exchanged, and clay dolls were especially given to the children. During the festival, no punishment was meted out. Schools and courts had a holiday; even war operations were brought to a halt. Slaves exchanged places with their masters and were permitted, without needing to fear punishment, to give free rein to the tongue.

The early Christians refused to participate in Roman worship, particularly worship of the emperor, which made them objects of intense persecution. They were uncompromising in their stand to "obey God as ruler rather than men," refusing to give to Roman rulers the worship that rightfully belonged to God.—Ac 5:29; Mr 12:17; see ROME (Religion).

Gods of Nations Contrasted With Jehovah. Today many of the gods mentioned in the Bible are little more than a name. Although their worshipers at times even sacrificed their own children to them, the false gods were unable to rescue those who looked to them for aid in time of need. (2Ki 17:31) Hence, in the face of his military successes, the king of Assyria, through his spokesman Rabshakeh, boasted: "Have the gods of the nations at all delivered each one his own land out of the hand of the king of Assyria? Where are the gods of Hamath and Arpad? Where are the gods of Sepharvaim, Hena and Ivvah? Have they delivered Samaria out of my hand? Who are there among all the gods of the lands that have delivered their land out of my hand, so that Jehovah should deliver Jerusalem out of my hand?" (2Ki 18:28, 31-35) But Jehovah did not fail his people as had those false gods. In one night the angel of Jehovah killed 185,000 in the camp of the Assyrians. Humiliated, the proud Assyrian monarch Sennacherib returned to Nineveh, later to be murdered by two of his sons in the temple of his god Nisroch. (2Ki 19:17-19, 35-37) Truly, "all the gods of the peoples are valueless gods; but as for Jehovah, he has made the very heavens."—Ps 96:5.

Not only do the false gods have the characteristics of their makers, but people also become much like the gods whom they worship. To illustrate: King Manasseh of Judah was devoted to false gods, even to the point of making his son pass through the fire. But Manasseh's zealous pursuit of false worship did not make him a better king. Rather, he proved to be like the bloodthirsty deities he worshiped, shedding innocent blood in very great quantity. (2Ki 21:1-6,

16) In sharp contrast with this, worshipers of the true God endeavor to be imitators of their Perfect Maker, displaying the fruitage of his spirit: love, joy, peace, long-suffering, kindness, goodness, faith, mildness, and self-control.—Eph 5:1; Ga 5:22, 23.

GOD THE GOD OF ISRAEL.

The name given by Jacob to the first altar that he built after he returned from Haran.

As a result of his encounter at Peniel with the angel of Jehovah, Jacob was given the name Israel, and after a peaceable meeting with his brother Esau, he dwelt at Succoth and then Shechem. Here he acquired a tract of land from the sons of Hamor and pitched his tent upon it. (Ge 32:24-30; 33:1-4, 17-19) "After that he set up there an altar and called it God the God of Israel," or "God Is the God of Israel." (Ge 33:20) In identifying himself by his newly given name Israel with the name of the altar, Jacob indicated his acceptance and appreciation of that name and of God's guiding him safely back into the Promised Land. The expression occurs only once in the Scriptures.

GOG.

The meaning of this name is uncertain.

1. A descendant of Reuben.—1Ch 5:3, 4.

2. The name is found in chapters 38 and 39 of Ezekiel and is there applied to the leader of a stormlike, multinational assault against God's people. The attack comes after Jehovah has gathered his people out of the nations and restored them to the previously devastated "mountains of Israel." Because they dwell in security, with no visible signs of protection, and because they enjoy abundant prosperity, Gog is drawn into waging a vicious, all-out attack upon them. He congregates a vast army from many nations for this purpose. But his assault sets off Jehovah's rage and brings terrible defeat and destruction upon Gog and his entire crowd. Their carcasses become food for birds and beasts, and their bones are buried in the valley that thereafter is called the Valley of Gog's Crowd (literally, Valley of Hamon-Gog).

The Assault's Source and Intent. The assault has a source far distant from the land of Israel. Gog is "of the land of Magog," situated in "the remotest parts of the north." (Eze 38:2, 15) He is the "head chieftain ["great prince," *AT;* "chief prince," *KJ, RS*] of Meshech and Tubal." (Eze 38:2, 3) Some translations here read "the prince of Rosh, Meshech, and Tubal" (*AS, JB*),

thus making "Rosh [Heb. for "head"]" refer to a country or people. No such land or people is mentioned elsewhere in the Bible, however. Meshech and Tubal, like Magog, are names given to sons of Japheth (Ge 10:2), and the three lands bearing these names lay to the N of Israel. (See MAGOG No. 2; MESHECH No. 1; TUBAL.) Other northern members of the attacking forces, also Japhetic, were Gomer and Togarmah (thought to be the progenitors of the ancient Cimmerians and Armenians, respectively). Japhetic Persia lay to the NE. But the conspiracy embraced southern Hamitic members also—Ethiopia and Put down in Africa. (Eze 38:4-6, 15) Gog's role, therefore, is as commander of a massive assault force that applies tremendous pressures designed to crush Jehovah's people as though they were in a vise.

Israel is described as "dwelling in the center of the earth." (Eze 38:12) Ancient Israel not only was located at a central point as regards the Eurasian and African continents but also was the center of pure worship of the true God and was counted by him as "the pupil of his eye."—De 32:9, 10; Zec 2:8.

Jehovah states that he will 'put hooks in Gog's jaws' and lead him to this attack. (Eze 38:4; compare 2Ki 19:20, 21, 28.) The prophecy clearly shows, however, that this is already Gog's desire, the scheme being a product of his own heart. (Eze 38:10, 11) Jehovah draws Gog out, nonetheless, by restoring and prospering his own name people. This incites Gog to manifest his malevolence toward God's people and he willingly advances into a course that brings swift destruction upon himself and all his associates. By the defeat and annihilation of Gog and his forces, Jehovah magnifies and sanctifies his own name before all observers.—Eze 38:12-23; 39:5-13, 21, 22; compare Joe 3:9-17.

Identification of Gog. The lands and peoples mentioned in the prophecy relating to Gog are known from the Bible and to some extent from secular history. But efforts to identify Gog with some historically known earthly ruler have not been successful. Most frequently suggested is Gyges, king of Lydia in western Asia Minor, called Guggu in the records of Assyrian monarch Ashurbanipal. (*Ancient Records of Assyria and Babylonia,* by D. Luckenbill, 1927, Vol. II, pp. 297, 351, 352) Gyges, however, had died decades before the writing of Ezekiel's prophecy. Hence, such identification is unacceptable. Additionally, the prophecy itself places Gog's attack in "the final part of the years," "in the final part of the days." (Eze 38:8, 16; compare Isa 2:2; Jer 30:24; 2Ti 3:1.) For these reasons, the name Gog is evidently cryptic or symbolic, not being that of any known human king or leader.

The evidence points to a fulfillment in what is elsewhere called "the time of the end." (Da 11:35; 12:9; compare Re 12:12.) Bible scholars and commentators generally recognize the prophecy as relating to the time of the Messianic Kingdom. As an example, *The New Schaff-Herzog Encyclopedia of Religious Knowledge* comments: "Gog appears as the leader of the last hostile attack of the world-powers upon the kingdom of God." (Edited by S. Jackson, 1956, Vol. V, p. 14) No fulfillment on natural Israel is known. The fulfillment in "the final part of the days" logically is with regard to spiritual Israel, the Christian congregation (Ro 2:28, 29; Ga 6:16), described by the apostle Paul as children of, and directed by, the "Jerusalem above." (Ga 4:26) These points aid in arriving at the identification of Gog.

Further aid is found in the book of Revelation. Prophetic visions there foretold a great increase in persecution against the Christian congregation on the part of the symbolic dragon, Satan the Devil. This was to follow his being cast down, with his demons, from the heavens to the region of the earth, an act accomplished by the Kingdom of God through Christ at the time of Jesus' beginning to exercise kingly authority. (Re 12:5-10, 13-17) The massing of earthly nations against God, his Son, and God's faithful servants on earth figures prominently in these visions, as does also the total defeat and desolation of such enemy forces. (Re 16:13-16; 17:12-14; 19:11-21) The feasting by birds on the corpses of such enemies of Christ's Kingdom rule likewise finds a correspondency here.—Compare Eze 39:4, 17-20 with Re 19:21.

The central figure, or leader, of the earth-wide assault against the Messianic Kingdom and its subjects, according to Revelation, is Satan the Devil. He is the only person in the Biblical record who can be said to fulfill adequately the description and role assigned to 'Gog of Magog' in the prophecy given to Ezekiel. The prophecy in Ezekiel concerning Gog therefore points to a vicious, earth-wide assault on God's people, an assault engineered and led by the abased Satan the Devil. This attack is what triggers the complete wiping out of such Satanic forces by means of God's awesome power.—Eze 38:18-22.

Burial of Gog's Crowd. The burial of "Gog and all his crowd" is in "the valley of those passing through on the east of the sea." (Eze 39:11) *An American Translation* here reads, "the valley of Abarim, east of the Dead Sea." The name Abarim is used at Numbers 33:47, 48 with reference to the mountains E of the Dead Sea. (See ABARIM.) There are two deep valleys, or gorges, in this region, the Arnon and the Zered. The Arnon is some 3 km (2 mi) wide at the top and is about 520 m (1,700 ft) deep. The Zered is an even more formidable canyon, its steep cliffs dropping some 1,190 m (3,900 ft). Either of these valleys may be used to represent this prophetic burial place, the Arnon being due E of the sea, while the Zered, at the SE, was the more traveled of the two. Or, since the picture presented is symbolic, no specific valley may be intended. This burial in a deep place by the Dead Sea likewise finds some parallel in Revelation's description of the disposal of the opposers of God's Kingdom by their being cast into the symbolic lake of fire, and by the abyssing of Satan.—Re 19:20; 20:1-3.

Is the Gog referred to in Revelation the same as the one in Ezekiel?

---

3. Revelation 20:8 also speaks of "Gog and Magog." Here, however, the reference is not to an individual commander, or ruler. Both names are shown to apply to "those nations in the four corners of the earth" who allow themselves to be misled by Satan after he is released from the symbolic "abyss." Since other texts show that the Millennial Rule of Christ brings an end to national rule and divisions (Da 2:44; 7:13, 14), it would appear that such "nations" are the product of rebellion against his earth-wide dominion. They advance "over the breadth of the earth" to encircle "the camp of the holy ones and the beloved city." This comes after the Millennial Rule over earth by Christ Jesus has reached its completion. —Re 20:2, 3, 7-9.

The use of the names "Gog and Magog" evidently serves to emphasize certain similarities between this post-Millennial situation and that of the earlier assault (prior to Satan's being abyssed). Both in Ezekiel and in Revelation, the opposers are numerous (those in Revelation being of an indefinite number, "as the sand of the sea"); the attack is the result of a widespread conspiracy and is directed against God's servants when they enjoy great prosperity. So, the use of "Gog and Magog" to describe those led into a post-Millennial rebellion is very fitting. Their end is absolute destruction.—Re 20:8-10, 14.

GOIIM (Goi′im) [Nations].

1. The realm of King Tidal, an ally of the Elamite king Chedorlaomer. (Ge 14:1-9) Although numerous suggestions have been made, no identification of its location has been established. In view of the meaning of the term and its translation in other texts (Jg 4:2; Isa 9:1) as a common noun ("nations") rather than a proper name, some suggest that Goiim was a collection of tribes with varied national backgrounds.—See TIDAL.

2. The domain W of the Jordan of a Canaanite king defeated by Joshua. He is spoken of as "the king of Goiim in Gilgal." (Jos 12:7, 23) Nothing is known of this Goiim except that Gilgal, possibly its seat, or center, is not the well-known Israelite campsite of the same name near the Jordan.

GOLAN (Go′lan). A city of Bashan in the territory of Manasseh, selected as a city of refuge. (De 4:41-43; Jos 20:2, 8) The Gershonite Levites were given the city for their dwelling. (Jos 21:27; 1Ch 6:71) Most scholars identify it with Sahm el Joulane, about 28 km (17 mi) E of the Sea of Galilee. A district to which it gave its name, today called The Golan but formerly Gaulanitis, is somewhat closer to the Sea of Galilee.

GOLD. The first and most frequently mentioned metal in the Bible. (Ge 2:11) From the beginning it has been a noble metal highly valued for its weight, rarity, durable nontarnishing luster, shimmering beauty, ductility, and malleability. A number of Hebrew terms refer to gold; included are *za·hav′* (Ex 25:11), *cha·ruts′* (Zec 9:3), *ke′them* (Ps 45:9), *paz* ("refined gold"; Ps 19:10), *seghohr′* ("pure gold"; Job 28:15), and *'oh·phir′* ("gold of Ophir"; Job 22:24). The Greek terms *khry·sos′* and *khry·si′on* of the Christian Greek Scriptures are used with reference to coins, ornaments, and the metal in general; they are also used in a metaphoric sense.—Mt 10:9; 1Pe 3:3; Mt 2:11; 1Co 3:12.

Gold's rarity gave it a monetary value that made it useful as a commercial medium of exchange and as a measure of wealth and prominence. (Ge 13:2; 1Ch 21:25; Es 8:15) Gold coinage was a late invention, however. The color and luster of gold and its resistance to oxidation, or tarnishing, make it especially valuable for jewelry and ornamentation of all kinds.—Ge 24:22; 41:42; Jg 8:24-26; Ps 45:9, 13.

When found in its native purity in gravel deposits and riverbeds, gold can easily be separated and recovered, because of its great weight. The book of Job mentions mining and refining operations.—Job 28:1, 2, 6.

Used in Tabernacle and Temple. Gold's malleability permits it to be hammered into countless shapes. In the construction of the tabernacle, gold was beaten into plates for overlay work and into thin sheets cut into thread that was woven into certain garments of the high priest. (Ex 25:31; 30:1-3; 37:1, 2; 39:2, 3) It was similarly used in the temple built by Solomon. (1Ki 6:21-35; 10:18; 2Ch 3:5-9) Alloying gold with other metal to increase its hardness extends its utility. This process was also employed in ancient Israel.—1Ki 10:16; see ELECTRUM.

A great quantity of gold was used in the tabernacle, the current value of this gold being estimated at about $11,269,000. (Ex 25:10-40; 38:24) However, in comparison with the amount of gold used, the wilderness tabernacle was only a miniature of Solomon's glorious temple. David had set aside no less than 100,000 talents of gold for that temple, valued today in excess of $38,-535,000,000. (1Ch 22:14) The lampstands and the temple's utensils—forks, bowls, pitchers, basins, cups, and so forth—were made of gold and silver; some utensils were of copper; the cherubs in the Most Holy, the altar of incense, and even the entire inside of the house were overlaid with gold.—1Ki 6:20-22; 7:48-50; 1Ch 28:14-18; 2Ch 3:1-13.

Solomon's Revenue. Large amounts of gold poured into Solomon's treasury from the king of Tyre (120 talents) and the queen of Sheba (120 talents), from annual tributes and taxes, and by means of his own merchant fleet. The account says: "The weight of the gold that came to Solomon in one year amounted up to six hundred and sixty-six talents of gold [c. $256,643,000]." That was apart from revenues from traders, governors, and so forth.—1Ki 9:14, 27, 28; 10:10, 14, 15.

Ophir was one place from which Solomon acquired fine gold. A pottery fragment said to be of the eighth century B.C.E. has been discovered that has inscribed on it: "Gold of Ophir to Beth Horon, 30 shekels."—1Ki 9:28; 10:11; Job 28:16; see OPHIR.

Disposition of Gold in Captured Cities. God commanded Israel that the graven images of the idol gods of the nations be burned in the fire: "You must not desire the silver and the gold upon them, nor indeed take it for yourself, for fear you may be ensnared by it; for it is a thing detestable to Jehovah your God. And you must not bring a detestable thing into your house and actually become a thing devoted to destruction like it. You should thoroughly loathe it and absolutely detest it, because it is something devoted to destruction." (De 7:25, 26) Idols and their appurtenances were therefore burned, and the gold and silver on them were sometimes ground to powder.—Ex 32:20; 2Ki 23:4.

Other gold and silver objects in captured cities could be taken after being processed with fire for cleansing. (Nu 31:22, 23) Jericho was an exception to this, for it was the firstfruits of the conquest of Canaan. Its gold and silver (except that on idols) had to be turned over to the priests, devoted to sanctuary use.—Jos 6:17-19, 24.

Wisdom, Faith, Better Than Gold. Though gold has great value, it, like other material riches, is not able to give life to its possessors (Ps 49:6-8; Mt 16:26), and no amount of gold can buy the true wisdom that comes from Jehovah. (Job 28: 12, 15-17, 28) His laws, commandments, and discipline are far more desirable than much refined gold. (Ps 19:7-10; 119:72, 127; Pr 8:10) Gold is powerless to deliver in the day of Jehovah's anger.—Zep 1:18.

Men of a materialistic society ridicule faith in God and call it impractical. Nonetheless, the apostle Peter points to faith's unexcelled durability and permanent value. He states that the tested quality of one's faith is of much greater value than gold, which can withstand fire yet can wear away and be destroyed by other means. Christians have to endure various trials that are sometimes grievous, but this serves to bring out the quality of their faith. (1Pe 1:6, 7) True faith can stand up under any tests.

Symbolic Use. Gold was spoken of by Job as a symbol of materialism, one of the things he knew he must avoid to please Jehovah. (Job 31: 24, 25) On the other hand, the beauty, preciousness, and purity of fine gold make it a fitting symbol in describing the holy city, New Jerusalem, and its broad way.—Re 21:18, 21.

Nebuchadnezzar's dream image had a head of gold, the rest of the image being made of less precious materials. Daniel interpreted the parts of the image as representing world powers, the head of gold being Nebuchadnezzar, that is, the imperial dynasty of Babylon's kings headed by Nebuchadnezzar. (Da 2:31-33, 37-40) Babylon is similarly symbolized as "a golden cup in the hand of Jehovah," useful to him as an executioner of his judgments on the nations.—Jer 51:7.

In the tabernacle built by Moses, gold was used in the enclosed compartments—the Holy Place, where the priests entered and performed duties, and the Most Holy, entered only by the high priest. Since the Most Holy with its golden ark of the covenant represented heaven, God's dwelling place, and since priests, but not ordinary Israelites, could enter the Holy Place, these things would logically represent things having to do with the heavens of God and with his "royal priesthood," that is, those with the heavenly calling, and their activity and duties toward God. (1Pe 2:9; Heb 9:1-5, 9, 11, 12, 23-25; 3:1) This priesthood is thus symbolically distinguished from people on earth to whom the priesthood ministers.

In encouraging the young man to serve his Creator while he still has strength and vigor, the wise writer of Ecclesiastes says that this should be done before "the golden bowl gets crushed." He apparently has reference to the bowllike cranium with its brain content, the crushing of which would deprive its possessor of life.—Ec 12:6, 7.

GOLGOTHA (Gol'go·tha) [Skull [Place]]. The place outside, although near, the city of Jerusalem, where Jesus Christ was impaled. (Mt 27:33; Joh 19:17-22; Heb 13:12) A road and a garden tomb were nearby. (Mt 27:39; Joh 19:41) "Golgotha," or "Skull Place," is also called "Calvary" (Lu 23:33, KJ, Dy), from the Latin calvaria (skull). The Biblical record does not state that Golgotha was on a hill, though it does mention the fact that some observed the impalement from a distance. —Mr 15:40; Lu 23:49.

In the fourth century C.E., Emperor Constantine assigned the task of determining the place of Jesus' impalement and his tomb to Bishop Macarius, who decided that Hadrian's then-existing temple of Aphrodite (Venus) had been erected on the site. Constantine therefore ordered the demolition of this temple and the construction of a basilica that later underwent expansion and modification, becoming the Church of the Holy Sepulchre. Archaeological excavations done since 1960 indicate that the area was used as a burial ground, and it is thought that this was true in the first century C.E. Thus the Church of the Holy Sepulchre now stands on one of the traditional sites of Golgotha and Jesus' tomb. Though located within the present walls of Jerusalem, the site is believed to have been outside the city walls in Jesus' day.

Another location that was proposed as the site of the impalement of Jesus is a promontory

230 m (755 ft) NE of the Damascus Gate, now known as Gordon's Calvary. It was suggested in 1842 as the true location of Golgotha and Jesus' tomb. In 1883 the location was endorsed by General C. G. Gordon, a British military hero. The identification was based on conjecture. On the basis of archaeological evidence available, Gabriel Barkay states that the nearby Garden Tomb that is frequently pointed out to tourists as being the burial place of Jesus was originally hewn and used some time in the eighth or seventh century B.C.E. That would not fit the description at John 19:41 of "a new memorial tomb, in which no one had ever yet been laid."—*Biblical Archaeology Review,* March/April 1986, p. 50.

Identification of Golgotha has often become an emotional religious issue. There is, however, no archaeological evidence that "Gordon's Calvary" is the place. As for the location marked by the Church of the Holy Sepulchre, its identification takes into account archaeological findings but is based largely on tradition that dates to the fourth century. Regarding the latter location, *Biblical Archaeology Review* (May/June 1986, p. 38) states: "We may not be absolutely certain that the site of the Holy Sepulchre Church is the site of Jesus' burial, but we certainly have no other site that can lay a claim nearly as weighty." So the identification remains conjectural.

GOLIATH (Go·li′ath).

The giant from the city of Gath, champion of the Philistine army, who was killed by David. Goliath towered to the extraordinary height of six cubits and a span (2.9 m; 9.5 ft). His copper coat of mail weighed 5,000 shekels (57 kg; 126 lb) and the iron blade of his spear weighed 600 shekels (6.8 kg; 15 lb). (1Sa 17:4, 5, 7) Goliath was one of the Rephaim; he may have been a mercenary soldier with the Philistine army.—1Ch 20:5, 8; see REPHAIM.

Not long after David's anointing by Samuel, and after Jehovah's spirit had left King Saul (1Sa 16:13, 14), the Philistines collected for war against Israel at Socoh and then encamped in Ephes-dammim. As the battle lines of the Philistines and Saul's army faced each other across the valley, the gigantic warrior Goliath emerged from the Philistine camp and loudly challenged Israel to supply a man to fight him in single combat, the outcome to determine which army should become the servant of the other. Morning and evening, for 40 days, the army of Israel, in great fear, was subjected to these taunts. No Israelite soldier had the courage to accept the challenge.—1Sa 17:1-11, 16.

In taunting the armies of the living God Jehovah, Goliath sealed his own doom. The young shepherd David, with God's spirit upon him, met Goliath's challenge. Goliath, preceded by his armor-bearer carrying a large shield, advanced, calling down evil upon David by his gods. To this David replied: "You are coming to me with a sword and with a spear and with a javelin, but I am coming to you with the name of Jehovah of armies, the God of the battle lines of Israel, whom you have taunted." (PICTURE, Vol. 1, p. 745) David slung a stone from his sling; it sank into Goliath's forehead, and he fell to the earth. David followed this up by standing on Goliath and cutting off his head with the giant's own sword. This was promptly followed by a signal rout and slaughter of the Philistines.—1Sa 17:26, 41-53.

"Then David took the head of the Philistine and brought it to Jerusalem, and his weapons he put in his tent." (1Sa 17:54) While it is true that the stronghold of Zion was not captured until later by David (2Sa 5:7), the city of Jerusalem itself had long been inhabited by Israelites, along with Jebusites. (Jos 15:63; Jg 1:8) Later on, David evidently turned Goliath's sword over to the sanctuary. This is indicated by the fact that Ahimelech the priest gave it to David when David was fleeing from Saul.—1Sa 21:8, 9.

A passage that has caused some difficulty is found at 2 Samuel 21:19, where it is stated: "Elhanan the son of Jaare-oregim the Bethlehemite got to strike down Goliath the Gittite, the shaft of whose spear was like the beam of loom workers." The parallel account at 1 Chronicles 20:5 reads: "Elhanan the son of Jair got to strike down Lahmi the brother of Goliath the Gittite, the shaft of whose spear was like the beam of loom workers."

Several suggestions have been made for an explanation of the problem. The Targum preserves a tradition that Elhanan is to be identified with David. The *Soncino Books of the Bible,* edited by A. Cohen (London, 1951, 1952), comment that there is no difficulty in the assumption that there were two Goliaths, commenting also that *Goliath* may have been a descriptive title like "Pharaoh," "Rabshakeh," "Sultan." The fact that one text refers to "Jaare-oregim," whereas the other reads "Jair," and also that only the account in Second Samuel contains the term "Bethlehemite [Heb., *behth hal·lach·mi′*]," while the Chronicles account alone contains the name "Lahmi [*′eth-Lach·mi′*]," has been suggested by the majority of commentators to be the result of a copyist's error.—See JAARE-OREGIM; LAHMI.

GOMER (Go'mer).

1. Grandson of Noah and first-named son of Japheth, born after the Flood. (Ge 10:1, 2; 1Ch 1:4, 5) He and his sons, Ashkenaz, Riphath, and Togarmah, are listed among "the families of the sons of Noah according to their family descents" from whom the nations were spread about after the Deluge.—Ge 10:3, 32.

The nation that descended from Gomer is historically associated with the ancient Cimmerians, an Aryan race who evidently settled in the region N of the Black Sea. In the eighth century B.C.E., during the reign of Assyrian King Sargon, they apparently were driven by the Scythians across the Caucasus (the mountainous region between the Black and Caspian Seas). The Cimmerians swept through Asia Minor, attacking the kingdom of Urartu (Ararat) and penetrating eastern Asia Minor, where the Armenian name for Cappadocia, *Gamirkʹ,* doubtless reflects their invasion. Faced with a strong Assyrian Empire to the E, the Cimmerians pushed westward and warred against the Phrygians and the Lydians. They were finally expelled from Lydia by Lydian King Alyattes (predecessor of Croesus).

Ezekiel's prophecy (the writing of which was evidently completed by about 591 B.C.E.) concerning the assault by "Gog of the land of Magog" against the regathered people of Jehovah lists "Gomer and all its bands" among Gog's forces along with Togarmah "of the remotest parts of the north, and all its bands."—Eze 38:2-8; see GOG No. 2; MAGOG No. 2; TOGARMAH.

2. The daughter of Diblaim who became the wife of Hosea in accord with Jehovah's instructions to that prophet. (Ho 1:2, 3) Gomer thereafter gave birth to three children, whose significant names were used by God to foretell the disastrous results of Israel's spiritual adultery in the form of idolatry. In relating the birth of the first child, a son named Jezreel, the account states that Gomer "bore to him [Hosea] a son." In connection with the births of the next two children, however, no reference is made to the prophet as the father, and this has been the basis for regarding them as probably illegitimate. (Ho 1:3-9) Hosea 3:1-3 appears to describe Gomer's being brought back from an adulterous course to the prophet, being purchased as though a slave, thus illustrating Israel's being received back by God on the basis of their repentance.

GOMORRAH (Go·mor'rah). One of "the cities of the District" probably located near the southern end of the Dead Sea. (Ge 13:12) Sodom and Gomorrah were apparently the chief of these cities. Their ruins are believed by many scholars to be presently submerged under the waters of the Dead Sea, though some others recently have claimed that the ruins of the cities may be identified with sites along wadis to the E and SE of the Dead Sea. In Abraham's time the region was described as "well-watered . . . like the garden of Jehovah." (Ge 13:10; see DISTRICT OF THE JORDAN.) During the time that Lot, Abraham's nephew, resided in this fertile District, King Birsha of Gomorrah along with the kings of four other cities of the District rebelled against the domination of Chedorlaomer of Elam and three other allied kings. They were attacked and fled, some of their soldiers falling into the numerous bitumen pits in the area. Sodom and Gomorrah were sacked by the Eastern kings, who took Lot captive.—Ge 14:1-12.

More than 14 years later, the outcry of complaint about the wickedness of Sodom and Gomorrah became so great that Jehovah sent angels to inspect the situation and then to destroy the cities by a rain of fire and sulfur.—Ge 18:20, 21; 19:24, 28.

The thoroughness of the destruction of these cities was afterward used as a symbol of complete and everlasting annihilation. (De 29:22, 23; Isa 1:9; 13:19; Jer 49:18) Jehovah figuratively expressed the depth of wickedness to which the rulers and people of Judah and Jerusalem had sunk when he addressed them through the prophet Isaiah: "Hear the word of Jehovah, you dictators of Sodom. Give ear to the law of our God, you people of Gomorrah."—Isa 1:1, 10; Jer 23:14.

The apostle Peter said that by reducing Sodom and Gomorrah to ashes, God condemned them, "setting a pattern for ungodly persons of things to come." (2Pe 2:6) This mention by Peter and references by Jesus Christ and Jude prove that Jesus and his disciples acknowledged that these cities of the District had actually existed and that they accepted the Biblical account of them as true. Though the *cities* underwent "the judicial punishment of everlasting fire" (Jude 7), Jesus indicated that people of Sodom and Gomorrah would experience a resurrection to stand for judgment. He contrasted them with a city that rejected his disciples in their preaching of the Kingdom good news, saying: "It will be more endurable for the land of Sodom and Gomorrah on Judgment Day than for that city."—Mt 10:7, 14, 15; see SODOM.

GOODNESS.

The quality or state of being good; moral excellence; virtue. Goodness is solid through and through, with no badness or rottenness. It is a positive quality and expresses itself in the performance of good and beneficial acts toward others. The most common words for "good" in the Bible are the Hebrew *tohv* and the Greek *a·ga·thos'; a·ga·thos'* is usually used in a moral or religious sense.

Jehovah's Goodness. Jehovah God is good in the absolute and consummate sense. The Scriptures say: "Good and upright is Jehovah" (Ps 25:8), and they exclaim: "O how great his goodness is!" (Zec 9:17) Jesus Christ, though he had this quality of moral excellence, would not accept "Good" as a title, saying to one who addressed him as "Good Teacher": "Why do you call me good? Nobody is good, except one, God." (Mr 10:17, 18) He thus recognized Jehovah as the ultimate standard of what is good.

When Moses asked to see His glory, Jehovah replied: "I myself shall cause all my goodness to pass before your face, and I will declare the name of Jehovah before you." Jehovah screened Moses from looking upon his face, but as he passed by (evidently by means of his angelic representative [Ac 7:53]) he declared to Moses: "Jehovah, Jehovah, a God merciful and gracious, slow to anger and abundant in loving-kindness and truth, preserving loving-kindness for thousands, pardoning error and transgression and sin, but by no means will he give exemption from punishment." —Ex 33:18, 19, 22; 34:6, 7.

Here goodness is seen to be a quality that involves mercy, loving-kindness, and truth but does not condone or cooperate in any way with badness. On this basis David could pray to Jehovah to forgive his sins 'for the sake of Jehovah's goodness.' (Ps 25:7) Jehovah's goodness, as well as his love, was involved in the giving of his Son as a sacrifice for sins. By this he provided a means for helping those who would want that which is truly good, and at the same time he condemned badness and laid the basis for fully satisfying justice and righteousness.—Ro 3:23-26.

A Fruit of the Spirit. Goodness is a fruit of God's spirit and of the light from his Word of truth. (Ga 5:22; Eph 5:9) It is to be cultivated by the Christian. Obedience to Jehovah's commands develops goodness; no man has goodness on his own merit. (Ro 7:18) The psalmist appeals to God as the Source of goodness: "Teach me goodness, sensibleness and knowledge themselves, for in your commandments I have exercised faith," and, "You are good and are doing good. Teach me your regulations."—Ps 119:66, 68.

Goodness Bestows Benefits. Goodness can also mean beneficence, the bestowing of beneficial things upon others. Jehovah desires to express goodness toward his people, as the apostle Paul prayed for the Christians in Thessalonica: "We always pray for you, that our God may count you worthy of his calling and perform completely all he pleases of goodness and the work of faith with power." (2Th 1:11) Many are the examples of God's abundant goodness to those who look to him. (1Ki 8:66; Ps 31:19; Isa 63:7; Jer 31:12, 14) Moreover, "Jehovah is good to all, and his mercies are over all his works." (Ps 145:9) With a purpose he extends good to all, that his goodness may bring many to serve him and that they may thereby gain life. Likewise, any individual exercising goodness is a blessing to his associates. —Pr 11:10.

As servants of God and imitators of him, Christians are commanded to prove what is God's good and perfect will for them (Ro 12:2); they are to cling to what is good (Ro 12:9), to do it (Ro 13:3), to work what is good (Ro 2:10), to follow after it (1Th 5:15), to be zealous for it (1Pe 3:13), to imitate what is good (3Jo 11), and to conquer evil with it (Ro 12:21). Their doing of good is to be especially extended to those related to them in the Christian faith; additionally, it is to be practiced toward all others.—Ga 6:10.

A Related Term. Similar to the Greek word for good (*a·ga·thos'*) is another word, *ka·los'*. The latter denotes that which is intrinsically good, beautiful, well adapted to its circumstances or ends (as fine ground, or soil; Mt 13:8, 23), and that which is of fine quality, including that which is ethically good, right, or honorable (as God's name; Jas 2:7). It is closely related in meaning to good, but may be distinguished by being translated "fine," "right," "honest," or "well."—Mt 3:10; Jas 4:17; Heb 13:18; Ro 14:21.

GOOD NEWS.

This refers to the good news of the Kingdom of God and of salvation by faith in Jesus Christ. It is called in the Bible "the good news of the kingdom" (Mt 4:23), "the good news of God" (Ro 15:16), "the good news about Jesus Christ" (Mr 1:1), "the good news of the undeserved kindness of God" (Ac 20:24), "the good news of peace" (Eph 6:15), and the "everlasting good news" (Re 14:6).

The Greek word translated "good news" ("gospel" in *KJ* and some other versions) is *eu·ag·ge'li·on*. "An evangelizer" (the English word being almost a transliteration of the Greek) is a preacher of the good news.—Ac 21:8; 2Ti 4:5.

Its Content. An idea of the content and scope of the good news can be gained from the above designations. It includes all the truths about which Jesus spoke and the disciples wrote. While men of old hoped in God and had faith through knowledge of Him, God's purposes were first "made clearly evident through the manifestation of our Savior, Christ Jesus, who has abolished death but has shed light upon life and incorruption through the good news."—2Ti 1:9, 10.

Centuries earlier God had declared the good news to Abraham, thereby indicating the means by which he purposed to provide the good news. He said: "By means of you all the nations will be blessed." (Ga 3:8) Later, through the prophet Isaiah, Jehovah spoke of the preaching of the good news. Jesus Christ read from this prophecy in the synagogue at Nazareth, afterward saying: "Today this scripture that you just heard is fulfilled." (Lu 4:16-21) Isaiah's prophecy described the purpose and effect of the good news to be preached, particularly from the time of Messiah's coming.—Isa 61:1-3.

Its Progress. At Jesus' birth the angel announced to the shepherds: "Have no fear, for, look! I am declaring to you good news of a great joy that all the people will have." (Lu 2:10) John the Baptizer prepared the way for Jesus' preaching of the good news, saying to the Jews: "Repent, for the kingdom of the heavens has drawn near." (Mt 3:1, 2) Jesus said of John's preaching: "From the days of John the Baptist until now the kingdom of the heavens is the goal toward which men press, and those pressing forward are seizing it."—Mt 11:12.

During Jesus' earthly ministry, he confined his preaching of the good news to the Jews and proselytes, saying: "I was not sent forth to any but to the lost sheep of the house of Israel." (Mt 15:24) When sending out the 12 apostles, he commanded them: "Do not go off into the road of the nations, and do not enter into a Samaritan city; but, instead, go continually to the lost sheep of the house of Israel." (Mt 10:5, 6) On one occasion he preached to a woman of the Samaritans, who were related to the Israelites, but this was not because he had gone into the city to preach. However, the response of the woman and others was so favorable that Jesus stayed with them for two days.—Joh 4:7-42.

After Jesus' death and resurrection, he gave his disciples the command: "Go therefore and make disciples of people of all the nations, baptizing them in the name of the Father and of the Son and of the holy spirit, teaching them to observe all the things I have commanded you." (Mt 28:19, 20) He also told them that their preaching would reach to "the most distant part of the earth." (Ac 1:8) But for about three and a half years afterward the holy spirit led the disciples to confine their preaching to Jews and Samaritans. Then Peter was sent by God to bring the good news to the household of the Roman army officer Cornelius. (Ac chaps 10, 11; 15:7) From that time on, the good news was declared to the greatest possible extent over the widest area.

Its Importance. The apostle Paul wrote with strong conviction about the provision for salvation that God had made through Jesus Christ. He declared that if anyone was to declare to the Galatians something beyond what they had learned, something that was actually a different teaching, "let him be accursed." Then, pointing to the source of the good news that he declared, Paul stated: "Neither did I receive it from man, nor was I taught it, except through revelation by Jesus Christ." (Ga 1:8, 11, 12) This strong declaration was necessary, for even then there were some who were trying to overthrow the true faith by preaching 'another good news.' (2Co 11:4; Ga 1:6, 7) Paul warned of an apostasy to come and stated that 'the mystery of lawlessness' was already at work; he admonished Christians to remember the purpose of the good news and to stand firm and maintain their hold on the spirit-guided traditions they had learned through the apostles.—2Th 2:3, 7, 14, 15; see TRADITION.

Faithfulness in holding on to and continuing to proclaim the good news was counted by Jesus as more important than one's present life, and Paul recognized that faithfully declaring it was vital. (Mr 8:35; 1Co 9:16; 2Ti 1:8) The individual might suffer the loss of his most cherished possessions, even undergoing persecutions but, in turn, would receive a hundredfold now, "houses and brothers and sisters and mothers and children and fields, . . . and in the coming system of things everlasting life."—Mr 10:29, 30.

The good news is the touchstone by which mankind is judged: Acceptance of and obedience to the good news result in salvation; rejection and disobedience bring destruction. (1Pe 4:5, 6, 17; 2Th 1:6-8) Particularly with this fact in view, the individual's motive in preaching the good news must be pure and he must preach it from the heart, out of love for those hearing. The apostles were so appreciative of the life-giving importance of the good news and were so fired with God's spirit and with love that they imparted not only the good news but also their "own souls" to those who listened to their preaching. (1Th 2:8) God provided that the proclaimers of the good news had the right to accept material help from those to whom they brought it. (1Co 9:11-14) But Paul and his close associates so cherished their privilege as bearers of the good news that they carefully avoided making financial gain therefrom, or even giving the appearance of doing so in connection with their preaching. The apostle Paul describes his course of action in this regard at 1 Corinthians 9:15-18 and 1 Thessalonians 2:6, 9.

Enemies. The good news has been bitterly fought, and the source of the enmity is identified by the apostle: "If, now, the good news we declare is in fact veiled, it is veiled among those who are perishing, among whom the god of this system of things has blinded the minds of the unbelievers, that the illumination of the glorious good news about the Christ, who is the image of God, might not shine through." (2Co 4:3, 4) The earliest enemies of the good news were the religious leaders of the Jews. Their enmity, however, resulted in good to the Gentiles, or people of the nations, in that it opened up the opportunity for Gentiles to be fellow partakers of "the promise in union with Christ Jesus through the good news."—Ro 11:25, 28; Eph 3:5, 6.

Enemies of the good news caused the Christians much suffering and required the apostles to put up a hard fight before rulers in defending and legally establishing the good news so that it might spread with the greatest possible freeness. —Php 1:7, 16; compare Mr 13:9-13; Ac 4:18-20; 5:27-29.

Jesus' Earthly Ministry and His Return. It is noteworthy that, for about six months before Jesus came to him for baptism, John the Baptizer preached: "Repent, for the kingdom of the heavens has drawn near," and when Jesus appeared, John pointed to Jesus as "the Lamb of God that takes away the sin of the world!" (Mt 3:1, 2; Joh 1:29) Thus he turned the people's attention toward the long-awaited Messianic King.—Ac 19:4.

While Jesus was on earth, he and his disciples announced: "The kingdom of the heavens has drawn near." (Mt 4:17; 10:7) Jesus, anointed as Christ, the King, said to the Pharisees, his enemies: "The kingdom of God is in your midst." (Lu 17:20, 21) This was the theme, or central point, of the good news during Jesus' earthly ministry. However, it is not reported that after Jesus' death the disciples proclaimed the Kingdom as having "drawn near" or as being at hand. Rather, the good news they preached was that after Jesus had laid down his life as the ransom price for salvation, he ascended to heaven and was then sitting at God's right hand. They also preached about Jesus' return at a later time and his Kingdom to come.—Heb 10:12, 13; 2Ti 4:1; Re 11:15; 12:10; 22:20; compare Lu 19:12, 15; Mt 25:31.

Jesus' disciples asked him, "What will be the sign of your presence and of the conclusion of the system of things?" In his answer Jesus enumerated certain things due to occur at that time. He said, among other things: "This good news of the kingdom will be preached in all the inhabited earth for a witness to all the nations; and then the end will come." (Mt 24:3, 14; Mr 13:10; compare Col 1:23.) In the Revelation given to the apostle John about 96 C.E., John saw an "angel flying in midheaven" who had "everlasting good news to declare as glad tidings to those who dwell on the earth, and to every nation and tribe and tongue and people, saying in a loud voice: 'Fear God and give him glory, because the hour of the judgment by him has arrived.'" (Re 14:6, 7) These inspired statements indicate that in the "last days" there would be an unparalleled proclamation of the good news of the Kingdom.

GOODWILL. Both the Hebrew *ra·tsohn'* and the Greek *eu·do·ki'a* and related forms of these words have reference to that which pleases or to one's being pleased, and they are translated "pleasure," "good pleasure," "liking," "approval," "goodwill," and so forth.

God's Goodwill. In the Bible the above terms are used with regard to the pleasure, approval, or goodwill of God. (Ps 51:18; 106:4; Eph 1:5, 9) God sets forth clearly what is required to please him, and he determines whom he will accept as his friends, as recipients of his goodwill. Those rejecting his Word or rebelling against him do not receive his goodwill but, rather, experience his displeasure.—Ps 2:5; Heb 3:16-19.

Man's Goodwill. The same words are also used with reference to the approval of men, or of goodwill on their part. (2Ch 10:7; Es 1:8; Ro

15:25, 26) The apostle Paul spoke of some who preached the Christ through goodwill. (Php 1:15) These sincere Christians were expressing goodwill toward the apostle and therefore also toward God and his Son, whom Paul was representing. Such ones would accordingly experience the goodwill of God. (Pr 8:35; 10:32; 11:27) Another example of the goodwill of man toward others is the apostle Paul's expression concerning his fleshly brothers, the Jews: "Brothers, the goodwill of my heart and my supplication to God for them are, indeed, for their salvation."—Ro 10:1.

"Men of Goodwill." When an angel announced the birth of Jesus, he appeared, not before the religious leaders of the Jews, but before humble shepherds. After he told the shepherds of the birth of the Messiah, an angelic host proclaimed: "Glory in the heights above to God, and upon earth peace among men of goodwill." (Lu 2:14) The angels were not proclaiming peace to God's enemies, who were not at peace with him. " 'There is no peace,' my God has said, 'for the wicked ones.' " (Isa 57:21) The *King James Version* renders Luke 2:14: "Glory to God in the highest, and on earth peace, good will toward men." But God was not here expressing goodwill toward men in general; neither did he mean that his peace was extended to those inclined toward him merely in a friendly and indulgent way. Rather, God had reference to those who would please him by genuine faith in him and who would become followers of his Son.

Modern translations harmonize with this view, making the matter clear. The *Revised Standard Version* reads: "Peace among men with whom he is pleased!" *The New English Bible* translates the phrase: "His peace for men on whom his favour rests." James Moffatt's translation renders it: "Peace on earth for men whom he favours!" and *An American Translation* reads: "Peace to the men he favors!" Other modern versions read similarly.

GOSHEN (Go'shen).

1. A region in Egypt where the Israelites resided for 215 years (1728-1513 B.C.E.). (Ge 45:10; 47:27) While the exact location of Goshen is uncertain, it appears to have lain in the eastern part of the Nile Delta, the entrance to Egypt proper. This is indicated by the fact that Joseph, leaving his Egyptian quarters, met his father (who was traveling from Canaan) at Goshen. (Ge 46:28, 29) Greek *Septuagint* renderings indicate that Goshen was in the vicinity of the Wadi Tumilat.

Pharaoh kept cattle at Goshen, and the Hebrews also pastured their flocks and herds there. (Ge 47:1, 4-6; 50:8) The description of the region as 'the very best of the land of Egypt' is apparently a relative term meaning the most fertile *pastoral* land, best suited for the particular needs of Jacob's family. Goshen may have been the same as "the land of Rameses." (Ge 47:6, 11) Beginning with the fourth blow on Egypt, Jehovah specifically singled out "Goshen" to be left unharmed.—Ex 8:22; 9:26.

2. A city in the mountainous region of Judah. (Jos 15:20, 48, 51) Some scholars tentatively identify it with Edh Dhahiriya, about 18 km (11 mi) SW of Hebron. "The land of Goshen" referred to at Joshua 10:41 and 11:16 was apparently a district in its vicinity. This district would take in the mountainous region between Hebron and the Negeb.

GOSSIP, SLANDER.
Gossip is idle personal talk; groundless rumor. Slander is defamation, generally malicious, whether oral or written.

Not all gossip is bad or damaging, though it can be. At times it may be commendatory about a person or persons; or it may be the mere relating of something trifling or unobjectionable about others, out of human interest. But it is easy to slip into hurtful or troublemaking talk, for gossip is idle talk. The Scriptures counsel against idle speech, pointing out that the tongue is difficult to tame and that it "is constituted a world of unrighteousness among our members, for it spots up all the body and sets the wheel of natural life aflame." Its destructiveness is further emphasized in that the Bible writer continues, "and it is set aflame by Gehenna." (Jas 3:6) The danger of loose, idle talk is emphasized many times. Such speech is connected with stupidity or foolishness (Pr 15:2); it is a snare and can bring the speaker to ruin. (Pr 13:3; 18:7) "In the abundance of words there does not fail to be transgression," says the proverb, counseling that keeping one's lips in check is discreet action. (Pr 10:19) "He that is keeping his mouth and his tongue is keeping his soul from distresses" is a warning against thoughtless, loose, or idle talk.—Pr 21:23.

"Out of the abundance of the heart the mouth speaks," said Jesus Christ. (Mt 12:34) Consequently, what one usually talks about is an index of that on which his heart is set. The Scriptures urge us to safeguard the heart and to think on and speak of the things that are true, serious, righteous, chaste, lovable, well spoken of, virtuous, and praiseworthy. (Pr 4:23; Php 4:8) Jesus

Christ said, "It is what proceeds out of his mouth that defiles a man," and he went on to name "wicked reasonings" and "false testimonies" among the things that proceed from the mouth but actually are out of the heart.—Mt 15:11, 19.

Gossip can lead to slander, becoming disastrous to the slanderer. The wisdom of the words at Ecclesiastes 10:12-14 is very evident: "The lips of the stupid one swallow him up. The start of the words of his mouth is foolishness, and the end afterward of his mouth is calamitous madness. And the foolish one speaks many words."

Gossip is talk that reveals something about the doings and the affairs of other persons. It may be unfounded rumor, even a lie, and although the gossiper may not know the untruthfulness of the rumor, he spreads it nevertheless, thereby making himself responsible for propagating a lie. It may be someone's faults and mistakes that the gossiper is talking about. But even if the things said are true, the gossiper is in the wrong and reveals lack of love. The proverb says: "The one covering over transgression is seeking love, and he that keeps talking about a matter is separating those familiar with one another."—Pr 17:9.

The apostle Paul gave strong advice to the overseer Timothy about the conduct of young widows who had no households to care for and who did not busy themselves in ministering to others. He said: "They also learn to be unoccupied, gadding about to the houses; yes, not only unoccupied, but also gossipers and meddlers in other people's affairs, talking of things they ought not." (1Ti 5:13) Such action is disorderly conduct. The same apostle spoke of some in the congregation at Thessalonica who were "walking disorderly among you, not working at all but meddling with what does not concern them." (2Th 3:11) The apostle Peter puts "a busybody in other people's matters" in very bad company —alongside a murderer, a thief, and an evildoer. —1Pe 4:15.

On the other hand, it is not gossip or slander and is not wrong to report conditions affecting a congregation to those having authority and responsibility to oversee and correct matters. This fact is demonstrated in the Scriptural record about the Christian congregation in ancient Corinth. There, dissensions and the paying of undue honor to men were creating sectarian attitudes, destroying the congregation's unity. Some members of the house of a certain Chloe who were aware of these things and were concerned about the congregation's spiritual welfare disclosed the fact to the absent apostle Paul, who acted quickly, writing corrective counsel to the congregation from Ephesus.—1Co 1:11.

What is the difference between gossip and slander?

While gossip can in some cases be more or less harmless (though it can become slander or lead into it), slander is always damaging and always causes hurt and contention. It may be with or without malicious motive. In either case, the slanderer is putting himself in a bad position before God, for "sending forth contentions among brothers" is among the things that God hates. (Pr 6:16-19) The Greek word for "slanderer" or "accuser" is di·a'bo·los. The word is also used in the Bible as a title of Satan "the Devil," the great slanderer of God. (Joh 8:44; Re 12:9, 10; Ge 3:2-5) This indicates the source of such defamatory accusation.

Slander constitutes a stumbling block to others, particularly to the one slandered. The law given by God to Israel commanded: "You must not go around among your people for the sake of slandering. You must not stand up against your fellow's blood." (Le 19:16) The seriousness of slander is here emphasized by pointing out that in some instances false charges might actually lead to execution. False witnesses have many times been instrumental in causing the death of innocent persons.—1Ki 21:8-13; Mt 26:59, 60.

Sometimes matters are confidential, but the slanderer delights in revealing them to others who have no right to know. (Pr 11:13) The slanderer gets pleasure in revealing things that cause sensation. The one listening to slander is also wrong and is damaging himself. (Pr 20:19; 26:22) A person may be turned away from his friends because of some defamatory remark about them made by a slanderer, and enmities and divisions may develop.—Pr 16:28.

The Scriptures foretell that the notable presence of slanderers would be one of the marks of "the last days." (2Ti 3:1-3) Such persons, men or women, if present among God's people, are to be reproved and corrected by responsible ones in the Christian congregation. (1Ti 3:11; Tit 2:1-5; 3Jo 9, 10) Slander, in causing contention (Pr 16:28), thus produces certain "works of the flesh" (such as hatreds, contentions, and divisions) that will prevent the slanderer and others he leads into wrongdoing from inheriting God's Kingdom. (Ga 5:19-21) Though the slanderer may be sly and deceitful, his badness will be uncovered in the congregation. (Pr 26:20-26) Jesus exposed the slanderous Judas (Joh 6:70) to his apostles and then dismissed Judas from his company. What then took place led to Judas' destruction. —Mt 26:20-25; Joh 13:21-27; 17:12.

A form of slander is *reviling*, the practice of which merits cutting off from the Christian congregation, for revilers are condemned by the Scriptures as unworthy of life. (1Co 5:11; 6:9, 10) Slander and reviling are often associated with rebellion against God or against those he has duly constituted and appointed to govern the congregation of his people. A case in point is that of Korah and his associates, who spoke in slanderous terms against Moses and Aaron in rebelling against God's arrangement. (Nu 16:1-3, 12-14) Jude calls attention to these rebellious ones and their end when he warns Christians against abusive speech, murmuring, complaining, and speaking "swelling things."—Jude 10, 11, 14-16.

GOURD [Heb., *paq·qu·'oth'*, plural]. The Hebrew word rendered "gourds" appears in the Bible only with reference to an incident occurring during a time of famine in Elisha's day. Someone had gathered some unfamiliar wild gourds and sliced them in with a stew. Upon tasting it, "the sons of the prophets" feared food poisoning and stopped eating, but Elisha miraculously saved the stew from being wasted.—2Ki 4:38-41.

Although a number of other suggestions have been made, the colocynth (*Citrullus colocynthis*), a plant related to the watermelon, is generally favored as the plant whose fruit probably corresponds to the "wild gourds" of the Scriptural record. The vine of the colocynth trails like the cucumber and also has similar foliage. The fruit is about the size of an orange; it has a thick, smooth rind with green and yellow mottlings, and it contains a very bitter and poisonous spongy pulp, from which the colocynth of medicine is derived. The characteristics of the colocynth would fit the Bible narrative of a wild gourd that was apparently poisonous, as suggested by its very taste. (2Ki 4:40) When most other plants have withered, it is still green and hence is a temptation to one unfamiliar with it.

The gourd-shaped ornaments (Heb., *peqa·'im'*) adorning the molten sea and the cedarwood paneling inside Solomon's temple may have been round like the fruit of the colocynth.—1Ki 6:18; 7:24; 2Ch 4:3.

GOVERNMENT. The authoritative direction and restraint exercised over the actions of men in communities, societies, and states. Also, the person, body of persons, or the organizations constituting the governing authority.

In the Christian Greek Scriptures forms of the word *ar·khe'* (beginning) are variously translated "principalities," "governments," "rulers," "Sovereignties." (*KJ; Dy; NW; AT; JB*) *Ky·ber'ne·sis* and *ky·ri·o'tes*, rendered "government" in some translations, more correctly mean "steering [guiding or directing]" and "lordship," respectively. In the Hebrew Scriptures, "government" is the English term sometimes used to translate *mem·sha·lah'*, "dominion" (Isa 22:21), and *mis·rah'*, "dominion" or "princely rule [or power]."—Isa 9:6.

The Bible reveals that there are invisible governments that are good, established by God (Eph 3:10), and those that are wicked, established by Satan and the demons. (Eph 6:12) Jesus Christ was the active agent of God in originally setting up all righteous governments and authorities, invisible and visible. (Col 1:15, 16) He has been placed by his Father Jehovah as head of all government (Col 2:8-10), and he must rule until all opposing governments, invisible and visible, are brought to nothing. (1Co 15:24) The apostle Paul indicated that there was a system of things to come in which there would be a government under the authority of Christ.—Eph 1:19-21.

World Governments. The Bible pictures world governments as "beasts" and says that they get their authority from the Dragon, Satan the Devil. God has permitted them to remain and has limited their scope and duration of rule, in harmony with his purpose.—Da chaps 7, 8; Re chaps 13, 17; Da 4:25, 35; Joh 19:11; Ac 17:26; 2Co 4:3, 4; see BEASTS, SYMBOLIC.

Christians and Governments. Jesus Christ and the early Christians did nothing to interfere with human governments of their day. (Joh 6:15; 17:16; 18:36; Jas 1:27; 4:4) They recognized the fact that some form of government is necessary for the existence of society, and they never fomented revolution or civil disobedience. (Ro 13:1-7; Tit 3:1) Jesus set forth the guiding principle for true worshipers of God to follow when he said: "Pay back, therefore, Caesar's things to Caesar, but God's things to God." (Mt 22:21) This principle enabled the early Christians (and Christians since then) to maintain a right balance as to relations with the two authorities, that of the civil governments and that of God. Jesus showed further that his position while on earth, and therefore that of his disciples, was not one of fighting against the "Caesar" governments but, rather, one of compliance with their regulations that did not conflict with God's law. Pilate himself recognized this fact when he said: "I find no fault in him." (Joh 18:38) The apostles followed Jesus' example.—Ac 4:19, 20; 5:29; 24:16; 25:10, 11, 18, 19, 25; 26:31, 32; see KINGDOM; SUPERIOR AUTHORITIES.

GOVERNOR.

Governors in Bible times generally had military and judicial powers and were responsible to see that the tribute, tax, or revenue to the king or superior ruler was paid by the jurisdictional districts or provinces that the governors ruled. (Lu 2:1, 2) Many of them put a heavy load on the people to supply food for themselves and their large body of attendants. —Ne 5:15-18.

King Solomon appointed governors over the districts of Israel. They are mentioned at 1 Kings 10:15 and may be the same as the 12 deputies of 1 Kings 4:7-19, whose duty it was to provide food for the king and his household, each for one month in the year.

Practically all the major powers of Bible times are spoken of as having rulers of the order of governors, either as local native rulers or as governors controlling occupied territories. (Syrian, 1Ki 20:24; Assyrian, Eze 23:5, 6, 12, 23; Babylonian, Jer 51:57; Persian, Ezr 8:36, Ne 2:7, 9; Arabian, 2Co 11:32; Roman, Lu 3:1) Joseph was a governor in a large sense, over all Egypt, subject only to the king. (Ge 41:40, 41; Ac 7:9, 10) Rabshakeh, an officer of King Sennacherib of Assyria, taunted Hezekiah about Jerusalem's weakness, saying that it would be unable to turn back even one of Sennacherib's lesser governors. But Rabshakeh failed to take into account the overwhelming force of Jehovah on Hezekiah's side.—Isa 36:4, 9; 37:36.

Nebuchadnezzar appointed Gedaliah to govern the remaining Israelites left in the land of Judah after carrying many of the people into exile in 607 B.C.E. Gedaliah was assassinated about two months later. (2Ki 25:8-12, 22, 25) As the 70-year period of exile neared its end, King Cyrus of Persia appointed Sheshbazzar (likely Zerubbabel) as governor of the Jews who returned to Jerusalem in 537 B.C.E. (Ezr 5:14; Hag 1:1, 14; 2:2, 21) Under King Artaxerxes of Persia, Nehemiah was made governor when he went back to rebuild the wall of Jerusalem, in 455 B.C.E.—Ne 5:14; see TIRSHATHA.

Under Roman rule, Judea was an imperial province; the governors there were directly responsible to the emperor for their actions. Pilate was the fifth of the line of governors of Judea. (Mt 27:2; Lu 3:1) Felix and Festus were Judea's 11th and 12th governors (if we do not count Publius Petronius and his successor Marsus, who, appointed as governors of Syria, at the same time managed the affairs of the Jews). (Ac 23:24-26; 24:27) These Roman governors had the power to order capital punishment, as we see in the case of Jesus, who was judged by Pilate.—Mt 27:11-14; Joh 19:10.

Governors of the nations in general were referred to by Jesus when he told his followers that they would be brought before such men to give a witness. Christians should not fear such rulers, though powerful, nor be worried about what to say when giving testimony before them. (Mt 10:18-20, 26) All such governors are part of the superior authorities to which Christians owe relative, not total, subjection. (Ro 13:1-7; Tit 3:1; 1Pe 2:13, 14; Ac 4:19, 20; 5:29; Mt 22:21) It was with the respect due the office of governor that Paul addressed Festus, before whom he was on trial, saying: "Your Excellency Festus." (Ac 26:25) However, in contrast with the apostles, who rendered respect and honor first to Jehovah, who governs all, the nation of Israel sank to the point where they accorded earthly governors more respect than they gave Jehovah. This circumstance was used by Jehovah in strong reproof to the nation through his prophet Malachi.—Mal 1:6-8; see SUPERIOR AUTHORITIES.

Matthew, quoting from Micah 5:2, shows that Bethlehem, though very insignificant as far as governing power in Judah was concerned, would become significant by reason of the fact that the greatest of governors would come from this city to shepherd Jehovah's people Israel. This prophecy finds its fulfillment in Christ Jesus the Great Governor under his Father, Jehovah God.—Mt 2:6.

GOVERNOR'S PALACE.

The Greek term prai·to′ri·on (from Lat., praetorium) designates the official residence of the Roman governors. In the governor's palace at Jerusalem, Pontius Pilate questioned Christ Jesus, and in its courtyard, Roman soldiers mocked him. (Mr 15:16; Joh 18:28, 33; 19:9) Some have identified the governor's palace with the Tower of Antonia, but others suggest that it was probably the palace built by Herod the Great. The following reasons have been presented in support of the latter view: (1) According to the first-century Jewish philosopher Philo (*The Embassy to Gaius,* 306, XXXIX), Herod's palace was called "the house of the governors," and it was there that Governor Pilate hung shields in honor of Tiberius Caesar. (2) The Jewish historian Josephus reports that the procurator Gessius Florus took up his quarters there. (*The Jewish War,* II, 301 [xiv, 8]) (3) Herod's palace in Caesarea served as the governor's palace in that city.—Ac 23:33-35.

The palace of Herod at Jerusalem was situated in the NW corner of the upper city, that is, of the southern part of the city. According to Josephus' description, it was surrounded by a 30-cubit-high (13 m; 44 ft) wall equipped with evenly spaced towers. Within the walls there were porticoes, courts, and groves of trees. The rooms were luxuriously furnished with gold, silver, and marble objects. There were bedchambers for a hundred guests.—*Jewish Antiquities,* XV, 318 (ix, 3); *The Jewish War,* V, 173-182 (iv, 4).

GOZAN (Go'zan). A name seemingly applied both to a place and to a river. At 2 Kings 19:12 and Isaiah 37:12, Gozan appears to embrace an area larger than a city, for its inhabitants are listed among the "nations" conquered by the Assyrians. Many scholars, evidently basing their conclusions on word similarities, believe that Gozan may correspond to Gauzanitis, a district of Mesopotamia referred to by Ptolemy and considered to be the same as the "Guzana" mentioned in Assyrian records. Ancient Guzana is commonly linked with modern Tell Halaf on the upper Khabur River, about 590 km (367 mi) ENE of the Sea of Galilee.

At 2 Kings 17:6 and 18:11 some translations read "Habor, the river of Gozan" (*AS, RS*), instead of "Habor at [or, by] the river Gozan" (*NW, Yg*), thus also making Gozan a place in these texts. But the rendering "Habor, the river of Gozan," does not harmonize with 1 Chronicles 5:26. In this passage Habor is listed between Halah and Hara; and Hara, not Habor, is listed before Gozan. This indicates that Habor and "the river of Gozan" (*AS*) are not synonymous. Hence, those who identify Gozan as a place throughout are obliged to reject the Chronicles reference. However, since the Hebrew allows for a consistent rendering of "river Gozan" in all three texts, there is reason to believe that it was in the vicinity of a river called Gozan that the king of Assyria settled some of the exiled Israelites of the northern kingdom. The Qezel Owzan of NW Iran has been suggested as a possible identification of "the river Gozan." It rises in the mountains SE of Lake Urmia (in what used to be the land of the Medes) and finally empties as the Sefid Rud or White River (the name applied to its lower course) into the SW section of the Caspian Sea. According to another view, the Gozan is a river of Mesopotamia.

GRAFTING. The process of joining the scion (shoot, twig) of a tree known to produce good fruit with the stock of another tree bearing inferior fruit so as to bring about a permanent union. Often grafting is done with a view to combining the advantageous characteristics of both scion (its good fruit) and stock (its vigor and strength). After grafted-in branches are established, though deriving nourishment from a different stock, they will produce the same kind of fruit as the tree from which they were taken.

The apostle Paul, writing to Christians in Rome, compared non-Jewish Christians to the branches of a wild olive that were grafted into the garden olive to replace natural branches that had been broken off. Such a procedure in grafting would, of course, be "contrary to nature." The natural branches corresponded to the Jews who, because of their lack of faith, lost out on their opportunity to be among those in line for Messiah's heavenly Kingdom. The grafting of wild olive branches, or non-Jewish Christians, into the garden olive to replace "natural branches" was no reason for those Gentiles to have lofty ideas, for only by faith could they maintain their position. Also, the grafting of branches from the wild olive into the garden olive illustrates the permanent union that has been effected between Jews and Gentiles as fellow members of "the Israel of God."—Ro 11:17-24; Ga 3:28; 6:16; compare Joh 15:1-6; see OLIVE.

GRAIN OFFERING. See OFFERINGS.

GRANARY. See STOREHOUSE.

GRANDPARENTS. Parents of one's father and/or one's mother. The term "grandparents," as well as "grandfather" and "grandmother," is rarely found in Bible translations. "Grandmother" at 1 Kings 15:10, 13 is translated from the same word as "mother" and is appropriately so rendered because Maacah was Asa's grandmother, not his mother. (1Ki 15:1, 2, 8) It appears that Maacah continued as the queen mother during Asa's reign until she was removed for her idolatry. (1Ki 15:13) Correspondingly, "father" on occasion indicated a grandfather or forefather. (Ge 28:13; 2Sa 9:7) Grandparents are also identified by such expressions as "the father of your mother" and "mother's father."—Ge 28:2; Jg 9:1.

"Children or grandchildren," the apostle says, should "keep paying a due compensation to their parents and grandparents [Gr., *pro·go'nois*]." (1Ti 5:4) Another form of the same word (*pro·go'non*) is rendered "forefathers" at 2 Timothy 1:3. Timothy's grandmother (Gr., *mam'me*) Lois is commended for having 'faith without hypocrisy,' and she apparently assisted in the development of Timothy's faith and spiritual growth.—2Ti 1:5; 3:14, 15.

GRAPE.   See Vine; Wine and Strong Drink.

GRASS.   Any of the plants belonging to the family Gramineae, the grasses, which include the cereal grains, the plants of meadow and pasture, sugarcane, and bamboo. However, even today, in common usage, this scientific classification is not strictly adhered to, and it is therefore unlikely that the ancient Hebrews differentiated between the true grasses and grasslike herbs.

Brought into existence during the third creative day (Ge 1:11-13), the grasses have served as a direct as well as an indirect source of food for man and the animals. Also, along with other plants, when in the sunlight they play a significant role in purifying the air, taking in sufficient carbon dioxide and giving off enough oxygen to balance the normal needs of humans and animals. The extensive root system of grasses serves as a deterrent to soil erosion. Appropriately, grass is referred to as one of Jehovah's provisions, as are also the sunlight and the rain that are so vital for grass to flourish.—Ps 104:14; 147:8; Zec 10:1; 2Sa 23:3, 4; Job 38:25-27; Mt 5:45.

The Israelites were very familiar with the withering of grass under the sun's intense heat during the dry season. So the transitoriness of man's life is fittingly likened to that of grass and is contrasted with the everlastingness of Jehovah and that of his "word" or "saying." (Ps 90:4-6; 103:15-17; Isa 40:6-8; 51:12; 1Pe 1:24, 25) Evildoers also are compared to grass that quickly withers. (Ps 37:1, 2) The haters of Zion as well as people about to be subjugated by military conquest are likened to shallow-rooted grass growing on earthen roofs, grass that withers even before being pulled up or that is scorched in the wake of the east wind.—Ps 129:5, 6; 2Ki 19:25, 26; Isa 37:26, 27.

A restoration prophecy foretold that the bones of God's servants would 'sprout like tender grass,'

that is, be invigorated with fresh strength.—Isa 66:14; compare Isa 58:9-11.

GRASSHOPPER   [Heb., *cha·ghav'*]. There is uncertainty as to the insect or insects designated by the Hebrew term *cha·ghav'*. However, since the fully developed, winged stage of locust (Heb., *'ar·beh'*) is mentioned along with the *cha·ghav'* at Leviticus 11:22 (as being clean for food), *cha·ghav'* may refer to a leaper rather than a flier. —See *NW* ftn.

The designation "grasshopper" is applied to any of numerous leaping insects of the families Acrididae (including the migratory locusts and the grasshoppers having short feelers) and Tettigoniidae (including the grasshoppers with long feelers).

Aside from its being listed as an insect clean for food and the references to its destructiveness to vegetation (2Ch 7:13), the grasshopper appears in an illustrative setting in Scripture. The unfaithful Israelite spies reported that in size they were as grasshoppers in comparison with the inhabitants of Canaan. (Nu 13:33) Men, especially those who oppose God, are as grasshoppers from Jehovah's standpoint and in view of his greatness. (Isa 40:22) In portraying the difficulties of old age, the congregator employed the figure of a grasshopper dragging itself along, thereby depicting the aged person as bent and stiff in figure, with arms thrust somewhat backward.—Ec 12:5; see Locust.

GRAVE.   A place of interment. Though today the term "grave" is generally understood to apply to an excavation in the earth for use as a place of burial, a common method of burial among the Hebrews and other Oriental peoples was by use of a natural cave or a rock-cut tomb, or vault. The Hebrew word *qe'ver* is the common word used to designate a burial place, a grave, or a graveyard. (Ge 23:7-9; Jer 8:1; 26:23) The related word *qevu·rah'* similarly may refer to an earthen grave or to a tomb excavated in rock.—Ge 35:20; 1Sa 10:2.

In Greek the common word for grave is *ta'phos* (Mt 28:1), and the verb form (*tha'pto*) means "bury." (Mt 8:21, 22) The word *mne'ma* (Lu 23: 53) refers to a tomb and the word *mne·mei'on* (Lu 23:55) refers to a memorial tomb.

Since these Hebrew and Greek words refer to an individual burial place or grave site, they are often used in the plural as referring to many such graves. They are, therefore, distinct from the Hebrew *she'ohl'* and its Greek equivalent *hai'des,* which refer to the common grave of mankind, or gravedom, and hence are always used in the singular. For this reason many modern translations have not followed the practice of the *King James Version,* in which *she'ohl'* and *hai'des* are alternately rendered by the words "hell," "grave," and "pit," but have instead simply transliterated them into English.—See HADES; SHEOL.

Nevertheless, since one's entry into Sheol is represented as taking place through burial in an individual grave or at a burial site, words pertaining to such places of interment are used as *parallel* though not *equivalent* terms with Sheol. —Job 17:1, 13-16; 21:13, 32, 33; Ps 88:3-12.

At Romans 3:13 the apostle Paul quotes Psalm 5:9, likening the throat of wicked and deceitful men to "an opened grave." As an opened grave is to be filled with the dead and with corruption, their throat opens for speech that is deadly and corrupt.—Compare Mt 15:18-20.

It was a custom to whitewash graves so that persons would not accidentally touch them and become unclean. The tombs near Jerusalem were whitewashed one month before Passover to prevent a person from becoming unclean at this special period of worship by accidentally touching a grave. Jesus used this custom as a basis for an illustration of the scribes and Pharisees as appearing righteous outwardly but inside being "full of hypocrisy and lawlessness."—Mt 23: 27, 28.

Although the grave is likened to a pit from which man rightly desires to be delivered, Job draws attention to the despair of those suffering persons who, lacking a clear hope or understanding of their Creator's purposes, seek death and "exult because they find a burial place." (Job 3:21, 22) Such attitude contrasts sharply with that of men who devoted their lives to their Creator's service and confidently embraced the promise of a resurrection.—Ps 16:9-11; Ac 24:15; Php 1:21-26; 2Ti 4:6-8; Heb 11:17-19; see BURIAL, BURIAL PLACES.

GRAVEL. Small stones or pebbles. In the Scriptures, "gravel" is used in an illustrative sense. The injurious aftereffects of gaining bread by falsehood are compared to having one's mouth filled with gravel. (Pr 20:17) Also, the severe treatment Jehovah meted out to unfaithful Jerusalem by means of the Babylonians is likened to 'breaking teeth with gravel.' (La 3:16) According to traditional Jewish thought, this was actually experienced by those taken into Babylonian exile. The tradition claims that they were forced to bake bread in pits dug in the ground and that, as a result, the bread contained grit.

GRAY-HEADEDNESS. Lightness of hair color caused by the reduction of pigment granules in the hair as a result of changes in body chemistry. There are infrequent cases of premature graying, but usually it accompanies older age. It is in this latter association that the Hebrew verb *siv* (grow gray) and more frequently the Hebrew noun *seh·vah'* (gray hairs, grayheadedness, old age) occur in the Bible. (Ru 4:15; 1Sa 12:2; 1Ki 2:6, 9; Job 15:10; Ps 71:18) Abraham, Gideon, and David lived to "a good old age [*seh·vah'*]."—Ge 15:15; 25:8; Jg 8:32; 1Ch 29:28.

The Bible recognizes both the beauty of youth and the splendor of old age. "The beauty of young men is their power, and the splendor of old men is their gray-headedness." (Pr 20:29) Especially is the latter true if such ones are found worshiping and serving Jehovah. "Grayheadedness is a crown of beauty when it is found in the way of righteousness." (Pr 16:31) "Those who are planted in the house of Jehovah, . . . they will still keep on thriving during grayheadedness." (Ps 92:13, 14) They will not be abandoned by their God. (Isa 46:4) Jehovah's law is: "Before gray hair you should rise up, and you must show consideration for the person of an old man."—Le 19:32.

Gray-headedness has nothing to do with the sex of individuals; neither is the natural color of the hair, whether blond, brunet, or red, a factor. Graying has long been recognized as beyond the power of man or medical science to prevent or remedy. This is a point Jesus Christ made after he said we should not swear by our heads.—Mt 5:36.

Hair dyes are not of modern discovery, for they were used by the Greeks and Romans. According to Josephus, it was reported that Herod the Great dyed his graying hair to hide his old age.—*Jewish Antiquities,* XVI, 233 (viii, 1).

GREAT CROWD. An expression that, in itself, is quite common in the Christian Greek Scriptures. "Great crowd(s)" is sometimes used with regard to the large groups of persons who heard Jesus Christ's public teaching. (Mt 14:14; 19:2; 20:29) After the vision of the destruction of the symbolic Babylon the Great, the apostle John heard "what was as a loud voice of a great crowd in heaven." (Re 19:1) At Revelation 7:9, however, "a great crowd" is mentioned whose identification has particularly been a matter of keen interest.

In this chapter, the apostle John first refers to the sealing of 144,000 slaves of God "out of every tribe of the sons of Israel." (Re 7:2-8) After this, he saw in a vision "a great crowd" out of all nations, tribes, peoples, and tongues. These ascribe their salvation to God and to the Lamb as they stand before God's throne. They have come out of "the great tribulation," they serve God in his temple, and he spreads his tent over them. All their hunger and thirst are to be ended and every tear is to be wiped from their eyes as his Son (the Lamb; Joh 1:29) guides them to the waters of life.—Re 7:9-17.

Popular Views. Various views have been advanced as to the significance and identification of this "great crowd." Many commentators view the 144,000 sealed ones, first mentioned, as members of "spiritual Israel" and believe that they symbolize the Christian congregation *while on earth.* They feel that the "great crowd" represents that same Christian congregation *in heaven,* after the individuals have died in faith and have been resurrected. Others hold that the 144,000 are literally from "every tribe of the sons of Israel" (Re 7:4), that is, *fleshly Jews who become Christians,* and they consider the "great crowd" to represent all the *Gentile* Christians. A consideration of Revelation chapter 7 and other related texts, however, reveals serious inconsistencies in these views, at the same time pointing to a different conclusion.

To hold that the 144,000 sealed ones are the members of the Christian congregation while on earth whereas the "great crowd" are the resurrected Christians in heaven does not harmonize with the other mention of the 144,000, in Revelation chapter 14. There the 144,000 are stationed with the Lamb on "Mount Zion." At Hebrews 12:18-24 the apostle Paul contrasts the experience of the Israelites at the earthly Mount Sinai with that of the Christians who have "approached a Mount Zion and a city of the living God, *heavenly* Jerusalem, and myriads of angels, in general assembly, and the congregation of the firstborn who have been enrolled in the heavens." Obviously, then, although Revelation 14:3 says that the 144,000 have been "bought from the earth," the context depicts them as being, not on earth, but in heaven with the heavenly Lamb, Christ Jesus. (Re 14:3, 4) This renders invalid the view that the 144,000 represent the Christian congregation while on earth in contrast with their being the "great crowd" in heaven.

Additionally, the way in which the apostle John introduces his vision of the "great crowd" indicates a clear distinction of identity between them and the 144,000 sealed ones. He states: "After these things [the account of the 144,000 sealed ones] I saw, and, look! a great crowd, which no man was able to number." (Re 7:9) He thus presents the "great crowd" as a separate entity and makes a definite contrast between the specific number of the 144,000 and the unnumbered "great crowd." They are also distinguished by their being, not "of the sons of Israel," but out of all nations, tribes, peoples, and tongues. They are not seen standing 'with the Lamb' as are the 144,000, at Revelation 14:1, but are "before the Lamb." These several factors all argue that the "great crowd" is separate and distinct from the 144,000 sealed ones.

On the other hand, the view that here Christians of Jewish stock are being distinguished from Gentile Christians runs counter to the apostle Paul's inspired statement that fleshly distinctions are of no consideration in the Christian congregation, its members being all one in union with Christ Jesus. (Ro 10:12; Ga 3:28) Jehovah, having 'fully reconciled both peoples [Jews and non-Jews] to himself in one body' through Christ, could hardly be expected to make a division between the two groups now by separating fleshly Jews from Gentiles in the vision given to John. (Eph 2:11-21; Ac 15:7-9) This is particularly evident when the divine principle stated by Paul is taken into account. The apostle wrote: "He is not a Jew who is one on the outside, nor is circumcision that which is on the outside upon the flesh. But he is a Jew who is one on the inside, and his circumcision is that of the heart by spirit." (Ro 2:28, 29) Why, too, would there be no mention of any 'sealing' of the Gentile Christians in this divine vision? And why would not the Gentile Christians be able to master the new song sung by the 144,000? (Re 14:3) It thus seems clear that the 144,000 sealed ones are of spiritual Israel, not fleshly Israel—hence include both Jewish and Gentile Christians.—Ga 6:16.

Their Identification. The key to the identification of the "great crowd" is found within the description of them in Revelation chapter 7 and in obviously parallel passages. Revelation 7:15-17 speaks of God as 'spreading his tent over them,' of their being guided to "fountains of waters of life," and of God's wiping "every tear from their eyes." At Revelation 21:2-4 we find parallel expressions: 'God's tent being with mankind,' his 'wiping every tear from their eyes,' and 'death being no more.' The vision there presented is concerning persons not in heaven, from where the 'New Jerusalem comes down,' but on earth, among mankind.

This poses the question: If the "great crowd" are persons who gain salvation and remain on earth, how could they be said to be 'standing before God's throne and before the Lamb'? (Re 7:9) The position of 'standing' is sometimes used in the Bible to indicate the holding of a favored or approved position in the eyes of the one in whose presence the individual or group stands. (Ps 1:5; 5:5; Pr 22:29, *AT*; Lu 1:19) In fact, in the previous chapter of Revelation, "the kings of the earth and the top-ranking ones and the military commanders and the rich and the strong ones and every slave and every free person" are depicted as seeking to hide themselves "from the face of the One seated on the throne and from the wrath of the Lamb, because the great day of their wrath has come, and who is able to stand?" (Re 6:15-17; compare Lu 21:36.) It thus appears that the "great crowd" is formed of those persons who have been preserved during that time of wrath and who have been able to "stand" as approved by God and the Lamb.

The Lamb's guiding them to "fountains of waters" of life" finds a parallel at Revelation 22:17, which says: "The spirit and the bride keep on saying: 'Come!' And let anyone hearing say: 'Come!' and let anyone thirsting come; let anyone that wishes take life's water free." The "bride" is clearly identified in the Scriptures as the anointed Christian congregation, espoused to the heavenly Bridegroom, Christ Jesus. (Eph 5:25-27; 2Co 11:2; Re 19:7-9; 21:9-11) The invitation to "take life's water free" presented by the heavenly "bride" class is obviously open to an unlimited number of persons, "anyone that wishes." Likewise unnumbered are the "great crowd," the vision at Revelation 7:9 thereby harmonizing with that at Revelation 22:17.

The sum of the evidence, therefore, points to the "great crowd" as representing all those persons who are not of the heavenly "bride" class, or 144,000 sealed ones, but who stand approved at the time of the "great tribulation" and are preserved alive on earth.—See CONGREGATION (The Christian Congregation of God); EARTH (Purpose); HEAVEN.

GREAT SEA. That immense body of water separating Europe and Africa, with Asia to its east. While the Hebrews called it the Great Sea, today it is commonly called by its Latin-based name, *Mediterranean,* meaning "in the Middle of the Land," for it is practically landlocked. This circumstance, plus the fact that hot winds off the Sahara Desert blow over it, results in a proportionately higher than usual evaporation rate and this, in turn, gives the water a higher specific gravity. That is why at the Strait of Gibraltar the lighter water of the Atlantic flows in near the surface and the heavier Mediterranean water empties out near the bottom. Ocean shipping may pass in and out of this "inland" sea only through narrow gateways—through the Strait of Gibraltar to the W, through the Dardanelles and Bosporus to the NE, and since the past century, through the Suez Canal to the SE.

It is not amiss today to call the Mediterranean the Great Sea, as ancient peoples did from the time of Moses onward, for it certainly measures up to all this name implies. (Nu 34:6, 7) Apart from its various arms that are also seas, the Mediterranean is about 3,540 km (2,200 mi) long, over 970 km (600 mi) wide at its greatest breadth, and it covers an area of about 2,510,-000 sq km (969,100 sq mi). Its deepest point is 5,093 m (16,709 ft).

The Italian and Greek peninsulas that jut down from the N create the Tyrrhenian, Ionian, Adriatic, and Aegean Seas, thus adding to the irregular shape and greatly increasing the length of the coastline. About middistance E and W, the sea narrows down to a width of about 150 km (90 mi) between Sicily and North Africa, and there the water is also comparatively shallow.

Ezekiel's prophecy speaks of "very many" fish in the Great Sea. (Eze 47:10) Fine coral and an abundance of sponge are found in these waters, in addition to more than 400 varieties of fish.

Bible writers not only used the name "Great Sea" (Jos 1:4; 9:1, 2; 15:12, 47; 23:4; Eze 47:15, 19, 20; 48:28) but they also referred to it by other comprehensive terms. To them this body of water was "the western sea," forming as it did the western boundary of their God-given land. (De 11:24; 34:1, 2) From the location of Jerusalem it was viewed as "the western sea" in contrast with "the eastern sea," that is, the Dead Sea. (Joe 2:20; Zec 14:8) Or it was called "the sea of the Philistines" (Ex 23:31) or simply "the Sea." —Nu 34:5.

From time immemorial, Phoenicians and other bold seafaring people traversed the Great Sea, discovered a number of its islands, and carried on trade between many of its port cities. The Bible mentions such islands as Arvad, Cauda, Chios, Cos, Crete, Cyprus, Malta, Patmos, Rhodes,

Samos, and Samothrace. Also, some of the coastal cities and sites on these islands and along the continental shores of the eastern section of the Great Sea are listed in the Bible, namely: Acco (Ptolemais), Achzib, Adramyttium, Alexandria, Amphipolis, Ashkelon, Attalia, Cnidus, Dor, Fair Havens, Gebal, Lasea, Patara, Phoenix, Puteoli, Rhegium, Salamis, Salmone, and Syracuse.

Jesus Christ visited the seaport regions of Tyre and Sidon (Mr 7:24, 31); Peter was in Joppa and Caesarea (Ac 10:5, 6, 24); Paul was in Paphos, Troas, Neapolis, Cenchreae, Ephesus, Assos, Mitylene, and Miletus (Ac 13:13; 16:11; 18:18, 19; 20:14, 15). The Great Sea is noted for its fierce storms that have resulted in numerous shipwrecks and much loss of life. Among the more fortunate were those who survived with Paul. —Ac 27:14, 15, 39-44.

GREAT TRIBULATION. See TRIBULATION.

GREECE, GREEKS. These names come from *Grai·koi′*, the name of a tribe in NW Greece. The Italians applied the name (Lat., *Graeci*) to the inhabitants of Greece as a whole. Eventually even Aristotle in his writings used the term in a similar way.

Another earlier name, Ionians, appears from the eighth century B.C.E. onward in Assyrian cuneiform records, as well as in Persian and Egyptian accounts. This name comes from that of Javan (Heb., *Ya·wan′*), son of Japheth and grandson of Noah. Javan was the Japhetic ancestor of the early peoples of Greece and the surrounding islands, as well as, evidently, of the early inhabitants of Cyprus, parts of southern Italy, Sicily, and Spain.—Ge 10:1, 2, 4, 5; 1Ch 1:4, 5, 7; see ELISHAH; JAVAN; KITTIM.

While "Ionian" now applies geographically to the sea between southern Italy and southern Greece, including the chain of islands along the W coast of Greece, the name once had a broader application more in harmony with the Hebrew Scriptures' use of "Javan." The prophet Isaiah, in the eighth century B.C.E., spoke of the time when the returned exiles of Judah would be sent to distant nations, including "Tubal and Javan, the faraway islands."—Isa 66:19.

In the Christian Greek Scriptures, the land is called *Hel·las′* ("Greece," Ac 20:2), and the people, *Hel′le·nes*. The Greeks themselves had used these names beginning several centuries before the Common Era and continue to do so. "Hellas" may have some connection with "Elishah," one of Javan's sons. (Ge 10:4) The name Achaia was also applied to central and southern Greece following the Roman conquest of 146 B.C.E.

The Land and Its Features. Greece occupied the southern part of the mountainous Balkan Peninsula and the islands near it, in the Ionian Sea on the W and in the Aegean Sea on the E. To the S lay the Mediterranean. The northern boundary is indeterminate, particularly so since in the earlier periods the Javanites of Greece were not consolidated into a particular nation. However, in later times "Greece" is understood to have reached to the regions of Illyria (corresponding roughly to western Yugoslavia and Albania) and Macedonia. In actuality, the Macedonians may have been of the same basic stock as those later called Greeks.

The land then, as now, was both rugged and rocky, with rough limestone mountains occupying some three fourths of the terrain. The mountain slopes were heavily wooded. The scarcity of fertile plains and valleys and the rockiness of the soil sharply reduced the agricultural capacities of the land. The mild climate, however, favored the growth of olives and grapes. Other products were barley, wheat, apples, figs, and pomegranates. Herds of sheep and goats found pasturage on the uncultivated areas. There were some mineral deposits—silver, zinc, copper, lead—and the mountains supplied abundant quantities of fine marble. The prophecy of Ezekiel (27:1-3, 13) includes Javan among those trading with Tyre and lists "articles of copper" among the products traded.

Maritime advantages. Travel by land was slow and difficult because of the mountains. Animal-drawn carts easily bogged down in the winter seasons. So the sea was the best avenue of Greek transportation and communication. The long, jagged coastline, deeply indented by bays and inlets, supplied abundant harbors and shelters for ships. Because of the several penetrating gulfs, few points within the ancient boundaries were more than 60 km (40 mi) distant from the sea. The southern part of mainland Greece, called the Peloponnesus, came close to being an island. Only a narrow neck of land, crossing between the Saronic Gulf and the Gulf of Corinth, connects the Peloponnesus with central Greece. (Today the Corinth Canal cuts through the narrow isthmus for about 6 km [3.5 mi] without locks, making the separation complete.)

The Javanites of Greece early became a seafaring people. The heel of Italy's "boot" lay only about 160 km (100 mi) across the Strait of Otranto from NW Greece. To the E, archipelagoes (chains of islands formed by submerged mountains with their tops rising above the water's surface) served as giant stepping-stones across the Aegean Sea to Asia Minor. At the NE corner of the Aegean a narrow passage, the Hellespont (also called the Dardanelles), led into the Sea of Marmara and then through the Bosporus strait into the Black Sea. Also, by sailing along the southern coast of Asia Minor, Greek ships early traveled to the shores of Syria and Palestine. A ship could cover as much as 100 km (60 mi) during a daylight period. The delivering of Paul's letters to the Thessalonians in Macedonia, likely written in Corinth, might therefore have taken a week or more, depending on weather conditions (and the number of ports stopped at along the way).

Greek influence and settlements were by no means limited to mainland Greece. The numerous islands studding the Ionian and Aegean Seas were considered as much a part of Greece as the mainland. Southern Italy and Sicily were included in what was called Great Hellas or, in Latin, *Graecia Magna*. The historical evidence indicates that the Javanites of Greece maintained contact and trade relations with those of Tarshish (Spain), far surpassing the Phoenicians in this regard. Similar association is found between the Greeks and the Javanites of Cyprus.

Origin of the Greek Tribes.   Modern historians offer various ideas on the origin of the Greek tribes and about their entry into the area. The popular view of successive "invasions" by northern tribes is largely based on Greek myths and archaeological conjecture. Actually, secular history concerning Greece does not begin until about the eighth century B.C.E. (the first Olympiad being celebrated in 776 B.C.E.), and a connected record is possible only from the fifth century B.C.E. onward. This was many centuries after the Flood and hence long after the dispersal of families because of the confusion of mankind's language at Babel. (Ge 11:1-9) During these many centuries other groups perhaps infiltrated the original stock of Javan and his sons, but for the period prior to the first millennium B.C.E., there are only theories of doubtful value.

Principal Greek tribes.   Among the principal tribes found in Greece were the *Achaeans* of Thessaly, the central Peloponnesus, and Boeotia; the *Aetolians* in W central Greece, the N part of the Peloponnesus, Elis, Aetolia, and the nearby islands; the *Dorians* of the eastern Peloponnesus,

the southern islands of the Aegean, and the SW part of Asia Minor; and the *Ionians* of Attica, the island of Euboea, the islands of the middle Aegean, and the W coasts of Asia Minor. However, any relationship between these tribes and the Macedonians in the earlier periods is uncertain.

Patriarchal Tradition and the City-States. The Greek-speaking tribes were quite independent, and even within the tribes the city-states that developed were likewise quite independent. Geographic features contributed to this. Many Greeks lived on islands, but on the mainland the majority lived in small valleys ringed by mountains. As to their early social structure, *The Encyclopedia Americana* offers this view: "The ultimate social unit was the patriarchal household. . . . The patriarchal tradition was strongly entrenched in Greek culture: the active citizens of a city-state (*polis*) were adult males only. The patriarchal family was enclosed within a series of concentric kinship circles—the clan (*genos*), the phratry [or group of families], the tribe." (1956, Vol. XIII, p. 377) This harmonizes quite well with the post-Flood patriarchal arrangement described in the Bible book of Genesis.

The pattern in Greece was somewhat similar to that of Canaan, where the various tribes (descended from Canaan) formed petty kingdoms, often based around a particular city. The Greek city-state was called a *po'lis.* This term seems to have applied originally to an acropolis, or fortified height, around which settlements developed. Later, it came to designate the entire area and the citizens forming the city-state. Most Greek city-states were small, usually having no more than 10,000 citizens (plus women, slaves, and children). At its height, in the fifth century B.C.E., Athens is said to have had only about 43,000 male citizens. Sparta had only about 5,000. Like the Canaanite petty kingdoms, the Greek city-states sometimes leagued together and also fought among themselves. The country remained politically fragmented until the time of Philip (II) of Macedon.

Democratic Experiments.   While knowledge of the governing methods of most Greek city-states is obscure, only those of Athens and Sparta being fairly well known, their governments evidently came to differ considerably from those of Canaan, Mesopotamia, or Egypt. At least during what may be termed secularly as the historical period, in place of kings the Greek city-states had magistrates, councils, and an assembly (*ek·kle·si'a*) of citizens. Athens experimented with direct democratic rule (the word "democracy" coming from Greek *de'mos,* meaning "people," and *kra'tos,* meaning "rule"). In this arrangement the entire body of citizens formed the legislature, speaking and voting in the assembly. The "citizens," however, were a minority, since women, foreign-born residents, and slaves did not hold citizenship rights. Slaves are thought to have formed as much as one third the population of many city-states, and doubtless their slave labor made possible the free time needed by the "citizens" to participate in the political assembly. It may be noted that the earliest reference to Greece in the Hebrew Scriptures, about the ninth century B.C.E., speaks of Judeans being sold by Tyre, Sidon, and Philistia as slaves to "the sons of the Greeks [literally, "Javanites" or "Ionians"]."—Joe 3:4-6.

Manufacturing and Trade. In addition to the principal activity of agriculture, the Greeks produced and exported many manufactured products. Greek vases became famous throughout the Mediterranean area; also important were articles of silver and gold and woolen fabrics. There were numerous small, independent shops owned by craftsmen, who had the help of a few laborers, slaves or freemen. In the Greek city of Corinth, the apostle Paul joined Aquila and Priscilla in the tentmaking trade, likely using fabric made from goat's hair, which was in good supply in Greece. (Ac 18:1-4) Corinth became a major commercial center because of its strategic position near the Gulf of Corinth and the Saronic Gulf. Other principal commercial cities were Athens and Aegina.

Grecian Culture and Arts. Greek education was restricted to males, and its principal aim was to produce "good citizens." But each city-state had its own concept of a good citizen. In Sparta education was almost entirely physical (contrast Paul's counsel to Timothy at 1Ti 4:8), young boys being taken from their parents at the age of 7 and assigned to barracks until the age of 30. In Athens the emphasis eventually came to be more strongly on literature, mathematics, and the arts. A trusted slave, called a *pai·da·go·gos',* accompanied the child to school, where training began at the age of six. (Note Paul's comparison of the Mosaic Law with a *pai·da·go·gos'* at Ga 3:23-25; see TUTOR.) Poetry was very popular in Athens, and pupils were required to memorize many poems. Though Paul's education was in Cilician Tarsus, he made use of a brief poetic quotation to

get his message across in Athens. (Ac 17:22, 28) Dramas, both tragedies and comedies, became popular.

Philosophy was assigned great importance in Athens and, in time, throughout Greece. Among the major philosophical groups were the *Sophists,* who held that truth was a matter of individual opinion; this view (similar to that of the Hindus) was opposed by such famous Greek philosophers as Socrates, his pupil Plato, and Plato's pupil Aristotle. Other philosophies dealt with the ultimate source of happiness. The *Stoics* held that happiness consists of living in accord with reason and that this alone matters. The *Epicureans* believed that pleasure is the true source of happiness. (Contrast Paul's statement to the Corinthians at 1Co 15:32.) Philosophers of these latter two schools were among those who engaged Paul in conversation at Athens, leading to his being brought to the Areopagus for a hearing. (Ac 17:18, 19) Another school of philosophy was that of the *Skeptics* who held that, in effect, nothing really mattered in life.

As a people, at least in later periods, the Greeks displayed an inquisitive trait and were characteristically fond of discussion and conversation about things that were novel. (Ac 17:21) They endeavored to solve some of the major questions of life and of the universe by process of human logic (and speculation). Thus, the Greeks considered themselves the intelligentsia of the ancient world. Paul's first letter to the Corinthians put such human wisdom and intellectualism in its proper place, when, among other things, he said: "If anyone among you thinks he is wise in this system of things, let him become a fool, that he may become wise. . . . 'Jehovah knows that the reasonings of the wise men are futile.'" (1Co 1:17-31; 2:4-13; 3:18-20) Despite all their philosophical debates and investigations, their writings show they found no genuine basis for hope. As Professors J. R. S. Sterrett and Samuel Angus point out: "No literature contains more pathetic laments over the sorrows of life, the passing of love, the deceitfulness of hope, and the ruthlessness of death."—*Funk and Wagnalls New Standard Bible Dictionary,* 1936, p. 313.

Greek Religion. The earliest knowledge of Greek religion comes through the epic poetry of Homer. Two epic poems, the *Iliad* and the *Odyssey,* are presumed by historians to have been written by him. The oldest papyrus portions of these poems are believed to date from sometime before 150 B.C.E. As George G. A. Murray, a professor of Greek, says of these early texts, they "differ 'wildly' from our vulgate," that is, from the text that has been popularly accepted in recent centuries. (*Encyclopædia Britannica*, 1942, Vol. 11, p. 689) Thus, unlike the Bible, there was no preservation of the integrity of Homeric texts, but they existed in an extremely fluid state, as Professor Murray demonstrates. The Homeric poems dealt with warrior heroes and gods who were very much like men.

There is evidence of Babylonian influence on Greek religion. One ancient Greek fable is nearly a literal translation of an Akkadian original.

Another poet, Hesiod, probably of the eighth century B.C.E., is credited with systematizing the multitude of Greek myths and legends. Together with the Homeric poems, Hesiod's *Theogony* formed the principal sacred writings, or theology, of the Greeks.

In considering the Greek myths, it is of interest to see how the Bible sheds light on their possible or even probable origin. As Genesis 6:1-13 shows, prior to the Flood, angelic sons of God came to earth, evidently materializing in human form, and cohabited with attractive women. They produced offspring who were called

Zeus. The Greek gods had human form and often were viewed as grossly immoral

Nephilim, or Fellers, that is, "those who cause others to fall down." The result of this unnatural union of spirit creatures with humans, and the hybrid race it produced, was an earth filled with immorality and violence. (Compare Jude 6; 1Pe 3:19, 20; 2Pe 2:4, 5; see NEPHILIM.) Like others of the post-Flood times, Javan, the progenitor of the Greek people, undoubtedly heard the account of pre-Flood times and circumstances, likely from his father Japheth, a survivor of the Flood. Note, now, what the writings attributed to Homer and Hesiod reveal.

The numerous gods and goddesses they described had human form and great beauty, though often being gigantic and superhuman. They ate, drank, slept, had sexual intercourse among themselves or even with humans, lived as families, quarreled and fought, seduced and raped. Though supposedly holy and immortal, they were capable of any type of deceit and crime. They could move among mankind either visibly or invisibly. Later Greek writers and philosophers sought to purge the accounts of Homer and Hesiod of some of the more vile acts attributed to the gods.

These accounts may reflect, although in greatly expanded, embellished, and distorted form, the authentic account of pre-Flood conditions found in Genesis. A further remarkable correspondency is that, in addition to the principal gods, the Greek legends describe demigods or heroes who were of both divine and human descent. These demigods were of superhuman strength but were mortal (Hercules being the only one of them granted the privilege of attaining immortality). The demigods thus bear a marked similarity to the Nephilim in the Genesis account.

Noting this basic correspondency, Orientalist E. A. Speiser would trace the theme of the Greek myths back to Mesopotamia. (*The World History of the Jewish People*, 1964, Vol. 1, p. 260) Mesopotamia was the location of Babylon and also the focus from which mankind spread after the confusion of man's language.—Ge 11:1-9.

The principal Greek gods were said to reside on the heights of Mount Olympus (2,920 m [9,570 ft] high), located S of the town of Beroea. (Paul was quite near Olympus' slopes when ministering to the Beroeans on his second missionary tour; Ac 17:10.) Among these Olympic gods were *Zeus* (called Jupiter by the Romans; Ac 28:11), the god of the sky; *Hera* (Roman Juno), Zeus' wife; *Ge* or *Gaea*, the goddess of the earth, also called the

Great Mother; *Apollo,* a solar god, a god of sudden death, shooting his deadly arrows from afar; *Artemis* (Roman Diana), the goddess of the hunt; the worship of another Artemis as a fertility goddess was prominent at Ephesus (Ac 19:23-28, 34, 35); *Ares* (Roman Mars), the god of war; *Hermes* (Roman Mercury), the god of travelers, of commerce, and of eloquence, the messenger of the gods (in Lystra, Asia Minor, the people called Barnabas "Zeus, but Paul Hermes, since he was the one taking the lead in speaking"; Ac 14:12); *Aphrodite* (Roman Venus), the goddess of fertility and love, considered to be the "sister of the Assyro-Babylonian Ishtar and the Syro-Phoenician Astarte" (*Greek Mythology,* by P. Hamlyn, London, 1963, p. 63); and numerous other gods and goddesses. Actually, each city-state seems to have had its own minor gods, worshiped according to local custom.

Festivals and games. Festivals played an important part in Greek religion. Athletic contests along with dramas, sacrifices, and prayers attracted persons from a wide area, and thus these festivals served as a bond for the politically divided city-states. Among the most prominent of these festivals were the Olympic Games (at Olympia), the Isthmian Games (held near Corinth), the Pythian Games (at Delphi), and the Nemean Games (near Nemea). The celebration of the Olympic Games every four years provided the basis for the Greek Era reckoning, each four-year period being called an Olympiad.—See GAMES.

Oracles, astrology, and shrines. Oracles, mediums through whom the gods supposedly revealed hidden knowledge, had many devotees. The most famous oracles occupied temples at Delos, Delphi, and Dodona. Here, for a price, individuals received answers to questions put to the oracle. The answers were usually ambiguous, needing interpretation by the priests. At Philippi in Macedonia, the girl with the art of prediction (from whom Paul caused a demon to withdraw) was acting as an oracle and 'furnishing her masters with much gain.' (Ac 16:16-19) Professor G. Ernest Wright traces modern astrology back through the Greeks to the diviners of Babylon. (*Biblical Archaeology,* 1963, p. 37) Healing shrines were also popular.

Philosophical teaching of immortality. Because the Grecian philosophers interested themselves in the ultimate questions of life, their views also served to shape the religious views of the people. Socrates, of the fifth century B.C.E.,

taught the immortality of the human soul. In *Phaedo* (64C, 105E), Plato quotes Socrates' conversation with two of his colleagues: "'Do we think there is such a thing as death? . . . We believe, do we not, that death is the separation of the soul from the body, and that the state of being dead is the state in which the body is separated from the soul and exists alone by itself and the soul is separated from the body and exists alone by itself? Is death anything other than this?' 'No, it is this,' he said. 'And the soul does not admit death?' 'No.'" Socrates continues, "'Then the soul is immortal.' 'Yes.'" Contrast this with Ezekiel 18:4 and Ecclesiastes 9:5, 10.

Temples and idols. In honor of the gods, magnificent temples were built, and to represent their gods, beautifully executed statues of marble and bronze were made. The ruins of some of the most famous of these temples are to be found on the Acropolis of Athens and include the Parthenon and the Erechtheum, along with the Propylaea. It was in this same city that Paul spoke to an audience, commented on the notable fear of the deities manifest in Athens, and plainly told his listeners that the Creator of heaven and earth "does not dwell in handmade temples" and that, as progeny of God, they should not imagine the Creator to be "like gold or silver or stone, like something sculptured by the art and contrivance of man."—Ac 17:22-29.

Period of the Persian Wars. The rise of the Medo-Persian Empire under Cyrus (who conquered Babylon in 539 B.C.E.) posed a threat to Greece. Cyrus had already conquered Asia Minor, including Greek colonies there. In Cyrus' third year (evidently as ruler of Babylon), Jehovah's angelic messenger informed Daniel that the fourth king of Persia would "rouse up everything against the kingdom of Greece." (Da 10:1; 11:1, 2) The third Persian king (Darius Hystaspis) put down a revolt of Greek colonies in 499 B.C.E. and prepared to invade Greece. The invading Persian fleet was wrecked by a storm in 492 B.C.E. Then, in 490, a large Persian force swept into Greece but was defeated by a small army of Athenians on the Plains of Marathon, NE of Athens. Darius' son Xerxes determined to avenge this defeat. As the foretold 'fourth king,' he roused up the entire empire to form a massive military force and in 480 B.C.E. crossed the Hellespont.

Though certain principal city-states of Greece now showed rare unity in their fight to stop the invasion, the Persian troops marched through north and central Greece, reached Athens, and burned its fortress height, the Acropolis. On the sea, however, the Athenians and supporting Greeks outmaneuvered and wrecked the Persian fleet (with its Phoenician and other allies) at Salamis. They followed up this victory with another defeat of the Persians on land at Plataea and yet another at Mycale, on the W coast of Asia Minor, after which the Persian forces abandoned Greece.

Athenian Supremacy. Athens now gained leadership in Greece by virtue of its strong navy. The period that followed, down to about 431 B.C.E., was the "Golden Age" of Athens, when the most renowned works of art and architecture were produced. Athens headed the Delian league of several Greek cities and islands. Because of resentment of Athenian preeminence by the Peloponnesian League, headed by Sparta, the Peloponnesian War broke out. It ran from 431 to 404 B.C.E., the Athenians finally suffering complete defeat at the hands of the Spartans. The rigid rule of Sparta lasted until about 371 B.C.E., and then Thebes gained superiority. Grecian affairs entered a period of political decay, though Athens continued to be the cultural and philosophical center of the Mediterranean. Finally, the emerging power of Macedonia under Philip II conquered Greece in 338 B.C.E., and Greece was unified under Macedonian control.

Greece Under Alexander the Great. Back in the sixth century B.C.E., Daniel had received a prophetic vision foretelling the overthrow of the Medo-Persian Empire by Greece. Philip's son Alexander had been educated by Aristotle and, after Philip's assassination, became the champion of the Greek-speaking peoples. In 334 B.C.E., Alexander set out to avenge Persian attacks on Greek cities on the W coast of Asia Minor. His lightning conquest of not only all Asia Minor but also Syria, Palestine, Egypt, and the entire Medo-Persian Empire as far as India fulfilled the prophetic picture at Daniel 8:5-7, 20, 21. (Compare Da 7:6.) By taking over control of Judah in 332 B.C.E., Greece now became the fifth successive world power insofar as the nation of Israel was concerned—Egypt, Assyria, Babylon, and Medo-Persia having been the previous four. By 328 B.C.E., Alexander's conquest was complete, and now the remaining portion of Daniel's vision saw fulfillment. Alexander died in Babylon in 323 B.C.E., and as foretold, his empire was subsequently split up into four dominions, none equaling the original empire in strength.—Da 8:8, 21, 22; 11:3, 4; see MAPS, Vol. 2, p. 334; ALEXANDER No. 1.

Before his death, however, Alexander had introduced Greek culture and the Greek language into all of his vast realm. Greek colonies were set up in many conquered lands. The city of Alexandria was built in Egypt and came to rival Athens as a center of learning. Thus was initiated the Hellenizing (or Grecizing) of much of the Mediterranean and Middle Eastern regions. Common Greek, or Koine, became the lingua franca, spoken by people of many nationalities. It was the language that Jewish scholars in Alexandria used in producing their translation of the Hebrew Scriptures, the *Septuagint.* Later, the Christian Greek Scriptures were recorded in Koine, and the international popularity of this language contributed to the rapid spread of the Christian good news throughout the Mediterranean area.—See GREEK.

Effect of Hellenization on the Jews. When Greece was divided among Alexander's generals, Judah became a border state between the Ptolemaic regime of Egypt and the Seleucid dynasty of Syria. First controlled by Egypt, the land was seized by the Seleucids in 198 B.C.E. In an effort to unite Judah with Syria in a Hellenic culture, Greek religion, language, literature, and attire were all promoted in Judah.

Greek colonies were founded throughout Jewish territory, including those at Samaria (thereafter called Sebaste), Acco (Ptolemais), and Bethshean (Scythopolis), as well as some set up on previously unsettled sites E of the Jordan River. (See DECAPOLIS.) A gymnasium was established in Jerusalem and attracted Jewish youths. Since Greek games were linked with Greek religion, the gymnasium served to corrupt Jewish adherence to Scriptural principles. Even the priesthood suffered considerable infiltration by Hellenism during this period. By this means, beliefs previously foreign to the Jews gradually began to take root; these included the pagan teaching of the immortality of the human soul and the idea of an underworld place of torment after death.

Antiochus Epiphanes' desecration of the temple at Jerusalem (168 B.C.E.) by introducing the worship of Zeus there marked the extreme point of Hellenization of the Jews and led to the Maccabean Wars.

In Alexandria, Egypt, where the Jewish sector occupied a considerable portion of the city, Hellenizing influence was also strong. (See ALEXANDRIA.) Some Alexandrian Jews allowed the popularity of Grecian philosophy to sway them. Certain Jewish writers felt obligated to try to accommodate Jewish beliefs to what was then the "modern trend." They tried to demonstrate that the current Grecian philosophical ideas were actually preceded by similar ideas in the Hebrew Scriptures or were even derived from them.

Roman Rule Over the Greek States. Macedonia and Greece (one of the four sections into which Alexander's empire had been divided) fell to the Romans in 197 B.C.E. The next year the Roman general proclaimed the "freedom" of all Greek cities. This meant no tribute was to be exacted, but Rome expected full cooperation with its wishes. Anti-Roman sentiment steadily developed. Macedonia warred against the Romans but was again defeated in 167 B.C.E. and about 20 years later became a Roman province. Led by Corinth, the Achaean League rebelled in 146 B.C.E., and Rome's armies marched into southern Greece and destroyed Corinth. The province of "Achaia" was formed and by 27 B.C.E. came to include all of southern and central Greece.—Ac 19:21; Ro 15:26; see ACHAIA.

The period of Roman rule was one of political and economic decline for Greece. Only Grecian culture continued strong and was widely adopted by the conquering Romans. They imported Greek statues and literature enthusiastically. Even entire temples were dismantled and shipped to Italy. Many of Rome's young men were educated in Athens and other Greek seats of learning. Greece, on the other hand, turned its thoughts inward and dwelt on its past, developing an antiquarian attitude.

"Hellenes" in the First Century C.E. At the time of Jesus Christ's ministry and that of his apostles, natives of Greece or those of Greek origin were still known as Hel'le·nes (singular, Hel'len). The Greeks referred to non-Greeks as "barbarians," meaning simply foreigners or those speaking a foreign tongue. The apostle Paul likewise contrasts "Greeks" and "Barbarians" at Romans 1:14.—See BARBARIAN.

In some instances Paul, however, also uses the term Hel'le·nes in a broader sense. Particularly as contrasted with the Jews, he refers to the Hel'le·nes, or Greeks, as representative of all the non-Jewish peoples. (Ro 1:16; 2:6, 9, 10; 3:9; 10:12; 1Co 10:32; 12:13) Thus at 1 Corinthians chapter 1, Paul evidently parallels "the Greeks" (vs 22) with "the nations" (vs 23). This was doubtless due to the prominence and preeminence of the Greek language and culture throughout the entire Roman Empire. In a sense, the Greeks 'headed the list' of non-Jewish peoples. This does not

mean that Paul or the other writers of the Christian Greek Scriptures used Hel'le·nes in a very loose sense so that by Hel'len they meant nothing more than a Gentile, as some commentators imply. Showing that Hel'le·nes was used to identify a distinct people, Paul, at Colossians 3:11, refers to the "Greek" as distinct from the "foreigner [bar'ba·ros]" and the "Scythian."

In harmony with the foregoing, Greek scholar Hans Windisch comments: "The sense of 'Gentile' [for the word Hel'len] cannot be proved, . . . either from Hellenistic Judaism or the NT." (Theological Dictionary of the New Testament, edited by G. Kittel; translator and editor, G. Bromiley, 1971, Vol. II, p. 516) Yet, he does present some evidence that Greek writers at times applied the term Hel'len to persons of other races who adopted the Greek language and culture—persons who were "Hellenized." So, in considering the Biblical references to Hel'le·nes, or Greeks, in many cases allowance must be made for the possibility at least that they were not such by birth or descent.

The "Grecian" woman of Syrophoenician nationality whose daughter Jesus healed (Mr 7: 26-30) was likely of Greek descent to be distinguished in this way. The "Greeks among those that came up to worship" at the Passover and who requested an interview with Jesus were evidently Greek proselytes to the Jewish religion. (Joh 12:20; note Jesus' prophetic statement in verse 32 as to 'drawing men of all sorts to himself.') Timothy's father and Titus are each called Hel'len. (Ac 16:1, 3; Ga 2:3) This may mean that they were of Greek descent. However, in view of the claimed tendency of some Greek writers to employ Hel'le·nes as referring to non-Greeks who were Greek speaking and of Greek culture, and in view of Paul's use of the term in the representative sense considered earlier, allowance can be made for the possibility that these persons were Greeks in this latter sense. Nevertheless, the fact that the Grecian woman was in Syrophoenicia, or that Timothy's father resided in Lystra of Asia Minor, or that Titus seems to have resided in Antioch of Syria, does not prove that they were not ethnically Greeks or descendants of such —for Greek colonists and immigrants were to be found in all these regions.

When Jesus told a group that he was going to 'go to him that sent him' and that "where I am [going] you cannot come," the Jews said among themselves: "Where does this man intend going, so that we shall not find him? He does not intend to go to the Jews dispersed among the Greeks and teach the Greeks, does he?" (Joh 7:32-36) By "the Jews dispersed among the Greeks" they evidently meant just that—not the Jews settled in Babylon but those scattered throughout the faraway Greek cities and lands to the west. The accounts of Paul's missionary travels reveal the remarkable number of Jewish immigrants there were in such Greek regions.

People of Greek ancestry are certainly meant at Acts 17:12 and 18:4, where events in the Greek cities of Beroea and Corinth are under discussion. This may also be true of "the Greeks" in Macedonian Thessalonica (Ac 17:4); in Ephesus on the western coast of Asia Minor, long colonized by Greeks and once the capital of Ionia (Ac 19:10, 17; 20:21); and even in Iconium in central Asia Minor (Ac 14:1). While the combination "Jews and Greeks" appearing in some of these texts might indicate that, like Paul, Luke there used "Greeks" as representative of non-Jewish peoples in general, actually only Iconium lay geographically outside the primary Grecian sphere.

Hellenists. In the book of Acts another term appears: *Hel·le·ni·stai'* (singular, *Hel·le·ni·stes'*). This term is not found either in Greek or in Hellenistic Jewish literature; hence, the meaning is not completely certain. However, most lexicographers believe it designates "Greek-speaking Jews" at Acts 6:1 and 9:29. In the first of these two texts, these *Hel·le·ni·stai'* are contrasted with the "Hebrew-speaking Jews" (*E·brai'oi* [Westcott and Hort Greek text]). On the day of Pentecost, 33 C.E., Jews and proselytes from many lands were present. That many such Greek-speaking persons came to the city is evidenced by the "Theodotus Inscription" found on the hill of Ophel in Jerusalem. Written in Greek, it states: "Theodotus, son of Vetenus, priest and archisynagogos [synagogue president], grandson of an archisynagogos, built the synagogue for the reading of the Law and for the teaching of the commandments and the guest house and the rooms and supplies of water as an inn for those who are in need when coming from abroad, which synagogue his fathers and the elders and Simonides founded." (*The Interpreter's Dictionary of the Bible*, edited by G. A. Buttrick, 1962, Vol. 4, p. 480) Some would connect this inscription with the "Synagogue of the Freedmen," members of which were among those responsible for the martyrdom of Stephen.—Ac 6:9; see FREEDMAN, FREEMAN.

The form of *Hel·le·ni·stai'* that appears in Acts 11:20, however, with reference to certain residents of Antioch, Syria, may refer to "Greek-speaking people" generally, rather than Greek-speaking Jews. This seems to be shown by the indication that, until the arrival of Christians of Cyrene and Cyprus, the preaching of the word in Antioch had been restricted to "Jews only." (Ac 11:19) So the *Hel·le·ni·stai'* there mentioned may mean persons of various nationalities who had been Hellenized, using the Greek language (and perhaps living according to Greek custom).—See ANTIOCH No. 1; CYRENE, CYRENIAN.

The apostle Paul visited Macedonia and Greece on both his second and third missionary tours. (Ac 16:11–18:11; 20:1-6) He spent time ministering in the important Macedonian cities of Philippi, Thessalonica, and Beroea and in the major Achaian cities of Athens and Corinth. (Ac 16:11, 12; 17:1-4, 10-12, 15; 18:1, 8) He devoted a year and a half to the ministry in Corinth on his second tour (Ac 18:11), during which time he wrote the two letters to the Thessalonians and possibly the one to the Galatians. On his third tour he wrote his letter to the Romans from Corinth. After his first imprisonment in Rome, Paul evidently again visited Macedonia, between 61 and 64 C.E., probably writing his first letter to Timothy and possibly his letter to Titus from there.

Through the early centuries of the Common Era, Greek culture continued to influence the Roman Empire, and Greece preserved its intellectual achievements, Athens possessing one of the chief universities in the Roman Empire. Constantine endeavored to fuse Christianity with certain pagan practices and teachings, and his own course set the stage for such fusion religion to become the official religion of the empire. This made Greece a part of Christendom.

Today Greece controls a land area of 131,-957 sq km (50,949 sq mi) and has a population of 9,967,000 (1985 estimate).

GREED. Inordinate or rapacious desire. The Hebrew verb *cha·madh'* and the Greek verb *e·pi·thy·me'o* both mean "desire." (Ps 68:16; Mt 13:17) Sometimes these words may, according to the context, convey a bad, selfish desire. (Ex 20:17; Ro 7:7) The Greek word *ple·o·ne·xi'a* literally means "a desire to have more" and is used in the Bible to denote "greediness" and "covetousness." —Eph 4:19; 5:3, ftn; Col 3:5.

Greed can manifest itself in love of money, desire for power or gain, or voraciousness for food and drink, sex, or other material things. The Scriptures warn Christians against this degrading trait and command that they should avoid association with anyone calling himself a Christian "brother" who practices greediness. (1Co 5:9-11) Greedy persons are classed with fornicators, idolaters, adulterers, men kept for unnatural purposes, thieves, drunkards, revilers, and extortioners, and indeed, greedy persons generally practice some of these things. If an individual does not turn away from his greediness, he will not inherit the Kingdom of God.—1Co 6:9, 10.

In condemnation of foolish talking and obscene jesting, the apostle Paul commands that fornication and uncleanness or greediness "not even be mentioned among you." This may mean that not only should such practices not exist among Christians but also that they should not even be a topic of their conversation for the purpose of gratifying the flesh.—Eph 5:3; compare Php 4:8.

Becomes Manifest in Actions. Greediness will manifest itself in some overt act that will reveal the individual's wrong and inordinate desire. The Bible writer James tells us that wrong desire, when it has become fertile, gives birth to sin. (Jas 1:14, 15) The greedy person can therefore be detected by his actions. The apostle Paul states that being a greedy person means being an idolater. (Eph 5:5) In his greedy desire such a one makes the thing desired his god, putting it above the service and worship of the Creator. —Ro 1:24, 25.

Alienates From God. Christians have come out from a world filled with all forms of bad conduct. Paul points out that not only are such things carried on but also that they are pursued with *greediness*, greedily sought after. Persons practicing these things are "alienated from the life that belongs to God." Those becoming Christians find that Christ their Exemplar was free of such things, and hence they must make their minds over, putting on the new Christian personality. (Eph 4:17-24; Ro 12:2) At the same time they are living among greedy persons of the world and must be careful to maintain cleanness as illuminators in the world.—1Co 5:9, 10; Php 2:14, 15.

Greediness for dishonest gain would disqualify a man from being a ministerial servant in the Christian congregation. (1Ti 3:8) Since such men are to stand before the congregation as examples, it follows that the principle would apply to all members of the congregation. (1Pe 5:2, 3) Especially is this seen to be true in the light of Paul's statement that greedy persons will not inherit the Kingdom.—Eph 5:5.

Covetousness. When greediness has as its object that which belongs to another, it becomes covetousness. In the Christian Greek Scriptures the same Greek words are used for "greediness" and "covetousness." Jesus Christ stated that covetousness defiles a man (Mr 7:20-23) and warned against it. He followed this warning with the illustration of the covetous rich man who, at death, no longer had benefit from or control of his wealth and was also in the lamentable state of not being "rich toward God." (Lu 12:15-21) Christians are told that their life is "hidden with the Christ" and that they must therefore deaden their body members as respects covetousness, hurtful desire, and all uncleannesses.—Col 3:3, 5.

GREEK. A language belonging to the Indo-European family of languages. (Hebrew is from the Semitic, another family of languages.) Greek is the language in which the Christian Scriptures were originally written (aside from Matthew's Gospel, which was written first in Hebrew) and in which also appeared the first complete translation of the Hebrew Scriptures, namely, the Greek *Septuagint*. It is an inflectional language, achieving variety in expression by means of stems, prefixes, and endings.

Koine. From about 300 B.C.E. to about 500 C.E. was the age of Koine, or common Greek, a mixture of differing Greek dialects of which Attic was the most influential. Koine became the international language. It had a very distinct advantage over the other languages of the day, in that it was almost universally known. Koine means common language, or dialect common to all. How widespread the use of Koine was can be seen from the fact that the decrees of the imperial governors and of the Roman senate were translated into Koine to be distributed throughout the Roman Empire. Accordingly, the charge posted above Jesus Christ's head at the time of his impalement was written not only in official Latin and in Hebrew but also in Greek (Koine). —Mt 27:37; Joh 19:19, 20.

Regarding the use of Greek in the land of Israel, one scholar comments: "Although the main body of the Jewish people rejected Hellenism and its ways, intercourse with the Greek peoples and the use of the Greek language was by no means eschewed. . . . The Palestinian teachers regarded the Greek translation of the Scriptures with favor, as an instrument for carrying the truth to the Gentiles." (*Hellenism*, by

N. Bentwich, 1919, p. 115) Of course, the primary reason for the Greek *Septuagint* was to benefit the Jews, especially those of the Dispersion, who no longer spoke the pure Hebrew but were familiar with Greek. Old Hebrew terms involving Jewish worship came to be replaced by terms Greek in origin. The word *sy·na·go·ge'*, meaning "a meeting together," is an example of the adoption of Greek words by the Jews.

Koine used by inspired Christian writers. Since the writers of the inspired Christian Scriptures were concerned with getting their message across with understanding to all the people, it was not the classical Greek but the Koine that they used. All these writers themselves were Jews. Though they were Semitic, they were not interested in the spread of Semitism, but in the truth of pure Christianity, and by means of the Greek language they could reach more people. They could better carry out their commission to "make disciples of people of all the nations." (Mt 28:19, 20) Also, the Koine was a fine instrument by which they could well express the subtle intricacies of thought that they desired to present.

The inspired Christian writers gave to Koine power, dignity, and warmth by reason of their exalted message. Greek words took on a richer, fuller, and more spiritual meaning in the contexts of the inspired Scriptures.

Alphabet. All present-day European alphabets stem either directly or indirectly from the Greek alphabet. However, the Greeks did not invent their alphabet; they borrowed it from the Semites. This is apparent from the fact that the Greek alphabetic letters (of about the seventh century B.C.E.) resembled the Hebrew characters (of about the eighth century B.C.E.). They also had the same general order, with a few exceptions. Additionally, the pronunciation of the names of some of the letters is very similar; for example: *al'pha* (Greek) and *'a'leph* (Hebrew); *be'ta* (Greek) and *behth* (Hebrew); *del'ta* (Greek) and *da'leth* (Hebrew); and many others. Koine had 24 letters. In adapting the Semitic alphabet to the Greek language, the Greeks made a valuable addition to it in that they took the surplus letters for which they had no corresponding consonants (*'a'leph, he', chehth, 'a'yin, waw,* and *yohdh*) and employed these to represent the vowel sounds *a, e* (short), *e* (long), *o, y,* and *i.*

Vocabulary. The Greek vocabulary is quite abundant and exact. The Greek writer has at his disposal sufficient words to enable him to make fine differentiation and to convey just the shade of meaning that he desires. To illustrate, the Greek makes a distinction between ordinary knowledge, *gno'sis* (1Ti 6:20), and intensified knowledge, *e·pi'gno·sis* (1Ti 2:4), and between *al'los* (Joh 14:16), meaning "another" of the same kind, and *he'te·ros,* meaning "another" of a different kind. (Ga 1:6) Many expressions in other languages have incorporated Greek words as well as basic roots that comprise Greek words, resulting in language that is more precise and specific in expression.

Nouns. Nouns are declined according to case, gender, and number. Related words, such as pronouns and adjectives, are declined to agree with their antecedents or that which they modify.

Case. Generally Koine is shown to have had five cases. (Some scholars enlarge this to eight.) In English there is usually no change in form for nouns except in the possessive case and in number. (Pronouns, however, are subject to more changes.) But in Koine each case usually requires a different form or ending, making the language much more complicated than English in this respect.

The Article. In English there are both a definite article ("the") and indefinite articles ("a," "an"). Koine has but a single article ὁ (*ho*), which is in some respects the equivalent of the definite article "the" in English. Whereas the English definite article "the" is never inflected, the Greek article is inflected as to case, gender, and number, just as the nouns are.

The Greek article is used not only to set off substantives, as with English, but also with infinitives, adjectives, adverbs, phrases, clauses, and even whole sentences. The use of the article with an adjective is found in the Greek at John 10:11, where the literal rendering would be: "I am the shepherd the fine [one]." This is stronger than merely "I am the fine shepherd." It is like putting "fine" in italics.

An example of the article being applied to an entire clause in Greek is found at Romans 8:26, where the phrase "what we should pray for as we need to" is preceded by the article in the neuter gender. Literally, the phrase would read *"the* for what we should pray." (*Int*) To get the thought across in English, it is helpful to add the words "problem of." The definite article focuses matters in such a way that the problem is brought together as a distinct issue. Thus, the rendering "For the [problem of] what we should pray for as we need to we do not know" (*NW*) gives more accurately the flavor of the writer's thought.

Verbs. Greek verbs are built from verbal roots primarily by means of stems and endings, or affixes and suffixes. They are conjugated according to voice, mood, tense, person, and number. In Greek they constitute a more difficult study than nouns. Better understanding of the Koine in recent years, particularly with regard to verbs, has enabled translators to bring out the real flavor and meaning of the Christian Greek Scriptures better than was possible in the older versions. Some of the more interesting features regarding Greek verbs and their influence on Bible understanding are considered in the following paragraphs.

Voice. English has only two voices for its verbs, namely, the active and passive voices, but Greek has also a distinctive "middle voice." In this voice, the subject participates in the results of the action or, at times, produces the action. The middle voice stresses the interest of the agent in the action of the verb.

The middle voice was also used with an intensive force. It served a purpose similar to italics in English. Paul said, after being told that bonds and tribulations awaited him when he got to Jerusalem: "Nevertheless, I do not make my soul of any account as dear to me, if only I may finish my course and the ministry that I received of the Lord Jesus." (Ac 20:22-24) Here the verb for "make," *poi·ou'mai,* is in the middle voice. Paul is saying, not that he does not value his life, but that the fulfilling of his ministry is far more important. That is *his* conclusion, regardless of what others may think.

The middle voice is used at Philippians 1:27: "Only behave [or, "carry on as citizens"] in a manner worthy of the good news about the Christ." The verb *po·li·teu'o·mai* is, in this text, in the middle voice, *po·li·teu'e·sthe,* "carry on as citizens," that is, *participate* in the activities of citizens, sharing in declaring the good news. Roman citizens generally took an active part in the affairs of the State, for Roman citizenship was highly prized, particularly in cities whose inhabitants had been given citizenship by Rome, as was the case in Philippi. So Paul is here telling Christians that they must not be inactive as merely being in the position of Christians, but they must participate in Christian activity. This is in harmony with his later words to them: "As for us, our citizenship exists in the heavens." —Php 3:20.

Tenses. Another important and distinctive characteristic of Greek, contributing to its exactness, is its use of verb tenses. Verbs and their tenses involve two elements: *kind* of action (the more important) and *time* of action (of less importance). There are three principal points of viewing action in the Greek language, each with modifying characteristics: (1) action as continuous ("to be doing"), represented basically in the *present* tense, the primary force of which is progressive action or that which habitually or successively recurs; (2) action as perfected or completed ("to have done"), the principal tense here being the *perfect;* (3) action as punctiliar, or momentary ("to do"), represented in the *aorist.* There are, of course, other tenses, such as the imperfect, the past perfect, and the future.

To illustrate the difference in the Greek tenses: At 1 John 2:1, the apostle John says: "If any man sin, we have an advocate with the Father" (*KJ*). The Greek verb for "sin" is in the aorist tense, hence the time of the action is punctiliar, or momentary. The aorist tense here points to one act of sinning, whereas the present infinitive would denote the condition of being a sinner or the continuous or progressive action in sinning. So John does not speak of someone carrying on a practice of sinning, but of one who does "commit a sin." (Compare Mt 4:9, where the aorist indicates that the Devil did not ask Jesus to do constant or continuous worship to him, but "an *act* of worship.")

But, if 1 John 3:6, 9 is read without taking into account the fact that the verb there is in the present tense, John seems to contradict his words above noted. The *King James Version* reads: "Whosoever abideth in him sinneth not," and, "Whosoever is born of God doth not commit sin." These renderings fail to carry over into English the continuous action denoted by the present tense of the Greek verbs used. Some modern translations, instead of saying here, "sinneth not" and "doth not commit sin," take note of the continuous action and render the verbs accordingly: "does not *practice* sin," "does not *carry on* sin" (*NW*); "*practices* sin," "*makes a practice* of sinning" (*CB*); "does not *habitually* sin," "does not *practice* sin" (*Ph*); "does not *continue* to sin" (*TEV*). Jesus commanded his followers at Matthew 6:33: "*Keep on,* then, seeking first the kingdom," indicating continuous effort, rather than merely "seek ye first the kingdom" (*KJ*).

In prohibitions, the present and aorist tenses

are likewise distinctly different. In the present tense a prohibition means more than not to do a thing. It means to *stop* doing it. Jesus Christ, en route to Golgotha, did not merely tell the women following him, "Do not weep," but, rather, since they were already weeping, he said: *"Stop weeping* for me." (Lu 23:28) Likewise to those selling doves in the temple, Jesus said: *"Stop making* the house of my Father a house of merchandise!" (Joh 2:16) In the Sermon on the Mount he said: *"Stop being anxious"* about what you will eat, drink, or wear. (Mt 6:25) On the other hand, in the aorist a prohibition was a command against doing something at any given time or moment. Jesus is shown as telling his hearers: "So, *never be anxious* [that is, do not be anxious at any moment] about the next day." (Mt 6:34) Here the aorist is used in order to indicate that the disciples should not be anxious at any time.

Another example of the need to take into consideration the Greek tense in translating is found at Hebrews 11:17. Some translations ignore the special significance in the tense of the verb. With reference to Abraham, the *King James Version* says: "He that had received the promises offered up his only begotten son." The Greek verb here translated "offered up" is in the imperfect tense, which may carry the thought that the action was intended or attempted, but not realized or accomplished. Hence, in harmony with what actually happened, the Greek verb is more appropriately rendered "attempted to offer up." Likewise, in Luke 1:59, speaking of the time of circumcision of the son of Zechariah and Elizabeth, the imperfect tense used indicates that instead of the rendering, *"They called* him Zacharias, after the name of his father" (*KJ*), the passage should read *"They were going to call* [the young child] by the name of its father, Zechariah" (*NW*). This is in harmony with what actually took place, namely, that he was given the name John, according to the angel Gabriel's instructions.—Lu 1:13.

Transliteration. This refers to the spelling of Greek words with letters of another alphabet. In most instances it is simply a letter-for-letter substitution, *b* for β, *g* for γ, and so on. This is also true of the Greek vowels, *a* for α, *e* for ε, *e* for η, *i* for ι, *o* for ο, *y* for υ, and *o* for ω.

Diphthongs. The above general rule of letter-for-letter substitution also applies to most diphthongs: *ai* for αι, *ei* for ει, *oi* for οι. The Greek letter *y'psi·lon* (υ) is an exception in the following instances: αυ is *au*, not *ay;* ευ is *eu*, not *ey;* ου is *ou*, not *oy;* υι is *ui*, not *yi;* ηυ is *eu*, not *ey.*

GREEK ALPHABET

Letter	Name	Transliteration and Pronunciation[1]
A α	Al'pha	a
B β	Be'ta	b
Γ γ	Gam'ma	g, hard, as in begin[2]
Δ δ	Del'ta	d
E ε	E'psi·lon	e, short, as in met
Z ζ	Ze'ta	z
H η	E'ta	e, long, as in they
Θ θ	The'ta	th
I ι	I·o'ta	i as in machine
K κ	Kap'pa	k
Λ λ	Lam'bda	l
M μ	My	m
N ν	Ny	n
Ξ ξ	Xi	x
O ο	O'mi·kron	o, short, as in lot
Π π	Pi	p
P ϱ	Rho	r
Σ σ, ς[3]	Sig'ma	s
T τ	Tau	t
Y υ	Y'psi·lon	y or u,[4] French u or German ü
Φ φ	Phi	ph as in phase
X χ	Khi	kh as in elkhorn
Ψ ψ	Psi	ps as in lips
Ω ω	O·me'ga	o, long, as in note

[1] Pronunciation shown here differs from modern Greek.
[2] Before κ, ξ, χ, or another γ, it is nasal and pronounced like *n* in think.
[3] Used only at the end of a word when *sig'ma* occurs.
[4] *Y'psi·lon* is *u* when it is part of a diphthong.

However, there are occasions when what may at first appear to be a diphthong will have a diaeresis (¨) over the second letter, as, for instance, αϋ, εϋ, οϋ, ηϋ, ωϋ, αϊ, οϊ. The diaeresis over an *i·o'ta* (ϊ) or *y'psi·lon* (ϋ) shows that it does not really form a diphthong with the vowel preceding it. Thus the *y'psi·lon* with a diaeresis is transliterated *y*, not *u*. The above examples would be *ay, ey, oy, ey, oy, ai, oi* respectively.

Some vowels (α, η, ω) have a small *i·o'ta* (ͺ) (called an *i·o'ta subscript*) written beneath them. In transliterating these Greek forms, the *i·o'ta* (or *i*) is placed not below the line, but next to and following the letter under which it appears. Thus ᾳ is *ai*, ῃ is *ei*, and ῳ is *oi*.

Accent marks. There are three types of accents in Greek: the acute (´), the circumflex (^), and the grave (`). In the Greek these appear over the vowel of the syllables they accentuate. However, in transliterations in this publication the accent mark comes at the end of the accented syllable and only one mark is used for all three types of Greek accents. Thus λόγος is marked *lo'gos;* ζῶον would be *zo'on.*

Syllables. As an aid to pronunciation, either a dot or the accent mark is used in transliterations to separate all syllables. A Greek word has as many syllables as it has vowels or diphthongs. Thus λόγος (*lo'gos*) has two vowels and therefore two syllables. The two vowels of a diphthong are in one syllable, not two. The word πνεῦμα (*pneu'ma*) has one diphthong (*eu*) and one other vowel (*a*) and thus has two syllables.

In syllable division the following rules have been observed: (1) When a single consonant occurs in the middle of a word, it is placed with the following vowel in the next syllable. Thus πατήρ would be *pa·ter'*. (2) Sometimes a combination of consonants appears in the middle of a Greek word. If this same combination of consonants can be used to start a Greek word, it may also begin a syllable. For instance, κόσμος would be divided *ko'smos*. The *sm* is kept with the second vowel. This is because many Greek words—like *Smyr'na*—open with those same two consonants. However, when a certain combination of consonants is found in the middle of a word and there is no Greek word beginning with that same combination, they are separated. Thus βύσσος is transliterated herein as *bys'sos*, since *ss* does not start any Greek word.

Breathing marks. A vowel at the beginning of a word requires either a "smooth" breathing mark ('), or a "rough" breathing mark ('). The "smooth" breathing mark (') may be disregarded in transliteration; the "rough" breathing mark (') calls for an *h* to be added at the start of the word. If the first letter is capitalized, these breathing marks occur before the word. In that case, 'I becomes *I*, while 'I is transliterated as *Hi*. When words begin with the small letters, the breathing marks appear over the first or, in the case of most diphthongs, over the second letter. Therefore αἰών becomes *ai·on'*, while ἁγνός is *ha·gnos'* and αἱρέομαι is *hai·re'o·mai*.

Additionally, the Greek letter *rho* (ϱ), transliterated *r*, always requires a "rough" breathing mark (') at the start of a word. So ϱαββεί is *rhab·bei'*.

GREEK SCRIPTURES. See CHRISTIAN GREEK SCRIPTURES; MANUSCRIPTS OF THE BIBLE.

GREEN. See COLORS.

GREENS. See BITTER GREENS.

GREETING. See ATTITUDES AND GESTURES.

GREYHOUND [Heb., *zar·zir' moth·na'yim*]. A very swift, keen-sighted dog, with a pointed muzzle, a slender streamlined body, and long, strong legs. There is considerable uncertainty, though, as to what is designated by the Hebrew expression, which literally means "the [animal] girded in at the hips (loins)." A number of Bible translations use "greyhound" in the main text at Proverbs 30:31, but in footnotes list "war-horse" and "rooster" as alternate renderings. (*AS, NW, Ro*) The reading "rooster" or "cock" (*AT, Dy, JB, Kx, Mo, RS*) has the support of the Greek *Septuagint* and the Latin *Vulgate*. "Greyhound" is an appropriate rendering, however, for it fits the description of an animal that does well with its "pacing." (Pr 30:29) The greyhound has been clocked at a speed of about 64 km/hr (40 mph). Also, the slenderness of the greyhound's lumbar regions, as if the animal were "girded in at the hips," would harmonize with what is considered to be the literal significance of the Hebrew designation.

GRIEF. See MOURNING.

GROUND. See EARTH.

GUARD. In the pre-Christian Scriptures the noun "guard" is drawn, in many instances, from the Hebrew verb *sha·mar'*, meaning "guard; keep; observe; watch." (Ge 3:24; 17:9; 37:11; 1Sa 26:15) The workmen rebuilding Jerusalem's wall under Nehemiah's direction served also as guards at night. (Ne 4:22, 23) Kings had runners accompanying their chariots as guards, as did Absalom and Adonijah when each tried to take the throne of Israel. (2Sa 15:1; 1Ki 1:5) Runners served under King Rehoboam as watchmen at the palace doors and kept guard over valued copper shields. (1Ki 14:27, 28) High Priest Jehoiada used runners at the temple, along with the Carian bodyguard, to protect young King Jehoash and to execute Athaliah.—2Ki 11:4-21; see CARIAN BODYGUARD; RUNNERS.

The Hebrew word *tab·bach'*, translated "cook" at 1 Samuel 9:23, meant, basically, "slaughterer" and gained the meaning "executioner"; it is elsewhere used with reference to the bodyguard of Pharaoh of Egypt and of King Nebuchadnezzar of Babylon. (Ge 37:36; 2Ki 25:8, 11, 20; Da 2:14) The Hebrew word *mish·ma''ath*, meaning, basically, "hearers" and rendered "subjects" in Isaiah 11:14, is used to refer to David's bodyguard (2Sa 23:23; 1Ch 11:25) and to the bodyguard of Saul, over which David had been chief.—1Sa 22:14.

It was the practice in Roman prisons to chain a prisoner to a soldier guard or, for maximum security, to two guards. (Ac 12:4, 6) However, during the apostle Paul's first imprisonment in

Rome, he was accorded the respect of being free from this form of restraint, having only a soldier guard living with him in his own hired house. (Ac 28:16, 30) During his second imprisonment he may have been chained to a guard.

To prevent the people from learning about Jesus' resurrection, the chief priests bribed Roman guards to circulate the lie that Jesus' followers had stolen his body.—Mt 27:62-66; 28:11-15; see SOLDIER.

The Roman Praetorian Guard was formed by Caesar Augustus in 13 B.C.E. to serve as imperial bodyguards. (Php 1:12, 13) Emperor Tiberius had this guard encamped permanently near the walls of Rome and by means of them held in check any unruliness of the people. This attached great importance to the commander of the guard, whose force came to amount to about 10,000 men. In time the Praetorian Guard became so powerful that it was able both to put emperors into office and to dethrone them.

Priests and Levites were organized under captains to guard the temple in Jerusalem.—See CAPTAIN OF THE TEMPLE.

GUARD, GATE OF THE.   See GATE, GATEWAY.

GUDGODAH   (Gud'go·dah). A wilderness encampment of the Israelites; probably the same as Hor-haggidgad. (De 10:6, 7; compare Nu 33:33.) Some, believing the name "Gudgodah" to be preserved in Wadi Khadakhid, suggest that this place may have been located on Wadi Khadakhid, about 65 km (40 mi) NNW of the Gulf of 'Aqaba. But this has been questioned, since the Hebrew consonants of Gudgodah do not actually correspond to those of Khadakhid. Concerning the order in which the Israelite camping sites are listed in Numbers and Deuteronomy, see BENE-JAAKAN.

GUEST.   See HOSPITALITY.

GUILT.   See LEGAL CASE.

GUILT OFFERING.   See OFFERINGS.

GULL   [Heb., sha'chaph]. One of the birds hunting prey or eating carrion that were prohibited as food according to God's law given to the Israelites.—Le 11:13, 16; De 14:12, 15.

Although the *King James Version* renders the Hebrew name of this bird as "cuckow" (cuckoo), this translation has generally been abandoned in favor of sea gull (sometimes called sea mew). (See CUCKOO.) Some lexicographers understand the name to be derived from a root meaning "be thin, slender, or lean," which might describe the gull from the standpoint of its trim appearance and the relative narrowness of the body as compared with the long, pointed wings. Others believe the Hebrew name *sha'chaph* is in imitation of the shrill cry made by this generally noisy bird. The older versions (*LXX, Vg*) also understood it to refer to the seagoing gull. The Hebrew term *sha'chaph* may be understood to be a generic term for a web-footed seabird resembling a gull. This group includes the true gulls, terns, skimmers, and skuas.

Gulls, members of the family Laridae, are generally powerful fliers, and in addition to swimming well, they rest and even sleep on the water. The gull alternately flaps its wings, soars, wheels, and glides downward to pick up food in the form of fish, insects, and practically any kind of offal and garbage (thus serving as a valuable scavenger in ports and harbors). Herring gulls carry mussels or other mollusks up into the air and then drop them on rocks to break them open and make possible the eating of their contents. Despite its avid appetite for carrion, the gull is exceptionally clean in its habits.

Several varieties of gulls, including the herring gull (*Larus argentatus*) and different types of the black-headed gull (*Larus ridibundus*), are found in Palestine along the Mediterranean seacoast and around the Sea of Galilee. Their color is usually white, though the back and upper side of the wings may be a pearl gray. The bill is strong and slightly curved. They usually live in colonies, nesting on cliff ledges or along the shores. Ranging in body size from that of a pigeon up to some 76 cm (30 in) in length, the gull's wingspan may be as much as 1.5 m (5 ft) across. A restless and seemingly tireless bird, the gull is able to continue flying even in stormy gales. Its abundant and overlapping feathers, as many as 6,544 being counted on a single large gull, keep the body warm and dry during sustained periods of rest in the water.

The tern, a member of the family Sternidae, is also abundant on Palestine's shores. It has a leaner body than the gull, is not a carrion eater, and has a forked tail and long tapering wings that are narrower than those of the gulls. Most terns are white, though generally wearing a black or gray cap. Feeding mainly on small fish, the tern hovers about and then darts quickly into the water with its long, straight, slender bill pointed downward to seize its prey. The tern is the greatest long-distance migrator of all birds, the arctic tern (*Sterna paradisaea*) covering as much as 35,400 km (22,000 mi) annually. Some terns, however, prefer the coastal waters of the warmer regions. Their rapid-moving, very graceful flight has earned them the name of swallows of the sea.

Like the falcon and the ibis, the gull was viewed as a sacred bird in ancient Egypt.

GULLOTH-MAIM (Gul'loth-ma'im) [Basins (Bowls) of Waters]. A site requested by Caleb's daughter at the time of her marriage to Othniel. (Jos 15:17-19; Jg 1:13-15) Many versions render *Gul·loth' ma'yim* as "springs of water," while "Upper *Gul·loth'* and Lower *Gul·loth'*" are generally translated 'upper springs and lower springs.' (See *JB, RS, Yg, KJ*.) It may be noted, however, that Caleb's daughter apparently did not simply desire "springs" from her father. She desired "a *field*," according to Joshua 15:18. Thus *Gul·loth' ma'yim* is sometimes rendered "well-watered land." (*Kx;* see also *Dy*.) Some scholars choose to leave it untranslated, simply employing the transliterations "Gullath-maim" (*AT*) or "Gulloth-maim." (*NW*) The exact location of Gulloth-maim is unknown.—See DEBIR No. 2.

GUNI (Gu'ni).

1. The second-named son of Naphtali, included among those of Jacob's household in Egypt. (Ge 46:24, 26; 1Ch 7:13) He founded the family of Gunites in the tribe of Naphtali.—Nu 26:48.

2. Ancestor of a prominent Gadite.—1Ch 5:11, 15.

GUNITES (Gu'nites). A family descended from Guni, a son of Naphtali.—Nu 26:48; Ge 46:24.

GUR. Ahaziah, king of Judah, was riding "on the way up to Gur, which is by Ibleam," when he was struck down at Jehu's orders. (2Ki 9:27) The location of Gur is now unknown.

The wounding of Ahaziah at Gur is not mentioned in the parallel account of his death at 2 Chronicles 22:8, 9, but it appears that the two accounts complement each other and must be combined to gain the full picture of the events. —See AHAZIAH No. 2.

GURBAAL (Gur·ba'al). A place inhabited by Arabs in King Uzziah's time. (2Ch 26:3, 7) Its exact site is unknown.

H

HAAHASHTARI (Ha·a·hash'ta·ri)[The Ahashtarite]. A descendant of Judah; son of Ashhur. —1Ch 4:1, 5, 6.

HABAIAH (Ha·bai'ah) [Jah Has Hidden]. A priest whose descendants returned from exile in Babylon. But as his "sons" were unable to establish their genealogy, they were barred from the priesthood and were not permitted to "eat from the most holy things until a priest stood up with Urim and Thummim."—Ezr 2:1, 2, 61-63; Ne 7:63-65.

HABAKKUK (Ha·bak'kuk) [Ardent Embrace]. Hebrew prophet of Judah and writer of the Bible book bearing his name. (Hab 1:1; 3:1) From the book's closing notation ("To the director on my stringed instruments") and the dirge in chapter 3, it has been inferred that Habakkuk was a Levitical temple musician. But the words following Habakkuk 3:19 do not make that certain, and dirges were also taken up by persons other than Levites. (2Sa 1:17, 18) While there are various traditions about Habakkuk, these are unreliable,

and the Scriptures themselves furnish no information concerning the prophet's parentage, tribe, circumstances in life, or his death. Evidence in the book of Habakkuk seems to indicate that he prophesied early in the reign of Jehoiakim, possibly before Nebuchadnezzar defeated the Egyptian army at Carchemish in 625 B.C.E.

HABAKKUK, BOOK OF. A book of the Hebrew Scriptures in eighth place among the so-called minor prophets in the Hebrew and *Septuagint* texts, as well as in common English Bibles. It is in two parts: (1) A dialogue between the writer and Jehovah (chaps 1, 2); (2) a prayer in dirges.—Chap 3.

Writer. The writer is identified in the book itself. The composition of both sections is ascribed to "Habakkuk the prophet."—1:1; 3:1; see HABAKKUK.

Canonicity. The canonicity of the book of Habakkuk is confirmed by ancient catalogs of the Hebrew Scriptures. While they do not mention it by name, the book evidently was embraced by

HIGHLIGHTS OF HABAKKUK

An answer to the question, Will God execute the wicked?

Written evidently about 628 B.C.E., when the Chaldeans were rising in prominence but before Jehoiakim became their vassal

Habakkuk cries out for help, asks how long God will allow the wicked to continue (1:1–2:1)

When Jehovah answers that He will raise up the Chaldeans as His instrument for punishment, Habakkuk cannot understand how the Holy One could countenance such a treacherous agent, one who makes a god of his war machine, whose dragnet gathers up men like fish, and who mercilessly kills peoples

The prophet waits for Jehovah's answer, recognizing that he is in line for reproof

Jehovah replies that he has an appointed time, pronounces woe upon the Chaldean agency (2:2-20)

Jehovah gives the assurance that even though there

might seem to be delay, the prophetic vision is "for the appointed time, and it keeps panting on to the end," eagerly moving toward its fulfillment

Pronouncements of woe indicate that the Chaldean instrumentality would not remain unpunished for plundering other nations, cutting off many peoples, building cities by bloodshed, making others drink the cup of shameful defeat, and engaging in idolatry

The prophet appeals for Jehovah to act and yet to show mercy during the coming day of distress (3:1-19)

Recalling past manifestations of Jehovah's power, the prophet is seized with fear and trembling, but he is determined to wait quietly for the day of distress, exulting in the God of his salvation

Even if the very means for supporting life were to fail, Habakkuk determines to rejoice in Jehovah as the God of salvation, the One who strengthens him

their references to the 'twelve Minor Prophets,' for otherwise the number 12 would be incomplete. The book's canonicity is unquestionably supported by quotations from it in the Christian Greek Scriptures. Though not referring to Habakkuk by name, Paul quoted Habakkuk 1:5 (*LXX*) while speaking to faithless Jews. (Ac 13:40, 41) He quoted from Habakkuk 2:4 ("But as for the righteous one, by his faithfulness he will keep living") when encouraging Christians to display faith.—Ro 1:16, 17; Ga 3:11; Heb 10:38, 39.

Among the Dead Sea Scrolls is a manuscript of Habakkuk (chaps 1, 2) in a pre-Masoretic Hebrew text with an accompanying commentary. It is noteworthy that in the text Jehovah's name is written in ancient Hebrew characters, whereas in the commentary the divine name is avoided, and instead, the Hebrew word 'El (meaning "God") is used.

Scholars believe that this scroll was written toward the end of the first century B.C.E. This makes it the oldest extant Hebrew manuscript of the book of Habakkuk. At Habakkuk 1:6 this manuscript reads "Chaldeans," thus confirming the correctness of the Masoretic text in showing that the Chaldeans (Babylonians) were the ones Jehovah would raise up as his agency.

Date and Setting. The statement "Jehovah is in his holy temple" (Hab 2:20) and the note that follows Habakkuk 3:19 ("To the director on my stringed instruments") indicate that Habakkuk prophesied before the temple built by Solomon in Jerusalem was destroyed in 607 B.C.E.

Also, Jehovah's declaration "I am raising up the Chaldeans" (1:6) and the prophecy's general tenor show that the Chaldeans, or Babylonians, had not yet desolated Jerusalem. But Habakkuk 1:17 may suggest that they had already begun to overthrow some nations. During the reign of Judah's good king Josiah (659-629 B.C.E.), the Chaldeans and Medes took Nineveh (in 632 B.C.E.), and Babylon was then on its way toward becoming a world power.—Na 3:7.

There are some who hold, in agreement with rabbinic tradition, that Habakkuk prophesied earlier, during the reign of King Manasseh of Judah. They believe that he was one of the prophets mentioned or alluded to at 2 Kings 21:10 and 2 Chronicles 33:10. They hold that the Babylonians were not yet a menace, which fact made Habakkuk's prophecy more unbelievable to the Judeans.—See Hab 1:5, 6.

On the other hand, in the early part of Jehoiakim's reign, Judah was within the Egyptian sphere of influence (2Ki 23:34, 35), and this could also be a time when God's raising up of the Chaldeans to punish the wayward inhabitants of Judah would be to them 'an activity they would not believe, though it was related.' (Hab 1:5, 6) Babylonian King Nebuchadnezzar defeated Pharaoh Necho at Carchemish in 625 B.C.E., in the fourth year of King Jehoiakim's reign. (Jer 46:2) So, Habakkuk may have prophesied and recorded the prophecy before that event, possibly completing the writing thereof about 628 B.C.E. in Judah. The use of the future tense regarding the

Chaldean threat evidently indicates a date earlier than Jehoiakim's vassalship to Babylon (620-618 B.C.E.).—2Ki 24:1.

Style. The style of writing is both forceful and moving. Vivid illustrations and comparisons are employed. (Hab 1:8, 11, 14, 15; 2:5, 11, 14, 16, 17; 3:6, 8-11) Commenting on Habakkuk's style, S. R. Driver said: "The literary power of Habakkuk is considerable. Though his book is a brief one, it is full of force; his descriptions are graphic and powerful; thought and expression are alike poetic." Such qualities are, of course, primarily due to divine inspiration.

The book of Habakkuk emphasizes Jehovah's supremacy over all nations (Hab 2:20; 3:6, 12), highlighting his universal sovereignty. It also places emphasis on the fact that the righteous live by faith. (2:4) It engenders reliance upon Jehovah, showing that he does not die (1:12), that he justly threshes the nations, and that he goes forth for the salvation of his people. (3:12, 13) For those exulting in him, Jehovah is shown to be the God of salvation and the Source of vital energy.—3:18, 19.

HABAZZINIAH (Hab·az·zi·ni'ah). A descendant of Jonadab the son of Rechab. "Jaazaniah the son of Jeremiah the son of Habazziniah" was one of the Rechabites tested by the prophet Jeremiah in the days of King Jehoiakim.—Jer 35:1-6.

HABOR (Ha'bor). A city or district to which the Assyrian king Tiglath-pileser III exiled numerous Israelites of the ten-tribe kingdom. (1Ch 5:26) Some scholars have linked this Habor with Abhar, a town located on the Qezel Owzan River of NW Iran about 210 km (130 mi) W of Tehran. At 2 Kings 17:6 and 18:11 some favor the reading "Habor, the river of Gozan" (*AS, RS*), and they suggest identifying the Habor with a tributary of the Euphrates, the Khabur River of SE Turkey and NE Syria. However, in agreement with 1 Chronicles 5:26, this phrase may instead be translated "Habor at [or, by] the river Gozan." —*NW, Yg;* see GOZAN.

HACALIAH (Hac·a·li'ah) [possibly, Wait for Jah; Keep in Expectation of Jah]. Governor Nehemiah's father.—Ne 1:1; 10:1.

HACHILAH (Hach·i'lah). A hill in the Wilderness of Ziph, where David and his men concealed themselves from King Saul. (1Sa 23:19; 26:1-3) Today its exact location is unknown.

HACHMONI (Hach'mo·ni) [possibly, Wise].

1. Ancestor of Zabdiel and his son Jashobeam. Jashobeam was the head one of David's top three mighty men and is called "the son of a Hachmonite." (1Ch 11:11; 27:2) "Hachmonite" is spelled "Tahchemonite" at 2 Samuel 23:8. If 1 Chronicles 12:6 refers to the same Jashobeam, the Hachmonites were descendants of the Levite Korah. —See JOSHEB-BASSHEBETH.

2. Father or ancestor of Jehiel. Jehiel was with King David's sons, presumably as a private instructor. (1Ch 27:32) Possibly the same as No. 1 above.

HACHMONITE. See HACHMONI No. 1.

HADAD (Ha'dad).

1. One of the 12 sons of Ishmael the son of Abraham and his concubine Hagar.—Ge 25:12-15; 1Ch 1:28-30.

2. Successor to the kingship of Edom after the death of Husham. "Hadad son of Bedad, who defeated the Midianites in the field of Moab," apparently ruled from the city of Avith.—Ge 36:31, 35, 36; 1Ch 1:46, 47.

3. Another king of Edom; husband of Mehetabel. Hadad succeeded Baal-hanan to the kingship, and "the name of his city was Pau." (1Ch 1:43, 50, 51) He is called Hadar at Genesis 36:39, which may be due to a scribal error, since the Hebrew letters corresponding to "r" (ר) and "d" (ד) are very similar.

4. An Edomite of the royal offspring and a troublemaker for Israel during Solomon's reign. While yet a child, Hadad, along with some of his father's servants, fled down to Egypt by way of Paran to escape Joab's slaughter of all the males of Edom. In Egypt, Hadad and those with him were kindly received, Pharaoh giving Hadad a house as well as food and land, and later even his own sister-in-law as a wife. By this woman, Hadad had a son named Genubath, who lived right in Pharaoh's house among the sons of Pharaoh. Upon learning that King David and Joab had died, Hadad returned to Edom and proved to be a resister to Solomon.—1Ki 11:14-22, 25.

5. Hadad is considered to be the chief deity of ancient Syria and is generally identified with Rimmon. The name Hadad appears as part of the names of certain Syrian kings, such as Benhadad (1Ki 15:18) and Hadadezer (1Ki 11:23), and also occurs in the name Hadadrimmon.—Zec 12:11; see HADADRIMMON.

HADADEZER (Had·ad·eʹzer) [Hadad Is a Helper]. Son of Rehob and king of Zobah, a Syrian (Aramaean) kingdom that is thought to have been situated N of Damascus (2Sa 8:3, 5; 1Ki 11:23; 1Ch 18:3, 5) and that included vassalages. (2Sa 10:19) Before being defeated by King David, Hadadezer had waged warfare against Toi (Tou) the king of Hamath.—2Sa 8:9, 10; 1Ch 18:9, 10.

After the Syrians who had been hired by the Ammonites to fight against David were defeated, Hadadezer strengthened his forces by enlisting additional Syrians from the region of the Euphrates. (2Sa 10:6, 15, 16; 1Ch 19:16) This may be alluded to at 2 Samuel 8:3 (compare 1Ch 18:3), where the reference seems to be to Hadadezer's seeking to put his control back again at the river Euphrates. On this, Cook's *Commentary* notes that the Hebrew literally means "to cause his hand to return" and states: "The exact force of the metaphor must . . . be decided by the context. If, as is most probable, this verse relates to the circumstances more fully detailed [at 2Sa 10:15-19], the meaning of the phrase here will be *when he* (Hadadezer) *went to renew his attack* (upon Israel), or *to recruit his strength against Israel, at the river Euphrates.*"

At Helam the forces of Hadadezer under the command of Shobach (Shophach) met those of David and were defeated. Immediately afterward, Hadadezer's vassals made peace with Israel. (2Sa 10:17-19; 1Ch 19:17-19) In the conflict 40,000 Syrian horsemen were killed. Perhaps in order to escape through rough terrain, these horsemen dismounted and were slain as footmen. This could account for their being called "horsemen" at 2 Samuel 10:18 and "men on foot" at 1 Chronicles 19:18. The difference in the number of Syrian charioteers killed in battle is usually attributed to scribal error, the lower figure of 700 charioteers being considered the correct one.

David also took much copper from Betah (apparently also called Tibhath) and Berothai (perhaps the same as Cun), two cities of Hadadezer's realm, and brought the gold shields belonging to Hadadezer's servants, probably the vassal kings, to Jerusalem. (2Sa 8:7, 8; 1Ch 18:7, 8; compare 2Sa 10:19.) David also captured many of Hadadezer's horses, horsemen, chariots, and footmen. The variation in the enumeration of these at 2 Samuel 8:4 and 1 Chronicles 18:4 may have arisen through scribal error. In the Greek *Septuagint* both passages indicate that 1,000 chariots and 7,000 horsemen were captured, and there-fore 1 Chronicles 18:4 perhaps preserves the original reading.

However, it may be noted that what are commonly viewed as scribal errors in the account of David's conflict with Hadadezer may simply reflect other aspects of the war or different ways of reckoning.

HADADRIMMON (Ha·dad·rimʹmon). Evidently a location in the valley plain of Megiddo. (Zec 12:11) Hadadrimmon is often identified with Rummana, a site about 7 km (4.5 mi) SSE of Megiddo.

The 'great wailing' at Hadadrimmon mentioned in Zechariah's prophecy perhaps alludes to the lamentation over King Josiah, killed in battle at Megiddo. (2Ki 23:29; 2Ch 35:24, 25) But some associate this lamentation with ritualistic mourning ceremonies like those for the false god Tammuz (compare Eze 8:14) and consider "Hadadrimmon" to be the composite name of a god. This is unlikely, especially since Jehovah's words, through Zechariah, are part of a prophecy concerning the Messiah. Hardly could idolatrous weeping ceremonies serve as a prophetic illustration; but the mourning for a faithful Judean king could well do so.—Compare Joh 19:37 and Re 1:7 with Zec 12:10-14.

HADAR (Haʹdar). Successor to the kingship of Edom after the death of Baal-hanan; also called Hadad.—Ge 36:31, 39; 1Ch 1:43, 50, 51; see HADAD No. 3.

HADASHAH (Ha·dashʹah) [New]. A Judean city in the Shephelah. (Jos 15:33, 37) Its exact ancient location is today unknown.

HADASSAH (Ha·dasʹsah) [Myrtle]. The cousin of Mordecai who replaced Persian Queen Vashti; better known by her Persian name Esther. —Es 2:7; see ESTHER.

HADES (Haʹdes). This is the common transliteration into English of the corresponding Greek word *haiʹdes.* It perhaps means "the unseen place." In all, the word "Hades" occurs ten times in the earliest manuscripts of the Christian Greek Scriptures.—Mt 11:23; 16:18; Lu 10:15; 16:23; Ac 2:27, 31; Re 1:18; 6:8; 20:13, 14.

The *King James Version* translates *haiʹdes* as "hell" in these texts, but the *Revised Standard Version* renders it "Hades," with the exception of Matthew 16:18, where "powers of death" is used, though the footnote reads "gates of Hades." "Hades" rather than "hell" is used in many modern translations.

The Greek *Septuagint* translation of the Hebrew Scriptures (from Genesis to Malachi) uses the word "Hades" 73 times, employing it 60 times to translate the Hebrew word *she'ohl'*, commonly rendered "Sheol." Luke, the divinely inspired writer of Acts, definitely showed Hades to be the Greek equivalent of Sheol when he translated Peter's quotation from Psalm 16:10. (Ac 2:27) Inversely, nine modern Hebrew translations of the Christian Greek Scriptures use the word "Sheol" to translate Hades at Revelation 20:13, 14; and the Syriac translation uses the related word *Shiul.*

In all but two cases in which the word Hades is used in the Christian Greek Scriptures it is related to death, either in the verse itself or in the immediate context; the two other instances are discussed in the following paragraph. Hades does not refer to a single grave (Gr., *ta'phos*), or to a single tomb (Gr., *mne'ma*), or to a single memorial tomb (Gr., *mne·mei'on*), but to the *common grave* of mankind, where the dead and buried ones are unseen. It thus signifies the same as the corresponding word "Sheol," and an examination of its use in all its ten occurrences bears out this fact.—See GRAVE; SHEOL.

In its first occurrence, at Matthew 11:23, Jesus Christ, in chiding Capernaum for its disbelief, uses Hades to represent the depth of debasement to which Capernaum would come down, in contrast with the height of heaven to which she assumed to exalt herself. A corresponding text is found at Luke 10:15. Note the similar way in which Sheol is used at Job 11:7, 8.

Jesus and Congregation Delivered. Concerning the Christian congregation, Jesus said, at Matthew 16:18, that "the gates of Hades ["powers of death," *RS*] will not overpower it." Similarly, King Hezekiah, when on the verge of death, said: "In the midst of my days I will go into the gates of Sheol." (Isa 38:10) It, therefore, becomes apparent that Jesus' promise of victory over Hades means that its "gates" will open to release the dead by means of a resurrection, even as was the case with Christ Jesus himself.

Since Hades refers to the common grave of mankind, a place rather than a condition, Jesus entered within "the gates of Hades" when buried by Joseph of Arimathea. On Pentecost of 33 C.E., Peter said of Christ: "Neither was he forsaken in Hades nor did his flesh see corruption. This Jesus God resurrected, of which fact we are all witnesses." (Ac 2:25-27, 29-32; Ps 16:10) Whereas "the gates of Hades" (Mt 16:18) were still holding David within their domain in Peter's day (Ac 2:29), they had swung open for Christ Jesus when his Father resurrected him out of Hades. Thereafter, through the power of the resurrection given him (Joh 5:21-30), Jesus is the Holder of "the keys of death and of Hades."—Re 1:17, 18.

Manifestly, the Bible Hades is not the imagined place that the ancient non-Christian Greeks described in their mythologies as a "dark, sunless region within the earth," for there was no resurrection from such mythological underworld.

Illustrative Use. At Revelation 6:8 Hades is figuratively pictured as closely following after the rider of the pale horse, personalized Death, to receive the victims of the death-dealing agencies of war, famine, plagues, and wild beasts.

The sea (which at times serves as a watery grave for some) is mentioned in addition to Hades (the common *earthen* grave), for the purpose of stressing the inclusiveness of *all* such dead ones when Revelation 20:13, 14 says that the sea, death, and Hades are to give up or be emptied of the dead in them. Thereafter, death and Hades (but not the sea) are cast into "the lake of fire," "the second death." They thereby figuratively 'die out' of existence, and this signifies the end of Hades (Sheol), the common grave of mankind, as well as of death inherited through Adam.

The remaining text in which Hades is used is found at Luke 16:22-26 in the account of "the rich man" and "Lazarus." The language throughout the account is plainly parabolic and cannot be construed literally in view of all the preceding texts. Note, however, that "the rich man" of the parable is spoken of as being *"buried"* in Hades, giving further evidence that Hades means the common grave of mankind.—See GEHENNA; TARTARUS.

HADID (Ha'did). An ancestral city of certain Benjamites returning from Babylonian exile (Ezr 2:1, 2, 33; Ne 7:6, 7, 37; 11:31, 34), commonly identified with el-Haditheh (Tel Hadid), an abandoned Arab village about 5 km (3 mi) ENE of Lod (Lydda). It is generally thought that Hadid is probably the same as the "Huditi" mentioned in the Karnak List of Thutmose III, and the "Adida" in the Apocryphal book of First Maccabees (12: 38; 13:13, *RS,* ecumenical edition), there described as being situated in the Shephelah and overlooking the coastal plain.

HADLAI (Had'lai) [Ceasing]. Father of the Amasa who was one of the heads of the sons of Ephraim in the days of King Pekah of Israel and King Ahaz of Judah.—2Ch 28:6, 12, 16.

HADORAM (Ha·do'ram).

1. A son of Joktan and descendant of Shem, listed among the founders of the post-Flood families. (Ge 10:21, 25-27, 32) This family settled in Arabia, possibly in Yemen.

2. Son of Hamath's King Tou. Hadoram was sent by his father to David with congratulations and gifts to mark Israel's victory over the king of Zobah. (1Ch 18:9-11) He is called Joram at 2 Samuel 8:10.

3. The superintendent of those conscripted for forced labor under Kings David, Solomon, and Rehoboam. When sent by Rehoboam to the rebellious northern tribes, Hadoram was stoned to death. (2Ch 10:18) He is called Adoram at 1 Kings 12:18 and 2 Samuel 20:24, and Adoniram at 1 Kings 4:6 and 5:14.

HADRACH (Ha'drach). A land against which Jehovah expressed a pronouncement through his prophet Zechariah. This prophecy, pronounced probably in 518 B.C.E., showed that Hadrach had incurred Jehovah's displeasure. It is mentioned in association with a number of cities surrounding Israel, such as Damascus, Hamath, Tyre, Sidon, and the Philistine cities of Ashkelon, Gaza, Ekron, and Ashdod.—Zec 9:1-8.

It may be that Hadrach was a city-state that exercised control over the area surrounding it. It is believed to be the Hatarikka of the Assyrian inscriptions, identified with the mound of Tell Afis, about 45 km (28 mi) SW of Aleppo. Assyrian King Tiglath-pileser III lists Hatarikka among the "19 districts belonging to Hamath."—*Ancient Near Eastern Texts*, edited by J. Pritchard, 1974, pp. 282, 283.

HA-ELEPH (Ha-e'leph) [The Ox; The Cow]. A city of Benjamin, the site of which is today unknown. (Jos 18:21, 28) Some scholars think that Ha-eleph may actually be part of the name of the preceding city, "Zelah." However, those who would combine "Zelah" with "Ha-eleph" thereby reduce the number of cities to 13, and this does not agree with the Bible's reference to 14 cities.

HAGAB (Ha'gab) [Grasshopper]. Ancestor of a family of Nethinim temple slaves. "The sons of Hagab" are mentioned among those returning with Zerubbabel in 537 B.C.E. from exile in Babylon. (Ezr 2:1, 2, 43, 46) The name Hagab, however, does not appear in the parallel list at Nehemiah 7:48.

HAGABAH (Hag'a·bah) [Grasshopper]. Ancestor of a family of Nethinim temple slaves. "The sons of Hagabah" were among those returning in 537 B.C.E. from exile in Babylon.—Ezr 2:1, 2, 43, 45; Ne 7:48.

HAGAR (Ha'gar). Sarah's Egyptian maidservant; later, Abraham's concubine and the mother of Ishmael. While in Egypt because of a famine in the land of Canaan, Abraham (Abram) came to have menservants and maidservants, and it may be that Hagar came to be Sarah's maidservant at this time.—Ge 12:10, 16.

Since Sarah (Sarai) remained barren, she requested that Abraham have relations with Hagar, giving her to Abraham as his wife. But upon becoming pregnant, Hagar began to despise her mistress to such an extent that Sarah voiced complaint to her husband. "So Abram said to Sarai: 'Look! Your maidservant is at your disposal. Do to her what is good in your eyes.' Then Sarai began to humiliate her so that she ran away from her." (Ge 16:1-6) At the fountain on the way to Shur, Jehovah's angel found Hagar and instructed her to return to her mistress and to humble herself under her hand. Moreover, she was told that Jehovah would greatly multiply her seed and that the son to be born to her was to be called Ishmael. Abraham was 86 years old when Ishmael was born.—Ge 16:7-16.

Years later, when Abraham prepared "a big feast on the day of Isaac's being weaned" at the age of about 5 years, Sarah noticed Hagar's son Ishmael, now about 19 years old, "poking fun." This was no innocent child's play. As implied by the next verse in the account, it may have involved a taunting of Isaac over heirship. Here Ishmael was making early manifestation of the antagonistic traits that Jehovah's angel foretold would be shown by him. (Ge 16:12) Apparently fearing for the future of her son Isaac, Sarah requested Abraham to drive out Hagar and her son. This displeased Abraham, but at Jehovah's direction he followed through on his wife's request. Early the next morning he dismissed Hagar with her son, giving her bread and a skin water bottle.—Ge 21:8-14.

Hagar wandered about in the wilderness of Beer-sheba. "Finally the water became exhausted . . . and she threw the child under one of the bushes." Ishmael's being referred to as a "child" is not an anachronism, for the Hebrew word *ye'-ledh* here rendered "child" also means "young man" and is so translated at Genesis 4:23. As to his being thrown under one of the bushes, although it was foretold that he would be "a zebra of a man," Ishmael may not have been very strong as a teenager. (Ge 16:12) Hence he may have given out first, necessitating his mother's supporting him. This would not be inconceivable, for women in those days, especially slave women, were accustomed to carrying heavy burdens in everyday life. It seems that in time Hagar also gave out, making it necessary for her to withdraw her support from him, depositing him, perhaps somewhat abruptly, under the nearest sheltering bush. Hagar herself sat down "about the distance of a bowshot" (a common Hebrew expression denoting the usual distance at which archers placed their targets) away from her son. —Ge 21:14-16.

God's angel then called to Hagar, telling her not to be afraid and that Ishmael would be constituted a great nation. Furthermore, God opened her eyes so that she saw a well of water, from which she filled the skin bottle and gave her son a drink. "God continued to be with the boy," and in time he became an archer and "took up dwelling in the wilderness of Paran." Hagar procured a wife for him from the land of Egypt.—Ge 21:17-21.

According to the apostle Paul, Hagar figured in a symbolic drama in which she represented the nation of fleshly Israel, bound to Jehovah by the Law covenant inaugurated at Mount Sinai, which covenant brought forth "children for slavery." Because of the sinful condition of the people, the nation was unable to keep the terms of that covenant. Under it the Israelites did not become a free people but were condemned as sinners worthy of death; hence, they were slaves. (Joh 8:34; Ro 8:1-3) Jerusalem of Paul's day corresponded to Hagar, for Jerusalem the capital, representing the organization of natural Israel, found herself in slavery with her children. Spirit-begotten Christians, though, are children of the "Jerusalem above," God's symbolic woman. This Jerusalem, like Sarah the freewoman, has never been in slavery. But just as Isaac was persecuted by Ishmael, so also the children of the "Jerusalem above," who have been set free by the Son, experienced persecution at the hands of the children of enslaved Jerusalem. However, Hagar and her son were driven out, representing Jehovah's casting off natural Israel as a nation.—Ga 4:21-31; see also Joh 8:31-40.

HAGGAI (Hag′gai) [[Born on a] Festival]. A Hebrew prophet in Judah and Jerusalem during Zerubbabel's governorship in the reign of Persian King Darius Hystaspis.—Hag 1:1; 2:1, 10, 20; Ezr 5:1, 2.

Jewish tradition holds that Haggai was a member of the Great Synagogue. From Haggai 2:10-19 it has been suggested that he may have been a priest. His name appears along with that of the prophet Zechariah in the superscriptions of Psalm 111 (112) in the Latin *Vulgate;* Psalms 125 and 126 in the Syriac *Peshitta;* 145 in the Greek *Septuagint,* the *Peshitta,* and the *Vulgate;* and 146, 147, and 148 in the *Septuagint* and the *Peshitta.* It is probable that Haggai was born in Babylon and that he returned to Jerusalem with Zerubbabel and the Jewish remnant in 537 B.C.E. But little is actually known about Haggai, for the Scriptures do not reveal the prophet's parentage, tribe, and so forth.

Haggai became the first postexilic prophet and was joined about two months later by Zechariah. (Hag 1:1; Zec 1:1) A halt to temple construction had been precipitated by enemy opposition but extended for some years by Jewish apathy and selfish pursuit of personal interests. Haggai kindled the zeal of the repatriated Jewish exiles for the resumption of temple construction. (Ezr 3:10-13; 4:1-24; Hag 1:4) Four God-given messages delivered by Haggai during about a four-month period in the second year of Darius Hystaspis (520 B.C.E.) and recorded by the prophet in the Bible book of Haggai were especially effective in initially moving the Jews to resume temple-building work. (Hag 1:1; 2:1, 10, 20; see HAGGAI, BOOK OF.) Haggai and Zechariah continued to urge them on in the work until the temple was completed toward the end of Darius' sixth year, in 515 B.C.E.—Ezr 5:1, 2; 6:14, 15.

HAGGAI, BOOK OF. An inspired book of the Hebrew Scriptures listed among the so-called minor prophets. It consists of four messages from Jehovah to Jews that had returned from Babylonian exile, urging them to finish rebuilding the temple in Jerusalem. Also being prophetic, the book foretold such things as the filling of Jehovah's house with glory and the overthrow of human kingdoms.—Hag 2:6, 7, 21, 22.

Writership and Canonicity. The writer was Haggai the prophet, who personally delivered each message found in the book. (Hag 1:1; 2:1, 10, 20; see HAGGAI.) While most of the ancient Scripture catalogs do not list the book of Haggai by name, it is evidently included in their references to the 'twelve Minor Prophets,' the number 12 thus being complete. The Jews have never questioned its right to a place among the Hebrew

HIGHLIGHTS OF HAGGAI

Four messages designed to motivate the Jews to move ahead with the rebuilding of Jehovah's temple

Written in Jerusalem 17 years after the Jews returned from exile, when temple building had not yet been completed

Message to people living in paneled houses, while Jehovah's house lies in ruins (1:1-15)

To those feeling that it is not the time for rebuilding the temple Jehovah makes clear that neglect of this work has led to the withdrawal of his blessing, so that harvests are poor and hired laborers receive meager wages

Zerubbabel, Joshua, and the rest of the people respond favorably; they are promised that Jehovah will be with them in the temple rebuilding work; temple work starts

Proclamation that Jehovah will fill his house with glory (2:1-9)

In the view of aged ones who had seen the glory of Solomon's temple, the new structure seems like nothing

Jehovah urges Zerubbabel, Joshua, and the rest of the people to be strong, not disheartened, to continue with the work, assuring them that the glory of the rebuilt temple will surpass that of the former one

People are shown that neglect of temple rebuilding has made them and all their work unclean before God (2:10-19)

Priests answer questions indicating that holiness cannot be transferred but uncleanness can

Jehovah encourages the people by informing that from the day the temple foundation is laid Jehovah will bestow his blessing, ending the poor harvests

Message to Zerubbabel about Jehovah's rocking heavens and earth (2:20-23)

When Jehovah rocks heavens and earth, even overthrowing the throne of kingdoms, the enemies will turn their weapons against themselves; thus no power will succeed in blocking temple rebuilding

Jehovah will make Zerubbabel like his own seal ring, thus guaranteeing that his position will be secure regardless of what may happen

---

Scriptures, and the canonicity of the book is definitely established by the quotation from Haggai 2:6 appearing at Hebrews 12:26.—Compare Hag 2:21.

Style. The language is simple and the meaning is made abundantly clear. Thought-provoking questions are sometimes posed. (Hag 1:4, 9; 2:3, 12, 13, 19) The book of Haggai contains strong reproof, encouragement, and hope-inspiring prophecy. The divine name, Jehovah, appears 35 times in its 38 verses, and it is clearly shown that the messages were from God, Haggai serving as His commissioned messenger.—1:13.

Date and Circumstances. The four messages recorded by Haggai were delivered at Jerusalem within about a four-month period in the second year of Persian King Darius Hystaspis (520 B.C.E.), the book apparently being completed in 520 B.C.E. (Hag 1:1; 2:1, 10, 20) Zechariah was prophesying for the same purpose during Haggai's prophetic activity.—Ezr 5:1, 2; 6:14.

Messages of Lasting Benefit. Among other things, the book of Haggai engenders faith in Jehovah, essential to God's servants. It shows that God is with his people (Hag 1:13; 2:4, 5), and it also urges them to put his interests first in life. (Hag 1:2-8; Mt 6:33) The book makes clear the fact that mere formalistic worship does not please Jehovah (Hag 2:10-17; compare Isa 29:13, 14; Mt 15:7-9) but that faithful actions harmonizing with the divine will are what result in bless-

ing. (Hag 2:18, 19; compare Pr 10:22.) The writer of the Bible book of Hebrews applies Haggai 2:6 as having a greater fulfillment in connection with God's Kingdom in the hands of Jesus Christ. —Heb 12:26-29.

HAGGI (Hag′gi) [[Born on a] Festival]. The second-named son of Gad; grandson of Jacob and ancestral head of the Haggites.—Ge 46:8, 16; Nu 26:4, 15.

HAGGIAH (Hag·gi′ah) [Festival of Jah; or, Jah Is My Festival]. Son of Shimea; a Levite of the family of Merari.—1Ch 6:16, 29, 30.

HAGGITES. See HAGGI.

HAGGITH (Hag′gith) [[Born on a] Festival]. A wife of David and the mother of Adonijah; her son schemed to get the kingship over Israel. —2Sa 3:2, 4; 1Ki 1:5, 11; 1Ch 3:1, 2.

HAGRI (Hag′ri) [Of (Belonging to) Hagar]. Father of Mibhar, one of David's mighty men. —1Ch 11:26, 38.

HAGRITE (Hag′rite) [possibly, Of (Belonging to) Hagar]. Apparently a pastoral people residing in tents E of Gilead. In the days of King Saul, the Israelites living E of the Jordan defeated the Hagrites, taking 100,000 captives, as well as thousands of camels, asses, and sheep. (1Ch 5:10, 18-22) The psalmist listed the Hagrites among other enemies of Israel, such as the Edomites,

Moabites, Ammonites, and Amalekites. (Ps 83:2-7) However, during David's rule, Jaziz the Hagrite was in charge of the royal flocks.—1Ch 27:31.

Many scholars believe that the Hagrites are probably the same as the *A·grai'oi* mentioned by the ancient geographers Strabo, Ptolemy, and Pliny. Whether they were descendants of Hagar, as some suppose, cannot be definitely established.

HAIL. A form of precipitation consisting of pellets of ice, or frozen rain. The Bible's references to the destructive nature of hail are confirmed by what has happened in different parts of the earth in more recent years. In 1985, a hailstorm in Brazil killed more than 20 persons and injured another 300. Severe thunderstorms can generate hail the size of eggs or even grapefruit. An unusually large hailstone picked up after a storm in Kansas (U.S.A.) on September 3, 1970, measured some 15 cm (6 in.) across. The large stones fall at speeds of about 160 km/hr (100 mph). Hail is particularly damaging to crops, with single hailstorms sometimes causing losses amounting to millions of dollars.

Used by Jehovah. Hail is one of the forces Jehovah has used at times to accomplish his word and to demonstrate his great power. (Ps 148:1, 8; Isa 30:30) The first recorded instance of this was the seventh plague upon ancient Egypt, a destructive hailstorm that ruined vegetation, shattered trees, and killed both men and beasts out in the field but did not affect the Israelites in Goshen. (Ex 9:18-26; Ps 78:47, 48; 105:32, 33) Later, in the Promised Land, when the Israelites, under Joshua, came to the aid of the Gibeonites, who were threatened by an alliance of five kings of the Amorites, Jehovah used great hailstones against the attacking Amorites. On this occasion more died from the hailstones than in battle with Israel.—Jos 10:3-7, 11.

Symbolic. Jehovah, however, did not spare unfaithful Israel from devastating hail. (Hag 2:17) Furthermore, through his prophet Isaiah, he foretold the overthrow of the ten-tribe kingdom by the Assyrians, comparing the conquering Assyrian forces to "a thunderous storm of hail." (Isa 28:1, 2) Similarly the Babylonians, like hail, were to sweep away Judah's "refuge of a lie," that is, Judah's alliance with Egypt for military help.—Isa 28:14, 17; 31:1-3.

In the book of Revelation, reference is made to hail in conjunction with the first of the seven angels with trumpets blowing his trumpet, and in connection with the opening of the heavenly temple sanctuary of God. (Re 8:2, 7; 11:19) Then, at the pouring out of the seventh bowl of God's anger, symbolic hailstones weighing about a talent (20.4 kg; 45 lb) descend upon wicked men. —Re 16:1, 17, 21.

'For the day of war.' In speaking to Job out of the windstorm, Jehovah indicated that he had reserved storehouses of hail for "the day of fight and war." (Job 38:1, 22, 23) Appropriately, therefore, hail is mentioned among the elements to be used against the attacking forces of "Gog."—Eze 38:18, 22.

HAIR. Historically, men and women in general have regarded their hair as ornamental, enhancing their attractiveness, and as a sign, in many cases, of strength and youth. Therefore, great care has been given to the hair.

Egyptians. The Egyptians had, probably, the most peculiar customs with regard to their hair. The men, especially priests and soldiers, shaved their heads and beards. Herodotus says that the Nile dwellers shaved the heads of the boys, leaving only a few locks on the sides and perhaps on the front and back. When the child reached maturity these were removed as being marks of childhood. For the men, it was a sign of mourning or slovenliness to let the hair and beard grow. For this reason Joseph, when taken out of prison, shaved before being brought into the presence of Pharaoh. (Ge 41:14) Egyptian men, however, sometimes wore wigs, and beards that they tied on. Some Egyptian monumental representations show men of high rank with long, well-cared-for hair; it is not discernible whether the hair is their own or is a wig.

Conversely, Egyptian women wore their natural hair long and plaited. Well-preserved, plaited hair has been found on a considerable number of Egyptian female mummies.

Assyrians, Babylonians, Romans. The Assyrian and Babylonian men, and Asians in general, wore their hair long. Assyrian reliefs show the men with close-combed hair, the ends falling on the shoulders in curls. Their beards were also long, sometimes divided into two or three tiers of curls, with the mustache trimmed and also curled. Some believe that the very long hair depicted on the monuments was partly false, an addition to the person's natural hair.

In ancient times the Romans evidently wore beards but, about the third century B.C.E., adopted the custom of shaving.

Hebrews. The practice among Hebrew men from the first was to let the beard grow, but it was kept well groomed; and they trimmed the hair to a moderate length. In Absalom's case, his hair grew so abundantly that when he cut it once a year, it weighed 200 shekels (2.3 kg; 5 lb), possibly made heavier by the use of oil or ointments. (2Sa 14:25, 26) God's law commanded Israelite men that they should not 'cut their side-locks short around,' nor destroy the "extremity" of their beards. This was not an injunction against trimming the hair or beard but was evidently to prevent imitation of pagan practices. (Le 19:27; Jer 9:25, 26; 25:23; 49:32) To neglect the hair or beard, likely leaving them untrimmed and untended, was a sign of mourning. (2Sa 19:24) In instructions to priests given through the prophet Ezekiel, God commanded that they clip, but not shave, the hair of their heads and that they not wear their hair loose when serving in the temple.—Eze 44:15, 20.

Hebrew women took care of their hair as a mark of beauty (Ca 7:5), letting it grow long. (Joh 11:2) For a woman to cut off her hair was a sign of mourning or distress. (Isa 3:24) When an Israelite soldier captured a virgin woman from an enemy city and desired to marry her, she was required first to cut off her hair and attend to her nails and to undergo a one-month period of mourning for her parents, since they would have been killed in the taking of the city.—De 21:10-13; 20:10-14.

In the diagnosis of leprosy, one factor that the priest had to consider was the color and condition of the hair on the affected part.—Le 13:1-46.

Christians. The apostles Peter and Paul were both impelled to counsel Christian women not to give undue attention to hairstyling and ornamentation, as was the custom of the day. Instead, they were admonished to focus their attention on adorning themselves with the incorruptible apparel of a quiet and mild spirit.—1Pe 3:3, 4; 1Ti 2:9, 10.

The apostle Paul also called attention to the situation and general practice among the people to whom he wrote and showed that it was natural for a man to have shorter hair than a woman. (See NATURE.) A woman having her hair shorn, or shaved off, was disgraced. God had given her long hair "instead of a headdress," but, Paul argued, a woman could not use this natural covering, which was a glory to her, to excuse herself from wearing a head covering, "a sign of authority," when praying or prophesying in the Christian congregation. By recognizing this fact and

wearing a covering in such circumstances, the Christian woman would be acknowledging theocratic headship and showing Christian subjection. She would thus glorify both her husbandly head and Jehovah God, the Head of all.—1Co 11:3-16.

Figurative Usage. Job cut the hair off his head as a symbol of the desolate condition he was in, with his children and property taken away.—Job 1:20.

Ezekiel was commanded to cut off the hair of his head and of his beard, divide it into thirds, and dispose of it in ways that would prophetically describe the distressing things that would happen to the inhabitants of Jerusalem in the execution of God's judgments against her. (Eze 5:1-13) Distress and affliction were also symbolized by pulling out the hair, or cutting it off. (Ezr 9:3; Jer 7:29; 48:37; Mic 1:16) Dishonor, contempt, or reproach could be expressed by pulling out the hair of another's head or face.—Ne 13:25; Isa 50:6.

The number of hairs on the human head (said to average about 100,000) was used to represent great numbers or innumerability. (Ps 40:12; 69:4) And the fineness of the hair was used figuratively for minuteness. (Jg 20:16) 'Not a hair of your head will perish (or, fall)' is a statement guaranteeing full and complete protection and safety. (Lu 21:18; 1Sa 14:45; 2Sa 14:11; 1Ki 1:52; Ac 27:34) A similar implication was denoted by Jesus Christ's words to his disciples as to God's care for them: "The very hairs of your head are all numbered."—Mt 10:30; Lu 12:7.

Gray-headedness merited respect (Pr 16:31; 20:29) and was used at times synonymously for age and for wisdom. (Job 15:9, 10; see GRAY-HEADEDNESS.) Jehovah, in a vision to Daniel, symbolically was represented as having white hair, "like clean wool," as "the Ancient of Days." (Da 7:9) The apostle John saw Jesus Christ represented in a vision as having hair "white as white wool."—Re 1:1, 14, 17, 18.

Animal Hair. Goat hair was used in making cloth. (Ex 26:7) John the Baptizer wore a garment of camel hair. (Mt 3:4; Mr 1:6) This type of garment was an official one for a prophet. (2Ki 1:8; compare Ge 25:25.) Rebekah placed goat hair on the hands and neck of Jacob to simulate Esau's hair.—Ge 27:16; see BEARD.

HAKKATAN   (Hak′ka·tan) [The Small One]. Father of the Johanan of the family of Azgad who, accompanied by 110 males, returned from Babylon with Ezra.—Ezr 8:1, 12.

HAKKOZ (Hak′koz) [The Thorn]. An Aaronic priest and head of the paternal house that in David's time was constituted the 7th of the 24 priestly divisions.—1Ch 24:3-7, 10.

After returning from Babylon in 537 B.C.E., "sons of Hakkoz" were among those who were disqualified from the priesthood because of being unable to establish their genealogy. They were among those forbidden to eat from "the most holy things until a priest stood up with Urim and Thummim." (Ezr 2:61-63; Ne 7:63-65) A descendant of Hakkoz is specifically referred to as sharing in rebuilding the walls of Jerusalem.—Ne 3:21.

HAKUPHA (Ha·ku′pha). Head of a family of Nethinim temple slaves. "The sons of Hakupha" are listed among those returning from Babylonian exile.—Ezr 2:1, 43, 51; Ne 7:6, 46, 53.

HALAH (Ha′lah). A place to which Assyrian monarchs transported Israelite captives. (2Ki 17:6; 18:11; 1Ch 5:26) Certain scholars believe that Obadiah 20 should perhaps read "exiles in Halah" rather than "exiles of this ["army," JB; "force," Ro, Yg; "host," AS, KJ] rampart." (NW) Whereas various identifications have been suggested, Halah's exact location remains unknown. Some associate it with the Hallahu mentioned in Akkadian texts.

HALAK, MOUNT (Ha′lak) [Smooth Mountain]. A mountain marking the southern geographic limit of Israel's conquest of the Promised Land under the leadership of Joshua. (Jos 11:16, 17; 12:7) Halak is generally identified with Jebel Halaq (Har He-Halaq), the last W Palestinian height on the road from Beer-sheba to the Arabah. The range that begins with Jebel Halaq divides the pastureland on the E from the sandy desert on the W. If this identification is correct, then the Biblical description of Halak as 'going up,' or 'rising,' toward Seir may mean that the broad side of this mountain, running from SW to NE, faces Seir.

HALHUL (Hal′hul). A city in the mountainous region of Judah. (Jos 15:20, 48, 58) The same name is still attached to a village and a conspicuous hill, about 6 km (3.5 mi) N of Hebron.

HALI (Ha′li) [Ornament]. A town on the boundary of Asher, listed between Helkath and Beten. (Jos 19:24, 25) While the location is uncertain, the site of Khirbet Ras ′Ali (Tel ′Alil), about 17 km (11 mi) ESE of Haifa, is suggested. This would place it on the eastern edge of the Plain of Acco.

HALLEL (Hal·lel′). A song of praise to Jehovah. Psalms 113 to 118 constitute what is known in Jewish writings as the "Egyptian Hallel." According to the Mishnah, this Hallel was sung at the temple and in the synagogues on the occasion of the Passover (Pesahim 10:5-7) and the festivals of Pentecost, Booths, and Dedication (Sukkah 4:8; Ta′anit 4:5). At the celebration of the Passover in the home, the first part of this Hallel (either Psalm 113 [according to the School of Shammai] or Psalms 113 and 114 [School of Hillel]) was recited after the second cup of wine had been poured and the significance of the Passover explained. The Hallel was brought to a conclusion over the fourth cup of wine. The "Great Hallel" (variously considered to be Psalm 136 only, Psalms 120-136, or Psalm 135:4–136:26) is said to have been sung on joyful occasions and by those who used a fifth cup of wine at the celebration of the Passover.

HALLELUJAH (Hal·le·lu′jah). A transliteration of the Hebrew expression ha·lelu-Yah′, appearing first at Psalm 104:35. In the New World Translation it is nearly always translated "praise Jah, you people." The expression occurs 24 times in the Hebrew Scriptures and, with the exception of Psalm 135:3 ("praise Jah," NW), introduces and/or concludes the Psalms in which it is found. (See Ps 112:1; 115:18; 146:1, 10; 147:1, 20; 148:1, 14; 149:1, 9; 150:1, 6.) This expression stands alongside "Amen" at the close of Book Four of Psalms (Ps 106:48), and a Greek form of it appears four times at Revelation 19:1-6, where the reference is to the joy experienced over the destruction of Babylon the Great and that associated with Jehovah's beginning to rule as King.—See JAH.

HALLOHESH (Hal·lo′hesh) [The Charmer; The Whisperer].

1. Father of Shallum. Hallohesh's son Shallum was "a prince of half the district of Jerusalem" who, with his daughters, did repair work on the wall of Jerusalem in 455 B.C.E.—Ne 3:12.

2. One of the headmen of the people whose descendant, if not he himself, attested to the confession contract drawn up in the days of Nehemiah; possibly the same as No. 1.—Ne 9:38; 10:1, 14, 24.

HAM.

1. One of Noah's three sons, born after 2470 B.C.E. (Ge 5:32; 7:6; 11:10) He was possibly the youngest son (Ge 9:24); however, he is listed in second place at Genesis 5:32; 6:10; and else-

where. At Genesis 10:21 Shem is called "the brother of Japheth the oldest." Some believe that the expression "youngest son" at Genesis 9:24 refers to Noah's grandson Canaan.—See CANAAN, CANAANITE No. 1.

Ham was the father of four sons, Cush, Mizraim, Put, and Canaan. (Ge 10:6; 1Ch 1:8) The Ethiopians, Egyptians, some Arabian and African tribes, and the Canaanites descended from these sons. While it is claimed that some of the Hamitic tribes and nations listed in Genesis chapter 10 spoke a Semitic language, this does not weigh against their being of Hamitic descent or their having originally spoken a Hamitic tongue. Many peoples adopted the language of their conquerors, of other peoples with whom they associated, or of the land to which they migrated.

Ham married before the Flood. Along with his wife, his father and mother, and his two brothers and their wives, he survived the Flood. (Ge 6:18; 7:13; 8:15, 16, 18; 1Pe 3:19, 20) Ham's sons were born after the Flood.

Sometime later he became involved in an incident that brought a curse on his son Canaan. Noah had become intoxicated with wine and had uncovered himself in his tent. Ham saw his father's nakedness, and instead of showing the proper respect for Noah, the family head and the servant and prophet whom God had made an instrument in the preservation of the human race, Ham told his two brothers of his discovery. Shem and Japheth exhibited the proper respect by walking backwards with a mantle to cover Noah so that they would not bring reproach by looking on their father's nakedness. Noah, on awakening, uttered a curse, not on Ham, but on Ham's son Canaan. In the accompanying blessing of Shem, which included a blessing for Japheth, Ham was passed over and ignored; only Canaan was mentioned as cursed and was prophetically foretold to become a slave to Shem and Japheth. —Ge 9:20-27.

It is possible that Canaan himself had been involved directly in the incident and that his father Ham had failed to correct him. Or Noah, speaking prophetically by inspiration, foresaw that the bad tendency in Ham, perhaps already manifest in his son Canaan, would be inherited by Canaan's offspring. The curse was partly fulfilled when the Semitic Israelites subjugated the Canaanites. Those who were not destroyed (for example, the Gibeonites [Jos 9]) were made slaves to Israel. Centuries later, the curse was further fulfilled when descendants of Ham's son Canaan came under the domination of the Japhetic world powers of Medo-Persia, Greece, and Rome.

Some persons have incorrectly held that the black race and enslavement of members of that race resulted from the curse pronounced upon Canaan. On the contrary, the descendants of Canaan, the cursed one, were not of the black race. The black race descended from Cush and possibly from Put, other sons of Ham who were not involved in the incident or the curse.

2. A city of the Zuzim E of the Jordan. (Ge 14:5) Defeat was inflicted on the city by the king of Elam in coalition with three other kings at the time they crushed the rebellion of the cities of the District in the Dead Sea area. (Ge 14:1-12) The order of the listing of Ham in Genesis 14:5, 6 seems to place it S of Ashteroth-karnaim and N of Shaveh-kiriathaim. The name of the city is preserved in that of the modern village of Ham on the Wadi er-Rejeileh (also called Wadi Ham) about 6 km (3.5 mi) SSW of Irbid in the 'Ajlun, and about 30 km (19 mi) SE of the S end of the Sea of Galilee. The ancient city itself appears to be the tell (Tell Ham) nearby.

3. In the Psalms, "Ham" is associated with Egypt, it being called "the land of Ham."—Ps 78:51; 105:23, 27; 106:21, 22; see EGYPT, EGYPTIAN.

HAMAN (Ha'man). Son of Hammedatha the Agagite. The designation "Agagite" may mean that Haman was a royal Amalekite. (Es 3:1; see AGAG No. 1; AGAGITE.) If, indeed, Haman was an Amalekite, this in itself would explain why he harbored such great hatred for the Jews, for Jehovah had decreed the eventual extermination of the Amalekites. (Ex 17:14-16) This was because they showed hatred for God and his people by taking the initiative to sally forth in attack on the Israelites when they were traveling through the wilderness.—Ex 17:8.

Haman was a servant of King Ahasuerus (Xerxes I) of Persia, who ruled early in the fifth century B.C.E. Haman was honored and appointed as prime minister over the Persian Empire. Enraged by the refusal of Mordecai the Jew to bow down to him, Haman plotted the destruction of Mordecai and all the Jews in the empire. He painted the Jews as undesirable in the empire, lawbreakers, having laws "different from all other people's." He added an economic appeal, saying to the king: "Let there be a writing that they be destroyed; and ten thousand silver talents [c. $66,060,000] I shall pay into the hands of those doing the work by bringing it into the king's treasury." The king gave Haman his signet ring and replied: "The silver is given to you, also the people, to do with them according to what is good in your own eyes."—Es 3:1-11.

Haman was greatly puffed up with pride because of receiving authority from the king to issue a decree for the annihilation and spoliation of the Jews and, additionally, because of later being invited to two banquets held by Queen Esther. (Es 3:12, 13; 5:4-12) But just when Haman thought he was about to realize his highest ambitions, matters were reversed for him. Egotistically expecting to be exalted, Haman experienced crushing humiliation when the king ordered him to conduct a public ceremony honoring the hated Mordecai, who had previously uncovered a plot against the king's life. (Es 6:1-12; 2:21-23) Haman's wise men and his wife took this as an omen that Haman would go down before the Jew Mordecai.—Es 6:13.

Haman's downfall was brought to a crashing climax during the second special banquet held by

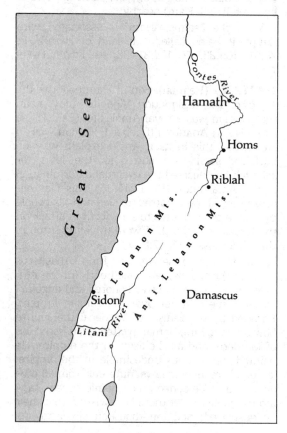

Queen Esther, who was Mordecai's cousin. (Es 2:7) Courageously, in Haman's presence, she made an appeal to the king. She revealed to the astonished king that his own interests were endangered; in fact, his queen's life was imperiled by a murderous plot. As the king's rage mounted, Esther boldly identified the now terrified prime minister as the dastardly plotter, "this bad Haman." (Es 7:1-6) Subsequently, the king ordered the murderous Haman to be hanged on the 22-m-high (73 ft) stake Haman had prepared for the hanging of Mordecai. (Es 7:7-10) In turn, Haman's house was given to Esther (Es 8:7), and Mordecai was made prime minister, with authorization to grant the Jews permission to defend themselves. (Es 8:2, 10-15) In two days of avenging themselves upon their foes, the Jews gained a smashing victory, killing over 75,000 of their enemies. Haman's ten sons were killed; then, on the next day, they were hung up before the people as a disgrace.—Es 9:1-17; see ESTHER; ESTHER, BOOK OF; MORDECAI No. 2; PURIM.

Haman manifested the traits of the Amalekites. He was obviously a worshiper of false gods, and he perhaps relied on astrologers when having lots cast to determine the auspicious day for the destruction of the Jews. (Es 3:7; see LOT, I.) He carried out "the works of the flesh," practicing idolatry, spiritism, manifesting his murderous hatred for the Jews, showing a proud, haughty, egotistical spirit with extreme jealousy and envy of others, especially the servants of God. (Ga 5:19-21) He practiced lying and deception (Es 3:8) and proved to be a cringing coward when his plans were foiled and he stood condemned. (Es 7:6-8) Haman showed himself to be a servant of God's Adversary, the Devil, according to the principle at Romans 6:16.

HAMATH (Ha′math), **HAMATHITE** (Ha′math·ite). The city of Hamath was the capital of a small Canaanite kingdom in Syria during the early history of Israel. The rich agricultural region surrounding it also took the same name. During Greek and Roman times the classical name of the city was Epiphania, so named by Antiochus IV (Epiphanes). Today it is called Hama, a shortened form of its original name.

The city of Hamath was located on the Orontes River, along important trade routes, 81 km (50 mi) inland from the Mediterranean, about 190 km (118 mi) N of Damascus and about 120 km (75 mi) S of Aleppo.

Though sometimes said to be of Hittite origin, Hamath was more likely founded by the *Ha-*

mathites, relatives of the Hittites and one of the 70 post-Flood families. Heth and Hamath, the forefathers of these two family lines, were listed as the 2nd and 11th sons respectively of Canaan the son of Ham.—Ge 10:6, 15-18; 1Ch 1:8, 13-16; see HITTITES.

"The Entering in of Hamath." The oldest account we have of Hamath tells how the 12 Israelite spies in the 16th century B.C.E. came up from the S as far as "the entering in of Hamath," an oft-repeated phrase thought to refer, not to the gates of the city itself but, rather, to the southern boundary of the territory over which it ruled. (Nu 13:21) It was to this limit that Joshua's conquest was pushed northward. (Jos 13:2, 5; Jg 3:1-3) Some scholars, however, suggest that the expression "as far as to the entering in of Hamath" (Jos 13:5) should possibly read "as far as Lebi-hamath (Lion of Hamath)," hence a definite place.—See *Vetus Testamentum,* Leiden, 1952, p. 114.

The exact location of this boundary (or place) is not certain. It was reckoned as the northern boundary of Israel's territory (Nu 34:8; 1Ki 8:65; 2Ki 14:25; 2Ch 7:8) and as bordering on Damascus. (Jer 49:23; Eze 47:15-17; 48:1; Zec 9:1, 2) Some think it was the southern extremity of the Coele-Syria Valley (also called the Beqa'), which runs between the Lebanon and Anti-Lebanon mountain ranges. Others say it was halfway between Baalbek and Riblah. Yet others suggest it was still farther N where the pass opens up between Homs and the sea.—Eze 47:20.

Relations With Israel. Toi (Tou) king of Hamath sent his son Joram (Hadoram) to congratulate King David for having defeated their common enemy Hadadezer. Hamath was then an independent kingdom. (2Sa 8:3, 9, 10; 1Ch 18:3, 9, 10) However, during Solomon's reign the kingdom of Hamath seems to have been under Israel's control, for Solomon built storage cities in that region. (2Ch 8:3, 4) After Solomon's death, Hamath gained its independence and remained independent except for a brief period in the ninth century B.C.E. when Jeroboam II temporarily brought it again under Israelite control. (2Ki 14: 28) About this time it was described as "populous Hamath."—Am 6:2.

In the eighth century B.C.E. Hamath and her neighbors, including the ten-tribe kingdom of Israel, were overrun by the Assyrians in their sweep to world domination. Assyria's policy was to exchange and relocate her captives, and so people of Hamath were brought in to replace inhabitants of Samaria who, in turn, were moved to Hamath and other places. (2Ki 17:24; 19:12, 13; Isa 10:9-11; 37:12, 13) In the high places of Samaria, the Hamathites then set up images of their god Ashima, even though this worthless god had proved to be helpless against the Assyrians.—2Ki 17:29, 30; 18:33, 34; Isa 36:18, 19.

According to an extant cuneiform inscription (British Museum 21946), after the battle of Carchemish in 625 B.C.E. (Jer 46:2), Nebuchadnezzar's forces overtook and destroyed the fleeing Egyptians in the district of Hamath. (*Assyrian and Babylonian Chronicles,* by A. K. Grayson, 1975, p. 99) In this same area, a few years earlier, Pharaoh Nechoh had taken King Jehoahaz captive. (2Ki 23:31-33) Then in 607 B.C.E., with the fall of Jerusalem, Zedekiah and other captives were taken to Riblah in the region of Hamath, and there before his eyes Zedekiah's sons, along with others of the nobility, were put to death. (2Ki 25:18-21; Jer 39:5, 6; 52:9, 10, 24-27) Nevertheless, God had promised that in due time he would restore a remnant of his captive people, including those in the land of Hamath.—Isa 11: 11, 12.

HAMATH-ZOBAH (Ha'math-zo'bah). This place was apparently conquered by Solomon and thus figuring in his only military engagement alluded to in Scripture. (2Ch 8:3) The exact identity of Hamath-zobah is uncertain. Hamath and Zobah may have been adjoining kingdoms (compare 1Ch 18:9; 2Ch 8:4), whence the compound name "Hamath-zobah." That two neighboring geographic locations may be joined in this way is illustrated by 1 Chronicles 6:78. The literal Hebrew of this text reads "the Jordan Jericho," or "the Jordan of Jericho," and is usually rendered "the Jordan at [by] Jericho."—*NW, RS, KJ.*

HAMMATH (Ham'math).

1. "The father" of the house of Rechab and an ancestor of certain Kenites.—1Ch 2:55.

2. [Place of a Hot (Spring)]. A fortified city of Naphtali. (Jos 19:32, 35) It is generally identified with Hammam Tabariyeh (Hame Teveriya), just S of Tiberias on the W side of the Sea of Galilee. The sulfurous spring there apparently gave Hammath its name. If, as most scholars believe, Hammoth-dor (Jos 21:32) and Hammon (1Ch 6:76) are alternate names for the same location, Hammath also functioned as a Levite city.

HAMMEDATHA (Ham·me·da'tha). An Agagite; father of Haman, who plotted the extermination of the Jews in the days of Mordecai and Esther.—Es 3:1, 6.

HAMMER. A tool used for pounding and driving; a mallet. Hammers were employed for driving in nails (Jer 10:4) and tent pins (Jg 4:21), in the quarrying operation for splitting stones by repeated pounding as well as in shaping and facing building stones (1Ki 6:7), and for shaping metal as in the making of idols.—Isa 41:7; 44:12.

The various materials used for making hammerheads included stone, metal, and wood. Likely the hammer, or mallet, used by Jael to drive the tent pin into the temples of Sisera was made of wood.—Jg 4:21; 5:26.

In a figurative sense the word of Jehovah's judgment is compared to a forge hammer that smashes the crag. (Jer 23:29) Also, in Jehovah's hand, Babylon was like a forge hammer, breaking nations and kingdoms in pieces.—Jer 50:23; compare Jer 25:8, 9, 17-26.

HAMMOLECHETH (Ham·mo′le·cheth) [The Queen]. The sister of Manasseh's grandson Gilead. She gave birth to Ishhod, Abi-ezer, and Mahlah.—1Ch 7:14, 17, 18.

HAMMON (Ham′mon) [meaning "Place of a Hot (Spring)"].

1. A city on the boundary of Asher. (Jos 19:24-28) It is generally identified with Umm el ′Awamid, on the Mediterranean seacoast, about 16 km (10 mi) SSW of Tyre.

2. A site in the territory of Naphtali given to the Levites (1Ch 6:71, 76); apparently the same as Hammath.—Jos 19:35; see HAMMATH No. 2.

HAMMOTH-DOR (Ham′moth-dor) [meaning "Hot (Springs) of Dor"]. A city of Naphtali given to Gershonite Levites. (Jos 21:27, 32) It is apparently the same as Hammath.—Jos 19:35; see HAMMATH No. 2.

HAMMUEL (Ham′mu·el). Son of Mishma of the tribe of Simeon.—1Ch 4:24-26.

HAMONAH (Ha·mo′nah) [meaning "Crowd (Multitude)"]. A symbolic city in the vicinity of the valley in which Gog and his crowd are to be buried, after their combined attack on God's people ends in defeat and mass slaughter. The city derives its name from that circumstance and is a memorial of Jehovah's victory over these foes. (Eze 39:16) A city implies an organized body of persons, here apparently relating to the organization for bone disposal described in Ezekiel 39:11-15.—See GOG No. 2.

HAMON-GOG (Ha′mon-Gog) [Gog's Crowd]. The English derivation of the Hebrew name of a valley, evidently symbolic, described as "the val-ley of those passing through on the east of the [Dead] sea." In this valley, Gog and all his forces are buried after their destruction by Jehovah.—Eze 39:11, 15, ftns; see GOG No. 2.

HAMOR (Ha′mor) [He-Ass]. A Hivite chieftain; father of Shechem. It was from the sons of Hamor that Jacob purchased a tract of land where he pitched his tent and then later set up an altar. After Shechem violated Jacob's daughter Dinah, both Shechem and his father Hamor were killed by Simeon and Levi, in avenging their sister.—Ge 33:18-20; 34:1, 2, 25, 26.

HAMSTRING. The hamstrings in quadrupeds are the back tendons above the hock of the hind legs. Hamstringing, the act of cutting these tendons, cripples the animal and renders it unfit for work or warfare. The arbitrariness of Jacob's sons Simeon and Levi found expression in their hamstringing bulls, likely when executing vengeance on the Hivites of Shechem. (Ge 49: 5, 6) In carrying out war operations, the Israelites hamstrung the horses of their enemies; on one occasion Joshua was specifically directed to do so by Jehovah. (Jos 11:6, 9; 2Sa 8:3, 4; 1Ch 18:3, 4) This was the simplest method of putting horses out of the battle, and after being disabled in this way, the horses undoubtedly were killed, destroyed along with the war chariots. By not appropriating to themselves the horses of their enemies and then using them in warfare, the Israelites would be safeguarded from being ensnared into relying on horses instead of on Jehovah for protection.—Compare De 17:16; Isa 31:1, 3.

HAMUL (Ha′mul) [meaning "Shown Compassion; Spared"], **HAMULITES** (Ha·mu′lites). The younger son of Perez and the grandson of Judah, from whom the Hamulites descended.—Ge 46: 12; Nu 26:21; 1Ch 2:5.

HAMUTAL (Ha·mu′tal) [possibly, Father-in-Law Is Dew]. Daughter of "Jeremiah from Libnah"; wife of King Josiah and mother of Jehoahaz and Mattaniah (Zedekiah), both of whom reigned as kings over Judah.—2Ki 23:30, 31; 24:17, 18; Jer 52:1.

HANAMEL (Han′a·mel). Son of Shallum the paternal uncle of the prophet Jeremiah. It was from Hanamel that the prophet bought the field that was in Anathoth at the time the Babylonians were laying siege to Jerusalem.—Jer 32:1-12.

HANAN (Ha′nan) [Showing Favor; Gracious].

1. One of "the sons of Shashak"; a Benjamite. —1Ch 8:1, 23-25.

2. Son of Maacah; one of the mighty men of David's military forces.—1Ch 11:26, 43.

3. One of the six sons of Azel; a descendant of King Saul.—1Ch 8:33-38; 9:44.

4. Son of Igdaliah, "a man of the true God." It was in the dining room of the sons of Hanan that the prophet Jeremiah tested the Rechabites' obedience to the command of their forefather Jehonadab not to drink wine.—Jer 35:3-6.

5. Head of a family of Nethinim temple slaves, members of which returned from Babylon with Zerubbabel in 537 B.C.E.—Ezr 2:1, 2, 43, 46; Ne 7:46, 49.

6. One of the Levites who assisted Ezra in explaining the Law to the congregation of Israel that was assembled in the public square before the Water Gate of Jerusalem. (Ne 8:1, 7) He may have been the same as No. 7 or No. 10.

7. A Levite whose descendant, if not he himself, attested by seal the "trustworthy arrangement" contracted during Nehemiah's governorship. (Ne 9:38; 10:1, 9, 10) If it was Hanan himself who sealed this agreement, he may be the same as No. 6 or No. 10.

8, 9. Two "heads of the people" whose descendants, if not they themselves, attested to the confession contract during Nehemiah's governorship.—Ne 9:38; 10:1, 14, 22, 26.

10. Son of Zaccur; a faithful Levite appointed by Nehemiah to distribute the due portions to the Levites, under the direction of Shelemiah, Zadok, and Pedaiah. (Ne 13:13) He may be the same as No. 6 or No. 7.

HANANEL. See TOWER.

HANANI (Ha·na′ni) [possibly a shortened form of Hananiah].

1. One of Heman's 14 sons. Hanani was designated by lot to lead the 18th group of musicians at the sanctuary in the time of King David.—1Ch 25:4-6, 9, 25.

2. The seer, or visionary, who rebuked King Asa of Judah for making an alliance with the king of Syria instead of relying upon Jehovah, and who was put in the house of the stocks because the king took offense at what he said. (2Ch 16:1-3, 7-10) Hanani apparently was the father of Jehu, the prophet who rebuked Baasha the king of Israel and Jehoshaphat the king of Judah.—1Ki 16:1-4, 7; 2Ch 19:2, 3; 20:34.

3. A priest of "the sons of Immer" among those dismissing their foreign wives in compliance with Ezra's exhortation.—Ezr 2:36, 37; 10: 10, 11, 20, 44.

4. Nehemiah's brother. At the time of his coming to Shushan, Hanani, along with other men of Judah, apprised Nehemiah of the condition of Jerusalem's wall. (Ne 1:2, 3) After the wall was rebuilt, Nehemiah put his brother Hanani and also Hananiah in command of Jerusalem.—Ne 7:1, 2.

5. A Levite priest and musician who participated in the procession arranged by Nehemiah at the inauguration of Jerusalem's wall.—Ne 12:31-36.

HANANIAH (Han·a·ni′ah) [meaning "Jehovah Has Shown Favor; Jehovah Has Been Gracious"].

1. Son of Shashak and head of a Benjamite house.—1Ch 8:1, 24, 25, 28.

2. One of the 14 sons of Heman and head of the 16th of the 24 service groups of Levitical musicians appointed by David to serve at the sanctuary.—1Ch 25:1, 4, 5, 8, 9, 23.

3. A high-ranking officer, 'prince,' in King Uzziah's army.—2Ch 26:11.

4. Father of the Zedekiah who was a prince during the reign of Jehoiakim the king of Judah. —Jer 36:12.

5. Son of Azzur; a false prophet from the Benjamite city of Gibeon who opposed Jehovah's prophet Jeremiah. During the reign of King Zedekiah of Judah, while Jeremiah encouraged the people to bring their necks under the yoke of the king of Babylon and thus keep living (Jer 27:12-14), Hananiah prophesied that Babylon's power would be broken within two years, that the Jewish exiles there would be released, and that all the confiscated utensils of the temple would be returned. To illustrate his point, Hananiah removed the wooden yoke from off Jeremiah's neck and broke it. Jehovah then commanded Jeremiah to inform Hananiah that the yoke bar of wood was to be replaced by an iron yoke and that Hananiah's death would occur within that year. True to the prophecy, the false prophet died in that year.—Jer 28.

6. Probably the grandfather of Irijah the officer at the gate of Benjamin who seized the prophet Jeremiah, falsely charging that he was attempting to desert to the Chaldeans.—Jer 37:1-15.

7. The Hebrew name of Shadrach, one of Daniel's three Jewish companions taken to Babylon in 617 B.C.E.—Da 1:6, 7; see SHADRACH.

8. Son of Zerubbabel and father of Pelatiah and Jeshaiah.—1Ch 3:19, 21.

9. A descendant of Bebai who was among those heeding Ezra's exhortation to dismiss their foreign wives.—Ezr 10:10, 11, 28, 44.

10. A Levite priest and head of the paternal house of Jeremiah during Nehemiah's governorship.—Ne 12:12, 26.

11. A member of the ointment mixers who did repair work on the wall of Jerusalem in Nehemiah's time.—Ne 3:8.

12. Son of Shelemiah; one who shared in repairing the wall of Jerusalem in 455 B.C.E.—Ne 3:30.

13. A priestly trumpeter who participated in the ceremonies arranged by Nehemiah at the inauguration of Jerusalem's wall.—Ne 12:31, 40, 41.

14. One of the heads of the people whose descendant, if not he himself, attested by seal the "trustworthy arrangement" contracted during Nehemiah's governorship.—Ne 9:38; 10:1, 14, 23.

15. The prince of the Castle, a trustworthy man fearing God more than many others. Nehemiah put him in command of Jerusalem along with Hanani.—Ne 7:2.

HAND. The terminal part of the arm. The "hand," as used in the Scriptures, at times includes the wrist, as at Genesis 24:22, 30, 47 and Ezekiel 16:11, where bracelets are said to be worn on the "hands," and at Judges 15:14, where mention is made of the fetters on Samson's "hands." The hand applies the power of the arm and directs it, so, in many cases where it appears in figurative speech, the idea of "applied power" can be associated with the word "hand." (Ex 7:4; 13:3; De 2:15; Lu 1:66) Since the human hand is very dexterous and versatile and a part of the body with which work is done, it is used symbolically in many Bible texts to denote a wide range of actions.

The common Hebrew term for "hand" is *yadh;* at times, the word *kaph* is rendered "hand," but it literally means "palm." (Job 22:30, ftn) The usual Greek term for "hand" is *kheir.*

Manual Gestures and Their Significance. The hands were employed in gestures to express various things. They were lifted in prayer, the palms usually turned toward heaven in appeal (2Ch 6:12; Ne 8:6); lifted in oaths (Ge 14:22); touched to the mouth in a form of salute (Job 31:27); clapped in joy, as in applause (2Ki 11:12) or in anger or derision (Nu 24:10; Job 27:23; Na 3:19); waved in threat (Isa 10:32); placed on top

of the head or on the loins in sadness or distress (2Sa 13:19; Jer 30:5, 6); washed with water in an attempt to denote ceremonial cleanness, innocence, or ridding oneself of responsibility.—Mt 15:1, 2; 27:24; contrast Ps 26:5, 6; 51:1, 2; see ATTITUDES AND GESTURES.

Figurative and Symbolic Usages. The hand was sometimes used to represent the person himself, as in David's appeal to Nabal for food: "Just give, please, whatever your hand may find." (1Sa 25:8) It also referred to one's general disposition or activity (Ge 16:12), or it denoted his responsibility to account for his actions.—Ge 9:5; Eze 3:18, 20.

The hands of the priests were filled with sacrifices by Moses at the time of their installation as part of the ceremony symbolically equipping them, 'filling their hands' with authority and power for the priesthood.—Le 8:25-27; see FILL HAND WITH POWER.

Jehovah assured Jacob that his son Joseph would "lay his hand upon your eyes," that is, close Jacob's eyes after he had died. (Ge 46:4) This privilege would ordinarily have been that of the firstborn. Hence these words not only assured Jacob that his beloved son Joseph would remain near him during the remaining years of the aged patriarch's life but also apparently foretold that the right of firstborn, lost by Reuben, would go to Joseph.

God is symbolically spoken of as using his "hand," that is, his applied power, in accomplishing work; a few of such instances are: creation (Ps 8:6; 102:25); destroying his enemies (Isa 25:10, 11); delivering his people (Ex 7:4, 5); exercising favor and power toward those seeking him (Ezr 8:22); making provision (Ps 104:28; 145:16); and offering help (Isa 11:11). Elihu declared that the powerful ones depart "by no hand," and the stone of Nebuchadnezzar's prophetic dream was cut out of a mountain "not by hands"; in each case the meaning was that the action occurred, not by human hands, but by the power of Jehovah.—Job 34:1, 20; Da 2:34, 44, 45.

'In, into, or under one's hand' means to be under such one's power or dominion (Ge 9:2; 41:35; Job 2:6; 1Pe 5:6; compare Ge 37:21), or it may mean "at your disposal" or 'in one's care' (Ge 16:6, compare *Le;* Ge 42:37, compare *RS;* Lu 23:46; Joh 10:28, 29). *"With uplifted hand"* denotes being vigorous, victorious (Ex 14:8); *'strengthening the hands'* means empowering or supplying and equipping (Ezr 1:6); *"weakening the hands,"* breaking down the morale (Jer 38:4); *'putting one's own life into his hand or palm,'* risking his life (1Sa 19:5; Job 13:14). *"Shaking hands"* was done in making a promise (Ezr 10:19) or in going surety for another (Pr 6:1-3; 17:18; 22:26); *'putting the hand to'* signifies undertaking (De 15:10, compare *KJ*); *'putting one's hand upon another's goods,'* stealing or improperly using such (Ex 22:7, 8, 10, 11); *'clean hands'* denote innocence (2Sa 22:21; compare Ps 24: 3, 4); *'blood filling the hands,'* murder (Isa 1:15; 59:3, 7); *'putting the hand over the mouth,'* keeping quiet (Jg 18:19); *'dropping the hands down,'* becoming discouraged (2Ch 15:7; see also Isa 35:3; Heb 12:12, 13); and *'opening up the hand,'* being generous (De 15:11).

"A little more *folding of the hands* in lying down" brings poverty to the lazy one. (Pr 6:9-11) He is described as being too weary to get his hand out of the banquet bowl to bring it back to his mouth. (Pr 26:15) The negligent person "working with a *slack hand* will be of little means," whereas the *diligent hand* will bring riches.—Pr 10:4.

Other Hebrew idiomatic expressions involving the hand are: *'put your hand with,'* meaning to cooperate with, be on the side of (Ex 23:1; 1Sa 22:17); *"by the hand of"* denotes under the guidance of (Ex 38:21) or by means of (Ex 4:13; Le 8:36; 10:11); *'his hand does not reach,'* or *'his hand is not attaining it,'* he does not have enough (financial) means (Le 14:21); *'what his hand shall get,'* what he can afford (Nu 6:21); *'hands of a sword,'* power of a sword (Job 5:20); *'hand of the tongue,'* power of the tongue (Pr 18:21); *'life of your hand,'* revival of your power (Isa 57:10); *'to shut the hand'* from one's brother, that is, to be closefisted as to helping him.—De 15:7, *KJ*.

Jehovah told the Israelites that they should tie his words "as a *sign upon* [*their*] *hand*" (De 6:6-8; 11:18) and that he had engraved Zion upon his palms (Isa 49:14-16), denoting constant remembrance and attention. With similar meaning, Jehovah tells the eunuchs who lay hold of his covenant that he will give them in his house "a monument" (or, place; literally, a "hand"). (Isa 56:4, 5) The Bible speaks of worshipers of God as writing upon their hands, symbolically, the words, "Belonging to Jehovah," thus denoting they are his slaves. (Isa 44:5) In the same way the "mark" of "the wild beast" in the right hand would symbolize one's giving attention, devotion, and active support to "the wild beast" and its "image," inasmuch as a person's hands are used

to do work in behalf of the one he serves.—Re 13:16, 17; 14:9, 10; 20:4.

Laying On of Hands. Aside from mere handling, *hands were laid on* a person or object for various purposes. The general meaning of the act, however, was that of a designation, a pointing out of the person or thing as being acknowledged, or recognized, in a certain way. During the ceremony at the installation of the priesthood, Aaron and his sons laid their hands on the head of the bull and the two rams to be sacrificed, thereby acknowledging that these animals were being sacrificed for them for the sake of their becoming priests of Jehovah God. (Ex 29: 10, 15, 19; Le 8:14, 18, 22) When appointing Joshua as his successor at God's command, Moses laid his hand on Joshua, who consequently was "full of the spirit of wisdom" and so was able to lead Israel properly. (De 34:9) Hands were laid on persons when designating them as receivers of a blessing. (Ge 48:14; Mr 10:16) Jesus Christ touched, or laid his hands on, some persons he healed. (Mt 8:3; Mr 6:5; Lu 13:13) The gift of the holy spirit was granted in some instances through the laying on of the hands of the apostles.—Ac 8:14-20; 19:6.

Appointments to service. In the Christian congregation appointments of mature men to positions or offices of responsibility were also made by the *laying on of hands* by those authorized to do so. (Ac 6:6; 1Ti 4:14) Because of the influence such appointed men would have and the example they would set, the apostle Paul admonished Timothy: "Never lay your hands hastily upon any man; neither be a sharer in the sins of others." This meant not to appoint a man without due consideration of his qualifications, lest the man fail to carry out the duties of his office properly, and Timothy thus share the blame for the difficulty caused.—1Ti 5:22.

The Right Hand. The *right hand* was considered to be of great importance, symbolically. Joseph was displeased when Jacob crossed his hands in order to lay his right hand on Ephraim, Joseph's younger son. But Jacob did this purposely, to give Ephraim the superior blessing. (Ge 48:13-20) To be on the right hand of a ruler was to have the most important position, next to the ruler himself (Ps 110:1; Ac 7:55, 56; Ro 8:34; 1Pe 3:22), or a position in his favor. (Mt 25:33) Jesus is spoken of in the vision of Revelation as having the seven stars of the seven congregations in his right hand. That is, all these bodies of elders have his favor and are under his full control, power, and direction.—Re 1:16, 20; 2:1.

For God to take hold of one's right hand would strengthen that one. (Ps 73:23) Usually the right hand of a warrior was his sword-wielding hand, and it was unprotected by the shield in the left hand. Therefore, a friend would stand or fight at his right hand as an upholder and protector. This circumstance is used metaphorically with regard to God's help and protection to those serving him.—Ps 16:8; 109:30, 31; 110:5; 121:5.

The writer of Ecclesiastes says: "The heart of the wise is at his right hand, but the heart of the stupid at his left hand." In other words, the wise one inclines toward a good, favorable path, but the stupid one inclines toward a bad course.—Ec 10:2.

Directions. The Hebrew expressions for "right hand" (Heb., ya·min') and "left hand" (Heb., semo'l') are also translated "south" and "north," respectively (Ge 14:15; Ps 89:12), since directions were reckoned from the standpoint of a person facing the E. Hence, S would be to his right.—1Sa 23:19, 24.

Other Uses. "Hand" (Heb., yadh) is also used for "side" (Ex 2:5; Ec 4:1), or 'at the side of' (Ne 3:4, 5, 7); for "coast" (Nu 24:24); and for the "tenons" of the tabernacle panel frames (Ex 26: 17; compare KJ, margin). The Hebrew word kaph (often rendered "palm" and "hand") is used for the "sole" of the foot (Ge 8:9), for cups ("spoons," KJ) of the tabernacle and of the temple (Ex 25:29; Nu 7:84, 86; 2Ki 25:14), and for "socket" (of one's thigh) or "hollow" (of a sling). (Ge 32:25, 32; 1Sa 25:29) Both yadh (hand) and kaph (palm; hand) are variously translated by yet other English terms.

"Handfuls," figuratively, stands for abundance (Ge 41:47), or "a handful" may mean only a little (1Ki 17:12) or a modest portion (Ec 4:6), according to the context.—See ARM; THUMB; WASHING OF HANDS.

HANDBREADTH. A linear measure approximately corresponding to the width of the hand at the base of the fingers. The handbreadth is reckoned at 7.4 cm (2.9 in.); four fingerbreadths equaled a handbreadth, and six handbreadths equaled a cubit. (Ex 25:25; 37:12; 1Ki 7:26; 2Ch 4:5; Eze 40:5, 43; 43:13) According to Psalm 39:5, David said: "You have made my days just a few"; however, "just handbreadths" appears in the Hebrew Masoretic text. (NW, ftn) Christ Jesus similarly employed the word "cubit": "Who of you by being anxious can add one cubit to his life span?"—Mt 6:27.

HANDCUFFS. See BOND.

HAND MILL. See MILL.

HANDSHAKE. See ATTITUDES AND GESTURES.

HANES (Ha'nes). A site mentioned at Isaiah 30:4 in Jehovah's denunciation of those seeking help from Egypt. (Isa 30:1-5) The location is uncertain.

There are various possible meanings given to the text. Some commentators believe the "envoys" are Jewish, sent to obtain Egyptian military aid, and that these arrive at Hanes on such a mission. Others suggest that the envoys are those of Pharaoh (mentioned in Isa 30:3) depicted as receiving the Jewish delegation when it reached Hanes. Whatever is the case, Jehovah showed that Egypt would be a vain source of help.—Isa 30:5.

HANGING. Under the law given by Jehovah to Israel, certain criminals might be hung upon a stake after being put to death, as "accursed of God," placed on public display as a warning example. A dead person thus hung was to be taken down before nightfall and buried; leaving him on the stake all night would defile the soil given to the Israelites by God. (De 21:22, 23) Israel followed this rule even if the one executed was not an Israelite.—Jos 8:29; 10:26, 27.

The two sons and five grandsons of Saul whom David turned over to the Gibeonites for execution were not buried before nightfall. They were left in the open from the start of the barley harvest (March-April) until rain came, evidently after the harvest season was completed. The reason the Gibeonites were allowed to follow a different procedure in this instance seems to be because a national sin had been committed by King Saul, who had put some of the Gibeonites to death, thus violating the covenant made with them by Joshua centuries earlier. (Jos 9:15) Now God had caused the land to suffer a three-year famine as evidence of his anger. Therefore the bodies of the hanged ones were left exposed until Jehovah indicated that his wrath had been appeased by ending the drought period with a downpour of rain. David then had the bones of the men buried, after which "God let himself be entreated for the land."—2Sa 21:1-14.

The narrative of the book of Esther reports the hanging of several persons. The same Hebrew word (ta·lah', meaning "hang; hang up") is used in each instance. It is specifically stated that

Haman's ten sons were killed by the Jews, then hanged the next day. (Es 9:7-10, 13, 14) The others hanged were evidently treated in the same manner, their dead bodies being exposed on high before the public because their crimes were offenses against the king. (Es 2:21-23; 7:9, 10) The same Hebrew word is used for the hanging of Pharaoh's chief baker.—Ge 40:22; 41:13.

The nations surrounding Israel were generally more cruel than the Israelites in their methods of inflicting punishment and of heaping reproach on those executed. When the armies of Babylon captured Jerusalem, they inflicted cruel punishments on the nobles, hanging some of the princes by "just their hand."—La 5:12.

Jesus Christ was hanged alive, nailed to a stake, on order of the Roman government in Palestine. (Joh 20:25, 27) The apostle Paul explains that the manner of Jesus' death was highly important to the Jews, for "Christ by purchase released us from the curse of the Law by becoming a curse instead of us, because it is written: 'Accursed is every man hanged upon a stake.'" —Ga 3:13; see IMPALEMENT.

In two cases of suicide recorded in the Bible, strangulation by hanging was employed. Ahithophel, David's traitorous counselor, strangled himself ("hanged himself," *LXX*). (2Sa 17:23) Ahithophel's action was prophetic of that of one of Jesus' apostles who proved to be traitorous, Judas Iscariot. (Ps 41:9; Joh 13:18) Judas hanged himself also. (Mt 27:5) Apparently the rope, or perhaps a branch of the tree on which Judas hanged himself, broke, "and pitching head foremost he noisily burst in his midst and all his intestines were poured out."—Ac 1:18.

HANNAH (Han'nah) [Favor, Grace]. Mother of the prophet Samuel. Hannah lived with her Levite husband Elkanah and his other wife Peninnah in Ramathaim-zophim in the mountainous region of Ephraim. In spite of Hannah's long barrenness, contrasted with Peninnah's bearing several children, Hannah was still Elkanah's more beloved wife. Peninnah taunted Hannah because of her barrenness, notably when Elkanah took his family for their yearly appearance at the tabernacle in Shiloh.—1Sa 1:1-8.

On one visit to Shiloh, Hannah vowed to Jehovah that if she could bear a son, she would give him to Jehovah, for His service. Seeing her lips move as she prayed inaudibly, High Priest Eli at first suspected that she had overindulged in wine and was drunk. But on learning of her sober

fervor and sincerity, he expressed the wish that Jehovah God would grant her petition. Indeed, she soon became pregnant. After giving birth to Samuel, she did not go to Shiloh again until Samuel was weaned. Then she presented him to Jehovah as she had promised, bringing an offering consisting of a three-year-old bull, an ephah of flour, and a large jar of wine. (1Sa 1:9-28) Each year thereafter, when she came to Shiloh, Hannah brought along a new sleeveless coat for her son. Eli again blessed her, and Jehovah again opened her womb so that in time she gave birth to three sons and two daughters.—1Sa 2:18-21.

Several desirable qualities are observed in Hannah. She was prayerful and humble, and she had a desire to please her husband. Each year she accompanied him to sacrifice at the tabernacle. She made a great sacrifice of her own, giving up the companionship of her son, to keep her word and show appreciation for Jehovah's kindness. She retained her motherly affection, as shown by her making a new coat for Samuel each year. The thoughts expressed in her song of thankfulness, when she and Elkanah presented Samuel for temple service, are quite similar to the sentiments voiced by Mary shortly after learning she was to mother the Messiah.—Lu 1:46-55.

HANNATHON (Han'na·thon) [possibly from a root meaning "show favor; be gracious"]. A boundary city of Zebulun. (Jos 19:10, 14) Most scholars tentatively identify Hannathon with Tell el-Bedeiwiyeh (Tel Hannaton), about 10 km (6 mi) NNW of Nazareth. Hannathon appears in the records of Assyrian King Tiglath-pileser III and also in the Amarna Tablets.

HANNIEL (Han'ni·el) [God Has Shown Favor; God Has Been Gracious; or, Favor (Grace) of God].

1. A chieftain selected by Jehovah to represent the tribe of Manasseh in dividing the land W of the Jordan among the nine and a half Israelite tribes settling there. Hanniel was a son of Ephod and a descendant of Joseph.—Nu 34:13, 17, 23.

2. Head of an Asherite house; son of Ulla. —1Ch 7:30, 39, 40.

HANOCH (Ha'noch) [One Trained Up; Inaugurated [that is, dedicated, initiated]].

1. A son of Midian the fourth-named son of Abraham by Keturah.—Ge 25:1, 2, 4; 1Ch 1:33.

2. A son of Jacob's firstborn Reuben and the forefather of the Hanochites.—Ge 46:8, 9; Ex 6:14; Nu 26:4, 5; 1Ch 5:3.

HANOCHITES (Ha′noch·ites) [Of (Belonging to) Hanoch]. A family descended from Hanoch, a son of Reuben.—Nu 26:4, 5; Ge 46:9.

HANUN (Ha′nun) [He Has Shown Favor; He Has Been Gracious].

1. Son of and successor to the throne of Nahash the king of Ammon. Because of the lovingkindness Nahash had exercised toward him, David sent messengers to comfort Hanun over the loss of his father. But Hanun, convinced by his princes that this was merely a subterfuge on David's part to spy out the city, dishonored David's servants by shaving off half their beards and cutting their garments in half to their buttocks and then sent them away. When the sons of Ammon saw that they had become foul smelling to David because of the humiliation meted out to his messengers, Hanun took the initiative to prepare for war and hired the Syrians to fight against Israel. In the ensuing conflicts the Ammonites and the Syrians were completely defeated by Israel; David subjected the surviving Ammonites of Rabbah to forced labor.—2Sa 10: 1–11:1; 12:26-31; 1Ch 19:1–20:3.

2. One who, with the inhabitants of Zanoah, repaired the Valley Gate and part of the wall of Jerusalem.—Ne 3:13.

3. "The sixth son of Zalaph"; he did repair work on the wall of Jerusalem.—Ne 3:30.

HAPHARAIM (Haph′a·ra′im) [Place of Digging]. A site on the territorial boundary of the tribe of Issachar. (Jos 19:17-19) It cannot be identified with certainty. However, most scholars tentatively locate it at et-Taiyiba, about 12 km (7.5 mi) NW of Beth-shean. Hapharaim also appears in a list of the Palestinian cities conquered by Egypt's King Shishak.

HAPPINESS. Happiness is a state of wellbeing that is characterized by relative permanence, by emotion ranging from mere contentment to deep and intense joy in living, and by a natural desire for it to continue. It thus differs from mere pleasure, which may come about simply through chance contact and stimulation.

The Hebrew word for "happy" is ′e′sher (Ps 40:4), while the related verb ′a·shar′ means "pronounce happy." (Ge 30:13) These Hebrew terms are used with reference to humans. They often denote the result of positive action, such as acting with consideration toward the lowly one or being in fear of Jehovah. (Ps 41:1; 112:1) The Greek word rendered "happy" is ma·ka′ri·os.

The happinesses described in the Psalms and Proverbs, and particularly those spoken of by Jesus Christ in his Sermon on the Mount, are often termed "beatitudes" or "blessednesses." However, "happiness" is a more exact rendering of the Bible terms used, for both Hebrew and Greek have distinct words for "bless" (Heb., ba·rakh′; Gr., eu·lo·ge′o). Furthermore, "blessed" carries the thought of the action of blessing, while "happy" brings to mind the state or condition that results from the blessing of God. Many modern versions render ′a·shar′ and ma·ka′ri·os as "happy," "happiness." (CK, JB, Ph, Ro, TEV, Yg, NW, and other versions) Ma·ka′ri·os is translated "happy" in KJ at Acts 26:2 and Romans 14:22.

Jehovah and Jesus Christ. Jehovah is "the happy God" and his Son Jesus Christ is called "the happy and only Potentate." (1Ti 1:11; 6:15) In spite of the fact that Jehovah's name and sovereignty have been challenged by the introduction of wickedness in both heaven and earth (see JEHOVAH), he is sure of the outworking of his purposes; nothing can be done beyond what his will permits. (Isa 46:10, 11; 55:10, 11) His longsuffering in permitting conditions that are within his power to change has been with a definite purpose or end in view; therefore he is happy. The apostle Paul writes: "God, although having the will to demonstrate his wrath and to make his power known, tolerated with much longsuffering vessels of wrath made fit for destruction, in order that he might make known the riches of his glory upon vessels of mercy, which he prepared beforehand for glory."—Ro 9:22-24.

Therefore, as the psalmist exclaims: "The glory of Jehovah will prove to be to time indefinite. Jehovah will rejoice in his works." (Ps 104:31) He is the greatest and foremost Giver, never changing or letting his generosity and merciful, loving attitude be turned to bitterness because of ingratitude on the part of creatures. "Every good gift and every perfect present is from above, for it comes down from the Father of the celestial lights, and with him there is not a variation of the turning of the shadow." (Jas 1:17) His Son, Jesus Christ, resting full confidence in his Father and always doing the things that please Him, is happy. (Joh 8:29) Even when undergoing trials and sufferings, Jesus had an inward joy.—Heb 12:2; compare Mt 5:10-12.

What is the basis for real happiness?

All the happinesses promised in the Bible are contingent upon a right relationship with God; all of them are realized on the basis of love of God and faithful service to him. True happiness cannot be achieved apart from obedience to Jehovah. His blessing is essential for happiness, as one of his 'good gifts' and 'perfect presents.'

Happiness does not find its source in amassing material wealth or power. Jesus said: "There is more happiness in giving than there is in receiving." (Ac 20:35) The one who gives consideration to the lowly one, thereby enjoying the happiness of giving, is promised: "Jehovah himself will guard him and preserve him alive. He will be pronounced happy in the earth." (Ps 41:1, 2) The things that contribute to true happiness are knowledge of Jehovah, wisdom from him, and even his correction and discipline. (Pr 2:6; 3:13, 18; Ps 94:12) The truly happy person trusts in Jehovah (Pr 16:20), delights in and walks in His law (Ps 1:1, 2; 112:1), observes justice (Ps 106:3), and fears God (Ps 128:1).

A Happy Nation. Happiness can be the lot of an entire nation or people if the nation truly follows Jehovah as its God and obeys his laws. (Ps 33:12; 144:15) The nation of Israel, after David's righteous administration and during the time that King Solomon followed Jehovah's law, was secure and happy, "like the grains of sand that are by the sea for multitude, eating and drinking and rejoicing." (1Ki 4:20, 25; 10:8; 2Ch 9:7) This demonstrates the influence of righteous rule on a nation. (Compare Pr 29:2, 18.) Jesus made clear the requirement for national happiness to the nationalistic Jews who thought that because they were the fleshly descendants of Abraham and Jacob they were the 'happy nation whose God is Jehovah.' (Ps 33:12) He plainly told them that the Kingdom of God would be taken from them and "given to a nation producing its fruits." (Mt 21:43) The apostle Peter later applied the term "nation" to the spiritual ones in union with Christ, saying: "You are 'a chosen race, a royal priesthood, a holy nation, a people for special possession, that you should declare abroad the excellencies' of the one that called you out of darkness into his wonderful light."—1Pe 2:9.

Christ's Counsel About Happiness. Jesus strikingly opened his Sermon on the Mount by enumerating nine happinesses, naming qualities that bring one into God's favor, with the prospect of inheriting the Kingdom of the heavens. (Mt 5:1-12) It is notable in these happinesses that neither the condition in which a person finds himself because of time and unforeseen occurrence nor the purely humanitarian acts a person might perform bring the blessing of happiness.

True happiness stems from those things that have to do with spirituality, the worship of God, and the fulfillment of God's promises. For example, Jesus says: "Blessed are the poor *in spirit* . . . " (*KJ*), or, more understandably rendered: "Happy are those conscious of their spiritual need, since the kingdom of the heavens belongs to them." (Mt 5:3) He goes on to say: "Happy are those who mourn, since they will be comforted." (Mt 5:4) It is evident that he does not have in mind *all* persons who mourn for any reason. The mourning would be because of their poor spiritual state, their sinful condition, and the distressing circumstances that have resulted from human sinfulness, as well as their hunger and thirst for righteousness. Such mourners would be observed and favored by God with his blessing of spiritual satisfaction, just as Jesus promises: "They will be filled."—Compare 2Co 7:10; Isa 61:1-3; Eze 9:4.

In the book of Revelation, Jesus Christ, through the angelic messenger, proclaims seven happinesses. (Re 1:3; 14:13; 16:15; 19:9; 20:6; 22:7; 22:14) The book declares, in its introduction: "Happy is he who reads aloud and those who hear the words of this prophecy, and who observe the things written in it" (Re 1:3), and in its conclusion says: "Happy are those who wash their robes, that the authority to go to the trees of life may be theirs and that they may gain entrance into the city [New Jerusalem] by its gates."—Re 22:14.

Take Delight in Jehovah. In summary, it is clear that those achieving real happiness are the "holy nation" of God (1Pe 2:9), along with all others associated with that nation who serve and obey Jehovah from the heart. The psalmist says: "Rejoice in Jehovah, O you righteous ones, and give thanks to his holy memorial." (Ps 97:12) The apostle Paul echoes this admonition in writing to the Christian congregation: "Always rejoice in the Lord. Once more I will say, Rejoice!" (Php 4:4) It is, therefore, not in one's wealth or wisdom, nor in one's accomplishments or might that a person can find happiness. It is in knowledge of Jehovah, who counsels: "Let not the wise man brag about himself because of his wisdom, and let not the mighty man brag about himself because of his mightiness. Let not the rich man brag about himself because of his riches. But let the one bragging about himself brag about himself because of this very thing, the having of insight and the having of knowledge of me, that I am Jehovah, the One exercising loving-kindness, justice and righteousness in the earth; for in these things I do take delight."—Jer 9:23, 24.

HAPPIZZEZ (Hap'piz·zez) [possibly from a root meaning "smash"]. An Aaronic priest designated by lot in David's time as chief of the 18th priestly division.—1Ch 24:1-7, 15.

HARA (Ha'ra). A site to which Assyrian King Tilgath-pilneser (Tiglath-pileser III) transported Israelite captives. (1Ch 5:26) Similar references (2Ki 17:6; 18:11) to a later Assyrian exile tell of Israelites' being taken to "the cities of the Medes" (Masoretic text) or "the mountains of the Medes." (*LXX*) Many scholars feel that the *Septuagint* reading may be the correct one and suggest that at 1 Chronicles 5:26 "Hara" (*Ha·ra'*, perhaps an Aramaic form of the Hebrew word for "mountain" [*har*]) became a proper name when the phrase "of the Medes" was inadvertently omitted. If this assumption is correct, "Hara" may have applied to "the mountains of the Medes" E of the Tigris River valley. However, some who consider the Gozan of 2 Kings 17:6 and 18:11 to be a place (as in *JB, RS*) and not a river believe that "Hara" possibly was a local designation for a mountainous region in Turkey.

HARADAH (Har·a'dah) [possibly, Trembling]. A site where the Israelites encamped while on their way to the land of Canaan. (Nu 33:24, 25) Its location is today unknown.

HARAN (Ha'ran).

1. Son of Terah and brother of Abram (Abraham) and Nahor. Haran fathered Lot and two daughters, Iscah and Milcah; the latter married her uncle Nahor. Haran died before Terah and Abram left Ur of the Chaldeans.—Ge 11: 26-31.

2. A descendant of Gershon through Shimei; tribe of Levi.—1Ch 23:6-9.

3. A son of Caleb by his concubine Ephah, and "father" of Gazez; tribe of Judah.—1Ch 2:3, 42, 46.

4. A city of northern Mesopotamia in which Abram (Abraham) resided temporarily; here Terah his father died. (Ge 11:31, 32; 12:4, 5; Ac 7:2-4) The name Haran also seems to have embraced the surrounding area, for Haran is listed among "the nations" conquered by the kings of Assyria.—2Ki 19: 11, 12.

Some time after leaving Haran, Abraham sent his oldest servant to his relatives (apparently residing at Haran or a nearby town, "the city of Nahor") to find a bride for his son Isaac. (Ge 24) Later, Jacob, Abraham's grandson, went to Haran to escape the wrath of his brother Esau and also to find a wife among the daughters of his uncle Laban. (Ge 27:42-46; 28:1, 2, 10) At a well, evidently near Haran, Jacob met Rachel.—Ge 29:4-12.

In the eighth century B.C.E., Assyrian King Sennacherib tried to intimidate Judean King Hezekiah with messages boasting about his forefathers' conquest of Haran and other places.—2Ki 19:8-13; Isa 37:8-13.

Assyrian sources seem to refer to Haran as Harranu (meaning "Road"), perhaps because of its being on the caravan route linking it with cities such as Nineveh, Asshur, Babylon, and Tyre, as well as the land of Egypt. (Compare Eze 27:23.) The name of the ancient city is preserved in modern Haran, situated where two wadis join to form a stream that reaches the Balikh River in the winter, about 110 km (68 mi) above where the Balikh empties into the Euphrates River. But some believe that the ancient site itself lies to the N of modern Haran. Certain scholars see evidence for patriarchal residence (as described in the Bible) in the correspondency of ancient place-

Present-day Haran preserves the name of the ancient city at or near which Abraham's servant found a wife for Isaac

names in this area to such personal names as Serug, Nahor, and Terah.—Ge 11:22-26.

HARARITE (Har'a·rite). The designation of certain mighty men of David. (2Sa 23:8, 11, 33; 1Ch 11:26, 34, 35) They were perhaps from the hill country of Judah.

HARBONA (Har·bo'na). One of Ahasuerus' seven court officials sent to convey to Queen Vashti the king's word for her to appear before him. Then, at the time that Haman's scheme to exterminate the Jews was exposed, Harbona's mentioning the 50-cubit stake Haman had made for Mordecai prompted Ahasuerus to order that Haman himself be hanged on it.—Es 1:10-12; 7:9, 10.

HARE [Heb., 'ar·ne'veth]. A gnawing animal of the Leporidae family, closely related to but larger than the rabbit. It differs from the latter in that its young are usually not born in an underground burrow, are active at birth, fully furred, and have open eyes. The hare is known by its divided lip, long ears, cocked tail, and its long hind limbs and feet, so useful for a speedy escape from its enemies. The fastest hares are said to attain a speed of as much as 70 km/hr (43 mph). The average length of the animals, of which there are numerous varieties, is about 0.6 m (2 ft). Their usual coloration is grayish or brownish.

The hare was prohibited as food under the Law given through Moses and is referred to as a chewer of the cud. (Le 11:4, 6; De 14:7) Hares and rabbits, of course, do not have a multichambered or multiparted stomach and do not regurgitate their food for rechewing, which characteristics are associated with the scientific classification of ruminants or cud chewers. Nevertheless, although the Hebrew term here used for chewing literally means "bringing up," the modern scientific classification was not the basis for what the Israelites in Moses' day understood 'cud chewing' to be. Hence, there is no foundation for judging the accuracy of the Bible statement by the restricted, relatively recent conception of what constitutes a cud-chewing animal, as done by many critics.

In the past, commentators with faith in the inspiration of the Bible record saw no error in the statement of the Law. Observed *The Imperial Bible-Dictionary:* "It is obvious that the hare does in repose chew over and over the food which it has some time taken; and this action has always

been popularly considered a chewing of the cud. Even our poet Cowper, a careful noticer of natural phenomena, who has recorded his observations on the three hares which he had domesticated, affirms that they 'chewed the cud all day till evening.'"—Edited by P. Fairbairn, London, 1874, Vol. I, p. 700.

Scientific observation of hares and rabbits in more recent years, however, indicates that even more than seeming cud chewing is involved. Writes François Bourlière (*The Natural History of Mammals,* 1964, p. 41): "The habit of 'refection,' or passing the food twice through the intestine instead of only once, seems to be a common phenomenon in the rabbits and hares. Domestic rabbits usually eat and swallow without chewing their night droppings, which form in the morning as much as half the total contents of the stomach. In the wild rabbit refection takes place twice daily, and the same habit is reported for the European hare. . . . It is believed that this habit provides the animals with large amounts of B vitamins produced by bacteria in the food within the large intestine." On the same point, the work *Mammals of the World* (by E. P. Walker, 1964, Vol. II, p. 647) notes: "This may be similar to 'chewing the cud' in ruminant mammals." —See CUD.

HAREPH (Ha'reph) [meaning "He Has Reproached (Taunted)"]. A descendant of Judah; son of Hur and the "father of Beth-gader."—1Ch 2:3, 50, 51; see BETH-GADER.

HARHAIAH (Har·hai'ah). Father of Uzziel. Harhaiah's son, a goldsmith, did repair work on the wall of Jerusalem under the direction of Nehemiah.—Ne 3:8.

HARHAS (Har'has). Grandfather of Shallum the husband of the prophetess Huldah. (2Ki 22:14) In the Masoretic text his name is given as Hasrah at 2 Chronicles 34:22.

HARHUR (Har'hur) [Burning Fever]. Ancestral head of a family of Nethinim temple slaves. "The sons of Harhur" are listed among those returning with Zerubbabel from Babylon in 537 B.C.E.—Ezr 2:1, 2, 43, 51; Ne 7:46, 53.

HARIM (Ha'rim) [Devoted; Banned].

1. An Aaronic priest selected by lot to head the 3rd of the 24 priestly divisions organized by David. (1Ch 24:1, 3, 7, 8) "Sons [or descendants] of Harim" are mentioned among the postexilic priests: 1,017 returned from Babylon

in 537 B.C.E. (Ezr 2:1, 2, 36, 39; Ne 7:42) Adna was the head of this paternal house in the following generation. (Ne 12:12, 15) Five "of the sons of Harim" took foreign wives but put them away in response to Ezra's exhortation to do so. (Ezr 10: 10, 11, 21, 44) A representative of the family (or possibly one of them bearing the same name) supported the covenant of faithfulness after Nehemiah's arrival in 455 B.C.E.—Ne 9:38; 10:1, 5, 8.

2. The founder of a nonpriestly family, 320 of whom returned from Babylon to Jerusalem with Zerubbabel. (Ezr 2:1, 2, 32; Ne 7:35) As with members of the priestly family of the same name (No. 1), eight descendants of this Harim also took foreign wives and dismissed them. (Ezr 10:25, 31, 32, 44) Likewise their representative attested the "trustworthy arrangement" contracted during Nehemiah's governorship. (Ne 9:38; 10:1, 14, 27) One "son" of Harim, Malchijah, helped repair Jerusalem's wall.—Ne 3:11.

HARIPH (Ha'riph) [meaning "He Has Reproached (Taunted)"]. Head of a family of which 112 males returned from Babylonian exile in 537 B.C.E.; also called Jorah. (Ne 7:6, 7, 24; Ezr 2:18) The name Hariph is again listed among the heads of the people, evidently being represented by a descendant, who attested by seal the confession contract made during Nehemiah's governorship.—Ne 9:38; 10:1, 14, 19.

HARIPHITE (Har'i·phite) [Of (Belonging to) Hariph or Haruph]. A designation applied to a Benjamite, Shephatiah, who joined David at Ziklag while David was still under restrictions because of Saul. Shephatiah's being called a Hariphite may mean that he was either a native of Hariph, or Haruph (a place of unknown location), or a descendant of a certain Hariph, or Haruph. —1Ch 12:1, 2, 5.

HARLOT. A prostitute. The term is usually applied to a female who engages in sex relations outside the marriage bond, especially if she customarily does this for some form of hire. In fact, the Greek term *por'ne* (harlot; fornicatrix; prostitute) comes from a root meaning "sell." (Re 17: 1, ftn) The Hebrew term *zoh·nah'* (harlot; prostitute) comes from the root verb *za·nah'*, meaning "play the harlot; have immoral intercourse; commit prostitution; fornicate."—See PROSTITUTE.

From the beginning, harlotry was condemned by God. The perfect marriage standard was established in Eden by God himself at the marriage of Adam and Eve, when He stated: "A man will

leave his father and his mother and he must stick to his wife and they must become one flesh." (Ge 2:24) Though God condemned harlotry, he did permit concubinage and polygamy, even among his servants, until his due time to reestablish the perfect marriage standard through Jesus Christ. Jesus quoted the above words of his Father, and the apostle Paul pointed out that this rule was binding on the Christian congregation. He showed that a Christian who violates this rule joins himself to a harlot, as "one body."—Mt 19:4-9; 1Co 6:16.

The early view of harlotry among God's servants is illustrated in the case of Judah the great-grandson of Abraham. While living as an alien resident in Canaan, where harlotry was tolerated, the family head Judah had relations with his son Er's widow Tamar, who was disguised as a harlot. When it was discovered that Tamar was pregnant from the act, it was reported to Judah: "Tamar your daughter-in-law has played the harlot, and here she is also pregnant by her harlotry." Judah then ordered her to be burned (that is, first put to death, then burned as detestable) because she was considered to be espoused to Judah's son Shelah. On discovering the full facts, Judah did not excuse himself for his act with a supposed harlot, but he said regarding Tamar: "She is more righteous than I am, for the reason that I did not give her to Shelah my son." He excused Tamar for thus acting to have offspring from Judah after Judah had failed to give her to his son Shelah in order that brother-in-law marriage might be performed toward her.—Ge 38:6-26.

Harlotry was condemned by the Law of God to Israel, although harlots existed in the land. (Pr 7) The Law strictly forbade prostitution of an Israelite girl. (Le 19:29; 21:9) Any Israelite girl who had committed fornication and who later married under the fraudulent claim of being a virgin was to be stoned to death. (De 22:20, 21) The payment that was obtained as the hire of a harlot was a disgusting thing and was unacceptable as a contribution to the sanctuary of Jehovah. This was in contrast with pagan practices wherein temple harlots were often a source of revenue. —De 23:18.

Rahab, a harlot of the pagan city of Jericho, displayed a right heart toward Jehovah and acted to assist the Israelite spies sent out by Joshua. For her faith, and works in harmony therewith, her life was spared. She later joined in honorable marriage with Salmon of the tribe of Judah and became an ancestress of Jesus Christ.—Jos chap 2; 6:22-25; Mt 1:1, 5; Jas 2:25.

When Jesus Christ was on earth, he scathingly denounced the unbelieving chief priests and older men of influence, declaring that tax collectors and harlots were going ahead of them into the Kingdom of God. (Mt 21:23, 31, 32) These despised persons were righthearted ones who received forgiveness through faith in Christ. Nevertheless, they had to clean up first from their harlotry, for those continuing to practice such immorality cannot inherit the Kingdom. —Ga 5:19-21; Eph 5:5.

Figurative Use. The term "harlot" is also used figuratively to apply to a professed worshiper of Jehovah, or to an organization or a nation that claims to worship him but that actually gives affection and worship to other gods. Jerusalem became a "harlot" in this sense. In fact, she went so far that she did what was not normal for harlots, namely, instead of receiving pay, she paid pagan nations to practice harlotry with her. —Eze 16:33, 34; see Eze 23, where Samaria (representing Israel) and Jerusalem (Judah) are likened to prostitutes.

Revelation symbolically depicts a harlot who rides on a scarlet-colored wild beast and has as a name on her forehead "Babylon the Great, the mother of the harlots and of the disgusting things of the earth." With her "the kings of the earth committed fornication."—Re 17:1-5; see BABYLON THE GREAT; FORNICATION.

HAR–MAGEDON (Har–Ma·ged′on) [from Heb., meaning "Mountain of Megiddo"]. This name is directly associated with "the war of the great day of God the Almighty." The term applies specifically to the condition, or situation, to which "the kings of the entire inhabited earth" are gathered in oppositon to Jehovah and his Kingdom by Jesus Christ. In a number of versions it is rendered "Armageddon." (Re 16:14, 16, AT; KJ; JB; RS; TEV) The name Har–Magedon, taken from Hebrew, means simply "Mountain of Megiddo."

There does not appear to have been a literal place called "Mountain of Megiddo," either inside or outside the Promised Land, before or during the days of the apostle John, who recorded the vision. Hence, Har–Magedon evidently draws its significance from the events associated with the ancient city of Megiddo.

Megiddo was situated a few miles SE of Mount Carmel, overlooking and dominating the Plain of Esdraelon (Jezreel) and controlling major N-S and E-W trade and military routes. Joshua first conquered this Canaanite city. (Jos 12:7, 8, 21) Near this site Jabin's army under command of Sisera was later destroyed. Jehovah there employed natural forces to assist the Israelite army under Barak. The account reads: "Barak went descending from Mount Tabor with ten thousand men behind him. And Jehovah began to throw Sisera and all his war chariots and all the camp into confusion by the edge of the sword before Barak. Finally Sisera got down off the chariot and took to flight on foot. And Barak chased after the war chariots and the camp as far as Harosheth of the nations, so that all the camp of Sisera fell by the edge of the sword. Not as much as one remained."—Jg 4:14-16.

After the victory, Barak and the prophetess Deborah broke out in song, which went, in part: "Kings came, they fought; it was then that the kings of Canaan fought in Taanach by the waters of Megiddo. No gain of silver did they take. From heaven did the stars fight, from their orbits they fought against Sisera. The torrent of Kishon washed them away, the torrent of ancient days, the torrent of Kishon. You went treading down strength, O my soul. It was then that the hoofs of horses pawed because of dashings upon dashings of his stallions."—Jg 5:19-22.

It was at Megiddo that King Ahaziah of Judah died after he was mortally wounded on orders of Jehu. (2Ki 9:27) There King Josiah of Judah was killed in an encounter with Pharaoh Nechoh. (2Ki 23:29, 30) Because of its commanding position, many other nations, according to secular history, warred around Megiddo. 'Jews, Gentiles, Saracens, crusaders, Egyptians, Persians, Druses, Turks, and Arabs have all pitched their tents on the plain of Esdraelon.'—Word Studies in the New Testament, by M. R. Vincent, 1957, Vol. II, p. 542.

The Revelation account depicts the combined forces of the kings of the earth as being gathered "to the place [Gr., form of to′pos] that is called in Hebrew Har–Magedon." (Re 16:16) In the Bible to′pos may refer to a literal location (Mt 14:13, 15, 35); to one's opportunity, or "chance" (Ac 25:16); or to a figurative realm, condition, or situation (Re 12:6, 14). In view of the context, it is to a "place" in the last-mentioned sense that earth's combined military powers are marching.

"The war of the great day of God the Almighty" at Har–Magedon was not some past event but is depicted in Revelation as future from the time of John's vision. The gathering of the kings to Har–Magedon is described as being a result of the pouring out of the sixth of the seven bowls containing the "last" plagues that will bring to a finish the anger of God. (Re 15:1; 16:1, 12) Also, indicating that the war at Har–Magedon is closely associated with Christ's presence is the warning of his coming as a thief, which is placed between verses 14 and 16 of Revelation chapter 16.

The global aspect of the war is emphasized in the context. There the opponents of Jehovah are identified as "the kings of the entire inhabited earth," who are mobilized by "expressions inspired by demons."—Re 16:14.

Farther on, John says: "And I saw the wild beast and the kings of the earth and their armies gathered together to wage the war with the one seated on the horse and with his army." (Re 19:19) This chapter identifies the leader of the heavenly armies, seated on a white horse, as one who is called "Faithful and True" and "The Word of God." (Re 19:11-13) Therefore, it is Jesus Christ, The Word, who acts as the commander of God's heavenly armies. (Joh 1:1; Re 3:14) Further showing that Christ leads the heavenly forces is the statement that the earthly forces "battle with the Lamb [who is Jesus Christ (Joh 1:29)], but, because he is Lord of lords and King of kings, the Lamb will conquer them. Also, those called and chosen and faithful with him will do so."—Re 17:13, 14.

Since the vision in Revelation chapter 19 reveals only armies in heaven as participating in the warfare as supporters of Jesus Christ, The Word of God, it indicates that none of Jehovah's Christian servants on earth will participate in the fighting. This is in harmony with the words of Jesus Christ at Matthew 26:52 that his disciples not resort to weapons of physical warfare. (Compare Ex 14:13, 14; 2Ch 20:15, 17, 22, 23; Ps 2:4-9.) The birds that fly in midheaven will dispose of the bodies of those slaughtered.—Re 19:11-21.

Har–Magedon is thus seen to be a fight, not merely among men, but one in which God's invisible armies take part. Its coming is certain and it will take place at the time set by Jehovah God, who "is doing according to his own will among the army of the heavens and the inhabitants of the earth."—Da 4:35; see also Mt 24:36.

HARMON (Har'mon). There is uncertainty as to what is designated by the Hebrew term transliterated "Harmon" (Am 4:3, *AS, NW, RS*), some

translators giving such widely differing renderings as "refuse heap" (*AT*) and "palace" (*KJ*). If the reading of the Greek *Septuagint* ("the mountain Remman") comes closer to the original Hebrew text, then perhaps "Harmon" refers to "the crag of Rimmon."—Jg 20:45, 47.

HARNEPHER (Har'ne·pher). Son of Zophah of the tribe of Asher.—1Ch 7:30, 36.

HAROD (Ha'rod) [Trembling]. A well (spring or fountain, as this is the usual meaning of the Hebrew word, although the Hebrew words for "well" and "fountain" are sometimes used interchangeably; compare Ge 16:7, 14; 24:11, 13), in the vicinity of which the Israelite army under Gideon's leadership encamped and where, later, the reduced force of 10,000 was put to the proof. Subsequently 300 men were selected to rout the Midianites. The earlier departure of 22,000 Israelites because of their being "afraid and trembling" may have been the reason for giving the well its name.—Jg 7:1-7.

The well of Harod has been traditionally identified with 'Ain Jalud (Mayan Harod), a spring rising on the NW spur of Mount Gilboa. Regarding 'Ain Jalud the noted scholar G. A. Smith observed: "It bursts some fifteen feet [less than 5 m] broad and two [0.6 m] deep from the foot of Gilboa, and mainly out of it, but fed also by the other two springs ['Ain el-Meiyiteh and 'Ain Tuba'un], it flows strongly enough to work six or seven mills. The deep bed and soft banks of this stream constitute a formidable ditch in front of the position on Gilboa, and render it possible for defenders of the latter to hold the spring at their feet in face of an enemy on the plain: and the spring is indispensable to them, for neither to the left, right, nor rear is other living water. . . . The stream, which makes it possible for the occupiers of the hill to hold also the well against the enemy on the plain, forbids them to be careless in using the water; for they drink in face of that enemy, and the reeds and shrubs which mark its course afford cover for hostile ambushes."—*The Historical Geography of the Holy Land,* London, 1968, p. 258.

HARODITE (Ha'rod·ite) [Of (Belonging to) Harod]. A resident of Harod or a person living near a place called Harod. The term is applied to Shammah and Elika, two of David's mighty men. (2Sa 23:8, 25) If "Shammah" and "Shammoth" are the same person, then the use of "Harorite" at 1 Chronicles 11:27 is possibly a scribal error for

"Harodite," the change perhaps arising from the similarity between the Hebrew letters "r" (ר) and "d" (ד).

HAROEH (Ha·ro'eh) [The Seer]. One listed in the genealogy of Judah as a son of Shobal. (1Ch 2:3, 52) Haroeh is generally thought to be the same as Reaiah.—1Ch 4:2; see REAIAH No. 1.

HARORITE (Ha'ro·rite). A term indicating the place from which Shammoth, one of David's mighty men, came. (1Ch 11:26, 27) "Harorite" may be an error for "Harodite."—2Sa 23:25; see HARODITE.

HAROSHETH (Ha·ro'sheth). A site, called fully "Harosheth of the nations," that served as military headquarters for Sisera, the army chief of the Canaanite king Jabin, who ruled in Hazor. (Jg 4:2, 13) Judge Barak pressed his victory over these enemy forces to this same point. (Jg 4:16) The name Harosheth (meaning "Woodland; Woody Thicket") seems to be preserved in el-Harithiyeh, near the western exit of the Plain of Jezreel and about 16 km (10 mi) NNW of Megiddo. However, scholars usually hold that the actual ancient site was at nearby Tell 'Amr (Tel Me'ammer).

HARP. The name of the first musical instrument mentioned in Scripture. (Ge 4:21, *AS, Fn, Kx, NW, Yg, Da*) The Hebrew word *kin·nohr'* (harp) is also rendered "lyre" in a number of Bible translations. (*JB, Mo, Ro, RS*) In about half of the 42 occurrences of *kin·nohr'* in the Bible, the translators of the *Septuagint* rendered it by the Greek *ki·tha'ra*. The *ki·tha'ra* was an instrument resembling the lyre (Gr., *ly'ra*), but it had a more shallow sounding board. Modern translations generally render *ki·tha'ra* in the Christian Greek Scriptures as "harp." (1Co 14:7; Re 5:8) Pictorial representations on Egyptian monuments indicate that ancient harps were of many styles and shapes, with a varying number of strings. In view of those points, some have suggested that *kin·nohr'* may have been a somewhat general term designating any instrument incorporating basic features of the ancient harp.

All that the Hebrew Scriptures definitely indicate about the *kin·nohr'* is that it was portable and comparatively light in weight, since it could be played in a procession, or even by a prostitute as she sang, walking through a city. (1Sa 10:5; 2Sa 6:5; Isa 23:15, 16) Some were made of "algum" wood. (1Ki 10:12) The strings may have been made from the small intestines of sheep, although perhaps spun vegetable fibers were also used.

David, who was skilled in playing the *kin·nohr'* "with his hand" (1Sa 16:16, 23), assigned this instrument a prominent place along with the 'stringed instrument' (*ne'vel*) in the orchestra that later played at Solomon's temple. (1Ch 25:1; 2Ch 29:25) When Nehemiah inaugurated Jerusalem's wall, the *kin·nohr'* added to the joy of the occasion. (Ne 12:27) Since the *kin·nohr'* was essentially a "pleasant" instrument of "exultation," its sound would cease at times of judgment or punishment. (Ps 81:2; Eze 26:13; Isa 24:8, 9) Saddened by their exile in Babylon, the Israelites had no inclination to play their harps, but they hung them upon poplar trees.—Ps 137:1, 2.

Because of the uncertainty surrounding the precise identity of the *kin·nohr'*, and especially the *ne'vel* (stringed instrument), any attempt to compare the two instruments is speculative. First Chronicles 15:20, 21 mentions "stringed instruments [*neva·lim'* (plural)] tuned to Alamoth, . . . harps [*kin·no·rohth'* (plural)] tuned to Sheminith." If "Alamoth" refers to a higher musical register and "Sheminith" to a lower tonal range, this could imply that the *kin·nohr'* was the larger, lower-pitched instrument. On the other hand, the reverse could be true (which is the general consensus) if, indeed, Alamoth and Sheminith are specifically here mentioned because of being exceptional tunings for these instruments. In any event, both instruments were portable.

At Daniel 3:5, 7, 10, 15, the Aramaic word *sab·bekha"* seems to refer to a "triangular harp" (*NW*), also rendered as "trigon" (*AT, JB, RS*) and "sambuca." (*Da*) The *sab·bekha"* is described by some as a small, shrill, triangular, four-stringed harp, which description harmonizes with the above renderings.—See STRINGED INSTRUMENT.

HARPOON. A barbed, spearlike instrument generally used in striking large fish. Reference is made to the harpoon only at Job 41:7, drawing attention to the armorlike quality of the skin of Leviathan (the crocodile), which resists penetration by an ordinary harpoon.

HARSHA (Har'sha) [possibly, Deaf; Keeping Silent]. Ancestral head of a family of Nethinim temple slaves, members of which returned from Babylon with Zerubbabel in 537 B.C.E.—Ezr 2:1, 2, 43, 52; Ne 7:54.

HARUM (Ha'rum). A man of the tribe of Judah.—1Ch 4:1, 8.

HARUMAPH (Ha·ru'maph) [probably, Having a Slit Nose]. Father (or forefather) of the Jedaiah who helped Nehemiah rebuild Jerusalem's wall.—Ne 3:10.

HARUZ (Ha'ruz) [possibly, Gold; or, Diligent]. A man from Jotbah; the grandfather of King Amon of Judah and the father of Meshullemeth the wife of King Manasseh.—2Ki 21:19, 20.

HARVEST. The gathering of crops; one of the things that will never cease "all the days the earth continues." (Ge 8:22) Harvesttime is accompanied by great rejoicing, although much hard work is, of course, required to gather the crops. (Ps 126:5, 6; Isa 9:3; 16:9, 10) Certain Biblical happenings were noted as occurring in relation to the time of harvest.—Ge 30:14; Jos 3:15; Jg 15:1; Ru 1:22; 2:23; 1Sa 6:13; 2Sa 21:9; 23:13.

Sabbaths and Jubilee. God's law to Israel outlined certain requirements and provisions regarding the harvest. Important as it was, the Israelites were not relieved of their obligation to observe the Sabbath, the Law making no provision for harvesting on that day in the event of an emergency. (Ex 34:21; compare Ne 13:15.) Since no sowing was to be done during the Sabbath year, as well as the Jubilee year, there would, of course, be no crops to gather in, with the exception of the growth from spilled kernels of the former harvest. But even this was not to be harvested by the owner, although he, his slaves and his hired laborers, settlers and alien residents, as well as domestic animals and wild beasts could eat of the land's produce.—Ex 23: 10, 11; Le 25:3-7, 11, 12, 20-22.

Firstfruits, and Care for Poor. The firstfruits of each harvest were to be presented to Jehovah. (Le 23:10, 11; De 26:1-4) The fruit of a tree was not to be gathered for personal use until its fifth year.—Le 19:23-25.

If hungry, an Israelite could enter the field or vineyard of another and eat of its produce to satisfaction, but he could not carry anything away in a container or use a sickle to cut the grain of his fellowman.—De 23:24, 25; compare Mt 12:1; Lu 6:1; see GLEANING.

At harvesttime, the Israelites were not to reap the edges of their fields completely nor to pick up the gleanings, as such leftovers of their grainfields and vineyards were designated for the afflicted one and the alien resident.—Le 19:9, 10; 23:22; De 24:19.

Weather. In the Promised Land in ancient times, as today, it rarely rained during harvesttime; in fact, when Jehovah let it rain and thunder in answer to Samuel's prayer, this proved to the Israelites that they had committed a great evil in asking for a human king. (1Sa 12:17-19; see also Pr 26:1.) But the Jordan River would overflow its banks because of the late rains in the early spring and the melting snows from the Lebanon Mountains.—Jos 3:15; 5:10, 11.

The weather is hot at harvesttime, making a cloud of dew most refreshing. (Isa 18:4) A drink chilled with snow from the mountains is welcome, and this, rather than a snowfall, is evidently what is referred to by the parallelism at Proverbs 25:13, since snow during harvesttime would be a calamity.

Flax, Barley, Wheat. In the vicinity of Jericho flax began to be harvested in the 12th month, Adar (February-March), or early in Nisan (March-April), the first month of the Hebrews' sacred year. The stalks of flax were pulled or hoed up and then laid out to dry. There were stalks of flax on Rahab's roof when she hid the spies (Jos 2:6) in the first days of Nisan.—Jos 2:16, 22, 23; 3:1, 2; 4:19.

Next came the barley harvest in the month of Nisan (March-April). The Israelites entered the Promised Land at the time of the barley harvest and began eating of the land's produce on Nisan 15. (Jos 3:15; 5:10, 11) While the barley harvest continued in the hills of Palestine, in the plains the wheat harvest followed (Ru 1:22; 2:23; 2Sa 21:9), commencing during the month of Ziv, or Iyyar (April-May).

Then, during the month of Sivan (May-June), the wheat harvest was under way in the uplands. Grasping the stalks of grain with one hand, the reapers cut them off with a sickle.—Compare De 23:25; Isa 17:5.

Grapes, Dates, Figs, Olives. The month of Tammuz (June-July) saw the first ripe grapes, with the harvest of grapes beginning in the month of Ab (July-August), at which time the olives were also ripe in the lowlands. During the month of Elul (August-September) the general vintage harvest was under way, the dates were ripe, pomegranates were ripening, and the summer figs were gathered. (Nu 13:23) The harvest had generally been completed by the month of Ethanim, or Tishri (September-October), although olives might still be gathered in northern Galilee in the month of Bul, or Heshvan (Marheshvan) (October-November). Olives were harvested by beating the tree branches with a stick. —De 24:20; see CALENDAR.

Festivals. Israel's three primary festivals were directly associated with the harvest. (Ex 23:14-17) The Festival of Unfermented Cakes, beginning on Nisan 15, coincided with the barley harvest. On Nisan 16, "the day after the sabbath" (not necessarily a weekly sabbath, as the initial day of the festival was designated a sabbath regardless of the day on which it fell), the high priest was to wave a sheaf of the firstfruits of the barley harvest to and fro before Jehovah.—Le 23:6-11.

The Festival of Weeks, or Pentecost, came on the 50th day from Nisan 16. This was at the time of the wheat harvest. Two leavened loaves of the firstfruits of the new grain were then to be presented as a wave offering to Jehovah. (Le 23:15-17) Evidently with reference to the seven weeks of harvesting between the Festival of Unfermented Cakes and the Festival of Pentecost, Jeremiah describes Jehovah as "the One who guards even the prescribed weeks of the harvest for us," preserving this period as a dry season, since rain would be damaging to the harvest. —Jer 5:24; compare Am 4:7.

The Festival of Booths, or of Ingathering, beginning on the 15th day of the seventh month Ethanim, or Tishri, brought the major part of the agricultural year to a joyful conclusion, as the harvesting had generally been completed by that time.—Le 23:33-36, 39-43; see FESTIVAL and the respective festivals under their own headings.

Figurative Usage. The return of people from exile and the gathering of persons for life are compared to harvesting (Ho 6:11; Mt 9:37, 38; Lu 10:2; Joh 4:35-38), as is the gathering and destruction of the wicked. (Jer 51:33; Re 14:17-20) Christ Jesus referred to "the conclusion of the system of things" as the harvest, at which time the angels, acting in the capacity of reapers, would gather out all weedlike ones and pitch them into "the fiery furnace," whereas the wheatlike ones would "shine as brightly as the sun in the kingdom of their Father." (Mt 13:24-30, 36-43) This harvesting work is carried on under the direction of Jesus Christ, for in the book of Revelation he, as 'someone like a son of man,' is depicted with a sharp sickle in his hand. —Re 14:14-16; see AGRICULTURE.

HASADIAH (Has·a·di'ah) [Loving-Kindness of Jah; Jah Is Loving-Kindness]. One of Zerubbabel's sons. The fact that the sons of Zerubbabel

are listed in two different groups (the first two names being separated from the other five by the mention of Shelomith in the genealogy of King David's descendants) may possibly mean that they were sons of different mothers.—1Ch 3:1, 19, 20.

HASHABIAH (Hash·a·bi'ah) [Jehovah Has Accounted (Considered)].

1. A Levite in the line of descent from Merari to the temple singer Ethan. (1Ch 6:31, 44-47) Possibly the same as No. 6.

2. Head of the 12th of the 24 groups into which David divided the Levite temple musicians; one of the six sons of Jeduthun and possibly a descendant of No. 1.—1Ch 25:1, 3, 19.

3. An administrator "for all the work of Jehovah and for the king's service" whom David assigned with his brothers over the territory W of the Jordan. He was a Levite, a descendant of Kohath's son Hebron. (1Ch 26:30; 23:12) Possibly the same as No. 4.

4. A prince and leader of the tribe of Levi during David's reign. (1Ch 27:16, 17, 22) Possibly the same as No. 3.

5. One of "the chiefs of the Levites" who contributed many animals for King Josiah's great Passover celebration.—2Ch 35:1, 9.

6. A Levite whose descendant resided in Jerusalem after the Babylonian exile. (1Ch 9:2, 3, 14; Ne 11:1, 4, 15, 20) Possibly the same as No. 1.

7. One of the chief priests whom Ezra entrusted with the transporting of precious materials from Babylon to Jerusalem in 468 B.C.E. (Ezr 8:24-30) He may be the same one mentioned in verse 19 and possibly the same as No. 9.

8. A Levite, perhaps a descendant of No. 1, who attested the national agreement of faithfulness in Nehemiah's day. (Ne 9:38; 10:1, 9, 11) Possibly he was the same as No. 10 or 11.

9. A priest heading the paternal house of Hilkiah during the tenure of High Priest Joiakim the successor of Jeshua. (Ne 12:10, 12, 21) Possibly the same as No. 7.

10. One of the heads of the Levites, serving during Joiakim's officiate.—Ne 12:23, 24, 26; see No. 8.

11. A Levite prince of half the district of Keilah who repaired a section of Jerusalem's wall for his district.—Ne 3:17; see No. 8.

12. A Levite of "the sons of Asaph" whose descendant was overseer of the Levites in postexilic Jerusalem.—Ne 11:22.

HASHABNAH (Ha·shab′nah) [shortened form of Hashabneiah]. One of the heads of the people whose descendant, if not he himself, attested by seal the confession contract made during Nehemiah's governorship.—Ne 9:38; 10:1, 14, 25.

HASHABNEIAH (Hash·ab·nei′ah) [possibly, Jah Has Accounted (Considered) Me].

1. Father of Hattush. The latter did repair work on Jerusalem's wall.—Ne 3:10.

2. One of eight Levites who called upon the sons of Israel to bless Jehovah and his glorious name and then reviewed God's dealings with Israel before the attestation by seal to the confession contract made during Nehemiah's governorship. (Ne 9:5, 38) Perhaps, as suggested by the reading in the Syriac *Peshitta,* he is identical with one of the Levites named Hashabiah, such as the one mentioned at Ezra 8:19 or at Nehemiah 10:11.

HASH-BADDANAH (Hash-bad′da·nah). One of seven men, possibly Levites, who stood to the left of Ezra as he read from the book of the Law to the congregation of Israel at the public square near the Water Gate of Jerusalem.—Ne 8:1-4.

HASHEM (Ha′shem). "The sons of Hashem the Gizonite" are listed among David's mighty men. (1Ch 11:26, 34) The corresponding list of the mighty men of David's military forces reads "the sons of Jashen."—2Sa 23:32.

HASHMONAH (Hash·mo′nah). An Israelite camping site, apparently between Mithkah and Moseroth. (Nu 33:29, 30) Its exact location is uncertain. Hashmonah has been linked with the Wadi Hashim near the suggested location of Kadesh-barnea, and according to another view, it may be the same as Azmon.—Nu 34:4, 5; see AZMON.

HASHUBAH (Ha·shu′bah) [Accounting; Consideration]. Son of Zerubbabel.—1Ch 3:19, 20.

HASHUM (Ha′shum). Ancestral head of a family of Israelites, members of which returned from Babylon with Zerubbabel in 537 B.C.E. (Ezr 2:1, 2, 19; Ne 7:22) Upon Ezra's arrival in Jerusalem in 468 B.C.E., seven men of "the sons of Hashum" dismissed their foreign wives. (Ezr 10: 33, 44) The family representative or one bearing the name Hashum stood to the left of Ezra as he read the book of the Law to the Israelites assembled at the public square before the Water Gate of Jerusalem. (Ne 8:1-4) Likewise a representative of the house of Hashum attested by seal the "trustworthy arrangement" contracted during Nehemiah's governorship.—Ne 9:38; 10:1, 14, 18.

HASSENAAH (Has·se·na′ah) [possibly, The Hated (One)]. "The sons of Hassenaah" rebuilt the Fish Gate at the time Jerusalem's walls were being repaired under Nehemiah's direction. (Ne 3:3) Hassenaah may be the same as Senaah, without the Hebrew definite article.—Ezr 2:35; Ne 7:38; see SENAAH.

HASSENUAH (Has·se·nu′ah).

1. Father of Hodaviah of the tribe of Benjamin. —1Ch 9:7.

2. Father or ancestor of a certain Judah, a Benjamite who was a contemporary of Nehemiah.—Ne 11:7, 9.

HASSHUB (Has′shub) [One Who Is Accounting (Considering)].

1. Son of Pahath-moab; one of those who did repair work when the wall of Jerusalem was being rebuilt under Nehemiah's direction.—Ne 3:11.

2. One who repaired a section of the wall of Jerusalem, evidently a section in front of his house.—Ne 3:23.

3. One of the heads of the people whose descendant, if not he himself, attested by seal the "trustworthy arrangement" contracted during Nehemiah's governorship.—Ne 9:38; 10:1, 14, 23.

4. A Merarite Levite; son of Azrikam and father of Shemaiah.—1Ch 9:14; Ne 11:15.

HASUPHA (Ha·su′pha). The forefather of a family of Nethinim, members of which returned from Babylon with Zerubbabel in 537 B.C.E. —Ezr 2:1, 2, 43; Ne 7:46.

HATE. In the Scriptures the word "hate" has several shades of meaning. It may denote intense hostility, sustained ill will often accompanied by malice. Such hate may become a consuming emotion seeking to bring harm to its object. "Hate" may also signify a strong dislike but without any intent to bring harm to the object, seeking instead to avoid it because of a feeling of loathing toward it. The Bible also employs the word "hate" to mean loving to a lesser degree. (Ge 29:31, 33; De 21:15, 16) For example, Jesus Christ said: "If anyone comes to me and does not hate his father and mother and wife and children and brothers and sisters, yes, and even his own soul, he cannot be my disciple." (Lu 14:26) Obviously Jesus did not mean that his followers were to feel hostility or loathing toward their families and toward themselves, as this would not be in agreement with the rest of the Scriptures.—Compare Mr 12:29-31; Eph 5:28, 29, 33.

God's law to Israel stated: "You must not hate your brother in your heart." (Le 19:17) One of the requirements for one presenting himself as an unintentional manslayer and seeking to gain safety in the cities of refuge was that he had not held hatred toward the one slain.—De 19:4, 11-13.

Hate One's Enemies? Jesus' counsel to love one's enemies is in full harmony with the spirit of the Hebrew Scriptures. (Mt 5:44) Faithful Job recognized that any feeling of malicious joy over the calamity of one intensely hating him would have been wrong. (Job 31:29) The Mosaic Law enjoined upon the Israelites the responsibility to come to the aid of other Israelites whom they might view as their enemies. (Ex 23:4, 5) Instead of rejoicing over the disaster of an enemy, God's servants are instructed: "If the one hating you is hungry, give him bread to eat; and if he is thirsty, give him water to drink."—Pr 24:17, 18; 25:21.

The idea that enemies were to be hated was one of the things added to God's law by the Jewish teachers of tradition. Since the Law directed that the Israelites love their neighbors (Le 19:18), these teachers inferred that this implied hating their enemies. "Friend" and "neighbor" came to be viewed as applying exclusively to Jews, whereas all others were considered to be natural enemies. In the light of their traditional understanding of "neighbor" and in view of tradition that fostered enmity toward the Gentiles, it can readily be seen why they added the unauthorized words "and hate your enemy" to the statement in God's law.—Mt 5:43.

The Christian, by contrast, is under obligation to love his enemies, that is, those who make themselves personal enemies. Such love (Gr., a·ga'pe) is not sentimentality, based on mere personal attachment, as is usually thought of, but is a moral or social love based on deliberate assent of the will as a matter of principle, duty, and propriety, sincerely seeking the other's good according to what is right. A·ga'pe (love) transcends personal enmities, never allowing these to cause one to abandon right principles and to retaliate in kind. As to those who oppose his

Christian course and persecute him, doing so in ignorance, the servant of God will even pray for such that their eyes might be opened to see the truth concerning God and His purposes.—Mt 5:44.

Proper Hatred. Nevertheless, under certain conditions and at certain times it is proper to hate. "There is . . . a time to love and a time to hate." (Ec 3:1, 8) Even of Jehovah it is said that he hated Esau. (Mal 1:2, 3) But this cannot be attributed to any arbitrariness on God's part. Esau proved himself unworthy of Jehovah's love by despising his birthright and selling it and hence also the divine promises and blessings attached thereto. Moreover, he purposed to kill his brother Jacob. (Ge 25:32-34; 27:41-43; Heb 12:14-16) God also hates lofty eyes, a false tongue, hands that are shedding innocent blood, a heart fabricating hurtful schemes, feet that are in a hurry to run to badness, a false witness, anyone sending forth contentions among brothers, in fact, everyone and everything standing in complete opposition to Jehovah and his righteous laws.—Pr 6:16-19; De 16:22; Isa 61:8; Zec 8:17; Mal 2:16.

What kind of hatred must servants of God cultivate?

In true loyalty to Jehovah, his servants hate what and whom he hates. (2Ch 19:2) "Do I not hate those who are intensely hating you, O Jehovah, and do I not feel a loathing for those revolting against you? With a complete hatred I do hate them. They have become to me real enemies." (Ps 139:21, 22) But this hate does not seek to inflict injury on others and is not synonymous with spite or malice. Rather, it finds expression in its utter abhorrence of what is wicked, avoiding what is bad and those intensely hating Jehovah. (Ro 12:9, 17, 19) Christians rightly hate those who are confirmed enemies of God, such as the Devil and his demons, as well as men who have deliberately and knowingly taken their stand against Jehovah.

While Christians have no love for those who turn the undeserved kindness of God into an excuse for loose conduct, they do not hate persons who become involved in wrongdoing but who are worthy of being shown mercy. Instead of hating the repentant wrongdoer, they hate the wicked act, yes, "even the inner garment that has been stained by the flesh."—Jude 4, 23.

Avoiding Improper Hatred. Upon becoming Christians, persons who formerly hated one another do so no longer. (Tit 3:3) The one hating his brother is still walking in darkness, and any claim on his part to be a lover of God would really be a lie. Hatred of one's brother is tantamount to murder.—1Jo 2:9, 11; 4:20; 3:15.

Sentimentality can cause one's view of love and hate to get out of balance, as was apparently true of David in connection with his son Absalom. (2Sa 18:33; 19:1-6) Thus, too, "the one holding back his rod is hating his son, but the one loving him is he that does look for him with discipline."—Pr 13:24.

By respecting the privacy of others and showing loving consideration, a person can avoid unnecessarily making himself an object of hatred. Hence the advice: "Make your foot rare at the house of your fellowman, that he may not have his sufficiency of you and certainly hate you."—Pr 25:17.

HATHACH (Ha'thach). A eunuch of King Ahasuerus, appointed to attend Queen Esther and through whom she communicated with Mordecai.—Es 4:5, 6, 9, 10.

HATHATH (Ha'thath). Son of Othniel the son of Kenaz, probably by Caleb's daughter Achsah. —1Ch 4:13; Jos 15:17.

HATIPHA (Ha·ti'pha) [Carried Off by Force]. Ancestor of a family of Nethinim temple slaves, members of which returned from Babylon with Zerubbabel in 537 B.C.E.—Ezr 2:1, 2, 43, 54; Ne 7:56.

HATITA (Ha·ti'ta). Ancestor of a family of temple gatekeepers, members of which returned from Babylon with Zerubbabel in 537 B.C.E. —Ezr 2:1, 2, 42; Ne 7:45.

HATTIL (Hat'til). A paternal head of sons of "the servants of Solomon" who returned to Jerusalem from Babylon with Zerubbabel.—Ezr 2:1, 2, 55, 57; Ne 7:59.

HATTUSH (Hat'tush).

1. A head priest who returned from Babylon with Zerubbabel in 537 B.C.E.—Ne 12:1, 2, 7.

2. Son of Shemaiah; a descendant of David through Solomon.—1Ch 3:1, 10, 22.

3. The head of the paternal house of the sons of David who returned with Ezra to Jerusalem in 468 B.C.E. (Ezr 8:1, 2) Possibly the same as No. 2.

4. Son of Hashabneiah; one who shared in repairing Jerusalem's wall in the days of Nehemiah.—Ne 3:10.

5. A priest or the forefather of one who, during Nehemiah's governorship, attested by seal the confession contract.—Ne 9:38; 10:1, 4, 8.

HAUGHTINESS. Disdainful pride; superciliousness; arrogance. Haughtiness is the opposite of humility. The Greek and Hebrew words translated "haughty" and "haughtiness" have the basic meaning of causing oneself to appear "high," "exalted," "lofty," "eminent." One who is haughty is, in his own esteem, superior, lifted up above his fellowmen. As a result, such a person usually claims honor and attention beyond what is due and treats others with disrespect and insolence.

A Condition of the Heart. Haughtiness is a bad quality or characteristic that is deeper than a mental conclusion. Jesus Christ named it along with murder, thievery, blasphemy, and other wrongdoing and said that "from inside, out of the heart of men," such things issue forth. (Mr 7:21, 22) Jesus' earthly mother Mary said of Jehovah: "He has scattered abroad those who are haughty in the intention of their hearts." (Lu 1:51) David appealed to Jehovah, saying: "My heart has not been haughty."—Ps 131:1; Isa 9:9; Da 5:20.

Even a person whose heart has been humble in service of God can become haughty because of gaining wealth or power or by reason of his beauty, success, wisdom, or the acclaim of others. King Uzziah of Judah was such a person. He ruled well and enjoyed Jehovah's blessing for many years. (2Ch 26:3-5) But the Bible record states: "However, as soon as he was strong, his heart became haughty even to the point of causing ruin, so that he acted unfaithfully against Jehovah his God and came into the temple of Jehovah to burn incense upon the altar of incense." (2Ch 26:16) Uzziah lifted himself up to perform priestly duties, which privilege God had expressly withheld from the kings of Israel, making kingship and priesthood separate.

At one time good King Hezekiah became, for a brief period, haughty in heart, and his haughtiness evidently infected the people he ruled. He had been exalted in rulership because of Jehovah's blessing, but he failed to appreciate and to recognize that all credit should have gone to God. The chronicler writes of him: "But according to the benefit rendered him Hezekiah made no return, for his heart became haughty and there came to be indignation against him and against Judah and Jerusalem." Happily, he recovered from this dangerous attitude. The account continues: "However, Hezekiah humbled himself for the haughtiness of his heart, he and the inhabitants of Jerusalem, and Jehovah's indignation did not come upon them in the days of Hezekiah." —2Ch 32:25, 26; compare Isa 3:16-24; Eze 28:2, 5, 17.

God Opposes Haughtiness. Not only are haughty ones distasteful to honest men but, more seriously, they also receive the opposition of Jehovah God. (Jas 4:6; 1Pe 5:5) Haughtiness is foolishness and a sin (Pr 14:3; 21:4), and Jehovah sets himself against the haughty to bring them low. (2Sa 22:28; Job 10:16; 40:11; Ps 18:27; 31:18, 23; Isa 2:11, 17) If not forsaken, haughtiness is sure to bring destruction. The ancient nation of Moab, which lifted itself up against God and his people, was brought to nothing. (Isa 16:6; 25:10, 11; Jer 48:29) Even the ten-tribe kingdom of Israel was not spared when it became haughty and insolent in heart.—Isa 9:8-12.

Guarding Against Haughtiness. A person should therefore watch carefully to keep haughtiness out of his heart. He should be especially on guard when he has achieved success in any endeavor or when he is given a higher or more responsible position. He ought to be mindful that "pride is before a crash, and a haughty spirit before stumbling." (Pr 16:18) If he lets haughtiness grow, it can come to control him to the extent that Jehovah will class him with those whom He gives up to a disapproved mental state, and who are deserving of death. (Ro 1:28, 30, 32) Such caution is especially appropriate in "the last days," when, as the apostle warned, haughtiness would be one of the distinguishing characteristics of those critical times.—2Ti 3:1, 2.

Additionally, the person desiring God's favor should avoid flattery, which tends to cultivate haughtiness in others. The proverb says: "An able-bodied man that is flattering his companion is spreading out a mere net for his steps." (Pr 29:5) Not only does the flatterer bring ruin to his companion ("a flattering mouth causes an overthrow"; Pr 26:28) but he also receives God's disfavor. The apostle Paul was careful to avoid both flattery and haughtiness.—1Th 2:5, 6.

HAURAN (Ha·u·ran′) [Grown Pale]. A boundary site in Ezekiel's vision of Israel's inheritance. (Eze 47:13, 15, 16, 18) According to some scholars it embraced approximately the same area earlier covered by the term "Bashan." (See BASHAN.) Hauran is apparently the district referred to in ancient Egyptian texts (*Huruna*) and Assyrian documents of Shalmaneser III (*Hauranu*). It also appears to correspond to the smaller region

called Auranitis in Greco-Roman times. The name Hauran is applied today to the rolling prairie of rich, red soil between Damascus and the Yarmuk.

HAVILAH (Hav′i·lah) [[Region of] Sand].

1. A land 'encircled' by the Pishon, one of the four rivers branching off from the river issuing out of Eden. It is further identified as a land of good gold, bdellium gum, and onyx stone. (Ge 2:10-12) Inasmuch as the Pishon River is no longer identifiable, the location of the land of Havilah remains uncertain. (See PISHON.) The description of its resources is considered by some to be typically Arabian, and it is associated by some with a region in Arabia. On the basis of the Biblical reference to "the *entire land* of Havilah," J. Simons suggests that the term "Havilah" may take in the entire Arabian Peninsula, though it is difficult to see how the Pishon River could have 'encircled' such an area.—*The Geographical and Topographical Texts of the Old Testament,* Leiden, 1959, pp. 40, 41.

2. According to Genesis 25:18, the Ishmaelites were "tabernacling from Havilah near Shur, which is in front of Egypt, as far as Assyria." This would require that Havilah, or at least a portion thereof, extend to or near the Sinai Peninsula, in which the Wilderness of Shur likely is located. (See SHUR.) The text evidently shows that the nomadic Ishmaelites ranged from the Sinai Peninsula clear across northern Arabia and into Mesopotamia. Similarly, when King Saul struck down the Amalekites "from Havilah as far as Shur, which is in front of Egypt" (1Sa 15:7), it would appear that the expression "from Havilah" points to a portion, probably the NW corner, of the Arabian Peninsula as representing one limit of the territory in which the Amalekites were centered, while the Wilderness of Shur in the Sinai Peninsula represented the other limit, or as expressed in *The Interpreter's Dictionary of the Bible,* "from the desert interior of the N Arabian Nejd to the region N of modern Suez in Egypt." (Edited by G. A. Buttrick, 1962, Vol. 1, p. 101) Thus, it would appear that it embraced at least the NW portion of the Arabian Peninsula and perhaps a much larger area.

3. A son of Cush the son of Ham. (Ge 10:6, 7) Many scholars view the name Havilah in this text as also representing a region, and the name may well have come to be applied to the area settled by the descendants of this son of Cush. Since the majority of Cush's descendants appear to have

migrated into Africa and Arabia following the breakup at Babel (Ge 11:9), it is generally suggested that the descendants of the Cushite Havilah are to be connected with the region called Haulan in ancient Sabean inscriptions. This region lay on the SW coast of Arabia to the N of modern-day Yemen. Additionally, some suggest that, in course of time, migrants of this tribe crossed the Red Sea to the area now known as Djibouti and Somalia in Africa, the ancient name possibly being preserved there in that of the Aualis. (A Dictionary of the Bible, edited by J. A. Hastings, 1903, Vol. II, p. 311) It is equally possible that the migration took place in a reverse direction, that is, from Africa to Arabia. The strait of the Red Sea, called Bab el-Mandeb, that separates Arabia from Djibouti in Africa is only about 30 km (19 mi) wide.

4. A son of Joktan and descendant of Shem through Arpachshad. (Ge 10:22-29) The names of certain others of Joktan's sons, such as Hazarmaveth and Ophir, are evidently connected with regions in S Arabia. Thus it seems likely that the Semitic Havilah and his descendants also settled in Arabia, though not necessarily in the south. Some would place him in the region identical with that of the Cushite Havilah; but the mere correspondency of the names is hardly basis for assuming that, in spite of their ethnological differences, they both gravitated to the same area. While the evidence connecting the Cushite Havilah with the region in SW Arabia known as Haulan (mentioned in No. 3) is not conclusive, hence possibly allowing for Haulan to be connected instead with the Semitic Havilah, Haulan's association with Africa and its proximity to Ethiopia (the land of Cush) would seem to favor its being linked with the Cushite Havilah. On this basis it would seem likely that the Havilah descended from Shem occupied territory more to the N of Arabia, perhaps providing the source for the name of the land referred to in No. 1.

HAVVOTH-JAIR   (Hav'voth-ja'ir) [Tent Villages of Jair]. Villages located in Manasseh's territory E of the Jordan. Since "Gilead" at times also denotes all of Israel's land E of the Jordan (Jos 22:9), this may explain why the Havvoth-jair are spoken of as being in Gilead (Nu 32:40, 41), although other texts locate the villages in Bashan.—De 3:14; Jos 13:29, 30.

Jair (a descendant of Judah through Hezron, but also reckoned as a descendant of Manasseh), a contemporary of Moses, is credited with capturing these "tent villages," evidently 23 in number, and naming them Havvoth-jair, after himself. (Nu 32:39-41; De 3:14; 1Ch 2:3, 21-23; see JAIR No. 1.) Years later, 30 cities in the possession of Judge Jair's 30 sons were known as Havvoth-jair. Some critics view this as a contradictory explanation about the origin of the name Havvoth-jair. However, the Judges account does not state that the name Havvoth-jair was first used in this later period. It simply indicates that at the time of the writing, the name still was in use and was applied to these 30 cities.—Jg 10:3, 4.

During the reign of Solomon, the tent villages of Jair were included in one of the districts placed under a deputy. (1Ki 4:7, 13) The 60 cities mentioned in 1 Kings 4:13 and in other texts (Jos 13:30; 1Ch 2:23) were at that time fortified cities of the Argob region in Bashan and possibly did not include the numerous rural towns. (Compare De 3:4, 5.) "The tent villages" of Jair may possibly have been distinct from the 60 cities, but this is uncertain.

At an unspecified time in Israel's history, Geshur and Syria captured the Havvoth-jair. —1Ch 2:23.

HAZAEL   (Haz'a·el) [God Beheld]. A notable king of Syria, Hazael apparently began to rule during the reign of King Jehoram of Israel (c. 917-905 B.C.E.). (2Ki 8:7-16) He died during the reign of King Jehoash of Israel (c. 859-845 B.C.E.). (2Ki 13:24, 25) Hazael was not of royal lineage but had merely been a high officer in the service of his predecessor, King Ben-hadad II of Syria.—2Ki 8:7-9.

Years prior to Hazael's reign, Jehovah had instructed Elijah to "anoint Hazael as king over Syria." The reason for the appointment was that Israel had sinned against God and Hazael was to execute punishment upon the nation.—1Ki 19:15-18.

Hazael was never literally anointed with oil, but the commission given to Elijah was nevertheless fulfilled by his successor Elisha the prophet. This occurred when Syrian King Ben-hadad II fell sick and sent Hazael to Syria's principal city Damascus. Hazael was to take a gift and to inquire of Elisha whether or not Ben-hadad would survive his sickness. Elisha said to Hazael: "Go, say to [Ben-hadad], 'You will positively revive,'" but the prophet continued, saying: "And Jehovah has shown me that he will positively die." He further said to Hazael: "Jehovah has shown me you as king over Syria." On Hazael's return, in reply to the king's question as to Elisha's answer,

Hazael said: "He said to me, 'You will positively revive'"; but then, on the next day, Hazael suffocated the king with a wet coverlet and began to rule in his place.—2Ki 8:7-15.

The words of Elisha to Hazael have been the subject of considerable conjecture. According to the margin of the Masoretic text, as well as the Greek *Septuagint,* the Latin *Vulgate,* the Syriac *Peshitta,* and 18 Hebrew manuscripts, the text reads: "Say to him, 'You *will*,'" whereas the main body of the Masoretic text says, "Say, 'You *will not*.'"

If the reading is taken that Hazael was told to tell Ben-hadad "'You will positively revive,'" Elisha's answer to Ben-hadad's inquiry may have been in the form of a riddle, meaning that Ben-hadad's sickness itself would not kill him but that he would nevertheless die (as he did, by the hand of Hazael). At any rate, Hazael verbally gave the king the first part of Elisha's answer: "You will positively revive," but the rest of the answer Hazael carried out in violent action.—2Ki 8:10.

Hazael Oppresses Israel. Shortly after becoming king, Hazael engaged in a war with the kings of Israel and Judah at Ramoth-gilead. At that time, King Jehoram of Israel was wounded at Ramah, but the outcome of the battle itself is not stated in the account. (2Ki 8:25-29; 2Ch 22:1-6) In the days of Jehoram's successor King Jehu of Israel, Hazael began to take Israel's land piece by piece, capturing Gilead and Bashan, E of the Jordan. (2Ki 10:32, 33) This apparently opened the way for his later invasion of the kingdom of Judah. Hazael took the city of Gath in Philistia and then set his face to go up against Jerusalem. King Jehoash of Judah, however, bought Hazael off by giving him valuable things from the temple and palace so that Hazael withdrew, sparing Jerusalem.—2Ki 12:17, 18.

Particularly during the reign of Jehu's son Jehoahaz of Israel, Hazael became a great oppressor of Israel, fulfilling what the prophet Elisha had foreseen—that Hazael would consign Israel's fortified places to the fire, kill their choice men with the sword, dash to pieces their children, and rip up their pregnant women. (2Ki 13:3, 22; 8:12) Yet, God did not allow Syria to crush Israel completely. (2Ki 13:4, 5) After Hazael's death, King Jehoash of Israel, in three victories, recaptured from Hazael's son Ben-hadad III the cities that Hazael had taken from King Jehoahaz, his father. (2Ki 13:23-25) Later King Jeroboam II of Israel "restored Damascus and Hamath to Judah in Israel."—2Ki 14:28.

In Ancient Inscriptions. Hazael is mentioned in a historical inscription found at a place now called Afis, about 40 km (25 mi) SW of Aleppo. The inscription calls Hazael "king of Aram." This inscription agrees with the Bible, that Hazael's son Ben-hadad III, here called "Barhadad," succeeded him as king of Syria.

The campaigns of Shalmaneser III against Syria are recorded in his annals, in which he recounts his victories over Hazael. In these annals, Hazael is called a commoner (literally, son of nobody), doubtless because he was not of royal descent but took the throne of Damascus by assassinating King Ben-hadad II. One of these inscriptions reads: "In the eighteenth year of my rule I crossed the Euphrates for the sixteenth time. Hazael of Damascus (*Imerisu*) put his trust upon his numerous army and called up his troops in great number, making the mountain Senir (Sa-ni-ru), a mountain, facing the Lebanon, to his fortress. I fought with him and inflicted a defeat upon him, killing with the sword 16,000 of his experienced soldiers. I took away from him 1,121 chariots, 470 riding horses as well as his camp. He disappeared to save his life (but) I followed him and besieged him in Damascus (*Di-mas-qi*), his royal residence. (There) I cut down his gardens (outside of the city, and departed). I marched as far as the mountains of Hauran (sade^e ^mat Ha-u-ra-ni), destroying, tearing down and burning innumerable towns, carrying booty away from them which was beyond counting."—*Ancient Near Eastern Texts,* edited by J. B. Pritchard, 1974, p. 280.

However, Shalmaneser III evidently failed to take Damascus itself. This was apparently left for Tiglath-pileser III to accomplish, in the days of Syrian King Rezin. This fulfilled Jehovah's prophecy through Amos: "I will send a fire onto the house of Hazael, and it must devour the dwelling towers of Ben-hadad. And I will break the bar of Damascus."—Am 1:4, 5; 2Ki 16:9.

HAZAIAH (Ha·zai'ah) [Jah Beheld]. A descendant of Judah's son Shelah.—Ne 11:4, 5; Nu 26:20.

HAZAR-ADDAR (Ha'zar-ad'dar) [Courtyard (Settlement) of Addar]. A city on the southern border of Judah, perhaps the same as the Addar near Kadesh-barnea.—Nu 34:4; Jos 15:3; see ADDAR No. 2.

HAZAR-ENAN (Ha'zar-e'nan), **HAZAR-ENON** (Ha'zar-e'non) [Courtyard (Settlement) of the Fountain (Spring)]. A site on the northern boundary of "the land of Canaan." (Nu 34:2, 7-10)

Ezekiel referred to Hazar-enon (Hazar-enan), along with Damascus and Hamath, in his forevision of the territory of Israel. (Eze 47:13, 17; 48:1) A positive identification of the site cannot be made at this time. However, most scholars tentatively locate it at Qaryatein, about 120 km (75 mi) NE of Damascus on the road to Palmyra.

HAZAR-GADDAH (Ha'zar-gad'dah) [Courtyard (Settlement) of Gaddah]. A city in southern Judah (Jos 15:21, 27); the location is unknown.

HAZARMAVETH (Ha·zar·ma'veth) [Courtyard (Settlement) of Death]. A descendant of Noah through Shem and Joktan. (Ge 10:1, 21, 25, 26; 1Ch 1:20) It is generally believed that Hazarmaveth's descendants settled the Hadhramaut region in southern Arabia. A connection between Hadhramaut and Hazarmaveth is suggested by the similarity of the consonants in the original Hebrew and Arabic names. The geographic limits of the Hadhramaut are not closely defined. It is approximately 880 km (550 mi) long and 240 km (150 mi) wide. The coastal plain is rather narrow, and then the land rises steeply, forming a stony plateau with an average elevation of between 900 and 1,200 m (3,000 and 4,000 ft). Many deep, cliff-lined torrent valleys cut through the high plateau. These valleys are very fertile. Palms and dates thrive; sheep, camels, asses, and cattle find pasture; and millet, alfalfa, indigo, cotton, and corn are among the crops grown there. Chief of the torrent valleys is the Wadi Hadhramaut. This stream begins its course some 480 km (300 mi) inland from the W coast of the Arabian Peninsula and gradually curves eastward for about 640 km (400 mi), finally emptying into the Arabian Sea as the Wadi Masila (the name applied to its lower course). The Hadhramaut region anciently played an important role because of its incense trade. But frankincense trees, once abundant, are now scarce there.

HAZAR-SHUAL (Ha'zar-shu'al) [Courtyard (Settlement) of the Fox]. An enclave city of Simeon in the S of Judah. (Jos 15:21, 28; 19:1-3; 1Ch 4:28) It was reoccupied after the Babylonian exile. (Ne 11:25-27) The location is uncertain; some scholars suggest an identification with Khirbet el-Watan, about 3 km (2 mi) ESE of Beer-sheba.

HAZAR-SUSAH (Ha'zar-su'sah) [Courtyard (Settlement) of the Mare]. A Simeonite enclave city in the southern part of Judah (Jos 19:1, 2, 5), also called Hazar-susim. (1Ch 4:31) A similar list of cities originally assigned to Judah has "Sansannah" in place of Hazar-susah. (Jos 15:21, 31)

Some view them as separate locations, placing Sansannah to the NNE of Beer-sheba and Hazar-susah about 26 km (16 mi) to the W of Beer-sheba at Sbalat Abu Susein, near the Plains of Philistia. A number of scholars, however, view it as probable that Hazar-susah is simply a secondary name for Sansannah, such secondary name, by its meaning, describing a notable function of the place. If it is the same as Sansannah, Hazar-susah may tentatively be identified with Khirbet esh-Shamsaniyat to the NNE of Beer-sheba, a short distance from the suggested site of Madmannah (likely Beth-marcaboth), mentioned before (Hazar-susah, Hazar-susim, or Sansannah) in the foregoing texts.—See BETH-MARCABOTH.

HAZAR-SUSIM. See HAZAR-SUSAH.

HAZAZON-TAMAR (Haz'a·zon-ta'mar)[Gravel [Slope] of the Palm Tree]. A city inhabited by Amorites and apparently located in the vicinity of the Low Plain of Siddim. King Chedorlaomer and his allies defeated the Amorites dwelling in Hazazon-tamar. (Ge 14:5-8) Centuries later the combined forces of Moab, Ammon, and the mountainous region of Seir came against Judah by way of "Hazazon-tamar, that is to say, En-gedi." (2Ch 20:2, 10, 11) Many scholars believe that the Genesis reference points to a location some distance S of En-gedi and therefore regard the words "that is to say, En-gedi," as a late addition. The name "Hazazon-tamar," however, appears to be preserved in the Wadi Hasasa (Nahal Hazezon) about 10 km (6 mi) N of the suggested site of En-gedi. Also, the meaning of Hazazon-tamar would fit the En-gedi region, described by Josephus as a place where "the finest palm-trees" are grown. (*Jewish Antiquities*, IX, 7 [i, 2]) So if the Genesis passage refers to a more southerly location, possibly there were two places called Hazazon-tamar: the one linked with En-gedi; the other perhaps the site SW of the Dead Sea that is called simply Tamar.—Eze 47:19; 48:28.

HAZER-HATTICON (Ha'zer-hat'ti·con). A site mentioned in Ezekiel's vision as on the boundary of Israel and "toward the boundary of Hauran." (Eze 47:13, 16) A site by this name is unknown; some consider it a scribal error for "Hazar-enon."—Eze 47:16, 17; see HAZAR-ENAN, HAZAR-ENON.

HAZEROTH (Ha·ze'roth) [Courtyards; Settlements]. Israel's last camping site before entering the wilderness of Paran. (Nu 11:35; 12:16; 33:17,

18; De 1:1) At Hazeroth, Miriam was stricken with leprosy after she and Aaron questioned Moses' authority and his taking of a Cushite wife. (Nu 11:35; 12:1-16) Most scholars connect Biblical Hazeroth with the oasis 'Ain Khadra, about 60 km (37 mi) NE of the traditional site of Mount Sinai.

HAZIEL (Ha'zi·el) [God Beheld]. Son of Shimei; a Gershonite Levite in the time of David. —1Ch 23:6-9.

HAZO (Ha'zo) [possibly a shortened form of Hazael, meaning "God Beheld"]. A nephew of Abraham; fifth-named son of Nahor and Milcah. —Ge 22:20-22.

HAZOR (Ha'zor) [Courtyard; Settlement].

1. The chief city of northern Canaan at the time of Israel's conquest under Joshua. (Jos 11: 10) Hazor has been identified with Tell el-Qedah (Tel Hazor) located about 11 km (7 mi) SSE of the suggested site of Kedesh. According to archaeologist Yigael Yadin, under whose direction excavations were carried out at the site from 1955 to

1958 and 1968 to 1969, the Hazor of Joshua's time covered an area of approximately 60 ha (150 acres) and could have accommodated from 25,000 to 30,000 inhabitants.

Jabin the king of Hazor led the united forces of northern Canaan against Joshua but suffered a humiliating defeat. Hazor itself was burned, the only city in that area built on a mound to be so treated. (Jos 11:1-13) Although later assigned to the tribe of Naphtali (Jos 19:32, 35, 36), Hazor, in the time of Deborah and Barak, was the seat of another powerful Canaanite king also called Jabin.—Jg 4:2, 17; 1Sa 12:9.

At a later period, Hazor, like Gezer and Megiddo, was fortified by King Solomon. (1Ki 9:15) Archaeological finds indicate that the gates of these three cities were of similar construction. Reporting on the excavations at Hazor, Yigael Yadin, in his work *The Art of Warfare in Biblical Lands* (1963, Vol. II, p. 288), writes: "As the first sign of the gate of this wall began to emerge from the dust and earth that were gently being scooped away, we were struck by its similarity to the 'Gate of Solomon' which had been discovered at Megiddo. Before proceeding further with the excavation, we made tentative markings of the

Ruins of gates at Hazor evidently dating to the time of Solomon

ground following our estimate of the plan of the gate on the basis of the Megiddo gate. And then we told the laborers to go ahead and continue removing the debris. When they had finished, they looked at us with astonishment, as if we were magicians or fortune-tellers. For there, before us, was the gate whose outline we had marked, a replica of the Megiddo gate. This proved not only that both gates had been built by Solomon but that both had followed a single master plan."

Over 200 years after Solomon's death, during the reign of Israelite King Pekah, the Assyrian king Tiglath-pileser III conquered Hazor and carried its inhabitants into exile.—2Ki 15:29.

2. A Judean city in the Negeb, perhaps to be linked with el-Jebariyeh, located some 24 km (15 mi) ENE of the suggested site of Kadesh-barnea (likely the same as Kedesh).—Jos 15: 21, 23.

3. Another name for Kerioth-hezron, a town of Judah that has generally been identified with Khirbet el-Qaryatein (Tel Qeriyyot), located about 20 km (12 mi) S of Hebron.—Jos 15: 21, 25.

4. A town located in the territory of Benjamin. (Ne 11:31, 33) Khirbet Hazzur, situated about 7 km (4.5 mi) NW of the Temple Mount in Jerusalem, has been suggested as a probable site.

5. A region in the Arabian Desert east of the Jordan mentioned in the prophecy of Jeremiah as being due for despoiling by King Nebuchadrezzar (Nebuchadnezzar) of Babylon.—Jer 49:28-33.

HAZOR-HADATTAH (Ha′zor-ha·dat′tah) [probably, The New Courtyard (Settlement)]. A city in the southern part of Judah. (Jos 15:21, 25) Its exact location is not known.

HAZZELELPONI (Haz·ze·lel·po′ni) [possibly, Offer Shadow to My Face]. Probably the daughter of "the father of Etam"; the sister of Jezreel, Ishma, and Idbash.—1Ch 4:1, 3.

HE′ [ה]. The fifth letter in the Hebrew alphabet. In speaking, he′ has a guttural sound somewhere between the softer ′a′leph and the harsher chehth. It thus corresponds generally to the English "h" and is similar to the sound of "h" in the word "behind." In the Hebrew, it appears at the beginning of each verse of Psalm 119:33-40. The letters he′ [ה] and chehth [ח] are very similar in form.—See HEBREW, II.

HEAD. The top of the human body; the location of the brain and the senses of sight, hearing, smell, and taste. The head (Heb., ro′sh; Gr., ke-

pha·le′) figures prominently in the Bible in both a literal and a figurative sense.

Crushing or Bruising. The book of Ecclesiastes contains a metaphoric description of the effects of old age, terminating in death. (Ec 12:1-7) The 'crushing of the golden bowl' describes the breaking down at death of the brain and its functions in the bowllike cranium of the head. Death or destruction are represented by the expression 'breaking the head' or 'wounding' the head. (Ps 68:21; 74:13, 14) The Bible's first prophecy (Ge 3:15) states that the 'seed of the woman,' after himself suffering a bruising of the heel, will bruise the serpent's head. In fulfillment, other texts show that the Serpent, Satan the Devil, is to be put into an abyss where he will be immobile for a thousand years and shortly thereafter is to be annihilated forever in "the lake of fire," "the second death."—Re 20:1-3, 7, 10, 14; 12:9.

'Lifting Up the Head.' King David, bowed in humiliation and trouble, looked to Jehovah as his Shield and the One 'lifting up his head,' enabling him to hold his head high again. (Ps 3:3; compare Lu 21:28.) In fulfillment of Joseph's interpretation of a dream, Pharaoh 'lifted up the head' of his chief cupbearer by restoring him to his former office. But Pharaoh 'lifted up [the] head from off' his chief baker, putting him to death.—Ge 40:13, 19-22.

Blessing, Anointing, Swearing. The head was the member of the body on which blessings were placed. (Ge 48:13-20; 49:26) God's favor, guidance, and wisdom are likened to a lamp shining on the head and a wreath of charm on the head. (Job 29:3; Pr 4:7-9) Anointing oil was poured on the head. (Le 8:12; Ps 133:2) In his Sermon on the Mount, Jesus counseled to 'grease the head' when fasting, so as to appear well groomed and not make a sanctimonious show of self-denial for public acclaim. (Mt 6:17, 18) Greasing the head of a guest with oil came to be one of the essential marks of hospitality. (Lu 7:46) The Jews developed a custom of swearing by their head (or life), a practice Jesus condemned.—Mt 5:36, 37; see OATH.

Representing the Person. The head as the governing member of the body was also used to represent the person himself. Jesus Christ's having "nowhere to lay down his head" meant he had no residence that he could call his own. (Mt 8:20) The head of a Nazirite was under a vow, his long hair attesting to the fact. (Nu 6:5, 18-20) The sins or errors of a person were spoken of as being *over his head.* (Ezr 9:6; Ps 38:4; compare Da 1:10.) David showed appreciation for reproof from the righteous, calling it *oil that his head would not want to refuse.* (Ps 141:5) When judgment catches up with the wicked person, he is said to be recompensed by having his *evil or his punishment come upon his own head.* (Jg 9:57; 1Sa 25:39; Jer 23:19; 30:23; Joe 3:4, 7; Ob 15; compare Ne 4:4.) One's *blood being on his own head* meant that an individual pursuing a wrong course of action worthy of bringing the death sentence was personally responsible for the loss of his life. (2Sa 1:16; 1Ki 2:37; Eze 33:2-4; Ac 18:6) To *bring back on his head the blood of those a person killed* would be to bring him to judgment for bloodguilt.—1Ki 2:32, 33.

Each year, the sins of the people were confessed by Israel's high priest, with his hands on the head of the goat for Azazel (transferring the sins to the goat), after which the animal was led into the wilderness to carry these errors off into oblivion. (Le 16:7-10, 21, 22) As other texts show, Jesus Christ personally 'carried our sicknesses and bore our pains' and 'bore the sins of many.' —Isa 53:4, 5; Heb 9:28; 1Pe 2:24.

The priests and others in whose behalf certain sacrifices were made *laid their hands on the head* of the animal in acknowledgment that the sacrifice was for them.—Le 1:2-4; 8:14; Nu 8:12.

Exaltation, Humiliation, and Contempt. Among some of the nations, soldiers were buried with their *swords under their heads,* that is, with military honors. (Eze 32:27) The wise man's *"eyes are in his head,"* that is, he sees where he is going. (Ec 2:14) *Dust, earth, or ashes put on the head* signified distress, mourning, or humiliation. (Jos 7:6; 1Sa 4:12; 2Sa 13:19) The psalmist, in recounting the testings and hardships on God's people, says that *men had ridden over Israel's head.* He apparently refers to the subjection under which God's people were brought by mere worldly men (the Hebrew word used is *'enohsh',* "mortal man") who were powerful, cruel, and haughty. (Ps 66:12; compare Isa 51:23.) To *bow down the head* was a sign of humility or of mourning (Isa 58:5), and to *wag, or shake, the head* was symbolic of derision, contempt, or astonishment.—Ps 22:7; Jer 18:15, 16; Mt 27:39, 40; Mr 15:29, 30.

Kindness to Enemies. The Bible recommends that a person treat his enemy kindly, "for by doing this you will *heap fiery coals upon his head."* (Ro 12:20; Pr 25:21, 22) This metaphor is drawn from the ancient process of smelting, where coals were heaped on top of the ore as well as being underneath. So exercising kindness will tend to soften the person and melt his hardness, separating evil impurities and bringing out the good in him.

Ruling Position. "Head" could refer to the chief member of a family, tribe, nation, or government. (Jg 11:8; 1Sa 15:17; 1Ki 8:1; 1Ch 5:24) "Family head" is, literally, "patriarch" (Gr., *pa·tri·ar'khes*). (Ac 2:29; 7:8, 9; Heb 7:4) "At the head" was used in the sense of leading. (Mic 2:13) Israel itself, if obedient to God, was to be at the *head of the nations,* on top, in that the nation would be free and prosperous, even having the people of other nations in their debt. (De 28:12, 13) If the Israelites disobeyed, the alien resident would lend to them, becoming head over them.—De 28:43, 44.

Seven heads of the dragon. The "dragon" seen in heaven in the apostle John's vision had seven heads. It is identified as the Devil. (Re 12:3, 9) Additionally, the "wild beast" on earth, which receives its power from the dragon, and also the "scarlet-colored wild beast" are both depicted as having seven heads, and these heads are clearly used to represent world powers. (Re 13:1; 17:3, 9, 10; compare Da 2:32, 37, 38, where King Nebuchadnezzar's dynasty is called a "head.") Hence, the seven diademed heads of the Dragon would evidently point to Satan's headship over the seven world powers of Bible prophecy.—Eph 6:12; see BEASTS, SYMBOLIC; GOG No. 2.

Head of the Christian Congregation. In the Christian congregation Jesus Christ is the Head of the congregation, which is his "body," of 144,000 members. (Eph 1:22, 23; Col 1:18; Re 14:1) Having immortality, he is the ever-living liaison member of the body of spirit-begotten Christians on earth at any given time, supplying all necessary things for them to grow spiritually and function to God's glory. (1Co 12:27; Eph 4:15, 16; Col 2:18, 19) As the material temple had a "headstone" (Zec 4:7), so Jesus is the headstone of a spiritual temple (Ac 4:8-11; 1Pe 2:7) and the head of all government and authority under God, who is the Head over all. (Col 2:10; 1Co 11:3) The Bible likens Christ's position as head of the congregation to that of a husband toward his wife, to impress upon human married couples the direction, love, and care the husband must exercise and the subjection that the wife must manifest within the marital union.—Eph 5:22-33.

The apostle Paul, drawing on the principle of the primary headship of God, the Head of Christ, and the relative headship of the man over the woman, sets forth the principle governing the Christian congregation, namely, that the woman should recognize the God-ordained headship of man by wearing a head covering, "a sign of authority," upon her head when praying or prophesying in the congregation.—1Co 11:3-16; see HAIR; HEADDRESS; HEADSHIP.

Other Uses. The Hebrew word for "head" is used to refer to the tops of pillars of the tabernacle, the courtyard, and the temple (Ex 36:37, 38; 38:17; 1Ki 7:16), as well as to the tops of mountains (Ge 8:5), of bushes or trees (1Ch 14:15), of a ladder (Ge 28:12), and of a scepter (Es 5:2), to cite a few examples. It is also applied to that which is the head of or the beginning of something, such as the head of rivers and of roads (Ge 2:10; Eze 21:21) as well as the first month ("the start [head] of the months" [Ex 12:2]). The Jewish name for their new year's day is Rosh Hashanah, literally meaning, "Head of the Year."—See ATTITUDES AND GESTURES.

HEADBAND. See HEADDRESS.

HEAD COVERING. Aside from being an item of dress, head covering has a spiritual significance among God's servants in connection with headship and subjection. The apostle Paul sets forth the God-ordained principle of headship operative in the Christian congregation, saying: "The head of every man is the Christ; in turn the head of a woman is the man; in turn the head of the Christ is God." (1Co 11:3) Paul points out that a head covering is "a sign of authority" that the woman should wear in acknowledging the headship of the man, submitting herself to proper theocratic authority, when she is praying or is prophesying in the congregation.—1Co 11:4-6, 10.

The apostle shows, conversely, that the man should not wear a head covering when taking the lead before the congregation, as when praying or prophesying. It is his normal position under God's arrangement. For the man to wear a head covering in these instances would bring shame upon his own head. It would also indicate disrespect for Jesus Christ as his head as well as for the Supreme Head, Jehovah God, for man is "God's image and glory," originally made as God's representative on earth. He should not obscure this fact by wearing a head covering. The man was created first, prior to the woman; the woman is "out of man" and was created "for the sake of the man." Her qualities are an expression of the man's honor and dignity, just as the man's qualities are a reflection of the honor and dignity of God. Therefore the Christian woman should be happy to acknowledge her subordinate position by the modesty and subjection she displays, and she should be willing to represent this visibly by wearing a veil or other material as a head covering. She should not try to usurp the man's place but should, rather, uphold his headship.—1Co 11:4, 7-10.

Paul calls attention to the naturally long hair of the women in the congregation to which he wrote as a continuous God-given reminder that the woman is by nature subject to the man. She should, therefore, acknowledge this when performing what are customarily the man's duties in the Christian congregation, and she should wear some form of head covering besides her hair, which she normally always has. She will thereby show that she recognizes the God-ordained headship principle and that she makes a distinction between her normal daily activities and the performing of special duties in the congregation when, for example, there is no qualified male member present, or when she is teaching others individually in a formal session for Bible study in the presence of her husband or a male member of the congregation.—1Co 11: 11-15.

As a powerful reason for the congregation of God to follow this procedure, the apostle points to the angels of God, who are "sent forth to minister for those who are going to inherit salvation." (Heb 1:13, 14) These mighty spirit persons are interested in and concerned with Christians' keeping their places within God's arrangement so that theocratic order and pure worship are maintained before God.—1Co 11:10.

The need for this counsel to the congregation at ancient Corinth is better understood when we realize that it was the general custom then for women always to be veiled in public. Only those of loose morals went unveiled. And the pagan priestesses at the temples evidently followed the practice of removing their veils and letting their hair hang disheveled when claiming to be under divine inspiration. Such a practice in the Christian congregation would be disgraceful and a flouting of Jehovah God's arrangement of headship and subjection. Paul concluded his argument by saying that if anyone disputed for any custom other than what Paul set forth, the congregation should nevertheless follow the apostle's counsel regarding the wearing of a head covering. This makes such instruction applicable at all times and places in the Christian congregation.—1Co 11:16.

The Hebrews in ancient times, aside from wearing a headdress as an article of apparel, would cover their heads to signify a condition of mourning. (2Sa 15:30; Jer 14:3) Women also showed modesty in this way. When Rebekah was about to meet Isaac, "she proceeded to take a headcloth and to cover herself," evidently as a symbol of her subjection to him as the one who was to become her husband.—Ge 24:65; see HEADDRESS; HEADSHIP.

HEADDRESS. Among the Hebrews, little emphasis was placed on a covering for the head as a regularly worn article of clothing. When necessary, the common people may at times have used the mantle or the robe for this purpose. Ornamental headdress, however, was often worn by men in official positions and by both men and women on festive or special occasions. The priests of Israel had their prescribed form of headgear.—Ex 28:4, 39, 40; see CROWN; DRESS.

Types of Headdress in Hebrew Scriptures. The head covering first mentioned in the Bible is the headcloth that Rebekah put on when she met Isaac. (Ge 24:65) The Hebrew word used here is *tsa·'iph'*, elsewhere translated "shawl." (Ge 38:14, 19) The wearing of this "headcloth" evidently signified Rebekah's subjection to her betrothed Isaac.

The turban (Heb., *mits·ne'pheth*) of the high priest was of fine linen, wrapped around the head, having a gold plate tied to its front with blue string. (Ex 28:36-39; Le 16:4) The ornamental headgear of the underpriests was also "wrapped" around the head, but a different Hebrew word (*migh·ba·'ah'*) is used for their headdress, indicating that it was different in form and perhaps not as elaborate as the high priest's turban. Nor did the underpriests' headgear have the gold plate.—Le 8:13.

Job mentions the turban in a figurative sense, likening his justice to a turban. (Job 29:14; compare Pr 1:9; 4:7-9.) Women sometimes wore turbans. (Isa 3:23) Here the Hebrew word is *tsa-niph'*. It is used in the expression "kingly turban" at Isaiah 62:3, and at Zechariah 3:5, for the high priest's headgear.

The *pe'er'*, evidently turbanlike, was worn by a bridegroom (Isa 61:10) and was a symbol of joyfulness. (Isa 61:3; compare Eze 24:17, 23.) This word is also used for the headdress of women (Isa 3:20) and for that of the priests.—Eze 44:18.

The headbands (Heb., *shevi·sim'*) seem to have been made of network. (Isa 3:18) The "pendant turbans" (Heb., *tevu·lim'*) described by Ezekiel as being on the heads of Chaldean warriors may have been highly colored and decorated.—Eze 23:14, 15.

Daniel's three young Hebrew companions, fully dressed and even wearing caps, were thrown into Nebuchadnezzar's furnace. The caps may have been worn to denote their title or rank. Some believe that they were conical in shape. —Da 3:21.

Ancient and Modern Headgear. Most of the representations on monuments and reliefs of Egypt, Babylon, and Assyria depict scenes of war and hunting, or of the royal palace or the temples. However, the Egyptians, particularly, have a good many illustrations of workmen plying various arts and trades. In these the kings, chieftains, and nobles are shown wearing widely varying forms of headdress, while the common people are often pictured without head covering, or sometimes with rather close-fitting headgear.

A very similar form of headdress in the Middle East today is the *kaffiyeh,* worn by the Bedouin. It consists of a square cloth folded so that three corners hang down over the back and shoulders. It is bound on with a cord around the head, leaving the face exposed and affording protection from sun and wind for the head and neck. It is possible that such a covering for the head was worn anciently by the Hebrews.

Head Covering and Feminine Subjection. The apostle Paul directed that women have on a head covering when praying or prophesying in the Christian congregation. The woman thereby acknowledged the headship principle, according to which the man is the head of the woman, Christ is man's head and, in turn, God is the head of Christ. Paul said that a woman's long hair is naturally given to her "instead of a headdress." The apostle was then writing to the Christians at Corinth, living among Europeans and Semites, with whom this natural distinction between males and females as to length of hair was the case. Slave women and those caught in fornication or adultery had their heads shaved. Paul pointed out that the long hair of a woman was a natural evidence of her womanly position under man's headship. The woman, seeing this natural reminder of her subjection, should, in consequence, wear a form of head covering as "a sign of authority" on her head when praying or prophesying in the congregation, thus demonstrating before others, including the angels, her personal recognition of the headship principle. (1Co 11:3-16) This had doubtless been the practice of prophetesses of ancient times, such as Deborah (Jg 4:4) and Anna (Lu 2:36-38), when they prophesied.—See HAIR.

HEADSHIP.

The basic principle of headship is set out at 1 Corinthians 11:3: "The head of every man is the Christ; in turn the head of a woman is the man; in turn the head of the Christ is God."

Man's Place. The first part of this counsel on headship applied to the man; he is not independent and without need to recognize a "head." Rather, he is obliged to follow the directions and pattern provided by his head, Christ. (1Jo 2:6) This is so not only in regard to his religious activities (Mt 28:19, 20) but also in his personal activities. For instance, if he is a family man, then out of respect for his own head, Christ, he should comply with the counsel to dwell with his wife according to knowledge, 'assigning her honor as to a weaker vessel,' and he should put forth an earnest effort to train his children properly. (1Pe 3:7; Eph 6:4) This counsel was provided in the Bible for all in Christ's congregation; so respect for headship is involved in a man's heeding it.—Eph 5:23.

As man had priority in human creation, he is given priority of position over the woman. (1Ti 2:12, 13) The woman was made from a rib taken from the man and was bone of his bones and flesh of his flesh. (Ge 2:22, 23) She was created for the sake of the man, not the man for her sake. (1Co 11:9) Therefore, the woman, in God's arrangement for the family, was always to be in subjection to her husband and was not to usurp his authority. (Eph 5:22, 23; 1Pe 3:1) Also, in the Christian congregation the woman is not to teach other dedicated men nor to exercise authority over them.—1Ti 2:12.

Among the Hebrews of ancient times the superior position occupied by the man in the family and in the tribal arrangement was recognized. Sarah was submissive, calling Abraham "lord," and is favorably mentioned for this recognition of his headship. (Ge 18:12; 1Pe 3:5, 6) Under the Law covenant the preferred position of the male was emphasized. Only the males were required by command to assemble for the three festivals of Jehovah at the place that God chose, although

women also attended. (De 16:16) The woman was ceremonially "unclean" twice as long after the birth of a baby girl as after that of a baby boy.—Le 12:2, 5.

Woman's Place. In ancient times, there were circumstances under which a woman put on a head covering to denote subjection. (Ge 24:65) Discussing the headship arrangement in the Christian congregation, the apostle Paul explained that if a woman prays or prophesies in the congregation, occupying a position God has assigned to the man, she should have on a head covering. In temporarily doing these things because no dedicated male Christian is present to do them, even though she may have long hair, the woman should not argue that her long hair is sufficient to denote her subjection. Instead, she should let her own actions demonstrate her submissiveness and her acknowledgment of man's headship. The Christian woman does this by wearing a head covering as "a sign of authority." This should be done "because of the angels," who observe the Christian's actions and who, as those ministering to the Christian congregation, are concerned with it. By wearing a head covering when necessary for spiritual reasons, the Christian woman acknowledges God's headship arrangement.—1Co 11:5-16; Heb 1:14.

This proper theocratic order in the congregation and in the family arrangement does not hinder the woman in serving God, nor does it impede her efforts in carrying out her family activities and responsibilities. It allows her full and Scriptural freedom to serve in her place, while still being pleasing to God in harmony with the principle: "God has set the members in the body, each one of them, just as he pleased." (1Co 12:18) Many women of ancient times had fine privileges while recognizing the headship of the man and enjoyed happy and satisfying lives. Among these were Sarah, Rebekah, Abigail, and Christian women such as Priscilla and Phoebe.

Responsibility. The exercise of authorized headship grants certain rights, but it also involves duties or obligations. 'Christ is head of the congregation' and so has the right to make decisions involving it and demonstrate authority over it. (Eph 5:23) But his headship also obliges him to accept the duty of caring for the congregation and bearing responsibility for his decisions. In a similar manner, a husband in exercising his headship has certain rights as to making final decisions and providing oversight. In addition, though, he has the duty to accept responsibility for his family. He has the primary obligation to provide materially and spiritually for his household.—1Ti 5:8.

The Christian man is to exercise his headship wisely, loving his wife as himself. (Eph 5:33) Jesus Christ exercises his headship over the Christian congregation in this manner. (Eph 5:28, 29) As head over his children, a father is not to irritate them but is to bring them up "in the discipline and mental-regulating of Jehovah." (Eph 6:4) And as shepherds of the flock of God, "older men" in the Christian congregation are not to lord it over God's "sheep" but are to remember their subjection to Jesus Christ and Jehovah God. (1Pe 5:1-4) Jesus Christ has always acted in accord with the headship principle, manifesting full recognition of his Father's headship in word and deed. Even after ruling the earth for a thousand years, he will acknowledge Jehovah's universal headship by handing the Kingdom over to Jehovah, subjecting "himself to the One who subjected all things to him, that God may be all things to everyone." (1Co 15:24-28; Joh 5:19, 30; 8:28; 14:28; Php 2:5-8) Christians, followers of Jesus Christ, also acknowledge Jehovah's supreme headship, addressing their prayers to him and recognizing him as Father and God Almighty.—Mt 6:9; Re 1:8; 11:16, 17; see FAMILY; HUSBAND.

HEALING.
The restoring of health to the sick; the making sound, or whole, that which is broken or injured; the curing of various diseases and defects; the returning of a person to the general state of well-being. The Hebrew verb *ra·pha'* and the Greek verb *i·a'o·mai* are the principal words in the Bible that describe such healing in both a literal and a figurative sense. The Greek verb *the·ra·peu'o* is rendered 'cure.' (Mt 4: 23, 24) Sometimes the healing was a gradual matter; at other times it was instantaneous.

Among the blessings Jehovah bestowed on all mankind is the regenerative power of their physical organisms, the ability of the body to heal itself when wounded or diseased. A physician may recommend certain measures to speed recovery, but in reality it is the God-given recuperative powers within the body that accomplish the healing. Hence, the psalmist David acknowledged that though he was born imperfect, his Creator was able to sustain him during illness and heal all his maladies. (Ps 51:5; 41:1-3; 103:2-4) Jehovah restored the bodily health of afflicted Job (Job 42:10) and God also provided physical healing for his people Israel.—Ex 15:26.

Of Jehovah it is written that he both wounds and heals, and he does this literally and figuratively. Hence, with him there is a time to wound and a time to heal. (De 32:39; compare Ec 3:1, 3.) Unfaithful Jehoram, king of Judah, for example, was punished by Jehovah with a physical disorder of the intestines for which there was no healing. (2Ch 21:16, 18, 19) Moses recognized that it was Jehovah who had stricken Miriam with leprosy; hence, he pleaded with the only One who could cure her, saying: "O God, please! Heal her, please!" (Nu 12:10, 13) In the matter of childbearing, Jehovah healed King Abimelech, his wife, and his slave girls after the crisis had passed involving Sarah and the seed of promise. —Ge 20:17, 18.

In the Bible, spiritual rather than physical breakdown, and spiritual healing in turn, are subjects of particular significance. Attention is called to the responsibility of natural Israel's leaders in these matters. "From the prophet even to the priest, each one [was] acting falsely" in Jeremiah's day, they at the same time making a pretense of healing the breakdown of God's people, claiming that all was well. (Jer 6:13, 14; 8:11) In this they were very much like Job's comforters, "physicians of no value."—Job 13:4.

In a few instances inanimate objects were healed, in the sense of being made whole again, like the torn-down altar Elijah mended. (1Ki 18: 30) Also, the prophet Elisha healed the waters near Jericho so that they no longer caused miscarriages. (2Ki 2:19-22) Jeremiah, however, shattered the potter's flask so completely that it was beyond repair, that is, beyond healing, and thus furnished a fine illustration. "In the same way," Jehovah declared, "I shall break this people and this city as someone breaks the vessel of the potter so that it is no more able to be repaired [a form of *ra·pha'*; literally, healed]."—Jer 19:11; compare 2Ch 36:15-17.

Jesus and His Fellow Healers. Jesus Christ recognized that "teaching . . . and preaching the good news of the kingdom" was of first importance in his ministry and that "curing every sort of disease and every sort of infirmity among the people" was secondary. That is why he felt pity for the crowds primarily "because they were skinned and thrown about like sheep without a shepherd."—Mt 4:23; 9:35, 36; Lu 9:11.

This Great Teacher also showed compassion on the multitudes that followed him because they hoped that he would heal their physical ailments. (Mt 12:15; 14:14; 19:2; Lu 5:15) His miraculous healing work served as a visible sign to his generation and gave added evidence of his Messiahship, as prophesied. (Mt 8:16, 17) It also foreshadowed the healing blessings that will be extended to mankind under God's Kingdom rule. (Re 21:3, 4) In a very real sense Jesus healed and restored the health of many persons—the lame, the maimed, the blind, the dumb (Mt 15:30, 31), the epileptic, the paralytic (Mt 4:24), a woman suffering from a hemorrhage (Mr 5:25-29), one with a withered hand (Mr 3:3-5), a man with dropsy (Lu 14:2-4), and on many occasions those who were demon possessed were released from their Satanic enslavement and bondage.—Mt 12: 22; 15:22-28; 17:15, 18; Mr 1:34; Lu 6:18; 8:26-36; 9:38-42; Ac 10:37, 38.

Jesus' manner of curing people took various forms at different times. "Get up, pick up your cot and walk," is all that Jesus said on one occasion, and a sick man near the pool of Bethzatha was cured. (Joh 5:2-9) In another instance, Jesus just spoke the word and the ailing one, though a distance away, was healed. (Mt 8:5-13) At other times he personally laid his hand on the sick one (Mt 8:14, 15) or touched a wound and healed it. (Lu 22:50, 51) Several diseased persons simply touched Jesus or even the fringe of his garment and were healed. (Mt 14:36; Mr 6:56; Lu 6:19; 8:43-47) And it made no difference that the persons had been afflicted with the disease for many years.—Mt 9:20-22; Lu 13:11-13; Joh 5:5-9.

Some persons opposed Jesus, not appreciating the wonderful healing work he was doing. The religious leaders were greatly angered when Jesus healed persons on the Sabbath. (Mt 12:9-14; Lu 14:1-6; Joh 5:10-16) On one such occasion Jesus silenced opponents by saying: "Hypocrites, does not each one of you on the sabbath untie his bull or his ass from the stall and lead it away to give it drink? Was it not due, then, for this woman who is a daughter of Abraham, and whom Satan held bound, look! eighteen years, to be loosed from this bond on the sabbath day?" —Lu 13:10-17.

It was not the application of Jesus' own power, knowledge, or wisdom that healed the sick. Neither was hypnotherapy, psychotherapy, or any similar method used. Rather, it was the spirit and power of Jehovah that effected such healing. (Lu 5:17; 9:43) Not all, however, were grateful enough to give God the glory for these cures. (Lu 17:12-18) Today, not everyone recognizes the everlasting healing benefits made available

through the ransom sacrifice of Christ.—1Pe 2:24.

Jesus delegated this divine power of healing to others who were closely associated with him in his ministry. When the 12 apostles were sent out, and later the 70 disciples, they were empowered to cure the sick. (Mt 10:5, 8; Lu 10:1, 8, 9) After Pentecost of 33 C.E., certain ones, including Peter, John, Philip, and Paul, were given this divine power to heal completely. (Ac 3:1-16; 4:14; 5:15, 16; 8:6, 7; 9:32-34; 28:8, 9) After Christianity became firmly rooted, and with the passing of the apostles off the scene, such "gifts of healings" also passed away.—1Co 12:8, 9, 28, 30; 13:8, 13.

It was important that the one performing the cure have full faith and confidence in Jehovah and acknowledge, as Jesus did, that the curing was accomplished by God's power. (Mt 17:14-20; Joh 5:19) It was not necessary, however, for the afflicted ones to have faith before being cured. (Joh 5:5-9, 13) Many, though, did have strong faith.—Mt 8:5-13; 15:28; Mr 5:34; Lu 7:1-10; 17:19; Ac 14:8-10; see FAITH.

Miraculous healing was to be a "sign" of divine backing. (Ac 4:22, 29, 30) Those who refused to recognize and acknowledge this sign were spiritually blind and deaf. (Isa 6:10; Joh 12:37-41) For the reason, then, that divine healings were to serve as a sign to unbelievers, they were not ordinarily performed in behalf of those who were already spirit-begotten Christians. So when Timothy had stomach trouble, instead of performing a miraculous cure, Paul recommended that he take a little wine for his ailment.—1Ti 5:23.

Spiritual Healing. On the other hand, true spiritual healing comes from Jehovah to repentant ones. It means a return to his favor and the enjoyment of his blessings once again. (Isa 19:22; 57:17-19; Jer 33:6) Such healing has the effect of strengthening the weak hands and wobbly knees, opening blind eyes, restoring hearing to the deaf, healing the lame, and giving speech to the dumb, in a spiritual way. (Isa 35:3-6) But those incorrigible in their apostasy never experience a healing, or restoration to good health and prosperity spiritually. (2Ch 36:15-17; Isa 6:10; Jer 30:12, 13; Ac 28:24-28) Similarly, there was to be no healing for Egypt, her Pharaoh, and for the "king of Assyria."—Jer 46:11; Eze 30:21; Na 3:18, 19.

The Scriptures prescribe the remedy for persons who are spiritually sick.—Heb 12:12, 13; Jas 5:14-16; Re 3:18.

HEARING. See EAR; OBEDIENCE.

HEART. The important organ of the body whose chief function is to pump the blood to nourish the body cells.—Le 17:14.

The heart is made prominent in the Scriptures, being mentioned about a thousand times in one way or another. The Hebrew (*lev, le·vav'*) and Greek (*kar·di'a*) words for "heart" are used by the Bible writers both literally and figuratively.

The Literal Heart. In comparatively few instances the Bible writers refer to the literal heart organ. Thus, when Jehu proceeded to shoot Jehoram "between the arms . . . the arrow came out at his heart."—2Ki 9:24; see also Ex 28:30.

The Figurative Heart. In the great majority of its occurrences in the Scriptures, the word "heart" is used *figuratively*. It is said to stand for "the central part in general, the inside, and so for *the interior man* as manifesting himself in all his various activities, in his desires, affections, emotions, passions, purposes, his thoughts, perceptions, imaginations, his wisdom, knowledge, skill, his beliefs and his reasonings, his memory and his consciousness."—*Journal of the Society of Biblical Literature and Exegesis,* 1882, p. 67.

So, in the Scriptures the figurative heart is not confined to being the seat of affection and motivation, nor is it limited to the intellect. "Among the Semites . . . all that was peculiar to man, in the category of feelings as well as intellect and will, was attributed to the heart." It is "the sum total of the interior man as opposed to the flesh, which is the exterior and tangible man."—*The Metaphorical Use of the Names of Parts of the Body in Hebrew and in Akkadian,* by E. Dhorme, Paris, 1963, pp. 113, 114, 128 (in French).

Not mere outward appearances but what a person really is inside is what counts with God, who is an examiner of hearts. (Pr 17:3; 24:12; Ps 17:3; 1Sa 16:7) So the Scriptures counsel: "More than all else that is to be guarded, safeguard your heart [the whole inner man], for out of it are the sources of life." (Pr 4:23) And Christian wives are urged to give primary attention, not to external adornment, but to "the *secret person of the heart* in the incorruptible apparel of the quiet and mild spirit, which is of great value in the eyes of God." —1Pe 3:3, 4.

In a number of cases in the Bible where the term "heart" occurs, it evidently focuses attention on the *thinking faculties,* but not in a sense that would isolate such faculties from the rest of what makes up the inner person. Moses urged the Israelites, "You must call back to your heart ["must recall to your mind," ftn] that Jehovah is

the true God." And later he told them, "Jehovah has not given you a heart ["mind," ftn] to know." (De 4:39; 29:4) Showing that at times the heart, as referred to in both the Hebrew Scriptures and the Christian Greek Scriptures, includes the intellect are instances where it is associated with "thinking" (Mt 9:4), "reasoning" (Mr 2:6), "understanding" (1Ki 3:12; Mr 6:52), and "knowledge" (Pr 15:14).

Motivation, the impelling force behind our conduct, is a further vital aspect of the inner person, as represented by the "heart." Thus, those making contributions for the construction of the tabernacle "came, everyone whose heart impelled him." (Ex 35:21, 26, 29; 36:2) Wicked Haman "emboldened himself" (literally, filled him as to his heart) to scheme against the Jews. (Es 7:5, ftn; Ac 5:3) Hebrews 4:12 explains that God's word of promise, like a sharp sword, is able to "discern thoughts and intentions of the heart." Jesus, too, indicated that from the heart springs the motivating force behind our conduct, whether it is good or bad. (Mt 15:19; Lu 6:45) With a view to our cultivating right motivations, the Bible warns us against allowing our dealings with others to be tainted by a desire for selfish gain (Jude 16) or permitting love of money, a craving for riches, to determine our course of life. (1Ti 6:9, 10; Pr 23:4, 5) Rather, it encourages us to cultivate genuine love for God as a basis for our service to him (1Jo 5:3; De 11:13) and self-sacrificing love as a guide in dealing with fellow believers (Joh 15:12, 13); it also encourages us to make a practice of loving others of our fellowmen as we do ourselves (Lu 10:27-37; Ga 6:10). Obviously, the cultivating of such motivations involves use of the thinking faculties.—Ps 119:2, 24, 111.

The condition of our figurative heart is reflected in our *disposition, our attitude,* whether proud or humble. (Pr 16:5; Mt 11:29) Our *feelings and emotions* are also part of that inner man. These include love (De 6:5; 1Pe 1:22), joy (De 28:47; Joh 16:22), pain and sorrow (Ne 2:2; Ro 9:2), hate (Le 19:17). Thus the heart can be "anxious" (Isa 35:4), "pierced" by affliction (Ps 109:22), 'melted' by fear of distresses (De 20:8). In the Christian Greek Scriptures, when the mind is mentioned along with the heart, "mind" refers to the intellect while "heart" refers to the emotions, desires, and feelings of the inner person. For example, Jesus said: "You must love Jehovah your God with your whole heart and with your whole soul and with your whole mind." (Mt 22:37) He thus showed that a person's desires, feelings, and emotions must express his love for God, but he must also express that love by the way he uses his mental faculties, as by taking in knowledge of God and Christ.—Joh 17:3.

All such functions, capabilities, emotions, and qualities are ascribed, not to the literal heart organ, but to the figurative heart as representing the total inner personality.

The Heart Can Be "Treacherous." Adam, although perfect, let his heart be enticed; he rejected the truth and turned away from God. (See Jas 1:14, 15.) Consequently, all humans, the offspring of fallen Adam, have been conceived in sin and brought forth in error. (Ps 51:5) After the Flood, God said regarding sinful mankind in general: "The inclination of the heart of man is bad from his youth up."—Ge 8:21.

God told the rebellious nation of Judah: "The heart is more treacherous than anything else and is desperate." (Jer 17:9) This constitutes a serious warning that those seeking to please God must give attention not merely to what other humans see but to the kind of person they really are, the inner man. A person may have been a Christian for many years, have a fine knowledge of the Bible, and feel confident that he can safely handle any situation that may arise. Yet, although he knows full well that an act is wrong and specifically condemned by God's law, the thoughts and desires that he has secretly cherished may entice him into sinful action.

For these reasons a Christian, though he knows the truth and may consider himself mature, must remember the treachery that his heart can display and must therefore exercise great care not to place himself in the way of temptation.—Mt 6:13; 1Co 10:8-12.

Serving With "a Complete Heart." The literal heart must be whole to function normally, but the figurative heart can be divided. David prayed: "*Unify my heart* to fear your name," suggesting that a person's heart could be divided with regard to its affections and fears. (Ps 86:11) Such a person may be "halfhearted"—lukewarmly worshiping God. (Ps 119:113; Re 3:16) An individual can also be of "a double heart" (literally, with a heart and a heart), trying to serve two masters, or deceptively saying one thing while thinking something else. (1Ch 12:33; Ps 12:2, ftn) Jesus strongly denounced such doublehearted hypocrisy.—Mt 15:7, 8.

One seeking to please God must be neither halfhearted nor doublehearted but must serve him with a *complete* heart. (1Ch 28:9) This re-

quires diligent effort in view of the heart's being desperate and inclined to badness. (Jer 17:9, 10; Ge 8:21) Of help in maintaining a complete heart are: heartfelt prayer (Ps 119:145; La 3:41), regular study of God's Word (Ezr 7:10; Pr 15:28), zealous participation in preaching the good news (compare Jer 20:9), and association with others whose hearts are complete toward Jehovah. —Compare 2Ki 10:15, 16.

What is meant by being in "want of heart"?

A number of times the Scriptures speak of a person's being in "want of heart." *Lexicon in Veteris Testamenti Libros* (by Koehler and Baumgartner, Leiden, 1958, p. 470) says that this means "without intelligence." *A Hebrew and English Lexicon of the Old Testament* by William Gesenius (translated by E. Robinson, 1836, p. 517) says that such a person is "void of understanding." "Want of heart" marks a person who is lacking good judgment or discernment. Thus, "want of heart" is contrasted with "understanding" (Pr 10:13) and "discernment." (Pr 11:12; 15: 21) In other cases the one in "want of heart" is shown to be "inexperienced," "foolish," lacking in wisdom. (Pr 7:7; 9:1-9, 16; 10:21) By using the term "heart," these scriptures show that positive qualities of the whole inner person are deficient.

That the expression "want of heart" includes the idea of lacking good judgment or discernment is evident from the context in which it is used in the Scriptures. At Proverbs 6:32 the wise man says that one committing adultery "is in want of heart." Other translations here read: "lacketh sense" (*Ro*), "has no sense" (*RS, JB*), "lacks judgment" (*NIV*), "is a senseless fool" (*NE*). The adulterer is "a senseless fool" in view of the bitter fruit of such sexual immorality. (Pr 1:2-4; 6:23-35; 7:7, 21-27) Outwardly he may appear to be a reputable person, but the inner man is seriously lacking in proper development.

Another proverb says: "A man that is wanting in heart ['lacking sense,' *Ro*] shakes hands [a gesture used to ratify an agreement], going full surety before his companion." (Pr 17:18) Perhaps swayed by sentimentality, such a man enters an agreement that could well result in loss of money and serious economic hardship for him. Though he may be well-intentioned or have praiseworthy motives, he nonetheless betrays a lack of good judgment.

In contrast to being in "want of heart," the proverbs also speak of a person's "acquiring heart." As Proverbs 19:8 says: "He that is acquiring heart is loving his own soul. He that is guarding discernment is going to find good." He is a person who gives serious attention to what he really is deep down inside. He uses his mind to acquire accurate knowledge of God and of his ways; he meditates on these things and seeks to apply them. He carefully molds his desires, affections, emotions, and goals in life in harmony with what he realizes will be approved by God. So doing, he benefits himself, demonstrating that he 'loves his own soul.' By thus building up the inner person, he 'guards discernment,' because he fortifies in wholesome ways those factors that powerfully influence his own ability to think clearly and act wisely.

God's Heart. Jehovah reveals that he has affections and emotions, the Bible describing him as having a "heart." At the time of the Flood "he felt hurt at his heart," regretting that men had rejected his righteous rule, making it necessary for him to turn from being their benefactor to becoming their destroyer. (Ge 6:6) By contrast, God's "heart" 'rejoices' when his servants are faithful. (Pr 27:11) Such a thing as the cruel offering up of humans as burnt sacrifices, practiced by some of the deviating Israelites, never had come up into God's heart, showing also that he could not be a God of eternal torment.—Jer 7:31; 19:5.

Center, or Midst, of a Thing. Because the literal heart is a central organ of the body, the term "heart" is at times applied to the center, or midst, of something, such as "the heart of the earth" (Mt 12:40), "the heart of the sea" (Ex 15:8; Jon 2:3), and "the heart of the big tree" (2Sa 18:14). At Deuteronomy 4:11 the expression "midheaven" literally means "the heart of the heavens."—See *NW* ftn.

Prophetic. The symbolic use of "heart" figures in a prophetic way at Daniel 7:4, where the lionlike beast representing the kingdom of Babylon was made to stand on two feet and was given "the heart of a man," that is, it no longer possessed the courageous "heart of the lion." (2Sa 17:10) It was then defeated by the symbolic "bear," Medo-Persia.—Da 7:5; see BEASTS, SYMBOLIC.

HEAVEN. The Hebrew *sha·ma'yim* (always in the plural), which is rendered "heaven(s)," seems to have the basic sense of that which is high or lofty. (Ps 103:11; Pr 25:3; Isa 55:9) The etymology of the Greek word for heaven (*ou·ra·nos'*) is uncertain.

Physical Heavens. The full scope of the physical heavens is embraced by the original-language term. The context usually provides sufficient information to determine which area of the physical heavens is meant.

Heavens of earth's atmosphere. "The heaven(s)" may apply to the full range of earth's atmosphere in which dew and frost form (Ge 27:28; Job 38:29), the birds fly (De 4:17; Pr 30:19; Mt 6:26), the winds blow (Ps 78:26), lightning flashes (Lu 17:24), and the clouds float and drop their rain, snow, or hailstones (Jos 10:11; 1Ki 18:45; Isa 55:10; Ac 14:17). "The sky" is sometimes meant, that is, the apparent or visual dome or vault arching over the earth.—Mt 16:1-3; Ac 1:10, 11.

This atmospheric region corresponds generally to the "expanse [Heb., *ra·qi'a'*]" formed during the second creative period, described at Genesis 1:6-8. It is evidently to this 'heaven' that Genesis 2:4; Exodus 20:11; 31:17 refer in speaking of the creation of "the heavens and the earth."—See EXPANSE.

When the expanse of atmosphere was formed, earth's surface waters were separated from other waters above the expanse. This explains the expression used with regard to the global Flood of Noah's day, that "all the springs of the vast watery deep were broken open and the floodgates of the heavens were opened." (Ge 7:11; compare Pr 8:27, 28.) At the Flood, the waters suspended above the expanse apparently descended as if by certain channels, as well as in rainfall. When this vast reservoir had emptied itself, such "floodgates of the heavens" were, in effect, "stopped up."—Ge 8:2.

Outer space. The physical "heavens" extend through earth's atmosphere and beyond to the regions of outer space with their stellar bodies, "all the army of the heavens"—sun, moon, stars, and constellations. (De 4:19; Isa 13:10; 1Co 15:40, 41; Heb 11:12) The first verse of the Bible describes the creation of such starry heavens prior to the development of earth for human habitation. (Ge 1:1) These heavens show forth God's glory, even as does the expanse of atmosphere, being the work of God's "fingers." (Ps 8:3; 19:1-6) The divinely appointed "statutes of the heavens" control all such celestial bodies. Astronomers, despite their modern equipment and advanced mathematical knowledge, are still unable to comprehend these statutes fully. (Job 38:33; Jer 33:

25) Their findings, however, confirm the impossibility of man's placing a measurement upon such heavens or of counting the stellar bodies. (Jer 31:37; 33:22; see STAR.) Yet they are numbered and named by God.—Ps 147:4; Isa 40:26.

"Midheaven" and 'extremities of heavens.'
The expression "midheaven" applies to the region within earth's expanse of atmosphere where birds, such as the eagle, fly. (Re 8:13; 14:6; 19:17; De 4:11 [Heb., "heart of the heavens"]) Somewhat similar is the expression "between the earth and the heavens." (1Ch 21:16; 2Sa 18:9) The advance of Babylon's attackers from "the extremity of the heavens" evidently means their coming to her from the distant horizon (where earth and sky appear to meet and the sun appears to rise and set). (Isa 13:5; compare Ps 19:4-6.) Similarly "from the four extremities of the heavens" apparently refers to four points of the compass, thus indicating a coverage of the four quarters of the earth. (Jer 49:36; compare Da 8:8; 11:4; Mt 24:31; Mr 13:27.) As the heavens surround the earth on all sides, Jehovah's vision of everything "under the whole heavens" embraces all the globe.—Job 28:24.

The cloudy skies. Another term, the Hebrew *sha'chaq,* is also used to refer to the "skies" or their clouds. (De 33:26; Pr 3:20; Isa 45:8) This word has the root meaning of something beaten fine or pulverized, as the "film of dust" (*sha'chaq*) at Isaiah 40:15. There is a definite appropriateness in this meaning, inasmuch as clouds form when warm air, rising from the earth, becomes cooled to what is known as the dewpoint, and the water vapor in it condenses into minute particles sometimes called water dust. (Compare Job 36:27, 28; see CLOUD.) Adding to the appropriateness, the visual effect of the blue dome of the sky is caused by the diffusion of the rays of the sun by gas molecules and other particles (including dust) composing the atmosphere. By God's formation of such atmosphere, he has, in effect, 'beaten out the skies hard like a molten mirror,' giving a definite limit, or clear demarcation, to the atmospheric blue vault above man.—Job 37:18.

"Heavens of the heavens." The expression "heavens of the heavens" is considered to refer to the highest heavens and would embrace the complete extent of the physical heavens, however vast, since the heavens extend out from the earth in all directions.—De 10:14; Ne 9:6.

Solomon, the constructor of the temple at Jerusalem, stated that the "heavens, yes, the heaven of the heavens" cannot contain God. (1Ki 8:27) As the Creator of the heavens, Jehovah's position is far above them all, and "his name alone is unreachably high. His dignity is above earth and heaven." (Ps 148:13) Jehovah measures the physical heavens as easily as a man would measure an object by spreading his fingers so that the object lies between the tips of the thumb and the little finger. (Isa 40:12) Solomon's statement does not mean that God has no specific place of residence. Nor does it mean that he is omnipresent in the sense of being literally everywhere and in everything. This can be seen from the fact that Solomon also spoke of Jehovah as hearing "from the heavens, your established place of dwelling," that is, the heavens of the spirit realm.—1Ki 8:30, 39.

Thus, in the physical sense, the term "heavens" covers a wide range. While it may refer to the farthest reaches of universal space, it may also refer to something that is simply high, or lofty, to a degree beyond the ordinary. Thus, those aboard storm-tossed ships are said to "go up to the heavens, . . . down to the bottoms." (Ps 107:26) So, too, the builders of the Tower of Babel intended to put up a structure with its "top in the heavens," a "skyscraper," as it were. (Ge 11:4; compare Jer 51:53.) And the prophecy at Amos 9:2 speaks of men as 'going up to the heavens' in a vain effort to elude Jehovah's judgments, evidently meaning that they would try to find escape in the high mountainous regions.

Spiritual Heavens. The same original-language words used for the physical heavens are also applied to the spiritual heavens. As has been seen, Jehovah God does not reside in the physical heavens, being a Spirit. However, since he is "the High and Lofty One" who resides in "the height" (Isa 57:15), the basic sense of that which is "lifted up" or "lofty" expressed in the Hebrew-language word makes it appropriate to describe God's "lofty abode of holiness and beauty." (Isa 63:15; Ps 33:13, 14; 115:3) As the Maker of the physical heavens (Ge 14:19; Ps 33:6), Jehovah is also their Owner. (Ps 115:15, 16) Whatever is his pleasure to do in them, he does, including miraculous acts.—Ps 135:6.

In many texts, therefore, the "heavens" stand for God himself and his sovereign position. His throne is in the heavens, that is, in the spirit realm over which he also rules. (Ps 103:19-21; 2Ch 20:6; Mt 23:22; Ac 7:49) From his supreme or ultimate position, Jehovah, in effect, 'looks down' upon the physical heavens and earth (Ps

14:2; 102:19; 113:6), and from this lofty position also speaks, answers petitions, and renders judgment. (1Ki 8:49; Ps 2:4-6; 76:8; Mt 3:17) So we read that Hezekiah and Isaiah, in the face of a grave threat, "kept praying . . . and crying to the heavens for aid." (2Ch 32:20; compare 2Ch 30: 27.) Jesus, too, used the heavens as representing God when asking the religious leaders whether the source of John's baptism was "from heaven or from men." (Mt 21:25; compare Joh 3:27.) The prodigal son confessed to having sinned "against heaven" as well as against his own father. (Lu 15:18, 21) "The kingdom of the heavens," then, means not merely that it is based in and rules from the spiritual heavens but also that it is "the kingdom of God."—Da 2:44; Mt 4:17; 21:43; 2Ti 4:18.

Also because of God's heavenly position, both men and angels raised hands or faces toward the heavens in calling upon him to act (Ex 9:22, 23; 10:21, 22), in swearing to an oath (Da 12:7), and in prayer (1Ki 8:22, 23; La 3:41; Mt 14:19; Joh 17:1). At Deuteronomy 32:40 Jehovah speaks of himself as 'raising his hand to heaven in an oath.' In harmony with Hebrews 6:13, this evidently means that Jehovah swears by himself.—Compare Isa 45:23.

Angelic dwelling place. The spiritual heavens are also the "proper dwelling place" of God's spirit sons. (Jude 6; Ge 28:12, 13; Mt 18:10; 24:36) The expression "army of the heavens," often applied to the stellar creation, sometimes describes these angelic sons of God. (1Ki 22:19; compare Ps 103:20, 21; Da 7:10; Lu 2:13; Re 19:14.) So, too, "the heavens" are personified as representing this angelic organization, "the congregation of the holy ones."—Ps 89:5-7; compare Lu 15:7, 10; Re 12:12.

Representing Rulership. We have seen that the heavens can refer to Jehovah God in his sovereign position. Thus, when Daniel told Nebuchadnezzar that the experience the Babylonian emperor was due to have would make him "know that the *heavens* are ruling," it meant the same as knowing "that the *Most High* is Ruler in the kingdom of mankind."—Da 4:25, 26.

However, aside from its reference to the Supreme Sovereign, the term "heavens" can also refer to other ruling powers that are exalted or lifted up above their subject peoples. The very dynasty of Babylonian kings that Nebuchadnezzar represented is described at Isaiah 14:12 as being starlike, a "shining one, son of the dawn." By the conquest of Jerusalem in 607 B.C.E., that Babylonian dynasty lifted its throne "above the stars of God," these "stars" evidently referring to the Davidic line of Judean kings (even as the Heir to the Davidic throne, Christ Jesus, is called "the bright morning star" at Re 22:16; compare Nu 24:17). By its overthrow of the divinely authorized Davidic throne, the Babylonian dynasty, in effect, exalted itself heaven high. (Isa 14:13, 14) This lofty grandeur and far-reaching dominion were also represented in Nebuchadnezzar's dream by a symbolic tree with its height 'reaching the heavens.'—Da 4:20-22.

New heavens and new earth. The connection of the "heavens" with ruling power aids in understanding the meaning of the expression "new heavens and a new earth" found at Isaiah 65:17; 66:22 and quoted by the apostle Peter at 2 Peter 3:13. Observing such relationship, M'Clintock and Strong's *Cyclopædia* (1891, Vol. IV, p. 122) comments: "In Isa. lxv, 17, a new heaven and a new earth signify a new government, new kingdom, new people."

Even as the "earth" can refer to a society of people (Ps 96:1; see EARTH), so, too, "heavens" can symbolize the superior ruling power or government over such "earth." The prophecy presenting the promise of "new heavens and a new earth," given through Isaiah, was one dealing initially with the restoration of Israel from Babylonian exile. Upon the Israelites' return to their homeland, they entered into a new system of things. Cyrus the Great was used prominently by God in bringing about that restoration. Back in Jerusalem, Zerubbabel (a descendant of David) served as governor, and Joshua as high priest. In harmony with Jehovah's purpose, this new governmental arrangement, or "new heavens," directed and supervised the subject people. (2Ch 36:23; Hag 1:1, 14) Thereby, as verse 18 of Isaiah chapter 65 foretold, Jerusalem became "a cause for joyfulness and her people a cause for exultation."

Peter's quotation, however, shows that a future fulfillment was to be anticipated, on the basis of God's promise. (2Pe 3:13) Since God's promise in this case relates to the presence of Christ Jesus, as shown at verse 4, the "new heavens and a new earth" must relate to God's Messianic Kingdom and its rule over obedient subjects. By his resurrection and ascension to God's right hand, Christ Jesus became "higher than the heavens" (Heb 7:26) in that he was thereby placed "far above every government and authority and power and lordship . . . not only in this system of things, but also in that to come."—Eph 1:19-21; Mt 28:18.

Christian followers of Jesus, as "partakers of the heavenly calling" (Heb 3:1), are assigned by God as "heirs" in union with Christ, through whom God purposed "to gather all things together again." "The things in the heavens," that is, those called to heavenly life, are the first to be thus gathered into unity with God through Christ. (Eph 1:8-11) Their inheritance is "reserved in the heavens." (1Pe 1:3, 4; Col 1:5; compare Joh 14:2, 3.) They are "enrolled" and have their "citizenship" in the heavens. (Heb 12:20-23; Php 3:20) They form the "New Jerusalem" seen in John's vision as "coming down out of heaven from God." (Re 21:2, 9, 10; compare Eph 5:24-27.) Since this vision is initially stated to be of "a new heaven and a new earth" (Re 21:1), it follows that both are represented in what is thereafter described. Hence the "new heaven" must correspond to Christ together with his "bride," the "New Jerusalem," and the "new earth" is seen in the 'peoples of mankind' who are their subjects and who receive the blessings of their rule, as depicted in verses 3 and 4.

Passing away of former heaven and earth. John's vision refers to the passing away of "the former heaven and the former earth." (Re 21:1; compare 20:11.) In the Christian Greek Scriptures, earthly governments and their peoples are shown to be subject to Satanic rule. (Mt 4:8, 9; Joh 12:31; 2Co 4:3, 4; Re 12:9; 16:13, 14) The apostle Paul referred to "the wicked spirit forces in the heavenly places," with their governments, authorities, and world rulers. (Eph 6:12) So the passing away of "the former heaven" indicates the end of political governments along with Satan and his demons. This identification of "the former heaven" harmonizes with the fact that shortly before the statement concerning the 'former heaven having passed away,' John had seen a vision of the complete defeat of Satan's forces and the casting of Satan into "the abyss." (Re 19:19–20:3) The earthly subjects of Satan's rule are destroyed prior to his abyssing, as shown at Revelation 19:17, 18. (Compare 1Jo 2:15-17.) The description of a fiery destruction of heaven and earth at 2 Peter 3:7-12 corresponds to the visions in Revelation.

Abasement of That Which Is Exalted. Because the heavens represent that which is elevated, the abasement of those things that are exalted is at times represented by the overthrow or the 'rocking' or 'agitating' of the heavens. Jehovah is said to have "thrown down from heaven to earth the beauty of Israel" at the time of its

desolation. That beauty included its kingdom and princely rulers and their power, and such beauty was devoured as by fire. (La 2:1-3) But Israel's conqueror, Babylon, later experienced an agitation of her own "heaven" and a rocking of her "earth" when the Medes and Persians overthrew Babylon and her heavenly gods proved false and unable to save her from the loss of her dominion over the land.—Isa 13:1, 10-13.

Similarly, it was prophesied that the heaven-high position of Edom would not save her from destruction and that Jehovah's sword of judgment would be drenched in her heights, or "heavens," with no help for her from any heavenly, or exalted, source. (Isa 34:4-7; compare Ob 1-4, 8.) Those making great boasts, wickedly speaking in an elevated style as if to "put their mouth in the very heavens," are certain to fall to ruin. (Ps 73:8, 9, 18; compare Re 13:5, 6.) The city of Capernaum had reason to feel highly favored because of the attention it received by Jesus and his ministry. However, since it failed to respond to his powerful works, Jesus asked, "Will you perhaps be exalted to heaven?" and foretold instead, "Down to Hades you will come."—Mt 11:23.

Darkening of the Heavens. The darkening of the heavens or of the stellar bodies is often used to represent the removal of prosperous, favorable conditions, and their being replaced by foreboding, gloomy prospects and conditions, like a time when dark clouds blot out all light day and night. (Compare Isa 50:2, 3, 10.) This use of the physical heavens in connection with the mental outlook of humans is somewhat similar to the old Arabic expression, "His heaven has fallen to the earth," meaning that one's superiority or prosperity is greatly diminished. Also similar is the modern German expression, *"Aus allen Himmeln fallen"* (literally, to fall out of all heavens), conveying the idea of bitter disappointment and utter disillusionment.

Upon Judah such a day of darkness came in fulfillment of Jehovah's judgment through his prophet Joel, and it reached its culmination in Judah's desolation by Babylon. (Joe 2:1, 2, 10, 30, 31; compare Jer 4:23, 28.) Any hope of help from a heavenly source seemed to have dried up, and as foretold at Deuteronomy 28:65-67, they came into "dread night and day," with no relief or hope by sunlit morning or by moonlit evening. Yet, by the same prophet, Joel, Jehovah warned enemies of Judah that they would experience the same situation when he executed judgment upon them. (Joe 3:12-16) Ezekiel and Isaiah used this same figurative picture in foretelling God's judgment on Egypt and on Babylon respectively. —Eze 32:7, 8, 12; Isa 13:1, 10, 11.

The apostle Peter quoted Joel's prophecy on the day of Pentecost when urging a crowd of listeners to "get saved from this crooked generation." (Ac 2:1, 16-21, 40) The unheeding ones of that generation saw a time of grave darkness when the Romans besieged and eventually ravaged Jerusalem less than 40 years later. Prior to Pentecost, however, Jesus had made a similar prophecy and showed it would have a fulfillment at the time of his presence.—Mt 24:29-31; Lu 21:25-27; compare Re 6:12-17.

Permanence of Physical Heavens. Eliphaz the Temanite said of God: "Look! In his holy ones he has no faith, and the heavens themselves are actually not clean in his eyes." However, Jehovah said to Eliphaz that he and his two companions had "not spoken concerning me what is truthful as has my servant Job." (Job 15:1, 15; 42:7) By contrast, Exodus 24:10 refers to the heavens as representing purity. Thus there is no cause stated in the Bible for God's destroying the physical heavens.

That the physical heavens are permanent is shown by the fact that they are used in similes relating to things that are everlasting, such as the peaceful, righteous results of the Davidic kingdom inherited by God's Son. (Ps 72:5-7; Lu 1:32, 33) Thus, texts such as Psalm 102:25, 26 that speak of the heavens as 'perishing' and as 'being replaced like a worn-out garment' are not to be understood in a literal sense.

At Luke 21:33, Jesus says that "heaven and earth will pass away, but my words will by no means pass away." The sense of this expression seems to be like that of Matthew 5:18: "Truly I say to you that *sooner would* heaven and earth pass away [or, "it is easier for heaven and earth to pass away"; Lu 16:17] than for one smallest letter or one particle of a letter to pass away from the Law by any means and not all things take place."

Psalm 102:25-27 stresses God's eternity and imperishability, whereas his physical creation of heavens and earth is perishable, that is, it *could be* destroyed—if such were God's purpose. Unlike God's eternal existence, the permanence of any part of his physical creation is not independent. As seen in the earth, the physical creation must undergo a continual renewing process if it is to endure or retain its existing form. That the physical heavens are dependent on God's will and sustaining power is indicated at Psalm 148, where, after referring to sun, moon, and stars, along with other parts of God's creation, verse 6 states that God "keeps them standing forever, to time indefinite. A regulation he has given, and it will not pass away."

The words of Psalm 102:25, 26 apply to Jehovah God, but the apostle Paul quotes them with reference to Jesus Christ. This is because God's only-begotten Son was God's personal Agent employed in creating the physical universe. Paul contrasts the Son's permanence with that of the physical creation, which God, if he so designed, could 'wrap up just as a cloak' and set aside. —Heb 1:1, 2, 8, 10-12; compare 1Pe 2:3, ftn.

Various Poetic and Figurative Expressions. Because the physical heavens play a vital part in sustaining and prospering life on earth—by sunshine, rain, dew, refreshing winds, and other atmospheric benefits—they are spoken of poetically as Jehovah's "good storehouse." (De 28:11, 12; 33:13, 14) Jehovah opens its "doors" to bless his servants, as when causing manna, "the grain of heaven," to descend upon the ground. (Ps 78:23, 24; Joh 6:31) The clouds are like "water jars" in the upper chambers of that storehouse, and the rain pours forth as by "sluices," certain factors, such as mountains or even God's miraculous intervention, causing water condensation and subsequent rainfall in specific regions. (Job 38:37; Jer 10:12, 13; 1Ki 18:41-45) On the other hand, the withdrawal of God's blessing at times resulted in the heavens over the land of Canaan being "shut up," becoming, in appearance, as hard and as nonporous as iron and having a copper-colored metallic brightness, with a dust-filled, rainless atmosphere.—Le 26:19; De 11:16, 17; 28:23, 24; 1Ki 8:35, 36.

This aids one in understanding the picture presented at Hosea 2:21-23. Having foretold the devastating results of Israel's unfaithfulness, Jehovah now tells of the time of her restoration and the resulting blessings. In that day, he says, "I shall answer the heavens, and they, for their part, will answer the earth; and the earth, for its part, will answer the grain and the sweet wine and the oil; and they, for their part, will answer Jezreel." Evidently this represents Israel's petition for Jehovah's blessing through the chain of things of Jehovah's creation here named. For that reason these things are viewed as personified, hence, as if able to make a request, or petition.

Israel asks for grain, wine, and oil; these products, in turn, seek their plant food and water from the earth; the earth, in order to supply this need, requires (or figuratively calls for) sun, rain, and dew from the heavens; and the heavens (till now "shut up" because of the withdrawal of God's blessing) can respond only if God accepts the petition and restores his favor to the nation, thereby putting the productive cycle in motion. The prophecy gives the assurance that he will do so.

At 2 Samuel 22:8-15, David apparently uses the figure of a tremendous storm to represent the effect of God's intervention on David's behalf, freeing him from his enemies. The fierceness of this symbolic storm agitates the foundation of the heavens, and they 'bend down' with dark low-lying clouds. Compare the literal storm conditions described at Exodus 19:16-18; also the poetic expressions at Isaiah 64:1, 2.

Jehovah, "the Father of the celestial lights" (Jas 1:17), is frequently spoken of as having 'stretched out the heavens,' just as one would a tent cloth. (Ps 104:1, 2; Isa 45:12) The heavens, both the expanse of atmosphere by day and the starry heavens by night, have the appearance of an immense domed canopy from the standpoint of humans on earth. At Isaiah 40:22 the simile is that of stretching out "fine gauze," rather than the coarser tent cloth. This expresses the delicate finery of such heavenly canopy. On a clear night the thousands of stars do, indeed, form a lacy web stretched over the black velvet background of space. It may also be noted that even the enormous galaxy known as the Via Lactea, or Milky Way, in which our solar system is located, has a filmy gauzelike appearance from earth's viewpoint.

It can be seen from the foregoing that the context must always be considered in determining the sense of these figurative expressions. Thus, when Moses called on "the heavens and the earth" to serve as witnesses to the things that he declared to Israel, it is obvious that he did not mean the inanimate creation but, rather, the intelligent residents inhabiting the heavens and the earth. (De 4:25, 26; 30:19; compare Eph 1:9, 10; Php 2:9, 10; Re 13:6.) This is also true of the rejoicing by the heavens and earth over Babylon's fall, at Jeremiah 51:48. (Compare Re 18:5; 19:1-3.) Likewise it must be the spiritual heavens that "trickle with righteousness," as described at Isaiah 45:8. In other cases the literal heavens are meant but are figuratively described as rejoicing

or shouting out loud. At Jehovah's coming to judge the earth, as described at Psalm 96:11-13, the heavens, along with the earth, sea, and the field, take on a gladsome appearance. (Compare Isa 44:23.) The physical heavens also praise their Creator, in the same way that a beautifully designed product brings praise to the craftsman producing it. In effect, they speak of Jehovah's power, wisdom, and majesty.—Ps 19:1-4; 69:34.

Ascension to Heaven. At 2 Kings 2:11, 12 the prophet Elijah is described as "ascending in the windstorm to the heavens." The heavens here referred to are the atmospheric heavens in which windstorms occur, not the spiritual heavens of God's presence. Elijah did not die at the time of such ascension, but he continued to live for a number of years after his heavenly transportation away from his successor Elisha. Nor did Elijah upon death ascend to the spiritual heavens, since Jesus, while on earth, clearly stated that "no man has ascended into heaven." (Joh 3:13; see ELIJAH No. 1 (Elisha Succeeds Him).) At Pentecost, Peter likewise said of David that he "did not ascend to the heavens." (Ac 2:34) In reality, there is nothing in the Scriptures to show that a heavenly hope was held out to God's servants prior to the coming of Christ Jesus. Such hope first appears in Jesus' expressions to his disciples (Mt 19:21, 23-28; Lu 12:32; Joh 14:2, 3) and was fully comprehended by them only after Pentecost of 33 C.E.—Ac 1:6-8; 2:1-4, 29-36; Ro 8:16, 17.

The Scriptures show that Christ Jesus was the first one to ascend from earth to the heavens of God's presence. (1Co 15:20; Heb 9:24) By such ascension and his presentation of his ransom sacrifice there, he 'opened the way' for those who would follow—the spirit-begotten members of his congregation. (Joh 14:2, 3; Heb 6:19, 20; 10:19, 20) In their resurrection these must bear "the image of the heavenly one," Christ Jesus, in order to ascend to the heavens of the spirit plane, for "flesh and blood" cannot inherit that heavenly Kingdom.—1Co 15:42-50.

How can persons in "heavenly places" still be on earth?

The apostle Paul in his letter to the Ephesians speaks of Christians then living on earth as though they were already enjoying a heavenly position, being raised up and "seated . . . together in the heavenly places in union with Christ Jesus." (Eph 1:3; 2:6) The context shows that anointed Christians are so viewed by God because of his having 'assigned them as heirs' with his Son in the heavenly inheritance. While yet on earth, they have been exalted, or 'lifted up,' by such assignment. (Eph 1:11, 18-20; 2:4-7, 22) These points also shed light on the symbolic vision at Revelation 11:12. Likewise it provides a key for understanding the prophetic picture contained at Daniel 8:9-12, where what has previously been shown to represent a political power is spoken of as "getting greater all the way to the army of the heavens," and even causing some of that army and of the stars to fall to the earth. At Daniel 12:3, those servants of God on earth at the foretold time of the end are spoken of as shining "like the stars to time indefinite." Note, too, the symbolic use of stars in the book of Revelation, chapters 1 through 3, where the context shows that such "stars" refer to persons who are obviously living on earth and undergoing earthly experiences and temptations, these "stars" being responsible for congregations under their care. —Re 1:20; 2:1, 8, 12, 18; 3:1, 7, 14.

The way to heavenly life. The way to heavenly life involves more than just faith in Christ's ransom sacrifice and works of faith in obedience to God's instructions. The inspired writings of the apostles and disciples show that there must also be a calling and choosing of one by God through his Son. (2Ti 1:9, 10; Mt 22:14; 1Pe 2:9) This invitation involves a number of steps, or actions, taken to qualify such a one for the heavenly inheritance; many of such steps are taken by God, others by the one called. Among such steps, or actions, are the declaring righteous of the called Christian (Ro 3:23, 24, 28; 8:33, 34); bringing him forth ('begetting him') as a spiritual son (Joh 1:12, 13; 3:3-6; Jas 1:18); his being baptized into Christ's death (Ro 6:3, 4; Php 3:8-11); anointing him (2Co 1:21; 1Jo 2:20, 27); sanctifying him (Joh 17:17). The called one must maintain integrity until death (2Ti 2:11-13; Re 2:10), and after he has proved faithful in his calling and selection (Re 17:14), he is finally resurrected to spirit life.—Joh 6:39, 40; Ro 6:5; 1Co 15:42-49; see ANOINTED, ANOINTING; DECLARE RIGHTEOUS; RESURRECTION; SANCTIFICATION.

Third Heaven. At 2 Corinthians 12:2-4 the apostle Paul describes one who was "caught away . . . to the third heaven" and "into paradise." Since there is no mention in the Scriptures of any other person having had such an experience, it seems likely that this was the apostle's own experience. Whereas some have endeavored to relate Paul's reference to the third heaven to the early rabbinic view that there were stages of heaven, even a

total of "seven heavens," this view finds no support in the Scriptures. As we have seen, the heavens are not referred to specifically as if divided into platforms or stages, but, rather, the context must be relied upon to determine whether reference is to the heavens within earth's atmospheric expanse, the heavens of outer space, the spiritual heavens, or something else. It therefore appears that the reference to "the third heaven" indicates the superlative degree of the rapture in which this vision was seen. Note the way words and expressions are repeated *three* times at Isaiah 6:3; Ezekiel 21:27; John 21:15-17; Revelation 4:8, evidently for the purpose of expressing an intensification of the quality or idea.

HEBER   (He'ber) [Partner].

1. Son of Beriah and grandson of Asher; ancestral head of the Heberites.—Ge 46:17; Nu 26:45; 1Ch 7:30-32.

2. The Kenite husband of Jael (the woman who put Jabin's army chief Sisera to death) and a descendant of Hobab, "whose son-in-law Moses was." Heber had evidently separated himself from the rest of the Kenites and was at peace with Jabin the king of Hazor.—Jg 4:11, 17, 21; 5:24.

3. A man of the tribe of Judah and "the father of Soco."—1Ch 4:1, 18.

4. Descendant of Elpaal; head of a paternal house of the tribe of Benjamin.—1Ch 8:1, 17, 18, 28.

HEBERITES   (He'ber·ites) [Of (Belonging to) Heber]. An Asherite family descended from Heber.—Nu 26:44, 45.

HEBREW, I.   The designation "Hebrew" is first used for Abram, distinguishing him thereby from his Amorite neighbors. (Ge 14:13) Thereafter, in virtually every case of its use, the term "Hebrew(s)" continues to be employed as a contrasting or distinguishing designation—the one speaking is of a non-Israelite nation (Ge 39:13, 14, 17; 41:12; Ex 1:16; 1Sa 4:6, 9), or is an Israelite addressing a foreigner (Ge 40:15; Ex 1:19; 2:7; Jon 1:9), or foreigners are mentioned (Ge 43:32; Ex 1:15; 2:11-13; 1Sa 13:3-7).

As the above texts show, the designation "Hebrew" was already familiar to the Egyptians in the 18th century B.C.E. This would seem to indicate that Abraham, Isaac, and Jacob had become quite well known over a wide area, thus making the appellative "Hebrew" a recognizable one. When Joseph spoke of "the land of the Hebrews"

(Ge 40:15) to two of Pharaoh's servants, he doubtless referred to the region around Hebron that his father and forefathers had long made a sort of base of operations. Some six centuries later the Philistines still spoke of the Israelites as "Hebrews." During the time of King Saul "Hebrews" and "Israel" were equivalent terms. (1Sa 13:3-7; 14:11; 29:3) In the ninth century B.C.E. the prophet Jonah identified himself as a Hebrew to sailors (possibly Phoenicians) on a boat out of the seaport of Joppa. (Jon 1:9) The Law also distinguished "Hebrew" slaves from those of other races or nationalities (Ex 21:2; De 15:12), and in referring to this, the book of Jeremiah (in the seventh century B.C.E.) shows the term "Hebrew" to be then the equivalent of "Jew."—Jer 34:8, 9, 13, 14.

In later periods Greek and Roman writers regularly called the Israelites either "Hebrews" or "Jews," not "Israelites."

Origin and Significance of the Term. The views as to the origin and significance of the term "Hebrew" generally can be resolved into the following:

One view holds that the name comes from the root word 'a·var', meaning "pass; pass by; pass over; cross." The term would then apply to Abraham as the one whom God took "from the other side of the River [Euphrates]." (Jos 24:3) The translators of the Greek Septuagint so understood the term and thus at Genesis 14:13 referred to Abraham as "the passer" rather than "the Hebrew." This theory is quite popular, yet not without problems. The ending for the term 'Iv·ri' (Hebrew) is the same as that used in other terms that are definitely patronymics, that is, names formed by the addition of a prefix or suffix indicating relationship to the name of one's father or parental ancestor. Thus, Moh·'a·vi' (Moabite) denotes primarily one descended from Moab (Moh·'av') rather than one from a geographic region; so too with 'Am·moh·ni' (Ammonite), Da·ni' (Danite), and many others.

Additionally, if "Hebrew" were to apply to Abraham solely on the basis of his having 'crossed over' the Euphrates, the term might seem to be a very general one, applicable to any person who did the same—and likely there were many such emigrants in the course of the centuries. With such an origin, the term could be distinctive only if Abraham's crossing of the Euphrates was recognized as being by divine call. That this fact should be acknowledged by pagans using the term is a matter for question, but it cannot be deemed impossible.

A second view, endorsed by some scholars, is that the name denotes those who are sojourners, that is, 'passing through,' as distinguished from those who are residents or settlers. (Compare the use of 'a·var' at Ge 18:5; Ex 32:27; 2Ch 30:10.) While the Israelites did lead a nomadic life for a time, this was not the case after the conquest of Canaan. Yet, the name Hebrew continued to apply to them. Another objection to this concept may be that it is so broad that it would include all nomadic groups. Since Jehovah is Biblically identified as "the God of the Hebrews," it is evident that this does not mean 'all the nomads,' inasmuch as many nomadic peoples were worshipers of false gods.—Ex 3:18; 5:3; 7:16; 9:1, 13; 10:3..

A third view that accords well with the Biblical evidence is that "Hebrew" ('Iv·ri') comes from the name Eber ('E'ver), that of the great-grandson of Shem and an ancestor of Abraham. (Ge 11:10-26) It is true that nothing is known about Eber aside from his family relationship as a link in the chain of descent from Shem to Abraham. There is no outstanding act or other personal feature recorded that might form the basis for Eber's name being used so prominently by his descendants. Nevertheless, it is to be noted that Eber is specifically singled out at Genesis 10:21, Shem there being spoken of as "the forefather of all the sons of Eber." That the name Eber was applied centuries after his death to a certain people or region is evident from Balaam's prophecy in the 15th century B.C.E. (Nu 24:24) The use of the name as a patronymic would also link the Israelites with a particular one of the "family descents" from Noah, as recorded at Genesis 10:1-32.

As with the other views already discussed, the question arises as to why "Hebrew," if derived from the name Eber, should be applied so specifically and distinctively to the Israelites. Eber had other descendants, through his son Joktan, who were not in the line of descent to Abraham (and Israel). (Ge 10:25-30; 11:16-26) It would seem that the term 'Iv·ri' (Hebrew) would apply to all such descendants who could lay rightful claim to Eber as their ancestor. Some scholars suggest that originally this may have been the case, but that, in course of time, the name came to be restricted to the Israelites as the most prominent of the Eberites, or Hebrews. This would not be without some parallel in the Bible record. Although there were many non-Israelite descendants of Abraham, including the Edomites, the Ishmaelites, and the descendants of Abraham through his wife Keturah, it is the Israelites who are distinctively called the "seed of Abraham."

(Ps 105:6; Isa 41:8; compare Mt 3:9; 2Co 11:22.) Of course, this was because of God's action toward them in connection with the Abrahamic covenant. But the very fact that God made them a nation and gave them the land of Canaan as an inheritance, as well as victories over many powerful enemies, would certainly distinguish the Israelites not only from other descendants of Abraham but also from all other descendants of Eber. There is the possibility, too, that many of such other descendants also lost their "Eberite" identity by intermarriage with other peoples.

It may well be, then, that Eber is singled out in the genealogical lists as a divine indication that the Noachian blessing pronounced upon Shem would find its fulfillment especially in the descendants of Eber, the subsequent facts showing the Israelites to be the prime recipients of that blessing. Such specific mention of Eber would also serve the purpose of indicating the line of descent of the promised Seed mentioned in Jehovah's prophecy at Genesis 3:15, Eber thereby becoming a specific link between Shem and Abraham. Such a connection would also harmonize well with the designation of Jehovah as "the God of the Hebrews."

Balaam's prophecy. The understanding of Balaam's prophecy at Numbers 24:24 depends upon whether Eber is there used as a geographic term indicating the 'land (or people) on the other side,' or as a patronymic applying especially to the Hebrews (Israelites). Most commentators recognize Kittim, from whose coast ships would come to afflict Assyria and Eber, according to the prophecy, as being primarily the ancient designation of Cyprus. However, as the articles CYPRUS and KITTIM show, Cyprus came under heavy Greek influence; also, the name Kittim may have a broader application, beyond the island of Cyprus, perhaps allowing for a further connection with Greece. So, most scholars consider the prophecy to relate to the Greek, or Macedonian, conquest of the Middle Eastern nations, including Assyria. Those holding that Eber is here used geographically consider the affliction upon Eber to mean that not only Assyria but all the Mesopotamian powers (the people 'on the other side') would be brought under Western domination. Those regarding Eber as designating the Hebrews, suggest that the foretold affliction came upon them after the death of Alexander the Great and under the line of Seleucid rulers, particularly Antiochus Epiphanes. Even as the name Assyria in this text is actually the name Asshur in Hebrew, so too it appears that "Eber" is indeed

a patronymic designating the Hebrews rather than merely a geographic designation.

Use in the Christian Greek Scriptures. In the Christian Greek Scriptures the term "Hebrew" is used particularly in designating the language spoken by the Jews (Joh 5:2; 19:13, 17, 20; Ac 21:40; 22:2; Re 9:11; 16:16), the language in which the resurrected and glorified Jesus addressed Saul of Tarsus. (Ac 26:14, 15) At Acts 6:1 Hebrew-speaking Jews are distinguished from Greek-speaking Jews.—See GREECE, GREEKS (Hellenists).

Paul described himself as, first, a Hebrew; second, an Israelite; and third, of the seed of Abraham. (2Co 11:22) 'Hebrew' may here be used to show his racial origin (compare Php 3:4, 5) and perhaps language; 'Israelite,' his natural membership in the nation God had originally established as His name people (compare Ro 9:3-5); and 'seed of Abraham,' his being among those inheriting the promised blessings of the Abrahamic covenant.

The "Habiru." In numerous cuneiform records dating from the beginning of the second millennium B.C.E., the Akkadian (Assyro-Babylonian) term *habiru,* or *hapiru,* occurs. The Habiru were active in southern Mesopotamia and Asia Minor as well as in the Haran and Mari areas. Likewise, in about 60 of the Amarna Tablets, found in Egypt, vassal Canaanite rulers writing to the Pharaoh of Egypt (then their overlord) complained, among other things, of the attacks against their cities by certain rulers in league with the "Habiru."

The "Habiru" appeared in Mesopotamia as agricultural workers, mercenary soldiers, marauders, slaves, and so forth. Whereas some scholars have endeavored to link the Habiru with the Israelite conquest of Canaan, the evidence does not support such a view. In this regard, *The New International Dictionary of Biblical Archaeology* remarked: "Since the first revelation of the Habiru in the Amarna texts late in the nineteenth century scholars have been tempted to associate the Habiru with the biblical *'ibrim* or 'Hebrews,' —a word that occurs thirty-four times in the OT, usually either by foreigners or in the presence of foreigners. . . . Most scholars reject any direct identification of the Hebrews with the Habiru in view of the following objections: (1) philological difficulties in the equation; (2) the probability that Habiru is an appellative term describing a class, whereas *'ibri* is an ethnic term; (3) the considerable differences in the distribution, activity, and character of the two groups."—Edited by E. Blaiklock and R. Harrison, 1983, pp. 223, 224.

The "Habiru" appear in Egyptian documents under the name 'apiru. They were employed as quarry workers, wine pressers, and stone haulers. Linguistically it is not possible to identify the Egyptian word 'apiru with the Hebrew word 'Iv·ri'. Moreover, documents mention "Habiru" as being in Egypt long after the Hebrews had left that land.

HEBREW, II.

The Hebrew language was used for the writing of the major part of the inspired Scriptures—39 books in all (according to the division of material as found in many translations), composing some three quarters of the total content of the Bible. A small portion of these books, however, was written in Aramaic.—See ARAMAIC.

In the Hebrew Scriptures, the name Hebrew is not applied to the language, the name there being applied only to individuals or to the people of Israel as a whole. Reference is made to "the Jews' language" (2Ki 18:26, 28), "Jewish" (Ne 13:24), and "the language of Canaan" (Isa 19:18), which, at that time (the eighth century B.C.E.), was primarily Hebrew. In the Christian Greek Scriptures, however, the name Hebrew is regularly applied to the language spoken by the Jews. —See HEBREW, I.

Origin of the Hebrew Language. Secular history does not reveal the origin of the Hebrew language—or, for that matter, of any of the most ancient languages known, such as Sumerian, Akkadian (Assyro-Babylonian), Aramaean, and Egyptian. This is because these tongues appear already fully developed in the earliest written records men have found. (See LANGUAGE.) The various views advanced by scholars concerning the origin and development of Hebrew—such as those claiming that Hebrew derived from Aramaic or from some Canaanite dialect—are therefore conjectural. The same may be said for attempts at explaining the derivation of many words found in the Hebrew Scriptures. Scholars frequently assign an Akkadian or an Aramaic source for many of these words. However, as Dr. Edward Horowitz comments: "In the field of etymology [the study of word origins] there are wide differences of opinion among scholars, even among the very best of them." He then cites examples of explanations by renowned scholars of the etymology of certain Hebrew words, in each case showing that other prominent scholars disagree, and then adds: "And so we have these never ending differences between equally highly respected authorities."—*How the Hebrew Language Grew*, 1960, pp. xix, xx.

The Bible is the only historical source giving reliable evidence of the origin of the language that we know as Hebrew. It was, of course, spoken by the Israelite descendants of "Abram the Hebrew" (Ge 14:13), who, in turn, was descended from Noah's son Shem. (Ge 11:10-26) In view of God's prophetic blessing on Shem (Ge 9:26), it is reasonable to believe that Shem's language was not affected when God confused the language of the disapproved people at Babel. (Ge 11:5-9) Shem's language would remain the same as it had been previously, the "one language" that had existed from Adam onward. (Ge 11:1) This would mean that the language that eventually came to be called Hebrew was the one original tongue of mankind. As stated, secular history knows no other.

Question of the Language's Stability. History is replete with examples of languages changing over long periods of time. The English spoken in the time of Alfred the Great (of the ninth century C.E.) would seem like a foreign tongue to most English-speaking people of today. It might, therefore, seem likely that the language originally spoken by Adam would have changed substantially by the time the writing of the Hebrew Scriptures began with Moses. The long life spans enjoyed in that 2,500-year period, however, would be a definite factor operating against such change. Thus, there was only one human link, namely, Methuselah, needed to connect Adam with the Flood survivors. Additionally, Shem, who was evidently a pre-Flood contemporary of Methuselah for a number of years, lived well into the lifetime of Isaac. And less than 150 years elapsed from the death of Isaac (1738 B.C.E.) until the birth of Moses (1593 B.C.E.). This overlapping of the lives of individuals several generations apart would serve to maintain uniformity of speech. Of course, the extent to which these human links, such as Shem and Abraham, lived in geographic proximity is not always known. Regular communication is an important factor in language stability.

That not all of Shem's descendants continued to speak the "one language" of pre-Flood times in its pure form is evident from the differences that developed among the Semitic languages, including Hebrew, Aramaic, Akkadian, and the various Arabic dialects. In the 18th century B.C.E. (about the year 1761 B.C.E.), Abraham's grandson and grandnephew used different terms in naming the heap of stones they had set up as a memorial or witness between them. Jacob, the father of the Israelites, called it "Galeed," while Laban, a resident in Syria or Aram (though not himself a descendant of Aram), used the Aramaean term "Jegar-sahadutha." (Ge 31:47) The dissimilarity of these two terms, however, does not necessarily indicate a major difference between Aramaean and Hebrew at this point, inasmuch as Jacob seems to have faced no particular problem in communication there in Syria. Undoubtedly, as new circumstances and situations arose and new artifacts were produced, certain words would be coined to describe such developments. Such terms might differ from place to place among geographically separated groups of the same language family, even while the actual structure of their language remained very much the same.

Among the Israelites themselves, some small variation in pronunciation developed, as is evident by the different pronunciation given the word "Shibboleth" by the Ephraimites during the period of the Judges (1473 to 1117 B.C.E.). (Jg 12:4-6) This, however, is no basis for claiming (as some have) that the Israelites then spoke separate dialects.

In the eighth century B.C.E., the difference between Hebrew and Aramaic had become wide enough to mark them as separate languages. This is seen when King Hezekiah's representatives requested the spokesmen of Assyrian King Sennacherib to "speak with your servants, please, in the Syrian [Aramaic] language, for we can listen; and do not speak with us in the Jews' language in the ears of the people that are on the wall." (2Ki 18:17, 18, 26) Although Aramaic was then the lingua franca of the Middle East and was used in international diplomatic communication, it was not understood by the majority of the Judeans. The earliest known non-Biblical written documents in Aramaic are from about the same period, and these confirm the distinction between the two languages.

Had both Hebrew and Aramaic diverged from the original "one language," or did one of them preserve the purity of that primary language? While the Bible does not specifically say, the implication is that the language in which Moses began the writing of the inspired Sacred Record was the same as that spoken by the first man.

If history was put in written form before the Flood, such history would contribute notably to the preservation of the purity of the original tongue. Even if that history were passed on by oral tradition, it would still serve to maintain the stability of the original speech. The extreme care that the Jews of later times showed in endeavoring to conserve the true form of the Sacred Record illustrates the concern that would surely have been shown in patriarchal times to transmit accurately the earliest record of God's dealings with men.

Further reason for believing that the Hebrew of the Bible accurately represents the "one language" of pre-Babel times is the remarkable stability of the Hebrew language during the thousand-year period in which the Hebrew Scriptures were written. As *The International Standard Bible Encyclopedia* states: "One of the most remarkable facts connected with the Hebrew of the O[ld] T[estament] is that, although its literature covers a period of over a thousand years, the language (grammar and vocabulary) of the oldest parts differs little from that of the latest."—Edited by G. W. Bromiley, 1982, Vol. 2, p. 659.

Knowledge of the Language Incomplete. In reality, knowledge of ancient Hebrew is by no means complete. As Professor Burton L. Goddard says: "In large measure, the O[ld] T[estament] Hebrew must be self explanatory." (*The Zondervan Pictorial Bible Dictionary*, edited by M. Tenney, 1963, p. 345) This is because so few other contemporaneous writings in the Hebrew language have been found that could contribute to an understanding of the word usage. Among those of any importance are the Gezer calendar (a simple list of agricultural operations thought to date from the tenth century B.C.E.; PICTURE, Vol. 1, p. 960), some ostraca (inscribed pieces of broken pottery) from Samaria (mainly orders and receipts for wine, oil, and barley and generally assigned to the early part of the eighth century B.C.E.), the Siloam inscription (found in a water tunnel of Jerusalem and believed to date from the reign of King Hezekiah [745-717 B.C.E.]), and the Lachish ostraca (probably from the latter part of the seventh century B.C.E.).

Additionally, there is a Phoenician inscription on the sarcophagus of King Ahiram in Byblos (Gebal), its language closely resembling Hebrew and thought to be from the start of the first millennium B.C.E.; also the Moabite Stone, apparently from the late tenth or early ninth century B.C.E. The language on the Moabite Stone is very similar to Hebrew, as might be expected in view of the Moabites' descent from Abraham's nephew Lot.—Ge 19:30-37.

The total of the information on all these inscriptions, however, is but a small fraction of that found in the Hebrew Scriptures.

The Hebrew Scriptures themselves, though covering a wide range of subjects and employing an extensive vocabulary, by no means contain all the words or expressions of ancient Hebrew. The Siloam inscription and the Lachish ostraca, for example, contain certain word and grammatical constructions that do not appear in the Hebrew Scriptures, yet these constructions are clearly of Hebrew origin. Undoubtedly the ancient vocabulary of the Hebrew-speaking people contained many more "root" words, plus thousands of words derived from these, than are known today.

Aside from those portions of the Bible definitely known to be written in Aramaic, there are quite a number of words and expressions found in the Hebrew Scriptures for which the original "roots" are unknown. Lexicographers classify many of these as "loanwords," claiming that Hebrew borrowed these from other Semitic tongues, such as Aramaic, Akkadian, or Arabic. This is speculation, however. As Edward Horowitz states: "But sometimes the borrowing is so ancient that scholars do not know which language did the borrowing and which was the original owner." (*How the Hebrew Language Grew,* pp. 3, 5) It seems more probable that such questioned terms are genuinely Hebrew and are further evidence of the incompleteness of modern knowledge of the scope of the ancient language.

Among the evidences pointing to a rich vocabulary in ancient Hebrew are writings from the start of the Common Era. These include non-Biblical religious writings forming part of the Dead Sea Scrolls, and also the Mishnah, a body of rabbinic writings in Hebrew dealing with Jewish tradition. Writing in *The Encyclopedia Americana* (1956, Vol. XIV, p. 57a), Professor Meyer Waxman says: "Biblical Hebrew . . . does not exhaust the entire stock of words, as is proved by the Mishnah, which employs hundreds of Hebrew words not found in the Bible." Of course, some of these could have been later additions or coined expressions, but doubtless many were part of the Hebrew vocabulary during the period of the writing of the Hebrew Scriptures.

When Did Hebrew Begin to Wane? It is popularly held that the Jews began to change over to Aramaic speech during their exile in

Babylon. The evidence for this, however, is not strong. Modern examples show that subjugated groups or immigrants can and frequently do retain their native tongue over periods far longer than 70 years. Particularly since the Jews had the divine promise of a return to their homeland, it may be expected that they would be little inclined to drop Hebrew in favor of either Akkadian (Assyro-Babylonian) or Aramaic, the lingua franca of that time. True, Aramaic passages and words are to be found in the exilic and postexilic books, such as Daniel, Ezra, and Esther. This is not unusual, however, inasmuch as those books include accounts of events taking place in Aramaic-speaking lands, as well as official correspondence, and they deal with a people subject to domination by foreign powers using Aramaic as a diplomatic language.

Nehemiah 8:8 describes the "putting of meaning" into and "giving understanding" in the reading of the Law. It has been suggested that Hebrew was not then perfectly understood by the returned exiles and that some Aramaic paraphrasing was done. However, the text itself points more to an exposition of the sense and application of what was being taught in the Law, rather than to some clarification of linguistic terminology or grammatical forms.—Compare Mt 13:14, 51, 52; Lu 24:27; Ac 8:30, 31.

Actually, there is no reference in the Bible to any abandonment of Hebrew as the daily tongue of the people. True, Nehemiah found certain Jews who had Ashdodite, Ammonite, and Moabite wives and whose children did not know "how to speak Jewish." But the mention of this factor in connection with Nehemiah's indignation at the Jews involved in these marriages with non-Israelites indicates that such slighting of Hebrew was strongly disapproved. (Ne 13:23-27) This might be expected in view of the importance given to the reading of God's Word, which was till then mainly in Hebrew.

The period from the close of the Hebrew canon (likely in the time of Ezra and Malachi in the fifth century B.C.E.) down till the start of the Common Era is not dealt with to any extent in the Bible. Secular records are also few. But even these give little support to a changeover from Hebrew to Aramaic on the part of the Jewish people. The evidence indicates that many of the Apocryphal books, such as Judith, Ecclesiasticus (not Ecclesiastes), Baruch, and First Maccabees, were written in Hebrew, and these works are generally viewed as dating from the last three centuries before the Common Era. As already mentioned, some of the non-Biblical writings among the Dead Sea Scrolls were also in Hebrew, and Hebrew was used in compiling the Jewish Mishnah after the beginning of the Common Era.

Because of these and related facts, Dr. William Chomsky states that the theory held by some Jewish and non-Jewish scholars that Aramaic had completely displaced Hebrew is without any foundation and has been effectively disproved. If anything, it is more likely that the Jews became a bilingual people, but with Hebrew prevailing as the preferred tongue. As Dr. Chomsky says of the Mishnaic Hebrew: "This language bears all the earmarks of a typical vernacular employed by peasants, merchants and artisans. . . . On the basis of the available evidence it seems fair to conclude that the Jews were generally conversant, during the period of the Second Commonwealth, especially its latter part, with both languages [Hebrew and Aramaic]. Sometimes they used one, sometimes another."—*Hebrew: The Eternal Language*, 1969, pp. 207, 210.

The strongest evidence, however, favoring the view that Hebrew continued as a living language down into the first century of the Common Era is found in the references to the Hebrew language in the Christian Greek Scriptures. (Joh 5:2; 19:13, 17, 20; 20:16; Re 9:11; 16:16) While many scholars hold that the term "Hebrew" in these references should instead read "Aramaic," there is good reason to believe that the term actually applies to the Hebrew language, as is shown in the article ARAMAIC. When the physician Luke says that Paul spoke to the people of Jerusalem in "the Hebrew language," it seems unlikely that he meant thereby the Aramaic or Syrian language. (Ac 21:40; 22:2; compare 26:14.) Since the Hebrew Scriptures earlier distinguished between Aramaic (Syrian) and "the Jews' language" (2Ki 18:26) and since the first-century Jewish historian Josephus, considering this passage of the Bible, speaks of "Aramaic" and "Hebrew" as distinct tongues (*Jewish Antiquities*, X, 8 [i, 2]), there seems to be no reason for the writers of the Christian Greek Scriptures to have said "Hebrew" if they meant Aramaic or Syrian.

That Aramaic was widely used throughout Palestine by that time is acknowledged. The use of Aramaic "Bar" (son), rather than Hebrew "Ben," in several names (such as Bartholomew and Simon Bar-jonah) is one evidence of familiarity with Aramaic. Of course, some Jews also had Greek names, as did Andrew and Philip, and this

would not of itself prove that their common speech was Greek, any more than Mark's Latin name would prove that this was the common language of his family. Evidently four languages were current in Palestine in the first century of the Common Era: the three mentioned in the Bible as appearing on the sign over the impaled Jesus' head (Hebrew, Latin, and Greek [Joh 19:19, 20]) and the fourth one, Aramaic. Of these, Latin was undoubtedly the least common.

Jesus may well have used Aramaic on occasion, as when speaking to the Syrophoenician woman. (Mr 7:24-30) Certain expressions recorded as spoken by him are generally considered to be of Aramaic origin. Yet, even here there is need for caution since the classifying of these expressions as Aramaic is not without question. For example, the words spoken by Jesus while impaled on the stake, "*E'li, E'li, la'ma sa·bach-tha'ni?*" (Mt 27:46; Mr 15:34), are usually considered to be Aramaic, perhaps of a Galilean dialect. However, *The Interpreter's Dictionary of the Bible* says: "Opinion is divided in regard to the original language of the saying and as to whether Jesus himself would more naturally have used Hebrew or Aramaic. . . . Documents indicate that a form of Hebrew, somewhat influenced by Aramaic, may have been in use in Palestine in the first century A.D." (Edited by G. A. Buttrick, 1962, Vol. 2, p. 86) In reality, the Greek transliteration of these words, as recorded by Matthew and Mark, does not allow for a positive identification of the original language used.

One further evidence for the continued use of Hebrew in apostolic times is the testimony that Matthew's Gospel was originally written by him in Hebrew.

It appears, then, that Hebrew began to wane primarily after, and as a result of, the destruction of Jerusalem and its temple and the scattering of its remaining inhabitants in the year 70 C.E. Nevertheless, its use was continued in the synagogues wherever the Jews spread. Particularly from about the sixth century C.E. onward, zealous efforts were made to maintain the purity of the Hebrew text of the Scriptures by those Jewish scholars known as the Masoretes. And particularly from the 16th century onward, interest in ancient Hebrew revived, and the following century saw intensive study of other Semitic tongues begin. This has contributed to a clarification of the understanding of the ancient language and has resulted in improved translations of the Hebrew Scriptures.

Hebrew Alphabet and Script. The Hebrew alphabet was composed of 22 consonants; several of these evidently can represent two sounds, giving a total of some 28 sounds. The vowel sounds were supplied by the reader, guided by the context, much as an English-speaking person fills in the vowels for such abbreviations as "bldg." (building), "blvd." (boulevard), and "hgt." (height). It is believed that the traditional pronunciation of the Hebrew Scriptures was kept alive and handed down by those specializing in reading the Law, Prophets, and Psalms for the instruction of the people. Then, in the second half of the first millennium C.E., the Masoretes devised a system of dots and dashes called vowel points, and these were inserted in the consonantal text. Additionally, certain accent marks were supplied to indicate stress, pause, connection between words and clauses, and musical notation.

The earliest Hebrew inscriptions known are recorded in an ancient script considerably different in form from the square-shaped Hebrew letters of later documents, such as those of the early centuries of the Common Era. The square-shaped style is often called "Aramaic," or "Assyrian." It is believed that the change from ancient Hebrew characters to square Hebrew characters took place during the Babylonian exile. However, as Ernst Würthwein says: "For a long while the Old Hebrew script remained in use beside the square script. The coins of the period of Bar Kochba's revolt (A.D. 132-135) bear Old Hebrew letters. Among the texts found in the Dead Sea caves are some written in the Old Hebrew script." —*The Text of the Old Testament*, 1979, p. 5.

Origen, a Christian writer of the second and third centuries C.E., stated that, in the more correct copies of the Greek translations of the Hebrew Scriptures, the Tetragrammaton, or sacred name of Jehovah, was written in ancient Hebrew letters. This has been confirmed by the discovery of fragmentary leather scrolls dated to the first century C.E., containing the "minor" prophets in Greek. In these scrolls the Tetragrammaton appears in the ancient Hebrew characters. (See *NW* appendix, p. 1563, Nos. 2-4.) Fragments from the late fifth or early sixth century C.E. of Aquila's Greek version also contain the divine name written in ancient Hebrew characters.—*NW* appendix, p. 1563, Nos. 7, 8.

Dr. Horowitz says: "It was the old Hebrew alphabet that the Greeks borrowed and passed on to Latin, and it is the old Hebrew alphabet that the Greek most closely resembles."—*How the Hebrew Language Grew*, p. 18.

Qualities and Characteristics. Hebrew is a very expressive language, lending itself to the vivid description of events. Its short sentences and simple conjunctions give movement and flow of thought. Hebrew poetry, which adds to these qualities those of parallelism and rhythm, is remarkably expressive and moving.

Hebrew is rich in metaphors. "Seashore," at Genesis 22:17, in Hebrew is, literally, "lip of the sea." Other expressions are the "face of the earth," the "head" of a mountain, the "mouth of a cave," and similar metaphoric expressions. That this use of human terms in no way indicates any animistic belief can be seen from reading the Scriptures themselves, for the utmost disdain is shown toward those who would worship trees and other objects.—Compare Isa 44:14-17; Jer 10:3-8; Hab 2:19.

The Hebrew vocabulary is composed of concrete words, words that involve the senses of seeing, hearing, feeling, tasting, and smelling. Thus, they paint mental pictures for the hearer or reader. Because of this concrete quality, some scholars say that Hebrew is lacking in abstract terms. There definitely are some abstract nouns in Biblical Hebrew, however. For instance, the noun *ma·chasha·vah'* (drawn from the root *cha·shav'*, meaning "think") is translated by such abstract terms as "thought, device, invention, scheme." *Ba·tach'* (a verb that means "trust") is the source of the noun *be'tach* (security). Nevertheless, as a general rule abstract ideas are carried by concrete nouns. Consider the root verb *ka·vedh'*, which means, basically, "be heavy" (as at Jg 20:34). At Ezekiel 27:25 this same verb is translated 'become glorious,' that is, literally, 'become heavy.' Correspondingly, from this root is drawn the noun *ka·vedh'*, which refers to the liver, one of the heaviest internal organs, and the noun *ka·vohdh'*, meaning "glory." (Le 3:4; Isa 66:12) This taking of the abstract from the concrete is further illustrated by *yadh*, meaning "hand" and also "care," "means," or "guidance" (Ex 2:19; Ge 42:37; Ex 35:29; 38:21); *'aph* refers to both "nostril" and "anger" (Ge 24:47; 27:45); *zeroh'a'*, "arm," also conveys the abstract concept of "strength" (Job 22:8, 9).

It is, in reality, this very quality of concreteness that makes the Hebrew Scriptures lend themselves so well to translation, for the sense of the terms is generally of a universal quality, meaning the same in virtually any language. Still, it is a challenge for the translator to reproduce in another language the peculiar charm, simplicity, manner of expression, and forcefulness of Hebrew, particularly in its verb forms.

Hebrew is remarkable for its brevity, the frame of its structure allowing for such terseness. Aramaic, the closest to Hebrew of the Semitic tongues, is by comparison more ponderous, roundabout, wordy. In translation, it is often necessary to use auxiliary words to bring out the vividness, picturesqueness, and dramatic action of the Hebrew verb. Though this detracts somewhat from the brevity, it conveys more fully the beauty and accuracy of the Hebrew text.

Hebrew Poetry. These very qualities, including the strong sense of reality, are also what make Hebrew peculiarly suited for poetry. Hebrew poetic lines are short—many are no more than two or three words—making the total effect one of strong impact. Professor James Muilenburg, a member of the *Revised Standard Version* translating committee, has fittingly noted: "Speech [in Hebrew poetry] is concentrated, and all the emphasis is placed upon the important words. The Hebrew text of Psalm 23 contains only fifty-five words; our modern western translations employ twice that number. Yet even in translation the economy of the original Hebrew is not lost. . . . Hebrew poetry is language that is alive in speech. . . . The Hebrew poet helps us to see, to hear, to feel. The physical sensations are fresh and alive . . . The poet thinks in pictures, and the pictures are drawn from the area of everyday life common to all men."—*An Introduction to the Revised Standard Version of the Old Testament,* 1952, pp. 63, 64.

To exemplify the terseness of Hebrew poetic language observe the first verse of Psalm 23 as found in the *New World Translation.* Those English words needed to translate each Hebrew word are separated with a diagonal stroke (/):

Jehovah/[is] my Shepherd./
I shall lack/nothing./

It can be seen that the English equivalent needs eight words to translate four Hebrew words. The "is" has been supplied to give sense to the English; in Hebrew, it is understood.

Primary forms of parallelism. The most important formal element in Hebrew poetry is parallelism, or rhythm that is achieved not by rhyme (as in English) but by logical thought; it has been termed "sense rhythm." Consider the two lines of Psalm 24:1:

To Jehovah belong the earth and that which
fills it,
The productive land and those dwelling in it.

The lines here quoted are said to be in *synonymous* parallelism, that is, the second line repeats a portion of the previous line, but in different words. The phrase "To Jehovah belong" is essential to both lines. However, the terms "the earth" and "the productive land" are poetic synonyms, as are "that which fills it" and "those dwelling in it."

Most contemporary scholars agree that there are two other primary styles of parallelism:

In *antithetic* parallelism, as its designation implies, each line expresses contrary thoughts. Psalm 37:9 illustrates this:

For evildoers themselves will be cut off,
But those hoping in Jehovah are the ones
that will possess the earth.

Then there is *synthetic* (or, *formal, constructive*) parallelism in which the second portion does not simply echo the same thought as the first or give a contrast. Rather, it enlarges and adds a new thought. Psalm 19:7-9 is an example of this:

The law of Jehovah is perfect,
bringing back the soul.
The reminder of Jehovah is trustworthy,
making the inexperienced one wise.
The orders from Jehovah are upright,
causing the heart to rejoice;
The commandment of Jehovah is clean,
making the eyes shine.
The fear of Jehovah is pure,
standing forever.
The judicial decisions of Jehovah are true;
they have proved altogether righteous.

Notice that the second part of each sentence or clause completes the thought; the whole verse, therefore, is a synthesis, that is, the result of bringing together two elements. Only with the second half-lines, such as "bringing back the soul" and "making the inexperienced one wise," does the reader learn how the 'law is perfect' and how the "reminder of Jehovah is trustworthy." In such a series of synthetic parallels, this division between the first and second part serves as a rhythmic break. There is thus, along with the progression of thought, the preservation of a certain verse structure, a parallel of form. It is for this reason sometimes called *formal* or *constructive* parallelism.

Miscellaneous forms of parallelism. A number of other styles of parallelism have been suggested, though they are considered to be only variants or combinations of the synonymous, antithetic, and synthetic. Three of these suggestions are: emblematic, stairlike, introverted.

Emblematic (or *comparative*) parallelism makes use of simile or metaphor. Consider Psalm 103:12:

> As far off as the sunrise is from the sunset,
> So far off from us he has put our transgressions.

In *stairlike* parallelism two, three, or even more lines may be used to repeat and advance the thought of the first. Psalm 29:1, 2 is an illustration of this:

> Ascribe to Jehovah, O you sons of strong ones,
> Ascribe to Jehovah glory and strength.
> Ascribe to Jehovah the glory of his name.

The *introverted* parallelism is more elaborate and may take in a number of verses. Observe this example from Psalm 135:15-18:

> (1) The idols of the nations are silver and gold,
> (2) The work of the hands of earthling man.
> (3) A mouth they have, but they can speak nothing;
> (4) Eyes they have, but they can see nothing;
> (5) Ears they have, but they can give ear to nothing.
> (6) Also there exists no spirit in their mouth.
> (7) Those making them will become just like them,
> (8) Everyone who is trusting in them.

This parallelism is explained by W. Trail in his work *Literary Characteristics and Achievements of the Bible* (1864, p. 170): "Here the first line introverts with the eighth—in the one we have the idols of the heathen, in the other those who put their trust in idols. The second line introverts with the seventh—in the one is the fabrication, in the other the fabricators. The third line introverts with the sixth—in the one there are mouths without articulation, in the other mouths without breath. The fourth line introverts with the fifth, where the introverted parallelism may be said to unite its two halves in a parallelism of synthesis—eyes without vision, ears without the sense of hearing."

A similar, but more simple, form is an inversion of words in adjoining lines, as in Isaiah 11:13b (*RS*):

> Ephraim shall not be jealous of Judah,
> and Judah shall not harass Ephraim.

Grammar

I. Verbs. Verbs are the most important part of speech in the Hebrew language. The simplest verbal form is the third person singular masculine of the perfect state; this is the form found in lexicons. The three consonants of this form usually constitute the root. The root is ordinarily triliteral in structure, that is, made up of three consonants, the usual arrangement in Semitic languages. Such triliteral roots serve as the source to which nearly all other words in the language can be traced.

The verbal root is the simplest stem of the verb. It is often referred to as the "pure stem." From this pure stem, six other stems are formed by adding prefixes, doubling certain letters, and making vowel changes. The seven verbal stems represent the verbal root idea in three degrees:

To show variations in person, number, and gender, certain prefixes and suffixes are attached to the verbal stems.

State. Verbs in English are viewed particularly from the standpoint of tense, or time: past, present, future. In Hebrew, however, the *condi-*

Simple	Intensive	Causative
(1) Active (qal)	(3) Active (pi'el)	(6) Active (hiph'il)
(2) Passive (niph'al)	(4) Passive (pu'al)	(7) Passive (hoph'al)
	(5) Reflexive (hithpa'el)	

	Simple	Intensive	Causative
Active	קָטַל *qa·tal'* he killed	קִטֵּל *qit·tel'* he killed (brutally)	הִקְטִיל *hiq·til'* he caused to kill
Passive	נִקְטַל *niq·tal'* he was killed	קֻטַּל *qut·tal'* he was killed (brutally)	הָקְטַל *hoq·tal'* he was caused to kill
Reflexive		הִתְקַטֵּל *hith·qat·tel'* he killed himself	

tion of the action, rather than the time involved, is the important thing. The action is viewed as either complete or incomplete.

If the verb portrays completed action, it is in the *perfect state*. For instance, Genesis 1:1 says: "In the beginning God *created* the heavens and the earth." The action was completed; God "created," that is, he finished creating the heavens and the earth.

If the action is viewed as incomplete, the verb is in the *imperfect state*. This can be illustrated by Exodus 15:1: "Moses and the sons of Israel *proceeded to sing*." Here we see that while the action had started (they "proceeded" to sing), it had not terminated and was thus "imperfect," unfinished.

Of course, since by its very character the Hebrew perfect state represents action as completed, it belongs most naturally to past time. Therefore, **ka·thav'** (a perfect-state active verb) means, basically, "(he) wrote" and it is often so translated. (2Ki 17:37; 2Ch 30:1; 32:17; Ezr 4:7; Es 8:5) The idea of action completed in the *past* can also be observed in the rendering "had written" (Es 9:23; Job 31:35; Jer 36:27). However, **ka·thav'** also may be rendered as "has written" (2Ch 26:22)—what would be called the present perfect in English. "Must write" is also used to translate this perfect-state verb and shows the certainty of the action's being carried out. (Nu 5:23; De 17:18) Both of these latter renderings correctly imply completed action, but not in past time. So, the active verb *of itself* does not necessarily convey a concept of time. The perfect state can portray action as completed at any period of time: past, present, or future; contrastingly, the imperfect, while also able to show action at any time period, always views it as incomplete.

Therefore, while the ancient Hebrews were obviously able to comprehend the idea of time, in their language it is accorded a secondary position. *The Essentials of Biblical Hebrew*, by K. Yates, states: "The time as understood in most modern languages is not the same as that of the Semitic mind. The discernment of the time of an action is not of vital importance to the Hebrew thought pattern. It is necessary for the Indo-germanic thinker only to fit the action into his overemphasized estimation of time. The understanding of the condition of the action as to its completeness or incompleteness was sufficient generally to the Semite and if not, there was some word of temporal or historical significance which would bring time into focus." (Revised by

J. Owens, 1954, p. 129) If, as the Bible indicates, Hebrew was the original tongue used in Eden, this lack of emphasis on verbal time may reflect the outlook of man in his perfection, when the prospect of everlasting life was before Adam and when life had not been reduced to a mere 70 or 80 years. Jehovah provided Hebrew as a perfectly satisfactory means of communication between God and men, as well as among humans.

For English translation the time feature of the verb is determined by the *context*. The context shows whether the action being narrated is viewed as having occurred earlier, as taking place now, or as yet to occur.

II. Nouns. As noted above, nearly all words, including nouns, can be traced back to a verbal root. The root can be seen in both the spelling of the noun and its meaning.

There are two genders: masculine and feminine. The feminine is generally distinguished by the termination *ah* (*ohth*, plural) attached to the noun, as *'ish·shah'* (woman), *su·sohth'* (mares [feminine plural]).

The three numbers in Hebrew are singular, plural, and dual. The dual (identified by the suffix *a'yim*) is customarily used for objects that appear as pairs, such as hands (*ya·dha'yim*) and ears (*'oz·na'yim*).

Personal pronouns may also be inseparably attached to nouns. Thus *sus* is "horse"; but *su·si'*, "my horse"; *su·sey'kha*, "your horses."

III. Adjectives. Adjectives, too, are derived from verb roots. Thus, the verb **ga·dhal'** (grow up, become great) is the root of the adjective **ga·dhohl'** (great). (The definite article in Hebrew is *ha* [the]. There is no indefinite article [a].)

An adjective may be used in either of two ways:

(1) It may be a *predicative adjective*. In this case it stands before its noun and agrees with it in gender and number. The phrase *tohv haq-qohl'* (literally, "good the voice") is translated "the voice is good," the verb "is" being supplied.

(2) Or, it may be used to *qualify* (modify). In this situation it stands after the noun, agreeing with it not only in gender and number but also in definiteness. Then *haq·qohl' hat·tohv'* (literally, "the voice the good") means "the good voice."

Transliteration. Transliteration has reference to replacing characters in the Hebrew alphabet with English letters. Hebrew is written from right to left, but for English readers it is transliterated to read from left to right. The accompanying chart and the following explanation set out some of the general rules followed in this work.

Concerning the consonants. It will be observed that five letters have final forms. These appear only at the end of words. Certain consonants (ב, ג, ד, כ, פ, ת) have both a soft and a hard sound, the latter being indicated by a dot in the bosom of the letter (בּ, גּ, דּ, כּ, פּ, תּ). However, a dot in one of these consonants also signifies that it is to be doubled if it is immediately preceded by a vowel. Thus גַּבַּי is *gab·bai'*. Most of the other letters (though they have only one sound) are also doubled by a dot in their bosom (for instance, זּ is *zz*). An exception is the letter *he'* (ה), which sometimes has a dot in it (הּ) when it appears at the end of a word; the *he'*, however, is never doubled.

The consonants *waw* and *yohdh* may be employed in forming vowels. The *waw* (ו) will occur with the vowel *choh'lem* (ֹ) above it to make what is called a fully formed *choh'lem* (וֹ), transliterated in this work as *oh*. The combination וּ serves as a *u* and at the beginning of a word always stands alone as a syllable; however, if there is an additional vowel point below the letter (וּ), the dot indicates the *waw* is to be doubled. Thus בַּוַּי is *baw·wai'*; בּוּז is *buz*.

In the final form of *kaph*, the *shewa''* (ְ) or *qa'mets* (ָ) is written within the bosom rather than below the letter: ךְ, ךָ.

Concerning the vowels. All the vowels in this chart appear below the line except *choh'lem* (ֹ), which is placed above, and *shu'req* (ּ), which, as noted above, appears in the bosom of *waw* (וּ = *u*).

Concerning the half vowels. The English equivalents shown above are meant only as approximations. The Hebrew pronunciation of these half vowels is, in each case, an extremely slight sound.

Under certain conditions, a *shewa''* is vocalized and transliterated as an *e*. However, when the *shewa''* follows a short vowel or when it stands under a consonant closing a syllable, it is silent and considered a syllable divider. Thus יִקְטֹל is *yiq·tol'*.

Syllables. In Hebrew every syllable begins with a consonant and includes (1) one full vowel or (2) one half vowel and a full vowel. Thus, קָטַל is made up of two syllables, one being קָ (*qa*) and the other טַל (*tal*). Both syllables contain a full vowel and begin with a consonant. On the other hand, בְּרִית (*berith'*) has only one syllable since

Character	Consonants	Equivalent
א	'A'leph	'
ב	Behth	b
ב		v
ג	Gi'mel	g
ג		gh
ד	Da'leth	d
ד		dh
ה	He'	h
ו	Waw	w
ז	Za'yin	z
ח	Chehth	ch
ט	Tehth	t
י	Yohdh	y
כ	Kaph	k
כ Final: ך		kh
ל	La'medh	l
מ Final: ם	Mem	m
נ Final: ן	Nun	n
ס	Sa'mekh	s
ע	'A'yin	'
פ	Pe'	p
פ Final: ף		ph
צ Final: ץ	Tsa·dheh'	ts
ק	Qohph	q
ר	Rehsh	r
שׂ	Sin	s
שׁ	Shin	sh
ת	Taw	t
ת		th

Full Vowels

ָ	(long)	Qa'mets	a as in awl
ַ		Pa'thach	a as in father
ֵ	(long)	Tse'reh	e as in they
ֶ		Se'ghohl	e as in men
ִ		Chi'req	i as in machine
ֹ	(long)	Choh'lem	o as in no
ָ		Qa'mets Cha·tuph'	o as in nor
ֻ		Qib·buts'	u as in full
וּ		Shu'req	u as in cruel

Half Vowels

ְ	Shewa''	e obscure, as in average; or silent, as in made
ֲ	Cha·teph' Pa'thach	a as in hat
ֱ	Cha·teph' Se'ghohl	e as in met
ֳ	Cha·teph' Qa'mets	o as in not

Special Combinations

ַי = ai		ִי = i
ָי = ai		וֹ = oh
ֵי = eh		וּ = u
ֶי = ey		ָיו = av

it contains only one full vowel (.=i); the *shewa",* e (:), is a half vowel.

There are two apparent exceptions to the rule of only consonants starting a syllable: (1) When a word opens with ‌ו (*u*). Then the *u* stands as a separate syllable. Thus וּבֵן is *u·ven';* וּשְׁמִי is *u·shemi'.* (2) With a "furtive *pa'thach."* This is the vowel *pa'thach* (ַ) placed under the consonants ה, ח, ע, when they appear at the end of a word; in this case the *pa'thach* is sounded before the consonant. Thus רוּחַ is *ru'ach,* and not *ru·cha'.*

Sometimes a small horizontal line called a maqqeph (‑), similar to an English hyphen, appears between words. This serves to combine two or more words so that they are treated as a single word with only the last word retaining its accent. Thus כָּל־אֲשֶׁר is *kol-'asher'.*

Accents. All Hebrew words are accented on the last or next to the last syllable. Most are accented on the last syllable.

In transliterations in this work a single dot separates syllables; the accent is placed after the stressed syllable, using an accent symbol to denote primary stress (').

HEBREWS, LETTER TO THE. An inspired letter of the Christian Greek Scriptures. Evidence indicates that it was written by the apostle Paul to the Hebrew Christians in Judea about 61 C.E. To those Hebrew Christians the letter was most timely. It had then been about 28 years since Jesus Christ's death and resurrection. In the earlier part of that period severe persecution had been brought upon these Jewish Christians in Jerusalem and Judea by the Jewish religious leaders, resulting in the death of some Christians and the scattering of most of the others from Jerusalem. (Ac 8:1) The scattered ones remained active in spreading the good news everywhere they went. (Ac 8:4) The apostles had stayed in Jerusalem and had held the remaining congregation together there, and it had grown, even under stiff opposition. (Ac 8:14) Then, for a time, the congregation entered into a period of peace. (Ac 9:31) Later, Herod Agrippa I caused the death of the apostle James, John's brother, and mistreated others of the congregation. (Ac 12:1-5) Sometime after this, there developed a material need among the Christians in Judea, giving opportunity for those in Achaia and Macedonia (in about 55 C.E.) to demonstrate their love and unity by sending aid. (1Co 16:1-3; 2Co 9:1-5) So the Jerusalem congregation had suffered many hardships.

Purpose of the Letter. The congregation in Jerusalem was comprised almost entirely of Jews and those who had been proselytes to the Jews' religion. Many of these had come to a knowledge of the truth after the time of the most bitter persecution. At the time the letter to the Hebrews was written, the congregation was enjoying comparative peace, for Paul told them: "You have never yet resisted as far as blood." (Heb 12:4) Nevertheless, the lessening of outright physical persecution to death did not mean that strong opposition from the Jewish religious leaders had ceased. The newer members of the congregation had to face the opposition just as the rest did. And some others were immature, not having made the progress toward maturity that they should have made in view of the time. (5:12) The opposition they faced daily from the Jews put their faith to a test. They needed to build up the quality of endurance.—12:1, 2.

Time was running out for Jerusalem. Neither the apostle Paul nor those in the congregation at Jerusalem knew when the foretold desolation would occur, but God did know. (Lu 21:20-24; Da 9:24, 27) The situation would call for the Christians there to be alert and to exercise faith so that they would flee from the city when they saw Jerusalem surrounded by encamped armies. All in the congregation needed to strengthen themselves for these momentous events. According to tradition, it was just about five years after the writing of this letter that Cestius Gallus' troops attacked the city and then withdrew. Four years after that, Jerusalem and its temple were leveled by the Romans under General Titus. But before either of these events took place, Jehovah had provided the inspired counsel that his servants needed.

Jewish opposition. The Jewish religious leaders, by lying propaganda, had done everything they could to stir up hatred against Christ's followers. Their determination to fight Christianity with every possible weapon is demonstrated by their actions, as recorded in Acts 22:22; 23:12-15, 23, 24; 24:1-4; 25:1-3. They and their supporters constantly harassed the Christians, evidently using arguments in an effort to break their loyalty to Christ. They attacked Christianity with what might seem to a Jew to be powerful reasoning, hard to answer.

At that time Judaism had much to offer in the way of tangible, material things and outward appearance. The Jews might say that these things proved Judaism superior and Christianity foolish. Why, they had told Jesus that the nation had as their father *Abraham,* to whom the promises were given. (Joh 8:33, 39) *Moses,* to whom God spoke "mouth to mouth," was God's great servant and prophet. (Nu 12:7, 8) The Jews had the *Law* and the words of the *prophets* from the beginning. 'Did not this very *antiquity* establish Judaism as the true religion?' they might ask. At the inaugurating of the Law covenant, God had spoken by means of *angels;* in fact, the Law was transmitted through angels by the hand of the mediator Moses. (Ac 7:53; Ga 3:19) On this occa-

sion God had given a fear-inspiring demonstration of *power* in shaking Mount Sinai; the loud sound of a horn, smoke, thunder, and lightning accompanied the glorious display.—Ex 19:16-19; 20:18; Heb 12:18-21.

Besides all these things of antiquity, there stood the magnificent *temple* with its *priesthood* instituted by Jehovah. Priests officiated at the temple, daily handling many *sacrifices.* Accompanying these things were the costly *priestly garments* and the splendor of the *services* conducted at the temple. 'Had not Jehovah com-

---

HIGHLIGHTS OF HEBREWS

A powerful treatise that fortified Hebrew Christians and enabled them to help sincere fellow countrymen during the final years of the Jewish system

Evidently written by the apostle Paul less than a decade before Jerusalem was destroyed in 70 C.E.

The superior position occupied by God's Son (1:1–3:6)

He is the unique Son, appointed heir, exact representation of his Father's very being, through whom all that was made is also sustained

Compared with the Son, angels are but servants. The Father calls him alone "my son," the Firstborn to whom even angels would do obeisance; of him and not of angels can it be said that his royal rule rests upon God as his throne, his permanence surpasses that of heavens and earth made through him, and his position is at the Father's right hand

If the Law conveyed through angels could not be disregarded without punishment, what was spoken by God through the Son, who is higher than angels, must be given extraordinary attention

Though lower than angels as a man, Jesus Christ was afterward exalted above them and granted dominion over the inhabited earth to come

Moses was an attendant in the house of God, but Jesus Christ is over the entire house

Entering God's rest still possible (3:7–4:13)

Because of disobedience and lack of faith, the Israelites who left Egypt failed to enter God's rest

Christians can enter God's rest, provided they avoid Israel's disobedience and exert themselves in a course of faithfulness

The living word promising entrance into God's rest is sharper than a sword, dividing (by a person's response to it) between what he may appear to be as a soul and what he really is as to his spirit

Superiority of Christ's priesthood and the new covenant (4:14–10:31)

Because of having been tested in all respects yet remaining sinless, Jesus Christ as high priest can sym-

pathize with sinful humans and deal compassionately with them

He is priest by God's appointment according to the manner of Melchizedek, whose priesthood was greater than the Levitical priesthood

Unlike Levite priests in Aaron's family, Jesus Christ possesses an indestructible life and thus requires no successors to continue his saving work; he is sinless and so does not need to present sacrifices for himself; he offered up his own body, not animals, and entered, not an earthly sanctuary, but heaven itself with the value of his outpoured blood, thereby validating the new covenant

The new covenant, with Jesus as Mediator, is superior to the Law covenant in that those in it have God's laws in their hearts and enjoy true forgiveness of sins

Appreciation for these benefits will move Christians to make public declaration of hope and to assemble regularly

Faith essential to please God (10:32–12:29)

Jehovah is displeased with those faithlessly shrinking back from him instead of enduring so as to receive what he has promised

The exemplary faith of integrity-keepers from Abel onward serves as encouragement to endurance in the Christian race, while considering closely Jesus Christ and his flawless course under suffering

The suffering that God permits to befall faithful Christians may be viewed as a form of discipline from him, designed to produce the peaceful fruit of righteousness

Exhortations to pursue a faithful course (13:1-25)

Manifest brotherly love, be hospitable, remember believers who are suffering, maintain marriage in honor, and be content with present things, confident of Jehovah's help

Imitate the faith of those taking the lead, and avoid succumbing to strange teachings

Be willing to bear reproach as Christ did; always offer to God sacrifice of praise through him

Be obedient to those taking the lead

manded that sacrifices for sin be brought to the sanctuary, and did not the *high priest,* the descendant of Moses' own brother *Aaron,* enter the *Most Holy* on the Day of Atonement with a sacrifice for the sins of the whole nation? On this occasion, did he not approach representatively into the very *presence of God?,'* the Jews might argue. (Le 16) 'Furthermore, was not the *kingdom* the possession of the Jews, with one (the Messiah, who would later come, as they said) to sit on the throne at *Jerusalem* to rule?'

If the letter to the Hebrews was being written to equip the Christians to answer objections that were actually being raised by the Jews, then those enemies of Christianity had contended in this way: 'What did this new "heresy" have to point to as evidence of its genuineness and of God's favor? Where was their temple, and where their priesthood? In fact, where was their leader? Was he of any importance among the leaders of the nation during his lifetime—this Jesus, a Galilean, a carpenter's son, with no rabbinic education? And did he not die an ignominious death? Where was his kingdom? And who were his apostles and followers? Mere fishermen and tax collectors. Furthermore, whom did Christianity draw, for the most part? The poor and lowly persons of the earth and, even worse, uncircumcised Gentiles, not of the seed of Abraham, were accepted. Why should anyone put his trust in this Jesus, who had been put to death as a blasphemer and a seditionist? Why listen to his disciples, men unlettered and ordinary?'—Ac 4:13.

Superiority of Christian system. Some of the immature Christians may have become neglectful of their salvation through Christ. (Heb 2:1-4) Or they may have been swayed by the unbelieving Jews who surrounded them. Coming to their aid with masterful argument, using the Hebrew Scriptures, on which the Jews claimed to rely, the apostle shows irrefutably the superiority of the Christian system of things and of the priesthood and kingship of Jesus Christ. He Scripturally demonstrates that Jesus Christ is the *Son* of God, greater than *angels* (1:4-6), than *Abraham* (7:1-7), than *Moses* (3:1-6), and than the *prophets* (1:1, 2). In fact, Christ is the appointed heir of all things, crowned with glory and honor and appointed over the works of Jehovah's hands.—1:2; 2:7-9.

As to priesthood, Christ's is far superior to the Aaronic priesthood of the tribe of Levi. It is dependent, not on inheritance from sinful flesh, but on an oath of God. (Heb 6:13-20; 7:5-17,

20-28) Why, though, did he endure such hardships and die a death of suffering? This was foretold as essential to mankind's salvation and to qualify him as High Priest and the one to whom God will subject all things. (2:8-10; 9:27, 28; compare Isa 53:12.) He had to become blood and flesh and die in order to emancipate all those who through fear of death were in slavery. Through his death he is able to bring to nothing the Devil, a thing no human priest could do. (Heb 2:14-16) He, having so suffered, is a High Priest who can sympathize with our weaknesses and can come to our help, having been tested in all respects.—2:17, 18; 4:15.

Moreover, argues the apostle, this High Priest "passed through the heavens" and appeared in the very presence of God, not in a mere earthly tent or building that was only pictorial of heavenly things. (Heb 4:14; 8:1; 9:9, 10, 24) He needed to appear only once with his perfect, sinless sacrifice, not over and over again. (7:26-28; 9:25-28) He has no successors, as did the Aaronic priests, but lives forever to save completely those to whom he ministers. (7:15-17, 23-25) Christ is Mediator of the better covenant foretold through Jeremiah, under which sins can really be forgiven and consciences can be made clean, things that the Law could never accomplish. The Ten Words, the basic laws of the Law covenant, were written on stone; the law of the new covenant, on hearts. This prophetic word of Jehovah by Jeremiah made the Law covenant obsolete, to vanish away in time.—8:6-13; Jer 31:31-34; De 4:13; 10:4.

It is true, the writer of Hebrews continues, that an awesome display of power was manifested at Sinai, demonstrating God's approval of the Law covenant. But even more forcefully God bore witness at the inauguration of the new covenant with signs, portents, and powerful works, along with distributions of holy spirit to all the members of the congregation assembled. (Heb 2:2-4; compare Ac 2:1-4.) And as to Christ's Kingship, his throne is in the heavens itself, far higher than that of the kings of the line of David who sat on the throne in earthly Jerusalem. (Heb 1:9) God is the foundation of Christ's throne, and his Kingdom cannot be shaken, as was the kingdom in Jerusalem in 607 B.C.E. (1:8; 12:28) Furthermore, God has gathered his people before something far more awe inspiring than the miraculous display at Mount Sinai. He has caused anointed Christians to approach the heavenly Mount Zion, and he will yet shake not only the earth but also the heaven.—12:18-27.

The letter to the Hebrews is of inestimable value to Christians. Without it, many of the realities concerning Christ as foreshadowed by the Law would be unclear. For example, the Jews had known all along from the Hebrew Scriptures that when their high priest went into the Most Holy compartment of the sanctuary in their behalf he was representing them before Jehovah. But they never appreciated this reality: Someday the real High Priest would actually appear in the heavens in Jehovah's very presence! And as we read the Hebrew Scriptures, how could we realize the tremendous significance of the account of Abraham's meeting with Melchizedek, or understand so clearly what this king-priest typified? This, of course, is to cite only two examples out of the many realities that we come to visualize in reading the letter.

The faith that the letter builds helps Christians to hold on to their hope by means of "the evident demonstration of realities though not beheld." (Heb 11:1) At a time when many persons rely on antiquity, on the material wealth and power of organizations, on the splendor of rites and ceremonies, and look to the wisdom of this world instead of to God, the divinely inspired letter to the Hebrews admirably helps to make the man of God "fully competent, completely equipped for every good work."—2Ti 3:16, 17.

Writership and Time, Place Written. Writership of the letter to the Hebrews has been widely ascribed to the apostle Paul. It was accepted as an epistle of Paul by early writers. The Chester Beatty Papyrus No. 2 (P^{46}) (of about 200 C.E.) contains Hebrews among nine of Paul's letters, and Hebrews is listed among "fourteen letters of Paul the apostle" in "The Canon of Athanasius," of the fourth century C.E.

The writer of Hebrews does not identify himself by name. Even though all his other letters do bear his name, this lack of identification of the writer would obviously not rule out Paul. Internal evidence in the letter strongly points to Paul as its writer and to Italy, probably Rome, as the place of writing. (Heb 13:24) It was in Rome, evidently during the years 59 to 61 C.E., that Paul was first imprisoned. Timothy was with Paul in Rome, being mentioned in the apostle's letters to the Philippians, the Colossians, and Philemon, written from Rome during that imprisonment. (Php 1:1; 2:19; Col 1:1, 2; Phm 1:1) This circumstance fits the remark at Hebrews 13:23 about Timothy's release from prison and the writer's desire to visit Jerusalem soon.

The time of writing was before the destruction of Jerusalem in 70 C.E., for the temple at Jerusalem still stood, with services being performed there, as is evident from the argument in the letter. And Paul's remark about Timothy's being released reasonably fixes the time of writing about nine years earlier, namely, 61 C.E., when it is thought that Paul himself was released from his first imprisonment.—Heb 13:23.

HEBREW SCRIPTURES. The 39 divinely inspired books from Genesis to Malachi, according to the common arrangement today, constitute the major portion of the Bible.

The books of the Hebrew Scriptures as they appear in most Bible versions may be divided into three sections: (1) *Historic,* Genesis to Esther, 17 books; (2) *Poetic,* Job to The Song of Solomon, 5 books; (3) *Prophetic,* Isaiah to Malachi, 17 books. Such divisions are rather general, since the historical section contains poetic portions (Ge 2:23; 4:23, 24; 9:25-27; Ex 15:1-19, 21; Jg 5) as well as prophetic (Ge 3:15; 22:15-18; 2Sa 7:11-16); the poetic section contains historical material (Job 1:1–2:13; 42:7-17) as well as prophetic (Ps 2:1-9; 110:1-7); and in the prophetic section historical information and poetic material are found (Isa 7:1, 2; Jer 37:11–39:14; 40: 7–43:7; Lam 1:1–5:22).

By combining and rearranging these same 39 books in a different order, the Jews counted only 24 or 22 books and, according to their traditional canon, arranged them as follows: First, there was the *Law* (Heb., *Toh·rah'*), also called the Pentateuch, consisting of (1) Genesis, (2) Exodus, (3) Leviticus, (4) Numbers, and (5) Deuteronomy. (See PENTATEUCH.) Second came the *Prophets* (Heb., *Nevi·'im'*), divided into the "Early Prophets," (6) Joshua, (7) Judges, (8) Samuel (First and Second together as one book), (9) Kings (First and Second as one book), and the "Later Prophets," subdivided into the "Major" Prophets, (10) Isaiah, (11) Jeremiah and (12) Ezekiel, and (13) Twelve "Minor" Prophets (a single book composed of Hosea, Joel, Amos, Obadiah, Jonah, Micah, Nahum, Habakkuk, Zephaniah, Haggai, Zechariah, and Malachi). The third section was called the *Holy Writings* (Hagiographa or, in Hebrew, *Kethu·vim'*), beginning with (14) Psalms, (15) Proverbs, and (16) Job; then came the "Five Megilloth" or five separate scrolls, namely (17) The Song of Solomon, (18) Ruth, (19) Lamentations, (20) Ecclesiastes, and (21) Esther, followed by (22) Daniel, (23) Ezra-Nehemiah (combined), and (24) Chronicles (First and Second together as one book). The book of Ruth was sometimes appended to Judges, and Lamentations to Jeremiah, to give 22 books, a total corresponding to the number of letters in the Hebrew alphabet, although this is not the usual arrangement in Hebrew Bibles today.

Not all the early catalogs had the books of the Hebrew Scriptures arranged in the above order. This is because at the time the individual books were in separate scrolls. To illustrate: In the Babylonian Talmud (*Bava Batra* 14*b*), it is stated: "Our Rabbis taught: The order of the Prophets is, Joshua, Judges, Samuel, Kings, Jeremiah, Ezekiel, Isaiah, and the Twelve Minor Prophets." (Translated by M. Simon and I. Slotki) This may explain why Jeremiah precedes Isaiah in a number of Hebrew manuscripts written in Germany and France.

The Writers. All the Hebrew Scriptures were written and compiled by Jews, members of the nation "entrusted with the sacred pronouncements of God." (Ro 3:1, 2) And, for the most part, these pre-Christian Scriptures were written in Hebrew, with the following limited portions in Aramaic: Genesis 31:47; Ezra 4:8 to 6:18 and 7:12-26; Jeremiah 10:11; Daniel 2:4b to 7:28. Aramaic words are also found in Job, certain Psalms, The Song of Solomon, Jonah, Esther, and in the Hebrew parts of Daniel. The book of Ezekiel likewise shows Aramaic influence.

Moses wrote and compiled the first five books of the Bible, and he was followed by some 38 other writers and compilers including Joshua, Samuel, David, Solomon, Isaiah, Jeremiah, Ezekiel, Daniel, Ezra, and Nehemiah. They lived over a period of 1,100 years, from the 16th to the 5th century B.C.E., and came from various occupations, such as that of shepherd, copyist, governor, king, prophet, and priest.

Some of the Bible writers were eyewitnesses of the incidents they recorded; Moses' wrote of his experiences before Pharaoh. (Ex 5:1–12:32) They gathered certain historical data from previous records through diligent research, as when compiling the genealogical records. (1Ch 1-9) But many things, such as knowledge concerning the assembly of angelic hosts in heaven and revelations in the field of prophecy, were matters beyond the realm of human knowledge and could be learned only by direct inspiration of God. This and the perfect unity of the whole, despite being the composite work of many writers extending over so long a period of time with their various

backgrounds, all attest to and demonstrate that Bible writers indeed "spoke from God as they were borne along by holy spirit."—2Pe 1:21.

Canon of Hebrew Scriptures. The books of the Hebrew Scriptures do not appear in our Bibles in the order in which they were written. Joel, Amos, and Jonah lived about two centuries or so before Jeremiah, Ezekiel, and Daniel. Nor do the titles of the books always disclose their writer. The book of Job, for instance, was apparently written by Moses; the book of Ruth, by Samuel. Details about the individual books, as to when and by whom each was written, are set out in the "Table of Bible Books in Order Completed" in the article BIBLE. See the articles on the individual books for contents, importance and significance, proof of authenticity, and other information.

The canon of the Hebrew Scriptures was well established when Jesus Christ was on earth, as is evidenced by his statements recorded in the Christian Greek Scriptures. For example, he referred to the three-section arrangement when he spoke of "all the things written in the *law* of Moses and in the *Prophets* and *Psalms*." (Lu 24:44) His followers wrote of or spoke of "the public reading of the Law and of the Prophets," "the Scriptures," "the law of Moses and the Prophets," "the holy Scriptures," and "the holy writings." —Ac 13:15; 18:24; 28:23; Ro 1:2; 2Ti 3:15; see CANON.

Noteworthy too is the fact that no Apocryphal writings were admitted into the Hebrew canon. From the days of Ezra and Malachi, in the fifth century B.C.E., the completed canon of the Hebrew Scriptures has been guarded and protected against the inclusion of any writings of questionable nature. (See APOCRYPHA.) Scrupulous care was exercised by the manuscript copyists called Sopherim, who at a later time were succeeded by the Masoretes.

Originally the Hebrew Scriptures were written without vowels or punctuation, and without our present chapter and verse divisions. In the second half of the first millennium C.E. the Masoretes, who were also very careful Bible copyists, established a system of vowel points and accent marks as an aid to reading and pronunciation.

Preservation and Transmission. The Jewish Sopherim (scribes), although meticulous as to avoiding errors in copying, made certain emendations, or corrections, in the text where, in their opinion, the original text seemed to show irreverence for God or disrespect for his representatives. In more than 140 instances the Jewish scribes changed the Tetragrammaton (the consonantal equivalent of the name Jehovah) to read either "Sovereign Lord" or "God."—See *NW* appendix, pp. 1562, 1569.

None of the original writings of the Hebrew Scriptures are extant today, but there are possibly 6,000 handwritten copies containing all or part of the Hebrew Scriptures. The Nash Papyrus, which contains small portions of Deuteronomy, and many of the Dead Sea Scrolls were copied before our Common Era. Besides copies of the Scriptures in Hebrew, many versions of the pre-Christian Scriptures have been made, either the whole or in part, in many languages. The first actual translation was the Greek *Septuagint,* which commenced about 280 B.C.E. Jerome's Latin *Vulgate* also contained an early translation of the Hebrew Scriptures. The *New World Translation* of the Hebrew Scriptures was based on the seventh, eighth, and ninth editions of Rudolf Kittel's *Biblia Hebraica,* which is the printed edition of Codex Leningrad B 19^A, the earliest complete manuscript of the Hebrew Scriptures.

Critics of the Bible have expended considerable effort in an attempt to discredit the Hebrew Scriptures, labeling them as either forgeries or simply folklore lacking historic authenticity. One line of attack has been to dissect the different Bible books in an effort to prove that they were written by different hands, as if a person were incapable of writing in more than one style. Such argument is altogether unsound, for persons who write poetry can also write prose, and vice versa. A lawyer who formulates a legal document easily and quickly shifts his style when relating some personal experience. When the critics claim that certain verses, which they label "J" and in which the name Jehovah occurs, were written by men other than the writers of the verses where the title "God" (Heb., *'Elo·him'*) appears, and which they designate as "E," they demonstrate shallow reasoning.

In pointing out the fallacy of the critics' claim, K. A. Kitchen, of the University of Liverpool, says: "Nowhere in the Ancient Orient is there anything which is definitely known to parallel the elaborate history of fragmentary composition and conflation [composite text] of Hebrew literature (or marked by just such criteria) as the documentary hypotheses would postulate. And conversely, any attempt to apply the criteria of the documentary theorists to Ancient Oriental compositions that have known histories but exhibit the same literary phenomena results in manifest absurdities."—*Ancient Orient and Old Testament,* 1968, p. 115.

Importance. The importance of the Hebrew Scriptures cannot be overemphasized, for without their law code, history, and prophecies, much in the Christian Greek Scriptures would be doubtful in meaning. (Lu 24:27, 44) "For all the things that were written aforetime were written for our instruction." "Now these things went on befalling them as examples, and they were written for a warning to us upon whom the ends of the systems of things have arrived." (Ro 15:4; 1Co 10:11) Hence, the Christian Bible writers repeatedly quoted from and alluded to the former Bible writings, in this way carrying foward and expanding many of the themes and promises set forth in the Hebrew Scriptures. In the Christian Greek Scriptures, The *New World Translation* presents as direct quotations 320 passages from the Hebrew Scriptures. According to a listing published by Westcott and Hort, the combined total of quotations and references is some 890.

Without the Hebrew Scriptures we would be lacking many details about man's origin, the cause of death, and the Edenic promise that the Serpent's head will be crushed by the seed of the woman. Without the Hebrew Scriptures we would not know many details about such things as the Noachian Flood, why blood is sacred, God's covenant with Abraham, how Jehovah fought for his covenant people, and the history of the pictorial theocratic kingdom.

HEBRON (He'bron).

1. Grandson of Levi and son of Kohath; forefather of "the sons of Hebron" or Hebronites.—Ex 6:16, 18; Nu 3:19, 27; 26:58; 1Ch 6:2, 18; 15:4, 9; 23:12, 19; 26:30-32.

2. Son of Mareshah and father of Korah, Tappuah, Rekem, and Shema; a descendant of Caleb of the tribe of Judah.—1Ch 2:42, 43.

3. [Place of Partnership]. An ancient city in the mountainous region of Judah that was built seven years before Zoan in Egypt. (Nu 13:22) Hebron is located about 30 km (19 mi) SSW of Jerusalem and lies over 900 m (3,000 ft) above sea level. It has the distinction of being one of the oldest still-inhabited locations in the Middle East. Hebron's ancient name "Kiriath-arba" (Town of Arba) appears to have been derived from its Anakim founder, Arba. (Ge 23:2; Jos 14:15) The city and its neighboring hills have long been famous for their vineyards, pomegranates, figs, olives, apricots, apples, and nuts. Blessed with

numerous springs and wells, Hebron is surrounded by miles of greenery.

The patriarchs Abraham, Isaac, and Jacob spent part of their alien residence at Hebron. (Ge 13:18; 35:27; 37:13, 14) Sarah died there and was buried in a cave at nearby Machpelah. This cave, purchased along with surrounding land by Abraham from Hittite Ephron, became a family burial place, where Abraham, Isaac, Rebekah, Leah, and Jacob were also buried.—Ge 23:2-20; 49:29-33; 50:13.

At the time Moses sent the 12 spies into the Promised Land, the giantlike descendants of Anak were inhabiting Hebron. (Nu 13:22, 28, 33) About 40 years later, Hoham the king of Hebron joined four other kings in an offensive against Gibeon, a city that had made peace with Joshua. The Israelites responded to Gibeon's appeal for aid and, with Jehovah's help, defeated the armies of the five kings that had come against Gibeon. Afterward these five kings, who had hidden themselves in a cave, were executed and their dead bodies hung upon stakes until evening.—Jos 10:1-27.

As Israel's campaign in southern Canaan continued, the inhabitants of Hebron, including their king (evidently Hoham's successor), were devoted to destruction. (Jos 10:36, 37) However, although the Israelites under Joshua broke the power of the Canaanites, it appears that they did not immediately establish garrisons to hold on to their conquests. Evidently while Israel was warring elsewhere, the Anakim reestablished themselves at Hebron, making it necessary for Caleb (or the sons of Judah under Caleb's leadership) to wrest the city from their control sometime afterward. (Jos 11:21-23; 14:12-15; 15:13, 14; Jg 1:10) Originally assigned to Caleb of the tribe of Judah, Hebron was afterward given a sacred status as a city of refuge. It also served as a priestly city. However, "the field of the city [Hebron]" and its settlements were Caleb's hereditary possession. —Jos 14:13, 14; 20:7; 21:9-13.

At Hebron, about four centuries later, the men of Judah anointed David as king. He ruled from there for seven and a half years, meanwhile becoming father to six sons, Amnon, Chileab (Daniel), Absalom, Adonijah, Shephatiah, and Ithream. (2Sa 2:1-4, 11; 3:2-5; 1Ch 3:1-4) Earlier, the inhabitants of Hebron evidently helped David when he was outlawed by King Saul. (1Sa 30:26, 31) Toward the close of David's reign at Hebron, Abner, the main supporter of the rival kingship of Saul's son Ish-bosheth (2Sa 2:8, 9), defected to David. Upon returning from a raid and learning that David had sent Abner away in peace, Joab directed messengers to bring Abner back and then personally killed him at Hebron, where Abner was afterward buried. (2Sa 3:12-27, 32) Later, Rechab and Baanah murdered Ish-bosheth and, expecting a reward, brought his head to David at Hebron, but he had them executed for their vile deed. (2Sa 4:5-12) Subsequently, David was anointed as king over all Israel, and he transferred his capital from Hebron to Jerusalem. —2Sa 5:1-9.

Some years later David's son Absalom returned to Hebron and there initiated his unsuccessful usurpation of his father's kingship. (2Sa 15:7-10) It was likely because of Hebron's historical importance as

Street scene in Hebron, which was one of Israel's ancient cities of refuge

onetime capital of Judah, as well as because of its being his native city, that Absalom chose this city as the starting point of his drive for the throne. Later, David's grandson, King Rehoboam, rebuilt Hebron. (2Ch 11:5-10) After the desolation of Judah by the Babylonians and the return of the Jewish exiles, some of the repatriated Jews settled at Hebron (Kiriath-arba).—Ne 11:25.

HEBRONITES (He′bron·ites) [Of (Belonging to) Hebron]. A Levite family descended from Kohath's son Hebron. (Ex 6:16, 18; Nu 3:27; 26: 58; 1Ch 26:23, 24) King David assigned 1,700 capable Hebronites to serve in administrative capacities over the region W of the Jordan and 2,700 over the territory E of the Jordan.—1Ch 26:30-32.

HEDGE. Orchards and vineyards were commonly surrounded by hedges, thick rows of thorny plants, to safeguard the area from thieves and the depredations of animals. (Isa 5:5) The Scriptures employ the expression "put up a hedge" in a figurative sense to denote the giving of protection. (Job 1:10) On the other hand, 'hedging in' is used to represent the rearing up of obstacles, or barriers, placing an individual or even a nation in a helpless and forsaken situation with no way out. (Job 3:23; Ho 2:6; compare Job 19:8; La 3:7-9.) With reference to the moral corruption existing among the Israelites of his day, Micah wrote that "their most upright one is worse than a thorn hedge," that is, prickly, hurtful, and injurious.—Mic 7:4.

HEEL. The back part of the foot below the ankle. This part of the human body was often referred to in a figurative way in the Bible. To hold or injure one's heel would retard, or hinder, him. Jacob grabbed the heel of his twin brother Esau as they came out of their mother's womb. (Ge 25:26) For this he was named Jacob, meaning "One Seizing the Heel; Supplanter," which had prophetic meaning. (Ge 27:36; Ho 12:2, 3) The family head Jacob, in blessing his fifth son Dan, foretold, favorably for Dan, that he would be like a serpent that lies in wait by the roadside and bites the heels of the horse, throwing off its rider. (Ge 49:17; see VIPER, HORNED.) The tribe of Dan was at the "heel" of things as the rear guard of Israel during their wilderness journey, inflicting damage on Israel's enemies.—Nu 10:25.

Unfaithful Jerusalem was likened in prophecy to a disreputable woman, to be punished by having her heels "treated violently," that is, to be forced to walk over rough terrain, painful to her heels; this occurred when Jerusalem was taken into exile to Babylon in 607 B.C.E.—Jer 13:22.

King David spoke figuratively of his traitorous companion Ahithophel, saying: "[He] has magnified his heel against me." (Ps 41:9) This had a prophetic fulfillment in Judas Iscariot, to whom Jesus applied the text, saying: "He that used to feed on my bread has lifted up his heel against me." (Joh 13:18) Thus the expression indicates a treacherous action, one threatening harm to the person against whom the heel is "magnified" or "lifted up."

The first recorded prophecy, at Genesis 3:15, foretold that the "serpent" would bruise the 'seed of the woman' in the heel. Though painful, a heel bruise is not permanently disabling. Jesus, the "seed" (Ga 3:16), was put to death by the earthly agents of the great Serpent, Satan the Devil (Re 12:9), but on the third day was recovered from this 'heel bruise' when his Father Jehovah resurrected him.—Ac 2:22-24; 10:40.

HEGAI (Heg′a·i). A eunuch of King Ahasuerus' court; the guardian of the women who prepared Esther with special beauty treatments before she was taken to the king.—Es 2:3, 8, 9, 15.

HEIFER [Heb., ʽegh·lah′; Gr., da·ma′lis]. A young cow that has not produced a calf.

A heifer was among the animals that Abraham cut into two parts, and he then saw "a smoking furnace and a fiery torch that passed in between these pieces." This was in connection with God's concluding of a covenant with him.—Ge 15:9-18.

In Israel a person who touched a human corpse, a human bone or grave, or who came into a tent in which lay a corpse, was unclean. He was required to undergo a specified cleansing procedure on pain of being "cut off from the midst of the congregation." In this procedure the ashes of a sound red cow on which no yoke had come were used. Water in which some of these ashes had been mixed was sprinkled on the unclean one. Paul makes reference to this procedure, showing that it only had the effect of sanctifying to the extent of cleanness of the flesh but that it typified the real cleansing of conscience through the sacrifice of Jesus Christ.—Nu 19:1-22; Heb 9:13, 14.

A young cow was also used when bloodguilt rested on a city because of a murder in which the murderer was unknown. The older men of the city nearest to the one found slain, accompanied by some of the priests of the sons of Levi, were required to take the young unworked cow and break its neck in an uncultivated torrent valley in which there was running water. Then the older men of that city were to wash their hands over the young cow and to appeal to God not to put bloodguilt on the city. God would hear the plea and relieve the city of the guilt of shedding innocent blood. Evidently the fact that the cow's neck was broken, instead of the cow's being slaughtered as a sin offering, indicated that, in symbol, the cow suffered the punishment that should have been borne by the unknown murderer, and this procedure did not serve in any way to benefit the murderer as expiation for his crime. To Jehovah God, who sees all, was left the judgment of the actual murderer. Of course, if the murderer should later be discovered, he would be put to death for murder, as the Law required. The ceremony involving the young cow would make the matter publicly known and would tend to assist in the uncovering of the murderer.—De 21:1-9; Nu 35:30-33.

The prophet Jeremiah spoke figuratively of the nation of Egypt, when settled prosperously and well fed in her land, as "a very pretty heifer" but foretold that her defeat was to come. (Jer 46:20, 21) The same prophet also likened the Babylonian conquerors of God's people to a heifer pawing in the tender grass, because of their exultation over their capture of Israel. (Jer 50:11) Hosea spoke of Ephraim, the ten-tribe kingdom, as having at one time been like a trained heifer, under God's instruction and blessing, having plenty, as a threshing animal was allowed to eat of the fruitage of its work, which was comparatively light.—Ho 10:11; De 25:4.

HEIR. See INHERITANCE.

HELAH (He′lah). One of Ashhur's two wives. Three of her sons are listed in the genealogies of Judah.—1Ch 4:1, 5, 7.

HELAM (He′lam). The site where David's army defeated the military forces of Syrian King Hadadezer under his army chief Shobach. (2Sa 10:15-19) Some scholars link it with "Alema" mentioned in the Apocryphal book of First Maccabees (5:26, *JB*). It may thus be the same as modern ′Alma, about 55 km (34 mi) due E of the Sea of Galilee.

HELBAH (Hel′bah). A city in the territory of the tribe of Asher. It is mentioned as being one of the towns from which the tribe of Asher did not drive out the Canaanite inhabitants. (Jg 1:31, 32) Some scholars consider it to be the same as

Ahlab and identify it with Khirbet el-Mahalib, about 6 km (3.5 mi) NE of Tyre. However, its exact location is not certain.

HELBON (Hel′bon). A place noted for its fine wine, which was highly valued by the city of Tyre. (Eze 27:18) Helbon is generally identified with the modern village of Halbun, about 20 km (12 mi) NNW of Damascus. The village lies in a narrow valley with terraced vineyards located far up the mountain slopes. In ancient times, not only Tyre but also Assyria, Babylonia, and Persia obtained the wine of Helbon.

HELDAI (Hel′dai) [possibly, Mole Rat].

1. The head of the 12th monthly service group that David organized; a descendant of Othniel. (1Ch 27:1, 15) Being a Netophathite, he is likely the mighty man called Heleb and Heled the son of Baanah the Netophathite.—2Sa 23:8, 29; 1Ch 11:26, 30.

2. A man who returned from Babylon and whose silver and gold went into the making of a crown for High Priest Joshua. (Zec 6:10, 11) This Heldai is called Helem in verse 14.

HELEB (He′leb). One of David's mighty men. (2Sa 23:8, 29) A son of Baanah the Netophathite, he is also called Heled in the Chronicles listing, and likely is the same as Heldai.—1Ch 11:30; 27:15.

HELED (He′led) [Duration of Life; System of Things; or, possibly, Mole Rat]. A mighty man in David's army. He was a son of Baanah the Netophathite. (1Ch 11:26, 30) He is also called Heleb in the parallel list and likely is the same as Heldai.—2Sa 23:29; 1Ch 27:15.

HELEK (He′lek) [a shortened form of Hilkiah, meaning "My Portion (Share) Is Jehovah"], **HELEKITES** (He′lek·ites). The second-listed son of Gilead, and great-grandson of Manasseh. He founded the family of the Helekites that was numbered in the census at the end of the Israelites' wilderness trek and that received an inheritance in Manasseh's territory.—Nu 26:3, 4, 29, 30; Jos 17:2.

HELEM (He′lem).

1. [Heb., *He′lem*]. A descendant of Asher whose family is listed in the genealogy of the tribe. (1Ch 7:35, 40) He is likely the same as Hotham of verse 32.

2. [Heb., *Che′lem*]. Also called Heldai, he was one who contributed gold and silver for High

Priest Joshua's crown after the remnant's return from Babylon.—Zec 6:10, 11, 14.

HELEPH (He'leph).

A site in Naphtali's inheritance. (Jos 19:32, 33) Its exact location is uncertain. However, some geographers tentatively place it at Khirbet 'Irbadeh (Horvat 'Arpad) about 5 km (3 mi) W of the NNE summit of Mount Tabor.

HELEZ (He'lez) [He Has Rescued].

1. One of David's mighty men, a Paltite or Pelonite. (2Sa 23:8, 26; 1Ch 11:26, 27) When David organized the monthly service groups, Helez was given charge of the seventh division. —1Ch 27:1, 10.

2. A descendant of Judah; son of a certain Azariah and father of Eleasah.—1Ch 2:3, 39.

HELI (He'li) [from Heb., meaning "High (Exalted)"].

Evidently the father of Mary and maternal grandfather of Jesus Christ. (Lu 3:23) Joseph's being called the "son of Heli" is understood to mean that he was the son-in-law of Heli. While not listing her, Luke evidently traces the natural descent of Jesus' mother Mary from David.—Lu 3:31; see GENEALOGY OF JESUS CHRIST.

HELKAI (Hel'kai) [shortened form of Hilkiah, meaning "My Portion (Share) Is Jehovah"].

A head of the priestly paternal house of Meraioth in the days of Joiakim the high priest.—Ne 12: 12, 15.

HELKATH (Hel'kath) [Smooth Place].

A city listed among the boundary sites of the tribe of Asher (Jos 19:24, 25, 31), later assigned to the Gershonites as a Levite city. (Jos 21:27, 30, 31) It appears at 1 Chronicles 6:75 with the variant spelling of Hukok. Its location is conjectural. Some have identified it with Khirbet el-Harbaj (Tel Regev), 18 km (11 mi) S of Acco and near the base of the Carmel mountain range. *The Illustrated Bible Dictionary* edited by J. D. Douglas (1980, Vol. 2, p. 634) considers as "perhaps even better, Tell el-Qasis," about 9 km (5.5 mi) S of Khirbet el-Harbaj, lying at the entrance to the Valley of Jezreel. Since the towns of Hali and Beten, mentioned after Helkath in the list at Joshua 19:24-26, are generally considered to have been in the southern part of the Plain of Acco, such identification with Tell el-Qasis (Tel Qashish) would indicate a boundary description beginning in the extreme SE corner of the Plain of Acco, rather than one beginning in the north and running south. Further identification of other towns is needed, however, to determine this.

HELKATH-HAZZURIM (Hel'kath-haz·zu'-rim) [Field of Flint Knives; or, by an emendation, Field of Sides].

A field near "the pool of Gibeon." Twenty-four young men, 12 representing the armies of Ish-bosheth and 12 from the servants of David, died there while 'putting on a combat.' The place was subsequently named from this incident.—2Sa 2:12-16.

HELL.

A word used in the *King James Version* (as well as in the Catholic *Douay Version* and most older translations) to translate the Hebrew *she'ohl'* and the Greek *hai'des*. In the *King James Version* the word "hell" is rendered from *she'ohl'* 31 times and from *hai'des* 10 times. This version is not consistent, however, since *she'ohl'* is also translated 31 times "grave" and 3 times "pit." In the *Douay Version she'ohl'* is rendered "hell" 64 times, "pit" once, and "death" once.

In 1885, with the publication of the complete *English Revised Version*, the original word *she'ohl'* was in many places transliterated into the English text of the Hebrew Scriptures, though, in most occurrences, "grave" and "pit" were used, and "hell" is found some 14 times. This was a point on which the American committee disagreed with the British revisers, and so, when producing the *American Standard Version* (1901) they transliterated *she'ohl'* in all 65 of its appearances. Both versions transliterated *hai'des* in the Christian Greek Scriptures in all ten of its occurrences, though the Greek word *Ge'en·na* (English, "Gehenna") is rendered "hell" throughout, as is true of many other modern translations.

Concerning this use of "hell" to translate these original words from the Hebrew and Greek, *Vine's Expository Dictionary of Old and New Testament Words* (1981, Vol. 2, p. 187) says: "HADES . . . It corresponds to 'Sheol' in the O.T. [Old Testament]. In the A.V. of the O.T. [Old Testament] and N.T. [New Testament], it has been unhappily rendered 'Hell.'"

Collier's Encyclopedia (1986, Vol. 12, p. 28) says concerning "Hell": "First it stands for the Hebrew Sheol of the Old Testament and the Greek Hades of the Septuagint and New Testament. Since Sheol in Old Testament times referred simply to the abode of the dead and suggested no moral distinctions, the word 'hell,' as understood today, is not a happy translation."

It is, in fact, because of the way that the word "hell" is understood today that it is such an unsatisfactory translation of these original Bible words. *Webster's Third New International Dictionary*, unabridged, under "Hell" says: "fr[om] . . .

helan to conceal." The word "hell" thus originally conveyed no thought of heat or torment but simply of a 'covered over or concealed place.' In the old English dialect the expression "helling potatoes" meant, not to roast them, but simply to place the potatoes in the ground or in a cellar.

The meaning given today to the word "hell" is that portrayed in Dante's *Divine Comedy* and Milton's *Paradise Lost,* which meaning is completely foreign to the original definition of the word. The idea of a "hell" of fiery torment, however, dates back long before Dante or Milton. The *Grolier Universal Encyclopedia* (1971, Vol. 9, p. 205) under "Hell" says: "Hindus and Buddhists regard hell as a place of spiritual cleansing and final restoration. Islamic tradition considers it as a place of everlasting punishment." The idea of suffering after death is found among the pagan religious teachings of ancient peoples in Babylon and Egypt. Babylonian and Assyrian beliefs depicted the "nether world . . . as a place full of horrors, . . . presided over by gods and demons of great strength and fierceness." Although ancient Egyptian religious texts do not teach that the burning of any individual victim would go on forever, they do portray the "Other World" as featuring "pits of fire" for "the damned."—*The Religion of Babylonia and Assyria,* by Morris Jastrow, Jr., 1898, p. 581; *The Book of the Dead,* with introduction by E. Wallis Budge, 1960, pp. 135, 144, 149, 151, 153, 161, 200.

"Hellfire" has been a basic teaching in Christendom for many centuries, it is understandable why *The Encyclopedia Americana* (1956, Vol. XIV, p. 81) said: "Much confusion and misunderstanding has been caused through the early translators of the Bible persistently rendering the Hebrew Sheol and the Greek Hades and Gehenna by the word hell. The simple transliteration of these words by the translators of the revised editions of the Bible has not sufficed to appreciably clear up this confusion and misconception." Nevertheless, such transliteration and consistent rendering does enable the Bible student to make an accurate comparison of the texts in which these original words appear and, with open mind, thereby to arrive at a correct understanding of their true significance.—See GEHENNA; GRAVE; HADES; SHEOL; TARTARUS.

HELMET.   See ARMS, ARMOR.

HELON   (He'lon) [from a root meaning "vital energy"]. A man of the tribe of Zebulun whose son Eliab was the chieftain of his tribe during Israel's trek through the wilderness.—Nu 1:4, 9, 16; 2:7; 7:24; 10:16.

HEMAM   (He'mam). Son of Lotan and descendant of Seir the Horite. (Ge 36:20, 22) The name is rendered as Homam in 1 Chronicles 1:39 according to the reading of the Masoretic text, but the Greek *Septuagint* gives the name as Hemam.

HEMAN   (He'man).

1. One of four wise men whose wisdom, though great, was surpassed by that of King Solomon. Heman, Calcol, and Darda are designated as "the sons of Mahol," an expression thought by some to refer to an association of dancers or musicians. (1Ki 4:31) At 1 Chronicles 2:3-6 Heman is identified as a descendant of Judah through Zerah. In the superscription to Psalm 88 he is called an "Ezrahite," which apparently is simply another word for "Zerahite."—See EZRAHITE.

2. Son of Joel and grandson of the prophet Samuel of the family of Kohathites; a Levite singer and cymbalist during the reigns of David and Solomon. (1Ch 6:33; 15:17-19; 2Ch 5:11, 12) The father of 14 sons and 3 daughters, he led his family in song at the house of Jehovah. However, he himself, along with Asaph and Jeduthun, was under the immediate control of the king.—1Ch 25:1, 4-6.

HEMDAN   (Hem'dan) [Desirable]. One of the sons of Dishon, who was a son of Seir the Horite. (Ge 36:20, 21, 26) The Horites were the original inhabitants of the mountainous regions of Seir until dispossessed by the descendants of Esau. (De 2:12, 21, 22) His name is variously rendered at 1 Chronicles 1:41 as "Hemdan" (*NW*), "Amram" (*KJ*), "Hamram" (*Dy*), and "Hamran" (*AS, RS*).

HEN, I   [Favor; Grace]. Son of a certain Zephaniah (not the prophet); one who returned from exile in Babylon. He is mentioned in connection with the grand crown that was to be placed on the head of Joshua the high priest and that would afterward come to belong to Hen and three others as a memorial in the temple of Jehovah.—Zec 6:11, 14.

Likely Hen is to be identified with the Josiah mentioned in Zechariah 6:10. The name Hen has been variously regarded as (1) a proper name, (2) an abbreviation or corruption of the name Josiah, and (3) a common noun. In the Syriac the name Josiah appears in both Zechariah 6:10 and 6:14, as it does in various modern translations.

(*Mo, La, AT*) While "to Hen the son of Zephaniah" is found in the main text of Zechariah 6:14 in the *American Standard Version,* an alternate reading is given in a footnote, which says: "Or, *for the kindness of the son* [of Zephaniah]." The rendering "Hen," as found in the *New World Translation* and others, is based on the Masoretic text.

HEN, II   [Gr., *or'nis*]. In the Hebrew Scriptures there is no apparent reference to the domestic chicken (*Gallus domesticus*), but in the Christian Greek Scriptures Jesus Christ referred to the hen gathering her chicks under her protective wings in his simile concerning his desire to gather unresponsive Jerusalem. (Mt 23:37; Lu 13:34) The Greek word there used (*or'nis*) is generic and hence may refer to any bird, wild or domesticated. But in Attic Greek it usually meant a hen, since this was the most common and useful of the domestic fowl. Jesus' reference to a son asking his father for an egg (Lu 11:11, 12) indicates that the domestic hen was common in Palestine at that time. (See COCK.) From the Greek *or'nis* (genitive: *or'ni·thos*) comes the English word "ornithology," the branch of zoology that deals with birds.

Certain rabbinic laws forbade the eating of eggs laid on the Sabbath day, since it was held that this constituted work on the part of the hen; some, however, allowed the eating of the eggs if the hen was one kept for eating and not for laying. (Babylonian Talmud, *Bezah* 2a, b) The Bible, however, contains no such rules.

HENA   (He'na). A city or region listed with Sepharvaim and Ivvah and conquered by the Assyrians. (2Ki 18:34; 19:13; Isa 37:13) The Greek *Septuagint* here uses *A·na,* the name of a town on the middle course of the Euphrates River. Some scholars, however, consider it more likely that Hena, along with Sepharvaim and Ivvah, lay in Syria.

HENADAD   (Hen'a·dad). A Levite whose descendants apparently served as supervisors in connection with the rebuilding of the temple by Zerubbabel. (Ezr 3:8, 9) Two of Henadad's descendants are specifically referred to as sharing in the repair of Jerusalem's wall, and one of his descendants attested by seal the confession contract made during Nehemiah's governorship. —Ne 3:17, 18, 24; 9:38; 10:1, 9.

HENNA   [Heb., *ko'pher*]. A shrub that bears clusters of small cream-colored, four-petal flowers at the tips of its branches; their strong fra-

grance is especially enjoyed by Middle Eastern peoples. Often a sprig of henna is put in bouquets, and women wear it in their hair and in their bosom. From ancient times henna has also been employed as a cosmetic.

This shrub (*Lawsonia inermis*), which still grows wild in Palestine, attains a maximum height of about 4 m (13 ft). It is mentioned only in The Song of Solomon (1:14; 4:13; 7:11).

Henna paste, which is made from pulverized leaves of the plant, is used as a cosmetic. When the paste is washed off, the stain, commonly an orange or reddish color, remains. Henna has been used to dye the nails of fingers and toes, fingertips, hands, feet, beards, hair, and even the manes and tails of horses, as well as skins and leather. The Hebrew root from which *ko'pher* is thought to be derived has been defined as "cover," seemingly indicative of its use as a dye. —Compare Ge 6:14.

HEPHER   (He'pher).
[1-3: He Has Searched Out]
   1. A son of Gilead and great-grandson of Manasseh; ancestor of the Hepherites. (Nu 26:29, 30, 32; 27:1) Hepher was the father of Zelophehad, known for having no sons but five daughters whose case set a legal precedent in handling hereditary possessions when there was no male offspring. —Nu 26:33; 27:1-11; Jos 17:2, 3.
   2. A descendant of Judah; son of Ashhur by his wife Naarah. —1Ch 4:1, 5, 6.
   3. A Mecherathite; one of David's outstanding warriors. —1Ch 11:26, 36.
   4. [Digging [that is, a waterpit]]. Apparently both a city and a district W of the Jordan. The king of the Canaanite city of Hepher was among those defeated by Joshua. (Jos 12:7, 8, 17) In the time of Solomon, the district of Hepher, as well as Socoh, were under the jurisdiction of an appointed deputy. (1Ki 4:7, 10) The exact location of ancient Hepher is not definitely known. Some suggest identifying it with Tell el-Ifshar (Tel Hefer), about 40 km (25 mi) NNE of Tel Aviv-Yafo.

HEPHERITES   (He'pher·ites) [Of (Belonging to) Hepher]. A Manassite family descended from Hepher. —Nu 26:29, 30, 32.

HEPHZIBAH   (Heph'zi·bah) [My Delight Is in Her].
   1. Wife of Hezekiah and mother of King Manasseh. —2Ki 20:21; 21:1.
   2. The name "Hephzi-bah" is applied to Jerusalem in a restoration prophecy, according to

certain Bible translations. (Isa 62:4, *AS, KJ, Ro*) Here others use expressions such as "My pleasure in her" (*Dy*), "my Delight" (*Mo*), and "My Delight Is in Her." (*NW, AT, RS*) It was foretold that Jehovah would find delight in this city as it became "a crown of beauty" in his hand.—Isa 62:1-4.

HERALD. A court official, used to make public proclamation of royal commands and decrees. The word appears at Daniel 3:4, where a herald is mentioned as declaring Nebuchadnezzar's decree for the people to worship the image he made. (See ftn.) When Daniel was to become third ruler in the kingdom of Babylon according to King Belshazzar's command, this fact was "heralded." (Da 5:29, ftn) In the ancient Greek games, a herald announced the name and country of each contestant and the name, country, and father of a victor.

The Greek verb translated "preach" is *ke·rys'so.* This Greek verb, which occurs many times in the Christian Greek Scriptures, may also be rendered "herald." The use of this word at Matthew 24:14 and Mark 13:10 indicates that the proclaimers of the good news of God's Kingdom would be acting like heralds.—See *NW* ftns; compare Mr 1:45; Re 5:2.

Ke·rys'so, in general, means "proclaim" (good or bad news), as distinguished from *eu·ag·ge·li'zo·mai,* "declare good news." Noah was a preacher (or herald, *ke'ryx*) to the antediluvian world, warning them. (2Pe 2:5) Christ preached (like a herald) to the spirits in prison, but not the good news.—1Pe 3:18, 19.

HERES (He'res) [Sun].
1. A mount (Heb., *har*) where Amorites kept dwelling despite Israel's conquest of Canaan. It is associated with the territory of the tribe of Dan. (Jg 1:34, 35) Most scholars consider it the equivalent of Ir-shemesh (which is evidently the same as Beth-shemesh on the boundary of Judah and Dan) mentioned at Joshua 19:41.—See BETH-SHEMESH No. 1.

2. Gideon returned from warring against the Midianites by "the pass that goes up to Heres." This place is unknown outside the Biblical reference at Judges 8:13. Some scholars therefore suggest that the Hebrew text may have originally read "before the sun [*ha·che'res*] was up," or "from up in the mountains," instead of "the pass that goes up to Heres."

HERESH (He'resh) [Deaf; Keeping Silent]. A Levite whose name appears in a list of those returning from exile in Babylon.—1Ch 9:1, 14, 15.

HERETH, FOREST OF (He'reth) [Engraved]. One of David's hiding places while pursued by Saul. (1Sa 22:5) "The forest of Hereth" was apparently named after a town in its locality. Its exact location in the land of Judah is uncertain.

HERMAS (Her'mas). One of the Christians in the congregation at Rome to whom Paul sent personal greetings.—Ro 16:14.

HERMES (Her'mes).
1. One of the Christians in the congregation at Rome to whom Paul sent personal greetings.—Ro 16:14.

2. A Greek god; the son of Zeus by Maia, identified by the Romans with their god of commerce, Mercury. Hermes was regarded as the messenger of the gods. He was believed to be the discreet counselor of the heroes and was considered to be the god of commerce, skillful speech, gymnastic skill, sleep, and dreams. It was believed that this god not only guided the living but also conducted the dead to Hades.

While the apostle Paul was at Lystra, the native people, after seeing the apostle cure a man lame from birth, identified Paul with the god Hermes, since Paul was the one "taking the lead in speaking." (Ac 14:8-13) This identification harmonizes with their conception of Hermes as a divine messenger and a god of skillful speech. That Hermes was worshiped by the people of Lystra is indicated by the following inscription found in that vicinity in 1909: "Toues Macrinus also called Abascantus and Batasis son of Bretasis having made in accordance with a vow at their own expense [a statue of] Hermes Most Great along with a sun-dial dedicated it to Zeus the sun-god." —*The International Standard Bible Encyclopaedia,* edited by J. Orr, 1960, Vol. III, p. 1944.

HERMOGENES (Her·mog'e·nes) [Born of Hermes]. One of two Christians in the district of Asia specifically mentioned by name as having turned away from Paul, possibly because of the violent persecution launched by Nero against the Christians after the burning of Rome in 64 C.E. —2Ti 1:15.

HERMON (Her'mon) [Devoted Thing; Banned Thing]. Hermon has been identified with the highest mountain in the vicinity of Palestine, called Jebel esh-Sheikh (possibly meaning "Mountain of the Old One [Gray Beard]") or

*The snow of Mount Hermon
helps to condense night vapors,
producing abundant dew for the land*

Jebel eth-Thalj (meaning "Mountain of the Snow") by the Arabs. These names evidently derive from the circumstance that Mount Hermon is snowcapped nearly the year around. Its snowy top might be said to resemble an old man's crown of white hair. In ancient times, this mountain was known to the Sidonians as "Sirion" and to the Amorites as "Senir." (De 3:8, 9) The latter name also seems to have been used to denote a part of the Anti-Lebanon Range. (1Ch 5:23) "Sion" (not Zion) was still another name applied to Mount Hermon. (De 4:47, 48) The psalmist mentioned Hermon along with Tabor as crying out joyfully in Jehovah's name.—Ps 89:12.

Forming the S end of the Anti-Lebanon Range, Mount Hermon rises 2,814 m (9,232 ft) above sea level and extends about 30 km (19 mi) from N to S. Its several peaks are connected by a plateau. (Ps 42:6) Mount Hermon is composed of limestone, although having outcroppings of basalt on the eastern and western sides. Its upper portion is completely bare with the exception of low shrubs in places. But lower down, there are firs, fruit trees, and shrubs. Vineyards occupy the lower slopes of the western and southern sides.

On a clear day, the top of Hermon affords a splendid view of much of Palestine. To the W can be seen the mountains of Lebanon, the Plain of Tyre, and the Mediterranean Sea; to the SW, Mount Carmel; to the S, the Jordan Valley with the Hula Basin and the Sea of Galilee; and to the E, the Plain of Damascus.

Mount Hermon's snowy head serves to condense the night vapors, thus producing abundant dew. "More copious dew," observed the 19th-century naturalist H. B. Tristram, "we never experienced. Everything was drenched with it, and the tents were small protection." (*The Land of Israel*, London, 1866, pp. 608, 609) The refreshing dew of Hermon preserves vegetation during the long rainless season. (Ps 133:3; see DEW.) The melting snows of Mount Hermon are the main source of the river Jordan.

Anciently, Mount Hermon was a haunt for wild animals, such as lions and leopards. (Ca 4:8) In recent times foxes, wolves, leopards, and Syrian bears have been reported there.

Mount Hermon became the northern limit of the Promised Land. (Jos 12:1; 13:2, 5, 8, 11) The Hivites, who resided at its base, were defeated by Joshua. (Jos 11:1-3, 8, 16, 17) This mountain may have been the scene for the transfiguration of Jesus Christ (Mt 17:1; Mr 9:2; Lu 9:28; 2Pe 1:18), for he was in nearby Caesarea Philippi shortly before this event.—Mr 8:27; see BAAL-HERMON; TRANSFIGURATION.

HEROD. The name of a family of political rulers over the Jews. They were Idumeans, Edomites. They were nominally Jews, for the Idumeans had had circumcision forced upon them by the Maccabean ruler John Hyrcanus I in about 125 B.C.E., according to Josephus.

Aside from the Bible's brief mention of the Herods, most of the information about them is contained in Josephus' history. The progenitor of the Herods was Antipater (Antipas) I, whom Alexander Jannaeus the Hasmonaean (Maccabean) king had made governor of Idumea. Antipater's son, also called Antipater or Antipas, was the father of Herod the Great. Josephus relates that the historian Nicholas of Damascus says Antipater (II) was of the stock of the principal Jews who came out of Babylon into the land of Judah. But Josephus says that Nicholas' assertion was merely to gratify Herod, who was actually an Edomite on both his father's side and his mother's.

Antipater II, a very rich man, was involved in politics and intrigue and had great ambitions for his sons. He supported John Hyrcanus II, the son of Alexander Jannaeus and Salome Alexandra, against Hyrcanus' brother Aristobulus for the position of Jewish high priest and king. Actually, though, Antipater was working ambitiously for himself and eventually received Roman citizenship and the governorship of Judea from Julius Caesar. Antipater appointed his first son Phasael as governor of Jerusalem and another son, Herod, governor of Galilee. His career ended when he was poisoned by an assassin.

1. Herod the Great, the second son of Antipater (Antipas) II by his wife Cypros. History bears out the truth of the Bible's brief glimpse of this man's character as unscrupulous, crafty, suspicious, immoral, cruel, and murderous. He possessed his father's ability as a diplomat and an opportunist. It must be said, however, that he showed ability as an organizer and a military commander. He is described by Josephus as a man of great physical strength, having skill in horsemanship and in the use of the javelin and the bow. (*The Jewish War,* I, 429, 430 [xxi, 13]) Probably his most outstanding beneficial trait was his ability as a builder.

He first distinguished himself in his governorship of Galilee by ridding his territory of robber bands. However, certain Jews were envious and, together with the mothers of the slain robbers, stirred up Hyrcanus II (then high priest) to summon Herod before the Sanhedrin on the charge that he ran ahead of that body by executing the robbers summarily instead of bringing them first to trial. Herod complied but boldly and disrespectfully appeared before them with a bodyguard, though as a professed proselyte he was subject to that court. For this insult to the Jewish high court he incurred the anger of the judges. According to Josephus, one judge, named Samaias (Simeon), was bold enough to stand up and speak, predicting that if Herod escaped punishment, he would in time kill those there sitting in judgment. But Hyrcanus was a passive, weak-willed man. Under pressure of Herod's intimidation, coupled with a letter from Sextus Caesar (a relative of Julius Caesar and then president of

Syria) threatening Hyrcanus if he did not dismiss the charges, Hyrcanus capitulated.—*Jewish Antiquities,* XIV, 168-176 (ix, 4).

King of Judea. Herod succeeded his father and, about 39 B.C.E., was made king of greater Judea by appointment of the Roman senate; but he was not able to establish himself as de facto king until three years later when he took Jerusalem and deposed Antigonus, son of Aristobulus. After this victory Herod took steps to maintain his position by persuading the Roman Mark Antony to kill Antigonus and by seeking out the principal members of Antigonus' party, 45 men in all, and putting them to death. Of the principal Pharisees, he spared only Samaias and Pollio, for he finally killed even John Hyrcanus II some years later. By thus slaughtering those who had sat in judgment upon him, he fulfilled the prediction of Samaias.

Ever an astute politician, Herod believed that his best interests lay in supporting Rome. But he had to be very diplomatic, frequently changing sides to keep pace with the shifting fortunes of the Roman rulers. Being a close friend of Sextus, Herod first supported Julius Caesar, then aligned himself with Caesar's assassin Cassius. He was able to get the favor of Mark Antony, the enemy of Cassius and avenger of Caesar, partly by means of large bribes. Later, when Octavius (Augustus Caesar) defeated Antony at the battle of Actium, Herod adroitly obtained Augustus' forgiveness for supporting Antony, and thereafter he retained the friendship of Augustus. Because of his support of Rome and his free use of money as gifts to the Caesars, along with his smoothness of speech, Herod always won out when complaints or charges against him were taken to Rome by the Jews or others, sometimes members of his own household.

The governorship of Galilee had been Herod's first dominion. Cassius had made him governor of Coele-Syria. Later, the Roman senate, at Antony's recommendation, had made him king of Judea. To this, Emperor Augustus now added Samaria, Gadara, Gaza, and Joppa, then the regions of Trachonitis, Batanaea, Auranitis, and Perea, an area east of the Jordan roughly corresponding to Gilead. Idumea was also under his dominion.

Temple and Other Building Works. As to Herod's building works, the rebuilding of the temple of Zerubbabel at Jerusalem is most noteworthy, particularly from a Biblical standpoint. It was constructed at tremendous cost and is described by Josephus as truly magnificent. (*Jewish*

Antiquities, XV, 395, 396 [xi, 3]) The Jews, because of their hatred and suspicion of Herod, would not permit him to tear down the existing temple beforehand, but he had to gather the building materials and have them on the ground before he could start any demolition. The temple sanctuary was rebuilt, according to Josephus, in 18 months. (*Jewish Antiquities,* XV, 421 [xi, 6]) Other main structures were erected in eight years. But in 30 C.E. the Jews stated that the temple was built in 46 years. This statement was made during a conversation with Jesus Christ near the time of the first Passover after Jesus' baptism. (Joh 2:13-20) According to Josephus (*Jewish Antiquities,* XV, 380 [xi, 1]), that work began in the 18th year of Herod's reign. If counted in the way that the Jews had viewed the regnal years of their kings, that could mean 18/17 B.C.E. Actually, work continued on the temple in the form of additions, and so forth, until six years before its destruction in 70 C.E.

Herod also was responsible for the construction of theaters, amphitheaters, hippodromes, citadels, fortresses, palaces, gardens, temples in honor of Caesar, aqueducts, monuments, and even cities. These cities he named after himself, his relatives, or the emperors of Rome. He built an artificial harbor at Caesarea that rivaled the seaport of Tyre. According to Josephus tremendous stones were laid in 20 fathoms (36 m; 120 ft) of water to make a mole about 60 m (200 ft) wide. (*Jewish Antiquities,* XV, 334, 335 [ix, 6]) Herod reconstructed the fortresses of Antonia and Masada, the latter being made most magnificent. His building achievements were spread to cities as far removed as Antioch in Syria and Rhodes (on the island of the same name).

Herod was extremely lavish in his entertainment and was free with gifts, particularly to Roman dignitaries. One of the chief complaints against him by the Jews was his building of amphitheaters such as the one at Caesarea, where he held Grecian and Roman games, including chariot races, gladiatorial fights, men fighting wild beasts, and other pagan festivities. So interested was he in keeping alive the Olympic Games that, while in Greece on a trip to Rome, he even became one of the combatants. Then he donated a great sum of money to perpetuate the games, as well as, incidentally, his own name. Being nominally a Jew, he called the Jews "my countrymen" and those who had returned from Babylon to build Zerubbabel's temple "my fathers." Nonetheless, his course of life was a complete denial of his claim to be a servant of Jehovah God.

Trouble in Family. Practically the entire family of the Herods was ambitious, suspicious, grossly immoral, and troublesome. Herod found his greatest difficulties and sorrows in his own family. His mother Cypros and his sister Salome constantly aggravated the situation. Herod had married Mariamne (I), the granddaughter of Hyrcanus II and daughter of Alexander who was son of Aristobulus. She was a strikingly beautiful woman, and Herod greatly loved her, but hatred developed between her and Herod's mother and sister. Herod was constantly envious, and he was suspicious that members of his family, particularly his sons, were plotting against him; in some cases his suspicions were justified. His greed for power and his suspicions now moved him to cause the murder of his wife Mariamne, three of his sons, his wife's brother and grandfather (Hyrcanus), several who had been his best friends, and many others. He employed torture to wring confessions from whomever he suspected of having information that would confirm his suspicions.

Relationship With the Jews. Herod tried to pacify the Jews by temple rebuilding and by giving them needed things in times of famine. At times he eased the taxes of some of his subjects. He even managed to get Augustus to grant the Jews privileges in various parts of the world. Yet his tyranny and cruelty outweighed this, and during most of his rule he had trouble with the Jews.

His Sickness and Death. Very possibly because of his licentious living, Herod was eventually afflicted with a loathsome disease accompanied by fever and, to quote Josephus, "an intolerable itching of the whole skin, continuous pains in the intestines, tumours in the feet as in dropsy, inflammation of the abdomen and gangrene of the privy parts, engendering worms, in addition to asthma, with great difficulty in breathing, and convulsions in all his limbs."—*The Jewish War,* I, 656 (xxxiii, 5).

It was during his fatal sickness that he ordered the slaughter of his scheming son Antipater. Also, knowing that the Jews would rejoice upon hearing of his own death, Herod commanded the most illustrious men of the Jewish nation to gather at a place called the Hippodrome, at Jericho, and there had them shut in. He then gave a command to those near him that, when he died, the news of his death should not be announced until these Jewish leaders were first killed. Then, said he, every family in Judea would certainly weep at his funeral. This order was never carried out. Herod's sister Salome and her husband Alexas freed these men and sent them to their homes.

Herod died at the age of about 70 years. He had made a will designating his son Antipas as his successor, but shortly before his death he added a codicil or made a new will appointing Archelaus to that position. Archelaus was acknowledged by the people and the army as king (the Bible says that Jesus' adoptive father Joseph heard that "Archelaus ruled as king of Judea instead of his father Herod"; Mt 2:22). But the action was con-

Ruins of multileveled palace built by Herod the Great atop Masada

tested by Antipas. After a hearing of the matter in Rome, Augustus Caesar upheld Archelaus. However, he constituted Archelaus an ethnarch and divided the territory formerly ruled over by Herod: half went to Archelaus; Antipas and Philip, two of Herod's other sons, were granted a share each in the other half.

Slaughter of Children. The Bible account of Herod's slaughter of all the boys two years of age and under in Bethlehem and its districts is in harmony with the other historical accounts of Herod and his wicked disposition. This occurred not long before Herod's death, for Jesus escaped by being taken down into Egypt by his parents, but they returned and settled in Galilee after Herod died. These two events were foretold by Jehovah through his prophets Jeremiah and Hosea.—Mt 2:1-23; Jer 31:15; Ho 11:1.

Date of His Death. A problem arises with regard to the time of Herod's death. Some chronologers hold that he died in the year 5 or 4 B.C.E. Their chronology is based to a large extent on Josephus' history. In dating the time that Herod was appointed king by Rome, Josephus uses a "consular dating," that is, he locates the event as occurring during the rule of certain Roman consuls. According to this, Herod's appointment as king would be in 40 B.C.E., but the data of another historian, Appianos, would place the event in 39 B.C.E. By the same method Josephus places Herod's capture of Jerusalem in 37 B.C.E., but he also says that this occurred 27 years after the capture of the city by Pompey (which was in 63 B.C.E.). (*Jewish Antiquities*, XIV, 487, 488 [xvi, 4]) His reference to that latter event would make the date of Herod's taking the city of Jerusalem 36 B.C.E. Now, Josephus says that Herod died 37 years from the time that he was appointed king by the Romans, and 34 years after he took Jerusalem. (*Jewish Antiquities*, XVII, 190, 191 [viii, 1]) This might indicate that the date of his death was 2 or perhaps 1 B.C.E.

It may be that the Jewish historian Josephus counted the reigns of the kings of Judea by the accession-year method, as had been done with the kings of the line of David. If Herod was appointed king by Rome in 40 B.C.E., his first regnal year could run from Nisan of 39 to Nisan of 38 B.C.E.; similarly, if counted from his capture of Jerusalem in 37 (or 36) B.C.E., his first regnal year could start in Nisan 36 (or 35) B.C.E. So if, as Josephus says, Herod died 37 years after his appointment by Rome and 34 years after his capture of Jerusalem, and if those years are counted in each case according to the regnal year, his

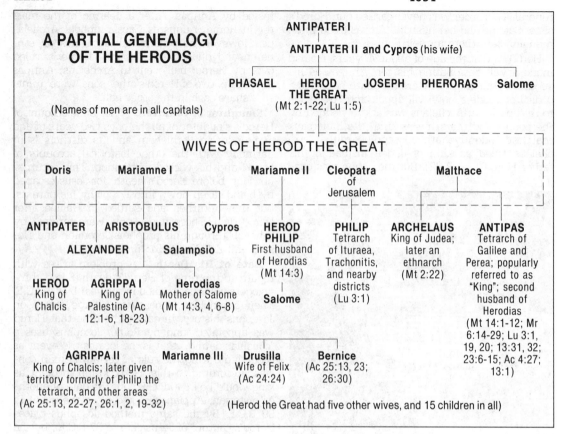

A PARTIAL GENEALOGY OF THE HERODS

(Names of men are in all capitals)

ANTIPATER I

ANTIPATER II and Cypros (his wife)

PHASAEL   **HEROD THE GREAT** (Mt 2:1-22; Lu 1:5)   **JOSEPH**   **PHERORAS**   Salome

WIVES OF HEROD THE GREAT

Doris	Mariamne I		Mariamne II	Cleopatra of Jerusalem	Malthace	

ANTIPATER   **ARISTOBULUS**   Cypros   **HEROD PHILIP**   **PHILIP**   **ARCHELAUS**   **ANTIPAS**

ALEXANDER   Salampsio

HEROD PHILIP
First husband of Herodias
(Mt 14:3)

PHILIP
Tetrarch of Ituraea, Trachonitis, and nearby districts
(Lu 3:1)

ARCHELAUS
King of Judea; later an ethnarch
(Mt 2:22)

ANTIPAS
Tetrarch of Galilee and Perea; popularly referred to as "King"; second husband of Herodias
(Mt 14:1-12; Mr 6:14-29; Lu 3:1, 19, 20; 13:31, 32; 23:6-15; Ac 4:27; 13:1)

HEROD
King of Chalcis

AGRIPPA I
King of Palestine (Ac 12:1-6, 18-23)

Herodias
Mother of Salome
(Mt 14:3, 4, 6-8)

Salome

AGRIPPA II
King of Chalcis; later given territory formerly of Philip the tetrarch, and other areas
(Ac 25:13, 22-27; 26:1, 2, 19-32)

Mariamne III

Drusilla
Wife of Felix
(Ac 24:24)

Bernice
(Ac 25:13, 23; 26:30)

(Herod the Great had five other wives, and 15 children in all)

---

death could have been in 1 B.C.E. Presenting an argument to this effect in *The Journal of Theological Studies,* W. E. Filmer writes that evidence from Jewish tradition indicates that Herod's death occurred on Shebat 2 (the month of Shebat falls in January-February of our calendar).—Edited by H. Chadwick and H. Sparks, Oxford, 1966, Vol. XVII, p. 284.

According to Josephus, Herod died not long after an eclipse of the moon and before a Passover. (*Jewish Antiquities,* XVII, 167 [vi, 4]; 213 [ix, 3]) Since there was an eclipse on March 11, 4 B.C.E. (March 13, Julian), some have concluded that this was the eclipse referred to by Josephus.

On the other hand, there was a total eclipse of the moon in 1 B.C.E., about three months before Passover, while the one in 4 B.C.E. was only partial. The total eclipse in 1 B.C.E. was on January 8 (January 10, Julian), 18 days before Shebat 2, the traditional day of Herod's death. Another eclipse (partial) occurred on December 27 of 1 B.C.E. (December 29, Julian).—See CHRONOLOGY (*Lunar eclipses*).

Another line of calculation centers around the age of Herod at the time of his death. Josephus says that he was about 70 years old. He says that at the time Herod received his appointment as governor of Galilee (which is generally dated 47 B.C.E.), he was 15 years old; but this has been understood by scholars to be an error, 25 years evidently being intended. (*Jewish Antiquities,* XVII, 148 [vi, 1]; XIV, 158 [ix, 2]) Accordingly, Herod's death occurred in 2 or 1 B.C.E. We must bear in mind, however, that Josephus has many inconsistencies in his dating of events and is therefore not the most reliable source. For the most reliable evidence, we must look to the Bible.

The available evidence indicates that Herod died likely in the year 1 B.C.E. The Bible historian Luke tells us that John came baptizing in the 15th year of Tiberius Caesar. (Lu 3:1-3) Augustus died on August 17, 14 C.E. On September 15, Tiberius was named emperor by the Roman Senate. The Romans did not use the accession-year system; consequently, the 15th year would run from the latter part of 28 C.E. to the latter part of 29 C.E.

John was six months older than Jesus and began his ministry (evidently in the spring of the year) ahead of Jesus as Jesus' forerunner, preparing the way. (Lu 1:35, 36) Jesus, whom the Bible indicates was born in the fall of the year, was about 30 years old when he came to John to be baptized. (Lu 3:21-23) Therefore he was baptized, most likely, in the fall, about October of 29 C.E. Counting back 30 years would bring us to the fall of 2 B.C.E. as the time of the human birth of the Son of God. (Compare Lu 3:1, 23 with Daniel's prophecy of the "seventy weeks" at Da 9:24-27.)—See SEVENTY WEEKS.

The astrologers who visited Jesus. The apostle Matthew tells us that after Jesus had been born in Bethlehem *"in the days of Herod* the king," astrologers from eastern parts came to Jerusalem, saying that they saw his star when they were in the east. Herod's fears and suspicions were immediately aroused, and he determined from the chief priests and scribes that the Christ was to be born in Bethlehem. Then he called in the astrologers and ascertained from them the time of the star's appearing.—Mt 2:1-7.

We note that this was sometime after Jesus' birth, for he was now not in the manger but with his parents in a house. (Mt 2:11; compare Lu 2:4-7.) After the astrologers failed to return to Herod with news of the young child's whereabouts, the king ordered the slaughter of all the children two years of age and under throughout Bethlehem and its districts. Jesus, in the meantime, was taken to Egypt by his parents because of God's warning. (Mt 2:12-18) The death of Herod could hardly have taken place before 1 B.C.E., for, in that case, Jesus (born about October 1, 2 B.C.E.) would have been less than three months old.

On the other hand, it would not be necessary for Jesus to be two years old when the killing of the children occurred; he could even have been less than a year old, for Herod calculated from the time that the star appeared to the astrologers while they were *in the east*. (Mt 2:1, 2, 7-9) This may well have been a period of some months, for if the astrologers came from the age-old center of astrology, Babylon or Mesopotamia, as is likely the case, it was a very long journey. It had taken the Israelites at least four months to make the trip when they were repatriated from Babylon in 537 B.C.E. Herod evidently concluded that by killing all babies up to two years of age he would be sure to get this one who was born "king of the Jews." (Mt 2:2) That Herod died not long after

these things took place is indicated by the fact that Jesus apparently did not stay in Egypt very long.—Mt 2:19-21.

We may conclude, therefore, that Bible chronology, astronomical data, and available historical records seem to point to the time of Herod's death as 1 B.C.E., or possibly even early in 1 C.E.

2. Herod Antipas, son of Herod the Great and Malthace, a Samaritan woman. He was brought up in Rome with his brother Archelaus. In Herod's will, Antipas had been named to receive the kingship, but Herod, at the last, changed his will, naming Archelaus instead. Antipas contested the will before Augustus Caesar, who upheld Archelaus' claim but divided the kingdom, giving Antipas the tetrarchy of Galilee and Perea. "Tetrarch," meaning 'ruler over one fourth' of a province, was a term applied to a minor district ruler or territorial prince. However, popularly he may have been called King, as was Archelaus.—Mt 14:9; Mr 6:14, 22, 25-27.

Antipas married the daughter of Aretas, king of Arabia, whose capital was at Petra. But on one of his trips to Rome, Antipas visited his half brother Herod Philip, the son of Herod the Great and Mariamne II (not Philip the tetrarch). While visiting, he became infatuated with Philip's wife Herodias, who was ambitious for position. He took her back to Galilee and married her, divorcing Aretas' daughter and sending her back to her home. This insulting action brought war. Aretas invaded Antipas' dominion and inflicted tremendous losses on him, to the extent that he was almost overthrown. Antipas was saved by an appeal to Rome that brought an order from the emperor for Aretas to halt the war.

Antipas gained high favor with Tiberius Caesar, the successor of Augustus. A builder like his father, but on a far smaller scale, Antipas built a city on Lake Gennesaret (the Sea of Galilee, or Tiberias) and named it Tiberias, after the emperor. (Joh 6:1, 23) Another city, Julias, he named for Augustus' wife, Julia (more commonly called Livia). He also constructed forts, palaces, and theaters.

Kills John the Baptizer. It was Herod Antipas' adulterous relationship with Herodias that brought reproof from John the Baptizer. John could properly correct Antipas on this matter, for Antipas was nominally a Jew and professedly under the Law. Antipas put John into prison, desiring to kill him, but was afraid of the people, who believed John was a prophet. Nevertheless, at a celebration of Antipas' birthday, Herodias' daughter so pleased him that he made an oath to give her whatever she asked. Herodias instructed her daughter to ask for John's head. Herod, though it was not pleasing to him, cravenly gave in to save face before those attending the celebration and because of his oath. (However, under the Law he would not be bound by an oath to perform an illegal act, such as murder.)—Mt 14:3-12; Mr 6:17-29.

Afterward, when Antipas heard of Jesus' ministry of preaching, healing, and casting out demons, he was frightened, fearing that Jesus was actually John who had been raised from the dead. Thereafter he greatly desired to see Jesus, apparently not to hear his preaching, but because he was not sure of this conclusion.—Mt 14:1, 2; Mr 6:14-16; Lu 9:7-9.

It was likely on an occasion when Jesus was passing through Perea on his way to Jerusalem that the Pharisees said to him: "Get out and be on your way from here, because Herod wants to kill you." It may be that Herod started this rumor, hoping to cause Jesus to flee out of his territory in fear, for Herod may have been afraid to be so bold as to raise his hand again to kill a prophet of God. Evidently referring to Herod's craftiness, Jesus in his reply called Herod "that fox."—Lu 13:31-33.

"The Leaven of Herod." It was during the rulership of Herod Antipas that Jesus warned his followers: "Keep your eyes open, look out for the leaven of the Pharisees and the leaven of Herod." (Mr 8:15) Both of these sects, the Pharisees and the Herodians, or party followers of Herod, opposed Jesus Christ and his teachings, and though they were at enmity with each other, both saw Christ as a common enemy and were united against him. The Herodians were more political than religious; it has been said that they claimed to follow the Law but maintained the opinion that it was lawful for the Jews to acknowledge a foreign prince (for the Herods were not true Jews, but Idumeans). The Herodians were very nationalistic and supported neither the idea of theocratic rule under Jewish kings nor Roman rule, but they wanted the restoration of the national kingdom under one or the other of the sons of Herod.

An example betraying their nationalistic "leaven" was the catch question that they, along with the Pharisees, used in an attempt to trap Jesus: "Is it lawful to pay head tax to Caesar or not? Shall we pay, or shall we not pay?" (Mr 12:13-15) Jesus called them "hypocrites," and showed that he was alert to look out for their "leaven," for his

reply disarmed them, foiling their intention either to bring an accusation of sedition or to arouse the people against him.—Mt 22:15-22.

Makes Fun of Jesus. On the last day of Jesus' earthly life, when he was brought before Pontius Pilate and Pilate heard that Jesus was a Galilean, Pilate sent him to Herod Antipas the district ruler (tetrarch) of Galilee (who was then in Jerusalem), for Pilate had experienced trouble with the Galileans. (Lu 13:1; 23:1-7) On seeing Jesus, Herod rejoiced, not because he was concerned with Jesus' welfare or wanted to make any real attempt to find out the truth or untruth of the charges brought against him by the priests and the scribes, but because he desired to see Jesus perform some sign. This, Jesus refused to do, and he was silent when Herod questioned him "with a good many words." Jesus knew that this appearance before Herod was forced on him only as a sort of mockery. Herod, disappointed in Jesus, discredited him and made fun of him by clothing him with a bright garment and sent him back to Pilate, who was the superior authority as far as Rome was concerned. Pilate and Herod had been enemies, possibly because of certain accusations that Herod had leveled against Pilate. But this move on Pilate's part pleased Herod and they became friends.—Lu 23:8-12.

After the release of Peter and John from custody shortly after Pentecost of 33 C.E., the disciples, in prayer to God, said: "Both Herod [Antipas] and Pontius Pilate with men of nations and with peoples of Israel were in actuality gathered together in this city against your holy servant Jesus . . . And now, Jehovah, give attention to their threats, and grant your slaves to keep speaking your word with all boldness."—Ac 4:23, 27-29.

At Acts 13:1 a Christian, Manaen, is spoken of as having been educated with Herod the district ruler. Since Antipas was brought up in Rome with a certain private citizen, the Bible statement may indicate that Manaen received his education in Rome.

Banished to Gaul. When Agrippa I was made king of Philip's tetrarchy by Gaius Caesar (Caligula), Antipas' wife Herodias reproached her husband, saying it was only because of slothfulness on his part that he did not receive kingship. She argued that since he was already a tetrarch, whereas, by contrast, Agrippa had formerly had no office at all, Antipas should go to Rome and request a kingship from Caesar. He finally yielded to his wife's persistent pressure. But Caligula was angered by Antipas' ambitious request and, giving heed to accusations from Agrippa, banished Antipas to Gaul (the city of Lyons, France); he finally died in Spain. Herodias, though she could have escaped punishment because of being Agrippa's sister, stuck with her husband, likely because of her pride. Antipas' tetrarchy and, after his exile, his money, as well as Herodias' estate, came to be given to Agrippa I. Thus Herodias was responsible for Antipas' two great calamities: his near defeat by King Aretas and his banishment.

3. Herod Agrippa I. Grandson of Herod the Great. He was a son of Aristobulus, who, in turn, was a son of Herod the Great by Mariamne I, granddaughter of High Priest Hyrcanus II. Aristobulus had been put to death by Herod the Great. Agrippa was the last of the Herods to become king of all Palestine, as his grandfather had been.

His Early Life.   Agrippa's position as "Herod the king" was attained by a number of maneuvers and the help of his friends in Rome. (Ac 12:1) Educated in Rome along with Emperor Tiberius' son Drusus and his nephew Claudius, he became a familiar figure in important circles there. He was extremely extravagant and reckless. Greatly in debt, even owing money to the Roman treasury, he left Rome and fled to Idumea. Eventually, with the help of his sister Herodias and his wife Cypros (daughter of Herod the Great's nephew, whose wife was Herod's daughter), he found residence for a while at Tiberias. A quarrel developed between him and Antipas, causing him to leave. He finally got back to Rome and into the good graces of Tiberius Caesar.

However, an injudicious statement got Agrippa into trouble with Emperor Tiberius. In an unguarded moment he expressed the wish to Gaius (Caligula), with whom he had cultivated a friendship, that he, Gaius, might soon be emperor. Overheard by Agrippa's servant, his remarks came to the ears of Tiberius, who cast Agrippa into prison. His life was in the balance for several months, but some months later Tiberius died and Caligula became emperor. He released Agrippa and elevated him to the position of king over the territories that his late uncle Philip had governed.

Favored by Roman Emperors.   Herodias, envious of her brother's position as king, persuaded her husband Herod Antipas, who was only a tetrarch, to make an appeal to the new emperor in Rome for a crown. But Agrippa outmaneuvered Antipas in the matter. Before Tiberius the emperor, he charged that Antipas had made alliances with Sejanus the conspirator against Tiberius and

with the Parthians, charges that Antipas could not deny. It led to Antipas' banishment. Antipas' territories of Galilee and Perea were added to Agrippa's kingdom. In one passage Josephus says that Caligula gave these dominions to Agrippa, and in two others that Claudius did so. Likely Caligula made the promise, and Claudius confirmed it.

On the occasion of the assassination of Caligula, dated by scholars as 41 C.E., Agrippa was in Rome. He was able to act as liaison, or negotiator, between the Senate and his friend, the new emperor Claudius. Claudius expressed his appreciation by awarding him the territory of Judea and Samaria as well as the kingdom of Lysanias. Agrippa now became ruler of about the same dominion that his grandfather Herod the Great had held. At this time Agrippa asked for and received the kingdom of Chalcis from Claudius, for his brother Herod. (This Herod receives mention in history only as king of Chalcis, a small territory on the W slope of the Anti-Lebanon mountains.)

Curries Jews' Favor; Persecutes Christians. Agrippa curried favor with the Jews, claiming to be a devoted adherent to Judaism. Caligula, claiming he was a god, had decided to erect a statue of himself in the temple at Jerusalem, but Agrippa adroitly persuaded him not to do it. Agrippa later began building a wall about the N suburb of Jerusalem. To Claudius this appeared to be a possible fortifying of the city against any Roman attack that might be made in the future. Consequently, Claudius ordered Agrippa to desist. Agrippa belied his claim of being a worshiper of God by supporting and arranging gladiatorial games and other pagan shows in the theater.

Agrippa was acceptable to the Jews because of his Hasmonaean descent on his grandmother Mariamne's side of the family. While championing the cause of the Jews under the Roman yoke, he also built up an unenviable record for persecution of Christians, who were generally hated by the unbelieving Jews. He "did away with James the brother of John by the sword." (Ac 12:1, 2) Seeing that this pleased the Jews, he arrested and imprisoned Peter. An angel's intervention, bringing about Peter's release, caused a great stir among Agrippa's soldiers and resulted in the punishment of Peter's guards.—Ac 12:3-19.

Executed by God's Angel.   Agrippa's rule came abruptly to an end. At Caesarea, during a festival in honor of Caesar, he robed himself in a magnificent royal garment and began giving a public address to an assembled audience of people from Tyre and Sidon, who were suing for peace with him. The audience responded by shouting: "A god's voice, and not a man's!" The Bible records his summary execution as a condemned hypocrite: "Instantly the angel of Jehovah struck him, because he did not give the glory to God; and he became eaten up with worms and expired."—Ac 12:20-23.

Chronologers place the death of King Herod Agrippa I in 44 C.E., at the age of 54 and after he had reigned three years over all Judea. He was survived by his son Herod Agrippa II and his daughters Bernice (Ac 25:13), Drusilla the wife of Governor Felix, and Mariamne III.—Ac 24:24.

4. Herod Agrippa II. Great-grandson of Herod the Great. He was the son of Herod Agrippa I and his wife Cypros. He was the end of the princes of the Herodian line, according to historians. Agrip-

Bronze coin depicting the head of Domitian and, on the reverse side, bearing the name King Agrippa (II)

pa had three sisters, named Bernice, Drusilla, and Mariamne III. (Ac 25:13; 24:24) He was reared in the imperial household in Rome. When he was only 17 years of age his father died, and Emperor Claudius' advisers thought him too young to assume rulership of the dominions of his father. Accordingly, Claudius assigned governors over the territories instead. After remaining in Rome for a time, Agrippa II was given the kingship over Chalcis, a small principality on the western slope of the Anti-Lebanon Range, after his uncle (Herod king of Chalcis) died.

It was not long afterward that Claudius appointed him king over the tetrarchies formerly belonging to Philip and Lysanias. (Lu 3:1) He was also given oversight of the temple of Jerusalem and was invested with the authority to appoint the Jewish high priests. His domains were further enlarged by Claudius' successor Nero, who grant-

ed him Tiberias and Taricheae in Galilee and Julias in Perea with its dependent towns.

Later, Agrippa turned his attention to building an addition to the palace that had been erected by the Hasmonaean kings in Jerusalem. Because he could now observe from this palace addition what went on in the temple courtyard, the Jews erected a wall blocking his view and also obstructing the view from a certain vantage point for the Roman guards. This displeased both Herod and Festus, but on appeal of the Jews to Nero, the emperor let the wall remain. Agrippa also beautified Caesarea Philippi (changing its name to Neronias in honor of Nero). Following his father's pattern, he built a theater at Berytus, in Phoenicia, expending vast sums on shows there.

Agrippa carried on an incestuous relationship with his sister Bernice, who had left her husband the king of Cilicia. This unclean, unscriptural relationship with his own sister brought great scandal upon him.—Le 18:9, 29; De 27:22.

When it became evident that the Jews' rebellion against the Roman yoke (66-70 C.E.) would only spell national disaster, Agrippa tried to persuade them to take a more moderate course. His appeals being of no avail, he forsook the Jews and attached himself to the Roman army, getting wounded by a slingstone in the actual fighting.

Paul's Defense Before Him. The Scriptures introduce King Herod Agrippa II and his sister Bernice at the time of their courtesy call on Governor Festus, in about the year 58 C.E. (Ac 25:13) Festus had succeeded Governor Felix. It was during the governorship of Felix that the apostle Paul had been accused by the Jews, but Felix, upon leaving office, desired to gain favor with the Jews and left Paul bound. (Ac 24:27) Incidentally, Felix was a brother-in-law of Agrippa, having married his sister Drusilla. (Ac 24:24) While Paul was awaiting further action on his appeal to Caesar (Ac 25:8-12), King Agrippa voiced to Governor Festus his desire to hear what Paul had to say. (Ac 25:22) Paul was glad to make his defense before Agrippa, whom he referred to as being "expert on all the customs as well as the controversies among Jews." (Ac 26:1-3) Paul's powerful argument moved Agrippa to say: "In a short time you would persuade me to become a Christian." To this Paul answered: "I could wish to God that whether in a short time or in a long time not only you but also all those who hear me today would become men such as I also am, with the exception of these bonds." (Ac 26:4-29) Agrippa and Festus determined that Paul was innocent but that, since he had appealed to Caesar, he had to be sent to Rome for trial.—Ac 26:30-32.

Following the destruction of Jerusalem in 70 C.E., Herod Agrippa with his sister Bernice moved to Rome, where he was given the office of praetor. Agrippa died childless in about 100 C.E.

5. Herod Philip. Son of Herod the Great by Mariamne II, daughter of High Priest Simon. Philip was the first husband of Herodias, who divorced him to marry his half brother Herod Antipas. He is mentioned incidentally in the Bible at Matthew 14:3; Mark 6:17, 18; and Luke 3:19.

The name Herod Philip is used to distinguish him from Philip the tetrarch, for the latter, according to Josephus, was also a son of Herod the Great by another wife, Cleopatra of Jerusalem.

Philip was apparently in line for succession to his father's throne, as next eldest after his half brothers Antipater, Alexander, and Aristobulus, all three of whom their father executed. Herod's earlier will listed him as in line after Antipas. But he was passed over in Herod's final will, the kingdom going to Archelaus. Josephus relates that Herod blotted Philip's name out of his will because Mariamne II, Philip's mother, had been aware of the plot of Antipater against Herod but had not revealed it.

Philip had a daughter, Salome, by Herodias. She was evidently the one who danced before Herod Antipas and, because of her mother's coaching, asked for the head of John the Baptizer.—Mt 14:1-13; Mr 6:17-29.

6. Philip the tetrarch. Son of Herod the Great by his wife Cleopatra of Jerusalem. He was brought up in Rome. He married Salome the daughter of Herod Philip and Herodias. When his father died, Augustus Caesar divided the kingdom, giving Philip the tetrarchy of Ituraea, Trachonitis, and other nearby districts, with a yearly revenue of 100 talents. (Perhaps Ituraea was added later and is therefore omitted by Josephus.) He ruled for more than 30 years. Josephus says: "In his conduct of the government he showed a moderate and easy-going disposition. Indeed, he spent all his time in the territory subject to him." Josephus goes on to say that Philip sat in judgment wherever he happened to be and heard cases without delay. He died at Julias and was buried with great pomp. Since he left no sons, Emperor Tiberius added his tetrarchy to the province of Syria.—*Jewish Antiquities,* XVIII, 106-108 (iv, 6).

Philip's name is mentioned once in the Bible in connection with the dating of John the Baptizer's ministry. (Lu 3:1) The text here, along with his torical information about the reigns of Augustus and Tiberius, shows that John's ministry began in 29 C.E.

HEROD, PARTY FOLLOWERS OF. These were evidently Jewish partisans or party followers of the Herodian dynasty, which received its authority from Rome. During Jesus Christ's earthly ministry Herod Antipas headed this dynasty.

There is no mention of the Herodians in secular history, and little Scriptural reference is made to them. (Mt 22:16; Mr 3:6; 12:13) However, there are strong objections to believing, as some do, that the Herodians were household domestics of Herod, that they were his soldiers, or that they were his court officials.

Politically, the Herodians stood on middle ground, opposed on the one hand by the Pharisees and Jewish zealots who advocated a Jewish kingdom completely independent of Roman control, and on the other hand by those who advocated complete absorption of Judea by the Roman Empire. Some of the Sadducees, rated as free thinkers and moderates in Judaism, probably belonged to the Herodian school of thought. This latter conclusion is drawn from the reports of Matthew and Mark as to Jesus' statement about leaven. According to Matthew 16:6, Jesus said, "Watch out for the leaven of the Pharisees and Sadducees," whereas Mark 8:15 says, "Look out for the leaven of the Pharisees and the leaven of Herod." Repeating the word "leaven" emphasized that there was a difference in the corrupt teachings of the two parties. Instead of "Herod," this latter text reads "Herodians" in some manuscripts, namely, the Chester Beatty Papyrus No. 1 (P[45]), the *Codex Washingtonianus I,* and the *Codex Koridethianus.*—*The Interpreter's Dictionary of the Bible,* edited by G. A. Buttrick, 1962, Vol. 2, p. 594; *Our Bible and the Ancient Manuscripts,* by Sir Frederic Kenyon, 1958, pp. 215, 216.

There is one thing certain: the party followers of Herod and the Pharisees, though openly opposed to one another in their political and Judaistic views, were solidly united in their violent opposition to Jesus. On at least two occasions these opposing parties consulted together on how best to do away with their common opponent. The first reported instance was shortly after Passover, 31 C.E., during Jesus' great Galilean ministry. Upon seeing Jesus restore a man's dried-up hand on the Sabbath, "the Pharisees went out and immediately began holding council with the party followers of Herod against him, in order to destroy him."—Mr 3:1-6; Mt 12:9-14.

The second reported occasion was nearly two years later, just three days before Jesus was put to death, when disciples of the Pharisees and party followers of Herod joined forces in putting Jesus to the test in the matter of taxation. These men were secretly hired "to pretend that they were righteous, in order that they might catch him in speech, so as to turn him over to the government and to the authority of the governor." (Lu 20:20) They prefaced their direct question about taxes with words of flattery designed to throw Jesus off guard. However, Jesus, perceiving their cunning wickedness, declared: "Why do you put me to the test, hypocrites?" He then completely silenced them by his answer on the matter of paying taxes.—Mt 22:15-22; Lu 20:21-26.

HERODIAS (He·ro′di·as). The wife of Herod Antipas, who, through her daughter Salome, requested and received the head of John the Baptizer in 32 C.E. (Mr 6:22-28) Her father Aristobulus, son of Herod the Great by his second wife Mariamne I, and her mother were first cousins. Her brother was Herod Agrippa I, who did away with the apostle James, the brother of John.—Ac 12:1, 2.

Herodias first married her half uncle, her father's half brother, another son of Herod the Great (by his third wife, Mariamne II), that son commonly being called Herod Philip to distinguish him from Philip the district ruler of Ituraea and Trachonitis. (Lu 3:1) This uncle-husband of Herodias, Herod Philip, fathered Salome, apparently her only child. However, Herodias divorced him and married his half brother Herod Antipas, also a son of her grandfather Herod the Great, by his fourth wife, Malthace. Herod Antipas, who was district ruler (literally, "the tetrarch") at the time, and whom Jesus Christ called "that fox" (Lu 13:31, 32), also divorced his first wife, a daughter of the Nabataean king Aretas of Arabia, in order to marry Herodias.

John the Baptizer, therefore, had reason to condemn this marriage of Herodias and Herod Antipas, it being both illegal and immoral under Jewish law, and for doing so he was thrown into prison and later beheaded. His fearless and righteous condemnation aroused the bitter hatred of Herodias, so she seized the first opportunity to have the prophet put to death.—Mt 14:1-11; Mr 6:16-28; Lu 3:19, 20; 9:9.

Herodias' brother Herod Agrippa I returned from Rome in 38 C.E., having been appointed king of Judea. This greatly vexed Herodias, for her husband, although he was a king's son, remained only a district ruler. She therefore did not cease pressuring her husband until he too went to Rome in hopes of also being crowned a king with a kingdom. Flavius Josephus tells that Herodias' brother Agrippa secretly sent letters to Emperor Caligula accusing Antipas of being in conspiracy with the Parthians. As a consequence, Antipas was sent in banishment to Gaul; he was accompanied by Herodias.—*Jewish Antiquities,* XVIII, 240-256 (vii, 1, 2); *The Jewish War,* II, 181-183 (ix, 6).

HERODION (He·ro′di·on). One to whom Paul sent personal greetings in his letter to the Christian congregation at Rome. Paul refers to Herodion as "my relative." (Ro 16:11) Some suggest that this may simply mean that Herodion was a fellow Jew rather than an immediate member of Paul's family, in view of the apostle's use of the designation "relatives" at Romans 9:3. However, since Paul does not refer to all the Jews to whom he sent greetings as "my relatives" (compare Ac 18:2; Ro 16:3), likely a closer relative is meant. —See ANDRONICUS.

HERON [Heb., ′ana·phah′]. A bird that, according to the Mosaic Law, was not to be eaten. (Le 11:13, 19; De 14:12, 18) The Hebrew name is considered by some to have been derived from a root word meaning "breathe hard," or possibly, "snort," likely in anger. Others suggest a closer connection of the name with the Hebrew word for "nose" (′aph), perhaps as descriptive of the bird's beak. Since the Bible says "the heron according to its kind" ("in its several species," *AT*), the Hebrew name may well include the different varieties to be found within the heron family (scientifically designated Ardeidae), such as the true heron, the egret, and the bittern. All these birds have long sharp bills, or beaks, and some are noted for the unusual raucous sound they make when disturbed or excited.

The birds of the heron family are basically waders, frequenting marshes, swamps, inland streams, and lakes. They have long slender necks and long, bare, extraordinarily thin legs, and long toes including a large hind toe. With a stately stride they wade along, searching for frogs, small crabs, or small reptiles; or else they stand motionless, patiently waiting for small fish to come within their range, whereupon a lightning thrust of the bird's long neck spears the fish with its pointed beak. Their large wings carry them in a rather slow majestic flight, legs stretched out behind but with the long neck doubled back so that the head rests between the shoulders, thus differing from the crane and the ibis that fly with their neck as well as their legs outstretched.

In Palestine there are several varieties of herons: the common or gray heron (*Ardea cinerea*), the goliath heron (*Ardea goliath*), and the purple heron (*Ardea purpurea*). They measure up to 1.5 m (59 in.) in length and are found around the Sea of Galilee, along the banks of the Jordan and the Kishon, in marshy regions, and along the seacoast.

Heron; a bird not to be eaten by the Israelites, according to the Law

Egrets are among the most graceful and beautiful birds of the heron family, often having pure white plumage. With a length of 50-90 cm (20-35 in.), egrets are common in Palestine. The cattle egret, or buff-backed heron (*Bubulcus ibis*), is frequently found in association with grazing cattle, feeding on available insects.

The bittern is a stouter, browner variety of heron, also found in Palestine in marshy regions. With a length of about 75 cm (30 in.), the Eurasian bittern (*Botaurus stellaris*) characteristically has plumage streaked with black, buff, and white; the underparts are a pale buff color with brown stripes, and the legs are yellowish green. This color combination harmonizes exactly with the marsh grass it inhabits, and when in danger, the bird stands motionless with neck and bill pointed upward. This, together with the vertical stripes, causes it to blend in perfectly with its surroundings in effective camouflage. Another variety found in Palestine is the little bittern (*Ixobrychus minutus*). Bitterns are also noted for the deep booming or pumping sound they make by expelling air from their gullets, the head and neck being violently contorted at the same time.

HESED (He′sed) [shortened form of Hasadiah, meaning "Loving-Kindness of Jah; Jah Is Loving-Kindness"]. An Israelite whose son was one of Solomon's 12 deputies, each being responsible to provide the king and his household with food one month in the year.—1Ki 4:7, 10.

HESHBON (Hesh′bon). A place identified with modern Hisban, a ruined city situated about 20 km (12 mi) SW of Rabbah (′Amman). It lies nearly midway between the Arnon and the Jabbok. (Jos 12:2) As yet no archaeological remains dating to the Canaanite period have been found there. A large ruined reservoir is located a short distance to the E of Heshbon, and about 180 m (600 ft) below the city there is a fountain that has formed a succession of pools.—Compare Ca 7:4; see BATH-RABBIM.

The Amorite king Sihon captured Heshbon from the Moabites and made it his royal residence. The Moabite defeat even provided the basis for a taunting proverbial saying, either of Amorite or Israelite origin. In the event this saying stemmed from the Amorites, it mocked the Moabites and memorialized King Sihon's victory. But, if originating with the Israelites, it signified that just as Sihon had wrested Heshbon from the Moabites, so Israel would take this and other cities from the Amorites. The taunt would then be that the victory of Sihon paved the way for the Israelites to take possession of land to which they would otherwise not have been entitled.—Nu 21:26-30; De 2:9.

When King Sihon refused to allow the Israelites under Moses to pass peacefully through his land and instead prepared to battle against them, Jehovah gave his people the victory over Sihon. Amorite cities, undoubtedly including Heshbon, were devoted to destruction. (De 2:26-36; 3:6; 29:7; Jg 11:19-22) Afterward the Reubenites rebuilt Heshbon (Nu 32:37), it being included among the cities that Moses gave to them. (Jos 13:15-17) As a border city between Reuben and Gad, Heshbon later became a part of Gad's territory and is named as one of the four Gadite cities assigned to the Levites.—Jos 21:38, 39; 1Ch 6:77, 80, 81.

At a later period Heshbon evidently came under Moabite control, as is indicated by the fact that both Isaiah and Jeremiah mention it in their pronouncements of doom against Moab. (Isa 15:4; 16:7-9; Jer 48:2, 34, 45) Jeremiah also refers to this city in a pronouncement against Ammon. (Jer 49:1, 3) Some commentators understand this to indicate that Heshbon had by then come into Ammonite hands. Others suggest that this may mean either that Heshbon of Moab would share the same fate as Ai or that a different Heshbon in the territory of Ammon is intended.

According to the Jewish historian Josephus, Heshbon was in the possession of the Jews in the time of Alexander Jannaeus (103-76 B.C.E.). Later, Herod the Great had jurisdiction over the city. —*Jewish Antiquities,* XIII, 395-397 (xv, 4); XV, 294 (viii, 5).

HESHMON (Hesh'mon). A city in the southern part of Judah (Jos 15:21, 27), the location of which is now unknown.

HESHVAN. See CALENDAR.

HETH. The second-listed son of Canaan and great-grandson of Noah through Ham. (Ge 10:1, 6, 15; 1Ch 1:13) Heth was ancestral father of the Hittites (1Ki 10:29; 2Ki 7:6; see HITTITES), one branch of which settled in the hill country of Judah. (Ex 3:8) It was in the vicinity of Hebron that Abraham purchased from Ephron the Hittite the field of Machpelah and the cave therein, as a burial place. (Ge 23:2-20; 25:8-10; 49:32) Of its 14 occurrences, the name Heth appears 10 times in connection with "the sons of Heth." Two of Esau's wives were from among "the daughters of Heth" (also called "the daughters of Canaan"), these wives being a source of grief to his parents. —Ge 26:34, 35; 27:46; 28:1, 6-8.

HETHLON (Heth'lon). A site, the approach to which lay on the northern border of the land of Israel, as seen in Ezekiel's vision. (Eze 47:13, 15; 48:1) Some scholars tentatively identify Hethlon with modern-day Haitla, about 35 km (22 mi) NE of Tripoli, Lebanon.

HEZEKIAH (Hez·e·ki'ah) [Jehovah Strengthens].

1. King of Judah, 745-717 B.C.E. He apparently became king when his father Ahaz died, in "the third year of Hoshea" king of Israel (perhaps meaning Hoshea's third year as tributary king under Tiglath-pileser III), counting his reign officially from Nisan of the following year (745 B.C.E.). (2Ki 18:1) Prophets contemporary with Hezekiah's reign were Isaiah, Hosea, and Micah. (Isa 1:1; Ho 1:1; Mic 1:1) Hezekiah was outstanding as a king who "kept sticking to Jehovah," doing what was right in Jehovah's eyes and following his commandments. From the beginning of his reign he proved himself zealous for the promotion of true worship, not only in Judah but in all the territory of Israel. In following the ways of Jehovah as David his forefather had done, it could be said of Hezekiah that "after him there proved to be no one like him among all the kings of Judah, even those who had happened to be prior to him." For this "Jehovah proved to be with him."—2Ki 18:3-7.

Literary Contributions. Hezekiah is also known for his interest in compiling some of the Proverbs of Solomon, as the introduction to the section now known as chapters 25 to 29 of Proverbs reads: "These also are the proverbs of Solomon that the men of Hezekiah the king of Judah transcribed." (Pr 25:1) He wrote the song of thanksgiving recorded at Isaiah 38:10-20 after Jehovah healed him of his deadly sickness. In it he mentions "my string selections." (Vs 20) Some believe that Hezekiah wrote Psalm 119. If correct, it would seem that this psalm was written when Hezekiah was a prince, not yet the king.

Situation at Hezekiah's Accession. When Hezekiah came to the throne the kingdom of Judah was under God's disfavor, for Hezekiah's father Ahaz had committed many detestable acts before Jehovah and had let the worship of false gods run unrestrained in Judah. Therefore, Jehovah had permitted the land to suffer at the hands of its enemies, particularly the second world power, Assyria. Ahaz had stripped the temple and the palace to provide a bribe for the king of Assyria. Worse yet, he had cut up the utensils of the temple, closed its doors, and made altars for himself "at every corner in Jerusalem," sacrificing to other gods. Ahaz, by an alliance, had placed his kingdom under the protection of the king of Assyria during his reign. (2Ki 16:7-9; 2Ch 28:24, 25) But Hezekiah, early in his reign, "proceeded to rebel against the king of Assyria."—2Ki 18:7.

At Hezekiah's accession to the throne of Judah, the northern ten-tribe kingdom of Israel was in even worse condition. For Israel's gross sins Jehovah had allowed them to come into dire straits, becoming tributary to Assyria, and it would not be long until Assyria would swallow up Israel and carry her people into exile.—2Ki 17:5-23.

His Zeal for True Worship. Hezekiah demonstrated his zeal for Jehovah's worship immediately on taking the throne at 25 years of age. His first act was to reopen and repair the temple. Then, calling together the priests and Levites, he said to them: "It is close to my heart to conclude a covenant with Jehovah the God of Israel." This was a covenant of faithfulness, as though the Law covenant, still in effect but neglected, was inaugurated anew in Judah. With great energy he proceeded to organize the Levites in their services, and he reestablished the arrangements for musical instruments and singing of praises. It was Nisan, the month for Passover to be celebrated, but the temple and the priests and Levites were unclean. By the 16th day of Nisan, the temple was cleansed and its utensils restored. Then a special atonement had to be made for all Israel. First, the princes brought sacrifices, sin offerings for the kingdom, the sanctuary, and the people, followed by thousands of burnt offerings by the people.—2Ch 29:1-36.

Since the people's uncleanness prevented their observance of the Passover at the regular time, Hezekiah took advantage of the law that allowed those who are unclean to celebrate the Passover one month later. He called not only Judah but also Israel by means of letters sent by runners throughout the land from Beer-sheba to Dan. The runners met with derision from many; but individuals, particularly from Asher, Manasseh, and Zebulun, humbled themselves to come, some from Ephraim and Issachar also attending. Besides this, many non-Israelite worshipers of Jehovah were on hand. It was likely a difficult matter for those in the northern kingdom who stood for

true worship to attend. They, like the messengers, would meet opposition and ridicule, inasmuch as the ten-tribe kingdom was in a decadent state, sunk in false worship and harassed by the Assyrian menace.—2Ch 30:1-20; Nu 9:10-13.

After the Passover, the Festival of Unfermented Cakes was held for seven days with such attendant joy that the entire congregation decided to extend it seven days longer. Even in such perilous times Jehovah's blessing prevailed so that "there came to be great rejoicing in Jerusalem, for from the days of Solomon the son of David the king of Israel there was none like this in Jerusalem."—2Ch 30:21-27.

That this was a real restoration and revival of true worship and not merely a transient emotional gathering is seen in what followed. Before their return home the celebrants went out and destroyed the sacred pillars, pulled down the high places and the altars, and cut down the sacred poles throughout Judah and Benjamin and even in Ephraim and Manasseh. (2Ch 31:1) Hezekiah set the example by crushing to pieces the copper serpent that Moses had made, because the people had made it an idol, burning sacrificial smoke to it. (2Ki 18:4) After the great festival Hezekiah ensured the continuation of true worship by organizing the priestly divisions and arranging for the support of the temple services; he admonished obedience to the Law as to the tithes and firstfruit contributions to the Levites and priests, to which the people responded wholeheartedly.—2Ch 31:2-12.

Assyrian Pressure Builds Up. During those strenuous times, when Assyria was sweeping everything in its path, Hezekiah trusted in Jehovah the God of Israel. He rebelled against the king of Assyria and struck down the Philistine cities, which had evidently become allied with Assyria. —2Ki 18:7, 8.

It was in Hezekiah's fourth year (742 B.C.E.) that Shalmaneser the king of Assyria began the siege of Samaria. In Hezekiah's sixth year (740 B.C.E.) Samaria was taken. The people of the ten-tribe kingdom were deported, and the Assyrians moved in others to occupy the land. (2Ki 18:9-12) This left the kingdom of Judah, representing God's theocratic government and true worship, like a small island surrounded by hostile enemies.

Sennacherib, the son of Sargon II, was ambitious to add the conquest of Jerusalem to his trophies of war, especially in view of the fact that Hezekiah had withdrawn from the alliance that had been entered into with Assyria by his father King Ahaz. In the 14th year of Hezekiah's reign (732 B.C.E.), Sennacherib "came up against all the fortified cities of Judah and proceeded to seize them." Hezekiah offered to buy Sennacherib off to save the threatened city of Jerusalem, whereupon Sennacherib demanded the enormous sum of 300 silver talents (c. $1,982,000) and 30 gold talents (c. $11,560,000). To pay this amount, Hezekiah was obliged to give all the silver that was found in the temple and the royal treasury, besides the precious metals that Hezekiah himself had caused to be overlaid on the temple doors and posts. This satisfied the king of Assyria, but only temporarily.—2Ki 18:13-16.

Building and Engineering Works. In the face of imminent attack by greedy Sennacherib, Hezekiah displayed wisdom and military strategy. He stopped up all the springs and water sources outside the city of Jerusalem so that, in the event of a siege, the Assyrians would be short on water supplies. He strengthened the city's fortifications and "made missiles in abundance and shields." But his trust was not in this military equipment, for in gathering together the military chieftains and the people, he encouraged them, saying: "Be courageous and strong. Do not be afraid nor be terrified because of the king of Assyria and on account of all the crowd that is with him; for with us there are more than there are with him. With him there is an arm of flesh, but with us there is Jehovah our God to help us and to fight our battles."—2Ch 32:1-8.

One of the outstanding engineering feats of ancient times was the aqueduct of Hezekiah. It ran from the well of Gihon, E of the northern part of the City of David, in a rather irregular course, extending some 533 m (1,749 ft) to the Pool of Siloam in the Tyropoeon Valley below the City of David but within a new wall added to the southern part of the city. (2Ki 20:20; 2Ch 32:30) An inscription in ancient Hebrew characters was found by archaeologists on the wall of the narrow tunnel, which had an average height of 1.8 m (6 ft). The inscription reads, in part: "And this was the way in which it was cut through:—While [. . .] (were) still [. . .] axe(s), each man toward his fellow, and while there were still three cubits to be cut through, [there was heard] the voice of a man calling to his fellow, for there was *an overlap* in the rock on the right [and on the left]. And when the tunnel was driven through, the quarrymen hewed (the rock), each man toward his fellow, axe against axe; and the water flowed from

the spring toward the reservoir for 1,200 cubits, and the height of the rock above the head(s) of the quarrymen was 100 cubits." (*Ancient Near Eastern Texts,* edited by J. B. Pritchard, 1974, p. 321) So the tunnel was cut through the rock from both ends, meeting in the middle—a real engineering accomplishment.

Sennacherib's Failure at Jerusalem. Fulfilling Hezekiah's expectations, Sennacherib determined to attack Jerusalem. While Sennacherib was with his army besieging the strongly fortified city of Lachish, he sent a part of his army along with a deputation of military chiefs to demand capitulation of Jerusalem. The spokesman for the group was Rabshakeh (not the man's name, but his military title), who spoke Hebrew fluently. He loudly ridiculed Hezekiah and taunted Jehovah, boasting that Jehovah could no more deliver Jerusalem than the gods of the other nations had been able to save the lands of their worshipers from the king of Assyria.—2Ki 18:13-35; 2Ch 32:9-15; Isa 36:2-20.

Hezekiah was greatly distressed but continued to trust in Jehovah and appealed to him at the temple, also sending some of the head ones of the people to the prophet Isaiah. Isaiah's reply, from Jehovah, was that Sennacherib would hear a report and would return to his own land, where eventually he would be slain. (2Ki 19:1-7; Isa 37:1-7) At this time Sennacherib had pulled away from Lachish to Libnah, where he heard that Tirhakah the king of Ethiopia had come out to fight against him. Nevertheless, Sennacherib sent letters by messenger to Hezekiah, continuing his threats and taunting Jehovah the God of Israel. On receipt of the highly reproachful letters, Hezekiah spread them before Jehovah, who again answered through Isaiah, taunting Sennacherib in return and assuring that the Assyrians would not enter Jerusalem. Jehovah said: "I shall certainly defend this city to save it for my own sake and for the sake of David my servant."—2Ki 19:8-34; Isa 37:8-35.

During the night Jehovah sent his angel, who destroyed 185,000 of the cream of Sennacherib's troops, "every valiant, mighty man and leader and chief in the camp of the king of Assyria, so that he went back with shame of face to his own land." Thus Sennacherib's threat to Jerusalem was effectually removed. Later "it came about that as he was bowing down at the house of Nisroch his god, Adrammelech and Sharezer, his own sons, struck him down with the sword." —2Ch 32:21; Isa 37:36-38.

Inscriptions have been discovered describing Sennacherib's defeat of the Ethiopian forces. These say: "As to Hezekiah, the Jew, he did not submit to my yoke, I laid siege to 46 of his strong cities . . . and conquered (them) . . . Himself I made a prisoner in Jerusalem, his royal residence, like a bird in a cage." (*Ancient Near Eastern Texts*, p. 288) He does not claim to have captured the city. This supports the Bible account of Hezekiah's revolt against Assyria and Sennacherib's failure to take Jerusalem. In the custom of the inscriptions of the pagan kings, to exalt themselves, Sennacherib in this inscription exaggerates the amount of silver paid by Hezekiah, as 800 talents, in contrast with the Bible's 300.

Miraculous Extension of Hezekiah's Life. Around the time of Sennacherib's threats against Jerusalem, Hezekiah was afflicted with a malignant boil. He was instructed by the prophet Isaiah to arrange his affairs in preparation for death. At that time Hezekiah did not as yet have a son, and it therefore appeared that the royal Davidic line was in danger of being broken. Hezekiah prayed to Jehovah fervently, with tears, whereupon Jehovah sent Isaiah back to inform Hezekiah that he would have 15 years added to his life. A miraculous sign was given, the shadow of the sun being caused to move ten steps backward on "the stairs of Ahaz." (See SUN.) In the third year after that, Hezekiah had a son called Manasseh, who later succeeded him on the throne.—2Ki 20:1-11, 21; 21:1; Isa 38:1-8, 21.

Hezekiah's Mistake and Repentance. The Scripture record states that "according to the benefit rendered him Hezekiah made no return, for his heart became haughty and there came to be indignation against him and against Judah and Jerusalem." (2Ch 32:25) The Bible does not say whether or not this haughtiness was connected with his unwise act in showing the entire treasure of his house and all his dominion to the messengers of the Babylonian king Berodach-baladan (Merodach-baladan) who were sent to Hezekiah after he recovered from his illness. Hezekiah may have displayed all this wealth to impress the king of Babylon as a possible ally against the king of Assyria. This, of course, could tend to excite the greed of the Babylonians. The prophet Isaiah was against any alliance with or dependence on God's age-old enemy Babylon. When Isaiah heard how Hezekiah had treated the Babylonian messengers, he uttered the inspired prophecy from Jehovah that the Babylonians in time would carry away everything to Babylon, including some of Hezekiah's descendants. Heze-

kiah, however, humbled himself and God kindly allowed that the calamity would not come in his days.—2Ki 20:12-19; 2Ch 32:26, 31; Isa 39:1-8.

In the days of the prophet Jeremiah, some of the heads of the people in Jerusalem spoke favorably of Hezekiah because of his giving attention to Micah of Moresheth, the prophet of Jehovah.—Jer 26:17-19.

2. An ancestor of the prophet Zephaniah, possibly King Hezekiah.—Zep 1:1.

3. A man of Israel whose descendants returned with Zerubbabel from the Babylonian exile. He was probably not the same person as King Hezekiah. (Ezr 2:1, 2, 16; Ne 7:6, 7, 21) It may have been a descendant of this Hezekiah who was one of the headmen of the people attesting by seal the "trustworthy arrangement" in Nehemiah's day.—Ne 9:38; 10:1, 14, 17.

HEZION (He′zi·on). Grandfather of the first King Ben-hadad of Syria mentioned in the Bible. (1Ki 15:18) Hezion is thought by some to be the person called Rezon at 1 Kings 11:23.

HEZIR (He′zir) [Pig; Boar].

1. The priest whose paternal house was chosen by lot for the 17th of the 24 priestly service divisions organized toward the end of David's reign.—1Ch 24:1, 3, 5-7, 15.

2. One of "the heads of the people" whose descendant, if not he himself, in Nehemiah's time supported the resolution to be true to Jehovah.—Ne 9:38; 10:1, 14, 20.

HEZRO (Hez′ro). A Carmelite; one of the mighty men of David's military forces.—2Sa 23:8, 35; 1Ch 11:26, 37.

HEZRON (Hez′ron) [Courtyard; Settlement].

1. Son of Reuben and ancestral head of "the Hezronites."—Ge 46:9; Ex 6:14; Nu 26:4-6; 1Ch 5:3.

2. Son of Perez and family head of the Judean "Hezronites"; ancestor of King David and of Jesus Christ. (Ge 46:12; Nu 26:20, 21; Ru 4:18-22; Mt 1:3; Lu 3:33) At the age of 60, Hezron took the daughter of Machir as wife and by her became father to Segub. (1Ch 2:21) His sons Jerahmeel, Ram, and Chelubai (Caleb) apparently were born earlier.—1Ch 2:9, 18, 25.

According to the reading of 1 Chronicles 2:24 in the Masoretic text, Hezron died at Caleb-ephrathah, and after this his widow Abijah bore Ashhur, the father of Tekoa. However, some scholars believe that the Masoretic text does not preserve the original reading, since Hezron is listed among the 70 "souls of the house of Jacob who came into Egypt" and so must have died in that land (Ge 46:12, 26, 27), and it seems to them unlikely that a place in Egypt bore the Hebrew name Caleb-ephrathah. Hence, many translators have emended 1 Chronicles 2:24 to correspond more to the readings of the Greek *Septuagint* and the Latin *Vulgate*. *The Jerusalem Bible* renders this text: "After Hezron's death, Caleb married Ephrathah, wife of Hezron his father, who bore him Ashhur, father of Tekoa." The translation by J. B. Rotherham reads: "And after the death of Hezron Caleb entered Ephrathah, and the wife of Hezron was Abiah who bare him Ashhur father of Tekoa." So, according to these alterations, "Ashhur" is either the "son" of Hezron by Abiah (Abijah) or the "son" of Caleb by Ephrathah.

3. A city on the southern border of Judah situated between Kadesh-barnea and Addar. (Jos 15:1-3) However, the parallel account at Numbers 34:4 does not list Hezron and Addar separately but reads "Hazar-addar," implying that Hezron, or Hazar, likely was near Addar, if not actually the same place.—See ADDAR No. 2.

HEZRONITES (Hez'ron·ites) [Of (Belonging to) Hezron]. This designation is applied both to the family descended from Reuben's son Hezron (Ge 46:9; Nu 26:4-6) and to the one descended from Judah's grandson Hezron.—Ge 46:12; Nu 26:21.

HIDDAI (Hid'dai). One of the mighty men in David's army. Hiddai was from the torrent valleys of Gaash in the mountainous region of Ephraim. (2Sa 23:8, 30; Jos 24:30) His name is given as Hurai at 1 Chronicles 11:32.

HIDDEKEL (Hid'de·kel). One of the four rivers branching off from the river issuing out of Eden. (Ge 2:10-14) The Hiddekel was known in Old Persian as the *Tigra,* from which comes the Greek name for the Tigris River. In Arabic it is known as the Shatt Dijla. It is called by some the twin river of the Euphrates, and together with this river, it waters the plains of Mesopotamia.

It was on the banks of the Tigris (Hiddekel) River that Daniel received the vision concerning the power struggle to be waged by "the king of the north" and "the king of the south." (Da 10:4, 5; 11:5, 6) After entering the Mesopotamian plains, the Tigris passes by the sites of many ancient cities. Opposite modern Mosul the ruins of ancient Nineveh lie on the river's E bank. On the same side, farther S, is the site of Calah, and below it, on the W bank, is found ancient Asshur. A short distance below Baghdad, on the W bank, are the ruins of Seleucia, ancient capital of the Seleucid dynasty of rulers.

The Tigris has its sources in central Armenia (the eastern part of modern Turkey). Of the Tigris' headstreams, the western is the more distant, rising on the southern slopes of the Anti-Taurus Mountains about 25 km (15 mi) SE of the city of Elazig and just a few miles from the source of the Euphrates River. It is thus evident that these two rivers could easily have had a single source before the global Flood produced topographical changes in the earth's surface. For the first 240 km (150 mi) the western source flows SE and is joined by other shorter eastern sources. Then, at a point south of the western end of Lake Van, the river takes a more southerly course. It passes through a deep gorge before finally emerging from the mountains onto the upper part of the Mesopotamian plain. From there to its junction with the Euphrates River, the Tigris is fed from the E by four tributary streams: the Great Zab, the Little Zab, the 'Adhaim, and the Diyala.

It is generally believed that, anciently, the Tigris and Euphrates had separate entrances into the sea, but that over the centuries the accumulation of silt has filled in the head of the gulf so that now the rivers unite. After their junction they form the wide stream called the Shatt-al-Arab, which flows some 160 km (100 mi) before emptying into the Persian Gulf.

The full length of the Tigris covers some 1,850 km (1,150 mi). It is a wide stream, at some points having a width of 366 m (400 yd), but is generally shallow, and above Baghdad it is navigable only by boats of shallow draft. A much swifter river than the Euphrates, the Tigris is only about two thirds the length of its "twin" and of lesser importance commercially.

HIEL (Hi'el) [shortened form of Ahiel, meaning "My Brother Is God; Brother of God"]. A Bethelite who rebuilt Jericho during Ahab's reign in the tenth century B.C.E. In fulfillment of the oath Joshua had pronounced at the destruction of Jericho over 500 years earlier, Hiel laid the foundation of the city at the forfeit of Abiram his firstborn and put up its doors at the forfeit of Segub his youngest child.—Jos 6:26; 1Ki 16: 33, 34.

HIERAPOLIS (Hi·e·rap'o·lis) [Holy City]. A city in the province of Asia. It was located on the northern edge of the Lycus Valley of Asia Minor, about 10 km (6 mi) N of Laodicea at modern Pamukkale, Turkey.

Although the apostle Paul apparently never visited Hierapolis, the effects of his long work at Ephesus (from the winter of 52/53 C.E. until after Pentecost in 55 C.E. [1Co 16:8]) radiated over 'all the district of Asia.' (Ac 19:1, 10) Christianity appears to have actually reached Hierapolis through the 'efforts' of Epaphras.—Col 4:12, 13.

While the city lacked political importance, it became prosperous in the peaceful Roman period as a center of devotion to Cybele. Her worship there was enhanced by two natural phenomena, mineral springs and the Plutonium, or Charonion, a deep, narrow chasm that emitted deadly fumes.

HIGGAION (Hig·ga′ion). A transliteration of the Hebrew expression *hig·ga·yohn′*, understood by lexicographers to denote a technical term of musical direction. (Ps 9:16) On the basis of the context in its appearances in the Hebrew text, it has been variously rendered as "soft utterance," "meditation," "thoughts," "melody," "sweet music," "resounding music," and "muttering(s)." (Ps 19:14; 92:3; La 3:62, *AT, Mo, NW, Ro, RS, Yg*) At Psalm 9:16, Higgaion may signify either a solemn, deep-toned harp interlude or a solemn pause conducive to meditation.

HIGH PLACES. The Hebrew word generally translated "high places" (*ba·mohth′*) is usually associated with worship, but it can also simply refer to elevations, hills, and mountains (2Sa 1:19, 25 [compare 1Sa 31:8]; Am 4:13; Mic 1:3], "high waves of the sea" (literally, high places of the sea) (Job 9:8), and heights, or "high places of the clouds" (Isa 14:14).

Evidently the expressions 'to ride upon earth's high places' and 'to tread upon the high places' are to be understood as signifying victorious subjugation of a land, for one controlling all the high places, that is, the hills and mountains of a country, is, in effect, the lord of the land.—De 32:13; 33:29.

Centers of False Worship. High places, or the sites or shrines where idolatry was engaged in, were to be found not only on hills and mountains but also in the valleys, in streambeds, in cities, and under the trees. (De 12:2; 1Ki 14:23; 2Ki 17:29; Eze 6:3) They were equipped with altars for sacrifice, incense stands, sacred poles, sacred pillars, and graven images. (Le 26:30; Nu 33:52; De 12:2, 3; Eze 6:6) At many of the high places, male and female prostitutes served. (1Ki 14:23, 24; Ho 4:13, 14) Frequently the high places

were the scenes of licentious rites, including ceremonial prostitution and child sacrifice.—Isa 57:5; Jer 7:31; 19:5.

There were also houses, or sanctuaries, of the high places where priests officiated and where the images of the deities were kept. (1Ki 12:31; 13:32; 2Ki 17:29, 32; 23:19, 20; Isa 16:12) Thus, the designation "high place" may at times refer to such a sanctuary rather than to an elevated site for worship. This is suggested by Ezekiel's reference to high places of varied colors. (Eze 16:16) Perhaps these high places were tentlike sanctuaries.

Before entering the Promised Land, the Israelites were commanded to destroy the sacred high places of the Canaanites and all the appendages of false worship associated therewith. (Nu 33:51, 52) But the Israelites failed to do this, and after the death of Joshua and the older generation, wholesale apostasy set in.—Jg 2:2, 8-13; Ps 78:58.

Not All High Places Condemned. According to Jehovah's law, sacrifices were to be offered only at the place he designated. In the days of Joshua, the Israelites recognized that the unauthorized building of an altar for burnt offering was, in effect, rebellion against Jehovah. (De 12:1-14; Jos 22:29) However, there are indications that, after the sacred Ark was removed from the tabernacle (1Sa 4:10, 11; 6:1, 10-14; 7: 1, 2), approved sacrificing at places other than the tent of meeting was done, not only under special circumstances but, in some cases, also on somewhat of a regular basis. (1Sa 7:7-9; 10:8; 11:14, 15; 16:4, 5; 1Ki 3:3; 1Ch 21:26-30) On the high place at an unnamed city in the land of Zuph, a structure had been erected where, it seems, the communion sacrifices could be eaten. The dining hall there accommodated about 30 men, if not more. Even the girls in the city were familiar with the sacrificial procedure there. (1Sa 9:5, 11-13, 22-25) It may also have been a practice for families to have a yearly sacrifice, not at the tabernacle, but in their own cities.—1Sa 20:6, 29.

The sacrificing on high places was excused on the ground that no house had been built to the name of Jehovah. Hence, Solomon had to sacrifice on the great high place at Gibeon, where the tabernacle was located at the time.—1Ki 3:2-4; 1Ch 16:37-40, 43; 21:29; 2Ch 1:3, 13; see ALTAR; OFFERINGS.

Solomon's Reign and Ten-Tribe Kingdom. Toward the latter part of his reign, King Solomon built high places for the false gods worshiped by his foreign wives. This contributed to the

Israelites' abandoning the true worship of Jehovah and serving false gods. Therefore, Jehovah, by means of his prophet Ahijah, indicated that ten tribes would be ripped away from the son of Solomon and that Jeroboam would rule over these.—1Ki 11:7, 8, 30-35.

Although Jeroboam had Jehovah's assurance that his kingship would be secure if he continued serving God in faithfulness, as soon as he became king he feared that the Israelites would revolt if they continued going up to Jerusalem for worship. For this reason he instituted calf worship at Dan and Bethel and there built high places. (1Ki 11:38; 12:26-33) As long as the ten-tribe kingdom existed, idolatrous worship continued at high places. "The sons of Israel went searching into the things that were not right toward Jehovah their God and kept building themselves high places in all their cities, from the tower of the watchmen clear to the fortified city."—2Ki 17:9.

Under inspiration, the prophet Amos foretold that the "high places of Isaac" would become desolated. The "high places of Isaac" evidently refer to the sacred high places where the Israelites of the ten-tribe kingdom, descendants of Isaac through Jacob, or Israel, practiced apostate worship. This is also indicated by the fact that the expression "high places of Isaac" runs parallel with 'sanctuaries of Israel.'—Am 7:9; see also Ho 10:2-10.

After the king of Assyria took the ten-tribe kingdom into exile, the high places continued to exist for a time, since the foreign peoples who were moved into the territory of Samaria by the king of Assyria continued employing the high places in their worship. (2Ki 17:24, 29-32) About 100 years after this, faithful King Josiah of Judah pulled down the altar and the high place at Bethel and desecrated the altar by burning human bones upon it. He also removed all the houses of the high places in the cities of Samaria, sacrificed (killed) all the priests of the high places, and burned human bones upon the altars. (2Ki 23:15-20) This fulfilled a prophecy uttered over 300 years earlier by an unnamed "man of God." —1Ki 13:1, 2.

In the Kingdom of Judah. King Rehoboam followed the apostasy of his father Solomon, and his subjects continued building high places and practicing licentious rites. (1Ki 14:21-24) Rehoboam's son and successor Abijam "went on walking in all the sins of his father."—1Ki 15:1-3.

Asa, who succeeded Abijam to the throne, served Jehovah in faithfulness and put forth decisive efforts to rid the kingdom of all appendages of false worship. (1Ki 15:11-13) "He removed from all the cities of Judah the high places and the incense stands." (2Ch 14:2-5) However, 1 Kings 15:14 and 2 Chronicles 15:17 apparently indicate that the high places were not removed. It may be that, although Asa removed the high places for worship of false gods, he left those at which the people worshiped Jehovah. Or, perhaps, high places cropped up again toward the end of his reign and were thereby present for his successor Jehoshaphat to destroy. But even during Jehosh-

High place at Gezer.
Sacred pillars were erected here

aphat's reign the high places did not fully disappear. (1Ki 22:42, 43; 2Ch 17:5, 6; 20:31-33) So entrenched was Judah's worship at high places that the reforms of both Asa and Jehoshaphat could not remove all of them permanently.

King Jehoram, unlike his father Jehoshaphat, made high places on the mountains of Judah. (2Ch 21:1, 11) The religious state of the kingdom remained in a degraded condition throughout the reigns of Ahaziah and the usurper Athaliah, the daughter of Ahab and Jezebel. (2Ki 8:25-27; 2Ch 22:2-4, 10) Although definite reforms to restore true worship were undertaken at the beginning of Jehoash's reign, apostasy set in once again after the death of High Priest Jehoiada, and the high places did not disappear. (2Ki 12:2, 3; 2Ch 24:17, 18) The high places continued to exist as centers of unlawful worship throughout the reigns of Kings Amaziah, Azariah (Uzziah), and Jotham. (2Ki 14:1-4; 15:1-4, 32-35) The next Judean king, Ahaz, not only sacrificed and made sacrificial smoke on the high places but even made his own son pass through the fire. (2Ki 16:2-4) He also made additional "high places for making sacrificial smoke to other gods."—2Ch 28:25.

During the days of King Hezekiah, another extensive purge was undertaken to remove the high places. (2Ki 18:1-4, 22; 2Ch 32:12) After the great Passover celebration held during his reign, the Israelites went throughout the cities of Judah and Benjamin and even in Ephraim and Manasseh breaking up the sacred pillars, cutting down the sacred poles, and pulling down the high places and the altars.—2Ch 30:21, 23; 31:1.

This restoration of true worship was short lived. Hezekiah's son Manasseh rebuilt the very high places that his father had destroyed. (2Ki 21:1-3; 2Ch 33:1-3) Manasseh caused the people to act even more wickedly than the pagan Canaanites whom Jehovah had annihilated. Hence, the Almighty determined to bring calamity upon Judah and Jerusalem. (2Ki 21:9-12) After being taken captive by the king of Assyria and brought to Babylon, Manasseh repented. Upon returning to Jerusalem, he took steps to remove the appendages of false worship. But the people continued offering sacrifices upon the unauthorized high places, not to false gods, however, but to Jehovah. (2Ch 33:10-17) Manasseh's successor, his son Amon, did not continue the reforms started by his father but made guiltiness increase. —2Ch 33:21-24.

Josiah, who succeeded Amon, distinguished himself by doing what was right in Jehovah's eyes and adhering to the law of Moses. He put out of business the foreign-god priests, who rendered up sacrificial smoke on the high places. He pulled down the high places not only throughout Judah but also in the cities of Samaria. The sites used for false worship were desecrated so that they could not be used to offend Jehovah.—2Ki 23:4-20; 2Ch 34:1-7.

The account of Josiah's making the high places that had been built by Solomon unfit for worship tends to confirm the conclusion that, although previous kings had torn down the high places, there was a revival of these. It seems only logical that faithful Kings Asa and Jehoshaphat had torn down these high places of false worship that dated from the reign of Solomon.

Although no further mention is made of high places in the Kings and Chronicles accounts after Josiah's thorough purge of all vestiges of false worship, the last four kings of Judah, namely, Jehoahaz, Jehoiakim, Jehoiachin, and Zedekiah, are reported as doing what was bad in Jehovah's eyes. (2Ki 23:31, 32, 36, 37; 24:8, 9, 18, 19) Apostate worship at high places was resumed by the Israelites. Hence, Jehovah, through his prophet Ezekiel, warned the nation of the dire consequences to come upon them: "I am bringing upon you a sword, and I shall certainly destroy your high places. And your altars must be made desolate and your incense stands must be broken, and I will cause your slain ones to fall before your dungy idols."—Eze 6:3, 4.

It is noteworthy that there is no record of any worship at high places after the return from Babylonian exile. As had been foretold, the faithful Jewish remnant had profited from the bitter experience and had come to know Jehovah.—Eze 6:9, 10.

HIGH PRIEST. The principal one who represented the people before God. He was also charged with supervision of all the other priests.

The Bible uses various terms to designate the high priest, namely, "the high [literally, great] priest" (Nu 35:25, 28; Jos 20:6, ftn), "the priest, the anointed one" (Le 4:3), "the chief [or, high; literally, head] priest" (2Ch 26:20, ftn; 2Ki 25:18, ftn), "the head" (2Ch 24:6), or simply, "the priest" (2Ch 26:17). In the latter case the context often makes clear that the high priest is meant. In the Christian Greek Scriptures, "chief priests" is evidently used to denote the principal men of the priesthood, which might include any ex-high priests who had been deposed and possibly, in

addition, the heads of the 24 priestly divisions.
—Mt 2:4; Mr 8:31.

The appointment of Aaron, Israel's first high priest, was from God. (Heb 5:4) The high priesthood of Israel was inaugurated in Aaron and passed down from father to oldest son, unless that son died or was disqualified, as in the case of Aaron's two oldest sons, who sinned against Jehovah and died. (Le 10:1, 2) King Solomon deposed a high priest in fulfillment of divine prophecy and put another qualified man of the line of Aaron in his place. (1Ki 2:26, 27, 35) Later on, when the nation was under Gentile rule, those Gentile rulers removed and appointed high priests according to their will. It seems, nonetheless, that the line of Aaron was quite well adhered to throughout the entire history of the nation down till Jerusalem's destruction in 70 C.E., although there may have been exceptions, such as Menelaus, also called Onias (*Jewish Antiquities*, XII, 238, 239 [v, 1]), whom 2 Maccabees 3:4, 5 and 4:23 indicates was a Benjamite.

Qualifications and Requirements for Office.
In harmony with the dignity of the office, the high priest's closeness to Jehovah in representing the nation before Him, and also the typical significance of the office, the requirements were rigid.

A list of disqualifying physical blemishes for all priests is set forth at Leviticus 21:16-23. Additional restrictions were placed on the high priest: He was to marry none other than a virgin of Israel; he was not to marry a widow. (Le 21:13-15) Furthermore, he was not allowed to defile himself for the dead, that is, he could not touch any human corpse, even that of his father or his mother, because that would make him unclean. He was neither to let his hair go ungroomed nor tear his garments for the dead.—Le 21:10-12.

The Bible does not specifically state the age of eligibility for high priest. While it gives a retirement age of 50 years for Levites, it does not mention any retirement for priests, and its record indicates that the high priest's appointment was for his lifetime. (Nu 8:24, 25) Aaron was 83 years old when he went with Moses before Pharaoh. His anointing as high priest apparently took place in the following year. (Ex 7:7) He was 123 years of age at the time of his death. During all this time he served, with no retirement. (Nu 20:28; 33:39) The provision of the cities of refuge takes note of the lifetime tenure of the high priest, in requiring that the unintentional manslayer remain in the city until the death of the high priest.—Nu 35:25.

Installation. Some indication of the office Jehovah had in mind for Aaron is seen in privileges given him soon after the Exodus from Egypt. In the wilderness on the way to Sinai, Aaron was the one commanded to take a jar of manna and to deposit it before the Testimony as something to be kept. This was before the tent of meeting or the ark of the covenant was yet in existence. (Ex 16:33, 34, ftn) Later, Aaron came to be the one in full charge of the sacred tent and its Ark. Aaron and two of his sons, with 70 of the older men of Israel, were specifically named as privileged to approach Mount Horeb, where they saw a vision of God.—Ex 24:1-11.

But Jehovah made his first actual statement of his purpose to separate Aaron and his sons for the priesthood when giving Moses instructions for making the priestly garments. (Ex 28) After these instructions were given, God outlined to Moses the procedure for installing the priesthood and then definitely made it known: "The priesthood must become theirs as a statute to time indefinite."—Ex 29:9.

In keeping with Jehovah's majesty and cleanness, Aaron and his sons could not perform priestly duties until they were sanctified and empowered by the installation service. (Ex 29) Moses, as mediator of the Law covenant, performed the installation. A sanctification ceremony, occupying the seven days of Nisan 1 to 7, 1512 B.C.E., saw the priesthood fully installed, their hands filled with power to act as priests. (Le 8) The next day, Nisan 8, an initial atonement service was performed for the nation (very much like the regular Day of Atonement services that were decreed to be celebrated annually on Tishri 10; this first performance of the priesthood is described in Leviticus 9). It was appropriate and necessary, for the people of Israel were in need of cleansing from their sins, including their recent transgression in connection with the golden calf. —Ex 32.

In installing the high priest, one of the significant acts Moses had to perform was the anointing of Aaron by pouring upon Aaron's head the sacred anointing oil specially compounded according to God's directions. (Le 8:1, 2, 12; Ex 30:22-25, 30-33; Ps 133:2) The later high priests, successors of Aaron, are spoken of as "anointed." While the Bible does not record an instance of their actual anointing with literal oil, it does set forth this law: "And the holy garments that are Aaron's will serve for his sons after him to anoint them in them and to fill their hand with power in

Garments of Israel's high priest

special garments of glory and beauty on certain occasions. Exodus chapters 28 and 39 describe both the design and the making of these garments under the direction of Moses as commanded by God. The innermost garment (except for the *linen drawers* reaching "from the hips and to the thighs," worn by all the priests "to cover the naked flesh"; Ex 28:42) was the *robe* (Heb., *kutto'neth*), made of fine (probably white) linen of checkerwork weave. This robe apparently had long sleeves and reached down to the ankles. It was likely woven in one piece. A sash of fine twisted linen woven with blue, reddish purple, and coccus scarlet thread went around the body, probably above the waist.—Ex 28:39; 39:29.

The *turban,* evidently different from the headdress of the underpriests, was also of fine linen. (Ex 28:39) Fastened to the forefront of the turban was a *shining plate of pure gold* with the words "Holiness belongs to Jehovah" engraved on it. (Ex 28:36) This plate was called "the holy sign of dedication."—Ex 29:6; 39:30.

Over the linen robe was the *blue sleeveless coat* (Heb., *me'il'*). It was also probably woven in one piece, with a strong border around the opening at the top to prevent tearing. The blue sleeveless coat was put on by slipping it over the head. This garment was shorter than the linen robe, and around its bottom hem were alternate golden bells and pomegranates made of blue, reddish-purple, and scarlet thread. The bells would be heard as the high priest went about his work in the sanctuary.—Ex 28:31-35.

The *ephod,* an apronlike garment made with front and back parts and reaching a short distance below the waist, was worn by all the priests and sometimes by persons not in the priesthood. (1Sa 2:18; 2Sa 6:14) But the ephod of the high priests' apparel of beauty was of special embroidered work. It was of fine twisted linen with wool dyed reddish purple, coccus scarlet material, and gold thread made from gold beaten into thin plates, then cut into threads. (Ex 39:2, 3) Shoulder pieces possibly extended down on each side in the back from the shoulders to the girdle. On top of the shoulder pieces were two gold settings, each with an onyx stone, and each stone having engraved on it six of the names of the sons of Israel (Jacob) in order of their birth. A girdle of the same material bound the ephod around the waist, the girdle being "upon" the ephod, possibly being fastened to the ephod as a part of it.—Ex 28:6-14.

The *breastpiece of judgment* was undoubtedly the most costly and glorious part of the high

them. Seven days the priest who succeeds him from among his sons and who comes into the tent of meeting to minister in the holy place will wear them."—Ex 29:29, 30.

Garments of Office. Besides wearing linen garments similar to those of the underpriests in his usual activities (Le 16:4), the high priest wore

priest's dress. It was made of the same material as the ephod, was rectangular in shape, the length being twice the width, but was doubled so that it formed a square about 22 cm (9 in.) on a side. The doubling made a sort of pocket or pouch. (See BREASTPIECE.) The breastpiece was adorned with 12 precious stones set in gold, each engraved with the name of one of the sons of Israel. These stones, of ruby, topaz, emerald, and other gems, were arranged in four rows. Two chains of gold, wreathed in a ropework pattern, were made on the breastpiece, and rings of gold were set in the corners; the top rings were fastened to the ephod's shoulder pieces by the gold chains. The two bottom rings were attached with blue strings to the shoulder pieces of the ephod, just above the girdle.—Ex 28:15-28.

The *Urim and the Thummim* were put by Moses "in the breastpiece." (Le 8:8) It is not known just what the Urim and the Thummim were. Some scholars consider them to have been lots that were cast or drawn from the breastpiece, by Jehovah's direction, giving, basically, a "yes" or "no" answer to a question. If so, they may have been placed in the "pouch" of the breastpiece. (Ex 28:30, *AT; Mo*) This is perhaps indicated in the text at 1 Samuel 14:41, 42. Yet others hold that the Urim and Thummim had to do with the stones in the breastpiece in some way, but this view seems less likely. Other references to the Urim and the Thummim are found at Numbers 27:21; Deuteronomy 33:8; 1 Samuel 28:6; Ezra 2:63; and Nehemiah 7:65.—See URIM AND THUMMIM.

These beautiful garments were worn by the high priest when he approached Jehovah with an inquiry on an important matter. (Nu 27:21; Jg 1:1; 20:18, 27, 28) Also, on the Day of Atonement, after the sin offerings were completed, he changed from his white linen garments to his garments of glory and beauty. (Le 16:23, 24) He apparently wore the latter on other occasions as well.

The instructions regarding Atonement Day, at Leviticus chapter 16, do not state specifically that the high priest, after putting on his glorious apparel, was to lift his hands and bless the people. However, in the record of the atonement service held on the day after the priesthood's installation, which follows closely the Atonement Day procedure, we read: "Then Aaron raised his hands toward the people and blessed them." (Le 9:22) Jehovah had shown what the blessing should be when he commanded Moses: "Speak to Aaron and his sons, saying, 'This is the way you should bless the sons of Israel, saying to them: "May Jehovah bless you and keep you. May Jehovah make his face shine toward you, and may he favor you. May Jehovah lift up his face toward you and assign peace to you."'"—Nu 6:23-27.

Responsibility and Duties. The dignity, seriousness, and responsibility of the high priest's office is emphasized by the fact that sins on his part could bring guiltiness upon the people. (Le 4:3) The high priest alone was to go into the Most Holy compartment of the sanctuary, and only on one day of the year, the Day of Atonement. (Le 16:2) When he went into the tent of meeting on that day, no other priest was allowed in the tent. (Le 16:17) He officiated over all the Atonement Day services. He made atonement for his house and for the people on special occasions (Le 9:7) and intervened before Jehovah in behalf of the people when Jehovah's anger blazed against them. (Nu 15:25, 26; 16:43-50) When questions of national importance arose, he was the one to approach Jehovah with Urim and Thummim. (Nu 27:21) He officiated at the slaughter and burning of the red cow, the ashes of which were used in the water for cleansing.—Nu 19:1-5, 9.

Evidently the high priest was able, as he desired, to take part in any priestly duty or ceremony. By King David's time the priesthood had grown large in number. So that all could serve, David arranged the priests in 24 divisions. (1Ch 24:1-18) This system continued for the duration of the priesthood's existence. However, the high priest was not restricted to certain times for service at the sanctuary, as were the underpriests, but could take part at any time. (The underpriests could assist at any time, but certain duties were reserved as the privilege of the priests of the particular division then on duty.) As was true with the underpriests, the festival seasons were the high priest's busiest periods.

The sanctuary, its service, and treasury were under the high priest's supervision. (2Ki 12:7-16; 22:4) In this responsibility, it appears that there was a secondary priest who was his chief assistant. (2Ki 25:18) In later times, this assistant, called the Sagan, would officiate for the high priest when for some reason the high priest was incapacitated. (*The Temple,* by A. Edersheim, 1874, p. 75) Eleazar, Aaron's son, had a special oversight assigned to him.—Nu 4:16.

The high priest was also the leader in the religious instruction of the nation.—Le 10:8-11; De 17:9-11.

He and the secular rulers (Joshua, the Judges, and, under the monarchy, the king) were the high courts of the nation. (De 17:9, 12; 2Ch 19:10, 11) After the Sanhedrin was formed (in later times), the high priest presided over that body. (Some traditions say that he did not preside in every case—only as he willed.) (Mt 26:57; Ac 5:21) High Priest Eleazar participated with Joshua in dividing the land among the 12 tribes.—Jos 14:1; 21:1-3.

The high priest's death had to be announced to the cities of refuge throughout the land; it meant the release of all persons who were confined to the boundaries of the cities of refuge for the guilt of accidental manslaughter.—Nu 35:25-29.

The High-Priestly Line. For the line of descent of the high priest and the names of those who actually served in this office, please see the accompanying chart. The Bible specifically names only a few as serving in that capacity, but it gives us genealogical records of Aaron's line. No doubt a good number of those listed in the genealogical tables served as high priests, even though the Bible does not have occasion to relate an account of their acts nor name them definitely as holding the office. The few it actually names as such are hardly enough to fill in the lapse of time, particularly between the priesthood's beginning in 1512 B.C.E. and Jerusalem's destruction in 607 B.C.E. Also, often there are names passed over in the genealogical tables, so unnamed ones may also have served in the office. The chart, therefore, is not intended to give a wholly complete and accurate list but may help the reader to obtain a better picture of the high-priestly line.

Melchizedek's Priesthood. The first priest mentioned in the Bible is Melchizedek, who was "priest of the Most High God" as well as king of Salem (Jerusalem). Abraham met this priest-king when he returned from defeating the three kings in league with Elamite King Chedorlaomer. Abraham showed he recognized the divine source of Melchizedek's authority by giving him a tenth of the fruits of his victory and by receiving Melchizedek's blessing. The Bible does not give the record of Melchizedek's ancestry, his birth, or his death. He had no predecessors or successors.—Ge 14:17-24; see MELCHIZEDEK.

The High Priesthood of Jesus Christ. The Bible book of Hebrews points out that Jesus Christ, since his resurrection and entry into heaven, is "a high priest according to the manner of Melchizedek forever." (Heb 6:20; 7:17, 21) To describe the greatness of Christ's priesthood and its superiority over the Aaronic priesthood, the writer shows that Melchizedek was both a king and a priest by designation of the Most High God, and not by inheritance. Christ Jesus, not of the tribe of Levi, but of Judah and of the line of David, did not inherit his office by descent from Aaron, but obtained it by direct appointment of God, as did Melchizedek. (Heb 5:10) In addition to the promise recorded at Psalm 110:4: "Jehovah has sworn (and he will feel no regret): 'You are a priest to time indefinite according to the manner of Melchizedek!'" which appointment makes him a heavenly King-Priest, Christ also possesses Kingdom authority by reason of his descent from David. In the latter case, he becomes the heir of the kingship promised in the Davidic covenant. (2Sa 7:11-16) He therefore holds in combination the offices of kingship and priesthood, as did Melchizedek.

In another way the surpassing excellence of Christ's high priesthood is shown, namely, in that Levi, the progenitor of the Jewish priesthood, in effect, gave tithes to Melchizedek, for Levi was still in the loins of Abraham when the patriarch gave a tenth to Salem's priest-king. Moreover, in that sense Levi was also blessed by Melchizedek, and the rule is that the lesser is blessed by the greater. (Heb 7:4-10) The apostle also calls attention to Melchizedek's being "fatherless, motherless, without genealogy, having neither a beginning of days nor an end of life" as being representative of the everlasting priesthood of Jesus Christ, who has been resurrected to "an indestructible life."—Heb 7:3, 15-17.

Nevertheless, although Christ does not get his priesthood from fleshly descent through Aaron, nor does he have a predecessor or successor in his office, he fulfills the things typified by the Aaronic high priest. The apostle makes this perfectly clear when he shows that the tentlike tabernacle constructed in the wilderness was a pattern of "the true tent, which Jehovah put up, and not man" and that the Levitical priests rendered "sacred service in a typical representation and a shadow of the heavenly things." (Heb 8:1-6; 9:11) He relates that Jesus Christ, who had, not animal sacrifices, but his own perfect body to offer, did away with the validity or need for animal sacrifices; Jesus then "passed through the heavens," "not with the blood of goats and of young bulls, but with his own blood, once for all time into the holy place and obtained an everlasting deliverance for us." (Heb 4:14; 9:12; 10:5, 6, 9) He went into the holy place typified by the Most Holy into which Aaron entered, namely, "heaven itself, now

ISRAEL'S HIGH-PRIESTLY LINE

Genealogies of the high priests are found at 1 Chronicles 6:1-15, 50-53 and Ezra 7:1-5. These do not contain all the names; some links are omitted, as is common in Hebrew genealogical tables. Josephus and the Jewish rabbis insert additional names, but their accuracy is open to question. Question marks after names in boldface type indicate those who may have served in the office of high priest (several very likely so) but who are listed only in the high-priestly line of descent in the Bible and are not specifically stated to have served as high priests.

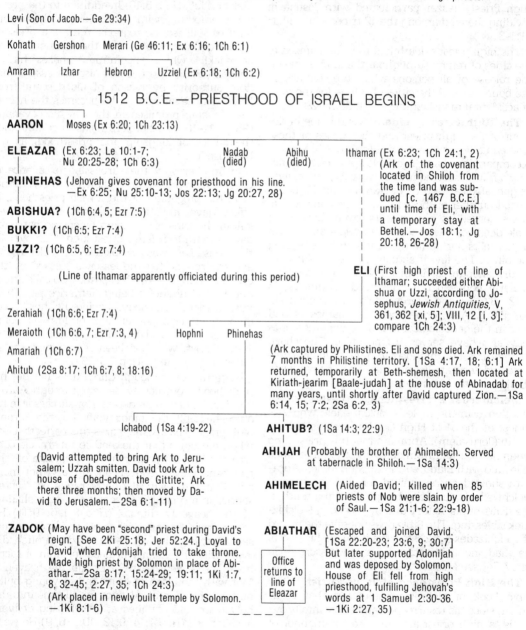

Levi (Son of Jacob.—Ge 29:34)

Kohath   Gershon   Merari (Ge 46:11; Ex 6:16; 1Ch 6:1)

Amram   Izhar   Hebron   Uzziel (Ex 6:18; 1Ch 6:2)

1512 B.C.E.—PRIESTHOOD OF ISRAEL BEGINS

AARON   Moses (Ex 6:20; 1Ch 23:13)

ELEAZAR (Ex 6:23; Le 10:1-7; Nu 20:25-28; 1Ch 6:3)   Nadab (died)   Abihu (died)   Ithamar (Ex 6:23; 1Ch 24:1, 2) (Ark of the covenant located in Shiloh from the time land was subdued [c. 1467 B.C.E.] until time of Eli, with a temporary stay at Bethel.—Jos 18:1; Jg 20:18, 26-28)

PHINEHAS (Jehovah gives covenant for priesthood in his line. —Ex 6:25; Nu 25:10-13; Jos 22:13; Jg 20:27, 28)

ABISHUA? (1Ch 6:4, 5; Ezr 7:5)

BUKKI? (1Ch 6:5; Ezr 7:4)

UZZI? (1Ch 6:5, 6; Ezr 7:4)

(Line of Ithamar apparently officiated during this period)

ELI (First high priest of line of Ithamar; succeeded either Abishua or Uzzi, according to Josephus, *Jewish Antiquities*, V, 361, 362 [xi, 5]; VIII, 12 [i, 3]; compare 1Ch 24:3)

Zerahiah (1Ch 6:6; Ezr 7:4)

Meraioth (1Ch 6:6, 7; Ezr 7:3, 4)   Hophni   Phinehas

Amariah (1Ch 6:7)

Ahitub (2Sa 8:17; 1Ch 6:7, 8; 18:16)

(Ark captured by Philistines. Eli and sons died. Ark remained 7 months in Philistine territory. [1Sa 4:17, 18; 6:1] Ark returned, temporarily at Beth-shemesh, then located at Kiriath-jearim [Baale-judah] at the house of Abinadab for many years, until shortly after David captured Zion.—1Sa 6:14, 15; 7:2; 2Sa 6:2, 3)

Ichabod (1Sa 4:19-22)   **AHITUB?** (1Sa 14:3; 22:9)

AHIJAH (Probably the brother of Ahimelech. Served at tabernacle in Shiloh.—1Sa 14:3)

(David attempted to bring Ark to Jerusalem; Uzzah smitten. David took Ark to house of Obed-edom the Gittite; Ark there three months; then moved by David to Jerusalem.—2Sa 6:1-11)

AHIMELECH (Aided David; killed when 85 priests of Nob were slain by order of Saul.—1Sa 21:1-6; 22:9-18)

ZADOK (May have been "second" priest during David's reign. [See 2Ki 25:18; Jer 52:24.] Loyal to David when Adonijah tried to take throne. Made high priest by Solomon in place of Abiathar.—2Sa 8:17; 15:24-29; 19:11; 1Ki 1:7, 8, 32-45; 2:27, 35; 1Ch 24:3) (Ark placed in newly built temple by Solomon. —1Ki 8:1-6)

ABIATHAR (Escaped and joined David. [1Sa 22:20-23; 23:6, 9; 30:7] But later supported Adonijah and was deposed by Solomon. House of Eli fell from high priesthood, fulfilling Jehovah's words at 1 Samuel 2:30-36. —1Ki 2:27, 35)

Office returns to line of Eleazar

AHIMAAZ? (2Sa 15:27, 36; 17:20; 1Ch 6:8)

AZARIAH (I)? (1Ki 4:2; 1Ch 6:9)

(The next three names, Amariah, Jehoiada, and Zechariah, are evidently links that were passed over at 1Ch 6:1-15)

AMARIAH (In King Jehoshaphat's time.—2Ch 19:11)

JEHOIADA (In the time of Ahaziah, Athaliah, and Jehoash.—2Ki 11:4–12:9; 2Ch 22:10–24:15)

ZECHARIAH? (Stoned to death, with King Jehoash's approval.—2Ch 24:20-22)

JOHANAN? (1Ch 6:10)

AZARIAH (II) (Probably the priest who resisted King Uzziah in his presumptuous act.—1Ch 6:10; 2Ch 26:17-20)

(The next two names, Urijah and Azariah, may be links that are omitted at 1Ch 6:1-15)

URIJAH? (The priest who built an altar like the pagan altar at Damascus, at King Ahaz' order.—2Ki 16:10-16)

AZARIAH (II or III) (Of the line of Zadok; served in King Hezekiah's time. He may be the same person as Azariah II, listed earlier, or another with the same name.—2Ch 31:10-13)

AMARIAH? (1Ch 6:11; Ezr 7:3)

AHITUB (Ne 11:11; 1Ch 6:11, 12; 9:11; Ezr 7:2)

MERAIOTH? (He was a priest, a descendant of Ahitub, but may not have served as high priest.—1Ch 9:11; Ne 11:11)

ZADOK? (1Ch 6:12; 9:11; Ezr 7:2; Ne 11:11)

SHALLUM? (Meshullam) (1Ch 6:12, 13; 9:11; Ezr 7:2; Ne 11:11)

HILKIAH (In King Josiah's time.—2Ki 22:4-14; 23:4; 1Ch 6:13; 2Ch 34:9-22)

AZARIAH (III or IV)? (1Ch 6:13, 14)

SERAIAH (Killed by Nebuchadnezzar at Riblah after Jerusalem's fall in 607 B.C.E. —2Ki 25:18-21; 1Ch 6:14; Ezr 7:1; Jer 52:24-27)

JEHOZADAK? (Taken into Babylonian exile by Nebuchadnezzar in 607 B.C.E. His son Jeshua [Joshua] and possibly other sons were born during the exile. He was, of course, unable to perform duties at the temple.—1Ch 6:14, 15; Ezr 3:2)

(Ark of the covenant disappears; not in later temples built in Jerusalem)

AFTER THE RETURN FROM EXILE

JOSHUA (Jeshua) (Returned in 537 B.C.E. with Zerubbabel.—Ezr 2:2; 3:2; Ne 12:10; Hag 1:1; Zec 3:1; 6:11)

JOIAKIM? (Ne 12:10, 12; held office at time of Ezra's return to Jerusalem, according to Josephus, *Jewish Antiquities*, XI, 121 [v, 1])

ELIASHIB (In Nehemiah's time.—Ne 3:20; 12:10, 22; 13:4, 6, 7)

JOIADA? (Ne 12:10, 11, 22; 13:28)

JOHANAN (Jonathan?) (Ne 12:11, 22, 23)

JADDUA? (Probably in or "down till" the days of Darius the Persian.—Ne 12:11, 22)

FROM THE TIME OF DARIUS (II) THE PERSIAN

(From this point the Apocryphal books of First and Second Maccabees and *Jewish Antiquities* [XI-XX], by Josephus, are the sources for the list of high priests down to the time of the Maccabees. Josephus names more as high priests than does First Maccabees. From the Maccabees to the destruction of Jerusalem in 70 C.E., the chief source is Josephus. The Bible names only three [Annas, Joseph Caiaphas, and Ananias]. The high-priestly line seems to have been adhered to, at least in the majority of cases, although pagan rulers deposed and appointed the high priests at will.)

ISRAEL'S HIGH-PRIESTLY LINE (*cont'd*)

ONIAS I
SIMON I
ELEAZAR
MANASSEH
ONIAS II   (Continued in column to the right) ▷

SIMON II
ONIAS III
JOSHUA (Gr., Jesus); also Jason
ONIAS (Called also Menelaus)
JAKIM (Called in Greek, Alcimus); also Jacimus

THE MACCABEAN PRIEST-KINGS

JONATHAN
SIMON (Jonathan's brother)
JOHN HYRCANUS
ARISTOBULUS I ▷

ALEXANDER JANNAEUS
HYRCANUS II (Aristobulus II seized temporary rule)
ANTIGONUS

AFTER HEROD THE GREAT BECAME KING (Mt 2:1)
(Appointed by Herod)

HANANEL (Latinized Gr., Ananelus)
ARISTOBULUS III
HANANEL (a second time)
JESUS (son of Phabet) ▷

SIMON (son of Boethus)
MATTHIAS (Mattathias) (son-in-law of Boethus)
JOAZAR (son of Boethus)

(Appointed by Archelaus, King of Judea — Mt 2:22)

ELEAZAR (son of Boethus) ▷

JESUS (son of Sie) (Joazar restored by the multitude)

(Appointed by Quirinius, Governor of Syria — Lu 2:2)

ANNAS (Ananus) (son of Seth) (Appointed by Quirinius; deposed by Valerius Gratus, governor of Judea, about 15 C.E. He was the father-in-law of Caiaphas. After being deposed, he continued to exercise great influence.—Lu 3:2; Joh 18:13, 24; Ac 4:6)

(Appointed by Valerius Gratus, Governor of Judea)

ISMAEL (son of Phabi)
ELEAZAR (son of Annas)
SIMON (son of Camithus)
JOSEPH CAIAPHAS (Officiated during Jesus' earthly ministry and the early part of the apostles' ministry. He presided as high priest over Jesus' trial before the Sanhedrin, in company with his father-in-law Annas. [Mt 26:3, 57; Lu 3:2; Joh 11:49, 51; 18:13, 14, 24, 28] He and Annas called Peter and John before them and commanded them to stop preaching. [Ac 4:6, 18] Caiaphas was the high priest who authorized Saul to receive letters to the synagogue at Damascus for the arrest of Christians.—Ac 9:1, 2, 14)

(Appointed by Vitellius, Governor of Syria)

JONATHAN (son of Annas) ▷

THEOPHILUS (son of Annas)

(Appointed by Herod Agrippa I)

SIMON (Cantheras) (son of Boethus)
MATTHIAS (Mattathias) (son of Annas) ▷

ELIONAEUS (son of Cantheras)

(Appointed by Herod, King of Chalcis)

JOSEPH (son of Camydus)
ANANIAS (son of Nedebaeus) (Presided over the Sanhedrin at Paul's trial.—Ac 23:2; 24:1)

(Appointed by Herod Agrippa II)

ISMAEL (son of Phabi)
JOSEPH (Cabi) (son of former high priest Simon)
ANNAS (Ananus) (son of Annas)
JESUS (son of Damnaeus)
JESUS (son of Gamaliel) ▷

MATTHIAS (Mattathias) (son of Theophilus)
PHANAS (Phannias or Phinehas; son of Samuel) (Made high priest not by Herod Agrippa but by the people during the war against Rome)

to appear before the person of God for us."—Heb 9:24.

The sacrifice of Jesus as the antitypical High Priest did not need to be repeated as did those of the Aaronic priests, because his sacrifice actually removed sin. (Heb 9:13, 14, 25, 26) Moreover, in the type, or shadow, no priest of the Aaronic priesthood could live long enough to save completely or bring to complete salvation and perfection all those to whom he ministered, but Christ "is able also to save completely those who are approaching God though him, because he is always alive to plead for them."—Heb 7:23-25.

In addition to making sacrifices, the high priest in Israel blessed the people and was their chief instructor in God's righteous laws. The same is true of Jesus Christ. On appearing before his Father in the heavens, he "offered one sacrifice for sins perpetually and sat down at the right hand of God, from then on awaiting until his enemies should be placed as a stool for his feet." (Heb 10:12, 13; 8:1) Therefore, "the second time that he appears it will be apart from sin and to those earnestly looking for him for their salvation." —Heb 9:28.

Jesus Christ's superiority as High Priest is seen in another sense also. Becoming a man of blood and flesh like his "brothers" (Heb 2:14-17), he was thoroughly tested; he suffered all manner of opposition, persecution, and finally, an ignominious death. As it is stated: "Although he was a Son, he learned obedience from the things he suffered; and after he had been made perfect he became responsible for everlasting salvation to all those obeying him." (Heb 5:8, 9) Paul explains benefits we can receive from his being thus tested: "For in that he himself has suffered when being put to the test, he is able to come to the aid of those who are being put to the test." (Heb 2:18) Those who call on him for help are assured of merciful and sympathetic consideration. "For," says Paul, "we have as high priest, not one who cannot sympathize with our weaknesses, but one who has been tested in all respects like ourselves, but without sin."—Heb 4:15, 16.

Christian Underpriests. Jesus Christ is the only priest "according to the manner of Melchizedek" (Heb 7:17), but like Aaron the high priest of Israel, Jesus Christ has a body of underpriests provided for him by his Father, Jehovah. These are promised joint heirship with him in the heavens, where they will also share as associate kings in his Kingdom. (Ro 8:17) They are known as "a royal priesthood." (1Pe 2:9) They are shown in the vision of the Bible book of Revelation singing a new song in which they say that Christ bought them with his blood and "made them to be a kingdom and priests to our God, and [that] they are to rule as kings over the earth." (Re 5:9, 10) Later in the vision these are shown to number 144,000. They also are described as having "been bought from the earth," as followers of the Lamb, "bought from among mankind as firstfruits to God and to the Lamb." (Re 14:1-4; compare Jas 1:18.) In this chapter of Revelation (14), warning is given with regard to the mark of the beast, showing that avoidance of this mark "means endurance for the holy ones." (Re 14:9-12) These 144,000 bought ones are the ones who endure faithfully, who come to life and rule as kings with Christ, and who "will be priests of God and of the Christ, and will rule as kings with him for the thousand years." (Re 20:4, 6) Jesus' high-priestly services bring them into this glorious position.

Beneficiaries of the Heavenly Priesthood. The vision of the New Jerusalem recorded in Revelation gives an indication of who will receive the ministrations of the great High Priest and those associated with him as heavenly underpriests. Aaron and his family, together with the priestly tribe of Levi, ministered to the people of the 12 tribes in the land of Palestine. As for the New Jerusalem, "the nations will walk by means of its light."—Re 21:2, 22-24.

See also PRIEST.

HIGHWAY, ROAD. The terms *mesil·lah'* (highway) and *de'rekh* (road) in Hebrew and the term *ho·dos'* (way; road) in Greek are all used to refer to a public way, track, or route, generally between towns or cities.—See WAY, THE.

From ancient times highways and roads, including several important trade routes, linked cities and kingdoms in the area of Palestine. (Nu 20:17-19; 21:21, 22; 22:5, 21-23; Jos 2:22; Jg 21:19; 1Sa 6:9, 12; 13:17, 18; see KING'S ROAD.) What is considered to have been the principal route led from Egypt to the Philistine cities of Gaza and Ashkelon and gradually bent northeastward in the direction of Megiddo. It continued to Hazor, N of the Sea of Galilee, and then led to Damascus. This route via Philistia was the shortest from Egypt to the Promised Land. But Jehovah kindly led the Israelites by another way so that they would not get disheartened by a Philistine attack.—Ex 13:17.

In the Promised Land the maintenance of a good road system took on added importance for the Israelites, as there was only one center of worship for the entire nation. Therefore many of the Israelites had to travel considerable distances each year to comply with the Law's requirement that all the males assemble for the three seasonal festivals. (De 16:16) Additionally, tithes, contributions, and any offerings, whether voluntary or obligatory, had to be presented at the place Jehovah would choose. (De 12:4-7) After Solomon's building the temple, that place was Jerusalem. So, as the Israelites traveled on the roads to and from Jerusalem, there were fine opportunities for fathers to teach God's law to their sons.—De 6:6, 7.

Attention also had to be given to maintaining the roads leading to the six cities of refuge. These roads had to be well marked and kept clear of obstacles that might impede the accidental manslayer's progress. (De 19:3) According to Jewish tradition, a signpost indicating the direction to the city of refuge was placed at every crossroad. —Babylonian Talmud, *Makkot* 10b.

Although the Bible gives no description of the ancient roads, it does contain allusions to their construction and maintenance. At times hills and other irregularities may have been leveled, and the roads cleared of stones and banked up. (Isa 40:3, 4; 57:14; 62:10) The historian Josephus claims that King Solomon paved the roads leading to Jerusalem with black stone.—*Jewish Antiquities*, VIII, 187 (vii, 4).

However, nothing definite is known about the structure of ancient roads until the days of the Roman Empire. The Romans distinguished themselves as road builders, linking their vast empire to facilitate the movement of their armies. Their roads were paved with flat stones, and the roadbeds usually consisted of three layers: (bottom) rubble, (middle) flat slabs set in mortar, and (top) concrete and crushed stone. The roads sloped from the center toward both sides and were equipped with milestones, curbstones, and drainage ditches. Also, wells could be found at convenient intervals. Running in nearly straight lines, Roman roads passed over hills rather than around them. The famous Roman highway, the Appian Way, measured some 5.5 m (18 ft) in width and was paved with large lava blocks. The apostle Paul, while en route to Rome as a prisoner, traveled over this road, parts of which are still used today.—Ac 28:15, 16; see APPIUS, MARKETPLACE OF.

The words of Isaiah 19:23 about the coming into existence of "a highway out of Egypt to Assyria" pointed forward to the friendly relations that would one day prevail between these two lands. In effecting the release of his people, Jehovah, as it were, made highways for them that led out of the lands of their captivity.—Isa 11:16; 35:8-10; 49:11-13; Jer 31:21.

HILEN (Hi'len). Apparently the same as Holon, one of the 13 priestly cities.—Jos 21:13-19; 1Ch 6:54-60; see HOLON No. 1.

HILKIAH (Hil·ki'ah) [My Portion (Share) Is Jehovah].

1. A Levite of the family of Merari; son of Amzi and forefather of the Ethan appointed by David as a singer at the sanctuary.—1Ch 6:31, 32, 44-46.

2. A Levite gatekeeper of the family of Merari who received this assignment in David's time; a son of Hosah.—1Ch 26:10-12.

3. Father of the Eliakim who was an official in King Hezekiah's court.—2Ki 18:37.

4. The high priest in the days of King Josiah; son of Shallum and father of Azariah; apparently a forefather of Ezra the copyist. (2Ki 22:3, 4; 1Ch 6:13; Ezr 7:1, 2, 6) Hilkiah, as high priest, figured prominently in the restoration of true worship undertaken by Josiah. During the course of the temple repair work, Hilkiah found the very "book of Jehovah's law by the hand of Moses." What made the find outstanding was most likely the manuscript's being the original book written by Moses. Hilkiah gave it to Shaphan the secretary, who took the manuscript to the king. Upon hearing Shaphan read the book, King Josiah dispatched a delegation headed by High Priest Hilkiah to Huldah the prophetess to inquire of Jehovah in behalf of the king and the people. —2Ki 22:3-14; 2Ch 34:14.

5. Father of Jeremiah the prophet; a priest in Anathoth in the land of Benjamin.—Jer 1:1.

6. Father of the Gemariah whom King Zedekiah sent along with Elasah to King Nebuchadnezzar in Babylon.—Jer 29:3.

7. A Levite priest who returned from Babylon with Zerubbabel.—Ne 12:1, 7.

8. One of those standing at Ezra's right hand on the occasion of his reading the Law to the people.—Ne 8:2-4.

9. The name of a priestly paternal house in the days of Nehemiah the governor.—Ne 12:12, 21, 26.

HILL. The Hebrew term *giv·'ah'* and the Greek term *bou·nos'* refer to a natural elevation of earth's surface, lower than a mountain. Rounded hills are especially noticeable in Judea, though they are also found in other parts of Palestine.

On occasion hills served as burial places and places for concealment. (Jos 24:33; 1Sa 23:19; 26:1) Homes and towns were frequently built on them, as was the house of Abinadab where the Ark was kept for some 70 years.—1Sa 7:1, 2.

In highlighting the greatness of the Almighty, the prophet Isaiah shows that Jehovah can, in effect, 'weigh the hills in the scales.' (Isa 40:12) The mountains and hills are described as "eternal" and "indefinitely lasting," but even greater permanence than this is ascribed to God's loving-kindness and covenant of peace.—Isa 54:10; Ge 49:26; De 33:15.

Before undertaking a journey, Eastern rulers would often send out men to prepare the way before them by removing stones, filling up depressions, smoothing out rough places, and, at times, even leveling hills. In a figurative sense, the hills were leveled in making possible the unhindered return of the Jews from Babylon to Jerusalem in 537 B.C.E. This was also prophetic of the preparatory work done by John the Baptizer before the appearance of the Messiah.—Isa 40:4; Lu 3:1-6.

It was often on hills that the Israelites, in imitation of the Canaanites, carried on idolatrous worship. (De 12:2; 1Ki 14:23; 2Ki 17:9, 10; Isa 65:7; Jer 2:20; 17:1-3; Eze 6:13; 20:28; Ho 4:13) This explains the prophetic response to the appeal for Israel to return to Jehovah: "Here we are! We have come to you, for you, O Jehovah, are our God. Truly the hills as well as the turmoil on the mountains belong to falsehood."—Jer 3:22, 23.

Most appropriately, therefore, both Isaiah and Micah foretold that "the mountain of the house of Jehovah" would become firmly established above the top of the mountains and would be lifted up above the hills. (Isa 2:2; Mic 4:1) In sharp contrast with this, those not doing Jehovah's will at the time of his executional work will "say to the mountains, 'Cover us!' and to the hills, 'Fall over us!'"—Ho 10:8; Lu 23:30; compare Isa 2:19; Re 6:16, 17.

HILLEL (Hil'lel) [possibly, He Has Flashed Forth [Light]; or, He Has Praised]. A Pirathonite, an inhabitant of the town of Pirathon in Ephraim. Hillel's son Abdon judged Israel for eight years. —Jg 12:13-15.

HIN. A liquid measure (Ex 30:24; Nu 28:14; Eze 45:24; 46:5, 7, 11); also used with reference to the container for measuring a hin. (Le 19:36) According to the Jewish historian Josephus, a hin equaled two Athenian choes; a bath equaled 72

sextarii. (*Jewish Antiquities,* III, 197 [viii, 3]; VIII, 57 [ii, 9]) Since other sources indicate that two Athenian choes amounted to 12 sextarii, the hin may be reckoned at one sixth of a bath measure or about 3.67 L (7.75 pt).

The Scriptures also mention fractions of a hin: a half, a third, a fourth, and a sixth; this last was the daily water ration allowed Ezekiel when depicting the severe condition to come upon Jerusalem under siege.—Ex 29:40; Le 23:13; Nu 15:4-7, 9, 10; 28:5, 7; Eze 4:11; 46:14.

HIND [Heb., *'ai·ya·lah'*; *'ai·ye'leth*]. A female deer; member of the Cervidae family. The hind is a slender, graceful creature, timid, surefooted, and swift. When heavy with young, the hinds retire to the recesses of the forest to give birth and then continue in seclusion, tenderly caring for and protecting the fawns until such time as they can care for themselves.—Job 39:1; Ps 29:9.

The gentle, graceful hind figures in the vivid imagery of the Bible. (Pr 5:18, 19; Ca 2:7; 3:5; see GAZELLE.) Allusion is made to the animal's swiftness and surefootedness, enabling it to escape from its enemies. (2Sa 22:1, 34; Ps 18:32, 33; Hab 3:19) Possibly with reference to skillfulness and swiftness in warfare, Jacob prophetically described the tribe of Naphtali as "a slender hind." (Ge 49:21) The psalmist, when deprived of free access to the sanctuary, compares his longing for God to the hind's yearning for water streams. (Ps 42:1-4) The picture of a hind forsaking her newborn fawn, so contrary to her well-known solicitude for her offspring under normal conditions, indicates the severity of the droughts upon Judah.—Jer 14:1, 2, 5.

HINNOM, VALLEY OF. A valley located on the S and SW of Jerusalem; it runs S from the vicinity of the modern Jaffa Gate, turns sharply E at the SW corner of the city, and runs along the S to meet the Tyropoeon and Kidron valleys at a point near the city's SE corner. It is also known as "the valley of the son(s) of Hinnom"; the "Valley," as in the expression "Valley Gate" (Jos 15:8; 2Ki 23:10; Ne 3:13); possibly "the low plain of the carcasses and of the fatty ashes" at Jeremiah 31:40. The individual after whom the valley may have been named is unknown, as is also the meaning of the name Hinnom.—PICTURE, Vol. 2, p. 949.

At the point just above Hinnom's convergence with the Tyropoeon and Kidron valleys, it widens out. Here was probably the location of Topheth. (2Ki 23:10) On the S side of the valley near its eastern extremity is the traditional site of Akeldama, the "Field of Blood," the potter's field purchased with Judas' 30 pieces of silver. (Mt 27: 3-10; Ac 1:18, 19) Farther up, the valley is quite narrow and deep, with many sepulcher chambers in its terraced cliffs.

The Valley of Hinnom formed a part of the boundary between the tribes of Judah and Benjamin, Judah's territory being to the S, placing Jerusalem in Benjamin's territory, as outlined at Joshua 15:1, 8; 18:11, 16. The valley is now known as the Wadi er-Rababi (Ge Ben Hinnom).

Apostate King Ahaz of Judah made sacrificial smoke and burned his son(s) in the fire in this valley. (2Ch 28:1-3) His grandson King Manasseh exceeded Ahaz, promoting wickedness on a grand scale, also making "his own sons pass through the fire in the valley of the son of Hinnom." (2Ch 33:1, 6, 9) King Josiah, Manasseh's grandson, put an end to this detestable practice in Topheth by defiling the place, desecrating it, thereby making it unfit for worship, possibly by scattering bones or refuse therein.—2Ki 23:10.

Jeremiah, who prophesied in the days of Kings Josiah, Jehoahaz, Jehoiakim, Jehoiachin, and Zedekiah, expressed Jehovah's judgment for the sins of the nation, one of the foremost being the abominable sacrifice of their children to Molech. He was commanded to take some of the older men of the people and the priests out the Gate of the Potsherds (Gate of the Ash-heaps), located at the SE corner of Jerusalem, to the Valley of Hinnom in the area of Topheth. There he declared Jehovah's pronouncement: "Look! there are days coming . . . when this place will be called no more Topheth and the valley of the son of Hinnom, but the valley of the killing." Then, smashing an earthenware flask before their eyes, he continued with Jehovah's judgment: "In the same way I shall break this people and this city . . . and in Topheth they will bury until there is no more place to bury." (Jer 19:1, 2, 6, 10, 11) In other words, the slaughter, not of sacrificial victims to Molech, but of the wicked by God's judgment, would be so great that some bodies would lie unburied in the valley. This would pollute it to an even greater degree than Josiah had done.

Jeremiah's prophetic words do not necessarily mean that such sacrifices to Molech were still going on in Jeremiah's time, but that Jehovah would punish the nation for their practices, past as well as present, and for the innocent blood shed by them, particularly the human sacrifices during Manasseh's reign. The prophet, in another pronouncement, told the nation that they would be punished for what Manasseh had done. (Jer 15:4; compare 2Ki 23:26; Jer 32:30-35.) Also, Jeremiah's declaration at chapter 19, verse 3, is parallel to the statement at 2 Kings 21:12. However, in Jeremiah's day the people certainly were carrying on with idolatries, which gave evidence that they had not repented in the least for the gross sins they shared in during Manasseh's reign. At Jeremiah 2:23, it may be Hinnom that Jeremiah refers to in calling Judah's attention to their idolatrous sins.

The gates in Jerusalem's wall that were situated on the Valley of Hinnom were, probably, the Corner Gate at the city's NW corner, the Valley Gate at its SW corner, and the Gate of the Potsherds near the point where the Valley of Hinnom joined the Tyropoeon and Kidron valleys. (2Ki 14:13; Ne 2:13; 12:31; Jer 19:2) Between the Corner Gate and the Valley Gate, the sides of the Valley of Hinnom are so steep as to make impractical the location of other gates along this portion of Jerusalem's wall. King Uzziah built towers by the Corner Gate and the Valley Gate, inasmuch as these would be the more vulnerable places along this part of the valley.—2Ch 26:9.

It was in this valley to the S of Jerusalem that Nehemiah made his night inspection tour, examining the city wall eastward from the Valley Gate to the Gate of the Ash-heaps, turning up the Kidron for a distance and then back to reenter the city by the Valley Gate. (Ne 2:13-15) In Nehemiah's time the Valley of Hinnom apparently marked the northern limits of the settlements of the sons of Judah (aside from those dwelling in Jerusalem).—Ne 11:25, 30.

In the Christian Greek Scriptures, the Valley of Hinnom is referred to by the equivalent Greek term Ge′en·na.—Mt 5:22; Mr 9:47; see GEHENNA.

HIPPOPOTAMUS. See BEHEMOTH.

HIPS. The exterior lumbar region and small of the back. The Hebrew word moth·na′yim is generally translated "hips" or "loins," although there is another Hebrew word that more specifically means "loins."—See LOINS.

A belt was often worn at the hips, especially by the soldier, who slipped a sheathed sword or dagger under the belt or fastened the sword sheath to it. (2Sa 20:8; Ne 4:18) The secretary wore his inkhorn at the hips, placed under his belt or sash. (Eze 9:2) Sackcloth was worn around the hips as a sign of mourning.—Ge 37:34; Am 8:10.

Before engaging in any form of vigorous physical activity, a person would 'gird up his hips,' often by pulling the ends of his loose, flowing garment between his legs and tucking those ends under his sash. The Israelites in Egypt ate the Passover with their hips girded, ready to march out of the land. Elijah was similarly prepared when he ran before Ahab's chariot.—Ex 12:11; 1Ki 18:46.

Figurative Usage. The muscles in the area of the hips play a major part in picking up and carrying heavy loads; hence the appropriateness of the statement at Psalm 66:11, "You have put pressure on our hips." Strengthening the hips would denote getting ready to exert power, as for a fight. (Na 2:1) The good wife is said to gird her hips with strength and invigorate her arms to carry out her multitudinous activities for the well-being of the household. (Pr 31:17) Conversely, those who have been reduced to a weakened condition by fear, distress, or defeat are said to have wobbling, or shaking, hips. (Ps 69:23; Eze 21:6; 29:7) To ungird the hips of kings means to take away their strength.—Isa 45:1.

Jehovah spoke of the houses of Israel and Judah as having been like a belt on his hips, so closely had he held them to himself, in order that they might become to him a praise and something beautiful. (Jer 13:11) Jesus Christ is prophetically pictured as reigning with righteousness as the belt of his hips and faithfulness as the belt of his loins. This may refer to the fact that all the active powers of Jesus Christ adhere unchangeably to righteousness and faithfulness. Like a belt that provides support, the moral quality of righteousness strengthens him in acting as Jehovah's appointed Judge.—Isa 11:1, 5.

HIRAH (Hi'rah). Judah's Adullamite companion.—Ge 38:1, 12.

HIRAM (Hi'ram) [possibly a shortened form of Ahiram, meaning "My Brother Is High (Exalted)"]. In the Masoretic text alternate spellings are found in certain passages: "Hirom" (1Ki 5:10, 18; 7:40a) and "Huram" (2Ch 2:3).

1. King of Tyre, and friendly contemporary of Kings David and Solomon in the 11th century B.C.E.

After David conquered the stronghold of Zion and set about to build a palace on the site, Hiram sent messengers to arrange a trade treaty between himself and David. Hiram then supplied David with cedar timber from the western slopes of Lebanon as well as craftsmen skilled in working with wood and stone.—2Sa 5:11; 1Ch 14:1.

Upon hearing that David had died and that Solomon was reigning in his stead, Hiram sent his servants to renew the friendship agreement. (1Ki 5:1) Solomon then enlisted the help of Hiram in supplying materials and some of the manpower necessary for the building of the great temple, at the same time bargaining to pay Hiram's labor force with large quantities of wheat, barley, wine, and oil. (1Ki 5:2-6; 2Ch 2:3-10) In turn, Hiram blessed Jehovah, and a covenant of friendship was concluded between the two nations.—1Ki 5:7-12; 2Ch 2:11-16.

At the end of Solomon's 20-year building project he gave Hiram 20 cities, but they proved most undesirable in Hiram's eyes. (1Ki 9:10-13; see CABUL No. 2.) Whether Hiram returned these same cities or gave Solomon other cities is not certain. (2Ch 8:1, 2) Nor is it certain whether Hiram's giving Solomon 120 talents of gold ($46,242,000) was subsequent to receiving the gift of cities or if it somehow figured in the exchange. —1Ki 9:14.

Hiram also shared with Solomon in another joint enterprise, in which the latter built a fleet of ships in the Gulf of 'Aqaba at Ezion-geber. Hiram then supplied experienced seamen to man them along with Solomon's servants. In addition to these ships that plied the waters off the E coast of Africa, Hiram and Solomon had other ships sailing as far as Tarshish, apparently at the western end of the Mediterranean. All together, these extensive operations on the high seas brought in a great deal of wealth—gold, silver, ivory, precious stones, valuable woods, and rarities like apes and peacocks.—1Ki 9:26-28; 10:11, 12, 22; 2Ch 8:18; 9:10, 21; see EZION-GEBER.

2. The skilled artisan who made many of the furnishings of Solomon's temple. His father was a Tyrian, but his mother was a widow "from the tribe of Naphtali" (1Ki 7:13, 14) "of the sons of Dan." (2Ch 2:13, 14) This apparent difference resolves itself if we take the view, as some scholars do, that she was born of the tribe of Dan, had been widowed by a first husband of the tribe of Naphtali, and then was remarried to a Tyrian.

Hiram, the king of Tyre (No. 1), sent this Hiram to supervise the special construction for Solomon because of his ability and experience in working with materials such as gold, silver, copper, iron, stone, and wood. Hiram was also unusually skilled in dyeing, engraving, and designing all sorts of devices. No doubt from childhood on he received some of his technical training in the industrial arts of the times from his Tyrian father, who himself was an accomplished craftsman in copper.—1Ki 7:13-45; 2Ch 2:13, 14; 4:11-16.

The king of Tyre apparently refers to this man as Hiram-abi, which seems to be an appellation literally meaning "Hiram My Father." (2Ch 2:13) By this the king did not mean that Hiram was his literal father but, perhaps, that he was the king's "counselor" or "master workman." Similarly, the expression Hiram-abiv (literally, "Hiram His Father") seems to mean 'Hiram is his (that is, the king's) master workman.'—2Ch 4:16.

HIRAM-ABI (Hi′ram-a′bi) [Hiram My Father]. An appellation applied to the "skillful man" whom the king of Tyre sent to make the furnishings of Solomon's temple. It evidently indicated that Hiram was "father" in the sense of being a master workman.—2Ch 2:13; see HIRAM No. 2.

HIRAM-ABIV (Hi′ram-a′biv) [Hiram His Father]. A term used in reference to the skilled craftsman sent from Tyre to supervise construction of the furnishings of Solomon's temple. It seems to indicate that Hiram was "father," not in a literal sense, but in that he was a master workman.—2Ch 4:16; see HIRAM No. 2.

HIRE, WAGES. Generally, compensation paid to laborers for their work or services. (Le 19:13) As a verb, "hire" means to employ someone (Mt 20:1) or to rent something. (Ex 22:14, 15; Ac 28:30) "Wages" may be synonymous with "reward." For example, King Nebuchadrezzar's (Nebuchadnezzar's) wages or reward for his service as Jehovah's executioner in destroying Tyre was the conquest of Egypt with all its wealth for him to plunder. (Eze 29:18, 19; see also Ru 2:12; Isa 61:8; 62:11.) In fulfillment of Zechariah 11:12, Judas Iscariot received 30 pieces of silver from the priests (if shekels, $66) as "wages" for betraying Jesus Christ. (Mt 26:14-16; 27:3-10; Ac 1:18; see BRIBE.) Also, "wages" at times denotes "recompense." "The wages sin pays is death."—Ro 6:23; see also Ps 109:20; Isa 65:6, 7.

Hire was paid not only in the form of money or silver (2Ch 24:11, 12; 25:6) but also in domestic animals, agricultural products, and so forth. Jacob's wages for 14 years of work were his two wives, Leah and Rachel. Additionally, he served six years for the agreed-upon part of Laban's flock. (Ge 29:15, 18, 27; 31:41) Leah, in giving her son's mandrakes to Rachel, "hired" Jacob to have relations with her, and for this reason she referred to the son born to her as "hireling's wages." (Ge 30:14-18) In the time of Jesus' earthly ministry, the usual daily wage for agricultural workers was evidently one denarius (74 cents).—Mt 20:2.

God's law to Israel required that hired laborers be paid at the close of the workday. (Le 19:13; De 24:14, 15) The Scriptures severely censure those dealing dishonestly with the wages of hired workers.—Jer 22:13; Mal 3:5; Jas 5:4.

Care must be exercised when hiring others to be sure that those hired are competent. Hence the proverb: "As an archer piercing everything is the one hiring someone stupid or the one hiring passersby."—Pr 26:10.

The hospitality and material assistance extended to those exclusively devoting themselves to the interests of pure worship may be referred to as wages due them, according to the principle: "The worker is worthy of his wages." (Lu 10:7; 1Ti 5:17, 18) The tithes of the Israelites constituted the wages of the Levites for their service at the sanctuary. (Nu 18:26, 30, 31) On the other hand, a righteous standing with God, and everlasting life, are not given as *wages* to those serving God, for they are *gifts* resulting from the undeserved kindness of God through Jesus Christ because His servants exercise faith in the ransom sacrifice of Christ.—Ro 4:2-8; 6:23.

Neglect of the sanctuary in the days of the prophet Haggai resulted in Jehovah's withholding his blessing so that those hiring themselves out were doing so for "a bag having holes," that is, the hire received was meager and quickly spent. (Hag 1:3-6) Then, with respect to the days before the restoration of the temple, Jehovah said through Zechariah: "For before those days there were no wages for mankind made to exist; and as for the wages of domestic animals, there was no such thing."—Zec 8:9, 10; see GIFTS, PRESENTS; GIFTS FROM GOD; HIRED LABORER.

In contrast with the Hebrew word *sa·khar′* (usually meaning hire in the sense of a wage paid for labor or services rendered), the Hebrew word *'eth·nan′*, from the root *na·than′* (give), is used in the Scriptures exclusively with reference to the hire gained from prostitution, literal or figurative. The latter is thus viewed as a gift rather than a wage earned by labor and is generally used in a bad sense. The Law forbade bringing into the sanctuary for a vow either "the hire of a harlot" or "the price of a dog," this latter likely referring to the hire of a male homosexual. (De 23:18) In view of this, the reference to Tyre's hire for prostitution to the nations becoming something holy to Jehovah evidently means that the Most High would sanctify Tyre's material gain therefrom in the sense of his seeing that it was used according to his will, causing it to result in benefit for his servants. (Isa 23:17, 18; compare Ne 13:16.) Both

Judah and Israel were guilty of prostituting themselves to other nations. (Eze 23:1-16; Ho 9:1; Mic 1:6, 7) But God specifically denounced Jerusalem for something unusual in this regard. Unlike harlots who receive hire, Jerusalem even gave hire to the nations committing prostitution with her.—Eze 16:26-34, 41.

HIRED LABORER.
One who (in contrast with a slave) received a wage for his work.

The Law required that such laborers be paid at the end of the workday. (Le 19:13; De 24:14, 15) At least by the first century C.E., it appears that the wages were agreed upon before the laborers ever began their work, that the workday was 12 hours long, from about six in the morning to six in the evening, and that the customary day's wage for vineyard workers was evidently a denarius (74 cents). (Mt 20:1-13) The Scriptural reference to "years of a hired laborer" seems to indicate that the duration of the work agreement, or contract, was also fixed.—Isa 16:14; 21:16.

Evidently in Israel many of the hired laborers were uncircumcised, for the Law prescribed that they not partake of the Passover, although circumcised slaves could do so, being viewed as members of an Israelite family. Likewise, while the hired laborers of a priest could not eat of the holy things, no such prohibition rested on circumcised slaves, as these were also actually members of the priest's household.—Ex 12:43-45; Le 22: 10, 11.

An Israelite who, because of financial reverses, had to sell himself into slavery to a fellow Israelite, or to an alien resident, a settler, or a member of the alien resident's family, was to be treated, not tyrannically, but with due consideration like a hired laborer. Then, if in his case it had not been possible to take advantage of the right of repurchase, he was to be set free from servitude either in the seventh year of his servitude or in the Jubilee year, depending upon which came first. —Ex 21:2; Le 25:39, 40, 47-49, 53; De 15:12; see SLAVE.

At times hired laborers were subjected to abuses from their employers. Through his prophet Malachi, Jehovah warned that He would become a speedy witness against those acting fraudulently with the wages of a wage worker.—Mal 3:5; see also Jas 5:4; HIRE, WAGES.

The hired laborer generally was anxious to see the close of the workday and to receive his wages. (Job 7:1, 2) He often did not properly have the interests of his employer fully at heart, as is evident from Jesus Christ's statement that, unlike the hired man who flees in the case of danger, he, as the Fine Shepherd, would surrender his soul in behalf of the sheep.—Joh 10:11-15; see also Jer 46:21.

HITTITES
(Hit′tites) [Of (Belonging to) Heth]. A people descended from Heth, the second-named son of Canaan. (Ge 10:15) They were therefore of Hamitic origin.—Ge 10:6.

Abraham had some dealings with the Hittites, who were residing in Canaan at the time of his moving there. Jehovah had promised to give to Abraham's seed the land of Canaan, which was inhabited by a number of nations, including the Hittite nation. (Ge 15:18-21) However, Jehovah told Abraham that "the error of the Amorites [a term often used generally for the nations in Canaan] has not yet come to completion." (Ge 15:16) Therefore Abraham respected the Hittite ownership of the land, and when his wife Sarah died, he bargained with Ephron the son of Zoar the Hittite for a cave in which to bury her.—Ge 23:1-20.

In Joshua's day the Hittites are described as inhabiting the land that covered an area "from the wilderness and this Lebanon to the great river, the river Euphrates, that is, all the land of the Hittites." (Jos 1:4) Apparently they lived mainly in the mountainous regions, which would include Lebanon and, possibly, areas in Syria. —Nu 13:29; Jos 11:3.

Under Noah's Curse. The descent of the Hittites from Canaan brought them under the curse placed by Noah upon Canaan, and when Israel subjugated them it was in fulfillment of Noah's words at Genesis 9:25-27. The religion of the Hittites was pagan, undoubtedly being phallic, as were the other Canaanite religions. When Abraham's grandson Esau married Hittite women, this was "a source of bitterness of spirit to Isaac and Rebekah," Esau's father and mother.—Ge 26:34, 35; 27:46.

God described the land that the Hittites and other associated nations occupied as "a land flowing with milk and honey." (Ex 3:8) But these nations had become so corrupt that their presence on the land defiled it. (Le 18:25, 27) Many are the warnings that God gave Israel as to the danger of association with them in their degraded, filthy practices. He lists many immoralities, forbidding the Israelites to engage in them, and then says: "Do not make yourselves unclean by any of these things, because by all these things the nations [including the Hittites] whom I am sending out from before you have made themselves unclean." —Le 18:1-30.

Destruction Decreed. The Hittites were one of the seven nations named as due to be devoted to destruction. These nations were described as "more populous and mighty" than Israel. So the seven nations at that time must have numbered more than three million persons, and the Hittites in their mountain stronghold would be a formidable foe. (De 7:1, 2) They manifested their enmity by assembling with the other nations of Canaan to fight Israel (led by Joshua) when they got news of Israel's crossing the Jordan and destroying the cities of Jericho and Ai. (Jos 9:1, 2; 24:11) The cities of the Hittites therefore should have been destroyed and their inhabitants wiped out so that they would not be a danger to Israel's loyalty to God and cause Israel to incur God's disfavor. (De 20:16-18) But Israel carried out God's command imperfectly. After Joshua passed off the scene they disobediently failed to clear out these nations, which remained as a thorn in the side and a constant harassment to them.—Nu 33:55, 56.

Later History. Because Israel did not obey God by destroying the Canaanite nations completely, God declared: "I, in turn, have said, 'I shall not drive them away from before you, and they must become snares to you, and their gods will serve as a lure to you.'" (Jg 2:3) It appears that those Canaanites remaining among Israel were tolerated and, in some rare instances, were even given positions of respect and responsibility. Also, it seems that, of the Canaanite nations, only the Hittites maintained prominence and strength as a nation.—1Ki 10:29; 2Ki 7:6.

Two Hittites were soldiers, possibly officers, in David's army, namely, Ahimelech and Uriah. Uriah was a man zealous for the victory of Israel over its enemies, and one who observed the Law. David had relations with Bath-sheba, the wife of Uriah, and subsequently had Uriah put into a dangerous position in battle, where he was killed. For this, David was punished by God.—1Sa 26:6; 2Sa 11:3, 4, 11, 15-17; 12:9-12.

King Solomon levied men from among the Hittites for slavish forced labor. (2Ch 8:7, 8) However, his foreign wives, among whom were Hittite women, caused Solomon to turn away from Jehovah his God. (1Ki 11:1-6) The Hittites are mentioned in the Bible as having kings and warring ability as late as the reign of King Jehoram of Israel (c. 917-905 B.C.E.). (2Ki 7:6) However, the Syrian, Assyrian, and Babylonian conquests of the land apparently shattered the Hittites as a power.

After the restoration of Israel from exile in 537 B.C.E., the people of Israel and even some of the priests and Levites married women of the Canaanite nations and gave their daughters to Canaanite men, among these being Hittites. This was in violation of God's law. For this, Ezra reproved them, moving them to an agreement to put away their foreign wives.—Ezr 9:1, 2; 10:14, 16-19, 44.

Figurative Use. Jehovah, speaking through the prophet Ezekiel, used the term "Hittite" in a figurative sense in speaking to Jerusalem. He said: "Your origin and your birth were from the land of the Canaanite. Your father was the Amorite, and your mother was a Hittite." (Eze 16:3) Jerusalem, the capital of the nation, upon which Jehovah placed his name was, when Israel entered the land, a city occupied by the Jebusites. But since the most prominent tribes were the Amorites and the Hittites, these are apparently used as representative of the nations of Canaan, including the Jebusites. Therefore the city had a lowly heritage, but Jehovah had caused it to be beautified. Through King David, sitting on "Jehovah's throne" (1Ch 29:23), with the ark of the covenant on Mount Zion, and finally, the glorious temple built by David's son Solomon, the fame of Jerusalem came to be spread about among the nations. But Jerusalem became like the Canaanite nations around her, corrupt and immoral, for which Jehovah finally brought desolation upon her.—Eze 16:14, 15.

Secular Attempts at Identification. Historians and archaeologists have tried to identify the Hittites of the Bible in secular history. Their primary basis for making identifications has been linguistic, the comparison of words apparently having similar sound or spelling.

In the Assyrian cuneiform texts, frequent reference is made to "Hatti" in a context that usually places it in Syria or Palestine. These may be references to the Biblical Hittites. However, on the basis of this term "Hatti," scholars try to identify the Bible Hittites with the so-called Hittite Empire that had its capital in Asia Minor, far to the N and W of the land of Canaan. This they try to do in the following manner, but in doing so they refer to three different groups of people.

Three Groups "Identified." In Anatolia (a part of what is now called Turkey) in Asia Minor, many ancient texts have been unearthed at Bogazköy, formerly called "Hattushash." It was the capital of a land that modern scholars have called Hatti and whose inhabitants spoke "Hattic." These early people were evidently overrun by conquerors who brought in a different language, which, according to scholars, was an Indo-European language. This language used cuneiform script and is called "cuneiform Hittite." Later a yet different Indo-European language using hieroglyphic script superseded the cuneiform script, and this language is referred to as "hieroglyphic Hittite." Some examples of texts in this language are said to have been found in both Asia Minor and northern Syria. Scholars say that these three languages represent three groups. But there is no proof that any of these were the Hittites of the Bible. Concerning so-called cuneiform Hittite, Martin Noth stated: "The term 'Hittite' is not found in the ancient texts, but was invented by modern students, resting on the historical connection between this language and the kingdom of *Hatti* in Asia Minor." He goes on to say regarding the "Hittite hieroglyphs": "The conventional term Hittite is irrelevant and confusing when applied to them." (*The Old Testament World,* 1966, p. 231) Another historian, E. A. Speiser, concludes: "The problem of the Hittites in the Bible is . . . complex. To begin with, there is the question as to which type of Hittites may be involved in any given Biblical passage: Hattians, Indo-European Hittites of the cuneiform records, or hieroglyphic Hittites."—*The World History of the Jewish People,* 1964, Vol. 1, p. 160.

From the foregoing it can be seen that any supposed identification of the Hittites of the Bible with the "Hittite Empire" that had as its capital city Hattushash is merely conjecture and has not been proved. Because of this uncertainty, references in this publication to the secular "Hittites" are generally set in quotation marks to remind the reader that such identification is not proved and that we do not feel the evidence is strong enough to view such identification as conclusive.

HIVITES (Hi′vites). A people descended from Canaan the son of Ham. (Ge 10:6, 15, 17; 1Ch 1:13, 15) Hivites inhabited the city of Shechem in the days of the patriarch Jacob. The sons of Jacob, led by Simeon and Levi, killed every male and plundered the city because Shechem the son of Hamor the chieftain had defiled their sister Dinah.—Ge 34:1-29.

When Israel entered the Promised Land, the Hivites constituted one of the seven Canaanite nations that God promised to drive out before them. (Ex 3:8, 17; 13:5; 23:23, 28; 33:2; 34:11) These nations were said to be more populous and mighty than Israel. (De 7:1) Moses commanded the Israelites to devote them to destruction, leaving none alive when capturing their cities, because of their detestable practices and their false

gods. Otherwise they would prove to be a snare and would cause Israel to come into God's disfavor.—Le 18:27, 28; De 18:9-13; 20:15-18.

The Bible records Joshua's total destruction of the cities of those nations. (Jos chaps 10, 11) Hivites residing "at the base of [Mount] Hermon in the land of Mizpah" were among the tribes joining the Canaanite kings against Joshua at the bidding of Jabin the king of Hazor. (Jos 11:1-3) Hivites are listed among those fighting against Israel and suffering defeat. (Jos 9:1, 2; 12:7, 8; 24:11) However, there was one group of the Hivite nation that was spared. (Jos 9:3, 7) This group was the Gibeonites, evidently representing three other Hivite cities as well. These alone feared Jehovah, recognizing that he was fighting for Israel. By a stratagem they managed to enter into a covenant with Israel's leaders and so were not killed but were made menial servants of Israel. (Jos 9:1-15, 24-27) This is one instance of the fulfillment of Noah's curse upon Canaan, in that the Gibeonites and their associates, though not destroyed, became slaves of the Semites.—Ge 9:25-27.

Jehovah indicated his approval of Israel's faithful keeping of their covenant with these Hivites by fighting for Gibeon's protection against the surrounding Canaanite nations that came against them as a result of their covenant with Israel. (Jos 10:1-14) From this time on the Gibeonites dwelt peaceably with Israel. (2Sa 21:1-6) They are called "Amorites" at 2 Samuel 21:2, but this is evidently because "Amorite" was a term often applied to the Canaanite nations in general, since the Amorites were one of the most powerful tribes. (See AMORITE.) At the time of Joshua's conquest, these approved Hivites resided in the city of Gibeon, located not far NW of Jerusalem, also in Chephirah, Beeroth, and Kiriath-jearim. Gibeon is described as 'a great city, like one of the royal cities, and greater than Ai, and all its men were mighty ones.'—Jos 10:2; 9:17.

After Joshua's death Israel failed to continue to clear out the Canaanite nations as God had commanded, but even intermarried with them. Hence, the Bible record reads: "Now these are the nations that Jehovah let stay so as by them to test Israel . . . The five axis lords of the Philistines, and all the Canaanites, even the Sidonians and the Hivites inhabiting Mount Lebanon from Mount Baal-hermon as far as to the entering in of Hamath . . . and they [the Israelites] took up serving their gods."—Jg 3:1-6.

This passage locates the Hivites as mountain dwellers in the Lebanon Range clear up to the northernmost part of the Promised Land. (Nu 34:8; Jos 11:1, 3) When Joab and his men took a census at King David's command, "they came to the fortress of Tyre and all the cities of the Hivites." (2Sa 24:7) Tyre was evidently just below the southern end of the Hivite territory.

During Solomon's nationwide building program, he used Canaanites, including Hivites, for forced labor under the direction of Israelite overseers. This further fulfilled Noah's prophetic curse on Canaan.—1Ki 9:20-23; 2Ch 8:7-10.

Hivites, Horites, and Hurrians. At Genesis 36:2 Zibeon, the grandfather of one of Esau's wives, is called a Hivite. But verses 20 and 24 list him as a descendant of Seir the Horite. The word "Horite" may be derived from the Hebrew *chor* ("hole") and may mean merely "cave dweller." This would eliminate any seeming discrepancy between the texts at Genesis 36:2 and verses 20, 24.—See HORITE.

Archaeologists have unearthed ancient writings that scholars have interpreted as proof that a nation called Hurrians inhabited the regions of Armenia, Anatolia, Syria, and parts of Palestine from patriarchal times; and they believe that this people included the Hivites, Horites, and Jebusites. They equate "Horite" with "Hivite" and believe that somehow the Hurrians came to be called Hivites. Their theory is based to a great extent on linguistic similarities, particularly in proper names. The name Horite is, therefore, generally thought by them to be related to "Hurrian" rather than to mean "cave dweller."

The Bible, however, seems to make a definite distinction between these tribes, and it does not mention the name Hurrian. Therefore it is wiser to await further evidence before accepting such identification as conclusive.

HIZKI (Hiz'ki) [shortened form of Hezekiah, meaning "Jehovah Strengthens"]. A Benjamite listed among the sons of Elpaal.—1Ch 8:1, 17, 18.

HIZKIAH (Hiz·ki'ah) [shortened form of Hezekiah, meaning "Jehovah Strengthens"]. One of the three sons of Neariah, a descendant of King Solomon.—1Ch 3:10, 23.

HOARFROST. A silvery-white deposit of ice needles formed by direct condensation at freezing temperatures. The ice crystals are long and needle shaped; usually they are perpendicular to the objects on which they occur and are most abundant along their edges. The moisture in the atmosphere freezes without passing through the liquid state, condensing on trees, plants, and other ob-

jects, usually in the night. It is often found on windows.

Jehovah speaks to Job of "the hoarfrost of heaven," doubtless because it is produced from the atmosphere by condensation. (Job 38:29) Of Jehovah, the psalmist says: "Hoarfrost he scatters just like ashes." (Ps 147:16) Jehovah gives forth the hoarfrost with as much ease as a man scatters ashes with his hand. It covers, or encrusts, such things as trees, grass, and houses with a covering, just as though ashes had been scattered over them by Jehovah's invisible hand.

The manna provided by Jehovah for the Israelites during their 40 years of wandering in the wilderness is described in this way at Exodus 16:14: "The layer of dew evaporated and here upon the surface of the wilderness there was a fine flaky thing, fine like hoarfrost upon the earth."

HOBAB (Ho'bab) [possibly, Cherished]. Moses' brother-in-law; son of Reuel (Jethro) and a Midianite, of the tribe of Kenites. (Nu 10:29; Ex 3:1; Jg 1:16) When the time came for the Israelites to move from the region of Mount Sinai toward the Promised Land, Moses requested that Hobab accompany them to serve as "eyes," or as a scout, for the nation because of his familiarity with the area. Although Hobab declined at first, apparently he did accompany the Israelites, for his descendants, the Kenites, took up dwelling in the Wilderness of Judah to the S of Arad and are mentioned as still living in that area in the time of Saul and David.—Nu 10:29-32; Jg 1:16; 1Sa 15:6; 27:10; 30:26, 29.

The Masoretic text of Judges 4:11, however, identifies Hobab as the father-in-law of Moses. (*NW, Yg, Ro, Da, JP, Mo, AT*) So the one name, Hobab, may designate two separate individuals, namely, Moses' father-in-law as well as his brother-in-law. That this is not out of the question is seen by the fact that more than one name is assigned to Moses' father-in-law.—Compare Ex 2:16-22; 3:1.

On the other hand, if Hobab was indeed only the name of the son of Reuel and hence was the name of only the brother-in-law of Moses, then the reference to Hobab as being Moses' father-in-law must mean that Hobab was viewed as the representative of his father Reuel, who was, in that case, likely then dead.—See JETHRO; KENITE.

HOBAH (Ho'bah). A site "north of Damascus" to which Abraham pursued the defeated armies under Chedorlaomer. (Ge 14:13-17) The Biblical location is associated by certain scholars with Hoba, a spring on the road between Palmyra and Damascus, where at least the ancient name appears to be preserved. Hoba, like other large springs near the desert, once may have had a village standing nearby.

HOD [Dignity]. Son of Zophah from the tribe of Asher. Hod was probably the head over one of the larger divisions of the army, having other chieftains under him.—1Ch 7:36, 37, 40.

HODAVIAH (Hod·a·vi′ah).

1. One of the seven sons of Elioenai, a descendant of King Solomon.—1Ch 3:10, 24.

2. One of the seven paternal heads of the half tribe of Manasseh.—1Ch 5:23, 24.

3. A Benjamite; "son of Hassenuah" and father, or ancestor, of Meshullam.—1Ch 9:7.

4. A Levite family head, 74 of whose "sons" (descendants) returned from Babylon in 537 B.C.E. and some of whom, if not all, served as supervisors in connection with the rebuilding of the temple. (Ezr 2:1, 2, 40; 3:9) Hodaviah is called Judah at Ezra 3:9 and Hodevah at Nehemiah 7:43.

HODESH (Ho′desh) [New Moon]. One of the wives of the Benjamite Shaharaim.—1Ch 8:1, 8, 9.

HODEVAH (Ho′de·vah). Forefather of certain Levites among those returning from Babylonian exile (Ne 7:6, 7, 43); alternate form of the name "Hodaviah."—Ezr 2:40; see HODAVIAH No. 4.

HODIAH (Ho·di′ah) [Dignity Is Jah].

1. A man who married the sister of a certain Naham. The name appears in the genealogy of Judah.—1Ch 4:1, 19.

2. A Levite who assisted Ezra in explaining the law of Jehovah to the congregation of Israel assembled before the Water Gate at the public square of Jerusalem, and evidently also one of those who called upon the sons of Israel to bless Jehovah and His glorious name and then reviewed God's dealings with His people. (Ne 8:1, 5, 7; 9:5) This Hodiah may be the same as either No. 3 or 4.

3, 4. The name of two Levites whose descendants, if not they themselves, attested by seal to the confession contract made during Nehemiah's governorship. If they personally did the sealing, then one of them could have been No. 2.—Ne 9:38; 10:1, 9, 10, 13.

5. One of "the heads of the people" whose descendant, if not he himself, attested to the confession contract in Nehemiah's day.—Ne 10:1, 14, 18.

HOE.   See FARMING IMPLEMENTS.

HOGLAH (Hog′lah). The third listed of Zelophehad's five daughters. Since her father had no sons, his inheritance was divided among the five daughters with the stipulation that they marry inside their own tribe of Manasseh, in order "that their inheritance might continue together with the tribe of the family of their father" and not "circulate from one tribe to another."—Nu 36:1-12; 26:33; 27:1-11; Jos 17:3, 4.

HOHAM (Ho′ham). King of Hebron; one of the five kings who went up to war against Gibeon because it had made peace with Joshua and the Israelites. These five kings were defeated when Joshua came to the aid of the Gibeonites. After being put to death, they were hung upon stakes until the evening and were thereafter thrown into a cave.—Jos 10:1-27.

HOLINESS.   The state or character of being holy. Holiness means "religious cleanness or purity; sacredness." Also, the original Hebrew qo′-dhesh conveys the thought of separateness, exclusiveness, or sanctification to God, who is holy; a state of being set aside to the service of God. In the Christian Greek Scriptures, the words rendered "holy" (ha′gi·os) and "holiness" (ha·gi·a·smos′ [also, "sanctification"]; ha·gi·o′tes; ha·gi·o·sy′ne) likewise denote separation to God; they also are used to refer to holiness as a quality of God and to purity or perfection in one's personal conduct.

Jehovah.   The quality of holiness belongs to Jehovah. (Ex 39:30; Zec 14:20) Christ Jesus addressed him as "Holy Father." (Joh 17:11) Those in the heavens are shown declaring: "Holy, holy, holy is Jehovah of armies," attributing to him holiness, cleanness in the superlative degree. (Isa 6:3; Re 4:8; compare Heb 12:14.) He is the Most Holy One, superior to all others in holiness. (Pr 30:3; here the plural form of the Hebrew word translated "Most Holy" is used to denote excellence and majesty.) The Israelites were frequently reminded that Jehovah is the Source of all holiness as they observed the words "Holiness belongs to Jehovah" that were engraved on the shining gold plate on the high priest's turban. This plate was called "the holy sign of dedication," showing that the high priest was set apart to a service of special holiness. (Ex 28:36; 29:6) In Moses' victory song after the deliverance through the Red Sea, Israel sang: "Who among the gods is like you, O Jehovah? Who is like you, proving yourself mighty in holiness?" (Ex 15:11; 1Sa 2:2) As an added guarantee of the carrying out of his word, Jehovah has even sworn by his holiness. —Am 4:2.

God's *name* is sacred, set apart from all defilement. (1Ch 16:10; Ps 111:9) His name Jehovah is to be held as holy, sanctified above all others. (Mt 6:9) Disrespect for his name merits the punishment of death.—Le 24:10-16, 23; Nu 15:30.

Since Jehovah God is the Originator of all righteous principles and laws (Jas 4:12) and is the basis of all holiness, any person or thing that is holy becomes so because of relationship with Jehovah and his worship. One cannot have understanding or wisdom unless he has knowledge of the Most Holy One. (Pr 9:10) Jehovah can be worshiped only in holiness. One claiming to worship him but practicing uncleanness is disgusting in his sight. (Pr 21:27) When Jehovah foretold that he would make the way clear for his people to return to Jerusalem from Babylonian exile, he said: "The Way of Holiness it will be called. The unclean one will not pass over it." (Isa 35:8) The small remnant that returned in 537 B.C.E. did so wholeheartedly to restore true worship, with right and holy motives, not for political or selfish considerations.—Compare the prophecy at Zec 14:20, 21.

Holy spirit. Jehovah's active force, or spirit, is subject to his control and always accomplishes his purpose. It is clean, pure, sacred, and set apart for God's good use. Therefore it is called "holy spirit" and "the spirit of holiness." (Ps 51:11; Lu 11:13; Ro 1:4; Eph 1:13) The holy spirit operating on a person is a force for holiness or cleanness. Any unclean or wrong practice constitutes a resisting or "grieving" of that spirit. (Eph 4:30) Though impersonal in itself, the holy spirit is expressive of God's holy personality and therefore can be 'grieved.' The practice of any wrongdoing tends to "put out the fire of the spirit." (1Th 5:19) If such practice is continued, God's holy spirit is, in effect, made to "feel hurt," and this may result in God's changing into an enemy of the rebellious one. (Isa 63:10) A person grieving the holy spirit may go so far as to blaspheme against it, which sin Jesus Christ said will not be forgiven in the present system of things nor in that to come.—Mt 12:31, 32; Mr 3:28-30; see SPIRIT.

Jesus Christ. Jesus Christ is, in a special sense, God's Holy One. (Ac 3:14; Mr 1:24; Lu 4:34) His holiness came from his Father when Jehovah created him as his only-begotten Son. He maintained his holiness as the closest one to his Father in the heavens. (Joh 1:1; 8:29; Mt 11:27) When his life was transferred to the womb of the virgin girl Mary, he was born as a holy human Son of God. (Lu 1:35) He is the only one who as a human maintained perfect, sinless holiness and who at the end of his earthly life was still "loyal, guileless, undefiled, separated from the sinners." (Heb 7:26) He was 'declared righteous' on his own merit. (Ro 5:18) A status of holiness before God is obtained by other humans only on the basis of Christ's holiness, and it is gained through faith in his ransom sacrifice. It is a "holy faith," which, if maintained, will serve in keeping one in God's love.—Jude 20, 21.

Other Persons. The entire nation of Israel was counted holy because of God's choosing and sanctifying of it, bringing the people exclusively into covenant relationship with him as a special property. He told them that if they obeyed him, they would be "a kingdom of priests and a holy nation." (Ex 19:5, 6) By obedience they would "indeed prove to be holy to [their] God." God admonished them: "You should prove yourselves holy, because I Jehovah your God am holy." (Nu 15:40; Le 19:2) The dietary, sanitary, and moral laws that God gave them were constant reminders to them of their separateness and holiness to God. The restrictions placed upon them by these laws were a strong force that greatly limited their association with their pagan neighbors, proving to be a protection to keep Israel holy. On the other hand, the nation would lose its holy status before God if disobedient to his laws.—De 28:15-19.

Although Israel as a nation was holy, certain individuals within the nation were considered holy in a special way. The priests, and particularly the high priest, were set aside for service at the sanctuary and represented the people before God. In such capacity they were holy and had to maintain sanctification in order to be able to carry out their service and to continue to be viewed as holy by God. (Le 21; 2Ch 29:34) The prophets and other inspired Bible writers were holy men. (2Pe 1:21) Women of ancient times who were faithful to God are called "holy" by the apostle Peter. (1Pe 3:5) Soldiers of Israel on a military campaign were considered holy, for the wars they fought were the wars of Jehovah. (Nu 21:14; 1Sa 21:5, 6) Every male firstborn of Israel was holy to Jehovah, since, at the time of the Passover in Egypt, the firstborn had been spared by Jehovah from death; they belonged to him. (Nu 3:12, 13; 8:17) For this reason each firstborn son had to be redeemed at the sanctuary. (Ex 13:1, 2; Nu 18:15, 16; Lu 2:22, 23) A person (man or woman) taking a vow to live as a Nazirite was holy during the period of the vow. This time was set apart as being fully devoted to some special service of Jehovah. The Nazirite had to observe certain legal requirements; a violation would make him unclean. He then had to make a special sacrifice to restore his status of holiness. The days prior to his becoming unclean did not count toward the fulfillment of his Naziriteship; he had to begin anew the carrying out of his vow.—Nu 6:1-12.

Places. A place is made holy by the presence of Jehovah. (When appearing to men, he manifested his presence by means of angels representing him; Ga 3:19.) Moses was on holy ground as he stood observing the burning bush from which an angel representing Jehovah spoke to him. (Ex 3:2-5) Joshua was reminded that he was on holy ground when an angel, the prince of the army of Jehovah, materialized and stood before him. (Jos 5:13-15) Peter, referring to the transfiguration of Christ and to Jehovah's speaking at that time, called the site "the holy mountain."—2Pe 1:17, 18; Lu 9:28-36.

The tabernacle courtyard was holy ground. According to tradition, the priests served there barefoot because they were serving at the sanctuary, which was associated with Jehovah's presence. The two compartments of the sanctuary were called "the Holy Place" and "the Most Holy," as they were progressively closer to the ark of the covenant. (Heb 9:1-3) The temple that later stood in Jerusalem was likewise holy. (Ps 11:4) Holiness applied to Mount Zion and Jerusalem because the sanctuary and "Jehovah's throne" were located there.—1Ch 29:23; Ps 2:6; Isa 27:13; 48:2; 52:1; Da 9:24; Mt 4:5.

The army of Israel was reminded to keep the camp clean from human excrement or other contamination, because "Jehovah your God is walking about within your camp . . . and your camp must prove to be holy, that he may see nothing indecent in you and certainly turn away from accompanying you." (De 23:9-14) Here physical cleanness is linked with holiness.

Periods of Time. Certain days or periods of time were set apart for Israel as holy. This was not because of any holiness intrinsic, or inherent, in the time periods themselves. It was because they were to be seasons of special observance in the worship of Jehovah. In setting aside these periods, God had in mind the people's welfare and their spiritual upbuilding. There were the weekly Sabbaths. (Ex 20:8-11) On these days the people could concentrate their attention on God's law and on teaching it to their children. Other days of

holy convention or Sabbath were: the first day of the seventh month (Le 23:24) and the Day of Atonement on the tenth day of the seventh month. (Le 23:26-32) The festival periods, and particularly certain days thereof, were observed as "holy conventions." (Le 23:37, 38) These festivals were Passover and the Festival of Unfermented Cakes (Le 23:4-8); Pentecost, or the Festival of Weeks (Le 23:15-21); and the Festival of Booths, or Ingathering.—Le 23:33-36, 39-43; see CONVENTION.

In addition, every seventh year was a sabbath year, a full year of holiness. During a sabbath year the land was to lie uncultivated; this provision, like the weekly Sabbath, gave the Israelites even more time to study Jehovah's law, to meditate on it, and to teach it to their children. (Ex 23:10, 11; Le 25:2-7) Finally, every 50th year was called a Jubilee, likewise counted as holy. This, too, was a sabbath year, but in addition it restored the nation economically to the theocratic status that God established at the time the land was apportioned. It was a holy year of freedom, rest, and refreshment.—Le 25:8-12.

Jehovah commanded that his people 'afflict their souls' on the Day of Atonement, a day of "holy convention." This meant that they should fast and should recognize and confess their sins as well as feel godly sorrow for them. (Le 16:29-31; 23:26-32) But no day holy to Jehovah was to be a day of weeping and sadness for his people. Rather, those days were to be days of rejoicing and declaring of praise to Jehovah for his marvelous provisions through his lovingkindness.—Ne 8:9-12.

Jehovah's holy rest day. The Bible shows us that God proceeded to rest from his creative works some 6,000 years ago, declaring the seventh "day" sacred, or holy. (Ge 2:2, 3) The apostle Paul shows that Jehovah's great rest day is a long period of time, when he speaks of the day as still being open so that by faith and obedience Christians can enter into its rest. As a holy day, it is a time of relief and rejoicing for Christians even in the midst of a weary, sin-stricken world.—Heb 4:3-10; see DAY.

Objects. Certain things were set aside for use in worship. Here also holiness came to them by reason of their sanctification for Jehovah's service; not that they had holiness of themselves, to be used as a charm or fetish. For example, one of the primary holy objects, the ark of the covenant, proved to be no charm when Eli's two wicked sons accompanied it into battle against the Philistines. (1Sa 4:3-11) The things made holy by God's decree included the altar of sacrifice (Ex 29:37), the anointing oil (Ex 30:25), the special incense (Ex 30:35, 37), the garments of the priesthood (Ex 28:2; Le 16:4), the showbread (Ex 25:30; 1Sa 21:4, 6), and all the furniture of the sanctuary. These latter items included the golden altar of incense, the table of showbread, and the lampstands, along with their utensils. Many of these items are listed at 1 Kings 7:47-51. These things were holy also in a greater sense in that they were patterns of heavenly things and served in a typical way for the benefit of those who are going to inherit salvation.—Heb 8:4, 5; 9:23-28.

The written Word of God is called "the holy Scriptures," or "holy writings." It was written under the influence of the holy spirit and has the power of sanctifying, or making holy, those who obey its commands.—Ro 1:2; 2Ti 3:15.

Animals and Produce. The firstborn males of cattle, sheep, and goats were counted as holy to Jehovah and were not to be redeemed. They were to be sacrificed, and a portion went to the sanctified priests. (Nu 18:17-19) The firstfruits and the tithe were holy, as were all sacrifices and all gifts sanctified to the service of the sanctuary. (Ex 28:38) All things holy to Jehovah were sacred and could not be considered lightly or used in a common, or profane, way. An example is the law regarding the tithe. If a man set aside the portion to be tithed, say, of his wheat crop, and then he or one of his household unintentionally took some of it for home use, such as cooking, the man was guilty of violating God's law respecting holy things. The Law required that he make compensation to the sanctuary of an equal amount plus 20 percent, besides offering up a sound ram of the flock as a sacrifice. Thus, great respect was engendered for the holy things belonging to Jehovah.—Le 5:14-16.

Christian Holiness. The Leader of Christians, the Son of God, when born as a human, was holy (Lu 1:35), and he maintained that sanctification, or holiness, throughout his earthly life. (Joh 17:19; Ac 4:27; Heb 7:26) This holiness was thorough, perfect, filling his every thought, word, and action. By maintaining his holiness even to a sacrificial death, he made it possible for others to attain holiness. Consequently, those called to be his footstep followers are called with "a holy calling." (2Ti 1:9) They become Jehovah's anointed ones, the spiritual brothers of Jesus Christ, and are called "holy ones" or "saints." (Ro 15:26; Eph 1:1; Php 4:21; compare KJ.) They receive holiness by faith in the ransom sacrifice of Christ. (Php 3:8, 9; 1Jo 1:7) Holiness, then, does not inhere in them, or belong to them, through their own merit, but it comes to them through Jesus Christ.—Ro 3:23-26.

The many Scriptural references to living members of the congregation as "holy ones," or "saints" (Dy, KJ), make it clear that a person is not made a holy one, or "saint," by men or by an organization, nor does such a one have to wait until after death to be made a "saint." He is a "holy one" by virtue of God's calling of him to joint heirship with Christ. He is holy in the eyes of God while he is on earth, with the hope of heavenly life in the spirit realm, wherein dwell Jehovah God and his Son, along with the holy angels.—1Pe 1:3, 4; 2Ch 6:30; Mr 12:25; Ac 7:56.

Clean conduct essential. Those who have this holy standing before Jehovah strive, with the help of God's spirit, to attain to the holiness of God and Christ. (1Th 3:12, 13) This requires study of God's Word of truth and the application of it to their lives. (1Pe 1:22) It requires response to Jehovah's discipline. (Heb 12:9-11) It follows that if a person is genuinely holy, he will pursue a course of holiness, cleanness, and moral uprightness. Christians are admonished to present their bodies to God as a sacrifice that is holy, just as acceptable sacrifices presented at the ancient sanctuary were holy. (Ro 12:1) Holiness in conduct is a command: "In accord with the Holy One who called you, do you also become holy yourselves in all your conduct, because it is written: 'You must be holy, because I am holy.'"—1Pe 1:15, 16.

Those who become members of the body of Christ are "fellow citizens of the holy ones and are members of the household of God." (Eph 2:19) They are likened to a holy temple of living stones for Jehovah and constitute "a royal priesthood, a holy nation, a people for special possession." (1Pe 2:5, 9) They must cleanse themselves of "every defilement of *flesh* and *spirit,* perfecting holiness in God's fear." (2Co 7:1) If a Christian practices habits that defile or damage his fleshly body, or make it filthy or unclean, or if he goes contrary to the Bible in doctrine or morals, he does not love or fear God and is turning away from holiness. One cannot carry on uncleanness and remain holy.

Holy things to be treated with respect. If a member of the temple class uses his body in an unclean way, he defiles and tears down not only himself but also God's temple, and "if anyone destroys the temple of God, God will destroy him; for the temple of God is holy, which temple you people are." (1Co 3:17) He has been redeemed by the blood of God's Holy One. (1Pe 1:18, 19) If anyone misuses what is holy to Jehovah, whether his own body or any other dedicated thing, or if he harms or commits offenses against another person who is holy to God, he will suffer punishment from God.—2Th 1:6-9.

God revealed to Israel his attitude toward such profane use of his holy possessions. This is seen in his law prohibiting the common, or profane, use of things set apart as holy for those under the Mosaic Law, for example, the firstfruits and the tithe. (Jer 2:3; Re 16:5, 6; Lu 18:7; 1Th 4:3-8; Ps 105:15; Zec 2:8) Also consider the punishment God brought upon Babylon for its malicious misuse of his temple vessels and of the people of his holy nation. (Da 5:1-4, 22-31; Jer 50:9-13) In view of this attitude of God, Christians are repeatedly commended for and reminded of the necessity to exercise loving, kind treatment toward Jehovah's holy ones, the spiritual brothers of Jesus Christ.—Ro 15:25-27; Eph 1:15, 16; Col 1:3, 4; 1Ti 5:9, 10; Phm 5-7; Heb 6:10; compare Mt 25:40, 45.

Counted holy in God's sight. Before Jesus came to earth and became the forerunner and opener of the way to heavenly life, faithful men and women were counted holy. (Heb 6:19, 20; 10:19, 20; 1Pe 3:5) So, too, "a great crowd" not included among the 144,000 "sealed" ones can have a status of holiness before God. Such are viewed as wearing clean garments, washed in the blood of Christ. (Re 7:2-4, 9, 10, 14; see GREAT CROWD.) In due time all who live in heaven and on earth will be holy, for "the creation itself also will be set free from enslavement to corruption and have the glorious freedom of the children of God." —Ro 8:20, 21.

Holiness blessed by Jehovah. Holiness on a person's part carries with it merit from God in the individual's family relationship. Thus, if a married person is a Christian, holy to God, this one's mate and the children of the union, if not themselves dedicated servants of God, benefit from the merit of the one who is holy. For this reason the apostle recommends: "If any brother has an unbelieving wife, and yet she is agreeable to dwelling with him, let him not leave her; and a woman who has an unbelieving husband, and yet he is agreeable to dwelling with her, let her not leave her husband. For the unbelieving husband is sanctified in relation to his wife, and the unbelieving wife is sanctified in relation to the brother; otherwise, your children would really be unclean, but now they are holy." (1Co 7:12-14) The clean, believing mate is therefore not unclean by relations with the unbelieving mate, and the family

as a unit is not viewed by God as unclean. Furthermore, the association of the believer with the family provides any unbelievers therein the finest of opportunities to become believers, to make over their personalities, and to present their bodies "a sacrifice living, holy, acceptable to God." (Ro 12:1; Col 3:9, 10) In the clean, holy atmosphere that the believer serving God can promote, the family is blessed.—See SANCTIFICATION (In Marriage).

HOLON   (Ho'lon) [Place of Sand].

1. A city in the mountainous region of Judah assigned to the priestly Kohathites (Jos 15:21, 48, 51; 21:9-19); apparently called Hilen at 1 Chronicles 6:58. Holon of Judah is tentatively identified with Khirbet 'Illin (Horvat 'Illit), about 17 km (11 mi) NNW of Hebron.

2. A Moabite city of the tableland, or "level country," E of the Jordan mentioned with other cities in a pronouncement against Moab. (Jer 48: 21) Its exact location is today unknown.

HOLY CONTRIBUTION.   A portion of land in Ezekiel's vision of the division of the Promised Land.

Each of the 12 tribes, with the exception of Levi (Ephraim and Manasseh standing for Joseph, thus making up the 12), was given an allotment running E and W across the land. South of the portion for Judah, which was the seventh allotment from the northern extremity, was an administrative strip of land. (Eze 48:1-8) The northern border of this strip ran along the southern border of Judah's allotment; it was bounded on the S by Benjamin's portion, which was the fifth allotment from the southern extremity. (Eze 48:23-28) This administrative strip was 25,000 cubits (13 km; 8 mi) wide from N to S. It was to be given by the people for governmental use.—Eze 48:8.

The sanctuary of Jehovah was located in the midst of a 25,000-cubit-square "contribution" within the administrative strip. The remainder of the strip to the E and W of this "contribution" consisted of two portions for the chieftain. (Eze 48:20-22; see CHIEFTAIN.) The square "contribution" was divided as follows: a strip along the northern boundary, 10,000 cubits (5.2 km; 3.2 mi) wide, for the nonpriestly Levites. None of this assignment of land was to be sold or exchanged, "for it is something holy to Jehovah." (Eze 48:13, 14) Bordering the Levite portion on the S was a 10,000-cubit strip, a "holy contribution for the priests." This priestly section contained Jehovah's sanctuary, or temple. (Eze 48:9-12) This left a strip 5,000 cubits (2.6 km;

1.6 mi) wide on the south. This section was "something profane for the city, for a dwelling place and for pasture ground." (Eze 48:15) In the center of this section was to be the city called "Jehovah Himself Is There." The city was 4,500 cubits (2.3 km; 1.4 mi) square, having 12 gates, with a pasture ground 250 cubits (130 m; 425 ft) wide all around it. The remaining portion of the 25,000-cubit square, namely 10,000 cubits to the E of the city and 10,000 cubits to the W (5,000 cubits wide), was also considered profane and was to be cultivated by the tribes of Israel to provide food for the city.—Eze 48:15-19, 30-35.

Thus, "the holy contribution" was actually 25,-000 cubits E to W and 20,000 cubits N to S. It consisted of two 10,000-cubit-wide strips, one assigned to the priests and the other to the Levites. The remainder of the 25,000-cubit-square contribution was "something profane," being used "for the city, for a dwelling place and for pasture ground."—Eze 48:10, 13-15, 18, 20, 21.

HOLY OF HOLIES.   See Most Holy.

HOLY ONES.   Those who are clean, particularly in a spiritual or moral sense; it also denotes persons set apart for the service of God, in heaven or on earth.

Jehovah himself, supreme in cleanness and righteousness, is the Most Holy One. (Ho 11:12) He is frequently called "the Holy One of Israel." (2Ki 19:22; Ps 71:22; 89:18) The apostle John says to fellow members of the Christian congregation: "You have an anointing from the *holy one.*" (1Jo 2:20) Jesus Christ is called "that holy and righteous one" referred to at Acts 3:14. Angels of Jehovah in heaven are holy ones, fully devoted to God's service, clean and righteous.—Lu 9:26; Ac 10:22.

In Ancient Times.   Humans on earth who have been set apart for the service of God have also been called "holy ones." (Ps 34:9) Israel, brought into covenant relationship with God, became his special property and was, as a nation, holy to him. That is why individuals of that nation who practiced uncleanness or wrongdoing brought defilement and Jehovah's disfavor upon the nation, unless action was taken to clear them out. Greedy, disobedient Achan is a case in point; his sin brought distress on Israel until he was discovered and stoned to death.—Jos 7.

Aaron, anointed with the holy anointing oil as the nation's high priest, was holy in a special, intensified sense. (Ps 106:16) Accordingly, the requirements of his office were very exacting. (Le

21:1-15; also note the disqualifying factors for all priests in verses 16-23; see High Priest.) A sin on the part of the high priest (for example, an error in judgment of a matter) could bring guiltiness upon the people and had to be atoned for by the sacrifice of a young bull, the same sacrifice required for a mistake of the entire assembly.—Le 4:3, 13, 14.

Christian Holy Ones.   Persons brought into relationship with God by means of the new covenant are sanctified, cleansed, and set apart for God's exclusive service by "the blood of the covenant," the shed blood of Jesus Christ. (Heb 10:29; 13:20) They are thereby constituted "holy ones" ("saints" in *KJ* and some other versions). Consequently, they do not become "holy ones," or "saints," by decree of a man or an organization, but by God, who brings them into covenant relationship with himself through the blood of Jesus Christ. The term "holy ones" applies to all those thus brought into union and joint heirship with Christ, not to a mere few considered to have exceptional holiness. It is also applied in the Bible to them from the beginning of their sanctified course on earth, not being deferred until after their death. Peter says they must be holy because God is holy. (1Pe 1:15, 16; Le 11:44) All the spiritual brothers of Christ in the congregations are frequently called "holy ones."—Ac 9:13; 26: 10; Ro 1:7; 12:13; 2Co 1:1; 13:13.

As the "wife" of Christ, the entire congregation is represented as wearing bright, clean, fine linen, which stands for "the righteous acts of the holy ones." (Re 19:7, 8) Against these, while they are on earth, Satan the Devil's symbolic political "wild beast" is seen in vision waging war. (Re 13:3, 7) Thereby the endurance of the holy ones is severely tested, but they conquer by observing the commandments of God and the faith of Jesus. —Re 13:10; 14:12.

Their hope.   In a parallel vision Daniel saw a wild beast making war upon God's holy ones; this was followed by a court scene in which "the Ancient of Days" gave judgment in favor of the holy ones and they were given an indefinitely lasting Kingdom, "the kingdom and the rulership and the grandeur of the kingdoms under all the heavens."—Da 7:21, 22, 27.

These "holy ones" do not exercise kingly authority while on earth but must await their being united with Christ in the heavens. (Eph 1:18-21) They must first be 'conquerors.' (Re 3:21; compare Re 2:26, 27; 3:5, 12.) They are to act as priests and to rule as kings with Christ during his

Thousand Year Reign. (Re 20:4, 6) The apostle Paul states that the holy ones will judge the world, as well as angels, evidently sharing in the execution of judgment on wicked ones.—1Co 6:2, 3; Re 2:26, 27.

Attack on "Camp of the Holy Ones." At Revelation 20:7-9 it is foretold that Satan the Devil will lead the nations in war against "the camp of the holy ones and the beloved city" after the end of the thousand years of Christ's reign. The prophecy evidently refers to an earthly rebellion against the sovereignty of God's kingdom over earth, which is an attack on the "holy ones." In this context these are evidently those of restored mankind who are maintaining their integrity to God and his Messianic King.—See HOLINESS.

HOLY PLACE.
A term applied in several ways in the Scriptures. (1) In general, it could be applied to the camp of Israel, to Jerusalem and the holy places within it; also, it was specifically used in reference to (2) the entire tent of meeting and, later, the temple; (3) the Most Holy, the innermost compartment of the tabernacle and, later, the temple; and (4) the first interior room of the tabernacle, as distinguished from the Most Holy compartment. In each appearance of the expression "holy place," the application intended can be determined from the context.

1. The *camp of Israel* (De 23:14); later, the land of Israel and the city of Jerusalem in particular. (Compare Mt 24:15 and Lu 21:20; notice the expression "holy city" at Mt 27:53.) God's sanctuary was located there, his name was placed there, and his people were counted holy. (Eze 21:2) The entire camp, and later the entire land that God gave to his people, was to be kept holy. Hence, anyone offering up a sacrifice to a false god or carrying on any unclean practices defiled God's sanctuary, which was located in their midst.—Le 20:3; compare Le 18:21, 30; 19:30; Nu 5:2, 3; Jer 32:34; Eze 5:11; 23:38.

2. The *tent of meeting* and, later, the *temple*. The entire arrangement, including the courtyard of the tabernacle and the temple courts, was a holy place. (Ex 38:24; 2Ch 29:5; Ac 21:28) The primary items located in the courtyard were the altar of sacrifice and the copper basin. These were holy objects. Only those persons ceremonially clean could enter into the tabernacle courtyard at any time; likewise, no one could go into the temple courts in an unclean state. For example, a woman in the unclean state could not touch any holy thing or come into the holy place. (Le

12:2-4) Evidently even a state of continued uncleanness on the part of the Israelites was considered to be a defiling of the tabernacle. (Le 15:31) Those presenting offerings for cleansing from leprosy brought their sacrifice only as far as the gate of the courtyard. (Le 14:11) No unclean person could partake of a communion sacrifice at the tabernacle or the temple, on pain of death.—Le 7:20, 21.

3. The *Most Holy*, the innermost compartment. At Leviticus 16:2 it is called "the holy place [Heb., *haq·qo'desh*, "holy"] inside the curtain." Paul apparently had this compartment in mind when he spoke of Jesus' entry into heaven, saying that he did not enter into a "holy place [Gr., *ha'gi·a*, "holies"] made with hands." (Heb 9:24) At Hebrews 10:19 Paul speaks of "the holy place" (*NW*); "the holiest" (*KJ*) (literally, the holies, or the holy places, the plural denoting excellence).

The Most Holy of the tabernacle contained only the golden ark of the covenant, surmounted by two golden cherubs with wings extended. (Ex 25:10-22; 26:33) The temple built by Solomon also contained two large cherubs of oil-tree wood overlaid with gold. (1Ki 6:23-28) Following the Babylonian exile, however, the sacred Ark was missing from the Most Holy.

In the Most Holy, the high priest was surrounded by embroidered cherubs on the tabernacle's inner covering and on the curtain. (Ex 26:1, 31, 33) In Solomon's temple, the walls and ceiling were of cedarwood covered with gold; cherubs, palm-tree figures, gourd-shaped ornaments, and blossoms were engraved on the walls.—1Ki 6:16-18, 29; 2Ch 3:7, 8.

4. The *first, larger compartment*, the *Holy Place*, or the *Holy*, as distinguished from the innermost compartment, the Most Holy. (Ex 26:33) This compartment was two thirds the total length of the structure. (1Ki 6:16, 17; 2Ch 3:3, 8) Inside the Holy Place of the tabernacle were located the golden lampstand on the S side of the room (Ex 25:31-40; 40:24, 25), the golden altar of incense at the W end in front of the curtain to the Most Holy (Ex 30:1-6; 40:26, 27), and the table of showbread on the N side (Ex 25:23-30; 40:22, 23; Heb 9:2, 3). Along with these were the accompanying golden utensils, including bowls, snuffers, and so forth. In the temple's Holy Place were the golden altar, the ten tables of showbread, and ten lampstands. The lampstands and tables were placed five on the right and five on the left.—1Ki 7:48-50; 2Ch 4:7, 8, 19, 20.

When inside the tabernacle's Holy Place, the

priest would see, between the parts of the panel frames of the walls, and on the ceiling, the colorful embroidered cherubs of the tabernacle's inner covering. (Ex 26:1, 15) Suspended from four golden pillars was the curtain to the Most Holy, likewise embroidered with cherubs. (Ex 26:31-33) The screen to the tabernacle entrance was also of colorful material. (Ex 26:36) In the temple, the walls of this room had carvings of cherubs, palm-tree figures, gourd-shaped ornaments, and garlands of blossoms, all covered with gold.—1Ki 6:17, 18, 22, 29.

Symbolic Significance. The arrangement that God set up for man's atonement through the sacrifice of Jesus Christ is called "the greater and more perfect tent not made with hands." Christ entered "once for all time into the holy place" of this great spiritual temple "and obtained an everlasting deliverance for us," writes the apostle Paul. (Heb 9:11, 12) On going into heaven and appearing before Jehovah, Christ entered into what was pictured by the innermost compartment of the tabernacle, namely, the Most Holy. (Heb 9:24, 25) Thus the tabernacle and its services served as "a typical representation and a shadow of the heavenly things."—Heb 8:5.

Christian underpriests. Inasmuch as the place where God dwells is a sanctuary, a holy place, the Christian congregation is also likened to a holy place, the temple of God. (1Co 3:17; Eph 2:21, 22) While on earth, the anointed followers of Jesus Christ are spoken of as "being built up a spiritual house for the purpose of a holy priesthood" and as constituting "a royal priesthood." (1Pe 2:5, 9) As the underpriests served in the courtyard and also in the Holy Place, so these Christian priests of God serve before his symbolic altar and also in the symbolic Holy Place. The priests of Israel had to be clean, so when they were preparing to serve in the Holy Place they washed themselves with water from the copper basin in the courtyard. (Ex 40:30-32) So, too, those Christians who have been declared righteous are said to be "washed clean." (1Co 6:11) The Israelite priests were surrounded by the figures of the cherubs on the tabernacle curtains as they carried out their duties there. This calls to mind the statement of the apostle to certain ones that are declared righteous that, while yet on earth, "[God] seated us together in the heavenly places in union with Christ Jesus." (Eph 2:4-6) As these Christians of the "royal priesthood" serve, they offer sacrifices of praise (Heb 13:15) and prayers to God (related to the incense; Re 8:4), eat the spiritual food God provides (as he provid-

ed the showbread for the priests; Mr 2:26), and enjoy light from God's Word of truth (as from the lampstand; Ps 119:105). The apostle Paul points out that they have the hope, through the sacrifice of Jesus Christ, of entering into the real "Most Holy," heaven itself.—Heb 6:19, 20; 9:24; 1Pe 1:3, 4; see HOLY CONTRIBUTION; MOST HOLY.

HOLY SPIRIT. See SPIRIT.

HOMAM (Ho'mam). Son of Horite Sheik Lotan; the same as Hemam.—Ge 36:20-22; 1Ch 1:39; see HEMAM.

HOMER.

A dry measure corresponding to the cor and equaling ten baths or ten ephahs. (Eze 45:11, 14) Based on the estimated volume of the bath measure, the ephah has been reckoned at 22 L (20 dry qt). The homer would therefore equal 220 L (200 dry qt). (Ho 3:2) In the wilderness, greedy Israelites gathered miraculously provided quail in such numbers that the "one collecting least gathered ten homers" (2,200 L; 2,000 dry qt; 62 bu). (Nu 11:32) The Scriptures also mention the homer as a measure for barley, seed, and wheat.—Le 27:16; Isa 5:10; Eze 45:13.

HONEY, HONEYCOMB.

Bee honey is a sweet, viscid fluid manufactured by bees. Honey is referred to in the Hebrew Scriptures by the words *no'pheth* (flowing honey, or comb honey) and *devash'*. This latter word may refer not only to bee honey but also to the syrup of fruits. (Le 2:11, ftn) In the Greek Scriptures *me'li* is used, along with the adjective *a'gri·os*, "wild," to denote the honey of wild bees.

The Honeycomb. The honeycomb is a marvel of engineering; it reveals the Creator's unparalleled wisdom and ability in putting such "engineering" and construction instinct in the honeybee. The hexagonal shape of the cells is ideal for holding the maximum quantity of honey with a minimum of beeswax, the material of which the cell walls are made. When a comb is being built, beeswax is made by special glands in the bee's body. It oozes through pores in the body, forming small white flakes. Using its legs, the bee moves the flakes to its jaws. It then chews the wax and places it in the part of the honeycomb being constructed. The walls of the comb are only one third of a millimeter ($\frac{1}{80}$ in.) thick but can support 30 times their weight.

Honeybees build their nests in a variety of places, including trees, rocks, and, in one case, even in the carcass of a dead animal, which evidently was no longer carrion but had been dried out by the sun. This was the lion's carcass from which Samson ate honey.—Jg 14:8, 9.

Honey. Bee honey is made from the nectar obtained from flowers and fruit. In the process of gathering the nectar and depositing it in the honeycomb, certain chemicals from the bee's body are added. Some of the water evaporates from the nectar, and the chemicals transform the nectar into honey. The color and flavor of honey vary according to the source of nectar. Honey is easily assimilated by the body and quickly converted into energy.

Most of the Bible's references to the honey of bees is to wild honey, such as John the Baptizer ate in the wilderness. (Mt 3:1, 4) The energy-giving property of honey is illustrated in the case of King Saul's son Jonathan who, exhausted from battle, tasted some honey. Immediately his eyes "began to beam." (1Sa 14:25-30) This energy food is listed among the provisions God supplied for his people in the wilderness. There, where few trees existed, the people were able to get honey to eat "out of a crag," that is, from the honeycombs that the bees built in rocky places.—De 32:13.

Illustrative Use. The curative properties of honey are compared to pleasant sayings and wisdom, not only because of its sweetness and fine taste but also because of its health-giving qualities. Pleasant sayings are healthful spiritually, just as honey is good for the physical body. The writer of Proverbs says: "Pleasant sayings are a honeycomb, sweet to the soul and a healing to the bones."—Pr 16:24; 24:13, 14.

The sweetness and enjoyment of eating honey is applied illustratively throughout the Scriptures. Examples are found at Ezekiel 3:2, 3 and Revelation 10:9. Comb honey is often mentioned, for it is considered superior in flavor, sweetness, and richness to honey that has been exposed to the air for a time. Emphasizing the goodness and pleasantness of the words spoken by the Shulammite girl, her shepherd lover speaks of them as "comb honey" that keeps dripping from her lips. (Ca 4:11) Jehovah's judicial decisions are so fine, healthful, and beneficial that they are even "sweeter than honey and the flowing honey of the combs." (Ps 19:9, 10) His sayings are 'smoother to the palate than honey to the mouth.'—Ps 119:103.

While honey is good, overeating of it can cause nausea (Pr 25:16), and this eating of too much honey is compared to people seeking out their own glory.—Pr 25:27.

Proverbs chapter 5 uses the sweetness of comb honey to illustrate the temptation to sexual immorality that the "strange woman" can bring to bear by her appeal to a man with her use of charm and smooth words. It constitutes a fine warning to Christians today. "As a honeycomb the lips of a strange woman keep dripping, and her palate is smoother than oil. But the aftereffect from her is as bitter as wormwood; it is as sharp as a two-edged sword. Her feet are descending to death," says the wise man. Her smooth, honeylike words and actions lead the man right up to the immoral act so that "all of a sudden he is going after her, like a bull that comes even to the slaughter."—Pr 5:3-5; 7:21, 22.

Honey of Fruits. The Hebrew word *devash'* can refer also to the juice, or syrup, of fruits —figs, dates, and so forth. Often the context enables the reader to determine whether or not bee honey is meant. Evidently the syrup of fruits is what is prohibited from being offered on the altar at Leviticus 2:11, because of its tendency to ferment. That bee honey is not meant here is indicated by the next verse, which included the prohibited "honey" as firstfruits to be offered to Jehovah. Since most of the honey used by the Israelites was wild honey, not a cultivated crop, the "honey" offered as firstfruits when Hezekiah motivated the people to support the priesthood was undoubtedly the juice or syrup of fruits. —2Ch 31:5.

A Land of Milk and Honey. The description of Palestine as "a land flowing with milk and honey," often repeated in the Scriptures, is apt, for not only was the land well supplied with the product of bees but also with the syrup of fruits. (Ex 3:8; Le 20:24; De 11:9; Jos 5:6) The latter is apparently referred to as being an item of trade exchanged for Tyre's merchandise.—Eze 27:2, 17; see BEE.

HONOR.
The principal Hebrew term denoting "honor" is *ka·vohdh'*, which literally means "heaviness." (Compare the use of related terms in 1Sa 4:18 and 2Sa 14:26.) So a person who is honored is regarded as being weighty, or amounting to something. In Greek, the noun *ti·me'* conveys the sense of "honor," "esteem," "value," "preciousness." Thus the verb *ti·ma'o* can also mean "set a price on" (Mt 27:9); the noun *ti·me'* can have the sense of "price," "value" (Mt 27:6; Ac 4:34); and the adjective *ti'mi·os* can mean "esteemed," "dear, or valuable," and "precious."—Ac 5:34; 20:24; 1Co 3:12.

Jehovah God and His Son. By reason of his Creatorship and Sovereignty, Jehovah God is deserving of honor, reverential regard or respect.

(1Ti 1:17; Heb 3:3, 4; Re 4:9-11) People render this honor by doing what is pleasing in his sight, as his Son did at all times. (Joh 8:29, 49) While the Law covenant was in effect, the Israelites could honor Jehovah by presenting their very best as sacrifices.—Pr 3:9; Mal 1:6-8.

Mere formalistic observance of the outward forms of worship does not constitute a true honoring of the Almighty. There also needs to be a real love for Jehovah's ways and a heartfelt desire to do his will. This was lacking among the religious leaders of Judaism in the time of Jesus' earthly ministry.—Mr 7:6; Isa 29:13.

Jesus Christ set the perfect example in honoring his Father, carrying out His will flawlessly to the point of laying down his life in sacrifice. (Mt 26:39; Joh 10:17, 18) Because he delighted to do the Father's will, his Father honored him by acknowledging him as His beloved and approved Son. (2Pe 1:17; Mt 17:5) After the completion of Jesus' earthly course, God conferred far greater honor and dignity upon his Son than Jesus had before his becoming a man. (Php 2:9-11) The case of Jesus Christ illustrates how the Most High will honor all who honor Him, recognizing them as His approved servants and blessing them beyond measure.—1Sa 2:30.

Since it was Jehovah God who highly exalted his Son, all who refuse to acknowledge Jesus Christ as the immortal King of kings and Lord of lords dishonor the Father. Because of who he is and what he has accomplished, the Son deserves honor and loyal support. (Joh 5:23; 1Ti 6:15, 16; Re 5:11-13) All who desire to be honored by the Son as his approved disciples must imitate his example and faithfully adhere to his teaching. —Ro 2:7, 10.

Other Persons to Be Honored. Whereas Jehovah God and his Son merit the greatest honor, there are relationships among humans that also call for honor. Children are to honor their parents by being obedient. (De 5:16; Eph 6:1, 2) When parents come into need, their adult offspring can show honor by responding willingly with material aid. (Mt 15:4-6; 1Ti 5:3, 4) Whereas the husband would honor his wife by treating her lovingly and with dignity, the wife would honor her husband by being in subjection and showing deep respect. (1Pe 3:1-7) Elders who worked hard in teaching were to be given "double honor," which evidently included material aid. (1Ti 5:17, 18) Christian slaves were to honor their masters by respectfully discharging the tasks assigned to them. (1Ti 6:1, 2) Rulers and others in authority should be given the honor, or respect, that their position requires. (Ro 13:7) Regardless of their station in life, people of all sorts, as part of God's creation, are deserving of honor.—1Pe 2:17.

Christians are to take the lead in showing honor to fellow believers. (Ro 12:10) This includes seeking not one's own advantage but that of others. (1Co 10:24) It calls for a willingness to perform humble tasks. (Lu 22:26; Joh 13:12-17) This fine spirit can be maintained by remembering that every believer is precious to God and that Christians need one another, just as each member of the human body is dependent on the others. —1Co 12:14-27.

While not being glory seekers, Christians are rightly concerned about maintaining an honorable standing before Jehovah God and his Son. This necessitates guarding against associations that corrupt and resisting the desires of the sinful flesh. Only by remaining morally and spiritually pure does one remain an honorable vessel for God's use. (1Th 4:3-8; 2Ti 2:20-22; Heb 13:4) Therein lies real honor.

HOOK. A curved or sharply angled piece of metal or other material, sometimes barbed.

Gold hooks were used in the tabernacle to fasten together the two large sections of the embroidered linen covering, and copper hooks for the two sections of the goat's hair covering. (Ex 26:1, 5, 6, 7, 10, 11; 36:13, 18; 39:33) The curtain between the Holy and the Most Holy was hung on hooks, evidently of gold (Ex 26:31-33), as was also the screen to the tabernacle entrance.—Ex 26:36, 37.

Fishhooks were used by ancient fishermen. (Hab 1:14, 15; Isa 19:1, 6-8; Mt 17:24-27) Butcher hooks are mentioned in the Bible. (Am 4:2) Hooks, possibly thorns, were also employed for leading animals, particularly wild beasts.—Eze 19:3, 4, 6, 9, ftn.

Human captives were sometimes led by hooks in the lips, nose, or tongue. An Assyrian pictorial representation shows the king holding three captives by cords fastened to hooks in their lips while he blinds one of them with a spear. It was, therefore, understandable to King Sennacherib of Assyria when Jehovah spoke figuratively to him through the prophet Isaiah: "I shall certainly put my hook in your nose and my bridle between your lips, and I shall indeed lead you back by the way by which you have come."—2Ki 19:20, 21, 28; Isa 37:29.

Jehovah figuratively spoke to Pharaoh of Egypt, in whom Israel had foolishly trusted for support against Babylon: "I will put hooks in your jaws . . .

And I will bring you up out of the midst of your Nile canals . . . And I will abandon you to the wilderness . . . And all the inhabitants of Egypt will have to know that I am Jehovah, for the reason that they proved to be, as a support, a reed to the house of Israel." (Eze 29:1-7) The language was fitting; the historian Herodotus (II, 70) stated that the Egyptians used a hook to capture the crocodile and draw it out of the water. Jehovah also foretold that he would put hooks in the jaws of "Gog of the land of Magog" and would bring him forth to the final attack upon God's people and to his own execution.—Eze 38:1-4; 39:1-4.

HOOPOE (hoo'poe) [Heb., *du·khi·phath'*]. About the size of a slender pigeon, the hoopoe (*Upupa epops*) is a somewhat cinnamon-colored bird, distinctively marked with alternate broad bars of white and black along its wings and back. Its most conspicuous feature is a crest of plumes, each feather ending in a white border tipped with black, the crest running from the base of the long, slender curved bill all the way to the back of the bird's head. Though colorfully and conspicuously dressed, the hoopoe is notably unclean in home and habits. Its diet of insects is obtained by probing with its sharp bill not only into the ground but also into dunghills and other filth. The nest gives off a disagreeable odor produced by secretions of the bird's oil glands, and it also becomes foul smelling due to the bird's failure to clean the nest of excrement. Thus, while not a bird of prey nor an eater of carrion, the hoopoe was included among the birds listed as unclean for food in the Mosaic Law.—Le 11:13, 19; De 14:12, 18.

Hoopoe, pretty bird with unclean habits

Found throughout southern Asia and Africa and parts of Europe, the hoopoe migrates to Palestine about the first of March and remains until the approach of winter, when it heads southward to Egypt and other parts of northern Africa.

The identification of this bird with "the lapwing," as in the *King James Version* (Le 11:19; De 14:18), is no longer followed by modern translations. The translators of the Greek *Septuagint* and the Latin *Vulgate* understood it to be "the hoopoe" (*e'pops*, LXX; *upupa*, Vg), and the Syriac and Arabic names for the hoopoe (Syriac, *qaqupha;* Arabic, *hudhudu*) also confirm this identification.

Some believe the Hebrew name for the hoopoe (*du·khi·phath'*) is intended to represent the peculiar, somewhat dovelike cry of the bird, as is clearly the case with its name in the other languages mentioned. Others would derive the name from the Hebrew verb meaning "pound" (compare Nu 11:8), noting the hoopoe's practice of probing the ground for its food.

HOPE. It can mean trust, reliance; desire accompanied with expectation of what is desired or belief that it is attainable; one on whom hopes are centered; a source of hopeful expectation, or promise; something that is hoped for, or an object of hope. The Hebrew root verb *qa·wah'*, from which come terms rendered "hope," basically means "wait for" with eager expectation. (Ge 49: 18) In the Christian Greek Scriptures, the sense of the Greek term *el·pis'* (hope) is "expectation of good."

No Real Hope Without God. True hope, as spoken of in the Bible, is superior to mere desire, which may have no foundation or prospect of fulfillment. It is also better than mere expectation, because that which is expected is not always desirable. The Bible shows that the people of the world in general have no real, solidly based hope; mankind is going into death, and without knowledge of a provision from a higher source there is no hope in what lies ahead. Solomon expressed the futility of man's situation without God's intervention as "the greatest vanity! . . . Everything is vanity."—Ec 12:8; 9:2, 3.

The faithful patriarch Job said that there is hope even for a tree to sprout again, but man, when he dies, is gone permanently. But Job then indicated that he was speaking of man on his own without help from God, for Job expressed the desire and hope that God would remember him. (Job 14:7-15) Similarly, the apostle Paul informs Christians that they, having the hope of resurrection, should not "sorrow just as the rest also do who have no hope." (1Th 4:13) Again, speaking to Gentile Christians, Paul points out to them that before coming to a knowledge of God's provision through Christ, they were alienated from the nation with which God had in the past been dealing, and as Gentiles they then "had no hope and were without God in the world."—Eph 2:12.

Expressions common among those who have no hope in God and his promise of a resurrection of the dead are similar to the words of the disobedient inhabitants of Jerusalem who, instead of showing repentance and sorrow when faced with the threat of destruction of their city as a judgment from God, abandoned themselves to sensual enjoyment. They said: "Let there be eating and drinking, for tomorrow we shall die." (Isa 22: 13) The apostle warns against becoming infected with the attitude of such hopeless ones.—1Co 15:32, 33.

Wrong Hopes. Paul was not denying that the people of the world have some reasonable hopes that they pursue, some of a commendable nature. Rather, he showed that, without God, a person's hopes are of no consequence; really, they are futile in the long run.

But besides the minor, common, normal human hopes there are bad ones. There are hopes that are wickedly entertained. In some instances these may appear to be fulfilled, but in actuality they are realized only in a temporary sense, for a proverb states: "The expectation of the righteous ones is a rejoicing, but the very hope of the wicked ones will perish." (Pr 10:28) Additionally, "When a wicked man dies, his hope perishes; and even expectation based on powerfulness has perished." (Pr 11:7) So, selfish hopes, and those based on a false foundation of materialism, on lies, on wrong dealings, or on the power or promises of men, are sure to be frustrated.

The Source of Hope. Jehovah God is the Source of true hope and the One able to fulfill all his promises and the hopes of those trusting in him. It is through his undeserved kindness that he has given mankind "comfort and good hope." (2Th 2:16) He has been the hope of righteous men in all ages. He was called "the hope of Israel" and "the hope of [Israel's] forefathers" (Jer 14:8; 17:13;

50:7), and many are the expressions of hope, trust, and confidence in him in the Hebrew Scriptures. In his loving-kindness toward his people, even when they were going into exile for disobedience to him, he said to them: "I myself well know the thoughts that I am thinking toward you, . . . thoughts of peace, and not of calamity, to give you a future and a hope." (Jer 29:11) Jehovah's promise kept alive the faith and hope of faithful Israelites during the Babylonian exile; it greatly strengthened men such as Ezekiel and Daniel, for Jehovah had said: "There exists a hope for your future, . . . and the sons will certainly return to their own territory." (Jer 31:17) That hope came to fruition when a faithful Jewish remnant returned in 537 B.C.E. to rebuild Jerusalem and its temple.—Ezr 1:1-6.

Hope of Reward Proper. The hope of the servant of God that he will receive a reward is not selfishness. For a true view and proper understanding of God, a person must know that loving-kindness and generosity are outstanding qualities of God; the individual must believe not only that God is but also "that he becomes the rewarder of those earnestly seeking him." (Heb 11:6) Hope keeps the Christian minister balanced and in God's service, knowing that Jehovah will provide his daily needs. The apostle Paul points this out, drawing on the principles set forth in the Law. Paul quotes the law at Deuteronomy 25:4: "You must not muzzle a bull while it is threshing." He then adds: "Really for our sakes it was written, because the man who plows ought to plow in hope and the man who threshes ought to do so in hope of being a partaker."—1Co 9:9, 10.

Essential to Faith. Hope is also essential to faith; it is the groundwork and basis for faith. (Heb 11:1) In turn, faith makes the hope brighter and stronger. The apostle Paul, in order to strengthen Christians, cites the fine example of Abraham. When Abraham and his wife Sarah were, from a human standpoint, beyond the hope of having children, it is said: "Although beyond hope, yet based on hope he had faith, that he might become the father of many nations in accord with what had been said: 'So your seed will be.'" Abraham knew that as far as producing children was concerned, his body and that of Sarah were "deadened." But he did not grow weak in faith. Why? "Because of the promise of God he did not waver in a lack of faith, but became powerful by his faith."—Ro 4:18-20.

The apostle then applies Abraham's example of faith and hope to Christians, concluding: "Let us exult, based on hope of the glory of God . . . and the hope does not lead to disappointment; because the love of God has been poured out into our hearts through the holy spirit, which was given us."—Ro 5:2, 5.

The Christian Hope. The hope of the Christian and, indeed, of mankind lies in Jesus Christ. The gaining of lasting life in heaven or on earth was not open to any of humankind until Christ Jesus "shed light upon life and incorruption through the good news." (2Ti 1:10) The spirit-begotten brothers of Christ are told that they have heavenly hopes because of the great mercy of God, who gave to them "a new birth to a living hope through the resurrection of Jesus Christ from the dead." (1Pe 1:3, 4; Col 1:5, 27; Tit 1:1, 2; 3:6, 7) This happy hope is to be realized "at the revelation of Jesus Christ." (1Pe 1:13, 21; Tit 2:13) Christ Jesus is therefore called "our hope" by the apostle Paul.—1Ti 1:1.

This hope of everlasting life and incorruption for those who are "partakers of the heavenly calling" (Heb 3:1) is solidly based and is something that can be confidently relied on. It is supported by two things in which it is impossible for God to lie, namely, his promise and his oath, and the hope resides with Christ, who is now immortal in the heavens. Therefore this hope is spoken of as "an anchor for the soul, both sure and firm, and it enters in within the curtain [as the high priest entered the Most Holy on the Day of Atonement], where a forerunner has entered in our behalf, Jesus, who has become a high priest according to the manner of Melchizedek forever." —Heb 6:17-20.

Must be developed and maintained. The necessity for Christians to hold on to the "one hope" (Eph 4:4) is constantly stressed in the Bible. It requires continued industriousness and the exercise of freeness of speech and "boasting" over the hope itself. (Heb 3:6; 6:11) Hope is developed by endurance under tribulation; this leads to an approved condition before God, from whom hope comes. (Ro 5:2-5) It is placed alongside faith and love as one of the three qualities characterizing the Christian congregation since the disappearance of the miraculous gifts of the spirit that were present in the first-century congregation.—1Co 13:13.

Qualities and benefits. Hope is indispensable to the Christian. It accompanies joy, peace, and power of holy spirit. (Ro 15:13) It promotes freeness of speech in the approach to God for his undeserved kindness and mercy. (2Co 3:12) It

enables the Christian to endure with rejoicing, no matter what the conditions may be. (Ro 12:12; 1Th 1:3) As a helmet protected the head of a warrior, so the hope of salvation protects the mental powers, enabling the Christian to maintain integrity. (1Th 5:8) Hope is a strengthening thing, because, while the anointed Christian yet on earth does not *possess* the reward of heavenly life, his desire with expectation is so strong that, despite severe trials and difficulties, he keeps on waiting patiently for the hoped-for thing with endurance.—Ro 8:24, 25.

Hope helps keep the Christian in a clean way of life, for he knows that God and Christ, in whom the hope lies, are pure and that he cannot hope to be like God and to receive the reward if he practices uncleanness or unrighteousness. (1Jo 3:2, 3) It is closely allied with the greatest quality, love, for one having the true love of God will also have hope in all of God's promises. And he will, additionally, hope the very best for his brothers in the faith, loving them and trusting their sincerity of heart in Christ.—1Co 13:4, 7; 1Th 2:19.

Superior to hope under the Law. Prior to the giving of the Law to Israel, the faithful forefathers of the nation had hope in God. (Ac 26:6, 7; Ge 22:18; Mic 7:20; 2Ti 1:3) They looked for God's provision for life. When the Law came, it appeared at first that here would be the fulfillment of their hope. But, on the contrary, the Law exposed all as sinners before God and, by making transgressions manifest, condemned all under it to death. (Ga 3:19; Ro 7:7-11) The Law itself was holy, not bad; yet by its very holiness and righteousness, it exposed the imperfections of those under it. (Ro 7:12) As foretold through the prophets, it was necessary for God to bring in "a better hope" through Jesus Christ, setting aside the Law and enabling those putting faith in Christ to draw near to God.—Heb 7:18, 19; 11:40; compare Jer 31:31-34.

Hope for all mankind. The undeserved kindness of God is further magnified in that the wonderful hope that he opened up for the spiritual brothers of Jesus Christ, to be joint heirs with him in the heavenly calling (Heb 3:1), is also closely tied in with a hope for all mankind who desire to serve God. The apostle Paul, after outlining the hope of those who have the expectation of becoming the heavenly "sons of God" and joint heirs with Christ, explains: "The eager expectation of the creation is waiting for the revealing of the sons of God. For the creation was subjected to futility, not by its own will but through him that subjected it, on the basis of hope that the creation itself also will be set free from enslavement to corruption and have the glorious freedom of the children of God."—Ro 8:14, 17, 19-21.

According to Paul's words at Romans 8:20, 21, Jehovah God did not destroy man's forefather Adam at the time of his sin, but he allowed men to be born from an imperfect father, with futility facing them not because of any deliberate fault of their own, but because of inherited imperfection. However, God did not leave them without hope but kindly set forth hope through the promised "seed" (Ge 3:15; 22:18), who is Jesus Christ. (Ga 3:16) Doubtless because the time of Messiah's first coming had been forecast in prophecy, the preaching of John the Baptizer roused the expectations of the nation of Israel. (Lu 3:15; Da 9:24-27) Jesus fulfilled that hope by his ministry, death, and resurrection. But the great hope for mankind in general, both the living and the dead, lies in the Kingdom of Christ, when he and his joint heirs serve as heavenly kings and priests. Then mankind exercising faith will eventually be released from the corruption of imperfection and sin and will come to the full status of "children of God." Their hope is reinforced by God's resurrection of his Son more than 1,900 years ago.—Ac 17:31; 23:6; 24:15.

Jehovah God has provided his Word the Bible with its instruction and examples, so that all men may have hope. (Ro 15:4; 1Co 10:11; 2Ti 3:16, 17) This hope has to be proclaimed to others by those possessing it; in so doing, the possessor of hope saves himself and those who listen to him.—1Pe 3:15; 1Ti 4:16.

HOPHNI (Hoph'ni) [from Egyptian, meaning "Tadpole"]. One of High Priest Eli's sons. Hophni and his brother Phinehas were "good-for-nothing men," guilty of sacrilegious conduct and gross immorality. (1Sa 1:3; 2:12-17, 22-25) Because of unfaithfulness while serving as priest at Jehovah's sanctuary, Jehovah judged Hophni worthy of death, which befell him at the time the Philistines captured the sacred Ark.—1Sa 2:34; 4:4, 11, 17; see PHINEHAS No. 2.

HOPHRA (Hoph'ra) [from Egyptian, meaning "The Heart of Ra [the sun-god] Endures"]. In the Greek *Septuagint* (Jer 51:30, corresponding to 44:30 in most versions), he is called *Ou·a·phre'*. Pharaoh Hophra is called Apries by Herodotus. Hophra is believed to have reigned for 19 years. However, according to Herodotus (II, 161), he reigned for 25 years.

After the Jews fled to Egypt in 607 B.C.E., Jehovah said by the mouth of Jeremiah: "Here I am giving Pharaoh Hophra, the king of Egypt, into the hand of his enemies and into the hand of those seeking for his soul." (Jer 44:1, 26, 30) This was to be a sign of imminent calamity to come over the Jews dwelling in Egypt. (Jer 44:29) According to Herodotus (II, 161-169), Hophra (Apries) undertook a disastrous expedition to Cyrene to help the Libyans against the Greeks in the sixth century B.C.E. Hophra's troops revolted against him and set up Ahmose II (Amasis) as rival king. Even then, Hophra was so arrogant that he "supposed that not even a god could depose him from his throne." However, he was taken prisoner and finally was killed by being strangled.

HOR [Heb., *Hor ha·har'*, "Hor the Mountain"].
1. The mountain near Moserah on the border of Edom where Aaron died shortly before Israel's entry into the Promised Land. With the assembly of Israel watching, Aaron, Moses, and Aaron's son Eleazar ascended Mount Hor. On the mountaintop Moses removed Aaron's priestly garments and clothed Eleazar with them. After this, Aaron died, and Moses and Eleazar probably buried him there.—Nu 20:22-29; De 32:50; compare De 10:6.

According to the historian Josephus, Mount Hor was one of the high mountains encompassing the Edomite city of Petra. (*Jewish Antiquities*, IV, 82, 83 [iv, 7]) Tradition has linked it with Jebel Harun (meaning "Mountain of Aaron"), a twin-topped, red sandstone mountain having an elevation of some 1,460 m (4,790 ft) and situated less than 5 km (3 mi) WSW of Petra. However, Jebel Harun does not seem to fit the Biblical description of Israel's coming from Kadesh (Kadesh-barnea) to Mount Hor "on the frontier of the land of Edom." (Nu 33:37-39, 41) Jebel Harun is not on Edom's border, but within that country. Thus for Israel to have reached this traditional site would have meant trespassing on Edom's territory. But this could not have occurred, since the Israelites had previously been denied passage through Edom. (Nu 20:14-22; De 2:5-8) Hence, many scholars favor as a possible identification the isolated, steep-sided white chalk Jebel Madurah (Har Zin [Hor Ha Har]), a mountain about 40 km (25 mi) SW of the Dead Sea, and about 60 km (37 mi) ENE of Kadesh.

2. A mountain marking the northern extremity of Canaan. (Nu 34:7, 8) No certain identification can be made. Some scholars believe that this Mount Hor (Heb., *Hor ha·har'*) may be the same

as Mount Hermon. Others suggest that it perhaps designates the entire Lebanon Range or a prominent peak thereof.

HORAM (Ho'ram). King of Gezer; one of the 31 kings defeated by the Israelites under the leadership of Joshua during the conquest of the Promised Land. Horam and all his host were killed when they came to the aid of Lachish at the time of Joshua's campaign against that city.—Jos 10: 33; 12:7, 8, 12, 24.

HOREB (Ho'reb) [Dry; Waste]. "The mountain of the true God," apparently the same as Mount Sinai. (1Ki 19:8; Ex 33:6) Generally, though, Horeb seems to designate the mountainous region around Mount Sinai, otherwise called the Wilderness of Sinai.—De 1:6, 19; 4:10, 15; 5:2; 9:8; 18:16; 29:1; 1Ki 8:9; 2Ch 5:10; Ps 106:19; Mal 4:4; compare Ex 3:1, 2; Ac 7:30; see SINAI Nos. 1 and 2.

At Horeb, Jehovah's angel appeared to Moses in the midst of the burning thornbush, commissioning him to lead Israel out of Egypt. (Ex 3:1-15) Later, while at Rephidim, the liberated Israelites complained about having no water to drink. Thereupon, at Jehovah's direction, Moses, accompanied by some of the older men of Israel, went to a rock in Horeb, evidently the mountainous region of Horeb, and struck the rock with his rod. Water miraculously began issuing forth from this rock. (Ex 17:1-6; compare Ps 105:41.) Centuries afterward, the prophet Elijah fled from vengeful Queen Jezebel to Horeb by way of Beer-sheba. —1Ki 19:2-8.

HOREM (Ho'rem) [possibly, Small Split Rock]. A fortified city of Naphtali. (Jos 19:35, 38, 39) Its location is unknown today.

HORESH (Ho'resh) [Wooded Place]. A site in the Wilderness of Ziph where David hid from Saul. Here also Jonathan acknowledged David as the next king of Israel, and the two men "concluded a covenant" of mutual support. (1Sa 23:15-19) Horesh is tentatively identified with modern-day Khirbet Khoreisa, about 9 km (5.5 mi) SSE of Hebron.

HOR-HAGGIDGAD (Hor-hag·gid'gad). An Israelite wilderness camping site. As discussed under the heading BENE-JAAKAN, a comparison of Numbers 33:31-33 with Deuteronomy 10:6, 7 seems to indicate that the Israelites passed through this same region twice, Hor-haggidgad being called "Gudgodah" on the later trip. (See GUDGODAH.) The exact location cannot be deter-

mined with certainty. Most scholars, however, tentatively identify Hor-haggidgad (Gudgodah) with a site on the Wadi Khadakhid, about 65 km (40 mi) NNW of the Gulf of 'Aqaba.

HORI (Ho'ri).

1. A descendant of Seir the Horite through Lotan.—Ge 36:20-22; 1Ch 1:39.

2. A Simeonite whose son Shaphat was one of the 12 spies sent out by Moses from the Wilderness of Paran.—Nu 13:2, 3, 5.

HORITE (Hor'ite). A people inhabiting the mountains of Seir in patriarchal times. They are called in the Bible "the sons of Seir the Horite." (Ge 36:20, 21, 29, 30) The Edomites "proceeded to dispossess them and to annihilate them from before them and to dwell in their place."—De 2:12, 22.

At Genesis 36:2, in the Masoretic text, the grandfather of one of Esau's wives is called "Zibeon the Hivite." At verses 20 and 24, however, he is shown to be a descendant of Seir the Horite. "Horite" may mean merely "cave dweller," from Hebrew chor ("hole"). This would make Zibeon a Hivite who was a cave dweller.

At Joshua 9:7 the Greek *Septuagint* calls the Gibeonites "Chorrean" (Horites) instead of "Hivites," but this apparently is an error, in view of the fact that the Gibeonites belonged to one of the seven Canaanite nations devoted to destruction (the Horites did not). The Masoretic text has "Hivites."—Jos 9:22-27; De 7:1, 2.

Hurrians. Many modern scholars now believe that the Horites are actually a people whom they call Hurrians. This conclusion is based primarily on linguistic similarities, particularly similarities in proper names in ancient tablets that were discovered in recent times over a wide area reaching from modern Turkey into Syria and Palestine. So they hold that the "Hurrians" came to be called Horites. But note E. A. Speiser's comments in *The World History of the Jewish People* (1964, Vol. 1, p. 159). He first advances this argument:

"Biblical Jebusites, too, proved to be Hurrians in disguise. They were of foreign stock (Jud. 19:12), a description borne out by the Jebusite personal name *Awarnah* (II Sam. 24:16, *K*ᵉ*thib*). A 14th century ruler of Jerusalem, or Jebus, bore a name containing the attested Hurrian element *Hepa*. Thus Jebusites and Hivites alike—two of the featured pre-Israelite nations—were merely subdivisions of the wide-spread Hurrian group." But then he adds:

"The above conclusion, however, must now be modified in one significant respect. The required change detracts nothing from the position of the local Hurrians in early Biblical times; but it does affect the automatic identification of Hurrians with Horites. . . . There is no archaeological evidence whatever for a Hurrian settlement in Edom or Transjordan. It follows, therefore, that the Biblical term *Hori*—much in the same manner as Cush—must have been used at one time in two distinct and unrelated meanings."

Therefore, though the scholars wish to use a name not found in the Bible to apply to a widespread people who, they say, include the Horites, Hivites, and Jebusites, they admit that, for example, there is no evidence of Hurrian population in Edom, where Biblical Horites lived. The Bible, then, in calling the pre-Edomite inhabitants of Seir "Horites" evidently restricts the name to that group in Seir.

HORMAH (Hor'mah) [A Devoting to Destruction]. A city in the southern part of the territory of Judah (1Ch 4:30), but possibly the name is applied to more than one site, the other being perhaps a place or region.

Following the return of the 12 Israelite spies to Kadesh (Nu 13:26), the Israelites at first refused to attempt an invasion of Canaan. Then, following Jehovah's condemnation of their rebellious attitude and lack of faith, they decided to attempt it, contrary to his instructions. They "got up early in the morning" to go up to the place that Jehovah mentioned. The record speaks of their endeavoring to "go up to the top of the mountain." (Nu 14:40) However, their statement about going up to "the place that Jehovah mentioned" may indicate "the mountainous region of the Amorites" referred to by Moses in his restatement of the events, rather than a particular mountain. (De 1:19-21, 41-43) The record does not indicate how far they traveled, nor does it specifically indicate whether the actions described took place during one day or not; but the text seems to indicate events occurring within a relatively short space of time.

Whatever was the case, the record shows that they were met by the Amalekites and Canaanites (at De 1:44, "Amorites," a term used to refer to the people of Canaan in general; compare Ge 48:22; Jos 24:15), and these defeated the Israelites, scattering them "as far as Hormah." (Nu 14:45) The account in Deuteronomy 1:44 says they were scattered "in Seir as far as Hormah." Seir was the territory of the Edomites, and their dominion then seems to have extended W of the

Wadi Arabah into the Negeb region. (Compare Nu 20:14, 16; Jos 11:17.) Following this defeat, the Israelites returned to Kadesh.—De 1:45, 46.

Their wandering period having ended, the Israelites again advanced toward Canaan and were attacked by the Canaanite king of Arad. (See ARAD No. 2.) Again we do not know how far to the S the king of Arad advanced before engaging in combat with the Israelites, but the Israelites, following a vow to Jehovah, gained the victory over this king and 'devoted his cities to destruction,' thereafter naming the place "Hormah." (Nu 21:1-3; see DEVOTED THING.) While Moses had already employed this name in the earlier account of the Canaanites' victory over Israel, it is probable that he did so in an anticipatory way, intending to refer to it later in the record, showing the origin of the name. (Nu 14:45) The Israelites did not settle in the region then, however, but traveled around Edom and turned N, eventually making their entry into Canaan by crossing the Jordan N of the Dead Sea.—Nu 21:4; 22:1.

At Joshua 12:14 "the king of Hormah" is listed next to the king of Arad among the 31 kings defeated by Joshua. It seems unlikely that this refers to the victory gained earlier while Moses was yet alive and Joshua was serving as military commander, since these victories are listed as though gained after Israel's crossing the Jordan into Canaan. (Jos 12:7, 8) Though this victory by Joshua is not specifically described, it may be included in the statement at Joshua 10:40-42. This would indicate that after Israel departed from that region in order to travel around the land of Edom, the Canaanites resettled the territory. While Joshua is shown to have defeated the king of Hormah, the record does not state that the Israelites then occupied the city of Hormah. —Compare the case of Gezer at Jos 12:12; Jg 1:29.

The city was included in the list of towns "at the extremity of the tribe of the sons of Judah toward the boundary of Edom in the south." (Jos 15:21, 30) However, it was assigned to the tribe of Simeon as an "enclave" city within Judah's territory. (Jos 19:1, 2, 4; compare 16:9.) Since the record only shows that Joshua defeated Hormah's king (not mentioning any conquest of the city), the tribes of Judah and Simeon thereafter combined their forces to "strike the Canaanites inhabiting Zephath and to devote it to destruction. Hence the name of the city was called Hormah." (Jg 1:17) Their naming of the city here simply may have been a confirmation or restatement of the name applied to it earlier. The use of the name Hormah back in Moses' time is considered by some to have been with reference to the entire district or region instead of the one city of Zephath. This would mean that the entire district was under ban, or devoted to destruction, whenever that destruction should eventually be accomplished.—Compare *Commentary on the Old Testament,* by C. F. Keil and F. Delitzsch, 1973, Vol. II, Joshua, Judges, Ruth, p. 256; see ZEPHATH.

The location of Hormah is uncertain. Various suggestions have been given, but since the proposed sites are all over 60 km (37 mi) N of Kadesh-barnea, from which the Israelites initially started out "early in the morning" (Nu 14:40), and since Hormah is stated to be the point to which they were scattered in defeat, evidently fleeing back toward Kadesh, such positions so far to the N would hardly seem to fit the Biblical account.

Though still a Simeonite city in David's time, Hormah was one of the places he visited during his exile as a fugitive and one of the cities to which he later sent gifts.—1Sa 30:26-31; 1Ch 4:24, 28-31.

HORN. Animal horns were used in Israel as vessels for oil, as drinking flasks, as inkhorns and containers for cosmetics, and as musical or signaling instruments.—1Sa 16:1, 13; 1Ki 1:39; Eze 9:2; see SECRETARY'S INKHORN.

Musical and Signaling Instruments. The Hebrew word *qe'ren* is the general designation for an animal's horn. (Ge 22:13) It is used once to refer to a wind instrument, namely, in the expression "horn [Heb., *qe'ren*] of the ram" in Joshua 6:5. This expression is put in parallel with the Hebrew word *shoh·phar'* (horn), a term always referring to a ram's horn used as a musical instrument. The modern *shoh·phar'* is a hollow ram's horn about 36 cm (14 in.) long, straightened by heat but curved upward at the bell end. It has a separate mouthpiece to facilitate blowing. The *shoh·phar'* of Bible times, it is thought, had no separate mouthpiece, and according to the Talmud, the ram's horn was not straightened but left crooked.

The *shoh·phar'* was basically used as a signaling instrument. It assembled the Israelite forces, sometimes sounded the "alarm signal" against a city to be attacked, and directed other maneuvers in warfare. (Jg 3:27; 6:34; 2Sa 2:28; Joe 2:1; Zep 1:16) In case of enemy attack, the *shoh·phar'* gave warning. (Ne 4:18-20) Being just a signaling instrument in battle, the sound of 300 of these horns would, under normal circumstances, indicate an army of considerable size. So when the Midianites heard the horns blown by everyone in Gideon's band of 300 men, "the whole camp got on the run," terror stricken.—Jg 7:15-22.

In addition to the horn's announcing every new moon, it proclaimed the year of Jubilee and added to the joyful spirit of other occasions. (Ps 81:3; Le 25:8-10; 2Sa 6:15; 2Ch 15:14) When Jehovah stated the terms of the Law covenant, the miraculous sound of a horn was one of the features of the spectacle at Mount Sinai. (Ex 19:16-19; 20:18) To proclaim the beginning and the end of the Sabbath with the *shoh·phar'* appears to have been a custom established before the Common Era.

Israelites of all stations seemed to know how to use the *shoh·phar'*. The priests blew it when marching around Jericho and likely were the ones who announced the Jubilee with it. (Jos 6:4, 5, 15, 16, 20; Le 25:8-10) Its being sounded by Ehud, by Gideon and his 300 men, and by Joab, as well as by the watchmen, who were not necessarily Levites, indicates general familiarity with the instrument.—Jg 3:27; 6:34; 7:22; 2Sa 2:28; Eze 33:2-6.

The Hebrew term *yoh·vel'* (ram) is used as a synonym of *shoh·phar'* in Exodus 19:13, where it is rendered "ram's horn." At Daniel 3:5, 7, 10, 15, *qe'ren* appears in Aramaic as part of the Babylonian orchestra.—See TRUMPET.

Horns of Altars. The horns of both the incense altar and the altar of sacrifice at the tabernacle were hornlike projections extending outward from the four corners. They were overlaid with the same material as the altar, either copper or gold. (Ex 27:2; 37:25, 26) The altars at Solomon's temple were probably patterned after those of the tabernacle.—1Ki 6:20, 22.

It was on the horns of the altar of sacrifice that Moses put some of the blood of the bull of the sin offering at the installation service to "purify the altar from sin." (Le 8:14, 15) According to Jehovah's direction, the priest was to put the blood of certain sacrifices on the horns of either one altar or the other, depending on the sacrifice offered. —Le 4:7, 18, 25, 30, 34; 16:18.

Jehovah said that the sins of Judah were engraved "on the horns of their altars" (Jer 17:1), making the altars unclean and their sacrifices unacceptable; and in Amos 3:14 Jehovah states his purpose to desecrate the altars for calf worship at Bethel by the cutting off of their horns.

The statement at Exodus 21:14 may mean that even a priest was to be executed for murder, or that the act of taking hold of the horns of the altar would not shield any willful murderer.—Compare 1Ki 2:28-34.

The altars seen in vision by Ezekiel and John had horns.—Eze 43:15; Re 9:13, 14.

Figurative Usage. An animal's horn (Heb., *qe'ren;* Gr., *ke'ras*) is a formidable weapon and Biblically was used quite often in a figurative sense, especially in the Hebrew Scriptures. Rulers and ruling dynasties, both the righteous and the wicked, were symbolized by horns, and their achieving of conquests was likened to pushing with the horns.—De 33:17; Da 7:24; 8:2-10, 20-24; Zec 1:18-21; Lu 1:69-71; Re 13:1, 11; 17:3, 12; see BEASTS, SYMBOLIC.

In one instance Jehovah, in assuring victory to his people, said he would 'change the horn of the daughter of Zion to iron.' (Mic 4:13) Whereas Jehovah raised up the horn of his people, or caused it to be exalted, the wicked are warned not to lift up their horn arrogantly, for the horns of the wicked will be cut down. (1Sa 2:10; Ps 75:4, 5, 10; 89:17; Am 6:12-14) In expression of his feeling of complete abandonment, Job sorrowfully states: "I have thrust my horn in the very dust." —Job 16:15.

"Horn" may also be used to describe an article shaped like a horn. At Ezekiel 27:15, the "horns of ivory" probably refer to elephant tusks. At Isaiah 5:1 the Hebrew phrase "a horn the son of oil [or, fatness]" evidently refers to "a fruitful hillside," the "horn" being used to represent the upward slope of the hill.—*NW,* ftn.

HORONAIM (Hor·o·na'im) [possibly, Two Holes [that is, caves]]. A place in Moab included among those against which Jehovah's judgment was directed. (Isa 15:1, 5; Jer 48:1, 3, 5, 34) Its exact location is uncertain. However, the possible meaning of its name has led some to identify Horonaim tentatively with el-'Iraq (meaning "Cave"), situated about 490 m (1,600 ft) below the level of the Moabite plateau and about 18 km (11 mi) E of the southern end of the Dead Sea. Horonaim may be the same as the "Hauronen" mentioned in the Moabite Stone as having been taken in battle by Mesha the king of Moab.

HORONITE (Hor'o·nite) [Of (Belonging to) Beth-horon or Horonaim]. A designation applied to Sanballat, one of the men opposing the work of Nehemiah. (Ne 2:10, 19) Some scholars think that Sanballat may have been from the Moabite city of Horonaim (Isa 15:5; Jer 48:3) and, in support of this, call attention to his being mentioned with Tobiah the Ammonite and Geshem the Arabian. But the view generally favored is that "Horonite" probably means a native, or inhabitant, of Beth-

horon. Both Upper and Lower Beth-horon were located in territory originally assigned to Ephraim.—Jos 16:1, 3, 5.

HORSE [Heb., *sus; re'khev* (chariot horses); *re'khesh* (team of horses; post horses); Gr., *hip'pos*]. Jehovah, the Creator of this animal, when reproving Job, described some of the horse's principal characteristics: its great strength, its snorting with its large nostrils, its pawing the ground in impatience, its excitement at the prospect of battle, and its not being terrified by the clashing of weapons. (Job 39:19-25) This familiar animal has, from ancient times, been closely associated with man, who has used the bridle and the whip to control it.—Ps 32:9; Pr 26:3; Jas 3:3.

Military Use. Apart from its use by kings, princes, and state officials, or for rapid communication systems (2Sa 15:1; Ec 10:7; Es 6:7, 8; 8:14; Jer 17:25; 22:4), the horse was used mainly in warfare in ancient times.—Pr 21:31; Isa 5:28; Jer 4:13; 8:16; 46:4, 9.

Horses, however, do not lend themselves well for military use in mountainous, rough terrain. (Am 6:12) Hence, when King Ahab of Israel defeated the army of Syria, Ben-hadad's servants offered the excuse that it was because the God of Israel was "a God of mountains" and not of the level plains, where horses and chariots operate to advantage. Nevertheless, Jehovah gave Israel the victory even in the plains.—1Ki 20:23-29.

The horse was such a formidable part of an effective fighting force that the mere sound of a large number of horses and chariots was enough to inspire fear and cause an army that considered itself outnumbered to resort to panicky flight. (2Ki 7:6, 7) The military might of Egypt, Assyria, Babylonia, Medo-Persia, and other nations largely depended on horses. (Isa 31:1, 3; Jer 6:22, 23; 50:35, 37, 41, 42; 51:27, 28; Eze 23:5, 6, 23; 26:7, 10, 11; Na 3:1, 2; Hab 1:6, 8) Repeatedly, horses, equipped with bridles, reins, head ornaments, saddlecloths, and other trappings, are depicted on ancient monuments.

God's chosen people of ancient times, the Israelites, though, were not to be like the Egyptians and other contemporary nations that considered horses and chariots indispensable to safety and independence. Israel's kings were forbidden to increase horses for themselves. (De 17:15, 16) Instead of trusting in military might, horses, and chariots, the Israelites were to look to Jehovah for help, and they were never to become fearful of the war equipment of their foes.—De 20:1-4; Ps 20:7; 33:17; Ho 1:7.

King David of Israel was mindful of Jehovah's prohibition against multiplying horses. In his victory over Hadadezer of Zobah, David could have added many horses to his army, but, instead, he kept only the number he deemed sufficient for his immediate purposes and ordered the remainder to be hamstrung.—2Sa 8:3, 4; 1Ch 18:3, 4; compare Jos 11:6, 9; see HAMSTRING.

From Solomon to the Return From Exile. However, David's son and successor, Solomon, began to accumulate thousands of horses. (1Ki 4:26 [here "forty thousand stalls of horses" is generally believed to be a scribal error for "four thousand"]; compare 2Ch 9:25.) From Egypt as well as other lands, King Solomon received horses (2Ch 9:28), and horses were among the gifts brought by those desiring to hear his wisdom. (1Ki 10:24, 25; 2Ch 9:23, 24) The animals were stabled in special chariot cities and also at Jerusalem. (1Ki 9:17-19; 10:26) The barley and straw furnished as fodder for the horses were supplied by the regional deputies in charge of providing food for the royal table.—1Ki 4:27, 28.

During Solomon's reign, royal merchants trafficked in horses and chariots. The price of a horse was 150 silver pieces ($330, if the silver pieces were shekels), and the price of a chariot was 600 silver pieces (c. $1,320, if shekels).—1Ki 10: 28, 29; 2Ch 1:16, 17.

In later years kings of Judah and Israel used horses in warfare. (1Ki 22:4; 2Ki 3:7) With reference to Judah, the prophet Isaiah stated that the land was filled with horses. (Isa 2:1, 7) Although at times in Israel's history conditions of drought, famine, and military reverses greatly reduced the number of horses (1Ki 17:1; 18:1, 2, 5; 2Ki 7:13, 14; 13:7; Am 4:10), the people still put their confidence in horses and looked to Egypt for military assistance. (Isa 30:16; 31:1, 3) Wicked kings of Judah even dedicated certain horses to the pagan cult of the sun, bringing them within the sacred precincts of the temple of Jehovah. (2Ki 23:11) The last Judean king, Zedekiah, rebelled against King Nebuchadnezzar of Babylon and then sent to Egypt for horses and military aid. (2Ch 36:11, 13; Eze 17:15) As a result, in fulfillment of prophecy, Judah went into exile.—Eze 17:16-21; Jer 52:11-14.

Horses are mentioned among the beasts of burden that would be used to transport God's scattered people to Jerusalem. (Isa 66:20) It is therefore notable that in the first fulfillment of the restoration prophecies, the returning Jews brought back 736 horses.—Ezr 2:1, 66; Ne 7:68.

Illustrative Use. In Scripture, the horse figures repeatedly in illustrative settings. The adulterous sons of faithless Jerusalem are likened to "horses seized with sexual heat." (Jer 5:7, 8) Unfaithful Jerusalem prostituted herself to the rulers of the pagan nations, lusting after them in the style of concubines belonging to those of inordinate sexual capacity, likened to male horses. (Eze 23:20, 21) The stubborn, unrepentant attitude of an apostate people is compared with the impetuous manner of a horse dashing into battle without regard for the consequences.—Jer 8:6.

The special attention and ornamentation lavished on a royal steed is the figure used to represent Jehovah's turning his favorable attention to his repentant people, making them like a victorious war horse.—Zec 10:3-6.

When Jehovah, through the prophet Joel, foretold a grievous plague to come upon those who professed to be his people, but who were in fact apostates, he described devouring pests having "the appearance of horses." (Joe 2:1-4) The apostle John received a similar vision of a great locust plague, with locusts 'resembling horses prepared for battle.'—Re 9:7.

John also saw armies of cavalry to the number of two myriads of myriads (200,000,000) empowered to execute the destructive judgments of God. The horses had death-dealing power in both their heads and their tails. All these horses apparently were under the direction of the four angels that had been bound at the Euphrates River.—Re 9:15-19.

Jehovah's invisible heavenly war equipment is represented by fiery horses and chariots. (2Ki 2:11, 12) Elisha, on one occasion, prayed for the eyes of his terrified attendant to be opened to see that "the mountainous region was full of horses and war chariots of fire all around Elisha" to protect him from the surrounding forces of Syrians sent out to capture him.—2Ki 6:17.

Centuries later Zechariah received a vision involving four chariots, the first with red horses, the second with black horses, the third with white horses, and the fourth with speckled, particolored horses. These are identified as "the four spirits of the heavens."—Zec 6:1-8; see also Zec 1:8-11.

Zechariah's prophecy about those doing military service against Jerusalem indicated that Jehovah would come to the rescue of his people and bring destruction upon the enemy and their horses. (Zec 14:12-15; see also Eze 38 and 39.) As one of the blessed results of that action, no more would the horse be used in warfare. Rather, it would be employed as an instrument of service to God's glory, as implied by the words: "There will prove to be upon the bells of the horse 'Holiness belongs to Jehovah!'" (Zec 14:20; compare Ex 28:36, 37.) Also, the cutting off of war chariot and horse denotes a restoration of peace.—Zec 9:10.

In the apostle John's symbolic vision, the glorified Jesus Christ is depicted as riding a white horse and as being accompanied by an army, all of whose members are seated on white horses. This vision was revealed to John as representing the righteousness and justice of the war that Christ will wage against all enemies on behalf of his God and Father, Jehovah. (Re 19:11, 14) Earlier, Christ's taking kingly action and the calamities that follow are represented by different horsemen and their mounts.—Re 6:2-8.

HORSE GATE. See GATE, GATEWAY.

HOSAH (Ho'sah).

1. A Merarite gatekeeper for the tent in which the ark of the covenant was put by David. (1Ch 16:1, 37, 38) He and his sons made up a division of gatekeepers assigned to the Shallecheth Gate on the W of the sanctuary.—1Ch 26:10-19.

2. A city in Asher apparently near Tyre, but otherwise unknown.—Jos 19:24, 29, 30.

HOSEA (Ho·se'a) [shortened form of Hoshaiah]. Hebrew prophet and writer of the Bible book of Hosea; identified merely as the son of Beeri. Hosea served as Jehovah's prophet during the reigns of Kings Uzziah, Jotham, Ahaz, and Hezekiah of Judah as well as Jeroboam II (son of Joash) of Israel, in the late ninth century and well into the eighth century B.C.E. (Ho 1:1) Prophets of the same general period included Amos, Isaiah, and Micah.—Am 1:1; Isa 1:1; Mic 1:1.

Hosea may be identified as a prophet (and probably a subject) of the ten-tribe northern kingdom of Israel. That kingdom was the principal object of the declarations in the book of Hosea. Whereas Judah was named therein only 15 times, and its capital city, Jerusalem, not even once, the book contains 44 references to Israel, 37 to Ephraim (Israel's dominant tribe), and 6 to Samaria, the capital of the northern kingdom. Most of the other locations mentioned in the book either were a part of the northern kingdom or were on its borders.—Ho 1:4, 5; 5:1, 8; 6:8, 9; 10:5, 8, 15; 12:11; 14:6, 7.

Hosea, nevertheless, apparently attached primary importance to the kings of Judah, mention-

ing all four who reigned there during his ministry, while listing only the one ruling in Israel when he began his work. (Ho 1:1) But, instead of indicating that the prophet came from, or was born in, Judah, this factor may show that Hosea, like other prophets of God, regarded only the Judean kings of David's family as rightful rulers over God's people, viewing the northern kingdom of Israel as a general religious and civil apostasy from Jehovah. Of course, this listing of rulers in both kingdoms facilitates more accurate dating of Hosea's prophetic activity.

HOSEA, BOOK OF. A book of the Hebrew Scriptures written by "Hosea the son of Beeri." (Ho 1:1) In it the writer's domestic life is paralleled with God's relationship to Israel. (Chaps 1-3) The book shows that mere formal religious ceremony does not find acceptance with Jehovah. (6:6) It also highlights God's mercy and lovingkindness.—2:19; 11:1-4; 14:4.

Time and Place of Composition. Hosea began serving as a prophet at a time when Judean King Uzziah (829-778 B.C.E.) and King Jeroboam II of Israel (c. 844-804 B.C.E.) were contemporaries, and thus no later than 804 B.C.E., the apparent end of Jeroboam's reign. (Ho 1:1) Hosea's prophetic ministry continued into the reign of King Hezekiah of Judah, whose kingship began about 745 B.C.E. Hence, it spanned no less than 59 years, though it doubtless covered some time in the reigns of Jeroboam II and Hezekiah, thus being somewhat longer. Although Hosea recorded a prophecy concerning Samaria's destruction (13:16), he did not report its fulfillment, which he probably would have done if the writing of the book had extended to 740 B.C.E., the date of Samaria's fall. Therefore, the book of Hosea was evidently written in the district of Samaria and completed sometime between 745 and 740 B.C.E.

Setting. The book of Hosea is concerned primarily with the northern ten-tribe kingdom of Israel (also called Ephraim after its dominant tribe, the names being used interchangeably in the book). When Hosea began to prophesy during King Jeroboam's reign, Israel enjoyed material prosperity. But the people had rejected knowledge of God. (Ho 4:6) Their wicked practices included acts of bloodshed, stealing, fornication, adultery, and the veneration of Baal and calf idols. (2:8, 13; 4:2, 13, 14; 10:5) After King Jeroboam died, prosperity ceased, and frightful conditions, marked by unrest and political assassination, came into existence. (2Ki 14:29–15:30) Faithful

Hosea also prophesied amid these circumstances. Finally, in 740 B.C.E., Samaria fell to the Assyrians, bringing the ten-tribe kingdom to its end. —2Ki 17:6.

Hosea's Wife and the Children. At Jehovah's command, Hosea took to himself "a wife of fornication and children of fornication." (Ho 1:2) This does not mean that the prophet married a prostitute or an immoral woman already having illegitimate children. It indicates that the woman would become adulterous and have such children after her marriage to the prophet. Hosea married Gomer, who "bore to him a son," Jezreel. (1:3, 4) Gomer later gave birth to a daughter, Loruhamah, and thereafter to a son named Lo-ammi, both evidently being fruits of her adultery, as no personal reference is made to the prophet in connection with their births. (1:6, 8, 9) Loruhamah means "[She Was] Not Shown Mercy," and the meaning of Lo-ammi is "Not My People," these names indicating Jehovah's disapproval of wayward Israel. On the other hand, the name of the firstborn child "Jezreel," meaning "God Will Sow Seed," is applied to the people favorably in a restoration prophecy.—2:21-23.

After the birth of these children, Gomer apparently abandoned Hosea for her paramours, but it is not said that the prophet divorced her. Evidently she was later forsaken by her lovers and fell into poverty and slavery, for Hosea 3:1-3 seems to indicate that the prophet purchased her as though she were a slave and took her back as a wife. His relationship with Gomer paralleled that of Jehovah with Israel, God being willing to take back his erring people after they repented of their spiritual adultery.—Ho 2:16, 19, 20; 3:1-5.

Some Bible scholars have viewed Hosea's marriage as visionary, as a trance, or a dream, never carried into action. However, the prophet did not say or indicate that a vision, or a dream, was involved. Others have considered the marriage to be an allegory or a parable. But Hosea did not use symbolic or figurative terminology when discussing it. Viewing this as an account of the actual marriage of Hosea to Gomer and of Gomer's literal restoration to the prophet gives force and significance to the application of these things historically and factually to Israel. It does not strain the plain Biblical account, and it harmonizes with Jehovah's choosing of Israel, the nation's subsequent spiritual adultery, and the people's restoration to God upon their repentance.

Style. Hosea's writing style is concise, even abrupt at times. There are rapid changes of thought. The book contains expressions of great feeling and power in the form of rebuke, warning, and exhortation, as well as tender pleas for repentance. And it contains excellent figures of speech. —Ho 4:16; 5:13, 14; 6:3, 4; 7:4-8, 11, 12; 8:7; 9:10; 10:1, 7, 11-13; 11:3, 4; 13:3, 7, 8, 15; 14:5-7.

HIGHLIGHTS OF HOSEA

Prophecies directed mainly to Israel (the northern kingdom, also called Ephraim) and emphasizing Jehovah's extraordinary mercy

Written by Hosea after 745 B.C.E., shortly before Israel was taken into exile by Assyria

---

Jehovah's dealings with Israel illustrated by Hosea's domestic life (1:1–3:5)

Hosea is told to marry a woman who thereafter proves to be adulterous, this illustrating Israel's unfaithfulness to Jehovah

By his wife Gomer, Hosea has a son named Jezreel. The next two children of Gomer, Lo-ruhamah (meaning "[She Was] Not Shown Mercy") and Lo-ammi (meaning "Not My People"), are evidently the fruitage of her adultery; the meanings of the names point to Jehovah's withdrawing mercy from Israel and his rejection of the unfaithful people

After experiencing divine judgment for faithlessly turning to Baal worship, Israel will be restored and again experience blessings, fulfilling the meaning of the name Jezreel (that is, "God Will Sow Seed")

Hosea is directed to take back his adulterous wife; he does so but restricts her activities, prohibiting fornication—indicative of Israel's situation until the time of returning to Jehovah

Prophetic judgments against Israel (and Judah) for unfaithfulness to Jehovah (4:1–13:16)

By engaging in fraud, murder, stealing, adultery, idolatry, and spiritual prostitution, the people show they have no knowledge of God; so they face an accounting

Israel's idolatry, moral corruption, and foolishly seeking political alliances with opposing powers (Egypt and Assyria), instead of relying on Jehovah for security, will lead to devastation of the land with the survivors' being taken away to Assyria

Appeal to return to Jehovah (14:1-9)

People are urged to petition Jehovah for pardon, to offer the bulls of their lips, and no longer to look to a military alliance and war horses for protection

Their return to Jehovah will result in healing, his loving them freely, and a flourishing condition under his blessing

Canonicity. The book of Hosea stands first in the order of the so-called minor prophets in common English Bibles, as well as in the ancient Hebrew and *Septuagint* texts. Jerome specified that one of the divisions of the Jews' sacred books was The Book of the Twelve Prophets, which evidently included the book of Hosea to fill out the number 12. Melito of the second century C.E. left a catalog including these books, as did Origen and others.

Harmony With Other Bible Books. This book harmonizes with thoughts expressed elsewhere in the Bible. (For instance, compare Ho 6:1 with De 32:39; Ho 13:6 with De 8:11-14; 32:15, 18.) The book of Hosea refers to occurrences recorded in other parts of the Scriptures, such as incidents involving Jacob (Ho 12:2-4, 12; Ge 25: 26; 32:24-29; 29:18-28; 31:38-41), Israel's Exodus from Egypt (Ho 2:15; 11:1; 12:13), her unfaithfulness in connection with Baal of Peor (Ho 9:10; Nu 25), and the nation's request for a human king (Ho 13:10, 11; 1Sa 8:4, 5, 19-22).

Use in the Christian Greek Scriptures. Twice Jesus Christ quoted from Hosea 6:6, using the words "I want mercy, and not sacrifice." (Mt 9:13; 12:7) He referred to Hosea 10:8 when pronouncing judgment on Jerusalem (Lu 23:30), and this statement was used at Revelation 6:16. Paul and Peter both made use of Hosea 1:10 and 2:23. (Ro 9:25, 26; 1Pe 2:10) Paul quoted from Hosea 13:14 (*LXX*) when discussing the resurrection, in asking: "Death, where is your victory? Death, where is your sting?"—1Co 15:55; compare also Hosea 14:2 with Hebrews 13:15.

Fulfilled Prophecies. The prophetic words of Hosea 13:16 concerning Samaria's fall were fulfilled. Hosea's prophecy also showed that Israel would be deserted by her lovers among the nations. (Ho 8:7-10) Indeed, they were of no assistance when Samaria was destroyed and inhabitants of Israel became Assyrian captives in 740 B.C.E.—2Ki 17:3-6.

Hosea's prophecy foretold that God would send a fire into the cities of Judah. (Ho 8:14) In the 14th year of King Hezekiah's reign, Assyrian King Sennacherib "came up against all the fortified cities of Judah and proceeded to seize them." (2Ki 18:13) However, Hosea also prophesied that Jehovah would save Judah. (Ho 1:7) This occurred when God frustrated Sennacherib's planned attack on Jerusalem, Jehovah's angel destroying 185,000 men of the Assyrian army in one night. (2Ki 19:34, 35) But a much more disastrous "fire" came when Jerusalem and the cities of Judah

were destroyed by King Nebuchadnezzar of Babylon in 607 B.C.E.—2Ch 36:19; Jer 34:6, 7.

Nonetheless, in keeping with inspired restoration prophecies found in the book of Hosea, a remnant of the people of Judah and Israel were gathered together and emerged from the land of exile, Babylonia, in 537 B.C.E. (Ho 1:10, 11; 2:14-23; 3:5; 11:8-11; 13:14; 14:1-8; Ezr 3:1-3) Paul used Hosea 1:10 and 2:23 to emphasize God's undeserved kindness as expressed toward "vessels of mercy," and Peter also employed these texts. These apostolic applications show that the prophecies also pertain to God's merciful gathering of a spiritual remnant.—Ro 9:22-26; 1Pe 2:10.

Messianic prophecy is also found in the book of Hosea. Matthew applied the words of Hosea 11:1 ("out of Egypt I called my son") to the child Jesus, who was taken into Egypt but was later brought back to Israel.—Mt 2:14, 15.

HOSHAIAH (Ho·shai'ah) [Saved by Jah; Jah Has Saved].

1. Father of Jezaniah or Azariah, who was a contemporary of the prophet Jeremiah. (Jer 42:1, 2; 43:2) In the Greek *Septuagint* the name Azariah appears instead of Jezaniah at Jeremiah 42:1.

2. Apparently a prince of Judah who participated in the procession arranged by Nehemiah at the inauguration of the wall of Jerusalem.—Ne 12:31, 32.

HOSHAMA (Hosh'a·ma) [possibly a shortened form of the name Jehoshama, meaning "Jehovah Has Heard (Listened)"]. One of the seven sons born to King Jehoiachin (Jeconiah) while in Babylonian exile.—1Ch 3:17, 18.

HOSHEA (Ho·she'a) [shortened form of Hoshaiah].

1. One of the 12 sent by Moses to spy out the Land of Promise in 1512 B.C.E.; son of Nun of the tribe of Ephraim. Moses, however, preferred to call him Jehoshua, meaning "Jehovah Is Salvation." (Nu 13:8, 16) In Greek the *Septuagint* has the name reading I·e·sous' (Jesus). As Moses' successor he was generally called by the shortened Hebrew form "Joshua."—Jos 1:1.

2. The tribal prince of Ephraim during David's reign; son of Azaziah.—1Ch 27:20, 22.

3. The Hebrew spelling of Hosea, Jehovah's prophet, who lived from the ninth into the eighth century B.C.E. during the reigns of Judah's kings Uzziah, Jotham, Ahaz, and Hezekiah.—Ho 1:1; see HOSEA.

4. Last king of the northern kingdom of Israel, which came to its end in 740 B.C.E.; son of Elah.

He did what was bad in Jehovah's sight, yet not to the same degree as his predecessors. (2Ki 17:1, 2) Hoshea had no hereditary claim to the throne, nor did he receive a special anointing from God to be king. Rather, it was by conspiracy against and murder of King Pekah that the usurper Hoshea gained the throne. Second Kings 15:30 states that Hoshea put Pekah to death and "began to reign in place of him in the twentieth year of Jotham." Since Judean King Jotham is credited with only 16 years (2Ki 15:32, 33; 2Ch 27:1, 8), this may refer to the 20th year counting from the start of Jotham's kingship, which would actually be the fourth year of the reign of Jotham's successor Ahaz.—See JOTHAM No. 3.

It appears that Hoshea was not fully recognized as king over Israel until sometime later, however. Second Kings 17:1 states that, in the 12th year of Ahaz, Hoshea "became king in Samaria over Israel for nine years." So, it may be that at this point Hoshea was able to establish full control from Samaria. Possibly Assyrian backing at this point aided him, for the records of Assyrian King Tiglath-pileser III make the claim that he put Hoshea on the throne.—See chart "Outstanding Dates During the Period of the Kings of Judah and of Israel" in CHRONOLOGY article.

Shalmaneser V, successor to Tiglath-pileser III, compelled Hoshea to pay tribute, but it was not long before Hoshea sent messengers to So the king of Egypt, appealing for assistance, and subsequently withheld tribute from the Assyrians. Upon learning of this secret conspiracy, Shalmaneser V put Hoshea in the house of detention and laid siege to Samaria. In 740 B.C.E., after a three-year siege, the city fell, its inhabitants were carried off into exile, and the split-off ten-tribe kingdom of Israel came to its end.—2Ki 17:3-6.

5. One of the heads of the people whose descendant, if not he himself, agreed to the Levitical proposal for a trustworthy arrangement in the time of Nehemiah.—Ne 9:5, 38; 10:1, 14, 23.

HOSPITALITY.
The cordial and generous reception and entertainment of guests or strangers. "Hospitality" is translated from the Greek *phi·lo·xe·ni'a,* literally meaning "love of (fondness for, or kindness to) strangers."

In Ancient Times. In patriarchal times, though Egyptians and others practiced hospitality, the Semites were most notable for this quality. Care for the traveler was viewed as an integral part of living, and great was the courtesy extended the visitor, whether a stranger, a friend, a relative, or an invited guest.

From the Bible accounts we learn that hospitality was customarily extended to a traveler. He was greeted by a kiss, particularly if a relative. (Ge 29:13, 14) His feet were washed by a member of the household, usually a servant (Ge 18:4), and his animals were fed and cared for. (Ge 24:15-25, 29-33) He was often asked to stay for the night and sometimes even for several days. (Ge 24:54; 19:2, 3) The visitor was regarded as under the householder's protection during his stay. (Ge 19:6-8; Jg 19:22-24) On departure, he might be escorted partway on his journey.—Ge 18:16.

The importance with which the extending of hospitality was viewed is seen in Reuel's remarks when his daughters spoke of the "Egyptian" traveler (actually Moses) who had helped them in watering their flock. Reuel exclaimed: "But where is he? Why is it that you have left the man behind? Call him, that he may eat bread."—Ex 2:16-20.

In the cities. It is evident from the Bible accounts that, particularly in the cities, non-Israelites might not always be hospitable toward Israelites. (Jg 19:11, 12) Also, in the cities hospitality was probably not offered as readily as in more isolated areas. However, a Levite man with his attendant and his concubine sat down after sunset in the public square of Gibeah, seemingly expecting to be offered a place to stay overnight. This indicates that hospitality, even in the cities, was quite common. (Jg 19:15) In this instance, the Levite man remarked that he had provisions for his party as well as for his animals. (Jg 19:19) He required shelter only. But the bad attitude of the Benjamites inhabiting this city made it inhospitable, as was verified by what later occurred.—Jg 19:26-28.

To servants of God. While hospitality was generally practiced, the fine hospitality depicted in the Bible accounts was undoubtedly because, in most instances, the ones showing hospitality were servants of Jehovah. Especially noticeable were the hospitality and respect shown to those who were prophets or special servants of God. Abraham stood by the three angels for whom he provided a meal, while they ate. This seems to have been a token of respect for the men whom Abraham recognized to be angelic representatives of Jehovah. (Ge 18:3, 7, 8) And just as Abraham "ran" to prepare for his guests, Manoah showed eagerness in preparing food for the man whom he thought to be a man of God, but who was actually an angel. (Jg 13:15-18, 21) A prominent woman of Shunem showed hospitality to

Elisha because, as she said: "Here, now, I well know that it is a holy man of God that is passing by us constantly."—2Ki 4:8-11.

Inhospitality condemned. Because the Ammonites and Moabites refused to extend hospitality to the nation of Israel when they were traveling toward the Promised Land, and the Moabites even hired Balaam to call down evil on them, Jehovah decreed that no Ammonite or Moabite man could be admitted to the congregation of Israel. (De 23:3, 4) In this instance it was, not a mere failure to display humanitarian hospitality, but a hatred of God and his people that moved the Ammonites and Moabites to inhospitality and hostility.

Jehovah, through the prophet Isaiah, condemned the people of Israel for their lack of hospitality, telling them that their fasting and bowing before Him was of no value when at the same time they were letting their brothers suffer lack of food, clothing, and shelter.—Isa 58:3-7.

In the First Century C.E. The practice of hospitality in the first century of the Common Era continued much as it had been carried on in earlier times, although conditions had somewhat altered the extent of its practice. The Samaritans and Jews were not on good terms, so hospitality between them was often lacking. (Joh 4:7-9; 8:48) Also, domination by foreign nations had increased enmities, and the country roads were beset by robbers. Even some inns were run by dishonest, inhospitable men.

Nevertheless, among the Jews, the same amenities as in times past were generally observed toward the guest. He was welcomed with a kiss, his head was anointed or greased with oil, and his feet were washed. At banquets the guests were usually seated according to rank and honor.—Lu 7:44-46; 14:7-11.

Toward Jesus' disciples. The Lord Jesus Christ said, when sending out the 12 and later the 70 to preach in Israel, that they would be received hospitably into the homes of those who appreciated the good news they preached. (Mt 10:5, 6, 11-13; Lu 10:1, 5-9) Though Jesus himself had "nowhere to lay down his head," he was entertained in homes of persons who recognized him as sent from God.—Mt 8:20; Lu 10:38.

Paul took it as an accepted fact that his Christian brother Philemon would provide hospitality for him upon his visit after being released from prison. This was not presuming upon Philemon, for Paul knew from past association with Philemon that he would be more than anxious to provide what he could. (Phm 21, 22) The apostle John, in his letter written about 98 C.E., pointed out that members of the Christian congregation were under obligation to assist the traveling representatives sent forth, "that we may become fellow workers in the truth." John also commended Gaius for his hospitality, saying that he had shown this spirit to those sent forth who were "strangers at that." That is, these were not previously personally known to Gaius but were, nevertheless, warmly treated because of the service they were rendering to the congregation.—3Jo 5-8.

A Mark of True Christianity. Genuine hospitality, from the heart, is a mark of true Christianity. After the outpouring of the holy spirit on the day of Pentecost, 33 C.E., many newly converted Christians remained in Jerusalem to learn more about the good news of the Kingdom before leaving for their homes in various parts of the earth. Hospitality was shown them by the Christians living in Jerusalem, who entertained them in their homes and even sold their possessions and considered all things to be held in common. (Ac 2:42-46) An organized arrangement was later set up by the apostles for distributing food to the needy widows among them.—Ac 6:1-6.

Hospitality is a requirement for Christians. Although many had undergone severe persecution and some had experienced the plundering of their belongings, Paul commanded: "Do not forget hospitality." (Heb 13:2; 10:34) Peter showed that it should be willingly extended, saying: "Be hospitable to one another without grumbling." (1Pe 4:9; compare 2Co 9:7.) Emphasizing their prior obligation to fellow believers, Paul wrote that fellow Christians were to "work what is good toward all, but especially toward those related to us in the faith."—Ga 6:10.

Hospitality was one of the important qualities requisite for those who would be appointed as overseers in the Christian congregations. (1Ti 3:2; Tit 1:7, 8) Also, Paul instructed Timothy, an overseer in Ephesus, that Christian widows put on the list for receiving material assistance from the congregation should be those who had "entertained strangers." (1Ti 5:9, 10) Evidently these women had made their homes open and available to Christian ministers or missionaries who visited or served the congregation, even though prior to this many of these visitors would naturally have been "strangers" to them. Lydia was such a woman. She was unusually hospitable, Luke reporting: "She just made us come."—Ac 16:14, 15.

A proof of faith. The disciple James points out that hospitality is essential as a work demonstrating one's faith. He says: "If a brother or a sister is in a naked state and lacking the food sufficient for the day, yet a certain one of you says to them: 'Go in peace, keep warm and well fed,' but you do not give them the necessities for their body, of what benefit is it? Thus, too, faith, if it does not have works, is dead in itself."—Jas 2:14-17.

Blessings. The Scriptures, in recommending hospitality, point out that great are the spiritual blessings received by the hospitable one. Paul says: "Do not forget hospitality, for through it some, unknown to themselves, entertained angels." (Heb 13:2; Ge 19:1-3, 6, 7; Jg 6:11-14, 22; 13:2, 3, 8, 11, 15-18, 20-22) Jesus himself stated the principle: "There is more happiness in giving than there is in receiving."—Ac 20:35.

Out of appreciation for Jesus' work, Matthew Levi spread a big reception feast for him and, in turn, was blessed by hearing Jesus answer the critical questions of the Pharisees and additionally relate one of his fine illustrations. Matthew's use of his house in this hospitable way provided the tax collectors and others with whom Matthew was acquainted an opportunity to receive a witness.—Lu 5:27-39.

After Zacchaeus had shown hospitality to Jesus because of his faith, he was immeasurably blessed by hearing Jesus say: "This day salvation has come to this house."—Lu 19:5-10.

In a prophecy concerning the time of his return in Kingdom glory, Jesus said that the people would be separated, just as sheep are separated from goats by a shepherd. This would be done on the basis of the treatment they would accord his "brothers," even though they did not see Jesus with their physical eyes. Those showing hospitality and kindness to Christ's "brothers" would be doing it because they recognized them to be brothers of Christ and sons of God. (Mt 25:31-46) In another statement he showed that not mere humanitarian hospitality would bring lasting reward from God but hospitality rendered to God's prophets because they are recognized as God's representatives, disciples belonging to Christ. —Mt 10:40-42; Mr 9:41, 42.

When Not to Be Extended. The Bible tells Christians that there are some to whom they should not extend hospitality. "Everyone that pushes ahead and does not remain in the teaching of the Christ does not have God. . . . If anyone comes to you and does not bring this teaching, never receive him into your homes or say a greeting to him. For he that says a greeting to him is a sharer in his wicked works." (2Jo 9-11) To keep such a one in the home or to fraternize with him would be dangerous to one's own spirituality and, in effect, would be condoning his course. It would be misleading to others and a reproach to the congregation. This principle is expressed also at Romans 16:17, 18; Matthew 7:15; 1 Corinthians 5:11-13.

Inns and Lodging Places. The ancient inn was apparently little more than a place of shelter for the traveler, providing also a place for his animals, similar to what has been termed a "caravansary." Such may have been the lodging place where Joseph's half brothers stayed on their journey back from Egypt to Canaan (Ge 42:27; 43:21) and where the angel appeared before Moses' wife Zipporah.—Ex 4:24.

It seems that prostitutes sometimes operated lodging places. Rahab the prostitute of Jericho lodged the two spies sent out by Joshua, and she showed kindness and hospitality to them by hiding them from their pursuers. (Jos 2:1-13) Samson lodged at the house of a prostitute woman in Gaza until midnight, waiting to humiliate the Philistines by carrying off the city gates.—Jg 16:1-3.

Some of the inns in Palestine during the first century C.E. were evidently more elaborate, perhaps providing not only shelter but also food and other services, at a designated charge. The hospitable Samaritan of Jesus' parable paid out of his own funds for the injured man's care at an inn. —Lu 10:30-35.

The Guest. In ancient times the guest, while treated with the utmost courtesy and honor, was expected to observe certain amenities and requirements. For example, it was considered among the vilest of acts to partake of another man's food and then betray him or bring harm to him. (Ps 41:9; Joh 13:18) The guest was not to presume upon his host or on the group gathered together by taking the seat of honor, or the place of prominence, but was to leave this for the host to determine. (Lu 14:7-11) Neither should he 'wear out his welcome,' by being at the home of his host too long or by going there too often. (Pr 25:17) It may be noted that Jesus always imparted spiritual blessings when enjoying the hospitality of his host. (Lu 5:27-39; 19:1-8) For a similar reason he told his disciples whom he sent out that when they reached a town, they should stay in the home where hospitality was extended them and not be "transferring from house to house." They should not be thus seeking a place where the householder could provide them with more comfort, entertainment, or material things.—Lu 10:1-7; Mr 6:7-11.

The apostle Paul, who did much traveling and who received hospitality from many of his Christian brothers, nevertheless, did not make himself a financial burden on any of them. Much of the time he worked at a secular occupation, and he set forth the law: "If anyone does not want to work, neither let him eat." (2Th 3:7-12; 1Th 2:6) By reason of this, Paul had an answer to the charges of the so-called superfine apostles in Corinth, who accused Paul of taking advantage of the Christians in the congregation there. (2Co 11:5, 7-10) He could boast in the fact that he provided the good news to them absolutely without cost, not even taking the things he had the right to as an apostle and a minister of God.—1Co 9:11-18.

Avoid Hypocritical Hospitality. A warning about accepting a hypocritical display of hospitality is given at Proverbs 23:6-8: "Do not feed yourself with the food of anyone of ungenerous eye [literally, "evil as to eye"], nor show yourself craving his tasty dishes. For as one that has calculated within his soul, so he is. 'Eat and drink,' he says to you, but his heart itself is not with you. Your morsel that you have eaten, you will vomit it out, and you will have wasted your pleasant words." Not being the kind that gives something freeheartedly, but expecting something back for what he gives, such a person calculates against you, inviting you in a hearty manner, but with some ulterior motive. By partaking of his food, and particularly if you crave his tasty dishes so as to desire to enjoy them again, you place yourself to some extent under his power. You may find it hard to refuse some request of his, and you may possibly get involved in difficulty. Then you will feel sick at ever having eaten with him, and the pleasant words that you expressed, hoping that they would promote spirituality and upbuilding friendship, will certainly have been wasted.—Compare Ps 141:4.

HOTHAM (Ho'tham) [Seal; Seal Ring].

1. Son of Heber from the tribe of Asher (1Ch 7:30-32); likely the same person as the Helem mentioned in 1 Chronicles 7:35.

2. An Aroerite whose sons Shama and Jeiel are listed among the mighty men of David's military forces.—1Ch 11:26, 44.

HOTHIR (Ho'thir) [from a root meaning "more than enough; overflow"]. One of the 14 sons of Heman who served under the direction of their father as musicians at the sanctuary. In David's time Hothir and his sons and brothers were constituted the 21st of the 24 service groups of musicians.—1Ch 25:1, 4-6, 28.

HOUR. The Greek word ho'ra (hour) is used in the Christian Greek Scriptures to denote a short period of time; a fixed, definite time; or a division of the day. No term for "hour" is found in the Hebrew Scriptures. The ancient Israelites may have divided the daytime into four parts. (Ne 9:3) Instead of designating certain hours, the Hebrew Scriptures use the expressions "morning," "noon," "midday," and "evening" as time markers for events. (Ge 24:11; 43:16; De 28:29; 1Ki 18:26) Also, perhaps more precise designations were "as soon as the sun shines forth" (Jg 9:33), "the breezy part of the day" (Ge 3:8), "the heat of the day" (Ge 18:1; 1Sa 11:11), and "the time of the setting of the sun" (Jos 10:27; Le 22:7). The Passover sacrifice was to be slaughtered "between the two evenings," which seems to mean a time after sunset and before deep twilight. (Ex 12:6) This view is supported by some scholars, as well as by the Karaite Jews and Samaritans, although the Pharisees and Rabbinists considered it to be the time between the beginning of the sun's descent and the real sunset.

God commanded that burnt offerings be made on the altar "in the morning," and "between the two evenings." Along with each of these, a grain offering was made. (Ex 29:38-42) So it came about that expressions such as "the going up of the grain offering," where the context indicates whether morning or evening (as at 1Ki 18:29, 36), and "the time of the evening gift offering" (Da 9:21) referred to a fairly well-defined time.

The night was divided into three periods called watches. Mention is made of "the night watches" (Ps 63:6), "the middle night watch" (Jg 7:19), and "the morning watch" (Ex 14:24; 1Sa 11:11).

The 24-Hour Day. Egypt has been credited with the division of the day into 24 hours, 12 for daylight, 12 for night. These hours would not always be of the same length from day to day, because of the change of seasons, making the daylight hours longer and the night hours shorter in summertime (except at the equator). Our modern-day division of the day into 24 hours of 60 minutes each results from a combination of Egyptian reckoning and Babylonian mathematics, a sexagesimal system (founded on the number 60). The practice of counting the day from midnight to midnight, thereby eliminating the seasonal variation in the length of the hours, was a later development, perhaps Roman.

In the First Century. In the first century C.E., the Jews used the count of 12 hours to the day, starting with sunrise. "There are twelve hours of daylight, are there not?" said Jesus. (Joh 11:9) Of course, this made the hours vary in length from one day to the next, according to the seasons; the only times that they were of the same length as our hours was at the time of the equinoxes. Evidently this slight variation, which would not be so great in Palestine, did not create any major inconvenience. The start of the day would correspond to about 6:00 a.m., our time. In the illustration of the workers in the vineyard, Jesus made mention of the 3rd hour, the 6th, 9th, 11th, and, one hour later, "evening" (which would be the 12th). These times would correspond to our 8:00 to 9:00 a.m., 11:00 a.m. to noon, 2:00 to 3:00 p.m., 4:00 to 5:00 p.m., and 5:00 to 6:00 p.m., respectively. (Mt 20:3, 5, 6, 8, 12; Ac 3:1; 10:9) Midnight and "cockcrowing" are time designations also used in the Christian Greek Scriptures. (Mr 13:35; Lu 11:5; Ac 20:7; 27:27; see COCKCROWING.) Under Roman domination the Jews seem to have adopted the Roman division of the night into four watches instead of the former three.—Lu 12:38; Mt 14:25; Mr 6:48.

A Seeming Discrepancy. Some have pointed to what appears to be a discrepancy between the statement at Mark 15:25, which says Jesus was impaled at "the third hour," and that at John 19:14, which indicates that by "about the sixth hour" Jesus' final trial before Pilate was just ending. John had access to Mark's account, and he certainly could have repeated the time stated by Mark. Therefore John must have had a reason for stating the hour differently from Mark.

Why the seeming discrepancy? A variety of suggestions have been offered. None of these satisfy all objections. We simply do not have enough information to explain with any certainty the reason for this difference between the accounts. Perhaps Mark's or John's reference to the hour was parenthetical, not in chronological order. Whatever the case, one thing is certain: Both writers were inspired by holy spirit.

The synoptic Gospels clearly indicate that by the sixth hour, or 12 noon, Jesus had already been hanging on the stake long enough for the soldiers to cast lots over his garments and for the chief priests, the scribes, the soldiers, and other passersby to speak abusively of him. They also indicate that about 3:00 p.m. Jesus expired. (Mt 27:38-45; Mr 15:24-33; Lu 23:32-44) The truly important thing to remember is that Jesus died for our sins on Nisan 14, 33 C.E.—Mt 27:46-50; Mr 15:34-37; Lu 23:44-46.

Other Uses. The word *ho′ra* is often used in the Christian Greek Scriptures to denote "immediately" or within a very short period. A woman who touched the fringe of Jesus' outer garment became well "from that hour." (Mt 9:22) "Hour" could refer to a special or momentous point of time not exactly specified or to the starting point of that time. For example, Jesus said: "Concerning that day and hour nobody knows" (Mt 24:36), "The hour is coming when everyone that kills you will imagine he has rendered a sacred service to God" (Joh 16:2), and, "The hour is coming when I will speak to you no more in comparisons" (Joh 16:25).

Again, "hour" might designate a general time of day, as when the disciples said to Jesus about the multitude of people that had followed him to a lonely place: "The place is lonely and the hour is already far advanced; send the crowds away." —Mt 14:15; Mr 6:35.

Figurative or Symbolic Use. Symbolically or figuratively used, "hour" means a relatively short period of time. Jesus said to the crowd who came out against him: "This is your hour and the authority of darkness." (Lu 22:53) The ten horns on the scarlet-colored wild beast are said to represent ten kings who are to receive authority as kings "one hour" with the wild beast. (Re 17:12) Of Babylon the Great, it is said: "In one hour your judgment has arrived!" (Re 18:10) In harmony with Jesus' words at Matthew 13:25, 38 concerning the wheat and the weeds, Paul's warnings at Acts 20:29 and 2 Thessalonians 2:3, 7 regarding the coming apostasy, and Peter's statement at 2 Peter 2:1-3, John, the last surviving apostle, could well say: "Young children, it is the last hour, and, just as you have heard that antichrist is coming, even now there have come to be many antichrists; from which fact we gain the knowledge that it is the last hour." It was a very short time, indeed, "the last hour," the final part of the apostolic period, after which the apostasy would spring forth in full bloom.—1Jo 2:18.

As recorded at Revelation 8:1-4, the apostle John saw, during a silence in heaven for "about a half hour," an angel with incense that he offered with the prayers of all the holy ones. This reminds one of the practice in the temple in Jerusalem "at the hour of offering incense." (Lu 1:10) Alfred Edersheim, in *The Temple* (1874, p. 138), presents the traditional Jewish account of this "hour": "Slowly the incensing priest and his assistants ascended the steps to the Holy Place . . . Next, one of the assistants reverently spread the coals on the golden altar; the other arranged the incense; and then the chief officiating priest was left alone within the Holy Place, to await the signal of the president before burning the incense. . . . As the president gave the word of command, which marked that 'the time of incense had come,' 'the whole multitude of the people without' withdrew from the inner court, and fell down before the Lord, spreading their hands in silent prayer. It is this most solemn period, when throughout the vast Temple buildings deep silence rested on the worshipping multitude, while within the sanctuary itself the priest laid the incense on the golden altar, and the cloud of 'odours' rose up before the Lord."

HOUSE. The word "house" as used in the Bible (Heb., *ba'yith;* Gr., *oi'kos* or *oi·ki'a*) may denote, among other things, (1) a household or all the offspring of one man (Ge 12:1; 17:13, 23; Ob 1:17, 18; Mic 1:5); (2) a dwelling house (Ge 19:2-4); (3) a jail or, figuratively, a country of enslavement (Ge 40:4, 14; Ex 13:3); (4) a dwelling place of animals and birds (Job 39:6; Ps 104:17); (5) a spiderweb (Job 8:14); (6) a royal residence or palace (2Sa 5:11; 7:2); (7) a priestly line (1Sa 2:35); (8) a royal dynasty (1Sa 25:28; 2Sa 7:11); (9) Jehovah's tabernacle or temple, both literal and as referred to in an illustrative way (Ex 23:19; 34:26; 1Ki 6:1; 1Pe 2:5); (10) the dwelling place of Jehovah, heaven itself (Joh 14:2); (11) the sanctuary of a false god (Jg 9:27; 1Sa 5:2; 1Ki 16:32; 2Ki 5:18); (12) the corruptible physical body of humans (Ec 12:3; 2Co 5:1-4); (13) the incorruptible spiritual body (2Co 5:1); (14) the common grave (Job 17:13; Ec 12:5); (15) an association of workers engaged in the same profession (1Ch 4:21); and (16) a building for housing official records of state (Ezr 6:1).

A form of the Hebrew word for house (*ba'yith*) often constitutes part of a proper name, as in Bethel (meaning "House of God") and Bethlehem (meaning "House of Bread").

Building Materials, Construction Methods. Anciently, as today, different types of dwellings existed. Construction techniques varied according to the time period, the economic circumstances of the builder, and the available materials. The builders of Babel, for instance, used brick instead of stone, and "bitumen served as mortar for them."—Ge 11:3.

Many of the Israelites began dwelling in the houses of the dispossessed Canaanites and likely followed similar construction methods for years afterward. (De 6:10, 11) Apparently stone houses were preferred (Isa 9:10; Am 5:11), as these were more substantial and safer from intruders than those built of mud brick. Robbers could readily gain access to mud houses by simply digging through a wall. (Compare Job 24:16.) However, in the lowlands, where little good-quality limestone and sandstone was available, sun-dried or, sometimes, kiln-baked mud bricks were used for the walls of dwellings. Sycamore, juniper, and, particularly in the better houses, cedar beams and rafters were used.—Ca 1:17; Isa 9:10.

Archaeologists have excavated the ruins of several kinds of ancient Palestinian dwellings. Often there was an oven in the courtyard and sometimes also a well or a cistern. (2Sa 17:18) The ruins of houses that have been found indicate considerable variation in size. One was only about 5 m (16 ft) square, whereas another measured 32 by 30 m (104 by 97 ft). Rooms often were from about 3.5 to 4.5 m (12 to 15 ft) square.

Some houses were built atop wide city walls. (Jos 2:15) But preferably they were constructed on a rock-mass (Mt 7:24), and generally mud-brick work was not started until two or three rows of stone had first been laid. When a house could not be erected on a rock-mass, often a solid foundation was laid, its depth below ground being equivalent to the height of the stone wall above ground. Some foundations were built with large uncut stones, and the cracks were filled with small rocks; others were constructed of hewn stones. The ruins of one mud-brick house excavated by archaeologists had stonework to a height of over 0.5 m (1.5 ft); in another the stone construction rose to a height of about 1 m (3 ft). The walls of some houses were about 1 m (3 ft) thick. Often a kind of whitewash was applied to the exterior walls (Eze 13:11, 15), and mud-brick walls on the street side were sometimes faced with pebbles to protect their surface.

Building stones were aligned and bonded with carefully smoothed and fitted cornerstones. (Compare Ps 118:22; Isa 28:16.) A mixture of clay and straw commonly served as mortar. At times this mixture included lime, ashes, pulverized pottery fragments, pounded shells, or limestone. It was applied to the bricks or stones to hold them together, and it was also used as a plaster for interior walls. (Le 14:41, 42) In some cases, however, stones were so accurately cut that mortar was not needed.

Floors. Floors, including those of the courtyard, consisted of beaten earth or were paved with stone, brick, or lime plaster. A depression in the floor commonly served as a fireplace, but braziers were used to heat the finer homes. (Jer

36:22, 23) Smoke escaped through a hole in the roof. (Ho 13:3) The rooms of palatial houses perhaps had wooden floors, like the temple.—1Ki 6:15.

Windows. Rectangular openings in the walls served as windows. At least some of these were large enough for a man to pass through. (Jos 2:15; 1Sa 19:12; Ac 20:9) Particularly the windows facing the street were equipped with lattices.—Jg 5:28; Pr 7:6.

Doors. Doors were commonly made of wood and turned on pivots (Pr 26:14) fitted into sockets in the wooden or stone lintel and threshold. Two upright wooden posts served as jambs. (Ex 12:22, 23) Although some houses had two entranceways, usually only one door led from the street into the courtyard, from which access could be gained to all the rooms of the house.

Interior decorations and furniture. In luxurious homes the walls of the rooms were paneled with cedar or other costly woods and were smeared with vermilion. (Jer 22:14; Hag 1:4) "The houses of ivory" of some wealthy ones evidently had rooms paneled with wood inlaid with ivory. (1Ki 22:39; Am 3:15) Aside from the various cooking utensils, vessels, baskets, and other household items, the furnishings of the home might include beds or divans, chairs, stools, tables, and lampstands. (Compare 2Sa 4:11; 2Ki 4:10; Ps 41:3; Mt 5:15.) The furniture in the homes of some wealthy persons was beautified with inlaid work of ivory, gold, and silver.—Compare Es 1:6; Am 3:12; 6:4.

Roof and upper chamber. Most roofs were flat, and the Law required that Israelite roofs be surrounded by a parapet to prevent accidents. (De 22:8) When a slight slope was given to the roof, this permitted the rain to run off. The roof rested on strong wooden beams laid from wall to wall. Smaller wooden rafters were placed across these beams and, in turn, were covered with branches, reeds, and the like. Next came a layer of earth several inches thick that was coated with a thick plaster of clay or of clay and lime. An opening could easily be dug through such an earthen roof, as was done by men who were endeavoring to get a paralytic into Jesus' presence so that he might be healed. (Mr 2:4) The beams of the roof often were supported by a row of upright wooden posts resting on stone bases. Grass could sprout from these roofs (Ps 129:6), and it was difficult to keep them from leaking. (Pr 19:13; 27:15; Ec 10:18) Probably before the rainy season began, roofs were repaired and rolled smooth to allow a better runoff of water.

The roofs were places of considerable activity in both peaceful and calamitous times. (Isa 22:1; Jer 48:38) From them announcements could be made or certain actions could quickly be brought to public notice. (2Sa 16:22; Mt 10:27) Flax was dried on the roofs (Jos 2:6), and there persons might converse (1Sa 9:25), walk in the cool evening (2Sa 11:2), engage in true or false worship (Jer 19:13; Zep 1:5; Ac 10:9), or even sleep (1Sa 9:26). During the Festival of Ingathering, booths were erected on the rooftops and in the courtyards of the houses.—Ne 8:16.

Often a roof chamber or upper chamber was built on the housetop. This was a pleasant, cool room that often served as a guest room. (Jg 3:20; 1Ki 17:19; 2Ki 1:2; 4:10) Of course, some homes were two-story buildings with a regular upper story. In a large upper chamber, either a roof chamber or a room of an upper story, Jesus celebrated the last Passover with his disciples and instituted the commemoration of the Lord's Evening Meal. (Lu 22:11, 12, 19, 20) And on the day of Pentecost, 33 C.E., some 120 disciples were apparently in an upper chamber of a house in Jerusalem when God's spirit was poured out upon them.—Ac 1:13-15; 2:1-4.

Usually outside stairs or, in the poorer homes, ladders led from the courtyard to the roof. Therefore, when necessary, a person on the housetop could leave without having to go into the house itself. Since many homes were built close together, it was often possible to walk from rooftop to rooftop. These factors may have some bearing on the meaning of Jesus' counsel at Matthew 24:17 and Mark 13:15. In the better homes an interior staircase gave access to the upper story.

The Law Protected Property Rights. It was Jehovah's purpose that his obedient people have the joy of living in their own houses. (Compare Isa 65:21.) For someone else to gain occupancy of the house of its builder was a calamity to fall upon disobedient ones. (De 28:30; La 5:2) And a man who had not yet inaugurated his new house was exempted from military service.—De 20:5, 6.

Certain provisions of God's law to Israel protected property rights. The Law condemned coveting another's possessions, including his house (Ex 20:17), and Jehovah, through his prophets, denounced the unlawful seizure of houses. (Mic 2:2; compare Ne 5:1-5, 11.) A creditor could not force his way into the house of his debtor and seize a pledge. (De 24:10, 11) An Israelite who sanctified his house to Jehovah could buy it back by paying 120 percent of its estimated value to the sanctuary. (Le 27:14, 15) Also, those who had to sell their houses retained repurchase rights, at least for a time. Houses in unwalled villages could be bought back by their original owners and had to be returned to them in the Jubilee year. But houses in walled cities became the permanent property of the buyer if they were not bought back within the allotted one-year period during which the repurchase right continued in force. The right of repurchase was permanent in the case of houses located in walled Levite cities. If not bought back earlier, all houses formerly belonging to Levites had to be returned to their original owners in the Jubilee year.—Le 25:29-33.

A Place for Spiritual Instruction. From earliest times the home functioned as a center for giving instruction in pure worship. God's law to Israel specifically commanded fathers to teach their sons when sitting in the house, as well as at other times. (De 6:6, 7; 11:19) Also, God's law was to be written, apparently figuratively, on the doorposts of their houses (De 6:9; 11:20), and the home was to be kept free from all appendages of idolatry. (De 7:26) In view of the fact that the home was used for such a sacred purpose, houses infected with "malignant leprosy" were to be torn down. (See LEPROSY.) The law concerning leprous houses would have reminded the Israelites that they could live only in homes that were clean from God's standpoint.—Le 14:33-57.

With the establishment of Christianity, preaching and teaching from house to house became a prominent part of true worship. (Ac 20:20) Jesus' followers availed themselves of the hospitality accorded them by 'deserving ones' or 'friends of peace,' and they stayed in the houses of such persons until completing their ministry in a particular city. (Mt 10:11; Lu 10:6, 7; see PREACHER, PREACHING ["From House to House"].) Often groups or congregations of Christians regularly met together in houses to consider God's Word. (Ro 16:5; 1Co 16:19; Col 4:15; Phm 2) But any who turned away from the teaching of the Christ were not welcomed in private homes.—2Jo 10.

HOUSE OF THE FOREST OF LEBANON.

A part of the complex of government buildings erected by King Solomon during his 13-year building program after he had finished the temple at Jerusalem (1027-1014 B.C.E.). The building was evidently used for the storage and display of valuable arms and utensils. This structure, located S of the temple, received its name either because it was constructed of cedar from Lebanon

or because its many large cedar pillars reminded one of the forests there.

The House of the Forest of Lebanon was 100 cubits (44 m; 146 ft) long, 50 cubits (22 m; 73 ft) wide, and 30 cubits (13 m; 44 ft) high. It appears to have had stone walls (1Ki 7:9), with cedar beams the ends of which were laid into the walls and were additionally supported by four rows of pillars ("four" in the Hebrew text; "three" in the Greek *Septuagint*). Above the pillars, there were evidently cedar-paneled chambers. Some suggested reconstructions of this house have three tiers of chambers above the pillars and these face an unroofed court in the middle of the building. The chambers were said to have "an illumination opening opposite an illumination opening in three tiers." This seems to have meant that, looking out over the court, there were openings or large windows that faced corresponding windows in the chambers on the opposite side of the court. Or, it possibly meant that there was a window in each chamber facing the court and one facing the outside. The entrances (likely the doorways leading to the chambers and perhaps between them) "were squared with the frame." They were therefore not arch-shaped or vaulted. The windows were of like shape.—1Ki 7:2-5.

A problem arises in regard to the number of rows of pillars, as mentioned in the foregoing. For the Hebrew text says that there were four rows and later speaks of 45 pillars, then says: "There were fifteen to a row." (1Ki 7:2, 3) Some have thought that the text here applies to the chambers in three tiers, 15 chambers to a row, and that there may have been a greater number of pillars placed in the four rows. Others prefer the *Septuagint* reading of "three" rows of pillars. A number of translations alter the reading of the text so that the "forty-five" refers to the beams rather than to the upright pillars, or columns.—See *NE, NAB, AT, AS.*

After Solomon finished the house, he placed in it 200 large shields of alloyed gold, each overlaid with 600 shekels of gold (worth c. $77,000), and 300 bucklers of alloyed gold, each plated with three minas of gold (worth c. $19,300). This would be over 21 million dollars' worth of gold on the shields and bucklers. Besides this, there was an unstated number of gold vessels used in the house. (1Ki 10:16, 17, 21; 2Ch 9:15, 16, 20) These gold shields were carried away by Shishak king of Egypt during the reign of Solomon's son Rehoboam. Rehoboam replaced them with shields of copper, which he committed to the control of the chiefs of the runners, the guards of the entrance of the king's house.—1Ki 14:25-28; 2Ch 12:9-11.

The House of the Forest of Lebanon is also called "the armory of the house of the forest" at Isaiah 22:8.

HOUSES OF THE SOUL.

This literally translated expression "houses of the soul" probably denotes "perfume receptacles." These may have been suspended from a chain or necklace and worn by 'the haughty daughters of Zion' around their necks.—Isa 3:16, 18, 20.

The Hebrew expression is *bat·teh' han·ne'-phesh. Ne'phesh* (soul) may, in this case, signify "that which is breathed" or "smelled," and *bat·teh'* (houses) can mean "receptacles."

HUKKOK (Huk'kok) [Engraved; Inscribed; Hewn Out]. A border city of Naphtali. (Jos 19:32, 34) Whereas some consider it to be too far N and E, present-day Huqoq has been identified with ancient Hukkok. This site lies about 7 km (4.5 mi) W of the northern end of the Sea of Galilee and overlooks the fertile Plain of Gennesaret.

HUKOK (Hu'kok) [Engraved; Inscribed; Hewn Out]. Apparently the same as Helkath, a border city in the territory of Asher that was assigned to the Gershonites of the tribe of Levi.—Jos 19:25; 21:31, 33; 1Ch 6:74, 75; see HELKATH.

HUL. A son of Aram. (Ge 10:23) At 1 Chronicles 1:17, though, Hul appears to be listed as a son of Shem. In the Alexandrine Manuscript and Hebrew manuscript Kennicott 175, 1 Chronicles 1:17 reads as does Genesis 10:23, having the phrase "and the sons of Aram" before listing Uz, Hul, Gether, and Mash. So, the omission of the words "and the sons of" at 1 Chronicles 1:17 in the Masoretic text may be due to scribal error. But this is not necessarily the case; in the Scriptures, "sons" can also include grandsons and even later descendants. (For what might be a comparable situation, see 1Ch 1:4, where Shem, Ham, and Japheth are not introduced as sons of Noah, perhaps because their relationship to Noah was so well known that the original writer felt it unnecessary to make the identification.)

The area settled by the descendants of Hul is not definitely known. Josephus identifies Hul (Urus) as the founder of Armenia. (*Jewish Antiquities,* I, 145 [vi, 4]) Others have suggested areas in Mesopotamia and elsewhere. Many favor the Hula region in the vicinity of the Biblical waters of Merom that lay N of the Sea of Galilee, since the name Hul seems to be preserved in "Hula" and also in "Ulatha," a town in that area mentioned by Josephus.

HULDAH (Hul'dah) [feminine form of Heled, meaning "Duration of Life; System of Things"; or, possibly, "Mole Rat"]. The wife of Shallum; a prophetess residing at Jerusalem during the reign of faithful King Josiah of Judah.

When Josiah heard the reading of "the very book of the law" found by Hilkiah the high priest during the temple repair work, he sent a delegation to inquire of Jehovah. They went to Huldah, who, in turn, relayed the word of Jehovah, indicating that all the calamities for disobedience recorded in the "book" would befall the apostate nation. Huldah added that Josiah, because of having humbled himself before Jehovah, would not have to look upon the calamity but would be gathered to his forefathers and be taken to his graveyard in peace.—2Ki 22:8-20; 2Ch 34:14-28.

Some consider Huldah's prophecy to be in error in view of Josiah's death in an unnecessary battle. (2Ki 23:28-30) However, the "peace" in which Josiah would be gathered to his graveyard is obviously in contrast with "the calamity" due to come upon Judah. (2Ki 22:20; 2Ch 34:28) Josiah died prior to the coming of that calamity in 609-607 B.C.E., when the Babylonians besieged and destroyed Jerusalem. Additionally, that the expression 'to be gathered to one's forefathers' does not necessarily exclude dying a violent death in warfare is indicated by the use of the comparable expression 'to lie down with one's forefathers' with reference to a death in battle as well as a nonviolent death.—Compare De 31:16; 1Ki 2:10; 22:34, 40.

HUMILITY. Freedom from pride or arrogance; lowliness of mind. It is not weakness but a state of mind that is pleasing to Jehovah.

In the Hebrew Scriptures, "humility" is drawn from a root word (*'a·nah'*) meaning "be afflicted; be humbled; be oppressed." Words drawn from this root are variously translated "humility," "meekness," "affliction," and so forth. Two other Hebrew verbs involving "humility" are *ka·na''* (literally, subdue [oneself]) and *sha·phel'* (literally, be or become low). In the Christian Greek Scriptures the word *ta·pei·no·phro·sy'ne* is translated "humility" and "lowliness of mind." It is drawn from the words *ta·pei·no'o,* "make low," and *phren,* "the mind."

A person can achieve a state of humility by reasoning on his relationship to God and to his fellowmen, as outlined in the Bible, and then practicing the principles learned. A Hebrew word, *hith·rap·pes',* translated "humble yourself," means, literally, "stamp yourself down." It well expresses the action described by the wise writer of Proverbs: "My son, if you have gone surety for your fellowman, . . . if you have been ensnared by the sayings of your mouth, . . . you have come into the palm of your fellowman: Go humble yourself [stamp yourself down] and storm your fellowman with importunities. . . . Deliver yourself." (Pr 6:1-5) In other words, throw away your pride, acknowledge your mistake, set matters straight, and seek forgiveness. Jesus admonished that a person humble himself before God like a child and that, instead of trying to be prominent, he minister to or serve his brothers.—Mt 18:4; 23:12.

Or, a person may learn humility by being brought low, humbled by experience. Jehovah told Israel that he humbled them by causing them to walk 40 years in the wilderness in order to put them to the test so as to know what was in their heart and to make them know that "not by bread alone does man live but by every expression of Jehovah's mouth does man live." (De 8:2, 3) Many of the Israelites no doubt profited from this severe experience and gained humility from it. (Compare Le 26:41; 2Ch 7:14; 12:6, 7.) If a person or a nation refuses to become humble or to accept humbling discipline, such will suffer humiliation in due time.—Pr 15:32, 33; Isa 2:11; 5:15.

Pleases God. Humility has great value in the eyes of Jehovah. Although God does not owe mankind anything, in undeserved kindness he is ready to show mercy and favor to those humbling themselves before him. Such ones show that they are not trusting or boasting in themselves but are looking to him and want to do his will. As the inspired Christian writers James and Peter say: "God opposes the haughty ones, but he gives undeserved kindness to the humble ones."—Jas 4:6; 1Pe 5:5.

Even those who have in the past practiced very bad things, if they truly humble themselves before Jehovah and beseech him for mercy, will be heard by him. By promoting false worship in the land, King Manasseh of Judah had seduced the inhabitants of Judah and Jerusalem "to do worse than the nations that Jehovah had annihilated from before the sons of Israel." Yet, after Jehovah had let him go into captivity to the king of Assyria, Manasseh "kept humbling himself greatly because of the God of his forefathers. And he kept praying to Him, so that He let himself be entreated by him and He heard his request for favor and restored him to Jerusalem to his kingship; and Manasseh came to know that Jehovah is the true God." Thus Manasseh learned humility.—2Ch 33:9, 12, 13; compare 1Ki 21:27-29.

Provides Right Guidance. One who humbles himself before God can expect to have God's guidance. Ezra had a heavy responsibility in leading back from Babylon to Jerusalem more than 1,500 men, besides the priests, the Nethinim, and the women and children. Additionally, they carried with them a great amount of gold and silver for beautifying the temple in Jerusalem. They needed protection on the journey, but Ezra did not want to ask the king of Persia for a military escort and thereby show reliance on human might. Besides, he had previously said to the king: "The hand of our God is over all those seeking him for good." Therefore he proclaimed a fast, so the people would humble themselves before Jehovah. They made request of God, and he listened and provided them with protection from enemy ambushes on the way so that they completed the hazardous trip successfully. (Ezr 8:1-14, 21-32) The prophet Daniel, in Babylonian exile, was highly favored by God's sending an angel to him with a vision, because Daniel humbled himself before God in his search for guidance and understanding.—Da 10:12.

Humility will guide a person in the proper path and will bring him into glory, for it is God who exalts one and puts down another. (Ps 75:7) "Before a crash the heart of a man is lofty, and before glory there is humility." (Pr 18:12; 22:4) So, one seeking glory by haughtiness will fail, as did King Uzziah of Judah, who became presumptuous and unlawfully usurped priestly duties: "As soon as he was strong, his heart became haughty even to the point of causing ruin, so that he acted unfaithfully against Jehovah his God and came into the temple of Jehovah to burn incense upon the altar of incense." When he became enraged at the priests for correcting him, he was stricken with leprosy. (2Ch 26:16-21) Lack of humility caused Uzziah to be misguided, to his downfall.

Aids One in Time of Adversity. Humility can aid one greatly in meeting the challenge of adversity. If calamity comes, humility enables a person to hold up and endure as well as to continue his service to God. King David underwent many adversities. He was hunted as an outlaw by King Saul. But he never complained against God or exalted himself above Jehovah's anointed one. (1Sa 26:9, 11, 23) When he sinned against Jehovah in the affair with Bath-sheba and was most severely reproved by God's prophet Nathan, he humbled himself before God. (2Sa 12:9-23) Afterward, when a certain Benjamite named Shimei began publicly calling down evil on David, and David's officer Abishai wanted to kill the man for so disrespecting the king, David displayed humility. He replied to Abishai: "Here my own son, who has come forth out of my own inward parts, is looking for my soul; and how much more now a Benjaminite! . . . Perhaps Jehovah will see with his eye, and Jehovah will actually restore to me goodness instead of his malediction this day." (2Sa 16:5-13) Later, David numbered the people, contrary to Jehovah's will. The account reads: "And David's heart began to beat him after he had so numbered the people. Consequently David said to Jehovah: 'I have sinned very much in what I have done. . . . I have acted very foolishly.'" (2Sa 24:1, 10) Although he suffered punishment, David was not removed as king; his humility played a large part in his restoration to Jehovah's favor.

A Quality of God. Jehovah God himself includes humility among his qualities. This is not because there is any inferiority on his part or any submission to others. Rather, he shows humility in exercising mercy and great compassion upon lowly sinners. That he deals with sinners at all and has provided his Son as a sacrifice for mankind's sins is an expression of his humility. Jehovah God has permitted evil for some 6,000 years and let mankind be brought forth, even though their father Adam had sinned. Through undeserved kindness, mercy was thereby shown to Adam's offspring, giving them opportunity for everlasting life. (Ro 8:20, 21) All of this displays, along with other fine qualities of God, his humility.

King David saw and appreciated this quality in God's undeserved kindness to him. After Jehovah had delivered him out of the hand of all his enemies, he sang: "You will give me your shield of salvation, and it is your humility that makes me great." (2Sa 22:36; Ps 18:35) Though in his great dignity he sits in his exalted place in the highest heavens, it can nevertheless be said of Jehovah: "Who is like Jehovah our God, him who is making his dwelling on high? He is condescending to look on heaven and earth, raising up the lowly one from the very dust; he exalts the poor one from the ashpit itself, to make him sit with nobles, with the nobles of his people."—Ps 113:5-8.

Jesus Christ's Humility. Jesus Christ, when on earth, set the greatest example of a humble servant of God. On the evening before his death, Jesus girded himself with a towel and washed and dried the feet of each of his 12 apostles, a service customarily performed by menials and slaves. (Joh 13:2-5, 12-17) He had told his disciples: "Whoever exalts himself will be humbled, and whoever humbles himself will be exalted." (Mt 23:12; Lu 14:11) The apostle Peter, present that night, remembered Jesus' fine example in living up to his words. He later admonished fellow believers: "All of you gird yourselves with lowliness of mind toward one another . . . Humble yourselves, therefore, under the mighty hand of God, that he may exalt you in due time."—1Pe 5:5, 6.

The apostle Paul encourages Christians to have the same mental attitude as Jesus Christ; he points to the high position of the Son of God in his prehuman existence in the heavens with his Father Jehovah, his willingly emptying himself, taking a slave's form, and coming to be in the likeness of men. Paul adds: "More than that, when he [Jesus] found himself in fashion as a man, he humbled himself and became obedient as far as death, yes, death on a torture stake." Jesus' own words as to the reward of humility are powerfully proved true in his own case, as the apostle goes on to say: "For this very reason also God exalted him to a superior position and kindly gave him the name that is above every other name."—Php 2:5-11.

More outstandingly, even with such a highly exalted position, when he wields 'all authority in heaven and on the earth' to bring about God's will concerning the earth (Mt 28:18; 6:10), Christ will still have the same humility at the end of his Thousand Year Reign. Thus, the Scriptures tell us: "When all things will have been subjected to him, then the Son himself will also subject himself to the One who subjected all things to him, that God may be all things to everyone."—1Co 15:28.

Jesus Christ said of himself: "I am mild-tempered and lowly in heart." (Mt 11:29) When he presented himself to the people of Jerusalem as their King, he fulfilled the prophecy that said of him: "Look! Your king himself comes to you. He is righteous, yes, saved; humble, and riding upon an ass, even upon a full-grown animal the son of a she-ass." (Zec 9:9; Joh 12:12-16) In his exalted heavenly position when he goes forth against the enemies of God, the command is prophetically given to him: "In your splendor go on to success; ride in the cause of truth and humility and righteousness." (Ps 45:4) Therefore, those who have humility can rejoice, even though they may have been crushed and mistreated by the proud and haughty. They can take comfort in the words: "Seek Jehovah, all you meek ones of the earth, who have practiced His own judicial decision. Seek righteousness, seek meekness. Probably you

may be concealed in the day of Jehovah's anger."
—Zep 2:3.

Jehovah's words to Israel before the destruction of Jerusalem warned the humble ones and comforted them in declaring that God would, nevertheless, act in their behalf in his due time. He said: "Then I shall remove from the midst of you your haughtily exultant ones; and you will never again be haughty in my holy mountain. And I shall certainly let remain in the midst of you a people humble and lowly, and they will actually take refuge in the name of Jehovah." (Zep 3:11, 12) Humility will actually result in the saving of many, as it is written: "The humble people you will save; but your eyes are against the haughty ones, that you may bring them low." (2Sa 22:28) Thus we have assurance that the King Jesus Christ, who rides in the cause of truth and humility and righteousness, will save his people who humble themselves before him and before his Father, Jehovah.

Christians Must Cultivate Humility. In counseling fellow Christians to put on the personality that "is being made new according to the image of the One who created it," the apostle Paul says: "Accordingly, as God's chosen ones, holy and loved, clothe yourselves with the tender affections of compassion, kindness, *lowliness of mind,* mildness, and long-suffering." (Col 3:10, 12) Citing the fine example of Christ, he admonishes them: 'With *lowliness of mind* consider that the others [of God's servants] are superior to you.' (Php 2:3) Again he appeals: "Be minded the same way toward others as to yourselves; do not be minding lofty things, but be led along with the lowly things. Do not become discreet in your own eyes."—Ro 12:16.

It is in the same vein that Paul tells the Christians in the city of Corinth: "For, though I am free from all persons, I have made myself the slave to all, that I may gain the most persons. And so to the Jews I became as a Jew, that I might gain Jews; to those under law I became as under law, though I myself am not under law, that I might gain those under law. To those without law I became as without law, although I am not without law toward God but under law toward Christ, that I might gain those without law. To the weak I became weak, that I might gain the weak. I have become all things to people of all sorts, that I might by all means save some." (1Co 9:19-22) It takes real humility to do this.

Works for peace. Humility promotes peace. A humble person does not fight his Christian brothers in order to establish his supposed personal "rights." The apostle argued that, though he had freedom to do all things, he would do only the things that are upbuilding, and if a brother's conscience was bothered by his personal actions, he would refrain from that practice.—Ro 14:19-21; 1Co 8:9-13; 10:23-33.

It also requires humility to keep the peace by putting into practice Jesus' counsel to forgive others their sins against us. (Mt 6:12-15; 18:21, 22) And when one person offends another, it tests his humility to obey the command to go to the other person and admit the wrong, asking forgiveness. (Mt 5:23, 24) Or when the offended person approaches him, only love coupled with humility will prompt one to acknowledge the wrong and act immediately to set matters straight. (Mt 18:15; Lu 17:3; compare Le 6:1-7.) But the results such humility brings in the way of peace to the individual and to the organization far outweigh the feeling of humiliation; also, his humble action further develops and strengthens in the individual the fine quality of humility.

Essential for unity in the congregation. Humility will help the Christian to be content with the things that he has, and it will help him to maintain joy and balance. The interdependency of the Christian congregation, as illustrated by the apostle at First Corinthians chapter 12, is based on obedience, humility, and submissiveness to God's organizational arrangement. Therefore, while the male members of the congregation are told: "If any man is reaching out for an office of overseer, he is desirous of a fine work," they are also told not to be ambitiously seeking a position of responsibility, for example, as teachers of the congregation, for these "shall receive heavier judgment."—1Ti 3:1; Jas 3:1.

All, men and women, should be submissive to those taking the lead and should wait on Jehovah for any appointments or assignments to responsibility, for it is from him that promotion comes. (Ps 75:6, 7) As some of the Levite sons of Korah said: "I have chosen to stand at the threshold in the house of my God rather than to move around in the tents of wickedness." (Ps 84:10) Such true humility takes time to develop. The Scriptures, in setting forth the qualifications for one who would be appointed to the office of overseer, specify that a newly converted man should not be appointed, "for fear that he might get puffed up with pride and fall into the judgment passed upon the Devil." —1Ti 3:6.

False Humility. Christians are warned against letting their humility be only on the surface. Anyone who takes delight in a mock humility can become "puffed up without proper cause by his fleshly frame of mind." A person who is truly humble will not think that the Kingdom of God or entering into it has to do with what one eats or drinks or what one refrains from eating or drinking. The Bible shows that a person may eat or drink or may refrain from partaking of certain things because he feels he should, from a health standpoint or for the sake of conscience. Yet if a person thinks that his having a favorable standing with God depends on whether or not he eats, drinks, or touches certain things or whether or not he observes certain religious days, he does not realize that his actions are "possessed of an appearance of wisdom in a self-imposed form of worship and mock humility, a severe treatment of the body; but they are of no value in combating the satisfying of the flesh."—Col 2:18, 23; Ro 14:17; Ga 3:10, 11.

False humility can actually result in developing haughtiness in the individual, for he may tend to think he is righteous on his own merit; or he may feel that he is accomplishing his ends, not realizing that he cannot deceive Jehovah. If haughtiness develops, he will in time be humbled in a way that he will not enjoy. He will be brought low, and it may be to his own destruction.—Pr 18:12; 29:23.

HUMTAH (Hum'tah) [Sand Lizard Place]. A city in the mountainous region of Judah. (Jos 15:20, 48, 54) Its location is no longer known.

HUNTING AND FISHING. Only after the Flood was man authorized to hunt and fish for food. (Ge 9:3, 4) But even in pre-Flood times men may have engaged in hunting to procure animal skins for making clothing and other items. —Compare Ge 3:21.

After the Deluge, Nimrod was the first man to distinguish himself as "a mighty hunter in opposition to Jehovah" (Ge 10:8, 9), undoubtedly one who hunted for sport, as did later kings of Assyria, Egypt, and other lands. There is no indication that the Israelites ever hunted for sport, although they did hunt animals such as gazelles and stags for food (1Ki 4:22, 23) and killed wild beasts in self-defense (Jg 14:5, 6) or in defense of domestic animals or of crops.—1Sa 17:34-36; Ca 2:15.

With reference to hunting, the Mosaic Law restated the post-Flood prohibition on eating blood. (Ge 9:4; Le 17:12-14; see BLOOD.) Additionally, certain wild animals were designated as unclean for food. (Le 11:2-20; De 14:3-20) Another law made it wrong for the Israelites to take both the mother bird and her offspring or eggs. In many cases, her attachment to her young would have made the mother bird easy game; however, she was to be sent away, likely allowing her to have more offspring.—De 22:6, 7.

Various implements and devices were employed for hunting, including bows and arrows (Ge 21:20; 27:3), slings (1Sa 17:34, 40; Job 41:1, 28), traps, nets, pits, and hooks (Ps 140:5; Eze 17:20; 19:4, 9). Swords, spears, darts, clubs, and javelins no doubt were also used.—Job 41:1, 26-29.

To capture animals, nets were often set up. Then a group of hunters would frighten the animals, commonly by making noise, so that these ran against the nets, which were so constructed that they would fall upon the animals. Also, pits were dug and then camouflaged with a thin cover of sticks and earth. Animals were trapped by being made to flee over the covering. In addition, snares that entangled the animals' feet were used, and a combination of pits and nets may also have been employed.—Compare Job 18:8-11; Jer 18:22; 48:42-44; see BIRDCATCHER; TRAP.

Fishing. Among the Hebrews fishing was an occupation; it is not mentioned as being done merely for sport. Fishermen used nets, harpoons, and spears, as well as hook and line. (Job 41:1, 7; Eze 26:5, 14; Hab 1:15, 17; Mt 17:27) Frequently fishing was done at night. Dragnets were let down from boats; then either they were hauled ashore or the catch of fish was emptied into the boats. Afterward the fish were sorted. Those fit for food according to the terms of the Law were kept; the unsuitable kinds were thrown away. (Mt 13:47, 48; Lu 5:5-7; Joh 21:6, 8, 11) A net much smaller than the dragnet may have been cast by fishermen wading in the water or standing on the shore.—See DRAGNET.

Fishing was strenuous work. It called for physical exertion, especially when the men had to draw in the nets filled with fish (Joh 21:6, 11) or row the boats against the wind. (Mr 6:47, 48) At times fishermen toiled all night without catching anything. (Lu 5:5; Joh 21:3) Afterward nets had to be dried and repaired.—Eze 47:10; Mt 4:21.

The fishermen Peter, Andrew, James, and John worked together as partners. (Mt 4:18, 21; Lu 5:3, 7, 10) On at least one occasion seven of Jesus' disciples, including Nathanael and Thomas, fished together. (Joh 21:2, 3) One of the two fishermen mentioned but not identified at John 21:2 may have been Peter's brother Andrew; the other perhaps was Philip, as suggested by the fact that his home was in Bethsaida (meaning "House of the Hunter (or, Fisherman)").—Joh 1:43, 44.

Figurative. Fishing may represent military conquest. (Am 4:2; Hab 1:14, 15) On the other hand, Jesus likened the work of making disciples to fishing for men. (Mt 4:19) Jeremiah 16:16, where the reference is to Jehovah's 'sending for many fishers and hunters,' may be understood either in a favorable or an unfavorable sense. If this text is directly related to verse 15, which speaks about the restoration of the Israelites to their land, then the allusion is to the searching out of the repentant Jewish remnant. Otherwise, the fishers and hunters are enemy forces sent out to find the unfaithful Israelites, thus allowing none of them to escape Jehovah's judgment. —Compare Eze 9:2-7.

HUPHAM (Hu'pham), **HUPHAMITES** (Hu'-pham·ites) [Of (Belonging to) Hupham]. Also called Huppim; Hupham was a "son," probably a later descendant, of Benjamin, and ancestral head of the Huphamites.—Ge 46:8, 21; Nu 26:39; see HUPPIM.

HUPPAH (Hup'pah) [Shelter]. Head of the 13th of the 24 priestly divisions David organized. —1Ch 24:1-3, 7, 13.

HUPPIM (Hup'pim). A son, or descendant, of Benjamin included in the list of those who came into Egypt with Jacob's household in 1728 B.C.E. or were born there during Jacob's lifetime. (Ge 46:8, 21) Other passages suggest that he was either a grandson or great-grandson through Bela and Iri. (1Ch 7:6, 7, 12; in 8:1-5 he is apparently called Huram.) Time barely allows for Benjamin to have had grandsons when entering Egypt, but Genesis 46:8 might be understood to indicate that all these souls had been born while Jacob was still alive even down in Egypt, not necessarily born before he and his household went there. (See BENJAMIN No. 1.) The family that Huppim (also called Hupham) founded, called Huphamites, is numbered among the tribe of Benjamin in the second wilderness census of the Israelites. (Nu 26:1-4, 38, 39) Huppim is mentioned also at 1 Chronicles 7:14, 15 in association with Manasseh, but the connection is unclear.

HUR.

1. A descendant of Judah; son of Caleb and Ephrath; grandfather of the craftsman Bezalel. Some of Hur's descendants may have settled in Bethlehem. (Ex 31:2; 35:30; 38:22; 1Ch 2:19, 20, 50, 51, 54; 4:1-4; 2Ch 1:5) Likely the same as No. 2.

2. A prominent associate of Moses and Aaron. When, shortly after leaving Egypt, Israel was attacked by the Amalekites, Hur accompanied Moses and Aaron to the top of a hill where he and Aaron supported Moses' hands until Jehovah gave Israel the victory over the Amalekites. (Ex 17:8-13) On one occasion not long thereafter, Moses and Joshua went up on Mount Sinai to receive more of the Law, leaving Hur and Aaron in charge of the camp. (Ex 24:12-14) He is likely the same Hur (No. 1) as the grandfather of the tabernacle craftsman Bezalel. Josephus wrote that Hur was Miriam's husband, but the Bible does not say anything about this.—*Jewish Antiquities*, III, 54 (ii, 4).

3. A king of Midian, one of five dominated by Amorite King Sihon until Israel, moving toward the Promised Land, defeated Sihon. (Jos 13:15, 16, 21; Nu 21:21-24) Afterward, Hur and his four compatriots apparently allied themselves with Moab's king Balak in opposition to Israel. (Nu 22:1-7) Later, as directed by Jehovah, the Israelites warred against the Midianites and killed Hur as well as his four allied Midianite kings and the greedy prophet Balaam.—Nu 31:1-8.

4. Father of Solomon's food deputy in the mountainous region of Ephraim.—1Ki 4:7, 8.

5. Father of Rephaiah. Hur's son Rephaiah helped Nehemiah rebuild Jerusalem's wall.—Ne 3:9.

HURAI (Hu'rai). One of David's mighty men; from the torrent valleys of Gaash. (1Ch 11:26, 32) He is called Hiddai at 2 Samuel 23:30.

HURAM (Hu'ram). Probably either a grandson or a great-grandson of Benjamin through Bela and Ir(i); apparently also called Huppim.—1Ch 7:6, 7, 12; 8:3-5; see HUPPIM.

HURI (Hu'ri). A Gadite descended through Buz. —1Ch 5:11, 14.

HUSBAND. A married man is denoted by the Hebrew term *'ish* (man) and the Greek term *a·ner'* (male person). (Ho 2:16, ftn; Ro 7:2, *Int*) Other Hebrew terms variously used with reference to a husband are *'a·dhohn'* (lord), *ba'al* (owner; master), and *re'a'* (companion; friend). (Ge 18:12; 20:3; Jer 3:20) In Israel a man who was engaged, or betrothed, was also spoken of as "husband" and the girl as "wife."—De 22:23, 24; Mt 1:18-20.

A man would betroth a woman or contract for future marriage by paying her father or guardians the bride-price, or purchase money. (Ex 22:16, 17) She then became his property. (Ex 20:17) The word *ba'al*, meaning "owner, master," applied to him, and the woman was called *be'u·lah'*, meaning "owned as a wife." (Ge 20:3; De 22:22; Isa 62:4) To the ancient nation of Israel, Jehovah said: "I myself have become the husbandly owner [a form of *ba˝al*] of you people."—Jer 3:14; Isa 62:4, 5; see INHERITANCE (Period of the Law).

In patriarchal times the husband served as priest and judge in the family, and throughout the Scriptures the husband and father was almost invariably accorded deep respect.—Ge 31:31, 32; Job 1:5; 1Pe 3:5, 6; compare De 21:18-21; Es 1:10-21.

Headship. A man, upon marrying a woman, brings her under a new law, "the law of her husband," according to which the husband can make rules and regulations for his family. (Ro 7:2, 3) He becomes her head to whom she should be subject. (Eph 5:21-24, 33) This is a relative headship, in view of the superior headships of God and Christ.—1Co 11:3.

The husband, while head of the house, is, nevertheless, required to render to his wife marriage dues, sex relations, for "the husband does not exercise authority over his own body, but his wife does." (1Co 7:3-5) He is also responsible for the spiritual and material welfare of his family. —Eph 6:4; 1Ti 5:8.

The headship of the husband places on him a weighty responsibility. While he is the owner of the wife, he has to recognize that she is precious in the eyes of God, especially so when she is a Christian. He is to love her as he loves himself, for she is "one flesh" with him.—Ge 2:24; Mt 19:4-6; Eph 5:28, 33.

Husbands are to exercise for their wives the same loving care that Christ does for the congregation. (Eph 5:25, 28-30, 33) They are to recognize that the wife is "a weaker vessel," assigning her honor, taking into consideration her physical and emotional makeup and vicissitudes. This is especially important if the couple are Christians, being fellow heirs of "the undeserved favor of life," in order for the husband's prayers not to be hindered. (1Pe 3:7) Even if the wife is not a believer, this gives the husband no excuse for divorce or separation. Rather, he should dwell with her if she is agreeable to it and realize that he may help her to become a believer and also work toward the salvation of the children.—1Co 7:12, 14, 16; see FAMILY; FATHER; MARRIAGE.

Divorce. Under the Mosaic Law a man could divorce his wife, but she could not divorce him. He was required to give her a written certificate of divorce. (De 24:1-4) Jesus Christ showed that such an arrangement for divorce in Israel was made as a *concession* out of regard for their

hardheartedness. (Mt 19:8) If, however, a man had seduced a virgin girl who was not engaged, she was to become his wife (unless her father refused to give her to him), and he was not allowed to divorce her all his days.—De 22:28, 29.

Both the Hebrew Scriptures and the Christian Greek Scriptures stress that the husband should limit his sex relations to his marriage mate (Pr 5:15-20) and that marriage must be kept honorable, for God will judge fornicators and adulterers. (Heb 13:4) During patriarchal times and under the Law, polygamy and concubinage were practiced by allowance from Jehovah, but in the Christian arrangement a man may have but one living wife. (Ge 25:5, 6; 29:18-28; De 21:15-17; Mt 19:5; Ro 7:2, 3; 1Ti 3:2) The only Christian ground for divorce and remarriage is "fornication."—Mt 19:9; see FORNICATION.

Illustrative Use. In view of the fact that the ancient nation of Israel was bound to Jehovah by means of the Law covenant, God was their "husbandly owner." (Jer 3:14) The apostle Paul speaks of Jehovah as the Father of anointed Christians, his spiritual sons, and of "the Jerusalem above" as their mother, indicating that Jehovah considers himself a husband to this Jerusalem.—Ga 4:6, 7, 26; compare Isa 54:5.

Jesus Christ is viewed as the Husband of the Christian congregation. (Eph 5:22, 23; Re 19:7; 21:2) This analogy highlights both his headship and his loving care for the congregation. He laid down his own life on behalf of his bride, and he continues to feed and cherish it.

HUSHAH (Hu′shah). Either a "son" of or a city "fathered" or "founded" by Ezer of the tribe of Judah. (1Ch 4:1, 4) If Hushah designates a city, then it was likely the home of one of David's mighty men, Sibbecai, who was probably also called Mebunnai. (1Ch 27:11; compare 2Sa 23:27; 1Ch 11:29.) Some regard Hushah as the name of a city and identify it with Husan, about 6 km (3.5 mi) W of Bethlehem.

HUSHAI (Hu′shai) [possibly a shortened form of Hoshabiah, meaning "Jehovah Has Accounted (Considered)"]. A loyal Archite friend of King David who helped thwart Absalom's rebellion. (1Ch 27:33) Hushai, with his robe ripped and dirt on his head, met the fleeing king on the Mount of Olives. He followed David's suggestion that he go back into the city, feign loyalty to Absalom, endeavor to frustrate Ahithophel's counsel, and keep David informed through the priests Zadok and Abiathar. (2Sa 15:30, 32-37) At first Absalom was suspicious, but Hushai succeeded in winning his confidence. (2Sa 16:16-19) When Absalom called for Hushai's opinion concerning the best military strategy, Hushai spoke contrary to Ahithophel and recommended a course that would in fact allow David time to get organized. Hushai presented his idea in a way that made it appear better to Absalom and his associates than Ahithophel's advice to attack immediately. Hushai then informed the priests of what had happened. (2Sa 17:1-16) Hushai's counsel frustrated that of Ahithophel, just as David had petitioned God, and thus 'Jehovah brought calamity upon Absalom.'—2Sa 15:31; 17:14; see FRIEND (Friend [Companion] of the King).

HUSHAM (Hu′sham). A native of the land of the Temanites who succeeded Jobab as king of Edom. (Ge 36:31, 34, 35; 1Ch 1:45, 46) This was "before any king reigned over the sons of Israel." —1Ch 1:43.

HUSHATHITE (Hu′shath·ite) [Of (Belonging to) Hushah]. A resident, or perhaps a descendant, of Hushah.—2Sa 21:18; 23:8, 27; 1Ch 11:26, 29; 20:4; 27:1, 11.

HUSHIM (Hu′shim).

1. Son of Dan (Ge 46:23), evidently called Shuham at Numbers 26:42.

2. A designation given to the sons of Aher of the tribe of Benjamin.—1Ch 7:6, 12.

3. Wife of the Benjamite Shaharaim and the mother of Abitub and Elpaal.—1Ch 8:1, 8, 11.

HYACINTH (hy′a·cinth). A deep-blue semi-precious stone; in Greek, hy·a′kin·thos. (Primarily the word referred to the flower by that name, probably describing the dark-blue iris.) The 11th of the foundation stones of New Jerusalem is said to be hyacinth.—Re 21:20.

Hyacinth blue (hyacinthine) is one of the colors of the breastplates in the description of the armies of cavalry, at Revelation 9:16, 17. The breastplates spoken of were probably those worn by the riders of the horses. Fire red and sulfur yellow are mentioned as the other two breastplate colors. In view of the later statement that the horses breathed out fire, smoke, and sulfur, the hyacinth blue may represent the darkness of smoke, which, along with fire and sulfur, may be destructive to life.

HYKSOS. See EGYPT, EGYPTIAN.

HYMENAEUS (Hy·me·nae′us) [named after Hymen, the Greek god of marriage]. An apostate from Christianity during the first century, Hyme-

naeus was identified by Paul as a blasphemer, full of "empty speeches that violate what is holy." In his deviation from the truth, Hymenaeus, along with a certain Philetus, taught false doctrine, subverting the faith of some. One of their false teachings was that 'the resurrection had already occurred' in their day. Evidently this was their teaching: that the resurrection was merely a spiritual one, of a symbolic kind, and that the dedicated Christians had already had their resurrection, that this was all there was to the matter and there was no further resurrection in the future under God's Messianic Kingdom.—2Ti 2:18; compare 1Co 15:12-23.

In Paul's first letter to Timothy, Hymenaeus' name is associated with another apostate, Alexander. The apostle states that he had handed Hymenaeus and Alexander "over to Satan," evidently referring to Paul's expelling or disfellowshipping them from the congregation.—1Ti 1:18-20; 2Ti 2:16, 17.

HYPOCRITE. A person who pretends to be what he is not; a person whose actions are out of harmony with his words.

Although words from the Hebrew root cha·neph′ are rendered "hypocrite" or "hypocrisy" in some translations, such as the King James Version, Douay, and Leeser, other translators have variously rendered these words "profane" (Yg), "impious" (Ro), "godless" (RS), and "apostate" (NW). According to A Hebrew and English Lexicon of the Old Testament by Brown, Driver, and Briggs (1980, pp. 337, 338), cha·neph′, when used as an adjective, may be defined as "profane, irreligious . . . , godless"; or, as a verb, "be polluted, profane . . . , inclining away from right." In the Scriptures cha·neph′ appears in parallel with those forgetting God (Job 8:13), the wicked (Job 20:5), evildoers (Isa 9:17), and it is used in contrast with the upright and innocent ones.—Job 17:8; see APOSTASY.

The Greek word rendered "hypocrite" (hy·po·kri·tes′) means "one who answers," as well as meaning a stage actor. Greek and Roman actors employed large masks with mechanical devices for amplifying the voice. Hence, the Greek word hy·po·kri·tes′ came to be used in a metaphoric sense to apply to one playing false, or one putting on a pretense. The same word appears in the Greek Septuagint at Job 34:30; 36:13. Hypocrites are "unfaithful ones" (compare Lu 12:46 with Mt 24:51), and "hypocrisy" (hy·po′kri·sis), as used in the Scriptures, may also denote "wickedness" and "cunning."—Compare Mt 22:18; Mr 12:15;

Lu 20:23; see also Ga 2:13, where *hy·po'kri·sis* is rendered "pretense."

Jesus Christ identified as hypocrites persons who make gifts of mercy with showy display, who pray and fast to be seen of men, and who pick on the strawlike faults of their brothers but do nothing about removing their own rafterlike faults. Christ classified as such those who claimed to be God's servants but who failed to discern the significance of the time in which they were living and the events that were occurring, while readily drawing conclusions from the appearance of earth and sky as to what the weather would be like.—Mt 6:2, 5, 16; 7:1-5; Lu 6:42; 12:54-56.

Not only did the Son of God while on earth denounce the religious leaders of Israel as hypocrites but he also stated his reasons for doing so. They rendered mere lip service to the Creator, making the word of God invalid because of their traditions. (Mt 15:1, 6-9; Mr 7:6, 7) Their actions were out of harmony with their words. (Mt 23:1-3) The scribes and Pharisees not only deliberately refused to avail themselves of the opportunity to enter the Kingdom of the heavens, but they added to their sin by trying to hinder others from doing so. They put forth every effort to convert someone, only to make him twice as much a subject for Gehenna as they were. They were sticklers for the little things of the Law but disregarded the weightier matters of it—justice, mercy, and faithfulness. As hypocrites, they possessed only a seemingly clean outward appearance; inside they were full of immoderateness. Like whitewashed graves, outwardly beautiful, they appeared righteous to men, but inside they were "full of hypocrisy and lawlessness." They built the graves of the prophets and decorated the memorial tombs of the righteous ones, claiming that they would not have shed the blood of such ones. However, their course of action proved them to be just like their murderous forefathers. (Mt 23:13-36) The teaching of the Pharisees and Sadducees was actually hypocrisy.—Mt 16:6, 12; Lu 12:1; see also Lu 13:11-17.

A striking example of a hypocritical course was that followed by the disciples of the Pharisees and the party followers of Herod when approaching Jesus on the tax question. First they resorted to flattery, saying: "Teacher, we know you are truthful and teach the way of God in truth." Then they posed the catch question: "Is it lawful to pay head tax to Caesar or not?" Appropriately Jesus referred to them as hypocrites, since they were not really desirous of getting an answer to their question but merely raised it with a view to trapping Jesus in his speech.—Mt 22:15-22; Lu 20:19-26; PICTURE, Vol. 2, p. 544.

A hypocritical course cannot be concealed indefinitely. (Lu 12:1-3) Hypocrites are condemned by God as unworthy of life everlasting. (Mt 24:48-51) Therefore, a Christian's love and faith must be without hypocrisy. (Ro 12:9; 2Co 6:4, 6; 1Ti 1:5) The wisdom from above is not hypocritical.—Jas 3:17.

HYSSOP [Heb., *'e·zohv'*; Gr., *hys'so·pos*]. The exact identification of hyssop is uncertain. The Hebrew and Greek terms may, in fact, embrace several different kinds of plants.

Some modern scholars say that the hyssop of the Hebrew Scriptures is probably marjoram (*Origanum maru*). This plant of the mint family is common in Palestine. Under favorable conditions it attains a height of 0.5 to 0.9 m (1.5 to 3 ft). Its branches and thick leaves are hairy, and as indicated at 1 Kings 4:33, it can be found growing in rock crevices and on walls.

Hyssop was used by the Israelites in Egypt to splash the blood of the Passover victim on the two doorposts and the upper part of the doorway of their houses. (Ex 12:21, 22) At the inauguration of the Law covenant, Moses employed hyssop in sprinkling the book of the Law and the people. (Heb 9:19) Hyssop also figured in the cleansing ceremony for persons or houses previously infected with leprosy (Le 14:2-7, 48-53; see CLEAN, CLEANNESS [Leprosy]) and in the preparation of the ashes to be used in "the water for cleansing," as well as in the spattering of this water on certain things and persons. (Nu 19:6, 9, 18) David thus appropriately prayed to be purified from sin with hyssop.—Ps 51:7.

The hyssop mentioned in connection with Jesus Christ's impalement (Joh 19:29) is thought by some to refer to durra, or Indian millet, a variety of common sorghum (*Sorghum vulgare*). It is a tall, small-grained plant with long, broad leaves. Since this plant commonly attains a height of at least 1.8 m (6 ft) in Palestine, it could have provided a stalk, or "reed," of sufficient length to convey the sponge of sour wine to Jesus' mouth. (Mt 27:48; Mr 15:36) Others think that even in this case hyssop may be marjoram and suggest that a bunch of marjoram may have been attached to the "reed" mentioned by Matthew and Mark. Still another view is that John 19:29 originally read *hys·soi'* (pike, javelin), not *hys·so'poi* (hyssop); hence the renderings "on a pike" (*AT*) and "on a spear" (*Mo*).

I

IBHAR (Ib'har) [May Jehovah Choose [Him]]. One of the sons born to King David in Jerusalem after he transferred his residence there from Hebron.—2Sa 5:13-15; 1Ch 14:4, 5.

IBLEAM (Ib'le·am) [possibly from a root meaning "swallow down"]. A city in the territory of Issachar but assigned with its dependent towns to Manasseh. The Manassites, however, failed to dispossess the Canaanites from Ibleam. (Jos 17:11-13; Jg 1:27) Ibleam appears to be the same as the Bileam in Manasseh given to the Kohathite Levites. (1Ch 6:70) But the parallel passage mentioning Levite cities in the territory of the half tribe of Manasseh (Jos 21:25) reads "Gath-rimmon" instead of "Bileam" or "Ibleam." Generally this is attributed to scribal error, "Gath-rimmon," the name of a city in Dan, probably having been inadvertently repeated from verse 24.

Ibleam has been identified with Khirbet Bel'a-meh, about 18 km (11 mi) SSE of Megiddo.

Near Ibleam, King Ahaziah of Judah was fatally struck down at the command of Jehu. (2Ki 9:27) Later, Jehu's dynasty ended with the assassination of Zechariah at Ibleam (according to the Lagardian edition of the *LXX*).—2Ki 15:10-12, *JB, NW, RS*.

IBNEIAH (Ib·ne'iah) [Jehovah Has Built]. Son of Jeroham; a Benjamite head of a paternal house returning from Babylonian exile.—1Ch 9:1-3, 7-9.

IBNIJAH (Ib·ni'jah) [Jehovah Has Built]. A Benjamite, forefather of a certain Meshullam. —1Ch 9:7, 8.

IBRI (Ib'ri) [A Hebrew]. Son of Jaaziah; a Merarite Levite of King David's time.—1Ch 24:27, 30, 31.

IBSAM (Ib'sam) [Perfumed; Balsam Oil; Spicy]. One of the sons of Tola; a paternal head of the tribe of Issachar.—1Ch 7:1, 2.

IBZAN (Ib'zan). The one who succeeded Jephthah as judge of Israel. Ibzan was the father of 30 sons and 30 daughters, indicating that he was a polygamist and evidently also a man of some means. He procured 30 daughters as wives for his sons. After judging for seven years, Ibzan died

and was buried in his native city of Bethlehem, likely the Bethlehem in Zebulun.—Jg 12:7-10; Jos 19:10, 14, 15; see BETHLEHEM No. 2.

ICE. Water in its solid state, produced by freezing. Both Elihu and Jehovah God called Job's attention to the marvel of ice, the Almighty saying: "Out of whose belly does the ice actually come forth . . . ? The very waters keep themselves hidden as by stone, and the surface of the watery deep makes itself compact." (Job 36:1; 37:10; 38:1, 29, 30) The formation of ice as here referred to is possible only because of a most unusual property of water. As the water in lakes and seas cools, it becomes heavier. The lighter, warmer water is displaced by the heavier water and rises to the top. But when the water as a whole reaches about 4° C. (39° F.), this process reverses. The water becomes lighter as it nears the freezing point and remains as a layer above the warmer water beneath. This upper layer then turns to ice, "makes itself compact." Being lighter than water, the ice keeps the waters beneath "hidden as by stone," thus protecting marine life. Were it not for this phenomenon, much of the water in the lakes and even the oceans would in time become solid ice, thus making the earth inhospitable to life.

The psalmist speaks of Jehovah's "throwing his ice like morsels." This evidently refers to hail or sleet.—Ps 147:17; see HAIL.

The Hebrew term for "ice" (*qe'rach*) is also used to refer to a temperature of freezing or below that as well as to "frost."—Jer 36:30.

ICHABOD (Ich'a·bod) [Where Is the Glory?]. Son of Phinehas born after the death of Phinehas; brother of Ahitub; grandson of High Priest Eli. The name Ichabod, given to him by his dying mother while giving birth, signified that glory had gone away from Israel in view of the capture of the Ark and the deaths of Phinehas and Eli. —1Sa 4:17-22; 14:3.

ICONIUM (I·co'ni·um). An ancient city of Asia Minor lying about 1,027 m (3,370 ft) above sea level. Iconium is presently known as Konya (Konia), located about 240 km (150 mi) S of Ankara on the SW edge of the central Turkish plateau. In the first century C.E., Iconium was one of the principal cities in the Roman province of Galatia and lay astride the main trade route from Ephesus to Syria.

The city had an influential Jewish population. Paul and Barnabas, after being forced to leave Pisidian Antioch, preached in the city of Iconium and in its synagogue, and there they helped many Jews and Greeks to become believers. But when an attempt was made to stone them, they fled from Iconium to Lystra. However, Jews from Antioch and Iconium soon came to Lystra and stirred up the crowds there so that they stoned Paul. Thereafter Paul and Barnabas went to Derbe and then courageously returned to Lystra, Iconium, and Antioch, strengthening the brothers and appointing "older men" to positions of responsibility in the congregations established in these cities.—Ac 13:50, 51; 14:1-7, 19-23.

Later, after the circumcision issue arose and was settled by the apostles and older men of the Jerusalem congregation, Paul may have revisited Iconium. It was on this second missionary journey that Paul took along Timothy, a young man having a fine reputation among the brothers at Lystra and Iconium.—Ac 16:1-5; 2Ti 3:10, 11.

Iconium was on the border between Phrygia and Lycaonia. This may explain why certain ancient writers, including Strabo and Cicero, assigned it to Lycaonia, whereas Xenophon called it the last city of Phrygia. From a geographic standpoint, Iconium belonged to Lycaonia, but as indicated by archaeological discoveries, it was Phrygian in culture and speech. Inscriptions found at the site in 1910 show that Phrygian was the language used there for two centuries after Paul's time. Appropriately, therefore, the writer of Acts did not include Iconium as part of Lycaonia, where the "Lycaonian tongue" was spoken.—Ac 14:6, 11.

IDALAH (I′da·lah). A boundary city of Zebulun. (Jos 19:14-16) While its exact location is unknown, some link Idalah with Khirbet el-Huwarah, 1.5 km (1 mi) SW of the suggested location of Bethlehem in Zebulun.

IDBASH (Id′bash) [from a root meaning "honey"]. A man of Judah, evidently a son of the founder of Etam.—1Ch 4:1, 3; see ETAM No. 3.

IDDO (Id′do).
[1-5: shortened form of Adaiah, meaning "Jehovah Has Decked [the nameholder]"]

1. Son of Joah; a Levite of the family of Gershom.—1Ch 6:19-21.

2. Father of Ahinadab, the one serving as Solomon's food deputy in Mahanaim.—1Ki 4:7, 14.

3. A visionary whose writings were consulted by the compiler of Chronicles for information concerning the affairs of Kings Solomon, Rehoboam, and Abijah. Iddo's writings are referred to as an "exposition," a "commentary," or a "midrash."—2Ch 9:29; 12:15; 13:22, ftn.

4. A prophet, father of Berechiah and grandfather of the prophet Zechariah. (Ezr 5:1; 6:14; Zec 1:1, 7) This Iddo may be the same as No. 5.

5. A priest listed among those returning to Jerusalem with Zerubbabel in 537 B.C.E. In the days of High Priest Joiakim the paternal house of Iddo was headed by Zechariah. (Ne 12:1, 4, 12, 16) He may be the same as No. 4.

6. [possibly from a root meaning "laud"; or from a different root meaning "know"]. Son of a certain Zechariah; prince of the half tribe of Manasseh in Gilead in King David's time.—1Ch 27: 21, 22.

7. Head of the Nethinim temple slaves residing at Casiphia, 220 of whom accompanied Ezra to Jerusalem in 468 B.C.E.—Ezr 8:17, 20.

IDOL, IDOLATRY. An idol is an image, a representation of anything, or a symbol that is an object of passionate devotion, whether material or imagined. Generally speaking, idolatry is the veneration, love, worship, or adoration of an idol. It is usually practiced toward a real or supposed higher power, whether such power is believed to have animate existence (as a human, an animal, or an organization) or is inanimate (as a force or lifeless object of nature). Idolatry generally involves some form, ceremony, or ritual.

The Hebrew terms used to refer to idols often highlighted the origin and inherent worthlessness of idols, or they were derogatory terms of contempt. Among these are words rendered "carved or graven image" (literally, something carved out); "molten statue, image, or idol" (literally, something cast or poured out); "horrible idol"; "vain idol" (literally, vanity); and "dungy idol." "Idol" is the usual rendering of the Greek word ei′do·lon.

Not All Images Are Idols. God's law not to form images (Ex 20:4, 5) did not rule out the making of all representations and statues. This is indicated by Jehovah's later command to make two golden cherubs on the cover of the Ark and to embroider representations of cherubs on the inner tent covering of ten tent cloths for the tabernacle and the curtain separating the Holy from the Most Holy. (Ex 25:18; 26:1, 31, 33) Likewise, the interior of Solomon's temple, the architectural plans for which were given to David by divine inspiration (1Ch 28:11, 12), was beautifully embellished with engraved carvings of cherubs, palm-tree figures, and blossoms. Two cherubs of oil-tree wood overlaid with gold stood in the Most Holy of that temple. (1Ki 6:23, 28, 29) The molten sea rested upon 12 copper bulls, and the sidewalls of the copper carriages for temple use were decorated with figures of lions, bulls, and cherubs. (1Ki 7:25, 28, 29) Twelve lions lined the steps leading up to Solomon's throne.—2Ch 9:17-19.

These representations, however, were not idols for worship. Only the officiating priests saw the representations of the tabernacle interior and, later, of the temple interior. No one but the high priest entered the Most Holy, and that only on the Day of Atonement. (Heb 9:7) Thus there was no danger of the Israelites' being ensnared into idolizing the golden cherubs in the sanctuary. These representations primarily served as a picture of the heavenly cherubs. (Compare Heb 9:24, 25.) That they were not to be venerated is evident from the fact that the angels themselves were not to be worshiped.—Col 2:18; Re 19:10; 22:8, 9.

Of course, there were times when images became idols, although not originally intended as objects of veneration. The copper serpent that Moses formed in the wilderness came to be worshiped, and therefore faithful King Hezekiah crushed it to pieces. (Nu 21:9; 2Ki 18:1, 4) The ephod made by Judge Gideon became "a snare" to him and to his household.—Jg 8:27.

Images as Aids in Worship. The Scriptures do not sanction the use of images as a means to address God in prayer. Such a practice runs counter to the principle that those seeking to serve Jehovah must worship him with spirit and truth. (Joh 4:24; 2Co 4:18; 5:6, 7) He tolerates no mixing of idolatrous practices with true worship, as is illustrated by his condemnation of calf worship, although the Israelites had attached his name thereto. (Ex 32:3-10) Jehovah does not share his glory with graven images.—Isa 42:8.

There is not a single instance in Scripture where faithful servants of Jehovah resorted to the use of visual aids to pray to God or engaged in a form of relative worship. Of course, some may cite Hebrews 11:21, which, according to the Catholic Douay Version, reads: "By faith Jacob, dying, blessed each of the sons of Joseph, and adored the top of his rod." Then in a footnote on this scripture it is held that Jacob paid relative honor and veneration to the top of Joseph's rod, and the comment is made: "Some translators, who are no friends to this relative honour, have corrupted the text, by translating it: *he worshipped, leaning*

upon the top of his staff." However, rather than being a corruption of the text, as this footnote maintains, this latter rendering and comparable variants thereof are in agreement with the sense of the Hebrew text at Genesis 47:31 and have been adopted even by a number of Catholic translations, including *The Jerusalem Bible.*

Forms of Idolatry. Acts of idolatry referred to in the Bible included such revolting practices as ceremonial prostitution, child sacrifice, drunkenness, and self-laceration to the point of causing blood to flow. (1Ki 14:24; 18:28; Jer 19:3-5; Ho 4:13, 14; Am 2:8) Idols were venerated by partaking of food and drink in festivals or ceremonies in their honor (Ex 32:6; 1Co 8:10), by bowing and sacrificing to them, by song and dance before them, and even by a kiss. (Ex 32:8, 18, 19; 1Ki 19:18; Ho 13:2) Idolatry was also committed by arranging a table of food and drink for false gods (Isa 65:11), by making drink offerings, sacrificial cakes, and sacrificial smoke (Jer 7:18; 44:17), and by weeping in religious ceremony (Eze 8:14). Certain actions, such as tatooing the flesh, making cuttings upon the flesh, imposing baldness on the forehead, cutting the sidelocks, and destroying the extremity of the beard, were prohibited by the Law, possibly, at least in part, because of being linked with prevailing idolatrous practices of neighboring peoples.—Le 19:26-28; De 14:1.

Then there are the more subtle forms of idolatry. Covetousness is idolatry (Col 3:5), since the object of an individual's cravings diverts affection from the Creator and thus, in effect, becomes an idol. Instead of serving Jehovah God in faithfulness, a person can become a slave to his belly, that is, to fleshly desire or appetite, and make this his god. (Ro 16:18; Php 3:18, 19) Since love for the Creator is demonstrated by obedience (1Jo 5:3), rebellion and pushing ahead presumptuously are comparable to acts of idolatry.—1Sa 15:22, 23.

Pre-Flood Idolatry. Idolatry had its beginning, not in the visible realm, but in the invisible. A glorious spirit creature developed the covetous desire to resemble the Most High. So strong was his desire that it alienated him from his God, Jehovah, and his idolatry caused him to rebel. —Job 1:6-11; 1Ti 3:6; compare Isa 14:12-14; Eze 28:13-15, 17.

Similarly, Eve constituted herself the first human idolater by coveting the forbidden fruit, this wrong desire leading her to disobey God's command. By allowing selfish desire to rival his love for Jehovah and then by disobeying him, Adam likewise became guilty of idolatry.—Ge 3:6, 17.

Since the rebellion in Eden, only a minority of

mankind have remained free from idolatry. During the lifetime of Adam's grandson Enosh, men apparently practiced a form of idolatry. "At that time a start was made of calling on the name of Jehovah." (Ge 4:26) But evidently this was no calling upon Jehovah in faith, something done by righteous Abel many years earlier and for which he suffered martyrdom at the hands of his brother Cain. (Ge 4:4, 5, 8) Apparently, what was started in the days of Enosh was a false form of worship in which Jehovah's name was misused or improperly applied. Either men applied Jehovah's name to themselves or to other men (through whom they pretended to approach God in worship), or else they applied the divine name to idol objects (as a visible, tangible aid in their attempt to worship the invisible God).

To what extent idolatry was practiced from the days of Enosh until the Flood, the Bible record does not reveal. The situation must have progressively deteriorated, because in Noah's day "Jehovah saw that the badness of man was abundant in the earth and every inclination of the thoughts of his heart was only bad all the time." Besides the inherited sinful inclination of man, the materialized angels, who had relations with the daughters of men, and the hybrid offspring of these unions, the Nephilim, exerted upon the world of that time a strong influence toward bad. —Ge 6:4, 5.

Idolatry in Patriarchal Times. Although the Flood of Noah's day destroyed all human idolaters, idolatry began anew, spearheaded by Nimrod, "a mighty hunter in opposition to Jehovah." (Ge 10:9) Doubtless under Nimrod's direction, the building of Babel and its tower (likely a ziggurat for use in idolatrous worship) began. The plans of those builders were frustrated when Jehovah confused their language. No longer being able to understand one another, they gradually left off building the city and scattered. However, the idolatry that began at Babel did not end there. Wherever those builders went they carried their false religious concepts.—Ge 11:1-9; see GODS AND GODDESSES.

The next city mentioned in the Scriptures, Ur of the Chaldeans, like Babel, was not devoted to the worship of the true God, Jehovah. Archaeological diggings there have revealed that the patron deity of that city was the moon-god Sin. It was in Ur that Terah, the father of Abram (Abraham), resided. (Ge 11:27, 28) Living in the midst of idolatry, Terah may have engaged in it, as is indicated centuries later by Joshua's words to the Israelites: "It was on the other side of the River [Euphrates]

that your forefathers dwelt a long time ago, Terah the father of Abraham and the father of Nahor, and they used to serve other gods." (Jos 24:2) But Abraham displayed faith in the true God, Jehovah.

Wherever Abraham, and later his descendants, went they met up with idolatry, influenced by the original apostasy at Babel. So there was an ever-present danger of being contaminated by such idolatry. Even those related to Abraham had idols. Laban, who was the father-in-law of Abraham's grandson Jacob, had teraphim, or family gods, in his possession. (Ge 31:19, 31, 32) Jacob himself found it necessary to instruct his household to put away all their foreign gods, and he hid the idols turned over to him. (Ge 35:2-4) Perhaps he disposed of them in this way so that none in his household might reuse the metal as something having special value on account of its previous idolatrous use. Whether Jacob initially melted or smashed the images is not stated.

Idolatry and God's Covenant People. As Jehovah had indicated to Abraham, his descendants, the Israelites, became alien residents in a land not theirs, namely Egypt, and suffered affliction there. (Ge 15:13) In Egypt they came in contact with rank idolatry, for image making ran riot in that country. Many of the deities worshiped there were represented by animal heads, among them being the cat-headed Bast, the cow-headed Hathor, the falcon-headed Horus, the jackal-headed Anubis (PICTURE, Vol. 1, p. 946), and the ibis-headed Thoth, to name but a few. Creatures of sea, air, and land were venerated, and at death "sacred" animals were mummified.

The Law that Jehovah gave to his people after liberating them from Egypt was explicitly directed against idolatrous practices so prevalent among the ancients. The second of the Ten Commandments expressly prohibited making for worship a carved image or a representation of anything in the heavens, on the earth, or in the waters. (Ex 20:4, 5; De 5:8, 9) In his final exhortations to the Israelites, Moses emphasized the impossibility of making an image of the true God and warned them to beware of the snare of idolatry. (De 4:15-19) To further safeguard the Israelites from becoming idolaters, they were commanded not to conclude any covenant with the pagan inhabitants of the land they were entering or to form marriage alliances with them, but to annihilate them. All existing appendages of idolatry—altars, sacred pillars, sacred poles, and graven images—were to be destroyed.—De 7:2-5.

Moses' successor Joshua assembled all the

tribes of Israel at Shechem and admonished them to remove the false gods and to serve Jehovah faithfully. The people agreed to do so and continued serving Jehovah during his lifetime and that of the older men who extended their days after Joshua. (Jos 24:14-16, 31) But thereafter wholesale apostasy set in. The people began worshiping Canaanite deities—Baal, Ashtoreth, and the sacred pole, or Asherah. Hence, Jehovah abandoned the Israelites into the hands of their enemies. However, when they repented, he mercifully raised up judges to deliver them.—Jg 2:11-19; 3:7; see ASHTORETH; BAAL No. 4; SACRED PILLAR; SACRED POLE.

Under the rule of the kings. During the reigns of Israel's first king, Saul, of his son Ish-bosheth, and of David, there is no mention of large-scale idolatry being engaged in by the Israelites. Nevertheless, there are indications that idolatry lingered on in the kingdom. Saul's own daughter, Michal, for instance, had a teraphim image in her possession. (1Sa 19:13; see TERAPHIM.) It was not until the latter part of the reign of David's son Solomon, however, that outright idolatry came to be practiced, the monarch himself, under the influence of his many foreign wives, giving the impetus to idolatry by sanctioning it. High places were built to Ashtoreth, Chemosh, and Milcom, or Molech. The people in general succumbed to false worship and began bowing down to these idol gods.—1Ki 11:3-8, 33; 2Ki 23:13; see CHEMOSH; MOLECH.

On account of this idolatry, Jehovah ripped ten tribes away from Solomon's son Rehoboam and gave these to Jeroboam. (1Ki 11:31-35; 12:19-24) Although assured that his kingdom would remain firm if he continued serving Jehovah in faithfulness, Jeroboam, on becoming king, instituted calf worship, fearing that the people would revolt against his rule if they continued going to Jerusalem for worship. (1Ki 11:38; 12:26-33) Idolatrous calf worship continued all the days the ten-tribe kingdom existed, with Tyrian Baalism being introduced during Ahab's reign. (1Ki 16:30-33) Not all apostatized, however. While Ahab reigned, there still was a remnant of 7,000 who had neither bent the knee to nor kissed Baal, and this at a time when Jehovah's prophets were being killed with the sword, doubtless at the instigation of Ahab's wife Jezebel.—1Ki 19:1, 2, 14, 18; Ro 11:4; see CALF (Calf Worship).

With the exception of Jehu's eradication of Baal worship (2Ki 10:20-28), there is no record of any religious reform being undertaken by a monarch of the ten-tribe kingdom. To the prophets repeat-

edly sent by Jehovah, the people and rulers of the northern kingdom gave no heed, so that finally the Almighty abandoned them into the hands of the Assyrians because of their sordid record of idolatry.—2Ki 17:7-23.

In the kingdom of Judah, the situation was not much different, aside from the reforms carried out by certain kings. Whereas a divided kingdom had come about as a direct result of idolatry, Solomon's son Rehoboam did not take to heart Jehovah's discipline and shun idolatry. As soon as his position was secure, he and all Judah with him apostatized. (2Ch 12:1) The people built high places, equipping these with sacred pillars and sacred poles, and engaged in ceremonial prostitution. (1Ki 14:23, 24) Although Abijam (Abijah) expressed faith in Jehovah at the time he warred against Jeroboam and was blessed with victory, to a large extent he imitated the sinful course of his father and predecessor on the throne, Rehoboam.—1Ki 15:1, 3; 2Ch 13:3-18.

The next two Judean kings, Asa and Jehoshaphat, served Jehovah in faithfulness and endeavored to rid the kingdom of idolatry. But Judah was so steeped in worship at high places that, despite the efforts of both of these kings to destroy them, the high places seem to have persisted secretly or they cropped up again.—1Ki 15:11-14; 22:42, 43; 2Ch 14:2-5; 17:5, 6; 20:31-33.

The reign of Judah's next king, Jehoram, commenced with bloodshed and began a new chapter in Judah's idolatry. This is attributed to his having idolatrous Ahab's daughter, Athaliah, as wife. (2Ch 21:1-4, 6, 11) The queen mother Athaliah also proved to be the counselor to Jehoram's son Ahaziah. Hence, during the rule of Ahaziah and that of the usurper Athaliah, idolatry continued with the approval of the crown.—2Ch 22:1-3, 12.

Early in the reign of Jehoash, following the execution of Athaliah, there was a restoration of true worship. But upon the death of High Priest Jehoiada, there was a return to idol worship at the instigation of Judah's princes. (2Ki 12:2, 3; 2Ch 24:17, 18) Jehovah therefore abandoned the Judean forces into the hands of the invading Syrians, and Jehoash was murdered by his own servants.—2Ch 24:23-25.

Undoubtedly the execution of God's judgment upon Judah and the violent death of Amaziah's father Jehoash made a deep impression upon Amaziah, so that he proceeded at first to do what was right in Jehovah's eyes. (2Ch 25:1-4) But after defeating the Edomites and taking their images, he began serving the gods of his vanquished foes. (2Ch 25:14) Retribution came when Judah was defeated by the ten-tribe kingdom and later when Amaziah was murdered by conspirators. (2Ch 25:20-24, 27) Although Azariah (Uzziah) and his son Jotham are reported generally to have done what was right in Jehovah's eyes, their subjects persisted in idolatry at the high places. —2Ki 15:1-4, 32-35; 2Ch 26:3, 4, 16-18; 27:1, 2.

During the kingship of Jotham's son Ahaz, Judah's religious state reached a new low. Ahaz began to practice idolatry on a scale never known before in Judah; he was the first-reported Judean king to have sacrificed his offspring in the fire as a false religious act. (2Ki 16:1-4; 2Ch 28:1-4) Jehovah chastised Judah by means of defeats at the hands of their enemies. Ahaz, instead of repenting, concluded that the gods of the kings of Syria were giving them the victory and therefore decided to sacrifice to these deities so that they might also help him. (2Ch 28:5, 23) Furthermore, the doors of Jehovah's temple were closed, and its utensils were cut to pieces.—2Ch 28:24.

While Ahaz did not benefit from Jehovah's discipline, his son Hezekiah did. (2Ch 29:1, 5-11) In the very first year of his becoming king, Hezekiah restored the true worship of Jehovah. (2Ch 29:3) His reign saw the destruction of appendages of false worship not only in Judah and Benjamin but also in Ephraim and Manasseh.—2Ch 31:1.

But Hezekiah's own son Manasseh completely revived idolatry. (2Ki 21:1-7; 2Ch 33:1-7) As to the reasons for this, the Bible record is silent. Manasseh, who began ruling as a 12-year-old, may have been wrongly directed initially by counselors and princes not exclusively devoted to Jehovah's service. Unlike Ahaz, though, Manasseh, as a captive in Babylon, repented upon receiving this severe discipline from Jehovah and undertook reforms upon returning to Jerusalem. (2Ch 33:10-16) His son Amon, however, reverted to sacrificing to the graven images.—2Ch 33:21-24.

Next came Josiah's rule and a thorough eradication of idolatry in Judah. The sites of idolatrous worship were desecrated there and even in the cities of Samaria. The foreign-god priests and those making sacrificial smoke to Baal, as well as to the sun, the moon, the constellations of the zodiac, and all the army of the heavens, were put out of business. (2Ki 23:4-27; 2Ch 34:1-5) Still this large-scale campaign against idolatry did not effect permanent reform. The last four Judean kings, Jehoahaz, Jehoiakim, Jehoiachin, and Zedekiah, persisted in idolatry.—2Ki 23:31, 32, 36,

37; 24:8, 9, 18, 19; see Astrologers; High Places; Zodiac.

The references to idolatry in the writings of the prophets further cast light on what occurred during the last years of the kingdom of Judah. Sites of idolatry, ceremonial prostitution, and child sacrifice continued to exist. (Jer 3:6; 17:1-3; 19:2-5; 32:29, 35; Eze 6:3, 4) Even Levites were guilty of practicing idolatry. (Eze 44:10, 12, 13) Ezekiel, transported in vision to Jerusalem's temple, there saw a detestable idol, "the symbol of jealousy," and the veneration of representations of creeping things and loathsome beasts, as well as the according of reverence to the false god Tammuz and the sun.—Eze 8:3, 7-16.

Despite the fact that the Israelites adored idols to the point of sacrificing their own children, they carried on a semblance of worshiping Jehovah and reasoned that no calamity would befall them. (Jer 7:4, 8-12; Eze 23:36-39) So empty-headed had the people in general become by reason of their pursuit of idolatry that when calamity did come and Jerusalem was desolated by the Babylonians in 607 B.C.E., in fulfillment of Jehovah's word, they attributed it to their failure to make sacrificial smoke and drink offerings to the "queen of the heavens."—Jer 44:15-18; see Queen of the Heavens.

Why Israel Turned to Idolatry. There were a number of factors that caused so many Israelites repeatedly to abandon true worship. Being one of the works of the flesh, idolatry appealed to the desires of the flesh. (Ga 5:19-21) Once settled in the Promised Land, the Israelites may have observed their pagan neighbors, whom they had failed to drive out entirely, having good success with their crops by reason of longer experience in working the land. Likely many made inquiry and heeded the advice of their Canaanite neighbors as to what was needed to please the Baal, or "owner," of each piece of land.—Ps 106:34-39.

Forming marriage alliances with idolaters was another inducement to apostatize. (Jg 3:5, 6) The unrestrained sexual indulgence associated with idolatry proved to be no little temptation. At Shittim on the Plains of Moab, for instance, thousands of Israelites yielded to immorality and engaged in false worship. (Nu 22:1; 25:1-3) To some, being able to give way to unrestrained drinking at the sanctuaries of false gods may have been tempting.—Am 2:8.

Then there was the attraction of supposedly learning what the future had in store, this stemming from a desire to be assured that all would go well. Examples of this are Saul's consulting a spirit medium and Ahaziah's sending to inquire of Baal-zebub the god of Ekron.—1Sa 28:6-11; 2Ki 1:2, 3.

The Folly of Idol Worship. Time and again the Scriptures call attention to the foolishness of relying on gods of wood, stone, or metal. Isaiah describes the manufacture of idols and shows the stupidity of a person who uses part of the wood of a tree to cook his food and to warm himself and then makes the remainder into a god to whom he looks for aid. (Isa 44:9-20) In the day of Jehovah's fury, wrote Isaiah, false worshipers would throw their worthless idols to the shrewmice and to the bats. (Isa 2:19-21) "Woe to the one saying to the piece of wood: 'O do awake!' to a dumb stone: 'O wake up!'" (Hab 2:19) Those making dumb idols will become just like them, that is, lifeless. —Ps 115:4-8; 135:15-18; see Re 9:20.

Viewpoint Toward Idolatry. Faithful servants of Jehovah have always regarded idols with abhorrence. In Scripture, false gods and idols are repeatedly referred to in contemptible terms, as being valueless (1Ch 16:26; Ps 96:5; 97:7), horrible (1Ki 15:13; 2Ch 15:16), shameful (Jer 11:13; Ho 9:10), detestable (Eze 16:36, 37), and disgusting (Eze 37:23). Often mention is made of "dungy idols," this expression being a rendering of the Hebrew word gil·lu·lim', which is related to a word meaning "dung." (1Ki 14:10; Zep 1:17) This term of contempt, first appearing at Leviticus 26:30, is found nearly 40 times in the book of Ezekiel alone, beginning with chapter 6, verse 4.

Faithful Job recognized that even if his heart became enticed in secrecy at beholding heavenly bodies such as the moon and his 'hand proceeded to kiss his mouth' (apparently alluding to throwing a kiss with the hand in an idolatrous practice), this would have constituted a denial of God, hence idolatry. (Job 31:26-28; compare De 4:15, 19.) With reference to a practicer of righteousness, Jehovah said through the prophet Ezekiel, "His eyes he did not raise to the dungy idols of the house of Israel," that is, to offer supplication to them or in expectation of help from them.—Eze 18:5, 6.

Another fine example of shunning idolatry was that of the three Hebrews, Shadrach, Meshach, and Abednego, who, although threatened with death in the fiery furnace, refused to bow before the image of gold erected by King Nebuchadnezzar in the Plain of Dura.—Da 3.

The early Christians heeded the inspired counsel: "Flee from idolatry" (1Co 10:14), and image makers viewed Christianity as a threat to their profitable business. (Ac 19:23-27) As testified to by secular historians, remaining free from idolatry often placed Christians living in the Roman Empire in a position similar to that of the three Hebrews. Acknowledging the divine character of the emperor as head of the state by offering a pinch of incense could have spared such Christians from death, but few compromised. Those early Christians fully appreciated that once they turned away from idols to serve the true God (1Th 1:9), a return to idolatry would mean their being debarred from the New Jerusalem and their losing out on the prize of life.—Re 21:8; 22:14, 15.

Servants of Jehovah must guard themselves from idols (1Jo 5:21), even today. It was foretold that great pressures would be brought to bear against all the inhabitants of the earth to worship the symbolic "wild beast" and its "image." None who persist in such idolatrous worship will receive God's gift of life everlasting. "Here is where it means endurance for the holy ones."—Re 13:15-17; 14:9-12; see DISGUSTING THING, LOATHSOME THING.

IDOLS, MEATS OFFERED TO. In the pagan world of the first century C.E., it was a common practice to offer meats to idols ceremonially. On such occasions parts of the sacrificial animal victim were placed on the idol altar, a portion went to the priests, and a portion went to the worshipers, who would use it for a meal or feast, either in the temple or in a private house. However, some of the flesh that had been offered to the idols was often turned over to the ma'kel·lon, or meat market, to be sold.

Many persons before becoming Christians had been accustomed to eating meats offered to idols with a feeling of reverence for the idol. (1Co 8:7) In so doing, these former pagans had been sharers with the demon god represented by the idol. (1Co 10:20) Quite fittingly, therefore, by formal letter from Jerusalem, the governing body of the early Christian congregation, under the guidance of the holy spirit, forbade such formal, religious eating of meats offered to idols, thus safeguarding Christians from idolatry in this regard.—Ac 15:19-23, 28, 29.

Christians, like those living in pagan Corinth, were faced with a number of questions in this matter. Could they conscientiously go into an idol temple and eat meat if they did so with no thought of honoring the idol? And, would there be any objection to buying from the ma'kel·lon meats that had been ceremonially offered to idols? Finally, how should a Christian handle this matter when eating as a guest in someone else's home?

Under inspiration Paul provided the Corinthian Christians with timely information to aid them in making the correct decisions. Although "an idol is nothing," it would not be advisable for a Christian to go to an idol temple to eat meat (even though his eating was not part of a religious ceremony), because he could thereby be giving spiritually weak observers the wrong impression. Such observers might conclude that the Christian was worshiping the idol, and they could be stumbled by this. It could lead such weaker ones to the point of actually eating meats sacrificed to idols in religious ceremony, in direct violation of the decree of the governing body. There was also the danger that the Christian eater would violate his own conscience and yield to idol worship.—1Co 8: 1-13.

Since the ceremonial offering of meats to idols produced no change in the meat, the Christian could, however, with a good conscience buy meat from a market that received some of its meat from religious temples. This meat had lost its "sacred" significance. It was just as good as any other meat, and the Christian was therefore not under obligation to make inquiry respecting its origin.—1Co 10:25, 26.

Furthermore, the Christian, upon being invited to a meal, did not have to make inquiry concerning the source of the meat but could eat it with a good conscience. If, however, an individual present at the meal were to remark that the meat had been "offered in sacrifice," then the Christian would refrain from eating it to avoid stumbling others.—1Co 10:27-29.

The words of the glorified Jesus Christ to John respecting the Christian congregations at Pergamum and Thyatira indicate that certain ones had failed to heed the apostolic decree in not keeping themselves clean from things sacrificed to idols. —Re 2:12, 14, 18, 20.

IDUMEA (Id·u·me′a) [from Greek, meaning "[Land] of the Edomites"]. In Maccabean and Roman times the geographic boundaries of Idumea did not include the heartland of ancient Edom, E of the Arabah, but embraced parts of what had formerly been Simeonite and Judean territory. As indicated by the Apocryphal book of First Maccabees (4:29, 61; 5:65, *JB*), Idumea included the region around Hebron as far N as Beth-zur, about 26 km (16 mi) SSW of Jerusalem. It is reported

that the Idumeans suffered a crushing defeat at the hands of Judas Maccabaeus. (1 Maccabees 5:3) Later, according to Josephus, John Hyrcanus I subdued all the Idumeans, allowing them to remain in the land on condition that they submit to circumcision and adhere to Jewish law. Rather than leave the country, the Idumeans complied with this condition. (*Jewish Antiquities*, XIII, 257, 258 [ix, 1]) Inhabitants of Idumea were among those who personally came to Jesus upon hearing of the "many things he was doing."—Mr 3:8; see EDOM, EDOMITES.

IEZER (Ie′zer) [shortened form of either Abiezer or Ahiezer], **IEZERITES** (Ie′zer·ites). Iezer is a shortened form of the name Abi-ezer, the prefix "Ab" (meaning "Father") being removed. He and his descendants, the Iezerites, were of "the sons of Gilead."—Nu 26:30; see ABI-EZER No. 1.

IGAL (I′gal) [May [God] Redeem (Repurchase); [God] Has Redeemed (Repurchased)].

1. Chieftain of the tribe of Issachar sent by Moses to spy out the land of Canaan.—Nu 13: 1-3, 7.

2. One of King David's mighty men; son of Nathan of Zobah.—2Sa 23:8, 36.

3. A man of the tribe of Judah who was of the royal line of David.—1Ch 3:1, 22.

IGDALIAH (Ig·da·li′ah) [Great Is Jehovah]. Father of Hanan.—Jer 35:3, 4.

IIM (I′im) [possibly, Heaps of Ruins]. A city in southern Judah. (Jos 15:21, 29) Its exact location is uncertain.

IJON (I′jon). One of the places taken by the military forces of Syria's King Ben-hadad I during the reign of Baasha. (1Ki 15:20, 21; 2Ch 16:4) Nearly two centuries later, Assyrian King Tiglathpileser III conquered Ijon and exiled its population. (2Ki 15:29) Geographers generally link Ijon with Tell ed-Dibbin about 15 km (9 mi) NNW of Dan. But some question this identification because surface exploration of the mound has not revealed any evidence of occupation in the period referred to in Scripture. However, those favoring the commonly proposed identification attribute the absence of such evidence at the base of Tell ed-Dibbin to the well-preserved ancient walls that have prevented spillage from the mound.

IKKESH (Ik′kesh) [Crooked]. The Tekoite whose son Ira was one of King David's mighty men. —2Sa 23:8, 26; 1Ch 11:26, 28; 27:9.

ILAI

ILAI (I'lai). An Ahohite; a mighty man of David's military forces, apparently called Zalmon in 2 Samuel 23:28.—1Ch 11:26, 29.

ILLEGITIMATE.

Not according to law. The Hebrew word for an illegitimate child is *mamzer'*, a word of uncertain etymology, possibly related to a Hebrew word rendered "ulcer" in Jeremiah 30:13 and Hosea 5:13 and to an Arabic word meaning "putrefy; cause nausea," pointing to corruptness.

At Deuteronomy 23:2 the Law reads: "No illegitimate son may come into the congregation of Jehovah. Even to the tenth generation none of his may come into the congregation of Jehovah." The number ten represents completeness; thus "the tenth" generation would mean that such ones could never come into the congregation. The same law is stated regarding the Ammonite and the Moabite, and there the words are added, "to time indefinite," which makes the point clear. However, the Ammonite and Moabite were precluded, not, as some say, because their forefathers were born of incest, but because of the attitude they showed toward Israel when that nation was on its journey toward the Promised Land.—De 23:3-6; see AMMONITES.

Fornication, adultery, and incest are detestable to Jehovah. Under the Law the adulterer and the incestuous one were to be put to death, and none of the daughters of Israel were to become prostitutes. (Le 18:6, 29; 19:29; 20:10; De 23:17) Furthermore, it would cause confusion and a breakdown of the family arrangement for the illegitimate son to inherit; he could have no inheritance in Israel.

Some commentators claim that Jephthah was an illegitimate son, but this is not correct. The Bible does not say that he was illegitimate; it says that "he was the son of a prostitute woman." (Jg 11:1) Like Rahab, who had been a prostitute but who married the Israelite Salmon, Jephthah's mother doubtless married honorably, and Jephthah was no more an illegitimate son than was the son of Salmon and Rahab, who was a fleshly ancestor of Jesus Christ. (Mt 1:5) Likely Jephthah's mother was a secondary wife of Gilead, and Jephthah may even have been Gilead's firstborn. He could not have been a member of the congregation of Israel had he been illegitimate, and his half brothers, who had driven him out, could not legally have asked him to become their head. (Jg 11:2, 6, 11) That Jephthah may have been the son of a secondary wife would not make him illegitimate. The son of a secondary wife had the same inheritance rights as the son of a favorite wife, as the Law states at Deuteronomy 21:15-17.

In the Christian Greek Scriptures, the word *no'thos* ('illegitimate child,' *NW;* 'bastard,' *KJ, Int*) is used once, at Hebrews 12:8. As shown by the context, the writer likens God to a father who disciplines his son out of love. The writer therefore says, "If you are without the discipline of which all have become partakers, you are really illegitimate children, and not sons." Those claiming to be spiritual sons of God but practicing sin and disobedience are cut off from the congregation of God and do not receive the discipline that God gives his legitimate sons to bring them to perfection.

Illegitimate Fire and Incense. At Leviticus 10:1 the Hebrew word *zar* (feminine, *za·rah';* literally, strange) is used with regard to "illegitimate fire, which [God] had not prescribed for them" but which Aaron's sons Nadab and Abihu presented before Jehovah and for which he executed them by fire. (Le 10:2; Nu 3:4; 26:61) Subsequently, Jehovah said to Aaron: "Do not drink wine or intoxicating liquor, you and your sons with you, when you come into the tent of meeting, that you may not die. It is a statute to time indefinite for your generations, both in order to make a distinction between the holy thing and the profane and between the unclean thing and the clean, and in order to teach the sons of Israel all the regulations that Jehovah has spoken to them by means of Moses." (Le 10:8-11) This seems to indicate that Nadab and Abihu were in a state of intoxication, which condition emboldened them to offer fire not prescribed. Such fire was likely illegal as to its time, place, or manner of offering, or it could have been incense other than of the composition described at Exodus 30:34, 35. Their inebriated condition did not excuse their sin.

The same word, *zar*, is used at Exodus 30:9, with reference to the burning of illegitimate incense on the altar of incense in the Holy Place. —See *NW* ftn.

ILLUSTRATIONS.

The Greek expression *pa·ra·bo·le'* (literally, a placing beside or together) has a wider latitude of meaning than the English "proverb" or "parable." However, "illustration" covers a wide range that can include "parable" and, in many cases, "proverb." A "proverb" embodies a truth in expressive language, often metaphorically, and a "parable" is a comparison or similitude, a short, usually fictitious, narrative from which a moral or spiritual truth is drawn.

That the Scriptures use the word *pa·ra·bo·le'* with a wider meaning than the English "parable" is shown at Matthew 13:34, 35, where Matthew points out that it had been foretold concerning Jesus Christ that he would speak with "illustrations" (*NW*), "parables" (*KJ, RS*). Psalm 78:2, quoted by Matthew in this connection, refers to "a proverbial saying" (Heb., *ma·shal'*), and for this term the Gospel writer employed the Greek word *pa·ra·bo·le'*. As the literal meaning of the Greek term implies, the *pa·ra·bo·le'* served as a means of teaching or communicating an idea, a method of explaining a thing by 'placing it beside' another similar thing. (Compare Mr 4:30.) Most English translations simply use the anglicized form "parable" to render the Greek term. However, this translation does not serve to convey the full meaning in every instance.

For example, at Hebrews 9:9 and 11:19 most translations find it necessary to resort to expressions other than "parable." In the first of these texts the tabernacle, or tent, used by Israel in the wilderness, is called by the apostle Paul "an illustration [*pa·ra·bo·le'*; "figure," *KJ*; "similitude," *Ro*; "symbolic," *AT, RS*] for the appointed time." In the second text Abraham is described by the apostle as having received Isaac back from the dead "in an illustrative way" (*NW*) (*en pa·ra·bo·lei'*; "figuratively speaking," *JB, RS*). The saying, "Physician, cure yourself," is also termed a *pa·ra·bo·le'*. (Lu 4:23) In view of this, a more basic term such as "illustration" (*NW*) serves for a consistent rendering of *pa·ra·bo·le'* in all cases.

Another related term is "allegory" (Gr., *al·le·go·ri'a*), which is a prolonged metaphor in which a series of actions are symbolic of other actions, while the characters often are types or personifications. Paul uses the Greek verb *al·le·go·re'o* (allegorize) at Galatians 4:24, concerning Abraham, Sarah, and Hagar. It is translated 'be an allegory' (*KJ*), 'be an allegorical utterance' (*AT*), and "stand as a symbolic drama" (*NW*).

The apostle John also used a distinct term (*pa·roi·mi'a*) that denotes "comparison" (Joh 10:6; 16:25, 29); it is variously translated "figure," "figurative language," "parable," "proverb," and "comparison" (*AT, KJ, NW*). Peter employed the same term with regard to the "proverb" of the dog returning to its vomit and the sow to rolling in the mire.—2Pe 2:22.

Effectiveness.   Illustrations or parables as a powerful teaching device are effective in at least five ways: (1) They arrest and hold attention; few things command interest like an experience or a story. Who is not familiar with the illustrations of the prodigal son and of the one lost sheep? (2) They stir up the thinking faculty; one of the best mental exercises is to search out the meaning of a comparison, to get the abstract truths thus presented. (3) They stir emotions and, by the usually evident practical application of the truths to the hearer, reach the conscience and the heart. (4) They aid memory; one can later reconstruct the story and make application of it. (5) They preserve the truth, for they are always applicable and understandable in any time and age. This is because they deal with life and natural things, whereas mere words may change in meaning. This is one reason why the Bible truths remain in full clarity today, just as they were at the time they were spoken or written.

Purposes.   The primary purpose of all illustrations is, as shown in the foregoing, to teach. But the illustrations of the Bible also serve other purposes:

(1) The fact that a person sometimes has to dig to get their full, deep, heart-reaching meaning tends to turn back those who do not love God but who have a mere surface interest and therefore do not desire the truth in their hearts. (Mt 13:13-15) God is not gathering such persons. Illustrations moved the humble ones to ask for further explanation; the proud refused to do so. Jesus said: "Let him that has ears listen," and though the majority of the crowds hearing Jesus went their way, the disciples would come and ask for explanation.—Mt 13:9, 36.

(2) Illustrations conceal truths from those who would misuse them and who desire to entrap God's servants. Jesus answered the Pharisees' catch question with the illustration of the tax coin, concluding: "Pay back, therefore, Caesar's things to Caesar, but God's things to God." His enemies were left to make the application themselves; but Jesus' disciples fully understood the principle of neutrality there set forth.—Mt 22:15-21.

(3) Because the hearer is left to apply the principles of the illustration to himself, it can carry to him a clear message of warning and rebuke, at the same time disarming him so that he has no ground to retaliate against the speaker. In other words, as the saying goes, 'If the shoe fits, wear it.' When the Pharisees criticized Jesus for eating with tax collectors and sinners, Jesus replied: "Persons in health do not need a physician, but the ailing do. Go, then, and learn what this means, 'I want mercy, and not sacrifice.' For I came to call, not righteous people, but sinners." —Mt 9:11-13.

(4) Even when being used to give correction to a person, illustrations can be used to sidestep prejudice on the part of the hearer, keeping his mind from being beclouded by such prejudice, and thereby accomplishing more than would a mere statement of fact. Such was the case when Nathan found a hearing ear in reproving King David for his sin in connection with Bath-sheba and Uriah. (2Sa 12:1-14) This was also the case when an illustration was used to get wicked King Ahab unknowingly to weigh the principles involved in his own disobedient action in sparing the life of King Ben-hadad of Syria, an enemy of God, and to utter a judgment condemning himself.—1Ki 20:34, 38-43.

(5) Illustrations can motivate persons to take action one way or another, to 'show their true colors,' as to whether or not they are genuine servants of God. When Jesus said: "He that feeds on my flesh and drinks my blood has everlasting life," "many of his disciples went off to the things behind and would no longer walk with him." In this way Jesus 'weeded out' those who did not really believe from the heart.—Joh 6:54, 60-66.

Proper Viewpoint and Approach. Bible illustrations have more than one aspect. They set forth and illuminate principles, and they often have a prophetic meaning and application. Moreover, some had a prophetic meaning for the time when they were spoken or shortly thereafter, and some were to have, in addition, a fulfillment in the distant future.

There are two general misconceptions that can hinder the understanding of the illustrations of the Bible. One is the viewing of all the illustrations as being merely good stories, examples, or lessons. The parable of the prodigal son, for instance, is considered by some to be a mere piece of fine literature; the illustration of the rich man and Lazarus, an example of reward and punishment after death.

In this connection it may also be remarked that the illustrations, although drawn from life and natural things, did not necessarily take place in actuality. Although some illustrations begin with expressions such as: "Once upon a time," "A man had," "There was a man," "A certain man was," or similar phrases, they were devised by the speaker under influence of God's spirit and were what they are called—illustrations, or parables. (Jg 9:8; Mt 21:28, 33; Lu 16:1, 19) Of Jesus Christ it is said: "All these things Jesus spoke to the crowds by illustrations. Indeed, without an illustration he would not speak to them."—Mt 13:34; Mr 4:33, 34.

A second obstacle to understanding is the drawing of too fine an application of the illustration, trying to make every detail of the narrative of the literal events fit symbolically by arbitrary application or interpretation.

The proper approach is made, first, by reading the context, ascertaining the setting in which the illustration was spoken, asking, What were the conditions and the circumstances? For instance, when the rulers and people of Israel were addressed as "dictators of Sodom" and "people of Gomorrah," it makes us think of a people who were gross sinners against Jehovah. (Isa 1:10; Ge 13:13; 19:13, 24) When the psalmist prays to Jehovah to do to the enemies of God and His people "as to Midian," it calls to mind the complete rout of those oppressors of God's people, over 120,000 being slain.—Ps 83:2, 3, 9-11; Jg 8:10-12.

Next, a knowledge of the Law, the customs and usages, and the idiom of the day is often helpful. For example, a knowledge of the Law helps us to understand the illustration of the dragnet. (Mt 13:47-50) The fact that fruit trees were taxed in Palestine during that time and that unproductive trees were cut down helps us to understand why Jesus caused an unfruitful fig tree to wither so as to use it for illustrative purposes.—Mt 21:18-22.

Finally, the factors in an illustration should not be given an arbitrary meaning, one gained from a private view or from philosophy. The rule is set forth for Christians: "No one has come to know the things of God, except the spirit of God. Now we received, not the spirit of the world, but the spirit which is from God, that we might know the things that have been kindly given us by God. These things we also speak, not with words taught by human wisdom, but with those taught by the spirit, as we *combine spiritual matters with spiritual words.*"—1Co 2:11-13.

An application of this rule can be demonstrated in connection with the prophetic illustration in Revelation chapter 6. A white horse is the first of four mentioned here. (Re 6:2) What does it symbolize? We can turn to other parts of the Bible as well as to the context to get its significance. Proverbs 21:31 says: "The horse is something prepared for the day of battle." White is often used to symbolize righteousness. God's throne of judgment is white; the armies in heaven are on white horses and are clothed in white, clean, fine linen. (Re 20:11; 19:14; compare Re 6:11; 19:8.) We could conclude, therefore, that the white horse represents righteous warfare.

The horseman on the black mount has a pair of scales, and foodstuffs are being weighed out. (Re

6:5, 6) Famine is here evidently pictured, for in the famine prophecy of Ezekiel he was told: "Your food that you will eat will be by weight . . . and they will have to eat bread by weight and in anxious care, and it will be by measure and in horror that they will drink water itself." (Eze 4:10, 16) Often by understanding Biblical symbolic usage, such as in the case of animals mentioned in illustrations, one can get help and spiritual light.—See BEASTS, SYMBOLIC.

A good number of illustrations are understood because of the Bible's own explanation, often followed by a narrative of events in fulfillment of them. Among these, to name two, are: Ezekiel's boring a hole through a wall and going out with his face covered (Eze 12:1-16; 2Ki 25:1-7, 11; Jer 52:1-15), as well as Abraham's attempting to sacrifice Isaac but receiving him back by God's intervention (these illustrations were also actual occurrences, carried out in dramalike manner). (Ge 22:9-13; Heb 11:19) Others, particularly many spoken by Jesus Christ, are explained afterward by Jesus himself. In many cases, the understanding of Bible illustrations is aided by modern events in fulfillment.

In the Hebrew Scriptures. The Hebrew prophets and Bible writers, moved by Jehovah's spirit, recorded countless apt illustrations. Illustrative language appears in Genesis, in Jehovah's promise that he would multiply Abraham's seed "like the stars of the heavens and like the grains of sand that are on the seashore." (Ge 22:15-18) To emphasize the sad plight to which sin had brought his people in Judah, Jehovah moved Isaiah to compare it to a loathsome physically diseased condition, saying: "The whole head is in a sick condition, and the whole heart is feeble. . . . Wounds and bruises and fresh stripes—they have not been squeezed out or bound up, nor has there been a softening with oil." (Isa 1:4-6) To King Nebuchadnezzar, Jehovah conveyed prophetic messages with visions of a huge image and a towering tree, and Daniel saw certain governments of earth depicted as beasts.—Da chaps 2, 4, 7.

Frequently the prophets used a word or an expression in speaking of a person or a group with a view to imparting its characteristics to the individual or the group, that is, metaphorically. For example, Jehovah is described as "the Rock of Israel," as a "crag," and as a "stronghold," thus conveying the idea that God is a solid source of security. (2Sa 23:3; Ps 18:2) Judah is said to be "a lion cub." (Ge 49:9) The Assyrians are said to be "the rod" for God's anger.—Isa 10:5.

On numerous occasions the prophets acted out the message they had been commissioned to deliver, thus reenforcing the impact of the spoken word. Jeremiah foretold calamity for Jerusalem and emphasized it by breaking a flask before the eyes of assembled older men of the people and of the priests. He foretold servitude to Babylon and made it vivid by sending bands and yoke bars to various kings. (Jer chaps 19, 27) Isaiah walked about naked and barefoot to emphasize to the Israelites that it would be in this manner that the Egyptians and the Ethiopians, to whom they were looking for help, would be led away into exile. (Isa 20) Ezekiel engraved an illustration of Jerusalem on a brick, built a siege rampart against it, put an iron griddle between himself and his model, and lay on his side facing it, to depict the coming siege of Jerusalem.—Eze 4.

At times stories were related to emphasize the point to be conveyed. Jotham did this to show the landowners of Shechem their folly in selecting so vile a man as Abimelech for their king. (Jg 9:7-20) In the book of Ezekiel an account was woven around two eagles and a vine, to illustrate the course of Judah in relation to Babylon and Egypt. (Eze 17) Similarly, Ezekiel used two sisters, Oholah and Oholibah, who became prostitutes, to illustrate the course of Samaria (the ten-tribe kingdom of Israel) and Jerusalem (Judah).—Eze 23.

The illustrations mentioned here are only a few of the many illustrations of the Hebrew Scriptures. Virtually every Bible writer and prophet used illustrations, some being given to them directly by God himself in the form of visions, some in words, and some by means of actual realities, as, for instance, the tabernacle, which is called "an illustration."—Heb 9:9.

In the Greek Scriptures. The Christian Greek Scriptures, too, are filled with vivid illustrations. Of Jesus Christ it was said, "Never has another man spoken like this." Of all humans who have ever lived on earth, he had the greatest resources of knowledge from which to draw. (Joh 7:46) He is the one through whom everything was made by God. (Joh 1:1-3; Col 1:15-17) He was intimately acquainted with all creation. Understandably, therefore, his comparisons were most apt and his portrayal of human emotions reflected deep understanding. He was like the wise man of old who said: "And besides the fact that the congregator had become wise, he also taught the people knowledge continually, and he pondered and made a thorough search, that he might arrange many proverbs in order. The congregator sought to find the delightful words and the writing of correct words of truth."—Ec 12:9, 10.

Jesus appropriately identified his disciples as "the salt of the earth" and "the light of the world." (Mt 5:13, 14) He urged them to "observe intently the birds of heaven" and to "take a lesson from the lilies of the field." (Mt 6:26-30) He likened himself to a shepherd who was willing to die for his sheep. (Joh 10:11-15) To Jerusalem he said: "How often I wanted to gather your children together, the way a hen gathers her chicks together under her wings! But you people did not want it." (Mt 23:37) Hypocritical religious leaders he called "blind guides, who strain out the gnat but gulp down the camel!" (Mt 23:24) And concerning a person who would stumble others, he declared: "It would be of more advantage to him if a millstone were suspended from his neck and he were thrown into the sea."—Lu 17:1, 2.

While the illustrations used by Jesus could be short, terse expressions similar to the proverbial sayings found in the Hebrew Scriptures, they were usually longer and often were of story length and character. Jesus generally drew his illustrations from the surrounding creation, from familiar customs of everyday life, from occasional happenings or not-impossible situations, and from recent events well known to his hearers.

Some of Jesus' prominent illustrations. In the material that follows, you will find helpful information concerning the background and context of 30 of the illustrations used by Jesus Christ in his earthly ministry and recorded by the Gospel writers:

(1) *The two debtors* (Lu 7:41-43). The purpose of the parable of the two debtors, one of whom owed ten times as much as the other, and the parable's application are found in the context, Luke 7:36-40, 44-50.

The illustration was prompted by the attitude of Jesus' host Simon toward the woman who came in and greased Jesus' feet with perfumed oil. The presence of such an uninvited person was not regarded as unusual, for it seems that on some occasions uninvited persons could enter the room during a meal and sit along the wall, from there conversing with those reclining at the table in the center of the room. Jesus made fitting application of the situation of the two debtors, pointing out that Simon had failed to provide water for his feet, to greet him with a kiss, and to grease his head with oil; these were courtesies customarily accorded a guest. But the woman

who had many sins showed the greater love and hospitality toward Jesus, even though she was not his hostess. He then told her: "Your sins are forgiven."

(2) *The sower* (Mt 13:3-8; Mr 4:3-8; Lu 8:5-8). There are no clues to the interpretation in the illustration itself, but the explanation is plainly given at Matthew 13:18-23; Mark 4:14-20; and Luke 8:11-15. Attention is focused on the circumstances affecting the soil, or heart, and the influences that can hinder the growth of the seed, or the word of the Kingdom.

Various means of sowing seed were used in those days. One common way was for the sower to carry a bag of seed tied across his shoulder and around his waist; others would form a pouch for the seed from a part of their outer garment. They would scatter the seed broadcast by hand as they walked. Seed was covered as soon as possible, before the crows and ravens could get it. But when the plowman left footpaths between fields unplowed, or if some seed fell on hard ground alongside the road, the birds ate up the seed that fell there. "The rocky places" were not spots where rocks were merely scattered in the soil; but, as Luke 8:6 says, the seed fell on "the rockmass," or a concealed rock ledge, on which there was very little soil. Plants from these seeds would soon wither in the sun. The soil where the thorns were had evidently been plowed, but it had not been cleaned of weeds, so they grew up and choked out the newly planted seeds. The stated yields of the productive seeds—a hundredfold, sixtyfold, and thirtyfold—are well within reason. The sowing of seed and the various types of soil were familiar to Jesus' hearers.

(3) *Weeds among the wheat* (Mt 13:24-30). Explanation is provided by Jesus, as recorded at Matthew 13:36-43, contrasting "the wheat" or "the sons of the kingdom" with "the weeds," "the sons of the wicked one."

Oversowing a wheat field with weeds is a deed of enmity not unknown in the Middle East. "The weeds" referred to are usually believed to be the poisonous bearded darnel (*Lolium temulentum*), its poisonous properties generally thought to stem from a fungus growing within these seeds. It has an appearance much like that of wheat until maturity, but then it can be readily identified. If eaten, it can result in dizziness and, under certain circumstances, even death. Since the roots of these weeds readily become intertwined with the roots of the wheat, to uproot them before harvest, even if they could be identified, would result in loss of wheat.

(4) The mustard grain (Mt 13:31, 32; Mr 4: 30-32; Lu 13:18, 19). It is stated that the subject is "the kingdom of the heavens." As shown in other texts, this can refer to some feature in connection with the Kingdom (even those falsely claiming to represent it) and is not limited to the approved membership of that Kingdom.—Mt 13: 47, 48; 25:1, 2.

The mustard grain was tiny and so it could be used to designate anything extremely small. (Lu 17:6) When fully developed, some mustard plants actually attain a height of 3 to 4.5 m (10 to 15 ft) and have sturdy branches, thus virtually becoming "a tree," as Jesus said. We are helped to identify the "tree" if we take note of the fact that the series of illustrations in which this one is included was introduced at Matthew 13:13-15 by a statement regarding a negative factor. It should also be noted that in the context "birds" are referred to in a negative sense; they are shown to represent "the wicked one."—Mt 13:4, 19; Lu 8:12.

(5) The leaven (Mt 13:33). Again, the subject is "the kingdom of the heavens." But, like the preceding illustration, this one is included in a series that the Bible introduces by a statement regarding failure of people to get the real sense of God's Word.—Mt 13:13-15.

The "three large measures" are three *sa'ta,* that is, three seahs, equaling a total of about 22 L (20 dry qt) of flour. The amount of leaven would be small in comparison, but just a little can affect everything around it. The leaven was usually a piece of fermented dough left over from the last baking. Leaven, it should be noted, is used in the Scriptures to represent false teaching, a corrupting influence.—Lu 12:1; 1Co 5:6-8.

(6) The hidden treasure (Mt 13:44). Spoken by Jesus, not to the crowds, but to his own disciples. (Mt 13:36) As stated in the text, the subject is "the kingdom of the heavens," which brings joy to the one finding it; it requires that he make changes and adjustments in his life and seek the Kingdom first, giving up everything for it.

(7) The merchant seeking pearls (Mt 13:45, 46). Spoken by Jesus to his disciples. He likens the Kingdom of the heavens to a fine pearl of such value that a man sells all his possessions to acquire it.

Pearls are precious gems found in shells of oysters and certain other mollusks. Not all pearls are "fine," however; some may be, not a translucent white, but yellow, or they may have a dusky tinge, or they may not be smooth. Among ancients in the Middle East, the pearl was prized

and brought delight to its owner. In this illustration, the merchant was seeking pearls; he had the discernment to appreciate the surpassing value of this one and he was willing to take the trouble to make all the arrangements needed and to part with all else to acquire it.—Compare Lu 14:33; Php 3:8.

(8) The dragnet (Mt 13:47-50). With this illustration Jesus describes a separating, or culling out, of those unfit for the Kingdom of the heavens. Verse 49 points to "the conclusion of the system of things" as the time when the fulfillment culminates. Since the dragnet gathered up both "fine" fish and "unsuitable" ones, the net itself must represent an arrangement that embraces those who are truly in line for the Kingdom as well as those who falsely claim to be.

A dragnet is a net of rope or flax cords designed to be drawn along the bottom of a body of water. By means of it all kinds of fish would be gathered. The illustration was most appropriate for Jesus' disciples, some of whom were fishermen. They well knew that some fish were unsuitable and had to be discarded because, not having fins and scales, they were unclean and could not be eaten, according to the Mosaic Law.—Le 11:9-12; De 14:9, 10.

(9) The unmerciful slave (Mt 18:23-35). The situation giving rise to Jesus' use of the illustration is set out in Matthew 18:21, 22, and the application is stated in verse 35. It emphasizes how small the debts of our fellowmen to us are in comparison with our debt to God. The illustration impresses upon us as sinful humans, for whom God forgives so great a debt by means of Christ's sacrifice, the need to show forgiveness for the relatively insignificant sins our fellowman commits against us.

A denarius equaled a day's wages; so 100 denarii, the smaller debt, equaled approximately one third of a year's wages. Ten thousand silver talents, the larger debt, equaled 60 million denarii, or wages that would require thousands of lifetimes to accumulate. The enormous size of the debt owed the king is indicated in that, according to Josephus, the provinces of Judea, Idumea, and Samaria and certain cities together paid taxes in his day amounting to 600 talents a year; Galilee and Perea paid 200. Jesus himself (in verse 35) states the principle expressed in the parable: "In like manner my heavenly Father will also deal with you if you do not forgive each one his brother from your hearts."

(10) The neighborly Samaritan (Lu 10:30-37). The setting, recorded at Luke 10:25-29, shows

that the illustration was given in reply to the question, "Who really is my neighbor?" The proper conclusion to be drawn from the illustration is shown in verses 36 and 37.

The road from Jerusalem to Jericho led through wild and lonely terrain that was the scene of frequent robberies. So bad was it that, in time, a garrison was stationed there to protect travelers. Jericho was about 23 km (14 mi) ENE of Jerusalem. To identify the "neighbor" toward whom the Law commanded the exercise of love, Jesus spoke of the reactions of a priest and of a Levite toward a man who had been robbed and left half-dead. The priests were men who were assigned to offer sacrifices at the temple in Jerusalem, and the Levites assisted them. The Samaritans recognized the Law as expressed in the Pentateuch, but the Jews were not neighborly toward them, in fact, they would have no dealings with them. (Joh 4:9) They viewed the Samaritans with great contempt (Joh 8:48), and there were those Jews who cursed them publicly in their synagogues and daily prayed to God that the Samaritans might not be partakers of eternal life. Oil and wine, poured into the wounds of the injured man, were often used for healing purposes. The two denarii that the Samaritan left with the innkeeper for the man's care equaled about two days' wages.—Mt 20:2.

(11) *The persistent friend* (Lu 11:5-8). The illustration was part of Jesus' reply to his disciples' request for instruction on how to pray. (Lu 11:1-4) As shown in verses 9 and 10, the point to be drawn from it is not that God is disturbed by our requests but that he expects us to *keep on asking.*

Hospitality is a duty in which people of the Middle East love to excel. Even though the guest arrived unexpectedly at midnight, perhaps due to the uncertainties of travel then, his host would feel compelled to provide food. Since it is often difficult to judge exactly how much bread a household will need to have baked, there was some borrowing among neighbors. In this case the neighbor had gone to bed. Since some homes, especially those of the poor, might consist of only one large room, his getting up would disturb the whole family, hence the man's reluctance to grant the request.

(12) *The unreasonable rich man* (Lu 12:16-21). The illustration was part of Jesus' reply to a man who asked him to arbitrate in a matter of inheritance. As shown in verse 15, the point emphasized is that "even when a person has an abundance his life does not result from the things he

possesses." Compare it with what Jesus went on to say to his disciples, beginning in verse 22.

The Law required that two parts of everything belonging to the father be inherited by his eldest son. (De 21:17) Apparently the dispute came about because of failure to respect this law; hence the warning against covetousness.

(13) *The unproductive fig tree* (Lu 13:6-9). Spoken late in 32 C.E., a full three years after Jesus' baptism. Report had just been made about Pilate's killing some Galileans. Jesus had also cited the case of the death of 18 upon whom the tower of Siloam fell and told the people that, unless they repented, they would all be destroyed. (Lu 13:1-5) Then he went on to use this illustration.

It was common to set both fig and olive trees in the vineyards at certain distances, so that when the vineyards had a bad year, there would still be some income. New trees grown from cuttings usually produce at least a few figs within two or three years. The parallel between the three years mentioned in the illustration and the three years of Jesus' ministry that had passed was evidently significant. The tree appeared from a distance to be productive but was deceptive. As a taxable item, it was a burden, hence it deserved to be destroyed.

(14) *The grand evening meal* (Lu 14:16-24). Verses 1-15 give the setting; at a meal the illustration was related to a fellow guest who said: "Happy is he who eats bread in the kingdom of God."

It was customary to notify those previously invited to a feast when the meal was actually ready. Those who begged off from this grand evening meal preferred to pursue other interests that would normally seem quite reasonable. However, their responses showed that they had no real desire to be present, nor did they have proper regard for the host. Most of the ones later invited, the poor, the crippled, the lame, the blind, and others finally brought in, were persons viewed by the world in general as unworthy.—Compare vs 13.

(15) *The one lost sheep* (Lu 15:3-7). Luke 15:1, 2 shows that the illustration was prompted by the muttering of the Pharisees and the scribes over the fact that Jesus welcomed sinners and tax collectors. Matthew 18:12-14 records a similar illustration used on a different occasion.

Tax collectors, particularly those who were Jews, were hated because their occupation was to gather taxes for the hated Romans. They were held in scorn. Jesus' illustration concerning the one lost sheep was one that his hearers would readily recognize from everyday life. A lost sheep is helpless; it is the shepherd who does the searching to recover it. The joy in heaven over the sinner who repents is in marked contrast with the muttering of the scribes and Pharisees over the concern that Jesus showed for such persons.

(*16*) *The lost drachma coin* (Lu 15:8-10). The setting is found in Luke 15:1, 2, and this illustration immediately follows the one concerning the one lost sheep. Verse 10 points out the application.

A drachma was worth 65 cents, almost a day's wages. However, this lost coin may have had special value as one of a set of ten, perhaps an heirloom or part of a prized string used for adornment. It was necessary to light a lamp to search, because the light opening in a home, if any, was usually quite small; and the sweeping would facilitate the search, because the floor was generally just clay.

(*17*) *The prodigal son* (Lu 15:11-32). The Pharisees and scribes were muttering because Jesus welcomed tax collectors and sinners and ate with them. Jesus replied by giving the illustrations of the one lost sheep and the lost coin, followed by this parable.

The inheritance of the younger son was half that of the elder brother, according to Jewish law. (De 21:17) As the younger son went to a far country, so the Jews viewed the tax collectors as having left them to take up service to Rome. To be forced to take up swineherding was degrading to a Jew, since these animals were unclean according to the Law. (Le 11:7) On his return home, the younger son asked to be accepted, not as a son, but as a hired man. Such a man was not even part of the estate, as were the slaves, but was an outsider hired, often for just a day at a time. (Mt 20:1, 2, 8) The father called for a robe, the best one, for the younger son. This was not merely a simple article of clothing, but it probably was a richly embroidered vestment of the sort presented to an honored guest. The ring and sandals were possibly tokens of dignity and of a free man.

(*18*) *The unrighteous steward* (Lu 16:1-8). The lesson to be drawn from the illustration is stated in verses 9-13. The steward is commended, not for his unrighteousness, but for his practical wisdom.

The steward was placed in charge of the affairs of his master; it was a position of great trust. (Ge 24:2; 39:4) In Jesus' illustration, the steward's being dismissed meant that he was being sent out of the house, with no means of support. His lowering of the debts of his master's debtors brought him no money but was done to win friends who might favor him in the future. One hundred bath measures of oil equaled 2,200 L (581 gal), and 100 cor measures of wheat came to 22,000 L (625 bu).

(*19*) *The rich man and Lazarus* (Lu 16:19-31). The setting, in Luke 16:14, 15, shows that the money-loving Pharisees were listening and sneering. But Jesus told them: "You are those who declare yourselves righteous before men, but God knows your hearts; because what is lofty among men is a disgusting thing in God's sight."

The "purple and linen" in which the rich man was decked out were comparable to garb worn only by princes, nobles, and priests. (Es 8:15; Ge 41:42; Ex 28:4, 5) They were very costly. Hades, where this rich man is said to have gone, is the common grave of dead mankind. That it cannot be concluded from this parable that Hades itself is a place of blazing fire is made clear at Revelation 20:14, where death and Hades are described as being hurled *into* "the lake of fire." The death of the rich man and his being in Hades must therefore be figurative, figurative death being mentioned elsewhere in the Scriptures. (Lu 9:60; Col 2:13; 1Ti 5:6) So the fiery torment was experienced while he was figuratively dead but actually alive as a human. Fire is used in God's Word to describe his fiery judgment messages (Jer 5:14; 23:29), and the work done by God's prophets in declaring his judgments is said to 'torment' those who oppose God and his servants.—Re 11:7, 10.

Lazarus is a Grecianized form of the Hebrew name Eleazar, which means "God Has Helped." The dogs that licked his sores were apparently scavengers that roamed the streets and were viewed as unclean. Lazarus' being in the bosom position of Abraham indicates that he was in a position of favor (compare Joh 1:18), this figure of speech being drawn from the practice of reclining at meals in such a way that one could lean back on the bosom of a friend.—Joh 13:23-25.

(*20*) *Good-for-nothing slaves* (Lu 17:7-10). Verse 10 shows the lesson to be drawn from the illustration.

Slaves who worked in the fields of their master also frequently served his evening meal. Not only was it the usual thing for them to wait until their master had eaten before they would do so, but often it was a matter of dispute as to which one of them would have the honor of waiting on him. It was not viewed as an extra burden but as something to which their master was entitled.

(*21*) *The widow and the judge* (Lu 18:1-8). As stated in verse 1, the illustration was "with regard to the need for them always to pray and not to give up." Verses 7 and 8 also show application. The illustration emphasizing prayer was particularly appropriate in view of what is stated in the preceding chapter, verses 20 to 37.

Apparently the judge was not connected with a Jewish tribunal. In the first century there were four Jewish courts: (1) the village court, consisting of three men; (2) a court consisting of seven older men of the village; (3) in Jerusalem there were lower courts consisting of 23 persons each, and such courts were established in cities of sufficient size elsewhere throughout Palestine; and (4) the principal court, the Great Sanhedrin, consisting of 71 members, with its seat at Jerusalem and with authority over the whole nation. (See COURT, JUDICIAL) But the judge of the illustration does not fit into the Jewish judicial arrangement in which at least a three-man court officiated; so he must have been one of the judges or police magistrates appointed by the Romans. It is plainly stated that he did not fear God nor was he constrained by concern over public opinion. The illustration does not say that God is like the unrighteous judge; rather, it contrasts God with the judge. If this judge would finally do what was right, how much more so would God! Persistence on the part of the widow moved the unrighteous judge to act; God's servants likewise must persist in prayer. God, who is righteous, will respond in answer to their prayer, causing justice to be done.

(*22*) *The self-righteous Pharisee and the penitent tax collector* (Lu 18:9-14). The setting and the objective of the illustration are found in verses 9 and 14 respectively.

Those who went to the temple to pray did not go into the Holy or the Most Holy, but they were permitted to enter the surrounding courts. These men, Jews, probably stood in the outer court, the Court of Women, as it was called. The Pharisees were proud and self-righteous, viewing other men with contempt. (Joh 7:47, 49) They fasted twice a week, though this was not required by the Mosaic Law. The days they chose for this, it is reported, were the regular market days when many people would be in town, when special services were held in the synagogues, and when the local Sanhedrin met; so their piety would be observed. (Mt 6:16; compare 10:17, ftn) The Jewish tax collectors were permitted to go to the temple, but they were hated for their service to Rome.

(*23*) *The workers paid a denarius* (Mt 20:1-16). The illustration is part of Jesus' answer to Peter's question in Matthew 19:27: "Look! We have left all things and followed you; what actually will there be for us?" Note also Matthew 19:30 and 20:16.

Grape-gathering time is a season of anxious concern for the owners of vineyards. Some workers are employed for the entire harvesttime; others are hired as the need becomes apparent. Payment of wages at the end of the day was in harmony with the Mosaic Law; it was a necessity for poor laborers. (Le 19:13; De 24:14, 15) A denarius, which was payment for the day's work, was a silver Roman coin. Its modern-day value would be 74 cents. In the first century C.E., the day, from sunrise to sunset, was divided by the Jews into 12 equal parts; so the 3rd hour would be about 8:00 to 9:00 a.m.; the 6th hour, about 11:00 a.m. to noon; the 9th hour, about 2:00 to 3:00 p.m.; and the 11th hour, about 4:00 to 5:00 p.m.

(*24*) *The minas* (Lu 19:11-27). Spoken as Jesus was on his way up to Jerusalem for the last time, 33 C.E. (Lu 19:1, 28) The reason for the illustration, as stated in verse 11, was that "they were imagining that the kingdom of God was going to display itself instantly."

It was a common thing in the Roman Empire for a person of noble birth to travel to Rome in quest of kingly power. Archelaus, the son of Herod the Great, had done this, but the Jews sent 50 ambassadors to the court of Augustus to bring charges against him and, if possible, thwart his quest for power. The silver mina that was initially given to each slave would be worth $65.40 in today's values but was equal to 88 days' wages then.

(*25*) *The two children* (Mt 21:28-31). Spoken in the temple at Jerusalem, the illustration was part of Jesus' reply to the questions in verse 23: "By what authority do you do these things? And who gave you this authority?" Having handled their questions, Jesus used some illustrations to show the religious leaders what kind of persons they really were.

Jesus points to the application of his illustration in verses 31 and 32. He indicates that the chief priests and the older men of influence to whom he was speaking were comparable to the first child, professing to serve God but actually failing to do so. On the other hand, the tax collectors and harlots who believed John the Baptizer were like the second child; at first they rudely refused to serve God but later felt regret and changed their course.

(*26*) *The murderous cultivators* (Mt 21:33-44; Mr 12:1-11; Lu 20:9-18). Spoken in the temple in Jerusalem, just three days before Jesus, God's Son, was killed. This illustration, too, was in answer to the question about the source of Jesus' authority. (Mr 11:27-33) Immediately after the illustration, the Gospel accounts state that the religious leaders realized that he was speaking about them.—Mt 21:45; Mr 12:12; Lu 20:19.

The fence around the vineyard might have been of stone (Pr 24:30, 31) or it might have been a hedge. (Isa 5:5) The wine vat was frequently excavated in the rock and consisted of two levels, the juice flowing from the upper one to the lower. The tower was a lookout place for the guard, who was to keep out thieves and animals. In some cases, the cultivators employed received a certain portion of the fruits. In other cases, the cultivators paid rent in money or agreed to give the owner a definite amount of the produce, the latter apparently being the case in the illustration. By murdering the son, the heir, they may have thought to seize the vineyard as their own, since the one who planted it was out of the country. In Isaiah 5:1-7 "the vineyard of Jehovah" is said to be "the house of Israel." As shown by the Gospel writers, Jesus quoted Psalm 118:22, 23 as a key to understanding the illustration.

(*27*) *The marriage feast for the king's son* (Mt 22:1-14). As indicated by verse 1, this illustration is a continuation of the discussion that precedes it and is part of Jesus' reply to the question about the authority by which he carried on his work. (Mt 21:23-27) For application, note verses 2 and 14.

Some months before this, Jesus had used a similar illustration concerning a grand evening meal to which many were invited; the invitees then showed preoccupation with other matters and disregard for their would-be host. (Lu 14:16-24) This time, just three days before his death, Jesus speaks not only of unwillingness to come but also of a murderous spirit on the part of some of those invited. Their murder of the king's representatives amounted to rebellion; so the king's armies destroyed the murderers and burned their city. This was a royal wedding, and it is likely that a special garment was provided by the royal host for his guests on an occasion such as this. If so, the failure of one of the guests to be clothed with the marriage garment indicated that he had spurned the garment provided by the king when it was offered to him.

(*28*) *The ten virgins* (Mt 25:1-13). This illustration concerning "the kingdom of the heavens" is part of Jesus' reply to the question of his disciples recorded in Matthew 24:3. The purpose of the illustration is plainly shown in Matthew 25:13.

In those days an important feature of the marriage ceremony was the solemn bringing of the bride from her father's home to the home of her bridegroom or the bridegroom's father. The bridegroom, arrayed in his best attire, would leave his house in the evening for the home of the bride's parents, escorted by his friends. From there, accompanied by musicians and singers and usually by persons bearing lamps, the procession moved toward the home of the bridegroom. The people along the route would take great interest in the procession; some would join it, particularly maids bearing lamps. (Jer 7:34; 16:9; Isa 62:5) The procession might be delayed until late, as there was no particular haste, so that some waiting along the way might get drowsy and fall asleep. The singing and exultation would be heard quite a distance ahead, those hearing it making the cry: "Here is the bridegroom!" Then, after the bridegroom and his entourage had gone into the house and closed the door, it was too late for tardy guests to enter. The lamps carried in the procession burned oil and required frequent refilling.

(*29*) *The talents* (Mt 25:14-30). This illustration about a man who was about to travel abroad was spoken by Jesus to four of his disciples just three days before his death, not long after which he was to ascend to heaven. It, too, is part of Jesus' reply to the question found at Matthew 24:3.—Mr 13:3, 4.

Unlike the illustration of the minas, in which each slave was given just one mina, here the talents are given "to each one according to his own ability." (Lu 19:11-27) The silver talent, which is apparently referred to here, would be as much as a laboring man could earn in 14 years in those days. The slaves should all have been interested in the master's estate and so should have traded diligently and wisely with the master's goods committed to their care. The least they should have done was to deposit the money with the bankers, so that, if they did not themselves want to increase their master's goods, the money would not lie completely idle but would earn interest. But the wicked and sluggish slave hid in the ground the talent committed to him, thereby, in effect, working against his master's interests.

(*30*) *The sheep and the goats* (Mt 25:31-46). As stated in verses 31, 32, 41, 46, what is here illustrated is the separating and judging of the people of the nations when the Son of man arrives in his glory. This illustration is part of Jesus' reply to his disciples' question concerning 'the sign of his presence and the conclusion of the system of things.'—Mt 24:3.

Sheep and goats commonly graze together in the Middle East, and the shepherd easily identifies the two kinds of animals when he wants to separate them. Jesus' reference to goats in this illustration is with no discredit to animals of that kind. (On the annual Day of Atonement the blood of a goat was used to make atonement for sin in behalf of Israel.) So the goats merely represent one class of people, and the sheep represent another class. The "right hand," where the "sheep" are put, is a place of honor. (Ac 2:33; Eph 1:19, 20) The "left," where the "goats" are put, represents a place of dishonor. (Compare Ec 10:2.) Notice that the "sheep," who are put on the right hand of the enthroned Son of man, are shown to be different from Jesus Christ's "brothers," to whom they did acts of kindness.—Mt 25:34-40; Heb 2:11, 12.

The book of Revelation. The book of Revelation concludes the Holy Scriptures with one of the most outstanding concentrations of illustrations found in the entire Bible. As the writer John himself relates, it was presented to him "in signs." (Re 1:1) Therefore, it can truthfully be said that, from beginning to end, the Bible is outstanding for its use of appropriate illustrations.

Illustrations by Christ's disciples. Besides recording the illustrations spoken by Jesus Christ, the Christian Bible writers also made good use of such. In the book of Acts, Luke records the fine illustrations used by the apostle Paul when talking to non-Jews in Athens. Paul referred to objects of devotion with which they were acquainted and to the writings of their own poets. (Ac 17:22-31) As a reading of the letter to the Hebrews will reveal, the same apostle (who is generally credited with writing this letter) freely used illustrations from the history of God's dealing with Israel. To those in Corinth, who were familiar with Greek sports, he likened the Christian course to a race. (1Co 9:24-27) Outstanding is the illustration of the olive tree, with its warning against complacency and its admonition to Christians to perform sacred service to God with their power of reason.—Ro 11:13-32; 12:1, 2.

Jesus' half brother James nicely wove into his writing common circumstances of daily life, referring to a man looking in a mirror, the bridle of

a horse, the rudder of a ship, and so forth, to drive home spiritual truths. (Jas 1:23, 24; 3:3, 4) Peter and Jude drew heavily on earlier inspired writings for incidents to illustrate the message that they were moved by holy spirit to convey. All these fine illustrations, directed by the spirit of God, serve their purpose toward making God's Word the Bible a living book.

ILLYRICUM (Il·lyr'i·cum). A Roman province with varying boundaries that roughly corresponded to what is today western Yugoslavia and part of Albania on the Adriatic Sea.

After three years of fighting, Emperor Tiberius completely subdued the Dalmatians in 9 C.E., and Dalmatia, Iapydia, and Liburnia became the Roman province of Illyricum. The name of the southern portion, Dalmatia, eventually came to designate the entire province.

At Romans 15:19 the apostle Paul speaks of preaching in a circuit "as far as Illyricum." Whether the original Greek is to be understood to mean that Paul actually preached in or merely up to Illyricum cannot be established with certainty.

IMAGE. Any representation or likeness of a person or thing.—Mt 22:20.

Whereas references to images in the Bible frequently relate to idolatry, this is not always the case. God, in creating man, said first, "Let us make man in our image [or, shadow, semblance], according to our likeness." (Ge 1:26, 27, ftn) Since God's Son stated that his Father is "a Spirit," this rules out any physical likeness between God and man. (Joh 4:24) Rather, man has qualities reflecting, or mirroring, those of his heavenly Maker, qualities that positively distinguish man from the animal creation. (See ADAM No. 1.) Though in the image of his Creator, man was not made to be an object of worship, or veneration.

Even as Adam's own son Seth (born to him in his imperfection, however) was in Adam's "likeness, in his image" (Ge 5:3), Adam's likeness to God originally identified him as God's earthly son. (Lu 3:38) Despite man's fall to imperfection, the fact of mankind's originally having been made in God's image was cited after the Noachian Flood as the basis for the divine law authorizing humans to serve as executioners in putting murderers to death. (Ge 9:5, 6; see AVENGER OF BLOOD.) In Christian instructions concerning feminine head covering, Christian men were told they ought not to wear such a covering, since the man "is God's image and glory," while the woman is man's glory.—1Co 11:7.

Has Jesus always reflected his Father's likeness to the same degree?

God's firstborn Son, who later became the man Jesus, is in his Father's image. (2Co 4:4) Inasmuch as that Son was obviously the one to whom God spoke in saying, "Let us make man in *our* image," this likeness of the Son to his Father, the Creator, existed from when the Son was created. (Ge 1:26; Joh 1:1-3; Col 1:15, 16) When on earth as a perfect man, he reflected his Father's qualities and personality to the fullest extent possible within human limitations, so he could say that "he that has seen me has seen the Father also." (Joh 14:9; 5:17, 19, 30, 36; 8:28, 38, 42) This likeness, however, was certainly heightened at the time of Jesus' resurrection to spirit life and his being granted "all authority . . . in heaven and on the earth" by his Father, Jehovah God. (1Pe 3:18; Mt 28:18) Since God then exalted Jesus to "a superior position," God's Son now reflected his Father's glory to an even greater degree than he had before leaving the heavens to come to earth. (Php 2:9; Heb 2:9) He is now "the exact representation of [God's] very being."—Heb 1:2-4.

All anointed members of the Christian congregation are foreordained by God to be "patterned after the image of his Son." (Ro 8:29) Christ Jesus is their model not only in their life pattern, as they follow in his footsteps and imitate his course and ways, but also in their death and resurrection. (1Pe 2:21-24; 1Co 11:1; Ro 6:5) Having borne the earthly "image of the one made of dust [Adam]," as spirit creatures they thereafter bear "the image of the heavenly one [the last Adam, Christ Jesus]." (1Co 15:45, 49) During their earthly life, they are privileged to "reflect like mirrors the glory of Jehovah" that shines to them from God's Son, being progressively transformed into the image conveyed by that glory-reflecting Son. (2Co 3:18; 4:6) God thereby creates in them a new personality, one that is a reflection, or image, of his own divine qualities.—Eph 4:24; Col 3:10.

Improper Use of Images. Whereas humans are to imitate and endeavor to mirror the qualities of their heavenly Father and model their lives after his Son, the veneration of physical images in worship is consistently condemned throughout the Scriptures. God's detestation of such practice was clearly expressed in the Law given to Israel. Not only carved images but the making of the "form" of anything in heaven, on earth, or in the sea as an object of religious worship was prohibited. (Ex 20:4, 5; Le 26:1; Isa 42:8) Such objects might be made of any substance, in any form —wood, metal, stone; carved, cast, hammered, hewn; in the figure of humans, animals, birds, inanimate objects, or just symbolic forms—but none were approved by God for veneration. The making of them was a 'ruinous act,' the committing of evil in Jehovah's eyes, a detestable and offensive thing bringing his curse upon those doing so. (De 4:16-19, 23-25; 27:15; Nu 33:52; Isa 40:19, 20; 44:12, 13; Eze 7:20) The decking of them with gold and silver would not make them less disgusting in God's sight nor prevent their being defiled and discarded as "mere dirt!"—De 7:5, 25; Isa 30:22.

Such use of images is shown to be inexcusable before God, since it goes contrary to all reason and intelligence and betrays foolish, empty-headed reasoning as well as a refusal to acknowledge obvious facts. (Isa 44:14-20; Jer 10:14; Ro 1:20-23) The images would prove to be of no benefit; giving no knowledge, guidance, or protection; being speechless, helpless, and lifeless, an eventual cause for shame. (Isa 44:9-11; 45:20; 46:5-7; Hab 2:18-20) Jehovah's prophetic declarations, accurately foretelling future events, thwarted any efforts of the unfaithful Israelites to attribute the outworking of such events to their idolatrous images.—Isa 48:3-7.

Despite God's clear pronouncements, the Israelites and others foolishly attempted to combine the use of religious images with the worship of the true God, Jehovah. (Ex 32:1-8; 1Ki 12:26-28; 2Ki 17:41; 21:7) A woman in the time of the Judges even sanctified certain silver pieces to Jehovah and then used them in the making of a religious image. (Jg 17:3, 4; 18:14-20, 30, 31) Prior to Jerusalem's destruction by the Babylonians, detestable religious images had been introduced into the temple area, and one such is described as a "symbol of jealousy," evidently referring to the incitement of God's jealousy by giving to an image the praise rightfully belonging to him.—Eze 8:3-12; Ex 20:5.

However, certain objects, formed in the image of plants, flowers, animals, and even cherubs, were made at Jehovah's command and hence were proper. While serving as symbolic representations in connection with God's worship, they themselves were given no veneration, or worship, as in the matter of prayer or sacrifice.—See IDOL, IDOLATRY.

Images in the Book of Daniel. In the second year of Nebuchadnezzar's kingship (evidently counting from the time of his conquest of Jerusalem in 607 B.C.E.), the Babylonian king had a dream, the effect of which greatly disturbed him, producing insomnia. He apparently did not recall the full contents of the dream, for he demanded of his wise men and priests that they reveal both the dream and its interpretation. Despite their boasted ability as revealers of secret things, the Babylonian wise men were unable to fulfill the royal request. This brought upon them the decree of death, and the lives of Daniel and his companions were likewise endangered. By divine help Daniel was able to reveal not only the dream but also its meaning. Daniel's expression of praise and thanksgiving upon receiving the revelation draws attention to Jehovah God as the Source of wisdom and might and as the one who is "changing times and seasons, removing kings and setting up kings." (Da 2:1-23) The dream was clearly the result of God's doing and served to illustrate in a prophetic way God's irresistible dominion over earth's affairs.

Nebuchadnezzar's dream was of an immense image, in human form. The body parts were of metal; from top to bottom, they were made of progressively less valuable but harder metals, beginning with gold and terminating with iron; the feet and toes, however, had clay mixed with the iron. The entire image was crushed to powder by a stone cut out of a mountain, the stone thereafter filling the entire earth.—Da 2:31-35.

What is the meaning of the parts of the dream image seen by Nebuchadnezzar?

The image obviously relates to domination of the earth and Jehovah God's purpose regarding such domination. This is made clear in Daniel's inspired interpretation. The golden head represented Nebuchadnezzar, the one who, by divine permission, had gained power as the dominant world ruler and, more importantly, had overthrown the typical kingdom of Judah. However, in saying, "You yourself are the head of gold," it does not seem that Daniel restricted the head's significance to Nebuchadnezzar alone. Since the other body parts represented kingdoms, the head evidently represented the *dynasty* of Babylonian kings from Nebuchadnezzar down till Babylon's fall in the time of King Nabonidus and his son Belshazzar.—Da 2:37, 38.

The kingdom represented by the silver breasts and arms would therefore be the Medo-Persian power, which overthrew Babylon in 539 B.C.E. It was "inferior" to the Babylonian dynasty but not in the sense of having a smaller area of dominion or of having less strength militarily or economically. Babylon's superiority may therefore relate to its having been the overthrower of the typical kingdom of God at Jerusalem, a distinction not held by Medo-Persia. The Medo-Persian dynasty of world rulers ended with Darius III (Codommanus), whose forces were thoroughly defeated by Alexander the Macedonian in 331 B.C.E. Greece is thus the power depicted by the image's belly and thighs of copper.—Da 2:39.

The Grecian, or Hellenic, dominion continued, though in divided form, until it was finally absorbed by the rising power of Rome. The Roman World Power thus appears in the image symbolized by the baser but harder metal, iron, found in the legs of the great image. Rome's strength to break and crush opposing kingdoms, indicated in the prophecy, is well known in history. (Da 2:40) Yet Rome alone cannot fulfill the requirements of being represented by the image's legs and feet, for the rule of the Roman Empire did not see the completion of the prophetic dream, namely, the coming of the symbolic stone cut out of the mountain as well as its crushing the entire image and thereafter filling the entire earth.

Thus, the expressions of some Bible commentators are much like those of M. F. Unger, who says: "Nebuchadnezzar's dream, as unravelled by Daniel, describes the course and end of 'the times of the Gentiles' (Luke 21:24; Rev. 16:19); that is, of the Gentile world power to be destroyed at the Second Coming of Christ. . . . The ten-toed form will be the condition of Gentile world domination at the time of the returning Smiting Stone (Dan. 2:34, 35). . . . At the first advent of Christ neither the sudden crushing blow took place nor did the ten-toed condition occur." (*Unger's Bible Dictionary*, 1965, p. 516) Daniel himself said to Nebuchadnezzar that the dream had to do with "what is to occur in the final part of the days" (Da 2:28), and since the symbolic stone is shown to represent the Kingdom of God, it may be expected that the domination pictured by the iron legs and feet of the image would extend down to the time of the establishment of that Kingdom and till the time it takes action to "crush and put an end to all these kingdoms."—Da 2:44.

History shows that, although the Roman Empire enjoyed an extension of life in the form of the Holy Roman Empire of the Germanic nation, it eventually gave way to the rising power of its onetime imperial subject, Britain. Because of their close affinity and general unity of action, Britain and the United States today are often referred to as the Anglo-American World Power, the present dominant power in world history.

The mixture of iron and clay in the toes of the great image graphically illustrates the condition due to be manifest in the final expression of political world domination. Clay is elsewhere used metaphorically in the Scriptures to stand for fleshly men, made of the dust of the earth. (Job 10:9; Isa 29:16; Ro 9:20, 21) Daniel's interpretation thus appears to equate the clay with "the offspring of mankind," the mixing in of which produces fragility in that which is symbolized by the image's ten toes. This points to a weakening and a lack of cohesion in the ironlike strength of the final form of world domination by earthly kingdoms. (Da 2:41-43) The common man would wield greater influence in affairs of government. "Ten" being used consistently in the Bible to express completeness (see NUMBER, NUMERAL), the ten toes apparently represent the entire global system of rulership at the time when God's Kingdom is established and takes action against the worldly powers.—Compare Re 17:12-14.

The golden image later set up by Nebuchadnezzar on the Plain of Dura is not directly related to the immense image of the dream. In view of its dimensions—60 cubits (27 m; 88 ft) high and only 6 cubits (2.7 m; 8.8 ft) broad (or a ratio of ten to one)—it does not seem likely to have been a statue in human form, unless it had a very high pedestal, one that was higher than the human statue itself. The human form has a ratio of only four to one as to height and breadth. So the image may have been more symbolic in nature, perhaps like the obelisks of ancient Egypt.—Da 3:1.

The Image of the Wild Beast. After a vision of a seven-headed wild beast that rises out of the sea, the apostle John saw the vision of a two-horned beast ascending out of the earth, speaking like a dragon and telling those who dwell on the earth "to make an image to the [seven-headed] wild beast." (Re 13:1, 2, 11-14) Beasts are consistently used in the Bible as symbols of political governments. The image of the seven-headed wild beast must therefore be some agency reflecting the characteristics and will of the globe-dominating political system represented by the seven-headed wild beast. Logically, it should also have seven heads and ten horns like the wild beast out of the sea that it represents. It is of interest to note, then, that another seven-headed beast, distinct from the wild beast out of the sea, is described at Revelation chapter 17. Its significance, as well as that of both the seven-headed wild beast and the two-horned beast, is considered under BEASTS, SYMBOLIC.

After its first mention in Revelation chapter 13,

the image of the beast is regularly referred to along with the wild beast, particularly in connection with the worship of that wild beast and the receiving of its mark. The image of the beast shares in these things.—Re 14:9-11; 15:2; 16:2; 19:20; 20:4; see MARK, II.

IMAGE OF THE BEAST.   See IMAGE.

IMLAH   (Im'lah) [May [God] Fill; or, May [God] Cause to Reign]. Father of Micaiah, a prophet of Jehovah contemporaneous with Kings Ahab and Jehoshaphat.—1Ki 22:8, 9; 2Ch 18:7, 8.

IMMANUEL   (Im·man'u·el) [With Us Is God]. A name first mentioned by the prophet Isaiah (7:14; 8:8) during the reign of Ahaz (761-746 B.C.E.). In Matthew 1:23, the only other occurrence, Immanuel is a name-title applied to Christ the Messiah.

In view of the circumstances under which the prophecy was given, Bible commentators have looked for an "Immanuel" in Isaiah's day, one who fittingly served then as a sign that 'God was with them.' In that eighth century B.C.E., Pekah and Rezin, the kings of Israel and Syria, were bent on overthrowing Ahaz, king of Judah, in order to put the son of Tabeel upon his throne. (Isa 7:1-6) Jehovah, however, remembered his kingdom covenant with David, the forefather of Ahaz, and sent his prophet with this reassuring message:

"Listen, please, O house of David. . . . Jehovah himself will give you men a sign: Look! The maiden herself will actually become pregnant, and she is giving birth to a son, and she will certainly call his name Immanuel. Butter and honey he will eat by the time that he knows how to reject the bad and choose the good. For before the boy will know how to reject the bad and choose the good, the ground of whose two kings you are feeling a sickening dread will be left entirely."—Isa 7:13-16.

Then, after telling about the birth of Isaiah's second son, Maher-shalal-hash-baz, the prophecy next describes how the threat to Judah would be removed. As an irresistible flood, the Assyrians would completely inundate Syria and the northern kingdom of Israel, not stopping until they had dangerously spread over the land of Judah, even "to fill the breadth of your land, O Immanuel!" Then, in poetic grandeur, the prophet Isaiah warns all those in opposition to Jehovah: If you gird yourselves for war, if you plan out a scheme, if you speak a word against Jehovah—"it will not stand, for *God is with us* [Immanuel]!" —Isa 8:5-10.

Some have suggested that in the type back there "Immanuel" was a third son of Isaiah, perhaps by a Jewish maiden who may have become a second wife of the prophet. Certain Jewish commentators endeavored to apply the prophecy to the birth of Ahaz' son Hezekiah. This, however, is ruled out, since the prophecy was uttered during Ahaz' reign (Isa 7:1), making Hezekiah at least nine years old at the time.—2Ki 16:2; 18:1, 2.

Another possible candidate was Isaiah's second son, mentioned in the next chapter, Maher-shalal-hash-baz, concerning whom it was said: "Before the boy will know how to call out, 'My father!' and 'My mother!' one will carry away the resources of Damascus and the spoil of Samaria before the king of Assyria." (Isa 8:1-4) Certainly this echoes what was said about Immanuel: "Before the boy will know how to reject the bad and choose the good, the ground of whose two kings [of Damascus and Samaria] you are feeling a sickening dread will be left entirely." (Isa 7:16) Also, the birth of Isaiah's second son is presented in close connection with the further prophecy involving Immanuel and, as Immanuel was to be a "sign," so also Isaiah said: "I and the children whom Jehovah has given me are as *signs.*"—Isa 7:14; 8:18.

The principal objection to this identification of Isaiah's second son as the Immanuel of Ahaz' day is on the grounds that Isaiah's wife is spoken of as "the prophetess," not as "the maiden," as well as the fact that she was already the mother of Isaiah's firstborn, Shear-jashub, hence no "maiden." (Isa 7:3; 8:3) It may be noted, however, that the Hebrew word here translated "maiden" is not *bethu·lah'*, meaning, specifically, "virgin," but is *'al·mah'*, having a broader reference to a young woman, who could be either a virgin maiden or a recently married woman. The singular *'al·mah'* also occurs in six other texts, more than one of which involves a virgin maiden.—Ge 24:43 (compare vs 16); Ex 2:8; Ps 68:25; Pr 30:19; Ca 1:3; 6:8.

The full and complete identity of Immanuel, of course, is found in the office and personage of the Lord Jesus Christ. The use, therefore, of the Hebrew word *'al·mah'* in the prophecy would accommodate both the type (if such was a young wife of Ahaz or of Isaiah) and the antitype (the betrothed and yet virgin Mary). In the case of Mary there was no question about her being a virgin when she became "pregnant by holy spirit," both Matthew and Luke recording this historical fact. (Mt 1:18-25; Lu 1:30-35) "All this actu-

ally came about for that to be fulfilled which was spoken by Jehovah through his prophet," Matthew observed. It was a *sign* that identified the long-awaited Messiah. So in keeping with these facts, Matthew's Gospel (quoting Isa 7:14) uses the Greek word *par·the'nos,* meaning "virgin," to translate *'al·mah',* saying: "Look! The virgin [*par·the'nos*] will become pregnant and will give birth to a son, and they will call his name Immanuel." (Mt 1:22, 23) In no way was this taking liberties or distorting the text. Over a century earlier, the Jewish translators of the Greek *Septuagint* had also used *par·the'nos* in rendering Isaiah 7:14.

This identity of Jesus Christ as Immanuel did not mean he was the incarnation of God, 'God in the flesh,' which proponents of the Trinity teaching claim is implied by the meaning of Immanuel, namely, "With Us Is God." It was a common practice among Jews to embody the word "God," even "Jehovah," in Hebrew names. Even today Immanuel is the proper name of many men; none of whom are incarnations of God.

If there seems to be a conflict between the angel's instructions to Mary ("you are to call his name Jesus") and Isaiah's prophecy ("she will certainly call his name Immanuel"), let it be remembered that Messiah was also to be called by yet other names. (Lu 1:31; Isa 7:14) For example, Isaiah 9:6 said concerning this one: "His name will be called Wonderful Counselor, Mighty God, Eternal Father, Prince of Peace." Yet none of these names were given to Mary's firstborn as personal names, neither when he was a babe nor after he took up his ministry. Rather, they were all prophetic title-names by which Messiah would be identified. Jesus lived up to the meaning of these names in every respect, and that is the sense in which they were prophetically given, to show his qualities and the good offices he would perform toward all those accepting him as Messiah. So also with his title Immanuel. He measured up to and fulfilled its meaning.

Worshipers of Jehovah have always desired God to be with them, on their side, backing them up in their undertakings, and often he reassures them that he is, sometimes giving them visible signs to this effect. (Ge 28:10-20; Ex 3:12; Jos 1:5, 9; 5:13–6:2; Ps 46:5-7; Jer 1:19) If today the personal identity of Immanuel in the days of Ahaz remains uncertain, it may be that Jehovah so directed in order not to distract the attention of later generations from the Greater Immanuel, when he put in his appearance as a sign from heaven. With the coming of his beloved Son to earth as the promised Messianic "seed" (Ge 3:15) and rightful heir to the throne of David, Jehovah was furnishing his greatest sign that he had not forsaken mankind or his Kingdom covenant. The title-name Immanuel, therefore, was particularly appropriate to Christ, for his presence was indeed a sign from heaven. And with this foremost representative of Jehovah among mankind, Matthew under inspiration could truly say, "With Us Is God."

IMMER (Im'mer).

1. A descendant of Aaron designated head of the 16th priestly division in David's time. (1Ch 24:1, 6, 14) Apparently 1,052 of his descendants returned with Zerubbabel from Babylon in 537 B.C.E. (Ezr 2:37; Ne 7:40) Two of "the sons of Immer" were among those putting away their foreign wives in Ezra's time.—Ezr 10:20, 44.

2. Father of Meshillemith (or Meshillemoth); possibly the same as No. 1.—1Ch 9:12; Ne 11:13.

3. Father of the priest Pashhur, an opposer of Jeremiah who had the prophet put in stocks. Jeremiah prophesied that Pashhur and all his house would be taken to Babylon. (Jer 20:1, 2, 6) If the designation "the son of Immer" is to be understood as denoting a descendant rather than an actual son, this Immer may be No. 1.

4. Father of Zadok, one who shared in repairing Jerusalem's wall. (Ne 3:29) This Immer may, however, be the same as No. 1, if the designation "the son of Immer" is to be regarded as meaning a descendant.

5. Seemingly a place in Babylonia from which certain priests returned who were unable to prove their genealogy.—Ezr 2:59; Ne 7:61.

IMMERSION. See BAPTISM.

IMMORTALITY.

The Greek word *a·tha·na·si'a* is formed by the negative prefix *a* followed by a form of the word for "death" (*tha'na·tos*). Thus, the basic meaning is "deathlessness," and refers to the quality of life that is enjoyed, its endlessness and indestructibility. (1Co 15:53, 54, ftn; 1Ti 6:16, ftn) The Greek word *a·phthar·si'a*, meaning "incorruption," refers to that which cannot decay or be corrupted, that which is imperishable.—Ro 2:7; 1Co 15:42, 50, 53; Eph 6:24; 2Ti 1:10.

The expressions "immortal" or "immortality" do not occur in the Hebrew Scriptures, which do show, however, that Jehovah God, as the Source of all life, is not subject to death, hence, is immortal. (Ps 36:7, 9; 90:1, 2; Hab 1:12) This fact is also emphatically stated by the Christian apostle Paul in referring to God as "the King of eternity, incorruptible."—1Ti 1:17.

As the article SOUL shows, the Hebrew Scriptures also make plain that man is not inherently immortal. References to the human soul (Heb., *ne'phesh*) as dying, heading for the grave, and being destroyed are numerous. (Ge 17:14; Jos 10:32; Job 33:22; Ps 22:29; 78:50; Eze 18:4, 20) The Christian Greek Scriptures, of course, are in harmony and likewise contain references to the death of the soul (Gr., *psy·khe'*). (Mt 26:38; Mr 3:4; Ac 3:23; Jas 5:20; Re 8:9; 16:3) Therefore the Christian Greek Scriptures do not dispute or alter the inspired teaching of the Hebrew Scriptures that man, the human soul, is mortal, subject to death. The Christian Greek Scriptures, however, do contain the revelation of God's purpose to grant immortality to certain of his servants.

How can Jesus be "the one alone having immortality"?

The first one described in the Bible as rewarded with the gift of immortality is Jesus Christ. That he did not possess immortality before his resurrection by God is seen from the inspired apostle's words at Romans 6:9: "Christ, now that he has been raised up from the dead, dies no more; death is master over him no more." (Compare Re 1:17, 18.) For this reason, when describing him as "the King of those who rule as kings and Lord of those who rule as lords," 1 Timothy 6:15, 16 shows that Jesus is distinct from all such other kings and lords in that he is "the one alone having immortality." The other kings and lords, because of being mortal, die, even as did also the high priests of Israel. The glorified Jesus, God's appointed High Priest after the order of Melchizedek, however, has "an *indestructible* life."—Heb 7:15-17, 23-25.

The word "indestructible" here translates the Greek term *a·ka·ta'ly·tos*, meaning, literally, "indissoluble." (Heb 7:16, ftn) The word is a compound of the negative prefix *a* joined to other words relating to a "loosening down," as in Jesus' statement regarding the loosening down or throwing down of the stones of the temple at Jerusalem (Mt 24:1, 2), as well as in Paul's reference to the loosening down of the earthly "tent" of Christians, that is, the dissolving of their earthly life in human bodies. (2Co 5:1) Thus, the immortal life granted Jesus upon his resurrection is not merely endless but is *beyond* deterioration or dissolution and is *beyond* destruction.

Kingdom Heirs Granted Immortality. For the anointed Christians called to reign with Christ in the heavens (1Pe 1:3, 4), the promise is that they share with Christ in the likeness of his resurrection. (Ro 6:5) Thus, as in the case of their Lord and Head, the anointed members of the Christian congregation who die faithful receive a resurrection to immortal spirit life, so that "this which is mortal puts on immortality." (1Co 15:50-54) As with Jesus, immortality in their case does not mean simply everlasting life, or mere freedom from death. That they, too, are granted "the power of an indestructible life" as fellow heirs with Christ is seen from the apostle Paul's association of incorruptibility with the immortality they attain. (1Co 15:42-49) Over them "the second death has no authority."—Re 20:6; see INCORRUPTION.

This grant of immortality to the Kingdom heirs is all the more remarkable, in view of the fact that even God's angels are shown to be mortal, despite their possessing spirit bodies, not carnal ones. Angelic mortality is evident in view of the judgment of death entered against the spirit son who became God's Adversary, or Satan, and also against those other angels who followed that satanic course and "did not keep their original position but forsook their own proper dwelling place." (Jude 6; Mt 25:41; Re 20:10, 14) So the grant of "indestructible life" (Heb 7:16) or "indissoluble life" to those Christians who gain the privilege of reigning with God's Son in the heavenly Kingdom marvelously demonstrates God's confidence in them.—See HEAVEN (The way to heavenly life); LIFE.

IMNA (Im'na) [[God] Has Held Back (Withheld)]. Son of Helem; a valiant, mighty man and head of a paternal house of the tribe of Asher. —1Ch 7:35, 40.

IMNAH (Im'nah) [May [God] Appoint (or, Number); [God] Has Appointed (or, Numbered)].

1. First-named son of Asher and forefather of the Imnites.—Ge 46:17; Nu 26:44; 1Ch 7:30.

2. The Levite whose son Kore was the gatekeeper to the east in temple service, in charge of the voluntary offerings of Jehovah, in Hezekiah's time.—2Ch 31:14.

IMNITES (Im'nites) [Of (Belonging to) Imnah]. A family of the tribe of Asher descended from Imnah.—Nu 26:44.

IMPALEMENT (im·pale'ment). In the literal sense, the fastening of a victim either dead or alive to a stake, or pole. The execution of Jesus Christ is the best-known case. (Lu 24:20; Joh 19:14-16; Ac 2:23, 36) Impalements by nations in ancient times were carried out in a variety of ways.

The Assyrians, noted for their savage warfare, impaled captives by hanging their nude bodies atop pointed stakes that were run up through the abdomens into the chest cavities of the victims. Several reliefs have been found on monuments, one such depicting the Assyrian assault and conquest of Lachish, on which this method of impalement is shown.—2Ki 19:8; PICTURE, Vol. 1, p. 958.

The Persians also used impalement as a form of punishment. Some say the Persians customarily first beheaded or flayed those they impaled. Darius the Great forbade interference with the rebuilding of the Jerusalem temple, and any violator of that decree was to be impaled (literally, raised up) on a timber pulled out of his own house. (Ezr 6:11) During the reign of Darius' son, Ahasuerus (Xerxes I), two of the palace doorkeepers were hanged, or impaled, on a stake, the usual punishment meted out to traitors by the Persians. (Es 2:21-23) Haman and his ten sons were similarly hanged on a stake. (Es 5:14; 6:4; 7:9, 10; 9:10, 13, 14, 25) Herodotus (III, 125, 159; IV, 43) also cites other examples of Persian impalements.

It was Jewish law that those guilty of such heinous crimes as blasphemy or idolatry were first killed by stoning, by beheading, or by some other method, and then their dead bodies were exposed on stakes, or trees, as warning examples to others. (De 21:22, 23; Jos 8:29; 10:26; 2Sa 21:6, 9) The Egyptians may also have first killed their criminals before fastening them to stakes, as is indicated by Joseph's prophetic words to Pharaoh's chief baker: "Pharaoh will lift up your head from off you *and* will certainly hang you upon a stake."—Ge 40:19, 22; 41:13.

The Greeks and Romans, it is said, adopted the practice of impalement from the Phoenicians, and not until the days of Constantine was it abolished in the empire. Very seldom was a Roman citizen impaled, for this was a punishment usually given slaves and criminals of the lowest sort. Impalement was looked upon by both Jews and Romans as a symbol of humiliation and shame, reserved for those accursed.—De 21:23; Ga 3:13; Php 2:8.

In the first century, if the Jews had the right to impale a person for religious reasons (a point on which there is some doubt), it is quite certain they could not do so for civil offenses; only a Roman official like Pontius Pilate had such authority. (Joh 18:31; 19:10) Nevertheless, the Jews, and especially their chief priests and rulers, bore the prime responsibility for Christ's impalement. —Mr 15:1-15; Ac 2:36; 4:10; 5:30; 1Co 2:8.

The Romans sometimes tied the victim to the

stake, in which case he might live for several days before his physical endurance was overcome by the torture of pain, thirst, hunger, and exposure to the sun. As in the case of Jesus, nailing the hands (and likely the feet also) of the accused to a stake was customary among the Romans. (Joh 20:25, 27; Lu 24:39; Ps 22:16, ftn; Col 2:14) Since the wrists have always been considered by anatomists as part of the hands, some medical men think the nails were driven between the small bones of the wrists to prevent the stripping out that could have occurred if they had been driven through the palms. (See *The Journal of the American Medical Association,* March 21, 1986, p. 1460.) This would be consistent with the Bible's own use of the word "hand" to include the wrist in such texts as Genesis 24:47, where bracelets are said to be worn on the "hands," and Judges 15:14, where reference is made to fetters that were on Samson's "hands."

The record does not say whether the evildoers impaled alongside Jesus were nailed or simply tied to the stakes. If only tied, this might explain why, when Jesus was found dead, they were still alive and had to have their legs broken. (Joh 19:32, 33) Death by suffocation soon followed the breaking of their legs, since, as some think, this would have prevented the raising of the body to ease tension of chest muscles. Of course, this is not a conclusive point on why the evildoers outlived Jesus, for they had not experienced the mental and physical torture inflicted on Jesus. He had previously undergone an all-night ordeal at the hands of his enemies, in addition to being beaten by the Roman soldiers, perhaps to the point that he could not carry his own torture stake, as was the custom.—Mr 14:32–15:21; Lu 22:39–23:26.

What does the original Greek reveal as to the shape of the instrument on which Jesus was put to death?

Most Bible translations say Christ was "crucified" rather than "impaled." This is because of the common belief that the torture instrument upon which he was hung was a "cross" made of two pieces of wood instead of a single pale, or stake. Tradition, not the Scriptures, also says that the condemned man carried only the crossbeam of the cross, called the *patibulum,* or *antenna,* instead of both parts. In this way some try to avoid the predicament of having too much weight for one man to drag or carry to Golgotha.

Yet, what did the Bible writers themselves say about these matters? They used the Greek noun *stau·ros'* 27 times and the verbs *stau·ro'o* 46 times, *syn·stau·ro'o* (the prefix *syn,* meaning "with") 5 times, and *a·na·stau·ro'o* (*a·na',* meaning "again") once. They also used the Greek word *xy'lon,* meaning "wood," 5 times to refer to the torture instrument upon which Jesus was nailed.

Stau·ros' in both the classical Greek and Koine carries no thought of a "cross" made of two timbers. It means only an upright stake, pale, pile, or pole, as might be used for a fence, stockade, or palisade. Says Douglas' *New Bible Dictionary* of 1985 under "Cross," page 253: "The Gk. word for 'cross' (*stauros;* verb *stauroo . . .*) means primarily an upright stake or beam, and secondarily a stake used as an instrument for punishment and execution."

The fact that Luke, Peter, and Paul also used *xy'lon* as a synonym for *stau·ros'* gives added evidence that Jesus was impaled on an upright stake without a crossbeam, for that is what *xy'lon* in this special sense means. (Ac 5:30; 10:39; 13:29; Ga 3:13; 1Pe 2:24) *Xy'lon* also occurs in the Greek *Septuagint* at Ezra 6:11, where it speaks of a single beam or timber on which a lawbreaker was to be impaled.

The *New World Translation,* therefore, faithfully conveys to the reader this basic idea of the Greek text by rendering *stau·ros'* as "torture stake," and the verb *stau·ro'o* as "impale," that is, to fasten on a stake, or pole. In this way there is no confusion of *stau·ros'* with the traditional ecclesiastical crosses. (See TORTURE STAKE.) The matter of one man like Simon of Cyrene bearing a torture stake, as the Scriptures say, is perfectly reasonable, for if it was 15 cm (6 in.) in diameter and 3.5 m (11 ft) long, it probably weighed little more than 45 kg (100 lb).—Mr 15:21.

Note what W. E. Vine says on this subject: "STAUROS (σταυρός) denotes, primarily, an upright pale or stake. On such malefactors were nailed for execution. Both the noun and the verb *stauroo,* to fasten to a stake or pale, are originally to be distinguished from the ecclesiastical form of a two beamed cross." Greek scholar Vine then mentions the Chaldean origin of the two-piece cross and how it was adopted from the pagans by Christendom in the third century C.E. as a symbol of Christ's impalement.—*Vine's Expository Dictionary of Old and New Testament Words,* 1981, Vol. 1, p. 256.

Significant is this comment in the book *The Cross in Ritual, Architecture, and Art:* "It is strange, yet unquestionably a fact, that in ages long before the birth of Christ, and since then in lands untouched by the teaching of the Church, the Cross has been used as a sacred symbol. . . . The Greek Bacchus, the Tyrian Tammuz, the Chaldean Bel, and the Norse Odin, were all symbolised to their votaries by a cruciform device."—By G. S. Tyack, London, 1900, p. 1.

The book *The Non-Christian Cross,* by J. D. Parsons (London, 1896), adds: "There is not a single sentence in any of the numerous writings forming the New Testament, which, in the original Greek, bears even indirect evidence to the effect that the stauros used in the case of Jesus was other than an ordinary stauros; much less to the effect that it consisted, not of one piece of timber, but of two pieces nailed together in the form of a cross. . . . It is not a little misleading upon the part of our teachers to translate the word stauros as 'cross' when rendering the Greek documents of the Church into our native tongue, and to support that action by putting 'cross' in our lexicons as the meaning of stauros without carefully explaining that that was at any rate not the primary meaning of the word in the days of the Apostles, did not become its primary signification till long afterwards, and became so then, if at all, only because, despite the absence of corroborative evidence, it was for some reason or other assumed that the particular stauros upon which Jesus was executed had that particular shape."—Pp. 23, 24; see also *The Companion Bible,* 1974, Appendix No. 162.

Figurative Usage. Not only do the Scriptures bear thorough witness concerning the physical impalement of the Lord Jesus Christ (1Co 1:13, 23; 2:2; 2Co 13:4; Re 11:8) but they also speak of impalement in a figurative, metaphoric sense, as at Galatians 2:20. Christians have put their old personality to death through faith in the impaled Christ. (Ro 6:6; Col 3:5, 9, 10) "Moreover, those who belong to Christ Jesus impaled the flesh together with its passions and desires," Paul writes, adding that through Christ "the world has been impaled to me and I to the world."—Ga 5:24; 6:14.

Apostates in effect "impale the Son of God afresh for themselves and expose him to public shame," doing so by their Judaslike rebellion against God's arrangement for salvation.—Heb 6:4-6.

IMPARTIALITY.
Freedom from bias or favoritism; fairness. Impartiality is a matter of not letting position, ability to speak well, wealth, a bribe, or, on the other hand, sentimentality for a poor or otherwise disadvantaged person sway one's judgment or actions in favor of the individual. Impartiality sees that all are treated in harmony with what is fair and just, according to what each deserves and needs.—Pr 3:27.

The Hebrew expression *na·sa'' pa·nim',* rendered 'treat with partiality,' literally means "lift up the face." (Le 19:15) An Oriental way of greeting was to bow humbly and turn one's face to the ground. As a sign of acknowledgment and recognition, the one greeted lifted up, or raised, the face of the one who had bowed. (Compare Ge 32: 20, where "give a kindly reception" renders the Hebrew phrase literally meaning "lift up the face.") The expression came to be used disparagingly when referring to corrupt preferential treatment. The Hebrew phrase *na·khar' pa·nim'* (rendered "be partial," but literally meaning "recognize the face") was similarly used. (De 1:17; 16:19) The Greek expression *lam·ba'no pro'so·pon* ('show partiality'; literally, "take or accept the face") is modeled on the Hebrew. (Lu 20:21; compare *Int.*) Compounded forms of these two verbs are rendered "partiality; favoritism" (Ro 2:11; Jas 2:1), 'show favoritism' (Jas 2:9), and "partial" (Ac 10:34).—Compare *Int.*

Jehovah Impartial. Jehovah says that he "treats none with partiality nor accepts a bribe." (De 10:17; 2Ch 19:7) The apostle Peter said, when God sent him to declare the good news to the uncircumcised Gentile Cornelius: "For a certainty I perceive that God is not partial, but in every nation the man that fears him and works righteousness is acceptable to him."—Ac 10:34, 35; Ro 2:10, 11.

Jehovah, the Creator and Supreme One, cannot be challenged on his decisions and actions. He can do as he pleases with what he has created and does not owe anyone anything. (Ro 9:20-24; 11:33-36; Job 40:2) He deals with individuals or groups, even nations, according to his purpose and his own appointed time. (Ac 17:26, 31) Nevertheless, God is impartial. He rewards each person, not according to his outward appearance or possessions, but according to what he is and what he does. (1Sa 16:7; Ps 62:12; Pr 24:12) His Son Jesus Christ follows the same impartial course.—Mt 16:27.

Not partial toward Israel. Some persons have held that Jehovah dealt partially by using and favoring Israel as his people of ancient times. However, an honest examination of his dealings with Israel will reveal that such a charge is erroneous. Jehovah chose and dealt with Israel, not because of their greatness and numbers, but because of his love and appreciation for the faith and loyalty of his friend Abraham, their forefather. (Jas 2:23) Also, he was long-suffering toward them because he had placed his name upon them. (De 7:7-11; Eze 36:22; De 29:13; Ps 105:8-10) While obedient, Israel was blessed above the nations not having the Law. When Israel was disobedient, God was patient and merciful, but he punished them, nevertheless. And though their position was a favored one, they were under weightier responsibility before God because of bearing God's name and because they were under the Law. For the Law carried curses against the one breaking it. It is written: "Cursed is the one who will not put the words of this law in force by doing them." (De 27:26) The Jews, by violating the Law, came under this curse, which was in addition to their condemnation as offspring of sinful Adam. (Ro 5:12) Therefore, to redeem the Jews from this special disability, Christ not only had to die but also had to die on a torture stake, as the apostle Paul argues at Galatians 3:10-13.

Thus, God exercised no partiality toward Israel. God was using Israel with the blessing of all nations in view. (Ga 3:14) By this means God was actually working toward the benefit of people of all nations in his due time. In harmony with this, the apostle remarks: "Is he the God of the Jews only? Is he not also of people of the nations? Yes, of people of the nations also, if truly God is one, who will declare circumcised people righteous as a result of faith and uncircumcised people righteous by means of their faith." (Ro 3:29, 30) Furthermore, in the ancient Jewish commonwealth, men from other nations could come under God's favor and blessing by worshiping Jehovah the God of Israel and keeping his law, as did the Gibeonites, the Nethinim (meaning "Given Ones"), and many alien residents.—Jos 9:3, 27; 1Ki 8:41-43; Ezr 8:20; Nu 9:14.

Although patient and merciful, repeatedly receiving Israel back when they repented, Jehovah finally cast them off as his name people. (Lu 13:35; Ro 11:20-22) The apostle's statement applies here: "He will render to each one according to his works: . . . wrath and anger, tribulation and distress, upon the soul of every man who works what is injurious, of the Jew first and also of the Greek; but glory and honor and peace for everyone who works what is good, for the Jew first and also for the Greek. For there is no partiality with God."—Ro 2:6-11.

So, while a superficial, short-range view of God's dealings might appear to reveal partiality, the deeper, long-range view brings to light marvelous impartiality and justice beyond anything man could have conceived. How finely he worked out matters so that all mankind would have opportunity to receive his favor and life!—Isa 55:8-11; Ro 11:33.

Not partial toward David. As Jehovah told Moses, he is a God who will by no means give exemption from punishment for wrongdoing. (Ex 34:6, 7; Col 3:25) Even in the case of his beloved servant David, with whom Jehovah had made a covenant for the kingdom, God made no exception. He punished David severely for his sins. After David's sin against God in the affair involving Bath-sheba and her husband Uriah, Jehovah told him: "Here I am raising up against you calamity out of your own house; and I will take your wives under your own eyes and give them to your fellowman, and he will certainly lie down with your wives under the eyes of this sun. Whereas you yourself acted in secret, I, for my part, shall do this thing in front of all Israel and in front of the sun."—2Sa 12:11, 12.

The Bible account reveals that David indeed suffered much trouble from his own family. (2Sa chaps 13-18; 1Ki 1) While God did not put him to death, out of respect for the kingdom covenant He had made with David (2Sa 7:11-16), David did suffer very great sorrows. As an earlier servant of God, Elihu, had said: "There is One who has not shown partiality to princes." (Job 34:19) However, based on the coming sacrifice of Jesus Christ, God could forgive the repentant David and yet maintain His own justice and righteousness. (Ro 3:25, 26) Through the sacrifice of his Son, God has a just and impartial basis on which to undo the death of Uriah and others, so that, ultimately, none suffer unjustly.—Ac 17:31.

Counsel to Judges. Jehovah gave strong counsel to the judges in Israel as to impartiality. Judges were under the strict command: "You must not be partial in judgment." (De 1:17; 16:19; Pr 18:5; 24:23) They were not to show partiality to a poor man merely because of his poorness, out of sentimentality or out of prejudice against the wealthy. Neither were they to favor a rich man because of his wealth, perhaps catering to him for favor, for a bribe, or through fear of his power or influence. (Le 19:15) God eventually condemned the unfaithful Levitical priesthood in Israel for violation of his law and, as he particularly pointed out, for showing partiality, since they acted as judges in the land.—Mal 2:8, 9.

In the Christian Congregation.

In the Christian congregation impartiality is a law; the showing of favoritism is a sin. (Jas 2:9) Those guilty of acts of favoritism become "judges rendering wicked decisions." (Jas 2:1-4) Such persons do not have the wisdom from above, which is free from partial distinctions. (Jas 3:17) Those in responsible positions in the congregation are under the serious obligation the apostle Paul placed on Timothy, an overseer: "I solemnly charge you before God and Christ Jesus and the chosen angels to keep these things without prejudgment, doing nothing according to a biased leaning." This would apply especially when judicial hearings are being conducted in the congregation.—1Ti 5:19-21.

'Admiring personalities for own benefit.' Violation of the principle of impartiality can result in the severest condemnation. Jesus' half brother Jude describes men who are "murmurers, complainers about their lot in life, proceeding according to their own desires, and their mouths speak swelling things, while they are *admiring personalities* for the sake of their own benefit." (Jude 16) These men are called "the ones that make separations, animalistic men, not having spirituality." (Jude 19) Such ones may sway others by their swelling words and their admiration of personalities, like the ones Paul describes who "slyly work their way into households and lead as their captives weak women loaded down with sins, led by various desires." (2Ti 3:6) Destruction awaits them.—Jude 12, 13.

"Worthy of double honor"—How? In view of these things, how can those in the Christian congregation reckon the older men who preside in a fine way "worthy of double honor, especially those who work hard in speaking and teaching"? (1Ti 5:17) This is, not because of the personalities of these men or their ability, but because of their diligence and hard work at the extra responsibilities placed upon them. God's arrangements and appointments are to be respected. Such men should receive special cooperation and support in getting the work of God's congregation accomplished. (Heb 13:7, 17) James the half brother of Jesus points out that teachers in the congregation are under weighty responsibility to God, receiving heavier judgment. (Jas 3:1) Therefore they deserve to be heard, obeyed, and given honor. For a similar reason the wife should honor and respect her husband, who is charged by God with responsibility for the household and is judged by Him accordingly. (Eph 5:21-24, 33) Such respect for men placed in responsible positions by God's arrangement is not partiality.

Respect for rulers. Christians are also told to respect rulers of human governments. This is not because of the personal qualities of these men, some of whom may be corrupt, nor is it because they may be in position to grant special favors. Christians respect rulers because God commands it; also because of the position of responsibility the office stands for. The apostle says: "Let every soul be in subjection to the superior authorities, for there is no authority except by God; the existing authorities stand placed in their relative positions by God. Therefore he who opposes the authority has taken a stand against the arrangement of God." (Ro 13:1, 2) These men, if they misuse their authority, must answer to God. The honor, or respect, due the office is rendered to the one filling that office by the Christian according to the rule: "Render to all their dues, to him who calls for the tax, the tax; to him who calls for the tribute, the tribute; to him who calls for fear, such fear; to him who calls for honor, such honor." (Ro 13:7) The honor rendered in this particular respect by the Christian above that accorded to ordinary citizens is not a showing of partiality.

IMRAH (Im′rah) [He Rebels]. Son of Zophah; a paternal head and also a head of chieftains of the tribe of Asher, a valiant, mighty man.—1Ch 7:36, 40.

IMRI (Im′ri) [shortened form of Amariah, meaning "Jehovah Has Said"].

1. Son of Bani of the tribe of Judah through Perez.—1Ch 9:4.

2. Father of the Zaccur who shared in rebuilding the wall of Jerusalem.—Ne 3:2.

INAUGURATION (in·au·gu·ra′tion). An initiation, with solemn ceremonies, of a structure, an arrangement, or a place. "Inaugurate" is translated from the Hebrew verb *cha·nakh′* (noun form, *chanuk·kah′*) and from the Greek verb *en·kai·ni′zo*, which primarily means "make new, or innovate," as by dedication. The Hebrew word *ne′zer*, the holy sign of dedication, is considered under the subject DEDICATION.

When the Mosaic Law covenant was put into operation, it was solemnly initiated by suitable ceremonies involving animal sacrifices and the sprinkling of blood on the altar, on the book, and on the people. This event was referred to by the apostle Paul as the act of inaugurating that covenant.—Ex 24:4-8; Heb 9:18-20.

By Paul's words "neither was the former covenant inaugurated [form of Gr. *en·kai·ni'zo*] without blood" (Heb 9:18), he indicates that the new covenant was similarly put into effect—inaugurated by Jesus' death, resurrection, and ascension into heaven, where Jesus presented the value of his human life and from where he thereafter poured out holy spirit upon his disciples. Since Jesus Christ was resurrected in the spirit, he could actually enter into the real "holy place," the heavens of Jehovah's presence, and with his ransom sacrifice make it possible for his anointed followers to enter also into heaven. Thus it could be said that he began, innovated, or inaugurated the way into the heavens, which provision would thereafter be used by others.—Heb 10:19, 20.

We also read of solemn ceremonies involving the offerings by the tribal chieftains at the inauguration of the tabernacle altar in the wilderness. (Nu 7:10, 11, 84-88) There was a special assembly for the inauguration of Solomon's temple and its great sacrificial altar.—1Ki 8:63; 2Ch 7:5, 9.

When the temple was rebuilt under Zerubbabel following the Babylonian exile, there were solemn initiation ceremonies in which hundreds of animals were sacrificed. (Ezr 6:16, 17) Later, the walls around the rebuilt Jerusalem were restored under the direction of Nehemiah, and again an elaborate inauguration festival was held, with two large thanksgiving choirs participating in the praising of Jehovah.—Ne 12:27-43.

In addition to these impressive national ceremonies of inauguration, we read of a man inaugurating, or initiating, his house (De 20:5), and the superscription of Psalm 30, ascribed to David, designates it as "A song of inauguration of the house."

When Nebuchadnezzar completed the erection of the huge image of gold on the Plain of Dura, he called together all the satraps, prefects, governors, counselors, treasurers, judges, police magistrates, and all administrators of the jurisdictional districts for the impressive ceremonies of inauguration. Nebuchadnezzar thus hoped to unite all his subjects in worship. The three young Hebrews present at this affair refused to compromise their worship of Jehovah by participating in this national religion.—Da 3:1-30.

To this day the Jews annually celebrate what they call Hanukkah in the month of December. This is in remembrance of the inauguration (Heb., *chanuk·kah'*) festival that followed the cleansing of the temple by Judas Maccabaeus in 165 B.C.E. after it had been polluted by Antiochus IV Epiphanes.—Joh 10:22; see FESTIVAL OF DEDICATION.

INCENSE. A compound of aromatic gums and balsams that will burn slowly, giving off a fragrant aroma. The Hebrew words *qeto'reth* and *qetoh·rah'* are from the root *qa·tar'*, meaning "make sacrificial smoke." The equivalent in the Christian Greek Scriptures is *thy·mi'a·ma.*

The sacred incense prescribed for use in the wilderness tabernacle was made of costly materials that the congregation contributed. (Ex 25:1, 2, 6; 35:4, 5, 8, 27-29) In giving the divine formula for this fourfold mixture, Jehovah said to Moses: "Take to yourself perfumes: stacte drops and onycha and perfumed galbanum and pure frankincense. There should be the same portion of each. And you must make it into an incense, a spice mixture, the work of an ointment maker, salted, pure, something holy. And you must pound some of it into fine powder and put some of it before the Testimony in the tent of meeting, where I shall present myself to you. It should be most holy to you people." Then, to impress upon them the exclusiveness and holiness of the incense, Jehovah added: "Whoever makes any like it to enjoy its smell must be cut off from his people."—Ex 30:34-38; 37:29.

At a later time the rabbinic Jews added other ingredients to the temple incense, Josephus saying it was made of 13 sweet-smelling spices. (*The Jewish War*, V, 218 [v, 5]) According to Maimonides, some of these extra items included amber, cassia, cinnamon, myrrh, saffron, and spikenard.

At the W end of the Holy compartment of the tabernacle, next to the curtain dividing it off from the Most Holy, was located "the altar of incense." (Ex 30:1; 37:25; 40:5, 26, 27) There was also a similar incense altar in Solomon's temple. (1Ch 28:18; 2Ch 2:4) Upon these altars, every morning and evening the sacred incense was burned. (Ex 30:7, 8; 2Ch 13:11) Once a year on the Day of Atonement coals from the altar were taken in a censer, or fire holder, together with two handfuls of incense, into the Most Holy, where the incense was made to smoke before the mercy seat of the ark of the testimony.—Le 16:12, 13.

High Priest Aaron initially offered the incense upon the altar. (Ex 30:7) However, his son Eleazar was given oversight of the incense and other tabernacle items. (Nu 4:16) It appears that the burning of incense, except on the Day of Atonement, was not restricted to the high priest, as underpriest Zechariah (father of John the Baptizer) is mentioned as handling this service. (Lu 1:8-11) Soon after the tabernacle service began to function, Aaron's two sons Nadab and Abihu were struck dead by Jehovah for attempting to offer up incense with "illegitimate fire." (Le 10:1, 2; compare Ex 30:9; see ABIHU.) Later, Korah and 250 others, all Levites but not of the priestly line, rebelled against the Aaronic priesthood. As a test they were instructed by Moses to take fire holders and burn incense at the tabernacle entrance so that Jehovah might indicate whether he accepted them as his priests. The group perished while in the act, their fire holders in hand. (Nu 16:6, 7, 16-18, 35-40) So, too, King Uzziah was stricken with leprosy when he presumptuously attempted to burn incense in the temple.—2Ch 26:16-21.

As time went on, the nation of Israel became so negligent in the prescribed worship of Jehovah that they closed the temple and burned incense on other altars. (2Ch 29:7; 30:14) Worse than that, they burned incense to other gods before whom they prostituted themselves, and in other ways they desecrated the holy incense, all of which was detestable in Jehovah's sight.—Eze 8:10, 11; 16:17, 18; 23:36, 41; Isa 1:13.

Significance. The Law covenant had a shadow of better things to come (Heb 10:1), and it seems that the burning of incense under that arrangement represented the acceptable prayers of God's faithful servants. The psalmist declared, "May my prayer be prepared as incense before you [Jehovah]." (Ps 141:2) Likewise, the highly symbolic book of Revelation describes those around God's heavenly throne as having "golden bowls that were full of incense, and the incense means the prayers of the holy ones." "A large quantity of incense was given him [an angel] to offer it with the prayers of all the holy ones upon the golden altar that was before the throne." (Re 5:8; 8:3, 4) In several respects the burning incense served as a fitting symbol of the prayers of the holy ones that are "offered up" (Heb 5:7) night and day (1Th 3:10), and are pleasant to Jehovah. —Pr 15:8.

Incense, of course, could not make the prayers of false worshipers acceptable to God. (Pr 28:9; Mr 12:40) On the other hand, the prayers of a righteous one are effectual. (Jas 5:16) So, too, when a plague from God broke out, Aaron quickly "put the incense on and began making atonement for the people."—Nu 16:46-48.

Not Burned by Christians. Though incense is burned today in certain religions of Christendom, as also in Buddhist temples, we find no basis in Scripture for such practice by Christians. Censers are not listed among church vessels for the first four centuries of the Common Era, and not until Gregory the Great (latter part of the sixth century) is there clear evidence of incense being used in church services. Obviously, this is because with the coming of Christ and the nailing of the Law covenant and its regulations to the torture stake (Col 2:14), and especially after the temple and its Aaronic priesthood were completely removed, the burning of incense in the worship of God ceased. No authorization for its use in the Christian congregation was given, and early Christians, like the Jews, never individually burned incense for religious purposes.

Early Christians also refused to burn incense in honor of the emperor, even though it cost them their lives. As Daniel P. Mannix observes: "Very few of the Christians recanted, although an altar with a fire burning on it was generally kept in the arena for their convenience. All a prisoner had to do was scatter a pinch of incense on the flame and he was given a Certificate of Sacrifice and turned free. It was also carefully explained to him that he was not worshiping the emperor; merely acknowledging the divine character of the emperor as head of the Roman state. Still, almost no Christians availed themselves of the chance to escape." —*Those About to Die,* 1958, p. 137.

Tertullian (second and third centuries C.E.) says that Christians would not even engage in the incense trade. (*On Idolatry,* chap. XI) This, however, is not the case with the incense merchants doing business with symbolic Babylon the Great. —Re 18:11, 13.

INCENSE, ALTAR OF. See ALTAR.

INCEST. See CRIME AND PUNISHMENT (Major crimes under the Law).

INCORRUPTION. The quality of a body that is not subject to decay, ruin, or destruction.

Direct references to incorruption are found only in the Christian Greek Scriptures. There the word translates the Greek *a·phthar·si'a,* formed of the negative prefix *a* and a form of *phthei'ro.* This latter word means "corrupt" (2Co 7:2) or "spoil" (1Co 15:33), hence to bring to a lower or inferior state; also "put to death" or "destroy." (2Pe 2:12) The adjective form *a'phthar·tos* (incorruptible) is also used.

Corruption and Corruptibility. In considering incorruption, it is helpful to analyze first the use of the Greek terms for corruption and corruptibility. Keep in mind that there is a difference between a thing's being corrupt and its being corrupt*ible,* that is, capable of being corrupted.

Corruption and corruptibility may relate both to things material and to things not material. The crown that Greek athletes sought was corruptible

—subject to decay, deterioration, or disintegration. (1Co 9:25) Even gold (dissoluble in aqua regia) and silver are corruptible. (1Pe 1:18; compare Jas 5:3.) Boats can be "wrecked" or, literally, "corrupted through" (from the intensive form *di-a·phthei'ro*), suffering breakdown of their structural form. (Re 8:9) The same Greek word is used with respect to the "ruining" of the earth. (Re 11:18) Man, the fleshly creature, is corruptible (Ro 1:23); in his imperfect state his body is subject to damaging diseases and eventually to dissolution in death, the body breaking down in decay. (Ac 13:36) As regards things not material, good habits can be corrupted, or spoiled, by bad associations (1Co 15:33); men may become mentally corrupted, turned away from sincerity, chastity, and truth (2Co 11:3; 1Ti 6:5; 2Ti 3:8), this resulting in moral decay, a corrupting of the individual's personality.—Eph 4:22; Jude 10.

Even perfect human bodies are corruptible, that is, they are not beyond ruin or destruction. For this reason, the apostle Paul could say that the resurrected Jesus was thereafter "destined no more *to return to corruption*" (Ac 13:34), that is, never to return to life in a corruptible human body. Only God's action prevented the fleshly body of his Son's earthly existence from seeing corruption in the grave. (Ac 2:31; 13:35-37) That body, however, was not preserved for the use of the resurrected Jesus, since the apostle Peter states that Jesus was "put to death in the flesh, but . . . made alive in the spirit." (1Pe 3:18) It thus seems evident that God disposed of that body miraculously, thereby not letting it see ruinous decay.—See BODY (Christ's Body of Flesh).

Angels, though spirit creatures, are shown to have corruptible bodies, inasmuch as they are declared to be subject to destruction.—Mt 25:41; 2Pe 2:4; compare Lu 4:33, 34.

Human enslavement to corruption. While Adam, even in his perfection, had a corruptible body, it was only because of his rebellion against God that he came into "enslavement to corruption" and passed this condition on to all of his offspring, the human race. (Ro 8:20-22) This enslavement to corruption results from sin or transgression (Ro 5:12) and produces bodily imperfection that leads to degradation, disease, aging, and death. For this reason, the one 'sowing with a view to the flesh reaps corruption from his flesh' and does not gain the everlasting life promised those who sow with a view to the spirit.—Ga 6:8; compare 2Pe 2:12, 18, 19.

Attainment of Incorruption by Christians. As noted, the Hebrew Scriptures make no direct reference to incorruption, and they regularly stress the mortality of the human soul. Thus, the apostle says of Christ Jesus that he "has shed light upon life and incorruption through the good news." (2Ti 1:10) Through Jesus, God revealed the sacred secret of his purpose to grant to anointed Christians the privilege of reigning with his Son in the heavens. (Lu 12:32; Joh 14:2, 3; compare Eph 1:9-11.) By resurrecting their Savior Jesus Christ from the dead, God has given such Christians the living hope of "an incorruptible and undefiled and unfading inheritance . . . reserved in the heavens." (1Pe 1:3, 4, 18, 19; compare 1Co 9:25.) Such ones are born again while yet in the flesh, that is, granted the position of spiritual sons of God, born of "incorruptible reproductive seed, through the word of the living and enduring God."—1Pe 1:23; compare 1Jo 3:1, 9.

Though dealt with by God as his spiritual sons and although having the promise of an incorruptible inheritance, these Christians called to the heavenly Kingdom do not possess immortality or incorruption while yet on earth in the flesh. This is seen from the fact that they are *"seeking* glory and honor and incorruptibleness by endurance in work that is good." (Ro 2:6, 7) The "incorruptibleness" sought evidently does not mean merely freedom from moral corruption. By following Christ's example and by faith in his ransom sacrifice, these Christians have already "escaped from the corruption that is in the world through lust" (2Pe 1:3, 4); they are "loving our Lord Jesus Christ in incorruptness" and 'showing incorruptness in their teaching.' (Eph 6:24; Tit 2:7, 8) The incorruptibleness (along with glory and honor) they seek by faithful endurance relates to their glorification at the time of their resurrection as actual spirit sons of God, and this is evident from Paul's first letter to the Corinthians.

Raised to Immortality and Incorruption. Christ Jesus entered into immortality upon his resurrection from the dead, thereafter possessing "an indestructible life." (1Ti 6:15, 16; Heb 7:15-17) As the "exact representation of [the] very being" of his Father, who is the incorruptible God (Heb 1:3; 1Ti 1:17), the resurrected Jesus also enjoys incorruptibility.

United with Jesus in the likeness of his resurrection, his joint heirs also are resurrected not merely to everlasting life as spirit creatures but to immortality and incorruption. Having lived, served faithfully, and died in corruptible human bodies, they now receive incorruptible spirit bodies, as Paul clearly states at 1 Corinthians 15: 42-54. Immortality therefore evidently refers to the quality of the life they enjoy, its endlessness and indestructibility, whereas incorruption apparently relates to the organism or body that God gives them, one that is inherently beyond decay, ruin, or destruction. It therefore appears that God grants them the power to be self-sustaining, not dependent upon outside sources of energy as are his other creatures, fleshly and spirit. This is a stirring evidence of God's confidence in them. Such independent and indestructible existence, however, does not remove them from God's control; and they, like their Head Christ Jesus, continue subject to their Father's will and directions. —1Co 15:23-28; see IMMORTALITY; SOUL.

INDIA (In'di·a). The exact area designated by the Bible name "India" is uncertain. (Es 8:9) Scholars generally suggest that it denotes the area drained by the Indus River and its tributaries, that is, the Punjab region and perhaps also Sind. The testimony of the historian Herodotus (III, 88, 94; IV, 44) indicates that "India" first became a part of the Persian Empire during the rule of Darius Hystaspis (521-486 B.C.E.). In the time of Ahasuerus (considered to be Xerxes I, son of Darius Hystaspis), India was the eastern limit of the empire.—Es 1:1.

Likely the Indus Valley was settled not long after the language of Babel's builders was confused. A comparison of the ancient civilization of the Indus Valley with that of Mesopotamia reveals the erection of structures like the ziggurat platforms of Mesopotamia, sculptures of the human figure with heads having the masklike features typical of ancient Mesopotamian sculpture, and pictographic signs that bear a resemblance to early Mesopotamian forms. Assyriologist Samuel N. Kramer has suggested that the Indus Valley was settled by a people who fled from Mesopotamia when the Sumerians took control of the area.

INDUSTRIOUSNESS. Steady and persevering activity; painstaking effort; diligence; zeal. Commonly the term implies lawful and useful labor. It is the opposite of slothfulness or idleness.

The Hebrew and Greek words in the Bible that are sometimes translated "industrious" or "industriousness" are more often rendered "earnest" or "earnestness," and other forms of such words are frequently translated "endeavor" or "do [one's] utmost."

Christians are admonished not to slack their hands or become weary in well doing. Paul said: "We desire each one of you to show the same industriousness [literally, "speed up"] so as to have the full assurance of the hope down to the end, in order that you may not become sluggish,

but be imitators of those who through faith and patience inherit the promises." (Heb 6:11, 12; compare Pr 10:4; 12:24; 18:9.) Jesus Christ told his disciples: "Exert yourselves vigorously to get in through the narrow door, because many, I tell you, will seek to get in but will not be able." (Lu 13:24) Paul himself was an example of such rigorous exertion. (Col 1:29; 2Th 3:7-9) Jehovah and his Son are, of course, the foremost examples of industriousness.—Joh 5:17; Isa 40:26.

To prevent their being inactive or unfruitful, Christians must 'contribute in response [to God's promises] all earnest effort' in supplying to their faith virtue, knowledge, self-control, endurance, godly devotion, brotherly affection, and love. (2Pe 1:4-8) This calls for the constant application of industrious perseverance (2Ti 2:15; Heb 4:11) and unflagging attention. (Heb 2:1) Much of the strength for this comes through the help of Jehovah's spirit. What could more strongly express the need for industriousness than the apostle Paul's counsel: "Do not loiter at your business. Be aglow with the spirit. Slave for Jehovah"? This requirement of industriousness applies to all ministers ("let us be at this ministry"), but with special force to those in positions in which they preside over meetings and activities in the congregation, for "he that presides, let him do it in real earnest."—Ro 12:7, 8, 11.

In the Christian congregation, needy ones receiving material help from the congregation must be industrious ones. The Scriptural rule is: "If anyone does not want to work, neither let him eat." The exhortation to those not working is that they get busy, "that by working with quietness they should eat food they themselves earn." (2Th 3:10-12) A professed Christian who refuses or neglects to provide for his household "has disowned the faith and is worse than a person without faith." (1Ti 5:8) Even widows who were needy, before being put on the congregation's list for regular provision of material assistance, had to have a record of Christian activity, having "diligently followed every good work."—1Ti 5: 9, 10.

Rewards of Industriousness. Rich rewards come to the industrious person both now and in the future. "The hand of the diligent one is what will make one rich." (Pr 10:4) "The hand of the diligent ones is the one that will rule." (Pr 12:24) Their soul "will be made fat." (Pr 13:4) The industrious wife is one whose "sons have risen up and proceeded to pronounce her happy; her owner rises up, and he praises her." Of her, it is proclaimed: "Give her of the fruitage of her hands, and let her works praise her even in the gates." (Pr 31:28, 31) Above all, the spiritual brothers of Christ are told: "Do your utmost to make the calling and choosing of you sure for yourselves; for if you keep on doing these things you will by no means ever fail. In fact, thus there will be richly supplied to you the entrance into the everlasting kingdom of our Lord and Savior Jesus Christ."—2Pe 1:10, 11.

INGATHERING, FESTIVAL OF.   See FESTIVAL OF BOOTHS.

INHERITANCE.   Any property passing at the owner's death to the heir or to those entitled to succeed; anything received from progenitors or predecessors as if by succession. The principal Hebrew verb used is na·chal' (noun, na·chalah'). It involves getting or giving an inheritance or hereditary possession, usually as a result of succession. (Nu 26:55; Eze 46:18) The verb ya·rash' is used at times in the sense "succeed as heir," but more often, "take possession" apart from succession. (Ge 15:3; Le 20:24) It also has the meaning "dispossess; drive away," involving military action. (De 2:12; 31:3) The Greek words having to do with inheritance are related to kle'ros, which originally meant "lot" but came to mean "share" and finally "inheritance."—Mt 27:35; Ac 1:17; 26:18.

In Israel the inheritance applied primarily to land possessions, although it was used with respect to movable property as well. The Bible speaks of the inheritance of things of a spiritual nature also. Spirit-begotten Christians are called "heirs indeed of God, but joint heirs with Christ." They look forward, if they remain faithful, to "the everlasting inheritance."—Ro 8:17; Heb 9:15.

Patriarchal Period.   The faithful Hebrew patriarchs Abraham, Isaac, and Jacob possessed no land, except for the field with the cave used as a burial place and the field near Shechem purchased by Jacob. (Ge 23:19, 20; 33:19) Concerning Abraham's residence in Canaan, the Christian martyr Stephen said: "Yet he did not give him any inheritable possession in it, no, not a footbreadth; but he promised to give it to him as a possession, and after him to his seed, while as yet he had no child." (Ac 7:5) The material inheritance that these men passed on consisted of their cattle and their movable goods. The firstborn son inherited a double portion (two parts) of the property as compared with that allotted to other sons. In the case of the patriarch Job, his daughters received

an inheritance in among their brothers. It is not stated whether this included land inheritance. —Job 42:15.

The father could transfer the birthright if he had a good reason, giving the firstborn's inheritance to a younger son. In the instances of this noted in the Bible, it was not through whim or favoritism, but there was a basis on which the father determined to make the change in the birthright inheritance. Ishmael, as Abraham's oldest son, was prospective heir for about 14 years. (Ge 16:16; 17:18-21; 21:5) But at Sarah's request and with Jehovah's approval, Abraham dismissed Ishmael, then about 19 years of age. Isaac then possessed the firstborn's right and later received everything that Abraham had, with the exception of gifts that Abraham gave to sons later born to him by Keturah. (Ge 21:8-13; 25:5, 6) Reuben the firstborn of Jacob lost his birthright inheritance by reason of fornication with his father's concubine. (Ge 49:3, 4; 1Ch 5:1, 2) Jacob gave the greater blessing to Ephraim, Joseph's younger son, rather than to Manasseh, the older.—Ge 48:13-19.

Concubinage was legal. In fact, in the Bible the concubine is sometimes designated "wife," and the man with whom she lives, "husband." Her father is called his father-in-law, and he is called her father's son-in-law. (Ge 16:3; Jg 19:3-5) The sons of concubines were legitimate and therefore had an inheritance status equal to that of the sons of a regular wife.

Before Abraham had any children, he spoke of his slave Eliezer as the prospective heir of his goods but was told by Jehovah that he would have a child as heir.—Ge 15:1-4.

Period of the Law.   Under the Law a father was prevented from constituting the son of a better-loved wife his firstborn at the expense of his actual firstborn from a wife less loved. He had to give to the firstborn a double portion of everything that he owned. (De 21:15-17) When there were no sons, the inheritance went to the daughters. (Nu 27:6-8; Jos 17:3-6) However, daughters who inherited land were required to marry only in the family of their father's tribe, in order to prevent the circulation of their inheritance from tribe to tribe. (Nu 36:6-9) If there were no children, the order of passing on the inheritance was to (1) brothers of the deceased, (2) his father's brothers, (3) the closest blood relation. (Nu 27:9-11) A wife received no inheritance from her husband. If there were no children, the wife was considered to be the owner of the land until it was redeemed by the one having the right of repurchase. In such case the wife was repurchased along with the property. (Ru 4:1-12) Under the law of brother-in-law marriage, the first child born to the woman by the repurchaser became heir of the deceased husband and carried on his name.—De 25:5, 6.

Hereditary lands. The inheritance of the sons of Israel was given to them by Jehovah, who outlined the boundaries of the land to Moses. (Nu 34:1-12; Jos 1:4) The sons of Gad, the sons of Reuben, and half of the tribe of Manasseh were granted their allotment of territory by Moses. (Nu 32:33; Jos 14:3) The rest of the tribes received their inheritance by lot at the direction of Joshua and Eleazar. (Jos 14:1, 2) In harmony with Jacob's prophecy at Genesis 49:5, 7, Simeon and Levi were not given a separate section of territory as inheritance. Simeon's territory consisted of land (along with enclave cities) inside the territory of Judah (Jos 19:1-9), while Levi was granted 48 cities throughout the entire territory of Israel. Since the Levites received the appointment to special service at the sanctuary, Jehovah was said to be their inheritance. They received the tithe as their portion or inheritance in return for their service. (Nu 18:20, 21; 35:6, 7) Families were given assignments within the territory of their tribe. As families would increase and sons would inherit, the land would be progressively divided up into smaller and smaller parcels.

Since land was kept in the possession of the same family from generation to generation, it could not be sold in perpetuity. The sale of land was, in effect, only the leasing of it for the value of crops it would produce, the purchase price being on a graduated scale according to the number of years until the next Jubilee, at which time all land possession would revert to the original owner if it had not been repurchased or redeemed prior to the Jubilee. (Le 25:13, 15, 23, 24) This regulation included houses in unwalled cities, which were regarded as part of the open field. As for a house in a walled city, the right of repurchase remained only for one year from the time of sale, at which time it became the property of the buyer. In the case of houses in Levite cities, the right of repurchase continued to time indefinite because the Levites had no inheritance of land.—Le 25:29-34.

The inviolability of the hereditary possession is illustrated in the case of Naboth's vineyard. Naboth refused either to sell it to the king or to exchange it for another vineyard; the crown did not have the right of eminent domain. (1Ki 21:2-6) A person could, however, *devote* a part of

his inheritance to Jehovah for the sanctuary. If so, it could not be redeemed, but it remained the property of the sanctuary and its priesthood. If a man wished to *sanctify* part of his property for the temporary use of the sanctuary, he could do so; and if he later wished to redeem it, he could do this by adding a fifth of its valuation. This doubtless protected the sanctuary treasury from loss and also created greater respect for the sanctuary and that which was offered in the worship of Jehovah. If the sanctified field was sold to another man, then in the Jubilee it would be as a field *devoted* and would not be returned to the original owner but would remain the property of the sanctuary and its priesthood.—Le 27:15-21, 28; see SANCTIFICATION (Sanctifying of Land).

From the foregoing it can be seen that wills had no place in Hebrew terminology or practice, the laws of inheritance obviating any necessity of such a document. Even movable property was disposed of by its owner during his lifetime or by the laws of inheritance at the time of his death. In Jesus' illustration of the prodigal son, the younger son, on request, received his share of the property before his father's death.—Lu 15:12.

Benefits of hereditary laws. The laws governing the hereditary possessions and the dividing of them into smaller portions as the population increased were in themselves a contributing factor to greater family unity. In a land such as Israel, consisting of much hill country, as in Judea, this was advantageous in that it caused the Israelites to make the optimum use of the land, even terracing hillsides, resulting in clothing the land with beauty and greenery, the olive, the fig tree, the palm, and the vine, providing food for a great population. The fact that every man was a possessor of land created a greater love for the soil on which he lived, promoted industriousness, and, along with the Jubilee regulation, restored the nation to its original theocratic status every 50th year. This helped maintain a balanced economy. However, as with other features of the Law, abuses eventually crept in.

As Jehovah had told Israel, he was the real Owner of the land. They were alien residents and settlers from his standpoint. Therefore, he was able to put them out of the land at any time he saw fit. (Le 25:23) Because of their many violations of God's law, they were sent into exile for 70 years under the power of Babylon and remained under Gentile domination even after their restoration in 537 B.C.E. Finally, in 70 C.E., the Romans took them completely off the land, selling thousands into slavery. Even their genealogical records were lost or destroyed.

Christian Inheritance. Jesus Christ, as the son of David, inherits the throne of David. (Isa 9:7; Lu 1:32) As the Son of God, he inherits heavenly kingship through the covenant Jehovah made with him. (Ps 110:4; Lu 22:28-30) Christ, therefore, inherits the nations, to break to pieces all opposers and to rule forever.—Ps 2:6-9.

The anointed members of the Christian congregation are spoken of as having a heavenly inheritance, sharing Jesus' inheritance as his "brothers." (Eph 1:14; Col 1:12; 1Pe 1:4, 5) This includes the earth.—Mt 5:5.

Because God redeemed Israel out of Egypt, they became his possession or "inheritance." (De 32:9; Ps 33:12; 74:2; Mic 7:14) They foreshadowed the "nation" of spiritual Israel, whom God considers his "inheritance" because he possesses them, having purchased them by means of the blood of his only-begotten Son, Jesus Christ.—1Pe 2:9; 5:2, 3; Ac 20:28.

Jesus Christ pointed out that persons who give up valuable things for the sake of his name and for the sake of the good news "will inherit everlasting life."—Mt 19:29; Mr 10:29, 30; see BIRTHRIGHT; BROTHER-IN-LAW MARRIAGE; FIRSTBORN, FIRSTLING.

INK. The Hebrew word *deyoh'*, found only at Jeremiah 36:18, may possibly be an Egyptian loanword. In the Christian Greek Scriptures, *me'lan* occurs only three times (2Co 3:3; 2Jo 12; 3Jo 13) and is the neuter form of the masculine adjective *me'las*, meaning "black."—Mt 5:36; Re 6:5, 12.

Generally speaking, inks were made of a pigment or coloring material dispersed in a medium containing gum, glue, or varnish that acted both as a carrying agent, or vehicle, and as a binder to hold the pigment on the surface to which it was applied. The oldest ink formulas, and the oldest specimens found, show that the pigment was a carbonaceous black, either in the form of amorphous soot obtained from burning oil or wood, or a crystalline charcoal from animal or vegetable sources. The pigments of red inks were iron oxides. Certain tinctures were also used by the ancients. Josephus says the copy of the Law sent to Ptolemy Philadelphus was written in gold letters. (*Jewish Antiquities*, XII, 89 [ii, 11]) If vegetable juices or dyes were ever used in inks, they long ago disappeared because of their perishable nature.

To make the best inks, much time was required to grind and disperse the pigments in their vehicles. The inks were then usually stored as dried cakes or bars, which were moistened sufficiently by the scribe as he applied the ink to his brush or reed.

The Chinese inks long enjoyed the reputation of having the deepest tone and being the most durable. Documents written in some of these inks can be soaked in water for several weeks without washing out. On the other hand, inks were also made so they could be erased with a wet sponge or damp cloth. This may have been the basis for Jehovah's saying, in a symbolic way, "Whoever has sinned against me, I shall wipe him out of my book."—Ex 32:33; see also Nu 5:23; Ps 109:13, 14.

INKHORN. See SECRETARY'S INKHORN.

INN. In Greek, *pan·do·khei'on*, literally meaning "a place where all are received or taken in," that is, where travelers could find accommodations for themselves and their animals. Perhaps ancient Middle Eastern inns resembled those built there in more recent times. These commonly consist of a walled square with only one entrance. Along the walls on a raised platform there are unfurnished rooms for sheltering travelers and goods, entrance being gained from the inner courtyard. The animals are left in the large court, which often has a centrally situated well. Innkeepers of ancient times furnished a few necessary provisions to travelers and cared for persons left in their charge, receiving compensation for their services.—Lu 10:33-35.

INSECTS. In the adult stage, these invertebrates are distinguished by a body consisting of three segments, head, thorax, and abdomen, with six legs, a pair of feelers, and generally two or four wings.

The picturesque language of the Bible refers to insects as 'going on all fours.' Obviously Moses was familiar with the fact that insects have six legs. So the reference is undoubtedly to their mode of travel rather than to the number of their legs. There are winged insects, including the bees, flies, and wasps, that walk with their six legs *in the manner of* four-legged animals. Other insects, such as the locusts, are equipped with two leaper legs and thus literally use the other four legs for crawling.—Le 11:20-23.

The more than 800,000 known varieties of insects present a panorama of contrast. While some are somberly colored, others are arrayed in bright hues and with beautiful designs. All the shades of the rainbow are represented. In size, insects vary from beetles that are small enough to get through the eye of a needle to curious "walking sticks" that measure more than 30 cm (1 ft) in length. Among the insects can be found organized communities, builders, agriculturists, manufacturers, long-distance fliers, expert jumpers, swimmers, and burrowers. Through study and observation, man can learn much from the insects, most importantly that they are God's creations, endowed with instinctive wisdom, not by chance, but by the Source of all wisdom, Jehovah.—Job 12:7-9.

Although many are inclined to view insects as pests that damage crops and man's possessions as well as spread disease, actually only a very small percentage of insects can be designated as harmful under present circumstances. The majority can be classified either as neutral or as directly or indirectly beneficial to man.

Insects stand in an important relationship to plants. It has been estimated that 85 percent of flowering plants are either completely or partly dependent on insect pollination. Insects also play a beneficial role as soil builders and scavengers. Dyes and shellac are produced from scale insects. In the Middle East, insects, such as locusts, have for centuries been used as an item of the diet. Were it not for the existence of insects, honey and silk would be unknown.

Insects indeed occupy an important place in relation to the rest of the earthly creation. Observed Carl D. Duncan, professor of entomology and botany: "It is not too much to say that insects determine the character of man's world to a far greater extent than he does himself, and that if they were suddenly to disappear completely the world would be changed so extensively that it is extremely doubtful that man would be able to maintain any sort of organized society whatever." —*Annual Report of the Smithsonian Institution,* 1947, p. 346.

INSIGHT. Essentially, insight is the ability to see into a situation. To act with insight is to act with prudence, discretion. According to Wilson's *Old Testament Word Studies,* the Hebrew verb *sa·khal'* means "to look at; to be prudent, circumspect; to act prudently, to be intelligent." (1978, p. 461) Thus, *sa·khal'* is rendered 'have insight' (Ps 14:2), 'act with discretion' (Pr 10:19), "act prudently" (1Sa 18:5), 'have success' (Pr 17:8), 'cause to show insight' (Pr 16:23). The noun *se'khel* is translated "insight" (Ps 111:10) and "discretion." —1Sa 25:3.

Insight is closely related to understanding, but there is a fine distinction between the two terms. Says the *Theological Wordbook of the Old Testament:* "While *bin* [understanding] indicates 'distinguishing between,' [*sa·khal'*] relates to an intelligent knowledge of the reason. There is the process of thinking through a complex arrangement of thoughts resulting in a wise dealing and use of good practical common sense. Another end result is the emphasis upon being successful." —Edited by R. L. Harris, 1980, Vol. 2, p. 877; see UNDERSTANDING.

In the Greek Scriptures, the verb *sy·ni'e·mi* is translated 'has insight' at Romans 3:11, where the apostle Paul quotes from Psalm 14:2. *Sy·ni'e·mi* is also rendered "get the sense of" (Mt 13:13-15), 'grasp' (Mt 16:12), "understand" (Ac 28:26), and 'perceive' (Eph 5:17).

Jehovah God gives insight to his servants by providing them with counsel and advice that they can use to direct their steps and control their actions. (Ps 32:8; compare Da 9:22.) He provides such wise guidance by means of his Word. To gain insight, though, a person must do more than read the Bible. He must appreciate it so as to be motivated to do all that God directs. (Jos 1:7, 8; 1Ki 2:3) Needed also is the help of God's spirit. (Ne 9:20; compare 1Ch 28:12, 19.) Once acquired, insight must be safeguarded. One can lose it by turning from God's ways.—Ps 36:1-3; Pr 21:16.

Insight can be displayed in various ways, resulting in blessings both to the one who has it and to others. The psalmist pronounces happy the one "acting with consideration [with insight] toward the lowly one." (Ps 41:1) A wife who is "discreet" (showing insight) is described as a blessing from Jehovah. (Pr 19:14) Insight, looking beyond the obvious, enables one to guard his mouth (Pr 10:19; 16:23) and to know when to keep silent. (Am 5:13) It also helps one to avoid anger and overlook transgression. (Pr 19:11) One who has insight accepts correction. (Ps 2:10) According to Proverbs 21:11, when a wise person obtains insight —that is, when he carefully considers available information and as a result acquires a clearer picture of a matter—he "gets knowledge," that is, he knows what to do regarding the matter, what conclusions to draw, what counsel to give.

INSPECTION GATE. See GATE, GATEWAY.

INSPIRATION. The quality or state of being moved by or produced under the direction of a spirit from a superhuman source. When that source is Jehovah, the result is a pronouncement or writings that are truly the word of God. The apostle Paul stated at 2 Timothy 3:16: "All Scripture is inspired of God." The phrase "inspired of God" translates the compound Greek word *the·o'pneu·stos,* meaning, literally, "God-breathed" or "breathed by God."

This is the only occurrence of this Greek term in the Scriptures. Its use here clearly identifies God as the Source and Producer of the Sacred Scriptures, the Bible. Their being "God-breathed" finds some parallel in the expression found in the Hebrew Scriptures at Psalm 33:6: "By the word of Jehovah the heavens themselves were made, and by the spirit [or breath] of his mouth all their army."

Results From the Operation of God's Spirit. The means or agency for the inspiration of "all Scripture" was God's holy spirit, or active force. (See SPIRIT.) That holy spirit operated toward or upon men to move them and guide them in setting down God's message. Thus, the apostle Peter says of Bible prophecy: "You know this first, that no prophecy of Scripture springs from any private interpretation. For prophecy was at no time brought by man's will, but men spoke from God as they were borne along by holy spirit." (2Pe 1:20, 21) The evidence shows that God's spirit operated on the minds and hearts of all the Bible writers to carry them along to the goal purposed by God. King David said: "The spirit of Jehovah it was that spoke by me, and his word was upon my tongue." (2Sa 23:2) When Jesus quoted Psalm 110, he said that David had written it "by inspiration [literally, in spirit]." (Mt 22:43) The parallel passage in Mark 12:36 reads "by the holy spirit."

Even as Jehovah's spirit moved men or qualified them to perform other divine assignments —the making of priestly garments and equipment for the tabernacle (Ex 28:3; 35:30-35), carrying the load of administration (De 34:9), leading military forces (Jg 3:9, 10; 6:33, 34)—so it enabled men to record the Scriptures. By means of that spirit, they could be given wisdom, understanding, knowledge, counsel, and power, beyond what was normal and according to their particular need. (Isa 11:2; Mic 3:8; 1Co 12:7, 8) David is stated to have received the architectural plan of the temple "by inspiration [literally, by the spirit]." (1Ch 28:12) Jesus assured his apostles that God's spirit would help them, teaching, guiding, and recalling to their minds the things they had heard from him, as well as revealing to them future things. (Joh 14:26; 16:13) This assured the truthfulness and accuracy of their Gospel accounts, including many lengthy quotations of Jesus' speeches, even though John's Gospel account, for example, was written scores of years after the death of Jesus.

Controlled by "the hand of Jehovah." The Bible writers, therefore, came under Jehovah's "hand," or guiding and controlling power. (2Ki 3:15, 16; Eze 3:14, 22) Even as Jehovah's "hand" could cause his servants to speak or to keep silent at appointed times (Eze 3:4, 26, 27; 33:22), so it could stimulate writing or act as a restraining force; it could prompt the writer to deal with certain matters or restrict him from including other material. The end product would, in every case, be that which Jehovah desired.

How Writers Received Divine Direction. As the apostle states, God spoke "in many ways" to his servants in pre-Christian times. (Heb 1:1, 2) In at least one case, that of the Ten Commandments, or Decalogue, the information was divinely supplied in written form, merely requiring copying into the scrolls or other material used by Moses. (Ex 31:18; De 10:1-5) In other cases, information was transmitted by verbal dictation, word for word. When presenting the large body of laws and statutes of God's covenant with Israel, Jehovah instructed Moses: "Write down for yourself these words." (Ex 34:27) The prophets also were often given specific messages to deliver, and these were then recorded, forming part of the Scriptures.—1Ki 22:14; Jer 1:7; 2:1; 11:1-5; Eze 3:4; 11:5.

Among still other methods used for conveying information to the Bible writers were dreams and visions. Dreams, or night visions as they were sometimes called, evidently superimposed a picture of God's message or purpose on the mind of the sleeping person. (Da 2:19; 7:1) Visions given while the person was conscious were an even more frequently used vehicle of communication of God's thoughts to the mind of the writer, the revelation being impressed pictorially upon the conscious mind. (Eze 1:1; Da 8:1; Re 9:17) Some visions were received when the person had fallen into a trance. Though conscious, the person apparently was so absorbed by the vision received during the trance as to be oblivious to all else around him.—Ac 10:9-17; 11:5-10; 22:17-21; see VISION.

Angelic messengers were used on many occasions to transmit the divine messages. (Heb 2:2) Such messengers played a larger part in the transmission of information than is at times apparent. Thus, whereas the Law given to Moses is presented as spoken by God, both Stephen and Paul show that God used his angels in transmitting that legal code. (Ac 7:53; Ga 3:19) Since the angels spoke in Jehovah's name, the message they presented could therefore properly be called "the word of Jehovah."—Ge 22:11, 12, 15-18; Zec 1:7, 9.

No matter what the particular means employed for the transmission of the messages, all parts of the Scriptures would be of the same quality, all of them being inspired, or "God-breathed."

Is the fact that Bible writers showed individuality in expression consistent with the Bible's being inspired by God?

The evidence indicates, however, that the men used by God to record the Scriptures were not merely automatons, simply recording dictated material. We read concerning the apostle John that the "God-breathed" Revelation was presented to him through God's angel "in signs" and that John then "bore witness to the word God gave and to the witness Jesus Christ gave, even to all the things he saw." (Re 1:1, 2) It was "by inspiration [literally, "in spirit"]" that John "came to be in the Lord's day" and he was told: "What you see write in a scroll." (Re 1:10, 11) So, God apparently saw good to allow Bible writers to use their mental faculties in selecting words and expressions to describe the visions they saw (Hab 2:2), while always exercising sufficient control and guidance over them so that the end product would be not only accurate and true but also such as suited Jehovah's purpose. (Pr 30:5, 6) That personal effort on the part of the writer was involved is shown by the statement at Ecclesiastes 12:9, 10, there being a pondering, searching, and arranging in order to present properly "delightful words and the writing of correct words of truth."—Compare Lu 1:1-4.

This doubtless explains why there are different styles of writing as well as expressions that apparently reflect the background of the individual writers. The natural qualifications of the writers may have been a factor in God's selection of them for their particular assignment; he may also have prepared them prior thereto to serve his particular purpose.

As evidence of this individuality of expression, Matthew, who had been a tax collector, makes numerous particularly specific references to numbers and money values. (Mt 17:27; 26:15; 27:3) Luke, "the beloved physician" (Col 4:14), on the other hand, uses distinctive expressions that reflect his medical background.—Lu 4:38; 5:12; 16:20.

Even where the writer speaks of receiving "the word of Jehovah" or a certain "pronouncement," it may be that this was transmitted, not word for word, but by giving the writer a mental picture of God's purpose, one that the writer would thereafter express in words. This is perhaps indicated by the writers' speaking at times of 'seeing' (rather than 'hearing') "the pronouncement" or "the word of Jehovah."—Isa 13:1; Mic 1:1; Hab 1:1; 2:1, 2.

The men used to write the Scriptures therefore cooperated with the operation of Jehovah's holy spirit. They were willing and submissive to God's guidance (Isa 50:4, 5), eager to know God's will and leading. (Isa 26:9) In many cases they had certain goals in mind (Lu 1:1-4) or were responding to an evident need (1Co 1:10, 11; 5:1; 7:1), and God directed them so that what they wrote coincided with and fulfilled his purpose. (Pr 16:9) As spiritual men, their hearts and minds were attuned to God's will, they 'had the mind of Christ' and so were not setting down mere human wisdom nor a "vision of their own heart," as false prophets did.—1Co 2:13-16; Jer 23:16; Eze 13:2, 3, 17.

It can be seen that the holy spirit would, indeed, have "varieties of operations" toward or upon these Bible writers. (1Co 12:6) A considerable portion of the information was humanly accessible to them, sometimes already existing in written form, as in the case of genealogies and certain historical accounts. (Lu 1:3; 3:23-38; Nu 21:14, 15; 1Ki 14:19, 29; 2Ki 15:31; 24:5; see BOOK.) Here God's spirit would operate to prevent inaccuracy or error from intruding into the Divine Record and also to guide in the selection of material to be included. Obviously, not everything stated by other persons and thereafter included in the Bible was inspired of God, but the *selection* of the material to be part of the Holy Scriptures and the *accurate recording* of it were under the direction of holy spirit. (See Ge 3:4, 5; Job 42:3; Mt 16:21-23.) In this way God has preserved in his inspired Word a record demonstrating what happens when people listen to him and work in harmony with his purpose, as well as the outcome when they think, speak, and act in ways that show disregard for God or ignorance of his righteous ways. On the other hand, the information concerning the prehuman history of the earth (Ge 1:1-26), heavenly events and activities (Job 1:6-12 and other texts), and prophecies, as well as revelations of God's purposes and of doctrines, was not humanly obtainable and would need to be transmitted supernaturally by God's spirit. As to wise sayings and counsel, even though the writer may have learned much from his personal experience in life and even more from his own study and application of those parts of the Scriptures already recorded, the operation of God's spirit would still be required to ensure the information's qualifying as part of the Word of God that is "alive and exerts power . . . and is able to discern thoughts and intentions of the heart." —Heb 4:12.

This may be seen by the expressions the apostle Paul makes in his first letter to the Corinthians. In giving counsel on marriage and singleness he says at one point: "But to the others I say, yes, I, not the Lord . . . " Again: "Now concerning virgins I have no command from the Lord, but I give my opinion." And finally, regarding a widowed woman, he states: "But she is happier if she remains as she is, according to my opinion. I certainly think I also have God's spirit." (1Co 7:12, 25, 40) The evident meaning of Paul's statements is that he could quote no direct teaching by the Lord Jesus on certain points. Hence Paul gave his personal opinion as a spirit-filled apostle. His counsel, however, was "God-breathed" and so came to form part of the Sacred Scriptures, having equal authority with the rest of those Scriptures.

There is clearly a distinction between the inspired writings of the Bible and other writings that, while manifesting a measure of the spirit's direction and guidance, are not properly classed with the Sacred Scriptures. As has been shown, in addition to the canonical books of the Hebrew Scriptures, there were other writings, such as official records concerning the kings of Judah and Israel, and these, in many cases, may have been drawn up by men devoted to God. They were even used in research done by those writers who were inspired to write part of the Sacred Scriptures. So, too, in apostolic times. In addition to the letters included in the Bible canon, there were doubtless many other letters written by the apostles and older men to the numerous congregations during the course of the years. While the writers were spirit-guided men, still God did not place his seal of guarantee distinguishing any such additional writings as part of the inerrant Word of God. The Hebrew noncanonical writings may have contained some error, and even the noncanonical writings of the apostles may have reflected to some degree the incomplete understanding that existed in the early years of the Christian congregation. (Compare Ac 15:1-32; Ga 2:11-14; Eph 4:11-16.) However, even as God by his spirit, or active force, granted to certain Christians the "discernment of inspired utterances," he could also guide the governing body of the Christian congregation in discerning which inspired writings were to be included in the canon of the Sacred Scriptures.—1Co 12:10; see CANON.

Recognition of Scriptures as Inspired. The evidence is clear that all the Sacred Scriptures, as progressively added to the Bible canon, were consistently recognized by God's servants, including Jesus and his apostles, as inspired. By "inspiration" is meant, not a mere heightening of the intellect and emotions to a higher degree of accomplishment or sensitivity (as is often said of secular artists or poets), but the production of writings that are inerrant and that have the same authority as if written by God himself. For this reason the prophets who contributed to the writing of the Hebrew Scriptures ceaselessly credited their messages to God, with the pronouncement, "This is what Jehovah has said," doing so over 300 times. (Isa 37:33; Jer 2:2; Na 1:12) Jesus and his apostles confidently quoted the Hebrew Scriptures as God's own word spoken through the assigned writers, hence as certain of fulfillment and as the final authority in any controversy. (Mt 4:4-10; 19:3-6; Lu 24:44-48; Joh 13:18; Ac 13:33-35; 1Co 15:3, 4; 1Pe 1:16; 2:6-9) They contained "the sacred pronouncements of God." (Ro 3:1, 2; Heb 5:12) After explaining in Hebrews 1:1 that God spoke to Israel through the prophets, Paul goes on to quote from several books of the Hebrew Scriptures, presenting the texts as though spoken personally by Jehovah God himself. (Heb 1:5-13) Compare similar references to the holy spirit at Acts 1:16; 28:25; Hebrews 3:7; 10:15-17.

Showing his full faith in the inerrancy of the Sacred Writings, Jesus said that "the Scripture cannot be nullified" (Joh 10:34, 35) and that "sooner would heaven and earth pass away than for one smallest letter or one particle of a letter to pass away from the Law by any means and not all things take place." (Mt 5:18) He told the Sadducees that they were in error regarding the resurrection because "you know neither the Scriptures nor the power of God." (Mt 22:29-32; Mr 12:24) He was willing to submit to arrest and death itself because of knowing that this was in fulfillment of the written Word of God, the Sacred Scriptures. —Mt 26:54; Mr 14:27, 49.

These statements, of course, apply to the pre-Christian Hebrew Scriptures. That the Christian Greek Scriptures were likewise presented and accepted as inspired is also clear (1Co 14:37; Ga 1:8, 11, 12; 1Th 2:13), the apostle Peter in one statement including Paul's letters with the rest of the

Scriptures. (2Pe 3:15, 16) Thus the entire body of the Scriptures comprise the unified and harmonious written Word of God.—Eph 6:17.

Authority of Copies and Translations. Absolute inerrancy is therefore to be attributed to the written Word of God. This is true of the original writings, none of which are known to exist today. The copies of those original writings and the translations made in many languages cannot lay claim to absolute accuracy. There is solid evidence and sound reason for believing, however, that the available manuscripts of the Sacred Scriptures do provide copies of the written Word of God in nearly exact form, the points in question having little bearing on the sense of the message conveyed. God's own purpose in preparing the Sacred Scriptures and the inspired declaration that "the saying of Jehovah endures forever" give assurance that Jehovah God has preserved the internal integrity of the Scriptures through the centuries.—1Pe 1:25.

What accounts for differences in wording of quotations made from the Hebrew Scriptures in the Christian Greek Scriptures?

In a number of cases the writers of the Christian Greek Scriptures evidently made use of the Greek *Septuagint* translation when quoting from the Hebrew Scriptures. At times the rendering of the *Septuagint,* as quoted by them, differs somewhat from the reading of the Hebrew Scriptures as now known (most translations today being based on the Hebrew Masoretic text dating back to about the tenth century C.E.). As an example, Paul's quotation of Psalm 40:6 contains the expression "but you prepared a body for me," an expression found in the *Septuagint.* (Heb 10:5, 6) The available Hebrew manuscripts of Psalm 40:6 have, in place of that expression, the words "these ears of mine you opened up." Whether the *original* Hebrew text contained the phrase found in the *Septuagint* cannot be stated with certainty. Whatever the case, God's spirit guided Paul in his quotation, and therefore these words have divine authorization. This does not mean that the entire *Septuagint* translation is to be viewed as inspired; but those portions quoted by the inspired Christian writers did become an integral part of God's Word.

In a few cases the quotations made by Paul and others differ from both the Hebrew and Greek texts as found in available manuscripts. The dif-

ferences are minor, however, and upon examination are seen to be the result of paraphrasing, epitomizing, the use of synonymous terms, or the addition of explanatory words or phrases. Genesis 2:7, for instance, says "the man came to be a living soul," whereas Paul in quoting this portion said: "It is even so written: 'The *first* man *Adam* became a living soul.'" (1Co 15:45) His addition of the words "first" and "Adam" served to emphasize the contrast he was making between Adam and Christ. The insertion was fully in accord with the facts recorded in the Scriptures and in no way perverted the sense or content of the text quoted. Those to whom Paul wrote had copies (or translations) of the Hebrew Scriptures older than those we have today and could investigate his quotations, in a way similar to that of the people of Beroea. (Ac 17:10, 11) The inclusion of these writings in the canon of the Sacred Scriptures by the Christian congregation of the first century gives evidence of their acceptance of such quotations as part of the inspired Word of God.—Compare also Zec 13:7 with Mt 26:31.

"Inspired Expressions"—True and False. The Greek word *pneu'ma* (spirit) is used in a special manner in some apostolic writings. At 2 Thessalonians 2:2, for example, the apostle Paul urges his Thessalonian brothers not to get excited or shaken from their reason "either through an inspired expression [literally, "spirit"] or through a verbal message or through a letter as though from us, to the effect that the day of Jehovah is here." It is clear that Paul uses the word *pneu'ma* (spirit) in connection with means of communication, such as the "verbal message" or "letter." For this reason Lange's *Commentary on the Holy Scriptures* (p. 126) says on this text: "By this the Apostle intends a spiritual suggestion, pretended prediction, utterance of a prophet." (Translated and edited by P. Schaff, 1976) Vincent's *Word Studies in the New Testament* states: "*By spirit.* By prophetic utterances of individuals in Christian assemblies, claiming the authority of divine revelations." (1957, Vol. IV, p. 63) Thus, while some translations simply render *pneu'ma* in this and similar cases as "spirit," other translations read "message of the Spirit" (*AT*), "prediction" (*JB*), "inspiration" (D'Ostervald; Segond [French]), "inspired expression" (*NW*).

Paul's words make it clear that there are true "inspired expressions" and false ones. He refers to both kinds at 1 Timothy 4:1 when saying that "the inspired utterance [from Jehovah's holy spirit] says definitely that in later periods of time some will fall away from the faith, paying attention to misleading inspired utterances and teachings of demons." This identifies the source of the false "inspired utterances" as the demons. This is supported by the vision given the apostle John in which he saw "three unclean inspired expressions," froglike in appearance, proceeding from the mouths of the dragon, the wild beast, and the false prophet, and which expressions he specifically states are "inspired by demons," serving to gather earth's kings to the war at Har–Magedon. —Re 16:13-16.

With good reason, then, John urged Christians to "test the inspired expressions to see whether they originate with God." (1Jo 4:1-3; compare Re 22:6.) He then went on to show that God's true inspired expressions were coming through the genuine Christian congregation, not through unchristian worldly sources. John's statement was, of course, inspired by Jehovah God, but even aside from this, John's letter had laid a solid foundation for making the straightforward statement: "He that gains the knowledge of God listens to us; he that does not originate with God does not listen to us. This is how we take note of the inspired expression of truth and the inspired expression of error." (1Jo 4:6) Far from being mere dogmatism, John had shown that he and other true Christians were manifesting the fruits of God's spirit, primarily love, and were proving by their right conduct and truthful speech that they were indeed "walking in the light" in union with God.—1Jo 1:5-7; 2:3-6, 9-11, 15-17, 29; 3:1, 2, 6, 9-18, 23, 24; contrast Tit 1:16.

INSTALLATION (in·stal·la'tion). The induction of the priesthood into office. The Hebrew word for "installation" (mil·lu·'im') literally means "a filling," that is, a filling of the hand with power, an empowering. (Ex 29:22, ftn; compare Eze 43: 26, ftn; see FILL HAND WITH POWER.) The same term is used for the "setting" of jewels.—1Ch 29:2.

Aaron and his sons were taken from the Kohathite family of the tribe of Levi to serve as the priesthood for Israel. (Ex 6:16, 18, 20; 28:1) Their installation occupied seven days, apparently falling on Nisan 1-7, 1512 B.C.E., while Israel was encamped at the foot of Mount Sinai in the Arabian Peninsula. (Ex 40:2, 12, 17) The tent of meeting had just been completed and set up on the first day of the month; the priestly family had been chosen by Jehovah; and now Moses, the brother of Aaron, as mediator of the Law covenant, was commanded to perform the ceremony of their sanctification and installation. Instructions for the procedure are given in Exodus chap-

ter 29, and the record of Moses' carrying out the ceremony is in Leviticus chapter 8.

On this first day, with Jehovah's presence represented by the pillar of cloud above the tabernacle (Ex 40:33-38), Moses assembled all the sacrificial items: the bull, the two rams, the basket of unfermented cakes, the anointing oil, and the priestly garments. As instructed, he called the congregation of Israel, which likely meant the older men as representatives of the entire congregation, to gather at the entrance of the tent of meeting, outside the curtain that surrounded the courtyard. Since they evidently could observe what took place in the courtyard, the gateway screen, 20 cubits (8.9 m; 29 ft) wide, was probably removed.—Le 8:1-5; Ex 27:16.

Moses washed Aaron and Aaron's sons Nadab, Abihu, Eleazar, and Ithamar (or, he commanded them to wash themselves) at the copper basin in the courtyard and put upon Aaron the glorious garments of the high priest. (Nu 3:2, 3) Now clothed in beautiful apparel, Aaron was invested with the garments representing the qualities and responsibilities of his office. Moses then anointed the tabernacle, all its furnishings and utensils, and the altar of burnt offering, as well as the basin and the utensils used in connection with them. This sanctified them, set them aside for the exclusive use and service of God for which they would now be employed. Finally Moses anointed Aaron by pouring the oil upon his head.—Le 8:6-12; Ex 30:22-33; Ps 133:2.

Bull of the Sin Offering. Following this, Moses clothed Aaron's sons, after which he caused Aaron and his sons to lay their hands on the head of the bull of the sin offering, their action signifying their acknowledgment of the offering as being for them, the priestly house. After slaughtering the bull, Moses put some of the blood on the altar and poured the rest out at the base of the altar, thus symbolizing cleansing from the defilement brought because of the sinful nature of the priests who officiated at the altar. The blood being put on the *horns* of the altar evidently signified that the *power* of the sacrificial arrangement lay in the shed blood of the sacrifice. (Heb 9:22) The sprinkling of the altar was likewise required in connection with other offerings. (Le 1:5, 11; 3:2; 4:6; 16:18) Notice, however, that this being 'ordination day' for the priesthood and not the national atonement day for sins, the bull's blood was not taken into the Most Holy. (See Le 16:14.) As with other sin offerings, the fat upon the intestines, the appendage of the liver, and the two kidneys with their fat were placed on the altar. (Le 4:8-10, 20,

26, 31) The rest of the bull, with its skin and dung, was taken outside the camp to be burned. —Le 8:13-17.

Sacrificial Rams. Then Aaron and his sons laid hands on the ram of the burnt offering, and it was slaughtered, some of its blood being sprinkled upon the altar. The ram was then cut into parts, washed, and burned on the altar; but this did not include the dung and the skin. (Le 7:8) As this ram of the burnt offering was offered up completely, nothing being retained for consumption by any human, so these priests were completely sanctified to Jehovah's holy, priestly service.—Le 8:18-21; compare Le 1:3-9.

The other ram, "the ram of the installation," after having the priests' hands laid upon it, was slaughtered. Here the blood was used differently. Some of it was put on the right earlobe, right thumb, and right big toe of Aaron and his sons; so the faculties represented by these body members were to be used fully in connection with the sacrificial feature of their ministry. The rest of the blood Moses sprinkled upon the altar.—Le 8:22-24.

The fat around the ram's organs, before being offered in the usual way, was placed, along with one of each of the three kinds of unfermented cakes taken from the basket, on the right leg of the ram. All of this was now put on the palms of Aaron and his sons and was waved before Jehovah by Moses, who evidently put his hands under the priests' hands to do so. This signified that their hands were 'filled with power,' that is, filled with sacrificial gifts and fully equipped and empowered for sacrificial duty. They were shown to be authorized not only to offer the fat portions on the altar but also to receive the gifts provided for their sustenance as Jehovah's abundant arrangement for his priesthood. The part of the ram waved, the right leg, usually went to the officiating priest as his portion. (Le 7:32-34; Nu 18:18) In this instance, it was all burned on the altar. Thus it was both presented (waved) before Jehovah and actually offered, acknowledging all of it as his bestowal upon the priesthood.—Le 8:25-28.

Moses, acting in a priestly capacity during the installation service, now received the breast from the installation ram as his own portion, after presenting it as a wave offering.—Le 8:29; see also Ex 29:26-28.

Some of the ram's blood with the anointing oil (apparently mixed) was spattered upon Aaron, his sons, and their garments, to sanctify them. This also identified them with the sacrificial of-

fice, as directed by God's spirit. There is no mention of Aaron's sons being anointed by pouring oil over the head, as Aaron had been.—Le 8:30.

At the entrance of the tent of meeting, Aaron and his sons were to boil the portion of the ram's flesh that had not been burned on the altar or given to Moses. They would eat it, along with the cakes remaining in the basket, but any of this food left over was to be burned the next morning. This emphasized the cleanness and also stressed the completeness of their sanctification and service (because what was eaten was free from any putrefaction or staleness, and remainders were *completely* disposed of). It is notable also that no leaven was in the cakes.—Le 8:31, 32; Ex 29:31-34.

Completion of the Installation. The installation took seven days, before the end of which the priesthood could not officiate in the fullest sense. On each of the days, a bull was sacrificed as a sin offering to purify the altar. During the entire seven days, day and night, the newly ordained priests had to man posts of duty at the entrance of the tent of meeting, keeping "the obligatory watch of Jehovah," that they might not die.—Le 8:33-36; Ex 29:35-42.

On the eighth day, fully equipped and installed in office, the priesthood officiated (without Moses' assistance) for the first time, performing an atonement service for the nation of Israel, especially in need of cleansing not only because of their natural sinfulness but also because of their recent disobedience in connection with the golden calf, which had brought Jehovah's displeasure. (Le 9:1-7; Ex 32:1-10) At the conclusion of this first service by the newly installed priesthood, Jehovah manifested his approval and confirmation of them in office by sending miraculous fire, doubtless from the pillar of cloud above the tabernacle, devouring the remainder of the sacrifice on the altar.—Le 9:23, 24.

The Bible gives no record of an installation ceremony for the successors of Aaron. Evidently the one installation service was sufficient to place the Aaronic house and all its male offspring in their priestly office once and for all, to continue to time indefinite, down until the installation in office of the true and everlasting high priest Jesus Christ.—Heb 7:12, 17; 9:11, 12; see HIGH PRIEST; PRIEST.

INSTRUCTION. Direction or teaching that calls for compliance. The Hebrew verb *ya·rah'* means "instruct; direct; teach." The Hebrew term *le'qach* (instruction) basically means "a taking."

(De 32:2; compare Jer 9:20, where the related verb occurs in the expression "may your ear take the word of his mouth.") The same term is rendered "persuasiveness" in Proverbs 16:21. The Greek *pai·deu'o* means "instruct; chastise; discipline," and the Greek *ka·te·khe'o* means "teach orally; instruct."

Jehovah is the "Grand Instructor" of his people (Isa 30:20), and those who receive his instruction are under obligation to act in harmony with it —they *"will* walk in his paths" and *"will have to* beat their swords into plowshares and their spears into pruning shears." (Isa 2:2, 3; Mic 4: 2, 3) Appreciating the value of Jehovah's instruction and having a desire to comply with it, his servants pray: "Instruct me, O Jehovah, about your way. I shall walk in your truth. Unify my heart to fear your name."—Ps 86:11; 27:11; 119:33.

In ancient Israel, Jehovah assigned the priests as instructors of his people. Emphasizing the importance of compliance with instruction received through this channel, Moses said: "You must do in accordance with the word that they will hand down to you from that place which Jehovah will choose; and you must be careful to do according to all that they instruct you. In accordance with the law that they will point out to you, and according to the judicial decision that they will say to you, you should do. You must not turn aside from the word that they will hand down to you, to the right or to the left." (De 17:10, 11; 24:8) To those in the Christian congregation, the apostle Paul wrote: "All the things that were written aforetime were written for our instruction, that through our endurance and through the comfort from the Scriptures we might have hope." (Ro 15:4) We do well, therefore, to search out the commandments, take note of the underlying principles, and learn well the lessons that are set forth throughout God's inspired Word and then comply with these in our own lives.—See PUBLIC INSTRUCTOR.

Instruction can be received even from the domestic animals and from the earth, as stated at Job 12:7-10. (Pr 6:6) In these, wise persons will see evidence of the handiwork of God and of the fact that all life is dependent upon God. Humans who fail to act in harmony with this abundant evidence are, as the apostle Paul wrote, "inexcusable."—Ro 1:20.

Those who became disciples of Jesus Christ addressed him as Instructor, thus acknowledging his authority and their responsibility to comply with his directions. (Lu 5:5; 9:33) A group of ten leprous men who implored Jesus for mercy likewise addressed him in this manner.—Lu 17:13.

Although instruction calls for compliance and is not merely for entertainment, it can be imparted in a refreshing way. Jehovah directed Moses to teach Israel a song in which he said: "My instruction will drip as the rain, my saying will trickle as the dew, as gentle rains upon grass." (De 32:2) To the Christian overseer Timothy, Paul wrote about "instructing with mildness those not favorably disposed; as perhaps God may give them repentance leading to an accurate knowledge of truth." (2Ti 2:25) Instruction can, however, involve discipline in the form of chastisement. Such discipline is not always easy to take, but when one responds to it, it will yield "peaceable fruit, namely, righteousness."—Heb 12:7-11.

Not all instruction is given by one whose motivation is proper, nor is the objective necessarily beneficial for the one who receives it. "Moses was instructed in all the wisdom of the Egyptians," but at the age of 40 he openly identified himself with the Hebrews and left behind what could have been his inheritance in the royal courts of Egypt. (Ac 7:22) Isaiah spoke of prophets in Israel who gave false instruction, and Micah wrote regarding priests who instructed "just for a price." (Mic 3:11; Isa 9:15) Some persons foolishly turned to molten statues for instruction. (Hab 2:18) The soldiers who had been guarding Jesus' tomb were willing, after they had been bribed, to comply with the instruction given them to lie regarding what had happened to Jesus' body.—Mt 28: 12-15.

INSTRUMENT. See STRINGED INSTRUMENT; LEVELING INSTRUMENT.

INTEGRITY. Moral soundness, completeness, one's being blameless and faultless.

The Hebrew terms relating to integrity (*tom, tum·mah', tam, ta·mim'*) have the root meaning of that which is "complete" or "whole." (Compare Le 25:30; Jos 10:13; Pr 1:12.) *Ta·mim'* is used several times to refer to physical completeness, or soundness, and freedom from impairment, for example, regarding sacrificial animals. (Ex 12:5; 29:1; Le 3:6) But more frequently these terms describe moral soundness or blamelessness.

When applied to God, *ta·mim'* may properly be translated "perfect," as in describing Jehovah's activity and works, his way, knowledge, and law. (De 32:4; Job 36:4; 37:16; Ps 18:30; 19:7) All these divine qualities and expressions manifest such unmatchable completeness and fullness, are so sound and free from defect, or fault, that they clearly identify their Source as the one true God. —Ro 1:20; see PERFECTION.

Significance of Human Integrity. In a few cases the Hebrew *tom* conveys simply the idea of honest motive, innocence as to wrong intention. (Compare Ge 20:5, 6; 2Sa 15:11.) But mainly these related Hebrew terms describe unswerving devotion to righteousness. Biblical usage and examples emphasize unbreakable devotion to a *person,* Jehovah God, and to his expressed will and purpose as the course of vital importance.

Involved in the supreme issue. The first human pair were given the opportunity to manifest integrity in Eden. The restriction regarding the tree of knowledge put to the test their devotion to their Creator. Under the pressure of outside influence from God's Adversary and his appeal to selfishness, they gave way to disobedience. Their shame, their reluctance to face their Creator, and their lack of candor in responding to his questions all gave evidence of their lack of integrity. (Compare Ps 119:1, 80.) Obviously, however, they were not the first to break integrity, since the spirit creature who led them into a rebellious course had already done so.—Ge 3:1-19; compare his course with the dirge pronounced against the king of Tyre at Eze 28:12-15; see SATAN.

Satan's rebellion, visibly initiated in Eden, produced an issue of universal importance—that of the rightfulness of God's sovereignty over all his creatures, his right to require full obedience of them. Since the issue was not one of superiority of power but, rather, was a moral issue, it could not be settled merely by the exercise of power, as by God's immediately crushing Satan and the human pair out of existence. This fact is an aid in understanding why wickedness and its author, Satan, have been allowed to continue so long. (See WICKEDNESS.) Since God's Adversary first drew upon humans for support and endorsement of his rebel course (the earliest evidence for any siding with Satan on the part of spirit sons of God not appearing until sometime prior to the Flood; Ge 6:1-5; compare 2Pe 2:4, 5), this made the question of man's integrity to God's sovereign will an essential part of the overall issue (though Jehovah's sovereignty is not itself dependent on the integrity of his creatures). Proof of this is seen in the case of Job.

Job. Job, who evidently lived in the period between the death of Joseph and the time of Moses, is described as a man who had "proved to be blameless [Heb., *tam*] and upright, and fearing God and turning aside from bad." (Job 1:1; see JOB.) That human integrity forms part of the issue between Jehovah God and Satan is clear from God's questioning his Adversary about Job when Satan appeared during an angelic assembly in the courts of heaven. Satan imputed false motive to Job's worship of God, alleging that Job served not out of pure devotion but for selfish benefits. He thereby placed in question Job's integrity to God. Permitted to divest Job of his vast possessions and even of his children, Satan failed to crack Job's integrity. (Job 1:6–2:3) He then claimed that Job was selfishly willing to endure the loss of possessions and children as long as he could save his own skin. (Job 2:4, 5) Thereafter stricken with a painful, consuming disease and subjected to dissuasion from his own wife as well as to disparaging criticism and slurs from companions who misrepresented God's standards and purposes (Job 2:6-13; 22:1, 5-11), Job's response was that he would not deny having been a man of integrity. "Until I expire I shall not take away my integrity from myself! On my justness I have laid hold, and I shall not let it go; my heart will not taunt me for any of my days." (Job 27:5, 6) His maintaining integrity demonstrated that God's Adversary was a liar.

Satan's challenging statements in Job's case show he held the position that all persons could be drawn away from God's side, that none served out of a purely unselfish motive. Thus humans, as well as God's spirit sons, have the remarkable privilege of contributing to the vindication and sanctification of God's name and demonstrating their support of Jehovah's sovereignty, doing so by a course of integrity. The ones "blameless in their way are a pleasure" to Jehovah.—Pr 11:20; contrast this with the false view advanced by Eliphaz at Job 22:1-3.

Basis for divine judgment. Having a favorable judgment from God is dependent on the creature's integrity-keeping course. (Ps 18:23-25) As King David wrote: "Jehovah himself will pass sentence on the peoples. Judge me, O Jehovah, according to my righteousness and according to my integrity in me. Please, may the badness of wicked ones come to an end, and may you establish the righteous one." (Ps 7:8, 9; compare Pr 2:21, 22.) Suffering Job expressed the confidence that "[Jehovah] will weigh me in accurate scales and God will get to know my integrity." (Job 31:6) Job thereafter lists about a dozen examples from actual life that, if true of him, would have demonstrated a lack of integrity.—Job 31:7-40.

What does integrity keeping include in the case of imperfect humans?

Since all men are imperfect and unable to measure up perfectly to God's standards, it is evident that their integrity does not mean perfection of action or of speech. Rather, the Scriptures show it means wholeness or completeness of heart devotion. David, through weakness, committed several serious wrongs, but he, nevertheless, 'walked with integrity of heart' (1Ki 9:4), for he accepted reproof and corrected his way. He thereby proved that his heart still retained genuine love for Jehovah God. (Ps 26:1-3, 6, 8, 11) As David later told his son Solomon: "Know the God of your father and serve him with a complete heart and with a delightful soul; for all hearts Jehovah is searching, and every inclination of the thoughts he is discerning." Solomon's heart, however, did not "prove to be complete with Jehovah his God like the heart of David his father."—1Ch 28:9; 1Ki 11:4; the word "complete" in these two texts is from another Hebrew term, sha·lem', as at Pr 11:1; 1Ki 15:14.

Integrity is therefore not restricted to any one aspect of human conduct; it does not apply just to matters obviously "religious." For God's servant it is a way of life in which the individual 'walks,' constantly searching to know Jehovah's will. (Ps 119:1-3) David shepherded the nation of Israel "according to the integrity of his heart," both in matters directly relating to Jehovah's worship and in his conduct of governmental affairs. He also desired that those around him and those acting as his ministers likewise be persons of integrity, "walking in a faultless way." (Ps 78:72; 101:2-7) One 'proves himself faultless' before God over a period of time, as did Noah, Abraham, and others.—Ge 6:9; 17:1; 2Sa 22:24.

Integrity requires uncompromising loyalty to God and adherence to righteousness, not merely under favorable conditions or circumstances, but under all conditions and at all times. After stressing that only the integrity-keeper, "speaking the truth in his heart," is acceptable to Jehovah, the psalmist says of such a one that "he has sworn to what is bad for himself, and yet he does not alter," that is, even if something he has solemnly agreed to turns out to be apparently against his personal interests, he still stays true to his agreement. (Ps 15:1-5; contrast Ro 1:31, 1Ti 1:10.) Integrity, then, is most evident when the individual's devotion is under test and he is pressured to abandon his righteous course. Though made a laughingstock by opposers (Job 12:4; compare Jer 20:7) or made the object of their bitter speech (Ps 64:3, 4), hatred, and violent persecution (Pr 29:10; Am 5:10), whether in sickness or in distressful adversity, a person must 'hold fast his integrity' as did Job, no matter what the cost.—Job 2:3.

Such an integrity-keeping course is possible, not by the individual's personal moral strength, but only through deep faith and trust in Jehovah and His saving power. (Ps 25:21) God's promise is that he will be a "shield" and "stronghold," guarding the way of those walking in integrity. (Pr 2:6-8; 10:29; Ps 41:12) Their constant concern for gaining Jehovah's approval brings stability to their lives, enabling them to follow a straight course to their goal. (Ps 26:1-3; Pr 11:5; 28:18) Though, as Job perplexedly observed, the blameless may suffer because of the rule of the wicked and may die along with the wicked, Jehovah assures that he is aware of the life of the faultless person and guarantees that such a person's inheritance will continue, his future will be peaceful, and he will come into the possession of good. (Job 9:20-22; Ps 37:18, 19, 37; 84:11; Pr 28:10) As in Job's case, it is being a man of integrity, rather than one's wealth, that makes one a person of genuine worth, meriting respect. (Pr 19:1; 28:6) Children privileged to have such a person for a parent are to be counted happy (Pr 20:7), receiving a splendid legacy in their father's life example, enjoying a share in his good name and the respect he gained.

In addition to the examples of Job and David, the Hebrew Scriptures are replete with other examples of men of integrity. Abraham showed unswerving loyalty to God in his willingness to sacrifice his son Isaac. (Ge 22:1-12) Daniel and his three companions provide sterling illustrations of integrity under test, in youth and in later life. (Da 1:8-17; 3:13-23; 6:4-23) At Hebrews chapter 11, the apostle Paul lists a long line of men of pre-Christian times who through faith displayed integrity under a wide variety of difficult circumstances.—Note particularly vss 33-38.

Integrity in the Christian Greek Scriptures. Whereas no exact word for "integrity" appears in the Christian Greek Scriptures, the idea pervades this entire portion of the Bible. God's Son, Jesus Christ, gave the finest example of integrity and of supreme trust in his heavenly Father's strength and care. He thereby was "made perfect" for his position as High Priest, as well as Anointed King of the heavenly Kingdom, one greater than David's. (Heb 5:7-9; 4:15; 7:26-28; Ac 2:34, 35) Integrity is embraced in the commandment Jesus singled out as the greatest of all—loving Jehovah

God with one's whole heart, mind, soul, and strength. (Mt 22:36-38) His injunction that "you must accordingly be perfect, as your heavenly Father is perfect" (Mt 5:48) also stressed a completeness of one's devotion to righteousness. (The Greek terms for perfection convey the idea of that which has been 'brought to completion' and so are somewhat similar in meaning to the Hebrew terms already discussed.)

Jesus' teachings emphasized purity of heart, singleness of outlook and intent, freedom from hypocrisy—all these being qualities that characterize integrity. (Mt 5:8; 6:1-6, 16-18, 22, 23; Lu 11:34-36) The apostle Paul showed the same concern as had David and earlier servants of God for proving blameless and faultless. He was free from any charge of corruption or deviousness in his ministry and in all his dealings with others.—2Co 4:1, 2; 6:3-10; 8:20, 21; 1Th 1:3-6.

Perseverance in a God-given commission in the face of opposition, and endurance of privations, persecution, and suffering for adhering to a course of godly devotion, also marked Paul and other early Christians as persons of integrity. —Ac 5:27-41; 2Co 11:23-27.

INTEREST.
The price or rate paid by a debtor for the use of what he borrows.

Already in the second millennium B.C.E., Babylon had a fully developed loan system. The Code of Hammurabi indicates a 20-percent interest rate on money and grain, and it stipulates that a merchant charging a higher rate would forfeit the amount lent. By contrast God's law to Israel prohibited making loans on interest to needy fellow Israelites. No one was to profit from another's financial reverses. (Ex 22:25; Le 25:36, 37; De 23:19) And Proverbs 28:8 indicates that fortunes acquired from interest wrongfully collected would eventually become the possession of "the one showing favor to the lowly ones."

Foreigners, however, could be charged interest by the Israelites. (De 23:20) Jewish commentators understand this to apply, not to cases of need, but to business loans. (*The Pentateuch and Haftorahs*, edited by J. H. Hertz, London, 1972, p. 849) Usually foreigners were in Israel only temporarily, often as merchants, and could reasonably be expected to pay interest, particularly since they would also be lending to others on interest.

Whereas upright Israelites obeyed God's law about making interest-free loans (Ps 15:5; Eze 18:5, 8, 17), lending on interest apparently became common and brought hardships on needy debtors. (Ne 5:1-11; Isa 24:2; Eze 18:13; 22:12) Jesus Christ, though, upheld God's law in this regard and gave it an even broader application, saying: "Continue . . . to lend without interest, not hoping for anything back." (Lu 6:34, 35) It would therefore be improper to withhold assistance from a person who because of continued adversity and through no fault of his own might be unable to repay a debt. But when the loan is not needed to relieve poverty, there would be no objection to a person's charging interest on a loan. Jesus himself, by having the wicked slave in one of his illustrations censured for failing to deposit his master's money with the bankers so as to draw interest, implied that receiving interest from invested capital is proper.—Mt 25:26, 27; Lu 19:22, 23.

INTERPRETATION.
In the Bible an interpreter may be either of two kinds. He may be a translator, one who conveys the meaning of words spoken or written in one language to persons reading or speaking another, and he can do this either orally or in writing. On the other hand, an interpreter may be one who explains Bible prophecy by giving others the meaning, significance, and understanding of prophetic dreams, visions, and messages of divine origin.

Translation. The confusion of man's language during the building of the Tower of Babel resulted in the human family's suddenly becoming a multilingual race. This, in turn, gave rise to a new profession, that of interpreter or translator. (Ge 11:1-9) Some five centuries later, in order to conceal his identity as their brother, Joseph employed a translator to interpret for him when speaking to his Hebrew brothers in the Egyptian language. (Ge 42:23) A form of the Hebrew word *lits* (deride; scorn) is rendered "interpreter" in this text. The same word is sometimes rendered 'spokesman' when referring to an envoy versed in a foreign language, as were "the spokesmen of the princes of Babylon" sent to converse with King Hezekiah of Judah.—2Ch 32:31.

The gift of speaking in foreign tongues was one of the manifestations of God's outpoured holy spirit upon the faithful disciples of Christ on Pentecost 33 C.E. However, this was no duplication of what occurred on the Plains of Shinar 22 centuries earlier. For, instead of replacing their original language with a new one, these disciples retained their mother tongue and at the same time were enabled to speak in the tongues of foreign-language groups about the magnificent things of God. (Ac 2:1-11) Along with this ability to speak in different tongues, other miraculous gifts of the spirit were bestowed on members of the early Christian congregation, including the gift of translating from one language to another. Christians were also given instruction on the proper use of this gift.—1Co 12:4-10, 27-30; 14:5, 13-28.

The most remarkable example of translation from one language to another is the rendering of the Bible into many, many tongues, a monumental task that has consumed centuries of time. Today this Book, the whole or in part, appears in well over 1,800 languages. However, none of such translations or their translators were inspired. Historically, such translation work dates back to the third century B.C.E. when work on the Greek *Septuagint* was begun in which the inspired Holy Scriptures in Hebrew and Aramaic, the 39 books as they are now reckoned, were rendered into the common Greek, or Koine, the international language of that time.

Bible writers of the 27 books that make up the Christian Greek Scriptures, which books completed the Bible's canon, often quoted from the Hebrew Scriptures. Apparently they sometimes used the Greek *Septuagint* instead of personally translating from the Hebrew text of the Scriptures. (Compare Ps 40:6 [39:7, *LXX*] with Heb 10:5.) They also made their own rather free translations, however, as is seen by comparing Hosea 2:23 with Romans 9:25. An example of where they paraphrased, instead of making a literal translation, may be noted by comparing Deuteronomy 30:11-14 with Romans 10:6-8.

These Bible writers often translated the names of persons, titles, places, and expressions for the benefit of their readers. They gave the meaning of such names as Cephas, Barnabas, Tabitha, Bar-Jesus, and Melchizedek (Joh 1:42; Ac 4:36; 9:36; 13:6, 8; Heb 7:1, 2); also the meaning of the titles Immanuel, Rabbi, and Messiah (Mt 1:23; Joh 1:38, 41); the meaning of places like Golgotha, Siloam, and Salem (Mr 15:22; Joh 9:7; Heb 7:2); and translations of the terms *"Tal'i·tha cu'mi"* and *"E'li, E'li, la'ma sa·bach·tha'ni?"*—Mr 5:41; 15:34.

Matthew first wrote his Gospel account in Hebrew, according to the ancient testimony of Jerome, Eusebius Pamphili, Origen, Irenaeus, and Papias. Who translated this Gospel later into Greek is not known. If Matthew did so himself, as some think, then it is the only known inspired translation of Scripture.

In classical Greek the word *her·me·neu'o* often means "explain, interpret." In the Christian Greek Scriptures it has the meaning "translate." (Joh 1:42; 9:7; Heb 7:2) It is similar to the name of the Greek god Hermes (Mercury), regarded by ancient mythologists not only as the messenger, envoy, and interpreter for the gods but also the patron of writers, speakers, and translators. The pagans in Lystra called Paul "Hermes, since he was the one taking the lead in speaking." (Ac 14:12) The prefix *me·ta'* implies "a change," and so, added to *her·me·neu'o,* the word *me·ther·me·neu'o·mai* results, a word that also occurs several times in the Bible. It means "change or translate from one language to another," and is always in the passive voice, as *"when* translated."—Mt 1:23.

Interpretation of Prophecy. *Di·er·me·neu'o* is a strengthened and intensified form of *her·me·neu'o.* It is usually used in reference to translating languages (Ac 9:36; 1Co 12:30), but it also signifies "explain fully; interpret fully." *Di·er·me·neu'o* was therefore the word Luke used in relating how Jesus on the road to Emmaus with two of his disciples commenced with the writings of Moses and the prophets and "interpreted to them things pertaining to himself in all the Scriptures." The two disciples were later telling others of the experience, how Jesus was "fully opening up the Scriptures" to them.—Lu 24:13-15, 25-32.

Dy·ser·me'neu·tos has an opposite meaning. It was used by Paul and is found only at Hebrews 5:11, meaning "hard to interpret," that is, "hard to be explained."—See *Int.*

Another Greek word rendered "interpretation" is *e·pi'ly·sis,* from the verb literally meaning "loosen up or release" (hence, explain or solve). True prophecy does not find its source in the expressed opinions or interpretations of men but, rather, originates with God. Hence Peter writes: "No prophecy of Scripture springs from any private interpretation [*e·pi·ly'se·os*] . . . but men spoke from God as they were borne along by holy spirit." (2Pe 1:20, 21) Thus, the Bible prophecies were never the product of astute deductions and predictions by men based on their personal analysis of human events or trends.

The meaning of some prophecies was obvious, hence requiring no interpretation, as when the prophet was used to foretell that the Judeans would 'go into captivity to the king of Babylon for seventy years' or that Babylon would become 'a desolate waste.' The *time* of the fulfillment, of course, was not always known, though in some cases this, too, was explicitly stated. Many prophecies or particular features of the prophecies, however, were only partially understood at the time of their being given, the full understanding or interpretation awaiting God's due time for their being made clear. This was true with some of the prophecies of Daniel and with regard to the Messiah and the sacred secret involving him.—Da 12:4, 8-10; 1Pe 1:10-12.

All of Egypt's magic-practicing priests and wise men were helpless when it came to interpreting Pharaoh's God-sent dreams. "There was no interpreter of them for Pharaoh." (Ge 41:1-8) It was then brought to Pharaoh's attention that Joseph had successfully interpreted the dreams of Pharaoh's chief cupbearer and chief baker. (Ge 40:5-22; 41:9-13) However, in that connection Joseph had taken no credit to himself but had called their attention to Jehovah as the Interpreter of dreams, saying, "Do not interpretations belong to God?" (Ge 40:8) So when called before Pharaoh to interpret the king's dream, Joseph declared: "I need not be considered! God will announce welfare to Pharaoh." (Ge 41:14-16) After hearing the interpretation, even Pharaoh acknowledged Joseph to be "one in whom the spirit of God" was found, for "God has caused you [Joseph] to know all this."—Ge 41:38, 39.

Similarly, Daniel was used by God to make known the interpretation of Nebuchadnezzar's dreams. After first praying to God for understanding of the secret and getting the answer in a night vision, Daniel was brought before the king both to recall the forgotten dream and then to give the interpretation. (Da 2:14-26) By way of an introduction, Daniel reminded the king that all his wise men, conjurers, magic-practicing priests, and astrologers were unable to interpret the dream. "However," Daniel continued, "there exists a God in the heavens who is a Revealer of secrets, . . . as for me, it is not through any wisdom that exists in me more than in any others alive that this secret is revealed to me, except to the intent that the interpretation may be made known to the king."—Da 2:27-30.

On a second occasion, when all the magic-practicing priests, conjurers, Chaldeans, and astrologers were unable to interpret the king's dream concerning the great tree that was cut down, Daniel was again called in, and again the divine origin of the prophecy was emphasized. In virtual acknowledgment of this fact, the king said to Daniel: "I myself well know that the spirit of the holy gods is in you," and "you are competent, because the spirit of holy gods is in you."—Da 4:4-18, 24.

Years later, on the very night in which Babylon fell to the Medes and Persians, this aging servant of Jehovah, Daniel, was once again called upon to interpret a divine message for a king. This time a mysterious hand had written MENE, MENE, TEKEL, PARSIN on the palace wall during Belshazzar's feast. All the wise men of Babylon proved unable to interpret the cryptic writing. The queen mother then recalled that Daniel was still available, the one "in whom there is the spirit of holy gods," as well as "illumination and insight and wisdom like the wisdom of gods." In interpreting the writing, which was really a prophecy in itself, Daniel once again magnified Jehovah as the God of true prophecy.—Da 5:1, 5-28.

INTERPRETER.   See INTERPRETATION.

INTESTINES.   The bowels or entrails. The Hebrew word qe'rev is used to describe the "interior parts," "inward parts," or "intestines" of men and of animals. (Ex 12:9; 29:13; Ps 5:9) It denotes that which is "inside" and is often used as a preposition, with the meaning "within; in the midst of."—Ge 25:22; De 17:20.

Another term that refers to the internal organs is the Hebrew me·'eh'. Always occurring in the plural (me·'im'), it is used for "intestines" in 2 Samuel 20:10 and 2 Chronicles 21:15, 18, 19. The word may denote the "inward parts" of a creature, as in the account of the large fish that swallowed Jonah. There it occurs twice and is shown in parallel with the "belly" of the large fish. (Jon 1:17; 2:1, 2) The reproductive system of humans may also be referred to by this Hebrew term. (Ge 15:4; Ru 1:11) Because of the evident link between the emotions and internal organs, the intestines, or bowels, were considered the seat of the deepest emotions.—Compare Isa 63:15; Jer 4:19; 31:20.

Physical food is assimilated by the intestines. This fact was metaphorically used to represent mental or spiritual digestion when, in vision, Ezekiel was told to eat a scroll, filling his intestines (Heb., me·'im') with it. Ezekiel was to gain spiritual strength by meditating upon and storing in his memory the words written in the scroll. He was thereby nourished spiritually and provided with a message to speak.—Eze 3:1-6; compare Re 10:8-10.

In the Christian Greek Scriptures, the word splag'khna, which literally means "intestines," is used once to refer to the literal intestines. (Ac 1:18) Elsewhere it is metaphorically used to denote "tender affections" and "tender compassions."—2Co 6:12; Php 1:8; 2:1; Col 3:12; 1Jo 3:17.

INTOXICATION.   See DRUNKENNESS.

IOB.   Third-named son of Issachar. (Ge 46:13) At Numbers 26:24 and 1 Chronicles 7:1, the name appears as Jashub.

IPHDEIAH (Iph·de′iah) [May Jah Redeem; Jah Has Redeemed]. Son of Shashak; a headman of the tribe of Benjamin.—1Ch 8:1, 25, 28.

IPHTAH (Iph′tah) [shortened form of Iphtah-el]. A city of Judah in the Shephelah. (Jos 15:20, 33, 43) Tarqumiya, about 10 km (6 mi) WNW of Hebron, has been suggested as a possible location.

IPHTAH-EL (Iph′tah-el) [May God Open; God Has Opened]. A valley on the boundary between the tribes of Zebulun and Asher. (Jos 19:10, 14, 24, 27) Various places NW of Nazareth have been proposed, but the exact location is uncertain.

IR [Full-Grown Ass]. 'Father' of Shuppim and Huppim (1Ch 7:12); probably the same as the Benjamite Iri.—1Ch 7:7.

IRA (I′ra) [Full-Grown Ass].

1. A Jairite listed among King David's leading officers as "a priest of David." (2Sa 20:26) Ira perhaps was a descendant of the Jair mentioned at Numbers 32:41, and therefore, in this case the designation "priest" may signify "chief minister," "prince." There is no Biblical evidence that the Jairites were Levites. However, if the reading of the Syriac *Peshitta* is correct, Ira may have been a priest from the Levite city of Jattir (Jathir). —Compare 2Sa 8:18; 1Ch 6:57; 18:17.

2. Son of Ikkesh the Tekoite; one of the mighty men of King David's military forces.—2Sa 23:24, 26; 1Ch 11:26, 28.

3. An Ithrite; another of King David's mighty men.—2Sa 23:38; 1Ch 11:40.

IRAD (I′rad). Grandson of Cain; forefather of the bigamist Lamech, and of Jabal and Tubal-cain.—Ge 4:17-23.

IRAM (I′ram) [possibly from a root meaning "full-grown ass"]. A sheik or chieftain of Esau (Edom).—Ge 36:43; 1Ch 1:54.

IRI (I′ri) [possibly from a root meaning "full-grown ass"]. Son of Bela; a paternal head and valiant, mighty man of Benjamin. (1Ch 7:7) Iri is probably the same as the Ir of 1 Chronicles 7:12.

IRIJAH (I·ri′jah) [Jah Sees]. "Son of Shelemiah the son of Hananiah"; the officer in charge of the Gate of Benjamin in Jerusalem who arrested Jeremiah on the false charge of intending to desert to the Babylonians.—Jer 37:13, 14.

IR-NAHASH (Ir-na′hash) [City of Nahash]. Seemingly a place fathered, or founded, by the Judean Tehinnah. (1Ch 4:1, 12) The exact location

of Ir-nahash is uncertain. Some scholars favor as a possible identification Deir Nahhas, about 20 km (12 mi) WNW of Hebron.

IRON. One of the oldest metals known to man. Today it is rated the most abundant, most useful, and cheapest of all metals. It is the fourth most plentiful element in the crust of the earth, while the earth's core is said to be nearly 90 percent iron. The Bible record reveals that it was used in the making of tools, nails, gates, weapons, fetters, instruments for writing, and even false gods.

Pure iron in commerce is uncommon. Pig iron contains about 3 percent carbon plus small amounts of other elements. Wrought iron has much less carbon. (Job 40:18) The many varieties of steel are simply iron alloyed with carbon and other additives to give them special characteristics. "Steel" in the *King James Version,* however, is a mistranslation for "copper." (2Sa 22:35; Job 20:24; Ps 18:34; Jer 15:12) Because of the crude furnaces and smelting methods, the iron in Bible times was never totally purified but was an alloy of carbon and other elements. Tubal-cain of the fourth millennium B.C.E. was the first person known to forge and work with iron.—Ge 4:22.

Meteoric iron was one type used at an early time by man. In Egyptian tombs iron beads have been found that have proved to be meteoric in composition. But man was not limited to that source of supply. He mined iron oxides and sulfides and smelted the same, notwithstanding the high temperatures needed to melt iron. (Job 28:2; Eze 22:20; see REFINE, REFINER.) However, its use was quite limited compared with copper and bronze, which could be worked cold. Nevertheless, iron doubtless was especially valued because of its great strength and utility. Iron was included among the spoils of war highly esteemed by the Israelites. (Nu 31:22; Jos 6:19, 24; 22:8) But more than captured iron was to be their portion. Moses promised that upon reaching Palestine, they would find iron deposits, and so it proved to be. (De 8:9) Other sources of iron mentioned in the Bible included Tarshish, as well as "Vedan and Javan from Uzal."—Eze 27:12, 19.

In their conquest of the Promised Land, the Israelites were confronted with war chariots equipped with iron scythes. (Jos 17:16, 18; Jg 1:19) At one point during Saul's reign, "there was not a smith [metalworker] to be found in all the land of Israel." Because of a ban imposed by the Philistines, only the king and his son Jonathan had a sword; Israel was forced to take all metal tools down to the Philistines to have them sharpened.—1Sa 13:19-22.

Later, however, King David gathered together huge quantities of iron for use in the temple construction. Under Solomon's reign there was contributed "iron worth a hundred thousand talents," or, according to many translations, "a hundred thousand talents of iron." (1Ch 22:14, 16; 29:2, 7) If the reference is to the *value* of the iron and if the talents were silver, then the iron was worth $660,600,000. If the reference is to the *weight* of the iron, then it amounted to about 3,420 metric tons (3,770 tons).

Figurative Usage. The iron furnace is a symbol of hard and hot oppression (De 4:20; 1Ki 8:51; Jer 11:4); iron yokes, unbreakable bondage. (De 28:48; Jer 28:13, 14) In a figurative sense iron symbolizes hardness (Le 26:19; De 28:23), stubbornness (Isa 48:4; Jer 6:28), strength (Jer 1:18; Da 7:7; Re 9:9), kingly power, and judicial authority (Ps 2:9; Re 2:27; 12:5; 19:15).

IRPEEL (Ir′pe·el) [May God Heal; God Has Healed]. A city of Benjamin. (Jos 18:21, 27) Some suggest as a possible identification Rafat, a village about 10 km (6 mi) NW of Jerusalem.

IR-SHEMESH (Ir-she′mesh) [City of the Sun]. A town on the boundary of Dan, listed between Eshtaol and Shaalabbin in Joshua 19:41, 42. It is possibly the same as Beth-shemesh of Joshua 15:10. If so, then it was later occupied by the tribe of Judah and assigned from that tribe as one of the 48 Levite cities.—Jos 21:16; 1Ch 6:59; Nu 35:6, 7; see BETH-SHEMESH No. 1.

IRU (I′ru) [possibly from a root meaning "full-grown ass"]. The first-named son of Caleb the spy; of Judah's tribe. (1Ch 4:15) Some scholars think that the name was really Ir and that the "u" was only the Hebrew conjunction *and*.

ISAAC (I′saac) [Laughter]. The only son of Abraham by his wife Sarah. Hence, a vital link in the line of descent leading to Christ. (1Ch 1:28, 34; Mt 1:1, 2; Lu 3:34) Isaac was weaned at about 5, was as good as offered up as a sacrifice at perhaps 25, was married at 40, became father to twin sons at 60, and died at the age of 180.—Ge 21:2-8; 22:2; 25:20, 26; 35:28.

The birth of Isaac was under the most unusual circumstances. Both his father and his mother were very old, his mother long before having stopped menstruating. (Ge 18:11) So when God told Abraham that Sarah would give birth to a son, he laughed over the prospect, saying: "Will a man a hundred years old have a child born, and

will Sarah, yes, will a woman ninety years old give birth?" (Ge 17:17) Upon learning what was to take place, Sarah laughed too. (See LAUGHTER.) Then, "at the appointed time" the following year, the child was born, proving that nothing is "too extraordinary for Jehovah." (Ge 18:9-15) Sarah then exclaimed: "God has prepared laughter for me," adding, "everybody hearing of it will laugh at me." And so, just as Jehovah had said, the boy was appropriately named Isaac, meaning "Laughter."—Ge 21:1-7; 17:19.

Being of Abraham's household and heir to the promises, Isaac was properly circumcised on the eighth day.—Ge 17:9-14, 19; 21:4; Ac 7:8; Ga 4:28.

How old was Isaac when he was weaned?

The day Isaac was weaned, Abraham prepared a big feast. Apparently on that occasion Sarah noticed Ishmael "poking fun" at his younger half brother Isaac. (Ge 21:8, 9) Some translations (*JB, Mo, RS*) say that Ishmael was only "playing" with Isaac, that is, in the sense of child's play. However, the Hebrew word *tsa·chaq′* can also have an offensive connotation. Thus, when this same word occurs in other texts (Ge 19:14; 39:14, 17), these translations render it "jesting" or "joking" and "insult."

Certain Targums, as well as the Syriac *Peshitta,* at Genesis 21:9, give Ishmael's remarks the sense of "deriding." Concerning *tsa·chaq′,* Cook's *Commentary* says: "It probably means in this passage, as it has generally been understood, 'mocking laughter.' As Abraham had laughed for joy concerning Isaac, and Sarah had laughed incredulously, so now Ishmael laughed in derision, and probably in a persecuting and tyrannical spirit." Deciding the matter, the inspired apostle Paul clearly shows that Ishmael's treatment of Isaac was affliction, *persecution,* not childlike play. (Ga 4:29) Certain commentators, in view of Sarah's insistence, in the next verse (Ge 21:10), that "the son of this slave girl is not going to be an heir with my son, with Isaac," suggest that Ishmael (14 years Isaac's senior) perhaps quarreled and taunted Isaac with regard to heirship.

Jehovah had told Abraham that as alien residents his seed would be afflicted for 400 years, which affliction ended with Israel's deliverance out of Egypt in 1513 B.C.E. (Ge 15:13; Ac 7:6) Four hundred years prior thereto would mark 1913 B.C.E. as the beginning of that affliction.

Consequently, this also fixes 1913 as the year Isaac was weaned, since timewise the two events, his being weaned and his being mistreated by Ishmael, are closely associated in the account. This means that Isaac was about five years old when weaned, having been born in 1918 B.C.E. Incidentally, his birth marked the beginning of the 450 years mentioned in Acts 13:17-20, which time period ended about 1467 B.C.E. when Joshua's campaign in Canaan concluded and the land was distributed to the various tribes.

Today, when so many women in the Western world refuse to nurse their babies, or nurse them for only six to nine months, a five-year period may seem inconceivably long. But Dr. D. B. Jelliffe reports that in many parts of the world children are not weaned until they are one and a half to two years old, and in Arabia it is customary for a mother to nurse her young anywhere from 13 to 32 months. Medically speaking, nursing, or lactation, may normally be continued until the next pregnancy is some few months advanced.—*Infant Nutrition in the Subtropics and Tropics,* Geneva, 1968, p. 38.

In the Middle Ages in Europe the average age for weaning was two years, and in the time of the Maccabees (first and second century B.C.E.) women nursed their sons for three years. (2 Maccabees 7:27) Four thousand years ago when people lived an unrushed life, and there was not the present-day pressure or necessity to telescope so much into the shortened life span, it is easy to understand why Sarah could have nursed Isaac for five years. Besides, he was Sarah's only child after many years of barrenness.

Willing to Be Sacrificed. After Isaac was weaned, nothing further is said of his childhood. The next notice we have of him is when God said to his father Abraham: "Take, please, your son, your only son whom you so love, Isaac, and make a trip to the land of Moriah and there offer him up as a burnt offering." (Ge 22:1, 2) After a three-day journey they came to the place selected by God. Isaac carried the wood; his father, the fire and the slaughtering knife. "But where is the sheep for the burnt offering?" Isaac asked. "God will provide himself the sheep" was the answer. —Ge 22:3-8, 14.

Reaching the site, they built an altar and laid the wood in place. Then Isaac was bound hand and foot and put atop the wood. As Abraham raised the knife, Jehovah's angel stayed his hand. Abraham's faith had not been misplaced; Jehovah provided a ram, there caught in the mountain thicket, that could be offered up for a burnt offer-

ing in the place of and as a substitute for Isaac. (Ge 22:9-14) Thus Abraham, reckoning "that God was able to raise him up even from the dead," did "in an illustrative way" receive Isaac back from the dead.—Heb 11:17-19.

This dramatic episode proved the faith and obedience not only of Abraham but also of his son Isaac. Jewish tradition, recorded by Josephus, says that Isaac was 25 years old at the time. At any rate, he was old enough and strong enough to carry a considerable quantity of wood up a mountain. So, he could have resisted his 125-year-old father when the time came to bind him if he had chosen to be rebellious against Jehovah's commandments. (*Jewish Antiquities,* I, 227 [xiii, 2]) Instead, Isaac submissively let his father proceed to offer him as a sacrifice in harmony with God's will. For this demonstration of Abraham's faith, Jehovah then repeated and enlarged upon his covenant with Abraham, which covenant was transferred by God to Isaac after the death of Isaac's father.—Ge 22:15-18; 26:1-5; Ro 9:7; Jas 2:21.

More important, a great prophetic picture was there enacted, portraying how Christ Jesus, the Greater Isaac, would in due time willingly lay down his human life as the Lamb of God for mankind's salvation.—Joh 1:29, 36; 3:16.

Marriage and Family. After the death of Isaac's mother his father concluded it was time the son got married. Abraham, however, was determined that Isaac would not marry a pagan Canaanite. So, under the patriarchal arrangement, Abraham sent his trusted household servant back to the relatives in Mesopotamia to pick a woman of Semitic origin who also worshiped Abraham's God Jehovah.—Ge 24:1-9.

The mission was bound to succeed, for from the very outset the whole matter of choice was placed in the hands of Jehovah. As it turned out, Isaac's cousin Rebekah proved to be God's choice, and she, in turn, willingly left her relatives and family to accompany the caravan back to the land of the Negeb where Isaac lived. The account tells of the meeting of the two for the first time and then says: "After that Isaac brought her into the tent of Sarah his mother. Thus he took Rebekah and she became his wife; and he fell in love with her, and Isaac found comfort after the loss of his mother." (Ge 24:10-67) Isaac being 40, the marriage took place in 1878 B.C.E.—Ge 25:20.

From the history of Isaac we learn that Rebekah continued barren for 20 years. This afforded Isaac the opportunity to show whether he, like his father, had faith in Jehovah's promise to bless all the families of the earth through a seed yet unborn, and this he did by continually entreating Jehovah for a son. (Ge 25:19-21) As in his own case, it was again demonstrated that the seed of promise would come, not through the natural course of events, but only through Jehovah's intervening power. (Jos 24:3, 4) Finally, in 1858 B.C.E., when Isaac was 60 years old, he was given the double blessing of twins, Esau and Jacob.—Ge 25:22-26.

Because of a famine, Isaac moved his family to Gerar in Philistine territory, being told by God not to go down to Egypt. It was on this occasion that Jehovah confirmed his purpose to carry out the Abrahamic promise through Isaac, repeating its terms: "I will multiply your seed like the stars of the heavens and I will give to your seed all these lands; and by means of your seed all nations of the earth will certainly bless themselves."—Ge 26:1-6; Ps 105:8, 9.

In this not too friendly Philistine country, Isaac, like his father Abraham, used strategy by claiming his wife was his sister. After a time, Jehovah's blessing on Isaac became a source of envy to the Philistines, making it necessary for him to move, first to the torrent valley of Gerar, and then to Beer-sheba, on the edge of the arid Negeb region. While here, the formerly hostile Philistines came seeking "an oath of obligation," or a treaty of peace, with Isaac, for as they acknowledged, "You now are the blessed of Jehovah." At this place his men struck water and Isaac called it Shibah. "That is why the name of the city is Beer-sheba [meaning "Well of the Oath; or, Well of Seven"], down to this day."—Ge 26:7-33; see BEER-SHEBA.

Isaac had always been fond of Esau, because he was the outdoor type, a hunter and a man of the field, and this meant game in Isaac's mouth. (Ge 25:28) So, with failing eyesight and a feeling he did not have long to live, Isaac prepared to give Esau the firstborn's blessing. (Ge 27:1-4) Whether he was unaware that Esau had sold his birthright to his brother Jacob and whether he failed to remember the divine decree, given before the two boys' birth, that "the older will serve the younger," is not known. (Ge 25:23, 29-34) Whatever the case, Jehovah remembered, and so did Rebekah, who quickly arranged things so that Jacob received the blessing. When Isaac learned of the ruse that had been used to accomplish this, he refused to change what was unmistakably Jehovah's will in the matter. Isaac also prophesied that Esau and his descendants would reside far away from the fertile fields, would live by the sword, and would finally break the yoke of servi-

tude to Jacob from off their necks.—Ge 27:5-40; Ro 9:10-13; see ESAU.

Subsequently, Isaac sent Jacob to Paddan-aram to make sure he did not marry a Canaanitess, as his brother Esau had done to the vexation of his parents. When Jacob returned many years later, Isaac was residing at Kiriath-arba, that is, Hebron, in the hill country. It was here in 1738 B.C.E., the year before his grandson Joseph was made prime minister of Egypt, that Isaac died at the age of 180, "old and satisfied with days." Isaac was buried in the cave of Machpelah where his parents and his wife were buried, and where later his son Jacob would be buried.—Ge 26:34, 35; 27:46; 28:1-5; 35:27-29; 49:29-32.

Significance of Other References to Isaac. Throughout the Bible, Isaac is mentioned dozens of times in the familiar expression "Abraham, Isaac and Jacob." Sometimes the point being made is in reference to Jehovah as the God these patriarchs worshiped and served. (Ex 3:6, 16; 4:5; Mt 22:32; Ac 3:13) At other times the reference is to the covenant Jehovah made with them. (Ex 2:24; De 29:13; 2Ki 13:23) Jesus also used this expression in an illustrative way. (Mt 8:11) In one instance Isaac, the patriarchal forefather, is mentioned in a Hebraic parallelism along with his descendants, the nation of Israel.—Am 7:9, 16.

Isaac as the seed of Abraham was pictorial of Christ, through whom everlasting blessings come. As it is written: "Now the promises were spoken to Abraham and to his seed. It says, not: 'And to seeds,' as in the case of many such, but as in the case of one: 'And to your seed,' who is Christ." And by extension, Isaac was also pictorial of those who "belong to Christ," who "are really Abraham's seed, heirs with reference to a promise." (Ga 3:16, 29) Furthermore, the two boys, Isaac and Ishmael, together with their mothers, "stand as a symbolic drama." Whereas natural Israel (like Ishmael) "was actually born in the manner of flesh," these making up spiritual Israel "are children belonging to the promise the same as Isaac was."—Ga 4:21-31.

Isaac is also numbered among the "so great a cloud of witnesses surrounding us," for he too was among those "awaiting the city having real foundations, the builder and maker of which city is God."—Heb 12:1; 11:9, 10, 13-16, 20.

ISAIAH (I·sa′iah) [Salvation of Jehovah]. A prophet, the son of Amoz (not the prophet Amos). He served Judah and Jerusalem in the days of Kings Uzziah, Jotham, Ahaz, and Hezekiah of Judah. (Isa 1:1) Kings Pekah and Hoshea were ruling in the northern kingdom of Israel, which ended in 740 B.C.E., during the time of Isaiah's prophetic service. Contemporary prophets were Micah, Hosea, and Oded. Isaiah evidently began his prophesying later than Hosea did and before Micah began.—2Ch 28:9; Ho 1:1; Mic 1:1.

During Isaiah's prophetic service to Judah, especially in the days of King Ahaz, the kingdom was in a deplorable moral state. It was full of revolt on the part of both princes and people, and in Jehovah's eyes the nation was sick in the heart and in the head. The rulers were called "dictators of Sodom" and the people likened to "people of Gomorrah." (Isa 1:2-10) Isaiah was told in advance that their ears would be unresponsive. Jehovah said that this situation would continue until the nation would come to ruin and that only "a tenth," "a holy seed," would be left like the stump of a massive tree. Isaiah's prophetic work must have comforted and strengthened the faith of that small number, even though the rest of the nation refused to take heed.—Isa 6:1-13.

Though concentrating on Judah, Isaiah also uttered prophecies concerning Israel and the nations round about, as they had a bearing on Judah's situation and history. He enjoyed a long term in the prophetic office, starting in about 778 B.C.E., when King Uzziah died, or possibly earlier, and continuing until sometime after the 14th year of Hezekiah's reign (732 B.C.E.).—Isa 36:1, 2; 37:37, 38.

Isaiah's Family. Isaiah was married. His wife is called "the prophetess" (Isa 8:3), which seems to mean more than merely the wife of a prophet. Evidently, like Deborah of the time of the Judges and like Huldah during Josiah's reign, she had a prophetic assignment from Jehovah. —Jg 4:4; 2Ki 22:14.

The Bible names two sons of Isaiah, given to him as "signs and as miracles in Israel." (Isa 8:18) Shear-jashub was old enough in the days of Ahaz to accompany his father when Isaiah delivered a message to that king. The name Shear-jashub means "A Mere Remnant (Those Remaining Over) Will Return." This name was prophetic in that, just as certainly as a son born to Isaiah was given that name, so the kingdom of Judah would in time be overthrown and only a mere remnant would return after a period of exile. (Isa 7:3; 10:20-23) This return of a small remnant took place in 537 B.C.E. when King Cyrus of Persia issued a decree liberating them from Babylon after an exile of 70 years.—2Ch 36:22, 23; Ezr 1:1; 2:1, 2.

Another son of Isaiah was named prior to conception, and the name was written on a tablet and attested to by reliable witnesses. Apparently the matter was kept secret until after the birth of the son, when the witnesses could come forward and testify to the prophet's foretelling of the birth, thereby proving the matter to have prophetic significance. The name given to the boy by God's command was Maher-shalal-hash-baz, meaning "Hurry, O Spoil! He Has Made Haste to the Plunder; or, Hurrying to the Spoil, He Has Made Haste to the Plunder." It was said that before this son would know how to call out, "My father!" and "My mother!" the threat to Judah existing from the conspiracy of Syria and the ten-tribe kingdom of Israel would be removed. —Isa 8:1-4.

The prophecy indicated that relief would come to Judah soon; relief did come when Assyria interfered with the campaign against Judah by King Rezin of Syria and King Pekah of Israel. The Assyrians captured Damascus and, later, in 740 B.C.E., despoiled and destroyed the kingdom of Israel, fully carrying out the prophetic meaning of the boy's name. (2Ki 16:5-9; 17:1-6) However, instead of trusting in Jehovah, King Ahaz tried to stave off the threat made by Syria and Israel, resorting to bribery of the king of Assyria to gain his protection. Because of this, Jehovah allowed Assyria to become a great threat to Judah and actually to flood into the land right up to Jerusalem itself, as Isaiah had warned.—Isa 7:17-20.

Isaiah spoke many times of "signs" that Jehovah would give, among them being his two sons and, in one instance, Isaiah himself. Jehovah commanded him to walk about naked and barefoot for three years as a sign and a portent against Egypt and against Ethiopia, signifying that they would be led captive by the king of Assyria.—Isa 20:1-6; compare Isa 7:11, 14; 19:20; 37:30; 38:7, 22; 55:13; 66:19.

Prophecies of Exile and Restoration. Isaiah was also privileged to foretell that Assyria would not be the nation to dethrone the kings of Judah and destroy Jerusalem, but that this would be done by Babylon. (Isa 39:6, 7) At the time when Assyria flooded Judah "up to the neck," Isaiah delivered the comforting message to King Hezekiah that the Assyrian forces would not be able to enter the city. (Isa 8:7, 8) Jehovah backed up His word by sending an angel to destroy 185,000 of the Assyrian army's mighty men and leaders, thus delivering Jerusalem.—2Ch 32:21.

The thing that undoubtedly gave Isaiah the greatest joy was the privilege accorded him by

Jehovah to speak and to write many prophecies of restoration of his beloved Jerusalem. Although Jehovah would allow the people to go into exile to Babylon because of rebellion and revolt against him, God would in time judge Babylon because she acted out of malice and intended to hold God's people in captivity forever. A number of Isaiah's prophecies are devoted to God's judgment on Babylon and the desolate ruin she would become, never to be rebuilt.—Isa 45:1, 2; chaps 13, 14, 46-48.

The restoration prophecies that are found throughout the book of Isaiah glorify Jehovah's undeserved kindness and mercy toward his people and toward all mankind. They foretell the time when Jerusalem would be elevated to a new position with Jehovah, a glory that would be seen by all nations, and when she would be a blessing to all nations. Jerusalem was indeed restored and rebuilt and was blessed by the presence of the Messiah, who "shed light upon life and incorruption through the good news." (2Ti 1:10) Jerusalem's restoration also had a greater and grander fulfillment to come.—Ro 15:4; 1Co 10:11; Ga 4:25, 26.

Effects of Isaiah's Work. Isaiah wrote not only the Bible book bearing his name but also evidently at least one historical book, the affairs of King Uzziah, which no doubt formed part of the official records of the nation. (2Ch 26:22) In faithfully carrying out the prophetic work assigned to him by Jehovah, he had a strong influence on the nation's history, particularly as a result of his counseling and guiding righteous King Hezekiah. Many of Isaiah's prophecies also have a larger fulfillment in the Messiah and his Kingdom. Isaiah's book is quoted or referred to many times in the Christian Greek Scriptures. In many instances the Christian writers make application of Isaiah's prophecies to Jesus Christ or point to a fulfillment of his prophecies in their day.

ISAIAH, BOOK OF.

The book of Isaiah outstandingly magnifies Jehovah as "the Holy One of Israel," applying this expression to him a total of 25 times. Also, it points with unmistakable clarity to the Messiah, or Anointed One, of Jehovah through whom deliverance would come to the people of God.

The very first verse of the book of Isaiah identifies its contents as "the vision of Isaiah the son of Amoz that he visioned concerning Judah and Jerusalem." So, although the book contains prophetic utterances concerning many nations, they are not to be viewed as a collection of disconnect-

ed pronouncements concerning these nations. Rather, these are a series of prophecies that had a direct effect on Judah and Jerusalem.

Historical Background. Isaiah 1:1 informs us that Isaiah visioned these things in the days of Uzziah, Jotham, Ahaz, and Hezekiah, kings of Judah. This was a period of severe international tension and one in which false religious attitudes had a profound effect on the people of Judah. Near the beginning of Isaiah's career King Uzziah died a leper because of his presumptuousness in taking over priestly duties. (2Ch 26:16, 19-21) It is reported that during the reign of Uzziah's son Jotham, while the king did what was right, "the people were yet acting ruinously."—2Ch 27:2; 2Ki 15:34.

Next came King Ahaz, who for 16 years set a bad example for the nation, carrying on Baal worship with its rites of human sacrifice. There was "great unfaithfulness toward Jehovah." (2Ch 28:1-4, 19) It was at this time that the allied kings of Syria and Israel besieged Jerusalem so that Ahaz, ignoring the counsel of Isaiah the prophet, sent to Tiglath-pileser III, the king of Assyria, for military assistance. (2Ki 16:5-8; Isa 7:1-12) By this Ahaz 'made flesh his arm, his heart turning away from Jehovah.' (Jer 17:5) Assyria agreed to an alliance, but, of course, was interested mainly in expanding its own power. The Assyrian army captured Damascus of Syria and apparently took into exile those inhabitants of religiously apostate Israel that lived E of the Jordan.—1Ch 5:26.

Later, when Samaria failed to pay tribute, it too was besieged and its inhabitants were deported. (2Ki 16:9; 17:4-6; 18:9-12) This ended the ten-tribe kingdom and left Judah surrounded on all sides by Gentile nations. Later Assyrian rulers kept up military operations in the W, assaulting cities of Judah and of surrounding nations. Sennacherib even demanded the capitulation of Jerusalem itself. But under the kingship of Hezekiah the situation there had changed. Hezekiah trusted in Jehovah, and Jehovah proved to be with him. —2Ki 18:5-7; Isa chaps 36, 37.

Isaiah undertook his service as a prophet during the reign of Uzziah, who began to rule in 829 B.C.E., and he continued as such into the time of Hezekiah's reign, which concluded by about 717 B.C.E. Isaiah, chapter 6, verse 1, refers to "the year that King Uzziah died" (c. 778 B.C.E.) as the time when Isaiah received the commission from Jehovah that is recorded in that chapter; though it may be that he had recorded the preceding information before that. Then in chapter 36, verse 1, reference is made to "the fourteenth year

*Isaiah 37:24–40:2 as it appears in
the Dead Sea Scroll. What is now numbered
chapter 40 is here shown beginning
on the last line of the column in which
chapter 39 concludes*

says that Pekah the king of Israel came against Jerusalem to war in the days of King Ahaz. Although Ahaz ruled from 761 to 746 B.C.E., Pekah's kingship ended by about 758 B.C.E.; so the incident must have occurred before that year. Further, Isaiah 14:28 dates a pronouncement concerning Philistia "in the year that King Ahaz died," which would be 746 B.C.E. These references assist in fixing the events in the book of Isaiah in the stream of time.

Unity of Writership. Certain Bible critics in modern times have contended that the book of Isaiah was not all written by Isaiah. Some claim that chapters 40 through 66 were written by an unidentified person who lived about the time of the end of the Jews' Babylonian exile. Other critics pare off additional portions of the book, theorizing that someone other than Isaiah must have written them. But the Bible itself does not agree with these contentions.

Inspired writers of the Christian Greek Scriptures credited both the material now designated chapters 1 to 39 and chapters 40 to 66 to "Isaiah the prophet." They *never* intimated that there were two persons who bore this name or that the name of the writer of part of the book was unknown. (For examples compare Mt 3:3 and 4:14-16 with Isa 40:3 and 9:1, 2; also Joh 12:38-41 with Isa 53:1 and 6:1, 10.) In addition to this, there are numerous other places where the Christian Greek Scripture writers specifically credit material quoted from the latter part of the book of Isaiah, not to an unidentified writer, but to "Isaiah the prophet." (Compare Mt 12:17-21 with Isa 42:1-4; Ro 10:16 with Isa 53:1.) Jesus Christ himself, when he read from "the scroll of the prophet Isaiah" at the synagogue in Nazareth, was reading from Isaiah 61:1, 2.—Lu 4:17-19.

of King Hezekiah" (732 B.C.E.), when Sennacherib sent an army against Jerusalem and was turned back. In addition to giving the account of the threatened siege and the delivery of Jerusalem, Isaiah tells of Sennacherib's return to Nineveh and his assassination. (Isa 37:36-38) If this bit of historical information was written by Isaiah and was not an insertion by a later hand, it may show that Isaiah prophesied for some time after Hezekiah's 14th year. The Assyrian and Babylonian chronological records (though their reliability is questionable) seem to indicate that Sennacherib ruled some 20 years after his campaign against Jerusalem. Jewish tradition, which can also be unreliable, says that Isaiah was sawn asunder at King Manasseh's order. (Whether Paul has reference to this at Hebrews 11:37, as some believe, has not been proved.)—Isa 1:1.

There are also a few other references that help to date the contents of specific portions of the book of Isaiah. For example, chapter 7, verse 1,

Furthermore, the Dead Sea Scroll of Isaiah (IQIs[a], believed to have been copied toward the end of the second century B.C.E.) contains evidence that the copyist who penned it knew nothing of any supposed division in the prophecy at the close of chapter 39. He began the 40th chapter on the last line of the column of writing that contains chapter 39.

The entire book of Isaiah has been passed down through the centuries as a single work, not as two or more. The continuity from chapter 39 to chapter 40 is evident in what is recorded at Isaiah 39:6, 7, which is an obvious transition to what follows.

Those who would credit the book to more than one writer do not feel that it was possible for Isaiah to have foretold nearly two centuries in advance that a ruler named Cyrus would liberate the exiled Jews; consequently they speculate that this was written at a later time, at least after Cyrus began his conquests. (Isa 44:28; 45:1) But they fail to grasp the import of this entire portion of the book, because the material specifically deals with foreknowledge, with the ability of God to tell in advance what would happen to his people. Nearly 200 years in advance this prophecy recorded the name of one not yet born who would conquer Babylon and liberate the Jews. Its fulfillment would definitely prove that it was of divine origin. It was not Isaiah's estimate of the

---

HIGHLIGHTS OF ISAIAH

Prophecies to stimulate Jehovah's servants to fear him, not the surrounding nations, and to look to him, the true God, for deliverance, with full confidence in his promises of salvation and restoration

Directed to Judah and Jerusalem by Isaiah during the years leading up to Sennacherib's unsuccessful efforts against Jerusalem in 732 B.C.E., and possibly some time afterward

The guilt of Judah and Jerusalem; Isaiah's commission (1:1–6:13)

Jehovah does not look favorably upon the sacrifices of people guilty of oppression, injustice, and bloodshed

Though judgment is to be executed on faithless ones, in time the mountain of Jehovah's house will be exalted and many people will turn to him

For Judah's disobedience, Jehovah to remove essentials for sustaining life (bread and water) and the basis for social stability

Arrogant women, decked out in finery, to be forced to wear the attire of captives

Israel, as a vineyard, has failed to produce fruits of justice and righteousness

Isaiah's lips are cleansed; he willingly responds to commission as prophet, to go to unresponsive people

Threatened enemy invasions and promise of relief (7:1–12:6)

Syro-Israelite effort to dethrone Ahaz to fail; confirmatory sign of Immanuel's birth given

Isaiah's son Maher-shalal-hash-baz to serve as sign that Damascus and Samaria will be ravaged by Assyria before the boy can say "My father!" and "My mother!"

Lasting relief to come by means of the Prince of Peace

Assyria, rod of Jehovah's anger, to be punished for insolence; Jerusalem to be delivered

Twig out of stump of Jesse to become a ruler having God's spirit, to rule in justice

Pronouncements of international desolations (13:1–23:18)

Babylon to be desolated, her "king" brought down to Sheol

Assyria's yoke to depart, Philistine root to die by famine, Moab to be desolated, and Damascus to be reduced to ruin

Egyptians and Ethiopians to be humiliated by Assyrians and taken into exile

Elam and Media to share in bringing about Babylon's fall

Tyre to be brought low, forgotten for 70 years

Forecast of salvation by Jehovah (24:1–35:10)

Jehovah to make a great banquet for all peoples and to swallow up death forever

Salvation by Jehovah to be the subject of a song

A king to reign for righteousness, and princes to rule for justice; peace and security to time indefinite

Edom to be desolated; Zion to rejoice over her own restoration

Jehovah provides deliverance from Assyria; Babylonian exile foretold (36:1–39:8)

Assyrians invade Judah; Jehovah saves Jerusalem in answer to Hezekiah's prayer; 185,000 Assyrians slain

Hezekiah shows treasures to Babylonian delegation; Isaiah announces coming exile to Babylon

Release from Babylon by the true God, restoration of Zion, Messiah to come (40:1–66:24)

Jerusalem to be restored by the All-Wise, All-Powerful Creator

Restoration of his people will vindicate Jehovah as the only God, the one who alone can foretell the future, to the shame of lifeless gods fashioned by men

Babylon's fall to Cyrus to pave way for rebuilding Jerusalem

Devastated Zion to be made like the garden of Jehovah

Jehovah's servant, the Messiah, to die for transgressions of others

Barren Zion to have many sons, and no weapon to succeed against her

Jehovah invites his people to rejoice in creation of new heavens and new earth, but wicked transgressors have no share

future, but, as he himself wrote, "this is what Jehovah has said." (Isa 45:1) Ascribing the writing of this portion of Isaiah to a writer in Cyrus' time would still not solve the problem for the critics. Why not? Because this portion of the book also foretold in detail events in the earthly life and ministry of the Messiah, Jesus Christ—things even farther in the future. The fulfillment of these prophecies seals the prophecy of Isaiah as divinely inspired and not a collection of the works of impostors.

Those who deny that Isaiah wrote chapters 40 through 66 usually, for like reasons, deny that he wrote chapter 13, concerning the fall of Babylon. Yet chapter 13 is introduced with the words: "The pronouncement against Babylon that Isaiah the son of Amoz saw in vision." Obviously, this is the same "Isaiah the son of Amoz" whose name appears in the opening verse of chapter 1.

Interrelationships. Isaiah's writings are extensively interwoven with many other parts of the Bible. A century or more after Isaiah's time, Jeremiah wrote the record found in the books of Kings, and it is interesting to observe that what is recorded at 2 Kings 18:13 to 20:19 is essentially the same as that found in Isaiah chapters 36 to 39. Not only do other prophets cover matters similar to those considered by Isaiah but there are numerous specific references made to the writings of Isaiah themselves by other Bible writers.

Among the most outstanding and most frequently quoted prophecies from the book of Isaiah are those foretelling details concerning the Messiah. As shown in the accompanying chart, many of these are specifically quoted and applied by the inspired writers of the Christian

Some Prophecies Applying to Jesus Christ

Isaiah Text		Christian Scriptures
7:14	Born from a maiden, a virgin girl	Mt 1:22, 23
9:7; 11:1-5, 10	Offspring of David son of Jesse	Lu 1:32, 33; Ro 15:8, 12
40:3-5	In connection with his coming, announcement was made: "Clear up the way of Jehovah, you people!"	Mt 3:1-3; Mr 1:1-4; Lu 3:3-6; Joh 1:23
61:1, 2	Anointed by Jehovah to tell good news to meek ones	Lu 4:17-21
9:1, 2	Brought light to Galilee	Mt 4:13-16
42:1-4	Made God's justice clear; did not crush those who were like a bruised reed	Mt 12:10-21
53:4, 5	Carried sicknesses of others; because of his wounds others were healed	Mt 8:16, 17; 1Pe 2:24
53:1	Not believed in	Joh 12:37, 38
53:12	Reckoned with lawless ones	Lu 22:37
8:14, 15; 28:16	Rejected, stone of stumbling, but became foundation cornerstone	1Pe 2:6-8

Other Instances in Which Events Fulfilling Isaiah's Prophecies Are Noted, but Where the Writer Makes No Reference to Isaiah

Isaiah Text		Christian Scriptures
50:6	Was insulted, slapped, spit on	Mt 26:67; Mr 14:65
53:7	Quiet and uncomplaining before accusers	Mt 27:12-14; Ac 8:28, 32-35
53:9	Buried in a rich man's grave	Mt 27:57-60
53:8, 11	Sacrificial death, to open the way for many to a righteous standing with God	Ro 4:25

Other Prophecies Fulfilled

A Few of the Many Events Prior to the First Century C.E. That Fulfilled Prophecies of Isaiah

Isaiah Text	
1:26-30; 24:1-6; 39:6, 7	Jerusalem destroyed; exile to Babylon
43:14; 44:26-28	Release from exile; Jerusalem restored; Cyrus an instrument used by Jehovah to accomplish this
23:1, 8, 13, 14	Mainland city of Tyre destroyed by Chaldeans under Nebuchadnezzar

Larger Fulfillments Now and in the Future

It is obvious, from a reading of the Bible, that many of Isaiah's prophecies have more than one fulfillment and that a great portion of the book is finding and is yet to find its final, major fulfillment. In the book of Revelation alone are many quotations or allusions to Isaiah's prophecies, some of which are here listed:

Isaiah Text		Revelation
21:9	Babylon has fallen!	18:2
40:10	Jehovah is coming with his reward	22:12
47:5, 7-9	Babylon, a harlot and mistress of kingdoms, suffers calamity	17:1, 2, 18; 18:7
48:20	God's people commanded to get out of Babylon	18:4
60:1, 3, 5, 11	New Jerusalem likened to ancient Jerusalem in its restored state	21:11, 24-26
66:22	Jehovah creates new heaven(s) and a new earth	21:1

Greek Scriptures. It is of interest to observe that Jesus Christ and his apostles quoted most frequently from Isaiah to make clear the identification of the Messiah.

This is by no means the full extent to which other inspired Bible writers quoted from the prophecy of Isaiah, but it highlights some of the prophecies for which Isaiah is most widely noted. These prophecies, along with all the rest of the book, magnify Jehovah, the Holy One of Israel, as the One who provides this salvation for his people through his anointed Son.

ISCAH (Is′cah). Daughter of Abraham's brother Haran, and sister of Lot. She was born before her uncle Abraham and the household left Ur of the Chaldees.—Ge 11:27-31.

ISCARIOT (Is·car′i·ot) [from Heb., possibly, Man From Kerioth]. The designation for the traitor apostle Judas (and his father Simon) that sets him apart from the other apostle also named Judas. (Mt 10:4; Lu 6:16; Joh 6:71) If "Iscariot" means, as is most commonly thought, "Man From Kerioth," then it likely identifies Simon and his son as being from the Judean town of Kerioth-hezron.—Jos 15:25; see JUDAS No. 4.

ISHBAH (Ish′bah) [May He Still (Calm)]. A descendant of Judah; father of Eshtemoa.—1Ch 4:1, 17.

ISHBAK (Ish′bak). The fifth listed of the six sons that Keturah bore to Abraham, which sons Abraham sent away with gifts but without a share of his inheritance.—Ge 25:1, 2, 5, 6; 1Ch 1:32.

ISHBI-BENOB (Ish′bi-be′nob). One of four Rephaim (the giant race of Canaanites) who were prominent during the last wars with Israel in David's reign. Ishbi-benob carried a copper spear weighing 300 shekels (3.4 kg; 7.5 lb) and was on the verge of killing David when fast-acting Abishai himself put the giant to death.—2Sa 21:15-17, 22.

ISH-BOSHETH (Ish-bo′sheth) [meaning "Man of Shame"]. Youngest of Saul's four sons and his successor to the throne. From the genealogical listings it appears that his name was also Eshbaal, meaning "Man of Baal." (1Ch 8:33; 9:39) However, elsewhere, as in Second Samuel, he is called Ish-bosheth, a name in which "baal" is replaced by "bosheth." (2Sa 2:10) This Hebrew word bo′-sheth is found at Jeremiah 3:24 and is rendered "shameful thing." (AS, AT, JP, NW, Ro, RS) In two other occurrences ba″al and bo′sheth are found

parallel and in apposition, in which the one explains and identifies the other. (Jer 11:13; Ho 9:10) There are also other instances where individuals similarly had "bosheth" or a form of it substituted for "baal" in their names, as, for example, "Jerubbesheth" for "Jerubbaal" (2Sa 11:21; Jg 6:32) and "Mephibosheth" for "Meribbaal," the latter being a nephew of Ish-bosheth.—2Sa 4:4; 1Ch 8:34; 9:40.

The reason for these double names or substitutions is not known. One theory advanced by some scholars attempts to explain the dual names as an alteration made when the common noun "baal" (owner; master) became more exclusively identified with the distasteful fertility god of Canaan, Baal. However, in the same Bible book of Second Samuel, where the account of Ish-bosheth appears, King David himself is reported as naming a place of battle Baal-perazim (meaning "Owner of Breakings Through"), in honor of the Lord Jehovah, for as he said: "Jehovah has broken through my enemies." (2Sa 5:20) Another view is that the name Ish-bosheth may have been prophetic of that individual's shameful death and the calamitous termination of Saul's dynasty.

After the death of Saul and his other sons on the battlefield at Gilboa, Abner, a relative of Saul and the chief of his forces, took Ish-bosheth across the Jordan to Mahanaim, where he was installed as king over all the tribes except Judah, which recognized David as king. At the time Ish-bosheth was 40 years old, and he is said to have reigned for two years. Since the Bible does not say exactly where this two-year reign fits in with the seven-and-a-half-year period when David ruled as king at Hebron, there is no way of resolving differences of opinion held by scholars on the point. However, it does seem more reasonable to think that Ish-bosheth was made king shortly after the death of his father (rather than five years later), in which case there would have been a lapse of about five years between his assassination and David's being installed as king over all Israel. —2Sa 2:8-11; 4:7; 5:4, 5.

Ish-bosheth's short rule was marked by both internal and external troubles. The war between his house and that of David "came to be long drawn out"; he lost 360 men to David's 20 in one engagement. (2Sa 2:12-31; 3:1) At the same time his relative Abner kept strengthening himself at the expense of Ish-bosheth, even to the point of having relations with one of Saul's concubines, which, according to Oriental custom, was tantamount to treason. When rebuked for this by Ish-bosheth, Abner withdrew his support and made a covenant with David, part of which stipulated the return of David's wife, Michal, who was Ish-bosheth's own sister. (2Sa 3:6-21) Abner's death at the hand of Joab further weakened Ish-bosheth's position, and shortly thereafter two of his own captains assassinated him while he was taking his midday siesta. (2Sa 3:22-27; 4:1, 2, 5-7) However, when these murderers, in seeking a reward, brought Ish-bosheth's head to David, he had them put to death and ordered the head interred in the tomb of Abner at Hebron.—2Sa 4:8-12.

Thus it was that the dynasty of Saul, which could have lasted "to time indefinite," came to its abrupt and humiliating end, not because of the sins of Ish-bosheth, but instead, because of those of his father. (1Sa 13:13; 15:26-29) It is true, Ish-bosheth was a weak ruler, one who gained and held the throne principally because of the strength of Abner. Nevertheless, David referred to him as "a righteous man."—2Sa 4:11.

ISHHOD (Ish'hod) [Man of Dignity]. A descendant of Manasseh whose mother was Hammolecheth.—1Ch 7:14, 18.

ISHI (Ish'i) [shortened form of Isaiah, meaning "Salvation of Jehovah"].

1. A descendant of Judah; son of Appaim and father of Sheshan.—1Ch 2:3, 31.

2. Another descendant of Judah.—1Ch 4:1, 20.

3. A leader and family head of the half tribe of Manasseh that lived E of the Jordan.—1Ch 5:23, 24.

4. A Simeonite whose four sons are noted in the Chronicles for having led 500 to victory against the Amalekites living in Mount Seir.—1Ch 4:42, 43.

ISHMA (Ish'ma) [shortened form of Ishmael]. An early descendant of Judah.—1Ch 4:1, 3.

ISHMAEL (Ish'ma·el) [God Hears (Listens)].

1. Son of Abraham by Sarah's Egyptian slave girl Hagar; born in 1932 B.C.E., his father being 86 years old at the time.—Ge 16:1-4, 11-16.

When informed that Sarah would also have a son from whom "kings of peoples" would come, Abraham petitioned God in behalf of his first-born: "O that Ishmael might live before you!" God's reply, after declaring that the future son Isaac would be the covenant heir, was: "As regards Ishmael I have heard you. Look! I will bless him and will make him fruitful and will multiply him very, very much. He will certainly produce twelve chieftains, and I will make him become a great nation." (Ge 17:16, 18-20) Ishmael was then circumcised, at the age of 13, along with his father and his father's servants.—Ge 17:23-27.

A year later Isaac was born; Ishmael was now 14. (Ge 16:16; 21:5) Five years after that, in 1913 B.C.E., on the day of Isaac's being weaned, Ishmael was caught "poking fun" at his younger half brother. (Ge 21:8, 9) This was no innocent child's play on the part of Ishmael. Rather, as implied by the next verse in the account, it may have involved a taunting of Isaac over heirship. The apostle Paul says these events were "a symbolic drama" and shows that the mistreatment of Isaac by the half-blooded Egyptian Ishmael was *persecution.* Hence, this was the beginning of the foretold 400 years of Israel's affliction that ended with deliverance from Egyptian bondage in 1513 B.C.E.—Ga 4:22-31; Ge 15:13; Ac 7:6; see ISAAC.

Ishmael's demonstration of scorn toward Isaac led to the dismissal of him and his mother from Abraham's household, but not without provisions for their journey. Abraham "took bread and a skin water bottle and gave it to Hagar, setting it upon her shoulder, and the child, and then dismissed her." (Ge 21:14) Some have interpreted this to mean that Ishmael, now 19 years old, was also placed on the back of Hagar, and indeed this is the way some translations read. (*JB, Mo,* Bagster's *LXX*) Certain scholars, however, consider the phrase "setting it upon her shoulder" as only parenthetical, inserted to explain how the bread and water were carried, and so, if this phrase is placed in parentheses or set off by commas, the difficulty is removed. Professors Keil and Delitzsch assert that the expression "and the child" depends upon the sentence's principal verb "took," not on the verb "gave" or the word "setting." This tie-in of "the child" with "took" is made by the conjunction "and." The thought, therefore, is this: Abraham *took* bread and water and gave them to Hagar (placing them on her shoulder) and *took* the child and also gave it to her.—*Commentary on the Old Testament,* 1973, Vol. I, The First Book of Moses, pp. 244, 245.

Hagar apparently lost her way in the wilderness of Beer-sheba, and so when the water ran out and Ishmael became exhausted, "she threw the child under one of the bushes." (Ge 21:14, 15) This expression "threw the child" does not mean Ishmael was a baby in arms. The Hebrew word *ye'ledh* (child) does not necessarily refer to an infant but is often applied to an adolescent boy or a young man. Hence, it was said of the youth Joseph (17 at the time) that he was sold into slavery over Reuben's protest, "Do not sin against the child [bai·ye′ledh]." Lamech likewise spoke of "a young man [ye′ledh]" as having wounded him. —Ge 42:22; 4:23; see also 2Ch 10:8.

Neither does Hagar's act of 'throwing' the child down imply she was carrying him in her arms or on her back, though she was evidently supporting her tired son. She apparently withdrew her support suddenly, as did those who brought lame and infirm ones to Jesus and "fairly threw them at his feet."—Mt 15:30.

In accord with the meaning of Ishmael's name, "God heard" his cry for help, provided the necessary water, and allowed him to live to become an archer. As a nomadic inhabitant of the Paran Wilderness, he fulfilled the prophecy that said of him: "He will become a zebra of a man. His hand will be against everyone, and the hand of everyone will be against him; and before the face of all his brothers he will tabernacle." (Ge 21:17-21; 16:12) Hagar found an Egyptian wife for her son, and he in time fathered 12 sons, chieftains and family heads of the promised "great nation" of Ishmaelites. Ishmael also had at least one daughter, Mahalath, who married Esau.—Ge 17:20; 21: 21; 25:13-16; 28:9; see ISHMAELITE.

At the age of 89 Ishmael assisted Isaac in burying their father Abraham. After that he lived another 48 years, dying in 1795 B.C.E. at the age of 137. (Ge 25:9, 10, 17) There is no record of Ishmael's being buried in the cave of Machpelah, the place of burial for Abraham and Isaac, along with their wives.—Ge 49:29-31.

2. A descendant of Saul through Jonathan; son of Azel of the tribe of Benjamin.—1Ch 8:33-38, 40; 9:44.

3. Father of Zebadiah who was appointed by Jehoshaphat to serve as a royal representative in judicial matters; of the tribe of Judah.—2Ch 19:8, 11.

4. One of "the chiefs of hundreds" who entered the covenant with High Priest Jehoiada for the overthrow of wicked Athaliah and the enthronement of Jehoash; son of Jehohanan.—2Ch 23:1, 12-15, 20; 24:1.

5. Ringleader of those who killed Governor Gedaliah only three months after the downfall of Jerusalem in 607 B.C.E.; son of Nethaniah of the royal line. At the time the governor's appointment was made by Nebuchadnezzar, Ishmael, son of Nethaniah, was in the field as one of the military chiefs. Later, he came to Gedaliah and apparently entered a sworn covenant of peace and support with the governor. Secretly, however,

Ishmael conspired with Baalis, the king of the Ammonites, to kill Gedaliah. Other military commanders, including Johanan, warned Gedaliah of Ishmael's mischief, but the governor, not believing the report, refused to grant Johanan permission to strike Ishmael down.—2Ki 25:22-24; Jer 40:7-16.

As a result, when Gedaliah was entertaining Ishmael and his band of ten men at a meal, they rose up and killed their host as well as the Jews and Chaldeans who were with him. The next day these assassins seized 80 men who had come from Shechem, Shiloh, and Samaria, killing all but 10 of them, and throwing their bodies into the great cistern built by King Asa. Ishmael and his men then took the remnant of those living in Mizpah captive and headed for Ammonite territory. On the way Johanan and his forces overtook and rescued the captives, but Ishmael and eight of his men escaped to their Ammonite sanctuary. —2Ki 25:25; Jer 41:1-18.

6. One of the priests of the paternal house of Pashhur who put away their foreign wives in the days of Ezra.—Ezr 10:22, 44.

ISHMAELITE (Ish′ma·el·ite) [Of (Belonging to) Ishmael]. A descendant of Ishmael, the firstborn son of Abraham by Hagar, the Egyptian handmaid of Sarah. (Ge 16:1-4, 11) Ishmael, in turn, married an Egyptian by whom he had 12 sons (Nebaioth, Kedar, Adbeel, Mibsam, Mishma, Dumah, Massa, Hadad, Tema, Jetur, Naphish, Kedemah), the chieftains of the various Ishmaelite clans. (Ge 21:21; 25:13-16) The Ishmaelites, therefore, were at the start one fourth Semitic and three fourths Hamitic, racially speaking.

As God had promised, the Ishmaelites grew to become "a great nation" that 'could not be numbered for multitude.' (Ge 17:20; 16:10) But instead of settling down (they built few cities), they preferred the nomadic life. Ishmael himself was "a zebra of a man," that is, a restless wanderer who roamed the Wilderness of Paran and lived by his bow and arrows. His descendants were likewise tent-dwelling Bedouin for the most part, a people who ranged over the Sinai Peninsula from "in front of Egypt," that is, to the E of Egypt and across northern Arabia as far as Assyria. They were noted for being a fierce, warlike people hard to get along with, even as it was said of their father Ishmael: "His hand will be against everyone, and the hand of everyone will be against him."—Ge 16:12; 21:20, 21; 25:16, 18.

In further describing the Ishmaelites, it is said: "In front of all his brothers he settled down [Heb., *na·phal'*]." (Ge 25:18) Similarly, the Midianites and their allies, it was said, "were plumped [*no·phelim'*, a participle form of *na·phal'*] in the low plain" in Israelite territory until Gideon's band forcefully routed them. (Jg 7:1, 12) Hence, when the Ishmaelites "settled down" it was evidently with the intent of holding on to the region until forcefully removed.

In the course of time it is quite likely that intermarriage between Ishmaelites and descendants of Abraham through Keturah (Ge 25:1-4) occurred, resulting in the inhabitants of sections of Arabia. Since Ishmael and Midian were half brothers, any intermarriage of their respective descendants with the amalgamation of their blood, habits, traits, and occupations could have given rise to an interchangeable usage of the terms "Ishmaelites" and "Midianites," as is noted in the description of the caravan that sold Joseph into Egyptian slavery. (Ge 37:25-28; 39:1) In the days of Gideon the hordes that invaded Israel were described as both Midianites and Ishmaelites, one of the identifying marks of the latter being their gold nose rings.—Jg 8:24; compare Jg 7:25 and 8:22, 26.

The animosity Ishmael had toward Isaac seems to have been handed down to his descendants, even to the extent of hating the God of Isaac, for the psalmist, in enumerating those that are "the very ones intensely hating" Jehovah, includes the Ishmaelites. (Ps 83:1, 2, 5, 6) There were, however, evidently exceptions. Under the organizational arrangement instituted by David, Obil, who is referred to as an Ishmaelite, had supervision over the camels of the king.—1Ch 27:30, 31.

Muhammad, who lived in the seventh century C.E., claimed to be an Ishmaelite descendant of Abraham.

ISHMAIAH (Ish·ma'iah) [May Jehovah Hear (Listen); Jehovah Has Heard (Listened)].

1. An outstanding Gibeonite warrior who joined David's army at Ziklag before Saul's death. (1Ch 12:1, 4) In this early list of David's "thirty" leading warriors, Ishmaiah is called their head, but the absence of his name in later lists suggests that he may have died in the meantime.—2Sa 23:8, 18, 19; 1Ch 11:10, 11, 20, 21.

2. The prince over the tribe of Zebulun in David's time; son of Obadiah.—1Ch 27:19, 22.

ISHMERAI (Ish'me·rai) [May Jehovah Guard]. A head among the Benjamites who lived in Jerusalem; son or descendant of Elpaal.—1Ch 8:1, 18, 28.

ISHPAH (Ish'pah) [taken from a root meaning "sweep bare"]. A head of the people among the Benjamites living in Jerusalem; son or descendant of Beriah.—1Ch 8:1, 16, 28.

ISHPAN (Ish'pan) [possibly, He Has Judged]. A Benjamite son or descendant of Shashak; one of the heads of the people living in Jerusalem.—1Ch 8:1, 22, 25, 28.

ISHTOB (Ish'tob) [Man of Tob]. One of the small kingdoms that provided fighting men for the sons of Ammon to use against David. The forces from "Ishtob" and their allies were defeated. (2Sa 10, *AT, KJ, NW, Yg*) Most translators and geographers consider that Ishtob should be rendered "men of Tob," referring to "the land of Tob" where Jephthah resided. (Jg 11:3-11; see 2Sa 10: 6, 8, *AS, JB, JP, RS.*) However, the reading "Ishtob" has the support of certain ancient versions. (*LXX; Sy; Vg*) The location of an ancient Ishtob is not now known.—See TOB.

ISHVAH (Ish'vah) [meaning, possibly, "Made Equal; Smoothed Out"]. The second of Asher's four sons. (Ge 46:17; 1Ch 7:30) Since he is not listed in the families of Asher, it is possible that he had no sons or that his line of descent soon died out.—Nu 26:44.

ISHVI (Ish'vi) [meaning, possibly, "Made Equal; Smoothed Out"].

1. Third-listed son of Asher and founder of the Ishvite family in that tribe.—Ge 46:17; Nu 26:44; 1Ch 7:30.

2. One of King Saul's sons.—1Sa 14:49.

ISHVITES (Ish'vites) [Of (Belonging to) Ishvi]. A family descended from Ishvi, a son of Asher. —Ge 46:17; Nu 26:44.

ISLAND, ISLE. The Hebrew term *'i* (plural, *'i·yim'*) is not restricted to a body of land smaller than a continent and completely surrounded by water (Isa 11:11; 24:15) but also designates dry land (Isa 42:15) or coastland(s). (Isa 20:6; 23:2, 6; Jer 2:10) Figuratively, the word *'i* applies to the inhabitants of such islands or coastlands. (Ge 10: 5, ftn; Isa 49:1, ftn; 59:18, ftn) Sometimes "islands" represent the most distant places and their inhabitants. (Isa 41:5; 66:19; Eze 39:6; see MAGOG No. 2.) Thus nothing will be too remote or isolated, like islands in the sea, to escape the effects of the symbolic earthquake on Babylon the Great. (Re 16:18-21; compare Re 6:12-14.) From Jehovah's standpoint, all the islands are as "mere fine dust."—Isa 40:15.

Among the islands specifically named in the Bible are Cyprus (Ac 13:4-6), Cos, Rhodes (Ac 21:1), Crete (Ac 27:7), Cauda (Ac 27:16), Malta (Ac 28:1), and Patmos (Re 1:9).

ISMACHIAH (Is·ma·chi′ah) [May Jehovah Support; Jehovah Has Supported]. One of the Levites selected as a commissioner in connection with the contributions for temple service during Hezekiah's reign.—2Ch 31:13.

ISRAEL (Is′ra·el) [Contender (Perseverer) With God; or, God Contends].

1. The name God gave to Jacob when he was about 97 years old. It was during the night that Jacob crossed the torrent valley of Jabbok on his way to meet his brother Esau that he began struggling with what turned out to be an angel. Because of Jacob's perseverance in the struggle, his name was changed to Israel as a token of God's blessing. In commemoration of these events, Jacob named the place Peniel or Penuel. (Ge 32:22-28; see JACOB No. 1.) Later, at Bethel the change in name was confirmed by God, and from then on to the end of his life Jacob was frequently called Israel. (Ge 35:10, 15; 50:2; 1Ch 1:34) Many of the more than 2,500 occurrences of the name Israel, however, are in reference to Jacob's descendants as a nation.—Ex 5:1, 2.

2. All the descendants of Jacob, collectively, at any one time. (Ex 9:4; Jos 3:7; Ezr 2:2b; Mt 8:10) As the offspring and descendants of Jacob's 12 sons, they were quite often called "the sons of Israel"; less often, "the house of Israel," "the people of Israel," the "men of Israel," "the state of Israel," or the "Israelites."—Ge 32:32; Mt 10:6; Ac 4:10; 5:35; Eph 2:12; Ro 9:4; see ISRAELITE.

In 1728 B.C.E. famine caused the household of Jacob to travel to Egypt, where, as alien residents, their descendants remained for 215 years. All the Israelites reckoned as "of the house of Jacob who came into Egypt," not counting the wives of Jacob's sons, were 70. But during their sojourn there they became a very large society of slaves, totaling perhaps some two or three million or more.—Ge 46:26, 27; Ex 1:7; see EXODUS.

On his deathbed Jacob blessed his 12 sons in this order: Reuben, Simeon, Levi, Judah, Zebulun, Issachar, Dan, Gad, Asher, Naphtali, Joseph, Benjamin; and through them the patriarchal tribal arrangement was continued. (Ge 49:2-28) However, during Israel's period of slavery the Egyptians set up their own overseer system, independent of the patriarchal establishment, designating certain ones from among the Israelites as officers. These kept count of the bricks produced and assisted the Egyptian overlords, who drove the Israelites to work. (Ex 5:6-19) Moses, on the other hand, when making known Jehovah's instructions to the congregation, did so through "the older men of Israel" who were the hereditary heads of the paternal houses. They were also the ones who accompanied him when appearing before Pharaoh.—Ex 3:16, 18; 4:29, 30; 12:21.

In due time, at the end of the predetermined 400-year period of affliction, in 1513 B.C.E., Jehovah crushed the dominating world power of Egypt and, with a great display of his Sovereign Almightiness, brought his people Israel out of slavery. With them came "a vast mixed company" of non-Israelites who were happy to cast their lot in with that of God's chosen people.—Ge 15:13; Ac 7:6; Ex 12:38.

Birth of the Nation. Under the covenant made with Abraham, the resultant congregation of Israel was viewed as a single individual, and, therefore, a close relative could reclaim or repurchase them from their slavery. Jehovah was that close relative by this legal covenant, indeed, their Father, and as the rightful Repurchaser he used punitive force to kill Pharaoh's firstborn for refusing to release God's "firstborn" son Israel. (Ex 4:22, 23; 6:2-7) Thus legally delivered from Egypt, Israel became the exclusive property of Jehovah. "You people only have I known out of all the families of the ground," he said. (Am 3:2; Ex 19:5, 6; De 7:6) God now saw fit, however, to deal with them, not strictly as a patriarchal society, but as the nation of Israel, which he created and to which he gave a theocratic government founded on the Law covenant as a constitution.

Within three months after Israel left Egypt it became an independent nation under the Law covenant inaugurated at Mount Sinai. (Heb 9:19, 20) The Ten Words, or Ten Commandments, written "by God's finger" formed the framework of that national code, to which some 600 other laws, statutes, regulations, and judicial decisions were added. This made it the most comprehensive set of laws possessed by any ancient nation, spelling out as it did in great detail the relationship between man and God, as well as between man and his fellowmen.—Ex 31:18; 34:27, 28.

As a pure theocracy, all judicial, legislative, and executive authority rested with Jehovah. (Isa 33:22; Jas 4:12) In turn, this Great Theocrat delegated certain administrative power to his appointed representatives. The law code itself even provided for an eventual dynasty of kings that would represent Jehovah in civil matters. These kings, however, were not absolute monarchs, since the priesthood was separate from the kingship and independent of it, and in reality the kings sat on "Jehovah's throne" as his representatives, subject to his directives and discipline.—De 17:14-20; 1Ch 29:23; 2Ch 26:16-21.

Under the constitutional code, worship of Jehovah was placed above everything else and dominated every part of the nation's life and activity. Idolatry was rank treason punishable by death. (De 4:15-19; 6:13-15; 13:1-5) The sacred tabernacle, and later the temple, with its prescribed sacrifices was the physical center of worship. The God-appointed priesthood had the Urim and Thummim, by means of which answers were received from Jehovah on important and difficult questions of life or death. (Ex 28:30) Regular assemblies of the men, women, and children were provided (compulsory for the men), and they helped to maintain the nation's spiritual health and unity.—Le 23:2; De 31:10-13.

Provisions were made for a system of judges over "tens," "fifties," "hundreds," and "thousands." In this way the cases of the people could be handled quickly, and appeals could be made on up to Moses, who could, when necessary, present the matter before Jehovah for final decision. (Ex 18:19-26; De 16:18) The military organization with its conscription of manpower and distribution of command also conformed to a similar numerical system.—Nu 1:3, 4, 16; 31:3-6, 14, 48.

The various civil, judicial, and military offices were filled by the hereditary heads of the tribes —the older men who were experienced, wise, and discreet. (De 1:13-15) These older men stood before Jehovah as representatives of the entire congregation of Israel, and through them Jehovah and Moses spoke to the people in general. (Ex 3:15, 16) They were men who patiently heard judicial cases, enforced the various features of the Law covenant (De 21:18-21; 22:15-21; 25:7-10), abided by the divine decisions already rendered (De 19:11, 12; 21:1-9), furnished military leadership (Nu 1:16), confirmed treaties already negotiated (Jos 9:15), and, as a committee under the headship of the high priest, discharged other responsibilities (Jos 22:13-16).

This new theocratic state of Israel with its centralized authority still retained the patriarchal arrangement of 12 tribal divisions. But in order to relieve the tribe of Levi of military service (so it could devote its time exclusively to religious matters) and still retain 12 tribes having 12 portions in the Promised Land, formal genealogical adjustments were made. (Nu 1:49, 50; 18:20-24) There was also the matter concerning the firstborn

rights. Reuben, Jacob's firstborn, was entitled to a double portion in the inheritance (compare De 21:17), but he forfeited this right by committing incestuous immorality with his father's concubine. (Ge 35:22; 49:3, 4) These vacancies, the vacancy of Levi among the 12 as well as the absence of one with firstborn rights, had to be filled.

In a comparatively simple way Jehovah adjusted both matters by a single act. Joseph's two sons, Ephraim and Manasseh, were advanced to full status as tribal heads. (Ge 48:1-6; 1Ch 5:1, 2) Again 12 tribes exclusive of Levi could be numbered, and also a double portion of the land was representatively given to Joseph the father of Ephraim and Manasseh. In this way the firstborn rights were taken away from Reuben, the firstborn of Leah, and given to Joseph, the firstborn of Rachel. (Ge 29:31, 32; 30:22-24) Now with these adjustments the names of the 12 (non-Levite) tribes of Israel were Reuben, Simeon, Judah, Issachar, Zebulun, Ephraim, Manasseh, Benjamin, Dan, Asher, Gad, and Naphtali.—Nu 1:4-15.

From Sinai to the Promised Land. Only 2 out of 12 spies sent into the Promised Land came back with faith strong enough to encourage their brothers to invade and conquer. Jehovah, therefore, determined that for this general lack of faith all those more than 20 years old who had come out of Egypt, with few exceptions, would die there in the wilderness. (Nu 13:25-33; 14:26-34) And so for 40 years that vast camp of Israel wandered about in the Sinai Peninsula. Even Moses and Aaron died without setting foot on the Promised Land. Soon after Israel came out of Egypt, a census showed there were 603,550 able-bodied men, but about 39 years later the new generation numbered 1,820 less, or 601,730.—Nu 1:45, 46; 26:51.

During Israel's nomadic wilderness life Jehovah was a wall of protection around them, a shield from their enemies. It was only when they rebelled against him that he allowed evil to befall them. (Nu 21:5, 6) Jehovah also provided for their every need. He gave them manna and water, gave them a sanitary code by which their health was protected, and even kept their shoes from wearing out. (Ex 15:23-25; 16:31, 35; De 29:5) But in spite of such loving and miraculous care on the part of Jehovah, Israel repeatedly murmured and complained; and from time to time rebels arose to challenge the theocratic appointments, making it necessary for Jehovah to discipline them severely, that the rest might learn to fear and obey their Grand Deliverer.—Nu 14:2-12; 16:1-3; De 9:24; 1Co 10:10.

Israel's 40-year trek through the wilderness was coming to an end when Jehovah gave the kings of the Amorites, Sihon and Og, into their hands. With this victory Israel fell heir to a great amount of territory E of the Jordan in which the tribes of Reuben and Gad and half the tribe of Manasseh settled down.—De 3:1-13; Jos 2:10.

Israel Under the Judges. Following Moses' death, Joshua led the Israelites across the Jordan in 1473 B.C.E. into the land described as "flowing with milk and honey." (Nu 13:27; De 27:3) Then, in a sweeping six-year campaign, they conquered the territory that had been controlled by 31 kings W of the Jordan, including such fortified cities as Jericho and Ai. (Jos 1 to 12) The coastal plains and certain enclave cities, like the Jebusite stronghold that later became the City of David, were exceptions. (Jos 13:1-6; 2Sa 5:6-9) These God-defying elements that were allowed to remain acted like thorns and thistles in the side of Israel, and intermarriage with them only increased the pain. For a period of more than 380 years, from the death of Joshua to their complete subjugation by David, such worshipers of false gods acted "as agents to test Israel so as to know whether they would obey Jehovah's commandments."—Jg 3:4-6.

The newly conquered territory was divided among the tribes of Israel by lot, as Jehovah had commanded Moses. Six "cities of refuge" were set aside for the safety of unintentional manslayers. These, and 42 other cities and their surrounding agricultural land, were allotted to the tribe of Levi.—Jos 13 to 21.

Each city appointed judges and officers in its gates for handling judicial affairs as provided under the Law covenant (De 16:18) as well as representative older men to administer the general interests of the city. (Jg 11:5) Although the tribes maintained their identity and inheritances, much of the centralized organizational control that had been exercised during the stay in the wilderness was gone. The song of Deborah and Barak, the events of Gideon's warfare, and the activities of Jephthah all reveal the problems of lack of unity in action that arose after Moses and his successor Joshua passed off the scene and the people failed to look to their invisible Head, Jehovah God, for guidance.—Jg 5:1-31; 8:1-3; 11:1–12:7.

With the death of Joshua and of the older men of his generation, the people began to vacillate in their faithfulness and obedience to Jehovah, like a great pendulum swinging to and fro between true and false worship. (Jg 2:7, 11-13, 18, 19) When they abandoned Jehovah and turned to serving the Baals, he removed his protection and allowed the nations around them to move in to pillage the land. Awakened by such oppression to the need for united action, wayward Israel appealed to Jehovah and he, in turn, raised up judges, or saviors, to deliver the people. (Jg 2:10-16; 3:15) There was a whole series of these valiant judges after Joshua, including Othniel, Ehud, Shamgar, Barak, Gideon, Tola, Jair, Jephthah, Ibzan, Elon, Abdon, and Samson.—Jg 3 to 16.

Each deliverance had a uniting effect on the nation. There were other uniting incidents too. On one occasion when a Levite's concubine had been wantonly ravished, 11 tribes acted in outraged unity against the tribe of Benjamin, reflecting a sense of national guilt and responsibility. (Jg chaps 19, 20) All the tribes were unitedly drawn to the ark of the covenant in the tabernacle at Shiloh. (Jos 18:1) They therefore felt the loss nationally when the Ark was captured by the Philistines because of the debauchery and misconduct of the priesthood at that time, especially on the part of High Priest Eli's sons. (1Sa 2:22-36; 4:1-22) With the death of Eli, and with Samuel becoming a prophet and judge of Israel, there was a unifying effect on Israel, as Samuel traveled in a circuit through Israel to handle the questions and disputes of the people.—1Sa 7:15, 16.

The United Kingdom. Samuel was extremely displeased when, in 1117 B.C.E., Israel pleaded: "Do appoint for us a king to judge us like all the nations." However, Jehovah told Samuel, "Listen to the voice of the people . . . for it is not you whom they have rejected, but it is I whom they have rejected from being king over them." (1Sa 8:4-9; 12:17, 18) Thereupon, Saul the Benjamite was picked as Israel's first king, and though he began his rule well enough, it was not long before his presumptuousness led to disobedience, disobedience, in turn, to rebellion, and rebellion to his finally consulting a spirit medium—so that after 40 years he proved a complete failure!—1Sa 10:1; 11:14, 15; 13:1-14; 15:22-29; 31:4.

David of the tribe of Judah, a 'man agreeable to Jehovah's heart' (1Sa 13:14; Ac 13:22), was anointed king in the place of Saul, and under his able leadership the nation's boundaries were extended to the limits promised, from "the river of Egypt to the great river, the river Euphrates." —Ge 15:18; De 11:24; 2Sa 8:1-14; 1Ki 4:21.

During David's 40-year reign various specialized offices were created in addition to the tribal arrangement. There was an inner circle of counselors surrounding the king himself, besides the older men of influence that served the centralized government. (1Ch 13:1; 27:32-34) Then there was the larger departmental staff of the government made up of tribal princes, chiefs, court officials, and military personnel having administrative responsibilities. (1Ch 28:1) For effective handling of certain matters, David appointed 6,000 Levites as judges and officers. (1Ch 23:3, 4) Other departments with their appointed overseers were established to look after the cultivation of the fields and to manage such things as the vineyards and wineries, the olive groves and oil supplies, and the livestock and the flocks. (1Ch 27:26-31) The king's financial interests were similarly cared for by a central treasury department separate from that supervising the treasures stored elsewhere, as in outlying cities and villages.—1Ch 27:25.

Solomon succeeded his father David as king in 1037 B.C.E. He reigned "over all the kingdoms from the River [Euphrates] to the land of the Philistines and to the boundary of Egypt" for 40 years. His reign was especially marked by peace and prosperity, for the nations round about kept "bringing gifts and serving Solomon all the days of his life." (1Ki 4:21) The wisdom of Solomon was proverbial, he being the wisest king of ancient times, and during his reign Israel reached the zenith of its power and glory. One of Solomon's grandest accomplishments was the building of the magnificent temple, the plans for which he had received from his inspired father David.—1Ki chaps 3 to 9; 1Ch 28:11-19.

And yet for all his glory, riches, and wisdom, Solomon ended up a failure, for he allowed his many foreign wives to turn him away from the pure worship of Jehovah to the profane practices of false religions. In the end Solomon died disapproved by Jehovah, and Rehoboam his son succeeded him.—1Ki 11:1-13, 33, 41-43.

Rehoboam, lacking wisdom and foresight, increased the already heavy government burdens on the people. This, in turn, caused the ten northern tribes to secede under Jeroboam, even as Jehovah's prophet had foretold. (1Ki 11:29-32; 12:12-20) Thus it was that the kingdom of Israel was divided in 997 B.C.E.

For details on the divided kingdom, see ISRAEL No. 3.

Israel After the Babylonian Exile. During the next 390 years following the death of Solomon and the breaking up of the united kingdom

and on down to the destruction of Jerusalem in 607 B.C.E., the term "Israel" usually applied only to the ten tribes under the rule of the northern kingdom. (2Ki 17:21-23) But with the return of a remnant of all 12 tribes from exile, and continuing on down to the second destruction of Jerusalem in 70 C.E., the term "Israel" once again embraced the whole of Jacob's descendants living at that time. Again the people of all 12 tribes were called "all Israel."—Ezr 2:70; 6:17; 10:5; Ne 12:47; Ac 2:22, 36.

Those who returned to Jerusalem with Zerubbabel and High Priest Joshua (Jeshua) in 537 B.C.E. included 42,360 males (and, undoubtedly, their wives and children; in addition to slaves and professional singers), and these began rebuilding Jehovah's house of worship. (Ezr 3:1, 2; 5:1, 2) Later others returned with Ezra in 468 B.C.E. (Ezr 7:1–8:36), and still later, in 455 B.C.E., no doubt others accompanied Nehemiah when he came to Jerusalem with the special assignment to rebuild the walls and gates of the city. (Ne 2:5-9) Many Israelites, however, remained scattered throughout the empire, as noted in the book of Esther.—Es 3:8; 8:8-14; 9:30.

While Israel did not return to its former sovereignty as an independent nation, yet it did become a Hebrew commonwealth with considerable freedom under Persian domination. Deputy rulers and governors (like Zerubbabel and Nehemiah) were appointed from among the Israelites themselves. (Ne 2:16-18; 5:14, 15; Hag 1:1) The older men of Israel and the tribal princes continued to act as counselors and representatives of the people. (Ezr 10:8, 14) The priestly organization was reestablished, based on the ancient genealogical records that had been carefully preserved, and with such Levitical arrangement once again in operation, the sacrifices and other requirements of the Law covenant were observed.—Ezr 2:59-63; 8:1-14; Ne 8:1-18.

With the fall of the Persian Empire and the rise of Grecian domination of the world, Israel found itself torn by the conflict between the Ptolemies of Egypt and the Seleucids of Syria. The latter, during the rule of Antiochus IV (Epiphanes), determined to eradicate Jewish worship and customs. His effort reached a climax in 168 B.C.E. when a pagan altar was erected atop the temple altar in Jerusalem and dedicated to the Greek god Zeus. This outrageous incident, however, had a reverse effect, for it was the spark that touched off the Maccabean uprising. Three years later, to the day, victorious Jewish leader Judas Maccabaeus re-dedicated the cleansed temple to Jehovah with a festival that has since been commemorated by the Jews as Hanukkah.

The century that followed was one of great internal disorder in which Israel was led farther and farther away from the tribal administrative provisions of the Law covenant. It was during this period when home rule by the Maccabeans or Hasmonaeans met with varying fortunes, and when the parties of the pro-Hasmonaean Saddu-cees and the anti-Hasmonaean Pharisees devel-oped. Finally Rome, by now the world power, was called upon to interfere. In response General Gnaeus Pompey was sent, and after a three-month siege he took Jerusalem in 63 B.C.E. and annexed Judea to the empire. Herod the Great was appointed king of the Jews by Rome in about 39 B.C.E., and about three years later he effec-tively crushed the Hasmonaean rule. Shortly be-fore Herod's death Jesus was born in 2 B.C.E., as "a glory of your people Israel."—Lu 2:32.

Rome's imperial authority over Israel during the first century C.E. was distributed among dis-trict rulers and governors, or procurators. The Bible mentions such district rulers as Philip, Lysa-nias, and Herod Antipas (Lu 3:1); as well as Governors Pontius Pilate, Felix, and Festus (Ac 23:26; 24:27); and Kings Agrippa I and II (Ac 12:1; 25:13). Internally, there still remained some semblance of the tribal genealogical arrange-ment, as is seen when Caesar Augustus had Isra-elites register in the respective cities of their paternal houses. (Lu 2:1-5) Among the people "the older men" and the priestly Levitical func-tionaries were still very influential (Mt 21:23; 26:47, 57; Ac 4:5, 23), though they had, to a large degree, substituted the traditions of men for the written requirements of the Law covenant.—Mt 15:1-11.

In such an atmosphere Christianity had its birth. First came John the Baptizer, the forerun-ner of Jesus, who turned many of the Israelites back to Jehovah. (Lu 1:16; Joh 1:31) Then Jesus and his apostles followed up in the rescue work, laboring as they did among "the lost sheep of the house of Israel," opening blind eyes to the false traditions of men and to the excelling benefits of pure worship of God. (Mt 15:24; 10:6) Yet, only a remnant accepted Jesus as Messiah and were saved. (Ro 9:27; 11:7) These were the ones that joyfully hailed him as the "King of Israel." (Joh 1:49; 12:12, 13) The majority, refusing to put faith in Jesus (Mt 8:10; Ro 9:31, 32), joined their

religious leaders in crying out: "Take him away! Take him away! Impale him!" "We have no king but Caesar."—Joh 19:15; Mr 15:11-15.

Time soon proved that this pretended solid fidelity to Caesar was false. Fanatical elements in Israel fomented one revolt after another, and each time the province suffered harsh Roman reprisals, reprisals that, in turn, increased the Jewish ha-tred of Roman rule. The situation finally became so explosive that the local Roman forces were no longer able to contain it and Cestius Gallus, gov-ernor of Syria, moved against Jerusalem with stronger forces to maintain Roman control.

After setting fire to Bezetha, N of the temple, Gallus encamped in front of the royal palace, SW of the temple. At that moment, Josephus says, he could have easily forced his way into the city; his delay, however, strengthened the insurgents. The advance units of the Romans then made a protec-tive covering, like the back of the tortoise, with their shields over themselves and began under-mining the walls. Again when the Romans were about to succeed, they withdrew in the fall of 66 C.E. Concerning this withdrawal, Josephus says: "Cestius . . . suddenly recalled his troops, renounced his hopes, without having suffered any reverse, and, contrary to all calculation, retired from the city." (The Jewish War, II, 540 [xix, 7]) This attack on the city, followed by the sudden withdrawal, furnished the signal and the oppor-tunity for the Christians there to 'flee to the mountains' as instructed by Jesus.—Lu 21:20-22.

The next year (67 C.E.) Vespasian set about putting down the Jewish uprising, but Nero's unexpected death in 68 opened the way for Ves-pasian to become emperor. So he returned to Rome in 69 and left his son Titus to continue the campaign, and the next year, 70 C.E., Jerusalem was entered and destroyed. Three years later the last Jewish stronghold at Masada fell to the Ro-mans. Josephus says that during the whole cam-paign against Jerusalem 1,100,000 Jews died, many from pestilence and famine, and 97,000 were taken captive, he says, many being scat-tered as slaves to all quarters of the empire.—The Jewish War, VI, 420 (ix, 3).

For the identity of "the twelve tribes of Israel" that are referred to at Matthew 19:28 and Luke 22:30, see TRIBE ("Judging the Twelve Tribes of Israel").

3. The tribes that twice formed a separate northern kingdom of Israel.

The first split in the national government came with the death of Saul in about 1078 B.C.E. The tribe of Judah recognized David as king, but the rest of the tribes made Saul's son Ish-bosheth king; two years later Ish-bosheth was assassinated. (2Sa 2:4, 8-10; 4:5-7) In time the breach was healed and David became king of all 12 tribes. —2Sa 5:1-3.

Later in David's reign, when the revolt by his son Absalom had been put down, all the tribes once again acknowledged David as king. Yet, in returning the king to his throne, a dispute arose over protocol, and in this matter the ten northern tribes called Israel were at odds with the men of Judah.—2Sa 19:41-43.

All 12 tribes were united in their support of David's son Solomon in his kingship. But upon his death in about 998 B.C.E. the second dividing of the kingdom occurred. Only the tribes of Benjamin and Judah supported King Rehoboam, who sat on his father Solomon's throne in Jerusalem. Israel, consisting of the ten other tribes to the N and E, picked Jeroboam to be their king.—1Ki 11:29-37; 12:1-24; MAP, Vol. 1, p. 947.

At first the capital of Israel was set up at Shechem. Later it was moved to Tirzah, and then during the reign of Omri it was moved to Samaria, where it remained for the next 200 years. (1Ki 12:25; 15:33; 16:23, 24) Jeroboam recognized that unified worship holds a people together, and so to keep the breakaway tribes from going to Jerusalem's temple to worship, he set up two golden calves, not at the capital, but at the two extremities of Israel's territory, one at Bethel in the south and the other at Dan in the north. He also installed a non-Levitical priesthood to lead and instruct Israel in worship of both the golden calves and the goat-shaped demons.—1Ki 12:28-33; 2Ch 11:13-15.

In Jehovah's eyes this was a very great sin that Jeroboam committed. (2Ki 17:21, 22) Had he remained faithful to Jehovah and not turned to such rank idolatry, God would have allowed his dynasty to continue, but as it turned out, his house lost the throne when his son Nadab was assassinated less than two years after Jeroboam's death.—1Ki 11:38; 15:25-28.

As the ruler went, so went the nation of Israel. Nineteen kings, not counting Tibni (1Ki 16:21, 22), reigned from 997 to 740 B.C.E. Only nine had their own sons succeed them, and only one had a dynasty extending to the fourth generation. Seven of Israel's kings ruled two years or less; some for only a few days. One committed suicide, four others met a premature death, and six others were assassinated by ambitious men who then

occupied the throne of their victims. Whereas the best of the whole lot, Jehu, pleased Jehovah by removing the vile Baal worship that Ahab and Jezebel had sponsored, yet "Jehu himself did not take care to walk in the law of Jehovah the God of Israel with all his heart"; he allowed Jeroboam's calf worship to continue throughout the land. —2Ki 10:30, 31.

Jehovah, for his part, was certainly long-suffering with Israel. During their 257-year history he continued to send his servants to warn the rulers and the people of their wicked ways, but to no avail. (2Ki 17:7-18) Among these devoted servants of God were the prophets Jehu (not the king), Elijah, Micaiah, Elisha, Jonah, Oded, Hosea, Amos, and Micah.—1Ki 13:1-3; 16:1, 12; 17:1; 22:8; 2Ki 3:11, 12; 14:25; 2Ch 28:9; Ho 1:1; Am 1:1; Mic 1:1.

Israel's problem of protecting herself against invasion was greater than Judah's, for though she had double the population, she also had nearly triple the land area to guard. In addition to warring against Judah from time to time, she was frequently at war on her northern and eastern frontiers with Syria and under pressure from Assyria. The final siege of Samaria was begun by Shalmaneser V in the seventh year of Hoshea's reign, but it took nearly three years before the city was taken by the Assyrians in 740 B.C.E. —2Ki 17:1-6; 18:9, 10.

The policy of the Assyrians, inaugurated by Shalmaneser's predecessor Tiglath-pileser III, was to remove captives from conquered territory and transplant in their place peoples from other parts of the empire. Thus, future uprisings were discouraged. In this instance the other national groups brought into Israel's territory eventually became intermingled both racially and religiously and were known thereafter as Samaritans.—2Ki 17:24-33; Ezr 4:1, 2, 9, 10; Lu 9:52; Joh 4:7-43.

With the fall of Israel the ten northern tribes were not completely lost, however. Some persons of these tribes evidently were left in Israel's territory by the Assyrians. Others no doubt fled from Israel's idolatry to Judah's territory prior to 740 B.C.E., and their descendants would have been among the captives taken to Babylon in 607 B.C.E. (2Ch 11:13-17; 35:1, 17-19) No doubt there were descendants also from among those taken captive by the Assyrians (2Ki 17:6; 18:11) who were numbered among the returning remnant that made up the 12 tribes of Israel in 537 B.C.E. and thereafter.—1Ch 9:2, 3; Ezr 6:17; Ho 1:11; compare Eze 37:15-22.

4. The Promised Land, or geographic territory assigned to the nation of Israel (all 12 tribes), in contrast with the territory of other nations (1Sa 13:19; 2Ki 5:2; 6:23), and over which Israelite kings ruled.—1Ch 22:2; 2Ch 2:17.

Following the division of the nation "the land of Israel" was at times used to designate the northern kingdom's territory, distinguishing it from that of Judah. (2Ch 30:24, 25; 34:1, 3-7) After the northern kingdom's fall the name of Israel was, in effect, kept alive by Judah, the only kingdom remaining of Israel's (Jacob's) descendants. Therefore, it is primarily with reference to the land of the Judean kingdom and its capital Jerusalem that the expression "soil of Israel" is used by the prophet Ezekiel. (Eze 12:19, 22; 18:2; 21:2, 3) This was the geographic area that was completely desolated for 70 years from and after 607 B.C.E. (Eze 25:3) but to which a faithful remnant would be regathered.—Eze 11:17; 20: 42; 37:12.

For a description of Israel's geographic and climatic characteristics, as well as its size, location, natural resources, and related features, see the article PALESTINE.

ISRAELITE   (Is′ra·el·ite) [Of (Belonging to) Israel]. A descendant of Jacob, whose name was changed to Israel. (2Sa 17:25; Joh 1:47; Ro 11:1; see ISRAEL No. 1.) As determined by the context, in the plural the term refers to the following: (1) Members of all the 12 tribes before the split in the kingdom (1Sa 2:14; 13:20; 29:1); (2) those of the 10-tribe northern kingdom (1Ki 12:19; 2Ki 3:24); (3) non-Levitical Jews returning from Babylonian exile (1Ch 9:1, 2); (4) Jews of the first century C.E.—Ac 13:16; Ro 9:3, 4; 2Co 11:22.

ISRAEL OF GOD.   This expression, found only once in Scripture, refers to spiritual Israel rather than to racial descendants of Jacob, whose name was changed to Israel. (Ge 32:22-28) The Bible speaks of "Israel in a fleshly way" (1Co 10:18), as well as spiritual Israel made up of those for whom descent from Abraham is not a requirement. (Mt 3:9) The apostle Paul, when using the expression "the Israel of God," shows that it has nothing to do with whether one is a circumcised descendant of Abraham or not.—Ga 6:15, 16.

The prophet Hosea foretold that God, in rejecting the nation of natural Israel in favor of this spiritual nation, which includes Gentiles, would say "to those not my people: 'You are my people.'" (Ho 2:23; Ro 9:22-25) In due time the Kingdom of God was taken away from the nation of natural

Jews and given to a spiritual nation bringing forth Kingdom fruitage. (Mt 21:43) To be sure, natural Jews were included in spiritual Israel. The apostles and others who received holy spirit at Pentecost in 33 C.E. (about 120), those added on that day (about 3,000), and those that later increased the number to about 5,000 were all Jews and proselytes. (Ac 1:13-15; 2:41; 4:4) But even at that, they were, as Isaiah described them, "a mere remnant" saved out of that cast-off nation. —Isa 10:21, 22; Ro 9:27.

Other scriptures elaborate on this matter. With the breaking off of some "natural branches" of the figurative olive tree, there was a grafting in of "wild" non-Israelite ones, so that there was no racial or class distinction among those that "are really Abraham's seed, heirs with reference to a promise." (Ro 11:17-24; Ga 3:28, 29) "Not all who spring from Israel are really 'Israel.'" "For he is not a Jew who is one on the outside, nor is circumcision that which is on the outside upon the flesh. But he is a Jew who is one on the inside, and his circumcision is that of the heart by spirit." (Ro 9:6; 2:28, 29) Natural Israel failed to produce the required number, so God "turned his attention to the nations to take out of them a people for his name" (Ac 15:14), concerning whom it was said, "You were once not a people, but are now God's people." (1Pe 2:10) The apostle Peter quoted what had been said to natural Israel and applied it to this spiritual Israel of God, saying it is in reality "a chosen race, a royal priesthood, a holy nation, a people for special possession."—Ex 19:5, 6; 1Pe 2:9.

The 12 tribes mentioned in Revelation chapter 7 must refer to this spiritual Israel for several valid reasons. The listing does not match that of natural Israel at Numbers chapter 1. Also Jerusalem's temple and priesthood and all the tribal records of natural Israel were permanently destroyed, lost forever, long before John had his vision in 96 C.E. But more important, John received his vision upon a background of the aforementioned developments from and after Pentecost 33 C.E. In the light of such events, John's vision of those standing on the heavenly Mount Zion with the Lamb (whom natural Israel had rejected) revealed the number of this spiritual Israel of God to be 144,000 "bought from among mankind."—Re 7:4; 14:1, 4.

ISSACHAR   (Is′sa·char) [He Is Wages [that is, a man of wages]].

1. The ninth son of Jacob and the fifth of Leah's seven children born in Paddan-aram. Leah viewed this son as Jehovah's reward or wages paid for her having allowed a maidservant to bear sons by her husband during a period when she was barren.—Ge 29:32–30:21; 35:23, 26; 1Ch 2:1.

Issachar was perhaps eight years old when his family moved to Canaan in 1761 B.C.E. After that nothing is known of his life aside from the recorded events in which, as one of "the sons of Jacob," he mutually participated. (Ge 34:5-7, 13, 27; 37:3-27; 42:1-3; 45:15) In 1728 B.C.E., when Issachar was about 41 years old, he moved to Egypt together with his sons Tola, Puvah (Puah), Iob (Jashub), and Shimron as part of the 'seventy souls' of Jacob's household.—Ge 46:13, 27; Ex 1:1-3; 1Ch 7:1.

When Jacob was on his deathbed, Issachar was the 5th of the 12 sons to receive his father's blessing: "Issachar is a strong-boned ass, lying down between the two saddlebags. And he will see that the resting-place is good and that the land is pleasant; and he will bend down his shoulder to bear burdens and he will become subject to slavish forced labor." (Ge 49:14, 15) In pronouncing this blessing, not only was Jacob pointing out certain individual characteristics and events in the personal life of Issachar but, as with the blessings bestowed on his brothers, Jacob was also foretelling tribal traits and conduct that would be displayed in the future by Issachar's descendants "in the final part of the days."—Ge 49:1.

2. One of the 12 tribes of Israel; descendants of Jacob through his son Issachar.

When the first census was taken after leaving Egypt, the number of able-bodied men 20 years old and upward who were fit for warfare among this tribe was 54,400. (Nu 1:17-19, 28, 29) A similar census about 39 years later showed the tribe had increased their registered ones to 64,-300, and in David's time the fighting force numbered 87,000. (Nu 26:23-25; 1Ch 7:5) There were 200 head ones of the tribe that went to Hebron in 1070 B.C.E. when David was made "king over all Israel."—1Ch 12:23, 32, 38.

In the layout of the great wilderness camp, the families of Issachar, together with those of their full-blood brother-tribe Zebulun, were situated on Judah's flanks on the E side of the tabernacle (Nu 2:3-8); when on the march this three-tribe division was assigned to take the lead. (Nu 10:14-16) Moses' parting blessings on the tribes grouped Issachar and Zebulun together (De 33:18), but a few years later they were separated when the

tribes were divided into two groups to hear the reading of blessings and cursings of the Law between the mountains of Gerizim and Ebal.—De 27:11-13; Jos 8:33-35; see EBAL, MOUNT.

In dividing up the Promised Land, Issachar was the fourth tribe chosen by lot to receive its inheritance, which proved to be mainly in the fertile Valley of Jezreel. Bounding Issachar were the tribal territories of Zebulun and Naphtali on the N, the Jordan River on the E, Manasseh's territory on the S, and on the W a portion of Asher's allotment. Mount Tabor lay along its northern boundary with Zebulun, while the city of Megiddo was near its SW border and Beth-shean was toward its SE boundary. Within this territory there were a number of Canaanite cities and their dependent settlements. (Jos 17:10; 19:17-23) It was here in this choice valley that the tribe of Issachar, according to Moses' blessing, 'rejoiced in their tents.'—De 33:18.

The likening of Jacob's son Issachar to "a strong-boned ass" evidently pointed to a quality reflected as well in the tribe descended from him. (Ge 49:14, 15) The land assigned them was indeed "pleasant," a fertile part of Palestine, good for agriculture. Issachar seems to have accepted well the hard labor involved in such work. Willingness is indicated by his 'bending down his shoulder to bear burdens.' So, while the tribe was not particularly outstanding, it apparently could be commended for taking on the load of responsibility that was its share.

Certain cities within Issachar's possession were designated as enclave cities belonging to the neighbor tribe of Manasseh, including the prominent cities of Megiddo and Beth-shean. (Jos 17:11) A number of towns in its territory, together with their surrounding pasture grounds, were also set aside for the tribe of Levi. (Jos 21:6, 28, 29; 1Ch 6:62, 71-73) Later, Issachar supplied its share (one twelfth of the annual needs) for the support of Solomon's court.—1Ki 4:1, 7, 17.

Among the prominent individuals of Issachar was Igal, the tribe's selected spy who joined others in advising Israel not to enter the Promised Land. (Nu 13:1-3, 7, 31-33) As chieftains of the tribe, Nethanel served after the Exodus (Nu 1:4, 8; 7:18; 10:15), Paltiel when Israel entered the Promised Land (Nu 34:17, 18, 26), and Omri during the reign of David.—1Ch 27:18, 22.

Issachar was listed among those that supported Judge Barak in the overthrow of Jabin's forces under Sisera. (Jg 4:2; 5:15) Later, for 23 years Tola of the tribe of Issachar was one of the judges of Israel. (Jg 10:1, 2) After the split-up of the united kingdom, Baasha of Issachar was the third ruler of the northern kingdom. A wicked man, Baasha murdered his predecessor to gain the throne and held it for 24 years. (1Ki 15:27, 28, 33, 34) Some 200 years later, Hezekiah the king of Judah invited those of the northern kingdom to join in keeping the Passover, and many from Issachar, in response, traveled up to Jerusalem for the celebration.—2Ch 30:1, 13, 18-20.

In the books of Ezekiel and Revelation, Issachar is enumerated with the other tribes and, in view of the prophetic nature of those visions, obviously has symbolic meaning.—Eze 48:25, 26, 33; Re 7:7.

3. A Levite gatekeeper; seventh son of Korahite Obed-edom. Issachar, together with his relatives, was assigned to guard duty on the S side of the sanctuary in Jerusalem.—1Ch 26:1-5, 13, 15.

ISSHIAH (Is·shi′ah) [Jehovah Makes Forget].

1. One of the headmen of the tribe of Issachar whose descendants helped make that tribe very numerous.—1Ch 7:1, 3, 4.

2. A warrior who joined David's forces at Ziklag; possibly a Korahite.—1Ch 12:1, 6.

3. A descendant of Kohath whose Levite sons were organized under David's reign.—1Ch 23:12, 20; 24:24, 25.

4. Another Levite of David's day, a descendant of Moses.—1Ch 23:14-17; 24:21.

ISSHIJAH (Is·shi′jah) [Jah Makes Forget]. One of the Levites who responded to Ezra's urging to send away their foreign wives and sons.—Ezr 10:31, 44.

ITALIAN BAND. A unit of the Roman army in which Cornelius of Caesarea served as a centurion. In the Bible's only reference to it, Cornelius is said to have been "an army officer of the Italian band, as it was called." (Ac 10:1) This was probably a cohort, so named to distinguish it from the regular Roman legions. A cohort in full strength consisted of about 600 men, that is, about one tenth the size of a legion. As its name implies, this cohort was probably made up of volunteers mustered in Italy, having Roman citizenship either as freeborn men or as freedmen.

The scripture does not say this Italian band was stationed at Caesarea. It only says that Cornelius, one of its army officers, had his home in Caesarea. —Ac 10:1, 2, 22, 24.

ITALY [possibly from Latin, *vitulus,* "calf"]. The boot-shaped peninsula extending out in a southeasterly direction from continental Europe into the Mediterranean Sea. From the Alps on the N to the "big toe" at the Strait of Messina in the S it is about 1,130 km (700 mi) long. It varies in width from 160 to 240 km (100 to 150 mi) and is bounded by the Adriatic Sea on the E and the Tyrrhenian Sea on the W. As a backbone down the middle of this peninsula is the Apennine mountain range, with fertile valleys running toward the coastal plains. The principal rivers are the Tiber and the Po. Italy is about the size of the Philippines.

Originally, according to Antiochus of Syracuse (of the fifth century B.C.E.), the name *Italia* applied only to the province of Calabria in the S where the *Itali* lived. This name seems to be a Grecized form of *Vitelia,* related to the Latin *vitulus,* meaning "calf." It was possibly applied to this region either because of its grazing lands and cattle or because its inhabitants supposed themselves to be descendants of their bull-god. By the first century C.E. the name Italy had been extended to cover much the same territory as it does today.

Over the centuries peoples of various origins migrated to this very fertile land. Italy's early history includes wars between those already there and waves of newcomers that periodically invaded the land. The peninsula thus served as a melting pot of languages, blood, and customs as these different national groups settled down and intermarried.

Christianity was brought to Italy at an early date, for on the day of Pentecost, 33 C.E., Italian proselytes as well as Jews from Rome witnessed the outpouring of holy spirit and listened to Peter's explanation; no doubt some of them were among the "about three thousand" baptized on that occasion. (Ac 2:1, 10, 41) Returning to Italy, they could have formed the nucleus of the Christian congregation in Rome to whom Paul some years later addressed one of his letters. (Ro 1:1-7) Aquila and Priscilla may have been of that congregation in Italy when ordered by Emperor Claudius, sometime in the year 49 or early 50 C.E., to leave the country. They arrived in Corinth shortly before Paul got there on his first visit to that city on his second missionary tour. —Ac 18:1, 2.

Cornelius, undoubtedly an Italian and an army officer of "the Italian band," had a home in Caesarea. (Ac 10:1) It was in Caesarea that Paul, at his trial before Festus, appealed his case to Caesar. He was then taken by boat to Myra, where, together with other prisoners, he was transferred to a grain boat from Alexandria that was headed for Italy. (Ac 25:6, 11, 12; 27:1, 5, 6) Shipwrecked on the voyage, they had to winter on the island of Malta. Then probably in the spring of 59 C.E., Paul first touched Italian soil at Rhegium on the "toe" of Italy, and shortly thereafter he disembarked at Puteoli on the Bay of Pozzuoli (Naples). Here, more than 160 km (100 mi) S of Rome, Paul stayed for a week with the local congregation before going on up to Rome via the Appian Way, along which, at "the Marketplace of Appius and Three Taverns," he was met by the brothers from Rome. (Ac 28:11-16) Likely, toward the end of Paul's first Roman imprisonment, or shortly after his release in about 61 C.E., he wrote the book of Hebrews while still in Italy.—Heb 13:24.

ITHAI (I'thai) [possibly a shortened form of Ithiel]. Son of Ribai from Gibeah in Benjamin's territory; one of the mighty men of David's military forces. (1Ch 11:26, 31) Apparently Ithai is called Ittai at 2 Samuel 23:29.

ITHAMAR (Ith'a·mar) [possibly, Father (or, Brother) of the Palm Tree]. The fourth listed of Aaron's sons. (Ex 6:23; Nu 26:60; 1Ch 6:3) After having supervised the inventory of tabernacle materials, Ithamar, with his father and brothers, was installed as a priest in the ceremony detailed at Exodus 29. (Ex 28:1; 38:21; 40:12-15) When his two older brothers, Nadab and Abihu, were later executed for offering "illegitimate fire," Ithamar and his third brother Eleazar were told not to mourn for them. Later, Ithamar and Eleazar received a greater portion of priestly duties as Jehovah progressively outlined these. (Le 10:1-20) Ithamar was made overseer of the various tabernacle services performed by the Gershonites and Merarites.—Nu 3:2-4; 4:28, 33; 7:8.

Ithamar's descendants continued as priests, and during the reigns of Saul, David, and Solomon, members of the house of Ithamar's descendant Eli temporarily officiated as high priest. When David organized the temple service, 8 of the 24 priestly divisions were of the house of Ithamar. (1Ch 24:1-6; 1Sa 14:3; 22:9; see HIGH PRIEST.) Sons of Ithamar were also enrolled among the paternal houses of Israel after the Babylonian exile.—Ezr 8:2.

ITHIEL (Ith'i·el) [probably, With Me Is God].
1. One of the hearers of what Agur spoke, as recorded in Proverbs chapter 30; possibly a son or disciple of Agur.—Pr 30:1.
2. A Benjamite whose descendant lived in Jerusalem in Nehemiah's time.—Ne 11:4, 7.

ITHLAH (Ith'lah) [possibly from a root meaning "hang"]. One of the border cities of Dan. (Jos 19:40, 42) Its location is uncertain.

ITHMAH (Ith'mah) [from a root meaning "fatherless boy"]. One of several of David's mighty men listed only in Chronicles; a Moabite.—1Ch 11:26, 46.

ITHNAN (Ith'nan). A city at the extremity of southern Judah (Jos 15:21, 23), the location of which is unknown.

ITHRA (Ith'ra) [from a root meaning "more than enough; overflow"]. Father of Amasa by David's sister or half sister Abigail. (2Sa 17:25) He is called Jether at 1 Chronicles 2:17.—See JETHER No. 6.

ITHRAN (Ith'ran) [from a root meaning "more than enough; overflow"].
1. A son of the Edomite sheik Dishon; descendant of Seir the Horite.—Ge 36:20, 21, 26; 1Ch 1:38, 41.
2. A descendant of Asher through Zophah. (1Ch 7:30, 37) Likely the same as Jether (spelled similarly in Hebrew) in the following verse.—See JETHER No. 4.

ITHREAM (Ith're·am) [from a root meaning "more than enough; overflow"]. David's sixth son, born in Hebron by his wife Eglah.—2Sa 3:5; 1Ch 3:1, 3.

ITHRITE (Ith'rite) [Of (Belonging to) Jether (or, Jethro)]. A family name in the tribe of Judah, connected with Kiriath-jearim. (1Ch 2:3, 52, 53) Two of David's mighty men, Ira and Gareb, came from this family.—2Sa 23:38; 1Ch 11:40.

ITTAI (It'tai) [shortened form of Ithiel].
1. A Gittite warrior, presumably from the Philistine city of Gath, who was very loyal to David. When David and his attendants were fleeing Jerusalem because of Absalom's rebellion, 600 Gittites, including Ittai, came along. David tried to dissuade Ittai from leaving the city, but the warrior expressed his great devotion in these terms: "As Jehovah is living and as my lord the king is living, in the place where my lord the king may come to be, whether for death or for life, there is where your servant will come to be!" David then permitted Ittai to continue accompanying him. —2Sa 15:18-22.

After numbering his forces, David appointed this non-Israelite Ittai, along with Joab and Abishai, as chiefs, each over one third of the army.—2Sa 18:2, 5, 12.

2. One of David's mighty men; a Benjamite and the son of Ribai of Gibeah. (2Sa 23:29) He is called Ithai at 1 Chronicles 11:31.

ITURAEA (It·u·rae'a). A small territory of varying and undefined boundaries located NE of the Sea of Galilee.

The name Ituraea is thought to derive from Ishmael's son Jetur, whose descendants residing E of the Jordan were defeated by the Israelites. (Ge 25:15, 16; 1Ch 1:31; 5:18-23) Toward the close of the second century B.C.E., the Maccabean king Aristobulus I successfully warred against Ituraea and added much of its territory to Judea. To remain in the country, the inhabitants of Ituraea had to submit to circumcision and obey Jewish law. (*Jewish Antiquities*, XIII, 318 [xi, 3]) Later, Ituraea was one of the territories comprising the tetrarchy of Philip, inherited from his father Herod the Great.—Lu 3:1.

IVORY. The creamy-white tusks of the elephant, hippopotamus, walrus, and other animals. Though hard, and having a density about three and a half times as great as seasoned cedarwood, it is highly elastic and is easily carved or tooled. Its fine grain gives it a pleasing touch and finish that has remarkable durability. The intersecting layers of dentin, alternating in shade, add to its utility a beauty all its own. "Ivory" is designated in Hebrew by the words *shen* (literally, tooth) and *shen·hab·bim'* (rendered "elephants' teeth" in the Greek *Septuagint*). The Greek term *e·le·phan'ti-nos* means "made of ivory."

Ivory has been associated with the luxuries of life—fine art, elegant furnishings, treasured riches. Solomon's ships, once every three years, brought great quantities of ivory from faraway places. (1Ki 10:22; 2Ch 9:21) Befitting his glory and greatness, Solomon "made a great ivory throne and overlaid it with refined gold." (1Ki 10:18; 2Ch 9:17) The Psalms mention "the grand ivory palace" in connection with stringed instruments of music. (Ps 45:8) In the lovely Song of Solomon the writer uses ivory as a metaphor and a simile to express beauty: "His abdomen is an ivory plate covered with sapphires," "Your neck is like an ivory tower." (Ca 5:14; 7:4) King Ahab also built himself a palace using costly ivory, making it a veritable "house of ivory." (1Ki 22:39) In the days of Amos houses and couches were constructed with ivory. (Am 3:15; 6:4) Archaeological findings confirm the rather extensive use of ivory by the nation of Israel and her neighbors.

Egypt too used this natural "plastic" in making such things as combs, fan handles, dishes, ointment boxes, chair legs, game boards, statuettes,

and sculptured works of art. The city of Tyre, in her great sea commerce, inlaid the prows of her ships with ivory. Ivory is also listed among the costly things of ancient Tyre's traders, as well as in the stock of "the traveling merchants of the earth" who weep over Babylon the Great's fall into destruction.—Eze 27:6, 15; Re 18:11, 12.

IVVAH (Iv'vah). One of the cities conquered by the Assyrians (2Ki 18:34; 19:13; Isa 37:13), likely the same as Avva.—2Ki 17:24.

IYE-ABARIM (I'ye-ab'a·rim) [Ruins of the Fords (Crossings); Ruins of the Borderland (Regions Beyond)]. One of Israel's wilderness encampments. Its exact location is uncertain, but it was evidently on the southern border of Moab and near the torrent valley of Zered. (Nu 21:11, 12; 33:44) Perhaps Iye-abarim marked the southernmost point of the Abarim region. (Nu 33:47, 48; see ABARIM.) Yohanan Aharoni suggests an identification with el-Medeiyineh at the ford of the Brook Zered, about 60 km (37 mi) S of Dibongad, the next encampment listed.—*The Land of the Bible*, 1979, pp. 202, 436.

IYIM (I'yim) [Heaps of Ruins]. Apparently an abbreviated form of Iye-abarim, a site on the border of Moab where the Israelites encamped. —Nu 33:44, 45.

IZHAR (Iz'har). Two names, spelled similarly in Hebrew, are rendered the same in English.

1. *Yits·har'*. The second listed of Kohath's four sons; therefore a grandson of Levi. (Ex 6:16, 18; Nu 3:17, 19; 1Ch 6:2, 18) One of Izhar's three sons, Korah, was executed in the wilderness for rebellion.—Ex 6:21; Nu 16:1, 32.

Izhar founded the Levite family of Izharites. (Nu 3:27) Under King David, some of the Izharites, whose headman was Shelomith, were appointed singers, officers, and judges, while others performed regular Levitical duties.—1Ch 6:31-38; 23:12, 18; 24:20-22; 26:23, 29; see AMMINADAB No. 2.

2. *Yits·char'* (in agreement with *Vg*). A descendant of Judah; a son of Ashhur and Helah. (1Ch 4:1, 5, 7) In the margin of the Masoretic text the name is spelled Zohar.

IZHARITES (Iz'har·ites) [Of (Belonging to) Izhar]. A Levite family of the Kohathites that descended from Izhar.—Nu 3:19, 27; 1Ch 24:22; 26:23, 29.

IZLIAH (Iz·li'ah). A leading Benjamite who lived in Jerusalem; son or descendant of Elpaal. —1Ch 8:1, 18, 28.

IZRAHIAH (Iz·ra·hi′ah) [Jah Shines Forth; Jah Flashes Forth].

1. A descendant of Issachar through Tola. —1Ch 7:1-5.

2. An overseer of the singers who helped celebrate the completion of Nehemiah's rebuilding of Jerusalem's wall.—Ne 12:42.

IZRAHITE (Iz′rah·ite). The designation of the man Shamhuth, chief of David's fifth service division that ministered to him. (1Ch 27:8) Shamhuth was of either the town or family of Izrah.

IZRI (Iz′ri) [Of (Belonging to) Jezer]. The leader of the fourth course of 12 musicians at Jehovah's sanctuary under David's reorganization. (1Ch 25:7, 8, 11) Without the Hebrew letter *yohdh* at the beginning, his name is spelled "Zeri" in verse 3, where he is identified as a son of Jeduthun.

IZZIAH (Iz·zi′ah) [Jah Spatters]. One of the sons of Parosh who, after hearing Ezra's counsel, sent away their foreign wives and sons.—Ezr 10:25, 44.

J

JAAKOBAH (Ja·a·ko′bah) [from a root meaning "seize the heel; supplant"]. One of the chieftains of Simeon who, in the days of Hezekiah, extended their territory into the fertile valley of Gedor by striking down its inhabitants.—1Ch 4:24, 36-41.

JAALA, JAALAH (Ja′a·la[h]) [(Female) Mountain Goat]. The founder of a family of Solomon's servants, some of whom, along with the Nethinim, returned from the Babylonian exile with Zerubbabel.—Ezr 2:2, 55-58; Ne 7:7, 57-60.

JAARE-OREGIM (Ja′a·re-or′e·gim). A name appearing only at 2 Samuel 21:19. It is generally believed that scribal error has given rise to this name and that the correct reading is preserved in the parallel text at 1 Chronicles 20:5. "Jaare" is considered to be an alteration of "Jair," and "oregim" (′o·reghim′, "weavers" or "loom workers") is thought to have been copied inadvertently from a line below in the same verse.

JAARESHIAH (Ja·a·re·shi′ah). A family head in the tribe of Benjamin; son or descendant of Jeroham. He and his household lived in Jerusalem.—1Ch 8:1, 27, 28.

JAASIEL (Ja·a·si′el) [May God Make; God Has Made].

1. One of the mighty men of David, listed only in Chronicles; a Mezobaite.—1Ch 11:26, 47.

2. Prince of the tribe of Benjamin during David's reign. He was the son of Abner, therefore probably a cousin of King Saul.—1Ch 27:21, 22.

JAASU (Ja′a·su) [shortened form of Jaasiel]. A son of Bani and one of the Jews who responded to Ezra's admonition by putting away their foreign wives and sons.—Ezr 10:34, 37, 44.

JAAZANIAH (Ja·az·a·ni′ah) [Jehovah Has Given Ear]. Toward the end of the kingdom of Judah it seems that this was a rather common name; all four men mentioned in the Bible by this name lived within the same short period of time. The name has also been found in the Lachish Letters, and on a seal found at Tell en-Nasbeh the words "Ya′azanyahu, servant [officer] of the king" appear. (*The Biblical Archaeologist,* 1947, p. 71) There is no direct evidence, however, that such an inscription identifies any of the following persons.

1. A leader of the Rechabites when the prophet Jeremiah tested their integrity by offering them wine, which they refused. Jaazaniah was the son of another Jeremiah.—Jer 35:3, 5, 6.

2. Son of Shaphan; the only individual named in Ezekiel's vision (612 B.C.E.) of the 70 men who offered incense before carved idolatrous symbols in the temple at Jerusalem.—Eze 8:1, 10, 11.

3. Son of Azzur; one of the 25 men seen in Ezekiel's vision standing at the eastern gate of Jehovah's temple. Jaazaniah and his companions were "scheming hurtfulness and advising bad counsel against this city," and Ezekiel was commanded to prophesy against them.—Eze 11:1-4.

4. A military chief of Judah in the brief period immediately following the destruction of Jerusalem by the Babylonians. Jaazaniah (Jezaniah, as his name was sometimes spelled) was one of several who readily supported the appointment of Governor Gedaliah. (2Ki 25:23; Jer 40:7, 8) He was presumably included when "all the chiefs of

the military forces" warned Gedaliah of Ishmael's threat on his life and, after Ishmael did assassinate Gedaliah, pursued Ishmael and recovered those he had taken prisoner. (Jer 40:13, 14; 41:11-16) Jezaniah was among those leaders who inquired of Jeremiah concerning what to do then, but rather than follow his advice, they led the few remaining ones down to Egypt. (2Ki 25:26; Jer 42:1-3, 8; 43:1-5) "Azariah the son of Hoshaiah" is possibly a brother of, but more likely the same as, Jaazaniah.—Jer 43:2.

JAAZIAH (Ja·a·zi'ah). A Merarite Levite, four of whose sons or descendants served during David's reign.—1Ch 24:26, 27, 31.

JAAZIEL (Ja·a'zi·el). A Levite musician in the second division that accompanied the ark of the covenant when it was transferred from Obed-edom's house to Jerusalem. (1Ch 15:18) In verse 20 he is called Aziel. According to 1 Chronicles 16:5, where he is called Jeiel (the first "Jeiel" in that verse), he was afterward assigned to regular duty as a musician before the Ark.

JABAL (Ja'bal). A descendant of Cain; son of Lamech and his first wife Adah. (Ge 4:17, 19, 20) Jabal is called "the founder of those who dwell in tents and have livestock." Jabal was not the first shepherd, for Abel had been one previously; but Jabal evidently began or was predominant in nomadic livestock raising as a way of life. He perhaps invented tents, which would be much easier to move than permanent dwellings when a certain pasturage gave out.

JABBOK, TORRENT VALLEY OF (Jab'-bok). One of the main torrent valleys, or wadis, E of the Jordan, first mentioned in Scripture with reference to Jacob's crossing "the ford of Jabbok" with his household. Also, near this ford Jacob grappled with an angel.—Ge 32:22-30.

Though the Jabbok's headwaters rise near 'Amman (ancient Rabbah), the wadi collects waters from several perennial streams and numerous winter torrents before flowing into the Jordan 39 km (24 mi) N of the Dead Sea. Only about 40 km (25 mi) separate the source of the torrent valley from its finish, but the Jabbok's semicircular course covers about 100 km (62 mi). Its modern Arabic name, Wadi Zarqa, literally means "Torrent Valley of Blue." Perhaps this name is derived from the gray-blue color that the Jabbok exhibits when seen from a distance. Small fish abound in its shallow, easily fordable waters.

Oleander bushes and many kinds of small trees line the deep fertile valley through which the Jabbok flows. This valley, with its steep sides, served as a natural boundary. (De 3:16) The first section of the torrent valley, running from S to N, once constituted a frontier between the Ammonites and the Amorites (Nu 21:24), whereas the section extending from W to E split Gilead in two and formed the boundary between the realms of Amorite Kings Sihon and Og. (De 2:37; Jos 12:2; Jg 11:13, 22) Today this same valley is one of the best routes for crossing the Jordan from what was anciently called Gilead.

JABESH (Ja'besh).

1. [possibly, Dried-Up Place]. A town in the northern section of Gilead. Also known as Jabesh-gilead, it is mentioned in the history of the judges and kings.—Jg 21:8; 1Sa 11:1; 1Ch 10:11, 12; see JABESH-GILEAD.

2. [possibly, Dried Up]. Father of Israel's King Shallum.—2Ki 15:10, 13, 14.

JABESH-GILEAD (Ja'besh-gil'e·ad) [possibly, Dried-Up Place of Gilead]. An ancient town in the tribal territory of Gad, E of the Jordan. Its exact location is not certain, although most scholars believe that it was a little E of the Jordan in the vicinity of Wadi Yabis (Jabesh), about 35 km (22 mi) S of the Sea of Galilee.

The first mention of Jabesh-gilead was in the days of the Judges, in connection with the retribution dealt out to the neighboring tribe of Benjamin for its condoning of gross immorality. (Jg 21:8) On that occasion when the Israelites practically exterminated the entire tribe of Benjamin (only 600 males escaped), it was found that not a man of Jabesh-gilead had participated in meting out this justified punishment. It was therefore determined that every man, woman, and child of Jabesh-gilead, with the exception of the virgins, should be put to death. The 400 virgins that were thus spared were then given as wives to the fugitive Benjamites so as to prevent extinction of the tribe.—Jg 20:1–21:14.

Some three centuries later, when all Israel was clamoring for a visible king like the other nations had, the Ammonites threatened to bore out the right eye of every male inhabitant of Jabesh-gilead, a threat that was removed only when Saul mustered a force of 330,000 and put the Ammonites to flight. (1Sa 11:1-15) Forty years later the Philistines defeated the Israelites and hung the decapitated bodies of Saul and his three sons on the wall of the public square inside Beth-shan. Upon hearing of this disgrace, valiant men of Jabesh-gilead made a daring night raid in which they removed the corpses, brought them to

Jabesh-gilead, burned the bodies, and gave the bones a respectful burial. They then fasted for seven days.—1Sa 31:8-13; 1Ch 10:8-12.

David, as the newly anointed king of Judah, sent commendations and blessing to the citizens of Jabesh-gilead for having extended loving-kindness in this way toward the fallen anointed one of Israel. (2Sa 2:4-7) Later, David had the bones of Saul and Jonathan brought from Jabesh-gilead and interred in Saul's family burial plot in Benjamite territory.—2Sa 21:12-14.

JABEZ (Ja′bez).

1. [from a root meaning "pain"]. A descendant of Judah named Jabez by his mother because of her pain in giving birth to him. Jabez proved himself to be more honorable than his brothers and, in answer to his prayer, experienced Jehovah's blessing and protection.—1Ch 4:1, 9, 10.

2. Apparently a Judean site, perhaps founded by No. 1. Jabez was the home of three families of scribes. (1Ch 2:55) Its exact location is today unknown.

JABIN (Ja′bin) [possibly, Discerning; Understanding; or, One Who Builds]. Perhaps a dynastic name or title of the Canaanite kings of Hazor.

1. The king of Hazor when Joshua invaded the Promised Land. Jabin formed a confederation of northern Canaanite kings, and these amassed against Israel a force "as numerous as the grains of sand . . . [including] very many horses and war chariots." When camped at the waters of Merom, their combined armies were defeated by Joshua's surprise attack and follow-up pursuit. Jabin was executed when Hazor itself was later captured and burned.—Jos 11:1-14; 12:7, 19.

2. A later Canaanite king who ruled from the restored Hazor; possibly a descendant of No. 1. Jabin's being called "the king of Canaan" might denote supremacy over the other Canaanite kings, granting him exceptional power and authority; it does appear that there were others at least allied with him. On the other hand, the expression might merely distinguish him from kings of other lands. Jabin's army, including 900 chariots with iron scythes, was under the command of Sisera, who takes greater prominence in the account than Jabin himself.—Jg 4:2, 3; 5:19, 20.

By Jehovah's permission, Jabin harshly oppressed apostate Israel 20 years. But on their calling to God for deliverance, Jehovah raised up Barak and Deborah to lead Israel to victory over Jabin's army. Sisera was killed by the wife of Heber the Kenite, who had been at peace with Jabin. (Jg 4:3-22) The Israelites continued warring against Jabin and finally put him to death. —Jg 4:23, 24; Ps 83:9, 10.

JABNEEL (Jab′ne·el) [May God Build; God Has Built].

1. A Judean boundary site (Jos 15:1, 11), probably the same as the Jabneh that King Uzziah (829-778 B.C.E.) wrested from the Philistines. (2Ch 26:6) Jabneel is identified with modern Yavne. Situated about 6 km (3.5 mi) from the Mediterranean Sea, Yavne stands on an isolated, sandy hill 20 km (12 mi) S of Joppa.

2. A boundary site of Naphtali. (Jos 19:32, 33) Although some suggest an identification of the Talmudic Jabneel with Khirbet Yamma, the Biblical Jabneel is identified with Tell en-Na′am (Tel Yin′am), near a spring, about 8 km (5 mi) SSW of Tiberias. The name is preserved in the present-day village of Yavne′el nearby.

JABNEH (Jab′neh) [May [God] Build; [God] Has Built]. A walled Philistine city that suffered defeat at the hands of Judah's King Uzziah. (2Ch 26:6) It is probably the same as Jabneel.—Jos 15:11; see JABNEEL No. 1.

JACAN (Ja′can) [related through a play on words to the name Achor, meaning "Ostracism; Trouble"]. Fifth named of Abihail's seven sons; a Gadite.—1Ch 5:13, 14.

JACHIN (Ja′chin) [May [Jehovah] Firmly Establish; [Jehovah] Has Firmly Established].

1. The fourth-listed son of Simeon. (Ge 46:10) He is apparently called Jarib at 1 Chronicles 4:24. His descendants, the Jachinites, comprised one of the Simeonite families in Israel.—Ex 6:15; Nu 26:12.

2. The priest whose paternal house was selected by lot to care for the 21st of the 24 priestly divisions that David organized. (1Ch 24:7, 17) One or more of his descendants (or of another priest of the same name) resided in Jerusalem after the Babylonian exile.—1Ch 9:3, 10; Ne 11:10.

3. The southernmost of the twin pillars standing in front of Solomon's temple.—1Ki 7:15-22; see BOAZ, II; CAPITAL.

JACHINITES (Ja′chin·ites) [Of (Belonging to) Jachin]. Descendants of Simeon's son Jachin.—Ge 46:10; Nu 26:12.

JACKAL [Heb., tan]. A kind of wild dog that has a long, pointed muzzle and a bushy tail, and closely resembles the fox. This animal (*Canis*

aureus) is still encountered in Palestine. Though the jackal may attack and kill fowl and even lambs and, in fact, live on almost anything, including fruit, it is basically a scavenger that feeds on carrion. Hence, the animal performs a beneficial service, since the carrion otherwise might provide a breeding place for germs. Jackals generally hunt at night, singly, in pairs, or in small packs. During the day they usually sleep in desolate places, holes in the ground, caves, abandoned buildings, or ruins.

Since jackals are denizens of wild, lonely, and even desertlike areas, the domain of the jackal is used figuratively in the Scriptures to represent a state of utter desolation, without human inhabitant. Various prophecies use this figure to forecast desolation for Jerusalem, the cities of Judah, Hazor, Babylon, and Edom. (Jer 9:11; 10:22; 49:33; 51:37; Isa 34:5, 13; Mal 1:3) The Bible also makes reference to the jackal's mournful wailing, or howling. (Isa 13:22; Mic 1:8) The jackal's cry begins at sunset and is a long-drawn-out wail, repeated three or four times, each repetition being slightly higher in key than the preceding one. Finally the wail ends in a series of short, loud, yelping barks.

In Scripture the jackal figures repeatedly in an illustrative setting. Job, in describing his own lamentable state, exclaims that he has become "a brother to jackals." (Job 30:29) In regard to a humiliating defeat of God's people, the psalmist, perhaps with reference to the battlefield where jackals congregate to feed upon those slain (compare Ps 68:23), mourned: "You have crushed us in the place of jackals." (Ps 44:19) Babylon's siege of Jerusalem in 607 B.C.E. brought the stress of famine, with the result that mothers treated their own offspring cruelly. Thus Jeremiah appropriately contrasted the cruelty "of my people" with the jackals' maternal care.—La 4:3, 10.

On account of the intense droughts on the land of Judah when it lacked Jehovah's blessing, zebras are depicted as snuffing up the wind, that is, panting for breath, like jackals. (Jer 14:1, 2, 6) On the other hand, with reference to the restoration of his people, Jehovah promised that the abiding place of jackals would come to have grass, reeds, and papyrus plants. And Jehovah's providing water for his people in the wilderness would cause animals such as the jackal to glorify him.—Isa 35:7; 43:20, 21.

JACOB (Ja′cob) [One Seizing the Heel; Supplanter].

1. Son of Isaac and Rebekah, and younger twin brother of Esau. Jacob's parents had been married for 20 years before the birth of these twins, their only children, in 1858 B.C.E. Isaac at the time was 60 years old. So, as in the case of Abraham, Isaac's prayers for offspring were answered only after his patience and faith in God's promises had been fully tested.—Ge 25:20, 21, 26; Ro 9:7-10.

In her pregnancy, Rebekah was distressed by the struggling of the twins within her womb, which, Jehovah explained, were the beginnings of two opposing nations. Furthermore, Jehovah declared that, contrary to custom, the older would serve the younger. Accordingly, the second-born Jacob was holding the heel of Esau at their birth; hence the name Jacob, meaning "One Seizing the Heel." (Ge 25:22-26) Jehovah thus demonstrated his ability to detect the genetic bent of the unborn and to exercise his foreknowledge and right to select beforehand whom he chooses for his purposes; yet he in no way predetermines the final destiny of individuals.—Ro 9:10-12; Ho 12:3.

In contrast to his father's favorite son Esau, who was a wild, restless, wandering type of huntsman, Jacob is described as "a blameless [Heb., *tam*] man, dwelling in tents," one who led a quiet pastoral life and was dependable to look after domestic affairs, one who was especially loved by his mother. (Ge 25:27, 28) This Hebrew word *tam* is used elsewhere to describe those approved of God. For example, "bloodthirsty men hate anyone blameless," yet Jehovah gives assurance that "the future of [the blameless] man will be peaceful." (Pr 29:10; Ps 37:37) The integrity keeper Job "proved to be blameless [Heb., *tam*] and upright."—Job 1:1, 8; 2:3.

Received Birthright and Blessing. Abraham did not die until his grandson Jacob was 15 years old, in 1843 B.C.E., and so the boy had ample opportunity to hear of God's oath-bound covenant directly from the lips of his grandfather as well as his father. (Ge 22:15-18) Jacob realized what a privilege it would be to participate in the fulfillment of such divine promises. Finally the opportunity presented itself legally to purchase from his brother the firstborn's birthright and all that went with it. (De 21:15-17) This opportunity arrived one day when Esau came in from the field exhausted and smelled the tasty stew his brother had cooked. "Quick, please," Esau exclaimed, "give me a swallow of the red—the red there, for I am tired!" Jacob's reply: "Sell me, first of all, your right as firstborn!" "Esau despised the birthright," and so the sale was quickly made and sealed with a solemn oath. (Ge 25:29-34; Heb 12:16) Reasons enough why Jehovah said, "I loved Jacob, but Esau I hated."—Ro 9:13; Mal 1:2, 3.

Was it proper for Jacob to impersonate Esau?

When Isaac was old and thought that he would soon die, he sent Esau out to hunt some venison, saying: "Let me eat, in order that my soul may bless you before I die." However, Rebekah overheard the conversation and quickly sent Jacob to get two kids of the goats so she could prepare a tasty dish for Isaac, and she said to Jacob: "You must bring it to your father and he must eat it, in order that he may bless you before his death." She even put the skins of the kids on Jacob's hands and neck to cause Isaac, when feeling Jacob, to conclude that he was Esau. When Jacob took the food in to his father, Isaac asked him: "Who are you, my son?" And Jacob answered: "I am Esau your firstborn." Legally, as Jacob well knew, he was entitled to act in the role of Esau, the firstborn of Isaac. Isaac felt Jacob to see if this was really Esau or not, and he said: "The voice is the voice of Jacob, but the hands are the hands of Esau." Nevertheless, matters worked out successfully, and as the account says, "He blessed him." (Ge 27:1-29) Had Rebekah and Jacob done the right thing?

There could be no doubt that Jacob was entitled to the blessing. Before the birth of the twins, Jehovah had said to Rebekah: "The older will serve the younger." (Ge 25:23) Later, in harmony with the inclination that Jehovah had already foreseen and that had caused him to love Jacob more than he did Esau, Esau sold his birthright to Jacob for just a bowl of stew.—Ge 25:29-34.

To what extent Isaac knew of these indications as to who should receive the blessing, the Bible account does not say. Exactly why Rebekah and Jacob handled the matter in the way they did, we do not know, except that both of them knew that the blessing belonged to Jacob. Jacob did not maliciously misrepresent himself in order to get something that did not rightfully belong to him. The Bible does not condemn what Rebekah and Jacob did. The outcome was that Jacob received the rightful blessing. Isaac himself evidently saw that Jehovah's will had been accomplished. Shortly after this, when sending Jacob off to Haran to get a wife, Isaac further blessed Jacob and specifically said: "God Almighty . . . will give to you the blessing of Abraham." (Ge 28:3, 4; compare Heb 11:20.) So we properly conclude that the outcome of the matter was what Jehovah purposed. The Bible states clearly the lesson that we should draw from this account, warning that we should be careful "that there may be no fornicator nor anyone not appreciating sacred things, like Esau, who in exchange for one meal gave away his rights as firstborn."—Heb 12:16.

Jacob's Move to Paddan-aram. (MAP, Vol. 1, p. 529) Jacob was 77 years old when he left Beer-sheba for the land of his foreparents, a land where he spent the next 20 years of his life. (Ge 28:10; 31:38) After traveling NNE about 100 km (62 mi) he stopped at Luz (Bethel) in the Judean hills for the night, using a stone for his pillow. There in his dreams he saw a ladder, or flight of stairs, reaching into the heavens, upon which angels were ascending and descending. At the top Jehovah was envisioned, and He now confirmed with Jacob the divine covenant made with Abraham and Isaac.—Ge 28:11-13; 1Ch 16:16, 17.

In this covenant Jehovah promised Jacob that He would watch over and keep him and would not forsake him until the land upon which he was lying had become his and his seed had become like the dust particles of the earth for numbers. Moreover, "by means of you and by means of your seed all the families of the ground will certainly bless themselves." (Ge 28:13-15) When Jacob fully realized the import of the night's experience he exclaimed: "How fear-inspiring this place is! This is nothing else but the house of God." He therefore changed the name of Luz to Bethel, meaning "House of God," and proceeded to set up a pillar and anoint it as a witness of these momentous events. In grateful response to God's promise of support, Jacob also vowed that without fail he would give to Jehovah a tenth of all he received.—Ge 28:16-22.

Traveling on, Jacob eventually met his cousin Rachel in the vicinity of Haran and was invited by her father Laban, the brother of Jacob's mother, to stay with them. Jacob fell in love with Rachel and bargained to work seven years for her father if he would give her to be his wife. The passing years seemed "to be like some few days," so deep was Jacob's love for Rachel. However, at the wedding Rachel's older sister Leah was deceitfully substituted, Laban explaining, "It is not customary . . . to give the younger woman before the firstborn." After celebrating this marriage for a week, Laban then gave Rachel also to Jacob as his wife upon the agreement that Jacob would work another seven years in payment for her. Laban also gave Leah and Rachel two maidservants, Zilpah and Bilhah respectively.—Ge 29:1-29; Ho 12:12.

Jehovah began building a great nation out of this marriage arrangement. Leah bore Jacob four sons in succession: Reuben, Simeon, Levi, and Judah. Rachel, seeing she continued barren, then gave her slave girl Bilhah to Jacob and, through her, got two sons, Dan and Naphtali. At this time Leah remained barren. So she too gave her slave girl Zilpah to Jacob and got two sons from this union, namely, Gad and Asher. Leah then began bearing children once again, giving birth first to Issachar, then to Zebulun, and then to a daughter named Dinah. Rachel at last became pregnant and gave birth to Joseph. As a consequence, in the comparatively short period of seven years, Jacob was blessed with many children.—Ge 29: 30–30:24.

Jacob Made Rich Before Leaving Haran. On completing his 14-year work contract for the acquisition of his wives, Jacob was anxious to return to his homeland. But Laban, seeing how Jehovah had blessed him because of Jacob, insisted that he continue overseeing his flocks; Jacob was even told to stipulate his own wages. In that part of the world the sheep and goats are generally of a solid color, the sheep being white, the goats black. Jacob therefore asked that only the sheep and goats with abnormal colors or markings be given to him—all the sheep dark brown in color and all the goats with any white marks. "Why, that is fine!" was Laban's reply. And to keep the wages as low as possible, Laban, at Jacob's suggestion, separated out of the flocks all the striped, speckled, and color-patched goats and the dark-brown young male sheep, which he gave to his own sons to look after, even putting a three-day distance between them, to prevent any interbreeding of the two flocks. Only abnormally colored ones born in the future would be Jacob's. —Ge 30:25-36.

So here Jacob started off tending only sheep of normal color and goats with no markings. However, he worked hard and did what he thought would increase the number of off-colored animals. He took green sapling staffs of the storax, almond, and plane trees, and peeled the barks of these in such a way as to give them a striped, spotty appearance. These he placed in the gutters of the animals' drinking troughs, apparently with the idea that if the animals looked at the stripes when in heat there would be a prenatal influence that would make the offspring mottled or abnormal in color. Jacob also took care to place the sticks in the troughs only when the stronger robust animals were in heat.—Ge 30:37-42.

Results? The offspring abnormally marked or colored, and therefore Jacob's wages, proved to be more numerous than those of normal solid color, which were to be Laban's. Since the desired results were obtained, Jacob probably thought his stratagem with the striped sticks was responsible. In this he no doubt shared the same misconception commonly held by many people, namely, that such things can have an effect on the offspring. However, in a dream his Creator instructed him otherwise.

In his dream Jacob learned that certain principles of genetics, and not the sticks, were responsible for his success. Whereas Jacob was tending only solid-colored animals, yet the vision revealed that the male goats were striped, speckled, and spotty. How could this be? Apparently they were hybrids even though of uniform color, the result of crossbreeding in Laban's flock before Jacob began being paid. So certain of these animals carried in their reproductive cells the hereditary factors for spotting and speckling future generations, according to the laws of heredity discovered by Gregor Mendel in the last century.—Ge 31:10-12.

During the six years that Jacob worked under this arrangement, Jehovah greatly blessed and prospered him by increasing not only his flocks but also the number of his servants, camels, and asses, and this in spite of the fact that Laban kept changing the agreed-upon wages. Finally, "the true God of Bethel" instructed Jacob to return to the Promised Land.—Ge 30:43; 31:1-13, 41.

Return to the Promised Land. Fearing that Laban would again attempt to prevent Jacob from leaving his service, Jacob secretly took his wives and children, and all that he owned, crossed the Euphrates River, and headed for Canaan. In contemplating this move, Jacob was probably grazing his flocks close to the Euphrates, as is indicated by Genesis 31:4, 21. At the time, Laban was out shearing his flocks and was not informed of Jacob's departure until three days after he had left. More time may have elapsed in which the shearing was completed and preparations were made to chase after Jacob with his forces. All together, this would have given Jacob sufficient time to drive his slow-moving flocks all the way down to the mountainous region of Gilead before Laban caught up with him, a distance from Haran of not less than 560 km (350 mi), a distance, however, that could easily have been covered in seven days by Laban and his kinsmen riding camels in hot pursuit.—Ge 31:14-23.

When Laban found the object of his pursuit

camped a few kilometers N of the Jabbok, he demanded that Jacob explain: Why had he left without allowing Laban to kiss his children and grandchildren good-bye, and why had he stolen Laban's gods? (Ge 31:24-30) The answer to the first question was rather obvious—fear that Laban would have prevented him from leaving. As to the second question, Jacob knew nothing of any theft, and a search failed to disclose that Rachel had indeed stolen the family teraphim and hidden them in her camel's saddle basket.—Ge 31:31-35.

One explanation for Rachel's actions, and Laban's concern, is this: "Possession of the household gods marked a person as the legitimate heir, which explains Laban's anxiety in Gen. 31:26 ff. to recover his household gods from Jacob."—*Ancient Near Eastern Texts,* edited by J. B. Pritchard, 1974, p. 220, ftn. 51.

Their quarrel peacefully settled, Jacob set up a stone pillar and then heaped up stones, which stood there for many years as a witness to the covenant of peace that these two had concluded with a ceremonial meal. The names given to this heap of stones were Galeed (meaning "Witness Heap") and The Watchtower.—Ge 31:36-55.

Jacob was now anxious to make peace also with his brother Esau, whom he had not seen for more than 20 years. To soften any lingering hatred his brother might still harbor, Jacob sent ahead of him costly gifts for Esau—hundreds of goats and sheep, and many camels, asses, and head of cattle. (Ge 32:3-21) Jacob had fled Canaan with practically nothing; now because of Jehovah's blessing he was returning a wealthy man.

Why did the angel with whom Jacob wrestled cause Jacob to limp?

During the night that Jacob's household crossed the Jabbok on the way S to meet Esau, Jacob had the most unusual experience of wrestling with an angel, and because of his perseverance his name was changed to Israel, meaning "Contender (Perseverer) With God; or, God Contends." (Ge 32:22-28) Thereafter both names often appear in Hebrew poetic parallelisms. (Ps 14:7; 22:23; 78:5, 21, 71; 105:10, 23) In this struggle the angel touched the socket of Jacob's thigh joint, and Jacob limped for the rest of his life—perhaps to teach him humility; a constant reminder not to be overly exalted because of his God-given prosperity or for having grappled with an angel. In commemoration of these momentous events Jacob

called the place Peniel or Penuel.—Ge 32:25, 30-32.

After the conclusion of the amiable meeting between Jacob and Esau, these twins, now about 97 years old, each went his separate way, presumably not to meet again until they jointly buried their father Isaac some 23 years later. Esau went S to Seir with his gifts, and Jacob turned N, recrossing the Jabbok.—Ge 33:1-17; 35:29.

Next 33 Years as Alien Resident. After he parted company with Esau, Jacob settled down in Succoth. This was the first place where Jacob stayed for any length of time after returning from Paddan-aram. How long he was here is not stated, but it may have been a number of years, for he built himself a permanent structure in which to live and also booths or covered stalls of some sort for his livestock.—Ge 33:17.

Jacob's next move was westward across the Jordan to the vicinity of Shechem, where he bought a tract of land from the sons of Hamor for "a hundred pieces of money [Heb., *qesi·tah'*]." (Ge 33:18-20; Jos 24:32) The value of that ancient money unit, the *qesi·tah',* is not known today, but a hundred of them, all together, may have amounted to a considerable sum of weighed-out silver, there being no coins in those days.

It was at Shechem that Jacob's daughter Dinah began associating with the Canaanite women, and this, in turn, opened the way for Shechem, the son of the chieftain Hamor, to violate her. In the wake of this episode matters soon developed beyond Jacob's control—his sons killed every male inhabitant of Shechem, took the women and children captive, appropriated all the property and wealth of the community, and made their father Jacob a stench to the inhabitants of the land.—Ge 34:1-31.

Jacob was then divinely directed to leave Shechem and move down to Bethel, which he did. However, before going, he had his household clean themselves up, change their garments, remove all their false gods (probably including Laban's teraphim) as well as the earrings possibly worn as amulets. These Jacob buried out of sight near Shechem.—Ge 35:1-4.

Bethel, the "House of God," was of special importance to Jacob, for here, perhaps some 30 years before, Jehovah had passed on to him the Abrahamic covenant. Now, after Jacob built an altar to this great God of his forefathers, Jehovah restated the covenant and also confirmed that Jacob's name had been changed to Israel. Jacob then erected a pillar over which he poured a drink offering and oil in commemoration of these momentous events. It was also while sojourning here at Bethel that his mother's nurse Deborah died and was buried.—Ge 35:5-15.

Again we do not know how long Jacob lived at Bethel. Upon leaving there and moving southward, and while yet some distance from Bethlehem (Ephrath), birth pains struck Rachel, and in the ordeal of giving birth to her second son, Benjamin, she died. Jacob buried his beloved Rachel there and erected a pillar to mark her grave. —Ge 35:16-20.

This man Israel, now blessed with a full complement of 12 sons from whom the 12 tribes of Israel would spring, traveled on farther south. His next campsite is described as "a distance beyond the tower of Eder," which places it somewhere between Bethlehem and Hebron. It was while residing there that his oldest son Reuben had sexual relations with his father's concubine Bilhah, the mother of Dan and Naphtali. Reuben may have thought his father Jacob was too old to do anything about it, but Jehovah disapproved, and for his incestuous act Reuben lost the firstborn's birthright.—Ge 35:21-26; 49:3, 4; De 27: 20; 1Ch 5:1.

Perhaps it was prior to his son Joseph's being sold into Egyptian slavery that Jacob moved his residence down to Hebron, where his aging father Isaac was still living, but the date of this move is not certain.—Ge 35:27.

One day Jacob sent Joseph (now 17 years old) out to see how his brothers were getting along tending their father's flocks. When he finally located them at Dothan about 100 km (62 mi) N of Hebron, they seized him and sold him to a caravan of traders headed for Egypt. This was in 1750 B.C.E. They then led their father to believe that Joseph had been killed by a wild beast. For many days Jacob sorrowed over the loss, refusing to be comforted, and saying: "I shall go down mourning to my son into Sheol!" (Ge 37:2, 3, 12-36) The death of his father Isaac in 1738 B.C.E. only added to his grief.—Ge 35:28, 29.

The Move to Egypt. About ten years after Isaac's death an extensive famine forced Jacob to send ten of his sons down to Egypt for cereals. Benjamin remained behind. Pharaoh's food administrator, Joseph, recognized his brothers and demanded that they bring their younger brother Benjamin back with them to Egypt. (Ge 41:57; 42:1-20) However, when told of the demand, Jacob at first refused to let him go, fearing harm might befall this beloved son of his old age; Benjamin at the time was at least 22 years old. (Ge

42:29-38) Only when the food obtained in Egypt had all been eaten did Jacob finally consent to let Benjamin go.—Ge 43:1-14; Ac 7:12.

With the reconciliation of Joseph and his brothers came the invitation for Jacob and his whole household, together with all their livestock and belongings, to move down to the fertile land of Goshen in Egypt's delta country, for the great famine was destined to last another five years. Pharaoh even provided wagons and food provisions for their assistance. (Ge 45:9-24) On the way down, Jehovah assured Jacob that this move had his blessing and approval. (Ge 46:1-4) All the souls counted as belonging to Jacob's household, including Manasseh, Ephraim, and others that may have been born in Egypt before Jacob died, were 70 in number. (Ge 46:5-27; Ex 1:5; De 10:22) This number did not include Leah, who had died in the Promised Land (Ge 49:31), or his unnamed daughters, or the wives of his sons. —Ge 46:26; compare Ge 37:35.

Soon after arriving in Egypt in 1728 B.C.E., Jacob was brought to Pharaoh's court and there he greeted the king with a blessing. Jacob described himself as an alien resident (the same as Abraham and Isaac, for like them he too had not inherited the God-promised land). Asked about his age, Jacob replied that he was 130 but that, compared with those of his forefathers, his days had been "few and distressing."—Ge 47:7-10.

Shortly before his death, Jacob blessed his grandsons, Joseph's sons, and, by divine guidance, put the younger Ephraim ahead of the older Manasseh. Then to Joseph, who would receive the firstborn's double portion of the inheritance, Jacob declared: "I do give you one shoulder of land more than to your brothers, which I took from the hand of the Amorites by my sword and by my bow." (Ge 48:1-22; 1Ch 5:1) Since Jacob had peaceably purchased the plot of ground near Shechem from the sons of Hamor (Ge 33:19, 20), it seems that this promise to Joseph was an expression of Jacob's faith, in which he prophetically spoke of the future conquest of Canaan by his descendants as if already accomplished by his own sword and bow. (See AMORITE.) Joseph's double portion of that conquered land consisted of the two allotments given to the tribes of Ephraim and Manasseh.

Before he died, Jacob summoned up enough strength to bless his 12 sons individually. (Ge 49:1-28) He showed faith in the outworking of Jehovah's purposes. (Heb 11:21) Because of his faith and because Jehovah specifically confirmed to him the Abrahamic covenant of blessing, the

Scriptures often refer to Jehovah as the God not only of Abraham and Isaac but also of Jacob.—Ex 3:6; 1Ch 29:18; Mt 22:32.

Finally, in 1711 B.C.E., after 17 years of residence in Egypt, Jacob died at the age of 147. (Ge 47:27, 28) Thus that period of history from the birth of Jacob to his death ended, a history that occupies more than half the pages of the book of Genesis. (Chaps 25-50) In accordance with Jacob's wish to be buried in Canaan, Joseph first had the Egyptian physicians embalm his father's body in preparation for the trip. A great funeral train, in keeping with the prominence of his son Joseph, then set out from Egypt. When it came into the region of the Jordan, there were seven days of mourning rites, after which Jacob's sons buried their father in the cave of Machpelah where Abraham and Isaac had been interred. —Ge 49:29-33; 50:1-14.

2. The prophets often used "Jacob" in a figurative sense, with reference to the nation descended from the patriarch. (Isa 9:8; 27:9; Jer 10:25; Eze 39:25; Am 6:8; Mic 1:5; Ro 11:26) Jesus, on one occasion, used the name Jacob figuratively when speaking of those who would be "in the kingdom of the heavens."—Mt 8:11.

3. The father of Joseph who was the husband of Mary, the mother of Jesus.—Mt 1:15, 16.

JACOB'S FOUNTAIN.

The "well" or "fountain" where Jesus Christ, while resting, conversed with a Samaritan woman. (Joh 4:5-30) It is considered to be Bir Ya'qub (Be'er Ya'aqov), situated about 2.5 km (1.5 mi) SE of modern-day Nablus, not far from Tell Balata, the site of Shechem. Jacob's fountain is a deep well, the water level of which never rises to the top. Measurements made in the last century indicate the well's depth to be about 23 m (75 ft). It is approximately 2.5 m (8 ft) wide, although narrowing at the top. Because the well is usually dry from about the end of May until the autumn rains, some reason that its water is derived from rain and percolation. But others believe that the well is also spring fed and therefore could also be called a fountain.

The Bible does not directly state that Jacob dug the well. However, it does indicate that Jacob had property in this vicinity. (Ge 33:18-20; Jos 24:32; Joh 4:5) And the Samaritan woman told Jesus that "Jacob . . . gave us the well and [he] . . . together with his sons and his cattle drank out of it." (Joh 4:12) So Jacob likely dug it or had it dug, perhaps to provide water for his large household and flocks, thereby preventing trouble with his neighbors, who doubtless already owned the oth-

er water sources in the region. Or, he may have needed a better and more permanent supply of water when other wells in the area dried up.

JADA (Ja'da) [probably a shortened form of Jedaiah, meaning "Jah Knows"]. A descendant of Judah through Jerahmeel. Jada is listed as a son of Onam and father of Jether and Jonathan.—1Ch 2:3, 25, 26, 28, 32.

JADDAI (Jad'dai). A son of Nebo; one of those who took non-Israelite wives but sent them away at the urging of Ezra. (Ezr 10:43, 44) Some translations read "Iddo" instead of "Jaddai."—*AS, AT, Mo, Ro*.

JADDUA (Jad'du·a) [from a root meaning "know"].

1. One of the headmen of Israel whose descendant, if not he himself, sealed the resolution of faithfulness during Nehemiah's governorship. —Ne 10:1, 14, 21.

2. The last of the Aaronic high-priestly line listed in the Hebrew Scriptures. Jaddua's being the fifth generation after Jeshua allows for him to have lived during "the kingship of Darius the Persian."—Ne 12:10, 11, 22; see DARIUS No. 3.

JADE. A hard, durable, usually green-colored ornamental stone used for jewelry and carvings; in Hebrew, *ya·shepheh'*. It occurs as two distinct minerals, "nephrite" and "jadeite." Nephrite (true jade) is the most common variety. It varies from translucent to opaque and is found in colors such as dark green, black, gray, yellow, and white. Jadeite is more valuable than nephrite because of its more attractive coloring and rarity. Jade is particularly suitable for engraving because of its composition.

A beautiful jade stone with the name of one of Israel's 12 tribes engraved upon it adorned "the breastpiece of judgment" worn by High Priest Aaron, occupying the third position in the fourth row of stones. (Ex 28:2, 15, 20, 21; 39:9, 13, 14) Jade was also included among the precious stones that decorated the "covering" of the king of Tyre. —Eze 28:12, 13.

JADON (Ja'don) [possibly a shortened form of Jaazaniah, meaning "Jehovah Has Given Ear"]. A Meronothite who helped Nehemiah rebuild Jerusalem's wall in 455 B.C.E. Jadon was apparently from the vicinity of Mizpah.—Ne 3:7.

Josephus calls the unnamed prophet in 1 Kings 13 "Jadon."—*Jewish Antiquities*, VIII, 231 (viii, 5).

JAEL (Ja'el) [Mountain Goat]. The wife of Heber the Kenite, hence a non-Israelite, and slayer of the Canaanite army chief Sisera.

With her husband, Jael tented near Kedesh, and there was peace between Heber and the Canaanite oppressors. (Jg 4:10, 11, 17, 21; see KEDESH No. 3.) After Sisera was defeated at Israel's hand, he fled to Heber's neutral encampment, where Jael invited him into her tent. She then covered him with a blanket. When he asked for water she gave him a banquet bowl of curdled milk to drink. After she again covered him up, he asked her to stand guard at the entrance of the tent. Thinking himself secure as her guest, the tired and weary Sisera soon fell fast asleep. Jael, who as a tent dweller was undoubtedly used to driving tent pins into the ground, then quietly came in to him armed with a hammer and a tent pin that she drove through his head into the earth. When the pursuer Barak arrived, she showed him the army chief, dead at "the hand of a woman," as Deborah foretold. (Jg 4:9, 17-22) Jael's courageous act against the enemy of Jehovah is extolled in the victory song of Deborah and Barak, which also pronounces Jael "most blessed among women." —Jg 5:6, 24-27.

JAGUR (Ja'gur) [possibly related to Aramaic word meaning "[stone] heap"]. A city in the southern part of Judah. (Jos 15:21) Jagur is possibly to be identified with Khirbet el Gharra (Tel 'Ira), about 14 km (8.5 mi) E of Beer-sheba.

JAH. A poetic shortened form of Jehovah, the name of the Most High God. (Ex 15:1, 2) This abbreviated form is represented by the first half of the Hebrew Tetragrammaton יהוה (*YHWH*), that is, the letters *yohdh* (י) and *he'* (ה), the tenth and fifth letters of the Hebrew alphabet respectively.

Jah occurs 50 times in the Hebrew Scriptures, 26 times alone, and 24 times in the expression "Hallelujah," which is, literally, a command to a number of people to "praise Jah." However, the presence of "Jah" in the original is completely ignored by certain popular versions. (*Dy, Mo, RS*) The *King James Version* and *An American Translation* have it only once, as "Jah" and "Yah" respectively. (Ps 68:4) In the *English Revised Version* it appears twice in the body of the text (Ps 68:4; 89:8), and in the *American Standard Version* the full form, Jehovah, is substituted throughout, but these latter two translations in practically every occurrence of the contracted form call it to our attention in footnotes. The *New World Translation* preserves for the reader all 50 occurrences of Jah, or Yah; and Rotherham's *Emphasised Bible,* 49 of them.

In the Christian Greek Scriptures "Jah" appears four times in the expression Hallelujah. (Re 19:1, 3, 4, 6) Most Bibles simply carry this Greek expression over into English untranslated, but G. W. Wade renders it, "Praise ye Jehovah," and the *New World Translation* reads, "Praise Jah, you people!"

In point of time "Jah" could not have been a primitive form of the divine name used earlier than the Tetragrammaton itself. The latter full form, Jehovah, occurs 165 times in the Masoretic text in the book of Genesis, but it was not until the account of events after the Exodus from Egypt that the shorter form first appeared.—Ex 15:2.

The single syllable Jah is usually linked with the more moving emotions of praise and song, prayer and entreaty, and is generally found where the subject theme dwells upon a rejoicing over victory and deliverance, or where there is an acknowledgment of God's mighty hand and power. Examples of this special usage are abundant. The phrase, "Praise Jah, you people!" (Hallelujah) appears as a doxology, that is, an expression of praise to God, in the Psalms, the first being at Psalm 104:35. In other psalms it may be at the beginning only (Ps 111, 112), occasionally within a psalm (135:3), sometimes at the end only (Ps 104, 105, 115-117), but often at both the beginning and the end (Ps 106, 113, 135, 146-150). In the book of Revelation heavenly personages repeatedly punctuate their praise of Jehovah with this expression. —Re 19:1-6.

The remaining instances where "Jah" appears also reflect exaltation in songs and petitions to Jehovah. There is the song of deliverance by Moses. (Ex 15:2) In those recorded by Isaiah a double emphasis is gained by combining both names, "Jah Jehovah." (Isa 12:2; 26:4) Hezekiah, in his poetic exultation after being miraculously healed when close to death, expressed heightened feelings by repetition of Jah. (Isa 38:9, 11) The contrast is drawn between the dead, who cannot praise Jah, and those determined to live a life of praise to him. (Ps 115:17, 18; 118:17-19) Still other psalms display a prayerful appreciation for deliverance, protection, and correction.—Ps 94:12; 118:5, 14.

JAHATH (Ja'hath).

1. A descendant of Judah. Jahath's two sons founded the families of the Zorathites.—1Ch 4:1, 2.

2. A Levite descended from Gershon (Gershom) through Libni, and an ancestor of Asaph. —Ex 6:17; 1Ch 6:1, 20, 39-43.

3. Another Levite descended from Gershon, but through Gershon's other son, Shimei. Jahath was the head over his brothers, and his sons became a paternal house.—1Ch 23:6, 7, 10, 11.

4. A Levite during David's reign; a descendant of Kohath's son Izhar through Shelomoth.—1Ch 6:18; 24:22.

5. One of four Levites, a Merarite, assigned to oversee the temple repair work that King Josiah promoted.—2Ch 34:12.

JAHAZ (Ja'haz). A city E of the Jordan and evidently situated N of the Arnon. It was probably wrested from the Moabites by Amorite King Sihon. (Nu 21:23-26) At Jahaz the Israelites defeated the forces of Sihon, and the city itself became a Reubenite possession. (De 2:32, 33; Jos 13:15, 18, 23; Jg 11:20, 21) Subsequently Jahaz was designated as a Levite city for the Merarites. (Jos 21:34, 36) Later in Israel's history the city came under Moabite control. On the Moabite Stone, King Mesha boasted of having taken Jahaz from the king of Israel with 200 warriors. Also, the prophets Isaiah and Jeremiah mention the city in pronouncements against Moab.—Isa 15:1, 4; Jer 48:1, 34.

Although scholars have suggested several possible sites for ancient Jahaz, its precise location remains unknown.

JAHAZIEL (Ja·ha·zi'el) [May God Behold; God Has Beheld].

1. Third-listed son of Hebron, a Kohathite of the tribe of Levi.—1Ch 23:6, 12, 19; 24:23.

2. One of the mighty men who joined David at Ziklag.—1Ch 12:1, 4.

3. One of the priests with trumpets stationed before the ark of the covenant after David had it brought to Jerusalem.—1Ch 16:1, 6.

4. The Levite who was empowered by Jehovah's spirit to speak words of encouragement to King Jehoshaphat and the congregation when they were threatened by a superior force of the enemy. "Here is what Jehovah has said to you, 'Do not you be afraid or be terrified because of this large crowd,'" Jahaziel declared, "'for the battle is not yours, but God's. . . . You will not need to fight in this instance. Take your position, stand still and see the salvation of Jehovah in your behalf.'" (2Ch 20:14-17) Jahaziel was the son of Zechariah, a descendant of Asaph of the Gershom (Gershon [Ge 46:11]) family of Levites, hence not a priest.—1Ch 6:39-43.

5. The father of Shecaniah, who was one of those returning to Jerusalem with Ezra in 468 B.C.E.—Ezr 8:1, 5.

JAHDAI (Jah'dai). A father of six sons listed among the descendants of Judah's great-grandson Caleb. Jahdai's exact relationship to Caleb is not given.—1Ch 2:3, 42, 47.

JAHDIEL (Jah'di·el) [possibly, May God Feel Glad]. One of the household heads of the half tribe of Manasseh residing E of the Jordan; a valiant, mighty man. Jahdiel's descendants "began to act unfaithfully" toward Jehovah, leading to eventual exile by the Assyrians.—1Ch 5:23-26.

JAHDO (Jah'do) [possibly, May He Feel Glad]. A name in the genealogy of Gad's tribe; son of Buz and father of Jeshishai.—1Ch 5:11, 14.

JAHLEEL (Jah'le·el). Third-listed son of Zebulun and founder of the family of Jahleelites in his father's tribe.—Ge 46:14; Nu 26:26.

JAHLEELITES (Jah'le·el·ites) [Of (Belonging to) Jahleel]. Descendants of Jahleel of the tribe of Zebulun.—Nu 26:26.

JAHMAI (Jah'mai). Head of a forefather's house in the tribe of Issachar; son of Tola.—1Ch 7:1, 2.

JAHZEEL (Jah'ze·el) [God Divides]. The first-listed son of Naphtali and founder of the Jahzeelite family in that tribe. (Ge 46:24; Nu 26:48) His name is also spelled Jahziel.—1Ch 7:13.

JAHZEELITES (Jah'ze·el·ites) [Of (Belonging to) Jahzeel]. Descendants of Jahzeel of the tribe of Naphtali.—Nu 26:48.

JAHZEIAH (Jah·zei'ah) [May Jah Behold; Jah Has Beheld]. One who perhaps opposed Ezra's proposal that the sons of Israel send away their foreign wives and the children born to them; son of Tikvah. (Ezr 10:3, 10, 11, 15) However, it has been suggested that this opposition of Jahzeiah and Jonathan was not against Ezra's suggestion but against the procedure adopted for carrying it out. According to the Greek *Septuagint* and Latin *Vulgate,* Jahzeiah and the others assisted rather than opposed Ezra. Hence, an alternate rendering of Ezra 10:15 says that Jonathan and Jahzeiah "were the ones that acted representatively in this behalf."—*NW* ftn; see also *KJ; AS,* ftn; *Dy; Kx.*

JAHZERAH (Jah'ze·rah). A priest whose descendant lived in Jerusalem after the Babylonian exile. (1Ch 9:12) He is probably the same as Ahzai in Nehemiah 11:13.

JAHZIEL (Jah′zi·el) [God Divides]. An alternate spelling of Jahzeel (Ge 46:24), who was the first-listed son of Naphtali.—1Ch 7:13.

JAIL. See PRISON.

JAILER. One having in his custody persons accused of breaking the law; a prison keeper. Two Greek words are translated in the Scriptures as jailer: *ba·sa·ni·stes′,* meaning "tormentor," and *de·smo·phy′lax,* a compound of *de·smos′* (band, fetter) and *phy′lax* (guard).

Jailers often inflicted cruel tortures on prisoners, hence were called *ba·sa·ni·stes′.* For example, debtors were sometimes thrown into prison for failing to pay what they owed. There the jailer might scourge and torture them, and they would not be released until, as Jesus said, they "paid over the last coin of very little value." (Mt 5:25, 26) This also was the point of Jesus' illustration about the unmerciful slave. When the master learned what his ungrateful slave had done, he "delivered him to the jailers [*ba·sa·ni·stais′*], until he should pay back all that was owing."—Mt 18:34, 35; compare Re 14:11, where "torment" is translated from *ba·sa·ni·smou′.*

If the prisoners escaped, jailers were held liable for the penalty imposed on the escapee, according to Roman custom. Hence, when Peter was set free from prison by an angel, we read that Herod "examined the guards and commanded them to be led off to punishment."—Ac 12:19.

In Philippi, Paul and Silas were dragged before the civil magistrates, who commanded that they be beaten with rods, and "after they had inflicted many blows upon them, they threw them into prison, ordering the jailer [*de·smo·phy′la·ki*] to keep them securely. Because he got such an order, he threw them into the inner prison and made their feet fast in the stocks." (Ac 16:22-24) Then in the middle of the night a great earthquake opened all the prison doors. This caused the jailer to imagine the prisoners had escaped, and realizing what severe punishment would be meted out to him if this were so, he was about to kill himself when Paul informed him that they were all there. These events, together with Paul's instructions, caused this jailer to exercise faith, and he and his household became baptized believers.—Ac 16:25-36.

JAIR (Ja′ir).

1. A descendant of Judah through his grandson Hezron. Hezron married a woman from the tribe of Manasseh. (1Ch 2:21, 22) Jair is reckoned as a descendant of Manasseh rather than Judah, likely because of his exploits in the territory of Manasseh, where he captured a number of tent cities and named them after himself, which name they kept for many generations.—Nu 32:41; De 3:14; Jos 13:30; 1Ki 4:13; see HAVVOTH-JAIR.

2. The seventh judge of Israel. Since he was a Gileadite of high standing and each of his 30 sons is connected with one of the above-mentioned tent cities of Jair, he was likely a descendant of No. 1 above. Jair judged Israel for 22 years, after which he died and was buried in Kamon.—Jg 10:3-5.

3. Father of Mordecai; tribe of Benjamin.—Es 2:5.

4. Father of the Elhanan who slew Goliath's brother Lahmi. (1Ch 20:5) The corresponding passage at 2 Samuel 21:19 evidently contains a copyist's error.—See LAHMI.

JAIRITE (Ja′ir·ite) [Of (Belonging to) Jair]. The designation of Ira the "priest of David." (2Sa 20:26) Perhaps Ira was a descendant of the Manassite Jair. But if the Syriac *Peshitta* is correct, he may have been a priest from the Levite city of Jattir.—See IRA No. 1.

JAIRUS (Ja′i·rus). A presiding officer of the synagogue (probably in Capernaum) whose only daughter Jesus resurrected.—Mt 9:18; Mr 5:22; Lu 8:41, 42.

When, in late 31 or early 32 C.E., Jairus' 12-year-old daughter became so ill that she was expected to die, her father sought out Jesus, fell at his feet, and implored him to come and cure her before it was too late. While leading Jesus to his home, Jairus surely must have been greatly encouraged by witnessing Jesus heal a woman subject for 12 years to a flow of blood. But how disheartening to receive word from messengers that his own little daughter had already died! Nonetheless, Jesus urged Jairus not to fear, but to exercise faith. Passing amid the noisy mourners who scorned and ridiculed Jesus' remark that the child was only sleeping, Jairus, his wife, and three apostles accompanied Jesus inside, where Jesus restored the girl to life. As might be expected, Jairus and his wife were "beside themselves with great ecstasy."—Mr 5:21-43; Mt 9:18-26; Lu 8:41-56.

JAKEH (Ja′keh). Father of Agur, the writer of what is recorded in Proverbs 30.—Pr 30:1.

JAKIM (Ja′kim) [shortened form of Jekamiah, meaning "Jah Has Raised Up"].

1. A descendant of Benjamin through Shimei, included in a list of heads of fathers' houses residing in Jerusalem.—1Ch 8:1, 19-21, 28.

2. The priest whose paternal house was selected by lot for the 12th of the 24 divisions of priestly temple service during David's reign. —1Ch 24:3, 5, 12.

JALAM (Ja'lam). A son of Esau by his wife Oholibamah. Jalam was born in Canaan but was soon taken to Edom (Seir), where he eventually became a sheik.—Ge 36:5, 6, 8, 14, 18; 1Ch 1:35.

JALON (Ja'lon). A descendant of Judah; one of "the sons of Ezrah."—1Ch 4:17.

JAMBRES (Jam'bres). A resister of Moses, presumably one of the Egyptian magicians in the court of Pharaoh.—2Ti 3:8; Ex 7:11; see JANNES.

JAMES [English equivalent of Jacob, meaning, "One Seizing the Heel; Supplanter"].

1. Father of the apostle Judas (not Judas Iscariot).—Lu 6:16; Ac 1:13.

2. Son of Zebedee; brother of John and one of the 12 apostles of Jesus Christ. (Mt 10:2) His mother, it seems, was Salome, as may be noted by comparing two accounts of the same event. One mentions "the mother of the sons of Zebedee," the other calls her "Salome." (Mt 27:55, 56; Mr 15:40, 41; see SALOME No. 1.) A further comparison of John 19:25 perhaps points to Salome as the fleshly sister of Mary, Jesus' mother. If so, James was a first cousin of Jesus.

James and his brother were working with their father in the fishing business in 30 C.E. when Jesus called them, together with associate fishermen Peter and Andrew, to be his disciples and "fishers of men." In answering Jesus' call, James and John left a fishing business that was a partnership with Peter and Andrew and that was large enough to employ hired men.—Mt 4:18-22; Mr 1:19, 20; Lu 5:7-10.

The next year, 31 C.E., when Jesus designated 12 of his disciples to be apostles, James was one of the group selected.—Mr 3:13-19; Lu 6:12-16.

Often Peter, James, and John were mentioned as being together in close company with Christ. For example, these three were the only ones present with Christ in the mount of transfiguration (Mt 17:1, 2), were the only apostles invited into the house to witness the resurrection of Jairus' daughter (Lu 8:51), and were the ones closest to Jesus in Gethsemane while he was praying that last night (Mr 14:32-34). Peter, James, and John, together with Andrew, were the ones that asked Jesus when the foretold destruction of Jerusalem's temple would be and what would be the

sign of his presence and of the conclusion of the system of things. (Mr 13:3, 4) James is always mentioned along with his brother John, and in the majority of instances he is mentioned first. This may indicate he was the older of the two. —Mt 4:21; 10:2; 17:1; Mr 1:19, 29; 3:17; 5:37; 9:2; 10:35, 41; 13:3; 14:33; Lu 5:10; 6:14; 8:51; 9:28, 54; Ac 1:13.

To James and his brother, Jesus gave the surname Boanerges, a Semitic term meaning "Sons of Thunder." (Mr 3:17) This may have been because of the energetic, fiery, and enthusiastic nature of these men. On one occasion, for example, when certain Samaritans were inhospitable toward Jesus, James and John wanted to call down fire from heaven to annihilate them. Although reproved by Jesus for suggesting such revenge, this attitude was indicative of their righteous indignation and also of their faith. (Lu 9:51-55) They also entertained ambitions of having the most prominent positions in the Kingdom, at the right and left hands of Jesus, and they apparently got their mother (possibly Jesus' aunt) to request such favors of him. After explaining that such decisions were made by the Father, Jesus took the occasion to point out that "whoever wants to be first among you must be your slave." —Mt 20:20-28.

James evidently died in 44 C.E. Herod Agrippa I had him executed with the sword. He was the first of the 12 apostles to die as a martyr.—Ac 12:1-3.

3. Another apostle of Jesus Christ and son of Alphaeus. (Mt 10:2, 3; Mr 3:18; Lu 6:15; Ac 1:13) It is generally believed and quite probable that Alphaeus was the same person as Clopas, in which event James' mother was Mary, the same Mary that was "the mother of James the Less and of Joses." (Joh 19:25; Mr 15:40; Mt 27:56) He may have been called James the Less because of being either smaller in physical stature or younger in age than the other apostle James, the son of Zebedee.

4. Son of Joseph and Mary, and half brother of Jesus. (Mr 6:3; Ga 1:19) Although not an apostle, it was evidently this James who was an overseer of the Christian congregation at Jerusalem (Ac 12:17) and who wrote the Bible book bearing his name. (Jas 1:1) He may have been next to Jesus in age, being the first named of Mary's four natural-born sons: James, Joseph, Simon, and Judas. (Mt 13:55; see BROTHER.) Paul implies in his letter to the Corinthians, written about the year 55 C.E., that James was married.—1Co 9:5.

It appears that during Jesus' ministry James was well acquainted with his brother's activity (Lu 8:19; Joh 2:12), but though apparently not opposed, he was not one of the disciples and followers of Christ. (Mt 12:46-50; Joh 7:5) He was probably with his nonbelieving brothers when they urged Jesus to go boldly up to the Festival of Tabernacles, at a time when the rulers of the Jews were seeking to kill him. (Joh 7:1-10) James also may have been numbered among the relatives that said of Jesus: "He has gone out of his mind." —Mr 3:21.

However, after the death of Jesus and prior to Pentecost 33 C.E., James was assembled for prayer together with his mother, brothers, and the apostles in an upper chamber in Jerusalem. (Ac 1:13, 14) It was evidently to this James that the resurrected Jesus appeared personally, as reported at 1 Corinthians 15:7, so convincing this onetime nonbeliever that He was indeed the Messiah. This reminds us of Jesus' personal appearance to Paul.—Ac 9:3-5.

Thereafter James became a prominent member and, apparently, an "apostle" of the Jerusalem congregation. (See APOSTLE [Congregational Apostleships].) Thus, at Paul's first visit with the Jerusalem brothers (about 36 C.E.), he says he spent 15 days with Peter but "saw no one else of the apostles, only James the brother of the Lord." (Ga 1:18, 19) Peter, after his miraculous release from prison, instructed the brothers at John Mark's home, "Report these things to James and the brothers," thereby indicating James' prominence. (Ac 12:12, 17) About 49 C.E. the issue of circumcision came before "the apostles and the older men" at Jerusalem. Following personal testimony by Peter, Barnabas, and Paul, James spoke, offering a decision that was approved and adopted by the assembly. (Ac 15:6-29; compare Ac 16:4.) Referring to that occasion, Paul says that James, Cephas, and John "seemed to be pillars" among those at Jerusalem. (Ga 2:1-9) At the close of a later missionary tour, Paul, in Jerusalem, reported on his ministry to James and "all the older men," and these then gave him certain counsel to follow. —Ac 21:15-26; see also Ga 2:11-14.

That it was this 'brother of Jesus' who wrote the book of James, and not one of the apostles by the same name (either the son of Zebedee or the son of Alphaeus), seems to be indicated at the beginning of his letter. There the writer identifies himself as "a slave of God and of the Lord Jesus Christ," rather than as an apostle. In a similar fashion his brother Judas (Jude) also identified

himself as "a slave of Jesus Christ, but a brother of James." (Jas 1:1; Jude 1) Both brothers humbly avoided identifying themselves as fleshly brothers of the Lord Jesus Christ.

His being called "James the Just" is based on traditions that say he was so designated because of his way of life. There is no record in the Scriptures of James' death. The secular historian Josephus, however, says that during the interval between the death of Governor Festus, about 62 C.E., and the arrival of his successor Albinus, the high priest, Ananus (Ananias), "convened the judges of the Sanhedrin and brought before them a man named James, the brother of Jesus who was called the Christ, and certain others. He accused them of having transgressed the law and delivered them up to be stoned."—*Jewish Antiquities*, XX, 200 (ix, 1).

JAMES, LETTER OF.

An inspired letter of the Christian Greek Scriptures. It is one of the so-called general letters because, like First and Second Peter, First John, and Jude (but unlike most of the apostle Paul's letters), it was not addressed to any specific congregation or person. This letter is addressed to "the twelve tribes that are scattered about."—Jas 1:1.

Writer. The writer calls himself simply "James, a slave of God and of the Lord Jesus Christ." (Jas 1:1) Jesus had two apostles named James (Mt 10:2, 3), but it is unlikely that either of these wrote the letter. One apostle, James the son of Zebedee, was martyred about 44 C.E. As the section on "Date and Place of Composition" shows, this would be very early for him to have been the writer. (Ac 12:1, 2) The other apostle James, the son of Alphaeus, is not prominent in the Scriptural record, and very little is known about him. The outspoken nature of the letter of James would seem to weigh against the writer's being James the son of Alphaeus, for he would likely have identified himself as one of the 12 apostles, in order to back up his strong words with apostolic authority.

Rather, evidence points to James the half brother of Jesus Christ, to whom the resurrected Christ evidently had made a special appearance, and who was prominent among the disciples. (Mt 13:55; Ac 21:15-25; 1Co 15:7; Ga 2:9) The writer of the letter of James identifies himself as "a slave of God and of the Lord Jesus Christ," in much the same way as did Jude, who introduced the letter of Jude by calling himself "a slave of Jesus Christ, but a brother of James." (Jas 1:1; Jude 1) Furthermore, the salutation of James' letter includes the term "Greetings!" in the same way as did the letter concerning circumcision that was sent to the congregations. In this latter instance it was apparently Jesus' half brother James who spoke prominently in the assembly of "the apostles and the older men" at Jerusalem.—Ac 15:13, 22, 23.

Canonicity. The letter of James is contained in the Vatican Manuscript No. 1209, as well as the Sinaitic and the Alexandrine Manuscripts of the fourth and fifth centuries C.E. The Syriac *Peshitta* includes it, and it is found in at least ten ancient catalogs before the Council of Carthage in 397 C.E. Early religious writers quoted from it, Origen, Cyril of Jerusalem, Jerome, and others recognizing the letter as authentic Scripture.

Date and Place of Composition. The letter gives no indication that Jerusalem's fall to the Romans (in 70 C.E.) had yet taken place. According to the Jewish historian Josephus, a high priest named Ananus, a Sadducee, was responsible for bringing James and others before the Sanhedrin and having them stoned to death. This event, Josephus writes, occurred after the death of the Roman procurator Festus, but before his successor Albinus arrived. (*Jewish Antiquities*, XX, 197-203 [ix, 1]) If so, and if the sources placing the death of Festus at about 62 C.E. are correct, then James must have written his letter sometime prior to that date.

Jerusalem was the probable place of composition, for that is where James resided.—Ga 1:18, 19.

To Whom Written. James wrote the letter to "the twelve tribes that are scattered about," literally, "the (ones) in the dispersion." (Jas 1:1, ftn) He here addresses his spiritual "brothers," those who hold to "the faith of our Lord Jesus Christ," primarily those living beyond Palestine. (1:2; 2:1, 7; 5:7) James bases much of his argument on the Hebrew Scriptures, but this does not prove that his letter was only for Jewish Christians, even as one's acquaintance with the Hebrew Scriptures in modern times does not prove that one is of Jewish descent. His reference to Abraham as "our father" (2:21) is in harmony with Paul's words at Galatians 3:28, 29, where he shows that one's being of the true seed of Abraham is not determined by whether one is a Jew or a Greek. Therefore, "the twelve tribes" addressed must be the spiritual "Israel of God."—Ga 6:15, 16.

Purpose. James' purpose in writing seems to have been twofold: (1) to exhort his fellow believers to display faith and endurance amid their trials, and (2) to warn them against sins resulting in divine disapproval.

Some had fallen into the snare of looking to those more prominent and rich and showing

---

HIGHLIGHTS OF JAMES

A letter emphasizing that faith has to be demonstrated by works

Written before 62 C.E., more than eight years prior to Jerusalem's destruction by the Romans

---

Christians enduring faithfully under trial have reason to be happy (1:1-18)

God will generously give us the wisdom needed to endure if we keep asking for it in faith

Never does God try us with evil things; but a person may be enticed into a wrong course by his own wrong desire

Everything that Jehovah provides is good

Worship that is acceptable to God requires right works to demonstrate one's faith (1:19–2:26)

Put away all badness and accept God's word with mildness; be a doer of the word and not merely a hearer

Learn to control the tongue, look after orphans and widows, and keep without spot from the world

Favoring the rich while disregarding the poor is a violation of "the kingly law" of love

A living faith is revealed by works, as is evident in the examples of Abraham and Rahab

Teachers have a great responsibility before Jehovah (3:1-18)

They, and all Christians, must learn to control the tongue

They can do this if they manifest wisdom from above

Worldly tendencies will affect our relationship with God (4:1–5:12)

Those guilty of fighting to attain their selfish aims or those condemning their brothers need to repent

Friendship with the world is enmity with God

Materialistic planning that ignores Jehovah's will is arrogant

Divine judgment is in store for rich, defrauding oppressors

A spirit of impatience and sighing under adversity must be guarded against while we wait for Jesus Christ to judge

To recover from spiritual sickness resulting from sin, the suffering one should call on elders for help (5:13-20)

An open confession of sin as well as prayers on behalf of the sinner by the elders will promote spiritual healing

To recover an erring brother is to save him from spiritual death

favoritism. (Jas 2:1-9) They failed to discern what they really were in God's eyes and were hearers of the word but not doers. (1:22-27) They had begun to use their tongues wrongly, and their cravings for sensual pleasure were causing fights among them. (3:2-12; 4:1-3) Their desire for material things had brought some into the position of being friends of the world and therefore, not chaste virgins, but spiritual "adulteresses," at enmity with God.—4:4-6.

James corrected them on the matter of being doers as well as hearers by showing from Scriptural examples that a man having real faith would manifest it by works in harmony with his faith. For example, one having true faith would not say to a brother naked and lacking food, "Go in peace, keep warm and well fed," and not give him the necessities. (Jas 2:14-26) Here James was not contradicting Paul by saying that one could earn salvation by works. Rather, he accepts faith as the basis for salvation but points out that there cannot be genuine faith that does not produce good works. This is in harmony with Paul's description of the fruitage of the spirit, at Galatians 5:22-24, and his counsel to put on the new personality, at Ephesians 4:22-24 and Colossians 3:5-10, as well as his admonition to do good and share with others, at Hebrews 13:16.

Style. James' letter has a strong prophetic tone and contains many figures of speech and similes, giving it a certain resemblance to Jesus Christ's discourses, such as the Sermon on the Mount. Like Jesus, James drew on physical things —the sea, vegetation, animals, boats, a farmer, the earth—to give colorful backing to his arguments on faith, control of the tongue, patience, and so forth. (Jas 1:6, 9-11; 3:3-12; 5:7) This, together with the use of pointed questions and more than 50 imperatives in this relatively short letter, made James' letter dynamic.

Relationship to Earlier Inspired Scripture. James quoted or referred to the Hebrew Scriptures with regard to man's creation (Jas 3:9; Ge 1:26); Abraham and Rahab (Jas 2:21-26; Ge 15:6; 22:9-12; Jos 2; Isa 41:8); Job (Jas 5:11; Job 1:13-22; 2:7-10; 42:10-17); the Law (Jas 2:8, 11; Ex 20:13, 14; Le 19:18; De 5:17, 18), and Elijah (Jas 5:17, 18; 1Ki 17:1; 18:1). There are many pointed examples of direct harmony with statements of Jesus Christ. To name a few: concerning persecution (Jas 1:2; Mt 5:10-12); asking for and receiving things from God (Jas 1:5, 17; Lu 11:9-13); being both hearers and doers (Jas 1:22; Mt 7:21-27); separateness from the world (Jas 4:4; Joh 17:14); not judging others (Jas 4:12; Lu 6:37); reliability of one's word (Jas 5:12; Mt 5:33-37).

James 4:5 has presented a problem because there is uncertainty about the verse(s) James quoted (or perhaps only referred to). This text reads: "Or does it seem to you that the scripture says to no purpose: 'It is with a tendency to envy that the spirit which has taken up residence within us keeps longing'?" It has been suggested that these words were drawn by James under divine inspiration from the general thought of such texts as Genesis 6:5; 8:21; Proverbs 21:10; and Galatians 5:17.

JAMIN   (Ja′min) [Right Hand].

1. The second-listed son of Simeon. (Ge 46:10; Ex 6:15; 1Ch 4:24) He founded the family of the Jaminites.—Nu 26:12.

2. A descendant of Judah through Hezron's grandson Ram.—1Ch 2:9, 25, 27.

3. A postexilic Levite who helped explain the Law to the people assembled in Jerusalem.—Ne 8:7.

JAMINITES   (Ja′min·ites) [Of (Belonging to) Jamin]. Descendants of Jamin of Simeon's tribe. —Nu 26:12.

JAMLECH   (Jam′lech) [May [God] Cause to Reign]. One of the chieftains of the tribe of Simeon who, in the days of King Hezekiah, extended their territory into the Valley of Gedor.—1Ch 4:24, 34, 38-41.

JANAI   (Ja′nai) [possibly, May [God] Answer; [God] Has Answered]. A Gadite residing in the territory of Bashan.—1Ch 5:11, 12.

JANIM   (Ja′nim). A city in the mountainous region of Judah. (Jos 15:20, 48, 53) Janim is tentatively identified with Beni Na′im, about 5 km (3 mi) ESE of Hebron.

JANNAI   (Jan′na·i). An ancestor of Jesus' mother Mary; the fifth generation prior to her. —Lu 3:24.

JANNES   (Jan′nes). A resister of Moses with whom Paul compares apostates who resist the truth. (2Ti 3:8, 9) Jannes and Jambres, whose 'madness became plain to all,' are not identified in the Hebrew Scriptures, but it is generally agreed that they were two of the leading men in Pharaoh's court, perhaps the magic-practicing priests who resisted Moses and Aaron on their numerous appearances there. (Ex 7:11, 12, 22; 8:17-19; 9:11)

The amount of tradition that agrees with this greatly outweighs what little there is to the contrary. Non-Christian sources, such as Numenius, Pliny the Elder, Lucius Apuleius, a Qumran writing, the Targum of Jonathan, and several apocryphal writings all mention one or both of these men.

JANOAH (Ja·no'ah) [from a root that means "rest; settle down"].

1. A boundary location of Ephraim usually identified with Khirbet Yanun, about 20 km (12 mi) SE of Samaria.—Jos 16:5-7.

2. A city in the ten-tribe kingdom taken by Tiglath-pileser III during Pekah's reign (c. 778-759 B.C.E.). Its inhabitants were deported to Assyria. (2Ki 15:29) The exact location of Janoah is uncertain. Although some identify it with Yanouh, about 10 km (6 mi) E of Tyre, this location is considered to be too far W of the other cities listed at 2 Kings 15:29. Most scholars favor Tell en-Na'meh, about 10 km (6 mi) NE of Kedesh in Galilee.

JAPHETH (Ja'pheth) [May He Grant Ample Space]. A son of Noah; brother of Shem and of Ham. Although usually listed last, Japheth appears to have been the eldest of the three sons, as the Hebrew text of Genesis 10:21 refers to "Japheth the oldest" ("elder," *KJ; Da; Yg; Le; AS,* ftn). Some translators, however, understand the Hebrew text here to refer instead to Shem as "the elder brother of Japheth." (*RS;* also *AT, JB, NE*) Considering Japheth to be Noah's eldest son would place the time of his birth at 2470 B.C.E. —Ge 5:32.

Japheth and his wife were among the eight occupants of the ark, thereby surviving the Flood. (Ge 7:13; 1Pe 3:20) Remaining childless until after the Flood, they thereafter produced seven sons: Gomer, Magog, Madai, Javan, Tubal, Meshech, and Tiras. (Ge 10:1, 2; 1Ch 1:5) These sons and also some grandsons are the ones from whom "the population of the isles of the nations ["coastland peoples," *RS*] was spread about in their lands, each according to its tongue, according to their families, by their nations." (Ge 10:3-5; 1Ch 1:6, 7) Historically, Japheth was the progenitor of the Aryan or Indo-European (Indo-Germanic) branch of the human family. The names of his sons and grandsons are found in ancient historical texts as relating to peoples and tribes residing mainly to the N and W of the Fertile Crescent. They appear to have spread from the Caucasus eastward into Central Asia and westward

through Asia Minor to the islands and coastlands of Europe and perhaps all the way to Spain. Arabian traditions claim that one of Japheth's sons was also the progenitor of the Chinese peoples.—See CHART and MAP, Vol. 1, p. 329.

As a result of Japheth's respectful action taken in company with his brother Shem on the occasion of their father's drunkenness, Japheth was the object of his father's blessing. (Ge 9:20-27) In that blessing, Noah requested for Japheth that God "grant ample space [Heb., *yapht*]" to him. This Hebrew expression is evidently derived from the same root word as the name Japheth (Heb., *Ye'pheth* or *Ya'pheth*) and appears to indicate that the meaning of Japheth's name would be fulfilled in a literal sense and that his descendants would spread out over a wide area. His 'residing in the tents of Shem' is thought by some to indicate a peaceful relationship between the Japhethites and the Semites. However, since history does not particularly present such a peaceful association, it may, rather, be connected prophetically with God's later promise to Shem's descendants Abraham, Isaac, and Jacob, that in their "seed" all the families of the earth (including those descended from Japheth) would be blessed. (Ge 22:15-18; 26:3, 4; 28:10, 13, 14; compare Ac 10:34-36; Ga 3:28, 29.) Canaan's 'becoming a slave' to the Japhethites finds fulfillment in the domination of the land of Canaan during the rule of the Medo-Persian Empire (a Japhetic power) and in the later conquests by the Greeks and the Romans, including the conquests of the Canaanite strongholds of Tyre and Sidon.

JAPHIA (Ja·phi'a).

[1, 2: May [God] Beam Forth; [God] Has Beamed Forth]

1. The king of Lachish who joined forces with four other Amorite kings to punish Gibeon for making peace with Israel. (Jos 10:3-5) Gibeon's call for help brought Joshua's forces on a rescue mission from Gilgal. During the ensuing battle, the Israelites trapped Japhia and his allied kings in a cave at Makkedah. Later he and the others were executed and their dead bodies hung on stakes until sunset, after which they were thrown into the cave where they had sought refuge.—Jos 10:6-27.

2. A son of David born at Jerusalem.—2Sa 5:14, 15; 1Ch 3:7; 14:6.

3. A boundary site of Zebulun. (Jos 19:10, 12) It is identified with modern Yafa (Yafia), less than 3 km (2 mi) SW of Nazareth.

JAPHLET (Japh'let) [May He Provide Escape; He Has Provided Escape]. A descendant of Asher through Beriah and Heber. Three "sons of Japhlet" are included in the genealogy.—1Ch 7:30-33.

JAPHLETITES (Japh'le·tites) [Of (Belonging to) Japhlet]. An ancient people occupying territory on Ephraim's boundary when the Israelites moved into the Promised Land. (Jos 16:3) There is no historical evidence linking the Japhletites with the descendant of Asher who was named Japhlet. (1Ch 7:30, 32) Secular history provides no additional information about them.

JAR. See VESSELS.

JARAH (Ja'rah). A descendant of Saul through Jonathan and, according to this genealogy, himself a father of three sons. (1Ch 9:39-42) He is called Jehoaddah at 1 Chronicles 8:36.

JARED (Ja'red). Father of Enoch and a pre-Flood ancestor of Jesus Christ; the fifth generation after Adam. (1Ch 1:2; Lu 3:37) Jared, the son of Mahalalel, lived 962 years (3566-2604 B.C.E.), second only to his grandson Methuselah in longevity. He had a number of sons and daughters, becoming father to Enoch at the age of 162.—Ge 5:15-20.

JARHA (Jar'ha). An Egyptian slave of Judah's descendant Sheshan. Since Sheshan had no sons, he gave his daughter in marriage to Jarha, enabling Jarha to father Attai and thus preserve Sheshan's family line through him.—1Ch 2:34, 35.

JARIB (Ja'rib) [May [God] Contend; [God] Has Conducted [Our] Legal Case].

1. A son of Simeon (1Ch 4:24), elsewhere apparently called Jachin.—Ge 46:10; see JACHIN No. 1.

2. One of the nine headmen whom Ezra sent to encourage Levites and Nethinim to come to the river Ahava and join the others on the journey to Jerusalem.—Ezr 8:15-20.

3. One of the listed relatives of the priests who "promised by shaking hands" that they would dismiss their foreign wives in response to Ezra's bidding.—Ezr 10:18, 19.

JARMUTH (Jar'muth) [from a root meaning "be high (exalted)"].

1. One of five Amorite cities involved in the attempted punitive expedition against the Gibeonites. Its king, Piram, and his allies were defeated by Joshua. Thereafter this city of the Shephelah was assigned to Judah. (Jos 10:3-5, 23-25;

12:7, 11; 15:20, 33, 35) After the Babylonian exile Judeans again resided at Jarmuth. (Ne 11:25, 29) Khirbet Yarmuk (Tel Yarmut), some 26 km (16 mi) WSW of Jerusalem, seems to be the ancient site. Situated on a hilltop, it overlooks the coastal plains as far as Gaza by the Mediterranean Sea.

2. A city in Issachar assigned to the Gershonites. (Jos 21:27-29) It is believed to be the same as Ramoth (1Ch 6:73) and Remeth.—Jos 19:21; see RAMOTH No. 1.

JAROAH (Ja·ro'ah). A descendant of Gad who resided in the territory of Bashan.—1Ch 5:11, 14.

JASHAR, BOOK OF. See BOOK.

JASHEN (Ja'shen) [possibly, Sleeping; Falling Asleep]. The expression "the sons of Jashen" is found in the list of David's mighty men. (2Sa 23:32) The parallel list at 1 Chronicles 11:34 calls him Hashem the Gizonite.

JASHOBEAM (Ja·sho'be·am) [possibly, The People Have Returned].

1. A Korahite warrior who joined David's forces at Ziklag. (1Ch 12:1, 6) Possibly the same as No. 2.

2. The head one of David's three most outstanding mighty men. Jashobeam once used his spear to fight off several hundred of the enemy and was also one of the three to force their way into the Philistine camp to get water for David from the cistern of Bethlehem. (1Ch 11:11, 15-19) In the course of events, Jashobeam was appointed head of the first monthly division of 24,000. (1Ch 27:1, 2) He was a son of Zabdiel; a Hachmonite. His name is spelled Josheb-basshebeth at 2 Samuel 23:8.—See JOSHEB-BASSHEBETH.

JASHUB (Ja'shub) [probably, He Has Returned].

1. The third-listed son of Issachar and founder of the Jashubite division of his tribe. (1Ch 7:1; Nu 26:23, 24) He is called Iob at Genesis 46:13.

2. One of "the sons of Bani" who, after returning from the Babylonian exile, took but then dismissed foreign wives.—Ezr 10:29, 44.

JASHUBI-LEHEM (Jash'u·bi-le'hem). Name in the genealogies of Judah, possibly a descendant of Shelah. However, some translators think this means "returned to Lehem," that is, "to Bethlehem."—1Ch 4:21, 22; *Dy, AT, JB, Mo.*

JASHUBITES (Jash'u·bites) [Of (Belonging to) Jashub]. Descendants of Issachar's son Jashub (Iob), and one of the four major family divisions of the tribe.—Nu 26:23-25; Ge 46:13.

JASON (Ja'son) [possibly from a root meaning "heal"]. A prominent Christian in Thessalonica who had 'received Paul and Silas hospitably' on their first journey into Macedonia. A mob of jealous Jews set about to take Paul and Silas from Jason's house, but, not finding them there, they took Jason instead and made him the principal defendant in charges of sedition against Caesar. Jason and the others with him were released after giving "sufficient security," perhaps in the form of bail.—Ac 17:5-10; 1Th 2:18.

In Paul's letter to the Romans, written from Corinth on his next trip through Macedonia and Greece, Jason is one whose greetings are included. (Ro 16:21) If he is the same person as the Jason in Thessalonica, he apparently had come to Corinth, possibly with Paul. He is called a 'relative' of Paul, which can mean that he was a fellow countryman, though the primary meaning of the Greek word is "blood relative of the same generation." If a close fleshly relative of Paul, he was naturally the one with whom Paul would stay in Thessalonica.

JASPER. Modern jasper is an opaque variety of quartz containing an admixture of iron oxide. Its colors, often arranged in layers, are white, red, yellow, brown, or black. Jasper is harder than glass and is found in metamorphic rocks in mass or as distinct crystals. The best grades are used for gemstones and can be highly polished. Some scholars, however, believe that, since the jasper (Gr., *i'a·spis*) at Revelation 21:11 is called "a most precious stone . . . shining crystal-clear," the ancient stone may have been of greater rarity and value than the comparatively inexpensive modern jasper, and brilliantly translucent rather than opaque. Some scholars have suggested that the Greek term in reality refers to the diamond.

A stone of jasper (Heb., *ya·halom'*) representing one of Israel's 12 tribes was placed in the last position in the second row of stones on Aaron's "breastpiece of judgment." (Ex 28:2, 15, 18, 21; 39:11) The jeweled "covering" worn by the king of Tyre was adorned with jasper. (Eze 28:12, 13) In the vision of Jehovah's heavenly throne of splendor, John observed that "the one seated is, in appearance, like a jasper stone and a precious red-colored stone." (Re 4:1-3, 10, 11) "The holy city, New Jerusalem," is described as having a radiance like "a jasper stone shining crystal-clear." The structure of the holy city's wall was jasper, as was the first foundation stone.—Re 21:2, 10, 11, 18, 19.

JATHNIEL (Jath'ni·el). One of the Levite gatekeepers for the house of Jehovah; the fourth son of Meshelemiah, a Korahite.—1Ch 26:1, 2.

JATTIR (Jat'tir) [from a root meaning "more than enough; overflow"]. A priestly city in the mountainous region of Judah. (Jos 15:20, 48; 21:9, 10, 14; 1Ch 6:54, 57) It was to Jattir that David sent a portion of the spoils of victory taken from Amalekite raiders. Perhaps this was in appreciation for hospitality and friendship accorded to him, a fugitive from King Saul.—1Sa 30:17-20, 26, 27, 31.

Jattir is usually identified with Khirbet 'Attir (Horvat Yattir), about 21 km (13 mi) SSW of Hebron.

JAVAN (Ja'van). Fourth-listed son of Japheth and the father of Elishah, Tarshish, Kittim, and Dodanim (or Rodanim). As post-Flood descendants of Noah, they are included among those populating "the isles of the nations," which phrase can also refer to the coastlands and not simply to islands surrounded by water. (Ge 10:2, 4, 5; 1Ch 1:5, 7) Historical evidence indicates that the descendants of Javan and his four sons settled in the islands and coastlands of the Mediterranean Sea from Cyprus (Kittim) to the western Mediterranean.—See DODANIM; ELISHAH; KITTIM; TARSHISH No. 1.

Javan (Heb., *Ya·wan'*) is identified as the progenitor of the ancient Ionians, called by some "the parent tribe of the Greeks." (*Commentary on the Old Testament*, by C. F. Keil and F. Delitzsch, 1973, Vol. I, The First Book of Moses, p. 163) The name *I·a'o·nes* is used by the poet Homer (of perhaps the eighth century B.C.E.) as referring to the early Greeks, and beginning with Sargon II (eighth century B.C.E.), the name *Jawanu* begins to appear in Assyrian inscriptions.

In course of time the name Ionia came to be restricted to Attica (the region around Athens), the western coast of Asia Minor (corresponding to the coasts of the later provinces of Lydia and Caria), and the neighboring islands of the Aegean Sea. The sea that lies between southern Greece and southern Italy still retains the name Ionian, and this name is acknowledged to be of very ancient origin, supporting the view that this form of the name of Javan once applied to the mainland of Greece as well as to the later smaller area designated "Ionia."

Following the Genesis account, the descendants of Javan first begin to be mentioned about the latter part of the ninth century B.C.E. by the prophet Joel. The prophet there condemns the Tyrians, Sidonians, and Philistines for selling the sons of Judah and Jerusalem in their slave trade with "the sons of the Greeks" (literally, "the Ionians"). (Joe 3:4-6) Isaiah, in the eighth century B.C.E., foretells that some of the Jews surviving God's expression of wrath would travel to many lands, including "Javan," there proclaiming Jehovah's glory.—Isa 66:19.

Slaves and copper articles were listed in the late seventh or early sixth century B.C.E. as items being supplied by "Javan, Tubal and Meshech [these latter places evidently being located in eastern Asia Minor or to the N thereof]" to the wealthy commercial center of Tyre. (Eze 27:13) Verse 19 of the same prophecy again mentions Javan, but the fact that the other places mentioned in the context are in Syria, Palestine, and Arabia has led some to view the appearance of the name there to be the result of a scribal error. Rather than reading "and Javan from Uzal," the Greek *Septuagint* renders Javan as "wine," thus reading, "and with wine. From Asel [Uzal]." (*LXX*, Thomson) The *Revised Standard Version* reads "and wine from Uzal." Others, however, suggest that Javan may here refer to a Greek colony located in Arabia or that it may perhaps be the name of an Arabian tribe or town.

In Daniel's prophecy "Javan" is usually rendered by translators as "Greece," since the historical fulfillment of Daniel's writings makes this meaning evident. (Da 8:21; 10:20; 11:2) So, likewise, Zechariah's prophecy (520-518 B.C.E.), foretelling the successful warfare of the 'sons of Zion' against Javan (Greece).—Zec 9:13.

JAVELIN.   See ARMS, ARMOR.

JAZER   (Ja′zer) [May [God] Help]. An Amorite city with dependent towns, located E of the Jordan. In the time of Moses, the Israelites took Jazer and the surrounding region. (Nu 21:25, 32) Originally granted to Gad and fortified by that tribe, Jazer was subsequently assigned to the Levites. (Nu 32:1, 3-5, 34, 35; Jos 13:24, 25; 21:34, 38, 39; 1Ch 6:77, 81) It was one of the places mentioned in connection with the route followed by Joab and the chiefs of the military forces when they took the census that David had ordered without having divine authorization. (2Sa 24:4, 5) Toward the close of David's reign certain mighty men of the Hebronites residing at Jazer were assigned administrative duties in Israel's territory E of the Jordan.—1Ch 26:31, 32.

In the eighth century B.C.E., Jazer was in Moabite hands. It seems that the region was then, if not already earlier, famous for its vine culture. Jazer and other Moabite cities were foretold to suffer future calamity.—Isa 16:8-10; Jer 48: 32, 33.

Various possible identifications have been suggested for ancient Jazer, but its precise location remains unknown.

JAZIZ   (Ja′ziz). The chief caretaker of King David's flocks; a Hagrite.—1Ch 27:31.

JEALOUS, JEALOUSY.   According to Biblical usage, "jealousy" may be a positive or a negative quality or emotion. (Pr 14:30; Zec 1:14) The Hebrew noun *qin·ʼah′* variously means "insistence on exclusive devotion; toleration of no rivalry; zeal; ardor; jealousy [righteous or sinful]; envying." The Greek *ze′los* has a similar meaning. —2Co 11:2; 12:20.

Jehovah's Jealousy.   Jehovah describes himself as "a God exacting exclusive devotion." (Ex 20:5, ftn; De 4:24; 5:9; 6:15) He also says: "Jehovah, whose name is Jealous, he is a jealous God." (Ex 34:14) Over what and with what kind of jealousy? Not with the envious, selfish jealousy of humans. It is a jealousy, a zeal or ardor for his holy name, concerning which he himself says: "I will show exclusive devotion for my holy name." —Eze 39:25.

For his name.   When one considers what God's name stands for, the reason for his "insistence on exclusive devotion" becomes clear. (Eze 5:13) His name represents all that is right and righteous. He is holy, clean, upright, loyal in the superlative degree. (Isa 6:3; Re 4:8; 16:5) His sovereignty is necessary to the existence of the universe, and allegiance to his sovereignty and laws is essential to the order and peace of all creation. (Pr 29:2; 1Co 14:33) His jealousy is therefore a pure, clean jealousy and is altogether for the benefit of his creatures, as their devotion brings him—the Creator, Provider, and Giver of all good things—no profit. (Job 41:11; Ps 145:16; Ro 11:35; Jas 1:17; Re 4:11) But in his devotion to righteousness his heart is made glad with loving appreciation when his servants stand firm for righteousness and give exclusive devotion to him. —Pr 23:15, 16; 27:11.

Those serving God can rely on him to establish righteousness, being confident in his zeal for his name. He illustrated his zeal in his dealings with ancient Israel, and he tells us of the destruction of earthly governments and the establishment of the government of the Prince of Peace with justice and righteousness, saying: "The very zeal of Jehovah of armies will do this."—Isa 9:6, 7; Zep 3:8, 9.

For righteousness. In his love of righteousness and his insistence on exclusive devotion, Jehovah is impartial. Moses warned God's covenant people Israel that if anyone forsook the covenant, "Jehovah's anger and his ardor [would] smoke against that man, . . . and Jehovah [would] indeed wipe out his name from under the heavens." (De 29:19-21) God told the apostate, idol-worshiping, immoral city of Jerusalem that he would judge her and give her "the blood of rage and jealousy." (Eze 16:38; 23:25) This occurred when the Babylonians destroyed the city and the temple upon which Jehovah's name had been placed, but which name they had grossly defamed. Nevertheless, his jealousy did not overshadow or flood out his purposes and his mercy, for Jehovah spared a remnant to return and rebuild the temple.

For his people. Because of his love for his people and because they bear his holy name, Jehovah is jealous for them with a fiery zeal. Just as a husband jealously protects his wife as precious to him, so Jehovah says: "He that is touching you is touching my eyeball." (Zec 2:8) Accordingly, because of the malicious acts of the nations toward his people, God foretold: "I will be jealous for Zion with great jealousy, and with great rage I will be jealous for her," also, that he would be zealous for his land and would show compassion upon his people.—Zec 8:2; 1:14; Joe 2:18.

Inciting Jehovah to jealousy. In his insistence on exclusive devotion, Jehovah is not one to be mocked. (Ga 6:7) Any one of his servants who refuses to give him wholehearted devotion, failing to love him with his whole heart, mind, soul, and strength, is trying to serve two masters. Jesus explained that the result of this course would be disastrous, for such a man would love one master and despise the other. (Mt 6:24) Such a person is "inciting [Jehovah] to jealousy." (De 32:16; 1Ki 14:22) In a vision given to Ezekiel, Jehovah showed him a "symbol of jealousy," evidently idolatrous, in the gateway to the temple. (Eze 8:3, 5) For Judah's turning away from exclusive devotion to him, Jehovah's jealousy burned against them.

The apostle Paul says to Christians: "You cannot be partaking of 'the table of Jehovah' and the table of demons. Or 'are we inciting Jehovah to jealousy'? We are not stronger than he is, are we?" (1Co 10:21, 22; De 32:21) He points out that if a Christian practices sin willfully after having

received the accurate knowledge of the truth, he can look forward only to judgment and "a fiery jealousy that is going to consume those in opposition."—Heb 10:26, 27.

Jesus Christ. The Son of God, being more intimate with his Father than any other of his creatures, and better able to emulate him and reveal him to others, could say: "He that has seen me has seen the Father also." (Joh 14:9; Mt 11:27; Joh 1:18) Consequently his zeal and jealousy for righteousness and his Father's name exceeded that of all others. (Heb 1:9; Ps 45:7) He at all times rendered exclusive devotion to Jehovah. (Mt 4:10; Joh 8:29) When on earth, his heart burned with heated zeal, with jealousy because of the defamation of Jehovah's name that was being brought by money-loving merchants in the temple. (Joh 2:13-17) Just as he there fulfilled the prophecy at Psalm 69:9, "Sheer zeal for your house has eaten me up," so his followers can be sure of his zeal for completely establishing everlasting righteousness, justice, and respect for Jehovah's name and sovereignty in fulfillment of the prophecy at Psalm 45:3-6.

Worshipers of God With Exclusive Devotion. All who have been true worshipers of God have exercised zeal for his service and jealousy for his name. The prophet Elijah, who did powerful works in turning many in Israel back from false worship to the worship of Jehovah, said: "I have been absolutely jealous for Jehovah the God of armies." (1Ki 19:10, 14) Phinehas demonstrated devotion that pleased God and saved Israel from extermination by his zeal in killing a chieftain of Israel who had contaminated the camp by bringing in filthy phallic Baal worship. This was because, as an Israelite and a priest, Phinehas was "tolerating no rivalry at all" toward Jehovah.—Nu 25:11; compare 2Ki 10:16.

The Christian congregation must exercise the same jealous watch, that no unclean thing should spring up as a "poisonous root" to cause trouble and defile many. (Heb 12:15) If anyone corrupt should slip in and try to defile others, the congregation must 'exercise earnestness, clearing itself before Jehovah with indignation and zeal.' They must 'remove the wicked man from among them.' —1Co 5:4, 5, 13; 2Co 7:11, 12.

It is good, therefore, for Christians to exercise "a godly jealousy" in behalf of fellow Christians. That is, they should be burning with the desire to do all they can to assist one another to maintain exclusive devotion to God and obedience to Christ. The apostle Paul likened those who were his spiritual brothers to a virgin engaged to Christ as his prospective bride. He was jealously protecting them so that they could be preserved unblemished for Christ. (2Co 11:2; compare Re 19:7, 8.) His zeal for them is demonstrated in many expressions in his letters to the Corinthian congregation and to others. And the jealousy that Christ himself has for his "bride" (Re 21:9) is shown in his strong statements to the congregations as recorded in Revelation, chapters 1 through 3.

Inciting to jealousy in a proper way. Jehovah showed mercy to the nation of Israel after all except a remnant had rejected the Messiah. The remnant of believing Jews was the beginning of the Christian congregation; Jehovah's favor was now upon it rather than the rejected Jewish nation. Jehovah demonstrated this change of dealing by signs and portents and powerful works. (Heb 2:3, 4) He opened the way for Gentiles to come into his favor. But he did not 'close the door' on Israel altogether. As the Scriptures point out: "Did they [all Israelites] stumble so that they fell completely? Never may that happen! But by their false step there is salvation to people of the nations, to incite them to jealousy." (Ro 11:11) This was what Jehovah, centuries beforehand, had said he was going to do, which resulted in the saving of some. (De 32:21; Ro 10:19) The apostle Paul, who earnestly sought the good of fellow Israelites, followed this principle, saying: "Forasmuch as I am, in reality, an apostle to the nations, I glorify my ministry, if I may by any means incite those who are my own flesh to jealousy and save some from among them."—Ro 11:13, 14; 10:1.

Misdirected Zeal. One may be sincerely zealous, or jealous, for a certain cause and yet be wrong and displeasing to God. That was true of many of the Jews of the first century. They looked for righteousness to come to them through their own works under the Mosaic Law. But Paul showed that their zeal was misdirected because of lack of accurate knowledge. Therefore they did not receive the real righteousness that comes from God. They would have to see their error and turn to God through Christ to receive righteousness and freedom from the condemnation of the Law. (Ro 10:1-10) Saul of Tarsus was one of such, being extremely zealous for Judaism to the point of excess, "persecuting the congregation of God and devastating it." He was scrupulously keeping the Law as "one who proved himself blameless." (Ga 1:13, 14; Php 3:6) Yet his jealousy for Judaism was a misdirected one. He was sincere of heart, for which reason Jehovah exercised undeserved

kindness through Christ in turning him to the way of true worship.—1Ti 1:12, 13.

Jealousy and Envy. A person who shows improper jealousy suspects others without adequate cause or resents the diversion to another of what he unjustifiably claims as his own. An envious person discontentedly desires or covets the good fortune and attainments of others. The context often determines the sense in which the Hebrew words usually translated "jealous" or "jealousy," but sometimes "envy," are used in the Bible. The same is true of the Greek word for "jealousy," but the Greek language also has a separate word, *phtho'nos*, for "envy."

In the Corinthian congregation of the first century, ambitious men had come in, calling attention to themselves, boasting in men, and they were bringing about strife in the congregation. The congregation was split into factions jealously looking to, exalting, and following men. Paul pointed out that such jealousy was fleshly, not spiritual. (1Co 3:3; 2Co 12:20) He explained that godly love is not jealous in an improper way but, rather, is trusting and hopeful, always acting in the interests of others.—1Co 13:4, 5, 7.

Jealousy of the kind that Paul spoke against in the Corinthian congregation is not righteous. It is not in behalf of exclusive devotion to Jehovah. Rather, it is a form of idolatry, demonic in origin, and it breeds envy and strife. The Bible repeatedly warns against it, showing that it affects the heart itself. Jesus' half brother James wrote: "If you have bitter jealousy and contentiousness in your hearts, do not be bragging and lying against the truth. This is not the wisdom that comes down from above, but is the earthly, animal, demonic. For where jealousy and contentiousness are, there disorder and every vile thing are."—Jas 3:14-16; Ro 13:13; Ga 5:19-21.

Jealousy of the wrong kind has a detrimental effect on one's physical health, for "a calm heart is the life of the fleshly organism, but jealousy is rottenness to the bones." (Pr 14:30) Jealousy results from harboring suspicion or resentment within oneself. It can be more destructive than rage or anger because it may be more deep-rooted, more lasting and persistent, and less easily assuaged. Usually reason is thrown to the winds. (Pr 27:4) And the jealousy of a man who is righteously enraged toward another who commits adultery with his wife will not accept any sort of excuse or ransom!—Pr 6:32-35.

The wrong kind of jealousy can bring a person to a point where he sins against God, as did the ten half brothers of Joseph. (Ge 37:11; Ac 7:9) It can lead to loss of life for an individual and others involved, as it did in the case of Dathan and Abiram and members of their households. (Ps 106:16, 17) Worse yet, jealousy prompted unbelieving Jews to commit serious crimes toward the apostles and, in addition, blasphemy and attempted murder.—Ac 13:45, 50; 14:19.

Marital Jealousy. Jealousy of one toward his (or her) mate is good if it is a proper jealousy, a zeal for the mate's benefit and well-being. But improper jealousy, or mistrust without foundation, is wrong and lacking love, and it can result in ruin to the marriage.—1Co 13:4, 7.

Under the Mosaic Law, provision was made for cases of jealousy where the husband suspected his wife of secret adultery. If there were not the required two witnesses to prove the accusation so that the human judges could act to apply the death sentence, the procedure prescribed by the Law was that the couple should present themselves before Jehovah's representative, the priest. This action constituted an appeal to Jehovah, who was aware of all the facts, for his judgment. If adulterous, the woman received, as a direct punishment from Jehovah, the loss of her procreative powers. If the husband's jealousy was unfounded, then he had to acknowledge her innocence by having sex relations with her so that she could bear a child.—Nu 5:11-31.

God's Servants Are Warned Against Rivalry. Rivalry or competition, so common in the present system of things, is not fitting. The writer of the book of Ecclesiastes says: "I myself have seen all the hard work and all the proficiency in work, that it means the rivalry [Heb., *qin·ʹath*] of one toward another; this also is vanity and a striving after the wind."—Ec 4:4; compare Ga 5:26.

By being jealous of others' successes, possessions, or accomplishments, the servant of God may develop envy and covetousness, even going so far as being envious of those who are bad but who prosper. The Scriptures warn that this should not be; though the time may seem long that they prosper, they will receive quick judgment at God's time, as it is written: "Do not show yourself heated up because of the evildoers. Do not be envious of those doing unrighteousness. For like grass they will speedily wither." (Ps 37:1, 2) Envy of such ones can lead a person into copying their violent ways, detestable to Jehovah. —Pr 3:31, 32; 23:17; 24:1, 19; compare Ps 73:2, 3, 17-19, 21-23.

JEARIM (Je·ʹa·rim) [Forests]. A mountain that marked part of Judah's N boundary and on which the town of Chesalon was apparently located. —Jos 15:10; see CHESALON.

JEATHERAI (Je·athʹe·rai). A Levite; descendant of Gershon (Gershom).—1Ch 6:1, 20, 21.

JEBERECHIAH (Je·berʹe·chiʹah) [meaning "Jehovah Blesses"]. Father of the Zechariah who witnessed Isaiah's writing of the prophetic name Maher-shalal-hash-baz, that of the prophet's own son, on a tablet.—Isa 8:1, 2.

JEBUS (Jeʹbus) [possibly from a root meaning "tread down; stamp down"], **JEBUSITE** (Jebʹu·site). Jebus was an ancient city of the Jebusites on the site now known as Jerusalem.

In the time of Abraham before the year 1900 B.C.E., this place was called Salem (meaning "Peace"), which is included in the name Jerusalem and may be a contraction of it. (Heb 7:2) Mention was made of Urusalim (Jerusalem) in the Amarna Tablets found in Egypt. And in the books of Joshua, Judges, and First Samuel, where events prior to the conquest of the city by David are mentioned, the site is often called Jerusalem. (Jos 10:1, 3, 5, 23; 12:10; 15:8, 63; 18:28; Jg 1:7, 8, 21; 19:10; 1Sa 17:54) In only two passages is it referred to as Jebus. (Jg 19:10, 11; 1Ch 11:4, 5) In Joshua 18:28 *Yevu·siʹ* appears in the Hebrew, the ending *i* indicating people, the inhabitants of the city.

It therefore seems evident to most scholars that Jerusalem (or, possibly, Salem) was the city's original name, and that only when occupied by the Jebusites was it occasionally called Jebus. It is also generally agreed that "Jebus" was not a contraction of Jerusalem but, rather, a contraction of Jebusites, the name of the occupants of the site for a time. After David's capture of this stronghold of Zion and the establishment of his royal residence there, it was sometimes referred to as the "City of David."—2Sa 5:7.

The Jebusites, who occupied this city and the surrounding area, were descendants of Ham and Canaan. (Ge 10:15, 16, 20; 1Ch 1:13, 14) When mentioned along with their relatives (Hittites, Girgashites, Amorites, Canaanites, Perizzites, Hivites), the Jebusites are generally listed last, perhaps because of being the least numerous. (De 7:1; Jg 3:5) They were classified as a mountain-dwelling people (Nu 13:29), and their land was said to be, figuratively, "a land flowing with milk and honey."—Ex 3:8, 17.

Jehovah promised Abraham that he would give the land of the Jebusites to him and to his seed.

(Ge 15:18-21; Ne 9:8) In carrying out this promise, Jehovah brought his chosen people out of Egypt, and as they crossed the Jordan, God sent his angel ahead, commanding that they show themselves strong and that they oust all those who resisted them. (Ex 13:3-5; 23:23; 33:1, 2) They were to conclude no covenant and no marriage alliance with the Jebusites and other Canaanites but, instead, were to devote them to total destruction, leaving no breathing thing alive, "in order that they may not teach you to do according to all their detestable things."—Ex 34:11-16; De 20:16-18.

Upon observing the Israelite successes in the takeover of the land—the capture of Jericho and Ai as well as the capitulation of the Gibeonites—the Jebusite king Adoni-zedek headed a confederacy of five kings who were determined to stop the invasion. (Jos 9:1, 2; 10:1-5) In the battle that ensued, in which Jehovah caused the sun and moon to stand still, the armies of the confederacy were defeated, the kings were captured and put to death, and their corpses were impaled on stakes for all to see. (Jos 10:6-27; 12:7, 8, 10) It may have been after this victory that the Israelites put the torch to Jebus, burning it to the ground.—Jg 1:8.

With the conclusion of Joshua's campaign of conquest in the S and central portions of the Promised Land, he turned his attention to the northern section W of the Jordan. Once again the Jebusites rallied to resist, this time under the banner of Jabin, the king of Hazor, and again Israel defeated them, with Jehovah's help. (Jos 11:1-8) Nevertheless, after the burning of Jebus and sometime before the dividing of the land, the Jebusites had control of the strategic heights of Jerusalem, which they held for 400 years.—Jos 15:63.

The city of Jebus was assigned to Benjamin when the land was apportioned out, and it lay on the immediate border between the tribal territories of Judah and Benjamin. (Jos 15:1-8; 18:11, 15, 16, 25-28) However, the Israelites did not drive out the Jebusites but, instead, allowed their sons and daughters to intermarry with these people, and they even took up worshiping the false gods of the Jebusites. (Jg 1:21; 3:5, 6) During this period it remained "a city of foreigners," in which a Levite once refused to stay overnight.—Jg 19:10-12.

Finally, in 1070 B.C.E., David conquered Zion, the stronghold of the Jebusites. (2Sa 5:6-9; 1Ch 11:4-8) Later David purchased the threshing floor to the N from a Jebusite named Araunah (Ornan),

and there he built an altar and offered up special sacrifices. (2Sa 24:16-25; 1Ch 21:15, 18-28) It was upon this site years later that Solomon built the costly temple. (2Ch 3:1) Thereafter, Solomon put the descendants of the Jebusites to work in the great building program, working them as slaves.—1Ki 9:20, 21; 2Ch 8:7, 8.

In the last reference we have to the Jebusites, we learn that as an ethnic group they were still present to contaminate the worship of the Israelites upon their return from Babylonian exile.—Ezr 9:1, 2.

JEBUSI. See JEBUS, JEBUSITE.

JECOLIAH (Je·co·li′ah) [Jehovah Has Been Able]. Mother of Judah's King Uzziah (Azariah), whom she bore in about 845 B.C.E. Jecoliah, wife of Amaziah, was from Jerusalem.—2Ki 15:1, 2; 2Ch 26:1, 3.

JECONIAH (Jec·o·ni′ah) [Jehovah Firmly Establishes]. King of Judah for only three months and ten days before being taken captive to Babylon by Nebuchadnezzar in 617 B.C.E.; son of Jehoiakim and grandson of good King Josiah. (1Ch 3:15-17; Es 2:6; Jer 24:1) His name is occasionally contracted to Coniah. (Jer 22:24; 37:1) In certain translations it is sometimes spelled Jechoniah (Mt 1:11, 12, *JB; Mo; RS*), but most often it occurs as Jehoiachin.—2Ki 24:6, 8-15; see JEHOIACHIN.

JEDAIAH (Je·da′iah). Two Hebrew names, different in spelling and meaning, are transliterated into English the same way.
[1, 2: Heb., *Yedha·yah′*]

1. A Simeonite whose descendant Ziza was a chieftain when Hezekiah ruled.—1Ch 4:24, 37, 38, 41.

2. A postexilic resident of Jerusalem who repaired the section of the city wall in front of his house; son of Harumaph.—Ne 3:10.
[3-8: Heb., *Yedha‘·yah′*, Jah Knows]

3. A paternal house of priests selected by lot for the 2nd of the 24 priestly groups into which David divided the priesthood.—1Ch 24:1, 6, 7.

Listed below are several postexilic priests designated by the name Jedaiah, some of whom were quite likely members of the same paternal house, but this is difficult to determine.

4. A priest, or possibly members of the above-mentioned paternal house, who resided in Jerusalem after the return from Babylon. Jedaiah's being called "the son of" Joiarib at Nehemiah 11:10 may be a copyist's addition, as is indicated by comparison with 1 Chronicles 9:10. Jedaiah and the other two (Joiarib or Jehoiarib and Jachin) at the beginning of the lists in Nehemiah and Chronicles are the same names as those of paternal houses in the time of David. (1Ch 24:6, 7, 17) So it may be that reference is simply to the paternal houses, indicating that they were represented, whereas the names following may be of individuals; or it could be that all the names are of individuals then living.—1Ch 9:10-12; Ne 11: 10-13.

5. Forefather of 973 priests who returned from Babylon with Zerubbabel. (Ezr 2:1, 2, 36; Ne 7:39) These are likely members of the same paternal house (No. 3), unless their being "of the house of Jeshua" refers to some connection with the high-priestly line.

6, 7. Two priests of this name are included in the list of those who returned with Jeshua and Zerubbabel in 537 B.C.E. (Ne 12:1, 6, 7) During the priesthood of Jeshua's successor Joiakim, each of the two is referred to as a paternal house, one represented by Uzzi and the other by Nethanel. (Ne 12:12, 19, 21) Whether either or both of these Jedaiahs are connected with the original paternal house (No. 3) cannot be determined.

8. One of the returned exiles from whom gold and silver were taken and made into a crown for High Priest Joshua. (Zec 6:10-14) No connection with the above priests is specifically indicated.

JEDIAEL (Je·di′a·el) [God Knows [This One]; Known of God].

1. A son of Benjamin. Jediael's descendants at one time numbered 17,200 valiant, mighty men. (1Ch 7:6, 10, 11) He is probably the same as Benjamin's son Ashbel.—Ge 46:21; see ASHBEL, ASHBELITES.

2. One of several warriors and leaders of the tribe of Manasseh who joined David's army while he was camped at Ziklag. (1Ch 12:20, 21) Possibly the same as No. 3.

3. One of David's mighty men; son of Shimri. —1Ch 11:26, 45; see No. 2.

4. A gatekeeper of the house of Jehovah, appointed during David's reign. He was the second son of Korahite Meshelemiah.—1Ch 26:1, 2.

JEDIDAH (Je·di′dah) [Beloved]. Wife of Amon and mother of King Josiah, whom she bore in 667 B.C.E.; daughter of Adaiah from Bozkath. —2Ki 21:24-26; 22:1.

JEDIDIAH (Jed·i·di′ah) [Beloved of Jah]. The name given by Jehovah's prophet Nathan to the second child of David and Bath-sheba. (2Sa 12:24,

25) The name reflected Jehovah's love and acceptance of the newborn infant, in contrast with His rejection of their earlier adulterine child, which died soon after birth. (2Sa 12:13-19) In usage the name Jedidiah did not, however, supersede the name Solomon.—See SOLOMON.

JEDUTHUN (Je·du′thun) [possibly from a root meaning "laud"].

1. A Levitical musician. Apparently Jeduthun had previously been called Ethan, for prior to the Ark's arrival in Jerusalem, "Ethan" is connected with the other musicians, Heman and Asaph, whereas afterward "Jeduthun" is in this same association. (1Ch 15:17, 19; 25:1) There is no ancestry of Jeduthun given; there is for Ethan. (1Ch 6:44-47) And there are no descendants of Ethan mentioned; there are for Jeduthun. (1Ch 9:16) Changing the name from Ethan [meaning "Enduring; Everflowing"] to Jeduthun [possibly from a root meaning "laud"] was certainly in line with the assignment he was given.—1Ch 16:41; see ETHAN No. 3.

Jeduthun and his family of musicians participated in several celebrations when "thanking and praising Jehovah" was in order (1Ch 25:3); for example, when the ark of the covenant was brought to Jerusalem. (1Ch 16:1, 41, 42) Of the 24 divisions into which David's reorganization separated the sanctuary musicians, the 2nd, 4th, 8th, 10th, 12th, and 14th lots fell to the six sons of Jeduthun, all working under their father's direction. (1Ch 25:1, 3, 6, 7, 9, 11, 15, 17, 19, 21) The sharing of these duties by Jeduthun, Asaph, and Heman meant that each of the three main branches of Levites (Merari, Gershom, and Kohath respectively) was represented among the temple musicians. (1Ch 6:31-47) All three groups praised Jehovah with music when Solomon inaugurated the temple. (2Ch 5:12, 13) Jeduthun's descendants are mentioned during the reign of Hezekiah and even among the exiles who returned from Babylon.—2Ch 29:1, 12, 14, 15; Ne 11:17.

Three of the psalms mention Jeduthun in their superscriptions. Two of them (Ps 39, 62) read "To the director of Jeduthun" ("after the manner of [the choir of] Jeduthun," Ro ftn on superscription of Ps 39), while the third (Ps 77) reads "To the director on Jeduthun." (NW; Ro; "upon," AT) In each case the composition of the psalm is attributed to someone else, the first two to David and the third to Asaph; so there is no suggestion that Jeduthun composed them, though he is elsewhere called "the visionary of the king" and it is also said that he "was prophesying with the harp." (2Ch 35:15; 1Ch 25:1, 3) Therefore, the superscriptions of these three psalms are evidently instructions for their performance, perhaps identifying a style or even a musical instrument that was somehow associated with Jeduthun, or that he or his sons may have invented, introduced, developed, or made common through usage.

2. A Levite whose son or descendant, Obed-edom, was a gatekeeper at the time David had the Ark brought to Jerusalem.—1Ch 16:1, 37, 38.

JEGAR-SAHADUTHA　(Je′gar-sa·ha·du′tha) [Aramaic, meaning "Witness Heap"]. The Aramaic (Syrian) expression that Laban used to designate the heap of stones on which he and Jacob ate a covenant meal. This stone heap called Jegar-sahadutha was to serve as "a witness" that neither of them would pass it to harm the other. Jacob called it by the Hebrew equivalent "Galeed."—Ge 31:25, 46-53; see GALEED.

JEHALLELEL　(Je·hal′le·lel) [possibly, God Has Flashed Forth [Light]].

1. Father of four sons listed in the genealogies of Judah.—1Ch 4:1, 16.

2. A Merarite Levite whose son helped cleanse the temple during Hezekiah's reign.—2Ch 29:1, 12, 15, 16.

JEHDEIAH　(Jeh·de′iah) [possibly, May Jehovah Feel Glad].

1. A Levite (or his paternal house) descended from Amram, involved in David's reorganization of the Levites.—1Ch 24:20, 31.

2. A Meronothite in charge of King David's she-asses.—1Ch 27:30.

JEHEZKEL　(Je·hez′kel) [May God Strengthen; God Has Strengthened]. The priest and head of the paternal house that was selected by lot for the 20th of the 24 rotating groups into which David had the priestly services divided.—1Ch 24:1, 3, 7, 16.

JEHIAH　(Je·hi′ah) [May He Live, O Jah!]. A Levite who acted as a gatekeeper for the Ark at the time of its transfer to Jerusalem.—1Ch 15:24, 25.

JEHIEL　(Je·hi′el) [May He Live, O God!].

1. A Levite in the second division of musicians that accompanied the ark of the covenant from Obed-edom's house to Jerusalem. (1Ch 15:17, 18, 20, 25, 28) Afterward, Jehiel and others were

appointed to play outside the tent in which the Ark rested.—1Ch 16:1, 4-6.

2. A Levite descendant of Gershon through Ladan; a "headman." (1Ch 23:6-8) Toward the close of David's reign, Jehiel(i) and his sons (or the paternal house called by his name) took care of the treasury belonging to Jehovah's house of worship.—1Ch 26:21, 22; 29:8.

3. Caretaker, perhaps an instructor, of David's sons; a son or descendant of Hachmoni.—1Ch 27:32.

4. A son of King Jehoshaphat. Jehiel and his brothers had received gifts of riches and cities from their father, but the kingship was to go to their eldest brother Jehoram. However, after Jehoshaphat died, all these brothers were slain by Jehoram.—2Ch 21:1-4, 12, 13.

5. A Levite who helped to dispose of the unclean objects that King Hezekiah had removed from the temple; descendant of Heman. (2Ch 29:12, 14-19) Probably the same as No. 6.

6. A Levite commissioner appointed to help care for the bounteous contributions that the people brought to the temple during Hezekiah's reign. (2Ch 31:12, 13) Probably the same as No. 5.

7. One of three "leaders of the house of the true God" who made generous contributions of animal victims for King Josiah's great Passover celebration.—2Ch 35:8.

8. A member of the paternal house of Joab whose son Obadiah returned with Ezra to Jerusalem.—Ezr 8:1, 9.

9. One whose son acknowledged to Ezra the great error of the people in taking foreign wives; descendant of Elam. (Ezr 10:2) The Jehiel at Ezra 10:26, included in the list of those who sent away their foreign wives and sons (Ezr 10:44), is possibly the same person, or at least another descendant of Elam.

10. One of the priests who had taken foreign wives but sent them away.—Ezr 10:21, 44.

JEHIELI　(Je·hi′e·li) [Of (Belonging to) Jehiel]. A Gershonite Levite who apparently served as an overseer of the sanctuary's treasury. (1Ch 26:20-22) He is elsewhere called "Jehiel."—1Ch 23:6-8; 29:8; see JEHIEL No. 2.

JEHIZKIAH　(Je·hiz·ki′ah) [meaning "May Jehovah Strengthen Me; Jehovah Has Strengthened Me"]. A leading Ephraimite who opposed Israel's making captives of their brothers from the southern kingdom when the Israelites under King Pekah defeated Judah, and who also gave material

assistance to the captives. Jehizkiah was the son of Shallum.—2Ch 28:6, 8, 12-15.

JEHOADDAH (Je·ho'ad·dah) [possibly, Jehovah Has Decked Himself]. A Benjamite descendant of Saul through Jonathan and Merib-baal (Mephibosheth). Three sons of Jehoaddah are included in the genealogy. (1Ch 8:33-36; 2Sa 9:6, 12) He is called Jarah at 1 Chronicles 9:42.

JEHOADDAN. See JEHOADDIN.

JEHOADDIN (Je·ho·ad'din) [Jehovah Is Pleasure]. Mother of Judah's King Amaziah; wife of Jehoash. (2Ki 14:1, 2) In the Hebrew text the name is *written* "Jehoaddin," with a marginal note saying it should be *read* as "Jehoaddan," as at 2 Chronicles 25:1.

JEHOAHAZ (Je·ho'a·haz) [May Jehovah Take Hold; Jehovah Has Taken Hold].

1. Variant spelling of the name of Ahaziah, who succeeded his father Jehoram as king of Judah in the late tenth century B.C.E. (2Ch 21:16, 17; 22:1) This alternate spelling, also found in the Masoretic text at 2 Chronicles 25:23, simply transposes the divine name to serve as the prefix instead of the suffix. Once this king of Judah is called Azariah.—2Ch 22:6b; see AHAZIAH No. 2.

2. Son and successor of King Jehu as king of Israel. For 17 years Jehoahaz reigned, from 876 to about 860 B.C.E. (2Ki 10:35; 13:1) When he succeeded his father to the throne, much of the realm was controlled by Syrian King Hazael of Damascus, who had seized from Jehu all of Israel's territory E of the Jordan River. (2Ki 10:32-34) And because Jehoahaz did what was bad in Jehovah's eyes, God allowed Hazael to continue to oppress Israel all the days of Jehoahaz, reducing his fighting force to a mere 50 horsemen, 10 chariots, and 10,000 foot soldiers. Finally, Jehoahaz sought Jehovah's favor, and because of the covenant with Abraham, Isaac, and Jacob, Jehovah did not allow Syria to bring Israel completely to ruin. (2Ki 13:2-7, 22, 23) Upon his death Jehoahaz was buried in Samaria and was succeeded on the throne by his son Jehoash.—2Ki 13:8, 9; 2Ch 25:17.

Certain translations, as well as the Masoretic text, spell the name Joahaz in 2 Kings 14:1.—See JOAHAZ No. 1.

3. Son and successor of Josiah as king of Judah. His mother's name was Hamutal. (2Ki 23:31) Ezra and Jeremiah, according to certain manuscripts, call him Shallum, which some suggest may have been his name prior to his accession to the throne. (1Ch 3:15; Jer 22:11) After the death of his father

at the hands of Pharaoh Nechoh of Egypt, Jehoahaz (though not the oldest of Josiah's living sons) was apparently the people's choice as successor to the throne. (2Ki 23:29, 30) In 2 Chronicles 36:2, where this same event is mentioned, certain translations (*AS, AT, JP, Ro*) have the shortened form Joahaz for Jehoahaz.—See JOAHAZ No. 3.

Jehoahaz was 23 years old when made king, and he ruled badly for three months in the early part of the year 628 B.C.E., until he was imprisoned at Riblah by Pharaoh. Later he was taken to Egypt, where he died in captivity, just as the prophet Jeremiah had foretold.—2Ki 23:31-34; Jer 22:10-12.

JEHOASH (Je·ho'ash).

1. King of Judah for 40 years, from 898 to 859 B.C.E. He was the youngest son of Judah's King Ahaziah; his mother was Zibiah from Beer-sheba. (2Ki 12:1; 1Ch 3:11) In the Masoretic text his name is often abbreviated to Joash.

The death of Ahaziah gave Athaliah, the wicked grandmother of Jehoash, an excuse to make herself queen. But to prevent anyone in the future from challenging her seizure of the throne, she killed off all the sons of Ahaziah with the exception of young Jehoash, who at the time was an infant less than a year old. He escaped the massacre because his aunt Jehosheba, the wife of High Priest Jehoiada, took him and his nurse and secretly hid them in the temple for six years.—2Ki 11:1-3; 2Ch 22:10-12.

When the child reached seven years of age, Jehoiada took into his confidence five chieftains to whom he revealed for the first time the legal heir to the throne. Jehoiada then armed the 500 men under the command of these chieftains with shields and weapons from the temple and instructed them to stand guard around Jehoash at the coronation ceremony in the temple courtyard. Anyone attempting to interfere was to be killed. (2Ki 11:4-12, 21; 2Ch 23:1-11) Upon hearing the people shouting, Athaliah came running, at the same time crying, "Conspiracy! Conspiracy!" She was quickly ushered out, and at the entry of the horse gate they put her to death. Jehoiada then made a covenant of faithfulness between Jehovah, the newly installed king, and the people, after which they tore down the house of Baal and destroyed its altars and images and even killed Mattan the priest of Baal.—2Ki 11:13-20; 2Ch 23:12-21.

Thereafter, as long as High Priest Jehoiada lived and acted as father and adviser to Jehoash, the young monarch prospered. Married by the time he was 21, he had two wives, one of whom was named Jehoaddan, and by these Jehoash became father to sons and daughters. In this way the line of David leading to the Messiah, which had come so near to being completely severed, was once again made strong.—2Ki 12:1-3; 2Ch 24:1-3; 25:1.

Jehovah's house was badly in need of repairs not merely because of age (now no more than 150 years old) but also because of neglect and plunder during the reign of Athaliah. As a consequence, Jehoash urged the Levites to raise the money for the restoration by going from city to city throughout Judah, but the response of the Levites was not wholehearted, and the work was not getting done. (2Ki 12:4-8; 2Ch 24:4-7) In time the arrangements for gathering and administering the funds were changed. The people responded well, and the repair work moved ahead to its completion.—2Ki 12:9-16; 2Ch 24:8-14.

After the death of faithful High Priest Jehoiada at the age of 130, the princes of the realm gradually turned King Jehoash and the people away from Jehovah to the worship of pagan idols and phallic "sacred poles." And when Jehovah raised up prophets to warn them, they refused to give heed. (2Ch 24:15-19) Jehoash went so far as to kill Zechariah, the very son of Jehoiada, because through him God reprovingly had asked: "Why are you overstepping the commandments of Jehovah?" Zechariah's dying words were: "Let Jehovah see to it and ask it back."—2Ch 24:20-22.

Retribution was not long in coming. With Jehovah's protection removed, a small military force of Syrians led by Hazael was able to invade Judah's territory, forcing Jehoash to give over the gold and treasures of the sanctuary, as well as his own possessions, leaving him a broken and diseased man. (2Ki 12:17, 18; 2Ch 24:23-25) Not long after that, two of his servants formed a conspiracy and put Jehoash to death at the comparatively young age of 47. They buried him in the City of David with his forefathers, and his son Amaziah reigned in his place.—2Ki 12:19-21; 2Ch 24:25-27.

2. King of Israel; son of Jehoahaz and grandson of Jehu. The shortened form of his name, Joash, also appears in the Masoretic text. (Ho 1:1; Am 1:1) He ruled for 16 years in the middle of the ninth century B.C.E. During the first part of the reign of this Jehoash (son of Jehoahaz) over the northern kingdom of Israel, Jehoash son of Ahaziah was king over the southern kingdom of Judah. —2Ki 13:10.

Jehoash generally did what was bad in Jehovah's eyes and allowed calf worship to continue throughout the land. Nevertheless, when the prophet Elisha was sick and near death Jehoash went down and wept over him, saying: "My father, my father, the war chariot of Israel and his horsemen!" (2Ki 13:11, 14) In response to the prophet's request, Jehoash shot an arrow out the window toward Syria and then beat the earth with his arrows. However, he only beat three times. Elisha was incensed at this, for had he continued to beat the earth five or six times, Elisha said, then Jehoash would have been completely victorious over the Syrians; but now, the prophet declared, he would enjoy only three partial victories. (2Ki 13:15-19) In Jehoash's three campaigns against the Syrians he did have a measure of success, recovering a number of Israelite cities that Ben-hadad's father Hazael had taken from the northern kingdom.—2Ki 13: 24, 25.

Jehoash also hired out a hundred thousand of his troops to the king of Judah to fight against the Edomites. However, on the advice of a "man of the true God" they were dismissed, and although they had been paid a hundred silver talents ($660,600) in advance, they were angered at being sent home, probably because of losing out on their anticipated share of the booty. So after their return N they plundered towns of the southern kingdom, from Samaria (perhaps their base of operations) as far as Beth-horon.—2Ch 25:6-10, 13.

It was probably in retaliation for this that the king of Judah provoked Jehoash to fight. In the battle that followed, Judean King Amaziah was captured at Beth-shemesh, and in the follow-up Jehoash's forces broke through the wall of Jerusalem, looting the temple and house of the king of their gold and silver and taking hostages back to Samaria. (2Ki 14:8-14; 2Ch 25:17-24) Finally, Jehoash died and was buried in Samaria, and his son Jeroboam II ruled in his place.—2Ki 13:12, 13; 14:15, 16.

JEHOHANAN (Je·ho·ha′nan) [Jehovah Has Shown Favor; Jehovah Has Been Gracious].

1. A Korahite gatekeeper during the reign of David; the sixth son of Meshelemiah.—1Ch 26:1-3.

2. An army chief under King Jehoshaphat, in direct charge of 280,000 men of Judah. (2Ch 17:12, 14-16) Possibly the same as No. 3.

3. Father of the Ishmael who stood up with Jehoiada and other chiefs to depose Athaliah and

put Jehoash on Judah's throne. (2Ch 23:1-3) Possibly the same as No. 2.

4. An Ephraimite whose son Azariah was a leader in that tribe around 760 B.C.E., when Kings Ahaz of Judah and Pekah of Israel were ruling.—2Ch 28:1, 6, 12.

5. Head of the priestly paternal house of Amariah during the days of Joiakim the successor of High Priest Jeshua.—Ne 12:10, 12, 13.

6. Son of Eliashib. Ezra retired to Jehohanan's temple dining hall to mourn over the unfaithfulness of the people.—Ezr 10:6.

7. One of four sons of Bebai who dismissed their foreign wives and sons in Ezra's day.—Ezr 10:28, 44.

8. Son of Nehemiah's antagonist Tobiah the Ammonite. Jehohanan married an Israelite girl. —Ne 6:17-19.

9. A priest positioned at the temple during the inauguration of Jerusalem's rebuilt wall.—Ne 12:40-42.

JEHOIACHIN   (Je·hoi′a·chin) [probably, Jehovah Has Firmly Established]. Son of Judean King Jehoiakim by Nehushta. (2Ki 24:6, 8; 2Ch 36:8) He is also called Jeconiah (a variant of Jehoiachin) and Coniah (a contraction of Jeconiah).—Es 2:6; Jer 28:4; 37:1.

At the age of 18 Jehoiachin became king and continued the bad practices of his father. (2Ki 24:8, 9; 2Ch 36:9, ftn) Jehoiachin's father, Jehoiakim, had been under subjection to Babylonian King Nebuchadnezzar but rebelled in his third year of such vassalage (618 B.C.E.). (2Ki 24:1) This resulted in a siege being laid against Jerusalem. The expression "during that time" (2Ki 24: 10) may refer, not to Jehoiachin's brief reign, but to the general period in which it fits, hence allowing for the siege to have begun during his father Jehoiakim's reign, as Daniel 1:1, 2 seems to indicate. It appears that Jehoiakim died during this siege and Jehoiachin ascended the throne of Judah. His rule ended, however, a mere three months and ten days later, when he surrendered to Nebuchadnezzar in 617 B.C.E. (in the month of Adar, according to a Babylonian chronicle). (2Ki 24:11, 12; 2Ch 36:9; *Assyrian and Babylonian Chronicles,* by A. Grayson, 1975, p. 102) In fulfillment of Jehovah's word through Jeremiah, he was taken into Babylonian exile. (Jer 22:24-27; 24:1; 27:19, 20; 29:1, 2) Other members of the royal household, court officials, craftsmen, and warriors were also exiled.—2Ki 24:14-16; see Nebuchadnezzar.

The record at 2 Kings 24:12-16 states that Nebuchadnezzar took these captives into exile, along with "all the treasures of the house of Jehovah and the treasures of the king's house." The account at Daniel 1:1, 2 refers to only "a part of the utensils" as being taken to Babylon. The explanation may be that the treasures referred to at Second Kings involved particularly the gold utensils, which are emphasized in that account, and that other utensils were allowed to remain. Another possibility is that, when Jerusalem yielded to the Babylonian siege (which came as a result of Jehoiakim's rebellion against the king of Babylon), "some of the utensils of the house of Jehovah" were taken to Babylon, and a short time later, when Jehoiachin himself was transferred to Babylon, other "desirable articles of the house of Jehovah" were taken along. This possibility is suggested by the account at 2 Chronicles 36:6-10. From the Chronicles account, it appears that Nebuchadnezzar, after successfully conquering Jerusalem, departed but then "sent and proceeded to bring [Jehoiachin] to Babylon with desirable articles of the house of Jehovah." In a similar way, ten years later, in the final conquest and destruction of Jerusalem (607 B.C.E.), Nebuchadnezzar retired to Riblah "in the land of Hamath," leaving the postconquest details to his chief of the bodyguard, Nebuzaradan.—2Ki 25:8-21.

While in Babylon, Jehoiachin fathered seven sons. (1Ch 3:16-18) In this way the royal line leading to the Messiah was preserved. (Mt 1:11, 12) But, as prophecy had indicated, none of Jehoiachin's descendants ever ruled from earthly Jerusalem. It therefore was as though Jehoiachin had been childless, with no offspring to succeed him as king.—Jer 22:28-30.

In the fifth year of Jehoiachin's exile, Ezekiel began his prophetic work. (Eze 1:2) About 32 years later, evidently in 580 B.C.E., Jehoiachin was released from prison by Nebuchadnezzar's successor Evil-merodach (Awil-Marduk) and given a position of favor above all the other captive kings. Thereafter he ate at Evil-merodach's table and received a daily allowance.—2Ki 25:27-30; Jer 52:31-34.

Babylonian administrative documents have been found listing rations for Jehoiachin and five of his sons.

JEHOIADA   (Je·hoi′a·da) [May Jehovah Know].

1. Father of the Benaiah who is almost always identified as "Benaiah the son of Jehoiada," and who was one of David's mighty men and also Solomon's army chief. (2Sa 23:8, 20, 22, 23; 1Ki

2:35) Jehoiada himself is connected with the priesthood, being called "the chief priest." He is referred to as "the leader of the sons of Aaron" and was among those flocking to David when he became king over all Israel at Hebron.—1Ch 27:5; 12:27, 38.

2. A counselor of King David; apparently a grandson of No. 1.—1Ch 27:33, 34.

3. High priest in the time of Jehoram, Ahaziah, Athaliah, and Jehoash. Jehoiada was married to King Jehoram's daughter Jehosheba, also called Jehoshabeath (the only recorded instance of a high priest marrying into the royal family). Jehoiada was noted especially for overthrowing Athaliah and elevating true worship in Judah. After Athaliah's ruling son Ahaziah was slain, she proceeded to kill off all the remaining royal offspring and placed herself on the throne. However, Jehosheba, herself a sister of Ahaziah though not necessarily Athaliah's daughter, took Ahaziah's infant son Jehoash away and kept him hidden for six years. In the seventh year, Jehoiada secured the support of the Levites, the chiefs of the Carian bodyguard and of the runners, as well as the heads of the paternal house of Israel. He then produced Jehoash, whom they proclaimed as king. Jehoiada next ordered Athaliah taken outside the temple grounds and slain.—2Ki 11:1-16; 2Ch 22:10–23:15.

Jehoiada thereafter wasted no time in advancing Jehovah's worship. He renewed Israel's covenant relationship with Jehovah, whereupon the people tore down the house of Baal and removed its altars, images, and priesthood. Jehoiada then restored full temple services. He had a strong influence for good upon the life of Jehoash. Jehoiada and the king repaired the temple and made various utensils for Jehovah's house. When, at the age of 130, Jehoiada finally died, he was given the exceptional honor of burial with the kings "because he had done good in Israel and with the true God and His house." Unfortunately, his good influence died with him, for Jehoash then listened to the princes of Judah and turned aside from Jehovah, even to the point of ordering the killing of Jehoiada's son Zechariah, who issued the unfaithful people a rebuke.—2Ki 11:17–12:16; 2Ch 23:16–24:22.

4. A priest who was replaced by Zephaniah the son of Maaseiah during Jeremiah's time.—Jer 29:24-27.

JEHOIAKIM (Je·hoi'a·kim) [possibly, Jehovah Raises Up]. One of the last Judean kings, son of Josiah by Zebidah, and originally called Eliakim.

(2Ki 23:34, 36; 1Ch 3:15) Jehoiakim's bad rule of about 11 years (628-618 B.C.E.) was marked by injustices, oppression, and murder. (2Ch 36:5; Jer 22:17; 52:2) Also, during his reign Judah experienced much harassment from Chaldean, Syrian, Moabite, and Ammonite marauder bands.—2Ki 24:2.

After the death of King Josiah, the people of Judah for some reason constituted Eliakim's younger brother Jehoahaz king. About three months later Pharaoh Necho (Nechoh) took King Jehoahaz captive and made 25-year-old Eliakim king, changing the new ruler's name to Jehoiakim. Necho also imposed a heavy fine on the kingdom of Judah. King Jehoiakim exacted the silver and gold for this fine from his subjects by taxation. (2Ki 23:34-36; 2Ch 36:3-5) Despite the financial burden that was therefore already on the people, Jehoiakim made plans for building a new, luxurious palace. Probably to keep down the cost, he oppressively withheld the laborers' wages. Consequently Jehovah, through Jeremiah, pronounced woe upon this wicked ruler, indicating that he would have the burial of a he-ass. —Jer 22:13-19.

Early in Jehoiakim's reign Jeremiah warned that unless the people repented, Jerusalem and her temple would be destroyed. Thereafter the prophet was threatened with death. However, the prominent man Ahikam stood up for Jeremiah and saved the prophet from harm. Previously, similar prophesying by Urijah had so enraged Jehoiakim that he had determined to kill him. Although fearful Urijah had fled to Egypt, he did not escape the king's wrath. Jehoiakim had had Urijah brought back and then had killed him with the sword.—Jer 26:1-24.

The fourth year of the reign of Jehoiakim (625 B.C.E.) saw Nebuchadnezzar defeat Pharaoh Necho in a battle over the domination of Syria-Palestine. The battle took place at Carchemish by the Euphrates, over 600 km (370 mi) N of Jerusalem. (Jer 46:1, 2) In that same year Jeremiah began dictating to his secretary Baruch the words Jehovah directed against Israel, Judah, and all the nations, recording messages that had begun to be delivered from the 13th year of Josiah's reign (at which time Jehoiakim had been about six years old) onward. Nearly a year later, in the ninth lunar month (Chislev, November/December), the scroll containing the dictated message was read before King Jehoiakim. As soon as Jehudi read three or four page-columns, that section was cut off and thrown into the fire burning in the brazier of the king's winter house. Thus the entire scroll was committed to the flames section by section. Jehoiakim ignored the pleas of three of his princes not to burn the roll. He particularly objected to the prophetic words that pointed to the desolation of Judah at the hands of Babylon's king. This suggests that Nebuchadnezzar had not yet come against Jerusalem and made Jehoiakim his vassal.—Jer 36:1-4, 21-29.

Second Kings 24:1 shows that Nebuchadnezzar brought pressure upon the Judean king "and so Jehoiakim became his servant [or vassal] for three years. However, he [Jehoiakim] turned back and rebelled against him [Nebuchadnezzar]." Evidently it is to this third year of Jehoiakim as a vassal king under Babylon that Daniel refers at Daniel 1:1. It could not be Jehoiakim's third year of his 11-year reign over Judah, for at that time Jehoiakim was a vassal, not to Babylon, but to Egypt's Pharaoh Necho. It was not until Jehoiakim's *fourth* year of rule over Judah that Nebuchadnezzar demolished Egyptian domination over Syria-Palestine by his victory at Carchemish (625 B.C.E. [apparently after Nisan]). (Jer 46:2) Since Jehoiakim's revolt against Babylon led to his downfall after about 11 years on the throne, the beginning of his three-year vassalage to Babylon must have begun toward the end of his eighth year of rule, or early in 620 B.C.E.

Daniel's account (1:1, 2) states that Nebuchadnezzar came against Jerusalem and laid siege to it and that Jehoiakim, along with some of the temple utensils, was given into the Babylonian king's hand. However, the account at 2 Kings 24:10-15 describes the siege of Jerusalem by the Babylonians and shows that Jehoiakim's son Jehoiachin, whose reign lasted only three months and ten days, was the one who finally capitulated and went out to the Babylonians. It therefore appears that Jehoiakim died during the siege of the city, perhaps in the early part thereof. Jehovah's prophecy through Jeremiah (22:18, 19; 36:30) indicated that Jehoiakim was not to receive a decent burial; his corpse was to lie unattended outside the gates of Jerusalem, exposed to the sun's heat by day and the frost by night. Just in what way Jehoiakim was 'given into the hand of Nebuchadnezzar' (Da 1:2) is not revealed. It may have been in the sense of his dying under siege and of his son's thereafter having to go out into captivity, so that Jehoiakim's line suffered the loss of the kingship at Nebuchadnezzar's hands. There is no way to confirm the Jewish tradition (recorded by Josephus) that Nebuchadnezzar killed Jehoiakim and commanded that his dead body be

thrown outside Jerusalem's walls. (*Jewish Antiquities*, X, 97 [vi, 3]) By whatever means Jehoiakim's death came, it appears that the copper fetters Nebuchadnezzar had brought along to bind Jehoiakim were not used as planned.—2Ch 36:6.

Following the siege of Jerusalem during Jehoiakim's "third year" (as vassal king), Daniel and other Judeans, including nobles and members of the royal family, were taken as exiles to Babylon. There being no record of an earlier Babylonian exile, this appears to place the event in the short reign of Jehoiachin, Jehoiakim's successor.—2Ki 24:12-16; Jer 52:28.

After Jehoiakim's son Jehoiachin surrendered, Nebuchadnezzar elevated Jehoiachin's uncle Zedekiah to the throne of Judah. (2Ch 36:9, 10) This fulfilled Jeremiah's prophecy that Jehoiakim would have no one sitting on the throne of David. (Jer 36:30) Jehoiakim's son Jehoiachin ruled a mere three months and ten days.

JEHOIARIB   (Je·hoi′a·rib) [May Jehovah Contend; Jehovah Has Conducted [Our] Legal Case]. The priest whose paternal house was selected by lot as first of the 24 priestly divisions organized during David's rule. (1Ch 24:1-3, 5-7) Some of the postexilic descendants of this paternal house, or another priest with the same name, lived in Jerusalem. (1Ch 9:3, 10) The name is spelled Joiarib in the parallel list at Nehemiah 11:10.

JEHONADAB   (Je·hon′a·dab) [Jehovah Is Willing (Noble; Generous)], **JONADAB** (Jon′a·dab) [shortened form of Jehonadab]. In the Hebrew text and many English translations, both spellings are used interchangeably for each of the two persons bearing the name.

1. David's nephew; son of his brother Shimeah. Jehonadab was "a very wise man" but crafty and shrewd. After inducing David's son Amnon to disclose to him his passion for his half sister Tamar, Jehonadab proposed the scheme by which Amnon violated her. After her full brother Absalom had Amnon killed in revenge, the report came to David that Absalom had killed all the king's sons, but Jehonadab was on hand to give assurance that Amnon alone was dead. (2Sa 13:3-5, 14, 22, 28-33) He is possibly the "Jonathan" at 2 Samuel 21:21 and 1 Chronicles 20:7.

2. Son of Rechab; companion of King Jehu. His encounter with Jehu was not accidental, for on Jehonadab's own initiative he was "coming to meet him," and in turn, he received Jehu's blessing. The subsequent events showed that Jehonadab was in complete agreement with Jehu's

determination to annihilate Baal worship out of Israel. At each proposal made by Jehu, Jehonadab quickly responded in the affirmative. "Is your heart upright with me?" Jehu asked. He answered, "It is." "Do give me your hand," Jehu said; and Jehonadab gave him his hand. Now in Jehu's chariot, Jehonadab was told, "Do go along with me and look upon my toleration of no rivalry toward Jehovah," and again he manifested willingness. Finally, when they got to Samaria, and all the worshipers of Baal were assembled, Jehonadab did not turn back but accompanied Jehu into the house of Baal and remained by his side during the slaughter that followed. At the same time Jehu demonstrated his complete trust and confidence in Jehonadab.—2Ki 10:15-28.

Nearly 300 years later, Jehonadab's descendants, the Rechabites, were used by Jeremiah at Jehovah's direction as an example of faithfulness to their forefather's commands, in contrast with the disobedience to God displayed by the people of Judah and Jerusalem. Jehonadab had instructed the Rechabites to live in tents, sow no seed, plant no vineyards, and take no wine. When Jeremiah offered them wine, they refused, referring back to the commandment of their ancestor Jehonadab. For such faithfulness Jehovah promised: "There will not be cut off from Jonadab the son of Rechab a man to stand before me always."—Jer 35:1-19.

JEHONATHAN (Je·hon'a·than) [Jehovah Has Given]. In Hebrew this name is often used interchangeably with Jonathan. Listed below are only those occurrences where it is rendered Jehonathan. For those occurrences where the shorter form appears, see JONATHAN.

1. One of the Levites sent by Jehoshaphat in the third year of his reign to teach Jehovah's law to the people of Judah.—2Ch 17:5, 7-9.

2. A secretary whose house was converted into a prison, where Jeremiah was kept in detention. (Jer 37:15, 20; 38:26) The house likely had subterranean quarters suitable for imprisonment.

3. Postexilic head of a paternal house of priests in the days of Jeshua's successor Joiakim.—Ne 12:10, 12, 18.

JEHORAM (Je·ho'ram) [Jehovah Is High (Exalted)]. A shortened form of the name is Joram.

1. One of two priests whom Jehoshaphat selected in 934 B.C.E., the third year of his reign, along with leading princes and Levites, to be traveling teachers of "the book of Jehovah's law."—2Ch 17:7-9.

2. Son of Ahab and Jezebel, who succeeded his older brother Ahaziah as the tenth king of the northern kingdom of Israel in about 917 B.C.E. He reigned 12 years. (2Ki 1:17, 18; 3:1; 9:22) This king of Israel should not be confused with the king of Judah by the same name, who was his brother-in-law. (See No. 3.) Though Jehoram removed the sacred pillar of Baal erected by his father, he continued to do "what was bad in Jehovah's eyes," clinging to calf worship instituted by Jeroboam.—1Ki 12:26-29; 16:33; 2Ki 3:2, 3.

King Jehoshaphat of Judah and the king of Edom joined Jehoram in an attack on Moab that proved successful because Jehovah deceived the enemy with an optical illusion. God's prophet Elisha instructed those of the camp of Israel to dig ditches in which to catch much-needed and divinely provided water. The next morning the reflection of the sunlight upon this water caused the Moabites to think the water was blood. Thinking the confederate camp of the three kings had killed off one another, the Moabites moved in to take the spoil, only to be slaughtered in great numbers.—2Ki 3:4-27.

Naaman, the army chief of Syria, came to Jehoram to be cured of leprosy, bearing a letter to that effect from the king of Syria. Jehoram, thinking the Syrian ruler was picking a quarrel, exclaimed, 'Am I God who can put to death and preserve alive and cure leprosy?' Elisha, however, requested that Jehoram send Naaman to him so that the Syrian army chief might know that the true God did have a prophet in the land, one capable of performing such cures.—2Ki 5:1-8.

In advance, Jehovah's prophet Elisha also informed Jehoram of Syrian military maneuvers. (2Ki 6:8-12) Certain Syrian assaults against Israel were divinely foiled during Jehoram's reign.—2Ki 6:13–7:20.

But despite such manifestations of God's loving-kindness, Jehoram, down to the day of his death, did not repent and turn to Jehovah with all his heart. Death came suddenly and in an unexpected way. Jehoram was at Jezreel recuperating from wounds received in battle with the Syrians. In time, he went out to meet Jehu, asking, "Is there peace, Jehu?" The negative answer made Jehoram turn to flee, but Jehu shot an arrow through his heart. Thus "this son of a murderer" (2Ki 6:32) was executed, his dead body being pitched into the field of Naboth.—2Ki 9:14-26.

3. The firstborn son of Jehoshaphat who, at the age of 32, became king of Judah. (2Ch 21:1-3, 5, 20) It appears that for a number of years Jehoram was in some way associated with his father in the kingship. (2Ki 1:17; 8:16) The eight years of rulership credited to Jehoram count from 913 B.C.E. (2Ki 8:17) So during these years both the northern and southern kingdoms had rulers with the same name. They were also brothers-in-law because Jehoram of Judah married Athaliah, the daughter of Ahab and Jezebel and sister of Jehoram of Israel.—2Ki 8:18, 25, 26; see No. 2 above.

At least partially because of the bad influence of his wife Athaliah, Jehoram did not pursue the righteous ways of his father Jehoshaphat. (2Ki 8:18) Not only did Jehoram murder his six brothers and some of the princes of Judah but he also turned his subjects away from Jehovah to false gods. (2Ch 21:1-6, 11-14) His whole reign was marred by both internal trouble and external strife. First, Edom rebelled; then Libnah revolted against Judah. (2Ki 8:20-22) In a letter to Jehoram, the prophet Elijah warned: "Look! Jehovah is dealing a great blow to your people and to your sons and to your wives and to all your goods." Moreover, you, King Jehoram, "will be with many sicknesses, with a malady of your intestines, until your intestines have come out because of the sickness day by day."—2Ch 21:12-15.

It all occurred just that way. Jehovah allowed Arabs and Philistines to overrun the land and take Jehoram's wives and sons captive. God permitted only Jehoram's youngest son, Jehoahaz (also called Ahaziah), to escape, a concession made, however, only for the sake of the Kingdom covenant made with David. "After all this Jehovah plagued [Jehoram] in his intestines with a sickness for which there was no healing." Two years later "his intestines came out" and he gradually died. So ended the life of this wicked man, who "went away without being desired." He was buried in the City of David, "but not in the burial places of the kings." Ahaziah his son became king in his stead.—2Ch 21:7, 16-20; 22:1; 1Ch 3:10, 11.

JEHOSHABEATH (Je·ho·shab′e·ath) [Jehovah Is Plenty]. Daughter of King Jehoram and wife of High Priest Jehoiada. She is also called Jehosheba.—2Ch 22:10-12; 2Ki 11:1-3; see JEHOSHEBA.

JEHOSHAPHAT (Je·hosh′a·phat) [Jehovah Is Judge].

1. Son of Ahilud serving as recorder during the reigns of David and Solomon.—2Sa 8:16; 20:24; 1Ki 4:3; 1Ch 18:15.

2. One of King Solomon's 12 deputies. For a month each year this "son of Paruah" supplied the food for the king and his household from the territory of Issachar.—1Ki 4:7, 17.

3. Son of Judean King Asa by Azubah the daughter of Shilhi. At the age of 35 Jehoshaphat succeeded his father to the throne and ruled for 25 years, from 936 B.C.E. (1Ki 22:42; 2Ch 20:31) His reign was contemporaneous with that of Israelite Kings Ahab, Ahaziah, and Jehoram. (1Ki 22:41, 51; 2Ki 3:1, 2; 2Ch 17:3, 4) It was marked by stability, prosperity, glory, and relative peace with neighboring lands. Jehoshaphat received presents from his subjects and tribute from the Philistines and Arabs.—2Ch 17:5, 10, 11.

Accomplishments. Jehoshaphat strengthened his position by putting military forces in Judah's fortified cities, as well as garrisons both in the land of Judah and in the Israelite territory captured by his father Asa. At Jerusalem a large body of valiant warriors served the royal interests; and in Judah, Jehoshaphat built fortified places and storage cities.—2Ch 17:1, 2, 12-19.

Unlike the Israelite kings of the northern kingdom, Jehoshaphat manifested great concern for true worship. (2Ch 17:4) He commissioned certain princes, Levites, and priests to teach Jehovah's law in the cities of Judah. (2Ch 17:7-9) Jehoshaphat also sanctified holy offerings (2Ki 12:18) and personally traveled throughout his realm, directing his subjects to return to Jehovah in faithfulness. (2Ch 19:4) Courageously Jehoshaphat continued the campaign against idolatry started by Asa. (1Ki 22:46; 2Ch 17:6) But improper worship at high places was so entrenched among the Israelites that Jehoshaphat's efforts did not permanently eradicate it.—1Ki 22:43; 2Ch 20:33.

Jehoshaphat's reign also witnessed the institution of a better judicial system. The king himself impressed upon the judges the importance of being impartial and free from bribery, since they were judging, not for man, but for Jehovah.—2Ch 19:5-11.

Jehoshaphat proved himself to be a king who relied on Jehovah. When Judah was threatened by the combined forces of Ammon, Moab, and the mountainous region of Seir, he humbly acknowledged the nation's weakness in the face of this danger and prayed to Jehovah for help. Thereafter Jehovah fought for Judah by striking confusion into the ranks of the enemy so that they slaughtered one another. Consequently the surrounding nations became fearful, and Judah continued to enjoy peace.—2Ch 20:1-30.

Relationship With the Ten-Tribe Kingdom.
Jehoshaphat maintained peace with the northern kingdom and unwisely formed a marriage alliance with Ahab. (1Ki 22:44; 2Ch 18:1) For this reason on several occasions he was drawn into other alliances with the kingdom of Israel.

During a visit in the northern kingdom sometime after the marriage of Ahab's daughter Athaliah to his firstborn Jehoram, Jehoshaphat agreed to accompany King Ahab in a military venture to recover Ramoth-gilead from the Syrians. However, before actually starting out, Jehoshaphat requested that Ahab inquire of Jehovah. Four hundred prophets assured Ahab of success. But Jehovah's true prophet Micaiah, hated by Ahab but called at Jehoshaphat's insistence, foretold certain defeat. Nevertheless, Jehoshaphat, perhaps so as not to go back on his original promise to accompany Ahab, went into battle dressed in his royal garments. Since Ahab had taken the precaution to disguise himself, the Syrians mistakenly concluded that Jehoshaphat was Israel's king and therefore subjected him to the heaviest attack. Jehoshaphat barely escaped with his life, and Ahab, despite the disguise, was mortally wounded. (1Ki 22:2-37; 2Ch 18) Upon returning to Jerusalem, Jehoshaphat was censured for unwisely allying himself with wicked Ahab, the visionary Jehu saying to him: "Is it to the wicked that help is to be given, and is it for those hating Jehovah that you should have love? And for this there is indignation against you from the person of Jehovah."—2Ch 19:2.

Later, Jehoshaphat became partner to King Ahaziah, Ahab's successor, in a shipbuilding enterprise at Ezion-geber on the Gulf of 'Aqaba. But Jehovah disapproved of this maritime alliance with wicked Ahaziah. Therefore, in fulfillment of prophecy, the ships were wrecked.—1Ki 22:48, 49; 2Ch 20:35-37; see AHAZIAH No. 1.

Sometime after this, Jehoshaphat joined Ahaziah's successor to the throne, Jehoram, and the king of Edom in a military offensive to put down Moabite King Mesha's revolt against the ten-tribe kingdom. But the armies of the alliance became entrapped in a waterless wilderness. Jehoshaphat therefore called for a prophet of Jehovah. Only out of regard for Jehoshaphat did the prophet Elisha seek divine inspiration, and his subsequent advice saved the three kings and their armies from disaster.—2Ki 3:4-25.

Jehoram Becomes King.   While Jehoshaphat was still alive he gave the kingship to his firstborn Jehoram, but to his other sons he gave precious gifts and fortified cities in Judah. (2Ki 8:16; 2Ch 21:3) Particularly after Jehoshaphat's death and burial in the City of David did the marriage alliance with the house of Ahab prove to be disastrous for the kingdom of Judah. Under the influence of Athaliah, Jehoram revived idolatrous practices.—1Ki 22:50; 2Ch 21:1-7, 11.

4. Father of Israelite King Jehu.—2Ki 9:2, 14.

JEHOSHAPHAT, LOW PLAIN OF.   Evidently a symbolic place, also called the "low plain of the decision." (Joe 3:2, 14) Since it relates to God's execution of judgment, it is appropriately designated as "the low plain of Jehoshaphat," for the name Jehoshaphat means "Jehovah Is Judge." Also, during Jehoshaphat's reign Jehovah delivered Judah and Jerusalem from the combined forces of Ammon, Moab, and the mountainous region of Seir, causing the enemy forces to become confused and to slaughter one another. —2Ch 20:1-29.

At the symbolic "low plain of Jehoshaphat" Jehovah judges the nations as worthy of execution on account of their mistreatment of his people. The low plain itself serves as a huge symbolic winepress for crushing the nations like bunches of grapes. To link "the low plain of Jehoshaphat" literally with the Kidron Valley, the Valley of Hinnom, or the Valley of Jezreel, as some have done, is hardly plausible. None of these valleys would be large enough to accommodate "all" the nations.—Joe 3:1-3, 12-14; compare Re 14:18-20.

JEHOSHEBA   (Je·hosh'e·ba) [Jehovah Is Plenty]. Wife of High Priest Jehoiada; daughter of King Jehoram of Judah, though not necessarily by his wife Athaliah. Her name is also spelled "Jehoshabeath." (2Ch 22:11) After the death of her brother (or half brother) King Ahaziah, Jehosheba took Ahaziah's infant son Jehoash into hiding to escape Athaliah's slaughter of the royal offspring. Jehoiada and Jehosheba kept their nephew hidden in their temple quarters for six years before Jehoiada brought him out to be proclaimed king. (2Ki 11:1-3; 2Ch 22:10-12) Jehosheba's action, along with that of her husband, providentially preserved the royal lineage from David to the Messiah.

JEHOSHUA   (Je·hosh'u·a) [Jehovah Is Salvation]. Son of Nun; an Ephraimite who succeeded Moses and led the Israelites into the Promised Land. His original name was Hoshea, but Moses called him Jehoshua, or Joshua (a short form of Jehoshua).—Nu 13:8, 16; De 34:9; Jos 1:1, 2; see JOSHUA No. 1.

Map Index

Reference numbers in this index have boldface type to indicate the volume, lightface type for the pages.

The names in parentheses in this index are usually alternate names of the same place or indications of the area in which the city or village is located.

Distances between locations, as stated in articles, are generally given in terms of air miles (km).

On maps in this publication, north is toward the top of page.

● on a map = city or village that can be located with reasonable certainty.

○ on a map = city or village concerning the location of which there is reasonable evidence but some uncertainty.

Abbreviations Used in This Publication

Bible Translations

AB	*The Amplified Bible* (1965), Zondervan Publishing House
An	*The Anchor Bible* (1964 and following years), W. F. Albright and D. N. Freedman, general editors
AS	*American Standard Version* (1901; as printed in 1944), American Revision Committee
AT	*The Complete Bible—An American Translation* (1939; as printed in 1951), J. M. Powis Smith and Edgar J. Goodspeed
BC	*Sagrada Biblia* (1947), José María Bover and Francisco Cantera Burgos, Madrid, Spain
BE	*The Bible in Basic English* (1949), Cambridge University Press
By	*The Bible in Living English* (1972), Steven T. Byington
CB	*The New Testament—A Translation in the Language of the People* (1937; as printed in 1950), Charles B. Williams
CC	*The New Testament* (1941; as printed in 1947), Confraternity of Christian Doctrine Revision
CK	*The New Testament—A New Translation in Plain English* (1963), Charles K. Williams
Da	*The 'Holy Scriptures'* (1949 Edition), J. N. Darby
Dy	*Challoner-Douay Version* (c. 1750; as printed in 1942)
ED	*The Emphatic Diaglott* (1864; as printed in 1942), Benjamin Wilson
ER	*English Revised Version* (1885; as printed in 1893), Cambridge University Press
Fn	*The Holy Bible in Modern English* (1903; as printed in 1935), Ferrar Fenton
Int	*The Kingdom Interlinear Translation of the Greek Scriptures* (1985 Edition)
JB	*The Jerusalem Bible* (1966), Alexander Jones, general editor
JP	*The Holy Scriptures According to the Masoretic Text* (1917; as printed in 1952), The Jewish Publication Society of America
KJ	*King James Version* (1611; as printed in 1942)
Kx	*The Holy Bible* (1956), Ronald A. Knox
La	*The Holy Bible From Ancient Eastern Manuscripts* (1957), George M. Lamsa
Le	*The Twenty-Four Books of the Holy Scriptures* (1853; as printed in 1914), Isaac Leeser
LXX	Greek *Septuagint* (originally produced in the third and second centuries B.C.E.), as edited by Alfred Rahlfs (1935)
LXX, Bagster	*The Septuagint With Apocrypha: Greek and English* (translation by L. C. L. Brenton, 1851; as printed in 1986)
LXX, Thomson	*The Septuagint Bible* (translation by Charles Thomson, 1808; revised by C. A. Muses, 1954)
Mo	*A New Translation of the Bible* (1935; as printed in 1954), James Moffatt
MR	*The Modern Reader's Bible* (1907; as printed in 1924), Richard G. Moulton, editor
NAB	*The New American Bible* (1970), Catholic Biblical Association of America
NAS	*New American Standard Bible* (1971), Lockman Foundation
NC	*Sagrada Biblia* (1944; as printed in 1972), Eloíno Nácar Fuster and Alberto Colunga
NE	*The New English Bible* (1970)
NIV	*The Holy Bible—New International Version* (1978)
NW	*New World Translation of the Holy Scriptures—With References* (1984)
Ph	*The New Testament in Modern English* (1958; as printed in 1976), J. B. Phillips
Ro	*The Emphasised Bible* (1902), Joseph B. Rotherham
RS	*Revised Standard Version* (1952; as printed in 1971)
Sd	*The Authentic New Testament* (1958), Hugh J. Schonfield
Sh	*The Holy Bible* (1892), Samuel Sharpe
Sp	*The New Testament of Our Lord and Saviour Jesus Christ* (1937; as printed in 1948), Francis Aloysius Spencer
Sy	Syriac *Peshitta*, originally produced in the fifth century C.E. (edited by S. Lee, London, 1826, and reprinted by United Bible Societies, 1979)
TC	*The Twentieth Century New Testament*, Revised Edition (1904)
TEV	*Today's English Version* (1976)
Vg	Latin *Vulgate* (originally produced c. 400 C.E. by Jerome; edited by R. Weber, Stuttgart, Germany, 1975)
VM	*La Santa Biblia*, Versión Moderna (1966), Sociedades Bíblicas en América Latina
We	*The New Testament in Modern Speech* (Fifth Edition, 1943; as printed in 1944), R. F. Weymouth; revised by J. A. Robertson
Yg	*The Holy Bible* (Revised Edition of 1887), Robert Young

Books of the Bible

Ac	Acts	Ho	Hosea	Ne	Nehemiah
Am	Amos	Isa	Isaiah	Nu	Numbers
Ca	Song of Solomon (Canticles)	Jas	James	Ob	Obadiah
		Jer	Jeremiah	1Pe	Peter, 1
1Ch	Chronicles, 1	Jg	Judges	2Pe	Peter, 2
2Ch	Chronicles, 2	Joe	Joel	Phm	Philemon
1Co	Corinthians, 1	1Jo	John, 1	Php	Philippians
2Co	Corinthians, 2	2Jo	John, 2	Pr	Proverbs
Col	Colossians	3Jo	John, 3	Ps	Psalms
Da	Daniel	Joh	John	Re	Revelation
De	Deuteronomy	Jon	Jonah	Ro	Romans
Ec	Ecclesiastes	Jos	Joshua	Ru	Ruth
Eph	Ephesians	1Ki	Kings, 1	1Sa	Samuel, 1
Es	Esther	2Ki	Kings, 2	2Sa	Samuel, 2
Ex	Exodus	La	Lamentations	1Th	Thessalonians, 1
Eze	Ezekiel	Le	Leviticus	2Th	Thessalonians, 2
Ezr	Ezra	Lu	Luke	1Ti	Timothy, 1
Ga	Galatians	Mal	Malachi	2Ti	Timothy, 2
Ge	Genesis	Mr	Mark	Tit	Titus
Hab	Habakkuk	Mt	Matthew	Zec	Zechariah
Hag	Haggai	Mic	Micah	Zep	Zephaniah
Heb	Hebrews	Na	Nahum		

Other Abbreviations

a.	after	in.	inch(es)	p.	page
a.m.	(ante meridiem), before noon	kg	kilogram(s)	par(s).	paragraph(s)
		kl	kiloliter(s)	pl.	plural
avdp	avoirdupois	km	kilometer(s)	p.m.	(post meridiem), after noon
b.	before	km/hr	kilometers per hour		
B.C.E.	before Common Era	L	liter(s)	pp.	pages
bu	bushel(s)	Lat.	Latin	pt	pint(s)
c.	about	lb	pound(s)	qt	quart(s)
C.	Celsius	lit.	literally	S	south
C.E.	Common Era	m	meter(s)	SE	southeast
chap(s)	chapter(s)	mg	milligram(s)	sec(s).	section(s)
cm	centimeter(s)	mi	mile(s)	sq	square
col.	column	ml	milliliter(s)	SSE	south-southeast
cu	cubic	mm	millimeter(s)	SSW	south-southwest
E	east	mph	miles per hour	Sup	superscription
ENE	east-northeast	MS(S)	manuscript(s)	SW	southwest
ESE	east-southeast	Mt(s).	Mount(ains)	t	troy
F.	Fahrenheit	N	north	T.V.	Torrent Valley
ft	foot/feet	NE	northeast	Vol(s).	Volume(s)
ftn(s)	footnote(s)	NNE	north-northeast	vs(s)	verse(s)
g	gram(s)	NNW	north-northwest	W	west
gal	gallon(s)	No(s).	number(s)	WNW	west-northwest
Gr.	Greek	NW	northwest	WSW	west-southwest
ha	hectare(s)	oz	ounce(s)	yd	yard
Heb.	Hebrew				

NOTE: All quotations from classical authors are from the Loeb Classical Library, unless otherwise indicated.

* archeology — ostraca (broken pieces of pottery) used in bible times inexpensive writing surface. could be used by the poorest classes. 7th C.E. ostraca bearing Bible texts have been discovered in Egypt. Suggesting one means by which common people had access to portions of the Bible. (The International Standard Bible Encyclopedia) (1986) WT 8-15-88 par 7.

Endsheet Pictures

Left-hand page

Upper left: Assyrian war chariots carrying religious standards

Upper right: Cyrus Cylinder, which records his capture of Babylon and his freeing of prisoners to return to their homelands

Lower left: Clay tablet reporting the capture of Jerusalem by Nebuchadnezzar II; 617 B.C.E.

Lower right: Ruins of gateway near the site of the audience hall of Darius I at Persepolis

Right-hand page

Babylon being invaded by soldiers of Cyrus the Great in 539 B.C.E.